THE NORTON ANTHOLOGY OF

AMERICAN

LITERATURE

SHORTER NINTH EDITION

VOLUME 1: BEGINNINGS TO 1865

Michael A. Elliott
ASA GRIGGS CANDLER PROFESSOR OF ENGLISH AND AMERICAN STUDIES
EMORY UNIVERSITY

Sandra M. Gustafson
PROFESSOR OF ENGLISH AND AMERICAN STUDIES
UNIVERSITY OF NOTRE DAME

Amy Hungerford
BIRD WHITE HOUSUM PROFESSOR OF ENGLISH AND AMERICAN STUDIES
AND DIRECTOR OF THE DIVISION OF THE HUMANITIES
YALE UNIVERSITY

Mary Loeffelholz
PROFESSOR OF ENGLISH
NORTHEASTERN UNIVERSITY

THE NORTON ANTHOLOGY OF
AMERICAN
LITERATURE

SHORTER NINTH EDITION

Robert S. Levine, *General Editor*

PROFESSOR OF ENGLISH AND
DISTINGUISHED UNIVERSITY PROFESSOR AND
DISTINGUISHED SCHOLAR–TEACHER
University of Maryland, College Park

VOLUME 1: BEGINNINGS TO 1865

W · W · NORTON & COMPANY
NEW YORK · LONDON

W. W. Norton & Company has been independent since its founding in 1923, when William Warder Norton and Mary D. Herter Norton first published lectures delivered at the People's Institute, the adult education division of New York City's Cooper Union. The firm soon expanded its program beyond the Institute, publishing books by celebrated academics from America and abroad. By midcentury, the two major pillars of Norton's publishing program— trade books and college texts—were firmly established. In the 1950s, the Norton family transferred control of the company to its employees, and today—with a staff of four hundred and a comparable number of trade, college, and professional titles published each year—W. W. Norton & Company stands as the largest and oldest publishing house owned wholly by its employees.

Editor: Julia Reidhead
Managing Editor, College: Marian Johnson
Manuscript Editors: Kurt Wildermuth, Harry Haskell,
Michael Fleming, Candace Levy, Tenyia Lee
Assistant Editor: Rachel Taylor
Media Editor: Carly Fraser Doria
Assistant Media Editor: Ava Bramson
Managing Editor, College Digital Media: Kim Yi
Media Project Editors: Kristin Sheerin, Cooper Wilhelm
Marketing Manager, Literature: Kimberly Bowers
Production Manager: Sean Mintus
Art Director: Debra Morton Hoyt
Cover Design: Tiani Kennedy
Photo Editor: Cat Abelman
Permissions Manager: Megan Jackson Schindel
Permissions Clearing: Margaret Gorenstein
Composition: Westchester Book Group

The Library of Congress has cataloged an earlier edition as follows:
Library of Congress Cataloging-in-Publication Data
Names: Levine, Robert S. (Robert Steven), 1953- editor.
Title: The Norton anthology of American literature / Robert S. Levine, general editor;
Michael A. Elliott, Sandra M. Gustafson, Amy Hungerford, Mary Loeffelholz.
Description: Ninth edition. | New York : W. W. Norton & Company, 2017. |
Includes bibliographical references and index.
Identifiers: LCCN 2016043347| ISBN 9780393935714 (pbk., v. a : alk. paper) |
ISBN 9780393264470 (pbk., v. b : alk. paper) | ISBN 9780393264487 (pbk., v. c :
alk. paper) | ISBN 9780393264494 (pbk., v. d : alk. paper) | ISBN 9780393264500
(pbk., v. e : alk. paper)
Subjects: LCSH: American literature. | United States—Literary collections.
Classification: LCC PS507 .N65 2016 | DDC 810.8—dc23 LC record available
at https://lccn.loc.gov/2016043347

This edition: ISBN 978-0-393-26452-4

W. W. Norton & Company, Inc., 500 Fifth Avenue, New York, NY 10110
www.wwnorton.com

W. W. Norton & Company Ltd., 15 Carlisle Street, London W1D 3BS

Contents

American Literature 1820–1865

Preface to the Shorter Ninth Edition

The Ninth Edition of *The Norton Anthology of American Literature* is the first for me as General Editor; for the Eighth Edition, I served as Associate General Editor under longstanding General Editor Nina Baym. On the occasion of a new general editorship, we have undertaken one of the most extensive revisions in our long publishing history. Three new section editors have joined the team: Sandra M. Gustafson, Professor of English and Concurrent Professor of American Studies at the University of Notre Dame, who succeeds Wayne Franklin and Philip Gura as editor of "American Literature, Beginnings to 1820"; Michael A. Elliott, Professor of English at Emory University, who succeeds Nina Baym, Robert S. Levine, and Jeanne Campbell Reesman as editor of "American Literature, 1865–1914"; and Amy Hungerford, Professor of English and American Studies at Yale University, who succeeds Jerome Klinkowitz and Patricia B. Wallace as editor of "American Literature since 1945." These editors join Robert S. Levine, editor of "American Literature, 1820–1865," and Mary Loeffelholz, editor of "American Literature, 1914–1945." Each editor, new or continuing, is a well-known expert in the relevant field or period and has ultimate responsibility for his or her section of the anthology, but we have worked closely from first to last to rethink all aspects of this new edition. Period introductions, author headnotes, thematic clusters, annotations, illustrations, and bibliographies have all been updated and revised. We have also added a number of new authors, selections, and thematic clusters. We are excited about the outcome of our collaboration and anticipate that, like the previous eight editions, this edition of *The Norton Anthology of American Literature* will continue to lead the field.

From the anthology's inception in 1979, the editors have had three main aims: first, to present a rich and substantial enough variety of works to enable teachers to build courses according to their own vision of American literary history (thus, teachers are offered more authors and more selections than they will probably use in any one course); second, to make the anthology self-sufficient by featuring many works in their entirety along with extensive selections for individual authors; third, to balance traditional interests with developing critical concerns in a way that allows for the complex, rigorous, and capacious study of American literary traditions. As early as 1979, we anthologized work by Anne Bradstreet, Mary Rowlandson, Sarah Kemble Knight, Phillis Wheatley, Margaret Fuller, Harriet Beecher Stowe, Frederick Douglass, Sarah Orne Jewett, Kate Chopin, Mary E. Wilkins Freeman, Booker T. Washington, Charles W. Chesnutt, Edith Wharton,

W. E. B. Du Bois, and other writers who were not yet part of a standard canon. Yet we never shortchanged writers—such as Franklin, Emerson, Whitman, Hawthorne, Melville, Dickinson, Hemingway, Fitzgerald, and Faulkner—whose work many students expected to read in their American literature courses, and whom most teachers then and now would not think of doing without.

The so-called canon wars of the 1980s and 1990s usefully initiated a review of our understanding of American literature, a review that has enlarged the number and diversity of authors now recognized as contributors to the totality of American literature. The traditional writers look different in this expanded context, and they also appear different according to which of their works are selected. Teachers and students remain committed to the idea of the literary—that writers strive to produce artifacts that are both intellectually serious and formally skillful—but believe more than ever that writers should be understood in relation to their cultural and historical situations. We address the complex interrelationships between literature and history in the period introductions, author headnotes, chronologies, and some of the footnotes. As in previous editions, we have worked with detailed suggestions from many teachers on how best to present the authors and selections. We have gained insights as well from the students who use the anthology. Thanks to questionnaires, face-to-face and phone discussions, letters, and email, we have been able to listen to those for whom this book is intended. For the Shorter Ninth Edition, we have drawn on the careful commentary of over 130 reviewers and reworked aspects of the anthology accordingly.

Our new materials continue the work of broadening the canon by representing new writers in depth, without sacrificing widely assigned writers, many of whose selections have been reconsidered, reselected, and expanded. Our aim is always to provide extensive enough selections to do the writers justice, including complete works wherever possible. Our Shorter Ninth Edition offers sixteen complete longer works, including such newly added works as Charles Brockden Brown's *Memoirs of Carwin the Biloquist* and James Baldwin's "Sonny's Blues." Two complete works—Eugene O'Neill's *Long Day's Journey into Night* and Tennessee Williams's *A Streetcar Named Desire*—are exclusive to *The Norton Anthology of American Literature*. Charles Brockden Brown, Louisa May Alcott, and Junot Díaz are among the writers added to the prior edition, and to this edition we have introduced George Saunders and Natasha Trethewey, among others. We have also expanded and in some cases reconfigured such central figures as Franklin, Hawthorne, Dickinson, Twain, and Hemingway, offering new approaches in the headnotes, along with some new selections. In fact, the headnotes and, in many cases, selections for such frequently assigned authors as William Bradford, Washington Irving, James Fenimore Cooper, William Cullen Bryant, Henry Wadsworth Longfellow, Ralph Waldo Emerson, Harriet Beecher Stowe, Mark Twain, William Dean Howells, Henry James, Kate Chopin, W. E. B. Du Bois, Edith Wharton, Willa Cather, and William Faulkner have been revised, updated, and in some cases entirely rewritten in light of recent scholarship. The Shorter Ninth Edition further expands its selections of women writers and writers from diverse ethnic, racial, and regional backgrounds—always with attention to the critical acclaim that recognizes their contributions to the American literary record. New and recently added writers such as Samson Occom, along with the figures represented in the new cluster "Native American Oral Literature," enable teachers to bring early Native American writing and oratory into their syllabi, or, should they prefer, to focus on these selections as a freestanding unit leading toward the moment after 1945 when Native writers fully entered the mainstream of literary activity.

We are pleased to continue our popular innovation of topical gatherings of short texts that illuminate the cultural, historical, intellectual, and literary concerns of their respective periods. Designed to be taught in a class period or two, or used as background, each of the nine clusters consists of brief, carefully excerpted primary and (in one case) secondary texts, about six to ten per cluster, and an introduction. Diverse voices—many new to the anthology—highlight a range of views current when writers of a particular time period were active, and thus allow students better to understand some of the large issues that were being debated at particular historical moments. For example, in "Slavery, Race, and the Making of American Literature," texts by David Walker, William Lloyd Garrison, Angelina Grimké, Sojourner Truth, James M. Whitfield, and Martin R. Delany speak to the great paradox of pre–Civil War America: the contradictory rupture between the realities of slavery and the nation's ideals of freedom.

The Shorter Ninth Edition strengthens this feature with seven new and revised clusters attuned to the requests of teachers. To help students address the controversy over race and aesthetics in *Adventures of Huckleberry Finn*, we have revised a cluster that shows what some of the leading critics of the past few decades thought was at stake in reading and interpreting slavery and race in Twain's canonical novel. The 1865–1914 section also features "Realism and Naturalism," and we continue to include the useful "Modernist Manifestos" in the section covering 1914–1945. We have added to the popular "Creative Nonfiction" in the post-1945 section new selections by David Foster Wallace, Hunter S. Thompson, and Joan Didion, which join texts by such writers as Jamaica Kincaid and Edwidge Danticat.

The Shorter Ninth Edition features an expanded illustration program, both of the black-and-white images, 107 of which are placed throughout the volumes, and of the color plates so popular in the last two editions. In selecting color plates—from Elizabeth Graham's embroidered map of Washington, D.C., at the start of the nineteenth century to Jeff Wall's "After 'Invisible Man'" at the beginning of the twenty-first—the editors aim to provide images relevant to literary works in the anthology while depicting arts and artifacts representative of each era. In addition, graphic works—segments from Art Spiegelman's canonical graphic novel, *Maus*, and a facsimile page of Emily Dickinson manuscript, along with the many new illustrations—open possibilities for teaching visual texts.

Period-by-Period Revisions

American Literature, Beginnings to 1820. Sandra M. Gustafson, the new editor for this period, has substantially revised this section. Prior editions broke this period into two historical sections, with two introductions and a dividing line at the year 1700; Gustafson has dropped that artificial divide to tell a more coherent and fluid story (in her new introduction) about the variety of American literatures during this long period. The section continues to feature narratives by early European explorers of the North American continent as they encountered and attempted to make sense of the diverse cultures they met, and as they sought to justify their aim of claiming the territory for Europeans. In addition to the standing material by John Smith and William Bradford, we include new material by Roger Williams and Charles Brockden Brown's *Memoirs of Carwin the Biloquist* (the complete "prequel" to his first novel, *Wieland*). We continue to offer substantial selections from Rowlandson's enormously influential *A Narrative of the Captivity and Restoration of Mrs. Mary Rowlandson* and Benjamin Franklin's *Autobiography* (which remains one of the most compelling works on the emergence of an "American" self). New and revised thematic clusters of texts highlight themes central to this long historical period. "Native American Oral Literature" features creation stories, trickster tales, oratory, and poetry from a spectrum of traditions, while "Native American Eloquence" collects speeches and accounts by Canassatego and Native American women (both new to the volume), Pontiac, Chief Logan (as cited by Thomas Jefferson), and Tecumseh, which, as a group, illustrate the centuries-long pattern of initial peaceful contact between Native Americans and whites mutating into bitter and violent conflict. The Native American presence in the volume is further expanded with increased representation of Samson Occom, which includes an excerpt from his sermon at the execution of Moses Paul. The new cluster "Ethnographic and Naturalist Writings" includes writings by Sarah Kemble Knight, William Bartram, and Hendrick Aupaumut. With this cluster, and a number of new selections and revisions in the other historical sections, the Ninth Edition pays greater attention to the impact of science on American literary traditions.

American Literature, 1820–1865. Under the editorship of Robert S. Levine, this section over the past several editions has become more diverse. Included here are the complete texts of Emerson's *Nature*, Douglass's *Narrative,* Whitman's *Song of Myself,* Melville's *Benito Cereno,* and Rebecca Harding Davis's *Life in the Iron Mills.* At the same time, aware of the important role of African American writers in the period, and the omnipresence of race and slavery as literary and political themes, we have recently added the major African American writer Frances E. W. Harper. A generous selection from Stowe's *Uncle Tom's Cabin,* and the cluster "Slavery, Race, and the Making of American Literature," also help remind students of how central slavery was to the literary and political life of the nation during this period. "Native Americans: Resistance and Removal" gathers oratory and writings—by Native Americans such as Black Hawk and whites such as Ralph Waldo Emerson—protesting Andrew Jackson's ruthless national policy of Indian removal. Political themes, far from diluting the literary imagination of American authors, served to inspire some of the most memorable writing of the pre–Civil War period.

Recently added prose fiction includes a chapter from Cooper's *The Last of the Mohicans.* Poetry by Emily Dickinson is now presented in the texts established by R. W. Franklin and includes a facsimile page from Fascicle 10. For this edition we have added several poems by Dickinson that were inspired by the Civil War. Other selections added to this edition include Poe's popular short story "The Cask of Amontillado."

American Literature, 1865–1914. Newly edited by Michael A. Elliott, this section includes expanded selections of key works, as well as new ones that illustrate how many of the struggles of this period prefigure our own. Complete longer works include Twain's *Adventures of Huckleberry Finn* and James's *Daisy Miller*. In the Eighth Edition, we introduced a section on the critical controversy surrounding race and the conclusion of *Adventures of Huckleberry Finn*. That section remains as important as ever, and new additions incorporate a recent debate about the value of an expurgated edition of the novel.

We have substantially revised clusters designed to give students a sense of the cultural context of the period. New selections in "Realism and Naturalism" demonstrate what was at stake in the debate over realism, among them a feminist response from Charlotte Perkins Gilman. We have also added fiction by African American authors, including Pauline Hopkins's "Talma Gordon." The 1865–1914 period saw a rise in immigration that helped to make the country what it is today. A newly added selection of poems by Emma Lazarus brings this theme into focus.

American Literature, 1914–1945. Edited by Mary Loeffelholz, "American Literature, 1914–1945" offers a number of complete longer works, including Eugene O'Neill's *Long Day's Journey into Night* (exclusive to the Norton Anthology). New selections by Zora Neale Hurston ("Sweat") and John Steinbeck ("The Chrysanthemums") further contribute to the volume's exploration of issues connected with racial and social geographies. Selections by Ezra Pound, T. S. Eliot, Marianne Moore, Hart Crane, and Langston Hughes encourage students and teachers to contemplate the interrelation of modernist aesthetics with ethnic, regional, and popular writing. In "Modernist Manifestos," F. T. Marinetti, Mina Loy, Ezra Pound, Willa Cather, William Carlos Williams, and Langston Hughes show how the manifesto as a form exerted a powerful influence on international modernism in all the arts. Other recent and new additions to this section include Faulkner's popular "A Rose for Emily," Gertrude Stein's introduction to *The Making of Americans*, Hemingway's "Hills Like White Elephants," and poems by Edwin Arlington Robinson.

American Literature since 1945. Amy Hungerford, the new editor of "American Literature since 1945," has revised the section to present a wider range of writing in poetry, prose, drama, and nonfiction. As before, the section offers the complete texts of Tennessee Williams's *A Streetcar Named Desire* (exclusive to this anthology), Arthur Miller's *Death of a Salesman*, and Allen Ginsberg's *Howl*. New to this edition is Don DeLillo. The selection from *White Noise*, one of DeLillo's most celebrated novels, tells what feels like a contemporary story about a nontraditional family navigating an environmental disaster in a climate saturated by mass media. Two newly added stories—Patricia Highsmith's "The Quest for *Blank Claveringi*" and George Saunders's "CivilWarLand in Bad Decline"—reveal the impact of science fiction, fantasy, horror, and (especially in the case of Saunders) mass media on literary fiction. Recognized literary figures in all genres, ranging from Elizabeth Bishop to Leslie Marmon Silko and Toni Morrison, continue to be richly represented. In response to instructors' requests, we now include Flannery O'Connor's "A Good Man Is Hard to Find" and James Baldwin's "Sonny's Blues."

One of the most distinctive features of twentieth- and twenty-first-century American literature is a rich vein of African American poetry. This edition adds a contemporary poet from this living tradition: Natasha Trethewey, whose selections include personal and historical elegies. Trethewey joins African American poets whose work has long helped define the anthology—Rita Dove, Gwendolyn Brooks, Robert Hayden, Audre Lorde, and others.

This edition gives even greater exposure to literary and social experimentation during the 1960s, 1970s, and beyond. To our popular cluster "Creative Nonfiction" we have added a new selection by Joan Didion, from "Slouching Towards Bethlehem," which showcases her revolutionary style of journalism as she comments on experiments with public performance and communal living during the 1960s. A new selection from David Foster Wallace in the same cluster pushes reportage on the Maine Lobster Festival into philosophical inquiry: how can we fairly assess the pain of other creatures? Standing authors in the anthology, notably John Ashbery and Amiri Baraka, fill out the section's survey of radical change in the forms, and social uses, of literary art.

We are delighted to offer this revised Shorter Ninth Edition to teachers and students, and we welcome your comments.

Additional Resources from the Publisher

We are also pleased to offer the Ninth Edition in an ebook format. The Digital Anthologies include all the content of the print volumes, with print-corresponding page and line numbers for seamless integration into the print-digital mixed classroom. Annotations are accessible with a click or a tap, encouraging students to use them with minimal interruption to their reading of the text. The e-reading platform facilitates active reading with a powerful annotation tool and allows students to do a full-text search of the anthology and read online or off. The Digital Editions can be accessed from any computer or device with an Internet browser and are available to students at a fraction of the print price at digital.wwnorton.com /americanlit9shorter. For exam copy access to the Digital Editions and for information on making the Digital Editions available through the campus bookstore or packaging the Digital Editions with the print anthology, instructors should contact their Norton representative.

To give instructors even more flexibility, Norton is making available the full list of 254 Norton Critical Editions. A Norton Critical Edition can be included with any volume at a discounted price (see your Norton representative for details). Each Norton Critical Edition gives students an authoritative, carefully annotated text accompanied by rich contextual and critical materials prepared by an expert in the subject. The publisher also offers the much-praised guide *Writing about American Literature*, by Karen Gocsik

(University of California–San Diego) and Coleman Hutchison (University of Texas–Austin), free with either volume.

In addition to the Digital Editions, for students using *The Norton Anthology of American Literature*, the publisher provides a wealth of free resources at digital.wwnorton.com/americanlit9shorter. There students will find more than fifty reading-comprehension quizzes on the period introductions and widely taught works with extensive feedback that points them back to the text. Ideal for self-study or homework assignments, Norton's sophisticated quizzing engine allows instructors to track student results and improvement. For over twenty-five works in the anthology, the sites also offer Close Reading Workshops that walk students step-by-step through analysis of a literary work. Each workshop prompts students to read, reread, consider contexts, and answer questions along the way, making these perfect assignments to build close-reading skills.

The publisher also provides extensive instructor-support materials. New to the Ninth Edition is an online Interactive Instructor's Guide at iig.wwnorton.com/americanlit9/full. Invaluable for course preparation, this resource provides hundreds of teaching notes, discussion questions, and suggested resources from the much-praised *Teaching with* The Norton Anthology of American Literature: *A Guide for Instructors* by Edward Whitley (Lehigh University). Also at this searchable and sortable site are quizzes, images, and lecture PowerPoints for each introduction, topic cluster, and twenty-five widely taught works. A PDF of *Teaching with NAAL* is available for download at wwnorton.com/instructors.

Finally, Norton Coursepacks bring high-quality digital media into a new or existing online course. The coursepack includes all the reading comprehension quizzes (customizable within the coursepack), the Writing about Literature video series, a bank of essay and exam questions, bulleted summaries of the period introductions, and "Making Connections" discussion or essay prompts to encourage students to draw connections across the anthology's authors and works. Coursepacks are available in a variety of formats, including Blackboard, Canvas, Desire2Learn, and Moodle, at no cost to instructors or students.

Editorial Procedures

As in past editions, editorial features—period introductions, headnotes, annotations, and bibliographies—are designed to be concise yet full and to give students necessary information without imposing a single interpretation. The editors have updated all apparatus in response to new scholarship: period introductions have been entirely or substantially rewritten, as have many headnotes. All selected bibliographies and each period's general-resources bibliographies, categorized by Reference Works, Histories, and Literary Criticism, have been thoroughly updated. The Ninth Edition retains two editorial features that help students place their reading in historical and cultural context—a Texts/Contexts timeline following each period introduction and a map on the front endpaper of each volume.

Whenever possible, our policy has been to reprint texts as they appeared in their historical moment. There is one exception: we have modernized most spellings and (very sparingly) the punctuation in Volume 1 on the principle that archaic spellings and typography pose unnecessary problems for beginning students. We have used square brackets to indicate titles supplied by the editors for the convenience of students. Whenever a portion of a text has been omitted, we have indicated that omission with three asterisks. If the omitted portion is important for following the plot or argument, we give a brief summary within the text or in a footnote. After each work, we cite the date of first publication on the right; in some instances, the latter is followed by the date of a revised edition for which the author was responsible. When the date of composition is known and differs from the date of publication, we cite it on the left.

The editors have benefited from commentary offered by hundreds of teachers throughout the country. Those teachers who prepared detailed critiques, or who offered special help in preparing texts, are listed under Acknowledgments, on a separate page. We also thank the many people at Norton who contributed to the Ninth Edition: Julia Reidhead, who supervised the Ninth Edition; Marian Johnson, managing editor, college; Carly Fraser Doria, media editor; manuscript editors Kurt Wildermuth, Michael Fleming, Harry Haskell, Candace Levy, and Tenyia Lee; Rachel Taylor and Ava Bramson, assistant editors; Sean Mintus, production manager; Cat Abelman, photo editor; Julie Tesser, photo researcher; Debra Morton Hoyt, art director; Tiani Kennedy, cover designer; Megan Jackson Schindel, permissions manager; and Margaret Gorenstein, who cleared permissions. We also wish to acknowledge our debt to the late George P. Brockway, former president and chairman at Norton, who invented this anthology, and to the late M. H. Abrams, Norton's advisor on English texts. All have helped us create an anthology that, more than ever, testifies to the continuing richness of American literary traditions.

ROBERT S. LEVINE, General Editor

Acknowledgments

Among our many critics, advisors, and friends, the following were of especial help toward the preparation of the Shorter Ninth Edition, either with advice or by providing critiques of particular periods of the anthology: Rolena Adorno (Yale University); M. Lee Alexander (William and Mary); John Allen (Milwaukee Area Technical College); Kathaleen Amende (Alabama State University); Dr. Andrew S. Andermatt (Paul Smith's College); Brian Anderson (Central Piedmont Community College); David L. Anderson (Butler County Community College); Peter Antelyes (Vassar College); Christopher Apap (Oakland University); Susanna Ashton (Clemson University); John Baffa (Morton College); Amy Bagwell (Central Piedmont Community College); Heidi Bauer (Lower Columbia College); Jenny Beaver (Rowan-Cabarrus Community College); Rebecca Belcher-Rankin (Olivet Nazarene University); Roger A. Berger (Everett Community College); Kyle Bishop (Southern Utah University); Susanne Bloomfield (University of Nebraska–Kearney); Anne Boyd Rioux (University of New Orleans); Alan Brown (University of West Alabama); Martin Brückner (University of Delaware); John Bruni (Grand Valley State University); Joanna Brooks (San Diego State University); Dr. Eugenia Bryan (Georgia Southwestern State University); Lisa Carl (North Carolina Central University); Allison Carpenter (Northampton Community College); Thomas Cassidy (South Carolina State University); Patrick Cesarini (University of South Alabama); Kathleen Chescattie (Harrisburg Area Community College); Lauren Coats (Louisiana State University); Tiffany Collins (Ogeechee Technical College); Josh Cohen (Emory University); Matt Cohen (University of Texas at Austin); James H. Cox (The University of Texas at Austin); Laura Dassow Walls (University of Notre Dame); Matthew Davis (University of Wisconsin–Stevens Point); Mike Davis (Beaufort Community College); Christopher G. Diller (Berry College); James J. Donahue (SUNY Potsdam); Philip J. Egan (Western Michigan University); Patrick Erben (University of West Georgia); Duncan Faherty (The City University of New York); Daniel Fineman (Occidental College); Edward Gallagher (Danville Area Community College); Armida Gilbert (Georgia Perimeter College); Paul Gilmore (Rutgers University); Cory R. Goehring (Waynesburg University); Mary Goodwin (National Taiwan Normal University); Jurgen E. Grandt (University of North Georgia–Gainesville Campus); James N. Green (Library Company of Philadelphia); Kathy Griffith Fish (University of the Cumberlands); Annemarie Hamlin (Central Oregon Community College); Matthew Hartman (Ball State University); Terry Heller (Coe College); Alexander Hollenberg (Sheridan College); Greg Horn (Southwest Virginia Community

College); Coleman Hutchison (University of Texas, Austin); S. Selina Jamil (Prince George's Community College); Joel J. Janicki (Soochow University); Gwendolyn Jones Harold (Clayton State University); Michael Joslin (Lees-McRae College); Cheung Kai Chong (Shih Shin University); Mark Kamrath (University of Central Florida); Kristi Key (Oklahoma Baptist University); Mabel Khawaja (Hampton University, Virginia); James Kirkpatrick (Central Piedmont Community College); Dawn Knopf (Clark College); Kristie Knotts; Jonathan Malcolm Lampley (Dalton State College); Andrew Lanham (Yale University); Marianne Layer (New River Community and Technical College); Richard Leith; Alfred J. López (Purdue University); Bridget Marshall (University of Massachusetts, Lowell); David McCracken (Coker College); John McGreevy (University of Notre Dame); Nancy McKinney (Illinois State University); Fiona McWilliam (University of Texas, San Antonio); Jim McWilliams (Dickinson State University); Christine Mihelich (Marywood University); Joshua Miller (University of Akron); Jesus Montano (Hope College); Laura Morgan Green (Northeastern University); David J. Nackley (Mohawk Valley Community College); Bernard G. Neff (Mount Aloysius College); David Neimeyer (Washington Adventist University); Lee Ogletree (Wiregrass Georgia Technical College); Dawn Oshiro (Kapiolani Community College); Jason Palmer; Martha H. Patterson (McKendree University); Jay Peterson (Atlantic Cape Community College); Christopher Phillips (Lafayette College); Roxanna Pisiak (Morrisville State College); Ben Railton (Fitchburg State University); Palmer Rampell (Yale University); Joseph Rezek (Boston University); Danielle Roach (Miami University); Marc Robinson (Yale University); J. B. Rollins (National Chung Cheng University); Shelbey Rosengarten (St. Petersburg College); Debby Rosenthal (John Carroll University); Phillip Round (University of Iowa); Karin Russell (Keiser University); Melissa Ryan (Alfred University); Claire Satlof (Valley Forge Military College); Gordon Sayre (University of Oregon); Judith Scheffler (West Chester University); William Scott Hanna (West Liberty University); Susan Scott Parrish (University of Michigan); Gabriela Serrano (Angelo State University); Marvin Jerome Severson (Kennesaw State University); Anna Shectman (Yale University); Lincoln Shlensky (University of Victoria); Kim Smith (Baker College); John Springer (University of Central Oklahoma); Kelsey Squire (Ohio Dominican University); Julia Stern (Northwestern University); Dorothy Stringer (Temple University); Kyle Taylor (West Georgia Technical College); Dorothy Terry (Tougaloo College); Jade Tsui-yu Lee (National Kaohsiung Normal University); Barbara Urban (Central Piedmont Community College); Kim Vanderlaan (California University of Pennsylvania); Joanne van der Woude (University of Groningen); Abram van Engen (Washington University); Susan VanZanten (Seattle Pacific University); Jeremy Voigt (Whatcom Community College); Bryan Waterman (New York University); Belinda Wheeler (Claflin University); Elizabeth Wiet (Yale University); Keith Wilhite (Siena College); Andrea N. Williams (The Ohio State University); K. Jamie Woodlief (West Chester University); Curtis A. Yehnert (Western Oregon University); Aiping Zhang (California State University, Chico).

THE NORTON ANTHOLOGY OF

AMERICAN

LITERATURE

SHORTER NINTH EDITION

VOLUME I: BEGINNINGS TO 1865

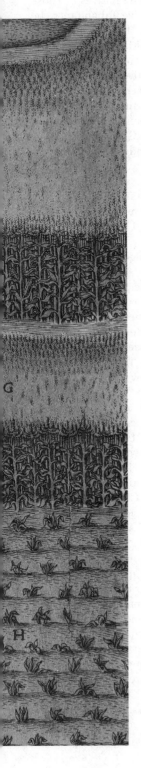

Beginnings
to 1820

QUESTIONS OF IDENTITY

In 1631, the English captain John Smith published *Advertisements for the Unexperienced Planters of New England, or Any Where: Or, the Path-way to Experience to Erect a Plantation*, the last and most polished of his works. Smith had been instrumental in the 1607 founding of Jamestown in Virginia, England's first long-lived American settlement, and he later provided guidance for both the Pilgrims who established Plymouth in 1620 and the Puritans who founded the Massachusetts Bay Colony 10 years later. Reading *Advertisements for the Unexperienced Planters* now, when anticolonial and independence movements have made colonization justly suspect, Smith's endorsement of English plantations in North America strikes a discordant note. Smith anticipated such objections, for he heard them from his contemporaries. "Many good religious devout men have made it a great question, as a matter in conscience, by what warrant they might goe to possesse those Countries, which are none of theirs, but the poore Salvages [i.e., savages']," he wrote. He considered the answer to this objection self-evident: "for God did make the world to be inhabited with mankind, and to have his name knowne to all Nations, and from generation to generation." Although hardly a pious man, Smith saw God's hand at work in England's seizing of the Americas.

On a more mundane level, the dense population and soil depletion in England seemed to Smith sufficient reason to take advantage of the fact that "here in Florida, Virginia, New-England, and Cannada, is more land than all the people in Christendome can

John White, **Indian Village of Secoton** (detail), 1585. For more information about this image, see the color insert in this volume.

manure [i.e., cultivate], and yet more to spare than all the natives of those Countries can use and culturate." The continent's native inhabitants, he enthused, would "sell you a whole Countrey" in exchange "for a copper kettle and a few toyes, as beads and hatchets." In his text, Smith did not consider that these "sales" might have been based on different concepts of property, nor did he dwell on the deadly epidemics that decimated Native societies following the arrival of Europeans. He based his arguments for colonization on the precedents available in sacred and secular history. Adam and Eve established a plantation, Smith argued, as did Noah and his family after the flood, and so on through "the Hebrewes, Lacedemonians, the Goths, Grecians, Romans, and the rest." Moreover Portugal and Spain had a one-hundred-and-forty-year lead on England in terms of colony formation, and they were wresting great wealth from the people of the Americas, who once had possessed the natural resources. It would be "neglect of our duty and religion" as well as "want of charity to those poore Salvages" to fail to challenge these Roman Catholic countries for control of the hemisphere, Smith concluded. The difficulty today of seeing European settlement as an expression of "charity" to the "Salvages" means that the "great question" raised by the "good religious devout men" opposed to colonization remains fresh and vital.

In 1805, the Seneca orator Sagoyewatha, or Red Jacket, offered a Native perspective on colonization in an address to the missionary Jacob Cram that can serve as a rebuttal of Smith. "There was a time when our forefathers owned this great island," Sagoyewatha told Cram. "Their seats extended from the rising to the setting sun. The Great Spirit had made it for the use of Indians." When "your forefathers" arrived, he continued, "they found friends and not enemies. They told us they had fled from their own country for fear of wicked men, and had come here to enjoy their religion. They asked us for a small seat. We took pity on them, granted their request; and they sat down amongst us." Sagoyewatha went on to describe the devastating impact on Native Americans of the strong alcohol introduced by Europeans and to relate how the once small colonial populations had grown and spilled over onto lands that the Natives had not meant to relinquish. He also challenged Cram on the relevance of Christianity to Native communities, which, he stressed, had their own religious traditions. In addition, Christianity hardly seemed a unifying force for good. "If there is but one religion," Sagoyewatha asked, "why do you white people differ so much about it? Why [are you] not all agreed, as you can all read the book [i.e., the Bible]?"

In his 1782 book *Letters from an American Farmer*, the French-born writer J. Hector St. John de Crèvecœur posed another resonant question: "What is an American?" Crèvecœur offered his most explicit answer to this question in Letter III, where he described "the American" as a "new man, who acts upon new principles; he must therefore entertain new ideas, and form new opinions." The American people were "a mixture of English, Scotch, Irish, French, Dutch, Germans and Swedes," he wrote, emphasizing that they farmed their own land and peacefully practiced various faiths, including Roman Catholicism, Quakerism, and several forms of Protestantism. Crèvecœur's description captured important aspects of late colonial society. In its early years, the American colonies were shaped by competing empires: the large ones— New Spain, New France, and the English colonies, including Virginia and New England—and more modest efforts, such as New Netherland and New

Sweden. In the eighteenth century, even as Britain consolidated its empire in North America, an influx of immigrants from Northern Europe produced in the mid-Atlantic colonies the particular mixture that Crèvecœur described. He contrasted this American "melting" of peoples with life in Europe, where national and religious divisions fueled chronic wars while lingering feudal systems and powerful states oppressed the common people.

Elsewhere in *Letters*, Crèvecœur complicated his idealized vision of America as a place where Europeans could liberate themselves from the constraints of the Old World. He noted the attractions of the frontier, a borderland where hunting surpassed agriculture as the dominant mode of life. In that contact zone, European Americans adopted the customs and habits of Native Americans even as they sought to supplant them. He also reported on the hierarchical plantation-based societies of the southern colonies, and the horrors inflicted there on enslaved African Americans. His description of a caged slave is one of the most unforgettable passages in the book. In these selections, the liberating potential of the New World is shown to have sharp limits, and the process of nation-formation to have negative ramifications as well as positive consequences.

Letters from an American Farmer proved an immediate sensation, for it offered insights into what the emerging nation might become, and how the result might affect Europe. Though Crèvecœur was probably a Loyalist supporter of British rule, his work was greeted enthusiastically by political radicals in England and Enlightenment philosophes in France, as well as by the American statesman Thomas Jefferson, who echoed Crèvecœur's enthusiasm for the yeoman farmer in his *Notes on the State of Virginia* (1787). After a period of relative neglect in the nineteenth century, Crèvecœur's vision of America was revived in 1908, when Israel Zangwill's "The Melting Pot," a play focused on recent waves of European immigration, became a smash hit. Readers embraced *Letters* as a classic of American literature presenting an archetype of American identity. Unfortunately, the resulting view of *Letters* highlighted the formation of white American identity while marginalizing nonwhites. In recent years, a more comprehensive approach to Crèvecœur's work has emphasized the sections on slavery and white/Native interactions on the frontier. *Letters from an American Farmer* offers today's readers vivid accounts of assumptions and contradictions that helped shape the early United States and its literature.

Nearly four decades after *Letters from an American Farmer* became one of the literary hits of the age of revolution, Washington Irving cast a backward look at this founding era in his tale "Rip Van Winkle." Irving was born in 1783, the year that the Treaty of Paris brought a formal close to the Revolutionary War, and he was named for the Virginia planter and slave owner who led the Continental Army to victory and later became the first president of the United States. Irving was one of the earliest American-born authors to win international literary celebrity, which he achieved as an expatriate writer living in England. The work that first made him famous was *The Sketch Book* (1819–20), a volume of stories and essays that includes his best-known tales, "Rip Van Winkle" and "The Legend of Sleepy Hollow." While these stories take place in the Catskill region of New York and there are two essays on Native American life and history, the bulk of the volume concerns English customs. This fact suggests the limits to revolutionary change in the literary world of Irving's day. Despite the ambition of many writers to create distinctly "American" works, the literature of the United States remained oriented toward England for decades after independence.

"Rip Van Winkle" emphasizes continuity more than transformation, and it highlights the checkered quality of human nature rather than its potential for radical new beginnings. Based on a German folktale and set in a sleepy Dutch village on the Hudson River shortly before the Revolution, the story features Rip, a slacker who embarks on a hunting expedition to evade his wife's demands. In the mountains, he mysteriously finds himself in the company of the English explorer Henry Hudson, who in 1609 traveled from New York Harbor as far as Albany, sailing up the river that now bears his name. Hudson and his men silently invite Rip to drink with them, and he soon falls into a deep and unnaturally prolonged sleep. When he returns to his village after a 20-year interval, the Revolution has passed, and Rip finds much that is unfamiliar, as well as things that are uncannily familiar yet somehow different. Frustrated, he bursts out, "Does nobody here know Rip Van Winkle?"—and a version of his younger self is pointed out to him. This person turns out to be the son he left at home two decades earlier, now grown up to be a man much like his father.

Irving invites his readers to consider the disorienting nature of social transformation. He particularly contrasts the quieter, slower colonial world with the bustle and clamor of the newly democratizing political culture. The story suggests that despite some obvious superficial differences, not very much has changed, and that some of the circumstances that have changed have not necessarily improved. These central themes are captured in Irving's description of how the image of King George III on the sign of the local inn has been repainted as George Washington. The sign offers a compelling symbol of how things can remain the same underneath even as external appearances transform. The excitement of radical change and the appeal of tradition and continuity that Irving explores in this story have been fertile themes for many American writers. Questions about the competing values and historical narratives that shape American identities were as relevant for Irving's readers as they had been two hundred years earlier for John Smith.

EXPLORING ORIGINS

The question of identity is often tied to the nature of origins. Most of the earliest surviving writings about the Americas are narratives of discovery, a vast and frequently fascinating category of works that includes Samuel de Champlain's chronicles of New France; Thomas Harriot's descriptions of Native customs and natural resources in the Chesapeake Bay region; and—of great interest to Washington Irving—the account of Henry Hudson's explorations written by Robert Juet, the sailor who later mutinied and set Hudson adrift in the bay that bears his name, never to be seen again. Irving's retelling of the Hudson story in his *History of New-York* (1809) greatly mutes the brutality in Juet's narrative to present a colonial history that is notably relaxed and genial, while explicitly marginalizing Native Americans. Virtually all colonization narratives tell a story that is closer to Juet's than to Irving's. These works show that while some elements of influence

Columbus Landing in the Indies, from *La Lettera dell'isole che ha
trovata nouovamenta il re di'spagna,* 1493. This woodcut was created
to accompany a metrical version, by the Florentine poet Giuliano
Dati, of the letter Columbus wrote describing his first voyage. The
image is interesting for its symbolic presentation of European
authority (in the person of Ferdinand of Spain) and its early
conceptualization of what the Taino Indians looked like.

and exchange were peaceful, conflict and violence were major forces shaping
this new world. Individually and collectively, these writings demonstrate that
"discovery" entailed a many-sided process of confrontation and exchange
among heterogeneous European, American, and, eventually, African peoples.
It was out of encounters such as the ones described in these narratives that
the hybrid cultural universe of the Atlantic world began to emerge.

In 1828, Irving published a biography of Christopher Columbus, the Genoese explorer who sailed across the Atlantic four times on behalf of the
Spanish Empire. Columbus's own writings provide a remarkable view into
the radical changes that his voyage of 1492 set in motion. His *Letter to Luis
de Santangel Regarding the First Voyage* (1493)—better known as the Letter
of Discovery—was the first printed account of the territory that Europeans
later came to call America. This riveting description of the unexpected
marvels that Columbus and his crew encountered in the West Indies circulated widely throughout Europe. Columbus lavished praise on the stunning
island mountains, the many different types of trees and beautiful forms of
vegetation, the rivers that appeared to be full of gold, and the fertile soil
promising agricultural riches. He described the indigenous population as
welcoming, loosely organized, and largely defenseless. And in a harbinger of

things to come, he told how "in the first island that I came to, I took some of them by force." He captured these Natives—and took some of them with him on the return voyage to Europe—with the idea that Europeans and Natives could learn to communicate through gestures and, eventually, language. Before long, however, captivity in the service of potentially peaceful exchange yielded to other types of coercion, including enslavement.

Perhaps it was one of Columbus's original captives who in 1494 returned home to relate tales of a new world full of "marvels"—that is, the marvels of Spain, which were as unfamiliar to his Native audience as the marvels of the West Indies were to Columbus's European readers. The man in question was a Taino Indian from the Bahamas, who had been baptized and renamed Diego Colón, after Columbus's son. (Colón is the Spanish version of the family's name.) Diego Colón and another captive served as translators for a large party of Spaniards, around fifteen hundred, who arrived in the Caribbean early in November 1493. In the words of the Spanish historian Andrés Bernáldez, who knew Columbus well and edited his papers, Colón regaled the other Natives with tales of "the things which he had seen in Castile and the marvels of Spain, . . . the great cities and fortresses and churches, . . . the people and horses and animals, . . . the great nobility and wealth of the sovereigns and great lords, . . . the kinds of food, . . . the festivals and tournaments [and] bull-fighting." Colón's story catches in miniature the extraordinary changes that began to occur as natives of Europe encountered natives of the Americas in a sustained way for the first time in recorded history.

Each group of peoples was of course the product and agent of its own history and brought a unique sense of "reality" to the encounter. For example, the year of Columbus's first voyage was also the year of the Spanish *Reconquista*, that is, the final defeat of the Islamic Moors of North Africa who had conquered Spain more than 700 years earlier. The *Reconquista* was just one phase of the centuries-long wars between Christian and Muslim empires that shaped European perceptions of, and actions in, the Americas. Captain John Smith had earned his military title fighting in southeastern Europe against the imperial forces of the Ottoman Turks, then at the height of their power. There were recognizably imperial states in the Americas as well. In the two centuries before Columbus's voyage, the Aztecs had consolidated an empire in present-day Mexico, and over the course of the fourteenth century the Inca Empire had expanded to encompass territory from what is now southern Colombia to Chile. Because of the Aztec and Inca presences, the view of European conquest as a contest of empires is particularly strong in Spanish accounts. The conquistador Hernán Cortés described the sophistication and wealth that existed in the Aztec capital, Tenochtitlán, before he ordered his forces to destroy it. In a more muted way, Smith portrayed English interactions with the Powhatan Indians as the product of their competing imperial projects, with Chief Powhatan undertaking to absorb the English newcomers within his expanding area of influence while Smith struggled to establish dominance.

When the Europeans arrived in the Americas, the indigenous people numbered between fifty million and one hundred million. Mass deaths among the indigenous communities facilitated European expansion. Almost literally from 1492, Native peoples started to die in large numbers. Whole populations plummeted as diseases such as smallpox, measles, and typhus spread throughout the Caribbean and then on the mainland of Central and South America. These diseases became even more lethal as a consequence of war, enslavement, brutal mistreatment, and despair. The rapid introduction of slavery of Native Americans by Europeans, which Columbus helped initiate, reflects both historical practices and contemporary developments. The word "slave" derives from "Slav," which refers to speakers of Slavic languages, in central and eastern Europe; many Slavs were taken as property by Spanish Muslims in the ninth century. Race-based slavery emerged shortly before Columbus's first voyage: the European slave trade in Africa began in 1441, and in 1452 Pope Nicholas V authorized the enslaving of non-Christians. In 1500 slavery was a common form of labor, with variants around the globe, including in Africa and the Americas. Columbus had intended to create a market in enslaved Americans, and a substantial number of Natives were taken as slaves, but ultimately this project failed because too many Native people died. Europeans began transporting small numbers of enslaved Africans to the Americas shortly after arriving there. Those numbers soon multiplied, and the social and cultural features of this new world became even more complex as the slaves introduced the arts and traditions of various African societies.

The impacts in the Americas of disease and of slavery can be seen in miniature in the history of the Caribbean island Hispaniola. The population of Hispaniola (estimated at between one hundred thousand and eight million in 1492) plunged following the Spanish occupation, partly through disease

New World Natives, from an anonymous German woodcut, c. 1505. The text accompanying this detailed early illustration comments on Native Americans and their customs, praising their physical appearance and healthfulness as well as their distaste for both private property and public government. Only in passing does it assert that they kill and eat their enemies, smoking the dead bodies above their fires, as on closer inspection the woodcut indicates.

and partly through abuses of the *encomienda* system, which gave individual Spaniards claims to Native labor and wealth. Faced with this sudden decline in Native workers, Spain introduced African slavery there as early as 1501. In 1522, the first major slave rebellion in the Americas took place on the island, when enslaved African Muslims killed nine Spaniards. From this point forward, slave resistance became commonplace. Nevertheless, by the mid-sixteenth century the Native population had been so completely displaced by African slaves that the Spanish historian Antonio de Herrera called the island "an effigy or an image of Ethiopia itself." Hispaniola was the leading edge of broader devastations and transformations; colonization, disease, and slavery had similarly sweeping effects in many parts of the Americas.

It would be inaccurate to picture indigenous Americans as merely victims suffering an inexorable decline. The motif of the "vanishing Indian" that became prominent in the early nineteenth century misrepresents historical realities, which involved unevenly textured cultural developments. Some indigenous Americans made shrewd use of the European presence to forward their own aims. In 1519, the disaffected Natives in the Aztec Empire threw in their lot with Cortés because they saw a chance to settle the score with their overlord, Montezuma. In New England, the Pequot War of 1637 involved a similar alignment on the English side of such tribes as the Narragansetts and the Mohegans, who had grievances with the militarily aggressive Pequots. The Powhatans of the Chesapeake Bay region and the Iroquois in the Northeast seized on European technology and the European market, adopting novel weaponry (the gun) and incorporating new trade goods into their networks as a means of consolidating advantages gained before the arrival of the colonists. Beginning in the eighteenth century, the Comanches built an empire that dominated other Native groups and contested European (and later United States and Mexican) power in the southern plains and southwestern regions of North America. Above all, Native societies were not static. Even as their populations shrank, indigenous Americans resisted, transformed, and exploited the cultural and social practices that Europeans and Africans brought to the Americas. Eventually, these resilient, resourceful peoples embraced writing and print to protect their communities, advance their interests, and convey their vital place in the world.

Meanwhile, the African population in the Americas was expanding. Although free blacks were a growing presence, most of the Africans were slaves who were often forced into heterogeneous groups that brought together members of various cultures speaking distinct languages. Under the harsh conditions of European domination, they created new forms of expression that retained ties to their cultures of origin. One notable instance of this dynamic process involves the West African figure of Esu Elegbara, the guardian of the crossroads and interpreter of the gods, who appears in works of verbal art created in African communities throughout the Americas. Esu features in narrative praise poems, divination verses, lyrical songs, and prose narratives and is particularly connected with matters of heightened (that is, "literary") language and interpretation. By the eighteenth century, many African Americans practiced Christianity, and the Bible provided a stock of characters and rhetorical postures that they used to articulate their experiences and worldviews and to advocate for their freedom.

LITERARY BACKGROUNDS AND
CONSEQUENCES OF 1492

Apart from the literatures of ancient Greece and Rome, few of the works now regarded as classics of European literature had been produced when Columbus sailed in 1492. Those that did exist can be grouped into a few genres. There were epic poems, such as *Beowulf* (English), *The Song of Roland* (French), and Dante's *Divine Comedy* (Italian); chivalric romances, including *Sir Gawain and the Green Knight* (English); shorter romances, such as the lais of Marie de France; story sequences, including the Italian writer Boccaccio's *Decameron* and the English poet Chaucer's *Canterbury Tales*; sacred lyric poems, such as by Hildegard of Bingen; and sonnets, notably those by the Italian poet Petrarch, who honed the form into a major genre that, during the Renaissance, Shakespeare made important to English literature. Aristotle's and Cicero's works were already widely known, and the revival of Greco-Roman classics that characterized the Renaissance was on the horizon. Augustine's *Confessions* was among the broadly influential works of sacred prose, while secular chronicles and histories attracted many readers. In 1300, Marco Polo's account of his travels to China began to circulate; *The Travels of Sir John Mandeville*, a fabulous account of a journey through the Middle East and beyond, appeared five or six decades later. Published in manuscript before the Gutenberg printing press was invented around 1440, both works are thought to have influenced Christopher Columbus's writings about his "new world."

Beginning with the publication in 1493 of Columbus's Letter of Discovery, the printing press became part of the engine driving European expansion in the Americas. Explorers and adventurers produced a large and intriguing body of literature that communicated the wonders of the new world, described Native societies with varying degrees of accuracy and appreciation, and offered explanations and justifications for numerous colonial projects. In some cases, notably that of the Spanish friar Bartolomé de las Casas, writers also testified about the atrocities being committed against Native peoples. Print increasingly made possible the dissemination of texts rich with imagery and practical knowledge, helping to stir individual imaginations and national ambitions with regard to the West Indies and the Americas and, in a few instances, seeking to limit the negative impact of colonization on indigenous Americans.

Cataclysms such as the devastation of the Indies and the Conquest of Mexico produced not only the Spanish narratives of Columbus, Cortés, and Las Casas but also Native responses. For example, in 1528 anonymous Native writers, working in the Nahuatl language of the Aztecs but using the Roman alphabet introduced by the Spanish, lamented the fall of their capital to Cortés:

> Broken spears lie in the roads;
> we have torn our hair in our grief.
> The houses are roofless now, and their walls
> are red with blood.

No one reading these four lines will easily glorify the conquest of Mexico or of the Americas more generally. Such testimonies offer an essential outlook on this painful history.

At the time of conquest Native Americans had rich oral cultures that valued memory over material means of preserving texts. There were some important exceptions. The Aztecs and a few other groups produced written works in their own languages, though Spanish conquerors destroyed many of the *amoxtli* and other types of Native "books." Many indigenous communities used visual records in subtle and sophisticated ways, with a notable example being the Andean quipu, a type of knotted string. North American recording devices included shellwork belts, known as *wampum*, and painted animal hides, tepees, and shields. The histories and rituals encoded in these devices were translated into spoken language in ways that had significant parallels in what is sometimes called print culture. Scripture was regularly interpreted and delivered in a sermon in much the same manner as a *wampum* belt might be "read" at a treaty conference. Again, a printed narrative might be read aloud, similar to the way that Native tales were recounted; while hymns and ballads were designed for singing and provided an early contact point between European and Native verbal artists.

In addition to taking diverse forms, early American literature reflects the linguistic and cultural range of the colonial world. Spanish, French, German and its variants, and other European languages are prominent in the written archive about North America. Dozens of Native languages left traces, which include evidence of at least eight creation narratives, with notable examples being the Iroquois creation story and the Winnebago trickster cycle included in this volume. Although English eventually became the main language in the United States, and thus the dominant medium of classic American literature, it was a late arrival in the Americas. Likewise, although the New England colonies, founded in the early seventeenth century, have conventionally been regarded as the central source of early American literature, the first North American settlements were established elsewhere many years earlier. The Spanish founded colonies at present-day St. Augustine, Florida (1565), and Santa Fe, New Mexico (1610), and Dutch settlers established New Netherland (1614), which came to include New York City and Albany (1614). All of these cities, which started as colonial outposts, are older than Boston (1630), which was not even the first permanent English settlement in North America. That distinction goes to the Jamestown colony, in Virginia (1607).

The writings of Thomas Harriot and John Smith about Virginia's Chesapeake Bay region are crucial to a full understanding of the English-language literature of the Americas. Harriot produced the first account of England's new world in *A Brief and True Report of the New Found Land of Virginia* (1588), which combines descriptions of marketable commodities, a detailed and often accurate description of Native beliefs and practices, and a narration of how Wingina, the Algonquian headman on Roanoke Island, interacted with the English colonizers and sought to understand the devastating effects of the illnesses that followed in their wake. As noted earlier, John Smith was an enthusiastic and prolific proselytizer for English colonization, instrumental in the establishment of Virginia and influential as well in the founding of

New England. Smith epitomized those proponents of colonization who came from the underclasses in their native countries, and he made a powerful case for the opportunities that America offered them. Energetic and confident, Smith could be subversive, even mutinous, in his writings as in his life. His works present a vision of America as a place where much that was genuinely new might be learned and created. This vision came to maturity in his writings about New England, and helped to shape what many regard as the most influential body of writings from the early period.

LITERARY NEW ENGLAND

The founding of Plymouth Plantation, in 1620, marks a new phase in the literary history of colonial North America. The first months of the Plymouth colony were inauspicious. After landing on the raw Massachusetts shore in November 1620, the Pilgrims braced for winter. They survived this "starving time" with the essential aid of the nearby Wampanoag Indians and their leader, Massasoit. From these "small beginnings," as the colony's leader, William Bradford, refers to them in *Of Plymouth Plantation* (c. 1630), grew a community that later came to be invested with a symbolic significance that far exceeded its size and remote location. The Pilgrims' religious motivation for leaving England is only part of the story. Backed by English investors, the seafaring migration was commercial as well as spiritual. Among the hundred people on the group's ship, the *Mayflower*, almost three times as many were secular settlers as were Separatist Puritans. The persistent tension between the material and spiritual goals of the Plymouth colonists appears in many early writings about the region. For instance, Thomas Morton portrays this conflict in values in *New English Canaan* (1637), where the Plymouth leaders appear not as holy men but as domineering and repressive antagonists of Morton's colony at Ma-re Mount. Morton also conveys a different sensibility about relations with the Natives, expressing little desire to convert them to Christianity and focusing instead on joining with them in May Day festivities. Although Morton probably overstated the ideological differences and minimized the economic rivalry with Plymouth, the contrast suggests a spectrum of colonial responses to their new environment.

Much larger than either Plymouth or Ma-re Mount was the Massachusetts Bay Colony, founded in 1630 by Puritans under John Winthrop. The Massachusetts Bay colonists initially wanted to retain their ties with the Church of England, leading to their designation as non-Separating Congregationalists, which distinguished them from the more radical Separatists at Plymouth. On other issues, they shared basic beliefs with the Pilgrims: both agreed with the Protestant Reformation leader Martin Luther that no pope or bishop had the right to impose any law on a Christian without consent, and both accepted the Reformation theologian John Calvin's view that God freely chose (or "elected") those he would save and those he would damn eternally.

Puritans have a grim reputation as religious zealots, prudes, and killjoys. These conceptions stem from the Calvinist doctrine of election. However,

A	In *Adam's* Fall We Sinned all.	
B	Thy Life to Mend This *Book* Attend.	
C	The *Cat* doth play And after flay.	
D	A *Dog* will bite A Thief at night.	
E	An *Eagles* flight Is out of fight.	
F	The Idle *Fool* Is whipt at School.	
G	As runs the *Glafs* Mans life doth pafs.	
H	My *Book* and *Heart* Shall never part.	
J	*Job* feels the Rod Yet bleffes GOD.	
K	Our *KING* the good No man of blood.	
L	The *Lion* bold The *Lamb* doth hold.	
M	The *Moon* gives light In time of night.	
N	*Nightingales* fing In Time of Spring.	
O	The *Royal Oak* it was the Tree That fav'd His Royal Majeftie.	
P	*Peter* denies His Lord and cries.	
Q	Queen *Efther* comes in Royal State To Save the JEWS from difmal Fate	
R	*Rachol* doth mour. For her firft born.	
S	*Samuel* anoints Whom God appoint:	
T	*Time* cuts down all Both great and fmall.	
U	*Uriah's* beauteous Wife Made *David* feek his Life.	
W	*Whales* in the Sea God's Voice obey.	
X	*Xerxes* the great did die, And fo muft you & I.	
Y	*Youth* forward flips Death fooneft nips.	
Z	*Zacheus* he Did climb the Tree His Lord to fee,	

The New-England Primer (1690). Like other Protestants, Puritans believed that the Bible should be accessible to all believers, and to that end *The New-England Primer* was designed for children learning to read. Benjamin Harris printed the first edition in Boston; a London edition appeared in 1701. Many more editions followed—though very few copies survived.

In the mid-eighteenth century, Benjamin Franklin's Philadelphia print shop sold nearly forty thousand copies of its own later version. This page is from *The New-England Primer, a Reprint of the Earliest Known Edition* (1899), edited by Paul Leicester Ford, which reproduces the one surviving, incomplete copy of the 1727 edition.

counter to the stereotype, Puritans did not necessarily consider most people damned before birth. Instead, they argued that Adam broke the "Covenant of Works"—the promise God made to Adam that he was immortal and could live in Paradise forever as long as he obeyed God's commandments—when he disobeyed and ate of the tree of knowledge of good and evil, thereby bringing sin and death into the world. Their central doctrine was the new "Covenant of Grace," a binding agreement that Jesus Christ made with all people who believed in him and that he sealed with his Crucifixion, promising them eternal life. The New England churches aspired to be more rigorous than others, and this idea of the covenant contributed to the feeling that they were a special few. When John Winthrop in *A Model of Christian Charity* (written 1630) expressed the ideals that he wanted the colonists to embrace, he wrote that the eyes of the world were on them and that they should strive to be an example for all, a "city upon a hill." In their respective histories of Plymouth and Massachusetts Bay, Bradford and Winthrop wished to record the actualization of the founding dream, which was first and foremost a dream of a purified community of mutually supporting Protestant Christians.

In keeping with the doctrine of election, Puritan ministers typically addressed themselves not to the hopelessly unregenerate but to the spiritually indifferent—that is, to the potentially "elect." They spoke to the heart more often than the mind, always distinguishing between heartfelt "saving faith" and "historical," or rational, understanding. While preachers sometimes sought to evoke fear by focusing on the terrors of hell, as the latter-day Puritan Jonathan Edwards famously did in his sermon "Sinners in the Hands of an Angry God" (1741), this method did not reflect the exclusive—or even the main—tenor of Puritan religious life. The considerable joy and love in Puritanism resulted directly from meditation on Christ's redeeming power. The minister-poet Edward Taylor conveys this element of Puritan experience in his rapturous litany of Christ's attributes: "He is altogether lovely in everything, lovely in His person, lovely in His natures, lovely in His properties, lovely in His offices, lovely in His titles, lovely in His practice, lovely in His purchases and lovely in His relations." All of Taylor's art considers the miraculous gift of the Incarnation,

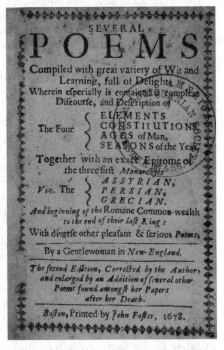

The Tenth Muse. Anne Bradstreet's first book appeared in London in 1650, with the title *The Tenth Muse, Lately Sprung up in America.* There were nine muses in the classical world. In 1678, this second edition of Bradstreet's poems was published in Boston.

reflecting his typically Puritan sensibility. Similar qualities are evident in the works of Anne Bradstreet, a Puritan and the first British North American writer to publish a volume of poetry. Bradstreet confessed her religious doubts to her children, but she emphasized that it was "upon this rock Christ Jesus" that she built her faith.

Religious emotion provided a unifying factor for diverse denominations, leading to the kind of melding that Crèvecœur would later find characteristic of American life. The closest thing in New England to Crèvecœur's ideal was in the Providence colony, which the Puritan theologian Roger Williams helped guide toward a more capacious understanding of religious freedom than was accepted in Plymouth or Massachusetts Bay. Williams insisted that "christenings make not Christians." In other words, as he interpreted the doctrine of election, rituals and displays meant less than inner faith. Accordingly, he helped make Providence a refuge for religious dissenters and outsiders, including Antinomians, Quakers, and Jews. He also worked hard—and for a time, successfully—to establish good relations with the region's Narragansett Indians. However, harmonious relations were shattered in 1675, when King Philip led the Wampanoags and their Narragansett allies to war against the colonies, with devastating effects on both sides. In her captivity narrative, the Puritan settler Mary Rowlandson movingly describes the mutual betrayal experienced by the indigenous people and the colonists.

Just over a decade after Rowland's captivity, King William's War became the first in a series of conflicts between New England and New France that culminated in 1763 with Britain's victory in the French and Indian War. During the intervening decades, colonists regularly fought alongside European troops and Native allies. European state politics informed the fighting, as did religious differences between Protestant England and Catholic France, which infused events that roiled Puritan communities, such as the Salem witchcraft crisis of 1692. That famous and, in a certain sense, defining crisis reflected complex transformations of colonial authority and identity. Though small in comparison to the witch trials that took place in Europe and the British Isles in roughly the same period, the tragic events at Salem, which culminated in the execution of twenty people, loom large in part because of their distinctive features and overdetermined meaning. The trials unfolded as the new royal charter transformed Massachusetts Bay from a colony to a province, shifting power to the metropolis. Meanwhile, rivals to Puritanism were becoming more visible, not only in New France, but also in other British colonies with different religious identities and competing understandings of the relationship between church and state. Maryland, established in 1634, had a strong association with both Catholicism and religious toleration, while Rhode Island, which had grown from Roger Williams's settlement at Providence, was granted a royal charter in 1663. The founding of the Quaker colony of Pennsylvania in 1681 posed an especially strong challenge to the Bay Colony, both because of the rapid growth of Philadelphia into a major hub and because of Quakerism's competing approach to Christian reform.

One of the most controversial features of Quakerism was its embrace of women's religious leadership. This issue resonated in the colony that had banished Anne Hutchinson in 1638 and, some two decades later, went on to execute Mary Dyer, a follower of Hutchinson who later embraced Quaker beliefs and returned to Massachusetts to challenge its authorities. In 1661, shortly after the end of the Commonwealth and the restoration of the monarchy, King Charles II rebuked the Bay Colony for executing Dyer and three male Quakers. Concerns about Puritan intolerance contributed to the new regime's approach to the Massachusetts charter, which unfolded over three decades even as the monarchy underwent a sustained period of instability that culminated in the Glorious Revolution of 1688, when the Catholic King James II was replaced by the Protestant monarchs William and Mary. All these developments contributed in important though indirect ways to the Salem proceedings.

Several men were executed during the Salem crisis, but the majority of the condemned were women. What's more, the first person to be accused was the enslaved woman Tituba, who was practicing folk rituals with a group of Puritan girls when the "afflictions" began. Probably an Indian from the South American mainland, Tituba had arrived in Salem by way of Barbados. In 1656, that island had been the immediate point of origin of the first Quaker evangelists to Massachusetts, who were accused of witchcraft and imprisoned. Though the Puritans understood what was happening to their community in different terms than those suggested here, focusing their fears on the presence of the devil in Massachusetts rather than on social, political, and religious pressures, their writings did at times reflect an awareness that many forces inflamed the crisis. The excerpt from Cotton Mather's *Wonders of the Invisible World* (1693) shows how an internationally renowned Puritan intellectual who was attuned to the new science sought to understand the nature of witchcraft, and gives some insight into this symbolically important moment in early American literary history.

ENLIGHTENMENT IDEALS

The Salem witch trials proved to be a watershed moment, tied to dramatic social and economic changes during the late colonial period. These shifts were gradually matched by transformations in intellectual life. By the early eighteenth century, scientists and philosophers in Europe and the Americas had posed great challenges to seventeenth-century beliefs. Many intellectuals now embraced the power of the human mind to comprehend the universe as never before. What is sometimes called the "modern era"— characterized principally by the gradual supplanting of religious worldviews by scientific and philosophical ideas anchored in experiential knowledge— emerged from efforts to conceive of human existence in new terms. These developments in science and philosophy, known generally as the Enlightenment, did not necessarily lead to secularization. For example, Isaac Newton and John Locke—respectively, the leading English scientist and philosopher of the age—both sought to resolve implicit conflicts between their work and Christian tradition. Newton's study of the laws of motion and gravity had the potential to undermine religious beliefs insofar as it revealed a natural order that was perhaps independent of divine power. Locke's theory of the human mind as a tabula rasa, or blank slate, endowed with powers of perception but without innate content, posed a direct challenge to established forms of Christianity by calling into question the idea of original sin.

Arguing that God worked in reasonable, not necessarily mysterious ways, these thinkers saw nothing heretical in contending that the universe was an orderly system whose laws humanity could comprehend through the application of reason.

Many Enlightenment scientists and philosophers deduced the existence of a supreme being from the construction of the universe rather than from the Bible, a view often called Deism. For many Deists, a harmonious universe could represent the beneficence of God, and this positivity extended to an optimistic view of human nature. Locke said that "our business" here on earth "is not to know all things, but those which concern our conduct," prompting his followers to consider human actions and motives as worthy objects of study. The philosophers of the Scottish Common Sense school built on Locke's insights about human faculties to propose that sympathy and sociability functioned as a kind of emotional glue that could unite communities no longer held together by shared beliefs and traditional structures of authority. Indeed, they claimed that one's supreme moral obligation was to relate to one's fellows through a natural power of sympathy. Adam Smith's *Theory of Moral Sentiments* (1759) was a notably influential contributor to this vein of social analysis. Meanwhile, earlier modes of thought—for instance, Bradford's and Winthrop's penchants for the allegorical and emblematic, with every natural and human event seen as a direct message from God—came to seem anachronistic and quaint.

Interest in ordinary individuals as part of nature and society led to developments in literature. While religiously themed works such as John Milton's *Paradise Lost* (1667) and John Bunyan's *Pilgrim's Progress* (1678) remained popular, the novel began to take a recognizably modern shape in the early eighteenth century. English novelists such as Aphra Behn, Daniel Defoe, Samuel Richardson, Henry Fielding, and Laurence Sterne portrayed emotions and experiences with increasing directness. In the colonies, the influences that were giving birth to the Anglophone novel also engendered new forms of descriptive naturalist and ethnographic writing, exemplified here in selections from Sarah Kemble Knight, Hendrick Aupaumut, and William Bartram. The same confluence of intellectual and social developments also gave rise to nonfiction works such as Benjamin Franklin's *Autobiography* (written between 1771 and 1790).

Modernity has often been characterized as a radical break from faith-based forms of thought. Consider, however, that both the religious Bunyan and the more secular Defoe were among Franklin's literary influences. From the old to the new there were substantial continuities, as well as shifts that were more gradual than immediate. In the first half of the eighteenth century, a number of religious revivals occurred in England and America, but they were fueled by the new emphasis on emotion as a defining component of human experience. For example, the religious fires that burned from 1734 until about 1750 in what became known as the Great Awakening were directly produced by the Locke-inspired cult of feeling that was reshaping narrative prose. Now ministers, echoing the Enlightenment philosophers, argued that humanity's greatest pleasure—indeed, its purpose—was to do good for others and that sympathetic emotions might guarantee future glory. These ideas, a small part of earlier religious thought, acquired a new salience in connection with revivalism.

The most significant figure in transatlantic revivalism was Jonathan Edwards, a leading minister and theologian who helped form this new culture with a series of "awakenings" in and around Northampton, Massachusetts. Edwards's description of these events in *A Faithful Narrative of the Surprising Work of God* (1737) was hugely influential on the movement. Having read Locke, Edwards believed that if his parishioners were to be awakened from their spiritual slumbers they had to experience religion viscerally, not just comprehend it intellectually. In a series of sermons and treatises, Edwards worked to rejuvenate the basic tenets of Calvinism, including that of unconditional election, the sixteenth-century doctrine most difficult for eighteenth-century minds to accept.

George Whitefield, c. 1741, by John Wollaston. Transatlantic revivalist George Whitefield preaching to a crowded meeting during the Great Awakening.

Edwards insisted that such doctrines made sense in terms of Enlightenment science, and he developed what one literary historian has called a "rhetoric of sensation" to persuade his listeners that God's sovereignty was not only the most reasonable doctrine but also the most "delightful" and that it revealed itself to him, in an almost sensuous way, as "exceeding pleasant, bright, and sweet." In carefully reasoned, calmly argued prose, Edwards brought many in his audience to accept that "if the great things of religion are rightly understood, they will affect the heart." This "heart religion," as it later came to be known, involved both the terrors of hell, which Edwards describes in the sermon "Sinners in the Hands of an Angry God," and the joy that his faith brought him, as he expresses it in his "Personal Narrative" (c. 1740). In Edwards's work, the pietist strains of Puritan writing—the embrace of emotion and its verbal expression—were amplified and brought close to similar developments in secular literature. For example, the English writer Samuel Richardson's novel *Pamela; or, Virtue Rewarded* (1740) was a favorite in the Edwards household.

The revivalists' styles of worship proved more welcoming to Native American and African American Christians than the Puritans' styles had been. Nonwhites had greater opportunities for literacy and training for the ministry, and mixed-race and nonwhite congregations were formed in increasing numbers. As a result, the Great Awakening fostered greater mingling of white, red, and black expressive styles in sacred song and speech—including hymnody, whose flourishing during the period also contributed to the growth of secular poetry—and led to the writing of some of the earliest

English-language literature by Native Americans and African Americans. The writers John Marrant, Samson Occom, Hendrick Aupamut, Olaudah Equiano, and Phillis Wheatley emerged from this evangelical melding of cultures. At the same time, a parallel "Indians Great Awakening" revived indigenous spiritual practices and helped catalyze the resistance of leaders such as Sagoyewatha, Pontiac, and Tecumseh to colonial military and cultural power.

PURSUING HAPPINESS

In the second half of the eighteenth century, religion continued to play a major role in many colonists' lives even as politics took on a new importance. After winning the French and Indian War in 1763, Britain consolidated its empire in North America. To help pay for its war debt, the monarchy heavily taxed the colonies. Colonial resentments about increasingly heavy-handed tax policies escalated until April 1775, when the Battles of Lexington and Concord, both in Massachusetts, began the American Revolutionary War against Britain. That summer, representatives from the thirteen British North American colonies convened a Second Continental Congress to take charge of the war effort. In the June 7, 1776, session of this Congress, Richard Henry Lee of Virginia brought a decade of colonial agitation to the boiling point by moving that "these united colonies are, and of a right ought to be, free and independent states." Another Virginian, Thomas Jefferson, led a committee—including John Adams of Massachusetts and Benjamin Franklin of Pennsylvania—that drafted a Declaration of Independence, which was issued on July 4. The heart of this document was the statement that "certain truths are self-evident, that all men are created equal, that they are endowed by their Creator with certain unalienable Rights, that among these are Life, Liberty and the pursuit of Happiness." These words reflect Jefferson's reading of the Scottish Common Sense philosophers, particularly Francis Hutcheson and Lord Kames (Henry Home), who built on Locke's work to argue that a moral sense is common to all humans. This universal sense of right and wrong justified the overthrow of tyrants, the restoration of political order, and the establishment of new covenants—not, as Bradford and Winthrop would have argued, for the glory of God, but, as the Declaration argued, for the individual's right to happiness on earth.

In January 1776 the young journalist Thomas Paine published his pamphlet *Common Sense*, which proved hugely influential in tipping the scales toward revolution. Though Paine probably did not choose his title to allude to the Scottish philosophers who were so important for Jefferson and other patriot leaders, his manifesto invoked similar ideas. In arguing that separation from England was the colonists' only reasonable course and that "the Almighty" had planted these feelings in us "for good and wise purposes," Paine appealed to basic tenets of the Enlightenment. He had emigrated from England to America in 1774 with a letter of recommendation from Benjamin Franklin. Franklin was, among many other things, a successful newspaper editor and printer, and Paine was quickly hired to edit the *Pennsylvania Magazine*, one of the new periodicals transforming the literary scene. The first newspaper in the colonies had appeared in 1704, and by the time of the

The Destruction of Tea at Boston Harbor, lithograph by Nathaniel Currier. The Boston Tea Party of 1763, when colonists, some disguised as Native Americans, protested a new British tax on tea and other commodities.

Revolution there were almost fifty papers and forty magazines. Paine's magazine work helped shape a plain style that proved effective in catalyzing revolution. He was the most prominent of a number of writers who took advantage of the transformation in print culture that was to make modern authorship possible.

After the former colonists' victory over the British in 1783, people from greatly different backgrounds and of varied nationalities now found reasons to call themselves "Americans." America, as Washington Irving would later note, was a "logocracy," a polity based in and governed by words, and the political events of the 1770s presented a distinctive opportunity for writers. The most significant works of the period are political writings, and among the most notable of these are the essays that the statesmen Alexander Hamilton, John Jay, and James Madison wrote for New York newspapers in 1787–88 in support of the new federal Constitution, which are collectively known as *The Federalist* or *The Federalist Papers*. The impact of the revolution on the rise of early national literature can also be seen in the career of Philip Freneau, who aspired to be a full-time writer, combining journalism with belles lettres. Though he failed to sustain himself with his pen, Freneau made numerous contributions to the literature of the Revolution. His volume *Poems Written Chiefly during the Late War* (1786) contains notable patriotic works, and his later political poetry includes a tribute to Thomas Paine.

Women writers, too, expressed a revolutionary political sensibility. In the most famous letter of her lively and informative correspondence with her husband, John, Abigail Adams exhorted the Second Continental Congress to "remember the Ladies" in the new code of laws they were then framing. John and his fellows largely failed to heed Abigail's call. However, inspired by

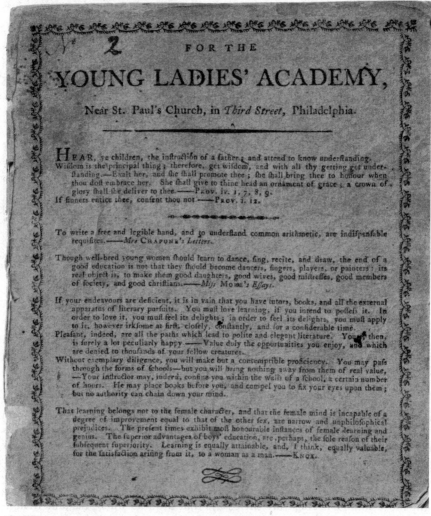

2

FOR THE

YOUNG LADIES' ACADEMY,

Near St. Paul's Church, in *Third Street*, Philadelphia.

HEAR, ye children, the instruction of a father; and attend to know understanding. Wisdom is the principal thing; therefore, get wisdom, and with all thy getting get understanding.—Exalt her, and she shall promote thee; she shall bring thee to honour when thou dost embrace her. She shall give to thine head an ornament of grace; a crown of glory shall she deliver to thee.——Prov. iv. 1, 7, 8, 9.
If sinners entice thee, consent thou not——Prov. i. 12.

To write a free and legible hand, and to understand common arithmetic, are indispensable requisites.——*Mrs* Chapone's *Letters*.

Though well-bred young women should learn to dance, sing, recite, and draw, the end of a good education is not that they should become dancers, singers, players, or painters; its real object is, to make them good daughters, good wives, good mistresses, good members of society, and good christians.——*Miss* More's *Essays*.

If your endeavours are deficient, it is in vain that you have tutors, books, and all the external apparatus of literary pursuits. You must love learning, if you intend to possess it. In order to love it, you must feel its delights; in order to feel its delights, you must apply to it, however irksome at first, closely, constantly, and for a considerable time. Pleasant, indeed, are all the paths which lead to polite and elegant literature. Young then, is surely a lot peculiarly happy —— Value duly the opportunities you enjoy, and which are denied to thousands of your fellow creatures. Without exemplary diligence, you will make but a contemptible proficiency. You may pass through the forms of schools—but you will bring nothing away from them of real value. —Your instructor may, indeed, confine you within the walls of a school, a certain number of hours. He may place books before you, and compel you to fix your eyes upon them; but no authority can chain down your mind.

That learning belongs not to the female character, and that the female mind is incapable of a degree of improvement equal to that of the other sex, are narrow and unphilosophical prejudices. The present times exhibit most honourable instances of female learning and genius. The superior advantages of boys' education, are, perhaps, the sole reason of their subsequent superiority. Learning is equally attainable, and, I think, equally valuable, for the satisfaction arising from it, to a woman as a man.——Knox.

Syllabus of lectures from the Young Ladies' Academy, in Philadelphia, 1787. Educational opportunities for girls expanded after the American Revolution. The Young Ladies' Academy opened in 1787, attracting great interest from leaders in what was then the nation's capital.

Enlightenment ideals of reason and equality, women such as Annis Boudinot Stockton, Judith Sargent Murray, Susanna Rowson, and Hannah Webster Foster wrote works exploring women's rights as citizens. Murray tackled the subject in her essays on the intellectual capacities of women, whereas Stockton's poems, as well as the writings of Rowson and Foster, explored the social and legal constraints on women and considered their right to be equal partners in the new nation's democratic experiment. Like such self-consciously "American" productions as Royall Tyler's play *The Contrast* (first performed 1787) and Franklin's *Autobiography*, these works mark the beginning of a new sense of national identity.

Not all the responses to the new order were enthusiastic or uncritical. For example, fiction offered an avenue for biting social critique. Often considered the first American novel, William Hill Brown's *The Power of Sympathy* was published in 1789, the year that the first government under the new Constitution was established. It tells an anti-utopian tale of incest and suicide. Charles Brockden Brown adapted the conventions of Gothic fiction to explore the dangers and limits of democratic republicanism in works such as his novella *Memoirs of Carwin, the Biloquist* (1803–05), a prequel to his better-known novel *Wieland; or The Transformation: An American Tale* (1798), which develops Carwin's story in tragic ways. Rowson's *Charlotte Temple* (1791) and Foster's *The Coquette* (1797) were important precursors of the many popular sentimental novels of the nineteenth century—most famously, Harriet Beecher Stowe's antislavery novel *Uncle Tom's Cabin* (1852)—that carried powerful social messages.

Perhaps the most hopeful aspects of the Revolution were represented by Benjamin Franklin, whose reputation continued to grow after his death, in 1790. As parts of his *Autobiography* appeared in print in 1791 and 1818— the full text finally became available in 1868—Franklin increasingly came to represent the promise of the Enlightenment in America. He was self-educated, social, assured, a man of the world, ambitious, public-spirited, speculative about the nature of the universe, and in matters of religion content "to observe the actual conduct of humanity rather than to debate supernatural matters that are unprovable"—a stance that John Locke had earlier endorsed. Franklin always presented himself as depending on first-hand experience, too worldly-wise to be caught off guard, and minding "the main chance" (i.e., for personal gain), as a Franklinian character in Tyler's *The Contrast* counsels. These aspects of Franklin's persona, however, belie another side of him and of the eighteenth century: an idealistic assumption about the common good. He absorbed this sense partly from the works of Cotton Mather, which he encountered during his Boston youth, and it forms the basis of the American Revolution's great public documents, especially the Declaration of Independence.

The Revolution established the United States as an independent nation with ideals such as freedom and equality that were both ambitious and deeply ambiguous. The only people who consistently possessed the right to vote in the new government were white men who owned property. Most African Americans were enslaved, and many Native communities were being pushed off their lands. Yet Revolutionary principles appealed to some writers who suffered from their limited application. In 1774, the year she was manumitted, the poet Phillis Wheatley wrote a letter to the Mohegan leader and Presbyterian minister Samson Occom that was later printed in a dozen colonial newspapers. Here Wheatley posited that "in every human Breast, God has implanted a Principle, which we call Love of Freedom; it is impatient of Oppression, and pants for Deliverance." Though they sometimes used language similar to Wheatley's, Revolutionary leaders held conflicting views about slavery. George Washington, the first U.S. president, freed his slaves in his will. Thomas Jefferson, the third president, liberated just five slaves, leaving the vast majority in bondage at his death. Benjamin Franklin owned slaves for many years. He embraced the antislavery cause late in life, and in 1787 became the president of the first abolitionist organization in the United States. John Adams, the second U.S. president, never owned slaves and sought to gradually end the system through legislation, an effort that succeeded in some places. Even Adams, however, was uneasy with the Quaker-led abolitionist movement, whose at times confrontational strategies he believed counterproductive. The rising urgency of the abolitionists reflected changing realities. After the inventor Eli Whitney patented the cotton gin in 1794, the slave system gained a new lease on its brutal life. The end of the Atlantic slave trade in 1807 led, not to slavery's eventual demise as Adams and many others in the founding generation had hoped, but to forms of enslavement that in some ways were even crueler than before.

The conditions for many Native Americans also worsened in the nineteenth century. Various eastern tribes had sided with the British during the Revolution, driven by their vulnerability to colonial expansion. After the British defeat, they were exposed to the vengeance and greed of white Americans. Entire tribes were systematically displaced from their traditional territories, pushed ever farther west, or forced onto reservations. In an effort to resist the United States' encroachments on Native territory, the confederacy headed by Shawnee leader Tecumseh sided with the British in the War of 1812, a two-and-a-half-year conflict that resolved issues left from the Revolution with a U.S. victory. Meanwhile, Tecumseh's confederation collapsed after American forces killed him in 1813. "Indian Removal" was vigorously debated in the 1820s, with anti-Removal activism emerging as a major social movement. Eventually the movement failed, and Removal became the policy of the federal government.

In 1820, freedom and equality remained future prospects for multitudes of Americans. Many white men still could not vote unless they owned property, though restrictions lessened more quickly over the next decade as universal white manhood suffrage became a reality. Women could not vote, and while the educational opportunities for white women were expanding, their legal status remained sharply limited. They were wards of their fathers until marriage, at which point their legal identities were merged with their husbands', so that they could not own property or keep any wages they earned. Yet many people embraced the idea that with the application of intelligence the principles of liberty could be extended and the human lot improved. This "progressive" or "perfectibilist" spirit was fostered in some places by newer liberal Churches such as the Unitarians and Universalists, as well as the more established Quakers. Imaginative energy flowed into extending the principles of liberty codified by the Revolutionary generation and correcting a variety of institutional and social injustices. In addition to the causes previously mentioned, post-Revolutionary social movements targeted the misuse of prisons, the use of capital punishment, the existence of war, and the treatment of the blind and disabled. Many works of literature reflected on this progressive sensibility, whether to foster it or to question its premises.

*

While at the start of the period covered in this volume "America" was merely notional—and its literature even more so—by 1820 "American literature" had come to mean something fairly specific: the poems, short stories, novels, essays, orations, plays, and other works produced by authors who hailed from, or resided in, the United States of America. As this list of genres suggests, "literature" itself had come to resemble its contemporary meaning more closely than it did in 1492. Printed works had become far more accessible, giving rise to an increasingly robust literary marketplace that featured both locally produced works and influential writings from across the Atlantic. Technological innovations such as the cylinder press created sweeping transformations in the book market, and new kinds of writers (women, African Americans, Native Americans, laborers) were finding outlets for their creations. All the while American literature continued to be shaped by its formation in the Atlantic world's crucible of cultures, its distinctive configuration of the sacred and the secular, the influence of the American Revolution, and the intertwined histories of empire and nation.

BEGINNINGS TO 1820

TEXTS	CONTEXTS
Peoples indigenous to the Americas orally perform and transmit various "literary" genres, including speeches, songs, and stories	
	1000–1300 Anasazi communities inhabit southwestern regions
	1492 Christopher Columbus arrives in the Bahamas • An estimated 4–7 million Native Americans in what is now the United States, including Alaska
1493 Columbus, **"Letter to Luis de Santangel Regarding the First Voyage"**	
	1500 Native American populations begin to be ravaged by European diseases • Enslaved Africans begin arriving in small numbers
	1514 Bartolomé de las Casas petitions Spanish Crown to treat Native American peoples as humanely as other subject populations
	1519–21 Cortés conquers Aztecs in Mexico
	1526 Spanish explorers bring first African slaves to South Carolina
	1539 First printing press in the Americas set up in Mexico City • Hernando de Soto invades Florida
1542 Álvar Núñez Cabeza de Vaca, *The Relation of Álvar Núñez Cabeza de Vaca*	
1552 Bartolomé de las Casas, *The Very Brief Relation of the Devastation of the Indies*	
	1558–1603 Reign of Elizabeth I
	1584 Walter Raleigh lands on "island" of Roanoke; names it "Virginia" for Queen Elizabeth (sometimes called the Virgin Queen)
	1603–13 Samuel de Champlain explores the Saint Lawrence River; founds Québec
	1607 Jamestown is established in Virginia • Powhatan confederacy saves colonists from starving; teaches them to plant tobacco
	1619 Twenty Africans arrive in Jamestown on a Dutch vessel as indentured servants; they are the first known Africans in a British colony
	1620 *Mayflower* drops anchor in Plymouth Harbor
	1621 First Thanksgiving, at Plymouth

Boldface titles indicate works in the anthology.

TEXTS	CONTEXTS
1624 John Smith, *The General History of Virginia, New England, and the Summer Isles*	
1630 John Winthrop, "A Model of Christian Charity" (pub. 1838)	1630–43 Immigration of English Puritans to Massachusetts Bay
1630–50 William Bradford writes *Of Plymouth Plantation* (pub. 1856)	1634 The first English settlers arrive in Maryland aboard *The Ark* and *The Dove*
1637 Thomas Morton, *New English Canaan*	1637 Pequot War
1640 Bay Psalm Book	1638 Anne Hutchinson banished from Bay Colony for challenging Puritan beliefs
1643 Roger Williams, *A Key into the Language of America*	1642–51 English Civil War
1650 Anne Bradstreet, *The Tenth Muse*	1649 Execution of Charles I
1662 Michael Wigglesworth, *The Day of Doom*	1660 Restoration of British monarchy
1673–1729 Samuel Sewall keeps his *Diary* (pub. 1878–82)	1663 Royal Charter granted to Rhode Island (and Providence Plantation)
	1675–76 King Philip's War destroys power of Native American tribes in New England
	1681 William Penn founds Pennsylvania
1682 Mary Rowlandson's *Narrative of the Captivity and Restoration*	
1682–1725 Edward Taylor writing his *Preparatory Meditations* (pub. 1939, 1960)	1689–97 King William's War (first of four colonial wars involving France, Britain, and Spain)
	1691 New royal charter creates the Province of Massachusetts Bay, which includes Plymouth
	1692 Salem witchcraft trials
1702 Cotton Mather, *Magnalia Christi Americana*	
	1718 French found New Orleans
	1726–56 The Great Awakening
1741 Jonathan Edwards, *Sinners in the Hands of an Angry God*	1741 Vitus Bering discovers Alaska
	1755–63 French and Indian Wars
1768 Samson Occom, *A Short Narrative of My Life* (pub. 1982)	
1771–90 Benjamin Franklin continues his *Autobiography* (Part I pub. 1818)	
1773 Phillis Wheatley, *Poems on Various Subjects*	1773 Boston Tea Party
1774–83 John and Abigail Adams exchange letters (pub. 1840, 1875)	
	1775–83 American Revolutionary War

TEXTS	CONTEXTS
1776 Thomas Paine, ***Common Sense***	1776 Declaration of Independence
1780s Annis Boudinot Stockton publishes poems in magazines and newspapers	
1782 J. Hector St. John de Crèvecoeur, ***Letters from an American Farmer***	
	1783 Britain opens "Old Northwest" (region south of Great Lakes) to United States after Treaty of Paris ends American Revolution
1786 Philip Freneau, ***Poems***	
1787 Thomas Jefferson, *Notes on the State of Virginia* • Royall Tyler, *The Contrast*	**1787** U.S. Constitution adopted
1787–88 ***The Federalist*** papers	
1789 Olaudah Equiano, ***The Interesting Narrative of the Life of Olaudah Equiano***	**1789** George Washington elected first president
1790 Judith Sargent Murray, ***On the Equality of the Sexes***	
	1791 Washington, D.C., established as U.S. capital
1797 Hannah Foster, *The Coquette*	
1803–05 Charles Brockden Brown, ***Memoirs of Carwin***	**1803** United States buys Louisiana Territory from France
	1812–14 War of 1812 (against England)
1819 Washington Irving, *Rip Van Winkle*	**1819** Spain exchanges the Florida Territory for U.S. assumption of $5 million in debts • Missouri asks to be admitted as a slave state, sparking a crisis resolved the next year through the Missouri Compromise

Native American Oral Literature

The languages, political economies, and religious beliefs of Native American peoples are extremely diverse, and so are their tales, orations, songs, chants, and other oral genres. Examples of oral works include the trickster tale cycles of the Winnebago Indians (or Ho-Chunks), Apache jokes, Hopi personal naming and grievance chants, Yaqui deer songs, and Yuman dream songs. Many genres have a religious or spiritual dimension, including Piman shamanic chants, Iroquois condolence rituals, Navajo curing and blessing chants, and Chippewa songs of the Great Medicine Society. Most of the works were not translated into alphabetic forms until long after the arrival of Europeans, and the circumstances of their initial creation and development are largely unknown. The use of written records in the precontact Americas was relatively circumscribed, and European conquerors systematically destroyed the bodies of writing in places such as Tenochtitlán (present-day Mexico City), leaving just a handful of the pictograph codices known as *amoxtli* to carry forward pre-Columbian practices. Other indigenous American recording devices include Andean *quipu*, which are colored, knotted strings used to represent a numeric system. In North America, painted hides or bark and wampum belts made of shell could serve as prompts for the recitation of tales or in treaty negotiations and other ceremonies. These nonalphabetic texts share some of the mnemonic and narrative functions of literature.

Although the term "literature" comes from the Latin *littera*, "letter," and so has been linked to alphabetic writing, all literature has roots in the oral arts. In keeping with Aristotle's *Poetics* (c. 335 B.C.E.), the earliest surviving work of literary theory, forms of Western literature have traditionally been grouped into lyric, which takes its name from the lyre, a stringed instrument used by the ancient Greeks to accompany a song or recitation; drama, which originated in the religious cultures of ancient Greece and the medieval Christian Church; and epic (more broadly, narrative), developed in and for oral performance. (The first works of Euro-American literature, the *Vinland Sagas* of the thirteenth century, are epics.) Rhetoric and oratory, which Aristotle treated separately from the other forms because of their prominent and distinctive place in ancient Greek culture, also involve the spoken word. There are parallels as well as differences between these Aristotelian genres and the types of oral literature created by the earliest American societies.

From first contact, Europeans were intrigued by indigenous oral performances and sought to translate them into alphabetic written forms. Christopher Columbus and the explorers who came after him described the formal speeches of Native leaders, even though they often did not understand their meaning. Over time, Native artists taught Europeans and European Americans to recognize other kinds of verbal art, such as creation tales and poetic songs. Eventually collaboration and indigenous authorship became more common. Today scholars are actively studying pre-Columbian history and art, and the sources and traditions of the most ancient texts from the American hemisphere are gradually coming to be better understood.

The archive of Native American oral genres continues to expand as new instances are identified in the written record or transcribed in a modern form. The selections in this cluster represent some genres that were common in the repertoires of many North American indigenous societies before 1820: creation and trickster tales, orations, and songs (here rendered as poems). Native American creation stories serve Native cultures much as the Book of Genesis serves the Judeo-Christian world: they posit a general outlook and offer perspectives on what life is and how to understand it. All Native peoples have stories of the earliest times; reprinted here is one from the Iroquois of the Northeast. Like creation stories, trickster tales are among the most ancient elements of Native American cultures, and they have survived because they provide both pleasure and instruction. The term "trickster" is often used to describe a wandering, bawdy, gluttonous, and obscene figure, a threat to order everywhere. Yet a trickster can also be a culture hero, one who long ago helped establish the order of the world that we know today, and in this way as well trickster tales resemble creation stories. The qualities of this paradoxical figure—both creator and destroyer of order—are on display in the selection from the Winnebago trickster cycle included in this section.

Oratory was the first Native American genre that Europeans recognized as a verbal art. Formalized speech is a common feature of human cultures, notably in diplomatic settings, whether a reception at a European court or a performance of an Iroquois condolence ritual. The formalized modes of address that Native Americans used in their early encounters with Europeans were often lavishly described in exploration narratives. One reason such scenes were central in Renaissance-era accounts is that the writers were imitating classical historiography, with its emphasis on oratory. As set pieces in their narratives, the writers included moving and aesthetically pleasing speeches based more or less loosely on memory and other sources. "Powhatan's Discourse of Peace and War," by John Smith, and "King Philip's Speech," by William Apess, are reconstructed works that provide narrative drama in their original contexts and stand alone as effective examples of Native eloquence.

The poems included here were transcribed by Euro-Americans in the eighteenth and early nineteenth centuries, reflecting an evolving approach to Native American oral genres. While the three recorders of these works served as diplomats and, in one case, as a missionary, they took an active interest in indigenous verbal arts. At the time, a ballad revival in Britain had awakened a curiosity about oral traditions and popular culture, a curiosity that fed into literary Romanticism. Transcriber-authors took indigenous forms from their ritual or other performance contexts and brought them in written form to non-Native audiences. These transcribers often collaborated with the artists to present something of the larger contexts and significances of the works to readers.

The selections in this cluster illustrate the variety of ways that Native American oral literature has been experienced historically, and suggest some of the pleasures and complexities involved in its reception today. Whether reconstructed from memory, recorded with the aid of a translator, or produced by Native authors, they provide insight into the verbal arts of pre-Columbian America as they have survived to the present. The more modern works included here were created with the involvement of indigenous verbal artists, and their sources can be traced to the period before 1820 covered by this volume.

Stories of the Beginning of the World

THE IROQUOIS CREATION STORY

The people known collectively as the Iroquois (as the French called them), or the Five Nations (as the English called them), were made up of the Mohawk, Seneca, Oneida, Onondaga, and Cayuga nations. This confederacy may have formed in the thirteenth or fourteenth century. In the eighteenth century, the Tuscarora of North Carolina joined the confederacy, which became the Six Nations. The heart of Iroquois country lies in what is now upstate New York, west of the Hudson River. At different times in its long history "the ambiguous Iroquois Empire," as one scholar has termed it, extended around Lake Ontario, including parts of what is now Canada, and south into present-day Pennsylvania. The Six Nations called themselves People of the Longhouse (*Haudenosaunee* in Seneca, *Kanosoni* in Mohawk), in reference to their primary type of dwelling. Their longhouses were about twenty feet wide and from forty to two hundred feet long, accommodating several families who shared cooking fires. The largest Iroquois towns included as many as two thousand people.

The Iroquois creation story exists in some twenty-five written or printed versions, making it one of the best-known instances of Native American oral literature. The Frenchman Gabriel Sagard first translated and transcribed the tale in 1623. Two centuries later, David Cusick became the first Native person to write it down. Cusick published the version included here on the eve of Andrew Jackson's election to the presidency, and he was well aware of Jackson's stated intention of "removing"

Atotarho. This is one of four engravings that David Cusick included in the second edition (1828) of *Sketches of the Ancient History of the Six Nations*. It shows the war chief of the Onondagas, Atotarho, said to be a sorcerer, with a twisted body and snakes in his hair. Several times Atotarho rejected pleas from the Great Peacemaker, Deganawidah, and his follower, Hiawatha, that he join them in uniting the Iroquois. Finally, after they healed him and combed the tangles from his hair, he agreed and became the traditional "firekeeper"—tender of the sacred fire—of the Iroquois Confederacy.

eastern Indians to lands west of the Mississippi. Perhaps because the Iroquois were under intensifying pressure from white settlement, Cusick's version emphasizes the conflict between the twins Enigorio, the good mind, and Enigonhahetgea, the bad mind. Although the story involves monsters and supernatural events, Cusick calls the work a history, because it tells the history of the Iroquois Confederacy.

David Cusick was born around 1780 on the Oneida Reservation in central New York, in Madison County, to a Tuscorora family. His father, Nicholas, an important leader among his people, was a Christian who had served on the American side during the Revolution. Educated by the missionary Samuel Kirkland, David Cusick became a physician and an artist. The woodcuts at the front of the second edition (1828) of his *Sketches of the Ancient History of the Six Nations* are his work. Cusick's *Sketches* was well known in its time and served as an important source for Henry Rowe Schoolcraft's influential *Notes on the Iroquois* (1847), which shaped the literary culture of the day. In his preface to that work, Schoolcraft wrote that "no nation of the widely spread red race of America, has displayed so high and heroic a love of liberty, united with the true art of government, and personal energy and stamina of character, as the Iroquois."

Part I of Cusick's *Sketches*, excerpted here, deals with the foundation and establishment of the Iroquois world. Parts II and III present the ancient Iroquois as defending themselves against both monsters and other tribes by means that may have resonated with the Iroquois defense against expansionist Americans.

The Iroquois Creation Story[1]

A Tale of the Foundation of the Great Island, Now North America;— the Two Infants Born, and the Creation of the Universe

Among the ancients there were two worlds in existence. The lower world was in great darkness;—the possession of the great monster; but the upper world was inhabited by mankind; and there was a woman conceived[2] and would have the twin born. When her travail drew near, and her situation seemed to produce a great distress on her mind, and she was induced by some of her relations to lay herself on a mattress which was prepared, so as to gain refreshments to her wearied body; but while she was asleep the very place sunk down towards the dark world.[3] The monsters of the great water were alarmed at her appearance of descending to the lower world; in consequence all the species of the creatures were immediately collected into where it was expected she would fall. When the monsters were assembled, and they made consultation, one of them was appointed in haste to search the great deep, in order to procure some earth, if it could be obtained; accordingly the monster descends, which succeeds, and returns to the place. Another requisition was presented, who would be capable to secure the woman from the terrors of the great water, but none was able to comply except a large turtle

---

1. The text is from the first edition of *Sketches of the Ancient History of the Six Nations* (1827).
2. I.e., a woman, known as Sky Woman, who became pregnant without sexual activity. "Mankind": humans, although they have different powers than those of humans as we understand them. "The great monster": or monsters, undefined

creatures. In other versions, the "monsters" are some type of familiar animal; here, Cusick conveys the mystery and danger in the unformed universe.
3. Other versions have Sky Woman either being pushed out of the upper world or accidentally falling.

came forward and made proposal to them to endure her lasting weight, which was accepted. The woman was yet descending from a great distance. The turtle executes upon the spot, and a small quantity of earth was varnished on the back part of the turtle. The woman alights on the seat prepared, and she receives a satisfaction.[4] While holding her, the turtle increased every moment and became a considerable island of earth, and apparently covered with small bushes. The woman remained in a state of unlimited darkness, and she was overtaken by her travail to which she was subject. While she was in the limits of distress one of the infants in her womb was moved by an evil opinion and he was determined to pass out under the side of the parent's arm, and the other infant in vain endeavoured to prevent his design.[5] The woman was in a painful condition during the time of their disputes, and the infants entered the dark world by compulsion, and their parent expired in a few moments. They had the power of sustenance without a nurse, and remained in the dark regions. After a time the turtle increased to a great Island and the infants were grown up, and one of them possessed with a gentle disposition, and named ENIGORIO, i.e. the good mind. The other youth possessed an insolence of character, and was named ENIGONHAHET-GEA, i.e. the bad mind.[6] The good mind was not contented to remain in a dark situation, and he was anxious to create a great light in the dark world; but the bad mind was desirous that the world should remain in a natural state. The good mind determines to prosecute his designs, and therefore commences the work of creation. At first he took the parent's head, (the deceased) of which he created an orb, and established it in the centre of the firmament, and it became of a very superior nature to bestow light to the new world, (now the sun) and again he took the remnant of the body and formed another orb, which was inferior to the light (now moon). In the orb a cloud of legs appeared to prove it was the body of the good mind, (parent). The former was to give light to the day and the latter to the night; and he also created numerous spots of light, (now stars): these were to regulate the days, nights, seasons, years, etc. Whenever the light extended to the dark world the monsters were displeased and immediately concealed themselves in the deep places, lest they should be discovered by some human beings. The good mind continued the works of creation, and he formed numerous creeks and rivers on the Great Island, and then created numerous species of animals of the smallest and the greatest, to inhabit the forests, and fishes of all kinds to inhabit the waters. When he had made the universe he was in doubt respecting some being to possess the Great Island; and he formed two images of the dust of the ground in his own likeness, male and female,

---

4. I.e., she lands safely, without harm.
5. Other versions of the story have Sky Woman give birth to a daughter, who again becomes supernaturally pregnant (perhaps by the spirit of the turtle), and it is *she* who conceives the twins. The twins argue even in the womb, the Evil Twin deciding not to be born in the normal way but to burst through his mother's side, which leads to her death. The theme of rival twins is widespread in the Americas.
6. More commonly, the Good Twin is called Tharonhiawagon (Sky-Grasper, Creator, or Upholder of the Heavens), and the Evil Twin is

named Tawiscaron (Evil-Minded, Flint, Ice, Patron of Winter, or various disasters). Cusick's Enigorio is a rough translation of the Tuscarora word for "good-minded" into Mohawk, and his Enigonhahetgea is an equally rough translation into Seneca, Onondaga, or Cayuga of the Tuscarora word for "bad-minded." Cusick has probably changed the Tuscarora words best known to him into these other Iroquois languages because they were considered to be more prestigious than Tuscarora, the Tuscaroras having only recently joined the Iroquois Confederacy.

and by his breathing into their nostrils he gave them the living souls, and named them EA-GWE-HOWE, i.e., a real people;[7] and he gave the Great Island all the animals of game for their maintenance and he appointed thunder to water the earth by frequent rains, agreeable of the nature of the system; after this the Island became fruitful and vegetation afforded the animals subsistence. The bad mind, while his brother was making the universe, went throughout the Island and made numerous high mountains and falls of water, and great steeps, and also creates various reptiles which would be injurious to mankind; but the good mind restored the Island to its former condition. The bad mind proceeded further in his motives and he made two images of clay in the form of mankind; but while he was giving them existence they became apes;[8] and when he had not the power to create mankind he was envious against his brother; and again he made two of clay. The good mind discovered his brother's contrivances, and aided in giving them living souls, (it is said these had the most knowledge of good and evil). The good mind now accomplishes the works of creation, notwithstanding the imaginations of the bad mind were continually evil; and he attempted to enclose all the animals of game in the earth, so as to deprive them from mankind; but the good mind released them from confinement, (the animals were dispersed, and traces of them were made on the rocks near the cave where it was closed). The good mind experiences that his brother was at variance with the works of creation, and feels not disposed to favor any of his proceedings, but gives admonitions of his future state. Afterwards the good mind requested his brother to accompany him, as he was proposed to inspect the game, etc., but when a short distance from their moninal residence,[9] the bad mind became so unmanly that he could not conduct his brother any more.[1] The bad mind offered a challenge to his brother and resolved that who gains the victory should govern the universe; and appointed a day to meet the contest. The good mind was willing to submit to the offer, and he enters the reconciliation with his brother; which he falsely mentions that by whipping with flags would destroy his temporal life;[2] and he earnestly solicits his brother also to notice the instrument of death, which he manifestly relates by the use of deer horns, beating his body he would expire. On the day appointed the engagement commenced, which lasted for two days: after pulling up the trees and mountains as the track of a terrible whirlwind, at last the good mind gained the victory by using the horns, as mentioned the instrument of death, which he succeeded in deceiving his brother and he crushed him in the earth; and the last words uttered from the bad mind were, that he would have equal power over the souls of mankind after death; and

7. Humans. "EA-GWE-HOWE": Tuscarora term used by speakers of all the languages of the Six Nations; today, it simply means Indian or Indians.
8. Cusick may have seen an ape or a depiction of apes (there are no apes native to the New World) and decided to name them as the creatures made by the Evil Twin in contrast to the humans made by the Good Twin. Some later renditions of the Iroquois creation story also refer to apes at this point in the narrative.
9. Cusick perhaps means their nominal (named

or designated) residence.
1. I.e., the Evil Twin became so rude and obnoxious that the Good Twin could not lead ("conduct") his brother to the appointed place any longer.
2. The Good Twin tells his brother that he can be killed by being beaten with corn stalks, rushes, reeds, or cattails. Cusick calls this a deception; other accounts treat it as a confession of weakness. Next, the Evil Twin admits that he would die if beaten with the antlers of deer.

he sinks down to eternal doom, and became the Evil Spirit.[3] After this tumult the good mind repaired to the battle ground, and then visited the people and retires from the earth.[4]

3. This event may reflect an awareness of the Christian belief in the devil as the ultimate evil spirit, ruler over the lower depths.

4. Other versions go on to say that the Good Twin teaches the people how to grow corn and how to avoid harm by means of prayer and ritual.

TRICKSTER TALES

FROM THE WINNEBAGO TRICKSTER CYCLE

The Winnebagos, or Ho-Chunks, came to their homelands—at the western end of what is now Green Bay, Wisconsin—from some more southeasterly location perhaps a thousand years ago. They lived by hunting and fishing; by planting corn, squash, and beans; and by gathering wild rice and berries. The French explorer Jean Nicolet is credited as their first European contact, in 1634. The English name "Winnebago" comes from the Algonquian people's name for the tribe, "people of the dirty water," which may simply refer to the strong smell of Wisconsin's Lake Winnebago and Fox River in the summer. The Ho-Chunks' name for themselves, "Ho-chungra," means "people of the parent speech," or "people of the Big Voice." Now geographically divided—mainly between Wisconsin and Nebraska—as a consequence of colonization and the provisions of nineteenth-century treaties, the Ho-Chunks claim that their ancestors played an important role in the creation and preservation of the large, mysterious earthen mounds that exist along the Mississippi River and throughout the Midwest.

Winnebago culture is rich in trickster tales. The story reprinted here comes from *The Trickster: A Study in American Indian Mythology* (1956), a collection of forty-nine Winnebago trickster stories edited by the American cultural anthropologist and folklorist Paul Radin. A student of the eminent anthropologist Franz Boas, Radin had begun collecting Winnebago stories in the early 1900s. He did not hear the tales narrated, nor did he know the identity of the narrator. Rather, as he notes, "an older individual" told the stories in Ho-Chunk to a Winnebago consultant, Sam Blowsnake, who wrote them down. Then Radin, Blowsnake, and another Winnebago man, Oliver LaMere, collaborated on the translation into English, which Radin, following Boas's methods, published in literate prose.

The tale of the trickster and the talking "laxative bulb" is widespread throughout Native American cultures. The trickster (or "the old man," as he is twice called here) interacts with plants and trees, sometimes defying them and at other times relying on them to get oriented. He also engages with humans, who foolishly listen to him and then suffer the consequences. The trickster plays the fool with the greatest vigor. His efforts to escape the consequences of his actions—and to recover from those consequences once his efforts fail—propel the narrative. To cleanse and restore himself, the trickster performs some hard and extremely unpleasant work that involves a reorientation toward the natural world. Apart from the entertainment value of its scatological humor and farcical elements, this story teaches numerous lessons, such as do not be gullible and do not think of yourself as superior to natural forces.

[Trickster and the Talking Bulb]

23

As he went wandering around aimlessly he suddenly heard someone speaking. He listened very carefully and it seemed to say, "He who chews me will defecate; he will defecate!" That was what it was saying. "Well, why is this person talking in this manner?" said Trickster. So he walked in the direction from which he had heard the speaking and again he heard, quite near him, someone saying: "He who chews me, he will defecate; he will defecate!" This is what was said. "Well, why does this person talk in such fashion?" said Trickster. Then he walked to the other side. So he continued walking along. Then right at his very side, a voice seemed to say, "He who chews me, he will defecate; he will defecate!" "Well, I wonder who it is who is speaking. I know very well that if I chew it, I will not defecate." But he kept looking around for the speaker and finally discovered, much to his astonishment, that it was a bulb on a bush. The bulb it was that was speaking. So he seized it, put it in his mouth, chewed it, and then swallowed it. He did just this and then went on.

"Well, where is the bulb gone that talked so much? Why, indeed, should I defecate? When I feel like defecating, then I shall defecate, no sooner. How could such an object make me defecate!" Thus spoke Trickster. Even as he spoke, however, he began to break wind. "Well this, I suppose, is what it meant. Yet the bulb said I would defecate, and I am merely expelling gas. In any case I am a great man even if I do expel a little gas!" Thus he spoke. As he was talking he again broke wind. This time it was really quite strong. "Well, what a foolish one I am. This is why I am called Foolish One, Trickster." Now he began to break wind again and again. "So this is why the bulb spoke as it did, I suppose." Once more he broke wind. This time it was very loud and his rectum began to smart. "Well, it surely is a great thing!" Then he broke wind again, this time with so much force, that he was propelled forward. "Well, well, it may even make me give another push, but it won't make me defecate," so he exclaimed defiantly. The next time he broke wind, the hind part of his body was raised up by the force of the explosion and he landed on his knees and hands. "Well, go ahead and do it again! Go ahead and do it again!" Then, again, he broke wind. This time the force of the expulsion sent him far up in the air and he landed on the ground, on his stomach. The next time he broke wind, he had to hang on to a log, so high was he thrown. However, he raised himself up and, after a while, landed on the ground, the log on top of him. He was almost killed by the fall. The next time he broke wind, he had to hold on to a tree that stood near by. It was a poplar and he held on with all his might yet, nevertheless, even then, his feet flopped up in the air. Again, and for the second time, he held on to it when he broke wind and yet he pulled the tree up by the roots. To protect himself, the next time, he went on until he came to a large tree, a large oak tree. Around this he put both his arms. Yet, when he broke wind, he was swung up and his toes struck against the tree. However, he held on.

After that he ran to a place where people were living. When he got there, he shouted, "Say, hurry up and take your lodge down, for a big warparty is upon you and you will surely be killed! Come let us get away!" He scared them all so much that they quickly took down their lodge, piled it on Trickster, and then got on him themselves. They likewise placed all the little dogs they had on top of Trickster.[1] Just then he began to break wind again and the force of the expulsion scattered the things on top of him in all directions. They fell far apart from one another. Separated, the people were standing about and shouting to one another; and the dogs, scattered here and there, howled at one another. There stood Trickster laughing at them till he ached.

Now he proceeded onward. He seemed to have gotten over his troubles. "Well, this bulb did a lot of talking," he said to himself, "yet it could not make me defecate." But even as he spoke he began to have the desire to defecate, just a very little. "Well, I suppose this is what it meant. It certainly bragged a good deal, however." As he spoke he defecated again. "Well, what a braggart it was! I suppose this is why it said this." As he spoke these last words, he began to defecate a good deal. After a while, as he was sitting down, his body would touch the excrement. Thereupon he got on top of a log and sat down there but, even then, he touched the excrement. Finally, he climbed up a log that was leaning against a tree. However, his body still touched the excrement, so he went up higher. Even then, however, he touched it so he climbed still higher up. Higher and higher he had to go. Nor was he able to stop defecating. Now he was on top of the tree. It was small and quite uncomfortable. Moreover, the excrement began to come up to him.

24

Even on the limb on which he was sitting he began to defecate. So he tried a different position. Since the limb, however, was very slippery he fell right down into the excrement. Down he fell, down into the dung. In fact he disappeared in it, and it was only with very great difficulty that he was able to get out of it. His raccoon-skin blanket was covered with filth, and he came out dragging it after him. The pack he was carrying on his back was covered with dung, as was also the box containing his penis.[2] The box he emptied and then placed it on his back again.

25

Then, still blinded by the filth, he started to run. He could not see anything. As he ran he knocked against a tree. The old man cried out in pain. He reached out and felt the tree and sang:

"Tree, what kind of a tree are you? Tell me something about yourself!"

And the tree answered, "What kind of a tree do you think I am? I am an oak tree. I am the forked oak tree that used to stand in the middle of the valley. I am that one," it said. "Oh, my, is it possible that there might be some water around here?" Trickster asked. The tree answered, "Go straight on." This is what it told him. As he went along he bumped up against another tree. He was knocked backwards by the collision. Again he sang:

"Tree, what kind of a tree are you? Tell me something about yourself!"

"What kind of a tree do you think I am? The red oak tree that used to stand at the edge of the valley, I am that one." "Oh, my, is it possible that there is

1. These actions are inappropriate responses to the supposed danger.
2. That the trickster carries his penis in a box was established in earlier stories. It is this box that he washes at the end of the next section of the story.

water around here?" asked Trickster. Then the tree answered and said, "Keep straight on," and so he went again. Soon he knocked against another tree. He spoke to the tree and sang:

"Tree, what kind of a tree are you? Tell me something about yourself!"

"What kind of a tree do you think I am? The slippery elm tree that used to stand in the midst of the others, I am that one." Then Trickster asked, "Oh, my, is it possible that there would be some water near here?" And the tree answered and said, "Keep right on." On he went and soon he bumped into another tree and he touched it and sang:

"Tree, what kind of a tree are you? Tell me something about yourself!"

"What kind of a tree do you think I am? I am the basswood tree that used to stand on the edge of the water. That is the one I am." "Oh, my, it is good," said Trickster. So there in the water he jumped and lay. He washed himself thoroughly.

It is said that the old man almost died that time, for it was only with the greatest difficulty that he found the water. If the trees had not spoken to him he certainly would have died. Finally, after a long time and only after great exertions, did he clean himself, for the dung had been on him a long time and had dried. After he had cleansed himself he washed his raccoon-skin blanket and his box.

ORATORY

POWHATAN'S DISCOURSE OF PEACE AND WAR

Powhatan was a powerful confederation of Indian tribes in the Chesapeake Bay region of present-day Virginia. In the early 1600s, the Powhatan confederacy occupied an area that was roughly one hundred miles on each side. They called the area Tsenacommacah, and it had a precontact population of roughly twenty-five thousand. By 1607, when Captain John Smith arrived with the expedition sent by the Virginia Company of London to establish Jamestown, the population had shrunk by some ten thousand people, largely from diseases borne to Tsenacommacah by previous Europeans. These colonists included a Spanish mission that had been briefly established there in 1571 and the English "lost colony" at Roanoke, which had vanished by 1590. Despite its diminished population, the Powhatan confederacy remained a regional power involved in far-flung trade networks. It included more than thirty tribes, each with its own chief, or werowance. The tribal alliance was held together mainly by marriage and in some cases by coercion.

Powhatan was the adopted name of the paramount chief, or mamanatowick, of the Powhatans at the time of Jamestown's settlement. His given name was Wahunsunacock, and he was the father of Pocohantas. Chief Powhatan was probably in his mid sixties when, in late 1607, he captured Smith and held him for under a month, which was long enough for Smith to learn a great deal about the Powhatans and their leader. (For more on Smith, see the selection of his writings later in this volume.) Smith and Chief Powhatan struck an alliance, and the English and the Powhatans became trading partners. The food and other assistance that the Powhatans supplied to Jamestown allowed the English colony to survive through its first winter, though more than half the men and boys in the small colony died even with their aid, leaving only thirty-eight of the original hundred and forty-four colonists. The metal tools, copper kettles, and glass beads provided by the English enabled the Powhatans to establish trade dominance over inland tribes.

"Powhatan's Discourse of Peace and War" appears in Smith's *General History of Virginia, New England, and the Summer Isles* (1624), as the opening speech in his account of the tense negotiations that led to this trade agreement. In the full text, Smith describes the speech as a "subtle discourse" intended to deceive and manipulate the English, to which he responded with considerable bluster and thinly veiled threats. Probably based at least in part on Smith's memories of these events, the discourse and the entire scene are informed by the conventions of classical historiography, which often features set speeches that distill key elements and add drama to the narrative. As reconstructed by Smith, Powhatan's speech makes a compelling case for peaceful relations, even as questions of its authenticity and sincerity add layers of complexity.

Powhatan's Discourse of Peace and War[1]

Captain Smith, you may understand that I having seen the death of all my people thrice, and not any one living of those three generations but my self;[2] I know the difference of peace and war better than any in my country. But now I am old and ere long must die, my brethren, namely Opitchapam, Opechancanough, and Kekataugh, my two sisters, and their two daughters, are distinctly each others successors. I wish their experience no less than mine, and your love to them no less than mine to you. But this bruit from Nandsamund,[3] that you are come to destroy my country, so much affrighteth all my people as they dare not visit you. What will it avail you to take that by force you may quickly have by love, or to destroy them that provide you food? What can you get by war, when we can hide our provisions and fly to the woods? whereby you must famish by wronging us your friends. And why are you thus jealous of our loves seeing us unarmed, and both do, and are willing still to feed you, with that you cannot get but by our labours? Think you I am so simple, not to know it is better to eat good meat, lie well, and sleep quietly with my women and children, laugh and be merry with you, have copper, hatchets, or what I want being your friend: than be forced to fly from all, to lie cold in the woods, feed upon acorns, roots, and such trash, and be so hunted by you, that I can neither rest, eat, nor sleep; but my tired men must watch, and if a twig but break, every one crieth there commeth Captain Smith: then must I fly I know not whither: and thus with miserable fear, end my miserable life, leaving my pleasures to such youths as you, which through your rash unadvisedness may quickly as miserably end, for want of that, you never know where to find. Let this therefore assure you of our loves, and every year our friendly trade shall furnish you with corn, and now also, if you would come in friendly manner to see us, and not thus with your guns and swords as to invade your foes.

1. The text is from John Smith, *The Generall Historie of Virginia, New-England, and the Summer Isles: With the Names of the Adventurers, Planters, and Governors from Their First Beginning, Ano: 1584. To This present 1624* (1624).

2. Powhatan refers to deaths from both disease and warfare.
3. Noise or rumor from Nansemond, another tribe of the Chesapeake region.

KING PHILIP'S SPEECH

King Philip was the English name adopted by the Wampanoag leader Metacom (c. 1638–1676), who led an alliance against the English colonies in Massachusetts, Rhode Island, and Connecticut in what became known as King Philip's War (1675–76). Philip was the son of Massassoit, who had maintained peaceful relations with the Plymouth colonists since their arrival in 1620. In 1662, when Philip became the leader of the Wampanoag alliance, longstanding grievances over land and regional governance had transformed the region into a powder keg. War erupted in 1675, after the Plymouth colony executed three Wampanoags. Philip's alliance exacted great costs on the English but was defeated after Philip was killed in the Great Swamp Fight of August 1676.

After the war, there was an outpouring of printed works giving English perspectives on the conflict, most famously the popular captivity narrative of Mary Rowlandson (reprinted later in this volume), which first appeared in 1682 and was republished many times. Rowlandson's descriptions of her interactions with Philip show him to have been in some measure generous and sympathetic toward her, even as he held her prisoner. Other reports on the war were less respectful toward the defeated leader, notably the account of Captain Benjamin Church, whose celebrity as a military hero arose partly from his role in Philip's death. In *Entertaining Passages Relating to Philip's War* (1716), Church described Philip's dead body as looking like that of "a doleful, great, naked, dirty beast" and told how he had ordered the corpse drawn and quartered. Philip's head was staked on a pole in Plymouth, where it remained for years.

It was the kind of dehumanization of Philip found in *Entertaining Passages* that the Pequot leader and Methodist minister William Apess set out to correct in 1836, when he delivered his "Eulogy on King Philip" at the Odeon in Boston. "King Philip's Speech" is from that eulogy. Speeches offering a Native American perspective on America's colonial wars had become a popular genre after Thomas Jefferson published "Chief Logan's Speech" (included in this volume). Claiming descent from Philip, Apess described him as a leading American, the equal of George Washington and Alexander the Great, a "hero of the wilderness" and martyr to a lost cause who deserved universal respect. By way of introduction, Apess explained that "this famous speech of Philip was calculated to arouse them to arms, to do the best they could in protecting and defending their rights."

King Philip's Speech[1]

BROTHERS,—You see this vast country before us, which the great Spirit gave to our fathers and us; you see the buffalo and deer that now are our support.—Brothers, you see these little ones, our wives and children, who are looking to us for food and raiment; and you now see the foe before you, that they have grown insolent and bold; that all our ancient customs are disregarded; the treaties made by our fathers and us are broken, and all of us insulted; our council fires disregarded, and all the ancient customs of our fathers; our brothers

---

1. The text is from *Eulogy on King Philip, as Pronounced at the Odeon, in Federal Street, Boston, by the Rev. William Apes[s], An Indian* (1836).

murdered before our eyes, and their spirits cry to us for revenge. Brothers, these people from the unknown world will cut down our groves, spoil our hunting and planting grounds, and drive us and our children from the graves of our fathers, and our council fires, and enslave our women and children.

POETRY

These three selections of early Native American poetry have been excerpted from prose accounts published between 1765 and 1820. They were chosen to illustrate various styles and sources. Interest in oral literatures was strong on both sides of the Atlantic in the eighteenth century, with works such as Thomas Percy's *Reliques of Ancient English Poetry* (1765) and Sir Walter Scott's *Minstrelsy of the Scottish Border* (1802) representing British traditions. In North America, the appeal of indigenous chants and songs for non-Native readers arose in part from a desire to establish a Native equivalent to the ancient poetry of the British isles that Percy and Scott had collected in their volumes. After the American Revolution, a new nationalism in search of local origins provided an additional motive for collecting and enjoying Native poetry.

The Cherokee war song included here appears as "A Translation of the War-Song. *Caw waw noo dee, &c.*" in *The Memoirs of Lieut. Henry Timberlake* (1765). Historically, the Cherokees occupied a broad territory in the Southeast, including areas of what are now the Carolinas, Georgia, and Tennessee. Timberlake had served in the Second Virginia Regiment under Colonel William Byrd, whose ethnographic and naturalist writings are excerpted elsewhere in this volume. Timberlake's *Memoirs* are a rich source of information about mid-eighteenth-century Cherokee culture and society. He had traveled to Tennessee to conduct peace negotiations in 1761, and he later accompanied Ostenaco and two other Cherokee chiefs to London. Of the songs printed in his volume, Timberlake wrote: "Both the ideas and verse are very loose in the original, and they are set to as loose a music, many composing both tunes and song off hand, according to the occasion; tho' some tunes, especially those taken from the northern Indians, are extremely pretty, and very like the Scotch."

The Reverend John Heckewelder, a Moravian missionary, printed the Lenape war song included here as "The Song of the Lenape Warriors Going Against the Enemy" in his *History, Manners, and Customs of the Indian Nations Who Once Inhabited Pennsylvania and the Neighbouring States* (1818). The Lenapes (also known as the Lenni Lenapes or Delaware Indians) were ancient inhabitants of the Middle Atlantic region, occupying parts of what later became several states, including New Jersey, Pennsylvania, and New York. Their diplomatic and mediation skills were widely admired. Heckewelder spent more than a decade as a missionary to the Lenape in Pennsylvania and Ohio, and he later worked for the United States Senate as a treaty negotiator. The novelist James Fenimore Cooper drew heavily on Heckewelder's *History* in his *Leatherstocking Tales*. Heckewelder's introduction to the song included here emphasizes the impossibility of capturing the vocal tones and musical accompaniment of the performance, which he compares to the difficulties of describing "the melodies of the ancient Greeks." He nevertheless reports how the performers sang the words "in short lines . . . most generally in detached parts, as time permits and as the occasion or their feelings prompt them. Their accent is very pathetic [i.e., sad], and the whole, in their language, produces considerable effect."

The two Cherokee songs of friendship included here are drawn from a letter written by Dr. Samuel L. Mitchill in 1817 to the secretary of the American Antiquarian Society (AAS), which was published three years later in *Archaeologia Americana*, a volume of the society's *Transactions*. In his letter, Mitchill describes how his interactions with the Osages and Cherokees during his service as the chairman of the U.S. Senate Committee on Indian Affairs led to the transcription of several songs and poems. Of the performance of the Cherokee songs of friendship he notes, "They repeat the song and chorus until they are tired." The words of these songs were written down for him by "Mr. Hicks, a Cherokee of the half blood, with his own hand," while they were in the company of several military officers and Double Head, a Cherokee warrior. Mitchill sent the songs to the AAS as part of an ongoing effort by that organization to record indigenous American history and culture.

Cherokee War Song[1]

Where'er the earth's enlighten'd by the sun,
Moon shines by night, grass grows, or waters run,
Be't known that we are going, like men, afar,
In hostile fields to wage destructive war;
Like men we go, to meet our country's foes,   5
Who, woman-like, shall fly our dreaded blows;
Yes, as a woman, who beholds a snake,
In gaudy horror, glisten thro' the brake,
Starts trembling back, and stares with wild surprize,
Or pale thro' fear, unconscious, panting, flies.[2]   10
Just so these foes, more tim'rous than the hind,
Shall leave their arms and only clothes behind;
Pinch'd by each blast, by ev'ry thicket torn,
Run back to their own nation, now its scorn:
Or in the winter, when the barren wood   15
Denies their gnawing entrails nature's food,
Let them sit down, from friends and country far,
And wish, with tears, they ne'er had come to war.
We'll leave our clubs,[3] dew'd with their country show'rs,
And, if they dare to bring them back to ours,   20
Their painted scalps shall be a step to fame,
And grace our own and glorious country's name.
Or if we warriors spare the yielding foe,
Torments at home the wretch must undergo.[4]

1. The text is from *The Memoirs of Lieut. Henry Timberlake (Who Accompanied Three Cherokee Indians to England in the Year 1762)* (1765).
2. "As the Indians fight naked, the vanquished are constrained to endure the rigours of the weather in their flight, and live upon roots and fruit, as they throw down their arms to accelerate their flight thro' the woods" [Timberlake's note].
3. "It is the custom of the Indians, to leave a club something of the form of a cricket-bat, but with their warlike exploits engraved on it, in their enemy's country, and the enemy accepts the defiance, by bringing this back to their country" [Timberlake's note].

4. "The prisoners of war are generally tortured by the women, at the party's return, to revenge the death of those that have perished by the wretch's countrymen. This savage custom has been so much mitigated of late, that the prisoners were only compelled to marry, and then generally allowed all the privileges of the natives. This lenity, however, has been a detriment to the nation; for many of these returning to their countrymen, have made them acquainted with the country-passes, weaknesses, and haunts of the Cherokees; besides that it gave the enemy greater courage to fight against them" [Timberlake's note].

But when we go, who knows which shall return, 25
When growing dangers rise with each new morn?
Farewell, ye little ones, ye tender wives,
For you alone we would conserve our lives!
But cease to mourn, 'tis unavailing pain,
If not fore-doom'd, we soon shall meet again. 30
But, O ye friends! in case your comrades fall,
Think that on you our deaths for vengeance call;
With uprais'd tomahawks pursue our blood,
And stain, with hostile streams, the conscious wood,
That pointing enemies may never tell 35
The boasted place where we, their victims, fell.[5]

Lenape War Song[1]

O poor me!
Who[2] am going out to fight the enemy,
And know not whether I shall return again,
To enjoy the embraces of my children
And my wife. 5
O poor creature!
Whose life is not in his own hands,
Who has no power over his own body,
But tries to do his duty
For the welfare of his nation. 10
O! thou Great Spirit above!
Take pity on my children
And on my wife!
Prevent their mourning on my account!
Grant that I may be successful in this attempt— 15
That I may slay my enemy,
And bring home the trophies of war
To my dear family and friends,
That we may rejoice together.
O! take pity on me! 20
Give me strength and courage to meet my enemy,
Suffer me to return again to my children,
To my wife
And to my relations!
Take pity on me and preserve my life 25
And I will make to thee a sacrifice.

5. "Their custom is generally to engrave their victory on some neighbouring tree, or set up some token of it near the field of battle; to this their enemies are here supposed to point to, as boasting their victory over them, and the slaughter that they made" [Timberlake's note].

1. The text is from *History, Manners, and Customs of The Indian Nations Who Once Inhabited Pennsylvania and the Neighbouring States* (1818; rev. ed. 1876).
2. Heckewelder wrote "Whom."

Two Cherokee Songs of Friendship[1]

Song the First

Can, nal, li, èh, ne-was-tu.
A friend you resemble.
Chorus. Yai, ne, noo, way. E,noo,way,hā.

Song the Second

Ti, nai, tau, nā, cla, ne-was-tu.
Brothers I think we are.
Chorus. Yai, ne, noo, way. E,noo,way,hā.

1. The texts are from "Letter from Dr. Samuel L. Mitchill," *Transactions and Collections of the American Antiquarian Society* (1820).

CHRISTOPHER COLUMBUS
1451–1506

In Washington Irving's widely read biography of Christopher Columbus, first published in 1828, the acclaimed American writer described the European adventurer as possessing an "ardent and enthusiastic imagination which threw a magnificence over his whole course of thought." "In his letters and journals," Irving observed, "instead of detailing circumstances with the technical precision of a mere navigator, he notices the beauties of nature with the enthusiasm of a poet or a painter." Popular travel narratives by Marco Polo and Sir John Mandeville probably influenced Columbus's plans for his historic first voyage and shaped his prose style, Irving remarked, and he described as well a "visionary" cast of mind that was evident in everything Columbus did. Summing up the meaning of the adventurer's dramatic life, Irving wrestled with the fact that the consequences of this visionary quality were often destructive to himself and those around him—not least due to his role in making slavery a central part of the encounter between Europe and the Americas.

Born into a family of wool workers near the Mediterranean port of Genoa, Columbus turned to the sea as a young man, developed a plan to find a commercially viable Atlantic route to Asia, and in 1492 won the support of the Spanish monarchs, Ferdinand and Isabella, for this "enterprise of the Indies." His unexpected discoveries led to three later voyages intended to establish Spanish power in the West Indies and in South America. What seemed an auspicious beginning was followed by a long series of disasters and disappointments. His willingness to enslave the natives, and his lack of interest in indigenous social and cultural forms, had devastating consequences. What had appeared to him to be friendly relations with the Taino Indians on the island of Hispaniola in 1492 turned sour as the settlers demanded gold and sexual partners from their hosts. On Columbus's return to the island in 1494, none of the Europeans remained alive. A new settlement fell into disorder while he was away in Cuba and Jamaica. In 1496, he was forced to return to Spain to clear his name of politically motivated charges made against him by European rivals involved in the colonies. A third voyage, begun in 1498, took him for the first time to the South American mainland. The lushness of nature there made him believe he was near paradise, but when he returned to Hispaniola, he discovered the Spanish settlers on that island in open rebellion against his authority. Able to reach a truce only at the expense of the Taino Indians, who were virtually enslaved by the rebels, Columbus soon found himself under arrest. He was sent in chains to Spain in 1500 to answer yet more charges. His last voyage, intended to restore his tarnished reputation, resulted in a long period of suffering in Panama and shipwreck in Jamaica. During this time, Columbus underwent a virtual breakdown, even suffering delusional periods. Rescued at last, he returned to Europe and died not long afterward. His discoveries in the West Indies were left in a state of violent disorder.

The supposed *Journal* of Columbus's first voyage is actually a summary prepared by the cleric and reformer Bartolomé de las Casas. However, several documents regarding the four voyages survive from Columbus's hand. His letter to Luis de Santangel, a court official who helped secure financing for the first voyage, provides a more authentic account. This so-called Letter of Discovery served as the basis for the first printed description of America, initially issued in 1493 and widely translated and reprinted across Europe. Here, Columbus writes of marvels in a manner that becomes entwined with the language of possession. A memorandum regarding the second voyage, intended by Columbus for the Spanish monarchs (whose responses to each point also survive), offers useful insights into the emerging ambiguities and problems of the Hispaniola colony. For the third and fourth voyages, three letters from Columbus, two sent to the Crown and one to a woman of the Spanish court, detail his deepening worldly and spiritual troubles. His emotional fragility and spiritual despair are effectively conveyed in the excerpt from his letter to Ferdinand and Isabella regarding his fourth voyage that is included here along with the letter to Santangel.

The following texts are from *Select Documents Illustrating the Four Voyages of Columbus* (1930–33), translated and edited by Cecil Jane.

Letter of Discovery

[At sea, February 15, 1493]

Sir,

As I know that you will be pleased at the great victory with which Our Lord has crowned my voyage, I write this to you, from which you will learn how in thirty-three days, I passed from the Canary Islands to the Indies with the fleet which the most illustrious king and queen our sovereigns gave to me. And there I found very many islands filled with people innumerable, and of them all I have taken possession for their highnesses, by proclamation made and with the royal standard unfurled, and no opposition was offered to me. To the first island which I found I gave the name *San Salvador*,[1] in remembrance of the Divine Majesty, Who has marvelously bestowed all this; the Indians call it "Guanahani." To the second I gave the name *Isla de Santa María de Concepción*; to the third, *Fernandina*; to the fourth, *Isabella*; to the fifth, *Isla Juana*,[2] and so to each one I gave a new name.

1. The precise identity of the Bahamian island Columbus named San Salvador is not known today, although many theories have been put forward, most positing that Watling Island is the likeliest site.

2. Of these four islands, only the identity of Juana (Cuba) is today certain.

When I reached Juana I followed its coast to the westward, and I found it to be so extensive that I thought that it must be the mainland, the province of Catayo.[3] And since there were neither towns nor villages on the seashore, but only small hamlets, with the people of which I could not have speech because they all fled immediately, I went forward on the same course, thinking that I should not fail to find great cities and towns. And at the end of many leagues,[4] seeing that there was no change and that the coast was bearing me northwards, which I wished to avoid since winter was already beginning and I proposed to make from it to the south, and as moreover the wind was carrying me forward, I determined not to wait for a change in the weather and retraced my path as far as a certain harbor known to me. And from that point I sent two men inland to learn if there were a king or great cities. They traveled three days' journey and found an infinity of small hamlets and people without number, but nothing of importance. For this reason they returned.

I understood sufficiently from other Indians, whom I had already taken, that this land was nothing but an island. And therefore I followed its coast eastwards for one hundred and seven leagues to the point where it ended. And from that cape I saw another island distant eighteen leagues from the former, to the east, to which I at once gave the name "Española."[5] And I went there and followed its northern coast, as I had in the case of Juana, to the eastward for one hundred and eighty-eight great leagues in a straight line. This island and all the others are very fertile to a limitless degree, and this island is extremely so. In it there are many harbors on the coast of the sea, beyond comparison with others which I know in Christendom, and many rivers, good and large, which is marvelous. Its lands are high, and there are in it very many sierras and very lofty mountains, beyond comparison with the island of Tenerife.[6] All are most beautiful, of a thousand shapes, and all are accessible and filled with trees of a thousand kinds and tall, and they seem to touch the sky. And I am told that they never lose their foliage, as I can understand, for I saw them as green and as lovely as they are in Spain in May, and some of them were flowering, some bearing fruit, and some in another stage, according to their nature. And the nightingale[7] was singing and other birds of a thousand kinds in the month of November there where I went. There are six or eight kinds of palm, which are a wonder to behold on account of their beautiful variety, but so are the other trees and fruits and plants. In it are marvelous pine groves, and there are very large tracts of cultivable lands, and there is honey, and there are birds of many kinds and fruits in great diversity. In the interior are mines of metals, and the population is without number. Española is a marvel.

The sierras and mountains, the plains and arable lands and pastures, are so lovely and rich for planting and sowing, for breeding cattle of every kind, for building towns and villages. The harbours of the sea here are such as cannot be believed to exist unless they have been seen, and so with the riv-

---

3. I.e., China (or "Cathay").
4. Renaissance units of measurement were inexact. Columbus's "league" was probably about four miles.
5. I.e., Hispaniola, where the countries of Haiti and the Dominican Republic are located.

6. The largest of the Canary Islands.
7. Not native to the Western Hemisphere. Nor is the honeybee, presumably the source of the honey mentioned below. The existence of gold in the rivers, also mentioned below, was purely conjectural.

ers, many and great, and good waters, the majority of which contain gold. In the trees and fruits and plants, there is a great difference from those of Juana. In this island, there are many spices and great mines of gold and of other metals.

The people of this island, and of all the other islands which I have found and of which I have information, all go naked, men and women, as their mothers bore them, although some women cover a single place with the leaf of a plant or with a net of cotton which they make for the purpose. They have no iron or steel or weapons, nor are they fitted to use them, not because they are not well built men and of handsome stature, but because they are very marvellously timorous. They have no other arms than weapons made of canes, cut in seeding time, to the ends of which they fix a small sharpened stick. And they do not dare to make use of these, for many times it has happened that I have sent ashore two or three men to some town to have speech, and countless people have come out to them, and as soon as they have seen my men approaching they have fled, even a father not waiting for his son. And this, not because ill has been done to anyone; on the contrary, at every point where I have been and have been able to have speech, I have given to them of all that I had, such as cloth and many other things, without receiving anything for it; but so they are, incurably timid. It is true that, after they have been reassured and have lost their fear, they are so guileless and so generous with all they possess, that no one would believe it who has not seen it. They never refuse anything which they possess, if it be asked of them; on the contrary, they invite anyone to share it, and display as much love as if they would give their hearts, and whether the thing be of value or whether it be of small price, at once with whatever trifle of whatever kind it may be that is given to them, with that they are content. I forbade that they should be given things so worthless as fragments of broken crockery and scraps of broken glass, and ends of straps, although when they were able to get them, they fancied that they possessed the best jewel in the world. So it was found that a sailor for a strap received gold to the weight of two and a half *castellanos*,[8] and others much more for other things which were worth much less. As for new *blancas*, for them they would give everything which they had, although it might be two or three *castellanos'* weight of gold or an *arroba*[9] or two of spun cotton. . . . They took even the pieces of the broken hoops of the wine barrels and, like savages, gave what they had, so that it seemed to me to be wrong and I forbade it. And I gave a thousand handsome good things, which I had brought, in order that they might conceive affection, and more than that, might become Christians and be inclined to the love and service of their highnesses and of the whole Castilian nation, and strive to aid us and to give us of the things which they have in abundance and which are necessary to us. And they do not know any creed and are not idolaters; only they all believe that power and good are in the heavens, and they are very firmly convinced that I, with these ships and men, came from the heavens, and in this belief they everywhere received me, after they had overcome their fear. And this does not come because they are ignorant; on the contrary, they are of a very acute intelligence and are men who navigate all

8. A *castellano* was a gold coin.
9. A *blanca* was a copper coin. An *arroba* was equal to twenty-five pounds.

those seas, so that it is amazing how good an account they give of everything, but it is because they have never seen people clothed or ships of such a kind.

And as soon as I arrived in the Indies, in the first island which I found, I took by force some of them, in order that they might learn and give me information of that which there is in those parts, and so it was that they soon understood us, and we them, either by speech or signs, and they have been very serviceable.[1] I still take them with me, and they are always assured that I come from Heaven, for all the intercourse[2] which they have had with me; and they were the first to announce this wherever I went, and the others went running from house to house and to the neighbouring towns, with loud cries of, "Come! Come to see the people from Heaven!" So all, men and women alike, when their minds were set at rest concerning us, came, so that not one, great or small, remained behind, and all brought something to eat and drink, which they gave with extraordinary affection. In all the island, they have very many canoes, like rowing *fustas*,[3] some larger, some smaller, and some are larger than a *fusta* of eighteen benches. They are not so broad, because they are made of a single log of wood, but a *fusta* would not keep up with them in rowing, since their speed is a thing incredible. And in these they navigate among all those islands, which are innumerable, and carry their goods. One of these canoes I have seen with seventy and eighty men in her, and each one with his oar.

In all these islands, I saw no great diversity in the appearance of the people or in their manners and language.[4] On the contrary, they all understand one another, which is a very curious thing, on account of which I hope that their highnesses will determine upon their conversion to our holy faith, towards which they are very inclined.

I have already said how I have gone one hundred and seven leagues in a straight line from west to east along the seashore of the island Juana, and as a result of that voyage, I can say that this island is larger than England and Scotland together,[5] for, beyond these one hundred and seven leagues, there remain to the westward two provinces to which I have not gone. One of these provinces they call "Avan,"[6] and there the people are born with tails; and these provinces cannot have a length of less than fifty or sixty leagues, as I could understand from those Indians whom I have and who know all the islands.

The other, Española, has a circumference greater than all Spain, from Colibre, by the sea-coast, to Fuenterabia in Vizcaya, since I voyaged along one side one hundred and eighty-eight great leagues in a straight line from west to east.[7] It is a land to be desired and, seen, it is never to be left. And in it, although of all I have taken possession for their highnesses and all are more richly endowed than I know how, or am able, to say, and I hold them all

---

1. No record exists of how many indigenous people Columbus took captive, but only seven survived the voyage to Spain. On the second voyage, one of these seven acted as interpreter.

2. Communication, exchange.

3. A *fusta* was a moderate-sized ship, smaller than a galley, with banks of oars and a single mast.

4. Columbus was mistaken about the single language, as he later discovered. In fact, there was considerable linguistic diversity.

5. Actually, Cuba occupies roughly forty-three thousand square miles, whereas England alone is more than fifty thousand square miles in area.

6. The Natives called one region of the island "Havana," and "Avan" may be Columbus's rendering of that name.

7. Again, Columbus overstates his comparison. The coastline of Spain and Portugal measures roughly nineteen hundred miles, whereas that of Española is about fifteen hundred miles. "Colibre": Collioure, in the Pyrenees; "Fuenterabia:" Hondarribia, a coastal town in northwestern Spain.

for their highnesses, so that they may dispose of them as, and as absolutely as, of the kingdoms of Castile, in this Española, in the situation most convenient and in the best position for the mines of gold and for all intercourse as well with the mainland here as with that there, belonging to the Grand Khan, where will be great trade and gain, I have taken possession of a large town, to which I gave the name *Villa de Navidad*,[8] and in it I have made fortifications and a fort, which now will by this time be entirely finished, and I have left in it sufficient men[9] for such a purpose with arms and artillery and provisions for more than a year, and a *fusta*, and one, a master of all seacraft, to build others, and great friendship with the king of that land, so much so, that he was proud to call me, and to treat me as, a brother. And even if he were to change his attitude to one of hostility towards these men, he and his do not know what arms are and they go naked, as I have already said, and are the most timorous people that there are in the world, so that the men whom I have left there alone would suffice to destroy all that land, and the island is without danger for their persons, if they know how to govern themselves.

In all these islands, it seems to me that all men are content with one woman, and to their chief or king they give as many as twenty. It appears to me that the women work more than the men. And I have not been able to learn if they hold private property; what seemed to me to appear was that, in that which one had, all took a share, especially of eatable things.

In these islands I have so far found no human monstrosities, as many expected,[1] but on the contrary the whole population is very well-formed, nor are they negroes as in Guinea, but their hair is flowing, and they are not born where there is intense force in the rays of the sun; it is true that the sun has there great power, although it is distant from the equinoctial line twenty-six degrees. In these islands, where there are high mountains, the cold was severe this winter, but they endure it, being used to it and with the help of meats which they eat with many and extremely hot spices. As I have found no monsters, so I have had no report of any, except in an island "Quaris,"[2] the second at the coming into the Indies, which is inhabited by a people who are regarded in all the islands as very fierce and who eat human flesh. They have many canoes with which they range through all the islands of India and pillage and take as much as they can. They are no more malformed than the others, except that they have the custom of wearing their hair long like women, and they use bows and arrows of the same cane stems, with a small piece of wood at the end, owing to lack of iron which they do not possess. They are ferocious among these other people who are cowardly to an excessive degree, but I make no more account of them than of the rest. These are those who have intercourse with the women of "Matinino,"[3] which is the first island met on the way from Spain to the Indies, in which there is not a man. These women engage in no

---

8. A site on the modern bay of Caracol, in Haiti. "Grand Khan": the Chinese emperor.
9. Columbus left approximately forty men at La Navidad.
1. Among those who expected to find human monstrosities was Pierre d'Ailly, a French theologian, philosopher, and cardinal. Columbus annotated his own copy of d'Ailly's cosmographic and astronomical writings, the *Imago Mundi* (written between 1410 and 1419 and printed sometime between 1480 and 1490).
2. Either Dominica or Maria Galante.
3. Now Martinique. "Intercourse": here, in the sexual sense.

feminine occupation, but use bows and arrows of cane, like those already mentioned, and they arm and protect themselves with plates of copper, of which they have much.

In another island, which they assure me is larger than Española, the people have no hair. In it, there is gold incalculable, and from it and from the other islands, I bring with me Indians as evidence.

In conclusion, to speak only of that which has been accomplished on this voyage, which was so hasty, their highnesses can see that I will give them as much gold as they may need, if their highnesses will render me very slight assistance; moreover, spice and cotton, as much as their highnesses shall command; and mastic, as much as they shall order to be shipped and which, up to now, has been found only in Greece, in the island of Chios, and the Seignory[4] sells it for what it pleases; and aloe wood, as much as they shall order to be shipped, and slaves, as many as they shall order to be shipped and who will be from the idolaters.[5] And I believe that I have found rhubarb and cinnamon, and I shall find a thousand other things of value, which the people whom I have left there will have discovered, for I have not delayed at any point, so far as the wind allowed me to sail, except in the town of Navidad, in order to leave it secured and well established, and in truth, I should have done much more, if the ships had served me, as reason demanded.

This is enough . . . [6] and the eternal God, our Lord, Who gives to all those who walk in His way triumph over things which appear to be impossible, and this was notably one; for, although men have talked or have written of these lands, all was conjectural, without suggestion of ocular evidence, but amounted only to this, that those who heard for the most part listened and judged it to be rather a fable than as having any vestige of truth. So that, since Our Redeemer has given this victory to our most illustrious king and queen, and to their renowned kingdoms, in so great a matter, for this all Christendom ought to feel delight and make great feasts and give solemn thanks to the Holy Trinity with many solemn prayers for the great exaltation which they shall have, in the turning of so many peoples to our holy faith, and afterwards for temporal benefits, for not only Spain but all Christians will have hence refreshment and gain.

This, in accordance with that which has been accomplished, thus briefly.

Done in the caravel, off the Canary Islands,[7] on the fifteenth of February, in the year one thousand four hundred and ninety-three.

At your orders.   El Almirante.[8]

---

4. The Genoese government. "Chios": an island, now part of Greece, that had been claimed by Genoa since 1346; Columbus may have visited there in 1474–75. "Mastic": a natural resin produced from the mastic tree, sometimes known as "the tears of Chios." The trade in mastic was controlled by a company that became a tributary to the Ottomans in 1453.
5. In 1452, Pope Nicholas V authorized the Portuguese to reduce any non-Christians to the status of slaves; two years later, he granted Portugal a monopoly of the slave trade with Africa. Spain ignored the monopoly status that Nicholas had granted to Portugal and began trading in African

slaves. On arriving in the West Indies, Columbus almost immediately began to take captives, and a bit later he participated in the enslavement of Native people. He eventually developed a plan for a slave trade in indigenous Americans.
6. There is a gap here in the original manuscript.
7. Columbus was in fact off Santa Maria, one of the islands in the Azores. "Caravel": a fast, light sailing ship, much used by the Portuguese for exploring the African coast. Two of the three ships on Columbus's first voyage, the Niña and the Pinta, were caravels.
8. The Admiral.

[Postscript]

After having written this, and being in the sea of Castile, there came on me so great a south-south-west wind, that I was obliged to lighten ship. But I ran here to-day into this port of Lisbon,[9] which was the greatest marvel in the world, whence I decided to write to their highnesses. In all the Indies, I have always found weather like May; where I went in thirty-three days and I had returned in twenty-eight, save for these storms which have detained me for fourteen days, beating about in this sea. Here all the sailors say that never has there been so bad a winter nor so many ships lost.

Done on the fourth day of March.

1493

From Letter to Ferdinand and Isabella Regarding the Fourth Voyage[1]

[Jamaica, July 7, 1503]

✳   ✳   ✳

Of Española, Paria,[2] and the other lands, I never think without weeping. I believed that their example would have been to the profit of others; on the contrary, they are in an exhausted state; although they are not dead, the infirmity is incurable or very extensive; let him who brought them to this state come now with the remedy if he can or if he knows it; in destruction, everyone is an adept. It was always the custom to give thanks and promotion to him who imperiled his person. It is not just that he who has been so hostile to this undertaking should enjoy its fruits or that his children should. Those who left the Indies, flying from toils and speaking evil of the matter and of me, have returned with official employment.[3] So it has now been ordained in the case of Veragua.[4] It is an ill example and without profit for the business and for justice in the world.

The fear of this, with other sufficient reasons, which I saw clearly, led me to pray your highnesses before I went to discover these islands and Terra Firma, that you would leave them to me to govern in your royal name. It pleased you; it was a privilege and agreement, and under seal and oath, and you granted me the title of viceroy and admiral and governor general of all. And you fixed the boundary, a hundred leagues beyond the Azores and the Cape Verde Islands, by a line passing from pole to pole, and you gave me wide power over this and over all that I might further discover. The document states this very fully.

---

9. Columbus's decision to go to Lisbon, Portugal, aroused suspicions in Spain, where Portugal was regarded as a major rival.
1. Written on Jamaica in 1503, this letter was hand carried from there to Hispaniola by Diego Mendez.
2. Paria was the mainland region of what is now Venezuela, near the island of Trinidad. Columbus,

who had first landed in South America ("Terra Firma," as he terms it later) in 1498, argued that the terrestrial paradise lay nearby.
3. Although it appears that Columbus has specific personal enemies in mind, it is not clear whom he means.
4. I.e., Panama, where Columbus was shipwrecked earlier in this voyage.

The other most important matter, which calls aloud for redress, remains inexplicable to this moment. Seven years I was at your royal court, where all to whom this undertaking was mentioned, unanimously declared it to be a delusion. Now all, down to the very tailors, seek permission to make discoveries. It can be believed that they go forth to plunder, and it is granted to them to do so, so that they greatly prejudice my honor and do very great damage to the enterprise. It is well to give to God that which is His due and to Caesar that which belongs to him.[5] This is a just sentiment and based on justice.

The lands which here obey Your Highnesses are more extensive and richer than all other Christian lands. After I, by the divine will, had placed them under your royal and exalted lordship, and was on the point of securing a very great revenue, suddenly, while I was waiting for ships to come to your high presence with victory and with great news of gold, being very secure and joyful, I was made a prisoner and with my two brothers was thrown into a ship, laden with fetters, stripped to the skin, very ill-treated, and without being tried or condemned. Who will believe that a poor foreigner could in such a place rise against Your Highnesses, without cause, and without the support of some other prince, and being alone among your vassals and natural subjects, and having all my children at your royal court?

I came to serve at the age of twenty-eight years, and now I have not a hair on my body that is not gray, and my body is infirm, and whatever remained to me from those years of service has been spent and taken away from me and sold, and from my brothers, down to my very coat, without my being heard or seen, to my great dishonor. It must be believed that this was not done by your royal command. The restitution of my honor, the reparation of my losses, and the punishment of him who did this, will spread abroad the fame of your royal nobility. The same punishment is due to him who robbed me of the pearls, and to him who infringed my rights as admiral.[6] Very great will be your merit, fame without parallel will be yours, if you do this, and there will remain in Spain a glorious memory of Your Highnesses, as grateful and just princes.

The pure devotion which I have ever borne to the service of Your Highnesses, and the unmerited wrong that I have suffered, will not permit me to remain silent, although I would fain do so; I pray Your Highnesses to pardon me. I am so ruined as I have said; hitherto I have wept for others; now, Heaven have mercy upon me, and may the earth weep for me. Of worldly goods, I have not even a *blanca*[7] for an offering in spiritual things. Here in the Indies I have become careless of the prescribed forms of religion. Alone in my trouble, sick, in daily expectation of death, and encompassed about by a million savages, full of cruelty and our foes, and so separated from the holy Sacraments of Holy Church, my soul will be forgotten if it here leaves my body. Weep for me, whoever has charity, truth, and justice.

---

5. Cf. "Render therefore unto Caesar the things which are Caesar's, and unto God the things that are God's" (Matthew 22.21).
6. The reference is to Alonso de Ojeda (1468–c.

1516), who had taken pearls—part of what was reserved to Columbus under his agreement with the Spanish Crown—from Paria to Española.
7. See n. 9, p. 47.

I did not sail upon this voyage to gain honor or wealth; this is certain, for already all hope of that was dead. I came to Your Highnesses with true devotion and with ready zeal, and I do not lie. I humbly pray Your Highnesses that if it please God to bring me forth from this place, that you will be pleased to permit me to go to Rome and to other places of pilgrimage. May the Holy Trinity preserve your life and high estate, and grant you increase of prosperity.

Done in the Indies in the island of Jamaica, on the seventh of July, in the year one thousand five hundred and three.

1505

JOHN SMITH
1580–1631

One of the most vivid episodes in the literature of colonial British North America is a scene from the writings of Captain John Smith that takes place at the "court" of Powhatan, the mamanatowick (or paramount chief) of the Algonquians in the Chesapeake Bay region. (For more on Powhatan, see the excerpt from "Powhatan's Discourse" earlier in this volume.) Smith was a leading member of the English company that had established the colony of Jamestown, in what is now Virginia. While on an expedition to discover the source of the Chickahominy River, he was taken captive by some of Powhatan's men. Arriving at Powhatan's residence at Werowocomoco—on the York River, north of Jamestown—Smith was greeted with an elaborate welcoming ceremony and feast. Soon afterward, however, he was suddenly dragged before Powhatan and threatened with execution. The mamanatowick's preteen daughter Mataoka, better known as Pocahontas (c. 1596–1617), pleaded with her father not to kill Smith. When her appeal appeared to be failing, she shielded Smith's head with her arms and saved his life—or so Smith claimed. Historians and anthropologists have speculated that what Smith describes as a rescue from execution was instead a ceremony designed to make Smith subordinate to Powhatan, thereby transforming Jamestown into a tributary of the Algonquian leader.

The romantic narrative about how Pocahontas rescued John Smith forms one of the central myths of English colonization. It emerges from a short passage in *The General History of Virginia, New England, and the Summer Isles* (1624), a historical compilation that Smith produced jointly with several other writers. In the years between Smith's return from Virginia in 1609 and the appearance of the *General History,* Smith had published other accounts of his Virginia adventures that mention Pocahontas. But the lines devoted to her "rescue" of him appear exclusively in the *General History.* That volume appeared seven years after she died on board a ship while returning from England with her husband—the white colonist John Rolfe—and their son, Thomas. By the time the *General History* was published in London, no one was available to corroborate Smith's account of his dramatic rescue or clarify its significance. The mythology that has grown out of these few brief lines, sometimes conflating the rescue of Smith with Pocahontas's subsequent marriage to Rolfe, is a striking example of how some colonial-era texts have accrued layers of meaning that extend well beyond the words on the page.

This scene is not the only romancelike feature of Smith's writings. The English adventurer deliberately cultivated an aura resembling that of a knight in a chivalric romance—but with important differences. Like Sir Walter Raleigh, the aristocratic English explorer and champion of colonization, Smith pursued adventure and glory. Unlike Raleigh, he was not an aristocrat but a farmer's son. This difference in status forms a major element in Smith's writings. He hailed from the east of England, where his father had a farm on the edge of the Lincolnshire Wolds, an area of considerable natural beauty. The young Smith found the countryside too quiet for his taste. Shortly after his father died in 1596, the restless sixteen-year-old went to the Netherlands to fight for Dutch independence from Philip II of Spain. The fight was part of the European wars of religion, which pitted Protestants against Roman Catholics and, on the eastern front, Christians against Muslims. Smith was one of many planters whose involvement in the colonization of the Americas was colored by experience in these often brutal conflicts. Following his tour of duty in the Netherlands, he fought in the Mediterranean, and he later joined the Austrian imperial army in its war against the Ottoman Empire, which at that time encompassed large swathes of southeastern Europe and the Middle East, as well as parts of North Africa. While fighting the Ottomans in Hungary, Smith earned promotion to the captain's rank that became an enduring part of his public persona. He claimed, apparently with at least some degree of truth, that he had defeated and beheaded a succession of three Turkish officers in single combat. The coat of arms that he was later awarded showed the three severed heads.

Eventually, Smith was wounded in battle, taken prisoner, and sold as a slave to a Turkish noblewoman. Smith described his developing attachment to this noblewoman in his semiautobiographical work, *The True Travels, Adventures, and Observations of Captaine John Smith, in Europe, Asia, Affrica, and America* (1630). The romance might have ended in marriage, with Smith converting to Islam and serving as an Ottoman bureaucrat. Instead, the Englishman killed the noblewoman's brother in ambiguous circumstances—Smith may have mistaken a form of training for mistreatment—and escaped. Smith later gave place names drawn from his Turkish adventures to areas in New England, such as Three Turks' Heads (near Cape Ann in Massachusetts), which John Winthrop mentioned in his journal account of the Puritans' arrival in 1630.

After returning to England in the winter of 1604–05, Smith began looking for his next adventure. The twenty-six-year-old veteran had an assertive personality and military experience that were attractive qualities to the members of the Virginia Company of London as they organized their 1606 expedition to establish what they hoped would be England's first permanent plantation in North America. But those qualities also carried liabilities. Smith sometimes used force unnecessarily, and his hard-to-control temper and stubborn self-reliance could make him a troublesome companion. He ran afoul of the people in charge of the expedition on the voyage to America in 1607, when he was placed under arrest and threatened with execution. Then, in a remarkable turn of events, his name was found on the list of council members that the company had designated to run the colony, which had been kept secret until the group's arrival. The company had recognized qualities in Smith that they believed would be useful to the group, and so despite his comparatively modest status and his propensity for challenging authority, they gave him a role in the Jamestown colony's leadership.

Smith set out to organize the men and explore and map the region. Many of the other colonists were from elite backgrounds, and they were often unwilling or unable to perform the hard and dangerous work that settlement demanded. The colonists who survived rampant illness, famine, warfare, and other mishaps increasingly came to value Smith's leadership, and in 1608 he was elected to the colony's highest office, becoming the equivalent of its governor. But official status offered little protection in the volatile colonial setting. When Smith returned to Jamestown after being held captive by Powhatan—the episode where he was "rescued" by Pocahontas—he was charged with the deaths of the two soldiers who had accompanied him on the expedition that ended in his capture. Smith was saved from hanging when the colonists were distracted by the fortuitous arrival of a fleet with much-needed supplies from England. Not long afterward, however, Smith's gunpowder bag mysteriously exploded in his lap while he napped on the deck of an exploring vessel—possibly because a disgruntled member of the company had thrown a match into the powder. Smith left Virginia in 1609, never to return.

Smith is most closely associated with the Virginia enterprise, but he also took an active interest in New England, and his works form an important bridge between these first two permanent English colonies in North America. In 1614 he voyaged to New England, and he, not the Puritans, gave the region its name. He offered the Pilgrims his services as a guide for their voyage in 1620, but they chose instead to put Smith's helpful books and maps in the hands of a more temperate military leader, Myles Standish. If not for this rejection and some unfortunate setbacks that prevented future voyages, Smith might have become more famous for this second aspect of his American career than for the first: he published more works on New England than on Virginia, seeing in the northern region great potential for "middling" English settlers. Smith's New England works have a strong ideological caste, in that they focus more on the idea of America and less on the many challenges of establishing plantations there, doubtless a reflection of his indirect involvement.

Smith published some nine books between 1608 and 1631, including his works on Virginia and New England, books for aspiring seamen, and *The True Travels*. Many of his writings have a distinctly Elizabethan caste to them, though with a difference. In his works, the heroic ideal of the elite adventurer, typified by Sir Walter Raleigh, gives way to the prototype of the independent self-made man. Tales of exploration, piracy, and military adventure had stirred Smith's youthful imagination, and he longed to create his own heroic narratives. Rather than simply reproduce heroic literary conventions, Smith actively transformed them. In contrast to Raleigh, who was associated with the high literary ideals embodied in Edmund Spenser's epic poem *The Faerie Queen* (1590), Smith wrote prose accounts addressed to the expanding market for popular printed works, which was driven in part by the public appetite for writings about the colonization effort. Though largely untutored in the finer points of style, he had an ear for a good story and a capacity for striking metaphors. Sprinkled with classical allusions and references to the popular theater, his writings also demonstrate his mastery of the humanistic genres of oratory, history, and descriptive travel writing.

The most lasting and influential contribution of his writings was a vision of England's colonies as places where people of all economic backgrounds could support themselves as small farmers, in healthful and pleasant circumstances, with greater liberty than might be possible elsewhere. The outlines of the yeoman farmer ideal that would be so important for Virginia's Thomas Jefferson emerge clearly in Smith's works. The negative aspects of this vision emerge as well in passages revealing how this figure comes to overshadow and dominate those who pursued other modes of life, notably America's indigenous inhabitants. Perhaps Smith's most salient quality as a writer is his special knack for illustrating the connections between the often sordid or brutal details of the colonization enterprise and the imaginative work that propelled it.

The following texts are from *Travels and Works of Captain John Smith* (1910), edited by Edward Arber and A. G. Bradley.

From The General History of Virginia, New England, and the Summer Isles[1]

From The Third Book[2]

FROM CHAPTER 2. WHAT HAPPENED TILL THE FIRST SUPPLY[3]

Being thus left to our fortunes, it fortuned that within ten days[4] scarce ten amongst us could either go, or well stand, such extreme weakness and sickness oppressed us. And thereat none need marvel, if they consider the cause and reason, which was this:

Whilst the ships stayed, our allowance was somewhat bettered, by a daily proportion of biscuit, which the sailors would pilfer to sell, give, or exchange with us, for money, Sassafras,[5] furs, or love. But when they departed, there remained neither tavern, beer house, nor place of relief, but the common kettle.[6] Had we been as free from all sins as [from] gluttony, and drunkenness, we might have been canonized for Saints; but our President would never have been admitted, for engrossing to his private [use], oatmeal, sack, oil, aqua vitae, beef, eggs, or what not, but the kettle;[7] that indeed he allowed equally to be distributed, and that was half a pint of wheat, and as much barley boiled with water for a man a day, and this having fried some twenty-six weeks in the ship's hold, contained as many worms as grains, so that we might truly call it rather so much bran then corn; our drink[8] was water, our lodgings castles in the air.

With this lodging and diet, our extreme toil in bearing and planting palisades, so strained and bruised us, and our continual labor in the extremity of the heat had so weakened us, as were cause sufficient to have made us as miserable in our native country, or any other place in the world.

From May, to September [1607], those that escaped, lived upon sturgeon, and sea crabs. Fifty in this time we buried, the rest seeing the President's[9] projects to escape these miseries in our pinnace by flight (who all this time had neither felt want nor sickness) so moved our dead spirits, as we deposed him and established Ratcliffe in his place, (Gosnold being dead, Kendall deposed). Smith newly recovered, Martin[1] and Ratcliffe were by his care

---

1. The Bermuda Islands.
2. The Third Book is titled "The Proceedings and Accidents of the English Colony in Virginia" and is derived from Smith's Virginia book of 1612.
3. The bulk of this chapter may have been written by Smith, although at its publication in 1612 it was credited solely to Thomas Studley, chief storekeeper of the colony. In 1624, Smith added to Studley's signature at the end of this section of the text not only his own initials but also the names of Robert Fenton and Edward Harrington as part authors. Studley died early in the first year, on August 28, 1607, four days after Harrington, so neither could have written much of what is partly attributed to them. Of Robert Fenton nothing is known.
4. By the end of June 1607, after Captain Christopher Newport (d. 1617) left to fetch new supplies from England. "Fortuned": happened.
5. The bark of the sassafras tree, sold for its supposed medicinal qualities, was a valuable commodity in London.
6. I.e., the communal resources.

7. I.e., President Edward Maria Wingfield (c. 1560–1613), a man of high connections in England, would not have been canonized because he diverted many supplies (everything except the contents of the common kettle) for his own use, including sack (wine) and aqua vitae (brandy).
8. "Drink," here used ironically, customarily referred to wine or beer. "Corn": grain.
9. I.e., Wingfield's.
1. Captain John Martin (c. 1567–1632?) was a colonist best known for his contentiousness. "Captain John Ratcliffe" was an alias of John Sicklemore, master of one of the vessels on the voyage over and a member of the local council. The most enigmatic figure in Jamestown, he was elected president of the council in September 1607, but later fell out with Smith. Captain Bartholomew Gosnold (ca. 1572–1607), who had explored New England before the first Jamestown voyage, probably had been responsible for Smith's recruitment to the venture. Captain George Kendall was executed for mutiny later in the year.

preserved and relieved, and the most of the soldiers recovered with the skillful diligence of Master Thomas Wotton our general surgeon.

But now was all our provision spent, the sturgeon gone, all helps abandoned, each hour expecting the fury of the savages, when God the patron of all good endeavors, in that desperate extremity so changed the hearts of the savages, that they brought such plenty of their fruits, and provision, as no man wanted.[2]

And now where some affirmed it was ill done of the Council to send forth men so badly provided, this incontradictable reason will show them plainly they are too ill advised to nourish such ill conceits: first, the fault of our going was our own; what could be thought fitting or necessary we had; but what we should find, or want, or where we should be, we were all ignorant, and supposing to make our passage in two months, with victual to live, and the advantage of the spring to work; we were at sea five months, where we both spent our victual and lost the opportunity of the time and season to plant, by the unskilfull presumption of our ignorant transporters, that understood not at all, what they undertook.

Such actions have ever since the world's beginning been subject to such accidents, and everything of worth is found full of difficulties: but nothing so difficult as to establish a commonwealth so far remote from men and means, and where men's minds are so untoward[3] as neither do well themselves, nor suffer others. But to proceed.

The new President and Martin, being little beloved, of weak judgment in dangers, and less industry in peace, committed the managing of all things abroad[4] to Captain Smith: who by his own example, good words, and fair promises, set some to mow, others to bind thatch, some to build houses, others to thatch them, himself always bearing the greatest task for his own share, so that in short time, he provided most of them lodgings, neglecting any for himself.

This done, seeing the savages' superfluity begin to decrease [Smith] (with some of his workmen) shipped himself in the shallop[5] to search the country for trade. The want of[6] the language, knowledge to manage his boat without sails, the want of a sufficient power (knowing the multitude of the savages), apparel for his men, and other necessaries, were infinite impediments yet no discouragement.

Being but six or seven in company he went down the river to Kecoughtan[7] where at first they scorned him as a famished man, and would in derision offer him a handful of corn, a piece of bread, for their swords and muskets, and such like proportions also for their apparel. But seeing by trade and courtesy there was nothing to be had, he made bold to try such conclusions as necessity enforced; though contrary to his commission, [he] let fly[8] his muskets, ran his boat on shore, whereat they all fled into the woods.

So marching towards their houses, they might see great heaps of corn: much ado he had to restrain his hungry soldiers from present taking of it,

2. I.e., was in want.
3. Intractable.
4. I.e., outside the colony's palisade.
5. An open boat.
6. Inability to speak.

7. A village near the mouth of the James River whose inhabitants, the Kecoughtans, were members of the Powhatan Confederacy.
8. Fired.

expecting as it happened that the savages would assault them, as not long after they did with a most hideous noise. Sixty or seventy of them, some black, some red, some white, some particoloured, came in a square order,[9] singing and dancing out of the woods, with their Okee (which was an Idol made of skins, stuffed with moss, all painted and hung with chains and copper) borne before them, and in this manner, being well armed with clubs, targets, bows and arrow, they charged the English that so kindly received them with their muskets loaded with pistol shot, that down fell their God, and divers[1] lay sprawling on the ground; the rest fled again to the woods, and ere long sent one of their Quiyoughkasoucks[2] to offer peace, and redeem their Okee.

Smith told them, if only six of them would come unarmed and load his boat, he would not only be their friend, but restore them their Okee, and give them beads, copper, and hatchets besides, which on both sides was to their contents[3] performed, and then they brought him venison, turkeys, wild fowl, bread, and what they had, singing and dancing in sign of friendship till they departed.

In his return he discovered the town and country of Warraskoyack.[4]

> Thus God unboundless by His power,
> Made them thus kind, would us devour.

Smith perceiving (notwithstanding their late misery) not any regarded but from hand to mouth[5] (the company being well recovered) caused the pinnace to be provided with things fitting to get provision for the year following, but in the interim he made three or four journeys and discovered the people of Chickahominy.[6] Yet what he carefully provided the rest carelessly spent.

Wingfield and Kendall living in disgrace * * * strengthened themselves with the sailors and other confederates, to regain their former credit and authority, or at least such means aboard the pinnace, (being fitted to sail as Smith had appointed for trade) to alter her course and to go for England.

Smith, unexpectedly returning, had the plot discovered to him, much trouble he had to prevent it, till with store of saker[7] and musket shot he forced them stay or sink in the river: which action cost the life of Captain Kendall.

These brawls are so disgustful, as some will say they were better forgotten, yet all men of good judgment will conclude, it were better their baseness should be manifest to the world, than the business bear the scorn and shame of their excused disorders.[8]

9. "Square order": formation. "Particoloured": i.e., painted for battle.
1. Several. "Targets": small shields. "So kindly": in such a way.
2. Smith elsewhere defines this term as referring to the "petty gods" of the Algonquian-speaking peoples, but here it may mean priests.
3. I.e., in mutual contentment.
4. A village on the south side of the James River.
5. I.e., none of the settlers, despite their recent sufferings, gave any thought to gathering a store of provision for the future.
6. The region along the Chickahominy River, which empties into the James River a short distance west of Jamestown.
7. Shot for a small cannon used in sieges and on shipboard. "Discovered": revealed.
8. I.e., it is necessary to recount these troubles and lay the blame on the responsible individuals (Wingfield and Kendall), rather than let the whole "business" of the colony suffer ill repute.

The President and Captain Archer[9] not long after intended also to have abandoned the country, which project also was curbed, and suppressed by Smith.

The Spaniard never more greedily desired gold then he victual,[1] nor his soldiers more to abandon the country, than he to keep it. But [he found] plenty of corn in the river of Chickahominy, where hundreds of savages in divers places stood with baskets expecting his coming.

And now the winter approaching, the rivers became so covered with swans, geese, ducks, and cranes that we daily feasted with good bread, Virginia peas, pumpkins, and putchamins, fish, fowl, and divers sorts of wild beasts as fat as we could eat them, so that none of our Tuftaffety humorists[2] desired to go for England.

But our comedies never endured long without a tragedy, some idle exceptions[3] being muttered against Captain Smith, for not discovering the head of Chickahominy river, and [he being] taxed by the council to be too slow in so worthy an attempt. The next voyage he proceeded so far that with much labor by cutting of trees asunder he made his passage, but when his barge could pass no farther, he left her in a broad bay out of danger of shot, commanding none should go ashore till his return; himself with two English and two savages went up higher in a canoe, but he was not long absent but his men went ashore, whose want of government gave both occasion and opportunity to the savages to surprise one George Cassen, whom they slew and much failed not to have cut off the boat and all the rest.[4]

Smith little dreaming of that accident, being got to the marshes at the river's head twenty miles in the desert,[5] had his two men slain (as is supposed) sleeping by the canoe, whilst himself by fowling sought them victual, who finding he was beset with 200 savages, two of them he slew, still defending himself with the aid of a savage his guide, whom he bound to his arm with his garters, and used him as a buckler,[6] yet he was shot in his thigh a little, and had many arrows that stuck in his clothes but no great hurt, till at last they took him prisoner.

When this news came to Jamestown, much was their sorrow for his loss, few expecting what ensued.

Six or seven weeks those barbarians kept him prisoner, many strange triumphs and conjurations they made of him, yet he so demeaned[7] himself amongst them, as he not only diverted them from surprising the fort, but procured his own liberty, and got himself and his company such estimation amongst them, that those savages admired him more than their owne Quiyoughkasoucks.

The manner how they used and delivered him, is as followeth:

The savages having drawn from George Cassen whither Captain Smith was gone, prosecuting that opportunity they followed him with 300 bowmen,

---

9. Gabriel Archer (c. 1575–1609?) had been an associate of Bartholomew Gosnold before the Jamestown voyage. Having gone back to England in 1608 as a confirmed opponent of Smith, he returned to Virginia the following year to head an anti-Smith faction but died during the starving time the next winter. Ratcliffe (Sicklemore) was still president.
1. I.e., Smith wanted to find food for the colonists as much as Spanish conquistadors wanted

to find gold.
2. Self-indulgent persons who might be given to wearing lace. "Putchamins": persimmons.
3. Objections.
4. I.e., only through fault of their own did they fail to wipe out Cassen's whole party. "Government": discipline.
5. Wilderness.
6. Shield. "Garters": laces used for tying clothing.
7. Behaved.

conducted by the King of Pamunkey, who in divisions searching the turnings of the river, found Robinson and Emry by the fireside; those they shot full of arrows and slew.[8] Then finding the Captain, as is said, that used the savage that was his guide as his shield (three of them being slain and divers other so galled)[9] all the rest would not come near him. Thinking thus to have returned to his boat, regarding them, as he marched, more than his way, [he] slipped up to the middle in an oozy creek and his savage with him, yet dared they not come to him till being near dead with cold, he threw away his arms. Then according to their composition[1] they drew him forth and led him to the fire, where his men were slain. Diligently they chafed his benumbed limbs.

He demanding for their captain, they showed him Opechancanough, King of Pamunkey, to whom he gave a round ivory double compass dial. Much they marveled at the playing of the fly[2] and needle, which they could see so plainly and yet not touch it because of the glass that covered them. But when he demonstrated by that globe-like jewell, the roundness of the earth, and skies, the sphere of the sun, moon, and stars, and how the sun did chase the night round about the world continually, the greatness of the land and sea, the diversity of nations, variety of complexions, and how we were to them antipodes,[3] and many other such like matters, they all stood as amazed with admiration.

Notwithstanding, within an hour after, they tied him to a tree, and as many as could stand about him prepared to shoot him, but the King holding up the compass in his hand, they all laid down their bows and arrows, and in a triumphant manner led him to Orapaks, where he was after their manner kindly feasted, and well used.[4]

Their order in conducting him was thus: Drawing themselves all in file, the King in the midst had all their pieces[5] and swords borne before him. Captain Smith was led after him by three great savages holding him fast by each arm, and on each side six went in file with their arrows nocked.[6] But arriving at the town (which was but only thirty or forty hunting houses made of mats, which they remove as they please, as we our tents), all the women and children staring to behold him, the soldiers first all in file performed the form of a Bissom[7] so well as could be, and on each flank, officers as sergeants to see them keep their orders. A good time they continued this exercise and then cast themselves in a ring, dancing in such several postures and singing and yelling out such hellish notes and screeches; being strangely painted, every one [had] his quiver of arrows and at his back a club, on his arm a fox or an otter's skin or some such matter for his vambrace, their heads and shoulders painted red, with oil and pocones mingled together, which scarlet-like color made an exceeding handsome show, his bow in his hand,

8. I.e., these are the two men mentioned above as having been killed while they slept by the canoe (the fireside being by the canoe). John Robinson was a "gentleman"; Thomas Emry was a carpenter. "King of Pamunkey": Opechanca-nough, Powhatan's younger half-brother (d. 1644) and Smith's captor, who led the Powhatan Confederacy's attack on the colonists in 1622 and as late as 1644 attempted one last time to expel them from the country.
9. Wounded.

1. Agreement for surrender.
2. Compass card.
3. On the opposite side of the globe.
4. Treated. "Orapaks": a village located farther inland, later the residence of Powhatan.
5. Guns.
6. Notched; i.e., with their arrows fitted on the bowstring ready for use.
7. From an Italian term denoting a snakelike formation.

and the skin of a bird with her wings abroad[8] dryed, tied on his head, a piece of copper, a white shell, a long feather with a small rattle growing at the tails of their snakes tied to it, or some such like toy. All this while, Smith and the King stood in the midst, guarded as before is said, and after three dances they all departed. Smith they conducted to a long house where thirty or forty tall fellows did guard him, and ere long more bread and venison was brought him than would have served twenty men. I think his stomach at that time was not very good; what he left they put in baskets and tied over his head. About midnight they set the meat again before him; all this time not one of them would eat a bit with him, till the next morning they brought him as much more, and then did they eat all the old, and reserved the new as they had done the other, which made him think they would fat him to eat him. Yet in this desperate estate, to defend him from the cold, one Maocassater brought him his gown, in requital[9] of some beads and toys Smith had given him at his first arrival in Virginia.

Two days after, a man would have slain him (but that the guard prevented it) for the death of his son, to whom they conducted him to recover the poor man then breathing his last. Smith told them that at Jamestown he had a water would do it, if they would let him fetch it, but they would not permit that, but made all the preparations they could to assault Jamestown, craving his advice, and for recompence he should have life, liberty, land, and women. In part of a table book[1] he wrote his mind to them at the fort, what was intended, how they should follow that direction to affright the messengers, and without fail send him such things as he wrote for. And an inventory with them. The difficulty and danger, he told the savages, of the mines, great guns, and other engines[2] exceedingly affrighted them, yet according to his request they went to Jamestown in as bitter weather as could be of frost and snow, and within three days returned with an answer.

But when they came to Jamestown, seeing men sally out as he had told them they would, they fled, yet in the night they came again to the same place where he had told them they should receive an answer and such things as he had promised them, which they found accordingly, and with which they returned with no small expedition to the wonder of them all that heard it, that he could either divine[3] or the paper could speak.

Then they led him to the Youghtanunds, the Mattapanients, the Piankatanks, the Nantaughtacunds, and Onawmanients upon the rivers of Rappahannock and Potomac, over all those rivers, and back again by divers other several nations,[4] to the King's habitation at Pamunkey where they entertained him with most strange and fearful conjurations:[5]

> As if near led to hell,
> Amongst the devils to dwell.

---

8. Outspread. "Vambrace": forearm protection. "Pocones": a vegetable dye.
9. Payment.
1. A notebook.
2. Weaponry.
3. Perform magic. "Expedition": speed.
4. Other Algonquian-speaking groups. The

named groups were part of the Powhatan Confederacy.
5. Incantations. However, Smith derived the following couplet from a translation of the ancient Roman writer Seneca published by Martin Fotherby in his philosophical treatise *Atheomastix* (1622).

Not long after, early in a morning, a great fire was made in a long house, and a mat spread on the one side as on the other; on the one they caused him to sit, and all the guard went out of the house, and presently came skipping in a great grim fellow all painted over with coal[6] mingled with oil, and many snakes' and weasels' skins stuffed with moss, and all their tails tied together so as they met on the crown of his head in a tassel, and round about the tassel was as a coronet of feathers, the skins hanging round about his head, back, and shoulders and in a manner covered his face, with a hellish voice, and a rattle in his hand. With most strange gestures and passions he began his invocation and environed[7] the fire with a circle of meal; which done, three more such like devils came rushing in with the like antic tricks, painted half black, half red, but all their eyes were painted white and some red strokes like mustaches along their cheeks. Round about him those fiends danced a pretty while, and then came in three more as ugly as the rest, with red eyes and white strokes over their black faces. At last they all sat down right against him, three of them on the one hand of the chief priest, and three on the other. Then all with their rattles began a song; which ended, the chief priest laid down five wheat corns; then straining his arms and hands with such violence that he sweat and his veins swelled, he began a short oration;[8] at the conclusion they all gave a short groan and then laid down three grains more. After that, began their song again, and then another oration, ever laying down so many corns as before till they had twice encircled the fire; that done, they took a bunch of little sticks prepared for that purpose, continuing still their devotion, and at the end of every song and oration they laid down a stick betwixt the divisions of corn. Till night, neither he nor they did either eat or drink, and then they feasted merrily with the best provisions they could make. Three days they used this ceremony; the meaning whereof, they told him, was to know if he intended them well or no. The circle of meal signified their country, the circles of corn the bounds of the sea, and the sticks his country. They imagined the world to be flat and round, like a trencher,[9] and they in the midst.

After this they brought him a bag of gunpowder, which they carefully preserved till the next spring, to plant as they did their corn, because they would be acquainted with the nature of that seed.

Opitchapam, the King's brother,[1] invited him to his house, where, with as many platters of bread, fowl, and wild beasts as did environ him, he bid him welcome, but not any of them would eat a bit with him but put up all the remainder in baskets.

At his return to Opechancanough's, all the King's women and their children, flocked about him for their parts,[2] as a due by custom, to be merry with such fragments:

But his waking mind in hideous dreams did oft see wondrous shapes,
Of bodies strange, and huge in growth, and of stupendous makes.[3]

---

6. I.e., charcoal.
7. Encircled.
8. Prayer. "Wheat corns": i.e., five kernels of Indian corn.
9. A flat, wooden dish.

1. Actually the chief's half-brother; he succeeded Powhatan in 1618.
2. Gifts.
3. From a translation of the ancient Roman writer Lucretius by Fotherby.

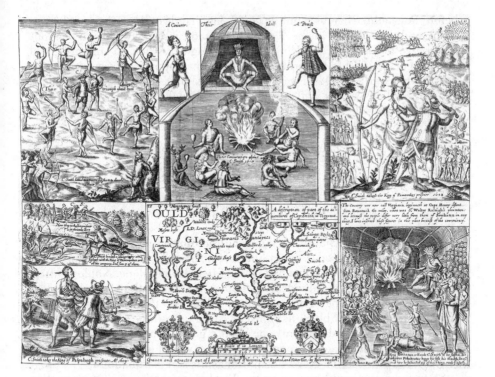

"Map of the old Virginia," by Robert Vaughan, from John Smith, *The General History of Virginia, New England, and the Summer Isles* (1624). This map of Old Virginia, the part of coastal North Carolina where the first English explorations and settlements took place in the 1580s, is surrounded by images portraying John Smith's warlike encounters around Jamestown some twenty years later. The panel in the lower right corner shows the intervention of Pocahontas in the supposed execution of Smith.

At last they brought him to Werowocomoco,[4] where was Powhatan, their Emperor. Here more than two hundred of those grim courtiers stood wondering at him, as [if] he had been a monster, till Powhatan and his train had put themselves in their greatest braveries.[5] Before a fire upon a seat like a bedstead, he sat covered with a great robe made of raccoon skins and all the tails hanging by. On either hand did sit a young wench of sixteen or eighteen years and along on each side [of] the house, two rows of men and behind them as many women, with all their heads and shoulders painted red, many of their heads bedecked with the white down of birds, but every one with something, and a great chain of white beads about their necks.

At his entrance before the King, all the people gave a great shout. The Queen of Appomattoc[6] was appointed to bring him water to wash his hands, and another brought him a bunch of feathers, instead of a towel to dry them; having feasted him after their best barbarous manner they could, a long consultation was held, but the conclusion was, two great stones were brought before Powhatan; then as many as could, laid hands on him, dragged him to them, and thereon laid his head and being ready with their clubs to beat out his brains, Pocahontas, the King's dearest daughter, when no entreaty could prevail, got his head in her arms and laid her own upon his to save him from death, whereat the Emperor was contented he should live to make him hatchets, and her bells, beads, and copper, for they thought him as well of all occupations as themselves.[7] For the King himself will make his own robes, shoes, bows, arrows, pots; plant, hunt, or do any thing so well as the rest.

> They say he bore a pleasant show,
> But sure his heart was sad.
> For who can pleasant be, and rest,
> That lives in fear and dread:
> And having life suspected, doth
> It still suspected lead.[8]

Two days after, Powhatan having disguised himself in the most fearfulest manner he could, caused Captain Smith to be brought forth to a great house in the woods and there upon a mat by the fire to be left alone. Not long after, from behind a mat that divided the house, was made the most dolefulest noise he ever heard; then Powhatan more like a devil than a man, with some two hundred more as black as himself, came unto him and told him now they were friends, and presently he should go to Jamestown, to send him two great guns and a grindstone for which he would give him the Country of Capahowasic and for ever esteem him as his son Nantaquoud.[9]

So to Jamestown with twelve guides Powhatan sent him. That night they quartered in the woods, he still expecting (as he had done all this long time of his imprisonment) every hour to be put to one death or other, for all their feasting. But almighty God (by His divine providence) had mollified the hearts of those stern barbarians with compassion. The next morning betimes they came to the fort, where Smith having used the savages with what kindness he could, he showed Rawhunt, Powhatan's trusty servant, two demiculverins[1] and a millstone to carry [to] Powhatan; they found them somewhat too heavy, but when they did see him discharge them, being loaded with stones, among the boughs of a great tree loaded with icickles, the ice and branches came so tumbling down that the poor savages ran away half dead with fear. But at last we regained some conference with them and gave them such toys and sent to Powhatan, his women, and children such presents as gave them in general full content.

Now in Jamestown they were all in combustion, the strongest preparing once more to run away with the pinnace; which with the hazard of his life, with saker falcon[2] and musket shot, Smith forced now the third time to stay or sink.

Some no better than they should be, had plotted with the President the next day to have put him to death by the Levitical[3] law, for the lives of

---

7. I.e., they thought him as variously skilled as themselves.
8. Derived from a translation of the ancient Greek playwright Euripides by Fotherby.
9. I.e., Powhatan would esteem him as highly as his own son Nantaquoud. Capahowasic was along the York River, near where Smith was held prisoner.
1. Large cannons.
2. Small artillery piece.
3. "And he that killeth any man shall surely be put to death" (Leviticus 24.17).

Robinson and Emry; pretending the fault was his that had led them to their ends: but he quickly took such order with such lawyers that he laid them by the heels till he sent some of them prisoners for England.

Now ever once in four or five days, Pocahontas with her attendants brought him so much provision that saved many of their lives, that else for all this had starved with hunger.

Thus from numb death our good God sent relief,
The sweet assuager of all other grief.[4]

His relation of the plenty he had seen, especially at Werowocomoco, and of the state and bounty of Powhatan (which till that time was unknown), so revived their dead spirits (especially the love of Pocahontas)[5] as all men's fear was abandoned.

Thus you may see what difficulties still crossed any good endeavor; and the good success of the business being thus oft brought to the very period of destruction; yet you see by what strange means God hath still delivered it.

* * *

From *The Fourth Book*

[SMITH'S FAREWELL TO VIRGINIA]

Thus far I have traveled in this Wilderness of Virginia, not being ignorant for all my pains this discourse will be wrested, tossed and turned as many ways as there is leaves;[6] that I have written too much of some, too little of others, and many such like objections. To such I must answer, in the Company's name I was requested to do it,[7] if any have concealed their approved experiences from my knowledge, they must excuse me: as for every fatherless or stolen relation,[8] or whole volumes of sophisticated rehearsals, I leave them to the charge of them that desire them. I thank God I never undertook anything yet [for which] any could tax me of carelessness or dishonesty, and what is he to whom I am indebted or troublesome?[9] Ah! were these my accusers but to change cases and places with me [for] but two years, or till they had done but so much as I, it may be they would judge more charitably of my imperfections. But here I must leave all to the trial of time, both myself, Virginia's preparations, proceedings and good events, praying to that great God the protector of all goodness to send them as good success as the goodness of the action[1] and country deserveth, and my heart desireth.

1624

---

4. The first line appears to be Smith's, inspired by Fotherby. The second comes from Fotherby's translation of a quotation from Euripides in a text by the ancient Greek writer Plutarch.
5. I.e., the evident affection of Pocahontas for Smith and the English was instrumental in reviving the colonists' spirits.
6. Pages.
7. Smith was not requested to write the whole *General History* by the Virginia Company, so it is

not clear what he means here. Possibly the discourse to which he refers is the brief summary of recommendations for the "reformation" of Virginia that ends the Fourth Book and that he drew up at the request of the royal commissioners charged with effecting that reformation.
8. I.e., anonymous or "fugitive" narratives. "Approved": proven.
9. I.e., and who is it that I have been a burden to?
1. Venture. "Events": results.

From A Description of New England

Who can desire more content, that hath small means; or but only his merit to advance his fortune, than to tread, and plant that ground he hath purchased by the hazard of his life? If he have but the taste of virtue and magnanimity, what to such a mind can be more pleasant, than planting and building a foundation for his posterity, got from the rude earth, by God's blessing and his own industry, without prejudice[1] to any? If he have any grain of faith or zeal in religion, what can he do less hurtful to any; or more agreeable to God, than to seek to convert those poor savages to know Christ, and humanity, whose labors with discretion will triple requite thy charge and pains? What so truly suits with honor and honesty, as the discovering things unknown? erecting towns, peopling countries, informing the ignorant, reforming things unjust, teaching virtue; and gaining to our native mother country a kingdom to attend her, finding employment for those that are idle, because they know not what to do: so far from wronging any, as to cause posterity to remember thee; and remembering thee, ever honor that remembrance with praise?

* * *

Then, who would live at home idly (or think in himself any worth to live) only to eat, drink, and sleep, and so die? Or by consuming that carelessly, [which] his friends got worthily? Or by using that miserably, that maintained virtue honestly? Or for being descended nobly, pine with the vain vaunt of great kindred, in penury?[2] Or (to maintain a silly show of bravery) toil out thy heart, soul, and time, basely, by shifts,[3] tricks, cards, and dice? Or by relating news of others' actions, shark[4] here or there for a dinner, or supper; deceive thy friends, by fair promises, and dissimulation, in borrowing where thou never intendest to pay; offend the laws, surfeit with excess, burden thy country, abuse thyself, despair in want, and then cozen[5] thy kindred, yea even thine own brother, and wish thy parents' death (I will not say damnation) to have their estates? though thou seest what honors, and rewards, the world yet hath for them will seek them and worthily deserve them.

* * *

Let this move you to embrace employment, for those whose educations, spirits, and judgments want but your purses; not only to prevent such accustomed dangers, but also to gain more thereby than you have. And you fathers that are either so foolishly fond, or so miserably covetous, or so wilfully ignorant, or so negligently careless, as that you will rather maintain your children in idle wantonness, till they grow your masters; or become so basely unkind, as they wish nothing but your deaths; so that both sorts grow dissolute: and although you would wish them anywhere to escape the gallows, and ease your cares; though they spend you here one, two, or three hundred pound a year; you would grudge to give half so much in adventure with them, to obtain an estate, which in a small time but with a little assistance of your

---

1. Harm. "Magnanimity": greatness of spirit.
2. I.e., live in poverty while claiming great ancestors.

3. Expedients. "Bravery": fine appearances.
4. Sponge.
5. Deceive. "Excess": overindulgence.

providence,[6] might be better than your own. But if an angel should tell you, that any place yet unknown can afford such fortunes; you would not believe him, no more than Columbus was believed there was any such land as is now the well-known abounding America; much less such large regions as are yet unknown, as well in America, as in Africa, and Asia, and Terra Incognita; where were courses for gentlemen (and them that would be so reputed) more suiting their qualities, than begging from their Prince's generous disposition, the labors of his subjects, and the very marrow of his maintenance.

I have not been so ill bred, but I have tasted of plenty and pleasure, as well as want and misery: nor doth necessity yet, or occasion of discontent, force me to these endeavors: nor am I ignorant what small thank I shall have for my pains; or that many would have the World imagine them to be of great judgment, that can but blemish these my designs, by their witty objections and detractions: yet (I hope) my reasons with my deeds, will so prevail with some, that I shall not want[7] employment in these affairs, to make the most blind see his own senselessness, and incredulity; hoping that gain will make them affect that, which religion, charity, and the common good cannot. It were but a poor device in me, to deceive myself; much more the king, state, my friends and country, with these inducements: which, seeing his Majesty hath given permission, I wish all sorts of worthy, honest, industrious spirits, would understand: and if they desire any further satisfaction, I will do my best to give it: Not to persuade them to go only;[8] but go with them: Not leave them there; but live with them there.

I will not say, but by ill providing and undue managing, such courses may be taken, [that] may make us miserable enough:[9] But if I may have the execution of what I have projected; if they want to eat, let them eat or never digest me.[1] If I perform what I say, I desire but that reward out of the gains [which] may suit my pains, quality, and condition. And if I abuse you with my tongue, take my head for satisfaction. If any dislike at the year's end, defraying their charge,[2] by my consent they should freely return. I fear not want of company sufficient, were it but known what I know of those countries; and by the proof of that wealth I hope yearly to return, if God please to bless me from such accidents, as are beyond my power in reason to prevent: For, I am not so simple to think, that ever any other motive than wealth, will ever erect there a commonwealth; or draw company from their ease and humors at home, to stay in New England to effect my purposes.

And lest any should think the toil might be insupportable, though these things may be had by labor, and diligence: I assure myself there are who delight extremely in vain pleasure, that take much more pains in England, to enjoy it, than I should do here to gain wealth sufficient: and yet I think they should not have half such sweet content: for, our pleasure here is still gains; in England charges and loss. Here nature and liberty affords us that freely, which in England we want, or it costeth us dearly. What pleasure can be more, than (being tired with any occasion[3] a-shore, in planting vines,

---

6. Provision.
7. Lack.
8. Alone.
9. I.e., he won't promise that even with bad management they'll succeed.

1. I.e., or never read Smith's works.
2. I.e., once they have paid the cost of their support for the year.
3. Task.

fruits, or herbs, in contriving their own grounds, to the pleasure of their own minds, their fields, gardens, orchards, buildings, ships, and other works, &c.) to recreate themselves before their own doors, in their own boats upon the sea; where man, woman and child, with a small hook and line, by angling, may take diverse sorts of excellent fish, at their pleasures? And is it not pretty sport, to pull up two pence, six pence, and twelve pence, as fast as you can haul and veer a line?[4] He is a very bad fisher [that] cannot kill in one day with his hook and line, one, two, or three hundred cods: which dressed and dried, if they be sold there for ten shillings the hundred (though in England they will give more than twenty) may not both the servant, the master, and merchant, be well content with this gain? If a man work but three days in seven, he may get more than he can spend, unless he will be excessive. Now that carpenter, mason, gardener, tailor, smith, sailor, forgers,[5] or what other, may they not make this a pretty recreation though they fish but an hour in a day, to take more than they eat in a week? or if they will not eat it, because there is so much better choice; yet sell it, or change it, with the fishermen, or merchants, for anything they want. And what sport doth yield a more pleasing content, and less hurt or charge than angling with a hook; and crossing the sweet air from isle to isle, over the silent streams of a calm sea? Wherein the most curious may find pleasure, profit, and content.

Thus, though all men be not fishers: yet all men, whatsoever, may in other matters do as well. For necessity doth in these cases so rule a commonwealth, and each in their several functions, as their labors in their qualities may be as profitable, because there is a necessary mutual use of all.

For Gentlemen, what exercise should more delight them, than ranging daily those unknown parts, using fowling and fishing, for hunting and hawking? and yet you shall see the wild hawks give you some pleasure, in seeing them stoop (six or seven after one another) an hour or two together, at the schools of fish in the fair harbors, as those ashore at a fowl; and never trouble nor torment yourselves, with watching, mewing,[6] feeding, and attending them: nor kill horse and man with running and crying, See you not a hawk?[7] For hunting also: the woods, lakes, and rivers afford not only chase sufficient, for any that delights in that kind of toil, or pleasure; but such beasts to hunt, that besides the delicacy of their bodies for food, their skins are so rich, as may well recompence thy daily labor, with a captains pay.

For laborers, if those that sow hemp, rape,[8] turnips, parsnips, carrots, cabbage, and such like; give twenty, thirty, forty, fifty shillings yearly for an acre of ground, and meat, drink, and wages to use it, and yet grow rich; when better, or at least as good ground, may be had, and cost nothing but labor; it seems strange to me, any such should there grow poor.

My purpose is not to persuade children [to go] from their parents; men from their wives; nor servants from their masters: only, such as with free consent may be spared: But that each parish, or village, in city, or country, that will but apparell their fatherless children, of thirteen or fourteen years of age, or young married people, that have small wealth to live on; here by their

---

4. I.e., fish.
5. I.e., ironworkers.
6. Keeping in a cage. "Stoop": swoop down.
7. Smith contrasts the delight of watching wild hawks hunt their prey in America with the tedious care that keepers of trained hawks in England must give their birds—as when such birds fly away and must be hunted for all over the countryside.
8. The rape plant.

labor may live exceedingly well: provided always that first there be a sufficient power to command them, houses to receive them, means to defend them, and meet provisions for them; for, any place may be overlain:[9] and it is most necessary to have a fortress (ere this grow to practice) and sufficient masters (as, carpenters, masons, fishers, fowlers, gardeners, husbandman, sawyers, smiths, spinsters, tailors, weavers, and such like) to take ten, twelve, or twenty, or as there is occasion, for apprentices. The masters by this may quickly grow rich; these may learn their trades themselves, to do the like; to a general and an incredible benefit, for king, and country, master, and servant.

1616

9. Overcome.

WILLIAM BRADFORD
1590–1657

William Bradford's *Of Plymouth Plantation* offered the first sustained treatment of New England's early history, and it helped shape enduring cultural narratives about the small settlement that a group of religious dissenters known as the Pilgrims established on the Massachusetts coast in 1620. Written between roughly 1630 and 1650, *Of Plymouth Plantation* casts a backward look on the Plymouth colony's early history and seeks meaning in its major episodes. As he composed his retrospective account, Bradford revised more immediate, journalistic-style narratives such as *Mourt's Relation* (1622), which Bradford coauthored with Edward Winslow, another Plymouth leader. He also incorporated and reworked his own notes. In the resulting narrative, Bradford portrays the uncertain and ambiguous emergence of providential meaning.

Bradford's life, with its many losses and dislocations as well as its strong if sometimes muted sense of purpose, provides a model of the Plymouth community. He was born in Yorkshire, in the northeast of England, a region still retaining marks of Viking invasions from centuries past. Bradford's father died when he was an infant, and he was passed among relatives and taught the arts of farming. His life changed at age twelve or thirteen, when he heard the sermons of Richard Clyfton. Clyfton was the Nonconformist minister of a small community in Scrooby, Nottinghamshire, a neighboring parish. Despite opposition from his uncles and grandparents, in 1606 Bradford left home and joined the community.

The members of the Scrooby church were known as "Separatists" because they were not sympathetic to the idea of a national Church, such as the one that King Henry VIII established in England after he broke with the pope. Separating from the Church of England was, however, by English law an act of treason, and many believers paid a high price for their dreams of purity. Other Puritan critics of the established Church, such as the non-Separating Congregationalists who eventually settled Boston, struck a middle path, retaining ties to the Church of England even as they developed a different organizational structure. Despite these differences, the churches at both Plymouth and the neighboring Massachusetts Bay Colony embraced John Calvin's Congregationalist model. Calvin (1509–1564), a French theologian, called upon Protestant reformers to set up "particular," independent churches, each founded on a formal covenant that would be sworn to by its members. In Congregational churches, God offered himself as a contractual partner to each believer in a contract freely initiated but perpetually binding. The model was twofold: the Old Testament covenant that God made with Adam and renewed through Jesus Christ, as well as the tight-knit communities of the early Christian churches.

Wishing to pursue their beliefs about church government more freely, the Scrooby community took up residence in the Netherlands, in Leiden (or Leyden), where Bradford joined them in 1609. But they suffered from continued government harassment, and with the Netherlands on the brink of war with Catholic Spain, the community took counsel from Captain John Smith and petitioned the English government for a grant of land in North America. In mid-September 1620, a portion of the congregation and a group of entrepreneurs sailed from Plymouth, England, for America. The rest of the congregation was expected to follow at some future time. The voyage on the *Mayflower* went relatively smoothly, though one person died, and there was some friction with the often less-than-godly mariners. The colonists' original grant was for land in the Virginia territory, but high seas prevented them from reaching that area and, after an initial foray at Cape Cod, they settled just north of the Cape at an area they named Plymouth, adapting the name that Smith gave to the region in his 1614 expedition. Soon after the *Mayflower's* arrival on the coast, Bradford's wife, Dorothy, fell overboard and drowned. However, little is known about this tragedy; strikingly, Bradford does not mention Dorothy's death in his journal or other writings.

In the second book of Bradford's history he describes the signing of the Mayflower Compact, a civil covenant designed to allow the temporal state to serve the devout citizen. It was the first of numerous "plantation covenants" intended both to protect the rights of citizens from the reach of established governments and to assert the community's authority to create its own "civil body politic" and make its own laws. The sense of communal purpose bolstered by the Compact helped sustain the Plymouth settlement through its difficult first months. Having arrived in winter and being inadequately provisioned, the company was decimated in the "Starving Time" that followed, losing half its members to disease and undernourishment. The colony's first governor, John Carver, was one of the fatalities, and Bradford was elected in Carver's place. As governor, Bradford was chief judge and jury, oversaw agriculture and trade, and made allotments of land. He also conferred with John Winthrop, a leader of neighboring Massachusetts Bay Colony, about matters of regional interest. Bradford served as governor for most of his remaining years.

Bradford was the first person to use the word "Pilgrims," from Hebrews 11.13 in the Geneva Bible, to describe the community of believers who sailed on the *Mayflower*. (The Geneva Bible, also known as the English Bible, was translated by Reformed English Protestants living in Switzerland; this version, used by Puritans, was outlawed by the Church of England.) For Bradford, as for the other members of this community, the decision to settle at Plymouth was the last step in their long journey to escape religious oppression in England. *Of Plymouth Plantation* situates their self-exile in the arc of Christian history as well as in the more recent events surrounding the Protestant Reformation, which sparked wars of religion that plagued England and the rest of Europe for generations. In the opening pages of his Plymouth history, Bradford invokes John Foxe's *Acts and Monuments* (1563), which relates the sufferings of Protestants under Mary Tudor, who as queen of England (1553–58) briefly reinstated Roman Catholicism and oversaw the execution by burning of some three hundred Protestants. Foxe's account, also known as *Foxe's Book of Martyrs*, was an iconic portrayal of Protestant oppression at the hands of Catholic authorities. The continued oppression of dissenters under Anglican rulers had driven the Plymouth colonists first to the Netherlands and then to America, where they hoped to find greater autonomy and opportunity.

This remote settlement was hardly isolated. Bradford locates Plymouth in an expanding network of relations with indigenous communities; with other English settlements, which had a mixture of commercial and religious imperatives; and with numerous European colonies. The latter included the neighboring Dutch colonies, which were Protestant; the more distant yet, ideologically speaking, more threatening French and Spanish colonies, which were Catholic; and the European colonies in the West Indies. Amid European colonization of the Americas, imperial rivalries, and religious conflicts, the Puritans sought to re-create the primitive simplicity of early Christianity.

Cotton Mather, in *Magnalia Christi America* (1702), his ecclesiastical history of New England, describes the self-educated Bradford as

> a person for study as well as action; and hence notwithstanding the difficulties which he passed in his youth, he attained unto a notable skill in languages. . . . But the Hebrew he most of all studied, because, he said, he would see with his own eyes the ancient oracles of God in their native beauty. . . . The crown of all his life was his holy, prayerful, watchful and fruitful walk with God, wherein he was exemplary.

The primitivist impulse animating Bradford and his companions made the success or failure of the Plymouth colony more than a worldly venture—it was a measure of their ability to interpret God's will as they found it in Scripture and to remake the world in its image.

However, the sense of unified purpose in the opening pages of Bradford's chronicle splinters as his account proceeds. Contributing to this fracture was the difficulty that the Plymouth community had in finding a suitable minister. The group's beloved pastor, John Robinson, died before he could cross the Atlantic. Several substitutes were inadequate or worse. Bradford relates the story of the Reverend John Lyford, who served the colony for years. A secret Anglican sympathizer, Lyford betrayed the colonists and was later implicated in misadventures and crimes, including a rape. The Reverend Roger Williams briefly served the Plymouth church but left after a few years for ideological reasons. Some of the other major episodes that tested Bradford and the community include the conflict with Thomas Morton; tensions involving other colonies; the war with the Pequot Indians; and, perhaps most challenging for Bradford, the drift of people away from Plymouth, drawn by economic opportunities, and the resulting divisions in the church. Finding that his lifelong search for a stable, like-minded community had once again been thwarted, the aging Bradford compared Plymouth to "an ancient mother, grown old and forsaken of her children."

Bradford composed his history at the height of the English Civil War, and it remained unpublished for over two centuries. The manuscript mysteriously disappeared around the time of the American Revolution. The first book (through chapter IX) had been copied into the Plymouth church records and was thus preserved, but the second book was believed lost. In 1855 the manuscript was located in the palace of the bishop of London, probably having been removed from Boston's Old South Church by British soldiers or the departing Tory governor, Thomas Hutchinson. After several decades of negotiations, the manuscript was returned to the United States in 1897 and deposited in the Massachusetts State Library.

Though not available in a printed edition until 1856, Bradford's manuscript was a major source for other historians and interpreters of the New England experience, such as Cotton Mather and Samuel Sewall. The incidents reported in Bradford's history continued to guide interpretations of the New England past even when the manuscript's location was unknown. In the early nineteenth century, the leading political thinker and orator Daniel Webster traced the origins of the U.S. Constitution to the Mayflower Compact, contributing to the formation of a narrative about the

Puritan sources of American democracy that influenced the French writer Alexis de Tocqueville's landmark study *Democracy in America* (1835, 1840). These developments in turn helped catalyze a literary reconsideration of the Puritan past. Some of the major events that Bradford describes in *Of Plymouth Plantation* were cast into fictional form by writers such as Nathaniel Hawthorne, whose story "The May-Pole of Merry Mount" (written 1835–36) portrays the conflict between the Plymouth colonists and Thomas Morton's settlement at Ma-re Mount, and Herman Melville, who gave the name of the Pequot Indians to his ill-fated ship in *Moby-Dick* (1851).

Perhaps the main reason for Plymouth's continued place in American memory today is its association with the Thanksgiving holiday. Thanksgiving feasts were common practices in early modern Europe, where they were held on special occasions to celebrate harvests and other important communal events, and this remained the practice in the colonies and United States well into the nineteenth century. President Abraham Lincoln initiated Thanksgiving Day as a national holiday in 1863, intending it as a unifying gesture in the midst of the Civil War. Seventy-six years later, President Franklin Delano Roosevelt moved the holiday from the last week of November to the previous week to help bolster retail sales during the Great Depression.

One striking thing about Bradford's narrative is how little his account of the "First Thanksgiving," in 1621, matches the popular image of that event, which features Puritans and Native Americans sharing the fruits of the land together. The vision of friendly cohabitation derives more directly from a passage in Bradford and Winslow's *Mourt's Relation*, which highlights the presence of the Wampanoag sachem (paramount chief) Massasoit and some ninety of his men, describes how "three days we entertained and feasted" them, and links the celebration to the "Covenant of Peace" between the colonists and the Natives. In recounting the same event decades later, Bradford does not mention the Natives, the peace covenant, or a feast. Instead, he stresses the natural bounty that the community enjoyed and insists on the truthfulness of his earlier reports regarding the land's potential. Though elsewhere Bradford mentions the peace agreement with Massasoit, far more memorable is his account of the burning of Mystic Fort, one of the worst colonial atrocities, where the Puritans slaughtered some four hundred Pequot men, women, and children, backed up by their Narragansett allies.

The differences between the two firsthand descriptions of the Plymouth colonists' first thanksgiving suggest Bradford's shifting priorities and audiences. Once the leading edge of radical Protestant colonization, the small plantation at Plymouth came, after 1630, to be overshadowed by Boston and the Massachusetts Bay Colony, and then by rapidly evolving events in England: civil war, the execution of King Charles I, and the establishment of the Commonwealth of England. Toward the end of the period when he revised his history, the future of New England was in doubt. The overthrow of the British monarchy made some Puritan colonists, notably including Winslow, decide to cast their fortunes with the new regime. Bradford oriented the events that he chronicled toward the changing scenes in England, New England, and the larger Atlantic world.

When Bradford wrote in his opening paragraph that his goal was to relate the main events of the Plymouth colony's short history, making them "manifest in a plain style, with singular regard unto the simple truth in all things," he knew that his work would include matter that he elsewhere described as "tedious and uncomfortable." The full history oscillates between passages of crisp, descriptive prose, sometimes embellished with claims of providential significance, and murky, drawn-out accounts of uncertain financial and political dealings. The uneven texture of the narrative registers the challenges that Bradford faced in both relating the flow of events during a volatile historical moment and trying to discern the signs of God's will in those events.

Of Plymouth Plantation[1]

From *Book I*

FROM CHAPTER I. [THE ENGLISH REFORMATION]

* * * When as by the travail and diligence of some godly and zealous preachers, and God's blessing on their labors, as in other places of the land, so in the North parts,[2] many became enlightened by the word of God, and had their ignorance and sins discovered[3] unto them, and began by His grace to reform their lives, and make conscience of their ways, the work of God was no sooner manifest in them, but presently they were both scoffed and scorned by the profane[4] multitude, and the ministers urged with the yoke of subscription,[5] or else must be silenced; and the poor people were so vexed with apparitors, and the pursuivants, and the commissary courts,[6] as truly their affliction was not small; which, notwithstanding, they bore sundry years with much patience, till they were occasioned (by the continuance and increase of these troubles, and other means which the Lord raised up in those days) to see further into things by the light of the word of God. How not only these base and beggarly ceremonies were unlawful, but also that the lordly and tyranous power of the prelates ought not to be submitted unto; which thus, contrary to the freedom of the gospel, would load and burden men's consciences, and by their compulsive power make a profane mixture of persons and things in the worship of God. And that their offices and callings, courts and canons, etc. were unlawful and anti-Christian; being such as have no warrant in the word of God; but the same that were used in popery, and still retained. Of which a famous author thus writeth in his Dutch commentaries: At the coming of King James into England,

> The new king (saith he) found there established the reformed religion, according to the reformed religion of King Edward VI. Retaining, or keeping still the spiritual state of the bishops, etc. after the old manner, much varying and differing from the reformed churches in Scotland, France, and the Netherlands, Embden, Geneva, etc. whose reformation is cut, or shaped much nearer the first Christian churches, as it was used in the Apostles' times.[7]

So many therefore of these professors[8] as saw the evil of these things, in these parts, and whose hearts the Lord had touched with heavenly zeal for his truth, they shook off this yoke of anti-Christian bondage, and as the Lord's free people, joined themselves (by a covenant of the Lord) into a

---

1. The text is adapted from William Bradford, *Bradford's History "Of Plimoth Plantation." From the Original Manuscript* (1897).
2. I.e., of England and Scotland.
3. Revealed.
4. Worldly.
5. I.e., threatened with forced compliance with the tenets of the Church of England.
6. "Apparitors . . . courts": the ecclesiastical courts and their officers.

7. Bradford quotes the Dutch historian Emanuel van Meteren's *General History of the Netherlands* (1608). King Edward VI reigned from 1547 to 1553. King James I reigned from 1603 to 1625. Most Puritans preferred the Calvinist system in Geneva or the Church of Scotland, which replaced a hierarchy of archbishops, bishops, and priests with a national assembly and a parish presbytery consisting of the ministers and elders.
8. Believers.

church estate, in the fellowship of the gospel, to walk in all his ways, made known, or to be made known unto them, according to their best endeavors, whatsoever it should cost them, the Lord assisting them. And that it cost them something this ensuing history will declare.

These people became two distinct bodies or churches, and in regard of distance of place did congregate severally; for they were of sundry towns and villages, some in Nottinghamshire, some of Lincolnshire, and some of Yorkshire, where they border nearest together. In one of these churches (besides others of note) was Mr. John Smith,[9] a man of able gifts, and a good preacher, who afterwards was chosen their pastor. But these afterwards falling into some errors in the Low Countries,[1] there (for the most part) buried themselves, and their names.

But in this other church (which must be the subject of our discourse) besides other worthy men, was Mr. Richard Clyfton, a grave and revered preacher, who by his pains and diligence had done much good, and under God had been a means of the conversion of many. And also that famous and worthy man Mr. John Robinson,[2] who afterwards was their pastor for many years, till the Lord took him away by death. Also Mr. William Brewster[3] a reverent man, who afterwards was chosen an elder of the church and lived with them till old age.

But after these things they could not long continue in any peaceable condition, but were hunted and persecuted on every side, so as their former afflictions were but as flea-bitings in comparison of these which now came upon them. For some were taken and clapped up in prison, others had their houses beset and watched night and day, and hardly escaped their hands;[4] and the most were fain to fly and leave their houses and habitations, and the means of their livelihood. Yet these and many other sharper things which afterward befell them, were no other than they looked for, and therefore were the better prepared to bear them by the assistance of God's grace and spirit. Yet seeing themselves thus molested, and that there was no hope of their continuance there, by a joint consent they resolved to go into the Low Countries, where they heard was freedom of religion for all men; as also how sundry from London, and other parts of the land, had been exiled and persecuted for the same cause, and were gone thither, and lived at Amsterdam, and in other places of the land. So after they had continued together about a year, and kept their meetings every Sabbath in one place or other, exercising the worship of God amongst themselves, notwithstanding all the diligence and malice of their adversaries, they seeing they could no longer continue in that condition, they resolved to get over into Holland as they could; which was in the year 1607 and 1608.

* * *

9. Not the soldier and explorer; a Cambridge University graduate who seceded from the Church of England in 1605.
1. The Netherlands.
2. Like John Smith and Richard Clyfton, a Cambridge graduate and a Separatist.
3. A church leader of the Pilgrims in both Leyden and Plymouth.
4. I.e., were nearly captured by the authorities.

CHAPTER IX. OF THEIR VOYAGE, AND HOW THEY PASSED THE SEA; AND OF THEIR SAFE ARRIVAL AT CAPE COD

September 6. These troubles being blown over,[5] and now all being compact together in one ship, they put to sea again with a prosperous wind, which continued divers days together, which was some encouragement unto them; yet, according to the usual manner, many were afflicted with seasickness. And I may not omit here a special work of God's providence. There was a proud and very profane young man, one of the seamen, of a lusty,[6] able body, which made him the more haughty; he would always be contemning the poor people in their sickness, and cursing them daily with grievous execrations, and did not let[7] to tell them, that he hoped to help to cast half of them overboard before they came to their journey's end, and to make merry with what they had; and if he were by any gently reproved, he would curse and swear most bitterly. But it pleased God before they came half seas over, to smite this young man with a grievous disease, of which he died in a desperate manner, and so was himself the first that was thrown overboard. Thus his curses lighted on his own head; and it was an astonishment to all his fellows, for they noted it to be the just hand of God upon him.

After they had enjoyed fair winds and weather for a season, they were encountered many times with cross winds, and met with many fierce storms, with which the ship was shroudly[8] shaken, and her upper works made very leaky; and one of the main beams in the midships was bowed and cracked, which put them in some fear that the ship could not be able to perform the voyage. So some of the chief of the company, perceiving the mariners to fear the sufficiency of the ship, as appeared by their mutterings, they entered into serious consultation with the master and other officers of the ship, to consider in time of the danger; and rather to return than to cast themselves into a desperate and inevitable peril. And truly there was great distraction and difference of opinion amongst the mariners themselves; fain would they do what could be done for their wages' sake (being now half the seas over) and on the other hand they were loath to hazard their lives too desperately. But in examining of all opinions, the master and others affirmed they knew the ship to be strong and firm underwater; and [as] for the buckling of the main beam, there was a great iron screw the passengers brought out of Holland, which would raise the beam into his place; the which being done, the carpenter and master affirmed that with a post put under it, set firm in the lower deck, and otherways bound, he would make it sufficient. And as for the decks and upper works they would caulk them as well as they could, and though with the working of the ship they would not long keep staunch,[9] yet there would otherwise be no great danger, if they did not overpress[1] her with sails. So they committed themselves to the will of God, and resolved to proceed. In sundry of these storms the winds were so fierce, and the seas so high, as

---

5. Some of Bradford's community sailed on the *Speedwell* from Delftshaven early in August 1620, but that ship's unseaworthiness forced their transfer to the *Mayflower*.
6. Strong, energetic.

7. Hesitate.
8. Shrewdly, in its original sense of badly or dangerously.
9. Watertight.
1. Overburden.

they could not bear a knot of sail, but were forced to hull,[2] for divers days together. And in one of them, as they thus lay at hull, in a mighty storm, a lusty young man (called John Howland) coming upon some occasion above the gratings, was, with a seele[3] of the ship thrown into [the] sea; but it pleased God that he caught hold of the topsail halyards, which hung overboard, and ran out at length; yet he held his hold (though he was sundry fathoms under water) till he was hauled up by the same rope to the brim of the water, and then with a boat hook and other means got into the ship again, and his life saved; and though he was something ill with it, yet he lived many years after, and became a profitable member both in church and commonwealth. In all this voyage there died but one of the passengers, which was William Butten, a youth, servant to Samuel Fuller, when they drew near the coast. But to omit other things (that I may be brief) after long beating at sea they fell with that land which is called Cape Cod; the which being made and certainly known to be it, they were not a little joyful. After some deliberation had amongst themselves and with the master of the ship, they tacked about and resolved to stand for the southward (the wind and weather being fair) to find some place about Hudson's River[4] for their habitation. But after they had sailed that course about half the day, they fell amongst dangerous shoals and roaring breakers, and they were so far entangled therewith as they conceived themselves in great danger; and the wind shrinking upon them withal, they resolved to bear up again for the Cape, and thought themselves happy to get out of those dangers before night overtook them, as by God's providence they did. And the next day they got into the Cape Harbor,[5] where they rid in safety. A word or two by the way of this cape; it was thus first named by Captain Gosnold and his company, Anno[6] 1602, and after by Captain Smith was called Cape James, but it retains the former name amongst seamen. Also that point which first showed those dangerous shoals unto them, they called Point Care, and Tucker's Terror, but the French and Dutch to this day call it Malabarr, by reason of those perilous shoals,[7] and the losses they have suffered there.

Being thus arrived in a good harbor and brought safe to land, they fell upon their knees and blessed the God of heaven, who had brought them over the vast and furious ocean, and delivered them from all the perils and miseries thereof, again to set their feet on the firm and stable earth, their proper element. And no marvel if they were thus joyful, seeing wise Seneca was so affected with sailing a few miles on the coast of his own Italy; as he affirmed, that he had rather remain twenty years on his way by land, than pass by sea to any place in a short time, so tedious and dreadful was the same unto him.[8]

But here I cannot but stay and make a pause, and stand half amazed at this poor people's present condition, and so I think will the reader, too, when he well considers the same. Being thus passed the vast ocean, and a sea of troubles before in their preparation (as may be remembered by that which went before), they had now no friends to welcome them, nor inns to enter-

2. Drift before the weather under very little sail.
3. Roll.
4. The Hudson River, in New York.
5. They arrived at present-day Provincetown Harbor on November 11, 1620, after sixty-five days at sea.

6. In the year (Latin).
7. The prefix *mal* means "bad," a reference to the dangerous sandbars.
8. Bradford cites *Moral Epistles to Lucilius*, by the Roman Stoic philosopher Seneca (4? B.C.E.–65 C.E.).

tain or refresh their weatherbeaten bodies, no houses or much less towns to repair to, to seek for succor. It is recorded in scripture as a mercy to the apostle and his shipwrecked company, that the barbarians showed them no small kindness in refreshing them,[9] but these savage barbarians, when they met with them (as after will appear) were readier to fill their sides full of arrows than otherwise. And for the season it was winter, and they that know the winters of that country know them to be sharp and violent, and subject to cruel and fierce storms, dangerous to travel to known places, much more to search an unknown coast. Besides, what could they see but a hideous and desolate wilderness, full of wild beasts and wild men? And what multitudes there might be of them they knew not. Neither could they, as it were, go up to the top of Pisgah,[1] to view from this wilderness a more goodly country to feed their hopes; for which way soever they turned their eyes (save upward to the heavens) they could have little solace or content in respect of any outward objects. For summer being done, all things stand upon them with a weatherbeaten face, and the whole country, full of woods and thickets, represented a wild and savage hue. If they looked behind them, there was the mighty ocean which they had passed, and was now as a main bar and gulf to separate them from all the civil parts of the world. If it be said they had a ship to succor them, it is true; but what heard they daily from the master and company? but that with speed they should look out a place with their shallop,[2] where they would be at some near distance; for the season was such as he would not stir from thence till a safe harbor was discovered by them where they would be, and he might go without danger; and that victuals consumed apace, but he must and would keep sufficient for themselves and their return. Yea, it was muttered by some, that if they got not a place in time, they would turn them and their goods ashore and leave them. Let it also be considered what weak hopes of supply and succor they left behind them, that might bear up their minds in this sad condition and trials they were under; and they could not but be very small. It is true, indeed, the affections and love of their brethren at Leyden was cordial and entire towards them, but they had little power to help them, or themselves; and how the case stood between them and the merchants at their coming away, hath already been declared. What could now sustain them but the spirit of God and His grace? May not and ought not the children of these fathers rightly say: "Our fathers were Englishmen which came over this great ocean, and were ready to perish in this wilderness; but they cried unto the Lord, and He heard their voice, and looked on their adversity,"[3] "Let them therefore praise the Lord, because He is good, and His mercies endure forever." "Yea, let them which have been redeemed of the Lord, show how He hath delivered them from the hand of the oppressor. When they wandered in the desert wilderness out of the way, and found no city to dwell in, both hungry, and thirsty, their soul was overwhelmed in them. Let them confess before the Lord His loving kindness, and His wonderful works before the sons of men."[4]

9. See Acts 28.1–2.
1. Mountain from which Moses saw the Promised Land (Deuteronomy 34.1–4).

2. Small vessel fitted with one or more masts.
3. Deuteronomy 26.6–8 [Bradford's note].
4. Psalm 107.1, 2, 4, 5, 8 [Bradford's note].

CHAPTER X. SHOWING HOW THEY SOUGHT OUT A PLACE OF HABITATION; AND WHAT BEFELL THEM THEREABOUT

Being thus arrived at Cape Cod the 11th of November, and necessity calling them to look out a place for habitation (as well as the master's and mariners' importunity), they having brought a large shallop with them out of England, stowed in quarters in the ship, they now got her out and set their carpenters to work to trim her up; but [she] being much bruised and shattered in the ship with foul weather, they saw she would be long in mending. Whereupon a few of them tendered themselves to go by land and discover those nearest places, whilst the shallop was in mending, and the rather because as they went into that harbor there seemed to be an opening some two or three leagues off,[5] which the master judged to be a river. It was conceived there might be some danger in the attempt, yet seeing them resolute, they were permitted to go, being sixteen of them, well armed, under the conduct of Captain Standish,[6] having such instructions given them as was thought meet. They set forth the 15th of November, and when they had marched about the space of a mile by the seaside, they espied five or six persons with a dog coming towards them, who were savages, but they fled from them, and ran up into the woods, and the English followed them, partly to see if they could speak with them, and partly to discover if there might not be more of them lying in ambush. But the Indians seeing themselves thus followed, they again forsook the woods, and ran away on the sands as hard[7] as they could, so as they could not come near them, but followed them by the track of their feet sundry miles, and saw that they had come the same way. So, night coming on, they made their rendezvous and set out their sentinels, and rested in quiet that night, and the next morning followed their track till they had headed a great creek, and so left the sands, and turned another way into the woods. But they still followed them by guess, hoping to find their dwellings, but they soon lost both them and themselves, falling into such thickets as were ready to tear their clothes and armor in pieces, but were most distressed for want of drink. But at length they found water and refreshed themselves, [it] being the first New England water they drunk of, and was now in their great thirst as pleasant unto them as wine or beer had been in foretimes. Afterwards they directed their course to come to the other shore, for they knew it was a neck of land they were to cross over, and so at length got to the seaside, and marched to this supposed river, and by the way found a pond of clear fresh water, and shortly after a good quantity of clear ground where the Indians had formerly set corn, and some of their graves. And proceeding further they saw new stubble where corn had been set the same year, also they found where lately a house had been, where some planks and a great kettle was remaining, and heaps of sand newly paddled with their hands, which they, digging up, found in them divers fair Indian baskets filled with corn, and some in ears, fair and good, of divers colors, which seemed to them a very goodly sight (having never seen any such before). This was near the place of that supposed river they came to seek, unto which they

---

5. This distance might have been six to nine miles.
6. Myles Standish (1584?–1656), a professional soldier who had fought in the Netherlands, was employed by the Pilgrims.
7. Fast.

went and found it to open itself into two arms with a high cliff of sand in the entrance, but more like to be creeks of salt water than any fresh, for aught they saw, and that there was good harborage for their shallop, leaving it further to be discovered by their shallop when she was ready. So their time limited them being expired, they returned to the ship, lest they should be in fear of their safety, and took with them part of the corn, and buried up the rest, and so like the men from Eshcol[8] carried with them of the fruits of the land, and showed their brethren, of which, and their return, they were marvelously glad, and their hearts encouraged.

After this, the shallop being got ready, they set out again for the better discovery of this place, and the master of the ship desired to go himself, so there went some thirty men, but found it to be no harbor for ships but only for boats. There was also found two of their houses covered with mats, and sundry of their implements in them, but the people were run away and could not be seen.[9] Also there was found more of their corn, and of their beans of various colors. The corn and beans they brought away, purposing to give them full satisfaction when they should meet with any of them (as about some six months afterward they did, to their good content). And here is to be noted a special providence of God, and a great mercy to this poor people, that here they got seed to plant them corn the next year, or else they might have starved, for they had none, nor any likelihood to get any till the season had been past (as the sequel did manifest). Neither is it likely they had had this, if the first voyage had not been made, for the ground was now all covered with snow, and hard frozen. But the Lord is never wanting unto his in their greatest needs; let his holy name have all the praise.

The month of November being spent in these affairs, and much foul weather falling in, the 6th of December they sent out their shallop again with ten of their principal men, and some seamen, upon further discovery, intending to circulate that deep bay of Cape Cod. The weather was very cold, and it froze so hard as the spray of the sea lighting on their coats, they were as if they had been glazed; yet that night betimes they got down into the bottom of the bay, and as they drew near the shore[1] they saw some ten or twelve Indians very busy about something. They landed about a league or two from them, and had much ado to put ashore anywhere, it lay so full of flats. [After their] being landed, it grew late, and they made themselves a barricade with logs and boughs as well as they could in the time, and set out their sentinel and betook them to rest, and saw the smoke of the fire the savages made that night. When morning was come they divided their company, some to coast along the shore in the boat, and the rest marched through the woods to see the land, if any fit place might be for their dwelling. They came also to the place where they saw the Indians the night before, and found they had been cutting up a great fish like a grampus,[2] being some two inches thick of fat like a hog, some pieces whereof they had left by the way; and the shallop found two more of these fishes dead on the sands, a thing usual after storms

8. In Numbers 13.23–26, scouts sent out by Moses to search the wilderness return after forty days with clusters of grapes picked near a brook they call Eschol.
9. Descendants of these Nauset Indians, the Wampanoag, today live on the reservation in Mashpee, Cape Cod.
1. Near present-day Eastham.
2. Probably a pilot whale.

in that place, by reason of the great flats of sand that lie off. So they ranged up and down all that day, but found no people, nor any place they liked. When the sun grew low, they hasted out of the woods to meet with their shallop, to whom they made signs to come to them into a creek hard by, the which they did at high water, of which they were very glad, for they had not seen each other all that day, since the morning. So they made them a barricado (as usually they did every night) with logs, stakes, and thick pine boughs, the height of a man, leaving it open to leeward, partly to shelter them from the cold and wind (making their fire in the middle, and lying round about it), and partly to defend them from any sudden assaults of the savages, if they should surround them.

So being very weary, they betook them to rest. But about midnight, they heard a hideous and great cry, and their sentinel called, "Arm! arm," so they bestirred them and stood to their arms, and shot off a couple of muskets, and then the noise ceased. They concluded it was a company of wolves, or such like wild beasts, for one of the seamen told them he had often heard such a noise in Newfoundland. So they rested till about five of the clock in the morning, for the tide, and their purpose to go from thence, made them be stirring betimes. So after prayer they prepared for breakfast, and it being day dawning, it was thought best to be carrying things down to the boat. But some said it was not best to carry the arms down, others said they would be the readier, for they had lapped them up in their coats from the dew. But some three or four would not carry theirs till they went themselves, yet as it fell out, the water being not high enough, they laid them down on the bankside, and came up to breakfast. But presently, all on the sudden, they heard a great and strange cry, which they knew to be the same voices they heard in the night, though they varied their notes, and one of their company being abroad came running in, and cried, "Men, Indians, Indians," and withal, their arrows came flying amongst them. Their men ran with all speed to recover their arms, as by the good providence of God they did. In the meantime, of those that were there ready, two muskets were discharged at them, and two more stood ready in the entrance of their rendezvous, but were commanded not to shoot till they could take full aim at them, and the other two charged again with all speed, for there were only four had arms there, and defended the barricado, which was first assaulted. The cry of the Indians was dreadful, especially when they saw their men run out of the rendezvous toward the shallop, to recover their arms, the Indians wheeling about upon them. But some running out with coats of mail on, and cutlasses in their hands, they soon got their arms, and let fly amongst them, and quickly stopped their violence. Yet there was a lusty man, and no less valiant, stood behind a tree within half a musket shot, and let his arrows fly at them. He was seen [to] shoot three arrows, which were all avoided. He stood three shots of a musket, till one taking full aim at him, made the bark or splinters of the tree fly about his ears, after which he gave an extraordinary shriek, and away they went all of them. They[3] left some to keep the shallop, and followed them about a quarter of a mile, and shouted once or twice, and shot off two or three pieces, and so returned. This they did, that they might conceive that they were not afraid of them or any way discouraged. Thus it pleased God to vanquish their ene-

3. The English.

mies, and give them deliverance; and by His special providence so to dispose that not any one of them were either hurt, or hit, though their arrows came close by them, and on every side them, and sundry of their coats, which hung up in the barricado, were shot through and through. Afterwards they gave God solemn thanks and praise for their deliverance, and gathered up a bundle of their arrows, and sent them into England afterward by the master of the ship, and called that place the "First Encounter." From hence they departed, and coasted all along, but discerned no place likely for harbor, and therefore hasted to a place that their pilot (one Mr. Coppin, who had been in the country before) did assure them was a good harbor, which he had been in, and they might fetch it before night, of which they were glad, for it began to be foul weather. After some hours' sailing, it began to snow and rain, and about the middle of the afternoon, the wind increased, and the sea became very rough, and they broke their rudder, and it was as much as two men could do to steer her with a couple of oars. But their pilot bade them be of good cheer, for he saw the harbor; but the storm increasing, and night drawing on, they bore what sail they could to get in, while they could see. But herewith they broke their mast in three pieces, and their sail fell overboard, in a very grown sea, so as they had like to have been cast away; yet by God's mercy they recovered themselves, and having the flood[4] with them, struck into the harbor. But when it came to, the pilot was deceived in the place, and said, the Lord be merciful unto them, for his eyes never saw that place before, and he and the master's mate would have run her ashore, in a cove full of breakers, before the wind. But a lusty seaman which steered, bade those which rowed, if they were men, about with her, or else they were all cast away, the which they did with speed. So he bid them be of good cheer and row lustily, for there was a fair sound before them, and he doubted not but they should find one place or other where they might ride in safety. And though it was very dark, and rained sore,[5] yet in the end they got under the lee of a small island, and remained there all that night in safety. But they knew not this to be an island till morning, but were divided in their minds: some would keep the boat for fear they might be amongst the Indians; others were so weak and cold, they could not endure, but got ashore, and with much ado got fire (all things being so wet) and the rest were glad to come to them, for after midnight the wind shifted to the northwest, and it froze hard. But though this had been a day and night of much trouble and danger unto them, yet God gave them a morning of comfort and refreshing (as usually He doth to His children), for the next day was a fair sunshining day, and they found themselves to be on an island secure from the Indians, where they might dry their stuff, fix their pieces,[6] and rest themselves, and gave God thanks for His mercies, in their manifold deliverances. And this being the last day of the week, they prepared there to keep the Sabbath. On Monday they sounded[7] the harbor, and found it fit for shipping, and marched into the land, and found divers cornfields, and little running brooks, a place (as they supposed) fit for situation. At least it was the best they could find, and the season, and their present necessity, made

4. Flood tide.
5. Heavily.
6. Weapons.
7. Measured the depth of.

them glad to accept of it. So they returned to their ship again with this news to the rest of their people, which did much comfort their hearts.

On the 15th of December they weighed anchor to go to the place they had discovered, and came within two leagues of it, but were fain to bear up again, but the 16th day the wind came fair, and they arrived safe in this harbor, and afterwards took better view of the place, and resolved where to pitch their dwelling,[8] and the 25th day began to erect the first house for common use to receive them and their goods.

From *Book II*

* * *

FROM CHAPTER XI.[1] THE REMAINDER OF ANNO 1620

I shall a little return back and begin with a combination[2] made by them before they came ashore, being the first foundation of their government in this place, occasioned partly by the discontented and mutinous speeches that some of the strangers[3] amongst them had let fall from them in the ship (that when they came ashore they would use their own liberty; for none had power to command them, the patent[4] they had being for Virginia, and not for New England, which belonged to another Government, with which the Virginia Company had nothing to do), and partly that such an act by them done (this their condition considered) might be as firm as any patent, and in some respects more sure.

The form was as followeth.

In the name of God, Amen. We whose names are underwritten, the loyal subjects of our dread sovereign Lord, King James, by the grace of God, of Great Britain, France, and Ireland king, defender of the faith, etc., having undertaken, for the glory of God, and advancement of the Christian faith, and honor of our king and country, a voyage to plant the first colony in the northern parts of Virginia, do by these presents solemnly and mutually in the presence of God, and one of another, covenant and combine ourselves together into a civil body politic, for our better ordering and preservation and furtherance of the ends aforesaid; and by virtue hereof to enact, constitute, and frame such just and equal laws, ordinances, acts, constitutions, and offices, from time to time, as shall be thought most meet and convenient for the general good of the Colony, unto which we promise all due submission and obedience. In witness whereof we have hereunder subscribed our names at Cape Cod the 11th of November, in the year of the reign of our sovereign lord, King James, of England, France, and Ireland the eighteenth, and of Scotland the fifty-fourth. Anno Domini[5] 1620.

After this they chose, or rather confirmed, Mr. John Carver[6] (a man godly and well approved amongst them) their governor for that year. And after they had provided a place for their goods, or common store, (which were

---

8. The landing, at Plymouth, occurred on December 21.
1. Bradford did not number the chapters in Book II.
2. A form of union.
3. Bradford's term for the voyagers who were not members of the Separatist church.
4. A document signed by a sovereign granting privileges to those named in it.
5. In the year of the Lord (Latin).
6. A tradesman, like Bradford, and an original member of the group that went to Holland.

long in unlading for want of boats, foulness of the winter weather, and sickness of divers)[7] and begun some small cottages for their habitation, as time would admit, they met and consulted of laws and orders, both for their civil and military government, as the necessity of their condition did require, still adding thereunto as urgent occasion in several times, and as cases did require.

[DIFFICULT BEGINNINGS]

In these hard and difficult beginnings they found some discontents and murmurings arise amongst some, and mutinous speeches and carriages[8] in other; but they were soon quelled and overcome by the wisdom, patience, and just and equal carriage of things by the governor and better part, which clave[9] faithfully together in the main. But that which was most sad and lamentable was, that in two or three months' time half of their company died, especially in January and February, being the depth of winter, and wanting houses and other comforts; being infected with the scurvy and other diseases, which this long voyage and their inaccommodate condition had brought upon them; so as there died sometimes two or three of a day, in the foresaid time; that of one hundred and odd persons, scarce fifty remained. And of these in the time of most distress, there was but six or seven sound persons, who, to their great commendations be it spoken, spared no pains, night nor day, but with abundance of toil and hazard of their own health, fetched them wood, made them fires, dressed them meat, made their beds, washed their loathsome clothes, clothed and unclothed them; in a word, did all the homely[1] and necessary offices for them which dainty and queasy stomachs cannot endure to hear named; and all this willingly and cheerfully, without any grudging in the least, showing herein their true love unto their friends and brethren, a rare example and worthy to be remembered. Two of these seven were Mr. William Brewster, their reverend elder, and Myles Standish, their captain and military commander, unto whom myself and many others were much beholden in our low and sick condition. And yet the Lord so upheld these persons, as in this general calamity they were not at all infected either with sickness or lameness. And what I have said of these, I may say of many others who died in this general visitation, and others yet living, that whilst they had health, yea, or any strength continuing, they were not wanting[2] to any that had need of them. And I doubt not but their recompense is with the Lord.

But I may not here pass by another remarkable passage not to be forgotten. As this calamity fell among the passengers that were to be left here to plant, and were hasted ashore and made to drink water, that the seamen might have the more beer, and one[3] in his sickness, desiring but a small can of beer, it was answered, that if he were their own father he should have none. The disease began to fall amongst them also, so as almost half of their company died before they went away, and many of their officers and lustiest men, as the boatswain, gunner, three quartermasters, the cook, and others. At which the master was something stricken and sent to the sick ashore and

---

7. Several people. "Unlading": unloading.
8. Attitudes.
9. Past tense of *cleave*: stuck closely. "Carriage": handling.

1. Intimate, domestic.
2. Lacking in attention.
3. Which was this author himself [Bradford's note].

told the governor he should send for beer for them that had need of it, though he drunk water homeward bound. But now amongst his company there was far another kind of carriage in this misery than amongst the passengers: for they that before had been boon companions in drinking and jollity in the time of their health and welfare, began now to desert one another in this calamity, saying they would not hazard their lives for them, they should be infected by coming to help them in their cabins, and so, after they came to die by it, would do little or nothing for them, but if they died let them die. But such of the passengers as were yet aboard showed them what mercy they could, which made some of their hearts relent, as the boatswain (and some others), who was a proud young man, and would often curse and scoff at the passengers. But when he grew weak, they had compassion on him and helped him; then he confessed he did not deserve it at their hands, he had abused them in word and deed. "O!" saith he, "you, I now see, show your love like Christians indeed one to another, but we let one another lie and die like dogs." Another lay cursing his wife, saying if it had not been for her he had never come [on] this unlucky voyage, and anon cursing his fellows, saying he had done this and that, for some of them, he had spent so much, and so much, amongst them, and they were now weary of him, and did not help him, having need. Another gave his companion all he had, if he died, to help him in his weakness; he went and got a little spice and made him a mess of meat once or twice, and because he died not so soon as he expected, he went amongst his fellows, and swore the rogue would cozen[4] him, he would see him choked before he made him any more meat; and yet the poor fellow died before morning.

[DEALINGS WITH THE NATIVES]

All this while the Indians came skulking about them, and would sometimes show themselves aloof off, but when any approached near them, they would run away. And once they stole away their tools where they had been at work, and were gone to dinner. But about the 16th of March a certain Indian came boldly amongst them, and spoke to them in broken English, which they could well understand, but marveled at it. At length they understood by discourse with him, that he was not of these parts, but belonged to the eastern parts, where some English ships came to fish, with whom he was acquainted, and could name sundry of them by their names, amongst whom he had got his language.[5] He became profitable to them in acquainting them with many things concerning the state of the country in the east parts where he lived, which was afterwards profitable unto them; as also of the people here, of their names, number, and strength; of their situation and distance from this place, and who was chief amongst them. His name was Samoset; he told them also of another Indian whose name was Squanto, a native of this place, who had been in England and could speak better English than himself. Being, after some time of entertainment and gifts, dismissed, a while after he came again, and five more with him, and they brought again all the tools that

4. Cheat. "Mess": meal.
5. The Abnaki chief Samoset had encountered English fishing vessels in southern Maine; he picked up his English there and may have come south with Captain Thomas Dermer (see the reference to him below).

were stolen away before, and made way for the coming of their great sachem,[6] called Massasoit, who, about four or five days after, came with the chief of his friends and other attendance, with the aforesaid Squanto. With whom, after friendly entertainment, and some gifts given him, they made a peace with him (which hath now continued this twenty-four years)[7] in these terms:

1. That neither he nor any of his, should injure or do hurt to any of their people.
2. That if any of his did any hurt to any of theirs, he should send the offender, that they might punish him.
3. That if anything were taken away from any of theirs, he should cause it to be restored, and they should do the like to his.
4. If any did unjustly war against him, they would aid him; if any did war against them, he should aid them.
5. He should send to his neighbors confederates, to certify them of this, that they might not wrong them, but might be likewise comprised in the conditions of peace.
6. That when their men came to them, they should leave their bows and arrows behind them.

After these things he returned to his place called Sowams, some forty mile from this place, but Squanto continued with them, and was their interpreter, and was a special instrument sent of God for their good beyond their expectation. He directed them how to set their corn, where to take fish, and to procure other commodities, and was also their pilot to bring them to unknown places for their profit, and never left them till he died. He was a native of this place, and scarce any left alive besides himself. He was carried away with divers others by one Hunt, a master of a ship, who thought to sell them for slaves in Spain; but he got away for England, and was entertained by a merchant in London, and employed to Newfoundland and other parts, and lastly brought hither into these parts by one Mr. Dermer, a gentleman employed by Sir Ferdinando Gorges and others, for discovery, and other designs in these parts. Of whom I shall say something, because it is mentioned in a book set forth Anno 1622 by the President and Council for New England,[8] that he made the peace between the savages of these parts and the English, of which this plantation, as it is intimated, had the benefit. But what a peace it was, may appear by what befell him and his men.

This Mr. Dermer was here the same year that these people came, as appears by a relation written by him, and given me by a friend, bearing date June 30, Anno 1620. And they came in November following, so there was but four months difference. In which relation to his honored friend, he hath these passages of this very place:

> I will first begin (saith he) with that place from whence Squanto, or Tisquantum, was taken away, which in Capt. Smith's map is called

6. Chief.
7. Bradford's aside indicates that, having begun his history in 1630, he was writing this part in 1644.
8. I.e., *A Brief Relation of the Discovery and Plan-* *tation of New England* (1622), by Gorges (c. 1566–1647), an English colonial entrepreneur. Gorges had a patent for settling in northern New England, but he hired explorers and did not travel to America.

Plymouth (and I would that Plymouth[9] had the like commodities). I would that the first plantation might here be seated, if there come to the number of fifty persons, or upward. Otherwise at Charlton,[1] because there the savages are less to be feared. The Pokanokets, which live to the west of Plymouth, bear an inveterate malice to the English, and are of more strength than all the savages from thence to Penobscot.[2] Their desire of revenge was occasioned by an Englishman, who having many of them on board, made a great slaughter with their murderers[3] and small shot, when as (they say) they offered no injury on their parts. Whether they were English or no, it may be doubted; yet they believe they were, for the French have so possessed them; for which cause Squanto cannot deny but they would have killed me when I was at Namasket, had he not entreated hard for me. The soil of the borders of this great bay, may be compared to most of the plantations which I have seen in Virginia. The land is of diverse sorts, for Patuxet is a hardy but strong soil, Nauset and Satucket are for the most part a blackish and deep mould, much like that where groweth the best tobacco in Virginia.[4] In the bottom of that great bay is store of cod and bass, or mullet, etc.

But above all he commends Pokanoket for the richest soil, and much open ground fit for English grain, etc.

Massachusetts is about nine leagues from Plymouth, and situate in the midst between both, is full of islands and peninsulas, very fertile for the most part.

(With sundry such relations which I forbear to transcribe, being now better known than they were to him.)

He was taken prisoner by the Indians at Monomoit[5] (a place not far from hence, now well known). He gave them what they demanded for his liberty, but when they had got what they desired, they kept him still and endeavored to kill his men, but he was freed by seizing on some of them, and kept them bound till they gave him a canoe's load of corn. Of which, see Purchas, lib. 9, fol. 1778.[6] But this was Anno 1619.

After the writing of the former relation he came to the Isle of Capawack[7] (which lies south of this place in the way to Virginia), and the foresaid Squanto with him, where he going ashore amongst the Indians to trade, as he used to do, was betrayed and assaulted by them, and all his men slain, but one that kept the boat; but himself got aboard very sore wounded, and they had cut off his head upon the cuddy of the boat, had not the man rescued him with a sword. And so they got away, and made shift to get into

---

9. Here, Dermer means Plymouth, England. John Smith published his *Description of New England* two years after his 1614 voyage. Tisquantum was Squanto's Indian name.
1. Near the mouth of the Charles River, in present-day Boston and Charlestown.
2. A large bay on Maine's central coast. "Pokanokets": the Wampanoags, the tribe of Massasoit.
3. Small cannons.
4. If Dermer was not lying about the soil, it has been much degraded since his visit. Patuxet ("at the little falls") was the Indian name for Plymouth. Nauset, named for the local Indian tribe,

was near present-day Eastham. Satucket ("near the mouth of the stream") was a Nauset village close to the town of Brewster.
5. Once a harbor near Orleans and Harwich.
6. Samuel Purchas (1577–1626) was an English clergyman and collector of travel writings, famous for compiling the four-volume work to which Bradford refers: *Purchas His Pilgrimes* (1625). "Lib.": abbreviation for *liber*: book (Latin). "Fol.": abbreviation for *folio*: sheet, or page (Latin). This reference is to p. 1778 in book 9 of vol. 4.
7. Martha's Vineyard.

Virginia, where he died, whether of his wounds or the diseases of the country, or both together, is uncertain. By all which it may appear how far these people were from peace, and with what danger this plantation was begun, save as the powerful hand of the Lord did protect them. These things were partly the reason why they[8] kept aloof and were so long before they came to the English. Another reason (as after themselves made known) was how about three years before, a French ship was cast away at Cape Cod, but the men got ashore, and saved their lives, and much of their victuals, and other goods. But after the Indians heard of it, they gathered together from these parts, and never left watching and dogging them till they got advantage, and killed them all but three or four which they kept, and sent from one sachem to another, to make sport with, and used them worse than slaves (of which the foresaid Mr. Dermer redeemed two of them) and they conceived this ship[9] was now come to revenge it.

Also, as after was made known, before they came to the English to make friendship, they got all the powachs[1] of the country, for three days together, in a horrid and devilish manner to curse and execrate them with their conjurations, which assembly and service they held in a dark and dismal swamp.

But to return. The spring now approaching, it pleased God the mortality began to cease amongst them, and the sick and lame recovered apace, which put as it were new life into them, though they had borne their sad affliction with much patience and contentedness, as I think any people could do. But it was the Lord which upheld them, and had beforehand prepared them; many having long borne the yoke, yea from their youth. Many other smaller matters I omit, sundry of them having been already published in a journal made by one of the company,[2] and some other passages of journeys and relations already published, to which I refer those that are willing to know them more particularly. And being now come to the 25th of March, I shall begin the year 1621.

*   *   *

FROM CHAPTER XIX. ANNO 1628

*   *   *

[MR. MORTON OF MERRYMOUNT]

About some three or four years before this time, there came over one Captain Wollaston, a man of pretty parts,[3] and with him three or four more of some eminency, who brought with them a great many servants, with provisions and other implements for to begin a plantation, and pitched themselves in a place within the Massachusetts [Bay Colony] which they called, after their Captain's name, Mount Wollaston.[4] Amongst whom was one Mr. Morton,[5] who, it should seem, had some small adventure of his own or other men's amongst them, but had little respect amongst them, and was slighted by

8. The Indians.
9. The *Mayflower.*
1. Medicine men.
2. *Mourt's Relation.*
3. I.e., of a clever nature.
4. Now Quincy, Massachusetts.
5. Very little is known of Captain Wollaston or Thomas Morton other than what Bradford tells. Wollaston may have been Richard Wollaston, a ship's captain and sometime pirate. Morton (c. 1579–1647) trained as a lawyer in London, moved to New England in the 1620s. He tangled with Bradford, partly because of his anti-Puritanism and more liberal version of colonialism, presented in his *New English Canaan* (1637), excerpted below. Morton named his settlement Ma-Re Mount, or "Hill by the Sea." The Puritans sarcastically called it Merrymount.

the meanest servants. Having continued there some time, and not finding things to answer their expectations, nor profit to arise as they looked for, Captain Wollaston takes a great part of the servants, and transports them to Virginia, where he puts them off at good rates, selling their time to other men;[6] and writes back to one Mr. Rasdall, one of his chief partners, and accounted their merchant, to bring another part of them to Virginia likewise, intending to put them off there as he had done the rest. And he, with the consent of the said Rasdall, appointed one Fitcher to be his lieutenant, and govern the remains of the plantation, till he or Rasdall returned to take further order thereabout. But this Morton abovesaid, having more craft than honesty (who had been a kind of pettifogger, of Furnivals Inn) in the other's absence, watches an opportunity (commons being but hard amongst them) and got some strong drink and other junkets, and made them a feast;[7] and after they were merry, he began to tell them, he would give them good counsel. "You see," saith he, "that many of your fellows are carried to Virginia; and if you stay till this Rasdall return, you will also be carried away and sold for slaves with the rest. Therefore I would advise you to thrust out this Lieutenant Fitcher; and I, having a part in the Plantation, will receive you as my partners and consociates; so may you be free from service, and we will converse, trade, plant, and live together as equals, and support and protect one another," or to like effect. This counsel was easily received; so they took opportunity, and thrust Lieutenant Fitcher out [of] doors, and would suffer him to come no more amongst them, but forced him to seek bread to eat, and other relief from his neighbors, till he could get passage for England. After this they fell to great licentiousness, and led a dissolute life, pouring out themselves into all profaneness. And Morton became lord of misrule,[8] and maintained (as it were) a school of Atheism. And after they had got some good into their hands, and got much by trading with the Indians, they spent it as vainly, in quaffing and drinking both wine and strong waters in great excess, and, as some reported, £10 worth in a morning. They also set up a maypole, drinking and dancing about it many days together, inviting the Indian women, for their consorts, dancing and frisking together, like so many fairies, or furies rather, and worse practices. As if they had anew revived and celebrated the feasts of the Roman Goddess Flora, or the beastly practices of the mad Bacchinalians.[9] Morton likewise (to show his poetry) composed sundry rhymes and verses, some tending to lasciviousness, and others to the detraction and scandal of some persons, which he affixed to this idle or idol maypole. They changed also the name of their place, and instead of calling it Mount Wollaston, they call it Merrymount, as if this jollity would have lasted ever. But this continued not long, for after Morton was sent for England (as follows to be declared) shortly after came over that worthy gen-

6. A servant was someone employed in agricultural or domestic labor; the servants in this case were indentured, meaning that their time had been purchased by their original employers (or masters) in exchange for their transportation to the colonies, and hence the remainder of their time could be sold to others.

7. The shifty lawyer ("pettifogger") Morton (who studied law at Furnivals Inn, one of London's Inns of Court), knowing that the settlers' ordinary food ("commons") was in short supply, threw a feast of alcohol and delicacies ("junkets") to win over the hearts and minds of the remaining servants.

8. The master of the carnival-like atmosphere of old English holidays, especially at Christmas.

9. At the ancient revels in honor of Bacchus, Roman god of wine, frenzied worshipers drank, danced, and even tore apart wild animals and devoured them. Flora, the Roman goddess of flowers and vegetation, was the center of a cult that put on risqué farces.

tleman, Mr. John Endicott, who brought over a patent under the broad seal, for the government of the Massachusetts, who visiting those parts caused that maypole to be cut down, and rebuked them for their profaneness, and admonished them to look there should be better walking; so they now, or others, changed the name of their place again, and called it Mount Dagon.[1]

Now to maintain this riotous prodigality and profuse excess, Morton, thinking himself lawless, and hearing what gain the French and fishermen made by trading of pieces,[2] powder, and shot to the Indians, he, as the head of this consortship, began the practise of the same in these parts; and first he taught them how to use them, to charge and discharge, and what proportion of powder to give the piece, according to the size or bigness of the same; and what shot to use for fowl, and what for deer. And having thus instructed them, he employed some of them to hunt and fowl for him, so as they became far more active in that employment than any of the English, by reason of their swiftness of foot, and nimbleness of body, being also quick-sighted, and by continual exercise well knowing the haunts of all sorts of game. So as when they saw the execution that a piece would do, and the benefit that might come by the same, they became mad, as it were, after them, and would not stick to give any price they could attain to for them, accounting their bows and arrows but baubles in comparison of them.

✳   ✳   ✳

This Morton having thus taught them the use of pieces, he sold them all he could spare, and he and his consorts determined to send for many out of England, and had by some of the ships sent for above a score. The which being known, and his neighbors meeting the Indians in the woods armed with guns in this sort, it was a terror unto them, who lived stragglingly,[3] and were of no strength in any place. And other places (though more remote) saw this mischief would quickly spread over all, if not prevented. Besides, they saw they should keep no servants, for Morton would entertain any, how vile soever, and all the scum of the country, or any discontents, would flock to him from all places, if this nest was not broken; and they should stand in more fear of their lives and goods (in short time) from this wicked and debauched crew, than from the savages themselves.

So sundry of the chief of the straggling plantations, meeting together, agreed by mutual consent to solicit those of Plymouth (who were then of more strength than them all) to join with them, to prevent the further growth of this mischief, and suppress Morton and his consorts before they grew to further head and strength. Those that joined in this action (and after contributed to the charge of sending him for England) were from Piscataqua, Naumkeag, Winnisimmett, Wessaguset, Nantasket, and other places where any English were seated. Those of Plymouth being thus sought to by their messengers and letters, and weighing both their reasons, and the common danger, were willing to afford them their help, though themselves had least cause of fear or hurt. So, to be short, they first resolved jointly to write to him, and in a friendly and neighborly way to admonish him to forbear these

---

1. According to Judges 16.23–31, the Philistines captured and tortured Samson, who brought down the temple of the Philistine god Dagon.

2. Guns.

3. In a scattered fashion.

courses, and sent a messenger with their letters to bring his answer. But he was so high as he scorned all advice, and asked who had to do with him; he had and would trade pieces with the Indians in despite of all, with many other scurillous terms full of disdain. They sent to him a second time, and bade him be better advised, and more temperate in his terms, for the country could not bear the injury he did; it was against their common safety, and against the King's proclamation. He answered in high terms as before, and that the King's proclamation was no law, demanding what penalty was upon it. It was answered, more than he could bear, His Majesty's displeasure. But insolently he persisted, and said the King was dead and his displeasure with him, and many the like things; and threatened withal that if any came to molest him, let them look to themselves, for he would prepare for them. Upon which they saw there was no way but to take him by force, and having so far proceeded, now to give over would make him far more haughty and insolent. So they mutually resolved to proceed, and obtained of the governor of Plymouth to send Captain Standish, and some other aid with him, to take Morton by force. The which accordingly was done. But they found him to stand stiffly in his defense, having made fast his doors, armed his consorts, set divers dishes of powder and bullets ready on the table; and if they had not been over-armed with drink, more hurt might have been done. They summoned him to yield, but he kept his house, and they could get nothing but scoffs and scorns from him; but at length, fearing they would do some violence to the house, he and some of his crew came out, but not to yield, but to shoot; but they were so steeled[4] with drink as their pieces were too heavy for them; himself with a carbine (over-charged and almost half filled with powder and shot, as was after found) had thought to have shot Captain Standish, but he stepped to him, and put by his piece, and took him. Neither was there any hurt done to any of either side, save that one was so drunk that he ran his own nose upon the point of a sword that one held before him as he entered the house, but he lost but a little of his hot blood.[5] Morton they brought away to Plymouth, where he was kept, till a ship went from the Isle of Shoals for England, with which he was sent to the Council of New England;[6] and letters written to give them information of his course and carriage; and also one was sent at their common charge to inform their Honors more particularly, and to prosecute against him. But he fooled of the messenger, after he was gone from hence, and though he went for England, yet nothing was done to him, not so much as rebuked, for aught was heard; but returned the next year. Some of the worst of the company were dispersed, and some of the more modest kept the house till he should be heard from. But I have been too long about so unworthy a person, and bad a cause.

*   *   *

---

4. Insensible.

5. In his own book, Morton refers to Standish as "Captain Shrimp" and says it would have been easy for him to destroy these "nine worthies" like "a flock of wild geese," but that he loathed violence and asked for his freedom to leave. He suggests that he was treated brutally because the Pilgrims wished to shame him before the Indian revelers.

6. The Council of New England was a joint stock company established by the British Crown in 1620. Its role was to colonize and govern New England. "Isle of Shoals": i.e., the Isles of Shoals, a group of small Atlantic islands straddling the borders of Maine and New Hampshire.

FROM CHAPTER XXIII. ANNO 1632

* * *

[PROSPERITY WEAKENS COMMUNITY]

Also the people of the plantation began to grow in their outward estates, by reason of the flowing of many people into the country, especially into the Bay of the Massachusetts, by which means corn and cattle rose to a great price, by which many were much enriched, and commodities grew plentiful; and yet in other regards this benefit turned to their hurt, and this accession of strength to their weakness. For now as their stocks increased, and the increase vendible,[7] there was no longer any holding them together, but now they must of necessity go to their great lots; they could not otherwise keep their cattle; and having oxen grown, they must have land for plowing and tillage. And no man now thought he could live, except he had cattle and a great deal of ground to keep them, all striving to increase their stocks. By which means they were scattered all over the bay, quickly, and the town, in which they lived compactly till now, was left very thin, and in a short time almost desolate. And if this had been all, it had been less, though too much; but the church must also be divided, and those that had lived so long together in Christian and comfortable fellowship must now part and suffer many divisions. First, those that lived on their lots on the other side of the bay (called Duxbury) they could not long bring their wives and children to the public worship and church meetings here, but with such burthen, as, growing to some competent number, they sued[8] to be dismissed and become a body of themselves; and so they were dismissed (about this time), though very unwillingly. But to touch this sad matter, and handle things together that fell out afterward: to prevent any further scattering from this place, and weakening of the same, it was thought best to give out some good farms to special persons, that would promise to live at Plymouth, and likely to be helpful to the church or commonwealth, and so tie the lands to Plymouth as farms for the same; and there they might keep their cattle and tillage by some servants, and retain their dwellings here. And so some special lands were granted at a place general, called Green's Harbor, where no allotments had been in the former division, a place very well meadowed, and fit to keep and rear cattle, good store. But alas! this remedy proved worse than the disease; for within a few years those that had thus got footing there rent themselves away, partly by force, and partly wearing the rest with importunity and pleas of necessity, so as they must either suffer them to go, or live in continual opposition and contention. And others still, as they conceived themselves straitened,[9] or to want accommodation, break away under one pretense or other, thinking their own conceived necessity, and the example of others, a warrant sufficient for them. And this, I fear, will be the ruin of New England, at least of the churches of God there, and will provoke the Lord's displeasure against them.

* * *

7. Salable.
8. Petitioned, requested.

9. Financially hampered.

JOHN WINTHROP
1588–1649

When Cotton Mather looked back on the founding years of the Massachusetts Bay Colony in *Magnalia Christi Americana* (1702)—the first attempt at a comprehensive history of the Puritan experiment—he identified John Winthrop as his model of the ideal earthly ruler. Mather came from a family of prominent Bay Colony ministers, and he was well placed to shape Winthrop's legacy. He did so using a number of sacred and secular analogies, labeling Winthrop "Nehemias Americanus" after Nehemiah, the biblical governor of Judea who rebuilt the wall of Jerusalem; describing him as a new Moses; and comparing him favorably to the Greek lawgiver Lycurgus and the devout Roman king Numa. Mather's praise for the man who led the Bay Colony in its early years reflects his era's approach to historical writing, which was strongly influenced by the work of the Greek historian Plutarch, supplemented with Roman and biblical texts. Mather's biography of the Puritan leader also underlines the status and skills that Winthrop brought to his position.

John Winthrop was the son of Adam Winthrop, a lawyer, and Anne Browne, the daughter of a tradesman. He was born in Groton, England, on an estate his father had purchased from King Henry VIII. It was a prosperous farm, and Winthrop had all the advantages of his father's social and economic position. He went to Cambridge University for two years—it is likely that he was first exposed to Puritan ideas there—and married at age seventeen. Unlike William Bradford and the Pilgrims, Winthrop was not a Separatist; that is, he wished to reform the Church of England from within rather than breaking with it and starting fresh. For Puritans like Winthrop, reform involved purging the national Church of the residual presence of Roman Catholicism, especially the hierarchy of the clergy and traditional practices such as kneeling at communion. For a time Winthrop thought of becoming a clergyman, but instead he turned to the practice of law.

In the 1620s, severe economic depression in England made Winthrop realize that he could not depend on the income from his father's estate and would need to find new means of support. The ascension to the throne of Charles I, who was known to be sympathetic to Roman Catholicism and impatient with Puritan reformers, also seemed an ominous sign. Winthrop was not alone in predicting that "God will bring some heavy affliction upon the land, and that speedily." He came to realize that if he antagonized the king by openly espousing the Puritan cause, he would lose everything. The only recourse seemed to be to obtain Charles's permission to emigrate. In March 1629, a group of enterprising merchants, all ardent Puritans, was able to get a charter for land in America from a Crown-approved joint stock company called the Council for New England. They called themselves "The Company of Massachusetts Bay in New England."

Winthrop was chosen governor in October 1629, and for the next twenty years most of the responsibility for the colony rested in his hands. An initial group of some seven hundred emigrants sailed from England with Winthrop on April 8, 1630, aboard the *Arbella*. It has long been believed that Winthrop delivered his sermon *A Model of Christian Charity* either just before departing from England or during the voyage. A review of the historical record suggests a far more ambiguous origin. There is no contemporary account of Winthrop delivering *A Model*, and there exists little evidence of its composition. The manuscript that survives is a copy made during Winthrop's lifetime, possibly incomplete, and of unknown provenance.

A Model of Christian Charity remains an iconic text despite its uncertain past. It sets out clearly and eloquently the ideals of a harmonious Christian community and reminds its audience members that they stand as an example to the world of the triumph or the failure of the Puritan enterprise. And in fact, events at the Massachusetts Bay Colony soon suggested that Winthrop's ideal of a selfless community was impossible to realize. In its first decade, the colony confronted basic differences over religious and civil liberties, social organization, and political structure. The colony also engaged in a brutal war with its Pequot neighbors.

Winthrop was governor for much of this decade, and he was closely involved with all of these conflicts. The frictions in the colony took a personal turn in 1645, when a group of leaders from the town of Hingham challenged Winthrop, then serving as deputy governor, over issues of local autonomy and representative government. Winthrop withstood the resulting impeachment threat and responded in the General Court with a trenchant speech distinguishing between natural liberty and civil or federal liberty, a distinction that remains a classic formulation. These and other disputes are detailed in the journal that he kept from 1630 until his death. Once the Winthrop family made the manuscript available to the colony's historians, including Cotton Mather and William Hubbard, the journal joined William Bradford's manuscript history, *Of Plymouth Plantation*, as a semiofficial history of New England.

Mather's account of Winthrop helped keep his memory alive. Beginning in 1790, when Noah Webster of dictionary fame published the first two volumes of Winthrop's journal, several New England intellectuals affiliated with the Massachusetts Historical Society (founded in 1791) worked to recover his words for future generations. James Savage published the first complete edition of the journal in 1825–26, though the achievement was marred when a fire at Savage's office destroyed the second volume of the manuscript. The first printed edition of *A Model of Christian Charity* appeared in the *Collections of the Massachusetts Historical Society* in 1838. Eventually, this little-known sermon acquired the status it has today, as an expression of the ideal suggested by its most resonant phrase, "a city upon a hill."

A Model of Christian Charity[1]

I

A MODEL HEREOF

God Almighty in His most holy and wise providence, hath so disposed of the condition of mankind, as in all times some must be rich, some poor, some high and eminent in power and dignity; others mean and in subjection.

THE REASON HEREOF

First, to hold conformity with the rest of His works, being delighted to show forth the glory of His wisdom in the variety and difference of the creatures; and the glory of His power, in ordering all these differences for the preservation and good of the whole; and the glory of His greatness, that as it is the glory of princes to have many officers, so this great King will have many stewards, counting Himself more honored in dispensing His gifts to man by man, than if He did it by His own immediate hands.

Secondly, that He might have the more occasion to manifest the work of His Spirit: first upon the wicked in moderating and restraining them, so that the rich and mighty should not eat up the poor, nor the poor and despised

---

1. The text is from Old South Leaflets, Old South Association, Old South Meetinghouse, Boston, Massachusetts, No. 207 (n.d.), edited by Samuel Eliot Morison.

rise up against their superiors and shake off their yoke; secondly in the regenerate,[2] in exercising His graces, in them, as in the great ones, their love, mercy, gentleness, temperance, etc., in the poor and inferior sort, their faith, patience, obedience, etc.

Thirdly, that every man might have need of other, and from hence they might be all knit more nearly together in the bonds of brotherly affection. From hence it appears plainly that no man is made more honorable than another or more wealthy, etc., out of any particular and singular respect to himself, but for the glory of his Creator and the common good of the creature, man. Therefore God still reserves the property of these gifts to Himself as [in] Ezekiel: 16.17. He there calls wealth His gold and His silver.[3] [In] Proverbs: 3.9, he claims their service as His due: honor the Lord with thy riches, etc.[4] All men being thus (by divine providence) ranked into two sorts, rich and poor; under the first are comprehended all such as are able to live comfortably by their own means duly improved; and all others are poor according to the former distribution.

There are two rules whereby we are to walk one towards another: justice and mercy. These are always distinguished in their act and in their object, yet may they both concur in the same subject in each respect; as sometimes there may be an occasion of showing mercy to a rich man in some sudden danger of distress, and also doing of mere justice to a poor man in regard of some particular contract, etc.

There is likewise a double law by which we are regulated in our conversation one towards another in both the former respects: the law of nature and the law of grace, or the moral law or the law of the Gospel, to omit the rule of justice as not properly belonging to this purpose otherwise than it may fall into consideration in some particular cases. By the first of these laws man as he was enabled so withal [is] commanded to love his neighbor as himself.[5] Upon this ground stands all the precepts of the moral law, which concerns our dealings with men. To apply this to the works of mercy, this law requires two things: first, that every man afford his help to another in every want or distress; secondly, that he performed this out of the same affection which makes him careful of his own goods, according to that of our Savior. Matthew: "Whatsoever ye would that men should do to you."[6] This was practiced by Abraham and Lot in entertaining the Angels and the old man of Gibeah.[7]

2. Humanity lost its natural innocence when Adam and Eve fell; that state is called unregenerate. When Jesus Christ came to ransom humankind from Adam and Eve's sin, he offered salvation for those who believed in him and who thus became regenerate, or saved.

3. "Thou hast also taken thy fair jewels made of my gold and of my silver, which I had given thee, and madest to thyself images of men, and didst commit whoredom with them." Textual evidence shows that Winthrop used the Geneva Bible, with occasional variants from the text of the 1599 edition. (The Geneva Bible, also known as the English Bible, was translated by Reformed English Protestants living in Switzerland; this version, used by the Puritans, was outlawed by the Church of England.)

4. "Honor the Lord with thy riches, and with the first fruits of all thine increase. So shall thy barns be filled with abundance, and thy presses

shall burst with new wine" (Proverbs 3.9–10).

5. Matthew 5.43, 19.19.

6. "Therefore whatsoever ye would that men should do to you: even so do ye to them: for this is the Law and the Prophets" (Matthew 7.12).

7. In Judges 19.16–21, an old citizen of Gibeah offered shelter to a traveling priest or Levite and defended him from enemies from a neighboring city. Abraham entertains the angels in Genesis 18: "Again the Lord appeared unto him in the plain of Mamre, as he sat in his tent door about the heat of the day. And he lifted up his eyes, and looked: and lo, three men stood by him, and when he saw them, he ran to meet them from the tent door, and bowed himself to the ground" (Genesis 18.1–2). Lot was Abraham's nephew, and he escaped the destruction of the city of Sodom because he defended from a mob two angels who were his guests (Genesis 19.1–14).

The law of grace or the Gospel hath some difference from the former, as in these respects: First, the law of nature was given to man in the estate of innocency; this of the Gospel in the estate of regeneracy. Secondly, the former propounds one man to another, as the same flesh and image of God; this as a brother in Christ also, and in the communion of the same spirit and so teacheth us to put a difference between Christians and others. *Do good to all, especially to the household of faith*: Upon this ground the Israelites were to put a difference between the brethren of such as were strangers though not of Canaanites.[8] Thirdly, the law of nature could give no rules for dealing with enemies, for all are to be considered as friends in the state of innocency, but the Gospel commands love to an enemy. Proof. If thine Enemy hunger, feed him; Love your Enemies, do good to them that hate you. Matthew: 5.44.

This law of the Gospel propounds likewise a difference of seasons and occasions. There is a time when a Christian must sell all and give to the poor, as they did in the Apostles' times.[9] There is a time also when a Christian (though they give not all yet) must give beyond their ability, as they of Macedonia, Corinthians: 2.8.[1] Likewise community of perils calls for extraordinary liberality, and so doth community in some special service for the Church. Lastly, when there is no other means whereby our Christian brother may be relieved in his distress, we must help him beyond our ability, rather than tempt God in putting him upon help by miraculous or extraordinary means.

This duty of mercy is exercised in the kinds, *giving, lending* and *forgiving*.—

Quest. What rule shall a man observe in giving in respect of the measure?

Ans. If the time and occasion be ordinary, he is to give out of his abundance. Let him lay aside as God hath blessed him. If the time and occasion be extraordinary, he must be ruled by them; taking this withal, that then a man cannot likely do too much, especially if he may leave himself and his family under probable means of comfortable subsistence.

Objection. A man must lay up for posterity, the fathers lay up for posterity and children and he "is worse than an infidel" that "provideth not for his own."

Ans. For the first, it is plain that it being spoken by way of comparison, it must be meant of the ordinary and usual course of fathers and cannot extend to times and occasions extraordinary. For the other place, the Apostle speaks against such as walked inordinately, and it is without question, that he is worse than an infidel who through his own sloth and voluptuousness shall neglect to provide for his family.

Objection. "The wise man's eyes are in his head" saith Solomon, "and foreseeth the plague,"[2] therefore we must forecast and lay up against evil times when he or his may stand in need of all he can gather.

Ans. This very argument Solomon useth to persuade to liberality, Ecclesiastes: "Cast thy bread upon the waters," and "for thou knowest not what evil

---

8. People who lived in Canaan, the biblical promised land for the Israelites.
9. "And they sold their possessions, and goods, and parted them to all men, as everyone had need" (Acts 2.45).
1. "We do you also to wit, brethren, of the grace of God bestowed upon the Churches of Macedonia. Because in great trial of affliction their joy abounded, and their most extreme poverty abounded unto their rich liberality. For to their power (I bear record) yea, and beyond their power they were willing. And prayed us with great instance that we would receive the grace, and fellowship of the ministering which is toward the Saints" (2 Corinthians 8.1–4).
2. Ecclesiastes 2.14. Solomon was the son of David and successor to David as king of Israel.

may come upon the land."[3] Luke: 16.9. "Make you friends of the riches of iniquity." [4] You will ask how this shall be? very well. For first he that gives to the poor, lends to the Lord and He will repay him even in this life an hundred fold to him or his—The righteous is ever merciful and lendeth and his seed enjoyeth the blessing; and besides we know what advantage it will be to us in the day of account when many such witnesses shall stand forth for us to witness the improvement of our talent.[5] And I would know of those who plead so much for laying up for time to come, whether they hold that to be Gospel, Matthew: 6.19: "Lay not up for yourselves treasures upon earth," [6] etc. If they acknowledge it, what extent will they allow it? if only to those primitive times, let them consider the reason whereupon our Savior grounds it. The first is that they are subject to the moth, the rust, the thief. Secondly, they will steal away the heart; where the treasure is there will the heart be also. The reasons are of like force at all times. Therefore the exhortation must be general and perpetual, with always in respect of the love and affection to riches and in regard of the things themselves when any special service for the church or particular distress of our brother do call for the use of them; otherwise it is not only lawful but necessary to lay up as Joseph[7] did to have ready upon such occasions, as the Lord (whose stewards we are of them) shall call for them from us. Christ gives us an instance of the first, when He sent his disciples for the ass, and bids them answer the owner thus, the Lord hath need of him.[8] So when the tabernacle was to be built He sends to His people to call for their silver and gold, etc.; and yields them no other reason but that it was for His work. When Elisha comes to the widow of Sareptah and finds her preparing to make ready her pittance for herself and family, He bids her first provide for Him; he challengeth first God's part which she must first give before she must serve her own family.[9] All these teach us that the Lord looks that when He is pleased to call for His right in anything we have, our own interest we have must stand aside till His turn be served. For the other, we need look no further than to that of John: 1: "He who hath this world's goods and seeth his brother to need and shuts up his compassion from him, how dwelleth the love of God in him," which comes punctually to this conclusion: if thy brother be in want and thou canst help him, thou needst not make doubt, what thou shouldst do, if thou lovest God thou must help him.

    Quest. What rule must we observe in lending?

    Ans. Thou must observe whether thy brother hath present or probable, or possible means of repaying thee, if there be none of these, thou must give him according to his necessity, rather than lend him as he requires. If he hath present means of repaying thee, thou art to look at him not as an act of mercy, but by way of commerce, wherein thou art to walk by the rule of

---

3. "Cast thy bread upon the waters: for after many days thou shalt find it. Give a portion to seven, and also to eight: for thou knowest not what evil shall be upon the earth" (Ecclesiastes 11.1–2).
4. The passage in Luke refers to a servant who is about to lose his job managing his boss's accounts. To guarantee that he will be welcome in the houses of his master's debtors, he cuts their bills in half. Jesus explains: "And I say unto you, Make you friends with the riches of iniquity, that when ye shall want, they may receive you into everlasting habitations" (Luke 16.9).
5. Originally a measure of money (as in the weight of gold).
6. "Lay not up treasures for yourselves upon the earth, where the moth and canker corrupt, and where thieves dig through and steal. But lay up treasures for yourselves in heaven, where neither the moth nor canker corrupteth, and where thieves neither dig through nor steal" (Matthew 6.19–20).
7. The son of Jacob and Rachel, who stored up the harvest in the seven good years before the famine (Genesis 41).
8. Matthew 21.5–7.
9. 1 Kings 17.8–24.

justice; but if his means of repaying thee be only probable or possible, then is he an object of thy mercy, thou must lend him, though there be danger of losing it, Deuteronomy: 15.7: "If any of thy brethren be poor," etc., "thou shalt lend him sufficient."[1] That men might not shift off this duty by the apparent hazard, He tells them that though the year of Jubilee[2] were at hand (when he must remit it, if he were not able to repay it before) yet he must lend him and that cheerfully: "It may not grieve thee to give him" saith He; and because some might object; "why so I should soon impoverish myself and my family," He adds "with all thy work,"[3] etc.; for our Savior, Matthew: 5.42: "From him that would borrow of thee turn not away."

Quest. What rule must we observe in forgiving?

Ans. Whether thou didst lend by way of commerce or in mercy, if he have nothing to pay thee, [you] must forgive, (except in cause where thou hast a surety or a lawful pledge) Deuteronomy: 15.2. Every seventh year the creditor was to quit that which he lent to his brother if he were poor as appears— verse 8: "Save when there shall be no poor with thee." In all these and like cases, Christ was a general rule, Matthew: 7.12: "Whatsoever ye would that men should do to you, do ye the same to them also."

Quest. What rule must we observe and walk by in cause of community of peril?

Ans. The same as before, but with more enlargement towards others and less respect towards ourselves and our own right. Hence it was that in the primitive church they sold all, had all things in common, neither did any man say that which he possessed was his own. Likewise in their return out of the captivity, because the work was great for the restoring of the church and the danger of enemies was common to all, Nehemiah exhorts the Jews to liberality and readiness in remitting their debts to their brethren, and disposing liberally of his own to such as wanted, and stand not upon his own due, which he might have demanded of them.[4] Thus did some of our forefathers in times of persecution in England, and so did many of the faithful of other churches, whereof we keep an honorable remembrance of them; and it is to be observed that both in Scriptures and later stories of the churches that such as have been most bountiful to the poor saints, especially in these extraordinary times and occasions, God hath left them highly commended to posterity, as Zacheus, Cornelius, Dorcas, Bishop Hooper, the Cuttler of Brussells and divers[5] others. Observe again that the Scripture gives no caution to restrain any from being over liberal this way; but all men to the liberal and cheerful practice hereof by the sweetest promises; as to instance one for many, Isaiah: 58.6: "Is not this the fast I have chosen to loose the bonds of

1. "If one of thy brethren with thee be poor within any of thy gates in thy land, which the Lord thy God giveth thee, thou shalt not harden thine heart, nor shut thine hand from thy poor brother: But thou shalt open thine hand unto him, and shalt lend him sufficient for his need which he hath" (Deuteronomy 15.7–8).
2. According to Mosaic law (Leviticus 25.8–13), the Jubilee year followed a cycle of seven sabbatical years. In the fiftieth year, the lands would lie fallow, all work would cease, and all debts would be canceled.
3. "Beware that there be not a wicked thought in thine heart, to say, The seventh year, the year of

freedom is at hand: therefore it grieveth thee to look on thy poor brother, and thou givest him nought, and he cry unto the Lord against thee, so that sin be in thee: Thou shalt give him, and let it not grieve thine heart to give unto him: for because of this the Lord thy God shall bless thee in all thy works, and in all that thou puttest thine hand to" (Deuteronomy 15.9–10).
4. Nehemiah was sent by King Artaxerxes to repair the walls of the city of Jerusalem; he saved the city as governor when he persuaded those lending money to charge no interest and to think first of the common good (see Nehemiah 3).
5. Various. The names are of Christian martyrs.

wickedness, to take off the heavy burdens, to let the oppressed go free and to break every yoke, to deal thy bread to the hungry and to bring the poor that wander into thy house, when thou seest the naked to cover them. And then shall thy light break forth as the morning, and thy health shall grow speedily, thy righteousness shall go before God, and the glory of the Lord shall embrace thee; then thou shalt call and the Lord shall answer thee" etc. [Verse] 10: "If thou pour out thy soul to the hungry, then shall thy light spring out in darkness, and the Lord shall guide thee continually, and satisfy thy soul in drought, and make fat thy bones; thou shalt be like a watered garden, and they shalt be of thee that shall build the old waste places" etc. On the contrary, most heavy curses are laid upon such as are straightened towards the Lord and His people, Judges: 5.[23]: "Curse ye Meroshe because ye came not to help the Lord," etc. Proverbs: [21.13]: "He who shutteth his ears from hearing the cry of the poor, he shall cry and shall not be heard." Matthew: 25: "Go ye cursed into everlasting fire" etc. "I was hungry and ye fed me not." 2 Corinthians: 9.6: "He that soweth sparingly shall reap sparingly."

Having already set forth the practice of mercy according to the rule of God's law, it will be useful to lay open the grounds of it also, being the other part of the commandment, and that is the affection from which this exercise of mercy must arise. The apostle[6] tells us that this love is the fulfilling of the law, not that it is enough to love our brother and so no further; but in regard of the excellency of his parts giving any motion to the other as the soul to the body and the power it hath to set all the faculties on work in the outward exercise of this duty. As when we bid one make the clock strike, he doth not lay hand on the hammer, which is the immediate instrument of the sound, but sets on work the first mover or main wheel, knowing that will certainly produce the sound which he intends. So the way to draw men to works of mercy, is not by force of argument from the goodness or necessity of the work; for though this course may enforce a rational mind to some present act of mercy, as is frequent in experience, yet it cannot work such a habit in a soul, as shall make it prompt upon all occasions to produce the same effect, but by framing these affections of love in the heart which will as natively bring forth the other, as any cause doth produce effect.

The definition which the Scripture gives us of love is this: "Love is the bond of perfection." First, it is a bond or ligament. Secondly it makes the work perfect. There is no body but consists of parts and that which knits these parts together gives the body its perfection, because it makes each part so contiguous to others as thereby they do mutually participate with each other, both in strength and infirmity, in pleasure and pain. To instance in the most perfect of all bodies: Christ and His church make one body. The several parts of this body, considered apart before they were united, were as disproportionate and as much disordering as so many contrary qualities or elements, but when Christ comes and by His spirit and love knits all these parts to Himself and each to other, it is become the most perfect and best proportioned body in the world. Ephesians: 4.16: "Christ, by whom all the body being knit together by every joint for the furniture thereof, according to the effectual power which is the measure of every perfection of parts," "a glorious body without spot or wrinkle," the ligaments hereof being Christ,

---

6. Saint Paul in his Epistle to the Romans 13.8.

or His love, for Christ is love (1 John: 4.8). So this definition is right: "Love is the bond of perfection."

From hence we may frame these conclusions. 1. First of all, true Christians are of one body in Christ, 1 Corinthians: 12.12, 27: "Ye are the body of Christ and members of their part." Secondly: The ligaments of this body which knit together are love. Thirdly: No body can be perfect which wants its proper ligament. Fourthly: All the parts of this body being thus united are made so contiguous in a special relation as they must needs partake of each other's strength and infirmity; joy and sorrow, weal and woe. 1 Corinthians: 12.26: "If one member suffers, all suffer with it, if one be in honor, all rejoice with it." Fifthly: This sensibleness and sympathy of each other's conditions will necessarily infuse into each part a native desire and endeavor to strengthen, defend, preserve and comfort the other.

To insist a little on this conclusion being the product of all the former, the truth hereof will appear both by precept and pattern. 1 John: 3.10: "Ye ought to lay down your lives for the brethren." Galatians: 6.2: "bear ye one another's burthens and so fulfill the law of Christ." For patterns we have that first of our Savior who out of His good will in obedience to His father, becoming a part of this body, and being knit with it in the bond of love, found such a native sensibleness of our infirmities and sorrows as He willingly yielded Himself to death to ease the infirmities of the rest of His body, and so healed their sorrows. From the like sympathy of parts did the apostles and many thousands of the saints lay down their lives for Christ. Again, the like we may see in the members of this body among themselves. Romans: 9. Paul could have been contented to have been separated from Christ, that the Jews might not be cut off from the body. It is very observable what he professeth of his affectionate partaking with every member: "who is weak" saith he "and I am not weak? who is offended and I burn not;"[7] and again, 2 Corinthians: 7.13. "therefore we are comforted because ye were comforted." Of Epaphroditus he speaketh,[8] Philippians: 2.30. that he regarded not his own life to do him service. So Phoebe[9] and others are called the servants of the church. Now it is apparent that they served not for wages, or by constraint, but out of love. The like we shall find in the histories of the church in all ages, the sweet sympathy of affections which was in the members of this body one towards another, their cheerfulness in serving and suffering together, how liberal they were without repining, harborers without grudging and helpful without reproaching; and all from hence, because they had fervent love amongst them, which only make the practice of mercy constant and easy.

The next consideration is how this love comes to be wrought. Adam in his first estate[1] was a perfect model of mankind in all their generations, and in him this love was perfected in regard of the habit. But Adam rent himself from his creator, rent all his posterity also one from another; whence it comes that every man is born with this principle in him, to love and seek himself only, and thus a man continueth till Christ comes and takes possession of the soul and infuseth another principle, love to God and our brother. And this latter having

---

7. 2 Corinthians 11.29.
8. Saint Paul tells the Philippians he will send them a spiritual guide: "But I supposed it necessary to send my brother Epaphroditus unto you my companion in labor, and fellow soldier, even your messenger, and he that ministered unto me such things as I wanted" (Philippians 2.25).
9. A Christian woman praised by Saint Paul in Romans 16.1.
1. I.e., in his innocence.

continual supply from Christ, as the head and root by which he is united, gets the predomining[2] in the soul, so by little and little expels the former. 1 John: 4.7. "love cometh of God and every one that loveth is born of God," so that this love is the fruit of the new birth, and none can have it but the new creature. Now when this quality is thus formed in the souls of men, it works like the spirit upon the dry bones. Ezekiel: 37: "bone came to bone." It gathers together the scattered bones, of perfect old man Adam,[3] and knits them into one body again in Christ, whereby a man is become again a living soul.

The third consideration is concerning the exercise of this love which is twofold, inward or outward. The outward hath been handled in the former preface of this discourse. For unfolding the other we must take in our way that maxim of philosophy *simile simili gaudet*, or like will to like [Latin]; for as it is things which are turned with disaffection to each other, the ground of it is from a dissimilitude arising from the contrary or different nature of the things themselves; for the ground of love is an apprehension of some resemblance in things loved to that which affects it. This is the cause why the Lord loves the creature, so far as it hath any of His image in it; He loves His elect because they are like Himself, He beholds them in His beloved son. So a mother loves her child, because she thoroughly conceives a resemblance of herself in it. Thus it is between the members of Christ. Each discerns, by the work of the spirit, his own image and resemblance in another, and therefore cannot but love him as he loves himself. Now when the soul, which is of a sociable nature, finds anything like to itself, it is like Adam when Eve was brought to him. She must have it one with herself. This is flesh of my flesh (saith the soul) and bone of my bone. She conceives a great delight in it, therefore she desires nearness and familiarity with it. She hath a great propensity to do it good and receives such content in it, as fearing the miscarriage of her beloved she bestows it in the inmost closet of her heart. She will not endure that it shall want any good which she can give it. If by occasion she be withdrawn from the company of it, she is still looking towards the place where she left her beloved. If she heard it groan, she is with it presently. If she find it sad and disconsolate, she sighs and moans with it. She hath no such joy as to see her beloved merry and thriving. If she see it wronged, she cannot bear it without passion. She sets no bounds to her affections, nor hath any thought of reward. She finds recompense enough in the exercise of her love towards it. We may see this acted to life in Jonathan and David.[4] Jonathan, a valiant man endowed with the spirit of Christ, so soon as he discovers the same spirit in David, had presently his heart knit to him by this lineament of love, so that it is said he loved him as his own soul. He takes so great pleasure in him, that he strips himself to adorn his beloved. His father's kingdom was not so precious to him as his beloved David. David shall have it with all his heart, himself desires no more but that he may be near to him to rejoice in his good. He chooseth to converse with him in the wilderness even to the hazard of his own life, rather than with the great courtiers in his father's palace. When he sees danger towards him, he spares neither rare pains nor peril to direct it. When injury was offered his beloved David, he would not bear it, though from his own father; and when they must

---

2. Predominance.
3. Jesus Christ has traditionally been called the New Adam to signify the redemption of human-

kind from the original sin of Old Adam.
4. The story of Jonathan and David is told in 1 Samuel 19 ff.

part for a season only, they thought their hearts would have broke for sorrow, had not their affections found vent by abundance of tears. Other instances might be brought to show the nature of this affection, as of Ruth and Naomi,[5] and many others; but this truth is cleared enough.

If any shall object that it is not possible that love should be bred or upheld without hope of requital, it is granted; but that is not our cause; for this love is always under reward. It never gives, but it always receives with advantage; first, in regard that among the members of the same body, love and affection are reciprocal in a most equal and sweet kind of commerce. Secondly, in regard of the pleasure and content that the exercise of love carries with it, as we may see in the natural body. The mouth is at all the pains to receive and mince the food which serves for the nourishment of all the other parts of the body, yet it hath no cause to complain; for first the other parts send back by several passages a due proportion of the same nourishment, in a better form for the strengthening and comforting the mouth. Secondly, the labor of the mouth is accompanied with such pleasure and content as far exceeds the pains it takes. So is it in all the labor of love among Christians. The party loving, reaps love again, as was showed before, which the soul covets more than all the wealth in the world. Thirdly: Nothing yields more pleasure and content to the soul than when it finds that which it may love fervently, for to love and live beloved is the soul's paradise, both here and in heaven. In the state of wedlock there be many comforts to bear out the troubles of that condition; but let such as have tried the most, say if there be any sweetness in that condition comparable to the exercise of mutual love.

From former considerations arise these conclusions.

First: This love among Christians is a real thing, not imaginary.

Secondly: This love is as absolutely necessary to the being of the body of Christ, as the sinews and other ligaments of a natural body are to the being of that body.

Thirdly: This love is a divine, spiritual nature free, active, strong, courageous, permanent; undervaluing all things beneath its proper object; and of all the graces, this makes us nearer to resemble the virtues of our Heavenly Father.

Fourthly: It rests in the love and welfare of its beloved. For the full and certain knowledge of these truths concerning the nature, use, and excellency of this grace, that which the Holy Ghost hath left recorded, 1 Corinthians: 13, may give full satisfaction, which is needful for every true member of this lovely body of the Lord Jesus, to work upon their hearts by prayer, meditation, continual exercise at least of the special [influence] of His grace, till Christ be formed in them and they in Him, all in each other, knit together by this bond of love.

II

It rests now to make some application of this discourse by the present design, which gave the occasion of writing of it. Herein are four things to be propounded: first the persons, secondly the work, thirdly the end, fourthly the means.

5. Naomi was Ruth's mother-in-law; when Ruth's husband died, she refused to leave Naomi (Ruth 1.16).

First, For the persons. We are a company professing ourselves fellow members of Christ, in which respect only though we were absent from each other many miles, and had our employments as far distant, yet we ought to account ourselves knit together by this bond of love, and live in the exercise of it, if we would have comfort of our being in Christ. This was notorious in the practice of the Christians in former times; as is testified of the Waldenses,[6] from the mouth of one of the adversaries *Æneas Sylvius* "mutuo [ament][7] penè antequam norunt," they used to love any of their own religion even before they were acquainted with them.

Secondly, for the work we have in hand. It is by a mutual consent, through a special overvaluing providence and a more than an ordinary approbation of the Churches of Christ, to seek out a place of cohabitation and consortship under a due form of government both civil and ecclesiastical. In such cases as this, the care of the public must oversway all private respects, by which, not only conscience, but mere civil policy, doth bind us. For it is a true rule that particular estates cannot subsist in the ruin of the public.

Thirdly. The end is to improve our lives to do more service to the Lord; the comfort and increase of the body of Christ whereof we are members; that ourselves and posterity may be the better preserved from the common corruptions of this evil world, to serve the Lord and work out our salvation under the power and purity of His holy ordinances.

Fourthly, for the means whereby this must be effected. They are twofold, a conformity with the work and end we aim at. These we see are extraordinary, therefore we must not content ourselves with usual ordinary means. Whatsoever we did or ought to have done when we lived in England, the same must we do, and more also, where we go. That which the most in their churches maintain as a truth in profession only, we must bring into familiar and constant practice, as in this duty of love. We must love brotherly without dissimulation; we must love one another with a pure heart fervently. We must bear one another's burthens. We must not look only on our own things, but also on the things of our brethren, neither must we think that the Lord will bear with such failings at our hands as he doth from those among whom we have lived; and that for three reasons.

First, In regard of the more near bond of marriage between Him and us, where-in He hath taken us to be His after a most strict and peculiar manner, which will make Him the more jealous of our love and obedience. So He tells the people of Israel, you only have I known of all the families of the earth, therefore will I punish you for your transgressions. Secondly, because the Lord will be sanctified in them that come near Him. We know that there were many that corrupted the service of the Lord, some setting up altars before His own, others offering both strange fire and strange sacrifices also; yet there came no fire from heaven or other sudden judgment upon them, as did upon Nadab and Abihu,[8] who yet we may think did not sin presumptu-

---

6. The Waldenses took their name from Pater Valdes, an early French reformer of the Church. They still survive as a religious community.
7. *Solent amare* is closer to the Latin than is *amant*, the suggestion of the original editor, Samuel Eliot Morison. Aeneas Sylvius Piccolomini (1405–1464), historian and scholar, became Pope Pius II.
8. "But Nadab and Abihu, the sons of Aaron, took either of them his censor, and put fire therein, and put incense thereupon, and offered strange fire before the Lord, which he had not commanded them. Therefore a fire went out from the Lord, and devoured them: so they died before the Lord" (Leviticus 10.1–2). Winthrop's point is that the chosen people are often punished more severely than unbelievers.

ously. Thirdly. When God gives a special commission He looks to have it strictly observed in every article. When He gave Saul a commission to destroy Amaleck, He indented with him upon certain articles,[9] and because he failed in one of the least, and that upon a fair pretense, it lost him the kingdom which should have been his reward if he had observed his commission.

Thus stands the cause between God and us. We are entered into covenant[1] with Him for this work. We have taken out a commission, the Lord hath given us leave to draw our own articles. We have professed to enterprise these actions, upon these and those ends, we have hereupon besought Him of favor and blessing. Now if the Lord shall please to hear us, and bring us in peace to the place we desire, then hath He ratified this covenant and sealed our commission, [and] will expect a strict performance of the articles contained in it; but if we shall neglect the observation of these articles which are the ends we have propounded, and, dissembling with our God, shall fall to embrace this present world and prosecute our carnal intentions, seeking great things for ourselves and our posterity, the Lord will surely break out in wrath against us; be revenged of such a perjured people and make us know the price of the breach of such a covenant.

Now the only way to avoid this shipwreck, and to provide for our posterity, is to follow the counsel of Micah,[2] to do justly, to love mercy, to walk humbly with our God. For this end, we must be knit together in this work as one man. We must entertain each other in brotherly affection, we must be willing to abridge ourselves of our superfluities, for the supply of other's necessities. We must uphold a familiar commerce together in all meekness, gentleness, patience and liberality. We must delight in each other, make other's conditions our own, rejoice together, mourn together, labor and suffer together, always having before our eyes our commission and community in the work, our community as members of the same body. So shall we keep the unity of the spirit in the bond of peace. The Lord will be our God, and delight to dwell among us as His own people, and will command a blessing upon us in all our ways, so that we shall see much more of His wisdom, power, goodness and truth, than formerly we have been acquainted with. We shall find that the God of Israel is among us, when ten of us shall be able to resist a thousand of our enemies; when He shall make us a praise and glory that men shall say of succeeding plantations, "the Lord make it like that of NEW ENGLAND." For we must consider that we shall be as a city upon a hill.[3] The eyes of all people are upon us, so that if we shall deal falsely with our God in this work we have undertaken, and so cause Him to withdraw His present help from us, we shall be made a story and a by-word through the world. We shall open the mouths of enemies to speak evil of the ways of God, and all professors for God's sake. We shall shame the faces of many of

9. I.e., made an agreement with him on parts of a contract. Saul was instructed to destroy the Amalekites and all they possessed, but he spared their sheep and oxen, and in doing so disobeyed God's commandment and was rejected as king (1 Samuel 15.1–34).
1. A legal contract. The Israelites entered into a covenant with God in which he promised to protect them if they kept his word and were faithful to him.
2. An eighth-century-B.C.E. prophet who, in the Book of Micah, speaks continually of God's judgment and the need to hope for salvation: "He hath showed thee, O man, what is good, and what the Lord requireth of thee: surely to do justly, and to love mercy, and to humble thyself, to walk with thy God" (Micah 6.8).
3. "Ye are the light of the world. A city that is set on an hill, cannot be hid. Neither do men light a candle, and put it under a bushel, but on a candlestick, and it giveth light unto all that are in the house" (Matthew 5.14–15).

God's worthy servants, and cause their prayers to be turned into curses upon us till we be consumed out of the good land whither we are agoing.

And to shut up this discourse with that exhortation of Moses, that faithful servant of the Lord, in his last farewell to Israel, Deuteronomy 30.[4] Beloved, there is now set before us life and good, death and evil, in that we are commanded this day to love the Lord our God, and to love one another, to walk in His ways and to keep His commandments and His ordinance and His laws, and the articles of our covenant with Him, that we may live and be multiplied, and that our Lord our God may bless us in the land whither we go to possess it. But if our hearts shall turn away, so that we will not obey, but shall be seduced, and worship other gods, our pleasures and profits, and serve them; it is propounded unto us this day, we shall surely perish out of the good land whither we pass over this vast sea to possess it.

> Therefore let us choose life,
> that we and our seed
> may live by obeying His
> voice and cleaving to Him,
> for He is our life and
> our prosperity.

1630   1838

4. "Behold, I have set before thee this day life and good, death and evil, In that I command thee this day, to love the Lord thy God, to walk in his ways, and to keep his commandment, and his ordinances, and his laws, that thou mayest live, and be multiplied, and that the Lord thy God may bless thee in the land, whither thou goest to possess it. But if thine heart turn away, so that thou wilt not obey, but shalt be seduced and worship other gods, and serve them, I pronounce unto you this day, that ye shall surely perish, ye shall not prolong your days in the land, whither thou passest over Jordan to possess it. I call heaven and earth to record this day against you, that I have set before you life and death, blessing and cursing: therefore choose life, that both thou and thy seed may live, By loving the Lord thy God, by obeying his voice, and by cleaving unto him: for he is thy life, and the length of thy days, that thou mayest dwell in the land which the Lord sware unto thy fathers, Abraham, Isaac, and Jacob, to give them" (Deuteronomy 30.15–20).

ROGER WILLIAMS
c. 1603–1683

Roger Williams is the preeminent figure associated with freedom of conscience and religious liberty in early New England. Banished from the Massachusetts Bay Colony in 1636 for spreading opinions that the colony's leadership considered dangerous, Williams went on to build Rhode Island into a model of inclusive self-government and a haven for religious minorities, opening it to dissenting refugees from the Puritan colonies and to the first Jewish and Quaker settlers in British North America. Williams also developed close relationships with indigenous leaders in the region, living at times in Native communities and mediating conflicts with other English colonies. In 1643, Williams produced *A Key into the Language of America*, a dictionary and cultural guide to the Algonquian peoples of New England that offers comparative social commentary, including reflections on the moral shortcomings of the English.

Williams was also a brilliant polemicist. A prominent genre in Williams's day, polemic involves a vigorous attack on an individual or an idea. Polemical writings on colonization and on religion contributed importantly to the rise of popular print culture in England. In controversial pamphlets such as "The Bloody Tenet of Persecution" (1644) and "The Hireling Ministry None of Christ's" (1652), Williams took strongly worded positions challenging many of the foundational assumptions of his Puritan neighbors. And in "Christenings Make Not Christians" (1645), Williams theorized about the formation of a truly consent-based religious community, which would not be restricted by race or cultural heritage, compelled by physical violence, or shaped by intellectual and emotional coercion. This work reveals a mind preoccupied with fundamental questions about human consciousness and will. In his life as in his writings, Williams pursued his understanding of liberty of conscience with striking integrity.

The son of a London merchant, Williams took an unexpected turn in 1617 when he met Sir Edward Coke, a leading legal thinker whose advocacy for the common law tradition and challenge to the authority of the king fundamentally shaped the era and transformed English law. Probably impressed by Williams's sharp intellect, Coke helped the young man get a first-rate education. After graduating from Cambridge University in 1627 and taking holy orders, Williams became involved in Church reform. Years later, he said that Archbishop William Laud, the preeminent clergyman in the Church of England under King Charles I, "pursued" him "out of this land." Laud required all clerics to pledge an oath of loyalty to the Church of England, sparking a crisis for dissenting clergy and contributing to the "Great Migration" of Puritans to New England.

In 1631 Williams arrived in Boston with his wife, Mary. He was at first a valued addition to the new colony at Massachusetts Bay, which badly needed men of his intellectual capabilities and educational attainments. Soon, however, Williams refused to minister at the prestigious First Church of Boston because he "durst not officiate to an unseparated people"—that is, a church that retained affiliations with the Anglican orthodoxy. This episode gave Massachusetts authorities their first taste of Williams's deep resistance to the established Church and his enormous confidence in matters of belief. Over the next four years, he ministered to the communities at Plymouth and then Salem. In 1635, while he was at Salem, the Bay Colony leaders accused him of holding "new and dangerous opinions against the authority of magistrates."

Williams had infuriated and threatened the leaders of Massachusetts by taking four positions, any one of which seriously undermined the theocracy that was at the heart of the Bay Colony government. He denied, first, that Massachusetts had a proper title to its land, arguing that King Charles I could not bestow a title to something that belonged to the Natives. Second, he argued that no unregenerate person (that is, anyone who had not been "born again") could be required either to pray or to swear a legal oath; third, that Massachusetts Bay Colony ministers, who had persuaded the king of England that they wished to remain part of the Church of England, should not only separate from the Church but repent that they had ever served it; and last, that civil authority was limited to civil matters and that magistrates had no jurisdiction over the soul. Williams wanted to create a barrier between Church and state to prevent Christianity from being contaminated by worldly interests. The position was disturbing to Separatist and non-Separatist alike, and it made Williams unwelcome in both Plymouth and Boston.

In his journal for January 1636, John Winthrop notes that when the governor of Massachusetts and his assistants met to reconsider the charge of divisiveness against Williams, they agreed that they could not wait until spring to banish him from the commonwealth. His opinions were dangerous and spreading, so they needed to send him back to England immediately. When they went to Salem to "carry him aboard the ship," however, they found he "had been gone 3 days before, but whither they could not learn." Williams had fled Massachusetts for Rhode Island—reportedly with

Winthrop's aid. He found shelter there with the Narragansett Indians and, from that time until his death almost fifty years later, Williams and Providence Plantation were synonymous with the spirit of religious liberty. In 1663, Rhode Island received a royal charter from King Charles II in which freedom of conscience was guaranteed, giving the colony an exceptional status in the English-speaking world.

The Massachusetts authorities did not cite Williams's attitude toward the American Indians in their charges against him, but in this regard as well, his position was antithetical to their own. From the beginning, he wrote, his "soul's desire was to do the natives good, and to that end to have their language." Although he was not interested in assimilating into their culture, Williams presented American Indians as no better or worse than the English "rogues" who dealt with them, and stressed that they possessed complex cultures with their own forms of civility. Williams knew that A Key into the Language of America would prove useful to those who wished to convert Native Americans to Christianity. He was not primarily interested in such efforts, and in "Christenings Make Not Christians" he argued against a line of thinking that promoted missionary work, which was ostensibly a central reason for the foundation of the Puritan colonies. Anyone not regenerate, Williams argued, was outside the people of God, and to refer to the American Indians as "heathen" was "improperly sinful" and "unchristianly."

He was greatly disappointed when, despite his efforts to befriend the Narragansetts, they burned the settlements at both Warwick and Providence during King Philip's War. By the time Williams died, the future looked grave for the Narragansetts. The great tribe would never recover from the losses incurred during that war. Despite this failure, Williams's efforts to separate religious and civil life, and to promote peaceful interactions among different groups, produced a lasting legacy. The Rhode Island charter offered a model that would be taken up in the U.S. Bill of Rights, which mandates the separation of Church and state and guarantees freedom of speech, of the press, and of assembly.

From A Key into the Language of America[1]

To My Dear and Well-Beloved Friends and Countrymen, in Old and New England

I present you with a key; I have not heard of the like, yet framed,[2] since it pleased God to bring that mighty continent of America to light. Others of my countrymen have often, and excellently, and lately written of the country (and none that I know beyond the goodness and worth of it).

This key, respects the native language of it, and happily may unlock some rarities concerning the natives themselves, not yet discovered.

I drew the materials in a rude lump at sea, as a private help to my own memory, that I might not, by my present absence, lightly lose what I had so dearly bought in some few years hardship, and charges among the barbarians. Yet being reminded by some, what pity it were to bury those materials in my grave at land or sea; and withal, remembering how oft I have been importuned by worthy friends of all sorts, to afford them some helps this way. I resolved (by the assistance of The Most High) to cast those materials into this key, pleasant and profitable for all, but especially for my friends residing in those parts.

---

1. The text is from the first edition (1643), reprinted by the Rhode Island and Providence Tercentenary Committee (1936).
2. Shaped.

A little key may open a box, where lies a bunch of keys.

With this I have entered into the secrets of those countries, wherever English dwell about two hundred miles, between the French and Dutch plantations; for want of this, I know what gross mistakes myself and others have run into.

There is a mixture of this language north and south, from the place of my abode, about six hundred miles; yet within the two hundred miles (aforementioned) their dialects do exceedingly differ; yet not so, but (within that compass) a man may, by this help, converse with thousands of natives all over the country: and by such converse it may please the Father of Mercies to spread civility, (and in His own most holy season) Christianity. For one candle will light ten thousand, and it may please God to bless a little leaven to season the mighty lump of those peoples and territories.

It is expected, that having had so much converse with these natives, I should write some little of them.

Concerning them (a little to gratify expectation) I shall touch upon four heads:

First, by what names they are distinguished.

Secondly, their original[3] and descent.

Thirdly, their religion, manners, customs, etc.

Fourthly, that great point of their conversion.

To the first, their names are of two sorts:

First, those of the English giving: as natives, savages, Indians, wildmen (so the Dutch call them *wilden*), Abergeny[4] men, pagans, barbarians, heathen.

Secondly, their names which they give themselves.

I cannot observe that they ever had (before the coming of the English, French or Dutch amongst them) any names to difference themselves from strangers, for they knew none; but two sorts of names they had, and have amongst themselves:

First, general, belonging to all natives, as Nínnuock, Ninnimissinnûwock, Eniskeetomparwog, which signifies Men, Folk, or People.

Secondly, particular names, peculiar to several nations, of them amongst themselves, as Nanhigganġuck, Massachusêuck, Cawasumsêuck, Cowwesġuck, Quintikóock, Qunnipiġuck, Pequttóog, etc.

They have often asked me, why we call them Indians, natives, etc. And understanding the reason, they will call themselves Indians, in opposition to English, etc.

For the second head proposed, their original and descent:

From Adam and Noah[5] that they spring, it is granted on all hands.

But for their later descent, and whence they came into those parts, it seems as hard to find, as to find the wellhead of some fresh stream, which running many miles out of the country to the salt ocean, hath met with many mixing streams by the way. They say themselves, that they have sprung and grown up in that very place, like the very trees of the wilderness.

They say that their great god Kautántowwìt created those parts, as I observed in the chapter of their religion.[6] They have no clothes, books, nor

---

3. Place of origin.
4. Aboriginal.
5. After the great flood described in the Bible,

only Noah and his family remained.
6. I.e., in Chapter XXI of Williams's *Key*, which has thirty-two chapters.

letters, and conceive their fathers never had; and therefore they are easily persuaded that the God that made Englishmen is a greater God, because He hath so richly endowed the English above themselves. But when they hear that about sixteen hundred years ago, England and the inhabitants thereof were like unto themselves, and since have received from God, clothes, books, etc. they are greatly affected with a secret hope concerning themselves.

Wise and judicious men, with whom I have discoursed, maintain their original to be northward from Tartaria:[7] and at my now taking ship, at the Dutch plantation, it pleased the Dutch Governor, (in some discourse with me about the natives), to draw their line from Iceland, because the name Sackmakan (the name for an Indian prince, about the Dutch) is the name for a prince in Iceland.

Other opinions I could number up: under favor I shall present (not mine opinion, but) my observations to the judgment of the wise.

First, others (and myself) have conceived some of their words to hold affinity with the Hebrew.

Secondly, they constantly anoint their heads as the Jews did.

Thirdly, they give dowries for their wives, as the Jews did.

Fourthly (and which I have not so observed amongst other nations as amongst the Jews, and these:) they constantly separate their women (during the time of their monthly sickness) in a little house alone by themselves four or five days, and hold it an irreligious thing for either father or husband or any male to come near them.

They have often asked me if it be so with women of other nations, and whether they are so separated: and for their practice they plead nature and tradition. Yet again I have found a greater affinity of their language with the Greek tongue.

2. As the Greeks and other nations, and ourselves call the seven stars (or Charles' Wain, the Bear,)[8] so do they Mosk or Paukunnawaw, the Bear.

3. They have many strange relations of one Wétucks, a man that wrought great miracles amongst them, and walking upon the waters, etc., with some kind of broken resemblance to the Son of God.

Lastly, it is famous that the Sowwest (Sowaniu) is the great subject of their discourse. From thence their traditions. There they say (at the southwest) is the court of their great god Kautántowwìt: at the southwest are their forefathers' souls: to the southwest they go themselves when they die; from the southwest came their corn, and beans out of their great god Kautántowwìt's field: and indeed the further northward and westward from us their corn will not grow, but to the southward better and better. I dare not conjecture in these uncertainties. I believe they are lost, and yet hope (in the Lord's holy season) some of the wildest of them shall be found to share in the blood of the Son of God. To the third head, concerning their religion, customs, manners etc. I shall here say nothing, because in those 32 chapters of the whole book, I have briefly touched those of all sorts, from their birth to their burials, and have endeavored (as the nature of the work would give way) to bring some short observations and applications home to Europe from America.

7. Mongolia.
8. I.e., the constellation known as Ursa Major (Great Bear), the Big Dipper, or Charlemagne's wagon ("wain").

Therefore fourthly, to that great point of their conversion, so much to be longed for, and by all New-English so much pretended,[9] and I hope in truth.

For myself I have uprightly labored to suit my endeavors to my pretenses: and of later times (out of desire to attain their language) I have run through varieties of intercourses[1] with them day and night, summer and winter, by land and sea, particular passages tending to this, I have related divers, in the chapter of their religion.

Many solemn discourses I have had with all sorts of nations of them, from one end of the country to another (so far as opportunity, and the little language I have could reach).

I know there is no small preparation in the hearts of multitudes of them. I know their many solemn confessions to myself, and one to another of their lost wandering conditions.

I know strong convictions upon the consciences of many of them, and their desires uttered that way.

I know not with how little knowledge and grace of Christ the Lord may save, and therefore, neither will despair, nor report much.

But since it hath pleased some of my worthy countrymen to mention (of late in print) Wequash, the Péquot captain, I shall be bold so far to second their relations, as to relate mine own hopes of him (though I dare not be so confident as others).

Two days before his death, as I passed up to Qunníhticut[2] River, it pleased my worthy friend Mr. Fenwick, (whom I visited at his house in Saybrook Fort at the mouth of that river) to tell me that my old friend Wequash lay very sick. I desired to see him, and himself was pleased to be my guide two miles where Wequash lay.

Amongst other discourse concerning his sickness and death (in which he freely bequeathed his son to Mr. Fenwick) I closed[3] with him concerning his soul: he told me that some two or three years before he had lodged at my house, where I acquainted him with the condition of all mankind, & his own in particular; how God created man and all things; how man fell from God, and of his present enmity against God, and the wrath of God against him until repentance. Said he, "your words were never out of my heart to this present;" and said he "me much pray to Jesus Christ." I told him so did many English, French, and Dutch, who had never turned to God, nor loved Him. He replied in broken English: "Me so big naughty heart, me heart all one stone!" Savory expressions using to breathe from compunct and broken hearts, and a sense of inward hardness and unbrokenness [sic]. I had many discourses with him in his life, but this was the sum of our last parting until our General Meeting.[4]

Now, because this is the great inquiry of all men: what Indians have been converted? what have the English done in those parts? what hopes of the Indians receiving the knowledge of Christ?

And because to this question, some put an edge from the boast of the Jesuits in Canada and Maryland, and especially from the wonderful conversions made by the Spaniards and Portugals in the West-Indies, besides what

---

9. Asserted, proffered (with none of the modern connotations of deceit).
1. Conversations.
2. Connecticut.
3. Came to the end of my talk.
4. I.e., until Judgment Day.

I have here written, as also, beside what I have observed in the chapter of their religion, I shall further present you with a brief additional discourse concerning this great point, being comfortably persuaded that that Father of Spirits, who was graciously pleased to persuade Japhet (the Gentiles) to dwell in the tents of Shem (the Jews),[5] will, in His holy season (I hope approaching), persuade these Gentiles of America to partake of the mercies of Europe, and then shall be fulfilled what is written by the prophet Malachi,[6] from the rising of the sun (in Europe) to the going down of the same (in America), My name shall be great among the Gentiles. So I desire to hope and pray,

Your unworthy countryman,
ROGER WILLIAMS

Directions for the Use of the Language

1. A dictionary or grammar way I had consideration of, but purposely avoided, as not so accommodate to the benefit of all, as I hope this form is.

2. A dialogue also I had thoughts of, but avoided for brevity's sake, and yet (with no small pains) I have so framed every chapter and the matter of it, as I may call it an implicit dialogue.

3. It is framed chiefly after the *Narragansett* dialect, because most spoken in the country, and yet (with attending to the variation of peoples and dialects) it will be of great use in all parts of the country.

4. Whatever your occasion be, either of travel, discourse, trading etc. turn to the table which will direct you to the proper chapter.

5. Because the life of all language is in the pronunciation, I have been at the pains and charges to cause the accents, tones or sounds to be affixed, (which some understand, according to the Greek language, acutes, graves, circumflexes) for example, in the second leaf[7] in the word *Ewò He*: the sound or tone must not be put on *E*, but *wò* where the grave accent is.

In the same leaf, in the word *Ascowequássin*, the sound must not be on any of the syllables, but on *quáss*, where the acute or sharp sound is.

In the same leaf in the word *Anspaumpmaûntam*, the sound must not be on any other syllable but *maûn*, where the circumflex or long sounding accent is.

6. The English for every Indian word or phrase stands in a straight line directly against the Indian: yet sometimes there are two words for the same thing (for their language is exceeding copious, and they have five or six words sometimes for one thing) and then the English stands against them both: for example in the second leaf:

Cowáunckamish & Cuckquénamish | I pray your favor.

---

5. Japhet was the third son of Noah and, in some traditions, the progenitor of the Indo-European race (see Genesis 9.18).
6. "For from the rising of the sun even unto the going down of the same my name shall be great among the Gentiles" (Malachi 1.11).
7. Page.

From *An Help to the Native Language of that Part of America Called New England*

FROM CHAPTER I. OF SALUTATION

1. The courteous pagan shall condemn
   Uncourteous Englishmen,
   Who live like foxes, bears and wolves,
   Or lion in his den.
2. Let none sing blessings to their souls,   5
   For that they courteous are:
   The wild barbarians with no more
   Than nature, go so far.
3. If nature's sons both wild and tame,
   Humane and courteous be: 10
   How ill becomes it Sons of God
   To want humanity?

FROM CHAPTER II. OF EATING AND ENTERTAINMENT

1. Coarse bread and water's most,[8] their fare,
   O England's diet fine;
   Thy cup runs ore[9] with plenteous store
   Of wholesome beer and wine.
2. Sometimes God gives them Fish or Flesh,   5
   Yet they're content without;
   And what comes in, they part to[1] friends
   And strangers round about.
3. God's providence is rich to his,
   Let none distrustful be;   10
   In wilderness, in great distress,
   These ravens have fed me.

FROM CHAPTER VI. OF THE FAMILY AND BUSINESS OF THE HOUSE

1. How busy are the sons of men?
   How full their heads and hands?
   What noise and tumults in our own,
   And eke[2] in Pagan lands?
2. Yet I have found less noise, more peace   5
   In wild America,
   Where women quickly build the house,
   And quickly move away.
[3] English and Indians busy are,
   In parts of their abode: 10
   Yet both stand idle, till God's call
   Set them to work for God. Mat. 20.7.[3]

8. Mostly.
9. Over.
1. Divide among.
2. Also (archaic).
3. "And about the eleventh hour he [Christ] went out, and found others standing idle, and said unto them, 'Why stand ye here all the day idle?' They said unto him, 'Because no man hath hired us.' He said unto them, 'Go ye also into the vineyard; and whatsoever is right, that shall ye receive'" (Matthew 20.6–7).

FROM CHAPTER XI. OF TRAVEL

1. God makes a path, provides a guide,
   And feeds in wilderness!
   His glorious name while breath remains,
   O that I may confess.
2. Lost many a time, I have had no guide,   5
   No house, but hollow tree!
   In stormy winter night no fire,
   No food, no company:
3. In him I have found a house, a bed,
   A table, company: 10
   No cup so bitter, but's made sweet,
   When God shall sweet'ning be.

FROM CHAPTER XVIII. OF THE SEA

[1] They see God's wonders that are call'ed
   Through dreadful seas to pass,
   In tearing winds and roaring seas,
   And calms as smooth as glass.
[2] I have in Europe's ships, oft been   5
   In King of terror's hand;
   When all have cried, "Now, now we sink,"
   Yet God brought safe to land.
[3] Alone 'mongst Indians in canoes,
   Sometime o'er-turn'd, I have been   10
   Half inch from death, in ocean deep,
   God's wonders I have seen.

ANNE BRADSTREET
c. 1612–1672

A nne Bradstreet produced the first sustained body of poetry in British North America. In Bradstreet's day, many people wrote and read poetry for pleasure, and poems were often included in prose works. (Consider John Smith's writings and Roger Williams's *A Key into the Language of America* [1643], which are excerpted above.) When Bradstreet's *The Tenth Muse* appeared in London in 1650, it became the first published volume of poems in English written by a resident of America. It was widely read in England and the colonies, notably by the New England minister-poet Edward Taylor, who had a copy of the second edition of Bradstreet's poems (1678) in his library.

Bradstreet's work continues to resonate with readers and writers. In the twentieth century, the American poets John Berryman, Susan Howe, and Adrienne Rich all wrote about Bradstreet and her work, inspired by her achievement. In her preface to the 1967 edition of Bradstreet's writings, Rich captured the drama of Bradstreet's life as a woman and a poet in the new British colonies: "To have written poems, the first good poems in America, while rearing eight children, lying frequently sick, keeping house at the edge of wilderness, was to have managed a poet's range and extension within confines as strict as any American poet has confronted." These circumstances, Rich continued, "forced into concentration and permanence a gifted energy that might, in another context, have spent itself in other, less enduring, directions."

Bradstreet's social position helped mitigate the "confines" that Rich described, and her English education provided intellectual resources that fueled her achievement. Her father, Thomas Dudley, manager of the country estate of the Puritan earl of Lincoln, enabled his daughter to receive an education superior to that of most young women of the time, including training in the classics. As a young girl, Bradstreet wrote poems to please her father. Her earliest surviving poems engage with such major literary works as Sir Walter Raleigh's *History of the World* (1614), as well as the writings of the leading English poets Sir Philip Sidney and Edmund Spenser and the French Protestant poet Guillaume de Salluste Du Bartas.

At sixteen she married Simon Bradstreet, a recent graduate of Cambridge University, who worked with Thomas Dudley. She continued to write poetry after their marriage. Simon assisted in preparing the Massachusetts Bay Company for its departure for America, and in 1630 the Bradstreets and the Dudleys sailed with John Winthrop's fleet. Bradstreet writes that when she first "came into this country" she "found a new world and new manners," at which her "heart rose" in resistance. "But after I was convinced it was the way of God, I submitted to it and joined the church at Boston."

Bradstreet's new circumstances posed many challenges and physical trials. As a child, she had endured a bout of rheumatic fever, which led to recurrent periods of severe fatigue. Even so, she eventually bore eight children. Simon's travels and her family's prominence doubtless placed demands on her as well. Her father served several terms as the Bay colony's governor and held other public offices. Her husband, who was secretary to the company and later governor of the colony, was involved in numerous diplomatic missions that took him away from home, including an extended trip to England in 1661. The frequent absence of her husband was one challenge among many. In 1666, she lost most of her worldly possessions when her house burned. She may also have lost manuscripts in the fire.

Like any good Puritan, Bradstreet routinely examined her conscience and wrestled to make sense of events, such as the house fire, in relation to a divine plan. According to one of the "Meditations" Bradstreet wrote for her children, she was troubled many times about the truth of the Scriptures, she never saw any convincing miracles, and she always wondered if the miracles she read about "were feigned." Eventually she came to believe that her eyes gave her the best evidence of God's existence. She is the first in a long line of American poets who took their consolation not from theology but from, as she wrote, the "wondrous works, that I see, the vast frame of the heaven and the earth, the order of all things, night and day, summer and winter, spring and autumn, the daily providing for this great household upon the earth, the preserving and directing of all to its proper end."

Bradstreet's poems circulated in manuscript until, without her knowledge, her brother-in-law John Woodbridge had them printed in London as *The Tenth Muse, Lately Sprung Up in America* (1650). Bradstreet expressed her ambivalence about the print publication of her work in the poem "The Author to Her Book," which she seems to have written in connection with a proposed second edition of *The Tenth Muse.* That volume was published posthumously, in Boston, as *Several Poems Compiled with Great Wit and Learning* (1678). This edition shows the growing influence of the *Bay Psalm Book* on Bradstreet's prosody and diction, and it includes a number of new poems in a more lyrical or elegiac vein that contrasts with her early works on public and philosophical themes. The more intimate poems highlight her concern for her family and home and reveal the pleasures that she took in everyday life.

The following texts are from *The Works of Anne Bradstreet* (1967), edited by Jeannine Hensley.

The Prologue

1

To sing of wars, of captains, and of kings,
Of cities founded, commonwealths begun,
For my mean[1] pen are too superior things:
Or how they all, or each their dates have run
Let poets and historians set these forth,   5
My obscure lines shall not so dim their worth.

2

But when my wond'ring eyes and envious heart
Great Bartas'[2] sugared lines do but read o'er,
Fool I do grudge the Muses[3] did not part
'Twixt him and me that overfluent store;   10
A Bartas can do what a Bartas will
But simple I according to my skill.

3

From schoolboy's tongue no rhet'ric we expect,
Nor yet a sweet consort[4] from broken strings,
Nor perfect beauty where's a main defect: 15
My foolish, broken, blemished Muse so sings,
And this to mend, alas, no art is able,
'Cause nature made it so irreparable.

4

Nor can I, like that fluent sweet tongued Greek,
Who lisped at first, in future times speak plain.[5]   20
By art he gladly found what he did seek,
A full requital of his striving pain.
Art can do much, but this maxim's most sure:
A weak or wounded brain admits no cure.

5

I am obnoxious to each carping tongue   25
Who says my hand a needle better fits,
A poet's pen all scorn I should thus wrong,
For such despite they cast on female wits:
If what I do prove well, it won't advance,
They'll say it's stol'n, or else it was by chance.   30

1. Humble.
2. Guillaume de Salluste Du Bartas (1544–1590), a French Protestant writer much admired by the Puritans. He was most famous as the author of *The Divine Weeks*, an epic poem recounting great moments in Christian history.
3. In Greek mythology, the nine goddesses of the arts and sciences. "Fool": i.e., like a fool.
4. Accord, harmony of sound.
5. The ancient Greek orator Demosthenes conquered a speech defect.

6

But sure the antique Greeks were far more mild
Else of our sex, why feigned they those nine
And poesy made Calliope's[6] own child;
So 'mongst the rest they placed the arts divine:
But this weak knot they will full soon untie.   35
The Greeks did nought, but play the fools and lie.

7

Let Greeks be Greeks, and women what they are;
Men have precedency and still excel,
It is but vain unjustly to wage war;
Men can do best, and women know it well   40
Preeminence in all and each is yours;
Yet grant some small acknowledgment of ours.

8

And oh ye high flown quills[7] that soar the skies,
And ever with your prey still catch your praise,
If e'er you deign these lowly lines your eyes   45
Give thyme or parsley wreath, I ask no bays;[8]
This mean and unrefined ore of mine
Will make your glist'ring gold but more to shine.

                                        1650

Contemplations

1

Some time now past in the autumnal tide,
When Phoebus[1] wanted but one hour to bed,
The trees all richly clad, yet void of pride,
Were gilded o'er by his rich golden head.
Their leaves and fruits seemed painted, but was true,   5
Of green, of red, of yellow, mixed hue;
Rapt were my senses at this delectable view.

2

I wist[2] not what to wish, yet sure thought I,
If so much excellence abide below,
How excellent is He that dwells on high,
Whose power and beauty by His works we know?   10

---

6. The muse of epic poetry.
7. Pens.
8. Garlands of laurel, used to crown a poet.

1. Apollo, the Greek and Roman sun god.
2. Knew.

Sure He is goodness, wisdom, glory, light,
That hath this under world so richly dight;[3]
More heaven than earth was here, no winter and no night.

3

Then on a stately oak I cast mine eye,   15
Whose ruffling top the clouds seemed to aspire;
How long since thou wast in thine infancy?
Thy strength, and stature, more thy years admire,
Hath hundred winters past since thou wast born?
Or thousand since thou brakest thy shell of horn?   20
If so, all these as nought, eternity doth scorn.

4

Then higher on the glistering Sun I gazed,
Whose beams was shaded by the leafy tree;
The more I looked, the more I grew amazed,
And softly said, "What glory's like to thee?"   25
Soul of this world, this universe's eye,
No wonder some made thee a deity;
Had I not better known, alas, the same had I.

5

Thou as a bridegroom from thy chamber rushes,
And as a strong man, joys to run a race;[4]   30
The morn doth usher thee with smiles and blushes;
The Earth reflects her glances in thy face.
Birds, insects, animals with vegative,[5]
Thy heat from death and dullness doth revive,
And in the darksome womb of fruitful nature dive.   35

6

Thy swift annual and diurnal course,
Thy daily straight and yearly oblique path,
Thy pleasing fervor and thy scorching force,
All mortals here the feeling knowledge hath.[6]
Thy presence makes it day, thy absence night,   40
Quaternal seasons ca025éd by thy might:
Hail creature, full of sweetness, beauty, and delight.

7

Art thou so full of glory that no eye
Hath strength thy shining rays once to behold?

3. Furnished, adorned.
4. The sun "is as a bridegroom coming out of his chamber, and rejoiceth as a strong man to run a race" (Psalm 19.5).
5. I.e., as well as plant life.
6. I.e., I know the feeling of (the sun).

And is thy splendid throne erect so high, 45
As to approach it, can no earthly mold?
How full of glory then must thy Creator be,
Who gave this bright light luster unto thee?
Admired, adored for ever, be that Majesty.

8

Silent alone, where none or[7] saw, or heard, 50
In pathless paths I lead my wand'ring feet,
My humble eyes to lofty skies I reared
To sing some song, my mazéd[8] Muse thought meet.
My great Creator I would magnify,
That nature had thus decked liberally; 55
But Ah, and Ah, again, my imbecility!

9

I heard the merry grasshopper then sing.
The black-clad cricket bear a second part;
They kept one tune and played on the same string,
Seeming to glory in their little art. 60
Shall creatures abject thus their voices raise
And in their kind resound their Maker's praise
Whilst I, as mute, can warble forth no higher lays?[9]

10

When present times look back to ages past,
And men in being fancy those[1] are dead, 65
It makes things gone perpetually to last,
And calls back months and years that long since fled.
It makes a man more aged in conceit[2]
Than was Methuselah,[3] or's grandsire great,
While of their persons and their acts his mind doth treat. 70

11

Sometimes in Eden fair he seems to be,
Sees glorious Adam there made lord of all,
Fancies the apple, dangle on the tree,
That turned his sovereign to a naked thrall.[4]
Who like a miscreant's driven from that place, 75
To get his bread with pain and sweat of face,
A penalty imposed on his backsliding race.

7. Either.
8. Amazed.
9. Short lyric or narrative poems intended to be sung.
1. I.e., those who.

2. Apprehension, the processes of thought.
3. Thought to have lived 969 years (Genesis 5.27).
4. Slave. For the story of Adam and Eve in Eden, where they ate the apple from the tree of the knowledge of good and evil, see Genesis 1–3.

12

Here sits our grandame in retired place,
And in her lap her bloody Cain new-born;
The weeping imp oft looks her in the face,   80
Bewails his unknown hap[5] and fate forlorn;
His mother sighs to think of Paradise,
And how she lost her bliss to be more wise,
Believing him that was, and is, father of lies.[6]

13

Here Cain and Abel come to sacrifice,   85
Fruits of the earth and fatlings[7] each do bring.
On Abel's gift the fire descends from skies,
But no such sign on false Cain's offering;
With sullen hateful looks he goes his ways,
Hath thousand thoughts to end his brother's days,   90
Upon whose blood his future good he hopes to raise.

14

There Abel keeps his sheep, no ill he thinks;
His brother comes, then acts his fratricide:
The virgin Earth of blood her first draught drinks,
But since that time she often hath been cloyed.   95
The wretch with ghastly face and dreadful mind
Thinks each he sees will serve him in his kind,
Though none on earth but kindred near then could he find.

15

Who fancies not his looks now at the bar,[8]
His face like death, his heart with horror fraught,   100
Nor malefactor ever felt like war,
When deep despair with wish of life hath fought,
Branded with guilt and crushed with treble woes,
A vagabond to Land of Nod[9] he goes.
A city builds, that walls might him secure from foes.   105

16

Who thinks not oft upon the father's ages,
Their long descent, how nephew's sons they saw,
The starry observations of those sages,
And how their precepts to their sons were law,
How Adam sighed to see his progeny,   110

---

5. Fortune, circumstances. As an adult, Eve's elder
son, Cain, slew his brother, Abel (Genesis 4.8).
6. Satan.
7. Animals fattened for slaughter.

8. I.e., at a (holy) tribunal; facing God's judgment.
9. An unidentified region east of Eden where
Cain dwelled after slaying Abel (Genesis 4.16).

Clothed all in his black sinful livery,
Who neither guilt nor yet the punishment could fly.

17

Our life compare we with their length of days
Who to the tenth of theirs doth now arrive?
And though thus short, we shorten many ways,   115
Living so little while we are alive;
In eating, drinking, sleeping, vain delight
So unawares comes on perpetual night,
And puts all pleasures vain unto eternal flight.

18

When I behold the heavens as in their prime,   120
And then the earth (though old) still clad in green,
The stones and trees, insensible of time,
Nor[1] age nor wrinkle on their front are seen;
If winter come and greenness then do fade,
A spring returns, and they more youthful made;   125
But man grows old, lies down, remains where once he's laid.

19

By birth more noble than those creatures all,
Yet seems by nature and by custom cursed,
No sooner born, but grief and care makes fall
That state obliterate he had at first;   130
Nor youth, nor strength, nor wisdom spring again,
Nor habitations long their names retain,
But in oblivion to the final day remain.

20

Shall I then praise the heavens, the trees, the earth
Because their beauty and their strength last longer?   135
Shall I wish there, or never to had birth,
Because they're bigger, and their bodies stronger?
Nay, they shall darken, perish, fade, and die,
And when unmade, so ever shall they lie,
But man was made for endless immortality.   140

21

Under the cooling shadow of a stately elm
Close sat I by a goodly river's side,
Where gliding streams the rocks did overwhelm,
A lonely place, with pleasures dignified.

1. Neither.

I once that loved the shady woods so well,   145
Now thought the rivers did the trees excel,
And if the sun would ever shine, there would I dwell.

22

While on the stealing stream I fixt mine eye,
Which to the longed-for ocean held its course,
I marked, nor crooks, nor rubs,[2] that there did lie   150
Could hinder aught,[3] but still augment its force.
"O happy flood," quoth I, "that holds thy race
Till thou arrive at thy beloved place,
Nor is it rocks or shoals that can obstruct thy pace,

23

Nor is't enough, that thou alone mayst slide   155
But hundred brooks in thy clear waves do meet,
So hand in hand along with thee they glide
To Thetis' house,[4] where all embrace and greet.
Thou emblem true of what I count the best,
O could I lead my rivulets to rest,   160
So may we press to that vast mansion, ever blest."

24

Ye fish, which in this liquid region 'bide,
That for each season have your habitation,
Now salt, now fresh where you think best to glide
To unknown coasts to give a visitation,   165
In lakes and ponds you leave your numerous fry;
So nature taught, and yet you know not why,
You wat'ry folk that know not your felicity.

25

Look how the wantons frisk to taste the air,
Then to the colder bottom straight they dive;   170
Eftsoon to Neptune's[5] glassy hall repair
To see what trade they great ones there do drive,
Who forage o'er the spacious sea-green field,
And take the trembling prey before it yield,
Whose armor is their scales, their spreading fins their shield.   175

26

While musing thus with contemplation fed,
And thousand fancies buzzing in my brain,

2. Difficulties.
3. Anything.
4. I.e., the sea, home of the sea nymph Thetis.

5. Roman god of the ocean. "Eftsoon": soon afterward.

The sweet-tongued Philomel[6] perched o'er my head
And chanted forth a most melodious strain
Which rapt me so with wonder and delight,   180
I judged my hearing better than my sight,
And wished me wings with her a while to take my flight.

27

"O merry Bird," said I, "that fears no snares,
That neither toils nor hoards up in thy barn,
Feels no sad thoughts nor cruciating[7] cares   185
To gain more good or shun what might thee harm.
Thy clothes ne'er wear, thy meat is everywhere,
Thy bed a bough, thy drink the water clear,
Reminds not what is past, nor what's to come dost fear."

28

"The dawning morn with songs thou dost prevent,[8]   190
Sets hundred notes unto thy feathered crew,
So each one tunes his pretty instrument,
And warbling out the old, begin anew,
And thus they pass their youth in summer season,
Then follow thee into a better region,   195
Where winter's never felt by that sweet airy legion."

29

Man at the best a creature frail and vain,
In knowledge ignorant, in strength but weak,
Subject to sorrows, losses, sickness, pain,
Each storm his state, his mind, his body break,   200
From some of these he never finds cessation,
But day or night, within, without, vexation,
Troubles from foes, from friends, from dearest, near'st relation.

30

And yet this sinful creature, frail and vain,
This lump of wretchedness, of sin and sorrow,   205
This weatherbeaten vessel wracked with pain,
Joys not in hope of an eternal morrow;
Nor all his losses, crosses, and vexation,
In weight, in frequency and long duration
Can make him deeply groan for that divine translation.[9]   210

6. I.e., the nightingale. In Greek mythology, Philomela, the daughter of King Attica, was transformed into a nightingale after her brother-in-law raped her and tore out her tongue.

7. I.e., excruciating, painful.
8. Anticipate.
9. Transformation.

31

The mariner that on smooth waves doth glide
Sings merrily and steers his bark with ease,
As if he had command of wind and tide,
And now become great master of the seas:
But suddenly a storm spoils all the sport,   215
And makes him long for a more quiet port,
Which 'gainst all adverse winds may serve for fort.

32

So he that saileth in this world of pleasure,
Feeding on sweets, that never bit of th' sour,
That's full of friends, of honor, and of treasure,   220
Fond fool, he takes this earth ev'n for heav'n's bower.
But sad affliction comes and makes him see
Here's neither honor, wealth, nor safety;
Only above is found all with security.

33

O Time the fatal wrack[1] of mortal things,   225
That draws oblivion's curtains over kings;
Their sumptuous monuments, men know them not,
Their names without a record are forgot,
Their parts, their ports, their pomp's[2] all laid in th' dust
Nor wit nor gold, nor buildings scape time's rust;   230
But he whose name is graved in the white stone[3]
Shall last and shine when all of these are gone.

1678

The Author to Her Book[1]

Thou ill-formed offspring of my feeble brain,
Who after birth didst by my side remain,
Till snatched from thence by friends, less wise than true,
Who thee abroad, exposed to public view,
Made thee in rags, halting to th' press to trudge,   5
Where errors were not lessened (all may judge).
At thy return my blushing was not small,
My rambling brat (in print) should mother call,
I cast thee by as one unfit for light,

1. Destroyer.
2. Vanity. "Parts": features. "Ports": places of refuge.
3. "To him that overcometh will I give to eat of the hidden manna and will give him a white stone, and in the stone a new name written, which no man knoweth saving he that receiveth it" (Revelation 2.17). "Scape": escape.
1. Bradstreet is thought to have written this poem in 1666, when the second edition of *The Tenth Muse* was contemplated.

Thy visage was so irksome in my sight;   10
Yet being mine own, at length affection would
Thy blemishes amend, if so I could:
I washed thy face, but more defects I saw,
And rubbing off a spot still made a flaw.
I stretched thy joints to make thee even feet,[2]   15
Yet still thou run'st more hobbling than is meet;
In better dress to trim thee was my mind,
But nought save homespun cloth i' th' house I find.
In this array 'mongst vulgars[3] may'st thou roam.
In critic's hands beware thou dost not come,   20
And take thy way where yet thou art not known;
If for thy father asked, say thou hadst none;
And for thy mother, she alas is poor,
Which caused her thus to send thee out of door.

1678

Before the Birth of One of Her Children

All things within this fading world hath end,
Adversity doth still our joys attend;
No ties so strong, no friends so dear and sweet,
But with death's parting blow is sure to meet.
The sentence past is most irrevocable,   5
A common thing, yet oh, inevitable.
How soon, my Dear, death may my steps attend,
How soon't may be thy lot to lose thy friend,
We both are ignorant, yet love bids me
These farewell lines to recommend to thee,   10
That when that knot's untied that made us one,
I may seem thine, who in effect am none.
And if I see not half my days that's due,
What nature would, God grant to yours and you;
The many faults that well you know I have   15
Let be interred in my oblivious grave;
If any worth or virtue were in me,
Let that live freshly in thy memory
And when thou feel'st no grief, as I no harms,
Yet love thy dead, who long lay in thine arms,   20
And when thy loss shall be repaid with gains
Look to my little babes, my dear remains.
And if thou love thyself, or loved'st me,
These O protect from stepdame's[1] injury.
And if chance to thine eyes shall bring this verse,   25
With some sad sighs honor my absent hearse;

2. I.e., metrical feet; thus to smooth out the lines.   1. I.e., stepmother's.
3. The common people.

And kiss this paper for thy love's dear sake,
Who with salt tears this last farewell did take.

1678

To My Dear and Loving Husband

If ever two were one, then surely we.
If ever man were loved by wife, then thee;
If ever wife was happy in a man,
Compare with me, ye women, if you can.
I prize thy love more than whole mines of gold   5
Or all the riches that the East doth hold.
My love is such that rivers cannot quench,
Nor ought but love from thee, give recompense.
Thy love is such I can no way repay,
The heavens reward thee manifold, I pray.   10
Then while we live, in love let's so persevere
That when we live no more, we may live ever.

1678

A Letter to Her Husband, Absent upon Public Employment

My head, my heart, mine eyes, my life, nay, more,
My joy, my magazine[1] of earthly store,
If two be one, as surely thou and I,
How stayest thou there, whilst I at Ipswich lie?[2]
So many steps, head from the heart to sever,   5
If but a neck, soon should we be together.
I, like the Earth this season, mourn in black,
My Sun is gone so far in's zodiac,
Whom whilst I 'joyed, nor storms, nor frost I felt,
His warmth such frigid colds did cause to melt.   10
My chilled limbs now numbed lie forlorn;
Return, return, sweet Sol, from Capricorn;[3]
In this dead time, alas, what can I more
Than view those fruits which through thy heat I bore?
Which sweet contentment yield me for a space,   15
True living pictures of their father's face.
O strange effect! now thou art southward gone,
I weary grow the tedious day so long;

1. Warehouse.
2. Ipswich, Massachusetts. Her husband may have been in England when she wrote this poem.

3. Capricorn, the tenth of the twelve signs of the zodiac, represents winter. "Sol": sun.

But when thou northward to me shalt return,
I wish my Sun may never set, but burn   20
Within the Cancer[4] of my glowing breast,
The welcome house of him my dearest guest.
Where ever, ever stay, and go not thence,
Till nature's sad decree shall call thee hence;
Flesh of thy flesh, bone of thy bone,   25
I here, thou there, yet both but one.

                                                                        1678

In Memory of My Dear Grandchild Elizabeth Bradstreet, Who Deceased August, 1665, Being a Year and a Half Old

1

Farewell dear babe, my heart's too much content,
Farewell sweet babe, the pleasure of mine eye,
Farewell fair flower that for a space was lent,
Then ta'en away unto eternity.
Blest babe, why should I once bewail thy fate,   5
Or sigh thy days so soon were terminate,
Sith[1] thou art settled in an everlasting state.

2

By nature trees do rot when they are grown,
And plums and apples thoroughly ripe do fall,
And corn and grass are in their season mown,   10
And time brings down what is both strong and tall.
But plants new set to be eradicate,
And buds new blown to have so short a date,
Is by His hand alone that guides nature and fate.

                                                                        1678

Here Follows Some Verses upon the Burning of Our House, July 10th, 1666

Copied Out of a Loose Paper

In silent night when rest I took
For sorrow near I did not look
I wakened was with thund'ring noise
And piteous shrieks of dreadful voice.

---

4. Cancer, the fourth sign of the zodiac,   1. Since.
represents summer.

That fearful sound of "Fire!" and "Fire!"   5
Let no man know is my desire.
I, starting up, the light did spy,
And to my God my heart did cry
To strengthen me in my distress
And not to leave me succorless.   10
Then, coming out, beheld a space
The flame consume my dwelling place.
And when I could no longer look,
I blest His name that gave and took,[1]
That laid my goods now in the dust.   15
Yea, so it was, and so 'twas just.
It was His own, it was not mine,
Far be it that I should repine;
He might of all justly bereft
But yet sufficient for us left.   20
When by the ruins oft I past
My sorrowing eyes aside did cast,
And here and there the places spy
Where oft I sat and long did lie:
Here stood that trunk, and there that chest,   25
There lay that store I counted best.
My pleasant things in ashes lie,
And them behold no more shall I.
Under thy roof no guest shall sit,
Nor at thy table eat a bit.   30
No pleasant tale shall e'er be told,
Nor things recounted done of old.
No candle e'er shall shine in thee,
Nor bridegroom's voice e'er heard shall be.
In silence ever shall thou lie,   35
Adieu, Adieu, all's vanity.[2]
Then straight I 'gin my heart to chide,
And did thy wealth on earth abide?
Didst fix thy hope on mold'ring dust?
The arm of flesh didst make thy trust?   40
Raise up thy thoughts above the sky
That dunghill mists away may fly.
Thou hast an house on high erect,
Framed by that mighty Architect,
With glory richly furnished,   45
Stands permanent though this be fled.
It's purchaséd and paid for too
By Him who hath enough to do.
A price so vast as is unknown
Yet by His gift is made thine own;   50

---

1. "The Lord gave, and the Lord hath taken away;   2. Empty, worthless. Cf. Ecclesiastes 1.2.
blessed be the name of the Lord" (Job 1.21).

There's wealth enough, I need no more,
Farewell, my pelf,[3] farewell my store.
The world no longer let me love,
My hope and treasure lies above.

1867

To My Dear Children

This book by any yet unread,
I leave for you when I am dead,
That being gone, here you may find
What was your living mother's mind.
Make use of what I leave in love,
And God shall bless you from above.
                                        A. B.

My dear children,

I, knowing by experience that the exhortations of parents take most effect when the speakers leave to speak,[1] and those especially sink deepest which are spoke latest, and being ignorant whether on my death bed I shall have opportunity to speak to any of you, much less to all, thought it the best, whilst I was able, to compose some short matters (for what else to call them I know not) and bequeath to you, that when I am no more with you, yet I may be daily in your remembrance (although that is the least in my aim in what I now do), but that you may gain some spiritual advantage by my experience. I have not studied in this you read to show my skill, but to declare the truth, not to set forth myself, but the glory of God. If I had minded the former, it had been perhaps better pleasing to you, but seeing the last is the best, let it be best pleasing to you.

The method I will observe shall be this: I will begin with God's dealing with me from my childhood to this day.

In my young years, about 6 or 7 as I take it, I began to make conscience of my ways, and what I knew was sinful, as lying, disobedience to parents, etc., I avoided it. If at any time I was overtaken with the like evils, it was as a great trouble, and I could not be at rest till by prayer I had confessed it unto God. I was also troubled at the neglect of private duties though too often tardy that way. I also found much comfort in reading the Scriptures, especially those places I thought most concerned my condition, and as I grew to have more understanding, so the more solace I took in them.

In a long fit of sickness which I had on my bed I often communed with my heart and made my supplication to the most High who set me free from that affliction.

But as I grew up to be about 14 or 15, I found my heart more carnal,[2] and sitting loose from God, vanity and the follies of youth take hold of me.

---

3. Possessions, usually in the sense of being falsely gained.

1. I.e., stop speaking.
2. I.e., worldly.

About 16, the Lord laid His hand sore upon me and smote me with the smallpox. When I was in my affliction, I besought the Lord and confessed my pride and vanity, and He was entreated of me and again restored me. But I rendered not to Him according to the benefit received.

After a short time I changed my condition and was married, and came into this country, where I found a new world and new manners, at which my heart rose. But after I was convinced it was the way of God, I submitted to it and joined to the church at Boston.

After some time I fell into a lingering sickness like a consumption together with a lameness, which correction I saw the Lord sent to humble and try me and do me good, and it was not altogether ineffectual.

It pleased God to keep me a long time without a child, which was a great grief to me and cost me many prayers and tears before I obtained one, and after him gave me many more of whom I now take the care, that as I have brought you into the world, and with great pains, weakness, cares, and fears brought you to this, I now travail[3] in birth again of you till Christ be formed in you.

Among all my experiences of God's gracious dealings with me, I have constantly observed this, that He hath never suffered me long to sit loose from Him, but by one affliction or other hath made me look home, and search what was amiss; so usually thus it hath been with me that I have no sooner felt my heart out of order, but I have expected correction for it, which most commonly hath been upon my own person in sickness, weakness, pains, sometimes on my soul, in doubts and fears of God's displeasure and my sincerity towards Him; sometimes He hath smote a child with a sickness, sometimes chastened by losses in estate,[4] and these times (through His great mercy) have been the times of my greatest getting and advantage; yea, I have found them the times when the Lord hath manifested the most love to me. Then have I gone to searching and have said with David, "Lord, search me and try me, see what ways of wickedness are in me, and lead me in the way everlasting,"[5] and seldom or never but I have found either some sin I lay under which God would have reformed, or some duty neglected which He would have performed, and by His help I have laid vows and bonds upon my soul to perform His righteous commands.

If at any time you are chastened of God, take it as thankfully and joyfully as in greatest mercies, for if ye be His, ye shall reap the greatest benefit by it. It hath been no small support to me in times of darkness when the Almighty hath hid His face from me that yet I have had abundance of sweetness and refreshment after affliction and more circumspection in my walking after I have been afflicted. I have been with God like an untoward[6] child, that no longer than the rod has been on my back (or at least in sight) but I have been apt to forget Him and myself, too. Before I was afflicted, I went astray, but now I keep Thy statutes.[7]

I have had great experience of God's hearing my prayers and returning comfortable answers to me, either in granting the thing I prayed for, or else in satisfying my mind without it, and I have been confident it hath been

---

3. Toil, labor.
4. Financial losses.
5. Cf. Psalm 139.23–24.

6. Unruly. "Circumspection": Prudence.
7. Cf. Psalm 119.8.

from Him, because I have found my heart through His goodness enlarged in thankfulness to Him.

I have often been perplexed that I have not found that constant joy in my pilgrimage and refreshing which I supposed most of the servants of God have, although He hath not left me altogether without the witness of His holy spirit, who hath oft given me His word and set to His seal that it shall be well with me. I have sometimes tasted of that hidden manna that the world knows not, and have set up my Ebenezer,[8] and have resolved with myself that against such a promise, such tastes of sweetness, the gates of hell shall never prevail; yet have I many times sinkings and droopings, and not enjoyed that felicity that sometimes I have done. But when I have been in darkness and seen no light, yet have I desired to stay myself upon the Lord, and when I have been in sickness and pain, I have thought if the Lord would but lift up the light of His countenance upon me, although He ground me to powder, it would be but light to me; yea, oft have I thought were I in hell itself and could there find the love of God toward me, it would be a heaven. And could I have been in heaven without the love of God, it would have been a hell to me, for in truth it is the absence and presence of God that makes heaven or hell.

Many times hath Satan troubled me concerning the verity of the Scriptures, many times by atheism how I could know whether there was a God; I never saw any miracles to confirm me, and those which I read of, how did I know but they were feigned? That there is a God my reason would soon tell me by the wondrous works that I see, the vast frame of the heaven and the earth, the order of all things, night and day, summer and winter, spring and autumn, the daily providing for this great household upon the earth, the preserving and directing of all to its proper end. The consideration of these things would with amazement certainly resolve me that there is an Eternal Being. But how should I know He is such a God as I worship in Trinity, and such a Savior as I rely upon? Though this hath thousands of times been suggested to me, yet God hath helped me over. I have argued thus with myself. That there is a God, I see. If ever this God hath revealed himself, it must be in His word, and this must be it or none. Have I not found that operation by it that no human invention can work upon the soul, hath not judgments befallen divers who have scorned and contemned it, hath it not been preserved through all ages maugre[9] all the heathen tyrants and all of the enemies who have opposed it? Is there any story but that which shows the beginnings of times, and how the world came to be as we see? Do we not know the prophecies in it fulfilled which could not have been so long foretold by any but God Himself?

When I have got over this block, then have I another put in my way, that admit this be the true God whom we worship, and that be his word, yet why may not the Popish religion be the right? They have the same God, the same Christ, the same word. They only interpret it one way, we another.

This hath sometimes stuck with me, and more it would, but the vain fooleries that are in their religion together with their lying miracles and cruel

---

8. In 1 Samuel 7.12, a stone monument to commemorate a victory over the Philistines. "Manna": the "bread from heaven" (Exodus 16.4) that fed the Israelites in the wilderness.
9. In spite of. "Divers": various (people). "Contemned": despised.

persecutions of the saints, which admit were they as they term them, yet not so to be dealt withal.

The consideration of these things and many the like would soon turn me to my own religion again.

But some new troubles I have had since the world has been filled with blasphemy and sectaries,[1] and some who have been accounted sincere Christians have been carried away with them, that sometimes I have said, "Is there faith upon the earth?" and I have not known what to think; but then I have remembered the works of Christ that so it must be, and if it were possible, the very elect should be deceived. "Behold," saith our Savior, "I have told you before."[2] That hath stayed my heart, and I can now say, "Return, O my Soul, to thy rest, upon this rock Christ Jesus will I build my faith, and if I perish, I perish"; but I know all the Powers of Hell shall never prevail against it. I know whom I have trusted, and whom I have believed, and that He is able to keep that I have committed to His charge.

Now to the King, immortal, eternal and invisible, the only wise God, be honor, and glory for ever and ever, Amen.

This was written in much sickness and weakness, and is very weakly and imperfectly done, but if you can pick any benefit out of it, it is the mark which I aimed at.

1867

1. Unbelievers, heretics.   2. Cf. John 13.19 and 14.29, Matthew 24.25.

MARY ROWLANDSON
c. 1637–1711

On June 20, 1675, the Wampanoag leader Metacom, who was sometimes called King Philip, organized the first of a series of attacks on New England settlements. These attacks, which lasted for more than a year, have become known as "King Philip's War." They were occasioned by the execution in Plymouth of three Wampanoag tribesmen, but the grievances behind them had been growing for decades. Crowded off their lands by the English colonists, the region's Algonquian communities, including the Wampanoag, had begun to experience severe food shortages. Metacom and his allies wanted to regain sovereignty over their territory and to stop further colonial expansion. By the end of the war, in August 1676, three thousand Native Americans were dead, including Metacom, who was killed by a Native ally of the English. Colonial leaders had sold Metacom's wife and children into slavery in the West Indies, along with many other prisoners of the war. The English had suffered major losses as well. More than twelve hundred houses had been burned, and about six hundred colonials were dead. The war to restore Native sovereignty in New England had instead sharply diminished it, though Metacom and his forces had posed an existential challenge to the colonies.

The most famous account of these attacks is *A Narrative of the Captivity and Restoration of Mrs. Mary Rowlandson,* written by the wife of the minister of the town of Lancaster, Massachusetts, fifty miles west of Boston. Rowlandson spent eleven weeks as the Wampanoag's captive. Born in Somersetshire, in the south of England, she moved to New England with her family in 1639. Her father, John White, became a wealthy landholder in the Massachusetts Bay Colony, and in 1653 he settled in Lancaster. Around 1656, she married the Reverend Joseph Rowlandson. The attack on Lancaster occurred on February 20, 1676, while Joseph was away from home. Several members of Rowlandson's family were killed in the attack, and she and three of her children were taken captive; her daughter Sarah was badly wounded and died a few days later. During her captivity, Rowlandson was separated from her older children and saw them only occasionally. She was ransomed and released on the second of May, and after several weeks her surviving children were returned. In 1677 she and Joseph moved to Wethersfield, Connecticut, where he died the next year. The town voted to pay her an annuity as their minister's widow. She married Captain Samuel Talcott in Wethersfield on August 6, 1679, and died in that Connecticut Valley town, thirty five years after her famous ordeal.

A
NARRATIVE
OF THE
CAPTIVITY, SUFFERINGS AND REMOVES
OF
Mrs. *Mary Rowlandfon,*

Who was taken Prifoner by the INDIANS with feveral others, and treated in the moft barbarous and cruel Manner by thofe vile Savages : With many other remarkable Events during her TRAVELS.

Written by her own Hand, for her private Ufe, and now made public at the earneft Defire of fome Friends, and for the Benefit of the afflicted.

BOSTON:
Printed and Sold at JOHN BOYLE's Printing-Office, next Door to the *Three Doves* in Marlborough-Street.

1773.

A Narrative. Mary Rowlandson, whose narrative first appeared in 1682, had refused to resist—or even try to escape from—her Native American captors. But in this illustration from around 1773, shortly before the beginning of the American Revolution, she has been given a gun and thus elevated into a defender of her realm —like the male patriots who at that time were opposing British policy.

Shortly after her release by the Wampanoags, Rowlandson began writing about her captivity, prompted by leading members of the clergy, including one who wrote a preface designed to find meaning for the colony in Rowlandson's experiences. (That anonymous author was probably Increase Mather, who is discussed in the headnote for his son, Cotton Mather, below.) Published in 1682, *A Narrative of the Captivity and Restoration of Mrs. Mary Rowlandson* became one of the most popular prose works of the seventeenth century in both British North America and England. The narrative combines high adventure with tragedy and exemplary piety, while also revealing complex psychological and social dynamics. Using "removes" (i.e., departures, movings from place to place) to structure her account, Rowlandson shows how she adjusted to the shock of the attack, the death of her daughter, and her own situation. As Rowlandson recovers and acclimates, she takes more interest in the unfamiliar people and activities around her, recognizing that some actions that initially seemed to reflect the "savagery" of her captors were instead necessitated by their desperate circumstances. She includes striking portrayals of Metacom, who treats her graciously; her master, Quinnapin, who becomes something of a protector for her; and Quinnapin's wife Weetamoo, the "squaw sachem," who treats her more harshly. She also vividly describes a "powwow" and other rituals and practices that were unfamiliar to her and many of her readers. She has some harsh words for "Praying Indians," that is, Native Christians who sided with Metacom against the English. Her closing reflections suggest her lingering trauma and her effort to make sense of her experiences as part of a divine plan. They offer some of the most moving passages about grief and acceptance in American literature.

Several editions of the narrative appeared around the time of the American Revolution, suggesting that part of the work's appeal is its connecting of an individual's experience to a group identity. Its continued popularity contributed to a revival of the genre of the captivity narrative in the early nineteenth century, as Indian Removal and westward expansion created new pressures on Native communities. One of the major descendants in the genre is *A Narrative of the Life of Mrs. Mary Jemison* (1824), the story of a captive white woman who made a life with the Iroquois. Rowlandson's narrative also exerted a lasting influence on American fiction, through works such as James Fenimore Cooper's *The Last of the Mohicans* (1826) and Catharine Maria Sedgwick's *Hope Leslie: Or, Early Times in the Massachusetts* (1827), which were inspired in part by the genre that Rowlandson so powerfully brought to life.

A Narrative of the Captivity and Restoration of Mrs. Mary Rowlandson[1]

On the tenth of February 1675,[2] came the Indians with great numbers upon Lancaster:[3] their first coming was about sunrising; hearing the noise of some guns, we looked out; several houses were burning, and the smoke ascending to heaven. There were five persons taken in one house; the father, and the mother and a sucking child, they knocked on the head; the other two they took and carried away alive. There were two others, who being out of their garrison[4] upon some occasion were set upon; one was knocked on the head, the other escaped; another there was who running along was shot and wounded, and fell down; he begged of them his life, promising them money (as they told me) but they would not hearken to him but knocked him in head, and stripped him naked, and split open his bowels.[5] Another, seeing many of the Indians about his barn, ventured and went out, but was quickly shot down. There were three others belonging to the same garrison who were killed; the Indians getting up upon the roof of the barn, had advantage to shoot down upon them over their fortification. Thus these murderous wretches went on, burning, and destroying before them.

1. The text is from *Original Narratives of Early American History, Narratives of Indian Wars 1675–1699* (1952), vol. 14, edited by C. H. Lincoln. All copies of Rowlandson's original edition have been lost. Like most modern editors, Lincoln reprints the second "Addition," first printed in Cambridge, Massachusetts, in 1682. The full title is *The sovereignty and goodness of GOD, together with the faithfulness of his promises displayed; being a narrative of the captivity and restoration of Mrs. Mary Rowlandson, commended by her, to all that desires to know the Lord's doings to, and dealings with her. Especially to her dear children and relations. The second Addition*

Corrected and amended. Written by her own hand for her private use, and now made public at the earnest desire of some friends, and for the benefit of the afflicted. Deut. 32.39. *See now that I, even I am he, and there is no god with me; I kill and I make alive, I wound and I heal, neither is there any can deliver out of my hand.*
2. Thursday, February 20, 1676, according to the Gregorian calendar, which was adopted in 1752.
3. Then a frontier town of about fifty families.
4. I.e., houses in the town where people gathered for defense.
5. Belly.

At length they came and beset our own house, and quickly it was the dole-fulest day that ever mine eyes saw. The house stood upon the edge of a hill; some of the Indians got behind the hill, others into the barn, and others behind anything that could shelter them; from all which places they shot against the house, so that the bullets seemed to fly like hail; and quickly they wounded one man among us, then another, and then a third. About two hours (according to my observation, in that amazing time) they had been about the house before they prevailed to fire it (which they did with flax and hemp, which they brought out of the barn, and there being no defense about the house, only two flankers[6] at two opposite corners and one of them not finished); they fired it once and one ventured out and quenched it, but they quickly fired it again, and that took. Now is the dreadful hour come, that I have often heard of (in time of war, as it was the case of others), but now mine eyes see it. Some in our house were fighting for their lives, others wal-lowing in their blood, the house on fire over our heads, and the bloody hea-then ready to knock us on the head, if we stirred out. Now might we hear mothers and children crying out for themselves, and one another, "Lord, what shall we do?" Then I took my children (and one of my sisters', hers) to go forth and leave the house: but as soon as we came to the door and appeared, the Indians shot so thick that the bullets rattled against the house, as if one had taken an handful of stones and threw them, so that we were fain to give back.[7] We had six stout dogs belonging to our garrison, but none of them would stir, though another time, if any Indian had come to the door, they were ready to fly upon him and tear him down. The Lord hereby would make us the more acknowledge His hand, and to see that our help is always in Him. But out we must go, the fire increasing, and coming along behind us, roaring, and the Indians gaping before us with their guns, spears, and hatchets to devour us. No sooner were we out of the house, but my brother-in-law (being before wounded, in defending the house, in or near the throat) fell down dead, whereat the Indians scornfully shouted, and hallowed,[8] and were presently upon him, stripping off his clothes, the bullets flying thick, one went through my side, and the same (as would seem) through the bowels and hand of my dear child in my arms. One of my elder sisters' children, named William, had then his leg broken, which the Indians perceiving, they knocked him on [his] head. Thus were we butchered by those merciless heathen, standing amazed, with the blood running down to our heels. My eldest sister being yet in the house, and seeing those woeful sights, the infidels hauling mothers one way, and children another, and some wallowing in their blood: and her elder son telling her that her son William was dead, and myself was wounded, she said, "And Lord, let me die with them," which was no sooner said, but she was struck with a bullet, and fell down dead over the threshold. I hope she is reap-ing the fruit of her good labors, being faithful to the service of God in her place. In her younger years she lay under much trouble upon spiritual accounts, till it pleased God to make that precious scripture take hold of her heart, "And he said unto me, my Grace is sufficient for thee" (2 Corinthians 12.9). More than twenty years after, I have heard her tell how sweet and com-fortable that place was to her. But to return: the Indians laid hold of us,

6. Projecting fortifications.
7. I.e., eager to return the gunfire.

8. Hollered, yelled.

pulling me one way, and the children another, and said, "Come go along with us"; I told them they would kill me: they answered, if I were willing to go along with them, they would not hurt me.

Oh the doleful sight that now was to behold at this house! "Come, behold the works of the Lord, what desolations he has made in the earth."[9] Of thirty-seven persons who were in this one house, none escaped either present death, or a bitter captivity, save only one, who might say as he, "And I only am escaped alone to tell the News" (Job 1.15). There were twelve killed, some shot, some stabbed with their spears, some knocked down with their hatchets. When we are in prosperity, Oh the little that we think of such dreadful sights, and to see our dear friends, and relations lie bleeding out their heart-blood upon the ground. There was one who was chopped into the head with a hatchet, and stripped naked, and yet was crawling up and down. It is a solemn sight to see so many Christians lying in their blood, some here, and some there, like a company of sheep torn by wolves, all of them stripped naked by a company of hell-hounds, roaring, singing, ranting, and insulting, as if they would have torn our very hearts out; yet the Lord by His almighty power preserved a number of us from death, for there were twenty-four of us taken alive and carried captive.

I had often before this said that if the Indians should come, I should choose rather to be killed by them than taken alive, but when it came to the trial my mind changed; their glittering weapons so daunted my spirit, that I chose rather to go along with those (as I may say) ravenous beasts, than that moment to end my days; and that I may the better declare what happened to me during that grievous captivity, I shall particularly speak of the several removes we had up and down the wilderness.

The First Remove

Now away we must go with those barbarous creatures, with our bodies wounded and bleeding, and our hearts no less than our bodies. About a mile we went that night, up upon a hill within sight of the town, where they intended to lodge. There was hard[1] by a vacant house (deserted by the English before, for fear of the Indians). I asked them whether I might not lodge in the house that night, to which they answered, "What, will you love English men still?" This was the dolefulest night that ever my eyes saw. Oh the roaring, and singing and dancing, and yelling of those black creatures in the night, which made the place a lively resemblance of hell. And as miserable was the waste that was there made of horses, cattle, sheep, swine, calves, lambs, roasting pigs, and fowl (which they had plundered in the town), some roasting, some lying and burning, and some boiling to feed our merciless enemies; who were joyful enough, though we were disconsolate. To add to the dolefulness of the former day, and the dismalness of the present night, my thoughts ran upon my losses and sad bereaved condition. All was gone, my husband gone (at least separated from me, he being in the Bay;[2] and to add to my grief, the Indians told me they would kill him as he came home-

---

9. Psalm 46.8.
1. Close.

2. I.e., Massachusetts Bay, or Boston.

ward), my children gone, my relations and friends gone, our house and home and all our comforts—within door and without—all was gone (except my life), and I knew not but the next moment that might go too. There remained nothing to me but one poor wounded babe, and it seemed at present worse than death that it was in such a pitiful condition, bespeaking compassion, and I had no refreshing for it, nor suitable things to revive it. Little do many think what is the savageness and brutishness of this barbarous enemy, Ay, even those that seem to profess more than others among them, when the English have fallen into their hands.

Those seven that were killed at Lancaster the summer before upon a Sabbath day, and the one that was afterward killed upon a weekday, were slain and mangled in a barbarous manner, by one-eyed John, and Marlborough's Praying Indians, which Capt. Mosely brought to Boston, as the Indians told me.[3]

The Second Remove[4]

But now, the next morning, I must turn my back upon the town, and travel with them into the vast and desolate wilderness, I knew not whither. It is not my tongue, or pen, can express the sorrows of my heart, and bitterness of my spirit that I had at this departure: but God was with me in a wonderful manner, carrying me along, and bearing up my spirit, that it did not quite fail. One of the Indians carried my poor wounded babe upon a horse; it went moaning all along, "I shall die, I shall die." I went on foot after it, with sorrow that cannot be expressed. At length I took it off the horse, and carried it in my arms till my strength failed, and I fell down with it. Then they set me upon a horse with my wounded child in my lap, and there being no furniture upon the horse's back, as we were going down a steep hill we both fell over the horse's head, at which they, like inhumane creatures, laughed, and rejoiced to see it, though I thought we should there have ended our days, as overcome with so many difficulties. But the Lord renewed my strength still, and carried me along, that I might see more of His power; yea, so much that I could never have thought of, had I not experienced it.

After this it quickly began to snow, and when night came on, they stopped, and now down I must sit in the snow, by a little fire, and a few boughs behind me, with my sick child in my lap; and calling much for water, being now (through the wound) fallen into a violent fever. My own wound also growing so stiff that I could scarce sit down or rise up; yet so it must be, that I must sit all this cold winter night upon the cold snowy ground, with my sick child in my arms, looking that every hour would be the last of its life; and having no Christian friend near me, either to comfort or help me. Oh, I may see the wonderful power of God, that my Spirit did not utterly sink under my affliction: still the Lord upheld me with His gracious and merciful spirit, and we were both alive to see the light of the next morning.

---

3. On August 30, 1675, Captain Samuel Mosely, encouraged by a number of people who were skeptical of converted American Indians, brought to Boston by force fifteen Christianized American Indians who lived on their own lands in Marlborough, Massachusetts, and accused them (probably unjustly) of an attack on the town of Lancaster on August 22.
4. West to Princeton, Massachusetts, near Mount Wachusett.

The Third Remove[5]

The morning being come, they prepared to go on their way. One of the Indians got up upon a horse, and they set me up behind him, with my poor sick babe in my lap. A very wearisome and tedious day I had of it; what with my own wound, and my child's being so exceeding sick, and in a lamentable condition with her wound. It may be easily judged what a poor feeble condition we were in, there being not the least crumb of refreshing that came within either of our mouths from Wednesday night to Saturday night, except only a little cold water. This day in the afternoon, about an hour by sun, we came to the place where they intended, viz.[6] an Indian town, called Wenimesset, northward of Quabaug. When we were come, Oh the number of pagans (now merciless enemies) that there came about me, that I may say as David, "I had fainted, unless I had believed, etc." (Psalm 27.13). The next day was the Sabbath. I then remembered how careless I had been of God's holy time; how many Sabbaths I had lost and misspent, and how evilly I had walked in God's sight; which lay so close unto my spirit, that it was easy for me to see how righteous it was with God to cut off the thread of my life and cast me out of His presence forever. Yet the Lord still showed mercy to me, and upheld me; and as He wounded me with one hand, so he healed me with the other. This day there came to me one Robert Pepper (a man belonging to Roxbury)[7] who was taken in Captain Beers's fight, and had been now a considerable time with the Indians; and up with them almost as far as Albany, to see King Philip, as he told me, and was now very lately come into these parts.[8] Hearing, I say, that I was in this Indian town, he obtained leave to come and see me. He told me he himself was wounded in the leg at Captain Beers's fight; and was not able some time to go, but as they carried him, and as he took oaken leaves and laid to his wound, and through the blessing of God he was able to travel again. Then I took oaken leaves and laid to my side, and with the blessing of God it cured me also; yet before the cure was wrought, I may say, as it is in Psalm 38.5–6, "My wounds stink and are corrupt, I am troubled, I am bowed down greatly, I go mourning all the day long." I sat much alone with a poor wounded child in my lap, which moaned night and day, having nothing to revive the body, or cheer the spirits of her, but instead of that, sometimes one Indian would come and tell me one hour that "your master will knock your child in the head," and then a second, and then a third, "your master will quickly knock your child in the head."

This was the comfort I had from them, miserable comforters are ye all, as he said.[9] Thus nine days I sat upon my knees, with my babe in my lap, till my flesh was raw again; my child being even ready to depart this sorrowful world, they bade me carry it out to another wigwam (I suppose because they would not be troubled with such spectacles) whither I went with a very heavy heart, and down I sat with the picture of death in my lap. About two hours in the night, my sweet babe like a lamb departed this life on Feb. 18, 1675.

---

5. February 12–27; they stopped at a Native American village on the Ware River, near New Braintree.
6. Abbreviation for *videlicet*: that is to say, namely (Latin).
7. A colonial town.

8. Captain Beers had attempted to save the garrison of Northfield, Massachusetts, on September 4, 1675. "Albany": then a colony in New York.
9. In Job 16.2, Job says: "I have heard many such things: miserable comforters are ye all."

It being about six years, and five months old. It was nine days from the first wounding, in this miserable condition, without any refreshing of one nature or other, except a little cold water. I cannot but take notice how at another time I could not bear to be in the room where any dead person was, but now the case is changed; I must and could lie down by my dead babe, side by side all the night after. I have thought since of the wonderful goodness of God to me in preserving me in the use of my reason and senses in that distressed time, that I did not use wicked and violent means to end my own miserable life. In the morning, when they understood that my child was dead they sent for me home to my master's wigwam (by my master in this writing, must be understood Quinnapin, who was a Sagamore,[1] and married King Philip's wife's sister; not that he first took me, but I was sold to him by another Narragansett Indian, who took me when first I came out of the garrison). I went to take up my dead child in my arms to carry it with me, but they bid me let it alone; there was no resisting, but go I must and leave it. When I had been at my master's wigwam, I took the first opportunity I could get to go look after my dead child. When I came I asked them what they had done with it; then they told me it was upon the hill. Then they went and showed me where it was, where I saw the ground was newly digged, and there they told me they had buried it. There I left that child in the wilderness, and must commit it, and myself also in this wilderness condition, to Him who is above all. God having taken away this dear child, I went to see my daughter Mary, who was at this same Indian town, at a wigwam not very far off, though we had little liberty or opportunity to see one another. She was about ten years old, and taken from the door at first by a Praying Ind. and afterward sold for a gun. When I came in sight, she would fall aweeping; at which they were provoked, and would not let me come near her, but bade me be gone; which was a heart-cutting word to me. I had one child dead, another in the wilderness, I knew not where, the third they would not let me come near to: "Me (as he said) have ye bereaved of my Children, Joseph is not, and Simeon is not, and ye will take Benjamin also, all these things are against me."[2] I could not sit still in this condition, but kept walking from one place to another. And as I was going along, my heart was even overwhelmed with the thoughts of my condition, and that I should have children, and a nation which I knew not, ruled over them. Whereupon I earnestly entreated the Lord, that He would consider my low estate, and show me a token for good, and if it were His blessed will, some sign and hope of some relief. And indeed quickly the Lord answered, in some measure, my poor prayers; for as I was going up and down mourning and lamenting my condition, my son came to me, and asked me how I did. I had not seen him before, since the destruction of the town, and I knew not where he was, till I was informed by himself, that he was amongst a smaller parcel of Indians, whose place was about six miles off. With tears in his eyes, he asked me whether his sister Sarah was dead; and told me he had seen his sister Mary; and prayed me, that I would not be troubled in reference to himself. The occasion of his coming to see me at this time, was this: there was, as I said, about six miles from us, a small plantation of Indians, where it seems he had been

1. A subordinate chief.　　　　2. Jacob's lamentation in Genesis 42.36.

during his captivity; and at this time, there were some forces of the Ind. gathered out of our company, and some also from them (among whom was my son's master) to go to assault and burn Medfield.[3] In this time of the absence of his master, his dame brought him to see me. I took this to be some gracious answer to my earnest and unfeigned desire. The next day, *viz.* to this, the Indians returned from Medfield, all the company, for those that belonged to the other small company, came through the town that now we were at. But before they came to us, Oh! the outrageous roaring and hooping[4] that there was. They began their din about a mile before they came to us. By their noise and hooping they signified how many they had destroyed (which was at that time twenty-three). Those that were with us at home were gathered together as soon as they heard the hooping, and every time that the other went over their number, these at home gave a shout, that the very earth rung again. And thus they continued till those that had been upon the expedition were come up to the Sagamore's wigwam; and then, Oh, the hideous insulting and triumphing that there was over some Englishmen's scalps that they had taken (as their manner is) and brought with them. I cannot but take notice of the wonderful mercy of God to me in those afflictions, in sending me a Bible. One of the Indians that came from [the] Medfield fight, had brought some plunder, came to me, and asked me, if I would have a Bible, he had got one in his basket. I was glad of it, and asked him, whether he thought the Indians would let me read? He answered, yes. So I took the Bible, and in that melancholy time, it came into my mind to read first the 28th chapter of Deuteronomy,[5] which I did, and when I had read it, my dark heart wrought on this manner: that there was no mercy for me, that the blessings were gone, and the curses come in their room,[6] and that I had lost my opportunity. But the Lord helped me still to go on reading till I came to Chap. 30, the seven first verses, where I found, there was mercy promised again, if we would return to Him by repentance;[7] and though we were scattered from one end of the earth to the other, yet the Lord would gather us together, and turn all those curses upon our enemies. I do not desire to live to forget this Scripture, and what comfort it was to me.

Now the Ind. began to talk of removing from this place, some one way, and some another. There were now besides myself nine English captives in this place (all of them children, except one woman). I got an opportunity to go and take my leave of them. They being to go one way, and I another, I asked them whether they were earnest with God for deliverance. They told me they did as they were able, and it was some comfort to me, that the Lord stirred up children to look to Him. The woman, *viz.* goodwife[8] Joslin, told me she should never see me again, and that she could find in her heart to run away. I wished her not to run away by any means, for we were near thirty miles from any English town, and she very big with child, and had but one week to reckon, and another child in her arms, two years old, and bad rivers there were to go over, and we were feeble, with our poor and coarse

3. This colonial town in Massachusetts was attacked on February 21.
4. Whooping.
5. A chapter concerned with blessings for obedience to God and curses for disobedience.
6. I.e., in place of the blessings.

7. "That then the Lord thy God will turn thy captivity, and have compassion upon thee, and will return and gather thee from all the nations" (Deuteronomy 30.3), referring to the Israelites' Babylonian captivity, or exile.
8. I.e., the mistress of a house.

entertainment.[9] I had my Bible with me, I pulled it out, and asked her whether she would read. We opened the Bible and lighted on Psalm 27, in which Psalm we especially took notice of that, *ver. ult.,* "Wait on the Lord, Be of good courage, and he shall strengthen thine Heart, wait I say on the Lord."[1]

The Twelfth Remove[2]

It was upon a Sabbath-day morning, that they prepared for their travel. This morning I asked my master whether he would sell me to my husband. He answered me "Nux," [3] which did much rejoice my spirit. My mistress, before we went, was gone to the burial of a papoose, and returning, she found me sitting and reading in my Bible; she snatched it hastily out of my hand, and threw it out of doors. I ran out and catched it up, and put it into my pocket, and never let her see it afterward. Then they packed up their things to be gone, and gave me my load. I complained it was too heavy, whereupon she gave me a slap in the face, and bade me go; I lifted up my heart to God, hoping the redemption was not far off; and the rather because their insolency grew worse and worse.

But the thoughts of my going homeward (for so we bent our course) much cheered my spirit, and made my burden seem light, and almost nothing at all. But (to my amazement and great perplexity) the scale was soon turned; for when we had gone a little way, on a sudden my mistress gives out; she would go no further, but turn back again, and said I must go back again with her, and she called her *sannup,* and would have had him gone back also, but he would not, but said he would go on, and come to us again in three days. My spirit was, upon this, I confess, very impatient, and almost outrageous.[4] I thought I could as well have died as went back; I cannot declare the trouble that I was in about it; but yet back again I must go. As soon as I had the opportunity, I took my Bible to read, and that quieting Scripture came to my hand, "Be still, and know that I am God" (Psalm 46.10). Which stilled my spirit for the present. But a sore time of trial, I concluded, I had to go through, my master being gone, who seemed to me the best friend that I had of an Indian, both in cold and hunger, and quickly so it proved. Down I sat, with my heart as full as it could hold, and yet so hungry that I could not sit neither; but going out to see what I could find, and walking among the trees, I found six acorns, and two chestnuts, which were some refreshment to me. Towards night I gathered some sticks for my own comfort, that I might not lie a-cold; but when we came to lie down they bade me to go out, and lie somewhere else, for they had company (they said) come in more than their own. I told them, I could not tell where to go, they bade me go look; I told them, if I went to another wigwam they would be angry, and send me home again. Then one of the company drew his sword, and told me he would run me through if I did not go presently. Then was I fain to stoop to this rude fellow, and to go out in the night, I knew not whither. Mine eyes have seen that fellow afterwards walking up and down Boston, under the appearance of a Friend Indian, and several others of the like cut. I went to one wigwam, and

9. Food. "One . . . reckon": i.e., before she was expected to give birth.
1. Verse 14. *"Ver. ult."*: last verse (Latin abbrev.)
2. Sunday, April 9.
3. Yes.
4. Outraged.

they told me they had no room. Then I went to another, and they said the same; at last an old Indian bade me to come to him, and his squaw gave me some ground nuts; she gave me also something to lay under my head, and a good fire we had; and through the good providence of God, I had a comfortable lodging that night. In the morning, another Indian bade me come at night, and he would give me six ground nuts, which I did. We were at this place and time about two miles from [the] Connecticut River. We went in the morning to gather ground nuts, to the river, and went back again that night. I went with a good load at my back (for they when they went, though but a little way, would carry all their trumpery[5] with them). I told them the skin was off my back, but I had no other comforting answer from them than this: that it would be no matter if my head were off too.

The Nineteenth Remove

They said, when we went out, that we must travel to Wachusett this day. But a bitter weary day I had of it, traveling now three days together, without resting any day between. At last, after many weary steps, I saw Wachusett hills, but many miles off. Then we came to a great swamp, through which we traveled, up to the knees in mud and water, which was heavy going to one tired before. Being almost spent, I thought I should have sunk down at last, and never got out; but I may say, as in Psalm 94.18, "When my foot slipped, thy mercy, O Lord, held me up." Going along, having indeed my life, but little spirit, Philip, who was in the company, came up and took me by the hand, and said, two weeks more and you shall be mistress again. I asked him, if he spake true? He answered, "Yes, and quickly you shall come to your master again; who had been gone from us three weeks." After many weary steps we came to Wachusett, where he was: and glad I was to see him. He asked me, when I washed me? I told him not this month. Then he fetched me some water himself, and bid me wash, and gave me the glass to see how I looked; and bid his squaw give me something to eat. So she gave me a mess of beans and meat, and a little ground nut cake. I was wonderfully revived with this favor showed me: "He made them also to be pitied of all those that carried them captives" (Psalm 106.46).

My master had three squaws, living sometimes with one, and sometimes with another one, this old squaw, at whose wigwam I was, and with whom my master had been those three weeks. Another was Weetamoo[6] with whom I had lived and served all this while. A severe and proud dame she was, bestowing every day in dressing herself neat as much time as any of the gentry of the land: powdering her hair, and painting her face, going with necklaces, with jewels in her ears, and bracelets upon her hands. When she had dressed herself, her work was to make girdles of wampum[7] and beads. The third squaw was a younger one, by whom he had two papooses. By the time I was refreshed by the old squaw, with whom my master was, Weetamoo's maid came to call me home, at which I fell aweeping. Then the old squaw told me, to encourage me, that if I wanted victuals, I should come to her,

---

5. Worthless things.
6. Rowlandson spells the name "Wattimore" here.

7. Beads of polished shells used by some American Indians as currency.

and that I should lie there in her wigwam. Then I went with the maid, and quickly came again and lodged there. The squaw laid a mat under me, and a good rug over me; the first time I had any such kindness showed me. I understood that Weetamoo thought that if she should let me go and serve with the old squaw, she would be in danger to lose not only my service, but the redemption pay[8] also. And I was not a little glad to hear this; being by it raised in my hopes, that in God's due time there would be an end of this sorrowful hour. Then came an Indian, and asked me to knit him three pair of stockings, for which I had a hat, and a silk handkerchief. Then another asked me to make her a shift, for which she gave me an apron.

Then came Tom and Peter,[9] with the second letter from the council, about the captives. Though they were Indians, I got them by the hand, and burst out into tears. My heart was so full that I could not speak to them; but recovering myself, I asked them how my husband did, and all my friends and acquaintance? They said, "They are all very well but melancholy." They brought me two biscuits, and a pound of tobacco. The tobacco I quickly gave away. When it was all gone, one asked me to give him a pipe of tobacco. I told him it was all gone. Then began he to rant and threaten. I told him when my husband came I would give him some. Hang him rogue[1] (says he), I will knock out his brains, if he comes here. And then again, in the same breath they would say that if there should come an hundred without guns, they would do them no hurt. So unstable and like madmen they were. So that fearing the worst, I durst not send to my husband, though there were some thoughts of his coming to redeem and fetch me, not knowing what might follow. For there was little more trust to them than to the master they served. When the letter was come, the Sagamores met to consult about the captives, and called me to them to inquire how much my husband would give to redeem me. When I came I sat down among them, as I was wont to do, as their manner is. Then they bade me stand up, and said they were the General Court.[2] They bid me speak what I thought he would give. Now knowing that all we had was destroyed by the Indians, I was in a great strait. I thought if I should speak of but a little it would be slighted, and hinder the matter; if of a great sum, I knew not where it would be procured. Yet at a venture I said, "Twenty pounds," yet desired them to take less. But they would not hear of that, but sent that message to Boston, that for twenty pounds I should be redeemed. It was a Praying Indian that wrote their letter for them. There was another Praying Indian, who told me, that he had a brother, that would not eat horse; his conscience was so tender and scrupulous (though as large as hell, for the destruction of poor Christians). Then he said, he read that Scripture to him, "There was a famine in Samaria, and behold they besieged it, until an ass's head was sold for fourscore pieces of silver, and the fourth part of a cab of dove's dung for five pieces of silver" (2 Kings 6.25). He expounded this place to his brother, and showed him that it was lawful to eat that in a famine which is not at another time. And now, says he, he will eat horse with any Indian of them all. There was another Praying Indian, who

---

8. I.e., the anticipated ransom money.
9. Christian Indians.
1. I.e., I'll hang that rogue.

2. In imitation of the colonial assembly of Massachusetts.

when he had done all the mischief that he could, betrayed his own father into the English hands, thereby to purchase his own life. Another Praying Indian was at [the] Sudbury fight,[3] though, as he deserved, he was afterward hanged for it. There was another Praying Indian, so wicked and cruel, as to wear a string about his neck, strung with Christians' fingers. Another Praying Indian, when they went to [the] Sudbury fight, went with them, and his squaw also with him, with her papoose at her back. Before they went to that fight they got a company together to powwow.[4] The manner was as followeth: there was one that kneeled upon a deerskin, with the company round him in a ring who kneeled, and striking upon the ground with their hands, and with sticks, and muttering or humming with their mouths. Besides him who kneeled in the ring, there also stood one with a gun in his hand. Then he on the deerskin made a speech, and all manifested assent to it; and so they did many times together. Then they bade him with the gun go out of the ring, which he did. But when he was out, they called him in again; but he seemed to make a stand; then they called the more earnestly, till he returned again. Then they all sang. Then they gave him two guns, in either hand one. And so he on the deerskin began again; and at the end of every sentence in his speaking, they all assented, humming or muttering with their mouths, and striking upon the ground with their hands. Then they bade him with the two guns go out of the ring again; which he did, a little way. Then they called him in again, but he made a stand. So they called him with greater earnestness; but he stood reeling and wavering as if he knew not whither he should stand or fall, or which way to go. Then they called him with exceeding great vehemency, all of them, one and another. After a little while he turned in, staggering as he went, with his arms stretched out, in either hand a gun. As soon as he came in they all sang and rejoiced exceedingly a while. And then he upon the deerskin, made another speech unto which they all assented in a rejoicing manner. And so they ended their business, and forthwith went to [the] Sudbury fight. To my thinking they went without any scruple, but that they should prosper, and gain the victory. And they went out not so rejoicing, but they came home with as great a victory. For they said they had killed two captains and almost an hundred men. One Englishman they brought along with them: and he said, it was too true, for they had made sad work at Sudbury, as indeed it proved. Yet they came home without that rejoicing and triumphing over their victory which they were wont to show at other times; but rather like dogs (as they say) which have lost their ears. Yet I could not perceive that it was for their own loss of men. They said they had not lost above five or six; and I missed none, except in one wigwam. When they went, they acted as if the devil had told them that they should gain the victory; and now they acted as if the devil had told them they should have a fall. Whether it were so or no, I cannot tell, but so it proved, for quickly they began to fall, and so held on that summer, till they came to utter ruin. They came home on a Sabbath day, and the Powwow[5] that kneeled upon the deerskin came home (I may say, without abuse) as black as the devil. When my master came home, he came to me and bid me make a shirt for his papoose, of a holland-laced pillowbere.[6] About that time there came an Indian to me

3. An attack on Sudbury, Massachusetts, April 18.
4. Confer.
5. Shaman.
6. Pillowcase.

and bid me come to his wigwam at night, and he would give me some pork and ground nuts. Which I did, and as I was eating, another Indian said to me, he seems to be your good friend, but he killed two Englishmen at Sudbury, and there lie their clothes behind you: I looked behind me, and there I saw bloody clothes, with bullet-holes in them. Yet the Lord suffered not this wretch to do me any hurt. Yea, instead of that, he many times refreshed me; five or six times did he and his squaw refresh my feeble carcass. If I went to their wigwam at any time, they would always give me something, and yet they were strangers that I never saw before. Another squaw gave me a piece of fresh pork, and a little salt with it, and lent me her pan to fry it in; and I cannot but remember what a sweet, pleasant, and delightful relish that bit had to me, to this day. So little do we prize common mercies when we have them to the full.

The Twentieth Remove[7]

It was their usual manner to remove, when they had done any mischief, lest they should be found out; and so they did at this time. We went about three or four miles, and there they built a great wigwam, big enough to hold an hundred Indians, which they did in preparation to a great day of dancing. They would say now amongst themselves, that the governor would be so angry for his loss at Sudbury, that he would send no more about the captives, which made me grieve and tremble. My sister being not far from the place where we now were, and hearing that I was here, desired her master to let her come and see me, and he was willing to it, and would go with her; but she being ready before him, told him she would go before, and was come within a mile or two of the place. Then he overtook her, and began to rant as if he had been mad, and made her go back again in the rain; so that I never saw her till I saw her in Charlestown.[8] But the Lord requited many of their ill doings, for this Indian her master, was hanged afterward at Boston. The Indians now began to come from all quarters, against their merry dancing day. Among some of them came one goodwife Kettle. I told her my heart was so heavy that it was ready to break. "So is mine too," said she, but yet said, "I hope we shall hear some good news shortly." I could hear how earnestly my sister desired to see me, and I as earnestly desired to see her; and yet neither of us could get an opportunity. My daughter was also now about a mile off, and I had not seen her in nine or ten weeks, as I had not seen my sister since our first taking. I earnestly desired them to let me go and see them: yea, I entreated, begged, and persuaded them, but to let me see my daughter; and yet so hard-hearted were they, that they would not suffer it. They made use of their tyrannical power whilst they had it; but through the Lord's wonderful mercy, their time was now but short.

On a Sabbath day, the sun being about an hour high in the afternoon, came Mr. John Hoar[9] (the council permitting him, and his own foreward spirit inclining him), together with the two forementioned Indians, Tom and

7. April 28 to May 2, to a camp at the southern end of Wachusett Lake, Princeton, Massachusetts.
8. Oldest neighborhood in Boston.
9. By the request of Rowlandson's husband, Hoar—a prominent lawyer and Indian missionary from Concord, Massachusetts—represented the colonial authorities at the negotiations for Rowlandson's release.

Peter, with their third letter from the council. When they came near, I was abroad. Though I saw them not, they presently called me in, and bade me sit down and not stir. Then they catched up their guns, and away they ran, as if an enemy had been at hand, and the guns went off apace. I manifested some great trouble, and they asked me what was the matter? I told them I thought they had killed the Englishman (for they had in the meantime informed me that an Englishman was come). They said, no. They shot over his horse and under and before his horse, and they pushed him this way and that way, at their pleasure, showing what they could do. Then they let them come to their wigwams. I begged of them to let me see the Englishman, but they would not. But there was I fain to sit their pleasure. When they had talked their fill with him, they suffered me to go to him. We asked each other of our welfare, and how my husband did, and all my friends? He told me they were all well, and would be glad to see me. Amongst other things which my husband sent me, there came a pound of tobacco, which I sold for nine shillings in money; for many of the Indians for want of tobacco, smoked hemlock, and ground ivy. It was a great mistake in any, who thought I sent for tobacco; for through the favor of God, that desire was overcome. I now asked them whether I should go home with Mr. Hoar? They answered no, one and another of them, and it being night, we lay down with that answer. In the morning Mr. Hoar invited the Sagamores to dinner; but when we went to get it ready we found that they had stolen the greatest part of the provision Mr. Hoar had brought, out of his bags, in the night. And we may see the wonderful power of God, in that one passage,[1] in that when there was such a great number of the Indians together, and so greedy of a little good food, and no English there but Mr. Hoar and myself, that there they did not knock us in the head, and take what we had, there being not only some provision, but also trading-cloth,[2] a part of the twenty pounds agreed upon. But instead of doing us any mischief, they seemed to be ashamed of the fact, and said, it were some matchit[3] Indian that did it. Oh, that we could believe that there is nothing too hard for God! God showed His power over the heathen in this, as He did over the hungry lions when Daniel was cast into the den.[4] Mr. Hoar called them betime[5] to dinner, but they ate very little, they being so busy in dressing themselves, and getting ready for their dance, which was carried on by eight of them, four men and four squaws. My master and mistress being two. He was dressed in his holland[6] shirt, with great laces sewed at the tail of it; he had his silver buttons, his white stockings, his garters were hung round with shillings, and he had girdles of wampum upon his head and shoulders. She had a kersey[7] coat, and covered with girdles of wampum from the loins upward. Her arms from her elbows to her hands were covered with bracelets; there were handfuls of necklaces about her neck, and several sorts of jewels in her ears. She had fine red stockings, and white shoes, her hair powdered and face painted red, that was always before black. And all the dancers were after the same manner. There were two others singing and knocking on a kettle for their music. They kept hopping up and

---

1. Incident.
2. Cloth used for barter.
3. Bad.
4. The prophet Daniel was cast into a den of lions, but they did not harm him (Daniel 6.1–29).
5. In good time; early.
6. Linen.
7. Coarse cloth woven from long wool and usually ribbed.

down one after another, with a kettle of water in the midst, standing warm upon some embers, to drink of when they were dry. They held on till it was almost night, throwing out wampum to the standers by. At night I asked them again, if I should go home? They all as one said no, except[8] my husband would come for me. When we were lain down, my master went out of the wigwam, and by and by sent in an Indian called James the Printer,[9] who told Mr. Hoar, that my master would let me go home tomorrow, if he would let him have one pint of liquors. Then Mr. Hoar called his own Indians, Tom and Peter, and bid them go and see whether he would promise it before them three; and if he would, he should have it; which he did, and he had it. Then Philip smelling the business called me to him, and asked me what I would give him, to tell me some good news, and speak a good word for me. I told him I could not tell what to give him. I would [give him] anything I had, and asked him what he would have? He said two coats and twenty shillings in money, and half a bushel of seed corn, and some tobacco. I thanked him for his love; but I knew the good news as well as the crafty fox. My master after he had had his drink, quickly came ranting into the wigwam again, and called for Mr. Hoar, drinking to him, and saying, he was a good man, and then again he would say, "hang him rogue." Being almost drunk, he would drink to him, and yet presently say he should be hanged. Then he called for me. I trembled to hear him, yet I was fain to go to him, and he drank to me, showing no incivility. He was the first Indian I saw drunk all the while that I was amongst them. At last his squaw ran out, and he after her, round the wigwam, with his money jingling at his knees. But she escaped him. But having an old squaw he ran to her; and so through the Lord's mercy, we were no more troubled that night. Yet I had not a comfortable night's rest; for I think I can say, I did not sleep for three nights together. The night before the letter came from the council, I could not rest, I was so full of fears and troubles, God many times leaving us most in the dark, when deliverance is nearest. Yea, at this time I could not rest night nor day. The next night I was overjoyed, Mr. Hoar being come, and that with such good tidings. The third night I was even swallowed up with the thoughts of things, *viz.* that ever I should go home again; and that I must go, leaving my children behind me in the wilderness; so that sleep was now almost departed from mine eyes.

On Tuesday morning they called their General Court (as they call it) to consult and determine, whether I should go home or no. And they all as one man did seemingly consent to it, that I should go home; except Philip, who would not come among them.

But before I go any further, I would take leave to mention a few remarkable passages of providence, which I took special notice of in my afflicted time.

1. Of the fair opportunity lost in the long march, a little after the fort fight, when our English army was so numerous, and in pursuit of the enemy, and so near as to take several and destroy them, and the enemy in such distress for food that our men might track them by their rooting in the earth for ground nuts, whilst they were flying for their lives. I say, that then our army should

8. Unless.
9. Wowaus, who assisted the Reverend John Eliot in his printing of the Bible.

want provision, and be forced to leave their pursuit and return homeward; and the very next week the enemy came upon our town, like bears bereft of their whelps, or so many ravenous wolves, rending us and our lambs to death. But what shall I say? God seemed to leave his People to themselves, and order all things for His own holy ends. Shall there be evil in the City and the Lord hath not done it?[1] They are not grieved for the affliction of Joseph, therefore shall they go captive, with the first that go captive.[2] It is the Lord's doing, and it should be marvelous in our eyes.

2. I cannot but remember how the Indians derided the slowness, and dullness of the English army, in its setting out. For after the desolations at Lancaster and Medfield, as I went along with them, they asked me when I thought the English army would come after them? I told them I could not tell. "It may be they will come in May," said they. Thus did they scoff at us, as if the English would be a quarter of a year getting ready.

3. Which also I have hinted before, when the English army with new supplies were sent forth to pursue after the enemy, and they understanding it, fled before them till they came to Banquaug river, where they forthwith went over safely; that that river should be impassable to the English. I can but admire to see the wonderful providence of God in preserving the heathen for further affliction to our poor country. They could go in great numbers over, but the English must stop. God had an over-ruling hand in all those things.

4. It was thought, if their corn were cut down, they would starve and die with hunger, and all their corn that could be found, was destroyed, and they driven from that little they had in store, into the woods in the midst of winter; and yet how to admiration did the Lord preserve them for His holy ends, and the destruction of many still amongst the English! strangely did the Lord provide for them; that I did not see (all the time I was among them) one man, woman, or child, die with hunger.

Though many times they would eat that, that[3] a hog or a dog would hardly touch; yet by that God strengthened them to be a scourge to His people.

The chief and commonest food was ground nuts. They eat also nuts and acorns, artichokes, lily roots, ground beans, and several other weeds and roots, that I know not.

They would pick up old bones, and cut them to pieces at the joints, and if they were full of worms and maggots, they would scald them over the fire to make the vermin come out, and then boil them, and drink up the liquor, and then beat the great ends of them in a mortar, and so eat them. They would eat horse's guts, and ears, and all sorts of wild birds which they could catch; also bear, venison, beaver, tortoise, frogs, squirrels, dogs, skunks, rattlesnakes; yea, the very bark of trees; besides all sorts of creatures, and provision which they plundered from the English. I can but stand in admiration to see the wonderful power of God in providing for such a vast number of our enemies in the wilderness, where there was nothing to be seen, but from hand to mouth. Many times in a morning, the generality of them would eat up all they had, and yet have some further supply against they wanted. It is

---

1. Amos 3.6.
2. Amos 6.6–7.

3. I.e., that which.

said, "Oh, that my People had hearkened to me, and Israel had walked in my ways, I should soon have subdued their Enemies, and turned my hand against their Adversaries" (Psalm 81.13–14). But now our perverse and evil carriages in the sight of the Lord, have so offended Him, that instead of turning His hand against them, the Lord feeds and nourishes them up to be a scourge to the whole land.

5. Another thing that I would observe is the strange providence of God, in turning things about when the Indians was at the highest, and the English at the lowest. I was with the enemy eleven weeks and five days, and not one week passed without the fury of the enemy, and some desolation by fire and sword upon one place or other. They mourned (with their black faces) for their own losses, yet triumphed and rejoiced in their inhumane, and many times devilish cruelty to the English. They would boast much of their victories; saying that in two hours time they had destroyed such a captain and his company at such a place; and boast how many towns they had destroyed, and then scoff, and say they had done them a good turn to send them to Heaven so soon. Again, they would say this summer that they would knock all the rogues in the head, or drive them into the sea, or make them fly the country; thinking surely, Agag-like, "The bitterness of Death is past."[4] Now the heathen begins to think all is their own, and the poor Christians' hopes to fail (as to man) and now their eyes are more to God, and their hearts sigh heavenward; and to say in good earnest, "Help Lord, or we perish." When the Lord had brought His people to this, that they saw no help in anything but Himself; then He takes the quarrel into His own hand; and though they had made a pit, in their own imaginations, as deep as hell for the Christians that summer, yet the Lord hurled themselves into it. And the Lord had not so many ways before to preserve them, but now He hath as many to destroy them.

But to return again to my going home, where we may see a remarkable change of providence. At first they were all against it, except my husband would come for me, but afterwards they assented to it, and seemed much to rejoice in it; some asked me to send them some bread, others some tobacco, others shaking me by the hand, offering me a hood and scarf to ride in; not one moving hand or tongue against it. Thus hath the Lord answered my poor desire, and the many earnest requests of others put up unto God for me. In my travels an Indian came to me and told me, if I were willing, he and his squaw would run away, and go home along with me. I told him no: I was not willing to run away, but desired to wait God's time, that I might go home quietly, and without fear. And now God hath granted me my desire. O the wonderful power of God that I have seen, and the experience that I have had. I have been in the midst of those roaring lions, and savage bears, that feared neither God, nor man, nor the devil, by night and day, alone and in company, sleeping all sorts together, and yet not one of them ever offered me the least abuse of unchastity to me, in word or action. Though some are ready to say I speak it for my own credit; but I speak it in the presence of God, and to His Glory. God's power is as great now, and as sufficient to save, as when He preserved Daniel in the lion's den; or the three children in the

---

4. 1 Samuel 15.32. Agag, king of Amalek, was defeated by Saul and thought himself spared, but was then slain by Samuel.

fiery furnace.[5] I may well say as his Psalm 107.12, "Oh give thanks unto the Lord for he is good, for his mercy endureth for ever." Let the redeemed of the Lord say so, whom He hath redeemed from the hand of the enemy, especially that I should come away in the midst of so many hundreds of enemies quietly and peaceably, and not a dog moving his tongue. So I took my leave of them, and in coming along my heart melted into tears, more than all the while I was with them, and I was almost swallowed up with the thoughts that ever I should go home again. About the sun going down, Mr. Hoar, and myself, and the two Indians came to Lancaster, and a solemn sight it was to me. There had I lived many comfortable years amongst my relations and neighbors, and now not one Christian to be seen, nor one house left standing. We went on to a farmhouse that was yet standing, where we lay all night, and a comfortable lodging we had, though nothing but straw to lie on. The Lord preserved us in safety that night, and raised us up again in the morning, and carried us along, that before noon, we came to Concord. Now was I full of joy, and yet not without sorrow; joy to see such a lovely sight, so many Christians together, and some of them my neighbors. There I met with my brother, and my brother-in-law, who asked me, if I knew where his wife was? Poor heart! he had helped to bury her, and knew it not. She being shot down by the house was partly burnt, so that those who were at Boston at the desolation of the town, and came back afterward, and buried the dead, did not know her. Yet I was not without sorrow, to think how many were looking and longing, and my own children amongst the rest, to enjoy that deliverance that I had now received, and I did not know whether ever I should see them again. Being recruited[6] with food and raiment we went to Boston that day, where I met with my dear husband, but the thoughts of our dear children, one being dead, and the other we could not tell where, abated our comfort each to other. I was not before so much hemmed in with the merciless and cruel heathen, but now as much with pitiful, tender-hearted and compassionate Christians. In that poor, and distressed, and beggarly condition I was received in; I was kindly entertained in several houses. So much love I received from several (some of whom I knew, and others I knew not) that I am not capable to declare it. But the Lord knows them all by name. The Lord reward them sevenfold into their bosoms of His spirituals, for their temporals.[7] The twenty pounds, the price of my redemption, was raised by some Boston gentlemen, and Mrs. Usher, whose bounty and religious charity, I would not forget to make mention of. Then Mr. Thomas Shepard of Charlestown received us into his house, where we continued eleven weeks; and a father and mother they were to us. And many more tender-hearted friends we met with in that place. We were now in the midst of love, yet not without much and frequent heaviness of heart for our poor children, and other relations, who were still in affliction. The week following, after my coming in, the governor and council sent forth to the Indians again; and that not without success; for they brought in my sister, and goodwife Kettle. Their not knowing where our children were was a sore trial to us still, and yet we were not without secret hopes that we should see them again. That which

---

5. Shadrach, Meshach, and Abednego refused to worship false gods and were cast into a fiery furnace but saved from death by an angel (Daniel 3.13–30).

6. Refreshed.

7. Worldly goods and gifts.

was dead lay heavier upon my spirit, than those which were alive and amongst the heathen: thinking how it suffered with its wounds, and I was no way able to relieve it; and how it was buried by the heathen in the wilderness from among all Christians. We were hurried up and down in our thoughts, sometime we should hear a report that they were gone this way, and sometimes that; and that they were come in, in this place or that. We kept inquiring and listening to hear concerning them, but no certain news as yet. About this time the council had ordered a day of public thanksgiving. Though I thought I had still cause of mourning, and being unsettled in our minds, we thought we would ride toward the eastward, to see if we could hear anything concerning our children. And as we were riding along (God is the wise disposer of all things) between Ipswich and Rowley we met with Mr. William Hubbard, who told us that our son Joseph was come in to Major Waldron's, and another with him, which was my sister's son. I asked him how he knew it? He said the major himself told him so. So along we went till we came to Newbury; and their minister being absent, they desired my husband to preach the thanksgiving for them; but he was not willing to stay there that night, but would go over to Salisbury, to hear further, and come again in the morning, which he did, and preached there that day. At night, when he had done, one came and told him that his daughter was come in at Providence. Here was mercy on both hands. Now hath God fulfilled that precious Scripture which was such a comfort to me in my distressed condition. When my heart was ready to sink into the earth (my children being gone, I could not tell whither) and my knees trembling under me, and I was walking through the valley of the shadow of death; then the Lord brought, and now has fulfilled that reviving word unto me: "Thus saith the Lord, Refrain thy voice from weeping, and thine eyes from tears, for thy Work shall be rewarded, saith the Lord, and they shall come again from the Land of the Enemy."[8] Now we were between them, the one on the east, and the other on the west. Our son being nearest, we went to him first, to Portsmouth, where we met with him, and with the Major also, who told us he had done what he could, but could not redeem him under seven pounds, which the good people thereabouts were pleased to pay. The Lord reward the major, and all the rest, though unknown to me, for their labor of love. My sister's son was redeemed for four pounds, which the council gave order for the payment of. Having now received one of our children, we hastened toward the other. Going back through Newbury my husband preached there on the Sabbath day; for which they rewarded him many fold.

On Monday we came to Charlestown, where we heard that the governor of Rhode Island had sent over for our daughter, to take care of her, being now within his jurisdiction; which should not pass without our acknowledgments. But she being nearer Rehoboth than Rhode Island, Mr. Newman went over, and took care of her and brought her to his own house. And the goodness of God was admirable to us in our low estate, in that He raised up passionate[9] friends on every side to us, when we had nothing to recompense any for their love. The Indians were now gone that way, that it was apprehended dangerous to go to her. But the carts which carried provision

---

8. Jeremiah 31.16. 9. Compassionate.

to the English army, being guarded, brought her with them to Dorchester, where we received her safe. Blessed be the Lord for it, for great is His power, and He can do whatsoever seemeth Him good. Her coming in was after this manner: she was traveling one day with the Indians, with her basket at her back; the company of Indians were got before her, and gone out of sight, all except one squaw; she followed the squaw till night, and then both of them lay down, having nothing over them but the heavens and under them but the earth. Thus she traveled three days together, not knowing whither she was going; having nothing to eat or drink but water, and green hirtle-berries.[1] At last they came into Providence, where she was kindly entertained by several of that town. The Indians often said that I should never have her under twenty pounds. But now the Lord hath brought her in upon free-cost, and given her to me the second time. The Lord make us a blessing indeed, each to others. Now have I seen that Scripture also fulfilled, "If any of thine be driven out to the outmost parts of heaven, from thence will the Lord thy God gather thee, and from thence will he fetch thee. And the Lord thy God will put all these curses upon thine enemies, and on them which hate thee, which persecuted thee" (Deuteronomy 30.4–7). Thus hath the Lord brought me and mine out of that horrible pit, and hath set us in the midst of tender-hearted and compassionate Christians. It is the desire of my soul that we may walk worthy of the mercies received, and which we are receiving.

Our family being now gathered together (those of us that were living), the South Church in Boston hired an house for us. Then we removed from Mr. Shephard's, those cordial friends, and went to Boston, where we continued about three-quarters of a year. Still the Lord went along with us, and provided graciously for us. I thought it somewhat strange to set up housekeeping with bare walls; but as Solomon says, "Money answers all things"[2] and that we had through the benevolence of Christian friends, some in this town, and some in that, and others; and some from England; that in a little time we might look, and see the house furnished with love. The Lord hath been exceeding good to us in our low estate, in that when we had neither house nor home, nor other necessaries, the Lord so moved the hearts of these and those towards us, that we wanted neither food, nor raiment for ourselves or ours: "There is a Friend which sticketh closer than a Brother" (Proverbs 18.24). And how many such friends have we found, and now living amongst? And truly such a friend have we found him to be unto us, in whose house we lived, viz. Mr. James Whitcomb, a friend unto us near hand, and afar off.

I can remember the time when I used to sleep quietly without workings in my thoughts, whole nights together, but now it is other ways with me. When all are fast about me, and no eye open, but His who ever waketh, my thoughts are upon things past, upon the awful dispensation of the Lord towards us, upon His wonderful power and might, in carrying of us through so many difficulties, in returning us in safety, and suffering none to hurt us. I remember in the night season, how the other day I was in the midst of thousands of enemies, and nothing but death before me. It is then hard work to persuade myself, that ever I should be satisfied with bread again. But now we are fed

---

1. Either blueberries or huckleberries. 2. Ecclesiastes 10.19.

with the finest of the wheat, and, as I may say, with honey out of the rock.[3] Instead of the husk, we have the fatted calf.[4] The thoughts of these things in the particulars of them, and of the love and goodness of God towards us, make it true of me, what David said of himself, "I watered my Couch with my tears" (Psalm 6.6). Oh! the wonderful power of God that mine eyes have seen, affording matter enough for my thoughts to run in, that when others are sleeping mine eyes are weeping.

I have seen the extreme vanity of this world:[5] One hour I have been in health, and wealthy, wanting nothing. But the next hour in sickness and wounds, and death, having nothing but sorrow and affliction.

Before I knew what affliction meant, I was ready sometimes to wish for it. When I lived in prosperity, having the comforts of the world about me, my relations by me, my heart cheerful, and taking little care for anything, and yet seeing many, whom I preferred before myself, under many trials and afflictions, in sickness, weakness, poverty, losses, crosses,[6] and cares of the world, I should be sometimes jealous least I should have my portion in this life, and that Scripture would come to my mind, "For whom the Lord loveth he chasteneth, and scourgeth every Son whom he receiveth" (Hebrews 12.6). But now I see the Lord had His time to scourge and chasten me. The portion of some is to have their afflictions by drops, now one drop and then another; but the dregs of the cup, the wine of astonishment, like a sweeping rain that leaveth no food, did the Lord prepare to be my portion. Affliction I wanted, and affliction I had, full measure (I thought), pressed down and running over. Yet I see, when God calls a person to anything, and through never so many difficulties, yet He is fully able to carry them through and make them see, and say they have been gainers thereby. And I hope I can say in some measure, as David did, "It is good for me that I have been afflicted."[7] The Lord hath showed me the vanity of these outward things. That they are the vanity of vanities, and vexation of spirit, that they are but a shadow, a blast, a bubble, and things of no continuance. That we must rely on God Himself, and our whole dependance must be upon Him. If trouble from smaller matters begin to arise in me, I have something at hand to check myself with, and say, why am I troubled? It was but the other day that if I had had the world, I would have given it for my freedom, or to have been a servant to a Christian. I have learned to look beyond present and smaller troubles, and to be quieted under them. As Moses said, "Stand still and see the salvation of the Lord" (Exodus 14.13).

1682

---

3. "He should have fed them also with the finest of the wheat: and with honey out of the rock should I have satisfied thee" (Psalm 81.16).
4. "And bring hither the fatted calf, and kill it; and let us eat, and be merry" (Luke 15.23).

5. Cf. Ecclesiastes 1.2. "Vanity": emptiness, futility.
6. Burdens.
7. Psalm 119.71.

EDWARD TAYLOR
c. 1642–1729

E dward Taylor's poetry was known only by a select circle in his own day. It was passed down in manuscript through his family for generations, until his great-grandson donated the manuscript volume to the Beinecke library, at Yale University, in 1883. Five decades later, the literary scholar Thomas H. Johnson located the manuscript there. After Johnson edited *The Poetical Works of Edward Taylor* (1939), the Puritan poet and his work became the object of sustained critical attention.

Taylor's lack of print publication in his lifetime did not mean that he thought his work unworthy. Manuscript publication remained a common practice long after the printing press had become widely available. In the seventeenth century, manuscript was a popular medium for coterie poetry, or poems shared exclusively with a small group of associates. The most eminent coterie poet may be John Donne (1572–1631), the Anglican minister whom many regard as the finest practitioner of Metaphysical poetry, an intellectual style that influenced Taylor. Donne authorized the print publication of just seven of his poems; his other 187 poems circulated exclusively in manuscript during his lifetime.

Even less of Taylor's poetry was printed in his own day—just a few fragments, notably the final two stanzas of "Upon Wedlock, and Death of Children," which Cotton Mather included at the end of a sermon that was published in London in 1689. Scholars think that Mather acquired those stanzas from a letter that Taylor wrote to his college friend Samuel Sewall, rather than from a compendium of poems. Taylor may have been less a coterie poet than a private one who wrote verses for his own satisfaction and inspiration. Yet he cared enough about future readers to copy his poems into a four-hundred-page leather-bound book, which he passed down to his descendants. Today, a number of pages from Taylor's manuscript can be viewed online at the Beinecke Library Web site.

As a youth, Taylor was schooled in English religious poetry, which he later adapted to his circumstances as the minister of a small New England village. He was probably born in Sketchly, Leicestershire County, England, and the dialect of that farming country gives some of his poems provincial charm. His father was a yeoman farmer—not a gentleman with a large estate but an independent land-holder with title to his farm. Taylor taught school for a time, perhaps after some university training. Then in 1668, rather than sign an oath of loyalty to the Church of England, he sailed to New England. He preferred self-exile in what he once called a "howling wilderness" to either compromising his religious principles as a Puritan or suffering the substantial legal consequences of refusing to do so. Once in Massachusetts, he attended Harvard College, where he prepared himself for the ministry.

In 1671 Taylor became the minister and physician in the frontier town of Westfield, Massachusetts, roughly a hundred miles west of Boston. After a delay caused partly by King Philip's War (1675–76; see the Mary Rowlandson headnote), he settled in and remained at Westfield for the rest of his life, also serving as a public servant. He married twice and had fourteen children, suffering the loss of many who died in infancy. Taylor also involved himself in the intellectual life and religious controver-sies of the colony. He strictly observed the "old" New England way, which called for a prospective church member to give a public account of conversion, and he fought against a movement to drop that requirement.

Taylor's grandson Ezra Stiles, who served as the president of Yale, described him as "a man of small stature, but firm; of quick Passions, yet serious and grave." Like most

Harvard-trained ministers, Taylor knew Latin, Hebrew, and Greek, and his peers regarded him as a good preacher. His extensive library included theology, such as works of Augustine, and religious histories including *Foxe's Book of Martyrs* (1563); natural sciences and history, including Sir Walter Raleigh's *History of the World* (1614); and a great many works by New England authors, including a substantial number of Cotton Mather's publications and the 1678 edition of Anne Bradstreet's poems.

Taylor worked in various poetic genres, including personal lyrics, elegies on the deaths of public figures, and translations of the psalms. His verses most closely resemble those of the early Metaphysical poet George Herbert. Delighting in puns, paradoxes, and a rich profusion of metaphors and images, the Metaphysical wits explored the nature of language and its capacity to express spiritual meanings, as Taylor does in "Huswifery" and *Preparatory Meditations*. Taylor's *God's Determinations* is a long poem in the tradition of the medieval debate. "Upon Wedlock, and Death of Children" uses knotty wordplay to express emotional pain and the search for meaning and solace. Other poems combine naturalistic detail with spiritual meaning in a more direct style. The following selections suggest Taylor's considerable range, which places him squarely in the distinguished tradition of seventeenth-century religious lyric poetry.

All of the following texts are from *Poems of Edward Taylor* (1960), edited by Donald E. Stanford.

From Preparatory Meditations[1]

Prologue

> Lord, Can a Crumb of Dust the Earth outweigh,
>   Outmatch all mountains, nay, the Crystal sky?
> Embosom in't designs that shall Display
>   And trace into the Boundless Deity?
>   Yea, hand a Pen whose moisture doth guide o'er   5
>   Eternal Glory with a glorious glore.[2]
>
> If it its Pen had of an Angel's Quill,
>   And sharpened on a Precious Stone ground tight,
> And dipped in liquid Gold, and moved by Skill
>   In Crystal leaves should golden Letters write,   10
>   It would but blot and blur, yea, jag, and jar
>   Unless Thou mak'st the Pen, and Scrivener.
>
> I am this Crumb of Dust which is designed
>   To make my Pen unto Thy Praise alone,

1. The full title is *Preparatory Meditations before my Approach to the Lord's Supper. Chiefly upon the Doctrine preached upon the Day of Administration [of Communion]*. Taylor administered communion once a month to those members of his congregation who had made a declaration of their faith. He wrote these meditations in private; they are primarily the result of his contemplation of the biblical texts that served as the basis for the communion sermon. A total of 217 meditations survive, dating from 1682 to 1725.
2. Glory (Scottish).

And my dull Fancy[3] I would gladly grind   15
    Unto an Edge on Zion's[4] Precious Stone.
And Write in Liquid Gold upon Thy Name
    My Letters till Thy glory forth doth flame.

Let not th' attempts break down my Dust, I pray,
    Nor laugh Thou them to scorn but pardon give.   20
Inspire this crumb of Dust till it display
    Thy Glory through't: and then Thy dust shall live.
    Its failings then Thou'lt overlook, I trust,
    They being Slips slipped from Thy Crumb of Dust.

Thy Crumb of Dust breathes two words from its breast,   25
    That Thou wilt guide its pen to write aright
To Prove Thou art, and that Thou art the best
    And show Thy Properties to shine most bright.
    And then Thy Works will shine as flowers on Stems
    Or as in Jewelry Shops, do gems.   30

c. 1682   1939

Meditation 8 (First Series)

John 6.51. I am the Living Bread.[1]

I kenning through Astronomy Divine
    The World's bright Battlement,[2] wherein I spy
A Golden Path my Pencil cannot line,
    From that bright Throne unto my Threshold lie.
    And while my puzzled thoughts about it pour,   5
    I find the Bread of Life in't at my door.

When that this Bird of Paradise[3] put in
    This Wicker Cage (my Corpse) to tweedle praise
Had pecked the Fruit forbade: and so did fling
    Away its Food; and lost its golden days;   10
    It fell into Celestial Famine sore:
    And never could attain a morsel more.

Alas! alas! Poor Bird, what wilt thou do?
    The Creatures' field no food for Souls e'er gave.

3. I.e., imagination.
4. In ancient Jerusalem, the hill on which King Solomon built his temple; the City of God on Earth.
1. "The Jews then murmured at him, because he said, I am the bread which came down from heaven. And they said, Is not this Jesus, the son of Joseph, whose father and mother we know? how is it then that he saith, I came down from heaven? Jesus therefore answered[,] . . . Verily, verily, I say unto you, He that believeth on me hath everlasting life. I am that bread of life" (John 6.41–48). Jesus offers a "New Covenant of Faith" in place of the "Old Covenant of Works," which Adam broke when he disobeyed God's commandment (Genesis 1–3).
2. I.e., discerning, by means of "divine astronomy," the towers of heaven. Taylor goes on to suggest an invisible golden path extends from this world to the gates of Heaven.
3. I.e., the soul, which is like a bird kept in the body's cage.

And if thou knock at Angels' doors they show   15
   An Empty Barrel: they no soul bread have.
   Alas! Poor Bird, the World's White Loaf is done.
   And cannot yield thee here the smallest Crumb.

In this sad state, God's Tender Bowels[4] run
   Out streams of Grace: and He to end all strife   20
The Purest Wheat in Heaven His dear-dear son
   Grinds, and kneads up into this Bread of Life.
   Which Bread of Life from Heaven down came and stands
   Dished on Thy Table up by Angels' Hands.

Did God mold up this Bread in Heaven, and bake,   25
   Which from His Table came, and to thine goeth?
Doth He bespeak thee thus, This Soul Bread take?
   Come Eat thy fill of this thy God's White Loaf?
   It's Food too fine for Angels, yet come, take
   And Eat thy fill. It's Heaven's Sugar Cake.   30

What Grace is this knead in this Loaf? This thing
   Souls are but petty things it to admire.
Ye Angels, help: This fill would to the brim
   Heav'ns whelmed-down[5] Crystal meal Bowl, yea and higher.
   This Bread of Life dropped in thy mouth, doth Cry: 35
   Eat, Eat me, Soul, and thou shalt never die.

June 8, 1684   1939

FROM GOD'S DETERMINATIONS[1]

The Preface

   Infinity, when all things it beheld
In Nothing, and of Nothing all did build,
Upon what Base was fixed the Lathe wherein
He turned this Globe, and riggalled[2] it so trim?
Who blew the Bellows of His Furnace Vast?   5
Or held the Mold wherein the world was Cast?

---

4. Here, the interior of the body, the heart, the intestines, or the location of sympathetic emotions.
5. Turned over.
1. The subject of this "debate" poem is made clear in the full title: *God's determinations touching His Elect* [i.e., those divinely chosen for salvation]: *and the Elect's combat in their conversion, and coming up to God in Christ, together with the comfortable effects thereof.* In this group of poems,

Taylor explores the progress of the human soul from the creation of the world and the fall from grace to the redemption of the Christian soul through Jesus Christ's Crucifixion: Christ's mercy triumphs over justice—the punishment that humanity deserves for disobedience—and the soul is finally carried to heaven to share in the joys of the Resurrection.
2. Grooved.

Who laid its Corner Stone?[3] Or whose Command?
Where stand the Pillars upon which it stands?
Who Laced and Filleted[4] the earth so fine,
With Rivers like green Ribbons Smaragdine?[5]   10
Who made the Sea's its Selvage,[6] and its locks
Like a Quilt Ball[7] within a Silver Box?
Who Spread its Canopy? Or Curtains Spun?
Who in this Bowling Alley bowled the Sun?
Who made it always when it rises set   15
To go at once both down, and up to get?
Who th' Curtain rods made for this Tapestry?
Who hung the twinkling Lanthorns[8] in the Sky?
Who? who did this? or who is He? Why, know
It's Only Might Almighty this did do.   20
His hand hath made this noble work which Stands
His Glorious Handiwork not made by hands.
Who spake all things from Nothing; and with ease
Can speak all things to Nothing, if He please.
Whose Little finger at His pleasure Can   25
Out mete[9] ten thousand worlds with half a Span:
Whose Might Almighty can by half a looks
Root up the rocks and rock the hills by the roots.
Can take this mighty World up in His hand,
And shake it like a Squitchen[1] or a Wand.   30
Whose single Frown will make the Heavens shake
Like as an aspen leaf the Wind makes quake.
Oh! what a might is this Whose single frown
Doth shake the world as it would shake it down?
Which All from Nothing fet,[2] from Nothing, All: 35
Hath All on Nothing set, lets Nothing fall.
Gave All to Nothing Man indeed, whereby
Through Nothing man all might Him Glorify.
In Nothing then embossed the brightest Gem
More precious than all preciousness in them.   40
But Nothing man did throw down all by Sin:
And darkened that lightsome Gem in him.
    That now his Brightest Diamond is grown
    Darker by far than any Coalpit Stone.

c. 1685   1939

3. "Where wast thou when I laid the foundations of the earth? declare, if thou hast understanding. Who hath laid the measures thereof, if thou knowest? or who hath stretched the line upon it? Whereupon are the foundations thereof fastened? or who laid the corner stone thereof; When the morning stars sang together, and all the sons of God shouted for joy? Or who shut up the sea with doors, when it brake forth, as if it had issued out of the womb?" (Job 38.4–8).

4. Encircled, bound around.
5. Emerald green.
6. The border of woven material that prevents unraveling.
7. A ball of wool that would unravel if it were not kept in a box.
8. Lanterns.
9. Outmeasure.
1. Switch.
2. Made.

Upon Wedlock, and Death of Children

A Curious Knot[1] God made in Paradise,
    And drew it out enameled[2] neatly Fresh.
It was the True-Love Knot, more sweet than spice,
    And set with all the flowers of Grace's dress.
    It's Wedden's[3] Knot, that ne're can be untied: 5
    No Alexander's Sword[4] can it divide.

The slips[5] here planted, gay and glorious grow:
    Unless an Hellish breath do singe their Plumes.
Here Primrose, Cowslips, Roses, Lilies blow[6]
    With Violets and Pinks that void[7] perfumes: 10
    Whose beauteous leaves o'erlaid with Honey Dew,
    And Chanting birds Chirp out sweet Music true.

When in this Knot I planted was, my Stock[8]
    Soon knotted, and a manly flower out brake.[9]
And after it, my branch again did knot,   15
    Brought out another Flower, its sweet-breathed mate.
    One knot gave one tother[1] the tother's place.
    Whence Chuckling smiles fought in each other's face.

But Oh! a glorious hand from glory came
    Guarded with Angels, soon did crop this flower[2]   20
Which almost tore the root up of the same,
    At that unlooked for, Dolesome, darksome hour.
    In Prayer to Christ perfumed it did ascend,
    And Angels bright did it to heaven 'tend.

But pausing on't, this sweet perfumed my thought: 25
    Christ would in Glory have a Flower, Choice, Prime,
And having Choice, chose this my branch forth brought.
    Lord take't. I thank Thee, Thou tak'st ought of mine:
    It is my pledge in glory, part of me
    Is now in it, Lord, glorified with Thee.   30

But praying o're my branch, my branch did sprout,
    And bore another manly flower, and gay,[3]
And after that another, sweet brake out,
    The which the former hand soon got away.

1. Flower bed.
2. Polished, shining.
3. I.e., wedding's.
4. Alexander the Great cut the Gordian knot devised by the king of Phyrgia when he learned that anyone who could undo it would rule Asia.
5. Cuttings.
6. Bloom.
7. Emit.

8. Stem, stalk.
9. I.e., broke out. Samuel Taylor was born on August 27, 1675, and lived to maturity.
1. To the other.
2. Elizabeth Taylor was born on December 27, 1676, and died on December 25, 1677.
3. James Taylor was born on October 12, 1678, and lived to maturity.

But Oh! the tortures, Vomit, screechings, groans,   35
  and six week's Fever would pierce hearts like stones.[4]

Grief o'er doth flow: and nature fault would find
  Were not Thy Will, my Spell, Charm, Joy, and Gem:
That as I said, I say, take, Lord, they're Thine.
  I piecemeal pass to Glory bright in them.   40
  In joy, may I sweet flowers for glory breed,
  Whether thou get'st them green, or lets them seed.

c. 1682   1939

Huswifery[1]

Make me, O Lord, Thy Spinning Wheel complete.[2]
  Thy Holy Word my Distaff make for me.
Make mine Affections Thy Swift Flyers neat
  And make my Soul Thy holy Spool to be.
  My conversation make to be Thy Reel   5
  And reel the yarn thereon spun of Thy Wheel.

Make me Thy Loom then, knit therein this Twine:
  And make Thy Holy Spirit, Lord, wind quills:[3]
Then weave the Web Thyself. The yarn is fine.
  Thine Ordinances make my Fulling Mills.[4]   10
  Then dye the same in Heavenly Colors Choice,
  All pinked with Varnished[5] Flowers of Paradise.

Then clothe therewith mine Understanding, Will,
  Affections, Judgment, Conscience, Memory,
My Words, and Actions, that their shine may fill   15
  My ways with glory and Thee glorify.
  Then mine apparel shall display before Ye
  That I am Clothed in Holy robes for glory.[6]

                                                                         1939

---

4. Abigail Taylor was born on August 6, 1681, and died on August 22, 1682.
1. Housekeeping; here, weaving.
2. In lines 2–6, Taylor refers to the working parts of a spinning wheel. "Distaff':' holds the raw wool or flax. "Flyers": regulate the spinning. "Spool": twists the yarn. "Reel": takes up the finished thread.
3. I.e., be like a spool or bobbin.
4. Where cloth is beaten and cleansed with fuller's earth, or soap.

5. Glossy, sparkling. "Pinked": adorned.
6. In Taylor's *Treatise Concerning the Lord's Supper*, he considers the significance of the sacrament of communion and takes as his text a passage from the New Testament: "And he saith unto him, Friend, how camest thou in hither not having a wedding garment? And he was speechless" (Matthew 22.12). Taylor argues that the wedding garment is the proper sign of the regenerate (spiritually reborn) Christian.

COTTON MATHER
1663–1728

Cotton Mather's writings represent the peak of New England Puritan intellectual life in its baroque phase: ornate, with a hint of decadence. The sense of a world-view a bit past its prime and straining to recover preeminence emerges from many accounts of his life and writings. Mather was the grandson of Richard Mather and John Cotton, leading first-generation ministers in the Massachusetts Bay Colony, and the son of another prominent minister, Increase Mather. These men published frequently on theology, church polity, history, and the natural sciences. Young Cotton Mather shouldered the burden of this inheritance, viewing it as a precious legacy for the colony and, indeed, all of humanity, but he did so at some personal cost. He stammered badly as a youth, and while he was able to overcome that debility well enough to become a minister, throughout his life he continued to suffer from nervous disorders that today we would probably call anxiety and depression. He had a reputation for being pushy and difficult, and he alienated people with extreme behavior, even when he acted with the best intentions.

Tutored by his father, this precocious eldest son of a distinguished family was admitted to Harvard College at the unusually young age of twelve. At Mather's graduation, in 1678, President Urian Oakes told the commencement audience that his hope was great that "in this youth, Cotton and Mather shall, in fact as well as name, join together and once more appear in life"—a reference to the young man's illustrious grandfathers. Later, the pressures associated with living up to his family heritage mounted. In 1685, his father began a long term as the president of Harvard, and for four years starting in the late 1680s he served as New England's envoy to England, where he renegotiated favorable terms for the colonial charter. These were remarkable accomplishments for any child to attempt to equal.

Mather remained for much of his adult life in his father's shadow. He studied medicine when it seemed that his stammer would prevent him from taking a pulpit, then began serving as his father's assistant pastor at Boston's Second Church after Increase became the president of Harvard. Cotton was later thwarted in his desire to follow his father into the Harvard presidency, a source of lingering bitterness to him. He finally became pastor at the Second Church after his father's death, only five years before he himself died. Frustrated professionally in certain ways, Mather devoted his considerable energy to the transatlantic republic of letters, involving himself in the major intellectual questions of his day and writing on a wide variety of topics.

Mather experienced further disappointment and tragedy in his personal life. His first two wives died, and his third wife became mentally ill. Of his fifteen children, only six survived to adulthood, and just two lived until his death. His extended family put uncomfortable demands on his financial resources. Despite these considerable responsibilities, he was passionately committed to the common good as he understood it, and he took great satisfaction in organizing societies for building churches, supporting schools for the children of slaves, and working to establish funds for indigent clergy. During Benjamin Franklin's early years in Boston, he learned a great deal from Mather about public service, and those insights became central to Franklin's life and writings.

Mather published over four hundred works. Some of his most engaging writings deal with the witchcraft trials at Salem, which exemplify central tensions between the Puritan worldview and an emerging, science-based modern order. Mather was only indirectly involved in the prosecutions. His writings on the subject, in works such as *The Wonders of the Invisible World* (1693), contain both an apocalyptic narrative of Satan's assaults on godly New England and more neutral descriptions of the supposed supernatural manifestations and the legal proceedings designed to stamp them out. Mather embraced the natural sciences warmly enough to earn election in 1713 into London's prestigious Royal Society, an organization founded in 1660 to promote scientific investigation of the natural world. His later writings included a medical compendium, and he took a public stand in favor of inoculation during Boston's smallpox epidemic in 1721–22. These facets of Mather's intellectual life are not as contradictory as they may appear. He studied the phenomena associated with witchcraft in much the same manner as he sought to understand other physical, mental, and spiritual phenomena.

While these publications suggest a major aspect of Mather's thought, his historical writings are what have earned him a significant place in American literary history. The title page of *Magnalia Christi Americana* (1702) describes this epic work as an "ecclesiastical history of New England." By the time Mather was writing his history of New England, however, the issues that seemed most pressing to his parishioners were political and social rather than theological. Mather defended the old order of church authority against the encroachment of an increasingly secular world, noting in a diary entry for 1700 that "there was hardly any but my father and myself to appear in defense of our invaded churches." But he also recast the Puritan perspective in ethical terms, producing what in essence were "conduct books." These works show him seeking to replace or augment the ever-fragile political power of the clergy with moral chastisement and persuasion. Here again, Mather shared an interest with Benjamin Franklin, whose *Poor Richard's Almanack* (1732–58) offers similar lessons in a more secular idiom. In a society adjusting to new realities, Mather was a worldly Puritan.

From The Wonders of the Invisible World[1]

[A People of God in the Devil's Territories]

The New Englanders are a people of God settled in those, which were once the devil's territories; and it may easily be supposed that the devil was exceedingly disturbed, when he perceived such a people here accomplishing the promise of old made unto our blessed Jesus, that He should have the utmost parts of the earth for His possession.[2] There was not a greater uproar among the Ephesians, when the Gospel was first brought among them,[3] than there was among the powers of the air (after whom those Ephesians walked) when first the silver trumpets of the Gospel here made the joyful sound. The devil thus irritated, immediately tried all sorts of methods

---

1. In May 1692, Governor William Phips of Massachusetts appointed a Court of Oyer and Terminer ("hear and determine") in the cases against some nineteen people in Salem accused of witchcraft. Mather had long been interested in the subject of witchcraft, and in this work, written at the request of the judges, he describes the case against the accused. Mather, like many others, saw the evidence of witchcraft as the devil's work, a last-ditch effort to undermine the Puritan ideal. He was skeptical of much of the evidence used against the accused, especially as the trials proceeded in the summer of 1692, but like a number

of prominent individuals in the community, he made no public protest. The work was first published in 1693; this text is from the reprint published by John Russell Smith in 1862.
2. After Jesus was baptized, he fasted in the desert for forty days; there, the devil tempted him and offered him the world (Luke 4).
3. Ephesus was an ancient city in Asia Minor, famous for its temples to the goddess Diana. When Saint Paul preached there, he received hostile treatment, and riots followed the sermons of missionaries who attempted to convert the Ephesians.

to overturn this poor plantation: and so much of the church, as was fled into this wilderness, immediately found the serpent cast out of his mouth a flood for the carrying of it away. I believe that never were more satanical devices used for the unsettling of any people under the sun, than what have been employed for the extirpation of the vine which God has here planted, casting out the heathen, and preparing a room before it, and causing it to take deep root, and fill the land, so that it sent its boughs unto the Atlantic Sea eastward, and its branches unto the Connecticut River westward, and the hills were covered with a shadow thereof. But all those attempts of hell have hitherto been abortive, many an Ebenezer[4] has been erected unto the praise of God, by his poor people here; and having obtained help from God, we continue to this day. Wherefore the devil is now making one attempt more upon us; an attempt more difficult, more surprising, more snarled with unintelligible circumstances than any that we have hitherto encountered; an attempt so critical, that if we get well through, we shall soon enjoy halcyon days with all the vultures of hell trodden under our feet. He has wanted his incarnate legions to persecute us, as the people of God have in the other hemisphere been persecuted: he has therefore drawn forth his more spiritual ones to make an attack upon us. We have been advised by some credible Christians yet alive, that a malefactor, accused of witchcraft as well as murder, and executed in this place more than forty years ago, did then give notice of an horrible plot against the country by witchcraft, and a foundation of witchcraft then laid, which if it were not seasonably discovered, would probably blow up, and pull down all the churches in the country. And we have now with horror seen the discovery of such a witchcraft! An army of devils is horribly broke in upon the place which is the center, and after a sort, the first-born of our English settlements: and the houses of the good people there are filled with the doleful shrieks of their children and servants, tormented by invisible hands, with tortures altogether preternatural. After the mischiefs there endeavored, and since in part conquered,[5] the terrible plague of evil angels hath made its progress into some other places, where other persons have been in like manner diabolically handled. These our poor afflicted neighbors, quickly after they become infected and infested with these demons, arrive to a capacity of discerning those which they conceive the shapes of their troublers; and notwithstanding the great and just suspicion that the demons might impose the shapes of innocent persons in their spectral exhibitions upon the sufferers (which may perhaps prove no small part of the witch-plot in the issue), yet many of the persons thus represented, being examined, several of them have been convicted of a very damnable witchcraft: yea, more than one [and] twenty have confessed, that they have signed unto a book, which the devil showed them, and engaged in his hellish design of bewitching and ruining our land. We know not, at least I know not, how far the delusions of Satan may be interwoven into some circumstances of the confessions; but one would think all the rules of understanding human affairs are at an end, if after so many most voluntary harmonious

---

4. Stone of help (Hebrew, literal trans.); a commemorative monument like the one Samuel erected to note victory over the Philistines (1 Samuel 7.12).

5. I.e., after the mischiefs were attempted there, and later partly overcome.

confessions, made by intelligent persons of all ages, in sundry towns, at several times, we must not believe the main strokes wherein those confessions all agree: especially when we have a thousand preternatural things every day before our eyes, wherein the confessors do acknowledge their concernment, and give demonstration of their being so concerned. If the devils now can strike the minds of men with any poisons of so fine a composition and operation, that scores of innocent people shall unite, in confessions of a crime, which we see actually committed, it is a thing prodigious, beyond the wonders of the former ages, and it threatens no less than a sort of a dissolution upon the world. Now, by these confessions 'tis agreed that the devil has made a dreadful knot of witches in the country, and by the help of witches has dreadfully increased that knot: that these witches have driven a trade of commissioning their confederate spirits to do all sorts of mischiefs to the neighbors, whereupon there have ensued such mischievous consequences upon the bodies and estates of the neighborhood, as could not otherwise be accounted for: yea, that at prodigious witch-meetings, the wretches have proceeded so far as to concert and consult the methods of rooting out the Christian religion from this country, and setting up instead of it perhaps a more gross diabolism than ever the world saw before. And yet it will be a thing little short of miracle, if in so spread a business as this, the devil should not get in some of his juggles,[6] to confound the discovery of all the rest.

* * *

But I shall no longer detain my reader from his expected entertainment, in a brief account of the trials which have passed upon some of the malefactors lately executed at Salem, for the witchcrafts whereof they stood convicted. For my own part, I was not present at any of them; nor ever had I any personal prejudice at the persons thus brought upon the stage; much less at the surviving relations of those persons, with and for whom I would be as hearty a mourner as any man living in the world: The Lord comfort them! But having received a command so to do,[7] I can do no other than shortly relate the chief matters of fact, which occurred in the trials of some that were executed, in an abridgment collected out of the court papers on this occasion put into my hands. You are to take the truth, just as it was; and the truth will hurt no good man. There might have been more of these, if my book would not thereby have swollen too big; and if some other worthy hands did not perhaps intend something further in these collections; for which cause I have only singled out four or five, which may serve to illustrate the way of dealing, wherein witchcrafts use to be concerned; and I report matters not as an advocate, but as an historian.

* * *

6. Tricks.
7. I.e., having been requested by the judges to write about the trials.

[The Trial of Martha Carrier]

AT THE COURT OF OYER AND TERMINER, HELD BY ADJOURNMENT
AT SALEM, AUGUST 2, 1692

I. Martha Carrier was indicted for the bewitching certain persons, according to the form usual in such cases, pleading not guilty to her indictment; there were first brought in a considerable number of the bewitched persons who not only made the court sensible[8] of an horrid witchcraft committed upon them, but also deposed that it was Martha Carrier, or her shape, that grievously tormented them, by biting, pricking, pinching and choking of them. It was further deposed that while this Carrier was on her examination before the magistrates, the poor people were so tortured that every one expected their death upon the very spot, but that upon the binding of Carrier they were eased. Moreover the look of Carrier then laid the afflicted people for dead; and her touch, if her eye at the same time were off them, raised them again: which things were also now seen upon her trial. And it was testified that upon the mention of some having their necks twisted almost round, by the shape of this Carrier, she replied, "It's no matter though their necks had been twisted quite off."

II. Before the trial of this prisoner, several of her own children had frankly and fully confessed not only that they were witches themselves, but that this their mother had made them so. This confession they made with great shows of repentance, and with much demonstration of truth. They related place, time, occasion; they gave an account of journeys, meetings and mischiefs by them performed, and were very credible in what they said. Nevertheless, this evidence was not produced against the prisoner at the bar,[9] inasmuch as there was other evidence enough to proceed upon.

III. Benjamin Abbot gave his testimony that last March was a twelvemonth,[1] this Carrier was very angry with him, upon laying out some land near her husband's: her expressions in this anger were that she would stick as close to Abbot as the bark stuck to the tree; and that he should repent of it afore seven years came to an end, so as Doctor Prescot should never cure him. These words were heard by others besides Abbot himself; who also heard her say, she would hold his nose as close to the grindstone[2] as ever it was held since his name was Abbot. Presently after this, he was taken with a swelling in his foot, and then with a pain in his side, and exceedingly tormented. It bred into a sore, which was lanced by Doctor Prescot, and several gallons of corruption[3] ran out of it. For six weeks it continued very bad, and then another sore bred in the groin, which was also lanced by Doctor Prescot. Another sore then bred in his groin, which was likewise cut, and put him to very great misery: he was brought unto death's door, and so remained until Carrier was taken, and carried away by the constable, from which [that] very day he began to mend, and so grew better every day, and is well ever since.

8. Aware.
9. I.e., the defendant in court.
1. I.e., a year ago last March.
2. I.e., literally, not metaphorically, press his

face against the revolving sandstone used for grinding, smoothing, etc.
3. Pus; infected matter. "Lanced": cut open.

Sarah Abbot also, his wife, testified that her husband was not only all this while afflicted in his body, but also that strange, extraordinary and unaccountable calamities befell his cattle; their death being such as they could guess at no natural reason for.

IV. Allin Toothaker testified that Richard, the son of Martha Carrier, having some difference with him, pulled him down by the hair of the head. When he rose again he was going to strike at Richard Carrier but fell down flat on his back to the ground, and had not power to stir hand or foot, until he told Carrier he yielded; and then he saw the shape of Martha Carrier go off his breast.

This Toothaker had received a wound in the wars; and he now testified that Martha Carrier told him he should never be cured. Just afore the apprehending of Carrier, he could thrust a knitting needle into his wound four inches deep; but presently after her being seized, he was thoroughly healed.

He further testified that when Carrier and he some times were at variance, she would clap her hands at him, and say he should get nothing by it; whereupon he several times lost his cattle, by strange deaths, whereof no natural causes could be given.

V. John Rogger also testified that upon the threatening words of this malicious Carrier, his cattle would be strangely bewitched; as was more particularly then described.

VI. Samuel Preston testified that about two years ago, having some difference with Martha Carrier, he lost a cow in a strange, preternatural, unusual manner; and about a month after this, the said Carrier, having again some difference with him, she told him he had lately lost a cow, and it should not be long before he lost another; which accordingly came to pass; for he had a thriving and well-kept cow, which without any known cause quickly fell down and died.

VII. Phebe Chandler testified that about a fortnight before the apprehension of Martha Carrier, on a Lordsday,[4] while the Psalm was singing in the Church, this Carrier then took her by the shoulder and shaking her, asked her, where she lived: she made her no answer, although as Carrier, who lived next door to her father's house, could not in reason but know who she was. Quickly after this, as she was at several times crossing the fields, she heard a voice, that she took to be Martha Carrier's, and it seemed as if it was over her head. The voice told her she should within two or three days be poisoned. Accordingly, within such a little time, one half of her right hand became greatly swollen and very painful; as also part of her face: whereof she can give no account how it came. It continued very bad for some days; and several times since she has had a great pain in her breast; and been so seized on her legs that she has hardly been able to go. She added that lately, going well to the house of God, Richard, the son of Martha Carrier, looked very earnestly upon her, and immediately her hand, which had formerly been poisoned, as is abovesaid, began to pain her greatly, and she had a strange burning at her stomach; but was then struck deaf, so that she could not hear any of the prayer, or singing, till the two or three last words of the Psalm.

---

4. Sunday.

VIII. One Foster, who confessed her own share in the witchcraft for which the prisoner stood indicted, affirmed that she had seen the prisoner at some of their witch-meetings, and that it was this Carrier, who persuaded her to be a witch. She confessed that the devil carried them on a pole to a witch-meeting; but the pole broke, and she hanging about Carrier's neck, they both fell down, and she then received an hurt by the fall, whereof she was not at this very time recovered.

IX. One Lacy, who likewise confessed her share in this witchcraft, now testified, that she and the prisoner were once bodily present at a witch-meeting in Salem Village; and that she knew the prisoner to be a witch, and to have been at a diabolical sacrament, and that the prisoner was the undoing of her and her children by enticing them into the snare of the devil.

X. Another Lacy, who also confessed her share in this witchcraft, now testified, that the prisoner was at the witch-meeting, in Salem Village, where they had bread and wine administered unto them.

XI. In the time of this prisoner's trial, one Susanna Sheldon in open court had her hands unaccountably tied together with a wheel-band[5] so fast that without cutting, it could not be loosed: it was done by a specter; and the sufferer affirmed it was the prisoner's.

Memorandum. This rampant hag, Martha Carrier, was the person of whom the confessions of the witches, and of her own children among the rest, agreed that the devil had promised her she should be Queen of Hebrews.

1692   1693

---

5. A strap that goes around a wheel.

JONATHAN EDWARDS
1703–1758

A pivotal figure in American literary history, the Puritan minister Jonathan Edwards created a fresh prose style that integrated contemporary theories of sensation with traditional Calvinist theology. Edwards spoke and wrote in a manner designed to give his audiences an almost visceral sense of spiritual realities. To appreciate his achievements as a religious writer, it may be helpful to consider how Edwards's focus on sensation distinguishes his prose from that of his older contemporary Cotton Mather. In many ways, Edwards and Mather were engaged in the same project, that is, updating the Calvinist tradition for their own time. Born forty years apart, both men were members of powerful New England religious dynasties, and they were also both active members of the Atlantic-world republic of letters, with an interest in the latest scientific ideas. As a writer, however, Mather frequently oriented himself toward the past, creating the baroque style that reached its apex in *Magnalia Christi Americana* (1702). Edwards focused instead on giving his audiences an immediate experience of "divine things" that could rival and even exceed the perceptions conveyed by the physical senses. The appeal of his rhetoric of sensation, as it has been called, was its capacity to make invisible things vividly present. Those things might be the theological tenets and spiritual experiences that Edwards held to be divine truths, or they might be the life stories of young girls and women (including his wife, Sarah Pierpont Edwards) that appealed to readers of the novel, a genre becoming prominent in Edwards's lifetime. Edwards is a central figure in American literary history, then, because of the way his works influenced the development of both religious and secular prose.

Born in East Windsor, Connecticut, a town not far from the major city of Hartford, Edwards was the son of the Reverend Timothy Edwards and Esther Stoddard Edwards. Edwards's mother was the daughter of the Reverend Solomon Stoddard, of Northampton, Massachusetts, one of the most influential figures in the religious life of New England. Stoddard's gifted grandson, the only male child in a family of eleven children, was groomed to be his heir. Studious and dutiful, Edwards showed remarkable gifts of observation and exposition from a young age. When he was eleven, he wrote an essay, still very readable, on the flying spider. At thirteen, he was admitted to Yale College, in New Haven; he stayed on to read theology for two years after his graduation. He was determined to perfect himself, and in one of his early notebooks he resolved "never to lose one moment of time, but to improve it in the most profitable way" he could. As a student, he always rose at four in the morning, studied thirteen hours a day, and reserved part of each day for walking. Edwards varied this routine little, even when—after two years in New York City, assisting at a Presbyterian church—he went to Northampton to assist his grandfather in his church. In 1727, he married Sarah Pierpont, a young woman from a leading New Haven clerical family. Two years later, Solomon Stoddard died, and Edwards succeeded him. In the twenty-four years that Edwards lived in Northampton, he fulfilled his duties as the pastor of a growing congregation and delivered brilliant sermons, wrote some of his most important books—concerned primarily with defining true religious experience—and raised his eleven children.

Until the mid-1740s, his relations with the town were harmonious. This period included the early years of the Great Awakening, when a spirit of revivalism transformed complacent believers all along the eastern seaboard, beginning in 1734. At first, Edwards could do no wrong. His meetinghouse was filled with converts, and his works describing the revivals were widely published and distributed on both sides of the Atlantic. But in his attempt to restore the church to the position of authority it held in the years of his grandfather's ministry, Edwards went too far. He berated people for becoming too secularized, named backsliders from his pulpit—including members of the best families in town—and tried to return to the old order of communion, permitting the sacrament to be taken only by those who had publicly declared themselves to be saved. Throughout the Connecticut River Valley, people were tired of religious controversy, and the hysterical behavior of a few fanatics turned many against the spirit of revivalism. On June 22, 1750, by a vote of two hundred to twenty, Edwards was dismissed from his church. Although the congregation had difficulty naming a successor, they preferred to have no sermons rather than let Edwards preach.

For the next seven years, Edwards served as missionary to the Housatonic Indians in Stockbridge, Massachusetts, a town thirty-five miles west of Northampton. Founded after the 1735 Treaty of Deerfield, Stockbridge was a product of the chronic imperial warfare—between British, French, and Native forces—that disrupted western New England throughout Edwards's lifetime. At Stockbridge, Edwards wrote his monumental treatises on free will and on true virtue as "that consent, propensity, and union of heart to Being in general, that is immediately exercised in a general good will." Edwards then received, very reluctantly, a call to become president of the College of New Jersey (later renamed Princeton University) after the Reverend Aaron Burr, Sr.—Edwards's son-in-law, who had been serving as the new college's president—died of fever and overwork. However, just three months after his arrival in Princeton, Edwards died of smallpox, the result of his inoculation to prevent infection.

All of Edwards's work is of a piece and, in essence, readily graspable. He was trying to restore to his congregation and to his readers that original sense of religious commitment that he felt had been lost since the first days of the Puritan exodus to America, and he wanted to do this by transforming his congregation from mere believers who understood the logic of Christian doctrine to converted Christians who were genuinely moved by the principles of their belief. Edwards wrote that he read the work of the English philosopher John Locke (1632–1704) with more pleasure "than the greedy miser finds when gathering up handfuls of silver and gold, from some newly discovered treasure." Locke confirmed Edwards's conviction that people must do more than comprehend religious ideas; they must be *moved* by them and come to know them experientially: the difference, as he says, is like that between reading the word "fire" and actually being burned. Basic to this newly felt belief is the recognition that nothing that an individual can do warrants his or her salvation, that people are motivated entirely by self-love, and only supernatural grace alters their natural depravity. Edwards says that he experienced several steps toward real Christian commitment but that his true conversion came only when he had achieved a "full and constant sense of the absolute sovereignty of God, and a delight in that sovereignty."

The word "delight" reminds us that Edwards was trying to inculcate and describe a religious feeling that approximates a physical sensation. He held that divine grace produced a new sense in the religious convert, which he sometimes analogized to taste. He believed this new sense would enable the convert to respond to God in more vital ways. "Delight" further links him to the transatlantic community of those who recognized sentiment as the basic emotion that connects individuals to one another. In his patient and lucid prose, Edwards became a master at the art of persuading his congregants and readers that they could—and *must*—possess an intense awareness of humanity's precarious condition and experience the joys and pleasures of grace.

Personal Narrative[1]

I had a variety of concerns and exercises about my soul from my childhood; but had two more remarkable seasons of awakening[2] before I met with that change, by which I was brought to those new dispositions, and that new sense of things, that I have since had. The first time was when I was a boy, some years before I went to college, at a time of remarkable awakening in my father's congregation. I was then very much affected[3] for many months, and concerned about the things of religion, and my soul's salvation; and was abundant in duties. I used to pray five times a day in secret, and to spend much time in religious talk with other boys; and used to meet with them to pray together. I experienced I know not what kind of delight in religion. My mind was much engaged in it, and had much self-righteous pleasure; and it was my delight to abound in religious duties. I, with some of my schoolmates joined together, and built a booth in a swamp, in a very secret and retired place, for a place of prayer. And besides, I had particular secret places of my own in the woods, where I used to retire by myself; and used to be from time to time much affected. My affections seemed to be lively and easily moved, and I seemed to be in my element, when engaged in religious duties. And I am ready to think, many are deceived with such affections, and such a kind of delight, as I then had in religion, and mistake it for grace.

But in process of time, my convictions and affections wore off; and I entirely lost all those affections and delights, and left off secret prayer, at least as to any constant performance of it; and returned like a dog to his vomit, and went on in ways of sin.[4]

Indeed, I was at some times very uneasy, especially towards the latter part of the time of my being at college.[5] Till it pleased God, in my last year at college, at a time when I was in the midst of many uneasy thoughts about the state of my soul, to seize me with a pleurisy;[6] in which he brought me nigh to the grave, and shook me over the pit of hell.

But yet, it was not long after my recovery, before I fell again into my old ways of sin. But God would not suffer me to go on with any quietness; but I had great and violent inward struggles: till after many conflicts with wicked inclinations, and repeated resolutions, and bonds that I laid myself under by a kind of vows to God, I was brought wholly to break off all former wicked ways, and all ways of known outward sin; and to apply myself to seek my salvation, and practice the duties of religion: but without that kind of affection and delight, that I had formerly experienced. My concern now wrought more by inward struggles and conflicts, and self-reflections. I made seeking

---

1. Because of Edwards's reference to an evening in January 1739, he must have written this essay after that date. Edwards's reasons for writing it are not known, and it was not published in his lifetime. After his death, his friend Samuel Hopkins had access to his manuscripts and prepared *The Life and Character of the Late Rev. Mr. Jonathan Edwards*, which was published in 1765. In that volume, the "Personal Narrative" appeared in section IV as the chapter "An Account of His Conversion, Experiences, and Religious Exercises, Given by Himself." The text here is from *Works of Jonathan Edwards* (1998), vol. 16, edited by George Claghorn.

2. I.e., spiritual awakenings, renewals. "Exercises": agitations.

3. Emotionally aroused, as opposed to merely understanding rationally the arguments for Christian faith.

4. "As a dog returneth to his vomit, so a fool returneth to his folly" (Proverbs 26.11).

5. Edwards was an undergraduate at Yale from 1716 to 1720 and a divinity student from 1720 to 1722.

6. A respiratory disorder.

my salvation the main business of my life. But yet it seems to me, I sought after a miserable manner: which has made me sometimes since to question, whether ever it issued in that which was saving;[7] being ready to doubt, whether such miserable seeking was ever succeeded. But yet I was brought to seek salvation, in a manner that I never was before. I felt a spirit to part with all things in the world, for an interest in Christ. My concern continued and prevailed, with many exercising things and inward struggles; but yet it never seemed to be proper to express my concern that I had, by the name of terror.

From my childhood up, my mind had been wont to be full of objections against the doctrine of God's sovereignty, in choosing whom He would to eternal life and rejecting whom he pleased; leaving them eternally to perish, and be everlastingly tormented in hell. It used to appear like a horrible doctrine to me. But I remember the time very well, when I seemed to be convinced, and fully satisfied, as to this sovereignty of God, and his justice in thus eternally disposing of men, according to his sovereign pleasure. But never could give an account, how, or by what means, I was thus convinced; not in the least imagining, in the time of it, nor a long time after, that there was any extraordinary influence of God's Spirit in it: but only that now I saw further, and my reason apprehended the justice and reasonableness of it. However, my mind rested in it; and it put an end to all those cavils and objections, that had till then abode with me, all the preceeding part of my life. And there has been a wonderful alteration in my mind, with respect to the doctrine of God's sovereignty, from that day to this; so that I scarce ever have found so much as the rising of an objection against God's sovereignty, in the most absolute sense, in showing mercy on whom he will show mercy, and hardening and eternally damning whom he will.[8] God's absolute sovereignty, and justice, with respect to salvation and damnation, is what my mind seems to rest assured of, as much as of anything that I see with my eyes; at least it is so at times. But I have oftentimes since that first conviction, had quite another kind of sense of God's sovereignty, than I had then. I have often since, not only had a conviction, but a *delightful* conviction. The doctrine of God's sovereignty has very often appeared, an exceeding pleasant, bright and sweet doctrine to me: and absolute sovereignty is what I love to ascribe to God. But my first conviction was not with this.

The first that I remember that ever I found anything of that sort of inward, sweet delight in God and divine things, that I have lived much in since, was on reading those words, 1 Tim. 1.17, "Now unto the King eternal, immortal, invisible, the only wise God, be honor and glory for ever and ever, Amen." As I read the words, there came into my soul, and was as it were diffused through it, a sense of the glory of the divine being, a new sense, quite different from anything I ever experienced before. Never any words of Scripture seemed to me as these words did. I thought with myself, how excellent a Being that was; and how happy I should be, if I might enjoy that God, and be wrapt[9] up to God in heaven, and be as it were swallowed up in him. I kept saying, and as it were singing over these words of Scripture to myself;

---

7. I.e., truly redeeming, capable of making the penitent a "saint."
8. "Therefore hath he mercy on whom he will have mercy, and whom he will he hardeneth" (Romans 9.18).
9. Lifted.

and went to prayer, to pray to God that I might enjoy him; and prayed in a manner quite different from what I used to do, with a new sort of affection. But it never came into my thought, that there was anything spiritual, or of a saving nature in this.

From about that time, I began to have a new kind of apprehensions and ideas of Christ, and the work of redemption, and the glorious way of salvation by him. I had an inward, sweet sense of these things, that at times came into my heart; and my soul was led away in pleasant views and contemplations of them. And my mind was greatly engaged, to spend my time in reading and meditating on Christ; and the beauty and excellency of his person, and the lovely way of salvation, by free grace in him. I found no books so delightful to me, as those that treated of these subjects. Those words (Cant. 2:1) used to be abundantly with me: "I am the rose of Sharon, the lily of the valleys." The words seemed to me, sweetly to represent, the loveliness and beauty of Jesus Christ. And the whole book of Canticles[1] used to be pleasant to me; and I used to be much in reading it, about that time. And found, from time to time, an inward sweetness, that used, as it were, to carry me away in my contemplations; in what I know not how to express otherwise, than by a calm, sweet abstraction of soul from all the concerns o[f] this world; and a kind of vision, or fixed ideas and imaginations, of being alone in the mountains, or some solitary wilderness, far from all mankind, sweetly conversing with Christ, and wrapt and swallowed up in God. The sense I had of divine things, would often of a sudden as it were, kindle up a sweet burning in my heart; an ardor of my soul, that I know not how to express.

Not long after I first began to experience these things, I gave an account to my father, of some things that had passed in my mind. I was pretty much affected by the discourse we had together. And when the discourse was ended, I walked abroad alone, in a solitary place in my father's pasture, for contemplation. And as I was walking there, and looked up on the sky and clouds; there came into my mind, a sweet sense of the glorious majesty and grace of God, that I know not how to express. I seemed to see them both in a sweet conjunction: majesty and meekness joined together: it was a sweet and gentle, and holy majesty; and also a majestic meekness; an awful sweetness; a high, and great, and holy gentleness.

After this my sense of divine things gradually increased, and became more and more lively, and had more of that inward sweetness. The appearance of everything was altered: there seemed to be, as it were, a calm, sweet cast, or appearance of divine glory, in almost everything. God's excellency, his wisdom, his purity and love, seemed to appear in everything; in the sun, moon and stars; in the clouds, and blue sky; in the grass, flowers, trees; in the water, and all nature; which used greatly to fix my mind. I often used to sit and view the moon, for a long time; and so in the daytime, spent much time in viewing the clouds and sky, to behold the sweet glory of God in these things: in the meantime, singing forth with a low voice, my contemplations of the Creator and Redeemer. And scarce anything, among all the works of nature, was so sweet to me as thunder and lightning. Formerly, nothing had been so terrible to me. I used to be a person uncommonly terrified with thunder: and it used to strike me with terror, when I saw a thunderstorm rising.

---

1. I.e., Song of Solomon.

But now, on the contrary, it rejoiced me. I felt God at the first appearance of a thunderstorm. And used to take the opportunity at such times, to fix myself to view the clouds, and see the lightnings play, and hear the majestic and awful voice of God's thunder: which often times was exceeding entertaining, leading me to sweet contemplations of my great and glorious God. And while I viewed, used to spend my time, as it always seemed natural to me, to sing or chant forth my meditations; to speak my thoughts in soliloquies, and speak with a singing voice.

I felt then a great satisfaction as to my good estate.[2] But that did not content me. I had vehement longings of soul after God and Christ, and after more holiness; wherewith my heart seemed to be full, and ready to break: which often brought to my mind, the words of the Psalmist, Ps. 119:28, "My soul breaketh for the longing it hath." I often felt a mourning and lamenting in my heart, that I had not turned to God sooner, that I might have had more time to grow in grace. My mind was greatly fixed on divine things; I was almost perpetually in the contemplation of them. Spent most of my time in thinking of divine things, year after year. And used to spend abundance of my time, in walking alone in the woods, and solitary places, for meditation, soliloquy and prayer, and converse with God. And it was always my manner, at such times, to sing forth my contemplations. And was almost constantly in ejaculatory[3] prayer, wherever I was. Prayer seemed to be natural to me; as the breath, by which the inward burnings of my heart had vent.

The delights which I now felt in things of religion, were of an exceeding different kind, from those forementioned, that I had when I was a boy. They were totally of another kind; and what I then had no more notion or idea of, than one born blind has of pleasant and beautiful colors. They were of a more inward, pure, soul-animating and refreshing nature. Those former delights, never reached the heart; and did not arise from any sight of the divine excellency of the things of God; or any taste of the soul-satisfying, and life-giving good, there is in them.

My sense of divine things seemed gradually to increase, till I went to preach at New York; which was about a year and a half after they began. While I was there, I felt them, very sensibly,[4] in a much higher degree, than I had done before. My longings after God and holiness, were much increased. Pure and humble, holy and heavenly Christianity, appeared exceeding amiable to me. I felt in me a burning desire to be in everything a complete Christian; and conformed to the blessed image of Christ: and that I might live in all things, according to the pure, sweet and blessed rules of the gospel. I had an eager thirsting after progress in these things. My longings after it, put me upon pursuing and pressing after them. It was my continual strife day and night, and constant inquiry, how I should be more holy, and live more holily, and more becoming a child of God, and disciple of Christ. I sought an increase of grace and holiness, and that I might live an holy life, with vastly more earnestness, than ever I sought grace, before I had it. I used to be continually examining myself, and studying and contriving for likely ways and means, how I should live holily, with far greater diligence and earnestness, than ever I pursued anything in my life: but with too great a

2. Condition of being.
3. I.e., exclaimed suddenly, blurted out spontaneously.
4. Feelingly.

dependence on my own strength, which afterwards proved a great damage to me. My experience had not then taught me, as it has done since, my extreme feebleness and impotence, every manner of way; and the innumerable and bottomless depths of secret corruption and deceit, that there was in my heart. However, I went on with my eager pursuit after more holiness; and sweet conformity to Christ.

The Heaven I desired was a heaven of holiness; to be with God, and to spend my eternity in divine love, and holy communion with Christ. My mind was very much taken up with contemplations on heaven, and the enjoyments of those there; and living there in perfect holiness, humility and love. And it used at that time to appear a great part of the happiness of heaven, that there the saints could express their love to Christ. It appeared to me a great clog and hindrance and burden to me, that what I felt within, I could not express to God, and give vent to, as I desired. The inward ardor of my soul, seemed to be hindered and pent up, and could not freely flame out as it would. I used often to think, how in heaven, this sweet principle should freely and fully vent and express itself. Heaven appeared to me exceeding delightful as a world of love. It appeared to me, that all happiness consisted in living in pure, humble, heavenly, divine love.

I remember the thoughts I used then to have of holiness. I remember I then said sometimes to myself, I do certainly know that I love holiness, such as the gospel prescribes. It appeared to me, there was nothing in it but what was ravishingly lovely. It appeared to me, to be the highest beauty and amiableness, above all other beauties: that it was a divine beauty; far purer than anything here upon earth; and that everything else, was like mire, filth and defilement, in comparison of it.

Holiness, as I then wrote down some of my contemplations on it, appeared to me to be of a sweet, pleasant, charming, serene, calm nature. It seemed to me, it brought an inexpressible purity, brightness, peacefulness and ravishment to the soul: and that it made the soul like a field or garden of God, with all manner of pleasant flowers; that is all pleasant, delightful and undisturbed; enjoying a sweet calm, and the gently vivifying beams of the sun. The soul of a true Christian, as I then wrote my meditations, appeared like such a little white flower, as we see in the spring of the year; low and humble on the ground, opening its bosom, to receive the pleasant beams of the sun's glory; rejoicing as it were, in a calm rapture; diffusing around a sweet fragrancy; standing peacefully and lovingly, in the midst of other flowers round about; all in like manner opening their bosoms, to drink in the light of the sun.

There was no part of creature-holiness, that I then, and at other times, had so great a sense of the loveliness of, as humility, brokenness of heart and poverty of spirit: and there was nothing that I had such a spirit to long for. My heart, as it were, panted after this to lie low before GOD, and in the dust; that I might be nothing, and that God might be all; that I might become as a little child.[5]

While I was there at New York, I sometimes was much affected with reflections on my past life, considering how late it was, before I began to be truly

---

5. "Verily I say unto you, Whosoever shall not receive the kingdom of God as a little child, he shall not enter therein" (Mark 10.15).

religious; and how wickedly I had lived till then: and once so as to weep abundantly, and for a considerable time together.

On January 12, 1722–3, I made a solemn dedication of myself to God, and wrote it down; giving up myself, and all that I had to God; to be for the future in no respect my own; to act as one that had no right to himself, in any respect. And solemnly vowed to take God for my whole portion and felicity; looking on nothing else as any part of my happiness, nor acting as if it were: and his law for the constant rule of my obedience; engaging to fight with all my might, against the world, the flesh and the devil, to the end of my life. But have reason to be infinitely humbled, when I consider, how much I have failed of answering my obligation.

I had then abundance of sweet religious conversation in the family where I lived, with Mr. John Smith, and his pious mother. My heart was knit in affection to those, in whom were appearances of true piety; and I could bear the thoughts of no other companions, but such as were holy, and the disciples of the blessed Jesus.

I had great longings for the advancement of Christ's kingdom in the world. My secret prayer used to be in great part taken up in praying for it. If I heard the least hint of anything that happened in any part of the world, that appeared to me, in some respect or other, to have a favorable aspect on the interest of Christ's kingdom, my soul eagerly catched at it; and it would much animate and refresh me. I used to be earnest to read public newsletters, mainly for that end; to see if I could not find some news favorable to the interest of religion in the world.

I very frequently used to retire into a solitary place, on the banks of Hudson's River, at some distance from the city, for contemplation on divine things, and secret converse with God; and had many sweet hours there. Sometimes Mr. Smith and I walked there together, to converse of the things of God; and our conversation used much to turn on the advancement of Christ's kingdom in the world, and the glorious things that God would accomplish for his church in the latter days.

I had then, and at other times, the greatest delight in the holy Scriptures, of any book whatsoever. Oftentimes in reading it, every word seemed to touch my heart. I felt an harmony between something in my heart, and those sweet and powerful words. I seemed often to see so much light, exhibited by every sentence, and such a refreshing ravishing food communicated, that I could not get along in reading. Used oftentimes to dwell long on one sentence, to see the wonders contained in it; and yet almost every sentence seemed to be full of wonders.

I came away from New York in the month of April 1723, and had a most bitter parting with Madam Smith and her son. My heart seemed to sink within me, at leaving the family and city, where I had enjoyed so many sweet and pleasant days. I went from New York to Weathersfield[6] by water. As I sailed away, I kept sight of the city as long as I could; and when I was out of sight of it, it would affect me much to look that way, with a kind of melancholy mixed with sweetness. However, that night after this sorrowful parting, I was greatly comforted in God at Westchester, where we went ashore to lodge: and had a pleasant time of it all the voyage to Saybrook.[7] It was sweet to me to think of

6. Wethersfield, Connecticut, is very close to Windsor.

7. Westchester and Saybrook are in New York and Connecticut, respectively.

meeting dear Christians in heaven, where we should never part more. At Saybrook we went ashore to lodge on Saturday, and there kept sabbath; where I had a sweet and refreshing season, walking alone in the fields.

After I came home to Windsor, remained much in a like frame of my mind, as I had been in at New York; but only sometimes felt my heart ready to sink, with the thoughts of my friends at New York. And my refuge and support was in contemplations on the heavenly state; as I find in my diary of May 1, 1723. It was my comfort to think of that state, where there is fulness of joy; where reigns heavenly, sweet, calm and delightful love, without alloy; where there are continually the dearest expressions of this love; where is the enjoyment of the persons loved, without ever parting; where these persons that appear so lovely in this world, will really be inexpressibly more lovely, and full of love to us. And how sweetly will the mutual lovers join together to sing the praises of God and the Lamb![8] How full will it fill us with joy, to think, that this enjoyment, these sweet exercises will never cease or come to an end; but will last to all eternity!

Continued much in the same frame in the general, that I had been in at New York, till I went to New Haven, to live there as Tutor of the College; having some special season of uncommon sweetness: particularly once at Bolton,[9] in a journey from Boston, walking out alone in the fields. After I went to New Haven, I sunk in religion; my mind being diverted from my eager and violent[1] pursuits after holiness, by some affairs that greatly perplexed and distracted my mind.

In September 1725, was taken ill at New Haven; and endeavoring to go home to Windsor, was so ill at the North Village, that I could go no further: where I lay sick for about a quarter of a year. And in this sickness, God was pleased to visit me again with the sweet influences of his spirit. My mind was greatly engaged there on divine, pleasant contemplations, and longings of soul. I observed that those who watched with me, would often be looking out for the morning, and seemed to wish for it. Which brought to my mind those words of the Psalmist, which my soul with sweetness made its own language, "My soul waiteth for the Lord more than they that watch for the morning: I say, more than they that watch for the morning."[2] And when the light of the morning came, and the beams of the sun came in at the windows, it refreshed my soul from one morning to another. It seemed to me to be some image of the sweet light of God's glory.

I remember, about that time, I used greatly to long for the conversion of some that I was concerned with. It seemed to me, I could gladly honor them, and with delight be a servant to them, and lie at their feet, if they were but truly holy.

But sometime after this, I was again greatly diverted in my mind, with some temporal concerns, that exceedingly took up my thoughts, greatly to the wounding of my soul: and went on through various exercises, that it would be tedious to relate, that gave me much more experience of my own heart, than ever I had before.

---

8. In the Book of Revelation, the symbol of Christ.
9. A town in Massachusetts, twenty-five miles from Boston.
1. I.e., intense, passionate, uncontrollable.
2. Psalm 130.6.

Since I came to this town, I have often had sweet complacency[3] in God in views of his glorious perfections, and the excellency of Jesus Christ. God has appeared to me, a glorious and lovely being, chiefly on the account of his holiness. The holiness of God has always appeared to me the most lovely of all his attributes. The doctrines of God's absolute sovereignty, and free grace, in showing mercy to whom he would show mercy; and man's absolute dependence on the operations of God's Holy Spirit, have very often appeared to me as sweet and glorious doctrines. These doctrines have been much my delight. God's sovereignty has ever appeared to me, as great part of his glory. It has often been sweet to me to go to God, and adore him as a sovereign God, and ask sovereign mercy of him.

I have loved the doctrines of the gospel: they have been to my soul like green pastures.[4] The gospel has seemed to me to be the richest treasure; the treasure that I have most desired, and longed that it might dwell richly in me. The way of salvation by Christ, has appeared in a general way, glorious and excellent, and most pleasant and beautiful. It has often seemed to me, that it would in a great measure spoil heaven, to receive it in any other way. That text has often been affecting and delightful to me, Is. 32:2, "A man shall be an hiding place from the wind, and a covert from the tempest," etc.

It has often appeared sweet to me, to be united to Christ; to have him for my head, and to be a member of his body: and also to have Christ for my teacher and prophet. I very often think with sweetness and longings and pantings of soul, of being a little child, taking hold of Christ, to be led by him through the wilderness of this world. That text, Matt. 18 at the beginning, has often been sweet to me, "Except ye be converted, and become as little children," etc. I love to think of coming to Christ, to receive salvation of him, poor in spirit, and quite empty of self; humbly exalting him alone; cut entirely off from my own root, and to grow into, and out of Christ: to have God in Christ to be all in all; and to live by faith in the Son of God, a life of humble, unfeigned confidence in him. That Scripture has often been sweet to me, Ps. 115:1, "Not unto us, O Lord, not unto us, but unto thy name give glory, for thy mercy, and for thy truth's sake." And those words of Christ, Luke 10:21, "In that hour Jesus rejoiced in spirit, and said, I thank thee, O Father, Lord of heaven and earth, that thou hast hid these things from the wise and prudent, and hast revealed them unto babes: even so Father, for so it seemed good in thy sight." That sovereignty of God that Christ rejoiced in, seemed to me to be worthy to be rejoiced in; and that rejoicing of Christ, seemed to me to show the excellency of Christ, and the spirit that he was of.

Sometimes only mentioning a single word, causes my heart to burn within me: or only seeing the name of Christ, or the name of some attribute of God. And God has appeared glorious to me, on account of the Trinity. It has made me have exalting thoughts of God, that he subsists in three persons; Father, Son, and Holy Ghost.

The sweetest joys and delights I have experienced, have not been those that have arisen from a hope of my own good estate; but in a direct view of

3. Contentment. "This town": Northampton.
4. Edwards alludes to Psalm 23.2: "He maketh me to lie down in green pastures: he leadeth me beside the still waters."

the glorious things of the gospel. When I enjoy this sweetness, it seems to carry me above the thoughts of my own safe estate. It seems at such times a loss that I cannot bear, to take off my eye from the glorious, pleasant object I behold without me, to turn my eye in upon myself, and my own good estate.

My heart has been much on the advancement of Christ's kingdom in the world. The histories of the past advancement of Christ's kingdom, have been sweet to me. When I have read histories of past ages, the pleasantest thing in all my reading has been, to read of the kingdom of Christ being promoted. And when I have expected in my reading, to come to any such thing, I have lotted[5] upon it all the way as I read. And my mind has been much entertained and delighted, with the Scripture promises and prophecies, of the future glorious advancement of Christ's kingdom on earth.

I have sometimes had a sense of the excellent fullness of Christ, and his meetness and suitableness as a Savior; whereby he has appeared to me, far above all, the chief of ten thousands.[6] And his blood and atonement has appeared sweet, and his righteousness sweet; which is always accompanied with an ardency of spirit, and inward strugglings and breathings and groanings, that cannot be uttered, to be emptied of myself, and swallowed up in Christ.

Once, as I rid out into the woods for my health, *anno*[7] 1737; and having lit from my horse in a retired place, as my manner commonly has been, to walk for divine contemplation and prayer; I had a view, that for me was extraordinary, of the glory of the Son of God; as mediator between God and man; and his wonderful, great, full, pure and sweet grace and love, and meek and gentle condescension.[8] This grace, that appeared to me so calm and sweet, appeared great above the heavens. The person of Christ appeared ineffably excellent, with an excellency great enough to swallow up all thought and conception. Which continued, as near as I can judge, about an hour; which kept me, the bigger part of the time, in a flood of tears, and weeping aloud. I felt withal, an ardency of soul to be, what I know not otherwise how to express, than to be emptied and annihilated; to lie in the dust, and to be full of Christ alone; to love him with a holy and pure love; to trust in him; to live upon him; to serve and follow him, and to be totally wrapt up in the fullness of Christ; and to be perfectly sanctified and made pure, with a divine and heavenly purity. I have several other times, had views very much of the same nature, and that have had the same effects.

I have many times had a sense of the glory of the third person in the Trinity, in his office of Sanctifier; in his holy operations communicating divine light and life to the soul. God in the communications of his Holy Spirit, has appeared as an infinite fountain of divine glory and sweetness; being full and sufficient to fill and satisfy the soul: pouring forth itself in sweet communications, like the sun in its glory, sweetly and pleasantly diffusing light and life.

I have sometimes had an affecting sense of the excellency of the word of God, as a word of life; as the light of life; a sweet, excellent, life-giving word:

---

5. Rejoiced.
6. "My beloved is white and ruddy, the chiefest among ten thousand" (Song of Solomon 5.10).

7. In the year (Latin).
8. Regard for those of lesser status.

accompanied with a thirsting after that word, that it might dwell richly in my heart.

I have often since I lived in this town, had very affecting views of my own sinfulness and vileness; very frequently so as to hold me in a kind of loud weeping, sometimes for a considerable time together: so that I have often been forced to shut myself up.[9] I have had a vastly greater sense of my wickedness, and the badness of my heart, since my conversion, than ever I had before. It has often appeared to me, that if God should mark iniquity against me, I should appear the very worst of all mankind; of all that have been since the beginning of the world of this time: and that I should have by far the lowest place in hell. When others that have come to talk with me about their soul concerns, have expressed the sense they have had of their own wickedness, by saying that it seemed to them, that they were as bad as the devil himself; I thought their expressions seemed exceeding faint and feeble, to represent my wickedness. I thought I should wonder, that they should content themselves with such expressions as these, if I had any reason to imagine, that their sin bore any proportion to mine. It seemed to me, I should wonder at myself, if I should express my wickedness in such feeble terms as they did.

My wickedness, as I am in myself, has long appeared to me perfectly ineffable, and infinitely swallowing up all thought and imagination; like an infinite deluge, or infinite mountains over my head. I know not how to express better, what my sins appear to me to be, than by heaping infinite upon infinite, and multiplying infinite by infinite. I go about very often, for this many years, with these expressions in my mind, and in my mouth, "Infinite upon infinite. Infinite upon infinite!" When I look into my heart, and take a view of my wickedness, it looks like an abyss infinitely deeper than hell. And it appears to me, that were it not for free grace, exalted and raised up to the infinite height of all the fullness and glory of the great Jehovah,[1] and the arm of his power and grace stretched forth, in all the majesty of his power, and in all the glory of his sovereignty; I should appear sunk down in my sins infinitely below hell itself, far beyond sight of everything, but the piercing eye of God's grace, that can pierce even down to such a depth, and to the bottom of such an abyss.

And yet, I ben't in the least inclined to think, that I have a greater conviction of sin than ordinary. It seems to me, my conviction of sin is exceeding small, and faint. It appears to me enough to amaze me, that I have no more sense of my sin. I know certainly, that I have very little sense of my sinfulness. That my sins appear to me so great, don't seem to me to be, because I have so much more conviction of sin than other Christians, but because I am so much worse, and have so much more wickedness to be convinced of. When I have had these turns of weeping and crying for my sins, I thought I knew in the time of it, that my repentance was nothing to my sin.

I have greatly longed of late, for a broken heart, and to lie low before God. And when I ask for humility of God, I can't bear the thoughts of being no more humble, than other Christians. It seems to me, that though their degrees of humility may be suitable for them; yet it would be a vile self-exaltation in

9. I.e., retire to his study.   1. The name used for God in the Old Testament.

me, not to be the lowest in humility of all mankind. Others speak of their longing to be humbled to the dust. Though that may be a proper expression for them, I always think for myself, that I ought to be humbled down below hell. 'Tis an expression that it has long been natural for me to use in prayer to God. I ought to lie infinitely low before God.

It is affecting to me to think, how ignorant I was, when I was a young Christian, of the bottomless, infinite depths of wickedness, pride, hypocrisy and deceit left in my heart.

I have vastly a greater sense, of my universal, exceeding dependence on God's grace and strength, and mere good pleasure, of late, than I used formerly to have; and have experienced more of an abhorrence of my own righteousness. The thought of any comfort or joy, arising in me, on any consideration, or reflection on my own amiableness, or any of my performances or experiences, or any goodness of heart or life, is nauseous and detestable to me. And yet I am greatly afflicted with a proud and self-righteous spirit; much more sensibly, than I used to be formerly. I see that serpent rising and putting forth its head, continually, everywhere, all around me.

Though it seems to me, that in some respects I was a far better Christian, for two or three years after my first conversion, than I am now; and lived in a more constant delight and pleasure: yet of late years, I have had a more full and constant sense of the absolute sovereignty of God, and a delight in that sovereignty; and have had more of a sense of the glory of Christ, as a mediator, as revealed in the Gospel. On one Saturday night in particular, had a particular discovery of the excellency of the gospel of Christ, above all other doctrines; so that I could not but say to myself; "This is my chosen light, my chosen doctrine": and of Christ, "This is my chosen prophet." It appeared to me to be sweet beyond all expression, to follow Christ, and to be taught and enlightened and instructed by him; to learn of him, and live to him.

Another Saturday night, January 1738–9, had such a sense, how sweet and blessed a thing it was, to walk in the way of duty, to do that which was right and meet to be done, and agreeable to the holy mind of God; that it caused me to break forth into a kind of a loud weeping, which held me some time; so that I was forced to shut myself up, and fasten the doors. I could not but as it were cry out, "How happy are they which do that which is right in the sight of God! They are blessed indeed, they are the happy ones!" I had at the same time, a very affecting sense, how meet and suitable it was that God should govern the world, and order all things according to his own pleasure; and I rejoiced in it, that God reigned, and that his will was done.

c. 1740   1765

A Divine and Supernatural Light[1]

IMMEDIATELY IMPARTED TO THE SOUL BY THE SPIRIT OF GOD, SHOWN TO BE BOTH A SCRIPTURAL AND RATIONAL DOCTRINE

Matthew 16.17

> And Jesus answered and said unto him, Blessed art thou, Simon Barjona;[2] for flesh and blood hath not revealed it unto thee, but my Father which is in heaven.

Christ addresses these words to Peter upon occasion of his professing his faith in Him as the Son of God. Our Lord was inquiring of His disciples, whom men said that He was; not that He needed to be informed, but only to introduce and give occasion to what follows. They answer that some said He was John the Baptist, and some Elias, and others Jeremias, or one of the prophets.[3] When they had thus given an account whom others said that He was, Christ asks them, whom they said that He was? Simon Peter, whom we find always zealous and forward, was the first to answer: he readily replied to the question, Thou art Christ, the Son of the living God.

Upon this occasion, Christ says as He does to him and of him in the text: in which we may observe.

1. That Peter is pronounced blessed on this account.—Blessed art thou— "Thou art an happy man, that thou art not ignorant of this, that I am Christ, the Son of the living God. Thou art distinguishingly happy. Others are blinded, and have dark and deluded apprehensions, as you have now given an account, some thinking that I am Elias, and some that I am Jeremias, and some one thing, and some another: but none of them thinking right, all of them are misled. Happy art thou, that art so distinguished as to know the truth in this matter."

2. The evidence of this his happiness declared, viz.,[4] That God, and He only, had revealed it to him. This is an evidence of his being blessed.

First. As it shows how peculiarly favored he was of God above others; q.d., "How highly favored art thou, that others, wise and great men, the scribes, Pharisees,[5] and rulers, and the nation in general, are left in darkness, to follow their own misguided apprehensions; and that thou shouldst be singled out, as it were, by name, that My heavenly Father should thus set His love on thee, Simon Bar-jona.—This argues thee blessed, that thou shouldst thus be the object of God's distinguishing love."

Secondly. It evidences his blessedness also, as it intimates that this knowledge is above any that flesh and blood can reveal. "This is such knowledge as only my Father which is in heaven can give. It is too high and excellent to be communicated by such means as other knowledge is. Thou art blessed, that thou knowest what God alone can teach thee."

---

1. Edwards delivered this sermon in Northampton; it was published the following year at the request of his congregation. The text here is from *The Works of Jonathan Edwards* (1829–30), vol. 6, edited by Sereno E. Dwight.
2. Simon, son of Jona; also known as the Apostle Peter.
3. Matthew 16.14. Elias is the name used in the New Testament for the prophet Elijah.
4. Abbreviation for *videlicet*: that is to say, namely (Latin).
5. A sect hostile to Jesus and known for their arrogance and pride (Matthew 9.9–13). "Scribes": interpreters of the Jewish law. "Q.d.": abbreviation for *quasi dicat*: as if he should say (Latin).

The original of this knowledge is here declared, both negatively and positively. Positively, as God is here declared the author of it. Negatively, as it is declared, that flesh and blood had not revealed it. God is the author of all knowledge and understanding whatsoever. He is the author of all moral prudence, and of the skill that men have in their secular business. Thus it is said of all in Israel that were wise-hearted and skilled in embroidering, that God had filled them with the spirit of wisdom. Exodus 28.3.[6]

God is the author of such knowledge; yet so that flesh and blood reveals it. Mortal men are capable of imparting the knowledge of human arts and sciences, and skill in temporal affairs. God is the author of such knowledge by those means: flesh and blood is employed as the mediate or second cause of it; He conveys it by the power and influence of natural means. But this spiritual knowledge, spoken of in the text, is what God is the author of, and none else: He reveals it, and flesh and blood reveals it not. He imparts this knowledge immediately, not making use of any intermediate natural causes, as He does in other knowledge.

What had passed in the preceding discourse naturally occasioned Christ to observe this; because the disciples had been telling how others did not know Him, but were generally mistaken about him, divided and confounded in their opinions of Him: but Peter had declared his assured faith, that He was the Son of God. Now it was natural to observe how it was not flesh and blood that had revealed it to him, but God; for if this knowledge were dependent on natural causes or means, how came it to pass that they, a company of poor fishermen, illiterate men, and persons of low education, attained to the knowledge of the truth, while the Scribes and Pharisees, men of vastly higher advantages, and greater knowledge and sagacity, in other matters, remained in ignorance? This could be owing only to the gracious distinguishing influence and revelation of the Spirit of God. Hence, what I would make the subject of my present discourse from these words, is this:

Doctrine

That there is such a thing as a spiritual and divine light, immediately imparted to the soul by God, of a different nature from any that is obtained by natural means. And on this subject I would,

    I. Show what this divine light is.
    II. How it is given immediately by God, and not obtained by natural means.
    III. Show the truth of the doctrine.
    And then conclude with a brief improvement.[7]

    I. I would show what this spiritual and divine light is. And in order to it would show,
    First, In a few things, what it is not. And here,
    1. Those convictions that natural men may have of their sin and misery, is not this spiritual and divine light. Men, in a natural condition, may have

---

6. This Bible passage refers to God's command to the people of Israel to make proper garments for Aaron's priesthood.

7. Literally, turning something to profit; here, the lesson to be learned.

convictions of the guilt that lies upon them, and of the anger of God, and their danger of divine vengeance. Such convictions are from the light of truth. That some sinners have a greater conviction of their guilt and misery than others is because some have more light, or more of an apprehension of truth than others. And this light and conviction may be from the Spirit of God; the Spirit convinces men of sin; but yet nature is much more concerned in it than in the communication of that spiritual and divine light that is spoken of in the doctrine; it is from the Spirit of God only as assisting natural principles, and not as infusing any new principles. Common grace differs from special in that it influences only by assisting of nature, and not by imparting grace, or bestowing anything above nature. The light that is obtained is wholly natural, or of no superior kind to what mere nature attains to, though more of that kind be obtained than would be obtained if men were left wholly to themselves; or, in other words, common grace only assists the faculties of the soul to do that more fully which they do by nature, as natural conscience or reason will by mere nature make a man sensible of guilt, and will accuse and condemn him when he has done amiss. Conscience is a principle natural to men; and the work that it doth naturally, or of itself, is to give an apprehension of right and wrong, and to suggest to the mind the relation that there is between right and wrong and a retribution. The Spirit of God, in those convictions which unregenerate men[8] sometimes have, assists conscience to do this work in a further degree than it would do if they were left to themselves. He helps it against those things that tend to stupify it, and obstruct its exercise. But in the renewing and sanctifying work of the Holy Ghost, those things are wrought in the soul that are above nature, and of which there is nothing of the like kind in the soul by nature; and they are caused to exist in the soul habitually, and according to such a stated constitution or law, that lays such a foundation for exercises in a continued course, as is called a principle of nature. Not only are remaining principles assisted to do their work more freely and fully, but those principles are restored that were utterly destroyed by the fall; and the mind thenceforward habitually exerts those acts that the dominion of sin had made it as wholly destitute of as a dead body is of vital acts.

The Spirit of God acts in a very different manner in the one case, from what He doth in the other. He may, indeed, act upon the mind of a natural man, but He acts in the mind of a saint[9] as an indwelling vital principle. He acts upon the mind of an unregenerate person as an extrinsic occasional agent; for, in acting upon them, He doth not unite himself to them: for, notwithstanding all His influences that they may possess, they are still sensual, having not the Spirit. Jude 19.[1] But He unites himself with the mind of a saint, takes him for His temple, actuates and influences him as a new supernatural principle of life and action. There is this difference, that the Spirit of God, in acting in the soul of a godly man, exerts and communicates Himself there in His own proper nature. Holiness is the proper nature

---

8. Those who are not yet saved.
9. Here, a living Christian who has passed from mere understanding of Christ's doctrine to heartfelt commitment; such people were often called "visible saints."

1. "These be they who separate themselves, sensual, having not the Spirit."

of the Spirit of God. The Holy Spirit operates in the minds of the godly, by uniting Himself to them, and living in them, and exerting His own nature in the exercise of their faculties. The Spirit of God may act upon a creature, and yet not in acting communicate Himself. The Spirit of God may act upon inanimate creatures, as, the Spirit moved upon the face of the waters,[2] in the beginning of the creation; so the Spirit of God may act upon the minds of men many ways, and communicate Himself no more than when He acts upon an inanimate creature. For instance, He may excite thoughts in them, may assist their natural reason and understanding, or may assist other natural principles, and this without any union with the soul, but may act, as it were, upon an external object. But as He acts in His holy influences and spiritual operations, He acts in a way of peculiar communication of Himself; so that the subject is thence denominated spiritual.

2. This spiritual and divine light does not consist in any impression made upon the imagination. It is no impression upon the mind, as though one saw anything with the bodily eyes. It is no imagination or idea of an outward light or glory, or any beauty of form or countenance, or a visible luster or brightness of any object. The imagination may be strongly impressed with such things; but this is not spiritual light. Indeed when the mind has a lively discovery of spiritual things, and is greatly affected with the power of divine light, it may, and probably very commonly doth, much affect the imagination; so that impressions of an outward beauty or brightness may accompany those spiritual discoveries. But spiritual light is not that impression upon the imagination, but an exceedingly different thing. Natural men may have lively impressions on their imaginations; and we cannot determine but that the devil, who transforms himself into an angel of light,[3] may cause imaginations of an outward beauty, or visible glory, and of sounds and speeches, and other such things; but these are things of a vastly inferior nature to spiritual light.

3. This spiritual light is not the suggesting of any new truths or propositions not contained in the word of God. This suggesting of new truths or doctrines to the mind, independent of any antecedent revelations of those propositions, either in word or writing, is inspiration; such as the prophets and apostles had, and such as some enthusiasts[4] pretend to. But this spiritual light that I am speaking of, is quite a different thing from inspiration. It reveals no new doctrine, it suggests no new proposition to the mind, it teaches no new thing of God, or Christ, or another world, not taught in the Bible, but only gives a due apprehension of those things that are taught in the word of God.

4. It is not every affecting[5] view that men have of religious things that is this spiritual and divine light. Men by mere principles of nature are capable of being affected with things that have a special relation to religion as well as other things. A person by mere nature, for instance, may be liable to be affected with the story of Jesus Christ, and the sufferings he underwent, as well as by any other tragical story. He may be the more affected with it from

---

2. Genesis 1.2.
3. Satan, a fallen angel, is also known as Lucifer (from the Latin for "bringing light" and originally associated with the morning star, Venus).
4. People who erroneously claim to be inspired by the spirit of God.
5. Emotionally arousing.

the interest he conceives mankind to have in it. Yea, he may be affected with it without believing it; as well as a man may be affected with what he reads in a romance, or sees acted in a stage play. He may be affected with a lively and eloquent description of many pleasant things that attend the state of the blessed in heaven, as well as his imagination be entertained by a romantic[6] description of the pleasantness of fairyland, or the like. And a common belief of the truth of such things, from education or otherwise, may help forward their affection. We read in Scripture of many that were greatly affected with things of a religious nature, who yet are there represented as wholly graceless, and many of them very ill[7] men. A person therefore may have affecting views of the things of religion, and yet be very destitute of spiritual light. Flesh and blood may be the author of this; one man may give another an affecting view of divine things with but common assistance; but God alone can give a spiritual discovery of them.—But I proceed to show.

Secondly, Positively what this spiritual and divine light is.

And it may be thus described: A true sense of the divine excellency of the things revealed in the word of God, and a conviction of the truth and reality of them thence arising. This spiritual light primarily consists in the former of these, viz., a real sense and apprehension of the divine excellency of things revealed in the word of God. A spiritual and saving conviction of the truth and reality of these things, arises from such a sight of their divine excellency and glory; so that this conviction of their truth is an effect and natural consequence of this sight of their divine glory. There is therefore in this spiritual light,

1. A true sense of the divine and superlative excellency of the things of religion; a real sense of the excellency of God and Jesus Christ, and of the work of redemption, and the ways and works of God revealed in the gospel. There is a divine and superlative glory in these things; an excellency that is of a vastly higher kind, and more sublime nature than in other things; a glory greatly distinguishing them from all that is earthly and temporal. He that is spiritually enlightened truly apprehends and sees it, or has a sense of it. He does not merely rationally believe that God is glorious, but he has a sense of the gloriousness of God in his heart. There is not only a rational belief that God is holy, and that holiness is a good thing, but there is a sense of the loveliness of God's holiness. There is not only a speculatively judging that God is gracious, but a sense how amiable God is on account of the beauty of this divine attribute.

There is a twofold knowledge of good of which God has made the mind of man capable. The first, that which is merely notional; as when a person only speculatively judges that anything is, which by the agreement of mankind, is called good or excellent, viz., that which is most to general advantage, and between which and a reward there is a suitableness,—and the like. And the other is, that which consists in the sense of the heart; as when the heart is sensible[8] of pleasure and delight in the presence of the idea of it. In the former is exercised merely the speculative faculty, or the

6. Fanciful, imaginary.
7. I.e., evil.

8. Aware.

understanding, in distinction from the will or disposition of the soul. In the latter, the will, or inclination, or heart, are mainly concerned.

Thus there is a difference between having an opinion, that God is holy and gracious, and having a sense of the loveliness and beauty of that holiness and grace. There is a difference between having a rational judgment that honey is sweet, and having a sense of its sweetness. A man may have the former, that knows not how honey tastes; but a man cannot have the latter unless he has an idea of the taste of honey in his mind. So there is a difference between believing that a person is beautiful, and having a sense of his beauty. The former may be obtained by hearsay, but the latter only by seeing the countenance. When the heart is sensible of the beauty and amiableness of a thing, it necessarily feels pleasure in the apprehension. It is implied in a person's being heartily sensible of the loveliness of a thing, that the idea of it is pleasant to his soul; which is a far different thing from having a rational opinion that it is excellent.

2. There arises from this sense of the divine excellency of things contained in the word of God, a conviction of the truth and reality of them; and that, either indirectly or directly.

First, Indirectly, and that two ways:

1. As the prejudices of the heart, against the truth of divine things, are hereby removed; so that the mind becomes susceptive of the due force of rational arguments for their truth. The mind of man is naturally full of prejudices against divine truth. It is full of enmity against the doctrines of the gospel; which is a disadvantage to those arguments that prove their truth, and causes them to lose their force upon the mind. But when a person has discovered to him the divine excellency of Christian doctrines, this destroys the enmity, removes those prejudices, sanctifies the reason, and causes it to lie open to the force of arguments for their truth.

Hence was the different effect that Christ's miracles had to convince the disciples, from what they had to convince the Scribes and Pharisees. Not that they had a stronger reason, or had their reason more improved; but their reason was sanctified, and those blinding prejudices, that the Scribes and Pharisees were under, were removed by the sense they had of the excellency of Christ, and his doctrine.

It not only removes the hindrances of reason, but positively helps reason. It makes even the speculative notions more lively. It engages the attention of the mind, with more fixedness and intenseness to that kind of objects; which causes it to have a clearer view of them, and enables it more clearly to see their mutual relations, and occasions it to take more notice of them. The ideas themselves that otherwise are dim and obscure are by this means impressed with the greater strength, and have a light cast upon them, so that the mind can better judge of them. As he that beholds objects on the face of the earth, when the light of the sun is cast upon them, is under greater advantage to discern them in their true forms and natural relations, than he that sees them in a dim twilight.

The mind, being sensible of the excellency of divine objects, dwells upon them with delight; and the powers of the soul are more awakened and enlivened to employ themselves in the contemplation of them, and exert themselves more fully and much more to the purpose. The beauty of the objects draws on the faculties, and draws forth their exercises; so that reason itself is under far greater advantages for its proper and free exercises, and to attain its proper end, free of darkness and delusion.—But,

Secondly, A true sense of the divine excellency of the things of God's word doth more directly and immediately convince us of their truth; and that because the excellency of these things is so superlative. There is a beauty in them so divine and godlike, that it greatly and evidently distinguishes them from things merely human, or that of which men are the inventors and authors; a glory so high and great, that when clearly seen, commands assent to their divine reality. When there is an actual and lively discovery of this beauty and excellency, it will not allow of any such thought as that it is the fruit of men's invention. This is a kind of intuitive and immediate evidence. They believe the doctrines of God's word to be divine, because they see a divine, and transcendent, and most evidently distinguishing glory in them; such a glory as, if clearly seen, does not leave room to doubt of their being of God, and not of men.

Such a conviction of the truths of religion as this, arising from a sense of their divine excellency, is included in saving faith. And this original of it is that by which it is most essentially distinguished from that common assent, of which unregenerate men are capable.

II. I proceed now to the second thing proposed, viz., to show how this light is immediately given by God, and not obtained by natural means. And here,

1. It is not intended that the natural faculties are not used in it. They are the subject of this light: and in such a manner, that they are not merely passive, but active in it. God, in letting in this light into the soul, deals with man according to his nature, and makes use of his rational faculties. But yet this light is not the less immediately from God for that; the faculties are made use of as the subject, and not as the cause. As the use we make of our eyes in beholding various objects, when the sun arises, is not the cause of the light that discovers those objects to us.

2. It is not intended that outward means have no concern in this affair. It is not in this affair, as in inspiration, where new truths are suggested; for, by this light is given only a due apprehension of the same truths that are revealed in the word of God, and therefore it is not given without the word. The gospel is employed in this affair. This light is the "light of the glorious gospel of Christ" (2 Corinthians 4.3–4).[9] The gospel is as a glass, by which this light is conveyed to us (1 Corinthians 13.12): "Now we see through a glass."[1]—But,

3. When it is said that this light is given immediately by God, and not obtained by natural means, hereby is intended that it is given by God without making use of any means that operate by their own power or natural force. God makes use of means; but it is not as mediate causes to produce this effect. There are not truly any second causes of it; but it is produced by God immediately. The word of God is no proper cause of this effect, but is made use of only to convey to the mind the subject matter of this saving

---

9. "But if our gospel be hid, it is hid to them that are lost: In whom the god of this world hath blinded the minds of them which believe not, lest the light of the glorious gospel of Christ, who is the image of God, should shine unto them."

1. "For now we see through a glass, darkly; but then face to face."

instruction: And this indeed it doth convey to us by natural force or influence. It conveys to our minds these doctrines; it is the cause of a notion of them in our heads, but not of the sense of their divine excellency in our hearts. Indeed a person cannot have spiritual light without the word. But that does not argue, that the word properly causes that light. The mind cannot see the excellency of any doctrine, unless that doctrine be first in the mind; but seeing the excellency of the doctrine may be immediately from the Spirit of God; though the conveying of the doctrine, or proposition, itself, may be by the word. So that the notions which are the subject matter of this light are conveyed to the mind by the word of God; but that due sense of the heart, wherein this light formally consists, is immediately by the Spirit of God. As, for instance, the notion that there is a Christ, and that Christ is holy and gracious, is conveyed to the mind by the word of God: But the sense of the excellency of Christ, by reason of that holiness and grace, is nevertheless, immediately the work of the Holy Spirit.—I come now,

III. To show the truth of the doctrine; that is, to show that there is such a thing as that spiritural light that has been described, thus immediately let into the mind by God. And here I would show, briefly, that this doctrine is both scriptural and rational.

First, It is scriptural. My text is not only full to the purpose, but it is a doctrine with which the Scripture abounds. We are there abundantly taught, that the saints differ from the ungodly in this; that they have the knowledge of God, and a sight of God, and of Jesus Christ. I shall mention but few texts out of many: 1 John 3.6: "Whosoever sinneth, hath not seen him, nor known him." 3 John 11: "He that doeth good, is of God: but he that doeth evil, hath not seen God." John 14.19: "The world seeth me no more; but ye see me." John 17.3: "And this is eternal life, that they might know thee, the only true God, and Jesus Christ whom thou hast sent." This knowledge, or sight of God and Christ, cannot be a mere speculative knowledge, because it is spoken of as that wherein they differ from the ungodly. And by these scriptures, it must not only be a different knowledge in degree and circumstances, and different in its effects, but it must be entirely different in nature and kind.

And this light and knowledge is always spoken of as immediately given of God; Matthew 11.25–27: "At that time, Jesus answered and said, I thank thee, O Father, Lord of heaven and earth, because thou hast hid these things from the wise and prudent, and hast revealed them unto babes. Even so, Father, for so it seemed good in thy sight. All things are delivered unto me of my Father: and no man knoweth the Father, save the Son, and he to whomsoever the Son will reveal him." Here this effect is ascribed exclusively to the arbitrary operation and gift of God bestowing this knowledge on whom He will, and distinguishing those with it who have the least natural advantage or means for knowledge, even babes, when it is denied to the wise and prudent. And imparting this knowledge is here appropriated to the Son of God, as His sole prerogative. And again, 2 Corinthians 4.6: "For God, who commanded the light to shine out of darkness, hath shined in our hearts, to give the light of the knowledge of the glory of God, in the face of Jesus Christ." This plainly shows, that there is a discovery of the divine superlative glory and excellency of God and Christ, peculiar to the saints: and, also, that it is as immediately from God, as light from the sun, and that it is the immediate effect of His power and will. For it is compared to God's creating the light by his powerful word in the beginning of the creation; and is said to be by the Spirit of the Lord, in the 18th verse of the preceding chapter. God is spoken of as giving the knowledge of Christ in conversion, as of what before was hidden and unseen; Galatians 1.15–16: "But when it pleased God, who separated me from my mother's womb, and called me by his grace, to reveal his son in me." The scripture also speaks plainly of such a knowledge of the word of God, as has been described as the immediate gift of God; Psalm 119.18: "Open thou mine eyes, that I may behold wondrous things out of thy law." What could the Psalmist mean, when he begged of God to open his eyes? Was he ever blind? Might he not have resort to the law, and see every word and sentence in it when he pleased? And what could he mean by those wondrous things? Were they the wonderful stories of the creation, and deluge, and Israel's passing through the Red Sea,[2] and the like? Were not his eyes open to read these strange things when he would? Doubtless, by wondrous things in God's law, he had respect to those distinguishing and wonderful excellencies, and marvelous manifestations of the divine perfections and glory contained in the commands and doctrines of the word, and those works and counsels of God that were there revealed. So the scripture speaks of a knowledge of God's dispensation, and covenant of mercy,[3] and way of grace towards His people, as peculiar to the saints, and given only by God; Psalm 25.14: "The secret of the Lord is with them that fear him; and he will show them his covenant."

And that a true and saving belief of the truth of religion is that which arises from such a discovery is, also, what the scripture teaches. As John 6.40: "And this is the will of him that sent me, that every one who seeth the Son, and believeth on him, may have everlasting life"; where it is plain that a true faith is what arises from a spiritual sight of Christ. And John 17.6–8: "I have manifested thy name unto the men which thou gavest me out of the world. Now, they have known, that all things whatsoever thou hast given me, are of thee. For I have given unto them the words which thou gavest me, and they have received them, and have known surely, that I came out from thee, and they have believed that thou didst send me"; where Christ's manifesting God's name to the disciples, or giving them the knowledge of God, was that whereby they knew that Christ's doctrine was of God, and that Christ Himself proceeded from Him, and was sent by Him. Again, John 12.44–46: "Jesus cried, and said, He that believeth on me, believeth not on me but on him that sent me. And he that seeth me, seeth him that sent me. I am come a light into the world, that whosoever believeth on me, should not abide in darkness." Their believing in Christ, and spiritually seeing Him, are parallel.

Christ condemns the Jews, that they did not know that He was the Messiah, and that His doctrine was true, from an inward distinguishing taste and relish of what was divine, in Luke 12.56–57. He having there blamed

---

2. The waters of the Red Sea divided for the Israelites in their exodus from Egypt (Exodus 14.21).
3. The agreement between Jesus Christ and those who believe in him that they would be saved; also known as the Covenant of Faith, as distinct from the Covenant of Works, which Adam broke.

the Jews, that, though they could discern the face of the sky and of the earth, and signs of the weather, that yet they could not discern those times—or, as it is expressed in Matthew, the signs of those times—adds, "yea, and why even of your ownselves, judge ye not what is right?" i.e., without extrinsic signs. Why have ye not that sense of true excellency, whereby ye may distinguish that which is holy and divine? Why have ye not that savor of the things of God, by which you may see the distinguishing glory, and evident divinity of me and my doctrine?

The apostle Peter mentions it as what gave him and his companions good and well-grounded assurance of the truth of the gospel, that they had seen the divine glory of Christ. 2 Peter 1.16: "For we have not followed cunningly devised fables, when we made known unto you the power and coming of our Lord Jesus Christ, but were eye-witnesses of his majesty." The apostle has respect to that visible glory of Christ which they saw in His transfiguration. That glory was so divine, having such an ineffable appearance and semblance of divine holiness, majesty, and grace, that it evidently denoted Him to be a divine person. But if a sight of Christ's outward glory might give a rational assurance of His divinity, why may not an apprehension of His spiritual glory do so too? Doubtless Christ's spiritual glory is in itself as distinguishing, and as plainly shows His divinity, as His outward glory— nay, a great deal more, for His spiritual glory is that wherein His divinity consists; and the outward glory of His transfiguration showed Him to be divine, only as it was a remarkable image or representation of that spiritual glory. Doubtless, therefore, he that has had a clear sight of the spiritual glory of Christ, may say, "I have not followed cunningly devised fables, but have been an eyewitness of His majesty, upon as good grounds as the apostle, when he had respect to the outward glory of Christ that he had seen." But this brings me to what was proposed next, viz., to show that,

Secondly, This doctrine is rational.[4]

1. It is rational to suppose, that there is really such an excellency in divine things—so transcendent and exceedingly different from what is in other things—that if it were seen, would most evidently distinguish them. We cannot rationally doubt but that things divine, which appertain to the supreme Being, are vastly different from things that are human; that there is a high, glorious, and godlike excellency in them that does most remarkably difference them from the things that are of men, insomuch that if the difference were but seen, it would have a convincing, satisfying influence upon anyone that they are divine. What reason can be offered against it unless we would argue that God is not remarkably distinguished in glory from men.

If Christ should now appear to any one as he did on the mount at His transfiguration,[5] or if He should appear to the world in His heavenly glory, as He will do at the Day of Judgment,[6] without doubt, His glory and majesty would be such as would satisfy everyone that He was a divine person, and that His religion was true; and it would be a most reasonable, and well grounded conviction too. And why may there not be that stamp of divinity

---

4. Capable of being grasped by the mind, understandable.
5. In Matthew 17.1–8, Christ appeared to Peter, James, and John shining "as the sun" and his garments "white as the light."
6. See Revelation 4.

or divine glory on the word of God, on the scheme and doctrine of the gospel, that may be in like manner distinguishing and as rationally convincing, provided it be but seen? It is rational to suppose, that when God speaks to the world, there should be something in His word vastly different from men's word. Supposing that God never had spoken to the world, but we had notice that He was about to reveal Himself from heaven and speak to us immediately Himself, or that He should give us a book of His own inditing;[7] after what manner should we expect that He would speak? Would it not be rational to suppose, that His speech would be exceeding different from men's speech, that there should be such an excellency and sublimity in His word, such a stamp of wisdom, holiness, majesty, and other divine perfections, that the word of men, yea of the wisest of men, should appear mean[8] and base in comparison of it? Doubtless it would be thought rational to expect this, and unreasonable to think otherwise. When a wise man speaks in the exercise of His wisdom, there is something in everything He says, that is very distinguishable from the talk of a little child. So, without doubt, and much more is the speech of God, to be distinguished from that of the wisest of men; agreeable to Jeremiah 23.28–29. God, having there been reproving the false prophets that prophesied in his name, and pretended that what they spake was His word, when indeed it was their own word, says, "The prophet that hath a dream, let him tell a dream; and he that hath my word let him speak my word faithfully: what is the chaff to the wheat? saith the Lord. Is not my word like as a fire? saith the Lord: and like a hammer that breaketh the rock in pieces?"

2. If there be such a distinguishing excellency in divine things, it is rational to suppose that there may be such a thing as seeing it. What should hinder but that it may be seen? It is no argument that there is no such distinguishing excellency, or that it cannot be seen, because some do not see it, though they may be discerning men in temporal matters. It is not rational to suppose, if there be any such excellency in divine things, that wicked men should see it. Is it rational to suppose that those whose minds are full of spiritual pollution, and under the power of filthy lusts, should have any relish or sense of divine beauty or excellency; or that their minds should be susceptive of that light that is in its own nature so pure and heavenly? It need not seem at all strange that sin should so blind the mind, seeing that men's particular natural tempers and dispositions will so much blind them in secular matters; as when men's natural temper is melancholy, jealous, fearful, proud, or the like.

3. It is rational to suppose that this knowledge should be given immediately by God, and not be obtained by natural means. Upon what account should it seem unreasonable that there should be any immediate communication between God and the creature? It is strange, that men should make any matter of difficulty of it. Why should not He that made all things still have something immediately to do with the things that He has made? Where lies the great difficulty, if we own the being of a God, and that He created all things out of nothing, of allowing some immediate influence of God on the creation still? And if it be reasonable to suppose it with respect

---

7. Composition.   8. Low, unethical.

to any part of the creation, it is especially so with respect to reasonable, intelligent creatures; who are next to God in the gradation of the different orders of beings, and whose business is most immediately with God; and reason teaches that man was made to serve and glorify his Creator. And if it be rational to suppose that God immediately communicates Himself to man in any affair, it is in this. It is rational to suppose that God would reserve that knowledge and wisdom, which is of such a divine and excellent nature, to be bestowed immediately by Himself, and that it should not be left in the power of second causes. Spiritual wisdom and grace is the highest and most excellent gift that ever God bestows on any creature; in this, the highest excellency and perfection of a rational creature consists. It is also immensely the most important of all divine gifts: it is that wherein man's happiness consists, and on which his everlasting welfare depends. How rational is it to suppose that God, however He has left lower gifts to second causes, and in some sort in their power, yet should reserve this most excellent, divine, and important of all divine communications in His own hands to be bestowed immediately by Himself, as a thing too great for second causes to be concerned in. It is rational to suppose that this blessing should be immediately from God, for there is no gift or benefit that is in itself so nearly related to the divine nature. Nothing which the creature receives is so much a participation of the Deity; it is a kind of emanation of God's beauty, and is related to God as the light is to the sun. It is, therefore, congruous and fit, that when it is given of God, it should be immediately from Himself, and by Himself, according to His own sovereign will.

It is rational to suppose, that it should be beyond man's power to obtain this light by the mere strength of natural reason; for it is not a thing that belongs to reason to see the beauty and loveliness of spiritual things; it is not a speculative thing, but depends on the sense of the heart. Reason, indeed, is necessary, in order to it, as it is by reason only that we are become the subjects of the means of it; which means, I have already shown to be necessary in order to it, though they have no proper causal influence in the affair.[9] It is by reason that we become possessed of a notion of those doctrines that are the subject matter of this divine light or knowledge; and reason may many ways be indirectly and remotely an advantage to it. Reason has also to do in the acts that are immediately consequent on this discovery: for, seeing the truth of religion from hence, is by reason, though it be but by one step, and the inference be immediate. So reason has to do in that accepting of and trusting in Christ that is consequent on it. But if we take reason strictly—not for the faculty of mental perception in general, but for ratiocination, or a power of inferring by arguments—the perceiving of spiritual beauty and excellency no more belongs to reason than it belongs to the sense of feeling to perceive colors, or to the power of seeing to perceive the sweetness of food. It is out of reason's province to perceive the beauty or loveliness of anything; such a perception does not belong to that faculty. Reason's work is to perceive truth and not excellency. It is not ratiocination that gives men the perception of the beauty and amiableness of a countenance, though it may be many ways indirectly an advantage to it; yet

---

9. I.e., it is through reason that God communicates grace via things and persons (i.e., "means").

it is no more reason that immediately perceives it than it is reason that perceives the sweetness of honey; it depends on the sense of the heart. Reason may determine that a countenance is beautiful to others, it may determine that honey is sweet to others, but it will never give me a perception of its sweetness.

I will conclude with a very brief improvement of what has been said.

First, this doctrine may lead us to reflect on the goodness of God, that has so ordered it, that a saving evidence of the truth of the Gospel is such as is attainable by persons of mean capacities and advantages, as well as those that are of the greatest parts and learning. If the evidence of the Gospel depended only on history and such reasonings as learned men only are capable of, it would be above the reach of far the greatest part of mankind. But persons with an ordinary degree of knowledge are capable, without a long and subtle train of reasoning, to see the divine excellency of the things of religion; they are capable of being taught by the Spirit of God, as well as learned men. The evidence that is this way obtained is vastly better and more satisfying than all that can be obtained by the arguings of those that are most learned and greatest masters of reason. And babes are as capable of knowing these things as the wise and prudent; and they are often hid from these when they are revealed to those. 1 Corinthians 1.26–27: "For ye see your calling, brethren, how that not many wise men, after the flesh, not many mighty, not many noble, are called. But God hath chosen the foolish things of the world."

Secondly, This doctrine may well put us upon examining ourselves, whether we have ever had this divine light let into our souls. If there be such a thing, doubtless it is of great importance whether we have thus been taught by the Spirit of God; whether the light of the glorious gospel of Christ, who is the image of God, hath shined unto us, giving us the light of the knowledge of the glory of God in the face of Jesus Christ; whether we have seen the Son, and believed on Him, or have that faith of gospel doctrines which arises from a spiritual sight of Christ.

Thirdly, All may hence be exhorted earnestly to seek this spiritual light. To influence and move to it, the following things may be considered.

1. This is the most excellent and divine wisdom that any creature is capable of. It is more excellent than any human learning; it is far more excellent than all the knowledge of the greatest philosophers or statesmen. Yea, the least glimpse of the glory of God in the face of Christ doth more exalt and ennoble the soul than all the knowledge of those that have the greatest speculative understanding in divinity without grace. This knowledge has the most noble object that can be, viz., the divine glory and excellency of God and Christ. The knowledge of these objects is that wherein consists the most excellent knowledge of the angels, yea, of God Himself.

2. This knowledge is that which is above all others sweet and joyful. Men have a great deal of pleasure in human knowledge, in studies of natural things; but this is nothing to that joy which arises from this divine light shining into the soul. This light gives a view of those things that are immensely the most exquisitely beautiful and capable of delighting the eye of the understanding. The spiritual light is the dawning of the light of glory in the heart. There is nothing so powerful as this to support persons in affliction, and to give the mind peace and brightness in this stormy and dark world.

3. This light is such as effectually influences the inclination and changes the nature of the soul. It assimilates our nature to the divine nature, and changes the soul into an image of the same glory that is beheld. 2 Corinthians 3.18: "But we all with open face, beholding as in a glass the glory of the Lord, are changed into the same image, from glory to glory, even as by the Spirit of the Lord." This knowledge will wean[1] from the world, and raise the inclination to heavenly things. It will turn the heart to God as the fountain of good, and to choose Him for the only portion. This light, and this only, will bring the soul to a saving close[2] with Christ. It conforms the heart to the gospel, mortifies its enmity and opposition against the scheme of salvation therein revealed; it causes the heart to embrace the joyful tidings, and entirely to adhere to, and acquiesce in, the revelation of Christ as our Savior; it causes the whole soul to accord and symphonize with it, admitting it with entire credit and respect, cleaving to it with full inclination and affection; and it effectually disposes the soul to give up itself entirely to Christ.

4. This light, and this only, has its fruit in an universal holiness of life. No merely notional or speculative understanding of the doctrines of religion will ever bring to this. But this light, as it reaches the bottom of the heart, and changes the nature, so it will effectually dispose to an universal obedience. It shows God as worthy to be obeyed and served. It draws forth the heart in a sincere love to God, which is the only principle of a true, gracious, and universal obedience, and it convinces of the reality of those glorious rewards that God has promised to them that obey Him.

1733   1734

Sinners in the Hands of an Angry God[1]

Deuteronomy 32.35

Their foot shall slide in due time.[2]

In this verse is threatened the vengeance of God on the wicked unbelieving Israelites, who were God's visible people, and who lived under the means of grace,[3] but who, notwithstanding all God's wonderful works towards them, remained (as in verse 28)[4] void of counsel, having no understanding in them. Under all the cultivations of heaven, they brought forth bitter and poisonous fruit, as in the two verses next preceding the text.[5] The expression I have

1. Draw us away.
2. Union.
1. Edwards delivered this sermon in Enfield, Connecticut, a town about thirty miles south of Northampton. According to Benjamin Trumbull's *A Complete History of Connecticut* (1797, 1818), Edwards read his sermon in a level voice with his sermon book in his left hand, and in spite of his calm, "there was such a breathing of distress, and weeping, that the preacher was obliged to speak to the people and desire silence, that he might be heard." The text here is from *The Works of Jonathan Edwards* (1829–30), vol. 7, edited by Sereno E. Dwight.
2. "To me belongeth vengeance, and recompense;

their foot shall slide in due time: for the day of their calamity is at hand, and the things that shall come upon them make haste."
3. I.e., the Ten Commandments.
4. "For they are a nation void of counsel, neither is there any understanding in them" (Deuteronomy 32.28).
5. "For their vine is of the vine of Sodom, and the fields of Gomorrah: their grapes are grapes of gall, their clusters are bitter: Their wine is the poison of dragons, and the cruel venom of asps" (Deuteronomy 32.32–33). Sodom and Gomorrah were wicked cities destroyed by a rain of fire and sulfur from heaven (Genesis 19.24).

chosen for my text, "Their foot shall slide in due time," seems to imply the following things, relating to the punishment and destruction to which these wicked Israelites were exposed.

1. That they were always exposed to destruction; as one that stands or walks in slippery places is always exposed to fall. This is implied in the manner of their destruction coming upon them, being represented by their foot sliding. The same is expressed, Psalm 73.18: "Surely thou didst set them in slippery places; thou castedst them down into destruction."

2. It implies that they were always exposed to sudden unexpected destruction. As he that walks in slippery places is every moment liable to fall, he cannot foresee one moment whether he shall stand or fall the next; and when he does fall, he falls at once without warning: which is also expressed in Psalm 73.18–19: "Surely thou didst set them in slippery places; thou castedst them down into destruction: How are they brought into desolation as in a moment!"

3. Another thing implied is, that they are liable to fall of themselves, without being thrown down by the hand of another; as he that stands or walks on slippery ground needs nothing but his own weight to throw him down.

4. That the reason why they are not fallen already, and do not fall now, is only that God's appointed time is not come. For it is said that when that due time, or appointed times comes, their foot shall slide. Then they shall be left to fall, as they are inclined by their own weight. God will not hold them up in these slippery places any longer, but will let them go; and then, at that very instant, they shall fall into destruction; as he that stands on such slippery declining ground, on the edge of a pit, he cannot stand alone, when he is let go he immediately falls and is lost.

The observation from the words that I would now insist upon is this. "There is nothing that keeps wicked men at any one moment out of hell, but the mere pleasure of God." By the mere pleasure of God, I mean His sovereign pleasure, His arbitrary will, restrained by no obligation, hindered by no manner of difficulty, any more than if nothing else but God's mere will had in the least degree, or in any respect whatsoever, any hand in the preservation of wicked men one moment. The truth of this observation may appear by the following considerations.

1. There is no want[6] of power in God to cast wicked men into hell at any moment. Men's hands cannot be strong when God rises up. The strongest have no power to resist Him, nor can any deliver[7] out of His hands. He is not only able to cast wicked men into hell, but He can most easily do it. Sometimes an earthly prince meets with a great deal of difficulty to subdue a rebel, who has found means to fortify himself, and has made himself strong by the numbers of his followers. But it is not so with God. There is no fortress that is any defense from the power of God. Though hand join in hand, and vast multitudes of God's enemies combine and associate themselves, they are easily broken in pieces. They are as great heaps of light chaff before the whirlwind; or large quantities of dry stubble before devouring flames. We find it easy to tread on and crush a worm that we see crawling on the earth; so it is easy for us to cut or singe a slender thread that any thing

---

6. Lack. 7. I.e., rescue others.

hangs by: thus easy is it for God, when he pleases, to cast His enemies down to hell. What are we, that we should think to stand before Him, at whose rebuke the earth trembles, and before whom the rocks are thrown down?

2. They deserve to be cast into hell; so that divine justice never stands in the way, it makes no objection against God's using His power at any moment to destroy them. Yea, on the contrary, justice calls aloud for an infinite punishment of their sins. Divine justice says of the tree that brings forth such grapes of Sodom, "Cut it down, why cumbereth it the ground?" Luke 13.7. The sword of divine justice is every moment brandished over their heads, and it is nothing but the hand of arbitrary mercy, and God's will, that holds it back.

3. They are already under a sentence of condemnation to hell. They do not only justly deserve to be cast down thither, but the sentence of the law of God, that eternal and immutable rule of righteousness that God has fixed between Him and mankind, is gone out against them, and stands against them; so that they are bound over[8] already to hell. John 3.18: "He that believeth not is condemned already." So that every unconverted man properly belongs to hell; that is his place; from thence he is, John 8.23: "Ye are from beneath." And thither he is bound; it is the place that justice, and God's word, and the sentence of his unchangeable law assign to him.

4. They are now the objects of that very same anger and wrath of God that is expressed in the torments of hell. And the reason why they do not go down to hell at each moment is not because God, in whose power they are, is not then very angry with them as He is with many miserable creatures now tormented in hell, who there feel and bear the fierceness of His wrath. Yea, God is a great deal more angry with great numbers that are now on earth: yea, doubtless, with many that are now in this congregation, who it may be are at ease, than He is with many of those who are now in the flames of hell.

So that it is not because God is unmindful of their wickedness, and does not resent it, that He does not let loose His hand and cut them off. God is not altogether such an one as themselves, though they may imagine Him to be so. The wrath of God burns against them, their damnation does not slumber; the pit is prepared, the fire is made ready, the furnace is now hot, ready to receive them; the flames do now rage and glow. The glittering sword is whet,[9] and held over them, and the pit hath opened its mouth under them.

5. The devil stands ready to fall upon them, and seize them as his own, at what moment God shall permit him. They belong to him; he has their souls in his possession, and under his dominion. The Scripture represents them as his goods, Luke 11.12.[1] The devils watch them; they are ever by them at their right hand; they stand waiting for them, like greedy hungry lions that see their prey, and expect to have it, but are for the present kept back. If God should withdraw His hand, by which they are restrained, they would in one moment fly upon their poor souls. The old serpent is gaping for them; hell opens its mouth wide to receive them; and if God should permit it, they would be hastily swallowed up and lost.

---

8. A legal phrase referring to the phase after an arraignment, when the accused is sent to trial. Here, it means condemned.

9. Sharpened.
1. "Or if he shall ask an egg, will he offer him a scorpion?"

6. There are in the souls of wicked men those hellish principles reigning that would presently kindle and flame out into hell fire, if it were not for God's restraints. There is laid in the very nature of carnal men a foundation for the torments of hell. There are those corrupt principles, in reigning power in them, and in full possession of them, that are seeds of hell fire. These principles are active and powerful, exceeding violent in their nature, and if it were not for the restraining hand of God upon them, they would soon break out, they would flame out after the same manner as the same corruptions, the same enmity does in the hearts of damned souls, and would beget the same torments as they do in them. The souls of the wicked are in Scripture compared to the troubled sea, Isaiah 57.20.[2] For the present, God restrains their wickedness by His mighty power, as He does the raging waves of the troubled sea, saying, "Hitherto shalt thou come, but no further;"[3] but if God should withdraw that restraining power, it would soon carry all before it. Sin is the ruin and misery of the soul; it is destructive in its nature; and if God should leave it without restraint, there would need nothing else to make the soul perfectly miserable. The corruption of the heart of man is immoderate and boundless in its fury; and while wicked men live here, it is like fire pent up by God's restraints, whereas if it were let loose, it would set on fire the course of nature; and as the heart is now a sink of sin, so if sin was not restrained, it would immediately turn the soul into a fiery oven, or a furnace of fire and brimstone.

7. It is no security to wicked men for one moment that there are no visible means of death at hand. It is no security to a natural[4] man that he is now in health and that he does not see which way he should now immediately go out of the world by any accident, and that there is no visible danger in any respect in his circumstances. The manifold and continual experience of the world in all ages, shows this is no evidence that a man is not on the very brink of eternity, and that the next step will not be into another world. The unseen, unthought-of ways and means of persons going suddenly out of the world are innumerable and inconceivable. Unconverted men walk over the pit of hell on a rotten covering, and there are innumerable places in this covering so weak that they will not bear their weight, and these places are not seen. The arrows of death fly unseen at noonday;[5] the sharpest sight cannot discern them. God has so many different unsearchable ways of taking wicked men out of the world and sending them to hell, that there is nothing to make it appear that God had need to be at the expense of a miracle, or go out of the ordinary course of His providence, to destroy any wicked man at any moment. All the means that there are of sinners going out of the world are so in God's hands, and so universally and absolutely subject to His power and determination, that it does not depend at all the less on the mere will of God whether sinners shall at any moment go to hell than if means were never made use of or at all concerned in the case.

8. Natural men's prudence and care to preserve their own lives, or the care of others to preserve them, do not secure them a moment. To this, divine

---

2. "But the wicked are like the troubled sea, when it cannot rest, whose waters cast up mire and dirt."
3. Job 38.11.

4. I.e., unregenerate, unsaved.
5. "Thou shalt not be afraid for the terror by night; nor for the arrow that flieth by day" (Psalm 91.5).

providence and universal experience do also bear testimony. There is this clear evidence that men's own wisdom is no security to them from death; that if it were otherwise we should see some difference between the wise and politic men of the world, and others, with regard to their liableness to early and unexpected death: but how is it in fact? Ecclesiastes 2.16: "How dieth the wise man? even as the fool."

9. All wicked men's pains and contrivance which they use to escape hell, while they continue to reject Christ, and so remain wicked men, do not secure them from hell one moment. Almost every natural man that hears of hell, flatters himself that he shall escape it; he depends upon himself for his own security; he flatters himself in what he has done, in what he is now doing, or what he intends to do. Every one lays out matters in his own mind how he shall avoid damnation, and flatters himself that he contrives well for himself, and that his schemes will not fail. They hear indeed that there are but few saved, and that the greater part of men that have died heretofore are gone to hell; but each one imagines that he lays out matters better for his own escape than others have done. He does not intend to come to that place of torment; he says within himself that he intends to take effectual care, and to order matters so for himself as not to fail.

But the foolish children of men miserably delude themselves in their own schemes, and in confidence in their own strength and wisdom; they trust to nothing but a shadow. The greater part of those who heretofore have lived under the same means of grace, and are now dead, are undoubtedly gone to hell; and it was not because they were not as wise as those who are now alive: it was not because they did not lay out matters as well for themselves to secure their own escape. If we could speak with them, and inquire of them, one by one, whether they expected when alive, and when they used to hear about hell, ever to be the subjects of that misery, we doubtless, should hear one and another reply, "No, I never intended to come here: I had laid out matters otherwise in my mind; I thought I should contrive well for myself: I thought my scheme good. I intended to take effectual care; but it came upon me unexpected; I did not look for it at that time, and in that manner; it came as a thief: Death outwitted me: God's wrath was too quick for me. Oh, my cursed foolishness! I was flattering myself, and pleasing myself with vain dreams of what I would do hereafter; and when I was saying, peace and safety, then suddenly destruction came upon me."

10. God has laid Himself under no obligation by any promise to keep any natural man out of hell one moment. God certainly has made no promises either of eternal life or of any deliverance or preservation from eternal death but what are contained in the covenant of grace,[6] the promises that are given in Christ, in whom all the promises are yea and amen. But surely they have no interest in the promises of the covenant of grace who are not the children of the covenant, who do not believe in any of the promises, and have no interest in the Mediator of the covenant.[7]

---

6. The original covenant God made with Adam is called the Covenant of Works; the second covenant Jesus Christ made with fallen humanity—declaring that if they believed in him they would be saved—is called the Covenant of Grace.

7. I.e., Christ, who mediated between God and humanity by taking upon himself the sins of the world and suffering for them.

So that, whatever some have imagined and pretended about promises made to natural men's earnest seeking and knocking,[8] it is plain and manifest that whatever pains a natural man takes in religion, whatever prayers he makes, till he believes in Christ, God is under no manner of obligation to keep him a moment from eternal destruction.

So that, thus it is that natural men are held in the hand of God, over the pit of hell; they have deserved the fiery pit, and are already sentenced to it; and God is dreadfully provoked. His anger is as great towards them as to those that are actually suffering the executions of the fierceness of His wrath in hell, and they have done nothing in the least to appease or abate that anger, neither is God in the least bound by any promise to hold them up one moment; the devil is waiting for them, hell is gaping for them, the flames gather and flash about them, and would fain lay hold on them, and swallow them up; the fire pent up in their own hearts is struggling to break out: and they have no interest in any Mediator, there are no means within reach that can be any security to them. In short, they have no refuge, nothing to take hold of; all that preserves them every moment is the mere arbitrary will, and uncovenanted, unobliged forbearance of an incensed God.

Application

The use of this awful[9] subject may be for awakening unconverted persons in this congregation. This that you have heard is the case of every one of you that are out of Christ. That world of misery, that lake of burning brimstone, is extended abroad under you. There is the dreadful pit of the glowing flames of the wrath of God; there is hell's wide gaping mouth open; and you have nothing to stand upon, nor any thing to take hold of; there is nothing between you and hell but the air; it is only the power and mere pleasure of God that holds you up.

You probably are not sensible[1] of this; you find you are kept out of hell, but do not see the hand of God in it; but look at other things, as the good state of your bodily constitution, your care of your own life, and the means you use for your own preservation. But indeed these things are nothing; if God should withdraw His hand, they would avail no more to keep you from falling, than the thin air to hold up a person that is suspended in it.

Your wickedness makes you as it were heavy as lead, and to tend downwards with great weight and pressure towards hell; and if God should let you go, you would immediately sink and swiftly descend and plunge into the bottomless gulf, and your healthy constitution, and your own care and prudence, and best contrivance, and all your righteousness, would have no more influence to uphold you and keep you out of hell, than a spider's web would have to stop a fallen rock. Were it not for the sovereign pleasure of God, the earth would not bear you one moment; for you are a burden to it; the creation groans with you; the creature is made subject to the bondage of your corruption, not willingly; the sun does not willingly shine upon you to give you light to serve sin and Satan; the earth does not willingly yield her increase

---

8. Matthew 7.7: "Ask, and it shall be given you; seek, and ye shall find; knock, and it shall be opened unto you." "Pretended": claimed.

9. Awe-inspiring.
1. Aware.

to satisfy your lusts; nor is it willingly a stage for your wickedness to be acted upon; the air does not willingly serve you for breath to maintain the flame of life in your vitals, while you spend your life in the service of God's enemies. God's creatures are good, and were made for men to serve God with, and do not willingly subserve to any other purpose, and groan when they are abused to purposes so directly contrary to their nature and end. And the world would spew you out, were it not for the sovereign hand of Him who hath subjected it in hope.[2] There are black clouds of God's wrath now hanging directly over your heads, full of the dreadful storm, and big with thunder; and were it not for the restraining hand of God, it would immediately burst forth upon you. The sovereign pleasure of God, for the present, stays His rough wind; otherwise it would come with fury, and your destruction would come like a whirlwind, and you would be like the chaff of the summer threshing floor.

The wrath of God is like great waters that are dammed for the present; they increase more and more, and rise higher and higher, till an outlet is given; and the longer the stream is stopped, the more rapid and mighty is its course when once it is let loose. It is true that judgment against your evil works has not been executed hitherto; the floods of God's vengeance have been withheld; but your guilt in the meantime is constantly increasing, and you are every day treasuring up more wrath; the waters are constantly rising, and waxing more and more mighty; and there is nothing but the mere pleasure of God that holds the waters back, that are unwilling to be stopped, and press hard to go forward. If God should only withdraw His hand from the floodgate, it would immediately fly open, and the fiery floods of the fierceness and wrath of God, would rush forth with inconceivable fury, and would come upon you with omnipotent power; and if your strength were ten thousand times greater than it is, yea, ten thousand times greater than the strength of the stoutest, sturdiest devil in hell, it would be nothing to withstand or endure it.

The bow of God's wrath is bent, and the arrow made ready on the string, and justice bends the arrow at your heart, and strains the bow, and it is nothing but the mere pleasure of God, and that of an angry God, without any promise or obligation at all, that keeps the arrow one moment from being made drunk with your blood. Thus all you that never passed under a great change of heart, by the mighty power of the Spirit of God upon your souls, all you that were never born again, and made new creatures, and raised from being dead in sin, to a state of new, and before altogether unexperienced light and life, are in the hands of an angry God. However you may have reformed your life in many things, and may have had religious affections, and may keep up a form of religion in your families and closets,[3] and in the house of God, it is nothing but His mere pleasure that keeps you from being this moment swallowed up in everlasting destruction. However unconvinced you may now be of the truth of what you hear, by and by you will be fully convinced of it. Those that are gone from being in the like circumstances with you see that it was so with them; for destruction came

---

2. Romans 8.20: "For the creature was made subject to vanity, not willingly, but because of Him who subjected it, in hope."

3. Studies; rooms for meditation. "Affections": feelings.

suddenly upon most of them; when they expected nothing of it and while they were saying, peace and safety: now they see that those things on which they depended for peace and safety, were nothing but thin air and empty shadows.

The God that holds you over the pit of hell, much as one holds a spider or some loathsome insect over the fire, abhors you, and is dreadfully provoked: His wrath towards you burns like fire; He looks upon you as worthy of nothing else but to be cast into the fire; He is of purer eyes than to bear to have you in His sight; you are ten thousand times more abominable in His eyes than the most hateful venomous serpent is in ours. You have offended Him infinitely more than ever a stubborn rebel did his prince; and yet it is nothing but His hand that holds you from falling into the fire every moment. It is to be ascribed to nothing else, that you did not go to hell the last night; that you was suffered to awake again in this world, after you closed your eyes to sleep. And there is no other reason to be given, why you have not dropped into hell since you arose in the morning, but that God's hand has held you up. There is no other reason to be given why you have not gone to hell, since you have sat here in the house of God, provoking His pure eyes by your sinful wicked manner of attending His solemn worship. Yea, there is nothing else that is to be given as a reason why you do not this very moment drop down into hell.

O sinner! Consider the fearful danger you are in: it is a great furnace of wrath, a wide and bottomless pit, full of the fire of wrath, that you are held over in the hand of that God, whose wrath is provoked and incensed as much against you, as against many of the damned in hell. You hang by a slender thread, with the flames of divine wrath flashing about it, and ready every moment to singe it, and burn it asunder; and you have no interest in any Mediator, and nothing to lay hold of to save yourself, nothing to keep off the flames of wrath, nothing of your own, nothing that you ever have done, nothing that you can do, to induce God to spare you one moment. And consider here more particularly.

1. Whose wrath it is: it is the wrath of the infinite God. If it were only the wrath of man, though it were of the most potent prince, it would be comparatively little to be regarded. The wrath of kings is very much dreaded, especially of absolute monarchs, who have the possessions and lives of their subjects wholly in their power, to be disposed of at their mere will. Proverbs 20.2: "The fear of a king is as the roaring of a lion: Whoso provoketh him to anger, sinneth against his own soul." The subject that very much enrages an arbitrary prince is liable to suffer the most extreme torments that human art can invent, or human power can inflict. But the greatest earthly potentates in their greatest majesty, and strength, and when clothed in their greatest terrors, are but feeble, despicable worms of the dust, in comparison of the great and almighty Creator and King of heaven and earth. It is but little that they can do, when most enraged, and when they have exerted the utmost of their fury. All the kings of the earth, before God, are as grasshoppers; they are nothing, and less than nothing: both their love and their hatred is to be despised. The wrath of the great King of kings, is as much more terrible than theirs, as His majesty is greater. Luke 12.4–5: "And I say unto you, my friends, Be not afraid of them that kill the body, and after that, have no more that they can do. But I will forewarn you whom you shall fear: fear

him, which after he hath killed, hath power to cast into hell: yea, I say unto you, Fear him."

2. It is the fierceness of His wrath that you are exposed to. We often read of the fury of God; as in Isaiah 59.18: "According to their deeds, accordingly he will repay fury to his adversaries." So Isaiah 66.15: "For behold, the Lord will come with fire, and with his chariots like a whirlwind, to render his anger with fury, and his rebuke with flames of fire." And in many other places. So, Revelation 19.15: we read of "the wine press of the fierceness and wrath of Almighty God."[4] The words are exceeding terrible. If it had only been said, "the wrath of God," the words would have implied that which is infinitely dreadful: but it is "the fierceness and wrath of God." The fury of God! the fierceness of Jehovah![5] Oh, how dreadful must that be! Who can utter or conceive what such expressions carry in them! But it is also "the fierceness and wrath of Almighty God." As though there would be a very great manifestation of His almighty power in what the fierceness of His wrath should inflict, as though omnipotence should be as it were enraged, and exerted, as men are wont to exert their strength in the fierceness of their wrath. Oh! then, what will be the consequence! What will become of the poor worms that shall suffer it! Whose hands can be strong? And whose heart can endure? To what a dreadful, inexpressible, inconceivable depth of misery must the poor creature be sunk who shall be the subject of this!

Consider this, you that are here present that yet remain in an unregenerate state. That God will execute the fierceness of His anger implies that He will inflict wrath without any pity. When God beholds the ineffable extremity of your case, and sees your torment to be so vastly disproportioned to your strength, and sees how your poor soul is crushed, and sinks down, as it were, into an infinite gloom; He will have no compassion upon you, He will not forbear the executions of His wrath, or in the least lighten His hand; there shall be no moderation or mercy, nor will God then at all stay His rough wind; He will have no regard to your welfare, nor be at all careful lest you should suffer too much in any other sense, than only that you shall not suffer beyond what strict justice requires. Nothing shall be withheld because it is so hard for you to bear. Ezekiel 8.18: "Therefore will I also deal in fury: mine eye shall not spare, neither will I have pity; and though they cry in mine ears with a loud voice, yet I will not hear them." Now God stands ready to pity you; this is a day of mercy; you may cry now with some encouragement of obtaining mercy. But when once the day of mercy is past, your most lamentable and dolorous cries and shrieks will be in vain; you will be wholly lost and thrown away of God as to any regard to your welfare. God will have no other use to put you to, but to suffer misery; you shall be continued in being to no other end; for you will be a vessel of wrath fitted to destruction; and there will be no other use of this vessel, but to be filled full of wrath. God will be so far from pitying you when you cry to Him, that it is said He will only "laugh and mock." Proverbs 1.25–26, etc.[6]

How awful are those words, Isaiah 63.3, which are the words of the great God: "I will tread them in mine anger, and will trample them in my fury,

---

4. "He treadeth the winepress of the fierceness and wrath of Almighty God."

5. The name used for God in the Old Testament.

6. "But ye have set at nought all my counsel, and would none of my reproof: I also will laugh at your calamity; I will mock you when your fear cometh."

and their blood shall be sprinkled upon my garments, and I will stain all my raiment." It is perhaps impossible to conceive of words that carry in them greater manifestations of these three things, viz.,[7] contempt, and hatred, and fierceness of indignation. If you cry to God to pity you, He will be so far from pitying you in your doleful case, or showing you the least regard or favor, that instead of that, He will only tread you under foot. And though He will know that you cannot bear the weight of omnipotence treading upon you, yet He will not regard that, but He will crush you under His feet without mercy; He will crush out your blood, and make it fly and it shall be sprinkled on His garments, so as to stain all His raiment. He will not only hate you, but He will have you in the utmost contempt: no place shall be thought fit for you, but under His feet to be trodden down as the mire of the streets.

3. The misery you are exposed to is that which God will inflict to that end, that He might show what that wrath of Jehovah is. God hath had it on His heart to show to angels and men both how excellent His love is, and also how terrible His wrath is. Sometimes earthly kings have a mind to show how terrible their wrath is, by the extreme punishments they would execute on those that would provoke them. Nebuchadnezzar, that mighty and haughty monarch of the Chaldean empire, was willing to show his wrath when enraged with Shadrach, Meshech, and Abednego; and accordingly gave orders that the burning fiery furnace should be heated seven times hotter than it was before; doubtless, it was raised to the utmost degree of fierceness that human art could raise it.[8] But the great God is also willing to show His wrath, and magnify His awful majesty and mighty power in the extreme sufferings of His enemies. Romans 9.22: "What if God, willing to show his wrath, and to make his power known, endure with much long-suffering the vessels of wrath fitted to destruction?" And seeing this is His design, and what He has determined, even to show how terrible the restrained wrath, the fury and fierceness of Jehovah is, He will do it to effect. There will be something accomplished and brought to pass that will be dreadful with a witness. When the great and angry God hath risen up and executed His awful vengeance on the poor sinner, and the wretch is actually suffering the infinite weight and power of His indignation, then will God call upon the whole universe to behold that awful majesty and mighty power that is to be seen in it. Isaiah 33.12–14: "And the people shall be as the burnings of lime, as thorns cut up shall they be burnt in the fire. Hear ye that are far off, what I have done; and ye that are near, acknowledge my might. The sinners in Zion are afraid; fearfulness hath surprised the hypocrites," etc.

Thus it will be with you that are in an unconverted state, if you continue in it; the infinite might, and majesty, and terribleness of the omnipotent God shall be magnified upon you, in the ineffable strength of your torments. You shall be tormented in the presence of the holy angels, and in the presence of the Lamb; and when you shall be in this state of suffering, the glorious inhabitants of heaven shall go forth and look on the awful spectacle, that they may see what the wrath and fierceness of the Almighty is; and when they have seen it, they will fall down and adore that great power and majesty.

7. Abbreviation for *videlicet*: that is to say, namely (Latin).
8. See Daniel 3.1–30.

Isaiah 66.23–24: "And it shall come to pass, that from one new moon to another, and from one sabbath to another, shall all flesh come to worship before me, saith the Lord. And they shall go forth and look upon the carcasses of the men that have transgressed against me; for their worm shall not die, neither shall their fire be quenched, and they shall be an abhorring unto all flesh."

4. It is everlasting wrath. It would be dreadful to suffer this fierceness and wrath of Almighty God one moment; but you must suffer it to all eternity. There will be no end to this exquisite horrible misery. When you look forward, you shall see a long forever, a boundless duration before you, which will swallow up your thoughts, and amaze your soul; and you will absolutely despair of ever having any deliverance, any end, any mitigation, any rest at all. You will know certainly that you must wear out long ages, millions of millions of ages, in wrestling and conflicting with this almighty merciless vengeance; and then when you have so done, when so many ages have actually been spent by you in this manner, you will know that all is but a point to what remains. So that your punishment will indeed be infinite. Oh, who can express what the state of a soul in such circumstances is! All that we can possibly say about it gives but a very feeble, faint representation of it; it is inexpressible and inconceivable: For "who knows the power of God's anger?"[9]

How dreadful is the state of those that are daily and hourly in the danger of this great wrath and infinite misery! But this is the dismal case of every soul in this congregation that has not been born again, however moral and strict, sober and religious, they may otherwise be. Oh that you would consider it, whether you be young or old! There is reason to think that there are many in this congregation now hearing this discourse that will actually be the subjects of this very misery to all eternity. We know not who they are, or in what seats they sit, or what thoughts they now have. It may be they are now at ease, and hear all these things without much disturbance, and are now flattering themselves that they are not the persons, promising themselves that they shall escape. If they knew that there was one person, and but one, in the whole congregation, that was to be the subject of this misery, what an awful thing would it be to think of! If we knew who it was, what an awful sight would it be to see such a person! How might all the rest of the congregation lift up a lamentable and bitter cry over him! But, alas! instead of one, how many is it likely will remember this discourse in hell? And it would be a wonder, if some that are now present should not be in hell in a very short time, even before this year is out. And it would be no wonder if some persons, that now sit here, in some seats of this meetinghouse, in health, quiet and secure, should be there before tomorrow morning. Those of you that finally continue in a natural condition, that shall keep out of hell longest will be there in a little time! your damnation does not slumber; it will come swiftly, and, in all probability, very suddenly upon many of you. You have reason to wonder that you are not already in hell. It is doubtless the case of some whom you have seen and known, that never deserved hell

---

9. "Who knoweth the power of thine anger? even according to thy fear, so is thy wrath" (Psalm 90.11).

more than you, and that heretofore appeared as likely to have been now alive as you. Their case is past all hope; they are crying in extreme misery and perfect despair; but here you are in the land of the living and in the house of God, and have an opportunity to obtain salvation. What would not those poor damned hopeless souls give for one day's opportunity such as you now enjoy!

And now you have an extraordinary opportunity, a day wherein Christ has thrown the door of mercy wide open, and stands in calling and crying with a loud voice to poor sinners; a day wherein many are flocking to Him, and pressing into the kingdom of God. Many are daily coming from the east, west, north and south; many that were very lately in the same miserable condition that you are in are now in a happy state, with their hearts filled with love to Him who has loved them, and washed them from their sins in His own blood, and rejoicing in hope of the glory of God. How awful is it to be left behind at such a day! To see so many others feasting, while you are pining and perishing! To see so many rejoicing and singing for joy of heart, while you have cause to mourn for sorrow of heart, and howl for vexation of spirit! How can you rest one moment in such a condition? Are not your souls as precious as the souls of the people at Suffield,[1] where they are flocking from day to day to Christ?

Are there not many here who have lived long in the world, and are not to this day born again? and so are aliens from the commonwealth of Israel,[2] and have done nothing ever since they have lived, but treasure up wrath against the day of wrath? Oh, sirs, your case, in an especial manner, is extremely dangerous. Your guilt and hardness of heart is extremely great. Do you not see how generally persons of your years are passed over and left, in the present remarkable and wonderful dispensation of God's mercy? You had need to consider yourselves, and awake thoroughly out of sleep. You cannot bear the fierceness and wrath of the infinite God. And you, young men, and young women, will you neglect this precious season which you now enjoy, when so many others of your age are renouncing all youthful vanities,[3] and flocking to Christ? You especially have now an extraordinary opportunity; but if you neglect it, it will soon be with you as with those persons who spent all the precious days of youth in sin, and are now come to such a dreadful pass in blindness and hardness. And you, children, who are unconverted, do not you know that you are going down to hell, to bear the dreadful wrath of that God, who is now angry with you every day and every night? Will you be content to be the children of the devil, when so many other children in the land are converted, and are become the holy and happy children of the King of kings?

And let every one that is yet out of Christ, and hanging over the pit of hell, whether they be old men and women, or middle-aged, or young people, or little children, now hearken to the loud calls of God's word and providence. This acceptable year of the Lord, a day of such great favors to some, will doubtless be a day of as remarkable vengeance to others. Men's hearts harden,

---

1. A town in the neighborhood [Edwards's note].   3. Cf. Ecclesiastes 1.2.
2. I.e., not among the chosen people, the saved.

and their guilt increases apace at such a day as this, if they neglect their souls; and never was there so great danger of such person being given up to hardness of heart and blindness of mind. God seems now to be hastily gathering in His elect[4] in all parts of the land; and probably the greater part of adult persons that ever shall be saved, will be brought in now in a little time, and that it will be as it was on the great outpouring of the Spirit upon the Jews in the apostles' days;[5] the election will obtain,[6] and the rest will be blinded. If this should be the case with you, you will eternally curse this day, and will curse the day that ever you was born, to see such a season of the pouring out of God's Spirit, and will wish that you had died and gone to hell before you had seen it. Now undoubtedly it is, as it was in the days of John the Baptist, the ax is in an extraordinary manner laid at the root of the trees,[7] that every tree which brings not forth good fruit, may be hewn down and cast into the fire.

Therefore, let everyone that is out of Christ, now awake and fly from the wrath to come. The wrath of Almighty God is now undoubtedly hanging over a great part of this congregation: Let everyone fly out of Sodom: "Haste and escape for your lives, look not behind you, escape to the mountain, lest you be consumed."[8]

Sunday, July 8, 1741.

1741

4. Those whom God has chosen to save.
5. In Acts 2, the Apostle Peter admonishes a crowd to repent and be converted, saying, "Save yourselves from this untoward generation. Then they that gladly received his word were baptized: and the same day there were added unto them about three thousand souls" (Acts 2.40–41).
6. I.e., during "the great outpouring of the

Spirit," as in a revival, the elect will respond positively to God's call.
7. "And now also the ax is laid unto the root of the trees: therefore every tree which bringeth not forth good fruit is hewn down, and cast into the fire" (Matthew 3.10).
8. Genesis 19.17.

BENJAMIN FRANKLIN
1706–1790

To a remarkable extent, the writings of Benjamin Franklin represent the metamorphosis of New England literary culture from "Puritan" to "Yankee." They also helped inaugurate the new national sensibility that emerged after the American Revolution. These regional and national transformations can be traced in *Poor Richard's Almanac*, in his political writings, and above all in *The Autobiography*, which presents the personal history and philosophy behind Franklinian self-fashioning. *The Autobiography* begins by tracing the family's origins to the English Midlands, where they were "franklins"—nonaristocractic landowners—and dissenting Protestants in a region profoundly disrupted by the English Civil Wars (1642–51). This family history of property ownership and concern for religious and civil liberties sets the stage for the life story that unfolds in sections, which Franklin produced from the eve of the American Revolution to shortly after the ratification of the United States Constitution and the inauguration of President George Washington. Because he was writing during these tumultuous times, when he was much occupied with public business, Franklin was able to carry his story only to his fifty-second year. Despite the narrative's incompleteness, Franklin's popular fame, the significance of his rise from obscure origins, and his lively prose style helped transform this loosely knit set of consecutive fragments into an iconic work.

Franklin's father, Josiah, was a maker of candles and soap who moved to Boston in 1682 from Ecton, Northamptonshire, England. He married Abiah Folger, whose father, Peter, was a poet, a linguist, and a missionary to the indigenous inhabitants of Nantucket Island. Benjamin was his father's youngest son in a family of seventeen children, and Josiah, who took pride in his Protestant ancestry, enrolled his son in Boston Grammar School as a preparation for the ministry. His plans were too financially ambitious, however, and Benjamin was forced to leave school and work for his father. The younger Franklin hated his father's occupation, however, and threatened to run away to sea.

A compromise was reached, and when Benjamin was twelve he was apprenticed to his brother James, a printer. This trade was a good fit for the young man, who loved books and reading and liked to write. In 1722, James unwittingly published his younger brother's first essay, when he printed an editorial left on his desk signed "Silence Dogood," the first in a series that Franklin produced over several months. The central theme of these letters is the promotion of the public interest, which Franklin had absorbed from Cotton Mather's *Essays to Do Good* (1710). When his brother was imprisoned in 1722 for offending Massachusetts officials, Franklin published the paper by himself.

The next year, however, Franklin broke with his brother and ran away to Philadelphia, an act of defiance that in his later telling accumulated symbolic power as a precursor to the Revolution. At seventeen, with little money in his pocket but already an expert printer, he made his way in the world, subject to numerous "errata"—as he liked to call his mistakes, using the publisher's term—but confident that he could profit from lessons learned. His most serious error was in trusting Pennsylvania governor Sir William Keith, who in 1724 sent him to London by falsely promising to sponsor a new newspaper. During his time in the British capital, Franklin worked as a typesetter and experimented with free thought, even publishing a pamphlet on the topic that he later had to explain in his *Autobiography*. He returned to the colonies two years later, at the very moment when print culture experienced a remarkable expansion and the printer came to play a major public role as a disseminator of information. Franklin, ever an astute businessman, turned this development to his advantage.

Franklin had an uncanny instinct for success and knew that commercialism demanded that anyone in business assume a public persona. He taught himself French, Spanish, Italian, and Latin and yet was shrewd enough to realize that people did not like to do business with merchants who put on airs. He dressed plainly and sometimes carried his own paper in a wheelbarrow through Philadelphia streets to assure prospective customers that he was hardworking and not above doing things for himself. By the time he was twenty-four, he was the sole owner of a successful printing shop as well as the editor and publisher of the *Pennsylvania Gazette*. He first offered his *Poor Richard's Almanac* for sale in 1733 and made it an American institution, preaching hard work and thrift, and filling it with maxims for achieving wealth.

Another of Franklin's popular writings was his pseudonymously published "Speech of Miss Polly Baker," which enjoyed transatlantic circulation and indicated his unusu-

Poor Richard, 1739.

AN

Almanack

For the Year of Chrift

1 7 3 9,

Being the Third after LEAP YEAR.

And makes fince the Creation.   Years
By the Account of the Eaftern *Greeks*   7247
By the Latin Church, when ☉ ent. ♈   6938
By the Computation of *W. W.*   5748
By the *Roman* Chronology   5688
By the *Jewifh* Rabbies   5500

Wherein is contained,

The Lunations, Eclipfes, Judgment of the Weather, Spring Tides, Planets Motions & mutual Afpeds, Sun and Moon's Rifing and Setting, Length of Days, Time of High Water, Fairs, Courts, and obfervable Days.

Fitted to the Latitude of Forty Degrees, and a Meridian of Five Hours Weft from *London,* but may without fenfible Error, ferve all the adjacent Places, even from *Newfoundland* to *South-Carolina.*

By *RICHARD SAUNDERS,* Philom.

PHILADELPHIA:
Printed and fold by *B. FRANKLIN,* at the New Printing-Office near the Market.

Almanac for 1739. Writing under the pseudonym Richard Saunders, Franklin became famous for the aphorisms included in his immensely popular *Poor Richard's Almanac.*

ally progressive views of women for his time. Franklin had already experimented with a female persona in his Silence Dogood letters, and in 1744 he had produced an edition of Samuel Richardson's novel *Pamela: or, Virtue Rewarded* (1740), which portrays a young servant woman who resists the sexual overtures of her master, until he eventually marries her. Franklin, who wanted to promote the growth of the colonial population, somewhat wryly turns the tables in Polly Baker's speech to the court, where she calls for a change in the laws that punished women who bore children outside of marriage and argues that in cases of illegitimate birth, men should share equal blame with women. These themes of the unjust and unequal punishment directed at women who violated the sexual norms of the day were emerging as central concerns in popular novels such as Richardson's *Clarissa* (1748), Susanna Rowson's *Charlotte Temple* (1791), and Hannah Webster Foster's *The Coquette* (1797). Franklin's interest in this issue was not purely intellectual or literary. In 1730, he had established a common-law marriage with Deborah Read, the daughter of his first landlady, and they went on to have two children. Around the time he married Read, Franklin fathered an illegitimate child, and Deborah accepted Franklin's son William into the household.

Before he retired from business at age forty-two, Franklin had founded a library, invented a stove, established a fire company, subscribed to an academy that would become the University of Pennsylvania, and served as secretary to the American Philosophical Society. In retirement, he intended to devote himself to public affairs and his lifelong passion for the natural sciences, especially the phenomena of sound, vapors, earthquakes, and electricity. Franklin's observations on electricity were published in London in 1751, and despite his disclaimers in *The Autobiography,* they won him the applause of British scientists. His inquiring mind was challenged most by the mechanics of the world's seemingly ordinary phenomena, and he was convinced that his mind's rational powers could solve riddles that had puzzled humankind for centuries. Franklin believed that people were naturally innocent, that all the mysteries that charmed the religious mind could be explained in ways that would promote human well-being, and that education, properly undertaken, would transform people's lives and set them free from the tyrannies of Church and monarchy. Franklin had no illusions about the "errata" of humankind, but his editorial metaphor—unlike, say, the word "sins"—suggests that human nature can progressively change.

Franklin's later years were spent at diplomatic tables in London, Paris, and Philadelphia, where his gift for irony served him well. He was a born diplomat—detached, adaptable, witty, urbane, charming, and clever—and of the slightly more than forty years left to him after his retirement, more than half were spent abroad. In 1757 he went to England to represent the colonies, and he stayed for five years. After a brief period in Philadelphia as a legislator, Franklin returned to England as a colonial representative, and there, in 1768, he began to doubt the possibility of compromise with the British government. "Parliament can make *all* laws for the colonies or *none*," he said, and "I think the arguments for the latter more numerous and weighty, than those for the former." When he returned to Philadelphia in May 1775, he was chosen as a representative to the Second Continental Congress, and he served on the committee to draft the Declaration of Independence. In October 1776, he was appointed minister to France, where he successfully negotiated a treaty of allegiance and became something of a cult hero. He was a member of the American delegation to the Paris peace conference, and he signed the Treaty of Paris in 1783, officially ending the Revolutionary War.

Franklin protested his too-long stay in Europe and returned to Philadelphia in 1785, serving as a delegate to the Constitutional Convention. At that time, he acted on the antislavery beliefs that he had come to embrace, joining and eventually serving as president for the Society for Promoting the Abolition of Slavery and the Relief of Negroes Unlawfully Held in Bondage in Philadelphia. By the time he died, he had become one of the most beloved Americans. Twenty thousand people attended his funeral, and editions of his works began appearing almost immediately. He remained a cultural hero well into the nineteenth century, and his reputation helped spawn rags-to-riches tales, such as those of Horatio Alger.

By the early twentieth century, Franklin had become a figure for intellectuals to diagnose rather than emulate. In his study *The Protestant Ethic and the Spirit of Capitalism* (1905), the German sociologist Max Weber criticized Franklin as a leading theorist of the secularized asceticism that Weber found at the heart of the capitalist economic system. In *Classic Studies in American Literature* (1923), the British novelist D. H. Lawrence, influenced by the psychoanalytic theories of Sigmund Freud, charged Franklin with indifference to the darker recesses of the soul. To these readers, Franklin's capacity for detachment suggests emotional and social inauthenticity, extending to the economic oppression of others and the repression of central elements of the self. Yet Franklin the secular ascetic was just one side of a man known for both his devotion to the public good at home and his high living at the French court. When Lawrence mocks the final precept in Franklin's "Art of Virtue"—to cultivate humility, Franklin writes, one should "imitate Jesus and Socrates"—he seemingly takes Franklin at face value, missing the ironic wit that makes Franklin's works so challenging and pleasurable. As is clear in *The Autobiography*, Franklin was a deliberate prose stylist who followed such distinguished British models as Joseph Addison and Richard Steele, John Bunyan, Daniel Defoe, and Jonathan Swift. A reading of Franklin's finest prose reveals a multifaceted and agile writer alert to the best and worst in humankind—including himself.

The Way to Wealth[1]

Preface to Poor Richard Improved

Courteous Reader,

I have heard that nothing gives an author so great pleasure, as to find his works respectfully quoted by other learned authors. This pleasure I have seldom enjoyed; for though I have been, if I may say it without vanity, an eminent author of almanacs annually now a full quarter of a century, my brother authors in the same way, for what reason I know not, have ever been very sparing in their applauses, and no other author has taken the least notice of me, so that did not my writings produce me some solid pudding, the great deficiency of praise would have quite discouraged me.

I concluded at length, that the people were the best judges of my merit; for they buy my works; and besides, in my rambles, where I am not personally known, I have frequently heard one or other of my adages repeated with "as Poor Richard says" at the end on 't; this gave me some satisfaction, as it showed not only that my instructions were regarded, but discovered likewise some respect for my authority; and I own, that to encourage the practice of remembering and repeating those wise sentences, I have sometimes quoted myself with great gravity.

Judge, then, how much I must have been gratified by an incident I am going to relate to you. I stopped my horse lately where a great number of people were collected at a vendue[2] of merchant goods. The hour of sale not being come, they were conversing on the badness of the times and one of the company called to a plain clean old man, with white locks, "Pray, Father Abraham, what think you of the times? Won't these heavy taxes quite ruin the country? How shall we be ever able to pay them? What would you advise us to?" Father Abraham stood up, and replied, "If you'd have my advice, I'll give it you in short, for a *word to the wise is enough, and many words won't fill a bushel*, as Poor Richard says." They joined in desiring him to speak his mind, and gathering round him, he proceeded as follows:

"Friends," says he, "and neighbors, the taxes are indeed very heavy, and if those laid on by the government were the only ones we had to pay, we might more easily discharge them; but we have many others, and much more grievous to some of us. We are taxed twice as much by our idleness, three times as much by our pride, and four times as much by our folly; and from these taxes the commissioners cannot ease or deliver us by allowing an abatement. However, let us hearken to good advice, and something may be done for us; *God helps them that help themselves*, as Poor Richard says, in his Almanac of 1733.

"It would be thought a hard government that should tax its people one-tenth part of their time, to be employed in its service. But idleness taxes many of us much more, if we reckon all that is spent in absolute sloth, or doing of nothing, with that which is spent in idle employments, or amusements, that

---

1. The text is from *The Writings of Benjamin Franklin* (1905), edited by Albert Henry Smyth. Franklin wrote this essay for the twenty-fifth anniversary issue of his *Almanac*, the first issue of which, under the fictitious editorship of "Richard Saunders," appeared in 1733. For this essay, Franklin brought together the best of his maxims in the guise of a speech by Father Abraham. It is frequently reprinted as "The Way to Wealth" but is also known by earlier titles: "Poor Richard Improved" and "Father Abraham's Speech."

2. Auction or sale.

amount to nothing. Sloth, by bringing on diseases, absolutely shortens life. *Sloth, like rust, consumes faster than labor wears; while the used key is always bright,* as Poor Richard says. *But dost thou love life, then do not squander time, for that's the stuff life is made of,* as Poor Richard says. How much more than is necessary do we spend in sleep, forgetting that *the sleeping fox catches no poultry* and that *there will be sleeping enough in the grave,* as Poor Richard says.

"*If time be of all things the most precious, wasting time must be,* as Poor Richard says, *the greatest prodigality;* since, as he elsewhere tells us, *lost time is never found again; and what we call time enough, always proves little enough:* let us then up and be doing, and doing to the purpose; so by diligence shall we do more with less perplexity. *Sloth makes all things difficult, but industry*[3] *all easy,* as Poor Richard says; *and he that riseth late must trot all day, and shall scarce overtake his business at night;* while *laziness travels so slowly, that poverty soon overtakes him,* as we read in Poor Richard, who adds, *drive thy business, let not that drive thee,* and *early to bed, and early to rise, makes a man healthy, wealthy, and wise.*

"So what signifies wishing and hoping for better times. We may make these times better, if we bestir ourselves. *Industry need not wish,* as Poor Richard says, *and he that lives upon hope will die fasting. There are no gains without pains; then help hands, for I have no lands,* or if I have, they are smartly taxed. And, as Poor Richard likewise observes, *he that hath a trade hath an estate; and he that hath a calling, hath an office of profit and honor;* but then the trade must be worked at, and the calling well followed, or neither the estate nor the office will enable us to pay our taxes. If we are industrious, we shall never starve; for, as Poor Richard says, *at the workingman's house hunger looks in, but dares not enter.* Nor will the bailiff or the constable enter, for *industry pays debts, while despair increaseth them,* says Poor Richard. What though you have found no treasure, nor has any rich relation left you a legacy, *diligence is the mother of good luck,* as Poor Richard says, and *God gives all things to industry. Then plow deep, while sluggards sleep, and you shall have corn to sell and to keep,* says Poor Dick. Work while it is called today, for you know not how much you may be hindered tomorrow, which makes Poor Richard says, *one today is worth two tomorrows,* and farther, *have you somewhat to do tomorrow, do it today.* If you were a servant, would you not be ashamed that a good master should catch you idle? Are you then your own master, *be ashamed to catch yourself idle,* as Poor Dick says. When there is so much to be done for yourself, your family, your country, and your gracious king, be up by peep of day; *let not the sun look down and say, inglorious here he lies.* Handle your tools without mittens; remember that *the cat in gloves catches no mice,* as Poor Richard says. 'Tis true there is much to be done, and perhaps you are weak-handed, but stick to it steadily; and you will see great effects, for *constant dropping*[4] *wears away stones,* and *by diligence and patience the mouse ate in two the cable;* and *little strokes fell great oaks,* as Poor Richard says in his Almanac, the year I cannot just now remember.

"Methinks I hear some of you say, 'must a man afford himself no leisure?' I will tell thee, my friend, what Poor Richard says, *employ thy time well, if thou*

3. I.e., industriousness.
4. I.e., of water.

meanest to gain leisure; and, since thou art not sure of a minute, throw not away an hour. Leisure is time for doing something useful; this leisure the diligent man will obtain, but the lazy man never; so that, as Poor Richard says *a life of leisure and a life of laziness are two things.*[5] Do you imagine that sloth will afford you more comfort than labor? No, for as Poor Richard says, *trouble springs from idleness, and grievous toil from needless ease. Many without labor, would live by their wits only, but they break for want of stock.* Whereas industry gives comfort, and plenty, and respect: *fly*[6] *pleasures, and they'll follow you. The diligent spinner has a large shift;*[7] *and now I have a sheep and a cow, everybody bids me good morrow;* all of which is well said by Poor Richard.

"But with our industry, we must likewise be steady, settled, and careful, and oversee our own affairs with our own eyes, and not trust too much to others; for, as Poor Richard says

> *I never saw an oft-removed tree,*
> *Nor yet an oft-removed family,*
> *That throve so well as those that settled be.*

And again, *three removes*[8] *is as bad as a fire;* and again, *keep thy shop, and thy shop will keep thee;* and again, *if you would have your business done, go; if not, send.* And again,

> *He that by the plow would thrive,*
> *Himself must either hold or drive.*

And again, *the eye of a master will do more work than both his hands;* and again, *want*[9] *of care does us more damage than want of knowledge;* and again, *not to oversee workmen is to leave them your purse open.* Trusting too much to others' care is the ruin of many; for, as the Almanac says, *in the affairs of this world, men are saved, not by faith, but by the want of it;* but a man's own care is profitable; for, saith Poor Dick, *learning is to the studious,* and *riches to the careful,* as well as *power to the bold,* and *heaven to the virtuous,* and farther, *if you would have a faithful servant, and one that you like, serve yourself.* And again, he adviseth to circumspection and care, even in the smallest matters, because sometimes *a little neglect may breed great mischief;* adding, *for want of a nail the shoe was lost; for want of a shoe the horse was lost; and for want of a horse the rider was lost, being overtaken and slain by the enemy; all for want of care about a horseshoe nail.*

"So much for industry, my friends, and attention to one's own business; but to these we must add frugality, if we would make our industry more certainly successful. A man may, if he knows not how to save as he gets, keep his nose all his life to the grindstone, and die not worth a groat[1] at last. *A fat kitchen makes a lean will,* as Poor Richard says; and

> *Many estates are spent in the getting,*
> *Since women for tea forsook spinning and knitting,*
> *And men for punch forsook hewing and splitting.*

---

5. I.e., two different things.　　　　8. Moves.
6. Flee.　　　　　　　　　　　　　　9. Lack.
7. Wardrobe.　　　　　　　　　　　1. A silver coin worth about four pence.

If you would be wealthy, says he, in another Almanac, *think of saving as well as of getting: the Indies have not made Spain rich, because her outgoes are greater than her incomes.*

"Away then with your expensive follies, and you will not then have so much cause to complain of hard times, heavy taxes, and chargeable families; for, as Poor Dick says,

> *Women and wine, game² and deceit,*
> *Make the wealth small and the wants great.*

And farther, *what maintains one vice would bring up two children.* You may think perhaps, that a little tea, or a little punch now and then, diet a little more costly, clothes a little finer, and a little entertainment now and then, can be no great matter; but remember what Poor Richard says, *many a little makes a mickle;* and farther, *Beware of little expenses; a small leak will sink a great ship;* and again, *who dainties³ love shall beggars prove;* and moreover, *fools make feasts, and wise men eat them.*

"Here you are all got together at this vendue of fineries and knicknacks. You call them goods; but if you do not take care, they will prove evils to some of you. You expect they will be sold cheap, and perhaps they may for less than they cost; but if you have no occasion for them, they must be dear to you. Remember what Poor Richard says; *buy what thou hast no need of, and ere long thou shalt sell thy necessaries.* And again, *at a great penny-worth pause a while:* he means, that perhaps the cheapness is apparent only, and not real; or the bargain, by straightening⁴ thee in thy business, may do thee more harm than good. For in another place he says, *many have been ruined by buying good pennyworths.* Again, Poor Richard says, *'tis foolish to lay out money in a purchase of repentance;* and yet this folly is practiced every day at vendues, for want of minding the Almanac. *Wise men,* as Poor Dick says, *learn by others' harms, fools scarcely by their own; but felix quem faciunt aliena pericula cautum.*⁵ Many a one, for the sake of finery on the back, have gone with a hungry belly, and half-starved their families. *Silks and satins, scarlet and velvets,* as Poor Richard says, *put out the kitchen fire.*

"These are not the necessaries of life; they can scarcely be called the conveniences; and yet only because they look pretty, how many want to have them! The artificial wants of mankind thus become more numerous than the natural; and, as Poor Dick says, *for one poor person, there are an hundred indigent.* By these, and other extravagancies, the genteel are reduced to poverty, and forced to borrow of those whom they formerly despised, but who through industry and frugality have maintained their standing; in which case it appears plainly, that *a plowman on his legs is higher than a gentleman on his knees,* as Poor Richard says. Perhaps they have had a small estate left them, which they knew not the getting of; they think, " 'Tis day, and will never be night"; that a little to be spent out of so much is not worth minding; *a child and a fool,* as Poor Richard says, *imagine twenty shillings and twenty years can never be spent* but, *always taking out of the meal-tub, and never putting in, soon comes to the bottom;* as Poor Dick says, *when the well's dry, they know the worth of water.* But this they might have known

---

2. Gambling.
3. Delicacies, luxuries. "Mickle": lot.

4. Restricting.
5. A Latin version of the proverb just quoted.

before, if they had taken his advice; *if you would know the value of money, go and try to borrow some; for, he that goes a-borrowing goes a-sorrowing;* and indeed so does he that lends to such people, when he goes to get it in again. Poor Dick farther advises, and says,

> Fond[6] *pride of dress is sure a very curse;*
> *E'er[7] fancy you consult, consult your purse.*

And again, *pride is as loud a beggar as want, and a great deal more saucy.* When you have bought one fine thing, you must buy ten more, that your appearance may be all of a piece; but Poor Dick says, *'tis easier to suppress the first desire, than to satisfy all that follow it.* And 'tis as truly folly for the poor to ape the rich, as for the frog to swell, in order to equal the ox.

> *Great estates may venture more,*
> *But little boats should keep near shore.*

'Tis, however, a folly soon punished; for *pride that dines on vanity sups on contempt,* as Poor Richard says. And in another place, *pride breakfasted with plenty, dined with poverty, and supped with infamy.* And after all, of what use is this pride of appearance, for which so much is risked so much is suffered? It cannot promote health, or ease pain; it makes no increase of merit in the person, it creates envy, it hastens misfortune.

> *What is a butterfly? At best*
> *He's but a caterpillar dressed.*
> *The gaudy fop's his picture just,*

as Poor Richard says.

"But what madness must it be to run in debt for these superfluities! We are offered, by the terms of this vendue, *six months' credit;* and that perhaps has induced some of us to attend it, because we cannot spare the ready money, and hope now to be fine without it. But, ah, think what you do when you run in debt; you give to another power over your liberty. If you cannot pay at the time, you will be ashamed to see your creditor; you will be in fear when you speak to him; you will make poor pitiful sneaking excuses, and by degrees come to lose your veracity, and sink into base downright lying; for, as Poor Richard says, *the second vice is lying, the first is running in debt.* And again, to the same purpose, *lying rides upon debt's back.* Whereas a free-born Englishman ought not to be ashamed or afraid to see or speak to any man living. But poverty often deprives a man of all spirit and virtue: *'tis hard for an empty bag to stand upright,* as Poor Richard truly says.

"What would you think of that prince, or that government, who should issue an edict forbidding you to dress like a gentleman or a gentlewoman, on pain of imprisonment or servitude? Would you not say, that you were free, have a right to dress as you please, and that such an edict would be a breach of your privileges, and such a government tyrannical? And yet you are about to put yourself under that tyranny, when you run in debt for such dress! Your creditor has authority, at his pleasure to deprive you of your liberty, by confining you in gaol[8] for life, or to sell you for a servant, if you should not be

6. Foolish. 8. Jail.
7. Every.

able to pay him! When you have got your bargain, you may, perhaps, think little of payment; but *creditors*, Poor Richard tells us, *have better memories than debtors*; and in another place says, *creditors are a superstitious sect, great observers of set days and times*. The day comes round before you are aware, and the demand is made before you are prepared to satisfy it, or if you bear your debt in mind, the term which at first seemed so long will, as it lessens, appear extremely short. Time will seem to have added wings to his heels as well as shoulders. *Those have a short Lent*, saith Poor Richard, *who owe money to be paid at Easter.*[9] Then since, as he says, *The borrower is a slave to the lender, and the debtor to the creditor,* disdain the chain, preserve your freedom; and maintain your independency: be industrious and free; be frugal and free. At present, perhaps, you may think yourself in thriving circumstances, and that you can bear a little extravagance without injury; but,

> For age and want, save while you may;
> No morning sun lasts a whole day,

as Poor Richard says. Gain may be temporary and uncertain, but ever while you live, expense is constant and certain; and *'tis easier to build two chimneys than to keep one in fuel*, as Poor Richard says. So, *rather go to bed supperless than rise in debt.*

> Get[1] *what you can, and what you get hold;*
> *'Tis the stone that will turn all your lead into gold,*

as Poor Richard says. And when you have got the philosopher's stone,[2] sure you will no longer complain of bad times, or the difficulty of paying taxes.

"This doctrine, my friends, is reason and wisdom; but after all, do not depend too much upon your own industry, and frugality, and prudence, though excellent things, for they may all be blasted without the blessing of heaven; and therefore, ask that blessing humbly, and be not uncharitable to those that at present seem to want it, but comfort and help them. Remember, Job[3] suffered, and was afterwards prosperous.

"And now to conclude, *experience keeps a dear[4] school, but fools will learn in no other, and scarce in that*; for it is true, *we may give advice, but we cannot give conduct*, as Poor Richard says: however, remember this, *they that won't be counseled, can't be helped*, as Poor Richard says: and farther, that, *if you will not hear reason, she'll surely rap your knuckles.*"

Thus the old gentleman ended his harangue. The people heard it, and approved the doctrine, and immediately practiced the contrary, just as if it had been a common sermon; for the vendue opened, and they began to buy extravagantly, notwithstanding his cautions and their own fear of taxes. I found the good man had thoroughly studied my almanacs, and digested all I had dropped on these topics during the course of five and twenty years. The frequent mention he made of me must have tired any one else, but my vanity was wonderfully delighted with it, though I was conscious that not a tenth part of the wisdom was my own, which he ascribed to me, but rather

9. In Christianity, Lent is the period of roughly six weeks before Easter. Poor Richard is saying debt would make that period feel shorter.
1. Earn.
2. A substance much sought by alchemists,

thought to transform base metals into gold.
3. The Old Testament patriarch whose faith was tested by suffering.
4. Expensive.

the gleanings I had made of the sense of all ages and nations. However, I resolved to be the better for the echo of it; and though I had at first determined to buy stuff for a new coat, I went away resolved to wear my old one a little longer. Reader, if thou wilt do the same, thy profit will be as great as mine. I am, as ever, thine to serve thee,

Richard Saunders
July 7, 1757

1757   1758

The Speech of Miss Polly Baker[1]

*The Speech of Miss Polly Baker, Before a Court of Judicature,
at Connecticut in New England, Where She Was Prosecuted
the Fifth Time for Having a Bastard Child; Which Influenced the
Court to Dispense with Her Punishment, and Induced One of Her
Judges to Marry Her the next Day*

May it please the Honourable Bench to indulge me a few Words: I am a poor unhappy Woman; who have no Money to Fee Lawyers to plead for me, being hard put to it to get a tolerable Living. I shall not trouble your Honours with long Speeches; for I have not the presumption to expect, that you may, by any Means, be prevailed on to deviate in your Sentence from the Law, in my Favour. All I humbly hope is, that your Honours would charitably move the Governor's Goodness on my Behalf, that my Fine may be remitted. This is the Fifth Time, Gentlemen, that I have been dragg'd before your Courts on the same Account; twice I have paid heavy Fines, and twice have been brought to public Punishment, for want of Money to pay those Fines. This may have been agreeable to the Laws; I do not dispute it: But since Laws are sometimes unreasonable in themselves, and therefore repealed; and others bear too hard on the Subject in particular Circumstances; and therefore there is left a Power somewhere to dispense with the Execution of them; I take the Liberty to say, that I think this Law, by which I am punished, is both unreasonable in itself, and particularly severe with regard to me, who have always lived an inoffensive Life in the Neighbourhood where I was born, and defy my Enemies (if I have any) to say I ever wrong'd Man, Woman, or Child. Abstracted from the Law, I cannot conceive (may it please your Honours) what the Nature of my Offence is. I have brought Five fine Children into the World, at the Risque of my Life: I have maintained them well by my own Industry, without burthening the Township, and could have done it better, if it had not been for the heavy Charges and Fines I have paid. Can it be a Crime (in the Nature of Things I mean) to add to the Number of the King's Subjects, in a new Country that really wants People? I own I should think it rather a Praise worthy, than a Punishable Action. I have debauch'd no other Woman's Husband, nor inticed any innocent Youth: These Things I never was charged with; nor has any one the least cause of Complaint against me, unless, perhaps the Minister, or the Justice, because I have had Children

---

1. The text is from *Gentleman's Magazine* (London), April 1747.

without being Married, by which they have miss'd a Wedding Fee. But, can even this be a Fault of mine? I appeal to your Honours. You are pleased to allow I don't want Sense; but I must be stupid to the last Degree, not to prefer the honourable State of Wedlock, to the Condition I have lived in. I always was, and still am, willing to enter into it; I doubt not my Behaving well in it, having all the Industry, Frugality, Fertility, and Skill in Oeconomy, appertaining to a good Wife's Character. I defy any Person to say I ever Refused an Offer of that Sort: On the contrary, I readily Consented to the only Proposal of Marriage that ever was made me, which was when I was a Virgin; but too easily confiding in the Person's Sincerity that made it, I unhappily lost my own Honour, by trusting to his; for he got me with Child, and then forsook me: That very Person you all know; he is now become a Magistrate of this County; and I had hopes he would have appeared this Day on the Bench, and have endeavoured to moderate the Court in my Favour; then I should have scorn'd to have mention'd it; but I must Complain of it as unjust and unequal, that my Betrayer and Undoer, the first Cause of all my Faults and Miscarriages (if they must be deemed such) should be advanced to Honour and Power, in the same Government that punishes my Misfortunes with Stripes and Infamy. I shall be told, 'tis like, that were there no Act of Assembly in the Case, the Precepts of Religion are violated by my Transgressions. If mine, then, is a religious Offence, leave it, Gentlemen, to religious Punishments. You have already excluded me from all the Comforts of your Church Communion: Is not that sufficient? You believe I have offended Heaven, and must suffer eternal Fire: Will not that be sufficient? What need is there, then, of your additional Fines and Whippings? I own, I do not think as you do; for, if I thought, what you call a Sin, was really such, I would not presumptuously commit it. But how can it be believed, that Heaven is angry at my having Children, when, to the little done by me towards it, God has been pleased to add his divine Skill and admirable Workmanship in the Formation of their Bodies, and crown'd it by furnishing them with rational and immortal Souls? Forgive me Gentlemen, if I talk a little extravagantly on these Matters; I am no Divine: But if you, great Men, (*)[2] must be making Laws, do not turn natural and useful Actions into Crimes, by your Prohibitions. Reflect a little on the horrid Consequences of this Law in particular: What Numbers of procur'd Abortions! and how many distress'd Mothers have been driven, by the Terror of Punishment and public Shame, to imbrue, contrary to Nature, their own trembling Hands in the Blood of their helpless Offspring! Nature would have induc'd them to nurse it up with a Parent's Fondness. 'Tis the Law therefore, 'tis the Law itself that is guilty of all these Barbarities and Murders. Repeal it then, Gentlemen; let it be expung'd for ever from your Books: And on the other hand, take into your wise Consideration, the great and growing Number of Batchelors in the Country, many of whom, from the mean Fear of the Expence of a Family, have never sincerely and honourably Courted a Woman in their Lives; and by their Manner of Living, leave unproduced (which I think is little better than Murder) Hundreds of their Posterity to the Thousandth Generation. Is not theirs a greater Offence against the Public Good, than mine? Compel them then, by a Law, either to Marry, or pay double the Fine

2. (*) Turning to some Gentlemen of the Assembly, then in Court [Franklin's note].

of Fornication every Year. What must poor young Women do, whom Custom has forbid to solicit the Men, and who cannot force themselves upon Husbands, when the Laws take no Care to provide them any, and yet severely punish if they do their Duty without them? Yes, Gentlemen, I venture to call it a Duty; 'tis the Duty of the first and great Command of Nature, and of Nature's God, *Increase and multiply*: A Duty, from the steady Performance of which nothing has ever been able to deter me; but for it's Sake, I have hazarded the Loss of the public Esteem, and frequently incurr'd public Disgrace and Punishment; and therefore ought, in my humble Opinion, instead of a Whipping, to have a Statue erected to my Memory.

1747

Remarks Concerning the Savages of North America[1]

Savages we call them, because their manners differ from ours, which we think the perfection of civility; they think the same of theirs.

Perhaps, if we could examine the manners of different nations with impartiality, we should find no people so rude, as to be without any rules of politeness; nor any so polite, as not to have some remains of rudeness.[2]

The Indian men, when young, are hunters and warriors; when old, counselors; for all their government is by counsel of the sages; there is no force, there are no prisons, no officers to compel obedience, or inflict punishment. Hence they generally study oratory, the best speaker having the most influence. The Indian women till the ground, dress the food, nurse and bring up the children, and preserve and hand down to posterity the memory of public transactions. These employments of men and women are accounted natural and honorable. Having few artificial wants, they have abundance of leisure for improvement by conversation. Our laborious manner of life, compared with theirs, they esteem slavish and base; and the learning, on which we value ourselves, they regard as frivolous and useless. An instance of this occurred at the Treaty of Lancaster, in Pennsylvania, *anno* 1744, between the government of Virginia and the Six Nations.[3] After the principal business was settled, the commissioners from Virginia acquainted the Indians by a speech, that there was at Williamsburg a college, with a fund for educating Indian youth; and that, if the Six Nations would send down half a dozen of their young lads to that college, the government would take care that they should be well provided for, and instructed in all the learning of the white people. It is one of the Indian rules of politeness not to answer a public proposition the same day that it is made; they think it would be treating it as a light matter, and that they show it respect by taking time to consider it, as of a matter important. They therefore deferred their answer till the day following; when their speaker began, by expressing their deep

1. The text is from *The Writings of Benjamin Franklin* (1905), edited by Albert Henry Smyth.
2. In Franklin's time, not only unmannerly behavior but also, more broadly, unsophisticated and uncivilized behavior. "Politeness": not just mannerly behavior but also sophisticated and civilized behavior.
3. The Iroquois confederacy, consisting of the Seneca, Cayuga, Oneida, Onondaga, Mohawk, and Tuscarora tribes. "*Anno*": in the year (Latin).

sense of the kindness of the Virginia government, in making them that offer; "for we know," says he, "that you highly esteem the kind of learning taught in those Colleges, and that the maintenance of our young men, while with you, would be very expensive to you. We are convinced, therefore, that you mean to do us good by your proposal; and we thank you heartily. But you, who are wise, must know that different nations have different conceptions of things; and you will therefore not take it amiss, if our ideas of this kind of education happen not to be the same with yours. We have had some experience of it; several of our young people were formerly brought up at the colleges of the northern provinces; they were instructed in all your sciences; but, when they came back to us, they were bad runners, ignorant of every means of living in the woods, unable to bear either cold or hunger, knew neither how to build a cabin, take a deer, or kill an enemy, spoke our language imperfectly, were therefore neither fit for hunters, warriors, nor counselors; they were totally good for nothing. We are however not the less obliged by your kind offer, though we decline accepting it; and, to show our grateful sense of it, if the gentlemen of Virginia will send us a dozen of their sons, we will take great care of their education, instruct them in all we know, and make *men* of them."

Having frequent occasions to hold public councils, they have acquired great order and decency in conducting them. The old men sit in the foremost ranks, the warriors in the next, and the women and children in the hindmost. The business of the women is to take exact notice of what passes, imprint it in their memories (for they have no writing), and communicate it to their children. They are the records of the council, and they preserve traditions of the stipulations in treaties 100 years back; which, when we compare with our writings, we always find exact. He that would speak, rises. The rest observe a profound silence. When he has finished and sits down, they leave him 5 or 6 minutes to recollect, that, if he has omitted anything he intended to say, or has anything to add, he may rise again and deliver it. To interrupt another, even in common conversation, is reckoned highly indecent. How different this from the conduct of a polite British House of Commons, where scarce a day passes without some confusion, that makes the speaker hoarse in calling to *order;* and how different from the mode of conversation in many polite companies of Europe, where, if you do not deliver your sentence with great rapidity, you are cut off in the middle of it by the impatient loquacity of those you converse with, and never suffered to finish it!

The politeness of these savages in conversation is indeed carried to excess, since it does not permit them to contradict or deny the truth of what is asserted in their presence. By this means they indeed avoid disputes; but then it becomes difficult to know their minds, or what impression you make upon them. The missionaries who have attempted to convert them to Christianity all complain of this as one of the great difficulties of their mission. The Indians hear with patience the truths of the Gospel explained to them, and give their usual tokens of assent and approbation; you would think they were convinced. No such matter. It is mere civility.

A Swedish minister, having assembled the chiefs of the Susquehanah Indians, made a sermon to them, acquainting them with the principal historical facts on which our religion is founded; such as the fall of our first parents by eating an apple, the coming of Christ to repair the mischief, His miracles and suffering, etc. When he had finished, an Indian orator stood up to thank him. "What you have told us," he says, "is all very good. It is indeed bad to eat apples. It is better to make them all into cider. We are much obliged by your kindness in coming so far, to tell us these things which you have heard from your mothers. In return, I will tell you some of those we have heard from ours. In the beginning, our fathers had only the flesh of animals to subsist on; and if their hunting was unsuccessful, they were starving. Two of our young hunters, having killed a deer, made a fire in the woods to broil some part of it. When they were about to satisfy their hunger, they beheld a beautiful young woman descend from the clouds, and seat herself on that hill, which you see yonder among the blue mountains. They said to each other, it is a spirit that has smelled our broiling venison, and wishes to eat of it; let us offer some to her. They presented her with the tongue; she was pleased with the taste of it, and said, 'Your kindness shall be rewarded; come to this place after thirteen moons, and you shall find something that will be of great benefit in nourishing you and your children to the latest generations.' They did so, and, to their surprise, found plants they had never seen before; but which, from that ancient time, have been constantly cultivated among us, to our great advantage. Where her right hand had touched the ground, they found maize; where her left hand had touched it, they found kidney-beans; and where her backside had sat on it, they found tobacco." The good missionary, disgusted with this idle tale, said, "What I delivered to you were sacred truths; but what you tell me is mere fable, fiction, and falsehood." The Indian, offended, replied, "My brother, it seems your friends have not done you justice in your education; they have not well instructed you in the rules of common civility. You saw that we, who understand and practice those rules, believed all your stories; why do you refuse to believe ours?"

When any of them come into our towns, our people are apt to crowd round them, gaze upon them, and incommode them, where they desire to be private; this they esteem great rudeness, and the effect of the want of instruction in the rules of civility and good manners. "We have," say they, "as much curiosity as you, and when you come into our towns, we wish for opportunities of looking at you, but for this purpose we hide ourselves behind bushes, where you are to pass, and never intrude ourselves into your company."

Their manner of entering one another's village has likewise its rules. It is reckoned uncivil in traveling strangers to enter a village abruptly, without giving notice of their approach. Therefore, as soon as they arrive within hearing, they stop and hollow,[4] remaining there till invited to enter. Two old men usually come out to them, and lead them in. There is in every village a vacant dwelling, called *the stranger's house.* Here they are placed, while the old men go round from hut to hut, acquainting the inhabitants, that strangers are arrived, who are probably hungry and weary; and every one sends them what he can spare of victuals, and skins to repose on. When the strangers are refreshed, pipes and tobacco are brought; and then, but not before, conversation begins, with inquiries who they are, whither bound, what news, etc.; and it usually ends with offers of service, if the strangers

---

4. Cry out; announce themselves.

have occasion of guides, or any necessaries for continuing their journey; and nothing is exacted for the entertainment.[5]

The same hospitality, esteemed among them as a principal virtue, is practiced by private persons; of which Conrad Weiser, our interpreter, gave me the following instances. He had been naturalized among the Six Nations, and spoke well the Mohawk language. In going through the Indian country, to carry a message from our Governor to the Council at Onondaga, he called at the habitation of Canassatego, an old acquaintance, who embraced him, spread furs for him to sit on, placed before him some boiled beans and venison, and mixed some rum and water for his drink. When he was well refreshed, and had lit his pipe, Canassatego began to converse with him; asked how he had fared the many years since they had seen each other; whence he then came; what occasioned the journey, etc. Conrad answered all his questions; and when the discourse began to flag, the Indian, to continue it, said, "Conrad, you have lived long among the white people, and know something of their customs; I have been sometimes at Albany, and have observed, that once in seven days they shut up their shops, and assemble all in the great house; tell me what it is for? What do they do there?" "They meet there," says Conrad, "to hear and learn *good things.*" "I do not doubt," says the Indian, "that they tell you so; they have told me the same; but I doubt the truth of what they say, and I will tell you my reasons. I went lately to Albany to sell my skins and buy blankets, knives, powder, rum, etc. You know I used generally to deal with Hans Hanson; but I was a little inclined this time to try some other merchant. However, I called first upon Hans, and asked him what he would give for beaver. He said he could not give any more than four shillings a pound; 'but,' says he, 'I cannot talk on business now; this is the day when we meet together to learn *good things,* and I am going to the meeting.' So I thought to myself, 'Since we cannot do any business today, I may as well go to the meeting too,' and I went with him. There stood up a man in black, and began to talk to the people very angrily. I did not understand what he said; but, perceiving that he looked much at me and at Hanson, I imagined he was angry at seeing me there; so I went out, sat down near the house, struck fire, and lit my pipe, waiting till the meeting should break up. I thought too, that the man had mentioned something of beaver, and I suspected it might be the subject of their meeting. So, when they came out, I accosted my merchant. 'Well, Hans,' says I, 'I hope you have agreed to give more than four shillings a pound.' 'No,' says he, 'I cannot give so much; I cannot give more than three shillings and sixpence.' I then spoke to several other dealers, but they all sung the same song,—three and sixpence,—three and sixpence. This made it clear to me, that my suspicion was right; and, that whatever they pretended of meeting to learn *good things,* the real purpose was to consult how to cheat Indians in the price of beaver. Consider but a little, Conrad, and you must be of my opinion. If they met so often to learn *good things,* they would certainly have learned some before this time. But they are still ignorant. You know our practice. If a white man, in traveling through our country, enters one of our cabins, we all treat him as I treat you; we dry him if he is wet, we warm him if he is cold, we give

5. I.e., hospitality.

him meat and drink, that he may allay his thirst and hunger; and we spread soft furs for him to rest and sleep on; we demand nothing in return. But, if I go into a white man's house at Albany, and ask for victuals and drink, they say, 'Where is your money?' and if I have none, they say, 'Get out, you Indian dog.' You see they have not yet learned those little *good things*, that we need no meetings to be instructed in, because our mothers taught them to us when we were children; and therefore it is impossible their meetings should be, as they say, for any such purpose, or have any such effect; they are only to contrive *the cheating of Indians in the price of beaver.*"[6]

1784

The Autobiography   Franklin worked on the manuscript of *The Autobiography* on four different occasions over a period of nineteen years. The first part is addressed to his son William Franklin (1731–1813), governor of New Jersey when Franklin was writing this section. Franklin was visiting the country home of Bishop Jonathan Shipley at Twyford, a village about fifty miles from London. He began writing on July 30 and finished on or about August 13, 1771. Franklin did not return to the manuscript until about thirteen years later, when he was living in France and serving as minister of the newly formed United States. He wrote the last two sections in August 1788 and the winter of 1789–90, stopping because of illness. The account goes up only to 1758, so it does not cover Franklin's great triumphs as a diplomat and public servant.

In 1791, the Paris publisher Jacques Buisson issued the first part of *The Autobiography* in a French translation. William Temple Franklin, Franklin's grandson and secretary, published a London edition of 1818 that included the first three parts in English. Temple Franklin had accidentally traded his handwritten manuscript of the full text for an incomplete copy. It was not until 1868 that the American lawyer and statesman John Bigelow published all four parts of the autobiography, in a more reliable edition based on a manuscript that he bought in France.

The text reprinted here is the first one taken directly from the manuscript (other editors have merely corrected earlier printed texts). It was established by J. A. Leo Lemay and Paul Zall for their 1986 Norton Critical Edition of *The Autobiography* and is here reprinted with permission. The text has been modernized only slightly. All manuscript abbreviations and symbols have been expanded. The editors omitted short dashes, which Franklin often wrote after sentences, and punctuation marks that "have been clearly superseded by revisions or additions." Careless slips have been corrected silently but are noted in the section on emendations in their text. Lemay and Zall generously let the editors of this anthology consult their footnotes and biographical sketches. Also helpful were the edition of Leonard W. Labaree et al. (1964) and Joyce E. Chaplin's revised Norton Critical Edition (2012).

6. "It is remarkable that in all ages and countries hospitality has been allowed as the virtue of those whom the civilized were pleased to call barbarians. The Greeks celebrated the Scythians for it. The Saracens possessed it eminently, and it is to this day the reigning virtue of the wild Arabs. St. Paul, too, in the relation of his voyage and shipwreck on the island of Melité says "the barbarous people showed us no little kindness; for they kindled a fire, and received us every one, because of the present rain, and because of the cold" [Franklin's note; the Apostle Paul relates his visit to Melita in Acts 28].

The Autobiography

[Part One]

TWYFORD, AT THE BISHOP OF ST. ASAPH'S 1771

Dear Son,

I have ever had a Pleasure in obtaining any little Anecdotes of my Ancestors. You may remember the Enquiries I made among the Remains of my Relations[1] when you were with me in England; and the Journey I took for that purpose. Now imagining it may be equally agreeable to you to know the Circumstances of *my* Life, many of which you are yet unacquainted with; and expecting a Week's uninterrupted Leisure in my present Country Retirement, I sit down to write them for you. To which I have besides some other Inducements. Having emerg'd from the Poverty and Obscurity in which I was born and bred, to a State of Affluence and some Degree of Reputation in the World, and having gone so far thro' Life with a considerable Share of Felicity, the conducting Means I made use of, which, with the Blessing of God, so well succeeded, my Posterity may like to know, as they may find some of them suitable to their own Situations, and therefore fit to be imitated. That Felicity, when I reflected on it, has induc'd me sometimes to say, that were it offer'd to my Choice, I should have no Objection to a Repetition of the same Life from its Beginning, only asking the Advantage Authors have in a second Edition to correct some Faults of the first. So would I if I might, besides correcting the Faults, change some sinister Accidents and Events of it for others more favorable, but tho' this were denied, I should still accept the Offer. However, since such a Repetition is not to be expected, the Thing most like living one's Life over again, seems to be a *Recollection* of that Life; and to make that Recollection as durable as possible, the putting it down in Writing. Hereby, too, I shall indulge the Inclination so natural in old Men, to be talking of themselves and their own past Actions, and I shall indulge it, without being troublesome to others who thro' respect to Age might think themselves oblig'd to give me a Hearing, since this may be read or not as any one pleases. And lastly, (I may as well confess it, since my Denial of it will be believ'd by no body) perhaps I shall a good deal gratify my own *Vanity*. Indeed I scarce ever heard or saw the introductory Words, *Without Vanity I may say,* etc. but some vain thing immediately follow'd. Most People dislike Vanity in others whatever Share they have of it themselves, but I give it fair Quarter wherever I meet with it, being persuaded that it is often productive of Good to the Possessor and to others that are within his Sphere of Action: And therefore in many Cases it would not be quite absurd if a Man were to thank God for his Vanity among the other Comforts of Life.

And now I speak of thanking God, I desire with all Humility to acknowledge, that I owe the mention'd Happiness of my past Life to his kind Providence, which led me to the Means I us'd and gave them Success. My Belief of This, induces me to *hope,* tho' I must not *presume,* that the same Goodness will still be exercis'd towards me in continuing that Happiness, or in

---

1. I.e., the remaining representatives of his family. Franklin and his son toured England in 1758 and visited ancestral homes at Ecton and Banbury.

enabling me to bear a fatal Reverso,[2] which I may experience as others have done, the Complexion of my future Fortune being known to him only: and in whose Power it is to bless to us even our Afflictions.

The Notes one of my Uncles (who had the same kind of Curiosity in collecting Family Anecdotes) once put into my Hands, furnish'd me with several Particulars, relating to our Ancestors. From those Notes I learned that the Family had liv'd in the same Village, Ecton in Northamptonshire, for 300 Years, and how much longer he knew not, (perhaps from the Time when the Name *Franklin* that before was the Name of an Order of People,[3] was assum'd by them for a Surname, when others took Surnames all over the Kingdom)[4] on a Freehold of about 30 Acres, aided by the Smith's Business which had continued in the Family till his Time, the eldest Son being always bred to that Business. A Custom which he and my Father both followed as to their eldest Sons. When I search'd the Register at Ecton, I found an Account of their Births, Marriages and Burials, from the Year 1555 only, there being no Register kept in that Parish at any time preceding. By that Register I perceiv'd that I was the youngest Son of the youngest Son for 5 Generations back. My Grandfather Thomas, who was born in 1598, lived at Ecton till he grew too old to follow Business longer, when he went to live with his Son John, a Dyer at Banbury in Oxfordshire, with whom my Father serv'd an Apprenticeship. There my Grandfather died and lies buried. We saw his Gravestone in 1758. His eldest Son Thomas liv'd in the House at Ecton, and left it with the Land to his only Child, a Daughter, who with her Husband, one Fisher of Wellingborough, sold it to Mr. Isted, now Lord of the Manor there.

My Grandfather had 4 Sons that grew up, viz., Thomas, John, Benjamin and Josiah. I will give you what Account I can of them at this distance from my Papers, and if those are not lost in my Absence, you will among them find many more Particulars. Thomas was bred a Smith under his Father, but being ingenious, and encourag'd in Learning (as all his Brothers likewise were,) by an Esquire[5] Palmer then the principal Gentleman in that Parish, he qualified himself for the Business of Scrivener,[6] became a considerable Man in the County Affairs, was a chief Mover of all public Spirited Undertakings for the County or Town of Northampton and his own Village, of which many Instances were told us at Ecton, and he was much taken Notice of and patroniz'd by the then Lord Halifax. He died in 1702, Jan. 6, old Stile,[7] just 4 Years to a Day before I was born. The Account we receiv'd of his Life and Character from some old People at Ecton, I remember struck you as something extraordinary from its Similarity to what you knew of mine. Had he died on the same Day, you said one might have suppos'd a Transmigration.[8]

John was bred a Dyer, I believe of Woollens. Benjamin was bred a Silk Dyer, serving an Apprenticeship at London. He was an ingenious Man.

2. I.e., a backhanded stroke; a term used in dueling with rapiers.
3. A "franklin" was a freeholder—a land owner not of noble birth.
4. Here a note [Franklin had intended to insert a note here].
5. An honorific originally extended to a young man of gentle birth but extended as a courtesy to any gentleman.
6. A professional copier of documents.

7. Until 1752, England used the Julian calendar, in which the new year began on March 25. Because the Julian calendar did not have leap years, it had fallen behind the astronomical year; the English skipped eleven days when adopting the Gregorian calendar. Franklin's birthday is either January 6, 1705–06, Old Style, or January 17, 1706, New Style.
8. The passage of the soul, upon death, to another's body.

I remember him well, for when I was a Boy he came over to my Father in Boston, and lived in the House with us some Years. He lived to a great Age. His Grandson Samuel Franklin now lives in Boston. He left behind him two Quarto[9] Volumes, Manuscript of his own Poetry, consisting of little occasional Pieces address'd to his Friends and Relations, of which the following sent to me, is a Specimen.[1] He had form'd a Shorthand of his own, which he taught me, but never practicing it I have now forgot it. I was nam'd after this Uncle, there being a particular Affection between him and my Father. He was very pious, a great Attender of Sermons of the best Preachers, which he took down in his Shorthand and had with him many Volumes of them. He was also much of a Politician, too much perhaps for his Station. There fell lately into my Hands in London a Collection he had made of all the principal Pamphlets relating to Public Affairs from 1641 to 1717. Many of the Volumes are wanting, as appears by the Numbering, but there still remains 8 Volumes Folio, and 24 in Quarto and Octavo. A Dealer in old Books met with them, and knowing me by my sometimes buying of him, he brought them to me. It seems my Uncle must have left them here when he went to America, which was above 50 Years since. There are many of his Notes in the Margins.

This obscure Family of ours was early in the Reformation, and continu'd Protestants thro' the Reign of Queen Mary,[2] when they were sometimes in Danger of Trouble on Account of their Zeal against Popery. They had got an English Bible,[3] and to conceal and secure it, it was fastened open with Tapes under and within the Frame of a Joint Stool.[4] When my Great Great Grandfather read in it to his Family, he turn'd up the Joint Stool upon his Knees, turning over the Leaves then under the Tapes. One of the Children stood at the Door to give Notice if he saw the Apparitor[5] coming, who was an Officer of the Spiritual Court. In that Case the Stool was turn'd down again upon its feet, when the Bible remain'd conceal'd under it as before. This Anecdote I had from my Uncle Benjamin. The Family continu'd all of the Church of England till about the End of Charles the Second's Reign,[6] when some of the Ministers that had been outed for Nonconformity, holding Conventicles[7] in Northamptonshire, Benjamin and Josiah adher'd to them, and so continu'd all their Lives. The rest of the Family remain'd with the Episcopal Church.

Josiah, my Father, married young, and carried his Wife with three Children unto New England, about 1682.[8] The Conventicles having been forbidden by Law, and frequently disturbed, induced some considerable Men of his Acquaintance to remove to that Country, and he was prevail'd with to accompany them thither, where they expected to enjoy their Mode of Religion

---

9. The terms "folio," "quarto," and "octavo" designate book sizes from large to small. A single sheet of paper folded once makes a folio, or four sides for printing; a quarto is obtained if the sheet is folded again; an octavo is the sheet folded once more.

1. Here insert it [Franklin's note, but he did not include the example].

2. Mary Tudor (1516–1558; reigned 1553–58) tried to restore Roman Catholicism as the national Church.

3. Also known as the "Geneva" version, translated by Reformed English Protestants living in

Switzerland; this version, used by the Puritans, was outlawed by the Church of England.

4. A small, four-legged stool.

5. An officer of an ecclesiastical court, in this case a court established to eliminate heresy.

6. Charles II (1630–1685) reigned from 1660 to 1685.

7. Secret and illegal meetings of Nonconformists, outlawed in 1664. Nonconformists refused to adopt the rituals and acknowledge the hierarchy of the Church of England.

8. More correctly, October 1683.

with Freedom. By the same Wife he had 4 Children more born there, and by a second Wife ten more, in all 17, of which I remember 13 sitting at one time at his Table, who all grew up to be Men and Women, and married. I was the youngest Son and the youngest Child but two, and was born in Boston, New England.

My Mother the second Wife was Abiah Folger, a Daughter of Peter Folger, one of the first Settlers of New England, of whom honorable mention is made by Cotton Mather, in his Church History of that Country, (entitled Magnalia Christi Americana) as a *godly learned Englishman,* if I remember the Words rightly.[9] I have heard that he wrote sundry small occasional Pieces, but only one of them was printed which I saw now many Years since. It was written in 1675, in the homespun Verse of that Time and People, and address'd to those then concern'd in the Government there. It was in favor of Liberty of Conscience, and in behalf of the Baptists, Quakers, and other Sectaries,[1] that had been under Persecution; ascribing the Indian Wars and other Distresses that had befallen the Country to that Persecution, as so many Judgments of God, to punish so heinous an Offence; and exhorting a Repeal of those uncharitable Laws. The whole appear'd to me as written with a good deal of Decent Plainness and manly Freedom. The six last concluding Lines I remember, tho' I have forgotten the two first of the Stanza, but the Purport of them was that his Censures proceeded from *Goodwill,* and therefore he would be known as the Author,

> because to be a Libeler, (says he)
> I hate it with my Heart.
> From Sherburne Town[2] where now I dwell,
> My Name I do put here,
> Without Offence, your real Friend,
> It is Peter Folgier.

My elder Brothers were all put Apprentices to different Trades. I was put to the Grammar School at Eight Years of Age, my Father intending to devote me as the Tithe[3] of his Sons to the Service of the Church. My early Readiness in learning to read (which must have been very early, as I do not remember when I could not read) and the Opinion of all his Friends that I should certainly make a good Scholar, encourag'd him in this Purpose of his. My Uncle Benjamin too approv'd of it, and propos'd to give me all his Shorthand Volumes of Sermons, I suppose as a Stock to set up with, if I would learn his Character.[4] I continu'd however at the Grammar School not quite one Year, tho' in that time I had risen gradually from the Middle of the Class of that Year to be the Head of it, and farther was remov'd into the next Class above it, in order to go with that into the third at the End of the Year. But my Father in the meantime, from a View of the Expense of a College Education which, having so large a Family, he could not well afford, and the mean Living many so educated were afterwards able to obtain, Reasons that he gave to his Friends in my Hearing, altered his first Intention, took me

---

9. Cotton Mather's ecclesiastical history was published in London in 1702; the quotation is properly "an Able Godly Englishman."
1. Sectarians; believers or followers of a particular religious teaching.

2. In the Island of Nantucket [Franklin's note].
3. I.e., as if his son were the tenth part of his income, traditionally given to the Church.
4. Here, his system of shorthand.

from the Grammar School, and sent me to a School for Writing and Arithmetic kept by a then famous Man, Mr. George Brownell, very successful in his Profession generally, and that by mild encouraging Methods. Under him I acquired fair Writing pretty soon, but I fail'd in the Arithmetic, and made no Progress in it.

At Ten Years old, I was taken home to assist my Father in his Business, which was that of a Tallow Chandler and Soap-Boiler.[5] A Business he was not bred to, but had assumed on his Arrival in New England and on finding his Dying Trade would not maintain his Family, being in little Request. Accordingly I was employed in cutting Wick for the Candles, filling the Dipping Mold, and the Molds for cast Candles, attending the Shop, going of Errands, etc. I dislik'd the Trade and had a strong Inclination for the Sea; but my Father declar'd against it; however, living near the Water, I was much in and about it, learned early to swim well, and to manage Boats, and when in a Boat or Canoe with other Boys I was commonly allow'd to govern,[6] especially in any case of Difficulty; and upon other Occasions I was generally a Leader among the Boys, and sometimes led them into Scrapes, of which I will mention one Instance, as it shows an early projecting[7] public Spirit, tho' not then justly conducted. There was a Salt Marsh that bounded part of the Mill Pond, on the Edge of which at Highwater, we us'd to stand to fish for Minnows. By much Trampling, we had made it a mere Quagmire. My Proposal was to build a Wharf there fit for us to stand upon, and I show'd my Comrades a large Heap of Stones which were intended for a new House near the Marsh, and which would very well suit our Purpose. Accordingly in the Evening when the Workmen were gone, I assembled a Number of my Playfellows, and working with them diligently like so many Emmets,[8] sometimes two or three to a Stone, we brought them all away and built our little Wharf. The next Morning the Workmen were surpris'd at Missing the Stones; which were found in our Wharf; Enquiry was made after the Removers; we were discovered and complain'd of; several of us were corrected by our Fathers; and tho' I pleaded the Usefulness of the Work, mine convinc'd me that nothing was useful which was not honest.

I think you may like to know something of his Person and Character. He had an excellent Constitution of Body, was of middle Stature, but well set and very strong. He was ingenious, could draw prettily, was skill'd a little in Music and had a clear pleasing Voice, so that when he play'd Psalm Tunes on his Violin and sung withal as he some times did in an Evening after the Business of the Day was over, it was extremely agreeable to hear. He had a mechanical Genius too, and on occasion was very handy in the Use of other Tradesmen's Tools. But his great Excellence lay in a sound Understanding, and solid Judgment in prudential Matters, both in private and public Affairs. In the latter indeed he was never employed, the numerous Family he had to educate and the Straitness of his Circumstances, keeping him close to his Trade, but I remember well his being frequently visited by leading People, who consulted him for his Opinion on Affairs of the Town or of the Church he belong'd to and show'd a good deal of Respect for his Judgment and Advice. He was also much consulted by private Persons about their Affairs

5. Maker of candles and soap.   7. Enterprising.
6. Steer.   8. Ants.

when any Difficulty occur'd, and frequently chosen an Arbitrator between contending Parties. At his Table he lik'd to have as often as he could, some sensible Friend or Neighbor, to converse with, and always took care to start some ingenious or useful Topic for Discourse, which might tend to improve the Minds of his Children. By this means he turn'd our Attention to what was good, just, and prudent in the Conduct of Life; and little or no Notice was ever taken of what related to the Victuals on the Table, whether it was well or ill drest, in or out of season, of good or bad flavor, preferable or inferior to this or that other thing of the kind; so that I was brought up in such a perfect Inattention to those Matters as to be quite Indifferent what kind of Food was set before me; and so unobservant of it, that to this Day, if I am ask'd I can scarce tell, a few Hours after Dinner, what I din'd upon. This has been a Convenience to me in traveling, where my Companions have been sometimes very unhappy for want of a suitable Gratification of their more delicate because better instructed Tastes and Appetites.

My Mother had likewise an excellent Constitution. She suckled all her 10 Children. I never knew either my Father or Mother to have any Sickness but that of which they died, he at 89 and she at 85 Years of age. They lie buried together at Boston, where I some Years since plac'd a Marble stone over their Grave with this Inscription:

Josiah Franklin
And Abiah his Wife
Lie here interred.
They lived lovingly together in Wedlock
Fifty-five Years.
Without an Estate or any gainful[9] Employment,
By constant Labor and Industry,
With God's Blessing,
They maintained a large Family
Comfortably;
And brought up thirteen Children,
And seven Grandchildren
Reputably.
From this Instance, Reader,
Be encouraged to Diligence in thy Calling,
And distrust not Providence.
He was a pious and prudent Man,
She a discreet and virtuous Woman.
Their youngest Son,
In filial Regard to their Memory,
Places this Stone.
J.F. born 1655—Died 1744. Ætat[1] 89
A.F. born 1667—died 1752——85.

By my rambling Digressions I perceive myself to be grown old. I us'd to write more methodically. But one does not dress for private Company as for a public Ball. 'Tis perhaps only Negligence.

---

9. Privileged. I.e., consistent and paid.   1. Abbreviation for *ætatis*: aged (Latin).

To return. I continu'd thus employ'd in my Father's Business for two Years, that is till I was 12 Years old; and my Brother John who was bred to that Business having left my Father, married and set up for himself at Rhode Island,[2] there was all Appearance that I was destin'd to supply his Place and be a Tallow Chandler. But my Dislike to the Trade continuing, my Father was under Apprehensions that if he did not find one for me more agreeable, I should break away and get to Sea, as his Son Josiah had done to his great Vexation. He therefore sometimes took me to walk with him, and see Joiners, Bricklayers, Turners, Braziers,[3] etc. at their Work, that he might observe my Inclination, and endeavor to fix it on some Trade or other on Land. It has ever since been a Pleasure to me to see good Workmen handle their Tools; and it has been useful to me, having learned so much by it, as to be able to do little Jobs myself in my House, when a Workman could not readily be got; and to construct little Machines for my Experiments while the Intention of making the Experiment was fresh and warm in my Mind. My Father at last fix'd upon the Cutler's Trade, and my Uncle Benjamin's Son Samuel who was bred to that Business in London being about that time establish'd in Boston, I was sent to be with him some time on liking. But his Expectations of a Fee with me displeasing my Father, I was taken home again.

From a Child I was fond of Reading, and all the little Money that came into my Hands was ever laid out in Books. Pleas'd with the Pilgrim's Progress, my first Collection was of John Bunyan's Works,[4] in separate little Volumes. I afterwards sold them to enable me to buy R. Burton's[5] Historical Collections; they were small Chapmen's Books[6] and cheap, 40 or 50 in all. My Father's little Library consisted chiefly of Books in polemic Divinity, most of which I read, and have since often regretted, that at a time when I had such a Thirst for Knowledge, more proper Books had not fallen in my Way, since it was now resolv'd I should not be a Clergyman. Plutarch's Lives[7] there was, in which I read abundently, and I still think that time spent to great Advantage. There was also a Book of Defoe's called an Essay on Projects and another of Dr. Mather's call'd Essays to do Good,[8] which perhaps gave me a Turn of Thinking that had an Influence on some of the principal future Events of my Life.

This Bookish Inclination at length determin'd my Father to make me a Printer, tho' he had already one Son, (James) of that Profession. In 1717 my Brother James return'd from England with a Press and Letters[9] to set up his Business in Boston. I lik'd it much better than that of my Father, but still had a Hankering for the Sea. To prevent the apprehended Effect of such an Inclination, my Father was impatient to have me bound[1] to my Brother.

2. John Franklin (1690–1756), Franklin's favorite brother, later became postmaster of Boston.
3. Woodworkers, bricklayers, latheworkers, brassworkers.
4. The English preacher John Bunyan (1628–1688) published Pilgrim's Progress in 1678; his literary works were enormously popular and available in cheap one-shilling editions. Pilgrim's Progress is an allegory in which the hero, Christian, flees the City of Destruction and makes his way to the Celestial City with the help of characters such as Mr. Worldly-Wiseman, Faithful, and Hopeful.

5. A pseudonym for Nathaniel Crouch (c. 1632–1725), a popularizer of British history.
6. Peddlers' books, hence inexpensive.
7. Parallel Lives, by the Greek biographer Plutarch (c. 46–120 c.e.), about noted Greek and Roman figures.
8. Cotton Mather's Bonifacius: An Essay upon the Good. Essay on Projects, by the English writer Daniel Defoe (1659?–1731), offers suggestions for economic improvement.
9. Type.
1. Apprenticed.

I stood out some time, but at last was persuaded and signed the Indentures,[2] when I was yet but 12 Years old. I was to serve as an Apprentice till I was 21 Years of Age, only I was to be allow'd Journeyman's Wages[3] during the last Year. In a little time I made great Proficiency in the Business, and became a useful Hand to my Brother. I now had Access to better Books. An Acquaintance with the Apprentices of Booksellers enabled me sometimes to borrow a small one, which I was careful to return soon and clean. Often I sat up in my Room reading the greatest Part of the Night, when the Book was borrow'd in the Evening and to be return'd early in the Morning lest it should be miss'd or wanted. And after some time an ingenious Tradesman[4] who had a pretty[5] Collection of Books, and who frequented our Printing-House, took Notice of me, invited me to his Library, and very kindly lent me such Books as I chose to read. I now took a Fancy to Poetry, and made some little Pieces. My Brother, thinking it might turn to account encourag'd me, and put me on composing two occasional Ballads. One was called the *Light House Tragedy,* and contain'd an Account of the drowning of Capt. Worthilake with his Two Daughters; the other was a Sailor Song on the Taking of *Teach* or Blackbeard the Pirate.[6] They were wretched Stuff, in the Grubstreet Ballad Style,[7] and when they were printed he sent me about the Town to sell them. The first sold wonderfully, the Event being recent, having made a great Noise. This flatter'd my Vanity. But my Father discourag'd me, by ridiculing my Performances, and telling me Verse-makers were generally Beggars; so I escap'd being a Poet, most probably a very bad one. But as Prose Writing has been of great Use to me in the Course of my Life, and was a principal Means of my Advancement, I shall tell you how in such a Situation I acquir'd what little Ability I have in that Way.

There was another Bookish Lad in the Town, John Collins by Name, with whom I was intimately acquainted. We sometimes disputed, and very fond we were of Argument, and very desirous of confuting one another. Which disputatious Turn, by the way, is apt to become a very bad Habit, making People often extremely disagreeable in Company, by the Contradiction that is necessary to bring it into Practice, and thence, besides souring and spoiling the Conversation, is productive of Disgusts and perhaps Enmities where you may have occasion for Friendship. I had caught it by reading my Father's Books of Dispute about Religion. Persons of good Sense, I have since observ'd, seldom fall into it, except Lawyers, University Men, and Men of all Sorts that have been bred at Edinburgh.[8] A Question was once some how or other started between Collins and me, of the Propriety of educating the Female Sex in Learning, and their Abilities for Study. He was of Opinion that it was improper; and that they were naturally unequal to it. I took the contrary Side, perhaps a little for Dispute sake. He was naturally more eloquent, had a ready Plenty of Words, and sometimes as I thought bore me

2. A contract binding him to work for his brother for nine years. James Franklin (1697–1735) had learned the printer's trade in England.
3. I.e., be paid for each day's work, having served his apprenticeship.
4. Mr. Matthew Adams [Franklin's note].
5. Exceptionally fine.
6. The full texts of these ballads are lost; George Worthylake, lighthouse keeper on Beacon Island,

Boston Harbor, and his wife and daughter were drowned on November 3, 1718. The pirate Blackbeard, Edward Teach, was killed off the Carolina coast on November 22, 1718.
7. Grub Street in London was inhabited by poor literary hacks who churned out poems of topical interest.
8. Scottish Presbyterians were noted for their argumentative nature.

down more by his Fluency than by the Strength of his Reasons. As we parted without settling the Point, and were not to see one another again for some time, I sat down to put my Arguments in Writing, which I copied fair and sent to him. He answer'd and I replied. Three or four Letters of a Side had pass'd, when my Father happen'd to find my Papers, and read them. Without entering into the Discussion, he took occasion to talk to me about the Manner of my Writing, observ'd that tho' I had the Advantage of my Antagonist in correct Spelling and pointing[9] (which I ow'd to the Printing-House) I fell far short in elegance of Expression, in Method and in Perspicuity, of which he convinc'd me by several Instances. I saw the Justice of his Remarks, and thence grew more attentive to the *Manner* in Writing, and determin'd to endeavor at Improvement.

About this time I met with an odd Volume of the Spectator.[1] I had never before seen any of them. I bought it, read it over and over, and was much delighted with it. I thought the Writing excellent, and wish'd if possible to imitate it. With that View, I took some of the Papers, and making short Hints of the Sentiment in each Sentence, laid them by a few Days, and then without looking at the Book, tried to complete the Papers again, by expressing each hinted Sentiment at length and as fully as it had been express'd before, in any suitable Words that should come to hand.

Then I compar'd my Spectator with the Original, discover'd some of my Faults and corrected them. But I found I wanted a Stock of Words or a Readiness in recollecting and using them, which I thought I should have acquir'd before that time, if I had gone on making Verses, since the continual Occasion for Words of the same Import but of different Length, to suit the Measure,[2] or of different Sound for the Rhyme, would have laid me under a constant Necessity of searching for Variety, and also have tended to fix that Variety in my Mind, and make me Master of it. Therefore I took some of the Tales and turn'd them into Verse: And after a time, when I had pretty well forgotten the Prose, turn'd them back again. I also sometimes jumbled my Collections of Hints into Confusion, and after some Weeks, endeavor'd to reduce them into the best Order, before I began to form the full Sentences, and complete the Paper. This was to teach me Method in the Arrangement of Thoughts. By comparing my Work afterwards with the original, I discover'd many faults and amended them; but I sometimes had the Pleasure of Fancying that in certain Particulars of small Import, I had been lucky enough to improve the Method or the Language and this encourag'd me to think I might possibly in time come to be a tolerable English Writer, of which I was extremely ambitious.

My Time for these Exercises and for Reading, was at Night after Work, or before Work began in the Morning; or on Sundays, when I contrived to be in the Printing-House alone, evading as much as I could the common Attendance on public Worship, which my Father used to exact of me when I was under his Care: And which indeed I still thought a Duty; tho' I could not, as it seemed to me, afford the Time to practice it.

---

9. Punctuation. Spelling and punctuation were not standardized at this time.
1. An English periodical published daily from March 1, 1711, to December 6, 1712, and revived in 1714. It contained essays by Joseph Addison (1672–1719) and Richard Steele (1672–1729) and addressed itself primarily to matters of literature and morality. Its aim was to "enliven morality with wit" and "temper wit with morality."
2. Meter.

When about 16 Years of Age, I happen'd to meet with a Book written by one Tryon,[3] recommending a Vegetable Diet. I determined to go into it. My Brother being yet unmarried, did not keep House, but boarded himself and his Apprentices in another Family. My refusing to eat Flesh occasioned an Inconveniency, and I was frequently chid for my singularity. I made myself acquainted with Tryon's Manner of preparing some of his Dishes, such as Boiling Potatoes or Rice, making Hasty Pudding,[4] and a few others, and then propos'd to my Brother, that if he would give me Weekly half the Money he paid for my Board, I would board myself. He instantly agreed to it, and I presently found that I could save half what he paid me. This was an additional Fund for buying Books: But I had another Advantage in it. My Brother and the rest going from the Printing-House to their Meals, I remain'd there alone, and dispatching presently my light Repast, (which often was no more than a Biscuit or a Slice of Bread, a Handful of Raisins or a Tart from the Pastry Cook's, and a Glass of Water) had the rest of the Time till their Return, for Study, in which I made the greater Progress from that greater Clearness of Head and quicker Apprehension which usually attend Temperance in Eating and Drinking. And now it was that being on some Occasion made asham'd of my Ignorance in Figures, which I had twice fail'd in learning when at School, I took Cocker's Book of Arithmetic,[5] and went thro' the whole by myself with great Ease. I also read Seller's and Sturmy's Books of Navigation,[6] and became acquainted with the little Geometry they contain, but never proceeded far in that Science. And I read about this Time Locke on Human Understanding and the Art of Thinking by Messrs. du Port Royal.[7]

While I was intent on improving my Language, I met with an English Grammar (I think it was Greenwood's[8]) at the End of which there were two little Sketches of the Arts of Rhetoric and Logic, the latter finishing with a Specimen of a Dispute in the Socratic Method.[9] And soon after I procur'd Xenophon's Memorable Things of Socrates,[1] wherein there are many Instances of the same Method. I was charm'd with it, adopted it, dropped my abrupt Contradiction and positive Argumentation, and put on the humble Enquirer and Doubter. And being then, from reading Shaftesbury and Collins, became a real Doubter in many Points of our Religious Doctrine,[2] I found this Method safest for myself and very embarrassing to those against whom I used it, therefore I took a Delight in it, practic'd it continually and grew very artful and expert in drawing People even of superior Knowledge into Concessions the Consequences of which they did not foresee, entangling

3. Thomas Tryon, whose *Way to Health, Wealth, and Happiness* appeared in 1682; a digest titled *Wisdom's Dictates* appeared in 1691.
4. I.e., cornmeal or oatmeal mush.
5. Edward Cocker's *Arithmetic*, published in 1677, was reprinted twenty times by 1700.
6. John Seller published *An Epitome of the Art of Navigation* in 1681. Samuel Sturmy published *The Mariner's Magazine: Or Sturmy's Mathematical and Practical Arts* in 1699.
7. The English philosopher John Locke (1632–1704) published *An Essay Concerning Human Understanding* in 1690. The philosophers Antoine Arnauld (1612–1694) and Pierre Nicole (1625?–1695), of Port Royal, France, published the English edition of *Logic: Or the Art of Thinking* in

1687. It was originally published in Latin in 1662.
8. James Greenwood wrote *An Essay towards a Practical English Grammar* (1711).
9. I.e., in the form of a debate or dialectic, as practiced by the Greek philosopher Socrates (c. 470–399 b.c.e.).
1. Work by the Greek historian Xenophon (434?–355 b.c.e.) translated by Edward Bysshe in 1712.
2. Anthony Ashley Cooper, third Earl of Shaftesbury (1671–1713), was a religious skeptic. Anthony Collins (1676–1729) argued that the world could satisfactorily be explained in terms of itself. Perhaps Franklin read Shaftesbury's *Characteristics of Men, Manners, Opinions, Times* (1711) and Collins's *A Discourse of Free Thinking* (1713).

them in Difficulties out of which they could not extricate themselves, and so obtaining Victories that neither myself nor my Cause always deserved. I continu'd this Method some few Years, but gradually left it, retaining only the Habit of expressing myself in Terms of modest Diffidence, never using when I advance any thing that may possibly be disputed, the Words, *Certainly, undoubtedly*, or any others that give the Air of Positiveness to an Opinion; but rather say, *I conceive*, or *I apprehend* a Thing to be so or so, *It appears to me*, or *I should think it so or so for such and such Reasons*, or *I imagine* it to be so, or *it is so if I am not mistaken*. This Habit I believe has been of great Advantage to me, when I have had occasion to inculcate my Opinions and persuade Men into Measures that I have been from time to time engag'd in promoting. And as the chief Ends of Conversation are to *inform*, or to be *informed*, to *please* or to *persuade*, I wish well-meaning sensible Men would not lessen their Power of doing Good by a Positive assuming Manner that seldom fails to disgust, tends to create Opposition, and to defeat every one of those Purposes for which Speech was given us, to wit, giving or receiving Information, or Pleasure: For If you would *inform*, a positive dogmatical Manner in advancing your Sentiments, may provoke Contradiction and prevent a candid Attention. If you wish Information and Improvement from the Knowledge of others and yet at the same time express yourself as firmly fix'd in your present Opinions, modest sensible Men, who do not love Disputation, will probably leave you undisturb'd in the Possession of your Error; and by such a Manner you can seldom hope to recommend yourself in *pleasing* your Hearers, or to persuade those whose Concurrence you desire. Pope says, judiciously.

> *Men should be taught as if you taught them not,*
> *And things unknown propos'd as things forgot,*

farther recommending it to us,

> To *speak tho' sure, with seeming Diffidence*.[3]

And he might have coupled with this Line that which he has coupled with another, I think less properly,

> *For want of Modesty is want of Sense.*

If you ask why *less properly*, I must repeat the Lines;

> "Immodest Words admit of *no* Defence;
> *For* Want of Modesty is Want of Sense."[4]

Now is not *Want of Sense*, (where a Man is so unfortunate as to want it) some Apology for his *Want of Modesty*? and would not the Lines stand more justly thus?

> Immodest Words admit *but this* Defence,
> That Want of Modesty is Want of Sense.

---

3. Franklin is quoting from memory lines 574–75 and 567 of *An Essay on Criticism*, by the English poet Alexander Pope (1688–1744). The first line should read, "Men must be taught as if you taught them not," and the third, "And speak, tho' sure, with seeming Diffidence."

4. Franklin is mistaken here: the lines are from Wentworth Dillon, fourth Earl of Roscommon (1633?–1685), from his *Essay on Translated Verse*, lines 113–14. The second line should read, "For want of decency is want of sense." "Want": lack.

This however I should submit to better Judgments.

My Brother had in 1720 or 21, begun to print a Newspaper. It was the second[5] that appear'd in America, and was called *The New England Courant*. The only one before it, was *The Boston News Letter*. I remember his being dissuaded by some of his Friends from the Undertaking, as not likely to succeed, one Newspaper being in their Judgment enough for America. At this time 1771 there are not less than five and twenty. He went on however with the Undertaking, and after having work'd in composing the Types and printing off the Sheets I was employ'd to carry the Papers thro' the Streets to the Customers. He had some ingenious Men among his Friends who amus'd themselves by writing little Pieces for this Paper, which gain'd it Credit, and made it more in Demand; and these Gentlemen often visited us. Hearing their Conversations, and their Accounts of the Approbation their Papers were receiv'd with, I was excited to try my Hand among them. But being still a Boy, and suspecting that my Brother would object to printing any Thing of mine in his Paper if he knew it to be mine, I contriv'd to disguise my Hand, and writing an anonymous Paper I put it in at Night under the Door of the Printing-House.

It was found in the Morning and communicated to his Writing Friends when they call'd in as Usual. They read it, commented on it in my Hearing, and I had the exquisite Pleasure, of finding it met with their Approbation, and that in their different Guesses at the Author none were named but Men of some Character among us for Learning and Ingenuity. I suppose now that I was rather lucky in my Judges: And that perhaps they were not really so very good ones as I then esteem'd them. Encourag'd however by this, I wrote and convey'd in the same Way to the Press several more Papers,[6] which were equally approv'd, and I kept my Secret till my small Fund of Sense for such Performances was pretty well exhausted, and then I discovered[7] it; when I began to be considered a little more by my Brother's Acquaintance, and in a manner that did not quite please him, as he thought, probably with reason, that it tended to make me too vain. And perhaps this might be one Occasion of the Differences that we began to have about this Time. Tho' a Brother, he considered himself as my Master, and me as his Apprentice; and accordingly expected the same Services from me as he would from another; while I thought he demean'd me too much in some he requir'd of me, who from a Brother expected more Indulgence, Our Disputes were often brought before our Father, and I fancy I was either generally in the right, or else a better Pleader, because the Judgment was generally in my favor. But my Brother was passionate and had often beaten me, which I took extremely amiss; and thinking my Apprenticeship very tedious, I was continually wishing for some Opportunity of shortening it, which at length offered in a manner unexpected.[8]

One of the Pieces in our Newspaper, on some political Point which I have now forgotten, gave Offence to the Assembly. He was taken up, censur'd and

---

5. Actually, the fifth; James Franklin's paper appeared on August 7, 1721.

6. The Silence Dogood letters (April 12–October 8, 1722), the earliest essay series in America.

7. Revealed.

8. I fancy his harsh and tyrannical Treatment of me, might be a means of impressing me with that Aversion to arbitrary Power that has stuck to me thro' my whole Life [Franklin's note].

Early American print shop. "The Printer hath metal Letters in a great number put into Boxes (5). The Compositor (1) taketh them out one by one, and according to the Copy (which he hath fastened before him in a Visorum [2]) composeth words in a Composing-stick (3) till a Line be made; he putteth these in a Galley (4) till a Page (6) be made, and those again in a Form (7), and he locketh them up in Iron Chases (8) with Quoins (9) lest they should drop out, and putteth them under the Press (10). Then the Press-man beateth it over with Printer's Ink, by means of Balls (11) spreadeth upon it the Papers put in the Frisket (12), which being put under the Spindle (14) on the Coffin (13) and pressed down with a Bar (15) he maketh to take impression." From *Comensius's Visible World* (1810), with thanks to James Green of the Library Company of Philadelphia.

imprison'd[9] for a Month by the Speaker's Warrant, I suppose because he would not discover his Author. I too was taken up and examin'd before the Council; but tho' I did not give them any Satisfaction, they contented themselves with admonishing me, and dismiss'd me; considering me perhaps as an Apprentice who was bound to keep his Master's Secrets. During my Brother's Confinement, which I resented a good deal, notwithstanding our private Differences, I had the Management of the Paper, and I made bold to give our Rulers some Rubs[1] in it, which my Brother took very kindly, while others began to consider me in an unfavorable Light, as a young Genius that had a Turn for Libeling and Satire.[2] My Brother's Discharge was accompanied with an Order of the House, (a very odd one) *that James Franklin should no longer print the Paper called the New England Courant.* There was a Consultation held in our Printing-House among his Friends what he should do

9. On June 11, 1722, the *Courant* hinted that there was collusion between local authorities and pirates raiding off Boston Harbor. James Franklin was jailed from June 12 to July 7. "Assembly": Massachusetts legislative body; the lower house, with representatives elected by towns of the Massachusetts General Court.

1. Insults, annoyances.

2. Satirizing.

in this Case. Some propos'd to evade the Order by changing the Name of the Paper; but my Brother seeing Inconveniences in that, it was finally concluded on as a better Way, to let it be printed for the future under the Name of *Benjamin Franklin*. And to avoid the Censure of the Assembly that might fall on him, as still printing it by his Apprentice, the Contrivance was, that my old Indenture should be return'd to me with a full Discharge on the Back of it, to be shown on Occasion; but to secure to him the Benefit of my Service I was to sign new Indentures for the Remainder of the Term, which were to be kept private. A very flimsy Scheme it was, but however it was immediately executed, and the Paper went on accordingly under my Name for several Months.[3] At length a fresh Difference arising between my Brother and me, I took upon me to assert my Freedom, presuming that he would not venture to produce the new Indentures. It was not fair in me to take this Advantage, and this I therefore reckon one of the first Errata of my Life: But the Unfairness of it weigh'd little with me, when under the Impressions of Resentment, for the Blows his Passion too often urg'd him to bestow upon me. Tho' he was otherwise not an ill-natur'd Man: Perhaps I was too saucy and provoking.

When he found I would leave him, he took care to prevent my getting Employment in any other Printing-House of the Town, by going round and speaking to every Master, who accordingly refus'd to give me Work. I then thought of going to New York as the nearest Place where there was a Printer: and I was the rather inclin'd to leave Boston, when I reflected that I had already made myself a little obnoxious to the governing Party; and from the arbitrary Proceedings of the Assembly in my Brother's Case it was likely I might if I stay'd soon bring myself into Scrapes; and farther that my indiscreet Disputations about Religion began to make me pointed at with Horror by good People, as an Infidel or Atheist; I determin'd on the Point: but my Father now siding with my Brother, I was sensible that if I attempted to go openly, Means would be used to prevent me. My Friend Collins therefore undertook to manage a little for me. He agreed with the Captain of a New York Sloop for my Passage, under the Notion of my being a young Acquaintance of his that had got a naughty Girl with Child, whose Friends would compel me to marry her, and therefore I could not appear or come away publicly. So I sold some of my Books to raise a little Money, was taken on board privately, and as we had a fair Wind, in three Days I found myself in New York near 300 Miles from home, a Boy of but 17, without the least Recommendation to or Knowledge of any Person in the Place, and with very little Money in my Pocket.

My Inclinations for the Sea, were by this time worn out, or I might now have gratified them. But having a Trade, and supposing myself a pretty good Workman, I offer'd my Service to the Printer of the Place, old Mr. William Bradford.[4] He could give me no Employment, having little to do, and Help enough already: But, says he, my Son at Philadelphia has lately lost his principal Hand, Aquila Rose, by Death. If you go thither I believe he may

---

3. The paper continued under Franklin's name until 1726, three years after he left Boston.
4. One of the first American printers (1663–1752)

and father of Andrew Bradford (1686–1742), Franklin's future competitor in Philadelphia.

employ you. Philadelphia was 100 Miles farther. I set out, however, in a Boat for Amboy;[5] leaving my Chest and Things to follow me round by Sea. In crossing the Bay we met with a Squall that tore our rotten Sails to pieces, prevented our getting into the Kill, and drove us upon Long Island.[6] In our Way a drunken Dutchman, who was a Passenger too, fell overboard; when he was sinking I reach'd thro' the Water to his shock Pate[7] and drew him up so that we got him in again. His Ducking sober'd him a little, and he went to sleep, taking first out of his Pocket a Book which he desir'd I would dry for him. It prov'd to be my old favorite Author Bunyan's Pilgrim's Progress in Dutch, finely printed on good Paper with copper Cuts,[8] a Dress better than I had ever seen it wear in its own Language. I have since found that it has been translated into most of the Languages of Europe, and suppose it has been more generally read than any other Book except perhaps the Bible. Honest John was the first that I know of who mix'd Narration and Dialogue, a Method of Writing very engaging to the Reader, who in the most interesting Parts finds himself as it were brought into the Company, and present at the Discourse. Defoe in his Crusoe, his Moll Flanders, Religious Courtship, Family Instructor, and other Pieces, has imitated it with Success.[9] And Richardson has done the same in his Pamela,[1] etc.

When we drew near the Island we found it was at a Place where there could be no Landing, there being a great Surf on the stony Beach. So we dropped Anchor and swung round towards the Shore. Some People came down to the Water Edge and hallow'd to us, as we did to them. But the Wind was so high and the Surf so loud, that we could not hear so as to understand each other. There were Canoes on the Shore, and we made Signs and hallow'd that they should fetch us, but they either did not understand us, or thought it impracticable. So they went away, and Night coming on, we had no Remedy but to wait till the Wind should abate, and in the mean time the Boatman and I concluded to sleep if we could, and so crowded into the Scuttle[2] with the Dutchman who was still wet, and the Spray beating over the Head of our Boat, leak'd thro' to us, so that we were soon almost as wet as he. In this Manner we lay all Night with very little Rest. But the Wind abating the next Day, we made a Shift to reach Amboy before Night, having been 30 hours on the Water without Victuals, or any Drink but a Bottle of filthy Rum: The Water we sail'd on being salt.

In the Evening I found myself very feverish, and went ill to Bed. But having read somewhere that cold Water drank plentifully was good for a Fever, I follow'd the Prescription, sweat plentifully most of the Night, my Fever left me, and in the Morning crossing the Ferry, proceeded on my Journey, on foot, having 50 Miles to Burlington,[3] where I was told I should find Boats that would carry me the rest of the Way to Philadelphia.

---

5. Perth Amboy, New Jersey.
6. In New York. "The Kill": the Kill van Kull, a narrow channel that separates Staten Island, New York, from New Jersey.
7. Shaggy head of hair.
8. Engravings. See n. 4, p. 473.
9. Defoe (see n. 8, p. 474) published *Robinson Crusoe* in 1719, *Moll Flanders* in 1722, *Religious Courtship* in 1772, and *The Family Instructor* in

1715–18.
1. The English writer Samuel Richardson (1689–1761) published his novel *Pamela: Or Virtue Rewarded* in 1740. Franklin reprinted it in 1744 and in doing so published the first novel in America.
2. An opening in a ship's deck, with a lid.
3. Then the capital of West Jersey, about eighteen miles north of Philadelphia.

It rain'd very hard all the Day, I was thoroughly soak'd, and by Noon a good deal tir'd, so I stopped at a poor Inn, where I stayed all Night, beginning now to wish I had never left home. I cut so miserable a Figure too, that I found by the Questions ask'd me I was suspected to be some runaway Servant, and in danger of being taken up on that Suspicion. However I proceeded the next Day, and got in the Evening to an Inn within 8 or 10 Miles of Burlington, kept by one Dr. Browne.[4]

He entered into Conversation with me while I took some Refreshment, and finding I had read a little, became very sociable and friendly. Our Acquaintance continu'd as long as he liv'd. He had been, I imagine, an itinerant Doctor, for there was no Town in England, or Country in Europe, of which he could not give a very particular Account. He had some Letters,[5] and was ingenious, but much of an Unbeliever, and wickedly undertook some Years after to travesty the Bible in doggerel Verse as Cotton had done Virgil.[6] By this means he set many of the Facts in a very ridiculous Light, and might have hurt weak minds if his Work had been publish'd: but it never was. At his House I lay that Night, and the next Morning reach'd Burlington. But had the Mortification to find that the regular Boats were gone a little before my coming, and no other expected to go till Tuesday, this being Saturday. Wherefore I return'd to an old Woman in the Town of whom I had bought Gingerbread to eat on the Water, and ask'd her Advice; she invited me to lodge at her House till a Passage by Water should offer; and being tired with my foot Traveling, I accepted the Invitation. She understanding I was a Printer, would have had me stay at that Town and follow my Business, being ignorant of the Stock necessary to begin with. She was very hospitable, gave me a Dinner of Ox Cheek with great Goodwill, accepting only of a Pot of Ale in return. And I thought myself fix'd till Tuesday should come. However walking in the Evening by the Side of the River a Boat came by, which I found was going towards Philadelphia with several People in her. They took me in, and as there was no Wind, we row'd all the Way; and about Midnight not having yet seen the City, some of the Company were confident we must have pass'd it, and would row no farther, the others knew not where we were, so we put towards the Shore, got into a Creek, landed near an old Fence with the Rails of which we made a Fire, the Night being cold, in October, and there we remain'd till Daylight. Then one of the Company knew the Place to be Cooper's Creek a little above Philadelphia, which we saw as soon as we got out of the Creek, and arriv'd there about 8 or 9 aClock, on the Sunday morning,[7] and landed at the Market Street Wharf.

I have been the more particular in this Description of my Journey, and shall be so of my first Entry into that City, that you may in your Mind compare such unlikely Beginning with the Figure I have since made there. I was in my working Dress, my best Clothes being to come round by Sea. I was dirty from my Journey; my Pockets were stuff'd out with Shirts and Stockings; I knew no Soul, nor where to look for Lodging. I was fatigu'd with Trav-

---

4. Dr. John Browne (c. 1667–1737), innkeeper in Bordentown, New Jersey, and a noted religious skeptic as well as physician.
5. I.e., formal education.
6. In *Scarronides*, the English writer Charles

Cotton (1630–1687) parodied the first and fourth books of the *Aeneid*, by the ancient Roman poet Virgil. Cotton's opening lines are: "I sing the Man (read it who list), / A Trojan true as ever pissed."
7. October 6, 1723.

eling, Rowing and Want of Rest. I was very hungry, and my whole Stock of Cash consisted of a Dutch Dollar and about a Shilling in Copper.[8] The latter I gave the People of the Boat for my Passage, who at first refus'd it on Account of my Rowing; but I insisted on their taking it, a Man being sometimes more generous when he has but a little Money than when he has plenty, perhaps thro' Fear of being thought to have but little. Then I walk'd up the Street, gazing about, till near the Market House I met a Boy with Bread. I had made many a Meal on Bread, and inquiring where he got it, I went immediately to the Baker's he directed me to in Second Street; and ask'd for Biscuit, intending such as we had in Boston, but they it seems were not made in Philadelphia, then I ask'd for a three-penny Loaf, and was told they had none such: so not considering or knowing the Difference of Money and the greater Cheapness nor the Names of his Bread, I bad him give me three pennyworth of any sort. He gave me accordingly three great Puffy Rolls. I was surpris'd at the Quantity, but took it, and having no Room in my Pockets, walk'd off, with a Roll under each Arm, and eating the other. Thus I went up Market Street as far as Fourth Street, passing by the Door of Mr. Read, my future Wife's Father, when she standing at the Door saw me, and thought I made as I certainly did a most awkward ridiculous Appearance. Then I turn'd and went down Chestnut Street and part of Walnut Street, eating my Roll all the Way, and coming round found myself again at Market Street Wharf, near the Boat I came in, to which I went for a Drought of the River Water, and being fill'd with one of my Rolls, gave the other two to a Woman and her Child that came down the River in the Boat with us and were waiting to go farther. Thus refresh'd I walk'd again up the Street, which by this time had many clean dress'd People in it who were all walking the same Way; I join'd them, and thereby was led into the great Meeting House of the Quakers near the Market. I sat down among them, and after looking round a while and hearing nothing said, being very drowsy thro' Labor and want of Rest the preceding Night, I fell fast asleep, and continu'd so till the Meeting broke up, when one was kind enough to rouse me. This was therefore the first House I was in or slept in, in Philadelphia.

Walking again down towards the River, and looking in the Faces of People, I met a young Quaker Man whose Countenance I lik'd, and accosting him requested he would tell me where a Stranger could get Lodging. We were then near the Sign of the Three Mariners. Here, says he, is one Place that entertains Strangers, but it is not a reputable House; if thee wilt walk with me, I'll show thee a better. He brought me to the Crooked Billet in Water Street. Here I got a Dinner. And while I was eating it, several sly Questions were ask'd me, as it seem'd to be suspected from my youth and Appearance, that I might be some Runaway. After Dinner my Sleepiness return'd: and being shown to a Bed, I lay down without undressing, and slept till Six in the Evening; was call'd to Supper; went to Bed again very early and slept soundly till the next Morning. Then I made myself as tidy as I could, and went to Andrew Bradford the Printer's. I found in the Shop the old Man his Father, whom I had seen at New York, and who traveling on horse back had got to Philadelphia before me. He introduc'd me to his Son, who receiv'd

8. Colonial money was extraordinarily heterogeneous, as Franklin's "stock" here begins to indicate.

me civilly, gave me a Breakfast, but told me he did not at present want a Hand, being lately supplied with one. But there was another Printer in town lately set up, one Keimer,[9] who perhaps might employ me; if not, I should be welcome to lodge at his House, and he would give me a little Work to do now and then till fuller Business should offer.

The old Gentleman said, he would go with me to the new Printer: And when we found him, Neighbor, says Bradford, I have brought to see you a young Man of your Business, perhaps you may want such a One. He ask'd me a few Questions, put a Composing Stick[1] in my Hand to see how I work'd, and then said he would employ me soon, tho' he had just then nothing for me to do. And taking old Bradford whom he had never seen before, to be one of the Townspeople that had a Goodwill for him, enter'd into a Conversation on his present Undertaking and Prospects; while Bradford not discovering[2] that he was the other Printer's Father; on Keimer's Saying he expected soon to get the greatest Part of the Business into his own Hands, drew him on by artful Questions and starting little Doubts, to explain all his Views, what Interest he relied on, and in what manner he intended to proceed. I who stood by and heard all, saw immediately that one of them was a crafty old Sophister,[3] and the other a mere Novice. Bradford left me with Keimer, who was greatly surpris'd when I told him who the old Man was.

Keimer's Printing-House I found, consisted of an old shatter'd Press and one small worn-out Font of English,[4] which he was then using himself, composing in it an Elegy on Aquila Rose[5] before-mentioned, an ingenious young Man of excellent Character much respected in the Town, Clerk of the Assembly,[6] and a pretty Poet. Keimer made Verses, too, but very indifferently. He could not be said to write them, for his Manner was to compose them in the Types directly out of his Head; so there being no Copy, but one Pair of Cases,[7] and the Elegy likely to require all the Letter, no one could help him. I endeavor'd to put his Press (which he had not yet us'd, and of which he understood nothing) into Order fit to be work'd with; and promising to come and print off his Elegy as soon as he should have got it ready, I return'd to Bradford's who gave me a little Job to do for the present, and there I lodged and dieted.[8] A few Days after Keimer sent for me to print off the Elegy. And now he had got another Pair of Cases, and a Pamphlet to reprint, on which he set me to work.

These two Printers I found poorly qualified for their Business. Bradford had not been bred to it, and was very illiterate; and Keimer tho' something of a Scholar, was a mere Compositor, knowing nothing of Presswork. He had been one of the French Prophets[9] and could act their enthusiastic Agitations. At this time he did not profess any particular Religion, but something of all on occasion; was very ignorant of the World, and had, as I afterwards found,

9. Samuel Keimer (c. 1688–1742), a printer in London before moving to Philadelphia.
1. An instrument of adjustable width in which type is set before being put on a galley (an oblong, single-column tray).
2. Revealing.
3. Trickster, rationalizer.
4. An oversized type, not usable for books and newspapers.
5. Journeyman printer (c. 1695–1723) for Andrew Bradford; his son Joseph apprenticed with Franklin.
6. One who has charge of the records, documents, and correspondence of any organized body (here, the Pennsylvania legislative council).
7. Two shallow trays that contain uppercase and lowercase type.
8. Boarded.
9. An English sect that preached doomsday and cultivated emotional fits.

a good deal of the Knave in his Composition. He did not like my Lodging at Bradford's while I work'd with him. He had a House indeed, but without Furniture, so he could not lodge me: But he got me a Lodging at Mr. Read's before-mentioned, who was the Owner of his House. And my Chest and Clothes being come by this time, I made rather a more respectable Appearance in the Eyes of Miss Read, than I had done when she first happen'd to see me eating my Roll in the Street.

I began now to have some Acquaintance among the young People of the Town, that were Lovers of Reading with whom I spent my Evenings very pleasantly and gaining Money by my Industry and Frugality, I lived very agreeably, forgetting Boston as much as I could, and not desiring that any there should know where I resided except my Friend Collins who was in my Secret, and kept it when I wrote to him. At length an Incident happened that sent me back again much sooner than I had intended.

I had a Brother-in-law, Robert Homes,[1] Master of a Sloop that traded between Boston and Delaware. He being at New Castle[2] 40 Miles below Philadelphia, heard there of me, and wrote me a Letter, mentioning the Concern of my Friends in Boston at my abrupt Departure, assuring me of their Goodwill to me, and that everything would be accommodated to my Mind if I would return, to which he exhorted me very earnestly. I wrote an Answer to his Letter, thank'd him for his Advice, but stated my Reasons for quitting Boston fully, and in such a Light as to convince him I was not so wrong as he had apprehended. Sir William Keith Governor of the Province,[3] was then at New Castle, and Captain Homes happening to be in Company with him when my Letter came to hand, spoke to him of me, and show'd him the Letter. The Governor read it, and seem'd surpris'd when he was told my Age. He said I appear'd a young Man of promising Parts, and therefore should be encouraged: The Printers at Philadelphia were wretched ones, and if I would set up there, he made no doubt I should succeed; for his Part, he would procure me the public Business, and do me every other Service in his Power. This my Brother-in-Law afterwards told me in Boston. But I knew as yet nothing of it; when one Day Keimer and I being at Work together near the Window, we saw the Governor and another Gentleman (which prov'd to be Colonel French, of New Castle) finely dress'd, come directly across the Street to our House, and heard them at the Door.

Keimer ran down immediately, thinking it a Visit to him. But the Governor enquir'd for me, came up, and with a Condescension[4] and Politeness I had been quite unus'd to, made me many Compliments, desired to be acquainted with me, blam'd me kindly for not having made myself known to him when I first came to the Place, and would have me away with him to the Tavern where he was going with Colonel French to taste as he said some excellent Madeira. I was not a little surpris'd, and Keimer star'd like a Pig poison'd. I went however with the Governor and Colonel French, to a Tavern the Corner of Third Street, and over the Madeira he propos'd my Setting up my Business, laid before me the Probabilities of Success, and both he and Colonel French assur'd me I should have their Interest and Influence

1. Ship's captain (d. before 1743), husband of Franklin's sister Mary.
2. City in Delaware.
3. Keith (1680–1749), lieutenant-governor of

Pennsylvania and Delaware from 1717 to 1726, fled to England in 1728 to escape creditors.
4. Disregard for difference in rank or station.

in procuring the Public-Business of both Governments. On my doubting whether my Father would assist me in it, Sir William said he would give me a Letter to him, in which he would state the Advantages, and he did not doubt of prevailing with him. So it was concluded I should return to Boston in the first Vessel with the Governor's Letter recommending me to my Father.

In the meantime the Intention was to be kept secret, and I went on working with Keimer as usual, the Governor sending for me now and then to dine with him, a very great Honor I thought it, and conversing with me in the most affable, familiar, and friendly manner imaginable. About the End of April 1724, a little Vessel offer'd for Boston. I took Leave of Keimer as going to see my Friends. The Governor gave me an ample Letter, saying many flattering things of me to my Father, and strongly recommending the Project of my setting up at Philadelphia, as a Thing that must make my Fortune. We struck on a Shoal in going down the Bay and sprung a Leak, we had a blustring time at Sea, and were oblig'd to pump almost continually, at which I took my Turn. We arriv'd safe however at Boston in about a Fortnight. I had been absent Seven Months and my Friends had heard nothing of me, for my Brother Homes was not yet return'd; and had not written about me. My unexpected Appearance surpris'd the Family; all were however very glad to see me and made me Welcome, except my Brother.

I went to see him at his Printing-House: I was better dress'd than ever while in his Service, having a genteel new Suit from Head to foot, a Watch, and my Pockets lin'd with near Five Pounds Sterling in Silver. He receiv'd me not very frankly, look'd me all over, and turn'd to his Work again. The Journeymen were inquisitive where I had been, what sort of a Country it was, and how I lik'd it? I prais'd it much, and the happy Life I led in it; expressing strongly my Intention of returning to it; and one of them asking what kind of Money we had there, I produc'd a handful of Silver and spread it before them, which was a kind of Raree-Show[5] they had not been us'd to, Paper being the Money of Boston. Then I took an Opportunity of letting them see my Watch: and lastly, (my Brother still grum and sullen) I gave them a Piece of Eight to drink[6] and took my Leave. This Visit of mine offended him extremely. For when my Mother some time after spoke to him of a Reconciliation, and of her Wishes to see us on good Terms together, and that we might live for the future as Brothers, he said, I had insulted him in such a Manner before his People that he could never forget or forgive it. In this however he was mistaken.

My Father receiv'd the Governor's Letter with some apparent Surprise; but said little of it to me for some Days; when Captain Homes returning, he show'd it to him, ask'd if he knew Keith, and what kind of a Man he was: Adding his Opinion that he must be of small Discretion, to think of setting a Boy up in Business who wanted yet 3 Years of being at Man's Estate. Homes said what he could in favor of the Project; but my Father was clear in the Impropriety of it; and at last gave a flat Denial to it. Then he wrote a civil Letter to Sir William thanking him for the Patronage he had so kindly offered me, but declining to assist me as yet in Setting up, I being in his Opinion

5. A sidewalk peep show. Silver coins were rare in the colonies.

6. A Spanish dollar with which they could buy drinks. "Grum": glum, morose.

too young to be trusted with the Management of a Business so important; and for which the Preparation must be so expensive.

My Friend and Companion Collins, who was a Clerk at the Post-Office, pleas'd with the Account I gave him of my new Country, determin'd to go thither also: And while I waited for my Father's Determination, he set out before me by Land to Rhode Island, leaving his Books which were a pretty Collection of Mathematics and Natural Philosophy,[7] to come with mine and me to New York where he propos'd to wait for me. My Father, tho' he did not approve Sir William's Proposition, was yet pleas'd that I had been able to obtain so advantageous a Character from a Person of such Note where I had resided, and that I had been so industrious and careful as to equip myself so handsomely in so short a time: therefore seeing no Prospect of an Accommodation between my Brother and me, he gave his Consent to my Returning again to Philadelphia, advis'd me to behave respectfully to the People there, endeavor to obtain the general Esteem, and avoid lampooning and libeling to which he thought I had too much Inclination; telling me, that by steady Industry and a prudent Parsimony, I might save enough by the time I was One and Twenty to set me up, and that if I came near the Matter he would help me out with the Rest. This was all I could obtain, except some small Gifts as Tokens of his and my Mother's Love, when I embark'd again for New York, now with their Approbation and their Blessing.

The Sloop putting in at Newport, Rhode Island, I visited my Brother John, who had been married and settled there some Years. He received me very affectionately, for he always lov'd me. A Friend of his, one Vernon, having some Money due to him in Pennsylvania, about 35 Pounds Currency, desired I would receive it for him, and keep it till I had his Directions what to remit it in. Accordingly he gave me an Order. This afterwards occasion'd me a good deal of Uneasiness. At Newport we took in a Number of Passengers for New York: Among which were two young Women, Companions, and a grave, sensible Matron-like Quaker-Woman with her Attendants. I had shown an obliging Readiness to do her some little Services which impress'd her I suppose with a degree of Goodwill towards me. Therefore when she saw a daily growing Familiarity between me and the two Young Women, which they appear'd to encourage, she took me aside and said, Young Man, I am concern'd for thee, as thou has no Friend with thee, and seems not to know much of the World, or of the Snares Youth is expos'd to; depend upon it those are very bad Women, I can see it in all their Actions, and if thee art not upon thy Guard, they will draw thee into some Danger: they are Strangers to thee, and I advise thee in a friendly Concern for thy Welfare, to have no Acquaintance with them. As I seem'd at first not to think so ill of them as she did, she mention'd some Things she had observ'd and heard that had escap'd my Notice; but now convinc'd me she was right. I thank'd her for her kind Advice, and promis'd to follow it. When we arriv'd at New York, they told me where they liv'd, and invited me to come and see them: but I avoided it. And it was well I did: For the next Day, the Captain miss'd a Silver Spoon and some other Things that had been taken out of his Cabin, and knowing that these were a Couple of Strumpets, he got a Warrant to search

7. I.e., natural science. "Determination": decision.

their Lodgings, found the stolen Goods, and had the Thieves punish'd. So tho' we had escap'd a sunken Rock which we scrap'd upon in the Passage, I thought this Escape of rather more Importance to me.

At New York I found my Friend Collins, who had arriv'd there some Time before me. We had been intimate from[8] Children, and had read the same Books together. But he had the Advantage of more time for Reading, and Studying and a wonderful Genius for Mathematical Learning in which he far outstripped me. While I liv'd in Boston most of my Hours of Leisure for Conversation were spent with him, and he continu'd a sober as well as an industrious Lad; was much respected for his Learning by several of the Clergy and other Gentlemen, and seem'd to promise making a good Figure in Life: but during my Absence he had acquir'd a Habit of Sotting with[9] Brandy; and I found by his own Account and what I heard from others, that he had been drunk every day since his Arrival at New York, and behav'd very oddly. He had gam'd too and lost his Money, so that I was oblig'd to discharge his Lodgings,[1] and defray his Expences to and at Philadelphia: Which prov'd extremely inconvenient to me. The then Governor of New York, Burnet,[2] Son of Bishop Burnet, hearing from the Captain that a young Man, one of his Passengers, had a great many Books, desired he would bring me to see him. I waited upon him accordingly, and should have taken Collins with me but that he was not sober. The Governor treated me with great Civility, show'd me his Library, which was a very large one, and we had a good deal of Conversation about Books and Authors. This was the second Governor who had done me the Honor to take Notice of me, which to a poor Boy like me was very pleasing.

We proceeded to Philadelphia. I received on the Way Vernon's Money, without which we could hardly have finish'd our Journey. Collins wish'd to be employ'd in some Counting House; but whether they discover'd his Dramming[3] by his Breath, or by his Behavior, tho' he had some Recommendations, he met with no Success in any Application, and continu'd Lodging and Boarding at the same House with me and at my Expense. Knowing I had that Money of Vernon's he was continually borrowing of me, still promising Repayment as soon as he should be in Business. At length he had got so much of it, that I was distress'd to think what I should do, in case of being call'd on to remit it. His Drinking continu'd, about which we sometimes quarrel'd, for when a little intoxicated he was very fractious. Once in a Boat on the Delaware with some other young Men, he refused to row in his Turn: I will be row'd home, says he. We will not row you, says I. You must, says he, or stay all Night on the Water, just as you please. The others said, Let us row; What signifies it? But my Mind being soured with his other Conduct, I continu'd to refuse. So he swore he would make me row, or throw me overboard; and coming along stepping on the Thwarts[4] towards me, when he came up and struck at me, I clapped my Hand under his Crotch, and rising, pitch'd him headforemost into the River. I knew he was a good Swimmer, and so was under little Concern about him; but before he could get round

8. I.e., since we were.
9. Getting stupefied on.
1. To pay the rent he owed.
2. William Burnet (1688–1729), governor of

New York and New Jersey from 1720 to 1728 and governor of Massachusetts from 1728 to 1729.
3. Drinking liquor.
4. The seat on which an oarsman sits.

to lay hold of the Boat, we had with a few Strokes pull'd her out of his Reach. And ever when he drew near the Boat, we ask'd if he would row, striking a few Strokes to slide her away from him. He was ready to die with Vexation, and obstinately would not promise to row; however seeing him at last beginning to tire, we lifted him in; and brought him home dripping wet in the Evening. We hardly exchang'd a civil Word afterwards; and a West India Captain who had a Commission to procure a Tutor for the Sons of a Gentleman at Barbados,[5] happening to meet with him, agreed to carry him thither. He left me then, promising to remit me the first Money he should receive in order to discharge the Debt. But I never heard of him after.

The Breaking into this Money of Vernon's was one of the first great Errata of my Life. And this Affair show'd that my Father was not much out in his Judgment when he suppos'd me too Young to manage Business of Importance. But Sir William, on reading his Letter, said he was too prudent. There was great Difference in Persons, and Discretion did not always accompany Years, nor was Youth always without it. And since he will not set you up, says he, I will do it myself. Give me an Inventory of the Things necessary to be had from England, and I will send for them. You shall repay me when you are able; I am resolv'd to have a good Printer here, and I am sure you must succeed. This was spoken with such an Appearance of Cordiality, that I had not the least doubt of his meaning what he said. I had hitherto kept the Proposition of my Setting up a Secret in Philadelphia, and I still kept it. Had it been known that I depended on the Governor, probably some Friend that knew him better would have advis'd me not to rely on him, as I afterwards heard it as his known Character to be liberal of Promises which he never meant to keep. Yet unsolicited as he was by me, how could I think his generous Offers insincere? I believ'd him one of the best Men in the World.

I presented him an Inventory of a little Printing-House, amounting by my Computation to about 100 Pounds Sterling. He lik'd it, but ask'd me if my being on the Spot in England to choose the Types and see that everything was good of the kind, might not be of some Advantage. Then, says he, when there, you may make Acquaintances and establish Correspondences in the Bookselling, and Stationery Way. I agreed that this might be advantageous. Then says he, get yourself ready to go with Annis;[6] which was the annual Ship, and the only one at that Time usually passing between London and Philadelphia. But it would be some Months before Annis sail'd, so I continu'd working with Keimer, fretting about the Money Collins had got from me, and in daily Apprehensions of being call'd upon by Vernon, which however did not happen for some Years after.

I believe I have omitted mentioning that in my first Voyage from Boston, being becalm'd off Block Island,[7] our People set about catching Cod and haul'd up a great many. Hitherto I had stuck to my Resolution of not eating animal Food; and on this Occasion, I consider'd with my Master Tryon, the taking every Fish as a kind of unprovok'd Murder, since none of them had or ever could do us any Injury that might justify the Slaughter. All this seem'd very reasonable. But I had formerly been a great Lover of Fish, and when

5. Island in the British West Indies.
6. Thomas Annis, captain of the *London Hope,* the boat on which Franklin sailed to London in

1724.
7. Off the coast of Rhode Island.

this came hot out of the Frying Pan, it smelt admirably well. I balanc'd some time between Principle and Inclination: till I recollected, that when the Fish were opened, I saw smaller Fish taken out of their Stomachs: Then, thought I, if you eat one another, I don't see why we mayn't eat you. So I din'd upon Cod very heartily and continu'd to eat with other People, returning only now and then occasionally to a vegetable Diet. So convenient a thing it is to be a *reasonable Creature,* since it enables one to find or make a Reason for everything one has a mind to do.

Keimer and I liv'd on a pretty good familiar Footing and agreed tolerably well: for he suspected nothing of my Setting up. He retain'd a great deal of his old Enthusiasms, and lov'd an Argumentation. We therefore had many Disputations. I us'd to work him so with my Socratic Method, and had trapann'd[8] him so often by Questions apparently so distant from any Point we had in hand, and yet by degrees led to the Point, and brought him into Difficulties and Contradictions, that at last he grew ridiculously cautious, and would hardly answer me the most common Question, without asking first, *What do you intend to infer from that?* However it gave him so high an Opinion of my Abilities in the Confuting Way, that he seriously propos'd my being his Colleague in a Project he had of setting up a new Sect. He was to preach the Doctrines, and I was to confound all Opponents. When he came to explain with me upon the Doctrines, I found several Conundrums[9] which I objected to, unless I might have my Way a little too, and introduce some of mine. Keimer wore his Beard at full Length, because somewhere in the Mosaic Law it is said, *thou shalt not mar the Corners of thy Beard.*[1] He likewise kept the seventh-day Sabbath; and these two Points were Essentials with him. I dislik'd both, but agreed to admit them upon Condition of his adopting the Doctrine of using no animal Food. I doubt, says he, my Constitution will not bear that. I assur'd him it would, and that he would be the better for it. He was usually a great Glutton, and I promis'd myself some Diversion in half-starving him. He agreed to try the Practice if I would keep him Company. I did so and we held it for three Months. We had our Victuals dress'd and brought to us regularly by a Woman in the Neighborhood, who had from me a List of 40 Dishes to be prepar'd for us at different times, in all which there was neither Fish Flesh nor Fowl, and the Whim suited me the better at this time from the Cheapness of it, not costing us about 18 Pence Sterling each, per Week. I have since kept several Lents most strictly, leaving the common Diet for that, and that for the common, abruptly, without the least Inconvenience: So that I think there is little in the Advice of making those Changes by easy Gradations. I went on pleasantly, but Poor Keimer suffer'd grievously, tir'd of the Project, long'd for the Flesh Pots of Egypt, and order'd a roast Pig.[2] He invited me and two Women Friends to dine with him, but it being brought too soon upon table, he could not resist the Temptation, and ate it all up before we came.

8. Trapped.
9. Puzzles, difficult questions.
1. "Ye shall not round the corners of your heads, neither shalt thou mar the corners of thy beard" (Leviticus 19.27). Keimer probably also wore his hair long. "Mosaic Law": ancient law as revealed to the prophet Moses and set out in the first five books of the Old Testament.

2. "And the whole congregation of the children of Israel murmured against Moses and [the prophet] Aaron in the wilderness: And the children of Israel said unto them, Would to God we had died by the hand of the Lord in the land of Egypt, when we sat by the flesh pots, and when we did eat bread to the full" (Exodus 16.2–3).

I had made some Courtship during this time to Miss Read. I had a great Respect and Affection for her, and had some Reason to believe she had the same for me: but as I was about to take a long Voyage, and we were both very young, only a little above 18, it was thought most prudent by her Mother to prevent our going too far at present, as a Marriage if it was to take place would be more convenient after my Return, when I should be as I expected set up in my Business. Perhaps too she thought my Expectations not so well founded as I imagined them to be.

My chief Acquaintances at this time were, Charles Osborne, Joseph Watson, and James Ralph;[3] All Lovers of Reading. The two first were Clerks to an eminent Scrivener or Conveyancer in the Town, Charles Brockden; the other was Clerk to a Merchant. Watson was a pious sensible young Man, of great integrity. The others rather more lax in their Principles of Religion, particularly Ralph, who as well as Collins had been unsettled by me, for which they both made me suffer. Osborne was sensible, candid, frank, sincere, and affectionate to his Friends; but in literary Matters too fond of Criticizing. Ralph, was ingenious, genteel in his Manners, and extremely eloquent; I think I never knew a prettier Talker. Both of them great Admirers of Poetry, and began to try their Hands in little Pieces. Many pleasant Walks we four had together, on Sundays into the Woods near Skuylkill,[4] where we read to one another and conferr'd on what we read. Ralph was inclin'd to pursue the Study of Poetry, not doubting but he might become eminent in it and make his Fortune by it, alledging that the best Poets must when they first began to write, make as many Faults as he did. Osborne dissuaded him, assur'd him he had no Genius for Poetry, and advis'd him to think of nothing beyond the Business he was bred to; that in the mercantile way tho' he had no Stock, he might by his Diligence and Punctuality recommend himself to Employment as a Factor,[5] and in time acquire wherewith to trade on his own Account. I approv'd the amusing oneself with Poetry now and then, so far as to improve one's Language, but no farther. On this it was propos'd that we should each of us at our next Meeting produce a Piece of our own Composing, in order to improve by our mutual Observations, Criticisms and Corrections. As Language and Expression was what we had in View, we excluded all Considerations of Invention,[6] by agreeing that the Task should be a Version of the 18th Psalm, which describes the Descent of a Deity.[7] When the Time of our Meeting drew nigh, Ralph call'd on me first, and let me know his Piece was ready. I told him I had been busy, and having little Inclination had done nothing. He then show'd me his Piece for my Opinion; and I much approv'd it, as it appear'd to me to have great Merit. Now, says he, Osborne never will allow the least Merit in any thing of mine, but makes 1000 Criticisms out of mere Envy. He is not so jealous of you. I wish therefore you would take this Piece, and produce it as yours. I will pretend not to have had time, and so produce nothing. We shall then see what he will say to it. It was agreed, and I immediately transcrib'd it that it might appear in my own hand. We met.

---

3. Brockden (1683–1769) arrived in Philadelphia in 1706. "Conveyancer": one who draws up leases and deeds.
4. A river at Philadelphia.

5. Business agent.
6. I.e., of originality.
7. "He bowed the heavens also, and came down: and darkness was under his feet" (Psalm 18.9).

Watson's Performance was read: there were some Beauties in it: but many Defects. Osborne's was read: It was much better. Ralph did it Justice, remark'd some Faults, but applauded the Beauties. He himself had nothing to produce. I was backward, seem'd desirous of being excus'd, had not had sufficient Time to correct; etc., but no Excuse could be admitted, produce I must. It was read and repeated; Watson and Osborne gave up the Contest; and join'd in applauding it immoderately. Ralph only made some Criticisms and propos'd some Amendments, but I defended my Text. Osborne was against Ralph, and told him he was no better a Critic than Poet; so he dropped the Argument. As they two went home together, Osborne express'd himself still more strongly in favor of what he thought my Production, having restrain'd himself before as he said, lest I should think it Flattery. But who would have imagin'd, says he, that Franklin had been capable of such a Performance; such Painting, such Force! such Fire! He has even improv'd the Original! In his common Conversation, he seems to have no Choice of Words; he hesitates and blunders; and yet, good God, how he writes!

When we next met, Ralph discover'd the Trick we had played him, and Osborne was a little laughed at. This Transaction fix'd Ralph in his Resolution of becoming a Poet. I did all I could to dissuade him from it, but he continu'd scribbling Verses, till *Pope* cur'd him. He became however a pretty good Prose Writer.[8] More of him hereafter. But as I may not have occasion again to mention the other two, I shall just remark here, that Watson died in my Arms a few Years after,[9] much lamented, being the best of our Set. Osborne went to the West Indies, where he became an eminent Lawyer and made Money, but died young.[1] He and I had made a serious Agreement, that the one who happen'd first to die, should if possible make a friendly Visit to the other, and acquaint him how he found things in that separate State. But he never fulfill'd his Promise.

The Governor, seeming to like my Company, had me frequently to his House; and his Setting me up was always mention'd as a fix'd thing. I was to take with me Letters recommendatory to a Number of his Friends, besides the Letter of Credit to furnish me with the necessary Money for purchasing the Press and Types, Paper, etc. For these Letters I was appointed to call at different times, when they were to be ready, but a future time was still[2] named. Thus we went on till the ship whose Departure too had been several times postponed was on the Point of sailing. Then when I call'd to take my Leave and receive the Letters, his Secretary, Dr. Bard,[3] came out to me and said the Governor was extremely busy, in writing, but would be down at New Castle before the Ship, and there the Letters would be delivered to me.

Ralph, tho' married and having one Child, had determined to accompany me in this Voyage. It was thought he intended to establish a Correspondence, and obtain Goods to sell on Commission. But I found afterwards, that thro'

---

8. Ralph (c. 1705–1762) became a well-known political journalist after trying his hand at poetry. In the second edition of the *Dunciad* (1728), a poem that attacks ignorance of all kinds, Alexander Pope (see n. 3, p. 478) responded to the slur against him in Ralph's poem *Sawney*. Pope wrote: "Silence, ye Wolves: while Ralph to Cynthia howls. / And makes Night hideous— Answer him ye Owls" (book 3, lines 159–60). In the 1742 edition, Pope included another dig at Ralph: "And see: The very Gazeteers give o'er, / Ev'n Ralph repents" (book 1, lines 215–16).
9. About 1728.
1. Osborne's dates are unknown.
2. Always.
3. Patrick Bard, or Baird, resided in Philadelphia as port physician after 1720.

some Discontent with his Wife's Relations, he purposed to leave her on their Hands, and never return again. Having taken leave of my Friends, and interchang'd some Promises with Miss Read, I left Philadelphia in the Ship, which anchor'd at New Castle. The Governor was there. But when I went to his Lodging, the Secretary came to me from him with the civilest Message in the World, that he could not then see me being engag'd in Business of the utmost Importance, but should send the Letters to me on board, wish'd me heartily a good Voyage and a speedy Return, etc. I return'd on board, a little puzzled, but still not doubting.

Mr. Andrew Hamilton, a famous Lawyer of Philadelphia, had taken Passage in the same Ship for himself and Son: and with Mr. Denham a Quaker Merchant,[4] and Messrs. Onion and Russel Masters of an Iron Work in Maryland, had engag'd the Great Cabin; so that Ralph and I were forc'd to take up with a Berth in the Steerage: And none on board knowing us, were considered as ordinary Persons. But Mr. Hamilton and his Son (it was James, since Governor) return'd from New Castle to Philadelphia the Father being recall'd by a great Fee to plead for a seized Ship. And just before we sail'd Colonel French coming on board, and showing me great Respect, I was more taken Notice of, and with my Friend Ralph invited by the other Gentlemen to come into the Cabin, there being now Room. Accordingly we remov'd thither.

Understanding that Colonel French had brought on board the Governor's Dispatches, I ask'd the Captain for those Letters that were to be under my Care. He said all were put into the Bag together; and he could not then come at them; but before we landed in England, I should have an Opportunity of picking them out. So I was satisfied for the present, and we proceeded on our Voyage. We had a sociable Company in the Cabin, and lived uncommonly well, having the Addition of all Mr. Hamilton's Stores, who had laid in plentifully. In this Passage Mr. Denham contracted a Friendship for me that continued during his Life. The Voyage was otherwise not a pleasant one, as we had a great deal of bad Weather.

When we came into the Channel, the Captain kept his Word with me, and gave me an Opportunity of examining the Bag for the Governor's Letters. I found none upon which my Name was put, as under my Care; I pick'd out 6 or 7 that by the Handwriting I thought might be the promis'd Letters, especially as one of them was directed to Basket[5] the King's Printer, and another to some Stationer. We arriv'd in London the 24th of December, 1724. I waited upon the Stationer who came first in my Way, delivering the Letter as from Governor Keith. I don't know such a Person, says he: but opening the Letter, O, this is from Riddlesden,[6] I have lately found him to be a complete Rascal, and I will have nothing to do with him, nor receive any Letters from him. So putting the Letter into my Hand, he turn'd on his Heel and left me to serve some Customer. I was surprised to find these were not the Governor's Letters. And after recollecting and comparing

4. Thomas Denham (d. 1728), merchant and benefactor, left Bristol, England, in 1715. In 1735, Andrew Hamilton (c. 1676–1741), a Scottish-born lawyer who lived in Philadelphia, successfully defended a newspaper publisher against a libel charge, establishing a precedent for freedom of the press in the colonies and earning the nickname "the Philadelphia lawyer" (now a catchphrase meaning an extremely competent lawyer). Hamilton's son James (c. 1710–1783) served as governor of Pennsylvania four times between 1748 and 1773.

5. John Baskett (d. 1742).

6. William Riddlesden (d. before 1733), well known in Maryland as a man of "infamy."

Circumstances, I began to doubt his Sincerity. I found my Friend Denham, and opened the whole Affair to him. He let me into Keith's Character, told me there was not the least Probability that he had written any Letters for me, that no one who knew him had the smallest Dependence on him, and he laughed at the Notion of the Governor's giving me a Letter of Credit, having as he said no Credit to give. On my expressing some Concern about what I should do: He advis'd me to endeavor getting some Employment in the Way of my Business. Among the Printers here, says he, you will improve yourself; and when you return to America, you will set up to greater Advantage.

We both of us happen'd to know, as well as the Stationer, that Riddlesden the Attorney, was a very Knave. He had half ruin'd Miss Read's Father by drawing him in to be bound[7] for him. By his Letter it appear'd, there was a secret Scheme on foot to the Prejudice of Hamilton, (Suppos'd to be then coming over with us,) and that Keith was concern'd in it with Riddlesden. Denham, who was a Friend of Hamilton's, thought he ought to be acquainted with it. So when he arriv'd in England, which was soon after, partly from Resentment and Ill-Will to Keith and Riddlesden, and partly from Goodwill to him: I waited on him, and gave him the Letter. He thank'd me cordially, the Information being of Importance to him. And from that time he became my Friend, greatly to my Advantage afterwards on many Occasions.

But what shall we think of a Governor's playing such pitiful Tricks, and imposing so grossly on a poor ignorant Boy! It was a Habit he had acquired. He wish'd to please everybody; and having little to give, he gave Expectations. He was otherwise an ingenious sensible Man, a pretty good Writer, and a good Governor for the People, tho' not for his Constituents the Proprietaries,[8] whose Instructions he sometimes disregarded. Several of our best Laws were of his Planning, and pass'd during his Administration.

Ralph and I were inseparable Companions. We took Lodgings together in Little Britain[9] at 3 shillings 6 pence per Week, as much as we could then afford. He found some Relations, but they were poor and unable to assist him. He now let me know his Intentions of remaining in London, and that he never meant to return to Philadelphia. He had brought no Money with him, the whole he could muster having been expended in paying his Passage. I had 15 Pistoles.[1] So he borrowed occasionally of me, to subsist while he was looking out for Business. He first endeavor'd to get into the Playhouse, believing himself qualified for an Actor; but Wilkes,[2] to whom he applied, advis'd him candidly not to think of that Employment, as it was impossible he should succeed in it. Then he propos'd to Roberts, a Publisher in Paternoster Row,[3] to write for him a Weekly Paper like the Spectator, on certain Conditions, which Roberts did not approve. Then he endeavor'd to get Employment as a Hackney Writer to copy for the Stationers and Lawyers about the Temple[4] but could find no Vacancy.

7. I.e., as a cosigner of a document and legally bound to be responsible for his debts.
8. Members of the Penn family, headed by William Penn (1644–1718), were the proprietors of Pennsylvania and its legal owners. "Constituents": those who appointed him their representative; in this case, the Penn family, which retained control of Pennsylvania until the Revolution.
9. A street in London near St. Paul's Cathedral.

1. Gold coins.
2. Robert Wilks (1665?–1732), an Irish actor, dominated London theater life from 1709 to 1730.
3. The center of the London printing business.
4. The Inner and Middle Temples were buildings in London that were centers for the legal profession. "Hackney Writer": copyist.

I immediately got into Work at Palmer's, then a famous Printing-House in Bartholomew Close;[5] and here I continu'd near a Year. I was pretty diligent; but spent with Ralph a good deal of my Earnings in going to Plays and other Places of Amusement. We had together consum'd all my Pistoles, and now just rubb'd on[6] from hand to mouth. He seem'd quite to forget his Wife and Child, and I by degrees my Engagements with Miss Read, to whom I never wrote more than one Letter, and that was to let her know I was not likely soon to return. This was another of the great Errata of my Life, which I should wish to correct if I were to live it over again. In fact, by our Expenses, I was constantly kept unable to pay my Passage.

At Palmer's I was employ'd in Composing for the second Edition of Wollaston's Religion of Nature.[7] Some of his Reasonings not appearing to me well-founded, I wrote a little metaphysical Piece, in which I made Remarks on them. It was entitled, A Dissertation on Liberty and Necessity, Pleasure and Pain. I inscrib'd it to my Friend Ralph. I printed a small Number. I occasion'd my being more consider'd by Mr. Palmer, as a young Man of some Ingenuity, tho' he seriously expostulated with me upon the Principles of my Pamplet which to him appear'd abominable.[8] My printing this Pamphlet was another Erratum.

While I lodg'd in Little Britain I made an Acquaintance with one Wilcox a Bookseller, whose Shop was at the next Door. He had an immense Collection of second-hand Books. Circulating Libraries were not then in Use; but we agreed that on certain reasonable Terms which I have now forgotten, I might take, read and return any of his Books. This I esteem'd a great Advantage, and I made as much Use of it as I could.

My Pamphlet by some means falling into the Hands of one Lyons,[9] a Surgeon, Author of a Book entitled The Infallibility of Human Judgment, it occasioned an Acquaintance between us; he took great Notice of me, call'd on me often, to converse on these Subjects, carried me to the Horns a pale Ale-House in [blank] Lane, Cheapside, and introduc'd me to Dr. Mandeville, Author of the Fable of the Bees[1] who had a Club there, of which he was the Soul, being a most facetious entertaining Companion. Lyons too introduc'd me to Dr. Pemberton, at Batson's Coffee House, who promis'd to give me an Opportunity some time or other of seeing Sir Isaac Newton,[2] of which I was extremely desirous; but this never happened.

I had brought over a few Curiosities among which the principal was a Purse made of the Asbestos, which purifies by Fire. Sir Hans Sloane heard of it, came to see me, and invited me to his House in Bloomsbury Square;

5. Just off Little Britain; a square known for its printers and typesetters.
6. Proceeded with difficulty.
7. The English philosopher William Wollaston's Religion of Nature Delineated was first printed privately in 1722. Its second edition (1724) sold so well that Franklin was here setting the type for a third edition (1725), not "the second edition."
8. By denying the existence of virtue and vice, Franklin opened himself to accusations of atheism.
9. William Lyons, a surgeon and author of The Infallibility, Dignity, and Excellence of Human

Judgment (1719).
1. Bernard Mandeville (c. 1670–1733), a Dutch physician and man of letters residing in London, published The Fable of the Bees in 1723.
2. English mathematician and physicist (1642–1727), best known for formulating theories of gravity, light, and color. Newton was president of the Royal Society, the British national academy of science, from 1703 to 1727. Henry Pemberton was a friend of Newton's and a member of the Society. Batson's, in Cornhill, was a favorite meeting place of physicians.

where he show'd me all his Curiosities,[3] and persuaded me to let him add that to the Number, for which he paid me handsomely.

In our House there lodg'd a young Woman, a Millener, who I think had a shop in the Cloisters.[4] She had been genteelly bred, was sensible and lively, and of most pleasing Conversation. Ralph read Plays to her in the Evenings, they grew intimate, she took another Lodging, and he follow'd her. They liv'd together some time, but he being still out of Business, and her Income not sufficient to maintain them with her Child, he took a Resolution of going from London, to try for a Country School, which he thought himself well qualified to undertake, as he wrote an excellent Hand, and was a Master of Arithmetic and Accounts. This however he deem'd a Business below him, and confident of future better Fortune when he should be unwilling to have it known that he once was so meanly employ'd, he chang'd his Name, and did me the Honor to assume mine. For I soon after had a Letter from him, acquainting me, that he was settled in a small Village in Berkshire, I think it was, where he taught reading and writing to 10 or a dozen Boys at 6 pence each per Week, recommending Mrs. T. to my Care, and desiring me to write to him directing for Mr. Franklin Schoolmaster at such a Place. He continu'd to write frequently, sending me large Specimens of an Epic Poem, which he was then composing, and desiring my Remarks and Corrections. These I gave him from time to time, but endeavor'd rather to discourage his Proceeding. One of Young's Satires was then just publish'd.[5] I copied and sent him a great Part of it, which set in a strong Light the Folly of pursuing the Muses with any Hope of Advancement by them. All was in vain. Sheets of the Poem continu'd to come by every Post. In the mean time Mrs. T. having on his Account lost her Friends and Business, was often in Distresses, and us'd to send for me, and borrow what I could spare to help her out of them. I grew fond of her Company, and being at this time under no Religious Restraints, and presuming on my Importance to her, I attempted Familiarities, (another Erratum) which she repuls'd with a proper Resentment, and acquainted him with my Behavior. This made a Breach between us, and when he return'd again to London, he let me know he thought I had cancel'd all the Obligations he had been under to me. So I found I was never to expect his Repaying me what I lent to him or advanc'd for him. This was however not then of much Consequence, as he was totally unable. And in the Loss of his Friendship I found myself reliev'd from a Burden. I now began to think of getting a little Money beforehand; and expecting better Work, I left Palmer's to work at Watts's[6] near Lincoln's Inn Fields, a still greater Printing-House. Here I continu'd all the rest of my Stay in London.

At my first Admission into this Printing-House, I took to working at Press, imagining I felt a Want of the Bodily Exercise I had been us'd to in America, where Presswork is mix'd with Composing.[7] I drank only Water; the other Workmen, near 50 in Number, were great Guzzlers of Beer. On occasion I carried up and down Stairs a large Form of Types[8] in each hand, when others

3. Sloane (1660–1753), a physician and naturalist, succeeded Newton as president of the Royal Society. His library and museum served as the basis for the present collection at the British Museum.
4. Probably near St. Bartholomew's Church, London.

5. The English poet Edward Young (1683–1765) published the first four parts of Love of Fame, the Universal Passion in 1725.
6. Press belonging to John Watts (c. 1678–1763).
7. I.e., the workers do both the printing and typesetting for it.
8. Type set and locked in metal frames.

carried but one in both Hands. They wonder'd to see from this and several Instances that the Water-American as they call'd me was *stronger* than themselves who drunk *strong*[9] Beer. We had an Alehouse Boy who attended always in the House to supply the Workmen. My Companion at the Press drank every day a Pint before Breakfast, a Pint at Breakfast with his Bread and Cheese; a Pint between Breakfast and Dinner; a Pint at Dinner; a Pint in the Afternoon about Six o'clock, and another when he had done his Day's Work. I thought it a detestable Custom. But it was necessary, he suppos'd, to drink *strong* Beer that he might be *strong* to labor. I endeavor'd to convince him that the Bodily Strength afforded by Beer could only be in proportion to the Grain or Flour of the Barley dissolved in the Water of which it was made; that there was more Flour in a Penny-worth of Bread, and therefore if he would eat that with a Pint of Water, it would give him more Strength than a Quart of Beer. He drank on however, and had 4 or 5 Shillings to pay out of his Wages every Saturday Night for that muddling Liquor; an Expense I was free from. And thus these poor Devils keep themselves always under.[1]

Watts after some Weeks desiring to have me in the Composing-Room, I left the Pressmen. A new *Bienvenu*[2] or Sum for Drink, being 5 Shillings, was demanded of me by the Compositors.[3] I thought it an Imposition, as I had paid below. The Master thought so too, and forbad my Paying it. I stood out two or three Weeks, was accordingly considered as an Excommunicate, and had so many little Pieces of private Mischief done me, by mixing my Sorts, transposing my Pages, breaking my Matter,[4] etc., etc. if I were ever so little out of the Room, and all ascrib'd to the Chapel[5] Ghost, which they said ever haunted those not regularly admitted, that notwithstanding the Master's Protection, I found myself oblig'd to comply and pay the Money; convinc'd of the Folly of being on ill Terms with those one is to live with continually. I was now on a fair Footing with them, and soon acquir'd considerable Influence. I propos'd some reasonable Alterations in their Chapel Laws, and carried them against all Opposition. From my Example a great Part of them, left their muddling Breakfast of Beer and Bread and Cheese, finding they could with me be supplied from a neighboring House with a large Porringer of hot Water-gruel, sprinkled with Pepper, crumb'd with Bread, and a Bit of Butter in it, for the Price of a Pint of Beer, viz., three halfpence. This was a more comfortable as well as cheaper Breakfast, and kept their Heads clearer. Those who continu'd sotting with Beer all day, were often, by not paying, out of Credit at the Alehouse, and us'd to make Interest with me to get Beer, *their Light,* as they phras'd it, *being out.* I watch'd the Pay table on Saturday Night, and collected what I stood engag'd for them, having to pay some times near Thirty Shillings a Week on their Accounts. This and my being esteem'd a pretty good Riggite,[6] that is a jocular verbal Satirist, supported my Consequence in the Society. My constant Attendance, (I never making a St. Monday),[7] recommended me to the Master; and my uncommon Quickness at Composing, occasion'd my being put upon all

---

9. With high alcohol content.
1. I.e., in poverty.
2. Welcome (French, literal trans.).
3. Typesetters. The workers set their own customs, practices, and fines.
4. Type set up for printing. "Sorts": type, letters.

5. "A Printing House is always called a Chapel by the Workmen" [Franklin's note].
6. One who makes fun of others.
7. Taking Monday off as if it were a religious holiday.

Work of Dispatch, which was generally better paid. So I went on now very agreeably.

My Lodging in Little Britain being too remote, I found another in Duke Street opposite to the Romish Chapel.[8] It was two pair of Stairs backwards at an Italian Warehouse. A Widow Lady kept the House; she had a Daughter and a Maid Servant, and a Journeyman who attended the Warehouse, but lodg'd abroad. After sending to enquire my Character at the House where I last lodg'd, she agreed to take me in at the same Rate, 3 Shillings 6 Pence per Week, cheaper as she said from the Protection she expected in having a Man lodge in the House. She was a Widow, an elderly Woman, had been bred a Protestant, being a Clergyman's Daughter, but was converted to the Catholic Religion by her Husband, whose Memory she much revered, had lived much among People of Distinction, and knew a 1000 Anecdotes of them as far back as the Times of Charles the second. She was lame in her Knees with the Gout, and therefore seldom stirr'd out of her Room, so sometimes wanted Company; and hers was so highly amusing to me that I was sure to spend an Evening with her whenever she desired it. Our Supper was only half an Anchovy each, on a very little Strip of Bread and Butter, and half a Pint of Ale between us. But the Entertainment was in her Conversation. My always keeping good Hours, and giving little Trouble in the Family, made her unwilling to part with me; so that when I talk'd of a Lodging I had heard of, nearer my Business, for 2 Shillings a Week, which, intent as I now was on saving Money, made some Difference; she bid me not think of it, for she would abate me two Shillings a Week for the future, so I remain'd with her at 1 Shilling 6 Pence as long as I stayed in London.

In a Garret of her House there lived a Maiden Lady of 70 in the most retired Manner, of whom my Landlady gave me this Account, that she was a Roman Catholic, had been sent abroad when young and lodg'd in a Nunnery with an Intent of becoming a Nun: but the Country not agreeing with her, she return'd to England, where there being no Nunnery, she had vow'd to lead the Life of a Nun as near as might be done in those Circumstances: Accordingly She had given all her Estate to charitable Uses, reserving only Twelve Pounds a year to live on, and out of this Sum she still gave a great deal in Charity, living herself on Watergruel only, and using no Fire but to boil it. She had lived many Years in that Garret, being permitted to remain there gratis by successive catholic Tenants of the House below, as they deem'd it a Blessing to have her there. A Priest visited her, to confess her every Day. I have ask'd her, says my Landlady, how she, as she liv'd, could possibly find so much Employment for a Confessor? O, says she, it is impossible to avoid *vain Thoughts*. I was permitted once to visit her: She was cheerful and polite, and convers'd pleasantly. The Room was clean, but had no other Furniture than a Mattress, a Table with a Crucifix and Book, a Stool, which she gave me to sit on, and a Picture over the Chimney of *St. Veronica*, displaying her Handkerchief with the miraculous Figure of Christ's bleeding Face on it,[9] which she explain'd to me with great

---

8. The Roman Catholic Chapel of St. Anselm and St. Cecilia.
9. According to tradition, as Christ bore the Cross, St. Veronica wiped his face with a cloth that miraculously retained the image of his face.

Seriousness. She look'd pale, but was never sick, and I give it as another Instance on how small an Income Life and Health may be supported.

At Watts's Printing-House I contracted an Acquaintance with an ingenious young Man, one Wygate, who having wealthy Relations, had been better educated than most Printers, was a tolerable Latinist, spoke French, and lov'd Reading. I taught him, and a Friend of his, to swim at twice going into the River, and they soon became good Swimmers. They introduc'd me to some Gentlemen from the Country who went to Chelsea by Water to see the College and Don Saltero's Curiosities.[1] In our Return, at the Request of the Company, whose Curiosity Wygate had excited, I stripped and leaped into the River, and swam from near Chelsea to Blackfriars,[2] performing on the Way many Feats of Activity both upon and under Water, that surpris'd and pleas'd those to whom they were Novelties. I had from a Child been ever delighted with this Exercise, had studied and practic'd all Thevenot's Motions and Positions,[3] added some of my own, aiming at the graceful and easy, as well as the Useful. All these I took this Occasion of exhibiting to the Company, and was much flatter'd by their Admiration. And Wygate, who was desirous of becoming a Master, grew more and more attach'd to me on that account, as well as from the Similarity of our Studies. He at length propos'd to me traveling all over Europe together, supporting ourselves every where by working at our Business. I was once inclin'd to it. But mentioning it to my good Friend Mr. Denham, with whom I often spent an Hour when I had Leisure, he dissuaded me from it; advising me to think only of returning to Pennsylvania, which he was now about to do.

I must record one Trait of this good Man's Character. He had formerly been in Business at Bristol, but fail'd in Debt to a Number of People, compounded[4] and went to America. There, by a close Application to Business as a Merchant, he acquir'd a plentiful Fortune in a few Years. Returning to England in the Ship with me, He invited his old Creditors to an Entertainment, at which he thank'd them for the easy Composition[5] they had favor'd him with, and when they expected nothing but the Treat, every Man at the first Remove[6] found under his Plate an Order on a Banker for the full Amount of the unpaid Remainder with Interest.

He now told me he was about to return to Philadelphia, and should carry over a great Quantity of Goods in order to open a Store there: He propos'd to take me over as his Clerk, to keep his Books (in which he would instruct me), copy his Letters, and attend the Store. He added, that as soon as I should be acquainted with mercantile Business he would promote me by sending me with a Cargo of Flour and Bread, etc., to the West Indies, and procure me Commissions from others; which would be profitable, and if I manag'd well, would establish me handsomely. The Thing pleas'd me, for I was grown tired of London, remember'd with Pleasure the happy Months I had spent in Pennsylvania, and wish'd again to see it. Therefore I immediately agreed,

1. I.e., the cabinets of curiosities in Don Saltero's, a coffeehouse in London's Chelsea district. "Don Saltero" was James Salter, a former servant of Sir Hans Sloane to whom Sloane had given many objects from his collection. "College": i.e., Chelsea Hospital, erected on the site of the former Chelsea College.

2. I.e., more than three miles.
3. I.e., in Melchisédech de Thevenot's *The Art of Swimming* (1699).
4. Settled part payment on his debts.
5. Conditions for accepting a declaration of bankruptcy.
6. I.e., the first time the plates were cleared.

on the Terms of Fifty Pounds a Year, Pennsylvania Money; less indeed than my then Gettings as a Compositor, but affording a better Prospect.

I now took Leave of Printing, as I thought for ever, and was daily employ'd in my new Business; going about with Mr. Denham among the Tradesmen, to purchase various Articles, and see them pack'd up, doing Errands, calling upon Workmen to dispatch, etc., and when all was on board, I had a few Days' Leisure. On one of these Days I was to my Surprise sent for by a great Man I knew only by Name, a Sir William Wyndham and I waited upon him. He had heard by some means or other of my Swimming from Chelsey to Blackfriars, and of my teaching Wygate and another young Man to swim in a few Hours. He had two Sons about to set out on their Travels; he wish'd to have them first taught Swimming; and propos'd to gratify me handsomely if I would teach them. They were not yet come to Town and my Stay was uncertain, so I could not undertake it. But from this Incident I thought it likely, that if I were to remain in England and open a Swimming School, I might get a good deal of Money. And it struck me so strongly, that had the Overture been sooner made me, probably I should not so soon have returned to America. After Many Years, you and I had something of more Importance to do with one of these Sons of Sir William Wyndham,[7] become Earl of Egremont, which I shall mention in its Place.

Thus I spent about 18 Months in London. Most Part of the Time, I work'd hard at my Business, and spent but little upon myself except in seeing Plays, and in Books. My Friend Ralph had kept me poor. He owed me about 27 Pounds; which I was now never likely to receive; a great Sum out of my small Earnings. I lov'd him notwithstanding, for he had many amiable Qualities. Tho' I had by no means improv'd my Fortune, I had pick'd up some very ingenious Acquaintance whose Conversation was of great Advantage to me, and I had read considerably.

We sail'd from Gravesend on the 23d of July 1726. For The Incidents of the Voyage, I refer you to my Journal, where you will find them all minutely related. Perhaps the most important Part of that Journal is the *Plan*[8] to be found in it which I formed at Sea for regulating my future Conduct in Life. It is the more remarkable, as being form'd when I was so young, and yet being pretty faithfully adhered to quite thro' to old Age. We landed in Philadelphia the 11th of October, where I found sundry Alterations. Keith was no longer Governor, being superseded by Major Gordon:[9] I met him walking the Streets as a common Citizen. He seem'd a little asham'd at seeing me, but pass'd without saying anything. I should have been as much asham'd at seeing Miss Read, had not her Friends despairing with Reason of my Return, after the Receipt of my Letter, persuaded her to marry another, one Rogers, a Potter, which was done in my Absence. With him however she was never happy, and soon parted from him, refusing to cohabit with him, or bear his Name. It being now said that he had another Wife. He was a worthless Fellow tho' an excellent Workman which was the Temptation to her Friends. He got into Debt, and ran away in 1727 or 28, went to the West Indies,

7. Franklin does not mention Charles Wyndham (1710–1763) again. Charles's father, Sir William (1687–1740), was an English statesman and Member of Parliament.

8. Only the outline and preamble of Franklin's *Plan* survive.
9. Patrick Gordon (1644–1736), deputy governor of Pennsylvania from 1726 to 1736.

and died there. Keimer had got a better House, a Shop well supplied with Stationery, plenty of new Types, a number of Hands tho' none good, and seem'd to have a great deal of Business.

Mr. Denham took a Store in Water Street, where we open'd our Goods. I attended the Business diligently, studied Accounts, and grew in a little Time expert at selling. We lodg'd and boarded together, he counsel'd me as a Father, having a sincere Regard for me: I respected and lov'd him: and we might have gone on together very happily: But in the Beginning of February 1726/7 when I had just pass'd my 21st Year, we both were taken ill. My Distemper was a Pleurisy, which very nearly carried me off: I suffered a good deal, gave up the Point[1] in my own mind, and was rather disappointed when I found myself recovering; regretting in some degree that I must now sometime or other have all that disagreeable Work to do over again. I forget what his Distemper was. It held him a long time, and at length carried him off. He left me a small Legacy in a nuncupative[2] Will, as a Token of his Kindness for me, and he left me once more to the wide World. For the Store was taken into the Care of his Executors, and my Employment under him ended: My Brother-in-law Homes, being now at Philadelphia, advis'd my Return to my Business. And Keimer tempted me with an Offer of large Wages by the Year to come and take the Management of his Printing-House that he might better attend his Stationer's Shop. I had heard a bad Character of him in London, from his Wife and her Friends, and was not fond of having any more to do with him. I tried for farther Employment as a Merchant's Clerk; but not readily meeting with any, I clos'd again with Keimer.

I found in *his* House these Hands; Hugh Meredith[3] a Welsh-Pennsylvanian, 30 Years of Age, bred to Country Work: honest, sensible, had a great deal of solid Observation, was something of a Reader, but given to drink: Stephen Potts,[4] a young Country Man of full Age, bred to the Same, of uncommon natural Parts[5] and great Wit and Humor, but a little idle. These he had agreed with at extreme low Wages, per Week, to be rais'd a Shilling every 3 Months, as they would deserve by improving in their Business, and the Expectation of these high Wages to come on hereafter was what he had drawn them in with. Meredith was to work at Press, Potts at Bookbinding, which he by Agreement, was to teach them, tho' he knew neither one nor t'other. John———a wild Irishman brought up to no Business, whose Service for 4 Years Keimer had purchas'd from the Captain of a Ship.[6] He too was to be made a Pressman. George Webb,[7] an Oxford Scholar, whose Time for 4 Years he had likewise bought, intending him for a Compositor: of whom more presently. And David Harry,[8] a Country Boy, whom he had taken Apprentice. I soon perceiv'd that the Intention of engaging me at Wages so much higher than he had been us'd to give, was to have these raw cheap Hands form'd thro' me, and as soon as I had instructed them, then, they being all articled to him, he should be able to do without me. I went on however, very cheerfully; put

---

1. End; i.e., resigned himself to death.
2. Oral.
3. Meredith (c. 1696–1749) was later a business partner of Franklin's.
4. Potts (d. 1758) was later a bookseller and an innkeeper.
5. I.e., handsome.

6. I.e., Keimer had paid for the Irishman's passage in exchange for his service.
7. Webb (1708–1736?) was later a member of Franklin's Junto (a small, select club for mutual improvement) and a printer.
8. A Welsh Quaker (1708–1760); later the first printer in Barbados.

his Printing-House in Order, which had been in great Confusion, and brought his Hands by degrees to mind their Business and to do it better.

It was an odd Thing to find an Oxford Scholar in the Situation of a bought Servant. He was not more than 18 Years of Age, and gave me this Account of himself; that he was born in Gloucester, educated at a Grammar School there, had been distinguish'd among the Scholars for some apparent Superiority in performing his Part when they exhibited Plays; belong'd to the Witty Club there, and had written some Pieces in Prose and Verse which were printed in the Gloucester Newspapers. Thence he was sent to Oxford; there he continu'd about a Year, but not well-satisfied, wishing of all things to see London and become a Player.[9] At length receiving his Quarterly Allowance of 15 Guineas,[1] instead of discharging his Debts, he walk'd out of Town, hid his Gown in a Furz Bush, and footed it to London, where having no Friend to advise him, he fell into bad Company, soon spent his Guineas, found no means of being introduc'd among the Players,[2] grew necessitous, pawn'd his Clothes and wanted Bread. Walking the Street very hungry, and not knowing what to do with himself, a Crimp's Bill was put into his Hand, offering immediate Entertainment and Encouragement to such as would bind themselves to serve in America. He went directly, sign'd the Indentures, was put into the Ship and came over; never writing a Line to acquaint his Friends what was become of him. He was lively, witty, good-natur'd and a pleasant Companion, but idle, thoughtless and imprudent to the last Degree.

John the Irishman soon ran away. With the rest I began to live very agreeably; for they all respected me, the more as they found Keimer incapable of instructing them, and that from me they learned something daily. We never work'd on a Saturday, that being Keimer's Sabbath. So I had two Days for Reading. My Acquaintance with ingenious People in the Town increased. Keimer himself treated me with great Civility and apparent Regard; and nothing now made me uneasy but my Debt to Vernon, which I was yet unable to pay, being hitherto but a poor Economist. He however kindly made no Demand of it.

Our Printing-House often wanted Sorts, and there was no Letter Founder[3] in America. I had seen Types cast at James's[4] in London, but without much Attention to the Manner: However I now contriv'd a Mold, made use of the Letters we had as Puncheons, struck the Matrices[5] in Lead, and thus supplied in a pretty tolerable way all Deficiencies. I also engrav'd several Things on occasion. I made the Ink, I was Warehouse-man and everything, in short quite a Factotum.[6]

But however serviceable I might be, I found that my Services became every Day of less Importance, as the other Hands improv'd in the Business. And when Keimer paid my second Quarter's Wages, he let me know that he felt them too heavy, and thought I should make an Abatement. He grew by degrees less civil, put on more of the Master, frequently found Fault, was captious and seem'd ready for an Out-breaking. I went on nevertheless with

9. Actor.
1. An evergreen shrub; gorse. "Gown": academic robe worn regularly by Oxford students. "15 Guineas": almost sixteen pounds.
2. An advertisement for free passage to the colonies for those who would work as indentured servants.
3. Foundry for type (sorts).
4. Thomas James's foundry.
5. Molds for casting type. "Puncheons": stamping tools.
6. Jack-of-all-trades.

a good deal of Patience, thinking that his encumber'd Circumstances were partly the Cause. At length a Trifle snapped our Connection. For a great Noise happening near the Courthouse, I put my Head out of the Window to see what was the Matter. Keimer being in the Street look'd up and saw me, call'd out to me in a loud Voice and angry Tone to mind my Business, adding some reproachful Words, that nettled me the more for their Publicity, all the Neighbors who were looking out on the same Occasion being Witnesses how I was treated. He came up immediately into the Printing-House, continu'd the Quarrel, high Words pass'd on both Sides, he gave me the Quarter's Warning we had stipulated, expressing a Wish that he had not been oblig'd to so long a Warning: I told him his Wish was unnecessary for I would leave him that Instant; and so taking my Hat walk'd out of Doors; desiring Meredith whom I saw below to take care of some Things I left, and bring them to my Lodging.

Meredith came accordingly in the Evening, when we talk'd my Affair over. He had conceiv'd a great Regard for me, and was very unwilling that I should leave the House while he remain'd in it. He dissuaded me from returning to my native Country[7] which I began to think of. He reminded me that Keimer was in debt for all he possess'd, that his Creditors began to be uneasy, that he kept his Shop miserably, sold often without Profit for ready Money, and often trusted without keeping Account. That he must therefore fail; which would make a Vacancy I might profit of. I objected my Want of Money. He then let me know, that his Father had a high Opinion of me, and from some Discourse that had pass'd between them, he was sure would advance Money to set us up, if I would enter into Partnership with him. My Time, says he, will be out with Keimer in the Spring. By that time we may have our Press and Types in from London: I am sensible I am no Workman. If you like it, Your Skill in the Business shall be set against the Stock I furnish; and we will share the Profits equally. The Proposal was agreeable, and I consented. His Father was in Town, and approv'd of it, the more as he saw I had great Influence with his Son, had prevail'd on him to abstain long from Dram-drinking, and he hop'd might break him of that wretched Habit entirely, when we came to be so closely connected. I gave an Inventory to the Father, who carried it to a Merchant; the Things were sent for; the Secret was to be kept till they should arrive, and in the mean time I was to get Work if I could at the other Printing-House. But I found no Vacancy there, and so remain'd idle a few Days, when Keimer, on a Prospect of being employ'd to print some Paper-money, in New Jersey, which would require Cuts and various Types that I only could supply, and apprehending Bradford might engage me and get the Job from him, sent me a very civil Message, that old Friends should not part for a few Words, the Effect of sudden Passion, and wishing me to return. Meredith persuaded me to comply, as it would give more Opportunity for his Improvement under my daily Instructions. So I return'd, and we went on more smoothly than for some time before. The New Jersey Job was obtain'd. I contriv'd a Copper-Plate Press for it, the first that had been seen in the Country. I cut several Ornaments and Checks for the Bills. We went together to Burlington,[8] where I executed the Whole to Satisfaction, and he

7. I.e., Boston.   8. City in New Jersey.

received so large a Sum for the Work, as to be enabled thereby to keep his Head much longer above Water.

At Burlington I made an Acquaintance with many principal People of the Province. Several of them had been appointed by the Assembly a Committee to attend the Press, and take Care that no more Bills were printed than the Law directed. They were therefore by Turns constantly with us, and generally he who attended brought with him a Friend or two for Company. My Mind having been much more improv'd by Reading than Keimer's, I suppose it was for that Reason my Conversation seem'd to be more valu'd. They had me to their Houses, introduc'd me to their Friends and show'd me much Civility, while he, tho' the Master, was a little neglected. In truth he was an odd Fish, ignorant of common Life, fond of rudely opposing receiv'd Opinions, slovenly to extreme dirtiness, enthusiastic[9] in some Points of Religion, and a little Knavish withal. We continu'd there near 3 Months, and by that time I could reckon among my acquired Friends, Judge Allen, Samuel Bustill, the Secretary of the Province, Isaac Pearson, Joseph Cooper and several of the Smiths, Members of Assembly, and Isaac Decow the Surveyor General. The latter was a shrewd sagacious old Man, who told me that he began for himself when young by wheeling Clay for the Brickmakers, learned to write after he was of Age, carried the Chain for Surveyors, who taught him Surveying, and he had now by his Industry acquir'd a good Estate; and says he, I foresee, that you will soon work this Man out of his Business and make a Fortune in it at Philadelphia. He had not then the least Intimation of my Intention to set up there or anywhere. These Friends were afterwards of great Use to me, as I occasionally was to some of them. They all continued their Regard for me as long as they lived.

Before I enter upon my public Appearance in Business, it may be well to let you know the then State of my Mind, with regard to my Principles and Morals, that you may see how far those influenc'd the future Events of my Life. My Parents had early given me religious Impressions, and brought me through my Childhood piously in the Dissenting Way.[1] But I was scarce 15 when, after doubting by turns of several Points as I found them disputed in the different Books I read, I began to doubt of Revelation itself. Some Books against Deism fell into my Hands; they were said to be the Substance of Sermons preached at Boyle's Lectures.[2] It happened that they wrought an Effect on me quite contrary to what was intended by them: For the Arguments of the Deists which were quoted to be refuted, appeared to me much Stronger than the Refutations. In short I soon became a thorough Deist. My Arguments perverted some others, particularly Collins and Ralph: but each of them having afterwards wrong'd me greatly without the least Compunction, and recollecting Keith's Conduct towards me, (who was another Freethinker) and my own towards Vernon and Miss Read which at Times gave me great Trouble, I began to suspect that this Doctrine tho' it might be true, was not very useful. My London pamphlet, which had for its Motto those Lines of Dryden

9. Highly emotional.
1. I.e., in the Congregational or Presbyterian way, as opposed to the Church of England way.
2. Robert Boyle (1627–1691), English physicist and chemist, endowed a series of lectures for discussing the existence of God and preaching against "infidels." Deism accepts a supreme being as the author of finite existence, but denies Christian doctrines of revelation and supernaturalism.

——*Whatever is, is right*
Tho' purblind Man Sees but a Part of
The Chain, the nearest Link,
His Eyes not carrying to the equal Beam,
That poizes all, above.[3]

And from the Attributes of God, his infinite Wisdom, Goodness and Power concluded that nothing could possibly be wrong in the World, and that Vice and Virtue were empty Distinctions, no such Things existing: appear'd now not so clever a Performance as I once thought it; and I doubted whether some Error had not insinuated itself unperceiv'd into my Argument, so as to infect all that follow'd, as is common in metaphysical Reasonings. I grew convinc'd that *Truth, Sincerity* and *Integrity* in Dealings between Man and Man, were of the utmost Importance to the Felicity of Life, and I form'd written Resolutions, (which still remain in my Journal Book) to practice them ever while I lived. Revelation had indeed no weight with me as such; but I entertain'd an Opinion, that tho' certain Actions might not be bad *because* they were forbidden by it, or good *because* it commanded them; yet probably those Actions might be forbidden *because* they were bad for us, or commanded *because* they were beneficial to us, in their own Natures, all the Circumstances of things considered. And this Persuasion, with the kind hand of Providence, or some guardian Angel, or accidental favorable Circumstances and Situations, or all together, preserved me (thro' this dangerous Time of Youth and the hazardous Situations I was sometimes in among Strangers, remote from the Eye and Advice of my Father) without any *willful* gross Immorality or Injustice that might have been expected from my Want of Religion. I say *willful*, because the Instances I have mentioned, had something of *Necessity* in them, from my Youth, Inexperience, and the Knavery of others. I had therefore a tolerable Character to begin the World with, I valued it properly, and determin'd to preserve it.

We had not been long return'd to Philadelphia, before the New Types arriv'd from London. We settled with Keimer, and left him by his Consent before he heard of it. We found a House to hire near the Market, and took it. To lessen the Rent, (which was then but 24 Pounds a Year tho' I have since known it let for 70) we took in Thomas Godfrey a Glazier,[4] and his Family, who were to pay a considerable Part of it to us, and we to board with them. We had scarce opened our Letters and put our Press in Order, before George House, an Acquaintance of mine, brought a Countryman to us; whom he had met in the Street enquiring for a Printer. All our Cash was now expended in the Variety of Particulars we had been obliged to procure, and this Countryman's Five Shillings, being our First Fruits and coming so seasonably, gave me more Pleasure than any Crown[5] I have since earn'd; and from the Gratitude I felt towards House, has made me often more ready than perhaps I should otherwise have been to assist young Beginners.

---

3. The first line is not from the English poet John Dryden (1631–1700) but from Alexander Pope's *Essay on Man* Epistle I, line 294; however, Dryden's line is close: "Whatever is, is in its Causes just." The rest of these lines are recalled accurately from Dryden's *Oedipus* (3.1.244–48).
4. Godfrey (1704–1749) set glass for window-panes. He was also an optician and inventor.
5. A coin worth five shillings.

There are Croakers in every Country always boding its Ruin. Such a one then lived in Philadelphia, a Person of Note, an elderly Man, with a wise Look and very grave Manner of Speaking. His Name was Samuel Mickle. This Gentleman, a Stranger to me, stopped one Day at my Door, and ask'd me if I was the young Man who had lately opened a new Printing-House: Being answer'd in the Affirmative; He said he was sorry for me; because it was an expensive Undertaking, and the Expense would be lost, for Philadelphia was a sinking[6] Place, the People already half Bankrupts or near being so; all Appearances of the contrary such as new Buildings and the Rise of Rents, being to his certain Knowledge fallacious, for they were in fact among the Things that would soon ruin us. And he gave me such a Detail of Misfortunes now existing or that were soon to exist, that he left me half-melancholy. Had I known him before I engag'd in this Business, probably I never should have done it. This Man continu'd to live in this decaying Place, and to declaim in the same Strain, refusing for many Years to buy a House there, because all was going to Destruction, and at last I had the Pleasure of seeing him give five times as much for one as he might have bought it for when he first began his Croaking.

I should have mention'd before, that in the Autumn of the preceding Year, I had form'd most of my ingenious Acquaintance into a Club, for mutual Improvement, which we call'd the Junto. We met on Friday Evenings. The Rules I drew up, requir'd that every Member in his Turn should produce one or more Queries on any Point of Morals, Politics or Natural Philosophy, to be discuss'd by the Company, and once in three Months produce and read an Essay of his own Writing on any Subject he pleased. Our Debates were to be under the Direction of a President, and to be conducted in the sincere Spirit of Enquiry after Truth, without fondness for Dispute, or Desire of Victory; and to prevent Warmth, all expressions of Positiveness[7] in Opinion, or of direct Contradiction, were after some time made contraband and prohibited under small pecuniary Penalties. The first Members were, Joseph Breintnall, a Copier of Deeds for the Scriveners; a good-natur'd friendly middle-ag'd Man, a great Lover of Poetry, reading all he could meet with, and writing some that was tolerable; very ingenious in many little Nicknackeries, and of sensible Conversation.[8] Thomas Godfrey, a self-taught Mathematician, great in his Way, and afterwards Inventor of what is now call'd Hadley's Quadrant.[9] But he knew little out of his way, and was not a pleasing Companion, as like most Great Mathematicians I have met with, he expected unusual Precision in everything said, or was forever denying or distinguishing upon Trifles, to the Disturbance of all Conversation. He soon left us. Nicholas Scull,[1] a Surveyor, afterwards Surveyor-General, Who lov'd Books, and sometimes made a few Verses. William Parsons, bred a Shoemaker, but loving Reading, had acquir'd a considerable Share of Mathematics, which he first studied with a View to Astrology that he afterwards laughed at. He

6. Economically declining.
7. Certainty. "Warmth": anger.
8. Breintnall (d. 1746) shared Franklin's interest in science.
9. Godfrey invented this instrument for measuring altitudes in navigation and astronomy—also known as the octant—around the same time as the English inventor John Hadley (1682–1744) did.
1. Nicholas Scull II (1687–1761).

also became Surveyor General.[2] William Maugridge, a Joiner,[3] and a most exquisite Mechanic, and a solid sensible Man. Hugh Meredith, Stephen Potts, and George Webb, I have Characteris'd before. Robert Grace,[4] a young Gentleman of some Fortune, generous, lively and witty, a Lover of Punning and of his Friends. And William Coleman, then a Merchant's Clerk, about my Age, who had the coolest clearest Head, the best Heart, and the exactest Morals, of almost any Man I ever met with. He became afterwards a Merchant of great Note, and one of our Provincial Judges: Our Friendship continued without Interruption to his Death, upwards of 40 Years.[5] And the Club continu'd almost as long and was the best School of Philosophy, Morals and Politics that then existed in the Province; for our Queries which were read the Week preceding their Discussion, put us on reading with Attention upon the several Subjects, that we might speak more to the purpose: and here too we acquired better Habits of Conversation, everything being studied in our Rules which might prevent our disgusting each other. From hence the long Continuance of the Club, which I shall have frequent Occasion to speak farther of hereafter; But my giving this Account of it here, is to show something of the Interest I had, everyone of these exerting themselves in recommending Business to us.

Breintnall particularly procur'd us from the Quakers, the Printing 40 Sheets of their History, the rest being to be done by Keimer: and upon this we work'd exceeding hard, for the Price was low. It was a Folio, Pro Patria Size, in Pica with Long Primer Notes.[6] I compos'd of it a Sheet a Day, and Meredith work'd it off at Press. It was often 11 at Night and sometimes later, before I had finish'd my Distribution[7] for the next day's Work: For the little Jobs sent in by our other Friends now and then put us back. But so determin'd I was to continue doing a Sheet a Day of the Folio, that one Night when having impos'd my Forms,[8] I thought my Day's Work over, one of them by accident was broken and two Pages reduc'd to Pie,[9] I immediately distributed and compos'd it over again before I went to bed. And this Industry visible to our Neighbors began to give us Character and Credit; particularly I was told, that mention being made of the new Printing Office at the Merchants' Every-night-Club, the general Opinion was that it must fail, there being already two Printers in the Place, Keimer and Bradford; but Doctor Baird (whom you and I saw many Years after at his native Place, St. Andrews in Scotland) gave a contrary Opinion; for the Industry of that Franklin, says he, is superior to anything I ever saw of the kind: I see him still at work when I go home from Club; and he is at Work again before his Neighbors are out of bed. This struck the rest, and we soon after had Offers from one of them to supply us with Stationery. But as yet we did not choose to engage in Shop Business.

2. Parsons (1701–1757) became surveyor general in 1741 and librarian of the Library Company—the first subscription library in North America, an offshoot of the Junto.
3. A ship's carpenter (d. 1766).
4. Franklin's landlord for thirty-seven years.
5. Coleman lived from 1704 to 1769.

6. A book, of large size, with the main text in twelve-point type and the notes in ten-point type.
7. I.e., of type, returning letters to their cases so they may be used again.
8. Locked the type into its form and readied it for printing.
9. A confused pile.

I mention this Industry the more particularly and the more freely, tho' it seems to be talking in my own Praise, that those of my Posterity who shall read it, may know the Use of that Virtue, when they see its Effects in my Favor throughout this Relation.

George Webb, who had found a Friend that lent him wherewith to purchase his Time of Keimer, now came to offer himself as a Journeyman to us. We could not then employ him, but I foolishly let him know, as a Secret, that I soon intended to begin a Newspaper, and might then have Work for him. My Hopes of Success as I told him were founded on this, that the then only Newspaper,[1] printed by Bradford was a paltry thing, wretchedly manag'd, no way entertaining; and yet was profitable to him. I therefore thought a good Paper could scarcely fail of good Encouragement. I requested Webb not to mention it, but he told it to Keimer, who immediately, to be beforehand with me, published Proposals for Printing one himself, on which Webb was to be employ'd. I resented this, and to counteract them, as I could not yet begin our Paper, I wrote several Pieces of Entertainment for Bradford's Paper, under the Title of the Busy Body which Breintnall continu'd some Months.[2] By this means the Attention of the Public was fix'd on that Paper, and Keimer's Proposals which we burlesqu'd and ridicul'd, were disregarded. He began his Paper however, and after carrying it on three Quarters of a Year, with at most only 90 Subscribers, he offer'd it to me for a Trifle, and I having been ready some time to go on with it, took it in hand directly, and it prov'd in a few Years extremely profitable to me.[3]

I perceive that I am apt to speak in the singular Number, though our Partnership still continu'd. The Reason may be, that in fact the whole Management of the Business lay upon me. Meredith was no Compositor, a poor Pressman, and seldom sober. My Friends lamented my Connection with him, but I was to make the best of it.

Our first Papers made a quite different Appearance from any before in the Province, a better Type and better printed: but some spirited Remarks of my Writing on the Dispute then going on between Governor Burnet[4] and the Massachusetts Assembly, struck the principal People, occasion'd the Paper and the Manager of it to be much talk'd of, and in a few Weeks brought them all to be our Subscribers. Their Example was follow'd by many, and our Number went on growing continually. This was one of the first good Effects of my having learned a little to scribble. Another was, that the leading Men, seeing a Newspaper now in the hands of one who could also handle a Pen, thought it convenient to oblige and encourage me. Bradford still printed the Votes and Laws and other Public Business. He had printed an Address of the House[5] to the Governor in a coarse blundering manner; We reprinted it elegantly and correctly, and sent one to every Member. They were sensible of the Difference, it strengthen'd the Hands of our Friends in the House, and they voted us their Printers for the Year ensuing.

Among my Friends in the House I must not forget Mr. Hamilton beforementioned,[6] who was then returned from England and had a Seat in it. He

---

1. The *American Weekly Mercury.*
2. From February 4, 1728, to September 25, 1729.
3. Franklin took over Keimer's *The Universal Instructor in All Arts and Sciences: and Pennsyl-* *vania Gazette* in October 1729 and shortened the name to the *Pennsylvania Gazette.*
4. See n. 2, p. 242.
5. I.e., the Pennsylvania Assembly.
6. See n. 4, p. 247.

interested himself[7] for me strongly in that Instance, as he did in many others afterwards, continuing his Patronage till his Death. Mr. Vernon about this time put me in mind of the Debt I ow'd him: but did not press me. I wrote him an ingenuous Letter of Acknowledgments, crav'd his Forbearance a little longer which he allow'd me, and as soon as I was able I paid the Principal with Interest and many Thanks. So that Erratum was in some degree corrected.

But now another Difficulty came upon me, which I had never the least Reason to expect. Mr. Meredith's Father, who was to have paid for our Printing-House according to the Expectations given me, was able to advance only one Hundred Pounds, Currency, which had been paid, and a Hundred more was due to the Merchant; who grew impatient and su'd us all. We gave Bail, but saw that if the Money could not be rais'd in time, the Suit must come to a Judgment and Execution, and our hopeful Prospects must with us be ruined, as the Press and Letters must be sold for Payment, perhaps at half-Price. In this Distress two true Friends whose Kindness I have never forgotten nor ever shall forget while I can remember anything, came to me separately unknown to each other, and without any Application from me, offering each of them to advance me all the Money that should be necessary to enable me to take the whole Business upon myself if that should be practicable, but they did not like my continuing the Partnership with Meredith, who as they said was often seen drunk in the Streets, and playing at low Games in Alehouses, much to our Discredit. These two Friends were *William Coleman* and *Robert Grace*.

I told them I could not propose a Separation while any Prospect remain'd of the Merediths fulfilling their Part of our Agreement. Because I thought myself under great Obligations to them for what they had done and would do if they could. But if they finally fail'd in their Performance, and our Partnership must be dissolv'd, I should then think myself at Liberty to accept the Assistance of my Friends. Thus the matter rested for some time. When I said to my Partner, perhaps your Father is dissatisfied at the Part you have undertaken in this Affair of ours, and is unwilling to advance for you and me what he would for you alone: If that is the Case, tell me, and I will resign the whole to you and go about my Business. No—says he, my Father has really been disappointed and is really unable; and I am unwilling to distress him farther. I see this is a Business I am not fit for. I was bred a Farmer, and it was a Folly in me to come to Town and put myself at 30 Years of Age an Apprentice to learn a new Trade. Many of our Welsh People are going to settle in North Carolina where Land is cheap: I am inclin'd to go with them, and follow my old Employment. You may find Friends to assist you. If you will take the Debts of the Company upon you, return to my Father the hundred Pound he has advanc'd, pay my little personal Debts, and give me Thirty Pounds and a new Saddle, I will relinquish the Partnership and leave the whole in your Hands. I agreed to this Proposal. It was drawn up in Writing, sign'd and seal'd immediately. I gave him what he demanded and he went soon after to Carolina; from whence he sent me next Year two long Letters, containing the best Account that had been given of that

---

7. "I got his Son once £500" [Franklin's note]. Franklin was able to get the legislature to pay Governor James Hamilton his salary when they were at odds with him.

Country, the Climate, Soil, Husbandry, etc., for in those Matters he was very judicious. I printed them in the Papers,[8] and they gave great Satisfaction to the Public.

As soon as he was gone, I recurr'd to my two Friends; and because I would not give an unkind Preference to either, I took half what each had offered and I wanted, of one, and half of the other; paid off the Company Debts, and went on with the Business in my own Name, advertising that the Partnership was dissolved. I think this was in or about the Year 1729.[9]

About this Time there was a Cry among the People for more Paper-Money, only 15,000 Pounds being extant in the Province and that soon to be sunk.[1] The wealthy Inhabitants oppos'd any Addition, being against all Paper Currency, from an Apprehension that it would depreciate as it had done in New England to the Prejudice of all Creditors. We had discuss'd this Point in our Junto, where I was on the Side of an Addition, being persuaded that the first small Sum struck in 1723 had done much good, by increasing the Trade, Employment, and Number of Inhabitants in the Province, since I now saw all the old Houses inhabited, and many new ones building, where as I remember'd well, that when I first walk'd about the Streets of Philadelphia, eating my Roll, I saw most of the Houses in Walnut Street between Second and Front Streets with Bills[2] on their Doors, to be let; and many likewise in Chestnut Street, and other Streets; which made me then think the Inhabitants of the City were one after another deserting it. Our Debates possess'd me so fully of the Subject, that I wrote and printed an anonymous Pamphlet on it, entitled, *The Nature and Necessity of a Paper Currency*.[3] It was well receiv'd by the common People in general; but the Rich Men dislik'd it; for it increas'd and strengthen'd the Clamor for more Money; and they happening to have no Writers among them that were able to answer it, their Opposition slacken'd, and the Point was carried by a Majority in the House. My Friends there, who conceiv'd I had been of some Service, thought fit to reward me, by employing me in printing the Money,[4] a very profitable Job, and a great Help to me. This was another Advantage gain'd by my being able to write. The Utility of this Currency became by Time and Experience so evident, as never afterwards to be much disputed, so that it grew soon to 55,000 Pounds, and in 1739 to 80,000 Pounds, since which it arose during War to upwards of 350,000 Pounds—Trade, Building and Inhabitants all the while increasing. Tho' I now think there are Limits beyond which the Quantity may be hurtful.

I soon after obtain'd, thro' my Friend Hamilton, the Printing of the New Castle Paper Money,[5] another profitable Job, as I then thought it; small Things appearing great to those in small Circumstances. And these to me were really great Advantages, as they were great Encouragements. He pro-

---

8. In the *Pennsylvania Gazette*, May 6 and 13, 1732.
9. More accurately, July 14, 1730.
1. Destroyed. In 1723, paper money had become so scarce that the Assembly issued new money secured by real estate mortgages; when the mortgages were paid off, the bills were "sunk." But by 1729, the value of the currency was so low that the money was recalled before the mortgages

were paid.
2. Signs.
3. *A Modest Inquiry into the Nature and Necessity of a Paper Currency* (April 3, 1729).
4. Franklin received the contract to print money in 1731.
5. I.e., for Delaware, which had a separate legislature but the same proprietary governor as Pennsylvania.

cured me also the Printing of the Laws and Votes of that Government which continu'd in my Hands as long as I follow'd the Business.

I now open'd a little Stationer's Shop.[6] I had in it Blanks of all Sorts the correctest that ever appear'd among us, being assisted in that by my Friend Breintnall; I had also Paper, Parchment, Chapmen's Books,[7] etc. One Whitmarsh a Compositor I had known in London, an excellent Workman now came to me and work'd with me constantly and diligently,[8] and I took an Apprentice the Son of Aquila Rose. I began now gradually to pay off the Debt I was under for the Printing-House. In order to secure my Credit and Character as a Tradesman, I took care not only to be in *Reality* Industrious and frugal, but to avoid all *Appearances* of the contrary. I dressed plainly; I was seen at no Places of idle Diversion; I never went out a-fishing or shooting; a Book, indeed, sometimes debauch'd me from my Work; but that was seldom, snug, and gave no Scandal: and to show that I was not above my Business, I sometimes brought home the Paper I purchas'd at the Stores, thro' the Streets on a Wheelbarrow. Thus being esteem'd an industrious thriving young Man, and paying duly for what I bought, the Merchants who imported Stationery solicited my Custom, others propos'd supplying me with Books, and I went on swimmingly. In the mean time Keimer's Credit and Business declining daily, he was at last forc'd to sell his Printing-House to satisfy his Creditors. He went to Barbados, and there lived some Years, in very poor Circumstances.

His Apprentice David Harry, whom I had instructed while I work'd with him, set up in his Place at Philadelphia, having bought his Materials. I was at first apprehensive of a powerful Rival in Harry, as his Friends were very able, and had a good deal of Interest. I therefore propos'd a Partnership to him; which he, fortunately for me, rejected with Scorn. He was very proud, dress'd like a Gentleman, liv'd expensively, took much Diversion and Pleasure abroad, ran in debt, and neglected his Business, upon which all Business left him; and finding nothing to do, he follow'd Keimer to Barbados; taking the Printing-House with him. There this Apprentice employ'd his former Master as a Journeyman. They quarrel'd often. Harry went continually behind-hand, and at length was forc'd to sell his Types, and return to his Country Work in Pennsylvania. The Person that bought them employ'd Keimer to use them, but in a few years he died. There remain'd now no Competitor with me at Philadelphia, but the old one, Bradford, who was rich and easy, did a little Printing now and then by straggling Hands, but was not very anxious about the Business. However, as he kept the Post Office, it was imagined he had better Opportunities of obtaining News, his Paper was thought a better Distributer of Advertisements than mine, and therefore had many more, which was a profitable thing to him and a Disadvantage to me. For tho' I did indeed receive and send Papers by the Post, yet the public Opinion was otherwise; for what I did send was by Bribing the Riders[9] who took them privately: Bradford being unkind enough to forbid it: which

6. In July 1730.
7. Inexpensive paper pamphlets.
8. Thomas Whitmarsh (d. 1733) moved to South Carolina the next year.

9. I.e., the postal riders, or carriers. Franklin bribed them to have his papers delivered on the same day as Andrew Bradford's.

occasion'd some Resentment on my Part; and I thought so meanly of him for it, that when I afterwards came into his Situation,[1] I took care never to imitate it.

I had hitherto continu'd to board with Godfrey who lived in Part of my House with his Wife and Children, and had one Side of the Shop for his Glazier's Business, tho' he work'd little, being always absorb'd in his Mathematics. Mrs. Godfrey projected a Match for me with a Relation's Daughter, took Opportunities of bringing us often together, till a serious Courtship on my Part ensu'd, the Girl being in herself very deserving. The old Folks encourag'd me by continual Invitations to Supper, and by leaving us together, till at length it was time to explain. Mrs. Godfrey manag'd our little Treaty. I let her know that I expected as much Money with their Daughter as would pay off my Remaining Debt for the Printing-House, which I believe was not then above a Hundred Pounds.[2] She brought me Word they had no such Sum to spare. I said they might mortgage their House in the Loan Office. The Answer to this after some Days was, that they did not approve the Match; that on Enquiry of Bradford they had been inform'd the Printing Business was not a profitable one, the Types would soon be worn out and more wanted, that S. Keimer and D. Harry had fail'd one after the other, and I should probably soon follow them; and therefore I was forbidden the House, and the Daughter shut up.

Whether this was a real Change of Sentiment, or only Artifice, on a Supposition of our being too far engag'd in Affection to retract, and therefore that we should steal a Marriage, which would leave them at Liberty to give or withhold what they pleas'd, I know not: But I suspected the latter, resented it, and went no more. Mrs. Godfrey brought me afterwards some more favorable Accounts of their Disposition, and would have drawn me on again: But I declared absolutely my Resolution to have nothing more to do with that Family. This was resented by the Godfreys, we differ'd, and they removed, leaving me the whole House, and I resolved to take no more Inmates. But this Affair having turn'd my Thoughts to Marriage, I look'd round me, and made Overtures of Acquaintance in other Places; but soon found that the Business of a Printer being generally thought a poor one, I was not to expect Money with a Wife unless with such a one, as I should not otherwise think agreeable. In the mean time, that hard-to-be-govern'd Passion of Youth, had hurried me frequently into Intrigues with low Women that fell in my Way, which were attended with some Expense and great Inconvenience, besides a continual Risk to my Health by a Distemper[3] which of all Things I dreaded, tho' by great good Luck I escaped it.

A friendly Correspondence as Neighbors and old Acquaintances, had continued between me and Mrs. Read's Family who all had a Regard for me from the time of my first Lodging in their House. I was often invited there and consulted in their Affairs, wherein I sometimes was of Service. I pitied poor Miss Read's unfortunate Situation, who was generally dejected, seldom

1. Franklin succeeded Bradford as postmaster of Philadelphia in October 1737.
2. Franklin's expectations were not unusual: marriage arrangements often hinged on agreeable financial considerations.
3. I.e., syphilis.

cheerful, and avoided Company. I consider'd my Giddiness and Inconstancy when in London as in a great degree the Cause of her Unhappiness; tho' the Mother was good enough to think the Fault more her own than mine, as she had prevented our Marrying before I went thither, and persuaded the other Match in my Absence. Our mutual Affection was revived, but there were now great Objections to our Union. That Match was indeed look'd upon as invalid, a preceding Wife being said to be living in England; but this could not easily be prov'd, because of the Distance, etc. And tho' there was a Report of his Death, it was not certain. Then, tho' it should be true, he had left many Debts which his Successor might be call'd upon to pay. We ventured however, over all these Difficulties, and I took her to Wife Sept. 1, 1730.[4] None of the Inconveniencies happened that we had apprehended, she prov'd a good and faithful Helpmate, assisted me much by attending the Shop, we throve together, and have ever mutually endeavor'd to make each other happy. Thus I corrected that great Erratum as well as I could.

About this Time our Club meeting, not at a Tavern, but in a little Room of Mr. Grace's set apart for that Purpose; a Proposition was made by me, that since our Books were often referr'd to in our Disquisitions upon the Queries, it might be convenient to us to have them all together where we met, that upon Occasion they might be consulted; and by thus clubbing our Books to a common Library, we should, while we lik'd to keep them together, have each of us the Advantage of using the Books of all the other Members, which would be nearly as beneficial as if each owned the whole. It was lik'd and agreed to, and we fill'd one End of the Room with such Books as we could best spare. The Number was not so great as we expected; and tho' they had been of great Use, yet some Inconveniencies occurring for want of due Care of them, the Collection after about a Year was separated, and each took his Books home again.

And now I set on foot my first Project of a public Nature, that for a Subscription Library. I drew up the Proposals, got them put into Form by our great Scrivener Brockden, and by the help of my Friends in the Junto, procur'd Fifty Subscribers of 40 Shillings each to begin with and 10 Shillings a Year for 50 Years, the Term our Company was to continue. We afterwards obtain'd a Charter, the Company being increas'd to 100. This was the Mother of all the North American Subscription Libraries now so numerous. It is become a great thing itself, and continually increasing. These Libraries have improv'd the general Conversation of the Americans, made the common Tradesmen and Farmers as intelligent as most Gentlemen from other Countries, and perhaps have contributed in some degree to the Stand so generally made throughout the Colonies in Defense of their Privileges.

Memo.

Thus far was written with the Intention express'd in the Beginning and therefore contains several little family Anecdotes of no Importance to others. What follows was written many Years after in compliance

---

4. Because there was no proof that John Rogers, Deborah Read's first husband, was dead, she and Franklin entered into a common-law marriage without civil ceremony.

with the Advice contain'd in these Letters, and accordingly intended for the Public. The Affairs of the Revolution occasion'd the Interruption.

[Part Two][1]

LETTER FROM MR. ABEL JAMES,[2] WITH NOTES ON MY LIFE, (RECEIVED IN PARIS)

My dear and honored Friend.

I have often been desirous of writing to thee, but could not be reconciled to the Thought that the Letter might fall into the Hands of the British,[3] lest some Printer or busy Body should publish some Part of the Contents and give our Friends Pain and myself Censure.

Some Time since there fell into my Hands to my great Joy about 23 Sheets in thy own handwriting containing an Account of the Parentage and Life of thyself, directed to thy Son ending in the Year 1730 with which there were Notes[4] likewise in thy writing, a Copy of which I enclose in Hopes it may be a means if thou continuedst it up to a later period, that the first and latter part may be put together; and if it is not yet continued, I hope thou wilt not delay it. Life is uncertain as the Preacher tells us, and what will the World say if kind, humane and benevolent Ben Franklin should leave his Friends and the World deprived of so pleasing and profitable a Work, a Work which would be useful and entertaining not only to a few, but to millions.

The Influence Writings under that Class have on the Minds of Youth is very great, and has no where appeared so plain as in our public Friends' Journals. It almost insensibly leads the Youth into the Resolution of endeavoring to become as good and as eminent as the Journalist. Should thine for Instance when published, and I think it could not fail of it, lead the Youth to equal the Industry and Temperance of thy early Youth, what a Blessing with that Class would such a Work be. I know of no Character living nor many of them put together, who has so much in his Power as Thyself to promote a greater Spirit of Industry and early Attention to Business, Frugality and Temperance with the American Youth. Not that I think the Work would have no other Merit and Use in the World, far from it, but the first is of such vast Importance, that I know nothing that can equal it.

The foregoing letter and the minutes accompanying it being shown to a friend, I received from him the following:

---

1. Franklin wrote the second part of his autobiography at the Hôtel de Valentenois, in Passy, a Paris suburb. He had been sent to Paris as one of the American representatives for the peace treaty that officially ended the war with Britain on September 3, 1783. Franklin remained in Paris until July 1785, when Thomas Jefferson succeeded him as a minister for trade agreements.

2. A Quaker merchant in Philadelphia (c. 1726–1790).
3. James wrote his letter in 1782, when Britain was still at war with the colonies.
4. Franklin's outline for his *Autobiography*, written in 1771; reprinted in the Yale University edition (1964).

LETTER FROM MR. BENJAMIN VAUGHAN[5]

My Dearest Sir, *Paris, January* 31, 1783.

When I had read over your sheets of minutes of the principal incidents of your life, recovered for you by your Quaker acquaintance; I told you I would send you a letter expressing my reasons why I thought it would be useful to complete and publish it as he desired. Various concerns have for some time past prevented this letter being written, and I do not know whether it was worth any expectation: happening to be at leisure however at present, I shall by writing at least interest and instruct myself; but as the terms I am inclined to use may tend to offend a person of your manners, I shall only tell you how I would address any other person, who was as good and as great as yourself, but less diffident. I would say to him, Sir, I *solicit* the history of your life from the following motives.

Your history is so remarkable, that if you do not give it, somebody else will certainly give it; and perhaps so as nearly to do as much harm, as your own management of the thing might do good.

It will moreover present a table of the internal circumstances of your country, which will very much tend to invite to it settlers of virtuous and manly minds. And considering the eagerness with which such information is sought by them, and the extent of your reputation, I do not know of a more efficacious advertisement than your Biography would give.

All that has happened to you is also connected with the detail of the manners and situation of *a rising* people; and in this respect I do not think that the writings of Caesar and Tacitus[6] can be more interesting to a true judge of human nature and society.

But these, Sir, are small reasons in my opinion, compared with the chance which your life will give for the forming of future great men; and in conjunction with your *Art of Virtue*,[7] (which you design to publish) of improving the features of private character, and consequently of aiding all happiness both public and domestic.

The two works I allude to, Sir, will in particular give a noble rule and example of *self-education*. School and other education constantly proceed upon false principles, and show a clumsy apparatus pointed at a false mark; but your apparatus is simple, and the mark a true one; and while parents and young persons are left destitute of other just means of estimating and becoming prepared for a reasonable course in life, your discovery that the thing is in many a man's private power, will be invaluable!

Influence upon the private character late in life, is not only an influence late in life, but a weak influence. It is in *youth* that we plant our chief habits and prejudices; it is in youth that we take our party[8] as to

---

5. English politician, the wealthy son (1751–1835) of a West Indies merchant and Maine mother; during the Paris peace talks, unofficial emissary between the British prime minister Lord Shelburne (1737–1805; in office 1782–83) and Franklin.
6. The Roman statesman historian Gaius Julius Caesar (100–44 B.C.E.) and Publius Cornelius

Tacitus (c. 56 C.E.–c. 120).
7. Vaughan is referring to Franklin's intention to write "a little work for the benefit of youth" to be called *The Art of Virtue*. Part Two of the *Autobiography* is, in part, a response to Vaughan's reminder.
8. Make our decision.

profession, pursuits, and matrimony. In youth therefore the turn is given; in youth the education even of the next generation is given; in youth the private and public character is determined: and the term of life extending from youth to age, life ought to begin well from youth; and more especially *before* we take our party as to our principal objects.

But your Biography will not merely teach self-education, but the education of *a wise man;* and the wisest man will receive lights and improve his progress, by seeing detailed the conduct of another wise man. And why are weaker men to be deprived of such helps, when we see our race has been blundering on in the dark, almost without a guide in this particular, from the farthest trace of time. Show then, Sir, how much is to be done, *both to sons and fathers;* and invite all wise men to become like yourself; and other men to become wise.

When we see how cruel statesmen and warriors can be to the humble race, and how absurd distinguished men can be to their acquaintance, it will be instructive to observe the instances multiply of pacific acquiescing manners; and to find how compatible it is to be great and *domestic;* enviable and yet *good-humored.*

The little private incidents which you will also have to relate, will have considerable use, as we want above all things, *rules of prudence in ordinary affairs;* and it will be curious to see how you have acted in these. It will be so far a sort of key to life, and explain many things that all men ought to have once explained to them, to give them a chance of becoming wise by foresight.

The nearest thing to having experience of one's own, is to have other people's affairs brought before us in a shape that is interesting; this is sure to happen from your pen. Your affairs and management will have an air of simplicity or importance that will not fail to strike; and I am convinced you have conducted them with as much originality as if you had been conducting discussions in politics or philosophy; and what more worthy of experiments and system, (its importance and its errors considered) than human life!

Some men have been virtuous blindly, others have speculated fantastically, and others have been shrewd to bad purposes; but you, Sir, I am sure, will give under your hand, nothing but what is at the same moment, wise, practical, and good.

Your account of yourself (for I suppose the parallel I am drawing for Dr. Franklin, will hold not only in point of character but of private history), will show that you are ashamed of no origin; a thing the more important, as you prove how little necessary all origin is to happiness, virtue, or greatness.

As no end likewise happens without a means, so we shall find, Sir, that even you yourself framed a plan by which you became considerable; but at the same time we may see that though the event is flattering, the means are as simple as wisdom could make them; that is, depending upon nature, virtue, thought, and habit.

Another thing demonstrated will be the propriety of every man's waiting for his time for appearing upon the stage of the world. Our sensations being very much fixed to the moment, we are apt to forget that more moments are to follow the first, and consequently that man should arrange his conduct so as to suit the *whole* of a life. Your attribution appears to have been applied to your *life,* and the passing moments of it have been enlivened with content and enjoyment, instead of being tormented with foolish impatience or regrets. Such a conduct is easy for those who make virtue and themselves their standard, and who try to keep themselves in countenance by examples of other truly great men, of whom patience is so often the characteristic.

Your Quaker correspondent, Sir (for here again I will suppose the subject of my letter resembling Dr. Franklin,) praised your frugality, diligence, and temperance, which he considered as a pattern for all youth: but it is singular that he should have forgotten your modesty, and your disinterestedness, without which you never could have waited for your advancement, or found your situation in the mean time comfortable; which is a strong lesson to show the poverty of glory, and the importance of regulating our minds.

If this correspondent had known the nature of your reputation as well as I do, he would have said; your former writings and measures would secure attention to your Biography, and Art of Virtue; and your Biography and Art of Virtue, in return, would secure attention to them. This is an advantage attendant upon a various character, and which brings all that belongs to it into greater play; and it is the more useful, as perhaps more persons are at a loss for the *means* of improving their minds and characters, than they are for the time or the inclination to do it.

But there is one concluding reflection, Sir, that will show the use of your life as a mere piece of biography. This style of writing seems a little gone out of vogue, and yet it is a very useful one; and your specimen of it may be particularly serviceable, as it will make a subject of comparison with the lives of various public cut-throats and intriguers, and with absurd monastic self-tormentors, or vain literary triflers. If it encourages more writings of the same kind with your own, and induces more men to spend lives fit to be written; it will be worth all Plutarch's Lives[9] put together.

But being tired of figuring to myself a character of which every feature suits only one man in the world, without giving him the praise of it; I shall end my letter, my dear Dr. Franklin, with a personal application to your proper self.

I am earnestly desirous then, my dear Sir, that you should let the world into the traits of your genuine character, as civil broils may otherwise tend to disguise or traduce it. Considering your great age, the caution of your character, and your peculiar style of thinking, it is not likely that any one besides yourself can be sufficiently master of the facts of your life, or the intentions of your mind.

Besides all this, the immense revolution of the present period, will necessarily turn our attention towards the author of it; and when virtuous principles have been pretended in it, it will be highly important to show that such have really influenced; and, as your own character will be the principal one to receive a scrutiny, it is proper (even for its effects

9. See n. 7, p. 227.

upon your vast and rising country, as well as upon England and upon Europe), that it should stand respectable and eternal. For the further-ance of human happiness, I have always maintained that it is necessary to prove that man is not even at present a vicious and detestable ani-mal; and still more to prove that good management may greatly amend him; and it is for much the same reason, that I am anxious to see the opinion established, that there are fair characters existing among the individuals of the race; for the moment that all men, without exception, shall be conceived abandoned, good people will cease efforts deemed to be hopeless, and perhaps think of taking their share in the scramble of life, or at least of making it comfortable principally for themselves.

Take then, my dear Sir, this work most speedily into hand: show your-self good as you are good, temperate as you are temperate; and above all things, prove yourself as one who from your infancy have loved jus-tice, liberty, and concord, in a way that has made it natural and consis-tent for you to have acted, as we have seen you act in the last seventeen years of your life. Let Englishmen be made not only to respect, but even to love you. When they think well of individuals in your native country, they will go nearer to thinking well of your country; and when your countrymen see themselves well thought of by Englishmen, they will go nearer to thinking well of England. Extend your views even further; do not stop at those who speak the English tongue, but after having set-tled so many points in nature and politics, think of bettering the whole race of men.

As I have not read any part of the life in question, but know only the character that lived it, I write somewhat at hazard. I am sure however, that the life, and the treatise I allude to (on the *Art of Virtue*), will nec-essarily fullfil the chief of my expectations; and still more so if you take up the measure of suiting these performances to the several views above stated. Should they even prove unsuccessful in all that a sanguine admirer of yours hopes from them, you will at least have framed pieces to interest the human mind; and whoever gives a feeling of pleasure that is innocent to man, has added so much to the fair side of a life other-wise too much darkened by anxiety, and too much injured by pain.

In the hope therefore that you will listen to the prayer addressed to you in this letter, I beg to subscribe myself, my dearest Sir, etc., etc.

Signed   BENJ. VAUGHAN.

CONTINUATION OF THE ACCOUNT OF MY LIFE.
BEGUN AT PASSY, 1784

It is some time since I receiv'd the above Letters, but I have been too busy till now to think of complying with the Request they contain. It might too be much better done if I were at home among my Papers, which would aid my Memory, and help to ascertain Dates. But my Return being uncertain, and having just now a little Leisure, I will endeavor to recollect and write what I can; if I live to get home, it may there be corrected and improv'd.

Not having any Copy here of what is already written, I know not whether an Account is given of the means I used to establish the Philadelphia public Library, which from a small Beginning is now become so considerable, though I remember to have come down to near the Time of that Transaction, 1730. I will therefore begin here, with an Account of it, which may be struck out if found to have been already given.

At the time I establish'd myself in Pennsylvania, there was not a good Bookseller's Shop in any of the Colonies to the Southward of Boston. In New York and Philadelphia the Printers were indeed Stationers, they sold only Paper, etc., Almanacs, Ballads, and a few common School Books. Those who lov'd Reading were oblig'd to send for their Books from England. The Members of the Junto had each a few. We had left the Alehouse where we first met, and hired a Room to hold our Club in. I propos'd that we should all of us bring our Books to that Room, where they would not only be ready to consult in our Conferences, but become a common Benefit, each of us being at Liberty to borrow such as he wish'd to read at home. This was accordingly done, and for some time contented us. Finding the Advantage of this little Collection, I propos'd to render the Benefit from Books more common by commencing a Public Subscription Library. I drew a Sketch of the Plan and Rules that would be necessary, and got a skillful Conveyancer Mr. Charles Brockden[1] to put the whole in Form of Articles of Agreement to be subscribed, by which each Subscriber engag'd to pay a certain Sum down for the first Purchase of Books and an annual Contribution for increasing them. So few were the Readers at that time in Philadelphia, and the Majority of us so poor, that I was not able with great Industry to find more than Fifty Persons, mostly young Tradesmen, willing to pay down for this purpose Forty shillings each, and Ten Shillings per Annum. On this little Fund we began. The Books were imported. The Library was open one Day in the Week for lending them to the Subscribers, on their Promissory Notes to pay Double the Value if not duly returned. The Institution soon manifested its Utility, was imitated by other Towns and in other Provinces, the Libraries were augmented by Donations, Reading became fashionable, and our People having no public Amusements to divert their Attention from Study became better acquainted with Books, and in a few Years were observ'd by Strangers to be better instructed and more intelligent than People of the same Rank generally are in other Countries.

When we were about to sign the above-mentioned Articles, which were to be binding on us, our Heirs, etc., for fifty Years, Mr. Brockden, the Scrivener, said to us, "You are young Men, but it is scarce probable that any of you will live to see the Expiration of the Term fix'd in this Instrument." A Number of us, however, are yet living: But the Instrument was after a few Years rendered null by a Charter that incorporated and gave Perpetuity to the Company.

The Objections, and Reluctances I met with in Soliciting the Subscriptions, made me soon feel the Impropriety of presenting oneself as the Proposer of any useful Project that might be suppos'd to raise one's Reputation in the smallest degree above that of one's Neighbors, when one has need of their Assistance to accomplish that Project. I therefore put myself as much as I could out of sight, and stated it as a Scheme of *a Number of Friends,* who had requested me to go about and propose it to such as they thought Lovers of Reading. In this way my Affair went on more smoothly, and I ever

---

1. Philadelphia's leading drafter of legal documents (1683–1769). "Conveyancer": an attorney who specializes in the transfer of real estate and property.

after practic'd it on such Occasions; and from my frequent Successes, can heartily recommend it. The present little Sacrifice of your Vanity will afterwards be amply repaid. If it remains a while uncertain to whom the Merit belongs, someone more vain than yourself will be encourag'd to claim it, and then even Envy will be dispos'd to do you Justice, by plucking those assum'd Feathers, and restoring them to their right Owner.

This Library afforded me the Means of Improvement by constant Study, for which I set apart an Hour or two each Day; and thus repair'd in some Degree the Loss of the Learned Education my Father once intended for me. Reading was the only Amusement I allow'd myself. I spent no time in Taverns, Games, or Frolics of any kind. And my Industry in my Business continu'd as indefatigable as it was necessary. I was in debt for my Printing-House, I had a young Family[2] coming on to be educated, and I had to contend with for Business two Printers who were establish'd in the Place before me. My Circumstances however grew daily easier: my original Habits of Frugality continuing. And My Father having among his Instructions to me when a Boy, frequently repeated a Proverb of Solomon, "*Seest thou a Man diligent in his Calling, he shall stand before Kings, he shall not stand before mean Men.*"[3] I from thence consider'd Industry as a Means of obtaining Wealth and Distinction, which encourag'd me: tho' I did not think that I should ever literally stand before Kings, which however has since happened; for I have stood before five,[4] and even had the honor of sitting down with one, the King of Denmark, to Dinner.

We have an English Proverb that says,

> He that would thrive
> Must ask his Wife,[5]

it was lucky for me that I had one as much dispos'd to Industry and Frugality as myself. She assisted me cheerfully in my Business, folding and stitching Pamphlets, tending Shop, purchasing old Linen Rags for the Paper-makers, etc., etc. We kept no idle Servants, our Table was plain and simple, our Furniture of the cheapest. For instance my Breakfast was a long time Bread and Milk, (no Tea,) and I ate it out of a two penny earthen Porringer[6] with a Pewter Spoon. But mark how Luxury will enter Families, and make a Progress, in Spite of Principle. Being Call'd one Morning to Breakfast, I found it in a China[7] Bowl with a Spoon of Silver. They had been bought for me without my Knowledge by my Wife, and had cost her the enormous Sum of three and twenty Shillings, for which she had no other Excuse or Apology to make, but that she thought 'her Husband deserv'd a Silver Spoon and China Bowl as well as any of his Neighbors. This was the first Appearance of Plate[8] and China in our House, which afterwards in a Course of Years as our Wealth increas'd, augmented gradually to several Hundred Pounds in Value.

---

2. Franklin had three children: William, born c. 1731; Francis, born in 1732; and Sarah, born in 1743.
3. Proverbs 22.29.
4. Louis XV and Louis XVI of France (reigned 1715–74 and 1774–92, respectively), George II and George III of England (reigned 1727–60 and 1760–1820, respectively), and Christian VI of Denmark (reigned 1730–46).
5. More commonly: "He that will thrive must ask leave of his wife."
6. Small bowl.
7. I.e., porcelain.
8. Silver.

I had been religiously educated as a Presbyterian, and tho' some of the Dogmas of that Persuasion, such as the Eternal Decrees of God, Election, Reprobation,[9] etc., appear'd to me unintelligible, others doubtful, and I early absented myself from the Public Assemblies of the Sect, Sunday being my Studying-Day, I never was without some religious Principles; I never doubted, for instance, the Existence of the Deity, that he made the World, and govern'd it by his Providence; that the most acceptable Service of God was the doing Good to Man; that our Souls are immortal; and that all Crime will be punished and Virtue rewarded either here or hereafter; these I esteem'd the Essentials of every Religion, and being to be found in all the Religions we had in our Country I respected them all, tho' with different degrees of Respect as I found them more or less mix'd with other Articles which without any Tendency to inspire, promote or confirm Morality, serv'd principally to divide us and make us unfriendly to one another. This Respect to all, with an Opinion that the worst had some good Effects, induc'd me to avoid all Discourse that might tend to lessen the good Opinion another might have of his own Religion; and as our Province increas'd in People and new Places of worship were continually wanted, and generally erected by voluntary Contribution, my Mite[1] for such purpose, whatever might be the Sect, was never refused.

Tho' I seldom attended any Public Worship, I had still an Opinion of its Propriety, and of its Utility when rightly conducted, and I regularly paid my annual Subscription for the Support of the only Presbyterian Minister or Meeting we had in Philadelphia. He us'd to visit me sometimes as a Friend, and admonish me to attend his Administrations, and I was now and then prevail'd on to do so, once for five Sundays successively. Had he been, *in my Opinion,* a good Preacher perhaps I might have continued, notwithstanding the occasion I had for the Sunday's Leisure in my Course of Study: But his Discourses were chiefly either polemic Arguments, or Explications of the peculiar Doctrines of our Sect, and were all to me very dry, uninteresting and unedifying, since not a single moral Principle was inculcated or enforc'd, their Aim seeming to be rather to make us Presbyterians than good Citizens. At length he took for his Text that Verse of the 4th Chapter of Philippians, *Finally, Brethren, Whatsoever Things are true, honest, just, pure, lovely, or of good report, if there be any virtue, or any praise, think on these Things;*[2] and I imagin'd in a Sermon on such a Text, we could not miss of having some Morality: But he confin'd himself to five Points only as meant by the Apostle, viz., 1. Keeping holy the Sabbath Day. 2. Being diligent in Reading the Holy Scriptures. 3. Attending duly the Public Worship. 4. Partaking of the Sacrament. 5. Paying a due Respect to God's Ministers. These might be all good Things, but as they were not the kind of good Things that I expected from that Text, I despaired of ever meeting with them from any other, was disgusted, and attended his Preaching no more. I had some Years before compos'd a little Liturgy or Form of Prayer for my own private Use, viz., in 1728, entitled, *Articles of Belief and Acts of Religion.*[3] I return'd to the Use

---

9. Punishment. "Election": God's determining who is to be saved and who is to be damned.
1. Small contribution.

2. A paraphrase of Philippians 4.8.
3. Only the first part of Franklin's two-part *Articles of Belief and Acts of Religion* survives.

of this, and went no more to the public Assemblies. My Conduct might be blameable, but I leave it without attempting farther to excuse it, my present purpose being to relate Facts, and not to make Apologies for them.

It was about this time that I conceiv'd the bold and arduous Project of arriving at moral Perfection. I wish'd to live without committing any Fault at anytime; I would conquer all that either Natural Inclination, Custom, or Company might lead me into. As I knew, or thought I knew, what was right and wrong, I did not see why I might not *always* do the one and avoid the other. But I soon found I had undertaken a Task of more Difficulty than I had imagined: While my Care was employ'd in guarding against one Fault, I was often surpris'd by another. Habit took the Advantage of Inattention. Inclination was sometimes too strong for Reason. I concluded at length, that the mere speculative Conviction that it was our Interest to be completely virtuous, was not sufficient to prevent our Slipping, and that the contrary Habits must be broken and good Ones acquired and established, before we can have any Dependence on a steady uniform Rectitude of Conduct. For this purpose I therefore contriv'd the following Method.

In the various Enumerations of the moral Virtues I had met with in my Reading, I found the Catalog more or less numerous, as different Writers included more or fewer Ideas under the same Name. Temperance, for Example, was by some confin'd to Eating and Drinking, while by others it was extended to mean the moderating every other Pleasure, Appetite, Inclination or Passion, bodily or mental, even to our Avarice and Ambition. I propos'd to myself, for the sake of Clearness, to use rather more Names with fewer Ideas annex'd to each, than a few Names with more Ideas; and I included after Thirteen Names of Virtues all that at that time occurr'd to me as necessary or desirable, and annex'd to each a short Precept, which fully express'd the Extent I gave to its Meaning.

These Names of Virtues with their Precepts were

1. TEMPERANCE.
Eat not to Dullness. Drink not to Elevation.

2. SILENCE.
Speak not but what may benefit others or yourself. Avoiding trifling Conversation.

3. ORDER.
Let all your Things have their Places. Let each Part of your Business have its Time.

4. RESOLUTION.
Resolve to perform what you ought. Perform without fail what you resolve.

5. FRUGALITY.
Make no Expense but to do good to others or yourself: i.e., Waste nothing.

6. INDUSTRY.
Lose no Time. Be always employ'd in something useful. Cut off all unnecessary Actions.

7. SINCERITY.

Use no hurtful Deceit. Think innocently and justly; and, if you speak; speak accordingly.

8. JUSTICE.

Wrong none, by doing Injuries or omitting the Benefits that are your Duty.

9. MODERATION.

Avoid Extremes. Forbear resenting Injuries so much as you think they deserve.

10. CLEANLINESS.

Tolerate no Uncleanness in Body, Clothes or Habitation.

11. TRANQUILITY.

Be not disturbed at Trifles, or Accidents common or unavoidable.

12. CHASTITY.

Rarely use Venery but for Health or Offspring; Never to Dullness, Weakness, or the Injury of your own or another's Peace or Reputation.

13. HUMILITY.

Imitate Jesus and Socrates.

My intention being to acquire the *Habitude*[4] of all these Virtues, I judg'd it would be well not to distract my Attention by attempting the whole at once, but to fix it on one of them at a time, and when I should be Master of that, then to proceed to another, and so on till I should have gone thro' the thirteen. And as the previous Acquisition of some might facilitate the Acquisition of certain others, I arrang'd them with that View as they stand above. *Temperance* first, as it tends to procure that Coolness and Clearness of Head, which is so necessary where constant Vigilance was to be kept up, and Guard maintained, against the unremitting Attraction of ancient Habits, and the Force of perpetual Temptations. This being acquir'd and establish'd, *Silence* would be more easy, and my Desire being to gain Knowledge at the same time that I improv'd in Virtue, and considering that in Conversation it was obtain'd rather by the Use of the Ears than of the Tongue, and therefore wishing to break a Habit I was getting into of Prattling, Punning and Joking, which only made me acceptable to trifling Company, I gave *Silence* the second Place. This, and the next, *Order,* I expected would allow me more Time for attending to my Project and my studies; RESOLUTION once become habitual, would keep me firm in my Endeavors to obtain all the subsequent Virtues; *Frugality* and *Industry,* by freeing me from my remaining Debt, and producing Affluence and Independence would make more easy the Practice of *Sincerity* and *Justice,* etc., etc. Conceiving then that agreeable to the Advice of Pythagoras[5] in his Golden Verses, daily Examination would be necessary, I contriv'd the following Method for conducting that Examination.

4. I.e., making these virtues an integral part of his nature.
5. Greek philosopher and mathematician (c. 580–c. 500 B.C.E.). Franklin added a note here: "Insert those Lines that direct it in a Note," and wished to include verses translated: "Let sleep not close your eyes till you have thrice examined the transactions of the day: where have I strayed, what have I done, what good have I omitted?"

I made a little Book in which I allotted a Page for each of the Virtues. I rul'd each Page with red Ink so as to have seven Columns, one for each Day of the Week, marking each Column with a Letter for the Day. I cross'd these Columns with thirteen red Lines, marking the Beginning of each Line with the first Letter of one of the Virtues, on which Line and in its proper Column I might mark by a little black Spot every Fault I found upon Examination, to have been committed respecting that Virtue upon that Day.

I determined to give a Week's strict Attention to each of the Virtues successively. Thus in the first Week my great Guard was to avoid every the least Offence against Temperance, leaving the other Virtues to their ordinary Chance, only marking every Evening the Faults of the Day. Thus if in the first Week I could keep my first Line marked T clear of Spots, I suppos'd the Habit of that Virtue so much strengthen'd and its opposite weaken'd, that I might venture extending my Attention to include the next, and for the following Week keep both Lines clear of Spots. Proceeding thus to the last, I could go thro' a Course complete in Thirteen Weeks, and four Courses in a Year. And like him who having a Garden to weed, does not attempt to eradicate all the bad Herbs at once, which would exceed his Reach and his Strength, but works on one of the Beds at a time, and having accomplish'd the first proceeds to a second; so I should have, (I hoped) the encouraging Pleasure of seeing on my Pages the Progress I made in Virtue, by clearing successively my Lines of their Spots, till in the End by a Number of Courses, I should be happy in viewing a clean Book after a thirteen Weeks' daily Examination.

This my little Book had for its Motto these Lines from *Addison's Cato,*

> *Here will I hold: If there is a Pow'r above us,*
> *(And that there is, all Nature cries aloud*
> *Thro' all her Works) he must delight in Virtue,*
> *And that which he delights in must be happy.*[6]

Another from *Cicero.*

> *O Vitæ Philosophia Dux! O Virtutum indagatrix, expultrixque vitiorum! Unus dies bene, et ex præceptis tuis actus, peccanti immortalitati est anteponendus.*[7]

Another from the Proverbs of Solomon speaking of Wisdom or Virtue;

> Length of Days is in her right hand, and in her Left Hand Riches and Honors; Her Ways are Ways of Pleasantness, and all her Paths are Peace.

III, 16, 17

And conceiving God to be the Fountain of Wisdom, I thought it right and necessary to solicit his Assistance for obtaining it; to this End I form'd the following little Prayer, which was prefix'd to my Tables of Examination, for daily Use.

---

6. *Cato, a Tragedy* 5.1.15–18, by the English writer Joseph Addison (1672–1719). Franklin also used these lines as an epigraph for his *Articles of Belief and Acts of Religion.*
7. From *Tusculan Disputations* 5.2.5, by the Roman philosopher and orator Marcus Tullius

Cicero (106–43 B.C.E.). Several lines are omitted after *vitiorum:* Oh, philosophy, guide of life: Oh, searcher out of virtues and expeller of vices! . . . One day lived well and according to thy precepts is to be preferred to an eternity of sin (Latin).

Form of the Pages

TEMPERANCE.

Eat not to Dulness.
Drink not to Elevation.

	S	M	T	W	T	F	S
T							
S	●	●		●		●	
O	●	●	●		●	●	●
R			●		●		
F		●			●		
I			●				
S							
J							
M							
Cl.							
T							
Ch							
H							

*O Powerful Goodness! bountiful Father! merciful Guide! Increase in me
that Wisdom which discovers my truest Interests; Strengthen my Resolutions to perform what that Wisdom dictates. Accept my kind Offices to
thy other Children, as the only Return in my Power for thy continual
Favors to me.*

I us'd also sometimes a little Prayer which I took from *Thomson's* Poems, viz.,

> *Father of Light and Life, thou Good supreme,*
> *O teach me what is good, teach me thy self!*
> *Save me from Folly, Vanity and Vice,*
> *From every low Pursuit, and fill my Soul*
> *With Knowledge, conscious Peace, and Virtue pure,*
> *Sacred, substantial, neverfading Bliss!*[8]

The Precept of *Order* requiring that *every Part of my Business should have
its allotted Time,* one Page in my little Book contain'd the following Scheme
of Employment for the Twenty-four Hours of a natural Day.

I enter'd upon the Execution of this Plan for Self-examination, and continu'd
it with occasional Intermissions for some time. I was surpris'd to find myself
so much fuller of Faults than I had imagined, but I had the Satisfaction of seeing them diminish. To avoid the Trouble of renewing now and then my little
Book, which by scraping out the Marks on the Paper of old Faults to make
room for new Ones in a new Course, became full of Holes: I transferr'd my
Tables and Precepts to the Ivory Leaves of a Memorandum Book, on which
the Lines were drawn with red Ink that made a durable Stain, and on those
Lines I mark'd my Faults with a black Lead Pencil, which Marks I could easily
wipe out with a wet Sponge. After a while I went thro' one Course only in a
Year, and afterwards only one in several Years; till at length I omitted them
entirely, being employ'd in Voyages and Business abroad with a Multiplicity of
Affairs, that interfered. But I always carried my little Book with me.

My Scheme of ORDER, gave me the most Trouble, and I found, that tho'
it might be practicable where a Man's Business was such as to leave him the
Disposition of his Time, that of a Journeyman Printer for instance, it was
not possible to be exactly observ'd by a Master, who must mix with the World,
and often receive People of Business at their own Hours. *Order* too, with
regard to Places for Things, Papers, etc., I found extremely difficult to
acquire. I had not been early accustomed to it, and having an exceeding good
Memory, I was not so sensible of the Inconvenience attending Want of
Method. This Article therefore cost me so much painful Attention and my
Faults in it vex'd me so much, and I made so little Progress in Amendment,
and had such frequent Relapses, that I was almost ready to give up the
Attempt, and content myself with a faulty Character in that respect. Like
the Man who in buying an Ax of a Smith my Neighbor, desired to have the
whole of its Surface as bright as the Edge; the Smith consented to grind it
bright for him if he would turn the Wheel. He turn'd while the Smith press'd
the broad Face of the Ax hard and heavily on the Stone, which made the
Turning of it very fatiguing. The Man came every now and then from the
Wheel to see how the Work went on; and at length would take his Ax as it

---

8. *The Seasons,* "Winter," lines 218–23, by the Scottish poet James Thomson (1700–1748).

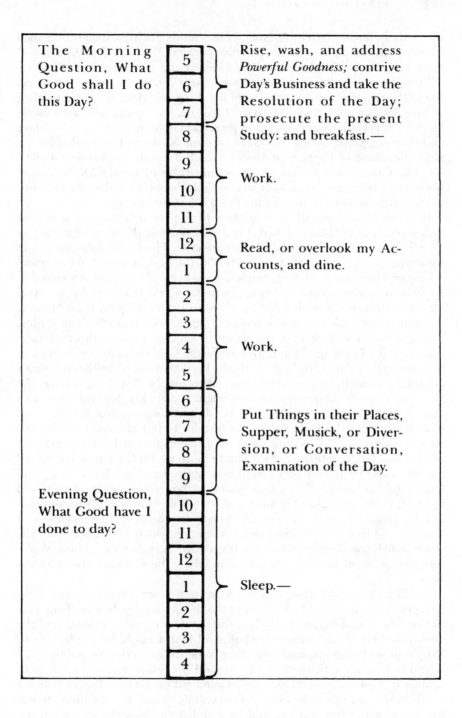

The Morning Question, What Good shall I do this Day?

5	Rise, wash, and address *Powerful Goodness;* contrive Day's Business and take the Resolution of the Day; prosecute the present Study: and breakfast.—
6	
7	
8	Work.
9	
10	
11	
12	Read, or overlook my Accounts, and dine.
1	
2	Work.
3	
4	
5	
6	Put Things in their Places, Supper, Musick, or Diversion, or Conversation, Examination of the Day.
7	
8	
9	
10	Sleep.—
11	
12	
1	
2	
3	
4	

Evening Question, What Good have I done to day?

was without farther Grinding. No, says the Smith, Turn on, turn on; we shall have it bright by and by; as yet 'tis only speckled. Yes, says the Man; but—I *think I like a speckled Ax best.*—And I believe this may have been the Case with many who having for want of some such Means as I employ'd found the Difficulty of obtaining good, and breaking bad Habits, in other Points of Vice and Virtue, have given up the Struggle, and concluded that *a speckled Ax was best.* For something that pretended to be Reason was every now and then suggesting to me, that such extreme Nicety as I exacted of myself might be a kind of Foppery in Morals, which if it were known would make me ridiculous; that a perfect Character might be attended with the Inconvenience of being envied and hated; and that a benevolent Man should allow a few Faults in himself, to keep his Friends in Countenance.

In Truth I found myself incorrigible with respect to *Order;* and now I am grown old, and my Memory bad, I feel very sensibly the want of it. But on the whole, tho' I never arrived at the Perfection I had been so ambitious of obtaining, but fell far short of it, yet I was by the Endeavor made a better and a happier Man than I otherwise should have been, if I had not attempted it; As those who aim at perfect Writing by imitating the engraved Copies,[9] tho' they never reach the wish'd for Excellence of those Copies, their Hand is mended by the Endeavor, and is tolerable while it continues fair and legible.

And it may be well my Posterity should be informed, that to this little Artifice, with the Blessing of God, their Ancestor ow'd the constant Felicity of his Life down to his 79th Year in which this is written. What Reverses may attend the Remainder is in the Hand of Providence: But if they arrive, the Reflection on past Happiness enjoy'd ought to help his Bearing them with more Resignation. To *Temperance* he ascribes his long-continu'd Health, and what is still left to him of a good Constitution. To *Industry* and *Frugality* the early Easiness of his Circumstances, and Acquisition of his Fortune, with all that Knowledge which enabled him to be an useful Citizen, and obtain'd for him some Degree of Reputation among the Learned. To *Sincerity* and *Justice* the Confidence of his Country, and the honorable Employs it conferr'd upon him. And to the joint Influence of the whole Mass of the Virtues, even in their imperfect State he was able to acquire them, all that Evenness of Temper, and that Cheerfulness in Conversation which makes his Company still sought for, and agreeable even to his younger Acquaintance. I hope therefore that some of my Descendants may follow the Example and reap the Benefit.

It will be remark'd[1] that, tho' my Scheme was not wholly without Religion there was in it no Mark of any of the distinguishing Tenets of any particular Sect. I had purposely avoided them; for being fully persuaded of the Utility and Excellency of my Method, and that it might be serviceable to People in all Religions, and intending some time or other to publish it, I would not have anything in it that should prejudice anyone of any Sect against it. I purposed writing a little Comment on each Virtue, in which I would have shown the Advantages of possessing it, and the Mischiefs attending its opposite Vice; and I should have called my Book the ART *of Virtue,* because it would have shown the *Means and Manner* of obtaining Virtue;

9. I.e., the models in the printed book.   1. Observed.

which would have distinguish'd it from the mere Exhortation to be good, that does not instruct and indicate the Means; but is like the Apostle's Man of verbal Charity, who only, without showing to the Naked and the Hungry *how* or where they might get Clothes or Victuals, exhorted them to be fed and clothed. *James II,* 15, 16.[2]

But it so happened that my Intention of writing and publishing this Comment was never fulfilled. I did indeed, from time to time put down short Hints of the Sentiments, Reasonings, etc., to be made use of in it; some of which I have still by me: But the necessary close Attention to private Business in the earlier part of Life, and public Business since, have occasioned my postponing it. For it being connected in my Mind with a *great and extensive Project* that required the whole Man to execute, and which an unforeseen Succession of Employs prevented my attending to, it has hitherto remain'd unfinish'd.

In this Piece it was my Design to explain and enforce this Doctrine, that vicious Actions are not hurtful because they are forbidden, but forbidden because they are hurtful, the Nature of Man alone consider'd: That it was therefore every one's Interest to be virtuous, who wish'd to be happy even in this World. And I should from this Circumstance (there being always in the World a Number of rich Merchants, Nobility, States and Princes, who have need of honest Instruments for the Management of their Affairs, and such being so rare) have endeavored to convince young Persons, that no Qualities were so likely to make a poor Man's Fortune as those of Probity and Integrity.

My List of Virtues contain'd at first but twelve: But a Quaker Friend having kindly inform'd me that I was generally thought proud; that my Pride show'd itself frequently in Conversation; that I was not content with being in the right when discussing any Point, but was overbearing and rather insolent; of which he convinc'd me by mentioning several Instances; I determined endeavoring to cure myself if I could of this Vice or Folly among the rest, and I added *Humility* to my List, giving an extensive Meaning to the Word. I cannot boast of much Success in acquiring the *Reality* of this Virtue; but I had a good deal with regard to the *Appearance* of it. I made it a Rule to forbear all direct Contradiction to the Sentiments of others, and all positive Assertion of my own. I even forbid myself, agreeable to the old Laws of our Junto, the Use of every Word or Expression in the Language that imported[3] a fix'd Opinion; such as *certainly, undoubtedly,* etc., and I adopted instead of them, I *conceive,* I *apprehend,* or I *imagine* a thing to be so or so, or it so appears to me at present. When another asserted something that I thought an Error, I denied myself the Pleasure of contradicting him abruptly, and of showing immediately some Absurdity in his Proposition; and in answering I began by observing that in certain Cases or Circumstances his Opinion would be right, but that in the present case there *appear'd* or *seem'd* to me some Difference, etc., I soon found the Advantage of this Change in my Manners. The Conversations I engag'd in went on more pleasantly. The modest way in which I propos'd my Opinions, procur'd

2. "If a brother or sister be naked, and destitute of daily food, And one of you say unto them, Depart in peace, be ye warmed and filled: notwithstanding ye give them not those things which are needful to the body; what doth it profit?"
3. Suggested.

them a readier Reception and less Contradiction; I had less Mortification when I was found to be in the wrong, and I more easily prevail'd with others to give up their Mistakes and join with me when I happen'd to be in the right. And this Mode, which I at first put on, with some violence to natural Inclination, became at length so easy and so habitual to me, that perhaps for these Fifty Years past no one has ever heard a dogmatical Expression escape me. And to this Habit (after my Character of Integrity) I think it principally owing, that I had early so much Weight with my Fellow Citizens, when I proposed new Institutions, or Alterations in the old; and so much Influence in public Councils when I became a Member. For I was but a bad Speaker, never eloquent, subject to much Hesitation in my choice of Words, hardly correct in Language, and yet I generally carried my Points.

In reality there is perhaps no one of our natural Passions so hard to subdue as *Pride*. Disguise it, struggle with it, beat it down, stifle it, mortify it as much as one pleases, it is still alive, and will every now and then peep out and show itself. You will see it perhaps often in this History. For even if I could conceive that I had completely overcome it, I should probably be proud of my Humility.

Thus far written at Passy, 1784.

1771–90   1868

SAMSON OCCOM
1723–1792

Born in a wigwam on Mohegan land near New London, Connecticut, Samson Occom (or Occum, as it is sometimes spelled) belonged to the northernmost branch of the Pequot tribe. When the religious revival known as the Great Awakening began, his mother, Sarah Occom, was among the first Mohegans to convert to evangelical, or New Light, Protestantism. In 1741, Occom himself converted to Christianity after hearing a sermon by the radical New Light preacher James Davenport. The following year, he was appointed to the Mohegan tribal council, where he served with his father, Joshua Occom. Two years later, he attended hearings in the Mason case, a land dispute between the state of Connecticut and the Mohegans where historic deeds and treaties played a large role. The case was decided in favor of Connecticut. Convinced that literacy was a crucial skill for defending native sovereignty in their historic domains, Occom sought out the Reverend Eleazar Wheelock, a Yale graduate and New Light minister who kept a small school at Lebanon Creek, in Mohegan territory. From 1743 until 1747, Occom studied English, Hebrew, Greek, and Latin with Wheelock. After completing his studies, he taught school for a short period, then prepared for the ministry under the Reverend Benjamin Pomeroy in Hebron, Connecticut.

In 1749, Occom moved to Montauk, at the southeastern tip of Long Island, New York. There, with the support of the local Montaukett community and the Boston branch of the Company for the Propagation of the Gospel in New England, he started a school for about thirty Native and white children. He married a Montaukett former pupil, Mary Fowler, in 1751, and together they formed a traditional home in a Montauk wigwam and started a family. After eleven years with the Montauks, during which time Occom served not only as a teacher but also as a healer, judge, and counselor, he was ordained by the presbytery of Suffolk, on Long Island. In 1761, he wrote *An Account of the Montauk Indians, on Long Island*, an early example of an indigenous author writing an ethnographic account of a Native community. That same year, he undertook a mission to the Iroquois, establishing a school in Oneida, in upstate New York, and recruiting students for Moor's Indian Charity School, a small institution that Wheelock had recently opened in Lebanon to help develop a Native ministry.

Occom went to England on a speaking tour with the Reverend Nathaniel Whitaker to raise funds for the Indian Charity School in 1765. Before his departure, Occom wrote a short autobiography to clarify some details about his background for the group sponsoring his trip. Over the next two years, he delivered some three hundred sermons across England, Scotland, and Ireland, while collecting around twelve thousand pounds for the school—an enormous sum of money for the time. During his stay in London, he testified in an appeal of the Mason land case. Wheelock had promised to care for Occom's family while he was away, but when Occom returned, he found his relations sickly and in extreme poverty.

In dire financial straits, alienated from Wheelock, and feeling vulnerable as an "Indian preacher" in the Presbyterian Church, Occom wrote a ten-page autobiography by way of self-justification. Dated September 17, 1768, *A Short Narrative of My Life* was not published until 1982. It provides fascinating details of the day-to-day life of a rural minister in eighteenth-century North America. Occom describes how he tended his garden, his animals, and his congregation, and how he preached to his Native parishioners and used innovative pedagogy to teach their children to read. He speculates that some of the criticisms leveled against him arose simply because "I am a poor Indian."

When Occom learned that Wheelock intended to use the money raised on the speaking tour to expand the Indian School into a college and move it to Hanover, New Hampshire, he angrily predicted to Wheelock that his college had too much "Grandeur for the Poor Indians, they'll never have much benefit of it." He was right. The newly renamed Dartmouth College soon ceased to focus on educating Native American students, and in 1773 Occom and Wheelock broke off their long relationship.

By that time, however, Occom had established himself as a public figure. On September 2, 1772, he preached at the execution of Moses Paul, a Wampanoag man convicted of murder. His sermon was densely packed with Scriptural allusions, and it addressed several audiences at once. Noting that he was preaching "at the earnest desire and invitation of the poor condemned Criminal," Occom called upon the assembled ministers to do the work of the Lord and exhorted his Native audience to avoid "the sin of drunkenness." *A Sermon, Preached at the Execution of Moses Paul, an Indian* was first printed on October 31 and went through three further editions by the end of the year. Nineteen editions were ultimately published, an extraordinary number for any work in this period.

Meanwhile, Occom preached widely, especially in New England, often to congregations of Native Christians. In 1774, he published his *Collection of Hymns and Spiritual Songs*, which included six hymns of his own composition. A prominent feature of Christian worship for centuries, hymns had become a source of friction between traditionalists and evangelical New Lights, who preferred the new hymns of the English theologians Isaac Watts and Charles Wesley to the older hymns in collections such as the *Bay Psalm Book*. Despite these tensions, hymn singing had become a central element of worship in Native Christian communities. Occom's hymnal appealed to a wide audience, appearing in four editions, the last in 1792. It had a lasting impact on the American tradition of hymnody.

A few months after Moses Paul's execution, Occom had attended the first organizational meeting of the Brotherton group, a pantribal movement to establish a Christian Indian town in Oneida territory. The aim of the town was to provide residents with a space where they could exercise self-governance, sheltered from white

The Reverend M^r. SAMSON OCCOM,

The first Indian Minister that ever was in Europe & who accompanied the Rev^d. Nathan^l Whitaker D.D. in an application to Great Britain for Charities to support of Rev^d. D^r. Whitocks Indian Academy & Missionaries among ye Native Savages of N^o. America.

Published according to Act of Parliament, Septr 20. 1768. by Henry Parker, at N° 82. in Cornhill, LONDON.

Samson Occom. Made during Occom's speaking tour of the British Isles, this famous print shows him pointing at a Bible. A bow and arrows hang directly above.

influence and encroachment. Occom was closely involved with the Brotherton community for over a decade. Shortly after moving his family to Brotherton in 1789, however, Occom became frustrated by conflicts within the community over the disposition of lands to whites. In 1791, the family moved to the Native Christian town of New Stockbridge, some fifteen miles northwest of Brotherton. When Occom died there the following year, of natural causes, three hundred indigenous people attended his funeral.

A Short Narrative of My Life[1]

From My Birth till I Received the Christian Religion

I was Born a Heathen and Brought up In Heathenism, till I was between 16 & 17 years of age, at a Place Calld Mohegan, in New London, Connecticut, in New England. My Parents Livd a wandering life, for did all the Indians at Mohegan, they Chiefly Depended upon Hunting, Fishing, & Fowling for their Living and had no Connection with the English, excepting to Traffic with them in their small Trifles; and they Strictly maintained and followed their Heathenish Ways, Customs & Religion, though there was Some Preaching among them. Once a Fortnight, in ye Summer Season, a Minister from New London used to come up, and the Indians to attend;[2] not that they regarded the Christian Religion, but they had Blankets given to them every Fall of the Year and for these things they would attend and there was a Sort of School kept, when I was quite young, but I believe there never was one that ever Learnt to read any thing,—and when I was about 10 Years of age there was a man who went about among the Indian Wigwams, and wherever he Could find the Indian Children, would make them read;[3] but the Children Used to take Care to keep out of his way;—and he used to Catch me Some times and make me Say over my Letters; and I believe I learnt Some of them. But this was Soon over too; and all this Time there was not one amongst us, that made a Profession of Christianity— Neither did we Cultivate our Land, nor kept any Sort of Creatures except Dogs, which we used in Hunting; and we Dwelt in Wigwams. These are a Sort of Tents, Covered with Matts, made of Flags.[4] And to this Time we were unaquainted with the English Tongue in general though there were a few, who understood a little of it.

From the Time of Our Reformation till I Left Mr. Wheelocks

When I was 16 years of age, we heard a Strange Rumor among the English, that there were Extraordinary Ministers Preaching from Place to Place and a Strange Concern among the White People.[5] This was in the Spring of the Year. But we Saw nothing of these things, till Some Time in the Summer, when Some Ministers began to visit us and Preach the Word of God; and the Common People all Came frequently and exhorted us to the things of God, which it pleased the Lord, as I humbly hope, to Bless and accompany with Divine Influence to the Conviction and Saving Conversion of a Number of us; amongst whom I was one that was Imprest with the things we had heard. These Preachers did not only come to us, but we frequently went to their meetings and Churches. After I was awakened[6] & converted, I went to all the meetings, I could come at; & Continued under Trouble of Mind about

---

1. The text is from *American Indian Nonfiction: An Anthology of Writings* (2007), edited by Bernd C. Peyer. Some of the bracketed insertions are Peyer's; others have been added for this anthology.
2. In 1729, the Harvard graduate and Congregationalist minister Eliphalet Adams occasionally preached to the Mohegans.

3. In 1733–38 the Yale graduate and Presbyterian minister Jonathan Barber occasionally taught the Mohegans.
4. I.e., woven mats, which were placed over birchbark frames.
5. I.e., the Great Awakening was underway.
6. I.e., awakened spiritually to a sense of sin.

6 months; at which time I began to Learn the English Letters; got me a Primer, and used to go to my English Neighbours frequently for Assistance in Reading, but went to no School. And when I was 17 years of age, I had, as I trust, a Discovery of the way of Salvation through Jesus Christ, and was enabl'd to put my trust in him alone for Life & Salvation. From this Time the Distress and Burden of my mind was removed, and I found Serenity and Pleasure of Soul, in Serving God. By this time I just began to Read in the New Testament without Spelling,—and I had a Stronger Desire Still to Learn to read the Word of God, and at the Same Time had an uncommon Pity and Compassion to my Poor Brethren According to the Flesh. I used to wish I was capable of Instructing my poor Kindred. I used to think, if I Could once Learn to Read I would Instruct the poor Children in Reading,—and used frequently to talk with our Indians Concerning Religion. This continued till I was in my 19th year: by this Time I Could Read a little in the Bible. At this Time my Poor Mother was going to Lebanon, and having had Some Knowledge of Mr. Wheelock and hearing he had a Number of English youth under his Tuition,[7] I had a great Inclination to go to him and be with him a week or a Fortnight, and Desired my Mother to Ask Mr. Wheelock whether he would take me a little while to Instruct me in Reading. Mother did so; and when She Came Back, She Said Mr. Wheelock wanted to See me as Soon as possible. So I went up, thinking I Should be back again in a few Days; when I got up there, he received me With kindness and Compassion and in Stead of Staying a Forthnight or 3 Weeks, I Spent 4 Years with him.—After I had been with him Some Time, he began to acquaint his Friends of my being with him, and of his Intentions of Educating me, and my Circumstances. And the good People began to give Some Assistance to Mr. Wheelock, and gave me Some old and Some New Clothes. Then he represented the Case to the Honorable Commissioners at Boston, who were Commission'd by the Honorable Society in London for Propagating the gospel among the Indians in New England and parts adjacent, and they allowed him 60 £ in old Tender, which was about 6 £ Sterling,[8] and they Continu'd it 2 or 3 years, I cant't tell exactly.—While I was at Mr. Wheelock's, I was very weakly and my Health much impaired, and at the End of 4 Years, I over Strained my Eyes to such a Degree, I Could not persue my Studies any Longer; and out of these 4 years I Lost Just about one year;—And was obliged to quit my Studies.

From the Time I left Mr. Wheelock till I Went to Europe

As soon as I left Mr. Wheelock, I endeavored to find Some Employ among the Indians; went to Nahantuck,[9] thinking they may want a School Master, but they had one; then went to Narraganset,[1] and they were Indifferent about a School, and went back to Mohegan, and heard a number of our Indians were going to Montauk, on Long Island, and I went with them, and the Indians there were very desirous to have me keep a School amongst them, and I Consented, and went back a while to Mohegan and Some time in November

7. Instruction.
8. Probably worth about $1,400 in present-day American currency.
9. A village of the Western Niantics, in present-

day East Lyme, Connecticut.
1. A village of the Narragansetts, in Charlestown, Rhode Island.

I went on the Island, I think it is 17 years ago last November. I agreed to keep School with them Half a Year, and left it with them to give me what they Pleased; and they took turns to Provide Food for me. I had near 30 Scholars this winter; I had an evening School too for those that could not attend the Day School—and began to Carry on their meetings, they had a Minister, one Mr. Horton, the Scotch Society's Missionary; but he Spent, I think two thirds of his Time at Sheenecock, 30 Miles from Montauk.[2] We met together 3 times for Divine Worship every Sabbath and once on every Wednesday evening. I [used] to read the Scriptures to them and used to expound upon Some particular Passages in my own Tongue. Visited the Sick and attended their Burials.—When the half year expired, they Desired me to Continue with them, which I complied with, for another half year, when I had fulfilled that, they were urgent to have me Stay Longer, So I continued amongst them till I was Married, which was about 2 years after I went there. And Continued to Instruct them in the Same manner as I did before. After I was married a while, I found there was need of a Support more than I needed while I was Single,—and made my Case Known to Mr. Buell[3] and to Mr. Wheelock, and also the Needy Circumstances and the Desires of these Indians of my Continuing amongst them, and the Commissioners were so good as to grant £15 a year Sterling—And I kept on in my Service as usual, yea I had additional Service; I kept School as I did before and Carried on the Religious Meetings as often as ever, and attended the Sick and their Funerals, and did what Writings they wanted, and often Sat as a Judge to reconcile and Decide their Matters Between them, and had visitors of Indians from all Quarters; and, as our Custom is, we freely Entertain all Visitors. And was fetched often from my Tribe and from others to see into their Affairs Both Religious, Temporal,—Besides my Domestic Concerns. And it Pleased the Lord to Increase my Family fast—and Soon after I was Married, Mr. Horton left these Indians and the Shenecock & after this I was [alone] and then I had the whole care of these Indians at Montauk, and visited the Shenecock Indians often. Used to set out Saturdays towards Night and come back again Mondays. I have been obliged to Set out from Home after Sun Set, and Ride 30 Miles in the Night, to Preach to these Indians. And Some Indians at Shenecock Sent their Children to my School at Montauk, I kept one of them Some Time, and had a Young Man a half year from Mohegan, a Lad from Nahantuck who was with me almost a year; and had little or nothing for keeping them.

My Method in the School was, as Soon as the Children got together, and took their proper Seats, I Prayed with them, then began to hear them. I generally began (after some of them Could Spell and Read,) With those that were yet in their Alphabets, So around, as they were properly Seated till I got through and I obliged them to Study their Books, and to help one another. When they could not make out a hard word they Brought it to me—and I usually heard them, in the Summer Season 8 Times a Day 4 in the morning, and in [the] after Noon.—In the Winter Season 6 Times a Day, As Soon as they could Spell, they were obliged to Spell when ever they wanted to go

2. The Presbyterian minister Azeriah Horton, a Yale graduate, ministered primarily to the Shinnecocks on Long Island and in Rhode Island.

3. Samuel Buell, the Presbyterian minister and Yale graduate, who preached at Occom's ordination, in 1759.

out. I concluded with Prayer; I generally heard my Evening Scholars 3 Times Round, And as they go out the School, every one, that Can Spell, is obliged to Spell a Word, and to go out Leisurely one after another. I Catechised 3 or 4 Times a Week according to the Assembly's [Shorter] Catechism, and many Times Proposed Questions of my own, and in my own Tongue. I found Difficulty with Some Children, who were Some what Dull,[4] most of these can soon learn to Say over their Letters, they Distinguish the Sounds by the Ear, but their Eyes can't Distinguish the Letters, and the way I took to cure them was by making an Alphabet on Small bits of paper, and glued them on Small Chips of Cedar after this manner A B & C. I put these on Letters in order on a Bench then point to one Letter and bid a Child to take notice of it, and then I order the Child to fetch me the Letter from the Bench; if he Brings the Letter, it is well, if not he must go again and again till he brings [the] right Letter. When they can bring any Letters this way, then I just Jumble them together, and bid them to set them in Alphabetical order, and it is a Pleasure to them; and they soon Learn their Letters this way.—I frequently Discussed or Exhorted my Scholars, in Religious matters.—My Method in our Religious Meetings was this; Sabbath Morning we Assemble together about 10 o'C and begin with Singing; we generally Sung Dr. Watt's Psalms or Hymns.[5] I distinctly read the Psalm or Hymn first, and then gave the meaning of it to them, after that Sing, then Pray, and Sing again after Prayer. Then proceed to Read from Suitable portion of Scripture, and so Just give the plain Sense of it in Familiar Discourse and apply it to them. So continued with Prayer and Singing. In the after Noon and Evening we Proceed in the Same Manner, and so in Wednesday Evening. Some Time after Mr. Horton left these Indians, there was a remarkable revival of religion among these Indians and many were hopefully converted to the Saving knowledge of God in Jesus. It is to be observed before Mr. Horton left these Indians they had Some Prejudices infused in their minds, by Some Enthusiastical Exhorters[6] from New England, against Mr. Horton, and many of them had left him, by this means he was Discouraged, and was disposed from[7] these Indians. And being acquainted with the Enthusiasts in New England & the make and the Disposition[8] of the Indians I took a mild way to reclaim them. I opposed them not openly but let them go on in their way, and whenever I had an opportunity, I would read Such pages of the Scriptures, and I thought would confound their Notions, and I would come to them with all Authority, Saying "these Saith the Lord"; and by this means, the Lord was pleased to Bless my poor Endeavours, and they were reclaimed, and Brought to hear almost any of the ministers.—I am now to give an Account of my Circumstances and manner of Living. I Dwelt in a Wigwam, a Small Hut with Small Poles and Covered with Matts made of Flags, and I was obligd to remove[9] twice a Year, about 2 miles Distance, by reason of the Scarcity of wood, for in one Neck of Land they Planted their Corn, and in another, they had their wood, and I was obligd to have my Corn carted and my Hay also,—and I got my Ground Plow'd every year, which Cost me about 12 shillings an acre; and I kept a Cow and a Horse, for which I paid 21

---

4. Somewhat slow to learn.
5. The works of the great English hymnodist Isaac Watts (1674–1748).
6. Enthusiastic lay preachers.

7. Turned away from.
8. Inclination.
9. Move.

shillings every year York currency, and went 18 miles to Mill for every Dust[1] of meal we used in my family. I Hired or Joined with my Neighbours to go to Mill, with a Horse or ox Cart, or on Horse Back, and Some time went myself. My Family Increasing fast, and my Visitors also. I was obligd to contrive every way to Support my Family; I took all opportunities, to get Some thing to feed my Family Daily. I Planted my own Corn, Potatoes, and Beans; I used to be out hoeing my Corn Some times before Sun Rise and after my School is Dismist,[2] and by this means I was able to raise my own Pork, for I was allowed to keep 5 Swine. Some mornings & Evenings I would be out with my Hook and Line to Catch fish, and in the Fall of Year and in the Spring, I used my gun, and fed my Family with Fowls. I Could more than pay for my Powder & Shot with Feathers. At other Times I Bound old Books for Easthampton People, made wooden Spoons and Ladles, Stocked Guns, & worked on Cedar to make Pails, [Piggins], and Churns & C.[3] Besides all these Difficulties I met with advers Providence, I bought a Mare, had it but a little while, and she fell into the Quick Sand and Died, After a while Bought another, I kept her about half year, and she was gone, and I never have heard of nor Seen her from that Day to this; it was Supposed Some Rogue Stole her. I got another and [it] Died with a Distemper, and last of all I Bought a Young Mare, and kept her till She had one Colt, and She broke her Leg and Died, and Presently after the [Colt] Died also. In the whole I Lost 5 Horse Kind; all these Losses helped to pull me down; and by this Time I got greatly in Debt, and acquainted my Circumstances to Some of my Friends, and they Represented my Case to the Commissioners of Boston, and Interceded with them for me, and they were pleased to vote 15 £ for my Help, and Soon after Sent a Letter to my good Friend at New London, acquainting him that they had Superseded their Vote; and my Friends were so good as to represent my Needy Circumstances Still to them, and they were so good at Last, as to Vote £ 15 and Sent it, for which I am very thankful; and the Revd Mr. Buell was so kind as to write in my behalf to the gentlemen of Boston; and he told me they were much Displeased with him, and heard also once again that they blamed me for being Extravagant; I Can't Conceive how these gentlemen would have me Live. I am ready to [forgive] their Ignorance, and I would wish they had Changed Circumstances with me but one month, that they may know, by experience what my Case really was; but I am now fully convinced, that it was not Ignorance, For I believe it can be proved to the world that these Same Gentlemen gave a young Missionary a Single man, *one Hundred Pounds* for one year, and fifty Pounds for an Interpreter, and thirty Pounds for an Introducer; so it Cost them one Hundred & Eighty Pounds in one Single Year, and they Sent too where there was no Need of a Missionary.

Now you See what difference they made between me and other missionaries; they gave me 180 Pounds for 12 years Service, which they gave for one years Services in another Mission.—In my Service (I speak like a fool,[4] but I am Constrained) I was my own Interpreter. I was both a School master and Minister to the Indians, yea I was their Ear, Eye & Hand, as Well as Mouth. I leave it with the World, as wicked as it is, to Judge, whether I ought

---

1. Particle, bit. "York": probably New York.
2. I.e., dismissed.
3. I.e., et cetera. "Piggins": small, wooden pails.
4. Cf. 2 Corinithians 11.23.

not to have had half as much, they gave a young man Just mentioned which would have been but £ 50 a year; and if they ought to have given me that, I am not under obligations to them, I owe them nothing at all; what can be the Reason that they used me after this manner? I can't think of any thing, but this as a Poor Indian Boy Said, Who was Bound out to an English Family, and he used to Drive Plow for a young man, and he whipt and Beat him allmost every Day, and the young man found fault with him, and Complained of him to his master and the poor Boy was Called to answer for himself before his master, and he was asked, what it was he did, that he was So Complained of and beat almost every Day. He Said, he did not know, but he Supposed it was because he could not drive any better; but says he, I Drive as well as I know how; and at other Times he Beats me, because he is of a mind to beat me; but says he believes he Beats me for the most of the Time "because I am an Indian".

So I am *ready* to Say, they have used me thus, because I Can't Influence the Indians so well as other missionaries; but I can assure them I have endeavoured to teach them as well as I know how;—but I *must Say*, "I believe it is because I am a poor Indian". I Can't help that God has made me So; I did not make my self so.

September 17, 1768   1982

From A Sermon at the Execution of Moses Paul, an Indian[1]

The ADDRESS

By the melancholy providence of God, and at the earnest desire and invitation of the poor condemned criminal,[2] I am here before this great concourse of people at this time, to give the last discourse to the poor miserable object who is to be executed this day before your eyes, for the due reward of his folly, and madness, and enormous wickedness. It is an unwelcome task to me to speak upon such an occasion; but since it is the desire of the poor man himself, in conscience I cannot deny him; I must endeavour to do the great work the dying man requests. I conclude that this great concourse of people have come together to see the execution of justice upon this poor Indian; and I suppose the biggest part of you look upon yourselves Christians, and as such I hope you will demean[3] yourselves; and that you will have suitable commiseration towards this poor object. Though you cannot in justice pray for his life to be continued in this world, you can pray earnestly for the salvation of his poor soul. Let this be therefore, the fervent exercise of our souls; for this is the last day we have to pray for him.—As for you that do not regard religion, it cannot

1. The text is from Samson Occom, *A Sermon at the Execution of Moses Paul, an Indian; Who had been guilty of Murder, Preached at New Haven in America* (1788).
2. Moses Paul, a Wampanoag man, was convicted of the murder of a white man, Moses Cook, and sentenced to death. Paul unsuccess-

fully appealed his conviction, charging the all-white jury with racial bias. Paul then wrote to Occom asking him to preach at his execution, which took place in 1772 at the Brick Meeting House in New Haven, Connecticut.
3. Behave.

be expected, that you will put up one petition for this miserable creature: yet I would intreat you seriously to consider the frailty of corrupt nature, and behave yourselves as becomes rational creatures.

And in a word, let us all be suitably affected with the melancholy occasion of the day, knowing that we are all dying creatures, and accountable unto God. Though this poor condemned criminal will in a few minutes know more than all of us, either in unutterable joy, or inconceivable woe; yet we shall certainly know as much as he, in a few days.

The sacred words that I have chosen to speak from upon this undesirable occasion, are found written in Romans vi. 23.

> FOR THE WAGES OF SIN IS DEATH, BUT THE GIFT OF GOD
> IS ETERNAL LIFE THROUGH JESUS CHRIST OUR LORD.

Death is called the King of Terrors, and it ought to be the subject of every man and woman's thoughts daily; because it is that unto which they are liable every moment of their lives: and therefore, it cannot be unseasonable to think, speak and hear of it at any time, and especially on this mournful occasion; for we must all come to it, how soon we cannot tell; whether we are prepared or not prepared, ready or not ready, whether death is welcome or not welcome, we must feel the force of it: whether we concern ourselves with death or not, it will concern itself with us. Seeing that this is the case with every one of us, what manner of persons ought we to be in all holy conversation and godliness; how ought men to exert themselves in preparation for death continually; for they know not what a day or an hour may bring forth, with respect to them. But, alas! according to the appearance of mankind in general, death is the least thought of. They go on from day to day, as if they were to live here for ever, as if this was the only life. They contrive, rack their inventions, disturb their rest, and even hazard their lives in all manner of dangers, both by sea and land; yea they leave no stone unturned that they may live in the world, and at the same time have little or no contrivance to die well: God and their souls are neglected, and heaven and eternal happiness are disregarded; Christ and his religion are despised—yet most of these very men intend to be happy when they come to die, not considering that there must be great preparation in order to die well. Yea there is none so fit to live as those that are fit to die; those that are not fit to die are not fit to live. Life and death are nearly connected: we generally own that it is a great and solemn thing to die. But I say again, how little do mankind realize these things? They are busy about the things of this world as if there was no death before them. Dr. Watts pictures them out to the life in his psalms:

See the vain race of mortals move	Some walk in honor's gaudy show,
Like shadows o'er the plain,	Some dig for golden ore,
They rage and strive, desire and love,	They toil for heirs they know not who,
But all their noise is vain.	And strait are seen no more.[4]

---

4. Psalm 39, "Teach Me the Measure of My Days," verses 3 and 4, by the English hymnodist Isaac Watts (1674–1748).

Eternal life is shamefully disregarded by men in general, and eternal death is chosen rather than life.[5] This is the general complaint of the bible from the beginning to the end. As long as Christ is neglected, life is refused, and as long as sin is cherished, death is chosen; and this seems to be the woful case of mankind of all nations, according to their appearance in these days; for it is too plain to be denied, that vice and immortality, and floods of iniquity are abounding every where amongst all nations, and all orders and ranks of men, and in every sect of people. Yea there is a great agreement and harmony among all nations, and from the highest to the lowest to practise sin and iniquity; and the pure religion of Jesus Christ is turned out of doors, and is dying without; or, in other words, the Lord Jesus Christ is turned out of doors by men in general, and even by his professed people. "He came to his own, and his own received him not."[6] But the devil is admitted, he has free access to the houses and hearts of the children of men: Thus life is refused and death is chosen.

But in further speaking upon our text, by divine assistance, I shall consider those two general propositions:

I. That sin is the cause of all the miseries that befall the children of men, both as to their bodies and souls, for time and eternity.

II. That eternal life and happiness is the free gift of God, through Jesus Christ our Lord.

In speaking to the first proposition, I shall first consider the nature of sin; and secondly, shall consider the consequences of sin, or the wages of sin, which is death.

First then, we are to describe the nature of sin.

Sin is the transgression of the law:—This is the scripture definition of sin. Now the law of God being holy, just and good; sin must be altogether unholy, unjust and evil. If I was to define sin, I should call it a contrariety to God; and as such it must be the vilest thing in the world; it is full of all evil; it is the evil of evils; the only evil, in which dwells no good thing; and is most destructive to God's creation, where ever it takes effect. It was sin that transformed the very angels of heaven into devils; and it was sin that caused hell to be made. If it had not been for sin, there never would have been such a thing as hell or devil, death or misery.

And if sin is such a thing as we have just described; it must be worse than the devils and hell itself.—Sin is full of deadly poison; it is full of malignity and hatred against God, against all his divine perfections and attributes, against his wisdom, against his power, against his holiness and goodness, against his mercy and justice, against his written law and gospel; yea, against his very being and existence. Were it in the power of sin, it would even dethrone God, and set itself on the throne.

*   *   *

2. I shall endeavour to shew the sad consequences or effects of sin upon the children of men.

Sin has poisoned them, and made them distracted or fools. The Psalmist says, The fool hath said in his heart, there is no God.[7] And Solomon, through

---

5. Cf. Deuteronomy 30.19.
6. John 1.11.
7. Psalm 14.1. "The Psalmist": David, the second

king of ancient Israel, traditionally considered the author of the Book of Psalms.

his Proverbs, calls ungodly sinners fools;[8] and their sin he calls their folly and foolishness. The Apostle James says, "But the tongue can no man tame, it is an unruly evil, full of deadly poison." It is the heart that is in the first place full of this "deadly poison." The tongue is only an interpreter of the heart. Sin has vitiated the whole man, both soul and body; all the powers are corrupted; it has turned the minds of men against all good, towards all evil. So poisoned are they, according to the Prophet Isaiah v. 20. "Wo unto them that call evil good, and good evil; that put darkness for light, and light for darkness; that put bitter for sweet, and sweet for bitter." And Christ Jesus saith in John iii. 19, 20. "And this is the condemnation, that light is come into the world, and men loved darkness rather than light, because their deeds were evil. For every one that doth evil hateth the light, neither cometh to the light, lest his deeds should be reproved." Sin has stupified mankind, they are now ignorant of God their maker; neither do they enquire after him. And they are ignorant of themselves, they know not what is good for them, neither do they understand their danger; and they have no fear of God before their eyes.

* * *

The next thing I shall consider, is the actual death of the body, or separation between soul and body. At the cessation of natural life, there is an end of all the enjoyments of this life: there is no more joy nor sorrow; no more hope nor fear, as to the body; no more contrivance and carrying on any business; no more merchandizing and trading; no more farming; no more buying and selling; no more building of any kind, no more contrivance at all to live in the world; no more flatteries nor frowns from the world; no more honor nor reproach; no more praise; no more good report, nor evil report; no more learning of any trades, arts or sciences in the world; no more sinful pleasures, they are all at an end; recreations, visiting, tavern haunting, music and dancing, chambering[9] and carousing, playing at dice and cards, or any game whatsoever; cursing and swearing, and profaning the holy name of God, drunkenness, fighting, debauchery, lying and cheating, in this world, must cease for ever. Not only so, sinners must bid an eternal farewell to all the world; bid farewell to all their beloved sins and pleasures: and the places and possessions that knew them once, shall know them no more for ever. And further, they must bid adieu to all sacred and divine things. They are obliged to leave the Bible, and all the ordinances thereof; and to bid farewell to preachers, and all sermons and all Christian people, and Christian conversation; they must bid a long farewell to sabbaths and seasons, and opportunities of worship; yea, an eternal farewell to God the Father, Son and Holy Ghost, and adieu to heaven and all happiness, to saints and all the inhabitants of the upper world. At your leisure please to read the destruction of Babylon; Rev. the 18th, most of that description will apply to the case of dying sinners.

Mean while, the poor departed soul must take up its lodging in sorrow, woe and misery, in the lake that burns with fire and brimstone, where the

8. James 3.8. Cf., e.g., Proverbs 14.9, 15.2, 26.4. "Solomon": a son of David who became a king of Israel, traditionally considered the author of the Book of Proverbs.

9. Illicit sexual intercourse.

worm dieth not, and the fire is not quenched; where a multitude of frightful deformed devils dwell, and the damned ghosts of Adam's race; where darkness, horror and despair reigns, where hope never comes, and where poor guilty naked souls will be tormented with exquisite torments, even the wrath of the Almighty poured out upon their damned souls; the smoke of their torments ascending up for ever and ever; and hellish groans, howlings, cries and shrieks all round them, and merciless devils upbraiding them for their folly and madness, and tormenting them incessantly.—And there they must endure the most unsatiable, fruitless desire, and the most overwhelming shame and confusion, and the most horrible fear, and the most doleful sorrow, and the most racking despair. When they cast their flaming eyes to heaven, with Dives in torments,[1] they behold an angry and frowning God, whose eyes are as a flaming fire, and they are struck with ten thousand darts of pain; and the sight of the happiness of the saints above, adds to their pains and aggravates their misery. And when they reflect upon their past folly and madness, in neglecting the great salvation in their day, it will pierce them with ten thousand inconceivable torments; it will as it were enkindle their hell afresh; and it will cause them to curse themselves bitterly, and curse the day in which they were born, and curse their parents that were the instruments of their being in the world; yea they will curse, bitterly curse; and with that very God that gave them their being, to be in the same condition with them in hell torments. This is what is called the second death, and it is the last death, and an eternal death to a guilty soul.

And O eternity, eternity, eternity! Who can measure it? Who can count the years thereof? Arithmetic must fail, the thoughts of men and angels are drowned in it; how shall we describe eternity? To what shall we compare it? Were it possible to employ a fly to carry off this globe by the small particles thereof, and to carry them to such a distance that it should return once in ten thousand years for another particle, and so continue until it has carried off all this globe, and framed them together in some unknown space, until it has made just such a world as this is; after all, eternity would remain the fame unexhausted duration. This must be the unavoidable portion of all impenitent sinners, let them be who they will, great or small, honorable or ignoble, rich or poor, bond or free. Negroes, Indians, English, or of what nations forever, all that die in their sins, must go to hell together, for the wages of sin is death.

The next thing that I was to consider is this:

II. That eternal life and happiness is the free gift of God, through Jesus Christ our Lord.

Under this proposition I shall endeavour to shew, what this life and happiness is.

The life that is mentioned in our text, begins with a *spiritual* life: it is the life of the soul, a restoration of soul from sin to holiness, from darkness to light, a translation from the kingdom and dominion of Satan, to the kingdom of God's grace. In other words, it is being restored to the image of God, and delivered from the image of Satan. And this life consists in union of the soul to God, and communion with God; a real participation of the divine

---

1. The parable of Dives the rich man and Lazarus appears in Luke 16.19–31.

nature, or in the apostle's words, it is Christ formed within us; "I live," says he, "yet not I, but Christ liveth in me."[2] And the apostle John saith, "God is love, and he that dwelleth in love, dwelleth in God, and God in him."[3] * * * This life is called eternal life, because God has planted a living principle in the soul; and whereas he was dead before, now he is made alive unto God; there is an active principle within him towards God, he now moves towards God in his religious devotions and exercises; is daily, comfortably and sweetly walking with God, in all his ordinances and commands; his delight is in the ways of God; he breathes towards God, a living breath, in praises, prayers, adorations and thanksgivings; his prayers are now heard in the heavens, and his praises delight the ears of the Almighty, and his thanksgivings are accepted. So alive is he now to God, that it is his meat and drink, yea more than his meat and drink, to do the will of his heavenly Father. It is his delight, his happiness and pleasure to serve God. He does not drag himself to his duties now, but he does them out of choice, and with alacrity of soul. Yea, so alive is he to God, that he gives up himself and all that he has entirely to God, to be for him and none other; his whole aim is to glorify God in all things, whether by life or death, all the same to him.

We have a bright example of this in St Paul. After he was converted, he was all alive to God; he regarded not himself, but was willing to spend, and be spent in the service of his God;[4] he was hated, reviled, despised, laughed at, and called by all manner of evil names; was scourged, stoned and imprisoned;— and all could not stop his activity towards God. He would boldly and courageously go on in preaching the gospel of the Lord Jesus Christ, to poor, lost, and undone sinners; he would do the work God set him about, in spite of all opposition he met with, either from men or devils, earth or hell; come death, or come life, none of these things moved him, because he was alive unto God. Though he suffered hunger and thirst, cold and heat, poverty and nakedness by day and by night, by sea and land, and was in danger all ways; yet he would serve God amidst all these dangers. Read his amazing account in 2 Cor. xi. 23. and on.

Another instance of marvellous love towards God, we have in Daniel. When there was a proclamation, sent by the king, to all his subjects, forbidding them to call upon their gods, for thirty days; which was done by envious men, that they might find occasion against Daniel, the servant of the Most High God; yet he having the life of God in his soul, regarded not the king's decree, but made his petitions to his God, as often as he used to do, though death was threatened to the disobedient. But he feared not the hell they had prepared; the den resembled hell, and the lions the devils. Thus Daniel and Paul went through fire and water, as the common saying is, because they had *eternal* life in their souls in an eminent manner; and they regarded not *this* life, for the cause and glory of God. And thus it has been in all ages with true Christians. Many of the fore-fathers of the English, in this country, had this life, and are gone the same way that the holy prophets and apostles went. Many of them went through all manner of sufferings for God; and a great number of them are gone home to heaven, in chariots of fire. I have seen the place in London, called Smithfield, where

2. Galatians 2.20. "The apostle": Jesus' apostle Paul.　　3. 1 John 4.16.

4. 2 Corinthians 12.15.

numbers were burnt to death for the religion of Jesus Christ.[5] And there is the same life in true Christians now in these days; and if there should persecutions arise in our day, I verily believe, true Christians would suffer with the same spirit and temper of mind, as those did, who suffered in days past.

We proceed to shew, that this life which we have described, is the free gift of God, through Jesus Christ our Lord.

Sinners have forfeited all mercy into the hand of divine justice, and have merited hell and damnation to themselves; for the wages of sin is everlasting death, but heaven and happiness is a free gift; it comes by favour; and all merit is excluded: and especially if we consider that we are fallen sinful creatures, and there is nothing in us that can recommend us to the favour of God. * * * And it is said, that this life is given in and through the Lord Jesus Christ. It could not be given in any other way, but in and through the death and sufferings of Christ; Christ himself is a gift, and he is the Christian's life. "For God so loved the world, that he gave his only begotten Son, that whosoever believeth in him should not perish, but have everlasting life."[6] The word says further, "For by grace ye are saved, through faith, and that not of yourselves, it is the gift of God."[7] This is given through Jesus Christ our Lord; Christ obtained it with his own blood, by the influence of his spirit he prepares us for it; and by his divine grace preserves us for it. In a word, he is all in all in our eternal salvation; all this is the free gift of God.

I have now gone through what I proposed from my text. And I shall now make some application of the whole.

First to the criminal in particular; and then to the auditory in general.[8]

My poor unhappy brother MOSES;

As it was your own desire that I should preach to you this last discourse, so I shall speak plainly to you.—You are the bone of my bone, and flesh of my flesh. You are an Indian, a despised creature; but you have despised yourself; yea, you have despised God more; you have trodden under foot his authority; you have despised his commands and precepts: and now, as God says, "be sure your sins will find you out;[9] so now, poor Moses, your sins have found you out, and they have overtaken you this day; the day of your death is now come; the King of Terrors is at hand; you have but a very few moments to breathe in this world.—The just laws of man, and the holy law of Jehovah, call aloud for the destruction of your mortal life; God says, "Whoso sheddeth man's blood, by man shall his blood be shed."[1] This is the ancient decree of heaven, and it is to be executed by man; nor have you the least gleam of hope of escape, for the unalterable sentence is past; the terrible day of execution is come; the unwelcome guard is about you; and the fatal instruments of death are now made ready; your coffin and your grave, your last lodging, are open ready to receive you.

Alas! poor Moses, now you know, by sad, by woful experience, the living truth of our text, that the wages of sin is death. You have been already dead; yea twice dead: by nature spiritually dead, and since the awful sentence of death has been past upon you, you have been dead to all the pleasures of

---

5. At this location, Protestants were executed during the reigns of Henry VIII (1509–47), Edward VI (1547–53), Mary I (1553–58), Elizabeth I (1558–1603), and James I (1603–1625).
6. John 3.16.
7. Ephesians 2.8.
8. The assembled listeners, including numerous clergymen.
9. Numbers 32.23.
1. Genesis 9.6.

this life: or all the pleasures, lawful or unlawful, have been dead to you: And death which is the wages of sin, is standing even on this side of your grave ready to put a final period to your mortal life; and just beyond the grave, eternal death awaits your poor soul, and the devils are ready to drag your miserable soul down to their bottomless den, where everlasting woe and horror reigns; the place is filled with doleful shrieks, howls and groans of the damned. Oh! to what a miserable, forlorn, and wretched condition, have your extravagant folly and wickedness brought you, i.e. if you die in your sins. And O! what manner of repentance ought you to manifest! How ought your heart to bleed for what you have done! How ought you to prostrate your soul before a bleeding God! And under self-condemnation, cry out, Ah Lord, ah Lord, what have I done!—Whatever partiality, injustice and error there may be among the judges of the earth, remember that you have deserved a thousand deaths, and a thousand hells, by reason of your sins, at the hands of a holy God. Should God come out against you in strict justice, alas! what could you say for yourself? for you have been brought up under the bright sunshine, and plain, and loud sound of the gospel; and you have had a good education; you can read and write well; and God has given you a good natural understanding: and therefore your sins are so much more aggravated. You have not sinned in such an ignorant manner as others have done; but you have sinned with both your eyes open as it were, under the light, even the glorious light of the gospel of the Lord Jesus Christ.—You have sinned against the light of your own conscience, against your knowledge and understanding; you have sinned against the pure and holy laws of God, and the just laws of men; you have sinned against heaven and earth; you have sinned against all the mercies and goodness of God; you have sinned against the whole Bible, against the Old and New-Testament; you have sinned against the blood of Christ, which is the blood of the everlasting covenant.[2] O poor Moses, see what you have done! and now repent, repent, I say again repent; see how the blood you shed cries against you, and the avenger of blood is at your heels. O fly, fly to the Blood of the Lamb of God, for the pardon of all your aggravated sins.

But let us now turn to a more pleasant theme.—Though you have been a great sinner, a heaven daring sinner; yet hark! O hear the joyful sound from heaven, even from the King of kings, and Lord of lords; that the gift of God is eternal life, through Jesus Christ our Lord. It is a free gift, and bestowed on the greatest sinners, and upon their true repentance towards God and faith in the Lord Jesus Christ, they shall be welcome to the life, which we have spoken of; it is granted upon free terms. He that hath no money may come; he that hath no righteousness, no goodness, may come; the call is to poor undone sinners; the call is not to the righteous, but sinners, inviting them to repentance. Hear the voice of the Son of the most high God, "Come unto me, all ye that labour and are heavy laden, and I will give you rest."[3] This is a call, a gracious call to you, poor Moses, under your present burdens and distresses. * * * O poor Moses, believe on the Lord Jesus Christ with all your heart, and thou shalt be saved eternally. Come just as you are, with all

2. In Calvinist theology, God established the Covenant of Works with Adam, who then broke it. Jesus Christ established the Covenant of Grace with those who believe in him and will thus be saved.
3. Matthew 11.28.

your sins and abominations, with all your blood-guiltiness, with all your condemnation, and lay hold of the hope set before you this day. This is the last day of salvation with your soul; you will be beyond the bounds of mercy in a few minutes more. O, what a joyful day will it be if you now openly believe in, and receive the Lord Jesus Christ; it would be the beginning of heavenly days with your poor soul; instead of a melancholy day, it would be a wedding day to your soul; it would cause the very angels in heaven to rejoice, and the saints on earth to be glad; it would cause the angels to come down from the realms above, and wait hovering about your gallows, ready to convey your soul to the heavenly mansions, there to take the possession of eternal glory and happiness, and join the heavenly choirs in singing the song of Moses and the Lamb; there to sit down forever with Abraham, Isaac and Jacob[4] in the kingdom of God's glory; and your shame and guilt shall be forever banished from the place, and all sorrow and fear forever fly away, and tears be wiped from your face; and there shall you forever admire the astonishing and amazing and infinite mercy of God in Christ Jesus, in pardoning such a monstrous sinner as you have been; there you will claim the highest note of praise, for the riches of free grace in Christ Jesus. But if you will not accept of a Saviour proposed to your acceptance in this last day of your life, you must this very day bid farewell to God the Father, Son and Holy Ghost, to heaven and all the saints and angels that are there; and you must bid all the saints in this lower world an eternal farewell, and even the whole world. And so I must leave you in the hands of God; and must turn to the whole auditory.

Sirs, We may plainly see, from what we have heard, and from the miserable object before us, into what a doleful condition sin has brought mankind, even into a state of death and misery. We are by nature as certainly under sentence of death from God, as this miserable man is, by the the just determination of man; and we are all dying creatures, this is the dreadful fruit of sin. O! let us then fly from all appearance of sin; let us fight against it with all our might; let us repent and turn to God, and believe on the Lord Jesus Christ, that we may live forever; let us all prepare for death, for we know not how soon, nor how suddenly we may be called out of the world.

Permit me *reverend gentlemen and fathers* in Israel, to speak a few words to you, though I am well sensible that I need to be taught the first principles of the oracles of God, by the least of you. But since the providence of God has so ordered it, that I must speak here on this occasion, I beg that you would not be offended nor be angry with me.

God has raised *you* up, from among your brethren, and has qualified, and authorised you to do his great work; and *you* are the servants of the Most High God, and ministers of the Lord Jesus, the Son of the living God: *you* are Christ's ambassadors; *you* are called Shepherds, watchmen, overseers, or bishops, and *you* are rulers of the temples of God, or of the assemblies of God's people; *you* are God's angels, and as such you have nothing to do but to wait upon God, and to do the work the Lord Jesus Christ your blessed Lord and Master has set you about, not fearing the face of any man, nor seeking to please men, but your Master. * * * But what need I speak any

---

4. The patriarchs of the Hebrew Bible.

more? Let us *all* attend, and hear the great Apostle of the Gentiles speaking unto us in Eph[esians] vi from the 10th verse and onward. "Finally, my brethren, be strong in the Lord, and in the power of his might; put on the whole armour of God, that ye may be able to stand against the wiles of the devil. For we wrestle not against flesh and blood, but against principalities, against powers, against the rulers of the darkness of this world, against spiritual wickedness in high places. Wherefore take unto you the whole armour of God, that ye may be able to stand in the evil day, and having done all to stand. Stand therefore, having your loins girt about with truth, and having on the breast-plate of righteousness; and your feet shod with the preparation of the gospel of peace: above all, taking the shield of faith, wherewith ye shall be able to quench all the fiery darts of the wicked; and take the helmet of salvation, and the sword of the spirit, which is the word of God; praying always with all prayer and supplication in the spirit, and watching thereunto with all perseverance, and supplication for all saints."

I shall now address myself to the *Indians*, my brethren and kindred according to the flesh.

MY POOR KINDRED,

You see the woful consequences of sin, by seeing this our poor miserable country-man now before us, who is to die this day for his sins and great wickedness. And it was the sin of drunkenness that has brought this destruction and untimely death upon him. There is a dreadful woe denounced from the Almighty against drunkards; and it is this sin, this abominable, this beastly and accursed sin of drunkenness, that has stript us of every desirable comfort in this life; by this we are poor, miserable and wretched; by this sin we have no name nor credit in the world among polite nations; for this sin we are despised in the world, and it is all right and just, for we despise ourselves more; and if we do not regard ourselves, who will regard us? And it is for our sins, and especially for that accursed, that most hateful sin of drunkenness that we suffer every day. For the love of strong drink we spend all that we have, and every thing we can get. By this sin we cannot have comfortable houses, nor any thing comfortable in our houses; neither food nor raiment, nor decent utensils. We are obliged to put up any sort of shelter just to screen us from the severity of the weather; and we go about with very mean,[5] ragged and dirty clothes, almost naked. And we are half starved, for most of the time obliged to pick up any thing to eat.—And our poor children are suffering every day for want[6] of the necessaries of life; they are very often crying for want of food, and we have nothing to give them; and in the cold weather they are shivering and crying, being pinched with the cold——All this is for the love of strong drink. And this is not all the misery and evil we bring on ourselves in this world; but when we are intoxicated with strong drink, we drown our rational powers, by which we are distinguished from the brutal creation; we unman ourselves, and bring ourselves not only level with the beasts of the field, but seven degrees beneath them; yea we bring ourselves level with the devils; I do not know but we make ourselves worse than the devils, for I never heard of drunken devils.

My poor kindred, do consider what a dreadful abominable sin drunkenness is. God made us men, and we choose to be beasts and devils; God made

5. Poor, shabby.   6. Lack.

us rational creatures, and we chuse to be fools. Do consider further, and behold a drunkard, and see how he looks, when he has drowned his reason; how deformed and shameful does he appear? He disfigures every part of him, both soul and body, which was made after the image of God. He appears with awful deformity, and his whole visage is disfigured; if he attempts to speak he cannot bring out his words distinct, so as to be understood; if he walks he reels and staggers to and fro, and tumbles down. And see how he behaves, he is now laughing, and then he is crying; he is singing, and the next minute he is mourning; and is all love to every one, and anon he is raging, and for fighting, and killing all before him, even the nearest and the dearest relations and friends: Yea nothing is too bad for a drunken man to do. He will do that which he would not do for the world, in his right mind.

Further, when a person is drunk, he is just good for nothing in the world; he is of no service to himself, to his family, to his neighbours, or his country; and how much more unfit is he to serve God: yet he is just as fit for the service of the devil.

Again, a man in drukenness is in all manner of dangers, he may be killed by his fellow-men, by wild beasts, and tame beasts; he may fall into the fire, into the water, or into a ditch; or he may fall down as he walks along, and break his bones or his neck; he may cut himself with edge tools.—Further, if he has any money or any thing valuable, he may lose it all, or may be robbed, or he may make a foolish bargain, and be cheated out of all he has.

I believe you know the truth of what I have just now said, many of you, by sad experience; yet you will go on still in your drunkenness. Though you have been cheated over and over again, and you have lost your substance by drunkenness, yet you will venture to go on in this most destructive sin. O fools when will ye be wise?—We all know the truth of what I have been saying, by what we have seen and heard of drunken deaths. How many have been drowned in our rivers, and how many have been frozen to death in the winter seasons! yet drunkards go on without fear and consideration: alas, alas! What will become of all such drunkards? Without doubt they must all go to hell, except they truly repent and turn to God. Drunkenness is so common amongst us, that even our young men and young women are not ashamed to get drunk. Our young men will get drunk as soon as they will eat when they are hungry—It is generally esteemed amongst men, more abominable for a woman to be drunk, than a man; and yet there is nothing more common amongst us than female drunkards. Women ought to be more modest than men; the holy scriptures recommend modesty to women in particular:—but drunken women have no modesty at all. It is more intolerable for a woman to get drunk, if, we consider further, that she is in great danger of falling into the hands of the sons of Belial,[7] or wicked men, and being shamefully treated by them.

And here I cannot but observe, we find in sacred writ, a woe denounced against men, who put their bottles to their neighbours' mouth to make them drunk, that they may see their nakedness;[8] and no doubt there are such devilish men now in our day, as there were in the days of old.

7. A name in the Hebrew Bible that later became identified with the devil.
8. See Genesis 9.22, where Ham sees the nakedness of his father, Noah. In some accounts, this led to the curse of Ham, which was said to explain the enslavement of Africans.

And to conclude, consider my poor kindred, you that are drunkards, into what a miserable condition you have brought yourselves. There is a dreadful woe thundering against you every day, and the Lord says, that drunkards shall not inherit the kingdom of God.

And now let me exhort you all to break off from your drunkenness, by a gospel repentance, and believe on the Lord Jesus and you shall be saved. Take warning by this doleful sight before us, and by all the dreadful judgments that have befallen poor drunkards. O let us all reform our lives, and live as becomes dying creatures, in time to come. Let us be persuaded that we are accountable creatures to God, and we must be called to an account in a few days. You that have been careless all your days, now awake to righteousness, and be concerned for your poor and never dying souls. Fight against all sins, and especially the sin that easily besets you, and behave in time to come as becomes rational creatures; and above all things, receive and believe on the Lord Jesus Christ, and you shall have eternal life; and when you come to die, your souls will be received into heaven, there to be with the Lord Jesus in eternal happiness, and with all the saints in glory; which God of his infinite mercy grant, through Jesus Christ our Lord. Amen.

September 2, 1772   1788

Hymns[1]

The Sufferings of Christ, or Throughout the Saviour's Life We Trace

Throughout the Saviour's Life we trace,
Nothing but Shame and deep Disgrace,
No period else is seen;
Till he a spotless Victim fell,
Tasting in Soul a painful Hell,   5
Caus'd by the Creature's Sin.
On the cold Ground methinks I see
My Jesus kneel, and pray for me;
For this I him adore;
Siez'd with a chilly sweat throughout,   10
Blood-drops did force their Passage out
Through ev'ry open'd Pore.
A pricking Thorn his Temples bore;
His Back with Lashes all was tore,
Till one the Bones might see;   15
Mocking, they push'd him here and there,
Marking his Way with Blood and Tear,

---

1. The texts are from Samson Occom, *A Choice Collection of Hymns and Spiritual Songs* (1774), as reprinted in *The Collected Writings of Samson Occom, Mohegan* (2006), edited by Joanna Brooks.

Press'd by the heavy Tree.[2]
Thus up the Hill he painful came,
Round him they mock, and make their Game,   20
At length his Cross they rear;
And can you see the mighty God,
Cry out beneath sin's heavy Load,
Without one thankful Tear?
Thus vailed in Humanity,   25
He dies in Anguish on the Tree;
What Tongue his Grief can tell?
The shudd'ring Rocks their Heads recline,
The mourning Sun refuse to shine,
When the Creator fell.[3]   30
Shout, Brethren, shout in songs divine,
He drank the Gall to give us Wine,[4]
To quench our parching Thirst;
Seraphs advance your Voices higher;
Bride of the Lamb,[5] unite the Choir,   35
And Laud thy precious Christ.

A Morning Hymn, or Now the Shades
of Night Are Gone

Now the shades of night are gone,
Now the morning light is come:
Lord, we would be thine to-day,
Drive the shades of sin away.
Make our souls as noon-day clear,   5
Banish every doubt and fear;
In thy vineyard, Lord, to-day
We would labor, we would pray.
Keep our haughty passions bound,
Rising up and sitting down,   10
Going out and coming in,[6]
Keep us safe from every sin.
When our work of life is past,
O receive us then at last;
Labor then will all be o'er,   15
Night of sin will be no more.

2. I.e., the cross that Jesus carried to the site of his Crucifixion.
3. During the three-hour period called the Crucifixion darkness, the sun disappeared as Jesus died on the cross.
4. According to the New Testament accounts of the Crucifixion, Jesus was offered unappetizing beverages while on the cross. E.g., in Matthew

27.34, he is offered a cup of gall (bile) mixed with vinegar (also translated as wine). However, John 2.1–11 describes the first miracle attributed to Jesus, earlier in his life: turning water into wine. Here, he performs a similar miracle.
5. Bride of Christ. The phrase is variously interpreted.
6. Cf. Psalm 121.8.

A Son's Farewell, or I Hear the Gospel's
Joyful Sound

I hear the gospel's joyful sound,
    An organ I shall be,
For to sound forth redeeming love,
    And sinner's misery.
Honor'd parents fare you well,   5
    My Jesus doth me call,
I leave you here with God until
    I meet you once for all.
My due affections I'll forsake,
    My parents and their house,   10
And to the wilderness betake,
    To pay the Lord my vows.
Then I'll forsake my chiefest mates,
    That nature could afford,
And wear the shield into the field,   15
    To wait upon the Lord.
Then thro' the wilderness I'll run,
    Preaching the gospel free;
O be not anxious for your son,
    The Lord will comfort me.   20
And if thro' preaching I shall gain
    True subjects to my Lord,
'Twill more than recompence my pain,
    To see them love the Lord.
My soul doth wish mount Zion[7] well,   25
    Whate'er becomes of me;
There my best friends and kindred dwell,
    And there I long to be.

---

7. Mount Zion is a hill in Jerusalem; by extension, it means Israel, the chosen people: here, the elect, or the faithful.

Ethnographic and Naturalist Writings

Broadly defined, the genre of literary ethnography is the written description of peoples, cultures, and societies. In this sense, literary ethnography involves a wide variety of styles and can be adapted to many different purposes. Descriptions of nature—naturalist writings, or natural histories as they are sometimes called—have a similarly multivalent character. Virtually all of the earliest "American" literature offers instances of ethnographic and naturalist writing, as the sustained European encounter with the Americas that began in 1492 provided writers with a treasure trove of new material. Descriptions of the land, its peoples, and its natural resources are central to narratives of contact and exploration, and they dominate promotional writings designed to encourage investment and colonization. Often enthusiastic in tone, such works typically describe marvels that can at first be puzzling, perhaps even a bit threatening, but are ultimately enticing.

A second register in these narratives, one that became more pronounced over time, involved a religiously inflected language of wonders and portents, sometimes associated with demonic influence. Drawing on folk beliefs as well as Christian traditions, works such as Cotton Mather's *Wonders of the Invisible World* (excerpted earlier in this volume) recorded observations in a quasi-scientific language influenced by the rise of empiricism—that is, the theory that all knowledge derives from sense experience—but they applied that language to events, or objects, that were not empirically observable in any direct way. Popular works in this vein appeared in early newspapers, almanacs, and broadsides, where occurrences such as earthquakes or the birth of misshapen fetuses ("monsters") were sometimes presented as curiosities but at other times interpreted as evidence of divine displeasure.

The eighteenth-century writings included in this cluster are distinguished from these earlier works by a deepening empiricism and a complexly self-reflective tone that is often manifested through humor. The empiricism and the humor align these works with English novels such as Daniel Defoe's *Robinson Crusoe* (1719) and Henry Fielding's *Joseph Andrews* (1742). Novelistic elements are especially prominent in the selection here by Sarah Kemble Knight. Her travel narrative, paying substantial attention to the communities and landscapes she encountered on her journey, offers a rich instance of an author seeking new ways to understand cultures and natural environments.

The final two selections have different emphases. William Bartram's charming "Anecdotes of a Crow" invites reflection on enduring questions about human and animal behavior. An instance of the popular naturalist essay, "Anecdotes of a Crow" shows the same interest in environment and social context that animates works such as J. Hector St. John de Crévecoeur's *Letters from an American Farmer* (1782), excerpted after this cluster. In "History of the Muh-he-con-nuk Indians," the Mahican writer Hendrick Aupaumut provides an insider's view of tribal traditions. Aupaumut's history signals the growing role of Native authors in representing indigenous communities.

SARAH KEMBLE KNIGHT

The Bostonian Sarah Kemble Knight (1666–1727) was a woman of many talents. She kept a boardinghouse and taught school (thus she was sometimes called Madam Knight) and supposedly numbered Benjamin Franklin and members of the Mather family among her pupils. She also taught penmanship, made copies of court records, and wrote letters for people having business with the courts. She educated herself about the law and had a reputation for skillfully settling estates. Such engagement in public affairs was not unusual; in the early eighteenth century, many women played significant economic roles.

While her husband was abroad in 1704, Knight settled her cousin Caleb Trowbridge's estate on behalf of his widow. To do so, she traveled to New Haven, Connecticut, on Monday, October 2, 1704. From there, she went to New York, and she returned home to Boston in March 1705. The journey was hazardous, not undertaken lightly in those years, and unusual for a woman traveling alone.

Like numerous classics of early American literature, *The Private Journal of a Journey from Boston to New York in the Year 1704* that Knight kept was not published until the nineteenth century, when it was transcribed from shorthand and edited by Theodore Dwight. It provides a striking contrast to the soul-searching journals of Knight's Puritan contemporaries, having more of a Yankee flavor. Her literary allusions and passages of poetry remind us that early Americans absorbed transatlantic literary models to express the most common and intimate details of their lives. A keen ethnographic observer of provincial America, Knight was a sharply humorous commentator on its sometimes crude or ridiculous features. Her journal depicts everyday life in the northeastern colonies at the turn of the eighteenth century, while revealing that its author shared some of her society's most troubling prejudices.

From The Private Journal of a Journey from Boston to New York in the Year 1704[1]

Saturday, October the Seventh

We set out early in the morning and being something unacquainted with the way, having asked it of some we met, they told us we must ride a mile or two and turn down a lane on the right hand, and by their direction we rode on but not yet coming to the turning, we met a young fellow and asked him how far it was to the lane which turned down towards Guilford.[2] He said we must ride a little further and turn down by the corner of Uncle Sam's lot. My guide vented his spleen at the lubber,[3] and we soon after came into the road, and keeping still on, without anything further remarkable, about two o'clock afternoon we arrived at New Haven, where I was received with all possible respects and civility. Here I discharged Mr. Wheeler with a reward

---

1. The text is from *The Journal of Madame Knight* (1920), edited by George P. Winship.

2. Town in Connecticut.
3. Clumsy fellow.

to his satisfaction, and took some time to rest after so long and toilsome a journey, and informed myself of the manners and customs of the place and at the same time employed myself in the affair I went there upon.

They are governed by the same laws as we in Boston (or little differing) throughout this whole colony of Connecticut, and much the same way of church government, and many of them good, sociable people, and I hope religious too. But a little too much independent in their principles, and, as I have been told, were formerly in their zeal very rigid in their administrations towards such as their laws made offenders, even to a harmless kiss or innocent merriment among young people, whipping being a frequent and counted an easy punishment, about which as other crimes, the judges were absolute in their sentences. They told me a pleasant story about a pair of justices in those parts, which I may not omit the relation of.

A negro slave belonging to a man in the town stole a hogshead[4] from his master and gave or sold it to an Indian, native of the place. The Indian sold it in the neighborhood, and so the theft was found out. Thereupon the heathen[5] was seized and carried to the justice's house to be examined. But his Worship (it seems) was gone into the field, with a brother in office to gather in his pompions.[6] Whither the malefactor is hurried, and complaint made and satisfaction in the name of justice demanded. Their Worships can't proceed in form without a bench: whereupon they order one to be immediately erected, which, for want of fitter materials, they made with pompions—which being finished, down sets their Worships, and the malefactor called and by the senior Justice interrogated after the following manner: You, Indian, why did you steal from this man? You shouldn't do so—it's a grandy wicked thing to steal. "Hol't, hol't," cries Justice junior. "Brother, you speak negro to him. I'll ask him." "You, sirrah, why did you steal this man's hogshead?" "Hogshead?" (replies the Indian), "Me no stomany."[7] "No?" says his Worship, and pulling off his hat, patted his own head with his hand, says, "Tatapa[8]you, Tatapa—you; all one this. Hogshead all one this." "Hah!" says Netop, "Now me stomany that." Whereupon the company fell into a great fit of laughter, even to roaring. Silence is commanded, but to no effect: for they continued perfectly shouting. "Nay," says his Worship in an angry tone, "If it be so, *take me off the bench.*"

Their diversions in this part of the country are on lecture days and training days[9] mostly: on the former there is riding from town to town.

And on training days the youth divert themselves by shooting at the target, as they call it (but it very much resembles a pillory[1]), where he that hits nearest the white has some yards of red ribbon presented him which being tied to his hatband, the two ends streaming down his back, he is led away in triumph with great applause as the winners of the Olympiack games. They generally marry very young: the males oftener, as I am told, under twenty than above. They generally make public weddings and have a way something

4. A large barrel or cask.
5. I.e., the Indian.
6. Pumpkins.
7. I.e., understand.
8. Equal to, the same as. The joke plays on the justice's head being the same as the head of a hog (a hog's head).

9. Days set aside for military exercises. "Lecture days": days when a less formal sermon was offered than the one prepared for Sundays.
1. A wooden frame on a post, with holes for the head and arms, used as public punishment for offenders.

singular (as they say) in some of them, *viz.* just before joining hands the bridegroom quits the place, who is soon followed by the bridesmen and, as it were, dragged back to duty—being the reverse to the former practice among us, to steel[2] man's pride.

There are great plenty of oysters all along by the seaside as far as I rode in the colony and those very good. And they generally lived very well and comfortably in their families. But too indulgent (especially the farmers) to their slaves, suffering too great familiarity from them, permitting them to sit at table and eat with them (as they say, to save time), and into the dish goes the black hoof as freely as the white hand. They told me that there was a farmer lived near the town where I lodged who had some difference with his slave concerning something the master had promised him and did not punctually perform, which caused some hard words between them. But at length they put the matter to arbitration and bound themselves to stand to the award of such as they named—which done, the arbitrators having heard the allegations of both parties, order the master to pay 40[3] to black face and acknowledge his fault. And so the matter ended, the poor master very honestly standing to[4] the award.

There are everywhere in the towns as I passed a number of Indians the natives of the country, and are the most savage[5] of all the savages of that kind that I had ever seen: little or no care taken (as I heard upon inquiry) to make them otherwise. They have in some places lands of their own, and governed by laws of their own making;—they marry many wives and at pleasure put them away, and on the least dislike or fickle humor, on either side. Saying *"stand away"* to one another is a sufficient divorce. And, indeed, those uncomely *"stand aways"* are too much in vogue among the English in this (indulgent colony) as their records plentifully prove, and that on very trivial matters, of which some have been told me, but are not proper to be related by a female pen, though some of that foolish sex have had too large a share in the story.

If the natives commit any crime on their own precincts among themselves the English takes no cognezens[6] of. But if on the English ground they are punishable by our laws. They mourn for their dead by blacking their faces and cutting their hair after an awkerd and frightful manner, but can't bear you should mention the names of their dead relations to them. They trade most for rum, for which they would hazard their very lives, and the English fit[7] them generally as well by seasoning it plentifully with water.

They give the title of merchant to every trader who rate their goods according to the time and spetia[8] they pay in: *viz.* pay, money, pay as money, and trusting. *Pay* is grain, pork, beef, &c. at the prices set by the General Court that year; *money* is pieces of eight, rials, or Boston or Bay shillings[9] (as they call them,) or good hard money, as sometimes silver coin is termed by them; also wampum, *viz.* Indian beads which serves for change. *Pay as money* is provisions, as aforesaid, one third cheaper than as the Assembly or General Court sets it, and *trust* as they and the merchant agree for time.

---

2. Fortify against.
3. Shillings, or two English pounds.
4. I.e., paying.
5. Unchristian.
6. Cognizance; recognition.
7. Fix; cheat.

8. Specie; actual coin or money. "Rate": calculate the price of.
9. Coin minted in the Massachusetts Bay Colony. "Pieces of eight": Spanish silver coins. "Rials": former English gold coins worth ten shillings.

Now, when the buyer comes to ask for a commodity, sometimes before the merchant answers that he has it, he says, *"Is your pay ready?"* Perhaps the chap replies "Yes." "What do you pay in?" says the merchant. The buyer having answered, then the price is set; as suppose he wants a sixpenny knife, in pay it is 12d[1]—in pay as money eight pence, and hard money its own price, *viz. 6d.* It seems a very intricate way of trade and what *Lex Mercatoria*[2] had not thought of.

Being at a merchant's house, in comes a tall country fellow, with his alfo-geos[3] full of tobacco; for they seldom lose their cud, but keep chewing and spitting as long as their eyes are open. He advanced to the middle of the room, makes an awkward nod, and spitting a large deal of aromatic tincture, he gave a scrape with his shovel-like shoe, leaving a small shovel full of dirt on the floor, made a full stop, hugging his own pretty body with his hands under his arms, stood staring round him like a cat let out of a basket. At last, like the creature Balaam rode on,[4] he opened his mouth and said: "Have you any ribinen for hatbands to sell, I pray?" The questions and answers about the pay being passed, the ribin is brought and opened. Bumpkin simpers, cries "It's confounded gay[5] I vow"; and beckning to the door, in comes Joan Tawdry,[6] dropping about 50 curtsies, and stands by him. He shows her the ribin. *"Law, you,"* says she, *"it's right gent,* do you take it, *tis dreadful[7] pretty."* Then she inquires *"Have you any hood silk[8] I pray?"* which being brought and bought, "Have you any *thread silk to sew it with?"* says she, which being accommodated with they departed. They generally stand after they come in a great while speechless, and sometimes don't say a word till they are asked what they want, which I impute to the awe they stand in of the merchants, who they are constantly almost indebted to, and must take what they bring without liberty to choose for themselves. But they serve them as well,[9] making the merchants stay long enough for their pay.

We may observe here the great necessity and benefit both of education and conversation; for these people have as large a portion of mother wit,[1] and sometimes a larger, than those who have been brought up in cities, but for want of improvements render themselves almost ridiculous, as above. I should be glad if they would leave such follies and am sure all that love clean houses (at least) would be glad on't too.[2]

They are generally very plain in their dress, throughout all the colony, as I saw, and follow one another in their modes, that you may know where they belong, especially the women, meet them where you will.

Their chief red-letter day is St. Election,[3] which is annually observed according to charter, to choose their government, a blessing they can never be thankful enough for, as they will find if ever it be their hard fortune to lose it. The present governor in Connecticut is the Honorable John Winthrop,

1. Twelve pence; "d" is from *denarius*, an ancient Roman coin.
2. The law of merchants (Latin).
3. Cheeks like saddlebags (from the Spanish *alforjas*: pouches).
4. I.e., talking, like the ass ridden by the Old Testament prophet Balaam (Numbers 22).
5. Vibrant; brilliant in color.
6. Slang for lower-class woman.
7. Extremely. "Gent": genteel, stylish. "Law": Lord.

8. Silk cloth suitable for a hood.
9. I.e., treat them equally badly.
1. Of native intelligence.
2. Knight criticizes country people for desiring luxuries and for chewing tobacco, which they spit in the house of the merchant where they go to purchase ribbons and such.
3. I.e., Election Day, which Knight mockingly suggests they treat as a sacred holiday.

A View of Fort George with the City of New York from the S.W. An engraving of New York from the southwest, showing the skyline (primarily church steeples) as it might have appeared to Sarah Kemble Knight in the early eighteenth century.

Esq.[4] A gentleman of an ancient and honorable family whose father was governor here sometime before, and his grandfather had been governor of the Massachusetts.[5] This gentleman is a very courteous and affable person, much given to hospitality, and has by his good services gained the affection of the people as much as any who had been before him in that post.

From *December the Sixth*

* * *

The city of New York is a pleasant, well-compacted place, situated on a commodious river which is a fine harbor for shipping. The buildings brick generally, very stately and high, though not altogether like ours in Boston. The bricks in some of the houses are of divers colors and laid in checkers,[6] being glazed look very agreeable. The inside of them are neat to admiration, the wooden work, for only the walls are plastered, and the sumers and gist[7] are planed and kept very white scowered as so is all the partitions if made of boards. The fireplaces have no jambs (as ours have) but the backs run flush with the walls, and the hearth is of tiles and is as far out into the room at the ends as before the fire, which is generally five foot in the lower rooms, and the piece over where the mantle tree should be is made as ours with joiners' work,[8] and as I suppose is fastened to iron rods inside. The house

4. Fitz-John Winthrop (1638–1707), governor of Connecticut 1698–1707.
5. John Winthrop (1606–1676), father of Fitz-John, governor of Connecticut 1659–76. John Winthrop (1588–1649), grandfather of Fitz-John, founding governor of Massachusetts Bay.
6. I.e., alternating. "Divers": various.
7. The main beams and joists.
8. Joiners were craftsmen who constructed things by joining pieces of wood together. Their work was more finished than a carpenter's. "Mantle tree": a wood beam over the opening of a fireplace.

where the vendue[9] was, had chimney corners like ours, and they and the hearths were laid with the finest tile that I ever see, and the staircases laid all with white tile which is ever clean, and so are the walls of the kitchen which had a brick floor. They were making great preparations to receive their governor, Lord Cornbury from the Jerseys,[1] and for that end raised the militia to guard him on shore to the fort.

They are generally of the Church of England and have a New England gentleman for their minister, and a very fine church set out with all customary requisites. There are also a Dutch and divers conventicles as they call them, *viz.* Baptist, Quakers, etc. They are not strict in keeping the Sabbath as in Boston and other places where I had been, but seem to deal with great exactness as far as I see or deal with. They are sociable to one another and courteous and civil to strangers and fare well in their houses. The English go very fashionable in their dress. But the Dutch, especially the middling sort, differ from our women, in their habit go loose,[2] wear French muchets which are like a cap and a headband in one, leaving their ears bare, which are set out with jewels of a large size and many in number. And their fingers hooped with rings, some with large stones in them of many colors as were their pendants in their ears, which you should see very old women wear as well as young.

They have vendues very frequently and make their earnings very well by them, for they treat with good liquor liberally, and the customers drink as liberally and generally pay for't as well, by paying for that which they bid up briskly for, after the sack[3] has gone plentifully about, though sometimes good penny worths' are got there. Their diversions in the winter is riding sleighs about three or four miles out of town, where they have houses of entertainment at a place called the Bowery,[4] and some go to friends' houses who handsomely treat them. Mr. Burroughs carried his spouse and daughter and myself out to one Madame Dowes, a gentlewoman that lived at a farm house, who gave us a handsome entertainment of five or six dishes and choice beer and metheglin,[5] cider, etc. all which she said was the produce of her farm. I believe we met 50 or 60 sleighs that day—they fly with great swiftness and some are so furious that they'll turn out of the path for none except a loaden cart. Nor do they spare for any diversion the place affords, and sociable to a degree, their tables being as free to their neighbors as to themselves.

Having here transacted the affair I went upon and some other that fell in the way, after about a fortnight's stay there I left New York with no little regret[.] * * *

1704   1825

9. Auction.
1. Edward Hyde (1661–1723), Viscount Cornbury, governor of New York and New Jersey 1701–08.
2. Are more casual in appearance. "Middling": middle class.

3. Wine; specifically, white wine imported from Spain or the Canaries.
4. Now a street in lower Manhattan.
5. A spiced variety of fermented beverage. The cider offered was probably also alcoholic.

WILLIAM BARTRAM

The son of the internationally famous botanist John Bartram, William Bartram (1739–1823) became an important naturalist in his own right. During his early years in Philadelphia, William accompanied his father on expeditions in the eastern American colonies to collect plants and served as an illustrator for his father's writings. He participated in the far-flung intellectual networks that included the local luminary Benjamin Franklin and the Swedish naturalist Carl von Linné, more familiarly known as Linnaeus, who developed the organism-naming system still used by biologists. For three years, Bartram attended the Philadelphia Academy (later the University of Pennsylvania). He then moved to the Cape Fear region of North Carolina to live with his uncle.

After France ceded Florida to England in 1765, Bartram traveled extensively in the southeastern United States, at first with his father and later on his own. In 1777, John Bartram died, leaving his botanical garden to William's brother, and William returned to Philadelphia to assist with its management. Among the Bartrams' most prominent customers were the United States presidents George Washington and Thomas Jefferson and the writer J. Hector St. John de Crèvecoeur.

William Bartram's most famous literary work derived from his journeys in the southeast. He published *Travels through North and South Carolina, East and West Florida, the Cherokee Country, the Extensive Territories of the Muscolgulges, or Creek Confederacy, and the Country of the Chactaws* in 1791. This account influenced numerous writers, including the eighteenth-century British Romantic poets Samuel Taylor Coleridge and William Wordsworth. In later years, Bartram continued to be active in naturalist circles and published several essays, including the following selection.

Anecdotes of an American Crow[1]

It is a difficult task to give a history of our Crow. And I hesitate not to aver, that it would require the pen of a very able biographer to do justice to his talents.

Before I enter on this subject minutely, it may be necessary to remark, that we do not here speak of the crow, collectively, as giving an account of the whole race[2] (since I am convinced, that these birds differ as widely as men do from each other, in point of talents and acquirements), but of a particular bird of that species, which I reared from the nest.

He was, for a long time, comparatively a helpless, dependent creature, having a very small degree of activity or vivacity, every sense seeming to be asleep, or in embryo, until he had nearly attained his finished dimensions, and figure, and the use of all his members. Then, we were surprised, and daily amused with the progressive developement of his senses, expanding and maturating as the wings of the youthful phalæna,[3] when disengaged from its nympha-shell.

These senses, however, seemed, as in man, to be only the organs or instruments of his intellectual powers, and of their effects, as directed towards the accomplishment of various designs, and the gratification of the passions.

1. The text is from *The Philadelphia Medical and Physical Journal*, Part 1, Vol. 1 (1804).
2. In the biological sense of a distinct population within a species.
3. Linnaeus's now obsolete term for most moths.

This was a bird of a happy temper, and good disposition. He was tractable and benevolent, docile and humble, whilst his genius demonstrated extraordinary acuteness, and lively sensations. All these good qualities were greatly in his favour, for they procured him friends and patrons, even among *men*, whose society and regard contributed to illustrate the powers of his understanding. But what appeared most extraordinary, he seemed to have the wit to select and treasure up in his mind, and the sagacity to practise, that kind of knowledge which procured him the most advantage and profit.

He had great talents, and a strong propensity to imitation. When I was engaged in weeding in the garden, he would often fly to me, and, after very attentively observing me in pulling up the small weeds and grass, he would fall to work, and with his strong beak, pluck up the grass; and the more so, when I complimented him with encouraging expressions. He enjoyed great pleasure and amusement in seeing me write, and would attempt to take the pen out of my hand, and my spectacles from my nose. The latter article he was so pleased with, that I found it necessary to put them out of his reach, when I had done using them. But, one time, in particular, having left them a moment, the crow being then out of my sight, recollecting the bird's mischievous tricks, I returned quickly, and found him upon the table, rifling my inkstand, books, and paper. When he saw me coming, he took up my spectacles, and flew off with them. I found it vain[4] to pretend to overtake him; but standing to observe his operations with my spectacles, I saw him settle down at the root of an apple-tree, where, after amusing himself, for awhile, I observed, that he was hiding them in the grass, and covering them with chips and sticks, often looking round about, to see whether I was watching him. When he thought he had sufficiently secreted them, he turned about, advancing towards me, at my call. When he had come near me, I ran towards the tree, to regain my property. But he, judging of my intentions, by my actions, flew, and arriving there before me, picked them up again, and flew off with them, into another apple-tree. I now almost despaired of ever getting them again. However, I returned back to a house, a little distance off, and there secreting myself, I had a full view of him, and waited to see the event. After some time had elapsed, during which I heard a great noise and talk from him, of which I understood not a word, he left the tree, with my spectacles dangling in his mouth, and alighted, with them, on the ground. After some time, and a great deal of caution and contrivance in choosing and rejecting different places, he hid them again, as he thought very effectually, in the grass, carrying and placing over them chips, dry leaves, &c., and often pushing them down with his bill. After he had finished this work, he flew up into a tree, hard by, and there continued a long time, talking to himself, and making much noise; bragging, as I supposed, of his achievements. At last, he returned to the house, where not finding me, he betook himself to other amusements. Having noted the place, where he had hid my spectacles, I hastened thither, and after some time recovered them.

This bird had an excellent memory. He soon learned the name which we had given him, which was Tom; and would commonly come when he was called, unless engaged in some favourite amusement, or soon after correction: for when he had run to great lengths in mischief, I was under the

4. Useless.

Timber rattler. William Bartram was a talented nature painter as well as being a naturalist writer. He encountered this timber rattler in the backwoods of colonial New Jersey.

Snapping turtle. Bartram produced this painting, which he titled "The great Mud Tortoise from Pennsylvania—called the snap[p]ing Turtle," around 1760.

necessity of whipping him; which I did with a little switch. He would, in general, bear correction with wonderful patience and humility, supplicating with piteous and penitent cries and actions. But sometimes, when chastisement became intolerable, he would suddenly start off, and take refuge in the next tree. Here he would console himself with chattering, and adjusting his feathers, if he was not lucky enough to carry off with him some of my property, such as a pen-knife, or a piece of paper; in this case, he would boast and brag very loudly. At other times, he would soon return, and with every token of penitence and submission, approach me for forgiveness and reconciliation. On these occasions, he would sometimes return, and settle on the ground, near my feet, and diffidently advance, with soft-soothing expressions, and a sort of circumlocution; and sit silently by me, for a considerable time. At other times, he would confidently come and settle upon my shoulder, and there solicit my favour and pardon, with soothing expressions, and caressing gesticulations; not omitting to tickle me about the neck, ears, &c.

Tom appeared to be influenced by a lively sense of domination (an attribute prevalent in the animal creation): but, nevertheless, his ambition, in this respect, seemed to be moderated by a degree of reason, or reflection. He was, certainly, by no means tyrannical, or cruel. It must be confessed, however, that he aimed to be master of every animal around him, in order to secure his independence and his self-preservation, and for the acquisition and defence of his natural rights. Yet, in general, he was peaceable and social with all the animals about him.

He was the most troublesome and teazing to a large dog, whom he could never conquer. This old dog, from natural fidelity, and a particular attachment, commonly lay down near me, when I was at rest, reading or writing under the shade of a pear-tree, in the garden, near the house. Tom (I believe from a passion of jealousy) would approach me, with his usual caresses, and flattery, and after securing my notice and regard, he would address the dog in some degree of complaisance, and by words and actions; and, if he could obtain access to him, would tickle him with his bill, jump upon him, and compose himself, for a little while. It was evident, however, that this seeming sociability was mere artifice to gain an opportunity to practise some mischievous trick; for no sooner did he observe the old dog to be dozing, than he would be sure to pinch his lips, and pluck his beard. At length, however, these bold and hazardous achievements had nearly cost him his life: for, one time, the dog being highly provoked, he made so sudden and fierce a snap, that the crow narrowly escaped with his head. After this, Tom was wary, and used every caution and deliberation in his approaches, examining the dog's eyes and movements, to be sure that he was really asleep, and at last would not venture nearer than his tail, and then by slow, silent, and wary steps, in a sideways, or oblique manner, spreading his legs, and reaching forward. In this position, he would pluck the long hairs of the dog's tail. But he would always take care to place his feet in such a manner as to be ready to start off, when the dog was roused and snapped at him.

1804

HENDRICK AUPAUMUT

Hendrick Aupaumut (1757–1830) produced one of the first ethnographies of a Native community written by an indigenous author: his "History of the Muh-he-con-nuk [Mahican] Indians" (1791). The path that led him to this project suggests many of the complexities facing Native American intellectuals in the eighteenth century.

Born in the Native Christian town of Stockbridge, Massachusetts, Aupaumut entered a community that had recently been ministered to by the Puritan divine Jonathan Edwards. Edwards served at Stockbridge from 1751 until late 1757, long enough to have baptized Aupaumut. Schooled by a Protestant minister, possibly Edwards's son Timothy, Aupaumut learned to speak, read, and write in English. In 1775 he wrote to Timothy Edwards, asking to borrow copies of some of his father's works, including the treatise on the freedom of the will that Edwards had written at Stockbridge.

When the Revolutionary War broke out, Aupaumut joined the Continental Army, forming a company along with other Stockbridge Indians. He earned a reputation as a good soldier, was commissioned as a captain, and saw extensive service, winning a commendation from George Washington, then the commanding general of the Continental Army. In the mid-1780s, Aupaumut led the Stockbridge community as it relocated to New Stockbridge, in central New York, where Samson Occom briefly joined him.

During the early 1790s, Aupaumut served as an emissary from President George Washington's administration to a pan-Indian alliance in the Great Lakes region of the Northwest Territory. His diplomatic initiatives continued for nearly two decades and were directed at finding peaceful resolutions to conflicts between the United States and Native communities. In the 1800s, he opposed Tecumseh's efforts to create a pantribal alliance to wage frontier warfare.

Even as Aupaumut pursued negotiated settlements between the United States and Indian groups on the western frontier, he began searching for land where the residents of New Stockbridge could relocate again, in order to be relieved of the pressures of white encroachment on their New York lands. In 1829, he joined the last group of Stockbridges to remove to the Fox River in Wisconsin, which is where he died.

In addition to numerous speeches and letters published during his lifetime, Aupaumut's writings include a narrative reporting on his diplomatic initiative to the Iroquois and Northwest tribes. The following selection is from the tribal history that he wrote in 1791, probably in connection with his proposal to serve as a negotiator for the Washington administration.

From History of the Muh-he-con-nuk Indians[1]

"Our ancestors, before they ever enjoyed Gospel revelation acknowledged one Supreme Being who dwells above, whom they styled Waun-theet Mon-nit-toow, or the Great, Good Spirit, the author of all things in heaven

---

1. The text is from Electa F. Jones, *Stockbridge, Past and Present; or, Records of an Old Mission Station* (1854).

and on earth and governs all events; and he is good to all his creatures. They also believed that there is an evil one, called Mton-toow or Wicked Spirit that loves altogether to do mischief; that he excites person or persons to tell a lie—angry, fight, hate, steal, to commit murder, and to be envious, malicious, and evil-talking; also excites nations to war with one another, to violated their friendship which the Great, Good Spirit given them to maintain for their mutual good, and their children after them.

"In order to please the Great, Good Spirit which they acknowledged to be their dependence, and on the other hand to withstand the evil one—therefore, the following custom was observed, which handed down to them by their fore-fathers, and considered as communicated to them by Good Spirit.

"The Head of each family—man or woman—would began with all ten-derness as soon as daylight, to waken up their children and teach them, as follows:—

"'My Children—you must remember that it is by the goodness of the Great, Good Spirit we are preserved through the night. My Children, you must listen to my words. If you wish to see many good days and evenings you must love to all men, and be kind to all people.

"'If you see any that are in distress, you must try to help them. Remem-ber that you will also be in distress some time or other. If you see any one hungry you must give him something to eat; though you should have but little cake, give him half of it, for you also liable to hunger. If you see one naked, you must cover him with your own raiment.[2] For you must consider that some future time you will also stand in need of such help; but if you will not assist, or have compassion for the poor, you will displease the Good Spirit; you will be called Uh-wu-theet, or hard-hearted and nobody will pity on you the time of your distress, but will mock at you.

*　*　*

"'My Children—at all times you must obey your Sachem and Chiefs,[3] in all good counsels they give; never to speak evil against them, for they have taken much pains in promoting your happiness. And if you do not observe this, you will be looked upon worse than the beasts are.'

"Thus they inculcate instruction to their children day after day until they are grown up; and after they are grown, yet they would teach them occa-sionally. And when young people have children they also teach theirs in like manner.—This custom is handed down from generation to another; at the same time it may be observed that there were some that did not take no pains to instruct their children, but would set bad examples before them, as well as there are such among civilized nations. But such men were roving about, and could not be contented to stay at one place.

"Our ancestors' Government was a Democratical. They had Wi-gow-wauw, or Chief Sachem, successively, as well as other nations had, chosen by the nation, whom they looked upon as conductor and promoter of their general welfare, and rendered him obedience as long as he behaved himself agree-ably to the office of a Sachem.[4] And this office was hereditary by the lineage

2. Cf. Matthew 25.34–40. Aupaumut may have purposefully highlighted similarities between Christian and Mahican beliefs.

3. Supreme leader and subordinates.
4. I.e., the Chief Sachem serves as long as he pleases the people.

of a female's offspring, but not on man's line, but on woman's part. That is—when Wi-gow-wauw is fallen by death, one of his Nephews, (if he has any) will be appointed to succeed his Uncle as a Sachem, and not any of his sons.[5]

The Sachem always have Woh-weet-quan-pe-chee, or Counselors, and one Mo-quau-pauw, or Hero, and one Mkhooh-que-thoth, or Owl, and one Un-nuh-kau-kun, or Messenger, or Runner; and the rest of the men are called young men. (But the Six Nations[6] call young men Warriors.) The Sachem is looked upon as a great tree under whose shade the whole nation is sit. His business is to contemplate the welfare of his people day and night—how to promote their peace and happiness. He also ever take pains to maintain and brighten the belt of friendship with all their allies. When he find any business of public nature, he is to call his counselors together to consult with them; and then they will determine what is good for the Nation. The Sachem must be a peaceable man—has nothing to do with wars—but he is at times go from house to house to exhort his people to live in unity and peace.

"The Sachem has no stated salary for his services; for it was a disgrace or reproach any man to ask reward for any of his public services; but whatever he does for his nation must be done out of friendship and good will. But it was the custom to help their Sachem voluntarily in building a long We-ko-wohm, or wigwam, all complete; and the hunters, when they returned from hunting each man give him a skin. The women also at times, some give him Mkith-non, or Muk-sens, some belts for the body, others garters, and some other ornaments—as wampum[7] to be for his own use. They are also to bring victuals to Sachem's to enable him to feed strangers;—for whenever strangers arrived at their fire-place[8] they are directed to go to Sachem's house. There they stay until their business is completed.

"The Sachem is allowed to keep Mno-ti, or peaceable bag, or bag of peace, containing about one bushel, some less.—This bag is made of Weeth-kuhn-pauk, or bitter sort of hemp; grows on intervals, about three or four feet long; and sometimes made of Wau-pon-nep-pauk, or white hemp, which grows by the side of rivers, or edge of marshes,—amazing strong and lasting—of which they make strings, and die part of the strings of different colors; then worked and made into bag of different marks. In this bag they keep various Squau-tho-won, or belts of wampum; also strings; which belts and strings they used to establish peace and friendship with different nations, and to use them on many occasions, and passed as coin. In this bag they keep all belts and strings which they received of their allies of different nations. This bag is, as it were, unmoveable; but it is always remain at Sachem's house, as hereditary with the office of a Sachem; and he is to keep the Pipe of Peace, made of red hard stone—a long stem to it. Besides this bag, they keep other smaller bags which they called Ne-mau-won-neh Mno-ti, or Scrip, which contains nourishment on journey, which they carry with them when they go out to hold treaties with other fire-places.[9] In such scrips they occasionally put belts and

5. I.e., the position was passed down through the female line, to the sons of the Chief Sachems' sisters.
6. The Iroquois Confederacy, consisting of the Mohawk, Oneida, Onondaga, Cayuga, Seneca, and Tuscarora tribes. Aupaumut compares the organizational structure of Mahican political society to that of the Iroquois, at a time when they were living in proximity to one another in central New York.
7. Currency, consisting of shells beaded on string. Wampum belts were also used to symbolize diplomatic agreements, similar to treaties.
8. I.e., a central spot, similar to a town center.
9. Here, meeting places for intertribal diplomacy.

strings for transacting business abroad. When they find the wampum will be fall short, besides what is kept in the bag, the Sachem and his counselors would sent their runner to gather, or collect wampum from their women, which business they called mauw-peen, or sitting into one place.

"The office of Counselors was not gotten by hereditary, but it was elective; therefore, the wise men were only entitled the office of Counselors. They are called Chiefs. Their business is to consult with their Sachems in promoting peace and happiness for their people. They will also at all times exhort young people to every good work.

"The title of Mo-quau-pauw, or Hero, is gotten only by merit; by remarkable conduct in the wars, by great courage and prudence. The business of Heroes in time of peace is to sit with their Sachem and Counselors in all their councils, and to confirm their agreements, but never to contradict them; for which they are beloved by their Sachem and Counselors, and by all their people. But when any warfare is sounded in their ears, then they will all meet together to hold a general Council: and when they find themselves under necessity of joining to such war, then the Sachem and Counselors will put the business in the hands of Heroes, exhorting them to be courageous and prudent, to take good care of their young men. But when the offers of peace is proposed, then the Hero will put the business in the hands of the Sachem and Counselors, who will cut or break the string of the bow, and bury the Puhwi, and by certain ceremony or emblem wipe off all tears and blood, and cleanse their beds, scattered all dark clouds, that they may enjoy pleasant days again.

"The office of Owl is come by merit also; who must have strong memory, and must be good speaker, and have strong voice. He is to sit by the side of his Sachem; his business is to proclaim the orders of his Sachem to the people with loud voice. And he is also to get up every morning as soon as daylight. In the first place he is to make noise like an Owl, then shouted to wake the people, and then ordered them to their respective lawful duties for the day.

"And the business of the Runner is to carry messages, or carry tidings; and he is always ready to run. He is to give notice to the people to attend. And when they go out another town to hold council, he is to run to inform the Chiefs that live in that town that his Chiefs will arrive—such a time. And when they hold treaty with any nation he is to light his Sachem's Pipe. And he must be man of veracity: for if he tell a falsehood, his feathers will be pulled off.

"Our Nation was divided into three clans or tribes, as Bear Tribe. Wolf Tribe, and Turtle Tribe. Our ancestors had particular opinion for each tribe to which they belonged. The Bear Tribe formerly considered as the head of the other tribes, and claims the title of hereditary office of Sachem. Yet they ever united as one family.

"And at the death of Sachem they considered as though their light is put out, and sitting under dark clouds, and in the situation of mourning, until another is appointed to succeed in the office; which must be done by the consent and approbation of the whole nation. Yet no other person has right to succeed but one of the nephews of the deceased Sachem, either the eldest, or the likeliest.

"One of the wisest of their Counselors is employed on such occasions. In the first place, when all things are ready, He will address the whole Nation as follows,—

"'My friends—grand-fathers, Uncles, Brothers, Cousins, attend. You also, my women—grand-mothers, Mothers, and Sisters, listen. You, the Children—you must also hear me attentively. It is the will of the Great, Wise, Good Spirit—our great tree has been fallen to the ground, and great darkness has been spread over our fire-place these many days, whereby we become as fatherless children. According to the custom of our good ancestors, and by the help of the Great Good Spirit. I now remove all dark clouds which hangs over our fire-place. [Strings of Wampum delivered.]

"'Again listen: I now raise your heads which has been hang downwards, and wipe off all your tears from your face, so that you may see clear, and open your ears that you may hear, and set your hearts right again, that you may understand distinctly.'" [Strings of Wampum again delivered.]

This ceremony has passed so entirely out of use that the Tribe are unable to give the remainder; indeed they have not retained even thus much of this interesting document. They, however, have retained their wampum. The *meaning* of a belt is remembered by the Indian Tribes in this manner. The whole body frequently assemble, and being seated, each piece is passed from hand to hand, every person repeating the words as he takes it. Then again the color conveys some idea. A blood-colored hatchet readily gives an impression of something warlike, while white speaks of peace.[1]

1791

1. Aupaumut describes a peace-building process resembling the Iroquois Condolence Ritual, a diplomatic ritual used by the Iroquois and other Native groups.

J. HECTOR ST. JOHN DE CRÈVECOEUR
1735–1813

J. Hector St. John de Crèvecoeur is a writer with a divided reputation, as well as a mysterious and fascinating past. Like Benjamin Franklin, another master of irony and disguise, Crèvecoeur rewards the reader's close attention but only rarely provides firm conclusions about the author's views and intentions. In "What Is an American?"—the most famous essay in his internationally acclaimed *Letters from an American Farmer* (1782)—Crèvecoeur offers an idealistic portrait of the soon-to-be United States, one that resonated with later depictions of the nation as a melting pot and a land of opportunity. Farmer James, Crèvecoeur's persona in the *Letters*, is at his happiest and most hopeful here, and these qualities have sometimes been taken as his creator's entire understanding of "the American, this new man." The full text of the *Letters* tells a different story. It includes a shocking depiction of a slave suffering a brutal punishment; and it ends with Farmer James having moved his family to a frontier Indian village out of despair over the fratricidal violence unleashed by the Revolution. The complexity of Crèvecoeur's stance toward Revolutionary-era American society is greatly magnified by the uncertainties surrounding the author's ultimate commitments. The uncertainties associated with the work itself are amplified by the differences between the English and French editions.

Born Michel-Guillaume Jean de Crèvecoeur in Caen, Normandy, the son of a minor nobleman, he was educated by Jesuits. However, he came to reject Catholicism as oppressive, and perhaps for this reason he broke with his father as a teenager, sailed to England, and lived there with distant relatives. In 1755 he traveled to French Canada. He enlisted in the Canadian militia, served the government as a surveyor and cartographer, and was wounded in the defense of Quebec during one of the major battles of the French and Indian War (1754–63). After his military career ended in 1759, he traveled to New York, where he was naturalized as a British colonial subject in 1765 and changed his name to Hector St. John. Sometimes he went by James Hector St. John, a moniker suggesting that he identified with his persona Farmer James. He later expanded his surname to St. John de Crèvecoeur and added an initial. For the next ten years, Crèvecoeur traveled extensively in the colonies as a surveyor and a trader with American Indians. In 1769, he married a wealthy Protestant woman, Mehetabel Tippet; bought land in Orange County, New York; and settled into life on his farm there, Pine Hill. The couple gave their three children names that evoked Crèvecoeur's French background; a daughter was named América-Francés. In his first year at Pine Hill, Crèvecoeur began to write a series of essays about America based on his travels and experience as a farmer.

The advent of the American Revolution prompted Crèvecoeur's wish to reestablish ownership of family lands in France. Although he seems to have held Loyalist sympathies and was suspected of being a British spy, he was arrested and imprisoned as an American spy in 1779, when he tried to sail from the British-held port of New York. (Some have suspected him of being a double agent.) His delayed departure was probably related to France's recognition of the United States and entrance into the war against Britain in 1778. Crèvecoeur reached London in 1780, and the following year he sold his manuscript to a publishing house there, leading to the 1782 edition of *Letters*. There is evidence to suggest that the British edition was partially rewritten by an unknown editor to draw out its republican themes. In France, Crèvecoeur reconciled with his father, then moved to Paris. There, he was celebrated by the French intellectuals known as the philosophes, who encouraged him to publish a French translation of the *Letters*. The text that appeared in 1784 was recast more favorably toward France.

In 1783, Crèvecoeur returned to the now victorious United States. He then learned that his farm had been burned in an Indian attack, his wife was dead, and his children were housed with strangers. After regaining custody of his children and moving to New York City, Crèvecoeur was made French consul to New York, Connecticut, and New Jersey. A great success as a diplomat, he was named an honorary citizen of several American cities; the town of St. Johnsbury, Vermont, was named in his honor; and he became an adopted member of the Oneida Nation. He returned to Paris in 1790, at the height of the French Revolution. Three years later, he retired to Normandy. His three-volume sequel to *Letters* (1801) was not well received. He died at his daughter's home outside Paris.

In the conceit that structures Crèvecoeur's work, Farmer James writes his letters in response to queries from an English visitor, who wishes to better understand America. The personal letter was a central genre in eighteenth-century literary culture, featured in epistolary novels as well as popular travelers' and naturalists' accounts, both factual and fictional. Works ranging from the French political philosopher Baron de Montesquieu's *Persian Letters* (1721) to the English poet Lady Mary Wortley Montagu's *Turkish Embassy Letters* (1763) to the English novelist Laurence Sterne's *A Sentimental Journey through France and Italy* (1768) embody aspects of the form as Crèvecoeur employed it. The American farmer was already a well-established figure in the political and social debates of the day, notably employed by the statesman John Dickinson in his *Letters from a Farmer in Pennsylvania* (1767–68).

Crèvecoeur's *Letters* engage the revolutionary-era debates over human nature and political organization vividly but unspecifically. He inserted himself into the same transatlantic debates over Americanness and its effects on humankind that Thomas Jefferson pursued in *Notes on the State of Virginia* (1785); but in contrast to Jefferson, with whom he later corresponded, Crèvecoeur's philosophical themes are woven through his work rather than presented discursively. This allusiveness distinguishes Crèvecoeur's *Letters* from the political writings of the day and lends the collection its lasting fascination.

From Letters from an American Farmer[1]

From *Letter III. What Is an American?*

I wish I could be acquainted with the feelings and thoughts which must agitate the heart and present themselves to the mind of an enlightened Englishman, when he first lands on this continent. He must greatly rejoice that he lived at a time to see this fair country discovered and settled; he must necessarily feel a share of national pride, when he views the chain of settlements which embellishes these extended shores. When he says to himself, this is the work of my countrymen, who, when convulsed by factions,[2] afflicted by a variety of miseries and wants, restless and impatient, took refuge here. They brought along with them their national genius,[3] to which they principally owe what liberty they enjoy, and what substance they possess. Here he sees the industry of his native country displayed in a new manner, and traces in their works the embryos of all the arts, sciences, and ingenuity which flourish in Europe. Here he beholds fair cities, substantial villages, extensive fields, an immense country filled with decent houses, good roads, orchards, meadows, and bridges, where an hundred years ago all was wild, woody, and uncultivated! What a train of pleasing ideas this fair spectacle must suggest; it is a prospect which must inspire a good citizen with the most heartfelt pleasure. The difficulty consists in the manner of viewing so extensive a scene. He is arrived on a new continent; a modern society offers itself to his contemplation, different from what he had hitherto seen. It is not composed, as in Europe, of great lords who possess everything, and of a herd of people who have nothing. Here are no aristocratical families, no courts, no kings, no bishops, no ecclesiastical dominion, no invisible power giving to a few a very visible one; no great manufacturers employing thousands, no great refinements of luxury. The rich and the poor are not so far removed from each other as they are in Europe. Some few towns excepted, we are all tillers of the earth, from Nova Scotia to West Florida. We are a people of cultivators, scattered over an immense territory, communicating with each other by means of good roads and navigable rivers, united by the silken bands of mild government, all respecting the laws, without dreading their power, because they are equitable. We are all animated with the spirit of an industry which is unfettered and unrestrained, because each person works for himself. If he travels through our rural districts he views not the

1. The text is from *Letters from an American Farmer*, edited by Albert Boni and Charles Boni (1925).

2. Disputes.
3. Spirit; distinctive character.

hostile castle, and the haughty mansion, contrasted with the clay-built hut and miserable cabin, where cattle and men help to keep each other warm, and dwell in meanness,[4] smoke, and indigence. A pleasing uniformity of decent competence appears throughout our habitations. The meanest of our log-houses is a dry and comfortable habitation. Lawyer or merchant are the fairest[5] titles our towns afford; that of a farmer is the only appellation of the rural inhabitants of our country. It must take some time ere he can reconcile himself to our dictionary, which is but short in words of dignity, and names of honor. There, on a Sunday, he sees a congregation of respectable farmers and their wives, all clad in neat homespun, well mounted, or riding in their own humble wagons. There is not among them an esquire, saving the unlettered magistrate. There he sees a parson as simple as his flock, a farmer who does not riot[6] on the labor of others. We have no princes, for whom we toil, starve, and bleed; we are the most perfect society now existing in the world. Here man is free as he ought to be; nor is this pleasing equality so transitory as many others are. Many ages will not see the shores of our great lakes replenished with inland nations, nor the unknown bounds of North America entirely peopled. Who can tell how far it extends? Who can tell the millions of men whom it will feed and contain? for no European foot has as yet traveled half the extent of this mighty continent!

The next wish of this traveler will be to know whence came all these people? They are a mixture of English, Scotch, Irish, French, Dutch, Germans and Swedes. From this promiscuous breed, that race now called Americans have arisen. The eastern provinces[7] must indeed be excepted, as being the unmixed descendants of Englishmen. I have heard many wish that they had been more intermixed also: for my part, I am no wisher, and think it much better as it has happened. They exhibit a most conspicuous figure in this great and variegated picture; they too enter for a great share in the pleasing perspective displayed in these thirteen provinces. I know it is fashionable to reflect on[8] them, but respect them for what they have done; for the accuracy and wisdom with which they have settled their territory; for the decency of their manners; for their early love of letters; their ancient college,[9] the first in this hemisphere; for their industry,[1] which to me who am but a farmer is the criterion of everything. There never was a people, situated as they are, who with so ungrateful a soil have done more in so short a time. Do you think that the monarchical ingredients which are more prevalent in other governments have purged them from all foul stains? Their histories assert the contrary.

In this great American asylum,[2] the poor of Europe have by some means met together, and in consequence of various causes; to what purpose should they ask one another what countrymen they are? Alas, two thirds of them had no country. Can a wretch who wanders about, who works and starves, whose life is a continual scene of sore affliction or pinching penury, can that man call England or any other kingdom his country? A country that had no bread for him, whose fields procured him no harvest, who met with nothing but the frowns of the rich, the severity of the laws, with jails and punish-

---

4. Poorness, shabbiness.
5. Most important.
6. I.e., indulge himself.
7. New England.
8. To censure or blame.

9. Harvard College, founded in 1636.
1. Industriousness.
2. Place of refuge (e.g., as from religious persecution).

ments; who owned not a single foot of the extensive surface of this planet? No! Urged by a variety of motives, here they came. Everything has tended to regenerate them; new laws, a new mode of living, a new social system; here they are become men: in Europe they were as so many useless plants, wanting vegetative mold and refreshing showers; they withered, and were mowed down by want, hunger, and war; but now by the power of transplantation, like all other plants they have taken root and flourished! Formerly they were not numbered in any civil lists[3] of their country, except in those of the poor; here they rank as citizens. By what invisible power has this surprising metamorphosis been performed? By that of the laws and that of their industry. The laws, the indulgent laws, protect them as they arrive, stamping on them the symbol of adoption; they receive ample rewards for their labors; these accumulated rewards procure them lands; those lands confer on them the title of freemen, and to that title every benefit is affixed which men can possibly require. This is the great operation daily performed by our laws. From whence proceed these laws? From our government. Whence the government? It is derived from the original genius and strong desire of the people ratified and confirmed by the crown. This is the great chain which links us all, this is the picture which every province exhibits, Nova Scotia excepted. There the crown has done all; either there were no people who had genius, or it was not much attended to: the consequence is that the province is very thinly inhabited indeed; the power of the crown in conjunction with the mosquitoes has prevented men from settling there. Yet some parts of it flourished once, and it contained a mild, harmless set of people. But for the fault of a few leaders, the whole were banished.[4] The greatest political error the crown ever committed in America was to cut off men from a country which wanted nothing but men!

What attachment can a poor European emigrant have for a country where he had nothing? The knowledge of the language, the love of a few kindred as poor as himself, were the only cords that tied him: his country is now that which gives him land, bread, protection, and consequence: *Ubi panis ibi patria*[5] is the motto of all emigrants. What then is the American, this new man? He is either a European, or the descendant of a European, hence that strange mixture of blood, which you will find in no other country. I could point out to you a family whose grandfather was an Englishman, whose wife was Dutch, whose son married a French woman, and whose present four sons have now four wives of different nations. *He* is an American, who, leaving behind him all his ancient prejudices and manners, receives new ones from the new mode of life he has embraced, the new government he obeys, and the new rank he holds. He becomes an American by being received in the broad lap of our great *Alma Mater.*[6] Here individuals of all nations are melted into a new race of men, whose labors and posterity will one day cause great changes in the world. Americans are the western pilgrims, who are carrying along with them that great mass of arts, sciences, vigor, and industry which began long since in the east; they will finish the great circle.

3. Recognized employees of the civil government: ambassadors, judges, secretaries, etc.
4. In 1755, as part of the French and Indian War, the French Acadians—settlers who had lived in Nova Scotia for about one hundred and twenty-five years—were banished by the British, who had taken the province in 1710.
5. Where there is bread, there is one's fatherland (Latin).
6. Dear mother (Latin, literal trans.).

The Americans were once scattered all over Europe; here they are incorporated into one of the finest systems of population which has ever appeared, and which will hereafter become distinct by the power of the different climates they inhabit. The American ought therefore to love this country much better than that wherein either he or his forefathers were born. Here the rewards of his industry follow with equal steps the progress of his labor; his labor is founded on the basis of nature, *self-interest*; can it want a stronger allurement? Wives and children, who before in vain demanded of him a morsel of bread, now, fat and frolicsome, gladly help their father to clear those fields whence exuberant crops are to arise to feed and to clothe them all; without any part being claimed, either by a despotic prince, a rich abbot, or a mighty lord. Here religion demands but little of him; a small voluntary salary to the minister, and gratitude to God; can he refuse these? The American is a new man, who acts upon new principles; he must therefore entertain new ideas, and form new opinions. From involuntary idleness, servile dependence, penury, and useless labor, he has passed to toils of a very different nature, rewarded by ample subsistence.—This is an American.

British America is divided into many provinces, forming a large association, scattered along a coast 1,500 miles extent and about 200 wide. This society I would fain examine, at least such as it appears in the middle provinces; if it does not afford that variety of tinges and gradations which may be observed in Europe, we have colors peculiar to ourselves. For instance, it is natural to conceive that those who live near the sea must be very different from those who live in the woods; the intermediate space will afford a separate and distinct class.

Men are like plants; the goodness and flavor of the fruit proceeds from the peculiar soil and exposition in which they grow. We are nothing but what we derive from the air we breathe, the climate we inhabit, the government we obey, the system of religion we profess, and the nature of our employment. Here you will find but few crimes; these have acquired as yet no root among us. I wish I was able to trace all my ideas; if my ignorance prevents me from describing them properly, I hope I shall be able to delineate a few of the outlines, which are all I propose.

Those who live near the sea feed more on fish than on flesh, and often encounter that boisterous element.[7] This renders them more bold and enterprising; this leads them to neglect the confined occupations of the land. They see and converse with a variety of people, their intercourse[8] with mankind becomes extensive. The sea inspires them with a love of traffic,[9] a desire of transporting produce from one place to another; and leads them to a variety of resources which supply the place of labor. Those who inhabit the middle settlements, by far the most numerous, must be very different; the simple cultivation of the earth purifies them, but the indulgences of the government, the soft remonstrances of religion, the rank of independent freeholders,[1] must necessarily inspire them with sentiments, very little known in Europe among people of the same class. What do I say? Europe has no such class of men; the early knowledge they acquire, the early bargains they make, give them a great degree of sagacity. As freemen they will

7. I.e., the sea.
8. Social experience.

9. Trade.
1. Nonaristocratic landowners.

be litigious; pride and obstinacy are often the cause of lawsuits; the nature of our laws and governments may be another. As citizens it is easy to imagine that they will carefully read the newspapers, enter into every political disquisition, freely blame or censure governors and others. As farmers they will be careful and anxious to get as much as they can, because what they get is their own. As northern men they will love the cheerful cup. As Christians, religion curbs them not in their opinions; the general indulgence leaves everyone to think for themselves in spiritual matters; the laws inspect our actions, our thoughts are left to God. Industry, good living, selfishness, litigiousness, country politics, the pride of freemen, religious indifference are their characteristics. If you recede still farther from the sea, you will come into more modern settlements; they exhibit the same strong lineaments, in a ruder appearance. Religion seems to have still less influence, and their manners are less improved.

Now we arrive near the great woods, near the last inhabited districts;[2] there men seem to be placed still farther beyond the reach of government, which in some measure leaves them to themselves. How can it pervade every corner; as they were driven there by misfortunes, necessity of beginnings, desire of acquiring large tracts of land, idleness, frequent want of economy,[3] ancient debts; the reunion of such people does not afford a very pleasing spectacle. When discord, want of unity and friendship; when either drunkenness or idleness prevail in such remote districts; contention, inactivity, and wretchedness must ensue. There are not the same remedies to these evils as in a long-established community. The few magistrates they have are in general little better than the rest; they are often in a perfect state of war; that of man against man, sometimes decided by blows, sometimes by means of the law; that of man against every wild inhabitant of these venerable woods, of which they are come to dispossess them. There men appear to be no better than carnivorous animals of a superior rank, living on the flesh of wild animals when they can catch them, and when they are not able, they subsist on grain. He who would wish to see America in its proper light, and have a true idea of its feeble beginnings and barbarous rudiments, must visit our extended line of frontiers where the last settlers dwell, and where he may see the first labors of settlement, the mode of clearing the earth, in all their different appearances; where men are wholly left dependent on their native tempers and on the spur of uncertain industry, which often fails when not sanctified by the efficacy of a few moral rules. There, remote from the power of example and check of shame, many families exhibit the most hideous parts of our society. They are a kind of forlorn hope, preceding by ten or twelve years the most respectable army of veterans which come after them. In that space, prosperity will polish some, vice and the law will drive off the rest, who uniting again with others like themselves will recede still farther; making room for more industrious people, who will finish their improvements, convert the loghouse into a convenient habitation, and rejoicing that the first heavy labors are finished, will change in a few years that hitherto barbarous country into a fine fertile, well-regulated district. Such is our progress, such is the march of the Europeans toward the interior parts of this

2. I.e., the frontier; the land west of the original colonies and east of the Mississippi.

3. I.e., they were improvident and spent beyond their means. "Want": lack.

continent. In all societies these are offcasts; this impure part serves as our precursors or pioneers; my father himself was one of that class,[4] but he came upon honest principles, and was therefore one of the few who held fast; by good conduct and temperance, he transmitted to me his fair inheritance, when not above one in fourteen of his contemporaries had the same good fortune.

Forty years ago his smiling country was thus inhabited; it is now purged, a general decency of manners prevails throughout, and such has been the fate of our best countries.

Exclusive of those general characteristics, each province has its own, founded on the government, climate, mode of husbandry, customs, and peculiarity of circumstances. Europeans submit insensibly to these great powers, and become, in the course of a few generations, not only Americans in general, but either Pennsylvanians, Virginians, or provincials under some other name. Whoever traverses the continent must easily observe those strong differences, which will grow more evident in time. The inhabitants of Canada, Massachusetts, the middle provinces, the southern ones will be as different as their climates; their only points of unity will be those of religion and language.

As I have endeavored to show you how Europeans become Americans, it may not be disagreeable to show you likewise how the various Christian sects introduced wear out, and how religious indifference becomes prevalent. When any considerable number of a particular sect happen to dwell contiguous to each other, they immediately erect a temple, and there worship the Divinity agreeably to their own peculiar ideas. Nobody disturbs them. If any new sect springs up in Europe it may happen that many of its professors[5] will come and settle in America. As they bring their zeal with them, they are at liberty to make proselytes if they can, and to build a meeting and to follow the dictates of their consciences; for neither the government nor any other power interferes. If they are peaceable subjects, and are industrious, what is it to their neighbors how and in what manner they think fit to address their prayers to the Supreme Being? But if the sectaries are not settled close together, if they are mixed with other denominations, their zeal will cool for want of fuel, and will be extinguished in a little time. Then the Americans become as to religion what they are as to country, allied to all. In them the name of Englishman, Frenchman, and European is lost, and in like manner, the strict modes of Christianity as practiced in Europe are lost also. This effect will extend itself still farther hereafter, and though this may appear to you as a strange idea, yet it is a very true one. I shall be able perhaps hereafter to explain myself better; in the meanwhile, let the following example serve as my first justification.

Let us suppose you and I to be traveling; we observe that in this house, to the right, lives a Catholic, who prays to God as he has been taught, and believes in transubstantiation;[6] he works and raises wheat, he has a large family of children, all hale and robust; his belief, his prayers offend nobody. About one mile farther on the same road, his next neighbor may be a good

---

4. Crèvecoeur's father, unlike Farmer John's, never went to America.
5. Believers.
6. The Roman Catholic doctrine that the sub-

stance of the bread and wine used in the sacrament of communion is changed at the consecration to the substance of the body and blood of Christ.

honest plodding German Lutheran, who addresses himself to the same God, the God of all, agreeably to the modes he has been educated in, and believes in consubstantiation;[7] by so doing he scandalizes nobody; he also works in his fields, embellishes the earth, clears swamps, etc. What has the world to do with his Lutheran principles? He persecutes nobody, and nobody persecutes him, he visits his neighbors, and his neighbors visit him. Next to him lives a seceder,[8] the most enthusiastic of all sectaries; his zeal is hot and fiery, but separated as he is from others of the same complexion, he has no congregation of his own to resort to, where he might cabal and mingle religious pride with worldly obstinacy. He likewise raises good crops, his house is handsomely painted, his orchard is one of the fairest in the neighborhood. How does it concern the welfare of the country, or of the province at large, what this man's religious sentiments are, or really whether he has any at all? He is a good farmer, he is a sober, peaceable, good citizen: William Penn[9] himself would not wish for more. This is the visible character, the invisible one is only guessed at, and is nobody's business. Next again lives a Low Dutchman, who implicitly believes the rules laid down by the synod of Dort.[1] He conceives no other idea of a clergyman than that of a hired man; if he does his work well he will pay him the stipulated sum; if not he will dismiss him, and do without his sermons, and let his church be shut up for years. But notwithstanding this coarse idea, you will find his house and farm to be the neatest in all the country; and you will judge by his wagon and fat horses that he thinks more of the affairs of this world than of those of the next. He is sober and laborious, therefore he is all he ought to be as to the affairs of this life; as for those of the next, he must trust to the great Creator. Each of these people instruct their children as well as they can, but these instructions are feeble compared to those which are given to the youth of the poorest class in Europe. Their children will therefore grow up less zealous and more indifferent in matters of religion than their parents. The foolish vanity, or rather the fury of making proselytes, is unknown here; they have no time, the seasons call for all their attention, and thus in a few years, this mixed neighborhood will exhibit a strange religious medley, that will be neither pure Catholicism nor pure Calvinism. A very perceptible indifference, even in the first generation, will become apparent; and it may happen that the daughter of the Catholic will marry the son of the seceder, and settle by themselves at a distance from their parents. What religious education will they give their children? A very imperfect one. If there happens to be in the neighborhood any place of worship, we will suppose a Quaker's meeting; rather than not show their fine clothes, they will go to it, and some of them may perhaps attach themselves to that society. Others will remain in a perfect state of indifference; the children of these zealous parents will not be able to tell what their religious principles are, and their grandchildren still less. The neighborhood of a place of worship generally leads them to it, and the action of going thither is the strongest evidence they can give of their attachment to any sect. The Quakers are the only people who retain a

7. As distinguished from transubstantiation; the doctrine that Christ's body is not present in or under the elements of bread and wine, but the bread and wine are signs of Christ's presence through faith.
8. One who dissents or withdraws from an established church.

9. English Quaker and founder of Pennsylvania (1644–1718).
1. An ecclesiastical assembly held in Dordrecht, or Dordt, Holland, in 1618 to settle disputes between Protestant Reformed churches. "Low Dutchman": someone from Holland, not Belgium.

fondness for their own mode of worship; for be they ever so far separated from each other, they hold a sort of communion with the society, and seldom depart from its rules, at least in this country. Thus all sects are mixed as well as all nations; thus religious indifference is imperceptibly disseminated from one end of the continent to the other; which is at present one of the strongest characteristics of the Americans. Where this will reach no one can tell, perhaps it may leave a vacuum fit to receive other systems. Persecution, religious pride, the love of contradiction are the food of what the world commonly calls religion. These motives have ceased here; zeal in Europe is confined; here it evaporates in the great distance it has to travel; there it is a grain of powder inclosed,[2] here it burns away in the open air, and consumes without effect.

But to return to our back settlers. I must tell you that there is something in the proximity of the woods which is very singular. It is with men as it is with the plants and animals that grow and live in the forests; they are entirely different from those that live in the plains. I will candidly tell you all my thoughts but you are not to expect that I shall advance any reasons. By living in or near the woods, their actions are regulated by the wildness of the neighborhood. The deer often come to eat their grain, the wolves to destroy their sheep, the bears to kill their hogs, the foxes to catch their poultry. This surrounding hostility immediately puts the gun into their hands; they watch these animals, they kill some; and thus by defending their property, they soon become professed hunters; this is the progress; once hunters, farewell to the plow. The chase renders them ferocious, gloomy, and unsociable; a hunter wants no neighbor, he rather hates them, because he dreads the competition. In a little time their success in the woods makes them neglect their tillage. They trust to the natural fecundity of the earth, and therefore do little; carelessness in fencing often exposes what little they sow to destruction; they are not at home to watch; in order therefore to make up the deficiency, they go oftener to the woods. That new mode of life brings along with it a new set of manners, which I cannot easily describe. These new manners, being grafted on the old stock, produce a strange sort of lawless profligacy, the impressions of which are indelible. The manners of the Indian natives are respectable, compared with this European medley. Their wives and children live in sloth and inactivity; and having no proper pursuits, you may judge what education the latter receive. Their tender minds have nothing else to contemplate but the example of their parents; like them they grow up a mongrel breed, half civilized, half savage, except nature stamps on them some constitutional propensities. That rich, that voluptuous sentiment is gone that struck them so forcibly; the possession of their freeholds[3] no longer conveys to their minds the same pleasure and pride. To all these reasons you must add their lonely situation, and you cannot imagine what an effect on manners the great distances they live from each other has! Consider one of the last settlements in its first view: of what is it composed? Europeans who have not that sufficient share of knowledge they ought to have, in order to prosper; people who have suddenly passed from oppression, dread of government, and fear of laws into the unlimited freedom of the woods. This

2. I.e., like gunpowder in a gun.
3. Parcels of land held outright for specified periods of time.

sudden change must have a very great effect on most men, and on that class particularly. Eating of wild meat, whatever you may think, tends to alter their temper: though all the proof I can adduce is that I have seen it: and having no place of worship to resort to, what little society this might afford is denied them. The Sunday meetings, exclusive of religious benefits, were the only social bonds that might have inspired them with some degree of emulation in neatness. Is it then surprising to see men thus situated, immersed in great and heavy labors, degenerate a little? It is rather a wonder the effect is not more diffusive. The Moravians[4] and the Quakers are the only instances in exception to what I have advanced. The first never settle singly, it is a colony of the society which emigrates; they carry with them their forms, worship, rules, and decency:[5] the others never begin so hard, they are always able to buy improvements,[6] in which there is a great advantage, for by that time the country is recovered from its first barbarity. Thus our bad people are those who are half cultivators and half hunters; and the worst of them are those who have degenerated altogether into the hunting state. As old plowmen and new men of the woods, as Europeans and new-made Indians, they contract the vices of both; they adopt the moroseness and ferocity of a native, without his mildness, or even his industry at home. If manners are not refined, at least they are rendered simple and inoffensive by tilling the earth; all our wants[7] are supplied by it, our time is divided between labor and rest, and leaves none of the commission of great misdeeds. As hunters it is divided between the toil of the chase, the idleness of repose, or the indulgence of inebriation. Hunting is but a licentious idle life, and if it does not always pervert good dispositions; yet, when it is united with bad luck, it leads to want:[8] want stimulates that propensity to rapacity and injustice, too natural to needy men, which is the fatal gradation. After this explanation of the effects which follow by living in the woods, shall we yet vainly flatter ourselves with the hope of converting the Indians? We should rather begin with converting our back-settlers; and now if I dare mention the name of religion, its sweet accents would be lost in the immensity of these woods. Men thus placed are not fit either to receive or remember its mild instructions; they want[9] temples and ministers, but as soon as men cease to remain at home, and begin to lead an erratic life, let them be either tawny or white, they cease to be its disciples.

* * *

Europe contains hardly any other distinctions but lords and tenants; this fair country alone is settled by freeholders, the possessors of the soil they cultivate, members of the government they obey, and the framers of their own laws, by means of their representatives. This is a thought which you have taught me to cherish; our difference from Europe, far from diminishing,

---

4. The Moravian Church, or Unity of Brethren, originated in Bohemia and Moravia in the fifteenth century. In the following two centuries, persecution forced groups of Moravians to emigrate to other lands.
5. The Moravians were family communities who gave up private property and were noted for their industry and thrift.
6. I.e., Quaker settlers had more money than the Moravians.
7. Needs.
8. Neediness, poverty.
9. Lack.

rather adds to our usefulness and consequence as men and subjects. Had our forefathers remained there, they would only have crowded it, and perhaps prolonged those convulsions which had shook it so long. Every industrious European who transports himself here may be compared to a sprout growing at the foot of a great tree; it enjoys and draws but a little portion of sap; wrench it from the parent roots, transplant it, and it will become a tree bearing fruit also. Colonists are therefore entitled to the consideration due to the most useful subjects; a hundred families barely existing in some parts of Scotland will here in six years cause an annual exportation of 10,000 bushels of wheat; 100 bushels being but a common quantity for an industrious family to sell, if they cultivated good land. It is here then that the idle may be employed, the useless become useful, and the poor become rich; but by riches I do not mean gold and silver, we have but little of those metals; I mean a better sort of wealth, cleared lands, cattle, good houses, good clothes, and an increase of people to enjoy them.

There is no wonder that this country has so many charms, and presents to Europeans so many temptations to remain in it. A traveler in Europe becomes a stranger as soon as he quits his own kingdom; but it is otherwise here. We know, properly speaking, no strangers; this is every person's country; the variety of our soils, situations, climates, governments, and produce hath something which must please everybody. No sooner does a European arrive, no matter of what condition, than his eyes are opened upon the fair prospect; he hears his language spoken, he retraces many of his own country manners, he perpetually hears the names of families and towns with which he is acquainted; he sees happiness and prosperity in all places disseminated; he meets with hospitality, kindness, and plenty everywhere; he beholds hardly any poor; he seldom hears of punishments and executions; and he wonders at the elegance of our towns, those miracles of industry and freedom. He cannot admire enough our rural districts, our convenient roads, good taverns, and our many accommodations; he involuntarily loves a country where everything is so lovely.

*   *   *

After a foreigner from any part of Europe is arrived, and become a citizen, let him devoutly listen to the voice of our great parent, which says to him, "Welcome to my shores, distressed European; bless the hour in which thou didst see my verdant fields, my fair navigable rivers, and my green mountains!—If thou wilt work, I have bread for thee; if thou wilt be honest, sober, and industrious, I have greater rewards to confer on thee—ease and independence. I will give thee fields to feed and clothe thee; a comfortable fireside to sit by, and tell thy children by what means thou hast prospered; and a decent bed to repose on. I shall endow thee beside with the immunities of a freeman. If thou wilt carefully educate thy children, teach them gratitude to God, and reverence to that government, the philanthropic government, which has collected here so many men and made them happy. I will also provide for thy progeny; and to every good man this ought to be the most holy, the most powerful, the most earnest wish he can possibly form, as well as the most consolatory prospect when he dies. Go thou and work and till; thou shalt prosper, provided thou be just, grateful, and industrious."

From *Letter IX. Description of Charles-Town; Thoughts on Slavery;*
on Physical Evil; A Melancholy Scene

Charles-Town is, in the north, what Lima is in the south;[1] both are capitals
of the richest provinces of their respective hemispheres: you may therefore
conjecture, that both cities must exhibit the appearances necessarily resulting from riches. Peru abounding in gold, Lima is filled with inhabitants who
enjoy all those gradations of pleasure, refinement, and luxury, which proceed from wealth. Carolina produces commodities, more valuable perhaps
than gold, because they are gained by greater industry; it exhibits also on
our northern stage, a display of riches and luxury, inferior indeed to the
former, but far superior to what are to be seen in our northern towns. Its
situation is admirable, being built at the confluence of two large rivers,
which receive in their course a great number of inferior streams; all navigable in the spring, for flat-boats. Here the produce of this extensive territory concenters; here therefore is the seat of the most valuable exportation;
their wharfs, their docks, their magazines,[2] are extremely convenient to
facilitate this great commercial business. The inhabitants are the gayest[3] in
America; it is called the center of our beau monde, and it [is] always filled
with the richest planters of the province, who resort hither in a quest of
health and pleasure. Here are always to be seen a great number of valetudi-
narians from the West Indies, seeking for the renovation of health, exhausted
by the debilitating nature of their sun, air, and modes of living. Many of
these West Indians have I seen, at thirty, loaded with the infirmities of old
age; for nothing is more common in those countries of wealth, than for persons to lose the abilities of enjoying the comforts of life, at a time when we
northern men just begin to taste the fruits of our labor and prudence. The
round of pleasure, and the expenses of those citizens' tables, are much
superior to what you would imagine: indeed the growth of this town and
province has been astonishingly rapid. It is [a] pity that the narrowness of
the neck[4] on which it stands prevents it from increasing; and which is the
reason why houses are so dear.[5] The heat of the climate, which is sometimes very great in the interior parts of the country, is always temperate in
Charles-Town; though sometimes when they have no sea breezes the sun is
too powerful. The climate renders excesses of all kinds very dangerous,
particularly those of the table; and yet, insensible or fearless of danger, they
live on, and enjoy a short and a merry life: the rays of their sun seem to urge
them irresistably to dissipation and pleasure: on the contrary, the women,
from being abstemious, reach to a longer period of life, and seldom die
without having had several husbands. An European at his first arrival must
be greatly surprised when he sees the elegance of their houses, their sumptuous furniture, as well as the magnificence of their tables. Can he imagine
himself in a country, the establishment of which is so recent?

The three principal classes of inhabitants are, lawyers, planters, and merchants; this is the province which has afforded to the first the richest spoils,
for nothing can exceed their wealth, their power, and their influence. They
have reached the *ne plus ultra* of worldly felicity; no plantation is secured,

1. Charles-Town (now Charleston), South Carolia;
Lima, Peru.
2. Warehouses.

3. Liveliest, most vibrant.
4. I.e., of the land, extending into the harbor.
5. Expensive.

no title is good, no will is valid, but what they dictate, regulate, and approve. The whole mass of provincial property is become tributary to this society; which, far above priests and bishops, disdain to be satisfied with the poor Mosaical portion of the tenth.[6] I appeal to the many inhabitants, who, while contending perhaps for their right to a few hundred acres, have lost by the mazes of the law their whole patrimony. These men are more properly law givers than interpreters of the law; and have united here, as well as in most other provinces, the skill and dexterity of the scribe with the power and ambition of the prince: who can tell where this may lead in a future day? The nature of our laws, and the spirit of freedom, which often tends to make us litigious, must necessarily throw the greatest part of the property of the colonies into the hands of these gentlemen. In another century, the law will possess in the north, what now the church possesses in Peru and Mexico.

While all is joy, festivity, and happiness in Charles-Town, would you imagine that scenes of misery overspread in the country? Their ears by habit are become deaf, their hearts are hardened; they neither see, hear, nor feel for the woes of their poor slaves, from whose painful labors all their wealth proceeds. Here the horrors of slavery, the hardship of incessant toils, are unseen; and no one thinks with compassion of those showers of sweat and of tears which from the bodies of Africans, daily drop, and moisten the ground they till. The cracks of the whip urging these miserable beings to excessive labor, are far too distant from the gay capital to be heard. The chosen race eat, drink, and live happy, while the unfortunate one grubs up the ground, raises indigo, or husks the rice; exposed to a sun full as scorching as their native one; without the support of good food, without the cordials of any cheering liquor. This great contrast has often afforded me subjects of the most afflicting meditation. On the one side, behold a people enjoying all that life affords most bewitching and pleasurable, without labor, without fatigue, hardly subjected to the trouble of wishing. With gold, dug from Peruvian mountains, they order vessels to the coasts of Guinea; by virtue of that gold, wars, murders, and devastations are committed in some harmless, peaceable African neighborhood, where dwelt innocent people, who even knew not but that all men were black. The daughter torn from her weeping mother, the child from the wretched parents, the wife from the loving husband; whose families swept away and brought through storms and tempests to this rich metropolis! There, arranged like horses at a fair, they are branded like cattle, and then driven to toil, to starve, and to languish for a few years on the different plantations of these citizens. And for whom must they work? For persons they know not, and who have no other power over them than that of violence; no other right than what this accursed metal has given them! Strange order of things! Oh, Nature, where are thou?—Are not these blacks thy children as well as we? On the other side, nothing is to be seen but the most diffusive misery and wretchedness, unrelieved even in thought or wish! Day after day they drudge on without any prospect of ever reaping for themselves; they are obliged to devote their lives, their limbs, their will, and every vital exertion to swell the wealth of masters; who look not upon them with half the kindness and affection with which they consider their dogs and

---

6. The practice of tithing (offering a tenth of one's worldly goods to God) was begun by the biblical patriarch Abraham (Genesis 14.20). It is "Mosaical" because the first five Books of the Old Testament (starting with Genesis) are traditionally ascribed to Moses.

horses. Kindness and affection are not the portion of those who till the earth, who carry the burdens, who convert the logs into useful boards. This reward, simple and natural as one would conceive it, would border on humanity; and planters must have none of it!

* * *

A clergyman settled a few years ago at George-Town,[7] and feeling as I do now, warmly recommended to the planters, from the pulpit, a relaxation of severity; he introduced the benignity of Christianity, and pathetically made use of the admirable precepts of that system to melt the hearts of his congregation into a greater degree of compassion toward their slaves than had been hitherto customary; "Sir (said one of his hearers) we pay you a genteel salary to read to us the prayers of the liturgy, and to explain to us such parts of the Gospel as the rule of the church directs; but we do not want you to teach us what we are to do with our blacks." The clergyman found it prudent to withhold any farther admonition. Whence this astonishing right, or rather this barbarous custom, for most certainly we have no kind of right beyond that of force? We are told, it is true, that slavery cannot be so repugnant to human nature as we at first imagine, because it has been practiced in all ages, and in all nations: the Lacedemonians[8] themselves, those great assertors of liberty, conquered the Helotes with the design of making them their slaves; the Romans, whom we consider as our masters in civil and military policy, lived in the exercise of the most horrid oppression; they conquered to plunder and to enslave. What a hideous aspect the face of the earth must then have exhibited! Provinces, towns, districts, often depopulated; their inhabitants driven to Rome, the greatest market in the world, and there sold by thousands! The Roman dominions were tilled by the hands of unfortunate people, who had once been, like their victors free, rich, and possessed of every benefit society can confer; until they became subject to the cruel right of war, and to lawless force. Is there then no superintending power who conducts the moral operations of the world, as well as the physical? The same sublime hand which guides the planets round the sun with so much exactness, which preserves the arrangement of the whole with such exalted wisdom and paternal care, and prevents the vast system from falling into confusion; doth it abandon mankind to all the errors, the follies, and the miseries, which their most frantic rage, and their most dangerous vices and passions can produce?

* * *

Everywhere one part of the human species are taught the art of shedding the blood of the other; of setting fire to their dwellings; of leveling the works of their industry: half of the existence of nations regularly employed in destroying other nations. What little political felicity is to be met with here and there, has cost oceans of blood to purchase; as if good was never to be the portion of unhappy man. Republics, kingdoms, monarchies, founded

---

7. Then a colony in South Carolina.
8. Lacedemonia was a country in the Peloponnese region of the ancient world. The inhabitants of its capital, Sparta—who were known as Spartans or Lacedemonians—enslaved the inhabitants of the town of Helos, who were known as Helotes.

either on fraud or successful violence, increase by pursuing the steps of the same policy, until they are destroyed in their turn, either by the influence of their own crimes, or by more successful but equally criminal enemies.

If from this general review of human nature, we descend to the examination of what is called civilized society; there the combination of every natural and artificial want, makes us pay very dear for what little share of political felicity we enjoy. It is a strange heterogeneous assemblage of vices and virtues, and of a variety of other principles, forever at war, forever jarring, forever producing some dangerous, some distressing extreme. Where do you conceive then that nature intended we should be happy? Would you prefer the state of men in the woods, to that of men in a more improved situation? Evil preponderates in both; in the first they often eat each other for want of food, and in the other they often starve each other for want of room. For my part, I think the vices and miseries to be found in the latter, exceed those of the former; in which real evil is more scarce, more supportable, and less enormous. Yet we wish to see the earth peopled; to accomplish the happiness of kingdoms, which is said to consist in numbers. Gracious God! to what end is the introduction of so many beings into a mode of existence in which they must grope amidst as many errors, commit as many crimes, and meet with as many diseases, wants, and sufferings!

The following scene will I hope account for these melancholy reflections, and apologize for the gloomy thoughts with which I have filled this letter: my mind is, and always has been, oppressed since I became a witness to it. I was not long since invited to dine with a planter who lived three miles from ——, where he then resided. In order to avoid the heat of the sun, I resolved to go on foot, sheltered in a small path, leading through a pleasant wood. I was leisurely traveling along, attentively examining some peculiar plants which I had collected, when all at once I felt the air strongly agitated; though the day was perfectly calm and sultry. I immediately cast my eyes toward the cleared ground, from which I was but at a small distance, in order to see whether it was not occasioned by a sudden shower; when at that instant a sound resembling a deep rough voice, uttered, as I thought, a few inarticulate monosyllables. Alarmed and surprised, I precipitately looked all round, when I perceived at about six rods distance something resembling a cage, suspended to the limbs of a tree; all the branches of which appeared covered with large birds of prey, fluttering about, and anxiously endeavoring to perch on the cage. Actuated by an involuntary motion of my hands, more than by any design of my mind, I fired at them; they all flew to a short distance, with a most hideous noise: when, horrid to think and painful to repeat, I perceived a Negro, suspended in the cage, and left there to expire! I shudder when I recollect that the birds had already picked out his eyes, his cheek bones were bare; his arms had been attacked in several places, and his body seemed covered with a multitude of wounds. From the edges of the hollow sockets and from the lacerations with which he was disfigured, the blood slowly dropped, and tinged the ground beneath. No sooner were the birds flown, than swarms of insects covered the whole body of this unfortunate wretch, eager to feed on his mangled flesh and to drink his blood. I found myself suddenly arrested by the power of affright and terror; my nerves were convulsed; I trembled, I stood motionless, involuntarily contemplating the fate of this Negro, in all its dismal latitude. The living specter, though deprived of his eyes, could still distinctly hear, and in his uncouth dialect begged me to give him some water to allay his thirst. Humanity herself would have recoiled back with horror; she would have balanced whether to lessen such reliefless distress, or mercifully with one blow to end this dreadful scene of agonizing torture! Had I had a ball in my gun, I certainly should have dispatched him; but finding myself unable to perform so kind an office, I sought, though trembling, to relieve him as well as I could. A shell ready fixed to a pole, which had been used by some Negroes, presented itself to me; filled it with water, and with trembling hands I guided it to the quivering lips of the wretched sufferer. Urged by the irresistible power of thirst, he endeavored to meet it, as he instinctively guessed its approach by the noise it made in passing through the bars of the cage. "Tankè, you whitè man, tankè you, putè somè poison and givè me." "How long have you been hanging there?" I asked him. "Two days, and me no die; the birds, the birds; aaah me!" Oppressed with the reflections which this shocking spectacle afforded me, I mustered strength enough to walk away, and soon reached the house at which I intended to dine. There I heard that the reason for this slave being thus punished was on account of his having killed the overseer of the plantation. They told me that the laws of self-preservation rendered such executions necessary; and supported the doctrine of slavery with the arguments generally made use of to justify the practice; with the repetition of which I shall not trouble you at present.

ADIEU.

c. 1769–80   1782

THOMAS PAINE
1737–1809

The author of two of the most popular books in eighteenth-century America, and the most persuasive rhetorician of the cause for independence, Thomas Paine was born in England and did not move to the colonies until he was thirty-seven years old and the rebellion was looming. Paine's early years prepared him to support the Revolution. The discrepancy between his high intelligence and the limitations imposed on him in England's hierarchical society made him long for a new social order. The son of a Quaker father and an Anglican mother, he once said that a sermon he heard at age eight convinced him of the cruelty inherent in Christianity and made him a rebel forever.

By the time he arrived in Philadelphia with letters of introduction from Benjamin Franklin, recommending him as an "ingenious, worthy young man," Paine had already led a remarkably full life. He attended grammar school until he was thirteen and was then apprenticed in his father's corset shop; at nineteen, he ran away from home to go to sea. From 1757 to 1774, he was, by turns, a corset maker, a tobacconist and grocer, a schoolteacher, and an exciseman (i.e., a government employee who taxed goods). Hoping to force Parliament to raise the salary of the excisemen, he engaged in some of the first efforts at labor organizing. His efforts failed, however, and he lost his job when he admitted that he had stamped goods as inspected when in fact they had not been examined. His first wife died less than a year after their marriage, and he was separated from his second wife after three years. Scandals about his private life and questions about his integrity provided his critics with ammunition for the rest of his life. Franklin was right, however, in recognizing Paine's genius; like Franklin, Paine was self-taught and curious about everything from the philosophy of law to natural science.

In Philadelphia, Paine transformed himself into a journalist. He quickly made his way in that city, first as a spokesman against slavery and then as the anonymous author of *Common Sense* (1776), the first pamphlet published in the colonies to urge immediate independence from Britain. Paine was obviously the right man in the right place at the right time. Relations with England were at their lowest ebb: Boston was under siege, and the Second Continental Congress had convened in Philadelphia. *Common Sense* sold phenomenally well and was quickly reprinted in cities along the eastern seaboard and in France, Germany, and England. Meanwhile, Paine enlisted in the Revolutionary Army and served as an aide-de-camp in battles in New York, New Jersey, and Pennsylvania. He followed the triumph of *Common Sense* with the first of sixteen pamphlets titled *The Crisis* (1776-83). The first *Crisis* paper ("These are the times that try men's souls") reportedly was read to General George Washington's troops at Trenton, New Jersey, and did much to shore up the spirits of the ultimately victorious Revolutionary soldiers.

After the war, Paine received a number of political appointments as rewards for his services as a writer for the American cause, but too indiscreet and hot-tempered for public employment, he misused his privileges and lost the most lucrative offices. In 1787, he returned to England, where he wrote his second-most successful work, *Rights of Man* (1791–92), an impassioned plea against hereditary monarchy. Paine was charged with treason and fled to France, where he was made a citizen and lionized as a spokesman for revolution. The horrors of the French Revolution, however, brought home to Paine that the overthrow of monarchy did not necessarily usher in enlightenment and order. When he protested the execution of Louis XVI, he was accused of sympathy with the Crown and imprisoned. He was saved from trial by the American ambassador, the future president James Monroe, who offered him renewed American citizenship and safe passage back to New York.

Paine spent the last years of his life in New York City and in New Rochelle, New York. During these years of unhappiness and impoverishment, his reputation suffered enormously as a result of his public rejection of organized religion in *The Age of Reason* (1794). Paine's attempt to define his beliefs was viewed as an attack on Christianity and, by extension, on conventional society. He was ridiculed and despised. Even George Washington, who had supported Paine's early writing, thought English criticism of him was "not a bad thing." Paine was buried on his farm at New Rochelle after his request for a Quaker gravesite was refused. Ten years later, an admirer exhumed his bones with the intention of having him reburied in England, but this plan came to nothing, and Paine's remains have never been found.

Paine's role in shaping American literature took numerous forms. He began his writing career in Philadelphia as the contributing editor of a magazine—then a new publication format—where he learned to address a wide audience, a skill that he turned to advantage in his polemical pamphlets. He made important contributions to the development of copyright and to the professionalization of authorship. But it was as a stylist of "plainness" that Paine made his greatest gift to American literature. Reflecting on his prose style, he said he needed no "ceremonious expressions." He wrote: "It is my design to make those who can scarcely read understand," to put arguments in a language "as plain as the alphabet," and to shape everything "to fit the powers of thinking and the turn of language to the subject, so as to bring out a clear conclusion that shall hit the point in question and nothing else."

Like Franklin, Thomas Jefferson admired Paine's use of the new populist rhetorical style then emerging to challenge the classical rhetoric associated with political elites. Having cut a controversial path through the age of democratic revolution, Paine inspired later radicals, such as the journalist and poet Walt Whitman (included later in this volume), who eulogized his hero in 1877: "That he labor'd well and wisely for the States in the trying period of their parturition, and in the seeds of their character, there seems to me no question. I dare not say how much of what our Union is owning and enjoying to day—its independence—its ardent belief in, and substantial practice of, radical human rights—and the severance of its government from all ecclesiastical and superstitious dominion—I dare not say how much of all this is owing to Thomas Paine, but I am inclined to think a good portion of it decidedly is."

From Common Sense[1]

Introduction

Perhaps the sentiments contained in the following pages are not yet sufficiently fashionable to procure them general favor; a long habit of not thinking a thing wrong gives it a superficial appearance of being right, and raises at first a formidable outcry in defence of custom. But the tumult soon subsides. Time makes more converts than reason.

As a long and violent abuse of power is generally the means of calling the right of it in question (and in matters too which might never have been thought of, had not the sufferers been aggravated into the inquiry), and as the King of England[2] hath undertaken in his own right, to support the Parliament in what he calls theirs, and as the good people of this country are grievously oppressed by the combination, they have an undoubted privilege to inquire into the pretensions of both, and equally to reject the usurpation of either.

In the following sheets, the author hath studiously avoided everything which is personal among ourselves. Compliments as well as censure to individuals make no part thereof. The wise and the worthy need not the triumph of a pamphlet; and those whose sentiments are injudicious or unfriendly will cease of themselves, unless too much pains is bestowed upon their conversions.

The cause of America is in a great measure the cause of all mankind. Many circumstances have, and will, arise which are not local, but universal, and through which the principles of all lovers of mankind are affected, and in the event of which their affections are interested. The laying a country desolate with fire and sword, declaring war against the natural rights of all mankind, and extirpating the defenders thereof from the face of the earth, is the concern of every man to whom nature hath given the power of feeling; of which class, regardless of party censure, is

THE AUTHOR

---

1. The full title is *Common Sense: Addressed to the Inhabitants of America, on the Following Interesting Subjects: viz.* [i.e., namely]: *I. Of the Origin and Design of Government in General; with Concise Remarks on the English Constitution. II. Of Monarchy and Hereditary Succession.*
III. Thoughts on the Present State of American Affairs. IV. Of the Present Ability of America; with some Miscellaneous Reflections. The text is from *The Writings of Thomas Paine* (1894–96), vol. 1, edited by M. D. Conway.
2. George III (1738–1820; reigned 1760–1820).

From *III. Thoughts on the Present State of American Affairs*

In the following pages I offer nothing more than simple facts, plain arguments, and common sense: and have no other preliminaries to settle with the reader, than that he will divest himself of prejudice and prepossession, and suffer his reason and his feelings to determine for themselves: that he will put on, or rather that he will not put off, the true character of a man, and generously enlarge his views beyond the present day.

Volumes have been written on the subject of the struggle between England and America. Men of all ranks have embarked in the controversy, from different motives, and with various designs; but all have been ineffectual, and the period of debate is closed. Arms as the last resource decide the contest; the appeal was the choice of the King, and the continent has accepted the challenge.

It hath been reported of the late Mr. Pelham[3] (who though an able minister was not without his faults) that on his being attacked in the House of Commons on the score that his measures were only of a temporary kind, replied, "they will last my time." Should a thought so fatal and unmanly possess the colonies in the present contest, the name of ancestors will be remembered by future generations with detestation.

The sun never shined on a cause of greater worth. 'Tis not the affair of a city, a county, a province, or a kingdom; but of a continent—of at least one eighth part of the habitable globe. 'Tis not the concern of a day, a year, or an age; posterity are virtually involved in the contest, and will be more or less affected even to the end of time, by the proceedings now. Now is the seed time of continental union, faith and honor. The least fracture now will be like a name engraved with the point of a pin on the tender rind of a young oak; the wound would enlarge with the tree, and posterity read it in full grown characters.

By referring the matter from argument to arms, a new era for politics is struck—a new method of thinking hath arisen. All plans, proposals, etc., prior to the nineteenth of April, i.e., to the commencement of hostilities,[4] are like the almanacs of the last year; which though proper then, are superseded and useless now. Whatever was advanced by the advocates on either side of the question then, terminated in one and the same point, viz., a union with Great Britain; the only difference between the parties was the method of effecting it; the one proposing force, the other friendship; but it hath so far happened that the first hath failed, and the second hath withdrawn her influence.

As much hath been said of the advantages of reconciliation, which, like an agreeable dream, hath passed away and left us as we were, it is but right that we should examine the contrary side of the argument, and inquire into some of the many material injuries which these colonies sustain, and always will sustain, by being connected with and dependent on Great Britain. To examine that connection and dependence, on the principles of nature and common sense, to see what we have to trust to, if separated, and what we are to expect, if dependent.

3. Henry Pelham (1696–1754; prime minister of Britain 1743–54).
4. On April 19, 1775, in the first armed conflict of the American Revolution, the Minutemen of Lexington, Massachusetts, defended their ammunition stores against the British.

I have heard it asserted by some, that as America has flourished under her former connection with Great Britain, the same connection is necessary towards her future happiness, and will always have the same effect. Nothing can be more fallacious than this kind of argument. We may as well assert that because a child has thrived upon milk, that it is never to have meat, or that the first twenty years of our lives is to become a precedent for the next twenty. But even this is admitting more than is true; for I answer roundly, that America would have flourished as much, and probably much more, had no European power taken any notice of her. The commerce by which she hath enriched herself are the necessaries of life, and will always have a market while eating is the custom of Europe.

But she has protected us, say some. That she hath engrossed[5] us is true, and defended the continent at our expense as well as her own, is admitted; and she would have defended Turkey from the same motive, viz., for the sake of trade and dominion.

Alas! we have been long led away by ancient prejudices and made large sacrifices to superstition. We have boasted the protection of Great Britain without considering that her motive was interest not attachment; and that she did not protect us from our enemies on our account; but from her enemies on her own account, from those who had no quarrel with us on any other account, and who will always be our enemies on the same account. Let Britain waive her pretensions to the continent, or the continent throw off the dependence, and we should be at peace with France and Spain, were they at war with Britain. The miseries of Hanover's last war[6] ought to warn us against connections.

It hath lately been asserted in Parliament, that the colonies have no relation to each other but through the parent country, i.e., that Pennsylvania and the Jerseys,[7] and so on for the rest, are sister colonies by the way of England; this is certainly a very roundabout way of proving relationship, but it is the nearest and only true way of proving enmity (or enemyship, if I may so call it). France and Spain never were, nor perhaps ever will be, our enemies as Americans, but as our being the subjects of Great Britain.

But Britain is the parent country, say some. Then the more shame upon her conduct. Even brutes do not devour their young, nor savages make war upon their families; wherefore, the assertion, if true, turns to her reproach; but it happens not to be true, or only partly so, and the phrase parent or mother country hath been jesuitically[8] adopted by the King and his parasites, with a low papistical design of gaining an unfair bias on the credulous weakness of our minds. Europe, and not England, is the parent country of America. This new world hath been the asylum for the persecuted lovers of civil and religious liberty from every part of Europe. Hither have they fled, not from the tender embraces of the mother, but from the cruelty of the monster; and it is so far true of England, that the same tyranny which drove the first emigrants from home, pursues their descendants still.

5. Dominated.
6. King George III was a descendant of the German House of Hanover. Paine is referring to the Seven Years' War (1756–63), which originally involved Prussia and Austria and grew to include all the major European powers. The war was settled in Britain's favor, but the North American component, the French and Indian War (1754–63), resulted in heavy colonial losses.
7. The province of New Jersey was divided into East and West Jersey.
8. I.e., cunningly (from the historical intrigues of the Jesuits, a Roman Catholic order of priests and brothers).

In this extensive quarter of the globe, we forget the narrow limits of three hundred and sixty miles (the extent of England) and carry our friendship on a larger scale; we claim brotherhood with every European Christian, and triumph in the generosity of the sentiment.

It is pleasant to observe by what regular gradations we surmount the force of local prejudices, as we enlarge our acquaintance with the world. A man born in any town in England divided into parishes, will naturally associate most with his fellow parishioners (because their interests in many cases will be common) and distinguish him by the name of neighbor; if he meet him but a few miles from home, he drops the narrow idea of a street, and salutes him by the name of townsman; if he travel out of the county and meet him in any other, he forgets the minor divisions of street and town, and calls him countryman, i.e., countyman: but if in their foreign excursions they should associate in France, or any other part of Europe, their local remembrance would be enlarged into that of Englishmen. And by a just parity of reasoning, all Europeans meeting in America, or any other quarter of the globe, are countrymen; for England, Holland, Germany, or Sweden, when compared with the whole, stand in the same places on the larger scale, which the divisions of street, town, and county do on the smaller ones; distinctions too limited for continental minds. Not one third of the inhabitants, even of this province,[9] are of English descent. Wherefore, I reprobate the phrase of parent or mother country applied to England only, as being false, selfish, narrow and ungenerous.

But, admitting that we were all of English descent, what does it amount to? Nothing. Britain, being now an open enemy, extinguishes every other name and title: and to say that reconciliation is our duty is truly farcical. The first King of England of the present line (William the Conqueror)[1] was a Frenchman, and half the peers of England are descendants from the same country; wherefore, by the same method of reasoning, England ought to be governed by France.

Much hath been said of the united strength of Britain and the colonies, that in conjunction they might bid defiance to the world: but this is mere presumption; the fate of war is uncertain, neither do the expressions mean anything; for this continent would never suffer itself to be drained of inhabitants to support the British arms in either Asia, Africa, or Europe.

Besides, what have we to do with setting the world at defiance? Our plan is commerce, and that, well attended to, will secure us the peace and friendship of all Europe; because it is the interest of all Europe to have America a free port. Her trade will always be a protection, and her barrenness of gold and silver secure her from invaders.

I challenge the warmest advocate for reconciliation to show a single advantage that this continent can reap by being connected with Great Britain. I repeat the challenge; not a single advantage is derived. Our corn[2] will fetch its price in any market in Europe, and our imported goods must be paid for buy them where we will.

But the injuries and disadvantages which we sustain by that connection, are without number; and our duty to mankind at large, as well as to our-

9. I.e., Pennsylvania.
1. William I (c. 1028–1087; reigned 1066–87) conquered England when he was duke of the

French region of Normandy, his homeland.
2. I.e., wheat, not what Americans now call corn.

selves, instruct us to renounce the alliance: because, any submission to, or dependence on, Great Britain tends directly to involve this continent in European wars and quarrels, and set us at variance with nations who would otherwise seek our friendship, and against whom we have neither anger nor complaint. As Europe is our market for trade, we ought to form no partial connection with any part of it. It is the true interest of America to steer clear of European contentions, which she never can do, while, by her dependence on Britain, she is made the makeweight in the scale of British politics.

Europe is too thickly planted with kingdoms to be long at peace, and whenever a war breaks out between England and any foreign power, the trade of America goes to ruin, because of her connection with Britain. The next war may not turn out like the last, and should it not, the advocates for reconciliation now will be wishing for separation then, because neutrality in that case would be a safer convoy than a man of war.[3] Everything that is right or reasonable pleads for separation. The blood of the slain, the weeping voice of nature cries, " 'Tis time to part." Even the distance at which the Almighty hath placed England and America is a strong and natural proof that the authority of the one over the other was never the design of Heaven. The time likewise at which the continent was discovered adds weight to the argument, and the manner in which it was peopled increases the force of it. The Reformation was preceded by the discovery of America: as if the Almighty graciously meant to open a sanctuary to the persecuted in future years, when home should afford neither friendship nor safety.

The authority of Great Britain over this continent is a form of government which sooner or later must have an end: and a serious mind can draw no true pleasure by looking forward, under the painful and positive conviction that what he calls "the present constitution" is merely temporary. As parents, we can have no joy, knowing that this government is not sufficiently lasting to insure anything which we may bequeath to posterity: and by a plain method of argument, as we are running the next generation into debt, we ought to do the work of it, otherwise we use them meanly and pitifully. In order to discover the line of our duty rightly, we should take our children in our hand, and fix our station a few years farther into life; that eminence will present a prospect which a few present fears and prejudices conceal from our sight.

Though I would carefully avoid giving unnecessary offense, yet I am inclined to believe that all those who espouse the doctrine of reconciliation may be included within the following descriptions.

Interested men who are not to be trusted, weak men who cannot see, prejudiced men who will not see, and a certain set of moderate men who think better of the European world than it deserves; and this last class, by an ill-judged deliberation, will be the cause of more calamities to this continent than all the other three.

It is the good fortune of many to live distant from the scene of present sorrow; the evil is not sufficiently brought to their doors to make them feel the precariousness with which all American property is possessed. But let our imaginations transport us a few moments to Boston;[4] that seat

---

3. A naval warship. "Like the last": the Seven Years' War ended in Britain's favor.

4. Boston was under British military occupation and was blockaded for six months.

of wretchedness will teach us wisdom, and instruct us forever to renounce a power in whom we can have no trust. The inhabitants of that unfortunate city, who but a few months ago were in ease and affluence, have now no other alternative than to stay and starve, or turn out to beg. Endangered by the fire of their friends if they continue within the city,[5] and plundered by the soldiery if they leave it, in their present situation they are prisoners without the hope of redemption, and in a general attack for their relief they would be exposed to the fury of both armies.

Men of passive tempers look somewhat lightly over the offenses of Great Britain, and, still hoping for the best, are apt to call out, "Come, come, we shall be friends again for all this." But examine the passions and feelings of mankind: bring the doctrine of reconciliation to the touchstone of nature, and then tell me whether you can hereafter love, honor, and faithfully serve the power that hath carried fire and sword into your land? If you cannot do all these, then are you only deceiving yourselves, and by your delay bringing ruin upon posterity. Your future connection with Britain, whom you can neither love nor honor, will be forced and unnatural, and, being formed only on the plan of present convenience, will in a little time fall into a relapse more wretched than the first. But if you say, you can still pass the violations over, then I ask, hath your house been burnt? Hath your property been destroyed before your face? Are your wife and children destitute of a bed to lie on, or bread to live on? Have you lost a parent or a child by their hands, and yourself the ruined and wretched survivor? If you have not, then are you not a judge of those who have. But if you have, and can still shake hands with the murderers, then are you unworthy the name of husband, father, friend, or lover, and whatever may be your rank or title in life, you have the heart of a coward, and the spirit of a sycophant.

This is not inflaming or exaggerating matters, but trying them by those feelings and affections which nature justifies, and without which we should be incapable of discharging the social duties of life, or enjoying the felicities of it. I mean not to exhibit horror for the purpose of provoking revenge, but to awaken us from fatal and unmanly slumbers, that we may pursue determinately some fixed object. 'Tis not in the power of Britain or of Europe to conquer America, if she doth not conquer herself by delay and timidity. The present winter is worth an age if rightly employed, but if lost or neglected the whole continent will partake of the misfortune; and there is no punishment which that man doth not deserve, be he who, or what, or where he will, that may be the means of sacrificing a season so precious and useful.

'Tis repugnant to reason, to the universal order of things, to all examples from former ages, to suppose that this continent can long remain subject to any external power. The most sanguine in Britain doth not think so. The utmost stretch of human wisdom cannot, at this time, compass a plan, short of separation, which can promise the continent even a year's security. Reconciliation is now a fallacious dream. Nature hath deserted the connection, and art cannot supply her place. For, as Milton wisely expresses, "never can true reconcilement grow where wounds of deadly hate have pierced so deep."[6]

---

5. I.e., liable to be caught in "friendly fire" from colonial rebels.

6. *Paradise Lost* 4.98–99, by the English poet John Milton (1608–1674).

* * *

A government of our own is our natural right: and when a man seriously reflects on the precariousness of human affairs, he will become convinced that it is infinitely wiser and safer to form a constitution of our own in a cool deliberate manner, while we have it in our power, than to trust such an interesting event to time and chance. If we omit it now, some Massanello[7] may hereafter arise, who, laying hold of popular disquietudes, may collect together the desperate and the discontented, and by assuming to themselves the powers of government, finally sweep away the liberties of the continent like a deluge. Should the government of America return again into the hands of Britain, the tottering situation of things will be a temptation for some desperate adventurer to try his fortune; and in such a case, what relief can Britain give? Ere she could hear the news, the fatal business might be done; and ourselves suffering like the wretched Britons under the oppression of the conqueror. Ye that oppose independence now, ye know not what ye do: ye are opening a door to eternal tyranny by keeping vacant the seat of government. There are thousands and tens of thousands, who would think it glorious to expel from the continent that barbarous and hellish power, which hath stirred up the Indians and the Negroes to destroy us; the cruelty hath a double guilt: it is dealing brutally by us, and treacherously by them.

To talk of friendship with those in whom our reason forbids us to have faith, and our affections wounded through a thousand pores instruct us to detest, is madness and folly. Every day wears out the little remains of kindred between us and them; and can there be any reason to hope, that as the relationship expires, the affection will increase, or that we shall agree better when we have ten times more and greater concerns to quarrel over than ever?

Ye that tell us of harmony and reconciliation, can ye restore to us the time that is past? Can ye give to prostitution its former innocence? Neither can ye reconcile Britain and America. The last cord now is broken, the people of England are presenting addresses against us. There are injuries which nature cannot forgive; she would cease to be nature if she did. As well can the lover forgive the ravisher of his mistress, as the continent forgive the murders of Britain. The Almighty hath implanted in us these unextinguishable feelings for good and wise purposes. They are the guardians of His image in our hearts. They distinguish us from the herd of common animals. The social compact would dissolve, and justice be extirpated from the earth, or have only a casual existence were we callous to the touches of affection. The robber and the murderer would often escape unpunished, did not the injuries which our tempers sustain provoke us into justice.

O! ye that love mankind! Ye that dare oppose not only the tyranny but the tyrant, stand forth! Every spot of the old world is overrun with oppression. Freedom hath been hunted round the globe. Asia and Africa have long expelled her. Europe regards her like a stranger, and England hath given her warning to depart. O! receive the fugitive, and prepare in time an asylum[8] for mankind.

1776

---

7. Thomas Anello, otherwise Massanello [i.e., Tommaso Aniello (1622–1647), known as Masaniello], a fisherman of Naples, who after spiriting up his countrymen in the public market place, against the oppression of the Spaniards, to whom the place was then subject, prompted them to revolt, and in the space of a day became King [Paine's note].
8. Refuge.

The Crisis, No. 1[1]

These are the times that try men's souls. The summer soldier and the sunshine patriot will, in this crisis, shrink from the service of their country; but he that stands it now, deserves the love and thanks of man and woman. Tyranny, like hell, is not easily conquered; yet we have this consolation with us, that the harder the conflict, the more glorious the triumph. What we obtain too cheap, we esteem too lightly: it is dearness[2] only that gives everything its value. Heaven knows how to put a proper price upon its goods; and it would be strange indeed if so celestial an article as freedom should not be highly rated. Britain, with an army to enforce her tyranny, has declared that she has a right (not only to tax) but "to bind us in all cases whatsoever,"[3] and if being bound in that manner is not slavery, then is there not such a thing as slavery upon earth. Even the expression is impious; for so unlimited a power can belong only to God.

Whether the independence of the continent was declared too soon, or delayed too long, I will not now enter into as an argument; my own simple opinion is, that had it been eight months earlier, it would have been much better. We did not make a proper use of last winter, neither could we, while we were in a dependent state. However, the fault, if it were one, was all our own;[4] we have none to blame but ourselves. But no great deal is lost yet. All that Howe has been doing for this month past is rather a ravage than a conquest, which the spirit of the Jerseys,[5] a year ago, would have quickly repulsed, and which time and a little resolution will soon recover.

I have as little superstition in me as any man living, but my secret opinion has ever been, and still is, that God Almighty will not give up a people to military destruction, or leave them unsupportedly to perish, who have so earnestly and so repeatedly sought to avoid the calamities of war, by every decent method which wisdom could invent. Neither have I so much of the infidel in me as to suppose that He has relinquished the government of the world, and given us up to the care of devils; and as I do not, I cannot see on what grounds the King of Britain can look up to heaven for help against us: a common murderer, a highwayman, or a housebreaker has as good a pretense as he.

'Tis surprising to see how rapidly a panic will sometimes run through a country. All nations and ages have been subject to them: Britain has trem-

1. Paine sometimes referred to this essay, the first of the sixteen Crisis pamphlets, as The American Crisis. In one week in 1776, he published three editions: one undated, one dated December 19, and the one reprinted here, dated December 23. The text is from The Writings of Thomas Paine (1894–96), vol. 1, edited by M. D. Conway.
2. Costliness.
3. Cf. the Second Continental Congress's "Declaration Setting Forth the Causes and Necessity of [the Massachusetts Assembly's] Taking Up Arms" (July 6, 1775): "By one statute [Parliament's Declaratory Act of 1766] it is declared that Parliament can 'of right make laws to bind us in all cases whatsoever.' What is to defend us

against so enormous, so unlimited a power?"
4. "The present winter is worth an age, if rightly employed; but, if lost or neglected, the whole continent will partake of the evil; and there is no punishment that man does not deserve, be he who, or what, or where he will, that may be the means of sacrificing a season so precious and useful" [Paine's note, taken from Common Sense]. Paine wanted an immediate declaration of independence, uniting the colonies and enlisting the aid of France and Spain.
5. The province of New Jersey was divided into East and West Jersey. Lord William Howe (1729–1814), commander of the British Army in America (1775–78).

bled like an ague[6] at the report of a French fleet of flat-bottomed boats; and in the fourteenth century the whole English army, after ravaging the kingdom of France, was driven back like men petrified with fear; and this brave exploit was performed by a few broken forces collected and headed by a woman, Joan of Arc.[7] Would that heaven might inspire some Jersey maid to spirit up her countrymen, and save her fair fellow sufferers from ravage and ravishment! Yet panics, in some cases, have their uses; they produce as much good as hurt. Their duration is always short; the mind soon grows through them, and acquires a firmer habit than before. But their peculiar advantage is that they are the touchstones of sincerity and hypocrisy, and bring things and men to light, which might otherwise have lain forever undiscovered. In fact, they have the same effect on secret traitors, which an imaginary apparition would have upon a private murderer. They sift out the hidden thoughts of man, and hold them up in public to the world. Many a disguised tory[8] has lately shown his head, that shall penitentially solemnize with curses the day on which Howe arrived upon the Delaware.[9]

As I was with the troops at Fort Lee, and marched with them to the edge of Pennsylvania, I am well acquainted with many circumstances, which those who live at a distance know but little or nothing of. Our situation there was exceedingly cramped, the place being a narrow neck of land between the North River[1] and the Hackensack. Our force was inconsiderable, being not one fourth so great as Howe could bring against us. We had no army at hand to have relieved the garrison, had we shut ourselves up and stood on our defense. Our ammunition, light artillery, and the best part of our stores had been removed on the apprehension that Howe would endeavor to penetrate the Jerseys, in which case Fort Lee could be of no use to us; for it must occur to every thinking man, whether in the army or not, that these kind of field forts are only for temporary purposes, and last in use no longer than the enemy directs his force against the particular object, which such forts are raised to defend. Such was our situation and condition at Fort Lee on the morning of the 20th of November, when an officer arrived with information that the enemy with 200 boats had landed about seven miles above: Major General Green,[2] who commanded the garrison, immediately ordered them under arms, and sent express to General Washington at the town of Hackensack, distant, by the way of the ferry, six miles. Our first object was to secure the bridge over the Hackensack, which laid up the river between the enemy and us, about six miles from us, and three from them. General Washington arrived in about three quarters of an hour, and marched at the head of the troops towards the bridge, which place I expected we should have a brush for; however, they did not choose to dispute it with us, and the greatest part of our troops went over the bridge, the rest over the ferry, except some which passed at a mill on a small creek, between the bridge and the ferry, and made their way through some marshy grounds up to the town of Hackensack, and there passed the river. We brought off as much baggage as

---

6. I.e., like one who is chilled.
7. Joan of Arc (1412–1431) led the French to victory over the English in 1429 (not "the fourteenth century").
8. Supporter of the king.
9. The Delaware River, which played a major part

in the 1776 battles—in New York, New Jersey, and Pennsylvania—that Paine details below.
1. The Hudson River.
2. Major General Nathanael Greene (1742–1786). Paine was his aide-de-camp.

the wagons could contain, the rest was lost. The simple object was to bring off the garrison, and march them on till they could be strengthened by the Jersey or Pennsylvania militia, so as to be enabled to make a stand. We staid four days at Newark, collected our outposts with some of the Jersey militia, and marched out twice to meet the enemy, on being informed that they were advancing, though our numbers were greatly inferior to theirs. Howe, in my little opinion, committed a great error in generalship in not throwing a body of forces off from Staten Island through Amboy, by which means he might have seized all our stores at Brunswick, and intercepted our march into Pennsylvania; but if we believe the power of hell to be limited, we must likewise believe that their agents are under some providential control.[3]

I shall not now attempt to give all the particulars of our retreat to the Delaware; suffice it for the present to say, that both officers and men, though greatly harassed and fatigued, frequently without rest, covering, or provision, the inevitable consequences of a long retreat, bore it with a manly and martial spirit. All their wishes centered in one, which was that the country would turn out and help them to drive the enemy back. Voltaire has remarked that King William never appeared to full advantage but in difficulties and in action;[4] the same remark may be made on General Washington, for the character fits him. There is a natural firmness in some minds which cannot be unlocked by trifles, but which, when unlocked, discovers a cabinet[5] of fortitude; and I reckon it among those kind of public blessings, which we do not immediately see, that God hath blessed him with uninterrupted health, and given him a mind that can even flourish upon care.

I shall conclude this paper with some miscellaneous remarks on the state of our affairs; and shall begin with asking the following question: Why is it that the enemy have left the New England provinces, and made these middle ones the seat of war? The answer is easy: New England is not infested with tories, and we are. I have been tender in raising the cry against these men, and used numberless arguments to show them their danger, but it will not do to sacrifice a world either to their folly or their baseness. The period is now arrived, in which either they or we must change our sentiments, or one or both must fall. And what is a tory? Good God! what is he? I should not be afraid to go with a hundred whigs[6] against a thousand tories, were they to attempt to get into arms. Every tory is a coward; for servile, slavish, self-interested fear is the foundation of toryism; and a man under such influence, though he may be cruel, never can be brave.

But, before the line of irrecoverable separation be drawn between us, let us reason the matter together: Your conduct is an invitation to the enemy, yet not one in a thousand of you has heart enough to join him. Howe is as much deceived by you as the American cause is injured by you. He expects you will all take up arms, and flock to his standard, with muskets on your shoulders. Your opinions are of no use to him, unless you support him personally, for 'tis soldiers, and not tories, that he wants.

3. The American losses were larger than Paine implies. General Howe took three thousand prisoners and a large store of military supplies when he captured Fort Lee.

4. The French writer François-Marie Arouet (1694–1778), known as Voltaire, made this remark about King William III of England (1650–1702) in his History of Louis the Fourteenth.

5. Storehouse.

6. Supporters of the Revolution.

I once felt all that kind of anger, which a man ought to feel, against the mean principles that are held by the tories: a noted one, who kept a tavern at Amboy,[7] was standing at his door, with as pretty a child in his hand, about eight or nine years old, as I ever saw, and after speaking his mind as freely as he thought was prudent, finished with this unfatherly expression, "Well! give me peace in my day." Not a man lives on the continent but fully believes that a separation must some time or other finally take place, and a generous parent should have said, "If there must be trouble, let it be in my day, that my child may have peace"; and this single reflection, well applied, is sufficient to awaken every man to duty. Not a place upon earth might be so happy as America. Her situation is remote from all the wrangling world, and she has nothing to do but to trade with them. A man can distinguish himself between temper and principle, and I am as confident, as I am that God governs the world, that America will never be happy till she gets clear of foreign dominion. Wars, without ceasing, will break out till that period arrives, and the continent must in the end be conqueror; for though the flame of liberty may sometimes cease to shine, the coal can never expire.

America did not, nor does not, want[8] force; but she wanted a proper application of that force. Wisdom is not the purchase of a day, and it is no wonder that we should err at the first setting off. From an excess of tenderness, we were unwilling to raise an army, and trusted our cause to the temporary defense of a well-meaning militia. A summer's experience has now taught us better; yet with those troops, while they were collected, we were able to set bounds to the progress of the enemy, and thank God! they are again assembling. I always considered militia as the best troops in the world for a sudden exertion, but they will not do for a long campaign. Howe, it is probable, will make an attempt on this city;[9] should he fail on this side of the Delaware, he is ruined: if he succeeds, our cause is not ruined. He stakes all on his side against a part on ours; admitting[1] he succeeds, the consequence will be that armies from both ends of the continent will march to assist their suffering friends in the middle states; for he cannot go everywhere, it is impossible. I consider Howe as the greatest enemy the tories have; he is bringing a war into their country, which, had it not been for him and partly for themselves, they had been clear of. Should he now be expelled, I wish with all the devotion of a Christian, that the names of whig and tory may never more be mentioned; but should the tories give him encouragement to come, or assistance if he come, I as sincerely wish that our next year's arms may expel them from the continent, and the congress appropriate their possessions to the relief of those who have suffered in well-doing. A single successful battle next year will settle the whole. America could carry on a two years' war by the confiscation of the property of disaffected persons, and be made happy by their expulsion. Say not that this is revenge; call it rather the soft resentment of a suffering people, who, having no object in view but the good of all, have staked their own all upon a seemingly doubtful event. Yet it is folly to argue against determined hardness; eloquence

---

7. Paine was stationed at Perth Amboy, New Jersey, while in the Continental Army.
8. Lack.

9. I.e., Philadelphia.
1. If.

may strike the ear, and the language of sorrow draw forth the tear of compassion, but nothing can reach the heart that is steeled with prejudice.

Quitting this class of men, I turn with the warm ardor of a friend to those who have nobly stood, and are yet determined to stand the matter out: I call not upon a few, but upon all: not on this state or that state, but on every state: up and help us; lay your shoulders to the wheel; better have too much force than too little, when so great an object is at stake. Let it be told to the future world that in the depth of winter, when nothing but hope and virtue could survive, that the city and the country, alarmed at one common danger, came forth to meet and to repulse it. Say not that thousands are gone, turn out your tens of thousands;[2] throw not the burden of the day upon Providence, but "show your faith by your works"[3] that God may bless you. It matters not where you live, or what rank of life you hold, the evil or the blessing will reach you all. The far and the near, the home counties and the back,[4] the rich and poor will suffer or rejoice alike. The heart that feels not now is dead: the blood of his children will curse his cowardice who shrinks back at a time when a little might have saved the whole, and made them happy. I love the man that can smile in trouble, that can gather strength from distress, and grow brave by reflection. 'Tis the business of little minds to shrink; but he whose heart is firm, and whose conscience approves his conduct, will pursue his principles unto death. My own line of reasoning is to myself as straight and clear as a ray of light. Not all the treasures of the world, so far as I believe, could have induced me to support an offensive war, for I think it murder; but if a thief breaks into my house, burns and destroys my property, and kills or threatens to kill me, or those that are in it, and to "bind me in all cases whatsoever" to his absolute will, am I to suffer it? What signifies it to me, whether he who does it is a king or a common man; my countryman or not my countryman; whether it be done by an individual villain, or an army of them? If we reason to the root of things we shall find no difference; neither can any just cause be assigned why we should punish in the one case and pardon in the other. Let them call me rebel, and welcome, I feel no concern from it; but I should suffer the misery of devils were I to make a whore of my soul by swearing allegiance to one whose character is that of a sottish, stupid, stubborn, worthless, brutish man. I conceive likewise a horrid idea in receiving mercy from a being, who at the last day shall be shrieking to the rocks and mountains to cover him, and fleeing with terror from the orphan, the widow, and the slain of America.

There are cases which cannot be overdone by language, and this is one. There are persons, too, who see not the full extent of the evil which threatens them; they solace themselves with hopes that the enemy, if he succeed, will be merciful. It is the madness of folly to expect mercy from those who have refused to do justice; and even mercy, where conquest is the object, is only a trick of war; the cunning of the fox is as murderous as the violence of the wolf, and we ought to guard equally against both. Howe's first object is, partly by threats and partly by promises, to terrify or seduce the people to

---

2. "Saul hath slain his thousands, and David his ten thousands" (1 Samuel 18.7).
3. "Shew me thy faith without thy works, and I will shew thee my faith by my works" (James 2.18).
4. I.e., the backwoods.

deliver up their arms and receive mercy. The ministry recommended the same plan to Gage, and this is what the tories call making their peace, "a peace which passeth all understanding"[5] indeed! A peace which would be the immediate forerunner of a worse ruin than any we have yet thought of. Ye men of Pennsylvania, do reason upon these things! Were the back counties to give up their arms, they would fall an easy prey to the Indians, who are all armed: this perhaps is what some tories would not be sorry for. Were the home counties to deliver up their arms, they would be exposed to the resentment of the back counties, who would then have it in their power to chastise their defection at pleasure. And were any one state to give up its arms, that state must be garrisoned by all Howe's army of Britons and Hessians[6] to preserve it from the anger of the rest. Mutual fear is the principal link in the chain of mutual love, and woe be to that state that breaks the compact. Howe is mercifully inviting you to barbarous destruction, and men must be either rogues or fools that will not see it. I dwell not upon the vapors of imagination: I bring reason to your ears, and, in language as plain as A, B, C, hold up truth to your eyes.

I thank God that I fear not. I see no real cause for fear. I know our situation well, and can see the way out of it. While our army was collected, Howe dared not risk a battle; and it is no credit to him that he decamped from the White Plains,[7] and waited a mean opportunity to ravage the defenseless Jerseys; but it is great credit to us, that, with a handful of men, we sustained an orderly retreat for near an hundred miles, brought off our ammunition, all our field pieces, the greatest part of our stores, and had four rivers to pass. None can say that our retreat was precipitate, for we were near three weeks in performing it, that the country[8] might have time to come in. Twice we marched back to meet the enemy, and remained out till dark. The sign of fear was not seen in our camp, and had not some of the cowardly and disaffected inhabitants spread false alarms through the country, the Jerseys had never been ravaged. Once more we are again collected and collecting; our new army at both ends of the continent is recruiting fast, and we shall be able to open the next campaign with sixty thousand men, well armed and clothed. This is our situation, and who will may know it. By perseverance and fortitude we have the prospect of a glorious issue; by cowardice and submission, the sad choice of a variety of evils—a ravaged country—a depopulated city—habitations without safety, and slavery without hope—our homes turned into barracks and bawdyhouses for Hessians, and a future race to provide for, whose fathers we shall doubt of. Look on this picture and weep over it! and if there yet remains one thoughtless wretch who believes it not, let him suffer it unlamented.

Common Sense

1776

---

5. "And the peace of God, which passeth all understanding, shall keep your hearts and minds through Christ Jesus" (Philippians 4.7). General Thomas Gage (1721–1787) commanded the British armies in America from 1763 to 1775, before Howe.

6. German mercenaries.
7. In New York, where, on October 28, 1776, General Howe successfully overcame Washington's troops but failed to take full advantage of his victory.
8. I.e., the local volunteers.

THOMAS JEFFERSON
1743–1826

I n June 1776, the Second Continental Congress met in Philadelphia to consider whether to declare their alliance of colonies independent of Great Britain. The delegates turned to a thirty-two-year-old representative from Virginia, Thomas Jefferson, to be the principal drafter of a statement that the full congress would then debate, amend, and vote to either accept or reject. Jefferson was an awkward speaker but a talented prose stylist, and his reputation as a writer had preceded him to Philadelphia. While serving in the Virginia House of Burgesses in 1774, he had written an influential and daring pamphlet, A Summary View of the Rights of British America, which denied all parliamentary authority over America and argued that ties to the British monarchy were voluntary and not irrevocable. On June 11, 1776, after some maneuvering by John Adams, Jefferson was chosen to head the committee charged with drafting a declaration of independence. The other members of the committee who helped Jefferson refine his draft were Adams, Benjamin Franklin, Roger Sherman, and Robert Livingston. On June 28, the draft declaration was presented to Congress, where it underwent some further modifications before it could pass unanimously, as it did on July 4. These alterations were a source of regret to Jefferson. In his Autobiography (1829), he included the original draft and indicated changes made by the Congress.

One of the omitted passages speaks to a central tension of Jefferson's legacy. Admired as a prophet of equality and liberty, he is also widely recognized as an owner of some two hundred slaves, including several men and women who were most likely his children with the enslaved woman Sally Hemings. This paradox in Jefferson's personal life resonates with a larger circumstance memorably captured by the English writer Samuel Johnson in his 1775 pamphlet "Taxation No Tyranny." "Why is it," Johnson asked, "we hear the loudest yelps for liberty among the drivers of negroes?" In his draft declaration, Jefferson seeks to turn the tables by blaming George III, "the christian king of Great Britain," for refusing to allow the colonists to limit the slave trade and inciting enslaved people "to rise in arms among us, . . . thus paying off former crimes committed against the LIBERTIES of one people, with crimes which he urges them to commit against the lives of another." In this formulation, Jefferson proposes an equivalence between the colonists, who are said to be resisting "slavery" to Great Britain, and those subjected to race-based chattel slavery. At the same time, he invokes the specter of racial warfare—of whites against the "merciless Indian savages" as well as black slaves—to unite the colonists against the Crown.

Jefferson wrote his Autobiography in 1821, and he may have been prompted to restore this passage of the draft declaration by a national crisis regarding whether to admit Missouri to the Union as a slave state and Maine as a free state. On March 3, 1820, the Missouri Compromise legislated a balance between free and slave states. Writing of the slave system in April 1820, he observed that "we have the wolf by the ear, and we can neither hold him, nor safely let him go. Justice is in one scale, and self-preservation in the other." As the restored text of the Declaration shows, Jefferson's fear of race war had long been a powerful—and powerfully distorting—factor in his thought. In the 1780s, it led him in Notes on the State of Virginia to support the colonization movement that sought to remove people of African descent from the United States.

Jefferson's complex stance is related to his roots in the Virginia planter society that had developed over the eighteenth century. He was born at the Shadwell plantation, in what is now Albemarle County, Virginia. His mother, Jane Randolph, came from one of the state's most prominent families. His father, Peter Jefferson, was a county official and surveyor. When Thomas was fourteen, his father died, and he inherited twenty-seven hundred acres of land and slaves to work it. Over the years he added to this expanse of property, which reached a peak of almost ten thousand acres.

In 1760 Jefferson entered the College of William and Mary, in Williamsburg, the capital of Virginia. There Jefferson met three men who strongly influenced his life: Governor Francis Fauquier, a fellow of the Royal Society, a famous scientific organization based in England; George Wythe, one of the best teachers of law in the colonies; and Dr. William Small, an emigrant from Scotland who introduced Jefferson to the Scottish Enlightenment, including the work of Francis Hutcheson, author of *An Inquiry into the Original of Our Ideas of Beauty and Virtue* (1725), and Henry Home, Lord Kames, author of *Essays on the Principles of Morality and Natural Religion* (1751), whose ideas shaped his aesthetic and political thought. Jefferson remained in Williamsburg to study law after graduation and was admitted to the bar in 1765.

Three years later he began clearing the mountaintop at his plantation, named Monticello, Italian for "little mountain." There, he eventually built the neoclassical mansion of his own design, completing the project in 1808. The year after he started his building project, he was elected to the Virginia House of Burgesses and began a prominent career in the legislature. After serving in the Continental Congress during the catalytic summer of 1776, he left to take up a seat in the Virginia House of Delegates that September. He was elected governor in 1779 and reelected the following year. Jefferson's term of office came to an ignominious end after the British captured Richmond in 1781. Jefferson and the legislature moved to Charlottesville, and he and the legislators barely escaped imprisonment when the pursuing British Army descended on them at Monticello. Jefferson's ensuing resignation and the lack of preparations for the defense of the city were held against him, and it was some time before he regained the confidence of Virginians.

From 1781 to late 1783, Jefferson withdrew from public life and remained for stretches of time at Monticello, completing his only book, *Notes on the State of Virginia*, a work of natural and social history that also presents Jefferson's thinking on a range of volatile issues, including slavery and race, religious liberty, and the economic basis of the future United States. He was elected to the Continental Congress in 1783, and in early 1784 he was among the Congressional delegates who signed the Treaty of Paris, ending the Revolutionary War. He was elected Minister to France in May 1784 and sailed from Boston on July 5 of that year. He returned to Monticello in 1789, and the following year George Washington appointed him to be the first secretary of state under the newly adopted Constitution. After three years, Jefferson retired once again and temporarily withdrew to Monticello. He ran for president in 1796, losing to John Adams and taking the office of vice president instead, as was then the practice. However, he won the watershed election of 1800, becoming the nation's third president and the first to be inaugurated in Washington, D.C. He named Benjamin Latrobe surveyor of public buildings and worked with Latrobe in planning a great city to be the new nation's capital.

When Jefferson returned to Monticello in 1809, his public life was over. In his later years, he kept up a copious correspondence. His exchanges with John Adams offer a study in contrasting personalities as well as fascinating insights into revolutionary history. On the Fourth of July, 1826—the fiftieth anniversary of the Declaration of Independence—Jefferson died a few hours before Adams, his longtime collaborator, rival, and correspondent. At the time of his death, he was deeply in debt, and his family was forced to sell Monticello. Despite the discomfort with the slave system that he frequently expressed, Jefferson ultimately freed a total of just seven of the people he held in bondage, all members of the extended Hemings family.

President of the United States, first secretary of state, minister to France, governor of Virginia, and congressman, Thomas Jefferson once said that he wished to be remembered for only three things: drafting the Declaration of Independence, writing and supporting the Virginia Statute for Religious Freedom (1786), and founding the University of Virginia (1819). Jefferson might well have included a number of other accomplishments in this list: a remarkable architect, he designed not just Monticello but also the Virginia state capitol and the original buildings for the University of Virginia; he had a library of some ten thousand volumes, which served as the basis for the Library of Congress, and a collection of paintings and sculpture that made him the greatest patron of the arts in the early United States; and he was known the world over for his spirit of scientific inquiry and as the creator of several remarkable inventions.

The three acts for which he wished to be remembered testify to Jefferson's lifelong passion to liberate the human mind from tyranny, whether imposed by the state, the Church, or human ignorance. The fact that he was unable to liberate his own mind from the tyranny of racialist thought remains part of his ambiguous legacy. The Declaration of Independence has directly influenced independence movements around the world, from Haiti to India and from Venezuela to Rhodesia. It offers an important argument for viewing "Life, Liberty and the pursuit of Happiness" as "unalienable Rights" best achieved through the exercise of popular government.

From The Autobiography of Thomas Jefferson[1]

From *The Declaration of Independence*

* * *

It appearing in the course of these debates, that the colonies of New York, New Jersey, Pennsylvania, Delaware, Maryland, and South Carolina were not yet matured for falling from the parent stem, but that they were fast advancing to that state, it was thought most prudent to wait a while for them, and to postpone the final decision to July 1st; but, that this might occasion as little delay as possible, a committee was appointed to prepare a Declaration of Independence. The committee were John Adams, Dr. Franklin, Roger Sherman, Robert R. Livingston, and myself. Committees were also appointed, at the same time, to prepare a plan of confederation for the colonies, and to state the terms proper to be proposed for foreign alliance. The committee for drawing the Declaration of Independence, desired me to do it. It was accordingly done, and being approved by them, I reported it to the House on Friday, the 28th of June, when it was read, and ordered to lie on the table.[2] On Monday, the 1st of July, the House resolved itself into a committee of the whole, and resumed the consideration of the original motion made by

1. On June 7, 1776, Richard Henry Lee of Virginia proposed to the Second Continental Congress, meeting in Philadelphia, that "these united Colonies are, and of a right ought to be, free and independent states." Lee's resolution was passed on July 2, and the Declaration was adopted on July 4 with the changes noted by Jefferson in this text, taken from his *Autobiography*. On August 2, a copy on parchment was signed by all the delegates but three, who signed later. The text is from *The Writings of Thomas Jefferson* (1903), edited by A. A. Lipscomb and A. E. Bergh.

2. A parliamentary procedure calling for the consideration of the proposal (British usage).

the delegates of Virginia, which, being again debated through the day, was carried in the affirmative by the votes of New Hampshire, Connecticut, Massachusetts, Rhode Island, New Jersey, Maryland, Virginia, North Carolina and Georgia. South Carolina and Pennsylvania voted against it. Delaware had but two members present, and they were divided. The delegates from New York declared they were for it themselves, and were assured their constituents were for it; but that their instructions having been drawn near a twelve-month before, when reconciliation was still the general object, they were enjoined by them to do nothing which should impede that object. They, therefore, thought themselves not justifiable in voting on either side, and asked leave to withdraw from the question: which was given them. The committee rose and reported their resolution to the House. Mr. Edward Rutledge, of South Carolina, then requested the determination might be put off to the next day, as he believed his colleagues, though they disapproved of the resolution, would then join in it for the sake of unanimity. The ultimate question, whether the House would agree to the resolution of the committee, was accordingly postponed to the next day, when it was again moved, and South Carolina concurred in voting for it. In the meantime, a third member had come post[3] from the Delaware counties, and turned the vote of that colony in favor of the resolution. Members of a different sentiment attending that morning from Pennsylvania also, her vote was changed, so that the whole twelve colonies who were authorized to vote at all, gave their voices for it; and, within a few days, the convention of New York approved of it, and thus supplied the void occasioned by the withdrawing of her delegates from the vote.

Congress proceeded the same day to consider the Declaration of Independence, which had been reported and lain on the table the Friday preceding, and on Monday referred to a committee of the whole. The pusillanimous idea that we had friends in England worth keeping terms with, still haunted the minds of many. For this reason, those passages which conveyed censures on the people of England were struck out, lest they should give them offense. The clause too, reprobating the enslaving the inhabitants of Africa, was struck out in complaisance to South Carolina and Georgia, who had never attempted to restrain the importation of slaves, and who, on the contrary, still wished to continue it. Our northern brethren also, I believe, felt a little tender under those censures; for though their people had very few slaves themselves, yet they had been pretty considerable carriers of them to others. The debates, having taken up the greater parts of the 2d, 3d, and 4th days of July, were, on the evening of the last, closed; the Declaration was reported by the committee, agreed to by the House, and signed by every member present, except Mr. Dickinson.[4] As the sentiments of men are known not only by what they receive, but what they reject also, I will state the form of the Declaration as originally reported. The parts struck out by Congress shall be distinguished by a black line drawn under them, and those inserted by them shall be placed in the margin, or in a concurrent column.

3. Posthaste: speedily.
4. John Dickinson of Pennsylvania, who opposed it.

A DECLARATION BY THE REPRESENTATIVES OF THE UNITED STATES OF
AMERICA, IN GENERAL CONGRESS ASSEMBLED.

When, in the course of human events, it becomes necessary
for one people to dissolve the political bands which have connected them with another, and to assume among the powers
of the earth the separate and equal station to which the laws
of nature and of nature's God entitle them, a decent respect
to the opinions of mankind requires that they should declare
the causes which impel them to the separation.

We hold these truths to be self evident: that all men are
created equal; that they are endowed by their Creator with   certain
inherent and inalienable rights; that among these are life, liberty, and the pursuit of happiness;[5] that to secure these rights,
governments are instituted among men, deriving their just
powers from the consent of the governed; that whenever any
form of government becomes destructive of these ends, it is
the right of the people to alter or to abolish it, and to institute
new government, laying its foundation on such principles,
and organizing its powers in such form, as to them shall seem
most likely to effect their safety and happiness. Prudence,
indeed, will dictate that governments long established should
not be changed for light and transient causes; and accordingly all experience hath shown that mankind are more disposed to suffer while evils are sufferable, than to right
themselves by abolishing the forms to which they are accustomed. But when a long train of abuses and usurpations,
begun at a distinguished[6] period and pursuing invariably the
same object, evinces a design to reduce them under absolute
despotism, it is their right, it is their duty to throw off such
government, and to provide new guards for their future security. Such has been the patient sufferance of these colonies;
and such is now the necessity which constrains them to
expunge their former systems of government. The history of   alter
the present king of Great Britain[7] is a history of unremitting
injuries and usurpations, among which appears no solitary   repeated
fact to contradict the uniform tenor of the rest, but all have in all having
direct object the establishment of an absolute tyranny over
these states. To prove this, let facts be submitted to a candid
world for the truth of which we pledge a faith yet unsullied by
falsehood.

He has refused his assent to laws the most wholesome and
necessary for the public good.

He has forbidden his governors to pass laws of immediate
and pressing importance, unless suspended in their opera-

5. Jefferson's phrase "life, liberty, and the pursuit of happiness" echoes "life, liberty, and property," from the English philosopher John Locke
(1632–1704). However, Jefferson may have been
more influenced by the Scottish Enlightenment

philosophers, particularly Hutcheson.
6. I.e., discernible.
7. King George III (1738–1820; reigned 1760–
1820).

tion till his assent should be obtained; and, when so suspended, he has utterly neglected to attend to them.

He has refused to pass other laws for the accommodation of large districts of people, unless those people would relinquish the right of representation in the legislature, a right inestimable to them, and formidable to tyrants only.

He has called together legislative bodies at places unusual, uncomfortable, and distant from the depository of their public records, for the sole purpose of fatiguing them into compliance with his measures.

He has dissolved representative houses repeatedly <u>and continually</u> for opposing with manly firmness his invasions on the rights of the people.

He has refused for a long time after such dissolutions to cause others to be elected, whereby the legislative powers, incapable of annihilation, have returned to the people at large for their exercise, the state remaining, in the meantime, exposed to all the dangers of invasion from without and convulsions within.

He has endeavored to prevent the population of these states; for that purpose obstructing the laws for naturalization of foreigners, refusing to pass others to encourage their migrations hither, and raising the conditions of new appropriations of lands.

He has <u>suffered</u> the administration of justice <u>totally to cease in some of these states</u> refusing his assent to laws for establishing judiciary powers. [obstructed by]

He has made <u>our</u> judges dependent on his will alone for the tenure of their offices, and the amount and payment of their salaries.

He has erected a multitude of new offices, <u>by a self-assumed power</u> and sent hither swarms of new officers to harass our people and eat out their substance.[8]

He has kept among us in times of peace standing armies <u>and ships of war</u> without the consent of our legislatures.

He has affected to render the military independent of, and superior to, the civil power.

He has combined with others[9] to subject us to a jurisdiction foreign to our constitutions and unacknowledged by our laws, giving his assent to their acts of pretended legislation for quartering large bodies of armed troops among us; for protecting them by a mock trial from punishment for any murders which they should commit on the inhabitants of these states; for cutting off our trade with all parts of the world; for imposing taxes on us without our consent; for depriving us [ ] of the benefits of trial by jury; for transporting us beyond seas to be tried for pretended offenses; for [in many cases]

---

8. I.e., consume the local people's food and other staple goods.   9. I.e., the British Parliament.

abolishing the free system of English laws in a neighboring province, establishing therein an arbitrary government, and enlarging its boundaries, so as to render it at once an example and fit instrument for introducing the same absolute rule into these states;[1] for taking away our charters, abolishing our most valuable laws, and altering fundamentally the forms of our governments; for suspending our own legislatures, and declaring themselves invested with power to legislate for us in all cases whatsoever. — colonies;

He has abdicated government here withdrawing his governors, and declaring us out of his allegiance and protection. — by declaring us out of his protection, and waging war against us.

He has plundered our seas, ravaged our coasts, burnt our towns, and destroyed the lives of our people.

He is at this time transporting large armies of foreign mercenaries[2] to complete the works of death, desolation and tyranny already begun with circumstances of cruelty and perfidy [ ] unworthy the head of a civilized nation. — scarcely paralleled in the most barbarous ages, and totally

He has constrained our fellow citizens taken captive on the high seas, to bear arms against their country, to become the executioners of their friends and brethren, or to fall themselves by their hands.

He has [ ] endeavored to bring on the inhabitants of our frontiers, the merciless Indian savages, whose known rule of warfare is an undistinguished destruction of all ages, sexes and conditions of existence. — excited domestic insurrection among us, and has

He has incited treasonable insurrections of our fellow citizens, with the allurements of forfeiture and confiscation of our property.

He has waged cruel war against human nature itself, violating its most sacred rights of life and liberty in the persons of a distant people who never offended him, captivating and carrying them into slavery in another hemisphere, or to incur miserable death in their transportation thither. This piratical warfare, the opprobrium of infidel powers, is the warfare of the christian king of Great Britain. Determined to keep open a market where men should be bought and sold, he has prostituted his negative[3] for suppressing every legislative attempt to prohibit or to restrain this execrable commerce. And that this assemblage of horrors might want no fact of distinguished die,[4] he is now exciting those very people to rise in arms among us, and to purchase that liberty of which he has deprived them, by murdering the people on whom he also obtruded them: thus paying off former crimes committed against the LIBERTIES of one people, with crimes which he urges them to commit against the lives of another.

1. The Quebec Act of 1774 recognized the Roman Catholic religion in Quebec and extended the borders of the province to the Ohio River; it restored French civil law and thus angered the New England colonies. It was often referred to as one of the "intolerable acts."
2. German soldiers hired by the king for colonial service.
3. I.e., vetoed legislation to end the slave trade.
4. Might lack nothing.

In every stage of these oppressions we have petitioned for redress in the most humble terms: our repeated petitions have been answered only by repeated injuries.

A prince[5] whose character is thus marked by every act which may define a tyrant is unfit to be the ruler of a [ ] people <u>who mean to be free. Future ages will scarcely believe that the hardiness of one man adventured,[6] within the short compass of twelve years only, to lay a foundation so broad and so undisguised for tyranny over a people fostered and fixed in principles of freedom.</u>

free

Nor have we been wanting in attentions[7] to our British brethren. We have warned them from time to time of attempts by their legislature to extend <u>a</u> jurisdiction over <u>these our states.</u> We have reminded them of the circumstances of our emigration and settlement here, <u>no one of which could warrant so strange a pretension: that these were effected at the expense of our own blood and treasure, unassisted by the wealth or the strength of Great Britain: that in constituting indeed our several forms of government, we had adopted one common king, thereby laying a foundation for perpetual league and amity with them: but that submission to their parliament was no part of our constitution, nor ever in idea, if history may be credited: and,</u> we [ ] appealed to their native justice and magnanimity <u>as well as to</u> the ties of our common kindred to disavow these usurpations which <u>were likely</u> <i>to</i> interrupt our connection and correspondence. They too have been deaf to the voice of justice and of consanguinity, <u>and when occasions have been given them, by the regular course of their laws, of removing from their councils the disturbers of our harmony, they have, by their free election, reestablished them in power. At this very time too, they are permitting their chief magistrate to send over not only soldiers of our common blood, but Scotch and foreign mercenaries to invade and destroy us. These facts have given the last stab to agonizing affection, and manly spirit bids us to renounce forever these unfeeling brethren. We must endeavor to forget our former love for them, and hold them as we hold the rest of mankind, enemies in war, in peace friends. We might have been a free and a great people together; but a communication of grandeur and of freedom, it seems, is below their dignity. Be it so, since they will have it. The road to happiness and to glory is open to us, too. We will tread it apart from them, and</u> acquiesce in the necessity which denounces[8] our eternal separation [ ]!

an unwarrantable / us

have
and we have
conjured
them by
would inevitably

and hold
them as we
hold the rest
of mankind,
enemies in
war, in peace
friends.

5. King George III.
6. Engaged.

7. Lacking attention.
8. Proclaims.

We therefore the representatives of the United States of America in General Congress assembled, do in the name, and by the authority of the good people of these <u>states reject and renounce all allegiance and subjection to the kings of Great Britain and all others who may hereafter claim by, through or under them; we utterly dissolve all political connection which may heretofore have subsisted between us and the people or parliament of Great Britain: and finally we do assert and declare these colonies to be free and independent states,</u> and that as free and independent states, they have full power to levy war, conclude peace, contract alliances, establish commerce, and to do all other acts and things which independent states may of right do.

And for the support of this declaration, we mutually pledge to each other our lives, our fortunes, and our sacred honor.

We, therefore, the representatives of the United States of America in General Congress assembled, appealing to the supreme judge of the world for the rectitude of our intentions, do in the name, and by the authority of the good people of these colonies, solemnly publish and declare, that these united colonies are, and of right ought to be free and independent states; that they are absolved from all allegiance to the British crown, and that all political connection between them and the state of Great Britain is, and ought to be, totally dissolved; and that as free and independent states, they have full power to levy war, conclude peace, contract alliances, establish commerce, and to do all other acts and things which independent states may of right do.

And for the support of this declaration, with a firm reliance on the protection of divine providence, we mutually pledge to each other our lives, our fortunes, and our sacred honor.

The Declaration thus signed on the 4th, on paper, was engrossed[9] on parchment, and signed again on the 2d of August.

1821   1829

9. Written in a legal hand.

THE FEDERALIST

When Richard Henry Lee, a Virginia delegate to the Continental Congress, proposed his resolution for independence from Britain on June 7, 1776, he also suggested that a "plan of confederation be prepared and transmitted to the respective colonies for their consideration and approbation." On July 12, 1776, the Articles of Confederation were presented to Congress. They were debated for a year and then ratified and adopted as the bylaws of the nation on March 1, 1781. The central question before the Constitutional Convention, meeting in Philadelphia six years later, was whether to salvage these articles through complicated amendments or to design a new national government. The Convention delegates decided on the latter and, in September 1787, received copies of the proposed Constitution, which they were to submit to their state legislatures for ratification. Advocates of the new Constitution, dubbed Federalists, and their Anti-Federalist opponents quickly rose to the occasion, and a great debate followed. Many feared what they saw as the loss of states' rights and the power of a large, impersonal federal government to dominate the lives of individual citizens, and they cited the absence of a bill of rights as a particular concern; others thought that the Constitution favored urban over rural populations; still others bemoaned the proposed end of the slave trade.

The debate took ten months, nowhere more seriously than in the state of New York, where adoption was not inevitable. The discussion there produced significant documents, the most enduring of which were the eighty-five essays that appeared in New York newspapers from October 1787 to April 1788 and were later collected in two volumes called *The Federalist*. These essays were written by Alexander

> In the PRESS,
> and speedily will be published,
> THE
> FEDERALIST,
> A Collection of Essays written in favor of the New Constitution.
> By a Citizen of New-York.
> Corrected by the Author, with Additions and Alterations.
> This work will be printed on a fine Paper and good Type, in one handsome Volume duodecimo, and delivered to subscribers at the moderate price of one dollar. A few copies will be printed on superfine royal writing paper, price ten shillings.
> No money required till delivery.
> To render this work more complete, will be added, without any additional expence,
> PHILO-PUBLIUS,
> AND THE
> Articles of the Convention,
> As agreed upon at Philadelphia, September 17th, 1787.

The Federalist. Beginning in 1787, Alexander Hamilton, James Madison, and John Jay wrote eighty-five essays in support of the new Constitution that eventually were published in book form as *The Federalist*.

Hamilton (1757–1804), a brilliant and quick-tempered man, born in the West Indies, who was an aide to General George Washington and, later, secretary of the Treasury; John Jay (1745–1829), who would be first chief justice of the United States Supreme Court and governor of the state of New York; and a Virginian, James Madison (1751–1836), a lawyer of distinction who would be fourth president of the United States. They used the pseudonym Publius (Latin for "public"), but the authorship was generally known.

As originally conceived, *The Federalist* had only one purpose: to persuade reluctant New Yorkers to adopt the proposed new Constitution. It did not set out to define the nature of government, yet it has proven to be far more lasting than most political treatises. Although authored individually, the essays comprising *The Federalist* share certain themes and rhetorical strategies, and they collectively respond to the writings of the ancient Greek philosopher Aristotle, the English thinkers Thomas Hobbes and John Locke, as well as David Hume and other Scottish Enlightenment philosophers. The text prominently registers the tension between the states and the union, which is sometimes referred to as "the empire," alluding to expectations that the nation would expand westward.

The underlying moral emphasis of *The Federalist* also marks the epochal shift in public authority away from the clergy to the legal profession. All three authors had studied law, and Hamilton and Jay had practiced it. Aspects of the legal culture then emerging to prominence in the early republic—including the authors' training in deliberative (or persuasive) and forensic (or judicial) rhetoric—are clearly visible in the text. Its essential argument is that individuals have a natural right to "liberty, dignity, and happiness" and that to ensure these rights government must "secure the public good, and private rights, against the dangers of a majority," at the same time preserving the "spirit and form of a popular government." This difficult balancing of interests that *The Federalist* argues for goes to the very heart of American democracy.

From The Federalist[1]

No. 1

[ALEXANDER HAMILTON]

To the People of the State of New York.   October 27, 1787
After an unequivocal experience of the inefficacy of the subsisting[2] federal government, you are called upon to deliberate on a new Constitution for the United States of America. The subject speaks its own importance; comprehending in its consequences nothing less than the existence of the Union, the safety and welfare of the parts of which it is composed, the fate of an empire, in many respects, the most interesting in the world. It has been frequently remarked that it seems to have been reserved to the people of this country, by their conduct and example, to decide the important question whether societies of men are really capable or not of establishing good government from reflection and choice, or whether they are forever destined to depend, for their political constitutions, on accident and force. If there be any truth in the remark, the crisis at which we are arrived may with propriety be regarded as the era in which that decision is to be made; and a wrong election of the part we shall act, may, in this view, deserve to be considered as the general misfortune of mankind.

This idea will add the inducements of philanthropy to those of patriotism to heighten the solicitude, which all considerate and good men must feel for the event. Happy will it be if our choice should be directed by a judicious estimate of our true interests, unperplexed and unbiased by considerations not connected with the public good. But this is a thing more ardently to be wished than seriously to be expected. The plan offered to our deliberations affects too many particular interests, innovates[3] upon too many local institutions, not to involve in its discussion a variety of objects foreign to its merits, and of views, passions and prejudices little favorable to the discovery of truth.

Among the most formidable of the obstacles which the new Constitution will have to encounter may readily be distinguished the obvious interest of a certain class of men in every state to resist all changes which may hazard a diminution of the power, emolument and consequence of the offices they hold under the state establishments—and the perverted ambition of another class of men, who will either hope to aggrandize themselves by the confu-

---

1. The text is from *The Federalist* (1961), edited by Jacob E. Cooke.

2. Existing, present.

3. Makes changes to.

sions of their country, or will flatter themselves with fairer prospects of elevation from the subdivision of the empire into several partial confederacies, than from its union under one government.

It is not, however, my design to dwell upon observations of this nature. I am well aware that it would be disingenuous to resolve indiscriminately the opposition of any set of men (merely because their situations might subject them to suspicion) into interested or ambitious views: candor will oblige us to admit, that even such men may be actuated by upright intentions; and it cannot be doubted that much of the opposition which has made its appearance, or may hereafter make its appearance, will spring from sources, blameless at least, if not respectable, the honest errors of minds led astray by preconceived jealousies and fears. So numerous indeed and so powerful are the causes, which serve to give a false bias to the judgment, that we upon many occasions see wise and good men on the wrong as well as on the right side of questions of the first magnitude to society. This circumstance, if duly attended to, would furnish a lesson of moderation to those, who are ever so much persuaded of their being in the right in any controversy. And a further reason for caution, in this respect, might be drawn from the reflection that we are not always sure that those who advocate the truth are influenced by purer principles than their antagonists. Ambition, avarice, personal animosity, party opposition, and many other motives, not more laudable than these, are apt to operate as well upon those who support as upon those who oppose the right side of a question. Were there not even these inducements to moderation, nothing could be more ill judged than that intolerant spirit, which has, at all times, characterized political parties. For, in politics as in religion, it is equally absurd to aim at making proselytes by fire and sword. Heresies in either can rarely be cured by persecution.

And yet however just these sentiments will be allowed to be, we have already sufficient indications that it will happen in this as in all former cases of great national discussion. A torrent of angry and malignant passions will be let loose. To judge from the conduct of the opposite parties, we shall be led to conclude that they will mutually hope to evince the justness of their opinions, and to increase the number of their converts by the loudness of their declamations, and by the bitterness of their invectives. An enlightened zeal for the energy and efficiency of government will be stigmatized, as the offspring of a temper fond of despotic power and hostile to the principles of liberty. An overscrupulous jealousy of danger to the rights of the people, which is more commonly the fault of the head than of the heart, will be represented as mere pretense and artifice; the bait for popularity at the expense of public good. It will be forgotten, on the one hand, that jealousy is the usual concomitant of violent love, and that the noble enthusiasm of liberty is too apt to be infected with a spirit of narrow and illiberal distrust. On the other hand, it will be equally forgotten that the vigor of government is essential to the security of liberty; that in the contemplation of a sound and well-informed judgment, their interest can never be separated; and that a dangerous ambition more often lurks behind the specious mask of zeal for the rights of the people than under the forbidding appearance of zeal for the firmness and efficiency of government. History will teach us that the former has been found a much more certain road to the introduction of despotism than the latter, and that of those men who have overturned the liberties of republics the greatest number have begun their career by paying an obsequious court to the people, commencing demagogues and ending tyrants.

In the course of the preceding observations I have had an eye, my fellow citizens, to putting you upon your guard against all attempts, from whatever quarter, to influence your decision in a matter of the utmost moment to your welfare by any impressions other than those which may result from the evidence of truth. You will, no doubt, at the same time, have collected from the general scope of them that they proceed from a source not unfriendly to the new Constitution. Yes, my countrymen, I own to you, that, after having given it an attentive consideration, I am clearly of opinion it is your interest to adopt it. I am convinced that this is the safest course for your liberty, your dignity, and your happiness. I effect not reserves, which I do not feel. I will not amuse you with an appearance of deliberation, when I have decided. I frankly acknowledge to you my convictions, and I will freely lay before you the reasons on which they are founded. The consciousness of good intentions disdains ambiguity. I shall not however multiply professions on this head. My motives must remain in the depository of my own breast: my arguments will be open to all, and may be judged of by all. They shall at least be offered in a spirit which will not disgrace the cause of truth.

I propose in a series of papers to discuss the following interesting particulars—the utility of the Union to your political prosperity—the insufficiency of the present confederation to preserve that Union—the necessity of a government at least equally energetic with the one proposed to the attainment of this object—the conformity of the proposed constitution to the true principles of republican government—its analogy to your own state constitution—and lastly, the additional security which its adoption will afford to the preservation of that species of government, to liberty and to property.

In the progress of this discussion I shall endeavor to give a satisfactory answer to all the objections which shall have made their appearance that may seem to have any claim to your attention.

It may perhaps be thought superfluous to offer arguments to prove the utility of the Union, a point, no doubt, deeply engraved on the hearts of the great body of the people in every state, and one, which it may be imagined, has no adversaries. But the fact is that we already hear it whispered in the private circles of those who oppose the new constitution that the thirteen states are of too great extent for any general system, and that we must of necessity resort to separate confederacies of distinct portions of the whole.[4] This doctrine will, in all probability, be gradually propagated, till it has votaries enough to countenance an open avowal of it. For nothing can be more evident, to those who are able to take an enlarged view of the subject, than the alternative of an adoption of the new Constitution, or a dismemberment of the Union. It will therefore be of use to begin by examining the advantages of that Union, the certain evils and the probable dangers to which every state will be exposed from its dissolution. This shall accordingly constitute the subject of my next address.

Publius

---

4. The same idea, tracing the arguments to their consequences, is held out in several of the late publications against the new Constitution [Publius's note].

No. 10

[JAMES MADISON]

To the People of the State of New York.   November 22, 1787

Among the numerous advantages promised by a well-constructed Union, none deserves to be more accurately developed than its tendency to break and control the violence of faction. The friend of popular governments never finds himself so much alarmed for their character and fate as when he contemplates their propensity to this dangerous vice. He will not fail therefore to set a due value on any plan which, without violating the principles to which he is attached, provides a proper cure for it. The instability, injustice and confusion introduced into the public councils have in truth been the mortal diseases under which popular governments have everywhere perished; as they continue to be the favorite and fruitful topics from which the adversaries to liberty derive their most specious declamations. The valuable improvements made by the American constitutions on the popular models, both ancient and modern, cannot certainly be too much admired; but it would be an unwarrantable partiality to contend that they have as effectually obviated the danger on this side as was wished and expected. Complaints are everywhere heard from our most considerate and virtuous citizens, equally the friends of public and private faith and of public and personal liberty; that our governments are too unstable; that the public good is disregarded in the conflicts of rival parties; and that measures are too often decided not according to the rules of justice and the rights of the minor party, but by the superior force of an interested and overbearing majority. However anxiously we may wish that these complaints had no foundation, the evidence of known facts will not permit us to deny that they are in some degree true. It will be found indeed, on a candid review of our situation, that some of the distresses under which we labor have been erroneously charged on the operation of our governments; but it will be found, at the same time, that other causes will not alone account for many of our heaviest misfortunes; and particularly, for that prevailing and increasing distrust of public engagements, and alarm for private rights, which are echoed from one end of the continent to the other. These must be chiefly, if not wholly, effects of the unsteadiness and injustice with which a factious spirit has tainted our public administrations.

By a faction I understand a number of citizens, whether amounting to a majority or minority of the whole, who are united and actuated by some common impulse of passion or of interest, adverse to the rights of other citizens, or to the permanent and aggregate interests of the community.

There are two methods of curing the mischiefs of faction: the one, by removing its causes; the other, by controlling its effects.

There are again two methods of removing the causes of faction: the one by destroying the liberty which is essential to its existence; the other, by giving to every citizen the same opinions, the same passions, and the same interests.

It could never be more truly said than of the first remedy, that it is worse than the disease. Liberty is to faction, what air is to fire, an aliment[5]

---

5. Nutriment; sustenance.

without which it instantly expires. But it could not be a less folly to abolish liberty, which is essential to political life, because it nourishes faction, than it would be to wish the annihilation of air, which is essential to animal life, because it imparts to fire its destructive agency.

The second expedient is as impracticable as the first would be unwise. As long as the reason of man continues fallible, and he is at liberty to exercise it, different opinions will be formed. As long as the connection subsists between his reason and his self-love, his opinions and his passions will have a reciprocal influence on each other; and the former will be objects to which the latter will attach themselves. The diversity in the faculties of men from which the rights of property originate is not less an insuperable obstacle to a uniformity of interests. The protection of these faculties is the first object of government. From the protection of different and unequal faculties of acquiring property, the possession of different degrees and kinds of property immediately results: and from the influence of these on the sentiments and views of the respective proprietors ensues a division of the society into different interests and parties.

The latent causes of faction are thus sown in the nature of man; and we see them everywhere brought into different degrees of activity, according to the different circumstances of civil society. A zeal for different opinions concerning religion, concerning government and many other points, as well of speculation as of practice; an attachment to different leaders ambitiously contending for pre-eminence and power; or to persons of other descriptions whose fortunes have been interesting to the human passions have in turn divided mankind into parties, inflamed them with mutual animosity, and rendered them much more disposed to vex and oppress each other than to cooperate for their common good. So strong is this propensity of mankind to fall into mutual animosities that where no substantial occasion presents itself, the most frivolous and fanciful distinctions have been sufficient to kindle their unfriendly passions and excite their most violent conflicts. But the most common and durable source of factions has been the various and unequal distribution of property. Those who hold and those who are without property have ever formed distinct interests in society. Those who are creditors and those who are debtors fall under a like discrimination. A landed interest, a manufacturing interest, a mercantile interest, a monied interest, with many lesser interests, grow up of necessity in civilized nations, and divide them into different classes, actuated by different sentiments and views. The regulation of these various and interfering interests forms the principal task of modern legislation, and involves the spirit of party and faction in the necessary and ordinary operations of government.

No man is allowed to be a judge in his own cause, because his interest would certainly bias his judgment and, not improbably, corrupt his integrity. With equal, nay with greater, reason a body of men are unfit to be both judges and parties at the same time; yet what are many of the most important acts of legislation but so many judicial determinations, not indeed concerning the rights of single persons, but concerning the rights of large bodies of citizens; and what are the different classes of legislators but advocates and parties to the causes which they determine? Is a law proposed concerning private debts? It is a question to which the creditors are parties on one side and the debtors on the other. Justice ought to hold the balance between them. Yet the parties are and must be themselves the judges; and the most numerous party, or, in other words, the most powerful faction, must be expected to prevail. Shall domestic manufactures be encouraged, and in what degree, by restrictions on foreign manufactures? are questions which would be differently decided by the landed and the manufacturing classes; and probably by neither, with a sole regard to justice and the public good. The apportionment of taxes on the various descriptions of property is an act which seems to require the most exact impartiality; yet, there is perhaps no legislative act in which greater opportunity and temptation are given to a predominant party to trample on the rules of justice. Every shilling with which they overburden the inferior number is a shilling saved to their own pockets.

It is in vain to say that enlightened statesmen will be able to adjust these clashing interests and render them all subservient to the public good. Enlightened statesmen will not always be at the helm; nor, in many cases, can such an adjustment be made at all, without taking into view indirect and remote considerations, which will rarely prevail over the immediate interest which one party may find in disregarding the rights of another, or the good of the whole.

The inference to which we are brought is that the *causes* of faction cannot be removed, and that relief is only to be sought in the means of controlling its *effects*.

If a faction consists of less than a majority, relief is supplied by the republican principle, which enables the majority to defeat its sinister views by regular vote. It may clog the administration, it may convulse the society, but it will be unable to execute and mask its violence under the forms of the Constitution. When a majority is included in a faction, the form of popular government on the other hand enables it to sacrifice to its ruling passion or interest both the public good and the rights of other citizens. To secure the public good and private rights against the danger of such a faction, and at the same time to preserve the spirit and the form of popular government, is then the great object to which our inquiries are directed. Let me add that it is the great desideratum[6] by which alone this form of government can be rescued from the opprobrium under which it has so long labored and be recommended to the esteem and adoption of mankind.

By what means is this object attainable? Evidently by one of two only. Either the existence of the same passion or interest in a majority at the same time must be prevented; or the majority, having such co-existent passion or interest, must be rendered, by their number and local situation, unable to concert and carry into effect schemes of oppression. If the impulse and the opportunity be suffered to coincide, we well know that neither moral nor religious motives can be relied on as an adequate control. They are not found to be such on the injustice and violence of individuals, and lose their efficacy in proportion to the number combined together; that is, in proportion as their efficacy becomes needful.

From this view of the subject, it may be concluded, that a pure democracy, by which I mean a society consisting of a small number of citizens who assemble and administer the government in person, can admit of no cure

6. Thing which is desired; that which is felt to be missing and needed (Latin).

for the mischiefs of faction. A common passion or interest will, in almost every case, be felt by a majority of the whole; a communication and concert[7] results from the form of government itself; and there is nothing to check the inducements to sacrifice the weaker party, or an obnoxious individual. Hence it is that such democracies have ever been spectacles of turbulence and contention; have ever been found incompatible with personal security, or the rights of property; and have in general been as short in their lives, as they have been violent in their deaths. Theoretic[8] politicians, who have patronized this species of government, have erroneously supposed that by reducing mankind to a perfect equality in their political rights, they would, at the same time, be perfectly equalized and assimilated in their possessions, their opinions, and their passions.

A republic, by which I mean a government in which the scheme of representation takes place, opens a different prospect, and promises the cure for which we are seeking. Let us examine the points in which it varies from pure democracy, and we shall comprehend both the nature of the cure, and the efficacy which it must derive from the Union.

The two great points of difference between a democracy and a republic are, first, the delegation of the government, in the latter, to a small number of citizens elected by the rest: secondly, the greater number of citizens, and greater sphere of country, over which the latter may be extended.

The effect of the first difference is, on the one hand, to refine and enlarge the public views by passing them through the medium of a chosen body of citizens, whose wisdom may best discern the true interest of their country, and whose patriotism and love of justice will be least likely to sacrifice it to temporary or partial considerations. Under such a regulation, it may well happen that the public voice pronounced by the representatives of the people will be more consonant to the public good than if pronounced by the people themselves convened for the purpose. On the other hand, the effect may be inverted. Men of factious tempers, of local prejudices, or of sinister designs may, by intrigue, by corruption or by other means, first obtain the suffrages,[9] and then betray the interests of the people. The question resulting is whether small or extensive republics are most favorable to the election of proper guardians of the public weal: and it is clearly decided in favor of the latter by two obvious considerations.

In the first place it is to be remarked that however small the republic may be, the representatives must be raised to a certain number in order to guard against the cabals[1] of a few; and that however large it may be, they must be limited to a certain number in order to guard against the confusion of a multitude. Hence the number of representatives in the two cases, not being in proportion to that of the constituents, and being proportionally greatest in the small republic, it follows, that if the proportion of fit characters be not less in the large than in the small republic, the former will present a greater option, and consequently a greater probability of a fit choice.

In the next place, as each representative will be chosen by a greater number of citizens in the large than in the small republic, it will be more difficult

7. Agreement, union.
8. Theoretical.

9. Votes.
1. Plots.

for unworthy candidates to practice with success the vicious arts, by which elections are too often carried; and the suffrages of the people being more free will be more likely to center on men who possess the most attractive merit, and the most diffusive and established characters.

It must be confessed that in this, as in most other cases, there is a mean, on both sides of which inconveniencies will be found to lie. By enlarging too much the number of electors, you render the representative too little acquainted with all their local circumstances and lesser interests; as by reducing it too much, you render him unduly attached to these, and too little fit to comprehend and pursue great and national objects. The federal Constitution forms a happy combination in this respect; the great and aggregate interests being referred to the national, the local, and, particular, to the state legislatures.

The other point of difference is the greater number of citizens and extent of territory which may be brought within the compass of republican, than of democratic government; and it is this circumstance principally which renders factious combinations less to be dreaded in the former than in the latter. The smaller the society, the fewer probably will be the distinct parties and interests composing it; the fewer the distinct parties and interests, the more frequently will a majority be found of the same party; and the smaller the number of individuals composing a majority, and smaller the compass within which they are placed, the more easily will they concert and execute their plans of oppression. Extend the sphere, and you take in a greater variety of parties and interests; you make it less probable that a majority of the whole will have a common motive to invade the rights of other citizens; or if such a common motive exists, it will be more difficult for all who feel it to discover their own strength, and to act in unison with each other. Besides other impediments, it may be remarked, that where there is a consciousness of unjust or dishonorable purposes, communication is always checked by distrust, in proportion to the number whose concurrence is necessary.

Hence it clearly appears that the same advantage which a republic has over a democracy, in controlling the effects of faction, is enjoyed by a large over a small republic—is enjoyed by the Union over the states composing it. Does this advantage consist in the substitution of representatives, whose enlightened views and virtuous sentiments render them superior to local prejudices, and to schemes of injustice? It will not be denied, that the representation of the Union will be most likely to possess these requisite endowments. Does it consist in the greater security afforded by a greater variety of parties, against the event of any one party being able to outnumber and oppress the rest? In an equal degree does the increased variety of parties, comprised within the Union, increase this security? Does it, in fine,[2] consist in the greater obstacles opposed to the concert and accomplishment of the secret wishes of an unjust and interested majority? Here, again, the extent of the Union gives it the most palpable advantage.

The influence of factious leaders may kindle a flame within their particular states, but will be unable to spread a general conflagration through the other states: a religious sect may degenerate into a political faction in a part

---

2. In short; to sum up.

of the confederacy,[3] but the variety of sects dispersed over the entire face of it must secure the national councils against any danger from that source: a rage for paper money, for an abolition of debts, for an equal division of property, or for any other improper or wicked project, will be less apt to pervade the whole body of the Union than a particular member of it; in the same proportion as such a malady is more likely to taint a particular county or district than an entire state.

In the extent and proper structure of the Union, therefore, we behold a republican remedy for the diseases most incident to republican government. And according to the degree of pleasure and pride we feel in being republicans, ought to be our zeal in cherishing the spirit, and supporting the character of Federalists.

Publius

1787   1788

3. Alliance, union.

OLAUDAH EQUIANO
1745?–1797

In 1789, *The Interesting Narrative of the Life of Olaudah Equiano, or Gustavus Vassa, the African* was published by Equiano in London, and it found an enthusiastic American audience when it was reprinted in New York two years later. Over the next five years *The Interesting Narrative* went through eight more editions, and it was reprinted on several occasions in the United States during the pre–Civil War period. This publication history suggests both the book's centrality to the antislavery cause and the powerful appeal of Equiano's narrative voice. No black person before the abolitionist Frederick Douglass (1817–1895) spoke so movingly to American readers about the inhumanity of slavery, and no work before Douglass's *Narrative* had such an impact on the antislavery movement. Incorporating the vocabulary and ideals of the Enlightenment—particularly the belief that sentiment linked all human beings and thus provided a basis for universal claims to human rights—Equiano made a powerful case for the countless disenfranchised and exploited workers whose labor fueled the new mercantilism. In American literature, replete with self-made figures who voyage from innocence to experience, Equiano's story stands in a class by itself, both for the challenges he faced and for the transformations he experienced. He defined himself as neither African American (his first owner in the New World was a Virginian) nor Anglo African (after he settled in London); instead, he came to exemplify the Atlantic Rim, presenting himself as someone who at various times called Africa, the Americas, and Europe his home.

Equiano wrote that he was born around 1745 in what is now Nigeria, in an otherwise unknown Ibo village called Essaka. He was sold to British slavers in 1756 and transported first to Barbadoes, in the West Indies, and then to a plantation in

Virginia. Recent scholarship has questioned these claims, suggesting that Equiano may have been born in the Carolinas. If this proves to be the case, it means that he made the decision to assume an African heritage for his life story, which then can be understood as an example of a witness narrative, that is, the testimony of someone from a marginalized group who speaks in the first person for the entire group's history. To make his life appear more representative, Equiano may have merged his experiences with those of the voiceless Africans who endured the horrors of the Middle Passage.

While the facts of his early life are uncertain, his account of his later years is corroborated by existing documents. He was with his second owner, Lieutenant Michael Henry Pascal, throughout the Seven Years' War (1756–63), in which England and France led opposing coalitions of nations. He was present at the siege of Fort Louisburg, on Cape Breton Island, Nova Scotia. Eventually, Equiano was sold to a Quaker merchant from Philadelphia, Robert King, who conducted much of his business in the West Indies. King often traded in "live cargo," or slaves, and Equiano saw much that made him grateful for his Quaker master's treatment of him, though he was also sensitive to the freedom being denied him. He saw the ugliest side of American life in both the North and the South. Even in Philadelphia, a city built on the premise of brotherly love, Equiano observed that the freed black was treated with profound contempt, "plundered" and "universally insulted," with no possibility of redress. King, however, did make it possible for Equiano to purchase his freedom in 1766. Having gained his liberty by paying forty pounds—money earned by carrying on his own business while managing King's—he never set foot on American soil again.

It was Equiano's intention to settle in London for the rest of his life. He made his living there as a free servant, a musician (he played the French horn), and a barber. Eventually Equiano's skill as a seaman, and his remarkable curiosity, made him yearn for new adventures. Before he died he had traveled as far as Turkey; attended the opera in Rome; participated in an expedition to search for a Northwest Passage through the arctic to the Pacific Ocean; and seen Jamaica, Honduras, and Nicaragua.

In 1783 Equiano brought to the British public's attention the case of the infamous ship *Zong*, whose owners had thrown one hundred and thirty-two shackled slaves overboard and later made insurance claims against their loss. He lectured widely on the abolition of slavery and urged a project to resettle poor blacks in Sierra Leone, Africa. He was given an official post in this undertaking, but lost it after he made accusations of corruption against British government officials. Although he spoke about his desire to return to Africa, it always lay beyond his reach. In a letter to his hosts in Birmingham, England, after he had lectured there, he wrote evocatively about an imagined scene:

> These acts of kindness and hospitality have filled me with a longing desire to see these worthy friends on my own estate in Africa, where the richest produce of it should be devoted to their entertainment. There they should partake of the luxuriant pineapples, and the well-flavored virgin palm-wine, and to heighten the bliss I would burn a certain tree, that would afford us light as clear and brilliant as the virtue of my guests.

In 1792 Equiano married Susanna Cullen, and their marriage was considered of sufficient public interest to be reported in the London *Gentleman's Magazine*. Five years later, he died of uncertain causes, and one of his daughters died shortly after.

From The Interesting Narrative of the Life of Olaudah Equiano, or Gustavas Vassa, the African, Written by Himself[1]

From *Chapter I*

I believe it is difficult for those who publish their own memoirs to escape the imputation of vanity; nor is this the only disadvantage under which they labor: it is also their misfortune, that what is uncommon is rarely, if ever, believed, and what is obvious we are apt to turn from with disgust, and to charge the writer with impertinence. People generally think those memoirs only worthy to be read or remembered which abound in great or striking events; those, in short, which in a high degree excite either admiration or pity: all others they consign to contempt and oblivion. It is therefore, I confess, not a little hazardous in a private and obscure individual, and a stranger too, thus to solicit the indulgent attention of the public; especially when I own[2] I offer here the history of neither a saint, a hero, nor a tyrant. I believe there are few events in my life, which have not happened to many: it is true the incidents of it are numerous; and, did I consider myself an European, I might say my sufferings were great: but when I compare my lot with that of most of my countrymen, I regard myself as a *particular favorite of Heaven,* and acknowledge the mercies of Providence in every occurrence of my life. If, then, the following narrative does not appear sufficiently interesting to engage general attention, let my motive be some excuse for its publication. I am not so foolishly vain as to expect from it either immortality or literary reputation. If it affords any satisfaction to my numerous friends, at whose request it has been written, or in the smallest degree promotes the interests of humanity, the ends for which it was undertaken will be fully attained, and every wish of my heart gratified. Let it therefore be remembered, that, in wishing to avoid censure, I do not aspire to praise.

That part of Africa, known by the name of Guinea, to which the trade for slaves is carried on, extends along the coast above 3400 miles, from Senegal to Angola, and includes a variety of kingdoms. Of these the most considerable is the kingdom of Benin, both as to extent and wealth, the richness and cultivation of the soil, the power of its king, and the number and warlike disposition of the inhabitants. It is situated nearly under the line,[3] and extends along the coast about 170 miles, but runs back into the interior part of Africa to a distance hitherto, I believe, unexplored by any traveler; and seems only terminated at length by the empire of Abyssinnia, near 1500 miles from its beginning. This kingdom is divided into many provinces or districts: in one of the most remote and fertile of which, I was born, in the year 1745, situated in a charming fruitful vale, named Essaka. The distance of this province from the capital of Benin and the sea coast must be very considerable: for I had never heard of white men or Europeans, nor of the sea; and our subjection to the king of Benin was little more than nominal;

---

1. The text is from the first edition, published in two volumes in 1789. The original paragraphing has been altered to facilitate reading.

2. Acknowledge.
3. I.e., the equator.

for every transaction of the government, as far as my slender observation extended, was conducted by the chief or elders of the place. The manners and government of a people who have little commerce with other countries, are generally very simple; and the history of what passes in one family or village, may serve as a specimen of the whole nation. My father was one of those elders or chiefs I have spoken of, and was styled Embrenche; a term, as I remember, importing the highest distinction, and signifying in our language a *mark* of grandeur. This mark is conferred on the person entitled to it, by cutting the skin across at the top of the forehead, and drawing it down to the eyebrows: and while it is in this situation applying a warm hand, and rubbing it until it shrinks up into a thick *weal* across the lower part of the forehead. Most of the judges and senators were thus marked; my father had long borne it: I had seen it conferred on one of my brothers, and I also was *destined* to receive it by my parents. Those Embrenche or chief men, decided disputes and punished crimes; for which purpose they always assembled together. The proceedings were generally short: and in most cases the law of retaliation prevailed.* * *

We are almost a nation of dancers, musicians and poets. Thus every great event, such as a triumphant return from battle, or other cause of public rejoicing, is celebrated in public dances, which are accompanied with songs and music suited to the occasion. The assembly is separated into four divisions, which dance either apart or in succession, and each with a character peculiar to itself. The first division contains the married men, who in their dances frequently exhibit feats of arms, and the representation of a battle. To these succeed the married women, who dance in the second division. The young men occupy the third: and the maidens the fourth. Each represents some interesting scene of real life, such as a great achievement, domestic employment, a pathetic[4] story, or some rural sport; and as the subject is generally founded on some recent event, it is therefore ever new. This gives our dances a spirit and variety which I have scarcely seen elsewhere.[5]

* * *

Chapter II

I hope the reader will not think I have trespassed on his patience in introducing myself to him, with some account of the manners and customs of my country. They had been implanted in me with great care, and made an impression on my mind, which time could not erase, and which all the adversity and variety of fortune I have since experienced, served only to rivet and record; for, whether the love of one's country be real or imaginary, or a lesson of reason, or an instinct of nature, I still look back with pleasure on the first scenes of my life, though that pleasure has been for the most part mingled with sorrow.

I have already acquainted the reader with the time and place of my birth. My father, besides many slaves, had a numerous family, of which seven lived to grow up, including myself and a sister, who was the only daughter.

4. Emotionally moving.
5. When I was in Smyrna I have frequently seen the Greeks dance after this manner [Equiano's note].

As I was the youngest of the sons, I became, of course, the greatest favorite with my mother, and was always with her; and she used to take particular pains to form my mind. I was trained up from my earliest years in the art of war: my daily exercise was shooting and throwing javelins; and my mother adorned me with emblems, after the manner of our greatest warriors. In this way I grew up till I was turned the age of eleven, when an end was put to my happiness in the following manner:—generally when the grown people in the neighborhood were gone far in the fields to labor, the children assembled together in some of the neighboring premises to play; and commonly some of us used to get up a tree to look out for any assailant, or kidnapper, that might come upon us—for they sometimes took those opportunities of our parents' absence, to attack and carry off as many as they could seize. One day as I was watching at the top of a tree in our yard, I saw one of those people come into the yard of our next neighbor but one to kidnap, there being many stout[6] young people in it. Immediately on this I gave the alarm of the rogue, and he was surrounded by the stoutest of them, who entangled him with cords, so that he could not escape till some of the grown people came and secured him. But, alas! ere long it was my fate to be thus attacked, and to be carried off, when none of the grown people were nigh. One day, when all our people were gone out to their works as usual, and only I and my dear sister were left to mind the house, two men and a woman got over our walls, and in a moment seized us both, and, without giving us time to cry out, or make resistance, they stopped our mouths, and ran off with us into the nearest wood. Here they tied our hands, and continued to carry us as far as they could, till night came on, when we reached a small house, where the robbers halted for refreshment, and spent the night. We were then unbound, but were unable to take any food; and, being quite overpowered by fatigue and grief, our only relief was some sleep, which allayed our misfortune for a short time. The next morning we left the house, and continued traveling all the day. For a long time we had kept the woods, but at last we came into a road which I believed I knew. I had now some hopes of being delivered; for we had advanced but a little way before I discovered some people at a distance, on which I began to cry out for their assistance; but my cries had no other effect than to make them tie me faster and stop my mouth, and then they put me into a large sack. They also stopped my sister's mouth, and tied her hands; and in this manner we proceeded till we were out of sight of these people. When we went to rest the following night, they offered us some victuals, but we refused it; and the only comfort we had was in being in one another's arms all that night, and bathing each other with our tears. But alas! we were soon deprived of even the small comfort of weeping together. The next day proved a day of greater sorrow than I had yet experienced; for my sister and I were then separated, while we lay clasped in each other's arms. It was in vain that we besought them not to part us; she was torn from me, and immediately carried away, while I was left in a state of distraction not to be described. I cried and grieved continually; and for several days did not eat any thing but what they forced into my mouth. At length, after many days traveling, during which I had often changed masters, I got into the hands of a chieftain, in a very pleasant country. This man had two wives and some children, and they

6. Strong.

all used[7] me extremely well, and did all they could to comfort me; particularly the first wife, who was something like my mother. Although I was a great many days' journey from my father's house, yet these people spoke exactly the same language with us. This first master of mine, as I may call him, was a smith,[8] and my principal employment was working his bellows, which were the same kind as I had seen in my vicinity. They were in some respects not unlike the stoves here in gentlemen's kitchens, and were covered over with leather; and in the middle of that leather a stick was fixed, and a person stood up, and worked it in the same manner as is done to pump water out of a cask with a hand pump. I believe it was gold he worked, for it was of a lovely bright yellow color, and was worn by the women on their wrists and ankles. I was there I suppose about a month, and they at last used to trust me some little distance from the house. This liberty I used in embracing every opportunity to inquire the way to my own home; and I also sometimes, for the same purpose, went with the maidens, in the cool of the evenings, to bring pitchers of water from the springs for the use of the house. I had also remarked where the sun rose in the morning, and set in the evening, as I had traveled along; and I had observed that my father's house was towards the rising of the sun. I therefore determined to seize the first opportunity of making my escape, and to shape my course for that quarter; for I was quite oppressed and weighed down by grief after my mother and friends; and my love of liberty, ever great, was strengthened by the mortifying circumstance of not daring to eat with the free-born children, although I was mostly their companion. While I was projecting my escape one day, an unlucky event happened, which quite disconcerted my plan, and put an end to my hopes. I used to be sometimes employed in assisting an elderly slave to cook and take care of the poultry; and one morning, while I was feeding some chickens, I happened to toss a small pebble at one of them, which hit it on the middle, and directly killed it. The old slave, having soon after missed the chicken, inquired after it; and on my relating the accident (for I told her the truth, for my mother would never suffer me to tell a lie), she flew into a violent passion, and threatened that I should suffer for it; and, my master being out, she immediately went and told her mistress what I had done. This alarmed me very much, and I expected an instant flogging, which to me was uncommonly dreadful, for I had seldom been beaten at home. I therefore resolved to fly; and accordingly I ran into a thicket that was hard by, and hid myself in the bushes. Soon afterwards my mistress and the slave returned, and, not seeing me, they searched all the house, but not finding me, and I not making answer when they called to me, they thought I had run away, and the whole neighborhood was raised in the pursuit of me. In that part of the country, as in ours, the houses and villages were skirted with woods, or shrubberies, and the bushes were so thick that a man could readily conceal himself in them, so as to elude the strictest search. The neighbors continued the whole day looking for me, and several times many of them came within a few yards of the place where I lay hid. I expected every moment, when I heard a rustling among the trees, to be found out, and punished by my master; but they never discovered me, though they were often so near that I even heard their

---

7. Treated.

8. A metalworker; here, a goldsmith.

conjectures as they were looking about for me; and I now learned from them that any attempts to return home would be hopeless. Most of them supposed I had fled towards home; but the distance was so great, and the way so intricate, that they thought I could never reach it, and that I should be lost in the woods. When I heard this I was seized with a violent panic, and abandoned myself to despair. Night, too, began to approach, and aggravated all my fears. I had before entertained hopes of getting home, and had determined when it should be dark to make the attempt; but I was now convinced it was fruitless, and began to consider that, if possibly I could escape all other animals, I could not those of the human kind; and that, not knowing the way, I must perish in the woods. Thus was I like the hunted deer—

> —"Every leaf and every whisp'ring breath,
> Convey'd a foe, and every foe a death."[9]

I heard frequent rustlings among the leaves, and being pretty sure they were snakes, I expected every instant to be stung by them. This increased my anguish, and the horror of my situation became now quite insupportable. I at length quitted the thicket, very faint and hungry, for I had not eaten or drank any thing all the day, and crept to my master's kitchen, from whence I set out at first, which was an open shed, and laid myself down in the ashes with an anxious wish for death, to relieve me from all my pains. I was scarcely awake in the morning, when the old woman slave, who was the first up, came to light the fire, and saw me in the fire place. She was very much surprised to see me, and could scarcely believe her own eyes. She now promised to intercede for me, and went for her master, who soon after came, and, having slightly reprimanded me, ordered me to be taken care of, and not ill treated.

Soon after this, my master's only daughter, and child by his first wife, sickened and died, which affected him so much that for some time he was almost frantic, and really would have killed himself, had he not been watched and prevented. However, in short time afterwards he recovered, and I was again sold. I was now carried to the left of the sun's rising, through many dreary wastes and dismal woods, amidst the hideous roarings of wild beasts. The people I was sold to used to carry me very often, when I was tired, either on their shoulders or on their backs. I saw many convenient well built sheds along the road, at proper distances, to accommodate the merchants and travelers, who lay in those buildings along with their wives, who often accompany them; and they always go well armed.

From the time I left my own nation, I always found somebody that understood me till I came to the sea coast. The languages of different nations did not totally differ, nor were they so copious as those of the Europeans, particularly the English. They were therefore, easily learned; and, while I was journeying thus through Africa, I acquired two or three different tongues. In this manner I had been traveling for a considerable time, when, one evening, to my great surprise, whom should I see brought to the house where I was but my dear sister! As soon as she saw me, she gave a loud shriek, and

---

9. Near quotation of lines 287–88 of "Cooper's Hill," a poem by the Anglo-Irish writer and statesman Sir John Denham (1615–1669).

ran into my arms—I was quite overpowered: neither of us could speak; but, for a considerable time, clung to each other in mutual embraces, unable to do any thing but weep. Our meeting affected all who saw us; and, indeed, I must acknowledge, in honor of those sable[1] destroyers of human rights, that I never met with any ill treatment, or saw any offered to their slaves, except tying them, when necessary, to keep them from running away. When these people knew we were brother and sister, they indulged us to be together; and the man, to whom I supposed we belonged, lay with us, he in the middle, while she and I held one another by the hands across his breast all night; and thus for a while we forgot our misfortunes, in the joy of being together; but even this small comfort was soon to have an end; for scarcely had the fatal morning appeared when she was again torn from me forever! I was now more miserable, if possible, than before. The small relief which her presence gave me from pain was gone, and the wretchedness of my situation was redoubled by my anxiety after her fate, and my apprehensions lest her sufferings should be greater than mine, when I could not be with her to alleviate them. Yes, thou dear partner of all my childish sports! thou sharer of my joys and sorrows! happy should I have ever esteemed myself to encounter every misery for you and to procure your freedom by the sacrifice of my own.—Though you were early forced from my arms, your image has been always riveted in my heart, from which neither time nor fortune have been able to remove it; so that, while the thoughts of your sufferings have damped my prosperity, they have mingled with adversity and increased its bitterness. To that Heaven which protects the weak from the strong, I commit the care of your innocence and virtues, if they have not already received their full reward, and if your youth and delicacy have not long since fallen victims to the violence of the African trader, the pestilential stench of a Guinea ship, the seasoning in the European colonies, or the lash and lust of a brutal and unrelenting overseer.

I did not long remain after my sister. I was again sold, and carried through a number of places, till after traveling a considerable time, I came to a town called Tinmah, in the most beautiful country I had yet seen in Africa. It was extremely rich, and there were many rivulets which flowed through it, and supplied a large pond in the center of the town, where the people washed. Here I first saw and tasted cocoa nuts, which I thought superior to any nuts I had ever tasted before; and the trees which were loaded, were also interspersed among the houses, which had commodious shades adjoining, and were in the same manner as ours, the insides being neatly plastered and whitewashed. Here I also saw and tasted for the first time, sugar cane. Their money consisted of little white shells, the size of the finger nail. I was sold here for one hundred and seventy-two of them, by a merchant who lived and brought me there. I had been about two or three days at his house, when a wealthy widow, a neighbor of his, came there one evening, and brought with her an only son, a young gentleman about my own age and size. Here they saw me; and, having taken a fancy to me, I was bought of the merchant, and went home with them. Her house and premises were situated close to one of those rivulets I have mentioned, and were the finest I ever saw in Africa: they were very extensive, and she had a number of slaves to attend her. The next

1. Black.

day I was washed and perfumed, and when mealtime came, I was led into the presence of my mistress, and ate and drank before her with her son. This filled me with astonishment; and I could scarce help expressing my surprise that the young gentleman should suffer[2] me, who was bound, to eat with him who was free; and not only so, but that he would not at any time either eat or drink till I had taken first, because I was the eldest, which was agreeable to our custom. Indeed, every thing here, and all their treatment of me, made me forget that I was a slave. The language of these people resembled ours so nearly, that we understood each other perfectly. They had also the very same customs as we. There were likewise slaves daily to attend us, while my young master and I, with other boys, sported with our darts and bows and arrows, as I had been used to do at home. In this resemblance to my former happy state, I passed about two months; and I now began to think I was to be adopted into the family, and was beginning to be reconciled to my situation, and to forget by degrees my misfortunes, when all at once the delusion vanished; for, without the least previous knowledge, one morning early, while my dear master and companion was still asleep, I was awakened out of my reverie to fresh sorrow, and hurried away even amongst the uncircumcised.

Thus, at the very moment I dreamed of the greatest happiness, I found myself most miserable; and it seemed as if fortune wished to give me this taste of joy only to render the reverse more poignant.—The change I now experienced, was as painful as it was sudden and unexpected. It was a change indeed, from a state of bliss to a scene which is inexpressible by me, as it discovered[3] to me an element I had never before beheld, and till then had no idea of, and wherein such instances of hardship and cruelty continually occurred, as I can never reflect on but with horror.

All the nations and people I had hitherto passed through, resembled our own in their manners, customs, and language: but I came at length to a country, the inhabitants of which differed from us in all those particulars. I was very much struck with this difference, especially when I came among a people who did not circumcise, and ate without washing their hands. They cooked also in iron pots, and had European cutlasses and cross bows, which were unknown to us, and fought with their fists among themselves. Their women were not so modest as ours, for they ate, and drank, and slept with their men. But above all, I was amazed to see no sacrifices or offerings among them. In some of those places the people ornamented themselves with scars, and likewise filed their teeth very sharp. They wanted sometimes to ornament me in the same manner, but I would not suffer them; hoping that I might some time be among a people who did not thus disfigure themselves, as I thought they did. At last I came to the banks of a large river which was covered with canoes, in which the people appeared to live with their household utensils, and provisions of all kinds. I was beyond measure astonished at this, as I had never before seen any water larger than a pond or a rivulet: and my surprise was mingled with no small fear when I was put into one of these canoes, and we began to paddle and move along the river. We continued going on thus till night, and when we came to land, and made fires on the banks, each family by themselves; some dragged their canoes on

2. Allow.   3. Revealed.

shore, others stayed and cooked in theirs, and laid in them all night. Those on the land had mats, of which they made tents, some in the shape of little houses; in these we slept; and after the morning meal, we embarked again and proceeded as before. I was often very much astonished to see some of the women, as well as the men, jump into the water, dive to the bottom, come up again, and swim about.—Thus I continued to travel, sometimes by land, sometimes by water, through different countries and various nations, till, at the end of six or seven months after I had been kidnapped, I arrived at the sea coast. It would be tedious and uninteresting to relate all the incidents which befell me during this journey, and which I have not yet forgotten; of the various hands I passed through, and the manners and customs of all the different people among whom I lived—I shall therefore only observe, that in all the places where I was, the soil was exceedingly rich; the pumpkins, eadas,[4] plaintains, yams, etc., etc., were in great abundance, and of incredible size. There were also vast quantities of different gums, though not used for any purpose, and every where a great deal of tobacco. The cotton even grew quite wild, and there was plenty of red-wood. I saw no mechanics[5] whatever in all the way, except such as I have mentioned. The chief employment in all these countries was agriculture, and both the males and females, as with us, were brought up to it, and trained in the arts of war.

The first object which saluted my eyes when I arrived on the coast, was the sea, and a slave ship, which was then riding at anchor, and waiting for its cargo. These filled me with astonishment, which was soon converted into terror, when I was carried on board. I was immediately handled, and tossed up to see if I were sound, by some of the crew; and I was now persuaded that I had gotten into a world of bad spirits, and that they were going to kill me. Their complexions, too, differing so much from ours, their long hair, and the language they spoke (which was very different from any I had ever heard), united to confirm me in this belief. Indeed, such were the horrors of my views and fears at the moment, that, if ten thousand worlds had been my own, I would have freely parted with them all to have exchanged my condition with that of the meanest[6] slave in my own country. When I looked round the ship too, and saw a large furnace[7] of copper boiling, and a multitude of black people of every description chained together, every one of their countenances expressing dejection and sorrow, I no longer doubted of my fate; and, quite overpowered with horror and anguish, I fell motionless on the deck and fainted. When I recovered a little, I found some black people about me, who I believed were some of those who had brought me on board, and had been receiving their pay; they talked to me in order to cheer me, but all in vain. I asked them if we were not to be eaten by those white men with horrible looks, red faces, and long hair. They told me I was not: and one of the crew brought me a small portion of spirituous liquor in a wine glass, but, being afraid of him, I would not take it out of his hand. One of the blacks, therefore, took it from him and gave it to me, and I took a little down my palate, which, instead of reviving me, as they thought it would, threw me into the greatest consternation at the strange feeling it produced,

4. Or eddoes, edible roots found in the tropics.
5. Artisans, manual workers.
6. Most poorly treated.
7. Smelting furnace.

having never tasted any such liquor before. Soon after this, the blacks who brought me on board went off, and left me abandoned to despair.

I now saw myself deprived of all chance of returning to my native country, or even the least glimpse of hope of gaining the shore, which I now considered as friendly; and I even wished for my former slavery in preference to my present situation, which was filled with horrors of every kind, still heightened by my ignorance of what I was to undergo. I was not long suffered to indulge my grief; I was soon put down under the decks, and there I received such a salutation in my nostrils as I had never experienced in my life: so that, with the loathsomeness of the stench, and crying together, I became so sick and low that I was not able to eat, nor had I the least desire to taste any thing. I now wished for the last friend, death, to relieve me; but soon, to my grief, two of the white men offered me eatables; and, on my refusing to eat, one of them held me fast by the hands, and laid me across, I think the windlass, and tied my feet, while the other flogged me severely. I had never experienced any thing of this kind before, and although not being used to the water, I naturally feared that element the first time I saw it, yet, nevertheless, could I have got over the nettings, I would have jumped over the side, but I could not; and besides, the crew used to watch us very closely who were not chained down to the decks, lest we should leap into the water; and I have seen some of these poor African prisoners most severely cut, for attempting to do so, and hourly whipped for not eating. This indeed was often the case with myself. In a little time after, amongst the poor chained men, I found some of my own nation, which in a small degree gave ease to my mind. I inquired of these what was to be done with us? They gave me to understand we were to be carried to these white people's country to work for them. I then was a little revived, and thought, if it were no worse than working, my situation was not so desperate; but still I feared I should be put to death, the white people looked and acted, as I thought, in so savage a manner; for I had never seen among any people such instances of brutal cruelty; and this not only shown towards us blacks, but also to some of the whites themselves. One white man in particular I saw, when we were permitted to be on deck, flogged so unmercifully with a large rope near the foremast, that he died in consequence of it; and they tossed him over the side as they would have done a brute. This made me fear these people the more; and I expected nothing less than to be treated in the same manner. I could not help expressing my fears and apprehensions to some of my countrymen; I asked them if these people had no country, but lived in this hollow place (the ship)? They told me they did not, but came from a distant one. "Then," said I, "how comes it in all our country we never heard of them?" They told me because they lived so very far off. I then asked where were their women? had they any like themselves? I was told they had. "And why," said I, "do we not see them?" They answered, because they were left behind. I asked how the vessel could go? they told me they could not tell; but that there was cloth put upon the masts by the help of the ropes I saw, and then the vessel went on; and the white men had some spell or magic they put in the water when they liked, in order to stop the vessel. I was exceedingly amazed at this account, and really thought they were spirits. I therefore wished much to be from amongst[8] them, for I

8. I.e., away from.

expected they would sacrifice me; but my wishes were vain—for we were so quartered that it was impossible for any of us to make our escape.

While we stayed on the coast I was mostly on deck; and one day, to my great astonishment, I saw one of these vessels coming in with the sails up. As soon as the whites saw it, they gave a great shout, at which we were amazed; and the more so, as the vessel appeared larger by approaching nearer. At last, she came to an anchor in my sight, and when the anchor was let go, I and my countrymen who saw it, were lost in astonishment to observe the vessel stop—and were now convinced it was done by magic. Soon after this the other ship got her boats out, and they came on board of us, and the people of both ships seemed very glad to see each other.—Several of the strangers also shook hands with us black people, and made motions with their hands, signifying I suppose, we were to go to their country, but we did not understand them.

At last, when the ship we were in had got in all her cargo, they made ready with many fearful noises, and we were all put under deck, so that we could not see how they managed the vessel. But this disappointment was the least of my sorrow. The stench of the hold while we were on the coast was so intolerably loathsome, that it was dangerous to remain there for any time, and some of us had been permitted to stay on the deck for the fresh air; but now that the whole ship's cargo were confined together, it became absolutely pestilential. The closeness of the place, and the heat of the climate, added to the number in the ship, which was so crowded that each had scarcely room to turn himself, almost suffocated us. This produced copious perspirations, so that the air soon became unfit for respiration, from a variety of loathsome smells, and brought on a sickness among the slaves, of which many died—thus falling victims to the improvident avarice, as I may call it, of their purchasers. This wretched situation was again aggravated by the galling of the chains, now become insupportable, and the filth of the necessary tubs,[9] into which the children often fell, and were almost suffocated. The shrieks of the women, and the groans of the dying, rendered the whole a scene of horror almost inconceivable. Happily perhaps, for myself, I was soon reduced so low here that it was thought necessary to keep me almost always on deck; and from my extreme youth I was not put in fetters. In this situation I expected every hour to share the fate of my companions, some of whom were almost daily brought upon deck at the point of death, which I began to hope would soon put an end to my miseries. Often did I think many of the inhabitants of the deep much more happy than myself. I envied them the freedom they enjoyed, and as often wished I could change my condition for theirs. Every circumstance I met with, served only to render my state more painful, and heightened my apprehensions, and my opinion of the cruelty of the whites.

One day they had taken a number of fishes; and when they had killed and satisfied themselves with as many as they thought fit, to our astonishment who were on deck, rather than give any of them to us to eat, as we expected, they tossed the remaining fish into the sea again, although we begged and prayed for some as well as we could, but in vain; and some of my countrymen, being pressed by hunger, took an opportunity, when they thought no one saw them, of trying to get a little privately; but they were discovered, and the

9. I.e., for excretion.

attempt procured them some very severe floggings. One day, when we had a smooth sea and moderate wind, two of my wearied countrymen who were chained together (I was near them at the time), preferring death to such a life of misery, somehow made through the nettings and jumped into the sea: immediately, another quite dejected fellow, who, on account of his illness, was suffered to be out of irons, also followed their example; and I believe many more would very soon have done the same, if they had not been prevented by the ship's crew, who were instantly alarmed. Those of us that were the most active, were in a moment put down under the deck, and there was such a noise and confusion amongst the people of the ship as I never heard before, to stop her, and get the boat out to go after the slaves. However, two of the wretches were drowned, but they got the other, and afterwards flogged him unmercifully, for thus attempting to prefer death to slavery. In this manner we continued to undergo more hardships than I can now relate, hardships which are inseparable from this accursed trade. Many a time we were near suffocation from the want of fresh air, which we were often without for whole days together. This, and the stench of the necessary tubs, carried off many.

During our passage, I first saw flying fishes, which surprised me very much; they used frequently to fly across the ship, and many of them fell on the deck. I also now first saw the use of the quadrant; I had often with astonishment seen the mariners make observations with it, and I could not think what it meant. They at last took notice of my surprise; and one of them, willing to increase it, as well as to gratify my curiosity, made me one day look through it. The clouds appeared to me to be land, which disappeared as they passed along. This heightened my wonder; and I was now more persuaded than ever, that I was in another world, and that every thing about me was magic. At last, we came in sight of the island of Barbadoes, at which the whites on board gave a great shout, and made many signs of joy to us. We did not know what to think of this; but as the vessel drew nearer, we plainly saw the harbor, and other ships of different kinds and sizes, and we soon anchored amongst them, off Bridgetown. Many merchants and planters now came on board, though it was in the evening. They put us in separate parcels,[1] and examined us attentively. They also made us jump, and pointed to the land, signifying we were to go there. We thought by this, we should be eaten by these ugly men, as they appeared to us; and, when soon after we were all put down under the deck again, there was much dread and trembling among us, and nothing but bitter cries to be heard all the night from these apprehensions, insomuch, that at last the white people got some old slaves from the land to pacify us. They told us we were not to be eaten, but to work, and were soon to go on land, where we should see many of our country people. This report eased us much. And sure enough, soon after we were landed, there came to us Africans of all languages.

We were conducted immediately to the merchant's yard, where we were all pent up together, like so many sheep in a fold, without regard to sex or age. As every object was new to me, every thing I saw filled me with surprise. What struck me first, was, that the houses were built with bricks and stories,[2] and in every other respect different from those I had seen in Africa; but I was still more astonished on seeing people on horseback. I did not know

---

1. Groups.   2. I.e., the buildings were two-storied.

what this could mean; and, indeed, I thought these people were full of nothing but magical arts. While I was in this astonishment, one of my fellow prisoners spoke to a countryman of his, about the horses, who said they were the same kind they had in their country. I understood them, though they were from a distant part of Africa; and I thought it odd I had not seen any horses there; but afterwards, when I came to converse with different Africans, I found they had many horses amongst them, and much larger than those I then saw.

We were not many days in the merchant's custody, before we were sold after their usual manner, which is this:—On a signal given (as the beat of a drum), the buyers rush at once into the yard where the slaves are confined, and make choice of that parcel they like best. The noise and clamor with which this is attended, and the eagerness visible in the countenances of the buyers, serve not a little to increase the apprehension of terrified Africans, who may well be supposed to consider them as the ministers of that destruction to which they think themselves devoted. In this manner, without scruple, are relations and friends separated, most of them never to see each other again. I remember, in the vessel in which I was brought over, in the men's apartment, there were several brothers, who, in the sale, were sold in different lots; and it was very moving on this occasion, to see and hear their cries at parting. O, ye nominal Christians![3] might not an African ask you— Learned you this from your God, who says unto you, Do unto all men as you would men should do unto you? Is it not enough that we are torn from our country and friends, to toil for your luxury and lust of gain? Must every tender feeling be likewise sacrificed to your avarice? Are the dearest friends and relations, now rendered more dear by their separation from their kindred, still to be parted from each other, and thus prevented from cheering the gloom of slavery, with the small comfort of being together, and mingling their sufferings and sorrows? Why are parents to lose their children, brothers their sisters, or husbands their wives? Surely, this is a new refinement in cruelty, which, while it has no advantage to atone for it, thus aggravates distress, and adds fresh horrors even to the wretchedness of slavery.

From *Chapter III*

I now totally lost the small remains of comfort I had enjoyed in conversing with my countrymen; the women too, who used to wash and take care of me were all gone different ways, and I never saw one of them afterwards.

I stayed in this island for a few days; I believe it could not be above a fortnight; when I, and some few more slaves, that were not salable amongst the rest, from very much fretting, were shipped off in a sloop for North America. On the passage we were better treated than when we were coming from Africa, and we had plenty of rice and fat pork. We were landed up a river a good way from the sea, about Virginia county, where we saw few or none of our native Africans, and not one soul who could talk to me. I was a few weeks weeding grass, and gathering stones in a plantation; and at last all my companions were distributed different ways, and only myself was left. I was now exceedingly miserable, and thought myself worse off than any of the rest of

---

3. Christians in name only.

my companions; for they could talk to each other, but I had no person to speak to that I could understand. In this state, I was constantly grieving and pining,[4] and wishing for death rather than any thing else. While I was in this plantation, the gentleman, to whom I suppose the estate belonged, being unwell, I was one day sent for to his dwelling house to fan him; when I came into the room where he was I was very much affrighted at some things I saw, and the more so as I had seen a black woman slave as I came through the house, who was cooking the dinner, and the poor creature was cruelly loaded with various kinds of iron machines; she had one particularly on her head, which locked her mouth so fast that she could scarcely speak; and could not eat nor drink. I was much astonished and shocked at this contrivance, which I afterwards learned was called the iron muzzle. Soon after I had a fan put in my hand, to fan the gentleman while he slept; and so I did indeed with great fear. While he was fast asleep I indulged myself a great deal in looking about the room, which to me appeared very fine and curious. The first object that engaged my attention was a watch which hung on the chimney, and was going. I was quite surprised at the noise it made, and was afraid it would tell the gentleman any thing I might do amiss; and when I immediately after observed a picture hanging in the room, which appeared constantly to look at me, I was still more affrighted, having never seen such things as these before. At one time I thought it was something relative to magic; and not seeing it move, I thought it might be some way the whites had to keep their great men when they died, and offer them libations as we used to do our friendly spirits. In this state of anxiety I remained till my master awoke, when I was dismissed out of the room, to my no small satisfaction and relief; for I thought that these people were all made up of wonders. In this place I was called Jacob; but on board the African Snow, I was called Michael. I had been some time in this miserable forlorn, and much dejected state, without having any one to talk to, which made my life a burden, when the kind and unknown hand of the Creator (who in very deed leads the blind in a way they know not) now began to appear, to my comfort; for one day the captain of a merchant ship, called the Industrious Bee, came on some business to my master's house. This gentleman, whose name was Michael Henry Pascal, was a lieutenant in the royal navy, but now commanded this trading ship, which was somewhere in the confines of the county many miles off. While he was at my master's house, it happened that he saw me, and liked me so well that he made a purchase of me. I think I have often heard him say he gave thirty or forty pounds sterling for me; but I do not remember which. However, he meant me for a present to some of his friends in England: and as I was sent accordingly from the house of my then master (one Mr. Campbell), to the place where the ship lay; I was conducted on horseback by an elderly black man (a mode of traveling which appeared very odd to me). When I arrived I was carried on board a fine large ship, loaded with tobacco, etc., and just ready to sail for England. I now thought my condition much mended; I had sails to lie on, and plenty of good victuals to eat; and everybody on board used me very kindly, quite contrary to what I had seen of any white people before; I therefore began to think that they were not all of the

4. Suffering.

same disposition. A few days after I was on board we sailed for England. I was still at a loss to conjecture my destiny. By this time, however, I could smatter a little imperfect English; and I wanted to know as well as I could where we were going. Some of the people of the ship used to tell me they were going to carry me back to my own country, and this made me very happy. I was quite rejoiced at the idea of going back; and thought if I could get home what wonders I should have to tell. But I was reserved for another fate, and was soon undeceived when we came within sight of the English coast. While I was on board this ship, my captain and master named me *Gustavus Vassa.* I at that time began to understand him a little, and refused to be called so, and told him as well as I could that I would be called Jacob; but he said I should not, and still called me Gustavus: and when I refused to answer to my new name, which I at first did, it gained me many a cuff; so at length I submitted, and by which I have been known ever since. The ship had a very long passage; and on that account we had very short allowance of provisions. Towards the last, we had only one pound and a half of bread per week, and about the same quantity of meat, and one quart of water a day. We spoke with only one vessel the whole time we were at sea, and but once we caught a few fishes. In our extremities the captain and people told me in jest they would kill and eat me; but I thought them in earnest, and was depressed beyond measure, expecting every moment to be my last. While I was in this situation, one evening they caught, with a good deal of trouble, a large shark, and got it on board. This gladdened my poor heart exceedingly, as I thought it would serve the people to eat instead of their eating me; but very soon, to my astonishment, they cut off a small part of the tail, and tossed the rest over the side. This renewed my consternation; and I did not know what to think of these white people, though I very much feared they would kill and eat me. There was on board the ship a young lad who had never been at sea before, about four or five years older than myself: his name was Richard Baker. He was a native of America, had received an excellent education, and was of a most amiable temper. Soon after I went on board, he showed me a great deal of partiality and attention, and in return I grew extremely fond of him. We at length became inseparable; and, for the space of two years, he was of very great use to me, and was my constant companion and instructor. Although this dear youth had many slaves of his own, yet he and I have gone through many sufferings together on shipboard; and we have many nights lain in each other's bosoms when we were in great distress. Thus such a friendship was cemented between us as we cherished till his death, which, to my very great sorrow, happened in the year 1759, when he was up the Archipelago, and on board his Majesty's ship the Preston: an event which I have never ceased to regret, as I lost at once a kind interpreter, an agreeable companion, and a faithful friend; who, at the age of fifteen, discovered a mind superior to prejudice; and who was not ashamed to notice, to associate with, and to be the friend and instructor of one who was ignorant, a stranger, of a different complexion, and a slave!

* * *

From *Chapter IV*

It was now between two and three years since I first came to England, a great part of which I had spent at sea; so that I became inured[5] to that service, and began to consider myself as happily situated, for my master treated me always extremely well; and my attachment and gratitude to him were very great. From the various scenes I had beheld on shipboard, I soon grew a stranger to terror of every kind, and was, in that respect at least, almost an Englishman. I have often reflected with surprise that I never felt half the alarm at any of the numerous dangers I have been in, that I was filled with at the first sight of the Europeans, and at every act of theirs, even the most trifling, when I first came among them, and for some time afterwards. That fear, however, which was the effect of my ignorance, wore away as I began to know them. I could now speak English tolerably well, and I perfectly understood every thing that was said. I not only felt myself quite easy with these new countrymen, but relished their society and manners. I no longer looked upon them as spirits, but as men superior to us; and therefore I had the stronger desire to resemble them, to imbibe their spirit, and imitate their manners. I therefore embraced every occasion of improvement, and every new thing that I observed I treasured up in my memory. I had long wished to be able to read and write; and for this purpose I took every opportunity to gain instruction, but had made as yet very little progress. However, when I went to London with my master, I had soon an opportunity of improving myself, which I gladly embraced. Shortly after my arrival, he sent me to wait upon the Miss Guerins, who had treated me with much kindness when I was there before;[6] and they sent me to school.

While I was attending these ladies, their servants told me I could not go to Heaven unless I was baptized. This made me very uneasy, for I had now some faint idea of a future state. Accordingly I communicated my anxiety to the eldest Miss Guerin, with whom I was become a favorite, and pressed her to have me baptized; when to my great joy, she told me I should. She had formerly asked my master to let me be baptized, but he had refused. However she now insisted on it; and he being under some obligation to her brother, complied with her request. So I was baptized in St. Margaret's church, Westminster, in February, 1759, by my present name. The clergyman at the same time, gave me a book, called a Guide to the Indians, written by the Bishop of Sodor and Man.[7] On this occasion, Miss Guerin did me the honor to stand as god-mother, and afterwards gave me a treat. I used to attend these ladies about the town, in which service I was extremely happy; as I had thus many opportunities of seeing London, which I desired of all things. I was sometimes, however, with my master at his rendezvous house,[8] which was at the foot of Westminster bridge. Here I used to enjoy myself in playing about the bridge stairs, and often in the waterman's wherries,[9] with other boys. On one of these occasions there was another boy with me in a wherry, and we went out into the current of the river; while we were there, two more

---

5. Accustomed.
6. Elizabeth Martha Guerin and Mary Guerin were Pascal's cousins. Toward the end of Chapter III, Equiano calls them "very amiable ladies, who took much notice and great care

of me."
7. Present-day Hebrides and the Isle of Man.
8. Private residence.
9. Small rowboats.

stout boys came to us in another wherry, and abusing us for taking the boat, desired me to get into the other wherry boat. Accordingly, I went to get out of the wherry I was in, but just as I had got one of my feet into the other boat, the boys shoved it off, so that I fell into the Thames; and, not being able to swim, I should unavoidably have been drowned, but for the assistance of some watermen who providentially came to my relief.

The Namur being again got ready for sea, my master, with his gang,[1] was ordered on board; and, to my no small grief, I was obliged to leave my school-master, whom I liked very much, and always attended while I stayed in London, to repair[2] on board with my master. Nor did I leave my kind patronesses, the Miss Guerins, without uneasiness and regret. They often used to teach me to read, and took great pains to instruct me in the principles of religion and the knowledge of God. I therefore parted from those amiable ladies with reluctance, after receiving from them many friendly cautions how to conduct myself, and some valuable presents.

When I came to Spithead,[3] I found we were destined for the Mediterranean, with a large fleet, which was now ready to put to sea. We only waited for the arrival of the Admiral, who soon came on board. And about the beginning of the spring of 1759, having weighed anchor, and got under way, sailed for the Mediterranean; and in eleven days, from the Land's End, we got to Gibralter. While we were here I used to be often on shore, and got various fruits in great plenty, and very cheap.

I had frequently told several people, in my excursions on shore, the story of my being kidnapped with my sister, and of our being separated, as I have related before; and I had as often expressed my anxiety for her fate, and my sorrow at having never met her again. One day, when I was on shore, and mentioning these circumstances to some persons, one of them told me he knew where my sister was, and if I would accompany him, he would bring me to her. Improbable as this story was, I believed it immediately, and agreed to go with him, while my heart leaped for joy; and, indeed, he conducted me to a black young woman, who was so like my sister, that at first sight, I really thought it was her; but I was quickly undeceived. And, on talking to her, I found her to be of another nation.

While we lay here, the Preston came in from the Levant.[4] As soon as she arrived, my master told me I should now see my old companion, Dick, who was gone in her when she sailed for Turkey. I was much rejoiced at this news, and expected every minute to embrace him; and when the captain came on board of our ship, which he did immediately after, I ran to inquire after my friend; but, with inexpressible sorrow, I learned from the boat's crew that the dear youth was dead! and that they had brought his chest, and all his other things, to my master. These he afterwards gave to me, and I regarded them as a memorial of my friend, whom I loved, and grieved for, as a brother.

* * *

After our ship was fitted out again for service, in September she went to Guernsey,[5] where I was very glad to see my old hostess, who was now a

1. I.e., crew.
2. Go; return. "Attended": visited.
3. On the southern coast of England; a common rendezvous for the British fleet.

4. The eastern shore of the Mediterranean. "Lay": i.e., remained, harbored.
5. One of the Channel Islands, in the English Channel.

widow, and my former little charming companion, her daughter. I spent some time here very happily with them, till October, when we had orders to repair to Portsmouth. We parted from each other with a great deal of affection; and I promised to return soon, and see them again, not knowing what all powerful fate had determined for me. Our ship having arrived at Portsmouth, we went into the harbor, and remained there till the latter end of November, when we heard great talk about a peace,[6] and, to our very great joy, in the beginning of December we had orders to go up to London with our ship, to be paid off. We received this news with loud huzzas, and every other demonstration of gladness; and nothing but mirth was to be seen throughout every part of the ship. I, too, was not without my share of the general joy on this occasion. I thought now of nothing but being freed, and working for myself, and thereby getting money to enable me to get a good education; for I always had a great desire to be able at least to read and write; and while I was on ship-board, I had endeavored to improve myself in both. While I was in the Etna, particularly, the captain's clerk taught me to write, and gave me a smattering of arithmetic, as far as the Rule of Three.[7] There was also one Daniel Queen, about forty years of age, a man very well educated, who messed[8] with me on board this ship, and he likewise dressed and attended the captain. Fortunately this man soon became very much attached to me, and took very great pains to instruct me in many things. He taught me to shave and dress hair a little, and also to read in the Bible, explaining many passages to me, which I did not comprehend. I was wonderfully surprised to see the laws and rules of my own country written almost exactly here; a circumstance which I believe tended to impress our manners and customs more deeply on my memory. I used to tell him of this resemblance, and many a time we have sat up the whole night together at this employment. In short, he was like a father to me, and some even used to call me after his name; they also styled me the black Christian. Indeed, I almost loved him with the affection of a son. Many things I have denied myself that he might have them; and when I used to play at marbles, or any other game, and won a few half-pence, or got any little money, which I sometimes did, for shaving any one, I used to buy him a little sugar or tobacco, as far as my stock of money would go. He used to say, that he and I never should part; and that when our ship was paid off, as I was as free as himself, or any other man on board, he would instruct me in his business, by which I might gain a good livelihood. This gave me new life and spirits; and my heart burned within me, while I thought the time long till I obtained my freedom. For though my master had not promised it to me, yet, besides the assurances I had received, that he had no right to detain me, he always treated me with the greatest kindness, and reposed in me an unbounded confidence; he even paid attention to my morals, and would never suffer me to deceive him, or tell lies, of which he used to tell me the consequences; and that if I did so, God would not love me. So that, from all this tenderness, I had never once supposed, in all my dreams of freedom, that he would think of detaining me any longer than I wished.

In pursuance of our orders, we sailed from Portsmouth for the Thames, and arrived at Deptford the 10th of December, where we cast anchor just as

---

6. I.e., to the Seven Years' War.
7. A method of finding a fourth (unknown) number from three given numbers. Etna was the name of the ship.
8. Took meals.

it was high water. The ship was up about half an hour, when my master ordered the barge to be manned; and all in an instant, without having before given me the least reason to suspect any thing of the matter, he forced me into the barge, saying, I was going to leave him, but he would take care I should not. I was so struck with the unexpectedness of this proceeding, that for some time I did not make a reply, only I made an offer to go for my books and chest of clothes, but he swore I should not move out of his sight, and if I did, he would cut my throat, at the same time taking his hanger.[9] I began, however, to collect myself, and plucking up courage, I told him I was free, and he could not by law serve me so. But this only enraged him the more: and he continued to swear, and said he would soon let me know whether he would or not, and at that instant sprung himself into the barge from the ship, to the astonishment and sorrow of all on board. The tide, rather unluckily for me, had just turned downward, so that we quickly fell down the river along with it, till we came among some outward-bound West Indiamen; for he was resolved to put me on board the first vessel he could get to receive me. The boat's crew, who pulled against their will, became quite faint, different times, and would have gone ashore, but he would not let them. Some of them strove then to cheer me, and told me he could not sell me, and that they would stand by me, which revived me a little, and I still entertained hopes; for, as they pulled along, he asked some vessels to receive me, but they would not. But, just as we had got a little below Gravesend, we came along side of a ship which was going away the next tide for the West Indies. Her name was the Charming Sally. Captain James Doran, and my master went on board, and agreed with him for me; and in a little time I was sent for into the cabin. When I came there, Captain Doran asked me if I knew him. I answered that I did not. "Then," said he, "you are now my slave." I told him my master could not sell me to him, nor to any one else. "Why," said he, "did not your master buy you?" I confessed he did. "But I have served him," said I, "many years, and he has taken all my wages and prize money, for I had only got one sixpence during the war; besides this I have been baptized, and by the laws of the land no man has a right to sell me." And I added that I had heard a lawyer and others at different times tell my master so. They both then said that those people who told me so were not my friends; but I replied, "It was very extraordinary that other people did not know the law as well as they." Upon this, Captain Doran said I talked too much English; and if I did not behave myself well, and be quiet, he had a method on board to make me. I was too well convinced of his power over me to doubt what he said; and my former sufferings in the slave ship presenting themselves to my mind, the recollection of them made me shudder. However, before I retired I told them that, as I could not get any right among men here, I hoped I should hereafter in Heaven; and I immediately left the cabin, filled with resentment and sorrow. The only coat I had with me my master took away with him, and said, "If your prize money had been £ 10,000, I had a right to it all, and would have taken it." I had about nine guineas, which, during my long seafaring life, I had scraped together from trifling perquisites and little ventures; and I hid it at that instant, lest my master should take that from me likewise, still hoping that by some means or other I

9. Small sword.

should make my escape to the shore; and indeed some of my old shipmates told me not to despair, for they would get me back again; and that, as soon as they could get their pay, they would immediately come to Portsmouth to me, where the ship was going. But, alas! all my hopes were baffled, and the hour of my deliverance was as yet far off. My master, having soon concluded his bargain with the captain, came out of the cabin, and he and his people got into the boat and put off. I followed them with aching eyes as long as I could, and when they were out of sight I threw myself on the deck, with a heart ready to burst with sorrow and anguish.

From *Chapter V*

* * *

About the middle of May, when the ship was got ready to sail for England, I all the time believing that fate's blackest clouds were gathering over my head, and expecting their bursting would mix me with the dead, Captain Doran sent for me ashore one morning, and I was told by the messenger that my fate was then determined. With trembling steps and fluttering heart, I came to the captain, and found with him one Mr. Robert King, a Quaker, and the first merchant in the place. The captain then told me my former master had sent me there to be sold; but that he had desired him to get me the best master he could, as he told him I was a very deserving boy, which Captain Doran said he found to be true; and if he were to stay in the West Indies, he would be glad to keep me himself; but he could not venture to take me to London, for he was very sure that when I came there I would leave him. I at that instant burst out a crying, and begged much of him to take me to England with him, but all to no purpose. He told me he had got me the very best master in the whole island, with whom I should be as happy as if I were in England, and for that reason he chose to let him have me, though he could sell me to his own brother-in-law for a great deal more money than what he got from this gentleman. Mr. King, my new master, then made a reply, and said the reason he had bought me was on account of my good character; and as he had not the least doubt of my good behavior, I should be very well off with him. He also told me he did not live in the West Indies, but at Philadelphia, where he was going soon; and, as I understood something of the rules of arithmetic, when we got there he would put me to school, and fit me for a clerk. This conversation relieved my mind a little, and I left those gentlemen considerably more at ease in myself than when I came to them; and I was very thankful to Captain Doran, and even to my old master, for the character[1] they had given me. A character which I afterwards found of infinite service to me. I went on board again, and took leave of all my shipmates, and the next day the ship sailed. When she weighed anchor, I went to the waterside and looked at her with a very wishful and aching heart, and followed her with my eyes until she was totally out of sight. I was so bowed down with grief, that I could not hold up my head for many months; and if my new master had not been kind to me, I believe I should have died under it at last. And, indeed, I soon found that he fully deserved the good

---

1. Favorable estimate, good reputation.

character which Captain Doran gave me of him; for he possessed a most amiable disposition and temper, and was very charitable and humane. If any of his slaves behaved amiss he did not beat or use them ill, but parted with them. This made them afraid of disobliging him; and as he treated his slaves better than any other man on the island, so he was better and more faithfully served by them in return. By this kind treatment I did at last endeavor to compose myself; and with fortitude, though moneyless, determined to face whatever fate had decreed for me. Mr. King soon asked me what I could do; and at the same time said he did not mean to treat me as a common slave. I told him I knew something of seamanship, and could shave and dress hair pretty well; and I could refine wines, which I had learned on shipboard, where I had often done it; and that I could write, and understood arithmetic tolerably well, as far as the Rule of Three. He then asked me if I knew any thing of gauging;[2] and, on my answering that I did not, he said one of his clerks should teach me to gauge.

Mr. King dealt in all manner of merchandize, and kept from one to six clerks. He loaded many vessels in a year; particularly to Philadelphia, where he was born; and was connected with a great mercantile house in that city. He had, besides, many vessels and droggers,[3] of different sizes, which used to go about the island; and others, to collect rum, sugar, and other goods. I understood pulling and managing those boats very well. And this hard work, which was the first that he set me to, in the sugar seasons used to be my constant employment. I have rowed the boat, and slaved at the oars, from one hour to sixteen in the twenty-four; during which I had fifteen pence sterling per day to live on, though sometimes only ten pence. However, this was considerably more than was allowed to other slaves that used to work often with me, and belonged to other gentlemen on the island. Those poor souls had never more than nine-pence per day, and seldom more than six-pence, from their masters or owners, though they earned them three or four pistareens.[4] For it is a common practice in the West Indies for men to purchase slaves, though they have not plantations themselves, in order to let them out to planters and merchants at so much a piece by the day, and they give what allowance they choose out of this product of their daily work to their slaves, for subsistence; this allowance is often very scanty. My master often gave the owners of the slaves two and a half of these pieces per day, and found the poor fellows in victuals himself,[5] because he thought their owners did not feed them well enough according to the work they did.

*　*　*

Once, for a few days, I was let out to fit[6] a vessel, and I had no victuals allowed me by either party; at last I told my master of this treatment, and he took me away from it. In many of the estates, on the different islands where I used to be sent for rum or sugar, they would not deliver it to me, or any other negro; he was therefore obliged to send a white man along with me to

---

2. Determining how fully loaded a ship is by measuring its depth in the water.
3. Slow West Indian vessels that sail along the coast.
4. These pistareens are of a value of a shilling [Equiano's note].
5. I.e., King was generous to the owners in terms of payment and to the slaves in terms of food.
6. Hired out to help equip.

those places; and then he used to pay him from six to ten pistareens a day. From being thus employed, during the time I served Mr. King, in going about the different estates on the island,[7] I had all the opportunity I could wish for, to see the dreadful usage of the poor men; usage that reconciled me to my situation, and made me bless God for the hands into which I had fallen.

I had the good fortune to please my master in every department in which he employed me; and there was scarcely any part of his business, or household affairs, in which I was not occasionally engaged. I often supplied the place[8] of a clerk, in receiving and delivering cargoes to the ships, in tending stores, and delivering goods. And besides this, I used to shave and dress my master when convenient, and take care of his horse; and when it was necessary, which was very often, I worked likewise on board of different vessels of his. By these means I became very useful to my master, and saved him, as he used to acknowledge, above a hundred pounds a year. Nor did he scruple to say I was of more advantage to him than any of his clerks; though their usual wages in the West Indies are from sixty to a hundred pounds current a year.

I have sometimes heard it asserted that a Negro cannot earn his master the first cost; but nothing can be further from the truth. I suppose nine tenths of the mechanics throughout the West Indies are Negro slaves; and I well know the coopers among them earn two dollars a day, the carpenters the same, and often times more; as also the masons, smiths, and fisherman, etc. And I have known many slaves whose masters would not take a thousand pounds current for them. But surely this assertion refutes itself; for, if it be true, why do the planters and merchants pay such a price for slaves? And, above all, why do those who make this assertion exclaim the most loudly against the abolition of the slave trade? So much are men blinded, and to such inconsistent arguments are they driven by mistaken interest! I grant, indeed, that slaves are sometimes, by half-feeding, half-clothing, over-working and stripes,[9] reduced so low, that they are turned out as unfit for service, and left to perish in the woods, or expire on the dunghill.

My master was several times offered, by different gentlemen, one hundred guineas for me, but he always told them he would not sell me, to my great joy. And I used to double my diligence and care, for fear of getting into the hands of those men who did not allow a valuable slave the common support of life. Many of them even used to find fault with my master for feeding his slaves so well as he did; although I often went hungry, and an Englishman might think my fare very indifferent;[1] but he used to tell them he always would do it, because the slaves thereby looked better and did more work.

While I was thus employed by my master, I was often a witness to cruelties of every kind, which were exercised on my unhappy fellow slaves. I used frequently to have different cargoes of new Negroes in my care for sale; and it was almost a constant practice with our clerks, and other whites, to commit violent depredations on the chastity of the female slaves; and these I was, though with reluctance, obliged to submit to at all times, being unable

---

7. Equiano remained in the West Indies from 1763 to 1766.
8. Held the position.

9. Lashes.
1. Poor, unsatisfactory.

to help them. When we have had some of these slaves on board my master's vessels, to carry them to other islands, or to America, I have known our mates to commit these acts most shamefully, to the disgrace, not of Christians only, but of men. I have even known them to gratify their brutal passion with females not ten years old; and these abominations, some of them practiced to such scandalous excess, that one of our captains discharged the mate and others on that account. And yet in Montserrat[2] I have seen a Negro man staked to the ground, and cut most shockingly, and then his ears cut off bit by bit, because he had been connected with a white woman, who was a common prostitute. As if it were no crime in the whites to rob an innocent African girl of her virtue; but most heinous in a black man only to gratify a passion of nature, where the temptation was offered by one of a different color, though the most abandoned woman of her species.

Another Negro man was half hanged, and then burnt, for attempting to poison a cruel overseer. Thus, by repeated cruelties, are the wretched first urged to despair, and then murdered, because they still retain so much of human nature about them as to wish to put an end to their misery, and retaliate on their tyrants! These overseers are indeed for the most part persons of the worst character of any denomination of men in the West Indies. Unfortunately, many humane gentlemen, but not residing on their estates, are obliged to leave the management of them in the hands of these human butchers, who cut and mangle the slaves in a shocking manner on the most trifling occasions, and altogether treat them in every respect like brutes. They pay no regard to the situation of pregnant women, nor the least attention to the lodging of the field Negroes. Their huts, which ought to be well covered, and the place dry where they take their little repose, are often open sheds, built in damp places; so that when the poor creatures return tired from the toils of the field, they contract many disorders, from being exposed to the damp air in this uncomfortable state, while they are heated, and their pores are open. This neglect certainly conspires with many others to cause a decrease in the births as well as in the lives of the grown Negroes. I can quote many instances of gentlemen who reside on their estates in the West Indies, and then the scene is quite changed; the Negroes are treated with lenity and proper care, by which their lives are prolonged, and their masters profited. To the honor of humanity, I knew several gentlemen who managed their estates in this manner, and they found that benevolence was their true interest. And, among many I could mention in several of the islands, I knew one in Montserrat whose slaves looked remarkably well, and never needed any fresh supplies of Negroes; and there are many other estates, especially in Barbadoes, which, from such judicious treatment, need no fresh stock of Negroes at any time. I have the honor of knowing a most worthy and humane gentleman, who is a native of Barbadoes, and his estates there.[3] This gentleman has written a treatise on the usage of his own slaves. He allows them two hours of refreshment at midday, and many other indulgencies and comforts, particularly in their lodging; and, besides this, he raises more provisions on his estate than they can destroy; so that by these attentions he saves the lives of his Negroes, and keeps them healthy, and as happy

2. An island in the West Indies, seven miles from Antigua.

3. Two of Equiano's notes identifying these men are omitted.

as the condition of slavery can admit. I myself, as shall appear in the sequel,[4] managed an estate, where, by those attentions, the Negroes were uncommonly cheerful and healthy, and did more work by half than by the common mode of treatment they usually do. For want,[5] therefore, of such care and attention to the poor Negroes, and otherwise oppressed as they are, it is no wonder that the decrease should require 20,000 new Negroes annually, to fill up the vacant places of the dead.

* * *

From *Chapter VI*

In the preceding chapter I have set before the reader a few of those many instances of oppression, extortion, and cruelty, which I have been a witness to in the West Indies; but were I to enumerate them all, the catalog would be tedious and disgusting. The punishments of the slaves on every trifling occasion are so frequent, and so well known, together with the different instruments with which they are tortured, that it cannot any longer afford novelty to recite them; and they are too shocking to yield delight either to the writer or the reader. I shall therefore hereafter only mention such as incidentally befell myself in the course of my adventures.

* * *

Some time in the year 1763, kind Providence seemed to appear rather more favorable to me. One of my master's vessels, a Bermudas sloop, about sixty tons burthen, was commanded by one captain Thomas Farmer, an Englishman, a very alert and active man, who gained my master a great deal of money by his good management in carrying passengers from one island to another; but very often his sailors used to get drunk and run away from the vessel, which hindered him in his business very much. This man had taken a liking to me, and many times begged of my master to let me go a trip with him as a sailor; but he would tell him he could not spare me, though the vessel sometimes could not go for want of hands, for sailors were generally very scarce in the island. However, at last, from necessity or force, my master was prevailed on, though very reluctantly, to let me go with this captain; but he gave him great charge to take care that I did not run away, for if I did he would make him pay for me. This being the case, the captain had for some time a sharp eye upon me whenever the vessel anchored; and as soon as she returned I was sent for on shore again. Thus was I slaving, as it were, for life, sometimes at one thing, and sometimes at another. So that the captain and I were nearly the most useful men in my master's employment. I also became so useful to the captain on ship-board, that many times, when he used to ask for me to go with him, though it should be but for twenty-four hours, to some of the islands near us, my master would answer he could not spare me, at which the captain would swear, and would not go the trip, and tell my master I was better to him on board than any three white men he had; for they used to behave ill in many respects, particularly in getting drunk; and then they frequently got the boat stove,[6] so as to hinder the vessel from coming back as

4. I.e., later.
5. Lack.

6. Put a hole in the boat.

soon as she might have done. This my master knew very well; and at last, by the captain's constant entreaties, after I had been several times with him, one day to my great joy, told me the captain would not let him rest, and asked whether I would go aboard as a sailor, or stay on shore and mind the stores, for he could not bear any longer to be plagued in this manner. I was very happy at this proposal, for I immediately thought I might in time stand some chance by being on board to get a little money, or possibly make my escape if I should be used ill. I also expected to get better food, and in greater abundance; for I had oftentimes felt much hunger, though my master treated his slaves, as I have observed, uncommonly well. I therefore, without hesitation, answered him, that I would go and be a sailor if he pleased. Accordingly I was ordered on board directly. Nevertheless, between the vessel and the shore, when she was in port, I had little or no rest, as my master always wished to have me along with him. Indeed he was a very pleasant gentleman, and but for my expectations on ship-board, I should not have thought of leaving him. But the captain liked me also very much, and I was entirely his right hand man. I did all I could to deserve his favor, and in return I received better treatment from him than any other, I believe, ever met with in the West Indies, in my situation.

After I had been sailing for some time with this captain, at length I endeavored to try my luck, and commence merchant. I had but a very small capital to begin with; for one single half bit,[7] which is equal to three pence in England, made up my whole stock. However, I trusted to the Lord to be with me; and at one of our trips to St. Eustatia,[8] a Dutch island, I bought a glass tumbler with my half bit, and when I came to Montserrat, I sold it for a bit, or six pence. Luckily we made several successive trips to St. Eustatia (which was a general mart for the West Indies, about twenty leagues from Montserrat), and in our next, finding my tumbler so profitable, with this one bit I bought two tumblers more; and when I came back, I sold them for two bits, equal to a shilling sterling. When we went again, I bought with these two bits four more of these glasses, which I sold for four bits on our return to Montserrat. And in our next voyage to St. Eustatia, I bought two glasses with one bit, and with the other three I bought a jug of Geneva,[9] nearly about three pints in measure. When we came to Montserrat, I sold the gin for eight bits, and the tumblers for two, so that my capital now amounted in all to a dollar, well husbanded[1] and acquired in the space of a month or six weeks, when I blessed the Lord that I was so rich. As we sailed to different islands, I laid this money out in various things occasionally, and it used to turn out to very good account, especially when we went to Guadaloupe, Grenada, and the rest of the French islands. Thus was I going all about the islands upwards of four years, and ever trading as I went, during which I experienced many instances of ill usage, and have seen many injuries done to other Negroes in our dealings with whites. And, amidst our recreations, when we have been dancing and merry-making, they, without cause, have molested and insulted us. Indeed, I was more than once obliged to look up to God on high, as I had advised the poor fisherman some time before. And I had not been long trading for myself in the manner I have related above, when I experienced the like

7. In the West Indies, a small silver coin worth a fraction of the Spanish dollar (Spanish dollars were common units of currency throughout the British colonies).

8. I.e., St. Eustatius, one of the Leeward Islands, in the West Indies.

9. A type of gin.

1. Managed.

trial in company with him as follows:—This man, being used to the water, was upon an emergency put on board of us by his master, to work as another hand, on a voyage to Santa Cruz; and at our sailing he had brought his little all for a venture, which consisted of six bits' worth of limes and oranges in a bag; I had also my whole stock, which was about twelve bits' worth of the same kind of goods, separate in two bags, for we had heard these fruits sold well in that island. When we came there, in some little convenient time, he and I went ashore to sell them; but we had scarcely landed, when we were met by two white men, who presently took our three bags from us. We could not at first guess what they meant to do, and for some time we thought they were jesting with us; but they too soon let us know otherwise, for they took our ventures immediately to a house hard by, and adjoining the fort, while we followed all the way begging of them to give us our fruits, but in vain. They not only refused to return them, but swore at us, and threatened if we did not immediately depart they would flog us well. We told them these three bags were all we were worth in the world, and that we brought them with us to sell when we came from Montserrat, and showed them the vessel. But this was rather against us, as they now saw we were strangers, as well as slaves. They still therefore swore, and desired us to be gone, and even took sticks to beat us; while we, seeing they meant what they said, went off in the greatest confusion and despair. Thus, in the very minute of gaining more by three times than I ever did by any venture in my life before, was I deprived of every farthing I was worth. An unsupportable misfortune! but how to help ourselves we knew not. In our consternation we went to the commanding officer of the fort, and told him how we had been served by his people, but we obtained not the least redress. He answered our complaints only by a volley of imprecations against us, and immediately took a horse-whip, in order to chastise us, so that we were obliged to turn out much faster than we came in. I now, in the agony of distress and indignation, wished that the ire of God in his forked lightning might transfix these cruel oppressors among the dead. Still, however, we persevered; went back again to the house, and begged and besought them again and again for our fruits, till at last some other people that were in the house asked if we would be contented if they kept one bag and gave us the other two. We, seeing no remedy whatever, consented to this; and they, observing one bag to have both kinds of fruit in it, which belonged to my companion, kept that; and the other two, which were mine, they gave us back. As soon as I got them, I ran as fast as I could, and got the first Negro man I could to help me off. My companion, however, stayed a little longer to plead; he told them the bag they had was his, and likewise all that he was worth in the world; but this was of no avail, and he was obliged to return without it. The poor old man wringing his hands, cried bitterly for his loss; and, indeed, he then did look up to God on high, which so moved me in pity for him, that I gave him nearly one-third of my fruits. We then proceeded to the markets to sell them; and Providence was more favorable to us than we could have expected, for we sold our fruits uncommonly well; I got for mine about thirty-seven bits. Such a surprising reverse of fortune in so short a space of time seemed like a dream, and proved no small encouragement for me to trust the Lord in any situation. My captain afterwards frequently used to take my part, and get me my right, when I have been plundered or used ill by these tender Christian depredators; among whom I have shuddered to observe the unceasing blasphemous execrations which are wantonly thrown out by persons of all ages and conditions, not only without occasion, but even as if they were indulgencies and pleasure.

* * *

The reader cannot but judge of the irksomeness of this situation to a mind like mine, in being daily exposed to new hardships and impositions, after having seen many better days, and been, as it were, in a state of freedom and plenty; added to which, every part of the world I had hitherto been in, seemed to me a paradise in comparison to the West Indies. My mind was therefore hourly replete with inventions and thoughts of being freed, and, if possible, by honest and honorable means; for I always remembered the old adage, and I trust it has ever been my ruling principle, that "honesty is the best policy;" and likewise that other golden precept—"To do unto all men as I would they should do unto me." However, as I was from early years a predestinarian, I thought whatever fate had determined must ever come to pass; and, therefore, if ever it were my lot to be freed, nothing could prevent me, although I should at present see no means or hope to obtain my freedom; on the other hand, if it were my fate not to be freed, I never should be so, and all my endeavors for that purpose would be fruitless. In the midst of these thoughts, I therefore looked up with prayers anxiously to God for my liberty; and at the same time used every honest means, and did all that was possible on my part to obtain it. In process of time, I became master of a few pounds, and in a fair way of making more, which my friendly captain knew very well; this occasioned him sometimes to take liberties with me; but whenever he treated me waspishly, I used plainly to tell him my mind, and that I would die before I would be imposed upon as other Negroes were, and that to my life had lost its relish when liberty was gone. This I said, although I foresaw my then well-being or future hopes of freedom (humanly speaking) depended on this man. However, as he could not bear the thoughts of my not sailing with him, he always became mild on my threats. I therefore continued with him; and, from my great attention to his orders and his business, I gained him credit, and through his kindness to me, I at last procured my liberty. While I thus went on, filled with the thoughts of freedom, and resisting oppression as well as I was able, my life hung daily in suspense, particularly in the surfs I have formerly mentioned, as I could not swim. These are extremely violent throughout the West Indies, and I was ever exposed to their howling rage and devouring fury in all the islands. I have seen them strike and toss a boat right up on end, and maim several on board. Once in the Grenada islands, when I and about eight others were pulling a large boat with two puncheons[2] of water in it, a surf struck us, and drove the boat, and all in it, about half a stone's throw, among some trees, and above the high water mark. We were obliged to get all the assistance we could from the nearest estate to mend the boat, and launch it into the water again. At Montserrat, one night, in pressing hard to get off the shore on board, the punt was overset with us four times, the first time I was very near being drowned; however, the jacket I had on kept me up above water a little space of time, when I called on a man near me, who was a good swimmer, and told him I could not swim; he then made

2. Large casks.

haste to me, and, just as I was sinking, he caught hold of me, and brought me to sounding, and then he went and brought the punt[3] also. As soon as we had turned the water out of her, lest we should be used ill for being absent, we attempted again three times more, and as often the horrid surfs served us as at first; but at last, the fifth time we attempted, we gained our point, at the imminent hazard of our lives. One day also, at Old Road, in Montserrat, our captain, and three men besides myself, were going in a large canoe in quest of rum and sugar, when a single surf tossed the canoe an amazing distance from the water, and some of us, near a stone's throw from each other. Most of us were very much bruised; so that I and many more often said, and really thought, that there was not such another place under the heavens as this. I longed, therefore, much to leave it, and daily wished to see my master's promise performed, of going to Philadelphia.

While we lay in this place, a very cruel thing happened on board our sloop, which filled me with horror; though I found afterwards such practices were frequent. There was a very clever and decent free young mulatto man, who sailed a long time with us; he had a free woman for his wife, by whom he had a child, and she was then living on shore, and all very happy. Our captain and mate, and other people on board, and several elsewhere, even the natives of Bermudas, all knew this young man from a child that he was always free, and no one had ever claimed him as their property. However, as might too often overcomes right in these parts, it happened that a Bermudas captain, whose vessel lay there for a few days in the road, came on board of us, and seeing the mulatto man, whose name was Joseph Clipson, he told him he was not free, and that he had orders from his master to bring him to Bermudas. The poor man could not believe the captain to be in earnest, but he was very soon undeceived, his men laying violent hands on him; and although he showed a certificate of his being born free in St. Kitts, and most people on board knew that he served his time to[4] boat building, and always passed for a free man, yet he was forcibly taken out of our vessel. He then asked to be carried ashore before the Secretary or Magistrates, and these infernal invaders of human rights promised him he should; but instead of that, they carried him on board of the other vessel. And the next day, without giving the poor man any hearing on shore, or suffering him even to see his wife or child, he was carried away, and probably doomed never more in this world to see them again. Nor was this the only instance of this kind of barbarity I was a witness to. I have since often seen in Jamaica and other islands, free men, whom I have known in America, thus villainously trepanned[5] and held in bondage. I have heard of two similar practices even in Philadelphia. And were it not for the benevolence of the Quakers in that city, many of the sable race, who now breathe the air of liberty, would, I believe, be groaning indeed under some planter's chains. These things opened my mind to a new scene of horror, to which I had been before a stranger. Hitherto I had thought slavery only dreadful, but the state of a free negro appeared to me now equally so at least, and in some respects even worse, for they live in constant alarm for their liberty; which is but nominal, for they are universally insulted and plundered, without the possibility of redress; for such is the equity of the West Indian laws, that no free Negro's

3. Narrow, flat-bottomed boat. "Sounding": i.e., where one could stand.
4. Was apprenticed at.
5. Trapped.

evidence will be admitted in their courts of justice. In this situation, is it surprising that slaves, when mildly treated, should prefer even the misery of slavery to such a mockery of freedom? I was now completely disgusted with the West Indies, and thought I never should be entirely free until I had left them.

* * *

About the latter end of the year 1764, my master bought a larger sloop, called the Prudence, about seventy or eighty tons, of which my captain had the command. I went with him in this vessel, and we took a load of new slaves for Georgia and Charlestown.[6] My master now left me entirely to the captain, though he still wished me to be with him; but I, who always much wished to lose sight of the West Indies, was not a little rejoiced at the thoughts of seeing any other country. Therefore, relying on the goodness of my captain, I got ready all the little venture I could; and, when the vessel was ready, we sailed, to my great joy. When we got to our destined places, Georgia and Charlestown, I expected I should have an opportunity of selling my little property to advantage. But here, particularly in Charlestown, I met with buyers, white men, who imposed on me as in other places. Notwithstanding, I was resolved to have fortitude, thinking no lot or trial too hard when kind Heaven is the rewarder.

We soon got loaded again, and returned to Montserrat; and there, amongst the rest of the islands, I sold my goods well; and in this manner I continued trading during the year 1764—meeting with various scenes of imposition, as usual. After this, my master fitted out his vessel for Philadelphia, in the year 1765; and during the time we were loading her, and getting ready for the voyage, I worked with redoubled alacrity, from the hope of getting money enough by these voyages to buy my freedom, in time, if it should please God; and also to see the town of Philadelphia, which I had heard a great deal about for some years past. Besides which, I had always longed to prove my master's promise the first day I came to him. In the midst of these elevated ideas, and while I was about getting my little stock of merchandize in readiness, one Sunday my master sent for me to his house. When I came there, I found him and the captain together; and, on my going in, I was struck with astonishment at his telling me he heard that I meant to run away from him when I got to Philadelphia. "And therefore," said he, "I must tell you again, you cost me a great deal of money, no less than forty pounds sterling; and it will not do to lose so much. You are a valuable fellow," continued he, "and I can get any day for you one hundred guineas, from many gentlemen in this island." And then he told me of Captain Doran's brother-in-law, a severe master, who ever wanted to buy me to make me his overseer. My captain also said he could get much more than a hundred guineas for me in Carolina. This I knew to be a fact; for the gentleman that wanted to buy me came off several times on board of us, and spoke to me to live with him, and said he would use me well. When I asked him what work he would put me to, he said, as I was a sailor, he would make me a captain of one of his rice vessels. But I refused; and fearing at the same time, by a sudden turn I saw in the captain's temper, he might mean to sell me, I told the gentleman I would not live with him on any condition, and that I certainly would run away with his vessel: but he said he did not fear that, as he

6. Charleston, South Carolina.

would catch me again, and then he told me how cruelly he would serve me if I should do so. My captain, however, gave him to understand that I knew something of navigation, so he thought better of it; and, to my great joy, he went away. I now told my master, I did not say I would run away in Philadelphia; neither did I mean it, as he did not use me ill, nor yet the captain; for if they did, I certainly would have made some attempts before now; but as I thought that if it were God's will I ever should be freed, it would be so, and, on the contrary, if it was not His will, it would not happen. So I hoped if ever I were freed, whilst I was used well, it should be by honest means; but as I could not help myself, he must do as he pleased; I could only hope and trust to the God of Heaven; and at that instant my mind was big with inventions, and full of schemes to escape. I then appealed to the captain, whether he ever saw any sign of my making the least attempt to run away, and asked him if I did not always come on board according to the time for which he gave me liberty; and, more particularly, when all our men left us at Guadeloupe, and went on board of the French fleet, and advised me to go with them, whether I might not, and that he could not have got me again. To my no small surprise, and very great joy, the captain confirmed every syllable that I had said, and even more; for he said he had tried different times to see if I would make any attempt of this kind, both at St. Eustatia and in America, and he never found that I made the smallest; but, on the contrary, I always came on board according to his orders; and he did really believe, if I ever meant to run away, that, as I could never have had a better opportunity, I would have done it the night the mate and all the people left our vessel at Guadeloupe. The captain then informed my master, who had been thus imposed on by our mate (though I did not know who was my enemy), the reason the mate had for imposing this lie upon him; which was, because I had acquainted the captain of the provisions the mate had given away or taken out of the vessel. This speech of the captain was like life to the dead to me, and instantly my soul glorified God; and still more so, on hearing my master immediately say that I was a sensible fellow, and he never did intend to use me as a common slave; and that but for the entreaties of the captain, and his character of me, he would not have let me go from the shores about as I had done. That also, in so doing, he thought by carrying one little thing or other to different places to sell, I might make money. That he also intended to encourage me in this, by crediting me with half a puncheon of rum and half a hogshead[7] of sugar at a time; so that, from being careful, I might have money enough, in some time, to purchase my freedom; and, when that was the case, I might depend upon it he would let me have it for forty pounds sterling money, which was only the same price he gave for me. This sound gladdened my poor heart beyond measure; though indeed it was no more than the very idea I had formed in my mind of my master long before, and I immediately made him this reply: "Sir, I always had that very thought of you, indeed I had, and that made me so diligent in serving you." He then gave me a large piece of silver coin, such as I never had seen or had before, and told me to get ready for the voyage, and he would credit me with a tierce[8] of sugar, and another of rum; he also said that he had two amiable sisters in Philadelphia, from whom I might get some necessary things. Upon this my noble captain desired

---

7. Large barrel.   8. A third of a barrel.

me to go aboard; and, knowing the African metal,[9] he charged me not to say any thing of this matter to any body; and he promised that the lying mate should not go with him any more. This was a change indeed: in the same hour to feel the most exquisite pain, and in the turn of a moment the fullest joy. It caused in me such sensations as I was only able to express in my looks; my heart was so overpowered with gratitude, that I could have kissed both of their feet. When I left the room, I immediately went, or rather flew, to the vessel; which being loaded, my master, as good as his word, trusted me with a tierce of rum, and another of sugar, when we sailed, and arrived safe at the elegant town of Philadelphia. I sold my goods here pretty well; and in this charming place I found every thing plentiful and cheap.

While I was in this place, a very extraordinary occurrence befell me. I had been told one evening of a wise woman, a Mrs. Davis, who revealed secrets, foretold events, etc., etc. I put little faith in this story at first, as I could not conceive that any mortal could foresee the future disposals of Providence, nor did I believe in any other revelation than that of the Holy Scriptures; however, I was greatly astonished at seeing this woman in a dream that night, though a person I never before beheld in my life. This made such an impression on me, that I could not get the idea the next day out of my mind, and I then became as anxious to see her as I was before indifferent. Accordingly in the evening, after we left off working, I inquired where she lived, and being directed to her, to my inexpressible surprise, beheld the very woman in the very same dress she appeared to me to wear in the vision. She immediately told me I had dreamed of her the preceding night; related to me many things that had happened with a correctness that astonished me, and finally told me I should not be long a slave. This was the more agreeable news; as I believed it the more readily from her having so faithfully related the past incidents of my life. She said I should be twice in very great danger of my life within eighteen months, which, if I escaped, I should afterwards go on well. So, giving me her blessing, we parted. After staying here sometime till our vessel was loaded, and I had bought in my little traffic, we sailed from this agreeable spot for Montserrat, once more to encounter the raging surfs.

* * *

We soon came to Georgia, where we were to complete our landing, and here worse fate than ever attended me; for one Sunday night, as I was with some negroes in their master's yard, in the town of Savannah, it happened that their master, one Doctor Perkins, who was a very severe and cruel man, came in drunk; and not liking to see any strange negroes in his yard, he and a ruffian of a white man, he had in his service, beset me in an instant, and both of them struck me with the first weapons they could get hold of. I cried out as long as I could for help and mercy; but, though I gave a good account of myself, and he knew my captain, who lodged hard[1] by him, it was to no purpose. They beat and mangled me in a shameful manner, leaving me near dead. I lost so much blood from the wounds I received, that I lay quite motionless, and was so benumbed that I could not feel any thing for many hours. Early in the morning, they took me away to the jail. As I did

9. I.e., character.   1. I.e., close.

not return to the ship all night, my captain, not knowing where I was, and being uneasy that I did not then make my appearance, made inquiry after me; and having found where I was, immediately came to me. As soon as the good man saw me so cut and mangled, he could not forbear weeping; he soon got me out of jail to his lodgings, and immediately sent for the best doctors in the place, who at first declared it as their opinion that I could not recover. My captain on this went to all the lawyers in the town for their advice, but they told him they could do nothing for me as I was a negro. He then went to Doctor Perkins, the hero who had vanquished me, and menaced him, swearing he would be revenged on him, and challenged him to fight.—But cowardice is ever the companion of cruelty—and the Doctor refused. However, by the skillfullness of one Dr. Brady of that place, I began at last to amend; but, although I was so sore and bad with the wounds I had all over me, that I could not rest in any posture, yet I was in more pain on account of the captain's uneasiness about me, than I otherwise should have been. The worthy man nursed and watched me all the hours of the night; and I was, through his attention and that of the doctor, able to get out of bed in about sixteen or eighteen days. All this time I was very much wanted on board, as I used frequently to go up and down the river for rafts, and other parts of our cargo, and stow them, when the mate was sick or absent. In about four weeks, I was able to go on duty, and in a fortnight after, having got in all our lading, our vessel set sail for Montserrat; and in less than three weeks we arrived there safe towards the end of the year. This ended my adventures in 1764, for I did not leave Montserrat again till the beginning of the following year.

From *Chapter VII*

Every day now brought me nearer my freedom, and I was impatient till we proceeded again to sea, that I might have an opportunity of getting a sum large enough to purchase it. I was not long ungratified; for, in the beginning of the year 1766, my master bought another sloop, named the Nancy, the largest I had ever seen. She was partly laden, and was to proceed to Philadelphia; our captain had his choice of three, and I was well pleased he chose this, which was the largest; for, from his having a large vessel, I had more room, and could carry a larger quantity of goods with me. Accordingly, when we had delivered our old vessel, the Prudence, and completed the lading of the Nancy, having made near three hundred per cent. by four barrels of pork I brought from Charlestown, I laid in as large a cargo as I could, trusting to God's providence to prosper my undertaking. With these views I sailed for Philadelphia. On our passage, when we drew near the land, I was for the first time surprised at the sight of some whales, having never seen any such large sea monsters before; and as we sailed by the land, one morning, I saw a puppy whale close by the vessel; it was about the length of a wherry boat, and it followed us all the day till we got within the Capes.[2] We arrived safe, and in good time at Philadelphia, and I sold my goods there chiefly to the Quakers. They always appeared to be a very honest, discreet sort of people, and never attempted to impose on[3] me; I therefore liked them, and ever after chose to deal with them in preference to any others.

2. Possibly Cape May, in southern New Jersey.   3. Cheat.

One Sunday morning, while I was here, as I was going to church, I chanced to pass a meetinghouse. The doors being open, and the house full of people, it excited my curiosity to go in. When I entered the house, to my great surprise, I saw a very tall woman standing in the midst of them, speaking in an audible voice something which I could not understand. Having never seen any thing of this kind before, I stood and stared about me for some time, wondering at this odd scene. As soon as it was over, I took an opportunity to make inquiry about the place and people, when I was informed they were called Quakers. I particularly asked what that woman I saw in the midst of them had said, but none of them were pleased to satisfy me; so I quitted them, and soon after, as I was returning, I came to a church crowded with people; the churchyard was full likewise, and a number of people were even mounted on ladders looking in at the windows. I thought this a strange sight, as I had never seen churches, either in England or the West Indies, crowded in this manner before. I therefore made bold to ask some people the meaning of all this, and they told me the Rev. Mr. George Whitefield was preaching. I had often heard of this gentleman, and had wished to see and hear him; but I never before had an opportunity. I now therefore resolved to gratify myself with the sight, and pressed in amidst the multitude. When I got into the church, I saw this pious man exhorting the people with the greatest fervor and earnestness, and sweating as much as I ever did while in slavery on Montserrat beach. I was very much struck and impressed with this; I thought it strange I had never seen divines exert themselves in this manner before, and was no longer at a loss to account for the thin congregations they preached to.

When we had discharged our cargo here, and were loaded again, we left this fruitful land once more, and set sail for Montserrat. My traffic had hitherto succeeded so well with me, that I thought, by selling my goods when we arrived at Montserrat, I should have enough to purchase my freedom. But as soon as our vessel arrived there, my master came on board, and gave orders for us to go to St. Eustatia, and discharge our cargo there, and from thence proceed for Georgia. I was much disappointed at this; but thinking, as usual, it was of no use to encounter with the decrees of fate, I submitted without repining, and we went to St. Eustatia. After we had discharged our cargo there, we took in a live cargo (as we call a cargo of slaves). Here I sold my goods tolerably well; but, not being able to lay out all my money in this small island to as much advantage as in many other places, I laid out only part, and the remainder I brought away with me net.[4] We sailed from hence for Georgia, and I was glad when we got there, though I had not much reason to like the place from my last adventure in Savannah; but I longed to get back to Montserrat and procure my freedom, which I expected to be able to purchase when I returned. As soon as we arrived here, I waited on my careful doctor, Mr. Brady, to whom I made the most grateful acknowledgments in my power, for his former kindness and attention during my illness.

* * *

When we had unladen the vessel, and I had sold my venture, finding myself master of about forty-seven pounds—I consulted my true friend, the captain, how I should proceed in offering my master the money for my freedom. He

4. In total, without further deductions.

told me to come on a certain morning, when he and my master would be at breakfast together. Accordingly, on that morning I went, and met the captain there, as he had appointed. When I went in I made my obeisance to my master, and with my money in my hand, and many fears in my heart, I prayed him to be as good as his offer to me, when he was pleased to promise me my freedom as soon as I could purchase it. This speech seemed to confound him, he began to recoil, and my heart that instant sunk within me. "What," said he, "give you your freedom? Why, where did you get the money? Have you got forty pounds sterling?" "Yes, sir," I answered. "How did you get it?" replied he. I told him, very honestly. The captain then said he knew I got the money honestly, and with much industry, and that I was particularly careful. On which my master replied, I got money much faster than he did; and said he would not have made me the promise he did if he had thought I should have got the money so soon. "Come, come," said my worthy captain, clapping my master on the back, "Come, Robert (which was his name), I think you must let him have his freedom;—you have laid your money out very well; you have received a very good interest for it all this time, and here is now the principal at last. I know Gustavus has earned you more than a hundred a year, and he will save you money, as he will not leave you.—Come, Robert, take the money." My master then said he would not be worse than his promise; and, taking the money, told me to go to the Secretary at the Register Office, and get my manumission drawn up. These words of my master were like a voice from Heaven to me. In an instant all my trepidation was turned into unutterable bliss; and I most reverently bowed myself with gratitude, unable to express my feelings, but by the overflowing of my eyes, and a heart replete with thanks to God, while my true and worthy friend, the captain, congratulated us both with a peculiar degree of heartfelt pleasure. As soon as the first transports of my joy were over, and that I had expressed my thanks to these my worthy friends, in the best manner I was able, I rose with a heart full of affection and reverence, and left the room, in order to obey my master's joyful mandate of going to the Register Office. As I was leaving the house I called to mind the words of the Psalmist,[5] in the 126th Psalm, and like him, "I glorified God in my heart, in whom I trusted." These words had been impressed on my mind from the very day I was forced from Deptford to the present hour, and I now saw them, as I thought, fulfilled and verified. My imagination was all rapture as I flew to the Register Office; and, in this respect, like the apostle Peter[6] (whose deliverance from prison was so sudden and extraordinary, that he thought he was in a vision), I could scarcely believe I was awake. Heavens! who could do justice to my feelings at this moment! Not conquering heroes themselves, in the midst of a triumph—Not the tender mother who has just regained her long lost infant, and presses it to her heart—Not the weary hungry, mariner, at the sight of the desired friendly port—Not the lover, when he once more embraces his beloved mistress, after she has been ravished from his arms! All within my breast was tumult, wildness, and delirium! My feet scarcely touched the ground, for they were

5. David, the second king of ancient Israel, traditionally considered the author of the biblical Book of Psalms.
6. "Acts xii.9" [Equiano's note]. "And he went out and followed him; and wist not that it was true which was done by the angel; but thought he saw a vision."

winged with joy; and, like Elijah, as he rose to Heaven,[7] they "were with light-ning sped as I went on." Every one I met I told of my happiness, and blazed about the virtue of my amiable master and captain.

When I got to the office and acquainted the Register with my errand, he congratulated me on the occasion, and told me he would draw up my manu-mission for half price, which was a guinea.[8] I thanked him for his kindness; and, having received it, and paid him, I hastened to my master to get him to sign it, that I might be fully released. Accordingly he signed the manumission that day; so that, before night, I, who had been a slave in the morning, trem-bling at the will of another, was become my own master, and completely free. I thought this was the happiest day I had ever experienced; and my joy was still heightened by the blessings and prayers of many of the sable race, par-ticularly the aged, to whom my heart had ever been attached with reverence.

*   *   *

As the form of my manumission has something peculiar in it, and expresses the absolute power and dominion one man claims over his fellow, I shall beg leave to present it before my readers at full length:

Montserrat.—To all men unto whom these presents[9] shall come: I, Robert King, of the parish of St. Anthony, in the said island, merchant, send greet-ing. Know ye, that I, the aforesaid Robert King, for and in consideration of the sum of seventy pounds current money of the said island,[1] to me in hand paid, and to the intent that a negro man slave, named Gustavus Vassa, shall and may become free, having manumitted, emancipated, enfranchised, and set free, and by these presents do manumit, emancipate, enfranchise, and set free, the aforesaid negro man slave, named Gustavus Vassa, for ever; hereby giving, granting, and releasing unto him, the said Gustavus Vassa, all right, title, dominion, sovereignty, and property, which, as lord and mas-ter over the aforesaid Gustavus Vassa, I had, or now have, or by any means whatsoever I may or can hereafter possibly have over him, the aforesaid negro, for ever. In witness whereof, I, the above said Robert King, have unto these presents set my hand and seal, this tenth day of July, in the year of our Lord one thousand seven hundred and sixty-six.

Robert King.

Signed, sealed, and delivered in the presence of Terry Legay, Montserrat.

Registered the within manumission at full length, this eleventh day of July, 1766, in liber[2] D.

Terry Legay, Register.

*   *   *

1789

---

7. God takes Elijah into heaven in 2 Kings 2.11.
8. A unit of British currency, equal to twenty-one shillings.
9. The present words; this document.
1. Because the exchange rate favored the West

Indians in this period, the forty pounds sterling that Equiano paid equaled seventy pounds in "local" currency.
2. Book (Latin).

JUDITH SARGENT MURRAY
1751–1820

J udith Sargent Murray addressed her most important subject—the independent
female mind—in her first published essay, "Desultory Thoughts upon the Utility
of Encouraging a Degree of Self-Complacency, Especially in Female Bosoms" (1784).
Writing under the pen name "Constantia," she advised young women that though a
"pleasing form is undoubtedly advantageous," a developed mind is far more mean-
ingful. An intellectual woman in a culture that regarded women as men's mental
inferiors, a professional writer in an era when almost no one—male or female—
made a living by writing, Murray went on to demonstrate the validity of her own
precepts.

Judith Sargent was born and spent much of her life in Gloucester, Massachusetts,
a coastal town about forty miles north of Boston. Her parents, Judith Saunders and
Winthrop Sargent, came from seafaring families. Along with her younger brother
Winslow, Judith was tutored by the local clergyman in college preparatory subjects
including Latin, Greek, and mathematics. Another distinctive feature of her
upbringing was her parents' liberal theology, which questioned the strict Calvinist
doctrine of election, that is, the belief that God had destined each soul to either
salvation or damnation. They embraced instead the teachings of the English Universalist James Relly, who proclaimed that salvation was available to anyone who
accepted Jesus Christ. Relly was sure that a rational God would never condemn
believers to hell. The Sargents and John Stevens, whom Judith married in 1769,
were thus ready to welcome Relly's greatest disciple, John Murray, who had left
England to preach in the eastern colonies, reaching Gloucester in 1774. In 1788,
about a year after the death of John Stevens in the West Indies, Judith Sargent
married John Murray. Meanwhile the first Universalist church in America had
been dedicated in Gloucester in 1780. The denomination went on to be a leader in
the effort to ordain women as ministers. As this suggests, Judith Sargent Murray's
advocacy of cultivating independent, intellectually alert women was highly compatible with her religious beliefs.

Murray's career as a writer began in earnest soon after she married Murray. In
an increasingly secular world, essays and novels with moral subtexts fashioned
readers into secular "congregations," and periodicals such as Boston's *Massachusetts
Magazine* and *The Gentleman's and Lady's Town and Country Magazine: or, Repository of Instruction and Entertainment*, where "The Utility of Encouraging a Degree
of Self-Complacency, Especially in Female Bosoms" first appeared, would supplant
or supplement many pulpits in the years to come. Eighteenth-century readers liked
a moral without the theology. But while Murray found an audience early on, it was
not easy for her to make a living by the pen. In the volatile world of print culture,
magazines changed hands frequently and many of them disappeared, while publishers assumed that contributors would be so eager to see their names in print that
no payment was necessary.

Murray's most important publication and her greatest financial success was a
three-volume compilation of her work, published in 1798 as *The Gleaner*, which she
dedicated to Abigail and John Adams. She seems to have published nothing new
from 1796 to 1802, when she offered some poems in a Boston publication that
hoped to take up where the defunct *Massachusetts Magazine* left off. Her major

"Keep within Compass," c. 1795. This engraving encourages women to remain outside the public sphere occupied by men. Judith Sargent Murray was among the thinkers of the time who challenged this view.

efforts during these years went to the care of her ailing and improvident husband and to editing his *Letters and Sketches of Sermons* (1812–13) and his posthumously published autobiography (1816). With her work on Murray's behalf completed, she left New England and made a final home with her daughter in Natchez, Mississippi, where she died in 1820.

At the beginning of her writing career, in 1779, Murray drafted "On the Equality of the Sexes," which offers a defense of women's intellectual abilities. The essay did not appear in print until 1790, the same year as the English writer Catherine Macaulay's similarly themed *Letters on Education*. Two years later the English writer Mary Wollstonecraft published *Vindication of the Rights of Woman*, a landmark political treatise and statement of women's rights. As these parallels suggest, Murray was at the forefront of the movement in the revolutionary Atlantic world to extend the promise of equality in the Declaration of Independence to women as well as men.

On the Equality of the Sexes[1]

Part I

That minds are not alike, full well I know,
This truth each day's experience will show.
To heights surprising some great spirits soar,
With inborn strength mysterious depths explore;
Their eager gaze surveys the path of light,   5
Confessed it stood to Newton's piercing sight.[2]
    Deep science, like a bashful maid retires,
And but[3] the *ardent* breast her worth inspires;
By perseverance the coy fair is won,
And Genius, led by Study, wears the crown.   10
    But some there are who wish not to improve,
Who never can the path of knowledge love,
Whose souls almost with the dull body one,
With anxious care each mental pleasure shun.
Weak is the leveled, enervated mind,   15
And but while here to vegetate designed.
The torpid spirit mingling with its clod
Can scarcely boast its origin from God.
Stupidly dull—they move progressing on—
They eat, and drink, and all their work is done,   20
While others, emulous of sweet applause,
Industrious seek for each event a cause,
Tracing the hidden springs whence knowledge flows,
Which nature all in beauteous order shows.
    Yet cannot I their sentiments imbibe   25
Who this distinction to the sex ascribe,
As if a woman's form must needs enroll
A weak, a servile, an inferior soul;
And that the guise of man must still proclaim
Greatness of mind, and him, to be the same.   30
Yet as the hours revolve fair proofs arise
Which the bright wreath of growing fame supplies,
And in past times some men have *sunk* so *low*,
That female records nothing *less* can show.
But imbecility[4] is still confined,   35
And by the lordly sex to us consigned.
They rob us of the power t'improve,
And then declare we only trifles love.
Yet haste the era when the world shall know
That such distinctions only dwell below.   40
The soul unfettered to no sex confined,
Was for the abodes of cloudless day designed.

---

1. The text is from *The Massachusetts Magazine, or, Monthly Museum of Knowledge and Rational Entertainment,* published in March and April 1790. Both the poem and the essay are by Murray.
2. Sir Isaac Newton (1642–1727), English scientist and philosopher, broke up white light into the colors of the spectrum by means of a prism and likewise recombined the colors.
3. And only.
4. Stupidity.

Meantime we emulate their manly fires,
Though erudition all their thoughts inspires,
Yet nature with *equality* imparts,   45
And *noble passions*, swell e'en *female hearts*.

Is it upon mature consideration we adopt the idea that nature is thus partial in her distributions? Is it indeed a fact that she hath yielded to one half of the human species so unquestionable a mental superiority? I know that to both sexes elevated understandings, and the reverse, are common. But, suffer me to ask, in what the minds of females are so notoriously deficient, or unequal? May not the intellectual powers be ranged under these four heads—imagination, reason, memory and judgment? The province of imagination hath long since been surrendered up to us, and we have been crowned undoubted sovereigns of the regions of fancy. Invention is perhaps the most arduous effort of the mind; this branch of imagination hath been particularly ceded to us, and we have been time out of mind invested with that creative faculty. Observe the variety of fashions (here I bar the contemptuous smile) which distinguish and adorn the female world; how continually are they changing, insomuch that they almost render the wise man's assertion problematical, and we are ready to say, *there is something new under the sun.*[5] Now what a playfulness, what an exuberance of fancy, what strength of inventive imagination, doth this continual variation discover?[6] Again, it hath been observed that if the turpitude of the conduct of our sex hath been ever so enormous, so extremely ready are we, that the very first thought presents us with an apology so plausible as to produce our actions even in an amiable light. Another instance of our creative powers is our talent for slander. How ingenious are we at inventive scandal? What a formidable story can we in a moment fabricate merely from the force of a prolific imagination? How many reputations in the fertile brain of a female have been utterly despoiled? How industrious are we at improving[7] a hint? Suspicion[8] how easily do we convert into conviction, and conviction, embellished by the power of eloquence, stalks abroad to the surprise and confusion of unsuspecting innocence. Perhaps it will be asked if I furnish these facts as instances of excellency in our sex. Certainly not; but as proofs of a creative faculty, of a lively imagination. Assuredly great activity of mind is thereby discovered, and was this activity properly directed what beneficial effects would follow. Is the needle and kitchen sufficient to employ the operations of a soul thus organized? I should conceive not. Nay, it is a truth that those very departments leave the intelligent principle vacant, and at liberty for speculation. Are we deficient in reason? We can only reason from what we know, and if an opportunity of acquiring knowledge hath been denied us, the inferiority of our sex cannot fairly be deduced from thence. Memory, I believe, will be allowed us in common, since every one's experience must testify that a loquacious old woman is as frequently met with as a communicative old man; their subjects are alike drawn from the fund of other times, and the transactions of their youth, or of maturer life, entertain, or perhaps fatigue you, in the evening of their lives. "But our judgment is not so strong—we do not distinguish so well."—Yet it

---

5. "There is no new thing under the sun" (Ecclesiastes 1.8).
6. Reveal.

7. Making use of.
8. Imagine.

may be questioned, from what doth this superiority in this determining faculty of the soul, proceed? May we not trace its source in the difference of education, and continued advantages? Will it be said that the judgment of a male of two years old is more sage than that of a female's of the same age? I believe the reverse is generally observed to be true. But from that period what partiality! How is the one exalted and the other depressed by the contrary modes of education which are adopted! The one is taught to aspire and the other is early confined and limited. As their years increase the sister must be wholly domesticated, while the brother is led by the hand through all the flowery paths of science. Grant that their minds are by nature equal, yet who shall wonder at the *apparent* superiority, if indeed custom becomes *second nature*; nay if it taketh place of nature, and that it doth the experience of each day will evince. At length arrived at womanhood, the uncultivated fair one feels a void which the employments allotted her are by no means capable of filling. What can she do? To books she may not apply; or if she doth, *to those only of the novel kind,*[9] lest she merit the appellation of a *learned lady*; and what ideas have been affixed to this term, the observation of many can testify. Fashion, scandal, and sometimes what is still more reprehensible are then called in to her relief; and who can say to what lengths the liberties she takes may proceed. Meantime she herself is most unhappy; she feels the want of a cultivated mind. Is she single, she in vain seeks to fill up time from sexual[1] employments or amusements. Is she united to a person whose soul nature made equal to her own, education hath set him so far above her that in those entertainments which are productive of such rational felicity she is not qualified to accompany him. She experiences a mortifying consciousness of inferiority which embitters every enjoyment. Doth the person to whom her adverse fate hath consigned her possess a mind incapable of improvement, she is equally wretched in being so closely connected with an individual whom she cannot but despise. Now was she permitted the same instructors as her brother (with an eye however to their particular departments) for the employment of a rational mind an ample field would be opened. In astronomy she might catch a glimpse of the immensity of the Deity and thence she would form amazing conceptions of the August and supreme Intelligence. In geography she would admire Jehovah in the midst of His benevolence; thus adapting this globe to the various wants and amusements of its inhabitants. In natural philosophy she would adore the infinite majesty of heaven, clothed in condescension[2] and as she traversed the reptile world, she would hail the goodness of a creating God. A mind thus filled would have little room for the trifles with which our sex are, with too much justice, accused of amusing themselves, and they would thus be rendered fit companions for those who should one day wear them as their crown. Fashions, in their variety, would then give place to conjectures, which might perhaps conduce to the improvement of the literary world; and there would be no leisure for slander or detraction. Reputation would not then be blasted, but serious speculations would occupy the lively imaginations of the sex. Unnecessary visits would be precluded, and that custom would only be indulged by way of relaxation, or to answer the demands of consanguinity and friendship. Females would

9. I.e., fiction.
1. Defined by gender roles.

2. A gracious disregard of its superiority. "Natural philosophy": i.e., natural science.

become discreet, their judgments would be invigorated, and their partners for life being circumspectly chosen, an unhappy Hymen[3] would then be as rare as is now the reverse.

Will it be urged that those acquirements would supersede our domestic duties? I answer that every requisite in female economy[4] is easily attained; and, with truth, I can add that when once attained they require no further *mental attention*. Nay, while we are pursuing the needle, or the superintendency of the family, I repeat, that our minds are at full liberty for reflection; that imagination may exert itself in full vigor; and that if a just foundation is early laid, our ideas will then be worthy of rational beings. If we were industrious we might easily find time to arrange them upon paper, or should avocations press too hard for such an indulgence, the hours allotted for conversation would at least become more refined and rational. Should it still be vociferated, "Your domestic employments are sufficient"—I would calmly ask, is it reasonable that a candidate for immortality, for the joys of heaven, an intelligent being, who is to spend an eternity in contemplating the works of Deity, should at present be so degraded as to be allowed no other ideas than those which are suggested by the mechanism of a pudding, or the sewing the seams of a garment? Pity that all such censurers of female improvement do not go one step further and deny their[5] future existence; to be consistent they surely ought.

Yes, ye lordly, ye haughty sex, our souls are by nature *equal* to yours; the same breath of God animates, enlivens, and invigorates us; and that we are not fallen lower than yourselves, let those witness who have greatly towered above the various discouragements by which they have been so heavily oppressed. And though I am unacquainted with the list of celebrated characters on either side, yet from the observations I have made in the contracted circle in which I have moved, I dare confidently believe that from the commencement of time to the present day there hath been as many females, as males, who, by the *mere force of natural powers*, have merited the crown of applause; who, *thus unassisted*, have seized the wreath of fame. I know there are [those] who assert that as the animal powers of the one sex are superior of course their mental faculties also must be stronger; thus attributing strength of mind to the transient organization of this earth born tenement.[6] But if this reasoning is just, man must be content to yield the palm[7] [to] many of the brute creation, since by not a few of his brethren of the field he is far surpassed in bodily strength. Moreover, was this argument admitted, it would prove too much, for ocular demonstration evinceth that there are many robust masculine ladies, and effeminate gentlemen. Yet I fancy that Mr. Pope, though clogged with an enervated body, and distinguished by a diminutive stature,[8] could nevertheless lay claim to greatness of soul, and perhaps there are many other instances which might be adduced to combat so unphilosophical an opinion. Do we not often see that when the clay built tabernacle[9] is well nigh dissolved, when it is just ready to mingle with the parent soil, the immortal inhabitant aspires to and even attaineth heights the most sublime and which were before wholly unexplored? Besides, were

3. Marriage. In classical mythology, Hymen is the god of marriage.
4. Housekeeping.
5. Women's.
6. I.e., of the human body.

7. The palm branch, a classical symbol of victory.
8. The English poet Alexander Pope (1688–1744) suffered an early illness that left his body deformed.
9. I.e., the body, which houses the soul.

we to grant that animal strength proved anything, taking into consideration the accustomed impartiality of nature, we should be induced to imagine that she had invested the female mind with superior strength as an equivalent for the bodily powers of man. But waving this however palpable advantage, for *equality only,* we wish to contend.

Part II

I am aware that there are many passages in the sacred oracles which seem to give the advantage to the other sex, but I consider all these as wholly metaphorical. Thus David was a man after God's own heart, yet see him enervated by his licentious passions! Behold him following Uriah to the death[1] and show me wherein could consist the immaculate Being's complacency. Listen to the curses which Job bestoweth upon the day of his nativity,[2] and tell me where is his perfection, where his patience—*literally* it existed not. David and Job were types of Him who was to come;[3] and the superiority of man, as exhibited in scripture, being also emblematical, all arguments deduced from thence of course fall to the ground. The exquisite delicacy of the female mind proclaimeth the exactness of its texture, while its nice[4] sense of honor announceth its innate, its native grandeur. And indeed, in one respect, the preeminence seems to be tacitly allowed us, for after an education which limits and confines, and employments and recreations which naturally tend to enervate the body and debilitate the mind, after we have from early youth been adorned with ribbons and other gewgaws,[5] dressed out like the ancient victims previous to a sacrifice, being taught by the care of our parents in collecting the most showy materials that the ornamenting [of] our exterior ought to be the principal object of our attention; after, I say, fifteen years thus spent, we are introduced into the world amid the united adulation of every beholder. Praise is sweet to the soul; we are immediately intoxicated by large draughts of flattery, which being plentifully administered, is to the pride of our hearts the most acceptable incense. It is expected that with the other sex we should commence immediate war, and that we should triumph over the machinations of the most artful. We must be constantly upon our guard; prudence and discretion must be our characteristics, and we must rise superior to, and obtain a complete victory over, those who have been long adding to the native strength of their minds by an unremitted study of men and books, and who have, moreover, conceived from the loose characters which they have seen portrayed in the extensive variety of their reading a most contemptible opinion of the sex. Thus unequal, we are, notwithstanding, forced to the combat, and the infamy which is consequent upon the smallest deviation in our conduct proclaims the high idea which was formed of our native strength; and thus, indirectly at least, is the preference acknowledged to be our due. And if we are allowed an equality of acquirement, let serious studies equally employ our minds and we

1. When King David lusted after Bathsheba, he contrived to send her husband, Uriah, into battle to be killed so that David might marry her. See 2 Samuel 11.3–27.
2. Although Job's faith survives many testings, he curses the day he was born (Job 3).
3. Medieval exegetes argued that Old Testa-
ment persons and events took on their full meaning in the New Testament. Job and David are thus, in their sufferings, types (i.e., prefigurations) of Jesus.
4. Refined. "Exactness": high finish or quality.
5. Trinkets.

will bid our souls arise to equal strength. We will meet upon even ground the despot man; we will rush with alacrity to the combat, and, crowned by success, we shall then answer the exalted expectations which are formed. Though sensibility, soft compassion, and gentle commiseration are inmates in the female bosom, yet against every deep laid art, altogether fearless of the event, we will set them in array; for assuredly the wreath of victory will encircle the spotless brow. If we meet an equal, a sensible friend, we will reward him with the hand of amity, and through life we will be assiduous to promote his happiness; but from every deep laid scheme for our ruin, retiring into ourselves, amid the flowery paths of science, we will indulge in all the refined and sentimental pleasures of contemplation. And should it still be urged that the studies thus insisted upon would interfere with our more peculiar department,[6] I must further reply that *early hours* and close application will do wonders; and to her who is from the first dawn of reason taught to fill up time rationally, both the requisites will be easy. I grant that niggard[7] fortune is too generally unfriendly to the mind; and that much of that valuable treasure, time, is necessarily expended upon the wants of the body; but it should be remembered that in embarrassed circumstances our companions have as little leisure for literary improvement as is afforded to us; for most certainly their provident care is at least as requisite as our exertions. Nay, we have even more leisure for sedentary pleasures, as our avocations are more retired, much less laborious, and, as hath been observed, by no means require that avidity of attention which is proper to the employments of the other sex. In high life, or, in other words, where the parties are in possession of affluence, the objection respecting time is wholly obviated, and, of course, falls to the ground. And it may also be repeated that many of those hours which are at present swallowed up in fashion and scandal might be redeemed were we habituated to useful reflections. But in one respect, O ye arbiters of our fate! we confess that the superiority is indubitably yours; you are by nature formed for our protectors; we pretend not to vie with you in bodily strength; upon this point we will never contend for victory. Shield us then, we beseech you, from external evils, and in return *we* will transact *your* domestic affairs. Yes, *your,* for are you not equally interested in those matters with ourselves? Is not the elegancy of neatness as agreeable to your sight as to ours; is not the well favored viand equally delightful to your taste; and doth not your sense of hearing suffer as much from the discordant sounds prevalent in an ill regulated family produced by the voices of children and many *et ceteras?*[8]

Constantia.

By way of supplement to the foregoing pages, I subjoin the following extract from a letter, wrote to a friend in the December of 1780.

And now assist me, O thou genius of my sex, while I undertake the arduous task of endeavoring to combat that vulgar, that almost universal error, which hath, it seems, enlisted even Mr. P—under its banners. The superiority of your sex hath, I grant, been time out of mind esteemed a truth incontrovertible; in consequence of which persuasion every plan of education hath

---

6. I.e., with duties belonging more particularly to women.

7. Stingy.

8. Unspecified other things (Latin).

been calculated to establish this favorite tenet. Not long since, weak and presuming as I was, I amused myself with selecting some arguments from nature, reason, and experience, against this so generally received idea. I confess that to sacred testimonies[9] I had not recourse. I held them to be merely metaphorical and thus regarding them, I could not persuade myself that there was any propriety in bringing them to decide in this *very important debate*. However, as you, sir, confine yourself entirely to the sacred oracles, I mean to bend the whole of my artillery against those supposed proofs which you have from thence provided, and from which you have formed an entrenchment *apparently* so invulnerable. And first, to begin with our great progenitors;[1] but here, suffer me to premise, that it is for mental strength I mean to contend, for with respect to animal powers, I yield them undisputed to that sex, which enjoys them in common with the lion, the tiger, and many other beasts of prey; therefore your observations respecting the *rib under the arm*,[2] *at a distance from the head*, etc., etc., in no sort militate against my view. Well, but the woman was first in the transgression. Strange how blind *self love* renders you men. Were you not wholly absorbed in a partial admiration of your own abilities, you would long since have acknowledged the force of what I am now going to urge. It is true some ignoramuses have absurdly enough informed us that the beauteous fair of paradise was seduced from her obedience by a malignant demon *in the guise of a baleful serpent*; but we, who are better informed, know that the fallen spirit presented himself to her view *a shining angel still*; for thus, saith the critics in the Hebrew tongue, ought the word to be rendered.[3] Let us examine her motive— Hark! the seraph declares that she shall attain a perfection of knowledge; for is there aught which is not comprehended under one or other of the terms *good* and *evil*. It doth not appear that she was governed by any one sensual appetite, but merely by a desire of adorning her mind. A laudable ambition fired her soul and a thirst for knowledge impelled the predilection so fatal in its consequences. Adam could not plead the same deception; assuredly he was not deceived; nor ought we to admire his superior strength, or wonder at his sagacity, when we so often confess that example is much more influential than precept. His gentle partner stood before him, a melancholy instance of the direful effects of disobedience; he saw her not possessed of that wisdom which she had fondly hoped to obtain, but he beheld the once blooming female disrobed of that innocence which had heretofore rendered her so lovely. To him, then, deception became impossible, as he had proof positive of the fallacy of the argument which the deceiver had suggested. What then could be his inducement to burst the barriers, and to fly directly in the face of that command, which *immediately* from the mouth of Deity *he* had received, since, I say, he could not plead that fascinating stimulus, the accumulation of knowledge, as indisputable conviction was so visibly portrayed before him. What mighty cause impelled him to sacrifice myriads of beings yet unborn, and by one impious act, which *he saw* would be productive of such fatal effects, entail undistinguished ruin upon a race of beings which

---

9. I.e., to the Bible.
1. Ancestors; here, Adam and Eve.
2. "And the rib, which the Lord God had taken from man, made he a woman, and brought her unto the man" (Genesis 2.22).

3. The earliest connection of Satan and light is in Isaiah 14.12: "How are thou fallen from heaven, O Lucifer, son of the morning!" *Lucifer* in Latin means "light bearer."

he was yet to produce. Blush, ye vaunters of fortitude, ye boasters of resolution, ye haughty lords of the creation; blush when ye remember that he was influenced by no other motive than a bare pusillanimous attachment to a woman! by sentiments so exquisitely soft that all his sons have from that period, when they have designed to degrade them, described as highly feminine. Thus it should seem that all the arts of the grand deceiver (since means adequate to the purpose are, I conceive, invariably pursued) were requisite to mislead our general mother, while the father of mankind forfeited his own, and relinquished the happiness of posterity, merely in compliance with the blandishments of a female. The subsequent subjection the apostle Paul explains as a figure; after enlarging upon the subject, he adds, *"This is a great mystery; but I speak concerning Christ and the church."*[4] Now we know with what consummate wisdom the unerring father of eternity hath formed his plans; all the types which he hath displayed he hath permitted *materially* to fail, in the very virtue for which *they* were famed. The reason for this is obvious; we might otherwise mistake his economy and render that honor to the creature which is due only to the creator. I know that Adam was a figure of Him who was to come.[5] The Grace contained in this figure is the reason of my rejoicing, and while I am very far from prostrating before the shadow, I yield joyfully in all things the preeminence to the Second Federal Head.[6] Confiding faith is prefigured by Abraham, yet he exhibits a contrast to affiance when he says of his fair companion, she is my sister.[7] Gentleness was the characteristic of Moses,[8] yet he hesitated not to reply to Jehovah Himself. With unsaintlike tongue he murmured at the waters of strife, and with rash hands he break the Tables which were inscribed by the finger of divinity.[9] David, dignified with the title of the man after God's own heart, and yet how stained was his life. Solomon was celebrated for wisdom, but folly is wrote in legible characters upon his almost every action.[1] Lastly, let us turn our eyes to man in the aggregate. He is manifested as the figure of strength, but that we may not regard him as any thing more than a figure, his soul is formed in no sort superior, but every way equal to the mind of her who is the emblem of weakness and whom he hails the gentle companion of his better days.

1790, 1995

4. Ephesians 5.32.
5. Adam prefigures Jesus.
6. Jesus is the "Second Federal Head" because he made a Covenant of Faith with humanity after Adam broke God's Covenant of Works. *Federal* comes from the Latin word meaning "compact" or "treaty."
7. When Abraham, the first patriarch and progenitor of the Hebrews, is about to enter Egypt with his wife, he fears the Egyptians will kill him to take her, so he asks her: "Say, I pray thee, thou art my sister: that it may be well with me for thy sake; and my soul shall live because of

thee" (Genesis 12.13). "Affiance": plighted faith; marriage.
8. The lawgiver who led the Israelites out of Egypt: "Now the man Moses was very meek, above all the men which were upon the face of the earth" (Numbers 12.3).
9. God inscribed the Ten Commandments on stone tablets ("Tables"), and Moses broke the first of those tablets (Exodus 32.19).
1. Solomon, third king of ancient Israel, was famously rich and wise, but worshiped false gods and failed to keep God's commandments (1 Kings 11.1–10).

PHILIP FRENEAU
1752–1832

I t has been said that Philip Freneau failed at almost everything he did. An accomplished journalist and political pamphleteer as well as a poet, Freneau did not fail at everything, but he was not able to support himself as a writer. His lack of success in this regard was partly a consequence of the immature print market in the United States. A generation later, Washington Irving and James Fenimore Cooper became the first American writers to support themselves with their pens.

Apart from the issue of the developing print market, there is the matter of Freneau's style. His most sympathetic readers believe that his genuine lyric gifts were always in conflict with his political pamphleteering. Another possibility emerges from the poems themselves, which reveal a writer poised between two eighteenth-century traditions: the neoclassical Augustan poetry exemplified by Alexander Pope, and the not-yet-fledged Romantic poetry inaugurated by Samuel Taylor Coleridge and William Wordsworth in their joint collection *Lyrical Ballads* (1798). Often characterized as a literary response to the age of democratic revolution, the Romantic poetics of Coleridge and Wordsworth called for the poet to be "a man speaking to men" in a natural sounding idiom and to employ freer verse forms than the heroic couplet (i.e., rhymed pairs of iambic pentameter lines) that was the mainstay of neoclassical poetry. Freneau, like his contemporary Phillis Wheatley (see her headnote, below), moved in the direction of Romantic themes and forms without accomplishing the transformation in poetics that his British contemporaries achieved.

Raised in Manhattan, Freneau had all the advantages of wealth and social position, which included an early introduction to the arts. Well-known writers and painters frequented the Freneau household. Educated in childhood by tutors, he entered the sophomore class at the College of New Jersey (now Princeton University) when he was just fifteen. At Princeton he became close friends with his roommate, James Madison, who would one day become the fourth president of the United States, and a classmate, Hugh Henry Brackenridge, who would become a judge and successful novelist. In their senior year Freneau and Brackenridge composed an ode, "On the Rising Glory of America," which Brackenridge read at commencement. It offers an early instance of Freneau's recurrent vision of a glorious future in which America fulfills the collective hope of humankind:

> Paradise anew
> Shall flourish, by no second Adam lost,
> No dangerous tree with deadly fruit shall grow,
> No tempting serpent to allure the soul
> From native innocence. . . . The lion and the lamb
> In mutual friendship linked, shall browse the shrub,
> And timorous deer with softened tigers stray
> O'er mead, or lofty hill, or grassy plain.

For a short time Freneau taught school, even as he hoped to make a career as a writer. When he was offered a position as secretary on a plantation in the West Indies in 1776, he sailed to St. Croix and remained there almost three years. On that island—where "Sweet orange groves in lonely valleys rise," as he put it—

Freneau wrote some of his most sensuous lyrics. As he remarks in "To Sir Toby" (1791), however, he could not talk only of "blossoms" and an "endless spring" in a land that abounded in poverty and misery, where the plantation owners grew wealthy on slave labor. In 1778 he returned home and enlisted as a seaman on a blockade runner; two years later he was captured at sea and imprisoned on the British ship *Scorpion,* anchored in New York harbor. He was treated cruelly, an experience he describes in "The British Prison Ship" (1781), his most popular poem with his contemporaries.

After Freneau regained his health, he moved to Philadelphia, where he worked in the post office and won his reputation as a journalist, satirist, and poet. As editor of the *Freeman's Journal,* Freneau wrote impassioned verse in support of the American Revolution, turned all his rhetorical gifts against loyalists to the British monarchy, and became identified as "the poet of the American Revolution." In 1791 Thomas Jefferson, then serving as secretary of state, hired Freneau as a translator in his department. At that point Philadelphia was the nation's capital, so Freneau remained in that city, devoting much of his time to editing the *National Gazette,* a newspaper associated with Jefferson's political party. That party, the Democratic-Republicans, favored a democratic republic rather than the strong federal government favored by the opposing Federalist party. Freneau had a sharp eye for anyone not sympathetic to the democratic cause. He strongly supported the French Revolution and had a special grudge against Alexander Hamilton, secretary of the Treasury, chief spokesman for the Federalists, who viewed the French Revolution skeptically. President George Washington, officially nonpartisan, found it ironic that "that rascal Freneau" should be employed by his administration when he attacked it outspokenly.

The *National Gazette* ceased publication in 1793, and after Jefferson resigned his office, Freneau left Philadelphia for good, alternating between ship's captain (a job that he had held on and off since 1778) and newspaper editor in New York and New Jersey. He spent his last years on his New Jersey farm, unable to make it self-supporting and with no hope of further employment. Year after year he sold off the land he had inherited from his father. Although he received a pension as a veteran of the American Revolution, he died impoverished and unknown, lost in a blizzard.

Freneau was a prolific writer of prose and poetry, addressing many topics including revolution and slavery, the fate of Native Americans, the sea, and nature. His best poems have a compelling lyricism. They reveal his interest in the beautiful, transient things of nature, and the conflict in his art between the sensuous and the didactic.

The following texts are from *The Poems of Freneau* (1929), edited by H. H. Clark, except as indicated.

The Wild Honey Suckle

Fair flower, that dost so comely grow,
Hid in this silent, dull retreat,
Untouched thy honeyed blossoms blow,[1]
Unseen thy little branches greet:
   No roving foot shall crush thee here,
   No busy hand provoke a tear.   5

By Nature's self in white arrayed,
She bade thee shun the vulgar[2] eye,

1. Bloom.   2. Common; unfeeling.

And planted here the guardian shade,
And sent soft waters murmuring by;   10
   Thus quietly thy summer goes,
   Thy days declining to repose.

Smit with those charms, that must decay,
I grieve to see your future doom;
They died—nor were those flowers more gay,   15
The flowers that did in Eden bloom;
   Unpitying frosts, and Autumn's power
   Shall leave no vestige of this flower.

From morning suns and evening dews
At first thy little being came: 20
If nothing once, you nothing lose,
For when you die you are the same;
   The space between, is but an hour,
   The frail duration of a flower.

1786

The Indian Burying Ground

In spite of all the learned have said,
I still my old opinion keep;
The *posture*, that *we* give the dead,
Points out the soul's eternal sleep.

Not so the ancients of these lands—   5
The Indian, when from life released,
Again is seated[1] with his friends,
And shares again the joyous feast.

His imaged birds, and painted bowl,
And venison, for a journey dressed,   10
Bespeak the nature of the soul,
Activity, that knows no rest.

His bow, for action ready bent,
And arrows, with a head of stone,
Can only mean that life is spent,   15
And not the old ideas gone.

Thou, stranger, that shalt come this way,
No fraud upon the dead commit—
Observe the swelling turf, and say
They do not *lie*, but here they *sit*.   20

---

1. The North American Indians bury their dead in a sitting posture; decorating the corpse with wampum, the images of birds, quadrupeds, etc.: And (if that of a warrior) with bows, arrows, tomahawks and other military weapons [Freneau's note].

Here still a lofty rock remains,
On which the curious eye may trace
(Now wasted, half, by wearing rains)
The fancies of a ruder race.

Here still an agéd elm aspires,   25
Beneath whose far-projecting shade
(And which the shepherd still admires)
The children of the forest played!

There oft a restless Indian queen
(Pale Sheba,[2] with her braided hair)   30
And many a barbarous form is seen
To chide the man that lingers there.

By midnight moons, o'er moistening dews,
In habit for the chase arrayed,
The hunter still the deer pursues,   35
The hunter and the deer, a shade![3]

And long shall timorous fancy see
The painted chief, and pointed spear,
And Reason's self shall bow the knee
To shadows and delusions here.   40

                                                    1788

On the Religion of Nature

The power, that gives with liberal hand
    The blessings man enjoys, while here,
And scatters through a smiling land
    Abundant products of the year;
        That power of nature, ever blessed,   5
        Bestowed religion with the rest.

Born with ourselves, her early sway
    Inclines the tender mind to take
The path of right, fair virtue's way
    Its own felicity to make.   10
        This universally extends
        And leads to no mysterious ends.

Religion, such as nature taught,
    With all divine perfection suits;
Had all mankind this system sought   15
    Sophists would cease their vain[1] disputes,

---

2. The queen who visited King Solomon to test
his renowned wisdom (1 Kings 10.1–13).

3. Has double meaning as shadow and spirit.
1. Pointless. "Sophists": teachers of philosophy.

And from this source would nations know
All that can make their heaven below.

This deals not curses on mankind,
 Or dooms them to perpetual grief,   20
If from its aid no joys they find,
 It damns them not for unbelief;
  Upon a more exalted plan
  Creatress nature dealt with man—

Joy to the day, when all agree   25
 On such grand systems to proceed,
From fraud, design, and error free,
 And which to truth and goodness lead:
  Then persecution will retreat
  And man's religion be complete.   30

1815

PHILLIS WHEATLEY
c. 1753–1784

Phillis Wheatley was either nineteen or twenty years old in September 1773, when her *Poems on Various Subjects, Religious and Moral* was published in London. At the time of the volume's publication, she was the object of considerable public attention because, in addition to being a child prodigy, Wheatley was an enslaved person. Her books included a testimonial from eighteen prominent citizens—including the governor of Massachusetts and the merchant and statesman John Hancock—who bore witness that "under the Disadvantage of serving as a Slave in a Family in this Town," Wheatley "had been examined and thought qualified to write them." While the circumstances and nature of the examination remain unclear, the need for such a testimonial indicates the obstacles that Wheatley faced in pursuing her literary art.

Born in Africa (probably in present-day Senegal or Gambia), she was captured by slavers and brought to Boston in 1761. A wealthy tailor, John Wheatley, purchased her as a companion for his wife, Susanna, and she was named after the vessel that carried her to America. Wheatley was fortunate in her surroundings, for Susanna Wheatley was sympathetic toward this frail and remarkably intelligent child. At a time when even few white women were given an education, Wheatley was taught to read and write, and before long she began to read Latin writers. She came to know the Bible well, and three English poets—John Milton, Alexander Pope, and Thomas Gray—strongly influenced her verse. The Wheatleys moved in a circle of enlightened Boston Christians, and Phillis was introduced to a community that was coming to view the keeping of slaves as incompatible with Christian life.

Wheatley became internationally famous after the publication of her poetic eulogy celebrating George Whitefield, the great English evangelist who made several visits to America, frequently toured New England, and died in Newburyport, Massachusetts, in 1770. In June 1773 she traveled to London in the company of the Wheatleys' son Nathaniel, partly for reasons of health and partly to seek support for her first book of poems. Benjamin Franklin and the lord mayor of London were among those who paid their respects. To her admirers, her literary gifts, intelligence, and piety exemplified the triumph of the human spirit over circumstance.

Just before her book could be published, Wheatley was called back to Boston by the news that Susanna Wheatley was dying. Early in the fall of 1773 she was granted manumission. Susanna Wheatley died in 1774. In the year that John Wheatley died, 1778,

Phillis Wheatley. This engraving—by Scipio Moorhead (see "To S. M.," on p. 428)—was the frontispiece to Wheatley's book.

Wheatley married John Peters, a freedman, about whom almost nothing is known other than that the Wheatleys did not like him, that he petitioned for a license to sell liquor in 1784, and that he may have been in debtor's prison when Phillis Wheatley died, having endured poverty and the loss of two children in her last years. On her deathbed her third child lay ill beside her and succumbed shortly after Wheatley herself. They were buried together in an unmarked grave. Five years earlier, Wheatley had run advertisements for her second volume of poetry, to include thirteen letters and thirty-three poems. Her hoped-for subscribers did not respond, however, so she never published that volume. Most of the poems and letters are lost.

Wheatley's poetry was rediscovered in the 1830s by the New England abolitionists, but she has never been better understood than at the present. Her recent critics have not only corrected a number of biographical errors but, more important, have provided a context in which her work can be more fully interpreted. This reconsideration shows Wheatley to be a bold and canny spokesperson for her faith and her politics. She early joined the cause of American independence and supported the abolition of slavery, anticipating her friend the Reverend Samuel Hopkins's complaint that when African Americans first heard the "sons of liberty" cry out for freedom they were shocked by the indifference to their own "abject slavery and utter wretchedness." In a public letter to the Presbyterian minister and Mohegan leader Samson Occom, Wheatley stressed that the exercise of slavery cannot be reconciled with a "principle" that God has implanted in every human breast, "Love of Freedom"; and in her poem addressed to the conservative Earl of Dartmouth, she wrote that there could be no justice anywhere if people in authority were deaf to the cries of human sorrow. She promoted the cause of American independence in her poem celebrating George Washington as well, perhaps with the idea that he might encourage greater support for the rights of African Americans.

In her prosody Wheatley employed the dominant neoclassical verse form of the heroic couplet, while the themes of her poetry—including spiritual and political liberty, the sublime wonders of nature, and the qualities of vision and imagination—

are more in keeping with the emerging Romantic tradition. A number of scholars have suggested that Wheatley's poetry includes allusions to her African childhood, some overt, others more subtle. Her work is enriched by the tension between traditional form and transformational ideas.

The following texts are from *The Poems of Phillis Wheatley* (1966, rev. 1989), edited by Julian D. Mason. Wheatley's spelling and punctuation have been retained.

On Being Brought from Africa to America

'Twas mercy brought me from my pagan land,
Taught my benighted soul to understand
That there's a God, that there's a Savior too:
Once I redemption neither sought nor knew.
Some view our sable[1] race with scornful eye,   5
"Their color is a diabolic dye."
Remember, Christians, Negroes, black as Cain,[2]
May be refined, and join the angelic train.

1773

To the Right Honourable William, Earl of Dartmouth,[1] His Majesty's Principal Secretary of State for North America, &c.

Hail, happy day, when, smiling like the morn,
Fair Freedom rose New England to adorn:
The northern clime beneath her genial ray,
Dartmouth, congratulates thy blissful sway:
Elate with hope her race no longer mourns,   5
Each soul expands, each grateful bosom burns,
While in thine hand with pleasure we behold
The silken reins, and Freedom's charms unfold.
Long lost to realms beneath the northern skies
She shines supreme, while hated faction dies: 10
Soon as appeared the Goddess[2] long desired,
Sick at the view, she[3] languished and expired;
Thus from the splendors of the morning light
The owl in sadness seeks the caves of night.

No more, America, in mournful strain   15
Of wrongs, and grievance unredressed complain,
No longer shalt thou dread the iron chain,

1. Black.
2. Cain slew his brother Abel and was "marked" by God for doing so. This mark has sometimes been taken to be the origin of dark-skinned peoples (Genesis 4.1–15).
1. William Legge, second Earl of Dartmouth

(1731–1801), was appointed secretary in charge of the American colonies in August 1772. He was sympathetic to the Methodist movement in England but not to the American Revolution.
2. Freedom.
3. Faction.

Which wanton Tyranny with lawless hand
Had made, and with it meant t' enslave the land.

Should you, my lord, while you peruse my song,   20
Wonder from whence my love of Freedom sprung,
Whence flow these wishes for the common good,
By feeling hearts alone best understood,
I, young in life, by seeming cruel fate
Was snatch'd from Afric's fancied happy seat: 25
What pangs excruciating must molest,
What sorrows labor in my parent's breast?
Steeled was that soul and by no misery moved
That from a father seized his babe beloved:
Such, such my case. And can I then but pray   30
Others may never feel tyrannic sway?

For favors past, great Sir, our thanks are due,
And thee we ask thy favors to renew,
Since in thy power,[4] as in thy will before,
To sooth the griefs, which thou did'st once deplore.   35
May heavenly grace the sacred sanction give
To all thy works, and thou forever live
Not only on the wings of fleeting Fame,
Though praise immortal crowns the patriot's name,
But to conduct to heavens refulgent fane,[5]   40
May fiery coursers sweep th' ethereal plain,[6]
And bear thee upwards to that blest abode,
Where, like the prophet,[7] thou shalt find thy God.

1773

To the University of Cambridge,[1] in New England

While an intrinsic ardor prompts to write,
The muses promise to assist my pen;
'Twas not long since I left my native shore
The land of errors, and Egyptian gloom:[2]
Father of mercy, 'twas Thy gracious hand   5
Brought me in safety from those dark abodes.

Students, to you 'tis given to scan the heights
Above, to traverse the ethereal space,
And mark the systems of revolving worlds.
Still more, ye sons of science[3] ye receive   10

4. I.e., since it is in thy power.
5. Heaven's shining temple.
6. The heavens. "Coursers": spirited horses.
7. In 2 Kings 11, a chariot of fire with fiery horses appears, and the prophet Elijah is taken up to heaven by a whirlwind.
1. Harvard.

2. "And Moses stretched forth his hand toward heaven; and there was a thick darkness in all the land of Egypt three days" (Exodus 10.22). "Errors": i.e., theological errors, because Africa was unconverted.
3. I.e., knowledge.

The blissful news by messengers from Heaven,
How Jesus' blood for your redemption flows.
See Him with hands out-stretched upon the cross;
Immense compassion in his bosom glows;
He hears revilers, nor resents their scorn: 15
What matchless mercy in the Son of God!
When the whole human race by sin had fallen,
He deigned to die that they might rise again,
And share with Him in the sublimest skies,
Life without death, and glory without end.   20

Improve[4] your privileges while they stay,
Ye pupils, and each hour redeem, that bears
Or good or bad report of you to Heaven.
Let sin, that baneful evil to the soul,
By you be shunned, nor once remit your guard;   25
Suppress the deadly serpent in its egg.
Ye blooming plants of human race divine,
An Ethiop[5] tells you 'tis your greatest foe;
Its transient sweetness turns to endless pain,
And in immense perdition sinks the soul.   30

1767   1773

On the Death of the Rev. Mr. George Whitefield, 1770[1]

Hail, happy saint, on thine immortal throne,
Possessed of glory, life, and bliss unknown;
We hear no more the music of thy tongue,
Thy wonted auditories[2] cease to throng.
Thy sermons in unequalled accents flow'd,   5
And every bosom with devotion glowed;
Thou didst in strains of eloquence refined
Inflame the heart, and captivate the mind.
Unhappy we the setting sun deplore,
So glorious once, but ah! it shines no more.   10

Behold the prophet in his towering flight!
He leaves the earth for heav'n's unmeasured height,
And worlds unknown receive him from our sight.
There Whitefield wings with rapid course his way,
And sails to Zion[3] through vast seas of day.   15
Thy prayers, great saint, and thine incessant cries
Have pierced the bosom of thy native skies.
Thou moon hast seen, and all the stars of light,
How he has wrestled with his God by night.

---

4. Take advantage of.
5. Ethiopian. In Wheatley's time, "Ethiopian" was a conventional name for the black peoples of Africa.

1. Whitefield, born in 1714, was the best-known revivalist in the eighteenth century.
2. I.e., thy customary listeners.
3. Here, the heavenly city of God.

He prayed that grace in every heart might dwell,   20
He longed to see America excel;
He charged[4] its youth that every grace divine
Should with full luster in their conduct shine;
That Savior, which his soul did first receive,
The greatest gift that even a God can give,   25
He freely offered to the numerous throng,
That on his lips with listening pleasure hung.

"Take Him, ye wretched, for your only good,
Take Him ye starving sinners, for your food;
Ye thirsty, come to this life-giving stream,   30
Ye preachers, take Him for your joyful theme;
Take Him my dear Americans, he said,
Be your complaints on His kind bosom laid:
Take Him, ye Africans, He longs for you,
Impartial Savior is His title due: 35
Washed in the fountain of redeeming blood,
You shall be sons, and kings, and priests to God."

Great *Countess*,[5] we Americans revere
Thy name, and mingle in thy grief sincere;
New England deeply feels, the orphans mourn,   40
Their more than father will no more return.

But, though arrested by the hand of death,
Whitefield no more exerts his laboring breath,
Yet let us view him in the eternal skies,
Let every heart to this bright vision rise;   45
While the tomb safe retains its sacred trust,
Till life divine re-animates his dust.

1770   1770, 1773

Thoughts on the Works of Providence

Arise, my soul, on wings enraptured, rise
To praise the monarch of the earth and skies,
Whose goodness and beneficence appear
As round its center moves the rolling year,
Or when the morning glows with rosy charms,   5
Or the sun slumbers in the ocean's arms:
Of light divine be a rich portion lent
To guide my soul, and favor my intent.
Celestial muse, my arduous flight sustain
And raise my mind to a seraphic[1] strain!   10

---

4. Exhorted.
5. Selina Shirley Hastings (c. 1707–1791), Countess of Huntingdon, head of a small society of
evangelical churches, was a strong supporter of
George Whitefield. Wheatley visited her in
England in 1773.
1. Angelic.

Adored for ever be the God unseen,
Which round the sun revolves this vast machine,
Though to His eye its mass a point appears:
Adored the God that whirls surrounding spheres,
Which first ordained that mighty Sol[2] should reign   15
The peerless monarch of the ethereal train:
Of miles twice forty millions is His height,
And yet His radiance dazzles mortal sight
So far beneath—from Him the extended earth
Vigor derives, and every flowery birth: 20
Vast through her orb she moves with easy grace
Around her Phoebus[3] in unbounded space;
True to her course the impetuous storm derides,
Triumphant o'er the winds, and surging tides.

Almighty, in these wond'rous works of Thine,   25
What Power, what Wisdom, and what Goodness shine!
And are Thy wonders, Lord, by men explored,
And yet creating glory unadored!

Creation smiles in various beauty gay,
While day to night, and night succeeds to day: 30
That Wisdom, which attends Jehovah's ways,
Shines most conspicuous in the solar rays:
Without them, destitute of heat and light,
This world would be the reign of endless night:
In their excess how would our race complain,   35
Abhorring life! how hate its lengthened chain!
From air adust[4] what numerous ills would rise?
What dire contagion taint the burning skies?
What pestilential vapors, fraught with death,
Would rise, and overspread the lands beneath?   40

Hail, smiling morn, that from the orient main[5]
Ascending dost adorn the heav'nly plain!
So rich, so various are thy beauteous dyes,
That spread through all the circuit of the skies,
That, full of thee, my soul in rapture soars,   45
And thy great God, the cause of all adores.[6]

O'er beings infinite His love extends,
His Wisdom rules them, and His Pow'r defends.
When tasks diurnal[7] tire the human frame,
The spirits faint, and dim the vital flame,   50
Then too that ever active bounty shines,
Which not infinity of space confines.
The sable[8] veil, that Night in silence draws,
Conceals effects, but shows the Almighty Cause,

2. The sun.
3. Apollo, the Greek sun god.
4. Dried up.
5. From the eastern ocean.

6. I.e., God created everything (including the "smiling morn").
7. Daily.
8. Black.

Night seals in sleep the wide creation fair,[9]   55
And all is peaceful but the brow of care.
Again, gay Phoebus, as the day before,
Wakes every eye, but what shall wake no more;
Again the face of nature is renewed,
Which still appears harmonious, fair, and good. 60
May grateful strains salute the smiling morn,
Before its beams the eastern hills adorn!

  Shall day to day, and night to night conspire
To show the goodness of the Almighty Sire?
This mental voice shall man regardless hear,   65
And never, never raise the filial prayer?
Today, O hearken, nor your folly mourn
For time mispent, that never will return.

  But see the sons of vegetation rise,
And spread their leafy banners to the skies.   70
All-wise Almighty providence we trace
In trees, and plants, and all the flowery race;
As clear as in the nobler frame of man,
All lovely copies of the Maker's plan.
The power the same that forms a ray of light,   75
That called creation from eternal night.
"Let there be light," He said. From his profound[1]
Old Chaos heard, and trembled at the sound:
Swift as the word, inspired by power divine,
Behold the light around its Maker shine,   80
The first fair product of the omnific[2] God,
And now through all his works diffused abroad.

  As reason's powers by day our God disclose,
So we may trace Him in the night's repose:
Say what is sleep? and dreams how passing strange! 85
When action ceases, and ideas range
Licentious and unbounded o'er the plains,
Where Fancy's[3] queen in giddy triumph reigns.
Hear in soft strains the dreaming lover sigh
To a kind fair,[4] or rave in jealousy;   90
On pleasure now, and now on vengeance bent,
The lab 'ring passions struggle for a vent.
What power, O man! thy reason then restores,
So long suspended in nocturnal hours?
What secret hand returns the mental train,   95
And gives improv'd thine active powers again?
From thee, O man, what gratitude should rise!
And, when from balmy sleep thou op'st thine eyes,
Let thy first thoughts be praises to the skies.

---

9. Beautiful.
1. Depths. "And God said, Let there be light: and there was light" (Genesis 1.3).
2. Omnificent: unlimited in creative power.
3. The imagination in its image-making aspect.
4. Woman.

How merciful our God who thus imparts   100
O'erflowing tides of joy to human hearts,
When wants and woes might be our righteous lot,
Our God forgetting, by our God forgot!

Among the mental powers a question rose,
"What most the image of the Eternal shows?"   105
When thus to Reason (so let Fancy rove)
Her great companion spoke, immortal Love.

"Say, mighty power, how long shall strife prevail,
And with its murmurs load the whispering gale?
Refer the cause to Recollection's shrine,   110
Who loud proclaims my origin divine,
The cause whence heaven and earth began to be,
And is not man immortalized by me?
Reason let this most causeless strife subside."
Thus Love pronounced, and Reason thus replied.   115

    "Thy birth, celestial queen! 'tis mine to own,
In thee resplendent is the Godhead shown;
Thy words persuade, my soul enraptured feels
Resistless beauty which thy smile reveals."
Ardent she spoke, and, kindling at her charms,   120
She clasped the blooming goddess in her arms.

    Infinite Love where'er we turn our eyes
Appears: this every creature's wants supplies;
This most is heard in Nature's constant voice,
This makes the morn, and this the eve rejoice;   125
This bids the fostering rains and dews descend
To nourish all, to serve one gen'ral end,
The good of man: yet man ungrateful pays
But little homage, and but little praise.
To him, whose works arrayed with mercy shine,   130
What songs should rise, how constant, how divine!

                                                                    1773

To S. M.,[1] a Young African Painter, on Seeing His Works

To show the laboring bosom's deep intent,
And thought in living characters to paint,
When first thy pencil did those beauties give,
And breathing figures learnt from thee to live,
How did those prospects give my soul delight,   5
A new creation rushing on my sight?
Still, wondrous youth! each noble path pursue,

1. Scipio Moorhead, a servant to the Reverend John Moorhead of Boston.

On deathless glories fix thine ardent view:
Still may the painter's and the poet's fire
To aid thy pencil, and thy verse conspire!   10
And may the charms of each seraphic[2] theme
Conduct thy footsteps to immortal fame!
High to the blissful wonders of the skies
Elate thy soul, and raise thy wishful eyes.
Thrice happy, when exalted to survey   15
That splendid city, crown'd with endless day,
Whose twice six gates[3] on radiant hinges ring:
Celestial Salem[4] blooms in endless spring.

   Calm and serene thy moments glide along,
And may the muse inspire each future song!   20
Still, with the sweets of contemplation blest,
May peace with balmy wings your soul invest!
But when these shades of time are chased away,
And darkness ends in everlasting day,
On what seraphic pinions shall we move,   25
And view the landscapes in the realms above?
There shall thy tongue in heavenly murmurs flow,
And there my muse with heavenly transport glow:
No more to tell of Damon's[5] tender sighs,
Or rising radiance of Aurora's[6] eyes,   30
For nobler themes demand a nobler strain,
And purer language on the ethereal plain.
Cease, gentle muse! the solemn gloom of night
Now seals the fair creation from my sight.

1773

To His Excellency General Washington[1]

Sir. I have taken the freedom to address your Excellency in the enclosed
poem, and entreat your acceptance, though I am not insensible of its inaccuracies. Your being appointed by the Grand Continental Congress to be
Generalissimo of the armies of North America, together with the fame of
your virtues, excite sensations not easy to suppress. Your generosity, therefore, I presume, will pardon the attempt. Wishing your Excellency all possible success in the great cause you are so generously engaged in. I am,

      Your Excellency's most obedient humble servant,
                    Phillis Wheatley

2. Angelic.
3. Heaven, like Jerusalem in antiquity, is
thought to have had twelve gates (as many gates
as tribes of Israel).
4. Heavenly Jerusalem.
5. In classical mythology, Damon pledged his
life for his friend Pythias.

6. The Roman goddess of the dawn.
1. This poem was first published in the *Pennsylvania Magazine* when Thomas Paine (see his
headnote, earlier in this volume) was editor.
After reading it, Washington invited Wheatley to
meet him in Cambridge, Massachusetts, in February 1776.

Providence, Oct. 26, 1775.[2]
His Excellency Gen. Washington.

Celestial choir! enthroned in realms of light,
Columbia's[3] scenes of glorious toils I write.
While freedom's cause her anxious breast alarms,
She flashes dreadful in refulgent arms.
See mother earth her offspring's fate bemoan,   5
And nations gaze at scenes before unknown!
See the bright beams of heaven's revolving light
Involved in sorrows and the veil of night!
    The goddess comes, she moves divinely fair,
Olive and laurel[4] binds her golden hair: 10
Wherever shines this native of the skies,
Unnumbered charms and recent graces rise.
    Muse! bow propitious while my pen relates
How pour her armies through a thousand gates,
As when Eolus[5] heaven's fair face deforms,   15
Enwrapped in tempest and a night of storms;
Astonished ocean feels the wild uproar,
The refluent surges beat the sounding shore;
Or thick as leaves in Autumn's golden reign,
Such, and so many, moves the warrior's train.   20
In bright array they seek the work of war,
Where high unfurled the ensign[6] waves in air.
Shall I to Washington their praise recite?
Enough thou know'st them in the fields of fight.
Thee, first in place and honors—we demand   25
The grace and glory of thy martial band.
Famed for thy valor, for thy virtues more,
Hear every tongue thy guardian aid implore!
    One century scarce performed its destined round,
When Gallic powers Columbia's fury found;[7]   30
And so may you, whoever dares disgrace
The land of freedom's heaven-defended race!
Fixed are the eyes of nations on the scales,
For in their hopes Columbia's arm prevails.
Anon Britannia droops the pensive head,   35
While round increase the rising hills of dead.
Ah! cruel blindness to Columbia's state!
Lament thy thirst of boundless power too late.
    Proceed, great chief, with virtue on thy side,
Thy every action let the goddess guide.   40
A crown, a mansion, and a throne that shine,
With gold unfading, WASHINGTON! be thine.

1775–76   1776, 1834

---

2. When the British occupied Boston in summer 1775, Wheatley and her former master's family moved to Providence, Rhode Island, for safety.
3. This reference to America as "the land Columbus found" is believed to be the first in print.
4. Classical emblems of victory.
5. Mythological ruler of the winds.
6. Flag or banner.
7. The French and Indian War (1754–63), between France and England, ended the French colonial empire in North America.

CHARLES BROCKDEN BROWN
1771–1810

Charles Brockden Brown had extraordinary insight into fiction's capacity to gauge emotional depths. Influenced by the gothic tradition in fiction—as exemplified by the work of English writers such as the political philosophers and novelists William Godwin and Mary Wollstonecraft—Brown used the emergent genre of the novel to test, celebrate, and sometimes reject the radical implications of revolutionary ideology. For Brown, the sentimental plots made popular by the English novelist Samuel Richardson and adapted by American novelists including Susanna Rowson and Hannah Webster Foster became a starting point for very different explorations. His fiction overturned readers' Enlightenment faith in the rationality of human behavior and indicated that the emotional and obsessive, as much as the logical, were basic elements of character. Brown thus began to explore a rich vein in American fiction that Edgar Allan Poe, Herman Melville, and Nathaniel Hawthorne mined in the nineteenth century with great success.

Brown was born into a Quaker family in Philadelphia, then the cultural and political center of the thirteen colonies and subsequently the first capital of the United States. (Benjamin Franklin mentions Brown's great-uncle in his *Autobiography*, and Brown was a member of the Belles Lettres Club, which sometimes met at Franklin's house.) During the American Revolution, Brown's father remained steadfast in the pacifist principles of the Quakers, refusing to bear arms or take a patriot oath, and he suffered the pillaging of his business and eight months of imprisonment in Virginia as a consequence. These events profoundly shaped Brown's attitudes toward revolution, which came to be reflected in his fiction. He prepared for a career in law, completing his schooling in 1787, the year that the Constitutional Convention met in Philadelphia. As the time approached for him to launch a legal career, however, he gravitated instead to the world of belles lettres. He might well have succeeded in Philadelphia, which by the 1790s had become a large, culturally sophisticated city where a writer could aspire to the newly possible profession of authorship.

Brown opted instead for New York City, where he met and befriended contemporaries who shared his intellectual ambitions. They included the Hartford wit and future president of Yale University, Timothy Dwight; the lexicographer Noah Webster; and Elihu Hubbard Smith, who in 1793 published the first anthology of American poetry. Encouraged by the Friendly Club, an association of young writers, physicians, and attorneys that met weekly for intellectual conversation, Brown read widely in English literature and published six novels in the gothic mode. *Wieland; or The Transformation: An American Tale* (1798), Brown's best-known work, is a tale of psychological and spiritual revolution, based on a true story about a man who believes God has instructed him to kill his family. In *Ormond* (1799) the main character, a freethinker recently returned from the Continent, tests the virtue of Constantia, who is an epitome of republican womanhood. *Edgar Huntly* (1799) capitalized on the public's continuing interest in tales of Indian captivity and the wilderness generally, even as Brown teased readers with a rational explanation—sleepwalking—for the strange behavior of one of his central characters. Brown turned to his home city for the setting of *Arthur Mervyn* (1799–1800), whose melodramatic plot has as its background Philadelphia's yellow fever outbreak of 1793.

Brown concluded his career as a novelist with the lesser-read sentimental novels *Clara Howard* and *Jane Talbot* (both 1801).

In 1827 Brown's novels were reissued in a uniform edition, making him the first American novelist to have this (posthumous) honor. In his lifetime, however, Brown abandoned the novel because he could not make a living by writing fiction. To augment his income he involved himself in other publishing ventures. Over the course of a decade, for example, he founded and edited *The Monthly Magazine and American Review* (1799–1800), *The Literary Magazine and American Register* (1803–07), and the *American Register, or General Repository of History, Politics, and Science* (1807–10), all of which provided outlets for his varied talents and ambitions. He contributed many essays to these and other journals, his most important effort being *Alcuin*, a lengthy dialogue on women's rights that shows Wollstonecraft's influence. *Alcuin* appeared first in the *Philadelphia Weekly Magazine* and was published as a book in 1798. His pamphlet *An Address to the Government of the United States on the Cession of Louisiana to the French* (1803) helped sway public opinion toward the purchase of the Louisiana Territory, and his translation of C. F. Volney's *A View of the Soil and Climate of the United States of America* (1804), with his own commentary, introduced this important French philosopher to many Americans. His work on *A Complete System of Geography* was interrupted by his death, from tuberculosis.

Although he is sometimes called America's first professional author, Brown did not enjoy the kind of success achieved a few years later by Washington Irving and James Fenimore Cooper, primarily because the technological infrastructure for the rapid production and widespread distribution of printed materials was not yet fully developed in the United States. Brown's significance thus resides in his ability to identify those topics—like the limits of rationality and the role of the senses in epistemology—that were of growing interest to an American and international readership and in his willingness to explore the implications of republican ideology on a range of psychological, philosophical, and social topics, including gender relations.

In his novella *Memoirs of Carwin the Biloquist*, Brown provides the early history of Frank Carwin, the mysterious character in his novel *Wieland; or The Transformation* who has an uncanny ability to project his voice while imitating the voices of others. (Biloquism as Brown uses the term is similar to what today is known as ventriloquism.) In *Wieland*, Carwin uses these powers in ways that fatally disrupt the Wieland family and their Enlightenment community. Brown began *Memoirs* while he was at work on *Wieland*, and he serialized the shorter work between November 1803 and March 1805 in his *Literary Magazine*. In certain ways *Memoirs* is directly tied to *Wieland*, especially in the novella's middle section, where Carwin obliquely addresses the young woman Clara, *Wieland*'s narrator, revealing that his memoirs explain and apologize for actions that may have contributed to the deaths of her relatives. But the interest of *Memoirs* goes well beyond this plot device, distilling major concerns that appear throughout Brown's fiction.

In the opening pages of *Memoirs*, Carwin describes his adolescent years, when intellectual curiosity and a love of reading, coupled with distaste for physical labor, bring him into conflict with his father, a domineering and socially conservative farmer. Language of all sorts is of particular interest to Carwin. He learns through experiment to throw his voice and to imitate the way others speak; he also teaches his dog, suggestively named "Damon" (similar to the classical "daemon," or godlike power) to understand his gestures and create the illusion of speech.

Shortly after Carwin moves in with an aunt in Philadelphia, he meets an Irishman named Ludloe, who guesses at his secret capability, or "art," as he calls it. Although Carwin resists full disclosure of his talent, Ludloe takes him to Dublin and begins grooming him to join a mysterious conspiratorial organization. Carwin's training involves an extended stay in Spain, where he studies the Roman Catholic

Church and learns about the Jesuits. After returning to Ireland, he is brought deeper into Ludloe's world when he is given access to his secret library. The novella concludes in the midst of things with a test of wills that involves Carwin's sense of self. Among the compelling themes that *Memoirs* explores in a transatlantic context are the interplay of power and perversity and the role of mystery in narrative. Through Carwin's biloquism, Brown examines the attractions and dangers of art in a democracy, while the figure of Ludloe speaks to a concern that is a pervasive theme in the literature of the early republic: the appeal and risks of social utopianism.

Memoirs of Carwin the Biloquist[1]

I was the second son of a farmer, whose place of residence was a western district of Pennsylvania. My eldest brother seemed fitted by nature for the employment to which he was destined. His wishes never led him astray from the hay-stack and the furrow. His ideas never ranged beyond the sphere of his vision, or suggested the possibility that to-morrow could differ from to-day. He could read and write, because he had no alternative between learning the lesson prescribed to him, and punishment. He was diligent, as long as fear urged him forward, but his exertions ceased with the cessation of this motive. The limits of his acquirements consisted in signing his name, and spelling out a chapter in the bible.

My character was the reverse of his. My thirst of knowledge was augmented in proportion as it was supplied with gratification. The more I heard or read, the more restless and unconquerable my curiosity became. My senses were perpetually alive to novelty, my fancy teemed with visions of the future, and my attention fastened upon every thing mysterious or unknown.

My father intended that my knowledge should keep pace with that of my brother, but conceived that all beyond the mere capacity to write and read was useless or pernicious. He took as much pains to keep me within these limits, as to make the acquisitions of my brother come up to them, but his efforts were not equally successful in both cases. The most vigilant and jealous scrutiny was exerted in vain: reproaches and blows, painful privations and ignominious penances had no power to slacken my zeal and abate my perseverance. He might enjoin upon me the most laborious tasks, set the envy of my brother to watch me during the performance, make the most diligent search after my books, and destroy them without mercy, when they were found; but he could not outroot my darling propensity. I exerted all my powers to elude his watchfulness. Censures and stripes[2] were sufficiently unpleasing to make me strive to avoid them. To affect[3] this desirable end, I was incessantly employed in the invention of stratagems and the execution of expedients.

My passion was surely not deserving of blame, and I have frequently lamented the hardships to which it subjected me; yet, perhaps, the claims which were made upon my ingenuity and fortitude were not without beneficial effects upon my character.

This contention lasted from the sixth to the fourteenth year of my age. My father's opposition to my schemes was incited by a sincere though

---

1. The text is from *The Literary Magazine and American Register* (1803–05).

2. Reprimands and blows.
3. Bring about.

unenlightened desire for my happiness. That all his efforts were secretly eluded or obstinately repelled, was a source of the bitterest regret. He has often lamented, with tears, what he called my incorrigible depravity, and encouraged himself to perseverance by the notion of the ruin that would inevitably overtake me if I were allowed to persist in my present career. Perhaps the sufferings which arose to him from the disappointment, were equal to those which he inflicted on me.

In my fourteenth year, events happened which ascertained[4] my future destiny. One evening I had been sent to bring cows from a meadow, some miles distant from my father's mansion. My time was limited, and I was menaced with severe chastisement if, according to my custom, I should stay beyond the period assigned.

For some time these menaces rung in my ears, and I went on my way with speed. I arrived at the meadow, but the cattle had broken the fence and escaped. It was my duty to carry home the earliest tidings of this accident, but the first suggestion was to examine the cause and manner of this escape. The field was bounded by cedar railing. Five of these rails were laid horizontally from post to post. The upper one had been broken in the middle, but the rest had merely been drawn out of the holes on one side, and rested with their ends on the ground. The means which had been used for this end, the reason why one only was broken, and that one the uppermost, how a pair of horns could be so managed as to effect that which the hands of man would have found difficult, supplied a theme of meditation.

Some accident recalled me from this reverie, and reminded me how much time had thus been consumed. I was terrified at the consequences of my delay, and sought with eagerness how they might be obviated.[5] I asked myself if there were not a way back shorter than that by which I had come. The beaten road was rendered circuitous by a precipice that projected into a neighbouring stream, and closed up a passage by which the length of the way would have been diminished one half: at the foot of the cliff the water was of considerable depth, and agitated by an eddy. I could not estimate the danger which I should incur by plunging into it, but I was resolved to make the attempt. I have reason to think, that this experiment, if it had been tried, would have proved fatal, and my father, while he lamented my untimely fate, would have been wholly unconscious that his own unreasonable demands had occasioned it.

I turned my steps towards the spot. To reach the edge of the stream was by no means an easy undertaking, so many abrupt points and gloomy hollows were interposed. I had frequently skirted and penetrated this tract, but had never been so completely entangled in the maze as now: hence I had remained unacquainted with a narrow pass, which, at the distance of an hundred yards from the river, would conduct me, though not without danger and toil, to the opposite side of the ridge.

This glen was now discovered, and this discovery induced me to change my plan. If a passage could be here effected, it would be shorter and safer than that which led through the stream, and its practicability was to be known only by experiment. The path was narrow, steep, and overshadowed by rocks. The sun was nearly set, and the shadow of the cliff above, obscured the passage almost as much as midnight would have done: I was accustomed to despise

---

4. Made certain.   5. Removed.

danger when it presented itself in a sensible[6] form, but, by a defect common in every one's education, goblins and spectres were to me the objects of the most violent apprehensions. These were unavoidably connected with solitude and darkness, and were present to my fears when I entered this gloomy recess.

These terrors are always lessened by calling the attention away to some indifferent[7] object. I now made use of this expedient, and began to amuse myself by hallowing as loud as organs of unusual compass and vigour would enable me. I uttered the words which chanced to occur to me, and repeated in the shrill tones of a Mohock[8] savage . . . "Cow! cow! come home! home!" . . . These notes were of course reverberated from the rocks which on either side towered aloft, but the echo was confused and indistinct.

I continued, for some time, thus to beguile the way, till I reached a space more than commonly abrupt, and which required all my attention. My rude ditty was suspended till I had surmounted this impediment. In a few minutes I was at leisure to renew it. After finishing the strain, I paused. In a few seconds a voice as I then imagined, uttered the same cry from the point of a rock some hundred feet behind me; the same words, with equal distinctness and deliberation, and in the same tone, appeared to be spoken. I was startled by this incident, and cast a fearful glance behind, to discover by whom it was uttered. The spot where I stood was buried in dusk, but the eminences were still invested with a luminous and vivid twilight. The speaker, however, was concealed from my view.

I had scarcely begun to wonder at this occurrence, when a new occasion for wonder, was afforded me. A few seconds, in like manner, elapsed, when my ditty[9] was again rehearsed, with a no less perfect imitation, in a different quarter. . . . To this quarter I eagerly turned my eyes, but no one was visible. . . . The station, indeed, which this new speaker seemed to occupy, was inaccessible to man or beast.

If I were surprized at this second repetition of my words, judge how much my surprise must have been augmented, when the same calls were a third time repeated, and coming still in a new direction. Five times was this ditty successively resounded, at intervals nearly equal, always from a new quarter, and with little abatement of its original distinctness and force.

A little reflection was sufficient to shew that this was no more than an echo of an extraordinary kind. My terrors were quickly supplanted by delight. The motives to dispatch were forgotten, and I amused myself for an hour, with talking to these cliffs: I placed myself in new positions, and exhausted my lungs and my invention in new clamours.

The pleasures of this new discovery were an ample compensation for the ill treatment which I expected on my return. By some caprice in my father I escaped merely with a few reproaches. I seized the first opportunity of again visiting this recess, and repeating my amusement; time, and incessant repetition, could scarcely lessen its charms or exhaust the variety produced by new tones and new positions.

The hours in which I was most free from interruption and restraint were those of moonlight. My brother and I occupied a small room above the

---

6. Perceptible.
7. Neutral.
8. A member of the Mohawk tribe (one of the original Five Nations of the Iroquois Confederacy, in western New York).
9. A short, simple song.

kitchen, disconnected, in some degree, with the rest of the house. It was the rural custom to retire early to bed and to anticipate the rising of the sun. When the moonlight was strong enough to permit me to read, it was my custom to escape from bed, and hie[1] with my book to some neighbouring eminence, where I would remain stretched on the mossy rock, till the sinking or beclouded moon, forbade me to continue my employment. I was indebted for books to a friendly person in the neighbourhood, whose compliance with my solicitations was prompted partly by benevolence and partly by enmity to my father, whom he could not more egregiously offend than by gratifying my perverse and pernicious curiosity.

In leaving my chamber I was obliged to use the utmost caution to avoid rousing my brother, whose temper disposed him to thwart me in the least of my gratifications. My purpose was surely laudable, and yet on leaving the house and returning to it, I was obliged to use the vigilance and circumspection of a thief.

One night I left my bed with this view. I posted first to my vocal glen, and thence scrambling up a neighbouring steep, which overlooked a wide extent of this romantic country, gave myself up to contemplation and the perusal of Milton's Comus.[2]

My reflections were naturally suggested by the singularity of this echo. To hear my own voice speak at a distance would have been formerly regarded as prodigious. To hear too, that voice, not uttered by another, by whom it might easily be mimicked, but by myself! I cannot now recollect the transition which led me to the notion of sounds, similar to these, but produced by other means than reverberation. Could I not so dispose my organs as to make my voice appear at a distance?

From speculation I proceeded to experiment. The idea of a distant voice, like my own, was intimately present to my fancy. I exerted myself with a most ardent desire, and with something like a persuasion that I should succeed. I started with surprise, for it seemed as if success had crowned my attempts. I repeated the effort, but failed. A certain position of the organs took place on the first attempt, altogether new, unexampled and as it were, by accident, for I could not attain it on the second experiment.

You[3] will not wonder that I exerted myself with indefatigable zeal to regain what had once, though for so short a space, been in my power. Your own ears have witnessed the success of these efforts. By perpetual exertion I gained it a second time, and now was a diligent observer of the circumstances attending it. Gradually I subjected these finer and more subtle motions to the command of my will. What was at first difficult, by exercise and habit, was rendered easy. I learned to accommodate my voice to all the varieties of distance and direction.

It cannot be denied that this faculty is wonderful and rare, but when we consider the possible modifications of muscular motion, how few of these are usually exerted, how imperfectly they are subjected to the will, and yet

---

1. Go quickly.
2. Formally titled *A Mask Presented at Ludlow Castle, 1634* (1637), this work by the English poet John Milton (1608–1674) takes its colloquial name from a central character modeled after the god of revelry.
3. The second-person address here is one of several indicators that *Memoirs* was conceived as an epistolary work.

that the will is capable of being rendered unlimited and absolute, will not our wonder cease?

We have seen men who could hide their tongues so perfectly that even an Anatomist, after the most accurate inspection that a living subject could admit, has affirmed the organ to be wanting, but this was effected by the exertion of muscles unknown and incredible to the greater part of mankind.

The concurrence of teeth, palate and tongue, in the formation of speech should seem to be indispensable, and yet men have spoken distinctly though wanting a tongue, and to whom, therefore, teeth and palate were superfluous. The tribe of motions requisite to this end, are wholly latent and unknown, to those who possess that organ.

I mean not to be more explicit. I have no reason to suppose a peculiar conformation or activity in my own organs, or that the power which I possess may not, with suitable directions and by steady efforts, be obtained by others, but I will do nothing to facilitate the acquisition. It is by far, too liable to perversion for a good man to desire to possess it, or to teach it to another.

There remained but one thing to render this instrument as powerful in my hands as it was capable of being. From my childhood, I was remarkably skilful at imitation. There were few voices whether of men or birds or beasts which I could not imitate with success. To add my ancient, to my newly acquired skill, to talk from a distance, and at the same time, in the accents of another, was the object of my endeavours, and this object, after a certain number of trials, I finally obtained.

In my present situation every thing that denoted intellectual exertion was a crime, and exposed me to invectives if not to stripes. This circumstance induced me to be silent to all others, on the subject of my discovery. But, added to this, was a confused belief, that it might be made, in some way instrumental to my relief from the hardships and restraints of my present condition. For some time I was not aware of the mode in which it might be rendered subservient to this end.

My father's sister was an ancient lady resident in Philadelphia, the relict of a merchant, whose decease left her the enjoyment of a frugal competence.[4] She was without children, and had often expressed her desire that her nephew Frank, whom she always considered as a sprightly and promising lad, should be put under her care. She offered to be at the expense of my education, and to bequeath to me at her death her slender patrimony.

This arrangement was obstinately rejected by my father, because it was merely fostering and giving scope to propensities, which he considered as hurtful, and because his avarice desired that this inheritance should fall to no one but himself. To me, it was a scheme of ravishing felicity, and to be debarred from it was a source of anguish known to few. I had too much experience of my father's pertinaciousness ever to hope for a change in his views; yet the bliss of living with my aunt, in a new and busy scene, and in the unbounded indulgence of my literary passion, continually occupied my thoughts: for a long time these thoughts were productive only of despondency and tears.

Time only enhanced the desirableness of this scheme; my new faculty would naturally connect itself with these wishes, and the question could not fail to occur whether it might not aid me in the execution of my favourite plan.

4. Small inheritance, enough to live on modestly. "Relict": widow.

A thousand superstitious tales were current in the family. Apparitions had been seen, and voices had been heard on a multitude of occasions. My father was a confident believer in supernatural tokens. The voice of his wife, who had been many years dead, had been twice heard at midnight whispering at his pillow. I frequently asked myself whether a scheme favourable to my views might not be built upon these foundations. Suppose (thought I) my mother should be made to enjoin upon him compliance with my wishes?

This idea bred in me a temporary consternation. To imitate the voice of the dead, to counterfeit a commission from heaven, bore the aspect of presumption and impiety. It seemed an offence which could not fail to draw after it the vengeance of the deity. My wishes for a time yielded to my fears, but this scheme in proportion as I meditated on it, became more plausible; no other occurred to me so easy and so efficacious. I endeavoured to persuade myself that the end proposed, was, in the highest degree praiseworthy, and that the excellence of my purpose would justify the means employed to attain it.

My resolutions were, for a time, attended with fluctuations and misgivings. These gradually disappeared, and my purpose became firm; I was next to devise the means of effecting my views, this did not demand any tedious deliberation. It was easy to gain access to my father's chamber without notice or detection, cautious footsteps and the suppression of breath would place me, unsuspected and unthought of, by his bed side. The words I should use, and the mode of utterance were not easily settled, but having at length selected these, I made myself by much previous repetition, perfectly familiar with the use of them.

I selected a blustering and inclement night, in which the darkness was augmented by a veil of the blackest clouds. The building we inhabited was slight in its structure, and full of crevices through which the gale found easy way, and whistled in a thousand cadencies. On this night the elemental music was remarkably sonorous, and was mingled not unfrequently with *thunder heard remote.*[5]

I could not divest myself of secret dread. My heart faultered with a consciousness of wrong. Heaven seemed to be present and to disapprove my work; I listened to the thunder and the wind, as to the stern voice of this disapprobation. Big drops stood on my forehead, and my tremors almost incapacitated me from proceeding.

These impediments however I surmounted; I crept up stairs at midnight, and entered my father's chamber. The darkness was intense and I sought with outstretched hands for his bed. The darkness, added to the trepidation of my thoughts, disabled me from making a right estimate of distances: I was conscious of this, and when I advanced within the room, paused.

I endeavoured to compare the progress I had made with my knowledge of the room, and governed by the result of this comparison, proceeded cautiously and with hands still outstretched in search of the foot of the bed. At this moment lightning flashed into the room: the brightness of the gleam was dazzling, yet it afforded me an exact knowledge of my situation. I had mistaken my way, and discovered that my knees nearly touched the bedstead, and that my hands at the next step, would have touched my father's cheek. His closed

5. Cf. Milton's *Paradise Lost* 2.477.

eyes and every line in his countenance, were painted, as it were, for an instant on my sight.

The flash was accompanied with a burst of thunder, whose vehemence was stunning. I always entertained a dread of thunder, and now recoiled, over-borne with terror. Never had I witnessed so luminous a gleam and so tremendous a shock, yet my father's slumber appeared not to be disturbed by it.

I stood irresolute and trembling; to prosecute my purpose in this state of mind was impossible. I resolved for the present to relinquish it, and turned with a view of exploring my way out of the chamber. Just then a light seen through the window, caught my eye. It was at first weak but speedily increased; no second thought was necessary to inform me that the barn, situated at a small distance from the house, and newly stored with hay, was in flames, in consequence of being struck by the lightning.

My terror at this spectacle made me careless of all consequences relative to myself. I rushed to the bed and throwing myself on my father, awakened him by loud cries. The family were speedily roused, and were compelled to remain impotent spectators of the devastation. Fortunately the wind blew in a contrary direction, so that our habitation was not injured.

The impression that was made upon me by the incidents of that night is indelible. The wind gradually rose into an hurricane; the largest branches were torn from the trees, and whirled aloft into the air; others were uprooted and laid prostrate on the ground. The barn was a spacious edifice, consisting wholly of wood, and filled with a plenteous harvest. Thus supplied with fuel, and fanned by the wind, the fire raged with incredible fury; meanwhile clouds rolled above, whose blackness was rendered more conspicuous by reflection from the flames; the vast volumes of smoke were dissipated in a moment by the storm, while glowing fragments and cinders were borne to an immense height, and tossed everywhere in wild confusion. Ever and anon the sable[6] canopy that hung around us was streaked with lightning, and the peals, by which it was accompanied, were deafening, and with scarcely any intermission.

It was, doubtless, absurd to imagine any connexion between this portentous scene and the purpose that I had meditated, yet a belief of this connexion, though wavering and obscure, lurked in my mind; something more than a coincidence merely casual, appeared to have subsisted between my situation, at my father's bed side, and the flash that darted through the window, and diverted me from my design. It palsied my courage, and strengthened my conviction, that my scheme was criminal.

After some time had elapsed, and tranquility was, in some degree, restored in the family, my father reverted to the circumstances in which I had been discovered on the first alarm of this event. The truth was impossible to be told. I felt the utmost reluctance to be guilty of a falsehood, but by falsehood only could I elude detection. That my guilt was the offspring of a fatal necessity, that the injustice of others gave it birth and made it unavoidable, afforded me slight consolation. Nothing can be more injurious than a lie, but its evil tendency chiefly respects our future conduct. Its direct consequences may be transient and few, but it facilitates a repetition, strengthens temptation, and grows into habit. I pretended some necessity had drawn me from my bed, and that discovering the condition of the barn, I hastened to inform my father.

6. Black.

Some time after this, my father summoned me to his presence. I had been previously guilty of disobedience to his commands, in a matter about which he was usually very scrupulous. My brother had been privy to my offence, and had threatened to be my accuser. On this occasion I expected nothing but arraignment and punishment. Weary of oppression, and hopeless of any change in my father's temper and views, I had formed the resolution of eloping from his house, and of trusting, young as I was, to the caprice of fortune. I was hesitating whether to abscond[7] without the knowledge of the family, or to make my resolutions known to them, and while I avowed my resolution, to adhere to it in spite of opposition and remonstrances, when I received this summons.

I was employed at this time in the field; night was approaching, and I had made no preparation for departure; all the preparation in my power to make, was indeed small; a few clothes made into a bundle, was the sum of my possessions. Time would have little influence in improving my prospects, and I resolved to execute my scheme immediately.

I left my work intending to seek my chamber, and taking what was my own, to disappear forever. I turned a stile that led out of the field into a bye path,[8] when my father appeared before me, advancing in an opposite direction; to avoid him was impossible, and I summoned my fortitude to a conflict with his passion.

As soon as we met, instead of anger and upbraiding, he told me, that he had been reflecting on my aunt's proposal, to take me under her protection, and had concluded that the plan was proper; if I still retained my wishes on that head, he would readily comply with them, and that, if I chose, I might set off for the city next morning, as a neighbour's wagon was preparing to go.

I shall not dwell on the rapture with which this proposal was listened to: it was with difficulty that I persuaded myself that he was in earnest in making it, nor could divine the reasons, for so sudden and unexpected a change in his maxims. . . . These I afterwards discovered. Some one had instilled into him fears, that my aunt, exasperated at his opposition to her request, respecting the unfortunate Frank, would bequeath her property to strangers; to obviate this evil, which his avarice prompted him to regard as much greater than any mischief, that would accrue to me, from the change of my abode, he embraced her proposal.

I entered with exultation and triumph on this new scene; my hopes were by no means disappointed. Detested labour was exchanged for luxurious idleness. I was master of my time, and the chooser of my occupations. My kinswoman, on discovering that I entertained no relish for the drudgery of colleges, and was contented with the means of intellectual gratification, which I could obtain under her roof, allowed me to pursue my own choice.

Three tranquil years passed away, during which, each day added to my happiness, by adding to my knowledge. My biloquial faculty was not neglected. I improved it by assiduous exercise; I deeply reflected on the use to which it might be applied. I was not destitute of pure intentions; I delighted not in evil; I was incapable of knowingly contributing to another's misery,

---

7. Leave secretly and in a hurry.
8. Private or little-used footway. "Stile": steps that allow people but not animals to climb over a fence or wall.

but the sole or principal end of my endeavours was not the happiness of others.

I was actuated by ambition. I was delighted to possess superior power; I was prone to manifest that superiority, and was satisfied if this were done, without much solicitude concerning consequences. I sported frequently with the apprehensions of my associates and threw out a bait for their wonder, and supplied them with occasions for the structure of theories. It may not be amiss to enumerate one or two adventures in which I was engaged.

I had taken much pains to improve the sagacity of a favourite Spaniel. It was my purpose, indeed, to ascertain to what degree of improvement the principles of reasoning and imitation could be carried in a dog. There is no doubt that the animal affixes distinct ideas to sounds. What are the possible limits of his vocabulary no one can tell. In conversing with my dog I did not use English words, but selected simple monosyllables. Habit likewise enabled him to comprehend my gestures. If I crossed my hands on my breast he understood the signal and laid down behind me. If I joined my hands and lifted them to my breast, he returned home. If I grasped one arm above the elbow he ran before me. If I lifted my hand to my forehead he trotted composedly behind. By one motion I could make him bark; by another I could reduce him to silence. He would howl in twenty different strains of mournfulness, at my bidding. He would fetch and carry with undeviating faithfulness.

His actions being thus chiefly regulated by gestures, that to a stranger would appear indifferent or casual, it was easy to produce a belief that the animal's knowledge was much greater than in truth, it was.

One day, in a mixed company, the discourse turned upon the unrivaled abilities of *Damon*.[9] Damon had, indeed, acquired in all the circles which I frequented, an extraordinary reputation. Numerous instances of his sagacity were quoted and some of them exhibited on the spot. Much surprise was excited by the readiness with which he appeared to comprehend sentences of considerable abstraction and complexity, though he in reality attended to nothing but the movements of hand or fingers with which I accompanied my words. I enhanced the astonishment of some and excited the ridicule of others, by observing that my dog not only understood English when spoken by others, but actually spoke the language himself, with no small degree of precision.

This assertion could not be admitted without proof; proof, therefore, was readily produced. At a known signal, Damon began a low interrupted noise, in which the astonished hearers clearly distinguished English words. A dialogue began between the animal and his master, which was maintained, on the part of the former, with great vivacity and spirit. In this dialogue the dog asserted the dignity of his species and capacity of intellectual improvement. The company separated, lost in wonder, but perfectly convinced by the evidence that had been produced.

On a subsequent occasion a select company was assembled at a garden, at a small distance from the city. Discourse glided through a variety of topics, till it lighted at length on the subject of invisible beings. From the speculations of philosophers we proceeded to the creations of the poet.

9. In Greek mythology, Damon and Pythias are men who represent an idealized friendship. The dog's name also evokes the Latin term *daemon*, which refers to a godlike power, often a benevolent nature spirit or a guardian spirit.

Some maintained the justness of Shakespeare's delineations of aerial beings, while others denied it. By no violent transition, Ariel[1] and his songs were introduced, and a lady, celebrated for her musical skill, was solicited to accompany her pedal harp with the song of "Five fathom deep thy father lies"[2] . . . She was known to have set, for her favourite instrument, all the songs of Shakespeare.

My youth made me little more than an auditor on this occasion. I sat apart from the rest of the company, and carefully noted every thing. The track which the conversation had taken, suggested a scheme which was not thoroughly digested when the lady began her enchanting strain.

She ended and the audience were mute with rapture. The pause continued, when a strain was wafted to our ears from another quarter. The spot where we sat was embowered by a vine. The verdant arch was lofty and the area beneath was spacious.

The sound proceeded from above. At first it was faint and scarcely audible; presently it reached a louder key, and every eye was cast up in expectation of beholding a face among the pendant clusters. The strain was easily recognized, for it was no other than that which Ariel is made to sing when finally absolved from the service of the wizard.

> In the Cowslip's bell I lie,
> On the Bat's back I do fly . . .
> After summer merrily, &c.[3]

Their hearts palpitated as they listened: they gazed at each other for a solution of the mystery. At length the strain died away at a distance, and an interval of silence was succeded by an earnest discussion of the cause of this prodigy. One supposition only could be adopted, which was, that the strain was uttered by human organs. That the songster was stationed on the roof of the arbour, and having finished his melody had risen into the viewless fields of air.

I had been invited to spend a week at this house: this period was nearly expired when I received information that my aunt was suddenly taken sick, and that her life was in imminent danger. I immediately set out on my return to the city, but before my arrival she was dead.

This lady was entitled to my gratitude and esteem; I had received the most essential benefits at her hand. I was not destitute of sensibility, and was deeply affected by this event: I will own, however, that my grief was lessened by reflecting on the consequences of her death, with regard to my own condition. I had been ever taught to consider myself as her heir, and her death, therefore, would free me from certain restraints.

My aunt had a female servant, who had lived with her for twenty years: she was married, but her husband, who as an artisan, lived apart from her: I had no reason to suspect the woman's sincerity and disinterestedness; but my aunt was no sooner consigned to the grave than a will was produced, in which Dorothy was named her sole and universal heir.

It was in vain to urge my expectations and my claims. . . . The instrument was legibly and legally drawn up. . . . Dorothy was exasperated by my opposition and surmises, and vigorously enforced her title. In a week after

---

1. In Shakespeare's *The Tempest*, a spirit bound to serve Prospero, a magician.

2. *The Tempest* 1.2.395, slightly misquoted.
3. *The Tempest* 5.1.89, 91–92.

the decease of my kinswoman, I was obliged to seek a new dwelling. As all my property consisted in my cloths and my papers, this was easily done.

My condition was now calamitous and forlorn. Confiding[4] in the acquisition of my aunt's patrimony, I had made no other provision for the future; I hated manual labour, or any task of which the object was gain. To be guided in my choice of occupations by any motive but the pleasure which the occupation was qualified to produce, was intolerable to my proud, indolent, and restive temper.

This resource was now cut off; the means of immediate subsistence were denied me: If I had determined to acquire the knowledge of some lucrative art, the acquisition would demand time, and, meanwhile, I was absolutely destitute of support. My father's house was, indeed, open to me, but I preferred to stifle myself with the filth of the kennel, rather than to return to it.

Some plan it was immediately necessary to adopt. The exigence of my affairs, and this reverse of fortune, continually occupied my thoughts; I estranged myself from society and from books, and devoted myself to lonely walks and mournful meditation.

One morning as I ranged along the bank of Schuylkill,[5] I encountered a person, by name Ludloe, of whom I had some previous knowledge. He was from Ireland; was a man of some rank and apparently rich: I had met with him before, but in mixed companies, where little direct intercourse had taken place between us. Our last meeting was in the arbour where Ariel was so unexpectedly introduced.

Our acquaintance merely justified a transient salutation; but he did not content himself with noticing me as I passed, but joined me in my walk and entered into conversation. It was easy to advert to the occasion on which we had last met, and to the mysterious incident which then occurred. I was solicitous to dive into his thoughts upon this head and put some questions which tended to the point that I wished.

I was somewhat startled when he expressed his belief, that the performer of this mystic strain was one of the company then present, who exerted, for this end, a faculty not commonly possessed. Who this person was he did not venture to guess, and could not discover, by the tokens which he suffered to appear, that his suspicions glanced at me.[6] He expatiated with great profoundness and fertility of ideas, on the uses to which a faculty like this might be employed. No more powerful engine, he said, could be conceived, by which the ignorant and credulous might be moulded to our purposes; managed by a man of ordinary talents, it would open for him the straightest and surest avenues to wealth and power.

His remarks excited in my mind a new strain of thoughts. I had not hitherto considered the subject in this light, though vague ideas of the importance of this art could not fail to be occasionally suggested: I ventured to inquire into his ideas of the mode, in which an art like this could be employed, so as to effect the purposes he mentioned.

He dealt chiefly in general representations. Men, he said, believed in the existence and energy of invisible powers, and in the duty of discovering and conforming to their will. This will was supposed to be sometimes made

4. Trusting.
5. River in Pennsylvania.

6. I.e., he did not speculate on the person's identity, nor did he indicate that he suspected me.

known to them through the medium of their senses. A voice coming from a quarter where no attendant form could be seen would, in most cases, be ascribed to supernal[7] agency, and a command imposed on them, in this manner, would be obeyed with religious scrupulousness. Thus men might be imperiously directed in the disposal of their industry, their property, and even of their lives. Men, actuated by a mistaken sense of duty, might, under this influence, be led to the commission of the most flagitious,[8] as well as the most heroic acts: If it were his desire to accumulate wealth, or institute a new sect, he should need no other instrument.

I listened to this kind of discourse with great avidity, and regretted when he thought proper to introduce new topics. He ended by requesting me to visit him, which I eagerly consented to do. When left alone, my imagination was filled with the images suggested by this conversation. The hopelessness of better fortune, which I had lately harboured, now gave place to cheering confidence. Those motives of rectitude which should deter me from this species of imposture, had never been vivid or stable, and were still more weakened by the artifices of which I had already been guilty. The utility or harmlessness of the end, justified, in my eyes, the means.

No event had been more unexpected, by me, than the bequest of my aunt to her servant. The will, under which the latter claimed, was dated prior to my coming to the city. I was not surprised, therefore, that it had once been made, but merely that it had never been cancelled or superseded by a later instrument. My wishes inclined me to suspect the existence of a later will, but I had conceived that, to ascertain its existence, was beyond my power.

Now, however, a different opinion began to be entertained. This woman like those of her sex and class was unlettered and superstitious. Her faith in spells and apparitions, was of the most lively kind. Could not her conscience be awakened by a voice from the grave! Lonely and at midnight, my aunt might be introduced, upbraiding her for her injustice, and commanding her to atone for it by acknowledging the claim of the rightful proprietor.

True it was, that no subsequent will might exist, but this was the fruit of mistake, or of negligence. She probably intended to cancel the old one, but this act might, by her own weakness, or by the artifices of her servant, be delayed till death had put it out of her power. In either case a mandate from the dead could scarcely fail of being obeyed.

I considered this woman as the usurper of my property. Her husband as well as herself, were laborious[9] and covetous; their good fortune had made no change in their mode of living, but they were as frugal and as eager to accumulate as ever. In their hands, money was inert and sterile, or it served to foster their vices.[1] To take it from them would, therefore, be a benefit both to them and to myself; not even an imaginary injury would be inflicted. Restitution, if legally compelled to it, would be reluctant and painful, but if enjoined by Heaven would be voluntary, and the performance of a seeming duty would carry with it, its own reward.

7. Heavenly, celestial.
8. Criminal, villainous.
9. Industrious.
1. Carwin offers several, not entirely compatible, reasons why Dorothy and her husband should not have inherited his aunt's fortune. His assertion about inert and sterile money refers to beliefs about the social value of allowing money to circulate, for instance by lending it out.

These reasonings, aided by inclination, were sufficient to determine me. I have no doubt but their fallacy would have been detected in the sequel,[2] and my scheme have been productive of nothing but confusion and remorse. From these consequences, however, my fate interposed, as in the former instance, to save me.

Having formed my resolution, many preliminaries to its execution were necessary to be settled. These demanded deliberation and delay; meanwhile I recollected my promise to Ludloe, and paid him a visit. I met a frank and affectionate reception. It would not be easy to paint the delight which I experienced in this man's society. I was at first oppressed with the sense of my own inferiority in age, knowledge and rank. Hence arose numberless reserves and incapacitating diffidences; but these were speedily dissipated by the fascinations of this man's address. His superiority was only rendered, by time, more conspicuous, but this superiority, by appearing never to be present to his own mind, ceased to be uneasy to me. My questions required to be frequently answered, and my mistakes to be rectified; but my keenest scrutiny, could detect in his manner, neither arrogance nor contempt. He seemed to talk merely from the overflow of his ideas, or a benevolent desire of imparting information.

My visits gradually became more frequent. Meanwhile my wants increased, and the necessity of some change in my condition became daily more urgent. This incited my reflections on the scheme which I had formed. The time and place suitable to my design, were not selected without much anxious inquiry and frequent waverings of purpose. These being at length fixed, the interval to elapse, before the carrying of my design into effect, was not without perturbation and suspense. These could not be concealed from my new friend and at length prompted him to inquire into the cause.

It was not possible to communicate the whole truth; but the warmth of his manner inspired me with some degree of ingenuousness.[3] I did not hide from him my former hopes and my present destitute condition. He listened to my tale with no expressions of sympathy, and when I had finished, abruptly inquired whether I had any objection to a voyage to Europe? I answered in the negative. He then said that he was preparing to depart in a fortnight and advised me to make up my mind to accompany him.

This unexpected proposal gave me pleasure and surprise, but the want of money occurred to me as an insuperable objection. On this being mentioned, Oho! said he, carelessly, that objection is easily removed, I will bear all expenses of your passage myself.

The extraordinary beneficence of this act as well as the air of uncautiousness attending it, made me doubt the sincerity of his offer, and when new declarations removed this doubt, I could not forbear expressing at once my sense of his generosity and of my own unworthiness.

He replied that generosity had been expunged from his catalogue as having no meaning or a vicious one. It was the scope of his exertions to be just. This was the sum of human duty, and he that fell short, ran beside, or outstripped justice was a criminal. What he gave me was my due or not my due. If it were my due, I might reasonably demand it from him and it was wicked to withhold

---

2. I.e., in what follows.   3. Frankness, trustfulness.

it. Merit on one side or gratitude on the other, were contradictory and unintelligible.

If I were fully convinced that this benefit was not my due and yet received it, he should hold me in contempt. The rectitude of my principles and conduct would be the measure of his approbation, and no benefit should he ever bestow which the receiver was not entitled to claim, and which it would not be criminal in him to refuse.

These principles were not new from the mouth of Ludloe, but they had, hitherto, been regarded as the fruits of a venturous speculation in my mind. I had never traced them into their practical consequences, and if his conduct on this occasion had not squared with his maxims, I should not have imputed to him inconsistency. I did not ponder on these reasonings at this time: objects of immediate importance engrossed my thoughts.

One obstacle to this measure was removed. When my voyage was performed how should I subsist in my new abode? I concealed not my perplexity and he commented on it in his usual manner. How did I mean to subsist, he asked, in my own country? The means of living would be, at least, as much within my reach there as here. As to the pressure of immediate and absolute want, he believed I should be exposed to little hazard. With talents such as mine, I must be hunted by a destiny peculiarly malignant, if I could not provide myself with necessaries wherever my lot were cast.

He would make allowances, however, for my diffidence and self-distrust, and would obviate my fears by expressing his own intentions with regard to me. I must be apprised, however, of his true meaning. He laboured to shun all hurtful and vicious things, and therefore carefully abstained from making or confiding *in promises*. It was just to assist me in this voyage, and it would probably be equally just to continue to me similar assistance when it was finished. That indeed was a subject, in a great degree, within my own cognizance. His aid would be proportioned to my wants and to my merits, and I had only to take care that my claims were just, for them to be admitted.

This scheme could not but appear to me eligible. I thirsted after an acquaintance with new scenes; my present situation could not be changed for a worse; I trusted to the constancy of Ludloe's friendship; to this at least it was better to trust than to the success of my imposture on Dorothy, which was adopted merely as a desperate expedient: finally I determined to embark with him.

In the course of this voyage my mind was busily employed. There were no other passengers beside ourselves, so that my own condition and the character of Ludloe, continually presented themselves to my reflections. It will be supposed that I was not a vague or indifferent observer.

There were no vicissitudes in the deportment or lapses in the discourse of my friend. His feelings appeared to preserve an unchangeable tenor, and his thoughts and words always to flow with the same rapidity. His slumber was profound and his wakeful hours serene. He was regular and temperate in all his exercises and gratifications. Hence were derived his clear perceptions and exuberant health.

This treatment of me, like all his other mental and corporal operations, was modelled by one inflexible standard. Certain scruples and delicacies were incident to my situation. Of the existence of these he seemed to be unconscious, and yet nothing escaped him inconsistent with a state of absolute equality.

I was naturally inquisitive as to his fortune and the collateral circumstances of his condition. My notions of politeness hindered me from making direct inquiries. By indirect means I could gather nothing but that his state was opulent and independent, and that he had two sisters whose situation resembled his own.

Though, in conversation, he appeared to be governed by the utmost candour; no light was let in upon the former transactions of his life. The purpose of his visit to America I could merely guess to be the gratification of curiosity.

My future pursuits must be supposed chiefly to occupy my attention. On this head I was destitute of all stedfast views. Without profession or habits of industry or sources of permanent revenue, the world appeared to me an ocean on which my bark was set afloat, without compass or sail. The world into which I was about to enter, was untried and unknown, and though I could consent to profit by the guidance I was unwilling to rely on the support of others.

This topic being nearest my heart, I frequently introduced into conversation with my friend; but on this subject he always allowed himself to be led by me, while on all others, he was zealous to point the way. To every scheme that I proposed he was sure to cause objections. All the liberal professions[4] were censured as perverting the understanding, by giving scope to the sordid motive of gain, or embuing the mind with erroneous principles. Skill was slowly obtained, and success, though integrity and independence must be given for it, dubious and instable. The mechanical trades were equally obnoxious; they were vicious by contributing to the spurious gratifications of the rich and multiplying the objects of luxury; they were destruction to the intellect and vigour of the artizan; they enervated his frame and brutalized his mind.

When I pointed out to him the necessity of some species of labour, he tacitly admitted that necessity, but refused to direct me in the choice of a pursuit, which though not free from defect should yet have the fewest inconveniences. He dwelt on the fewness of our actual wants, the temptations which attend the possession of wealth, the benefits of seclusion and privacy, and the duty of unfettering our minds from the prejudices which govern the world.

His discourse tended merely to unsettle my views and increase my perplexity. This effect was so uniform that I at length desisted from all allusions to this theme and endeavoured to divert my own reflections from it. When our voyage should be finished, and I should actually tread this new stage, I believed that I should be better qualified to judge of the measures to be taken by me.

At length we reached Belfast. From thence we immediately repaired to Dublin. I was admitted as a member of his family. When I expressed my uncertainty as to the place to which it would be proper for me to repair, he gave me a blunt but cordial invitation to his house. My circumstances allowed me no option and I readily complied. My attention was for a time engrossed by a diversified succession of new objects. Their novelty however disappearing,

---

4. Professions requiring special training in the arts and sciences; they include law, architecture, and medicine. The mechanical trades, mentioned below, require knowledge of tools and machinery.

left me at liberty to turn my eyes upon myself and my companion, and here my reflections were supplied with abundant food.

His house was spacious and commodious, and furnished with profusion and elegance. A suite of apartments was assigned to me, in which I was permitted to reign uncontrolled and access was permitted to a well furnished library. My food was furnished in my own room, prepared in the manner which I had previously directed. Occasionally Ludloe would request my company to breakfast, when an hour was usually consumed in earnest or sprightly conversation. At all other times he was invisible, and his apartments, being wholly separate from mine, I had no opportunity of discovering in what way his hours were employed.

He defended this mode of living as being most compatible with liberty. He delighted to expatiate on the evils of cohabitation.[5] Men, subjected to the same regimen, compelled to eat and sleep and associate at certain hours, were strangers to all rational independence and liberty. Society would never be exempt from servitude and misery, till those artificial ties which held human beings together under the same roof were dissolved. He endeavoured to regulate his own conduct in pursuance of these principles, and to secure to himself as much freedom as the present regulations of society would permit. The same independence which he claimed for himself he likewise extended to me. The distribution of my own time, the selection of my own occupations and companions should belong to myself.

But these privileges, though while listening to his arguments I could not deny them to be valuable, I would have willingly dispensed with. The solitude in which I lived became daily more painful. I ate and drank, enjoyed clothing and shelter, without the exercise of forethought or industry; I walked and sat, went out and returned for as long and at what seasons I thought proper, yet my condition was a fertile source of discontent.

I felt myself removed to a comfortless and chilling distance from Ludloe. I wanted to share in his occupations and views. With all his ingenuousness of aspect and overflow of thoughts, when he allowed me his company, I felt myself painfully bewildered with regard to his genuine condition and sentiments.

He had it in his power to introduce me to society, and without an introduction, it was scarcely possible to gain access to any social circle or domestic fireside. Add to this, my own obscure prospects and dubious situation. Some regular intellectual pursuit would render my state less irksome, but I had hitherto adopted no scheme of this kind.

Time tended, in no degree, to alleviate my dissatisfaction. It increased till the determination became at length formed of opening my thoughts to Ludloe. At the next breakfast interview which took place, I introduced the subject, and expatiated without reserve, on the state of my feelings. I concluded with intreating him to point out some path in which my talents might be rendered useful to himself or to mankind.

After a pause of some minutes, he said, What would you do? You forget the immaturity of your age. If you are qualified to act a part in the theatre of life, step forth; but you are not qualified. You want knowledge, and with this you ought previously to endow yourself. . . . Means, for this end, are

---

5. Living with others in a shared arrangement.

within your reach. Why should you waste your time in idleness, and torment yourself with unprofitable wishes? Books are at hand . . . books from which most sciences and languages can be learned. Read, analyze, digest; collect facts, and investigate theories: ascertain the dictates of reason, and supply yourself with the inclination and the power to adhere to them. You will not, legally speaking, be a man in less than three years. Let this period be devoted to the acquisition of wisdom. Either stay here, or retire to an house I have on the banks of Killarney,[6] where you will find all the conveniences of study.

I could not but reflect with wonder at this man's treatment of me. I could plead none of the rights of relationship; yet I enjoyed the privileges of a son. He had not imparted to me any scheme, by pursuit of which I might finally compensate him for the expense to which my maintainance and education would subject him. He gave me reason to hope for the continuance of his bounty. He talked and acted as if my fortune were totally disjoined from his; yet was I indebted to him for the morsel which sustained my life. Now it was proposed to withdraw myself to studious leisure, and romantic solitude. All my wants, personal and intellectual, were to be supplied gratuitously and copiously. No means were prescribed by which I might make compensation for all these benefits. In conferring them he seemed to be actuated by no view to his own ultimate advantage. He took no measures to secure my future services.

I suffered these thoughts to escape me, on this occasion, and observed that to make my application successful, or useful, it was necessary to pursue some end. I must look forward to some post which I might hereafter occupy beneficially to myself or others; and for which all the efforts of my mind should be bent to qualify myself.

These hints gave him visible pleasure; and now, for the first time, he deigned to advise me on this head. His scheme, however, was not suddenly produced. The way to it was circuitous and long. It was his business to make every new step appear to be suggested by my own reflections. His own ideas were the seeming result of the moment, and sprung out of the last idea that was uttered. Being hastily taken up, they were, of course, liable to objection. These objections, sometimes occurring to me and sometimes to him, were admitted or contested with the utmost candour. One scheme went through numerous modifications before it was proved to be ineligible, or before it yielded place to a better. It was easy to perceive, that books alone were insufficient to impart knowledge: that man must be examined with our own eyes to make us acquainted with their nature: that ideas collected from observation and reading, must correct and illustrate each other: that the value of all principles, and their truth, lie in their practical effects. Hence, gradually arose the usefulness of travelling, of inspecting the habits and manners of a nation, and investigating, on the spot, the causes of their happiness and misery. Finally, it was determined that Spain was more suitable than any other, to the views of a judicious traveller.

My language, habits, and religion were mentioned as obstacles to close and extensive views; but these difficulties successively and slowly vanished. Converse with books, and natives of Spain, a steadfast purpose and

6. I.e., in the region of the Lakes of Killarney, in southwestern Ireland.

unwearied diligence would efface all differences between me and a Castilian with respect to speech.[7] Personal habits were changeable, by the same means. The bars to unbounded intercourse, rising from the religion of Spain being irreconcilably opposite to mine, cost us no little trouble to surmount, and here the skill of Ludloe was eminently displayed.

I had been accustomed to regard as unquestionable, the fallacy of the Romish faith.[8] This persuasion was habitual and the child of prejudice, and was easily shaken by the artifices of this logician. I was first led to bestow a kind of assent on the doctrines of the Roman church; but my convictions were easily subdued by a new species of argumentation, and, in a short time, I reverted to my ancient disbelief, so that, if an exterior conformity to the rights of Spain were requisite to the attainment of my purpose, that conformity must be dissembled.

My moral principles had hitherto been vague and unsettled. My circumstances had led me to the frequent practice of insincerity; but my transgressions as they were slight and transient, did not much excite my previous reflections, or subsequent remorse. My deviations, however, though rendered easy by habit, were by no means sanctioned by my principles. Now an imposture, more profound and deliberate, was projected; and I could not hope to perform well my part, unless steadfastly and thoroughly persuaded of its rectitude.

My friend was the eulogist[9] of sincerity. He delighted to trace its influence on the happiness of mankind; and proved that nothing but the universal practice of this virtue was necessary to the perfection of human society. His doctrine was splendid and beautiful. To detect its imperfections was no easy task; to lay the foundations of virtue in utility, and to limit, by that scale, the operation of general principles; to see that the value of sincerity, like that of every other mode of action, consisted in its tendency to good, and that, therefore the obligation to speak truth was not paramount or intrinsical: that my duty is modelled on a knowledge and foresight of the conduct of others; and that, since men in their actual state, are infirm and deceitful, a just estimate of consequences may sometimes make dissimulation my duty were truths that did not speedily occur. The discovery, when made, appeared to be a joint work. I saw nothing in Ludloe but proofs of candour, and a judgment incapable of bias.

The means which this man employed to fit me for his purpose, perhaps owed their success to my youth and ignorance. I may have given you exaggerated ideas of his dexterity and address. Of that I am unable to judge. Certain it is, that no time or reflection has abated my astonishment at the profoundness of his schemes, and the perseverance with which they were pursued by him. To detail their progress would expose me to the risk of being tedious, yet none but minute details would sufficiently display his patience and subtlety.

It will suffice to relate, that after a sufficient period of preparation and arrangements being made for maintaining a copious intercourse with Ludloe,

---

7. On the Iberian peninsula, Castilian Spanish is the dominant form of the language. "A Castilian": a resident of Castile, a region in north-central Spain.
8. I.e., Roman Catholicism.
9. One who speaks in praise.

I embarked for Barcelona.[1] A restless curiosity and vigorous application have distinguished my character in every scene. Here was spacious field for the exercise of all my energies. I sought out a preceptor[2] in my new religion. I entered into the hearts of priests and confessors, the *hidalgo* and the peasant, the monk and the prelate, the austere and voluptuous devotee were scrutinized in all their forms.[3]

Man was the chief subject of my study, and the social sphere that in which I principally moved; but I was not inattentive to inanimate nature, nor unmindful of the past. If the scope of virtue were to maintain the body in health, and to furnish its highest enjoyments to every sense, to increase the number, and accuracy, and order of our intellectual stores, no virtue was ever more unblemished than mine. If to act upon our conceptions of right, and to acquit ourselves of all prejudice and selfishness in the formation of our principles, entitle us to the testimony of a good conscience, I might justly claim it.

I shall not pretend to ascertain my rank in the moral scale. Your notions of duty differ widely from mine. If a system of deceit, pursued merely from the love of truth; if voluptuousness, never gratified at the expense of health, may incur censure, I am censurable. This, indeed, was not the limit of my deviations. Deception was often unnecessarily practised, and my biloquial faculty did not lie unemployed. What has happened to yourselves may enable you, in some degree, to judge of the scenes in which my mystical[4] exploits engaged me. In none of them, indeed, were the effects equally disastrous, and they were, for the most part, the result of well digested projects.

To recount these would be an endless task. They were designed as mere specimens of power, to illustrate the influence of superstition: to give sceptics the consolation of certainty: to annihilate the scruples of a tender female, or facilitate my access to the bosoms of courtiers and monks.

The first achievement of this kind took place in the convent of the Escurial.[5] For some time the hospitality of this brotherhood allowed me a cell in that magnificent and gloomy fabric. I was drawn hither chiefly by the treasures of Arabian literature, which are preserved here in the keeping of a learned Maronite, from Lebanon.[6] Standing one evening on the steps of the great altar this devout friar expatiated on the miraculous evidences of his religion; and, in a moment of enthusiasm, appealed to San Lorenzo[7] whose martyrdom was displayed before us. No sooner was the appeal made than the saint, obsequious to the summons, whispered his responses from the shrine, and commanded the heretic to tremble and believe. This event was reported to the convent. With whatever reluctance, I could not refuse my testimony to its truth, and its influence on my faith was clearly shewn in my subsequent conduct.

---

1. Coastal city in northeastern Spain.
2. Teacher, tutor.
3. Carwin refers to types of Spanish Catholics, including the *hidalgo*, or gentleman; the prelate, a bishop or other high-ranking Church dignitary; and the female worshipper, or devotee, who might be self-denying ("austere") or sensuous ("voluptuous").
4. Relating to spiritual mysteries or to religious mysticism.

5. Built in the late sixteenth century by Philip II, the Royal Site of San Lorenzo de El Escorial is a historic residence of the king of Spain that encompasses a monastery, museum, and school.
6. The Maronite Church is an eastern rite Catholic Church that uses Aramaic (the language spoken by the historical Jesus) in parts of its worship service.
7. Saint Lawrence, a third-century Christian martyr.

A lady of rank, in Seville, who had been guilty of many unauthorized indulgences,[8] was, at last, awakened to remorse, by a voice from Heaven, which she imagined had commanded her to expiate her sins by an abstinence from all food for thirty days. Her friends found it impossible to outroot this persuasion, or to overcome her resolution even by force. I chanced to be one in a numerous company where she was present. This fatal illusion was mentioned, and an opportunity afforded to the lady of defending her scheme. At a pause in the discourse, a voice was heard from the ceiling, which confirmed the truth of her tale; but, at the same time revoked the command, and, in consideration of her faith, pronounced her absolution. Satisfied with this proof, the auditors dismissed their unbelief, and the lady consented to eat.

In the course of a copious correspondence with Ludloe, the observations I had collected were given. A sentiment, which I can hardly describe, induced me to be silent on all adventures connected with my bivocal projects. On other topics, I wrote fully, and without restraint. I painted, in vivid hues, the scenes with which I was daily conversant, and pursued, fearlessly, every speculation on religion and government that occurred. This spirit was encouraged by Ludloe, who failed not to comment on my narrative, and multiply deductions from my principles.

He taught me to ascribe the evils that infest society to the errors of opinion. The absurd and unequal distribution of power and property gave birth to poverty and riches, and these were the sources of luxury and crimes. These positions were readily admitted; but the remedy for these ills, the means of rectifying these errors were not easily discovered. We have been inclined to impute them to inherent defects in the moral constitution of men: that oppression and tyranny grow up by a sort of natural necessity, and that they will perish only when the human species is extinct. Ludloe laboured to prove that this was, by no means, the case: that man is the creature of circumstances: that he is capable of endless improvement: that his progress has been stopped by the artificial impediment of government: that by the removal of this, the fondest dreams of imagination will be realized.

From detailing and accounting for the evils which exist under our present institutions, he usually proceeded to delineate some scheme of Utopian felicity, where the empire of reason should supplant that of force: where justice should be universally understood and practised; where the interest of the whole and of the individual should be seen by all to be the same; where the public good should be the scope of all activity; where the tasks of all should be the same, and the means of subsistence equally distributed.

No one could contemplate his pictures without rapture. By their comprehensiveness and amplitude they filled the imagination. I was unwilling to believe that in no region of the world, or at no period could these ideas be realized. It was plain that the nations of Europe were tending to greater depravity, and would be the prey of perpetual vicissitude. All individual attempts at their reformation would be fruitless. He therefore who desired the diffusion of right principles, to make a just system be adopted by a whole community, must pursue some extraordinary method.

---

8. In Roman Catholicism, an indulgence is a way to reduce punishment for sins; it can be granted for, e.g., saying a specific prayer or visiting a certain shrine. Unauthorized indulgences are issued without the Pope's grant of authority. "Seville": city and province in south-central Spain.

In this state of mind I recollected my native country, where a few colonists from Britain had sown the germ of populous and mighty empires.[9] Attended, as they were, into their new abode, by all their prejudices, yet such had been the influence of new circumstances, of consulting for their own happiness, of adopting simple forms of government, and excluding nobles and kings from their system, that they enjoyed a degree of happiness far superior to their parent state.

To conquer the prejudices and change the habits of millions, are impossible. The human mind, exposed to social influences, inflexibly adheres to the direction that is given to it; but for the same reason why men, who begin in error will continue, those who commence in truth, may be expected to persist. Habit and example will operate with equal force in both instances.

Let a few, sufficiently enlightened and disinterested, take up their abode in some unvisited region. Let their social scheme be founded in equity, and how small soever their original number may be, their growth into a nation is inevitable. Among other effects of national justice, was to be ranked the swift increase of numbers. Exempt from servile obligations and perverse habits, endowed with property, wisdom, and health, hundreds will expand, with inconceivable rapidity into thousands and thousands, into millions; and a new race, tutored in truth, may, in a few centuries, overflow the habitable world.

Such were the visions of youth! I could not banish them from my mind. I knew them to be crude; but believed that deliberation would bestow upon them solidity and shape. Meanwhile I imparted them to Ludloe.

In answer to the reveries and speculations which I sent to him respecting this subject, Ludloe informed me, that they had led his mind into a new sphere of meditation. He had long and deeply considered in what way he might essentially promote my happiness. He had entertained a faint hope that I would one day be qualified for a station like that to which he himself had been advanced. This post required an elevation and stability, of views which human beings seldom reach, and which could be attained by me only by a long series of heroic labours. Hitherto every new stage in my intellectual progress had added vigour to his hopes, and he cherished a stronger belief than formerly that my career would terminate auspiciously. This, however, was necessarily distant. Many preliminaries must first be settled; many arduous accomplishments be first obtained; and my virtue be subjected to severe trials. At present it was not in his power to be more explicit; but if my reflections suggested no better plan, he advised me to settle my affairs in Spain, and return to him immediately. My knowledge of this country would be of the highest use, on the supposition of my ultimately arriving at the honours to which he had alluded; and some of these preparatory measures could be taken only with his assistance, and in his company.

This intimation was eagerly obeyed, and, in a short time, I arrived at Dublin. Meanwhile my mind had copious occupation in commenting on my friend's letter. This scheme, whatever it was, seemed to be suggested by my mention of a plan of colonization, and my preference of that mode of producing extensive and permanent effects on the condition of mankind. It was easy therefore to conjecture that this mode had been pursued under some mysterious modifications and conditions.

9. The colonies of British North America.

It had always excited my wonder that so obvious an expedient had been overlooked. The globe which we inhabit was very imperfectly known. The regions and nations unexplored, it was reasonable to believe, surpassed in extent, and perhaps in populousness, those with which we were familiar. The order of Jesuits[1] had furnished an example of all the errors and excellencies of such a scheme. Their plan was founded on erroneous notions of religion and policy, and they had absurdly chosen a scene[2] within reach of the injustice and ambition of an European tyrant.

It was wise and easy to profit by their example. Resting on the two props of fidelity and zeal, an association might exist for ages in the heart of Europe, whose influence might be felt, and might be boundless, in some region of the southern hemisphere; and by whom a moral and political structure might be raised, the growth of pure wisdom, and totally unlike those fragments of Roman and Gothic barbarism, which cover the face of what are called the civilized nations.[3] The belief now rose in my mind that some such scheme had actually been prosecuted, and that Ludloe was a coadjutor.[4] On this supposition, the caution with which he approached to his point, the arduous probation which a candidate for a part on this stage must undergo, and the rigours of that test by which his fortitude and virtue must be tried, were easily explained. I was too deeply imbued with veneration for the effects of such schemes, and too sanguine in my confidence in the rectitude of Ludloe, to refuse my concurrence in any scheme by which my qualifications might at length be raised to a due point.

Our interview was frank and affectionate. I found him situated just as formerly. His aspect, manners, and deportment were the same. I entered once more on my former mode of life, but our intercourse became more frequent. We constantly breakfasted together, and our conversation was usually prolonged through half the morning.

For a time our topics were general. I thought proper to leave to him the introduction of more interesting themes: this, however, he betrayed no inclination to do. His reserve excited some surprise, and I began to suspect that whatever design he had formed with regard to me, had been laid aside. To ascertain this question, I ventured, at length, to recall his attention to the subject of his last letter, and to enquire whether subsequent reflection had made any change in his views.

He said that his views were too momentous to be hastily taken up, or hastily dismissed; the station, my attainment of which depended wholly on myself, was high above vulgar heads, and was to be gained by years of solicitude and labour. This, at least, was true with regard to minds ordinarily constituted; I, perhaps, deserved to be regarded as an exception, and might be able to accomplish in a few months that for which others were obliged to toil during half their lives.

Man, continued he, is the slave of habit. Convince him to-day that his duty leads straight forward: he shall advance, but at every step his belief shall fade;

---

1. Or the Society of Jesus, a male religious congregation of the Catholic Church.
2. Paraguay [Brown's note]. Beginning in the seventeenth century, Jesuit missionaries tried to establish model communities of Paraguayan natives. The effort generated tensions with colonial officials, leading to the Jesuits' being expelled from Spanish America in 1767.
3. Possible reference to the Bavarian Illuminati, a secret society founded in 1776 that was devoted to spreading rationalist thought and eradicating religious influence on the state.
4. Helper, assistant.

habit will resume its empire, and to-morrow he shall turn back, or betake himself to oblique paths.

We know not our strength till it be tried. Virtue, till confirmed by habit, is a dream. You are a man imbued by errors, and vincible[5] by slight temptations. Deep enquiries must bestow light on your opinions, and the habit of encountering and vanquishing temptation must inspire you with fortitude. Till this be done, you are unqualified for that post, in which you will be invested with divine attributes, and prescribe the condition of a large portion of mankind.

Confide not in the firmness of your principles, or the stedfastness of your integrity. Be always vigilant and fearful. Never think you have enough of knowledge, and let not your caution slumber for a moment, for you know not when danger is near.

I acknowledged the justice of his admonitions, and professed myself willing to undergo any ordeal which reason should prescribe. What, I asked, were the conditions, on the fulfilment of which depended my advancement to the station he alluded to? Was it necessary to conceal from me the nature and obligations of this rank?

These enquiries sunk him more profoundly into meditation than I had ever before witnessed. After a pause, in which some perplexity was visible, he answered:

I scarcely know what to say. As to promises, I claim them not from you. We are now arrived at a point, in which it is necessary to look around with caution, and that consequences should be fully known. A number of persons are leagued together for an end of some moment. To make yourself one of these is submitted to your choice. Among the conditions of their alliance are mutual fidelity and secrecy.

Their existence depends upon this: their existence is known only to themselves. This secrecy must be obtained by all the means which are possible. When I have said thus much, I have informed you, in some degree, of their existence, but you are still ignorant of the purpose contemplated by this association, and of all the members, except myself. So far no dangerous disclosure is yet made: but this degree of concealment is not sufficient. Thus much is made known to you, because it is unavoidable. The individuals which compose this fraternity are not immortal, and the vacancies occasioned by death must be supplied from among the living. The candidate must be instructed and prepared, and they are always at liberty to recede. Their reason must approve the obligations and duties of their station, or they are unfit for it. If they recede, one duty is still incumbent upon them: they must observe an inviolable silence. To this they are not held by any promise. They must weigh consequences, and freely decide; but they must not fail to number among these consequences their own death.

Their death will not be prompted by vengeance. The executioner will say, he that has once revealed the tale is likely to reveal it a second time; and, to prevent this, the betrayer must die. Nor is this the only consequence: to prevent the further revelation, he, to whom the secret was imparted, must likewise perish. He must not console himself with the belief that his tresspass will be unknown. The knowledge cannot, by human means, be withheld from

5. Capable of being overcome.

this fraternity. Rare, indeed, will it be that his purpose to disclose is not discovered before it can be effected, and the disclosure prevented by his death.

Be well aware of your condition. What I now, or may hereafter mention, mention not again. Admit not even a doubt as to the propriety of hiding it from all the world. There are eyes who will discern this doubt amidst the closest folds of your heart, and your life will instantly be sacrificed.

At present be the subject dismissed. Reflect deeply on the duty which you have already incurred. Think upon your strength of mind, and be careful not to lay yourself under impracticable obligations. It will always be in your power to recede. Even after you are solemnly enrolled a member, you may consult the dictates of your own understanding, and relinquish your post; but while you live, the obligation to be silent will perpetually attend you.

We seek not the misery or death of any one, but we are swayed by an immutable calculation. Death is to be abhorred, but the life of the betrayer is productive of more evil than his death: his death, therefore, we choose, and our means are instantaneous and unerring.

I love you. The first impulse of my love is to dissuade you from seeking to know more. Your mind will be full of ideas; your hands will be perpetually busy to a purpose into which no human creature, beyond the verge of your brotherhood, must pry. Believe me, who have made the experiment, that compared with this task, the task of inviolable secrecy, all others are easy. To be dumb will not suffice; never to know any remission in your zeal or your watchfulness will not suffice. If the sagacity of others detect your occupations, however strenuously you may labour for concealment, your doom is ratified, as well as that of the wretch whose evil destiny led him to pursue you.

Yet if your fidelity fail not, great will be your recompence. For all your toils and self-devotion, ample will be the retribution.[6] Hitherto you have been wrapt in darkness and storm; then will you be exalted to a pure and unruffled element. It is only for a time that temptation will environ you, and your path will be toilsome. In a few years you will be permitted to withdraw to a land of sages, and the remainder of your life will glide away in the enjoyments of beneficence and wisdom.

Think deeply on what I have said. Investigate your own motives and opinions, and prepare to submit them to the test of numerous hazards and experiments.

Here my friend passed to a new topic. I was desirous of reverting to this subject, and obtaining further information concerning it, but he assiduously repelled all my attempts, and insisted on my bestowing deep and impartial attention on what had already been disclosed. I was not slow to comply with his directions. My mind refused to admit any other theme of contemplation than this.

As yet I had no glimpse of the nature of this fraternity. I was permitted to form conjectures, and previous incidents bestowed but one form upon my thoughts. In reviewing the sentiments and deportment of Ludloe, my belief continually acquired new strength. I even recollected hints and ambiguous allusions in his discourse, which were easily solved, on the supposition of the existence of a new model of society, in some unsuspected corner of the world.

6. Reward.

I did not fully perceive the necessity of secrecy; but this necessity perhaps would be rendered apparent, when I should come to know the connection that subsisted between Europe and this imaginary colony. But what was to be done? I was willing to abide by these conditions. My understanding might not approve of all the ends proposed by this fraternity, and I had liberty to withdraw from it, or to refuse to ally myself with them. That the obligation of secrecy should still remain, was unquestionably reasonable.

It appeared to be the plan of Ludloe rather to damp than to stimulate my zeal. He discouraged all attempts to renew the subject in conversation. He dwelt upon the arduousness of the office to which I aspired, the temptations to violate my duty with which I should be continually beset, the inevitable death with which the slightest breach of my engagements would be followed, and the long apprenticeship which it would be necessary for me to serve, before I should be fitted to enter into this conclave.

Sometimes my courage was depressed by these representations . . . . My zeal, however, was sure to revive; and at length Ludloe declared himself willing to assist me in the accomplishment of my wishes. For this end, it was necessary, he said, that I should be informed of a second obligation, which every candidate must assume. Before any one could be deemed qualified, he must be thoroughly known to his associates. For this end, he must determine to disclose every fact in his history, and every secret of his heart. I must begin with making these confessions, with regard to my past life, to Ludloe, and must continue to communicate, at stated seasons, every new thought, and every new occurrence, to him. This confidence was to be absolutely limitless: no exceptions were to be admitted, and no reserves to be practised; and the same penalty attended the infraction of this rule as of the former. Means would be employed, by which the slightest deviation, in either case, would be detected, and the deathful consequence would follow with instant and inevitable expedition. If secrecy were difficult to practise, sincerity, in that degree in which it was here demanded, was a task infinitely more arduous, and a period of new deliberation was necessary before I should decide. I was at liberty to pause: nay, the longer was the period of deliberation which I took, the better; but, when I had once entered this path, it was not in my power to recede. After having solemnly avowed my resolution to be thus sincere in my confession, any particle of reserve or duplicity would cost me my life.

This indeed was a subject to be deeply thought upon. Hitherto I had been guilty of concealment with regard to my friend. I had entered into no formal compact, but had been conscious [of] a kind of tacit obligation to hide no important transaction of my life from him. This consciousness was the source of continual anxiety. I had exerted, on numerous occasions, my bivocal faculty,[7] but, in my intercourse with Ludloe, had suffered not the slightest intimation to escape me with regard to it. This reserve was not easily explained. It was, in a great degree, the product of habit; but I likewise considered that the efficacy of this instrument depended upon its existence being unknown. To confide the secret to one, was to put an end to my privilege: how widely the knowledge would thenceforth be diffused, I had no power to foresee.

---

7. A variant term for ventriloquism.

Each day multiplied the impediments to confidence. Shame hindered me from acknowledging my past reserves. Ludloe, from the nature of our intercourse, would certainly account my reserve, in this respect, unjustifiable, and to excite his indignation or contempt was an unpleasing undertaking. Now, if I should resolve to persist in my new path, this reserve must be dismissed: I must make him master of a secret which was precious to me beyond all others; by acquainting him with past concealments, I must risk incurring his suspicion and his anger. These reflections were productive of considerable embarrassment.

There was, indeed, an avenue by which to escape these difficulties, if it did not, at the same time, plunge me into greater. My confessions might, in other respects, be unbounded, but my reserves, in this particular, might be continued. Yet should I not expose myself to formidable perils? Would my secret be for ever unsuspected and undiscovered?

When I considered the nature of this faculty, the impossibility of going farther than suspicion, since the agent could be known only by his own confession, and even this confession would not be believed by the greater part of mankind, I was tempted to conceal it.

In most cases, if I had asserted the possession of this power, I should be treated as a liar; it would be considered as an absurd and audacious expedient to free myself from the suspicion of having entered into compact with a dæmon, or of being myself an emissary of the grand foe.[8] Here, however, there was no reason to dread a similar imputation, since Ludloe had denied the preternatural pretensions of these airy sounds.

My conduct on this occasion was nowise influenced by the belief of any inherent sanctity in truth. Ludloe had taught me to model myself in this respect entirely with a view to immediate consequences. If my genuine interest, on the whole, was promoted by veracity, it was proper to adhere to it; but, if the result of my investigation were opposite, truth was to be sacrificed without scruple.

Meanwhile, in a point of so much moment, I was not hasty to determine. My delay seemed to be, by no means, unacceptable to Ludloe, who applauded my discretion, and warned me to be circumspect. My attention was chiefly absorbed by considerations connected with this subject, and little regard was paid to any foreign occupation or amusement.

One evening, after a day spent in my closet,[9] I sought recreation by walking forth. My mind was chiefly occupied by the review of incidents which happened in Spain. I turned my face towards the fields, and recovered not from my reverie, till I had proceeded some miles on the road to Meath.[1] The night had considerably advanced, and the darkness was rendered intense, by the setting of the moon. Being somewhat weary, as well as undetermined in what manner next to proceed, I seated myself on a grassy bank beside the road. The spot which I had chosen was aloof from passengers, and shrouded in the deepest obscurity.

Some time elapsed, when my attention was excited by the slow approach of an equipage.[2] I presently discovered a coach and six horses, but unattended,

8. I.e., Satan.
9. Apartment or small room.
1. County in Ireland, northwest of Dublin.
2. A carriage.

except by coachman and postillion,[3] and with no light to guide them on their way. Scarcely had they passed the spot where I rested, when some one leaped from beneath the hedge, and seized the head of the fore-horses. Another called upon the coachman to stop, and threatened him with instant death if he disobeyed. A third drew open the coach-door, and ordered those within to deliver their purses. A shriek of terror showed me that a lady was within, who eagerly consented to preserve her life by the loss of her money.

To walk unarmed in the neighbourhood of Dublin, especially at night, has always been accounted dangerous. I had about me the usual instruments of defence. I was desirous of rescuing this person from the danger which surrounded her, but was somewhat at a loss how to effect my purpose. My single strength was insufficient to contend with three ruffians. After a moment's debate, an expedient was suggested, which I hastened to execute.

Time had not been allowed for the ruffian who stood beside the carriage to receive the plunder, when several voices, loud, clamorous, and eager, were heard in the quarter whence the traveller had come. By trampling with quickness, it was easy to imitate the sound of many feet. The robbers were alarmed, and one called upon another to attend. The sounds increased, and, at the next moment, they betook themselves to flight, but not till a pistol was discharged. Whether it was aimed at the lady in the carriage, or at the coachman, I was not permitted to discover, for the report affrighted the horses, and they set off at full speed.

I could not hope to overtake them: I knew not whither the robbers had fled, and whether, by proceeding, I might not fall into their hands. . . . . . These considerations induced me to resume my feet, and retire from the scene as expeditiously as possible. I regained my own habitation without injury.

I have said that I occupied separate apartments from those of Ludloe. To these there were means of access without disturbing the family. I hasted[4] to my chamber, but was considerably surprized to find, on entering my apartment, Ludloe seated at a table, with a lamp before him.

My momentary confusion was greater than his. On discovering who it was, he assumed his accustomed looks, and explained appearances, by saying, that he wished to converse with me on a subject of importance, and had therefore sought me at this secret hour, in my own chamber. Contrary to his expectation, I was absent. Conceiving it possible that I might shortly return, he had waited till now. He took no further notice of my absence, nor manifested any desire to know the cause of it, but proceeded to mention the subject which had brought him hither. These were his words.

You have nothing which the laws permit you to call your own. Justice entitles you to the supply of your physical wants, from those who are able to supply them; but there are few who will acknowledge your claim, or spare an atom of their superfluity to appease your cravings. That which they will not spontaneously give, it is not right to wrest from them by violence. What then is to be done?

Property is necessary to your own subsistence. It is useful, by enabling you to supply the wants of others. To give food, and clothing, and shelter, is

3. Rider of the leading left-hand horse.
4. I.e., hastened.

to give life, to annihilate temptation, to unshackle virtue, and propagate felicity. How shall property be gained?

You may set your understanding or your hands at work. You may weave stockings, or write poems, and exchange them for money; but these are tardy[5] and meager schemes. The means are disproportioned to the end, and I will not suffer you to pursue them. My justice will supply your wants.

But dependence on the justice of others is a precarious condition. To be the object is a less ennobling state than to be the bestower of benefit. Doubtless you desire to be vested with competence and riches, and to hold them by virtue of the law, and not at the will of a benefactor. . . . He paused as if waiting for my assent to his positions. I readily expressed my concurrence, and my desire to pursue any means compatible with honesty. He resumed.

There are various means, besides labour, violence, or fraud. It is right to select the easiest within your reach. It happens that the easiest is at hand. A revenue of some thousands a year, a stately mansion in the city, and another in Kildare,[6] old and faithful domestics, and magnificent furniture, are good things. Will you have them?

A gift like that, replied I, will be attended by momentous conditions. I cannot decide upon its value, until I know these conditions.

The sole condition is your consent to receive them. Not even the airy obligation of gratitude will be created by acceptance. On the contrary, by accepting them, you will confer the highest benefit upon another.

I do not comprehend you. Something surely must be given in return.

Nothing. It may seem strange that, in accepting the absolute control of so much property, you subject yourself to no conditions; that no claims of gratitude or service will accrue; but the wonder is greater still. The law equitably enough fetters the gift with no restraints, with respect to you that receive it; but not so with regard to the unhappy being who bestows it. That being must part, not only with property but liberty. In accepting the property, you must consent to enjoy the services of the present possessor. They cannot be disjoined.

Of the true nature and extent of the gift, you should be fully apprized. Be aware, therefore, that, together with this property, you will receive absolute power over the liberty and person of the being who now possesses it. That being must become your domestic slave; be governed, in every particular, by your caprice.

Happily for you, though fully invested with this power, the degree and mode in which it will be exercised will depend upon yourself. . . . . You may either totally forbear the exercise, or employ it only for the benefit of your slave. However injurious, therefore, this authority may be to the subject of it, it will, in some sense, only enhance the value of the gift to you.

The attachment and obedience of this being will be chiefly evident in one thing. Its duty will consist in conforming, in every instance, to your will. All the powers of this being are to be devoted to your happiness; but there is one relation between you, which enables you to confer, while exacting, pleasure. . . . . This relation is *sexual*. Your slave is a woman; and the bond, which transfers her property and person to you, is . . . *marriage*.

5. Slow, sluggish.
6. Town and county southwest of Dublin.

My knowledge of Ludloe, his principles, and reasonings, ought to have precluded that surprise which I experienced at the conclusion of his discourse. I knew that he regarded the present institution of marriage as a contract of servitude, and the terms of it unequal and unjust. When my surprise had subsided, my thoughts turned upon the nature of his scheme. After a pause of reflection, I answered:

Both law and custom have connected obligations with marriage, which, though heaviest on the female, are not light upon the male. Their weight and extent are not immutable and uniform; they are modified by various incidents, and especially by the mental and personal qualities of the lady.

I am not sure that I should willingly accept the property and person of a woman decrepit with age, and enslaved by perverse habits and evil passions: whereas youth, beauty, and tenderness would be worth accepting, even for their own sake, and disconnected with fortune.

As to altar vows, I believe they will not make me swerve from equity. I shall exact neither service nor affection from my spouse. The value of these, and, indeed, not only the value, but the very existence, of the latter depends upon its spontaneity. A promise to love tends rather to loosen than strengthen the tie.

As to myself, the age of illusion is past. I shall not wed, till I find one whose moral and physical constitution will make personal fidelity easy. I shall judge without mistiness or passion, and habit will come in aid of an enlightened and deliberate choice.

I shall not be fastidious in my choice. I do not expect, and scarcely desire, much intellectual similitude between me and my wife. Our opinions and pursuits cannot be in common. While women are formed by their education, and their education continues in its present state, tender hearts and misguided understandings are all that we can hope to meet with.

What are the character, age, and person of the woman to whom you allude? and what prospect of success would attend my exertions to obtain her favour?

I have told you she is rich.[7] She is a widow, and owes her riches to the liberality of her husband, who was a trader of great opulence, and who died while on a mercantile adventure to Spain. He was not unknown to you. Your letters from Spain often spoke of him. In short, she is the widow of Benington, whom you met at Barcelona. She is still in the prime of life; is not without many feminine attractions; has an ardent and credulent[8] temper: and is particularly given to devotion. This temper it would be easy to regulate according to your pleasure and your interest, and I now submit to you the expediency of an alliance with her.

I am a kinsman, and regarded by her with uncommon deference; and my commendations, therefore, will be of great service to you, and shall be given.

I will deal ingenuously[9] with you. It is proper you should be fully acquainted with the grounds of this proposal. The benefits of rank, and property, and independence, which I have already mentioned as likely to accrue to you from this marriage, are solid and valuable benefits; but these are not the sole advantages, and to benefit you, in these respects, is not my whole view.

7. The speaker is Ludloe.
8. Credulous.

9. Candidly, sincerely.

No. My treatment of you henceforth will be regulated by one principle. I regard you only as one undergoing a probation or apprenticeship; as subjected to trials of your sincerity and fortitude. The marriage I now propose to you is desirable, because it will make you independent of me. Your poverty might create an unsuitable bias in favour of proposals, one of whose effects would be to set you beyond fortune's reach. That bias will cease, when you cease to be poor and dependent.

Love is the strongest of all human delusions. That fortitude, which is not subdued by the tenderness and blandishments of woman, may be trusted; but no fortitude, which has not undergone that test, will be trusted by us.

This woman is a charming enthusiast. She will never marry but him whom she passionately loves. Her power over the heart that loves her will scarcely have limits. The means of prying into your transactions, of suspecting and sifting your thoughts, which her constant society with you, while sleeping and waking, her zeal and watchfulness for your welfare, and her curiosity, adroitness, and penetration will afford her, are evident. Your danger, therefore, will be imminent. Your fortitude will be obliged to have recourse, not to flight, but to vigilance. Your eye must never close.

Alas! what human magnanimity can stand this test! How can I persuade myself that you will not fail? I waver between hope and fear. Many, it is true, have fallen, and dragged with them the author of their ruin, but some have soared above even these perils and temptations, with their fiery energies unimpaired, and great has been, as great ought to be, their recompence.

But you are doubtless aware of your danger. I need not repeat the consequences of betraying your trust, the rigour of those who will judge your fault, the unerring and unbounded scrutiny to which your actions, the most secret and indifferent, will be subjected.

Your conduct, however, will be voluntary. At your own option be it, to see or not to see this woman. Circumspection, deliberation, forethought, are your sacred duties and highest interest.

Ludloe's remarks on the seductive and bewitching powers of women, on the difficulty of keeping a secret which they wish to know, and to gain which they employ the soft artillery of tears and prayers, and blandishments and menaces, are familiar to all men, but they had little weight with me, because they were unsupported by my own experience. I had never had any intellectual or sentimental connection with the sex. My meditations and pursuits had all led a different way, and a bias had gradually been given to my feelings, very unfavourable to the refinements of love. I acknowledge, with shame and regret, that I was accustomed to regard the physical and sensual consequences of the sexual relation as realities, and every thing intellectual, disinterested, and heroic, which enthusiasts connect with it as idle dreams. Besides, said I, I am yet a stranger to the secret, on the preservation of which so much stress is laid, and it will be optional with me to receive it or not. If, in the progress of my acquaintance with Mrs. Benington, I should perceive any extraordinary danger in the gift, cannot I refuse, or at least delay to comply with any new conditions from Ludloe? Will not his candour and his affection for me rather commend than disapprove my diffidence? In fine, I resolved to see this lady.

She was, it seems, the widow of Benington, whom I knew in Spain. This man was an English merchant settled at Barcelona, to whom I had been commended by Ludloe's letters, and through whom my pecuniary supplies were furnished. . . . . Much intercourse and some degree of intimacy had taken place between us, and I had gained a pretty accurate knowledge of his character. I had been informed, through different channels, that his wife was much his superior in rank, that she possessed great wealth in her own right, and that some disagreement of temper or views occasioned their separation. She had married him for love, and still doted on him: the occasions for separation having arisen, it seems, not on her side but on his. As his habits of reflection were nowise friendly to religion, and as hers, according to Ludloe, were of the opposite kind, it is possible that some jarring had arisen between them from this source. Indeed, from some casual and broken hints of Benington, especially in the latter part of his life, I had long since gathered this conjecture. . . . . Something, thought I, may be derived from my acquaintance with her husband favourable to my views.

I anxiously waited for an opportunity of acquainting Ludloe with my resolution. On the day of our last conversation, he had made a short excursion from town, intending to return the same evening, but had continued absent for several days. As soon as he came back, I hastened to acquaint him with my wishes.

Have you well considered this matter, said he. Be assured it is of no trivial import. The moment at which you enter the presence of this woman will decide your future destiny. Even putting out of view the subject of our late conversations, the light in which you shall appear to her will greatly influence your happiness, since, though you cannot fail to love her, it is quite uncertain what return she may think proper to make. Much, doubtless, will depend on your own perseverance and address, but you will have many, perhaps insuperable obstacles to encounter on several accounts, and especially in her attachment to the memory of her late husband. As to her devout temper, this is nearly allied to a warm imagination in some other respects, and will operate much more in favour of an ardent and artful lover, than against him.

I still expressed my willingness to try my fortune with her.

Well, said he, I anticipated your consent to my proposal, and the visit I have just made was to her. I thought it best to pave the way, by informing her that I had met with one for whom she had desired me to look out. You must know that her father was one of these singular men who set a value upon things exactly in proportion to the difficulty of obtaining or comprehending them. His passion was for antiques, and his favourite pursuit during a long life was monuments in brass, marble, and parchment, of the remotest antiquity. He was wholly indifferent to the character or conduct of our present sovereign and his ministers, but was extremely solicitous about the name and exploits of a king of Ireland that lived two or three centuries before the flood. He felt no curiosity to know who was the father of his wife's child, but would travel a thousand miles, and consume months, in investigating which son of Noah it was that first landed on the coast of Munster.[1] He would give a hundred guineas[2] from the mint for a piece of

---

1. Province of southwestern Ireland. According to some legends, the biblical patriarch Noah's son Japhet or Japeth is the father of the Gaels in Ireland. In other legends, the father of this Irish people is Bith, a son of Noah who does not appear in the Bible.
2. British gold coins, in use from 1663 to 1817.

old decayed copper no bigger than his nail, provided it had awkward characters upon it, too much defaced to be read. The whole stock of a great bookseller was, in his eyes, a cheap exchange for a shred of parchment, containing half a homily written by St. Patrick.[3] He would have gratefully given all his patrimonial domains to one who should inform him what pendragon or druid it was who set up the first stone on Salisbury plain.[4]

This spirit, as you may readily suppose, being seconded by great wealth and long life, contributed to form a very large collection of venerable lumber[5] which, though beyond all price to the collector himself, is of no value to his heiress but so far as it is marketable. She designs to bring the whole to auction, but for this purpose a catalogue and description are necessary. Her father trusted to a faithful memory, and to vague and scarcely legible memorandums, and has left a very arduous task to any one who shall be named to the office. It occurred to me, that the best means of promoting your views was to recommend you to this office.

You are not entirely without the antiquarian frenzy yourself. The employment, therefore, will be somewhat agreeable to you for its own sake. It will entitle you to become an inmate of the same house, and thus establish an incessant intercourse between you, and the nature of the business is such, that you may perform it in what time, and with what degree of diligence and accuracy you please.

I ventured to insinuate that, to a woman of rank and family, the character of a hireling[6] was by no means a favourable recommendation.

He answered, that he proposed, by the account he should give of me, to obviate[7] every scruple of that nature. Though my father was no better than a farmer, it is not absolutely certain but that my remoter ancestors had princely blood in their veins: but as long as proofs of my low extraction did not impertinently intrude themselves, my silence, or, at most, equivocal surmises, seasonably made use of, might secure me from all inconveniences on the score of birth. He should represent me, and I was such, as his friend, favourite, and equal, and my passion for antiquities should be my principal inducement to undertake this office, though my poverty would make no objection to a reasonable pecuniary recompense.

Having expressed my acquiescence in his measures, he thus proceeded: My visit was made to my kinswoman, for the purpose, as I just now told you, of paving your way into her family; but, on my arrival at her house, I found nothing but disorder and alarm. Mrs. Benington, it seems, on returning from a longer ride than customary, last Thursday evening, was attacked by robbers. Her attendants related an imperfect tale of somebody advancing at the critical moment to her rescue. It seems, however, they did more harm than good; for the horses took to flight and overturned the carriage, in consequence of which Mrs. Benington was severely bruised. She has kept her bed ever since, and a fever was likely to ensue, which has only left her out of danger to-day.

As the adventure before related, in which I had so much concern, occurred at the time mentioned by Ludloe, and as all other circumstances

---

3. Fifth-century bishop known as the primary patron saint of Ireland.
4. Plateau in central England; the location of Stonehenge and other prehistoric monuments. "Pendragon": the title given to several traditional kings of the Britons, including King Arthur.

"Druid": member of an educated, priestly class among the Iron Age Celts.
5. Old and useless things.
6. A person paid to undertake menial work.
7. Remove.

were alike, I could not doubt that the person whom the exertion of my mysterious powers had relieved was Mrs. Benington: but what an ill-omened interference was mine! The robbers would probably have been satisfied with the few guineas[8] in her purse, and, on receiving these, would have left her to prosecute her journey in peace and security, but, by absurdly offering a succor,[9] which could only operate upon the fears of her assailants, I endangered her life, first by the desperate discharge of a pistol, and next by the fright of the horses. . . . My anxiety, which would have been less if I had not been, in some degree, myself the author of the evil, was nearly removed by Ludloe's proceeding to assure me that all danger was at an end, and that he left the lady in the road to perfect health. He had seized the earliest opportunity of acquainting her with the purpose of his visit, and had brought back with him her cheerful acceptance of my services. The next week was appointed for my introduction.

With such an object in view, I had little leisure to attend to any indifferent object. My thoughts were continually bent upon the expected introduction, and my impatience and curiosity drew strength, not merely from the character of Mrs. Benington, but from the nature of my new employment. Ludloe had truly observed, that I was infected with somewhat of this antiquarian mania myself, and I now remembered that Benington had frequently alluded to this collection in possession of his wife. My curiosity had then been more than once excited by his representations, and I had formed a vague resolution of making myself acquainted with this lady and her learned treasure, should I ever return to Ireland. . . . Other incidents had driven this matter from my mind.

Meanwhile, affairs between Ludloe and myself remained stationary. Our conferences, which were regular and daily, related to general topics, and though his instructions were adapted to promote my improvement in the most useful branches of knowledge, they never afforded a glimpse towards that quarter where my curiosity was most active.

The next week now arrived, but Ludloe informed me that the state of Mrs. Benington's health required a short excursion into the country, and that he himself proposed to bear her company. The journey was to last about a fortnight, after which I might prepare myself for an introduction to her.

This was a very unexpected and disagreeable trial to my patience. The interval of solitude that now succeeded would have passed rapidly and pleasantly enough, if an event of so much moment were not in suspense. Books, of which I was passionately fond, would have afforded me delightful and incessant occupation, and Ludloe, by way of reconciling me to unavoidable delays, had given me access to a little closet, in which his rarer and more valuable books were kept.

All my amusements, both by inclination and necessity, were centered in myself and at home. Ludloe appeared to have no visitants, and though frequently abroad, or at least secluded from me, had never proposed my introduction to any of his friends, except Mrs. Benington. My obligations to him were already too great to allow me to lay claim to new favors and indulgences, nor, indeed, was my disposition such as to make society needful to my happiness. My character had been, in some degree, modeled by the

8. British gold coins, in use from 1663 to 1817.
9. Aid, help.

faculty which I possessed. This deriving all its supposed value from impenetrable secrecy, and Ludloe's admonitions tending powerfully to impress me with the necessity of wariness and circumspection in my general intercourse with mankind, I had gradually fallen into sedate, reserved, mysterious, and unsociable habits. My heart wanted not a friend.

In this temper of mind, I set myself to examine the novelties which Ludloe's private book-cases contained. 'Twill be strange, thought I, if his favorite volumes do not show some marks of my friend's character. To know a man's favorite or most constant studies cannot fail of letting in some little light upon his secret thoughts, and though he would not have given me the reading of these books, if he had thought them capable of unveiling more of his concerns than he wished, yet possibly my ingenuity may go one step farther than he dreams of. You shall judge whether I was right in my conjectures.

The books which composed this little library were chiefly the voyages and travels of the missionaries of the sixteenth and seventeenth centuries. Added to these were some works upon political economy and legislation. Those writers who have amused themselves with reducing their ideas to practice, and drawing imaginary pictures of nations or republics, whose manners or government came up to their standard of excellence, were, all of whom I had ever heard, and some I had never heard of before, to be found in this collection. A translation of Aristotle's republic, the political romances of sir Thomas Moore, Harrington, and Hume,[1] appeared to have been much read, and Ludloe had not been sparing of his marginal comments. In these writers he appeared to find nothing but error and absurdity; and his notes were introduced for no other end than to point out groundless principles and false conclusions. . . . The style of these remarks was already familiar to me. I saw nothing new in them, or different from the strain of those speculations with which Ludloe was accustomed to indulge himself in conversation with me.

After having turned over the leaves of the printed volumes, I at length lighted on a small book of maps, from which, of course, I could reasonably expect no information, on that point about which I was most curious. It was an atlas, in which the maps had been drawn by the pen. None of them contained any thing remarkable, so far as I, who was indeed a smatterer in geography, was able to perceive, till I came to the end, when I noticed a map, whose prototype I was wholly unacquainted with. It was drawn on a pretty large scale, representing two islands, which bore some faint resemblance, in their relative proportions, at least, to Great Britain and Ireland. In shape they were widely different, but as to size there was no scale by which to measure them. From the great number of subdivisions, and from signs, which apparently represented towns and cities, I was allowed to infer, that the country was at least as extensive as the British isles. This map was apparently unfinished, for it had no names inscribed upon it.

I have just said, my geographical knowledge was imperfect. Though I had not enough to draw the outlines of any country by memory, I had still sufficient to recognize what I had before seen, and to discover that none of the

---

1. David Hume (1711–1776), Scottish philosopher, author of the essay "The Idea of a Perfect Commonwealth"; Plato (not Aristotle), ancient Greek philosopher, author of the dialogue *Republic*; Sir Thomas More (1478–1535), English statesman, author of the combination of fictional and political philosophy *Utopia*; James Harrington (1611–1677), English statesman, author of the work of political philosophy *The Commonwealth of Oceana*.

larger islands in our globe resembled the one before me. Having such and so strong motives to curiosity, you may easily imagine my sensations on surveying this map. Suspecting, as I did, that many of Ludloe's intimations alluded to a country well known to him, though unknown to others, I was, of course, inclined to suppose that this country was now before me.

In search of some clue to this mystery, I carefully inspected the other maps in this collection. In a map of the eastern hemisphere I soon observed the outlines of islands, which, though on a scale greatly diminished, were plainly similar to that of the land above described.

It is well known that the people of Europe are strangers to very nearly one half of the surface of the globe.[2] From the south pole up to the equator, it is only the small space occupied by southern Africa and by South America with which we are acquainted. There is a vast extent, sufficient to receive a continent as large as North America, which our ignorance has filled only with water. In Ludloe's maps nothing was still to be seen, in these regions, but water, except in that spot where the transverse parallels of the southern tropic and the 150th degree east longitude intersect each other.[3] On this spot were Ludloe's islands placed, though without any name or inscription whatever.

I needed not to be told that this spot had never been explored by any European voyager, who had published his adventures. What authority had Ludloe for fixing a habitable land in this spot? and why did he give us nothing but the courses of shores and rivers, and the site of towns and villages, without a name?

As soon as Ludloe had set out upon his proposed journey of a fortnight, I unlocked his closet, and continued rummaging among these books and maps till night. By that time I had turned over every book and almost every leaf[4] in this small collection, and did not open the closet again till near the end of that period. Meanwhile I had many reflections upon this remarkable circumstance. Could Ludloe have intended that I should see this atlas? It was the only book that could be styled a manuscript on these shelves, and it was placed beneath several others, in a situation far from being obvious and forward to the eye or the hand. Was it an oversight in him to leave it in my way, or could he have intended to lead my curiosity and knowledge a little farther onward by this accidental disclosure? In either case how was I to regulate my future deportment toward him? Was I to speak and act as if this atlas had escaped my attention or not? I had already, after my first examination of it, placed the volume exactly where I found it. On every supposition I thought this was the safest way, and unlocked the closet a second time, to see that all was precisely in the original order. . . . How was I dismayed and confounded on inspecting the shelves to perceive that the atlas was gone. This was a theft, which, from the closet being under lock and key, and the key always in my own pocket, and which, from the very nature of the thing stolen, could not be imputed to any of the domestics. After a few moments a suspicion occurred, which was soon changed into certainty by applying to the housekeeper, who told me that Ludloe had returned,

---

2. "The reader must be reminded that the incidents of this narrative are supposed to have taken place before the voyages of Bougainville and Cook"—EDITOR [Brown's note]. The French admiral Louis-Antoine, Comte de Bougainville (1729–1811) and the English captain James Cook (1728–1779) undertook separate explorations in the Pacific Ocean in the late 1760s.
3. I.e., at what we know as the approximate location of Australia.
4. Page.

apparently in much haste, the evening of the day on which he had set out upon his journey, and just after I had left the house, that he had gone into the room where this closet of books was, and, after a few minutes' stay, came out again and went away. She told me also, that he had made general enquiries after me, to which she had answered, that she had not seen me during the day, and supposed that I had spent the whole of it abroad. From this account it was plain, that Ludloe had returned for no other purpose but to remove this book out of my reach. But if he had a double key to this door, what should hinder his having access, by the same means, to every other locked up place in the house?

This suggestion made me start with terror. Of so obvious a means for possessing a knowledge of every thing under his roof, I had never been till this moment aware. Such is the infatuation which lays our most secret thoughts open to the world's scrutiny. We are frequently in most danger when we deem ourselves most safe, and our fortress is taken sometimes through a point, whose weakness nothing, it should seem, but the blindest stupidity could overlook.

My terrors, indeed, quickly subsided when I came to recollect that there was nothing in any closet or cabinet of mine which could possibly throw light upon subjects which I desired to keep in the dark. The more carefully I inspected my own drawers, and the more I reflected on the character of Ludloe, as I had known it, the less reason did there appear in my suspicions; but I drew a lesson of caution from this circumstance, which contributed to my future safety.

From this incident I could not but infer Ludloe's unwillingness to let me so far into his geographical secret, as well as the certainty of that suspicion, which had very early been suggested to my thoughts, that Ludloe's plans of civilization had been carried into practice in some unvisited corner of the world. It was strange, however, that he should betray himself by such an inadvertency. One who talked so confidently of his own powers, to unveil any secret of mine, and, at the same time, to conceal his own transactions, had surely committed an unpardonable error in leaving this important document in my way. My reverence, indeed, for Ludloe was such, that I sometimes entertained the notion that this seeming oversight was, in truth, a regular contrivance to supply me with a knowledge, of which, when I came maturely to reflect, it was impossible for me to make any ill use. There is no use in relating what would not be believed; and should I publish to the world the existence of islands in the space allotted by Ludloe's maps to these *incognitæ*,[5] what would the world answer? That whether the space described was sea or land was of no importance. That the moral and political condition of its inhabitants was the only topic worthy of rational curiosity. Since I had gained no information upon this point; since I had nothing to disclose but vain and fantastic surmises; I might as well be ignorant of every thing. Thus, from secretly condemning Ludloe's imprudence, I gradually passed to admiration of his policy. This discovery had no other effect than to stimulate my curiosity; to keep up my zeal to prosecute the journey I had commenced under his auspices.

I had hitherto formed a resolution to stop where I was in Ludloe's confidence: to wait till the success should be ascertained of my projects with

5. Unknown territories (Latin).

respect to Mrs. Benington, before I made any new advance in the perilous and mysterious road into which he had led my steps. But, before this tedious fortnight had elapsed, I was grown extremely impatient for an interview, and had nearly resolved to undertake whatever obligation he should lay upon me.

This obligation was indeed a heavy one, since it included the confession of my vocal powers. In itself the confession was little. To possess this faculty was neither laudable nor culpable, nor had it been exercised in a way which I should be very much ashamed to acknowledge. It had led me into many insincerities and artifices, which, though not justifiable by any creed, was entitled to some excuse, on the score of youthful ardour and temerity. The true difficulty in the way of these confessions was the not having made them already. Ludloe had long been entitled to this confidence, and, though the existence of this power was venial or wholly innocent, the obstinate concealment of it was a different matter, and would certainly expose me to suspicion and rebuke. But what was the alternative? To conceal it. To incur those dreadful punishments awarded against treason in this particular. Ludloe's menaces still rung in my ears, and appalled my heart. How should I be able to shun them? By concealing from every one what I concealed from him? How was my concealment of such a faculty to be suspected or proved? Unless I betrayed myself, who could betray me?

In this state of mind, I resolved to confess myself to Ludloe in the way that he required, reserving only the secret of this faculty. Awful, indeed, said I, is the crisis of my fate. If Ludloe's declarations are true, a horrid catastrophe awaits me: but as fast as my resolutions were shaken, they were confirmed anew by the recollection—Who can betray me but myself? If I deny, who is there can prove? Suspicion can never light upon the truth. If it does, it can never be converted into certainty. Even my own lips cannot confirm it, since who will believe my testimony?

By such illusions was I fortified in my desperate resolution. Ludloe returned at the time appointed. He informed me that Mrs. Benington expected me next morning. She was ready to depart for her country residence, where she proposed to spend the ensuing summer, and would carry me along with her. In consequence of this arrangement, he said, many months would elapse before he should see me again. You will indeed, continued he, be pretty much shut up from all society. Your books and your new friend will be your chief, if not only companions. Her life is not a social one, because she has formed extravagant notions of the importance of lonely worship and devout solitude. Much of her time will be spent in meditation upon pious books in her closet.[6] Some of it in long solitary rides in her coach, for the sake of exercise. Little will remain for eating and sleeping, so that unless you can prevail upon her to violate her ordinary rules for your sake, you will be left pretty much to yourself. You will have the more time to reflect upon what has hitherto been the theme of our conversations. You can come to town when you want to see me. I shall generally be found in these apartments.

In the present state of my mind, though impatient to see Mrs. Benington, I was still more impatient to remove the veil between Ludloe and myself. After some pause, I ventured to enquire if there was any impediment to

6. Private room.

my advancement in the road he had already pointed out to my curiosity and ambition.

He replied, with great solemnity, that I was already acquainted with the next step to be taken in this road. If I was prepared to make him my confessor, as to the past, the present, and the future, *without exception or condition*, but what arose from defect of memory, he was willing to receive my confession.

I declared myself ready to do so.

I need not, he returned, remind you of the consequences of concealment or deceit. I have already dwelt upon these consequences. As to the past, you have already told me, perhaps, all that is of any moment to know. It is in relation to the future that caution will be chiefly necessary. Hitherto your actions have been nearly indifferent to the ends of your future existence. Confessions of the past are required, because they are an earnest[7] of the future character and conduct. Have you then—but this is too abrupt. Take an hour to reflect and deliberate. Go by yourself; take yourself to severe task, and make up your mind with a full, entire, and unfailing resolution; for the moment in which you assume this new obligation will make you a new being. Perdition or felicity will hang upon that moment.

This conversation was late in the evening. After I had consented to postpone this subject, we parted, he telling me that he would leave his chamber door open, and as soon as my mind was made up I might come to him.

I retired accordingly to my apartment, and spent the prescribed hour in anxious and irresolute reflections. They were no other than had hitherto occurred, but they occurred with more force than ever. Some fatal obstinacy, however, got possession of me, and I persisted in the resolution of concealing *one thing*. We become fondly attached to objects and pursuits, frequently for no conceivable reason but the pain and trouble they cost us. In proportion to the danger in which they involve us do we cherish them. Our darling potion is the poison that scorches our vitals.

After some time, I went to Ludloe's apartment. I found him solemn, and yet benign, at my entrance. After intimating my compliance with the terms prescribed, which I did, in spite of all my labor for composure, with accents half faltering, he proceeded to put various questions to me, relative to my early history.

I knew there was no other mode of accomplishing the end in view, but by putting all that was related in the form of answers to questions; and when meditating on the character of Ludloe, I experienced excessive uneasiness as to the consummate art and penetration which his questions would manifest. Conscious of a purpose to conceal, my fancy invested my friend with the robe of a judicial inquisitor, all whose questions should aim at extracting the truth, and entrapping the liar.

In this respect, however, I was wholly disappointed. All his inquiries were general and obvious.—They betokened curiosity, but not suspicion; yet there were moments when I saw, or fancied I saw, some dissatisfaction betrayed in his features; and when I arrived at that period of my story which terminated with my departure, as his companion, for Europe, his pauses were, I thought, a little longer and more museful than I liked. At this period,

7. A pledge.

our first conference ended. After a talk, which had commenced at a late hour, and had continued many hours, it was time to sleep, and it was agreed that next morning the conference should be renewed.

On retiring to my pillow, and reviewing all the circumstances of this interview, my mind was filled with apprehension and disquiet. I seemed to recollect a thousand things, which showed that Ludloe was not fully satisfied with my part in this interview. A strange and nameless mixture of wrath and of pity appeared, on recollection, in the glances which, from time to time, he cast upon me. Some emotion played upon his features, in which, as my fears conceived, there was a tincture of resentment and ferocity. In vain I called my usual sophistries to my aid. In vain I pondered on the inscrutable nature of my peculiar faculty. In vain I endeavoured to persuade myself, that, by telling the truth, instead of entitling myself to Ludloe's approbation, I should only excite his anger, by what he could not but deem an attempt to impose upon his belief an incredible tale of impossible events. I had never heard or read of any instance of this faculty. I supposed the case to be absolutely singular, and I should be no more entitled to credit in proclaiming it, than if I should maintain that a certain billet[8] of wood possessed the faculty of articulate speech. It was now, however, too late to retract. I had been guilty of a solemn and deliberate concealment. I was now in the path in which there was no turning back, and I must go forward.

The return of day's encouraging beams in some degree quieted my nocturnal terrors, and I went, at the appointed hour, to Ludloe's presence. I found him with a much more cheerful aspect than I expected, and began to chide myself, in secret, for the folly of my late[9] apprehensions.

After a little pause, he reminded me, that he was only one among many, engaged in a great and arduous design. As each of us, continued he, is mortal, each of us must, in time, yield his post to another.—Each of us is ambitious to provide himself a successor, to have his place filled by one selected and instructed by himself. All our personal feelings and affections are by no means intended to be swallowed up by a passion for the general interest; when they can be kept alive and be brought into play, in subordination and subservience to the *great end*, they are cherished as useful, and revered as laudable; and whatever austerity and rigor you may impute to my character, there are few more susceptible of personal regards than I am.

You cannot know, till *you* are what *I* am, what deep, what all-absorbing interest I have in the success of my tutorship on this occasion. Most joyfully would I embrace a thousand deaths, rather than that you should prove a recreant.[1] The consequences of any failure in your integrity will, it is true, be fatal to yourself: but there are some minds, of a generous texture, who are more impatient under ills they have inflicted upon others, than of those they have brought upon themselves; who had rather perish, themselves, in infamy, than bring infamy or death upon a benefactor.

Perhaps of such noble materials is your mind composed. If I had not thought so, you would never have been an object of my regard, and therefore, in the motives that shall impel you to fidelity, sincerity, and perseverance, some regard to my happiness and welfare will, no doubt, have place.

8. Thick piece (of wood).
9. Recent.

1. Coward; one unfaithful to a belief, apostate.

And yet I exact nothing from you on this score. If your own safety be insufficient to control you, you are not fit for us. There is, indeed, abundant need of all possible inducements to make you faithful. The task of concealing nothing from me must be easy. That of concealing every thing from others must be the only arduous one. The *first* you can hardly fail of performing, when the exigence requires it, for what motive can you possibly have to practice evasion or disguise with me? You have surely committed no crime; you have neither robbed, nor murdered, nor betrayed. If you have, there is no room for the fear of punishment or the terror of disgrace to step in, and make you hide your guilt from me. You cannot dread any further disclosure, because I can have no interest in your ruin or your shame: and what evil could ensue the confession of the foulest murder, even before a bench of magistrates, more dreadful than that which will inevitably follow the practice of the least concealment to me, or the least undue disclosure to others?

You cannot easily conceive the emphatical solemnity with which this was spoken. Had he fixed piercing eyes on me while he spoke; had I perceived him watching my looks, and laboring to penetrate my secret thoughts, I should doubtless have been ruined: but he fixed his eyes upon the floor, and no gesture or look indicated the smallest suspicion of my conduct. After some pause, he continued, in a more pathetic tone, while his whole frame seemed to partake of his mental agitation.

I am greatly at a loss by what means to impress you with a full conviction of the truth of what I have just said. Endless are the sophistries by which we seduce ourselves into perilous and doubtful paths. What we do not see, we disbelieve, or we heed not. The sword may descend upon our infatuated head from above, but we who are, meanwhile, busily inspecting the ground at our feet, or gazing at the scene around us, are not aware or apprehensive of its irresistible coming. In this case, it must not be seen before it is felt, or before the time comes when the danger of incurring it is over. I cannot withdraw the veil, and disclose to your view the exterminating angel. All must be vacant and blank, and the danger that stands armed with death at your elbow must continue to be totally invisible, till that moment when its vengeance is provoked or unprovokable. I will do my part to encourage you in good, or intimidate you from evil. I am anxious to set before you all the motives which are fitted to influence your conduct; but how shall I work on your convictions?

Here another pause ensued, which I had not courage enough to interrupt. He presently resumed.

Perhaps you recollect a visit which you paid, on Christmas day, in the year——, to the cathedral church at Toledo.[2] Do you remember?

A moment's reflection recalled to my mind all the incidents of that day. I had good reason to remember them. I felt no small trepidation when Ludloe referred me to that day, for, at the moment, I was doubtful whether there had not been some bivocal agency exerted on that occasion. Luckily, however, it was almost the only similar occasion in which it had been wholly silent.

I answered in the affirmative. I remember them perfectly.

And yet, said Ludloe, with a smile that seemed intended to disarm this declaration of some of its terrors, I suspect your recollection is not as exact

---

2. City in central Spain, whose cathedral is one of the great examples of Gothic architecture.

as mine, nor, indeed, your knowledge as extensive. You met there, for the first time, a female, whose nominal uncle, but real father, a dean of that ancient church, resided in a blue stone house, the third from the west angle of the square of St. Jago.

All this was exactly true.

This female, continued he, fell in love with you. Her passion made her deaf to all the dictates of modesty and duty, and she gave you sufficient intimations, in subsequent interviews at the same place, of this passion; which, she being fair and enticing, you were not slow in comprehending and returning. As not only the safety of your intercourse, but even of both your lives, depended on being shielded even from suspicion, the utmost wariness and caution was observed in all your proceedings. Tell me whether you succeeded in your efforts to this end.

I replied, that, at the time, I had no doubt but I had.

And yet, said he, drawing something from his pocket, and putting it into my hand, there is the slip of paper, with the preconcerted[3] emblem inscribed upon it, which the infatuated girl dropped in your sight, one evening, in the left aisle of that church. That paper you imagined you afterwards burnt in your chamber lamp. In pursuance of this token, you deferred your intended visit, and next day the lady was accidentally drowned, in passing a river. Here ended your connection with her, and with her was buried, as you thought, all memory of this transaction.

I leave you to draw your own inference from this disclosure. Meditate upon it when alone. Recall all the incidents of that drama, and labour to conceive the means by which my sagacity has been able to reach events that took place so far off, and under so deep a covering. If you cannot penetrate these means, learn to reverence my assertions, that I cannot be deceived; and let sincerity be henceforth the rule of your conduct towards me, not merely because it is right, but because concealment is impossible.

We will stop here. There is no haste required of us. Yesterday's discourse will suffice for to-day, and for many days to come. Let what has already taken place be the subject of profound and mature reflection. Review, once more, the incidents of your early life, previous to your introduction to me, and, at our next conference, prepare to supply all those deficiences occasioned by negligence, forgetfulness, or design on our first. There must be some. There must be many. The whole truth can only be disclosed after numerous and repeated conversations. These must take place at considerable intervals, and when *all* is told, then shall you be ready to encounter the final ordeal, and load yourself with heavy and terrific sanctions.

I shall be the proper judge of the completeness of your confession.— Knowing previously, and by unerring means, your whole history, I shall be able to detect all that is deficient, as well as all that is redundant. Your confessions have hitherto adhered to the truth, but deficient they are, and they must be, for who, at a single trial can detail the secrets of his life? whose recollection can fully serve him at an instant's notice? who can free himself, by a single effort, from the dominion of fear and shame? We expect no miracles of fortitude and purity from our disciples. It is our discipline, our

---

3. Predetermined.

wariness, our laborious preparation that creates the excellence we have among us. We find it not ready made.

I counsel you to join Mrs. Benington without delay. You may see me when and as often as you please. When it is proper to renew the present topic, it shall be renewed. Till then we will be silent.—Here Ludloe left me alone, but not to indifference or vacuity. Indeed I was overwhelmed with the reflections that arose from this conversation. So, said I, I am still saved, if I have wisdom enough to use the opportunity, from the consequences of past concealments. By a distinction which I had wholly overlooked, but which could not be missed by the sagacity and equity of Ludloe, I have praise for telling the truth, and an excuse for withholding some of the truth. It was, indeed, a praise to which I was entitled, for I have made no *additions* to the tale of my early adventures. I had no motive to exaggerate or dress out in false colours. What I sought to conceal, I was careful to exclude entirely, that a lame or defective narrative might awaken no suspicions.

The allusion to incidents at Toledo confounded and bewildered all my thoughts. I still held the paper he had given me. So far as memory could be trusted, it was the same which, an hour after I had received it, I burnt, as I conceived, with my own hands. How Ludloe came into possession of this paper; how he was apprised of incidents, to which only the female mentioned and myself were privy; which she had too good reason to hide from all the world, and which I had taken infinite pains to bury in oblivion, I vainly endeavoured to conjecture.

To be continued.

1803–1805

Native American Eloquence: Negotiation and Resistance

The eloquence of Native American orators impressed Europeans from the early years of contact. Exploration narratives often included descriptions of Native speakers and sometimes offered versions of what they were purported to have said, as in John Smith's report on his negotiations with Powhatan in the "Native American Oral Traditions" cluster. By the eighteenth century, as interest in political oratory and classical republicanism grew, white readers came to recognize the eloquent Indian as a literary type, and Indian speeches figured prominently in schoolbooks such as the popular elocution manuals designed to teach young American citizens to engage in public affairs. Meanwhile, oratory remained a central form of verbal art in indigenous communities, and it was an important element in formal exchanges with white Americans. The words of Native orators appeared in official state documents, treaty proceedings, and ethnographic and historical works, and orations attributed to Native speakers appeared in novels, poems, and plays. The literary fashion for Native eloquence was grounded in real practices and closely tied to matters of political exigency. The vogue reached a peak in the 1820s, when debates over Indian Removal gave added urgency to the Native resistance expressed in a number of widely circulated speeches.

The selections included here exemplify some seventy years of written or printed representations of Native eloquence. A speech by the Iroquois leader Canassatego, which achieved strikingly wide circulation on both sides of the Atlantic, shows him to be a consummate diplomat as he argues for indigenous sovereignty. Two decades later Pontiac, citing a charismatic prophet of the Delawares, attempts to persuade Huron and Pottawatomi leaders to join his Ottawa people in armed resistance to the British, in much the same way that the Shawnee leader Tecumseh later seeks to forge an Indian alliance against the expansionist Americans. The Mingo warrior Logan explains the reasons for his violent resistance to the colonists whom his people had earlier welcomed. Finally, a group of Cherokee women diplomats marshal the rhetoric of political motherhood to call for peaceful and friendly relations.

Before the nineteenth century, published texts of Native American oratory were almost all produced by hands other than those of the orators themselves—the works of Samson Occom and Hendrick Aupaumut, both included in this volume, are important exceptions—and they vary in authenticity and accuracy. Some widely reprinted speeches are now known to be largely or entirely invented, while others approximate the speaker's actual words. Somewhere between these extremes are speeches that might be called "bicultural composites," probably based on what an Indian person said but rendered in an English text that owes much to translators, transcribers, editors, and publishers. No known fabrications have been included here, and the provenance of each speech is indicated as specifically as possible.

CANASSATEGO

anassatego (b. c. 1680; sometimes Canasatego) was an Onondaga Indian. The Onondagas—whose traditional homeland is in central New York, near present-day Syracuse—were one of the original Five (later Six) Nations of the Iroquois (or Haudenosaunee) League. Canassatego had no apparent connection to the hereditary sachems, or leaders, of the Onondagas, but around 1740, in the years leading to the final struggle between France and England for control of North America, he rose to prominence as a negotiator of several important treaties between the Iroquois and the English colonies. He probably achieved this status through his skills as an orator and a political tactician. His influence depended partly on his close relationship with Conrad Weiser (1696–1760), a German-born translator and Indian agent who cultivated a reputation as an honest broker between Pennsylvania authorities and the Iroquois leadership. Canassatego first appears in the written record for 1742, when he played a significant role in the negotiations with the Pennsylvania government over compensation for land. He played a larger role in the Lancaster Treaty proceedings of 1744, the source for the selection included here, and in meetings at Albany (1745) and Philadelphia (1749). He died in 1750, possibly a victim of poison. His successor was an ally of France and a professed Roman Catholic, indicating that schisms existed within Canassatego's Onondaga community.

The printed version of the Lancaster Treaty of 1744 circulated widely in the colonies and in England. Benjamin Franklin, the Pennsylvania colony's official printer, laid out the text of the treaty proceedings to resemble a printed play and sent copies to his business partners in London, New York, and Annapolis. A second edition appeared in Williamsburg, Virginia. Whatever literary appeal the proceedings had was closely tied to the significance of its content, which highlighted the central place of the Iroquois in the imperial contest between England and France. Canassatego used his position of relative power on this occasion to demand compensation for land that the Iroquois claimed after defeating the Susquehanna Indians. The colonial governments were reluctant to fulfill these claims, arguing that they had previously purchased the land from the Susquehannas. In the following speech, which was probably translated by Weiser, Canassatego asserts the priority of indigenous claims to sovereignty over those of the English.

Speech at Lancaster[1]

* * *

Brother, the Governor of Maryland,
When you mentioned the Affair of the Land Yesterday, you went back to old Times, and told us, you had been in Possession of the Province of *Maryland* above One Hundred Years; but what is One Hundred Years in Comparison of the Length of Time since our Claim began since we came out of this Ground? For we must tell you, that long before One Hundred Years our Ancestors came out of this very Ground, and their Children have remained here ever

---

1. The text is from A Treaty, Held at the Town of Lancaster, in Pennsylvania: by the Honourable the Lieutenant-governor of the Province, and the Honourable the Commissioners for the Provinces of Virginia and Maryland, with the Indians of the Six Nations, in June, 1744 (printed and sold by Benjamin Franklin, 1744).

since. You came out of the Ground in a Country that lies beyond the Seas, there you may have a just Claim, but here you must allow us to be your elder Brethren, and the Lands to belong to us long before you knew any thing of them. It is true, that above One Hundred Years ago the *Dutch* came here in a Ship, and brought with them several Goods; such as Awls, Knives, Hatchets, Guns, and many other Particulars, which they gave us; and when they had taught us how to use their Things, and we saw what sort of People they were, we were so well pleased with them, that we tied their Ship to the Bushes on the Shore;[2] and afterwards, liking them still better the longer they staid with us, and thinking the Bushes too tender, we removed the Rope, and tied it to the Trees; and as the Trees were liable to be blown down by high Winds, or to decay of themselves, we, from the Affection we bore them, again removed the Rope, and tied it to a strong and big Rock [*here the Interpreter said, They mean the* Oneido *Country*] and not content with this, for its further Security we removed the Rope to the big Mountain [*here the Interpreter says they mean the* Onandago *Country*] and there we tied it very fast, and rowll'd[3] Wampum about it; and, to make it still more secure, we stood upon the Wampum, and sat down upon it, to defend it, and to prevent any Hurt coming to it, and did our best Endeavours that it might remain uninjured for ever. During all this Time the New-comers, the *Dutch*, acknowledged our Right to the Lands, and sollicited us, from Time to Time, to grant them Parts of our Country, and to enter into League and Covenant with us, and to become one People with us.

After this the *English* came into the Country, and, as we were told, became one People with the *Dutch*.[4] About two Years after the Arrival of the *English*, an *English* Governor came to *Albany*, and finding what great Friendship subsisted between us and the *Dutch*, he approved it mightily, and desired to make as strong a League, and to be upon as good Terms with us as the *Dutch* were, with whom he was united, and to become one People with us: And by his further Care in looking into what had passed between us, he found that the Rope which tied the Ship to the great Mountain was only fastened with Wampum, which was liable to break and rot, and to perish in a Course of Years; he therefore told us, he would give us a Silver Chain, which would be much stronger, and would last for ever. This we accepted, and fastened the Ship with it, and it has lasted ever since. Indeed we have had some small Differences with the *English*, and, during these Misunderstandings, some of their young Men would, by way of Reproach, be every now and then telling us, that we should have perished if they had not come into the Country and furnished us with Strowds[5] and Hatchets, and Guns, and other Things necessary for the Support of Life; but we always gave them to understand that they were mistaken, that we lived before they came amongst us, and as well, or better, if we may believe what our Forefathers have told us. We had then Room enough, and Plenty of Deer, which was easily caught; and tho' we had not Knives, Hatchets, or Guns, such as we have now, yet we had Knives of Stone, and Hatchets of Stone, and Bows and Arrows, and those served our Uses as well then as the *English* ones do

---

2. The following passage uses metaphors that suggest Iroquois control over their alliance with the Dutch. In this passage, the addition of wampum enhances the strength and importance of the ties between the Iroquois and the Dutch.

3. Rolled.
4. The British seized New Amsterdam from the Dutch in 1664, renaming it New York.
5. Blankets made of stroud, a coarse woolen fabric.

now. We are now straitened, and sometimes in want of Deer, and liable to many other Inconveniences since the *English* came among us, and particularly from that Pen-and-Ink Work that is going on at the Table (*pointing to the Secretary*) and we will give you an Instance of this. Our Brother *Onas*,[6] a great while ago, came to *Albany* to buy the *Sasquahannah* Lands of us, but our Brother, the Governor of *New-York*, who, as we suppose, had not a good understanding with our Brother *Onas*, advised us not to sell him any Land, for he would make an ill Use of it; and, pretending to be our good Friend, he advised us, in order to prevent *Onas's*, or any other person's imposing upon us, and that we might always have our Land when we should want it, to put it into his Hands; and told us, he would keep it for our life, and never open his Hands, but keep them close shut, and not part with any of it, but at our Request. Accordingly we trusted him, and put our Land into his Hands, and charged him to keep it safe for our Use; but, some Time after, he went to *England*, and carried our Land with him, and there sold it to our Brother *Onas* for a large Sum of Money; and when, at the Instance of our Brother *Onas*, we were minded to sell him some Lands, he told us, we had sold the *Sasquahannah* Lands already to the Governor of *New-York*, and that he had bought them from him in *England*; tho', when he came to understand how the Governor of *New-York* had deceived us, he very generously paid us for our Lands over again.

Tho' we mention this Instance of an Imposition put upon us by the Governor of *New-York*, yet we must do the *English* the Justice to say, we have had their hearty Assistances in our Wars with the *French*, who were no sooner arrived amongst us than they began to render us uneasy, and to provoke us to War, and we have had several Wars with them; during all which we constantly received Assistance from the *English*, and, by their Means, we have always been able to keep up our Heads against their Attacks.

We now come nearer home. We have had your Deeds interpreted to us, and we acknowledge them to be good and valid, and that the *Conestogoe* or *Sasquahannah Indians* had a Right to sell those Lands to you, for they were then theirs; but since that Time we have conquered them, and their Country now belongs to us, and the Lands we demanded Satisfaction for are no Part of the Lands comprized in those Deeds; they are the *Cohongorontas* Lands; those, we are sure, you have not possessed One Hundred Years, no, nor above Ten Years, and we made our Demands so soon as we knew your People were settled in those Parts. These have never been sold, but remain still to be disposed of; and we are well pleased to hear you are provided with Goods, and do assure you of our Willingness to treat with you for those unpurchased Lands; in Confirmation whereof, we present you with this Belt of Wampum.

Which was received with the usual Ceremonies.

6. Originally a name given to William Penn (1644–1718), the founder of Pennsylvania, "Brother Onas" was later used to refer to any governor of Pennsylvania. "Onas" means feather, and, by extension, a quill pen.

PONTIAC

ontiac (1720?–1769) was an Ottawa Indian, born in the area between Lake Erie and Lake Huron, near present-day Detroit. "Ottawa" derives from the Algonquian word for commerce or trade, and in the eighteenth century the Ottawas had strong trading and diplomatic alliances with the French. But in 1760 the British defeated the French at Fort Detroit, and in 1762, Sir Jeffrey Amherst (1717–1797), commander-in-chief of British forces in North America, turned command of Detroit over to Henry Gladwin (1730–1791), a man who shared Amherst's contempt for Indians. Gladwin continued his predecessor's policies of refusing to supply food, arms, and, critically, gunpowder to the Indians as the French had done. He also discarded the French policy of treating Indians as allies in favor of treating them as subjects of the British Crown.

Pontiac is said to have given the speech printed here to an assembly of Ottawa, Huron, and Pottawatomi leaders on April 27, 1763. He relates the vision of Neolin, the Delaware prophet, who around 1760 began to preach the necessity of abandoning European customs and returning to traditional Native practices. Neolin's nativist message spread widely, catalyzing resistance to the expanding British presence that followed their defeat of the French. Pontiac does not seem to have encountered the Delaware prophet, but he knew Neolin's message, which led him to organize what non-Indians called a "conspiracy" against the British. He allegedly gave this speech to persuade other tribes to join the Ottawas in his resistance movement.

All reprintings of Pontiac's speech derive from Francis Parkman's *The Conspiracy of Pontiac* (1851). Parkman, a leading romantic historian, gives as his source for the speech the *"Pontiac, MS."* taken from the *"M'Dougal, MSS."* This information seems to point to Lieutenant John McDougall, who was intimately involved with the history of this period—indeed, he was taken prisoner by the Indians and managed to escape. But no manuscript by him has been found. Did McDougall hear Pontiac speak? If so, who translated and transcribed Pontiac's words? The historical record is silent. Pontiac's speech can be understood as a bicultural composite, on the assumption—a guess—that there is a strong likelihood that he spoke words to this effect based on his knowledge of the Delaware prophet.

Speech at Detroit

*   *   *

"A Delaware Indian," said Pontiac, "conceived an eager desire to learn wisdom from the Master of Life; but, being ignorant where to find him, he had recourse to fasting, dreaming, and magical incantations. By these means it was revealed to him, that, by moving forward in a straight, undeviating course, he would reach the abode of the Great Spirit. He told his purpose to no one; and having provided the equipments of a hunter,—gun, powderhorn, ammunition, and a kettle for preparing his food,—he set out on his errand. For some time he journeyed on in high hope and confidence. On the evening of the eighth day, he stopped by the side of a brook at the edge of a meadow, where he began to make ready his evening meal, when, looking up, he saw three large openings in the woods before him, and three well-beaten paths which entered them. He was much surprised; but his wonder increased, when, after it had grown dark, the three paths were more clearly visible than ever. Remembering the important object of his journey, he could neither rest nor sleep; and, leaving his fire, he crossed the meadow, and entered the largest of the three openings. He had advanced but a short distance into the forest, when a bright flame sprang out of the ground before him, and arrested his steps. In great amazement, he turned back, and entered the second path, where the same wonderful phenomenon again encountered him; and now, in terror and bewilderment, yet still resolved to persevere, he took the last of the three paths. On this he journeyed a whole day without interruption, when at length, emerging from the forest, he saw before him a vast mountain, of dazzling whiteness. So precipitous was the ascent, that the Indian thought it hopeless to go farther, and looked around him in despair: at that moment, he saw, seated at some distance above, the figure of a beautiful woman arrayed in white who arose as he looked upon her, and thus accosted him: 'How can you hope, encumbered as you are, to succeed in your design? Go down to the foot of the mountain, throw away your gun, your ammunition, your provisions, and your clothing; wash yourself in the stream which flows there, and you will then be prepared to stand before the Master of Life.' The Indian obeyed, and again began to ascend among the rocks, while the woman, seeing him still discouraged, laughed at his faintness of heart, and told him that, if he wished for success, he must climb by the aid of one hand and one foot only. After great toil and suffering, he at length found himself at the summit. The woman had disappeared, and he was left alone. A rich and beautiful plain lay before him, and at a little distance he saw three great villages, far superior to the squalid wigwams of the Delawares. As he approached the largest, and stood hesitating whether he should enter, a man gorgeously attired stepped forth, and, taking him by the hand, welcomed him to the celestial abode. He then conducted him into the presence of the Great Spirit, where the Indian stood confounded at the unspeakable splendor which surrounded him. The Great Spirit bade him be seated, and thus addressed him:—

"'I am the Maker of heaven and earth, the trees, lakes, rivers, and all things else. I am the Maker of mankind; and because I love you, you must do my will. The land on which you live I have made for you, and not for others. Why do you suffer the white men to dwell among you? My children, you have forgotten the customs and traditions of your forefathers. Why do you not clothe yourselves in skins, as they did, and use the bows and arrows, and the stone-pointed lances, which they used? You have bought guns, knives, kettles, and blankets, from the white men, until you can no longer do without them; and, what is worse, you have drunk the poison fire-water, which turns you into fools. Fling all these things away; live as your wise forefathers lived before you. And as for these English,—these dogs dressed in red,[1] who have come to rob you of your hunting-grounds, and drive away the game,—you must lift the hatchet against them. Wipe them from the face of the earth, and then you will win my favor back again, and once more be happy and prosperous. The children of your great father, the King of France,[2] are not like the English. Never forget that they are your brethren. They are very dear to me, for they love the red men, and understand the true mode of worshiping me.'"

1. British soldiers wore red jackets. 2. Louis XV (1710–1774).

The Great Spirit next gave his hearer various precepts of morality and religion, such as the prohibition to marry more than one wife; and a warning against the practice of magic, which is worshipping the devil. A prayer, embodying the substance of all that he had heard, was then presented to the Delaware. It was cut in hieroglyphics upon a wooden stick, after the custom of his people; and he was directed to send copies of it to all the Indian villages.

*　　*　　*

LOGAN

Although he was a person of considerable renown, the exact origins and identity of the man known as Chief Logan (1725?–1780) are not entirely clear. He was a Mingo—the term widely used for Iroquoian Natives living outside their nations' homelands—of either Oneida or Cayuga background. His Indian name was probably Tachnedorus, but he was known in English as John Logan. In 1774 agents of Virginia governor Lord Dunmore provoked a brief "war" with the aim of appropriating Native lands. A particularly brutal event of this war was the Yellow Creek massacre, on the upper Ohio River. Daniel Greathouse led a party that killed and scalped nine Indians, among them Logan's pregnant sister, who was mutilated along with her unborn child. At the end of the war, Logan was asked to attend a treaty meeting with Dunmore. He refused, but apparently sent a message through John Gibson that eventually was transformed into a speech in English. Gibson, although married to Logan's sister, had fought against the Indians in this war (and lost his wife and unborn child; his daughter survived). He would have understood whichever Iroquoian language Logan spoke.

Thomas Jefferson said he heard Logan's speech directly from Gibson and that he wrote it down in his memo book. The speech first appeared in print in the *Pennsylvania Journal* on January 20, 1775, based on a copy sent by James Madison. (How Madison got the speech is unknown.) Jefferson's text is almost identical to the Madison version. The mystery surrounding the text deepens in light of the discrepancies between the historical facts as they have been uncovered and various statements attributed to Logan. Logan is said to have asserted that Michael Cresap perpetrated the massacre, not Daniel Greathouse. And while Logan claims to have no surviving kin, he was later killed by a nephew.

Jefferson included Logan's speech in "Query VI. Productions Mineral, Vegetable, and Animal" of *Notes on the State of Virginia* (1787). In that volume Jefferson argued that the American Indians were not inherently inferior to Europeans and offered a strong defense of their "genius," pointing especially to their capacity for noble oratory. To illustrate this claim, but also to confirm the notion that Indians were a "vanishing race," he quoted Chief Logan's speech. When skeptics asserted that the speech was a fraud, Jefferson printed twenty-three pages of affidavits testifying to its authenticity in the 1801 edition of *Notes*. Nonetheless, it remains unclear just how much of this speech represents words that Logan actually spoke. Known as "Logan's Lament," the speech became famous, appearing, for example, in the fourth and fifth editions of the *McGuffey Readers*, textbooks widely used in nineteenth-century classrooms. It is the most famous instance of Indian oratory as a popular nineteenth-century American literary genre.

From Chief Logan's Speech[1]

Notes on the State of Virginia, Query VI

* * *

I may challenge the whole orations of Demosthenes and Cicero,[2] and of any more eminent orator, if Europe has furnished more eminent, to produce a single passage, superior to the speech of Logan, a Mingo chief, to Lord Dunmore,[3] when governor of this state. And, as a testimony of their talents in this line, I beg leave to introduce it, first stating the incidents necessary for understanding it. In the spring of the year 1774, a robbery was committed by some Indians on certain land-adventurers on the river Ohio. The whites in that quarter, according to their custom, undertook to punish this outrage in a summary way. Captain Michael Cresap, and a certain Daniel Great-house,[4] leading on these parties, surprised, at different times, traveling and hunting parties of the Indians, having their women and children with them, and murdered many. Among these were unfortunately the family of Logan, a chief celebrated in peace and war, and long distinguished as the friend of the whites. This unworthy return provoked his vengeance. He accordingly signalized himself in the war which ensued. In the autumn of the same year a decisive battle was fought at the mouth of the Great Kanhaway, between the collected forces of the Shawanese, Mingoes, and Delawares, and a detachment of the Virginia militia. The Indians were defeated, and sued for peace. Logan however disdained to be seen among the suppliants. But, lest the sincerity of a treaty should be distrusted, from which so distinguished a chief absented himself, he sent by a messenger[5] the following speech to be delivered to Lord Dunmore.

"I appeal to any white man to say, if ever he entered Logan's cabin hungry, and he gave him not meat; if ever he came cold and naked, and he clothed him not. During the course of the last long and bloody war, Logan remained idle in his cabin, an advocate for peace. Such was my love for the whites, that my countrymen pointed as they passed, and said, 'Logan is the friend of white men.' I had even thought to have lived with you, but for the injuries of one man. Col. Cresap, the last spring, in cold blood, and unprovoked, murdered all the relations of Logan, not sparing even my women and children. There runs not a drop of my blood in the veins of any living creature. This called on me for revenge. I have sought it: I have killed many: I have fully glutted my vengeance. For my country, I rejoice at the beams of peace. But do not harbor a thought that mine is the joy of fear. Logan never felt fear. He will not turn on his heel to save his life. Who is there to mourn for Logan?—Not one."

---

1. The text is from Thomas Jefferson, *Notes on the State of Virginia* (1787), edited by William Peden (1954).
2. The two most renowned classical orators. Demosthenes (c. 385–322 B.C.E.) was an Athenian. Marcus Tullius Cicero (106–43 B.C.E.) was a Roman.
3. John Murray, Earl of Dunmore (1732–1809), was the colonial governor of Virginia from 1771 to 1775.
4. Maryland-born settler in Virginia (c. 1752–1775). Cresap (1724–1775), Maryland-born soldier and settler.
5. John Gibson (1740–1882), Pennsylvania-born soldier and settler.

CHEROKEE WOMEN

In traditional matriarchal Cherokee society, women held authority within their families, supervised land usage, occupied political offices such as Beloved Woman (or Ghighua), and participated in diplomacy. Motherhood was an organizing concept used to ground women's claims to power. The diplomatic rhetoric of Cherokee women often focused on the physical and emotional bonds between mothers and children as a compelling reason to sustain peaceful relations with rival powers. In this address of September 8, 1787, to Benjamin Franklin, then serving as the governor of Pennsylvania and as a delegate to the Constitutional Convention, several representatives of the Cherokee Women's Council ask Congress to pay attention to their desire for peace.

To Governor Benjamin Franklin[1]

Brother,
I am in hopes my Brothers & the Beloved men near the water side will heare from me. This day I filled the pipes that they smoaked in piece,[2] and I am in hopes the smoake has Reached up to the skies above. I here send you a piece of the same Tobacco, and am in hopes you & your Beloved men will smoake it in Friendship—and I am glad in my heart that I am the mother of men that will smoak it in piece.
Brother,
I am in hopes if you Rightly consider it that woman is the mother of All—and that woman Does not pull Children out of Trees or Stumps nor out of old Logs, but out of their Bodies, so that they ought to mind what a woman says, and look upon her as a mother—and I have Taken the privelage to Speak to you as my own Children, & the same as if you had sucked my Breast—and I am in hopes you have a beloved woman amongst you who will help to put her Children Right if they do wrong, as I shall do the same—the great men have all promised to Keep the path clear & straight, as my Children shall Keep the path clear & white so that the Messengers shall go & come in safety Between us—the old people is never done Talking to their Children—which makes me say so much as I do. The Talk you sent to me was to talk to my Children, which I have done this day, and they all liked my Talk well, which I am in hopes you will heare from me Every now & then that I keep my Children in piece—tho' I am a woman giving you this Talk, I am in hopes that you and all the Beloved men in Congress will pay particular Attention to it, as I am Delivering it to you from the Bottom of my heart, that they will Lay this on the white stool in Congress, wishing them all well & success in all their undertakings—I hold fast the good Talk I Received from you my Brother, & thanks you kindly for your good Talks, & your presents, & the kind usage you gave to my son.
From KATTEUHA, The Beloved woman of Chota.[3]
[Indorsed by Kaattahee, Scolecutta, and Kaattahee, Cherokee Indian Women.]

1. The text is from *Transatlantic Feminisms in the Age of Revolutions* (2012), edited by Lisa L. Moore, Joanna Brooks, and Caroline Wigginton.
2. I.e., peace (as in "keep my Children in piece," below).
3. Cherokee town in Tennessee. Katteuha's identity is unknown.

TECUMSEH

I n 1846 the historian Henry Trumbull called Tecumseh (1775?–1813) "the most extraordinary Indian that has appeared in history." In 1961 the historian Alvin Josephy echoed Trumbull in denominating Tecumseh "the Greatest Indian." These high estimates are noteworthy in part because Tecumseh was unwaveringly hostile to the white Americans who relentlessly encroached on the lands of his people, the Shawnees, in areas of the Old Northwest Territory, present-day Ohio and Indiana. In the Treaty of Fort Wayne in 1809, the Shawnees—despite the opposition of Tecumseh and his charismatic brother, Tenkswatawa, known as the Prophet—ceded huge tracts of land to the United States. In response Tecumseh attempted to organize a multitribal resistance to the Americans. A turning point came in 1811, when William Henry Harrison (1773–1841), then governor of the Indiana Territory, decisively defeated the Prophet's forces at Tippecanoe (near present-day Lafayette). (In 1840, Harrison would be elected president of the United States, with James Tyler as his vice president, running on the slogan "Tippecanoe and Tyler too!") Tecumseh was not present at the battle. The defeat left the Prophet's followers disillusioned, and Tecumseh had no further success in bringing the tribes together in resistance. He fought on the side of the British in the War of 1812 and was killed at the Battle of the Thames, in southern Ontario.

The brief speech printed here derives from the captivity narrative of John Dunn Hunter, published in 1823. Hunter, born about 1802, was taken captive by Osage Indians when he was no more than two or three years old and lived among them until about 1816. He claimed to have heard Tecumseh speak to the Osages in 1811 or 1812. Although Tecumseh's visit to the Osages has not been substantiated, it is quite possible that he spoke to them and that the young and impressionable John Dunn Hunter was there. This bicultural composite was crafted by Hunter, who wrote that he was deeply moved by the words of "this untutored native of the forest . . . as no audience . . . either in ancient or modern times ever before witnessed."

Speech to the Osages[1]

When the Osages and distinguished strangers had assembled, Tecumseh arose; and after a pause of some minutes, in which he surveyed his audience in a very dignified, though respectfully complaisant and sympathizing manner, he commenced as follows:

Brothers—We all belong to one family; we are all children of the Great Spirit; we walk in the same path; slake our thirst at the same spring; and now affairs of the greatest concern lead us to smoke the pipe around the same council fire!

Brothers—We are friends; we must assist each other to bear our burdens. The blood of many of our fathers and brothers has run like water on the ground, to satisfy the avarice of the white men. We, ourselves, are threatened with a great evil; nothing will pacify them but the destruction of all the red men.

1. The text is from John Dunn Hunter, *Memoirs of a Captivity among the Indians of North America* (1823), edited by Richard Drinnon (1973).

Brothers—When the white men first set foot on our grounds, they were hungry; they had no place on which to spread their blankets, or to kindle their fires. They were feeble; they could do nothing for themselves. Our fathers commiserated their distress, and shared freely with them whatever the Great Spirit had given his red children. They gave them food when hungry, medicine when sick, spread skins for them to sleep on, and gave them grounds, that they might hunt and raise corn. Brothers, the white people are like poisonous serpents: when chilled, they are feeble and harmless; but invigorate them with warmth, and they sting their benefactors to death.

The white people came among us feeble; and now we have made them strong, they wish to kill us, or drive us back, as they would wolves and panthers.

Brothers—The white men are not friends to the Indians: at first, they only asked for land sufficient for a wigwam; now, nothing will satisfy them but the whole of our hunting grounds, from the rising to the setting sun.

Brothers—The white men want more than our hunting grounds; they wish to kill our warriors; they would even kill our old men, women, and little ones.

Brothers—Many winters ago, there was no land; the sun did not rise and set: all was darkness. The Great Spirit made all things. He gave the white people a home beyond the great waters. He supplied these grounds with game, and gave them to his red children; and he gave them strength and courage to defend them.

Brothers—My people wish for peace; the red men all wish for peace: but where the white people are, there is no peace for them, except it be on the bosom of our mother.[2]

Brothers—The white men despise and cheat the Indians; they abuse and insult them; they do not think the red men sufficiently good to live.

The red men have borne many and great injuries; they ought to suffer them no longer. My people will not; they are determined on vengeance; they have taken up the tomahawk; they will make it fat with blood; they will drink the blood of the white people.

Brothers—My people are brave and numerous; but the white people are too strong for them alone. I wish you to take up the tomahawk with them. If we all unite, we will cause the rivers to stain the great waters with their blood.

Brothers—If you do not unite with us, they will first destroy us, and then you will fall an easy prey to them. They have destroyed many nations of red men because they were not united, because they were not friends to each other.

Brothers—The white people send runners[3] amongst us; they wish to make us enemies, that they may sweep over and desolate our hunting grounds, like devastating winds, or rushing waters.

Brothers—Our Great Father, over the great waters, is angry with the white people, our enemies. He will send his brave warriors against them; he will send us rifles, and whatever else we want—he is our friend, and we are his children.

Brothers—Who are the white people that we should fear them? They cannot run fast, and are good marks to shoot at: they are only men; our

2. The earth.   3. Messengers.

fathers have killed many of them: we are not squaws, and we will stain the earth red with their blood.

Brothers—The Great Spirit is angry with our enemies; he speaks in thunder, and the earth swallows up villages, and drinks up the Mississippi. The great waters will cover their lowlands; their corn cannot grow; and the Great Spirit will sweep those who escape to the hills from the earth with his terrible breath.

Brothers—We must be united; we must smoke the same pipe; we must fight each other's battles; and more than all, we must love the Great Spirit: he is for us; he will destroy our enemies, and make all his red children happy.

American Literature
1820–1865

AN AMERICAN RENAISSANCE?

This volume of *The Norton Anthology of American Literature* presents works by Ralph Waldo Emerson, Edgar Allan Poe, Frederick Douglass, Nathaniel Hawthorne, Herman Melville, Walt Whitman, Emily Dickinson, Henry David Thoreau, Harriet Beecher Stowe, and their contemporaries—the writers generally regarded as central to our understanding of American literary traditions from the nineteenth century to the present day. The writers in this volume, particularly those who began publishing after 1830, are often celebrated as a group for having sparked a literary renaissance that helped American writing to achieve its first significant maturity. But the authors of this period were not always valued so highly by literary historians. In the early decades of the twentieth century, American literature was generally not taught in American universities, or else it was taught in subordinate relation to English literature, which was viewed as having an infinitely superior literary tradition. Among the important critical books that helped change this situation was F. O. Matthiessen's *American Renaissance: Art and Expression in the Age of Emerson and Whitman* (1941). Matthiessen gave American literature what had always been integral to the study of English literature: a Renaissance. England may have had Spenser, Shakespeare, and Donne, but America, Matthiessen proclaimed, had Emerson, Thoreau, Hawthorne, Melville, and Whitman. According to Matthiessen, the "Renaissance" was inspired by Emerson and came into its own in the 1850s with the writings of Hawthorne, Melville,

George Innes, **The Lackawanna Valley** (detail), 1855. For more information about this painting, see the color insert in this volume.

Thoreau, and Whitman. These and other key writers have an important place in this anthology, which owes a large debt to mid-twentieth-century formulations of the literary significance of the antebellum period.

Nevertheless, over the past several decades, the idea of an American Renaissance has come under considerable challenge. For instance, critics have noted that Matthiessen and others who helped to establish American literature as a field of study tended to exclude the significant contributions of women and minority writers, especially African Americans, and consequently closed off consideration of the wide range of writing developing in the United States during this time. Matthiessen and those who followed in his wake over the next several decades generally had little interest in popular authors of the period, such as the poets Lydia Sigourney and Henry Wadsworth Longfellow or the novelists Fanny Fern and Harriet Beecher Stowe, and little interest as well in publications outside of Massachusetts and New York. Recent critics have also faulted exponents of an American Renaissance for failing to attend to slavery, immigration, and other political and social contexts, all of which had a significant influence on the writing of the time, and for overemphasizing the separateness of English and American literary traditions, given that writers on both sides of the Atlantic were working in the same language and reading each other's works.

And yet, granting all of the shortcomings of the concept of an American Renaissance, one could say about the term what Benjamin Franklin in his *Autobiography* says about his efforts to subdue his pride: "Disguise it, struggle with it, beat it down, stifle it, mortify it as much as one pleases, it is still alive, and will every now and then peep out and show itself." For better or worse, the notion of an American Renaissance has continued to exert an enormous influence on the way that the literature of this period is understood, even though the idea of a literal renaissance (or rebirth) makes little sense in relation to a national literary tradition that was still in the process of coming into being.

The idea of an American Renaissance has been so influential in part because the literature of this period truly was crucial to the development of American literary traditions, at once building on writings that had preceded it and pointing to future possibilities. When this literature is viewed in much broader contexts and appreciated in its full complexity, its centrality to American literary history becomes even more evident. But the literature of the 1830s through the 1850s, which is the focus of Matthiessen's volume, cannot be disconnected from the decades immediately preceding it, a time when many U.S. cultural commentators were calling on Americans to produce literary texts worthy of a great nation. The American literary renaissance could be viewed retrospectively as a fulfillment of the repeated calls, from the 1770s on, for such an exemplary literature. Ironically, however, it was during the 1820s rather than the 1850s that critics of the time generally agreed that the United States *had* produced writers worthy of a great nation and agreed as well on the identity of its most important writers—namely, Washington Irving, William Cullen Bryant, James Fenimore Cooper, and Catharine Maria Sedgwick. No such consensus existed in the 1850s, as writers like Melville, Thoreau, Whitman, and even Hawthorne had relatively small readerships, while Dickinson (who kept most of her poems in manuscript) was basically unknown. The 1820s can be seen as the first great culmination of American literary nationalism, a decade that helped spawn the "Renaissance" to come.

AMERICAN LITERARY NATIONALISM AND THE 1820s

From the moment of the successful outcome of the American Revolution, literary nationalism had an important place in the emergent culture of the new nation. Convinced that a sign of a great nation was the existence of a great national literature, patriotic writers of the early republic attempted to produce "American" works as quickly as possible; such epic poems as Timothy Dwight's *The Conquest of Canaan* (1785) and Joel Barlow's *The Columbiad* (1807) can be seen as simultaneously bombastic and impressive achievements along these lines. From a different but still highly nationalistic perspective, Charles Brockden Brown proclaimed in the preface to his 1799 novel *Edgar Huntly* that he would make use of native materials—"incidents of Indian hostility, and the perils of the western wilderness"—to show how the United States offers "themes to the moral painter" that "differ essentially from those which exist in Europe." But even as writers of the early republic boldly sought to produce distinctively American works, there was a sense during the 1790s and early 1800s—a period haunted by the French Revolution's Reign of Terror and the subsequent Napoleonic Wars—that American nationality was provisional, vulnerable, fragile. The War of 1812, which emerged from ongoing conflicts with England, can therefore be seen as a war that, at least in part, spoke to Americans' desires to put an end to national anxiety by in effect reenacting the American Revolution against England and winning a victory once and for all. When English troops stormed the District of Columbia in 1814 and burned the Capitol and the White House, Americans' grim sense of vulnerability was underscored. But all that changed when Andrew Jackson's outnumbered troops defeated the English army at New Orleans in 1815, shortly after a peace treaty had officially ended the second major war between the two nations. From New Orleans there emerged a national mythology of the republican hero—the anti-aristocratic, antimonarchical

Gen. Andrew Jackson: The Hero of New Orleans. Lithograph. New York. N. Currier, c. 1835–56. Courtesy of the Library of Congress, Prints and Photographs Division.

person from an obscure background—who incarnated the strengths and virtues of the U.S. nation. The immediate beneficiary of that mythology, Andrew Jackson, would achieve further acclaim among his (white) contemporaries for fighting the Indians in the southeastern region that would become the state of Florida in 1845. When he was eventually elected president in 1828, he was regarded as the incarnation of the democratic spirit of the age, despite being a slaveholder committed to removing Indians from the nation. Jacksonian democratic ideals, with all of their conflicts and contradictions, would have an enormous impact on the writing emerging in the United States over the next several decades.

Well before 1828, however, the optimistic nationalism that found expression after the War of 1812 led to renewed efforts to develop a distinctively American literature worthy of a democratic republic that sought to take its place among the great nations of the world. Calls for a new American literature appeared regularly in the pages of the *North American Review*, an influential journal founded in Boston shortly after the war ended in 1815. In the journal's November 1815 issue, for instance, the critic Walter Channing urged his countrymen to produce "a literature of our own," even as he worried over the difficulties of developing such a literature in relation to English literary traditions. As the critic Edward Tyrell Channing remarked in an 1816 issue of the journal, a national literature "will have but feeble claims to excellence and distinction, when it stoops to put on foreign ornament and manner, and to adopt from other nations, images, allusions, and a metaphorical language, which are perfectly unmeaning and sickly out of their birth-place." Similarly, in his 1818 *An Essay on American Poetry*, the critic Solyman Brown asserted that Americans could not claim to have won the War of 1812 until that victory manifested itself in the production of a distinctively American literature: "The proudest freedom to which a nation can aspire, not excepting even political independence, is found in complete emancipation from literary thralldom." From the perspective of British literary nationalists, such emancipation would be slow in coming, given that, as they regularly maintained, American literature would always be overshadowed and subsumed by the long literary tradition of the parent country. Making just such an argument, the English critic Sydney Smith, in an oft-quoted attack on American literary nationalists, sarcastically demanded in an 1820 issue of the *Edinburgh Review*: "In the four quarters of the globe, who reads an American book?" As it turned out, Smith posed his question at an inopportune moment, for Americans could gloatingly respond that thousands of people in the United States and England were beginning to read American books. Not only were Charles Brockden Brown's novels of the 1790s achieving a new popularity in England but, right around the time of Smith's attack, the publication of Irving's *The Sketch Book* (1819–20), Bryant's *Poems* (1821), and Cooper's *The Spy* (1821) and *The Pioneers* (1823) suggested to many in the United States, England, and elsewhere that a worthy American literature *had* begun to take its place among the literatures of the more established nations.

It is worth underscoring, however, that during the 1820s Americans took pride in a literature that they regarded not necessarily as distinct from but rather in conversation with English literary traditions. Given the language that the countries shared, most American literary nationalists simply hoped that American writers could take their places alongside their British siblings or cousins. After all, literate Americans delighted in Spenser's *The Faerie Queen*, Shakespeare's plays, Milton's *Paradise Lost*, the essays of Joseph Addison and Richard Steele, and the poetry of Alexander Pope; and in the early decades of the nineteenth century they were reading the Romantic poets Wordsworth and Byron (among others) and, beginning in 1814 with the publication of *Waverley*, the historical novels of Walter Scott. Moreover, Irving's *The Sketch Book* had important sources in the essays of Addison and Steele; Bryant's poetry had important sources in Wordsworth; and Cooper's novels had important sources in Scott. Cooper objected to being termed the "American Scott," but the label would ultimately have been viewed as testimony to his novelistic mastery. For the most part, American writers of this time had a sophisticated understanding of their relationship to British and other literary traditions and would have regarded as nonsense the idea that they were expected to create a completely separate American literature.

They would also have regarded as nonsense the idea that American literature should be uncritically patriotic. One of the more notable features of the acclaimed 1820s writings of Irving, Bryant, and Cooper (along with the writings of their contemporaries such as Sedgwick, Sigourney, and Lydia Maria Child) was just how critical these writings could be of early national culture. Much of Irving's *The Sketch Book* is set in Europe, and though an often playfully ironic narrative voice of the American traveler holds the volume together, that persona is generally reverential toward the European historical past while casting a skeptical eye on a boastful U.S. nation that seems to have little interest in art and history. In his historical fictions of that decade, Cooper is similarly skeptical of U.S. claims to progress, presenting a demythified vision of the American Revolution in *The Spy*, and in *The Pioneers* depicting democratic energies as sometimes a threat to orderly government and the natural environment. In Cooper, as in Bryant, Sedgwick, and other writers of the period, visions of historical progress were tempered by the notion, widely disseminated during the Enlightenment and beyond, that all mighty nations must eventually fall. At a time when Indian removal was becoming national policy on the basis that, as many Americans believed, the day of the Indian was over, Cooper and Bryant suggested in works like *The Last of the Mohicans* (1826) and "The Prairies" (1834) that the U.S. nation was equally subject to the historical cycle of rise and decline. Taking a very different perspective, the Native American writer William Apess argued that Indian removal displayed the intolerance and racism of a nation destined to remain mired in conflict.

Adding to uncertainty about the future of the United States was the fact that the very shape, size, and demographic character of the nation were in flux. Jefferson's acquisition of the Louisiana Territory from France in 1803 doubled the size of the nation's total acreage, but its borders remained ill-defined, and the purchase soon raised difficult questions about how to balance the admission of free states and slave states in the expanding republic. The Missouri Compromise of 1820 appeared to resolve the political question by admitting Missouri as a slave state and Maine as a free state, and banning slavery in the northern reaches of the Louisiana Territory, but sectional conflict on slavery, states' rights, internal improvements, national tariffs, and other matters would continue to intensify in the wake of a compromise that was supposed to put an end to such conflicts. The assertion by South Carolina's legislature in 1832 of its right to "nullify" federal policies was one among many signs of the lack of national consensus during the two decades (1815–1835) that have been celebrated by some historians as the era of good feelings.

Still, in the wake of the War of 1812, there was a shared belief among a number of writers of the time that, as Brockden Brown had suggested back in the 1790s, the United States had the potential to develop a distinctive (though not separate) national literature. Authors such as Irving, Cooper, and Bryant placed a special emphasis on the importance of the natural landscape for the development of national character, finding in the relatively unspoiled vast lands of the continent a nurturing ground for the spiritual growth of a nation that, they sometimes suggested, could possibly emerge as "better" than any of those of long-settled Europe. These writers shared the vision of the popular Hudson River landscape painters of the antebellum period, New Yorkers like Thomas Cole and Asher Durand, who regularly portrayed individuals dwarfed by mountains and forests in a vast and unsettled nature where God's spirit could be apprehended. Cole may have identified republican decline as the ultimate historical reality (see his 1836 *The Course of Empire: Desolation* in the color insert to this volume), but most writers and artists of the period, including Cole, imagined that decline as hundreds, if not thousands, of years away. The American literary nationalism of the 1820s, like the American literary nationalism of the 1790s, explored difficult questions about the nation's future, about its strengths and vulnerabilities, and about its character and potential as a democratic republic. But the emergence of internationally acclaimed writers like Irving, Bryant, and Cooper also helped open up new literary opportunities for American writers, even as they would continue to have to compete with English writers for markets and prestige.

THE LITERARY MARKETPLACE IN AN EXPANDING NATION

By the second decade of the nineteenth century, Americans had easy access to contemporary British literature and criticism. Crossing the Atlantic on sailing ships and by the late 1830s on steamers, books or magazines first published in London could be distributed or republished almost immediately in the larger coastal cities—Boston, New York, Philadelphia, and Charleston. Volumes of poetry by the Scottish poet Robert Burns and by the English Romantics (Wordsworth, Coleridge, Byron, Shelley, Keats, and others), then Tennyson, and a little later Elizabeth Barrett Browning and Robert Browning were reprinted in the United States within months of their initial publication. Sir Walter Scott's historical novels were immensely popular in the United States (as a young man, Hawthorne dreamed of becoming an American Scott), and during the 1840s and 1850s crowds of Charles Dickens fans would congregate at the docks to greet steamships arriving in New York City with the latest installment of one of his serialized novels.

Geography and modes of transportation bore directly on publishing practices in the United States during this period. In 1800 there were few publishing firms; writers who wanted to publish a book generally took the handwritten manuscript to a local printer. They paid job rates to have it printed and made their own arrangements for distribution and sales, frequently having signed up committed purchasers beforehand in what was then called the "subscription" system. During the 1820s publishing centers began to develop in the major seaports, which could receive the latest British books by the fastest ships; these publishers shipped hastily reprinted copies inland by river traffic. The leading publishing towns were New York and Philadelphia; the Erie Canal, completed in 1825, gave New York an advantage in distributing books west to Ohio. Boston remained peripheral to the publishing industry until railroad connections to the West developed during the 1840s. Despite the aggressive merchandizing techniques of a few firms, a national market for American literature was slow to develop.

Besides the technical problems of book distribution across the nation's huge expanse, economic interests of American publishers and booksellers were sometimes (but not always) antithetical to the interests of American writers. A national copyright law became effective in the United States in 1790, but not until 1891 did U.S. writers get international copyright protection and foreign writers receive similar protection in the United States. For most of the century, American publishers routinely pirated English writers, paying nothing to Scott, Dickens, and other popular writers for works sold widely in inexpensive editions throughout the United States. American readers benefited from the situation, but the availability to publishers of texts that they did not have to purchase or pay royalties on made it perpetually difficult for U.S. writers to be paid for their work in their home country. As a result, there were relatively few professional authors in the United States before the Civil War. Bryant supported himself as a newspaper editor; Hawthorne received various political appointments over his lifetime; Emerson lived on a legacy from his first wife and on his well-compensated lectures; the financially struggling Melville spent the last several decades of his life working in the New York custom house; for most of his career, Longfellow taught languages at Harvard.

To survive economically, some American writers attempted to line up contracts with British publishers. But Irving's apparent conquest of the British publishing system, by which he received large sums for *The Sketch Book* and succeeding volumes, proved to be a short-term solution that worked mostly for Irving. Cooper and others followed in Irving's path for a time and were paid by magnanimous British publishers under a system whereby works first printed in Great Britain were presumed to hold a British copyright. But this practice was ruled illegal by a British judge in 1849, making it even harder for American writers to stake a claim to the British market, though Melville and other writers continued to make the effort and occasionally met with success. Some of the American authors who did best in England were antislavery writers, for the English apparently could not get enough of works that held their former colony up to shame. Frederick Douglass and William Wells Brown found a significant audience in Great Britain (the first African American novel, Wells Brown's *Clotel* [1853], was published *only* in England), and there were few writers more admired and widely read in England than Harriet Beecher Stowe.

Nevertheless, authorship and publishing were far from moribund in the antebellum United States, and Hawthorne, for one, came to envy the sales figures of such popular women writers as Susan Warner, Maria Susanna Cummins, and Fanny Fern. (Cummins's 1854 novel *The Lamplighter*, for instance, sold over one hundred thousand copies.) The period from 1820 to 1865 saw a dizzying growth in the nation's population and territorial reach; dramatic technological developments that would allow publishers to bring out works in ever-greater numbers at ever-greater profits; increasing urbanization (which helped enlarge readership in key profitable markets); and the expansion of railroads, canals, and other forms of transportation that would allow for more extensive and economical forms of distribution. The nation's population of approximately four million in 1790 jumped to thirty million by 1860, in part because of the massive emigration from Ireland and elsewhere in Europe that occurred during the 1840s and 1850s. Territorial space available to this burgeoning population dramatically increased following the war with Mexico (1846–48), which, as a result of the 1848 Treaty of Guadalupe Hidalgo, added 1.2 million square miles of land to the 1.8 million square miles that the nation held before the war; this is the area that would become Texas, California, Arizona, Nevada, and Utah, and parts of New Mexico, Colorado, and Wyoming. Beginning in the 1820s and continuing through the nineteenth century, there were ongoing efforts to connect and extend U.S. territory through the development of roads, canals, and railroads. Travel literature to the West (or what we now call the Midwest), such as Caroline Kirkland's *A New Home—Who'll Follow?* (1839) and Margaret Fuller's *Summer on the Lakes* (1843), became an increasingly popular genre. Richard Henry Dana in *Two Years before the Mast* (1840) and Francis Parkman in *The Oregon Trail* (1849) would write popular accounts of their respective travels to the Pacific Northwest. Dana's and Parkman's writings especially resonated with readers during the 1850s, the heyday of California immigration following the discovery of gold in California in the late 1840s.

There was also an increasing interest in urban writings, in large part because of the tremendous rise in the populations of Boston, Philadelphia, and New York brought about mostly by Irish immigration but also by an influx of native-born rural people to the cities from the farms, which suffered massive failures during the economic depression of the 1850s. Taken together, the growth of U.S. cities and the ongoing expansion of the nation's territorial reach contributed to one of the most significant developments of the time for those writers aspiring to professional authorship: the dramatic growth of newspaper and magazine publishing from the early years of the nineteenth century to the 1860s. Between 1800 and 1825, approximately four hundred newspapers were founded, and that number went into the thousands by 1860. Before 1825 there were approximately a hundred magazines published in the United States; by 1850 there were about six hundred. More than the typical U.S. book publisher, the proliferating newspapers and magazines provided writers with forums for their poetry and fiction, along with personal essays, travel writing, political reportage, and other writings suitable for daily, weekly, and monthly presses. Poe, Sigourney, Fuller, Hawthorne, Fern, and many other writers worked on their craft and developed their reputations with the help of their periodical publications.

Among the most popular magazines of the time were the mass-market *Graham's* and *Godey's Lady's Book*, both published in Philadelphia. Poe published stories and sketches in these journals, as did many women writers.

The *Lady's Book*, in fact, though published by Louis A. Godey, was edited for some forty years by the novelist and essayist Sarah J. Hale, whose editorial role in one of the major journals of the day points to the key place of women in the antebellum literary marketplace. Despite traditional notions that imaginative literature and creative writing could be harmful to women by overstimulating their imaginations and undermining their status as domestic beings, women found ways to enter the literary marketplace. Much writing by women of the antebellum period addressed domesticity head-on, sometimes, as with Fuller, criticizing the idea of separate cultural spheres for men and women; but more often, as with Stowe, showing how women could have an impact on the culture from within the home. But even with her emphasis on the cultural power of domesticity, Stowe, like Fuller, fully embraced the public sphere of authorship. Just about all of the women writers represented in this anthology made an important mark on the periodical culture of the time, and some used their connections to magazines and newspapers to develop as professional authors who were able to live on earnings from their writings. Child, Fuller, Fern, and Rebecca Harding Davis all had newspaper columns, and Fern was paid lavishly for hers; Child and Fuller served as editors of journals. Stowe got her start as an antislavery reformer writing sketches and short stories for regional newspapers.

"A Reading Party." Plate from *Godey's Lady's Book*, 1846.

"RENAISSANCE," REFORM, CONFLICT

Various reform movements, such as antislavery, temperance, women's rights, and even nativist anti-Catholicism (an extreme manifestation of Protestant evangelical reform), contributed to the proliferation of print during the antebellum period. As a theme and focus of cultural debate, reform emerged as a crucial constituent of the antebellum writings traditionally associated with the American Renaissance. Recognizing the centrality of reform to his cultural moment, Emerson declared in "Man the Reformer" (1841) that "the doctrine of Reform had never such scope as at the present hour." Though he emphasized self-culture and personal reform over public initiatives, by the 1840s Emerson had begun to link himself to activist reform movements. In "Emancipation in the West Indies" (1844), for example, he called on the "great masses of men" to take a larger role in opposing slavery, and he would remain firmly committed to antislavery reform up to the time of the Civil War. He also offered occasional remarks on the value of temperance (one of the most popular reform movements of the antebellum period); and in 1855 he addressed a women's rights convention in support of women's suffrage, which he would continue to endorse.

Emersonian reform also had literary implications. Rejecting the literary nationalism of the 1820s as imitative and timid, Emerson in "The American Scholar" (1837) called on those Americans with a "love of letters" to "lead in a new age" of men "inspired by the Divine Soul which also inspires all men." Trained as a Unitarian minister, Emerson had broken with the church by the time he began to publish his lectures and essays, having absorbed some of the major ideas of the European Romantics on the creative powers of the individual mind, the regenerative value of nature, the limits of historical associations and traditions, and the stultifying effects of established institutions. Ironically, in "The American Scholar" and his other writings of the time, Emerson drew on major philosophical and aesthetic ideas circulating in Europe to write as a literary reformer exhorting Americans to break their dependency on the "courtly muses of Europe."

Emerson's attacks on the Unitarian and other established churches for what he described as their refusal to honor the possibility of the miraculous in the here and now, and his affirmations of the near god-like powers of the creative imagination, helped popularize what literary historians have termed the Transcendentalist movement. In various ways, Emersonian Transcendentalism (which was never really a formalized movement) helped to inspire the writings of Fuller, Thoreau, Whitman, and many other writers. Even authors like Poe, Hawthorne, Melville, and Dickinson, who were skeptical of Emersonian optimism, arguably exhibited the influence of Emerson, who himself could be skeptical of Transcendentalism (for the dark side of the ecstasies of *Nature*, see his "Experience" [1844], which presents the individual as forever skating on surfaces). In the wake of Emerson's influential essays of the 1830s and 1840s, much writing of the antebellum period grappled with questions about the value of history, the ability of the individual to apprehend the godhead directly, the capacity of language to achieve and convey knowledge, and the difficulties of making sense of a universe in which meaning derives from individual creative insights rather than received authority. The fictional worlds of *The Scarlet Letter* and *Moby-Dick*, works that are obsessed with the problematics of interpretation, whether of the letter *A* or a whale, have a profoundly different feel from the more consensual, commonsensical fictional worlds of Irving, Sedgwick, and Cooper.

Antebellum writing taken as a whole is much too varied and conflicted to be viewed simply through the lens of Emerson's New England–based transcendental reformism. For instance, there was much excitement during the early national and antebellum periods, including among Emerson and his circle, about the ameliorative potential of science and technology as it was developing in transatlantic and global contexts. There were also competing notions about what actually constituted reform or "improvement." Proslavery, not just antislavery, could be regarded in a reform context; many Southerners, for instance, looked back to the founding of the nation and believed that the Constitution favored states' rights over what they regarded as the encroaching authoritarianism of the federal government, as Nathaniel Beverley Tucker made clear in his 1836 novel *The Partisan Leader: A Tale of the Future*. Reformism, particularly in the context of an expanding nation with its multiple constituencies and agendas, could be as much a source of conflict as of consensus.

Antebellum reform movements based in the North were often directed by Protestant-based organizations concerned with maintaining their cultural authority during a time of increasing class and ethnic diversity. Protestant evangelical reform could be taken to unattractive extremes in the period's pervasive anti-Catholic nativism. But concerns about the poor and working-class immigrants also had an important place in antebellum urban reform movements, as writers sought to expose readers to the plight of the impoverished in order to prompt philanthropic interventions. The fact that women had such a significant place in urban reform movements is not surprising, given that another major reform effort of the antebellum period centered on women's rights. In "The Great Lawsuit" (1843), excerpted in this volume, Margaret Fuller drew on the Declaration of Independence and Emersonian transcendental reform, among other sources, to make the case that women should have greater opportunities for education and participation in the public sphere, including the right to "represent themselves"—that is, to vote. In 1848, at the first women's rights convention in Seneca Falls, New York, Elizabeth Cady Stanton's "Declaration of Sentiments" invoked Jefferson's Declaration, substituting male for British tyrannical authority to show how the nation's social institutions and legal codes mainly served the interests of America's white male citizenry. That same year, the New York State Legislature, in response to critics like Stanton, passed the nation's most liberalized married women's property act, which made it legal for women to maintain control over the property they brought to their marriages. In most states, however, married women remained without legal rights to property for decades to come.

For good reason, many women writers of the period addressed questions of power: how to use power from within the domestic sphere, how to gain power in the public sphere, how to fend off unchecked patriarchal power.

DECLARATION OF SENTIMENTS

When, in the course of human events, it becomes necessary for one portion of the family of man to assume among the people of the earth a position different from that which they have hitherto occupied, but one to which the laws of nature and of nature's God entitle them, a decent respect to the opinions of mankind requires that they should declare the causes that impel them to such a course.

We hold these truths to be self-evident; that all men and women are created equal; that they are endowed by their Creator with certain inalienable rights; that among these are life, liberty, and the pursuit of happiness; that to secure these rights governments are instituted, deriving their just powers from the consent of the governed. Whenever any form of Government becomes destructive of these ends, it is the right of those who suffer from it to refuse allegiance to it, and to insist upon the institution of a new government, laying its foundation on such principles, and organizing its powers in such form as to them shall seem most likely to effect their safety and happiness. Prudence, indeed, will dictate that governments long established should not be changed for light and transient causes; and accordingly, all experience hath shown that mankind are more disposed to suffer, while evils are sufferable, than to right themselves, by abolishing the forms to which they are accustomed. But when a long train of abuses and usurpations, pursuing invariably the same object, evinces a design to reduce them under absolute despotism, it is their duty to throw off such government, and to provide new guards for their future security. Such has been the patient sufferance of the women under this government, and such is now the necessity which constrains them to demand the equal station to which they are entitled.

From the opening of the "**Declaration of Sentiments**,"
by Elizabeth Cady Stanton, in *Report of the Woman's Rights Convention Held at Seneca Falls, N.Y., July 19th and 20th, 1848.*

The danger posed by patriarchal power was a central theme of both antislavery and temperance reform. Sigourney and Stowe were two of the most prominent antislavery writers who supported the temperance movement, as they saw drinking as an activity that lured men away from their homes and into the saloons, transforming them into drunken hooligans. Inspired by the popular temperance writings of Timothy Shay Arthur, women authors regularly depicted drunken husbands or fathers as men who became driven by their animal passions, to the point where these "slaves to the bottle" became slaves to their own bodies. Such imagery and cultural concerns informed Child's antislavery story "The Quadroons" (1842), Stowe's antislavery novels *Uncle Tom's Cabin* (1852) and *Dred* (1856), and many other popular fictions by women and men alike, including Poe's "The Black Cat" (1843). Walt Whitman, who began his career by writing a temperance novel, *Franklin Evans; or The Inebriate* (1842), emphasized in *Song of Myself* the virtues of a natural intoxication in the pleasures of body and nature.

A number of writers of the antebellum period, including Whitman, took as one of their main subjects the anguishing paradox that the nation that boastfully presented itself as the bastion of freedom and equality was implicated in ongoing national crimes: the near-genocide of the American Indians, the enslavement of black people, and an expansionism that ignored other national sovereignties. Because the war with Mexico of 1846–1848 was understood by many Americans as consistent with the nation's "manifest destiny" to expand across the continent, only a small minority of American writers voiced more than perfunctory opposition; the best known of these dissenters was Thoreau, who spent a night in the Concord, Massachusetts, jail in symbolic protest against being taxed to support a war that he believed was mainly intended to enlarge the domain of slavery. The Native American writer John Rollin Ridge decried whites' racism against Native Americans and Mexican Americans in 1850s California, which achieved statehood in 1850 as a direct result of the war with Mexico. In his sensationalist novel *The Life and Adventures of Joaquín Murieta* (1854), Ridge portrayed a Mexican-American killer intent on taking bloody revenge against such racists. Emerson and Child had earlier dissented about the nation's treatment of Native Americans during the 1830s, when most writers were silent about the federal government's forced removal of southeastern Indian tribes from their homelands to territory west of the Mississippi River, as permitted by the Indian Removal Act of 1830. American destiny plainly required a little practical callousness, most whites felt, or if not callousness, then the worst kind of sympathy: a lament for "vanishing" Indians who were being killed off all the more quickly or at least without remorse because of such sentimental acquiescence. Native American spokespersons and authors like Black Hawk and William Apess questioned whites' constant interventions into Indian affairs; they were particularly critical of whites' deceptive treaties and land-grabbing policies. (For more on Native American dissent, see the section in this anthology titled "Native Americans: Removal and Resistance.") Of the major antebellum writers who were not Native American, only Child kept a critical eye over the decades on the white power, as opposed to the presumed providential inevitability, that was relentlessly working to shrink Indian lands and confuse extinction with extermination.

The vast majority of white Americans of the time accepted what they thought of as the destined "extinction" of the Native Americans. There was much more conflict over the practice of slavery, which Melville called "man's foulest crime." The antislavery campaign became increasingly influential in the Northeast, and, unsurprisingly, resistance to slavery and critiques of whites' antiblack racism were among the principal topics of antebellum African American writing. Describing his own former enslavement, the lecturer and author Frederick Douglass displayed a powerful capacity to stir his auditors and readers, in large part through his ability to make whites sympathize with the situation of blacks. The reformist potential of sympathy is one of the crucial themes of his novella, "The Heroic Slave" (1853), and of Frances Harper's antislavery poetry. Harper and Douglass were both inspired by Stowe's *Uncle Tom's Cabin* (1852), the best-selling novel of the antebellum period. Twentieth-century attacks on this novel for its supposed bad faith would have made little sense to Harper and Douglass. William Wells Brown may have been more skeptical of Stowe, as his ironically conceived novel *Clotel* suggests, but even he praised Stowe in the pages of William Lloyd Garrison's antislavery newspaper, the *Liberator*.

A politics of antislavery had an important place in the careers of a number of the writers represented in this anthology, ranging from Sigourney to Longfellow, Child to Stowe, Emerson to Melville. (See also the section on "Slavery, Race, and the Making of American Literature.") When the Fugitive Slave Act of 1850 was enforced in Boston in 1851 (by Melville's father-in-law, Chief Justice Lemuel Shaw), Thoreau in his journals expressed his outrage that Massachusetts citizens were being compelled to return escaping slaves to their Southern masters; after another famous case in 1854, he wrote his most scathing speech, "Slavery in Massachusetts," for delivery at a Fourth of July counterceremony at which a copy of the Constitution was burned. In that speech he summed up the disillusionment that many of his generation shared, presenting Massachusetts as a type of hell. More obliquely than Thoreau, Melville explored slavery in "Benito Cereno" (1855) as an index to the white supremacism that he regarded as a stain on the national character. At his bitterest, he felt in the mid-1850s that "free Ameriky" was "intrepid, unprincipled, reckless, predatory, with boundless ambition, civilized in externals but a savage at heart." In response to antislavery criticism, Southerners passionately defended the institution of slavery in such works as George Fitzhugh's *Sociology for the South* (1854) and Caroline Lee Hentz's *The Planter's Northern Bride* (1854), one of several anti–*Uncle Tom's Cabin* novels published during the 1850s.

John Brown's violent raid on Harpers Ferry in 1859, a failed effort to initiate a slave rebellion in the South, drew eloquent defenses from Emerson, Thoreau, Douglass, Stowe, and Child, though most in the North and across the country condemned Brown as a radical who threatened to bring the nation into a bloody civil war. With the outbreak of the Civil War, Douglass, Wells Brown, Child, Stowe, and other major writers of the period sought to present the war as, in the spirit of John Brown, a holy war against slavery that might redeem the millennial promise of the nation, which is to say, as the fulfillment of the promise of reform going back to Emerson and, as Lincoln himself suggested in his "Address Delivered at the Dedication of the Cemetery at Gettysburg" (1863), to the principles of the Declaration of Independence itself. The idea of the United States as an exceptional nation because it had been set aside for an exceptional destiny proved almost impossible to overcome, even in moments when the country marched into bloody internal conflict. When the war began on April 12, 1861, with Confederate guns opening fire on Fort Sumter, in South Carolina's Charleston Harbor, few understood what lay ahead; Northerners and Southerners alike expected the war to last only a few months. Visiting Boston and Concord in 1862, fresh from the newly formed West Virginia (the portion of the slave state Virginia that had chosen to stay with the Union), Rebecca Harding Davis saw that Emerson had little notion of the suffering involved in the war. Shortly before he died, Hawthorne, who had remained committed to the Democrats' vision of Union even at the price of retaining slavery for the foreseeable future, published a jaded account of the war, "Chiefly about War Matters," in the *Atlantic Monthly* of July 1862. While mocking Lincoln as a leader, the essay raised pointed questions about Americans' failure to anticipate that a war of this nature would bring unimagined bloodshed, eventually killing over six hundred thousand Americans before Robert E. Lee's surrender to Ulysses S. Grant at Appomattox, Virginia, on April 9, 1865.

Among the most notable literary responses to the Civil War from writers who had published during the antebellum period were two poetry collections: Whitman's *Drum-Taps* (1865) and Melville's *Battle-Pieces* (1866). (More privately at home, Dickinson was spurred to tragic lyricism by the deaths of young Amherst students she had known.) After a small run of his *Drum-Taps* had been sold, Whitman held back the edition for a sequel mainly consisting of newly written poems on the just-assassinated Lincoln, among them his great elegy "When Lilacs Last in the Dooryard Bloom'd." Both Whitman and Melville looked ahead as well as backward, Whitman calling "reconciliation" the "word over all," and Melville urging in his "Supplement" to *Battle-Pieces* that the victorious North "be Christians toward our fellow-whites, as well as philanthropic toward the blacks, our fellow-men." But Melville's emphasis on Northern whites' responsibility to show charity and "kindliness" toward Southern whites, who he remarked "stand nearer to us in nature," was problematic, for it pointed to the racism that contributed to the nation's larger failure to follow through on the reformist potential of the Civil War. By the time she died, Child was lamenting Reconstruction's failure to educate and offer economic uplift to the former slaves. In *Democratic Vistas* (1870), Whitman railed against the political corruption and materialism on display in the immediate wake of the Civil War. Though he worked for several

"Burial Trench at Gettysburg." Photograph by Timothy H. O'Sullivan (1840–1882).

Republican administrations, Douglass became disillusioned by the resurgence of segregationist practices and antiblack violence, most notably lynching, after the end of Reconstruction in 1877. A year before his death, in one of his greatest speeches, "The Lessons of the Hour" (1894), he called on the nation, as he had in "What to the Slave Is the Fourth of July?" (1852), to live up to its founding ideals of "human brotherhood and the self-evident truths of liberty and equality," proclaiming that if Americans were only willing to do that, "your problem will be solved" and "your Republic will stand and flourish forever." With his insistence on the unbounded potential of every individual and his critique of the racist and materialistic nation of the 1890s, Douglass rearticulated some of the same arguments that he had made in 1845 and that Emerson had made in the 1830s and 1840s. Viewed from this reformist perspective, the cultural work of what many continue to call the "American Renaissance" would remain in process.

THE SMALL AND LARGE WORLD OF AMERICAN WRITERS, 1820–1865

An anthology organized mainly by a national literature, a specific time period, and an array of major authors presented in the chronological order of their birthdates might seem artificially closed off from literature of other eras and nations. But close attention to nation and chronology is not meant to cut off conversations among the writers included here and those of other periods and nations. On the contrary, such attention can provide a foundation for developing complex conversations in different and broader contexts. Nevertheless, it is important to underscore that the era has a real existence of its own in literary terms: the authors in this anthology often *were* in conversation with one another; their world was relatively small and the number of instances of direct and indirect influences, counterinfluences, productive friendships, productive rejections of influences and friendships, and so on, are stunning. Sedgwick read Cooper's *The Last of the Mohicans* and wrote a "response" in *Hope Leslie*, emphasizing domestic and interracial possibilities in ways she thought Cooper did not. Whitman and Bryant were on friendly terms in New York City, even as Whitman was turning against the studied meditative verse of his compatriot; Child and John Greenleaf Whittier were long-time friends in the antislavery cause. Emerson was friends with Fuller and Thoreau, both of whom were influenced by his writings, and though he did not meet Whitman until after the publication of the first edition of *Leaves of Grass* (1855), Emerson's theorizing on poetry in "The Poet," which implicitly attacked Poe's ideas on poetry, had a pronounced influence not only on Whitman but also on Dickinson and many other American poets. While in Massachusetts during the early 1840s, Douglass imbibed the spirit of Emersonian self-reliance, and his *Narrative* presented his own variations on Emerson's notion of the divinity of self. Douglass inspired Stowe, who, while working on *Uncle Tom's Cabin*, wrote Douglass asking for more precise descriptions of a slave plantation and, after the publication of *Uncle Tom's Cabin*, met with him at her home in Andover and took pleasure in the fact that Douglass was one of her greatest champions. As much as Douglass admired *Uncle Tom's Cabin*, however, he pointed to problems with Stowe's conception of race in his novella of slave rebellion, "The Heroic Slave," which may have had an influence on Melville's novella of slave rebellion, "Benito Cereno." There is evidence that Douglass influenced Melville's conception of black music and dance in *Moby-Dick*; and it is worth noting that Douglass printed an excerpt from Melville's first novel, *Typee* (1846), in his newspaper the *North Star*.

Melville engaged the work of his American contemporaries, championing Cooper and Francis Parkman in the late 1840s, writing several sketches in the mode of Irving, parodying Sedgwick, and responding both positively and negatively to Emerson. He called Emerson a "deep diver" and yet at times found him naively optimistic; in *Moby-Dick* he posits the specter of an indifferent and even hostile nature in which it would be next to impossible, even suicidal, for an individual to become what Emerson termed a "transparent eyeball." Melville dedicated *Moby-Dick* to Hawthorne, whom he met at a picnic in 1850 and idolized at the time, writing an essay on American literary nationalism in his honor, "Hawthorne and His Mosses" (1850); Hawthorne and Melville mutually influenced one another during the early 1850s. At around the same time, the African American writer William Wells Brown was reading the short stories of Lydia Maria Child and almost word for word used one of those stories, "The Quadroons," to establish the plot of his novel *Clotel*. Frances Harper knew Wells Brown and his work and also took inspiration from such popular poets as Sigourney, Longfellow, and Whittier, who wrote powerful antislavery poems. Poe, who admired Sigourney, knew and attacked many of the celebrated writers of the day, such as Longfellow and Hawthorne, even as his poetry inspired some of Whitman's poetry, most notably "Out of the Cradle Endlessly Rocking" (1859), and his short stories influenced Hawthorne, whose fiction, much as Poe would have wanted to deny it, influenced his own: there are close connections between Hawthorne's "Young Goodman Brown" (1835), Poe's "The Fall of the House of Usher" (1839), and Hawthorne's *The House of the Seven Gables* (1851). Stowe thought highly of Hawthorne; and Harriet Jacobs, who may have known of Hawthorne's work, esteemed *Uncle Tom's Cabin* and wrote directly to Stowe asking for help in editing her autobiographical *Incidents in the Life of a Slave Girl* (1861). When Stowe refused, Jacobs got the editorial support of Child, whose fiction earlier had had an impact on Wells Brown. After escaping from slavery, Jacobs lived in New York City in the household of the brother of the best-selling writer Fanny Fern, Nathaniel Parker Willis, whom Fern satirized as "Hyacinth" in her most popular novel, *Ruth Hall* (1855). Fern admired Whitman, Irving, and Hawthorne; and Hawthorne praised Fern in a letter to his editor and friend William Ticknor. Hawthorne also praised Rebecca Harding Davis, who claimed Hawthorne as one of her most important influences. After reading Davis's "Life in the Iron-Mills" (1861), Hawthorne considered traveling to Wheeling, Virginia, to meet her, but was happy when she chose to visit him at his home in Concord, Massachusetts. Louisa May Alcott borrowed books from Emerson, got nature lessons from Thoreau, and read (and was influenced by) the fiction of her neighbor Hawthorne. Dickinson, whose family subscribed to numerous newspapers and magazines, and who ordered books by mail from Boston, read just about all of these authors and wrote a "private" poetry that was often in conversation with the work of her contemporaries.

Most of the writers represented in this anthology also ranged beyond the borders of the United States. Washington Irving was in England when *The Sketch Book* was published, and he remained abroad for over a decade, serving as a U.S. diplomat in Spain; at the height of his early career, Cooper traveled to France in 1826 and remained in Europe for the next seven years. Two decades later, Margaret Fuller traveled to Italy and participated in the Roman Revolution of the late 1840s; and in the early 1850s Hawthorne became U.S. consul in Liverpool and remained in Europe for nearly eight years. Travel abroad was central to Poe's, Emerson's, and Longfellow's educations; Stowe made a grand tour of Europe during the 1850s; and Douglass, Jacobs, and many other African Americans spent significant time in England. Melville toured England and later the Holy Land. All of these writers had friends abroad, regarded the literature of the United States as part of a larger world literature, and, accordingly, read widely, particularly in English and other European literatures.

Numerous U.S. authors of this period also had significant interests in the literatures of the southern Americas. Because of his fascination with Christopher Columbus, which culminated in his best-selling biography of 1828 and several other works about Spanish America, Irving was perhaps the most celebrated U.S. author to read widely in writings south of the national borders, but authors ranging from Hawthorne to Dickinson exhibited a curiosity about the Caribbean and Central and South America. Douglass's "The Heroic Slave" and Melville's "Benito Cereno" are compelling examples of works that look beyond the southern borders of the United States. Whitman also had a capacious hemispheric perspective on the Americas, and in the twentieth century he would find some of his most enthusiastic readers in Chile, Argentina, and Mexico.

As far as literary matters are concerned, all of the writers in this anthology were interested in much more than the contemporary. A glance at the footnotes in this volume will reveal the enormous influence of classics from ancient Greece and Rome, Greek and Roman myth, Indian and Asian religions (which is especially true for Thoreau), the English Renaissance (especially Shakespeare), Milton, English and German Romantics, the Bible, and a range of popular and classic literature from Scandinavian and numerous other countries. And yet even as many of these writers had an imaginative vision that took them beyond national borders and the limits of any period chronology, they were aware that they resided in a relatively new nation lacking literary traditions, and that there was a burden on them to establish such traditions. Melville's essay "Hawthorne and His Mosses" is among the period's notable examples of such literary nationalist ambition, which was neither insular nor separatist. As Melville remarks when comparing Hawthorne to Shakespeare: "Now I do not say that Nathaniel of Salem is greater than William of Avon, or as great. But the difference between the two men is by no means immeasurable." Melville, who resented British condescension toward American writers, aspired for parity between English and American literary traditions rather than a separation of American from English literature. With his emphasis on the democratic individual, Whitman was capable of a more hyperbolic American literary nationalism than any of the other writers in this volume, so it is ironic that the great majority of his most enthusiastic late nineteenth-century readers lived in England.

In addition to making claims for an American literary nationalism, the writers in this anthology sought to *create* American literary traditions. They did so by looking back to earlier colonial literatures and claiming them as "American." Many of the colonial texts that we now read as canonical, such as works by John Winthrop and William Bradford, were first republished in the nineteenth century and owe some of their current status to their recovery by early national and antebellum writers. Linking their nineteenth-century writings to the colonial past, Cooper, Hawthorne, Whittier, and many others created a sense of a continuously unfolding national history and literature that came to a fruition of sorts in the nineteenth century.

Crucial to the 1820–65 period of American literary history, then, was a pronounced sense among a number of its authors about their role not just in consolidating traditions but also in creating new traditions that would develop from their writings. Such an orientation is most pronounced in Whitman, whose poetry regularly imagines future readers and writers, but it is arguably a central impulse behind much of the literature of the period. In this respect, it should be kept in mind that a number of the writers represented in this anthology were somewhat neglected when they first began publishing, and that their greatest impact was not on the writing of their own time but on writing to come. In important ways, the 1820–65 period represents a dynamic moment in American literary history that is anything but hermetic. Irving and Bryant began their careers before 1820, and Melville, Douglass, Harper, Whitman, Alcott, Davis, Dickinson, Wells Brown, and other "antebellum" writers continued to thrive in the years following the Civil War (some of Melville's and Whitman's major late writings are included in this volume). Like Whitman, authors such as Thoreau, Melville, and Dickinson found their most enthusiastic readers in the twentieth century, and it is the twentieth-century response to these major authors that helped to shape our understanding of the period. Melville and Dickinson, for instance, weren't really "discovered" until the 1920s and 1930s, when they had an immediate impact on writers living then. Even those who were fairly well known during the nineteenth century—Poe, Hawthorne, Douglass, and others—came to be much better known in the twentieth century (Douglass's 1845 *Narrative*, for instance, was not republished after the early 1850s until 1960) and in some ways exerted an influence on twentieth-century literature and culture more significant than what they exerted on their nineteenth-century contemporaries. The point that should be emphasized at the close of this introduction is that the diverse writings published circa 1820–65 continue to remain foundational to the study of American literature not only because of what they accomplished within their own moment but also because, as Whitman says about himself, they ultimately cannot be contained within that moment and even within a national frame. The literature of this period encompasses multitudes and continues to write its (and our) literary futures.

AMERICAN LITERATURE 1820–1865

TEXTS	CONTEXTS
1815 Founding of the *North American Review*	**1815** Treaty of Ghent, ending the second war with England; before news of the treaty reaches Andrew Jackson, he leads American troops to victory over the British at the Battle of New Orleans
1817 William Cullen Bryant, "Thanatopsis"	
1820 Washington Irving, *The Sketch Book*	**1820** Missouri Compromise admits Missouri as a slave state, Maine as a free state, and excludes slavery in the Louisiana Territory north of latitude 36° 30'
1821 Bryant, *Poems*	**1821** Sequoyah (George Guess) invents syllabary in which Cherokee language can be written
1823 James Fenimore Cooper, *The Pioneers*	**1823** Monroe Doctrine warns all European powers not to establish new colonies on either American continent
	1825 Erie Canal opens, connecting Great Lakes region with the Atlantic
1826 Cooper, **The Last of the Mohicans**	
1827 David Cusick, *Sketches of Ancient History of the Six Nations* • Lydia Sigourney, *Poems* • Catharine Sedgwick, *Hope Leslie*	**1827** Baltimore & Ohio, first U.S. railroad • the African American newspaper *Freedom's Journal* is founded
	1827–28 Cherokee Nation ratifies its new constitution • the newspaper *The Cherokee Phoenix* founded
1828–30 Cherokee Council composes **Memorials** to Congress	
1829 William Apess, *A Son of the Forest* • David Walker, **Appeal**	**1829–37** President Andrew Jackson encourages westward migration of white population
	1830 Congress passes Indian Removal Act, allowing Jackson to negotiate treaties with the eastern tribes for their relocation west of the Mississippi
1831 Edgar Allan Poe, **Poems**	**1831** William Lloyd Garrison starts *The Liberator*, antislavery journal • Nat Turner leads a slave rebellion in Southampton County, Virginia; approximately sixty whites are killed and two hundred blacks are killed in retaliation
1833 Black Hawk, **Life**	
1835 William Gilmore Simms, *The Yemassee: A Romance of Carolina*	
1836 Ralph Waldo Emerson, **Nature**	
1837 Nathaniel Hawthorne, *Twice-Told Tales*	**1837** Financial panic: failures of numerous banks lead to severe unemployment that persists into the early 1840s

Boldface titles indicate works in the anthology.

TEXTS	CONTEXTS
	1838 Around this time, Underground Railroad begins aiding slaves escaping north, often to Canada
	1838–39 "Trail of Tears": Cherokees forced from their homelands by federal troops
1839 Caroline Stansbury Kirkland, *A New Home—Who'll Follow?*	
1840 Richard Henry Dana Jr., *Two Years before the Mast*	**1840** Founding of the Washingtonian Temperance Society; temperance quickly emerges as one of the most popular social reform movements of the period
1843 Margaret Fuller, **"The Great Lawsuit"** • Lydia Maria Child, *Letters from New-York*	
	1844 Samuel Morse invents telegraph
1845 Edgar Allan Poe, **"The Raven"** • Frederick Douglass, ***Narrative of the Life of Frederick Douglass***	**1845** United States annexes Texas
	1846 David Wilmot, a congressman from Pennsylvania, proposes in Congress that slavery be banned in territories gained from the Mexican War; his proviso is defeated
	1846–48 United States wages war against Mexico; Treaty of Guadalupe Hidalgo cedes entire Southwest to United States
1847 Henry Wadsworth Longfellow, *Evangeline*	**1847** Brigham Young leads Mormons from Nauvoo, Illinois, to Salt Lake, Utah Territory
	1848 Seneca Falls Convention inaugurates campaign for women's rights
	1848–49 Beginning years of the California Gold Rush, which brings hundreds of thousands of new settlers to California
1850 Nathaniel Hawthorne, *The Scarlet Letter*	**1850** Fugitive Slave Act of the Compromise of 1850 obliges free states to return escaped slaves to slaveholders • California becomes the 31st state
1851 Herman Melville, *Moby-Dick*	
1852 Harriet Beecher Stowe, ***Uncle Tom's Cabin***	
1853 William Wells Brown, *Clotel*	
1854 Henry David Thoreau, ***Walden*** • Frances Ellen Watkins Harper, *Poems on Miscellaneous Subjects* • John Rollin Ridge, *The Life and Adventures of Joaquín Murieta*	**1854** Republican Party formed, consolidating antislavery factions • Kansas-Nebraska Act approved by Congress; the act repeals the Missouri Compromise, making it legal for the white voting residents of a territory to determine whether it should be admitted as a slave or free state

TEXTS	CONTEXTS
1855 Walt Whitman, *Leaves of Grass* • Fanny Fern (Sarah Willis Parton), *Ruth Hall*	
	1857 Supreme Court *Dred Scott* decision denies citizenship to African Americans
1858 Abraham Lincoln, *"A House Divided"*	
1859 E.D.E.N. Southworth, *The Hidden Hand*	**1859** John Brown leads attack on Harpers Ferry
1860–65 Emily Dickinson writes several hundred **poems**	**1860** Short-lived Pony Express runs from Missouri to California
1861 Harriet Jacobs, *Incidents in the Life of a Slave Girl* • Rebecca Harding Davis, *Life in the Iron-Mills*	**1861** South Carolina batteries fire on U.S. fort, initiating the Civil War; Southern states secede from the Union and found the Confederate States of America
	1861–65 Civil War
1862 Elizabeth Stoddard, *The Morgesons*	
	1863 Emancipation Proclamation • Battle of Gettysburg
	1865 Thirteenth Amendment abolishes slavery in the United States
1866 John Greenleaf Whittier, *Snow-Bound: A Winter Idyl*	**1866** Completion of two successful trans-atlantic cables • Civil Rights Act
	1868 Fourteenth Amendment grants citizenship to those born or naturalized in the United States
1868–69 Louisa May Alcott, *Little Women*	
	1869 First transcontinental railroad completed; Central Pacific construction crews composed largely of Chinese laborers

WASHINGTON IRVING
1783–1859

Washington Irving had an unusually long and varied career, publishing his first satirical essays in 1802, when he was nineteen, and his last book, a five-volume life of George Washington, just a few months before he died at age seventy-six. Celebrated by Americans for his contributions to a burgeoning national literature, Irving also became the first American writer of the nineteenth century to achieve an international literary reputation. He created two of the most popular and enduring figures in American culture, Rip Van Winkle and Sleepy Hollow's Ichabod Crane, who figure in paintings, comic books, plays, films, and other media. Although he was regarded as a genial and comic writer, Irving regularly addressed darker and more complex themes of historical transformation and personal dislocation. His innovative travel sketches blurred the line between the personal essay and fiction, and he is considered one of the "inventors" of the modern short story. During a time in which there were no international copyright agreements, he managed to secure simultaneous British and American copyrights for his work. His canny understanding of the literary marketplace helped him become the first American able to support himself solely through his writing.

Irving was born in New York City on April 3, 1783, the last of eleven children of a Scottish-born father and English-born mother. He read widely in English literature at home, modeling his early prose on *The Spectator*, a daily paper published in 1711–12 by Joseph Addison and Richard Steele. Among the many other writers he delighted in were Shakespeare, Oliver Goldsmith, and Laurence Sterne. His brothers enjoyed writing poems and essays as companionable recreation, and, inspired by their example, he wrote a series of satirical essays on the theater and New York society under the pseudonym "Jonathan Oldstyle." Nine of these essays were published in his brother Peter's newspaper, the *Morning Chronicle*, during 1802–03.

When Irving showed signs of tuberculosis in 1804, his brothers sent him abroad for a two-year tour of Europe. On his return in 1806, he studied law with Josiah Hoffman, a former New York State attorney general, and he was admitted to the bar soon afterward. More important for his literary career, he and his brother William (along with William's brother-in-law, James Kirke Paulding) started a satirical magazine, *Salmagundi* (the name of a spicy hash), which ran from 1807 to 1808 with poems, sketches, and essays on a range of topics. In 1808 Irving began work on *A History of New-York from the Beginning of the World to the End of the Dutch Dynasty*, at first conceiving it as a parody of Samuel Lathem Mitchell's *The Picture of New York* (1807), then taking on a variety of satiric targets, including President Thomas Jefferson, whom he portrayed as an early Dutch governor of New Amsterdam, William the Testy. Narrated by the comical invented character Diedrich Knickerbocker, who dabbles in historical research, *A History of New York* (1809) brought Irving his first literary celebrity once his authorship of the pseudonymously published work was recognized. That same year Hoffman's daughter Matilda, to whom Irving was engaged, died suddenly from tuberculosis. Most biographers attribute Irving's lifelong bachelorhood to his grief over Matilda's death. However, her death freed him from the commitment he had made to her father to devote himself to the law, which he hated; and in the figure of his most famous alter ego, the genial bachelor Geoffrey Crayon, and even in his most famous fictional creation, Rip Van Winkle, there are hints that the single life suited Irving just fine.

In May 1815, Irving moved to Europe, and he remained there for seventeen years. At first he worked in Liverpool, England, with his brother Peter, an importer of English hardware, but in 1818, shortly after their mother died in New York, Peter went bankrupt. Grief-stricken, and yet grateful to be freed from the responsibilities of working for the family firm, Irving once again took up writing. He met Sir Walter Scott, an admirer of the Knickerbocker *History*, who directed him to the wealth of unused literary material in German folktales. There, Irving found sources for tales such as "Rip Van Winkle" and "The Legend of Sleepy Hollow." Some passages in "Rip Van Winkle," for instance, closely paraphrase J. C. C. N. Omar's "Peter Klaus" (1800), which also depicts a protagonist sleeping for twenty years. Irving began sending sections of *The Sketch Book* to the United States for publication in what would turn out to be seven installments published from 1819 to 1820. When the two-volume complete *Sketch Book* was printed in England in 1820, it made Irving even more famous and brought him the friendship of many of the leading British writers of the time. As Irving knew, part of his success derived from British reviewers' pleasure that a book by an American, as the Scottish literary critic Frances Jeffrey wrote in the *Edinburgh Review*, "should be written throughout with the greatest care and accuracy, and worked up to great purity and beauty of diction, on the model of the most elegant and polished of our native writers." Addison lay behind Irving's depiction of English country life, and Oliver Goldsmith influenced his sketch of Westminster Abbey. But among *The Sketch Book*'s graceful tributes to English scenes and characters were the two immensely popular tales set in rural New York, "Rip Van Winkle" and "The Legend of Sleepy Hollow," as well as "Traits of Indian Character" and "Philip of Pokanoket," a tribute to the Wampanoag leader who led the alliance against the English in 1675.

Irving's next two books, *Bracebridge Hall* (1822) and *Tales of a Traveller* (1824), were less successful, and in 1824 he accepted an invitation from the American minister to Spain to work with original manuscripts in Madrid to produce an account of Columbus's voyages. In 1828 he published *The Life and Voyages of Christopher Columbus*, which became the basis for standard schoolroom accounts of Columbus during the nineteenth and early twentieth centuries. Out of Irving's Spanish years came also *The Conquest of Granada* (1829), *Voyages and Discoveries of the Companions of Columbus* (1831), and *The Alhambra* (1832), which soon became known as "the Spanish Sketch Book."

In 1829 Irving was appointed secretary to the American legation in London. When he finally returned to the United States in 1832, critics wondered openly about whether this much admired "native" writer had become Europeanized. Setting out to reclaim his Americanness, Irving proclaimed his love for his country and headed west, taking a horseback journey into what is now Oklahoma. His travels and research resulted in three major works on the American West: *A Tour on the Prairies* (1835); *Astoria* (1836), an account of John Jacob Astor's fur-trading colony in Oregon; and *The Adventures of Captain Bonneville, U.S.A.* (1837), a narrative of explorations in the Rockies and the Far West.

In the late 1830s Irving bought and began refurbishing a house near Tarrytown, along the Hudson River north of New York City. But before settling down, in 1842 he accepted an appointment as minister to Spain and returned to Europe, spending four years in Madrid. After his return to the United States in 1846, he arranged with G. P. Putnam to publish a collected edition of his writings; he also prepared a biography of Oliver Goldsmith (1849). Irving's main work after 1850 was his long-contemplated life of George Washington, which he regarded as his greatest literary accomplishment. He collapsed just after finishing the last of its five volumes, and he died a few months later, on November 28, 1859.

Cooper, Hawthorne, and many other American writers were inspired by the success of *The Sketch Book*. Although Melville, in his essay on Hawthorne's *Mosses from an Old Manse*, declared his preference for creative geniuses over adept imitators such as

Irving, he could not escape Irving's influence, which emerges both in his short stories and in a late poem, "Rip Van Winkle's Lilacs." From the beginning, many readers identified with Rip as a counterhero, an anti–Benjamin Franklin who made a success of failure. Subsequent generations have responded profoundly to Irving's pervasive theme of mutability, especially his portrayal of the bewildering rapidity of change in American life.

The Author's Account of Himself[1]

> I am of this mind with Homer, that as the snaile that crept out of her shel was turned eftsoones into a toad, and thereby was forced to make a stoole to sit on; so the traveller that stragleth from his owne country is in a short time transformed into so monstrous a shape, that he is faine to alter his mansion with his manners, and to live where he can, not where he would.
>
> Lyly's *Euphues*.[2]

I was always fond of visiting new scenes, and observing strange characters and manners. Even when a mere child I began my travels, and made many tours of discovery into foreign parts and unknown regions of my native city, to the frequent alarm of my parents, and the emolument of the town-crier. As I grew into boyhood, I extended the range of my observations. My holiday afternoons were spent in rambles about the surrounding country. I made myself familiar with all its places famous in history or fable. I knew every spot where a murder or robbery had been committed, or a ghost been seen. I visited the neighbouring villages, and added greatly to my stock of knowledge, by noting their habits and customs, and conversing with their sages and great men. I even journeyed one long summer's day to the summit of the most distant hill, from whence I stretched my eye over many a mile of terra incognita,[3] and was astonished to find how vast a globe I inhabited.

This rambling propensity strengthened with my years. Books of voyages and travels became my passion, and in devouring their contents, I neglected the regular exercises of the school. How wistfully would I wander about the pier heads in fine weather, and watch the parting ships, bound to distant climes—with what longing eyes would I gaze after their lessening sails, and waft myself in imagination to the ends of the earth.

Farther reading and thinking, though they brought this vague inclination into more reasonable bounds, only served to make it more decided. I visited various parts of my own country; and had I been merely a lover of fine scenery, I should have felt little desire to seek elsewhere for its gratification: for on no country have the charms of nature been more prodigally lavished. Her mighty lakes, like oceans of liquid silver; her mountains, with their bright aerial tints; her valleys, teeming with wild fertility; her tremendous cataracts, thundering in their solitudes; her boundless plains, waving with spontaneous verdure; her broad deep rivers, rolling in solemn silence to the ocean; her trackless forests, where vegetation puts forth all its magnificence; her

---

1. The text is taken from the May 1819 first installment of *The Sketch Book of Geoffrey Crayon, Gent.* (For *The Sketch Book* and some of his subsequent essays and books, Irving adopted the pseudonym of Geoffrey Crayon.)
2. From *Euphues and His England* (1580), by the English writer John Lyly (1554–1606).
3. Unknown land (Latin).

skies, kindling with the magic of summer clouds and glorious sunshine:—no, never need an American look beyond his own country for the sublime and beautiful of natural scenery.

But Europe held forth all the charms of storied and poetical association. There were to be seen the masterpieces of art, the refinements of highly cultivated society, the quaint peculiarities of ancient and local custom. My native country was full of youthful promise; Europe was rich in the accumulated treasures of age. Her very ruins told the history of times gone by, and every mouldering stone was a chronicle. I longed to wander over the scenes of renowned achievement—to tread, as it were, in the footsteps of antiquity—to loiter about the ruined castle—to meditate on the falling tower—to escape, in short, from the commonplace realities of the present, and lose myself among the shadowy grandeurs of the past.

I had, beside all this, an earnest desire to see the great men of the earth. We have, it is true, our great men in America: not a city but has an ample share of them. I have mingled among them in my time, and been almost withered by the shade into which they cast me; for there is nothing so baleful to a small man as the shade of a great one, particularly the great man of a city. But I was anxious to see the great men of Europe; for I had read in the works of various philosophers, that all animals degenerated in America, and man among the number.[4] A great man of Europe, therefore, thought I, must be as superior to a great man of America, as a peak of the Alps to a highland of the Hudson; and in this idea I was confirmed, by observing the comparative importance and swelling magnitude of many English travellers among us; who, I was assured, were very little people in their own country. I will visit this land of wonders, therefore, thought I, and see the gigantic race from which I am degenerated.

It has been either my good or evil lot to have my roving passion gratified. I have wandered through different countries, and witnessed many of the shifting scenes of life. I cannot say that I have studied them with the eye of a philosopher, but rather with the sauntering gaze with which humble lovers of the picturesque stroll from the window of one print shop to another; caught sometimes by the delineations of beauty, sometimes by the distortions of caricature, and sometimes by the loveliness of landscape. As it is the fashion for modern tourists to travel pencil in hand, and bring home their port folios filled with sketches, I am disposed to get up a few for the entertainment of my friends. When I look over, however, the hints and memorandums I have taken down for the purpose, my heart almost fails me to find how my idle humour has led me aside from the great objects studied by every regular traveller who would make a book. I fear I shall give equal disappointment with an unlucky landscape painter, who had travelled on the continent, but following the bent of his vagrant inclination, had sketched in nooks, and corners, and by-places. His sketch book was accordingly crowded with cottages, and landscapes, and obscure ruins; but he had neglected to paint St. Peter's, or the

4. In the late 18th century, some Europeans argued that the North American environment caused humans to degenerate physically. These arguments were made most forcefully by the French naturalist Georges-Louis Leclerc, Comte de Buffon (1707–1788). Thomas Jefferson refuted de Buffon in his 1787 *Notes on the State of Virginia*.

Coliseum; the cascade of Terni, or the bay of Naples;[5] and had not a single glacier or volcano in his whole collection.

1819

Rip Van Winkle[1]

The following Tale was found among the papers of the late Diedrich Knickerbocker, an old gentleman of New-York, who was very curious in the Dutch history of the province, and the manners of the descendants from its primitive settlers. His historical researches, however, did not lay so much among books, as among men; for the former are lamentably scanty on his favourite topics; whereas he found the old burghers, and still more, their wives, rich in that legendary lore, so invaluable to true history. Whenever, therefore, he happened upon a genuine Dutch family, snugly shut up in its low-roofed farm house, under a spreading sycamore, he looked upon it as a little clasped volume of black-letter,[2] and studied it with the zeal of a book-worm.

The result of all these researches was a history of the province, during the reign of the Dutch governors, which he published some years since. There have been various opinions as to the literary character of his work, and, to tell the truth, it is not a whit better than it should be. Its chief merit is its scrupulous accuracy, which, indeed, was a little questioned, on its first appearance, but has since been completely established[3]; and it is now admitted into all historical collections, as a book of unquestionable authority.

The old gentleman died shortly after the publication of his work, and now, that he is dead and gone, it cannot do much harm to his memory, to say, that his time might have been much better employed in weightier labours. He, however, was apt to ride his hobby his own way; and though it did now and then kick up the dust a little in the eyes of his neighbours, and grieve the spirit of some friends, for whom he felt the truest deference and affection; yet his errors and follies are remembered "more in sorrow than in anger,"[4] and it begins to be suspected, that he never intended to injure or offend. But however his memory may be appreciated by critics, it is still held dear among many folk, whose good opinion is well worth having; particularly certain biscuit bakers, who have gone so far as to imprint his likeness on their new year cakes, and have thus given him a chance for immortality,

---

5. The locale of Mount Vesuvius and the ruins of Pompeii. Other popular tourist sites listed here are St. Peter's Basilica (built 1506–1626) in Vatican City; the Roman Colosseum (built c. 70–86 C.E.); and the Cascata delle Marmore, a man-made waterfall built near Terni (60 miles north of Rome) in 271 B.C.E.
1. "Rip Van Winkle" was the last of the sketches printed in the May 1819 first installment of *The Sketch Book*, the source of the present text.
2. Typeface in early printed books, resembling medieval script; such books, because of their value, were often equipped with clasps so they could be shut tightly and even locked.
3. Irving comically alludes to the deliberate inaccuracies of his Knickerbocker *History of New-York* (1809).
4. Shakespeare's *Hamlet* 1.2.231. To this quotation Irving appended the following footnote: "Vide [see] the excellent discourse of G. C. Verplanck, Esq. before the New-York Historical Society." If Irving's friend Gulian C. Verplanck ever made such an address about a fictional character, it would have been in fun.

almost equal to being stamped on a Waterloo medal, or a Queen Anne's farthing.[5]

Rip Van Winkle
A Posthumous Writing of Diedrich Knickerbocker

By Woden, God of Saxons,
From whence comes Wensday, that is Wodensday,
Truth is a thing that ever I will keep
Unto thylke day in which I creep into
My sepulchre—

—CARTWRIGHT[6]

Whoever has made a voyage up the Hudson, must remember the Kaatskill mountains.[7] They are a dismembered branch of the great Appalachian family, and are seen away to the west of the river, swelling up to a noble height, and lording it over the surrounding country. Every change of season, every change of weather, indeed, every hour of the day, produces some change in the magical hues and shapes of these mountains, and they are regarded by all the good wives, far and near, as perfect barometers. When the weather is fair and settled, they are clothed in blue and purple, and print their bold outlines on the clear evening sky; but some times, when the rest of the landscape is cloudless, they will gather a hood of gray vapours about their summits, which, in the last rays of the setting sun, will glow and light up like a crown of glory.

At the foot of these fairy mountains, the voyager may have descried the light smoke curling up from a village, whose shingle roofs gleam among the trees, just where the blue tints of the upland melt away into the fresh green of the nearer landscape. It is a little village of great antiquity, having been founded by some of the Dutch colonists, in the early times of the province, just about the beginning of the government of the good Peter Stuyvesant,[8] (may he rest in peace!) and there were some of the houses of the original settlers standing within a few years, with lattice windows, gable fronts surmounted with weathercocks, and built of small yellow bricks brought from Holland.

In that same village, and in one of these very houses, (which, to tell the precise truth, was sadly time worn and weather beaten,) there lived many years since, while the country was yet a province of Great Britain, a simple good natured fellow, of the name of Rip Van Winkle. He was a descendant of the Van Winkles who figured so gallantly in the chivalrous days of Peter Stuyvesant, and accompanied him to the siege of Fort Christina. He inherited, however, but little of the martial character of his ancestors. I have observed that he was a simple good natured man; he was moreover a kind neighbour, and an obedient, henpecked husband. Indeed, to the latter

5. Waterloo medals were minted liberally after the defeat there of Napoléon Bonaparte (1769–1821), emperor of France, in 1815. Farthings (tiny coins) from the reign of Anne (1665–1714), queen of Great Britain 1702–14, were commonly but wrongly considered rare.
6. From the play *The Ordinary* 3.1.1050–54, by the English writer William Cartwright (1611–1643). "Woden": Old English for "Odin," the chief Norse god.
7. Catskill Mountains, a range in southeastern New York.
8. Last governor of the Dutch province of New Netherlands (1592–1672); in 1655 (as mentioned in the next paragraph), his troops defeated Swedish colonists at Fort Christina, near what is now Wilmington, Delaware.

circumstance might be owing that meekness of spirit which gained him such universal popularity; for those men are most apt to be obsequious and conciliating abroad, who are under the discipline of shrews at home. Their tempers, doubtless, are rendered pliant and malleable in the fiery furnace of domestic tribulation, and a curtain lecture[9] is worth all the sermons in the world for teaching the virtues of patience and long suffering. A termagant[1] wife may, therefore, in some respects, be considered a tolerable blessing; and if so, Rip Van Winkle was thrice blessed.

Certain it is, that he was a great favourite among all the good wives of the village, who, as usual with the amiable sex, took his part in all family squabbles, and never failed, whenever they talked those matters over in their evening gossippings, to lay all the blame on Dame Van Winkle. The children of the village, too, would shout with joy whenever he approached. He assisted at their sports, made their playthings, taught them to fly kites and shoot marbles, and told them long stories of ghosts, witches, and Indians. Whenever he went dodging about the village, he was surrounded by a troop of them, hanging on his skirts, clambering on his back, and playing a thousand tricks on him with impunity; and not a dog would bark at him throughout the neighbourhood.

The great error in Rip's composition was an insuperable aversion to all kinds of profitable labour. It could not be for the want of assiduity or perseverance; for he would sit on a wet rock, with a rod as long and heavy as a Tartar's[2] lance, and fish all day without a murmur, even though he should not be encouraged by a single nibble. He would carry a fowling piece on his shoulder, for hours together, trudging through woods and swamps, and up hill and down dale, to shoot a few squirrels or wild pigeons. He would never even refuse to assist a neighbour in the roughest toil, and was a foremost man at all country frolicks for husking Indian corn, or building stone fences; the women of the village, too, used to employ him to run their errands, and to do such little odd jobs as their less obliging husbands would not do for them;—in a word, Rip was ready to attend to any body's business but his own; but as to doing family duty, and keeping his farm in order, it was impossible.

In fact, he declared it was no use to work on his farm; it was the most pestilent little piece of ground in the whole country; every thing about it went wrong, and would go wrong, in spite of him. His fences were continually falling to pieces; his cow would either go astray, or get among the cabbages; weeds were sure to grow quicker in his fields than any where else; the rain always made a point of setting in just as he had some out-door work to do. So that though his patrimonial estate had dwindled away under his management, acre by acre, until there was little more left than a mere patch of Indian corn and potatoes, yet it was the worst conditioned farm in the neighbourhood.

His children, too, were as ragged and wild as if they belonged to nobody. His son Rip, an urchin begotten in his own likeness, promised to inherit the habits, with the old clothes of his father. He was generally seen trooping like a colt at his mother's heels, equipped in a pair of his father's cast-off

9. Archaic term for when a wife says no to her husband's sexual entreaties after the curtains around the four-poster bed have been drawn for the night.

1. Harsh-tempered; nagging.
2. Refers to medieval warriors of northern and central Asia.

galligaskins,[3] which he had much ado to hold up with one hand, as a fine lady does her train in bad weather.

Rip Van Winkle, however, was one of those happy mortals, of foolish, well-oiled dispositions, who take the world easy, eat white bread or brown, which ever can be got with least thought or trouble, and would rather starve on a penny than work for a pound. If left to himself, he would have whistled life away, in perfect contentment; but his wife kept continually dinning in his ears about his idleness, his carelessness, and the ruin he was bringing on his family. Morning, noon, and night, her tongue was incessantly going, and every thing he said or did was sure to produce a torrent of household eloquence. Rip had but one way of replying to all lectures of the kind, and that, by frequent use, had grown into a habit. He shrugged his shoulders, shook his head, cast up his eyes, but said nothing. This, however, always provoked a fresh volley from his wife, so that he was fain to draw off his forces, and take to the outside of the house—the only side which, in truth, belongs to a henpecked husband.

Rip's sole domestic adherent was his dog Wolf, who was as much henpecked as his master; for Dame Van Winkle regarded them as companions in idleness, and even looked upon Wolf with an evil eye, as the cause of his master's so often going astray. True it is, in all points of spirit befitting an honourable dog, he was as courageous an animal as ever scoured the woods—but what courage can withstand the ever-during and all-besetting terrors of a woman's tongue? The moment Wolf entered the house, his crest fell, his tail drooped to the ground, or curled between his legs, he sneaked about with a gallows air, casting many a sidelong glance at Dame Van Winkle, and at the least flourish of a broomstick or ladle, would fly to the door with yelping precipitation.

Times grew worse and worse with Rip Van Winkle as years of matrimony rolled on; a tart temper never mellows with age, and a sharp tongue is the only edge tool that grows keener by constant use. For a long while he used to console himself, when driven from home, by frequenting a kind of perpetual club of the sages, philosophers, and other idle personages of the village, that held its sessions on a bench before a small inn, designated by a rubicund portrait of his majesty George the Third.[4] Here they used to sit in the shade, of a long lazy summer's day, talk listlessly over village gossip, or tell endless sleepy stories about nothing. But it would have been worth any statesman's money to have heard the profound discussions that sometimes took place, when by chance an old newspaper fell into their hands, from some passing traveller. How solemnly they would listen to the contents, as drawled out by Derrick Van Bummel, the schoolmaster, a dapper learned little man, who was not to be daunted by the most gigantic word in the dictionary; and how sagely they would deliberate upon public events some months after they had taken place.

The opinions of this junto[5] were completely controlled by Nicholas Vedder, a patriarch of the village, and landlord of the inn, at the door of which he took his seat from morning till night, just moving sufficiently to avoid the sun, and keep in the shade of a large tree; so that the neighbours could tell the hour by his movements as accurately as by a sun dial. It is true, he was

3. Loose, wide trousers.
4. King of Great Britain (1738–1820; reigned 1760–1820).
5. Ruling committee (Spanish).

rarely heard to speak, but smoked his pipe incessantly. His adherents, however, (for every great man has his adherents,) perfectly understood him, and knew how to gather his opinions. When any thing that was read or related displeased him, he was observed to smoke his pipe vehemently, and send forth short, frequent, and angry puffs; but when pleased, he would inhale the smoke slowly and tranquilly, and emit it in light and placid clouds, and sometimes taking the pipe from his mouth, and letting the fragrant vapour curl about his nose, would gravely nod his head in token of perfect approbation.

From even this strong hold the unlucky Rip was at length routed by his termagant wife, who would suddenly break in upon the tranquillity of the assemblage, call the members all to nought, nor was that august personage, Nicholas Vedder himself, sacred from the daring tongue of this terrible virago, who charged him outright with encouraging her husband in habits of idleness.

Poor Rip was at last reduced almost to despair; and his only alternative to escape from the labour of the farm and the clamour of his wife, was to take gun in hand, and stroll away into the woods. Here he would sometimes seat himself at the foot of a tree, and share the contents of his wallet[6] with Wolf, with whom he sympathised as a fellow sufferer in persecution. "Poor Wolf," he would say, "thy mistress leads thee a dogs' life of it; but never mind, my lad, while I live thou shalt never want a friend to stand by thee!" Wolf would wag his tail, look wistfully in his master's face, and if dogs can feel pity, I verily believe he reciprocated the sentiment with all his heart.

In a long ramble of the kind on a fine autumnal day, Rip had unconsciously scrambled to one of the highest parts of the Kaatskill mountains. He was after his favourite sport of squirrel shooting, and the still solitudes had echoed and re-echoed with the reports of his gun. Panting and fatigued, he threw himself, late in the afternoon, on a green knoll, covered with mountain herbage, that crowned the brow of a precipice. From an opening between the trees, he could overlook all the lower country for many a mile of rich woodland. He saw at a distance the lordly Hudson, far, far below him, moving on its silent but majestic course, the reflection of a purple cloud, or the sail of a lagging bark, here and there sleeping on its glassy bosom, and at last losing itself in the blue highlands.

On the other side he looked down into a deep mountain glen, wild, lonely, and shagged, the bottom filled with fragments from the impending cliffs, and scarcely lighted by the reflected rays of the setting sun. For some time Rip lay musing on this scene, evening was gradually advancing, the mountains began to throw their long blue shadows over the valleys, he saw that it would be dark long before he could reach the village, and he heaved a heavy sigh when he thought of encountering the terrors of Dame Van Winkle.

As he was about to descend, he heard a voice from a distance, hallooing, "Rip Van Winkle! Rip Van Winkle!" He looked around, but could see nothing but a crow winging its solitary flight across the mountain. He thought his fancy must have deceived him, and turned again to descend, when he heard the same cry ring through the still evening air; "Rip Van Winkle! Rip Van Winkle!"—at the same time Wolf bristled up his back, and giving a low growl,

6. Knapsack.

skulked to his master's side, looking fearfully down into the glen. Rip now felt a vague apprehension stealing over him; he looked anxiously in the same direction, and perceived a strange figure slowly toiling up the rocks, and bending under the weight of something he carried on his back. He was surprised to see any human being in this lonely and unfrequented place, but supposing it to be some one of the neighbourhood in need of his assistance, he hastened down to yield it.

On nearer approach, he was still more surprised at the singularity of the stranger's appearance. He was a short square built old fellow, with thick bushy hair, and a grizzled beard. His dress was of the antique Dutch fashion—a cloth jerkin[7] strapped round the waist—several pair of breeches, the outer one of ample volume, decorated with rows of buttons down the sides, and bunches at the knees. He bore on his shoulder a stout keg, that seemed full of liquor, and made signs for Rip to approach and assist him with the load. Though rather shy and distrustful of this new acquaintance, Rip complied with his usual alacrity, and mutually relieving each other, they clambered up a narrow gully, apparently the dry bed of a mountain torrent. As they ascended, Rip every now and then heard long rolling peals, like distant thunder, that seemed to issue out of a deep ravine, or rather cleft between lofty rocks, toward which their rugged path conducted. He paused for an instant, but supposing it to be the muttering of one of those transient thunder showers which often take place in mountain heights, he proceeded. Passing through the ravine, they came to a hollow, like a small amphitheatre, surrounded by perpendicular precipices, over the brinks of which impending trees shot their branches, so that you only caught glimpses of the azure sky, and the bright evening cloud. During the whole time, Rip and his companion had laboured on in silence; for though the former marvelled greatly what could be the object of carrying a keg of liquor up this wild mountain, yet there was something strange and incomprehensible about the unknown, that inspired awe, and checked familiarity.

On entering the amphitheatre, new objects of wonder presented themselves. On a level spot in the centre was a company of odd-looking personages playing at nine-pins. They were dressed in a quaint, outlandish fashion: some wore short doublets,[8] others jerkins, with long knives in their belts, and most had enormous breeches, of similar style with that of the guide's. Their visages, too, were peculiar: one had a large head, broad face, and small piggish eyes; the face of another seemed to consist entirely of nose, and was surmounted by a white sugarloaf hat, set off with a little red cockstail.[9] They all had beards, of various shapes and colours. There was one who seemed to be the commander. He was a stout old gentleman, with a weather-beaten countenance; he wore a laced doublet, broad belt and hanger,[1] high crowned hat and feather, red stockings, and high heeled shoes, with roses in them. The whole group reminded Rip of the figures in an old Flemish painting, in the parlour of Dominie[2] Van Schaick, the village parson, and which had been brought over from Holland at the time of the settlement.

What seemed particularly odd to Rip, was, that though these folks were evidently amusing themselves, yet they maintained the gravest faces, the

7. Jacket fitted tightly at the waist.
8. Male jackets covering from the neck to the upper thighs, where they hooked to stockings.

9. Feather. "Sugarloaf": cone-shaped.
1. Short, curved sword.
2. Minister.

most mysterious silence, and were, withal, the most melancholy party of pleasure he had ever witnessed. Nothing interrupted the stillness of the scene, but the noise of the balls, which, whenever they were rolled, echoed along the mountains like rumbling peals of thunder.

As Rip and his companion approached them, they suddenly desisted from their play, and stared at him with such fixed statue-like gaze, and such strange, uncouth, lack lustre countenances, that his heart turned within him, and his knees smote together. His companion now emptied the contents of the keg into large flagons, and made signs to him to wait upon the company. He obeyed with fear and trembling; they quaffed the liquor in profound silence, and then returned to their game.

By degrees, Rip's awe and apprehension subsided. He even ventured, when no eye was fixed upon him, to taste the beverage, which he found had much of the flavour of excellent Hollands.[3] He was naturally a thirsty soul, and was soon tempted to repeat the draught. One taste provoked another, and he reiterated his visits to the flagon so often, that at length his senses were overpowered, his eyes swam in his head, his head gradually declined, and he fell into a deep sleep.

On awaking, he found himself on the green knoll from whence he had first seen the old man of the glen. He rubbed his eyes—it was a bright sunny morning. The birds were hopping and twittering among the bushes, and the eagle was wheeling aloft, and breasting the pure mountain breeze. "Surely," thought Rip, "I have not slept here all night." He recalled the occurrences before he fell asleep. The strange man with the keg of liquor—the mountain ravine—the wild retreat among the rocks—the wo-begone party at nine-pins—the flagon—"Oh! that flagon! that wicked flagon!" thought Rip—"what excuse shall I make to Dame Van Winkle?"

He looked round for his gun, but in place of the clean well-oiled fowling-piece, he found an old firelock lying by him, the barrel encrusted with rust, the lock falling off, and the stock worm-eaten. He now suspected that the grave roysters[4] of the mountain had put a trick upon him, and having dosed him with liquor, had robbed him of his gun. Wolf, too, had disappeared, but he might have strayed away after a squirrel or partridge. He whistled after him, shouted his name, but all in vain; the echoes repeated his whistle and shout, but no dog was to be seen.

He determined to revisit the scene of the last evening's gambol,[5] and if he met with any of the party, to demand his dog and gun. As he arose to walk he found himself stiff in the joints, and wanting in his usual activity. "These mountain beds do not agree with me," thought Rip, "and if this frolick should lay me up with a fit of the rheumatism, I shall have a blessed time with Dame Van Winkle." With some difficulty he got down into the glen: he found the gully up which he and his companion had ascended the preceding evening, but to his astonishment a mountain stream was now foaming down it, leaping from rock to rock, and filling the glen with babbling murmurs. He, however, made shift to scramble up its sides, working his toilsome way through thickets of birch, sassafras, and witch hazle, and sometimes tripped up or

---

3. Gin made in Holland.
4. Revelers.
5. Frolicking or cavorting.

entangled by the wild grape vines that twisted their coils and tendrils from tree to tree, and spread a kind of network in his path.

At length he reached to where the ravine had opened through the cliffs, to the amphitheatre; but no traces of such opening remained. The rocks presented a high impenetrable wall, over which the torrent came tumbling in a sheet of feathery foam, and fell into a broad deep basin, black from the shadows of the surrounding forest. Here, then, poor Rip was brought to a stand. He again called and whistled after his dog; he was only answered by the cawing of a flock of idle crows, sporting high in air about a dry tree that overhung a sunny precipice; and who, secure in their elevation, seemed to look down and scoff at the poor man's perplexities. What was to be done? the morning was passing away, and Rip felt famished for his breakfast. He grieved to give up his dog and gun; he dreaded to meet his wife; but it would not do to starve among the mountains. He shook his head, shouldered the rusty firelock, and, with a heart full of trouble and anxiety, turned his steps homeward.

As he approached the village, he met a number of people, but none that he knew, which somewhat surprised him, for he had thought himself acquainted with every one in the country round. Their dress, too, was of a different fashion from that to which he was accustomed. They all stared at him with equal marks of surprise, and whenever they cast eyes upon him, invariably stroked their chins. The constant recurrence of this gesture, induced Rip, involuntarily, to do the same, when, to his astonishment, he found his beard had grown a foot long!

He had now entered the skirts of the village. A troop of strange children ran at his heels, hooting after him, and pointing at his gray beard. The dogs, too, not one of which he recognized for his old acquaintances, barked at him as he passed. The very village seemed altered: it was larger and more populous. There were rows of houses which he had never seen before, and those which had been his familiar haunts had disappeared. Strange names were over the doors—strange faces at the windows—every thing was strange. His mind now began to misgive him, that both he and the world around him were bewitched. Surely this was his native village, which he had left but the day before. There stood the Kaatskill mountains—there ran the silver Hudson at a distance—there was every hill and dale precisely as it had always been—Rip was sorely perplexed—"That flagon last night," thought he, "has addled my poor head sadly!"

It was with some difficulty he found the way to his own house, which he approached with silent awe, expecting every moment to hear the shrill voice of Dame Van Winkle. He found the house gone to decay—the roof fallen in, the windows shattered, and the doors off the hinges. A half starved dog, that looked like Wolf, was skulking about it. Rip called him by name, but the cur snarled, showed his teeth, and passed on. This was an unkind cut indeed—"My very dog," sighed poor Rip, "has forgotten me!"

He entered the house, which, to tell the truth, Dame Van Winkle had always kept in neat order. It was empty, forlorn, and apparently abandoned. This desolateness overcame all his connubial fears—he called loudly for his wife and children—the lonely chambers rung for a moment with his voice, and then all again was silence.

He now hurried forth, and hastened to his old resort, the little village inn—but it too was gone. A large rickety wooden building stood in its place, with great gaping windows, some of them broken, and mended with old hats and petticoats, and over the door was painted, "The Union Hotel, by Jonathan Doolittle." Instead of the great tree that used to shelter the quiet little Dutch inn of yore, there now was reared a tall naked pole, with something on top that looked like a red night cap,[6] and from it was fluttering a flag, on which was a singular assemblage of stars and stripes—all this was strange and incomprehensible. He recognised on the sign, however, the ruby face of King George, under which he had smoked so many a peaceful pipe, but even this was singularly metamorphosed. The red coat was changed for one of blue and buff,[7] a sword was stuck in the hand instead of a sceptre, the head was decorated with a cocked hat, and underneath was painted in large characters, GENERAL WASHINGTON.

There was, as usual, a crowd of folk about the door, but none that Rip recollected. The very character of the people seemed changed. There was a busy, bustling, disputatious tone about it, instead of the accustomed phlegm and drowsy tranquillity. He looked in vain for the sage Nicholas Vedder, with his broad face, double chin, and fair long pipe, uttering clouds of tobacco smoke instead of idle speeches; or Van Bummel, the schoolmaster, doling forth the contents of an ancient newspaper. In place of these, a lean bilious looking fellow, with his pockets full of handbills, was haranguing vehemently about rights of citizens—election—members of congress—liberty—Bunker's hill—heroes of seventy-six—and other words, that were a perfect Babylonish jargon[8] to the bewildered Van Winkle.

The appearance of Rip, with his long grizzled beard, his rusty fowling piece, his uncouth dress, and the army of women and children that had gathered at his heels, soon attracted the attention of the tavern politicians. They crowded around him, eyeing him from head to foot, with great curiosity.[9] The orator bustled up to him, and drawing him partly aside, inquired "which side he voted?" Rip stared in vacant stupidity. Another short but busy little fellow pulled him by the arm, and raising on tiptoe, inquired in his ear, "whether he was Federal or Democrat."[1] Rip was equally at a loss to comprehend the question; when a knowing, self-important old gentleman, in a sharp cocked hat, made his way through the crowd, putting them to the right and left with his elbows as he passed, and planting himself before Van Winkle, with one arm akimbo, the other resting on his cane, his keen eyes and sharp hat penetrating, as it were, into his very soul, demanded, in an austere tone, "what brought him to the election with a gun on his shoulder, and a mob at his heels, and whether he meant to breed a riot in the village?" "Alas! gentlemen," cried Rip, somewhat dismayed, "I am a poor quiet man, a native of the place, and a loyal subject of the King, God bless him!"

Here a general shout burst from the bystanders—"A tory! a tory! a spy! a refugee! hustle him! away with him!" It was with great difficulty that the self-important man in the cocked hat restored order; and having assumed a

---

6. Limp, close-fitting cap adopted during the French Revolution as a symbol of liberty (such caps were worn by freed slaves in ancient Rome). The pole is a "liberty pole"—i.e., a tall flagstaff topped by a liberty cap.
7. Colors of the Revolutionary uniform.
8. Irving conflates the story of Babel (Genesis 11.1–9) with the Babylonian captivity of the Jewish people (see, e.g., the Book of Jeremiah). "Bunker's hill": i.e., Bunker Hill, site, in Boston, of an early battle in the American Revolution.

9. For a contemporary painting depicting Rip Van Winkle's appearance in his village, see John Quidor's *The Return of Rip Van Winkle* (1829) in the color plates section of this volume.
1. Political parties that developed in the Washington administration (1789–97), with Secretary of the U.S. Treasury Alexander Hamilton (1755–1804) leading the Federalists and Secretary of State Thomas Jefferson (1743–1826) leading the Democrats.

tenfold austerity of brow, demanded again of the unknown culprit, what he came there for, and whom he was seeking. The poor man humbly assured them that he meant no harm; but merely came there in search of some of his neighbours, who used to keep about the tavern.

"Well—who are they?—name them."

Rip bethought himself a moment, and inquired, "where's Nicholas Vedder?"

There was a silence for a little while, when an old man replied, in a thin piping voice, "Nicholas Vedder? why he is dead and gone these eighteen years! There was a wooden tombstone in the church yard that used to tell all about him, but that's rotted and gone too."

"Where's Brom Dutcher?"

"Oh he went off to the army in the beginning of the war; some say he was killed at the battle of Stoney-Point—others say he was drowned in a squall, at the foot of Antony's Nose.[2] I don't know—he never came back again."

"Where's Van Bummel, the schoolmaster?"

"He went off to the wars too, was a great militia general, and is now in Congress."

Rip's heart died away, at hearing of these sad changes in his home and friends, and finding himself thus alone in the world. Every answer puzzled him, too, by treating of such enormous lapses of time, and of matters which he could not understand: war—congress—Stoney-Point;—he had no courage to ask after any more friends, but cried out in despair, "does nobody here know Rip Van Winkle?"

"Oh, Rip Van Winkle!" exclaimed two or three, "Oh, to be sure! that's Rip Van Winkle yonder, leaning against the tree."

Rip looked, and beheld a precise counterpart of himself, as he went up the mountain: apparently as lazy, and certainly as ragged. The poor fellow was now completely confounded. He doubted his own identity, and whether he was himself or another man. In the midst of his bewilderment, the man in the cocked hat demanded who he was, and what was his name?

"God knows," exclaimed he, at his wit's end; "I'm not myself—I'm somebody else—that's me yonder—no—that's somebody else, got into my shoes—I was myself last night, but I fell asleep on the mountain, and they've changed my gun, and every thing's changed, and I'm changed, and I can't tell what's my name, or who I am!"

The bystanders began now to look at each other, nod, wink significantly, and tap their fingers against their foreheads. There was a whisper, also, about securing the gun, and keeping the old fellow from doing mischief. At the very suggestion of which, the self-important man in the cocked hat retired with some precipitation. At this critical moment a fresh likely woman pressed through the throng to get a peep at the graybearded man. She had a chubby child in her arms, which, frightened at his looks, began to cry. "Hush, Rip," cried she, "hush, you little fool, the old man won't hurt you." The name of the child, the air of the mother, the tone of her voice, all awakened a train of recollections in his mind.

"What is your name, my good woman?" asked he.

---

2. I.e., Anthony's Nose, a mountain near West Point. "Stoney-Point": i.e., Stoney Point, site of a Revolutionary-era British fort that was captured and briefly held by the Continental Army.

"Judith Gardenier."

"And your father's name?"

"Ah, poor man, his name was Rip Van Winkle; it's twenty years since he went away from home with his gun, and never has been heard of since—his dog came home without him; but whether he shot himself, or was carried away by the Indians, nobody can tell. I was then but a little girl."

Rip had but one question more to ask; but he put it with a faltering voice: "Where's your mother?"

Oh, she too had died but a short time since; she broke a blood vessel in a fit of passion at a New-England pedlar.

There was a drop of comfort, at least, in this intelligence. The honest man could contain himself no longer.—He caught his daughter and her child in his arms.—"I am your father!" cried he—"Young Rip Van Winkle once—old Rip Van Winkle now!—Does nobody know poor Rip Van Winkle!"

All stood amazed, until an old woman, tottering out from among the crowd, put her hand to her brow, and peering under it in his face for a moment, exclaimed, "Sure enough! it is Rip Van Winkle—it is himself. Welcome home again, old neighbour—Why, where have you been these twenty long years?"

Rip's story was soon told, for the whole twenty years had been to him but as one night. The neighbours stared when they heard it; some were seen to wink at each other, and put their tongues in their cheeks; and the self-important man in the cocked hat, who, when the alarm was over, had returned to the field, screwed down the corners of his mouth, and shook his head—upon which there was a general shaking of the head throughout the assemblage.

It was determined, however, to take the opinion of old Peter Vanderdonk, who was seen slowly advancing up the road. He was a descendant of the historian of that name,[3] who wrote one of the earliest accounts of the province. Peter was the most ancient inhabitant of the village, and well versed in all the wonderful events and traditions of the neighbourhood. He recollected Rip at once, and corroborated his story in the most satisfactory manner. He assured the company that it was a fact, handed down from his ancestor the historian, that the Kaatskill mountains had always been haunted by strange beings. That it was affirmed that the great Hendrick Hudson, the first discoverer of the river and country, kept a kind of vigil there every twenty years, with his crew of the Half-moon, being permitted in this way to revisit the scenes of his enterprize, and keep a guardian eye upon the river, and the great city called by his name.[4] That his father had once seen them in their old Dutch dresses playing at nine pins in a hollow of the mountain; and that he himself had heard, one summer afternoon, the sound of their balls, like long peals of thunder.

To make a long story short, the company broke up, and returned to the more important concerns of the election. Rip's daughter took him home to live with her; she had a snug, well-furnished house, and a stout cheery farmer for a husband, whom Rip recollected for one of the urchins that used to

3. The Dutch-born lawyer Adriaen Van der Donck (c. 1618–c. 1655), a landowner in New Netherlands, published his promotional history of the colony in 1655.

4. Actually, a small town on the east bank of the Hudson River. "Hendrick Hudson": Henry Hudson (d. 1611), English navigator in the service of the Dutch.

climb upon his back. As to Rip's son and heir, who was the ditto of himself, seen leaning against the tree, he was employed to work on the farm; but evinced an hereditary disposition to attend to any thing else but his business.

Rip now resumed his old walks and habits; he soon found many of his former cronies, though all rather the worse for the wear and tear of time; and preferred making friends among the rising generation, with whom he soon grew into great favour.

Having nothing to do at home, and being arrived at that happy age when a man can do nothing with impunity, he took his place once more on the bench, at the inn door, and was reverenced as one of the patriarchs of the village, and a chronicle of the old times "before the war." It was some time before he could get into the regular track of gossip, or could be made to comprehend the strange events that had taken place during his torpor. How that there had been a revolutionary war—that the country had thrown off the yoke of old England—and that, instead of being a subject of his Majesty George the Third, he was now a free citizen of the United States. Rip, in fact, was no politician; the changes of states and empires made but little impression on him. But there was one species of despotism under which he had long groaned, and that was—petticoat government. Happily, that was at an end; he had got his neck out of the yoke of matrimony, and could go in and out whenever he pleased, without dreading the tyranny of Dame Van Winkle. Whenever her name was mentioned, however, he shook his head, shrugged his shoulders, and cast up his eyes; which might pass either for an expression of resignation to his fate, or joy at his deliverance.

He used to tell his story to every stranger that arrived at Mr. Doolittle's hotel. He was observed, at first, to vary on some points every time he told it, which was, doubtless, owing to his having so recently awaked. It at last settled down precisely to the tale I have related, and not a man, woman, or child in the neighbourhood, but knew it by heart. Some always pretended to doubt the reality of it, and insisted that Rip had been out of his head, and that this was one point on which he always remained flighty. The old Dutch inhabitants, however, almost universally gave it full credit. Even to this day they never hear a thunder storm of a summer afternoon, about the Kaatskill, but they say Hendrick Hudson and his crew are at their game of nine pins; and it is a common wish of all henpecked husbands in the neighbourhood, when life hangs heavy on their hands, that they might have a quieting draught out of Rip Van Winkle's flagon.

NOTE

The foregoing tale, one would suspect, had been suggested to Mr. Knickerbocker by a little German superstition about Charles V.[5] and the Kypphauser mountain; the subjoined note, however, which he had appended to the tale, shows that it is an absolute fact, narrated with his usual fidelity:

"The story of Rip Van Winkle may seem incredible to many, but nevertheless I give it my full belief, for I know the vicinity of our old Dutch settle-

5. Irving later changed "Charles V." (Holy Roman emperor, 1519–56) to "The Emperor Frederick *der Rothbart*" (i.e., Frederick Barbarossa; Holy Roman emperor, 1152–90). ("Rothbart" and "Barbarossa" both mean "redbeard.") In either form, this allusion is to a source other than the actual one, the story "Peter Klaus" in the folktales of J. C. C. N. Otmar (1800).

ments to have been very subject to marvellous events and appearances. Indeed, I have heard many stranger stories than this, in the villages along the Hudson; all of which were too well authenticated to admit of a doubt. I have even talked with Rip Van Winkle myself, who, when last I saw him, was a very venerable old man, and so perfectly rational and consistent on every other point, that I think no conscientious person could refuse to take this into the bargain; nay, I have seen a certificate on the subject taken before a country justice, and signed with a cross, in the justice's own hand writing. The story, therefore, is beyond the possibility of doubt.   D.K."

1819

JAMES FENIMORE COOPER
1789–1851

The author of thirty-two novels, a history of the American navy, five travel books, and two major works of social criticism, James Fenimore Cooper was among the most important writers of his time—a writer who helped chart the future course of American fiction. He wrote novels of manners, transatlantic and European fiction, and several historical novels on the American Revolution. A pioneering author of sea fiction, he had a significant influence on Herman Melville. But Cooper remains best known for the five historical novels of the Leatherstocking series, which are set between 1740 and the early 1800s. These novels—*The Pioneers* (1823), *The Last of the Mohicans* (1826), *The Prairie* (1827), *The Pathfinder* (1840), and *The Deerslayer* (1841)—explore the imperial, racial, and social conflicts central to the emergence of the United States; and their evocative portrayals of the frontiersman Natty Bumppo and his Indian friend Chingachgook helped to develop what the British novelist and critic D. H. Lawrence influentially called "the myth of America." Central to that myth is the image of a nation founded through conflict and dispossession that nonetheless managed to sustain belief in its youthful innocence.

Cooper was born on September 15, 1789, in Burlington, New Jersey, and in 1790 moved with his parents to Cooperstown, on Otsego Lake in central New York, a town founded and developed by his father, Judge William Cooper. A two-term member of Congress known for his energetic entrepreneurship and ardent Federalism, the judge hoped to educate his son to manage the family settlements, sending him first to an academy in Albany and then to Yale, where the thirteen-year-old Cooper became known as a prankster. Expelled from Yale because of misconduct in 1805, Cooper (at his father's insistence) became a sailor in 1806 and was commissioned as a midshipman in the U.S. Navy in 1808. One year later, when Judge Cooper unexpectedly died, leaving behind an apparently large fortune for his heirs, the twenty-year-old Cooper seemed set for life. He resigned from the navy and, in 1811, married Susan DeLancey, whose prominent New York State family had lost considerable possessions by siding with the British during the Revolution but still owned lands in Westchester County. For several years Cooper oversaw properties in Westchester County and Cooperstown. But the family fortunes steadily diminished. In 1819, with the death of an older brother, Cooper became the person primarily responsible for the debt-ridden

Cooper estate. A failure at managing the "real" Cooperstown, Cooper through his authorship of the Leatherstocking novels may well have sought to take imaginative possession of the New York lands he could never oversee with the skill of his father.

Cooper began his writing career in 1820, in large part in an effort to earn enough money to pay his debts. According to family lore, he bet his wife that he could write a better novel than the British novel of manners the two had been reading together. The result was *Precaution* (1820), a leaden novel of British high society modeled on Jane Austen's *Persuasion* (1818). Following that insignificant start, Cooper turned to the historical romance as popularized by the Scottish writer Sir Walter Scott, and produced *The Spy* (1821), the first important novel about the American Revolution. Its success led him to move to New York City and embark on a successful literary career. He founded a literary society there, the Bread and Cheese Club, and became the center of a circle that included notable painters of the Hudson River School as well as writers (William Cullen Bryant among them) and professionals. In 1823 he published *The Pioneers*, the first of the Leatherstocking novels featuring Natty Bumppo. Cooper had not written *The Pioneers* with the intention of inaugurating a series, but response to Natty Bumppo was so positive that he returned to him three years later with *The Last of the Mohicans*, consolidating his creation of one of the most popular characters in world literature. With his previous novels, Cooper had assumed the financial risk of paying printers and doing the bulk of the promotion. *Mohicans* was the first of his novels published by the Philadelphia firm of Carey and Lea, which paid him $5,000 (around $85,000 in today's value) for the novel. Although Cooper was never financially secure, this new arrangement helped him to pay off his family's debts.

In 1826, at the height of his fame, Cooper sailed for Europe with his wife and their five children. In Paris, where he became intimate with the aged Lafayette, he wrote *The Prairie* (1827) and *Notions of the Americans* (1828), a defense of the United States against criticism by European travelers. Smarting under the half-complimentary, half-patronizing epithet of "The American Scott," he wrote three historical novels set in medieval Europe—*The Bravo* (1831), *The Heidenmauer* (1832), and *The Headsman* (1833)—as a realistic corrective to what he regarded as Sir Walter Scott's glorifications of the past. On his return to the United States in 1833, Cooper was so angered by the negative reception of these novels that he renounced novel writing in *Letter to His Countrymen* (1834). Subsequently, at Cooperstown he gave notice that a point of land on Otsego Lake where the townspeople had been picnicking was private property and not to be used without his permission. Newspapers began attacking him as a would-be aristocrat poisoned by his residence abroad, and for years Cooper embroiled himself in lawsuits designed not to gain damages for libels but to tame the vitriolic press. Even while pursuing these legal efforts, Cooper continued to write book after book—social and political satires growing out of his experiences with the press, a political primer on the dangers of an unchecked, demagogic democracy (*The American Democrat* [1838]), and (silently retracting his 1834 renunciation of fiction writing) a series of sociopolitical novels and two additional Leatherstocking novels: *The Pathfinder* (1840) and *The Deerslayer* (1841). His monumental *History of the Navy of the United States of America* (1839) became the focus of new quarrels and a new lawsuit, and controversy continued to surround Cooper when he published his "Littlepage" novels—*Satanstoe* (1845), *The Chainbearer* (1845), and *The Redskins* (1846)—which supported landowners over tenants in the controversy known as the Anti-Rent War, and his anti-utopian novel *The Crater* (1847), which imagined the demise of the American republic as a result of demagogues' assaults on the Constitution. When Herman Melville reviewed Cooper's last great sea novel, *The Sea Lions* (1849), in the April 1849 issue of the *Literary World*, he lambasted "those who more for fashion's sake than anything else, have of late joined in decrying our national novelist" and concluded by warmly recommending what he termed one of Cooper's "happiest" novels.

Cooper died on September 14, 1851, a day before his sixty-second birthday. At a memorial commemoration on February 25, 1852, Washington Irving declared that the death of Cooper "left a space in our literature which will not be easily supplied"; Emerson spoke of "an old debt to him of happy days, on the first appearance of the *Pioneers*"; and the historian Francis Parkman proclaimed that of "all American writers, Cooper is the most original and the most thoroughly national." Throughout the century and into the next, Cooper's Leatherstocking novels had an incalculable vogue in the United States and abroad. Major European writers as diverse as Honoré de Balzac and Leo Tolstoy were profoundly moved by *The Pioneers* and the subsequent Natty Bumppo novels, while the novelist Joseph Conrad proclaimed that Cooper "wrote as well as any novelist of the time." Dissenting from such adulation, Mark Twain asserted in his classic essay "Fenimore Cooper's Literary Offenses" (1895) that Cooper's English is "a crime against the language." Nevertheless, the Leatherstocking novels are probably the books that most influenced Twain's own *Huckleberry Finn* and many other frontier and western novels published after the appearance of *Mohicans* in 1826. Twain's account of Huck's flight from society and his friendship with the runaway slave Jim drew on what continues to appeal to modern readers of Cooper: the profound dramatizations of such key American conflicts as natural rights versus legal rights, order versus change, wilderness versus established society, and—especially—the possibilities of democratic freedom and interracial friendship as exemplified by the enduring image of Natty Bumppo and Chingachgook on the vanishing frontier.

The Last of the Mohicans

The second novel in the Leatherstocking series, *The Last of the Mohicans; A Narrative of 1757* (1826), depicts Natty Bumppo, also known as Hawk-eye, as a wilderness scout in the British colony of New York at the time of the French and Indian War (1754–63). At the center of the novel is a fictionalized account of the August 10, 1757, massacre at Fort William Henry, in which perhaps hundreds of British colonists were killed or injured by the Huron Indians and other tribes allied with the French general Montcalm. According to Cooper, the ineptness of the British general Webb left the colonists vulnerable to the retaliatory violence of the Indians. By drawing on this historical incident, Cooper suggests that the colonists' progress toward independence required the departure from North America of both the French and the British military as well as any other European power aspiring to rule the continent. Published a few years before President Andrew Jackson initiated his Indian removal policies, the novel at first glance seems to reinforce the idea that progress required the "extinction" or expulsion of the Indians. But at the heart of the novel is a poignant interracial friendship between the white man, Natty Bumppo, and the Mohican, Chingachgook, suggestive of Cooper's unhappiness with the brutalities that

The cover of an 1836 British printing of *The Last of the Mohicans* (1826).

would eventually result in the death of Chingachgook's heroic son Uncas, "the last of the Mohicans." In Cooper's complex historical vision, progress always comes at a price, and the overall novel laments the sufferings of the Mohicans, whom Cooper presents as committed to the highest moral and ethical standards.

The chapter reprinted here comes from the beginning of the novel. Major Duncan Heyward is escorting the daughters of the British Lieutenant Colonel Munro, Alice and Cora, to Fort William Henry, which at the time is under the command of Munro himself. Unbeknownst to Heyward and the daughters, the Huron Magua, who offers himself as a guide in the wilderness, had once been flogged by Munro, and now vengefully wishes to capture the daughters. Natty, Chingachgook, and Uncas will eventually help the daughters reunite with their father. At this early point in the novel, however, before they have even met the Munro party, the friends Natty and Chingachgook discuss the colonial history of the Americas and convey the differing historical perspectives of the English and the Native Americans.

FROM THE LAST OF THE MOHICANS

From Volume I

Chapter III

[NATTY BUMPPO AND CHINGACHGOOK; STORIES OF THE FATHERS]

> Before these fields were shorn and tilled,
> Full to the brim our rivers flowed;
> The melody of waters filled
> The fresh and boundless wood;
> And torrents dashed, and rivulets played,
> And fountains spouted in the shade.
> *Bryant*[1]

Leaving the unsuspecting Heyward, and his confiding companions, to penetrate still deeper into a forest that contained such treacherous inmates, we must use an author's privilege, and shift the scene a few miles to the westward of the place where we have last seen them.

On that day, two men might be observed, lingering on the banks of a small but rapid stream, within an hour's journey of the encampment of Webb, like those who awaited the appearance of an absent person, or the approach of some expected event. The vast canopy of woods spread itself to the margin of the river, overhanging the water, and shadowing its dark glassy current with a deeper hue. The rays of the sun were beginning to grow less fierce, and the intense heat of the day was lessened, as the cooler vapours of the springs and fountains rose above their leafy beds, and rested in the atmosphere. Still that breathing silence, which marks the drowsy sultriness of an American landscape in July, pervaded the secluded spot, interrupted, only, by the low voices of the men in question, an occasional and lazy tap of a reviving wood-pecker, the discordant cry of some gaudy jay, or a swelling on the ear, from the dull roar of a distant water-fall.

---

1. From "An Indian at the Burial-Place of His Fathers" (1824), by William Cullen Bryant (1794–1878).

These feeble and broken sounds were, however, too familiar to the foresters, to draw their attention from the more interesting matter of their dialogue. While one of these loiterers showed the red skin and wild accoutrements of a native of the woods, the other exhibited, through the mask of his rude and nearly savage equipments, the brighter, though sun-burnt and long-faded complexion of one who might claim descent from an European parentage. The former was seated on the end of a mossy log, in a posture that permitted him to heighten the effect of his earnest language, by the calm but expressive gestures of an Indian, engaged in debate. His body, which was nearly naked, presented a terrific emblem of death, drawn in intermingled colours of white and black. His closely shaved head, on which no other hair than the well known and chivalrous scalping tuft was preserved, was without ornament of any kind, with the exception of a solitary Eagle's plume, that crossed his crown, and depended[2] over the left shoulder. A tomahawk and scalping-knife, of English manufacture, were in his girdle; while a short military rifle, of that sort with which the policy of the whites armed their savage allies, lay carelessly across his bare and sinewy knee. The expanded chest, full-formed limbs, and grave countenance of this warrior, would denote that he had reached the vigour of his days, though no symptoms of decay appeared to have yet weakened his manhood.

The frame of the white man, judging by such parts as were not concealed by his clothes, was like that of one who had known hardships and exertion from his earliest youth. His person, though muscular, was rather attenuated than full; but every nerve and muscle appeared strung and indurated,[3] by unremitted exposure and toil. He wore a hunting-shirt of forest-green, fringed with faded yellow, and a summer cap, of skins which had been shorn of their fur. He also bore a knife in a girdle of wampum, like that which confined the scanty garments of the Indian, but no tomahawk. His moccasins were ornamented after the gay fashion of the natives, while the only part of his under dress which appeared below the hunting-frock, was a pair of buckskin leggings, that laced at the sides, and were gartered above the knees, with the sinews of a deer. A pouch and horn completed his personal accoutrements, though a rifle of a great length, which the theory of the more ingenious whites had taught them, was the most dangerous of all fire-arms, leaned against a neighbouring sapling. The eye of the hunter, or scout, whichever he might be, was small, quick, keen, and restless, roving while he spoke, on every side of him, as if in quest of game, or distrusting the sudden approach of some lurking enemy. Notwithstanding these symptoms of habitual suspicion, his countenance was not only without guile, but at the moment at which he is introduced was charged with an expression of sturdy honesty.

"Even your traditions make the case in my favour, Chingachgook," he said, speaking in the tongue which was known to all the natives who formerly inhabited the country between the Hudson and the Potomack,[4] and of which we shall give a free translation for the benefit of the reader; endeavouring,

2. Hung down. "Scalping tuft": Cooper supplied the following note to the 1831 edition of *Mohicans*: "The North American warrior caused the hair to be plucked from his whole body; a small tuft, only, was left on the crown of his head, in order that his enemy might avail himself of it, in wrenching the scalp in the event of his fall. The scalp was the only admissible trophy of victory. Thus, it was deemed more important to obtain the scalp than to kill the man. . . ."
3. Hardened.
4. Potomac; river flowing from the Alleghenies to the Chesapeake Bay.

at the same time, to preserve some of the peculiarities, both of the individual and of the language. "Your fathers came from the setting sun, crossed the big river,[5] fought the people of the country, and took the land; and mine came from the red sky of the morning, over the salt lake, and did their work much after the fashion that had been set them by yours; then let God judge the matter between us, and friends, spare their words!"

"My fathers fought with the naked red-man!" returned the Indian, sternly, in the same language. "Is there no difference, Hawk-eye, between the stone-headed arrow of the warrior, and the leaden bullet with which you kill?"

"There is reason in an Indian, though nature has made him with a red skin!" said the white man, shaking his head, like one on whom such an appeal to his justice was not thrown away. For a moment he appeared to be conscious of having the worst of the argument, then rallying again, he answered to the objection of his antagonist in the best manner his limited information would allow: "I am no scholar, and I care not who knows it; but judging from what I have seen at deer chaces, and squirrel hunts, of the sparks below, I should think a rifle in the hands of their grandfathers, was not so dangerous as a hickory bow, and a good flint-head might be, if drawn with Indian judgment, and sent by an Indian eye."

"You have the story told by your fathers," returned the other, coldly waving his hand, in proud disdain. "What say your old men? do they tell the young warriors, that the pale-faces met the red-men, painted for war and armed with the stone hatchet or wooden gun?"

"I am not a prejudiced man, nor one who vaunts himself on his natural privileges, though the worst enemy I have on earth, and he is an Iroquois, daren't deny that I am genuine white," the scout replied, surveying, with secret satisfaction, the faded colour of his bony and sinewy hand; "and I am willing to own that my people have many ways, of which, as an honest man, I can't approve. It is one of their customs to write in books what they have done and seen, instead of telling them in their villages, where the lie can be given to the face of a cowardly boaster, and the brave soldier can call on his comrades to witness for the truth of his words. In consequence of this bad fashion, a man who is too conscientious to misspend his days among the women, in learning the names of black marks, may never hear of the deeds of his fathers, nor feel a pride in striving to outdo them. For myself, I conclude all the Bumppos could shoot; for I have a natural turn with a rifle, which must have been handed down from generation to generation, as our holy commandments tell us, all good and evil gifts are bestowed; though I should be loth to answer for other people in such a matter. But every story has its two sides; so I ask you, Chingachgook, what passed when our fathers first met?"

A silence of a minute succeeded, during which the Indian sat mute; then, full of the dignity of his office, he commenced his brief tale, with a solemnity that served to heighten its appearance of truth.

"Listen, Hawk-eye, and your ears shall drink no lies. 'Tis what my fathers have said, and what the Mohicans have done." He hesitated a single instant,

---

5. Cooper supplied the following note to the 1831 edition of *Mohicans*: "The Mississippi. The scout alludes to a tradition which is very popular among the tribes of the Atlantic states. Evidence of their Asiatic origin is deduced from the circumstance, though great uncertainty hangs over the whole history of the Indians."

and bending a cautious glance towards his companion, he continued in a manner that was divided between interrogation and assertion—"does not this stream at our feet, run towards the summer, until its waters grow salt, and the current flows upward!"

"It can't be denied, that your traditions tell you true in both these matters," said the white man; "for I have been there, and have seen them; though, why water, which is so sweet in the shade, should become bitter in the sun, is an alteration for which I have never been able to account."

"And the current!" demanded the Indian, who expected his reply with that sort of interest that a man feels in the confirmation of testimony, at which he marvels even while he respects it; "the fathers of Chingachgook have not lied!"

"The Holy Bible is not more true, and that is the truest thing in nature. They call this up-stream current the tide, which is a thing soon explained, and clear enough. Six hours the waters run in, and six hours they run out, and the reason is this; when there is higher water in the sea than in the river, it runs in, until the river gets to be highest, and then it runs out again."

"The waters in the woods, and on the great lakes, run downward until they lie like my hand," said the Indian, stretching the limb horizontally before him, "and then they run no more."

"No honest man will deny it," said the scout, a little nettled at the implied distrust of his explanation of the mystery of the tides; "and I grant that it is true on the small scale, and where the land is level. But every thing depends on what scale you look at things. Now, on the small scale, the 'arth is level; but on the large scale it is round. In this manner, pools and ponds, and even the great fresh water lakes, may be stagnant, as you and I both know they are, having seen them; but when you come to spread water over a great tract, like the sea, where the earth is round, how in reason can the water be quiet? You might as well expect the river to lie still on the brink of those black rocks a mile above us, though your own ears tell you that it is tumbling over them at this very moment!"

If unsatisfied by the philosophy of his companion, the Indian was far too dignified to betray his unbelief. He listened like one who was convinced, and resumed his narrative in his former solemn manner.

"We came from the place where the sun is hid at night, over great plains where the buffaloes live, until we reached the big river. There we fought the Alligewi,[6] till the ground was red with their blood. From the banks of the big river to the shores of the salt lake, there were none to meet us. The Maquas[7] followed at a distance. We said the country should be ours from the place where the water runs up no longer, on this stream, to a river, twenty suns' journey toward the summer. The land we had taken like warriors, we kept like men. We drove the Maquas into the woods with the bears. They only tasted salt at the licks; they drew no fish from the great lake: we threw them the bones."

"All this I have heard and believe," said the white man, observing that the Indian paused; "but it was long before the English came into the country."

6. Alleghanys, who, according to the Mohicans' tradition, were identical with the Cherokees.   7. Iroquois.

"A pine grew then, where this chestnut now stands. The first pale faces who came among us spoke no English. They came in a large canoe, when my fathers had buried the tomahawk with the red men around them. Then, Hawk-eye," he continued, betraying his deep emotion, only by permitting his voice to fall to those low, guttural tones, which render his language, as spoken at times, so very musical; "then, Hawk-eye, we were one people, and we were happy. The salt lake gave us its fish, the wood its deer, and the air its birds. We took wives who bore us children; we worshipped the Great Spirit; and we kept the Maquas beyond the sound of our songs of triumph!"

"Know you any thing of your own family, at that time?" demanded the white. "But you are a just man for an Indian! and as I suppose you hold their gifts, your fathers must have been brave warriors, and wise men at the council fire."

"My tribe is the grandfather of nations," said the native, "but I am an unmixed man. The blood of chiefs is in my veins, where it must stay for ever. The Dutch landed, and gave my people the fire-water;[8] they drank until the heavens and the earth seemed to meet, and they foolishly thought they had found the Great Spirit. Then they parted with their land. Foot by foot, they were driven back from the shores, until I, that am a chief and a Sagamore,[9] have never seen the sun shine but through the trees, and have never visited the graves of my fathers."

"Graves bring solemn feelings over the mind," returned the scout, a good deal touched at the calm suffering of his companion; "and often aid a man in his good intentions, though, for myself, I expect to leave my own bones unburied, to bleach in the woods, or to be torn asunder by the wolves. But where are to be found your race, which came to their kin in the Delaware country, so many summers since?"

"Where are the blossoms of those summers!—fallen, one by one: so all of my family departed, each in his turn, to the land of spirits. I am on the hill-top, and must go down into the valley; and when Uncas follows in my footsteps, there will no longer be any of the blood of the Sagamores, for my boy is the last of the Mohicans."

"Uncas is here!" said another voice, in the same soft, guttural tones, near his elbow; "who wishes Uncas?"

The white man loosened his knife in its leathern sheath, and made an involuntary movement of the hand towards his rifle, at this sudden interruption, but the Indian sat composed, and without turning his head at the unexpected sounds.

At the next instant, a youthful warrior passed between them, with a noiseless step, and seated himself on the bank of the rapid stream. No exclamation of surprise escaped the father, nor was any question made or reply given for several minutes, each appearing to await the moment, when he might speak, without betraying a womanish curiosity or childish impatience. The white man seemed to take counsel from their customs, and relinquishing his grasp of the rifle, he also remained silent and reserved. At length Chingachgook turned his eyes slowly towards his son, and demanded—

"Do the Maquas dare to leave the print of their moccasins in these woods?"

8. Alcoholic beverages.   9. Leader among chiefs.

"I have been on their trail," replied the young Indian, "and know that they number as many as the fingers of my two hands; but they lie hid like cowards."

"The thieves are outlying for scalps and plunder!" said the white man, whom we shall call Hawk-eye, after the manner of his companions. "That busy Frenchman, Montcalm, will send his spies into our very camp, but he will know what road we travel!"

"'Tis enough!" returned the father, glancing his eye towards the setting sun; "they shall be driven like deer from their bushes. Hawk-eye, let us eat to-night, and show the Maquas that we are men tomorrow."

"I am as ready to do the one as the other," replied the scout; "but to fight the Iroquois,'tis necessary to find the skulkers; and to eat,'tis necessary to get the game—talk of the devil and he will come; there is a pair of the biggest antlers I have seen this season, moving the bushes below the hill! Now, Uncas," he continued in a half whisper, and laughing with a kind of inward sound, like one who had learnt to be watchful, "I will bet my charger three times full of powder, against a foot of wampum,[1] that I take him atwixt the eyes, and nearer to the right than to the left."

"It cannot be!" said the young Indian, springing to his feet with youthful eagerness; "all but the tips of his horns are hid!"

"He's a boy!" said the white man, shaking his head while he spoke, and addressing the father. "Does he think when a hunter sees a part of the creatur, he can't tell where the rest of him should be!"

Adjusting his rifle, he was about to make an exhibition of that skill, on which he so much valued himself, when the warrior struck up the piece with his hand, saying,

"Hawk-eye! will you fight the Maquas?"

"These Indians know the nature of the woods, as it might be by instinct!" returned the scout, dropping his rifle, and turning away like a man who was convinced of his error. "I must leave the buck to your arrow, Uncas, or we may kill a deer for them thieves, the Iroquois, to eat."

The instant the father seconded this intimation by an expressive gesture of the hand, Uncas threw himself on the ground, and approached the animal with wary movements. When, within a few yards of the cover, he fitted an arrow to his bow with the utmost care, while the antlers moved, as if their owner snuffed an enemy in the tainted air. In another moment the twang of the bow was heard, a white streak was seen glancing into the bushes, and the wounded buck plunged from the cover, to the very feet of his hidden enemy. Avoiding the horns of the infuriated animal, Uncas darted to his side, and passed his knife across the throat, when bounding to the edge of the river, it fell, dying the waters with its blood to a great distance.

"'Twas done with Indian skill," said the scout, laughing inwardly, but with vast satisfaction; "and was a pretty sight to behold! Though an arrow is a near shot, and needs a knife to finish the work."

"Hugh!" ejaculated his companion, turning quickly, like a hound who scented his game.

"By the Lord, there is a drove of them!" exclaimed the hunting scout, whose eyes began to glisten with the ardour of his usual occupation; "if they come within range of a bullet, I will drop one, though the whole Six

1. Beads or other articles used as currency.

Nations[2] should be lurking within sound! What do you hear, Chingach-gook? for to my ears the woods are dumb."

"There is but one deer, and he is dead," said the Indian, bending his body, till his ear nearly touched the earth. "I hear the sounds of feet!"

"Perhaps the wolves have driven that buck to shelter, and are following in his trail."

"No. The horses of white men are coming!" returned the other, raising himself with dignity, and resuming his seat on the log with all his former composure. "Hawk-eye, they are your brothers; speak to them."

"That will I, and in English that the king needn't be ashamed to answer," returned the hunter, speaking in the language of which he boasted; "but I see nothing, nor do I hear the sounds of man or beast; 'tis strange that an Indian should understand white sounds better than a man, who, his very enemies will own, has no cross[3] in his blood, although he may have lived with the red skins long enough to be suspected! Ha! there goes something like the crack-ing of a dry stick, too—now I hear the bushes move—yes, yes, there is a tramping that I mistook for the falls—and—but here they come themselves; God keep them from the Iroquois!"

1826

2. A formal tribal alliance, also known as the Iro-quois Confederacy, of the Mohawks, Oneidas, Onondagas, Cayugas, Senecas, and Tuscaroras in the area of what is now upstate New York.

3. In this and other novels of the Leatherstock-ing series, Natty Bumppo insists on his pure whiteness.

WILLIAM CULLEN BRYANT
1794–1878

William Cullen Bryant made his mark on American poetry in 1821 with the publication of a slim volume, *Poems*, whose lyrical meditations on nature and death brought him international recognition as a poet worthy of being considered alongside William Wordsworth. He continued to publish poetry in miscellanies and newspapers, while bringing out volumes of his new and collected poems throughout his long lifetime. Though he never again received the critical acclaim that he had in 1821, he became increasingly popular and had many admirers. In an 1846 issue of the *Brooklyn Eagle*, for instance, Walt Whitman criticized the "literary quacks" who failed to appreciate "this beautiful poet," describing him as "a poet who, to our mind, stands among the first in the world." That same year, Poe proclaimed in the widely read *Godey's Lady's Book* that "Mr. Bryant has genius, and that of a marked character" and lamented that his talent "has been overlooked by modern schools." In part Bryant was overlooked because he refused to promote himself. Unlike Poe, Emerson, and Whitman, who all wrote poetic manifestos celebrating their own approaches to poetry, Bryant quietly published his work without making large claims for its importance. For much of his adult life he worked as a newspaper editor com-mitted first to the Jacksonian Democratic party and then to the Free Soil and

Republican parties. The poetry he continued to write and publish took on an increasingly public aspect, adding political topics of the day to his subject matter.

Bryant was born in the rural town of Cummington, Massachusetts. Encouraged by his parents, he learned Greek and Latin as a child. In 1807, when he was twelve, he published his first poem in the *Hampshire Gazette* in Northampton, Massachusetts; in 1808, he wrote a long anti-Jefferson poem, *The Embargo; or, Sketches of the Times: A Satire by a Youth of Thirteen*, which his Federalist father printed as a pamphlet. Bryant entered Williams College in 1810, but left after seven months with the hope of transferring to Yale. When his father revealed that he could no longer afford Bryant's college expenses, he continued to write poetry while preparing for a legal career by working in the law office of a family friend. He was admitted to the bar in 1815.

In July 1815, Bryant wrote "To a Waterfowl" and soon after wrote the first, shorter version of "Thanatopsis," the poem that established his reputation. Bryant's mother had taught him a harsh Calvinism. "Thanatopsis," however, conveys a pantheistic view of God in nature indicative of the increasing influence of liberal Protestantism, particularly Unitarianism, on Bryant's imagination. In his early teens Bryant was attracted to the pensive gloom of such eighteenth-century British graveyard poets as Robert Blair ("The Grave" [1743]) and Thomas Gray ("Elegy Written in a Country Churchyard" [1750]). His reading of Wordsworth's *Lyrical Ballads* (1798) influenced his prosody and inspired his own continuing development from a neoclassical to a Romantic poet who discerned moral lessons and a divine presence in the American landscape. Bryant's ever-supportive father sponsored the publication of the early version of "Thanatopsis" in the 1817 *North American Review*; the 1821 version concludes with a fervent injunction to trust in self and nature, thereby anticipating (and perhaps helping to inspire) Emerson's writings of the 1830s and 1840s.

Bryant would have liked to support himself as a poet, but this was impossible at the time, so in 1816 he opened a law partnership; he worked as a lawyer into the mid-1820s. In 1821 he married Frances Fairchild; the couple had two daughters. That same year he was invited to deliver the Phi Beta Kappa poem at Harvard College's commencement. He read a long poem on the progress of liberty, "The Ages," whose favorable reception induced him to publish his *Poems* later that year. Buoyed by the book's success, Bryant embarked on a practical kind of literary career by moving to New York City to edit the *New-York Review and Atheneum Magazine*. Welcomed as a celebrity, he embraced metropolitan life, becoming an early member of James Fenimore Cooper's Bread and Cheese Club and developing a close friendship with Catharine Sedgwick. She dedicated her second novel, *Redwood* (1823), to him and he favorably reviewed it in the April 1825 *North American Review*. Though the *New-York Review* failed, Bryant stayed in New York as an editorial assistant on the New York *Evening Post*. By 1829 he was the newspaper's part owner and editor-in-chief, a position he would keep for nearly fifty years. A Jacksonian Democrat, Bryant championed the rights of labor unions, the virtues of free trade, prison reform, the importance of international copyright protection for authors, and antislavery. His loathing of slavery eventually prompted him to lead the anti-slavery Free-Soil movement within the Democratic Party, and then leave the party altogether. In the mid-1850s he helped form the Republican Party and in 1860 was an influential supporter of Abraham Lincoln.

As he and his newspaper prospered, Bryant traveled widely in the United States and abroad. In 1850 he brought out *Letters of a Traveller*, the first of three collections of his travel writings. He also published more than ten volumes of poetry between 1832 and 1876. His best known public poem was "The Death of Lincoln," which he wrote shortly after the assassination; it was read to thousands gathered at New York City's Union Square the day before Lincoln's body arrived for a viewing. Bryant's wife, Frances, died in 1866, but he held on to his editorship at the *Evening Post*. In his seventies he began the remarkably ambitious project of translating Homer. His blank-verse version of the *Iliad* appeared in 1870 and his *Odyssey* followed in 1872.

The 1876 publication of his collected *Poems* crowned his career. Two years later, he died of the consequences of a fall after he gave a speech at the unveiling of a statue of the Italian patriot and revolutionary Giuseppe Mazzini in Central Park. In New York City flags were lowered to half-staff, and Bryant was mourned as a great poet and editor.

Thanatopsis[1]

To him who in the love of Nature holds
Communion with her visible forms, she speaks
A various language; for his gayer hours
She has a voice of gladness, and a smile
And eloquence of beauty, and she glides   5
Into his darker musings, with a mild
And gentle sympathy, that steals away
Their sharpness, ere he is aware. When thoughts
Of the last bitter hour come like a blight
Over thy spirit, and sad images   10
Of the stern agony, and shroud, and pall,
And breathless darkness, and the narrow house,
Make thee to shudder, and grow sick at heart;—
Go forth under the open sky, and list[2]
To Nature's teachings, while from all around—   15
Earth and her waters, and the depths of air,—
Comes a still voice—Yet a few days, and thee
The all-beholding sun shall see no more
In all his course; nor yet in the cold ground,
Where thy pale form was laid, with many tears,   20
Nor in the embrace of ocean shall exist
Thy image. Earth, that nourished thee, shall claim
Thy growth, to be resolv'd to earth again;
And, lost each human trace, surrend'ring up
Thine individual being, shalt thou go   25
To mix forever with the elements,
To be a brother to th' insensible rock
And to the sluggish clod, which the rude swain
Turns with his share,[3] and treads upon. The oak
Shall send his roots abroad, and pierce thy mould. 30
Yet not to thy eternal resting place
Shalt thou retire alone—nor couldst thou wish
Couch more magnificent. Thou shalt lie down
With patriarchs of the infant world—with kings,
The powerful of the earth—the wise, the good,   35
Fair forms, and hoary seers of ages past,
All in one mighty sepulchre.—The hills
Rock-ribb'd and ancient as the sun,—the vales

1. From *Poems* (1821); a shorter version appeared in the September 1817 issue of the *North American Review*.
2. Listen.
3. Plowshare. "Swain": farmer.

Stretching in pensive quietness between;
The venerable woods—rivers that move   40
In majesty, and the complaining brooks
That make the meadows green; and pour'd round all,
Old ocean's grey and melancholy waste,—
Are but the solemn decorations all
Of the great tomb of man. The golden sun,   45
The planets, all the infinite host of heaven,
Are shining on the sad abodes of death,
Through the still lapse of ages. All that tread
The globe are but a handful to the tribes
That slumber in its bosom.—Take the wings   50
Of morning—and the Barcan desert[4] pierce,
Or lose thyself in the continuous woods
Where rolls the Oregan,[5] and hears no sound,
Save his own dashings—yet—the dead are there,
And millions in those solitudes, since first   55
The flight of years began, have laid them down
In their last sleep—the dead reign there alone.—
So shalt thou rest—and what if thou shalt fall
Unnoticed by the living—and no friend
Take note of thy departure? All that breathe   60
Will share thy destiny. The gay will laugh
When thou art gone, the solemn brood of care
Plod on, and each one as before will chase
His favourite phantom; yet all these shall leave
Their mirth and their employments, and shall come,   65
And make their bed with thee. As the long train
Of ages glide away, the sons of men,
The youth in life's green spring, and he who goes
In the full strength of years, matron, and maid,
The bow'd with age, the infant in the smiles   70
And beauty of its innocent age cut off,—
Shall one by one be gathered to thy side,
By those, who in their turn shall follow them.
So live, that when thy summons comes to join
The innumerable caravan, that moves   75
To the pale realms of shade, where each shall take
His chamber in the silent halls of death,
Thou go not, like the quarry-slave at night,
Scourged to his dungeon, but sustain'd and sooth'd
By an unfaltering trust, approach thy grave,   80
Like one who wraps the drapery of his couch
About him, and lies down to pleasant dreams.

1817   1821

4. In Barca (northeast Libya).
5. An early variant spelling of Oregon; now the Columbia River.

To a Waterfowl[1]

Whither, 'midst falling dew,
While glow the heavens with the last steps of day,
Far, through their rosy depths, dost thou pursue
    Thy solitary way?

Vainly the fowler's eye   5
Might mark thy distant flight to do thee wrong,
As, darkly painted on the crimson sky,
    Thy figure floats along.

Seek'st thou the plashy[2] brink
Of weedy lake, or marge of river wide,   10
Or where the rocking billows rise and sink
    On the chafed ocean side?

There is a Power whose care
Teaches thy way along that pathless coast,—
The desert and illimitable air,—   15
    Lone wandering, but not lost.

All day thy wings have fann'd
At that far height, the cold thin atmosphere:
Yet stoop not, weary, to the welcome land,
    Though the dark night is near.   20

And soon that toil shall end,
Soon shalt thou find a summer home, and rest,
And scream among thy fellows; reeds shall bend
    Soon o'er thy sheltered nest.

Thou'rt gone, the abyss of heaven   25
Hath swallowed up thy form; yet, on my heart
Deeply hath sunk the lesson thou hast given,
    And shall not soon depart.

He, who, from zone to zone,
Guides through the boundless sky thy certain flight,   30
In the long way that I must tread alone,
    Will lead my steps aright.

1818   1821

---

1. From *Poems* (1821); an earlier version appeared in the May 1818 issue of the *North American Review*.
2. Marshy.

The Prairies[1]

These are the Gardens of the Desert, these
The unshorn fields, boundless and beautiful,
And fresh as the young earth, ere man had sinned—
The Prairies. I behold them for the first,
And my heart swells, while the dilated sight   5
Takes in the encircling vastness. Lo! they stretch
In airy undulations, far away,
As if the ocean, in his gentlest swell,
Stood still, with all his rounded billows fixed,
And motionless for ever.—Motionless?—   10
No—they are all unchained again. The clouds
Sweep over with their shadows, and beneath
The surface rolls and fluctuates to the eye;
Dark hollows seem to glide along and chase
The sunny ridges. Breezes of the South!   15
Who toss the golden and the flame-like flowers,
And pass the prairie-hawk that, poised on high,
Flaps his broad wings, yet moves not—ye have played
Among the palms of Mexico and vines
Of Texas, and have crisped the limpid brooks   20
That from the fountains of Sonora[2] glide
Into the calm Pacific—have ye fanned
A nobler or a lovelier scene than this?
Man hath no part in all this glorious work:
The hand that built the firmament hath heaved   25
And smoothed these verdant swells, and sown their slopes
With herbage, planted them with island groves,
And hedged them round with forests. Fitting floor
For this magnificent temple of the sky—
With flowers whose glory and whose multitude   30
Rival the constellations! The great heavens
Seem to stoop down upon the scene in love,—
A nearer vault, and of a tenderer blue,
Than that which bends above the eastern hills.
    As o'er the verdant waste I guide my steed,   35
Among the high rank grass that sweeps his sides,
The hollow beating of his footstep seems
A sacrilegious sound. I think of those
Upon whose rest he tramples. Are they here—
The dead of other days!—and did the dust   40
Of these fair solitudes once stir with life
And burn with passion? Let the mighty mounds[3]
That overlook the rivers, or that rise
In the dim forest crowded with old oaks,
Answer. A race, that long has passed away,   45

---

1. From the first printing in *Poems* (1834). Bryant wrote the poem over a year after visiting his brothers in Illinois during 1832.
2. River in northwest Mexico.

3. The burial mounds common in Illinois. Bryant follows a contemporary theory that they were built by a culture older than the American Indians.

Built them;—a disciplined and populous race
Heaped, with long toil, the earth, while yet the Greek
Was hewing the Pentelicus[4] to forms
Of symmetry, and rearing on its rock
The glittering Parthenon. These ample fields   50
Nourished their harvests, here their herds were fed,
When haply by their stalls the bison lowed,
And bowed his maned shoulder to the yoke.
All day this desert murmured with their toils,
Till twilight blushed and lovers walked, and wooed   55
In a forgotten language, and old tunes,
From instruments of unremembered form,
Gave the soft winds a voice. The red man came—
The roaming hunter tribes, warlike and fierce,
And the mound-builders vanished from the earth.   60
The solitude of centuries untold
Has settled where they dwelt. The prairie wolf
Hunts in their meadows, and his fresh dug den
Yawns by my path. The gopher mines the ground
Where stood their swarming cities. All is gone—   65
All—save the piles of earth that hold their bones—
The platforms where they worshipped unknown gods—
The barriers which they builded from the soil
To keep the foe at bay—till o'er the walls
The wild beleaguerers broke, and, one by one,   70
The strong holds of the plain were forced, and heaped
With corpses. The brown vultures of the wood
Flocked to those vast uncovered sepulchres,
And sat, unscared and silent, at their feast.
Haply some solitary fugitive,   75
Lurking in marsh and forest, till the sense
Of desolation and of fear became
Bitterer than death, yielded himself to die.
Man's better nature triumphed. Kindly words
Welcomed and soothed him; the rude conquerors   80
Seated the captive with their chiefs. He chose
A bride among their maidens. And at length
Seemed to forget,—yet ne'er forgot,—the wife
Of his first love, and her sweet little ones
Butchered, amid their shrieks, with all his race.   85
   Thus change the forms of being. Thus arise
Races of living things, glorious in strength,
And perish, as the quickening breath of God
Fills them, or is withdrawn. The red man too—
Has left the blooming wilds he ranged so long,   90
And, nearer to the Rocky Mountains, sought
A wider hunting ground. The beaver builds
No longer by these streams, but far away,
On waters whose blue surface ne'er gave back

4. Greek mountain from which a fine white marble was quarried, including that used in building the Parthenon, the temple of Athena on the Acropolis in Athens.

The white man's face—among Missouri's springs,   95
And pools whose issues swell the Oregan,[5]
He rears his little Venice.[6] In these plains
The bison feeds no more. Twice twenty leagues
Beyond remotest smoke of hunter's camp,
Roams the majestic brute, in herds that shake   100
The earth with thundering steps—yet here I meet
His ancient footprints stamped beside the pool.
    Still this great solitude is quick with life.
Myriads of insects, gaudy as the flowers
They flutter over, gentle quadrupeds,   105
And birds, that scarce have learned the fear of man
Are here, and sliding reptiles of the ground,
Startlingly beautiful. The graceful deer
Bounds to the wood at my approach. The bee,
A more adventurous colonist than man,   110
With whom he came across the eastern deep,
Fills the savannas with his murmurings,
And hides his sweets, as in the golden age,
Within the hollow oak. I listen long
To his domestic hum, and think I hear   115
The sound of that advancing multitude
Which soon shall fill these deserts. From the ground
Comes up the laugh of children, the soft voice
Of maidens, and the sweet and solemn hymn
Of Sabbath worshippers. The low of herds   120
Blends with the rustling of the heavy grain
Over the dark-brown furrows. All at once
A fresher wind sweeps by, and breaks my dream,
And I am in the wilderness alone.

                                                                 1834

---

5. The Columbia River.   6. I.e., builds a city in the water.

WILLIAM APESS
1798–1839

L ittle is known of William Apess's early life other than what he reports in *A Son of the Forest* (1829), the first extensive autobiography published by a Native American. His grandfather, says Apess, was a white man who married the granddaughter of the Wampanoag leader King Philip, or Metacom, whose death at the hands of the English colonists in 1676 brought an end to King Philip's War. Philip increasingly occupied Apess's thoughts during his lifetime, serving as the subject of his last published work. Apess's father, although of mixed blood, joined the Pequot tribe and married an Indian woman who may have been part African American. Born in

1798 in the rural town of Colrain, Massachusetts, Apess by the late 1820s and early 1830s had emerged as a notable reformist leader, arguing for the rights of Native American peoples while developing pointed critiques of the racism of white America. His speeches were noted in William Lloyd Garrison's widely read abolitionist newspaper, *The Liberator*, and may have had an impact on Frederick Douglass's early writings. More important, Apess, through his defiant and questioning rhetoric, helped to set the terms of cultural debate for Native Americans of his own time and beyond.

In *A Son of the Forest*, Apess details the pains of his early life. When he was three he was taken into the home of his poor, alcoholic maternal grandparents, where he was severely beaten. At four or five, he was sold as an indentured laborer. His first master allowed him to attend school for six years, which constituted his entire formal education; this master also introduced him to Christianity. Apess served as a soldier in the abortive American attack on Montreal in the War of 1812 and converted to evangelical Methodism after leaving the army. At the conclusion of *A Son of the Forest*, Apess writes that he achieved an "exhorter's" license from his church, enabling him to earn a living as an itinerant preacher; only later would he realize his goal of ordination as a Methodist minister.

A fervent Christian, Apess early understood Christianity as incompatible with any form of race prejudice, thereby presaging the position of a number of Christian abolitionists of the 1840s and 1850s. In 1833, Apess went to preach at Mashpee, the only remaining Indian town in Massachusetts. There he became involved in the Mashpee people's struggle to preserve their resources and rights, which were threatened by the overseers imposed on them by the Commonwealth of Massachusetts. The Mashpee eventually drew up petitions, probably composed by Apess, requiring that no whites cut wood or hay on Mashpee lands without the Indians' consent. As the petition proclaimed, "We, as a tribe, will rule ourselves, and have the right to do so; for all men are born free and equal, says the Constitution of the Country." Such unprecedented assertiveness on the part of the Indians alarmed the governor of Massachusetts, who announced his readiness to put down the "Mashpee Revolt" with troops. Apess's version of the controversy appears in his *Indian Nullification of the Unconstitutional Laws of Massachusetts, Relative to the Marshpee* [sic] *Tribe; or, The Pretended Riot Explained* (1835). A year before the book appeared, the Mashpee case was won when the state legislature granted the tribe the same rights of self-governance that other Massachusetts townships possessed.

Apess's career as a preacher and an author came to a close with his "Eulogy on King Philip," delivered in 1836 at the Odeon in Boston, one of the city's largest public lecture halls, and published that same year. In the "Eulogy," Apess meditates on his distant relation, naming Philip the foremost man that America had thus far produced. He reminds his audience, descendants of the Pilgrims, of the crimes of their ancestors: although "you and I have to rejoice that we have not to answer for our fathers' crimes; neither shall we do right to charge them one to another." Nonetheless, he notes, "in vain have I looked for the Christian to take me by the hand and bid me welcome to his cabin, as my fathers did them [the Christians], before we were born." Apess concludes that a "different course must be pursued. . . . And while you ask yourselves, 'What do they, the Indians, want?' you have only to look at the unjust laws made for them and say, 'They want what I want'": justice and Christian fellowship. Shortly after delivering this eulogy, Apess left the ministry and began to disappear from the public record. The evidence suggests that he moved to New York City in 1837, married a woman named Elizabeth, and died in debt, of what was described as "apoplexy," on April 10, 1839.

The selection that follows is the final chapter of *The Experiences of Five Christian Indians of the Pequot Tribe*, published in 1833, the year Apess came to Mashpee. The first of the "experiences" described in *Experiences of Five Christian Indians* is Apess's own, an account of his life and conversion that repeats some of the material in *A Son of the Forest* but intensifies considerably his condemnation of the Euro-American treatment of Native peoples. Apess concludes this book with the text reprinted here, "An Indian's Looking-Glass for the White Man," a searing indictment of race prejudice against people of color generally and Native Americans in particular.

An Indian's Looking-Glass for the White Man[1]

Having a desire to place a few things before my fellow creatures who are travelling with me to the grave, and to that God who is the maker and preserver both of the white man and the Indian, whose abilities are the same, and who are to be judged by one God, who will show no favor to outward appearances, but will judge righteousness. Now I ask if degradation has not been heaped long enough upon the Indians? And if so, can there not be a compromise; is it right to hold and promote prejudices? If not, why not put them all away? I mean here amongst those who are civilized. It may be that many are ignorant of the situation of many of my brethren within the limits of New England. Let me for a few moments turn your attention to the reservations in the different states of New England, and, with but few exceptions, we shall find them as follows: The most mean, abject, miserable race of beings in the world—a complete place of prodigality and prostitution.

Let a gentleman and lady of integrity and respectability visit these places, and they would be surprised; as they wandered from one hut to the other they would view with the females who are left alone, children half starved, and some almost as naked as they came into the world. And it is a fact that I have seen them as much so—while the females are left without protection, and are seduced by white men, and are finally left to be common prostitutes for them, and to be destroyed by that burning, fiery curse, that has swept millions, both of red and white men, into the grave with sorrow and disgrace—Rum. One reason why they are left so is, because their most sensible and active men are absent at sea. Another reason is, because they are made to believe they are minors and have not the abilities given them from God, to take care of themselves, without it is to see to a few little articles, such as baskets and brooms. Their land is in common stock, and they have nothing to make them enterprising.

Another reason is because those men who are Agents,[2] many of them are unfaithful, and care not whether the Indians live or die; they are much imposed upon by their neighbors who have no principle. They would think it no crime to go upon Indian lands and cut and carry off their most valuable timber, or any thing else they chose; and I doubt not but they think it clear gain. Another reason is because they have no education to take care of themselves; if they had, I would risk them to take care of their own property.

Now I will ask, if the Indians are not called the most ingenious people amongst us? And are they not said to be men of talents? And I would ask, could there be a more efficient way to distress and murder them by inches than the way they have taken? And there is no people in the world but who

1. The text is from William Apes, *The Experiences of Five Christian Indians of the Pequot Tribe* (Boston: James B. Dow, 1833).

2. Those appointed by the Commonwealth of Massachusetts to oversee Indian affairs in such towns as Mashpee.

may be destroyed in the same way. Now if these people are what they are held up in our view to be, I would take the liberty to ask why they are not brought forward and pains taken to educate them? to give them all a common education, and those of the brightest and first-rate talents put forward and held up to office. Perhaps some unholy, unprincipled men would cry out, the skin was not good enough; but stop friends—I am not talking about the skin, but about principles. I would ask if there cannot be as good feelings and principles under a red skin as there can be under a white? And let me ask, is it not on the account of a bad principle, that we who are red children have had to suffer so much as we have? And let me ask, did not this bad principle proceed from the whites or their forefathers? And I would ask, is it worth while to nourish it any longer? If not, then let us have a change; although some men no doubt will spout their corrupt principles against it, that are in the halls of legislation and elsewhere. But I presume this kind of talk will seem surprising and horrible. I do not see why it should so long as they (the whites) say that they think as much of us as they do of themselves.

This I have heard repeatedly, from the most respectable gentlemen and ladies—and having heard so much precept, I should now wish to see the example. And I would ask who has a better right to look for these things than the naturalist[3] himself—the candid man would say none.

I know that many say that they are willing, perhaps the majority of the people, that we should enjoy our rights and privileges as they do. If so, I would ask why are not we protected in our persons and property throughout the Union? Is it not because there reigns in the breast of many who are leaders, a most unrighteous, unbecoming and impure black principle, and as corrupt and unholy as it can be—while these very same unfeeling, self-esteemed characters pretend to take the skin as a pretext to keep us from our unalienable and lawful rights? I would ask you if you would like to be disfranchised from all your rights, merely because your skin is white, and for no other crime? I'll venture to say, these very characters who hold the skin to be such a barrier in the way, would be the first to cry out, injustice! awful injustice!

But, reader, I acknowledge that this is a confused world, and I am not seeking for office; but merely placing before you the black inconsistency that you place before me—which is ten times blacker than any skin that you will find in the Universe. And now let me exhort you to do away that principle, as it appears ten times worse in the sight of God and candid men, than skins of color—more disgraceful than all the skins that Jehovah ever made. If black or red skins, or any other skin of color is disgraceful to God, it appears that he has disgraced himself a great deal—for he has made fifteen colored people to one white, and placed them here upon this earth.

Now let me ask you, white man, if it is a disgrace for to eat, drink and sleep with the image of God, or sit, or walk and talk with them? Or have you the folly to think that the white man, being one in fifteen or sixteen, are the only beloved images of God? Assemble all nations together in your imagination, and then let the whites be seated amongst them, and then let us look for the whites, and I doubt not it would be hard finding them; for to the rest of the nations, they are still but a handful. Now suppose these

3. I.e., the American Indian; a play on the view of Indians as children of nature or "sons of the forest."

skins were put together, and each skin had its national crimes written upon it—which skin do you think would have the greatest? I will ask one question more. Can you charge the Indians with robbing a nation almost of their whole Continent, and murdering their women and children, and then depriving the remainder of their lawful rights, that nature and God require them to have? And to cap the climax, rob another nation to till their grounds, and welter out their days under the lash with hunger and fatigue under the scorching rays of a burning sun?[4] I should look at all the skins, and I know that when I cast my eye upon that white skin, and if I saw those crimes written upon it, I should enter my protest against it immediately, and cleave to that which is more honorable. And I can tell you that I am satisfied with the manner of my creation, fully—whether others are or not.

But we will strive to penetrate more fully into the conduct of those who profess to have pure principles, and who tell us to follow Jesus Christ and imitate him and have his Spirit. Let us see if they come any where near him and his ancient disciples. The first thing we are to look at, are his precepts, of which we will mention a few. 'Thou shalt love the Lord thy God with all thy heart, with all thy soul, with all thy mind, and with all thy strength. The second is like unto it. Thou shalt love thy neighbor as thyself. On these two precepts hang all the law and the prophets.'—Matt. xxii. 37, 38, 39, 40. 'By this shall all men know that they are my disciples, if ye have love one to another.'—John xiii. 35. Our Lord left this special command with his followers, that they should love one another.

Again, John in his Epistles says, 'He who loveth God, loveth his brother also.'—iv. 21. 'Let us not love in word but in deed.'—iii. 18. 'Let your love be without dissimulation. See that ye love one another with a pure heart fervently.'—1. Peter, viii. 22. 'If any man say, I love God, and hateth his brother, he is a liar.'—John iv. 20. 'Whosoever hateth his brother is a murderer, and no murderer hath eternal life abiding in him.' The first thing that takes our attention, is the saying of Jesus, 'Thou shalt love,' &c. The first question I would ask my brethren in the ministry, as well as that of the membership, What is love, or its effects? Now if they who teach are not essentially affected with pure love, the love of God, how can they teach as they ought? Again, the holy teachers of old said, 'Now if any man have not the spirit of Christ, he is none of his.'—Rom. viii. 9. Now my brethren in the ministry, let me ask you a few sincere questions. Did you ever hear or read of Christ teaching his disciples that they ought to despise one because his skin was different from theirs? Jesus Christ being a Jew, and those of his Apostles certainly were not whites,—and did not he who completed the plan of salvation complete it for the whites as well as for the Jews, and others? And were not the whites the most degraded people on the earth at that time, and none were more so; for they sacrificed their children to dumb idols![5] And did not St. Paul labor more abundantly for building up a Christian nation amongst you than any of the Apostles. And you know as well as I that you are not indebted to a principle beneath a white skin for your religious services, but to a colored one.

4. The reference is to the "nation" of Africa.
5. The ancient Hebrews considered various Middle Eastern peoples idolators whose practices were said to include child sacrifice.

What then is the matter now; is not religion the same now under a colored skin as it ever was? If so I would ask why is not a man of color respected; you may say as many say, we have white men enough. But was this the spirit of Christ and his Apostles? If it had been, there would not have been one white preacher in the world—for Jesus Christ never would have imparted his grace or word to them, for he could forever have withheld it from them. But we find that Jesus Christ and his Apostles never looked at the outward appearances. Jesus in particular looked at the hearts, and his Apostles through him being discerners of the spirit, looked at their fruit without any regard to the skin, color or nation; as St. Paul himself speaks, 'Where there is neither Greek nor Jew, circumcision nor uncircumcision, Barbarian nor Scythian, bond nor free—but Christ is all and in all.'[6] If you can find a spirit like Jesus Christ and his Apostles prevailing now in any of the white congregations, I should like to know it. I ask, is it not the case that everybody that is not white is treated with contempt and counted as barbarians? And I ask if the word of God justifies the white man in so doing? When the prophets prophesied, of whom did they speak? When they spoke of heathens, was it not the whites and others who were counted Gentiles? And I ask if all nations with the exception of the Jews were not counted heathens? and according to the writings of some, it could not mean the Indians, for they are counted Jews.[7] And now I would ask, why is all this distinction made among these Christian societies? I would ask what is all this ado about Missionary Societies, if it be not to Christianize those who are not Christians? And what is it for? To degrade them worse, to bring them into society where they must welter out their days in disgrace merely because their skin is of a different complexion. What folly it is to try to make the state of human society worse than it is. How astonished some may be at this—but let me ask, is it not so? Let me refer you to the churches only. And my brethren, is there any agreement? Do brethren and sisters love one another?—Do they not rather hate one another. Outward forms and ceremonies, the lusts of the flesh, the lusts of the eye and pride of life is of more value to many professors,[8] than the love of God shed abroad in their hearts, or an attachment to his altar, to his ordinances or to his children. But you may ask who are the children of God? perhaps you may say none but white. If so, the word of the Lord is not true.

I will refer you to St. Peter's precepts—Acts 10. 'God is no respecter of persons'—&c. Now if this is the case, my white brother, what better are you than God? And if no better, why do you who profess his gospel and to have his spirit, act so contrary to it? Let me ask why the men of a different skin are so despised, why are not they educated and placed in your pulpits? I ask if his services well performed are not as good as if a white man performed them? I ask if a marriage or a funeral ceremony, or the ordinance of the Lord's house would not be as acceptable in the sight of God as though he was white? And if so, why is it not to you? I ask again, why is it not as acceptable to have men to exercise their office in one place as well as in another? Perhaps you will say that if we admit you to all of these privileges you will want more. I expect that I can guess what that is—Why, say you, there would be intermarriages. How that would be I am not able to say—and if it should

---

6. Colossians 3.11.
7. A reference to the notion that Native Americans were descended from the ten lost tribes

of Israel.
8. I.e., those who profess the Christian faith.

be, it would be nothing strange or new to me; for I can assure you that I know a great many that have intermarried, both of the whites and the Indians—and many are their sons and daughters—and people too of the first respectability. And I could point to some in the famous city of Boston and elsewhere. You may now look at the disgraceful act in the statute law passed by the Legislature of Massachusetts, and behold the fifty pound fine levied upon any Clergyman or Justice of the Peace that dare to encourage the laws of God and nature by a legitimate union in holy wedlock between the Indians and whites. I would ask how this looks to your law makers. I would ask if this corresponds with your sayings—that you think as much of the Indians as you do of the whites. I do not wonder that you blush many of you while you read; for many have broken the ill-fated laws made by man to hedge up the laws of God and nature. I would ask if they who have made the law have not broken it—but there is no other state in New England that has this law but Massachusetts; and I think as many of you do not, that you have done yourselves no credit.

But as I am not looking for a wife, having one of the finest cast, as you no doubt would understand while you read her experience and travail of soul in the way to heaven, you will see that it is not my object. And if I had none, I should not want any one to take my right from me and choose a wife for me; for I think that I or any of my brethren have a right to choose a wife for themselves as well as the whites—and as the whites have taken the liberty to choose my brethren, the Indians, hundreds and thousands of them as partners in life, I believe the Indians have as much right to choose their partners amongst the whites if they wish. I would ask you if you can see any thing inconsistent in your conduct and talk about the Indians? And if you do, I hope you will try to become more consistent. Now if the Lord Jesus Christ, who is counted by all to be a Jew, and it is well known that the Jews are a colored people,[9] especially those living in the East, where Christ was born—and if he should appear amongst us, would he not be shut out of doors by many, very quickly? and by those too, who profess religion?

By what you read, you may learn how deep your principles are. I should say they were skin deep. I should not wonder if some of the most selfish and ignorant would spout a charge of their principles now and then at me. But I would ask, how are you to love your neighbors as yourself? Is it to cheat them? is it to wrong them in any thing? Now to cheat them out of any of their rights is robbery. And I ask, can you deny that you are not robbing the Indians daily, and many others? But at last you may think I am what is called a hard and uncharitable man. But not so. I believe there are many who would not hesitate to advocate our cause; and those too who are men of fame and respectability—as well as ladies of honor and virtue. There is a Webster, an Everett, and a Wirt,[1] and many others who are distinguished characters—besides an host of my fellow citizens, who advocate our cause daily. And how I congratulate such noble

9. Refers to the belief that Moses and the biblical Hebrews, including Jesus, were people of color.
1. William Wirt (1772–1834), lawyer, politician, orator, and writer; he served as attorney general under President James Monroe and was nominated by the Whig Party for president. Daniel Webster (1782–1852), orator, legislator, statesman, and interpreter of the Constitution; he served as con-gressman from New Hampshire, senator from Massachusetts, and secretary of state under presidents William Henry Harrison and John Tyler. Edward Everett (1794–1865), the first Eliot Professor of Greek at Harvard and the editor of the prestigious North American Review; he served in Congress and as governor of Massachusetts.

spirits—how they are to be prized and valued; for they are well calculated to promote the happiness of mankind. They well know that man was made for society, and not for hissing stocks[2] and outcasts. And when such a principle as this lies within the hearts of men, how much it is like its God—and how it honors its Maker—and how it imitates the feelings of the good Samaritan, that had his wounds bound up, who had been among thieves and robbers.

Do not get tired, ye noble-hearted—only think how many poor Indians want their wounds done up daily; the Lord will reward you, and pray you stop not till this tree of distinction shall be leveled to the earth, and the mantle of prejudice torn from every American heart—then shall peace pervade the Union.

1833

2. Those who are laughed at or hissed at (i.e., laughingstocks).

RALPH WALDO EMERSON
1803–1882

R alph Waldo Emerson is arguably the most influential American writer of the nineteenth century—the writer with whom numerous other significant writers of the time sought to come to terms. Without Emerson's inspirational essays on nonconformity, self-reliance, and anti-institutionalism, Henry David Thoreau's and Margaret Fuller's careers may have followed different paths; and without Emerson's call for an American bard whose poetry "speaks somewhat wildly" in addressing the nation's "ample geography," Whitman's great poetry might never have been written. Though Melville rejected Emerson's optimism, satirizing him in *The Confidence-Man* (1857) as a philosophical con man, he termed him a "deep diver" as well; Emerson's conception of nature as a sign of spirit permeates Melville's dynamic representations of the whale and the natural world in *Moby-Dick* (1851). Emerson's persisting influence on late-nineteenth- and twentieth-century American writers is evident in astonishing permutations, on figures as diverse as Emily Dickinson, Louisa May Alcott, William James, Theodore Dreiser, Robert Frost, John Dewey, and his namesake Ralph Waldo Ellison.

Emerson was born in Boston on May 25, 1803, the son of a Unitarian minister and the second of five surviving boys. He was eight years old when his father died. Determined to send as many sons as she could to Harvard—the traditional route for ministers-in-training—Emerson's mother kept a succession of boardinghouses. Around this time, Emerson's brilliant, eccentric aunt, Mary Moody Emerson (1774–1863), stepped in to become his principal educator and inspiration, guiding his reading and challenging his thinking over the next several decades. In the more conventional setting of Boston Public Latin School, where he was sent at age nine, and Harvard College, which he attended from 1817 to 1821, Emerson showed no particular promise. Graduating from Harvard thirtieth in a class of fifty-nine, Emerson served, as he put it, as "a hopeless Schoolmaster" in several Boston-area schools. Turning to the study of theology in 1825 at Harvard's Divinity School, he began preaching as a Unitarian in October 1826, and early in 1829 he was ordained by the Unitarians as a junior pastor at Boston's Second Church. In July of that year, he was promoted to pastor.

Led in the 1820s by William Ellery Channing (1780–1842), Boston Unitarianism accepted the Bible as the revelation of God's intentions but no longer held that human beings were innately depraved. In his 1828 sermon "Likeness to God," Channing came close to suggesting that Jesus was not a god but rather the highest expression of humanity. Emerson was deeply influenced by Channing, and his skepticism toward historical Christianity was strengthened by his exposure to the German "higher criticism," which regarded the Judeo-Christian Bible as a document produced in a specific historical time, rather than as the direct word of God, and interpreted biblical miracles as stories comparable to the myths of other cultures. Emerson was gradually developing a greater faith in individual moral sentiment and intuition than in revealed religion.

In 1831 Emerson faced a personal crisis: his wife, Ellen Tucker Emerson, whom he had married in 1829, died of tuberculosis on February 8, at the age of nineteen. Grief-stricken, Emerson wrote his aunt Mary: "My angel is gone to heaven this morning & I am alone in the world." Emerson also faced a spiritual crisis, perhaps precipitated by the death of Ellen, as his thinking developed into a full-fledged disillusionment with his position as pastor and with Unitarianism itself. Early in 1832 Emerson notified his church that he had become so skeptical of the validity of the Lord's Supper that he could no longer administer the sacrament, regarding it, as he remarked in his journal, as "worship in the dead forms of our forefathers." He resigned his pastorate on December 22, 1832, and on Christmas Day sailed for Europe, where he would remain until October 1833. During his European tour, he called on a number of well-known writers, in Italy meeting Walter Savage Landor, in England Samuel Coleridge and William Wordsworth, and in Scotland Thomas Carlyle, with whom he began a lifelong intellectual friendship.

Shortly after his return from Europe in late 1833, Emerson settled a legal dispute with the Tucker family and received the first installment of his wife's legacy. Soon he was assured of more than a thousand dollars annually, a considerable sum for that time. Without the need to produce a constant income, he began a new careeer as a lecturer, speaking around New England in the lyceums—public halls that brought a variety of speakers and performers to cities and smaller towns. In 1835, after a ten-month courtship, he married Lydia Jackson of Plymouth, and they moved to rural Concord, Massachusetts, where the Emerson family had property. There, Emerson completed his first book, *Nature*, which was published anonymously and at Emerson's own expense in 1836.

As the reviewers understood, *Nature* was not a Christian book but one influenced by a range of idealistic philosophies, ancient and modern, going back to Plato and more recently refashioned by a number of European Romantics. Although the favorable reception of *Nature* in England encouraged some American journalists to take Emerson seriously as an intellectual force, Emerson's immediate reward was having the book become the unofficial manifesto for a number of his philosophically inclined friends, who, over the next eight years, would meet irregularly and informally in Emerson's study and elsewhere. Termed "Transcendentalists" by mocking outsiders, the group was composed mainly of ministers who rejected the view of the philosopher John Locke (1643–1704) that the mind was a merely passive receptor of sense impressions, endorsing Samuel Coleridge's and other Romantics' alternative conception of the mind as actively intuitive and creative. Participants included the educators Bronson Alcott (1799–1888) and Elizabeth Palmer Peabody (1804–1894), the abolitionist and Unitarian minister Theodore Parker (1810–1860), the Unitarian minister (later an influential American Catholic) Orestes A. Brownson (1803–1876), Margaret Fuller, and Henry David Thoreau. The group began its own journal, *The Dial* (1840–44), edited for the most part by Emerson, Fuller, and Thoreau.

Nature reached a smaller audience than did many of Emerson's lectures, which were often written up in newspapers; his formal Harvard addresses to the Phi Beta Kappa Society in 1837 on the American scholar and to the Divinity School graduates in 1838 on the state of Christianity were both printed as pamphlets. Conservative ministers attacked "The Divinity School Address" for its rejection of historical Christianity and its bold questioning of the claims made for Christ as a divine savior. But with the publication of *Essays* (1841), Emerson's lasting reputation began to take shape. Far more than *Nature*, this book was directed to a popular audience. The twelve essays in the volume had been tried out, in whole or in part, in his lectures, so that their final form was shaped by the responses of his many audiences.

Early in 1842 Emerson's first son, Waldo, died at the age of five, a loss from which Emerson never fully recovered. Writing in his journal the day after Waldo's death, he expressed his grief and confusion: "Sorrow makes us all children again[,] destroys all differences of intellect[.] The wisest know nothing[.]" For the philosopher of idealism who had argued that the world can be apprehended mainly through intuition, the death of a beloved son pushed him toward the skepticism expressed most powerfully in "Experience" (1844), an essay presenting individuals as perpetually skating on surfaces. At the conclusion of the essay, however, Emerson, in an anticipation of the American school of pragmatism that he would profoundly influence, insisted on the importance of continuing to act in the world, however elusive and tragic that world might be.

Emerson continued to work steadily on essays derived from his extensive journals and his lecturing. In 1844 he brought out a second series of essays, including his influential "The Poet," which grappled with aesthetic issues of form and meter and foretold—indeed provided the blueprints for—the style and subject matter of some of the great national poets to come. Meter does not make the argument, he wrote, in striking contrast to his contemporary Edgar Allan Poe, but the argument (or poetic idea or vision) makes its own meter; thus he inspired Whitman to break with poetic tradition by introducing the idea of "open form" poetry. Emerson lectured in Boston, across the Northeast, in the South, and even (after the completion of the transcontinental railroad in 1869) in California, giving more than fifteen hundred lectures over the course of his career. These as much as his essays helped develop his reputation.

As Emerson's reputation continued to grow, he gained modest recognition for his own poems, which he collected at the end of 1846. In 1847–48 he took a second trip to Europe, delivering approximately seventy lectures in England and Scotland. One eventual result of that tour was the publication in 1856 of *English Traits*, an inquiry into the supposed racial, historical, and cultural characteristics of Anglo-Saxonism. (Like many thinkers of the time, Emerson accepted the idea of racial differences and hierarchies.) Two other books emerged from his lectures: *Representative Men* (1850), which examined exemplary intellectual and cultural figures, such as Shakespeare and Napoleon; and *The Conduct of Life* (1860), which examined tensions between thought and delimiting worldly forces, even as Emerson reaffirmed the power of self-culture and the individual mind.

Precisely because he so valued individual self-culture, Emerson was skeptical of social reforms that required group participation. In the early 1840s he refused to participate in the reformist, socialistic community Brook Farm in West Roxbury, Massachusetts, which drew a number of the Transcendentalists associated with *The Dial*. Abolitionism did engage his attention, however, and in 1844 he delivered a passionate antislavery address, "Emancipation of the Negroes in the British West Indies," at the Concord Court House on August 1, 1844. Appalled by the Fugitive Slave Act of 1850, Emerson became more fervent in his views during the 1850s, offering scathing attacks on Northern supporters of what he termed "this filthy law." In his 1855 "Lecture on Slavery," presented before the Massachusetts Anti-Slavery Society at the Tremont Temple in Boston, Emerson declaimed against the "outrage of giving back a stolen and plundered man to his thieves." Valuing individual rights and believing in the individual mind (or soul) as divine, Emerson regarded slavery as abhorrent. He also argued in favor of women's rights. In 1855, the same year he attacked slavery at Boston's Tremont Temple, he spoke before a women's rights convention to support women's right to vote, to "hold their property as men do theirs," and to "enter a school as freely as a church." Although Emerson never achieved national prominence as a social reformer, his lectures and essays motivated many of his admirers to become political and social activists.

Emerson's contemporary reputation rested on his lectures and essays, but all along he had been producing another major body of writings, his journals, which he called his "savings bank." The journals were not published in full until the late twentieth century, under the title *Journals and Miscellaneous Notebooks.* A historical record of responses to people and events, the journals, as critics are increasingly recognizing, are among the best accounts of the intellectual and spiritual life of a nineteenth-century American writer. Following the Civil War, Emerson cut back on his writing, partly for health reasons (as he aged he began to display the symptoms of memory loss). But he had his vigorous moments. In 1871 he traveled to California, and in late 1872 and into 1873, following a fire that severely damaged his house, he traveled to Europe and Egypt with his daughter Ellen and met with Carlyle one last time. Upon his return to Concord, he lectured occasionally there and in Boston. He died on April 27, 1882, and was buried in Concord's Sleepy Hollow Cemetery.

In a journal entry of 1836, Emerson wrote: "There is creative reading as well as creative writing." As a creative writer, Emerson attempted to get his whole philosophy into every essay, and even into single sentences. At the same time, he was skeptical of the capacity of language to embody truths, so he presented his essays as epistemological quests of sorts that, in the twistings and turnings and circlings of his thought, made enormous demands on his readers. Emerson's language can be elliptical and sometimes maddeningly abstract, but there is no American writer who placed greater importance on the reader's active interpretive role in generating new meanings and new ways of seeing the world. Emerson's respect for the independent spirit of his readers, his prompting of readers to trust their ideas and take them in new and even different directions—the main point of "Self-Reliance," perhaps his most famous essay—may in fact be the key to his broad literary and cultural influence.

Nature[1]

> "Nature is but an image or imitation of wisdom, the last thing of
> the soul; nature being a thing which doth only do, but not know."
> —PLOTINUS[2]

Introduction

Our age is retrospective. It builds the sepulchres of the fathers. It writes biographies, histories, and criticism. The foregoing generations beheld God and nature face to face; we, through their eyes. Why should not we also

1. *Nature* was published anonymously in 1836 by James Monroe and Company of Boston, paid for by Emerson himself (the company published a thousand copies for Emerson's approximately one hundred–dollar payment). The text used here is that of the first 1836 edition. A few obvious typographical errors have been corrected; and the changes that Emerson himself made in presentation copies to the opening of Chapter 4 have been adopted. Otherwise, the occasional oddities of punctuation, spelling, and subject–verb agreements that appeared in the 1836 text remain in this reprinting.
2. Emerson found the motto from the Roman philosopher Plotinus (205?–270?) in his copy of Ralph Cudworth's *The True Intellectual System of the Universe* (1820).

enjoy an original relation to the universe? Why should not we have a poetry and philosophy of insight and not of tradition, and a religion by revelation to us, and not the history of theirs? Embosomed for a season in nature, whose floods of life stream around and through us, and invite us by the powers they supply, to action proportioned to nature, why should we grope among the dry bones of the past,[3] or put the living generation into masquerade out of its faded wardrobe? The sun shines to-day also. There is more wool and flax in the fields. There are new lands, new men, new thoughts. Let us demand our own works and laws and worship.

Undoubtedly we have no questions to ask which are unanswerable. We must trust the perfection of the creation so far, as to believe that whatever curiosity the order of things has awakened in our minds, the order of things can satisfy. Every man's condition is a solution in hieroglyphic to those inquiries he would put. He acts it as life, before he apprehends it as truth. In like manner, nature is already, in its forms and tendencies, describing its own design. Let us interrogate the great apparition, that shines so peacefully around us. Let us inquire, to what end is nature?

All science has one aim, namely, to find a theory of nature. We have theories of races and of functions, but scarcely yet a remote approximation to an idea of creation. We are now so far from the road to truth, that religious teachers dispute and hate each other, and speculative men are esteemed unsound and frivolous. But to a sound judgment, the most abstract truth is the most practical. Whenever a true theory appears, it will be its own evidence. Its test is, that it will explain all phenomena. Now many are thought not only unexplained but inexplicable; as language, sleep, dreams, beasts, sex.

Philosophically considered, the universe is composed of Nature and the Soul. Strictly speaking, therefore, all that is separate from us, all which Philosophy distinguishes as the NOT ME,[4] that is, both nature and art, all other men and my own body, must be ranked under this name, NATURE. In enumerating the values of nature and casting up their sum, I shall use the word in both senses;—in its common and in its philosophical import. In inquiries so general as our present one, the inaccuracy is not material; no confusion of thought will occur. *Nature*, in the common sense, refers to essences unchanged by man; space, the air, the river, the leaf. *Art* is applied to the mixture of his will with the same things, as in a house, a canal, a statue, a picture. But his operations taken together are so insignificant, a little chipping, baking, patching, and washing, that in an impression so grand as that of the world on the human mind, they do not vary the result.

Chapter I. Nature

To go into solitude, a man needs to retire as much from his chamber as from society. I am not solitary whilst I read and write, though nobody is with me. But if a man would be alone, let him look at the stars. The rays that come from those heavenly worlds, will separate between him and vulgar things. One might think the atmosphere was made transparent with this design, to

3. An echo of Ezekiel 37.1–14, especially 37.4, where God tells Ezekiel to "Prophesy upon these bones, and say unto them, O ye dry bones, hear the word of the Lord."

4. Emerson draws on Thomas Carlyle's *Sartor Resartus* (1833–34) for his idea of "NOT ME," which Carlyle presents as similar to the German philosophical concept of "everything but the self."

give man, in the heavenly bodies, the perpetual presence of the sublime. Seen in the streets of cities, how great they are! If the stars should appear one night in a thousand years, how would men believe and adore; and pre- serve for many generations the remembrance of the city of God which had been shown! But every night come out these preachers of beauty, and light the universe with their admonishing smile.

The stars awaken a certain reverence, because though always present, they are always inaccessible; but all natural objects make a kindred impres- sion, when the mind is open to their influence. Nature never wears a mean appearance. Neither does the wisest man extort all her secret, and lose his curiosity by finding out all her perfection. Nature never became a toy to a wise spirit. The flowers, the animals, the mountains, reflected all the wis- dom of his best hour, as much as they had delighted the simplicity of his childhood.

When we speak of nature in this manner, we have a distinct but most poetical sense in the mind. We mean the integrity of impression made by manifold natural objects. It is this which distinguishes the stick of timber of the wood-cutter, from the tree of the poet. The charming landscape which I saw this morning, is indubitably made up of some twenty or thirty farms. Miller owns this field, Locke that, and Manning the woodland beyond. But none of them owns the landscape. There is a property in the horizon which no man has but he whose eye can integrate all the parts, that is, the poet. This is the best part of these men's farms, yet to this their land-deeds give them no title.

To speak truly, few adult persons can see nature. Most persons do not see the sun. At least they have a very superficial seeing. The sun illuminates only the eye of the man, but shines into the eye and the heart of the child. The lover of nature is he whose inward and outward senses are still truly adjusted to each other; who has retained the spirit of infancy even into the era of manhood.[5] His intercourse with heaven and earth, becomes part of his daily food. In the presence of nature, a wild delight runs through the man, in spite of real sorrows. Nature says,—he is my creature, and maugre[6] all his impertinent griefs, he shall be glad with me. Not the sun or the sum- mer alone, but every hour and season yields its tribute of delight; for every hour and change corresponds to and authorizes a different state of the mind, from breathless noon to grimmest midnight. Nature is a setting that fits equally well a comic or a mourning piece. In good health, the air is a cordial of incredible virtue. Crossing a bare common, in snow puddles, at twilight, under a clouded sky, without having in my thoughts any occur- rence of special good fortune, I have enjoyed a perfect exhilaration. Almost I fear to think how glad I am. In the woods too, a man casts off his years, as the snake his slough, and at what period soever of life, is always a child. In the woods, is perpetual youth. Within these plantations of God, a decorum and sanctity reign, a perennial festival is dressed, and the guest sees not how he should tire of them in a thousand years. In the woods, we return to reason and faith. There I feel that nothing can befal me in life,—no disgrace,

---

5. An echo of Samuel Taylor Coleridge's *Bio- graphia Literaria* (1817), ch. 4, in which Coleridge defines the character and privilege of genius as the ability to carry the feelings of childhood into adulthood.
6. Despite (archaic).

Shortly after the publication of *Nature*, Emerson's friend, the artist
and poet Christopher Cranch (1813–1893), depicted him as a
"transparent eye-ball" in "Illustrations of the New Philosophy"
(c. 1836).

no calamity, (leaving me my eyes,) which nature cannot repair. Standing on
the bare ground,—my head bathed by the blithe air, and uplifted into infinite space,—all mean egotism vanishes. I become a transparent eye-ball.
I am nothing. I see all. The currents of the Universal Being circulate through
me; I am part or particle of God. The name of the nearest friend sounds then
foreign and accidental. To be brothers, to be acquaintances,—master or servant, is then a trifle and a disturbance. I am the lover of uncontained and
immortal beauty. In the wilderness, I find something more dear and connate[7]
than in streets or villages. In the tranquil landscape, and especially in the
distant line of the horizon, man beholds somewhat as beautiful as his own
nature.

The greatest delight which the fields and woods minister, is the suggestion of an occult relation between man and the vegetable. I am not alone
and unacknowledged. They nod to me and I to them. The waving of the
boughs in the storm, is new to me and old. It takes me by surprise, and yet
is not unknown. Its effect is like that of a higher thought or a better emotion coming over me, when I deemed I was thinking justly or doing right.

7. Related.

Yet it is certain that the power to produce this delight, does not reside in nature, but in man, or in a harmony of both. It is necessary to use these pleasures with great temperance. For, nature is not always tricked in holiday attire, but the same scene which yesterday breathed perfume and glittered as for the frolic of the nymphs, is overspread with melancholy today. Nature always wears the colors of the spirit. To a man laboring under calamity, the heat of his own fire hath sadness in it. Then, there is a kind of contempt of the landscape felt by him who has just lost by death a dear friend. The sky is less grand as it shuts down over less worth in the population.

Chapter II. Commodity

Whoever considers the final cause[8] of the world, will discern a multitude of uses that enter as parts into that result. They all admit of being thrown into one of the following classes; Commodity; Beauty; Language; and Discipline.

Under the general name of Commodity, I rank all those advantages which our senses owe to nature. This, of course, is a benefit which is temporary and mediate, not ultimate, like its service to the soul. Yet although low, it is perfect in its kind, and is the only use of nature which all men apprehend. The misery of man appears like childish petulance, when we explore the steady and prodigal provision that has been made for his support and delight on this green ball which floats him through the heavens. What angels invented these splendid ornaments, these rich conveniences, this ocean of air above, this ocean of water beneath, this firmament of earth between? this zodiac of lights, this tent of dropping clouds, this striped coat of climates, this fourfold year? Beasts, fire, water, stones, and corn serve him. The field is at once his floor, his work-yard, his play-ground, his garden, and his bed.

> "More servants wait on man
> Than he'll take notice of."———[9]

Nature, in its ministry to man, is not only the material, but is also the process and the result. All the parts incessantly work into each other's hands for the profit of man. The wind sows the seed; the sun evaporates the sea; the wind blows the vapor to the field; the ice, on the other side of the planet, condenses rain on this; the rain feeds the plant; the plant feeds the animal; and thus the endless circulations of the divine charity nourish man.

The useful arts are but reproductions or new combinations by the wit of man, of the same natural benefactors. He no longer waits for favoring gales, but by means of steam, he realizes the fable of Æolus's bag,[1] and carries the two and thirty winds in the boiler of his boat. To diminish friction, he paves the road with iron bars, and, mounting a coach with a ship-load of men, animals, and merchandise behind him, he darts through the country, from town to town, like an eagle or a swallow through the air. By the aggregate of these aids, how is the face of the world changed, from the era of Noah to that of Napoleon! The private poor man hath cities, ships, canals, bridges,

8. In the sense of "purpose."
9. From "Man" (1633), by the English poet George Herbert (1593–1633), quoted at length in chapter VIII, "Prospects."
1. In Homer's *Odyssey* 10, Aeolus, the god of winds, gives Odysseus a bag containing favorable winds, but they create a storm when his unwary sailors let them all out at once. "Realizes": brings into real existence.

built for him. He goes to the post-office, and the human race run on his errands; to the book-shop, and the human race read and write of all that happens, for him; to the court-house, and nations repair his wrongs. He sets his house upon the road, and the human race go forth every morning, and shovel out the snow, and cut a path for him.

But there is no need of specifying particulars in this class of uses. The catalogue is endless, and the examples so obvious, that I shall leave them to the reader's reflection, with the general remark, that this mercenary benefit is one which has respect to a farther good. A man is fed, not that he may be fed, but that he may work.

Chapter III. Beauty

A nobler want of man is served by nature, namely, the love of Beauty.

The ancient Greeks called the world κασμος[2] beauty. Such is the constitution of all things, or such the plastic[3] power of the human eye, that the primary forms, as the sky, the mountain, the tree, the animal, give us a delight *in and for themselves*; a pleasure arising from outline, color, motion, and grouping. This seems partly owing to the eye itself. The eye is the best of artists. By the mutual action of its structure and of the laws of light, perspective is produced, which integrates every mass of objects, of what character soever, into a well colored and shaded globe, so that where the particular objects are mean and unaffecting, the landscape which they compose, is round and symmetrical. And as the eye is the best composer, so light is the first of painters. There is no object so foul that intense light will not make beautiful. And the stimulus it affords to the sense, and a sort of infinitude which it hath, like space and time, make all matter gay. Even the corpse hath its own beauty. But beside this general grace diffused over nature, almost all the individual forms are agreeable to the eye, as is proved by our endless imitations[4] of some of them, as the acorn, the grape, the pine-cone, the wheat-ear, the egg, the wings and forms of most birds, the lion's claw, the serpent, the butterfly, sea-shells, flames, clouds, buds, leaves, and the forms of many trees, as the palm.

For better consideration, we may distribute the aspects of Beauty in a threefold manner.

1. First, the simple perception of natural forms is a delight. The influence of the forms and actions in nature, is so needful to man, that, in its lowest functions, it seems to lie on the confines of commodity and beauty. To the body and mind which have been cramped by noxious work or company, nature is medicinal and restores their tone. The tradesman, the attorney comes out of the din and craft[5] of the street, and sees the sky and the woods, and is a man again. In their eternal calm, he finds himself. The health of the eye seems to demand a horizon. We are never tired, so long as we can see far enough.

But in other hours, Nature satisfies the soul purely by its loveliness, and without any mixture of corporeal benefit. I have seen the spectacle of morning from the hill-top over against my house, from day-break to sun-rise, with

2. Cosmos, or order (Greek).
3. Creative.
4. As in architectural and furniture design and decoration.
5. Craftiness, materialism.

emotions which an angel might share. The long slender bars of cloud float like fishes in the sea of crimson light. From the earth, as a shore, I look out into that silent sea. I seem to partake its rapid transformations: the active enchantment reaches my dust, and I dilate and conspire with[6] the morning wind. How does Nature deify us with a few and cheap elements! Give me health and a day, and I will make the pomp of emperors ridiculous. The dawn is my Assyria; the sun-set and moon-rise my Paphos, and unimaginable realms of faerie, broad noon shall be my England of the senses and the understanding; the night shall be my Germany of mystic philosophy and dreams.[7]

Not less excellent, except for our less susceptibility in the afternoon, was the charm, last evening, of a January sunset. The western clouds divided and subdivided themselves into pink flakes modulated with tints of unspeakable softness; and the air had so much life and sweetness, that it was a pain to come within doors. What was it that nature would say? Was there no meaning in the live repose of the valley behind the mill, and which Homer or Shakspeare could not re-form for me in words? The leafless trees become spires of flame in the sunset, with the blue east for their background, and the stars of the dead calices of flowers, and every withered stem and stubble rimed[8] with frost, contribute something to the mute music.

The inhabitants of cities suppose that the country landscape is pleasant only half the year. I please myself with observing the graces of the winter scenery, and believe that we are as much touched by it as by the genial influences of summer. To the attentive eye, each moment of the year has its own beauty, and in the same field, it beholds, every hour, a picture which was never seen before, and which shall never be seen again. The heavens change every moment, and reflect their glory or gloom on the plains beneath. The state of the crop in the surrounding farms alters the expression of the earth from week to week. The succession of native plants in the pastures and roadsides, which make the silent clock by which time tells the summer hours, will make even the divisions of the day sensible to a keen observer. The tribes of birds and insects, like the plants punctual to their time, follow each other, and the year has room for all. By water-courses, the variety is greater. In July, the blue pontederia or pickerel-weed blooms in large beds in the shallow parts of our pleasant river,[9] and swarms with yellow butterflies in continual motion. Art cannot rival this pomp of purple and gold. Indeed the river is a perpetual gala, and boasts each month a new ornament.

But this beauty of Nature which is seen and felt as beauty, is the least part. The shows of day, the dewy morning, the rainbow, mountains, orchards in blossom, stars, moonlight, shadows in still water, and the like, if too eagerly hunted, become shows merely, and mock us with their unreality. Go out of the house to see the moon, and 't is mere tinsel; it will not please as when its light shines upon your necessary journey. The beauty that shimmers in the yellow afternoons of October, who ever could clutch it? Go forth to find it, and it is gone: 't is only a mirage as you look from the windows of the diligence.

---

6. Breathe with.
7. Emerson is contrasting the rational empiricism of Scottish Common Sense philosophy with the mystical idealism of post-Kantian German philosophy. "Assyria": an ancient Near Eastern empire. "Paphos": an ancient city in Cyprus (site of worship of Aphrodite).
8. Coated. "Calices": i.e., calyxes; the outer whorls of leaves or sepals at the bases of flowers.
9. The Concord River.

2. The presence of a higher, namely, of the spiritual element is essential to its perfection. The high and divine beauty which can be loved without effeminacy, is that which is found in combination with the human will, and never separate. Beauty is the mark God sets upon virtue. Every natural action is graceful. Every heroic act is also decent,[1] and causes the place and the bystanders to shine. We are taught by great actions that the universe is the property of every individual in it. Every rational creature has all nature for his dowry and estate. It is his, if he will. He may divest himself of it; he may creep into a corner, and abdicate his kingdom, as most men do, but he is entitled to the world by his constitution. In proportion to the energy of his thought and will, he takes up the world into himself. "All those things for which men plough, build, or sail, obey virtue;" said an ancient historian.[2] "The winds and waves," said Gibbon,[3] "are always on the side of the ablest navigators." So are the sun and moon and all the stars of heaven. When a noble act is done,—perchance in a scene of great natural beauty; when Leonidas and his three hundred martyrs consume one day in dying, and the sun and moon come each and look at them once in the steep defile of Thermopylæ; when Arnold Winkelried,[4] in the high Alps, under the shadow of the avalanche, gathers in his side a sheaf of Austrian spears to break the line for his comrades; are not these heroes entitled to add the beauty of the scene to the beauty of the deed? When the bark of Columbus nears the shore of America;—before it, the beach lined with savages, fleeing out of all their huts of cane; the sea behind; and the purple mountains of the Indian Archipelago around, can we separate the man from the living picture? Does not the New World clothe his form with her palm-groves and savannahs as fit drapery? Ever does natural beauty steal in like air, and envelope great actions. When Sir Harry Vane[5] was dragged up the Tower-hill, sitting on a sled, to suffer death, as the champion of the English laws, one of the multitude cried out to him, "You never sate on so glorious a seat." Charles II., to intimidate the citizens of London, caused the patriot Lord Russel[6] to be drawn in an open coach, through the principal streets of the city, on his way to the scaffold. "But," to use the simple narrative of his biographer, "the multitude imagined they saw liberty and virtue sitting by his side." In private places, among sordid objects, an act of truth or heroism seems at once to draw to itself the sky as its temple, the sun as its candle. Nature stretcheth out her arms to embrace man, only let his thoughts be of equal greatness. Willingly does she follow his steps with the rose and the violet, and bend her lines of grandeur and grace to the decoration of her darling child. Only let his thoughts be of equal scope, and the frame will suit the picture. A virtuous man, is in unison with her works, and makes the central figure of the visible sphere. Homer, Pindar, Socrates, Phocion,[7] associate themselves fitly in our

1. Beautiful.
2. Sallust (1st century B.C.E.), Roman historian, in "The Conspiracy of Cataline," ch. 2.
3. Edward Gibbon (1737–1794), English historian, from *The Decline and Fall of the Roman Empire*, ch. 68.
4. Arnold von Winkelried, a Swiss hero, was killed (1386) in a battle against the Austrians at Sempach, from *The Decline and Fall of the Roman Empire*, ch. 68. Leonidas, king of Sparta, was killed (c. 480 B.C.E.) defending the pass at Thermopylae against the Persian army led by Xerxes.
5. English Puritan leader (1613–1662) who was

executed for treason by the Restoration government because he was suspected of conspiring against King Charles II (1630–1685).
6. William Lord Russel (1639–1683) was executed by English authorities for allegedly plotting to kill Charles II.
7. Athenian statesman and general of the 4th century B.C.E. Emerson knew of him from Plutarch's *Lives*. Pindar was a Greek lyric poet of the 5th and 6th centuries B.C.E. Socrates was a Greek philosopher of the 5th century B.C.E.

memory with the whole geography and climate of Greece. The visible heavens and earth sympathize with Jesus. And in common life, whosoever has seen a person of powerful character and happy genius, will have remarked how easily he took all things along with him,—the persons, the opinions, and the day, and nature became ancillary to a man.

3. There is still another aspect under which the beauty of the world may be viewed, namely, as it becomes an object of the intellect. Beside the relation of things to virtue, they have a relation to thought. The intellect searches out the absolute order of things as they stand in the mind of God, and without the colors of affection. The intellectual and the active powers seem to succeed each other in man, and the exclusive activity of the one, generates the exclusive activity of the other. There is something unfriendly in each to the other, but they are like the alternate periods of feeding and working in animals; each prepares and certainly will be followed by the other. Therefore does beauty, which, in relation to actions, as we have seen comes unsought, and comes because it is unsought, remain for the apprehension and pursuit of the intellect; and then again, in its turn, of the active power. Nothing divine dies. All good is eternally reproductive. The beauty of nature reforms itself in the mind, and not for barren contemplation, but for new creation.

All men are in some degree impressed by the face of the world. Some men even to delight. This love of beauty is Taste. Others have the same love in such excess, that, not content with admiring, they seek to embody it in new forms. The creation of beauty is Art.

The production of a work of art throws a light upon the mystery of humanity. A work of art is an abstract or epitome of the world. It is the result or expression of nature, in miniature. For although the works of nature are innumerable and all different, the result or the expression of them all is similar and single. Nature is a sea of forms radically alike and even unique. A leaf, a sun-beam, a landscape, the ocean, make an analogous impression on the mind. What is common to them all,—that perfectness and harmony, is beauty. Therefore the standard of beauty, is the entire circuit of natural forms,—the totality of nature; which the Italians expressed by defining beauty "il piu nell' uno."[8] Nothing is quite beautiful alone: nothing but is beautiful in the whole. A single object is only so far beautiful as it suggests this universal grace. The poet, the painter, the sculptor, the musician, the architect seek each to concentrate this radiance of the world on one point, and each in his several work to satisfy the love of beauty which stimulates him to produce. Thus is Art, a nature passed through the alembic[9] of man. Thus in art, does nature work through the will of a man filled with the beauty of her first works.

The world thus exists to the soul to satisfy the desire of beauty. Extend this element to the uttermost, and I call it an ultimate end. No reason can be asked or given why the soul seeks beauty. Beauty, in its largest and profoundest sense, is one expression for the universe. God is the all-fair. Truth, and goodness, and beauty, are but different faces of the same All. But beauty in nature is not ultimate. It is the herald of inward and eternal beauty, and

8. The many in one (Italian); a borrowing from Coleridge.

9. A distilling apparatus.

is not alone a solid and satisfactory good. It must therefore stand as a part and not as yet the last or highest expression of the final cause of Nature.

Chapter IV. Language

A third use which Nature subserves to man is that of Language. Nature is the vehicle of thought, and in a simple, double, and threefold degree.

1. Words are signs of natural facts.
2. Particular natural facts are symbols of particular spiritual facts.
3. Nature is the symbol of spirit.

1. Words are signs of natural facts. The use of natural history is to give us aid in supernatural history. The use of the outer creation is to give us language for the beings and changes of the inward creation. Every word which is used to express a moral or intellectual fact, if traced to its root, is found to be borrowed from some material appearance. *Right* originally means *straight*; *wrong* means *twisted*. *Spirit* primarily means *wind*; *transgression*, the crossing of a *line*; *supercilious*, the *raising of the eye-brow*. We say the *heart* to express emotion, the *head* to denote thought; and *thought* and *emotion* are, in their turn, words borrowed from sensible things, and now appropriated to spiritual nature. Most of the process by which this transformation is made, is hidden from us in the remote time when language was framed; but the same tendency may be daily observed in children. Children and savages use only nouns or names of things, which they continually convert into verbs, and apply to analogous mental acts.

2. But this origin of all words that convey a spiritual import,—so conspicuous a fact in the history of language,—is our least debt to nature. It is not words only that are emblematic; it is things which are emblematic. Every natural fact is a symbol of some spiritual fact.[1] Every appearance in nature corresponds to some state of the mind, and that state of the mind can only be described by presenting that natural appearance as its picture. An enraged man is a lion, a cunning man is a fox, a firm man is a rock, a learned man is a torch. A lamb is innocence; a snake is subtle spite; flowers express to us the delicate affections. Light and darkness are our familiar expression for knowledge and ignorance; and heat for love. Visible distance behind and before us, is respectively our image of memory and hope.

Who looks upon a river in a meditative hour, and is not reminded of the flux of all things? Throw a stone into the stream, and the circles that propagate themselves are the beautiful type of all influence. Man is conscious of a universal soul within or behind his individual life, wherein, as in a firmament, the natures of Justice, Truth, Love, Freedom, arise and shine. This universal soul, he calls Reason: it is not mine or thine or his, but we are its; we are its property and men.[2] And the blue sky in which the private earth is buried, the sky with its eternal calm, and full of everlasting orbs, is the type of Reason. That which, intellectually considered, we call Reason, considered in relation to nature, we call Spirit. Spirit is the Creator. Spirit hath life in

---

1. This passage invokes the doctrine of correspondences between the spiritual and natural worlds developed by the Swedish theologian and mystic Emanuel Swedenborg (1688–1772).
2. By *reason*, Emerson means something like the

intuitive powers of the mind; by *understanding*, he means logical and empirical reasoning. For Emerson, a suprarational reason is the higher faculty. Emerson probably derived these terms from Samuel Taylor Coleridge's *Biographia Literaria* (1817).

itself. And man in all ages and countries, embodies it in his language, as the FATHER.

It is easily seen that there is nothing lucky or capricious in these analogies, but that they are constant, and pervade nature. These are not the dreams of a few poets, here and there, but man is an analogist, and studies relations in all objects. He is placed in the centre of beings, and a ray of relation passes from every other being to him. And neither can man be understood without these objects, nor these objects without man. All the facts in natural history taken by themselves, have no value, but are barren like a single sex. But marry it to human history, and it is full of life. Whole Floras, all Linnæus' and Buffon's[3] volume, are but dry catalogues of facts; but the most trivial of these facts, the habit of a plant, the organs, or work, or noise of an insect, applied to the illustration of a fact in intellectual philosophy, or, in any way associated to human nature, affects us in the most lively and agreeable manner. The seed of a plant,—to what affecting analogies in the nature of man, is that little fruit made use of, in all discourse, up to the voice of Paul, who calls the human corpse a seed,—"It is sown a natural body; it is raised a spiritual body."[4] The motion of the earth round its axis, and round the sun, makes the day, and the year. These are certain amounts of brute light and heat. But is there no intent of an analogy between man's life and the seasons? And do the seasons gain no grandeur or pathos from that analogy? The instincts of the ant are very unimportant considered as the ant's; but the moment a ray of relation is seen to extend from it to man, and the little drudge is seen to be a monitor, a little body with a mighty heart, then all its habits, even that said to be recently observed, that it never sleeps, become sublime.

Because of this radical[5] correspondence between visible things and human thoughts, savages, who have only what is necessary, converse in figures. As we go back in history, language becomes more picturesque, until its infancy, when it is all poetry; or, all spiritual facts are represented by natural symbols. The same symbols are found to make the original elements of all languages. It has moreover been observed, that the idioms of all languages approach each other in passages of the greatest eloquence and power. And as this is the first language, so is it the last. This immediate dependence of language upon nature, this conversion of an outward phenomenon into a type of somewhat in human life, never loses its power to affect us. It is this which gives that piquancy to the conversation of a strong-natured farmer or back-woodsman, which all men relish.

Thus is nature an interpreter, by whose means man converses with his fellow men. A man's power to connect his thought with its proper symbol, and so utter it, depends on the simplicity of his character, that is, upon his love of truth and his desire to communicate it without loss. The corruption of man is followed by the corruption of language. When simplicity of character and the sovereignty of ideas is broken up by the prevalence of secondary desires, the desire of riches, the desire of pleasure, the desire of power, the desire of praise,—and duplicity and falsehood take place of simplicity

---

3. French naturalist (1707–1788). Linnæus was Carl von Linné (1707–1778), Swedish botanist. Both were developing systems of classification for natural objects.
4. 1 Corinthians 15.44.
5. Fundamental (literally "from the root").

and truth, the power over nature as an interpreter of the will, is in a degree lost; new imagery ceases to be created, and old words are perverted to stand for things which are not; a paper currency is employed when there is no bullion in the vaults. In due time, the fraud is manifest, and words lose all power to stimulate the understanding or the affections. Hundreds of writers may be found in every long-civilized nation, who for a short time believe, and make others believe, that they see and utter truths, who do not of themselves clothe one thought in its natural garment, but who feed unconsciously upon the language created by the primary writers of the country, those, namely, who hold primarily on nature.

But wise men pierce this rotten diction and fasten words again to visible things; so that picturesque language is at once a commanding certificate that he who employs it, is a man in alliance with truth and God. The moment our discourse rises above the ground line of familiar facts, and is inflamed with passion or exalted by thought, it clothes itself in images. A man conversing in earnest, if he watch his intellectual processes, will find that always a material image, more or less luminous, arises in his mind, contemporaneous with every thought, which furnishes the vestment of the thought. Hence, good writing and brilliant discourse are perpetual allegories. This imagery is spontaneous. It is the blending of experience with the present action of the mind. It is proper creation. It is the working of the Original Cause through the instruments he has already made.

These facts may suggest the advantage which the country-life possesses for a powerful mind, over the artificial and curtailed life of cities. We know more from nature than we can at will communicate. Its light flows into the mind evermore, and we forget its presence. The poet, the orator, bred in the woods, whose scenes have been nourished by their fair and appeasing changes, year after year, without design and without heed,—shall not lose their lesson altogether, in the roar of cities or the broil of politics. Long hereafter, amidst agitation and terror in national councils,—in the hour of revolution,—these solemn images shall reappear in their morning lustre, as fit symbols and words of the thoughts which the passing events shall awaken. At the call of a noble sentiment, again the woods wave, the pines murmur, the river rolls and shines, and the cattle low upon the mountains, as he saw and heard them in his infancy. And with these forms, the spells of persuasion, the keys of power are put into his hands.

3. We are thus assisted by natural objects in the expression of particular meanings. But how great a language to convey such pepper-corn[6] informations! Did it need such noble races of creatures, this profusion of forms, this host of orbs in heaven, to furnish man with the dictionary and grammar of his municipal speech? Whilst we use this grand cipher to expedite the affairs of our pot and kettle, we feel that we have not yet put it to its use, neither are able. We are like travellers using the cinders of a volcano to roast their eggs. Whilst we see that it always stands ready to clothe what we would say, we cannot avoid the question, whether the characters are not significant of themselves. Have mountains, and waves, and skies, no significance but what we consciously give them, when we employ them as emblems of our thoughts? The world is emblematic. Parts of speech are metaphors because

6. Ordinary, everyday.

the whole of nature is a metaphor of the human mind. The laws of moral nature answer to those of matter as face to face in a glass. "The visible world and the relation of its parts, is the dial plate of the invisible."[7] The axioms of physics translate the laws of ethics.[8] Thus, "the whole is greater than its part;" "reaction is equal to action;" "the smallest weight may be made to lift the greatest, the difference of weight being compensated by time;" and many the like propositions, which have an ethical as well as physical sense. These propositions have a much more extensive and universal sense when applied to human life, than when confined to technical use.

In like manner, the memorable words of history, and the proverbs of nations, consist usually of a natural fact, selected as a picture or parable of a moral truth. Thus; A rolling stone gathers no moss; A bird in the hand is worth two in the bush; A cripple in the right way, will beat a racer in the wrong; Make hay whilst the sun shines; 'T is hard to carry a full cup even; Vinegar is the son of wine; The last ounce broke the camel's back; Long-lived trees make roots first;—and the like.[9] In their primary sense these are trivial facts, but we repeat them for the value of their analogical import. What is true of proverbs, is true of all fables, parables, and allegories.

This relation between the mind and matter is not fancied by some poet, but stands in the will of God, and so is free to be known by all men. It appears to men, or it does not appear. When in fortunate hours we ponder this miracle, the wise man doubts, if, at all other times, he is not blind and deaf;

> ——"Can these things be,
> And overcome us like a summer's cloud,
> Without our special wonder?"[1]

for the universe becomes transparent, and the light of higher laws than its own, shines through it. It is the standing problem which has exercised the wonder and the study of every fine genius since the world began; from the era of the Egyptians and the Brahmins, to that of Pythagoras, of Plato, of Bacon, of Leibnitz,[2] of Swedenborg. There sits the Sphinx at the road-side, and from age to age, as each prophet comes by, he tries his fortune at reading her riddle.[3] There seems to be a necessity in spirit to manifest itself in material forms; and day and night, river and storm, beast and bird, acid and alkali, preëxist in necessary Ideas in the mind of God, and are what they are by virtue of preceding affections, in the world of spirit. A Fact is the end or last issue of spirit. The visible creation is the terminus or the circumference of the invisible world. "Material objects," said a French philosopher,

7. Emerson copied the Swedenborg quotation from the New Jerusalem Magazine (July 1832).
8. Adapted from Mme. De Staël's "Germany" (1813): "Even a mathematical axiom is a moral rule."
9. Proverbs drawn from several writers, including Francis Bacon, The Advancement of Learning (1605), and Scottish theologian Robert Leighton (1611–1684), Select Works (1832).
1. Shakespeare's Macbeth 3.4.110–12.
2. Gottfried Wilhelm Leibnitz (1646–1716), German mathematician who championed philosophical idealism and symbolic logic. Pythagorus (c. 582–ca. 507 B.C.E.), Greek philosopher

who believed in the transmigration of souls. Plato (c. 427–347 B.C.E.), Greek philosopher who was the founder of philosophical idealism. Sir Francis Bacon (1561–1626), English philosopher who developed inductive and empirical approaches to science.
3. In Greek mythology, a winged monster with a lion's body and head of a woman, who challenged those entering Thebes with a riddle; when they answered incorrectly, she killed them. But when Oedipus answered correctly, the Sphinx was so distraught that she killed herself, much to the delight of the Theban people, who named Oedipus their king.

"are necessarily kinds of *scoriæ* of the substantial thoughts of the Creator, which must always preserve an exact relation to their first origin; in other words, visible nature must have a spiritual and moral side."[4]

This doctrine is abstruse, and though the images of "garment," "scoriæ," "mirror," &c., may stimulate the fancy, we must summon the aid of subtler and more vital expositors to make it plain. "Every scripture is to be interpreted by the same spirit which gave it forth,"—is the fundamental law of criticism.[5] A life in harmony with nature, the love of truth and of virtue, will purge the eyes to understand her text. By degrees we may come to know the primitive sense of the permanent objects of nature, so that the world shall be to us an open book, and every form significant of its hidden life and final cause.

A new interest surprises us, whilst, under the view now suggested, we contemplate the fearful extent and multitude of objects; since "every object rightly seen, unlocks a new faculty of the soul."[6] That which was unconscious truth, becomes, when interpreted and defined in an object, a part of the domain of knowledge,—a new amount to the magazine[7] of power.

Chapter V. Discipline

In view of this significance of nature, we arrive at once at a new fact, that nature is a discipline. This use of the world includes the preceding uses, as parts of itself.

Space, time, society, labor, climate, food, locomotion, the animals, the mechanical forces, give us sincerest lessons, day by day, whose meaning is unlimited. They educate both the Understanding and the Reason. Every property of matter is a school for the understanding,—its solidity or resistance, its inertia, its extension, its figure, its divisibility. The understanding adds, divides, combines, measures, and finds everlasting nutriment and room for its activity in this worthy scene. Meantime, Reason transfers all these lessons into its own world of thought, by perceiving the analogy that marries Matter and Mind.

1. Nature is a discipline of the understanding in intellectual truths. Our dealing with sensible objects is a constant exercise in the necessary lessons of difference, of likeness, of order, of being and seeming, of progressive arrangement; of ascent from particular to general; of combination to one end of manifold forces. Proportioned to the importance of the organ to be formed, is the extreme care with which its tuition is provided,—a care pretermitted[8] in no single case. What tedious training, day after day, year after year, never ending, to form the common sense; what continual reproduction of annoyances, inconveniences, dilemmas; what rejoicing over us of little men; what disputing of prices, what reckonings of interest,—and all to form the Hand of the mind;—to instruct us that "good thoughts are no better than good dreams, unless they be executed!"[9]

4. From the French Swedenborgian Guillaume Oegger's "The True Messiah" (1829), which Emerson had seen in a manuscript translation, perhaps by Elizabeth Peabody. *Scoriæ*: i.e., scoria; slag or refuse left after metal has been smelted from ore.
5. From the English Quaker George Fox (1624–1691). Emerson's probable source for this quote is William Sewel's *History of the Rise, Increase, and Progress of the Christian People called Quakers* (1722).
6. From Coleridge's *Aids to Reflection* (1829).
7. Storehouse.
8. Neglected. "Tuition": guardianship.
9. Adapted from Bacon's "Of Great Place," in *Essays* (1625).

The same good office is performed by Property and its filial systems of debt and credit. Debt, grinding debt, whose iron face the widow, the orphan, and the sons of genius fear and hate;—debt, which consumes so much time, which so cripples and disheartens a great spirit with cares that seem so base, is a preceptor whose lessons cannot be foregone, and is needed most by those who suffer from it most. Moreover, property, which has been well compared to snow,—"if it fall level to-day, it will be blown into drifts tomorrow,"—is merely the surface action of internal machinery, like the index on the face of a clock. Whilst now it is the gymnastics of the understanding, it is hiving in the foresight of the spirit, experience in profounder laws.

The whole character and fortune of the individual is affected by the least inequalities in the culture of the understanding; for example, in the perception of differences. Therefore is Space, and therefore Time, that man may know that things are not huddled and lumped, but sundered and individual. A bell and a plough have each their use, and neither can do the office of the other. Water is good to drink, coal to burn, wool to wear; but wool cannot be drunk, nor water spun, nor coal eaten. The wise man shows his wisdom in separation, in gradation, and his scale of creatures and of merits, is as wide as nature. The foolish have no range in their scale, but suppose every man is as every other man. What is not good they call the worst, and what is not hateful, they call the best.

In like manner, what good heed, nature forms in us! She pardons no mistakes. Her yea is yea, and her nay, nay.

The first steps in Agriculture, Astronomy, Zoölogy, (those first steps which the farmer, the hunter, and the sailor take,) teach that nature's dice are always loaded; that in her heaps and rubbish are concealed sure and useful results.

How calmly and genially the mind apprehends one after another the laws of physics! What noble emotions dilate the mortal as he enters into the counsels of the creation, and feels by knowledge the privilege to BE! His insight refines him. The beauty of nature shines in his own breast. Man is greater that he can see this, and the universe less, because Time and Space relations vanish as laws are known.

Here again we are impressed and even daunted by the immense Universe to be explored. 'What we know, is a point to what we do not know.'[1] Open any recent journal of science, and weigh the problems suggested concerning Light, Heat, Electricity, Magnetism, Physiology, Geology, and judge whether the interest of natural science is likely to be soon exhausted.

Passing by many particulars of the discipline of nature we must not omit to specify two.

The exercise of the Will or the lesson of power is taught in every event. From the child's successive possession of his several senses up to the hour when he saith, "thy will be done!"[2] he is learning the secret, that he can reduce under his will, not only particular events, but great classes, nay the whole series of events, and so conform all facts to his character. Nature is thoroughly mediate. It is made to serve. It receives the dominion of man as

---

1. A saying ascribed both to Sir Isaac Newton (1642–1727), English mathematician and philosopher, and to Bishop Joseph Butler (1692–1752), English moralist.
2. Matthew 6.10 and 26.42.

meekly as the ass on which the Saviour rode.[3] It offers all its kingdoms to man as the raw material which he may mould into what is useful. Man is never weary of working it up. He forges the subtle and delicate air into wise and melodious words, and gives them wing as angels of persuasion and command. More and more, with every thought, does his kingdom stretch over things, until the world becomes, at last, only a realized will,—the double of the man.

2. Sensible objects conform to the premonitions of Reason and reflect the conscience. All things are moral; and in their boundless changes have an unceasing reference to spiritual nature. Therefore is nature glorious with form, color, and motion, that every globe in the remotest heaven; every chemical change from the rudest crystal up to the laws of life; every change of vegetation from the first principle of growth in the eye of a leaf, to the tropical forest and antediluvian[4] coal-mine; every animal function from the sponge up to Hercules,[5] shall hint or thunder to man the laws of right and wrong, and echo the Ten Commandments. Therefore is nature always the ally of Religion: lends all her pomp and riches to the religious sentiment. Prophet and priest, David, Isaiah,[6] Jesus, have drawn deeply from this source.

This ethical character so penetrates the bone and marrow of nature, as to seem the end for which it was made. Whatever private purpose is answered by any member or part, this is its public and universal function, and is never omitted. Nothing in nature is exhausted in its first use. When a thing has served an end to the uttermost, it is wholly new for an ulterior service. In God, every end is converted into a new means. Thus the use of Commodity, regarded by itself, is mean and squalid. But it is to the mind an education in the great doctrine of Use, namely, that a thing is good only so far as it serves; that a conspiring of parts and efforts to the production of an end, is essential to any being. The first and gross manifestation of this truth, is our inevitable and hated training in values and wants, in corn and meat.

It has already been illustrated, in treating of the significance of material things, that every natural process is but a version of a moral sentence. The moral law lies at the centre of nature and radiates to the circumference. It is the pith and marrow of every substance, every relation, and every process. All things with which we deal, preach to us. What is a farm but a mute gospel? The chaff and the wheat, weeds and plants, blight, rain, insects, sun,—it is a sacred emblem from the first furrow of spring to the last stack which the snow of winter overtakes in the fields. But the sailor, the shepherd, the miner, the merchant, in their several resorts, have each an experience precisely parallel and leading to the same conclusions. Because all organizations are radically alike. Nor can it be doubted that this moral sentiment which thus scents the air, and grows in the grain, and impregnates the waters of the world, is caught by man and sinks into his soul. The moral influence of nature upon every individual is that amount of truth which it illustrates to him. Who can estimate this? Who can guess how much firmness the sea-beaten rock has taught the fisherman? how much tranquillity

---

3. Matthew 21.5.
4. Before the Flood, which destroyed all living creatures not in Noah's ark (Genesis 6–9).
5. Roman name for the Greek mythological hero

Heracles, renowned for feats of strength.
6. Old Testament prophet. David was the second king of Israel.

has been reflected to man from the azure sky, over whose unspotted deeps the winds forevermore drive flocks of stormy clouds, and leave no wrinkle or stain? how much industry and providence and affection we have caught from the pantomime of brutes? What a searching preacher of self-command is the varying phenomenon of Health!

Herein is especially apprehended the Unity of Nature,—the Unity in Variety,—which meets us everywhere. All the endless variety of things make a unique, an identical impression. Xenophanes[7] complained in his old age, that, look where he would, all things hastened back to Unity. He was weary of seeing the same entity in the tedious variety of forms. The fable of Proteus has a cordial[8] truth. Every particular in nature, a leaf, a drop, a crystal, a moment of time is related to the whole, and partakes of the perfection of the whole. Each particle is a microcosm, and faithfully renders the likeness of the world.

Not only resemblances exist in things whose analogy is obvious, as when we detect the type of the human hand in the flipper of the fossil saurus, but also in objects wherein there is great superficial unlikeness. Thus architecture is called 'frozen music,' by De Stael and Goethe.[9] 'A Gothic church,' said Coleridge,[1] 'is a petrified religion.' Michael Angelo maintained, that, to an architect, a knowledge of anatomy is essential.[2] In Haydn's[3] oratorios, the notes present to the imagination not only motions, as, of the snake, the stag, and the elephant, but colors also; as the green grass. The granite is differenced in its laws only by the more or less of heat, from the river that wears it away. The river, as it flows, resembles the air that flows over it; the air resembles the light which traverses it with more subtile currents; the light resembles the heat which rides with it through Space. Each creature is only a modification of the other; the likeness in them is more than the difference, and their radical law is one and the same. Hence it is, that a rule of one art, or a law of one organization, holds true throughout nature. So intimate is this Unity, that, it is easily seen, it lies under the undermost garment of nature, and betrays its source in universal Spirit. For, it pervades Thought also. Every universal truth which we express in words, implies or supposes every other truth. *Omne verum vero consonat.*[4] It is like a great circle on a sphere, comprising all possible circles; which, however, may be drawn, and comprise it, in like manner. Every such truth is the absolute Ens[5] seen from one side. But it has innumerable sides.

The same central Unity is still more conspicuous in actions. Words are finite organs of the infinite mind. They cannot cover the dimensions of what is in truth. They break, chop, and impoverish it. An action is the perfection and publication of thought. A right action seems to fill the eye, and to be related to all nature. "The wise man, in doing one thing, does all; or, in the one thing he does rightly, he sees the likeness of all which is done rightly."[6]

---

7. Greek philosopher of 5th and 6th centuries B.C.E. who taught the unity of all existence.
8. Vital, heartwarming. Proteus was a sea god who could change his shape to evade any captor.
9. Johann Wolfgang von Goethe (1749–1832), in his *Conversations with Eckermann.* Mme. de Staël (1766–1817), in *Corinne,* book 4, chapter 3.
1. In his "Lecture on the General Character of the Gothic Mind in the Middle Ages" (1836).

2. From the sketch of Michelangelo (1475–1564) in *Lives of Eminent Persons* (1833).
3. Joseph Haydn (1732–1809), Austrian composer.
4. Every truth is consonant with every other truth (Latin).
5. Abstract being (Latin).
6. Paraphrase of Goethe's *Wilhelm Meister* (1795–96).

Words and actions are not the attributes of mute and brute nature. They introduce us to that singular form which predominates over all other forms. This is the human. All other organizations appear to be degradations of the human form. When this organization appears among so many that surround it, the spirit prefers it to all others. It says, 'From such as this, have I drawn joy and knowledge. In such as this, have I found and beheld myself. I will speak to it. It can speak again. It can yield me thought already formed and alive.' In fact, the eye,—the mind,—is always accompanied by these forms, male and female; and these are incomparably the richest informations[7] of the power and order that lie at the heart of things. Unfortunately, every one of them bears the marks as of some injury; is marred and superficially defective. Nevertheless, far different from the deaf and dumb nature around them, these all rest like fountain-pipes on the unfathomed sea of thought and virtue whereto they alone, of all organizations, are the entrances.

It were a pleasant inquiry to follow into detail their ministry to our education, but where would it stop? We are associated in adolescent and adult life with some friends, who, like skies and waters, are coextensive with our idea; who, answering each to a certain affection of the soul, satisfy our desire on that side; whom we lack power to put at such focal distance from us, that we can mend or even analyze them. We cannot chuse but love them. When much intercourse with a friend has supplied us with a standard of excellence, and has increased our respect for the resources of God who thus sends a real person to outgo our ideal; when he has, moreover, become an object of thought, and, whilst his character retains all its unconscious effect, is converted in the mind into solid and sweet wisdom,—it is a sign to us that his office is closing, and he is commonly withdrawn from our sight in a short time.

Chapter VI. Idealism

Thus is the unspeakable but intelligible and practicable meaning of the world conveyed to man, the immortal pupil, in every object of sense. To this one end of Discipline, all parts of nature conspire.

A noble doubt perpetually suggests itself, whether this end be not the Final Cause of the Universe; and whether nature outwardly exists. It is a sufficient account of that Appearance we call the World, that God will teach a human mind, and so makes it the receiver of a certain number of congruent sensations, which we call sun and moon, man and woman, house and trade. In my utter impotence to test the authenticity of the report of my senses, to know whether the impressions they make on me correspond with outlying objects, what difference does it make, whether Orion[8] is up there in heaven, or some god paints the image in the firmament of the soul? The relations of parts and the end of the whole remaining the same, what is the difference, whether land and sea interact, and worlds revolve and intermingle without number or end,—deep yawning under deep,[9] and galaxy balancing galaxy, throughout absolute space, or, whether, without relations

7. Products of the inward, form-giving capacity.
8. Constellation named for the mythical Greek hunter.

9. From Psalm 42.7: "Deep calleth unto deep at the noise of thy waterspouts: all thy waves and thy billows are gone over me."

of time and space, the same appearances are inscribed in the constant faith of man. Whether nature enjoy a substantial existence without, or is only in the apocalypse[1] of the mind, it is alike useful and alike venerable to me. Be it what it may, it is ideal to me, so long as I cannot try the accuracy of my senses.

The frivolous make themselves merry with the Ideal theory,[2] as if its consequences were burlesque; as if it affected the stability of nature. It surely does not. God never jests with us, and will not compromise the end of nature, by permitting any inconsequence in its procession. Any distrust of the permanence of laws, would paralyze the faculties of man. Their permanence is sacredly respected, and his faith therein is perfect. The wheels and springs of man are all set to the hypothesis of the permanence of nature. We are not built like a ship to be tossed, but like a house to stand. It is a natural consequence of this structure, that, so long as the active powers predominate over the reflective, we resist with indignation any hint that nature is more short-lived or mutable than spirit. The broker, the wheelwright, the carpenter, the tollman, are much displeased at the intimation.

But whilst we acquiesce entirely in the permanence of natural laws, the question of the absolute existence of nature, still remains open. It is the uniform effect of culture on the human mind, not to shake our faith in the stability of particular phenomena, as of heat, water, azote;[3] but to lead us to regard nature as a phenomenon, not a substance; to attribute necessary existence to spirit; to esteem nature as an accident and an effect.

To the senses and the unrenewed understanding, belongs a sort of instinctive belief in the absolute existence of nature. In their view, man and nature are indissolubly joined. Things are ultimates, and they never look beyond their sphere. The presence of Reason mars this faith. The first effort of thought tends to relax this despotism of the senses, which binds us to nature as if we were a part of it, and shows us nature aloof, and, as it were, afloat. Until this higher agency intervened, the animal eye sees, with wonderful accuracy, sharp outlines and colored surfaces. When the eye of Reason opens, to outline and surface are at once added, grace and expression. These proceed from imagination and affection, and abate somewhat of the angular distinctness of objects. If the Reason be stimulated to more earnest vision, outlines and surfaces become transparent, and are no longer seen; causes and spirits are seen through them. The best, the happiest moments of life, are these delicious awakenings of the higher powers, and the reverential withdrawing of nature before its God.

Let us proceed to indicate the effects of culture. 1. Our first institution[4] in the Ideal philosophy is a hint from nature herself.

Nature is made to conspire with spirit to emancipate us. Certain mechanical changes, a small alteration in our local position apprizes us of a dualism. We are strangely affected by seeing the shore from a moving ship, from a balloon, or through the tints of an unusual sky. The least change in our point of view, gives the whole world a pictorial air. A man who seldom rides, needs

1. Revelation (Greek).
2. The idea that the mind cannot know anything except its own ideas and thus cannot know material things in themselves is associated with Bishop George Berkeley (1685–1753), whose writings were an important influence on Emerson.
3. Nitrogen.
4. Instruction. "Effects of culture": in the sense of the effects of awakening thought.

only to get into a coach and traverse his own town, to turn the street into a puppet-show. The men, the women,—talking, running, bartering, fighting,—the earnest mechanic, the lounger, the beggar, the boys, the dogs, are unrealized[5] at once, or, at least, wholly detached from all relation to the observer, and seen as apparent, not substantial beings. What new thoughts are suggested by seeing a face of country quite familiar, in the rapid movement of the railroad car! Nay, the most wonted objects, (make a very slight change in the point of vision,) please us most. In a camera obscura,[6] the butcher's cart, and the figure of one of our own family amuse us. So a portrait of a well-known face gratifies us. Turn the eyes upside down, by looking at the landscape through your legs, and how agreeable is the picture, though you have seen it any time these twenty years!

In these cases, by mechanical means, is suggested the difference between the observer and the spectacle,—between man and nature. Hence arises a pleasure mixed with awe; I may say, a low degree of the sublime is felt from the fact, probably, that man is hereby apprized, that, whilst the world is a spectacle, something in himself is stable.

2. In a higher manner, the poet communicates the same pleasure. By a few strokes he delineates, as on air, the sun, the mountain, the camp, the city, the hero, the maiden, not different from what we know them, but only lifted from the ground and float before the eye. He unfixes the land and the sea, makes them revolve around the axis of his primary thought, and disposes them anew. Possessed himself by a heroic passion, he uses matter as symbols of it. The sensual man conforms thoughts to things; the poet conforms things to his thoughts.[7] The one esteems nature as rooted and fast; the other, as fluid, and impresses his being thereon. To him, the refractory world is ductile and flexible; he invests dusts and stones with humanity and makes them the words of the Reason. The imagination may be defined to be, the use which the Reason makes of the material world. Shakspeare possesses the power of subordinating nature for the purposes of expression, beyond all poets. His imperial muse tosses the creation like a bauble from hand to hand, to embody any capricious shade of thought that is uppermost in his mind. The remotest spaces of nature are visited, and the farthest sundered things are brought together, by a subtile spiritual connexion. We are made aware that magnitude of material things is merely relative, and all objects shrink and expand to serve the passion of the poet. Thus, in his sonnets, the lays of birds, the scents and dyes of flowers, he finds to be the *shadow* of his beloved; time, which keeps her from him, is his *chest*; the suspicion she has awakened, is her *ornament*;[8]

> The ornament of beauty is Suspect,
> A crow which flies in heaven's sweetest air.[9]

His passion is not the fruit of chance; it swells, as he speaks, to a city, or a state.

---

5. Made unsubstantial. "Mechanic": manual laborer.
6. Dark chamber or box with a lens or opening through which an image is projected in natural colors onto an opposite surface.
7. From Bacon's "The Advancement of Learning"

(2.4.2), but more directly from William Hazlitt's adaptation.
8. Emerson summarizes Shakespeare's Sonnet 98 and refers to Sonnet 65 ("Shall Time's best jewel from Time's chest lie hid?").
9. Shakespeare's Sonnet 70.

> No, it was builded far from accident;
> It suffers not in smiling pomp, nor falls
> Under the brow of thralling discontent;
> It fears not policy, that heretic,
> That works on leases of short numbered hours,
> But all alone stands hugely politic.[1]

In the strength of his constancy, the Pyramids[2] seem to him recent and transitory. And the freshness of youth and love dazzles him with its resemblance to morning.

> Take those lips away
> Which so sweetly were forsworn;
> And those eyes,—the break of day,
> Lights that do mislead the morn.[3]

The wild beauty of this hyperbole, I may say, in passing, it would not be easy to match in literature.

This transfiguration which all material objects undergo through the passion of the poet,—this power which he exerts, at any moment, to magnify the small, to micrify the great,—might be illustrated by a thousand examples from his Plays. I have before me the Tempest, and will cite only these few lines.

> PROSPERO.   The strong based promontory
> Have I made shake, and by the spurs plucked up
> The pine and cedar.[4]

Prospero calls for music to sooth the frantic Alonzo, and his companions;

> A solemn air, and the best comforter
> To an unsettled fancy, cure thy brains
> Now useless, boiled within thy skull.

Again;

> The charm dissolves space
> And, as the morning steals upon the night,
> Melting the darkness, so their rising senses
> Begin to chase the ignorant fumes that mantle
> Their clearer reason.

> Their understanding
> Begins to swell: and the approaching tide
> Will shortly fill the reasonable shores
> That now lie foul and muddy.

The perception of real affinities between events, (that is to say, of *ideal* affinities, for those only are real,) enables the poet thus to make free with

---

1. Shakespeare's Sonnet 124.
2. Shakespeare's Sonnet 123: "No, Time, thou shalt not boast that I do change: / Thy pyramids built up with newer might / To me are nothing novel, nothing strange: / They are but dressings of a former sight."
3. From Shakespeare's *Measure for Measure* 5.1.1–4.
4. Shakespeare's *The Tempest* 5.1.46–48; later quotations are from 5.1.58–60, 64–68, and 79–82.

the most imposing forms and phenomena of the world, and to assert the predominance of the soul.

3. Whilst thus the poet delights us by animating[5] nature like a creator, with his own thoughts, he differs from the philosopher only herein, that the one proposes Beauty as his main end; the other Truth. But, the philosopher, not less than the poet, postpones the apparent order and relations of things to the empire of thought. "The problem of philosophy," according to Plato, "is, for all that exists conditionally, to find a ground unconditioned and absolute."[6] It proceeds on the faith that a law determines all phenomena, which being known, the phenomena can be predicted. That law, when in the mind, is an idea. Its beauty is infinite. The true philosopher and the true poet are one, and a beauty, which is truth, and a truth, which is beauty, is the aim of both. Is not the charm of one of Plato's or Aristotle's definitions, strictly like that of the Antigone of Sophocles?[7] It is, in both cases, that a spiritual life has been imparted to nature; that the solid seeming block of matter has been pervaded and dissolved by a thought; that this feeble human being has penetrated the vast masses of nature with an informing soul, and recognised itself in their harmony, that is, seized their law. In physics, when this is attained, the memory disburthens itself of its cumbrous catalogues of particulars, and carries centuries of observation in a single formula.

Thus even in physics, the material is ever degraded before the spiritual. The astronomer, the geometer, rely on their irrefragable analysis, and disdain the results of observation. The sublime remark of Euler[8] on his law of arches, "This will be found contrary to all experience, yet it is true;" had already transferred nature into the mind, and left matter like an outcast corpse.

4. Intellectual science has been observed to beget invariably a doubt of the existence of matter. Turgot[9] said, "He that has never doubted the existence of matter, may be assured he has no aptitude for metaphysical inquiries." It fastens the attention upon immortal necessary uncreated natures, that is, upon Ideas; and in their beautiful and majestic presence, we feel that our outward being is a dream and a shade. Whilst we wait in this Olympus of gods, we think of nature as an appendix to the soul. We ascend into their region, and know that these are the thoughts of the Supreme Being. "These are they who were set up from everlasting, from the beginning, or ever the earth was. When he prepared the heavens, they were there; when he established the clouds above, when he strengthened the fountains of the deep. Then they were by him, as one brought up with him. Of them took he counsel."[1]

Their influence is proportionate. As objects of science, they are accessible to few men. Yet all men are capable of being raised by piety or by passion, into their region. And no man touches these divine natures, without becoming, in some degree, himself divine. Like a new soul, they renew the body. We become physically nimble and lightsome; we tread on air; life is no longer irksome, and we think it will never be so. No man fears age or misfortune or death, in their serene company, for he is transported out of

---

5. Giving life to.
6. Emerson draws this quotation from Coleridge's "The Friend" (1818).
7. Greek dramatist of the 5th century B.C.E.; in his tragedy *Antigone* the title character chooses death rather than violate her sacred duty to perform funeral rites for her slain brother.

8. Leonhard Euler (1707–1783), Swiss mathematician and physicist. Emerson took the quotation from Coleridge's *Aids to Reflection* (1829).
9. Anne Robert Jacques Turgot (1727–1781), French economist and author of a book on proofs of the existence of God.
1. Cf. Proverbs 8.23–30.

the district of change. Whilst we behold unveiled the nature of Justice and Truth, we learn the difference between the absolute and the conditional or relative. We apprehend the absolute. As it were, for the first time, *we exist*. We become immortal, for we learn that time and space are relations of matter; that, with a perception of truth, or a virtuous will, they have no affinity.

5. Finally, religion and ethics, which may be fitly called,—the practice of ideas, or the introduction of ideas into life,—have an analogous effect with all lower culture, in degrading nature and suggesting its dependence on spirit. Ethics and religion differ herein; that the one is the system of human duties commencing from man; the other, from God. Religion includes the personality of God; Ethics does not. They are one to our present design. They both put nature under foot. The first and last lesson of religion is, "The things that are seen, are temporal; the things that are unseen are eternal."[2] It puts an affront upon nature. It does that for the unschooled, which philosophy does for Berkeley and Viasa.[3] The uniform language that may be heard in the churches of the most ignorant sects, is,—'Contemn the unsubstantial shows of the world; they are vanities, dreams, shadows, unrealities; seek the realities of religion.' The devotee flouts nature. Some theosophists[4] have arrived at a certain hostility and indignation towards matter, as the Manichean and Plotinus. They distrusted in themselves any looking back to these flesh-pots of Egypt. Plotinus was ashamed of his body.[5] In short, they might all better say of matter, what Michael Angelo said of external beauty, "it is the frail and weary weed, in which God dresses the soul, which he has called into time."[6]

It appears that motion, poetry, physical and intellectual science, and religion, all tend to affect our convictions of the reality of the external world. But I own there is something ungrateful in expanding too curiously the particulars of the general proposition, that all culture tends to imbue us with idealism. I have no hostility to nature, but a child's love to it. I expand and live in the warm day like corn and melons. Let us speak her fair. I do not wish to fling stones at my beautiful mother, nor soil my gentle nest. I only wish to indicate the true position of nature in regard to man, wherein to establish man, all right education tends; as the ground which to attain is the object of human life, that is, of man's connexion with nature. Culture inverts the vulgar views of nature, and brings the mind to call that apparent, which it uses to call real, and that real, which it uses to call visionary. Children, it is true, believe in the external world. The belief that it appears only, is an afterthought, but with culture, this faith will as surely arise on the mind as did the first.

The advantage of the ideal theory over the popular faith, is this, that it presents the world in precisely that view which is most desirable to the mind. It is, in fact, the view which Reason, both speculative and practical, that is, philosophy and virtue, take. For, seen in the light of thought, the world always is phenomenal;[7] and virtue subordinates it to the mind. Idealism sees the world in God. It beholds the whole circle of persons and things, of actions

2. 2 Corinthians 4.18.
3. Reputed author of the Vedas, the ancient sacred literature of Hinduism. George Berkeley (1685–1753), Irish idealist philosopher.
4. In the broad sense of those who attempt to establish direct contact with divine principle through contemplation and revelation.
5. Plotinus was associated with Neoplatonism, a doctrine merging features from Greek philosophies with those of Judaism and Christianity.
6. Michelangelo's Sonnet 51 (c. 1530).
7. Only an appearance.

and events, of country and religion, not as painfully accumulated, atom after atom, act after act, in an aged creeping Past, but as one vast picture, which God paints on the instant eternity, for the contemplation of the soul. Therefore the soul holds itself off from a too trivial and microscopic study of the universal tablet. It respects the end too much, to immerse itself in the means. It sees something more important in Christianity, than the scandals of ecclesiastical history or the niceties of criticism; and, very incurious concerning persons or miracles, and not at all disturbed by chasms of historical evidence, it accepts from God the phenomenon, as it finds it, as the pure and awful form of religion in the world. It is not hot and passionate at the appearance of what it calls its own good or bad fortune, at the union or opposition of other persons. No man is its enemy. It accepts whatsoever befalls, as part of its lesson. It is a watcher more than a doer, and it is a doer, only that it may the better watch.

Chapter VII. Spirit

It is essential to a true theory of nature and of man, that it should contain somewhat progressive. Uses that are exhausted or that may be, and facts that end in the statement, cannot be all that is true of this brave lodging wherein man is harbored, and wherein all his faculties find appropriate and endless exercise. And all the uses of nature admit of being summed in one, which yields the activity of man an infinite scope. Through all its kingdoms, to the suburbs and outskirts of things, it is faithful to the cause whence it had its origin. It always speaks of Spirit. It suggests the absolute. It is a perpetual effect. It is a great shadow pointing always to the sun behind us.

The aspect of nature is devout. Like the figure of Jesus, she stands with bended head, and hands folded upon the breast. The happiest man is he who learns from nature the lesson of worship.

Of that ineffable essence which we call Spirit, he that thinks most, will say least. We can foresee God in the coarse and, as it were, distant phenomena of matter; but when we try to define and describe himself, both language and thought desert us, and we are as helpless as fools and savages. That essence refuses to be recorded in propositions, but when man has worshipped him intellectually, the noblest ministry of nature is to stand as the apparition[8] of God. It is the great organ through which the universal spirit speaks to the individual, and strives to lead back the individual to it.

When we consider Spirit, we see that the views already presented do not include the whole circumference of man. We must add some related thoughts.

Three problems are put by nature to the mind; What is matter? Whence is it? and Whereto? The first of these questions only, the ideal theory answers. Idealism saith: matter is a phenomenon, not a substance. Idealism acquaints us with the total disparity between the evidence of our own being, and the evidence of the world's being. The one is perfect, the other, incapable of any assurance; the mind is a part of the nature of things; the world is a divine dream, from which we may presently awake to the glories and certainties of day. Idealism is a hypothesis to account for nature by other principles than those of carpentry and chemistry. Yet, if it only deny the existence of matter,

8. Visible state.

it does not satisfy the demands of the spirit. It leaves God out of me. It leaves me in the splendid labyrinth of my perceptions, to wander without end. Then the heart resists it, because it baulks the affections in denying substantive being to men and women. Nature is so pervaded with human life, that there is something of humanity in all, and in every particular. But this theory makes nature foreign to me, and does not account for that consanguinity which we acknowledge to it.

Let it stand then, in the present state of our knowledge, merely as a useful introductory hypothesis, serving to apprize us of the eternal distinction between the soul and the world.

But when, following the invisible steps of thought, we come to inquire, Whence is matter? and Whereto? many truths arise to us out of the recesses of consciousness. We learn that the highest is present to the soul of man, that the dread universal essence, which is not wisdom, or love, or beauty, or power, but all in one, and each entirely, is that for which all things exist, and that by which they are; that spirit creates; that behind nature, throughout nature, spirit is present; that spirit is one and not compound; that spirit does not act upon us from without, that is, in space and time, but spiritually, or through ourselves. Therefore, that spirit, that is, the Supreme Being, does not build up nature around us, but puts it forth through us, as the life of the tree puts forth new branches and leaves through the pores of the old. As a plant upon the earth, so a man rests upon the bosom of God: he is nourished by unfailing fountains, and draws, at his need, inexhaustible power. Who can set bounds to the possibilities of man? Once inspire the infinite, by being admitted to behold the absolute natures of justice and truth, and we learn that man has access to the entire mind of the Creator, is himself the creator in the finite. This view, which admonishes me where the sources of wisdom and power lie, and points to virtue as to

> "The golden key
> Which opes the palace of eternity,"[9]

carries upon its face the highest certificate of truth, because it animates me to create my own world through the purification of my soul.

The world proceeds from the same spirit as the body of man. It is a remoter and inferior incarnation of God, a projection of God in the unconscious. But it differs from the body in one important respect. It is not, like that, now subjected to the human will. Its serene order is inviolable by us. It is therefore, to us, the present expositor of the divine mind. It is a fixed point whereby we may measure our departure. As we degenerate, the contrast between us and our house is more evident. We are as much strangers in nature, as we are aliens from God. We do not understand the notes of the birds. The fox and the deer run away from us; the bear and tiger rend us. We do not know the uses of more than a few plants, as corn and the apple, the potato and the vine. Is not the landscape, every glimpse of which hath a grandeur, a face of him? Yet this may show us what discord is between man and nature, for you cannot freely admire a noble landscape, if laborers are digging in the field hard by. The poet finds something ridiculous in his delight, until he is out of the sight of men.

9. From Milton's *Comus* 13–14.

Chapter VIII. Prospects

In inquiries respecting the laws of the world and the frame of things, the highest reason is always the truest. That which seems faintly possible—it is so refined, is often faint and dim because it is deepest seated in the mind among the eternal verities. Empirical science is apt to cloud the sight, and, by the very knowledge of functions and processes, to bereave the student of the manly contemplation of the whole. The savant[1] becomes unpoetic. But the best read naturalist who lends an entire and devout attention to truth, will see that there remains much to learn of his relation to the world, and that it is not to be learned by any addition or subtraction or other comparison of known quantities, but is arrived at by untaught sallies of the spirit, by a continual self-recovery, and by entire humility. He will perceive that there are far more excellent qualities in the student than preciseness and infallibility; that a guess is often more fruitful than an indisputable affirmation, and that a dream may let us deeper into the secret of nature than a hundred concerted experiments.

For, the problems to be solved are precisely those which the physiologist and the naturalist omit to state. It is not so pertinent to man to know all the individuals of the animal kingdom, as it is to know whence and whereto is this tyrannizing unity in his constitution, which evermore separates and classifies things, endeavouring to reduce the most diverse to one form. When I behold a rich landscape, it is less to my purpose to recite correctly the order and super-position of the strata, than to know why all thought of multitude is lost in a tranquil sense of unity. I cannot greatly honor minuteness in details, so long as there is no hint to explain the relation between things and thoughts; no ray upon the *metaphysics* of conchology, of botany, of the arts, to show the relation of the forms of flowers, shells, animals, architecture, to the mind, and build science upon ideas. In a cabinet[2] of natural history, we become sensible of a certain occult recognition and sympathy in regard to the most bizarre forms of beast, fish, and insect. The American who has been confined, in his own country, to the sight of buildings designed after foreign models, is surprised on entering York Minster or St. Peter's at Rome, by the feeling that these structures are imitations also,— faint copies of an invisible archetype. Nor has science sufficient humanity, so long as the naturalist overlooks that wonderful congruity which subsists between man and the world; of which he is lord, not because he is the most subtile inhabitant, but because he is its head and heart, and finds something of himself in every great and small thing, in every mountain stratum, in every new law of color, fact of astronomy, or atmospheric influence which observation or analysis lay open. A perception of this mystery inspires the muse of George Herbert, the beautiful psalmist of the seventeenth century. The following lines are part of his little poem on Man.[3]

> "Man is all symmetry,
> Full of proportions, one limb to another,
>   And to all the world besides.
>   Each part may call the farthest, brother;

---

1. Learned person.
2. Display case, or room containing many display cases.
3. Stanzas 1–4 and 6 of "Man" (1633).

For head with foot hath private amity,
    And both with moons and tides.

    "Nothing hath got so far
But man hath caught and kept it as his prey;
    His eyes dismount the highest star;
    He is in little all the sphere.
Herbs gladly cure our flesh, because that they
    Find their acquaintance there.

    "For us, the winds do blow.
The earth doth rest, heaven move, and fountains flow;
    Nothing we see, but means our good,
    As our delight, or as our treasure;
The whole is either our cupboard of food,
    Or cabinet of pleasure.

    "The stars have us to bed;
Night draws the curtain; which the sun withdraws.
    Music and light attend our head.
    All things unto our flesh are kind,
In their descent and being; to our mind,
    In their ascent and cause.

    "More servants wait on man
Than he'll take notice of. In every path,
    He treads down that which doth befriend him
    When sickness makes him pale and wan.
Oh mighty love! Man is one world, and hath
    Another to attend him."

The perception of this class of truths makes the eternal attraction which draws men to science, but the end is lost sight of in attention to the means. In view of this half-sight of science, we accept the sentence of Plato, that, "poetry comes nearer to vital truth than history."[4] Every surmise and vaticination[5] of the mind is entitled to a certain respect, and we learn to prefer imperfect theories, and sentences, which contain glimpses of truth, to digested systems which have no one valuable suggestion. A wise writer will feel that the ends of study and composition are best answered by announcing undiscovered regions of thought, and so communicating, through hope, new activity to the torpid spirit.

I shall therefore conclude this essay with some traditions of man and nature, which a certain poet[6] sang to me; and which, as they have always been in the world, and perhaps reappear to every bard, may be both history and prophecy.

'The foundations of man are not in matter, but in spirit. But the element of spirit is eternity. To it, therefore, the longest series of events, the oldest

---

4. In copying two quotations from the *Edinburgh Review* Emerson blurred the attributions; here he quotes not from Plato, but from section 9 of Aristotle's *Poetics*.
5. Foretelling, prophesying.

6. Perhaps a joking reference to Bronson Alcott (1799–1888), Emerson's neighbor and Trancendentalist friend, who authored his own "Orphic Sayings" (though these poetic passages are by Emerson).

chronologies are young and recent. In the cycle of the universal man, from whom the known individuals proceed, centuries are points, and all history is but the epoch of one degradation.

'We distrust and deny inwardly our sympathy with nature. We own and disown our relation to it, by turns. We are, like Nebuchadnezzar, dethroned, bereft of reason, and eating grass like an ox.[7] But who can set limits to the remedial force of spirit?

'A man is a god in ruins. When men are innocent, life shall be longer, and shall pass into the immortal, as gently as we awake from dreams. Now, the world would be insane and rabid, if these disorganizations should last for hundreds of years. It is kept in check by death and infancy. Infancy is the perpetual Messiah, which comes into the arms of fallen men, and pleads with them to return to paradise.

'Man is the dwarf of himself. Once he was permeated and dissolved by spirit. He filled nature with his overflowing currents. Out from him sprang the sun and moon; from man, the sun; from woman, the moon. The laws of his mind, the periods of his actions externized themselves into day and night, into the year and the seasons. But, having made for himself this huge shell, his waters retired; he no longer fills the veins and veinlets; he is shrunk to a drop. He sees, that the structure still fits him, but fits him colossally. Say, rather, once it fitted him, now it corresponds to him from far and on high. He adores timidly his own work. Now is man the follower of the sun, and woman the follower of the moon. Yet sometimes he starts in his slumber, and wonders at himself and his house, and muses strangely at the resemblance betwixt him and it. He perceives that if his law is still paramount, if still he have elemental power, "if his word is sterling yet in nature," it is not conscious power, it is not inferior but superior to his will. It is Instinct.' Thus my Orphic poet sang.

At present, man applies to nature but half his force. He works on the world with his understanding alone. He lives in it, and masters it by a penny-wisdom; and he that works most in it, is but a half-man and whilst his arms are strong and his digestion good, his mind is imbruted and he is a selfish savage. His relation to nature, his power over it, is through the understanding; as by manure; the economic use of fire, wind, water, and the mariner's needle; steam, coal, chemical agriculture; the repairs of the human body by the dentist and the surgeon. This is such a resumption of power, as if a banished king should buy his territories inch by inch, instead of vaulting at once into his throne. Meantime, in the thick darkness, there are not wanting gleams of a better light,—occasional examples of the action of man upon nature with his entire force,—with reason as well as understanding. Such examples are; the traditions of miracles in the earliest antiquity of all nations; the history of Jesus Christ; the achievements of a principle, as in religious and political revolutions, and in the abolition of the Slave-trade; the miracles of enthusiasm,[8] as those reported of Swedenborg, Hohenlohe, and the Shakers;[9] many obscure and yet contested facts, now arranged under the

---

7. The Babylonian king Nebuchadnezzar (d. 562 B.C.E.) "was driven from men, and did eat grass as oxen" (Daniel 4.33).
8. State of supernatural ecstasy or possession.
9. A Protestant millenarian sect known for its commitments to sexual equality and celibacy, the

Shakers were founded in England in 1747 and moved to America in 1774; like the Quakers, they preached the importance of attending to one's inner light. Leopold Franz Emmerich, prince of Hohenlohe (1794–1849), reputed miracle healer.

name of Animal Magnetism;[1] prayer; eloquence, self-healing; and the wisdom of children. These are examples of Reason's momentary grasp of the sceptre, the exertions of a power which exists not in time or space, but an instantaneous in-streaming causing power. The difference between the actual and the ideal force of man is happily figured by the schoolmen,[2] in saying, that the knowledge of man is an evening knowledge, *vespertina cognitio*, but that of God is a morning knowledge, *matutina cognitio*.

The problem of restoring to the world original and eternal beauty, is solved by the redemption of the soul. The ruin or the blank, that we see when we look at nature, is in our own eye. The axis of vision is not coincident with the axis of things, and so they appear not transparent but opake. The reason why the world lacks unity, and lies broken and in heaps, is, because man is disunited with himself. He cannot be a naturalist, until he satisfies all the demands of the spirit. Love is as much its demand, as perception. Indeed, neither can be perfect without the other. In the uttermost meaning of the words, thought is devout, and devotion is thought. Deep calls unto deep.[3] But in actual life, the marriage is not celebrated. There are innocent men who worship God after the tradition of their fathers, but their sense of duty has not yet extended to the use of all their faculties. And there are patient naturalists, but they freeze their subject under the wintry light of the understanding. Is not prayer also a study of truth,—a sally of the soul into the unfound infinite? No man ever prayed heartily, without learning something. But when a faithful thinker, resolute to detach every object from personal relations, and see it in the light of thought, shall, at the same time, kindle science with the fire of the holiest affections, then will God go forth anew into the creation.

It will not need, when the mind is prepared for study, to search for objects. The invariable mark of wisdom is to see the miraculous in the common. What is a day? What is a year? What is summer? What is woman? What is a child? What is sleep? To our blindness, these things seem unaffecting. We make fables to hide the baldness of the fact and conform it, as we say, to the higher law of the mind. But when the fact is seen under the light of an idea, the gaudy fable fades and shrivels. We behold the real higher law. To the wise, therefore, a fact is true poetry, and the most beautiful of fables. These wonders are brought to our own door. You also are a man. Man and woman, and their social life, poverty, labor, sleep, fear, fortune, are known to you. Learn that none of these things is superficial, but that each phenomenon hath its roots in the faculties and affections of the mind. Whilst the abstract question occupies your intellect, nature brings it in the concrete to be solved by your hands. It were a wise inquiry for the closet,[4] to compare, point by point, especially at remarkable crises in life, our daily history, with the rise and progress of ideas in the mind.

So shall we come to look at the world with new eyes. It shall answer the endless inquiry of the intellect,—What is truth? and of the affections,—What is good? by yielding itself passive to the educated Will. Then shall come to pass what my poet said; 'Nature is not fixed but fluid. Spirit alters, moulds, makes it. The immobility or bruteness of nature, is the absence of

---

1. Hypnotism.
2. Medieval scholastic philosophers.

3. Psalm 42.7.
4. The scholar's private workroom.

spirit; to pure spirit, it is fluid, it is volatile, it is obedient. Every spirit builds itself a house; and beyond its house, a world; and beyond its world, a heaven. Know then, that the world exists for you. For you is the phenomenon perfect. What we are, that only can we see. All that Adam had, all that Cæsar could, you have and can do. Adam called his house, heaven and earth; Cæsar called his house, Rome; you perhaps call yours, a cobler's trade; a hundred acres of ploughed land; or a scholar's garret. Yet line for line and point for point, your dominion is as great as theirs, though without fine names. Build, therefore your own world. As fast as you can conform your life to the pure idea in your mind, that will unfold its great proportions. A correspondent revolution in things will attend the influx of the spirit. So fast will disagreeable appearances, swine, spiders, snakes, pests, mad-houses, prisons, enemies, vanish; they are temporary and shall be no more seen. The sordor and filths of nature, the sun shall dry up, and the wind exhale. As when the summer comes from the south, the snow-banks melt, and the face of the earth becomes green before it, so shall the advancing spirit create its ornaments along its path, and carry with it the beauty it visits, and the song which enchants it; it shall draw beautiful faces, and warm hearts, and wise discourse, and heroic acts, around its way, until evil is no more seen. The kingdom of man over nature, which cometh not with observation,[5]—a dominion such as now is beyond his dream of God,—he shall enter without more wonder than the blind man feels who is gradually restored to perfect sight.'

1836

The American Scholar[1]

Mr. President, and Gentlemen,

I greet you on the re-commencement of our literary year.[2] Our anniversary is one of hope, and, perhaps, not enough of labor. We do not meet for games of strength or skill, for the recitation of histories, tragedies and odes, like the ancient Greeks; for parliaments of love and poesy, like the Troubadours;[3] nor for the advancement of science, like our cotemporaries in the British and European capitals. Thus far, our holiday has been simply a friendly sign of the survival of the love of letters amongst a people too busy to give to letters any more. As such, it is precious as the sign of an indestructible instinct. Perhaps the time is already come, when it ought to be, and will be something else; when the sluggard intellect of this continent will look from under its iron lids and fill the postponed expectation of the world with something better than the exertions of mechanical skill. Our day of dependence, our long apprenticeship to the learning of other lands, draws to a close. The millions that around us are rushing into life, cannot always be fed on the sere remains of

5. Luke 17.20.
1. The text printed here is that of the first publication (1837) as a pamphlet titled *An Oration, Delivered before the Phi Beta Kappa Society at Cambridge, August 31, 1837.* By changing the title to "The American Scholar" when he republished it in *Nature, Addresses, and Lectures* (1849), Emer-

son made clear that he was addressing a larger audience than this first group.
2. Also a reference to the academic year traditionally beginning in September.
3. Poets of southern France, especially Provence, in the 12th and 13th centuries.

foreign harvests. Events, actions arise, that must be sung, that will sing themselves. Who can doubt that poetry will revive and lead in a new age, as the star in the constellation Harp which now flames in our zenith, astronomers announce, shall one day be the pole-star[4] for a thousand years.

In the light of this hope, I accept the topic which not only usage, but the nature of our association, seem to prescribe to this day,—the AMERICAN SCHOLAR. Year by year, we come up hither to read one more chapter of his biography. Let us inquire what new lights, new events and more days have thrown on his character, his duties and his hopes.

It is one of those fables, which out of an unknown antiquity, convey an unlooked for wisdom, that the gods, in the beginning, divided Man into men, that he might be more helpful to himself;[5] just as the hand was divided into fingers, the better to answer its end.

The old fable covers a doctrine ever new and sublime; that there is One Man,—present to all particular men only partially, or through one faculty; and that you must take the whole society to find the whole man. Man is not a farmer, or a professor, or an engineer, but he is all. Man is priest, and scholar, and statesman, and producer, and soldier. In the *divided* or social state, these functions are parcelled out to individuals, each of whom aims to do his stint of the joint work, whilst each other performs his. The fable implies that the individual to possess himself, must sometimes return from his own labor to embrace all the other laborers. But unfortunately, this original unit, this fountain of power, has been so distributed to multitudes, has been so minutely subdivided and peddled out, that it is spilled into drops, and cannot be gathered. The state of society is one in which the members have suffered amputation from the trunk, and strut about so many walking monsters,—a good finger, a neck, a stomach, an elbow, but never a man.

Man is thus metamorphosed into a thing, into many things. The planter, who is Man sent out into the field to gather food, is seldom cheered by any idea of the true dignity of his ministry. He sees his bushel and his cart, and nothing beyond, and sinks into the farmer, instead of Man on the farm. The tradesman scarcely ever gives an ideal worth to his work, but is ridden by the routine of his craft, and the soul is subject to dollars. The priest becomes a form; the attorney, a statute-book; the mechanic, a machine; the sailor, a rope of a ship.

In this distribution of functions, the scholar is the delegated intellect. In the right state, he is, *Man Thinking*. In the degenerate state, when the victim of society, he tends to become a mere thinker, or, still worse, the parrot of other men's thinking.

In this view of him, as Man Thinking, the whole theory of his office[6] is contained. Him nature solicits, with all her placid, all her monitory pictures. Him the past instructs. Him the future invites. Is not, indeed, every man a student, and do not all things exist for the student's behoof? And, finally, is not the true scholar the only true master? But, as the old oracle said, "All things have two handles. Beware of the wrong one."[7] In life, too often, the

---

4. The North Star. "Harp": Lyra, a northern constellation, which includes the bright star Vega.
5. Emerson knew one such fable from Plato's *Symposium*.

6. Function.
7. From the Greek philosopher Epictetus (c. 50–c. 138 C.E.), who taught that the true good is within oneself.

scholar errs with mankind and forfeits his privilege. Let us see him in his school, and consider him in reference to the main influences he receives.

I. The first in time and the first in importance of the influences upon the mind is that of nature. Every day, the sun; and, after sunset, night and her stars. Ever the winds blow; ever the grass grows. Every day, men and women, conversing, beholding and beholden. The scholar must needs stand wistful and admiring before this great spectacle. He must settle its value in his mind. What is nature to him? There is never a beginning, there is never an end to the inexplicable continuity of this web of God, but always circular power returning into itself. Therein it resembles his own spirit, whose beginning, whose ending he never can find—so entire, so boundless. Far, too, as her splendors shine, system on system shooting like rays, upward, downward, without centre, without circumference,—in the mass and in the particle nature hastens to render account of herself to the mind. Classification begins. To the young mind, every thing is individual, stands by itself. By and by, it finds how to join two things, and see in them one nature; then three, then three thousand; and so, tyrannized over by its own unifying instinct, it goes on tying things together, diminishing anomalies, discovering roots running under ground, whereby contrary and remote things cohere, and flower out from one stem. It presently learns, that, since the dawn of history, there has been a constant accumulation and classifying of facts. But what is classification but the perceiving that these objects are not chaotic, and are not foreign, but have a law which is also a law of the human mind? The astronomer discovers that geometry, a pure abstraction of the human mind, is the measure of planetary motion. The chemist finds proportions and intelligible method throughout matter: and science is nothing but the finding of analogy, identity in the most remote parts. The ambitious soul sits down before each refractory fact; one after another, reduces all strange constitutions, all new powers, to their class and their law, and goes on forever to animate the last fibre of organization, the outskirts of nature, by insight.

Thus to him, to this school-boy under the bending dome of day, is suggested, that he and it proceed from one root; one is leaf and one is flower; relation, sympathy, stirring in every vein. And what is that Root? Is not that the soul of his soul?—A thought too bold—a dream too wild. Yet when this spiritual light shall have revealed the law of more earthly natures,—when he has learned to worship the soul, and to see that the natural philosophy that now is, is only the first gropings of its gigantic hand, he shall look forward to an ever expanding knowledge as to a becoming creator. He shall see that nature is the opposite of the soul, answering to it part for part. One is seal, and one is print. Its beauty is the beauty of his own mind. Its laws are the laws of his own mind. Nature then becomes to him the measure of his attainments. So much of nature as he is ignorant of, so much of his own mind does he not yet possess. And, in fine, the ancient precept, "Know thyself," and the modern precept, "Study nature," become at last one maxim.

II. The next great influence[8] into the spirit of the scholar, is, the mind of the Past,—in whatever form, whether of literature, of art, of institutions,

8. Inflowing.

that mind is inscribed. Books are the best type of the influence of the past, and perhaps we shall get at the truth—learn the amount of this influence more conveniently—by considering their value alone.

The theory of books is noble. The scholar of the first age received into him the world around; brooded thereon; gave it the new arrangement of his own mind, and uttered it again. It came into him—life; it went out from him—truth. It came to him—short-lived actions; it went out from him—immortal thoughts. It came to him—business; it went from him—poetry. It was—dead fact; now, it is quick[9] thought. It can stand, and it can go. It now endures, it now flies, it now inspires.[1] Precisely in proportion to the depth of mind from which it issued, so high does it soar, so long does it sing.

Or, I might say, it depends on how far the process had gone, of transmuting life into truth. In proportion to the completeness of the distillation, so will the purity and imperishableness of the product be. But none is quite perfect. As no air-pump can by any means make a perfect vacuum, so neither can any artist entirely exclude the conventional, the local, the perishable from his book, or write a book of pure thought that shall be as efficient, in all respects, to a remote posterity, as to cotemporaries, or rather to the second age. Each age, it is found, must write its own books; or rather, each generation for the next succeeding. The books of an older period will not fit this.

Yet hence arises a grave mischief. The sacredness which attaches to the act of creation,—the act of thought,—is instantly transferred to the record. The poet chanting, was felt to be a divine man. Henceforth the chant is divine also. The writer was a just and wise spirit. Henceforward it is settled, the book is perfect; as love of the hero corrupts into worship of his statue. Instantly, the book becomes noxious. The guide is a tyrant. We sought a brother, and lo, a governor. The sluggish and perverted mind of the multitude, always slow to open to the incursions of Reason, having once so opened, having once received this book, stands upon it, and makes an outcry, if it is disparaged. Colleges are built on it. Books are written on it by thinkers, not by Man Thinking; by men of talent, that is, who start wrong, who set out from accepted dogmas, not from their own sight of principles. Meek young men grow up in libraries, believing it their duty to accept the views which Cicero, which Locke, which Bacon have given, forgetful that Cicero, Locke and Bacon were only young men in libraries when they wrote these books.[2]

Hence, instead of Man Thinking, we have the bookworm. Hence, the book-learned class, who value books, as such; not as related to nature and the human constitution, but as making a sort of Third Estate[3] with the world and the soul. Hence, the restorers of readings, the emendators, the bibliomaniacs of all degrees.

This is bad; this is worse than it seems. Books are the best of things, well used; abused, among the worst. What is the right use? What is the one end which all means go to effect? They are for nothing but to inspire. I had better never see a book than to be warped by its attraction clean out of my own

9. Living. "Business": busyness, activity.
1. Breathes in. "Go": walk.
2. As a young man Marcus Tullius Cicero (106–43 B.C.E.), Roman statesman, was renowned for his oratory. John Locke (1632–1704), English philosopher and political thinker, wrote *Essay Concerning Human Understanding* (1690) before he

was forty. Sir Francis Bacon (1561–1626), English statesman and philosopher, is best known for his essays.
3. The term "Third Estate" is based on an obsolete social classification: first the clergy, second the nobility, third the common people.

orbit, and made a satellite instead of a system. The one thing in the world of value, is, the active soul,—the soul, free, sovereign, active. This every man is entitled to; this every man contains within him, although in almost all men, obstructed, and as yet unborn. The soul active sees absolute truth; and utters truth, or creates. In this action, it is genius; not the privilege of here and there a favorite, but the sound estate of every man. In its essence, it is progressive. The book, the college, the school of art, the institution of any kind, stop with some past utterance of genius. This is good, say they,—let us hold by this. They pin me down. They look backward and not forward. But genius always looks forward. The eyes of man are set in his forehead, not in his hindhead. Man hopes. Genius creates. To create,—to create,—is the proof of a divine presence. Whatever talents may be, if the man create not, the pure efflux[4] of the Deity is not his:—cinders and smoke, there may be, but not yet flame. There are creative manners, there are creative actions, and creative words; manners, actions, words, that is, indicative of no custom or authority, but springing spontaneous from the mind's own sense of good and fair.

On the other part, instead of being its own seer, let it receive always from another mind its truth, though it were in torrents of light, without periods of solitude, inquest and self-recovery, and a fatal disservice is done. Genius is always sufficiently the enemy of genius by over-influence. The literature of every nation bear me witness. The English dramatic poets have Shakspearized now for two hundred years.

Undoubtedly, there is a right way of reading,—so it be sternly subordinated. Man Thinking must not be subdued by his instruments. Books are for the scholar's idle times. When he can read God directly, the hour is too precious to be wasted in other men's transcripts of their readings. But when the intervals of darkness come, as come they must,—when the soul seeth not, when the sun is hid, and the stars withdraw their shining,—we repair to the lamps which were kindled by their ray to guide our steps to the East again, where the dawn is. We hear that we may speak. The Arabian proverb says, "A fig tree looking on a fig tree, becometh fruitful."

It is remarkable, the character of the pleasure we derive from the best books. They impress us ever with the conviction that one nature wrote and the same reads. We read the verses of one of the great English poets, of Chaucer, of Marvell, of Dryden,[5] with the most modern joy,—with a pleasure, I mean, which is in great part caused by the abstraction of all *time* from their verses. There is some awe mixed with the joy of our surprise, when this poet, who lived in some past world, two or three hundred years ago, says that which lies close to my own soul, that which I also had well nigh thought and said. But for the evidence thence afforded to the philosophical doctrine of the identity of all minds, we should suppose some pre-established harmony, some foresight of souls that were to be, and some preparation of stores for their future wants, like the fact observed in insects, who lay up food before death for the young grub they shall never see.

I would not be hurried by any love of system, by any exaggeration of instincts, to underrate the Book. We all know, that as the human body can

4. Flowing forth.
5. English poets: Geoffrey Chaucer (1340–1400),

Andrew Marvell (1621–1678), and John Dryden (1631–1700).

be nourished on any food, though it were boiled grass and the broth of shoes, so the human mind can be fed by any knowledge. And great and heroic men have existed, who had almost no other information than by the printed page. I only would say, that it needs a strong head to bear that diet. One must be an inventor to read well. As the proverb says, "He that would bring home the wealth of the Indies, must carry out the wealth of the Indies." There is then creative reading, as well as creative writing. When the mind is braced by labor and invention, the page of whatever book we read becomes luminous with manifold allusion. Every sentence is doubly significant, and the sense of our author is as broad as the world. We then see, what is always true, that as the seer's hour of vision is short and rare among heavy days and months, so is its record, perchance, the least part of his volume. The discerning will read in his Plato or Shakspeare, only that least part,—only the authentic utterances of the oracle,—and all the rest he rejects, were it never so many times Plato's and Shakspeare's.

Of course, there is a portion of reading quite indispensable to a wise man. History and exact science he must learn by laborious reading. Colleges, in like manner, have their indispensable office,—to teach elements. But they can only highly serve us, when they aim not to drill, but to create; when they gather from far every ray of various genius to their hospitable halls, and, by the concentrated fires, set the hearts of their youth on flame. Thought and knowledge are natures in which apparatus and pretension avail nothing. Gowns, and pecuniary foundations, though of towns of gold, can never countervail the least sentence or syllable of wit.[6] Forget this, and our American colleges will recede in their public importance whilst they grow richer every year.

III. There goes in the world a notion that the scholar should be a recluse, a valetudinarian,[7]—as unfit for any handiwork or public labor, as a penknife for an axe. The so called "practical men" sneer at speculative men, as if, because they speculate or *see*, they could do nothing. I have heard it said that the clergy,—who are always more universally than any other class, the scholars of their day,—are addressed as women: that the rough, spontaneous conversation of men they do not hear, but only a mincing and diluted speech. They are often virtually disfranchised; and, indeed, there are advocates for their celibacy. As far as this is true of the studious classes, it is not just and wise. Action is with the scholar subordinate, but it is essential. Without it, he is not yet man. Without it, thought can never ripen into truth. Whilst the world hangs before the eye as a cloud of beauty, we can not even see its beauty. Inaction is cowardice, but there can be no scholar without the heroic mind. The preamble of thought, the transition through which it passes from the unconscious to the conscious, is action. Only so much do I know, as I have lived. Instantly, we know whose words are loaded with life, and whose not.

The world,—this shadow of the soul, or *other me*, lies wide around. Its attractions are the keys which unlock my thoughts and make me acquainted with myself. I launch eagerly into this resounding tumult. I grasp the hands of those next me, and take my place in the ring to suffer and to work, taught

6. Intelligence. "Gowns": academic robes.   7. Invalid.

by an instinct that so shall the dumb abyss be vocal with speech. I pierce its order; I dissipate its fear; I dispose of it within the circuit of my expanding life. So much only of life as I know by experience, so much of the wilderness have I vanquished and planted, or so far have I extended my being, my dominion. I do not see how any man can afford, for the sake of his nerves and his nap, to spare any action in which he can partake. It is pearls and rubies to his discourse. Drudgery, calamity, exasperation, want, are instructers in eloquence and wisdom. The true scholar grudges every opportunity of action past by, as a loss of power.

It is the raw material out of which the intellect moulds her splendid products. A strange process too, this, by which experience is converted into thought, as a mulberry leaf is converted into satin.[8] The manufacture goes forward at all hours.

The actions and events of our childhood and youth are now matters of calmest observation. They lie like fair pictures in the air. Not so with our recent actions,—with the business which we now have in hand. On this we are quite unable to speculate. Our affections as yet circulate through it. We no more feel or know it, than we feel the feet, or the hand, or the brain of our body. The new deed is yet a part of life,—remains for a time immersed in our unconscious life. In some contemplative hour, it detaches itself from the life like a ripe fruit, to become a thought of the mind. Instantly, it is raised, transfigured; the corruptible has put on incorruption.[9] Always now it is an object of beauty, however base its origin and neighborhood. Observe, too, the impossibility of antedating this act. In its grub state, it cannot fly, it cannot shine,—it is a dull grub. But suddenly, without observation, the self-same thing unfurls beautiful wings, and is an angel of wisdom. So is there no fact, no event, in our private history, which shall not, sooner or later, lose its adhesive inert form, and astonish us by soaring from our body into the empyrean.[1] Cradle and infancy, school and playground, the fear of boys, and dogs, and ferules,[2] the love of little maids and berries, and many another fact that once filled the whole sky, are gone already; friend and relative, profession and party, town and country, nation and world, must also soar and sing.

Of course, he who has put forth his total strength in fit actions, has the richest return of wisdom. I will not shut myself out of this globe of action and transplant an oak into a flower pot, there to hunger and pine; nor trust the revenue of some single faculty, and exhaust one vein of thought, much like those Savoyards,[3] who, getting their livelihood by carving shepherds, shepherdesses, and smoking Dutchmen, for all Europe, went out one day to the mountain to find stock, and discovered that they had whittled up the last of their pine trees. Authors we have in numbers, who have written out their vein, and who, moved by a commendable prudence, sail for Greece or Palestine, follow the trapper into the prairie, or ramble round Algiers to replenish their merchantable stock.[4]

8. A form of silk produced by silkworms, which feed on mulberry leaves.
9. "For this corruptible must put on incorruption, and this mortal must put on immortality" (1 Corinthians 15.53).
1. The highest reaches of heaven.
2. Rods used for punishing children.
3. Savoy is in the western Alps, where France, Italy, and Switzerland converge.
4. Likely references to Emerson's contemporaries: Nathaniel Parker Willis (1806–1867), editor and travel writer; Washington Irving, whose A Tour on the Prairies appeared in 1835; and James Fenimore Cooper, whose The Prairie was published in 1827.

If it were only for a vocabulary the scholar would be covetous of action. Life is our dictionary. Years are well spent in country labors; in town—in the insight into trades and manufactures; in frank intercourse with many men and women; in science; in art; to the one end of mastering in all their facts a language, by which to illustrate and embody our perceptions. I learn immediately from any speaker how much he has already lived, through the poverty or the splendor of his speech. Life lies behind us as the quarry from whence we get tiles and copestones for the masonry of to-day. This is the way to learn grammar. Colleges and books only copy the language which the field and the workyard made.

But the final value of action, like that of books, and better than books, is, that it is a resource. That great principle of Undulation in nature, that shows itself in the inspiring and expiring of the breath; in desire and satiety; in the ebb and flow of the sea, in day and night, in heat and cold, and as yet more deeply ingrained in every atom and every fluid, is known to us under the name of Polarity,—these "fits of easy transmission and reflection," as Newton[5] called them, are the law of nature because they are the law of spirit.

The mind now thinks; now acts; and each fit reproduces the other. When the artist has exhausted his materials, when the fancy no longer paints, when thoughts are no longer apprehended, and books are a weariness,—he has always the resource to *live*. Character is higher than intellect. Thinking is the function. Living is the functionary. The stream retreats to its source. A great soul will be strong to live, as well as strong to think. Does he lack organ or medium to impart his truths? He can still fall back on this elemental force of living them. This is a total act. Thinking is a partial act. Let the grandeur of justice shine in his affairs. Let the beauty of affection cheer his lowly roof. Those "far from fame" who dwell and act with him, will feel the force of his constitution in the doings and passages of the day better than it can be measured by any public and designed display. Time shall teach him that the scholar loses no hour which the man lives. Herein he unfolds the sacred germ of his instinct screened from influence. What is lost in seemliness is gained in strength. Not out of those on whom systems of education have exhausted their culture, comes the helpful giant to destroy the old or to build the new, but out of unhandselled[6] savage nature, out of terrible Druids and Berserkirs, come at last Alfred[7] and Shakspear.

I hear therefore with joy whatever is beginning to be said of the dignity and necessity of labor to every citizen. There is virtue yet in the hoe and the spade, for learned as well as for unlearned hands. And labor is every where welcome; always we are invited to work; only be this limitation observed, that a man shall not for the sake of wider activity sacrifice any opinion to the popular judgments and modes of action.

I have now spoken of the education of the scholar by nature, by books, and by action. It remains to say somewhat of his duties.

5. From the *Optics* (1704) of Sir Isaac Newton (1642–1727), English scientist and mathematician.
6. A handsel is a gift to express good wishes at the outset of some enterprise; apparently Emerson uses "unhandselled" to mean something like unauspicious.
7. The enlightened 9th-century king of the West Saxons. "Terrible Druids and Berserkirs": uncivilized Celts and Anglo-Saxons.

They are such as become Man Thinking. They may all be comprised in self-trust. The office of the scholar is to cheer, to raise, and to guide men by showing them facts amidst appearances. He plies the slow, unhonored, and unpaid task of observation. Flamsteed and Herschel, in their glazed[8] observatory, may catalogue the stars with the praise of all men, and the results being splendid and useful, honor is sure. But he, in his private observatory, cataloguing obscure and nebulous stars of the human mind, which as yet no man has thought of as such,—watching days and months, sometimes, for a few facts; correcting still his old records;—must relinquish display and immediate fame. In the long period of his preparation, he must betray often an ignorance and shiftlessness in popular arts, incurring the disdain of the able who shoulder him aside. Long he must stammer in his speech; often forego the living for the dead. Worse yet, he must accept—how often! poverty and solitude. For the ease and pleasure of treading the old road, accepting the fashions, the education, the religion of society, he takes the cross of making his own, and, of course, the self accusation, the faint heart, the frequent uncertainty and loss of time which are the nettles and tangling vines in the way of the self-relying and self-directed; and the state of virtual hostility in which he seems to stand to society, and especially to educated society. For all this loss and scorn, what offset? He is to find consolation in exercising the highest functions of human nature. He is one who raises himself from private considerations, and breathes and lives on public and illustrious thoughts. He is the world's eye. He is the world's heart. He is to resist the vulgar prosperity that retrogrades ever to barbarism, by preserving and communicating heroic sentiments, noble biographies, melodious verse, and the conclusions of history. Whatsoever oracles the human heart in all emergencies, in all solemn hours has uttered as its commentary on the world of actions,—these he shall receive and impart. And whatsoever new verdict Reason from her inviolable seat pronounces on the passing men and events of to-day,—this he shall hear and promulgate.

These being his functions, it becomes him to feel all confidence in himself, and to defer never to the popular cry. He and he only knows the world. The world of any moment is the merest appearance. Some great decorum, some fetish of a government, some ephemeral trade, or war, or man, is cried up by half mankind and cried down by the other half, as if all depended on this particular up or down. The odds are that the whole question is not worth the poorest thought which the scholar has lost in listening to the controversy. Let him not quit his belief that a popgun is a popgun, though the ancient and honorable of the earth affirm it to be the crack of doom. In silence, in steadiness, in severe abstraction, let him hold by himself; add observation to observation; patient of neglect, patient of reproach, and bide his own time,—happy enough if he can satisfy himself alone that this day he has seen something truly. Success treads on every right step. For the instinct is sure that prompts him to tell his brother what he thinks. He then learns that in going down into the secrets of his own mind, he has descended into the secrets of all minds. He learns that he who has mastered any law in his private thoughts, is master to that extent of all men whose language he

---

8. Glass-roofed. John Flamsteed (1646–1719), English astronomer, first royal astronomer at Greenwich Observatory. Sir William Herschel (1738–1822), German-born English astronomer.

speaks, and of all into whose language his own can be translated. The poet in utter solitude remembering his spontaneous thoughts and recording them, is found to have recorded that which men in "cities vast" find true for them also. The orator distrusts at first the fitness of his frank confessions,—his want of knowledge of the persons he addresses,—until he finds that he is the complement of his hearers;—that they drink his words because he fulfils for them their own nature; the deeper he dives into his privatest secretest presentiment,—to his wonder he finds, this is the most acceptable, most public, and universally true. The people delight in it; the better part of every man feels, This is my music: this is myself.

In self-trust, all the virtues are comprehended. Free should the scholar be,—free and brave. Free even to the definition of freedom, "without any hindrance that does not arise out of his own constitution." Brave; for fear is a thing which a scholar by his very function puts behind him. Fear always springs from ignorance. It is a shame to him if his tranquillity, amid dangerous times, arise from the presumption that like children and women, his is a protected class; or if he seek a temporary peace by the diversion of his thoughts from politics or vexed questions, hiding his head like an ostrich in the flowering bushes, peeping into microscopes, and turning rhymes, as a boy whistles to keep his courage up. So is the danger a danger still: so is the fear worse. Manlike let him turn and face it. Let him look into its eye and search its nature, inspect its origin—see the whelping of this lion,—which lies no great way back; he will then find in himself a perfect comprehension of its nature and extent; he will have made his hands meet on the other side, and can henceforth defy it, and pass on superior. The world is his who can see through its pretension. What deafness, what stone-blind custom, what overgrown error you behold, is there only by sufferance,—by your sufferance. See it to be a lie, and you have already dealt it its mortal blow.

Yes, we are the cowed,—we the trustless. It is a mischievous notion that we are come late into nature; that the world was finished a long time ago. As the world was plastic and fluid in the hands of God, so it is ever to so much of his attributes as we bring to it. To ignorance and sin, it is flint. They adapt themselves to it as they may; but in proportion as a man has anything in him divine, the firmament flows before him, and takes his signet[9] and form. Not he is great who can alter matter, but he who can alter my state of mind. They are the kings of the world who give the color of their present thought to all nature and all art, and persuade men by the cheerful serenity of their carrying the matter, that this thing which they do, is the apple which the ages have desired to pluck, now at last ripe, and inviting nations to the harvest. The great man makes the great thing. Wherever Macdonald sits, there is the head of the table.[1] Linnæus makes botany the most alluring of studies and wins it from the farmer and the herb-woman. Davy, chemistry: and Cuvier,[2] fossils. The day is always his, who works in it with serenity and great aims. The unstable estimates of men crowd to him

9. Seal.
1. An old proverb says, "Where Macgregor sits, there is the head of the table"; Emerson substitutes another typical name for a Scottish chief.
2. Georges Cuvier (1769–1832), French pioneer in comparative anatomy and paleontology. Carl von Linné ("Linnæus") (1707–1778), Swedish botanist. Sir Humphry Davy (1778–1829), English chemist.

whose mind is filled with a truth, as the heaped waves of the Atlantic follow the moon.

For this self-trust, the reason is deeper than can be fathomed,—darker than can be enlightened. I might not carry with me the feeling of my audience in stating my own belief. But I have already shown the ground of my hope, in adverting to the doctrine that man is one. I believe man has been wronged: he has wronged himself. He has almost lost the light that can lead him back to his prerogatives. Men are become of no account. Men in history, men in the world of to-day are bugs, are spawn, and are called "the mass" and "the herd." In a century, in a millennium, one or two men; that is to say—one or two approximations to the right state of every man. All the rest behold in the hero or the poet their own green and crude being— ripened; yes, and are content to be less, so *that* may attain to its full stature. What a testimony—full of grandeur, full of pity, is borne to the demands of his own nature, by the poor clansman, the poor partisan, who rejoices in the glory of his chief. The poor and the low find some amends to their immense moral capacity, for their acquiescence in a political and social inferiority. They are content to be brushed like flies from the path of a great person, so that justice shall be done by him to that common nature which it is the dearest desire of all to see enlarged and glorified. They sun themselves in the great man's light, and feel it to be their own element. They cast the dignity of man from their downtrod selves upon the shoulders of a hero, and will perish to add one drop of blood to make that great heart beat, those giant sinews combat and conquer. He lives for us, and we live in him.

Men such as they are, very naturally seek money or power; and power because it is as good as money,—the "spoils," so called, "of office." And why not? for they aspire to the highest, and this, in their sleep-walking, they dream is highest. Wake them, and they shall quit the false good and leap to the true, and leave government to clerks and desks. This revolution is to be wrought by the gradual domestication of the idea of Culture. The main enterprise of the world for splendor, for extent, is the upbuilding of a man. Here are the materials strown along the ground. The private life of one man shall be a more illustrious monarchy,—more formidable to its enemy, more sweet and serene in its influence to its friend, than any kingdom in history. For a man, rightly viewed, comprehendeth the particular natures of all men. Each philosopher, each bard, each actor, has only done for me, as by a delegate, what one day I can do for myself. The books which once we valued more than the apple of the eye, we have quite exhausted. What is that but saying that we have come up with the point of view which the universal mind took through the eyes of that one scribe; we have been that man, and have passed on. First, one; then another; we drain all cisterns, and waxing greater by all these supplies, we crave a better and more abundant food. The man has never lived that can feed us ever. The human mind cannot be enshrined in a person who shall set a barrier on any one side to this unbounded, unboundable empire. It is one central fire which flaming now out of the lips of Etna, lightens the capes of Sicily; and now out of the throat of Vesuvius,[3] illuminates the towers and vineyards of Naples. It is

3. Active volcanoes in eastern Sicily and southern Italy.

one light which beams out of a thousand stars. It is one soul which animates all men.

But I have dwelt perhaps tediously upon this abstraction of the Scholar. I ought not to delay longer to add what I have to say, of nearer reference to the time and to this country.

Historically, there is thought to be a difference in the ideas which predominate over successive epochs, and there are data for marking the genius of the Classic, of the Romantic, and now of the Reflective or Philosophical age. With the views I have intimated of the oneness or the identity of the mind through all individuals, I do not much dwell on these differences. In fact, I believe each individual passes through all three. The boy is a Greek; the youth, romantic; the adult, reflective. I deny not, however, that a revolution in the leading idea may be distinctly enough traced.

Our age is bewailed as the age of Introversion. Must that needs be evil? We, it seems, are critical. We are embarrassed with second thoughts. We cannot enjoy any thing for hankering to know whereof the pleasure consists. We are lined with eyes. We see with our feet. The time is infected with Hamlet's unhappiness,—

> "Sicklied o'er with the pale cast of thought."[4]

Is it so bad then? Sight is the last thing to be pitied. Would we be blind? Do we fear lest we should outsee nature and God, and drink truth dry? I look upon the discontent of the literary class as a mere announcement of the fact that they find themselves not in the state of mind of their fathers, and regret the coming state as untried; as a boy dreads the water before he has learned that he can swim. If there is any period one would desire to be born in,—is it not the age of Revolution; when the old and the new stand side by side, and admit of being compared; when the energies of all men are searched by fear and by hope; when the historic glories of the old, can be compensated by the rich possibilities of the new era? This time, like all times, is a very good one, if we but know what to do with it.

I read with joy some of the auspicious signs of the coming days as they glimmer already through poetry and art, through philosophy and science, through church and state.

One of these signs is the fact that the same movement which effected the elevation of what was called the lowest class in the state, assumed in literature a very marked and as benign an aspect. Instead of the sublime and beautiful, the near, the low, the common, was explored and poetised. That which had been negligently trodden under foot by those who were harnessing and provisioning themselves for long journies into far countries, is suddenly found to be richer than all foreign parts. The literature of the poor, the feelings of the child, the philosophy of the street, the meaning of household life, are the topics of the time. It is a great stride. It is a sign—is it not? of new vigor, when the extremities are made active, when currents of warm life run into the hands and the feet. I ask not for the great, the remote, the romantic; what is doing in Italy or Arabia; what is Greek art, or Provençal Minstrelsy;[5] I embrace the common, I explore and sit at the feet

---

4. Shakespeare's *Hamlet* 3.1.85.
5. Music of the medieval troubadours of Provence, in southeastern France.

of the familiar, the low. Give me insight into to-day, and you may have the antique and future worlds. What would we really know the meaning of? The meal in the firkin;[6] the milk in the pan; the ballad in the street; the news of the boat; the glance of the eye; the form and the gait of the body;—show me the ultimate reason of these matters;—show me the sublime presence of the highest spiritual cause lurking, as always it does lurk, in these suburbs and extremities of nature; let me see every trifle bristling with the polarity that ranges it instantly on an eternal law; and the shop, the plough, and the ledger, referred to the like cause by which light undulates and poets sing;—and the world lies no longer a dull miscellany and lumber room,[7] but has form and order; there is no trifle; there is no puzzle; but one design unites and animates the farthest pinnacle and the lowest trench.

This idea has inspired the genius of Goldsmith, Burns, Cowper, and in a newer time, of Goethe, Wordsworth, and Carlyle.[8] This idea they have differently followed and with various success. In contrast with their writing, the style of Pope, of Johnson, of Gibbon,[9] looks cold and pedantic. This writing is blood-warm. Man is surprised to find that things near are not less beautiful and wondrous than things remote. The near explains the far. The drop is a small ocean. A man is related to all nature. This perception of the worth of the vulgar, is fruitful in discoveries. Goethe, in this very thing the most modern of the moderns, has shown us, as none ever did, the genius of the ancients.

There is one man of genius who has done much for this philosophy of life, whose literary value has never yet been rightly estimated;—I mean Emanuel Swedenborg.[1] The most imaginative of men, yet writing with the precision of a mathematician, he endeavored to engraft a purely philosophical Ethics on the popular Christianity of his time. Such an attempt, of course, must have difficulty which no genius could surmount. But he saw and showed the connexion between nature and the affections of the soul. He pierced the emblematic or spiritual character of the visible, audible, tangible world. Especially did his shade-loving muse hover over and interpret the lower parts of nature; he showed the mysterious bond that allies moral evil to the foul material forms, and has given in epical parables a theory of insanity, of beasts, of unclean and fearful things.

Another sign of our times, also marked by an analogous political movement is, the new importance given to the single person. Every thing that tends to insulate the individual,—to surround him with barriers of natural respect, so that each man shall feel the world is his, and man shall treat with man as a sovereign state with a sovereign state;—tends to true union as well as greatness. "I learned," said the melancholy Pestalozzi,[2] "that no

---

6. Small wooden vessel.
7. Junk room.
8. Emerson contrasts the so-called pre-Romantics Oliver Goldsmith (1730–1794), Robert Burns (1759–1796), and William Cowper (1731–1800) with the Romantics Johann Wolfgang von Goethe (1749–1832), William Wordsworth (1770–1850), and Thomas Carlyle (1795–1881).
9. The 18th-century British writers Alexander Pope (1688–1744), Samuel Johnson (1709–

1784), and Edward Gibbon (1737–1794).
1. Swedish scientist, theologian, and mystic (1688–1772). Emerson was inspired by Swedenborg's notion of the correspondence between the natural and spiritual worlds.
2. Johann Heinrich Pestalozzi (1746–1827), Swiss educator who was an early advocate of kindergarten education. His theories influenced several of Emerson's friends.

man in God's wide earth is either willing or able to help any other man."
Help must come from the bosom alone. The scholar is that man who must
take up into himself all the ability of the time, all the contributions of the
past, all the hopes of the future. He must be an university of knowledges. If
there be one lesson more than another which should pierce his ear, it is,
The world is nothing, the man is all; in yourself is the law of all nature, and
you know not yet how a globule of sap ascends; in yourself slumbers the
whole of Reason; it is for you to know all, it is for you to dare all. Mr. President and Gentlemen, this confidence in the unsearched might of man,
belongs by all motives, by all prophecy, by all preparation, to the American
Scholar. We have listened too long to the courtly muses of Europe. The
spirit of the American freeman is already suspected to be timid, imitative,
tame. Public and private avarice make the air we breathe thick and fat. The
scholar is decent, indolent, complaisant. See already the tragic consequence.
The mind of this country taught to aim at low objects, eats upon itself. There
is no work for any but the decorous and the complaisant. Young men of the
fairest promise, who begin life upon our shores, inflated by the mountain
winds, shined upon by all the stars of God, find the earth below not in unison with these,—but are hindered from action by the disgust which the
principles on which business is managed inspire, and turn drudges, or die
of disgust,—some of them suicides. What is the remedy? They did not yet
see, and thousands of young men as hopeful now crowding to the barriers
for the career, do not yet see, that if the single man plant himself indomita-
bly on his instincts, and there abide, the huge world will come round to him.
Patience—patience;—with the shades of all the good and great for company; and for solace, the perspective of your own infinite life; and for work,
the study and the communication of principles, the making those instincts
prevalent, the conversion of the world. Is it not the chief disgrace in the
world, not to be an unit;—not to be reckoned one character;—not to yield
that peculiar fruit which each man was created to bear, but to be reckoned
in the gross, in the hundred, or the thousand, of the party, the section, to
which we belong; and our opinion predicted geographically, as the north, or
the south. Not so, brothers and friends,—please God, ours shall not be so.
We will walk on our own feet; we will work with our own hands; we will
speak our own minds. Then shall man be no longer a name for pity, for
doubt, and for sensual indulgence. The dread of man and the love of man
shall be a wall of defence and a wreath of love around all. A nation of men
will for the first time exist, because each believes himself inspired by the
Divine Soul which also inspires all men.

1837

Self-Reliance[1]

Ne te quæsiveris extra.[2]

"Man is his own star, and the soul that can
Render an honest and a perfect man,
Command all light, all influence, all fate,
Nothing to him falls early or too late.
Our acts our angels are, or good or ill,
Our fatal shadows that walk by us still."
—Epilogue to Beaumont and Fletcher's
Honest Man's Fortune[3]

Cast the bantling[4] on the rocks,
Suckle him with the she-wolf's teat:
Wintered with the hawk and fox,
Power and speed be hands and feet.

I read the other day some verses written by an eminent painter[5] which were original and not conventional. Always the soul hears an admonition in such lines, let the subject be what it may. The sentiment they instil is of more value than any thought they may contain. To believe your own thought, to believe that what is true for you in your private heart, is true for all men,— that is genius. Speak your latent conviction and it shall be the universal sense; for always the inmost becomes the outmost,—and our first thought is rendered back to us by the trumpets of the Last Judgment. Familiar as the voice of the mind is to each, the highest merit we ascribe to Moses, Plato, and Milton, is that they set at naught books and traditions, and spoke not what men but what they thought. A man should learn to detect and watch that gleam of light which flashes across his mind from within, more than the lustre of the firmament of bards and sages. Yet he dismisses without notice his thought, because it is his. In every work of genius we recognize our own rejected thoughts: they come back to us with a certain alienated majesty. Great works of art have no more affecting lesson for us than this. They teach us to abide by our spontaneous impression with good humored inflexibility then most when the whole cry of voices is on the other side. Else, to-morrow a stranger will say with masterly good sense precisely what we have thought and felt all the time, and we shall be forced to take with shame our own opinion from another.

There is a time in every man's education when he arrives at the conviction that envy is ignorance; that imitation is suicide; that he must take himself for better, for worse, as his portion; that though the wide universe is full of good, no kernel of nourishing corn can come to him but through his toil bestowed on that plot of ground which is given to him to till. The power which resides in him is new in nature, and none but he knows what that is which he can do, nor does he know until he has tried. Not for nothing one face, one character, one fact makes much impression on him, and another none. It is not

---

1. First published in *Essays* (1841), the source of the present text.
2. The Roman poet Persius (34–62 C.E.), *Satire* 1.7: "Do not search outside yourself" (Latin), i.e., do not imitate.
3. Published in 1647, the play by the Jacobean dramatists Francis Beaumont (1584–1616) and John Fletcher (1579–1625) was written in 1613.
4. Baby. The stanza is Emerson's.
5. Probably the American painter Washington Alston (1779–1847), whose poetry Emerson praised in a journal entry of September 20, 1837.

without preëstablished harmony, this sculpture in the memory. The eye was placed where one ray should fall, that it might testify of that particular ray. Bravely let him speak the utmost syllable of his confession. We but half express ourselves, and are ashamed of that divine idea which each of us represents. It may be safely trusted as proportionate and of good issues, so it be faithfully imparted, but God will not have his work made manifest by cowards. It needs a divine man to exhibit any thing divine. A man is relieved and gay when he has put his heart into his work and done his best; but what he has said or done otherwise, shall give him no peace. It is a deliverance which does not deliver. In the attempt his genius deserts him; no muse befriends; no invention, no hope.

Trust thyself: every heart vibrates to that iron string. Accept the place the divine Providence has found for you; the society of your contemporaries, the connexion of events. Great men have always done so and confided themselves childlike to the genius of their age, betraying their perception that the Eternal was stirring at their heart, working through their hands, predominating in all their being. And we are now men, and must accept in the highest mind the same transcendent destiny; and not pinched in a corner, not cowards fleeing before a revolution, but redeemers and benefactors, pious aspirants to be noble clay plastic under the Almighty effort, let us advance and advance on Chaos and the Dark.

What pretty oracles nature yields us on this text in the face and behavior of children, babes and even brutes. That divided and rebel mind, that distrust of a sentiment because our arithmetic has computed the strength and means opposed to our purpose, these have not. Their mind being whole, their eye is as yet unconquered, and when we look in their faces, we are disconcerted. Infancy conforms to nobody: all conform to it, so that one babe commonly makes four or five out of the adults who prattle and play to it. So God has armed youth and puberty and manhood no less with its own piquancy and charm, and made it enviable and gracious and its claims not to be put by, if it will stand by itself. Do not think the youth has no force because he cannot speak to you and me. Hark! in the next room, who spoke so clear and emphatic? Good Heaven! it is he! it is that very lump of bashfulness and phlegm which for weeks has done nothing but eat when you were by, that now rolls out these words like bell-strokes. It seems he knows how to speak to his contemporaries. Bashful or bold, then, he will know how to make us seniors very unnecessary.

The nonchalance of boys who are sure of a dinner, and would disdain as much as a lord to do or say aught to conciliate one, is the healthy attitude of human nature. How is a boy the master of society; independent, irresponsible, looking out from his corner on such people and facts as pass by, he tries and sentences them on their merits, in the swift summary way of boys, as good, bad, interesting, silly, eloquent, troublesome. He cumbers himself never about consequences, about interests: he gives an independent, genuine verdict. You must court him: he does not court you. But the man is, as it were, clapped into jail by his consciousness. As soon as he has once acted or spoken with eclat, he is a committed person, watched by the sympathy or the hatred of hundreds whose affections must now enter into his account. There is no Lethe[6] for this. Ah, that he could pass again into his neutral,

---

6. Oblivion-producing water from the river of the underworld in Greek mythology.

godlike independence! Who can thus lose all pledge, and having observed, observe again from the same unaffected, unbiased, unbribable, unaffrighted innocence, must always be formidable, must always engage the poet's and the man's regards. Of such an immortal youth the force would be felt. He would utter opinions on all passing affairs, which being seen to be not private but necessary, would sink like darts into the ear of men, and put them in fear.

These are the voices which we hear in solitude, but they grow faint and inaudible as we enter into the world. Society everywhere is in conspiracy against the manhood of every one of its members. Society is a joint-stock company[7] in which the members agree for the better securing of his bread to each shareholder, to surrender the liberty and culture of the eater. The virtue in most request is conformity. Self-reliance is its aversion. It loves not realities and creators, but names and customs.

Whoso would be a man must be a nonconformist. He who would gather immortal palms[8] must not be hindered by the name of goodness, but must explore if it be goodness. Nothing is at last sacred but the integrity of our own mind. Absolve you to yourself, and you shall have the suffrage of the world. I remember an answer which when quite young I was prompted to make to a valued adviser who was wont to importune me with the dear old doctrines of the church. On my saying, What have I to do with the sacredness of traditions, if I live wholly from within? my friend suggested—"But these impulses may be from below, not from above." I replied, 'They do not seem to me to be such; but if I am the devil's child, I will live then from the devil.' No law can be sacred to me but that of my nature. Good and bad are but names very readily transferable to that or this; the only right is what is after my constitution, the only wrong what is against it. A man is to carry himself in the presence of all opposition as if every thing were titular and ephemeral but he. I am ashamed to think how easily we capitulate to badges and names, to large societies and dead institutions. Every decent and well-spoken individual affects and sways me more than is right. I ought to go upright and vital, and speak the rude truth in all ways. If malice and vanity wear the coat of philanthropy, shall that pass? If an angry bigot assumes this bountiful cause of Abolition, and comes to me with his last news from Barbadoes,[9] why should I not say to him, 'Go love thy infant; love thy wood-chopper: be good-natured and modest: have that grace; and never varnish your hard, uncharitable ambition with this incredible tenderness for black folk a thousand miles off. Thy love afar is spite at home.' Rough and graceless would be such greeting, but truth is handsomer than the affectation of love. Your goodness must have some edge to it—else it is none. The doctrine of hatred must be preached as the counteraction of the doctrine of love when that pules[1] and whines. I shun father and mother and wife and brother, when my genius calls me.[2] I would write on the lintels of the door-post, *Whim*.[3] I hope it is somewhat

---

7. Business for which the capital is held by its joint owners in transferable shares.

8. Great honors.

9. Island in the eastern Caribbean where slavery was officially abolished in 1834. Despite his apparent skepticism here, Emerson became increasingly committed to abolitionism during the 1840s.

1. Whimpers.

2. For shunning family to obey a divine command, see Matthew 10.34–37.

3. See Exodus 12 for God's instructions to Moses on marking with blood the "two side posts" and the "upper door post" (or lintel) of houses so that God would spare those within when He came to "smite all the firstborn in the land of Egypt, both man and beast."

better than whim at last, but we cannot spend the day in explanation. Expect me not to show cause why I seek or why I exclude company. Then, again, do not tell me, as a good man did to-day, of my obligation to put all poor men in good situations. Are they *my* poor? I tell thee, thou foolish philanthropist, that I grudge the dollar, the dime, the cent I give to such men as do not belong to me and to whom I do not belong. There is a class of persons to whom by all spiritual affinity I am bought and sold; for them I will go to prison, if need be; but your miscellaneous popular charities; the education at college of fools; the building of meeting-houses to the vain end to which many now stand; alms to sots; and the thousandfold Relief Societies;—though I confess with shame I sometimes succumb and give the dollar, it is a wicked dollar which by-and-by I shall have the manhood to withhold.

Virtues are in the popular estimate rather the exception than the rule. There is the man *and* his virtues. Men do what is called a good action, as some piece of courage or charity, much as they would pay a fine in expiation of daily non-appearance on parade. Their works are done as an apology or extenuation of their living in the world,—as invalids and the insane pay a high board. Their virtues are penances. I do not wish to expiate, but to live. My life is not an apology, but a life. It is for itself and not for a spectacle. I much prefer that it should be of a lower strain, so it be genuine and equal, than that it should be glittering and unsteady. I wish it to be sound and sweet, and not to need diet and bleeding.[4] My life should be unique; it should be an alms, a battle, a conquest, a medicine. I ask primary evidence that you are a man, and refuse this appeal from the man to his actions. I know that for myself it makes no difference whether I do or forbear those actions which are reckoned excellent. I cannot consent to pay for a privilege where I have intrinsic right. Few and mean as my gifts may be, I actually am, and do not need for my own assurance or the assurance of my fellows any secondary testimony.

What I must do, is all that concerns me, not what the people think. This rule, equally arduous in actual and in intellectual life, may serve for the whole distinction between greatness and meanness. It is the harder, because you will always find those who think they know what is your duty better than you know it. It is easy in the world to live after the world's opinion; it is easy in solitude to live after our own; but the great man is he who in the midst of the crowd keeps with perfect sweetness the independence of solitude.

The objection to conforming to usages that have become dead to you, is, that it scatters your force. It loses your time and blurs the impression of your character. If you maintain a dead church, contribute to a dead Bible-Society, vote with a great party either for the Government or against it, spread your table like base housekeepers,—under all these screens, I have difficulty to detect the precise man you are. And, of course, so much force is withdrawn from your proper life. But do your thing, and I shall know you. Do your work, and you shall reinforce yourself. A man must consider what a blindman's-bluff is this game of conformity. If I know your sect, I anticipate your argument. I hear a preacher announce for his text and topic the expediency of one of the institutions of his church. Do I not know beforehand that not possibly can he say a new and spontaneous word? Do I not know that with all this ostentation of examining the grounds of the institution, he will do no such thing? Do

---

4. The old medical treatment of bloodletting.

I not know that he is pledged to himself not to look but at one side; the permitted side, not as a man, but as a parish minister? He is a retained attorney, and these airs of the bench are the emptiest affectation. Well, most men have bound their eyes with one or another handkerchief, and attached themselves to some one of these communities of opinion. This conformity makes them not false in a few particulars, authors of a few lies, but false in all particulars. Their every truth is not quite true. Their two is not the real two, their four not the real four: so that every word they say chagrins us, and we know not where to begin to set them right. Meantime nature is not slow to equip us in the prison-uniform of the party to which we adhere. We come to wear one cut of face and figure, and acquire by degrees the gentlest asinine expression. There is a mortifying experience in particular which does not fail to wreak itself also in the general history; I mean, "the foolish face of praise,"[5] the forced smile which we put on in company where we do not feel at ease in answer to conversation which does not interest us. The muscles, not spontaneously moved, but moved by a low usurping wilfulness, grow tight about the outline of the face and make the most disagreeable sensation, a sensation of rebuke and warning which no brave young man will suffer twice.

For non-conformity the world whips you with its displeasure. And therefore a man must know how to estimate a sour face. The bystanders look askance on him in the public street or in the friend's parlor. If this aversation had its origin in contempt and resistance like his own, he might well go home with a sad countenance; but the sour faces of the multitude, like their sweet faces, have no deep cause,—disguise no god, but are put on and off as the wind blows, and a newspaper directs. Yet is the discontent of the multitude more formidable than that of the senate and the college. It is easy enough for a firm man who knows the world to brook the rage of the cultivated classes. Their rage is decorous and prudent, for they are timid as being very vulnerable themselves. But when to their feminine rage the indignation of the people is added, when the ignorant and the poor are aroused, when the unintelligent brute force that lies at the bottom of society is made to growl and mow,[6] it needs the habit of magnanimity and religion to treat it godlike as a trifle of no concernment.

The other terror that scares us from self-trust is our consistency; a reverence for our past act or word, because the eyes of others have no other data for computing our orbit than our past acts, and we are loath to disappoint them.

But why should you keep your head over your shoulder? Why drag about this monstrous corpse of your memory, lest you contradict somewhat you have stated in this or that public place? Suppose you should contradict yourself; what then? It seems to be a rule of wisdom never to rely on your memory alone, scarcely even in acts of pure memory, but bring the past for judgment into the thousand-eyed present, and live ever in a new day. Trust your emotion. In your metaphysics you have denied personality to the Deity: yet when the devout motions of the soul come, yield to them heart and life, though they should clothe God with shape and color. Leave your theory as Joseph his coat in the hand of the harlot, and flee.[7]

---

5. Alexander Pope's "Epistle to Dr. Arbuthnot" (1735), line 212.
6. Grimace.

7. When Potiphar's wife demanded that Joseph sleep with her, "he left his garment in her hand, and fled" (Genesis 39.12).

A foolish consistency is the hobgoblin of little minds, adored by little statesmen and philosophers and divines. With consistency a great soul has simply nothing to do. He may as well concern himself with his shadow on the wall. Out upon your guarded lips! Sew them up with packthread, do. Else, if you would be a man, speak what you think to-day in words as hard as cannon balls, and to-morrow speak what to-morrow thinks in hard words again, though it contradict every thing you said to-day. Ah, then, exclaim the aged ladies, you shall be sure to be misunderstood. Misunderstood! It is a right fool's word. Is it so bad then to be misunderstood? Pythagoras was misunderstood, and Socrates, and Jesus, and Luther, and Copernicus, and Galileo, and Newton,[8] and every pure and wise spirit that ever took flesh. To be great is to be misunderstood.

I suppose no man can violate his nature. All the sallies of his will are rounded in by the law of his being as the inequalities of Andes and Himmaleh[9] are insignificant in the curve of the sphere. Nor does it matter how you gauge and try him. A character is like an acrostic or Alexandrian stanza;[1]—read it forward, backward, or across, it still spells the same thing. In this pleasing contrite wood-life which God allows me, let me record day by day my honest thought without prospect or retrospect, and, I cannot doubt, it will be found symmetrical, though I mean it not, and see it not. My book should smell of pines and resound with the hum of insects. The swallow over my window should interweave that thread or straw he carries in his bill into my web also. We pass for what we are. Character teaches above our wills. Men imagine that they communicate their virtue or vice only by overt actions and do not see that virtue or vice emit a breath every moment.

Fear never but you shall be consistent in whatever variety of actions, so they be each honest and natural in their hour. For of one will, the actions will be harmonious, however unlike they seem. These varieties are lost sight of when seen at a little distance, at a little height of thought. One tendency unites them all. The voyage of the best ship is a zigzag line of a hundred tacks. This is only microscopic criticism. See the line from a sufficient distance, and it straightens itself to the average tendency. Your genuine action will explain itself and will explain your other genuine actions. Your conformity explains nothing. Act singly, and what you have already done singly, will justify you now. Greatness always appeals to the future. If I can be great enough now to do right and scorn eyes, I must have done so much right before, as to defend me now. Be it how it will, do right now. Always scorn appearances, and you always may. The force of character is cumulative. All the foregone days of virtue work their health into this. What makes the majesty of the heroes of the senate and the field, which so fills the imagination? The consciousness of a train of great days and victories behind. There they all stand and shed an united light on the advancing actor. He is attended as by a visible escort of angels to every man's eye. That is it which throws

8. Sir Isaac Newton (1642–1727), English mathematician and scientist who developed the laws of gravity and motion. Pythagorus (c. 582–c. 507 B.C.E.), Greek philosopher and mathematician who elaborated a theory of numbers. Martin Luther (1483–1546), German leader of the Protestant Reformation. Nicholas Copernicus (1473–1543), Polish astronomer who argued that the planets revolve around a stationary sun. Galileo Galilei (1564–1662), Italian astronomer, mathematician, and physicist who supported the Copernican system and laid the foundations for modern science.
9. Mountain ranges in South America and Asia.
1. A palindrome, reading the same backward as forward.

thunder into Chatham's voice, and dignity into Washington's port, and America into Adams's[2] eye. Honor is venerable to us because it is no ephemeris. It is always ancient virtue. We worship it to-day, because it is not of to-day. We love it and pay it homage, because it is not a trap for our love and homage, but is self-dependent, self-derived, and therefore of an old immaculate pedigree, even if shown in a young person.

I hope in these days we have heard the last of conformity and consistency. Let the words be gazetted[3] and ridiculous henceforward. Instead of the gong for dinner, let us hear a whistle from the Spartan fife.[4] Let us bow and apologize never more. A great man is coming to eat at my house. I do not wish to please him: I wish that he should wish to please me. I will stand here for humanity, and though I would make it kind, I would make it true. Let us affront and reprimand the smooth mediocrity and squalid contentment of the times, and hurl in the face of custom, and trade, and office, the fact which is the upshot of all history, that there is a great responsible Thinker and Actor moving wherever moves a man; that a true man belongs to no other time or place, but is the centre of things. Where he is, there is nature. He measures you, and all men, and all events. You are constrained to accept his standard. Ordinarily every body in society reminds us of somewhat else or of some other person. Character, reality, reminds you of nothing else. It takes place of the whole creation. The man must be so much that he must make all circumstances indifferent,—put all means into the shade. This all great men are and do. Every true man is a cause, a country, and an age; requires infinite spaces and numbers and time fully to accomplish his thought;—and posterity seem to follow his steps as a procession. A man Cæsar is born, and for ages after, we have a Roman Empire. Christ is born, and millions of minds so grow and cleave to his genius, that he is confounded with virtue and the possible of man. An institution is the lengthened shadow of one man; as, the Reformation, of Luther; Quakerism, of Fox; Methodism, of Wesley; Abolition, of Clarkson.[5] Scipio,[6] Milton called "the height of Rome;" and all history resolves itself very easily into the biography of a few stout and earnest persons.

Let a man then know his worth, and keep things under his feet. Let him not peep or steal, or skulk up and down with the air of a charity-boy, a bastard, or an interloper, in the world which exists for him. But the man in the street finding no worth in himself which corresponds to the force which built a tower or sculptured a marble god, feels poor when he looks on these. To him a palace, a statue, or a costly book have an alien and forbidding air, much like a gay equipage, and seem to say like that, 'Who are you, sir?' Yet they all are his, suitors for his notice, petitioners to his faculties that they will come out and take possession. The picture waits for my verdict: it is not to command me, but I am to settle its claims to praise. That popular fable of the sot

---

2. Probably John Quincy Adams (1767–1848), sixth president of the United States and, afterward, long-time member of the House of Representatives, known as "Old Man Eloquence." William Pitt, first Earl of Chatham (1708–1778), English statesman and great orator. George Washington (1732–1799), first president of the United States. "Port": carriage or physical bearing.

3. Printed in a newspaper or other public forum.

4. The Spartans were known for their military discipline and willingness to endure physical hardships.

5. These founders are George Fox (1624–1691), John Wesley (1703–1791), and Thomas Clarkson (1760–1846).

6. Scipio Africanus (237–183 B.C.E.), the conqueror of Carthage.

who was picked up dead drunk in the street, carried to the duke's house, washed and dressed and laid in the duke's bed, and, on his waking, treated with all obsequious ceremony like the duke, and assured that he had been insane,[7]—owes its popularity to the fact, that it symbolizes so well the state of man, who is in the world a sort of sot, but now and then wakes up, exercises his reason, and finds himself a true prince.

Our reading is mendicant and sycophantic. In history, our imagination makes fools of us, plays us false. Kingdom and lordship, power and estate are a gaudier vocabulary than private John and Edward in a small house and common day's work: but the things of life are the same to both: the sum total of both is the same. Why all this deference to Alfred, and Scanderbeg, and Gustavus?[8] Suppose they were virtuous: did they wear out virtue? As great a stake depends on your private act to-day, as followed their public and renowned steps. When private men shall act with vast views, the lustre will be transferred from the actions of kings to those of gentlemen.

The world has indeed been instructed by its kings, who have so magnetized the eyes of nations. It has been taught by this colossal symbol the mutual reverence that is due from man to man. The joyful loyalty with which men have every where suffered the king, the noble, or the great proprietor to walk among them by a law of his own, make his own scale of men and things, and reverse theirs, pay for benefits not with money but with honor, and represent the Law in his person, was the hieroglyphic by which they obscurely signified their consciousness of their own right and comeliness, the right of every man.

The magnetism which all original action exerts is explained when we inquire the reason of self-trust. Who is the Trustee? What is the aboriginal Self on which a universal reliance may be grounded? What is the nature and power of that science-baffling star, without parallax,[9] without calculable elements, which shoots a ray of beauty even into trivial and impure actions, if the least mark of independence appear? The inquiry leads us to that source, at once the essence of genius, the essence of virtue, and the essence of life, which we call Spontaneity or Instinct. We denote this primary wisdom as Intuition, whilst all later teachings are tuitions. In that deep force, the last fact behind which analysis cannot go, all things find their common origin. For the sense of being which in calm hours rises, we know not how, in the soul, is not diverse from things, from space, from light, from time, from man, but one with them, and proceedeth obviously from the same source whence their life and being also proceedeth. We first share the life by which things exist, and afterwards see them as appearances in nature, and forget that we have shared their cause. Here is the fountain of action and the fountain of thought. Here are the lungs of that inspiration which giveth man wisdom, of that inspiration of man which cannot be denied without impiety and atheism. We lie in the lap of immense intelligence, which makes us organs of its activity and receivers of its truth. When we discern justice, when we discern

7. See the "Induction" to Shakespeare's *The Taming of the Shrew.*
8. National heroes: Alfred (849–899), of England; Scanderbeg (1404?–1468), of Albania; and Gustavus (1594–1632), of Sweden.

9. An apparent change in the direction of an object caused by a change in the position from which it is observed. Emerson means without an observational position.

truth, we do nothing of ourselves, but allow a passage to its beams. If we ask whence this comes, if we seek to pry into the soul that causes,—all metaphysics, all philosophy is at fault. Its presence or its absence is all we can affirm. Every man discerns between the voluntary acts of his mind, and his involuntary perceptions. And to his involuntary perceptions, he knows a perfect respect is due. He may err in the expression of them, but he knows that these things are so, like day and night, not to be disputed. All my wilful actions and acquisitions are but roving;—the most trivial reverie, the faintest native emotion are domestic and divine. Thoughtless people contradict as readily the statement of perceptions as of opinions, or rather much more readily; for, they do not distinguish between perception and notion. They fancy that I choose to see this or that thing. But perception is not whimsical, but fatal. If I see a trait, my children will see it after me, and in course of time, all mankind,— although it may chance that no one has seen it before me. For my perception of it is as much a fact as the sun.

The relations of the soul to the divine spirit are so pure that it is profane to seek to interpose helps. It must be that when God speaketh, he should communicate not one thing, but all things; should fill the world with his voice; should scatter forth light, nature, time, souls from the centre of the present thought; and new date and new create the whole. Whenever a mind is simple, and receives a divine wisdom, then old things pass away,—means, teachers, texts, temples fall; it lives now and absorbs past and future into the present hour. All things are made sacred by relation to it,—one thing as much as another. All things are dissolved to their centre by their cause, and in the universal miracle petty and particular miracles disappear. This is and must be. If, therefore, a man claims to know and speak of God, and carries you backward to the phraseology of some old mouldered nation in another country, in another world, believe him not. Is the acorn better than the oak which is its fulness and completion? Is the parent better than the child into whom he has cast his ripened being? Whence then this worship of the past? The centuries are conspirators against the sanity and majesty of the soul. Time and space are but physiological colors which the eye maketh, but the soul is light; where it is, is day; where it was, is night; and history is an impertinence and an injury, if it be anything more than a cheerful apologue or parable of my being and becoming.

Man is timid and apologetic. He is no longer upright. He dares not say 'I think,' 'I am,' but quotes some saint or sage. He is ashamed before the blade of grass or the blowing rose. These roses under my window make no reference to former roses or to better ones; they are for what they are; they exist with God to-day. There is no time to them. There is simply the rose; it is perfect in every moment of its existence. Before a leaf-bud has burst, its whole life acts; in the full-blown flower, there is no more; in the leafless root, there is no less. Its nature is satisfied, and it satisfies nature, in all moments alike. There is no time to it. But man postpones or remembers; he does not live in the present, but with reverted eye laments the past, or, heedless of the riches that surround him, stands on tiptoe to foresee the future. He cannot be happy and strong until he too lives with nature in the present, above time.

This should be plain enough. Yet see what strong intellects dare not yet hear God himself, unless he speak the phraseology of I know not what David, or Jeremiah, or Paul.[1] We shall not always set so great a price on a few texts, on a few lines. We are like children who repeat by rote the sentences of grandames and tutors, and, as they grow older, of the men of talents and character they chance to see,—painfully recollecting the exact words they spoke; afterwards, when they come into the point of view which those had who uttered these sayings, they understand them, and are willing to let the words go; for, at any time, they can use words as good, when occasion comes. So was it with us, so will it be, if we proceed. If we live truly, we shall see truly. It is as easy for the strong man to be strong, as it is for the weak to be weak. When we have new perception, we shall gladly disburthen the memory of its hoarded treasures as old rubbish. When a man lives with God, his voice shall be as sweet as the murmur of the brook and the rustle of the corn.

And now at last the highest truth on this subject remains unsaid; probably, cannot be said; for all that we say is the far off remembering of the intuition. That thought, by what I can now nearest approach to say it, is this. When good is near you, when you have life in yourself,—it is not by any known or appointed way; you shall not discern the foot-prints of any other; you shall not see the face of man; you shall not hear any name;—the way, the thought, the good shall be wholly strange and new. It shall exclude all other being. You take the way from man not to man. All persons that ever existed are its fugitive ministers. There shall be no fear in it. Fear and hope are alike beneath it. It asks nothing. There is somewhat low even in hope. We are then in vision. There is nothing that can be called gratitude nor properly joy. The soul is raised over passion. It seeth identity and eternal causation. It is a perceiving that Truth and Right are. Hence it becomes a Tranquillity out of the knowing that all things go well. Vast spaces of nature; the Atlantic Ocean, the South Sea; vast intervals of time, years, centuries, are of no account. This which I think and feel, underlay that former state of life and circumstances, as it does underlie my present, and will always all circumstance, and what is called life, and what is called death.

Life only avails, not the having lived. Power ceases in the instant of repose; it resides in the moment of transition from a past to a new state; in the shooting of the gulf; in the darting to an aim. This one fact the world hates, that the soul *becomes*; for, that forever degrades the past; turns all riches to poverty; all reputation to a shame; confounds the saint with the rogue; shoves Jesus and Judas equally aside. Why then do we prate of self-reliance? Inasmuch as the soul is present, there will be power not confident but agent. To talk of reliance, is a poor external way of speaking. Speak rather of that which relies, because it works and is. Who has more soul than I, masters me, though he should not raise his finger. Round him I must revolve by the gravitation of spirits; who has less, I rule with like facility. We fancy it rhetoric when we speak of eminent virtue. We do not yet see that virtue is Height, and that a man or a company of men plastic and permeable to principles, by the law of nature must overpower and ride all cities, nations, kings, rich men, poets, who are not.

This is the ultimate fact which we so quickly reach on this as on every topic, the resolution of all into the ever blessed ONE. Virtue is the governor,

---

1. Biblical authors of the Book of Psalms, the Book of Jeremiah, and various New Testament Epistles, respectively.

the creator, the reality. All things real are so by so much of virtue as they contain. Hardship, husbandry, hunting, whaling, war, eloquence, personal weight, are somewhat, and engage my respect as examples of the soul's presence and impure action. I see the same law working in the nature for conservation and growth. The poise of a planet, the bended tree recovering itself from the strong wind, the vital resources of every vegetable and animal, are also demonstrations of the self-sufficing, and therefore self-relying soul. All history from its highest to its trivial passages is the various record of this power.

Thus all concentrates; let us not rove; let us sit at home with the cause. Let us stun and astonish the intruding rabble of men and books and institutions by a simple declaration of the divine fact. Bid them take the shoes from off their feet,[2] for God is here within. Let our simplicity judge them, and our docility to our own law demonstrate the poverty of nature and fortune beside our native riches.

But now we are a mob. Man does not stand in awe of man, nor is the soul admonished to stay at home, to put itself in communication with the internal ocean, but it goes abroad to beg a cup of water of the urns of men. We must go alone. Isolation must precede true society. I like the silent church before the service begins, better than any preaching. How far off, how cool, how chaste the persons look, begirt each one with a precinct or sanctuary. So let us always sit. Why should we assume the faults of our friend, or wife, or father, or child, because they sit around our hearth, or are said to have the same blood? All men have my blood, and I have all men's. Not for that will I adopt their petulance or folly, even to the extent of being ashamed of it. But your isolation must not be mechanical, but spiritual, that is, must be elevation. At times the whole world seems to be in conspiracy to importune you with emphatic trifles. Friend, client, child, sickness, fear, want, charity, all knock at once at thy closet door and say, 'Come out unto us.'—Do not spill thy soul; do not all descend; keep thy state; stay at home in thine own heaven; come not for a moment into their facts, into their hubbub of conflicting appearances, but let in the light of thy law on their confusion. The power men possess to annoy me, I give them by a weak curiosity. No man can come near me but through my act. "What we love that we have, but by desire we bereave ourselves of the love."[3]

If we cannot at once rise to the sanctities of obedience and faith, let us at least resist our temptations, let us enter into the state of war, and wake Thor and Woden,[4] courage and constancy in our Saxon breasts. This is to be done in our smooth times by speaking the truth. Check this lying hospitality and lying affection. Live no longer to the expectation of these deceived and deceiving people with whom we converse. Say to them, O father, O mother, O wife, O brother, O friend, I have lived with you after appearances hitherto. Henceforward I am the truth's. Be it known unto you that henceforward I obey no law less than the eternal law. I will have no covenants but proximities. I shall endeavor to nourish my parents, to support my family, to be the chaste husband of one wife,—but these relations I must fill after a new and

---

2. In Exodus 3.5, God commands Moses "to put off thy shoes from off thy feet, for the place whereon thou standest is holy ground."
3. In his notebook, Emerson attributed this quotation to the German poet and dramatist Fried-

rich Schiller (1759–1805).
4. Norse gods, here taken as ancestral gods of the Anglo-Saxon as well, associated respectively with courage and endurance.

unprecedented way. I appeal from your customs. I must be myself. I cannot break myself any longer for you, or you. If you can love me for what I am, we shall be the happier. If you cannot, I will still seek to deserve that you should. I must be myself. I will not hide my tastes or aversions. I will so trust that what is deep is holy, that I will do strongly before the sun and moon whatever inly rejoices me, and the heart appoints. If you are noble, I will love you; if you are not, I will not hurt you and myself by hypocritical attentions. If you are true, but not in the same truth with me, cleave to your companions; I will seek my own. I do this not selfishly, but humbly and truly. It is alike your interest and mine and all men's, however long we have dwelt in lies, to live in truth. Does this sound harsh to-day? You will soon love what is dictated by your nature as well as mine, and if we follow the truth, it will bring us out safe at last.—But so you may give these friends pain. Yes, but I cannot sell my liberty and my power, to save their sensibility. Besides, all persons have their moments of reason when they look out into the region of absolute truth; then will they justify me and do the same thing.

The populace think that your rejection of popular standards is a rejection of all standard, and mere antinomianism;[5] and the bold sensualist will use the name of philosophy to gild his crimes. But the law of consciousness abides. There are two confessionals, in one or the other of which we must be shriven. You may fulfil your round of duties by clearing yourself in the *direct*, or, in the *reflex* way. Consider whether you have satisfied your relations to father, mother, cousin, neighbor, town, cat, and dog; whether any of these can upbraid you. But I may also neglect this reflex standard, and absolve me to myself. I have my own stern claims and perfect circle. It denies the name of duty to many offices that are called duties. But if I can discharge its debts, it enables me to dispense with the popular code. If any one imagines that this law is lax, let him keep its commandment one day.

And truly it demands something godlike in him who has cast off the common motives of humanity, and has ventured to trust himself for a task-master. High be his heart, faithful his will, clear his sight, that he may in good earnest be doctrine, society, law to himself, that a simple purpose may be to him as strong as iron necessity is to others.

If any man consider the present aspects of what is called by distinction *society*, he will see the need of these ethics. The sinew and heart of man seem to be drawn out, and we are become timorous desponding whimperers. We are afraid of truth, afraid of fortune, afraid of death, and afraid of each other. Our age yields no great and perfect persons. We want men and women who shall renovate life and our social state, but we see that most natures are insolvent; cannot satisfy their own wants, have an ambition out of all proportion to their practical force, and so do lean and beg day and night continually. Our housekeeping is mendicant, our arts, our occupations, our marriages, our religion we have not chosen, but society has chosen for us. We are parlor soldiers. The rugged battle of fate, where strength is born, we shun.

If our young men miscarry in their first enterprizes, they lose all heart. If the young merchant fails, men say he is *ruined*. If the finest genius studies at one of our colleges, and is not installed in an office within one year afterwards in the cities or suburbs of Boston or New York, it seems to his friends and

5. Doctrine of salvation by faith alone.

to himself that he is right in being disheartened and in complaining the rest of his life. A sturdy lad from New Hampshire or Vermont, who in turn tries all the professions, who *teams it, farms it, peddles*, keeps a school, preaches, edits a newspaper, goes to Congress, buys a township, and so forth, in successive years, and always, like a cat, falls on his feet, is worth a hundred of these city dolls. He walks abreast with his days, and feels no shame in not 'studying a profession,' for he does not postpone his life, but lives already. He has not one chance, but a hundred chances. Let a stoic arise who shall reveal the resources of man, and tell men they are not leaning willows, but can and must detach themselves; that with the exercise of self-trust, new powers shall appear; that a man is the word made flesh, born to shed healing to the nations, that he should be ashamed of our compassion, and that the moment he acts from himself, tossing the laws, the books, idolatries, and customs out of the window,—we pity him no more but thank and revere him,—and that teacher shall restore the life of man to splendor, and make his name dear to all History.

It is easy to see that a greater self-reliance,—a new respect for the divinity in man,—must work a revolution in all the offices and relations of men; in their religion; in their education; in their pursuits; their modes of living; their association; in their property; in their speculative views.

1. In what prayers do men allow themselves! That which they call a holy office, is not so much as brave and manly. Prayer looks abroad and asks for some foreign addition to come through some foreign virtue, and loses itself in endless mazes of natural and supernatural, and mediatorial and miraculous. Prayer that craves a particular commodity—any thing less than all good, is vicious. Prayer is the contemplation of the facts of life from the highest point of view. It is the soliloquy of a beholding and jubilant soul. It is the spirit of God pronouncing his works good. But prayer as a means to effect a private end, is theft and meanness. It supposes dualism and not unity in nature and consciousness. As soon as the man is at one with God, he will not beg. He will then see prayer in all action. The prayer of the farmer kneeling in his field to weed it, the prayer of the rower kneeling with the stroke of his oar, are true prayers heard throughout nature, though for cheap ends. Caratach, in Fletcher's Bonduca, when admonished to inquire the mind of the god Audate, replies,

> "His hidden meaning lies in our endeavors,
> Our valors are our best gods."[6]

Another sort of false prayers are our regrets. Discontent is the want of self-reliance; it is infirmity of will. Regret calamities, if you can thereby help the sufferer; if not, attend your own work, and already the evil begins to be repaired. Our sympathy is just as base. We come to them who weep foolishly, and sit down and cry for company, instead of imparting to them truth and health in rough electric shocks, putting them once more in communication with the soul. The secret of fortune is joy in our hands. Welcome evermore to gods and men is the self-helping man. For him all doors are flung wide. Him all tongues greet, all honors crown, all eyes follow with desire. Our love goes

6. Lines 1294–95; the play by the English playwright John Fletcher (1579–1625) was produced around 1614.

out to him and embraces him, because he did not need it. We solicitously and apologetically caress and celebrate him, because he held on his way and scorned our disapprobation. The gods love him because men hated him. "To the persevering mortal," said Zoroaster,[7] "the blessed Immortals are swift."

As men's prayers are a disease of the will, so are their creeds a disease of the intellect. They say with those foolish Israelites, 'Let not God speak to us, lest we die. Speak thou, speak any man with us, and we will obey.'[8] Everywhere I am bereaved of meeting God in my brother, because he has shut his own temple doors, and recites fables merely of his brother's, or his brother's brother's God. Every new mind is a new classification. If it prove a mind of uncommon activity and power, a Locke, a Lavoisier, a Hutton, a Bentham, a Spurzheim,[9] it imposes its classification on other men, and lo! a new system. In proportion always to the depth of the thought, and so to the number of the objects it touches and brings within reach of the pupil, is his complacency. But chiefly is this apparent in creeds and churches, which are also classifications of some powerful mind acting on the great elemental thought of Duty, and man's relation to the Highest. Such is Calvinism, Quakerism, Swedenborgianism.[1] The pupil takes the same delight in subordinating every thing to the new terminology that a girl does who has just learned botany, in seeing a new earth and new seasons thereby. It will happen for a time, that the pupil will feel a real debt to the teacher,—will find his intellectual power has grown by the study of his writings. This will continue until he has exhausted his master's mind. But in all unbalanced minds, the classification is idolized, passes for the end, and not for a speedily exhaustible means, so that the walls of the system blend to their eye in the remote horizon with the walls of the universe; the luminaries of heaven seem to them hung on the arch their master built. They cannot imagine how you aliens have any right to see,—how you can see; 'It must be somehow that you stole the light from us.' They do not yet perceive, that, light unsystematic, indomitable, will break into any cabin, even into theirs. Let them chirp awhile and call it their own. If they are honest and do well, presently their neat new pinfold[2] will be too strait and low, will crack, will lean, will rot and vanish, and the immortal light, all young and joyful, million-orbed, million-colored, will beam over the universe as on the first morning.

2. It is for want of self-culture that the idol of Travelling, the idol of Italy, of England, of Egypt, remains for all educated Americans. They who made England, Italy, or Greece venerable in the imagination, did so not by rambling round creation as a moth round a lamp, but by sticking fast where they were, like an axis of the earth. In manly hours, we feel that duty is our place, and that the merrymen of circumstance should follow as they may. The soul is no traveller: the wise man stays at home with the soul, and when his

---

7. Religious prophet of ancient Persia.
8. See the fearful words of the Hebrews after God gave Moses the Ten Commandments, Exodus 20.19: "And they said unto Moses, Speak thou with us, and we will hear: but let not God speak with us, lest we die."
9. These innovators are John Locke (1632–1704), English philosopher; Antoine Lavoisier (1743–1797), French chemist; James Hutton (1726–1797), Scottish geologist; Jeremy Bentham (1748–1832), English philosopher; and Johann

Kaspar Spurzheim (1776–1832), German physician whose work led to the pseudoscience of phrenology, assessing character by interpreting the bumps on the skull.
1. Three widely varying religious movements founded by or based on the teachings of, respectively, John Calvin (1509–1564), French theologian; George Fox (1624–1691), English clergyman; and Emanuel Swedenborg (1688–1772), Swedish scientist and theologian.
2. Enclosure for animals.

necessities, his duties, on any occasion call him from his house, or into foreign lands, he is at home still, and is not gadding abroad from himself, and shall make men sensible by the expression of his countenance, that he goes the missionary of wisdom and virtue, and visits cities and men like a sovereign, and not like an interloper or a valet.

I have no churlish objection to the circumnavigation of the globe, for the purposes of art, of study, and benevolence, so that the man is first domesticated, or does not go abroad with the hope of finding somewhat greater than he knows. He who travels to be amused, or to get somewhat which he does not carry, travels away from himself, and grows old even in youth among old things. In Thebes, in Palmyra,[3] his will and mind have become old and dilapidated as they. He carries ruins to ruins.

Travelling is a fool's paradise. We owe to our first journeys the discovery that place is nothing. At home I dream that at Naples, at Rome, I can be intoxicated with beauty, and lose my sadness. I pack my trunk, embrace my friends, embark on the sea, and at last wake up in Naples, and there beside me is the stern Fact, the sad self, unrelenting, identical, that I fled from. I seek the Vatican, and the palaces. I affect to be intoxicated with sights and suggestions, but I am not intoxicated. My giant goes with me wherever I go.

3. But the rage of travelling is itself only a symptom of a deeper unsoundness affecting the whole intellectual action. The intellect is vagabond, and the universal system of education fosters restlessness. Our minds travel when our bodies are forced to stay at home. We imitate; and what is imitation but the travelling of the mind? Our houses are built with foreign taste; our shelves are garnished with foreign ornaments; our opinions, our tastes, our whole minds lean, and follow the Past and the Distant, as the eyes of a maid follow her mistress. The soul created the arts wherever they have flourished. It was in his own mind that the artist sought his model. It was an application of his own thought to the thing to be done and the conditions to be observed. And why need we copy the Doric or the Gothic model?[4] Beauty, convenience, grandeur of thought, and quaint expression are as near to us as to any, and if the American artist will study with hope and love the precise thing to be done by him, considering the climate, the soil, the length of the day, the wants of the people, the habit and form of the government, he will create a house in which all these will find themselves fitted, and taste and sentiment will be satisfied also.

Insist on yourself; never imitate. Your own gift you can present every moment with the cumulative force of a whole life's cultivation; but of the adopted talent of another, you have only an extemporaneous, half possession. That which each can do best, none but his Maker can teach him. No man yet knows what it is, nor can, till that person has exhibited it. Where is the master who could have taught Shakspeare? Where is the master who could have instructed Franklin, or Washington, or Bacon, or Newton? Every great man is an unique. The Scipionism[5] of Scipio is precisely that part he could not borrow. If any body will tell me whom the great man imitates in the original crisis when he performs a great act, I will tell him who else than himself can

3. Ruins of ancient cities in Egypt and Syria, respectively.
4. I.e., ancient Greek or medieval European architecture.
5. I.e., the essence of the man.

teach him. Shakspeare will never be made by the study of Shakspeare. Do that which is assigned thee, and thou canst not hope too much or dare too much. There is at this moment, there is for me an utterance bare and grand as that of the colossal chisel of Phidias,[6] or trowel of the Egyptians, or the pen of Moses, or Dante, but different from all these. Now possibly will the soul all rich, all eloquent, with thousand-cloven tongue, deign to repeat itself; but if I can hear what these patriarchs say, surely I can reply to them in the same pitch of voice: for the ear and the tongue are two organs of one nature. Dwell up there in the simple and noble regions of thy life, obey thy heart, and thou shalt reproduce the Foreworld again.

4. As our Religion, our Education, our Art look abroad, so does our spirit of society. All men plume themselves on the improvement of society, and no man improves.

Society never advances. It recedes as fast on one side as it gains on the other. Its progress is only apparent, like the workers of a treadmill. It undergoes continual changes: it is barbarous, it is civilized, it is christianized, it is rich, it is scientific; but this change is not amelioration. For every thing that is given, something is taken. Society acquires new arts and loses old instincts. What a contrast between the well-clad, reading, writing, thinking American, with a watch, a pencil, and a bill of exchange in his pocket, and the naked New Zealander, whose property is a club, a spear, a mat, and an undivided twentieth of a shed to sleep under. But compare the health of the two men, and you shall see that his aboriginal strength the white man has lost. If the traveller tell us truly, strike the savage with a broad axe, and in a day or two the flesh shall unite and heal as if you struck the blow into soft pitch, and the same blow shall send the white to his grave.

The civilized man has built a coach, but has lost the use of his feet. He is supported on crutches, but loses so much support of muscle. He has got a fine Geneva watch, but he has lost the skill to tell the hour by the sun. A Greenwich nautical almanac he has, and so being sure of the information when he wants it, the man in the street does not know a star in the sky. The solstice he does not observe; the equinox he knows as little; and the whole bright calendar of the year is without a dial in his mind. His notebooks impair his memory; his libraries overload his wit; the insurance office increases the number of accidents; and it may be a question whether machinery does not encumber; whether we have not lost by refinement some energy, by a christianity entrenched in establishments and forms, some vigor of wild virtue. For every stoic was a stoic;[7] but in Christendom where is the Christian?

There is no more deviation in the moral standard than in the standard of height or bulk. No greater men are now than ever were. A singular equality may be observed between the great men of the first and of the last ages; nor can all the science, art, religion and philosophy of the nineteenth century avail to educate greater men than Plutarch's heroes,[8] three or four and twenty centuries ago. Not in time is the race progressive. Phocion, Socrates, Anaxagoras, Diogenes,[9] are great men, but they leave no class. He who is

---

6. Greek sculptor of the 5th century B.C.E.
7. Emerson refers particularly to the Stoics, members of the Greek school of philosophy founded by Zeno about 308 B.C.E. It taught the ideal of a calm, self-controlled existence in which every occurrence is accepted as fated.

8. The lives of famous Greeks and Romans written by Plutarch (46?–120? C.E.), Greek biographer.
9. Four Greek philosophers: Phocion (402?–317 B.C.E.), Socrates (470?–399 B.C.E.), Anaxagoras (500?–428 B.C.E.), and Diogenes (412?–323 B.C.E.).

really of their class will not be called by their name, but be wholly his own man, and, in his turn the founder of a sect. The arts and inventions of each period are only its costume, and do not invigorate men. The harm of the improved machinery may compensate its good. Hudson and Behring[1] accomplished so much in their fishing-boats, as to astonish Parry and Franklin,[2] whose equipment exhausted the resources of science and art. Galileo, with an opera-glass, discovered a more splendid series of facts than any one since. Columbus found the New World in an undecked boat. It is curious to see the periodical disuse and perishing of means and machinery which were introduced with loud laudation, a few years or centuries before. The great genius returns to essential man. We reckoned the improvements of the art of war among the triumphs of science, and yet Napoleon conquered Europe by the Bivouac,[3] which consisted of falling back on naked valor, and disencumbering it of all aids. The Emperor held it impossible to make a perfect army, says Las Cases,[4] "without abolishing our arms, magazines, commissaries, and carriages, until in imitation of the Roman custom, the soldier should receive his supply of corn, grind it in his hand-mill, and bake his bread himself."

Society is a wave. The wave moves onward, but the water of which it is composed, does not. The same particle does not rise from the valley to the ridge. Its unity is only phenomenal. The persons who make up a nation today, next year die, and their experience with them.

And so the reliance on Property, including the reliance on governments which protect it, is the want of self-reliance. Men have looked away from themselves and at things so long, that they have come to esteem what they call the soul's progress, namely, the religious, learned, and civil institutions, as guards of property, and they deprecate assaults on these, because they feel them to be assaults on property. They measure their esteem of each other, by what each has, and not by what each is. But a cultivated man becomes ashamed of his property, ashamed of what he has, out of new respect for his being. Especially, he hates what he has, if he see that it is accidental,—came to him by inheritance, or gift, or crime; then he feels that it is not having; it does not belong to him, has no root in him, and merely lies there, because no revolution or no robber takes it away. But that which a man is, does always by necessity acquire, and what the man acquires is permanent and living property, which does not wait the beck of rulers, or mobs, or revolutions, or fire, or storm, or bankruptcies, but perpetually renews itself wherever the man is put. "Thy lot or portion of life," said the Caliph Ali,[5] "is seeking after thee; therefore be at rest from seeking after it." Our dependence on these foreign goods leads us to our slavish respect for numbers. The political parties meet in numerous conventions; the greater the concourse, and with each new uproar of announcement, The delegation from Essex![6] The Democrats from New Hampshire! The Whigs of Maine! the young patriot feels himself stronger than before by a new thousand of eyes and arms. In like manner the

---

1. Vitus Jonassen Bering (1680–1741), Danish navigator who explored the northern Pacific Ocean. Henry Hudson (d. 1611), English navigator (sometimes in service of the Dutch).
2. Sir William Edward Perry (1790–1855) and Sir John Franklin (1786–1847), English explorers of the Arctic.

3. Temporary military camp.
4. Comte Emmanuel de Las Cases (1766–1842), author of a book recording his conversations with the exiled Napoleon at St. Helena.
5. Fourth Muslim caliph of Mecca (602?–661).
6. County in Massachusetts.

reformers summon conventions, and vote and resolve in multitude. But not so, O friends! will the God deign to enter and inhabit you, but by a method precisely the reverse. It is only as a man puts off from himself all external support, and stands alone, that I see him to be strong and to prevail. He is weaker by every recruit to his banner. Is not a man better than a town? Ask nothing of men, and in the endless mutation, thou only firm column must presently appear the upholder of all that surrounds thee. He who knows that power is in the soul, that he is weak only because he has looked for good out of him and elsewhere, and so perceiving, throws himself unhesitatingly on his thought, instantly rights himself, stands in the erect position, commands his limbs, works miracles; just as a man who stands on his feet is stronger than a man who stands on his head.

So use all that is called Fortune. Most men gamble with her, and gain all, and lose all, as her wheel rolls. But do thou leave as unlawful these winnings, and deal with Cause and Effect, the chancellors of God. In the Will work and acquire, and thou hast chained the wheel of Chance, and shalt always drag her after thee. A political victory, a rise of rents, the recovery of your sick, or the return of your absent friend, or some other quite external event, raises your spirits, and you think good days are preparing for you. Do not believe it. It can never be so. Nothing can bring you peace but yourself. Nothing can bring you peace but the triumph of principles.

1841

The Poet[1]

A moody child and wildly wise
Pursued the game with joyful eyes,
Which chose, like meteors, their way,
And rived the dark with private ray:
They overleapt the horizon's edge,
Searched with Apollo's privilege;
Through man, and woman, and sea, and star,
Saw the dance of nature forward far;
Through worlds, and races, and terms, and times,
Saw musical order, and pairing rhymes.

Olympian bards who sung
Divine ideas below,
Which always find us young,
And always keep us so.

Those who are esteemed umpires of taste, are often persons who have acquired some knowledge of admired pictures or sculptures, and have an inclination for whatever is elegant; but if you inquire whether they are beautiful souls, and whether their own acts are like fair pictures, you learn that they are selfish and sensual. Their cultivation is local, as if you should rub

---

1. First published in *Essays, Second Series* (1844), the source of the present text, "The Poet" contains the fullest elaboration of Emerson's aesthetic ideas and his most incisive comments on contemporary poetry and criticism. The first prefatory poem is from one of Emerson's uncompleted poems, and the second is from his "Ode to Beauty" (1843).

a log of dry wood in one spot to produce fire, all the rest remaining cold. Their knowledge of the fine arts is some study of rules and particulars, or some limited judgment of color or form, which is exercised for amusement or for show. It is a proof of the shallowness of the doctrine of beauty, as it lies in the minds of our amateurs, that men seem to have lost the perception of the instant dependence of form upon soul. There is no doctrine of forms in our philosophy. We were put into our bodies, as fire is put into a pan, to be carried about; but there is no accurate adjustment between the spirit and the organ, much less is the latter the germination of the former. So in regard to other forms, the intellectual men do not believe in any essential dependence of the material world on thought and volition. Theologians think it a pretty air-castle to talk of the spiritual meaning of a ship or a cloud, of a city or a contract, but they prefer to come again to the solid ground of historical evidence; and even the poets are contented with a civil and conformed manner of living, and to write poems from the fancy, at a safe distance from their own experience. But the highest minds of the world have never ceased to explore the double meaning, or, shall I say, the quadruple, or the centuple, or much more manifold meaning, of every sensuous fact: Orpheus, Empedocles, Heraclitus, Plato, Plutarch, Dante, Swedenborg,[2] and the masters of sculpture, picture, and poetry. For we are not pans and barrows, nor even porters of the fire and torchbearers, but children of the fire, made of it, and only the same divinity transmuted, and at two or three removes, when we know least about it. And this hidden truth, that the foundations whence all this river of Time, and its creatures, floweth, are intrinsically ideal and beautiful, draws us to the consideration of the nature and functions of the Poet, or the man of Beauty, to the means and materials he uses, and to the general aspect of the art in the present time.

The breadth of the problem is great, for the poet is representative. He stands among partial men for the complete man, and apprises us not of his wealth, but of the commonwealth. The young man reveres men of genius, because, to speak truly, they are more himself than he is. They receive of the soul as he also receives, but they more. Nature enhances her beauty, to the eye of loving men, from their belief that the poet is beholding her shows at the same time. He is isolated among his contemporaries, by truth and by his art, but with this consolation in his pursuits, that they will draw all men sooner or later. For all men live by truth, and stand in need of expression. In love, in art, in avarice, in politics, in labor, in games, we study to utter our painful secret. The man is only half himself, the other half is his expression.

Notwithstanding this necessity to be published, adequate expression is rare. I know not how it is that we need an interpreter; but the great majority of men seem to be minors, who have not yet come into possession of their own, or mutes, who cannot report the conversation they have had with nature. There is no man who does not anticipate a supersensual utility in the sun, and stars, earth, and water. These stand and wait to render him a peculiar service. But there is some obstruction, or some excess of phlegm in our constitution, which does not suffer them to yield the due effect. Too feeble

---

2. Emanuel Swedenborg (1688–1772), Swedish scientist and mystic. Orpheus, a legendary Greek poet. Empedocles (5th century B.C.E.), Heraclitus (6th century B.C.E.), and Plato (4th century B.C.E.) were Greek philosophers. Plutarch (1st century), Greek biographer. Dante (1265–1321), Italian poet.

fall the impressions of nature on us to make us artists. Every touch should thrill. Every man should be so much an artist, that he could report in conversation what had befallen him. Yet, in our experience, the rays or appulses[3] have sufficient force to arrive at the senses, but not enough to reach the quick, and compel the reproduction of themselves in speech. The poet is the person in whom these powers are in balance, the man without impediment, who sees and handles that which others dream of, traverses the whole scale of experience, and is representative of man, in virtue of being the largest power to receive and to impart.

For the Universe has three children, born at one time, which reappear, under different names, in every system of thought, whether they be called cause, operation, and effect; or, more poetically, Jove, Pluto, Neptune;[4] or, theologically, the Father, the Spirit, and the Son; but which we will call here, the Knower, the Doer, and the Sayer. These stand respectively for the love of truth, for the love of good, and for the love of beauty. These three are equal. Each is that which he is essentially, so that he cannot be surmounted or analyzed, and each of these three has the power of the others latent in him, and his own patent.

The poet is the sayer, the namer, and represents beauty. He is a sovereign, and stands on the centre. For the world is not painted or adorned, but is from the beginning beautiful; and God has not made some beautiful things, but Beauty is the creator of the universe. Therefore the poet is not any permissive potentate, but is emperor in his own right. Criticism is infested with a cant of materialism, which assumes that manual skill and activity is the first merit of all men, and disparages such as say and do not, overlooking the fact that some men, namely, poets, are natural sayers, sent into the world to the end of expression, and confounds them with those whose province is action, but who quit it to imitate the sayers. But Homer's words are as costly and admirable to Homer, as Agamemnon's victories are to Agamemnon.[5] The poet does not wait for the hero or the sage, but, as they act and think primarily, so he writes primarily what will and must be spoken, reckoning the others, though primaries also, yet, in respect to him, secondaries and servants; as sitters or models in the studio of a painter, or as assistants who bring building materials to an architect.

For poetry was all written before time was, and whenever we are so finely organized that we can penetrate into that region where the air is music, we hear those primal warblings, and attempt to write them down, but we lose ever and anon a word, or a verse, and substitute something of our own, and thus miswrite the poem. The men of more delicate ear write down these cadences more faithfully, and these transcripts, though imperfect, become the songs of the nations. For nature is as truly beautiful as it is good, or as it is reasonable, and must as much appear, as it must be done, or be known. Words and deeds are quite indifferent modes of the divine energy. Words are also actions, and actions are a kind of words.

The sign and credentials of the poet are, that he announces that which no man foretold. He is the true and only doctor;[6] he knows and tells; he is

---

3. Energies.
4. In Roman mythology, the supreme god, god of the underworld, and god of the sea, respectively.

5. Emerson is comparing the author (Homer) with his character (Agamemnon, in *The Iliad*).
6. Teacher and healer.

the only teller of news, for he was present and privy to the appearance which he describes. He is a beholder of ideas, and an utterer of the necessary and causal. For we do not speak now of men of poetical talents, or of industry and skill in metre, but of the true poet. I took part in a conversation the other day, concerning a recent writer of lyrics, a man of subtle mind, whose head appeared to be a music-box of delicate tunes and rhythms, and whose skill, and command of language, we could not sufficiently praise. But when the question arose, whether he was not only a lyrist, but a poet, we were obliged to confess that he is plainly a contemporary, not an eternal man. He does not stand out of our low limitations, like a Chimborazo under the line,[7] running up from the torrid base through all the climates of the globe, with belts of the herbage of every latitude on its high and mottled sides; but this genius is the landscape-garden of a modern house, adorned with fountains and statues, with well-bred men and women standing and sitting in the walks and terraces. We hear, through all the varied music, the ground-tone of conventional life. Our poets are men of talents who sing, and not the children of music. The argument is secondary, the finish of the versus is primary.

For it is not metres, but a metre-making argument, that makes a poem,—a thought so passionate and alive, that, like the spirit of a plant or an animal, it has an architecture of its own, and adorns nature with a new thing. The thought and the form are equal in the order of time, but in the order of genesis the thought is prior to the form. The poet has a new thought: he has a whole new experience to unfold; he will tell us how it was with him, and all men will be the richer in his fortune. For, the experience of each new age requires a new confession, and the world seems always waiting for its poet. I remember, when I was young, how much I was moved one morning by tidings that genius had appeared in a youth who sat near me at table. He had left his work, and gone rambling none knew whither, and had written hundreds of lines, but could not tell whether that which was in him was therein told: he could tell nothing but that all was changed,—man, beast, heaven, earth, and sea. How gladly we listened! how credulous! Society seemed to be compromised. We sat in the aurora of a sunrise which was to put out all the stars. Boston seemed to be at twice the distance it had the night before, or was much farther than that. Rome,—what was Rome! Plutarch and Shakspeare were in the yellow leaf, and Homer no more should be heard of. It is much to know that poetry has been written this very day, under this very roof, by your side. What! that wonderful spirit has not expired! these stony moments are still sparkling and animated! I had fancied that the oracles were all silent, and nature had spent her fires, and behold! all night, from every pore, these fine auroras have been streaming. Every one has some interest in the advent of the poet, and no one knows how much it may concern him. We know that the secret of the world is profound, but who or what shall be our interpreter, we know not. A mountain ramble, a new style of face, a new person, may put the key into our hands. Of course, the value of genius to us is in the veracity of its report. Talent may frolic and juggle; genius realizes and adds. Mankind, in good earnest, have availed so far in understanding themselves and their work, that the foremost watchman on the peak announces

7. Equator. Chimborazo is a mountain in Ecuador.

his news. It is the truest word ever spoken, and the phrase will be the fittest, most musical, and the unerring voice of the world for that time.

All that we call sacred history attests that the birth of a poet is the principal event in chronology. Man, never so often deceived, still watches for the arrival of a brother who can hold him steady to a truth, until he has made it his own. With what joy I begin to read a poem, which I confide in as an inspiration! And now my chains are to be broken; I shall mount above these clouds and opaque airs in which I live,—opaque, though they seem transparent,—and from the heaven of truth I shall see and comprehend my relations. That will reconcile me to life, and renovate nature, to see trifles animated by a tendency, and to know what I am doing. Life will no more be a noise; now I shall see men and women, and know the signs by which they may be discerned from fools and satans. This day shall be better than my birth-day: then I became an animal: now I am invited into the science of the real. Such is the hope, but the fruition is postponed. Oftener it falls, that this winged man, who will carry me into the heaven, whirls me into the clouds, then leaps and frisks about with me from cloud to cloud, still affirming that he is bound heavenward; and I, being myself a novice, am slow in perceiving that he does not know the way into the heavens, and is merely bent that I should admire his skill to rise, like a fowl or a flying fish, a little way from the ground or the water; but the all-piercing, all-feeding, and ocular[8] air of heaven, that man shall never inhabit. I tumble down again soon into my old nooks, and lead the life of exaggerations as before, and have lost my faith in the possibility of any guide who can lead me thither where I would be.

But leaving these victims of vanity, let us, with new hope, observe how nature, by worthier impulses, has ensured the poet's fidelity to his office of announcement and affirming, namely, by the beauty of things, which becomes a new, and higher beauty, when expressed. Nature offers all her creatures to him as a picture-language. Being used as a type, a second wonderful value appears in the object, far better than its old value, as the carpenter's stretched cord, if you hold your ear close enough, is musical in the breeze. "Things more excellent than every image," says Jamblichus,[9] "are expressed through images." Things admit of being used as symbols, because nature is a symbol, in the whole, and in every part. Every line we can draw in the sand, has expression; and there is no body without its spirit or genius. All form is an effect of character; all condition, of the quality of the life; all harmony, of health; (and, for this reason, a perception of beauty should be sympathetic, or proper only to the good.) The beautiful rests on the foundations of the necessary. The soul makes the body, as the wise Spenser teaches:—

> "So every spirit, as it is most pure,
> And hath in it the more of heavenly light,
> So it the fairer body doth procure
> To habit in, and it more fairly dight,
> With cheerful grace and amiable sight.
> For, of the soul, the body form doth take,
> For soul is form, and doth the body make."[1]

8. Visible.
9. Neoplatonic philosopher of the 4th century c.e. (Neoplatonism is a mystical religious system combining features of Platonic and other Greek philosophies with features of Judaism and Christianity.)
1. "An Hymn in Honour of Beauty" (1596), by the English poet Edmund Spenser (1552–1599).

Here we find ourselves, suddenly, not in a critical speculation, but in a holy place, and should go very warily and reverently. We stand before the secret of the world, there where Being passes into Appearance, and Unity into Variety.

The Universe is the externisation of the soul. Wherever the life is, that bursts into appearance around it. Our science is sensual, and therefore superficial. The earth, and the heavenly bodies, physics, and chemistry, we sensually treat, as if they were self-existent; but these are the retinue of that Being we have. "The mighty heaven," said Proclus,[2] "exhibits, in its transfigurations, clear images of the splendor of intellectual perceptions; being moved in conjunction with the unapparent periods of intellectual natures." Therefore, science always goes abreast with the just elevation of the man, keeping step with religion and metaphysics; or, the state of science is an index of our self-knowledge. Since everything in nature answers to a moral power, if any phenomenon remains brute and dark, it is that the corresponding faculty in the observer is not yet active.

No wonder, then, if these waters be so deep, that we hover over them with a religious regard. The beauty of the fable proves the importance of the sense; to the poet, and to all others; or, if you please, every man is so far a poet as to be susceptible of these enchantments of nature: for all men have the thoughts whereof the universe is the celebration. I find that the fascination resides in the symbol. Who loves nature? Who does not? Is it only poets, and men of leisure and cultivation, who live with her? No; but also hunters, farmers, grooms, and butchers, though they express their affection in their choice of life, and not in their choice of words. The writer wonders what the coachman or the hunter values in riding, in horses, and dogs. It is not superficial qualities. When you talk with him, he holds these at as slight a rate as you. His worship is sympathetic; he has no definitions, but he is commanded in nature, by the living power which he feels to be there present. No imitation, or playing of these things, would content him; he loves the earnest of the northwind, of rain, of stone, and wood, and iron. A beauty not explicable, is dearer than a beauty which we can see to the end of. It is nature the symbol, nature certifying the supernatural, body overflowed by life, which he worships, with coarse, but sincere rites.

The inwardness, and mystery, of this attachment, drives men of every class to the use of emblems. The schools of poets, and philosophers, are not more intoxicated with their symbols, than the populace with theirs. In our political parties, compute the power of badges and emblems. See the great ball which they roll from Baltimore to Bunker hill! In the political processions, Lowell goes in a loom, and Lynn in a shoe, and Salem in a ship.[3] Witness the ciderbarrel, the log-cabin, the hickory-stick, the palmetto,[4] and all the cognizances of party. See the power of national emblems. Some stars, lilies, leopards, a crescent, a lion, an eagle, or other figure, which came into

---

2. Greek Neoplatonic philosopher (411–485).
3. Towns are symbolized by major products. "The great ball": as a campaign stunt, William Henry Harrison's supporters during the 1840 presidential campaign rolled huge balls at rallies to cries of "Keep the ball a-rolling."
4. Allusions to the 1840 presidential election.

Harrison's "Log Cabin and Hard Cider" campaign, which emphasized the candidate's humble roots while offering free alcohol to his supporters, helped him defeat Martin Van Buren. South Carolina, nicknamed the Palmetto State for its palm-like trees, claimed to be the birthplace of Andrew Jackson ("Old Hickory").

credit God knows how, on an old rag of bunting, blowing in the wind, on a fort, at the ends of the earth, shall make the blood tingle under the rudest, or the most conventional exterior. The people fancy they hate poetry, and they are all poets and mystics!

Beyond this universality of the symbolic language, we are apprised of the divineness of this superior use of things, whereby the world is a temple, whose walls are covered with emblems, pictures, and commandments of the Deity, in this, that there is no fact in nature which does not carry the whole sense of nature; and the distinctions which we make in events, and in affairs, of low and high, honest and base, disappear when nature is used as a symbol. Thought makes every thing fit for use. The vocabulary of an omniscient man would embrace words and images excluded from polite conversation. What would be base, or even obscene, to the obscene, becomes illustrious, spoken in a new connexion of thought. The piety of the Hebrew prophets purges their grossness. The circumcision is an example of the power of poetry to raise the low and offensive. Small and mean things serve as well as great symbols. The meaner the type by which a law is expressed, the more pungent it is, and the more lasting in the memories of men: just as we choose the smallest box, or case, in which any needful utensil can be carried. Bare lists of words are found suggestive, to an imaginative and excited mind; as it is related of Lord Chatham, that he was accustomed to read in Bailey's Dictionary,[5] when he was preparing to speak in Parliament. The poorest experience is rich enough for all the purposes of expressing thought. Why covet a knowledge of new facts? Day and night, house and garden, a few books, a few actions, serve us as well as would all trades and all spectacles. We are far from having exhausted the significance of the few symbols we use. We can come to use them yet with a terrible simplicity. It does not need that a poem should be long. Every word was once a poem. Every new relation is a new word. Also, we use defects and deformaties to a sacred purpose, so expressing our sense that the evils of the world are such only to the evil eye. In the old mythology, mythologists observe, defects are ascribed to divine natures, as lameness to Vulcan, blindness to Cupid, and the like, to signify exuberances.

For, as it is dislocation and detachment from the life of God, that makes things ugly, the poet, who re-attaches things to nature and the Whole,— re-attaching even artificial things, and violations of nature, to nature, by a deeper insight,—disposes very easily of the most disagreeable facts. Readers of poetry see the factory-village, and the railway, and fancy that the poetry of the landscape is broken up by these; for these works of art are not yet consecrated in their reading; but the poet sees them fall within the great Order not less than the bee-hive, or the spider's geometrical web. Nature adopts them very fast into her vital circles, and the gliding train of cars she loves like her own. Besides, in a centred mind, it signifies nothing how many mechanical inventions you exhibit. Though you add millions, and never so surprising, the fact of mechanics has not gained a grain's weight. The spiritual fact remains

---

5. Nathan (or Nathaniel) Bailey (d. 1742) published *An Universal Etymological English Dictionary* (1721), which ran through many editions. Lord Chatham was William Pitt (1708–1778), English statesman famous for his oratory.

unalterable, by many or by few particulars; as no mountain is of any appreciable height to break the curve of the sphere. A shrewd country-boy goes to the city for the first time, and the complacent citizen is not satisfied with his little wonder. It is not that he does not see all the fine houses, and know that he never saw such before, but he disposes of them as easily as the poet finds place for the railway. The chief value of the new fact, is to enhance the great and constant fact of Life, which can dwarf any and every circumstance, and to which the belt of wampum, and the commerce of America, are alike.

The world being thus put under the mind for verb and noun, the poet is he who can articulate it. For, though life is great, and fascinates, and absorbs,—and though all men are intelligent of the symbols through which it is named,—yet they cannot originally use them. We are symbols, and inhabit symbols; workmen, work, and tools, words and things, birth and death, all are emblems; but we sympathize with the symbols, and, being infatuated with the economical uses of things, we do not know that they are thoughts. The poet, by an ulterior intellectual perception, gives them a power which makes their old use forgotten, and puts eyes, and a tongue, into every dumb and inanimate object. He perceives the independence of the thought on the symbol, the stability of the thought, the accidency and fugacity of the symbol. As the eyes of Lyncæus[6] were said to see through the earth, so the poet turns the world to glass, and shows us all things in their right series and procession. For, through that better perception, he stands one step nearer to things, and sees the flowing or metamorphosis; perceives that thought is multiform; that within the form of every creature is a force impelling it to ascend into a higher form; and, following with his eyes the life, uses the forms which express that life, and so his speech flows with the flowing of nature. All the facts of the animal economy, sex, nutriment, gestation, birth, growth, are symbols of the passage of the world into the soul of man, to suffer there a change, and re-appear a new and higher fact. He uses forms according to the life, and not according to the form. This is true science. The poet alone knows astronomy, chemistry, vegetation, and animation, for he does not stop at these facts, but employs them as signs. He knows why the plain, or meadow of space, was strown with these flowers we call suns, and moons, and stars; why the great deep is adorned with animals, with men, and gods; for, in every word he speaks he rides on them as the horses of thought.

By virtue of this science the poet is the Namer, or Language-maker, naming things sometimes after their appearance, sometimes after their essence, and giving to every one its own name and not another's, thereby rejoicing the intellect, which delights in detachment or boundary. The poets made all the words, and therefore language is the archives of history, and, if we must say it, a sort of tomb of the muses. For, though the origin of most of our words is forgotten, each word was at first a stroke of genius, and obtained currency, because for the moment it symbolized the world to the first speaker and to the hearer. The etymologist finds the deadest word to have been once a brilliant picture. Language is fossil poetry. As the limestone of the continent consists of infinite masses of the shells of animalcules, so language is made

6. In Greek mythology, a keen-sighted crewman who sailed with Jason in search of the Golden Fleece.

up of images, or tropes, which now, in their secondary use, have long ceased to remind us of their poetic origin. But the poet names the thing because he sees it, or comes one step nearer to it than any other. This expression, or naming, is not art, but a second nature, grown out of the first, as a leaf out of a tree. What we call nature, is a certain self-regulated motion, or change; and nature does all things by her own hands, and does not leave another to baptise her, but baptises herself; and this through the metamorphosis again. I remember that a certain poet[7] described it to me thus:

> Genius is the activity which repairs the decays of things, whether wholly or partly of a material and finite kind. Nature, through all her kingdoms, insures herself. Nobody cares for planting the poor fungus: so she shakes down from the gills of one agaric[8] countless spores, any one of which, being preserved, transmits new billions of spores to-morrow or next day. The new agaric of this hour has a chance which the old one had not. This atom of seed is thrown into a new place, not subject to the accidents which destroyed its parent two rods off. She makes a man; and having brought him to ripe age, she will no longer run the risk of losing this wonder at a blow, but she detaches from him a new self, that the kind may be safe from accidents to which the individual is exposed. So when the soul of the poet has come to ripeness of thought, she detaches and sends away from it its poems or songs,—a fearless, sleepless, deathless progeny, which is not exposed to the accidents of the weary kingdom of time: a fearless, vivacious offspring, clad with wings (such was the virtue of the soul out of which they came), which carry them fast and far, and infix them irrecoverably into the hearts of men. These wings are the beauty of the poet's soul. The songs, thus flying immortal from their mortal parent, are pursued by clamorous flights of censures, which swarm in far greater numbers, and threaten to devour them; but these last are not winged. At the end of a very short leap they fall plump down, and rot, having received from the souls out of which they came no beautiful wings. But the melodies of the poet ascend, and leap, and pierce into the deeps of infinite time.

So far the bard taught me, using his freer speech. But nature has a higher end, in the production of new individuals, than security, namely, *ascension*, or, the passage of the soul into higher forms. I knew, in my younger days, the sculptor who made the statue of the youth which stands in the public garden. He was, as I remember, unable to tell directly, what made him happy, or unhappy, but by wonderful indirections he could tell. He rose one day, according to his habit, before the dawn, and saw the morning break, grand as the eternity out of which it came, and, for many days after, he strove to express this tranquillity, and, lo! his chisel had fashioned out of marble the form of a beautiful youth, Phosphorus,[9] whose aspect is such, that, it is said, all persons who look on it become silent. The poet also resigns himself to his mood, and that thought which agitated him is expressed, but *alter idem*,[1] in a manner totally new. The expression is organic, or, the new type which things themselves take when liberated. As, in the sun, objects paint their

---

7. A private joke: the poet is Emerson himself.
8. Fungus, such as a mushroom.

9. Greek god associated with the morning star.
1. The same yet different (Latin).

images on the retina of the eye, so they, sharing the aspiration of the whole universe, tend to paint a far more delicate copy of their essence in his mind. Like the metamorphosis of things into higher organic forms, is their change into melodies. Over everything stands its dæmon, or soul, and, as the form of the thing is reflected by the eye, so the soul of the thing is reflected by a melody. The sea, the mountain-ridge, Niagara, and every flower-bed, pre-exist, or super-exist, in pre-cantations,[2] which sail like odors in the air, and when any man goes by with an ear sufficiently fine, he overhears them, and endeavors to write down the notes, without diluting or depraving them. And herein is the legitimation of criticism, in the mind's faith, that the poems are a corrupt version of some text in nature, with which they ought to be made to tally. A rhyme in one of our sonnets should not be less pleasing than the iterated nodes of a seashell, or the resembling difference of a group of flowers. The pairing of the birds is an idyl, not tedious as our idyls are; a tempest is a rough ode, without falsehood or rant: a summer, with its harvest sown, reaped, and stored, is an epic song, subordinating how many admirably executed parts. Why should not the symmetry and truth that modulate these, glide into our spirits, and we participate the invention of nature?

This insight, which expresses itself by what is called Imagination, is a very high sort of seeing, which does not come by study, but by the intellect being where and what it sees, by sharing the path, or circuit of things through forms, and so making them translucid to others. The path of things is silent. Will they suffer a speaker to go with them? A spy they will not suffer; a lover, a poet, is the transcendency of their own nature,—him they will suffer. The condition of true naming, on the poet's part, is his resigning himself to the divine *aura*[3] which breathes through forms, and accompanying that.

It is a secret which every intellectual man quickly learns, that, beyond the energy of his possessed and conscious intellect, he is capable of a new energy (as of an intellect doubled on itself), by abandonment to the nature of things; that, beside his privacy of power as an individual man, there is a great public power, on which he can draw, by unlocking, at all risks, his human doors, and suffering the ethereal tides to roll and circulate through him: then he is caught up into the life of the Universe, his speech is thunder, his thought is law, and his words are universally intelligible as the plants and animals. The poet knows that he speaks adequately, then, only when he speaks somewhat wildly, or, "with the flower of the mind;" not with the intellect, used as an organ, but with the intellect released from all service, and suffered to take its direction from its celestial life; or, as the ancients were wont to express themselves, not with intellect alone, but with the intellect inebriated by nectar. As the traveller who has lost his way, throws his reins on his horse's neck, and trusts to the instinct of the animal to find his road, so must we do with the divine animal who carries us through this world. For if in any manner we can stimulate this instinct, new passages are opened for us into nature, the mind flows into and through things hardest and highest, and the metamorphosis is possible.

This is the reason why bards love wine, mead,[4] narcotics, coffee, tea, opium, the fumes of sandal-wood and tobacco, or whatever other species of

2. Prophetic incantations or spells.
3. I.e., all-pervading spirit.

4. A beverage made from fermented honey, malt, yeast, and water.

animal exhilaration. All men avail themselves of such means as they can, to add this extraordinary power to their normal powers; and to this end they prize conversation, music, pictures, sculpture, dancing, theatres, travelling, war, mobs, fires, gaming, politics, or love, or science, or animal intoxication, which are several coarser or finer *quasi*-mechanical substitutes for the true nectar, which is the ravishment of the intellect by coming nearer to the fact. These are auxiliaries to the centrifugal tendency of a man, to his passage out into free space, and they help him to escape the custody of that body in which he is pent up, and of that jail-yard of individual relations in which he is enclosed. Hence a great number of such as were professionally expressors of Beauty, as painters, poets, musicians, and actors, have been more than others wont to lead a life of pleasure and indulgence; all but the few who received the true nectar; and, as it was a spurious mode of attaining freedom, as it was an emancipation not into the heavens, but into the freedom of baser places, they were punished for that advantage they won, by a dissipation and deterioration. But never can any advantage be taken of nature by a trick. The spirit of the world, the great calm presence of the creator, comes not forth to the sorceries of opium or of wine. The sublime vision comes to the pure and simple soul in a clean and chaste body. That is not an inspiration which we owe to narcotics, but some counterfeit excitement and fury. Milton says, that the lyric poet may drink wine and live generously, but the epic poet, he who shall sing of the gods, and their descent unto men, must drink water out of a wooden bowl.[5] For poetry is not 'Devil's wine,' but God's wine. It is with this as it is with toys. We fill the hands and nurseries of our children with all manner of dolls, drums, and horses, withdrawing their eyes from the plain face and sufficing objects of nature, the sun, and moon, the animals, the water, and stones, which should be their toys. So the poet's habit of living should be set on a key so low and plain, that the common influences should delight him. His cheerfulness should be the gift of the sunlight; the air should suffice for his inspiration, and he should be tipsy with water. That spirit which suffices quiet hearts, which seems to come forth to such from every dry knoll of sere grass, from every pine-stump, and half-imbedded stone, on which the dull March sun shines, comes forth to the poor and hungry, and such as are of simple taste. If thou fill thy brain with Boston and New York, with fashion and covetousness, and wilt stimulate thy jaded senses with wine and French coffee, thou shalt find no radiance of wisdom in the lonely waste of the pinewoods.

If the imagination intoxicates the poet, it is not inactive in other men. The metamorphosis excites in the beholder an emotion of joy. The use of symbols has a certain power of emancipation and exhilaration for all men. We seem to be touched by a wand, which makes us dance and run about happily, like children. We are like persons who come out of a cave or cellar into the open air. This is the effect on us of tropes,[6] fables, oracles, and all poetic forms. Poets are thus liberating gods. Men have really got a new sense, and found within their world, another world, or nest of worlds; for, the meta-morphosis once seen, we divine that it does not stop. I will not now consider how much this makes the charm of algebra and the mathematics, which also have their tropes, but it is felt in every definition; as, when Aristotle defines

---

5. In Milton's "Sixth Latin Elegy" (1629).   6. Figures of speech.

space to be an immovable vessel, in which things are contained;—or, when Plato defines a *line* to be a flowing point; or, *figure* to be a bound of solid; and many the like. What a joyful sense of freedom we have, when Vitruvius announces the old opinion of artists, that no architect can build any house well, who does not know something of anatomy. When Socrates, in Charmides, tells us that the soul is cured of its maladies by certain incantations, and that these incantations are beautiful reasons, from which temperance is generated in souls; when Plato calls the world an animal; and Timæus affirms that the plants also are animals; or affirms a man to be a heavenly tree, growing with his root, which is his head, upward; and, as George Chapman, following him, writes,—

> "So in our tree of man, whose nervie root
> Springs in his top;"

when Orpheus speaks of hoariness as "that white flower which marks extreme old age;" when Proclus calls the universe the statue of the intellect; when Chaucer, in his praise of 'Gentilesse,' compares good blood in mean condition to fire, which, though carried to the darkest house betwixt this and the mount of Caucasus, will yet hold its natural office, and burn as bright as if twenty thousand men did it behold; when John saw, in the apocalypse, the ruin of the world through evil, and the stars fall from heaven, as the figtree casteth her untimely fruit; when Æsop reports the whole catalogue of common daily relations through the masquerade of birds and beasts;—we take the cheerful hint of the immortality of our essence, and its versatile habit and escapes, as when the gypsies say, "it is in vain to hang them, they cannot die."[7]

The poets are thus liberating gods. The ancient British bards had for the title of their order, "Those who are free throughout the world." They are free, and they make free. An imaginative book renders us much more service at first, by stimulating us through its tropes, than afterward, when we arrive at the precise sense of the author. I think nothing is of any value in books, excepting the transcendental and extraordinary. If a man is inflamed and carried away by his thought, to that degree that he forgets the authors and the public, and heeds only this one dream, which holds him like an insanity, let me read his paper, and you may have all the arguments and histories and criticism. All the value which attaches to Pythagoras, Paracelsus, Cornelius Agrippa, Cardan, Kepler, Swedenborg, Schelling, Oken,[8] or any other who introduces questionable facts into his cosmogony, as angels, devils, magic, astrology, palmistry, mesmerism,[9] and so on, is the certificate we have of departure from routine, and that here is a new witness. That also is the best success in conversation, the magic of liberty, which puts the world, like

---

7. Vitruvius Pollio (50?–26 B.C.E.), Roman writer on architecture. *Charmides* and *Timaeus* are two of Plato's Dialogues. The Chapman quotation is from his dedication to his translation of Homer. Chaucer's praise of "gentilesse" is in "The Wife of Bath's Tale." John's vision is in Revelation 6.13. The Greek Aesop in the 6th century B.C.E. wrote beast fables that commented on human foibles. The saying attributed to gypsies comes from the English travel writer George Borrow's *The Zincali* (1841).

8. Lorenz Oken (1779–1851), German naturalist. Pythagoras (6th century B.C.E.), Greek mathematician and mystic philosopher. Paracelsus (1493–1541), German alchemist. Agrippa (1486–1535), German physician. Girolamo Cardano (1501–1576), Italian mathematician. Johannes Kepler (1571–1630), German astronomer. Swedenborg, see n. 2, p. 254. Friedrich Wilhelm Joseph von Schelling (1775–1854), German philosopher.
9. Hypnotism.

a ball, in our hands. How cheap even the liberty then seems; how mean to study, when an emotion communicates to the intellect the power to sap and upheave nature; how great the perspective! nations, times, systems, enter and disappear, like threads in tapestry of large figure and many colors; dream delivers us to dream, and, while the drunkenness lasts, we will sell our bed, our philosophy, our religion, in our opulence.

There is good reason why we should prize this liberation. The fate of the poor shepherd, who, blinded and lost in the snowstorm, perishes in a drift within a few feet of his cottage door, is an emblem of the state of man. On the brink of the waters of life and truth, we are miserably dying. The inaccessibleness of every thought but that we are in, is wonderful. What if you come near to it,—you are as remote, when you are nearest, as when you are farthest. Every thought is also a prison; every heaven is also a prison. Therefore we love the poet, the inventor, who in any form, whether in an ode, or in an action, or in looks and behavior, has yielded us a new thought. He unlocks our chains, and admits us to a new scene.

This emancipation is dear to all men, and the power to impart it, as it must come from greater depth and scope of thought, is a measure of intellect. Therefore all books of the imagination endure, all which ascend to that truth, that the writer sees nature beneath him, and uses it as his exponent.[1] Every verse or sentence, possessing this virtue, will take care of its own immortality. The religions of the world are the ejaculations[2] of a few imaginative men.

But the quality of the imagination is to flow, and not to freeze. The poet did not stop at the color, or the form, but read their meaning; neither may he rest in this meaning, but he makes the same objects exponents of his new thought. Here is the difference betwixt the poet and the mystic, that the last nails a symbol to one sense, which was a true sense for a moment, but soon becomes old and false. For all symbols are fluxional; all language is vehicular and transitive, and is good, as ferries and horses are, for conveyance, not as farms and houses are, for homestead. Mysticism consists in the mistake of an accidental and individual symbol for an universal one. The morning-redness happens to be the favorite meteor to the eyes of Jacob Behmen,[3] and comes to stand to him for truth and faith; and he believes should stand for the same realities to every reader. But the first reader prefers as naturally the symbol of a mother and child, or a gardener and his bulb, or a jeweller polishing a gem. Either of these, or of a myriad more, are equally good to the person to whom they are significant. Only they must be held lightly, and be very willingly translated into the equivalent terms which others use. And the mystic must be steadily told,—All that you say is just as true without the tedious use of that symbol as with it. Let us have a little algebra, instead of this trite rhetoric,—universal signs, instead of these village symbols,—and we shall both be gainers. The history of hierarchies seems to show, that all religious error consisted in making the symbol too stark and solid, and, at last, nothing but an excess of the organ of language.

Swedenborg, of all men in the recent ages, stands eminently for the translator of nature into thought. I do not know the man in history to whom

---

1. Means of expounding his beliefs.
2. Throwings forth.

3. German mystic (1575–1624).

things stood so uniformly for words. Before him the metamorphosis continually plays. Everything on which his eye rests, obeys the impulses of moral nature. The figs become grapes whilst he eats them. When some of his angels affirmed a truth, the laurel twig which they held blossomed in their hands. The noise which, at a distance, appeared like gnashing and thumping, on coming nearer was found to be the voice of disputants. The men, in one of his visions, seen in heavenly light, appeared like dragons, and seemed in darkness: but, to each other, they appeared as men, and, when the light from heaven shone into their cabin, they complained of the darkness, and were compelled to shut the window that they might see.

There was this perception in him, which makes the poet or seer, an object of awe and terror, namely, that the same man, or society of men, may wear one aspect to themselves and their companions, and a different aspect to higher intelligences. Certain priests, whom he describes as conversing very learnedly together, appeared to the children, who were at some distance, like dead horses: and many the like misappearances. And instantly the mind inquires, whether these fishes under the bridge, yonder oxen in the pasture, those dogs in the yard, are immutably fishes, oxen, and dogs, or only so appear to me, and perchance to themselves appear upright men; and whether I appear as a man to all eyes. The Brahmins[4] and Pythagoras propounded the same question, and if any poet has witnessed the transformation, he doubtless found it in harmony with various experiences. We have all seen changes as considerable in wheat and caterpillars. He is the poet, and shall draw us with love and terror, who sees, through the flowing vest, the firm nature, and can declare it.

I look in vain for the poet whom I describe. We do not, with sufficient plainness, or sufficient profoundness, address ourselves to life, nor dare we chaunt our own times and social circumstance. If we filled the day with bravery, we should not shrink from celebrating it. Time and nature yield us many gifts, but not yet the timely man, the new religion, the reconciler, whom all things await. Dante's praise is, that he dared to write his autobiography in colossal cipher, or into universality. We have yet had no genius in America, with tyrannous eye, which knew the value of our incomparable materials, and saw, in the barbarism and materialism of the times, another carnival of the same gods whose picture he so much admires in Homer; then in the middle age; then in Calvinism. Banks and tariffs, the newspaper and caucus, methodism and unitarianism, are flat and dull to dull people, but rest on the same foundations of wonder as the town of Troy, and the temple of Delphos,[5] and are as swiftly passing away. Our logrolling, our stumps and their politics, our fisheries, our Negroes, and Indians, our boasts,[6] and our repudiations, the wrath of rogues, and the pusillanimity of honest men, the northern trade, the southern planting, the western clearing, Oregon, and Texas, are yet unsung. Yet America is a poem in our eyes; its ample geography dazzles the imagination, and it will not wait long for metres. If I have not

---

4. The highest social caste in Hindu culture, from which all priests are drawn.
5. The home of the Delphic oracle, or prophetess, in Greece. Troy is the site of the Trojan War in Asia Minor.
6. The common correction for the 1st edition's "boats." "Logrolling" seems to be used in the metaphorical sense of exchanging political favors. "Stumps" refers to the practice political orators had of addressing audiences from any makeshift platform, even a tree stump.

found that excellent combination of gifts in my countrymen which I seek, neither could I aid myself to fix the idea of the poet by reading now and then in Chalmers's collection of five centuries of English poets.[7] These are wits, more than poets, though there have been poets among them. But when we adhere to the ideal of the poet, we have our difficulties even with Milton and Homer. Milton is too literary, and Homer too literal and historical.

But I am not wise enough for a national criticism, and must use the old largeness a little longer, to discharge my errand from the muse to the poet concerning his art.

Art is the path of the creator to his work. The paths, or methods, are ideal and eternal, though few men ever see them, not the artist himself for years, or for a lifetime, unless he comes into the conditions. The painter, the sculptor, the composer, the epic rhapsodist, the orator, all partake one desire, namely, to express themselves symmetrically and abundantly, not dwarfishly and fragmentarily. They found or put themselves in certain conditions, as, the painter and sculptor before some impressive human figures; the orator, into the assembly of the people; and the others, in such scenes as each has found exciting to his intellect; and each presently feels the new desire. He hears a voice, he sees a beckoning. Then he is apprised, with wonder, what herds of dæmons hem him in. He can no more rest; he says, with the old painter, "By God, it is in me, and must go forth of me." He pursues a beauty, half seen, which flies before him. The poet pours out verses in every solitude. Most of the things he says are conventional, no doubt; but by and by he says something which is original and beautiful. That charms him. He would say nothing else but such things. In our way of talking, we say, "That is yours, this is mine;" but the poet knows well that it is not his; that it is as strange and beautiful to him as to you; he would fain hear the like eloquence at length. Once having tasted this immortal ichor,[8] he cannot have enough of it, and, as an admirable creative power exists in these intellections, it is of the last importance that these things get spoken. What a little of all we know is said! What drops of all the sea of our science are bailed up! and by what accident it is that these are exposed, when so many secrets sleep in nature! Hence the necessity of speech and song; hence these throbs and heart-beatings in the orator, at the door of the assembly, to the end, namely, that thought may be ejaculated as Logos, or Word.

Doubt not, O Poet, but persist. Say, "It is in me, and shall out." Stand there, baulked and dumb, stuttering and stammering, hissed and hooted, stand and strive, until, at last, rage draw out of thee that *dream*-power which every night shows thee is thine own; a power transcending all limit and privacy, and by virtue of which a man is the conductor of the whole river of electricity. Nothing walks, or creeps, or grows, or exists, which must not in turn arise and walk before him as exponent of his meaning. Comes he to that power, his genius is no longer exhaustible. All the creatures, by pairs and by tribes, pour into his mind as into a Noah's ark, to come forth again to people a new world. This is like the stock of air for our respiration, or for the combustion of our fireplace, not a measure of gallons, but the entire atmosphere if wanted. And therefore the rich poets, as Homer, Chaucer, Shakspeare, and

7. A popular collection of poetry compiled by Alexander Chalmers (1759–1834), Scottish journalist and biographer.

8. In Greek myth, blood of the gods, but Emerson may mean nectar, the drink of the gods.

Raphael,[9] have obviously no limits to their works, except the limits of their lifetime, and resemble a mirror carried through the street, ready to render an image of every created thing.

O poet! a new nobility is conferred in groves and pastures, and not in castles, or by the sword-blade, any longer. The conditions are hard, but equal. Thou shalt leave the world, and know the muse only. Thou shalt not know any longer the times, customs, graces, politics, or opinions of men, but shalt take all from the muse. For the time of towns is tolled from the world by funereal chimes, but in nature the universal hours are counted by succeeding tribes of animals and plants, and by growth of joy on joy. God wills also that thou abdicate a manifold and duplex life, and that thou be content that others speak for thee. Others shall be thy gentlemen, and shall represent all courtesy and worldly life for thee; others shall do the great and resounding actions also. Thou shalt lie close hid with nature, and canst not be afforded to the Capitol or the Exchange.[1] The world is full of renunciations and apprenticeships, and this is thine: thou must pass for a fool and a churl for a long season. This is the screen and sheath in which Pan[2] has protected his well-beloved flower, and thou shalt be known only to thine own, and they shall console thee with tenderest love. And thou shalt not be able to rehearse the names of thy friends in thy verse, for an old shame before the holy ideal. And this is the reward: that the ideal shall be real to thee; and the impressions of the actual world shall fall like summer rain, copious, but not troublesome, to thy invulnerable essence. Thou shalt have the whole land for thy park and manor, the sea for thy bath and navigation, without tax and without envy; the woods and the rivers thou shalt own; and thou shalt possess that wherein others are only tenants and boarders. Thou true land-lord! sea-lord! air-lord! Wherever snow falls, or water flows, or birds fly, wherever day and night meet in twilight, wherever the blue heaven is hung by clouds, or sown with stars, wherever are forms with transparent boundaries, wherever are outlets into celestial space, wherever is danger, and awe, and love, there is Beauty, plenteous as rain, shed for thee, and though thou shouldest walk the world over, thou shalt not be able to find a condition inopportune or ignoble.

1844

Each and All[1]

Little thinks, in the field, yon red-cloaked clown[2]
Of thee from the hill-top looking down;
The heifer that lows in the upland farm,
Far-heard, lows not thine ear to charm;
The sexton, tolling his bell at noon   5
Deems not that great Napoleon

---

9. Raphael Sanzio (1483–1520), renowned painter of the Italian Renaissance.
1. Stock exchange.
2. In Greek myth, the god of woods and fields, represented with goat's legs, horns, and ears.

1. First published in *Western Messenger* (February 1839) as "Each in All." The text is from Emerson's *Poems* (1847).
2. Rustic.

Stops his horse, and lists with delight,
Whilst his files sweep round yon Alpine height;
Nor knowest thou what argument
Thy life to thy neighbor's creed has lent.   10
All are needed by each one;
Nothing is fair or good alone.
I thought the sparrow's note from heaven,
Singing at dawn on the alder bough;
I brought him home, in his nest at even;[3]   15
He sings the song, but it cheers not now,
For I did not bring home the river and sky;—
He sang to my ear,—they sang to my eye,
The delicate shells lay on the shore;
The bubbles of the latest wave   20
Fresh pearls to their enamel gave;
And the bellowing of the savage sea
Greeted their safe escape to me.
I wiped away the weeds and foam,
I fetched my sea-born treasures home;   25
But the poor, unsightly, noisome[4] things
Had left their beauty on the shore;
With the sun, and the sand, and the wild uproar.
The lover watched his graceful maid,
As 'mid the virgin train she strayed,   30
Nor knew her beauty's best attire
Was woven still by the snow-white choir.
At last she came to his hermitage,
Like the bird from the woodlands to the cage;—
The gay enchantment was undone,   35
A gentle wife, but fairy none.
Then I said, 'I covet truth;
Beauty is unripe childhood's cheat;
I leave it behind with the games of youth.'—
As I spoke, beneath my feet   40
The ground-pine curled its pretty wreath,
Running over the club-moss burrs;
I inhaled the violet's breath;
Around me stood the oaks and firs;
Pine-cones and acorns lay on the ground;   45
Over me soared the eternal sky,
Full of light and of deity;
Again I saw, again I heard,
The rolling river, the morning bird;—
Beauty through my senses stole;   50
I yielded myself to the perfect whole.

1839, 1847

3. Evening.   4. Having an offensive smell.

Brahma[1]

If the red slayer think he slays,
    Or if the slain think he is slain,
They know not well the subtle ways
    I keep, and pass, and turn again.

Far or forgot to me is near;   5
    Shadow and sunlight are the same;
The vanished gods to me appear;
    And one to me are shame and fame.

They reckon ill who leave me out;
    When me they fly, I am the wings;   10
I am the doubter and the doubt,
    And I the hymn the Brahmin[2] sings.

The strong gods pine for my abode,
    And pine in vain the sacred Seven;[3]
But thou, meek lover of the good!   15
    Find me, and turn thy back on heaven.

1857

---

1. The text is from the November 1857 *Atlantic Monthly*. "Brahma": the creator god of sacred Hindu texts.
2. Members of the highest Hindu caste; originally the priests responsible for officiating at religious rites.
3. Seers or saints of ancient Hindu poetry.

Native Americans:
Removal and Resistance

J ust as the great majority of Native American peoples had fought on the side of the British during the Revolutionary War, so too did many Native peoples take the British side in the War of 1812. The reason, at base, was straightforward: Native Americans risked losing much more of their land and their autonomy at the hands of the colonials (1776), later the Americans (1812), than they did at the hands of the British. When the Treaty of Ghent ending the war with Britain was signed in 1814, the United States could at last feel no longer threatened by any European nation; but the American threat to Native nations was substantially increased.

President James Monroe invited Indian people to the White House in 1822, but things were to be different under his successor, Andrew Jackson. Jackson, who had fought against the Seminoles and Creeks in Florida, was elected president in 1828. "Indian removal"—the relocation of the southeastern tribes to lands west of the Mississippi—was an important part of his agenda. The Cherokees of Georgia were a major target for removal. By the time of Jackson's election, the Cherokees had a written language, a constitution modeled after that of the United States, and the first newspaper, the *Cherokee Phoenix*, to publish both in an indigenous language and in English. Although the Cherokees, in "memorials" to Congress and in editorials and articles in their newspaper, spoke out strongly against Jackson's removal policy, Congress nonetheless passed the Indian Removal Act in 1830, granting the president the authority to enter into treaties with the eastern tribes for their removal west of the Mississippi River. Finally, in 1838—in spite of frantic protest by many, including Ralph Waldo Emerson—the Cherokees were indeed forcibly removed by federal troops under General Winfield Scott. They were sent on what would be called the Trail of Tears to "Indian Country," present-day Oklahoma, a march in winter during which some four thousand people died, out of a population of about thirteen thousand.

Between the passage of the Removal Act and the Trail of Tears came the removal under different auspices of Black Hawk's Sauk people, the consequence of the so-called Black Hawk War of 1832, the last Indian war fought (for the most part) east of the Mississippi. Black Hawk's account of some of these matters, documenting removal and resistance, is included here.

BLACK HAWK

A member of the Sauk Nation, Black Hawk (1767?–1838) was born at Saukenuk on the Rock River in western Illinois. The town was destroyed by American militiamen during the Revolutionary War, and this act may well have initiated Black Hawk's lifelong distrust of and distaste for the Americans. In 1804, when the United States took control of the Louisiana Purchase from France, the Sauk chief Quashquame and some few others were persuaded to sign a treaty at St. Louis ceding

Sauk lands east of the Mississippi to the federal government. The signers of the treaty believed that they would be permitted to remain on their lands forever in spite of the sale. They did not understand that the document they had signed permitted them to remain only until the government sold or otherwise disposed of those lands. In 1816 Black Hawk and other Sauk chiefs signed another treaty, this one confirming the provisions of the 1804 treaty, but again, as Black Hawk insists, they had no clear idea of what was involved.

By the 1820s, settlers had begun to press into Sauk territory on the Rock River, and by 1829, submitting to the pressures put on them by the advancing Americans, many Sauk agreed to remove west of the Mississippi. The few who remained were forced west by U.S. troops under the command of General Edmund Gaines. Nonetheless, in 1832 Black Hawk led a party back to the Rock River, surely knowing that American opposition would ensue, yet determined to reestablish his people on their traditional homelands. His hopes in this endeavor were strengthened by a half-Sauk, half-Winnebago man named Wabokieshiek or White Cloud, known as the Winnebago Prophet, who had told Black Hawk that the return would be supported by Pottawatomi allies as well as by some English from Canada. This was not at all the case.

Governor John Reynolds of Illinois proclaimed Black Hawk's return "an invasion of the state" and called up five brigades of volunteers (the young Abraham Lincoln was among them) to join General Gaines, who had orders to force Black Hawk and his people back across the Mississippi. The federal and Illinois troops pursued Black Hawk and his people from the end of June until August 1832. They caught up with them as they were attempting a retreat to the western shore of the Mississippi. The steamboat *Warrior*, chartered by the U.S. Army, fired on Black Hawk's party as they attempted to cross the river, continuing to fire even as Black Hawk himself waved a white flag of surrender. Finally, on August 2, at Bad Axe, a junction of the Mississippi and the Bad Axe River in what is today Wisconsin, the remaining Sauk were attacked in a battle that turned into a massacre, with some three hundred of Black Hawk's band—many of them women and children—killed, and hundreds taken prisoner. Eight American soldiers died.

Black Hawk was imprisoned and taken east, where he twice met President Jackson. Returned, finally, to his people, he participated in the production of the *Life of Ma-ka-tai-me-she-kia-kiak, or Black Hawk . . . with an account of the cause and general history of the late war . . . dictated by himself*, a narrative of his life published in Cincinnati in 1833. It is not clear whether Black Hawk himself initiated the project— if he did, it was probably at the urging of many who had spoken with him in the East—or whether the initiator was John Barton Patterson, a young and ambitious local newspaper editor. Also involved in the making of Black Hawk's autobiography was Antoine LeClaire, part Pottawatomi, part French, who served as Black Hawk's interpreter. Upon the autobiography's publication, there was a predictable questioning of its authenticity. Roger Nichols's work convincingly makes the case that Black Hawk did indeed narrate the greater part of what we have, even managing, despite the cumbersome division of labor, to produce what Neil Schmitz has called "a Sauk history advocating a Sauk politics."

The selection printed here, from the 1833 text published by J. B. Patterson in Cincinnati, presents Black Hawk's strong sense of himself, his ties to his people, and his broad critique of the Americans.

From Life of Ma-ka-tai-me-she-kia-kiak, or Black Hawk

* * *

The great chief at St. Louis having sent word for us to go down and confirm the treaty of peace, we did not hesitate, but started immediately, that we might smoke the *peace-pipe* with him. On our arrival, we met the great chiefs in council. They explained to us the words of our Great Father at Washington, accusing us of heinous crimes and divers misdemeanors, particularly in not coming down when first invited. We knew very well that our *Great Father had deceived us*, and thereby *forced* us to join the British, and could not believe that he had put this speech into the mouths of these chiefs to deliver to us. I was not a civil chief, and consequently made no reply: but our chiefs told the commissioners that "what they had said was a *lie!*—that our Great Father had sent no such speech, he knowing the situation in which we had been placed had been *caused by him!*" The white chiefs appeared very angry at this reply, and said they "would break off the treaty with us, and *go to war*, as they would not be insulted."

Our chiefs had no intention of insulting them, and told them so—"that they merely wished to explain to them that *they had told a lie*, without making them angry; in the same manner that the whites do, when they do not believe what is told them!" The council then proceeded, and the pipe of peace was smoked.

Here, for the first time, I touched the goose quill to the treaty—not knowing, however, that, by that act, I consented to give away my village. Had that been explained to me, I should have opposed it, and never would have signed their treaty, as my recent conduct will clearly prove.[1]

What do we know of the manner of the laws and customs of the white people? They might buy our bodies for dissection, and we would touch the goose quill to confirm it, without knowing what we are doing. This was the case with myself and people in touching the goose quill the first time.

* * *

I returned to my hunting ground, after an absence of one moon. * * * In a short time we came up to our village, and found that the whites had not left it—but that others had come, and that the greater part of our corn-fields had been enclosed. When we landed, the whites appeared displeased because we had come back. We repaired the lodges that had been left standing, and built others. Ke-o-kuck came to the village; but his object was to persuade others to follow him to the Ioway. He had accomplished nothing towards making arrangements for us to remain, or to exchange other lands for our village. There was no more friendship existing between us. I looked upon him as a coward, and no brave, to abandon his village to be occupied by strangers. What *right* had these people to our village, and our fields, which the Great Spirit had given us to live upon?

1. The treaty of May 13, 1816, in which the Sauk of the Rock River reaffirmed the treaty of 1804. But as is clear from Black Hawk's account, misunderstandings persisted.

My reason teaches me that *land cannot be sold*. The Great Spirit gave it to his children to live upon, and cultivate, as far as is necessary for their subsistence; and so long as they occupy and cultivate it, they have the right to the soil—but if they voluntarily leave it, then any other people have a right to settle upon it. Nothing can be sold, but such things as can be carried away.

In consequence of the improvements of the intruders on our fields, we found considerable difficulty to get ground to plant a little corn. Some of the whites permitted us to plant small patches in the fields they had fenced, keeping all the best ground for themselves. Our women had great difficulty in climbing their fences, (being unaccustomed to the kind,) and were ill-treated if they left a rail down.

One of my old friends thought he was safe. His corn-field was on a small island of Rock river. He planted his corn; it came up well—but the white man saw it!—he wanted the island, and took his team over, ploughed up the corn, and re-planted it for himself! The old man shed tears; not for himself, but the distress his family would be in if they raised no corn.

The white people brought whisky into our village, made our people drunk, and cheated them out of their horses, guns, and traps! This fraudulent system was carried to such an extent that I apprehended serious difficulties might take place, unless a stop was put to it. Consequently, I visited all the whites and begged them not to sell whisky to my people. One of them continued the practice openly. I took a party of my young men, went to his house, and took out his barrel and broke in the head and turned out the whisky. I did this for fear some of the whites might be killed by my people when drunk.

Our people were treated badly by the whites on many occasions. At one time, a white man beat one of our women cruelly, for pulling a few suckers of corn out of his field, to suck, when hungry! At another time, one of our young men was beat with clubs by two white men for opening a fence which crossed our road, to take his horse through. His shoulder blade was broken, and his body badly bruised, from which he soon after *died!*

Bad, and cruel, as our people were treated by the whites, not one of them was hurt or molested by any of my band. I hope this will prove that we are a peaceable people—having permitted ten men to take possession of our corn-fields; prevent us from planting corn; burn and destroy our lodges; ill-treat our women; and *beat to death* our men, without offering resistance to their barbarous cruelties. This is a lesson worthy for the white man to learn: to use forbearance when injured.

We acquainted our agent daily with our situation, and through him, the great chief at St. Louis—and hoped that something would be done for us. The whites were *complaining* at the same time that *we* were *intruding* upon *their rights!* THEY made themselves out the *injured* party, and *we* the *intruders!* and called loudly to the great war chief to protect *their* property!

How smooth must be the language of the whites, when they can make right look like wrong, and wrong like right.

During this summer, I happened at Rock Island, when a great chief arrived, (whom I had known as the great chief of Illinois, [governor Cole,] in company with another chief, who, I have been told, is a great writer, [judge Jas. Hall]. I called upon them and begged to explain to them the grievances under which me and my people were laboring, hoping that they could do something for us. The great chief, however, did not seem disposed to council with me. He said he was no longer the great chief of Illinois—that his children had selected another father in his stead, and that he now only ranked as they did. I was surprised at this talk, as I had always heard that he was a good, brave, and great chief. But the white people never appear to be satisfied. When they get a good father, they hold councils, (at the suggestion of some bad, ambitious man, who wants the place himself,) and conclude, among themselves, that this man, or some other equally ambitious, would make a better father than they have, and nine times out of ten they don't get as good a one again.

I insisted on explaining to these two chiefs the true situation of my people. They gave their assent: I rose and made a speech, in which I explained to them the treaty made by Quàsh-quà-me, and three of our braves, according to the manner the trader and others had explained it to me. I then told them that Quàsh-quà-me and his party *denied*, positively, having ever sold my village; and that, as I had never known them to *lie*, I was determined to keep it in possession.

I told them that the white people had already entered our village, *burnt our lodges, destroyed our fences, ploughed up our corn, and beat our people:* that they had brought *whisky* into our country, *made our people drunk,* and taken from them their *horses, guns,* and *traps;* and that I had borne all this injury, without suffering any of my braves to raise a hand against the whites.

My object in holding this council, was to get the opinion of these two chiefs, as to the best course for me to pursue. I had appealed in vain, time after time, to our agent, who regularly represented our situation to the great chief at St. Louis, whose duty it was to call upon our Great Father to have justice done to us; but instead of this, we are told *that the white people want our country, and we must leave it to them!*

I did not think it possible that our Great Father wished us to leave our village, where we had lived so long, and where the bones of so many of our people had been laid. The great chief said that, as he was no longer a chief, he could do nothing for us; and felt sorry that it was not in his power to aid us—nor did he know how to advise us. Neither of them could do any thing for us; but both evidently appeared very sorry. It would give me great pleasure, at all times, to take these two chiefs by the hand.

That fall I paid a visit to the agent, before we started to our hunting grounds, to hear if he had any good news for me. He had news! He said that the land on which our village stood was now ordered to be sold to individuals; and that, when sold, *our right* to remain, by treaty, would be at an end, and that if we returned next spring, we would be *forced* to remove!

1833

PETALESHARO

Petalesharo (1797?–1874)—the name means "generous chief" or "man chief"— was a Skidi (also called Loup) Pawnee, one of four bands of the Pawnee Nation, which occupied lands in the old Missouri Territory. From October 1821 until March 1822, he was one of several Native people brought to Washington for an extended visit. During that time, the *National Daily Intelligencer* published an article called "Anecdote of a Pawnee Chief," which told of Petalesharo's successful efforts, in 1817 and 1820, to prevent young women captured from other tribes from being sacrificed in the Morning Star Ceremony. (The Skidi Pawnees were one of the very few tribes north of what is now the Mexican border to practice human sacrifice.) This account made him a most sought-after person. Petalesharo was one of the first Native people to be painted by Charles Bird King for the McKenney-Hall Indian Gallery (the paintings were reproduced in the gallery's *History of the Indian Tribes of North America* published in 1838–44); he was also painted by Samuel F.B. Morse, better known for his invention of Morse code.

The speeches printed here were delivered on February 4, 1822, at a conference attended by President James Monroe. They were first published by James Buchanan, British consul for the state of New York, in his *Sketches of the North American Indians* (1824). The first, which is identified as having been delivered by "The Pawnee Chief," is the speech usually referred to as "Petalesharo's Speech." But it is followed in Buchanan by a speech assigned to a "Pawnee Loup Chief," a more likely designation for Petalesharo. Although the date and the occasion for both of these are certain, it is not clear who translated and transcribed the speeches—and, it should be stressed, we do not know whether "Petalesharo's Speech" was in fact delivered by him or by an unnamed "Pawnee Chief." The speaker, whoever he may be, like Red Jacket (and others) before him, offers a "separatist" view of religion and culture, asserting that while the Great Father of the whites may be fine for them, "there is still *another* Great Father . . . *the Father of us all*," and it is to him that Native peoples continue to adhere. The second speech combines what is probably intended simply as good advice for the whites with a warrior's brief statement of his prowess.

The text is from Buchanan's *Sketches of the North American Indians* (1824).

Speech of the Pawnee Chief

My Great Father:—I have travelled a great distance to see you—I have seen you and my heart rejoices. I have heard your words—they have entered one ear and shall not escape the other, and I will carry them to my people as pure as they came from your mouth.

My Great Father:—I am going to speak the truth. The Great Spirit looks down upon us, and I call *Him* to witness all that may pass between us on this occasion. If I am here now and have seen your people, your houses, your vessels on the big lake, and a great many wonderful things far beyond my comprehension, which appear to have been made by the Great Spirit and placed in your hands, I am indebted to my Father here, who invited me from home, under whose wings I have been protected.[1] Yes, my Great Father, I have travelled with your chief; I have followed him, and trod in his tracks; but there is still *another* Great Father *to whom I am much indebted—it is the Father of us all.* Him who made us and placed us on this earth. I feel grateful to the Great Spirit for strengthening my heart for such an undertaking, and for preserving the life which he gave me. The Great Spirit made us all—he made my skin red, and yours white; he placed us on this earth, and intended that we should live differently from each other.

He made the whites to cultivate the earth, and feed on domestic animals; but he made us, red skins, to rove through the uncultivated woods and plains; to feed on wild animals; and to dress with their skins. He also intended that we should go to war—to take scalps—*steal horses from* and triumph over our enemies—cultivate peace at home, and promote the happiness of each other. I believe there are no people of any colour on this earth who do not believe in the Great Spirit—in rewards, and in punishments. We worship him, but we worship him not as you do. We differ from you in appearance and manners as well as in our customs; and we differ from you in our religion; we have no large houses as you have to worship the Great Spirit in; if we had them to-day, we should want others to-morrow, for we have not, like you, a fixed habitation—we have no settled home except our villages, where we remain but two moons in twelve. We, like animals, rove through the country, whilst you whites reside between us and heaven but still, my Great Father, we love the Great Spirit—we acknowledge his supreme power—our peace, our health, and our happiness depend upon him, and our lives belong to him—he made us and he can destroy us.

My Great Father:—Some of your good chiefs, as they are called (missionaries,) have proposed to send some of their good people among us to change our habits, to make us work and live like the white people. I will not tell a lie—I am going to tell the truth. You love your country—you love your people—you love the manner in which they live, and you think your people brave.—I am like you, my Great Father, I love my country—I love my people— I love the manner in which we live, and think myself and warriors brave. Spare me then, my Father; let me enjoy my country, and pursue the buffalo, and the beaver, and the other wild animals of our country, and I will trade their skins with your people. I have grown up, and lived thus long without work—I am in hopes you will suffer me to die without it. We have plenty of buffalo, beaver, deer and other wild animals—we have also an abundance of horses—we have every thing we want—we have plenty of land, if you will keep your people off of it. My father has a piece on which he lives (Council Bluffs) and we wish him to enjoy it—we have enough without it—but we wish him to live near us to give us good counsel—to keep our ears and eyes open that we may continue to pursue the right road—the road to happiness. He settles all differences between us and the whites, between the red skins themselves—he makes the whites do justice to the red skins, and he makes the red skins do justice to the whites. He saves the effusion of human blood, and restores peace and happiness on the land. You have already sent us a

---

1. Pointing to Major O'Fallon [Buchanan's note].

father; it is enough he knows us and we know him—we have confidence in him—we keep our eye constantly upon him, and since we have heard your words, we will listen more attentively to *his*.

It is too soon, my Great Father, to send those good men among us. *We are not starving yet*—we wish you to permit us to enjoy the chase until the game of our country is exhausted—until the wild animals become extinct. Let us exhaust our present resources before you make us toil and interrupt our happiness—let me continue to live as I have done, and after I have passed to the Good or Evil Spirit from off the wilderness of my present life, the subsistence of my children may become so precarious as to need and embrace the assistance of those good people.

There was a time when we did not know the whites—our wants were then fewer than they are now. They were always within our control—we had then seen nothing which we could not get. Before our intercourse with the *whites* (who have caused such a destruction in our game,) we could lie down to sleep, and when we awoke we would find the buffalo feeding around our camp—but now we are killing them for their skins, and feeding the wolves with their flesh, to make our children cry over their bones.

Here, My Great Father, is a pipe which I present you, as I am accustomed to present pipes to all the red skins in peace with us. It is filled with such tobacco as we were accustomed to smoke before we knew the white people. It is pleasant, and the spontaneous growth of the most remote parts of our country. I know that the robes, leggins, mockasins, bear-claws, &c., are of little value to you, but we wish you to have them deposited and preserved in some conspicuous part of your lodge, so that when we are gone and the sod turned over our bones, if our children should visit this place, as we do now, they may see and recognize with pleasure the deposites of their fathers; and reflect on the times that are past.

Speech of the Pawnee Loup Chief

My Great Father:—Whenever I see a white man amongst us without a protector, I tremble for him. I am aware of the ungovernable disposition of some of our young men, and when I see an inexperienced white man, I am always afraid they will make me cry. I now begin to love your people, and, as I love my own people too, I am unwilling that any blood should be spilt between us. You are unacquainted with our fashions, and we are unacquainted with yours; and when any of your people come among us, I am always afraid that they will be struck on the head like dogs, as we should be here amongst you, but for our father in whose tracks we tread. When your people come among us, they should come as we come among you, with some one to protect them, whom we know and who knows us. Until this chief came amongst us, three winters since, we roved through the plains only thirsting for each other's blood—we were blind—we could not see the right road, and we hunted to destroy each other. We were always feeling for obstacles, and every thing we felt we thought one. Our warriors were always going to and coming from war. I myself have killed and scalped in every direction. I have often triumphed over my enemies.

ELIAS BOUDINOT

Elias Boudinot (1804?–1839) was born at Oothcaloga, a Cherokee "progressive" town, in northwestern Georgia. His birth name was Gallegina, and he was also called Buck Watie. His father, Oo'watie, or David Watie, sent him at the age of six to a nearby Moravian mission school, where he continued until he was seventeen, at which time he set out north for another mission school, this one in Cornwall, Connecticut. It was on this trip that Buck Watie met the elderly Elias Boudinot, who had been a member of the Continental Congress and was at the time president of the American Bible Society. Consistent with an old Cherokee practice of changing names and with a newer Cherokee practice of adopting the names of prominent whites, Buck Watie became Elias Boudinot.

Although his uncle was the "progressive" assimilationist Major Ridge, whose picture says a good deal about him (see the color insert to this volume), and his younger brother, Stand Watie, joined white Southerners to become the last Confederate general to surrender to the North in the Civil War, Boudinot opposed removal until some time in 1832. In what is probably his best-known work, "An Address to the Whites," delivered in Philadelphia in 1826, Boudinot makes the same case that the "Memorial" of the Cherokee Council would make to Congress opposing removal: he insists that not only are his people able to attain Christianity and "civilization" but that they are well on the way to those attainments. About two years after the passage of the Indian Removal Act in 1830 and, in particular, once Georgia had instituted a lottery to dispose of Cherokee lands to white citizens of the state, Boudinot concluded that further resistance to removal was hopeless.

In 1835, he, his uncle Major Ridge, and a small number of wealthy Cherokee planters met at New Echota, where, on December 29, they signed the Treaty of New Echota, agreeing to exchange Cherokee lands in the southeast for land in Indian Country, present-day Oklahoma. Boudinot and his family went west before the Trail of Tears and so were already established when the last of the Cherokee people to survive the forced march arrived in Indian Country in early spring 1839. In June of that year, several Cherokees came to Boudinot to ask for medicine. Two followed him as he led them to the mission dispensary and then attacked him with a knife and a tomahawk, leaving him to die. That same day, his relatives Major Ridge and John Ridge were also killed for their part in signing the treaty. The murderers very likely acted in accord with a traditional practice of vengeance, taking lives in recompense for the lives of those who had died on the trail, and also in accord with a law passed by the Cherokee Council in 1829 making it a capital crime to cede Cherokee lands.

The selection printed here is from the first issue of the *Cherokee Phoenix*, dated February 21, 1828. Boudinot edited the paper until 1832, when the Cherokee Council asked him to withdraw because of his support for removal. The *Phoenix* was the first American newspaper to print an Indian language (in the syllabary that the Cherokee silversmith Sequoyah [c. 1770–1843] had invented in 1821); it also printed articles in English. Boudinot alerts his readers, white and Indian, to the fact that "the design of this paper . . . is [for] the benefit of the Cherokees."

From the Cherokee Phoenix

To the Public

FEBRUARY 21, 1828

We are happy in being able, at length, to issue the first number of our paper, although after a longer delay than we anticipated. This delay has been owing to unavoidable circumstances, which, we think, will be sufficient to acquit us, and though our readers and patrons may be wearied in the expectation of gratifying their eyes on this paper of no ordinary novelty, yet we hope their patience will not be so exhausted, but that they will give it a calm perusal and pass upon it a candid judgment. It is far from our expectation that it will meet with entire and universal approbation, particularly from those who consider learning and science necessary to the merits of newspapers. Such must not expect to be gratified here, for the merits, (if merits they can be called,) on which our paper is expected to exist, are not alike with those which keep alive the political and religious papers of the day. We lay no claim to extensive information; and we sincerely hope, this public disclosure will save us from the severe criticisms, to which our ignorance of many things, will frequently expose us, in the future of our editorial labors.— Let the public but consider our motives, and the design of this paper, which is, the benefit of the Cherokees, and we are sure, those who wish well to the Indian race, will keep out of view all failings and deficiencies of the Editor, and give a prompt support to the first paper ever published in an Indian country, and under the direction of some remnants of those, who by the most mysterious course of providence, have dwindled into oblivion. To prevent us from the like destiny, is certainly a laudable undertaking, which the Christian, the Patriot, and the Philanthropist will not be ashamed to aid. Many are now engaged, by various means and with various success, in attempting to rescue, not only us, but all our kindred tribes, from the impending danger which has been so fatal to our forefathers; and we are happy to be in a situation to tender them our public acknowledgments for their unwearied efforts. Our present undertaking is intended to be nothing more than a feeble auxiliary to these efforts. Those therefore, who are engaged for the good of the Indians of every tribe, and who pray that salvation, peace, and the comforts of civilized life may be extended to every Indian fire side on this continent, will consider us as co-workers together in their benevolent labors. To them we make our appeal for patronage, and pledge ourselves to encourage and assist them, in whatever appears to be for the benefit of the Aborigines.

In the commencement of our labours, it is due to our readers that we should acquaint them with the general principles, which we have prescribed to ourselves as rules in conducting this paper. These principles we shall accordingly state briefly. It may, however, be proper to observe that the establishment which has been lately purchased, principally with the charities of our white brethren, is the property of the Nation, and that the paper, which is now offered to the public, is patronized by, and under the direction of, the Cherokee Legislature, as will be seen in the Prospectus already before the public. As servants, we are bound to that body, from which, however, we have not received any instructions, but are left at liberty to form such regulations

The masthead of the *Cherokee Phoenix,* the first newspaper in both a Native language and English, illustrates the complex cultural and political situation of the Cherokee Nation at the time. The two words on either side of the phoenix are in the Cherokee syllabary invented by Sequoyah. They are pronounced roughly *Tsa-la-gi Tsi-le-hi-sa-ni.* The first word means "Cherokee"—as in the English below it—but the second word—unlike the English below it—does not mean "Phoenix" (there is no word in Cherokee for "phoenix"), but, rather, "I was down and I have risen" or "I will rise again" (the latter invokes both a phoenix *and* Christ). In putting the word PROTECTION between the bird's wings, the Cherokees mean to remind the federal government of its responsibility to protect them from the threats of the state of Georgia.

for our conduct as will appear to us most conducive to the interests of the people, for whose benefit, this paper has been established.

As the Phoenix is a national newspaper, we shall feel ourselves bound to devote it to national purposes. "The laws and public documents of the Nation," and matters relating to the welfare and condition of the Cherokees as a people, will be faithfully published in English and Cherokee.

As the liberty of the press is so essential to the improvement of the mind, we shall consider our paper, a *free paper,* with, however, proper and usual restrictions. We shall reserve to ourselves the liberty of rejecting such communications as tend to evil, and such as are too intemperate and too personal. But the columns of this paper shall always be open to free and temperate discussions on matters of politics, religion, &c.

We shall avoid as much as possible, controversy on disputed doctrinal points in religion. Though we have our particular belief on this important subject, and perhaps are as strenuous upon it, as some of our brethren of a different faith, yet we conscientiously think, & in this thought we are supported by men of judgment that it would be injudicious, perhaps highly pernicious, to introduce to this people, the various minor differences of Christians. Our object is not sectarian, and if we had a wish to support, in our paper, the denomination with which we have the honor and privilege of being connected, yet we know our incompetency for the task.

We will not unnecessarily intermeddle with the politics and affairs of our neighbors. As we have no particular interest in the concerns of the surrounding states, we shall only expose ourselves to contempt and ridicule by improper intrusion. And though at times, we should do ourselves injustice, to be silent, on matters of great interest to the Cherokees, yet we will not return railing for railing, but consult mildness, for we have been taught to believe, that "A soft answer turneth away wrath; but grievous words stir up anger." The unpleasant controversy existing with the state of Georgia, of which, many of our readers are aware, will frequently make our situation trying, by having hard sayings and threatenings thrown out against us, a specimen of which will be found in our next. We pray God that we may be delivered from such spirit.

In regard to the controversy with Georgia, and the present policy of the General Government, in removing, and concentrating the Indians, out of the limits of any state, which, by the way, appears to be gaining strength, we will invariably and faithfully state the feelings of the majority of our people. Our views, as a people, on this subject, have been sadly misrepresented. These views we do not wish to conceal, but are willing that the public should know what we think of this policy, which, in our opinion, if carried into effect, will prove pernicious to us.

* * *

In fine, we shall pay a sacred regard to truth, and avoid, as much as possible, that partiality to which we shall be exposed. In relating facts of a local nature, whether political, moral, or religious, we shall take care that exaggeration shall not be our crime. We shall also feel ourselves bound to correct all mistatements, relating to the present condition of the Cherokees.

How far we shall be successful in advancing the improvement of our people, is not now for us to decide. We hope, however, our efforts will not be altogether in vain.—Now is the moment when mere speculation on the practicability of civilizing us is out of the question. Sufficient and repeated evidence has been given, that Indians can be reclaimed from a savage state, and that with proper advantages, they are as capable of improvement in mind as any other people; and let it be remembered, notwithstanding the assertions of those who talk to the contrary, that this improvement can be made, not only by the Cherokees, but by all the Indians, *in their present locations*. We are rendered bold in making this assertion, by considering the history of our people within the last fifteen years. There was a time within our remembrance, when darkness was sadly prevalent, and ignorance abounded amongst us—when strong and deep rooted prejudices were directed against many things relating to civilized life—and when it was thought a disgrace, for a Cherokee to appear in the costume of a white man. We mention these things not by way of boasting, but to shew our readers that it is not a visionary thing to attempt to civilize and christianize all the Indians, but highly practicable.

* * *

We would now commit our feeble efforts to the good will and indulgence of the public, praying that God will attend them with his blessing, and hoping for that happy period, when all the Indian tribes of America shall arise, Phoenix like, from their ashes, and when the terms, "Indian depredation," "warwhoop," "scalping knife" and the like, shall become obsolete, and for ever be "buried deep under ground."

THE CHEROKEE MEMORIALS

I n 1828, Andrew Jackson, largely on his reputation as an Indian fighter, was elected president of the United States. In 1829, gold was discovered in Dahlonega on the western boundary of the Cherokee Nation in the state of Georgia. Georgia had for some time wished to rid itself of its Indian population, and the time seemed right to press the issue. Bills for the removal of the eastern Indians were introduced in both houses of Congress early in 1830; debate on the Removal Bill had begun in the House on February 24.

Anticipating these developments, the Cherokee Council had prepared a "memorial"—essentially a petition to Congress—as early as November 1829, which was received by the House in February of the following year, shortly before the official debate began. The memorial was probably authored for the most part by the clerk of the council, John Ridge, who had not yet broken with the "traditionalist" Cherokees, led by the principal chief John Ross, who were firmly opposed to removal. The memorial begins with what must be an intentional, although unstated, reference to the Declaration of Independence. Whereas the Declaration made known to the world the "long rain of abuses and usurpations" for which the British king George III was responsible, the Cherokee memorial establishes the wrongs done by his namesake state, Georgia, petitioning the Congress of the United States—the same body that had adopted the Declaration—for redress of grievances. Although the American colonists had had to *declare* their independence, the Cherokees instead *affirm* theirs. As they demonstrate, they have always been treated by the American colonials and the United States as a sovereign nation.

Acknowledging that Georgia and the president have the power to force them to unfamiliar land west of the Mississippi, the Cherokee Council insists that the use of such power would lead to an unjust and unhappy fate for the Cherokee Nation. In the florid language of the period, the council offers its vision of Cherokee advancement "in civilized life . . . science and Christian knowledge," on the lands they have long occupied.

This vision did not prevail. Basing his authority on the Treaty of New Echota— signed in 1835 by a minority of Cherokees—Jackson ordered the Cherokees to remove by the spring of 1838. Some moved west before that date. But the vast majority of the eastern Cherokee Nation refused to leave their homes. Thus it was that federal troops under the command of General Winfield Scott came to enforce the treaty. In the fall and winter of 1838–39, some thirteen thousand Cherokees were driven westward on what has come to be known as the Trail of Tears. Roughly one-third of them, about four thousand people, died en route. The survivors reached Indian Country, in what would eventually become Oklahoma, in the early spring of 1839.

Memorial of the Cherokee Council, November 5, 1829

To the Honorable Senate and House of Representatives of the
United States of America in Congress assembled:

We, the representatives of the people of the Cherokee nation, in general council convened, compelled by a sense of duty we owe to ourselves and nation, and confiding in the justice of your honorable bodies, address and make known to you the grievances which disturb the quiet repose and harmony of our citizens, and the dangers by which we are surrounded. Extraordinary as this course may appear to you, the circumstances that have imposed upon us this duty we deem sufficient to justify the measure; and our safety as individuals, and as a nation, require that we should be heard by the immediate representatives of the people of the United States, whose humanity and magnanimity, by permission and will of Heaven, may yet preserve us from ruin and extinction.

The authorities of Georgia have recently and unexpectedly assumed a doctrine, horrid in its aspect, and fatal in its consequences to us, and utterly at variance with the laws of nations, of the United States, and the subsisting treaties between us, and the known history of said State, of this nation, and of the United States. She claims the exercise of sovereignty over this nation; and has threatened and decreed the extension of her jurisdictional limits over our people. The Executive of the United States, through the Secretary of War,[1] in a letter to our delegation of the 18th April last, has recognised this right to be abiding in, and possessed by, the State of Georgia; by the Declaration of Independence, and the treaty of peace concluded between the United States and Great Britain in 1783; and which it is urged vested in her all the rights of sovereignty pertaining to Great Britain, and which, in time previously, she claimed and exercised, within the limits of what constituted the "thirteen United States." It is a subject of vast importance to know whether the power of self-government abided in the Cherokee nation at the discovery of America, three hundred and thirty-seven years ago; and whether it was in any manner affected or destroyed by the charters of European potentates. It is evident from facts deducible from known history, that the Indians were found here by the white man, in the enjoyment of plenty and peace, and all the rights of soil and domain, inherited from their ancestors from time immemorial, well furnished with kings, chiefs, and warriors, the bulwarks of liberty, and the pride of their race. Great Britain established with them relationships of friendship and alliance, and at no time did she treat them as subjects, and as tenants at will, to her power. In war she fought them as a separate people, and they resisted her as a nation. In peace, she spoke the language of friendship, and they replied in the voice of independence, and frequently assisted her as allies, at their choice to fight her enemies in their own way and discipline, subject to the control of their own chiefs, and unaccountable to European officers and military law. Such was the connexion of this nation to Great Britain, to wit, that of friendship, and not allegiance, to the period of the declaration of Independence by the United States, and during the Revolutionary contest, down to the treaty of peace between the United States and Great Britain, forty-six years ago, when she abandoned all hopes of conquest, and at the same time abandoned her Cherokee allies to the difficulties in which they had been involved, either to continue the war, or procure peace on the best terms they could, and close the scenes of carnage and blood, that had so long

---

1. I.e., John Eaton. President Andrew Jackson (the "Executive of the United States") believed that treating the Indians as sovereign nations was a mistake and that Indian occupancy of lands within the United States was simply owing to the generosity and goodwill of the federal government and the states in question.

been witnessed and experienced by both parties. Peace was at last concluded at Hopewell, in '85, under the administration of Washington, by "the Commissioners, Plenipotentiaries of the United States in Congress assembled"; and the Cherokees were received "into the favor and protection of the United States of America." It remains to be proved, under a view of all these circumstances, and the knowledge we have of history, how our right to self-government was affected and destroyed by the Declaration of Independence, which never noticed the subject of Cherokee sovereignty; and the treaty of peace, in '83, between Great Britain and the United States, to which the Cherokees were not a party; but maintained hostilities on their part to the treaty of Hopewell, afterwards concluded. If, as it is stated by the Hon. Secretary of War, that the Cherokees were mere tenants at will,[2] and only permitted to enjoy possession of the soil to pursue game; and if the States of North Carolina and Georgia were sovereigns in truth and in right over us; why did President Washington send "Commissioners Plenipotentiaries" to treat with the subjects of those States? Why did they permit the chiefs and warriors to enter into treaty, when, if they were subjects, they had grossly rebelled and revolted from their allegiance? And why did not those sovereigns make their lives pay the forfeit of their guilt, agreeably to the laws of said States? The answer must be plain—they were not subjects, but a distinct nation, and in that light viewed by Washington, and by all the people of the Union, at that period. In the first and second articles of the Hopewell treaty, and the third article of the Holston treaty,[3] the United States and the Cherokee nation were bound to a mutual exchange of prisoners taken during the war; which incontrovertibly proves the possession of sovereignty by *both* contracting parties. It ought to be remembered too, in the conclusions of the treaties to which we have referred, and most of the treaties subsisting between the United States and this nation, that the phraseology, composition, etc. was always written by the Commissioners, on the part of the United States, for obvious reasons: as the Cherokees were unacquainted with letters. Again, in the Holston treaty, eleventh article, the following remarkable evidence is contained that our nation is not under the jurisdiction of any State: "If any citizen or inhabitant of the United States, or of either of the territorial districts of the United States, shall go into any town, settlement, or territory, belonging to the Cherokees, and shall there commit any crime upon, or trespass against, the person or property of any peaceable and friendly Indian or Indians, which, *if committed within the jurisdiction of any State, or within the jurisdiction of either of the*

---

2. I.e., the will of the states and the federal government "to allow" the Cherokees to live on their own ancestral lands. These lands came into the possession of the United States as a result of the Declaration of Independence and victory in the Revolutionary War. The Treaty of Hopewell, signed November 28, 1785, was the first treaty between the Cherokees and the United States enacted after the Revolutionary War. It established the boundaries of Cherokee lands and was negotiated as an agreement between two sovereign nations. The Cherokees refer to the treaty to show that they were formerly recognized as an independent nation and should still be treated as

such. This argument remains in force today.
3. Signed July 2, 1791, this treaty gave the federal government (not the states) exclusive right to regulate all citizens' trade with the Cherokees and redrew the boundaries, much encroached on by the settlers, of Cherokee lands. It also affirmed "Perpetual peace between the United States and the Cherokee Nation," and forbade non-Cherokee persons from hunting on or traversing Cherokee lands without a passport issued by the federal government. The Cherokees cite this as further evidence of their having been treated as a sovereign nation in the past.

said districts, against a citizen or any white inhabitant thereof, would be punishable by the laws of such State or district, such offender or offenders shall be proceeded against in the same manner as if the offence had been committed *within the jurisdiction of the State or district* to which he or they may belong, against a citizen or white inhabitant thereof." The power of a State may put our national existence under its feet, and coerce us into her jurisdiction; but it would be contrary to legal right, and the plighted faith of the United States' Government. It is said by Georgia and the Honorable Secretary of War, that one sovereignty cannot exist within another, and, therefore, we must yield to the stronger power; but is not this doctrine favorable to our Government, which does not interfere with that of any other? Our sovereignty and right of enforcing legal enactments, extend no further than our territorial limits, and that of Georgia is, and has always terminated at, her limits. The constitution of the United States (article 6) contains these words: "All treaties made under the authority of the United States shall be the supreme law of the land, and the judges in every State shall be bound thereby, any thing in the laws or constitution of any State to the contrary notwithstanding." The sacredness of treaties, made under the authority of the United States, is paramount and supreme, stronger than the laws and constitution of any State. The jurisdiction, then, of our nation over its soil is settled by the laws, treaties, and constitution of the United States, and has been exercised from time out of memory.

Georgia has objected to the adoption, on our part, of a constitutional form of government, and which has in no wise violated the intercourse and connexion which bind us to the United States, its constitution, and the treaties thereupon founded, and in existence between us. As a distinct nation, notwithstanding any unpleasant feelings it might have created to a neighboring State, we had a right to improve our Government, suitable to the moral, civil, and intellectual advancement of our people; and had we anticipated any notice of it, it was the voice of encouragement by an approving world. We would, also, while on this subject, refer your attention to the memorial and protest submitted before your honorable bodies, during the last session of Congress, by our delegation then at Washington.

Permit us, also, to make known to you the aggrieved and unpleasant situation under which we are placed by the claim which Georgia has set up to a large portion of our territory, under the treaty of the Indian Springs concluded with the late General M'Intosh[4] and his party; and which was declared void, and of no effect, by a subsequent treaty between the Creek Nation and the United States, at Washington City. The President of the United States, through the Secretary of War, assured our delegation, that, so far as he understood the Cherokees had rights, protection should be afforded; and, respecting the intrusions on our lands, he had been advised, "and instructions had been forwarded to the agent of the Cherokees, directing

4. General William McIntosh was a Creek Indian leader who signed the Treaty of Indian Springs on February 12, 1785. The treaty ceded Creek lands to the state of Georgia and agreed to the removal of the Creeks to west of the Mississippi. But the Creeks had earlier denied McIntosh's right to act on their behalf and did not honor the treaty. McIntosh was assassinated, and John Ridge and David Vann were engaged to negotiate a new treaty, the "subsequent treaty" referred to later in the sentence.

him to cause their removal; and earnestly hoped, that, on this matter, all cause for future complaint would cease, and the order prove effectual." In consequence of the agent's neglecting to comply with the instructions, and a suspension of the order made by the Secretary afterwards, our border citizens are at this time placed under the most unfortunate circumstances, by the intrusions of citizens of the United States, and which are almost daily increasing, in consequence of the suspension of the once contemplated "effectual order." Many of our people are experiencing all the evils of personal insult, and, in some instances, expulsion from their homes, and loss of property, from the unrestrained intruders let loose upon us, and the encouragement they are allowed to enjoy, under the last order to the agent for this nation, which amounts to a suspension of the force of treaties, and the wholesome operation of the intercourse laws[5] of the United States. The reason alleged by the War Department for this suspension is, that it had been requested so to do, until the claim the State of Georgia has made to a portion of the Cherokee country be determined; and the intruders are to remain unmolested within the border limits of this nation. We beg leave to protest against this unprecedented procedure. If the State of Georgia has a claim to any portion of our lands, and is entitled by law and justice to them, let her seek through a legal channel to establish it; and we do hope that the United States will not suffer her to take possession of them forcibly, and investigate her claim afterwards.

Arguments to effect the emigration of our people, and to escape the troubles and disquietudes incident to a residence contiguous to the whites, have been urged upon us, and the arm of protection has been withheld, that we may experience still deeper and ampler proofs of the correctness of the doctrine; but we still adhere to what is right and agreeable to ourselves; and our attachment to the soil of our ancestors is too strong to be shaken. We have been invited to a retrospective view of the past history of Indians, who have melted away before the light of civilization, and the mountains of difficulties that have opposed our race in their advancement in civilized life. We have done so; and, while we deplore the fate of thousands of our complexion and kind, we rejoice that our nation stands and grows a lasting monument of God's mercy, and a durable contradiction to the misconceived opinion that the aborigines are incapable of civilization. The opposing mountains, that cast fearful shadows in the road of Cherokee improvement, have dispersed into vernal clouds; and our people stand adorned with the flowers of achievement flourishing around them, and are encouraged to secure the attainment of all that is useful in science and Christian knowledge.

Under the fostering care of the United States we have thus prospered; and shall we expect approbation, or shall we sink under the displeasure and rebukes of our enemies?

We now look with earnest expectation to your honorable bodies for redress, and that our national existence may not be extinguished before a prompt and effectual interposition is afforded in our behalf. The faith of your Government is solemnly pledged for our protection against all illegal oppressions, so long as we remain firm to our treaties; and that we have, for

5. Laws regulating trade.

a long series of years, proved to be true and loyal friends, the known history of past events abundantly proves. Your Chief Magistrate himself[6] has borne testimony of our devotedness in supporting the cause of the United States, during their late conflict with a foreign foe. It is with reluctant and painful feelings that circumstances have at length compelled us to seek from you the promised protection, for the preservation of our rights and privileges. This resort to us is a last one, and nothing short of the threatening evils and dangers that beset us could have forced it upon the nation but it is a right we surely have, and in which we cannot be mistaken—that of appealing for justice and humanity to the United States, under whose kind and fostering care we have been led to the present degree of civilization, and the enjoyment of its consequent blessings. Having said thus much, with patience we shall await the final issue of your wise deliberations.

6. John Marshall, chief justice of the Supreme Court.

RALPH WALDO EMERSON

Ralph Waldo Emerson (1803–1882) was perhaps the most important American thinker of the first half of the nineteenth century and a strong influence on Thoreau and Walt Whitman, among others. Although he knew some of the New England abolitionists, he did not himself become active in the cause until the 1850s. In regard to the American Indians, Emerson seems to have shared the general eastern distaste for President Andrew Jackson's removal policies, although it is only in his letter to Jackson's successor, Martin Van Buren, reprinted here, that he committed himself publicly to the Cherokees' cause.

Emerson seems to have learned of the imminent removal of the Cherokees only on April 19, 1838, writing in his journal, "I can do nothing. Why shriek? Why strike ineffectual blows?" Yet the following day he composed the first draft of his letter to Van Buren, noting in his journal, "The amount of [it], [to] be sure, is merely a Scream but sometimes a scream is better than a thesis." The following day he recorded his sense that this was "A deliverance that does not deliver the soul." Clearly, writing this letter was not an easy thing for him to do.

The letter does not seem ever to have been sent directly to Van Buren. Under the heading of "Communication," it was published, "with some reluctance" on the part of the proprietors of the *National Daily Intelligencer*, in the issue of May 14, 1838, next appearing on May 19 in the *Yeoman's Gazette* in Concord. The earliest version we have been able to find is from the *New Bedford Mercury* of May 25, 1838, the source of the text below.

Letter to Martin Van Buren

President of the United States

CONCORD, Mass. 23d April, 1838.

Sir—The seat you fill, places you in a relation of credit and dearness to every citizen. By right, and natural position, every citizen is your friend. Before any acts contrary to his own judgement or interest have repelled the affections of any man, each may look with trust and loving anticipations to your government. Each has the highest right to call your attention to such subjects as are of a public nature and properly belong to the chief magistrate; and the good magistrate will feel a joy in meeting such confidence. In this belief, and at the instance of a few of my friends and neighbors, I crave of your patience a short hearing for their sentiments and my own; and the circumstance that my name will be utterly unknown to you, will only give the fairer chance to your equitable construction of what I have to say.

Sir, my communication respects the sinister rumours that fill this part of the country concerning the Cherokee people. The interest always felt in the Aboriginal Population—an interest naturally growing as that decays—has been heightened in regard to this tribe. Even in our distant state, some good rumor of their worth and civility has arrived. We have learned with joy their improvement in social arts. We have read their newspapers. We have seen some of them in our schools and colleges. In common with the great body of the American people we have witnessed with sympathy the painful labors of these red men to redeem their own race from the doom of eternal inferiority, and to borrow and domesticate in the tribe, the arts and customs of the caucasian race. And notwithstanding the unaccountable apathy with which of late years the Indians have been sometimes abandoned to their enemies, it is not to be doubted that it is the good pleasure and the understanding of all humane persons in the republic—of the men and the matrons sitting in the thriving independent families all over the land, that they shall be duly cared for, that they shall taste justice and love from all to whom we have delegated the office of dealing with them.

The newspapers now inform us, that, in December 1835, a treaty contracting for the exchange of all the Cherokee territory, was pretended to be made by an agent on the part of the United States with some persons appearing on the part of the Cherokees; that the fact afterwards transpired that these deputies did by no means represent the will of the nation, and that out of eighteen thousand souls composing the nation, fifteen thousand six hundred and sixty eight have protested against the so called Treaty. It now appears that the Government of the United States choose to hold the Cherokees to this sham treaty, and are proceeding to execute the same. Almost the entire Cherokee nation stand up and say, "This is not our act. Behold us. Here are we. Do not mistake that handful of deserters for us," and the American President and his Cabinet, the Senate and the House of Representatives neither hear these men nor see them, and are contracting to put this nation into carts and boats and to drag them over mountains and rivers to a wilderness at a vast distance beyond the Mississippi.—And a paper purporting to be an army order, taxes a month from this day, as the hour for this doleful removal.

In the name of God, Sir, we ask you if this be so? Do the newspapers rightly inform us? Men and women with pale and perplexed faces meet one another in streets and churches here, and ask if this be so? We have inquired if this be a gross misrepresentation from the party opposed to the Government and anxious to blacken it with the people. We have looked in newspapers of different parties, and find a horrid confirmation of the tale. We are slow to believe it. We hoped the Indians were misinformed and their remonstrance was premature, and will turn out to be a needless act of terror. The piety, the principle that is left in these United States,—if only its coarsest form, a regard to the speech of men, forbid us to entertain it as a fact. Such a dereliction of all faith and virtue, such a denial of justice and such deafness to screams for mercy, were never heard of in times of peace, and in the dealing of a nation with its own allies and wards, since the earth was made. Sir, does this Government think that the people of the United States are become savage and mad? From their mind are the sentiments of love and of a good nature wiped clean out? The soul of man, the justice, the mercy, that is the heart's heart in all men from Maine to Georgia, does abhor this business.

In speaking thus the sentiments of my neighbors and my own, perhaps I overstep the bounds of decorum. But would it not be a higher indecorum, coldly to argue a matter like this? We only state the fact that a crime is projected that confounds our understandings by its magnitude,—a crime that really deprives us as well as the Cherokees of a country, for how could we call the conspiracy that should crush these poor Indians, our Government, or the land that was cursed by their parting and dying imprecations, our country, any more? You, Sir, will bring down that renowned chair in which you sit into infamy, if your seal is set to this instrument of perfidy, and the name of this nation, hitherto the sweet omen of religion and liberty, will stink to the world.

You will not do us the injustice of connecting this remonstrance with any sectional or party feeling.—It is in our hearts the simplest commandment of brotherly love. We will not have this great and solemn claim upon national and human justice huddled aside under the flimsy plea of its being a party act. Sir, to us the questions upon which the government and the people have been agitated during the past year touching the prostration of the currency and of trade, seem but motes in comparison. The hard times, it is true, have brought this discussion home to every farmhouse and poor man's house in this town; but it is the chirping of grasshoppers beside the immortal question whether justice shall be done by the race of civilized, to the race of savage man; whether all the attributes of reason, of civility, of justice, and even of mercy, shall be put off by the American people, and so vast an outrage upon the Cherokee nation, and upon human nature, shall be consummated.

One circumstance lessens the reluctance with which I intrude at this time on your attention, my conviction that the government ought to be admonished of a new historical fact which the discussion of this question has disclosed, namely that there exists in a great part of the northern people, a gloomy diffidence in the *moral* character of the government. On the broaching of this question, a general expression of despondency,—of disbelief that any good will accrue from a remonstrance on an act of fraud and robbery— appeared in those men to whom we naturally turn for aid and counsel. Will the American Government steal? Will it lie? Will it kill?—we ask triumphantly. Our wise men shake their heads dubiously. Our counsellers and old statesmen here, say, that ten years ago, they would have staked their life on the affirmation that the proposed Indian measures could not be executed, that the unanimous country would put them down. And now the steps of this crime follow each other so fast,—at such fatally quick time,—that the millions of virtuous citizens, whose agents the Government are, have no place to interpose, and must shut their eyes until the last howl and wailing of these poor tormented villages and tribes shall afflict the ear of the world.

I will not hide from you as an indication of this alarming distrust that a letter addressed as mine is, and suggesting to the mind of the Executive the plain obligations of man, has a burlesque character in the apprehension of some of my friends. I, sir, will not beforehand treat you with contumely of this distrust. I will at least state to you this fact and show you how plain and humane people whose love would be honor, regard the policy of the Government, and what injurious inferences they draw as to the mind of the Governors. A man with your experience in affairs must have seen cause to appreciate the futility of opposition to the moral sentiment. However feeble the sufferer, and however great the oppressor, it is in the nature of things that the blow should recoil on the aggressor. For God is in the sentiment, and it cannot be withstood. The potentate and the people perish before it; but with it, and as its executors, they are omnipotent.

I write thus, Sir, to inform you of the state of mind these Indian tidings have awakened here, and to pray with one voice more that you whose hands are strong with the delegated power of fifteen millions of men will avert with that might the terrific injury which threatens the Cherokee tribe.

With great respect, Sir,
I am your fellow-citizen,
Ralph Waldo Emerson

NATHANIEL HAWTHORNE
1804–1864

I n 1879, the author Henry James called Nathaniel Hawthorne "the most valuable example of American genius," expressing the widely held belief that he was the most significant fiction writer of the antebellum period. Readers continue to celebrate Hawthorne for his prose style, his perceptive renderings of New England history, his psychological acuity, and his vivid characterizations—especially of female characters. Still, for many, he remains tantalizingly elusive, a writer who—as he remarked in the "Custom-House" introduction to The Scarlet Letter—wished to keep "the inmost Me behind its veil." He was, to be sure, a deeply private man, but the elusiveness of his fiction stems from a deliberate aesthetic of ambiguity, a refusal to "stick a pin through a butterfly" (as he put it in the preface to The House of the Seven Gables) by imposing a single moral on a story. Withholding interpretation—or offering multiple and conflicting interpretations—Hawthorne not only makes readers do their own interpretive work but also shows how interpretation is often a form of self-expression.

Hawthorne was born on July 4, 1804, in Salem, Massachusetts. His prominent Puritan ancestors on the Hawthorne side of the family were among the first settlers of Massachusetts and included a judge in the Salem witchcraft trials of 1692. The men in his mother's family, the Mannings, were tradesmen and businessmen. When Hawthorne's sea-captain father died in Surinam of yellow fever in 1808, his mother, Elizabeth Manning Hawthorne, moved with her three children into the Manning family's commodious house in Salem. There, with his mother, sisters, grandparents, two aunts, and five uncles, Hawthorne discovered his love of reading, displaying particular interest as a boy in John Bunyan's Puritan allegory *The Pilgrim's Progress*. In 1813 he injured his foot in an accident, was fitted with a protective boot and crutches and, while remaining home from school during the long recuperation period, continued to read extensively. By his midteens he was reading the British novelists Henry Fielding, Tobias Smollett, William Godwin, and Sir Walter Scott, while forming an ambition, as he wrote his sister Elizabeth when he was sixteen, of "becoming an Author, and relying for support upon my pen." Hawthorne enjoyed long visits to the Manning properties at Sebago Lake, Maine, and at age seventeen enrolled at Bowdoin College in Brunswick, Maine. At Bowdoin he developed what would become lifelong friendships with Horatio Bridge, the future president Franklin Pierce, and other members of the nascent Democratic Party. These friends would later help further his literary career by providing him with patronage jobs and funds. The poet Henry Wadsworth Longfellow, another Bowdoin classmate, belonged to the more conservative Federalist Society. At the graduation ceremonies in 1825, Longfellow spoke of the possibility that "Our Native Writers" could achieve lasting fame; and twelve years later he would enthusiastically review Hawthorne's *Twice-Told Tales* in the prestigious *North American Review*, calling the collection of tales and sketches a "sweet, sweet book."

During the years between Hawthorne's graduation from Bowdoin in 1825 and the publication of *Twice-Told Tales* in 1837, Hawthorne seems to have lived quietly at home in Salem with his mother and sisters. He read extensively in colonial histories and documents, which would become important sources for such historical tales as "My Kinsman, Major Molineux" (1832) and "Young Goodman Brown" (1835), while keeping a close eye on his contemporary world, which would supply him with material for such popular sketches as "Little Annie's Ramble" (1835) and "A Rill from the Town Pump" (1835). In 1828 Hawthorne published his first novel, *Fanshawe*, at his own expense. Set at a college resembling Bowdoin, the novel was reviewed so negatively that he attempted to suppress its distribution. Over the next several years Hawthorne tried unsuccessfully to find a publisher for collections of the tales he was writing. He may have destroyed one collection, "Seven Tales of My Native Land"; in 1829 he failed to find a publisher for a volume called "Provincial Tales," which included "The Gentle Boy" and perhaps "My Kinsman, Major Molineux." A proposed third volume called "The Story Teller," in which the title character wandered about New England telling his stories in dramatic settings and circumstances, also foundered.

During the early 1830s, however, Hawthorne managed to publish a number of tales and sketches in the literary annuals that were issued every fall as Christmas gifts. Still, he received only a few dollars for each tale and no recognition, since publication in the annuals was anonymous. In 1836 he edited the *American Magazine of Useful and Entertaining Knowledge*, a job he secured through the Boston publisher Samuel Goodrich, whose annual, *The Token*, regularly published his tales. That same year, with the help of his sister Elizabeth, he wrote a children's reference work for Goodrich, *Peter Parley's Universal History on the Basis of Geography*. Unbeknownst to Hawthorne, his Bowdoin friend Horatio Bridge persuaded Goodrich to publish a collection of Hawthorne's tales by promising to repay any losses. This volume, *Twice-Told Tales*, appeared in March 1837 and was favorably reviewed in England as well as the United States. A notebook entry written sometime in 1836 was only a little premature: "In this dismal and sordid chamber FAME was won."

There is considerable uncertainty about Hawthorne's private affairs around the time of the publication of *Twice-Told Tales*. According to family lore, he may have challenged the future editor of the *Democratic Review*, John O'Sullivan, to a duel over Mary Silsbee of Salem. (During the 1840s O'Sullivan would publish over twenty of Hawthorne's stories in his journal.) Hawthorne may have also been enamored of Elizabeth Peabody, a Salemite who would become a major force in American educational reform as well as other progressive causes, and to whom he presented a copy of *Twice-Told Tales* in the fall of 1837. Sometime in late 1837 or 1838 Hawthorne met Elizabeth's youngest sister, Sophia Peabody, a painter whose migraine headaches often made her a virtual invalid; they were secretly engaged within a few months of the meeting. To save money for married life, Hawthorne accepted a patronage appointment as salt and coal measurer at the Boston Custom House during 1839 and 1840, and then invested some of his limited funds in the utopian community Brook Farm, located in West Roxbury, Massachusetts, where he spent seven months in 1841. During this period he published several children's books on colonial and revolutionary history—*Grandfather's Chair* (1841), *Famous Old People* (1841), *Liberty Tree* (1841), and *Biographical Stories for Children* (1842)—along with a revised and expanded edition of *Twice-Told Tales* (1842). He and Sophia Peabody were married in 1842; the couple rented a house in Concord named the "Old Manse" (owned by Emerson's family) and became friends with the notable writers and intellectuals of the area—Emerson, Thoreau, Margaret Fuller, and Ellery Channing, among others. The Hawthornes' first child, Una, was born in 1844. While a hoped-for novel failed to materialize, Hawthorne continued to publish sketches and tales, but with a more pronounced focus on social reform, science, and technology. In 1845, he edited his friend Bridge's *Journal of an African Cruiser*, but little money came of this enterprise, and Hawthorne had to move his family back to Salem to live with his mother and sisters. The following year he published *Mosses from an Old Manse*, which added a number of his recent periodical publications to some earlier work.

The Hawthornes' second child, Julian, was born in 1846. Desperately in need of money, Hawthorne turned to his Democratic friends. The Democrats' local party leader, the historian George Bancroft, found work for Hawthorne as surveyor of the Salem Custom House, a position that Hawthorne assumed in April 1846. The work was not demanding, but the routine stifled Hawthorne's creative energies. Even though he wrote little in these years, Hawthorne resented being thrown out of office by the new Whig administration in June 1849 and was pleased that his ouster led to a furious controversy in the newspapers. He then spent a summer of "great diversity and severity of emotion" (as he wrote in a journal entry of 1855), climaxed by his mother's death on July 31. In September he was at work on *The Scarlet Letter*, which he planned as a long tale to make up half a volume called "Old Time Legends; together with Sketches, Experimental and Ideal." Besides the long introduction, "The Custom-House," which was Hawthorne's means of revenging himself on the Salem Whigs who had "decapitated" him, he planned to include several tales. On the lookout for New England novelistic talent, James Fields, the young associate of the publisher William D. Ticknor, persuaded Hawthorne to drop the stories. The novel was published by the Boston house of Ticknor, Reed, and Fields in 1850.

Although some reviewers denounced *The Scarlet Letter* as licentious or morbid for its treatment of adultery, the novel was nevertheless a literary success in the United States and Great Britain, and Hawthorne was celebrated for his brilliant prose style and uncanny ability to re-create the past. Hawthorne used the setting of Puritan Boston to address the politics of revolution, community, and government central to the emerging nation; he also used the setting to explore matters of sexuality, gender, and psychology in their historical complexity. In this dark novel of love and revenge, Hawthorne evokes emotional sympathy for the heroine, Hester Prynne, even as he appears to condemn her actions. Despite the appearance of condemnation, Hester, for many readers over the years, has emerged as more vibrantly alive and appealing than the male characters of the novel. Hester's status as heroine was apparent from the beginning; as the feminist-abolitionist Jane Swisshelm observed in her 1850 review of the novel, if Hawthorne wanted to teach a lesson about the putative sins of Hester, "he had better try again. For our part if we knew there was such another woman as Hester Prynne in Boston now, we should travel all the way there to pay our respects." Strong women characters—Hepzibah in *The House of the Seven Gables* (1851), Zenobia (modeled on Margaret Fuller) in *The Blithedale Romance* (1852), and Miriam in *The Marble Faun* (1860)—would remain central to Hawthorne's long fictions. Though some recent commentators have reviled Hawthorne for his 1855 complaint to his publisher Ticknor about the "d——d mob of scribbling women," the fact is that, as evidenced by such stories as "The Birthmark" and "Rappaccini's Daughter" and all of the novels, few writers of the mid-nineteenth century were more insightful about the damage patriarchal culture can do to women.

Following the publication of *The Scarlet Letter*, the Hawthornes moved to Lenox, Massachusetts, in the Berkshire Mountains, in part to escape from the controversy surrounding the satirical "Custom-House" sketch, which had angered many in Salem. During a year and a half in Lenox, Hawthorne developed a complicated friendship with Herman Melville, who championed Hawthorne as a great American writer in his 1850 "Hawthorne and His Mosses" and dedicated *Moby-Dick* to him. Hawthorne, over time, pulled back from Melville, and their paths seldom crossed after 1852, when the Hawthornes moved to West Newton and then back to Concord. Hawthorne was especially productive during the early 1850s, publishing *The House of the Seven Gables*, a romance with a contemporary Salem setting, and *The Blithedale Romance*, which drew on Hawthorne's experiences at Brook Farm. Hawthorne also published *The Snow-Image and Other Twice-Told Tales* (1852), two books of tales and myths for children (*A Wonder-Book* [1852] and *The Tanglewood Tales* [1853]), and *The Life of Franklin Pierce*, a presidential campaign biography for his Bowdoin friend. The victorious Pierce appointed Hawthorne American consul at Liverpool, a job that again pulled Hawthorne away from his writing but that helped him support a family augmented by the birth of a third child in 1850, his daughter Rose.

At Liverpool (1853–57) Hawthorne, an industrious consul, was particularly concerned to gain greater protections for American sailors from abusive officers. Hawthorne resigned the position early in 1857 after Pierce failed to gain the Democrats' nomination for a second term, and remained in Europe to travel with his family. A stay in Italy—starting in the miserably cold early months of 1858—turned into a nightmare when malaria nearly killed his daughter Una. Hawthorne kept a minutely detailed tourist's account of his travels in Italy, and he drew on these notebooks for the romance he began in Florence in 1858 and finished late in 1859 after his return to England. This novel, inspired by the statue of a faun attributed to the classical Greek sculptor Praxiteles, was published in London in February 1860 as *Transformation* and one month later in the United States under Hawthorne's preferred title, *The Marble Faun*. Acclaimed by reviewers, the novel proved to be especially popular with American travelers to Rome later in the nineteenth century, who enjoyed using it as a guidebook.

The Hawthornes returned to their Concord home, which Hawthorne had named The Wayside, in June 1860. Hawthorne's final years in the United States were an unhappy time for him. Una remained sickly, and Hawthorne's own health began to decline. Increasingly depressed, he began a romance about an American claimant to an ancestral English estate, then put it aside to begin a romance about the search for an elixir of life, and then put that one aside as well to start another. Meanwhile, the Jacksonian Democrat Hawthorne was baffled and disturbed by the coming of the Civil War, regarding the Northern declaration of war not as an idealistic campaign to bring about the end of slavery, which he viewed as an evil, but as a frenzied form of aggression. Following a visit to Washington, D.C., in which he met Abraham Lincoln, Hawthorne published "Chiefly about War-Matters" in the July 1862 issue of the *Atlantic Monthly*; the essay satirized Lincoln and conveyed Hawthorne's critique of a nation gone mad with war. Fields, the editor of the *Atlantic*, paid well for this and other of Hawthorne's contributions, but Hawthorne was increasingly unable to respond to Fields's demands. In 1863 Hawthorne published *Our Old Home*, a collection of his English sketches, which he loyally dedicated to Franklin Pierce, who, because of his Southern sympathies, was now anathema to many Northerners. Harriet Beecher Stowe expressed disbelief that Hawthorne would dedicate a book to "that arch-traitor Pierce"; and according to Annie Fields, the wife of Hawthorne's publisher, Emerson and many others who received complimentary copies of the book reported that they had cut out the dedication page. Suffering from health problems, a frail and somewhat isolated Hawthorne embarked on a trip to New Hampshire with his friend Pierce early in May 1864, and died in his sleep, at a hotel, later that month. He was buried in the Sleepy Hollow Cemetery at Concord. Emerson, Longfellow, Fields, James Russell Lowell, and Oliver Wendell Holmes were among his pallbearers.

My Kinsman, Major Molineux[1]

After the kings of Great Britain had assumed the right of appointing the colonial governors,[2] the measures of the latter seldom met with the ready and general approbation, which had been paid to those of their predecessors, under the original charters. The people looked with most jealous scrutiny to the exercise of power, which did not emanate from themselves, and they usually rewarded the rulers with slender gratitude, for the compliances, by which, in softening their instructions from beyond the sea, they had incurred the reprehension of those who gave them. The annals of Massachusetts Bay will inform us, that of six governors, in the space of about forty years from the surrender of the old charter, under James II, two were imprisoned by a popular insurrection; a third, as Hutchinson[3] inclines to believe, was driven from the province by the whizzing of a musket ball; a fourth, in the opinion of the same historian, was hastened to his grave by continual bickerings with the house of representatives; and the remaining two, as well as their successors, till the Revolution, were favored with few and brief intervals of peaceful sway. The inferior members of the court party,[4] in times of high political excitement, led scarcely a more desirable life. These remarks may serve as preface to the following adventures, which chanced

1. The text is that of the first printing in *The Token* (1832). Hawthorne included the story in his final collection, *The Snow-Image, and Other Twice-Told Tales* (1852).
2. In 1684 King Charles II (r. 1660–85) annulled the original Massachusetts Charter, which had allowed the colony to elect its own governor. King James II (r. 1685–88) appointed the colony's first royal governor in 1685.
3. Thomas Hutchinson (1711–1780), the last

royal governor. The particular annals, or year-by-year histories, that Hawthorne has in mind are *The History of the Colony and Province of Massachusetts-Bay* (1764, 1767) by Hutchinson. James II (1633–1701) reigned briefly (1685–88) before being exiled to France in the Glorious Revolution (1688–89), which helped to establish the Parliament as the ruling governmental power in England.
4. The pro-Crown party.

upon a summer night, not far from a hundred years ago. The reader, in order to avoid a long and dry detail of colonial affairs, is requested to dispense with an account of the train of circumstances, that had caused much temporary inflammation of the popular mind.

It was near nine o'clock of a moonlight evening, when a boat crossed the ferry with a single passenger, who had obtained his conveyance, at that unusual hour, by the promise of an extra fare. While he stood on the landing-place, searching in either pocket for the means of fulfilling his agreement, the ferryman lifted a lantern, by the aid of which, and the newly risen moon, he took a very accurate survey of the stranger's figure. He was a youth of barely eighteen years, evidently country-bred, and now, as it should seem, upon his first visit to town. He was clad in a coarse grey coat, well worn, but in excellent repair; his under garments[5] were durably constructed of leather, and sat tight to a pair of serviceable and well-shaped limbs; his stockings of blue yarn, were the incontrovertible handiwork of a mother or a sister; and on his head was a three-cornered hat, which in its better days had perhaps sheltered the graver brow of the lad's father. Under his left arm was a heavy cudgel, formed of an oak sapling, and retaining a part of the hardened root; and his equipment was completed by a wallet,[6] not so abundantly stocked as to incommode the vigorous shoulders on which it hung. Brown, curly hair, well-shaped features, and bright, cheerful eyes, were nature's gifts, and worth all that art could have done for his adornment.

The youth, one of whose names was Robin, finally drew from his pocket the half of a little province-bill[7] of five shillings, which, in the depreciation of that sort of currency, did but satisfy the ferryman's demand, with the surplus of a sexangular piece of parchment valued at three pence. He then walked forward into the town, with as light a step, as if his day's journey had not already exceeded thirty miles, and with as eager an eye, as if he were entering London city, instead of the little metropolis of a New England colony. Before Robin had proceeded far, however, it occurred to him, that he knew not whither to direct his steps; so he paused, and looked up and down the narrow street, scrutinizing the small and mean wooden buildings, that were scattered on either side.

'This low hovel cannot be my kinsman's dwelling,' thought he, 'nor yonder old house, where the moonlight enters at the broken casement; and truly I see none hereabouts that might be worthy of him. It would have been wise to inquire my way of the ferryman, and doubtless he would have gone with me, and earned a shilling from the Major for his pains. But the next man I meet will do as well.'

He resumed his walk, and was glad to perceive that the street now became wider, and the houses more respectable in their appearance. He soon discerned a figure moving on moderately in advance, and hastened his steps to overtake it. As Robin drew nigh, he saw that the passenger was a man in years, with a full periwig of grey hair, a wide-skirted coat of dark cloth, and silk stockings rolled about his knees. He carried a long and polished cane, which he struck down perpendicularly before him, at every step; and at regular intervals he uttered two successive hems, of a peculiarly solemn and

5. Clothes worn on the lower part of the body.   7. Local paper money.
6. Knapsack.

sepulchral[8] intonation. Having made these observations, Robin laid hold of the skirt of the old man's coat, just when the light from the open door and windows of a barber's shop, fell upon both their figures.

'Good evening to you, honored Sir,' said he, making a low bow, and still retaining his hold of the skirt. 'I pray you to tell me whereabouts is the dwelling of my kinsman, Major Molineux?'

The youth's question was uttered very loudly; and one of the barbers, whose razor was descending on a well-soaped chin, and another who was dressing a Ramillies wig,[9] left their occupations, and came to the door. The citizen, in the meantime, turned a long favored countenance upon Robin, and answered him in a tone of excessive anger and annoyance. His two sepulchral hems, however, broke into the very centre of his rebuke, with most singular effect, like a thought of the cold grave obtruding among wrathful passions.

'Let go my garment, fellow! I tell you. I know not the man you speak of. What! I have authority, I have—hem, hem—authority; and if this be the respect you show your betters, your feet shall be brought acquainted with the stocks,[1] by daylight, tomorrow morning!'

Robin released the old man's skirt, and hastened away, pursued by an ill-mannered roar of laughter from the barber's shop. He was at first considerably surprised by the result of his question, but, being a shrewd youth, soon thought himself able to account for the mystery.

'This is some country representative,' was his conclusion, 'who has never seen the inside of my kinsman's door, and lacks the breeding to answer a stranger civilly. The man is old, or verily—I might be tempted to turn back and smite him on the nose. Ah, Robin, Robin! even the barber's boys laugh at you, for choosing such a guide! You will be wiser in time, friend Robin.'

He now became entangled in a succession of crooked and narrow streets, which crossed each other, and meandered at no great distance from the water-side. The smell of tar was obvious to his nostrils, the masts of vessels pierced the moonlight above the tops of the buildings, and the numerous signs, which Robin paused to read, informed him that he was near the centre of business. But the streets were empty, the shops were closed, and lights were visible only in the second stories of a few dwelling-houses. At length, on the corner of a narrow lane, through which he was passing, he beheld the broad countenance of a British hero swinging before the door of an inn, whence proceeded the voices of many guests. The casement of one of the lower windows was thrown back, and a very thin curtain permitted Robin to distinguish a party at supper, round a well-furnished table. The fragrance of good cheer steamed forth into the outer air, and the youth could not fail to recollect, that the last remnant of his travelling stock of provision had yielded to his morning appetite, and that noon had found, and left him, dinnerless.

'Oh, that a parchment three-penny might give me a right to sit down at yonder table,' said Robin, with a sigh. 'But the Major will make me welcome to the best of his victuals; so I will even step boldly in, and inquire my way to his dwelling.'

He entered the tavern, and was guided by the murmur of voices, and fumes of tobacco, to the public room. It was a long and low apartment, with oaken

---

8. Gloomy.
9. Elaborately braided wig named for Ramillies, Belgium.

1. Wood-framed instrument of punishment with holes for confining the ankles and sometimes the wrists as well.

walls, grown dark in the continual smoke, and a floor, which was thickly sanded, but of no immaculate purity. A number of persons, the larger part of whom appeared to be mariners, or in some way connected with the sea, occupied the wooden benches, or leather-bottomed chairs, conversing on various matters, and occasionally lending their attention to some topic of general interest. Three or four little groups were draining as many bowls of punch, which the great West India trade[2] had long since made a familiar drink in the colony. Others, who had the aspect of men who lived by regular and laborious handicraft, preferred the insulated bliss of an unshared potation, and became more taciturn under its influence. Nearly all, in short, evinced a predilection for the Good Creature in some of its various shapes, for this is a vice, to which, as the Fast-day[3] sermons of a hundred years ago will testify, we have a long hereditary claim. The only guests to whom Robin's sympathies inclined him, were two or three sheepish countrymen, who were using the inn somewhat after the fashion of a Turkish Caravansary; they had gotten themselves into the darkest corner of the room, and, heedless of the Nicotian[4] atmosphere, were supping on the bread of their own ovens, and the bacon cured in their own chimney-smoke. But though Robin felt a sort of brotherhood with these strangers, his eyes were attracted from them, to a person who stood near the door, holding whispered conversation with a group of ill-dressed associates. His features were separately striking almost to grotesqueness, and the whole face left a deep impression in the memory. The forehead bulged out into a double prominence, with a vale between; the nose came boldly forth in an irregular curve, and its bridge was of more than a finger's breadth; the eyebrows were deep and shaggy, and the eyes glowed beneath them like fire in a cave.

While Robin deliberated of whom to inquire respecting his kinsman's dwelling, he was accosted by the innkeeper, a little man in a stained white apron, who had come to pay his professional welcome to the stranger. Being in the second generation from a French protestant, he seemed to have inherited the courtesy of his parent nation; but no variety of circumstance was ever known to change his voice from the one shrill note in which he now addressed Robin.

'From the country, I presume, Sir?' said he, with a profound bow. 'Beg to congratulate you on your arrival, and trust you intend a long stay with us. Fine town here, Sir, beautiful buildings, and much that may interest a stranger. May I hope for the honor of your commands in respect to supper?'

'The man sees a family likeness! the rogue has guessed that I am related to the Major!' thought Robin, who had hitherto experienced little superfluous civility.

All eyes were now turned on the country lad, standing at the door, in his worn three-cornered hat, grey coat, leather breeches, and blue yarn stockings, leaning on an oaken cudgel, and bearing a wallet on his back. Robin replied to the courteous innkeeper, with such an assumption of consequence, as befitted the Major's relative.

'My honest friend,' he said, 'I shall make it a point to patronise your house on some occasion, when—' here he could not help lowering his voice— 'I may have more than a parchment three-pence in my pocket. My present business,' continued he, speaking with lofty confidence, 'is merely to inquire the way to the dwelling of my kinsman, Major Molineux.'

There was a sudden and general movement in the room, which Robin interpreted as expressing the eagerness of each individual to become his guide. But the innkeeper turned his eyes to a written paper on the wall, which he read, or seemed to read, with occasional recurrences to the young man's figure.

'What have we here?' said he, breaking his speech into little dry fragments, "Left the house of the subscriber, bounden servant,[5] Hezekiah Mudge—had on when he went away, grey coat, leather breeches, master's third best hat. One pound currency reward to whoever shall lodge him in any jail in the province." 'Better trudge, boy, better trudge.'

Robin had begun to draw his hand towards the lighter end of the oak cudgel, but a strange hostility in every countenance, induced him to relinquish his purpose of breaking the courteous innkeeper's head. As he turned to leave the room, he encountered a sneering glance from the bold-featured personage whom he had before noticed; and no sooner was he beyond the door, than he heard a general laugh, in which the innkeeper's voice might be distinguished, like the dropping of small stones in a kettle.

'Now is it not strange,' thought Robin, with his usual shrewdness, 'is it not strange, that the confession of an empty pocket, should outweigh the name of my kinsman, Major Molineux? Oh, if I had one of these grinning rascals in the woods, where I and my oak sapling grew up together, I would teach him that my arm is heavy, though my purse be light!'

On turning the corner of the narrow lane, Robin found himself in a spacious street, with an unbroken line of lofty houses on each side, and a steepled building at the upper end, whence the ringing of a bell announced the hour of nine. The light of the moon, and the lamps from numerous shop windows, discovered people promenading on the pavement, and amongst them, Robin hoped to recognise his hitherto inscrutable relative. The result of his former inquiries made him unwilling to hazard another, in a scene of such publicity, and he determined to walk slowly and silently up the street, thrusting his face close to that of every elderly gentleman, in search of the Major's lineaments. In his progress, Robin encountered many gay and gallant figures. Embroidered garments, of showy colors, enormous periwigs, gold-laced hats, and silver hilted swords, glided past him and dazzled his optics. Travelled youths, imitators of the European fine gentlemen of the period, trod jauntily along, half-dancing to the fashionable tunes which they hummed, and making poor Robin ashamed of his quiet and natural gait. At length, after many pauses to examine the gorgeous display of goods in the shop windows, and after suffering some rebukes for the impertinence of his scrutiny into people's faces, the Major's kinsman found himself near the steepled building, still unsuccessful in his search. As yet, however, he had seen only one side of the thronged street; so Robin crossed, and continued the same

---

5. A person bound, or "indentured," by contract to servitude for seven years (or another set period), usually in repayment for transportation to the colonies.

sort of inquisition down the opposite pavement, with stronger hopes than the philosopher seeking an honest man,[6] but with no better fortune. He had arrived about midway towards the lower end, from which his course began, when he overheard the approach of some one, who struck down a cane on the flag-stones at every step, uttering, at regular intervals, two sepulchral hems.

'Mercy on us!' quoth Robin, recognising the sound.

Turning a corner, which chanced to be close at his right hand, he hastened to pursue his researches, in some other part of the town. His patience was now wearing low, and he seemed to feel more fatigue from his rambles since he crossed the ferry, than from his journey of several days on the other side. Hunger also pleaded loudly within him, and Robin began to balance the propriety of demanding, violently and with lifted cudgel, the necessary guidance from the first solitary passenger, whom he should meet. While a resolution to this effect was gaining strength, he entered a street of mean appearance, on either side of which, a row of ill-built houses was straggling towards the harbor. The moonlight fell upon no passenger along the whole extent, but in the third domicile which Robin passed, there was a half-opened door, and his keen glance detected a woman's garment within.

'My luck may be better here,' said he to himself.

Accordingly, he approached the door, and beheld it shut closer as he did so; yet an open space remained, sufficing for the fair occupant to observe the stranger, without a corresponding display on her part. All that Robin could discern was a strip of scarlet petticoat, and the occasional sparkle of an eye, as if the moonbeams were trembling on some bright thing.

'Pretty mistress,'—for I may call her so with a good conscience, thought the shrewd youth, since I know nothing to the contrary—'my sweet pretty mistress, will you be kind enough to tell me whereabouts I must seek the dwelling of my kinsman, Major Molineux?'

Robin's voice was plaintive and winning, and the female, seeing nothing to be shunned in the handsome country youth, thrust open the door, and came forth into the moonlight. She was a dainty little figure, with a white neck, round arms, and a slender waist, at the extremity of which her scarlet petticoat jutted out over a hoop, as if she were standing in a balloon. Moreover, her face was oval and pretty, her hair dark beneath the little cap, and her bright eyes possessed a sly freedom, which triumphed over those of Robin.

'Major Molineux dwells here,' said this fair woman.

Now her voice was the sweetest Robin had heard that night, the airy counterpart of a stream of melted silver; yet he could not help doubting whether that sweet voice spoke gospel truth. He looked up and down the mean street, and then surveyed the house before which they stood. It was a small, dark edifice of two stories, the second of which projected over the lower floor; and the front apartment had the aspect of a shop for petty commodities.

'Now truly I am in luck,' replied Robin, cunningly, 'and so indeed is my kinsman, the Major, in having so pretty a housekeeper. But I prithee trouble him to step to the door; I will deliver him a message from his friends in the country, and then go back to my lodgings at the inn.'

<hr>

6. Diogenes, the Greek philosopher (412?–323 B.C.E.), carried a lantern about in daytime in his search for an honest man.

'Nay, the Major has been a-bed this hour or more,' said the lady of the scarlet petticoat; 'and it would be to little purpose to disturb him to night, seeing his evening draught was of the strongest. But he is a kind-hearted man, and it would be as much as my life's worth, to let a kinsman of his turn away from the door. You are the good old gentleman's very picture, and I could swear that was his rainy-weather hat. Also, he has garments very much resembling those leather—But come in, I pray, for I bid you hearty welcome in his name.'

So saying, the fair and hospitable dame took our hero by the hand; and though the touch was light, and the force was gentleness, and though Robin read in her eyes what he did not hear in her words, yet the slender waisted woman, in the scarlet petticoat, proved stronger than the athletic country youth. She had drawn his half-willing footsteps nearly to the threshold, when the opening of a door in the neighborhood, startled the Major's housekeeper, and, leaving the Major's kinsman, she vanished speedily into her own domicile. A heavy yawn preceded the appearance of a man, who, like the Moonshine of Pyramus and Thisbe, carried a lantern,[7] needlessly aiding his sister luminary in the heavens. As he walked sleepily up the street, he turned his broad, dull face on Robin, and displayed a long staff, spiked at the end.

'Home, vagabond, home!' said the watchman, in accents that seemed to fall asleep as soon as they were uttered. 'Home, or we'll set you in the stocks by peep of day!'

'This is the second hint of the kind,' thought Robin. 'I wish they would end my difficulties, by setting me there to-night.'

Nevertheless, the youth felt an instinctive antipathy towards the guardian of midnight order, which at first prevented him from asking his usual question. But just when the man was about to vanish behind the corner, Robin resolved not to lose the opportunity, and shouted lustily after him—

'I say, friend! will you guide me to the house of my kinsman, Major Molineux?'

The watchman made no reply, but turned the corner and was gone; yet Robin seemed to hear the sound of drowsy laughter stealing along the solitary street. At that moment, also, a pleasant titter saluted him from the open window above his head; he looked up, and caught the sparkle of a saucy eye; a round arm beckoned to him, and next he heard light footsteps descending the staircase within. But Robin, being of the household of a New England clergyman, was a good youth, as well as a shrewd one; so he resisted temptation, and fled away.

He now roamed desperately, and at random, through the town, almost ready to believe that a spell was on him, like that, by which a wizard of his country, had once kept three pursuers wandering, a whole winter night, within twenty paces of the cottage which they sought. The streets lay before him, strange and desolate, and the lights were extinguished in almost every house. Twice, however, little parties of men, among whom Robin distinguished individuals in outlandish attire, came hurrying along, but though on both occasions they paused to address him, such intercourse did not at all enlighten his perplexity. They did but utter a few words in some language

7. In the play-within-a-play in Shakespeare's *A Midsummer Night's Dream* 5.1, the character Moonshine carries a lantern representing the moonlight that shines on the lovers Pyramus and Thisbe.

of which Robin knew nothing, and perceiving his inability to answer, bestowed a curse upon him in plain English, and hastened away. Finally, the lad determined to knock at the door of every mansion that might appear worthy to be occupied by his kinsman, trusting that perseverance would overcome the fatality which had hitherto thwarted him. Firm in this resolve, he was passing beneath the walls of a church, which formed the corner of two streets, when, as he turned into the shade of its steeple, he encountered a bulky stranger, muffled in a cloak. The man was proceeding with the speed of earnest business, but Robin planted himself full before him, holding the oak cudgel with both hands across his body, as a bar to further passage.

'Halt, honest man, and answer me a question,' said he, very resolutely, 'Tell me, this instant, whereabouts is the dwelling of my kinsman, Major Molineux?'

'Keep your tongue between your teeth, fool, and let me pass,' said a deep, gruff voice, which Robin partly remembered. 'Let me pass, I say, or I'll strike you to the earth!'

'No, no, neighbor!' cried Robin, flourishing his cudgel, and then thrusting its larger end close to the man's muffled face. 'No, no, I'm not the fool you take me for, nor do you pass, till I have an answer to my question. Whereabouts is the dwelling of my kinsman, Major Molineux?'

The stranger, instead of attempting to force his passage, stept back into the moonlight, unmuffled his own face and stared full into that of Robin.

'Watch here an hour, and Major Molineux will pass by,' said he.

Robin gazed with dismay and astonishment, on the unprecedented physiognomy of the speaker. The forehead with its double prominence, the broadhooked nose, the shaggy eyebrows, and fiery eyes, were those which he had noticed at the inn, but the man's complexion had undergone a singular, or more properly, a two-fold change. One side of the face blazed of an intense red, while the other was black as midnight, the division line being in the broad bridge of the nose; and a mouth, which seemed to extend from ear to ear, was black or red, in contrast to the color of the cheek. The effect was as if two individual devils, a fiend of fire and a fiend of darkness, had united themselves to form this infernal visage. The stranger grinned in Robin's face, muffled his party-colored features, and was out of sight in a moment.

'Strange things we travellers see!' ejaculated Robin.

He seated himself, however, upon the steps of the church-door, resolving to wait the appointed time for his kinsman's appearance. A few moments were consumed in philosophical speculations, upon the species of the *genus homo*, who had just left him, but having settled this point shrewdly, rationally, and satisfactorily, he was compelled to look elsewhere for amusement. And first he threw his eyes along the street; it was of more respectable appearance than most of those into which he had wandered, and the moon, 'creating, like the imaginative power, a beautiful strangeness in familiar objects,' gave something of romance to a scene, that might not have possessed it in the light of day. The irregular, and often quaint architecture of the houses, some of whose roofs were broken into numerous little peaks; while others ascended, steep and narrow, into a single point; and others again were square; the pure milk-white of some of their complexions, the aged darkness of others, and the thousand sparklings, reflected from bright substances in the plastered walls of many; these matters engaged Robin's attention for awhile, and then began to grow wearisome. Next he endeavored to define the forms of distant objects, starting away with almost ghostly indistinctness, just as his eye appeared to grasp them; and finally he took a minute survey of an edifice, which stood on the opposite side of the street, directly in front of the church-door, where he was stationed. It was a large square mansion, distinguished from its neighbors by a balcony, which rested on tall pillars, and by an elaborate gothic window, communicating therewith.

'Perhaps this is the very house I have been seeking,' thought Robin.

Then he strove to speed away the time, by listening to a murmur, which swept continually along the street, yet was scarcely audible, except to an unaccustomed ear like his; it was a low, dull, dreamy sound, compounded of many noises, each of which was at too great a distance to be separately heard. Robin marvelled at this snore of a sleeping town, and marvelled more, whenever its continuity was broken, by now and then a distant shout, apparently loud where it originated. But altogether it was a sleep-inspiring sound, and to shake off its drowsy influence, Robin arose, and climbed a window-frame, that he might view the interior of the church. There the moonbeams came trembling in, and fell down upon the deserted pews, and extended along the quiet aisles. A fainter, yet more awful radiance, was hovering round the pulpit, and one solitary ray had dared to rest upon the opened page of the great bible. Had Nature, in that deep hour, become a worshipper in the house, which man had builded? Or was that heavenly light the visible sanctity of this place, visible because no earthly and impure feet were within the walls? The scene made Robin's heart shiver with a sensation of loneliness, stronger than he had ever felt in the remotest depths of his native woods; so he turned away, and sat down again before the door. There were graves around the church, and now an uneasy thought obtruded into Robin's breast. What if the object of his search, which had been so often and so strangely thwarted, were all the time mouldering in his shroud? What if his kinsman should glide through yonder gate, and nod and smile to him in passing dimly by?

'Oh, that any breathing thing were here with me!' said Robin.

Recalling his thoughts from this uncomfortable track, he sent them over forest, hill, and stream, and attempted to imagine how that evening of ambiguity and weariness, had been spent by his father's household. He pictured them assembled at the door, beneath the tree, the great old tree, which had been spared for its huge twisted trunk, and venerable shade, when a thousand leafy brethren fell. There, at the going down of the summer sun, it was his father's custom to perform domestic worship, that the neighbors might come and join with him like brothers of the family, and that the wayfaring man might pause to drink at that fountain, and keep his heart pure by freshening the memory of home. Robin distinguished the seat of every individual of the little audience; he saw the good man in the midst, holding the scriptures in the golden light that shone from the western clouds; he beheld him close the book, and all rise up to pray. He heard the old thanksgivings for daily mercies, the old supplications for their continuance, to which he had so often listened in weariness, but which were now among his dear remembrances. He perceived the slight inequality of his father's voice when he came to speak of the Absent One; he noted how his mother turned her face to the broad and knotted trunk, how his elder brother scorned, because the beard was rough upon his upper lip, to permit his features to be moved; how his younger sister drew down a low hanging branch before her eyes; and how the little one of all, whose sports had hitherto broken the decorum of the scene, understood the prayer for her playmate, and burst into clamorous grief. Then he saw them go in at the door; and when Robin would have entered also, the latch tinkled into its place, and he was excluded from his home.

'Am I here, or there?' cried Robin, starting; for all at once, when his thoughts had become visible and audible in a dream, the long, wide, solitary street shone out before him.

He aroused himself, and endeavored to fix his attention steadily upon the large edifice which he had surveyed before. But still his mind kept vibrating between fancy and reality; by turns, the pillars of the balcony lengthened into the tall, bare stems of pines, dwindled down to human figures, settled again in their true shape and size, and then commenced a new succession of changes. For a single moment, when he deemed himself awake, he could have sworn that a visage, one which he seemed to remember, yet could not absolutely name as his kinsman's, was looking towards him from the Gothic window. A deeper sleep wrestled with, and nearly overcame him, but fled at the sound of footsteps along the opposite pavement. Robin rubbed his eyes, discerned a man passing at the foot of the balcony, and addressed him in a loud, peevish, and lamentable cry.

'Halloo, friend! must I wait here all night for my kinsman, Major Molineux?'

The sleeping echoes awoke, and answered the voice; and the passenger, barely able to discern a figure sitting in the oblique shade of the steeple, traversed the street to obtain a nearer view. He was himself a gentleman in his prime, of open, intelligent, cheerful and altogether prepossessing countenance. Perceiving a country youth, apparently homeless and without friends, he accosted him in a tone of real kindness, which had become strange to Robin's ears.

'Well, my good lad, why are you sitting here?' inquired he. 'Can I be of service to you in any way?'

'I am afraid not, Sir,' replied Robin, despondingly; 'yet I shall take it kindly, if you'll answer me a single question. I've been searching half the night for one Major Molineux; now, Sir, is there really such a person in these parts, or am I dreaming?'

'Major Molineux! The name is not altogether strange to me,' said the gentleman smiling. 'Have you any objection to telling me the nature of your business with him?'

Then Robin briefly related that his father was a clergyman, settled on a small salary, at a long distance back in the country, and that he and Major Molineux were brothers' children. The Major, having inherited riches, and acquired civil and military rank, had visited his cousin in great pomp a year or two before; had manifested much interest in Robin and an elder brother, and, being childless himself, had thrown out hints respecting the future establishment of one of them in life. The elder brother was destined to succeed to the farm, which his father cultivated, in the interval of sacred duties; it was therefore determined that Robin should profit by his kinsman's generous intentions, especially as he had seemed to be rather the favorite, and was thought to possess other necessary endowments.

'For I have the name of being a shrewd youth,' observed Robin, in this part of his story.

'I doubt not you deserve it,' replied his new friend, good naturedly; 'but pray proceed.'

'Well, Sir, being nearly eighteen years old, and well grown, as you see,' continued Robin, raising himself to his full height, 'I thought it high time to begin the world. So my mother and sister put me in handsome trim, and my father gave me half the remnant of his last year's salary, and five days ago I started for this place, to pay the Major a visit. But would you believe it, Sir? I crossed the ferry a little after dusk, and have yet found nobody that would show me the way to his dwelling; only an hour or two since, I was told to wait here, and Major Molineux would pass by.'

'Can you describe the man who told you this?' inquired the gentleman.

'Oh, he was a very ill-favored fellow, Sir,' replied Robin, 'with two great bumps on his forehead, a hook nose, fiery eyes, and, what struck me as the strangest, his face was of two different colors. Do you happen to know such a man, Sir?'

'Not intimately,' answered the stranger, 'but I chanced to meet him a little time previous to your stopping me. I believe you may trust his word, and that the Major will very shortly pass through this street. In the mean time, as I have a singular curiosity to witness your meeting, I will sit down here upon the steps, and bear you company.'

He seated himself accordingly, and soon engaged his companion in animated discourse. It was but of brief continuance, however, for a noise of shouting, which had long been remotely audible, drew so much nearer, that Robin inquired its cause.

'What may be the meaning of this uproar?' asked he. 'Truly, if your town be always as noisy, I shall find little sleep, while I am an inhabitant.'

'Why, indeed, friend Robin, there do appear to be three or four riotous fellows abroad to-night,' replied the gentleman. 'You must not expect all the stillness of your native woods, here in our streets. But the watch will shortly be at the heels of these lads, and—'

'Aye, and set them in the stocks by peep of day,' interrupted Robin, recollecting his own encounter with the drowsy lantern-bearer. 'But, dear Sir, if I may trust my ears, an army of watchmen would never make head against such a multitude of rioters. There were at least a thousand voices went to make up that one shout.'

'May not one man have several voices, Robin, as well as two complexions?' said his friend.

'Perhaps a man may; but heaven forbid that a woman should!' responded the shrewd youth, thinking of the seductive tones of the Major's housekeeper.

The sounds of a trumpet in some neighboring street, now became so evident and continual, that Robin's curiosity was strongly excited. In addition to the shouts, he heard frequent bursts from many instruments of discord, and a wild and confused laughter filled up the intervals. Robin rose from the steps, and looked wistfully towards a point, whither several people seemed to be hastening.

'Surely some prodigious merrymaking is going on,' exclaimed he. 'I have laughed very little since I left home, Sir, and should be sorry to lose an opportunity. Shall we just step round the corner by that darkish house, and take our share of the fun?'

'Sit down again, sit down, good Robin,' replied the gentleman, laying his hand on the skirt of the grey coat. 'You forget that we must wait here for your kinsman; and there is reason to believe that he will pass by, in the course of a very few moments.'

The near approach of the uproar had now disturbed the neighborhood; windows flew open on all sides; and many heads, in the attire of the pillow, and confused by sleep suddenly broken, were protruded to the gaze of whoever had leisure to observe them. Eager voices hailed each other from house to house, all demanding the explanation, which not a soul could give. Half-dressed men hurried towards the unknown commotion, stumbling as they went over the stone steps, that thrust themselves into the narrow foot-walk. The shouts, the laughter, and the tuneless bray, the antipodes of music, came onward with increasing din, till scattered individuals, and then denser bodies, began to appear round a corner, at a distance of a hundred yards.

'Will you recognise your kinsman, Robin, if he passes in this crowd?' inquired the gentleman.

'Indeed, I can't warrant it, Sir; but I'll take my stand here, and keep a bright look out,' answered Robin, descending to the outer edge of the pavement.

A mighty stream of people now emptied into the street, and came rolling slowly towards the church. A single horseman wheeled the corner in the midst of them, and close behind him came a band of fearful wind-instruments, sending forth a fresher discord, now that no intervening buildings kept it from the ear. Then a redder light disturbed the moonbeams, and a dense multitude of torches shone along the street, concealing by their glare whatever object they illuminated. The single horseman, clad in a military dress, and bearing a drawn sword, rode onward as the leader, and, by his fierce and variegated countenance, appeared like war personified; the red of one cheek was an emblem of fire and sword; the blackness of the other betokened the mourning which attends them. In his train, were wild figures in the Indian dress, and many fantastic shapes without a model, giving the whole march a visionary air, as if a dream had broken forth from some feverish brain, and were sweeping visibly through the midnight streets. A mass of people, inactive, except as applauding spectators, hemmed the procession in, and several women ran along the sidewalks, piercing the confusion of heavier sounds, with their shrill voices of mirth or terror.[8]

'The double-faced fellow has his eye upon me,' muttered Robin, with an indefinite but uncomfortable idea, that he was himself to bear a part in the pageantry.

The leader turned himself in the saddle, and fixed his glance full upon the country youth, as the steed went slowly by. When Robin had freed his eyes from those fiery ones, the musicians were passing before him, and the torches were close at hand; but the unsteady brightness of the latter formed a veil which he could not penetrate. The rattling of wheels over the stones

8. Though set during the 1730s, the actions of the mob resemble those of the Boston Sons of Liberty during the Stamp Act crisis in 1765.

sometimes found its way to his ear, and confused traces of a human form appeared at intervals, and then melted into the vivid light. A moment more, and the leader thundered a command to halt; the trumpets vomited a horrid breath, and held their peace; the shouts and laughter of the people died away, and there remained only an universal hum, nearly allied to silence. Right before Robin's eyes was an uncovered cart. There the torches blazed the brightest, there the moon shone out like day, and there, in tar-and-feathery dignity, sate his kinsman, Major Molineux!

He was an elderly man, of large and majestic person, and strong, square features, betokening a steady soul; but steady as it was, his enemies had found the means to shake it. His face was pale as death, and far more ghastly; the broad forehead was contracted in his agony, so that the eyebrows formed one dark grey line; his eyes were red and wild, and the foam hung white upon his quivering lip. His whole frame was agitated by a quick, and continual tremor, which his pride strove to quell, even in those circumstances of overwhelming humiliation. But perhaps the bitterest pang of all was when his eyes met those of Robin; for he evidently knew him on the instant, as the youth stood witnessing the foul disgrace of a head that had grown grey in honor. They stared at each other in silence, and Robin's knees shook, and his hair bristled, with a mixture of pity and terror. Soon, however, a bewildering excitement began to seize upon his mind; the preceding adventures of the night, the unexpected appearance of the crowd, the torches, the confused din, and the hush that followed, the spectre of his kinsman reviled by that great multitude, all this, and more than all, a perception of tremendous ridicule in the whole scene, affected him with a sort of mental inebriety. At that moment a voice of sluggish merriment saluted Robin's ears; he turned instinctively, and just behind the corner of the church stood the lantern-bearer, rubbing his eyes, and drowsily enjoying the lad's amazement. Then he heard a peal of laughter like the ringing of silvery bells; a woman twitched his arm, a saucy eye met his, and he saw the lady of the scarlet petticoat. A sharp, dry cachinnation[9] appealed to his memory, and, standing on tiptoe in the crowd, with his white apron over his head, he beheld the courteous little innkeeper. And lastly, there sailed over the heads of the multitude a great, broad laugh, broken in the midst by two deep sepulchral hems; thus—

'Haw, haw, haw—hem, hem—haw, haw, haw, haw!'

The sound proceeded from the balcony of the opposite edifice, and thither Robin turned his eyes. In front of the Gothic window stood the old citizen, wrapped in a wide gown, his grey periwig exchanged for a nightcap, which was thrust back from his forehead, and his silk stockings hanging down about his legs. He supported himself on his polished cane in a fit of convulsive merriment, which manifested itself on his solemn old features, like a funny inscription on a tomb-stone. Then Robin seemed to hear the voices of the barbers; of the guests of the inn; and of all who had made sport of him that night. The contagion was spreading among the multitude, when, all at once, it seized upon Robin, and he sent forth a shout of laughter that echoed through the street; every man shook his sides, every man emptied his lungs, but Robin's shout was the loudest there. The cloud-spirits peeped from their silvery islands,

9. Loud laughter.

as the congregated mirth went roaring up the sky! The Man in the Moon heard the far bellow; 'Oho,' quoth he, 'the old Earth is frolicsome to-night!'

When there was a momentary calm in that tempestuous sea of sound, the leader gave the sign, and the procession resumed its march. On they went, like fiends that throng in mockery round some dead potentate, mighty no more, but majestic still in his agony. On they went, in counterfeited pomp, in senseless uproar, in frenzied merriment, trampling all on an old man's heart. On swept the tumult, and left a silent street behind.

$$• \quad • \quad • \quad • \quad •$$

'Well, Robin, are you dreaming?' inquired the gentleman, laying his hand on the youth's shoulder.

Robin started, and withdrew his arm from the stone post, to which he had instinctively clung, while the living stream rolled by him. His cheek was some-what pale, and his eye not quite so lively as in the earlier part of the evening.

'Will you be kind enough to show me the way to the Ferry?' said he, after a moment's pause.

'You have then adopted a new subject of inquiry?' observed his companion, with a smile.

'Why, yes, Sir,' replied Robin, rather dryly. 'Thanks to you, and to my other friends, I have at last met my kinsman, and he will scarce desire to see my face again. I begin to grow weary of a town life, Sir. Will you show me the way to the Ferry?'

'No, my good friend Robin, not to-night, at least,' said the gentleman. 'Some few days hence, if you continue to wish it, I will speed you on your journey. Or, if you prefer to remain with us, perhaps, as you are a shrewd youth, you may rise in the world, without the help of your kinsman, Major Molineux.'

1832

Young Goodman Brown[1]

Young goodman Brown came forth, at sunset, into the street of Salem village,[2] but put his head back, after crossing the threshold, to exchange a parting kiss with his young wife. And Faith, as the wife was aptly named, thrust her own pretty head into the street, letting the wind play with the pink ribbons of her cap, while she called to goodman Brown.

['Dearest heart,' whispered she, softly and rather sadly, when her lips were close to his ear, 'pr'y thee, put off your journey until sunrise, and sleep in your own bed to-night. A lone woman is troubled with such dreams and such thoughts, that she's afeard of herself, sometimes. Pray, tarry with me this night, dear husband, of all nights in the year!]

'My love and my Faith,' replied young goodman Brown, 'of all nights in the year, this one night must I tarry away from thee. My journey, as thou callest

1. The text is that of the first publication in the *New-England Magazine* (April 1835). Hawthorne reprinted the story in *Mosses from an Old Manse* (1846). "Goodman": title used to address a

man of humble birth.
2. In Massachusetts; the site of the witchcraft trials and executions of 1692.

it, forth and back again, must needs be done 'twixt now and sunrise. What, my sweet, pretty wife, dost thou doubt me already, and we but three months married!'

'Then, God bless you!' said Faith, with the pink ribbons, 'and may you find all well, when you come back.'

'Amen!' cried goodman Brown. 'Say thy prayers, dear Faith, and go to bed at dusk, and no harm will come to thee.'

So they parted; and the young man pursued his way, until, being about to turn the corner by the meeting-house, he looked back, and saw the head of Faith still peeping after him, with a melancholy air, in spite of her pink ribbons.

'Poor little Faith!' thought he, for his heart smote him. 'What a wretch am I, to leave her on such an errand! She talks of dreams, too. Methought, as she spoke, there was trouble in her face, as if a dream had warned her what work is to be done to-night. But, no, no! 't would kill her to think it. Well; she's a blessed angel on earth; and after this one night, I'll cling to her skirts and follow her to Heaven.'

With this excellent resolve for the future, goodman Brown felt himself justified in making more haste on his present evil purpose. He had taken a dreary road, darkened by all the gloomiest trees of the forest, which barely stood aside to let the narrow path creep through, and closed immediately behind. It was all as lonely as could be; and there is this peculiarity in such a solitude, that the traveler knows not who may be concealed by the innumerable trunks and the thick boughs overhead; so that, with lonely footsteps, he may yet be passing through an unseen multitude.

'There may be a devilish Indian behind every tree,' said goodman Brown, to himself; and he glanced fearfully behind him, as he added, 'What if the devil himself should be at my very elbow!'

His head being turned back, he passed a crook of the road, and looking forward again, beheld the figure of a man, in grave and decent attire, seated at the foot of an old tree. He arose, at goodman Brown's approach, and walked onward, side by side with him.

'You are late, goodman Brown,' said he. 'The clock of the Old South was striking as I came through Boston; and that is full fifteen minutes agone.'[3]

'Faith kept me back awhile,' replied the young man, with a tremor in his voice, caused by the sudden appearance of his companion, though not wholly unexpected.

It was now deep dusk in the forest, and deepest in that part of it where these two were journeying. As nearly as could be discerned, the second traveler was about fifty years old, apparently in the same rank of life as goodman Brown, and bearing a considerable resemblance to him, though perhaps more in expression than features. Still, they might have been taken for father and son. And yet, though the elder person was as simply clad as the younger, and as simple in manner too, he had an indescribable air of one who knew the world, and would not have felt abashed at the governor's dinnertable, or in king William's[4] court, were it possible that his affairs should

3. Boston's Old South Church, built in 1669, was approximately sixteen miles from Salem. That the "figure" could make the journey from Old South to Salem in fifteen minutes suggests supernatural powers.

4. Beginning in 1689, King William III (1650–1702) ruled England with his wife, Queen Mary II, until her death in 1694.

call him thither. But the only thing about him, that could be fixed upon as remarkable, was his staff, which bore the likeness of a great black snake, so curiously wrought, that it might almost be seen to twist and wriggle itself, like a living serpent. This, of course, must have been an ocular deception, assisted by the uncertain light.

'Come, goodman Brown!' cried his fellow-traveler, 'this is a dull pace for the beginning of a journey. Take my staff, if you are so soon weary.'

'Friend,' said the other, exchanging his slow pace for a full stop, 'having kept covenant by meeting thee here, it is my purpose now to return whence I came. I have scruples, touching the matter thou wot'st[5] of.'

'Sayest thou so?' replied he of the serpent, smiling apart. 'Let us walk on, nevertheless, reasoning as we go, and if I convince thee not, thou shalt turn back. We are but a little way in the forest, yet.'

'Too far, too far!' exclaimed the goodman, unconsciously resuming his walk. 'My father never went into the woods on such an errand, nor his father before him. We have been a race of honest men and good Christians, since the days of the martyrs.[6] And shall I be the first of the name of Brown, that ever took this path, and kept'—

'Such company, thou wouldst say,' observed the elder person, interpreting his pause. 'Good, goodman Brown! I have been as well acquainted with your family as with ever a one among the Puritans; and that's no trifle to say. I helped your grandfather, the constable, when he lashed the Quaker woman so smartly through the streets of Salem.[7] And it was I that brought your father a pitch-pine knot, kindled at my own hearth, to set fire to an Indian village, in king Philip's[8] war. They were my good friends, both; and many a pleasant walk have we had along this path, and returned merrily after midnight. I would fain be friends with you, for their sake.'

'If it be as thou sayest,' replied goodman Brown, 'I marvel they never spoke of these matters. Or, verily, I marvel not, seeing that the least rumor of the sort would have driven them from New-England. We are a people of prayer, and good works, to boot, and abide no such wickedness.'

'Wickedness or not,' said the traveler with the twisted staff, 'I have a very general acquaintance here in New-England. The deacons of many a church have drunk the communion wine with me; the selectmen, of divers towns, make me their chairman; and a majority of the Great and General Court[9] are firm supporters of my interest. The governor and I, too—but these are state-secrets.'

'Can this be so!' cried goodman Brown, with a stare of amazement at his undisturbed companion. 'Howbeit, I have nothing to do with the governor and council; they have their own ways, and are no rule for a simple husbandman,[1] like me. But, were I to go on with thee, how should I meet the eye of that

---

5. Wotest; to know (archaic).
6. I.e., during the reign of the Catholic Mary Tudor of England (r. 1553–58), called "Bloody Mary" for her persecution of Protestants. Common reading in New England was John Foxe's *Acts and Monuments* (1563), soon known as the *Book of Martyrs*; it concluded with detailed accounts of martyrdom under Mary.
7. Hawthorne's paternal great-great-grandfather, William Hathorne (1606–1681), had ordered the

whipping of a Quaker woman in Salem. Hawthorne mentions this incident in "The Custom-House" preface to *The Scarlet Letter*.
8. Leader of the Wampanoag Indians, Metacomet (d. 1676), called Philip by the English, led a bloody and ultimately unsuccessful war (1675–76) against the New England colonists.
9. The legislature.
1. Usually, farmer; here, man of ordinary status.

good old man, our minister, at Salem village? Oh, his voice would make me tremble, both Sabbath-day and lecture-day!'[2]

Thus far, the elder traveler had listened with due gravity, but now burst into a fit of irrepressible mirth, shaking himself so violently, that his snake-like staff actually seemed to wriggle in sympathy.

'Ha! ha! ha!' shouted he, again and again; then composing himself, 'Well, go on, goodman Brown, go on; but, pr'y thee, don't kill me with laughing!'

[Well, then, to end the matter at once,' said goodman Brown, considerably nettled, 'there is my wife, Faith. It would break her dear little heart; and I'd rather break my own!]

['Nay, if that be the case,' answered the other, 'e'en go thy ways, goodman Brown. I would not, for twenty old women like the one hobbling before us, that Faith should come to any harm.']

As he spoke, he pointed his staff at a female figure on the path, in whom goodman Brown recognized a very pious and exemplary dame, who had taught him his catechism, in youth, and was still his moral and spiritual adviser, jointly with the minister and deacon Gookin.[3]

'A marvel, truly, that goody Cloyse[4] should be so far in the wilderness, at night-fall!' said he. 'But, with your leave, friend, I shall take a cut through the woods, until we have left this Christian woman behind. Being a stranger to you, she might ask whom I was consorting with, and whither I was going.'

'Be it so,' said his fellow-traveler. 'Betake you to the woods, and let me keep the path.'

Accordingly, the young man turned aside, but took care to watch his companion, who advanced softly along the road, until he had come within a staff's length of the old dame. She, meanwhile, was making the best of her way, with singular speed for so aged a woman, and mumbling some indistinct words, a prayer, doubtless, as she went. The traveler put forth his staff, and touched her withered neck with what seemed the serpent's tail.

'The devil!' screamed the pious old lady.

'Then goody Cloyse knows her old friend?' observed the traveler, confronting her, and leaning on his writhing stick.

'Ah, forsooth, and is it your worship, indeed?' cried the good dame. 'Yea, truly is it, and in the very image of my old gossip, goodman Brown, the grandfather of the silly fellow that now is. But, would your worship believe it? my broomstick hath strangely disappeared, stolen, as I suspect, by that unhanged witch, goody Cory,[5] and that, too, when I was all anointed with the juice of smallage and cinque-foil and wolf's-bane'[6]—

'Mingled with fine wheat and the fat of a new-born babe,' said the shape of old goodman Brown.

'Ah, your worship knows the receipt,'[7] cried the old lady, cackling aloud. 'So, as I was saying, being all ready for the meeting, and no horse to ride on, I made up my mind to foot it; for they tell me, there is a nice young man to

---

2. Midweek sermon day, Wednesday or Thursday.
3. Daniel Gookin (1612–1687), colonial magistrate who looked after Indian affairs. Throughout the story Hawthorne uses historical names associated with Salem and the witchcraft trial.
4. Sarah Cloyce was accused of witchcraft and imprisoned during the Salem witch trials; she was released when the trials were suspended. "Goody": i.e., goodwife; the polite title for a mar-

ried woman of humble rank.
5. A woman named Martha Cory was hanged for witchcraft on September 22, 1692.
6. Plants associated with witchcraft. "Smallage": wild celery or parsley. "Cinque-foil": a five-lobed plant of the rose family (from the Latin for "five fingers"). "Wolf's-bane": hooded, poisonous plant known as monkshood (*bane* means "poison").
7. Recipe.

be taken into communion to-night. But now your good worship will lend me your arm, and we shall be there in a twinkling.'

'That can hardly be,' answered her friend. 'I may not spare you my arm, goody Cloyse, but here is my staff, if you will.'

[So saying, he threw it down at her feet, where, perhaps, it assumed life, being one of the rods which its owner had formerly lent to the Egyptian Magi.[8] Of this fact, however, goodman Brown could not take cognizance. He had cast up his eyes in astonishment, and looking down again, beheld neither goody Cloyse nor the serpentine staff, but his fellow-traveler alone, who waited for him as calmly as if nothing had happened.]

'That old woman taught me my catechism!' said the young man; and there was a world of meaning in this simple comment.

They continued to walk onward, while the elder traveler exhorted his companion to make good speed and persevere in the path, discoursing so aptly, that his arguments seemed rather to spring up in the bosom of his auditor, than to be suggested by himself. As they went, he plucked a branch of maple, to serve for a walking-stick, and began to strip it of the twigs and little boughs, which were wet with evening dew. The moment his fingers touched them, they became strangely withered and dried up, as with a week's sunshine. Thus the pair proceeded, at a good free pace, until suddenly, in a gloomy hollow of the road, goodman Brown sat himself down on the stump of a tree, and refused to go any farther.

'Friend,' said he, stubbornly, 'my mind is made up. Not another step will I budge on this errand. What if a wretched old woman do choose to go to the devil, when I thought she was going to Heaven! Is that any reason why I should quit my dear Faith, and go after her?'

'You will think better of this, by-and-by,' said his acquaintance, composedly. 'Sit here and rest yourself awhile; and when you feel like moving again, there is my staff to help you along.'

Without more words, he threw his companion the maple stick, and was as speedily out of sight, as if he had vanished into the deepening gloom. The young man sat a few moments, by the roadside, applauding himself greatly, and thinking with how clear a conscience he should meet the minister, in his morning-walk, nor shrink from the eye of good old deacon Gookin. And what calm sleep would be his, that very night, which was to have been spent so wickedly, but purely and sweetly now, in the arms of Faith! Amidst these pleasant and praiseworthy meditations, goodman Brown heard the tramp of horses along the road, and deemed it advisable to conceal himself within the verge of the forest, conscious of the guilty purpose that had brought him thither, though now so happily turned from it.

On came the hoof-tramps and the voices of the riders, two grave old voices, conversing soberly as they drew near. These mingled sounds appeared to pass along the road, within a few yards of the young man's hiding-place; but owing, doubtless, to the depth of the gloom, at that particular spot, neither the travelers nor their steeds were visible. Though their figures brushed the small boughs by the way-side, it could not be seen that they intercepted, even for a moment, the faint gleam from the strip of bright sky, athwart which they

8. Exodus 7.11 describes the magicians of Egypt who duplicated Aaron's feat of casting down his rod before Pharaoh and making it turn into a serpent.

must have passed. Goodman Brown alternately crouched and stood on tip-toe, pulling aside the branches, and thrusting forth his head as far as he durst, without discerning so much as a shadow. It vexed him the more, because he could have sworn, were such a thing possible, that he recognized the voices of the minister and deacon Gookin, jogging along quietly, as they were wont to do, when bound to some ordination or ecclesiastical council. While yet within hearing, one of the riders stopped to pluck a switch.

'Of the two, reverend Sir,' said the voice like the deacon's, 'I had rather miss an ordination-dinner than to-night's meeting. They tell me that some of our community are to be here from Falmouth and beyond, and others from Connecticut and Rhode-Island; besides several of the Indian powows,[9] who, after their fashion, know almost as much deviltry as the best of us. Moreover, there is a goodly young woman to be taken into communion.'

'Mighty well, deacon Gookin!' replied the solemn old tones of the minister. 'Spur up, or we shall be late. Nothing can be done, you know, until I get on the ground.'

The hoofs clattered again, and the voices, talking so strangely in the empty air, passed on through the forest, where no church had ever been gathered, nor solitary Christian prayed. Whither, then, could these holy men be journeying, so deep into the heathen wilderness? Young goodman Brown caught hold of a tree, for support, being ready to sink down on the ground, faint and overburthened with the heavy sickness of his heart. He looked up to the sky, doubting whether there really was a Heaven above him. Yet, there was the blue arch, and the stars brightening in it.

'With Heaven above, and Faith below, I will yet stand firm against the devil!' cried goodman Brown.

While he still gazed upward, into the deep arch of the firmament, and had lifted his hands to pray, a cloud, though no wind was stirring, hurried across the zenith, and hid the brightening stars. The blue sky was still visible, except directly overhead, where this black mass of cloud was sweeping swiftly northward. Aloft in the air, as if from the depths of the cloud, came a confused and doubtful sound of voices. Once, the listener fancied that he could distinguish the accents of town's-people of his own, men and women, both pious and ungodly, many of whom he had met at the communion-table, and had seen others rioting at the tavern. The next moment, so indistinct were the sounds, he doubted whether he had heard aught but the murmur of the old forest, whispering without a wind. Then came a stronger swell of those familiar tones, heard daily in the sunshine, at Salem village, but never, until now, from a cloud of night. There was one voice, of a young woman, uttering lamentations, yet with an uncertain sorrow, and entreating for some favor, which, perhaps, it would grieve her to obtain. And all the unseen multitude, both saints and sinners, seemed to encourage her onward.

—'Faith!' shouted goodman Brown, in a voice of agony and desperation; and the echoes of the forest mocked him, crying—'Faith! Faith!' as if bewildered wretches were seeking her, all through the wilderness.

The cry of grief, rage, and terror, was yet piercing the night, when the unhappy husband held his breath for a response. There was a scream,

9. Medicine men; usually spelled "pow-wow" and later used to refer to any conference or gathering. Falmouth is a town on Cape Cod, about seventy miles from Salem.

drowned immediately in a louder murmur of voices, fading into far-off laughter, as the dark cloud swept away, leaving the clear and silent sky above goodman Brown. But something fluttered lightly down through the air, and caught on the branch of a tree. The young man seized it, and beheld a pink ribbon.

'My Faith is gone!' cried he, after one stupefied moment. 'There is no good on earth; and sin is but a name. Come, devil! for to thee is this world given.'

And maddened with despair, so that he laughed loud and long, did goodman Brown grasp his staff and set forth again, at such a rate, that he seemed to fly along the forest-path, rather than to walk or run. The road grew wilder and drearier, and more faintly traced, and vanished at length, leaving him in the heart of the dark wilderness, still rushing onward, with the instinct that guides mortal man to evil. The whole forest was peopled with frightful sounds; the creaking of the trees, the howling of wild beasts, and the yell of Indians; while, sometimes, the wind tolled like a distant church-bell, and sometimes gave a broad roar around the traveler, as if all Nature were laughing him to scorn. But he was himself the chief horror of the scene, and shrank not from its other horrors.

'Ha! ha! ha!' roared goodman Brown, when the wind laughed at him. 'Let us hear which will laugh loudest! Think not to frighten me with your deviltry! Come witch, come wizard, come Indian powow, come devil himself! and here comes goodman Brown. You may as well fear him as he fear you!'

In truth, all through the haunted forest, there could be nothing more frightful than the figure of goodman Brown. On he flew, among the black pines, brandishing his staff with frenzied gestures, now giving vent to an inspiration of horrid blasphemy, and now shouting forth such laughter, as set all the echoes of the forest laughing like demons around him. The fiend in his own shape is less hideous, than when he rages in the breast of man. Thus sped the demoniac on his course, until, quivering among the trees, he saw a red light before him, as when the felled trunks and branches of a clearing have been set on fire, and throw up their lurid blaze against the sky, at the hour of midnight. He paused, in a lull of the tempest that had driven him onward, and heard the swell of what seemed a hymn, rolling solemnly from a distance, with the weight of many voices. He knew the tune; it was a familiar one in the choir of the village meeting-house. The verse died heavily away, and was lengthened by a chorus, not of human voices, but of all the sounds of the benighted wilderness, pealing in awful harmony together. Goodman Brown cried out; and his cry was lost to his own ear, by its unison with the cry of the desert.

In the interval of silence, he stole forward, until the light glared full upon his eyes. At one extremity of an open space, hemmed in by the dark wall of the forest, arose a rock, bearing some rude, natural resemblance either to an altar or a pulpit, and surrounded by four blazing pines, their tops a flame, their stems untouched, like candles at an evening meeting. The mass of foliage, that had overgrown the summit of the rock, was all on fire, blazing high into the night, and fitfully illuminating the whole field. Each pendent twig and leafy festoon was in a blaze. As the red light arose and fell, a numerous congregation alternately shone forth, then disappeared in shadow, and again grew, as it were, out of the darkness, peopling the heart of the solitary woods at once.

'A grave and dark-clad company!' quoth goodman Brown.

In truth, they were such. Among them, quivering to-and-fro, between gloom and splendor, appeared faces that would be seen, next day, at the council-board of the province, and others which, Sabbath after Sabbath, looked devoutly heavenward, and benignantly over the crowded pews, from the holiest pulpits in the land. Some affirm, that the lady of the governor was there. At least, there were high dames well known to her, and wives of honored husbands, and widows, a great multitude, and ancient maidens, all of excellent repute, and fair young girls, who trembled, lest their mothers should espy them. Either the sudden gleams of light, flashing over the obscure field, bedazzled goodman Brown, or he recognized a score of the church-members of Salem village, famous for their especial sanctity. Good old deacon Gookin had arrived, and waited at the skirts of that venerable saint, his revered pastor. But, irreverently consorting with these grave, reputable, and pious people, these elders of the church, these chaste dames and dewy virgins, there were men of dissolute lives and women of spotted fame, wretches given over to all mean and filthy vice, and suspected even of horrid crimes. It was strange to see, that the good shrank not from the wicked, nor were the sinners abashed by the saints. Scattered, also, among their pale-faced enemies, were the Indian priests, or powows, who had often scared their native forest with more hideous incantations than any known to English witchcraft.

'But, where is Faith?' thought goodman Brown; and, as hope came into his heart, he trembled.

Another verse of the hymn arose, a slow and solemn strain, such as the pious love, but joined to words which expressed all that our nature can conceive of sin, and darkly hinted at far more. Unfathomable to mere mortals is the lore of fiends. Verse after verse was sung, and still the chorus of the desert swelled between, like the deepest tone of a mighty organ. And, with the final peal of that dreadful anthem, there came a sound, as if the roaring wind, the rushing streams, the howling beasts, and every other voice of the unconverted wilderness, were mingling and according with the voice of guilty man, in homage to the prince of all. The four blazing pines threw up a loftier flame, and obscurely discovered shapes and visages of horror on the smoke-wreaths, above the impious assembly. At the same moment, the fire on the rock shot redly forth, and formed a glowing arch above its base, where now appeared a figure. With reverence be it spoken, the apparition bore no slight similitude, both in garb and manner, to some grave divine of the New-England churches.

'Bring forth the converts!' cried a voice, that echoed through the field and rolled into the forest.

—At the word, goodman Brown stept forth from the shadow of the trees, and approached the congregation, with whom he felt a loathful brotherhood, by the sympathy of all that was wicked in his heart. He could have well nigh sworn, that the shape of his own dead father[1] beckoned him to advance, looking downward from a smoke-wreath, while a woman, with dim features of despair, threw out her hand to warn him back. Was it his mother? But

---

1. The Salem witch trials came to focus on the question of "specter evidence"—whether the devil could take on the "shape" of innocent people. If he could, then many supposed appearances of the accused might have been impersonations. An increasing suspicion of the value of spectral evidence was among the factors leading to the suspension of the trials.

he had no power to retreat one step, nor to resist, even in thought, when the minister and good old deacon Gookin, seized his arms, and led him to the blazing rock. Thither came also the slender form of a veiled female, led between goody Cloyse, that pious teacher of the catechism, and Martha Carrier, who had received the devil's promise to be queen of hell.[2] A rampant hag was she! And there stood the proselytes, beneath the canopy of fire.

'Welcome, my children,' said the dark figure, 'to the communion of your race![3] Ye have found, thus young, your nature and your destiny. My children, look behind you!'

They turned; and flashing forth, as it were, in a sheet of flame, the fiend-worshippers were seen; the smile of welcome gleamed darkly on every visage.

'There,' resumed the sable form, 'are all whom ye have reverenced from youth. Ye deemed them holier than yourselves, and shrank from your own sin, contrasting it with their lives of righteousness, and prayerful aspirations heavenward. Yet, here are they all, in my worshipping assembly! This night it shall be granted you to know their secret deeds; how hoary-bearded elders of the church have whispered wanton words to the young maids of their households; how many a woman, eager for widow's weeds, has given her husband a drink at bed-time, and let him sleep his last sleep in her bosom; how beardless youths have made haste to inherit their fathers' wealth; and how fair damsels—blush not, sweet ones!—have dug little graves in the garden, and bidden me, the sole guest, to an infant's funeral. By the sympathy of your human hearts for sin, ye shall scent out all the places—whether in church, bed-chamber, street, field, or forest—where crime has been committed, and shall exult to behold the whole earth one stain of guilt, one mighty blood-spot. Far more than this! It shall be yours to penetrate, in every bosom, the deep mystery of sin, the fountain of all wicked arts, and which, inexhaustibly supplies more evil impulses than human power—than my power, at its utmost!—can make manifest in deeds. And now, my children, look upon each other.'

They did so; and, by the blaze of the hell-kindled torches, the wretched man beheld his Faith, and the wife her husband, trembling before that unhallowed altar.

'Lo! there ye stand, my children,' said the figure, in a deep and solemn tone, almost sad, with its despairing awfulness, as if his once angelic nature could yet mourn for our miserable race. 'Depending upon one another's hearts, ye had still hoped, that virtue were not all a dream. Now are ye undeceived! Evil is the nature of mankind. Evil must be your only happiness. Welcome, again, my children, to the communion of your race!'

'Welcome!' repeated the fiend-worshippers, in one cry of despair and triumph.

And there they stood, the only pair, as it seemed, who were yet hesitating on the verge of wickedness, in this dark world. A basin was hollowed, naturally, in the rock. Did it contain water, reddened by the lurid light? or was it blood? or, perchance, a liquid flame? Herein did the Shape of Evil dip his hand, and prepare to lay the mark of baptism upon their foreheads, that they

---

2. During her trial, the historical Martha Carrier told of how the devil promised that she could become the queen of hell; she was convicted and hanged for witchcraft on August 19, 1692.

3. The *New-England Magazine* erroneously printed "grave," corrected to "race" in *Mosses from an Old Manse* (1846).

Beginnings to 1820

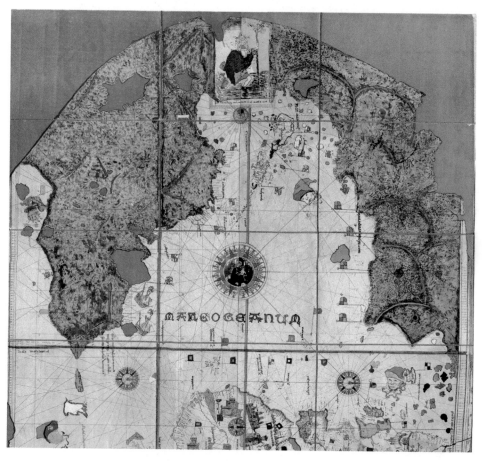

A Portion of the Mappa Mundi (World Map) by Juan de la Cosa, 1500

The oldest known cartographic representation of the Americas was made by Juan de la Cosa, a Spanish mariner, conquistador, and mapmaker. As pilot of the *Niña* during Columbus's second voyage (1494–95), de la Cosa learned about New World space firsthand. He also accompanied Columbus on his third voyage, and in 1499 he was the first pilot for the expedition of Alonso de Ojeda and Amerigo Vespucci. De la Cosa's map, measuring three feet by six feet, embraces the entire known world but is most notable for its attempt to portray and conceptualize the land that would come to be called the "New World" or "America." Hovering to the west (at the top) is a mystical figure of Columbus as Saint Christopher—the humble ferryman who carried Christ over the water on his back and thus supplied de la Cosa with a fitting metaphor for the looming Christianization of the Americas. The green area represents the western continents. Cuba, rendered as an island, shows up with remarkable clarity, below and to the right of the image of Columbus/Saint Christopher. The western edge of Europe is visible at the bottom.

René de Laudonnière and Chief Athore, Jacques Le Moyne de Morgues, 1564

When Protestant French colonists under Jean Ribault landed in Florida in the early 1560s, they erected two columns, decorated with the arms of the French king, that were intended to project their claim over the region. Jacques Le Moyne de Morgues, who as mapmaker and artist accompanied Ribault's successor, René de Laudonnière, on a second French expedition, here portrays the moment when the local Indian chief, Athore, took René de Laudonnière to Ribault's column. This engraving shows the native people "worshipping this stone as an idol," having placed before it offerings of fruit, edible roots, medicinal herbs, precious oils, and artifacts such as baskets and a bow and quiver. The artist, who escaped when the Spanish wiped out the French colony in 1565, settled in London, where he became an associate of Sir Walter Raleigh and the English artist-explorer John White.

The French Reach Port Royal, Theodor de Bry, 1591

Theodor de Bry, the first great illustrator of European voyages to the Americas, established the visual language through which generations of Old World inhabitants perceived the New World. In this engraving, based on a lost watercolor by Jacques Le Moyne de Morgues, de Bry shows the French fleet under Jean de Ribault reaching the coast of South Carolina at present-day St. Helena Sound, near Beaufort, in the spring of 1562. The representation of the Indian village, with its lush surroundings (pumpkins and grapes grow wild; deer, turkeys, and geese abound), offers an alluring image of America as paradise.

Indian Village of Secoton, John White, 1585

The English painter John White left an impressive visual record of places, people, and natural facts observed during several voyages to the New World in the 1580s. Collaborator at one time with the writer Thomas Harriot, White is known especially for his images of Native American life. This composite rendering of a village on the mainland of present-day North Carolina, just inside Pamlico Sound, is intended to show a wide array of Native customs and activities, from hunting and planting to everyday behavior and religious rites.

Elizabeth Clarke Freake and Baby Mary, unknown artist, 1671–74

Elizabeth Clarke (1642–1713), the daughter of a prosperous Boston merchant, was married in 1661 to the English-born lawyer John Freake, with whom she had eight children. Her portrait (like her husband's) was painted in 1671 by an unknown English-trained artist (now called "the Freake painter") who is believed to be responsible for several surviving portraits executed in a surprisingly rich style in the Boston area in the 1670s. When the Freakes' last child, Mary, was born in 1674, the artist or his successor added her to the portrait of Elizabeth, creating a composite of family life especially notable for the fineness of the clothes worn by the well-to-do mother.

Page from William Byrd's "Secret Diary"

For many years Byrd (1674–1744) kept an account of his daily life, both on his Virginia plantation, Westover, and on trips to London. Much of the diary was written in a code—developed by William Mason and published in 1707—designed for gentlemen to keep such writing from prying eyes. In terse but informative entries, Byrd discusses all facets of plantation life, from his religious exercises to the oversight of his many slaves. Most striking are his matter-of-fact records of his sexual encounters with slave women.

Hummingbird, from *The Natural History of Carolina, Florida and the Bahama Islands,* Mark Catesby, 1731–43

The British artist Mark Catesby produced the first large-scale natural history of the New World's flora and fauna, with which he was familiar from visits there between 1712 and 1719. In addition to birds he depicted reptiles, fish, and plant life, and in the text he discussed insects and the soil's and water's suitability for agriculture, among other topics. The engraving here is of what Catesby considered one of the New World's true wonders, the tiny ruby-throated hummingbird, near what he called a "trumpet flower." Before the development of color-printing technologies such as lithography, reproductions of this kind, including Catesby's, were hand-colored.

Benjamin Franklin Drawing Electricity from the Sky, Benjamin West, 1805

This allegorical depiction of Franklin conducting his famous experiment with a kite during a thunderstorm in the 1750s, and thereby demonstrating that lightning was electricity, suggests the almost mythic status he had achieved by the early nineteenth century, when his *Autobiography* became immensely popular. It also makes a claim for the importance of Americans to scientific inquiry in the Western world. Benjamin West (1738–1820), one of the most important American painters of this period and the first to be widely appreciated in England, made this sketch for a larger painting that he never completed. Notice the scientific apparatus to the left of Franklin. This orrery, which shows the relative positions of the planets, is being studied by childlike figures with oddly adult faces.

The Old Plantation, c. 1790–1800

This watercolor depicts slave life on an antebellum Southern plantation and is particularly important for its representation of slave quarters and of the slaves' social music. At right one man plays a gourd banjo and another keeps time with two sticks, or "bones." The man in the middle and two women do a ritual dance, probably reflecting West African cultural influences. The head wraps also reflect African influence.

Declaration of Independence, John Trumbull, c. 1817–19

This painting, measuring twelve feet by eighteen feet, depicts *the* iconic moment in American political history, the signing of the Declaration of Independence, in Philadelphia. In the center are the men who drafted the Declaration (l. to r., John Adams, Roger Sherman, Thomas Jefferson, and Benjamin Franklin), with Jefferson presenting the document to John Hancock, president of the Continental Congress. About two-thirds of the fifty-six signers are also depicted. Trumbull (1756–1843), who studied in England with the great American artist Benjamin West, is known primarily for his paintings of scenes from American history. Although completed several decades after the event it memorializes, this painting is a good example of American artists' and writers' attempts, after the War of 1812, to play a role in creating a unique and heroic American history.

Exhuming the Mastodon, Charles Wilson Peale, 1806–08

Peale (1741–1827) was the patriarch of a family of American artists, including his sons Rembrandt and Raphael, renowned for their portraits and still lifes. Like many eighteenth-century Americans (Thomas Jefferson included), Peale had a deep interest in natural history; he established in Philadelphia his own museum of scientific curiosities—a collection of specimens not arranged by any particular scientific method. In the early nineteenth century he organized an expedition to the Hudson Valley, in New York, to recover the recently discovered bones of a mastodon, which he and his son Rembrandt later mounted for display. This striking painting illustrates the elaborate excavation, with the apparatus in the center removing earth from the pit where the bones lie buried. Peale supervises at right. The fascination of the subject lay in its proof of America's long early history.

Elizabeth Graham's Embroidery Map

This *Plan of the City of Washington* (1800–1803) was worked in silk embroidery on linen by Elizabeth Graham, of Baltimore, Maryland, when she was about thirteen. The plan of the new capital city was originally designed by Pierre L'Enfant in 1791 and engraved by James Thackara and John Vallance in 1792. Graham decorated the map with oval cartouches showing George Washington and the figures of Justice, Hope, and Liberty, combining patriotic themes with the decorative arts.

The Return of Rip Van Winkle, John Quidor, 1829

A friend of Washington Irving, Quidor (1801–1881) depicted a key scene near the end of "Rip Van Winkle" (1819), capturing the fantastic quality of Rip's return to his village in New York's Catskill Mountains after sleeping through the American Revolution. In the background, the American flag and the image of George Washington on the tavern's sign suggest the post-Revolutionary moment. Rip appears both confused and in control amidst the curious crowd.

Major Ridge, a Cherokee Chief,
Charles Bird King, 1836–44

Major Ridge, a "progressive" Cherokee leader, signed the Cherokee Memorial of 1830 opposing Indian removal. But in 1835, having concluded that resistance to President Jackson's Indian removal program was futile, he, along with other members of his family, signed the Treaty of New Echota, which provided a legal basis for the forcible removal of the Cherokees in 1838. During a visit to Washington, he was painted by Charles Bird King (1785–1862), who produced portraits of a number of the prominent Indian leaders that visited the capital. He was assassinated by Cherokee opponents of the New Echota treaty on June 22, 1839.

The War Dance by the Ojibway Indians, George Catlin, 1835–37

Catlin (1796–1872), the most prolific and famous painter of Indians and Indian scenes in the nineteenth century, was in large part responsible for shaping white people's ideas of Indians and Indian culture. He painted portraits of renowned Native leaders such as the Seneca Red Jacket and the Sac leader Black Hawk, and he also painted scenes of traditional and ceremonial tribal life like this war dance of the "Ojibway." The Ojibwe, also known as the Chippewa, were one of the largest and most powerful North American tribes. Jane Johnston Schoolcraft belonged to the Ojibwe nation on her mother's side. Traditional Chippewa songs would be recorded by Frances Densmore early in the twentieth century.

The Course of Empire: Consummation of Empire, Thomas Cole, 1836

In the early 1830s Cole (1801–1848), the leader of the Hudson River school of New York landscape painters, was commissioned to do the five allegorical scenes that he titled *The Course of Empire.* Like James Fenimore Cooper and a number of other writers of the time, Cole feared that all republics, including the United States, followed patterns of cyclical history in which a rise is inevitably followed by a decline. In this painting, the third in the series, Cole draws on classical Roman imagery to portray the decadence and corruption that he feared would be ushered in by an increasingly urbanized United States.

The Course of Empire: Desolation, Thomas Cole, 1836

In *Destruction,* the fourth painting in *The Course of Empire,* Cole depicts the allegorical republic at the moment of its apocalyptic demise. In *Desolation,* the final painting, nature reasserts its domination. Humans have vanished from the scene; new trees have grown on the blighted landscape; birds nest atop a Corinthian column. Viewed in relation to *The Pastoral State,* the first in the series, *Desolation* suggests that the cycle of human rise and decline is on the verge of starting anew. Most of Cole's viewers regarded the series as a challenge, convinced that the United States could muster the virtue to resist the corrupting forces of decline.

War News from Mexico, Richard Caton Woodville, 1848

Working at the time in Germany, Woodville (1822–1855) sent this painting to be exhibited in New York City. In a small town where a post office shares space with an "American Hotel," eight white men gather to read the news about the war with Mexico (1846–48). The excitement of the principal reader is offset by the excluded white woman in the shadows and by the seated black workingman and black girl, perhaps his daughter, who seem to convey a muted knowingness about the consequences of a war that promised to extend the realm of slavery.

Uncle Tom and Little Eva, Robert Scott Duncanson, 1853

Commissioned by a Detroit abolitionist to depict a scene from Harriet Beecher Stowe's best-selling *Uncle Tom's Cabin* (1852), the free-born African American landscapist Duncanson (1821–1872) wanted to show that interracial human kindness and spirituality, not violence, would help to end slavery. In this scene, based on a black-and-white engraving in the novel's first edition, Little Eva teaches Uncle Tom to read the family Bible in a lush tropical setting near Louisiana's Lake Pontchartrain. Eva points toward the heavens, declaring, "I'm going there . . . before long." The glimmering sky suggests her impending salvation.

Shake Hands?, Lily Martin Spencer, 1854

The first female genre painter in the nineteenth-century United States, Spencer (1822–1902) achieved great popular success with this painting. In a kitchen replete with chicken, cabbage, and apples, a self-possessed and thoroughly happy woman extends a dough-covered hand. Typically a male gesture of equality, the proffered handshake boldly suggests the woman's sense that she is equal to anyone who might be viewing her. That the painting could be interpreted both as a celebration of women's domesticity and as a radical statement about women's equality no doubt contributed to its popularity. It toured several cities and in 1857 was lithographed for wide distribution.

The Lackawanna Valley, George Innes, 1855

In the early 1850s Innes (1825–1894) was commissioned by the Delaware, Lackawanna and Western Railroad to celebrate its development in the Northeast. In this scene just past a roundhouse in Scranton, Pennsylvania, the train, with its smoke and forward energy, seems at first glance to be intruding onto a bucolic landscape. Overall, though, Innes, perhaps because he was under commission, sought to depict nature and machine as organically integrated. The golden glow of the painting, along with the reclining youthful figure who is unthreatened by the approaching train, conveys a hopeful sense that this is the dawn of a glorious new era in U.S. civilization.

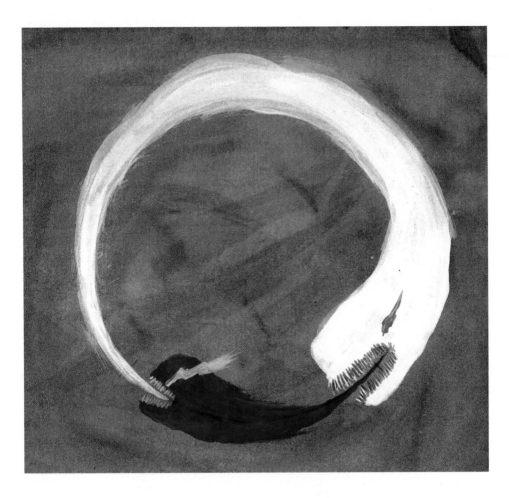

"Aye, he's chasing me now; not I him—that's bad . . . ," Matt Kish, 2011

In 2009, the Ohio-based artist Matt Kish (b. 1969) undertook the ambitious project of creating an image a day in response to selected text from each page of the Signet Edition of *Moby-Dick*. Reproductions of his artwork can be found in his *Moby-Dick in Pictures: One Drawing for Every Page* (2011), one of the most provocative engagements with *Moby-Dick* in recent years. In this image, inspired by Ahab's remark about Moby Dick in the final chapter of the novel, Ahab is imagined as something other than human.

might be partakers of the mystery of sin, more conscious of the secret guilt of others, both in deed and thought, than they could now be of their own. The husband cast one look at his pale wife, and Faith at him. What polluted wretches would the next glance shew them to each other, shuddering alike at what they disclosed and what they saw!

'Faith! Faith!' cried the husband. 'Look up to Heaven, and resist the Wicked One!'

Whether Faith obeyed, he knew not. Hardly had he spoken, when he found himself amid calm night and solitude, listening to a roar of the wind, which died heavily away through the forest. He staggered against the rock and felt it chill and damp, while a hanging twig, that had been all on fire, besprinkled his cheek with the coldest dew.

The next morning, young goodman Brown came slowly into the street of Salem village, staring around him like a bewildered man. The good old minister was taking a walk along the graveyard, to get an appetite for breakfast and meditate his sermon, and bestowed a blessing, as he passed, on goodman Brown. He shrank from the venerable saint, as if to avoid an anathema. Old deacon Gookin was at domestic worship, and the holy words of his prayer were heard through the open window. 'What God doth the wizard pray to?' quoth goodman Brown. Goody Cloyse, that excellent old Christian, stood in the early sunshine, at her own lattice, catechising a little girl, who had brought her a pint of morning's milk. Goodman Brown snatched away the child, as from the grasp of the fiend himself. Turning the corner by the meeting-house, he spied the head of Faith, with the pink ribbons, gazing anxiously forth, and bursting into such joy at sight of him, that she skipt along the street, and almost kissed her husband before the whole village. But, goodman Brown looked sternly and sadly into her face, and passed on without a greeting.

Had goodman Brown fallen asleep in the forest, and only dreamed a wild dream of a witch-meeting?

Be it so, if you will. But, alas! it was a dream of evil omen for young goodman Brown. A stern, a sad, a darkly meditative, a distrustful, if not a desperate man, did he become, from the night of that fearful dream. On the Sabbath-day, when the congregation were singing a holy psalm, he could not listen, because an anthem of sin rushed loudly upon his ear, and drowned all the blessed strain. When the minister spoke from the pulpit, with power and fervid eloquence, and, with his hand on the open bible, of the sacred truths of our religion, and of saint-like lives and triumphant deaths, and of future bliss or misery unutterable, then did goodman Brown turn pale, dreading, lest the roof should thunder down upon the gray blasphemer and his hearers. Often, awakening suddenly at midnight, he shrank from the bosom of Faith, and at morning or eventide, when the family knelt down at prayer, he scowled, and muttered to himself, and gazed sternly at his wife, and turned away. And when he had lived long, and was borne to his grave, a hoary corpse, followed by Faith, an aged woman, and children and grandchildren, a goodly procession, besides neighbors, not a few, they carved no hopeful verse upon his tomb-stone; for his dying hour was gloom.

1835

The May-Pole of Merry Mount[1]

> There is an admirable foundation for a philosophic romance, in the curious history of the early settlement of Mount Wallaston, or Merry Mount. In the slight sketch here attempted, the facts, recorded on the grave pages of our New England annalists, have wrought themselves, almost spontaneously, into a sort of allegory. The masques, mummeries, and festive customs, described in the text, are in accordance with the manners of the age. Authority, on these points may be found in Strutt's Book of English Sports and Pastimes.[2]

Bright were the days at Merry Mount, when the May-Pole was the banner-staff of that gay colony! They who reared it, should their banner be triumphant, were to pour sun-shine over New England's rugged hills, and scatter flower-seeds throughout the soil. Jollity and gloom were contending for an empire. Midsummer eve[3] had come, bringing deep verdure to the forest, and roses in her lap, of a more vivid hue than the tender buds of Spring. But May, or her mirthful spirit, dwelt all the year round at Merry Mount, sporting with the Summer months, and revelling with Autumn, and basking in the glow of Winter's fireside. Through a world of toil and care, she flitted with a dreamlike smile, and came hither to find a home among the lightsome hearts of Merry Mount.

Never had the May-Pole been so gaily decked as at sunset on mid-summer eve. This venerated emblem was a pine tree, which had preserved the slender grace of youth, while it equalled the loftiest height of the old wood monarchs. From its top streamed a silken banner, colored like the rainbow. Down nearly to the ground, the pole was dressed with birchen boughs, and others of the liveliest green, and some with silvery leaves, fastened by ribbons that fluttered in fantastic knots of twenty different colors, but no sad ones. Garden flowers, and blossoms of the wilderness, laughed gladly forth amid the verdure, so fresh and dewy, that they must have grown by magic on that happy pine tree. Where this green and flowery splendor terminated, the shaft of the May-Pole was stained with the seven brilliant hues of the banner at its top. On the lowest green bough hung an abundant wreath of roses, some that had been gathered in the sunniest spots of the forest, and others, of still richer blush, which the colonists had reared from English seed. Oh, people of the Golden Age, the chief of your husbandry, was to raise flowers!

But what was the wild throng that stood hand in hand about the May-Pole? It could not be, that the Fauns and Nymphs, when driven from their classic

---

1. The text is that of the first printing in *The Token* (1836). Hawthorne included the story in *Twice-Told Tales* (1837). "May-pole": in English tradition, the tall pole placed in a village around which flower-bedecked people danced to celebrate May Day (the coming of spring). Puritans condemned the custom as pagan.
2. Joseph Strutt, *The Sports and Pastimes of the People of England* (1801). Hawthorne also knew Nathaniel Morton's *New England Memorial* (1669), which drew on William Bradford's manuscript history *Of Plymouth Plantation*. Hawthorne's tale works loosely with the historical conflict between the colony of fur traders at

Mount Wollaston, now Quincy, Massachusetts, and the religious leaders of Plymouth and Salem from 1625 to 1630. Thomas Morton (c. 1579–1647), one of the traders, had dubbed Mount Wollaston "Merry Mount" and in 1627 encouraged the use of the maypole. In 1628 John Endicott (1589?–1665), the governor of the Massachusetts Bay Colony, led an expedition that cut down the maypole shortly after Morton was deported to England for trafficking firearms to the Indians. Morton presents his side of the conflict in *New English Canaan* (1637).
3. June 20, the day before the longest day of the year.

groves and homes of ancient fable, had sought refuge, as all the persecuted did, in the fresh woods of the West. These were Gothic monsters, though perhaps of Grecian ancestry. On the shoulders of a comely youth, uprose the head and branching antlers of a stag; a second, human in all other points, had the grim visage of a wolf; a third, still with the trunk and limbs of a mortal man, showed the beard and horns of a venerable he-goat. There was the likeness of a bear erect, brute in all but his hind legs, which were adorned with pink silk stockings. And here again, almost as wondrous, stood a real bear of the dark forest, lending each of his fore paws to the grasp of a human hand, and as ready for the dance as any in that circle. This inferior nature rose half-way, to meet his companions as they stooped. Other faces wore the similitude of man or woman, but distorted or extravagant, with red noses pendulous before their mouths, which seemed of awful depth, and stretched from ear to ear in an eternal fit of laughter. Here might be seen the Salvage Man,[4] well known in heraldry, hairy as a baboon, and girdled with green leaves. By his side, a nobler figure, but still a counterfeit, appeared an Indian hunter, with feathery crest and wampum belt. Many of this strange company wore fools-caps, and had little bells appended to their garments, tinkling with a silvery sound, responsive to the inaudible music of their gleesome spirits. Some youths and maidens were of soberer garb, yet well maintained their places in the irregular throng, by the expression of wild revelry upon their features. Such were the colonists of Merry Mount, as they stood in the broad smile of sunset, round their venerated May-Pole.

Had a wanderer, bewildered in the melancholy forest, heard their mirth, and stolen a half-affrighted glance, he might have fancied them the crew of Comus,[5] some already transformed to brutes, some midway between man and beast, and the others rioting in the flow of tipsey jollity that foreran the change. But a band of Puritans, who watched the scene, invisible themselves, compared the masques to those devils and ruined souls, with whom their superstition peopled the black wilderness.

Within the ring of monsters, appeared the two airiest forms, that had ever trodden on any more solid footing than a purple and golden cloud. One was a youth, in glistening apparel, with a scarf of the rainbow pattern crosswise on his breast. His right hand held a gilded staff, the ensign[6] of high dignity among the revellous, and his left grasped the slender fingers of a fair maiden, not less gaily decorated than himself. Bright roses glowed in contrast with the dark and glossy curls of each, and were scattered round their feet, or had sprung up spontaneously there. Behind this lightsome couple, so close to the May-Pole that its boughs shaded his jovial face, stood the figure of an English priest, canonically dressed, yet decked with flowers, in Heathen fashion, and wearing a chaplet of the native vine leaves. By the riot of his rolling eye, and the pagan decorations of his holy garb, he seemed the wildest monster there, and the very Comus of the crew.

'Votaries of the May-Pole,' cried the flower-decked priest, 'merrily, all day long, have the woods echoed to your mirth. But be this your merriest hour,

---

4. Person clad in foliage to represent a savage, as in medieval and Renaissance pageantry.
5. The god of revelry, here associated with Milton's *Comus* (1634), whose magical potions turn unsuspecting travelers in the woods into monstrous figures who join his crew.
6. Sign, token.

my hearts! Lo, here stand the Lord and Lady of the May, whom I, a clerk[7] of Oxford, and high priest of Merry Mount, am presently to join in holy matrimony. Up with your nimble spirits, ye morrice-dancers, green-men, and glee-maidens,[8] bears and wolves, and horned gentlemen! Come; a chorus now, rich with the old mirth of Merry England, and the wilder glee of this fresh forest; and then a dance, to show the youthful pair what life is made of, and how airily they should go through it! All ye that love the May-Pole, lend your voices to the nuptial song of the Lord and Lady of the May!'

This wedlock was more serious than most affairs of Merry Mount, where jest and delusion, trick and fantasy, kept up a continual carnival. The Lord and Lady of the May, though their titles must be laid down at sunset, were really and truly to be partners for the dance of life, beginning the measure that same bright eve. The wreath of roses, that hung from the lowest green bough of the May-Pole, had been twined for them, and would be thrown over both their heads, in symbol of their flowery union. When the priest had spoken, therefore, a riotous uproar burst from the rout of monstrous figures.

'Begin you the stave,[9] reverend Sir,' cried they all; 'and never did the woods ring to such a merry peal, as we of the May-Pole shall send up!'

Immediately a prelude of pipe, cittern,[1] and viol, touched with practised minstrelsy, began to play from a neighboring thicket, in such a mirthful cadence, that the boughs of the May-Pole quivered to the sound. But the May Lord, he of the gilded staff, chancing to look into his Lady's eyes, was wonderstruck at the almost pensive glance that met his own.

'Edith, sweet Lady of the May,' whispered he, reproachfully, 'is your wreath of roses a garland to hang above our graves, that you look so sad? Oh, Edith, this is our golden time! Tarnish it not by any pensive shadow of the mind; for it may be, that nothing of futurity will be brighter than the mere remembrance of what is now passing.'

'That was the very thought that saddened me! How came it in your mind too?' said Edith, in a still lower tone than he; for it was high treason to be sad at Merry Mount. 'Therefore do I sigh amid this festive music. And besides, dear Edgar, I struggle as with a dream, and fancy that these shapes of our jovial friends are visionary, and their mirth unreal, and that we are no true Lord and Lady of the May. What is the mystery in my heart?'

Just then, as if a spell had loosened them, down came a little shower of withering rose leaves from the May-Pole. Alas, for the young lovers! No sooner had their hearts glowed with real passion, than they were sensible of something vague and unsubstantial in their former pleasures, and felt a dreary presentiment of inevitable change. From the moment that they truly loved, they had subjected themselves to earth's doom of care, and sorrow, and troubled joy, and had no more a home at Merry Mount. That was Edith's mystery. Now leave we the priest to marry them, and the masquers to sport round the May-Pole, till the last sunbeam be withdrawn from its summit, and the shadows of the forest mingle gloomily in the dance. Meanwhile, we may discover who these gay people were.

7. In Anglican usage, lay minister who assists the parish clergyman.
8. Women singers. "Morrice-dancers": participants in an English folk dance. "Green-men": men bedecked in greenery.
9. Stanza or verse.
1. Guitar with pear-shaped body.

Two hundred years ago, and more, the old world and its inhabitants became mutually weary of each other. Men voyaged by thousands to the West; some to barter glass beads, and such like jewels, for the furs of the Indian hunter; some to conquer virgin empires; and one stern band to pray. But none of these motives had much weight with the colonists of Merry Mount. Their leaders were men who had sported so long with life, that when Thought and Wisdom came, even these unwelcome guests were led astray, by the crowd of vanities which they should have put to flight. Erring Thought and perverted Wisdom were made to put on masques, and play the fool. The men of whom we speak, after losing the heart's fresh gaiety, imagined a wild philosophy of pleasure, and came hither to act out their latest day-dream. They gathered followers from all that giddy tribe, whose whole life is like the festal days of soberer men. In their train were minstrels, not unknown in London streets; wandering players, whose theatres had been the halls of noblemen; mummeries, rope-dancers, and mountebanks,[2] who would long be missed at wakes, church-ales, and fairs; in a word, mirth-makers of every sort, such as abounded in that age, but now began to be discountenanced by the rapid growth of Puritanism. Light had their footsteps been on land, and as lightly they came across the sea. Many had been maddened by their previous troubles into a gay despair; others were as madly gay in the flush of youth, like the May Lord and his Lady; but whatever might be the quality of their mirth, old and young were gay at Merry Mount. The young deemed themselves happy. The elder spirits, if they knew that mirth was but the counterfeit of happiness, yet followed the false shadow wilfully, because at least her garments glittered brightest. Sworn triflers of a life-time, they would not venture among the sober truths of life, not even to be truly blest.

All the hereditary pastimes of Old England were transplanted hither. The King of Christmas was duly crowned, and the Lord of Misrule[3] bore potent sway. On the eve of Saint John,[4] they felled whole acres of the forest to make bonfires, and danced by the blaze all night, crowned with garlands, and throwing flowers into the flame. At harvest time, though their crop was of the smallest, they made an image with the sheaves of Indian corn, and wreathed it with autumnal garlands, and bore it home triumphantly. But what chiefly characterized the colonists of Merry Mount, was their veneration for the May-Pole. It has made their true history a poet's tale. Spring decked the hallowed emblem with young blossoms and fresh green boughs; Summer brought roses of the deepest blush, and the perfected foliage of the forest; Autumn enriched it with that red and yellow gorgeousness, which converts each wildwood leaf into a painted flower; and Winter silvered it with sleet, and hung it round with icicles, till it flashed in the cold sunshine, itself a frozen sunbeam. Thus each alternate season did homage to the May-Pole, and paid it a tribute of its own richest splendor. Its votaries danced round it, once, at least, in every month; sometimes they called it their religion, or their altar; but always, it was the banner-staff of Merry Mount.

Unfortunately, there were men in the new world, of a sterner faith than these May-Pole worshippers. Not far from Merry Mount was a settlement of

---

2. Showmen who "mount benches" to sell medicines or (as here) to tell stories or do tricks. "Mummeries": masked actors. "Rope-dancers": tightrope walkers.

3. Person appointed to preside over the traditional Christmas revelry.

4. Midsummer eve.

Puritans, most dismal wretches, who said their prayers before daylight, and then wrought in the forest or the cornfield, till evening made it prayer time again. Their weapons were always at hand, to shoot down the straggling savage. When they met in conclave, it was never to keep up the old English mirth, but to hear sermons three hours long, or to proclaim bounties on the heads of wolves and the scalps of Indians. Their festivals were fast-days, and their chief pastime the singing of psalms. Woe to the youth or maiden, who did but dream of a dance! The selectman nodded to the constable; and there sat the light-heeled reprobate in the stocks; or if he danced, it was round the whipping-post, which might be termed the Puritan May-Pole.

A party of these grim Puritans, toiling through the difficult woods, each with a horse-load of iron armor to burthen his footsteps, would sometimes draw near the sunny precincts of Merry Mount. There were the silken colonists, sporting round their May-Pole; perhaps teaching a bear to dance, or striving to communicate their mirth to the grave Indian; or masquerading in the skins of deer and wolves, which they had hunted for that especial purpose. Often, the whole colony were playing at blindman's bluff, magistrates and all with their eyes bandaged, except a single scape-goat, whom the blinded sinners pursued by the tinkling of the bells at his garments. Once, it is said, they were seen following a flower-decked corpse, with merriment and festive music, to his grave. But did the dead man laugh? In their quietest times, they sang ballads and told tales, for the edification of their pious visiters; or perplexed them with juggling tricks; or grinned at them through horse-collars; and when sport itself grew wearisome, they made game of their own stupidity, and began a yawning match. At the very least of these enormities, the men of iron shook their heads and frowned so darkly, that the revellers looked up, imagining that a momentary cloud had overcast the sunshine, which was to be perpetual there. On the other hand, the Puritans affirmed, that, when a psalm was pealing from their place of worship, the echo, which the forest sent them back, seemed often like the chorus of a jolly catch, closing with a roar of laughter. Who but the fiend, and his fond slaves, the crew of Merry Mount, had thus disturbed them! In due time, a feud arose, stern and bitter on one side, and as serious on the other as any thing could be, among such light spirits as had sworn allegiance to the May-Pole. The future complexion of New England was involved in this important quarrel. Should the grisly saints establish their jurisdiction over the gay sinners, then would their spirits darken all the clime, and make it a land of clouded visages, of hard toil, of sermon and psalm, forever. But should the banner-staff of Merry Mount be fortunate, sunshine would break upon the hills, and flowers would beautify the forest, and late posterity do homage to the May-Pole!

After these authentic passages from history, we return to the nuptials of the Lord and Lady of the May. Alas! we have delayed too long, and must darken our tale too suddenly. As we glanced again at the May-Pole, a solitary sun-beam is fading from the summit, and leaves only a faint golden tinge, blended with the hues of the rainbow banner. Even that dim light is now withdrawn, relinquishing the whole domain of Merry Mount to the evening gloom, which has rushed so instantaneously from the black surrounding woods. But some of these black shadows have rushed forth in human shape.

Yes: with the setting sun, the last day of mirth had passed from Merry Mount. The ring of gay masquers was disordered and broken; the stag lowered his antlers in dismay; the wolf grew weaker than a lamb; the bells of the morrice-dancers tinkled with tremulous affright. The Puritans had played a characteristic part in the May-Pole mummeries. Their darksome figures were intermixed with the wild shapes of their foes, and made the scene a picture of the moment, when waking thoughts start up amid the scattered fantasies of a dream. The leader of the hostile party stood in the centre of the circle, while the rout of monsters cowered around him, like evil spirits in the presence of a dread magician. No fantastic foolery could look him in the face. So stern was the energy of his aspect, that the whole man, visage, frame, and soul, seemed wrought of iron, gifted with life and thought, yet all of one substance with his head-piece and breast-plate. It was the Puritan of Puritans; it was Endicott himself![5]

'Stand off, priest of Baal!'[6] said he, with a grim frown, and laying no reverent hand upon the surplice. 'I know thee, Blackstone![7] Thou art the man, who couldst not abide the rule even of thine own corrupted church,[8] and hast come hither to preach iniquity, and to give example of it in thy life. But now shall it be seen that the Lord hath sanctified this wilderness for his peculiar people. Woe unto them that would defile it! And first for this flower-decked abomination, the altar of thy worship!'

And with his keen sword, Endicott assaulted the hallowed May-Pole. Nor long did it resist his arm. It groaned with a dismal sound; it showered leaves and rose-buds upon the remorseless enthusiast; and finally, with all its green boughs, and ribbons, and flowers, symbolic of departed pleasures, down fell the banner-staff of Merry Mount. As it sank, tradition says, the evening sky grew darker, and the woods threw forth a more sombre shadow.

'There,' cried Endicott, looking triumphantly on his work, 'there lies the only May-Pole in New England! The thought is strong within me, that, by its fall, is shadowed forth the fate of light and idle mirth-makers, amongst us and our posterity. Amen, saith John Endicott!'

'Amen!' echoed his followers.

But the votaries of the May-Pole gave one groan for their idol. At the sound, the Puritan leader glanced at the crew of Comus, each a figure of broad mirth, yet, at this moment, strangely expressive of sorrow and dismay.

'Valiant captain,' quoth Peter Palfrey, the Ancient[9] of the band, 'what order shall be taken with the prisoners?'

'I thought not to repent me of cutting down a May-Pole,' replied Endicott, 'yet now I could find in my heart to plant it again, and give each of these bestial pagans one other dance round their idol. It would have served rarely for a whipping-post!'

'But there are pine trees enow,' suggested the lieutenant.

'True, good Ancient,' said the leader. 'Wherefore, bind the heathen crew, and bestow on them a small matter of stripes apiece, as earnest[1] of our future

5. John Endicott (c. 1588–1665) served as the first governor of the Massachusetts Bay Colony from 1629 to 1630; he was succeeded by John Winthrop.
6. The slaying of the prophets of the fertility god Baal is described in 1 Kings 18.
7. "Did Governor Endicott speak less positively, we should suspect a mistake here. The Reverend Mr. Blackstone, though an eccentric, is not known to have been an immoral man. We rather doubt his identity with the priest of Merry Mount" [Hawthorne's note]. An eccentric clergyman, William Blackstone was known for quarreling with both the Merry Mounters and the Puritans.
8. The Anglican Church.
9. Lieutenant or standard bearer. Palfrey (d. 1663), one of the first English settlers of Salem, which had broken away from the Plymouth Colony in 1629.
1. Pledge.

justice. Set some of the rogues in the stocks to rest themselves, so soon as Providence shall bring us to one of our own well-ordered settlements, where such accommodations may be found. Further penalties, such as branding and cropping of ears, shall be thought of hereafter.'

'How many stripes for the priest?' inquired Ancient Palfrey.

'None as yet,' answered Endicott, bending his iron frown upon the culprit. 'It must be for the Great and General Court[2] to determine, whether stripes and long imprisonment, and other grievous penalty, may atone for his transgressions. Let him look to himself! For such as violate our civil order, it may be permitted us to show mercy. But woe to the wretch that troubleth our religion!'

'And this dancing bear,' resumed the officer. 'Must he share the stripes of his fellows?'

'Shoot him through the head!' said the energetic Puritan. 'I suspect witchcraft in the beast.'

'Here be a couple of shining ones,' continued Peter Palfrey, pointing his weapon at the Lord and Lady of the May. 'They seem to be of high station among these mis-doers. Methinks their dignity will not be fitted with less than a double share of stripes.'

Endicott rested on his sword, and closely surveyed the dress and aspect of the hapless pair. There they stood, pale, downcast, and apprehensive. Yet there was an air of mutual support, and of pure affection, seeking aid and giving it, that showed them to be man and wife, with the sanction of a priest upon their love. The youth, in the peril of the moment, had dropped his gilded staff, and thrown his arm about the Lady of the May, who leaned against his breast, too lightly to burthen him, but with weight enough to express that their destinies were linked together, for good or evil. They looked first at each other, and then into the grim captain's face. There they stood, in the first hour of wedlock, while the idle pleasures, of which their companions were the emblems, had given place to the sternest cares of life, personified by the dark Puritans. But never had their youthful beauty seemed so pure and high, as when its glow was chastened by adversity.

'Youth,' said Endicott, 'ye stand in an evil case, thou and thy maiden wife. Make ready presently; for I am minded that ye shall both have a token to remember your wedding-day!'

'Stern man,' exclaimed the May Lord, 'How can I move thee? Were the means at hand, I would resist to the death. Being powerless, I entreat! Do with me as thou wilt; but let Edith go untouched!'

'Not so,' replied the immitigable zealot. 'We are not wont to show an idle courtesy to that sex, which requireth the stricter discipline. What sayest thou, maid? Shall thy silken bridegroom suffer thy share of the penalty, besides his own?'

'Be it death,' said Edith, 'and lay it all on me!'

Truly, as Endicott had said, the poor lovers stood in a woeful case. Their foes were triumphant, their friends captive and abased, their home desolate, the benighted wilderness around them, and a rigorous destiny, in the shape of the Puritan leader, their only guide. Yet the deepening twilight could not

---

2. Massachusetts legislature.

altogether conceal, that the iron man was softened; he smiled, at the fair spectacle of early love; he almost sighed, for the inevitable blight of early hopes.

'The troubles of life have come hastily on this young couple,' observed Endicott. 'We will see how they comport themselves under their present trials, ere we burthen them with greater. If, among the spoil, there be any garments of a more decent fashion, let them be put upon this May Lord and his Lady, instead of their glistening vanities. Look to it, some of you.'

'And shall not the youth's hair be cut?' asked Peter Palfrey, looking with abhorrence at the love-lock and long glossy curls of the young man.

'Crop it forthwith, and that in the true pumpkin shell fashion,'[3] answered the captain. 'Then bring them along with us, but more gently than their fellows. There be qualities in the youth, which may make him valiant to fight, and sober to toil, and pious to pray; and in the maiden, that may fit her to become a mother in our Israel,[4] bringing up babes in better nurture than her own hath been. Nor think ye, young ones, that they are the happiest, even in our lifetime of a moment, who misspend it in dancing round a May-Pole!'

And Endicott, the severest Puritan of all who laid the rock-foundation of New England, lifted the wreath of roses from the ruin of the May-Pole, and threw it, with his own gauntleted hand, over the heads of the Lord and Lady of the May. It was a deed of prophecy. As the moral gloom of the world overpowers all systematic gaiety, even so was their home of wild mirth made desolate amid the sad forest. They returned to it no more. But, as their flowery garland was wreathed of the brightest roses that had grown there, so, in the tie that united them, were intertwined all the purest and best of their early joys. They went heavenward, supporting each other along the difficult path which it was their lot to tread, and never wasted one regretful thought on the vanities of Merry Mount.

1835

The Minister's Black Veil[1]

A Parable[2]

BY THE AUTHOR OF 'SIGHTS FROM A STEEPLE'

The sexton stood in the porch of Milford[3] meeting-house, pulling lustily at the bell-rope. The old people of the village came stooping along the street. Children, with bright faces, tript merrily beside their parents, or mimicked a graver gait, in the conscious dignity of their Sunday clothes. Spruce bachelors looked sidelong at the pretty maidens, and fancied that the sabbath

3. Roundhead style; relatively close-cropped in Puritan fashion.
4. Endicott makes the standard 17th-century Puritan identification of the New England settlers with the biblical Jews, whom he regarded as another persecuted, God-chosen group.
1. The text is that of the first printing in *The Token* (1836). Hawthorne reprinted the story in *Twice-Told Tales* (1837).
2. Another clergyman in New-England,

Mr. Joseph Moody, of York, Maine, who died about eighty years since, made himself remarkable by the same eccentricity that is here related of the Reverend Mr. Hooper. In his case, however, the symbol had a different import. In early life he had accidentally killed a beloved friend; and from that day till the hour of his own death, he hid his face from men [Hawthorne's note].
3. Town southwest of Boston.

sunshine made them prettier than on week-days. When the throng had mostly streamed into the porch, the sexton began to toll the bell, keeping his eye on the Reverend Mr. Hooper's door. The first glimpse of the clergyman's figure was the signal for the bell to cease its summons.

'But what has good Parson Hooper got upon his face?' cried the sexton in astonishment.

All within hearing immediately turned about, and beheld the semblance of Mr. Hooper, pacing slowly his meditative way towards the meeting-house. With one accord they started, expressing more wonder than if some strange minister were coming to dust the cushions of Mr. Hooper's pulpit.

'Are you sure it is our parson?' inquired Goodman Gray of the sexton.

'Of a certainty it is good Mr. Hooper,' replied the sexton. 'He was to have exchanged pulpits with Parson Shute of Westbury; but Parson Shute sent to excuse himself yesterday, being to preach a funeral sermon.'

The cause of so much amazement may appear sufficiently slight. Mr. Hooper, a gentlemanly person of about thirty, though still a bachelor, was dressed with due clerical neatness, as if a careful wife had starched his band,[4] and brushed the weekly dust from his Sunday's garb. There was but one thing remarkable in his appearance. Swathed about his forehead, and hanging down over his face, so low as to be shaken by his breath, Mr. Hooper had on a black veil. On a nearer view, it seemed to consist of two folds of crape,[5] which entirely concealed his features, except the mouth and chin, but probably did not intercept his sight, farther than to give a darkened aspect to all living and inanimate things. With this gloomy shade before him, good Mr. Hooper walked onward, at a slow and quiet pace, stooping somewhat and looking on the ground, as is customary with abstracted men, yet nodding kindly to those of his parishioners who still waited on the meeting-house steps. But so wonder-struck were they, that his greeting hardly met with a return.

'I can't really feel as if good Mr. Hooper's face was behind that piece of crape,' said the sexton.

'I don't like it,' muttered an old woman, as she hobbled into the meeting-house. 'He has changed himself into something awful, only by hiding his face.'

'Our parson has gone mad!' cried Goodman Gray, following him across the threshold.

A rumor of some unaccountable phenomenon had preceded Mr. Hooper into the meeting-house, and set all the congregation astir. Few could refrain from twisting their heads towards the door; many stood upright, and turned directly about; while several little boys clambered upon the seats, and came down again with a terrible racket. There was a general bustle, a rustling of the women's gowns and shuffling of the men's feet, greatly at variance with that hushed repose which should attend the entrance of the minister. But Mr. Hooper appeared not to notice the perturbation of his people. He entered with an almost noiseless step, bent his head mildly to the pews on each side, and bowed as he passed his oldest parishioner, a white-haired great-grandsire, who occupied an arm-chair in the centre of the aisle. It was strange to observe, how slowly this venerable man became conscious of something singular in

4. Collar of a clerical gown.   5. Crepe; a light, semitransparent fabric.

the appearance of his pastor. He seemed not fully to partake of the prevailing wonder, till Mr. Hooper had ascended the stairs, and showed himself in the pulpit, face to face with his congregation, except for the black veil. That mysterious emblem was never once withdrawn. It shook with his measured breath as he gave out the psalm; it threw its obscurity between him and the holy page, as he read the Scriptures; and while he prayed, the veil lay heavily on his uplifted countenance. Did he seek to hide it from the dread Being whom he was addressing?

Such was the effect of this simple piece of crape, that more than one woman of delicate nerves was forced to leave the meeting-house. Yet perhaps the pale-faced congregation was almost as fearful a sight to the minister, as his black veil to them.

Mr. Hooper had the reputation of a good preacher, but not an energetic one: he strove to win his people heavenward, by mild persuasive influences, rather than to drive them thither, by the thunders of the Word. The sermon which he now delivered, was marked by the same characteristics of style and manner, as the general series of his pulpit oratory. But there was something, either in the sentiment of the discourse itself, or in the imagination of the auditors, which made it greatly the most powerful effort that they had ever heard from their pastor's lips. It was tinged, rather more darkly than usual, with the gentle gloom of Mr. Hooper's temperament. The subject had reference to secret sin, and those sad mysteries which we hide from our nearest and dearest, and would fain conceal from our own consciousness, even forgetting that the Omniscient can detect them. A subtle power was breathed into his words. Each member of the congregation, the most innocent girl, and the man of hardened breast, felt as if the preacher had crept upon them, behind his awful veil, and discovered their hoarded iniquity of deed or thought. Many spread their clasped hands on their bosoms. There was nothing terrible in what Mr. Hooper said; at least, no violence; and yet, with every tremor of his melancholy voice, the hearers quaked. An unsought pathos came hand in hand with awe. So sensible were the audience of some unwonted attribute in their minister, that they longed for a breath of wind to blow aside the veil, almost believing that a stranger's visage would be discovered, though the form, gesture, and voice were those of Mr. Hooper.

At the close of the services, the people hurried out with indecorous confusion, eager to communicate their pent-up amazement, and conscious of lighter spirits, the moment they lost sight of the black veil. Some gathered in little circles, huddled closely together, with their mouths all whispering in the centre; some went homeward alone, wrapt in silent meditation; some talked loudly, and profaned the Sabbath-day with ostentatious laughter. A few shook their sagacious heads, intimating that they could penetrate the mystery; while one or two affirmed that there was no mystery at all, but only that Mr. Hooper's eyes were so weakened by the midnight lamp, as to require a shade. After a brief interval, forth came good Mr. Hooper also, in the rear of his flock. Turning his veiled face from one group to another, he paid due reverence to the hoary heads, saluted the middle-aged with kind dignity, as their friend and spiritual guide, greeted the young with mingled authority and love, and laid his hands on the little children's heads to bless them. Such was always his custom on the Sabbath-day. Strange and bewildered looks repaid him for his courtesy. None, as on former occasions, aspired to the honor of walking by their pastor's side. Old Squire Saunders, doubtless by an accidental lapse of memory, neglected to invite Mr. Hooper to his table, where the good clergyman had been wont to bless the food, almost every Sunday since his settlement. He returned, therefore, to the parsonage, and, at the moment of closing the door, was observed to look back upon the people, all of whom had their eyes fixed upon the minister. A sad smile gleamed faintly from beneath the black veil, and flickered about his mouth, glimmering as he disappeared.

'How strange,' said a lady, 'that a simple black veil, such as any woman might wear on her bonnet, should become such a terrible thing on Mr. Hooper's face!'

'Something must surely be amiss with Mr. Hooper's intellects,' observed her husband, the physician of the village. 'But the strangest part of the affair is the effect of this vagary, even on a sober-minded man like myself. The black veil, though it covers only our pastor's face, throws its influence over his whole person, and makes him ghost-like from head to foot. Do you not feel it so?'

'Truly do I,' replied the lady; 'and I would not be alone with him for the world. I wonder he is not afraid to be alone with himself!'

'Men sometimes are so,' said her husband.

The afternoon service was attended with similar circumstances. At its conclusion, the bell tolled for the funeral of a young lady. The relatives and friends were assembled in the house, and the more distant acquaintances stood about the door, speaking of the good qualities of the deceased, when their talk was interrupted by the appearance of Mr. Hooper, still covered with his black veil. It was now an appropriate emblem. The clergyman stepped into the room where the corpse was laid, and bent over the coffin, to take a last farewell of his deceased parishioner. As he stooped, the veil hung straight down from his forehead, so that, if her eye-lids had not been closed for ever, the dead maiden might have seen his face. Could Mr. Hooper be fearful of her glance, that he so hastily caught back the black veil? A person, who watched the interview between the dead and living, scrupled not to affirm, that, at the instant when the clergyman's features were disclosed, the corpse had slightly shuddered, rustling the shroud and muslin cap, though the countenance retained the composure of death. A superstitious old woman was the only witness of this prodigy. From the coffin, Mr. Hooper passed into the chambers of the mourners, and thence to the head of the staircase, to make the funeral prayer. It was a tender and heart-dissolving prayer, full of sorrow, yet so imbued with celestial hopes, that the music of a heavenly harp, swept by the fingers of the dead, seemed faintly to be heard among the saddest accents of the minister. The people trembled, though they but darkly understood him, when he prayed that they, and himself, and all of mortal race, might be ready, as he trusted this young maiden had been, for the dreadful hour that should snatch the veil from their faces. The bearers went heavily forth, and the mourners followed, saddening all the street, with the dead before them, and Mr. Hooper in his black veil behind.

'Why do you look back?' said one in the procession to his partner.

'I had a fancy,' replied she, 'that the minister and the maiden's spirit were walking hand in hand.'

'And so had I, at the same moment,' said the other.

That night, the handsomest couple in Milford village were to be joined in wedlock. Though reckoned a melancholy man, Mr. Hooper had a placid cheerfulness for such occasions, which often excited a sympathetic smile, where livelier merriment would have been thrown away. There was no quality of his disposition which made him more beloved than this. The company at the wedding awaited his arrival with impatience, trusting that the strange awe, which had gathered over him throughout the day, would now be dispelled. But such was not the result. When Mr. Hooper came, the first thing that their eyes rested on was the same horrible black veil, which had added deeper gloom to the funeral, and could portend nothing but evil to the wedding. Such was its immediate effect on the guests, that a cloud seemed to have rolled duskily from beneath the black crape, and dimmed the light of the candles. The bridal pair stood up before the minister. But the bride's cold fingers quivered in the tremulous hand of the bridegroom, and her death-like paleness caused a whisper, that the maiden who had been buried a few hours before, was come from her grave to be married. If ever another wedding were so dismal, it was that famous one, where they tolled the wedding-knell.[6] After performing the ceremony, Mr. Hooper raised a glass of wine to his lips, wishing happiness to the new-married couple, in a strain of mild pleasantry that ought to have brightened the features of the guests, like a cheerful gleam from the hearth. At that instant, catching a glimpse of his figure in the looking-glass, the black veil involved his own spirit in the horror with which it overwhelmed all others. His frame shuddered—his lips grew white—he spilt the untasted wine upon the carpet—and rushed forth into the darkness. For the Earth, too, had on her Black Veil.

The next day, the whole village of Milford talked of little else than Parson Hooper's black veil. That, and the mystery concealed behind it, supplied a topic for discussion between acquaintances meeting in the street, and good women gossiping at their open windows. It was the first item of news that the tavern-keeper told to his guests. The children babbled of it on their way to school. One imitative little imp covered his face with an old black handkerchief, thereby so affrighting his playmates, that the panic seized himself, and he well nigh lost his wits by his own waggery.

It was remarkable, that, of all the busy-bodies and impertinent people in the parish, not one ventured to put the plain question to Mr. Hooper, wherefore he did this thing. Hitherto, whenever there appeared the slightest call for such interference, he had never lacked advisers, nor shown himself averse to be guided by their judgment. If he erred at all, it was by so painful a degree of self-distrust, that even the mildest censure would lead him to consider an indifferent action as a crime. Yet, though so well acquainted with this amiable weakness, no individual among his parishioners chose to make the black veil a subject of friendly remonstrance. There was a feeling of dread, neither plainly confessed nor carefully concealed, which caused each to shift the responsibility upon another, till at length it was found expedient to send a deputation of the church, in order to deal with Mr. Hooper about the mystery, before it should grow into a scandal. Never did an embassy so

6. A reference to Hawthorne's "The Wedding Knell," which appeared in *The Token* for 1836 along with this story.

ill discharge its duties. The minister received them with friendly courtesy, but became silent, after they were seated, leaving to his visitors the whole burthen[7] of introducing their important business. The topic, it might be supposed, was obvious enough. There was the black veil, swathed round Mr. Hooper's forehead, and concealing every feature above his placid mouth, on which, at times, they could perceive the glimmering of a melancholy smile. But that piece of crape, to their imagination, seemed to hang down before his heart, the symbol of a fearful secret between him and them. Were the veil but cast aside, they might speak freely of it, but not till then. Thus they sat a considerable time, speechless, confused, and shrinking uneasily from Mr. Hooper's eye, which they felt to be fixed upon them with an invisible glance. Finally, the deputies returned abashed to their constituents, pronouncing the matter too weighty to be handled, except by a council of the churches, if, indeed, it might not require a general synod.

But there was one person in the village, unappalled by the awe with which the black veil had impressed all beside herself. When the deputies returned without an explanation, or even venturing to demand one, she, with the calm energy of her character, determined to chase away the strange cloud that appeared to be settling round Mr. Hooper, every moment more darkly than before. As his plighted wife, it should be her privilege to know what the black veil concealed. At the minister's first visit, therefore, she entered upon the subject, with a direct simplicity, which made the task easier both for him and her. After he had seated himself, she fixed her eyes steadfastly upon the veil, but could discern nothing of the dreadful gloom that had so over-awed the multitude: it was but a double fold of crape, hanging down from his forehead to his mouth, and slightly stirring with his breath.

'No,' said she aloud, and smiling, 'there is nothing terrible in this piece of crape, except that it hides a face which I am always glad to look upon. Come, good sir, let the sun shine from behind the cloud. First lay aside your black veil: then tell me why you put it on.'

Mr. Hooper's smile glimmered faintly.

'There is an hour to come,' said he, 'when all of us shall cast aside our veils. Take it not amiss, beloved friend, if I wear this piece of crape till then.'

'Your words are a mystery too,' returned the young lady. 'Take away the veil from them, at least.'

'Elizabeth, I will,' said he, 'so far as my vow may suffer me. Know, then, this veil is a type[8] and a symbol, and I am bound to wear it ever, both in light and darkness, in solitude and before the gaze of multitudes, and as with strangers, so with my familiar friends. No mortal eye will see it withdrawn. This dismal shade must separate me from the world: even you, Elizabeth, can never come behind it!'

'What grievous affliction hath befallen you,' she earnestly inquired, 'that you should thus darken your eyes for ever?'

'If it be a sign of mourning,' replied Mr. Hooper, 'I, perhaps, like most other mortals, have sorrows dark enough to be typified by a black veil.'

'But what if the world will not believe that it is the type of an innocent sorrow?' urged Elizabeth. 'Beloved and respected as you are, there may be

7. Burden.
8. Object that symbolically embodies or reveals a religious idea.

whispers, that you hide your face under the consciousness of secret sin. For the sake of your holy office, do away this scandal!'

The color rose into her cheeks, as she intimated the nature of the rumors that were already abroad in the village. But Mr. Hooper's mildness did not forsake him. He even smiled again—that same sad smile, which always appeared like a faint glimmering of light, proceeding from the obscurity beneath the veil.

'If I hide my face for sorrow, there is cause enough,' he merely replied; 'and if I cover it for secret sin, what mortal might not do the same?'

And with this gentle, but unconquerable obstinacy, did he resist all her entreaties. At length Elizabeth sat silent. For a few moments she appeared lost in thought, considering, probably, what new methods might be tried, to withdraw her lover from so dark a fantasy, which, if it had no other meaning, was perhaps a symptom of mental disease. Though of a firmer character than his own, the tears rolled down her cheeks. But, in an instant, as it were, a new feeling took the place of sorrow: her eyes were fixed insensibly on the black veil, when, like a sudden twilight in the air, its terrors fell around her. She arose, and stood trembling before him.

'And do you feel it then at last?' said he mournfully.

She made no reply, but covered her eyes with her hand, and turned to leave the room. He rushed forward and caught her arm.

'Have patience with me, Elizabeth!' cried he passionately. 'Do not desert me, though this veil must be between us here on earth. Be mine, and hereafter there shall be no veil over my face, no darkness between our souls! It is but a mortal veil—it is not for eternity! Oh, you know not how lonely I am and how frightened to be alone behind my black veil. Do not leave me in this miserable obscurity for ever!'

'Lift the veil but once, and look me in the face,' said she.

'Never! It cannot be!' replied Mr. Hooper.

'Then, farewell!' said Elizabeth.

She withrew her arm from his grasp, and slowly departed, pausing at the door, to give one long, shuddering gaze, that seemed almost to penetrate the mystery of the black veil. But, even amid his grief, Mr. Hooper smiled to think that only a material emblem had separated him from happiness, though the horrors which it shadowed forth, must be drawn darkly between the fondest of lovers.

From that time no attempts were made to remove Mr. Hooper's black veil, or, by a direct appeal, to discover the secret which it was supposed to hide. By persons who claimed a superiority to popular prejudice, it was reckoned merely an eccentric whim, such as often mingles with the sober actions of men otherwise rational, and tinges them all with its own semblance of insanity. But with the multitude, good Mr. Hooper was irreparably a bugbear.[9] He could not walk the street with any peace of mind, so conscious was he that the gentle and timid would turn aside to avoid him, and that others would make it a point of hardihood to throw themselves in his way. The impertinence of the latter class compelled him to give up his customary walk, at sunset, to the burial ground; for when he leaned pensively over the gate,

9. Object of dread.

there would always be faces behind the grave-stones, peeping at his black veil. A fable went the rounds, that the stare of the dead people drove him thence. It grieved him, to the very depth of his kind heart, to observe how the children fled from his approach, breaking up their merriest sports, while his melancholy figure was yet afar off. Their instinctive dread caused him to feel, more strongly than aught else, that a preternatural horror was interwoven with the threads of the black crape. In truth, his own antipathy to the veil was known to be so great, that he never willingly passed before a mirror, nor stooped to drink at a still fountain, lest, in its peaceful bosom, he should be affrighted by himself. This was what gave plausibility to the whispers, that Mr. Hooper's conscience tortured him for some great crime, too horrible to be entirely concealed, or otherwise than so obscurely intimated. Thus, from beneath the black veil, there rolled a cloud into the sunshine, an ambiguity of sin or sorrow, which enveloped the poor minister, so that love or sympathy could never reach him. It was said, that ghost and fiend consorted with him there. With self-shudderings and outward terrors, he walked continually in its shadow, groping darkly within his own soul, or gazing through a medium that saddened the whole world. Even the lawless wind, it was believed, respected his dreadful secret, and never blew aside the veil. But still good Mr. Hooper sadly smiled, at the pale visages of the worldly throng as he passed by.

Among all its bad influences, the black veil had the one desirable effect, of making its wearer a very efficient clergyman. By the aid of his mysterious emblem—for there was no other apparent cause—he became a man of awful power, over souls that were in agony for sin. His converts always regarded him with a dread peculiar to themselves, affirming, though but figuratively, that, before he brought them to celestial light, they had been with him behind the black veil. Its gloom, indeed, enabled him to sympathize with all dark affections. Dying sinners cried aloud for Mr. Hooper, and would not yield their breath till he appeared; though ever, as he stooped to whisper consolation, they shuddered at the veiled face so near their own. Such were the terrors of the black veil, even when death had bared his visage! Strangers came long distances to attend service at his church, with the mere idle purpose of gazing at his figure, because it was forbidden them to behold his face. But many were made to quake ere they departed! Once, during Governor Belcher's administration, Mr. Hooper was appointed to preach the election sermon.[1] Covered with his black veil, he stood before the chief magistrate, the council, and the representatives, and wrought so deep an impression, that the legislative measures of that year, were characterized by all the gloom and piety of our earliest ancestral sway.

In this manner Mr. Hooper spent a long life, irreproachable in outward act, yet shrouded in dismal suspicions; kind and loving, though unloved, and dimly feared; a man apart from men, shunned in their health and joy, but ever summoned to their aid in mortal anguish. As years wore on, shedding their snows above his sable veil, he acquired a name throughout the New-England churches, and they called him Father Hooper. Nearly all his parishioners, who were of mature age when he was settled, had been borne away

---

1. Sermon preached at the start of a governor's term. Jonathan Belcher (1682–1757) was governor of Massachusetts and New Hampshire (1730–41).

by many a funeral: he had one congregation in the church, and a more crowded one in the church-yard; and having wrought so late into the evening, and done his work so well, it was now good Father Hooper's turn to rest.

Several persons were visible by the shaded candlelight, in the death-chamber of the old clergyman. Natural connections he had none. But there was the decorously grave, though unmoved physician, seeking only to mitigate the last pangs of the patient whom he could not save. There were the deacons, and other eminently pious members of his church. There, also, was the Reverend Mr. Clark, of Westbury, a young and zealous divine, who had ridden in haste to pray by the bed-side of the expiring minister. There was the nurse, no hired handmaiden of death, but one whose calm affection had endured thus long, in secresy, in solitude, amid the chill of age, and would not perish, even at the dying hour. Who, but Elizabeth! And there lay the hoary head of good Father Hooper upon the death-pillow, with the black veil still swathed about his brow and reaching down over his face, so that each more difficult gasp of his faint breath caused it to stir. All through life that piece of crape had hung between him and the world: it had separated him from cheerful brotherhood and woman's love, and kept him in that saddest of all prisons, his own heart; and still it lay upon his face, as if to deepen the gloom of his darksome chamber, and shade him from the sunshine of eternity.

For some time previous, his mind had been confused, wavering doubtfully between the past and the present, and hovering forward, as it were, at intervals, into the indistinctness of the world to come. There had been feverish turns, which tossed him from side to side, and wore away what little strength he had. But in his most convulsive struggles, and in the wildest vagaries of his intellect, when no other thought retained its sober influence, he still showed an awful solicitude lest the black veil should slip aside. Even if his bewildered soul could have forgotten, there was a faithful woman at his pillow, who, with averted eyes, would have covered that aged face, which she had last beheld in the comeliness of manhood. At length the death-stricken old man lay quietly in the torpor of mental and bodily exhaustion, with an imperceptible pulse, and breath that grew fainter and fainter, except when a long, deep, and irregular inspiration seemed to prelude the flight of his spirit.

The minister of Westbury approached the bedside.

'Venerable Father Hooper,' said he, 'the moment of your release is at hand. Are you ready for the lifting of the veil, that shuts in time from eternity?'

Father Hooper at first replied merely by a feeble motion of his head; then, apprehensive, perhaps, that his meaning might be doubtful, he exerted himself to speak.

'Yea,' said he, in faint accents, 'my soul hath a patient weariness until that veil be lifted.'

'And is it fitting,' resumed the Reverend Mr. Clark, 'that a man so given to prayer, of such a blameless example, holy in deed and thought, so far as mortal judgment may pronounce; is it fitting that a father in the church should leave a shadow on his memory, that may seem to blacken a life so pure? I pray you, my venerable brother, let not this thing be! Suffer us to be gladdened by your triumphant aspect, as you go to your reward. Before the veil of eternity be lifted, let me cast aside this black veil from your face!'

And thus speaking, the reverend Mr. Clark bent forward to reveal the mystery of so many years. But, exerting a sudden energy, that made all the beholders stand aghast, Father Hooper snatched both his hands from beneath the bed-clothes, and pressed them strongly on the black veil, resolute to struggle, if the minister of Westbury would contend with a dying man.

'Never!' cried the veiled clergyman. 'On earth, never!'

'Dark old man!' exclaimed the affrighted minister, 'with what horrible crime upon your soul are you now passing to the judgment?'

Father Hooper's breath heaved; it rattled in his throat; but, with a mighty effort, grasping forward with his hands, he caught hold of life, and held it back till he should speak. He even raised himself in bed; and there he sat, shivering with the arms of death around him, while the black veil hung down, awful, at that last moment, in the gathered terrors of a life-time. And yet the faint, sad smile, so often there, now seemed to glimmer from its obscurity, and linger on Father Hooper's lips.

'Why do you tremble at me alone?' cried he, turning his veiled face round the circle of pale spectators. 'Tremble also at each other! Have men avoided me, and women shown no pity, and children screamed and fled, only for my black veil? What, but the mystery which it obscurely typifies, has made this piece of crape so awful? When the friend shows his inmost heart to his friend; the lover to his best-beloved; when man does not vainly shrink from the eye of his Creator, loathsomely treasuring up the secret of his sin; then deem me a monster, for the symbol beneath which I have lived, and die! I look around me, and lo! on every visage a black veil!'

While his auditors shrank from one another, in mutual affright, Father Hooper fell back upon his pillow, a veiled corpse, with a faint smile lingering on the lips. Still veiled, they laid him in his coffin, and a veiled corpse they bore him to the grave. The grass of many years has sprung up and withered on that grave, the burial-stone is moss-grown, and good Mr. Hooper's face is dust; but awful is still the thought, that it mouldered beneath the black veil!

1836

The Birth-Mark[1]

In the latter part of the last century, there lived a man of science—an eminent proficient in every branch of natural philosophy—who, not long before our story opens, had made experience of a spiritual affinity, more attractive than any chemical one. He had left his laboratory to the care of an assistant, cleared his fine countenance from the furnace-smoke, washed the stain of acids from his fingers, and persuaded a beautiful woman to become his wife. In those days, when the comparatively recent discovery of electricity, and other kindred mysteries of nature, seemed to open paths into the region of miracle, it was not unusual for the love of science to rival the love of woman, in its depth and absorbing energy. The higher intellect, the imagi-

---

1. First published in the *Pioneer* (March 1843), the source of the present text; the reprinting in *Mosses from an Old Manse* (1846) contains a few variants as well as two corrections (adopted and noted here).

nation, the spirit, and even the heart, might all find their congenial aliment in pursuits which, as some of their ardent votaries[2] believed, would ascend from one step of powerful intelligence to another, until the philosopher should lay his hand on the secret of creative force, and perhaps make new worlds for himself. We know not whether Aylmer possessed this degree of faith in man's ultimate control over nature. He had devoted himself, however, too unreservedly to scientific studies, ever to be weaned from them by any second passion. His love for his young wife might prove the stronger of the two; but it could only be by intertwining itself with his love of science, and uniting the strength of the latter to its own.

Such a union accordingly took place, and was attended with truly remarkable consequences, and a deeply impressive moral. One day, very soon after their marriage, Aylmer sat gazing at his wife, with a trouble in his countenance that grew stronger, until he spoke.

"Georgiana," said he, "has it never occurred to you that the mark upon your cheek might be removed?"

"No, indeed," said she, smiling; but perceiving the seriousness of his manner, she blushed deeply. "To tell you the truth, it has been so often called a charm, that I was simple enough to imagine it might be so."

"Ah, upon another face, perhaps it might," replied her husband. "But never on yours! No, dearest Georgiana, you came so nearly perfect from the hand of Nature, that this slightest possible defect—which we hesitate whether to term a defect or a beauty—shocks me, as being the visible mark of earthly imperfection."

"Shocks you, my husband!" cried Georgiana, deeply hurt; at first reddening with momentary anger, but then bursting into tears. "Then why did you take me from my mother's side? You cannot love what shocks you!"

To explain this conversation, it must be mentioned, that, in the centre of Georgiana's left cheek, there was a singular mark, deeply interwoven, as it were, with the texture and substance of her face. In the usual state of her complexion,—a healthy, though delicate bloom,—the mark wore a tint of deeper crimson, which imperfectly defined its shape amid the surrounding rosiness. When she blushed, it gradually became more indistinct, and finally vanished amid the triumphant rush of blood, that bathed the whole cheek with its brilliant glow. But, if any shifting emotion caused her to turn pale, there was the mark again, a crimson stain upon the snow, in what Aylmer sometimes deemed an almost fearful distinctness. Its shape bore not a little similarity to the human hand, though of the smallest pigmy size. Georgiana's lovers were wont to say, that some fairy, at her birth-hour, had laid her tiny hand upon the infant's cheek, and left this impress there, in token of the magic endowments that were to give her such sway over all hearts. Many a desperate swain would have risked life for the privilege of pressing his lips to the mysterious hand. It must not be concealed, however, that the impression wrought by this fairy sign-manual varied exceedingly; according to the difference of temperament in the beholders. Some fastidious persons—but they were exclusively of her own sex—affirmed that the Bloody Hand, as they chose to call it, quite destroyed the effect of Georgiana's beauty, and rendered her countenance even hideous. But it would be as reasonable to say,

---

2. Devoted admirers. "Aliment": nourishment.

that one of those small blue stains, which sometimes occur in the purest statuary marble, would convert the Eve of Powers[3] to a monster. Masculine observers, if the birth-mark did not heighten their admiration, contented themselves with wishing it away, that the world might possess one living specimen of ideal loveliness, without the semblance of a flaw. After his marriage—for he thought little or nothing of the matter before—Aylmer discovered that this was the case with himself.

Had she been less beautiful—if Envy's self could have found aught else to sneer at—he might have felt his affection heightened by the prettiness of this mimic hand, now vaguely portrayed, now lost, now stealing forth again, and glimmering to-and-fro with every pulse of emotion that throbbed within her heart. But, seeing her otherwise so perfect, he found this one defect grow more and more intolerable, with every moment of their united lives. It was the fatal flaw of humanity, which Nature, in one shape or another, stamps ineffaceably on all her productions, either to imply that they are temporary and finite, or that their perfection must be wrought by toil and pain. The Crimson Hand expressed the ineludible gripe,[4] in which mortality clutches the highest and purest of earthly mould, degrading them into kindred with the lowest, and even with the very brutes, like whom their visible frames return to dust. In this manner, selecting it as the symbol of his wife's liability to sin, sorrow, decay, and death, Aylmer's sombre imagination was not long in rendering the birth-mark a frightful object, causing him more trouble and horror than ever Georgiana's beauty, whether of soul or sense, had given him delight.

At all the seasons which should have been their happiest, he invariably, and without intending it—nay, in spite of a purpose to the contrary—reverted to this one disastrous topic. Trifling as it at first appeared, it so connected itself with innumerable trains of thought, and modes of feeling, that it became the central point of all. With the morning twilight, Aylmer opened his eyes upon his wife's face, and recognised the symbol of imperfection; and when they sat together at the evening hearth, his eyes wandered stealthily to her cheek, and beheld, flickering with the blaze of the wood fire, the spectral Hand that wrote mortality, where he would fain have worshipped. Georgiana soon learned to shudder at his gaze. It needed but a glance, with the peculiar expression that his face often wore, to change the roses of her cheek into a deathlike paleness, amid which the Crimson Hand was brought strongly out, like a bas-relief[5] of ruby on the whitest marble.

Late, one night, when the lights were growing dim, so as hardly to betray the stain on the poor wife's cheek, she herself, for the first time, voluntarily took up the subject.

"Do you remember, my dear Aylmer," said she, with a feeble attempt at a smile—"have you any recollection of a dream, last night, about this odious Hand?"

"None!—none whatever!" replied Aylmer, starting; but then he added in a dry, cold tone, affected for the sake of concealing the real depth of his emotion:—"I might well dream of it; for, before I fell asleep, it had taken a pretty firm hold of my fancy."

3. *Eve before the Fall*, a sculpture by the American Hiram Powers (1805–1873).

4. Grip (variant spelling).
5. Low-relief; slightly raised.

"And you did dream of it," continued Georgiana, hastily; for she dreaded lest a gush of tears should interrupt what she had to say—"A terrible dream! I wonder that you can forget it. Is it possible to forget this one expression?— 'It is in her heart now—we must have it out!'—Reflect, my husband; for by all means I would have you recall that dream."

The mind is in a sad state, when Sleep, the all-involving, cannot confine her spectres within the dim region of her sway, but suffers them to break forth, affrighting this actual life with secrets that perchance belong to a deeper one. Aylmer now remembered his dream. He had fancied himself, with his servant Aminadab, attempting an operation for the removal of the birth-mark. But the deeper went the knife, the deeper sank the Hand, until at length its tiny grasp appeared to have caught hold of Georgiana's heart; whence, however, her husband was inexorably resolved to cut or wrench it away.

When the dream had shaped itself perfectly in his memory, Aylmer sat in his wife's presence with a guilty feeling. Truth often finds its way to the mind close-muffled in robes of sleep, and then speaks with uncompromising directness of matters in regard to which we practise an unconscious self-deception, during our waking moments. Until now, he had not been aware of the tyrannizing influence acquired by one idea over his mind, and of the lengths which he might find in his heart to go, for the sake of giving himself peace.

"Aylmer," resumed Georgiana, solemnly, "I know not what may be the cost to both of us, to rid me of this fatal birth-mark. Perhaps its removal may cause cureless deformity. Or, it may be, the stain goes as deep as life itself. Again, do we know that there is a possibility, on any terms, of unclasping the firm gripe of this little Hand, which was laid upon me before I came into the world?"

"Dearest Georgiana, I have spent much thought upon the subject," hastily interrupted Aylmer—"I am convinced of the perfect practicability of its removal."

"If there be the remotest possibility of it," continued Georgiana, "let the attempt be made, at whatever risk. Danger is nothing to me; for life—while this hateful mark makes me the object of your horror and disgust—life is a burthen[6] which I would fling down with joy. Either remove this dreadful Hand, or take my wretched life! You have deep science! All the world bears witness of it. You have achieved great wonders! Cannot you remove this little, little mark, which I cover with the tips of two small fingers? Is this beyond your power, for the sake of your own peace, and to save your poor wife from madness?"

"Noblest—dearest—tenderest wife!" cried Aylmer, rapturously. "Doubt not my power. I have already given this matter the deepest thought—thought which might almost have enlightened me to create a being less perfect than yourself. Georgiana, you have led me deeper than ever into the heart of science. I feel myself fully competent to render this dear cheek as faultless as its fellow; and then, most beloved, what will be my triumph, when I shall have corrected what Nature left imperfect, in her fairest work! Even Pygmalion,[7] when his sculptured woman assumed life, felt not greater ecstasy than mine will be."

6. Burden.
7. In Greek myth, a king and sculptor who fell so deeply in love with his statue that Aphrodite granted his prayers and gave it life.

"It is resolved, then," said Georgiana, faintly smiling,—"And, Aylmer, spare me not, though you should find the birth-mark take refuge in my heart at last."

Her husband tenderly kissed her cheek—her right cheek—not that which bore the impress of the Crimson Hand.

The next day, Aylmer apprized his wife of a plan that he had formed, whereby he might have opportunity for the intense thought and constant watchfulness, which the proposed operation would require; while Georgiana, likewise, would enjoy the perfect repose essential to its success. They were to seclude themselves in the extensive apartments occupied by Aylmer as a laboratory, and where, during his toilsome youth, he had made discoveries in the elemental powers of nature, that had roused the admiration of all the learned societies in Europe. Seated calmly in this laboratory, the pale philosopher had investigated the secrets of the highest cloud-region, and of the profoundest mines; he had satisfied himself of the causes that kindled and kept alive the fires of the volcano; and had explained the mystery of fountains, and how it is that they gush forth, some so bright and pure, and others with such rich medicinal[8] virtues, from the dark bosom of the earth. Here, too, at an earlier period, he had studied the wonders of the human frame, and attempted to fathom the very process by which Nature assimilates all her precious influences from earth and air, and from the spiritual world, to create and foster Man, her masterpiece. The latter pursuit, however, Aylmer had long laid aside, in unwilling recognition of the truth, against which all seekers sooner or later stumble, that our great creative Mother, while she amuses us with apparently working in the broadest sunshine, is yet severely careful to keep her own secrets, and, in spite of her pretended openness, shows us nothing but results. She permits us, indeed, to mar, but seldom to mend, and, like a jealous patentee, on no account to make. Now, however, Aylmer resumed these half-forgotten investigations; not, of course, with such hopes or wishes as first suggested them; but because they involved much physiological truth, and lay in the path of his proposed scheme for the treatment of Georgiana.

As he led her over the threshold of the laboratory, Georgiana was cold and tremulous. Aylmer looked cheerfully into her face, with intent to reassure her, but was so startled with the intense glow of the birth-mark upon the whiteness of her cheek, that he could not restrain a strong convulsive shudder. His wife fainted.

"Aminadab! Aminadab!" shouted Aylmer, stamping violently on the floor.

Forthwith, there issued from an inner apartment a man of low stature, but bulky frame, with shaggy hair hanging about his visage, which was grimed with the vapors of the furnace. This personage had been Aylmer's underworker during his whole scientific career, and was admirably fitted for that office by his great mechanical readiness, and the skill with which, while incapable of comprehending a single principle, he executed all the practical details of his master's experiments. With his vast strength, his shaggy hair, his smoky aspect, and the indescribable earthiness that incrusted him, he seemed to represent man's physical nature; while Aylmer's slender figure, and pale, intellectual face, were no less apt a type of the spiritual element.

---

8. This 1846 reading replaces the 1843 *medical.*

"Throw open the door of the boudoir, Aminadab," said Aylmer, "and burn a pastille."[9]

"Yes, master," answered Aminadab, looking intently at the lifeless form of Georgiana; and then he muttered to himself;—"If she were my wife, I'd never part with that birth-mark."

When Georgiana recovered consciousness, she found herself breathing an atmosphere of penetrating fragrance, the gentle potency of which had recalled her from her deathlike faintness. The scene around her looked like enchantment. Aylmer had converted those smoky, dingy, sombre rooms, where he had spent his brightest years in recondite pursuits, into a series of beautiful apartments, not unfit to be the secluded abode of a lovely woman. The walls were hung with gorgeous curtains, which imparted the combination of grandeur and grace, that no other species of adornment can achieve; and as they fell from the ceiling to the floor, their rich and ponderous folds, concealing all angles and straight lines, appeared to shut in the scene from infinite space. For aught Georgiana knew, it might be a pavilion among the clouds. And Aylmer, excluding the sunshine, which would have interfered with his chemical processes, had supplied its place with perfumed lamps, emitting flames of various hue, but all uniting in a soft, empurpled radiance. He now knelt by his wife's side, watching her earnestly, but without alarm; for he was confident in his science, and felt that he could draw a magic circle round her, within which no evil might intrude.

"Where am I?—Ah, I remember!" said Georgiana, faintly; and she placed her hand over her cheek, to hide the terrible mark from her husband's eyes.

"Fear not, dearest!" exclaimed he, "Do not shrink from me! Believe me, Georgiana, I even rejoice in this single imperfection, since it will be such rapture to remove it."

"Oh, spare me!" sadly replied his wife—"Pray do not look at it again. I never can forget that convulsive shudder."

In order to soothe Georgiana, and, as it were, to release her mind from the burthen of actual things, Aylmer now put in practice some of the light and playful secrets, which science had taught him among its profounder lore. Airy figures, absolutely bodiless ideas, and forms of unsubstantial beauty, came and danced before her, imprinting their momentary footsteps on beams of light. Though she had some indistinct idea of the method of these optical phenomena, still the illusion was almost perfect enough to warrant the belief, that her husband possessed sway over the spiritual world. Then again, when she felt a wish to look forth from her seclusion, immediately, as if her thoughts were answered, the procession of external existence flitted across a screen. The scenery and the figures of actual life were perfectly represented, but with that bewitching, yet indescribable difference, which always makes a picture, an image, or a shadow, so much more attractive than the original. When wearied of this, Aylmer bade her cast her eyes upon a vessel, containing a quantity of earth. She did so, with little interest at first, but was soon startled, to perceive the germ of a plant, shooting upward from the soil. Then came the slender stalk—the leaves gradually unfolded themselves—and amid them was a perfect and lovely flower.

9. A tablet burned to perfume the air.

"It is magical!" cried Georgiana, "I dare not touch it."

"Nay, pluck it," answered Aylmer, "pluck it, and inhale its brief perfume while you may. The flower will wither in a few moments, and leave nothing save its brown seed-vessels—but thence may be perpetuated a race as ephemeral as itself."

But Georgiana had no sooner touched the flower than the whole plant suffered a blight, its leaves turning coal-black, as if by the agency of fire.

"There was too powerful a stimulus," said Aylmer thoughtfully.

To make up for this abortive experiment, he proposed to take her portrait by a scientific process of his own invention. It was to be effected by rays of light striking upon a polished plate of metal. Georgiana assented—but, on looking at the result, was affrighted to find the features of the portrait blurred and indefinable; while the minute figure of a hand appeared where the cheek should have been. Aylmer snatched the metallic plate, and threw it into a jar of corrosive acid.

Soon, however, he forgot these mortifying failures. In the intervals of study and chemical experiment, he came to her, flushed and exhausted, but seemed invigorated by her presence, and spoke in glowing language of the resources of his art. He gave a history of the long dynasty of the Alchemists, who spent so many ages in quest of the universal solvent, by which the Golden Principle might be elicited from all things vile and base.[1] Aylmer appeared to believe, that, by the plainest scientific logic, it was altogether within the limits of possibility to discover this long-sought medium; but, he added, a philosopher who should go deep enough to acquire the power, would attain too lofty a wisdom to stoop to the exercise of it. Not less singular were his opinions in regard to the Elixir Vitæ.[2] He more than intimated, that it was at his option to concoct a liquid that should prolong life for years—perhaps interminably— but that it would produce a discord in nature, which all the world, and chiefly the quaffer of the immortal nostrum, would find cause to curse.

"Aylmer, are you in earnest?" asked Georgiana, looking at him with amazement and fear; "it is terrible to possess such power, or even to dream of possessing it!"

"Oh, do not tremble, my love!" said her husband, "I would not wrong either you or myself, by working such inharmonious effects upon our lives. But I would have you consider how trifling, in comparison, is the skill requisite to remove this little Hand."

At the mention of the birth-mark, Georgiana, as usual, shrank, as if a red-hot iron had touched her cheek.

Again Aylmer applied himself to his labors. She could hear his voice in the distant furnace-room, giving directions to Aminadab, whose harsh, uncouth, misshapen tones were audible in response, more like the grunt or growl of a brute than human speech. After hours of absence, Aylmer re-appeared, and proposed that she should now examine his cabinet of chemical products, and natural treasures of the earth. Among the former he showed her a small vial, in which, he remarked, was contained a gentle, yet most powerful fragrance, capable of impregnating all the breezes that blow across a kingdom.

---

1. The goal of many alchemists was to turn base metal into gold.

2. Elixir of life (Latin); a potion with the power to prolong life indefinitely.

They were of inestimable value, the contents of that little vial; and, as he said so, he threw some of the perfume into the air, and filled the room with piercing and invigorating delight.

"And what is this?" asked Georgiana, pointing to a small crystal globe, containing a gold-colored liquid. "It is so beautiful to the eye, that I could imagine it the Elixir of Life."

"In one sense it is," replied Aylmer, "or rather the Elixir of Immortality. It is the most precious poison that ever was concocted in this world. By its aid, I could apportion the lifetime of any mortal at whom you might point your finger. The strength of the dose would determine whether he were to linger out years, or drop dead in the midst of a breath. No king, on his guarded throne, could keep his life, if I, in my private station, should deem that the welfare of millions justified me in depriving him of it."

"Why do you keep such a terrific drug?" inquired Georgiana in horror.

"Do not mistrust me, dearest!" said her husband, smiling; "its virtuous potency is yet greater than its harmful one. But, see! here is a powerful cosmetic. With a few drops of this, in a vase of water, freckles may be washed away as easily as the hands are cleansed. A stronger infusion would take the blood out of the cheek, and leave the rosiest beauty a pale ghost."

"Is it with this lotion that you intend to bathe my cheek?" asked Georgiana anxiously.

"Oh, no!" hastily replied her husband—"this is merely superficial. Your case demands a remedy that shall go deeper."

In his interviews with Georgiana, Aylmer generally made minute inquiries as to her sensations, and whether the confinement of the rooms, and the temperature of the atmosphere, agreed with her. These questions had such a particular drift, that Georgiana began to conjecture that she was already subjected to certain physical influences, either breathed in with the fragrant air, or taken with her food. She fancied, likewise—but it might be altogether fancy—that there was a stirring up of her system,—a strange, indefinite sensation creeping through her veins, and tingling, half painfully, half pleasurably, at her heart. Still, whenever she dared to look into the mirror, there she beheld herself, pale as a white rose, and with the crimson birth-mark stamped upon her cheek. Not even Aylmer now hated it so much as she.

To dispel the tedium of the hours which her husband found it necessary to devote to the processes of combination and analysis, Georgiana turned over the volumes of his scientific library. In many dark old tomes, she met with chapters full of romance and poetry. They were the works of the philosophers of the middle ages, such as Albertus Magnus, Cornelius Agrippa, Paracelsus, and the famous friar who created the prophetic Brazen Head.[3] All these antique naturalists stood in advance of their centuries, yet were imbued with some of their[4] credulity, and therefore were believed, and perhaps imagined themselves, to have acquired from the investigation of nature a power above nature, and from physics a sway over the spiritual world.

3. I.e., Roger Bacon (1214?–1294), English Franciscan monk interested in science and alchemy, who fashioned a head of bronze said to predict changes in climate and health. Magnus (1206?–1280), German theologian and alchemist. Agrippa (1486–1535), German theologian and writer. Philippus Aureolus Paracelsus (1493–1541), Swiss alchemist and physician.
4. This 1846 reading replaces the 1843 *its*.

Hardly less curious and imaginative were the early volumes of the Transactions of the Royal Society,[5] in which the members, knowing little of the limits of natural possibility, were continually recording wonders, or proposing methods whereby wonders might be wrought.

But, to Georgiana, the most engrossing volume was a large folio from her husband's own hand, in which he had recorded every experiment of his scientific career, with its original aim, the methods adopted for its development, and its final success or failure, with the circumstances to which either event was attributable. The book, in truth, was both the history and emblem of his ardent, ambitious, imaginative, yet practical and laborious, life. He handled physical details, as if there were nothing beyond them; yet spiritualized them all, and redeemed himself from materialism, by his strong and eager aspiration towards the infinite. In his grasp, the veriest clod of earth assumed a soul. Georgiana, as she read, reverenced Aylmer, and loved him more profoundly than ever, but with a less entire dependence on his judgment than heretofore. Much as he had accomplished, she could not but observe that his most splendid successes were almost invariably failures, if compared with the ideal at which he aimed. His brightest diamonds were the merest pebbles, and felt to be so by himself, in comparison with the inestimable gems which lay hidden beyond his reach. The volume, rich with achievements that had won renown for its author, was yet as melancholy a record as ever mortal hand had penned. It was the sad confession, and continual exemplification, of the short-comings of the composite man—the spirit burthened with clay and working in matter—and of the despair that assails the higher nature, at finding itself so miserably thwarted by the earthly part. Perhaps every man of genius, in whatever sphere, might recognise the image of his own experience in Aylmer's journal.

So deeply did these reflections affect Georgiana, that she laid her face upon the open volume, and burst into tears. In this situation she was found by her husband.

"It is dangerous to read in a sorcerer's books," said he, with a smile, though his countenance was uneasy and displeased. "Georgiana, there are pages in that volume, which I can scarcely glance over and keep my senses. Take heed lest it prove as detrimental to you!"

"It has made me worship you more than ever," said she.

"Ah! wait for this one success," rejoined he, "then worship me if you will. I shall deem myself hardly unworthy of it. But, come! I have sought you for the luxury of your voice. Sing to me, dearest!"

So she poured out the liquid music of her voice to quench the thirst of his spirit. He then took his leave, with a boyish exuberance of gaiety, assuring her that her seclusion would endure but a little longer, and that the result was already certain. Scarcely had he departed, when Georgiana felt irresistibly impelled to follow him. She had forgotten to inform Aylmer of a symptom, which, for two or three hours past, had begun to excite her attention. It was a sensation in the fatal birth-mark, not painful, but which induced a restlessness throughout her system. Hastening after her husband, she intruded, for the first time, into the laboratory.

5. The Royal Society of London, chartered in 1662 to advance scientific inquiry.

The first thing that struck her eye was the furnace, that hot and feverish worker, with the intense glow of its fire, which, by the quantities of soot clustered above it, seemed to have been burning for ages. There was a distilling apparatus in full operation. Around the room were retorts,[6] tubes, cylinders, crucibles, and other apparatus of chemical research. An electrical machine stood ready for immediate use. The atmosphere felt oppressively close, and was tainted with gaseous odors, which had been tormented forth by the processes of science. The severe and homely simplicity of the apartment, with its naked walls and brick pavement, looked strange, accustomed as Georgiana had become to the fantastic elegance of her boudoir. But what chiefly, indeed almost solely, drew her attention, was the aspect of Aylmer himself.

He was pale as death, anxious, and absorbed, and hung over the furnace as if it depended upon his utmost watchfulness whether the liquid, which it was distilling, should be the draught of immortal happiness or misery. How different from the sanguine and joyous mien that he had assumed for Georgiana's encouragement!

"Carefully now, Aminadab! Carefully, thou human machine! Carefully, thou man of clay!" muttered Aylmer, more to himself than his assistant. "Now, if there be a thought too much or too little, it is all over!"

"Hoh! hoh!" mumbled Aminadab—"look, master, look!"

Aylmer raised his eyes hastily, and at first reddened, then grew paler than ever, on beholding Georgiana. He rushed towards her, and seized her arm with a gripe that left the print of his fingers upon it.

"Why do you come hither? Have you no trust in your husband?" cried he impetuously. "Would you throw the blight of that fatal birth-mark over my labors? It is not well done. Go, prying woman, go!"

"Nay, Aylmer," said Georgiana, with the firmness of which she possessed no stinted endowment, "it is not you that have a right to complain. You mistrust your wife! You have concealed the anxiety with which you watch the development of this experiment. Think not so unworthily of me, my husband! Tell me all the risk we run; and fear not that I shall shrink, for my share in it is far less than your own!"

"No, no, Georgiana!" said Aylmer impatiently, "it must not be."

"I submit," replied she, calmly. "And, Aylmer, I shall quaff whatever draught you bring me; but it will be on the same principle that would induce me to take a dose of poison, if offered by your hand."

"My noble wife," said Aylmer, deeply moved, "I knew not the height and depth of your nature, until now: Nothing shall be concealed. Know, then, that this Crimson Hand, superficial as it seems, has clutched its grasp, into your being, with a strength of which I had no previous conception. I have already administered agents powerful enough to do aught except to change your entire physical system. Only one thing remains to be tried. If that fail us, we are ruined!"

"Why did you hesitate to tell me this?" asked she.

"Because, Georgiana," said Aylmer, in a low voice, "there is danger!"

"Danger? There is but one danger—that this horrible stigma shall be left upon my cheek!" cried Georgiana. "Remove it! remove it!—whatever be the cost—or we shall both go mad!"

6. Glass vessels used for distillation.

"Heaven knows, your words are too true," said Aylmer, sadly. "And now, dearest, return to your boudoir. In a little while, all will be tested."

He conducted her back, and took leave of her with a solemn tenderness, which spoke far more than his words how much was now at stake. After his departure, Georgiana became wrapt in musings. She considered the character of Aylmer, and did it completer justice than at any previous moment. Her heart exulted, while it trembled, at his honorable love, so pure and lofty that it would accept nothing less than perfection, nor miserably make itself contented with an earthlier nature than he had dreamed of. She felt how much more precious was such a sentiment, than that meaner kind which would have borne with the imperfection for her sake, and have been guilty of treason to holy love, by degrading its perfect idea to the level of the actual. And, with her whole spirit, she prayed, that, for a single moment, she might satisfy his highest and deepest conception. Longer than one moment, she well knew, it could not be; for his spirit was ever on the march—ever ascending—and each instant required something that was beyond the scope of the instant before.

The sound of her husband's footsteps aroused her. He bore a crystal goblet, containing a liquor colorless as water, but bright enough to be the draught of immortality. Aylmer was pale; but it seemed rather the consequence of a highly wrought state of mind, and tension of spirit, than of fear or doubt.

"The concoction of the draught has been perfect," said he, in answer to Georgiana's look. "Unless all my science have deceived me, it cannot fail."

"Save on your account, my dearest Aylmer," observed his wife, "I might wish to put off this birth-mark of mortality by relinquishing mortality itself, in preference to any other mode. Life is but a sad possession to those who have attained precisely the degree of moral advancement at which I stand. Were I weaker and blinder, it might be happiness. Were I stronger, it might be endured hopefully. But, being what I find myself, methinks I am of all mortals the most fit to die."

"You are fit for heaven without tasting death!" replied her husband. "But why do we speak of dying? The draught cannot fail. Behold its effect upon this plant!"

On the window-seat there stood a geranium, diseased with yellow blotches, which had overspread all its leaves. Aylmer poured a small quantity of the liquid upon the soil in which it grew. In a little time, when the roots of the plant had taken up the moisture, the unsightly blotches began to be extinguished in a living verdure.

"There needed no proof," said Georgiana, quietly. "Give me the goblet. I joyfully stake all upon your word."

"Drink, then, thou lofty creature!" exclaimed Aylmer, with fervid admiration. "There is no taint of imperfection on thy spirit. Thy sensible frame, too, shall soon be all perfect!"

She quaffed the liquid, and returned the goblet to his hand.

"It is grateful," said she with a placid smile. "Methinks it is like water from a heavenly fountain; for it contains I know not what of unobtrusive fragrance and deliciousness. It allays a feverish thirst, that had parched me for many days. Now, dearest, let me sleep. My earthly senses are closing over my spirit, like the leaves round the heart of a rose, at sunset."

She spoke the last words with a gentle reluctance, as if it required almost more energy than she could command to pronounce the faint and lingering syllables. Scarcely had they loitered through her lips, ere she was lost in slumber. Aylmer sat by her side, watching her aspect with the emotions proper to a man, the whole value of whose existence was involved in the process now to be tested. Mingled with this mood, however, was the philosophic investigation, characteristic of the man of science. Not the minutest symptom escaped him. A heightened flush of the cheek—a slight irregularity of breath—a quiver of the eye-lid—a hardly perceptible tremor through the frame—such were the details which, as the moments passed, he wrote down in his folio volume. Intense thought had set its stamp upon every previous page of that volume; but the thoughts of years were all concentrated upon the last.

While thus employed, he failed not to gaze often at the fatal Hand, and not without a shudder. Yet once, by a strange and unaccountable impulse, he pressed it with his lips. His spirit recoiled, however, in the very act, and Georgiana, out of the midst of her deep sleep, moved uneasily and murmured, as if in remonstrance. Again, Aylmer resumed his watch. Nor was it without avail. The Crimson Hand, which at first had been strongly visible upon the marble paleness of Georgiana's cheek, now grew more faintly outlined. She remained not less pale than ever; but the birth-mark, with every breath that came and went, lost somewhat of its former distinctness. Its presence had been awful; its departure was more awful still. Watch the stain of the rainbow fading out of the sky; and you will know how that mysterious symbol passed away.

"By Heaven, it is well nigh gone!" said Aylmer to himself, in almost irrepressible ecstasy. "I can scarcely trace it now. Success! Success! And now it is like the faintest rose-color. The slightest flush of blood across her cheek would overcome it. But she is so pale!"

He drew aside the window-curtain, and suffered the light of natural day to fall into the room, and rest upon her cheek. At the same time, he heard a gross, hoarse chuckle, which he had long known as his servant Aminadab's expression of delight.

"Ah, clod! Ah, earthly mass!" cried Aylmer, laughing in a sort of frenzy. "You have served me well! Matter and Spirit—Earth and Heaven—have both done their part in this! Laugh, thing of the senses! You have earned the right to laugh."

These exclamations broke Georgiana's sleep. She slowly unclosed her eyes, and gazed into the mirror, which her husband had arranged for that purpose. A faint smile flitted over her lips, when she recognised how barely perceptible was now that Crimson Hand, which had once blazed forth with such disastrous brilliancy as to scare away all their happiness. But then her eyes sought Aylmer's face, with a trouble and anxiety that he could by no means account for.

"My poor Aylmer!" murmured she.

"Poor? Nay, richest! Happiest! Most favored!" exclaimed he. "My peerless bride, it is successful! You are perfect!"

"My poor Aylmer!" she repeated, with a more than human tenderness. "You have aimed loftily!—you have done nobly! Do not repent, that, with so high and pure a feeling, you have rejected the best that earth could offer. Aylmer—dearest Aylmer—I am dying!"

Alas, it was too true! The fatal Hand had grappled with the mystery of life, and was the bond by which an angelic spirit kept itself in union with a mortal frame. As the last crimson tint of the birth-mark—that sole token of human imperfection—faded from her cheek, the parting breath of the now perfect woman passed into the atmosphere, and her soul, lingering a moment near her husband, took its heavenward flight. Then a hoarse, chuckling laugh was heard again! Thus ever does the gross Fatality of Earth exult in its invariable triumph over the immortal essence, which, in this dim sphere of half-development, demands the completeness of a higher state. Yet, had Aylmer reached a profounder wisdom, he need not thus have flung away the happiness, which would have woven his mortal life of the self-same texture with the celestial. The momentary circumstance was too strong for him; he failed to look beyond the shadowy scope of Time, and living once for all in Eternity, to find the perfect Future in the present.

1843, 1846

HENRY WADSWORTH LONGFELLOW
1807–1882

Henry Wadsworth Longfellow was the most beloved American poet of the nineteenth century. His narrative poems *Evangeline* (1847), *The Song of Hiawatha* (1855), and *The Courtship of Miles Standish* (1858) went through numerous editions, and his collections of lyrics—*The Seaside and the Fireside* (1850), *Tales of a Wayside Inn* (1863), and many others—were also enormously popular. In Great Britain, Longfellow outsold England's poet laureate Alfred, Lord Tennyson; and shortly after Longfellow's death in 1882, he became the first American-born poet enshrined in Westminster Abbey's famed Poets' Corner. As literary modernism took hold in the twentieth century, Longfellow came to be seen as an unadventurous, timid poet; but such an assessment unfairly diminishes the achievement of a writer who saw value in working with (rather than against) established forms and traditions. Viewed in relation to his own culture and his own poetic aspirations, Longfellow exhibited a metrical complexity, a mastery of sound and atmosphere, a progressive social conscience, and a melancholy outlook for which his soothing words were especially appropriate, as though the poet were comforting himself as well as his audience.

Longfellow was born in Portland, Maine (then still a part of Massachusetts), on February 27, 1807, the second of eight children. Both of his parents encouraged his early interest in reading and writing, but when he was sent to Bowdoin College in 1821, the expectation was that the fourteen-year-old Longfellow would eventually become a lawyer like his father. Graduating at age eighteen in the class of 1825, which also included Nathaniel Hawthorne and the future president Franklin Pierce, Longfellow made the risky vocational decision to pursue his interest in literature. He was aided in this ambition by a college trustee who donated money to Bowdoin to hire Longfellow as a professor of modern languages, provided that Longfellow agreed to use his own funds to study languages in Europe. Supported by his father, Longfellow spent three years abroad, traveling in Germany, Italy, France, and Spain (where he met Washington Irving, the American writer he most admired). Returning to the United States in 1829 with a new fluency in four languages, the twenty-two-year-old Longfellow assumed the professorship at Bowdoin. In 1831 he married Mary Storer Potter; four years later he was appointed the Smith Professor of Modern Languages and Belles Lettres at Harvard University, with the understanding that he would need to improve his skills in Germanic languages. To that end, he traveled to Europe with his wife in 1835; while in Holland, Mary died of complications from a miscarriage. Just before returning to the United States in 1836, Longfellow toured Switzerland and Austria, meeting and falling in love with Fanny Appleton, the daughter of the wealthy Boston industrialist Nathan Appleton. After a seven-year courtship, they married in 1843. As a wedding gift, Longfellow's father-in-law bought the couple Craigie House in Cambridge, a mansion abutting Harvard Yard where Longfellow himself had been renting rooms.

Longfellow's first published poem appeared in Maine's *Portland Gazette* on November 17, 1820, when he was thirteen years old. He published poems and prose while in college, but in his initial years as a professor he focused on publishing scholarly articles in the *North American Review*, along with language textbooks and translations of European poetry. But he soon returned to his principal interest, which was writing his own poetry, publishing his first volume, *Voices of the Night*, in 1839. Other poetic volumes quickly followed, including *Ballads and Other Poems* (1841), *Poems on Slavery* (1842), and *The Belfrey of Bruges and Other Poems* (1846). Longfellow's great commercial breakthrough came with the publication of his 1847 narrative poem *Evangeline*, which went through six printings in nine weeks. *Evangeline* weaves a tragic love story into a poetic narrative of the British dispossession of an Acadian French settlement in Nova Scotia during the French and Indian War (1756–63). At a time of increasing modernization, Longfellow tapped into the cultural nostalgia for times past that would also come to inform his popular Indian poetic narrative, *Hiawatha*. During these years Longfellow also published short and long prose pieces. Inspired by Irving's *Sketch Book* he brought out a collection of travel sketches, *Outre-Mer*, in 1835. In 1839 he published a two-volume prose romance, *Hyperion*; another prose romance, *Kavanagh*, appeared in 1849.

As a poet and a teacher, Longfellow took pride in his cosmopolitanism and transatlanticism. Rejecting the call by American literary nationalists for writing that drew mainly on native sources, Longfellow in his poetry worked with a wide range of sources—Homer and Virgil, for instance, for the hexameters of *Evangeline*, and Finnish mythologies and folk meter for *Hiawatha*. At Harvard, he taught European literatures of many periods and nationalities; he also published *The Poets and Poetry of Europe* (1845; rev. ed. 1871), a book of translations for the general reading public.

In 1854, Longfellow resigned from Harvard to devote himself completely to writing, editing, and translating. When he published *Hiawatha* one year after his resignation, the excellent sales (around thirty thousand copies in the first six months of publication) earned him his annual Harvard salary ($1,800) many times over. His 1858 *The Courtship of Miles Standish and Other Poems* sold twenty-five thousand copies in the United States over the first two months of publication, and ten thousand copies in London on its first day of publication. By the 1870s Longfellow's annual income from his writing was around $15,000, an enormous sum at that time and over $100,000 at today's value.

As with his first marriage, tragedy struck unexpectedly. In 1861 Fanny Longfellow burned to death when her dress caught fire while she was melting wax to preserve locks of her daughters' hair. Longfellow himself nearly died when he tried to smother the flames. In his grief Longfellow turned to translating the *Divine Comedy* of Dante, making the labor the occasion for regular meetings with friends such as James Russell Lowell and the young William Dean Howells; the volumes were published between 1865 and 1871. Longfellow made one last visit to Europe in 1868–69, during which Queen Victoria gave him a private audience and Oxford awarded him an honorary doctoral degree. On his return, he continued with his various writing and editing projects. His long religious poem *Christus: A Mystery*, the labor of many years, was published in 1872, and a number of other poetic volumes followed over the next decade, including a thirty-one-volume anthology, *Poems of Place* (1877–89). Longfellow died a month after his seventy-fifth birthday, on March 24, 1882. At the time he was working on a long poem about Michelangelo; *Michael Angelo: A Fragment* was published posthumously in 1883. One year later his bust was unveiled in Poets' Corner.

A Psalm of Life[1]

Life that shall send
A challenge to its end,
And when it comes, say, 'Welcome, friend.'[2]

What the Heart of the Young Man Said to the Psalmist

I

Tell me not, in mournful numbers,[3]
  Life is but an empty dream!
For the soul is dead that slumbers,
  And things are not what they seem.

II

Life is real—life is earnest—   5
  And the grave is not its goal:
Dust thou art, to dust returnest,
  Was not spoken of the soul.

III

Not enjoyment, and not sorrow,
  Is our destin'd end or way;   10
But to *act*, that each to-morrow
  Find us farther than to-day.

IV

Art is long, and time is fleeting,
  And our hearts, though stout and brave,
Still, like muffled drums, are beating   15
  Funeral marches to the grave.

---

1. The text is that of the first publication, in the *Knickerbocker: or, New-York Monthly Magazine* (September 1838). The poem was collected in *Voices of the Night* (1839).

2. Adapted from "Wishes to His Supposed Mistress" by the English poet Richard Crashaw (c. 1613–1649).

3. Meters, rhythms.

V

In the world's broad field of battle,
   In the bivouac of Life,
Be not like dumb, driven cattle!
   Be a hero in the strife!   20

VI

Trust no Future, howe'er pleasant!
   Let the dead Past bury its dead!
Act—act in the glorious Present!
   Heart within, and God o'er head!

VII

Lives of great men all remind us   25
   We can make *our* lives sublime,
And, departing, leave behind us
   Footsteps on the sands of time.

VIII

Footsteps, that, perhaps another,
   Sailing o'er life's solemn main,   30
A forlorn and shipwreck'd brother,
   Seeing, shall take heart again.

IX

Let us then be up and doing,
   With a heart for any fate;
Still achieving, still pursuing,   35
   Learn to labor and to wait.

                         1838, 1839

The Slave Singing at Midnight[1]

Loud he sang the psalm of David![2]
He, a Negro and enslaved,
Sang of Israel's victory,
Sang of Zion, bright and free.

In that hour, when night is calmest,   5
Sang he from the Hebrew Psalmist,
In a voice so sweet and clear
That I could not choose but hear,

---

1. From *Poems on Slavery* (1842).
2. Many of the psalms of the Old Testament have been attributed to David, the second of the Israelite kings, who reigned from c. 1000 B.C.E. to c. 962 B.C.E.

Songs of triumph, and ascriptions,
Such as reached the swart Egyptians,   10
When upon the Red Sea coast
Perished Pharaoh and his host.[3]

And the voice of his devotion
Filled my soul with strange emotion;
For its tones by turns were glad,   15
Sweetly solemn, wildly sad.

Paul and Silas, in their prison,
Sang of Christ, the Lord arisen,
And an earthquake's arm of might
Broke their dungeon-gates at night.[4]   20

But, alas! what holy angel
Brings the Slave this glad evangel?
And what earthquake's arm of might
Breaks his dungeon-gates at night?

1842

The Jewish Cemetery at Newport[1]

How strange it seems! These Hebrews in their graves.
  Close by the street of this fair sea-port town;
Silent beside the never-silent waves,
  At rest in all this moving up and down!

The trees are white with dust, that o'er their sleep   5
  Wave their broad curtains in the south-wind's breath,
While underneath such leafy tents they keep
  The long, mysterious Exodus of Death.

And these sepulchral stones, so old and brown,
  That pave with level flags[2] their burial-place,   10
Are like the tablets of the Law, thrown down
  And broken by Moses at the mountain's base.[3]

The very names recorded here are strange,
  Of foreign accent, and of different climes;

---

3. The Israelites escaped from slavery when the Red Sea divided to let them pass and then closed to drown Pharaoh and his army (Exodus 15).
4. See Acts 16.19–34 on the miraculous escape from prison of the Christian leaders Paul and Silas.
1. First published in *Putnam's Monthly Magazine* (July 1854), the source of the present text. The first Jewish settlers arrived in Newport, Rhode Island, in 1658, encouraged by the relatively tolerant religious attitudes of local leaders. During the colonial period, Newport had the second largest Jewish community in North America. The Touro Synagogue, the oldest still standing in the United States, dates from 1763. Longfellow visited Newport's Jewish Cemetery in July 1852.
2. Flagstones.
3. "Moses' anger waxed hot, and he cast the tablets out of his hands, and brake them beneath the mount" (Exodus 32.19).

Alvares and Rivera[4] interchange 15
    With Abraham and Jacob of old times.

"Blessed be God! for he created Death!"
    The mourners said: "and Death is rest and peace."
Then added, in the certainty of faith:
    "And giveth Life, that never more shall cease." 20

Closed are the portals of their Synagogue,
    No Psalms of David now the silence break,
No Rabbi reads the ancient Decalogue[5]
    In the grand dialect the Prophets spake.

Gone are the living, but the dead remain, 25
    And not neglected, for a hand unseen,
Scattering its bounty, like a summer rain,
    Still keeps their graves and their remembrance green.

How came they here? What burst of Christian hate;
    What persecution, merciless, and blind, 30
Drove o'er the sea,—that desert, desolate—
    These Ishmaels and Hagars[6] of mankind?

They lived in narrow streets and lanes obscure,
    Ghetto or Judenstrass,[7] in mirk and mire;
Taught in the school of patience to endure 35
    The life of anguish and the death of fire.

All their lives long, with the unleavened bread
    And bitter herbs[8] of exile and its fears,
The wasting famine of the heart they fed,
    And slaked its thirst with marah[9] of their tears. 40

Anathema maranatha![1] was the cry
    That rang from town to town, from street to street;
At every gate the accursed Mordecai[2]
    Was mocked, and jeered, and spurned by Christian feet.

Pride and humiliation hand in hand 45
    Walked with them through the world, where'er they went;
Trampled and beaten were they as the sand,
    And yet unshaken as the continent.

4. The Newport Jews were Sephardims, immigrants from Spain and Portugal, where they had acquired local names.
5. The Ten Commandments.
6. Outcasts. From Genesis 21, where Hagar, the concubine of Abraham, and their son, Ishmael, are driven from his household at the instigation of his wife, Sarah, after the birth of their son, Isaac.
7. Street of the Jews (German). "Ghetto": a section of a city to which Jews were restricted.
8. Foods eaten at Passover in remembrance of the exodus from slavery in Egypt.
9. Bitter water; see Exodus 15.22–25, which describes how the Hebrews, after crossing the Red Sea, came to Marah, where they found the water too bitter to drink until God showed Moses how to sweeten it with a tree.
1. "If any man love not the Lord Jesus Christ, let him be Anathema Maranatha" (1 Corinthians 16.22).
2. A Jewish leader abused by the Persians (Esther 2.5–6).

For in the back-ground, figures vague and vast,
   Of patriarchs and of prophets rose sublime,   50
And all the great traditions of the Past
   They saw reflected in the coming time.

And thus for ever with reverted look,
   The mystic volume of the world they read,
Spelling it backward like a Hebrew book,[3]   55
   Till Life became a Legend of the Dead.

But ah! what once has been shall be no more!
   The groaning earth in travail and in pain
Brings forth its races, but does not restore,
   and the dead nations never rise again.   60

1854

3. Hebrew is read from right to left.

JOHN GREENLEAF WHITTIER
1807–1892

John Greenleaf Whittier was born to a Quaker family on December 17, 1807, on a farm near Haverhill, Massachusetts. Although no longer persecuted in New England, Quakers were still a people apart, and Whittier grew up with a sense of being different from most of his neighbors. Labor on the debt-ridden farm overstrained his health in adolescence, and thereafter throughout his long life he suffered from intermittent physical collapses. At fourteen, having had only a meager education in a household suspicious of non-Quaker literature, he found in the Scottish poet Robert Burns (1759–1796) an initial source of inspiration. Like Burns, Whittier began writing poems that employed regional dialect, dealt with homely subjects, and displayed a democratic social conscience. His first poem was published in 1826 in a local newspaper run by another young man, William Lloyd Garrison (1805–1879), whose dedication to the antislavery movement was to affect Whittier's life profoundly. In 1827 Garrison helped persuade Whittier's father that the young poet deserved a formal education, and Whittier supported himself through two terms at Haverhill Academy. In 1836, six years after his father's death, Whittier and his mother and sisters moved from the farm to a house in nearby Amesbury, Massachusetts, which he owned until his death.

In his twenties Whittier became editor of various newspapers, some of regional importance. The turning point of his career came in 1833, when Garrison brought him into the abolitionist movement. In June 1833 Whittier published an antislavery pamphlet, *Justice and Expediency*, and later that year he helped found the American

Anti-Slavery Society. In the tradition of such antislavery Quakers as Anthony Bene-zet (1713–1784) and John Woolman (1720–1793), Whittier believed that there was only one practicable and just scheme of emancipation: "Immediate abolition of slav-ery; an immediate acknowledgment of the great truth, that man cannot hold property in man; an immediate surrender of baneful prejudice to Christian love; an immediate practical obedience to the command of Jesus Christ: 'Whatsoever ye would that men should do unto you, do even so to them'" (*Justice and Expediency*). In an effort to disseminate his views to the widest possible audience, Whittier published over a hun-dred antislavery poems and quickly emerged as the most popular poet of the aboli-tionist movement. His antislavery poetry was collected in 1837 in an unauthorized volume, *Poems Written during the Progress of the Abolition Question in the United States*, funded by abolitionists; one year later he oversaw the publication of *Poems* (1838), which included most of his antislavery poetry up to that time. That same year Whittier, in disguise, joined an antiabolitionist mob to save some of his papers as his office was being ransacked and burned.

From the 1830s through the 1850s, Whittier was a working editor and writer asso-ciated with abolitionist newspapers such as the Washington, D.C., weekly *National Era*, which serialized Harriet Beecher Stowe's *Uncle Tom's Cabin* from 1851 to 1852. During this time he published several additional volumes of poetry, including *Lays of My Home* (1843) and *The Chapel of Hermits and Other Poems* (1853), along with a serialized novel about New England's colonial past, *Leaves from Margaret Smith's Journal* (*National Era*, 1848–49). Like Nathaniel Hawthorne, Whittier had a keen interest in New England history. His first book, *Legends of New England* (1831), had explored New England's past in sketches and verse. In 1847 he published a sequel of sorts, the prose work *The Supernaturalism of New England*, which Hawthorne reviewed favorably in the New York monthly *Literary World*, terming it "no unworthy contribution from a poet to that species of literature which only a poet should meddle with." The New England writings of Hawthorne, Whittier, Catharine Sedgwick, and Stowe would have an important influence on the emergence of local-color regional-ism later in the century.

Despite his wide-ranging interests in poetry, prose, and editing, Whittier well into the 1850s was generally regarded (contemptuously by some) as simply an abolitionist poet. His reputation underwent a change in the late 1850s, when abolitionism had become more accepted in the North, and when his poetry and humorous folk leg-ends began to appear in the new (and very popular) *Atlantic Monthly*. With the out-break of the Civil War, the nonviolent Quaker Whittier, whose progressive antislavery poems had contributed to northern militancy, became increasingly troubled by the carnage on the battlefield and sought refuge in a domestic poetry that recaptured an idealized, harmonic past. Grief-stricken at the death of his younger sister Elizabeth in 1865, he began work on *Snow-Bound*, which James T. Fields published as a book in 1866. In the aftermath of the Civil War, at a time of national mourning, readers responded enthusiastically to Whittier's nostalgic evocation of a historical moment when houses were not divided and all was mostly well with the world. Suddenly the poet on the margins emerged, along with Longfellow, as one of the nation's most beloved poets. Whittier earned over $10,000 from the sales of *Snow-Bound*, an enormous sum for that time, and his subsequent volume, *The Tent on the Beach* (1867), was even more enthusiastically received, selling out its first printing of twenty thousand copies within the first three weeks of publication. During the final decades of his life, Whittier was regaled with honors, and even had a college in Iowa and a town in California named after him. On the occasion of his seventieth birthday, Stowe declared that Whittier's "life had been a consecration, his songs an inspiration, to all that is highest and best." In 1888 he helped edit a seven-volume edition of his collected works; his last volume, *At Sundown* (1890), was privately printed for friends. He died from a stroke in Hampton Falls, New Hampshire, on September 7, 1892.

Snow-Bound: A Winter Idyl[1]

To the memory of the household it describes, this poem is dedicated by the author.

"As the Spirits of Darkness be stronger in the dark, so Good Spirits which be Angels of Light are augmented not only by the Divine light of the Sun, but also by our common Wood Fire: and as the celestial Fire drives away dark spirits, so also this our Fire of Wood doth the same."
                    —COR. AGRIPPA, *Occult Philosophy*, Book I. chap. v.[2]

> "Announced by all the trumpets of the sky,
> Arrives the snow; and, driving o'er the fields,
> Seems nowhere to alight; the whited air
> Hides hills and woods, the river and the heaven,
> And veils the farm-house at the garden's end.
> The sled and traveller stopped, the courier's feet
> Delayed, all friends shut out, the housemates sit
> Around the radiant fireplace, enclosed
> In a tumultuous privacy of storm."
>   —EMERSON[3]

The sun that brief December day
Rose cheerless over hills of gray,
And, darkly circled, gave at noon
A sadder light than waning moon.

Slow tracing down the thickening sky   5
Its mute and ominous prophecy,
A portent seeming less than threat,
It sank from sight before it set.
A chill no coat, however stout,
Of homespun stuff could quite shut out,   10
A hard, dull bitterness of cold,
    That checked, mid-vein, the circling race
    Of life-blood in the sharpened face,
The coming of the snow-storm told.

The wind blew east: we heard the roar   15
Of Ocean on his wintry shore,
And felt the strong pulse throbbing there
Beat with low rhythm our inland air.

---

1. The text followed here is that of the 1st edition (1866). In a prefatory note to the 1891 edition, Whittier remarked that the "inmates of the family at the Whittier homestead who are referred to in the poem were my father, mother, my brother and two sisters, and my uncle and aunt, both unmarried. In addition, there was the district schoolmaster who boarded with us. The 'not unfeared, half-unwelcome guest' was Harriet Livermore, daughter of Judge Livermore, of New Hampshire, a young woman of fine natural ability, enthusiastic, eccentric." Harriet Livermore (1788–1868) became a well-known preacher, an unusual career for a woman at the time. A millenarian, she warned of a coming Apocalypse.
2. Heinrich Cornelius Agrippa (1486–1525) was a German physician and student of occult science. In his 1891 prefatory note, Whittier said that his family owned a 1651 edition of Agrippa's *Three Books of Occult Philosophy* (1532).
3. The opening of Emerson's "The Snow-Storm" (1841).

Meanwhile we did our nightly chores,—
Brought in the wood from out of doors,   20
Littered the stalls, and from the mows
Raked down the herd's-grass for the cows;
Heard the horse whinnying for his corn;
And, sharply clashing horn on horn,
Impatient down the stanchion rows   25
The cattle shake their walnut bows;[4]
While, peering from his early perch
Upon the scaffold's pole of birch,
The cock his crested helmet bent
And down his querulous challenge sent.   30

Unwarmed by any sunset light
The gray day darkened into night,
A night made hoary with the swarm
And whirl-dance of the blinding storm,
As zigzag wavering to and fro   35
Crossed and recrossed the wingéd snow:
And ere the early bed-time came
The white drift piled the window-frame,
And through the glass the clothes-line posts
Looked in like tall and sheeted ghosts.   40

So all night long the storm roared on:
The morning broke without a sun;
In tiny spherule traced with lines
Of Nature's geometric signs,
In starry flake, and pellicle,[5]   45
All day the hoary meteor fell;
And, when the second morning shone,
We looked upon a world unknown,
On nothing we could call our own.
Around the glistening wonder bent   50
The blue walls of the firmament,
No cloud above, no earth below,—
A universe of sky and snow!
The old familiar sights of ours
Took marvellous shapes; strange domes and towers   55
Rose up where sty or corn-crib stood,
Or garden wall, or belt of wood;
A smooth white mound the brush-pile showed,
A fenceless drift what once was road;
The bridle-post an old man sat   60
With loose-flung coat and high cocked hat;
The well-curb had a Chinese roof;
And even the long sweep,[6] high aloof,

---

4. Stanchions (here made of walnut and shaped
like a bow) are adjustable braces set a few inches
from stationary posts; they are pulled aside at the
top to let a cow's head pass, then fixed against the
neck so the cow cannot back out while being
milked or fed.
5. A thin crust of crystals.
6. I.e., a well sweep; a pole attached to a pivot,
with a bucket at one end for raising water.

In its slant splendor, seemed to tell
Of Pisa's leaning miracle.   65

A prompt, decisive man, no breath
Our father wasted: "Boys, a path!"
Well pleased, (for when did farmer boy
Count such a summons less than joy?)
Our buskins[7] on our feet we drew;   70
   With mittened hands, and caps drawn low,
    To guard our necks and ears from snow,
We cut the solid whiteness through.
And, where the drift was deepest, made
A tunnel walled and overlaid   75
With dazzling crystal: we had read
Of rare Aladdin's wondrous cave,
And to our own his name we gave,
With many a wish the luck were ours
To test his lamp's supernal powers.   80
We reached the barn with merry din,
And roused the prisoned brutes within.
The old horse thrust his long head out,
And grave with wonder gazed about;
The cock his lusty greeting said,   85
And forth his speckled harem led;
The oxen lashed their tails, and hooked,
And mild reproach of hunger looked;
The hornéd patriarch of the sheep,
Like Egypt's Amun[8] roused from sleep,   90
Shook his sage head with gesture mute,
And emphasized with stamp of foot.

All day the gusty north-wind bore
The loosening drift its breath before;
Low circling round its southern zone,   95
The sun through dazzling snow-mist shone.
No bell the hush of silence broke,
No neighboring chimney's social smoke
Curled over woods of snow-hung oak.
A solitude made more intense   100
By dreary voicéd elements,
The shrieking of the mindless wind,
The moaning tree-boughs swaying blind,
And on the glass the unmeaning beat
Of ghostly finger-tips of sleet.   105
Beyond the circle of our hearth
No welcome sound of toil or mirth
Unbound the spell, and testified
Of human life and thought outside.
We minded that the sharpest ear   110
The buried brooklet could not hear,

---

7. High-cut shoes, like a half boot.   8. Egyptian god with a ram's head.

The music of whose liquid lip
Had been to us companionship,
And, in our lonely life, had grown
To have an almost human tone.   115

As night drew on, and, from the crest
Of wooded knolls that ridged the west,
The sun, a snow-blown traveller, sank
From sight beneath the smothering bank,
We piled, with care, our nightly stack   120
Of wood against the chimney-back,—
The oaken log, green, huge, and thick,
And on its top the stout back-stick;
The knotty forestick laid apart,
And filled between with curious art   125
The ragged brush; then, hovering near,
We watched the first red blaze appear,
Heard the sharp crackle, caught the gleam
On whitewashed wall and sagging beam,
Until the old, rude-furnished room   130
Burst, flower-like, into rosy bloom;
While radiant with a mimic flame
Outside the sparkling drift became,
And through the bare-boughed lilac-tree
Our own warm hearth seemed blazing free.   135
The crane and pendent trammels[9] showed,
The Turks' heads[1] on the andirons glowed;
While childish fancy, prompt to tell
The meaning of the miracle,
Whispered the old rhyme: *"Under the tree,*   140
When fire outdoors burns merrily,
There the witches are making tea."
The moon above the eastern wood
Shone at its full; the hill-range stood
Transfigured in the silver flood,   145
Its blown snows flashing cold and keen,
Dead white, save where some sharp ravine
Took shadow, or the sombre green
Of hemlocks turned to pitchy black
Against the whiteness at their back.   150
For such a world and such a night
Most fitting that unwarming light,
Which only seemed where'er it fell
To make the coldness visible.

Shut in from all the world without,   155
We sat the clean-winged hearth about.
Content to let the north-wind roar
In baffled rage at pane and door,

9. Pot hooks hanging from the crane, or movable   1. A favorite ornamentation, turbanlike knots in
arm.   wrought iron.

While the red logs before us beat
The frost-line back with tropic heat;   160
And ever, when a louder blast
Shook beam and rafter as it passed,
The merrier up its roaring draught
The great throat of the chimney laughed.
The house-dog on his paws outspread   165
Laid to the fire his drowsy head,
The cat's dark silhouette on the wall
A couchant[2] tiger's seemed to fall;
And, for the winter fireside meet,
Between the andirons' straddling feet,   170
The mug of cider simmered slow,
The apples sputtered in a row,
And, close at hand, the basket stood
With nuts from brown October's wood.

What matter how the night behaved?   175
What matter how the north-wind raved?
Blow high, blow low, not all its snow
Could quench our hearth-fire's ruddy glow.
O Time and Change!—with hair as gray
As was my sire's that winter day,   180
How strange it seems, with so much gone
Of life and love, to still live on!
Ah, brother! only I and thou
Are left of all that circle now,—
The dear home faces whereupon   185
That fitful firelight paled and shone.
Henceforward, listen as we will,
The voices of that hearth are still;
Look where we may, the wide earth o'er,
Those lighted faces smile no more.   190
We tread the paths their feet have worn,
   We sit beneath their orchard-trees,
   We hear, like them, the hum of bees
And rustle of the bladed corn;
We turn the pages that they read,   195
   Their written words we linger o'er,
But in the sun they cast no shade,
No voice is heard, no sign is made,
   No step is on the conscious floor!
Yet Love will dream, and Faith will trust,   200
(Since He who knows our need is just,)
That somehow, somewhere, meet we must.
Alas for him who never sees
The stars shine through his cypress-trees!
Who, hopeless, lays his dead away,   205
Nor looks to see the breaking day
Across the mournful marbles[3] play!

2. Lying on stomach with head raised.   3. I.e., the gravestones.

Who hath not learned, in hours of faith,
    The truth to flesh and sense unknown,
That Life is ever lord of Death,   210
    And Love can never lose its own!

We sped the time with stories old,
Wrought puzzles out, and riddles told,
Or stammered from our school-book lore
"The Chief of Gambia's golden shore."[4]   215
How often since, when all the land
Was clay in Slavery's shaping hand,
As if a trumpet called, I've heard
Dame Mercy Warren's rousing word:
"*Does not the voice of reason cry,*   220
    Claim the first right which Nature gave,
From the red scourge of bondage fly,
    Nor deign to live a burdened slave!"
Our father rode again his ride
On Memphremagog's[5] wooded side;   225
Sat down again to moose and samp[6]
In trapper's hut and Indian camp;
Lived o'er the old idyllic ease
Beneath St. François'[7] hemlock-trees;
Again for him the moonlight shone   230
On Norman cap and bodiced zone;[8]
Again he heard the violin play
Which led the village dance away,
And mingled in its merry whirl
The grandam and the laughing girl.   235
Or, nearer home, our steps he led
Where Salisbury's[9] level marshes spread
    Mile-wide as flies the laden bee;
Where merry mowers, hale and strong,
Swept, scythe on scythe, their swaths along   240
    The low green prairies of the sea.
We shared the fishing off Boar's Head,
    And round the rocky Isles of Shoals[1]
    The hake-broil on the drift-wood coals;
The chowder on the sand-beach made,   245
Dipped by the hungry, steaming hot,
With spoons of clam-shell from the pot.
We heard the tales of witchcraft old,
And dream and sign and marvel told
To sleepy listeners as they lay   250
Stretched idly on the salted hay,

4. From "The African Chief," a widely reprinted antislavery poem by the Bostonian Sarah Wentworth Morton (1759–1846). In lines 220–23 Whittier quotes the poem but misidentifies the author as the Massachusetts historian Mercy Otis Warren (1728–1814).
5. A lake between Vermont and Quebec.
6. Cornmeal mush.
7. Village north of Lake Memphremagog.
8. Whittier's father is recalling the traditional clothes of women in French-Canadian settlements. (A "zone" is a belt or bodice.)
9. Nearby town in northeastern Massachusetts.
1. Off the New Hampshire coast.

Adrift along the winding shores,
When favoring breezes deigned to blow
The square sail of the gundalow[2]
And idle lay the useless oars.   255

Our mother, while she turned her wheel
Or run the new-knit stocking-heel,
Told how the Indian hordes came down
At midnight on Cochecho[3] town,
And how her own great-uncle bore   260
His cruel scalp-mark to fourscore.
Recalling, in her fitting phrase,
    So rich and picturesque and free,
    (The common unrhymed poetry
Of simple life and country ways,)   265
The story of her early days,—
She made for us the sunset shine
Aslant the tall columnar pine;
The river at her father's door
Its rippled moanings whispered o'er;   270
We heard the hawks at twilight play,
The boat-horn on Piscataqua,[4]
The loon's weird laughter far away.
So well she gleaned from earth and sky
That harvest of the ear and eye,   275
We almost felt the gusty air
That swept her native wood-paths bare,
Heard the far thresher's rhythmic flail,
The flapping of the fisher's sail,
Or saw, in sheltered cove and bay,   280
The ducks' black squadron anchored lay,
Or heard the wild geese calling loud
Beneath the gray November cloud.

Then, haply, with a look more grave,
And soberer tone, some tale she gave   285
From painful Sewell's[5] ancient tome,
Beloved in every Quaker home,
Of faith fire-winged by martyrdom,
Or Chalkley's Journal,[6] old and quaint,—
Gentlest of skippers, rare sea-saint!—   290
Who, when the dreary calms prevailed,
And water-butt and bread-cask failed,
And cruel, hungry eyes pursued
His portly presence mad for food,
With dark hints muttered under breath   295

---

2. Flat-bottomed boat.
3. Settlement near Dover, New Hampshire, on the Cochecho River.
4. I.e., foghorn on the Piscataqua River.
5. William Sewell or Sewel (1650–1725), author of a history of the Quakers. The history made painful reading because of the persecution and martyrdom many Quakers had suffered.
6. The *Journal* of the Quaker sea captain and preacher Thomas Chalkley (1675–1741) was published in 1747.

Of casting lots for life or death,
Offered, if Heaven withheld supplies,
To be himself the sacrifice.
Then, suddenly, as if to save
The good man from his living grave, 300
A ripple on the water grew,
A school of porpoise flashed in view.
"Take, eat," he said, "and be content;[7]
These fishes in my stead are sent
By Him who gave the tangled ram 305
To spare the child of Abraham."[8]
Our uncle, innocent of books,
But rich in lore of fields and brooks,
The ancient teachers never dumb
Of Nature's unhoused lyceum,[9] 310
In moons and tides and weather wise,
He read the clouds as prophecies,
And foul or fair could well divine,
By many an occult hint and sign,
Holding the cunning-warded[1] keys 315
To all the woodcraft mysteries;
Himself to Nature's heart so near
That all her voices in his ear
Of beast or bird had meanings clear,
Like Apollonius of old, 320
Who knew the tales the sparrows told,
Or Hermes,[2] who interpreted
What the sage cranes of Nilus[3] said;
A simple, guileless, childlike man,
Content to live where life began; 325
Strong only on his native grounds,
The little world of sights and sounds
Whose girdle was the parish bounds,
Whereof his fondly partial pride
The common features magnified, 330
As Surrey hills to mountains grew
In White of Selborne's[4] loving view,—
He told how teal and loon he shot,
And how the eagle's eggs he got,
The feats on pond and river done, 335
The prodigies of rod and gun;
Till, warming with the tales he told,
Forgotten was the outside cold,
The bitter wind unheeded blew,
From ripening corn the pigeons flew, 340
The partridge drummed i' the wood, the mink

---

7. Matthew 26.26: "Take, eat: this is my body" (Jesus's words at Passover).
8. See Genesis 22.13.
9. Lecture hall.
1. Carefully guarded.
2. Hermes Trismegistus (3rd century C.E.), legendary author of Egyptian books of magic. Apollonius (1st century C.E.), Greek mystic.
3. Nile River.
4. Gilbert White (1720–1793), English naturalist who lived in the county of Surrey, in southern England, and wrote *The Natural History and Antiquities of Selborne* (1789).

Went fishing down the river-brink.
In fields with bean or clover gay,
The woodchuck, like a hermit gray,
Peered from the doorway of his cell;   345
The muskrat plied the mason's trade,
And tier by tier his mud-walls laid;
And from the shagbark overhead
The grizzled squirrel dropped his shell.

Next, the dear aunt, whose smile of cheer   350
And voice in dreams I see and hear,—
The sweetest woman ever Fate
Perverse denied a household mate,
Who, lonely, homeless, not the less
Found peace in love's unselfishness,   355
And welcome wheresoe'er she went,
A calm and gracious element,
Whose presence seemed the sweet income
And womanly atmosphere of home,—
Called up her girlhood memories,   360
The huskings and the apple-bees,
The sleigh-rides and the summer sails,
Weaving through all the poor details
And homespun warp of circumstance
A golden woof-thread of romance.   365
For well she kept her genial mood
And simple faith of maidenhood;
Before her still a cloud-land lay,
The mirage loomed across her way;
The morning dew, that dries so soon   370
With others, glistened at her noon;
Through years of toil and soil and care
From glossy tress to thin gray hair,
All unprofaned she held apart
The virgin fancies of the heart.   375
Be shame to him of woman born
Who hath for such but thought of scorn.
There, too, our elder sister plied
Her evening task the stand beside;
A full, rich nature, free to trust,   380
Truthful and almost sternly just,
Impulsive, earnest, prompt to act,
And make her generous thought a fact,
Keeping with many a light disguise
The secret of self-sacrifice.   385
O heart sore-tried! thou hast the best
That Heaven itself could give thee,—rest,
Rest from all bitter thoughts and things!
    How many a poor one's blessing went
    With thee beneath the low green tent   390
Whose curtain never outward swings!

As one who held herself a part
Of all she saw, and let her heart
   Against the household bosom lean,
Upon the motley-braided mat 395
Our youngest and our dearest sat,
Lifting her large, sweet, asking eyes,
   Now bathed within the fadeless green
And holy peace of Paradise.
O, looking from some heavenly hill, 400
   Or from the shade of saintly palms,
   Or silver reach of river calms,
Do those large eyes behold me still?
With me one little year ago:—
The chill weight of the winter snow 405
   For months upon her grave has lain;
And now, when summer south-winds blow
   And brier and harebell bloom again,
I tread the pleasant paths we trod,
I see the violet-sprinkled sod 410
Whereon she leaned, too frail and weak
The hillside flowers she loved to seek,
Yet following me where'er I went
With dark eyes full of love's content.
The birds are glad; the brier-rose fills 415
The air with sweetness; all the hills
Stretch green to June's unclouded sky;
But still I wait with ear and eye
For something gone which should be nigh,
A loss in all familiar things, 420
In flower that blooms, and bird that sings.
And yet, dear heart! remembering thee,
   Am I not richer than of old?
Safe in thy immortality,
   What change can reach the wealth I hold? 425
   What chance can mar the pearl and gold
Thy love hath left in trust with me?
And while in life's late afternoon,
   Where cool and long the shadows grow,
I walk to meet the night that soon 430
   Shall shape and shadow overflow,
I cannot feel that thou art far,
Since near at need the angels are;
And when the sunset gates unbar,
   Shall I not see thee waiting stand, 435
And, white against the evening star,
   The welcome of thy beckoning hand?

Brisk wielder of the birch and rule,
The master of the district school
Held at the fire his favored place, 440
Its warm glow lit a laughing face

Fresh-hued and fair, where scarce appeared
The uncertain prophecy of beard.
He played the old and simple games
Our modern boyhood scarcely names,   445
Sang songs, and told us what befalls
In classic Dartmouth's college halls.
Born the wild Northern hills among,
From whence his yeoman father wrung
By patient toil subsistence scant,   450
Not competence and yet not want,
He early gained the power to pay
His cheerful, self-reliant way;
Could doff at ease his scholar's gown
To peddle wares from town to town;   455
Or through the long vacation's reach
In lonely lowland districts teach,
Where all the droll experience found
At stranger hearths in boarding round,
The moonlit skater's keen delight,   460
The sleigh-drive through the frosty night,
The rustic party, with its rough
Accompaniment of blind-man's-buff,
And whirling plate,[5] and forfeits paid,
His winter task a pastime made.   465
Happy the snow-locked homes wherein
He tuned his merry violin,
Or played the athlete in the barn,
Or held the good dame's winding yarn,
Or mirth-provoking versions told   470
Of classic legends rare and old,
Wherein the scenes of Greece and Rome
Had all the commonplace of home,
And little seemed at best the odds
'Twixt Yankee pedlers and old gods;   475
Where Pindus-born Araxes[6] took
The guise of any grist-mill brook,
And dread Olympus[7] at his will
Became a huckleberry hill.

A careless boy that night he seemed;   480
    But at his desk he had the look
And air of one who wisely schemed,
    And hostage from the future took
    In trainéd thought and lore of book.
Large-brained, clear-eyed,—of such as he   485
Shall Freedom's young apostles be,
Who, following in War's bloody trail,

---

5. Children's game of keeping a plate spinning on edge for as long as possible. "Blind-man's-buff": variant name for blind man's bluff, another children's game.

6. A Greek river, "born" in the Pindus Mountains.

7. Mountain that was the home of the gods in Greek mythology.

Shall every lingering wrong assail;
All chains from limb and spirit strike,
Uplift the black and white alike;   490
Scatter before their swift advance
The darkness and the ignorance,
The pride, the lust, the squalid sloth,
Which nurtured Treason's monstrous growth,
Made murder pastime, and the hell   495
Of prison-torture possible;
The cruel lie of caste refute,
Old forms recast, and substitute
For Slavery's lash the freeman's will,
For blind routine, wise-handed skill;   500
A school-house plant on every hill,
Stretching in radiate nerve-lines thence
The quick wires of intelligence;[8]
Till North and South together brought
Shall own the same electric thought,   505
In peace a common flag salute,
And, side by side in labor's free
And unresentful rivalry,
Harvest the fields wherein they fought.

Another guest[9] that winter night   510
Flashed back from lustrous eyes the light.
Unmarked by time, and yet not young,
The honeyed music of her tongue
And words of meekness scarcely told
A nature passionate and bold,   515
Strong, self-concentred, spurning guide,
Its milder features dwarfed beside
Her unbent will's majestic pride.
She sat among us, at the best,
A not unfeared, half-welcome guest,   520
Rebuking with her cultured phrase
Our homeliness of words and ways.
A certain pard-like,[1] treacherous grace
  Swayed the lithe limbs and drooped the lash,
  Lent the white teeth their dazzling flash;   525
  And under low brows, black with night,
  Rayed out at times a dangerous light;
The sharp heat-lightnings of her face
Presaging ill to him whom Fate
Condemned to share her love or hate.   530
A woman tropical, intense
In thought and act, in soul and sense,
She blended in a like degree
The vixen and the devotee,
Revealing with each freak or feint   535

8. Information, communication (the imagery is
from the telegraph, then still a recent development).

9. The boarder Harriet Livermore.
1. Leopardlike.

The temper of Petruchio's Kate,[2]
The raptures of Siena's saint.[3]
Her tapering hand and rounded wrist
Had facile power to form a fist;
The warm, dark languish of her eyes   540
Was never safe from wrath's surprise.
Brows saintly calm and lips devout
Knew every change of scowl and pout;
And the sweet voice had notes more high
And shrill for social battle-cry.   545

Since then what old cathedral town
Has missed her pilgrim staff and gown,
What convent-gate has held its lock
Against the challenge of her knock!
Through Smyrna's[4] plague-husked thoroughfares,   550
Up sea-set Malta's rocky stairs,
Gray olive slopes of hills that hem
Thy tombs and shrines, Jerusalem,
Or startling on her desert throne
The crazy Queen of Lebanon[5]   555
With claims fantastic as her own,
Her tireless feet have held their way;
And still, unrestful, bowed, and gray,
She watches under Eastern skies,
    With hope each day renewed and fresh,   560
    The Lord's quick coming in the flesh,
Whereof she dreams and prophesies!

Where'er her troubled path may be,
    The Lord's sweet pity with her go!
The outward wayward life we see,   565
    The hidden springs we may not know.
Nor is it given us to discern
    What threads the fatal sisters[6] spun,
    Through what ancestral years has run
The sorrow with the woman born,   570
What forged her cruel chain of moods,
What set her feet in solitudes,
    And held the love within her mute,
What mingled madness in the blood,
    A life-long discord and annoy,   575
    Water of tears with oil of joy,
And hid within the folded bud
    Perversities of flower and fruit.
It is not ours to separate

---

2. The heroine of Shakespeare's *Taming of the Shrew.*
3. St. Catharine (1347–1380) of Siena, in Tuscany, Italy.
4. Now Izmir in Turkey.
5. Lady Hester Stanhope (1776–1839), an Englishwoman who in 1810 settled in Lebanon, where she attempted to rule like a dictator over a small area. Whittier remarked in his 1891 preface to "Snow-Bound" that Harriet Livermore lived with Stanhope for a while before they quarreled over interpretations of Christ's Second Coming.
6. In Greek mythology the goddesses of destiny, the Fates.

The tangled skein of will and fate,   580
To show what metes and bounds should stand
Upon the soul's debatable land,
And between choice and Providence
Divide the circle of events;
But He who knows our frame is just,[7]   585
   Merciful, and compassionate,
And full of sweet assurances
And hope for all the language is,
That He remembereth we are dust!

At last the great logs, crumbling low,   590
Sent out a dull and duller glow,
The bull's-eye watch[8] that hung in view,
Ticking its weary circuit through,
Pointed with mutely-warning sign
Its black hand to the hour of nine.   595
That sign the pleasant circle broke:
My uncle ceased his pipe to smoke,
Knocked from its bowl the refuse gray
And laid it tenderly away,
Then roused himself to safely cover   600
The dull red brands with ashes over.
And while, with care, our mother laid
The work aside, her steps she stayed
One moment, seeking to express
Her grateful sense of happiness   605
For food and shelter, warmth and health,
And love's contentment more than wealth,
With simple wishes (not the weak,
Vain prayers which no fulfilment seek,
But such as warm the generous heart,   610
O'er-prompt to do with Heaven its part)
That none might lack, that bitter night,
For bread and clothing, warmth and light.

Within our beds awhile we heard
The wind that round the gables roared,   615
With now and then a ruder shock,
Which made our very bedsteads rock.
We heard the loosened clapboards tost,
The board-nails snapping in the frost;
And on us, through the unplastered wall,   620
Felt the light sifted snow-flakes fall.
But sleep stole on, as sleep will do
When hearts are light and life is new;
Faint and more faint the murmurs grew,
Till in the summer-land of dreams   625
They softened to the sound of streams,

7. Psalm 103.14: "For he knoweth our frame; he   8. Watch with a thick glass face.
remembereth that we are dust."

Low stir of leaves, and dip of oars,
And lapsing waves on quiet shores.

Next morn we wakened with the shout
Of merry voices high and clear;   630
And saw the teamsters[9] drawing near
To break the drifted highways out.
Down the long hillside treading slow
We saw the half-buried oxen go,
Shaking the snow from heads uptost,   635
Their straining nostrils white with frost.
Before our door the straggling train
Drew up, an added team to gain.
The elders threshed their hands a-cold,
    Passed, with the cider-mug, their jokes   640
    From lip to lip; the younger folks
Down the loose snow-banks, wrestling, rolled,
Then toiled again the cavalcade
    O'er windy hill, through clogged ravine,
    And woodland paths that wound between   645
Low drooping pine-boughs winter-weighed.
From every barn a team afoot,
At every house a new recruit,
Where, drawn by Nature's subtlest law,
Haply the watchful young men saw   650
Sweet doorway pictures of the curls
And curious eyes of merry girls,
Lifting their hands in mock defence
Against the snow-ball's compliments,
And reading in each missive tost   655
The charm with Eden never lost.
We heard once more the sleigh-bells' sound;
    And, following where the teamsters led,
The wise old Doctor went his round,
Just pausing at our door to say,   660
In the brief autocratic way
Of one who, prompt at Duty's call,
Was free to urge her claim on all,
    That some poor neighbor sick abed
At night our mother's aid would need.   665
For, one in generous thought and deed,
    What mattered in the sufferer's sight
    The Quaker matron's inward light,
The Doctor's mail[1] of Calvin's creed?
All hearts confess the saints elect   670
    Who, twain in faith, in love agree,
And melt not in an acid sect
    The Christian pearl of charity!

---

9. Those driving teams of oxen to plow snow.
1. Armor, with the suggestion that the French Protestant reformer John Calvin's (1509–1564) doctrines of predestination and Original Sin are less humane than the "whole armor of God" that Paul enjoins Christians to put on in Ephesians 6.11–17.

So days went on: a week had passed
Since the great world was heard from last.   675
The Almanac we studied o'er,
Read and reread our little store,
Of books and pamphlets, scarce a score;
One harmless novel, mostly hid
From younger eyes, a book forbid,   680
And poetry, (or good or bad,
A single book was all we had,)
Where Ellwood's meek, drab-skirted Muse,
    A stranger to the heathen Nine,[2]
    Sang, with a somewhat nasal whine,   685
The wars of David and the Jews.
At last the floundering carrier bore
The village paper to our door.
Lo! broadening outward as we read,
To warmer zones the horizon spread;   690
In panoramic length unrolled
We saw the marvels that it told.
Before us passed the painted Creeks,[3]
    And daft McGregor on his raids
    In dim Floridian everglades.[4]   695
And up Taygetos winding slow
Rode Ypsilanti's Mainote Greeks,
A Turk's head at each saddle-bow![5]
Welcome to us its week-old news,
Its corner for the rustic Muse,   700
    Its monthly gauge of snow and rain,
Its record, mingling in a breath
The wedding knell and dirge of death;
Jest, anecdote, and love-lorn tale,
The latest culprit sent to jail;   705
Its hue and cry of stolen and lost,
Its vendue[6] sales and goods at cost,
    And traffic calling loud for gain.
We felt the stir of hall and street,
The pulse of life that round us beat;   710
The chill embargo of the snow
Was melted in the genial glow;
Wide swung again our ice-locked door,
And all the world was ours once more!

2. Thomas Ellwood (1639–1714), English Quaker, wrote the *Davideis* (1712). Whittier has an essay on him in *Old Portraits and Modern Sketches* (1850). Here, Ellwood's source of inspiration wears "drab" Quaker clothes made of brownish yellow homespun, and knows nothing of the nine Greek goddesses who traditionally inspire artists and scientists.
3. Tribe of American Indians from Alabama who were subdued by Andrew Jackson in the Creek War (1813–14) and forced to resettle in present-day Oklahoma.

4. The Scottish adventurer Gregor McGregor (1786–1845) fought alongside Simón Bolívar (1783–1830) for the liberation of Venezuela from Spain, then in 1817 took possession of the Spanish-owned Amelia Island, off the Florida coast.
5. The Greek Revolutionary patriot Alexander Ypsilanti (1792–1828) defeated the Turks at Mount Taygetos in 1820; his saddle ornaments are heads of Turkish soldiers.
6. Auction.

Clasp, Angel of the backward look   715
  And folded wings of ashen gray
  And voice of echoes far away,
The brazen covers of thy book;
The weird palimpsest[7] old and vast,
Wherein thou hid'st the spectral past;   720
Where, closely mingling, pale and glow
The characters of joy and woe;
The monographs of outlived years,
Or smile-illumed or dim with tears,
  Green hills of life that slope to death,   725
And haunts of home, whose vistaed trees
Shade off to mournful cypresses
  With the white amaranths[8] underneath.
Even while I look, I can but heed
  The restless sands' incessant fall,   730
Importunate hours that hours succeed,
Each clamorous with its own sharp need,
  And duty keeping pace with all.
Shut down and clasp the heavy lids;
I hear again the voice that bids   735
The dreamer leave his dream midway
For larger hopes and graver fears:
Life greatens in these later years,
The century's aloe[9] flowers to-day!

Yet, haply, in some lull of life,   740
Some Truce of God which breaks its strife,
The worldling's eyes shall gather dew,
  Dreaming in throngful city ways
Of winter joys his boyhood knew;
And dear and early friends—the few   745
Who yet remain—shall pause to view
  These Flemish pictures[1] of old days;
Sit with me by the homestead hearth,
And stretch the hands of memory forth
  To warm them at the wood-fire's blaze!   750
And thanks untraced to lips unknown
Shall greet me like the odors blown
From unseen meadows newly mown,
Or lilies floating in some pond,
Wood-fringed, the wayside gaze beyond;   755
The traveller owns the grateful sense
Of sweetness near, he knows not whence,
And, pausing, takes with forehead bare
The benediction of the air.

1866

---

7. Parchment with earlier writing still visible beneath later writing.
8. Flowers associated with immortality.
9. The century plant, fabled to bloom only once every hundred years.
1. Dutch (Flemish) painters from the 17th century were known for their realistic domestic scenes.

EDGAR ALLAN POE
1809–1849

The facts of Poe's life, the most melodramatic of any of the major American writers of his generation, have been hard to determine; lurid legends about him circulated even before he died, some spread by Poe himself. Two days after Poe's death his supposed friend Rufus Griswold, a prominent anthologizer of American literature to whom Poe had entrusted his literary papers, began a campaign of character assassination, writing a vicious obituary and rewriting Poe's correspondence so as to alienate the public as well as his friends. Griswold's false claims and forgeries, unexposed for many years, significantly shaped Poe's reputation for decades.

Yet biographers now possess much reliable information about Poe's life. His mother, Elizabeth Arnold, was a prominent actress, touring the Eastern Seaboard in a profession that was then considered disreputable. In 1806, as a teenage widow, she married David Poe Jr., another actor. Edgar, the couple's second of three children, was born in Boston on January 19, 1809; a year later, David Poe deserted the family. In December 1811, Elizabeth Poe died at twenty-four while performing in Richmond, Virginia; the evidence suggests that her husband died soon afterward at the age of twenty-seven.

The disruptions of Poe's first two years were followed by years of security after John Allan, a young Richmond tobacco merchant, and his wife, Frances, took him in; his siblings (William Henry, born 1807, and Rosalie, born 1810) were sent to different foster parents. The Allans, who were childless, renamed the boy Edgar Allan and raised him as their son, but they never adopted him legally. Poe accompanied the family to England in 1815, where he attended good schools until the collapse of the London tobacco market forced the Allans back to Richmond in 1820. In 1824 Allan's firm failed and hostilities developed between Poe and his foster father. Allan lost interest in supporting Poe financially; even after inheriting all the property of a wealthy bachelor uncle, including several slave plantations, he provided only minimal funds to Poe for studying at the University of Virginia in 1826. Poe was a good student and wrote poetry on the side, but he ran into debt and began to drink. He gambled to pay his debts, instead losing as much as $2,000 (around $30,000 in current value). Allan refused to honor the debt, and Poe had to leave the university before his first year was completed. In March 1827, after another quarrel between the two, Allan ordered Poe out of the house.

The eighteen-year-old outcast Poe went first to Baltimore, and then moved north to his birthplace, where he paid for the printing of *Tamerlane and Other Poems*, "By a Bostonian," in 1827. Even before its publication, "Edgar A. Perry" (he had changed his name to avoid creditors) had joined the army. Released from the army with the rank of sergeant major, Poe now sought Allan's influence to help him get into the military academy at West Point. While waiting for the appointment, Poe condensed *Tamerlane*, revised other poems, and added new ones to make up a second volume, *Al Aaraaf, Tamerlane, and Minor Poems*, published in Baltimore in December 1829. In a short but favorable review, the influential New England critic John Neal declared that Poe could become "*foremost* in the rank of *real* poets."

Admitted to West Point in June 1830, Poe quickly became known for his conviviality and skills in mathematics and French. Despite renewed conflict with Allan, he believed himself the heir to Allan's great fortune. But his expectations were dashed when Allan, less than two years after the death of Frances Allan, married the

Edgar Allan Poe. Daguerreotype, 1848.

thirty-year-old Louisa Patterson in October 1830 and had a son in 1831 (in fact when Allan died in 1834, Poe was not mentioned in the will). The disillusioned Poe began to miss classes and roll calls and, as he anticipated, was expelled from school. Supportive friends among the cadets collected funds to publish his *Poems*, which appeared in May 1831. In this third book of his poetry Poe revised some earlier poems and for the first time included versions of both "To Helen" and "Israfel."

Poe's mature career—from his twenty-first year to his death in his fortieth year—was spent in four literary centers: Baltimore, Richmond, Philadelphia, and New York. The Baltimore years—mid-1831 to late 1835—were marked by hard work and comparative sobriety. Poe lived in poverty among his once-prosperous relatives, including his aunt Maria Poe Clemm and her daughter, Virginia. Poe's first story, "Metzengerstein," was published anonymously in the *Philadelphia Saturday Courier*, in January 1832; other stories appeared in the same paper throughout the year. Over the next two years, Poe placed stories and poems in the *Baltimore Saturday Visiter*. In January 1834 he made a significant breakthrough, publishing his tale "The Visionary" in *Godey's Lady's Book*, a popular Philadelphia monthly edited by Sarah J. Hale, for many years the nation's most prominent woman of letters. The writer and editor John P. Kennedy, who had read Poe's submissions to the *Saturday Visiter*, introduced the increasingly well-known Poe to Thomas W. White, publisher of the new Richmond-based *Southern Literary Messenger*. In August 1835, Poe became White's editorial assistant, moving back to Richmond where, for the next seventeen months, he played a significant role in the operations of the journal. Not only his stories and poems but also his often slashing reviews appeared in the *Messenger*, gaining him a reputation as the "Tomahawk Man," as White called him. Relations between Poe and White deteriorated when Poe resumed drinking. Returning to Baltimore briefly, Poe secretly married Virginia Clemm, and later publicly wed the thirteen-year-old Virginia in a May 1836 ceremony in Richmond.

Hoping to make the *Southern Literary Messenger* a nationally esteemed publication, Poe had to negotiate between the proslavery views of white Virginians and the growing opposition to such views in the North. As a result, though the journal did occasionally print proslavery pieces (including an anonymous defense of slavery in a review of April 1836 that was long attributed to Poe but was almost certainly not written by him), it usually adopted a middle-of-the-road position linking slavery to states' rights rather than God's will. In Poe's writings overall, slavery and race remain highly problematical. Like many white writers of the time, Poe sometimes resorted to racial stereotypes, and he sometimes conveyed his fears of the possibilities of black violence. For the most part, however, the perverse killers of his tales are white men. Critics continue to debate Poe's views on slavery and race. Although he spent years in the South and even held hopes for inheriting the property of a slaveholder, the fact is that his relative silence on the political debate on slavery makes him notably different from most southern intellectuals of the time—William Gilmore Simms, Nathaniel Beverly Tucker, and many others—who went on record with their proslavery views.

White fired Poe early in 1837, citing Poe's drinking, his demands for a higher salary, and his regular clashes with White about the day-to-day operations of the journal. Poe then moved, with his aunt (now his mother-in-law as well) and his wife, to New York City, where Mrs. Clemm ran a boarding house to support them all. In Richmond he had written a short novel, *The Narrative of Arthur Gordon Pym*, of which White had run two installments in the *Messenger* early in 1837. *Harper's* published it in July 1838, but it earned him little money. (It is now regarded as one of Poe's major works.) In 1838 Poe moved to Philadelphia, where, despite extreme poverty, he continued writing. In May 1839 he got his first steady job in more than two years, as co-editor of *Burton's Gentleman's Magazine*. There, in a job that paid him a small salary, he published book reviews and stories, including "The Fall of the House of Usher" and "William Wilson." Late in 1839, the Philadelphia firm of Lea and Blanchard published *Tales of the Grotesque and Arabesque*, a collection of the twenty-five stories Poe had written to that date. The mostly good reviews did not lead to good sales; the country was in the midst of an economic depression.

By the late 1830s, Poe was at the height of his powers as a writer of tales, though his personal and professional life continued to be unstable. William Burton fired him for drinking in May 1840 but recommended him to George Graham, who had bought out *Burton's* and created a new magazine called *Graham's*. Throughout 1841, Poe was with *Graham's* as a co-editor, courting subscribers by writing articles on cryptography—the art and science of code breaking. He also published "The Murders in the Rue Morgue," the first of what he termed his "tales of ratiocination" featuring detective August Dupin, a tale that many critics regard as the earliest example of detective fiction. In January 1842, Virginia Poe, not yet twenty, began hemorrhaging from her lungs while singing; she lived as a tubercular invalid only five more years. Poe continued reviewing for *Graham's*, but he resigned from the magazine in May 1842 after a dispute with Graham. His hope of his own journal—to be called the *Stylus*—was never realized.

In April 1844, Poe again moved his family to New York City, working as an editor on the *New York Evening Mirror*. Poe's most successful year was 1845. The February issue of *Graham's* contained an essay by James Russell Lowell declaring Poe a man of "genius"; and Poe's most popular work, "The Raven," appeared in the February *American Review* after advance publication in the *New York Evening Mirror*. One new literary acquaintance, the influential editor Evert A. Duyckinck, selected a dozen of Poe's stories for a collection brought out by Wiley & Putnam in June and arranged for the same firm to publish *The Raven and Other Poems* in November. Poe lectured on the poets of America and became a principal reviewer for a new weekly, the *Broadway Journal*, which also reprinted most of Poe's stories and poems. Still hoping to have his own magazine, in which he could be free of editorial interference, he purchased the *Broadway Journal* only to see it fail in January 1846.

While the tempo of Poe's life speeded up, with ever more literary feuds and drinking bouts, he maintained an undiminished commitment to his writing. During 1847, the year that Virginia died from tuberculosis, Poe was seriously ill himself. In 1848 he published *Eureka*, a philosophical prose work that presented God as the force behind all matter, and all matter as seeking a return to oneness. He also published "Ulalume," a poem inspired by his grief at the loss of Virginia. In 1848 he fell in love with the poet Sarah Helen Whitman, who refused his initial proposal, then agreed to a December 1848 marriage, and finally broke off the relationship. In his final year, during a two-month stay in Richmond, Poe joined a temperance society and got engaged to Elmira Royster Shelton, a widow whom he had known in his childhood. On a subsequent trip to Baltimore, Poe was found senseless near a polling place on Election Day (October 3). Taken to a hospital, he died on October 7, 1849, "of congestion of the brain." His poem "Annabel Lee" was published posthumously later that year.

Much of Poe's collected writings consists of his criticism, representing his abiding ambition to become a powerful critic and influence the course of American literary history. Just as he had modeled his poems and first tales on British examples (or British imitations of the German), he took his critical concepts from treatises on aesthetics by late-eighteenth-century Scottish Common Sense philosophers, who emphasized the aesthetic importance of moral sympathy. Later, he modified his approach with borrowings from A. W. Schlegel, Coleridge, and other Romantics, who emphasized the importance of intuitively conceived notions of the beautiful. But despite modulations in his theories, Poe's critical principles were consistent: he thought poetry should appeal only to the sense of beauty; informational poetry, poetry of ideas, or any sort of didactic poetry was, in his view, illegitimate. Holding that true poetic emotion was a vague sensory state inspired by the work of art itself, he set himself against realistic details in poetry, although the prose tale, with truth as one object, could profit from the discreet use of specifics. He believed that poems and tales should be short enough to be read in one sitting; otherwise the unity of effect would be dissipated. In his most famous artistic treatise, "The Philosophy of Composition," Poe makes clear that, unlike Emerson, he remains skeptical of the possibilities of transcendental vision untethered by the material realities of body and aesthetic form. In crucial ways, then, Poe split with Emerson and other Transcendentalists in arguing that the vision that comes to the artist and reader is inextricably linked to the formal qualities of the work of art itself.

Poe's reputation today rests not on his criticism, however, but on his poetry and tales. He has had immense influence on poets and prose writers both in the United States and abroad; among those who have followed his lead are such modernists as T. S. Eliot and William Faulkner. The tales have proven hard to classify—are they burlesque exaggerations of popular forms of fiction, or serious attempts to contribute to or alter those forms, or both of these at the same time? Poe's own comments deliberately obscured his intentions. Responding to a query from his literary admirer John P. Kennedy in 1836, who labeled his work "seriotragicomic," he said that most of his tales "were *intended* for half banter, half satire—although I might not have fully acknowledged this to be their aim even to myself." At the core of this and others of Poe's comments on his fiction is the pragmatism of a professional writer who recognized the advent of a mass market and wanted to succeed in it. He worked hard at structuring his tales of aristocratic madmen, self-tormented murderers, neurasthenic necrophiliacs, and other deviant types so as to produce, as he wrote in "The Philosophy of Composition," the greatest possible *effect* on his readers. Poe, more than most, understood his audience—its distractedness, its fascination with the new and short-lived, its anomie and confusion—and sought ways to gain its attention for stories that, aside from their shock value, regularly addressed compelling philosophical, cultural, psychological, and scientific issues: the place of irrationality, violence, and repression in human consciousness and social institutions; the alienation and dislocations attending democratic mass culture and the modernizing forces of the time; the tug and pull of the material and corporeal; the absolutely terrifying dimensions of one's own mind; and new ideas about technology and the physical universe. Seriously as he took the writing of his tales, Poe always put his highest stock in poetry, which he called a "passion" and not merely a "purpose." As he remarked in "The Philosophy of Composition," poetry, even more than fiction, provides the possibility of taking the reader out of body, in effect out of time, through "that intense and pure elevation of *soul*" which can come with "the contemplation of the beautiful." In a life that was often a tangled mess, the pursuit of the beautiful in works of art motivated Poe's writing to the very end.

The Raven[1]

By —— Quarles

[*The following lines from a correspondent—besides the deep quaint strain of the sentiment, and the curious introduction of some ludicrous touches amidst the serious and impressive, as was doubtless intended by the author—appear to us one of the most felicitous specimens of unique rhyming which has for some time met our eye. The resources of English rhythm for varieties of melody, measure, and sound, producing corresponding diversities of effect, have been thoroughly studied, much more perceived, by very few poets in the language. While the classic tongues, especially the Greek, possess, by power of accent, several advantages for versification over our own, chiefly through greater abundance of spondaic feet,[2] we have other and very great advantages of sound by the modern usage of rhyme. Alliteration is nearly the only effect of that kind which the ancients had in common with us. It will be seen that much of the melody of "The Raven" arises from alliteration, and the studious use of similar sounds in unusual places. In regard to its measure, it may be noted that if all the verses were like the second, they might properly be placed merely in short lines, producing a not uncommon form; but the presence in all the others of one line— mostly the second in the verse—which flows continuously, with only an aspirate pause in the middle, like that before the short line in the Sapphic Adonic,[3] while the fifth has at the middle pause no similarity of sound with any part besides, gives the versification an entirely different effect. We could wish the capacities of our noble language, in prosody, were better understood.—Ed. Am. Rev.*]

Once upon a midnight dreary, while I pondered, weak and weary,
Over many a quaint and curious volume of forgotten lore,
While I nodded, nearly napping, suddenly there came a tapping,
As of some one gently rapping, rapping at my chamber door.
"'Tis some visiter," I muttered, "tapping at my chamber door—   5
                Only this, and nothing more."

Ah, distinctly I remember it was in the bleak December,
And each separate dying ember wrought its ghost upon the floor.
Eagerly I wished the morrow;—vainly I had tried to borrow
From my books surcease of sorrow—sorrow for the lost Lenore—   10
For the rare and radiant maiden whom the angels name Lenore—
                Nameless here for evermore.

1. This printing of Poe's most famous poem is taken from the *American Review: A Whig Journal of Politics, Literature, Art and Science* 1 (February 1845), where it was first set in type from Poe's manuscript; the *New York Evening Mirror* printed the poem on January 29, 1845, probably from the proof sheets of the *American Review*. The prefatory paragraph, signed as if it were by the editor of the *American Review*, is retained here because Poe most likely wrote some or all of it himself. Many minor variations appear in later texts.
2. A spondee is a metrical foot consisting of two stressed syllables.
3. A Greek lyric form. An adonic is a dactyl (a foot with one long syllable and two short ones) followed by a spondee.

And the silken sad uncertain rustling of each purple curtain
Thrilled me—filled me with fantastic terrors never felt before;
So that now, to still the beating of my heart, I stood repeating   15
"'Tis some visiter entreating entrance at my chamber door—
Some late visiter entreating entrance at my chamber door;—
       This it is, and nothing more."

Presently my soul grew stronger; hesitating then no longer,
"Sir," said I, "or Madam, truly your forgiveness I implore;   20
But the fact is I was napping, and so gently you came rapping,
And so faintly you came tapping, tapping at my chamber door,
That I scarce was sure I heard you"—here I opened wide the door;—
       Darkness there, and nothing more.

Deep into that darkness peering, long I stood there wondering, fearing,   25
Doubting, dreaming dreams no mortal ever dared to dream before;
But the silence was unbroken, and the darkness gave no token,
And the only word there spoken was the whispered word, "Lenore!"
This I whispered, and an echo murmured back the word, "Lenore!"
       Merely this, and nothing more.   30

Then into the chamber turning, all my soul within me burning,
Soon I heard again a tapping somewhat louder than before.
"Surely," said I, "surely that is something at my window lattice;
Let me see, then, what thereat is, and this mystery explore—
Let my heart be still a moment and this mystery explore;—   35
       'Tis the wind, and nothing more!"

Open here I flung the shutter, when, with many a flirt and flutter,
In there stepped a stately raven of the saintly days of yore;
Not the least obeisance made he; not an instant stopped or stayed he;
But, with mien of lord or lady, perched above my chamber door—   40
Perched upon a bust of Pallas[4] just above my chamber door—
       Perched, and sat, and nothing more.

Then this ebony bird beguiling my sad fancy into smiling,
By the grave and stern decorum of the countenance it wore,
"Though thy crest be shorn and shaven, thou," I said, "art sure no craven,   45
Ghastly grim and ancient raven wandering from the Nightly shore—
Tell me what thy lordly name is on the Night's Plutonian[5] shore!"
       Quoth the raven, "Nevermore."

Much I marvelled this ungainly fowl to hear discourse so plainly,
Though its answer little meaning—little relevancy bore;   50
For we cannot help agreeing that no sublunary[6] being
Ever yet was blessed with seeing bird above his chamber door—
Bird or beast upon the sculptured bust above his chamber door,
       With such name as "Nevermore."

4. Athena, the Greek goddess of wisdom and the arts.
5. Black, as in the underworld ruled by Pluto in Greek mythology.
6. Earthly, beneath the moon.

But the raven, sitting lonely on the placid bust, spoke only   55
That one word, as if his soul in that one word he did outpour.
Nothing farther then he uttered—not a feather then he fluttered—
Till I scarcely more than muttered, "Other friends have flown before—
On the morrow *he* will leave me, as my hopes have flown before."
                    Quoth the raven, "Nevermore."   60

Wondering at the stillness broken by reply so aptly spoken,
"Doubtless," said I, "what it utters is its only stock and store,
Caught from some unhappy master whom unmerciful Disaster
Followed fast and followed faster—so, when Hope he would adjure,
Stern Despair returned, instead of the sweet Hope he dared adjure—   65
                    That sad answer, "Nevermore!"[7]

But the raven still beguiling all my sad soul into smiling,
Straight I wheeled a cushioned seat in front of bird, and bust, and door;
Then upon the velvet sinking, I betook myself to linking
Fancy unto fancy, thinking what this ominous bird of yore—   70
What this grim, ungainly, ghastly, gaunt, and ominous bird of yore
                    Meant in croaking "Nevermore."

This I sat engaged in guessing, but no syllable expressing
To the fowl whose fiery eyes now burned into my bosom's core;
This and more I sat divining, with my head at ease reclining   75
On the cushion's velvet lining that the lamplight gloated o'er,
But whose velvet violet lining with the lamplight gloating o'er,
                    She shall press, ah, nevermore!

Then, methought, the air grew denser, perfumed from an unseen censer
Swung by angels whose faint foot-falls tinkled on the tufted floor.   80
"Wretch," I cried, "thy God hath lent thee—by these angels he hath sent thee
Respite—respite and Nepenthe[8] from thy memories of Lenore!
Let me quaff this kind Nepenthe and forget this lost Lenore!"
                    Quoth the raven, "Nevermore."

"Prophet!" said I, "thing of evil!—prophet still, if bird or devil!—   85
Whether Tempter sent, or whether tempest tossed thee here ashore,
Desolate, yet all undaunted, on this desert land enchanted—
On this home by Horror haunted—tell me truly, I implore—
Is there—*is* there balm in Gilead?[9]—tell me—tell me, I implore!"
                    Quoth the raven, "Nevermore."   90

"Prophet!" said I, "thing of evil!—prophet still, if bird or devil!
By that Heaven that bends above us—by that God we both adore—
Tell this soul with sorrow laden if, within the distant Aidenn,[1]

---

7. This stanza concluded in the 1845 volume with these lines: "Followed faster till his songs one burden bore— / Till the dirges of his Hope that melancholy burden bore / Of 'Never—nevermore.'"
8. Drug that induces oblivion.
9. An echo of the ironic words in Jeremiah 8.22: "Is there no balm in Gilead; is there no physician there?" Gilead is a mountainous area east of the Jordan River between the Sea of Galilee and the Dead Sea; evergreens growing there were a source of medicinal resins.
1. One of Poe's vaguely evocative place names, designed to suggest Eden.

It shall clasp a sainted maiden whom the angels name Lenore—
Clasp a rare and radiant maiden whom the angels name Lenore." 95
        Quoth the raven, "Nevermore."

"Be that word our sign of parting, bird or fiend!" I shrieked, upstarting—
"Get thee back into the tempest and the Night's Plutonian shore!
Leave no black plume as a token of that lie thy soul hath spoken!
Leave my loneliness unbroken—quit the bust above my door! 100
Take thy beak from out my heart, and take thy form from off my door!"
        Quoth the raven, "Nevermore."

And the raven, never flitting, still is sitting, still is sitting
On the pallid bust of Pallas just above my chamber door;
And his eyes have all the seeming of a demon that is dreaming, 105
And the lamp-light o'er him streaming throws his shadow on the floor;
And my soul from out that shadow that lies floating on the floor
        Shall be lifted—nevermore!

             1845

Annabel Lee[1]

It was many and many a year ago,
  In a kingdom by the sea
That a maiden there lived whom you may know
  By the name of ANNABEL LEE;
And this maiden she lived with no other thought 5
  Than to love and be loved by me.

I was a child and *she* was a child,
  In this kingdom by the sea;
But we loved with a love that was more than love—
  I and my ANNABEL LEE— 10
With a love that the wingèd seraphs of heaven
  Coveted her and me.

And this was the reason that, long ago,
  In this kingdom by the sea,
A wind blew out of a cloud, chilling 15
  My beautiful ANNABEL LEE;
So that her highborn kinsmen came
  And bore her away from me,
To shut her up in a sepulchre
  In this kingdom by the sea. 20

The angels, not half so happy in heaven,
  Went envying her and me—

---

1. The text is that of the first printing, in an article by Rufus Griswold in the *New York Tribune* (October 9, 1849), signed "Ludwig," which was printed two days after Poe's death.

Yes!—that was the reason (as all men know,
    In this kingdom by the sea)
That the wind came out of the cloud by night,   25
    Chilling and killing my ANNABEL LEE.

But our love it was stronger by far than the love
    Of those who were older than we—
    Of many far wiser than we—
And neither the angels in heaven above,   30
    Nor the demons down under the sea,
Can ever dissever my soul from the soul
    Of the beautiful ANNABEL LEE:

For the moon never beams, without bringing me dreams
    Of the beautiful ANNABEL LEE;   35
And the stars never rise, but I feel the bright eyes
    Of the beautiful ANNABEL LEE:
And so, all the night tide, I lie down by the side
Of my darling—my darling—my life and my bride,
    In her sepulchre there by the sea—   40
    In her tomb by the sounding sea.

1849

Ligeia[1]

> *And the will therein lieth, which dieth not. Who knoweth the mysteries of the will, with its vigour? For God is but a great will pervading all things by nature of its intentness. Man doth not yield himself to the angels, nor unto death utterly, save only through the weakness of his feeble will.*
>
> —Joseph Glanvill[2]

I cannot, for my soul, remember how, when, or even precisely where I first became acquainted with the lady Ligeia. Long years have since elapsed, and my memory is feeble through much suffering: or, perhaps, I cannot *now* bring these points to mind, because, in truth, the character of my beloved, her rare learning, her singular yet placid cast of beauty, and the thrilling and enthralling eloquence of her low, musical language, made their way into my heart by paces, so steadily and stealthily progressive, that they have been unnoticed and unknown. Yet I know that I met her most frequently in some large, old, decaying city near the Rhine. Of her family—I have surely heard her speak—that they are of a remotely ancient date cannot be doubted. Ligeia! Buried in studies of a nature, more than all else, adapted to deaden impressions of the outward world, it is by that sweet word alone—by Ligeia, that I

---

1. "Ligeia" was first published in the *American Museum* 1 (September 1838), the source of the present text. Poe later revised the tale slightly and added to it the poem "The Conqueror Worm."
2. Like many of Poe's epigraphs (often added after

first publication), this one is fabricated. Joseph Glanvill (1636–1680) was one of the Cambridge Platonists, 17th-century English religious philosophers who tried to reconcile Christianity and Renaissance science.

bring before mine eyes in fancy the image of her who is no more. And now, while I write, a recollection flashes upon me that I have *never known* the paternal name of her who was my friend and my betrothed, and who became the partner of my studies, and eventually the wife of my bosom. Was it a playful charge on the part of my Ligeia? or was it a test of my strength of affection that I should institute no inquiries upon this point? or was it rather a caprice of my own—a wildly romantic offering on the shrine of the most passionate devotion? I but indistinctly recall the fact itself—what wonder that I have utterly forgotten the circumstances which originated or attended it? And indeed, if ever that spirit which is entitled *Romance*—if ever she, the wan, and the misty-winged *Ashtophet*[3] of idolatrous Egypt, presided, as they tell, over marriages ill-omened, then most surely she presided over mine.

There is one dear topic, however, on which my memory faileth me not. It is the person of Ligeia. In stature she was tall, somewhat slender, and in her latter days even emaciated. I would in vain attempt to pourtray the majesty, the quiet ease of her demeanour, or the incomprehensible lightness and elasticity of her footfall. She came and departed like a shadow. I was never made aware of her entrance into my closed study save by the dear music of her low sweet voice, as she placed her delicate hand upon my shoulder. In beauty of face no maiden ever equalled her. It was the radiance of an opium dream—an airy and spirit-lifting vision more wildly divine than the phantasies which hovered about the slumbering souls of the daughters of Delos.[4] Yet her features were not of that regular mould which we have been falsely taught to worship in the classical labors of the Heathen. "There is no exquisite[5] beauty," saith Verülam, Lord Bacon, speaking truly of all the forms and *genera* of beauty, "without some *strangeness* in the proportions." Yet, although I saw that the features of Ligeia were not of classic regularity, although I perceived that her loveliness was indeed "exquisite," and felt that there was much of "strangeness" pervading it, yet I have tried in vain to detect the irregularity, and to trace home my own perception of "the strange." I examined the contour of the lofty and pale forehead—it was faultless—how cold indeed that word when applied to a majesty so divine! The skin rivaling the purest ivory, the commanding breadth and repose, the gentle prominence of the regions above the temples, and then the raven-black, the glossy, the luxuriant and naturally-curling tresses, setting forth the full force of the Homeric epithet, "hyacinthine;"[6] I looked at the delicate outlines of the nose—and nowhere but in the graceful medallions of the Hebrews had I beheld a similar perfection. There was the same luxurious smoothness of surface, the same scarcely perceptible tendency to the aquiline, the same harmoniously curved nostril speaking the free spirit. I regarded the sweet mouth. Here was indeed the triumph of all things heavenly—the magnificent turn of the short upper lip—the soft, voluptuous repose of the under—the dimples which sported, and the colour which spoke—the teeth glancing back, with a brilliancy almost startling, every ray of the holy light which fell upon them in her serene, and placid, yet most exultingly radiant of all smiles. I scrutinized the formation

---

3. Variant of Ashtoreth, Phoenician goddess of fertility.
4. Probably the maidens attending Artemis, goddess of wild nature and the hunt; she was born on Delos, a Greek island in the Aegean Sea.

5. In his essay "Of Beauty" Francis Bacon, Baron Verulam (1561–1626), wrote "excellent," not "exquisite."
6. In the *Odyssey*, Homer compares Odysseus's curly hair to the flowering hyacinth plant.

of the chin—and here, too, I found the gentleness of breadth, the softness and the majesty, the fulness and the spirituality, of the Greek, the contour which the God Apollo revealed but in a dream to Cleomenes, the son of the Athenian.[7] And then I peered into the large eyes of Ligeia.

For eyes we have no models in the remotely antique. It might have been, too, that in these eyes of my beloved lay the secret to which Lord Verülam alludes. They were, I must believe, far larger than the ordinary eyes of our race. They were even far fuller than the fullest of the Gazelle eyes of the tribe of the valley of Nourjahad.[8] Yet it was only at intervals—in moments of intense excitement—that this peculiarity became more than slightly noticeable in Ligeia. And at such moments was her beauty—in my heated fancy thus it appeared perhaps—the beauty of beings either above or apart from the earth—the beauty of the fabulous Houri[9] of the Turk. The colour of the orbs was the most brilliant of black, and far over them hung jetty lashes of great length. The brows, slightly irregular in outline, had the same hue. The "strangeness," however, which I have found in the eyes of my Ligeia was of a nature distinct from the formation, or the colour, or the brilliancy of the feature, and must, after all, be referred to the *expression*. Ah, word of no meaning! behind whose vast latitude of mere sound we intrench our ignorance of so much of the spiritual. The expression of the eyes of Ligeia! How, for long hours have I pondered upon it! How have I, through the whole of a mid-summer night, struggled to fathom it! What was it—that something more profound than the well of Democritus[1]—which lay far within the pupils of my beloved? What *was* it? I was possessed with a passion to discover. Those eyes! those large, those shining, those divine orbs! they became to me twin stars of Leda,[2] and I to them devoutest of astrologers. Not for a moment was the unfathomable meaning of their glance, by day or by night, absent from my soul.

There is no point, among the many incomprehensible anomalies of the science of mind, more thrillingly exciting than the fact—never, I believe noticed in the schools—that in our endeavours to recall to memory something long forgotten we often find ourselves *upon the very verge* of remembrance without being able, in the end, to remember. And thus, how frequently, in my intense scrutiny of Ligeia's eyes, have I felt approaching the full knowledge of the secret of their expression—felt it approaching—yet not quite be mine—and so at length utterly depart. And (strange, oh strangest mystery of all!) I found, in the commonest objects of the universe, a circle of analogies to that expression. I mean to say that, subsequently to the period when Ligeia's beauty passed into my spirit, there dwelling as in a shrine, I derived from many existences in the material world, a sentiment, such as I felt always aroused within me by her large and luminous orbs. Yet not the more could I define that sentiment, or analyze, or even steadily view it. I recognized it, let me repeat, sometimes in the commonest objects of the universe. It has

7. Classical Greek sculptor whose name is affixed to the Venus de' Medici. The god Apollo was the patron of artists.
8. From the Asian romance *The History of Nourjahad* (1767), by the English writer Frances Sheridan (1724–1766).
9. Beautiful maiden waiting in paradise for the devout Muslim.

1. Greek philosopher (5th century B.C.E.); one of his proverbs is "Truth lies at the bottom of a well."
2. Queen of Sparta whom Zeus, in the form of a swan, raped, thereby begetting Helen of Troy and (according to some versions) the twin sons Castor and Pollux, whom Zeus transformed into the constellation Gemini.

flashed upon me in the survey of a rapidly-growing vine—in the contemplation of a moth, a butterfly, a chrysalis, a stream of running water. I have felt it in the ocean, in the falling of a meteor. I have felt it in the glances of unusually aged people. And there are one or two stars in heaven—(one especially, a star of the sixth magnitude, double and changeable, to be found near the large star in Lyra)[3] in a telescopic scrutiny of which I have been made aware of the feeling. I have been filled with it by certain sounds from stringed instruments, and not unfrequently by passages from books. Among innumerable other instances, I well remember something in a volume of Joseph Glanvill, which, perhaps merely from its quaintness—who shall say?—never failed to inspire me with the sentiment.—"And the will therein lieth, which dieth not. Who knoweth the mysteries of the will, with its vigor? For God is but a great will pervading all things by nature of its intentness. Man doth not yield him to the angels, nor unto death utterly, but only through the weakness of his feeble will."

Length of years, and subsequent reflection, have enabled me to trace, indeed, some remote connexion between this passage in the old English moralist and a portion of the character of Ligeia. An *intensity* in thought, action, or speech was possibly, in her, a result, or at least an index, of that gigantic volition which, during our long intercourse, failed to give other and more immediate evidence of its existence. Of all women whom I have ever known, she, the outwardly calm, the ever placid Ligeia, was the most violently a prey to the tumultuous vultures of stern passion. And of such passion I could form no estimate, save by the miraculous expansion of those eyes which at once so delighted and appalled me, by the almost magical melody, modulation, distinctness and placidity of her very low voice, and by the fierce energy, (rendered doubly effective by contrast with her manner of utterance) of the words which she uttered.

I have spoken of the learning of Ligeia: it was immense—such as I have never known in woman. In all the classical tongues was she deeply proficient, and as far as my own acquaintance extended in regard to the modern dialects of Europe, I have never known her at fault. Indeed upon any theme of the most admired, because simply the most abstruse, of the boasted erudition of the academy, have I *ever* found Ligeia at fault? How singularly, how thrillingly, this one point in the nature of my wife has forced itself, at this late period, only, upon my attention! I said her knowledge was such as I had never known in woman. Where breathes the man who, like her, has traversed, and successfully, *all* the wide areas of moral, natural, and mathematical science? I saw not then what I now clearly perceive, that the acquisitions of Ligeia were gigantic, were astounding—yet I was sufficiently aware of her infinite supremacy to resign myself, with a childlike confidence, to her guidance through the chaotic world of metaphysical investigation at which I was most busily occupied during the earlier years of our marriage. With how vast a triumph—with how vivid a delight—with how much of all that is ethereal in hope—did I *feel*, as she bent over me, in studies but little sought for—but less known that delicious vista by slow but very perceptible degrees expanding before me, down whose long, gorgeous, and all untrodden path I might

3. The lesser star is epsilon Lyrae, the large one Vega or alpha Lyrae.

at length pass onward to the goal of a wisdom too divinely precious not to be forbidden!

How poignant, then, must have been the grief with which, after some years, I beheld my well-grounded expectations take wings to themselves and flee away! Without Ligeia I was but as a child groping benighted. Her presence, her readings alone, rendered vividly luminous the many mysteries of the transcendentalism in which we were immersed. Letters, lambent and golden, grew duller than Saturnian[4] lead wanting the radiant lustre of her eyes. And now those eyes shone less and less frequently upon the pages over which I poured. Ligeia grew ill. The wild eye blazed with a too—too glorious effulgence; the pale fingers became of the transparent waxen hue of the grave—and the blue veins upon the lofty forehead swelled and sunk impetuously with the tides of the most gentle emotion. I saw that she must die— and I struggled desperately in spirit with the grim Azrael.[5] And the struggles of the passionate Ligeia were, to my astonishment, even more energetic than my own. There had been much in her stern nature to impress me with the belief that, to her, death would have come without its terrors—but not so. Words are impotent to convey any just idea of the fierceness of resistance with which Ligeia wrestled with the dark shadow. I groaned in anguish at the pitiable spectacle. I would have soothed—I would have reasoned; but in the intensity of her wild desire for life—for life—*but* for life, solace and reason were alike the uttermost of folly. Yet not for an instant, amid the most convulsive writhings of her fierce spirit, was shaken the external placidity of her demeanor. Her voice grew more gentle—grew more low—yet I would not wish to dwell upon the wild meaning of the quietly-uttered words. My brain reeled as I hearkened, entranced, to a melody more than mortal—to assumptions and aspirations which mortality had never before known.

That Ligeia loved me, I should not have doubted; and I might have been easily aware that, in a bosom such as hers, love would have reigned no ordinary passion. But in death only, was I fully impressed with the intensity of her affection. For long hours, detaining my hand, would she pour out before me the overflowings of a heart whose more than passionate devotion amounted to idolatry. How had I deserved to be so blessed by such confessions.—How had I deserved to be so cursed with the removal of my beloved in the hour of her making them? But upon this subject I cannot bear to dilate. Let me say only, that in Ligeia's more than womanly abandonment to a love, alas, all unmerited, all unworthily bestowed; I at length recognised the principle of her longing, with so wildly earnest a desire for the life which was now fleeing so rapidly away. It is this wild longing—it is this eager intensity of desire for life—*but* for life—that I have no power to pourtray—no utterance capable to express. Methinks I again behold the terrific struggles of her lofty, her nearly idealized nature, with the might and the terror, and the majesty of the great Shadow. But she perished. The giant *will* succumbed to a power more stern. And I thought, as I gazed upon the corpse, of the wild passage in Joseph Glanvill. "The will therein lieth, which dieth not. Who knoweth the mysteries of the will, with its vigor? For God is but a great

---

4. Sluggish; in alchemy *saturnus* is the name for lead.

5. The Angel of Death (in Judaism and Islam).

will pervading all things by nature of its intentness. Man doth not yield him to the angels, *nor unto death utterly*, save only through the weakness of his feeble will."

She died—and I, crushed into the very dust with sorrow, could no longer endure the lonely desolation of my dwelling in the dim and decaying city by the Rhine. I had no lack of what the world terms wealth—Ligeia had brought me far more, very far more, than falls ordinarily to the lot of mortals. After a few months, therefore, of weary and aimless wandering, I purchased, and put in some repair, an abbey, which I shall not name, in one of the wildest and least frequented portions of fair England. The gloomy and dreary grandeur of the building, the almost savage aspect of the domain, the many melancholy and time-honored memories connected with both, had much in unison with the feelings of utter abandonment which had driven me into that remote and unsocial region of the country. Yet, although the external abbey, with its verdant decay hanging about it suffered but little alteration, I gave way with a child-like perversity, and perchance with a faint hope of alleviating my sorrows, to a display of more than regal magnificence within. For such follies even in childhood I had imbibed a taste, and now they came back to me as if in the dotage of grief. Alas, I now feel how much even of incipient madness might have been discovered in the gorgeous and fantastic draperies, in the solemn carvings of Egypt, in the wild cornices and furniture of Arabesque,[6] in the bedlam patterns of the carpets of tufted gold! I had become a bounden slave in the trammels of opium, and my labors and my orders had taken a colouring from my dreams. But these absurdities I must not pause to detail. Let me speak only of that one chamber, ever accursed, whither, in a moment of mental alienation, I led from the altar as my bride—as the successor of the unforgotten Ligeia—the fair-haired and blue-eyed lady Rowena Trevanion, of Tremaine.

There is not any individual portion of the architecture and decoration of that bridal chamber which is not now visibly before me. Where were the souls of the haughty family of the bride, when, through thirst of gold, they permitted to pass the threshold of an apartment *so* bedecked, a maiden and a daughter so beloved? I have said that I minutely remember the details of the chamber—yet I am sadly forgetful on topics of deep moment—and here there was no system, no keeping, in the fantastic display, to take hold upon the memory. The room lay in a high turret of the castellated abbey, was pentagonal in shape, and of capacious size. Occupying the whole southern face of the pentagon was the sole window—an immense sheet of unbroken glass from Venice—a single pane, and tinted of a leaden hue, so that the rays of either the sun or moon, passing through it, fell with a ghastly lustre upon the objects within. Over the upper portion of this huge window extended the open trellice-work of an aged vine which clambered up the massy walls of the turret. The ceiling, of gloomy-looking oak, was excessively lofty, vaulted, and elaborately fretted with the wildest and most grotesque specimens of a semi-Gothic, semi-druidical[7] device. From out the most central recess of this melancholy vaulting, depended, by a single chain of gold, with long links, a

6. Ornamental style employing intricate patterns of lines and figures.

7. Druids are the legendary priests, or wizards, of ancient Britain and Ireland. "Fretted": ornamented with intersecting patterns.

huge censer of the same metal, Arabesque in pattern, and with many perforations so contrived that there writhed in and out of them, as if endued with a serpent vitality, a continual succession of parti-coloured fires. Some few ottomans and golden candelabras of Eastern figure were in various stations about—and there was the couch, too, the bridal couch, of an Indian model, and low, and sculptured of solid ebony, with a canopy above. In each of the angles of the chamber, stood on end a gigantic sarcophagus of black granite, from the tombs of the kings over against Luxor,[8] with their aged lids full of immemorial sculpture. But in the draping of the apartment lay, alas! the chief phantasy of all. The lofty walls—gigantic in height—even unproportionally so, were hung from summit to foot, in vast folds with a heavy and massy looking tapestry—tapestry of a material which was found alike as a carpet on the floor, as a covering for the ottomans, and the ebony bed, as a canopy for the bed, and as the gorgeous volutes[9] of the curtains which partially shaded the window. This material was the richest cloth of gold. It was spotted all over, at irregular intervals, with Arabesque figures, of about a foot in diameter, and wrought upon the cloth in patterns of the most jetty black. But these figures partook of the true character of the Arabesque only when regarded from a single point of view. By a contrivance now common, and indeed traceable to a very remote period of antiquity, they were made changeable in aspect. To one entering the room they bore the appearance of ideal monstrosities; but, upon a farther advance, this appearance suddenly departed; and, step by step, as the visitor moved his station in the chamber, he saw himself surrounded by an endless succession of the ghastly forms which belong to the superstition of the Northman, or arise in the guilty slumbers of the monk. The phantasmagoric effect was vastly heightened by the artificial introduction of a strong continual current of wind behind the draperies—giving a hideous and uneasy vitality to the whole.

In halls such as these—in a bridal chamber such as this, I passed, with the lady of Tremaine, the unhallowed hours of the first month of our marriage—passed them with but little disquietude. That my wife dreaded the fierce moodiness of my temper—that she shunned me, and loved me but little, I could not help perceiving—but it gave me rather pleasure than otherwise. I loathed her with a hatred belonging more to demon than to man. My memory flew back, (oh, with what intensity of regret!) to Ligeia, the beloved, the beautiful, the entombed. I revelled in recollections of her purity, of her wisdom, of her lofty, her ethereal nature, of her passionate, her idolatrous love. Now, then, did my spirit fully and freely burn with more than all the fires of her own. In the excitement of my opium dreams (for I was habitually fettered in the iron shackles of the drug)[1] I would call aloud upon her name, during the silence of the night, or among the sheltered recesses of the glens by day, as if, by the wild eagerness, the solemn passion, the consuming intensity of my longing for the departed Ligeia, I could restore the departed Ligeia to the pathways she had abandoned upon earth.

About the commencement of the second month of the marriage, the lady Rowena was attacked with sudden illness from which her recovery was slow.

8. In Egypt, near Thebes; site of famous ruins.
9. Scroll-like ornaments.

1. The *American Museum* has no punctuation after "dreams" or "drug" in this sentence; parentheses are added to the present text.

The fever which consumed her, rendered her nights uneasy, and, in her per-turbed state of half-slumber, she spoke of sounds, and of motions, in and about the chamber of the turret which had no origin save in the distemper of her fancy, or, perhaps, in the phantasmagoric influences of the chamber itself. She became at length convalescent—finally well. Yet but a brief period elapsed, ere a second more violent disorder again threw her upon a bed of suffering—and from this attack her frame, at all times feeble, never alto-gether recovered. Her illnesses were, after this period, of alarming charac-ter, and of more alarming recurrence, defying alike the knowledge and the great exertions of her medical men. With the increase of the chronic dis-ease which had thus, apparently, taken too sure hold upon her constitution to be eradicated by human means, I could not fail to observe a similar increase in the nervous irritability of her temperament, and in her excitability by trivial causes of fear. Indeed reason seemed fast tottering from her throne. She spoke again, and now more frequently and pertinaciously, of the sounds, of the slight sounds, and of the unusual motions among the tapestries, to which she had formerly alluded. It was one night near the closing in of Sep-tember, when she pressed this distressing subject with more than usual emphasis upon my attention. She had just awakened from a perturbed slum-ber, and I had been watching, with feelings half of anxiety, half of a vague terror, the workings of her emaciated countenance. I sat by the side of her ebony bed, upon one of the ottomans of India. She partly arose, and spoke, in an earnest low whisper, of sounds which she *then* heard, but which I could not hear, of motions which she *then* saw, but which I could not per-ceive. The wind was rushing hurriedly behind the tapestries, and I wished to show her (what, let me confess it, I could not *all* believe) that those faint, almost articulate, breathings, and the very gentle variations of the figures upon the wall, were but the natural effects of that customary rushing of the wind. But a deadly pallor overspreading her face, had proved to me that my exertions to re-assure her would be fruitless. She appeared to be fainting, and no attendants were within call. I remembered where was deposited a decanter of some light wine which had been ordered by her physicians, and hastened across the chamber to procure it. But, as I stepped beneath the light of the censer, two circumstances of a startling nature attracted my attention. I had felt that some palpable object had passed lightly by my person; and I saw that there lay a faint, indefinite shadow upon the golden carpet in the very middle of the rich lustre, thrown from the censer. But I was wild with the excitement of an immoderate dose of opium, and heeded these things but little, nor spoke of them to Rowena. Finding the wine, I re-crossed the chamber, and poured out a goblet-ful, which I held to the lips of the fainting lady. But she had now partially recovered, and took, herself, the vessel, while I sank upon the ottoman near me, with my eyes rivetted upon her person. It was then that I became distinctly aware of a gentle foot-fall upon the car-pet, and near the couch; and, in a second thereafter, as Rowena was in the act of raising the wine to her lips, I saw, or may have dreamed that I saw, fall within the goblet, as if from some invisible spring in the atmosphere of the room, three or four large drops of a brilliant and ruby colored fluid. If this I saw—not so Rowena. She swallowed the wine unhesitatingly, and I forbore to speak to her of a circumstance which must, after all, I considered, have been but the suggestion of a vivid imagination, rendered morbidly active by the terror of the lady, by the opium, and by the hour.

Yet I cannot conceal it from myself, after this period, a rapid change for the worse took place in the disorder of my wife, so that, on the third subsequent night, the hands of her menials prepared her for the tomb, and on the fourth, I sat alone, with her shrouded body, in that fantastical chamber which had received her as my bride. Wild visions, opium engendered, flitted, shadow-like, before me. I gazed with unquiet eye upon the sarcophagi in the angles of the room, upon the varying figures of the drapery, and upon the writhing of the parti-colored fires in the censer overhead. My eyes then fell, as I called to mind the circumstances of a former night, to the spot beneath the glare of the censer where I had beheld the faint traces of the shadow. It was there, however, no longer, and, breathing with greater freedom, I turned my glances to the pallid and rigid figure upon the bed. Then rushed upon me a thousand memories of Ligeia—and then came back upon my heart, with the turbulent violence of a flood, the whole of that unutterable woe with which I had regarded *her* thus enshrouded. The night waned; and still, with a bosom full of bitter thoughts of the one only and supremely beloved, I remained with mine eyes rivetted upon the body of Rowena.

It might have been midnight, or perhaps earlier, or later, for I had taken no note of time, when a sob, low, gentle, but very distinct, startled me from my revery. I *felt* that it came from the bed of ebony—the bed of death. I listened in an agony of superstitious terror—but there was no repetition of the sound; I strained my vision to detect any motion in the corpse, but there was not the slightest perceptible. Yet I could not have been deceived. I had heard the noise, however faint, and my whole soul was awakened within me, as I resolutely and perseveringly kept my attention rivetted upon the body. Many minutes elapsed before any circumstance occurred tending to throw light upon the mystery. At length it became evident that a slight, a very faint, and barely noticeable tinge of colour had flushed up within the cheeks, and along the sunken small veins of the eyelids. Through a species of unutterable horror and awe, for which the language of mortality has no sufficiently energetic expression, I felt my brain reel, my heart cease to beat, my limbs grow rigid where I sat. Yet a sense of duty finally operated to restore my self-possession. I could no longer doubt that we had been precipitate in our preparations for interment—that Rowena still lived. It was necessary that some immediate exertion be made; yet the turret was altogether apart from the portion of the Abbey tenanted by the servants—there were none within call, and I had no means of summoning them to my aid without leaving the room for many minutes—and this I could not venture to do. I therefore struggled alone in my endeavors to call back the spirit still hovering. In a short period it became evident however, that a relapse had taken place; the color utterly disappeared from both eyelid and cheek, leaving a wanness even more than that of marble; the lips became doubly shrivelled and pinched up in the ghastly expression of death; a coldness surpassing that of ice, overspread rapidly the surface of the body, and all the usual rigorous stiffness immediately supervened. I fell back with a shudder upon the ottoman from which I had been so startlingly aroused, and again gave myself up to passionate waking visions of Ligeia.

An hour thus elapsed when, (could it be possible?) I was a second time aware of some vague sound issuing from the region of the bed. I listened—in extremity of horror. The sound came again—it was a sigh. Rushing to the corpse, I saw—distinctly saw—a tremor upon the lips. In a minute after they slightly relaxed, disclosing a bright line of the pearly teeth. Amazement now struggled in my bosom with the profound awe which had hitherto reigned therein alone. I felt that my vision grew dim, that my brain wandered, and it was only by a convulsive effort that I at length succeeded in nerving myself to the task which duty thus, once more, had pointed out. There was now a partial glow upon the forehead, upon the cheek and throat—a perceptible warmth pervaded the whole frame—there was even a slight pulsation at the heart. The lady lived; and with redoubled ardour I betook myself to the task of restoration. I chafed, and bathed the temples, and the hands, and used every exertion which experience, and no little medical reading, could suggest. But in vain. Suddenly, the colour fled, the pulsation ceased, the lips resumed the expression of the dead, and, in an instant afterwards, the whole body took upon itself the icy chillness, the livid hue, the intense rigidity, the sunken outline, and each and all of the loathsome peculiarities of that which has been, for many days, a tenant of the tomb.

And again I sunk into visions of Ligeia—and again (what marvel that I shudder while I write?) *again* there reached my ears a low sob from the region of the ebony bed. But why shall I minutely detail the unspeakable horrors of that night? Why shall I pause to relate how, time after time, until near the period of the grey dawn, this hideous drama of revivification was repeated, and how each terrific relapse was only into a sterner and apparently more irredeemable death? Let me hurry to a conclusion.

The greater part of the fearful night had worn away, and the corpse of Rowena once again stirred—and now more vigorously than hitherto, although arousing from a dissolution more appalling in its utter hopelessness than any. I had long ceased to struggle or to move, and remained sitting rigidly upon the ottoman, a helpless prey to a whirl of violent emotions, of which extreme awe was perhaps the least terrible, the least consuming. The corpse, I repeat, stirred, and now more vigorously than before. The hues of life flushed up with unwonted energy into the countenance—the limbs relaxed—and, save that the eyelids were yet pressed heavily together, and that the bandages and draperies of the grave still imparted their charnel character to the figure, I might have dreamed that Rowena had indeed shaken off, utterly, the fetters of Death. But if this idea was not, even then, altogether adopted, I could, at least, doubt no longer, when, arising from the bed, tottering, with feeble steps, with closed eyes, and with the air of one bewildered in a dream, the lady of Tremaine stood bodily and palpably before me.

I trembled not—I stirred not—for a crowd of unutterable fancies connected with the air, the demeanour of the figure, rushing hurriedly through my brain, sent the purple blood ebbing in torrents from the temples to the heart. I stirred not—but gazed upon her who was before me. There was a mad disorder in my thoughts—a tumult unappeasable. Could it, indeed, be the *living* Rowena who confronted me? Why, *why* should I doubt it? The bandage lay heavily about the mouth—but then it was the mouth of the breathing lady of Tremaine. And the cheeks—there were the roses as in her noon of health—yes, these were indeed the fair cheeks of the living lady of Tremaine.

And the chin, with its dimples, as in health, was it not hers?—but—but *had she then grown taller since her malady?* What inexpressible madness seized me with that thought? One bound, and I had reached her feet! Shrinking from my touch, she let fall from her head, unloosened, the ghastly cerements[2] which had confined it, and there streamed forth, into the rushing atmosphere of the chamber, huge masses of long and dishevelled hair. *It was blacker than the raven wings of the midnight!* And now the eyes opened of the figure which stood before me. "Here then at least," I shrieked aloud, "can I never—can I never be mistaken—these are the full, and the black, and the wild eyes of the lady—of the lady Ligeia!"

1838

The Fall of the House of Usher[1]

During the whole of a dull, dark, and soundless day in the autumn of the year, when the clouds hung oppressively low in the heavens, I had been passing alone, on horseback, through a singularly dreary tract of country; and at length found myself, as the shades of the evening drew on, within view of the melancholy House of Usher. I know not how it was—but, with the first glimpse of the building, a sense of insufferable gloom pervaded my spirit. I say insufferable; for the feeling was unrelieved by any of that half-pleasurable, because poetic, sentiment, with which the mind usually receives even the sternest natural images of the desolate or terrible. I looked upon the scene before me—upon the mere house, and the simple landscape features of the domain—upon the bleak walls—upon the vacant eye-like windows—upon a few rank sedges—and upon a few white trunks of decayed trees—with an utter depression of soul which I can compare to no earthly sensation more properly than to the after-dream of the reveller upon opium—the bitter lapse into common life—the hideous dropping off of the veil. There was an iciness, a sinking, a sickening of the heart—an unredeemed dreariness of thought which no goading of the imagination could torture into aught of the sublime. What was it—I paused to think—what was it that so unnerved me in the contemplation of the House of Usher? It was a mystery all insoluble; nor could I grapple with the shadowy fancies that crowded upon me as I pondered. I was forced to fall back upon the unsatisfactory conclusion, that while, beyond doubt, there *are* combinations of very simple natural objects which have the power of thus affecting us, still the reason, and the analysis, of this power, lie among considerations beyond our depth. It was possible, I reflected, that a mere different arrangement of the particulars of the scene, of the details of this picture, would be sufficient to modify, or perhaps to annihilate its capacity for sorrowful impression; and, acting upon this idea, I reined my horse to the precipitous brink of a black and lurid tarn[2] that lay in unruffled lustre by the dwelling, and gazed down—but with a shudder even

2. Shrouds.
1. The text is that of the first publication in *Burton's Gentleman's Magazine, and American* *Monthly Review* 5 (September 1839).
2. A small lake, usually in the mountains.

more thrilling than before—upon the re-modelled and inverted images of the gray sedge, and the ghastly tree-stems, and the vacant and eye-like windows.

Nevertheless, in this mansion of gloom I now proposed to myself a sojourn of some weeks. Its proprietor, Roderick Usher, had been one of my boon companions in boyhood; but many years had elapsed since our last meeting. A letter, however, had lately reached me in a distant part of the country—a letter from him—which, in its wildly importunate nature, had admitted of no other than a personal reply. The MS. gave evidence of nervous agitation. The writer spoke of acute bodily illness—of a pitiable mental idiosyncrasy which oppressed him—and of an earnest desire to see me, as his best, and indeed, his only personal friend, with a view of attempting, by the cheerfulness of my society, some alleviation of his malady. It was the manner in which all this, and much more, was said—it was the apparent *heart* that went with his request—which allowed me no room for hesitation—and I accordingly obeyed, what I still considered a very singular summons, forthwith.

Although, as boys, we had been even intimate associates, yet I really knew little of my friend. His reserve had been always excessive and habitual. I was aware, however, that his very ancient family had been noted, time out of mind, for a peculiar sensibility of temperament, displaying itself, through long ages, in many works of exalted art, and manifested, of late, in repeated deeds of munificent yet unobtrusive charity, as well as in a passionate devotion to the intricacies, perhaps even more than to the orthodox and easily recognizable beauties, of musical science. I had learned, too, the very remarkable fact, that the stem of the Usher race, all time-honored as it was, had put forth, at no period, any enduring branch; in other words, that the entire family lay in the direct line of descent, and had always, with very trifling and very temporary variation, so lain. It was this deficiency, I considered, while running over in thought the perfect keeping of the character of the premises with the accredited character of the people, and while speculating upon the possible influence which the one, in the long lapse of centuries, might have exercised upon the other—it was this deficiency, perhaps, of collateral issue, and the consequent undeviating transmission, from sire to son, of the patrimony with the name, which had, at length, so identified the two as to merge the original title of the estate in the quaint and equivocal appellation of the "House of Usher"—an appellation which seemed to include, in the minds of the peasantry who used it, both the family and the family mansion.

I have said that the sole effect of my somewhat childish experiment, of looking down within the tarn, had been to deepen the first singular impression. There can be no doubt that the consciousness of the rapid increase of my superstition—for why should I not so term it?—served mainly to accelerate the increase itself. Such, I have long known, is the paradoxical law of all sentiments having terror as a basis. And it might have been for this reason only, that, when I again uplifted my eyes to the house itself, from its image in the pool, there grew in my mind a strange fancy—a fancy so ridiculous, indeed, that I but mention it to show the vivid force of the sensations which oppressed me. I had so worked upon my imagination as really to believe that around about the whole mansion and domain there hung an atmosphere peculiar to themselves and their immediate vicinity—an atmosphere which had no affinity with the air of heaven, but which had reeked up from the decayed trees, and the gray walls, and the silent tarn, in the form of an inelastic vapor or gas—dull, sluggish, faintly discernible, and leaden-hued. <u>Shaking off from my spirit what *must* have been a dream, I scanned more narrowly the real aspect of the building.</u> Its principal feature seemed to be that of an excessive antiquity. The discoloration of ages had been great. Minute fungi overspread the whole exterior, hanging in a fine tangled web-work from the eaves. Yet all this was apart from any extraordinary dilapidation. No portion of the masonry had fallen; and there appeared to be a wild inconsistency between its still perfect adaptation of parts, and the utterly porous, and evidently decayed condition of the individual stones. In this there was much that reminded me of the specious totality of old wood-work which has rotted for long years in some neglected vault, with no disturbance from the breath of the external air. Beyond this indication of extensive decay, however, the fabric gave little token of instability. Perhaps the eye of a scrutinizing observer might have discovered a barely perceptible fissure, which, extending from the roof of the building in front, made its way down the wall in a zigzag direction, until it became lost in the sullen waters of the tarn.

Noticing these things, I rode over a short causeway to the house. A servant in waiting took my horse, and I entered the Gothic archway of the hall. A valet, of stealthy step, thence conducted me, in silence, through many dark and intricate passages in my progress to the studio of his master. Much that I encountered on the way contributed, I know not how, to heighten the vague sentiments of which I have already spoken. While the objects around me—while the carvings of the ceilings, the sombre tapestries of the walls, the ebon blackness of the floors, and the phantasmagoric armorial trophies which rattled as I strode, were but matters to which, or to such as which, I had been accustomed from my infancy—while I hesitated not to acknowledge how familiar was all this—I still wondered to find how unfamiliar were the fancies which ordinary images were stirring up. On one of the staircases, I met the physician of the family. His countenance, I thought, wore a mingled expression of low cunning and perplexity. He accosted me with trepidation and passed on. The valet now threw open a door and ushered me into the presence of his master.

The room in which I found myself was very large and excessively lofty. The windows were long, narrow, and pointed, and at so vast a distance from the black oaken floor as to be altogether inaccessible from within. Feeble gleams of encrimsoned light made their way through the trellised panes, and served to render sufficiently distinct the more prominent objects around; the eye, however, struggled in vain to reach the remoter angles of the chamber, or the recesses of the vaulted and fretted ceiling. Dark draperies hung upon the walls. The general furniture was profuse, comfortless, antique, and tattered. Many books and musical instruments lay scattered about, but failed to give any vitality to the scene. I felt that I breathed an atmosphere of sorrow. An air of stern, deep, and irredeemable gloom hung over and pervaded all.

Upon my entrance, Usher arose from a sofa upon which he had been lying at full length, and greeted me with a vivacious warmth which had much in it, I at first thought of an overdone cordiality—of the constrained effort of the ennuyé[3] man of the world. A glance, however, at his countenance convinced

3. Bored (French).

me of his perfect sincerity. We sat down; and for some moments, while he spoke not, I gazed upon him with a feeling half of pity, half of awe. Surely, man had never before so terribly altered, in so brief a period, as had Roderick Usher! It was with difficulty that I could bring myself to admit the identity of the wan being before me with the companion of my early boyhood. Yet the character of his face had been at all times remarkable. A cadaverousness of complexion; an eye large, liquid, and luminous beyond comparison; lips somewhat thin and very pallid, but of a surpassingly beautiful curve; a nose of a delicate Hebrew model, but with a breadth of nostril unusual in similar formations; a finely moulded chin, speaking, in its want of prominence, of a want of moral energy; hair of a more than web-like softness and tenuity; these features, with an inordinate expansion above the regions of the temple, made up altogether a countenance not easily to be forgotten. And now in the mere exaggeration of the prevailing character of these features, and of the expression they were wont to convey, lay so much of change that I doubted to whom I spoke. The now ghastly pallor of the skin, and the now miraculous lustre of the eye, above all things startled and even awed me. The silken hair, too, had been suffered to grow all unheeded, and as, in its wild gossamer texture, it floated rather than fell about the face, I could not, even with effort, connect its arabesque expression with any idea of simple humanity.

In the manner of my friend I was at once struck with an incoherence—an inconsistency; and I soon found this to arise from a series of feeble and futile struggles to overcome an habitual trepidancy, an excessive nervous agitation. For something of this nature I had indeed been prepared, no less by his letter, than by reminiscences of certain boyish traits, and by conclusions deduced from his peculiar physical conformation and temperament. His action was alternately vivacious and sullen. His voice varied rapidly from a tremulous indecision (when the animal spirits seemed utterly in abeyance) to that species of energetic concision—that abrupt, weighty, unhurried, and hollow-sounding enunciation—that leaden, self-balanced and perfectly modulated guttural utterance, which may be observed in the moments of the intensest excitement of the lost drunkard, or the irreclaimable eater of opium.

It was thus that he spoke of the object of my visit, of his earnest desire to see me, and of the solace he expected me to afford him. He entered, at some length, into what he conceived to be the nature of his malady. It was, he said, a constitutional and a family evil, and one for which he despaired to find a remedy—a mere nervous affection, he immediately added, which would undoubtedly soon pass off. It displayed itself in a host of unnatural sensations. Some of these, as he detailed them, interested and bewildered me—although, perhaps, the terms, and the general manner of the narration had their weight. He suffered much from a morbid acuteness of the senses; the most insipid food was alone endurable; he could wear only garments of certain texture; the odors of all flowers were oppressive; his eyes were tortured by even a faint light; and there were but peculiar sounds, and these from stringed instruments, which did not inspire him with horror.

To an anomalous species of terror I found him a bounden slave. "I shall perish," said he, "I *must* perish in this deplorable folly. Thus, thus, and not otherwise, shall I be lost. I dread the events of the future, not in themselves, but in their results. I shudder at the thought of any, even the most trivial, incident, which may operate upon this intolerable agitation of soul. I have, indeed, no abhorrence of danger, except in its absolute effect—in terror. In this unnerved—in this pitiable condition—I feel that I must inevitably abandon life and reason together in my struggles with some fatal demon of fear."

I learned, moreover, at intervals, and through broken and equivocal hints, another singular feature of his mental condition. He was enchained by certain superstitious impressions in regard to the dwelling which he tenanted, and from which, for many years, he had never ventured forth—in regard to an influence whose supposititious force was conveyed in terms too shadowy here to be restated—an influence which some peculiarities in the mere form and substance of his family mansion, had, by dint of long sufferance, he said, obtained over his spirit—an effect which the *physique* of the gray walls and turrets, and of the dim tarn into which they all looked down, had, at length, brought about upon the *morale* of his existence.

He admitted, however, although with hesitation, that much of the peculiar gloom which thus afflicted him could be traced to a more natural and far more palpable origin—to the severe and long-continued illness—indeed to the evidently approaching dissolution—of a tenderly beloved sister; his sole companion for long years—his last and only relative on earth. "Her decease," he said, with a bitterness which I can never forget, "would leave him (him the hopeless and the frail) the last of the ancient race of the Ushers." As he spoke, the lady Madeline (for so was she called) passed slowly through a remote portion of the apartment, and, without having noticed my presence, disappeared. I regarded her with an utter astonishment not unmingled with dread. Her figure, her air, her features—all, in their very minutest development were those—were identically (I can use no other sufficient term) were identically those of the Roderick Usher who sat beside me. A feeling of stupor oppressed me, as my eyes followed her retreating steps. As a door, at length, closed upon her exit, my glance sought instinctively and eagerly the countenance of the brother—but he had buried his face in his hands, and I could only perceive that a far more than ordinary wanness had overspread the emaciated fingers through which trickled many passionate tears.

The disease of the lady Madeline had long baffled the skill of her physicians. A settled apathy, a gradual wasting away of the person, and frequent although transient affections of a partially cataleptical[4] character, were the unusual diagnosis. Hitherto she had steadily borne up against the pressure of her malady, and had not betaken herself finally to bed; but, on the closing in of the evening of my arrival at the house, she succumbed, as her brother told me at night with inexpressible agitation, to the prostrating power of the destroyer—and I learned that the glimpse I had obtained of her person would thus probably be the last I should obtain—that the lady, at least while living, would be seen by me no more.

For several days ensuing, her name was unmentioned by either Usher or myself; and, during this period, I was busied in earnest endeavors to alleviate the melancholy of my friend. We painted and read together—or I listened, as if in a dream, to the wild improvisations of his speaking guitar. And thus, as a closer and still closer intimacy admitted me more unreservedly into

---

4. A condition characterized by a loss of sensation and muscular paralysis.

the recesses of his spirit, the more bitterly did I perceive the futility of all attempt at cheering a mind from which darkness, as if an inherent positive quality, poured forth upon all objects of the moral and physical universe, in one unceasing radiation of gloom.

I shall ever bear about me, as Moslemin their shrouds at Mecca, a memory of the many solemn hours I thus spent alone with the master of the House of Usher. Yet I should fail in any attempt to convey an idea of the exact character of the studies, or of the occupations, in which he involved me, or led me the way. An excited and highly distempered ideality threw a sulphurous lustre over all. His long improvised dirges will ring for ever in my ears. Among other things, I bear painfully in mind a certain singular perversion and amplification of the wild air of the last waltz of Von Weber.[5] From the paintings over which his elaborate fancy brooded, and which grew, touch by touch, into vaguenesses at which I shuddered the more thrillingly, because I shuddered knowing not why, from these paintings (vivid as their images now are before me) I would in vain endeavor to educe more than a small portion which should lie within the compass of merely written words. By the utter simplicity, by the nakedness, of his designs, he arrested and over-awed attention. If ever mortal painted an idea, that mortal was Roderick Usher. For me at least—in the circumstances then surrounding me—there arose out of the pure abstractions which the hypochondriac contrived to throw upon his canvas, an intensity of intolerable awe, no shadow of which felt I ever yet in the contemplation of the certainly glowing yet too concrete reveries of Fuseli.[6]

One of the phantasmagoric conceptions of my friend, partaking not so rigidly of the spirit of abstraction, may be shadowed forth, although feebly, in words. A small picture presented the interior of an immensely long and rectangular vault or tunnel, with low walls, smooth, white, and without interruption or device. Certain accessory points of the design served well to convey the idea that this excavation lay at an exceeding depth below the surface of the earth. No outlet was observed in any portion of its vast extent, and no torch, or other artificial source of light was discernible—yet a flood of intense rays rolled throughout, and bathed the whole in a ghastly and inappropriate splendor.

I have just spoken of that morbid condition of the auditory nerve which rendered all music intolerable to the sufferer, with the exception of certain effects of stringed instruments. It was, perhaps, the narrow limits to which he thus confined himself upon the guitar, which gave birth, in great measure, to the fantastic character of his performances. But the fervid *facility* of his impromptus could not be so accounted for. They must have been, and were, in the notes, as well as in the words of his wild fantasias, (for he not unfrequently accompanied himself with rhymed verbal improvisations,) the result of that intense mental collectedness and concentration to which I have previously alluded as observable only in particular moments of the highest artificial excitement. The words of one of these rhapsodies I have easily borne away in memory. I was, perhaps, the more forcibly impressed with it, as he

5. Carl Maria von Weber (1786–1826), influential German composer of the Romantic school. "The Last Waltz of Von Weber" was composed by Carl Gottlieb Reissiger (1798–1859).

6. Henry Fuseli (1741–1825), Swiss painter noted for his interest in the supernatural.

gave it, because, in the under or mystic current of its meaning, I fancied that I perceived, and for the first time, a full consciousness on the part of Usher, of the tottering of his lofty reason upon her throne. The verses, which were entitled "The Haunted Palace," ran very nearly, if not accurately, thus:[7]

I

In the greenest of our valleys,
    By good angels tenanted,
Once a fair and stately palace—
    Snow-white palace—reared its head.
In the monarch Thought's dominion—
    It stood there!
Never seraph spread a pinion
    Over fabric half so fair.

II

Banners yellow, glorious, golden,
    On its roof did float and flow;
(This—all this—was in the olden
    Time long ago)
And every gentle air that dallied,
    In that sweet day,
Along the ramparts plumed and pallid,
    A winged odor went away.

III

Wanderers in that happy valley
    Through two luminous windows saw
Spirits moving musically
    To a lute's well-tunéd law,
Round about a throne, where sitting
    (Porphyrogene!)[8]
In state his glory well befitting,
    The sovereign of the realm was seen.

IV

And all with pearl and ruby glowing
    Was the fair palace door,
Through which came flowing, flowing, flowing,
    And sparkling evermore,
A troop of Echoes whose sole duty
    Was but to sing,
In voices of surpassing beauty,
    The wit and wisdom of their king.

---

7. In the original printing this note appeared at the end of the story: "The ballad of 'The Haunted Palace,' introduced in this tale, was published separately, some months ago, in the Baltimore 'Museum.'"

8. Born to the purple; of royal birth.

V

But evil things, in robes of sorrow,
    Assailed the monarch's high estate;
(Ah, let us mourn, for never morrow
    Shall dawn upon him, desolate!)
And, round about his home, the glory
    That blushed and bloomed
Is but a dim-remembered story
    Of the old time entombed.

VI

And travellers now within that valley,
    Through the red-litten windows, see
Vast forms that move fantastically
    To a discordant melody;
While, like a rapid ghastly river,
    Through the pale door,
A hideous throng rush out forever,
    And laugh—but smile no more.

    I well remember that suggestions arising from this ballad led us into a train of thought wherein there became manifest an opinion of Usher's which I mention not so much on account of its novelty, (for other men have thought thus,) as on account of the pertinacity with which he maintained it. This opinion, in its general form, was that of the sentience of all vegetable things. But, in his disordered fancy, the idea had assumed a more daring character, and trespassed, under certain conditions, upon the kingdom of inorganization. I lack words to express the full extent, or the earnest *abandon* of his persuasion. The belief, however, was connected (as I have previously hinted) with the gray stones of the home of his forefathers. The condition of the sentience had been here, he imagined, fulfilled in the method of collocation of these stones—in the order of their arrangement, as well as in that of the many fungi which overspread them, and of the decayed trees which stood around—above all, in the long undisturbed endurance of this arrangement, and in its reduplication in the still waters of the tarn. Its evidence—the evidence of the sentience—was to be seen, he said, (and I here started as he spoke,) in *the gradual yet certain condensation of an atmosphere of their own about the waters and the walls*. The result was discoverable, he added, in that silent, yet importunate and terrible influence which for centuries had moulded the destinies of his family, and which made *him* what I now saw him—what he was. Such opinions need no comment, and I will make none.

    Our books—the books which, for years, had formed no small portion of the mental existence of the invalid—were, as might be supposed, in strict keeping with this character of phantasm. We pored together over such works as the Ververt et Chartreuse of Gresset; the Belphegor of Machiavelli; the Selenography of Brewster; the Heaven and Hell of Swedenborg; the Subterranean Voyage of Nicholas Klimm de Holberg; the Chiromancy of Robert Flud, of Jean D'Indaginé, and of De la Chambre; the Journey into the Blue

Distance of Tieck; and the City of the Sun of Campanella.[9] One favorite volume was a small octavo edition of the Directorium Inquisitorium, by the Dominican Eymeric de Gironne; and there were passages in Pomponius Mela, about the old African Satyrs and Œgipans, over which Usher would sit dreaming for hours. His chief delight, however, was found in the earnest and repeated perusal of an exceedingly rare and curious book in quarto Gothic—the manual of a forgotten church—the *Vigilae Mortuorum secundum Chorum Ecclesiae Maguntinae.*[1]

I could not help thinking of the wild ritual of this work, and of its probable influence upon the hypochondriac, when, one evening, having informed me abruptly that the lady Madeline was no more, he stated his intention of preserving her corpse for a fortnight, previously to its final interment, in one of the numerous vaults within the main walls of the building. The worldly reason, however, assigned for this singular proceeding, was one which I did not feel at liberty to dispute. The brother had been led to his resolution (so he told me) by considerations of the unusual character of the malady of the deceased, of certain obtrusive and eager inquiries on the part of her medical men, and of the remote and exposed situation of the burial ground of the family. I will not deny that when I called to mind the sinister countenance of the person whom I met upon the staircase, on the day of my arrival at the house, I had no desire to oppose what I regarded as best but a harmless, and not by any means an unnatural precaution.[2]

At the request of Usher, I personally aided him in the arrangements for the temporary entombment. The body having been encoffined, we two alone bore it to its rest. The vault in which we placed it (and which had been so long unopened that our torches, half smothered in its oppressive atmosphere, gave us little opportunity for investigation) was small, damp, and utterly without means of admission for light; lying, at great depth, immediately beneath that portion of the building in which was my own sleeping apartment. It had been used, apparently, in remote feudal times, for the worst purposes of a donjon[3] keep, and, in later days, as a place of deposit for powder, or other highly combustible substance, as a portion of its floor, and the whole interior of a long archway through which we reached it, were carefully sheathed with copper. The door, of massive iron, had been, also, similarly protected. Its immense weight caused an unusually sharp grating sound, as it moved upon its hinges.

9. *The City of the Sun* by the Italian Tommaso Campanella (1568–1639) is a famous utopian work. Jean Baptiste Gresset (1709–1777) wrote the anticlerical *Vairvert* and *Ma Chartreuse*. In *Belphegor*, by Niccolò Machiavelli (1469–1527), a demon comes to earth to prove that women damn men to hell. Sir David Brewster (1781–1868), Scottish physicist who studied optics and light. Emanuel Swedenborg (1688–1772), Swedish scientist and mystic. Ludwig Holberg (1684–1754), Danish dramatist and historian, described a voyage to the land of death and back. The English physician Robert Flud (1574–1637) and two Frenchmen, Jean D'Indaginé (fl. early 16th century) and Maria Cireau de la Chambre (1594–1669), all wrote on chiromancy (palm reading). The German Ludwig Tieck (1773–1853) wrote *Das alte Buch; oder Reise ins Blaue hinein*, which narrates a journey to another world.

1. A book called *The Vigils of the Dead, According to the Church-Choir of Mayence* was printed in Switzerland around 1500. Nicholas Eymeric de Gerone, who was inquisitor-general for Castile in 1356, recorded procedures for torturing heretics. Pomponius Mela (1st century) was a Roman whose widely used book on geography (printed in Italy in 1471) described strange beasts ("œgipans" are African goat-men).

2. The shortage of corpses for dissection had led to the new profession of "resurrection men," who dug up fresh corpses and sold them to medical students and surgeons.

3. Dungeon.

Having deposited our mournful burden upon tressels[4] within this region of horror, we partially turned aside the yet unscrewed lid of the coffin, and looked upon the face of the tenant. The exact similitude between the brother and sister even here again startled and confounded me. Usher, divining, perhaps, my thoughts, murmured out some few words from which I learned that the deceased and himself had been twins, and that sympathies of a scarcely intelligible nature had always existed between them. Our glances, however, rested not long upon the dead—for we could not regard her unawed. The disease which had thus entombed the lady in the maturity of youth, had left, as usual in all maladies of a strictly cataleptical character, the mockery of a faint blush upon the bosom and the face, and that suspiciously lingering smile upon the lip which is so terrible in death. We replaced and screwed down the lid, and, having secured the door of iron, made our way, with toil, into the scarcely less gloomy apartments of the upper portion of the house.

And now, some days of bitter grief having elapsed, an observable change came over the features of the mental disorder of my friend. His ordinary manner had vanished. His ordinary occupations were neglected or forgotten. He roamed from chamber to chamber with hurried, unequal, and objectless step. The pallor of his countenance had assumed, if possible, a more ghastly hue—but the luminousness of his eye had utterly gone out. The once occasional huskiness of his tone was heard no more; and a tremulous quaver, as if of extreme terror, habitually characterized his utterance.— There were times, indeed, when I thought his unceasingly agitated mind was laboring with an oppressive secret, to divulge which he struggled for the necessary courage. At times, again, I was obliged to resolve all into the mere inexplicable vagaries of madness, as I beheld him gazing upon vacancy for long hours, in an attitude of the profoundest attention, as if listening to some imaginary sound. It was no wonder that his condition terrified—that it infected me. I felt creeping upon me, by slow yet certain degrees, the wild influences of his own fantastic yet impressive superstitions.

It was, most especially, upon retiring to bed late in the night of the seventh or eighth day after the entombment of the lady Madeline, that I experienced the full power of such feelings. Sleep came not near my couch—while the hours waned and waned away. I struggled to reason off the nervousness which had dominion over me. I endeavored to believe that much, if not all of what I felt, was due to the phantasmagoric influence of the gloomy furniture of the room—of the dark and tattered draperies, which, tortured into motion by the breath of a rising tempest, swayed fitfully to and fro upon the walls, and rustled uneasily about the decorations of the bed. But my efforts were fruitless. An irrepressible tremor gradually pervaded my frame; and, at length, there sat upon my very heart an incubus[5] of utterly causeless alarm. Shaking this off with a gasp and a struggle, I uplifted myself upon the pillows, and, peering earnestly within the intense darkness of the chamber, harkened—I know not why, except that an instinctive spirit prompted me— to certain low and indefinite sounds which came, through the pauses of the storm, at long intervals, I knew not whence. Overpowered by an intense

---

4. Trestles; braced supports.
5. An evil spirit supposed to lie upon people in their sleep.

sentiment of horror, unaccountable yet unendurable, I threw on my clothes with haste, for I felt that I should sleep no more during the night, and endeavored to arouse myself from the pitiable condition into which I had fallen, by pacing rapidly to and fro through the apartment.

I had taken but few turns in this manner, when a light step on an adjoining staircase arrested my attention. I presently recognized it as that of Usher. In an instant afterwards he rapped, with a gentle touch, at my door, and entered, bearing a lamp. His countenance was, as usual, cadaverously wan—but there was a species of mad hilarity in his eyes—an evidently restrained hysteria in his whole demeanor. His air appalled me—but any thing was preferable to the solitude which I had so long endured, and I even welcomed his presence as a relief.

"And you have not seen it?" he said abruptly, after having stared about him for some moments in silence—"you have not then seen it?—but, stay! you shall." Thus speaking, and having carefully shaded his lamp, he hurried to one of the gigantic casements, and threw it freely open to the storm.

The impetuous fury of the entering gust nearly lifted us from our feet. It was, indeed, a tempestuous yet sternly beautiful night, and one wildly singular in its terror and its beauty. A whirlwind had apparently collected its force in our vicinity; for there were frequent and violent alterations in the direction of the wind; and the exceeding density of the clouds (which hung so low as to press upon the turrets of the house) did not prevent our perceiving the life-like velocity with which they flew careering from all points against each other, without passing away into the distance. I say that even their exceeding density did not prevent our perceiving this—yet we had no glimpse of the moon or stars—nor was there any flashing forth of the lightning. But the under surfaces of the huge masses of agitated vapor, as well as all terrestrial objects immediately around us, were glowing in the unnatural light of a faintly luminous and distinctly visible gaseous exhalation which hung about and enshrouded the mansion.

"You must not—you shall not behold this!" said I, shudderingly, to Usher, as I led him, with a gentle violence, from the window to a seat. "These appearances, which bewilder you, are merely electrical phenomena not uncommon—or it may be that they have their ghastly origin in the rank miasma of the tarn. Let us close this casement—the air is chilling and dangerous to your frame. Here is one of your favorite romances. I will read, and you shall listen—and so we will pass away this terrible night together."

The antique volume which I had taken up was the "Mad Trist" of Sir Launcelot Canning[6]—but I had called it a favorite of Usher's more in sad jest than in earnest; for, in truth, there is little in its uncouth and unimaginative prolixity which could have had interest for the lofty and spiritual ideality of my friend. It was, however, the only book immediately at hand; and I indulged a vague hope that the excitement which now agitated the hypochondriac might find relief (for the history of mental disorder is full of similar anomalies) even in the extremeness of the folly which I should read. Could I have judged, indeed, by the wild, overstrained air of vivacity with which he harkened, or apparently harkened, to the words of the tale, I might have well congratulated myself upon the success of my design.

6. Not a real book. "Trist" here means meeting, or prearranged or fated encounter.

I had arrived at that well-known portion of the story where Ethelred, the hero of the Trist, having sought in vain for peaceable admission into the dwelling of the hermit, proceeds to make good an entrance by force. Here, it will be remembered, the words of the narrative run thus—

"And Ethelred, who was by nature of a doughty heart, and who was now mighty withal, on account of the powerfulness of the wine which he had drunken, waited no longer to hold parley with the hermit, who, in sooth, was of an obstinate and maliceful turn, but, feeling the rain upon his shoulders, and fearing the rising of the tempest, uplifted his mace outright, and, with blows, made quickly room in the plankings of the door for his gauntleted hand, and now pulling therewith sturdily, he so cracked, and ripped, and tore all asunder, that the noise of the dry and hollow-sounding wood alarummed and reverberated throughout the forest."

At the termination of this sentence I started, and, for a moment, paused; for it appeared to me (although I at once concluded that my excited fancy had deceived me)—it appeared to me that, from some very remote portion of the mansion or of its vicinity, there came, indistinctly, to my ears, what might have been, in its exact similarity of character, the echo (but a stifled and dull one certainly) of the very cracking and ripping sound which Sir Launcelot had so particularly described. It was, beyond doubt, the coincidence alone which had arrested my attention; for, amid the rattling of the sashes of the casements, and the ordinary commingled noises of the still increasing storm, the sound, in itself, had nothing, surely, which should have interested or disturbed me. I continued the story.

"But the good champion Ethelred, now entering within the door, was sore enraged and amazed to perceive no signal of the maliceful hermit; but, in the stead thereof, a dragon of scaly and prodigious demeanor, and of a fiery tongue, which sate in guard before a palace of gold, with a floor of silver; and upon the wall there hung a shield of shining brass with this legend enwritten—

> Who entereth herein, a conqueror hath bin,
> Who slayeth the dragon, the shield he shall win.

And Ethelred uplifted his mace, and struck upon the head of the dragon, which fell before him, and gave up his pesty breath, with a shriek so horrid and harsh, and withal so piercing, that Ethelred had fain to close his ears with his hands against the dreadful noise of it, the like whereof was never before heard."

Here again I paused abruptly, and now with a feeling of wild amazement—for there could be no doubt whatever that, in this instance, I did actually hear (although from what direction it proceeded I found it impossible to say) a low and apparently distant, but harsh, protracted, and most unusual screaming or grating sound—the exact counterpart of what my fancy had already conjured up as the sound of the dragon's unnatural shriek as described by the romancer.

Oppressed, as I certainly was, upon the occurrence of this second and most extraordinary coincidence, by a thousand conflicting sensations, in which wonder and extreme terror were predominant, I still retained sufficient presence of mind to avoid exciting, by any observation, the sensitive nervousness of my companion. I was by no means certain that he had noticed the sounds in question; although, assuredly, a strange alteration had, during the last few minutes, taken place in his demeanor. From a position fronting my own, he had gradually brought round his chair, so as to sit with his face to the door of the chamber, and thus I could but partially perceive his features, although I saw that his lips trembled as if he were murmuring inaudibly. His head had dropped upon his breast—yet I knew that he was not asleep, from the wide and rigid opening of the eye, as I caught a glance of it in profile. The motion of his body, too, was at variance with his idea—for he rocked from side to side with a gentle yet constant and uniform sway. Having rapidly taken notice of all this, I resumed the narrative of Sir Launcelot, which thus proceeded:—

"And now, the champion, having escaped from the terrible fury of the dragon, bethinking himself of the brazen shield, and of the breaking up of the enchantment which was upon it, removed the carcass from out of the way before him, and approached valorously over the silver pavement of the castle to where the shield was upon the wall; which in sooth tarried not for his full coming, but fell down at his feet upon the silver floor, with a mighty great and terrible ringing sound."

No sooner had these syllables passed my lips, than—as if a shield of brass had indeed, at the moment, fallen heavily upon a floor of silver—I became aware of a distinct, hollow, metallic, and clangorous, yet apparently muffled reverberation. Completely unnerved, I started convulsively to my feet, but the measured rocking movement of Usher was undisturbed. I rushed to the chair in which he sat. His eyes were bent fixedly before him, and throughout his whole countenance there reigned a more than stony rigidity. But, as I laid my hand upon his shoulder, there came a strong shudder over his frame; a sickly smile quivered about his lips; and I saw that he spoke in a low, hurried, and gibbering murmur, as if unconscious of my presence. Bending closely over his person, I at length drank in the hideous import of his words.

"Not hear it?—yes, I hear it, and *have* heard it. Long—long—long—many minutes, many hours, many days, have I heard it—yet I dared not—oh, pity me, miserable wretch that I am!—I dared not—I *dared* not speak! *We have put her living in the tomb!* Said I not that my senses were acute?—I *now* tell you that I heard her first feeble movements in the hollow coffin. I heard them—many, many days ago—yet I dared not—*I dared not speak!* And now—to-night—Ethelred—ha! ha!—the breaking of the hermit's door, and the death-cry of the dragon, and the clangor of the shield—say, rather, the rending of the coffin, and the grating of the iron hinges, and her struggles within the coppered archway of the vault! Oh whither shall I fly? Will she not be here anon? Is she not hurrying to upbraid me for my haste? Have I not heard her footsteps on the stair? Do I not distinguish that heavy and horrible beating of her heart? Madman!"—here he sprung violently to his feet, and shrieked out his syllables, as if in the effort he were giving up his soul—"Madman! *I tell you that she now stands without the door!*"

As if in the superhuman energy of his utterance there had been found the potency of a spell—the huge antique pannels to which the speaker pointed, threw slowly back, upon the instant, their ponderous and ebony jaws. It was the work of the rushing gust—but then without those doors there *did* stand the lofty and enshrouded figure of the lady Madeline of Usher. There was blood upon her white robes, and the evidence of some bitter struggle upon every portion of her emaciated frame. For a moment she remained trembling and reeling to and fro upon the threshold—then, with a low moaning cry, fell heavily inward upon the person of her brother, and in her horrible and now final death-agonies, bore him to the floor a corpse, and a victim to the terrors he had dreaded.

From that chamber, and from that mansion, I fled aghast. The storm was still abroad in all its wrath as I found myself crossing the old causeway. Suddenly there shot along the path a wild light, and I turned to see whence a gleam so unusual could have issued—for the vast house and its shadows were alone behind me. The radiance was that of the full, setting, and blood-red moon, which now shone vividly through that once barely-discernible fissure, of which I have before spoken, as extending from the roof of the building, in a zig-zag direction, to the base. While I gazed, this fissure rapidly widened—there came a fierce breath of the whirlwind—the entire orb of the satellite burst at once upon my sight—my brain reeled as I saw the mighty walls rushing asunder—there was a long tumultuous shouting sound like the voice of a thousand waters—and the deep and dank tarn at my feet closed sullenly and silently over the fragments of the *"House of Usher."*

1839

The Tell-Tale Heart[1]

Art is long and Time is fleeting,
And our hearts, though stout and brave,
Still, like muffled drums, are beating
Funeral marches to the grave.
—Longfellow[2]

True!—nervous—very, very dreadfully nervous I had been, and am; but why *will* you say that I am mad? The disease had sharpened my senses—not destroyed—not dulled them. Above all was the sense of hearing acute. I heard all things in the heaven and in the earth. I heard many things in hell. How, then, am I mad? Harken! and observe how healthily—how calmly I can tell you the whole story.

It is impossible to say how first the idea entered my brain; but, once conceived, it haunted me day and night. Object there was none. Passion there was none. I loved the old man. He had never wronged me. He had never given me insult. For his gold I had no desire. I think it was his eye!—yes, it was this! He had the eye of a vulture—a pale blue eye, with a film over it. Whenever it fell upon me, my blood ran cold; and so, by degrees—very gradually—I made up my mind to take the life of the old man, and thus rid myself of the eye forever.

Now this is the point. You fancy me mad. Madmen know nothing. But you should have seen *me*. You should have seen how wisely I proceeded—with what caution—with what foresight—with what dissimulation I went to

---

1. First published in *The Pioneer* (January 1843), the source of the present text.

2. Henry Wadsworth Longfellow's "A Psalm of Life" (1838), lines 13–16.

work! I was never kinder to the old man than during the whole week before I killed him. And every night, about midnight, I turned the latch of his door and opened it—oh so gently! And then, when I had made an opening sufficient for my head, I first put in a dark lantern,[3] all closed, closed, so that no light shone out, and then I thrust in my head. Oh, you would have laughed to see how cunningly I thrust it in! I moved it slowly—very, very slowly, so that I might not disturb the old man's sleep. It took me an hour to place my whole head within the opening so far that I could see the old man as he lay upon his bed. Ha!—would a madman have been so wise as this? And then, when my head was well in the room, I undid the lantern cautiously—oh, so cautiously (for the hinges creaked)—I undid it just so much that a single thin ray fell upon the vulture eye. And this I did for seven long nights—every night just at midnight—but I found the eye always closed; and so it was impossible to do the work; for it was not the old man who vexed me, but his Evil Eye. And every morning, when the day broke, I went boldly into his chamber, and spoke courageously to him, calling him by name in a hearty tone, and inquiring how he had passed the night. So you see he would have been a very profound old man, indeed, to suspect that every night, just at twelve, I looked in upon him while he slept.

Upon the eighth night I was more than usually cautious in opening the door. A watch's minute-hand moves more quickly than did mine. Never, before that night, had I *felt* the extent of my own powers—of my sagacity. I could scarcely contain my feelings of triumph. To think that there I was, opening the door, little by little, and the old man not even to dream of my secret deeds or thoughts. I fairly chuckled at the idea. And perhaps the old man heard me; for he moved in the bed suddenly, as if startled. Now you may think that I drew back—but no. His room was as black as pitch with the thick darkness, (for the shutters were close fastened, through fear of robbers,) and so I knew that he could not see the opening of the door, and I kept on pushing it steadily, steadily.

I had got my head in, and was about to open the lantern, when my thumb slipped upon the tin fastening, and the old man sprang up in the bed, crying out—"Who's there?"

I kept quite still and said nothing. For another hour I did not move a muscle, and in the meantime I did not hear the old man lie down. He was still sitting up in the bed, listening;—just as I have done, night after night, hearkening to the death-watches[4] in the wall.

Presently I heard a slight groan, and I knew that it was the groan of mortal terror. It was not a groan of pain, or of grief—oh, no!—it was the low, stifled sound that arises from the bottom of the soul when overcharged with *awe*. I knew the sound well. Many a night, just at midnight, when all the world slept, it has welled up from my own bosom, deepening, with its dreadful echo, the terrors that distracted me. I say I knew it well. I knew what the old man felt, and pitied him, although I chuckled at heart. I knew that he had been lying awake ever since the first slight noise, when he had turned in the bed. His fears had been, ever since, growing upon him. He

3. Lantern with a single opening and sliding panel that can cut off the light.
4. Beetles that make a hollow clicking sound by striking their heads against the wood into which they burrow.

had been trying to fancy them causeless, but could not. He had been saying to himself—"It is nothing but the wind in the chimney—it is only a mouse crossing the floor," or "it is merely a cricket which has made a single chirp." Yes, he had been trying to comfort himself with these suppositions; but he had found all in vain. *All in vain*; because death, in approaching the old man, had stalked with his black shadow before him, and the shadow had now reached and enveloped the victim. And it was the mournful influence of the unperceived shadow that caused him to feel—although he neither saw nor heard me—to *feel* the presence of my head within the room.

When I had waited a long time, very patiently, without hearing the old man lie down, I resolved to open a little—a very, very little crevice in the lantern. So I opened it—you cannot imagine how stealthily, stealthily—until, at length, a single dim ray, like the thread of the spider, shot from out the crevice and fell full upon the vulture eye.

It was open—wide, wide open—and I grew furious as I gazed upon it. I saw it with perfect distinctness—all a dull blue, with a hideous veil over it that chilled the very marrow in my bones; but I could see nothing else of the old man's face or person; for I had directed the ray, as if by instinct, precisely upon the damned spot.

And now—have I not told you that what you mistake for madness is but over acuteness of the senses?—now, I say, there came to my ears *a low, dull, quick sound—much such a sound as a watch makes when enveloped in cotton*. I knew *that* sound well, too. It was the beating of the old man's heart. It increased my fury, as the beating of a drum stimulates the soldier into courage.

But even yet I refrained and kept still. I scarcely breathed. I held the lantern motionless. I tried how steadily I could maintain the ray upon the eye. Meantime the hellish tattoo[5] of the heart increased. It grew quicker, and louder and louder every instant. The old man's terror *must* have been extreme! It grew louder, I say, louder every moment:—do you mark me well? I have told you that I am nervous:—so I am. And now, at the dead hour of night, and amid the dreadful silence of that old house, so strange a noise as this excited me to uncontrollable wrath. Yet, for some minutes longer, I refrained and kept still. But the beating grew louder, *louder*! I thought the heart must burst! And now a new anxiety seized me—the sound would be heard by a neighbor! The old man's hour had come! With a loud yell, I threw open the lantern and leaped into the room. He shrieked once—once only. In an instant I dragged him to the floor, and pulled the heavy bed over him. I then sat upon the bed and smiled gaily, to find the deed so far done. But, for many minutes, the heart beat on, with a muffled sound. This, however, did not vex me; it would not be heard through the walls. At length it ceased. The old man was dead. I removed the bed and examined the corpse. Yes, he was stone, stone dead. I placed my hand upon the heart and held it there many minutes. There was no pulsation. The old man was stone dead. His eye would trouble *me* no more.

If, still, you think me mad, you will think so no longer when I describe the wise precautions I took for the concealment of the body. The night waned, and I worked hastily, but in silence. First of all I dismembered the

5. Drumbeat.

corpse. I cut off the head and the arms and the legs. I then took up three planks from the flooring of the chamber, and deposited all between the scantlings.[6] I then replaced the boards so cleverly, so cunningly, that no human eye—not even *his*—could have detected anything wrong. There was nothing to wash out—no stain of any kind—no blood-spot whatever. I had been too wary for that. A tub had caught all—ha! ha!

When I had made an end of these labors, it was four o'clock—still dark as midnight. As the bell sounded the hour, there came a knocking at the street door. I went down to open it with a light heart,—for what had I *now* to fear? There entered three men, who introduced themselves, with perfect suavity, as officers of the police. A shriek had been heard by a neighbor during the night; suspicion of foul play had been aroused; information had been lodged at the police-office, and they (the officers) had been deputed to search the premises.

I smiled,—for *what* had I to fear? I bade the gentlemen welcome. The shriek, I said, was my own in a dream. The old man, I mentioned, was absent in the country. I took my visiters all over the house. I bade them search—search *well*. I led them, at length, to *his* chamber. I showed them his treasures, secure, undisturbed. In the enthusiasm of my confidence, I brought chairs into the room, and desired them *here* to rest from their fatigues; while I myself, in the wild audacity of my perfect triumph, placed my own seat upon the very spot beneath which reposed the corpse of the victim.

The officers were satisfied. My *manner* had convinced them. I was singularly at ease. They sat, and, while I answered cheerily, they chatted of familiar things. But, ere long, I felt myself getting pale and wished them gone. My head ached, and I fancied a ringing in my ears: but still they sat and still chatted. The ringing became more distinct:—I talked more freely, to get rid of the feeling; but it continued and gained definitiveness—until, at length, I found that the noise was *not* within my ears.

No doubt I now grew *very* pale;—but I talked more fluently, and with a heightened voice. Yet the sound increased—and what could I do? It was *a low, dull, quick sound—much such a sound as a watch makes when enveloped in cotton*. I gasped for breath—and yet the officers heard it not. I talked more quickly—more vehemently;—but the noise steadily increased. I arose, and argued about trifles, in a high key and with violent gesticulations;—but the noise steadily increased. Why *would* they not be gone? I paced the floor to and fro, with heavy strides, as if excited to fury by the observations of the men;—but the noise steadily increased. Oh God! what *could* I do? I foamed—I raved—I swore! I swung the chair upon which I had sat, and grated it upon the boards;—but the noise arose over all and continually increased. It grew louder—louder—*louder*! And still the men chatted pleasantly, and smiled. Was it possible they heard not? Almighty God! no, no! They heard!—they suspected!—they *knew*!—they were making a mockery of my horror!—this I thought, and this I think. But anything better than this agony! Anything was more tolerable than this derision! I could bear those hypocritical smiles no longer! I felt that I must scream or die!—and now—again!—hark! louder! louder! louder! *louder*!—

6. Small planks.

"Villains!" I shrieked, "dissemble no more! I admit the deed!—tear up the planks!—here, here!—it is the beating of his hideous heart!"

1843

The Black Cat[1]

For the most wild, yet most homely narrative which I am about to pen, I neither expect nor solicit belief. Mad indeed would I be to expect it, in a case where my very senses reject their own evidence. Yet, mad am I not—and very surely do I not dream. But to-morrow I die, and to-day I would unburthen my soul. My immediate purpose is to place before the world, plainly, succinctly, and without comment, a series of mere household events. In their consequences, these events have terrified—have tortured—have destroyed me. Yet I will not attempt to expound them. To me, they have presented little but Horror—to many they will seem less terrible than *barroques.*[2] Hereafter, perhaps, some intellect may be found which will reduce my phantasm to the commonplace—some intellect more calm, more logical, and far less excitable than my own, which will perceive, in the circumstances I detail with awe, nothing more than an ordinary succession of very natural causes and effects.

From my infancy I was noted for the docility and humanity of my disposition. My tenderness of heart was even so conspicuous as to make me the jest of my companions. I was especially fond of animals, and was indulged by my parents with a great variety of pets. With these I spent most of my time, and never was so happy as when feeding and caressing them. This peculiarity of character grew with my growth, and, in my manhood, I derived from it one of my principal sources of pleasure. To those who have cherished an affection for a faithful and sagacious dog, I need hardly be at the trouble of explaining the nature or the intensity of the gratification thus derivable. There is something in the unselfish and self-sacrificing love of a brute, which goes directly to the heart of him who has had frequent occasion to test the paltry friendship and gossamer fidelity of mere *Man.*

I married early, and was happy to find in my wife a disposition not uncongenial with my own. Observing my partiality for domestic pets, she lost no opportunity of procuring those of the most agreeable kind. We had birds, gold-fish, a fine dog, rabbits, a small monkey, and *a cat.*

This latter was a remarkably large and beautiful animal, entirely black, and sagacious to an astonishing degree. In speaking of his intelligence, my wife, who at heart was not a little tinctured with superstition, made frequent allusion to the ancient popular notion, which regarded all black cats as witches in disguise. Not that she was ever *serious* upon this point—and I mention the matter at all for no better reason than that it happens, just now, to be remembered.

---

1. First published in the August 1843 *United States Saturday Post*, a Philadelphia weekly, and reprinted here from *Tales* (1845).
2. Odd (French).

Pluto[3]—this was the cat's name—was my favorite pet and playmate. I alone fed him, and he attended me wherever I went about the house. It was even with difficulty that I could prevent him from following me through the streets.

Our friendship lasted, in this manner, for several years, during which my general temperament and character—through the instrumentality of the Fiend Intemperance—had (I blush to confess it) experienced a radical alteration for the worse. I grew, day by day, more moody, more irritable, more regardless of the feelings of others. I suffered myself to use intemperate language to my wife. At length, I even offered her personal violence. My pets, of course, were made to feel the change in my disposition. I not only neglected, but ill-used them. For Pluto, however, I still retained sufficient regard to restrain me from maltreating him, as I made no scruple of maltreating the rabbits, the monkey, or even the dog, when by accident, or through affection, they came in my way. But my disease grew upon me—for what disease is like Alcohol!—and at length even Pluto, who was now becoming old, and consequently somewhat peevish—even Pluto began to experience the effects of my ill temper.

One night, returning home, much intoxicated, from one of my haunts about town, I fancied that the cat avoided my presence. I seized him; when, in his fright at my violence, he inflicted a slight wound upon my hand with his teeth. The fury of a demon instantly possessed me. I knew myself no longer. My original soul seemed, at once, to take its flight from my body; and a more than fiendish malevolence, gin-nurtured, thrilled every fibre of my frame. I took from my waistcoat-pocket a pen-knife, opened it, grasped the poor beast by the throat, and deliberately cut one of its eyes from the socket! I blush, I burn, I shudder, while I pen the damnable atrocity.

When reason returned with the morning—when I had slept off the fumes of the night's debauch—I experienced a sentiment half of horror, half of remorse, for the crime of which I had been guilty; but it was, at best, a feeble and equivocal feeling, and the soul remained untouched. I again plunged into excess, and soon drowned in wine all memory of the deed.

In the meantime the cat slowly recovered. The socket of the lost eye presented, it is true, a frightful appearance, but he no longer appeared to suffer any pain. He went about the house as usual, but, as might be expected, fled in extreme terror at my approach. I had so much of my old heart left, as to be at first grieved by this evident dislike on the part of a creature which had once so loved me. But this feeling soon gave place to irritation. And then came, as if to my final and irrevocable overthrow, the spirit of PERVERSE-NESS. Of this spirit philosophy takes no account. Yet I am not more sure that my soul lives, than I am that perverseness is one of the primitive impulses of the human heart—one of the indivisible primary faculties, or sentiments, which give direction to the character of Man. Who has not, a hundred times, found himself committing a vile or a silly action, for no other reason than because he knows he should *not*? Have we not a perpetual inclination, in the teeth of our best judgment, to violate that which is *Law*, merely because we understand it to be such? This spirit of perverseness, I say, came to my final overthrow. It was this unfathomable longing of the soul *to vex itself*—to offer

3. In Roman mythology, god of the dead and ruler of the underworld.

violence to its own nature—to do wrong for the wrong's sake only—that urged me to continue and finally to consummate the injury I had inflicted upon the unoffending brute. One morning, in cool blood, I slipped a noose about its neck and hung it to the limb of a tree;—hung it with the tears streaming from my eyes, and with the bitterest remorse at my heart;—hung it *because* I knew that it had loved me, and *because* I felt it had given me no reason of offence;—hung it *because* I knew that in so doing I was committing a sin—a deadly sin that would so jeopardize my immortal soul as to place it—if such a thing were possible—even beyond the reach of the infinite mercy of the Most Merciful and Most Terrible God.

On the night of the day on which this cruel deed was done, I was aroused from sleep by the cry of fire. The curtains of my bed were in flames. The whole house was blazing. It was with great difficulty that my wife, a servant, and myself, made our escape from the conflagration. The destruction was complete. My entire worldly wealth was swallowed up, and I resigned myself thenceforward to despair.

I am above the weakness of seeking to establish a sequence of cause and effect, between the disaster and the atrocity. But I am detailing a chain of facts—and wish not to leave even a possible link imperfect. On the day succeeding the fire, I visited the ruins. The walls, with one exception, had fallen in. This exception was found in a compartment wall, not very thick, which stood about the middle of the house, and against which had rested the head of my bed. The plastering had here, in great measure, resisted the action of the fire—a fact which I attributed to its having been recently spread. About this wall a dense crowd were collected, and many persons seemed to be examining a particular portion of it with very minute and eager attention. The words "strange!" "singular!" and other similar expressions, excited my curiosity. I approached and saw, as if graven in *bas relief*[4] upon the white surface, the figure of a gigantic *cat*. The impression was given with an accuracy truly marvellous. There was a rope about the animal's neck.

When I first beheld this apparition—for I could scarcely regard it as less—my wonder and my terror were extreme. But at length reflection came to my aid. The cat, I remembered, had been hung in a garden adjacent to the house. Upon the alarm of fire, this garden had been immediately filled by the crowd—by some one of whom the animal must have been cut from the tree and thrown, through an open window, into my chamber. This had probably been done with the view of arousing me from sleep. The falling of other walls had compressed the victim of my cruelty into the substance of the freshly-spread plaster; the lime of which, with the flames, and the *ammonia* from the carcass, had then accomplished the portraiture as I saw it.

Although I thus readily accounted to my reason, if not altogether to my conscience, for the startling fact just detailed, it did not the less fail to make a deep impression upon my fancy. For months I could not rid myself of the phantasm of the cat; and, during this period, there came back into my spirit a half-sentiment that seemed, but was not, remorse. I went so far as to regret the loss of the animal, and to look about me, among the vile haunts which I now habitually frequented, for another pet of the same species, and of somewhat similar appearance, with which to supply its place.

4. Low relief (French); the slight projection from a flat sculptural background.

One night as I sat, half stupified, in a den of more than infamy, my attention was suddenly drawn to some black object, reposing upon the head of one of the immense hogsheads[5] of Gin, or of Rum, which constituted the chief furniture of the apartment. I had been looking steadily at the top of this hogshead for some minutes, and what now caused me surprise was the fact that I had not sooner perceived the object thereupon. I approached it, and touched it with my hand. It was a black cat—a very large one—fully as large as Pluto, and closely resembling him in every respect but one. Pluto had not a white hair upon any portion of his body; but this cat had a large, although indefinite splotch of white, covering nearly the whole region of the breast.

Upon my touching him, he immediately arose, purred loudly, rubbed against my hand, and appeared delighted with my notice. This, then, was the very creature of which I was in search. I at once offered to purchase it of the landlord; but this person made no claim to it—knew nothing of it— had never seen it before.

I continued my caresses, and, when I prepared to go home, the animal evinced a disposition to accompany me. I permitted it to do so; occasionally stooping and patting it as I proceeded. When it reached the house it domesticated itself at once, and became immediately a great favorite with my wife.

For my own part, I soon found a dislike to it arising within me. This was just the reverse of what I had anticipated; but—I know not how or why it was—its evident fondness for myself rather disgusted and annoyed. By slow degrees, these feelings of disgust and annoyance rose into the bitterness of hatred. I avoided the creature; a certain sense of shame, and the remembrance of my former deed of cruelty, preventing me from physically abusing it. I did not, for some weeks, strike, or otherwise violently ill use it; but gradually—very gradually—I came to look upon it with unutterable loathing, and to flee silently from its odious presence, as from the breath of a pestilence.

What added, no doubt, to my hatred of the beast, was the discovery, on the morning after I brought it home, that, like Pluto, it also had been deprived of one of its eyes. This circumstance, however, only endeared it to my wife, who, as I have already said, possessed, in a high degree, that humanity of feeling which had once been my distinguishing trait, and the source of many of my simplest and purest pleasures.

With my aversion to this cat, however, its partiality for myself seemed to increase. It followed my footsteps with a pertinacity which it would be difficult to make the reader comprehend. Whenever I sat, it would crouch beneath my chair, or spring upon my knees, covering me with its loathsome caresses. If I arose to walk it would get between my feet and thus nearly throw me down, or, fastening its long and sharp claws in my dress, clamber, in this manner, to my breast. At such times, although I longed to destroy it with a blow, I was yet withheld from so doing, partly by a memory of my former crime, but chiefly—let me confess it at once—by absolute *dread* of the beast.

This dread was not exactly a dread of physical evil—and yet I should be at a loss how otherwise to define it. I am almost ashamed to own—yes, even in this felon's cell, I am almost ashamed to own—that the terror and horror with which the animal inspired me, had been heightened by one of the merest

5. Large casks.

chimæras[6] it would be possible to conceive. My wife had called my attention, more than once, to the character of the mark of white hair, of which I have spoken, and which constituted the sole visible difference between the strange beast and the one I had destroyed. The reader will remember that this mark, although large, had been originally very indefinite; but, by slow degrees—degrees nearly imperceptible, and which for a long time my Reason struggled to reject as fanciful—it had, at length, assumed a rigorous distinctness of outline. It was now the representation of an object that I shudder to name—and for this, above all, I loathed, and dreaded, and would have rid myself of the monster *had I dared*—it was now, I say, the image of a hideous—of a ghastly thing—of the GALLOWS!—oh, mournful and terrible engine of Horror and of Crime—of Agony and of Death!

And now was I indeed wretched beyond the wretchedness of mere Humanity. And *a brute beast*—whose fellow I had contemptuously destroyed—*a brute beast* to work out for *me*—for me a man, fashioned in the image of the High God—so much of insufferable wo! Alas! neither by day nor by night knew I the blessing of Rest any more! During the former the creature left me no moment alone; and, in the latter, I started, hourly, from dreams of unutterable fear, to find the hot breath of *the thing* upon my face, and its vast weight—an incarnate Night-Mare that I had no power to shake off—incumbent eternally upon my *heart*!

Beneath the pressure of torments such as these, the feeble remnant of the good within me succumbed. Evil thoughts became my sole intimates—the darkest and most evil of thoughts. The moodiness of my usual temper increased to hatred of all things and of all mankind; while, from the sudden, frequent, and ungovernable outbursts of a fury to which I now blindly abandoned myself, my uncomplaining wife, alas! was the most usual and the most patient of sufferers.

One day she accompanied me, upon some household errand, into the cellar of the old building which our poverty compelled us to inhabit. The cat followed me down the steep stairs, and, nearly throwing me headlong, exasperated me to madness. Uplifting an axe, and forgetting, in my wrath, the childish dread which had hitherto stayed my hand, I aimed a blow at the animal which, of course, would have proved instantly fatal had it descended as I wished. But this blow was arrested by the hand of my wife. Goaded, by the interference, into a rage more than demoniacal, I withdrew my arm from her grasp and buried the axe in her brain. She fell dead upon the spot, without a groan.

This hideous murder accomplished, I set myself forthwith, and with entire deliberation, to the task of concealing the body. I knew that I could not remove it from the house, either by day or by night, without the risk of being observed by the neighbors. Many projects entered my mind. At one period I thought of cutting the corpse into minute fragments, and destroying them by fire. At another, I resolved to dig a grave for it in the floor of the cellar. Again, I deliberated about casting it in the well in the yard—about packing it in a box, as if merchandize, with the usual arrangements, and so getting a porter to take it from the house. Finally I hit upon what I considered a far better

---

6. Illusions.

expedient than either of these. I determined to wall it up in the cellar—as the monks of the middle ages are recorded to have walled up their victims.

For a purpose such as this the cellar was well adapted. Its walls were loosely constructed, and had lately been plastered throughout with a rough plaster, which the dampness of the atmosphere had prevented from hardening. Moreover, in one of the walls was a projection, caused by a false chimney, or fireplace, that had been filled up, and made to resemble the rest of the cellar. I made no doubt that I could readily displace the bricks at this point, insert the corpse, and wall the whole up as before, so that no eye could detect any thing suspicious.

And in this calculation I was not deceived. By means of a crow-bar I easily dislodged the bricks, and, having carefully deposited the body against the inner wall, I propped it in that position, while, with little trouble, I re-laid the whole structure as it originally stood. Having procured mortar, sand, and hair, with every possible precaution, I prepared a plaster which could not be distinguished from the old, and with this I very carefully went over the new brick-work. When I had finished, I felt satisfied that all was right. The wall did not present the slightest appearance of having been disturbed. The rubbish on the floor was picked up with the minutest care. I looked around triumphantly, and said to myself—"Here at least, then, my labor has not been in vain."

My next step was to look for the beast which had been the cause of so much wretchedness; for I had, at length, firmly resolved to put it to death. Had I been able to meet with it, at the moment, there could have been no doubt of its fate; but it appeared that the crafty animal had been alarmed at the violence of my previous anger, and forebore to present itself in my present mood. It is impossible to describe, or to imagine, the deep, the blissful sense of relief which the absence of the detested creature occasioned in my bosom. It did not make its appearance during the night—and thus for one night at least, since its introduction into the house, I soundly and tranquilly slept; aye, *slept* even with the burden of murder upon my soul!

The second and the third day passed, and still my tormentor came not. Once again I breathed as a freeman. The monster, in terror, had fled the premises forever! I should behold it no more! My happiness was supreme! The guilt of my dark deed disturbed me but little. Some few inquiries had been made, but these had been readily answered. Even a search had been instituted—but of course nothing was to be discovered. I looked upon my future felicity as secured.

Upon the fourth day of the assassination, a party of the police came, very unexpectedly, into the house, and proceeded again to make rigorous investigation of the premises. Secure, however, in the inscrutability of my place of concealment, I felt no embarrassment whatever. The officers bade me accompany them in their search. They left no nook or corner unexplored. At length, for the third or fourth time, they descended into the cellar. I quivered not in a muscle. My heart beat calmly as that of one who slumbers in innocence. I walked the cellar from end to end. I folded my arms upon my bosom, and roamed easily to and fro. The police were thoroughly satisfied and prepared to depart. The glee at my heart was too strong to be restrained. I burned to say if but one word, by way of triumph, and to render doubly sure their assurance of my guiltlessness.

"Gentlemen," I said at last, as the party ascended the steps, "I delight to have allayed your suspicions. I wish you all health, and a little more courtesy. By the bye, gentlemen, this—this is a very well constructed house." [In the rabid desire to say something easily, I scarcely knew what I uttered at all.]—"I may say an *excellently* well constructed house. These walls—are you going, gentlemen?—these walls are solidly put together;" and here, through the mere phrenzy of bravado, I rapped heavily, with a cane which I held in my hand, upon that very portion of the brick-work behind which stood the corpse of the wife of my bosom.

But may God shield and deliver me from the fangs of the Arch-Fiend! No sooner had the reverberation of my blows sunk into silence, than I was answered by a voice from within the tomb!—by a cry, at first muffled and broken, like the sobbing of a child, and then quickly swelling into one long, loud, and continuous scream, utterly anomalous and inhuman—a howl—a wailing shriek, half of horror and half of triumph, such as might have arisen only out of hell, conjointly from the throats of the damned in their agony and of the demons that exult in the damnation.

Of my own thoughts it is folly to speak. Swooning, I staggered to the opposite wall. For one instant the party upon the stairs remained motionless, through extremity of terror and of awe. In the next, a dozen stout arms were toiling at the wall. It fell bodily. The corpse, already greatly decayed and clotted with gore, stood erect before the eyes of the spectators. Upon its head, with red extended mouth and solitary eye of fire, sat the hideous beast whose craft had seduced me into murder, and whose informing voice had consigned me to the hangman. I had walled the monster up within the tomb!

1843, 1845

The Purloined Letter[1]

At Paris, just after dark one gusty evening in the autumn of 18—, I was enjoying the twofold luxury of meditation and a meerschaum,[2] in company with my friend C. Auguste Dupin, in his little back library, or book-closet, *au troisième,*[3] No. 33, *Rue Dunôt, Faubourg St. Germain.* For one hour at least we had maintained a profound silence; while each, to any casual observer, might have seemed intently and exclusively occupied with the curling eddies of smoke that oppressed the atmosphere of the chamber. For myself, however, I was mentally discussing certain topics which had formed matter for conversation between us at an earlier period of the evening; I mean the affair of the Rue Morgue, and the mystery attending the murder of Marie Roget.[4] I looked upon it, therefore, as something of coincidence, when the door of our apartment was thrown open and admitted our old acquaintance, Monsieur G——, the Prefect of the Parisian police.

1. The text is that of the first publication in *The Gift*, a Philadelphia annual dated 1845 but for sale late in 1844. Historians of detective fiction usually cite Poe's three stories about C. Auguste Dupin as the first of the genre. This is the third Dupin story, the others being "The Murders in the Rue Morgue" (1841) and "The Mystery of Marie Rôget" (1842).
2. Tobacco pipe.
3. Actually the fourth floor (because the French do not count the first, the *rez-de-chaussée*).
4. The earlier cases solved by Dupin.

We gave him a hearty welcome; for there was nearly half as much of the entertaining as of the contemptible about the man, and we had not seen him for several years. We had been sitting in the dark, and Dupin now arose for the purpose of lighting a lamp, but sat down again, without doing so, upon G.'s saying that he had called to consult us, or rather to ask the opinion of my friend, about some official business which had occasioned a great deal of trouble.

"If it is any point requiring reflection," observed Dupin, as he forebore to enkindle the wick, "we shall examine it to better purpose in the dark."

"That is another of your odd notions," said the Prefect, who had a fashion of calling every thing "odd" that was beyond his comprehension, and thus lived amid an absolute legion of "oddities."

"Very true," said Dupin, as he supplied his visiter with a pipe, and rolled towards him a very comfortable chair.

"And what is the difficulty now?" I asked. "Nothing more in the assassination way, I hope?"

"Oh no; nothing of that nature. The fact is, the business is *very* simple indeed, and I make no doubt that we can manage it sufficiently well ourselves; but then I thought Dupin would like to hear the details of it, because it is so excessively *odd*."

"Simple and odd," said Dupin.

"Why, yes; and not exactly that, either. The fact is, we have all been a good deal puzzled because the affair *is* so simple, and yet baffles us altogether."

"Perhaps it is the very simplicity of the thing which puts you at fault," said my friend.

"What nonsense you *do* talk!" replied the Prefect, laughing heartily.

"Perhaps the mystery is a little *too* plain," said Dupin.

"Oh, good heavens! who ever heard of such an idea?"

"A little *too* self-evident."

"Ha! ha! ha!—ha! ha! ha!—ho! ho! ho!" roared out our visiter, profoundly amused, "oh, Dupin, you will be the death of me yet!"

"And what, after all, *is* the matter on hand?" I asked.

"Why, I will tell you," replied the Prefect, as he gave a long, steady, and contemplative puff, and settled himself in his chair. "I will tell you in a few words; but, before I begin, let me caution you that this is an affair demanding the greatest secrecy, and that I should most probably lose the position I now hold, were it known that I confided it to any one."

"Proceed," said I.

"Or not," said Dupin.

"Well, then; I have received personal information, from a very high quarter, that a certain document of the last importance, has been purloined from the royal apartments. The individual who purloined it is known; this beyond a doubt; he was seen to take it. It is known, also, that it still remains in his possession."

"How is this known?" asked Dupin.

"It is clearly inferred," replied the Prefect, "from the nature of the document, and from the non-appearance of certain results which would at once arise from its passing *out* of the robber's possession;—that is to say, from his employing it as he must design in the end to employ it."

"Be a little more explicit," I said.

"Well, I may venture so far as to say that the paper gives its holder a certain power in a certain quarter where such power is immensely valuable." The Prefect was fond of the cant of diplomacy.

"Still I do not quite understand," said Dupin.

"No? Well; the disclosure of the document to a third person, who shall be nameless, would bring in question the honour of a personage of most exalted station; and this fact gives the holder of the document an ascendancy over the illustrious personage whose honour and peace are so jeopardized."

"But this ascendancy," I interposed, "would depend upon the robber's knowledge of the loser's knowledge of the robber. Who would dare—"

"The thief," said G, "is the—Minister D——, who dares all things, those unbecoming as well as those becoming a man. The method of the theft was not less ingenious than bold. The document in question—a letter, to be frank—had been received by the personage robbed while alone in the royal boudoir. During its perusal she was suddenly interrupted by the entrance of the other exalted personage from whom especially it was her wish to conceal it. After a hurried and vain endeavour to thrust it in a drawer, she was forced to place it, open as it was, upon a table. The address, however, was uppermost, and the contents thus unexposed, the letter escaped notice. At this juncture enters the Minister D——. His lynx eye immediately perceives the paper, recognises the handwriting of the address, observes the confusion of the personage addressed, and fathoms her secret. After some business transactions, hurried through in his ordinary manner, he produces a letter somewhat similar to the one in question, opens it, pretends to read it, and then places it in close juxtaposition to the other. Again he converses, for some fifteen minutes, upon the public affairs. At length, in taking leave, he takes also from the table the letter to which he had no claim. Its rightful owner saw, but, of course, dared not call attention to the act, in the presence of the third personage who stood at her elbow. The minister decamped; leaving his own letter—one of no importance—upon the table."

"Here, then," said Dupin to me, "you have precisely what you demand to make the ascendancy complete—the robber's knowledge of the loser's knowledge of the robber."

"Yes," replied the Prefect; "and the power thus attained has, for some months past, been wielded, for political purposes, to a very dangerous extent. The personage robbed is more thoroughly convinced, every day, of the necessity of reclaiming her letter. But this, of course, cannot be done openly. In fine, driven to despair, she has committed the matter to me."

"Than whom," said Dupin, amid a perfect whirlwind of smoke, "no more sagacious agent could, I suppose, be desired, or even imagined."

"You flatter me," replied the Prefect; "but it is possible that some such opinion may have been entertained."

"It is clear," said I, "as you observe, that the letter is still in possession of the minister; since it is this possession, and not any employment, of the letter, which bestows the power. With the employment the power departs."

"True," said G——; "and upon this conviction I proceeded. My first care was to make thorough search of the minister's hotel; and here my chief embarrassment lay in the necessity of searching without his knowledge.

Beyond all things, I have been warned of the danger which would result from giving him reason to suspect our design."

"But," said I, "you are quite *au fait*[5] in these investigations. The Parisian police have done this thing often before."

"O yes; and for this reason I did not despair. The habits of the minister gave me, too, a great advantage. He is frequently absent from home all night. His servants are by no means numerous. They sleep at a distance from their master's apartments, and, being chiefly Neapolitans, are readily made drunk. I have keys, as you know, with which I can open any chamber or cabinet in Paris. For three months a night has not passed, during the greater part of which I have not been engaged, personally, in ransacking the D——Hotel. My honour is interested, and, to mention a great secret, the reward is enormous. So I did not abandon the search until I had become fully satisfied that the thief is a more astute man than myself. I fancy that I have investigated every nook and corner of the premises in which it is possible that the paper can be concealed."

"But is it not possible," I suggested, "that although the letter may be in possession of the minister, as it unquestionably is, he may have concealed it elsewhere than upon his own premises?"

"This is barely possible," said Dupin. "The present peculiar condition of affairs at court, and especially of those intrigues in which D—— is known to be involved, would render the instant availability of the document—its susceptibility of being produced at a moment's notice—a point of nearly equal importance with its possession."

"Its susceptibility of being produced?" said I.

"That is to say, of being *destroyed*," said Dupin.

"True," I observed; "the paper is clearly then upon the premises. As for its being upon the person of the minister, we may consider that as out of the question."

["Entirely," said the Prefect. "He has been twice waylaid, as if by footpads, and his person rigorously searched under my own inspection."

"You might have spared yourself this trouble," said Dupin. "D——, I presume, is not altogether a fool, and, if not, must have anticipated these waylayings, as a matter of course."

"Not *altogether* a fool," said G——, "but then he's a poet, which I take to be only one remove from a fool."]

"True;" said Dupin, after a long and thoughtful whiff from his meerschaum, "although I have been guilty of certain doggerel myself."

"Suppose you detail," said I, "the particulars of your search."

"Why the fact is, we took our time, and we searched *every where*. I have had long experience in these affairs. I took the entire building, room by room; devoting the nights of a whole week to each. We examined, first, the furniture of each apartment. We opened every possible drawer; and I presume you know that, to a properly trained police agent, such a thing as a *secret* drawer is impossible. Any man is a dolt who permits a 'secret' drawer to escape him in a search of this kind. The thing is *so* plain. There is a certain

5. Informed about (French).

amount of bulk—of space—to be accounted for in every cabinet. Then we have accurate rules. The fiftieth part of a line could not escape us. After the cabinets we took the chairs. The cushions we probed with the fine long needles you have seen me employ. From the tables we removed the tops."

"Why so?"

"Sometimes the top of a table, or other similarly arranged piece of furniture, is removed by the person wishing to conceal an article; then the leg is excavated, the article deposited within the cavity, and the top replaced. The bottoms and tops of bed-posts are employed in the same way."

"But could not the cavity be detected by sounding?" I asked.

"By no means, if, when the article is deposited, a sufficient wadding of cotton be placed around it. Besides, in our case, we were obliged to proceed without noise."

"But you could not have removed—you could not have taken to pieces *all* articles of furniture in which it would have been possible to make a deposit in the manner you mention. A letter may be compressed into a thin spiral roll, not differing much in shape or bulk from a large knitting-needle, and in this form it might be inserted into the rung of a chair, for example. You did not take to pieces all the chairs?"

"Certainly not; but we did better—we examined the rungs of every chair in the hotel, and, indeed, the jointings of every description of furniture, by the aid of a most powerful microscope.[6] Had there been any traces of recent disturbance we should not have failed to detect it *instanter*.[7] A single grain of gimlet-dust, or sawdust, for example, would have been as obvious as an apple. Any disorder in the glueing—any unusual gaping in the joints—would have sufficed to insure detection."

"Of course you looked to the mirrors, between the boards and the plates, and you probed the beds and the bed-clothes, as well as the curtains and carpets."

"That of course; and when we had absolutely completed every particle of the furniture in this way, then we examined the house itself. We divided its entire surface into compartments, which we numbered, so that none might be missed; then we scrutinized each individual square inch throughout the premises, including the two houses immediately adjoining, with the microscope, as before."

"The two houses adjoining!" I exclaimed; "you must have had a great deal of trouble."

"We had; but the reward offered is prodigious."

"You include the *grounds* about the houses?"

"All the grounds are paved with brick. They gave us comparatively little trouble. We examined the moss between the bricks, and found it undisturbed."

"And the roofs?"

"We surveyed every inch of the external surface, and probed carefully beneath every tile."

"You looked among D——'s papers, of course, and into the books of the library?"

6. A powerful magnifying glass.   7. Instantly (Latin).

"Certainly; we opened every package and parcel; we not only opened every book, but we turned over every leaf in each volume, not contenting ourselves with a mere shake, according to the fashion of some of our police officers. We also measured the thickness of every book-*cover*, with the most accurate admeasurement, and applied to them the most jealous scrutiny of the microscope. Had any of the bindings been recently meddled with, it would have been utterly impossible that the fact should have escaped observation. Some five or six volumes, just from the hands of the binder, we carefully probed, longitudinally, with the needles."

"You explored the floors beneath the carpets?"

"Beyond doubt. We removed every carpet, and examined the boards with the microscope."

"And the paper on the walls?"

"Yes."

"You looked into the cellars?"

"We did; and, as time and labour were no objects, we dug up every one of them to the depth of four feet."

"Then," I said, "you have been making a miscalculation, and the letter is *not* upon the premises, as you suppose."

"I fear you are right there," said the Prefect. "And now, Dupin, what would you advise me to do?"

"To make a thorough re-search of the premises."

"That is absolutely needless," replied G——. "I am not more sure that I breathe than I am that the letter is not at the Hotel."

"I have no better advice to give you," said Dupin. "You have, of course, an accurate description of the letter?"

"Oh yes!"—And here the Prefect, producing a memorandum-book, proceeded to read aloud a minute account of the internal, and especially of the external, appearance of the missing document. Soon after finishing the perusal of this description, he took his departure, more entirely depressed in spirits than I had ever known the good gentleman before.

In about a month afterwards he paid us another visit, and found us occupied very nearly as before. He took a pipe and a chair, and entered into some ordinary conversation. At length I said,—

"Well, but G——, what of the purloined letter? I presume you have at last made up your mind that there is no such thing as overreaching the Minister?"

"Confound him, say I—yes; I made the re-examination, however, as Dupin suggested—but it was all labour lost, as I knew it would be."

"How much was the reward offered, did you say?" asked Dupin.

"Why, a very great deal—a *very* liberal reward—I don't like to say how much, precisely; but one thing I *will* say, that I wouldn't mind giving my individual check for fifty thousand francs to any one who could obtain me that letter. The fact is, it is becoming of more and more importance every day; and the reward has been lately doubled. If it were trebled, however, I could do no more than I have done."

"Why, yes," said Dupin, drawlingly, between the whiffs of his meerschaum, "I really—think, G——, you have not exerted yourself—to the utmost in this matter. You might—do a little more, I think, eh?"

"How?—in what way?"

"Why—puff, puff—you might—puff, puff—employ counsel in the matter, eh?—puff, puff, puff. Do you remember the story they tell of Abernethy?"[8]

"No; hang Abernethy!"

"To be sure! hang him and welcome. But, once upon a time, a certain rich miser conceived the design of spunging upon this Abernethy for a medical opinion. Getting up, for this purpose, an ordinary conversation in a private company, he insinuated his case to the physician, as that of an imaginary individual.

"'We will suppose,' said the miser, 'that his symptoms are such and such; now, doctor, what would *you* have directed him to take?'

"'Take!' said Abernethy, 'why, take *advice*, to be sure.'"

"But," said the Prefect, a little discomposed, "*I am perfectly* willing to take advice, and to pay for it. I would *really* give fifty thousand francs, every *centime* of it, to any one who would aid me in the matter!"

"In that case," replied Dupin, opening a drawer, and producing a checkbook, "you may as well fill me up a check for the amount mentioned. When you have signed it, I will hand you the letter."

I was astounded. The Prefect appeared absolutely thunder-stricken. For some minutes he remained speechless and motionless, looking incredulously at my friend with open mouth, and eyes that seemed starting from their sockets; then, apparently recovering himself in some measure, he seized a pen, and after several pauses and vacant stares, finally filled up and signed a check for fifty thousand francs, and handed it across the table to Dupin. The latter examined it carefully and deposited it in his pocket-book; then, unlocking an *escritoire*,[9] took thence a letter and gave it to the Prefect. This functionary grasped it in a perfect agony of joy; opened it with a trembling hand, cast a rapid glance at its contents, and then, scrambling and struggling to the door, rushed at length unceremoniously from the room and from the house, without having uttered a solitary syllable since Dupin had requested him to fill up the check.

When he had gone, my friend entered into some explanations.

"The Parisian police," he said, "are exceedingly able in their way. They are persevering, ingenious, cunning, and thoroughly versed in the knowledge which their duties seem chiefly to demand. Thus when G—— detailed to us his mode of searching the premises at the Hotel D——, I felt the entire confidence in his having made a satisfactory investigation—so far as his labours extended."

"So far as his labours extended?" said I.

"Yes," said Dupin. "The measures adopted were not only the best of their kind, but carried out to absolute perfection. Had the letter been deposited within the range of their search, these fellows would, beyond a question, have found it."

I merely laughed—but he seemed quite serious in all that he said.

"The measures, then," he continued, "were good in their kind, and well executed; their defect lay in their being inapplicable to the case, and to the man. A certain set of highly ingenious resources are, with the Prefect, a sort

8. Probably the English surgeon John Abernethy (1764–1831).

9. Writing desk (French).

of Procrustean bed,[1] to which he forcibly adapts his designs. But he perpetually errs by being too deep or too shallow, for the matter in hand; and many a schoolboy is a better reasoner than he. I knew one about eight years of age, whose success at guessing in the game of 'even and odd' attracted universal admiration. This game is simple, and is played with marbles. One player holds in his hand a number of these toys; and demands of another whether that number is even or odd. If the guess is right, the guesser wins one; if wrong, he loses one. The boy to whom I allude won all the marbles of the school. Of course he had some principle of guessing; and this lay in mere observation and admeasurement of the astuteness of his opponents. For example, an arrant simpleton is his opponent, and, holding up his closed hand, asks, 'are they even or odd?' Our schoolboy replies 'odd,' and loses; but upon the second trial he wins, for he then says to himself, 'the simpleton had them even upon the first trial, and his amount of cunning is just sufficient to make him have them odd upon the second; I will therefore guess odd;'—he guesses odd, and wins. Now, with a simpleton a degree above the first, he would have reasoned thus: 'this fellow finds that in the first instance I guessed odd, and, in the second, he will propose to himself, upon the first impulse, a simple variation from even to odd, as did the first simpleton; but then a second thought will suggest that this is too simple a variation, and finally he will decide upon putting it even as before. I will therefore guess even;'—he guesses even, and wins. Now this mode of reasoning in the schoolboy, whom his fellows termed 'lucky,'—what, in its last analysis, is it?"

"It is merely," I said, "an identification of the reasoner's intellect with that of his opponent."

"It is," said Dupin; "and, upon inquiring of the boy by what means he effected the *thorough* identification in which his success consisted, I received answer as follows: 'When I wish to find out how wise, or how stupid, or how good, or how wicked is any one, or what are his thoughts at the moment, I fashion the expression of my face, as accurately as possible, in accordance with the expression of his, and then wait to see what thoughts or sentiments arise in my mind or heart, as if to match or correspond with the expression.' This response of the schoolboy lies at the bottom of all the spurious profundity which has been attributed to Rochefoucault, to La Bougive, to Machiavelli, and to Campanella."[2]

"And the identification," I said, "of the reasoner's intellect with that of his opponent, depends, if I understand you aright, upon the accuracy with which the opponent's intellect is admeasured."

"For its practical value it depends upon this," replied Dupin; "and the Prefect and his cohort fail so frequently, first, by default of this identification, and, secondly, by ill-admeasurement, or rather through non-admeasurement, of the intellect with which they are engaged. They consider only their *own* ideas of ingenuity; and, in searching for any thing hidden, advert only to the

---

1. Procrustes, legendary Greek bandit, made his victims fit the bed he bound them to, either by stretching them to the required length or by hacking off any surplus length in the feet and legs.
2. Philosophers of the 15th to 16th centuries who depicted human behavior as ultimately motivated by selfishness. Duc de la Rochefou-
cauld (1613–1680) and Jean de la Bruyère (1645–1696), French moralists. Niccolò Macchiavelli (1469–1527) and Tommaso Campanella (1568–1639), Italian philosophers. Poe used a variant spelling for Rochefoucauld, and his printer probably misread "La Bruyère" as "La Bougive."

modes in which *they* would have hidden it. They are right in this much—that their own ingenuity is a faithful representative of that of *the mass;* but when the cunning of the individual felon is diverse in character from their own, the felon foils them, of course. This always happens when it is above their own, and very usually when it is below. They have no variation of principle in their investigations; at best, when urged by some unusual emergency—by some extraordinary reward—they extend or exaggerate their old modes of *practice,* without touching their principles. What, for example, in this case of D——, has been done to vary the principle of action? What is all this boring, and probing, and sounding, and scrutinizing with the microscope, and dividing the surface of the building into registered square inches—what is it all but an exaggeration *of the application* of the one principle or set of principles of search, which are based upon the one set of notions regarding human ingenuity, to which the Prefect, in the long routine of his duty, has been accustomed? Do you not see he has taken it for granted that *all* men proceed to conceal a letter,—not exactly in a gimlet-hole bored in a chair-leg—but, at least, in *some* out-of-the-way hole or corner suggested by the same tenor of thought which would urge a man to secrete a letter in a gimlet-hole bored in a chair-leg? And do you not see also, that such *recherchés*[3] nooks for concealment are adapted only for ordinary occasions, and would be adopted only by ordinary intellects; for, in all cases of concealment, a disposal of the article concealed—a disposal of it in this *recherché* manner,—is, in the very first instance, presumed and presumable; and thus its discovery depends, not at all upon the acumen, but altogether upon the mere care, patience, and determination of the seekers; and where the case is of importance—or, what amounts to the same thing in the policial eyes, when the reward is of magnitude, the qualities in question have *never* been known to fail. You will now understand what I meant in suggesting that, had the purloined letter been hidden any where within the limits of the Prefect's examination—in other words, had the principle of its concealment been comprehended within the principles of the Prefect—its discovery would have been a matter altogether beyond question. This functionary, however, has been thoroughly mystified; and the remote source of his defeat lies in the supposition that the Minister is a fool, because he has acquired renown as a poet. All fools are poets; this the Prefect *feels*; and he is merely guilty of a *non distributio medii*[4] in thence inferring that all poets are fools."

"But is this really the poet?" I asked. "There are two brothers, I know; and both have attained reputation in letters. The Minister I believe has written learnedly on the Differential Calculus. He is a mathematician, and no poet."

"You are mistaken; I know him well; he is both. As poet *and* mathematician, he would reason well; as poet, profoundly; as mere mathematician, he could not have reasoned at all, and thus would have been at the mercy of the Prefect."

"You surprise me," I said, "by these opinions, which have been contradicted by the voice of the world. You do not mean to set at naught the well-digested idea of centuries. The mathematical reason has been long regarded as *the* reason *par excellence*."

---

3. Out of the ordinary, esoteric (French).   4. A logical fallacy (Latin).

"'Il y a à parier,' replied Dupin, quoting from Chamfort, 'que toute idée publique, toute convention reçue, est une sottise, car elle a convenue au plus grand nombre.'[5] The mathematicians, I grant you, have done their best to promulgate the popular error to which you allude, and which is none the less an error for its promulgation as truth. With an art worthy a better cause, for example, they have insinuated the term 'analysis' into application to algebra. The French are the originators of this particular deception; but if a term is of any importance—if words derive any value from applicability— then 'analysis' conveys 'algebra' about as much as, in Latin, *ambitus* implies 'ambition,' *religio* 'religion,' or *homines honesti*, a set of *honourable* men."

"You have a quarrel on hand, I see," said I, "with some of the algebraists of Paris; but proceed."

"I dispute the availability, and thus the value, of that reason which is culti- vated in any especial form other than the abstractly logical. I dispute, in par- ticular, the reason educed by mathematical study. The mathematics are the science of form and quantity; mathematical reasoning is merely logic applied to observation upon form and quantity. The great error lies in supposing that even the truths of what is called *pure* algebra, are abstract or general truths. And this error is so egregious that I am confounded at the universality with which it has been received. Mathematical axioms are *not* axioms of general truth. What is true of *relation*—of form and quantity—is often grossly false in regard to morals, for example. In this latter science it is very usually *untrue* that the aggregated parts are equal to the whole. In chemistry also the axiom fails. In the consideration of motive it fails; for two motives, each of a given value, have not, necessarily, a value when united, equal to the sum of their values apart. There are numerous other mathematical truths which are only truths within the limits of *relation*. But the mathematician argues, from his *finite truths*, through habit, as if they were of absolutely general applicabil- ity—as the world indeed imagines them to be. Bryant,[6] in his very learned 'Mythology,' mentions an analogous source of error, when he says that 'although the Pagan fables are not believed, yet we forget ourselves continu- ally, and make inferences from them as existing realities.' With the algebra- ist, however, who are Pagans themselves, the 'Pagan fables' *are* believed, and the inferences are made, not so much through lapse of memory, as through an unaccountable addling of the brains. In short, I never yet encountered the mere mathematician who could be trusted out of equal roots, or one who did not clandestinely hold it as a point of his faith x^2+px was absolutely and unconditionally equal to q. Say to one of these gentlemen, by way of experi- ment, if you please, that you believe occasions may occur where x^2+px is *not* altogether equal to q, and, having made him understand what you mean, get out of his reach as speedily as convenient, for, beyond doubt, he will endeav- our to knock you down.

"I mean to say," continued Dupin, while I merely laughed at his last observations, "that if the Minister had been no more than a mathematician, the Prefect would have been under no necessity of giving me this check.

5. The odds are that every common notion, every accepted convention, is nonsense, because it has suited itself to the majority (French). Sébastien Roch Nicolas Chamfort (1741–1794), author of *Maximes et Pensées.*

6. Jacob Bryant (1715–1804), English scholar who wrote *A New System, or an Analysis of Antient Mythology* (1774–76).

Had he been no more than a poet, I think it probable that he would have foiled us all. I knew him, however, as both mathematician and poet, and my measures were adapted to his capacity, with reference to the circumstances by which he was surrounded. I knew him as a courtier, too, and as a bold *intriguant.* Such a man, I considered, could not fail to be aware of the ordinary policial modes of action. He could not have failed to anticipate—and events have proved that he did not fail to anticipate—the waylayings to which he was subjected. He must have foreseen, I reflected, the secret investigations of his premises. His frequent absences from home at night, which were hailed by the Prefect as certain aids to his success, I regarded only as *ruses,* to afford opportunity for thorough search to the police, and thus the sooner to impress them with the conviction to which G——, in fact, did finally arrive—the conviction that the letter was not upon the premises. I felt, also, that the whole train of thought, which I was at some pains in detailing to you just now, concerning the invariable principle of policial action in searches for articles concealed—I felt that this whole train of thought would necessarily pass through the mind of the Minister. It would imperatively lead him to despise all the ordinary *nooks* of concealment. *He* could not, I reflected, be so weak as not to see that the most intricate and remote recess of his hotel would be as open as his commonest closets to the eyes, to the probes, to the gimlets, and to the microscopes of the Prefect. I saw, in fine, that he would be driven, as a matter of course, to *simplicity,* if not deliberately induced to it as a matter of choice. You will remember, perhaps how desperately the Prefect laughed when I suggested, upon our first interview, that it was just possible this mystery troubled him so much on account of its being so *very* self-evident."

"Yes," said I, "I remember his merriment well. I really thought he would have fallen into convulsions."

"The material world," continued Dupin, "abounds with very strict analogies to the immaterial; and thus some colour of truth has been given to the rhetorical dogma, that metaphor, or simile, may be made to strengthen an argument, as well as to embellish a description. The principle of the *vis inertiæ*,[7] for example, with the amount of *momentum* proportionate with it and consequent upon it, seems to be identical in physics and metaphysics. It is not more true in the former, that a large body is with more difficulty set in motion than a smaller one, and that its subsequent *impetus* is commensurate with this difficulty, than it is, in the latter, that intellects of the vaster capacity, while more forcible, more constant, and more eventful in their movements than those of inferior grade, are yet the less readily moved, and more embarrassed and full of hesitation in the first few steps of their progress. Again: have you ever noticed which of the street signs, over the shop-doors, are the most attractive of attention?"

"I have never given the matter a thought," I said.

"There is a game of puzzles," he resumed, "which is played upon a map. One party playing requires another to find a given word—the name of town, river, state, or empire—any word, in short, upon the motley and perplexed surface of the chart. A novice in the game generally seeks to embarrass his opponents by giving them the most minutely lettered names;

7. The power of inertia (Latin).

but the adept selects such words as stretch, in large characters, from one end of the chart to the other. These, like the over-largely lettered signs and placards of the street, escape observation by dint of being excessively obvious; and here the physical oversight is precisely analogous with the moral inapprehension by which the intellect suffers to pass unnoticed those considerations which are too obtrusively and too palpably self-evident. But this is a point, it appears, somewhat above or beneath the understanding of the Prefect. He never once thought it probable, or possible, that the Minister had deposited the letter immediately beneath the nose of the whole world, by way of best preventing any portion of that world from perceiving it.

"But the more I reflected upon the daring, dashing, and discriminating ingenuity of D——; upon the fact that the document must always have been *at hand*, if he intended to use it to good purpose; and upon the decisive evidence, obtained by the Prefect, that it was not hidden within the limits of that dignitary's ordinary search—the more satisfied I became that, to conceal this letter, the Minister had resorted to the comprehensive and sagacious expedient of not attempting to conceal it at all.

"Full of these ideas, I prepared myself with a pair of green spectacles, and called one fine morning, quite by accident, at the ministerial hotel. I found D—— at home, yawning, lounging, and dawdling as usual, and pretending to be in the last extremity of *ennui*.[8] He is, perhaps, the most really energetic human being now alive—but that is only when nobody sees him.

"To be even with him, I complained of my weak eyes, and lamented the necessity of the spectacles, under cover of which I cautiously and thoroughly surveyed the whole apartment, while seemingly intent only upon the conversation of my host.

"I paid especial attention to a large writing-table near which he sat, and upon which lay confusedly, some miscellanous letters and other papers, with one or two musical instruments and a few books. Here, however, after a long and very deliberate scrutiny, I saw nothing to excite particular suspicion.

"At length my eyes, in going the circuit of the room, fell upon a trumpery fillagree card-rack of pasteboard, that hung dangling by a dirty blue riband, from a little brass knob just beneath the middle of the mantel-piece. In this rack, which had three or four compartments, were five or six visiting-cards, and a solitary letter. This last was much soiled and crumpled. It was torn nearly in two, across the middle—as if a design, in the first instance, to tear it entirely up as worthless, had been altered, or stayed, in the second. It had a large black seal, bearing the D—— cipher *very* conspicuously, and was addressed, in a diminutive female hand, to D——, the minister himself. It was thrust carelessly, and even, as it seemed, contemptuously, into one of the uppermost divisions of the rack.

"No sooner had I glanced at this letter, than I concluded it to be that of which I was in search. To be sure, it was, to all appearance, radically different from the one of which the Prefect had read us so minute a description. Here the seal was large and black, with the D—— cipher; there, it was small and red, with the ducal arms of the S—— family. Here, the address, to the

8. Boredom (French).

minister, was diminutive and feminine; there, the superscription, to a certain royal personage, was markedly bold and decided; the size alone formed a point of correspondence. But, then, the *radicalness* of these differences, which was excessive; the dirt, the soiled and torn condition of the paper, so inconsistent with the *true* methodical habits of D——, and so suggestive of a design to delude the beholder into an idea of the worthlessness of the document; these things, together with the hyper-obtrusive situation of this document, full in the view of every visiter, and thus exactly in accordance with the conclusions to which I had previously arrived; these things, I say, were strongly corroborative of suspicion, in one who came with the intention to suspect.

"I protracted my visit as long as possible, and, while I maintained a most animated discussion with the minister, upon a topic which I knew well had never failed to interest and excite him, I kept my attention really riveted upon the letter. In this examination, I committed to memory its external appearance and arrangement in the rack; and also fell, at length, upon a discovery which set at rest whatever trivial doubt I might have entertained. In scrutinizing the edges of the paper, I observed them to be more *chafed* than seemed necessary. They presented the *broken* appearance which is manifested when a stiff paper, having been once folded and pressed with a folder, is refolded in a reversed direction, in the same creases or edges which had formed the original fold. This discovery was sufficient. It was clear to me that the letter had been turned, as a glove, inside out, re-directed, and re-sealed. I bade the minister good morning and took my departure at once, leaving a gold snuff-box upon the table.

"The next morning I called for the snuff-box, when we resumed, quite eagerly, the conversation of the preceding day. While thus engaged, however, a loud report, as if of a pistol, was heard immediately beneath the windows of the hotel, and was succeeded by a series of fearful screams, and the shoutings of a terrified mob. D—— rushed to a casement, threw it open, and looked out. In the meantime, I stepped to the card-rack, took the letter, put it in my pocket, and replaced it by a *fac-simile*, which I had carefully prepared at my lodgings—imitating the D—— cipher, very readily, by means of a seal formed of bread.

"The disturbance in the street had been occasioned by the frantic behaviour of a man with a musket. He had fired it among a crowd of women and children. It proved, however, to have been without ball, and the fellow was suffered to go his way as a lunatic or a drunkard. When he had gone, D—— came from the window, whither I had followed him immediately upon securing the object in view. Soon afterwards I bade him farewell. The pretended lunatic was a man in my own pay."

"But what purpose had you," I asked, "in replacing the letter by a *fac-simile*? Would it not have been better, at the first visit, to have seized it openly, and departed?"

"D——," replied Dupin, "is a desperate man, and a man of nerve. His hotel, too, is not without attendants devoted to his interests. Had I made the wild attempt you suggest, I should never have left the ministerial presence alive. The good people of Paris would have heard of me no more. But I had an object apart from these considerations. You know my political prepossessions. In this matter, I act as a partisan of the lady concerned.

For eighteen months the minister has had her in his power. She has now him in hers—since, being unaware that the letter is not in his possession, he will proceed with his exactions as if it was. Thus will he inevitably commit himself, at once, to his political destruction. His downfall, too, will not be more precipitate than awkward. It is all very well to talk about the *facilis descensus Averni*;[9] but in all kinds of climbing, as Catalini[1] said of singing, it is far more easy to get up than to come down. In the present instance I have no sympathy—at least no pity for him who descends. He is that *monstrum horrendum*,[2] an unprincipled man of genius. I confess, however, that I should like very well to know the precise character of his thoughts, when, being defied by her whom the Prefect terms 'a certain personage,' he is reduced to opening the letter which I left for him in the card-rack."

"How? did you put any thing particular in it?"

"Why—it did not seem altogether right to leave the interior blank—that would have been insulting. To be sure, D——, at Vienna once, did me an evil turn, which I told him, quite good-humouredly, that I should remember. So, as I knew he would feel some curiosity in regard to the identity of the person who had outwitted him, I thought it a pity not to give him a clue. He is well acquainted with my MS., and I just copied into the middle of the blank sheet the words—

> "'—Un dessein si funeste,
> S'il n'est digne d'Atrée, est digne de Thyeste.'

They are to be found in Crébillon's 'Atrée.'"[3]

1844

The Cask of Amontillado[1]

The thousand injuries of Fortunato I had borne as I best could, but when he ventured upon insult I vowed revenge. You, who so well know the nature of my soul, will not suppose, however, that I gave utterance to a threat. *At length* I would be avenged; this was a point definitively settled—but the very definitiveness with which it was resolved precluded the idea of risk. I must not only punish but punish with impunity. A wrong is unredressed when retribution overtakes its redresser. It is equally unredressed when the avenger fails to make himself felt as such to him who has done the wrong.

It must be understood that neither by word nor deed had I given Fortunato cause to doubt my good will. I continued, as was my wont, to smile in

---

9. From Virgil's *Aeneid*, book 6: "The descent to Avernus [Hell] is easy."
1. Angelica Catalani (1780–1849), Italian singer.
2. "Dreadful monstrosity" (Virgil's epithet for Polyphemus, the one-eyed man-eating giant, in book 3 of the *Aeneid*).
3. Prosper Jolyot de Crébillon (1674–1762) wrote *Atrée et Thyeste* (1707), in which the Greek mythological figure Thyestes seduces the wife of his

brother Atreus, the king of Mycenae; in revenge Atreus murders the three sons of Thyestes and cooks them up to serve to their father at a feast. The quotation reads: "So baneful a scheme, / if not worthy of Atreus, is worthy of Thyestes" (French).
1. The text is that of the first publication, in *Godey's Magazine and Lady's Book* 33 (November 1846).

his face, and he did not perceive that my smile *now* was at the thought of his immolation.

He had a weak point—this Fortunato—although in other regards he was a man to be respected and even feared. He prided himself upon his connoisseurship in wine. Few Italians have the true virtuoso spirit. For the most part their enthusiasm is adopted to suit the time and opportunity, to practice imposture upon the British and Austrian *millionaires*. In painting and gemmary, Fortunato, like his countrymen, was a quack, but in the matter of old wines he was sincere. In this respect I did not differ from him materially;—I was skilful in the Italian vintages myself, and bought largely whenever I could.

It was about dusk, one evening during the supreme madness of the carnival season, that I encountered my friend. He accosted me with excessive warmth, for he had been drinking much. The man wore motley.[2] He had on a tight-fitting parti-striped dress, and his head was surmounted by the conical cap and bells. I was so pleased to see him that I thought I should never have done wringing his hand.

I said to him—"My dear Fortunato, you are luckily met. How remarkably well you are looking to-day. But I have received a pipe of what passes for Amontillado,[3] and I have my doubts."

"How?" said he. "Amontillado? A pipe? Impossible! And in the middle of the carnival!"

"I have my doubts," I replied; "and I was silly enough to pay the full Amontillado price without consulting you in the matter. You were not to be found, and I was fearful of losing a bargain."

"Amontillado!"

"I have my doubts."

"Amontillado!"

"And I must satisfy them."

"Amontillado!"

"As you are engaged, I am on my way to Luchresi. If any one has a critical turn it is he. He will tell me——"

"Luchresi cannot tell Amontillado from Sherry."

"And yet some fools will have it that his taste is a match for your own."

"Come, let us go."

"Whither?"

"To your vaults."

"My friend, no; I will not impose upon your good nature. I perceive you have an engagement. Luchresi——"

"I have no engagement;—come."

"My friend, no. It is not the engagement, but the severe cold with which I perceive you are afflicted. The vaults are insufferably damp. They are encrusted with nitre."[4]

"Let us go, nevertheless. The cold is merely nothing. Amontillado! You have been imposed upon. And as for Luchresi, he cannot distinguish Sherry from Amontillado."

2. A multicolored costume worn by clowns and jesters.

3. A light Spanish sherry. "Pipe": a large barrel.
4. Niter; potassium nitrate.

Thus speaking, Fortunato possessed himself of my arm; and putting on a mask of black silk and drawing a *roquelaire*[5] closely about my person, I suffered him to hurry me to my palazzo.

There were no attendants at home; they had absconded to make merry in honour of the time. I had told them that I should not return until the morning, and had given them explicit orders not to stir from the house. These orders were sufficient, I well knew, to insure their immediate disappearance, one and all, as soon as my back was turned.

I took from their sconces two flambeaux,[6] and giving one to Fortunato, bowed him through several suites of rooms to the archway that led into the vaults. I passed down a long and winding staircase, requesting him to be cautious as he followed. We came at length to the foot of the descent, and stood together upon the damp ground of the catacombs of the Montresors.

The gait of my friend was unsteady, and the bells upon his cap jingled as he strode.

"The pipe," said he.

"It is farther on," said I; "but observe the white web-work which gleams from these cavern walls."

He turned towards me, and looked into my eyes with two filmy orbs that distilled the rheum of intoxication.

"Nitre?" he asked, at length.

"Nitre," I replied. "How long have you had that cough?"

"Ugh! ugh! ugh!—ugh! ugh! ugh!—ugh! ugh! ugh!—ugh! ugh! ugh!—ugh! ugh! ugh!"

My poor friend found it impossible to reply for many minutes.

"It is nothing," he said, at last.

"Come," I said, with decision, "we will go back; your health is precious. You are rich, respected, admired, beloved; you are happy, as once I was. You are a man to be missed. For me it is no matter. We will go back; you will be ill, and I cannot be responsible. Besides, there is Luchresi——"

"Enough," he said; "the cough is a mere nothing; it will not kill me. I shall not die of a cough."

"True—true," I replied; "and, indeed, I had no intention of alarming you unneccessarily—but you should use all proper caution. A draught of this Medoc[7] will defend us from the damps."

Here I knocked off the neck of a bottle which I drew from a long row of its fellows that lay upon the mould.

"Drink," I said, presenting him the wine.

He raised it to his lips with a leer. He paused and nodded to me familiarly, while his bells jingled.

"I drink," he said, "to the buried that repose around us."

"And I to your long life."

He again took my arm, and we proceeded.

"These vaults," he said, "are extensive."

"The Montresors," I replied, "were a great and numerous family."

"I forget your arms."

---

5. A knee-length cloak.
6. Flaming torches. "Sconces": holders.

7. Red wine from the Bordeaux region of France.

"A huge human foot d'or, in a field azure; the foot crushes a serpent rampant whose fangs are imbedded in the heel."[8]

"And the motto?"

"*Nemo me impune lacessit.*"[9]

"Good!" he said.

The wine sparkled in his eyes and the bells jingled. My own fancy grew warm with the Medoc. We had passed through long walls of piled skeletons, with casks and puncheons[1] intermingling, into the inmost recesses of the catacombs. I paused again, and this time I made bold to seize Fortunato by an arm above the elbow.

"The nitre!" I said; "see, it increases. It hangs like moss upon the vaults. We are below the river's bed. The drops of moisture trickle among the bones. Come, we will go back ere it is too late. Your cough——"

"It is nothing," he said; "let us go on. But first, another draught of the Medoc."

I broke and reached him a flaçon of De Grâve.[2] He emptied it at a breath. His eyes flashed with a fierce light. He laughed and threw the bottle upwards with a gesticulation I did not understand.

I looked at him in surprise. He repeated the movement—a grotesque one.

"You do not comprehend?" he said.

"Not I," I replied.

"Then you are not of the brotherhood."

"How?"

"You are not of the masons."[3]

"Yes, yes," I said; "yes, yes."

"You? Impossible! A mason?"

"A mason," I replied.

"A sign," he said, "a sign."

"It is this," I answered, producing from beneath the folds of my *roquelaire* a trowel.

"You jest," he exclaimed, recoiling a few paces. "But let us proceed to the Amontillado."

"Be it so," I said, replacing the tool beneath the cloak and again offering him my arm. He leaned upon it heavily. We continued our rout in search of the Amontillado. We passed through a range of low arches, descended, passed on, and descending again, arrived at a deep crypt, in which the foulness of the air caused our flambeaux rather to glow than flame.

At the most remote end of the crypt there appeared another less spacious. Its walls had been lined with human remains, piled to the vault overhead, in the fashion of the great catacombs of Paris. Three sides of this interior crypt were still ornamented in this manner. From the fourth side the bones had been thrown down, and lay promiscuously upon the earth, forming at one point a mound of some size. Within the wall thus exposed by the displacing of the bones, we perceived a still interior crypt or recess, in depth about four

8. On the coat of arms the golden foot is in a blue background; the foot crushes a serpent whose head is reared up and biting.

9. No one insults me with impunity (Latin).

1. Large casks.

2. A Bordeaux wine.

3. International and secretive fraternal organization thought to have originated among stonemasons and cathedral builders in the Middle Ages, whose members identified themselves to each other through hand signs.

feet, in width three, in height six or seven. It seemed to have been constructed for no especial use within itself, but formed merely the interval between two of the colossal supports of the roof of the catacombs, and was backed by one of their circumscribing walls of solid granite.

It was in vain that Fortunato, uplifting his dull torch, endeavoured to pry into the depth of the recess. Its termination the feeble light did not enable us to see.

"Proceed," I said; "herein is the Amontillado. As for Luchresi——"

"He is an ignoramus," interrupted my friend, as he stepped unsteadily forward, while I followed immediately at his heels. In an instant he had reached the extremity of the niche, and finding his progress arrested by the rock, stood stupidly bewildered. A moment more and I had fettered him to the granite. In its surface were two iron staples, distant from each other about two feet, horizontally. From one of these depended a short chain, from the other a padlock. Throwing the links about his waist, it was but the work of a few seconds to secure it. He was too much astounded to resist. Withdrawing the key I stepped back from the recess.

"Pass your hand," I said, "over the wall; you cannot help feeling the nitre. Indeed, it is *very* damp. Once more let me *implore* you to return. No? Then I must positively leave you. But I will first render you all the little attentions in my power."

"The Amontillado!" ejaculated my friend, not yet recovered from his astonishment.

"True," I replied; "the Amontillado."

As I said these words I busied myself among the pile of bones of which I have before spoken. Throwing them aside, I soon uncovered a quantity of building stone and mortar. With these materials and with the aid of my trowel, I began vigorously to wall up the entrance of the niche.

I had scarcely laid the first tier of the masonry when I discovered that the intoxication of Fortunato had in great measure worn off. The earliest indication I had of this was a low moaning cry from the depth of the recess. It was *not* the cry of a drunken man. There was then a long and obstinate silence. I laid the second tier, and the third, and the fourth; and then I heard the furious vibration of the chain. The noise lasted for several minutes, during which, that I might hearken to it with the more satisfaction, I ceased my labours and sat down upon the bones. When at last the clanking subsided, I resumed the trowel, and finished without interruption the fifth, the sixth, and the seventh tier. The wall was now nearly upon a level with my breast. I again paused, and holding the flambeaux over the mason-work, threw a few feeble rays upon the figure within.

A succession of loud and shrill screams, bursting suddenly from the throat of the chained form, seemed to thrust me violently back. For a brief moment I hesitated, I trembled. Unsheathing my rapier, I began to grope with it about the recess; but the thought of an instant reassured me. I placed my hand upon the solid fabric of the catacombs and felt satisfied. I reapproached the wall. I replied to the yells of him who clamoured. I re-echoed, I aided, I surpassed them in volume and in strength. I did this, and the clamourer grew still.

It was now midnight, and my task was drawing to a close. I had completed the eighth, the ninth and the tenth tier. I had finished a portion of the last and the eleventh; there remained but a single stone to be fitted and plastered in. I struggled with its weight; I placed it partially in its destined position. But now there came from out the niche a low laugh that erected the hairs upon my head. It was succeeded by a sad voice, which I had difficulty in recognizing as that of the noble Fortunato. The voice said—

"Ha! ha! ha!—he! he! he!—a very good joke, indeed—an excellent jest. We will have many a rich laugh about it at the palazzo—he! he! he!—over our wine—he! he! he!"

"The Amontillado!" I said.

"He! he! he!—he! he! he!—yes, the Amontillado. But is it not getting late? Will not they be awaiting us at the palazzo—the Lady Fortunato and the rest? Let us be gone."

"Yes," I said, "let us be gone."

"*For the love of God, Montresor!*"

"Yes," I said, "for the love of God!"

But to these words I hearkened in vain for a reply. I grew impatient. I called aloud—

"Fortunato!"

No answer. I called again—

"Fortunato!"

No answer still. I thrust a torch through the remaining aperture and let it fall within. There came forth in return only a jingling of the bells. My heart grew sick; it was the dampness of the catacombs that made it so. I hastened to make an end of my labour. I forced the last stone into its position; I plastered it up. Against the new masonry I re-erected the old rampart of bones. For the half of a century no mortal has disturbed them. *In pace requiescat!*[4]

1846

The Philosophy of Composition[1]

Charles Dickens, in a note[2] now lying before me, alluding to an examination I once made of the mechanism of "Barnaby Rudge," says—"By the way, are you aware that Godwin wrote his 'Caleb Williams' backwards? He first involved his hero in a web of difficulties, forming the second volume, and then, for the first, cast about him for some mode of accounting for what had been done."[3]

I cannot think this the *precise* mode of procedure on the part of Godwin—and indeed what he himself acknowledges, is not altogether in accordance with Mr. Dickens' idea—but the author of "Caleb Williams" was too good an artist not to perceive the advantage derivable from at least a somewhat simi-

4. May he rest in peace! (Latin).
1. Poe wrote this as a lecture in hopes of capitalizing on the success of "The Raven." Poe, an advocate of rational composition rather than Romantic effusions, here presents an account of how he wrote "The Raven" that may or may not be factual. In a letter of August 9, 1846, Poe called the essay his "best specimen of analysis." The text here is that of the first printing, in *Graham's*

Magazine (April 1846).
2. Letter dated March 6, 1842.
3. William Godwin makes this claim in his 1832 preface to *Caleb Williams* (first published in 1794). As *Barnaby Rudge* was being serialized in 1842, Poe published an analysis of the novel that identified the murderer and correctly predicted the ending.

lar process. Nothing is more clear than that every plot, worth the name, must be elaborated to its *dénouement*[4] before any thing be attempted with the pen. It is only with the *dénouement* constantly in view that we can give a plot its indispensable air of consequence, or causation, by making the incidents, and especially the tone at all points, tend to the development of the intention.

There is a radical error, I think, in the usual mode of constructing a story. Either history affords a thesis—or one is suggested by an incident of the day—or, at best, the author sets himself to work in the combination of striking events to form merely the basis of his narrative—designing, generally, to fill in with description, dialogue, or autorial comment, whatever crevices of fact, or action, may, from page to page, render themselves apparent.

I prefer commencing with the consideration of an *effect*. Keeping originality *always* in view—for he is false to himself who ventures to dispense with so obvious and so easily attainable a source of interest—I say to myself, in the first place, "Of the innumerable effects, or impressions, of which the heart, the intellect, or (more generally) the soul is susceptible, what one shall I, on the present occasion, select?" Having chosen a novel, first, and secondly a vivid effect, I consider whether it can best be wrought by incident or tone—whether by ordinary incidents and peculiar tone, or the converse, or by peculiarity both of incident and tone—afterward looking about me (or rather within) for such combinations of event, or tone, as shall best aid me in the construction of the effect.

I have often thought how interesting a magazine paper might be written by any author who would—that is to say, who could—detail, step by step, the processes by which any one of his compositions attained its ultimate point of completion. Why such a paper has never been given to the world, I am much at a loss to say—but, perhaps, the autorial vanity has had more to do with the omission than any one other cause. Most writers—poets in especial—prefer having it understood that they compose by a species of fine frenzy[5]—an ecstatic intuition—and would positively shudder at letting the public take a peep behind the scenes, at the elaborate and vacillating crudities of thought—at the true purposes seized only at the last moment—at the innumerable glimpses of idea that arrived not at the maturity of full view—at the fully matured fancies discarded in despair as unmanageable—at the cautious selections and rejections—at the painful erasures and interpolations—in a word, at the wheels and pinions—the tackle for scene-shifting—the step-ladders and demon-traps—the cock's feathers, the red paint and the black patches, which, in ninety-nine cases out of the hundred, constitute the properties of the literary *histrio*.[6]

I am aware, on the other hand, that the case is by no means common, in which an author is at all in condition to retrace the steps by which his conclusions have been attained. In general, suggestions, having arisen pell-mell, are pursued and forgotten in a similar manner.

---

4. The final revelation showing the outcome, or untying, of the plot. From *dénouer* (French), "to untie."
5. The character Theseus's description of the poet in Shakespeare's *A Midsummer Night's Dream* 5.1.12: "The poet's eye, in a fine frenzy rolling, / Doth glance from heaven to earth, from earth to heaven / And as imagination bodies forth / The forms of things unknown, the poet's pen / Turns them to shapes, and gives to airy nothing / A local habitation and a name."
6. Artist (Latin).

For my own part, I have neither sympathy with the repugnance alluded to, nor, at any time, the least difficulty in recalling to mind the progressive steps of any of my compositions; and, since the interest of an analysis, or reconstruction, such as I have considered a *desideratum*,[7] is quite independent of any real or fancied interest in the thing analyzed, it will not be regarded as a breach of decorum on my part to show the *modus operandi*[8] by which some one of my own works was put together. I select "The Raven," as the most generally known. It is my design to render it manifest that no one point in its composition is referrible either to accident or intuition—that the work proceeded, step by step, to its completion with the precision and rigid consequence of a mathematical problem.

Let us dismiss, as irrelevant to the poem *per se*, the circumstance—or say the necessity—which, in the first place, gave rise to the intention of composing *a* poem that should suit at once the popular and the critical taste.

We commence, then, with this intention.

The initial consideration was that of extent. If any literary work is too long to be read at one sitting, we must be content to dispense with the immensely important effect derivable from unity of impression—for, if two sittings be required, the affairs of the world interfere, and every thing like totality is at once destroyed. But since, *ceteris paribus*,[9] no poet can afford to dispense with *any thing* that may advance his design, it but remains to be seen whether there is, in extent, any advantage to counterbalance the loss of unity which attends it. Here I say no, at once. What we term a long poem is, in fact, merely a succession of brief ones—that is to say, of brief poetical effects. It is needless to demonstrate that a poem is such, only inasmuch as it intensely excites, by elevating, the soul; and all intense excitements are, through a psychal necessity, brief. For this reason, at least one half of the "Paradise Lost"[1] is essentially prose—a succession of poetical excitements interspersed, *inevitably*, with corresponding depressions—the whole being deprived, through the extremeness of its length, of the vastly important artistic element, totality, or unity, of effect.

It appears evident, then, that there is a distinct limit, as regards length, to all works of literary art—the limit of a single sitting—and that, although in certain classes of prose composition, such as "Robinson Crusoe,"[2] (demanding no unity,) this limit may be advantageously overpassed, it can never properly be overpassed in a poem. Within this limit, the extent of a poem may be made to bear mathematical relation to its merit—in other words, to the excitement or elevation—again in other words, to the degree of the true poetical effect which it is capable of inducing; for it is clear that the brevity must be in direct ratio of the intensity of the intended effect:— this, with one proviso—that a certain degree of duration is absolutely requisite for the production of any effect at all.

Holding in view these considerations, as well as that degree of excitement which I deemed not above the popular, while not below the critical, taste, I

---

7. Something to be desired (Latin).
8. Method of procedure (Latin).
9. Other things being equal (Latin).
1. For Poe, John Milton's blank verse epic (1667)

of some 10,500 lines is much too long to be poetry all the way through.
2. Daniel Defoe's novel of shipwreck in the Caribbean (1719).

reached at once what I conceived the proper *length* for my intended poem—a length of about one hundred lines. It is, in fact, a hundred and eight.

My next thought concerned the choice of an impression, or effect, to be conveyed: and here I may as well observe that, throughout the construction, I kept steadily in view the design of rendering the work *universally* appreciable. I should be carried too far out of my immediate topic were I to demonstrate a point upon which I have repeatedly insisted, and which, with the poetical, stands not in the slightest need of demonstration—the point, I mean, that Beauty is the sole legitimate province of the poem. A few words, however, in elucidation of my real meaning, which some of my friends have evinced a disposition to misrepresent. That pleasure which is at once the most intense, the most elevating, and the most pure, is, I believe, found in the contemplation of the beautiful. When, indeed, men speak of Beauty, they mean, precisely, not a quality, as is supposed, but an effect—they refer, in short, just to that intense and pure elevation of *soul*—*not* of intellect, or of heart—upon which I have commented, and which is experienced in consequence of contemplating "the beautiful." Now I designate Beauty as the province of the poem, merely because it is an obvious rule of Art that effects should be made to spring from direct causes—that objects should be attained through means best adapted for their attainment—no one as yet having been weak enough to deny that the peculiar elevation alluded to, is *most readily* attained in the poem. Now the object, Truth, or the satisfaction of the intellect, and the object, Passion, or the excitement of the heart, are, although attainable, to a certain extent, in poetry, far more readily attainable in prose. Truth, in fact, demands a precision, and Passion, a *homeliness* (the truly passionate will comprehend me) which are absolutely antagonistic to that Beauty which, I maintain, is the excitement, or pleasurable elevation, of the soul. It by no means follows from any thing here said, that passion, or even truth, may not be introduced, and even profitably introduced, into a poem—for they may serve in elucidation, or aid the general effect, as do discords in music, by contrast—but the true artist will always contrive, first, to tone them into proper subserviency to the predominant aim, and, secondly, to enveil them, as far as possible, in that Beauty which is the atmosphere and the essence of the poem.

Regarding, then, Beauty as my province, my next question referred to the *tone* of its highest manifestation—and all experience has shown that this tone is one of *sadness.* Beauty of whatever kind, in its supreme development, invariably excites the sensitive soul to tears. Melancholy is thus the most legitimate of all the poetical tones.

The length, the province, and the tone, being thus determined, I betook myself to ordinary induction, with the view of obtaining some artistic piquancy which might serve me as a key-note in the construction of the poem—some pivot upon which the whole structure might turn. In carefully thinking over all the usual artistic effects—or more properly *points,* in the theatrical sense—I did not fail to perceive immediately that no one had been so universally employed as that of the *refrain.* The universality of its employment sufficed to assure me of its intrinsic value, and spared me the necessity of submitting it to analysis. I considered it, however, with regard to its susceptibility of improvement, and soon saw it to be in a primitive condition. As commonly used, the *refrain*, or burden, not only is limited to lyric verse, but depends for its impression upon the force of monotone—both in sound and thought. The pleasure is deduced solely from the sense of identity—of repetition. I resolved to diversify, and so vastly heighten, the effect, by adhering, in general, to the monotone of sound, while I continually varied that of thought: that is to say, I determined to produce continuously novel effects, by the variation *of the application* of the *refrain*—the *refrain* itself remaining, for the most part, unvaried.

These points being settled, I next bethought me of the *nature* of my *refrain*. Since its application was to be repeatedly varied, it was clear that the *refrain* itself must be brief, for there would have been an insurmountable difficulty in frequent variations of application in any sentence of length. In proportion to the brevity of the sentence, would, of course, be the facility of the variation. This led me at once to a single word as the best *refrain*.

The question now arose as to the *character* of the word. Having made up my mind to a *refrain*, the division of the poem into stanzas was, of course, a corollary: the *refrain* forming the close to each stanza. That such a close, to have force, must be sonorous and susceptible of protracted emphasis, admitted no doubt: and these considerations inevitably led me to the long *o* as the most sonorous vowel, in connection with *r* as the most producible consonant.

The sound of the *refrain* being thus determined, it became necessary to select a word embodying this sound, and at the same time in the fullest possible keeping with that melancholy which I had predetermined as the tone of the poem. In such a search it would have been absolutely impossible to overlook the word "Nevermore." In fact, it was the very first which presented itself.

The next *desideratum* was a pretext for the continuous use of the one word "nevermore." In observing the difficulty which I at once found in inventing a sufficiently plausible reason for its continuous repetition, I did not fail to perceive that this difficulty arose solely from the pre-assumption that the word was to be so continuously or monotonously spoken by *a human* being—I did not fail to perceive, in short, that the difficulty lay in the reconciliation of this monotony with the exercise of reason on the part of the creature repeating the word. Here, then, immediately arose the idea of a *non*-reasoning creature capable of speech; and, very naturally, a parrot, in the first instance, suggested itself, but was superseded forthwith by a Raven, as equally capable of speech, and infinitely more in keeping with the intended *tone*.

I had now gone so far as the conception of a Raven—the bird of ill omen—monotonously repeating the one word, "Nevermore," at the conclusion of each stanza, in a poem of melancholy tone, and in length about one hundred lines. Now, never losing sight of the object *supremeness*, or perfection, at all points, I asked myself—"Of all melancholy topics, what, according to the *universal* understanding of mankind, is the *most* melancholy?" Death—was the obvious reply. "And when," I said, "is this most melancholy of topics most poetical?" From what I have already explained at some length, the answer, here also, is obvious—"When it most closely allies itself to *Beauty*: the death, then, of a beautiful woman is, unquestionably, the most poetical topic in the world—and equally is it beyond doubt that the lips best suited for such topic are those of a bereaved lover."

I had now to combine the two ideas, of a lover lamenting his deceased mistress and a Raven continuously repeating the word "Nevermore"—I had to combine these, bearing in mind my design of varying, at every turn, the *application* of the word repeated; but the only intelligible model of such combination is that of imagining the Raven employing the word in answer to the queries of the lover. And here it was that I saw at once the opportunity afforded for the effect on which I had been depending—that is to say, the effect of the *variation of application*. I saw that I could make the first query propounded by the lover—the first query to which the Raven should reply "Nevermore"—that I could make this first query a commonplace one—the second less so—the third still less, and so on—until at length the lover, startled from his original *nonchalance* by the melancholy character of the word itself—by its frequent repetition—and by a consideration of the ominous reputation of the fowl that uttered it—is at length excited to superstition, and wildly propounds queries of a far different character—queries whose solution he has passionately at heart—propounds them half in superstition and half in that species of despair which delights in self-torture—propounds them not altogether because he believes in the prophetic or demoniac character of the bird (which, reason assures him, is merely repeating a lesson learned by rote) but because he experiences a phrenzied pleasure in so modeling his questions as to receive from the *expected* "Nevermore" the most delicious because the most intolerable of sorrow. Perceiving the opportunity thus afforded me—or, more strictly, thus forced upon me in the progress of the construction—I first established in mind the climax, or concluding query—that to which "Nevermore" should be in the last place an answer—that in reply to which this word "Nevermore" should involve the utmost conceivable amount of sorrow and despair.

Here then the poem may be said to have its beginning—at the end, where all works of art should begin—for it was here, at this point of my preconsiderations, that I first put pen to paper in the composition of the stanza:

> "Prophet," said I, "thing of evil! prophet still if bird or devil!
> By that heaven that bends above us—by that God we both adore,
> Tell this soul with sorrow laden, if within the distant Aidenn,
> It shall clasp a sainted maiden whom the angels name Lenore—
> Clasp a rare and radiant maiden whom the angels name Lenore."
> Quoth the raven "Nevermore."

I composed this stanza, at this point, first that, by establishing the climax, I might the better vary and graduate, as regards seriousness and importance, the preceding queries of the lover—and, secondly, that I might definitely settle the rhythm, the metre, and the length and general arrangement of the stanza—as well as graduate the stanzas which were to precede, so that none of them might surpass this in rhythmical effect. Had I been able, in the subsequent composition, to construct more vigorous stanzas, I should, without scruple, have purposely enfeebled them, so as not to interfere with the climacteric effect.

And here I may as well say a few words of the versification. My first object (as usual) was originality. The extent to which this has been neglected, in versification, is one of the most unaccountable things in the world. Admitting that there is little possibility of variety in mere *rhythm*, it is still clear that the possible varieties of metre and stanza are absolutely infinite—and yet, *for centuries, no man, in verse, has ever done, or ever seemed to think of doing, an original thing.* The fact is, originality (unless in minds of very unusual force) is by no means a matter, as some suppose, of impulse or intuition. In general, to be found, it must be elaborately sought, and although a positive merit of the highest class, demands in its attainment less of invention than negation.

Of course, I pretend to no originality in either the rhythm or metre of the "Raven." The former is trochaic—the latter is octameter acatalectic, alternating with heptameter catalectic repeated in the *refrain* of the fifth verse, and terminating with tetrameter catalectic. Less pedantically—the feet employed throughout (trochees) consist of a long syllable followed by a short: the first line of the stanza consists of eight of these feet—the second of seven and a half (in effect two-thirds)—the third of eight—the fourth of seven and a half—the fifth the same—the sixth three and a half. Now, each of these lines, taken individually, has been employed before, and what originality the "Raven" has, is in their *combination into stanza*; nothing even remotely approaching this combination has ever been attempted. The effect of this originality of combination is aided by other unusual, and some altogether novel effects, arising from an extension of the application of the principles of rhyme and alliteration.

The next point to be considered was the mode of bringing together the lover and the Raven—and the first branch of this consideration was the *locale*. For this the most natural suggestion might seem to be a forest, or the fields—but it has always appeared to me that a close *circumscription of space* is absolutely necessary to the effect of insulated incident:—it has the force of a frame to a picture. It has an indisputable moral power in keeping concentrated the attention, and, of course, must not be confounded with mere unity of place.

I determined, then, to place the lover in his chamber—in a chamber rendered sacred to him by memories of her who had frequented it. The room is represented as richly furnished—this in mere pursuance of the ideas I have already explained on the subject of Beauty, as the sole true poetical thesis.

The *locale* being thus determined, I had now to introduce the bird—and the thought of introducing him through the window, was inevitable. The idea of making the lover suppose, in the first instance, that the flapping of the wings of the bird against the shutter, is a "tapping" at the door, originated in a wish to increase, by prolonging, the reader's curiosity, and in a desire to admit the incidental effect arising from the lover's throwing open the door, finding all dark, and thence adopting the half-fancy that it was the spirit of his mistress that knocked.

I made the night tempestuous, first, to account for the Raven's seeking admission, and secondly, for the effect of contrast with the (physical) serenity within the chamber.

I made the bird alight on the bust of Pallas,[3] also for the effect of contrast between the marble and the plumage—it being understood that the bust was absolutely *suggested* by the bird—the bust of *Pallas* being chosen, first, as most in keeping with the scholarship of the lover, and, secondly, for the sonorousness of the word, Pallas, itself.

About the middle of the poem, also, I have availed myself of the force of contrast, with a view of deepening the ultimate impression. For example,

---

3. Pallas Athena, the Greek goddess of wisdom and the arts.

an air of the fantastic—approaching as nearly to the ludicrous as was admissible—is given to the Raven's entrance. He comes in "with many a flirt and flutter."

Not the *least obeisance made he*—not a moment stopped or stayed he,
But with *mien of lord or lady*, perched above my chamber door.

In the two stanzas which follow, the design is more obviously carried out:—

Then this ebony bird beguiling my sad fancy into smiling
By the *grave and stern decorum of the countenance it wore*,
"Though thy *crest be shorn and shaven* thou," I said, "art sure no craven,
Ghastly grim and ancient Raven wandering from the nightly shore—
Tell me what thy lordly name is on the Night's Plutonian shore!"
        Quoth the Raven "Nevermore."

———

Much I marvelled *this ungainly fowl* to hear discourse so plainly,
Though its answer little meaning—little relevancy bore;
For we cannot help agreeing that no living human being
Ever yet was blessed with seeing bird above his chamber door—
Bird or beast upon the sculptured bust above his chamber door,
       With such name as "Nevermore."

The effect of the *dénouement* being thus provided for, I immediately drop the fantastic for a tone of the most profound seriousness:—this tone commencing in the stanza directly following the one last quoted, with the line,

But the Raven, sitting lonely on that placid bust, spoke only, etc.

From this epoch the lover no longer jests—no longer sees any thing even of the fantastic in the Raven's demeanor. He speaks of him as a "grim, ungainly, ghastly, gaunt, and ominous bird of yore," and feels the "fiery eyes" burning into his "bosom's core." This revolution of thought, or fancy, on the lover's part, is intended to induce a similar one on the part of the reader—to bring the mind into a proper frame for the *dénouement*—which is now brought about as rapidly and as *directly* as possible.

With the *dénouement* proper—with the Raven's reply, "Nevermore," to the lover's final demand if he shall meet his mistress in another world—the poem, in its obvious phase, that of a simple narrative, may be said to have its completion. So far, every thing is within the limits of the accountable—of the real. A raven, having learned by rote the single word "Nevermore," and having escaped from the custody of its owner, is driven, at midnight, through the violence of a storm, to seek admission at a window from which a light still gleams—the chamber-window of a student, occupied half in poring over a volume, half in dreaming of a beloved mistress deceased. The casement being thrown open at the fluttering of the bird's wings, the bird itself perches on the most convenient seat out of the immediate reach of the student, who, amused by the incident and the oddity of the visiter's demeanor, demands of it, in jest and without looking for a reply, its name. The raven addressed, answers with its customary word, "Nevermore"—a word which finds immediate echo in the melancholy heart of the student, who, giving utterance aloud to certain thoughts suggested by the occasion, is again startled by the fowl's repetition of "Nevermore." The student now guesses the state of the case, but is impelled, as I have before explained, by the human thirst for self-torture, and in part by superstition, to propound such queries to the bird as will bring him, the lover, the most of the luxury of sorrow, through the anticipated answer "Nevermore." With the indulgence, to the utmost extreme, of this self-torture, the narration, in what I have termed its first or obvious phase, has a natural termination, and so far there has been no overstepping of the limits of the real.

But in subjects so handled, however skilfully, or with however vivid an array of incident, there is always a certain hardness or nakedness, which repels the artistical eye. Two things are invariably required—first, some amount of complexity, or more properly, adaptation; and, secondly, some amount of suggestiveness—some under current, however indefinite of meaning. It is this latter, in especial, which imparts to a work of art so much of that *richness* (to borrow from colloquy a forcible term) which we are too fond of confounding with *the ideal*. It is the *excess* of the suggested meaning—it is the rendering this the upper instead of the under current of the theme—which turns into prose (and that of the very flattest kind) the so called poetry of the so called transcendentalists.

Holding these opinions, I added the two concluding stanzas of the poem—their suggestiveness being thus made to pervade all the narrative which has preceded them. The under-current of meaning is rendered first apparent in the lines—

"Take thy beak from out *my heart,* and take thy form from off my door!"
Quoth the Raven "Nevermore!"

It will be observed that the words, "from out my heart," involve the first metaphorical expression in the poem. They, with the answer, "Nevermore," dispose the mind to seek a moral in all that has been previously narrated. The reader begins now to regard the Raven as emblematical—but it is not until the very last line of the very last stanza, that the intention of making him emblematical of *Mournful and Never-ending Remembrance* is permitted distinctly to be seen:

And the Raven, never flitting, still is sitting, still is sitting,
On the pallid bust of Pallas just above my chamber door;
And his eyes have all the seeming of a demon's that is dreaming,
And the lamplight o'er him streaming throws his shadow on the floor;
And my soul *from out that shadow* that lies floating on the floor
Shall be lifted—nevermore.

1846

ABRAHAM LINCOLN
1809–1865

Abraham Lincoln, the sixteenth president of the United States (1861–65), presided over the bloodiest war in U.S. history—one that preserved the Union and ended slavery. He was also one of the era's great prose stylists. Drawing on his boyhood in Kentucky and Indiana and his young manhood in rural Illinois, he used American traditions of ordinary speech and backwoods humor to great political effect and, in so doing, placed these regional traits at the center of American discourse. At the same time, he was passionately committed to the egalitarian principles of the Declaration of Independence and the spiritual ideals of the Bible, and he would regularly invoke both the Declaration and the Bible when contesting slavery and imagining the future of the United States. His vision of a national house divided by slavery was of a piece with Harriet Beecher Stowe's domestic and millennial vision, though in his late Civil War speeches, Lincoln was far more magnanimous toward the South than most antislavery writers. With his assassination in 1865, Lincoln, who had been reviled by many in the North and South, came to be regarded almost mystically as a Christlike figure whose death held out the promise that the great bloodletting of the war would give birth to a redeemed nation.

Lincoln was born on February 12, 1809, in a cabin in Hardin County, Kentucky. His father, Thomas Lincoln, and his mother, Mary Hanks, were barely literate; Lincoln himself attended school only sporadically—probably for no more than a year altogether. Although his access to books was limited, his memory was remarkable; years later he was able to draw on his childhood reading of the King James Bible, Aesop's *Fables*, John Bunyan's *Pilgrim's Progress*, Daniel Defoe's *Robinson Crusoe*, and Mason Locke Weems's *Life of George Washington*. Lincoln never lost his love of reading, adding John Stuart Mill, Lord Byron, Robert Burns, and especially Shakespeare to his list of favorites.

Lincoln spent his impoverished youth in Kentucky and southern Indiana, where his father farmed for a living. His mother died when he was nine, but his stepmother, who soon joined the family with children of her own, seems to have singled him out for special affection; Lincoln later spoke of her as his "angel mother." In 1830 the family moved to Illinois. After trying various jobs, Lincoln decided in the early 1830s to prepare for a career in law. In 1834 he was elected to the first of four terms as an Illinois state legislator. He passed the state bar examination in 1836 and moved the next year to the new state capital in Springfield, where he prospered as a lawyer. In 1842 he married Mary Todd, from a wealthy Kentucky family then residing in Springfield. The couple had four sons, only one of whom survived to adulthood.

The political and historical developments of the 1840s and 1850s that would result in Lincoln's election were complicated, but the central issue was whether slavery would be permitted in the new territories, which eventually would become states. Lincoln was elected to the U.S. Congress in 1846; always concerned with mediating rather than inflaming disputes, he voted against abolitionist measures, which he believed might eventually threaten the Union. At the same time, recalling his own remarkable rise from poverty, he insisted that new territories be kept free as "places for poor people to go and better their condition." He also joined an unsuccessful vote to censure President Polk for engaging in the war against Mexico (1846–48), a war he and many of his legislative colleagues believed to be both unjustified and unconstitutional. He did not run for reelection and it appeared that his political career had come to an end.

By 1854 the two major political parties of the time—the Whigs (to which Lincoln belonged) and the Democrats—had compromised on the extension of slavery into new territories and states. Strong antislavery elements in both parties, however, established independent organizations; and when, in 1854, the Republican Party was organized, Lincoln soon joined it. His new party lost the presidential election of 1856 to the Democrats, but in 1858 Lincoln reentered political life as the Republican candidate in the Illinois senatorial election. He opposed the Democrat Stephen A. Douglas, who had earlier sponsored the Kansas-Nebraska Bill, which left it to new territories to establish their status as slave or free when they achieved statehood. Lincoln may have won the famous series of debates with Douglas, but he lost the election. More important for the future, though, he had gained national recognition for his principled opposition to the extension of slavery and found a theme commensurate with his rapidly intensifying powers of thought and expression. As the "House Divided" speech suggests, Lincoln now added to the often biting satirical humor, and to the logic and natural grace of his earlier utterances, a resonance and moral purpose that mark his emergence as a national political leader and as a master of language.

This reputation was enhanced by the Cooper Union Address in 1860, his first in the East, in which Lincoln disputed the idea that slavery was endorsed by the Founding Fathers; and at the Republican presidential convention he won nomination on the third ballot. Lincoln was elected president of the United States in November 1860; but before he took office on March 4, 1861, seven southern states had seceded from the Union to form the Confederacy. Little more than a month after his inauguration, the Civil War had begun. True to his long-standing commitment, he devoted himself to the preservation of the Union. To do this he had to develop an overall war strategy, devise a workable command system, and find the right personnel to execute his plans. All of this he was to accomplish by trial and error in the early months of the war. As months turned to years, he had to garner popular support for his purposes by using his extraordinary political and oratorical skills in times of high passion and internal division; in two of his most famous speeches, the Gettysburg Address and the Second Inaugural, he offered an almost biblical vision of a divided, suffering nation that would one day reunite to bring forth "a new birth of freedom." Frederick Douglass, with whom Lincoln met three times at the White House, called the Second Inaugural a "sacred effort."

Lincoln committed himself by degrees to the elimination of slavery throughout the country. Initially, he wished only to contain it; next, he proceeded cautiously with the 1863 Emancipation Proclamation, which freed only the slaves of the seceded southern states; finally, he took the leading role in the passage of the Thirteenth Amendment, which outlawed slavery everywhere and forever in the United States. Elected to a second term in 1864, he had served scarcely a month of his new term when he was assassinated, while attending a play, by the actor John Wilkes Booth. He died on April 15, 1865. In subsequent weeks, mournful crowds gathered at the various stops of Lincoln's funeral train to pay homage to their fallen leader. Whitman spoke for the multitudes when he eulogized him in "When Lilacs Last in the Dooryard Bloom'd" (1865) as "the sweetest, wisest soul of all my days and lands."

Address Delivered at the Dedication of the Cemetery at Gettysburg, November 19, 1863[1]

Four score and seven years ago our fathers brought forth on this continent, a new nation, conceived in Liberty, and dedicated to the proposition that all men are created equal.

Now we are engaged in a great civil war, testing whether that nation, or any nation so conceived and so dedicated, can long endure. We are met on a great battle-field of that war. We have come to dedicate a portion of that field, as a final resting place for those who here gave their lives that that nation might live. It is altogether fitting and proper that we should do this.

But, in a larger sense, we can not dedicate—we can not consecrate—we can not hallow—this ground. The brave men, living and dead, who struggled here, have consecrated it, far above our poor power to add or detract. The world will little note, nor long remember what we say here, but it can never forget what they did here. It is for us the living, rather, to be dedicated here to the unfinished work which they who fought here have thus far so nobly advanced. It is rather for us to be here dedicated to the great task remaining before us—that from these honored dead we take increased devotion to that cause for which they gave the last full measure of devotion—that we here highly resolve that these dead shall not have died in vain—that this nation, under God, shall have a new birth of freedom—and that government of the people, by the people, for the people, shall not perish from the earth.

ABRAHAM LINCOLN

1863

Second Inaugural Address, March 4, 1865[1]

At this second appearing to take the oath of the presidential office, there is less occasion for an extended address than there was at the first. Then a statement, somewhat in detail, of a course to be pursued, seemed fitting and proper. Now, at the expiration of four years, during which public declarations have been constantly called forth on every point and phase of the great contest which still absorbs the attention, and engrosses the energies of the nation, little that is new could be presented. The progress of our arms, upon which all else chiefly depends, is as well known to the public as to myself; and it is, I trust, reasonably satisfactory and encouraging to all. With high hope for the future, no prediction in regard to it is ventured.

1. The source of the text printed here is the facsimile reproduced in W. F. Barton's *Lincoln at Gettysburg* (1930). Lincoln delivered the address approximately four months after the three-day battle between Robert E. Lee, with seventy thousand Southern troops, and George Gordon Meade, with more than ninety thousand Northern troops. The North was victorious in a battle that left over six thousand dead and thousands injured. Lincoln spoke at Cemetery Hill, which held the Union dead.

1. The text is based on photostats of the original manuscript, owned by the Abraham Lincoln Association. A little more than a month after Lincoln delivered this address, the Civil War came to an end at Appomattox, Virginia, on April 9, when Robert E. Lee formally surrendered to Ulysses S. Grant. Shortly after that, on April 14, Lincoln was fatally shot while attending a play at Ford's Theater in Washington, D.C.

On the occasion corresponding to this four years ago, all thoughts were anxiously directed to an impending civil war. All dreaded it—all sought to avert it. While the inaugural address was being delivered from this place, devoted altogether to *saving* the Union without war, insurgent agents were in the city seeking to *destroy* it without war—seeking to dissol[v]e the Union, and divide effects, by negotiation. Both parties deprecated war; but one of them would *make* war rather than let the nation survive; and the other would *accept* war rather than let it perish. And the war came.

One eighth of the whole population were colored slaves, not distributed generally over the Union, but localized in the Southern part of it. These slaves constituted a peculiar and powerful interest. All knew that this interest was, somehow, the cause of the war. To strengthen, perpetuate, and extend this interest was the object for which the insurgents would rend the Union, even by war; while the government claimed no right to do more than to restrict the territorial enlargement of it. Neither party expected for the war, the magnitude, or the duration, which it has already attained. Neither anticipated that the *cause* of the conflict might cease with, or even before, the conflict itself should cease. Each looked for an easier triumph, and a result less fundamental and astounding. Both read the same Bible, and pray to the same God; and each invokes His aid against the other. It may seem strange that any men should dare to ask a just God's assistance in wringing their bread from the sweat of other men's faces; but let us judge not that we be not judged. The prayers of both could not be answered; that of neither has been answered fully. The Almighty has his own purposes. "Woe unto the world because of offences! for it must needs be that offences come; but woe to that man by whom the offence cometh!"[2] If we shall suppose that American Slavery is one of those offences which, in the providence of God, must needs come, but which, having continued through His appointed time, He now wills to remove, and that He gives to both North and South, this terrible war, as the woe due to those by whom the offence came, shall we discern therein any departure from those divine attributes which the believers in a Living God always ascribe to Him? Fondly do we hope—fervently do we pray—that this mighty scourge of war may speedily pass away. Yet, if God wills that it continue, until all the wealth piled by the bond-man's two hundred and fifty years of unrequited toil shall be sunk, and until every drop of blood drawn with the lash, shall be paid by another drawn with the sword, as was said three thousand years ago, so still it must be said "the judgments of the Lord, are true and righteous altogether."[3]

With malice toward none; with charity for all; with firmness in the right, as God gives us to see the right, let us strive on to finish the work we are in; to bind up the nation's wounds; to care for him who shall have borne the battle, and for his widow, and his orphan—to do all which may achieve and cherish a just and lasting peace, among ourselves, and with all nations.

1865

---

2. Matthew 18.7.   3. Psalm 19.9.

MARGARET FULLER
1810–1850

I n their six-volume *History of Woman Suffrage* (1881), the U.S. feminists Elizabeth Cady Stanton, Susan B. Anthony, and Matilda Joslyn Gage declared that Margaret Fuller "possessed more influence upon the thought of American women than any woman previous to her time." When she died tragically at the age of forty, she had published approximately three hundred essays and reviews—emerging as one of the best literary critics of her day—as well as a major travel narrative, an important book on women's rights that predated the first women's suffrage convention by several years, and a collection of her writings. She had also edited the *Dial* (the semi-official journal of the Transcendentalists) and become one of the first female columnists and the first female overseas journalist for a U.S. daily newspaper, Horace Greeley's *New York Tribune*. She not only argued for the intellectual equality of women to men but, in her writings and personal life, presented herself as an example of women's abilities. At a time when no institutions of higher learning were open to women, her richly allusive writings displayed a knowledge of literary traditions, history, religion, and political and legal thought that one would associate with a university-educated scholar or teacher; and at a time when women were expected to remain within the domestic sphere—and never under any circumstances to compete with men—her activist public presence and confident persona troubled and fascinated her male friends. Influenced by Emerson's philosophy of self-culture and self-reliance, which she extended to women, Fuller continually challenged herself to move in new directions.

Sarah Margaret Fuller was born at Cambridgeport (now part of Cambridge), Massachusetts, on May 23, 1810, the first of the nine children of Margarett Crane and Timothy Fuller. Her father, a lawyer and four-term congressman, supervised her education, teaching her Latin, Greek, French, and Italian in a rigorous regime involving long hours of study and drill. In an autobiographical account written when she was thirty years old, Fuller complained of the nightmares and headaches that accompanied what she termed her "unnatural" childhood; but a few years later, in "The Great Lawsuit" (1843), she praised the father of "Miranda" (Fuller's fictionalized self-portrait in the essay) for regarding her "as a living mind" and thus freeing her from the culture's strictures against developing female intellect. By the time she was ten, she had read extensively in Virgil, Cicero, Tacitus, Shakespeare, and numerous other classic writers. In 1824, her parents sent her to Miss Susan Prescott's Young Ladies' Seminary in Groton, Massachusetts, a sort of finishing school, which she left after a year, returning to live with her family in Cambridge. During the late 1820s she began to read such influential European Romantics as the French novelist and political theorist Germaine de Staël and the German novelist, dramatist, and poet Johann Wolfgang von Goethe. Timothy Fuller moved the family to a farm in Groton in 1833, thus removing Margaret from the Cambridge environment she had come to find so stimulating. She continued with her self-education, however, translating Goethe's drama *Torquato Tasso* and publishing her first essay, "In Defense of Brutus," in an 1834 issue of the *Boston Daily Advertiser & Patriot*.

Fuller wanted to become a full-time writer and translator—activities then opening up to women—but those plans had to be abandoned when her father died of cholera in October 1835. Her mother was sickly, and the bulk of the responsibility for financially supporting the family fell to Fuller. Setting aside her own ambitions, she turned to teaching, first at Bronson Alcott's progressive co-educational Temple School in Boston, and then at the prestigious Greene Street School in Providence, Rhode Island. In her little spare time, she continued her writing and translating, placing several reviews and essays in the *Western Messenger*, and publishing a translation of *Eckermann's Conversations with Goethe* in 1839. Realizing that she would not be able to devote herself to her literary interests while holding a full-time teaching job, she resigned from Greene Street School in 1839 and moved back to Cambridge. To support herself, she established her "Conversations"—paid seminars for elite women of the Boston and Cambridge area in which dialogue, rather than rote learning or lecture, was the dominant pedagogy. These meetings anticipated the women's book-club movement of later in the century and were fondly remembered for years afterward by their participants. Over the next six years the group addressed such topics as Greek mythology, the fine arts, ethics, education, demonology, philosophical idealism, and the intellectual potential of women.

A friend of Emerson's since she first sought him out in 1836, Fuller edited the *Dial* from its founding in 1840 to 1842, while continuing to translate works by and about Goethe. In 1842 she resigned her editorship but kept on with her "Conversations" and writing. She did her first significant traveling in 1843, spending four months with friends touring the Great Lakes, Illinois, and the Wisconsin Territory. Upon her return, she researched the history of the old Northwest territories, wrote over thirty poems, and in 1844 brought out her first full-length book, *Summer on the Lakes, in 1843*, a volume of historical meditations, poetry, and travel narrative, which Edgar Allan Poe hailed as "remarkable." The New York editor Horace Greeley was so impressed with the book that he offered Fuller the position of full-time literary editor of the *New York Tribune*.

Fuller moved to New York City in late 1844, and during the next two years published over two hundred essays in the *Tribune*, including influential reviews of Poe, Hawthorne, Melville, and Frederick Douglass. (She republished a number of these reviews in her 1846 *Papers on Literature and Art*.) She also wrote columns on public questions—what we would now call investigative reporting—addressing such matters as the condition of the female prisoners she had visited in New York's Sing Sing Prison in late 1844. In 1845 Greeley published her *Woman in the Nineteenth Century*, which expanded her 1843 *Dial* essay "The Great Lawsuit: Man *versus* Men. Woman *versus* Women" into a full-length book. Taken together, the essay and book meditate powerfully on the ways that cultural constructions of gender limited both female and male potential. Providing examples of strong heroines and goddesses from history, literature, and mythology, she sought to inspire women readers to imagine greater possibilities for themselves. She also linked the situation of white domestic women to the situation of the slave, thus developing an overlapping critique of slavery and patriarchy.

Margaret Fuller, from a daguerreotype made in July 1846. This is the only known photograph of Fuller.

Lydia Maria Child declared in an 1845 review of *Woman in the Nineteenth Century* that Fuller raised important questions about whether under current conditions love is "a mockery, and marriage a sham." By the late nineteenth century both the book and "The Great Lawsuit" had emerged as landmarks in the history of feminist thought in the United States.

In August 1846, Fuller sailed for Europe, having arranged with Greeley to send back regular dispatches at the rate of ten dollars per column. Arriving first in England, she met the writer and philosopher Thomas Carlyle, whom she had long admired but who disappointed her by his reactionary political views and his cold response to the Italian revolutionary Giuseppe Mazzini, then a political refugee in England. In Paris she met the French woman novelist George Sand and the exiled Polish poet and revolutionary Adam Mickiewicz. She next went to Italy, at the time not a unified country but a collection of states—some independent, some controlled by the pope, and some controlled by Austria. Soon after settling in Rome she became romantically involved with Giovanni Angelo Ossoli, a nobleman eleven years her junior who supported the revolutionary cause of Italian unification (Risorgimento) led by Giuseppe Garibaldi and Mazzini. Her dispatches to the *Tribune* recorded her increasing preoccupation with the developing Italian revolution, which she linked to American ideals of republicanism that harked back to the original Roman republic, long her political ideal.

In December of 1847 Fuller became pregnant, but as a Protestant her marriage to the Catholic Ossoli seemed out of the question because of the opposition of his family and the difficulties of getting permission in Italy for an interfaith marriage. Through a dismal rainy season, she covered political events for the *Tribune,* and when cities of northern Italy revolted against the Austrians in March 1848, Fuller described to her New York readers the joyous response of the Roman citizens. Emerson wrote from England urging her to return home before war broke out, but she was not ready to tell her Massachusetts connections about her pregnancy, and chose instead to wait for the child's birth in the countryside near Rome. Ossoli, who had become a member of the civic guard, was with her when their son, Angelo, was born on September 5. Leaving the baby with a wet nurse—a common practice for the era—Fuller returned to Rome late in November in time to cover the flight of the pope and, early in 1849, the arrival of the Italian nationalist Garibaldi, the proclamation of the Roman Republic, and Mazzini's arrival in Rome as well. The republic lasted less than a year: French troops entered Rome on June 30, 1849, and quickly restored the pope to power. During the bloody siege, Fuller served as the director of the Hospital of the Fate Bene Fratelli, doing heroic work for the wounded revolutionaries.

After the defeat of the republican forces, Fuller moved to Florence with Angelo and Ossoli and began to work on a history of the short-lived Roman Republic. She may have married Ossoli, as his sister later claimed and as she herself stated in some of her letters home. But there was doubt about this among her friends, who may have been just as alarmed by her marriage to a Catholic as by what they regarded as her profligate sexual behavior as an unmarried woman. Convinced that she and Ossoli would have better economic prospects in the United States, Fuller arranged passage home, and on May 17, 1850, the three sailed for the United States. On July 19, two months and two days later—sailing ships took many weeks to cross the Atlantic—the ship was wrecked within sight of land off Fire Island, New York, and all three perished. Angelo's body washed ashore. A trunk containing some of Fuller's papers was later recovered, but not her history of Rome. Thoreau traveled to the site and sought vainly for her body; at home, Emerson wrote mournfully in his journal, "I have lost in her my audience." Hawthorne, who had been friends with Fuller during the 1840s, may have had her in mind when creating Hester Prynne in *The Scarlet Letter* (1850). Wishing to memorialize her career and yet confused about how to present this unconventional woman to a general audience, Fuller's male friends brought out *Memoirs of Margaret Fuller Ossoli* in 1852, which emphasized her eccentricities, egotism, and aloofness. But if her refusal to stay within feminine bounds disturbed her male contemporaries, that very nonconformity—an instance of Emerson's own teachings, after all—had been crucial to her achievements as an intellectual and writer.

From The Great Lawsuit:
Man *versus* Men. Woman *versus* Women[1]

[FOUR KINDS OF EQUALITY]

Where the thought of equality has become pervasive, it shows itself in four kinds.

The household partnership. In our country the woman looks for a "smart but kind" husband, the man for a "capable, sweet tempered" wife.

The man furnishes the house, the woman regulates it. Their relation is one of mutual esteem, mutual dependence. Their talk is of business, their affection shows itself by practical kindness. They know that life goes more smoothly and cheerfully to each for the other's aid; they are grateful and content. The wife praises her husband as a "good provider," the husband in return compliments her as a "capital housekeeper." This relation is good as far as it goes.

Next comes a closer tie which takes the two forms, either of intellectual companionship, or mutual idolatry. The last, we suppose, is to no one a pleasing subject of contemplation. The parties weaken and narrow one another; they lock the gate against all the glories of the universe that they may live in a cell together. To themselves they seem the only wise, to all others steeped in infatuation, the gods smile as they look forward to the crisis of cure, to men the woman seems an unlovely syren, to women the man an effeminate boy.

The other form, of intellectual companionship, has become more and more frequent. Men engaged in public life, literary men, and artists have often found in their wives companions and confidants in thought no less than in feeling. And, as in the course of things the intellectual development of woman has spread wider and risen higher, they have, not unfrequently, shared the same employment. As in the case of Roland and his wife, who were friends in the household and the nation's councils, read together, regulated home affairs, or prepared public documents together indifferently.

It is very pleasant, in letters begun by Roland and finished by his wife, to see the harmony of mind and the difference of nature, one thought, but various ways of treating it.

This is one of the best instances of a marriage of friendship. It was only friendship, whose basis was esteem; probably neither party knew love, except by name.

Roland was a good man, worthy to esteem and be esteemed, his wife as deserving of admiration as able to do without it. Madame Roland is the fairest

---

1. Reprinted from the *Boston Dial* (July 1843). In 1845 Fuller published a revised, expanded version of this work under the title *Woman in the Nineteenth Century*.

specimen we have yet of her class, as clear to discern her aim, as valiant to pursue it, as Spenser's Britomart,[2] austerely set apart from all that did not belong to her, whether as woman or as mind. She is an antetype of a class to which the coming time will afford a field, the Spartan[3] matron, brought by the culture of a book-furnishing age to intellectual consciousness and expansion.

Self-sufficing strength and clear-sightedness were in her combined with a power of deep and calm affection. The page of her life is one of unsullied dignity.

Her appeal to posterity is one against the injustice of those who committed such crimes in the name of liberty. She makes it in behalf of herself and her husband. I would put beside it on the shelf a little volume, containing a similar appeal from the verdict of contemporaries to that of mankind, that of Godwin in behalf of his wife, the celebrated, the by most men detested Mary Wolstonecraft.[4] In his view it was an appeal from the injustice of those who did such wrong in the name of virtue.

Were this little book interesting for no other cause, it would be so for the generous affection evinced under the peculiar circumstances. This man had courage to love and honor this woman in the face of the world's verdict, and of all that was repulsive in her own past history. He believed he saw of what soul she was, and that the thoughts she had struggled to act out were noble. He loved her and he defended her for the meaning and intensity of her inner life. It was a good fact.

Mary Wolstonecraft, like Madame Dudevant[5] (commonly known as George Sand) in our day, was a woman whose existence better proved the need of some new interpretation of woman's rights, than anything she wrote. Such women as these, rich in genius, of most tender sympathies, and capable of high virtue and a chastened harmony, ought not to find themselves by birth in a place so narrow, that in breaking bonds they become outlaws. Were there as much room in the world for such, as in Spenser's poem for Britomart, they would not run their heads so wildly against its laws. They find their way at last to purer air, but the world will not take off the brand it has set upon them. The champion of the rights of woman found in Godwin one who pleads her own cause like a brother. George Sand smokes, wears male attire, wishes to be addressed as Mon frère;[6] perhaps, if she found those who were as brothers indeed, she would not care whether she were brother or sister.

We rejoice to see that she, who expresses such a painful contempt for men in most of her works, as shows she must have known great wrong from them, in La Roche Mauprat[7] depicting one raised, by the workings of love, from the depths of savage sensualism to a moral and intellectual life. It was love for a pure object, for a steadfast woman, one of those who, the Italian said, could make the stair to heaven.

Women like Sand will speak now, and cannot be silenced; their characters and their eloquence alike foretell an era when such as they shall easier learn

2. In Spenser's *The Fairie Queene*, the female knight Britomart represents chastity.
3. Resembling the ancient Greeks known for their austerity and military valor.
4. *Memoirs of the Author of "A Vindication of the Rights of Woman"* (1798) by the English author William Godwin (1756–1836). Mary Wollstonecraft (1759–1797) married Godwin shortly before her death in childbirth.
5. Amandine Aurore Lucile Dudevant (1804–1876), French Romantic novelist who adopted a male pen name, wore male clothing, and had a succession of male lovers.
6. Old friend and colleague (French); literally, "my brother."
7. An 1837 drama by George Sand.

to lead true lives. But though such forebode, not such shall be the parents of it. Those who would reform the world must show that they do not speak in the heat of wild impulse; their lives must be unstained by passionate error; they must be severe lawgivers to themselves. As to their transgressions and opinions, it may be observed, that the resolve of Eloisa to be only the mistress of Abelard, was that of one who saw the contract of marriage a seal of degradation.[8] Wherever abuses of this sort are seen, the timid will suffer, the bold protest. But society is in the right to outlaw them till she has revised her law, and she must be taught to do so, by one who speaks with authority, not in anger and haste.

If Godwin's choice of the calumniated authoress of the "Rights of Woman," for his honored wife, be a sign of a new era, no less so is an article of great learning and eloquence, published several years since in an English review, where the writer, in doing full justice to Eloisa, shows his bitter regret that she lives not now to love him, who might have known better how to prize her love than did the egotistical Abelard.

These marriages, these characters, with all their imperfections, express an onward tendency. They speak of aspiration of soul, of energy of mind, seeking clearness and freedom. Of a like promise are the tracts now publishing by Goodwyn Barmby[9] (the European Pariah as he calls himself) and his wife Catharine. Whatever we may think of their measures, we see them in wedlock, the two minds are wed by the only contract that can permanently avail, of a common faith, and a common purpose.

We might mention instances, nearer home, of minds, partners in work and in life, sharing together, on equal terms, public and private interests, and which have not on any side that aspect of offence which characterizes the attitude of the last named; persons who steer straight onward, and in our freer life have not been obliged to run their heads against any wall. But the principles which guide them might, under petrified or oppressive institutions, have made them warlike, paradoxical, or, in some sense, Pariahs. The phenomenon is different, the last the same, in all these cases. Men and women have been obliged to build their house from the very foundation. If they found stone ready in the quarry, they took it peaceably, otherwise they alarmed the country by pulling down old towers to get materials.

These are all instances of marriage as intellectual companionship. The parties meet mind to mind, and a mutual trust is excited which can buckler them against a million. They work together for a common purpose, and, in all these instances, with the same implement, the pen.

A pleasing expression in this kind is afforded by the union in the names of the Howitts.[1] William and Mary Howitt we heard named together for years, supposing them to be brother and sister; the equality of labors and reputation, even so, was auspicious, more so, now we find them man and wife. In his late work on Germany, Howitt mentions his wife with pride, as one among the constellation of distinguished English women, and in a graceful, simple manner.

---

8. In her famous letters written in the 12th century, Eloisa steadfastly refused to marry Abelard, because marriage would force him to give up his teaching of theology within the Church.
9. English publisher (1820–1881) of socialist tracts who founded the London Communist Propaganda Society in 1841.
1. William Howitt (1792–1879) and Mary Howitt (1799–1888), prolific British authors and translators.

In naming these instances we do not mean to imply that community of employment is an essential to union of this sort, more than to the union of friendship. Harmony exists no less in difference than in likeness, if only the same key-note govern both parts. Woman the poem, man the poet; woman the heart, man the head; such divisions are only important when they are never to be transcended. If nature is never bound down, nor the voice of inspiration stifled, that is enough. We are pleased that women should write and speak, if they feel the need of it, from having something to tell; but silence for a hundred years would be as well, if that silence be from divine command, and not from man's tradition.

While Goetz von Berlichingen[2] rides to battle, his wife is busy in the kitchen; but difference of occupation does not prevent that community of life, that perfect esteem, with which he says,

"Whom God loves, to him gives he such a wife!"

Manzoni thus dedicates his Adelchi.[3]

"To his beloved and venerated wife, Enrichetta Luigia Blondel, who, with conjugal affections and maternal wisdom, has preserved a virgin mind, the author dedicates this Adelchi, grieving that he could not, by a more splendid and more durable monument, honor the dear name and the memory of so many virtues."

The relation could not be fairer, nor more equal, if she too had written poems. Yet the position of the parties might have been the reverse as well; the woman might have sung the deeds, given voice to the life of the man, and beauty would have been the result, as we see in pictures of Arcadia[4] the nymph singing to the shepherds, or the shepherd with his pipe allures the nymphs, either makes a good picture. The sounding lyre requires not muscular strength, but energy of soul to animate the hand which can control it. Nature seems to delight in varying her arrangements, as if to show that she will be fettered by no rule, and we must admit the same varieties that she admits.

I have not spoken of the higher grade of marriage union, the religious, which may be expressed as pilgrimage towards a common shrine. This includes the others; home sympathies, and household wisdom, for these pilgrims must know how to assist one another to carry their burdens along the dusty way; intellectual communion, for how sad it would be on such a journey to have a companion to whom you could not communicate thoughts and aspirations, as they sprang to life, who would have no feeling for the more and more glorious prospects that open as we advance, who would never see the flowers that may be gathered by the most industrious traveler. It must include all these. Such a fellow pilgrim Count Zinzendorf[5] seems to have found in his countess of whom he thus writes:

---

2. German knight (1481–1562), a sort of Robin Hood, familiar to Fuller from Goethe's play *Göetz von Berlichingen* (1773).
3. A tragedy (1822) by Alessandro Manzoni (1785–1873), Italian writer.
4. Pastoral district of the Peloponnesus in Greece, symbolic of rustic simplicity and contentment.

5. Nikolas Ludwig, Count von Zinzendorf (1700–1760), German leader of the Moravian Church, or the Bohemian Brethren, a Catholic heretical group founded in Bohemia around 1722, influential both in Europe and in the Moravian settlements in the American colonies, which he visited.

"Twenty-five years' experience has shown me that just the help-mate whom I have is the only one that could suit my vocation, Who else could have so carried through my family affairs? Who lived so spotlessly before the world? Who so wisely aided me in my rejection of a dry morality? Who so clearly set aside the Pharisaism[6] which, as years passed, threatened to creep in among us? Who so deeply discerned as to the spirits of delusion which sought to bewilder us? Who would have governed my whole economy so wisely, richly, and hospitably when circumstances commanded? Who have taken indifferently the part of servant or mistress, without on the one side affecting an especial spirituality, on the other being sullied by any worldly pride? Who, in a community where all ranks are eager to be on a level, would, from wise and real causes, have known how to maintain inward and outward distinctions? Who, without a murmur, have seen her husband encounter such dangers by land and sea? Who undertaken with him and sustained such astonishing pilgrimages? Who amid such difficulties always held up her head, and supported me? Who found so many hundred thousands and acquitted them on her own credit? And, finally, who, of all human beings, would so well understand and interpret to others my inner and outer being as this one, of such nobleness in her way of thinking, such great intellectual capacity, and free from the theological perplexities that enveloped me?"

An observer[7] adds this testimony.

"We may in many marriages regard it as the best arrangement, if the man has so much advantage over his wife that she can, without much thought of her own, be, by him, led and directed, as by a father. But it was not so with the Count and his consort. She was not made to be a copy; she was an original; and, while she loved and honored him, she thought for herself on all subjects with so much intelligence, that he could and did look on her as a sister and friend also."

Such a woman is the sister and friend of all beings, as the worthy man is their brother and helper.

[THE GREAT RADICAL DUALISM]

The especial genius of woman I believe to be electrical in movement, intuitive in function, spiritual in tendency. She is great not so easily in classification, or re-creation, as in an instinctive seizure of causes, and a simple breathing out of what she receives that has the singleness of life, rather than the selecting or energizing of art.

More native to her is it to be the living model of the artist, than to set apart from herself any one form in objective reality; more native to inspire and receive the poem than to create it. In so far as soul is in her completely developed, all soul is the same; but as far as it is modified in her as woman,

---

6. Self-righteous hypocrisy, from the Jewish sect whom Jesus condemned as whitened sepulchres (Matthew 23.27), "which indeed appear beautiful outward, but are within full of dead men's bones, and of all uncleanness."
7. Spangenberg [Fuller's note]. August Gotlieb Spangenberg (1704–1792), successor to Count von Zinzendorf. See p. 809, n. 5.

it flows, it breathes, it sings, rather than deposits soil, or finishes work, and that which is especially feminine flushes in blossom the face of earth, and pervades like air and water all this seeming solid globe, daily renewing and purifying its life. Such may be the especially feminine element, spoken of as Femality. But it is no more the order of nature that it should be incarnated pure in any form, than that the masculine energy should exist unmingled with it in any form.

Male and female represent the two sides of the great radical dualism. But, in fact, they are perpetually passing into one another. Fluid hardens to solid, solid rushes to fluid. There is no wholly masculine man, no purely feminine woman.

History jeers at the attempts of physiologists to bind great original laws by the forms which flow from them. They make a rule; they say from observation what can and cannot be. In vain! Nature provides exceptions to every rule. She sends women to battle, and sets Hercules spinning;[8] she enables women to bear immense burdens, cold, and frost; she enables the man, who feels maternal love, to nourish his infant like a mother. Of late she plays still gayer pranks. Not only she deprives organizations, but organs, of a necessary end. She enables people to read with the top of the head, and see with the pit of the stomach. Presently she will make a female Newton, and a male Syren.[9]

Man partakes of the feminine in the Apollo, woman of the Masculine as Minerva.

Let us be wise and not impede the soul. Let her work as she will. Let us have one creative energy, one incessant revelation. Let it take what form it will, and let us not bind it by the past to man or woman, black or white. Jove sprang from Rhea, Pallas from Jove.[1] So let it be.

If it has been the tendency of the past remarks to call woman rather to the Minerva side,—if I, unlike the more generous writer, have spoken from society no less than the soul,—let it be pardoned. It is love that has caused this, love for many incarcerated souls, that might be freed could the idea of religious self-dependence be established in them, could the weakening habit of dependence on others be broken up.

Every relation, every gradation of nature, is incalculably precious, but only to the soul which is poised upon itself, and to whom no loss, no change, can bring dull discord, for it is in harmony with the central soul.

If any individual live too much in relations, so that he becomes a stranger to the resources of his own nature, he falls after a while into a distraction, or imbecility, from which he can only be cured by a time of isolation, which gives the renovating fountains time to rise up. With a society it is the same. Many minds, deprived of the traditionary or instinctive means of passing a cheerful existence, must find help in self-impulse or perish. It is therefore that while any elevation, in the view of union, is

8. I.e., sets the strongest men to domestic tasks.
9. In this inversion of sexual stereotypes, a male would be as alluring as the Syrens (or Sirens), Greek sea nymphs who lured mariners into shipwreck on the rocks surrounding their island. Isaac Newton (1642–1727), English mathematician.
1. In Greek mythology, Rhea, the sister and wife of Cronus, and mother of Zeus (known to the Romans as Jove). Pallas Athena sprang from Jove's skull, fully grown and fully armed.

to be hailed with joy, we shall not decline celibacy as the great fact of the time. It is one from which no vow, no arrangement, can at present save a thinking mind. For now the rowers are pausing on their oars, they wait a change before they can pull together. All tends to illustrate the thought of a wise contemporary. Union is only possible to those who are units. To be fit for relations in time, souls, whether of man or woman, must be able to do without them in the spirit.

It is therefore that I would have woman lay aside all thought, such as she habitually cherishes, of being taught and led by men. I would have her, like the Indian girl, dedicate herself to the Sun, the Sun of Truth, and go no where if his beams did not make clear the path. I would have her free from compromise, from complaisance, from helplessness, because I would have her good enough and strong enough to love one and all beings, from the fulness, not the poverty of being.

Men, as at present instructed, will not help this work, because they also are under the slavery of habit. I have seen with delight their poetic impulses. A sister is the fairest ideal, and how nobly Wordsworth, and even Byron, have written of a sister.[2]

There is no sweeter sight than to see a father with his little daughter. Very vulgar men become refined to the eye when leading a little girl by the hand. At that moment the right relation between the sexes seems established, and you feel as if the man would aid in the noblest purpose, if you ask him in behalf of his little daughter. Once two fine figures stood before me, thus. The father of very intellectual aspect, his falcon eye softened by affection as he looked down on his fair child, she the image of himself, only more graceful and brilliant in expression. I was reminded of Southey's Kehama,[3] when lo, the dream was rudely broken. They were talking of education, and he said.

"I shall not have Maria brought too forward. If she knows too much, she will never find a husband; superior women hardly ever can."

"Surely," said his wife, with a blush, "you wish Maria to be as good and wise as she can, whether it will help her to marriage or not."

"No," he persisted, "I want her to have a sphere and a home, and some one to protect her when I am gone."

It was a trifling incident, but made a deep impression. I felt that the holiest relations fail to instruct the unprepared and perverted mind. If this man, indeed, would have looked at it on the other side, he was the last that would have been willing to have been taken himself for the home and protection he could give, but would have been much more likely to repeat the tale of Alcibiades[4] with his phials.

But men do *not* look at both sides, and women must leave off asking them and being influenced by them, but retire within themselves, and explore the groundwork of being till they find their peculiar secret. Then when they come forth again, renovated and baptized, they will know how to turn all dross to gold, and will be rich and free though they live in a hut, tranquil, if

2. Fuller alludes to the various tributes by William Wordsworth to his sister Dorothy and Lord Byron to his half-sister Augusta Leigh.
3. *The Curse of Kehama* (1810), by the English writer Robert Southey (1774–1843).
4. Athenian general (c. 450–404 B.C.E.), who was convicted for drunkenly imitating sacred rituals.

in a crowd. Then their sweet singing shall not be from passionate impulse, but the lyrical overflow of a divine rapture, and a new music shall be elucidated from this many-chorded world.

Grant her then for a while the armor and the javelin.[5] Let her put from her the press of other minds and meditate in virgin loneliness. The same idea shall reappear in due time as Muse, or Ceres,[6] the all-kindly, patient Earth-Spirit.

I tire every one with my Goethean illustrations. But it cannot be helped.

Goethe, the great mind which gave itself absolutely to the leadings of truth, and let rise through him the waves which are still advancing through the century, was its intellectual prophet. Those who know him, see, daily, his thought fulfilled more and more, and they must speak of it, till his name weary and even nauseate, as all great names have in their time. And I cannot spare the reader, if such there be, his wonderful sight as to the prospects and wants of women.

As his Wilhelm grows in life and advances in wisdom, he becomes acquainted with women of more and more character, rising from Mariana to Macaria.[7]

Macaria, bound with the heavenly bodies in fixed revolutions, the centre of all relations, herself unrelated, expresses the Minerva side.

Mignon, the electrical, inspired lyrical nature.

All these women, though we see them in relations, we can think of as unrelated. They all are very individual, yet seem nowhere restrained. They satisfy for the present, yet arouse an infinite expectation.

The economist Theresa, the benevolent Natalia, the fair Saint, have chosen a path, but their thoughts are not narrowed to it. The functions of life to them are not ends, but suggestions.

Thus to them all things are important, because none is necessary. Their different characters have fair play, and each is beautiful in its minute indications, for nothing is enforced or conventional, but everything, however slight, grows from the essential life of the being.

Mignon and Theresa wear male attire when they like, and it is graceful for them to do so, while Macaria is confined to her arm chair behind the green curtain, and the Fair Saint could not bear a speck of dust on her robe.

All things are in their places in this little world because all is natural and free, just as "there is room for everything out of doors." Yet all is rounded in by natural harmony which will always arise where Truth and Love are sought in the light of freedom.

Goethe's book bodes an era of freedom like its own, of "extraordinary generous seeking," and new revelations. New individualities shall be developed in the actual world, which shall advance upon it as gently as the figures come out upon his canvass.

A profound thinker has said "no married woman can represent the female world, for she belongs to her husband. The idea of woman must be represented by a virgin."

---

5. The weapons of Athena, Greek goddess of wisdom.
6. The Roman goddess of agriculture.
7. Feminine characters in Johann Wolfgang von Goethe's *Wilhelm Meister's Apprenticeship* (1796); other female characters from the same book are named just below.

But that is the very fault of marriage, and of the present relation between the sexes, that the woman does belong to the man, instead of forming a whole with him. Were it otherwise there would be no such limitation to the thought.

Woman, self-centred, would never be absorbed by any relation; it would be only an experience to her as to man. It is a vulgar error that love, *a* love to woman is her whole existence; she also is born for Truth and Love in their universal energy. Would she but assume her inheritance, Mary would not be the only Virgin Mother. Not Manzoni[8] alone would celebrate in his wife the virgin mind with the maternal wisdom and conjugal affections. The soul is ever young, ever virgin.

And will not she soon appear? The woman who shall vindicate their birthright for all women; who shall teach them what to claim, and how to use what they obtain? Shall not her name be for her era Victoria, for her country and her life Virginia?[9] Yet predictions are rash; she herself must teach us to give her the fitting name.

1843

---

8. Another allusion to the preface to Manzoni's *Adelchi.*
9. I.e., shall not her character include power (such us made Victoria so fit a name for a queen) and purity?

Slavery, Race, and the Making of American Literature

I n 1820 the English critic Sidney Smith became exasperated by the boasting of American literary nationalists, and in the pages of the *Edinburgh Review* he famously asked: "In the four quarters of the globe, who reads an American book? or goes to an American play? or looks at an American picture or statue?" His questions about Americans' self-proclaimed literary, cultural, and national superiority culminated with the most withering question of all: "Finally, under which of the old tyrannical governments of Europe is every sixth man a Slave, whom his fellow-creatures may buy and sell and torture?" For Smith, the making of American literature and culture could not be separated from the making of the nation itself. The paradoxical fact that a nation founded on the principles of equality would develop into a slaveholding republic was not lost on writers of the early national and antebellum period. The vast majority of antebellum writers confronted issues of slavery and race at some point during their careers. Whether central to their writings, as was the case with Frederick Douglass, early Harriet Beecher Stowe, William Wells Brown, and others, or of peripheral interest, as was true, say, for Catharine Maria Sedgwick and Fanny Fern, slavery could not be ignored. Tensions between the realities of slavery and the ideals of freedom inform much writing of the period.

The selections on slavery and race offered here take off from Thomas Jefferson, author of the first draft of the Declaration of Independence, who coined many of its most memorable phrases. Jefferson's *Notes on the State of Virginia* celebrated the democratic ideals of the Declaration while making clear that he regarded those ideals as best realized by whites. In the classificatory and hierarchical mode of the Enlightenment period, he presents black people as inferior to white people. Though he leaves the question of race open to further empirical analysis, his observations nevertheless helped give rise to the racial ethnological "science" of the nineteenth century, which invariably presented whites as superior to blacks. African American writers regularly sought to counter such claims, and in his *Appeal*, David Walker directly responds, or talks back, to Jefferson. Much African American writing of the period, and indeed much antislavery writing of the period, as we can see from the selections by Samuel Cornish and John Russwurm, and William Lloyd Garrison, sought to abolish slavery, improve the condition of the free blacks, and challenge the hierarchical claims of the racial ethnologists by invoking (or reclaiming) the principles of the Declaration. These principles were also insisted on by writers such as Emerson, Melville, Thoreau, and Whitman as they prodded readers to comprehend their own "enslavement" to cultural conventions. As Ishmael remarks at the opening of *Moby-Dick*: "Who aint a slave?" For many women writers of the period, slavery also raised questions about patriarchy and women's rights. As the selections from Angelina Grimké and Sojourner Truth suggest, women reformers saw themselves as especially qualified to contest slavery, which they regarded both as a specific institution in the slave South and as one of many manifestations of patriarchal power.

The best-selling literary work of the antebellum period was Stowe's antislavery novel *Uncle Tom's Cabin*; published in 1852, it sold around one million copies by the end of the decade. Inspired by feminist-abolitionists like Grimké, Stowe emphasized the importance of women to antislavery reform. In the manner of David Walker, Douglass, and numerous other African American writers, she lamented the unfinished work of the American Revolution by having the rebellious slave George Harris invoke the ideals of the Declaration. Like many Americans of the time, Stowe, even in a novel attacking slavery, seemed to accept notions of racial difference, presenting whites as unduly aggressive and blacks as domestic and religious to an extreme. The novel polarized the nation, spawning numerous other antislavery works in the North, along with a number of proslavery, anti–Uncle Tom's Cabin writings in the South. The debates on slavery exerted an especially strong influence on the literature of the 1840s and 1850s. Melville wrote a novella, "Benito Cereno," about a slave rebellion; Whitman in "Song of Myself" imagined himself offering succor to a fugitive slave; and Thoreau in "Slavery in Massachusetts" conceived of a Massachusetts that supported the Fugitive Slave Act of 1850 as a version of hell. Race, too, infused writings of the period, even texts that may not seem to be overtly about race. If whiteness was the culture's default and "superior" category of human existence, then, for many white writers blackness posed the threat (and sometimes appeal) of a dangerous otherness. Thus Poe's "The Black Cat" or Hawthorne's presentation of the "black" Chillingworth and Mistress Hibbens in The Scarlet Letter may well be inflected by anxieties about race.

In 1857, the Supreme Court ruled in the case of Dred Scott v. Sanford that blacks could never become U.S. citizens and were inferior to whites. That ruling, which robbed Jefferson's Declaration of Independence of its ambiguities and potential, made clear that the debates on slavery and race were debates about the nation. In the final selections here, the black nationalists James M. Whitfield and Martin R. Delany, as if anticipating the Dred Scott decision, develop African diasporic perspectives that look beyond the borders of the United States. In "Stanzas for the First of August," Whitfield likens African Americans to the emancipated blacks from the British West Indies, while in his 1854 "Political Destiny," Delany suggests that disenfranchised African Americans should consider emigrating to the southern Americas. In a similar vein, William Wells Brown depicts the surviving characters in Clotel choosing to live in Europe; and in Frederick Douglass's "The Heroic Slave," the black rebel Madison Washington is celebrated by the blacks of Nassau. And though Harriet Jacobs manages to escape from slavery to New York City, she presents herself at the end of Incidents in the Life of a Slave Girl as continuing to live in a "free" state that is not as hospitable to black people as England. Most African American leaders committed themselves to the Civil War effort, but the problems raised by slavery and racism in the antebellum period would continue to engage writers of the Reconstruction era and beyond.

THOMAS JEFFERSON

The Declaration of Independence, drafted in 1776 by the Virginian Thomas Jefferson (1743–1826), declared that "all men are created equal." Those resonant words helped inspire the American Revolution and the subsequent development of the nation's democratic institutions. Several years after drafting the Declaration, Jefferson explored the possibility of ending slavery in Virginia, and at various times in his life he wrote about slavery as an evil, remarking in his 1787 Notes on the State of Virginia, for example, that the "whole commerce between master and slave is a perpetual exercise of the most boisterous passions, the most unremitting despotism on the one part, and degrading submission on the other." Yet Jefferson, the nation's third president (1801–09), was a slaveowner who, recent DNA evidence suggests, had at least one child with his slave Sally Hemings; at his death, he manumitted only slaves in the Hemings family. Some therefore view him as a hypocrite who celebrated human liberty while defending Southerners' rights to enslave black people; others regard him as a visionary Founding Father who, despite being influenced by the racist ideologies current in his day, gave the nation's democratic ideals their most powerful written expression. At the time that he wrote *Notes on the State of Virginia*, a book intended primarily for European readers, Jefferson disapproved of slavery, but his antislavery views were grounded in beliefs in whites' superiority to blacks. In later life, as he became economically dependent on his slaves, he became more of a defender of the South's rights to own slaves, though he hoped for a national future in which slavery would come to an end and blacks would be colonized to other countries. As the subsequent selection from David Walker makes clear, the free blacks of the antebellum period were particularly troubled by Jefferson's writings, even as they sought to reinvigorate the principles of his Declaration. The selection from *Notes* is taken from *The Works of Thomas Jefferson* (1904), ed. Paul Leicester Ford.

From Notes on the State of Virginia

* * *

It will probably be asked, Why not retain and incorporate the blacks into the state, and thus save the expence of supplying by importation of white settlers, the vacancies they will leave?[1] Deep rooted prejudices entertained by the whites; ten thousand recollections, by the blacks, of the injuries they have sustained; new provocations; the real distinctions which nature has made; and many other circumstances will divide us into parties, and produce convulsions, which will probably never end but in the extermination of the one or the other race.—To these objections, which are political, may be added others, which are physical and moral. The first difference which strikes us is that of colour. Whether the black of the negro resides in the reticular membrane between the skin and scarfskin,[2] or in the scarfskin itself; whether it proceeds from the colour of the blood, the colour of the bile, or from that of some other secretion, the difference is fixed in nature, and is as real as if its seat and cause were better known to us. And is this difference of no importance? Is it not the foundation of a greater or less share of beauty in the two races? Are not the fine mixtures of red and white, the expressions of every passion by greater or less suffusions of colour in the one, preferable to that eternal monotony, which reigns in the countenances, that immovable veil of black which covers all the emotions of the other race? Add to these, flowing hair, a more elegant symmetry of form, their own judgment in favour of the whites, declared by their preference of them as uniformly as in the preference of the Oran ootan[3] for the black woman over those of his own species. The circumstance of superior beauty, is thought worthy attention in the propagation of our horses, dogs, and other domestic animals; why not in that of man? Besides those of colour, figure and hair, there are other physical distinctions proving a difference of race. They have less hair on the face and body. They secrete less by the kidnies, and more by the glands of the skin, which gives them a very strong and disagreeable odour. This

1. In the text, Jefferson had just proposed the possibility of emancipating some of the slaves and shipping them "to other parts of the world."

2. The outermost layer of skin.
3. Orangutan.

greater degree of transpiration, renders them more tolerant of heat, and less so of cold than the whites. Perhaps too a difference of structure in the pulmonary apparatus, which a late ingenious experimentalist[4] has discovered to be the principal regulator of animal heat, may have disabled them from extricating, in the act of inspiration, so much of that fluid from the outer air, or obliged them in expiration, to part with more of it. They seem to require less sleep. A black after hard labour through the day, will be induced by the slightest amusements to sit up till midnight or later, though knowing he must be out with the first dawn of the morning. They are at least as brave, and more adventuresome. But this may perhaps proceed from a want of forethought, which prevents their seeing a danger till it be present. When present, they do not go through it with more coolness or steadiness than the whites. They are more ardent after their female; but love seems with them to be an eager desire, than a tender delicate mixture of sentiment and sensation. Their griefs are transient. Those numberless afflictions, which render it doubtful whether heaven has given life to us in mercy or in wrath, are less felt, and sooner forgotten with them. In general, their existence appears to participate more of sensation than reflection. To this must be ascribed their disposition to sleep when abstracted from their diversions, and unemployed in labour. An animal whose body is at rest, and who does not reflect, must be disposed to sleep of course. Comparing them by their faculties of memory, reason, and imagination, it appears to me that in memory they are equal to the whites; in reason much inferior, as I think one could scarcely be found capable of tracing and comprehending the investigations of Euclid:[5] and that in imagination they are dull, tasteless, and anomalous. It would be unfair to follow them to Africa for this investigation. We will consider them here, on the same stage with the whites, and where the facts are not apochryphal on which a judgment is to be formed. It will be right to make great allowances for the difference of condition, of education, of conversation, of the sphere in which they move. Many millions of them have been brought to, and born in America. Most of them, indeed, have been confined to tillage, to their own homes, and their own society: yet many have been so situated, that they might have availed themselves of the conversation of their masters; many have been brought up to the handicraft arts, and from that circumstance have always been associated with the whites. Some have been liberally educated, and all have lived in countries where the arts and sciences are cultivated to a considerable degree, and have had before their eyes samples of the best works from abroad. The Indians, with no advantages of this kind, will often carve figures on their pipes not destitute of design and merit. They will crayon out an animal, a plant, or a country, so as to prove the existence of a germ in their minds which only wants cultivation. They astonish you with strokes of the most sublime oratory; such as prove their reason and sentiment strong, their imagination glowing and elevated. But never yet could I find that a black had uttered a thought above the level of plain narration; never seen even an elementary trait of painting or sculpture. In music they are more generally gifted than the whites, with accurate

---

4. Adair Crawford (1748–1795), an English chemist best known for his *Experiments and* *Observations on Animal Heat* (1779).
5. Greek mathematician, c. 300 B.C.E.

ears for tune and time, and they have been found capable of imagining a small catch.[6] Whether they will be equal to the composition of a more extensive run of melody, or of complicated harmony, is yet to be proved. Misery is often the parent of the most affecting touches in poetry.—Among the blacks is misery enough, God knows, but no poetry. Love is the peculiar œstrum[7] of the poet. Their love is ardent, but it kindles the senses only, not the imagination. Religion, indeed, has produced a Phyllis Whately;[8] but it could not produce a poet. The compositions published under her name are below the dignity of criticism.

* * *

To justify a general conclusion, requires many observations, even where the subject may be submitted to the Anatomical knife, to Optical glasses, to analysis by fire or by solvents. How much more then where it is a faculty, not a substance, we are examining; where it eludes the research of all the senses; where the conditions of its existence are various and variously combined; where the effects of those which are present or absent bid defiance to calculation; let me add too, as a circumstance of great tenderness, where our conclusion would degrade a whole race of men from the rank in the scale of beings which their Creator may perhaps have given them. To our reproach it must be said, that though for a century and a half we have had under our eyes the races of black and of red men, they have never yet been viewed by us as subjects of natural history. I advance it, therefore, as a suspicion only, that the blacks, whether originally a distinct race, or made distinct by time and circumstances, are inferior to the whites in the endowments both of body and mind.

1785

6. The instrument proper to them is the Banjar, which they brought hither from Africa, and which is the original of the guitar, its chords being precisely the four lower chords of the guitar [Jefferson's note].

7. Passionate impulse.
8. Jefferson refers to the African American poet Phillis Wheatley (1753–1784), whose *Poems* (1773) was popular in England, going through at least four printings.

DAVID WALKER

Central to the development of African American writing of the antebellum period was a willingness to critique national ideologies and practices. Frederick Douglass's "What to the Slave Is the Fourth of July?" (1852), for example, pointed to the failure of the nation to live up to the ideals of the Declaration of Independence. Two decades before Douglass's most famous speech, David Walker (c. 1790–1830), a free black in Boston, maintained that the nation failed to live up to those ideals because the author of the Declaration was a racist. In *David Walker's Appeal, in Four Articles, Together with a Preamble, to the Colored Citizens of the World, But in Particular, and Very Expressly to those of the United States of America* (1829), Walker argued for African Americans' rights to freedom and dignity in the United

States; in developing his argument, he challenged assumptions about black inferiority, particularly as set forth in Jefferson's *Notes on the State of Virginia*. Though Jefferson had died three years before the publication of the *Appeal*, Walker structured much of his text as a debate with Jefferson, and he hoped to use his text to create black community in the North and the South. To that end, he waged an unconventional campaign to smuggle the book into the South, sending some copies through the mail while entrusting others to intermediaries, including white sailors. The book became notorious for its militant assertion that blacks, when faced with possible enslavement, should "kill or be killed." While the volume appalled and terrified whites, it inspired black abolitionists such as Henry Highland Garnet (1815–1882), who in his 1843 "Address to the Slaves" exhorted the slaves to violently resist the masters. But the volume's main intention was not to push blacks into a race war (unless whites offered no other choice) but to argue for blacks' rights to U.S. citizenship. In 1848 the *Appeal* was republished as part of a volume titled *Walker's Appeal, With a Brief Sketch of His Life. By Henry Highland Garnet. And also Garnet's Address to the Slaves of the United States of America*, from which the selection below is taken.

From David Walker's Appeal in Four Articles

My beloved brethren: The Indians of North and of South America—the Greeks—the Irish subjected under the king of Great Britain—the Jews that ancient people of the Lord—the inhabitants of the islands of the sea—in fine, all the inhabitants of the earth, (except however, the sons of Africa) are called *men*, and of course are, and ought to be free. But *we*, (coloured people) and our children are *brutes!!* and of course are and ought to be SLAVES to the American people and their children forever! to dig their mines and work their farms; and thus go on enriching them, from one generation to another with our blood and our tears!!

I promised in a preceding page to demonstrate to the satisfaction of the most incredulous, that we, (coloured people of these United States of America) are the *most wretched, degraded* and abject set of beings that ever *lived* since the world began, and that the white Americans having reduced us to the wretched state of *slavery*, treat us in that condition *more cruel* (they being an enlightened and christian people) than any heathen nation did any people whom it had reduced to our condition. These affirmations are so well confirmed in the minds of all unprejudiced men who have taken the trouble to read histories, that they need no elucidation from me.

* * *

I have been for years troubling the pages of historians to find out what our fathers have done to the *white Christians of America*, to merit such condign punishment as they have inflicted on them, and do continue to inflict on us their children. But I must aver, that my researches have hitherto been to no effect. I have therefore come to the immovable conclusion, that they (Americans) have, and do continue to punish us for nothing else, but for enriching them and their country. For I cannot conceive of any thing else. Nor will I ever believe otherwise until the Lord shall convince me.

The world knows, that slavery as it existed among the Romans, (which was the primary cause of their destruction) was, comparatively speaking, no more than a *cypher*, when compared with ours under the Americans. Indeed, I should not have noticed the Roman slaves, had not the very learned and penetrating Mr. Jefferson said, "When a master was murdered, all his slaves in the same house or within hearing, were condemned to death."[1]—Here let me ask Mr. Jefferson, (but he is gone to answer at the bar of God, for the deeds done in his body while living,) I therefore ask the whole American people, had I not rather die, or be put to death than to be a slave to any tyrant, who takes not only my own, but my wife and children's lives by the inches? Yea, would I meet death with avidity far! far!! in preference to such *servile submission* to the murderous hands of tyrants. Mr. Jefferson's very severe remarks on us have been so extensively argued upon by men whose attainments in literature, I shall never be able to reach, that I would not have meddled with it, were it not to solicit each of my brethren, who has the spirit of a man, to buy a copy of Mr. Jefferson's "Notes on Virginia," and put it in the hand of his son. For let no one of us suppose that the refutations which have been written by our white friends are enough—they are *whites*—we are *blacks*. We, and the world wish to see the charges of Mr. Jefferson refuted by the blacks *themselves*, according to their chance: for we must remember that what the whites have written respecting this subject, is other men's labors and did not emanate from the blacks. I know well, that there are some talents and learning among the coloured people of this country, which we have not a chance to develope, in consequence of oppression; but our oppression ought not to hinder us from acquiring all we can.—For we will have a chance to develope them by and by. God will not suffer us, always to be oppressed. Our sufferings will come to an *end*, in spite of all the Americans this side of *eternity*. Then we will want all the learning and talents among ourselves, and perhaps more, to govern ourselves.—"Every dog must have its day,"[2] the American's is coming to an end.

But let us review Mr. Jefferson's remarks respecting us some further. Comparing our miserable fathers, with the learned philosophers of Greece, he says: "Yet notwithstanding these and other discouraging circumstances among the Romans, their slaves were often their rarest artists. They excelled too in science, insomuch as to be usually employed as tutors to their master's children; Epictetus, Terence and Phædrus, were slaves,—but they were of the race of whites. It is not their *condition* then, but *nature*, which has produced the distinction."[3] See this, my brethren!! Do you believe that this assertion is swallowed by millions of the whites? Do you know that Mr. Jefferson was one of as great characters as ever lived among the whites? See his writings for the world, and public labors for the United States of America. Do you believe that the assertions of such a man, will pass away into oblivion unobserved by this people and the world? If you do you are much mistaken—See how the American people treat us—have we souls in our bodies? are we men who have any spirits at all? I know that there are many *swell-bellied* fellows among us whose greatest object is to fill their stomachs. Such I do not mean—I am after those who know and feel, that we are MEN as well as other people; to them, I say, that unless we try to refute Mr. Jefferson's arguments respecting us, we will only establish them.

1. See his notes on Virginia [Walker's note].
2. Attributed to John Heywood (1497?–1580?),

English writer of proverbs and epigrams.
3. See his notes on Virginia [Walker's note].

But the slaves among the Romans. Every body who has read history, knows, that as soon as a slave among the Romans obtained his freedom, he could rise to the greatest eminence in the State, and there was no law instituted to hinder a slave from buying his freedom. Have not the Americans instituted laws to hinder us from obtaining our freedom. Do any deny this charge? Read the laws of Virginia, North Carolina, &c. Further: have not the Americans instituted laws to prohibit a man of colour from obtaining and holding any office whatever, under the government of the United States of America? Now, Mr. Jefferson tells us that our condition is not so hard, as the slaves were under the Romans!!!!

It is time for me to bring this article to a close. But before I close it, I must observe to my brethren that at the close of the first Revolution in this country with Great Britain, there were but thirteen States in the Union, now there are twenty-four, most of which are slave-holding States, and the whites are dragging us around in chains and hand-cuffs to their new States and Territories to work their mines and farms, to enrich them and their children, and millions of them believing firmly that we being a little darker than they, were made by our creator to be an inheritance to them and their children forever—the same as a parcel of *brutes!!*

Are we MEN!!—I ask you, O my brethren! are we MEN? Did our creator make us to be slaves to dust and ashes like ourselves? Are they not dying worms as well as we? Have they not to make their appearance before the tribunal of heaven, to answer for the deeds done in the body, as well as we? Have we any other master but Jesus Christ alone? Is he not their master as well as ours?—What right then, have we to obey and call any other master, but Himself? How we could be so *submissive* to a gang of men, whom we cannot tell whether they are as *good* as ourselves or not, I never could conceive. However, this is shut up with the Lord and we cannot precisely tell—but I declare, we judge men by their works.

The whites have always been an unjust, jealous unmerciful, avaricious and blood thirsty set of beings, always seeking after power and authority.—We view them all over the confederacy of Greece, where they were first known to be any thing, (in consequence of education) we see them there, cutting each other's throats—trying to subject each other to wretchedness and misery, to effect which they used all kinds of deceitful, unfair and unmerciful means. We view them next in Rome, where the spirit of tyranny and deceit rated still higher.—We view them in Gaul, Spain and in Britain—in fine, we view them all over Europe, together with what were scattered about in Asia and Africa, as heathens, and we see them acting more like devils than accountable men. But some may ask, did not the blacks of Africa, and the mulattoes of Asia, go on in the same way as did the whites of Europe. I answer no—they never were half so avaricious, deceitful and unmerciful as the whites, according to their knowledge.

But we will leave the whites or Europeans as heathens and take a view of them as christians, in which capacity we see them as cruel, if not more so than ever. In fact, take them as a body, they are ten times more cruel, avaricious and unmerciful than ever they were; for while they were heathens they were bad enough it is true, but it is positively a fact that they were not quite so audacious as to go and take vessel loads of men, women and children, and in cold blood and through devilishness, throw them into the sea, and murder them in all kind of ways. While they were heathens, they were too ignorant for such barbarity. But being christians, enlightened and sensible, they are completely prepared for such hellish cruelties. Now suppose God were to give them more sense, what would they do. If it were possible would they not *dethrone* Jehovah and seat themselves upon his throne? I therefore, in the name and fear of the Lord God of heaven and of earth, divested of prejudice either on the side of my colour or that of the whites, advance my suspicion, whether they are *as good by nature* as we are or not. Their actions, since they were known as a people, have been the reverse, I do indeed suspect them, but this, as I before observed, is shut up with the Lord, we cannot exactly tell, it will be proved in succeeding generations.

1829

SAMUEL E. CORNISH AND JOHN B. RUSSWURM

n March 1827, the New York Presbyterian minister Samuel Cornish (1795–1858) and the Jamaican-born John Russwurm (1799–1851), a classmate of Nathaniel Hawthorne's at Bowdoin College, established the first African American newspaper, *Freedom's Journal*, in New York City. This was a promising time for such a newspaper, for July 4, 1827, saw the official end of slavery in New York State. In their editorial statement "To Our Patrons," published in the newspaper's first issue of March 16, 1827 (the source of the text below), Cornish and Russwurm underscored just how important it was for African Americans to be able to plead their "own cause" in their own newspaper. Over the two years of the life of the newspaper, the editors printed essays, political treatises, fiction, and poetry by African American writers; and over the next several decades, African American newspapers such as the *Colored American* (1838–42), the *North Star* (1847–51), *Frederick Douglass' Paper* (1851–59), and the *Weekly Anglo-African* (1859–62) provided important print forums for the development of black writing in the United States. David Walker published in *Freedom's Journal* and helped to distribute it; James Whitfield published his poetry in a number of black journals; Martin Delany had a short-lived newspaper called the *Mystery* (1843); and Frederick Douglass developed a more independent voice once he broke from William Lloyd Garrison and began to articulate his own perspectives in the *North Star*, which he coedited with Delany. As scholars have come to realize, some of the most vital African American writing of the nineteenth century can be found in black newspapers and journals.

To Our Patrons

In presenting our first number to our Patrons, we feel all the diffidence of persons entering upon a new and untried line of business. But a moment's reflection upon the noble objects, which we have in view by the publication of this Journal; the expediency of its appearance at this time, when so many schemes are in action concerning our people—encourage us to come boldly before an enlightened publick. For we believe, that a paper devoted to the dissemination of useful knowledge among our brethren, and to their moral and religious improvement, must meet with the cordial approbation of every friend to humanity.

The peculiarities of this Journal, render it important that we should advertise to the world the motives by which we are actuated, and the objects which we contemplate.

We wish to plead our own cause. Too long have others spoken for us. Too long has the publick been deceived by misrepresentations, in things which concern us dearly, though in the estimation of some mere trifles; for though there are many in society who exercise towards us benevolent feelings; still (with sorrow we confess it) there are others who make it their business to enlarge upon the least trifle, which tends to the discredit of any person or colour; and pronounce anathemas and denounce our whole body for the misconduct of this guilty one. We are aware that there are many instances of vice among us, but we avow that it is because no one has taught its subjects to be virtuous: many instances of poverty, because no sufficient efforts accommodated to minds contracted by slavery, and deprived of early education have been made, to teach them how to husband their hard earnings, and to secure to themselves comforts.

Education being an object of the highest importance to the welfare of society, we shall endeavour to present just and adequate views of it, and to urge upon our brethren the necessity and expediency of training their children, while young, to habits of industry, and thus forming them for becoming useful members of society. It is surely time that we should awake from this lethargy of years, and make a concentrated effort for the education of our youth. We form a spoke in the human wheel, and it is necessary that we should understand our dependence on the different parts, and theirs on us, in order to perform our part with propriety.

Though not desirous of dictating, we shall feel it our incumbent duty to dwell occasionally upon the general principles and rules of economy. The world has grown too enlightened, to estimate any man's character by his personal appearance. Though all men acknowledge the excellency of Franklin's maxims,[1] yet comparatively few practise upon them. We may deplore when it is too late, the neglect of these self evident truths, but it avails little to mourn. Ours will be the task of admonishing our brethren on these points.

The civil rights of a people being of the greatest value, it shall ever be our duty to vindicate our brethren, when oppressed, and to lay the case before the publick. We shall also urge upon our brethren (who are qualified by the laws of the different states) the expediency of using their elective franchise; and of making an independent use of the same. We wish them not to become the tools of party.

And as much time is frequently lost, and wrong principles instilled, by the perusal of works of trivial importance, we shall consider it a part of our duty to recommend to our young readers, such authors as will not only enlarge

1. The maxims about self-help of Benjamin Franklin (1706–1790), which can be found in *Poor Richard's Almanac* (1732–58) and his posthumously published *Autobiography*.

their stock of useful knowledge, but such as will also serve to stimulate them to higher attainments in science.

We trust also, that through the columns of the FREEDOM'S JOURNAL, many practical pieces, having for their bases, the improvement of our brethren, will be presented to them, from the pens of many of our respected friends, who have kindly promised their assistance.

It is our earnest wish to make our Journal a medium of intercourse between our brethren in the different states of this great confederacy: that through its columns an expression of our sentiments, on many interesting subjects which concern us, may be offered to the publick: that plans which apparently are beneficial may be candidly discussed and properly weighed; if worthy, receive our cordial approbation; if not, our marked disapprobation.

Useful knowledge of every kind, and every thing that relates to Africa, shall find a ready admission into our columns; and as that vast continent becomes daily more known, we trust that many things will come to light, proving that the natives of it are neither so ignorant nor stupid as they have generally been supposed to be.

And while these important subjects shall occupy the columns of the FREEDOM'S JOURNAL, we would not be unmindful of our brethren who are still in the iron fetters of bondage. They are our kindred by all the ties of nature; and though but little can be effected by us, still let our sympathies be poured forth, and our prayers in their behalf, ascend to Him who is able to succour them.

From the press and the pulpit we have suffered much by being incorrectly represented. Men whom we equally love and admire have not hesitated to represent us disadvantagously, without becoming personally acquainted with the true state of things, nor discerning between virtue and vice among us. The virtuous part of our people feel themselves sorely aggrieved under the existing state of things—they are not appreciated.

Our vices and our degradation are ever arrayed against us, but our virtues are passed by unnoticed. And what is still more lamentable, our friends, to whom we concede all the principles of humanity and religion, from these very causes seem to have fallen into the current of popular feeling and are imperceptibly floating on the stream—actually living in the practice of prejudice, while they abjure it in theory, and feel it not in their hearts. Is it not very desirable that such should know more of our actual condition, and of our efforts and feelings, that in forming or advocating plans for our amelioration, they may do it more understandingly? In the spirit of candor and humility we intend by a simple representation of facts to lay our case before the publick, with a view to arrest the progress of prejudice, and to shield ourselves against the consequent evils. We wish to conciliate all and to irritate none, yet we must be firm and unwavering in our principles, and persevering in our efforts.

If ignorance, poverty and degradation have hitherto been our unhappy lot; has the Eternal decree gone forth, that our race alone, are to remain in this state, while knowledge and civilization are shedding their enlivening rays over the rest of the human family? The recent travels of Denham and Clapperton in the interior of Africa, and the interesting narrative which they have published; the establishment of the republic of Hayti after years of sanguinary warfare; its subsequent progress in all the arts of civilization;

and the advancement of liberal ideas in South America, where despotism has given place to free governments, and where many of our brethren now fill important civil and military stations, prove the contrary.[2]

The interesting fact that there are FIVE HUNDRED THOUSAND free persons of colour, one half of whom might peruse, and the whole be benefited by the publication of the Journal; that no publication, as yet, has been devoted exclusively to their improvement—that many selections from approved standard authors, which are within the reach of few, may occasionally be made—and more important still, that this large body of our citizens have no public channel—all serve to prove the real necessity, at present, for the appearance of the FREEDOM'S JOURNAL.

It shall ever be our desire to conduct the editorial department of our paper as to give offence to none of our patrons; as nothing is farther from us than to make it the advocate of any partial views, either in politics or religion. What few days we can number, have been devoted to the improvement of our brethren; and it is our earnest wish that the remainder may be spent in the same delightful service.

In conclusion, whatever concerns us as a people, will ever find a ready admission into the FREEDOM'S JOURNAL, interwoven with all the principal news of the day.

And while every thing in our power shall be performed to support the character of our Journal, we would respectfully invite our numerous friends to assist by their communications, and our coloured brethren to strengthen our hands by their subscriptions, as our labour is one of common cause, and worthy of their consideration and support. And we do most earnestly solicit the latter, that if at any time we should seem to be zealous, or too pointed in the inculcation of any important lesson, they will remember, that they are equally interested in the cause in which we are engaged, and attribute our zeal to the peculiarities of our situation, and our earnest engagedness in their well-being.

THE EDITORS

1827

2. References to the Central and South American independence movements in which various countries broke from Spanish rule during the 1810s and 1820s. Haiti emerged as an independent nation in 1804, after breaking from France in a violent war lasting several years. "Denham and Clapperton": the English soldier Dixon Denham (1786–1828) and the Scottish naval officer Bain Hugh Clapperton (1788–1827) published their *Narrative of Travels and Discoveries in Northern and Central Africa in the Years 1822, 1823, and 1824* in 1826.

WILLIAM LLOYD GARRISON

Born in Newburyport, Massachusetts, the white abolitionist William Lloyd Garrison (1805–1879) worked on the antislavery newspaper the *Genius of Universal Emancipation* during the late 1820s. In 1831 he established his own antislavery newspaper, the *Liberator*, which—published in Boston from January 1831 to December 1865—became the most influential antislavery newspaper of the time. The only near competitors were Frederick Douglass's the *North Star* and *Frederick Douglass' Paper*. In his newspaper editorials and other writings, Garrison advocated moral persuasion over violence, condemned the Constitution as a proslavery document, rejected union with slaveholders, and—most important—called for the immediate (not gradual) emancipation of the slaves. In 1833 he organized the American Anti-Slavery Society, which remained one of the most effective antislavery organizations of the period. Under its auspices, he published Douglass's *Narrative* in 1845; but Douglass broke with him around 1850 when he became convinced that Garrison's view of the Constitution as a proslavery document was incorrect. Garrison's antislavery activities, particularly the publication of his newspaper, infuriated Southerners and contributed to the increasingly heated sectional tensions of the antebellum period. That Nat Turner's bloody slave rebellion in Southampton, Virginia, occurred just months after Garrison began publishing the *Liberator* was not lost on his southern critics, who called for the suppression of the newspaper and other antislavery publications. In the editorial "To the Public," which appeared in the January 1, 1831, inaugural issue of the *Liberator*, the source of the selection printed here, Garrison invokes the Declaration of Independence of the Southerner Jefferson to argue for the need to fulfill the mandate of the American Revolution by bringing equality to all.

To the Public

In the month of August, I issued proposals for publishing "THE LIBERATOR" in Washington city; but the enterprise, though hailed in different sections of the country, was palsied by public indifference. Since that time, the removal of the Genius of Universal Emancipation[1] to the Seat of Government has rendered less imperious the establishment of a similar periodical in that quarter.

During my recent tour for the purpose of exciting the minds of the people by a series of discourses on the subject of slavery, every place that I visited gave fresh evidence of the fact, that a greater revolution in public sentiment was to be effected in the free states—*and particularly in New-England*—than at the south. I found contempt more bitter, opposition more active, detraction more relentless, prejudice more stubborn, and apathy more frozen, than among slave owners themselves. Of course, there were individual exceptions to the contrary. This state of things afflicted, but did not dishearten me. I determined, at every hazard, to lift up the standard of emancipation in the eyes of the nation, *within sight of Bunker Hill[2] and in the birth place of liberty*. That standard is now unfurled; and long may it float unhurt by the spoliations of time or the missiles of a desperate foe—yea, till every chain be broken, and every bondman set free! Let southern oppressors tremble—let their secret abettors tremble—let their northern apologists tremble—let all the enemies of the persecuted blacks tremble.

I deem the publication of my original Prospectus unnecessary, as it has obtained a wide circulation. The principles therein inculcated will be steadily pursued in this paper, excepting that I shall not array myself as the political

---

1. An antislavery newspaper edited by Benjamin Lundy (1789–1839). Garrison served as an editor from 1829 to 1830.

2. The site of a famous Revolutionary War battle in Boston on June 17, 1775.

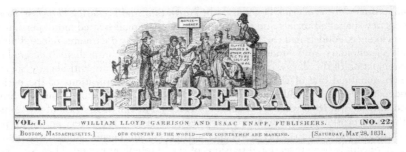

The Liberator. Detail from the masthead of Garrison's antislavery paper, May 28, 1831.

partisan of any man. In defending the great cause of human rights, I wish to derive the assistance of all religions and of all parties.

Assenting to the "self-evident truth" maintained in the American Declaration of Independence, "that all men are created equal, and endowed by their Creator with certain inalienable rights—among which are life, liberty and the pursuit of happiness," I shall strenuously contend for the immediate enfranchisement of our slave population. In Park-street Church, on the Fourth of July, 1829, in an address on slavery, I unreflectingly assented to the popular but pernicious doctrine of *gradual* abolition. I seize this opportunity to make a full and unequivocal recantation, and thus publicly to ask pardon of my God, of my country, and of my brethren the poor slaves, for having uttered a sentiment so full of timidity, injustice and absurdity. A similar recantation, from my pen, was published in the Genius of Universal Emancipation at Baltimore, in September, 1829. My conscience is now satisfied.

I am aware, that many object to the severity of my language; but is there not cause for severity? I *will be* as harsh as truth, and as uncompromising as justice. On this subject, I do not wish to think, or speak, or write, with moderation. No! no! Tell a man whose house is on fire, to give a moderate alarm; tell him to moderately rescue his wife from the hands of the ravisher; tell the mother to gradually extricate her babe from the fire into which it has fallen;—but urge me not to use moderation in a cause like the present. I am in earnest—I will not equivocate—I will not excuse—I will not retreat a single inch—AND I WILL BE HEARD. The apathy of the people is enough to make every statue leap from its pedestal, and to hasten the resurrection of the dead.

It is pretended, that I am retarding the cause of emancipation by the coarseness of my invective, and the precipitancy of my measures. *The charge is not true.* On this question my influence,—humble as it is,—is felt at this moment to a considerable extent, and shall be felt in coming years—not perniciously, but beneficially—not as a curse, but as a blessing; and posterity will bear testimony that I was right. I desire to thank God, that he enables me to disregard "the fear of man which bringeth a snare,"[3] and to speak his truth in its simplicity and power. And here I close with this fresh dedication:

---

3. Proverbs 29.25.

Oppression! I have seen thee, face to face,
And met thy cruel eye and cloudy brow;
But thy soul-withering glance I fear not now—
For dread to prouder feelings doth give place
Of deep abhorrence! Scorning the disgrace
Of slavish knees that at thy footstool bow
I also kneel—but with far other vow
Do hail thee and thy hord of hirelings base:—
I swear, while life-blood warms my throbbing veins,
Still to oppose and thwart, with heart and hand,
Thy brutalising sway—till Afric's chains
Are burst, and Freedom rules the rescued land,—
Trampling Oppression and his iron rod:
Such is the vow I take—SO HELP ME GOD![4]

1831

4. The poem is by Garrison.

ANGELINA E. GRIMKÉ

Born and raised in a slaveholding family in Charleston, South Carolina, Angelina E. Grimké (1805–1879) moved to Philadelphia in the 1820s and by the 1830s was a fervent supporter of Garrisonian abolitionism. At a time when women in her social class were expected to remain at home and embrace the private realm of domesticity, she was regarded as a particularly shocking cultural figure for her boldness in lecturing on abolitionism before mixed audiences of men and women. She found that her work in antislavery led her to champion women's rights as well. As she remarked in 1838: "The investigation of the rights of the slave has led me to a better understanding of my own." Other women writers of the period, such as Lydia Maria Child and Margaret Fuller, also saw connections between the causes of antislavery and women's rights. In *Appeal to the Christian Women of the South* (1836), the source of the selection printed here, Grimké, somewhat in the manner of Harriet Beecher Stowe in *Uncle Tom's Cabin*, urges Southern women to use their influence within the home to help bring about the end of slavery. Challenging key tenets of the proslavery argument, including the notion that emancipation would lead to a racial war of extermination (an argument that Jefferson made in *Notes in the State of Virginia*), Grimké in effect calls on Southern women to rebel against their own "enslavement" to patriarchy.

From Appeal to the Christian Women of the South

* * *

I have thus, I think, clearly proved to you seven propositions, viz.: First, that slavery is contrary to the declaration of our independence. Second, that it is contrary to the first charter of human rights given to Adam, and renewed to

Noah. Third, that the fact of slavery having been the subject of prophecy, furnishes *no* excuse whatever to slavedealers. Fourth, that no such system existed under the patriarchal dispensation. Fifth, that *slavery never* existed under the Jewish dispensation; but so far otherwise, that every servant was placed under the *protection of law*, and care taken not only to prevent all *involuntary* servitude, but all *voluntary perpetual* bondage. Sixth, that slavery in America reduces a *man* to a *thing*, a "chattel personal," *robs him* of *all* his rights as a *human being*, fetters both his mind and body, and protects the *master* in the most unnatural and unreasonable power, whilst it *throws him out* of the protection of law. Seventh, that slavery is contrary to the example and precepts of our holy and merciful Redeemer, and of his apostles.

But perhaps you will be ready to query, why appeal to *women* on this subject? *We* do not make the laws which perpetuate slavery. *No* legislative power is vested in *us*; *we* can do nothing to overthrow the system, even if we wished to do so. To this I reply, I know you do not make the laws, but I also know that *you are the wives and mothers, the sisters and daughters of those who do*; and if you really suppose *you* can do nothing to overthrow slavery, you are greatly mistaken. You can do much in every way: four things I will name. 1st. You can read on this subject. 2d. You can pray over this subject. 3d. You can speak on this subject. 4th You can *act* on this subject. I have not placed reading before praying, because I regard it more important, but because, in order to pray aright, we must understand what we are praying for; it is only then we can "pray with the understanding and the spirit also."

1. Read then on the subject of slavery. Search the Scriptures daily, whether the things I have told you are true. Other books and papers might be a great help to you in this investigation, but they are not necessary, and it is hardly probable that your Committees of Vigilance[1] will allow you to have any other. The *Bible* then is the book I want you to read in the spirit of inquiry, and the spirit of prayer. Even the enemies of Abolitionists, acknowledge that their doctrines are drawn from it. In the great mob in Boston,[2] last autumn, when the books and papers of the Anti-Slavery Society, were thrown out of the windows of their office, one individual laid hold of the Bible and was about tossing it out to the ground, when another reminded him that it was the Bible he had in his hand. "O! 'tis all one," he replied, and out went the sacred volume, along with the rest. We thank him for the acknowledgment. Yes, "*it is all one*," for our books and papers are mostly commentaries on the Bible, and the Declaration. Read the *Bible* then, it contains the words of Jesus, and they are spirit and life. Judge for yourselves whether *he sanctioned* such a system of oppression and crime.

2. Pray over this subject. When you have entered into your closets, and shut to the doors, then pray to your father, who seeth in secret, that he would open your eyes to see whether slavery is *sinful*, and if it is, that he would enable you to bear a faithful, open and unshrinking testimony against it, and to do whatsoever your hands find to do, leaving the consequences entirely to him, who still says to us whenever we try to reason away duty from the fear of consequences, "*What is that to thee, follow thou me.*"[3] Pray also for that

---

1. Groups of Southern whites who attempted to suppress abolitionist writings.
2. In October 1835, a mob attacked William

Lloyd Garrison and the English abolitionist George Thompson (1804–1878).
3. John 21.22.

"Am I not a Woman . . . ?" In the early nineteenth century, British antislavery advocates popularized the image of the kneeling slave, with the caption "Am I not a Man and a Brother?" This image from George Bourne's *Slavery Illustrated in Its Effects upon Women* (1837) suggests the increasing interconnections between antislavery and the campaign for women's rights.

poor slave, that he may be kept patient and submissive under his hard lot, until God is pleased to open the door of freedom to him without violence or bloodshed. Pray too for the master that his heart may be softened, and he made willing to acknowledge, as Joseph's brethren did, "Verily we are guilty concerning our brother," before he will be compelled to add in consequence of Divine judgment, "therefore is all this evil come upon us."[4] Pray also for all your brethren and sisters who are laboring in the righteous cause of Emancipation in the Northern States, England and the world. There is great encouragement for prayer in these words of our Lord. "Whatsoever ye shall ask the Father *in my name*, he *will give* it to you"[5]—Pray then without ceasing, in the closet and the social circle.

3. Speak on this subject. It is through the tongue, the pen, and the press, that truth is principally propagated. Speak then to your relatives, your friends, your acquaintances on the subject of slavery; be not afraid if you are conscientiously convinced it is *sinful*, to say so openly, but calmly, and to let your sentiments be known. If you are served by the slaves of others, try to ameliorate their condition as much as possible; never aggravate their faults, and thus add fuel to the fire of anger already kindled, in a master and mistress's bosom; remember their extreme ignorance, and consider them as your Heavenly Father does the *less* culpable on this account, even when they do wrong things. Discountenance *all* cruelty to them, all starvation, all corporal chastisement; these may brutalize and *break* their spirits, but will never bend them to willing, cheerful obedience. If possible, see that they are comfortably and *seasonably* fed, whether in the house or the field; it is unreasonable and cruel to expect slaves to wait for their breakfast until eleven o'clock, when they rise at five or six. Do all you can, to induce their owners to clothe them well, and to allow them many little indulgences which would contribute to their comfort. Above all, try to persuade your husband, father, brothers and sons, that *slavery is a crime against God and man*, and that it is a great sin to keep *human beings* in such abject ignorance; to deny them the privilege of learning to read and write. The Catholics are universally condemned, for denying the Bible to the

4. Cf. Genesis 42.21. 5. John 16.23.

common people, but, *slaveholders must not* blame them, for *they* are doing the *very same thing*, and for the very same reason, neither of these systems can bear the light which bursts from the pages of that Holy Book. And lastly, endeavour to inculcate submission on the part of the slaves, but whilst doing this be faithful in pleading the cause of the oppressed.

> "Will *you* behold unheeding,
> Life's holiest feelings crushed,
> Where *woman's* heart is bleeding,
> Shall *woman's* voice be hushed?"[6]

4. Act on this subject. Some of you *own* slaves yourselves. If you believe slavery is *sinful*, set them at liberty, "undo the heavy burdens and let the oppressed go free."[7] If they wish to remain with you, pay them wages, if not let them leave you. Should they remain teach them, and have them taught the common branches of an English education; they have minds and those minds, *ought to be improved*. So precious a talent as intellect, never was given to be wrapt in a napkin and buried in the earth. It is the *duty* of all, as far as they can, to improve their own mental faculties, because we are commanded to love God with *all our minds*, as well as with all our hearts, and we commit a great sin, if we *forbid or prevent* that cultivation of the mind in others, which would enable them to perform this duty.

1836

6. From "Think of Our Country's Glory," by Elizabeth Margaret Chandler (1807–1834), in *Poetical Works* (1836).
7. Isaiah 58.6.

SOJOURNER TRUTH

Born a slave in Ulster County in upstate New York, Sojourner Truth (1797–1883) emerged as one of the nation's most flamboyant advocates of the rights of African Americans and women. At least five of her children were sold into slavery before New York State abolished slavery in 1827, and though she never learned to read or write, she successfully sued for the return of one of her sons in 1829. In 1843 she had a visionary experience that left her convinced God wanted her to speak the truth about the evils of Americans' sins against blacks and women. Like Angelina Grimké, she regularly spoke before mixed audiences of men and women, presenting the causes of antislavery and women's rights as inextricably intertwined. With the publication of the *Narrative of Sojourner Truth* in 1850, a life history that she dictated to Oliver Gilbert, she gained even greater renown. Harriet Beecher Stowe regarded Truth an inspiring example of the black Christian woman as antipatriarchal reformer, and she was not alone in being influenced by newspaper reports of Truth's dramatic speeches. In the summer of 1851, Truth addressed a women's rights convention in Akron, Ohio. The account that follows is from the June 21, 1851, issue of the *Anti-Slavery Bugle*.

Speech to the Women's Rights Convention
in Akron, Ohio, 1851

One of the most unique and interesting speeches of the Convention was made by Sojourner Truth, an emancipated slave. It is impossible to transfer it to paper, or convey any adequate idea of the effect it produced upon the audience. Those only can appreciate it who saw her powerful form, her whole-souled, earnest gestures, and listened to her strong and truthful tones. She came forward to the platform and addressing the President said with great simplicity:

May I say a few words? Receiving an affirmative answer, she proceeded: I want to say a few words about this matter. I am a woman's rights. I have as much muscle as any man, and can do as much work as any man. I have plowed and reaped and husked and chopped and mowed, and can any man do more than that? I have heard much about the sexes being equal; I can carry as much as any man, and can cut as much too, if I can get it. I am as strong as any man that is now. As for intellect, all I can say is, if woman have a pint and man a quart—why cant she have her little pint full? You need not be afraid to give us our rights for fear we will take too much,—for we cant take more than our pint'll hold. The poor men seem to be all in confusion, and dont know what to do. Why children, if you have woman's rights give it to her and you will feel better. You will have your own rights, and they wont be so much trouble. I cant read, but I can hear. I have heard the bible and have learned that Eve caused man to sin. Well if woman upset the world, do give her a chance to set it rightside up again. The Lady has spoken about Jesus, how he never spurned woman from him, and she was right. When Lazarus[1] died, Mary and Martha came to him with faith and love and besought him to raise their brother. And Jesus wept—and Lazarus came forth. And how came Jesus into the world? Through God who created him and woman who bore him. Man, where is your part? But the women are coming up blessed be God and a few of the men are coming up with them. But man is in a tight place, the poor slave is on him, woman is coming on him, and he is surely between a hawk and a buzzard.

1851

1. Restored to life by Jesus (John 11.1–44).

JAMES M. WHITFIELD

B orn free in Exeter, New Hampshire, James M. Whitfield (1822–1871) moved in the late 1830s to Buffalo, New York, where he soon became a leader of Buffalo's African American community. A barber by trade, he participated in black reading societies and helped to organize antislavery protests, where he often recited his poetry. While attending African American conventions in the late 1840s and early 1850s, he met a number of more nationally based African American leaders, including Frederick Douglass and Martin Delany. In 1853 James S. Leavitt of Buffalo published Whitfield's only book of poems, *America and Other Poems*, which was dedicated to Delany. Douglass, for his part, had previously published several of Whitfield's poems in the *North Star* and *Frederick Douglass' Paper*, and he printed a favorable review of *America* in the July 15, 1853, issue of *Frederick Douglass' Paper*. However, around that time Whitfield and Douglass broke on the matter of black emigration. Whitfield accepted Delany's view that blacks should consider emigrating to Central America (see the selection by Delany), while Douglass wanted blacks to work for equality and citizenship within the United States. A debate between Whitfield and Douglass's associate editors appeared over several issues of *Frederick Douglass' Paper* and was reprinted in *Arguments, Pro and Con, on the Call for a National Emigration Convention* (1854). Although there is evidence that Whitfield considered emigrating to Haiti in 1859 or 1860, instead he moved to San Francisco in 1861, where he continued to work as a barber and write poetry. At an anniversary celebration of the Emancipation Proclamation in 1867, Whitfield read his poetry to the thousands of attendees at San Francisco's Platt's Hall.

Whitfield's *America* offers a complex view of the United States and of "America" itself, with poems about U.S. leaders, such as the antislavery advocate and sixth president John Quincy Adams, and other poems about black rebels of the Americas, such as Cinque, who led the famous 1839 slave revolt on the Cuban slave ship *Amistad*. The volume also includes an ode on the unfulfilled promises of the Fourth of July and the poem printed below on West Indies emancipation, which Whitfield initially read at a First of August celebration in Buffalo in 1849. For many African Americans, England's declaration on August 1, 1834, of the abolition of slavery in the British West Indies (which includes the present-day Caribbean nations of Jamaica, Barbados, Antigua, Guyana, and many others) offered an occasion for mass celebrations in the United States that expressed diasporic longings for black freedom throughout the Americas. The poem is taken from *America* (1853), which is reprinted in *The Works of James M. Whitfield* (2011), ed. Robert S. Levine and Ivy G. Wilson.

Stanzas for the First of August

From bright West Indies' sunny seas,
   Comes, borne upon the balmy breeze,
The joyous shout, the gladsome tone,
   Long in those bloody isles unknown,
Bearing across the heaving wave   5
The song of the unfettered slave.

No charging squadrons shook the ground,
   When freedom here her claims obtained;
No cannon, with tremendous sound,
   The noble patriot's cause maintained: 10
No furious battle-charger neighed,
No brother fell by brother's blade.

None of those desperate scenes of strife,
   Which mark the warrior's proud career,
The awful waste of human life,   15
   Have ever been enacted here;

But truth and justice spoke from heaven,
And slavery's galling chain was riven.

'T was moral force which broke the chain,
   That bound eight hundred thousand men;   20
And when we see it snapped in twain,
   Shall we not join in praises then?—
And prayers unto Almighty God,
Who smote to earth the tyrant's rod?

And from those islands of the sea,   25
   The scenes of blood and crime and wrong,
The glorious anthem of the free,
   Now swells in mighty chorus strong;
Telling th' oppressed, where'er they roam,
Those islands now are freedom's home.   30

1853

MARTIN R. DELANY

During the antebellum period, a number of African American leaders argued that the United States would forever remain a nation of slavery and white supremacy and that beneath the contradictions in Jefferson's vision lay the reality that he and others among the nation's founders never intended for blacks to become citizens of the new republic. Angered and disillusioned by the Compromise of 1850, with its infamous Fugitive Slave Act requiring all citizens to assist in returning escaped slaves to their "owners," the black Pittsburgh leader Martin R. Delany (1812–1885) broke with his friend Frederick Douglass, with whom he had co-edited the antislavery newspaper the *North Star*, and began to call for African American emigration. In 1854 he convened a National Emigration Convention of Colored People in Cleveland; his address at the convention, "Political Destiny," counseled African Americans to emigrate to Central or South America or to the Caribbean. His emigrationist vision inspired a number of African Americans, including William Wells Brown, who, in the wake of the Supreme Court's 1857 *Dred Scott* decision declaring that blacks could never become citizens of the United States, advocated African American emigration to Haiti. During the late 1850s and early 1860s, Delany worked on an initiative to establish a black colony in Africa; he also serialized a novel, *Blake* (1859, 1861–62), which focused on black insurrectionism in the Americas. With the outbreak of the Civil War, however, most black emigrationists, including Delany and Wells Brown, soon committed themselves to the Union cause, which they regarded as the cause of antislavery. Delany himself became the first black major in the Union Army. For the remainder of his life, however, he remained tempted by the prospect of black emigration to Africa. The text of his 1854 emigrationist speech is taken from *Proceedings of the National Emigration Convention of Colored People* (1854).

From Political Destiny of the Colored Race on the American Continent

* * *

Let it then be understood, as a great principle of political economy, that no people can be free who themselves do not constitute an essential part of the *ruling element* of the country in which they live. Whether this element be founded upon a true or false, a just or an unjust basis; this position in community is necessary to personal safety. The liberty of no man is secure, who controls not his own political destiny. What is true of an individual, is true of a family; and that which is true of a family, is also true concerning a whole people. To suppose otherwise, is that delusion which at once induces its victim, through a period of long suffering, patiently to submit to every species of wrong; trusting against probability, and hoping against all reasonable grounds of expectation, for the granting of privileges and enjoyment of rights, which never will be attained. This delusion reveals the true secret of the power which holds in peaceable subjection, all the oppressed in every part of the world.

A people, to be free, must necessarily be *their own rulers*: that is, *each individual* must, in himself, embody the *essential ingredient*—so to speak—of the *sovereign principle* which composes the *true basis* of his liberty. This principle, when not exercised by himself, may, at his pleasure, be delegated to another—his true representative.

Said a great French writer: "A free agent, in a free government, should be his own governor;"[1] that is, he must possess within himself the *acknowledged right to govern*: this constitutes him a *governor*, though he may delegate to another the power to govern himself.

No one, then, can delegate to another a power he never possessed; that is, he cannot *give an agency* in that which he never had a right. Consequently, the colored man in the United States, being deprived of the right of inherent sovereignty, cannot *confer* a suffrage, because he possesses none to confer. Therefore, where there is no suffrage, there can neither be *freedom* nor *safety* for the disfranchised. And it is a futile hope to suppose that the agent of another's concerns will take a proper interest in the affairs of those to whom he is under no obligations. Having no favors to ask or expect, he therefore has none to lose.

In other periods and parts of the world—as in Europe and Asia—the people being of one common, direct origin of race, though established on the presumption of difference by birth, or what was termed *blood*, yet the distinction between the superior classes and common people, could only be marked by the difference, in the dress and education of the two classes. To effect this, the interposition of government was necessary; consequently, the costume and education of the people became a subject of legal restriction, guarding carefully against the privileges of the common people.

In Rome, the Patrician and Plebeian were orders in the ranks of her people—all of whom were termed citizens (*cives*)—recognized by the laws of the country; their dress and education being determined by law, the better to

1. The most likely source is *Principles of Politics* (1815), by Benjamin Constant (1767–1830), French-Swiss political theorist.

fix the distinction. In different parts of Europe, at the present day, if not the same, the distinction among the people is similar, only on a modified—and in some kingdoms—probably more tolerant or deceptive policy.

In the United States, our degradation being once—as it has in a hundred instances been done—legally determined, our color is sufficient, independently of costume, education, or other distinguishing marks, to keep up that distinction.

In Europe, when an inferior is elevated to the rank of equality with the superior class, the law first comes to his aid, which, in its decrees, entirely destroys his identity as an inferior, leaving no trace of his former condition visible.

In the United States, among the whites, their color is made, by law and custom, the mark of distinction and superiority; while the color of the blacks is a badge of degradation, acknowledged by statute, organic law, and the common consent of the people.

With this view of the case—which we hold to be correct—to elevate to equality the degraded subject of law and custom, it can only be done, as in Europe, by an entire destruction of the identity of the former condition of the applicant. Even were this desirable—which we by no means admit—with the deep seated prejudices engendered by oppression, with which we have to contend, ages incalculable might reasonably be expected to roll around, before this could honorably be accomplished; otherwise, we should encourage and at once commence an indiscriminate concubinage and immoral commerce, of our mothers, sisters, wives and daughters, revolting to think of, and a physical curse to humanity.

If this state of things be to succeed, then, as in Egypt, under the dread of the inscrutable approach of the destroying angel, to appease the hatred of our oppressors, as a license to the passions of every white, let the lintel of each door of every black man, be stained with the blood of virgin purity and unsullied matron fidelity. Let it be written along the cornice in capitals, "The *will* of the white man is the rule of my household."[2] Remove the protection to our chambers and nurseries, that the places once sacred may henceforth become the unrestrained resort of the vagrant and rabble, always provided that the licensed commissioner of lust shall wear the indisputable impress of a *white* skin.

But we have fully discovered and comprehended the great political disease with which we are affected, the cause of its origin and continuance; and what is now left for us to do is to discover and apply a sovereign remedy—a healing balm to a sorely diseased body—a wrecked but not entirely shattered system. We propose for this disease a remedy. That remedy is Emigration. This Emigration should be well advised, and like remedies applied to remove the disease from the physical system of man, skillfully and carefully applied, within the proper time, directed to operate on that part of the system, whose greatest tendency shall be, to benefit the whole.

1854

2. Exodus 12.21–23 describes Moses instructing the Israelites to put the blood of the lamb just above their doorposts so God would know not to smite them.

HARRIET BEECHER STOWE
1811–1896

The author of the best-selling novel of the pre–Civil War period, Harriet Beecher
Stowe was born in Litchfield, Connecticut, the seventh child and fourth daughter of Lyman Beecher, an eminent evangelical Calvinist minister, and Roxana Foote
Beecher. After bearing two more children, Roxana died when Harriet was four; typically for this era, Lyman remarried quickly. Harriet Beecher found her stepmother
aloof and overly formal, and continued to grieve for her mother. The family eventually
numbered thirteen children, among whom Harriet was especially close to her brothers
Henry Ward (1813–1887) and Charles (1815–1900), her sister Catharine (1800–
1878), and her half-sister Isabella (1822–1907). Profoundly influenced by Lyman
Beecher's ambitions to shape the nation along the lines of his Protestant evangelical vision, many of the children grew up to take on leadership roles in the culture.
The men became ministers; the women became writers, teachers, and reformers.
Catharine was a pioneer in women's education and teacher training; Isabella turned
to suffragism and women's rights; Harriet wrote the most influential antislavery
novel in the nation's history.

Between 1819 and 1824, Harriet Beecher studied at Sarah Pierce's Litchfield
Female Academy, one of the earliest schools in the nation to offer serious academic
training to women. Pierce (1806–1863) believed that properly trained women were
ultimately destined (as she phrased it in a commencement address) to "instruct and
enlighten the world." In 1823, Catharine Beecher, who had also attended Pierce's
school, joined with another sister, Mary, to found a girls' academy in Hartford, Connecticut. Harriet Beecher began to study there in 1824 and became a teacher at the
academy in 1827.

In 1832 the Beecher family moved to Cincinnati, where Lyman Beecher assumed
the presidency of the new Lane Theological Seminary, convinced of the importance
of doing Protestant evangelical work in the western states. Working with her father
and her sister Harriet, Catharine Beecher founded the Western Female Institute in
order to train "Protestant young women" to teach the children of farmers and workers in the burgeoning schools of the Midwest. Although the Beechers regretted
leaving their beloved New England, they became part of an active home-based cultural life (scholars call this a "parlor culture") in Cincinnati, at that time the largest
city in the West. Harriet Beecher began to write short stories in 1834. That same
year she became acutely aware of the controversy over slavery when a number of Lane
students, including the soon-to-be prominent abolitionist Theodore Dwight Weld,
rebelled against Lyman Beecher's lukewarm antislavery position—he supported shipping free American blacks to a colony in Africa—and withdrew from the seminary.

In 1836, a year that saw major antiabolitionist riots in Cincinnati, Harriet Beecher
married Calvin Stowe, a professor of biblical literature at Lane who was one of the
best Hebrew scholars of his day. Because his salary was small and the Stowes began to
rear a large family very quickly—twin girls (Eliza and Harriet) were born in 1836, a
son (Henry) in 1838—Harriet Beecher Stowe continued to write for money even
though she found childbirth extremely debilitating. Her first book—a collection of
stories titled *The Mayflower*—appeared in 1843. Her first antislavery sketch, "Immediate Emancipation," appeared in 1845. The death of her baby boy Samuel, who succumbed to cholera in 1849 before he was a year old, was a great blow and infused
her writing with sympathy for people who were helpless in the face of great personal

loss. Although she had little firsthand knowledge of slavery, she had become increasingly interested in the abolitionist cause; now her deep sorrow forged an emotional link with the oppressed that was to push *Uncle Tom's Cabin* far beyond the standard abolitionist tract.

In 1849 Calvin Stowe accepted a position at Bowdoin College, in Maine, and the Stowes moved to New England in 1850. (In 1851, when the family moved again, he went to Andover Theological Seminary in Massachusetts.) Passage of the Fugitive Slave Act in 1850—which made it a federal crime to assist an escaping slave—had outraged Harriet Beecher Stowe and many other Northerners, who regarded the new law as having further implicated the North in the practice of slavery. For, if it was now a crime to help escaping slaves anywhere in the nation, one could no longer see slavery as simply a southern institution. Fired by this development, she began writing *Uncle Tom's Cabin*, which was serialized during 1851–52 in the Washington, D.C., weekly antislavery journal, the *National Era*. In this setting, the novel was well received, but its audience was limited to adherents of the abolitionist cause.

The novel had an entirely different effect when it appeared in book form in 1852. It sold around three thousand copies the day of publication and more than three hundred thousand copies by the end of the year. (Comparable figures for today's population would have to be more than ten times larger.) As a reviewer in the *Literary World* put it: "No literary work of any character or merit, whether of poetry or prose, or imagination or observation, fancy or fact, truth or fiction, that has ever been written since there have been writers or readers, has ever commanded so great a popular success." Between 1852 and 1860 it was reprinted in twenty-two languages. The novel helped push abolitionism from the margins to the mainstream, and thus moved the nation closer to Civil War—an outcome that, in fact, Stowe had hoped to avert by her depictions of slave suffering. Her aim had been to inspire voluntary emancipation by demonstrating the evil and unchristian nature of slavery.

Uncle Tom's Cabin made Stowe a national and international celebrity. When she traveled to Europe in 1853 she was entertained and feted wherever she went. As a means of authenticating aspects of *Uncle Tom's Cabin*, she had published the book-length *Key to Uncle Tom's Cabin* before setting sail. Over the next several years she met with a number of black abolitionists, including Frederick Douglass, and came to regret that the ending of *Uncle Tom's Cabin*, where a number of the novel's prominent black characters choose to emigrate to Africa, seemed to support colonization (the policy of relocating free blacks to Africa). In her next antislavery novel, *Dred; A Tale of the Great Dismal Swamp* (1856), she depicted slave rebels who, following the death of their leader, made their way to New York and Canada. Though not as popular as *Uncle Tom's Cabin*, the novel nonetheless sold several hundred thousand copies and was praised by the British novelist George Eliot as "rare in both its intensity and range of power."

As the Civil War approached, Stowe continued to write on behalf of abolitionism in the *New York Independent* while turning to novels focused on New England culture and history. She made a pioneering contribution to regional writing in such books as *The Minister's Wooing* (1859), *The Pearl of Orr's Island* (1862), *Oldtown Folks* (1869), and *Poganuc People* (1878). Much of the power of these novels derives from Stowe's profoundly ambivalent tributes to the old New England character and its ways of life in the prerailroad days. She deplored New England's doctrinal severity, yet admired the region's close sense of community, which she strove to depict in meticulous, nostalgic detail. These novels developed the figure of an innocent young woman whose religious intuitions resist the bookish theologies of male religious authorities. A historical novel, *Agnes of Sorrento* (1862), which drew on her travels in Italy, featured the same kind of heroine in a fifteenth-century setting.

In 1863 Calvin Stowe retired, and the Stowes moved to Hartford, Connecticut. In this same year she became an Episcopalian, abandoning the rigors of Calvinism with which she had struggled for so long. Her life contained many sorrows; only three of her seven children—the twins and the youngest child, Charles, born in 1850— outlived her. Calvin Stowe died in 1886; in her last decade, Harriet Beecher Stowe suffered greatly from physical illness and mental exhaustion.

When the modernist movement championed a critical ethos of understatement and antisentimentality, denying that politics had any place in serious literature, *Uncle Tom's Cabin* became a target of critical abuse. Overtly emotional, fearlessly political, and appealing to the widest possible audience, it represented literary values that modernism abhorred. More recently the novel's racial politics have come under fire, as some have objected to the extent to which it draws on stereotypes. But if it had not been so much a part of its own time, *Uncle Tom's Cabin* could never have achieved its effects, and reconsideration of the novel has helped revive appreciation for literature that is politically engaged and popularly effective. Understanding the importance of this novel in American culture also reminds readers of how central women were to literary life before the Civil War, and how openly they engaged with topics that, supposedly, were outside their sphere.

The text is that of the first American edition of *Uncle Tom's Cabin* (1852).

From Uncle Tom's Cabin; or, Life among the Lowly[1]

Volume I

CHAPTER VII. THE MOTHER'S STRUGGLE[2]

It is impossible to conceive of a human creature more wholly desolate and forlorn than Eliza, when she turned her footsteps from Uncle Tom's cabin.

Her husband's suffering and dangers, and the danger of her child, all blended in her mind, with a confused and stunning sense of the risk she was running, in leaving the only home she had ever known, and cutting loose from the protection of a friend whom she loved and revered. Then there was the parting from every familiar object,—the place where she had grown up, the trees under which she had played, the groves where she had walked many an evening in happier days, by the side of her young husband,— everything, as it lay in the clear, frosty starlight, seemed to speak reproachfully to her, and ask her whither could she go from a home like that?

But stronger than all was maternal love, wrought into a paroxysm of frenzy by the near approach of a fearful danger. Her boy was old enough to have walked by her side, and, in an indifferent case, she would only have led him by the hand; but now the bare thought of putting him out of her arms made her shudder, and she strained him to her bosom with a convulsive grasp, as she went rapidly forward.

The frosty ground creaked beneath her feet, and she trembled at the sound; every quaking leaf and fluttering shadow sent the blood backward to her heart, and quickened her footsteps. She wondered within herself at the strength that seemed to be come upon her; for she felt the weight of her boy

1. The novel follows the fortunes of two slaves from the Shelby plantation in Kentucky. The first plot concerns Tom, about thirty-five years old and a devout Christian; the second concerns Eliza, a young mother. "Uncle" refers to an honored person in the community who is not necessarily a relative.
2. At this point in the novel, Eliza has decided to run away with her son, Harry, rather than let him be sold to Haley. She has alerted Tom to his impending sale; he chooses to remain and allow himself to be sold to protect the other slave families on the plantation. As he knows, others would be sold in his place if he escaped.

╺as if it had been a feather, and every flutter of fear seemed to increase the supernatural power that bore her on, while from her pale lips burst forth, in frequent ejaculations, the prayer to a Friend above—"Lord, help! Lord, save me!"╗

If it were *your* Harry, mother, or your Willie, that were going to be torn from you by a brutal trader, to-morrow morning,—if you had seen the man, and heard that the papers were signed and delivered, and you had only from twelve o'clock till morning to make good your escape,—how fast could *you* walk? How many miles could you make in those few brief hours, with the darling at your bosom,—the little sleepy head on your shoulder,—the small, soft arms trustingly holding on to your neck?

For the child slept. At first, the novelty and alarm kept him waking; but his mother so hurriedly repressed every breath or sound, and so assured him that if he were only still she would certainly save him, that he clung quietly round her neck, only asking, as he found himself sinking to sleep,

"Mother, I don't need to keep awake, do I?"

"No, my darling; sleep, if you want to."

"But, mother, if I do get asleep, you won't let him get me?"

"No! so may God help me!" said his mother, with a paler cheek, and a brighter light in her large dark eyes.

"You're *sure*, an't you, mother?"

"Yes, *sure*!" said the mother, in a voice that startled herself; for it seemed to her to come from a spirit within, that was no part of her; and the boy dropped his little weary head on her shoulder, and was soon asleep. How the touch of those warm arms, the gentle breathings that came in her neck, seemed to add fire and spirit to her movements! It seemed to her as if strength poured into her in electric streams, from every gentle touch and movement of the sleeping, confiding child. Sublime is the dominion of the mind over the body, that, for a time, can make flesh and nerve impregnable, and string the sinews like steel, so that the weak become so mighty.

The boundaries of the farm, the grove, the wood-lot, passed by her dizzily, as she walked on; and still she went, leaving one familiar object after another, slacking not, pausing not, till reddening daylight found her many a long mile from all traces of any familiar objects upon the open highway.

She had often been, with her mistress, to visit some connections, in the little village of T——, not far from the Ohio river, and knew the road well. To go thither, to escape across the Ohio river, were the first hurried outlines of her plan of escape; beyond that, she could only hope in God.

When horses and vehicles began to move along the highway, with that alert perception peculiar to a state of excitement, and which seems to be a sort of inspiration, she became aware that her headlong pace and distracted air might bring on her remark and suspicion. She therefore put the boy on the ground, and, adjusting her dress and bonnet, she walked on at as rapid a pace as she thought consistent with the preservation of appearances. In her little bundle she had provided a store of cakes and apples, which she used as expedients for quickening the speed of the child, rolling the apple some yards before them, when the boy would run with all his might after it; and this ruse, often repeated, carried them over many a half-mile.

After a while, they came to a thick patch of woodland, through which murmured a clear brook. As the child complained of hunger and thirst, she climbed over the fence with him; and, sitting down behind a large rock which concealed them from the road, she gave him a breakfast out of her little package. The boy wondered and grieved that she could not eat; and when, putting his arms round her neck, he tried to wedge some of his cake into her mouth, it seemed to her that the rising in her throat would choke her.

"No, no, Harry darling! mother can't eat till you are safe! We must go on— on—till we come to the river!" And she hurried again into the road, and again constrained herself to walk regularly and composedly forward.

She was many miles past any neighborhood where she was personally known. If she should chance to meet any who knew her, she reflected that the well-known kindness of the family would be of itself a blind to suspicion, as making it an unlikely supposition that she could be a fugitive. As she was also so white as not to be known as of colored lineage, without a critical survey, and her child was white also, it was much easier for her to pass on unsuspected.

On this presumption, she stopped at noon at a neat farmhouse, to rest herself, and buy some dinner for her child and self; for, as the danger decreased with the distance, the supernatural tension of the nervous system lessened, and she found herself both weary and hungry.

The good woman, kindly and gossipping, seemed rather pleased than otherwise with having somebody come in to talk with; and accepted, without examination, Eliza's statement, that she "was going on a little piece, to spend a week with her friends,"—all which she hoped in her heart might prove strictly true.

An hour before sunset, she entered the village of T——, by the Ohio river, weary and foot-sore, but still strong in heart. Her first glance was at the river, which lay, like Jordan, between her and the Canaan[3] of liberty on the other side.

It was now early spring, and the river was swollen and turbulent; great cakes of floating ice were swinging heavily to and fro in the turbid waters. Owing to the peculiar form of the shore on the Kentucky side, the land bending far out into the water, the ice had been lodged and detained in great quantities, and the narrow channel which swept round the bend was full of ice, piled one cake over another, thus forming a temporary barrier to the descending ice, which lodged, and formed a great, undulating raft, filling up the whole river, and extending almost to the Kentucky shore.

Eliza stood, for a moment, contemplating this unfavorable aspect of things, which she saw at once must prevent the usual ferry-boat from running, and then turned into a small public house on the bank, to make a few inquiries.

The hostess, who was busy in various fizzing and stewing operations over the fire, preparatory to the evening meal, stopped, with a fork in her hand, as Eliza's sweet and plaintive voice arrested her.

"What is it?" she said.

"Isn't there any ferry or boat, that takes people over to B——, now?" she said.

"No, indeed!" said the woman; "the boats has stopped running."

---

3. In the Bible, the promised land for the Israelites, who wandered in the desert for forty years. The Jordan is the river they had to cross to get there.

Eliza's look of dismay and disappointment struck the woman, and she said, inquiringly,

"May be you're wanting to get over?—anybody sick? Ye seem mighty anxious?"

"I've got a child that's very dangerous,"[4] said Eliza. "I never heard of it till last night, and I've walked quite a piece to-day, in hopes to get to the ferry."

"Well, now, that's onlucky," said the woman, whose motherly sympathies were much aroused; "I'm re'lly consarned for ye. Solomon!" she called, from the window, towards a small back building. A man, in leather apron and very dirty hands, appeared at the door.

"I say, Sol," said the woman, "is that ar man going to tote them bar'ls over to-night?"

"He said he should try, if't was any way prudent," said the man.

"There's a man a piece down here, that's going over with some truck[5] this evening, if he durs'to; he'll be in here to supper to-night, so you'd better set down and wait. That's a sweet little fellow," added the woman, offering him a cake.

But the child, wholly exhausted, cried with weariness.

"Poor fellow! he isn't used to walking, and I've hurried him on so," said Eliza.

"Well, take him into this room," said the woman, opening into a small bedroom, where stood a comfortable bed. Eliza laid the weary boy upon it, and held his hands in hers till he was fast asleep. For her there was no rest. As a fire in her bones, the thought of the pursuer urged her on; and she gazed with longing eyes on the sullen, surging waters that lay between her and liberty.

Here we must take our leave of her for the present, to follow the course of her pursuers.

Though Mrs. Shelby had promised that the dinner should be hurried on table, yet it was soon seen, as the thing has often been seen before, that it required more than one to make a bargain. So, although the order was fairly given out in Haley's hearing, and carried to Aunt Chloe[6] by at least half a dozen juvenile messengers, that dignitary only gave certain very gruff snorts, and tosses of her head, and went on with every operation in an unusually leisurely and circumstantial manner.

For some singular reason, an impression seemed to reign among the servants generally that Missis would not be particularly disobliged by delay; and it was wonderful what a number of counter accidents occurred constantly, to retard the course of things. One luckless wight contrived to upset the gravy; and then gravy had to be got up *de novo*,[7] with due care and formality, Aunt Chloe watching and stirring with dogged precision, answering shortly, to all suggestions of haste, that she "warn't a going to have raw gravy on the table, to help nobody's catchings." One tumbled down with the water, and had to go to the spring for more; and another precipitated the butter into the path of events; and there was from time to time giggling news brought

---

4. I.e., dangerously ill.
5. Goods.
6. Tom's wife, the Shelbys' cook. The entire household works together to delay Haley's depar-

ture in pursuit of Eliza.
7. From the beginning (Latin). "Wight": serving person, slave.

into the kitchen that "Mas'r Haley was mighty oneasy, and that he couldn't sit in his cheer no ways, but was a walkin' and stalkin' to the winders and through the porch."

"Sarves him right!" said Aunt Chloe, indignantly. "He'll get wus nor oneasy, one of these days, if he don't mend his ways. *His* master'll be sending for him, and then see how he'll look!"

"He'll go to torment, and no mistake," said little Jake.

"He desarves it!" said Aunt Chloe, grimly; "he's broke a many, many, many hearts,—I tell ye all!" she said, stopping, with a fork uplifted in her hands; "it's like what Mas'r George reads in Ravelations,[8]—souls a callin' under the altar! and a callin' on the Lord for vengeance on sich!—and by and by the Lord he'll hear 'em—so he will!"

Aunt Chloe, who was much revered in the kitchen, was listened to with open mouth; and, the dinner being now fairly sent in, the whole kitchen was at leisure to gossip with her, and to listen to her remarks.

"Sich 'll be burnt up forever, and no mistake; won't ther?" said Andy.

"I'd be glad to see it, I'll be boun'," said little Jake.

"Chil'en!" said a voice, that made them all start. It was Uncle Tom, who had come in, and stood listening to the conversation at the door.

"Chil'en!" he said, "I'm afeard you don't know what ye're sayin'. Forever is a *dre'ful* word, chil'en; it's awful to think on 't. You oughtenter wish that ar to any human crittur."

"We wouldn't to anybody but the soul-drivers,"[9] said Andy; "nobody can help wishing it to them, they's so awful wicked."

"Don't natur herself kinder cry out on em?" said Aunt Chloe. "Don't dey tear der suckin' baby right off his mother's breast, and sell him, and der little children as is crying and holding on by her clothes,—don't dey pull 'em off and sells em? Don't dey tear wife and husband apart?" said Aunt Chloe, beginning to cry, "when it's jest takin' the very life on 'em?—and all the while does they feel one bit,—don't dey drink and smoke, and take it oncommon easy? Lor, if the devil don't get them, what's he good for?" And Aunt Chloe covered her face with her checked apron, and began to sob in good earnest.

"Pray for them that 'spitefully use you, the good book says," says Tom.[1]

"Pray for 'em!" said Aunt Chloe; "Lor, it's too tough! I can't pray for 'em."

"It's natur, Chloe, and natur's strong," said Tom, "but the Lord's grace is stronger; besides, you oughter think what an awful state a poor crittur's soul's in that'll do them ar things,—you oughter thank God that you an't *like* him, Chloe. I'm sure I'd rather be sold, ten thousand times over, than to have all that ar poor crittur's got to answer for."

"So'd I, a heap," said Jake. "Lor, *shouldn't* we cotch it, Andy?"

Andy shrugged his shoulders, and gave an acquiescent whistle.

"I'm glad Mas'r didn't go off this morning, as he looked to," said Tom; "that ar hurt me more than sellin', it did. Mebbe it might have been natural for him, but 't would have come desp't hard on me, as has known him from a baby; but I've seen Mas'r, and I begin ter feel sort o' reconciled to the Lord's

---

8. The Book of Revelation, which contains symbolic prophecies of the end of the world. George is the Shelbys' son, who in Chapter IV reads the Bible to the slaves.
9. Slave owners or traders.

1. From Matthew 5.44: "Love your enemies, bless them that curse you, do good to them that hate you, and pray for them which despitefully use you, and persecute you."

will now. Mas'r couldn't help hisself; he did right, but I'm feared things will be kinder goin' to rack, when I'm gone. Mas'r can't be spected to be a pryin' round everywhar, as I've done, a keepin' up all the ends. The boys all means well, but they's powerful car'less. That ar troubles me."

The bell here rang, and Tom was summoned to the parlor.

"Tom," said his master, kindly, "I want you to notice that I give this gentleman bonds to forfeit a thousand dollars if you are not on the spot when he wants you; he's going to-day to look after his other business, and you can have the day to yourself. Go anywhere you like, boy."

"Thank you, Mas'r," said Tom.

"And mind yerself," said the trader, "and don't come it over your master with any o' yer nigger tricks; for I'll take every cent out of him, if you an't thar. If he'd hear to me, he wouldn't trust any on ye—slippery as eels!"

"Mas'r," said Tom,—and he stood very straight,—"I was jist eight years old when ole Missis put you into my arms, and you wasn't a year old. 'Thar,' says she, 'Tom, that's to be *your* young Mas'r; take good care on him,' says she. And now I jist ask you, Mas'r, have I ever broke word to you, or gone contrary to you, 'specially since I was a Christian?"

Mr. Shelby was fairly overcome, and the tears rose to his eyes.

"My good boy," said he, "the Lord knows you say but the truth; and if I was able to help it, all the world shouldn't buy you."

"And sure as I am a Christian woman," said Mrs. Shelby, "you shall be redeemed as soon as I can any way bring together means. Sir," she said to Haley, "take good account of who you sell him to, and let me know."

"Lor, yes, for that matter," said the trader, "I may bring him up in a year, not much the wuss for wear, and trade him back."

"I'll trade with you then, and make it for your advantage," said Mrs. Shelby.

"Of course," said the trader, "all's equal with me; li'ves trade 'em up as down, so I does a good business. All I want is a livin', you know, ma'am; that's all any on us wants, I s'pose."

Mr. and Mrs. Shelby both felt annoyed and degraded by the familiar impudence of the trader, and yet both saw the absolute necessity of putting a constraint on their feelings. The more hopelessly sordid and insensible he appeared, the greater became Mrs. Shelby's dread of his succeeding in recapturing Eliza and her child, and of course the greater her motive for detaining him by every female artifice. She therefore graciously smiled, assented, chatted familiarly, and did all she could to make time pass imperceptibly.

At two o'clock Sam and Andy brought the horses up to the posts, apparently greatly refreshed and invigorated by the scamper of the morning.

Sam was there new oiled from dinner, with an abundance of zealous and ready officiousness. As Haley approached, he was boasting, in flourishing style, to Andy, of the evident and eminent success of the operation, now that he had "farly come to it."

"Your master, I s'pose, don't keep no dogs," said Haley, thoughtfully, as he prepared to mount.

"Heaps on 'em," said Sam, triumphantly; "thar's Bruno—he's a roarer! and, besides that, 'bout every nigger of us keeps a pup of some natur or uther."

"Poh!" said Haley,—and he said something else, too, with regard to the said dogs, at which Sam muttered,

"I don't see no use cussin' on 'em, no way."

"But your master don't keep no dogs (I pretty much know he don't) for trackin' out niggers."

Sam knew exactly what he meant, but he kept on a look of earnest and desperate simplicity.

"Our dogs all smells round considable sharp. I spect they's the kind, though they han't never had no practice. They's *far*[2] dogs, though, at most anything, if you'd get 'em started. Here, Bruno," he called, whistling to the lumbering Newfoundland, who came pitching tumultuously toward them.

"You go hang!" said Haley, getting up. "Come, tumble up now."

Sam tumbled up accordingly, dexterously contriving to tickle Andy as he did so, which occasioned Andy to split out into a laugh, greatly to Haley's indignation, who made a cut at him with his riding-whip.

"I's 'stonished at yer, Andy," said Sam, with awful gravity. "This yer's a seris bisness, Andy. Yer mustn't be a makin' game. This yer an't no way to help Mas'r."

"I shall take the straight road to the river," said Haley, decidedly, after they had come to the boundaries of the estate. "I know the way of all of 'em,—they makes tracks for the underground."[3]

"Sartin," said Sam, "dat's de idee. Mas'r Haley hits de thing right in de middle. Now, der's two roads to de river,—de dirt road and der pike,—which Mas'r mean to take?"

Andy looked up innocently at Sam, surprised at hearing this new geographical fact, but instantly confirmed what he said, by a vehement reiteration.

"Cause," said Sam, "I'd rather be 'clined to 'magine that Lizy'd take de dirt road, bein' it 's the least travelled."

Haley, notwithstanding that he was a very old bird, and naturally inclined to be suspicious of chaff, was rather brought up by this view of the case.

"If yer warn't both on yer such cussed liars, now!" he said, contemplatively, as he pondered a moment.

The pensive, reflective tone in which this was spoken appeared to amuse Andy prodigiously, and he drew a little behind, and shook so as apparently to run a great risk of falling off his horse, while Sam's face was immovably composed into the most doleful gravity.

"Course," said Sam, "Mas'r can do as he 'd ruther; go de straight road, if Mas'r thinks best,—it's all one to us. Now, when I study 'pon it, I think de straight road do best, *deridedly*."

"She would naturally go a lonesome way," said Haley, thinking aloud, and not minding Sam's remark.

"Dar an't no sayin'," said Sam; "gals is pecular; they never does nothin' ye thinks they will; mose gen'lly the contrar. Gals is nat'lly made contrary; and so, if you thinks they've gone one road, it is sartin you'd better go t' other, and then you'll be sure to find 'em. Now, my private 'pinion is, Lizy took der dirt road; so I think we'd better take de straight one."

---

2. Fair.
3. The Underground Railroad, the informal, secretive network of individuals whose homes were used by slaves escaping from the South to Canada.

This profound generic view of the female sex did not seem to dispose Haley particularly to the straight road; and he announced decidedly that he should go the other, and asked Sam when they should come to it.

"A little piece ahead," said Sam, giving a wink to Andy with the eye which was on Andy's side of the head; and he added, gravely, "but I've studded on de matter, and I'm quite clar we ought not to go dat ar way. I nebber been over it no way. It's despit lonesome, and we might lose our way,—whar we'd come to, de Lord only knows."

"Nevertheless," said Haley, "I shall go that way."

"Now I think on 't, I think I hearn 'em tell that dat ar road was all fenced up and down by der creek, and thar, an't it, Andy?"

Andy wasn't certain; he'd only "hearn tell" about that road, but never been over it. In short, he was strictly noncommittal.

Haley, accustomed to strike the balance of probabilities between lies of greater or lesser magnitude, thought that it lay in favor of the dirt road aforesaid. The mention of the thing he thought he perceived was involuntary on Sam's part at first, and his confused attempts to dissuade him he set down to a desperate lying on second thoughts, as being unwilling to implicate Eliza.

When, therefore, Sam indicated the road, Haley plunged briskly into it, followed by Sam and Andy.

Now, the road, in fact, was an old one, that had formerly been a thoroughfare to the river, but abandoned for many years after the laying of the new pike. It was open for about an hour's ride, and after that it was cut across by various farms and fences. Sam knew this fact perfectly well,—indeed, the road had been so long closed up, that Andy had never heard of it. He therefore rode along with an air of dutiful submission, only groaning and vociferating occasionally that 't was "desp't rough, and bad for Jerry's foot."

"Now, I jest give yer warning," said Haley, "I know yer; yer won't get me to turn off this yer road, with all yer fussin'—so you shet up!"

"Mas'r will go his own way!" said Sam, with rueful submission, at the same time winking most portentously to Andy, whose delight was now very near the explosive point.

Sam was in wonderful spirits,—professed to keep a very brisk look-out,— at one time exclaiming that he saw "a gal's bonnet" on the top of some distant eminence, or calling to Andy "if that thar wasn't 'Lizy' down in the hollow;" always making these exclamations in some rough or craggy part of the road, where the sudden quickening of speed was a special inconvenience to all parties concerned, and thus keeping Haley in a state of constant commotion.

After riding about an hour in this way, the whole party made a precipitate and tumultuous descent into a barn-yard belonging to a large farming establishment. Not a soul was in sight, all the hands being employed in the fields; but, as the barn stood conspicuously and plainly square across the road, it was evident that their journey in that direction had reached a decided finale.

"Wan't dat ar what I told Mas'r?" said Sam, with an air of injured innocence. "How does strange gentleman spect to know more about a country dan de natives born and raised?"

"You rascal!" said Haley, "you knew all about this."

"Didn't I tell yer I *know'd*, and yer wouldn't believe me? I telled Mas'r 't was all shet up, and fenced up, and I didn't spect we could get through,—Andy heard me."

It was all too true to be disputed, and the unlucky man had to pocket his wrath with the best grace he was able, and all three faced to the right about, and took up their line of march for the highway.

In consequence of all the various delays, it was about three-quarters of an hour after Eliza had laid her child to sleep in the village tavern that the party came riding into the same place. Eliza was standing by the window, looking out in another direction, when Sam's quick eye caught a glimpse of her. Haley and Andy were two yards behind. At this crisis, Sam contrived to have his hat blown off, and uttered a loud and characteristic ejaculation, which startled her at once; she drew suddenly back; the whole train swept by the window, round to the front door.

A thousand lives seemed to be concentrated in that one moment to Eliza. Her room opened by a side door to the river. She caught her child, and sprang down the steps towards it. The trader caught a full glimpse of her, just as she was disappearing down the bank; and throwing himself from his horse, and calling loudly on Sam and Andy, he was after her like a hound after a deer. In that dizzy moment her feet to her scarce seemed to touch the ground, and a moment brought her to the water's edge. Right on behind they came; and, nerved with strength such as God gives only to the desperate, with one wild cry and flying leap, she vaulted sheer over the turbid current by the shore, on to the raft of ice beyond. It was a desperate leap—impossible to anything but madness and despair; and Haley, Sam, and Andy, instinctively cried out, and lifted up their hands, as she did it.

The huge green fragment of ice on which she alighted pitched and creaked as her weight came on it, but she staid there not a moment. With wild cries and desperate energy she leaped to another and still another cake;—stumbling—leaping—slipping—springing upwards again! Her shoes are gone—her stockings cut from her feet—while blood marked every step; but she saw nothing, felt nothing, till dimly, as in a dream, she saw the Ohio side, and a man helping her up the bank.

"Yer a brave gal, now, whoever ye ar!" said the man, with an oath.

Eliza recognized the voice and face of a man who owned a farm not far from her old home.

"O, Mr. Symmes!—save me—do save me—do hide me!" said Eliza.

"Why, what's this?" said the man. "Why, if 'tan't Shelby's gal!"

"My child!—this boy!—he'd sold him! There is his Mas'r," said she, pointing to the Kentucky shore. "O, Mr. Symmes, you've got a little boy!"

"So I have," said the man, as he roughly, but kindly, drew her up the steep bank. "Besides, you're a right brave gal. I like grit, wherever I see it."

When they had gained the top of the bank, the man paused.

"I'd be glad to do something for ye," said he; "but then there's nowhar I could take ye. The best I can do is to tell ye to go *thar*," said he, pointing to a large white house which stood by itself, off the main street of the village. "Go thar; they're kind folks. Thar's no kind o' danger but they'll help you,—they're up to all that sort o' thing."

"The Lord bless you!" said Eliza, earnestly.

"No 'casion, no 'casion in the world," said the man. "What I've done's of no 'count."

"And, oh, surely, sir, you won't tell any one!"

"Go to thunder, gal! What do you take a feller for? In course not," said the man. "Come, now, go along like a likely, sensible gal, as you are. You've arnt your liberty, and you shall have it, for all me."

The woman folded her child to her bosom, and walked firmly and swiftly away. The man stood and looked after her.

"Shelby, now, mebbe won't think this yer the most neighborly thing in the world; but what's a feller to do? If he catches one of my gals in the same fix, he's welcome to pay back. Somehow I never could see no kind o' critter a strivin' and pantin', and trying to clar theirselves, with the dogs arter 'em, and go agin 'em. Besides, I don't see no kind of 'casion for me to be hunter and catcher for other folks, neither."

So spoke this poor, heathenish Kentuckian, who had not been instructed in his constitutional relations,[4] and consequently was betrayed into acting in a sort of Christianized manner, which, if he had been better situated and more enlightened, he would not have been left to do.

Haley had stood a perfectly amazed spectator of the scene, till Eliza had disappeared up the bank, when he turned a blank, inquiring look on Sam and Andy.

"That ar was a tolable fair stroke of business," said Sam.

"The gal's got seven devils in her, I believe!" said Haley. "How like a wildcat she jumped!"

"Wal, now," said Sam, scratching his head, "I hope Mas'r'll 'scuse us tryin' dat ar road. Don't think I feel spry enough for dat ar, no way!" and Sam gave a hoarse chuckle.

"You laugh!" said the trader, with a growl.

"Lord bless you, Mas'r, I couldn't help it, now," said Sam, giving way to the long pent-up delight of his soul. "She looked so curi's, a leapin' and springin'—ice a crackin'—and only to hear her,—plump! ker chunk! ker splash! Spring! Lord! how she goes it!" and Sam and Andy laughed till the tears rolled down their cheeks.

"I'll make ye laugh t'other side yer mouths!" said the trader, laying about their heads with his riding-whip.

Both ducked, and ran shouting up the bank, and were on their horses before he was up.

"Good-evening, Mas'r!" said Sam, with much gravity. "I berry much spect Missis be anxious 'bout Jerry. Mas'r Haley won't want us no longer. Missis wouldn't hear of our ridin' the critters over Lizy's bridge to-night;" and, with a facetious poke into Andy's ribs, he started off, followed by the latter, at full speed,—their shouts of laughter coming faintly on the wind.

＊　＊　＊

---

4. Allusion to the Fugitive Slave Act, recently passed by Congress as part of the Compromise of 1850, which made it a federal crime to aid fugitive slaves.

CHAPTER IX. IN WHICH IT APPEARS THAT A SENATOR IS BUT A MAN

The light of the cheerful fire shone on the rug and carpet of a cosey parlor, and glittered on the sides of the tea-cups and well-brightened tea-pot, as Senator Bird[5] was drawing off his boots, preparatory to inserting his feet in a pair of new handsome slippers, which his wife had been working for him while away on his senatorial tour. Mrs. Bird, looking the very picture of delight, was superintending the arrangements of the table, ever and anon mingling admonitory remarks to a number of frolicsome juveniles, who were effervescing in all those modes of untold gambol and mischief that have astonished mothers ever since the flood.

"Tom, let the door-knob alone,—there's a man! Mary! Mary! don't pull the cat's tail,—poor pussy! Jim, you mustn't climb on that table,—no, no!—You don't know, my dear, what a surprise it is to us all, to see you here to-night!" said she, at last, when she found a space to say something to her husband.

"Yes, yes, I thought I'd just make a run down, spend the night, and have a little comfort at home. I'm tired to death, and my head aches!"

Mrs. Bird cast a glance at a camphor-bottle,[6] which stood in the half-open closet, and appeared to meditate an approach to it, but her husband interposed.

"No, no, Mary, no doctoring! a cup of your good hot tea, and some of our good home living, is what I want. It's a tiresome business, this legislating!"

And the senator smiled, as if he rather liked the idea of considering himself a sacrifice to his country.

"Well," said his wife, after the business of the tea-table was getting rather slack, "and what have they been doing in the Senate?"

Now, it was a very unusual thing for gentle little Mrs. Bird ever to trouble her head with what was going on in the house of the state, very wisely considering that she had enough to do to mind her own. Mr. Bird, therefore, opened his eyes in surprise, and said,

"Not very much of importance."

"Well; but is it true that they have been passing a law forbidding people to give meat and drink to those poor colored folks that come along?[7] I heard they were talking of some such law, but I didn't think any Christian legislature would pass it!"

"Why, Mary, you are getting to be a politician, all at once."

"No, nonsense! I wouldn't give a fip for all your politics, generally, but I think this is something downright cruel and unchristian. I hope, my dear, no such law has been passed."

"There has been a law passed forbidding people to help off the slaves that come over from Kentucky, my dear; so much of that thing has been done by these reckless Abolitionists, that our brethren in Kentucky are very strongly excited, and it seems necessary, and no more than Christian and kind, that something should be done by our state to quiet the excitement."

---

5. An Ohio state senator, returning from a session in Columbus, the state capital.
6. During the 19th century, camphor, a compound from a tree of the same name, was used for pain relief.
7. Such a state law would have added force to the federal Fugitive Slave Act.

"And what is the law? It don't forbid us to shelter these poor creatures a night, does it, and to give 'em something comfortable to eat, and a few old clothes, and send them quietly about their business?"

"Why, yes, my dear; that would be aiding and abetting, you know."

Mrs. Bird was a timid, blushing little woman, of about four feet in height, and with mild blue eyes, and a peach-blow[8] complexion, and the gentlest, sweetest voice in the world;—as for courage, a moderate-sized cock-turkey had been known to put her to rout at the very first gobble, and a stout house-dog, of moderate capacity, would bring her into subjection merely by a show of his teeth. Her husband and children were her entire world, and in these she ruled more by entreaty and persuasion than by command or argument. There was only one thing that was capable of arousing her, and that provocation came in on the side of her unusually gentle and sympathetic nature;—anything in the shape of cruelty would throw her into a passion, which was the more alarming and inexplicable in proportion to the general softness of her nature. Generally the most indulgent and easy to be entreated of all mothers, still her boys had a very reverent remembrance of a most vehement chastisement she once bestowed on them, because she found them leagued with several graceless boys of the neighborhood, stoning a defenceless kitten.

"I'll tell you what," Master Bill used to say, "I was scared that time. Mother came at me so that I thought she was crazy, and I was whipped and tumbled off to bed, without any supper, before I could get over wondering what had come about; and, after that, I heard mother crying outside the door, which made me feel worse than all the rest. I'll tell you what," he'd say, "we boys never stoned another kitten!"

On the present occasion, Mrs. Bird rose quickly, with very red cheeks, which quite improved her general appearance, and walked up to her husband, with quite a resolute air, and said, in a determined tone,

"Now, John, I want to know if you think such a law as that is right and Christian?"

"You won't shoot me, now, Mary, if I say I do!"

"I never could have thought it of you, John; you didn't vote for it?"

"Even so, my fair politician."

"You ought to be ashamed, John! Poor, homeless, houseless creatures! It's a shameful, wicked, abominable law, and I'll break it, for one, the first time I get a chance; and I hope I *shall* have a chance, I do! Things have got to a pretty pass, if a woman can't give a warm supper and a bed to poor, starving creatures, just because they are slaves, and have been abused and oppressed all their lives, poor things!"

"But, Mary, just listen to me. Your feelings are all quite right, dear, and interesting, and I love you for them; but, then, dear, we mustn't suffer our feelings to run away with our judgment; you must consider it's not a matter of private feeling,—there are great public interests involved,—there is such a state of public agitation rising, that we must put aside our private feelings."

"Now, John, I don't know anything about politics, but I can read my Bible; and there I see that I must feed the hungry, clothe the naked, and comfort the desolate; and that Bible I mean to follow."

8. Peach blossom.

"But in cases where your doing so would involve a great public evil—"

"Obeying God never brings on public evils. I know it can't. It's always safest, all round, to *do as He* bids us."

"Now, listen to me, Mary, and I can state to you a very clear argument, to show—"

"O, nonsense, John! you can talk all night, but you wouldn't do it. I put it to you, John,—would *you* now turn away a poor, shivering, hungry creature from your door, because he was a runaway? *Would* you, now?"

Now, if the truth must be told, our senator had the misfortune to be a man who had a particularly humane and accessible nature, and turning away anybody that was in trouble never had been his forte; and what was worse for him in this particular pinch of the argument, was, that his wife knew it, and, of course, was making an assault on rather an indefensible point. So he had recourse to the usual means of gaining time for such cases made and provided; he said "ahem," and coughed several times, took out his pocket-handkerchief, and began to wipe his glasses. Mrs. Bird, seeing the defenceless condition of the enemy's territory, had no more conscience than to push her advantage.

"I should like to see you doing that, John—I really should! Turning a woman out of doors in a snow-storm, for instance; or, may be you'd take her up and put her in jail, wouldn't you? You would make a great hand at that!"

"Of course, it would be a very painful duty," began Mr. Bird, in a moderate tone.

"Duty, John! don't use that word! You know it isn't a duty—it can't be a duty! If folks want to keep their slaves from running away, let 'em treat 'em well,—that's my doctrine. If I had slaves (as I hope I never shall have), I'd risk their wanting to run away from me, or you either, John. I tell you folks don't run away when they are happy; and when they do run, poor creatures! they suffer enough with cold and hunger and fear, without everybody's turning against them; and, law or no law, I never will, so help me God!"

"Mary! Mary! My dear, let me reason with you."

"I hate reasoning, John,—especially reasoning on such subjects. There's a way you political folks have of coming round and round a plain right thing; and you don't believe in it yourselves, when it comes to practice. I know *you* well enough, John. You don't believe it's right any more than I do; and you wouldn't do it any sooner than I."

At this critical juncture, old Cudjoe, the black man-of-all-work, put his head in at the door, and wished "Missis would come into the kitchen;" and our senator, tolerably relieved, looked after his little wife with a whimsical mixture of amusement and vexation, and, seating himself in the arm-chair, began to read the papers.

After a moment, his wife's voice was heard at the door, in a quick, earnest tone,—"John! John! I do wish you'd come here, a moment."

He laid down his paper, and went into the kitchen, and started, quite amazed at the sight that presented itself:—A young and slender woman, with garments torn and frozen, with one shoe gone, and the stocking torn away from the cut and bleeding foot, was laid back in a deadly swoon upon two chairs. There was the impress of the despised race on her face, yet none could help feeling its mournful and pathetic beauty, while its stony sharpness, its cold, fixed, deathly aspect, struck a solemn chill over him. He drew his breath short, and stood in silence. His wife, and their only colored domestic, old Aunt Dinah, were busily engaged in restorative measures; while old Cudjoe had got the boy on his knee, and was busy pulling off his shoes and stockings, and chafing his little cold feet.

"Sure, now, if she an't a sight to behold!" said old Dinah, compassionately; "'pears like 'twas the heat that made her faint. She was tol'able peart when she cum in, and asked if she couldn't warm herself here a spell; and I was just a askin' her where she cum from, and she fainted right down. Never done much hard work, guess, by the looks of her hands."

"Poor creature!" said Mrs. Bird, compassionately, as the woman slowly unclosed her large, dark eyes, and looked vacantly at her. Suddenly an expression of agony crossed her face, and she sprang up, saying, "O, my Harry! Have they got him?"

The boy, at this, jumped from Cudjoe's knee, and, running to her side, put up his arms. "O, he's here! he's here!" she exclaimed.

"O, ma'am!" said she, wildly, to Mrs. Bird, "do protect us! don't let them get him!"

"Nobody shall hurt you here, poor woman," said Mrs. Bird, encouragingly. "You are safe; don't be afraid."

"God bless you!" said the woman, covering her face and sobbing; while the little boy, seeing her crying, tried to get into her lap.

With many gentle and womanly offices, which none knew better how to render than Mrs. Bird, the poor woman was, in time, rendered more calm. A temporary bed was provided for her on the settle,[9] near the fire; and, after a short time, she fell into a heavy slumber, with the child, who seemed no less weary, soundly sleeping on her arm; for the mother resisted, with nervous anxiety, the kindest attempts to take him from her; and, even in sleep, her arm encircled him with an unrelaxing clasp, as if she could not even then be beguiled of her vigilant hold.

Mr. and Mrs. Bird had gone back to the parlor, where, strange as it may appear, no reference was made, on either side, to the preceding conversation; but Mrs. Bird busied herself with her knitting-work, and Mr. Bird pretended to be reading the paper.

"I wonder who and what she is!" said Mr. Bird, at last, as he laid it down.

"When she wakes up and feels a little rested, we will see," said Mrs. Bird.

"I say, wife!" said Mr. Bird, after musing in silence over his newspaper.

"Well, dear!"

"She couldn't wear one of your gowns, could she, by any letting down, or such matter? She seems to be rather larger than you are."

A quite perceptible smile glimmered on Mrs. Bird's face, as she answered, "We'll see."

Another pause, and Mr. Bird again broke out,

"I say, wife!"

"Well! What now?"

"Why, there's that old bombazin[1] cloak, that you keep on purpose to put over me when I take my afternoon's nap; you might as well give her that,— she needs clothes."

---

9. A small sofa.

1. Fabric woven of silk and wool.

At this instant, Dinah looked in to say that the woman was awake, and wanted to see Missis.

Mr. and Mrs. Bird went into the kitchen, followed by the two eldest boys, the smaller fry having, by this time, been safely disposed of in bed.

The woman was now sitting up on the settle, by the fire. She was looking steadily into the blaze, with a calm, heartbroken expression, very different from her former agitated wildness.

"Did you want me?" said Mrs. Bird, in gentle tones. "I hope you feel better now, poor woman!"

A long-drawn, shivering sigh was the only answer; but she lifted her dark eyes, and fixed them on her with such a forlorn and imploring expression, that the tears came into the little woman's eyes.

"You needn't be afraid of anything; we are friends here, poor woman! Tell me where you came from, and what you want," said she.

"I came from Kentucky," said the woman.

"When?" said Mr. Bird, taking up the interrogatory.

"To-night."

"How did you come?"

"I crossed on the ice."

"Crossed on the ice!" said every one present.

"Yes," said the woman, slowly, "I did. God helping me, I crossed on the ice; for they were behind me—right behind—and there was no other way!"

"Law, Missis," said Cudjoe, "the ice is all in broken-up blocks, a swinging and a tetering up and down in the water!"

"I know it was—I know it!" said she, wildly; "but I did it! I wouldn't have thought I could,—I didn't think I should get over, but I didn't care! I could but die, if I didn't. The Lord helped me; nobody knows how much the Lord can help 'em, till they try," said the woman, with a flashing eye.

"Were you a slave?" said Mr. Bird.

"Yes, sir; I belonged to a man in Kentucky."

"Was he unkind to you?"

"No, sir; he was a good master."

"And was your mistress unkind to you?"

"No, sir—no! my mistress was always good to me."

"What could induce you to leave a good home, then, and run away, and go through such dangers?"

The woman looked up at Mrs. Bird, with a keen, scrutinizing glance, and it did not escape her that she was dressed in deep mourning.

"Ma'am," she said, suddenly, "have you ever lost a child?"

The question was unexpected, and it was a thrust on a new wound; for it was only a month since a darling child of the family had been laid in the grave.

Mr. Bird turned around and walked to the window, and Mrs. Bird burst into tears; but, recovering her voice, she said,

"Why do you ask that? I have lost a little one."

"Then you will feel for me. I have lost two, one after another,—left 'em buried there when I came away; and I had only this one left. I never slept a night without him; he was all I had. He was my comfort and pride, day and night; and, ma'am, they were going to take him away from me,—to *sell* him,—sell him down south, ma'am, to go all alone,—a baby that had never been away from his mother in his life! I couldn't stand it, ma'am. I knew I never should be good for anything, if they did; and when I knew the papers were signed, and he was sold, I took him and came off in the night; and they chased me,—the man that bought him, and some of Mas'r's folks,—and they were coming down right behind me, and I heard 'em. I jumped right on to the ice; and how I got across, I don't know,—but, first I knew, a man was helping me up the bank."

The woman did not sob nor weep. She had gone to a place where tears are dry; but every one around her was, in some way characteristic of themselves, showing signs of hearty sympathy.

The two little boys, after a desperate rummaging in their pockets, in search of those pocket-handkerchiefs which mothers know are never to be found there, had thrown themselves disconsolately into the skirts of their mother's gown, where they were sobbing, and wiping their eyes and noses, to their hearts' content;—Mrs. Bird had her face fairly hidden in her pocket-handkerchief; and old Dinah, with tears streaming down her black, honest face, was ejaculating, "Lord have mercy on us!" with all the fervor of a camp-meeting;—while old Cudjoe, rubbing his eyes very hard with his cuffs, and making a most uncommon variety of wry faces, occasionally responded in the same key, with great fervor. Our senator was a statesman, and of course could not be expected to cry, like other mortals; and so he turned his back to the company, and looked out of the window, and seemed particularly busy in clearing his throat and wiping his spectacle-glasses, occasionally blowing his nose in a manner that was calculated to excite suspicion, had any one been in a state to observe critically.

"How came you to tell me you had a kind master?" he suddenly exclaimed, gulping down very resolutely some kind of rising in his throat, and turning suddenly round upon the woman.

"Because he *was* a kind master; I'll say that of him, any way;—and my mistress was kind; but they couldn't help themselves. They were owing money; and there was some way, I can't tell how, that a man had a hold on them, and they were obliged to give him his will. I listened, and heard him telling mistress that, and she begging and pleading for me,—and he told her he couldn't help himself, and that the papers were all drawn;—and then it was I took him and left my home, and came away. I knew 'twas no use of my trying to live, if they did it; for 't 'pears like this child is all I have."

"Have you no husband?"

"Yes, but he belongs to another man. His master is real hard to him, and won't let him come to see me, hardly ever; and he's grown harder and harder upon us, and he threatens to sell him down south;—it's like I'll never see *him* again!"

The quiet tone in which the woman pronounced these words might have led a superficial observer to think that she was entirely apathetic; but there was a calm, settled depth of anguish in her large, dark eye, that spoke of something far otherwise.

"And where do you mean to go, my poor woman?" said Mrs. Bird.

"To Canada, if I only knew where that was. Is it very far off, is Canada?" said she, looking up, with a simple, confiding air, to Mrs. Bird's face.

"Poor thing!" said Mrs. Bird, involuntarily.

"Is't a very great way off, think?" said the woman, earnestly.

"Much further than you think, poor child!" said Mrs. Bird; "but we will try to think what can be done for you. Here, Dinah, make her up a bed in your own room, close by the kitchen, and I'll think what to do for her in the morning. Meanwhile, never fear, poor woman; put your trust in God; he will protect you."

Mrs. Bird and her husband reentered the parlor. She sat down in her little rocking-chair before the fire, swaying thoughtfully to and fro. Mr. Bird strode up and down the room, grumbling to himself, "Pish! pshaw! confounded awkward business!" At length, striding up to his wife, he said,

"I say, wife, she'll have to get away from here, this very night. That fellow will be down on the scent bright and early to-morrow morning; if 'twas only the woman, she could lie quiet till it was over; but that little chap can't be kept still by a troop of horse and foot, I'll warrant me; he'll bring it all out, popping his head out of some window or door. A pretty kettle of fish it would be for me, too, to be caught with them both here, just now! No; they'll have to be got off to-night."

"To-night! How is it possible?—where to?"

"Well, I know pretty well where to," said the senator, beginning to put on his boots, with a reflective air; and, stopping when his leg was half in, he embraced his knee with both hands, and seemed to go off in deep meditation.

"It's a confounded awkward, ugly business," said he, at last, beginning to tug at his boot-straps again, "and that's a fact!" After one boot was fairly on, the senator sat with the other in his hand, profoundly studying the figure of the carpet. "It will have to be done, though, for aught I see,—hang it all!" and he drew the other boot anxiously on, and looked out of the window.

Now, little Mrs. Bird was a discreet woman,—a woman who never in her life said, "I told you so!" and, on the present occasion, though pretty well aware of the shape her husband's meditations were taking, she very prudently forbore to meddle with them, only sat very quietly in her chair, and looked quite ready to hear her liege lord's intentions, when he should think proper to utter them.

"You see," he said, "there's my old client, Van Trompe, has come over from Kentucky, and set all his slaves free; and he has bought a place seven miles up the creek, here, back in the woods, where nobody goes, unless they go on purpose; and it's a place that isn't found in a hurry. There she'd be safe enough; but the plague of the thing is, nobody could drive a carriage there to-night, but *me*."

"Why not? Cudjoe is an excellent driver."

"Ay, ay, but here it is. The creek has to be crossed twice; and the second crossing is quite dangerous, unless one knows it as I do. I have crossed it a hundred times on horseback, and know exactly the turns to take. And so, you see, there's no help for it. Cudjoe must put in the horses, as quietly as may be, about twelve o'clock, and I'll take her over; and then, to give color to the matter, he must carry me on to the next tavern, to take the stage[2] for Columbus, that comes by about three or four, and so it will look as if I had had the carriage only for that. I shall get into business bright and early in the morning. But I'm thinking I shall feel rather cheap there, after all that's been said and done; but, hang it, I can't help it!"

2. Stagecoach.

"Your heart is better than your head, in this case, John," said the wife, laying her little white hand on his. "Could I ever have loved you, had I not known you better than you know yourself?" And the little woman looked so handsome, with the tears sparkling in her eyes, that the senator thought he must be a decidedly clever fellow, to get such a pretty creature into such a passionate admiration of him; and so, what could he do but walk off soberly, to see about the carriage. At the door, however, he stopped a moment, and then coming back, he said, with some hesitation,

"Mary, I don't know how you'd feel about it, but there's that drawer full of things—of—of—poor little Henry's." So saying, he turned quickly on his heel, and shut the door after him.

His wife opened the little bed-room door adjoining her room, and, taking the candle, set it down on the top of a bureau there; then from a small recess she took a key, and put it thoughtfully in the lock of a drawer, and made a sudden pause, while two boys, who, boy like, had followed close on her heels, stood looking, with silent, significant glances, at their mother. And oh! mother that reads this, has there never been in your house a drawer, or a closet, the opening of which has been to you like the opening again of a little grave? Ah! happy mother that you are, if it has not been so.

Mrs. Bird slowly opened the drawer. There were little coats of many a form and pattern, piles of aprons, and rows of small stockings; and even a pair of little shoes, worn and rubbed at the toes, were peeping from the folds of a paper. There was a toy horse and wagon, a top, a ball,—memorials gathered with many a tear and many a heart-break! She sat down by the drawer, and, leaning her head on her hands over it, wept till the tears fell through her fingers into the drawer; then suddenly raising her head, she began, with nervous haste, selecting the plainest and most substantial articles, and gathering them into a bundle.

"Mamma," said one of the boys, gently touching her arm, "are you going to give away *those* things?"

"My dear boys," she said, softly and earnestly, "if our dear, loving little Henry looks down from heaven, he would be glad to have us do this. I could not find it in my heart to give them away to any common person—to anybody that was happy; but I give them to a mother more heart-broken and sorrowful than I am; and I hope God will send his blessings with them!"

There are in this world blessed souls, whose sorrows all spring up into joys for others; whose earthly hopes, laid in the grave with many tears, are the seed from which spring healing flowers and balm for the desolate and the distressed. Among such was the delicate woman who sits there by the lamp, dropping slow tears, while she prepares the memorials of her own lost one for the outcast wanderer.

After a while, Mrs. Bird opened a wardrobe, and, taking from thence a plain, serviceable dress or two, she sat down busily to her work-table, and, with needle, scissors, and thimble, at hand, quietly commenced the "letting down" process which her husband had recommended, and continued busily at it till the old clock in the corner struck twelve, and she heard the low rattling of wheels at the door.

"Mary," said her husband, coming in, with his overcoat in his hand, "you must wake her up now; we must be off."

Mrs. Bird hastily deposited the various articles she had collected in a small plain trunk, and locking it, desired her husband to see it in the carriage, and then proceeded to call the woman. Soon, arrayed in a cloak, bonnet, and shawl, that had belonged to her benefactress, she appeared at the door with her child in her arms. Mr. Bird hurried her into the carriage, and Mrs. Bird pressed on after her to the carriage steps. Eliza leaned out of the carriage, and put out her hand,—a hand as soft and beautiful as was given in return. She fixed her large, dark eyes, full of earnest meaning, on Mrs. Bird's face, and seemed going to speak. Her lips moved,—she tried once or twice, but there was no sound,—and pointing upward, with a look never to be forgotten, she fell back in the seat, and covered her face. The door was shut, and the carriage drove on.

What a situation, now, for a patriotic senator, that had been all the week before spurring up the legislature of his native state to pass more stringent resolutions against escaping fugitives, their harborers and abettors!

Our good senator in his native state had not been exceeded by any of his brethren at Washington, in the sort of eloquence which has won for them immortal renown! How sublimely he had sat with his hands in his pockets, and scouted³ all sentimental weakness of those who would put the welfare of a few miserable fugitives before great state interests!

He was as bold as a lion about it, and "mightily convinced" not only himself, but everybody that heard him;—but then his idea of a fugitive was only an idea of the letters that spell the word,—or, at the most, the image of a little newspaper picture of a man with a stick and bundle, with "Ran away from the subscriber" under it. The magic of the real presence of distress,—the imploring human eye, the frail, trembling human hand, the despairing appeal of helpless agony,—these he had never tried. He had never thought that a fugitive might be a hapless mother, a defenceless child,—like that one which was now wearing his lost boy's little well-known cap; and so, as our poor senator was not stone or steel,—as he was a man, and a downright noblehearted one, too,—he was, as everybody must see, in a sad case for his patriotism. And you need not exult over him, good brother of the Southern States; for we have some inklings that many of you, under similar circumstances, would not do much better. We have reason to know, in Kentucky, as in Mississippi, are noble and generous hearts, to whom never was tale of suffering told in vain. Ah, good brother! is it fair for you to expect of us services which your own brave, honorable heart would not allow you to render, were you in our place?

Be that as it may, if our good senator was a political sinner, he was in a fair way to expiate it by his night's penance. There had been a long continuous period of rainy weather, and the soft, rich earth of Ohio, as every one knows, is admirably suited to the manufacture of mud,—and the road was an Ohio railroad of the good old times.

"And pray, what sort of a road may that be?" says some eastern traveller, who has been accustomed to connect no ideas with a railroad, but those of smoothness or speed.

Know, then, innocent eastern friend, that in benighted regions of the west, where the mud is of unfathomable and sublime depth, roads are made

---

3. Mocked.

of round rough logs, arranged transversely side by side, and coated over in their pristine freshness with earth, turf, and whatsoever may come to hand, and then the rejoicing native calleth it a road, and straightway essayeth to ride thereupon. In process of time, the rains wash off all the turf and grass aforesaid, move the logs hither and thither, in picturesque positions, up, down and crosswise, with divers chasms and ruts of black mud intervening.

Over such a road as this our senator went stumbling along, making moral reflections as continuously as under the circumstances could be expected,—the carriage proceeding along much as follows,—bump! bump! bump! slush! down in the mud!—the senator, woman and child, reversing their positions so suddenly as to come, without any very accurate adjustment, against the windows of the down-hill side. Carriage sticks fast, while Cudjoe on the outside is heard making a great muster among the horses. After various ineffectual pullings and twitchings, just as the senator is losing all patience, the carriage suddenly rights itself with a bounce,—two front wheels go down into another abyss, and senator, woman, and child, all tumble promiscuously on to the front seat,—senator's hat is jammed over his eyes and nose quite unceremoniously, and he considers himself fairly extinguished;—child cries, and Cudjoe on the outside delivers animated addresses to the horses, who are kicking, and floundering, and straining, under repeated cracks of the whip. Carriage springs up, with another bounce,—down go the hind wheels,—senator, woman, and child, fly over on to the back seat, his elbows encountering her bonnet, and both her feet being jammed into his hat, which flies off in the concussion. After a few moments the "slough" is passed, and the horses stop, panting;—the senator finds his hat, the woman straightens her bonnet and hushes her child, and they brace themselves firmly for what is yet to come.

For a while only the continuous bump! bump! intermingled, just by way of variety, with divers side plunges and compound shakes; and they begin to flatter themselves that they are not so badly off, after all. At last, with a square plunge, which puts all on to their feet and then down into their seats with incredible quickness, the carriage stops,—and, after much outside commotion, Cudjoe appears at the door.

"Please, sir, it's powerful bad spot, this yer. I don't know how we's to get clar out. I'm a thinkin' we'll have to be a gettin' rails."[4]

The senator despairingly steps out, picking gingerly for some firm foothold; down goes one foot an immeasurable depth,—he tries to pull it up, loses his balance, and tumbles over into the mud, and is fished out, in a very despairing condition, by Cudjoe.

But we forbear, out of sympathy to our readers' bones. Western travellers, who have beguiled the midnight hour in the interesting process of pulling down rail fences, to pry their carriages out of mud holes, will have a respectful and mournful sympathy with our unfortunate hero. We beg them to drop a silent tear, and pass on.

It was full late in the night when the carriage emerged, dripping and bespattered, out of the creek, and stood at the door of a large farm-house.

---

4. A reference to the practice of removing boards from rail fences to make tracks to enable a carriage or cart to get out of the mud.

It took no inconsiderable perseverance to arouse the inmates; but at last the respectable proprietor appeared, and undid the door. He was a great, tall, bristling Orson of a fellow,[5] full six feet and some inches in his stockings, and arrayed in a red flannel hunting-shirt. A very heavy *mat* of sandy hair, in a decidedly tousled condition, and a beard of some days' growth, gave the worthy man an appearance, to say the least, not particularly prepossessing. He stood for a few minutes holding the candle aloft, and blinking on our travellers with a dismal and mystified expression that was truly ludicrous. It cost some effort of our senator to induce him to comprehend the case fully; and while he is doing his best at that, we shall give him a little introduction to our readers.

Honest old John Van Trompe was once quite a considerable land-holder and slave-owner in the State of Kentucky. Having "nothing of the bear about him but the skin,"[6] and being gifted by nature with a great, honest, just heart, quite equal to his gigantic frame, he had been for some years witnessing with repressed uneasiness the workings of a system equally bad for oppressor and oppressed. At last, one day, John's great heart had swelled altogether too big to wear his bonds any longer; so he just took his pocket-book out of his desk, and went over into Ohio, and bought a quarter of a township of good, rich land, made out free papers for all his people,—men, women, and children,—packed them up in wagons, and sent them off to settle down; and then honest John turned his face up the creek, and sat quietly down on a snug, retired farm, to enjoy his conscience and his reflections.

"Are you the man that will shelter a poor woman and child from slave-catchers?" said the senator, explicitly.

"I rather think I am," said honest John, with some considerable emphasis.

"I thought so," said the senator.

"If there's anybody comes," said the good man, stretching his tall, muscular form upward, "why here I'm ready for him: and I've got seven sons, each six foot high, and they'll be ready for 'em. Give our respects to 'em," said John; "tell 'em it's no matter how soon they call,—make no kinder difference to us," said John, running his fingers through the shock of hair that thatched his head, and bursting out into a great laugh.

Weary, jaded, and spiritless, Eliza dragged herself up to the door, with her child lying in a heavy sleep on her arm. The rough man held the candle to her face, and uttering a kind of compassionate grunt, opened the door of a small bedroom adjoining to the large kitchen where they were standing, and motioned her to go in. He took down a candle, and lighting it, set it upon the table, and then addressed himself to Eliza.

"Now, I say, gal, you needn't be a bit afeard, let who will come here. I'm up to all that sort o' thing," said he, pointing to two or three goodly rifles over the mantel-piece; "and most people that know me know that 't wouldn't be healthy to try to get anybody out o' my house when I'm agin it. So *now* you jist go to sleep now, as quiet as if yer mother was a rockin' ye," said he, as he shut the door.

6. A strong, wild man; from the story of "Orson and Valentine," an early French romance that appeared in English around 1550. Orson is the lost son of a king; abandoned in the woods, he was raised by a bear.

6. As recorded in James Boswell's *Life of Samuel Johnson* (1791), the Anglo-Irish author Oliver Goldsmith (1730–1794) proclaimed that the great English author and critic Johnson (1709–1784) "had nothing of the bear but his skin."

"Why, this is an uncommon handsome un," he said to the senator. "Ah, well; handsome uns has the greatest cause to run, sometimes, if they has any kind o' feelin, such as decent women should. I know all about that."

The senator, in a few words, briefly explained Eliza's history.

"O! ou! aw! now, I want to know?" said the good man, pitifully; "sho! now sho! That's natur now, poor crittur! hunted down now like a deer,—hunted down, jest for havin' natural feelin's, and doin' what no kind o' mother could help a doin'! I tell ye what, these yer things make me come the nighest to swearin', now, o' most anything," said honest John, as he wiped his eyes with the back of a great, freckled, yellow hand. "I tell yer what, stranger, it was years and years before I'd jine the church, 'cause the ministers round in our parts used to preach that the Bible went in for these ere cuttings up,—and I couldn't be up to 'em with their Greek and Hebrew, and so I took up agin 'em, Bible and all. I never jined the church till I found a minister that was up to 'em all in Greek and all that, and he said right the contrary; and then I took right hold, and jined the church,—I did now, fact," said John, who had been all this time uncorking some very frisky bottled cider, which at this juncture he presented.

"Ye'd better jest put up here, now, till daylight," said he, heartily, "and I'll call up the old woman, and have a bed got ready for you in no time."

"Thank you, my good friend," said the senator, "I must be along, to take the night stage for Columbus."

"Ah! well, then, if you must, I'll go a piece with you, and show you a cross road that will take you there better than the road you came on. That road's mighty bad."

John equipped himself, and, with a lantern in hand, was soon seen guiding the senator's carriage towards a road that ran down in a hollow, back of his dwelling. When they parted, the senator put into his hand a ten-dollar bill.

"It's for her," he said, briefly.

"Ay, ay," said John, with equal conciseness.

They shook hands, and parted.

* * *

CHAPTER XII. SELECT INCIDENT OF LAWFUL TRADE

"In Ramah there was a voice heard,—weeping, and lamentation, and great mourning; Rachel weeping for her children, and would not be comforted."[7]

Mr. Haley and Tom jogged onward in their wagon, each, for a time, absorbed in his own reflections. Now, the reflections of two men sitting side by side are a curious thing,—seated on the same seat, having the same eyes, ears, hands and organs of all sorts, and having pass before their eyes the same objects,—it is wonderful what a variety we shall find in these same reflections!

As, for example, Mr. Haley: he thought first of Tom's length, and breadth, and height, and what he would sell for, if he was kept fat and in good case till he got him into market. He thought of how he should make out his gang;

7. Paraphrase of Jeremiah 31.15.

he thought of the respective market value of certain supposititious men and women and children who were to compose it, and other kindred topics of the business; then he thought of himself, and how humane he was, that whereas other men chained their "niggers" hand and foot both, he only put fetters on the feet, and left Tom the use of his hands, as long as he behaved well; and he sighed to think how ungrateful human nature was, so that there was even room to doubt whether Tom appreciated his mercies. He had been taken in so by "niggers" whom he had favored; but still he was astonished to consider how good-natured he yet remained!

As to Tom, he was thinking over some words of an unfashionable old book, which kept running through his head again and again, as follows: "We have here no continuing city, but we seek one to come; wherefore God himself is not ashamed to be called our God; for he hath prepared for us a city."[8] These words of an ancient volume, got up principally by "ignorant and unlearned men," have, through all time, kept up, somehow, a strange sort of power over the minds of poor, simple fellows, like Tom. They stir up the soul from its depths, and rouse, as with trumpet call, courage, energy, and enthusiasm, where before was only the blackness of despair.

Mr. Haley pulled out of his pocket sundry newspapers, and began looking over their advertisements, with absorbed interest. He was not a remarkably fluent reader, and was in the habit of reading in a sort of recitative half-aloud, by way of calling in his ears to verify the deductions of his eyes. In this tone he slowly recited the following paragraph:

> "EXECUTOR'S SALE,—NEGROES!—Agreeably to order of court, will be sold, on Tuesday, February 20, before the Court-house door, in the town of Washington, Kentucky, the following negroes: Hagar, aged 60; John, aged 30; Ben, aged 21; Saul, aged 25; Albert, aged 14. Sold for the benefit of the creditors and heirs of the estate of Jesse Blutchford, Esq.
>
> > SAMUEL MORRIS,
> > THOMAS FLINT,
> > > *Executors.*"

"This yer I must look at," said he to Tom, for want of somebody else to talk to.

"Ye see, I'm going to get up a prime gang to take down with ye, Tom; it'll make it sociable and pleasant like,—good company will, ye know. We must drive right to Washington[9] first and foremost, and then I'll clap you into jail, while I does the business."

Tom received this agreeable intelligence quite meekly; simply wondering, in his own heart, how many of these doomed men had wives and children, and whether they would feel as he did about leaving them. It is to be confessed, too, that the naïve, off-hand information that he was to be thrown into jail by no means produced an agreeable impression on a poor fellow who had always prided himself on a strictly honest and upright course of life. Yes, Tom, we must confess it, was rather proud of his honesty, poor fellow,—not having very much else to be proud of;—if he had belonged to some of the higher walks of society, he, perhaps, would never have been reduced to such straits. However, the day wore on, and the evening saw Haley and Tom

---

8. Amalgam of Hebrews 11.16 and Hebrews 13.14.

9. Washington, Kentucky; upriver from New Orleans.

comfortably accommodated in Washington,—the one in a tavern, and the other in a jail.

About eleven o'clock the next day, a mixed throng was gathered around the court-house steps,—smoking, chewing, spitting, swearing, and conversing, according to their respective tastes and turns,—waiting for the auction to commence. The men and women to be sold sat in a group apart, talking in a low tone to each other. The woman who had been advertised by the name of Hagar was a regular African in feature and figure. She might have been sixty, but was older than that by hard work and disease, was partially blind, and somewhat crippled with rheumatism. By her side stood her only remaining son, Albert, a bright-looking little fellow of fourteen years. The boy was the only survivor of a large family, who had been successively sold away from her to a southern market. The mother held on to him with both her shaking hands, and eyed with intense trepidation every one who walked up to examine him.

"Don't be feard, Aunt Hagar," said the oldest of the men, "I spoke to Mas'r Thomas 'bout it, and he thought he might manage to sell you in a lot both together."

"Dey needn't call me worn out yet," said she, lifting her shaking hands. "I can cook yet, and scrub, and scour,—I'm wuth a buying, if I do come cheap;—tell em dat ar,—you *tell* em," she added, earnestly.

Haley here forced his way into the group, walked up to the old man, pulled his mouth open and looked in, felt of his teeth, made him stand and straighten himself, bend his back, and perform various evolutions to show his muscles; and then passed on to the next, and put him through the same trial. Walking up last to the boy, he felt of his arms, straightened his hands, and looked at his fingers, and made him jump, to show his agility.

"He an't gwine to be sold widout me!" said the old woman, with passionate eagerness; "he and I goes in a lot together; I's rail strong yet, Mas'r, and can do heaps o' work,—heaps on it, Mas'r."

"On plantation?" said Haley, with a contemptuous glance. "Likely story!" and, as if satisfied with his examination, he walked out and looked, and stood with his hands in his pocket, his cigar in his mouth, and his hat cocked on one side, ready for action.

"What think of 'em?" said a man who had been following Haley's examination, as if to make up his own mind from it.

"Wal," said Haley, spitting, "I shall put in, I think, for the youngerly ones and the boy."

"They want to sell the boy and the old woman together," said the man.

"Find it a tight pull;—why, she's an old rack o' bones,—not worth her salt."

"You wouldn't, then?" said the man.

"Anybody'd be a fool 't would. She's half blind, crooked with rheumatis, and foolish to boot."

"Some buys up these yer old critturs, and ses there's a sight more wear in 'em than a body'd think," said the man, reflectively.

"No go, 't all," said Haley; "wouldn't take her for a present,—fact,—I've *seen*, now."

"Wal, 'tis kinder pity, now, not to buy her with her son,—her heart seems so sot on him,—s'pose they fling her in cheap."

"Them that's got money to spend that ar way, it's all well enough. I shall bid off on that ar boy for a plantation-hand;—wouldn't be bothered with her, no way,—not if they'd give her to me," said Haley.

"She'll take on desp't," said the man.

"Nat'lly, she will," said the trader, coolly.

The conversation was here interrupted by a busy hum in the audience; and the auctioneer, a short, bustling, important fellow, elbowed his way into the crowd. The old woman drew in her breath, and caught instinctively at her son.

"Keep close to yer mammy, Albert,—close,—dey'll put us up togedder," she said.

"O, mammy, I'm feared they won't," said the boy.

"Dey must, child; I can't live, no ways, if they don't," said the old creature, vehemently.

The stentorian tones of the auctioneer, calling out to clear the way, now announced that the sale was about to commence. A place was cleared, and the bidding began. The different men on the list were soon knocked off at prices which showed a pretty brisk demand in the market; two of them fell to Haley.

"Come, now, young un," said the auctioneer, giving the boy a touch with his hammer, "be up and show your springs, now."

"Put us two up togedder, togedder,—do please, Mas'r," said the old woman, holding fast to her boy.

"Be off," said the man, gruffly, pushing her hands away; "you come last. Now, darkey, spring;" and, with the word, he pushed the boy toward the block, while a deep, heavy groan rose behind him. The boy paused, and looked back; but there was no time to stay, and, dashing the tears from his large, bright eyes, he was up in a moment.

His fine figure, alert limbs, and bright face, raised an instant competition, and half a dozen bids simultaneously met the ear of the auctioneer. Anxious, half-frightened, he looked from side to side, as he heard the clatter of contending bids,—now here, now there,—till the hammer fell. Haley had got him. He was pushed from the block toward his new master, but stopped one moment, and looked back, when his poor old mother, trembling in every limb, held out her shaking hands toward him.

"Buy me too, Mas'r, for de dear Lord's sake!—buy me,—I shall die if you don't!"

"You'll die if I do, that's the kink of it," said Haley,—"no!" And he turned on his heel.

The bidding for the poor old creature was summary. The man who had addressed Haley, and who seemed not destitute of compassion, bought her for a trifle, and the spectators began to disperse.

The poor victims of the sale, who had been brought up in one place together for years, gathered round the despairing old mother, whose agony was pitiful to see.

"Couldn't dey leave me one? Mas'r allers said I should have one,—he did," she repeated over and over, in heartbroken tones.

"Trust in the Lord, Aunt Hagar," said the oldest of the men, sorrowfully.

"What good will it do?" said she, sobbing passionately.

"Mother, mother,—don't! don't!" said the boy. "They say you's got a good master."

"I don't care,—I don't care. O, Albert! oh, my boy! you's my last baby. Lord, how ken I?"

"Come, take her off, can't some of ye?" said Haley, dryly; "don't do no good for her to go on that ar way."

The old men of the company, partly by persuasion and partly by force, loosed the poor creature's last despairing hold, and, as they led her off to her new master's wagon, strove to comfort her.

"Now!" said Haley, pushing his three purchases together, and producing a bundle of handcuffs, which he proceeded to put on their wrists; and fastening each handcuff to a long chain, he drove them before him to the jail.

A few days saw Haley, with his possessions, safely deposited on one of the Ohio boats. It was the commencement of his gang, to be augmented, as the boat moved on, by various other merchandise of the same kind, which he, or his agent, had stored for him in various points along shore.

The La Belle Rivière,[1] as brave and beautiful a boat as ever walked the waters of her namesake river, was floating gayly down the stream, under a brilliant sky, the stripes and stars of free America waving and fluttering over head; the guards crowded with well-dressed ladies and gentlemen walking and enjoying the delightful day. All was full of life, buoyant and rejoicing;— all but Haley's gang, who were stored, with other freight, on the lower deck, and who, somehow, did not seem to appreciate their various privileges, as they sat in a knot, talking to each other in low tones.

"Boys," said Haley, coming up, briskly, "I hope you keep up good heart, and are cheerful. Now, no sulks, ye see; keep stiff upper lip, boys; do well by me, and I'll do well by you."

The boys addressed responded the invariable "Yes, Mas'r," for ages the watchword of poor Africa; but it's to be owned they did not look particularly cheerful; they had their various little prejudices in favor of wives, mothers, sisters, and children, seen for the last time,—and though "they that wasted them required of them mirth,"[2] it was not instantly forthcoming.

"I've got a wife," spoke out the article enumerated as "John, aged thirty," and he laid his chained hand on Tom's knee,—"and she don't know a word about this, poor girl!"

"Where does she live?" said Tom.

"In a tavern a piece down here," said John; "I wish, now, I *could* see her once more in this world," he added.

Poor John! It *was* rather natural; and the tears that fell, as he spoke, came as naturally as if he had been a white man. Tom drew a long breath from a sore heart, and tried, in his poor way, to comfort him.

And over head, in the cabin, sat fathers and mothers, husbands and wives; and merry, dancing children moved round among them, like so many little butterflies, and everything was going on quite easy and comfortable.

"O, mamma," said a boy, who had just come up from below, "there's a negro trader on board, and he's brought four or five slaves down there."

"Poor creatures!" said the mother, in a tone between grief and indignation.

"What's that?" said another lady.

"Some poor slaves below," said the mother.

"And they've got chains on," said the boy.

1. The Beautiful River (French).   2. Paraphrase of Psalms 137.3.

"What a shame to our country that such sights are to be seen!" said another lady.

"O, there's a great deal to be said on both sides of the subject," said a genteel woman, who sat at her state-room door sewing, while her little girl and boy were playing round her. "I've been south, and I must say I think the negroes are better off than they would be to be free."

"In some respects, some of them are well off, I grant," said the lady to whose remark she had answered. "The most dreadful part of slavery, to my mind, is its outrages on the feelings and affections,—the separating of families, for example."

"That *is* a bad thing, certainly," said the other lady, holding up a baby's dress she had just completed, and looking intently on its trimmings; "but then, I fancy, it don't occur often."

"O, it does," said the first lady, eagerly; "I've lived many years in Kentucky and Virginia both, and I've seen enough to make any one's heart sick. Suppose, ma'am, your two children, there, should be taken from you, and sold?"

"We can't reason from our feelings to those of this class of persons," said the other lady, sorting out some worsteds on her lap.

"Indeed, ma'am, you can know nothing of them, if you say so," answered the first lady, warmly. "I was born and brought up among them. I know they *do* feel, just as keenly,—even more so, perhaps,—as we do."

The lady said "Indeed!" yawned, and looked out the cabin window, and finally repeated, for a finale, the remark with which she had begun,—"After all, I think they are better off than they would be to be free."

"It's undoubtedly the intention of Providence that the African race should be servants,—kept in a low condition," said a grave-looking gentleman in black, a clergyman, seated by the cabin door. "'Cursed be Canaan; a servant of servants shall he be,' the scripture says."[3]

"I say, stranger, is that ar what that text means?" said a tall man, standing by.

"Undoubtedly. It pleased Providence, for some inscrutable reason, to doom the race to bondage, ages ago; and we must not set up our opinion against that."

"Well, then, we'll all go ahead and buy up niggers," said the man, "if that's the way of Providence,—won't we, Squire?" said he, turning to Haley, who had been standing, with his hands in his pockets, by the stove, and intently listening to the conversation.

"Yes," continued the tall man, "we must all be resigned to the decrees of Providence. Niggers must be sold, and trucked round, and kept under; it's what they's made for. 'Pears like this yer view's quite refreshing, an't it, stranger?" said he to Haley.

"I never thought on 't," said Haley. "I couldn't have said as much, myself; I ha'nt no larning. I took up the trade just to make a living; if 't an't right, I calculated to 'pent on 't in time, *ye* know."

"And now you'll save yerself the trouble, won't ye?" said the tall man. "See what 't is, now, to know scripture. If ye'd only studied yer Bible, like this yer good man, ye might have know'd it before, and saved ye a heap o' trouble.

---

3. Genesis 9.25, from the story of Noah and his son Ham; a passage cited by proslavery writers to justify slavery on the assumption that Africans were Ham's descendants.

Ye could jist have said, 'Cussed be'—what's his name?—'and 't would all have come right.'" And the stranger, who was no other than the honest drover whom we introduced to our readers in the Kentucky tavern,[4] sat down, and began smoking, with a curious smile on his long, dry face.

A tall, slender young man, with a face expressive of great feeling and intelligence, here broke in, and repeated the words, "'All things whatsoever ye would that men should do unto you, do ye even so unto them.'[5] I suppose," he added, "*that* is scripture, as much as 'Cursed be Canaan.'"

"Wal, it seems quite *as* plain a text, stranger," said John the drover, "to poor fellows like us, now;" and John smoked on like a volcano.

The young man paused, looked as if he was going to say more, when suddenly the boat stopped, and the company made the usual steamboat rush, to see where they were landing.

"Both them ar chaps parsons?" said John to one of the men, as they were going out.

The man nodded.

As the boat stopped, a black woman came running wildly up the plank, darted into the crowd, flew up to where the slave gang sat, and threw her arms round that unfortunate piece of merchandise before enumerated— "John, aged thirty," and with sobs and tears bemoaned him as her husband.

But what needs tell the story, told too oft,—every day told,—of heartstrings rent and broken,—the weak broken and torn for the profit and convenience of the strong! It needs not to be told;—every day is telling it,—telling it, too, in the ear of One who is not deaf, though he be long silent.

The young man who had spoken for the cause of humanity and God before stood with folded arms, looking on this scene. He turned, and Haley was standing at his side. "My friend," he said, speaking with thick utterance, "how can you, how dare you, carry on a trade like this? Look at those poor creatures! Here I am, rejoicing in my heart that I am going home to my wife and child; and the same bell which is a signal to carry me onward towards them will part this poor man and his wife forever. Depend upon it, God will bring you into judgment for this."

The trader turned away in silence.

"I say, now," said the drover, touching his elbow, "there's differences in parsons, an't there? 'Cussed be Canaan' don't seem to go down with this 'un, does it?"

Haley gave an uneasy growl.

"And that ar an't the worse on 't," said John; "mabbe it won't go down with the Lord, neither, when ye come to settle with Him, one o' these days, as all on us must, I reckon."

Haley walked reflectively to the other end of the boat.

"If I make pretty handsomely on one or two next gangs," he thought, "I reckon I'll stop off this yer; it's really getting dangerous." And he took out his pocket-book, and began adding over his accounts,—a process which many gentlemen besides Mr. Haley have found a specific[6] for an uneasy conscience.

---

4. Mr. Symmes was introduced at the end of chapter III. "Drover": cattle driver, farmer.

5. From Sermon on the Mount (Matthew 7.12).
6. Healing tonic.

The boat swept proudly away from the shore, and all went on merrily, as before. Men talked, and loafed, and read, and smoked. Women sewed, and children played, and the boat passed on her way.

One day, when she lay to for a while at a small town in Kentucky, Haley went up into the place on a little matter of business.

Tom, whose fetters did not prevent his taking a moderate circuit, had drawn near the side of the boat, and stood listlessly gazing over the railings. After a time, he saw the trader returning, with an alert step, in company with a colored woman, bearing in her arms a young child. She was dressed quite respectably, and a colored man followed her, bringing along a small trunk. The woman came cheerfully onward, talking, as she came, with the man who bore her trunk, and so passed up the plank into the boat. The bell rung, the steamer whizzed, the engine groaned and coughed, and away swept the boat down the river.

The woman walked forward among the boxes and bales of the lower deck, and, sitting down, busied herself with chirruping to her baby.

Haley made a turn or two about the boat, and then, coming up, seated himself near her, and began saying something to her in an indifferent undertone.

Tom soon noticed a heavy cloud passing over the woman's brow; and that she answered rapidly, and with great vehemence.

"I don't believe it,—I won't believe it!" he heard her say. "You're jist a foolin with me."

"If you won't believe it, look here!" said the man, drawing out a paper; "this yer's the bill of sale, and there's your master's name to it; and I paid down good solid cash for it, too, I can tell you,—so, now!"

"I don't believe Mas'r would cheat me so; it can't be true!" said the woman, with increasing agitation.

"You can ask any of these men here, that can read writing. Here!" he said, to a man that was passing by, "jist read this yer, won't you! This yer gal won't believe me, when I tell her what 't is."

"Why, it's a bill of sale, signed by John Fosdick," said the man, "making over to you the girl Lucy and her child. It's all straight enough, for aught I see."

The woman's passionate exclamations collected a crowd around her, and the trader briefly explained to them the cause of the agitation.

"He told me that I was going down to Louisville, to hire out as cook to the same tavern where my husband works,—that's what Mas'r told me, his own self; and I can't believe he'd lie to me," said the woman.

"But he has sold you, my poor woman, there's no doubt about it," said a good-natured looking man, who had been examining the papers; "he has done it, and no mistake."

"Then it's no account talking," said the woman, suddenly growing quite calm; and, clasping her child tighter in her arms, she sat down on her box, turned her back round, and gazed listlessly into the river.

"Going to take it easy, after all!" said the trader. "Gal's got grit, I see."

The woman looked calm, as the boat went on; and a beautiful soft summer breeze passed like a compassionate spirit over her head,—the gentle breeze, that never inquires whether the brow is dusky or fair that it fans. And she saw sunshine sparkling on the water, in golden ripples, and heard gay voices, full of ease and pleasure, talking around her everywhere; but her heart lay as if a great stone had fallen on it. Her baby raised himself up against her, and stroked her cheeks with his little hands; and, springing up and down, crowing and chatting, seemed determined to arouse her. She strained him suddenly and tightly in her arms, and slowly one tear after another fell on his wondering, unconscious face; and gradually she seemed, and little by little, to grow calmer, and busied herself with tending and nursing him.

The child, a boy of ten months, was uncommonly large and strong of his age, and very vigorous in his limbs. Never, for a moment, still, he kept his mother constantly busy in holding him, and guarding his springing activity.

"That's a fine chap!" said a man, suddenly stopping opposite to him, with his hands in his pockets. "How old is he?"

"Ten months and a half," said the mother.

The man whistled to the boy, and offered him part of a stick of candy, which he eagerly grabbed at, and very soon had it in a baby's general depository, to wit, his mouth.

"Rum fellow!" said the man. "Knows what's what!" and he whistled, and walked on. When he had got to the other side of the boat, he came across Haley, who was smoking on top of a pile of boxes.

The stranger produced a match, and lighted a cigar, saying, as he did so, "Decentish kind o' wench you've got round there, stranger."

"Why, I reckon she *is* tol'able fair," said Haley, blowing the smoke out of his mouth.

"Taking her down south?" said the man.

Haley nodded, and smoked on.

"Plantation hand?" said the man.

"Wal," said Haley, "I'm fillin' out an order for a plantation, and I think I shall put her in. They told me she was a good cook; and they can use her for that, or set her at the cotton-picking. She's got the right fingers for that; I looked at 'em. Sell well, either way;" and Haley resumed his cigar.

"They won't want the young 'un on a plantation," said the man.

"I shall sell him, first chance I find," said Haley, lighting another cigar.

"S'pose you'd be selling him tol'able cheap," said the stranger, mounting the pile of boxes, and sitting down comfortably.

"Don't know 'bout that," said Haley; "he's a pretty smart young 'un,—straight, fat, strong; flesh as hard as a brick!"

"Very true, but then there's all the bother and expense of raisin'."

"Nonsense!" said Haley; "they is raised as easy as any kind of critter there is going; they an't a bit more trouble than pups. This yer chap will be running all round, in a month."

"I've got a good place for raisin', and I thought of takin' in a little more stock," said the man. "One cook lost a young 'un last week,—got drownded in a wash-tub, while she was a hangin' out clothes,—and I reckon it would be well enough to set her to raisin' this yer."

Haley and the stranger smoked a while in silence, neither seeming willing to broach the test question of the interview. At last the man resumed:

"You wouldn't think of wantin' more than ten dollars for that ar chap, seeing you *must* get him off yer hand, any how?"

Haley shook his head, and spit impressively.

"That won't do, no ways," he said, and began his smoking again.

"Well, stranger, what will you take?"

"Well, now," said Haley, "I *could* raise that ar chap myself, or get him raised; he's oncommon likely and healthy, and he'd fetch a hundred dollars, six months hence; and, in a year or two, he'd bring two hundred, if I had him in the right spot;—so I shan't take a cent less nor fifty for him now."

"O, stranger! that's rediculous, altogether," said the man.

"Fact!" said Haley, with a decisive nod of his head.

"I'll give thirty for him," said the stranger, "but not a cent more."

"Now, I'll tell ye what I will do," said Haley, spitting again, with renewed decision. "I'll split the difference, and say forty-five; and that's the most I will do."

"Well, agreed!" said the man, after an interval.

"Done!" said Haley. "Where do you land?"

"At Louisville," said the man.

"Louisville," said Haley. "Very fair, we get there about dusk. Chap will be asleep,—all fair,—get him off quietly, and no screaming,—happens beautiful,—I like to do everything quietly,—I hates all kind of agitation and fluster." And so, after a transfer of certain bills had passed from the man's pocket-book to the trader's, he resumed his cigar.

It was a bright, tranquil evening when the boat stopped at the wharf at Louisville. The woman had been sitting with her baby in her arms, now wrapped in a heavy sleep. When she heard the name of the place called out, she hastily laid the child down in a little cradle formed by the hollow among the boxes, first carefully spreading under it her cloak; and then she sprung to the side of the boat, in hopes that, among the various hotel-waiters who thronged the wharf, she might see her husband. In this hope, she pressed forward to the front rails, and, stretching far over them, strained her eyes intently on the moving heads on the shore, and the crowd pressed in between her and the child.

"Now's your time," said Haley, taking the sleeping child up, and handing him to the stranger. "Don't wake him up, and set him to crying, now; it would make a devil of a fuss with the gal." The man took the bundle carefully, and was soon lost in the crowd that went up the wharf.

When the boat, creaking, and groaning, and puffing, had loosed from the wharf, and was beginning slowly to strain herself along, the woman returned to her old seat. The trader was sitting there,—the child was gone!

"Why, why,—where?" she began, in bewildered surprise.

"Lucy," said the trader, "your child's gone; you may as well know it first as last. You see, I know'd you couldn't take him down south; and I got a chance to sell him to a first-rate family, that'll raise him better than you can."

The trader had arrived at that stage of Christian and political perfection which has been recommended by some preachers and politicians of the north, lately, in which he had completely overcome every humane weakness and prejudice. His heart was exactly where yours, sir, and mine could be brought, with proper effort and cultivation. The wild look of anguish and utter despair that the woman cast on him might have disturbed one less practised; but he was used to it. He had seen that same look hundreds of times. You can get used to such things, too, my friend; and it is the great object of recent efforts to make our whole northern community used to them, for the glory of the Union. So the trader only regarded the mortal anguish which he saw working in those dark features, those clenched hands, and suffocating breathings, as necessary incidents of the trade, and merely calculated whether she was going to scream, and get up a commotion on the boat; for, like other supporters of our peculiar institution, he decidedly disliked agitation.

But the woman did not scream. The shot had passed too straight and direct through the heart, for cry or tear.

Dizzily she sat down. Her slack hands fell lifeless by her side. Her eyes looked straight forward, but she saw nothing. All the noise and hum of the boat, the groaning of the machinery, mingled dreamily to her bewildered ear; and the poor, dumb-stricken heart had neither cry nor tear to show for its utter misery. She was quite calm.

The trader, who, considering his advantages, was almost as humane as some of our politicians, seemed to feel called on to administer such consolation as the case admitted of.

"I know this yer comes kinder hard, at first, Lucy," said he; "but such a smart, sensible gal as you are, won't give way to it. You see it's *necessary*, and can't be helped!"

"O! don't, Mas'r, don't!" said the woman, with a voice like one that is smothering.

"You're a smart wench, Lucy," he persisted; "I mean to do well by ye, and get ye a nice place down river; and you'll soon get another husband,—such a likely gal as you—"

"O! Mas'r, if you *only* won't talk to me now," said the woman, in a voice of such quick and living anguish that the trader felt that there was something at present in the case beyond his style of operation. He got up, and the woman turned away, and buried her head in her cloak.

The trader walked up and down for a time, and occasionally stopped and looked at her.

"Takes it hard, rather," he soliloquized, "but quiet, tho';—let her sweat a while; she'll come right, by and by!"

Tom had watched the whole transaction from first to last, and had a perfect understanding of its results. To him, it looked like something unutterably horrible and cruel, because, poor, ignorant black soul! he had not learned to generalize, and to take enlarged views. If he had only been instructed by certain ministers of Christianity, he might have thought better of it, and seen in it an every-day incident of a lawful trade; a trade which is the vital support of an institution which some American divines tell us has no evils but such as are inseparable from any other relations in social and domestic life. But Tom, as we see, being a poor, ignorant fellow, whose reading had been confined entirely to the New Testament, could not comfort and solace himself with views like these. His very soul bled within him for what seemed to him the *wrongs* of the poor suffering thing that lay like a crushed reed on the boxes; the feeling, living, bleeding, yet immortal *thing*, which American state law coolly classes with the bundles, and bales, and boxes, among which she is lying.

Tom drew near, and tried to say something; but she only groaned. Honestly, and with tears running down his own cheeks, he spoke of a heart of love in the skies, of a pitying Jesus, and an eternal home; but the ear was deaf with anguish, and the palsied heart could not feel.

Night came on,—night calm, unmoved, and glorious, shining down with her innumerable and solemn angel eyes, twinkling, beautiful, but silent. There was no speech nor language, no pitying voice nor helping hand, from that distant sky. One after another, the voices of business or pleasure died away; all on the boat were sleeping, and the ripples at the prow were plainly heard. Tom stretched himself out on a box, and there, as he lay, he heard, ever and anon, a smothered sob or cry from the prostate creature,—"O! what shall I do? O Lord! O good Lord, do help me!" and so, ever and anon, until the murmur died away in silence.

At midnight, Tom waked, with a sudden start. Something black passed quickly by him to the side of the boat, and he heard a splash in the water. No one else saw or heard anything. He raised his head,—the woman's place was vacant! He got up, and sought about him in vain. The poor bleeding heart was still, at last, and the river rippled and dimpled just as brightly as if it had not closed above it.

Patience! patience! ye whose hearts swell indignant at wrongs like these. Not one throb of anguish, not one tear of the oppressed, is forgotten by the Man of Sorrows, the Lord of Glory. In his patient, generous bosom he bears the anguish of a world. Bear thou, like him, in patience, and labor in love; for sure as he is God, "the year of his redeemed *shall* come."[7]

The trader waked up bright and early, and came out to see to his live stock. It was now his turn to look about in perplexity.

"Where alive is that gal?" he said to Tom.

Tom, who had learned the wisdom of keeping counsel, did not feel called on to state his observations and suspicions, but said he did not know.

"She surely couldn't have got off in the night at any of the landings, for I was awake, and on the look-out, whenever the boat stopped. I never trust these yer things to other folks."

This speech was addressed to Tom quite confidentially, as if it was something that would be specially interesting to him. Tom made no answer.

The trader searched the boat from stem to stern, among boxes, bales and barrels, around the machinery, by the chimneys, in vain.

"Now, I say, Tom, be fair about this yer," he said, when, after a fruitless search, he came where Tom was standing. "You know something about it, now. Don't tell me,—I know you do. I saw the gal stretched out here about ten o'clock, and ag'in at twelve, and ag'in between one and two; and then at four she was gone, and you was sleeping right there all the time. Now, you know something,—you can't help it."

"Well, Mas'r," said Tom, "towards morning something brushed by me, and I kinder half woke; and then I hearn a great splash, and then I clare woke up, and the gal was gone. That's all I know on 't."

The trader was not shocked nor amazed; because, as we said before, he was used to a great many things that you are not used to. Even the awful presence of Death struck no solemn chill upon him. He had seen Death many times,—met him in the way of trade, and got acquainted with him,—and he only thought of him as a hard customer, that embarrassed his property operations very unfairly; and so he only swore that the gal was a baggage, and that he was devilish unlucky, and that, if things went on in this way, he

7. Paraphrase of Isaiah 63.4.

should not make a cent on the trip. In short, he seemed to consider himself an ill-used man, decidedly; but there was no help for it, as the woman had escaped into a state which *never will* give up a fugitive,—not even at the demand of the whole glorious Union. The trader, therefore, sat discontentedly down, with his little account-book, and put down the missing body and soul under the head of *losses!*

"He's a shocking creature, isn't he,—this trader? so unfeeling! It's dreadful, really!"

"O, but nobody thinks anything of these traders! They are universally despised,—never received into any decent society."

But who, sir, makes the trader? Who is most to blame? The enlightened, cultivated, intelligent man, who supports the system of which the trader is the inevitable result, or the poor trader himself? You make the public sentiment that calls for his trade, that debauches and depraves him, till he feels no shame in it; and in what are you better than he?

Are you educated and he ignorant, you high and he low, you refined and he coarse, you talented and he simple?

In the day of a future Judgment, these very considerations may make it more tolerable for him than for you.

In concluding these little incidents of lawful trade, we must beg the world not to think that American legislators are entirely destitute of humanity, as might, perhaps, be unfairly inferred from the great efforts made in our national body to protect and perpetuate this species of traffic.

Who does not know how our great men are outdoing themselves, in declaiming against the *foreign* slave-trade. There are a perfect host of Clarksons[8] and Wilberforces risen up among us on that subject, most edifying to hear and behold. Trading negroes from Africa, dear reader, is so horrid! It is not to be thought of! But trading them from Kentucky,— that's quite another thing!

* * *

Volume II

FROM CHAPTER XXVI. DEATH[9]

Weep not for those whom the veil of the tomb,
In life's early morning, hath bid from our eyes.[1]

* * *

"Mamma," said Eva, "I want to have some of my hair cut off,—a good deal of it."

"What for?" said Marie.

"Mamma, I want to give some away to my friends, while I am able to give it to them myself. Won't you ask aunty to come and cut it for me?"

8. The English abolitionist Thomas Clarkson (1760–1846), who with his countryman William Wilberforce was an architect of the 1807 act of Parliament abolishing the slave trade. A similar act was passed by the U.S. Congress the same year; it prohibited importation of slaves from abroad, which allowed the trade to flourish within the United States.
9. Two years have passed. To escape the hot New Orleans summer, St. Clare has brought his family and slaves to his villa at Lake Pontchartrain in southeastern Louisiana. Eva, who has been showing signs of serious illness, has declared to Tom that she would be happy to die if her death would bring an end to the sufferings of the slaves.
1. From "Weep Not for Those" (1816), by the Irish poet Thomas Moore (1779–1852).

Marie raised her voice, and called Miss Ophelia, from the other room.

The child half rose from her pillow as she came in, and, shaking down her long golden-brown curls, said, rather playfully, "Come, aunty, shear the sheep!"

"What's that?" said St. Clare, who just then entered with some fruit he had been out to get for her.

"Papa, I just want aunty to cut off some of my hair;—there's too much of it, and it makes my head hot. Besides, I want to give some of it away."

Miss Ophelia came, with her scissors.

"Take care,—don't spoil the looks of it!" said her father; "cut underneath, where it won't show. Eva's curls are my pride."

"O, papa!" said Eva, sadly.

"Yes, and I want them kept handsome against the time I take you up to your uncle's plantation, to see Cousin Henrique," said St. Clare, in a gay tone.

"I shall never go there, papa;—I am going to a better country. O, do believe me! Don't you see, papa, that I get weaker, every day?"

"Why do you insist that I shall believe such a cruel thing, Eva?" said her father.

"Only because it is *true*, papa: and, if you will believe it now, perhaps you will get to feel about it as I do."

St. Clare closed his lips, and stood gloomily eying the long, beautiful curls, which, as they were separated from the child's head, were laid, one by one, in her lap. She raised them up, looked earnestly at them, twined them around her thin fingers, and looked, from time to time, anxiously at her father.

"It's just what I've been foreboding!" said Marie; "it's just what has been preying on my health, from day to day, bringing me downward to the grave, though nobody regards it. I have seen this, long. St. Clare, you will see, after a while, that I was right."

"Which will afford you great consolation, no doubt!" said St. Clare, in a dry, bitter tone.

Marie lay back on a lounge, and covered her face with her cambric handkerchief.

Eva's clear blue eye looked earnestly from one to the other. It was the calm, comprehending gaze of a soul half loosed from its earthly bonds; it was evident she saw, felt, and appreciated, the difference between the two.

She beckoned with her hand to her father. He came, and sat down by her.

"Papa, my strength fades away every day, and I know I must go. There are some things I want to say and do,—that I ought to do; and you are so unwilling to have me speak a word on this subject. But it must come; there's no putting it off. Do be willing I should speak now!"

"My child, I *am* willing!" said St. Clare, covering his eyes with one hand, and holding up Eva's hand with the other.

"Then, I want to see all our people together. I have some things I *must* say to them," said Eva.

"*Well,*" said St. Clare, in a tone of dry endurance.

Miss Ophelia despatched a messenger, and soon the whole of the servants were convened in the room.

Eva lay back on her pillows; her hair hanging loosely about her face, her crimson cheeks contrasting painfully with the intense whiteness of her complexion and the thin contour of her limbs and features, and her large, soul-like eyes fixed earnestly on every one.

The servants were struck with a sudden emotion. The spiritual face, the long locks of hair cut off and lying by her, her father's averted face, and Marie's sobs, struck at once upon the feelings of a sensitive and impressible race; and, as they came in, they looked one on another, sighed, and shook their heads. There was a deep silence, like that of a funeral.

Eva raised herself, and looked long and earnestly round at every one. All looked sad and apprehensive. Many of the women hid their faces in their aprons.

"I sent for you all, my dear friends," said Eva, "because I love you. I love you all; and I have something to say to you, which I want you always to remember. . . . I am going to leave you. In a few more weeks, you will see me no more—"

Here the child was interrupted by bursts of groans, sobs, and lamentations, which broke from all present, and in which her slender voice was lost entirely. She waited a moment, and then, speaking in a tone that checked the sobs of all, she said,

"If you love me, you must not interrupt me so. Listen to what I say. I want to speak to you about your souls. . . . Many of you, I am afraid, are very careless. You are thinking only about this world. I want you to remember that there is a beautiful world, where Jesus is. I am going there, and you can go there. It is for you, as much as me. But, if you want to go there, you must not live idle, careless, thoughtless lives. You must be Christians. You must remember that each one of you can become angels, and be angels forever. . . . If you want to be Christians, Jesus will help you. You must pray to him; you must read—"

The child checked herself, looked piteously at them, and said, sorrowfully,

"O, dear! you *can't* read,—poor souls!" and she hid her face in the pillow and sobbed, while many a smothered sob from those she was addressing, who were kneeling on the floor, aroused her.

"Never mind," she said, raising her face and smiling brightly through her tears, "I have prayed for you; and I know Jesus will help you, even if you can't read. Try all to do the best you can; pray every day; ask Him to help you, and get the Bible read to you whenever you can; and I think I shall see you all in heaven."

"Amen," was the murmured response from the lips of Tom and Mammy, and some of the elder ones, who belonged to the Methodist church. The younger and more thoughtless ones, for the time completely overcome, were sobbing, with their heads bowed upon their knees.

"I know," said Eva, "you all love me."

"Yes; oh, yes! indeed we do! Lord bless her!" was the involuntary answer of all.

"Yes, I know you do! There isn't one of you that hasn't always been very kind to me; and I want to give you something that, when you look at, you shall always remember me. I'm going to give all of you a curl of my hair; and, when you look at it, think that I loved you and am gone to heaven, and that I want to see you all there."

It is impossible to describe the scene, as, with tears and sobs, they gathered round the little creature, and took from her hands what seemed to them a last mark of her love. They fell on their knees; they sobbed, and prayed, and kissed the hem of her garment; and the elder ones poured forth words of endearment, mingled in prayers and blessings, after the manner of their susceptible race.

As each one took their gift, Miss Ophelia, who was apprehensive for the effect of all this excitement on her little patient, signed to each one to pass out of the apartment.

At last, all were gone but Tom and Mammy.

"Here, Uncle Tom," said Eva, "is a beautiful one for you. O, I am so happy, Uncle Tom, to think I shall see you in heaven,—for I'm sure I shall; and Mammy,—dear, good, kind Mammy!" she said, fondly throwing her arms round her old nurse,—"I know you'll be there, too."

"O, Miss Eva, don't see how I can live without ye, no how!" said the faithful creature. "'Pears like it's just taking everything off the place to oncet!"[2] and Mammy gave way to a passion of grief.

Miss Ophelia pushed her and Tom gently from the apartment, and thought they were all gone; but, as she turned, Topsy was standing there.

"Where did you start up from?" she said, suddenly.

"I was here," said Topsy, wiping the tears from her eyes. "O, Miss Eva, I've been a bad girl; but won't you give *me* one, too?"

"Yes, poor Topsy! to be sure, I will. There—every time you look at that, think that I love you, and wanted you to be a good girl!"

"O, Miss Eva, I *is* tryin!" said Topsy, earnestly; "but, Lor, it's so hard to be good! 'Pears like I an't used to it, no ways!"

"Jesus knows it, Topsy; he is sorry for you; he will help you."

Topsy, with her eyes hid in her apron, was silently passed from the apartment by Miss Ophelia; but, as she went, she hid the precious curl in her bosom.

* * *

Eva had been unusually bright and cheerful, that afternoon, and had sat raised in her bed, and looked over all her little trinkets and precious things, and designated the friends to whom she would have them given; and her manner was more animated, and her voice more natural, than they had known it for weeks. Her father had been in, in the evening, and had said that Eva appeared more like her former self than ever she had done since her sickness; and when he kissed her for the night, he said to Miss Ophelia,— "Cousin, we may keep her with us, after all; she is certainly better;" and he had retired with a lighter heart in his bosom than he had had there for weeks.

But at midnight,—strange, mystic hour!—when the veil between the frail present and the eternal future grows thin,—then came the messenger!

There was a sound in that chamber, first of one who stepped quickly. It was Miss Ophelia, who had resolved to sit up all night with her little charge, and who, at the turn of the night, had discerned what experienced nurses significantly call "a change." The outer door was quickly opened, and Tom, who was watching outside, was on the alert, in a moment.

"Go for the doctor, Tom! lose not a moment," said Miss Ophelia; and, stepping across the room, she rapped at St. Clare's door.

2. At once (colloquial).

"Cousin," she said, "I wish you would come."

Those words fell on his heart like clods upon a coffin. Why did they? He was up and in the room in an instant, and bending over Eva, who still slept.

What was it he saw that made his heart stand still? Why was no word spoken between the two? Thou canst say, who hast seen that same expression on the face dearest to thee;—that look indescribable, hopeless, unmistakable, that says to thee that thy beloved is no longer thine.

On the face of the child, however, there was no ghastly imprint,—only a high and almost sublime expression,—the overshadowing presence of spiritual natures, the dawning of immortal life in that childish soul.

They stood there so still, gazing upon her, that even the ticking of the watch seemed too loud. In a few moments, Tom returned, with the doctor. He entered, gave one look, and stood silent as the rest.

"When did this change take place?" said he, in a low whisper, to Miss Ophelia.

"About the turn of the night," was the reply.

Marie, roused by the entrance of the doctor, appeared, hurriedly, from the next room.

"Augustine! Cousin!—O!—what!" she hurriedly began.

"Hush!" said St. Clare, hoarsely; *"she is dying!"*

Mammy heard the words, and flew to awaken the servants. The house was soon roused,—lights were seen, footsteps heard, anxious faces thronged the verandah, and looked tearfully through the glass doors; but St. Clare heard and said nothing,—he saw only *that look* on the face of the little sleeper.

"O, if she would only wake, and speak once more!" he said; and, stooping over her, he spoke in her ear,—"Eva, darling!"

The large blue eyes unclosed,—a smile passed over her face;—she tried to raise her head, and to speak.

"Do you know me, Eva?"

"Dear papa," said the child, with a last effort, throwing her arms about his neck. In a moment they dropped again; and, as St. Clare raised his head, he saw a spasm of mortal agony pass over the face,—she struggled for breath, and threw up her little hands.

"O, God, this is dreadful!" he said, turning away in agony, and wringing Tom's hand, scarce conscious what he was doing. "O, Tom, my boy, it is killing me!"

Tom had his master's hands between his own; and, with tears streaming down his dark cheeks, looked up for help where he had always been used to look.

"Pray that this may be cut short!" said St. Clare,—"this wrings my heart."

"O, bless the Lord! it's over,—it's over, dear Master!" said Tom; "look at her."

The child lay panting on her pillows, as one exhausted,—the large clear eyes rolled up and fixed. Ah, what said those eyes, that spoke so much of heaven? Earth was past, and earthly pain; but so solemn, so mysterious, was the triumphant brightness of that face, that it checked even the sobs of sorrow. They pressed around her, in breathless stillness.

"Eva," said St. Clare, gently.

She did not hear.

"O, Eva, tell us what you see! What is it?" said her father.

A bright, a glorious smile passed over her face, and she said, brokenly,—
"O! love,—joy,—peace!" gave one sigh, and passed from death unto life!

"Farewell, beloved child! the bright, eternal doors have closed after thee;
we shall see thy sweet face no more. O, woe for them who watched thy
entrance into heaven, when they shall wake and find only the cold gray sky
of daily life, and thou gone forever!"

* * *

1852

HARRIET JACOBS
c. 1813–1897

The first African American woman known to have authored a slave narrative in
the United States, Harriet Jacobs was born into slavery in Edenton, North Carolina. Her father was a skilled carpenter who was permitted to hire himself out, and
her parents were allowed to live together even though they had different masters;
therefore, as a child Jacobs was unaware that she was a slave. Her mother's death
and a change of owners for both Jacobs and her father brought her into the family
of Dr. and Mrs. James Norcom in 1825. There, as she grew to adulthood, she was
sexually threatened by the doctor and abused by his jealous wife. As a defense
against this treatment, Jacobs became involved with an unmarried white attorney,
Samuel Tredwell Sawyer, with whom she had two children: Joseph, born in 1829,
and Louisa Matilda, born in 1833. When Norcom sent her to a country plantation
in 1835, she escaped back to Edenton, hiding for perhaps seven years in an attic
crawl space in the home of her maternal grandmother, who had been emancipated
some years earlier. While Jacobs was in hiding, Sawyer purchased, but did not
emancipate, their two children. Jacobs finally escaped to the North in 1842, and
later both her children came north as well. Life in the North remained insecure
and perilous, however, because slave catchers were constantly hunting down
escaped slaves to return them to the South, which they could do more aggressively
after 1850 with the Fugitive Slave Act on their side.

For much of the next two decades Jacobs worked in the family of Nathaniel Parker
Willis (1806–1867), one of the era's most popular writers and editors (and the brother
of the popular writer Fanny Fern). She took care of his children and became particularly close to his second wife, Cornelia Grinnell Willis, a staunch abolitionist. In
1852 Cornelia Willis arranged to purchase Jacobs from Norcom's daughter, Jacobs's
legal owner; then she emancipated Jacobs, who continued to work for Willis after he
became a widower.

Jacobs spent most of 1849 in Rochester, New York, working for the Anti-Slavery
Office run by her younger brother, who had also escaped slavery. She read through
a large body of antislavery writings and also came to know a number of abolitionists, including many white women, among them the Quaker Amy Post, who became
a mentor to her and in whose house she lived for nine months while her brother was
away on lecture tours. Jacobs wanted to contribute her life story to the abolitionist
cause in a way that would capture the attention of Northern white women in partic-

ular, to show them how slavery debased and demoralized women, at once subjecting them to white male lust and also depriving them of the right to make homes for their families. Yet this topic was difficult to discuss in an era when extreme sexual prudery was the norm, when standards of female sexual "purity" could result in blaming the unmarried slave mother rather than the man whose victim she was. In *Incidents in the Life of a Slave Girl* Jacobs tried to do more than create sympathy for her plight; she sought to win the respect and admiration of her readers for the courage with which she forestalled abuse and for the independence with which she chose a lover rather than having one forced on her. Her description of hiding in the attic, her emphasis on family life and maternal values, and her account of the difficulties of fugitive slaves in the North differentiate the book from the numerous slave narratives produced in the twenty years before the Civil War.

Encouraged by the success of Harriet Beecher Stowe's *Uncle Tom's Cabin* (1852)—one of whose heroines is the slave concubine Cassy—Jacobs began work on her narrative around 1853 and finished it by 1858. She was not successful in finding a publisher for it, however, until Lydia Maria Child (1802–1880), the well-known woman of letters and abolitionist, agreed to write a preface for it. Child became interested in the project, putting much editorial work into the manuscript; and when the contracted publishers went bankrupt, she arranged for its publication. The book came out under the pseudonym "Linda Brent" in 1861; it was sold by antislavery societies in the Northeast, was published in England in 1862, and received several favorable reviews. The outbreak of the Civil War made its message less pressing, however; and it sank from notice until the 1980s, when renewed interest in writings by African American women and superb archival scholarship by Jean Fagin Yellin, establishing that this was an autobiographical narrative and not a novel, brought belated acclaim to the work.

During and after the war Jacobs worked with the Quakers in their efforts to help freed slaves through direct aid and by organizing schools, orphanages, and nursing homes. She ran a boardinghouse in Cambridge, Massachusetts, and later moved to Washington, D.C., with her daughter. She is buried in Mount Auburn Cemetery in Cambridge.

From Incidents in the Life of a Slave Girl[1]

I. Childhood

I was born a slave; but I never knew it till six years of happy childhood had passed away. My father was a carpenter, and considered so intelligent and skilful in his trade, that, when buildings out of the common line were to be erected, he was sent for from long distances, to be head workman. On condition of paying his mistress two hundred dollars a year, and supporting himself, he was allowed to work at his trade, and manage his own affairs. His strongest wish was to purchase his children; but, though he several times offered his hard earnings for that purpose, he never succeeded. In complexion my parents were a light shade of brownish yellow, and were termed mulattoes. They lived together in a comfortable home; and, though we were all slaves, I was so fondly shielded that I never dreamed I was a piece of merchandise, trusted to them for safe keeping, and liable to be demanded of them at any moment. I had one brother, William, who was two years younger

1. The text is that of the 1861 edition, published in Boston.

than myself—a bright, affectionate child. I had also a great treasure in my maternal grandmother, who was a remarkable woman in many respects. She was the daughter of a planter in South Carolina, who, at his death, left her mother and his three children free, with money to go to St. Augustine,[2] where they had relatives. It was during the Revolutionary War; and they were captured on their passage, carried back, and sold to different purchasers. Such was the story my grandmother used to tell me; but I do not remember all the particulars. She was a little girl when she was captured and sold to the keeper of a large hotel.[3] I have often heard her tell how hard she fared during childhood. But as she grew older she evinced so much intelligence, and was so faithful, that her master and mistress could not help seeing it was for their interest to take care of such a valuable piece of property. She became an indispensable personage in the household, officiating in all capacities, from cook and wet nurse to seamstress. She was much praised for her cooking; and her nice crackers became so famous in the neighborhood that many people were desirous of obtaining them. In consequence of numerous requests of this kind, she asked permission of her mistress to bake crackers at night, after all the household work was done; and she obtained leave to do it, provided she would clothe herself and her children from the profits. Upon these terms, after working hard all day for her mistress, she began her midnight bakings, assisted by her two oldest children. The business proved profitable; and each year she laid by a little, which was saved for a fund to purchase her children. Her master died, and the property was divided among his heirs. The widow had her dower[4] in the hotel, which she continued to keep open. My grandmother remained in her service as a slave; but her children were divided among her master's children. As she had five, Benjamin, the youngest one, was sold, in order that each heir might have an equal portion of dollars and cents. There was so little difference in our ages that he seemed more like my brother than my uncle. He was a bright, handsome lad, nearly white; for he inherited the complexion my grandmother had derived from Anglo-Saxon ancestors. Though only ten years old, seven hundred and twenty dollars were paid for him. His sale was a terrible blow to my grandmother; but she was naturally hopeful, and she went to work with renewed energy, trusting in time to be able to purchase some of her children. She had laid up three hundred dollars, which her mistress one day begged as a loan, promising to pay her soon. The reader probably knows that no promise or writing given to a slave is legally binding; for, according to Southern laws, a slave, *being* property, can *hold* no property. When my grandmother lent her hard earnings to her mistress, she trusted solely to her honor. The honor of a slaveholder to a slave!

To this good grandmother I was indebted for many comforts. My brother Willie and I often received portions of the crackers, cakes, and preserves, she made to sell; and after we ceased to be children we were indebted to her for many more important services.

2. During the Revolutionary War, a British port town in what is now Florida.
3. John Horniblow, who ran the King's Arms hotel in Edenton, North Carolina. Jacobs's grandmother's legal name was Margaret (Molly) Horniblow (c. 1771–1853); as was typical for the era,

Molly received the surname of her owner. *Incidents* never mentions a grandfather, and no information has been recovered relating to the paternal parentage of Molly's children.
4. Inheritance from her husband's estate.

Such were the unusually fortunate circumstances of my early childhood. When I was six years old, my mother died, and then, for the first time, I learned, by the talk around me, that I was a slave. My mother's mistress was the daughter of my grandmother's mistress. She was the foster sister of my mother; they were both nourished at my grandmother's breast. In fact, my mother had been weaned at three months old, that the babe of the mistress might obtain sufficient food. They played together as children; and, when they became women, my mother was a most faithful servant to her whiter foster sister. On her death-bed her mistress promised that her children should never suffer for any thing; and during her lifetime she kept her word. They all spoke kindly of my dead mother, who had been a slave merely in name, but in nature was noble and womanly. I grieved for her, and my young mind was troubled with the thought who would now take care of me and my little brother. I was told that my home was now to be with her mistress; and I found it a happy one. No toilsome or disagreeable duties were imposed upon me. My mistress was so kind to me that I was always glad to do her bidding, and proud to labor for her as much as my young years would permit. I would sit by her side for hours, sewing diligently, with a heart as free from care as that of any free-born white child. When she thought I was tired, she would send me out to run and jump; and away I bounded, to gather berries or flowers to decorate her room. Those were happy days—too happy to last. The slave child had no thought for the morrow; but there came that blight, which too surely waits on every human being born to be a chattel.

When I was nearly twelve years old, my kind mistress sickened and died. As I saw the cheek grow paler, and the eye more glassy, how earnestly I prayed in my heart that she might live! I loved her; for she had been almost like a mother to me. My prayers were not answered. She died, and they buried her in the little churchyard, where, day after day, my tears fell upon her grave.

I was sent to spend a week with my grandmother. I was now old enough to begin to think of the future; and again and again I asked myself what they would do with me. I felt sure I should never find another mistress so kind as the one who was gone. She had promised my dying mother that her children should never suffer for any thing; and when I remembered that, and recalled her many proofs of attachment to me, I could not help having some hopes that she had left me free. My friends were almost certain it would be so. They thought she would be sure to do it, on account of my mother's love and faithful service. But, alas! we all know that the memory of a faithful slave does not avail much to save her children from the auction block.

After a brief period of suspense, the will of my mistress was read, and we learned that she had bequeathed me to her sister's daughter, a child of five years old. So vanished our hopes. My mistress had taught me the precepts of God's Word: "Thou shalt love thy neighbor as thyself."[5] "Whatsoever ye would that men should do unto you, do ye even so unto them."[6] But I was her slave, and I suppose she did not recognize me as her neighbor. I would give much to blot out from my memory that one great wrong. As a child, I loved my mistress; and, looking back on the happy days I spent with her, I try to

---

5. Mark 12.31.   6. Matthew 7.12.

think with less bitterness of this act of injustice. While I was with her, she taught me to read and spell; and for this privilege, which so rarely falls to the lot of a slave, I bless her memory.

She possessed but few slaves; and at her death those were all distributed among her relatives. Five of them were my grandmother's children, and had shared the same milk that nourished her mother's children. Notwithstanding my grandmother's long and faithful service to her owners, not one of her children escaped the auction block. These God-breathing machines are no more, in the sight of their masters, than the cotton they plant, or the horses they tend.

* * *

VII. The Lover

Why does the slave ever love? Why allow the tendrils of the heart to twine around objects which may at any moment be wrenched away by the hand of violence? When separations come by the hand of death, the pious soul can bow in resignation, and say, "Not my will, but thine be done, O Lord!"[7] But when the ruthless hand of man strikes the blow, regardless of the misery he causes, it is hard to be submissive. I did not reason thus when I was a young girl. Youth will be youth. I loved, and I indulged the hope that the dark clouds around me would turn out a bright lining. I forgot that in the land of my birth the shadows are too dense for light to penetrate. A land

> "Where laughter is not mirth; nor thought the mind;
> Nor words a language; no e'en men mankind.
> Where cries reply to curses, shrieks to blows,
> And each is tortured in his separate hell."[8]

There was in the neighborhood a young colored carpenter; a free born man. We had been well acquainted in childhood, and frequently met together afterwards. We became mutually attached, and he proposed to marry me. I loved him with all the ardor of a young girl's first love. But when I reflected that I was a slave, and that the laws gave no sanction to the marriage of such, my heart sank within me. My lover wanted to buy me; but I knew that Dr. Flint was too wilful and arbitrary a man to consent to that arrangement. From him, I was sure of experiencing all sorts of opposition, and I had nothing to hope from my mistress.[9] She would have been delighted to have got rid of me, but not in that way. It would have relieved her mind of a burden if she could have seen me sold to some distant state, but if I was married near home I should be just as much in her husband's power as I had previously been,—for the husband of a slave has no power to protect her.[1] Moreover, my mistress, like many others, seemed to think that slaves had no right to any family ties of their own; that they were created merely to wait upon the family of the mistress. I once heard her abuse a young slave girl, who told her that a colored man wanted to make her his wife. "I will have you peeled and pickled, my lady," said she, "if I ever hear you mention

7. Matthew 26.39.
8. From *The Lament of Tasso* 4.7–10 (1817), by the English poet George Gordon, Lord Byron (1788–1824).
9. Dr. Flint is the father of Brent's owner, Emily

Flint, who is a child at this time, giving Flint and his wife (whom Brent refers to as her mistress) legal power.
1. Flint has been attempting to coerce Brent into sexual relations.

that subject again. Do you suppose that I will have you tending *my* children with the children of that nigger?" The girl to whom she said this had a mulatto child, of course not acknowledged by its father. The poor black man who loved her would have been proud to acknowledge his helpless offspring.

Many and anxious were the thoughts I revolved in my mind. I was at a loss what to do. Above all things, I was desirous to spare my lover the insults that had cut so deeply into my own soul. I talked with my grandmother about it, and partly told her my fears. I did not dare to tell her the worst. She had long suspected all was not right, and if I confirmed her suspicions I knew a storm would rise that would prove the overthrow of all my hopes.

This love-dream had been my support through many trials; and I could not bear to run the risk of having it suddenly dissipated. There was a lady in the neighborhood, a particular friend of Dr. Flint's, who often visited the house. I had a great respect for her, and she had always manifested a friendly interest in me. Grandmother thought she would have great influence with the doctor. I went to this lady, and told her my story. I told her I was aware that my lover's being a free-born man would prove a great objection; but he wanted to buy me; and if Dr. Flint would consent to that arrangement, I felt sure he would be willing to pay any reasonable price. She knew that Mrs. Flint disliked me; therefore, I ventured to suggest that perhaps my mistress would approve of my being sold, as that would rid her of me. The lady listened with kindly sympathy, and promised to do her utmost to promote my wishes. She had an interview with the doctor, and I believe she pleaded my cause earnestly; but it was all to no purpose.

How I dreaded my master now! Every minute I expected to be summoned to his presence; but the day passed, and I heard nothing from him. The next morning, a message was brought to me: "Master wants you in his study." I found the door ajar, and I stood a moment gazing at the hateful man who claimed a right to rule me, body and soul. I entered, and tried to appear calm. I did not want him to know how my heart was bleeding. He looked fixedly at me, with an expression which seemed to say, "I have half a mind to kill you on the spot." At last he broke the silence, and that was a relief to both of us.

"So you want to be married, do you?" said he, "and to a free nigger."

"Yes, sir."

"Well, I'll soon convince you whether I am your master, or the nigger fellow you honor so highly. If you *must* have a husband, you may take up with one of my slaves."

What a situation I should be in, as the wife of one of *his* slaves, even if my heart had been interested!

I replied, "Don't you suppose, sir, that a slave can have some preference about marrying? Do you suppose that all men are alike to her?"

"Do you love this nigger?" said he, abruptly.

"Yes, sir."

"How dare you tell me so!" he exclaimed, in great wrath. After a slight pause, he added, "I supposed you thought more of yourself; that you felt above the insults of such puppies."

I replied, "If he is a puppy I am a puppy, for we are both of the negro race. It is right and honorable for us to love each other. The man you call a puppy never insulted me, sir; and he would not love me if he did not believe me to be a virtuous woman."

He sprang upon me like a tiger, and gave me a stunning blow. It was the first time he had ever struck me; and fear did not enable me to control my anger. When I had recovered a little from the effects, I exclaimed, "You have struck me for answering you honestly. How I despise you!"

There was silence for some minutes. Perhaps he was deciding what should be my punishment; or, perhaps, he wanted to give me time to reflect on what I had said, and to whom I had said it. Finally, he asked, "Do you know what you have said?"

"Yes, sir; but your treatment drove me to it."

"Do you know that I have a right to do as I like with you,—that I can kill you, if I please?"

"You have tried to kill me, and I wish you had; but you have no right to do as you like with me."

"Silence!" he exclaimed, in a thundering voice. "By heavens, girl, you forget yourself too far! Are you mad? If you are, I will soon bring you to your senses. Do you think any other master would bear what I have borne from you this morning? Many masters would have killed you on the spot. How would you like to be sent to jail for your insolence?"

"I know I have been disrespectful, sir," I replied; "but you drove me to it; I couldn't help it. As for the jail, there would be more peace for me there than there is here."

"You deserve to go there," he said, "and to be under such treatment, that you would forget the meaning of the word *peace*. It would do you good. It would take some of your high notions out of you. But I am not ready to send you there yet, notwithstanding your ingratitude for all my kindness and forbearance. You have been the plague of my life. I have wanted to make you happy, and I have been repaid with the basest ingratitude; but though you have proved yourself incapable of appreciating my kindness, I will be lenient towards you, Linda. I will give you one more chance to redeem your character. If you behave yourself and do as I require, I will forgive you and treat you as I always have done; but if you disobey me, I will punish you as I would the meanest slave on my plantation. Never let me hear that fellow's name mentioned again. If I ever know of your speaking to him, I will cowhide you both; and if I catch him lurking about my premises, I will shoot him as soon as I would a dog. Do you hear what I say? I'll teach you a lesson about marriage and free niggers! Now go, and let this be the last time I have occasion to speak to you on this subject."

Reader, did you ever hate? I hope not. I never did but once; and I trust I never shall again. Somebody has called it "the atmosphere of hell;" and I believe it is so.

For a fortnight the doctor did not speak to me. He thought to mortify me; to make me feel that I had disgraced myself by receiving the honorable addresses of a respectable colored man, in preference to the base proposals of a white man. But though his lips disdained to address me, his eyes were very loquacious. No animal ever watched its prey more narrowly than he watched me. He knew that I could write, though he had failed to make me read his letters; and he was now troubled lest I should exchange letters with another man. After a while he became weary of silence; and I was sorry for it. One morning, as he passed through the hall, to leave the house, he contrived to thrust a note into my hand. I thought I had better read it, and spare myself the vexation of having him read it to me. It expressed regret for the blow he had given me, and reminded me that I myself was wholly to blame for it. He hoped I had become convinced of the injury I was doing myself by incurring his displeasure. He wrote that he had made up his mind to go to Louisiana; that he should take several slaves with him, and intended I should be one of the number. My mistress would remain where she was; therefore I should have nothing to fear from that quarter. If I merited kindness from him, he assured me that it would be lavishly bestowed. He begged me to think over the matter, and answer the following day.

The next morning I was called to carry a pair of scissors to his room. I laid them on the table, with the letter beside them. He thought it was my answer, and did not call me back. I went as usual to attend my young mistress to and from school. He met me in the street, and ordered me to stop at his office on my way back. When I entered, he showed me his letter, and asked me why I had not answered it. I replied, "I am your daughter's property, and it is in your power to send me, or take me, wherever you please." He said he was very glad to find me so willing to go, and that we should start early in the autumn. He had a large practice in the town, and I rather thought he had made up the story merely to frighten me. However that might be, I was determined that I would never go to Louisiana with him.

Summer passed away, and early in the autumn, Dr. Flint's eldest son was sent to Louisiana to examine the country, with a view to emigrating. That news did not disturb me. I knew very well that I should not be sent with *him*. That I had not been taken to the plantation before this time, was owing to the fact that his son was there. He was jealous of his son; and jealousy of the overseer had kept him from punishing me by sending me into the fields to work. Is it strange that I was not proud of these protectors? As for the overseer, he was a man for whom I had less respect than I had for a bloodhound.

Young Mr. Flint did not bring back a favorable report of Louisiana, and I heard no more of that scheme. Soon after this, my lover met me at the corner of the street, and I stopped to speak to him. Looking up, I saw my master watching us from his window. I hurried home, trembling with fear. I was sent for, immediately, to go to his room. He met me with a blow. "When is mistress to be married?" said he, in a sneering tone. A shower of oaths and imprecations followed. How thankful I was that my lover was a free man! that my tyrant had no power to flog him for speaking to me in the street!

Again and again I revolved in my mind how all this would end. There was no hope that the doctor would consent to sell me on any terms. He had an iron will, and was determined to keep me, and to conquer me. My lover was an intelligent and religious man. Even if he could have obtained permission to marry me while I was a slave, the marriage would give him no power to protect me from my master. It would have made him miserable to witness the insults I should have been subjected to. And then, if we had children, I knew they must "follow the condition of the mother."[2] What a terrible blight that would be on the heart of a free, intelligent father! For *his* sake, I felt that I ought not to link his fate with my own unhappy destiny. He was going to Savannah to see about a little property left him by an uncle; and hard as

2. In Southern law, the mother's legal status as slave or free determined the legal status of the child.

it was to bring my feelings to it, I earnestly entreated him not to come back. I advised him to go to the Free States, where his tongue would not be tied, and where his intelligence would be of more avail to him. He left me, still hoping the day would come when I could be bought. With me the lamp of hope had gone out. The dream of my girlhood was over. I felt lonely and desolate.

Still I was not stripped of all. I still had my good grandmother, and my affectionate brother. When he put his arms round my neck, and looked into my eyes, as if to read there the troubles I dared not tell, I felt that I still had something to love. But even that pleasant emotion was chilled by the reflection that he might be torn from me at any moment, by some sudden freak of my master. If he had known how we love each other, I think he would have exulted in separating us. We often planned together how we could get to the north. But, as William remarked, such things are easier said than done. My movements were very closely watched, and we had no means of getting any money to defray our expenses. As for grandmother, she was strongly opposed to her children's undertaking any such project. She had not forgotten poor Benjamin's sufferings[3] and she was afraid that if another child tried to escape, he would have a similar or a worse fate. To me, nothing seemed more dreadful than my present life. I said to myself, "William *must* be free. He shall go to the north, and I will follow him." Many a slave sister has formed the same plans.

*　*　*

X. A Perilous Passage in the Slave Girl's Life

After my lover went away, Dr. Flint contrived a new plan. He seemed to have an idea that my fear of my mistress was his greatest obstacle. In the blandest tones, he told me that he was going to build a small house for me, in a secluded place, four miles away from the town. I shuddered; but I was constrained to listen, while he talked of his intention to give me a home of my own, and to make a lady of me. Hitherto, I had escaped my dreaded fate, by being in the midst of people. My grandmother had already had high words with my master about me. She had told him pretty plainly what she thought of his character, and there was considerable gossip in the neighborhood about our affairs, to which the open-mouthed jealousy of Mrs. Flint contributed not a little. When my master said he was going to build a house for me, and that he could do it with little trouble and expense, I was in hopes something would happen to frustrate his scheme; but I soon heard that the house was actually begun. I vowed before my Maker that I would never enter it. I had rather toil on the plantation from dawn till dark; I had rather live and die in jail, than drag on, from day to day, through such a living death. I was determined that the master, whom I so hated and loathed, who had blighted the prospects of my youth, and made my life a desert, should not, after my long struggle with him, succeed at last in trampling his victim under his feet. I would do any thing, every thing, for the sake of defeating him. What *could* I do? I thought and thought, till I became desperate, and made a plunge into the abyss.

3. One of Brent's uncles, caught attempting to escape, was jailed for six months, then sold to a trader. He eventually escaped to New York City but never saw his mother again.

And now, reader, I come to a period in my unhappy life, which I would gladly forget if I could. The remembrance fills me with sorrow and shame. It pains me to tell you of it; but I have promised to tell you the truth, and I will do it honestly, let it cost me what it may. I will not try to screen myself behind the plea of compulsion from a master; for it was not so. Neither can I plead ignorance or thoughtlessness. For years, my master had done his utmost to pollute my mind with foul images, and to destroy the pure principles inculcated by my grandmother, and the good mistress of my childhood. The influences of slavery had had the same effect on me that they had on other young girls; they had made me prematurely knowing, concerning the evil ways of the world. I knew what I did, and I did it with deliberate calculation.

But, O, ye happy women, whose purity has been sheltered from childhood, who have been free to choose the objects of your affection, whose homes are protected by law, do not judge the poor desolate slave girl too severely! If slavery had been abolished, I, also, could have married the man of my choice; I could have had a home shielded by the laws; and I should have been spared the painful task of confessing what I am now about to relate; but all my prospects had been blighted by slavery. I wanted to keep myself pure; and, under the most adverse circumstances, I tried hard to preserve my self-respect; but I was struggling alone in the powerful grasp of the demon Slavery; and the monster proved too strong for me. I felt as if I was forsaken by God and man; as if all my efforts must be frustrated; and I became reckless in my despair.

I have told you that Dr. Flint's persecutions and his wife's jealousy had given rise to some gossip in the neighborhood. Among others, it chanced that a white unmarried gentleman had obtained some knowledge of the circumstances in which I was placed. He knew my grandmother, and often spoke to me in the street. He became interested for me, and asked questions about my master, which I answered in part. He expressed a great deal of sympathy, and a wish to aid me. He constantly sought opportunities to see me, and wrote to me frequently. I was a poor slave girl, only fifteen years old.

So much attention from a superior person was, of course, flattering; for human nature is the same in all. I also felt grateful for his sympathy, and encouraged by his kind words. It seemed to me a great thing to have such a friend. By degrees, a more tender feeling crept into my heart. He was an educated and eloquent gentleman; too eloquent, alas, for the poor slave girl who trusted in him. Of course I saw whither all this was tending. I knew the impassable gulf between us; but to be an object of interest to a man who is not married, and who is not her master, is agreeable to the pride and feelings of a slave, if her miserable situation has left her any pride or sentiment. It seems less degrading to give one's self, than to submit to compulsion. There is something akin to freedom in having a lover who has no control over you, except that which he gains by kindness and attachment. A master may treat you as rudely as he pleases, and you dare not speak; moreover, the wrong does not seem so great with an unmarried man, as with one who has a wife to be made unhappy. There may be sophistry in all this; but the condition of a slave confuses all principles of morality, and, in fact, renders the practice of them impossible.

When I found that my master had actually begun to build the lonely cottage, other feelings mixed with those I have described. Revenge, and calculations of interest, were added to flattered vanity and sincere gratitude for kindness. I knew nothing would enrage Dr. Flint so much as to know that I favored another; and it was something to triumph over my tyrant even in that small way. I thought he would revenge himself by selling me, and I was sure my friend, Mr. Sands, would buy me.[4] He was a man of more generosity and feeling than my master, and I thought my freedom could be easily obtained from him. The crisis of my fate now came so near that I was desperate. I shuddered to think of being the mother of children that should be owned by my old tyrant. I knew that as soon as a new fancy took him, his victims were sold far off to get rid of them; especially if they had children. I had seen several women sold, with his babies at the breast. He never allowed his offspring by slaves to remain long in sight of himself and his wife. Of a man who was not my master I could ask to have my children well supported; and in this case, I felt confident I should obtain the boon. I also felt quite sure that they would be made free. With all these thoughts revolving in my mind, and seeing no other way of escaping the doom I so much dreaded, I made a headlong plunge. Pity me, and pardon me, O virtuous reader! You never knew what it is to be a slave; to be entirely unprotected by law or custom; to have the laws reduce you to the condition of a chattel, entirely subject to the will of another. You never exhausted your ingenuity in avoiding the snares, and eluding the power of a hated tyrant; you never shuddered at the sound of his footsteps, and trembled within hearing of his voice. I know I did wrong. No one can feel it more sensibly than I do. The painful and humiliating memory will haunt me to my dying day. Still, in looking back, calmly, on the events of my life, I feel that the slave woman ought not to be judged by the same standard as others.

The months passed on. I had many unhappy hours. I secretly mourned over the sorrow I was bringing on my grandmother, who had so tried to shield me from harm. I knew that I was the greatest comfort of her old age, and that it was a source of pride to her that I had not degraded myself, like most of the slaves. I wanted to confess to her that I was no longer worthy of her love; but I could not utter the dreaded words.

As for Dr. Flint, I had a feeling of satisfaction and triumph in the thought of telling *him*. From time to time he told me of his intended arrangements, and I was silent. At last, he came and told me the cottage was completed, and ordered me to go to it. I told him I would never enter it. He said, "I have heard enough of such talk as that. You shall go, if you are carried by force; and you shall remain there."

I replied, "I will never go there. In a few months I shall be a mother."

He stood and looked at me in dumb amazement, and left the house without a word. I thought I should be happy in my triumph over him. But now that the truth was out, and my relatives would hear of it, I felt wretched. Humble as were their circumstances, they had pride in my good character. Now, how could I look them in the face? My self-respect was gone! I had resolved that I would be virtuous, though I was a slave. I had said, "Let the storm beat! I will brave it till I die." And now, how humiliated I felt!

I went to my grandmother. My lips moved to make confession, but the words stuck in my throat. I sat down in the shade of a tree at her door and

---

4. Brent misjudged Flint, who becomes even more possessive when he learns of her relationship with Sands.

began to sew. I think she saw something unusual was the matter with me. The mother of slaves is very watchful. She knows there is no security for her children. After they have entered their teens she lives in daily expectation of trouble. This leads to many questions. If the girl is of a sensitive nature, timidity keeps her from answering truthfully, and this well-meant course has a tendency to drive her from maternal counsels. Presently, in came my mistress, like a mad woman, and accused me concerning her husband. My grandmother, whose suspicions had been previously awakened, believed what she said. She exclaimed, "O Linda! has it come to this? I had rather see you dead than to see you as you now are. You are a disgrace to your dead mother." She tore from my fingers my mother's wedding ring and her silver thimble. "Go away!" she exclaimed, "and never come to my house, again." Her reproaches fell so hot and heavy, that they left me no chance to answer. Bitter tears, such as the eyes never shed but once, were my only answer. I rose from my seat, but fell back again, sobbing. She did not speak to me; but the tears were running down her furrowed cheeks, and they scorched me like fire. She had always been so kind to me! So kind! How I longed to throw myself at her feet, and tell her all the truth! But she had ordered me to go, and never to come there again. After a few minutes, I mustered strength, and started to obey her. With what feelings did I now close that little gate, which I used to open with such an eager hand in my childhood! It closed upon me with a sound I never heard before.

Where could I go? I was afraid to return to my master's. I walked on recklessly, not caring where I went, or what would become of me. When I had gone four or five miles, fatigue compelled me to stop. I sat down on the stump of an old tree. The stars were shining through the boughs above me. How they mocked me, with their bright, calm light! The hours passed by, and as I sat there alone a chilliness and deadly sickness came over me. I sank on the ground. My mind was full of horrid thoughts. I prayed to die; but the prayer was not answered. At last, with great effort I roused myself, and walked some distance further, to the house of a woman who had been a friend of my mother. When I told her why I was there, she spoke soothingly to me; but I could not be comforted. I thought I could bear my shame if I could only be reconciled to my grandmother. I longed to open my heart to her. I thought if she could know the real state of the case, and all I had been bearing for years, she would perhaps judge me less harshly. My friend advised me to send for her. I did so; but days of agonizing suspense passed before she came. Had she utterly forsaken me? No. She came at last. I knelt before her, and told her the things that had poisoned my life; how long I had been persecuted; that I saw no way of escape; and in an hour of extremity I had become desperate. She listened in silence. I told her I would bear any thing and do any thing, if in time I had hopes of obtaining her forgiveness. I begged of her to pity me, for my dead mother's sake. And she did pity me. She did not say, "I forgive you;" but she looked at me lovingly, with her eyes full of tears. She laid her old hand gently on my head, and murmured, "Poor child! Poor child!"

*   *   *

XIV. Another Link to Life

I had not returned to my master's house since the birth of my child. The old man raved to have me thus removed from his immediate power; but his wife vowed, by all that was good and great, she would kill me if I came back; and he did not doubt her word. Sometimes he would stay away for a season. Then he would come and renew the old threadbare discourse about his forbearance and my ingratitude. He labored, most unnecessarily, to convince me that I had lowered myself. The venomous old reprobate had no need of descanting on that theme. I felt humiliated enough. My unconscious babe was the ever-present witness of my shame. I listened with silent contempt when he talked about my having forfeited *his* good opinion; but I shed bitter tears that I was no longer worthy of being respected by the good and pure. Alas! slavery still held me in its poisonous grasp. There was no chance for me to be respectable. There was no prospect of being able to lead a better life.

Sometimes, when my master found that I still refused to accept what he called his kind offers, he would threaten to sell my child. "Perhaps that will humble you," said he.

Humble *me*! Was I not already in the dust?[5] But his threat lacerated my heart. I knew the law gave him power to fulfill it; for slaveholders have been cunning enough to enact that "the child shall follow the condition of the *mother*," not of the *father*; thus taking care that licentiousness shall not interfere with avarice. This reflection made me clasp my innocent babe all the more firmly to my heart. Horrid visions passed through my mind when I thought of his liability to fall into the slave trader's hands. I wept over him, and said, "O my child! perhaps they will leave you in some cold cabin to die, and then throw you into a hole, as if you were a dog."

When Dr. Flint learned that I was again to be a mother, he was exasperated beyond measure. He rushed from the house, and returned with a pair of shears. I had a fine head of hair; and he often railed about my pride of arranging it nicely. He cut every hair close to my head, storming and swearing all the time. I replied to some of his abuse, and he struck me. Some months before, he had pitched me down stairs in a fit of passion; and the injury I received was so serious that I was unable to turn myself in bed for many days. He then said, "Linda, I swear by God I will never raise my hand against you again;" but I knew that he would forget his promise.

After he discovered my situation, he was like a restless spirit from the pit. He came every day; and I was subjected to such insults as no pen can describe. I would not describe them if I could; they were too low, too revolting. I tried to keep them from my grandmother's knowledge as much as I could. I knew she had enough to sadden her life, without having my troubles to bear. When she saw the doctor treat me with violence, and heard him utter oaths terrible enough to palsy a man's tongue, she could not always hold her peace. It was natural and motherlike that she should try to defend me; but it only made matters worse.

When they told me my new-born babe was a girl, my heart was heavier than it had ever been before. Slavery is terrible for men; but it is far more

5. Job 42.6.

terrible for women. Superadded to the burden common to all, *they* have wrongs, and sufferings, and mortifications peculiarly their own.

Dr. Flint had sworn that he would make me suffer, to my last day, for this new crime against *him*, as he called it; and as long as he had me in his power he kept his word. On the fourth day after the birth of my babe, he entered my room suddenly, and commanded me to rise and bring my baby to him. The nurse who took care of me had gone out of the room to prepare some nourishment, and I was alone. There was no alternative. I rose, took up my babe, and crossed the room to where he sat. "Now stand there," said he, "till I tell you to go back!" My child bore a strong resemblance to her father, and to the deceased Mrs. Sands, her grandmother. He noticed this; and while I stood before him, trembling with weakness, he heaped upon me and my little one every vile epithet he could think of. Even the grandmother in her grave did not escape his curses. In the midst of his vituperations I fainted at his feet. This recalled him to his senses. He took the baby from my arms, laid it on the bed, dashed cold water in my face, took me up, and shook me violently, to restore my consciousness before any one entered the room. Just then my grandmother came in, and he hurried out of the house. I suffered in consequence of this treatment; but I begged my friends to let me die, rather than send for the doctor. There was nothing I dreaded so much as his presence. My life was spared; and I was glad for the sake of my little ones. Had it not been for these ties to life, I should have been glad to be released by death, though I had lived only nineteen years.

Always it gave me a pang that my children had no lawful claim to a name. Their father offered his; but, if I had wished to accept the offer, I dared not while my master lived. Moreover, I knew it would not be accepted at their baptism. A Christian name they were at least entitled to; and we resolved to call my boy for our dear good Benjamin, who had gone far away from us.

My grandmother belonged to the church, and she was very desirous of having the children christened. I knew Dr. Flint would forbid it, and I did not venture to attempt it. But chance favored me. He was called to visit a patient out of town, and was obliged to be absent during Sunday. "Now is the time," said my grandmother; "we will take the children to church, and have them christened."

When I entered the church, recollections of my mother came over me, and I felt subdued in spirit. There she had presented me for baptism, without any reason to feel ashamed. She had been married, and had such legal rights as slavery allows a slave. The vows had at least been sacred to *her*, and she had never violated them. I was glad she was not alive, to know under what different circumstances her grandchildren were presented for baptism. Why had my lot been so different from my mother's? *Her* master had died when she was a child; and she remained with her mistress till she married. She was never in the power of any master; and thus she escaped one class of the evils that generally fall upon slaves.

When my baby was about to be christened, the former mistress of my father stepped up to me, and proposed to give it her Christian name. To this I added the surname of my father, who had himself no legal right to it; for my grandfather on the paternal side was a white gentleman. What tangled skeins are the genealogies of slavery![6] I loved my father; but it mortified me to be obliged to bestow his name on my children.

When we left the church, my father's old mistress invited me to go home with her. She clasped a gold chain around my baby's neck. I thanked her for this kindness; but I did not like the emblem. I wanted no chain to be fastened on my daughter, not even if its links were of gold. How earnestly I prayed that she might never feel the weight of slavery's chain, whose iron entereth into the soul.

* * *

XXI. The Loophole of Retreat[7]

A small shed had been added to my grandmother's house years ago. Some boards were laid across the joists at the top, and between these boards and the roof was a very small garret, never occupied by any thing but rats and mice. It was a pent roof, covered with nothing but shingles, according to the southern custom for such buildings. The garret was only nine feet long and seven wide. The highest part was three feet high, and sloped down abruptly to the loose board floor. There was no admission for either light or air. My uncle Phillip, who was a carpenter, had very skilfully made a concealed trap-door, which communicated with the storeroom. He had been doing this while I was waiting in the swamp. The storeroom opened upon a piazza. To this hole I was conveyed as soon as I entered the house. The air was stifling; the darkness total. A bed had been spread on the floor. I could sleep quite comfortably on one side; but the slope was so sudden that I could not turn on the other without hitting the roof. The rats and mice ran over my bed; but I was weary, and I slept such sleep as the wretched may, when a tempest has passed over them. Morning came. I knew it only by the noises I heard; for in my small den day and night were all the same. I suffered for air even more than for light. But I was not comfortless. I heard the voices of my children. There was joy and there was sadness in the sound. It made my tears flow. How I longed to speak to them! I was eager to look on their faces; but there was no hole, no crack, through which I could peep. This continued darkness was oppressive. It seemed horrible to sit or lie in a cramped position day after day, without one gleam of light. Yet I would have chosen this, rather than my lot as a slave, though white people considered it an easy one; and it was so compared with the fate of others. I was never cruelly over-worked; I was never lacerated with the whip from head to foot; I was never so beaten and bruised that I could not turn from one side to the other; I never had my heel-strings cut to prevent my running away; I was never chained to a log and forced to drag it about, while I toiled in the fields from morning till night; I was never branded with hot iron, or torn by bloodhounds. On the contrary, I had always been kindly treated, and tenderly cared for, until I came into the hands of Dr. Flint. I had never wished for freedom till then. But though my life in slavery was comparatively devoid of hardships, God pity the woman who is compelled to lead such a life!

6. Jacobs stresses her mixed-race parentage not to claim that she is really white but to show the arbitrariness and absurdity of racial distinctions. 7. From *The Task* 4.88–90, a popular long poem (1785) by the English poet William Cowper

(1731–1800). By this point in the narrative Brent has escaped from the Flint household and is hiding in a crawl space beneath the roof of her grandmother's house. The account states that she remains there for seven years.

My food was passed up to me through the trap-door my uncle had contrived; and my grandmother, my uncle Phillip, and aunt Nancy would seize such opportunities as they could, to mount up there and chat with me at the opening. But of course this was not safe in the daytime. It must all be done in darkness. It was impossible for me to move in an erect position, but I crawled about my den for exercise. One day I hit my head against something, and found it was a gimlet.[8] My uncle had left it sticking there when he made the trap-door. I was as rejoiced as Robinson Crusoe[9] could have been at finding such a treasure. It put a lucky thought into my head. I said to myself, "Now I will have some light. Now I will see my children." I did not dare to begin my work during the daytime, for fear of attracting attention. But I groped round; and having found the side next the street, where I could frequently see my children, I struck the gimlet in and waited for evening. I bored three rows of holes, one above another; then I bored out the interstices between. I thus succeeded in making one hole about an inch long and an inch broad. I sat by it till late into the night, to enjoy the little whiff of air that floated in. In the morning I watched for my children. The first person I saw in the street was Dr. Flint. I had a shuddering, superstitious feeling that it was a bad omen. Several familiar faces passed by. At last I heard the merry laugh of children, and presently two sweet little faces were looking up at me, as though they knew I was there, and were conscious of the joy they imparted. How I longed to *tell* them I was there!

My condition was now a little improved. But for weeks I was tormented by hundreds of little red insects, fine as a needle's point, that pierced through my skin, and produced an intolerable burning. The good grandmother gave me herb teas and cooling medicines, and finally I got rid of them. The heat of my den was intense, for nothing but thin shingles protected me from the scorching summer's sun. But I had my consolations. Through my peeping-hole I could watch the children, and when they were near enough, I could hear their talk. Aunt Nancy brought me all the news she could hear at Dr. Flint's. From her I learned that the doctor had written to New York to a colored woman, who had been born and raised in our neighborhood, and had breathed his contaminating atmosphere. He offered her a reward if she could find out any thing about me. I know not what was the nature of her reply; but he soon after started for New York in haste, saying to his family that he had business of importance to transact. I peeped at him as he passed on his way to the steamboat. It was a satisfaction to have miles of land and water between us, even for a little while; and it was a still greater satisfaction to know that he believed me to be in the Free States. My little den seemed less dreary than it had done. He returned, as he did from his former journey to New York, without obtaining any satisfactory information. When he passed our house next morning, Benny was standing at the gate. He had heard them say that he had gone to find me, and he called out, "Dr. Flint, did you bring my mother home? I want to see her." The doctor stamped his foot at him in a rage, and exclaimed, "Get out of the way, you little damned rascal! If you don't, I'll cut off your head."

---

8. Small tool for boring holes.
9. Hero of a novel of the same name (1719) by the English writer Daniel Defoe (1660–1731) about a man shipwrecked on a desert island.

Benny ran terrified into the house, saying, "You can't put me in jail again. I don't belong to you now." It was well that the wind carried the words away from the doctor's ear. I told my grandmother of it, when we had our next conference at the trap-door; and begged of her not to allow the children to be impertinent to the irascible old man.

Autumn came, with a pleasant abatement of heat. My eyes had become accustomed to the dim light, and by holding my book or work in a certain position near the aperture I contrived to read and sew. That was a great relief to the tedious monotony of my life. But when winter came, the cold penetrated through the thin shingle roof, and I was dreadfully chilled. The winters there are not so long, or so severe, as in northern latitudes; but the houses are not built to shelter from cold, and my little den was peculiarly comfortless. The kind grandmother brought me bed-clothes and warm drinks. Often I was obliged to lie in bed all day to keep comfortable; but with all my precautions, my shoulders and feet were frostbitten. O, those long, gloomy days, with no object for my eye to rest upon, and no thoughts to occupy my mind, except the dreary past and the uncertain future! I was thankful when there came a day sufficiently mild for me to wrap myself up and sit at the loophole to watch the passers by. Southerners have the habit of stopping and talking in the streets, and I heard many conversations not intended to meet my ears. I heard slave-hunters planning how to catch some poor fugitive. Several times I heard allusions to Dr. Flint, myself, and the history of my children, who, perhaps, were playing near the gate. One would say, "I wouldn't move my little finger to catch her, as old Flint's property." Another would say, "I'll catch *any* nigger for the reward. A man ought to have what belongs to him, if he *is* a damned brute." The opinion was often expressed that I was in the Free States. Very rarely did any one suggest that I might be in the vicinity. Had the least suspicion rested on my grandmother's house, it would have been burned to the ground. But it was the last place they thought of. Yet there was no place, where slavery existed, that could have afforded me so good a place of concealment.

Dr. Flint and his family repeatedly tried to coax and bribe my children to tell something they had heard said about me. One day the doctor took them into a shop, and offered them some bright little silver pieces and gay handkerchiefs if they would tell where their mother was. Ellen shrank away from him, and would not speak; but Benny spoke up, and said, "Dr. Flint, I don't know where my mother is. I guess she's in New York; and when you go there again, I wish you'd ask her to come home, for I want to see her; but if you put her in jail, or tell her you'll cut her head off, I'll tell her to go right back."

* * *

XLI. Free at Last[1]

Mrs. Bruce, and every member of her family, were exceedingly kind to me. I was thankful for the blessings of my lot, yet I could not always wear a cheerful countenance. I was doing harm to no one; on the contrary, I was doing all the good I could in my small way; yet I could never go out to breathe God's

---

1. This is the final chapter of *Incidents*. Having escaped from the South on a ship headed to Philadelphia, Brent finds employment with the Bruce family of New York City, but she remains in constant fear of being returned to the South under the provisions of the Fugitive Slave Act of 1793.

free air without trepidation at my heart. This seemed hard; and I could not think it was a right state of things in any civilized country.

From time to time I received news from my good old grandmother. She could not write; but she employed others to write for her. The following is an extract from one of her last letters:—

> "Dear Daughter: I cannot hope to see you again on earth; but I pray to God to unite us above, where pain will no more rack this feeble body of mine; where sorrow and parting from my children will be no more.[2] God has promised these things if we are faithful unto the end. My age and feeble health deprive me of going to church now; but God is with me here at home. Thank your brother for his kindness. Give much love to him, and tell him to remember the Creator in the days of his youth,[3] and strive to meet me in the Father's kingdom. Love to Ellen and Benjamin. Don't neglect him. Tell him for me, to be a good boy. Strive, my child, to train them for God's children. May he protect and provide for you, is the prayer of your loving old mother."

These letters both cheered and saddened me. I was always glad to have tidings from the kind, faithful old friend of my unhappy youth; but her messages of love made my heart yearn to see her before she died, and I mourned over the fact that it was impossible. Some months after I returned from my flight to New England, I received a letter from her, in which she wrote, "Dr. Flint is dead. He has left a distressed family. Poor old man! I hope he made his peace with God."

I remembered how he had defrauded my grandmother of the hard earnings she had loaned; how he had tried to cheat her out of the freedom her mistress had promised her, and how he had persecuted her children; and I thought to myself that she was a better Christian than I was, if she could entirely forgive him. I cannot say, with truth, that the news of my old master's death softened my feelings towards him. There are wrongs which even the grave does not bury. The man was odious to me while he lived, and his memory is odious now.

His departure from this world did not diminish my danger. He had threatened my grandmother that his heirs should hold me in slavery after he was gone; that I never should be free so long as a child of his survived. As for Mrs. Flint, I had seen her in deeper afflictions than I supposed the loss of her husband would be, for she had buried several children; yet I never saw any signs of softening in her heart. The doctor had died in embarrassed circumstances, and had little to will to his heirs, except such property as he was unable to grasp. I was well aware what I had to expect from the family of Flints; and my fears were confirmed by a letter from the south, warning me to be on my guard, because Mrs. Flint openly declared that her daughter could not afford to lose so valuable a slave as I was.

I kept close watch of the newspapers for arrivals; but one Saturday night, being much occupied, I forgot to examine the Evening Express as usual. I went down into the parlor for it, early in the morning, and found the boy about to kindle a fire with it. I took it from him and examined the list of

---

2. Paraphrase of Revelation 21.4.   3. Ecclesiastes 12.1.

arrivals. Reader, if you have never been a slave, you cannot imagine the acute sensation of suffering at my heart, when I read the names of Mr. and Mrs. Dodge,[4] at a hotel in Courtland Street. It was a third-rate hotel, and that circumstance convinced me of the truth of what I had heard, that they were short of funds and had need of my value, as *they* valued me; and that was by dollars and cents. I hastened with the paper to Mrs. Bruce. Her heart and hand were always open to every one in distress, and she always warmly sympathized with mine. It was impossible to tell how near the enemy was. He might have passed and repassed the house while we were sleeping. He might at that moment be waiting to pounce upon me if I ventured out of doors. I had never seen the husband of my young mistress, and therefore I could not distinguish him from any other stranger. A carriage was hastily ordered; and, closely veiled, I followed Mrs. Bruce, taking the baby again with me into exile. After various turnings and crossings, and returnings, the carriage stopped at the house of one of Mrs. Bruce's friends, where I was kindly received. Mrs. Bruce returned immediately, to instruct the domestics what to say if any one came to inquire for me.

It was lucky for me that the evening paper was not burned up before I had a chance to examine the list of arrivals. It was not long after Mrs. Bruce's return to her house, before several people came to inquire for me. One inquired for me, another asked for my daughter Ellen, and another said he had a letter from my grandmother, which he was requested to deliver in person.

They were told, "She *has* lived here, but she has left."

"How long ago?"

"I don't know, sir."

"Do you know where she went?"

"I do not, sir." And the door was closed.

This Mr. Dodge, who claimed me as his property, was originally a Yankee pedler in the south; then he became a merchant, and finally a slaveholder. He managed to get introduced into what was called the first society, and married Miss Emily Flint. A quarrel arose between him and her brother, and the brother cowhided him. This led to a family feud, and he proposed to remove to Virginia. Dr. Flint left him no property, and his own means had become circumscribed, while a wife and children depended upon him for support. Under these circumstances, it was very natural that he should make an effort to put me into his pocket.

I had a colored friend, a man from my native place, in whom I had the most implicit confidence. I sent for him, and told him that Mr. and Mrs. Dodge had arrived in New York. I proposed that he should call upon them to make inquiries about his friends at the south, with whom Dr. Flint's family were well acquainted. He thought there was no impropriety in his doing so, and he consented. He went to the hotel, and knocked at the door of Mr. Dodge's room, which was opened by the gentleman himself, who gruffly inquired, "What brought you here? How came you to know I was in the city?"

"Your arrival was published in the evening papers, sir; and I called to ask Mrs. Dodge about my friends at home. I didn't suppose it would give any offence."

---

4. Dodge is the married name of Emily Flint, Brent's legal owner.

"Where's that negro girl, that belongs to my wife?"

"What girl, sir?"

"You know well enough. I mean Linda, that ran away from Dr. Flint's plantation, some years ago. I dare say you've seen her, and know where she is."

"Yes, sir, I've seen her, and know where she is. She is out of your reach, sir."

"Tell me where she is, or bring her to me, and I will give her a chance to buy her freedom."

"I don't think it would be of any use, sir. I have heard her say she would go to the ends of the earth, rather than pay any man or woman for her freedom, because she thinks she has a right to it. Besides, she couldn't do it, if she would, for she has spent her earnings to educate her children."

This made Mr. Dodge very angry, and some high words passed between them. My friend was afraid to come where I was; but in the course of the day I received a note from him. I supposed they had not come from the south, in the winter, for a pleasure excursion; and now the nature of their business was very plain.

Mrs. Bruce came to me and entreated me to leave the city the next morning. She said her house was watched, and it was possible that some clew to me might be obtained. I refused to take her advice. She pleaded with an earnest tenderness, that ought to have moved me; but I was in a bitter, disheartened mood. I was weary of flying from pillar to post. I had been chased during half my life, and it seemed as if the chase was never to end. There I sat, in that great city, guiltless of crime, yet not daring to worship God in any of the churches. I heard the bells ringing for afternoon service, and, with contemptuous sarcasm, I said, "Will the preachers take for their text, 'Proclaim liberty to the captive, and the opening of prison doors to them that are bound'?[5] or will they preach from the text, 'Do unto others as ye would they should do unto you'?"[6] Oppressed Poles and Hungarians could find a safe refuge in that city; John Mitchell[7] was free to proclaim in the City Hall his desire for "a plantation well stocked with slaves;" but there I sat, an oppressed American, not daring to show my face. God forgive the black and bitter thoughts I indulged on that Sabbath day! The Scripture says, "Oppression makes even a wise man mad;"[8] and I was not wise.

I had been told that Mr. Dodge said his wife had never signed away her right to my children, and if he could not get me, he would take them. This it was, more than any thing else, that roused such a tempest in my soul. Benjamin was with his uncle William in California, but my innocent young daughter had come to spend a vacation with me. I thought of what I had suffered in slavery at her age, and my heart was like a tiger's when a hunter tries to seize her young.

Dear Mrs. Bruce! I seem to see the expression of her face, as she turned away discouraged by my obstinate mood. Finding her expostulations unavailing, she sent Ellen to entreat me. When ten o'clock in the evening arrived and Ellen had not returned, this watchful and unwearied friend became

5. Isaiah 61.1.
6. Matthew 7.12.
7. Irish American (1815–1875) who founded the proslavery New York newspaper *The Citizen* and who argued that free blacks would take the jobs of

Irish workers. "Poles and Hungarians": following the failed European revolutions of 1848, many political refugees settled in New York City and New England.
8. Ecclesiastes 7.7.

anxious. She came to us in a carriage, bringing a well-filled trunk for my journey—trusting that by this time I would listen to reason. I yielded to her, as I ought to have done before.

The next day, baby and I set out in a heavy snow storm, bound for New England again. I received letters from the City of Iniquity,[9] addressed to me under an assumed name. In a few days one came from Mrs. Bruce, informing me that my new master was still searching for me, and that she intended to put an end to this persecution by buying my freedom. I felt grateful for the kindness that prompted this offer, but the idea was not so pleasant to me as might have been expected. The more my mind had become enlightened, the more difficult it was for me to consider myself an article of property; and to pay money to those who had so grievously oppressed me seemed like taking from my sufferings the glory of triumph. I wrote to Mrs. Bruce, thanking her, but saying that being sold from one owner to another seemed too much like slavery; that such a great obligation could not be easily cancelled; and that I preferred to go to my brother in California.

Without my knowledge, Mrs. Bruce employed a gentleman in New York to enter into negotiations with Mr. Dodge. He proposed to pay three hundred dollars down, if Mr. Dodge would sell me, and enter into obligations to relinquish all claim to me or my children forever after. He who called himself my master said he scorned so small an offer for such a valuable servant. The gentleman replied, "You can do as you choose, sir. If you reject this offer you will never get any thing; for the woman has friends who will convey her and her children out of the country."

Mr. Dodge concluded that "half a loaf was better than no bread," and he agreed to the proffered terms. By the next mail I received this brief letter from Mrs. Bruce: "I am rejoiced to tell you that the money for your freedom has been paid to Mr. Dodge. Come home to-morrow. I long to see you and my sweet babe."

My brain reeled as I read these lines. A gentleman near me said, "It's true; I have seen the bill of sale." "The bill of sale!" Those words struck me like a blow. So I was *sold* at last! A human being *sold* in the free city of New York! The bill of sale is on record, and future generations will learn from it that women were articles of traffic in New York, late in the nineteenth century of the Christian religion. It may hereafter prove a useful document to antiquaries, who are seeking to measure the progress of civilization in the United States. I well know the value of that bit of paper; but much as I love freedom, I do not like to look upon it. I am deeply grateful to the generous friend who procured it, but I despise the miscreant who demanded payment for what never rightfully belonged to him or his.

I had objected to having my freedom bought, yet I must confess that when it was done I felt as if a heavy load had been lifted from my weary shoulders. When I rode home in the cars I was no longer afraid to unveil my face and look at people as they passed. I should have been glad to have met Daniel Dodge himself; to have had him seen me and known me, that he might have mourned over the untoward circumstances which compelled him to sell me for three hundred dollars.

9. New York City, because it was the center of activity for hunters of fugitive slaves.

When I reached home, the arms of my benefactress were thrown round me, and our tears mingled. As soon as she could speak, she said, "O Linda, I'm *so* glad it's all over! You wrote to me as if you thought you were going to be transferred from one owner to another. But I did not buy you for your services. I should have done just the same, if you had been going to sail for California tomorrow. I should, at least, have the satisfaction of knowing that you left me a free woman."

My heart was exceedingly full. I remembered how my poor father had tried to buy me, when I was a small child, and how he had been disappointed. I hoped his spirit was rejoicing over me now. I remembered how my good old grandmother had laid up her earnings to purchase me in later years, and how often her plans had been frustrated. How that faithful, loving old heart would leap for joy, if she could look on me and my children now that we were free! My relatives had been foiled in all their efforts, but God had raised me up a friend among strangers, who had bestowed on me the precious, long-desired boon. Friend! It is a common word, often lightly used. Like other good and beautiful things, it may be tarnished by careless handling; but when I speak of Mrs. Bruce as my friend, the word is sacred.

My grandmother lived to rejoice in my freedom; but not long after, a letter came with a black seal. She had gone "where the wicked cease from troubling, and the weary are at rest."[1]

Time passed on, and a paper came to me from the south, containing an obituary notice of my uncle Phillip. It was the only case I ever knew of such an honor conferred upon a colored person. It was written by one of his friends, and contained these words: "Now that death has laid him low, they call him a good man and a useful citizen; but what are eulogies to the black man, when the world has faded from his vision? It does not require man's praise to obtain rest in God's kingdom." So they called a colored man a *citizen*! Strange words to be uttered in that region![2]

Reader, my story ends with freedom; not in the usual way, with marriage.[3] I and my children are now free! We are as free from the power of slaveholders as are the white people of the north; and though that, according to my ideas, is not saying a great deal, it is a vast improvement in *my* condition. The dream of my life is not yet realized. I do not sit with my children in a home of my own. I still long for a hearthstone of my own, however humble. I wish it for my children's sake far more than for my own. But God so orders circumstances as to keep me with my friend Mrs. Bruce. Love, duty, gratitude, also bind me to her side. It is a privilege to serve her who pities my oppressed people, and who has bestowed the inestimable boon of freedom on me and my children.

It has been painful to me, in many ways, to recall the dreary years I passed in bondage. I would gladly forget them if I could. Yet the retrospection is not altogether without solace; for with those gloomy recollections come tender memories of my good old grandmother, like light, fleecy clouds floating over a dark and troubled sea.

1861

1. Job 3.17.
2. Free blacks in North Carolina did not have the legal status of citizens.

3. Allusion to the way popular novels of the period typically ended with a happy marriage.

HENRY DAVID THOREAU
1817–1862

Henry David Thoreau aspired to write great literature by adventuring at home, traveling, as he put it, a good deal in Concord, Massachusetts. "As travelers go around the world and report natural objects and phenomena, so let another stay at home and report the phenomena of his own life," he remarked in a journal entry of August 1851. Known by some of his Concord neighbors as the Harvard graduate who never lived up to his potential, Thoreau presented himself in *Walden* as an exemplary figure who—by virtue of his philosophical questionings, economic good sense, nonconformity, and appreciative observation of the natural world—could serve as a model for others. Thoreau infuriated and inspired his Massachusetts neighbors and audiences while he lived; since his death, his writings have continued to provoke generations of readers to contemplate their obligations to society, nature, and themselves.

The third of four children of Cynthia (Dunbar) and John Thoreau, a storekeeper who opened a pencil-making business in the early 1820s, Thoreau was born in Concord on July 12, 1817. His sister Helen, five years his senior, was an important teacher in his childhood years; his brother, John, two years his senior, was his closest friend; and his sister Sophia, two years his junior, cared for him at the end of his life. Because Henry was regarded as the more academically promising of the two brothers, the family, which was struggling economically (his mother ran their home as a boarding-house to produce additional income), decided that he would be the one son to attend Harvard. Thoreau began his studies there in 1833, excelling in languages but otherwise failing to distinguish himself. After his 1837 graduation he returned to Concord, where he taught briefly at a local elementary school before resigning in protest when he was instructed to flog some of his students. In 1838 he took a teaching and administrative position at the private Concord Academy, where a year later John joined him as a teacher and co-director of the school. The brothers had to close the Concord Academy in 1841 because of John's poor health. Paralyzed by tetanus from a razor cut, John died in Thoreau's arms on January 1, 1842. The grief at the loss of his beloved brother would inspire his elegiac *A Week on the Concord and Merrimack Rivers* (1849), which memorialized a two-week boating trip that the brothers took in 1839.

Thoreau met his fellow Concordian, Ralph Waldo Emerson, in 1836. Emerson, fourteen years his senior, became the most important influence and friendship in his life. Thoreau attended the informal meetings of the New England Transcendentalists that convened irregularly in Emerson's study and there met such people as Margaret Fuller and the education reformers Elizabeth Peabody and Bronson Alcott (father of Louisa May). With Emerson's encouragement, Thoreau also began to keep a journal, which served him as a sourcebook for some of his published writings and lectures, eventually growing to nearly two million words. In 1840, Thoreau commenced his efforts to make a name for himself as a published writer. He placed a poem and an essay in the inaugural issue of the *Dial*, the journal founded by the Concord Transcendentalist circle and edited by Margaret Fuller (and at times by Thoreau himself); he would publish over thirty essays, poems, and translations in the journal before it ceased operations in 1844. He never stopped reading, although contemporary writers meant little to him except for Emerson and Thomas Carlyle, whom he regarded as one of the great prophets of the era. He steeped himself in the classics—Greek, Latin, and English—and read the sacred writings of the Hindus in translation; they are an enormous influence on the cosmic vision of *Walden*.

Early in 1844 Thoreau delivered his first series of lectures, "The Conservative and the Reformer," in Boston's Armory Hall. To his great embarrassment, during a camping trip in April of that year, he accidentally set fire to the Concord woods near Walden Pond, burning approximately three hundred acres. Shortly after the fire, Thoreau decided to begin what he termed his "experiment" at Walden, building a cabin on land that Emerson owned near the pond and taking up residence there on July 4, 1845—a symbolic moment of personal liberation aligned with the celebration of national freedom. One of Thoreau's major goals in moving to the pond was to write a book about his 1839 boating journey with his brother (which he completed before he left after two years, two months, and two days). Only a couple of miles from town, his cabin became the destination of many local visitors, and he often went back to Concord for meals and conversation. During his time at Walden, Thoreau also spent one night of 1846 in the local jail when, in protest against what he regarded as the proslavery agenda of the war against Mexico, he refused to pay his poll tax. That experience would inspire "Resistance to Civil Government" (1849), which in due time would become a world-famous essay on the relationship of the individual to the state.

In 1849 Thoreau published the book he had drafted at Walden as *A Week on the Concord and Merrimack Rivers*, a work that mixes naturalist meditations, personal reflections, poetry, and scripture. Barely noticed by reviewers and readers, it sold fewer than three hundred of the thousand copies printed. Thoreau had subsidized the publication through his royalties, and in 1853, when he received the unsold books, he wrote in his journal: "I have now a library of nearly nine hundred volumes, over seven hundred of which I wrote myself." Despite the critical and financial setback of *A Week*, Thoreau worked intensively on *Walden* between 1847 and its publication in 1854. The prestigious Boston firm of Ticknor and Fields published the book in a small print run of two thousand copies, and by 1859 most of these copies had been sold. Encouraged by the relatively good reviews and sales, Thoreau over the next few years attempted to work up books from his Cape Cod travels of 1849 and 1850 and his Maine travels of 1857, bringing out sections of the Cape Cod manuscript in the 1855 *Putnam's Monthly Magazine*. None of the other books that Thoreau published or projected has achieved the influence and reputation of *Walden*, where Thoreau's whole literary character emerges—his love of nature, his rhetorical inventiveness, his humor, his philosophical adventurousness, his everyday nonconformity. In it he becomes, in the highest sense, a fully employed public servant, offering readers the fruits of his experience, thought, and artistic dedication.

His writing and lectures brought Thoreau a small but widening circle of admirers. His earlier journals had combined naturalistic observations with moral commentary; in the 1850s they increasingly recorded his observations of nature without comment and in great detail as he sought to understand the daily and seasonal rhythms of nature. Inspired by his reading during the early 1850s of the German naturalist Alexander von Humboldt (1769–1859) and the English naturalist Charles Darwin (1809–1882), he made himself into what critic Laura Dassow Walls has called "a scientific seer, walking, recording, measuring, and weaving the details of nature into meaning." Professors at Harvard, such as the geologist Louis Agassiz, found his scientific vision of interest. At the same time, Thoreau emerged as one of the most outspoken abolitionists in the Concord area. In 1854, the year of *Walden*'s publication, he delivered his best-known antislavery speech, "Slavery in Massachusetts," at a rally in Framingham, Massachusetts, protesting the arrest of the fugitive slave Anthony Burns. Thoreau achieved his greatest prominence as an antislavery speaker with his defense of John Brown immediately after Brown's arrest at Harpers

Ferry in October 1859. Before large audiences in Concord, Boston, and Worcester, Thoreau honored Brown's revolutionary antislavery aims. He thus welcomed the Civil War, with its promise of ridding the nation of slavery, even as he faced the difficulties of declining health brought on by tuberculosis, the great nineteenth-century killer of young adults. (His sister Helen had died of the disease in 1849.) In May 1861 Thoreau traveled to Minnesota with the hope of recovering his health, and there he collected botanical specimens and observed the Sioux Indians of the region. His health continuing to deteriorate, he returned to Concord and worked with his sister Sophia to prepare what he recognized would be posthumously published writings. He was forty-four when he died at Concord on May 6, 1862. The little fame he had achieved was as a social experimenter who applied Emerson's theoretical transcendentalism to daily life, and as John Brown's champion.

Between June 1862, the month after Thoreau's death, and November 1863, the Boston-based *Atlantic Monthly* published the essays "Walking," "Autumn Tints," "Wild Apples," "Life without Principle," and "Night and Moonlight." In 1862 Ticknor and Fields reissued *A Week* and *Walden* (which never again went out of print) and attempted to capitalize on the growing interest in Thoreau by publishing five new books: *Excursions* (1863), *The Maine Woods* (1864), *Cape Cod* (1864), *Letters to Various Persons* (1865), and *A Yankee in Canada, with Anti-Slavery and Reform Papers* (1866). An expanded version of Emerson's eulogy for Thoreau, published in the *Atlantic Monthly* for August 1863, confirmed Thoreau's growing reputation. By the early twentieth century, Thoreau was becoming widely recognized as a social philosopher, naturalist, and writer with few peers. In 1906 his journals were published for the first time in chronological order, in fourteen volumes as part of a twenty-volume set of his complete works. That same year, Mahatma Gandhi, in his African exile, read "Resistance to Civil Government" and later acknowledged its important influence on his thinking about how best to achieve Indian independence. Later in the century, Martin Luther King Jr. would similarly attest to the crucial influence of Thoreau on his adoption of nonviolent civil disobedience as a key to the civil rights movement.

By the middle of the twentieth century, Thoreau's literary reputation equaled or surpassed Emerson's, with *Walden* regarded as one of the masterpieces of American literature. It is a work that powerfully affected environmentalists like John Muir and Aldo Leopold, who greatly admired Thoreau for his concerns about the natural habitat; contemporary writers like Edward Abbey and Annie Dillard also cite him frequently. As crucial as environmental concerns, and even antislavery, were to Thoreau, however, he always insisted that all principled action had to be undertaken by the individual rather than through groups. It is important to recall that Thoreau described *Walden* as an "experiment"—an account of one possible way of viewing, representing, and acting in the world. In *Walden*'s punning wordplay, richly allusive sentences, and (with its numerous references to a panoply of Eastern and Western texts) truly global textual vision, Thoreau more than anything else attempted to push his readers to think—to "wake . . . up," as he put it in the book's epigraph. Life is short and life is miraculous, Thoreau insists, and it is incumbent on each individual to figure out how best to respond to the circumstances of the moment. Though there are considerable differences between Thoreau and Emerson, the most provocative literary expression of Emerson's call for self-reliance may well be Thoreau's bragging, visionary, down-to-earth *Walden*.

Resistance to Civil Government[1]

I heartily accept the motto,—"That government is best which governs least;"[2] and I should like to see it acted up to more rapidly and systematically. Carried out, it finally amounts to this, which also I believe,—"That government is best which governs not at all;" and when men are prepared for it, that will be the kind of government which they will have. Government is at best but an expedient; but most governments are usually, and all governments are sometimes, inexpedient. The objections which have been brought against a standing army, and they are many and weighty, and deserve to prevail, may also at last be brought against a standing government. The standing army is only an arm of the standing government. The government itself, which is only the mode which the people have chosen to execute their will, is equally liable to be abused and perverted before the people can act through it. Witness the present Mexican war, the work of comparatively a few individuals using the standing government as their tool; for, in the outset, the people would not have consented to this measure.[3]

This American government,—what is it but a tradition, though a recent one, endeavoring to transmit itself unimpaired to posterity, but each instant losing some of its integrity? It has not the vitality and force of a single living man; for a single man can bend it to his will. It is a sort of wooden gun to the people themselves; and, if ever they should use it in earnest as a real one against each other, it will surely split. But it is not the less necessary for this; for the people must have some complicated machinery or other, and hear its din, to satisfy that idea of government which they have. Governments show thus how successfully men can be imposed on, even impose on themselves, for their own advantage. It is excellent, we must all allow; yet this government never of itself furthered any enterprise, but by the alacrity with which it got out of its way. It does not keep the country free. It does not settle the West. It does not educate. The character inherent in the American people has done all that has been accomplished; and it would have done somewhat more, if the government had not sometimes got in its way. For government is an expedient by which men would fain succeed in letting one another alone; and, as has been said, when it is most expedient, the governed are most let alone by it. Trade and commerce, if they were not made of India rubber, would never manage to bounce over the obstacles which legislators are continually putting in their way; and, if one were to judge these men wholly by the effects of their actions, and not partly by their intentions, they would deserve to be

---

1. "Resistance to Civil Government" is reprinted here from its first appearance, in *Aesthetic Papers* (1849), edited by the educational reformer Elizabeth Peabody (1804–1894). Thoreau had delivered a version of the essay as a lecture in January and again in February 1848 at the Concord Lyceum, under the title "The Rights and Duties of the Individual in Relation to Government." After his death it was reprinted in *A Yankee in Canada, with Anti-Slavery and Reform Papers* (1866) as "Civil Disobedience." That title, although commonly used, may not be authorial; the title of the first printing, as Thoreau indicates, was a play on "The Duty of Submission to Civil Government Explained," the title of a chapter in *Principles of Moral and Political Philosophy* (1785), by the English theologian and moralist William Paley (1743–1805).
2. These words appeared on the masthead of the *Democratic Review*, the New York magazine that published two early Thoreau pieces in 1843.
3. The Mexican War (1846–48) was criticized by Whigs and some Democrats as an "executive's war" because President Polk commenced hostilities without a congressional declaration of war. Many New Englanders, including Thoreau, regarded the war as part of the South's effort to extend the territorial domain of slavery.

classed and punished with those mischievous persons who put obstructions on the railroads.

But, to speak practically and as a citizen, unlike those who call themselves no-government men, I ask for, not at once no government, but *at once* a better government. Let every man make known what kind of government would command his respect, and that will be one step toward obtaining it.

After all, the practical reason why, when the power is once in the hands of the people, a majority are permitted, and for a long period continue, to rule, is not because they are most likely to be in the right, nor because this seems fairest to the minority, but because they are physically the strongest. But a government in which the majority rule in all cases cannot be based on justice, even as far as men understand it. Can there not be a government in which majorities do not virtually decide right and wrong, but conscience?—in which majorities decide only those questions to which the rule of expediency is applicable? Must the citizen ever for a moment, or in the least degree, resign his conscience to the legislator? Why has every man a conscience, then? I think that we should be men first, and subjects afterward. It is not desirable to cultivate a respect for the law, so much as for the right. The only obligation which I have a right to assume, is to do at any time what I think right. It is truly enough said,[4] that a corporation has no conscience; but a corporation of conscientious men is a corporation *with* a conscience. Law never made men a whit more just; and, by means of their respect for it, even the well-disposed are daily made the agents of injustice. A common and natural result of an undue respect for law is, that you may see a file of soldiers, colonel, captain, corporal, privates, powder-monkeys and all, marching in admirable order over hill and dale to the wars, against their wills, aye, against their common sense and consciences, which makes it very steep marching indeed, and produces a palpitation of the heart. They have no doubt that it is a damnable business in which they are concerned; they are all peaceably inclined. Now, what are they? Men at all? or small moveable forts and magazines, at the service of some unscrupulous man in power? Visit the Navy Yard, and behold a marine, such a man as an American government can make, or such as it can make a man with its black arts, a mere shadow and reminiscence of humanity, a man laid out alive and standing, and already, as one may say, buried under arms with funeral accompaniments, though it may be

> "Not a drum was heard, nor a funeral note,
>   As his corse to the ramparts we hurried;
> Not a soldier discharged his farewell shot
>   O'er the grave where our hero we buried."[5]

The mass of men serve the State thus, not as men mainly, but as machines, with their bodies. They are the standing army, and the militia, jailers, constables, *posse comitatus*,[6] &c. In most cases there is no free exercise whatever of the judgment or of the moral sense; but they put themselves on a level with wood and earth and stones; and wooden men can perhaps be

---

4. By the English jurist Sir Edward Coke (1552–1634), in a famous legal decision of 1612.
5. From the Irish poet Charles Wolfe's "Burial of Sir John Moore at Corunna" (1817). "Corse": corpse.
6. Sheriff's posse (Latin).

manufactured that will serve the purpose as well. Such command no more respect than men of straw, or a lump of dirt. They have the same sort of worth only as horses and dogs. Yet such as these even are commonly esteemed good citizens. Others, as most legislators, politicians, lawyers, ministers, and office-holders, serve the State chiefly with their heads; and, as they rarely make any moral distinctions, they are as likely to serve the devil, without intending it, as God. A very few, as heroes, patriots, martyrs, reformers in the great sense, and *men*, serve the State with their consciences also, and so necessarily resist it for the most part; and they are commonly treated by it as enemies. A wise man will only be useful as a man, and will not submit to be "clay," and "stop a hole to keep the wind away,"[7] but leave that office to his dust at least:—

> "I am too high-born to be propertied,
> To be a secondary at control,
> Or useful serving-man and instrument
> To any sovereign state throughout the world."[8]

He who gives himself entirely to his fellow-men appears to them useless and selfish; but he who gives himself partially to them is pronounced a benefactor and philanthropist.

How does it become a man to behave toward this American government to-day? I answer that he cannot without disgrace be associated with it. I cannot for an instant recognize that political organization as *my* government which is the *slave's* government also.

All men recognize the right of revolution; that is, the right to refuse allegiance to and to resist the government, when its tyranny or its inefficiency are great and unendurable. But almost all say that such is not the case now. But such was the case, they think, in the Revolution of '75. If one were to tell me that this was a bad government because it taxed certain foreign commodities brought to its ports, it is most probable that I should not make an ado about it, for I can do without them: all machines have their friction; and possibly this does enough good to counterbalance the evil. At any rate, it is a great evil to make a stir about it. But when the friction comes to have its machine, and oppression and robbery are organized, I say, let us not have such a machine any longer. In other words, when a sixth of the population of a nation which has undertaken to be the refuge of liberty are slaves, and a whole country is unjustly overrun and conquered by a foreign army, and subjected to military law, I think that it is not too soon for honest men to rebel and revolutionize. What makes this duty the more urgent is the fact, that the country so overrun is not our own, but ours is the invading army.

Paley, a common authority with many on moral questions, in his chapter on the "Duty of Submission to Civil Government," resolves all civil obligation into expediency; and he proceeds to say, "that so long as the interest of the whole society requires it, that is, so long as the established government cannot be resisted or changed without public inconveniency, it is the will of God that the established government be obeyed, and no longer."—"This principle being admitted, the justice of every particular case of resistance is

---

7. Shakespeare's *Hamlet* 5.1.236–37.   8. Shakespeare's *King John* 5.1.79–82.

reduced to a computation of the quantity of the danger and grievance on the one side, and of the probability and expense of redressing it on the other." Of this, he says, every man shall judge for himself. But Paley appears never to have contemplated those cases to which the rule of expediency does not apply, in which a people, as well as an individual, must do justice, cost what it may. If I have unjustly wrested a plank from a drowning man, I must restore it to him though I drown myself.[9] This, according to Paley, would be inconvenient. But he that would save his life, in such a case, shall lose it.[1] This people must cease to hold slaves, and to make war on Mexico, though it cost them their existence as a people.

In their practice, nations agree with Paley; but does any one think that Massachusetts does exactly what is right at the present crisis?

> "A drab of state, a cloth-o'-silver slut,
> To have her train borne up, and her soul trail in the dirt."[2]

Practically speaking, the opponents to a reform in Massachusetts are not a hundred thousand politicians at the South, but a hundred thousand merchants and farmers here,[3] who are more interested in commerce and agriculture than they are in humanity, and are not prepared to do justice to the slave and to Mexico, *cost what it may.* I quarrel not with far-off foes, but with those who, near at home, co-operate with, and do the bidding of those far away, and without whom the latter would be harmless. We are accustomed to say, that the mass of men are unprepared; but improvement is slow, because the few are not materially wiser or better than the many. It is not so important that many should be as good as you, as that there be some absolute goodness somewhere; for that will leaven the whole lump.[4] There are thousands who are *in opinion* opposed to slavery and to the war, who yet in effect do nothing to put an end to them; who, esteeming themselves children of Washington and Franklin, sit down with their hands in their pockets, and say that they know not what to do, and do nothing; who even postpone the question of freedom to the question of free-trade, and quietly read the prices-current along with the latest advices[5] from Mexico, after dinner, and, it may be, fall asleep over them both. What is the price-current of an honest man and patriot to-day? They hesitate, and they regret, and sometimes they petition; but they do nothing in earnest and with effect. They will wait, well disposed, for others to remedy the evil, that they may no longer have it to regret. At most, they give only a cheap vote, and a feeble countenance and God-speed, to the right, as it goes by them. There are nine hundred and ninety-nine patrons of virtue to one virtuous man; but it is easier to deal with the real possessor of a thing than with the temporary guardian of it.

All voting is a sort of gaming, like chequers or backgammon, with a slight moral tinge to it, a playing with right and wrong, with moral questions; and betting naturally accompanies it. The character of the voters is not staked. I cast my vote, perchance, as I think right; but I am not vitally concerned that

---

9. A problem in situational ethics cited by Cicero (106–43 B.C.E.) in *De Officiis* 3.
1. Matthew 10.39; Luke 9.24.
2. Cyril Tourneur (1575?–1626), *The Revenger's Tragedy* 3.4.
3. Thoreau refers to the economic alliance of southern cotton growers with northern shippers, farmers, and manufacturers.
4. 1 Corinthians 5.6: "Know ye not that a little leaven leaventh the whole lump?"
5. New dispatches. "Children of Washington and Franklin": i.e., patriotic Americans, children of rebels and revolutionaries.

that right should prevail. I am willing to leave it to the majority. Its obligation, therefore, never exceeds that of expediency. Even voting *for the right* is *doing* nothing for it. It is only expressing to men feebly your desire that it should prevail. A wise man will not leave the right to the mercy of chance, nor wish it to prevail through the power of the majority. There is but little virtue in the action of masses of men. When the majority shall at length vote for the abolition of slavery, it will be because they are indifferent to slavery, or because there is but little slavery left to be abolished by their vote. *They* will then be the only slaves. Only *his* vote can hasten the abolition of slavery who asserts his own freedom by his vote.

I hear of a convention to be held at Baltimore,[6] or elsewhere, for the selection of a candidate for the Presidency, made up chiefly of editors, and men who are politicians by profession; but I think, what is it to any independent, intelligent, and respectable man what decision they may come to, shall we not have the advantage of his wisdom and honesty, nevertheless? Can we not count upon some independent votes? Are there not many individuals in the country who do not attend conventions? But no: I find that the respectable man, so called, has immediately drifted from his position, and despairs of his country, when his country has more reason to despair of him. He forthwith adopts one of the candidates thus selected as the only *available* one, thus proving that he is himself *available* for any purposes of the demagogue. His vote is of no more worth than that of any unprincipled foreigner or hireling native, who may have been bought. Oh for a man who is a *man*, and, as my neighbor says, has a bone in his back which you cannot pass your hand through! Our statistics are at fault: the population has been returned too large. How many *men* are there to a square thousand miles in this country? Hardly one. Does not America offer any inducement for men to settle here? The American has dwindled into an Odd Fellow,—one who may be known by the development of his organ of gregariousness, and a manifest lack of intellect and cheerful self-reliance; whose first and chief concern, on coming into the world, is to see that the alms-houses are in good repair; and, before yet he has lawfully donned the virile garb,[7] to collect a fund for the support of the widows and orphans that may be; who, in short, ventures to live only by the aid of the mutual insurance company, which has promised to bury him decently.

It is not a man's duty, as a matter of course, to devote himself to the eradication of any, even the most enormous wrong; he may still properly have other concerns to engage him; but it is his duty, at least, to wash his hands of it, and, if he gives it no thought longer, not to give it practically his support. If I devote myself to other pursuits and contemplations, I must first see, at least, that I do not pursue them sitting upon another man's shoulders. I must get off him first, that he may pursue his contemplations too. See what gross inconsistency is tolerated. I have heard some of my townsmen say, "I should like to have them order me out to help put down an insurrection of the slaves, or to march to Mexico,—see if I would go;" and yet these very men have each,

6. The Democratic convention was held in Baltimore in May 1848.
7. Adult clothes allowed for a Roman boy on reaching the age of fourteen. The Independent Order of Odd Fellows, a benevolent fraternal organization, was chosen by Thoreau for the satirical value of its name; in his view the archetypal American is not the individualist, the genuine odd fellow, but the conformist.

directly by their allegiance, and so indirectly, at least, by their money, furnished a substitute. The soldier is applauded who refuses to serve in an unjust war by those who do not refuse to sustain the unjust government which makes the war; is applauded by those whose own act and authority he disregards and sets at nought; as if the State were penitent to that degree that it hired one to scourge it while it sinned, but not to that degree that it left off sinning for a moment. Thus, under the name of order and civil government, we are all made at last to pay homage to and support our own meanness. After the first blush of sin, comes its indifference; and from immoral it becomes, as it were, *un*moral, and not quite unnecessary to that life which we have made.

The broadest and most prevalent error requires the most disinterested virtue to sustain it. The slight reproach to which the virtue of patriotism is commonly liable, the noble are most likely to incur. Those who, while they disapprove of the character and measures of a government, yield to it their allegiance and support, are undoubtedly its most conscientious supporters, and so frequently the most serious obstacles to reform. Some are petitioning the State to dissolve the Union, to disregard the requisitions of the President. Why do they not dissolve it themselves,—the union between themselves and the State,—and refuse to pay their quota into its treasury? Do not they stand in the same relation to the State, that the State does to the Union? And have not the same reasons prevented the State from resisting the Union, which have prevented them from resisting the State?

How can a man be satisfied to entertain an opinion merely, and enjoy *it*? Is there any enjoyment in it, if his opinion is that he is aggrieved? If you are cheated out of a single dollar by your neighbor, you do not rest satisfied with knowing that you are cheated, or with saying that you are cheated, or even with petitioning him to pay you your due; but you take effectual steps at once to obtain the full amount, and see that you are never cheated again. Action from principle,—the perception and the performance of right,—changes things and relations; it is essentially revolutionary, and does not consist wholly with any thing which was. It not only divides states and churches, it divides families; aye, it divides the *individual*, separating the diabolical in him from the divine.

Unjust laws exist: shall we be content to obey them, or shall we endeavor to amend them, and obey them until we have succeeded, or shall we transgress them at once? Men generally, under such a government as this, think that they ought to wait until they have persuaded the majority to alter them. They think that, if they should resist, the remedy would be worse than the evil. But it is the fault of the government itself that the remedy *is* worse than the evil. *It* makes it worse. Why is it not more apt to anticipate and provide for reform? Why does it not cherish its wise minority? Why does it cry and resist before it is hurt? Why does it not encourage its citizens to be on the alert to point out its faults, and *do* better than it would have them? Why does it always crucify Christ, and excommunicate Copernicus and Luther,[8] and pronounce Washington and Franklin rebels?

8. Thoreau cites as announcers of new truths Copernicus (1473–1543), the Polish astronomer who died too soon after the publication of his new system of astronomy to be excommunicated from the Catholic Church for writing it, and Martin Luther (1483–1546), the German leader of the Protestant Reformation who was excommunicated.

One would think, that a deliberate and practical denial of its authority was the only offence never contemplated by government; else, why has it not assigned its definite, its suitable and proportionate penalty? If a man who has no property refuses but once to earn nine shillings[9] for the State, he is put in prison for a period unlimited by any law that I know, and determined only by the discretion of those who placed him there; but if he should steal ninety times nine shillings from the State, he is soon permitted to go at large again.

If the injustice is part of the necessary friction of the machine of government, let it go, let it go: perchance it will wear smooth,—certainly the machine will wear out. If the injustice has a spring, or a pulley, or a rope, or a crank, exclusively for itself, then perhaps you may consider whether the remedy will not be worse than the evil; but if it is of such a nature that it requires you to be the agent of injustice to another, then, I say, break the law. Let your life be a counter friction to stop the machine. What I have to do is to see, at any rate, that I do not lend myself to the wrong which I condemn.

As for adopting the ways which the State has provided for remedying the evil, I know not of such ways. They take too much time, and a man's life will be gone. I have other affairs to attend to. I came into this world, not chiefly to make this a good place to live in, but to live in it, be it good or bad. A man has not every thing to do, but something; and because he cannot do *every thing*, it is not necessary that he should do *something* wrong. It is not my business to be petitioning the governor or the legislature any more than it is theirs to petition me; and, if they should not hear my petition, what should I do then? But in this case the State has provided no way: its very Constitution is the evil. This may seem to be harsh and stubborn and unconciliatory; but it is to treat with the utmost kindness and consideration the only spirit that can appreciate or deserves it. So is all change for the better, like birth and death which convulse the body.

I do not hesitate to say, that those who call themselves abolitionists should at once effectually withdraw their support, both in person and property, from the government of Massachusetts, and not wait till they constitute a majority of one, before they suffer the right to prevail through them. I think that it is enough if they have God on their side, without waiting for that other one. Moreover, any man more right than his neighbors, constitutes a majority of one already.[1]

I meet this American government, or its representative the State government, directly, and face to face, once a year, no more, in the person of its tax-gatherer; this is the only mode in which a man situated as I am necessarily meets it; and it then says distinctly, Recognize me; and the simplest, the most effectual, and, in the present posture of affairs, the indispensablest mode of treating with it on this head, of expressing your little satisfaction with and love for it, is to deny it then. My civil neighbor, the tax-gatherer,[2] is the very man I have to deal with,—for it is, after all, with men and not with parchment that I quarrel,—and he has voluntarily chosen to be an agent of

---

9. Because of sporadic coin shortages, the British shilling was still in use in parts of the United States during the 1840s; it was valued at approximately 20 U.S. cents. The amount of the tax, assessed on adult male citizens, was $1.50, approximately $30 in today's currency.

1. John Knox (1505?–1572), the Scottish religious reformer, said that "a man with God is always in the majority."
2. Sam Staples, who sometimes assisted Thoreau in his surveying.

the government. How shall he ever know well what he is and does as an officer of the government, or as a man, until he is obliged to consider whether he shall treat me, his neighbor, for whom he has respect, as a neighbor and well-disposed man, or as a maniac and disturber of the peace, and see if he can get over this obstruction to his neighborliness without a ruder and more impetuous thought or speech corresponding with his action? I know this well, that if one thousand, if one hundred, if ten men whom I could name,—if ten *honest* men only,—aye, if *one* HONEST man, in this State of Massachusetts, *ceasing to hold slaves*, were actually to withdraw from this copartnership, and be locked up in the county jail therefor, it would be the abolition of slavery in America. For it matters not how small the beginning may seem to be: what is once well done is done for ever. But we love better to talk about it: that we say is our mission. Reform keeps many scores of newspapers in its service, but not one man. If my esteemed neighbor, the State's ambassador,[3] who will devote his days to the settlement of the question of human rights in the Council Chamber, instead of being threatened with the prisons of Carolina, were to sit down the prisoner of Massachusetts, that State which is so anxious to foist the sin of slavery upon her sister,—though at present she can discover only an act of inhospitality to be the ground of a quarrel with her,—the Legislature would not wholly waive the subject the following winter.

Under a government which imprisons any unjustly, the true place for a just man is also a prison. The proper place to-day, the only place which Massachusetts has provided for her freer and less desponding spirits, is in her prisons, to be put out and locked out of the State by her own act, as they have already put themselves out by their principles. It is there that the fugitive slave, and the Mexican prisoner on parole, and the Indian come to plead the wrongs of his race, should find them; on that separate, but more free and honorable ground, where the State places those who are not *with* her but *against* her,—the only house in a slave-state in which a free man can abide with honor. If any think that their influence would be lost there, and their voices no longer afflict the ear of the State, that they would not be as an enemy within its walls, they do not know by how much truth is stronger than error, nor how much more eloquently and effectively he can combat injustice who has experienced a little in his own person. Cast your whole vote, not a strip of paper merely, but your whole influence. A minority is powerless while it conforms to the majority; it is not even a minority then; but it is irresistible when it clogs by its whole weight. If the alternative is to keep all just men in prison, or give up war and slavery, the State will not hesitate which to choose. If a thousand men were not to pay their tax-bills this year, that would not be a violent and bloody measure, as it would be to pay them, and enable the State to commit violence and shed innocent blood. This is, in fact, the definition of a peaceable revolution, if any such is possible. If the tax-gatherer, or any other public officer, asks me, as one has done, "But what shall I do?" my answer is, "If you really wish to do any thing, resign your office." When the subject has refused allegiance, and the officer has resigned his office,

---

3. Samuel Hoar (1778–1856), local political figure who as agent of the state of Massachusetts had been expelled from Charleston, South Carolina, in 1844 while interceding on behalf of imprisoned black seamen from Massachusetts.

then the revolution is accomplished. But even suppose blood should flow. Is there not a sort of blood shed when the conscience is wounded? Through this wound a man's real manhood and immortality flow out, and he bleeds to an everlasting death. I see this blood flowing now.

I have contemplated the imprisonment of the offender, rather than the seizure of his goods,—though both will serve the same purpose,—because they who assert the purest right, and consequently are most dangerous to a corrupt State, commonly have not spent much time in accumulating property. To such the State renders comparatively small service, and a slight tax is wont to appear exorbitant, particularly if they are obliged to earn it by special labor with their hands. If there were one who lived wholly without the use of money, the State itself would hesitate to demand it of him. But the rich man—not to make any invidious comparison—is always sold to the institution which makes him rich. Absolutely speaking, the more money, the less virtue; for money comes between a man and his objects, and obtains them for him; and it was certainly no great virtue to obtain it. It puts to rest many questions which he would otherwise be taxed to answer; while the only new question which it puts is the hard but superfluous one, how to spend it. Thus his moral ground is taken from under his feet. The opportunities of living are diminished in proportion as what are called the "means" are increased. The best thing a man can do for his culture when he is rich is to endeavour to carry out those schemes which he entertained when he was poor. Christ answered the Herodians according to their condition. "Show me the tribute-money," said he;—and one took a penny out of his pocket;—If you use money which has the image of Cæsar on it, and which he has made current and valuable, that is, *if you are men of the State*, and gladly enjoy the advantages of Cæsar's government, then pay him back some of his own when he demands it: "Render therefore to Cæsar that which is Cæsar's, and to God those things which are God's,"[4]—leaving them no wiser than before as to which was which; for they did not wish to know.

When I converse with the freest of my neighbors, I perceive that, whatever they may say about the magnitude and seriousness of the question, and their regard for the public tranquillity, the long and the short of the matter is, that they cannot spare the protection of the existing government, and they dread the consequences of disobedience to it to their property and families. For my own part, I should not like to think that I ever rely on the protection of the State. But, if I deny the authority of the State when it presents its tax-bill, it will soon take and waste all my property, and so harass me and my children without end. This is hard. This makes it impossible for a man to live honestly and at the same time comfortably in outward respects. It will not be worth the while to accumulate property; that would be sure to go again. You must hire or squat somewhere, and raise but a small crop, and eat that soon. You must live within yourself, and depend upon yourself, always tucked up and ready for a start, and not have many affairs. A man may grow rich in Turkey even, if he will be in all respects a good subject of the Turkish government. Confucious said,—"If a State is governed by the principles of reason, poverty and misery are subjects of shame; if a State is not governed by the

---

4. Matthew 22.16–21. In their attempt to entrap Jesus, the Pharisees (a Jewish sect that held to Mosaic law) were using secular government functionaries of Herod, the king of Judea.

principles of reason, riches and honors are the subjects of shame."[5] No: until I want the protection of Massachusetts to be extended to me in some distant southern port, where my liberty is endangered, or until I am bent solely on building up an estate at home at peaceful enterprise, I can afford to refuse allegiance to Massachusetts, and her right to my property and life. It costs me less in every sense to incur the penalty of disobedience to the State, than it would to obey. I should feel as if I were worth less in that case.

Some years ago, the State met me in behalf of the church, and commanded me to pay a certain sum toward the support of a clergyman whose preaching my father attended, but never I myself. "Pay it," it said, "or be locked up in the jail." I declined to pay. But, unfortunately, another man saw fit to pay it. I did not see why the schoolmaster should be taxed to support the priest, and not the priest the schoolmaster; for I was not the State's schoolmaster, but I supported myself by voluntary subscription. I did not see why the lyceum should not present its tax-bill, and have the State to back its demand, as well as the church. However, at the request of the selectmen, I condescended to make some such statement as this in writing:—"Know all men by these presents, that I, Henry Thoreau, do not wish to be regarded as a member of any incorporated society which I have not joined." This I gave to the town-clerk; and he has it. The State, having thus learned that I did not wish to be regarded as a member of that church, has never made a like demand on me since; though it said that it must adhere to its original presumption that time. If I had known how to name them, I should then have signed off in detail from all the societies which I never signed on to; but I did not know where to find a complete list.

I have paid no poll-tax for six years.[6] I was put into a jail[7] once on this account, for one night; and, as I stood considering the walls of solid stone, two or three feet thick, the door of wood and iron, a foot thick, and the iron grating which strained the light, I could not help being struck with the foolishness of that institution which treated me as if I were mere flesh and blood and bones, to be locked up. I wondered that it should have concluded at length that this was the best use it could put me to, and had never thought to avail itself of my services in some way. I saw that, if there was a wall of stone between me and my townsmen, there was a still more difficult one to climb or break through, before they could get to be as free as I was. I did not for a moment feel confined, and the walls seemed a great waste of stone and mortar. I felt as if I alone of all my townsmen had paid my tax. They plainly did not know how to treat me, but behaved like persons who are underbred. In every threat and in every compliment there was a blunder; for they thought that my chief desire was to stand the other side of that stone wall. I could not but smile to see how industriously they locked the door on my meditations, which followed them out again without let or hinderance, and *they* were really all that was dangerous. As they could not reach me, they had resolved to punish my body; just as boys, if they cannot come at some person against whom they have a spite, will abuse his dog. I saw that the State was half-witted, that it was timid as a lone woman with her silver spoons, and that it did not know its friends from its foes, and I lost all my remaining respect for it, and pitied it.

5. Confucius's *Analects* 8.13.
6. I.e., since 1840.

7. The Middlesex County jail in Concord, a large three-story building.

Thus the State never intentionally confronts a man's sense, intellectual or moral, but only his body, his senses. It is not armed with superior wit or honesty, but with superior physical strength. I was not born to be forced. I will breathe after my own fashion. Let us see who is the strongest. What force has a multitude? They only can force me who obey a higher law than I. They force me to become like themselves. I do not hear of *men* being *forced* to live this way or that by masses of men. What sort of life were that to live? When I meet a government which says to me, "Your money or your life," why should I be in haste to give it my money? It may be in a great strait, and not know what to do: I cannot help that. It must help itself; do as I do. It is not worth the while to snivel about it. I am not responsible for the successful working of the machinery of society. I am not the son of the engineer. I perceive that, when an acorn and a chestnut fall side by side, the one does not remain inert to make way for the other, but both obey their own laws, and spring and grow and flourish as best they can, till one, perchance, overshadows and destroys the other. If a plant cannot live according to its nature, it dies; and so a man.

The night in prison was novel and interesting enough. The prisoners in their shirt-sleeves were enjoying a chat and the evening air in the doorway, when I entered. But the jailer said, "Come, boys, it is time to lock up;" and so they dispersed, and I heard the sound of their steps returning into the hollow apartments. My room-mate was introduced to me by the jailer, as "a first-rate fellow and a clever man." When the door was locked, he showed me where to hang my hat, and how he managed matters there. The rooms were whitewashed once a month; and this one, at least, was the whitest, most simply furnished, and probably the neatest apartment in the town. He naturally wanted to know where I came from, and what brought me there; and, when I had told him, I asked him in my turn how he came there, presuming him to be an honest man, of course; and, as the world goes, I believe he was. "Why," said he, "they accuse me of burning a barn; but I never did it." As near as I could discover, he had probably gone to bed in a barn when drunk, and smoked his pipe there; and so a barn was burnt. He had the reputation of being a clever man, had been there some three months waiting for his trial to come on, and would have to wait as much longer; but he was quite domesticated and contented since he got his board for nothing, and thought that he was well treated.

He occupied one window, and I the other; and I saw, that if one stayed there long, his principal business would be to look out the window. I had soon read all the tracts that were left there, and examined where former prisoners had broken out, and where a grate had been sawed off, and heard the history of the various occupants of that room; for I found that even here there was a history and a gossip which never circulated beyond the walls of the jail. Probably this is the only house in the town where verses are composed, which are afterward printed in a circular form, but not published. I was shown quite a long list of verses which were composed by some young men who had been detected in an attempt to escape, who avenged themselves by singing them.

I pumped my fellow-prisoner as dry as I could, for fear I should never see him again; but at length he showed me which was my bed, and left me to blow out the lamp.

It was like travelling into a far country, such as I had never expected to behold, to lie there for one night. It seemed to me that I never had heard the town-clock strike before, nor the evening sounds of the village; for we slept with the windows open, which were inside the grating. It was to see my native village in the light of the middle ages, and our Concord was turned into a Rhine stream, and visions of knights and castles passed before me. They were the voices of old burghers that I heard in the streets. I was an involuntary spectator and auditor of whatever was done and said in the kitchen of the adjacent village-inn,—a wholly new and rare experience to me. It was a closer view of my native town. I was fairly inside of it. I never had seen its institutions before. This is one of its peculiar institutions; for it is a shire town.[8] I began to comprehend what its inhabitants were about.

In the morning, our breakfasts were put through the hole in the door, in small oblong-square tin pans, made to fit, and holding a pint of chocolate, with brown bread, and an iron spoon. When they called for the vessels again, I was green enough to return what bread I had left; but my comrade seized it, and said that I should lay that up for lunch or dinner. Soon after, he was let out to work at haying in a neighboring field, whither he went every day, and would not be back till noon; so he bade me good-day, saying that he doubted if he should see me again.

When I came out of prison,—for some one interfered, and paid the tax,[9]—I did not perceive that great changes had taken place on the common, such as he observed who went in a youth, and emerged a tottering and gray-headed man; and yet a change had to my eyes come over the scene,—the town, and State, and country,—greater than any that mere time could effect. I saw yet more distinctly the State in which I lived. I saw to what extent the people among whom I lived could be trusted as good neighbors and friends; that their friendship was for summer weather only; that they did not greatly purpose to do right; that they were a distinct race from me by their prejudices and superstitions, as the Chinamen and Malays are; that, in their sacrifices to humanity, they ran no risks, not even to their property; that, after all, they were not so noble but they treated the thief as he had treated them, and hoped, by a certain outward observance and a few prayers, and by walking in a particular straight though useless path from time to time, to save their souls. This may be to judge my neighbors harshly; for I believe that most of them are not aware that they have such an institution as the jail in their village.

It was formerly the custom in our village, when a poor debtor came out of jail, for his acquaintances to salute him, looking through their fingers, which were crossed to represent the grating of a jail window, "How do ye do?" My neighbors did not thus salute me, but first looked at me, and then at one another, as if I had returned from a long journey. I was put into jail as I was going to the shoemaker's to get a shoe which was mended. When I was let out the next morning, I proceeded to finish my errand, and, having put on my mended shoe, joined a huckleberry party, who were impatient to put themselves under my conduct; and in

---

8. Comparable to county seat. 9. The identity of this person is unknown.

half an hour,—for the horse was soon tackled,[1]—was in the midst of a huckleberry field, on one of our highest hills, two miles off; and then the State was nowhere to be seen.

This is the whole history of "My Prisons."[2]

I have never declined paying the highway tax, because I am as desirous of being a good neighbor as I am of being a bad subject; and, as for supporting schools, I am doing my part to educate my fellow-countrymen now. It is for no particular item in the tax-bill that I refuse to pay it. I simply wish to refuse allegiance to the State, to withdraw and stand aloof from it effectually. I do not care to trace the course of my dollar, if I could, till it buys a man, or a musket to shoot one with,—the dollar is innocent,—but I am concerned to trace the effects of my allegiance. In fact, I quietly declare war with the State, after my fashion, though I will still make what use and get what advantage of her I can, as is usual in such cases.

If others pay the tax which is demanded of me, from a sympathy with the State, they do but what they have already done in their own case, or rather they abet injustice to a greater extent than the State requires. If they pay the tax from a mistaken interest in the individual taxed, to save his property or prevent his going to jail, it is because they have not considered wisely how far they let their private feelings interfere with the public good.

This, then, is my position at present. But one cannot be too much on his guard in such a case, lest his action be biassed by obstinacy, or an undue regard for the opinions of men. Let him see that he does only what belongs to himself and to the hour.

I think sometimes, Why, this people mean well; they are only ignorant; they would do better if they knew how; why give your neighbors this pain to treat you as they are not inclined to? But I think, again, this is no reason why I should do as they do, or permit others to suffer much greater pain of a different kind. Again, I sometimes say to myself, When many millions of men, without heat, without ill-will, without personal feeling of any kind, demand of you a few shillings only, without the possibility, such is their constitution, of retracting or altering their present demand, and without the possibility, on your side, of appeal to any other millions, why expose yourself to this overwhelming brute force? You do not resist cold and hunger, the winds and the waves, thus obstinately; you quietly submit to a thousand similar necessities. You do not put your head into the fire. But just in proportion as I regard this as not wholly a brute force, but partly a human force, and consider that I have relations to those millions as to so many millions of men, and not of mere brute or inanimate things, I see that appeal is possible, first and instantaneously, from them to the Maker of them, and, secondly, from them to themselves. But, if I put my head deliberately into the fire, there is no appeal to fire or to the Maker of fire, and I have only myself to blame. If I could convince myself that I have any right to be satisfied with men as they are, and to treat them accordingly, and not according, in some respects, to my requisitions and expectations of what they and I ought to be, then, like a good Mussulman[3] and fatalist, I should endeavor to be satisfied with things

1. Harnessed.
2. An allusion to the title of a book (1832) by the Italian poet Silvio Pellico (1789–1854) describing his years of hard labor in Austrian prisons.
3. Muslim.

as they are, and say it is the will of God. And, above all, there is this difference between resisting this and a purely brute or natural force, that I can resist this with some effect; but I cannot expect, like Orpheus,[4] to change the nature of the rocks and trees and beasts.

I do not wish to quarrel with any man or nation. I do not wish to split hairs, to make fine distinctions, or set myself up as better than my neighbors. I seek rather, I may say, even an excuse for conforming to the laws of the land. I am but too ready to conform to them. Indeed I have reason to suspect myself on this head; and each year, as the tax-gatherer comes round, I find myself disposed to review the acts and position of the general and state governments, and the spirit of the people, to discover a pretext for conformity. I believe that the State will soon be able to take all my work of this sort out of my hands, and then I shall be no better a patriot than my fellow-countrymen. Seen from a lower point of view, the Constitution, with all its faults, is very good; the law and the courts are very respectable; even this State and this American government are, in many respects, very admirable and rare things, to be thankful for, such as a great many have described them; but seen from a point of view a little higher, they are what I have described them; seen from a higher still, and the highest, who shall say what they are, or that they are worth looking at or thinking of at all?

However, the government does not concern me much, and I shall bestow the fewest possible thoughts on it. It is not many moments that I live under a government, even in this world. If a man is thought-free, fancy-free, imagination-free, that which *is not* never for a long time appearing *to be* to him, unwise rulers or reformers cannot fatally interrupt him.

I know that most men think differently from myself; but those whose lives are by profession devoted to the study of these or kindred subjects, content me as little as any. Statesmen and legislators, standing so completely within the institution, never distinctly and nakedly behold it. They speak of moving society, but have no resting-place without it. They may be men of a certain experience and discrimination, and have no doubt invented ingenious and even useful systems, for which we sincerely thank them; but all their wit and usefulness lie within certain not very wide limits. They are wont to forget that the world is not governed by policy and expediency. Webster[5] never goes behind government, and so cannot speak with authority about it. His words are wisdom to those legislators who contemplate no essential reform in the existing government; but for thinkers, and those who legislate for all time, he never once glances at the subject. I know of those whose serene and wise speculations on this theme would soon reveal the limits of his mind's range and hospitality. Yet, compared with the cheap professions of most reformers, and the still cheaper wisdom and eloquence of politicians in general, his are almost the only sensible and valuable words, and we thank Heaven for him. Comparatively, he is always strong, original, and, above all, practical. Still his quality is not wisdom, but prudence. The lawyer's truth is not Truth, but consistency, or a consistent expediency. Truth is always in harmony with herself, and is not concerned chiefly to reveal the justice that

---

4. In Greek mythology, Orpheus's singing and playing of the lyre charmed animals and moved even rocks and trees to dance.

5. Daniel Webster (1782–1852), prominent Massachusetts Whig politician, at the time a senator.

may consist with wrong-doing. He well deserves to be called, as he has been called, the Defender of the Constitution. There are really no blows to be given by him but defensive ones. He is not a leader, but a follower. His leaders are the men of '87.[6] "I have never made an effort," he says, "and never propose to make an effort; I have never countenanced an effort, and never mean to countenance an effort, to disturb the arrangement as originally made, by which the various States came into the Union."[7] Still thinking of the sanction which the Constitution gives to slavery, he says, "Because it was a part of the original compact,—let it stand." Notwithstanding his special acuteness and ability, he is unable to take a fact out of its merely political relations, and behold it as it lies absolutely to be disposed of by the intellect,—what, for instance, it behoves a man to do here in America to-day with regard to slavery, but ventures, or is driven, to make some such desperate answer as the following, while professing to speak absolutely, and as a private man,—from which what new and singular code of social duties might be inferred?—"The manner," says he, "in which the government of those States where slavery exists are to regulate it, is for their own consideration, under their responsibility to their constituents, to the general laws of propriety, humanity, and justice, and to God. Associations formed elsewhere, springing from a feeling of humanity, or any other cause, having nothing whatever to do with it. They have never received any encouragement from me, and they never will."[8]

They who know of no purer sources of truth, who have traced up its stream no higher, stand, and wisely stand, by the Bible and the Constitution, and drink at it there with reverence and humility; but they who behold where it comes trickling into this lake or that pool, gird up their loins once more, and continue their pilgrimage toward its fountain-head.

No man with a genius for legislation has appeared in America. They are rare in the history of the world. There are orators, politicians, and eloquent men, by the thousand; but the speaker has not yet opened his mouth to speak, who is capable of settling the much-vexed questions of the day. We love eloquence for its own sake, and not for any truth which it may utter, or any heroism it may inspire. Our legislators have not yet learned the comparative value of free-trade and of freedom, of union, and of rectitude, to a nation. They have no genius or talent for comparatively humble questions of taxation and finance, commerce and manufactures and agriculture. If we were left solely to the wordy wit of legislators in Congress for our guidance, uncorrected by the seasonable experience and the effectual complaints of the people, America would not long retain her rank among the nations. For eighteen hundred years, though perchance I have no right to say it, the New Testament has been written; yet where is the legislator who has wisdom and practical talent enough to avail himself of the light which it sheds on the science of legislation?

The authority of government, even such as I am willing to submit to,— for I will cheerfully obey those who know and can do better than I, and in many things even those who neither know nor can do so well,—is still an impure one: to be strictly just, it must have the sanction and consent of the

---

6. The authors of the U.S. Constitution.
7. From Webster's speech "The Admission of Texas" (December 22, 1845).

8. These extracts have been inserted since the Lecture was read [Thoreau's note]. He is referring to the quotation beginning "The manner."

governed. It can have no pure right over my person and property but what I concede to it. The progress from an absolute to a limited monarchy, from a limited monarchy to a democracy, is a progress toward a true respect for the individual. Is a democracy, such as we know it, the last improvement possible in government? Is it not possible to take a step further towards recognizing and organizing the rights of man? There will never be a really free and enlightened State, until the State comes to recognize the individual as a higher and independent power, from which all its own power and authority are derived, and treats him accordingly. I please myself with imagining a State at last which can afford to be just to all men, and to treat the individual with respect as a neighbor; which even would not think it inconsistent with its own repose, if a few were to live aloof from it, not meddling with it, nor embraced by it, who fulfilled all the duties of neighbors and fellow-men. A State which bore this kind of fruit, and suffered it to drop off as fast as it ripened, would prepare the way for a still more perfect and glorious State, which also I have imagined, but not yet anywhere seen.

1849, 1866

WALDEN;

OR,

LIFE IN THE WOODS.

By HENRY D. THOREAU,

AUTHOR OF "A WEEK ON THE CONCORD AND MERRIMACK RIVERS."

I do not propose to write an ode to dejection, but to brag as lustily as chanticleer in the morning, standing on his roost, if only to wake my neighbors up. — Page 92.

BOSTON:

TICKNOR AND FIELDS.

M DCCC LIV.

Walden. Title page of the first edition (1854); the drawing is by Thoreau's sister Sophia.

Walden, or Life in the Woods[1]

I do not propose to write an ode to dejection, but to brag as lustily as chanticleer in the morning, standing on his roost, if only to wake my neighbors up.

1. Economy

When I wrote the following pages, or rather the bulk of them, I lived alone, in the woods, a mile from any neighbor, in a house which I had built myself, on the shore of Walden Pond, in Concord, Massachusetts, and earned my living by the labor of my hands only. I lived there two years and two months. At present I am a sojourner in civilized life again.

I should not obtrude my affairs so much on the notice of my readers if very particular inquiries had not been made by my townsmen concerning my mode of life, which some would call impertinent, though they do not appear to me at all impertinent, but, considering the circumstances, very natural and pertinent. Some have asked what I got to eat; if I did not feel lonesome; if I was not afraid; and the like. Others have been curious to learn what portion of my income I devoted to charitable purposes; and some, who have large families, how many poor children I maintained. I will therefore ask those of my readers who feel no particular interest in me to pardon me if I undertake to answer some of these questions in this book. In most books, the I, or first person, is omitted; in this it will be retained; that, in respect to egotism, is the main difference. We commonly do not remember that it is, after all, always the first person that is speaking. I should not talk so much about myself if there were any body else whom I knew as well. Unfortunately, I am confined to this theme by the narrowness of my experience. Moreover, I, on my side, require of every writer, first or last, a simple and sincere account of his own life, and not merely what he has heard of other men's lives; some such account as he would send to his kindred from a distant land; for if he has lived sincerely, it must have been in a distant land to me. Perhaps these pages are more particularly addressed to poor students. As for the rest of my readers, they will accept such portions as apply to them. I trust that none will stretch the seams in putting on the coat, for it may do good service to him whom it fits.

I would fain say something, not so much concerning the Chinese and Sandwich Islanders[2] as you who read these pages, who are said to live in New England; something about your condition, especially your outward condition or circumstances in this world, in this town, what it is, whether it is necessary that it be as bad as it is, whether it cannot be improved as well as not. I have travelled a good deal in Concord; and every where, in shops, and offices, and fields, the inhabitants have appeared to me to be doing penance in a thousand

---

1. Thoreau began writing *Walden* early in 1846, some months after he began living at Walden Pond, and by late 1847, when he moved back into the village of Concord, he had drafted roughly half the book. Between 1852 and 1854 he rewrote the manuscript several times and substantially enlarged it. The text printed here is that of the 1st edition (1854), with a few printer's errors corrected on the basis of Thoreau's set of marked proofs, his corrections in his copy of *Walden*, and scholars' comparisons of the printed book and the manuscript drafts.
2. Hawaiians.

remarkable ways. What I have heard of Brahmins sitting exposed to four fires and looking in the face of the sun; or hanging suspended, with their heads downward, over flames; or looking at the heavens over their shoulders "until it becomes impossible for them to resume their natural position, while from the twist of the neck nothing but liquids can pass into the stomach;" or dwelling, chained for life, at the foot of a tree; or measuring with their bodies, like caterpillars, the breadth of vast empires; or standing on one leg on the tops of pillars,—even these forms of conscious penance are hardly more incredible and astonishing than the scenes which I daily witness.[3] The twelve labors of Hercules[4] were trifling in comparison with those which my neighbors have undertaken; for they were only twelve, and had an end; but I could never see that these men slew or captured any monster or finished any labor. They have no friend Iolas to burn with a hot iron the root of the hydra's head, but as soon as one head is crushed, two spring up.

I see young men, my townsmen, whose misfortune it is to have inherited farms, houses, barns, cattle, and farming tools; for these are more easily acquired than got rid of. Better if they had been born in the open pasture and suckled by a wolf,[5] that they might have seen with clearer eyes what field they were called to labor in. Who made them serfs of the soil? Why should they eat their sixty acres, when man is condemned to eat only his peck of dirt? Why should they begin digging their graves as soon as they are born? They have got to live a man's life, pushing all these things before them, and get on as well as they can. How many a poor immortal soul have I met well nigh crushed and smothered under its load, creeping down the road of life, pushing before it a barn seventy-five feet by forty, its Augean stables never cleansed, and one hundred acres of land, tillage, mowing, pasture, and wood-lot! The portionless, who struggle with no such unnecessary inherited encumbrances, find it labor enough to subdue and cultivate a few cubic feet of flesh.

But men labor under a mistake. The better part of the man is soon ploughed into the soil for compost. By a seeming fate, commonly called necessity, they are employed, as it says in an old book, laying up treasures which moth and rust will corrupt and thieves break through and steal.[6] It is a fool's life, as they will find when they get to the end of it, if not before. It is said that Deucalion and Pyrrha created men by throwing stones over their heads behind them:[7]—

> Inde genus durum sumus, experiensque laborum,
> Et documenta damus quâ simus origine nati.[8]

3. For his information on religious self-torture among high-caste Hindus in India, Thoreau drew on *The History of India* (1817) by James Mill (1773–1836).

4. Son of Zeus and Alcmene, this half-mortal could become a god only by performing twelve labors, each apparently impossible. The second labor, the slaying of the Lernaean hydra, a many-headed sea monster, is referred to just below. (Hercules' friend Iolas helped by searing the stump each time Hercules cut off one of the heads, which otherwise would have regenerated.) The seventh labor, mentioned in the following paragraph, was the cleansing of Augeas's filthy stables in one day,

a feat Hercules accomplished by diverting two nearby rivers through the stables.

5. Roman myth tells of how Romulus and Remus, the founders of Rome, were suckled by a wolf.

6. Matthew 6.19.

7. According to Greek mythology, Deucalion and Pyrrha repopulated the earth by throwing stones behind them over their shoulders. The stones thrown by Deucalion turned into men, and the stones thrown by Pyrrha turned into women.

8. From *Metamorphoses*, by the Roman poet Ovid (43 B.C.E.–18 C.E.), and translated by Sir Walter Raleigh (1554?–1618) in his *History of the World* (1614).

Or, as Raleigh rhymes it in his sonorous way,—

"From thence our kind hard-hearted is, enduring pain and care,
Approving that our bodies of a stony nature are."

So much for a blind obedience to a blundering oracle, throwing the stones over their heads behind them, and not seeing where they fell.

Most men, even in this comparatively free country, through mere ignorance and mistake, are so occupied with the factitious cares and superfluously coarse labors of life that its finer fruits cannot be plucked by them. Their fingers, from excessive toil, are too clumsy and tremble too much for that. Actually, the laboring man has not leisure for a true integrity day by day; he cannot afford to sustain the manliest relations to men; his labor would be depreciated in the market. He has no time to be any thing but a machine. How can he remember well his ignorance—which his growth requires—who has so often to use his knowledge? We should feed and clothe him gratuitously sometimes, and recruit him with our cordials, before we judge of him. The finest qualities of our nature, like the bloom on fruits, can be preserved only by the most delicate handling. Yet we do not treat ourselves nor one another thus tenderly.

Some of you, we all know, are poor, find it hard to live, are sometimes, as it were, gasping for breath. I have no doubt that some of you who read this book are unable to pay for all the dinners which you have actually eaten, or for the coats and shoes which are fast wearing or are already worn out, and have come to this page to spend borrowed or stolen time, robbing your creditors of an hour. It is very evident what mean and sneaking lives many of you live, for my sight has been whetted by experience; always on the limits, trying to get into business and trying to get out of debt, a very ancient slough, called by the Latins, *æs alienum*, another's brass, for some of their coins were made of brass; still living, and dying, and buried by this other's brass; always promising to pay, promising to pay, to-morrow, and dying to-day, insolvent; seeking to curry favor, to get custom, by how many modes, only not state-prison offences; lying, flattering, voting, contracting yourselves into a nutshell of civility, or dilating into an atmosphere of thin and vaporous generosity, that you may persuade your neighbor to let you make his shoes, or his hat, or his coat, or his carriage, or import his groceries for him; making yourselves sick, that you may lay up something against a sick day, something to be tucked away in an old chest, or in a stocking behind the plastering, or, more safely, in the brick bank; no matter where, no matter how much or how little.

I sometimes wonder that we can be so frivolous, I may almost say, as to attend to the gross but somewhat foreign form of servitude called Negro Slavery, there are so many keen and subtle masters that enslave both north and south. It is hard to have a southern overseer; it is worse to have a northern one; but worst of all when you are the slave-driver of yourself. Talk of a divinity in man! Look at the teamster on the highway, wending to market by day or night; does any divinity stir within him? His highest duty to fodder and water his horses! What is his destiny to him compared with the shipping interests? Does not he drive for Squire Make-a-stir?[9] How godlike, how immortal, is he? See how he cowers and sneaks, how vaguely all the day he fears, not being

9. An allegorical name modeled on those in John Bunyan's *Pilgrim's Progress* (1678, 1684).

immortal nor divine, but the slave and prisoner of his own opinion of himself, a fame won by his own deeds. Public opinion is a weak tyrant compared with our own private opinion. What a man thinks of himself, that it is which determines, or rather indicates, his fate. Self-emancipation even in the West Indian provinces of the fancy and imagination,—what Wilberforce[1] is there to bring that about? Think, also, of the ladies of the land weaving toilet cushions against the last day, not to betray too green an interest in their fates! As if you could kill time without injuring eternity.

The mass of men lead lives of quiet desperation. What is called resignation is confirmed desperation. From the desperate city you go into the desperate country, and have to console yourself with the bravery of minks and muskrats. A stereotyped but unconscious despair is concealed even under what are called the games and amusements of mankind. There is no play in them, for this comes after work. But it is a characteristic of wisdom not to do desperate things.

When we consider what, to use the words of the catechism, is the chief end of man,[2] and what are the true necessaries and means of life, it appears as if men had deliberately chosen the common mode of living because they preferred it to any other. Yet they honestly think there is no choice left. But alert and healthy natures remember that the sun rose clear. It is never too late to give up our prejudices. No way of thinking or doing, however ancient, can be trusted without proof. What every body echoes or in silence passes by as true to-day may turn out to be falsehood to-morrow, mere smoke of opinion, which some had trusted for a cloud that would sprinkle fertilizing rain on their fields. What old people say you cannot do you try and find that you can. Old deeds for old people, and new deeds for new. Old people did not know enough once, perchance, to fetch fresh fuel to keep the fire a-going; new people put a little dry wood under a pot, and are whirled round the globe with the speed of birds, in a way to kill old people, as the phrase is. Age is no better, hardly so well, qualified for an instructor as youth, for it has not profited so much as it has lost. One may almost doubt if the wisest man has learned any thing of absolute value by living. Practically, the old have no very important advice to give the young, their own experience has been so partial, and their lives have been such miserable failures, for private reasons, as they must believe; and it may be that they have some faith left which belies that experience, and they are only less young than they were. I have lived some thirty years on this planet, and I have yet to hear the first syllable of valuable or even earnest advice from my seniors. They have told me nothing, and probably cannot tell me any thing, to the purpose. Here is life, an experiment to a great extent untried by me; but it does not avail me that they have tried it. If I have any experience which I think valuable, I am sure to reflect that this my Mentors[3] said nothing about.

One farmer says to me, "You cannot live on vegetable food solely, for it furnishes nothing to make bones with;" and so he religiously devotes a part

---

1. William Wilberforce (1759–1833), English philanthropist, was instrumental in helping to abolish the slave trade (1807) and end slavery in the British Empire (1833).
2. From the Westminster Shorter Catechism in the *New England Primer*: "What is the chief end of man? Man's chief end is to glorify God and to enjoy him forever."
3. From Mentor, in Homer's *Odyssey*: the friend whom Odysseus entrusted with the education of his son, Telemachus.

of his day to supplying his system with the raw material of bones; walking all the while he talks behind his oxen, which, with vegetable-made bones, jerk him and his lumbering plough along in spite of every obstacle. Some things are really necessaries of life in some circles, the most helpless and diseased, which in others are luxuries merely, and in others still are entirely unknown.

The whole ground of human life seems to some to have been gone over by their predecessors, both the heights and the valleys, and all things to have been cared for. According to Evelyn, "the wise Solomon prescribed ordinances for the very distances of trees; and the Roman prætors have decided how often you may go into your neighbor's land to gather the acorns which fall on it without trespass, and what share belongs to that neighbor."[4] Hippocrates[5] has even left directions how we should cut our nails; that is, even with the ends of the fingers, neither shorter nor longer. Undoubtedly the very tedium and ennui which presume to have exhausted the variety and the joys of life are as old as Adam. But man's capacities have never been measured; nor are we to judge of what he can do by any precedents, so little has been tried. Whatever have been thy failures hitherto, "be not afflicted, my child, for who shall assign to thee what thou hast left undone?"[6]

We might try our lives by a thousand simple tests; as, for instance, that the same sun which ripens my beans illumines at once a system of earths like ours. If I had remembered this it would have prevented some mistakes. This was not the light in which I hoed them. The stars are the apexes of what wonderful triangles! What distant and different beings in the various mansions of the universe are contemplating the same one at the same moment! Nature and human life are as various as our several constitutions. Who shall say what prospect life offers to another? Could a greater miracle take place than for us to look through each other's eyes for an instant? We should live in all the ages of the world in an hour; ay, in all the worlds of the ages. History, Poetry, Mythology!—I know of no reading of another's experience so startling and informing as this would be.

The greater part of what my neighbors call good I believe in my soul to be bad, and if I repent of any thing, it is very likely to be my good behavior. What demon possessed me that I behaved so well? You may say the wisest thing you can old man,—you who have lived seventy years, not without honor of a kind,—I hear an irresistible voice which invites me away from all that. One generation abandons the enterprises of another like stranded vessels.

I think that we may safely trust a good deal more than we do. We may waive just so much care of ourselves as we honestly bestow elsewhere. Nature is as well adapted to our weakness as to our strength. The incessant anxiety and strain of some is a well nigh incurable form of disease. We are made to exaggerate the importance of what work we do; and yet how much is not done by us! or, what if we had been taken sick? How vigilant we are! determined not to live by faith if we can avoid it; all the day long on the alert, at night we unwillingly say our prayers and commit ourselves to uncertainties. So

---

4. *Silva; or a Discourse of Forest-Trees* (1664), by the English writer John Evelyn (1620–1706), who called for the reforestation of lands cleared for estates. "Prætors": in the Roman Republic, high elected magistrates.
5. Influential Greek physician (460?–377? B.C.E.),
who emphasized the importance of doctors making an ethical commitment to the care of their patients (known as the "Hippocratic Oath").
6. From H. H. Wilson's translation of the *Vishnu Purana* (1840), a Hindu religious text.

thoroughly and sincerely are we compelled to live, reverencing our life, and denying the possibility of change. This is the only way, we say; but there are as many ways as there can be drawn radii from one centre. All change is a miracle to contemplate; but it is a miracle which is taking place every instant. Confucius said, "To know that we know what we know, and that we do not know what we do not know, this is true knowledge."[7] When one man has reduced a fact of the imagination to be a fact to his understanding, I foresee that all men will at length establish their lives on that basis.

Let us consider for a moment what most of the trouble and anxiety which I have referred to is about, and how much it is necessary that we be troubled, or, at least, careful. It would be some advantage to live a primitive and frontier life, though in the midst of an outward civilization, if only to learn what are the gross necessaries of life and what methods have been taken to obtain them; or even to look over the old day-books of the merchants, to see what it was that men most commonly bought at the stores, what they stored, that is, what are the grossest groceries. For the improvements of ages have had but little influence on the essential laws of man's existence; as our skeletons, probably, are not to be distinguished from those of our ancestors.

By the words *necessary of life*, I mean whatever, of all that man obtains by his own exertions, has been from the first, or from long use has become, so important to human life that few, if any, whether from savageness, or poverty, or philosophy, ever attempt to do without it. To many creatures there is in this sense but one necessary of life, Food. To the bison of the prairie it is a few inches of palatable grass, with water to drink; unless he seeks the Shelter of the forest or the mountain's shadow. None of the brute creation requires more than Food and Shelter. The necessaries of life for man in this climate may, accurately enough, be distributed under the several heads of Food, Shelter, Clothing, and Fuel; for not till we have secured these are we prepared to entertain the true problems of life with freedom and a prospect of success. Man has invented, not only houses, but clothes and cooked food; and possibly from the accidental discovery of the warmth of fire, and the consequent use of it, at first a luxury, arose the present necessity to sit by it. We observe cats and dogs acquiring the same second nature. By proper Shelter and Clothing we legitimately retain our own internal heat; but with an excess of these, or of Fuel, that is, with an external heat greater than our own internal, may not cookery properly be said to begin? Darwin, the naturalist, says of the inhabitants of Tierra del Fuego, that while his own party, who were well clothed and sitting close to a fire, were far from too warm, these naked savages, who were farther off, were observed, to his great surprise, "to be streaming with perspiration at undergoing such a roasting."[8] So, we are told, the New Hollander[9] goes naked with impunity, while the European shivers in his clothes. Is it impossible to combine the hardiness of these savages with the intellectualness of the civilized man? According to Liebig,[1] man's body is a stove, and food the fuel which keeps up the internal combustion in the lungs. In cold weather we eat more, in warm less. The animal heat is the

---

7. From *Analects* 2:17, by the Chinese philosopher Confucius (551?–479 B.C.E.).
8. Charles Darwin (1809–1882), *Journal of Researches* (1839).
9. Australian aborigine.
1. Justus, Baron von Liebig (1803–1873), German chemist, author of *Organic Chemistry* (1840).

result of a slow combustion, and disease and death take place when this is too rapid; or for want of fuel, or from some defect in the draught, the fire goes out. Of course the vital heat is not to be confounded with fire; but so much for analogy. It appears, therefore, from the above list, that the expression, *animal life*, is nearly synonymous with the expression, *animal heat*; for while Food may be regarded as the Fuel which keeps up the fire within us,— and Fuel serves only to prepare that Food or to increase the warmth of our bodies by addition from without,—Shelter and Clothing also serve only to retain the *heat* thus generated and absorbed.

The grand necessity, then, for our bodies, is to keep warm, to keep the vital heat in us. What pains we accordingly take, not only with our Food, and Clothing, and Shelter, but with our beds, which are our night-clothes, robbing the nests and breasts of birds to prepare this shelter within a shelter, as the mole has its bed of grass and leaves at the end of its burrow! The poor man is wont to complain that this is a cold world; and to cold, no less physical than social, we refer directly a great part of our ails. The summer, in some climates, makes possible to man a sort of Elysian[2] life. Fuel, except to cook his Food, is then unnecessary; the sun is his fire, and many of the fruits are sufficiently cooked by its rays; while Food generally is more various, and more easily obtained, and Clothing and Shelter are wholly or half unnecessary. At the present day, and in this country, as I find by my own experience, a few implements, a knife, an axe, a spade, a wheelbarrow, &c., and for the studious, lamplight, stationery, and access to a few books, rank next to necessaries, and can all be obtained at a trifling cost. Yet some, not wise, go to the other side of the globe, to barbarous and unhealthy regions, and devote themselves to trade for ten or twenty years, in order that they may live,—that is, keep comfortably warm,—and die in New England at last. The luxuriously rich are not simply kept comfortably warm, but unnaturally hot; as I implied before, they are cooked, of course *à la mode*.[3]

Most of the luxuries, and many of the so called comforts of life, are not only not indispensable, but positive hinderances to the elevation of mankind. With respect to luxuries and comforts, the wisest have ever lived a more simple and meager life than the poor. The ancient philosophers, Chinese, Hindoo, Persian, and Greek, were a class than which none has been poorer in outward riches, none so rich in inward. We know not much about them. It is remarkable that *we* know so much of them as we do. The same is true of the more modern reformers and benefactors of their race. None can be an impartial or wise observer of human life but from the vantage ground of what *we* should call voluntary poverty. Of a life of luxury the fruit is luxury, whether in agriculture, or commerce, or literature, or art. There are nowadays professors of philosophy, but not philosophers. Yet it is admirable to profess because it was once admirable to live. To be a philosopher is not merely to have subtle thoughts, nor even to found a school, but so to love wisdom as to live according to its dictates, a life of simplicity, independence, magnanimity, and trust. It is to solve some of the problems of life, not only theoretically, but practically. The success of great scholars and thinkers is commonly a courtier-like success, not kingly, not manly. They make shift to live merely by conformity,

2. In Greek mythology, Elysium is the home of the blessed after death.

3. According to the latest fashion (French).

practically as their fathers did, and are in no sense the progenitors of a nobler race of men. But why do men degenerate ever? What makes families run out? What is the nature of the luxury which enervates and destroys nations? Are we sure that there is none of it in our own lives? The philosopher is in advance of his age even in the outward form of his life. He is not fed, sheltered, clothed, warmed, like his contemporaries. How can a man be a philosopher and not maintain his vital heat by better methods than other men?

When a man is warmed by the several modes which I have described, what does he want next? Surely not more warmth of the same kind, as more and richer food, larger and more splendid houses, finer and more abundant clothing, more numerous incessant and hotter fires, and the like. When he has obtained those things which are necessary to life, there is another alternative than to obtain the superfluities; and that is, to adventure on life now, his vacation from humbler toil having commenced. The soil, it appears, is suited to the seed, for it has sent its radicle downward, and it may now send its shoot upward also with confidence. Why has man rooted himself thus firmly in the earth, but that he may rise in the same proportion into the heavens above?—for the nobler plants are valued for the fruit they bear at last in the air and light, far from the ground, and are not treated like the humbler esculents,[4] which, though they may be biennials, are cultivated only till they have perfected their root, and often cut down at top for this purpose, so that most would not know them in their flowering season.

I do not mean to prescribe rules to strong and valiant natures, who will mind their own affairs whether in heaven or hell, and perchance build more magnificently and spend more lavishly than the richest, without ever impoverishing themselves, not knowing how they live,—if, indeed, there are any such, as has been dreamed; nor to those who find their encouragement and inspiration in precisely the present condition of things, and cherish it with the fondness and enthusiasm of lovers,—and, to some extent, I reckon myself in this number; I do not speak to those who are well employed, in whatever circumstances, and they know whether they are well employed or not;—but mainly to the mass of men who are discontented, and idly complaining of the hardness of their lot or of the times, when they might improve them. There are some who complain most energetically and inconsolably of any, because they are, as they say, doing their duty. I also have in my mind that seemingly wealthy, but most terribly impoverished class of all, who have accumulated dross, but know not how to use it, or get rid of it, and thus have forged their own golden or silver fetters.

If I should attempt to tell how I have desired to spend my life in years past, it would probably surprise those of my readers who are somewhat acquainted with its actual history; it would certainly astonish those who know nothing about it. I will only hint at some of the enterprises which I have cherished.

In any weather, at any hour of the day or night, I have been anxious to improve the nick of time, and notch it on my stick too;[5] to stand on the meeting of two eternities, the past and future, which is precisely the present moment; to toe that line. You will pardon some obscurities, for there are more secrets in my trade than in most men's, and yet not voluntarily kept,

4. Edibles.
5. Allusion to Daniel Defoe's *Robinson Crusoe*

(1719), a novel Thoreau much admired. Crusoe kept track of time by cutting notches on wood.

but inseparable from its very nature. I would gladly tell all that I know about it, and never paint "No Admittance" on my gate.

I long ago lost a hound, a bay horse, and a turtle-dove,[6] and am still on their trail. Many are the travellers I have spoken concerning them, describing their tracks and what calls they answered to. I have met one or two who had heard the hound, and the tramp of the horse, and even seen the dove disappear behind a cloud, and they seemed as anxious to recover them as if they had lost them themselves.

To anticipate, not the sunrise and the dawn merely, but, if possible, Nature herself! How many mornings, summer and winter, before yet any neighbor was stirring about his business, have I been about mine! No doubt, many of my townsmen have met me returning from this enterprise, farmers starting for Boston in the twilight, or woodchoppers going to their work. It is true, I never assisted the sun materially in his rising, but, doubt not, it was of the last importance only to be present at it.

So many autumn, ay, and winter days, spent outside the town, trying to hear what was in the wind, to hear and carry it express! I well-nigh sunk all my capital in it, and lost my own breath into the bargain, running in the face of it. If it had concerned either of the political parties, depend upon it, it would have appeared in the Gazette with the earliest intelligence.[7] At other times watching from the observatory of some cliff or tree, to telegraph any new arrival; or waiting at evening on the hill-tops for the sky to fall, that I might catch something, though I never caught much, and that, manna-wise,[8] would dissolve again in the sun.

For a long time I was reporter to a journal, of no very wide circulation, whose editor has never yet seen fit to print the bulk of my contributions, and, as is too common with writers, I got only my labor for my pains.[9] However, in this case my pains were their own reward.

For many years I was self-appointed inspector of snow storms and rain storms, and did my duty faithfully; surveyor, if not of highways, then of forest paths and all across-lot routes, keeping them open, and ravines bridged and passable at all seasons, where the public heel had testified to their utility.

I have looked after the wild stock of the town, which give a faithful herdsman a good deal of trouble by leaping fences; and I have had an eye to the unfrequented nooks and corners of the farm; though I did not always know whether Jonas or Solomon worked in a particular field to-day; that was none of my business. I have watered the red huckleberry, the sand cherry and the nettle tree, the red pine and the black ash, the white grape and the yellow violet, which might have withered else in dry seasons.

In short, I went on thus for a long time, I may say it without boasting, faithfully minding my business, till it became more and more evident that my townsmen would not after all admit me into the list of town officers, nor make my place a sinecure with a moderate allowance. My accounts, which

6. Symbols of elusive ideas, or ideals, whose exact meanings have not been determined.
7. News. "Gazette": newspaper.
8. In Exodus 16, manna is the bread that God rained from heaven so the Israelites could survive in the desert on their way from Egypt to the Promised Land.
9. Thoreau puns on the common usage of *journal* to mean a daily newspaper as well as a diary. Thoreau himself is the negligent or too demanding editor.

I can swear to have kept faithfully, I have, indeed, never got audited, still less accepted, still less paid and settled. However, I have not set my heart on that.

Not long since, a strolling Indian went to sell baskets at the house of a well-known lawyer in my neighborhood. "Do you wish to buy any baskets?" he asked. "No, we do not want any," was the reply. "What!" exclaimed the Indian as he went out the gate, "do you mean to starve us?" Having seen his industrious white neighbors so well off,—that the lawyer had only to weave arguments, and by some magic wealth and standing followed, he had said to himself; I will go into business; I will weave baskets; it is a thing which I can do. Thinking that when he had made the baskets he would have done his part, and then it would be the white man's to buy them. He had not discovered that it was necessary for him to make it worth the other's while to buy them, or at least make him think that it was so, or to make something else which it would be worth his while to buy. I too had woven a kind of basket of a delicate texture, but I had not made it worth any one's while to buy them.[1] Yet not the less, in my case, did I think it worth my while to weave them, and instead of studying how to make it worth men's while to buy my baskets, I studied rather how to avoid the necessity of selling them. The life which men praise and regard as successful is but one kind. Why should we exaggerate any one kind at the expense of the others?

Finding that my fellow-citizens were not likely to offer me any room in the court house, or any curacy or living[2] any where else, but I must shift for myself, I turned my face more exclusively than ever to the woods, where I was better known. I determined to go into business at once, and not wait to acquire the usual capital, using such slender means as I had already got. My purpose in going to Walden Pond was not to live cheaply nor to live dearly there, but to transact some private business with the fewest obstacles; to be hindered from accomplishing which for want of a little common sense, a little enterprise and business talent, appeared not so sad as foolish.

I have always endeavored to acquire strict business habits; they are indispensable to every man. If your trade is with the Celestial Empire,[3] then some small counting house on the coast, in some Salem harbor, will be fixture enough. You will export such articles as the country affords, purely native products, much ice and pine timber and a little granite, always in native bottoms. These will be good ventures. To oversee all the details yourself in person; to be at once pilot and captain, and owner and underwriter; to buy and sell and keep the accounts; to read every letter received, and write or read every letter sent; to superintend the discharge of imports night and day; to be upon many parts of the coast almost at the same time;—often the richest freight will be discharged upon a Jersey shore,[4]—to be your own telegraph, unweariedly sweeping the horizon, speaking all passing vessels bound coastwise; to keep up a steady despatch of commodities, for the supply of such a distant and exorbitant market; to keep yourself informed of the state of the markets, prospects of war and peace every where, and anticipate the tendencies of trade and civilization,—taking advantage of the results of all exploring expeditions, using

1. A reference to Thoreau's poorly selling first book, *A Week on the Concord and Merrimack Rivers* (1849).
2. A church office with a fixed, steady income.
3. China, from the belief that the Chinese emperors were sons of heaven.
4. I.e., by shipwreck on the way to New York.

new passages and all improvements in navigation;—charts to be studied, the position of reefs and new lights and buoys to be ascertained, and ever, and ever, the logarithmic tables to be corrected, for by the error of some calculator the vessel often splits upon a rock that should have reached a friendly pier,—there is the untold fate of La Perouse;—universal science to be kept pace with, studying the lives of all great discoverers and navigators, great adventurers and merchants from Hanno[5] and the Phœnicians down to our day; in fine, account of stock to be taken from time to time, to know how you stand. It is a labor to task the faculties of a man,—such problems of profit and loss, of interest, of tare and tret,[6] and gauging of all kinds in it, as demand a universal knowledge.

I have thought that Walden Pond would be a good place for business, not solely on account of the railroad and the ice trade; it offers advantages which it may not be good policy to divulge; it is a good port and a good foundation. No Neva[7] marshes to be filled; though you must every where build on piles of your own driving. It is said that a flood-tide, with a westerly wind, and ice in the Neva, would sweep St. Petersburg from the face of the earth.

As this business was to be entered into without the usual capital, it may not be easy to conjecture where those means, that will still be indispensable to every such undertaking, were to be obtained. As for Clothing, to come at once to the practical part of the question, perhaps we are led oftener by the love of novelty, and a regard for the opinions of men, in procuring it, than by a true utility. Let him who has work to do recollect that the object of clothing is, first, to retain the vital heat, and secondly, in this state of society, to cover nakedness, and he may judge how much of any necessary or important work may be accomplished without adding to his wardrobe. Kings and queens who wear a suit but once, though made by some tailor or dress-maker to their majesties, cannot know the comfort of wearing a suit that fits. They are no better than wooden horses to hang the clean clothes on. Every day our garments become more assimilated to ourselves, receiving the impress of the wearer's character, until we hesitate to lay them aside, without such delay and medical appliances and some such solemnity even as our bodies. No man ever stood the lower in my estimation for having a patch in his clothes; yet I am sure that there is greater anxiety, commonly, to have fashionable, or at least clean and unpatched clothes, than to have a sound conscience. But even if the rent is not mended, perhaps the worst vice betrayed is improvidence. I sometimes try my acquaintances by such tests as this;—who could wear a patch, or two extra seams only, over the knee? Most behave as if they believed that their prospects for life would be ruined if they should do it. It would be easier for them to hobble to town with a broken leg than with a broken pantaloon. Often if an accident happens to a gentleman's legs, they can be mended; but if a similar accident happens to the legs of his pantaloons, there is no help for it; for he considers, not what is truly respectable, but what is respected. We know but few men,

---

5. Carthaginian navigator (6th–5th centuries B.C.E.), credited with opening the coast of west Africa to trade. Jean François de Galaup, comte de la Pérouse (1741–1788), French explorer of the western Pacific.

6. Terms from shipping: "tare" is the deduction to the purchaser for the weight of the container; "tret" is the deduction for any damages.

7. A river in Russia.

a great many coats and breeches. Dress a scarecrow in your last shift, you standing shiftless by, who would not soonest salute the scarecrow? Passing a cornfield the other day, close by a hat and coat on a stake, I recognized the owner of the farm. He was only a little more weather-beaten than when I saw him last. I have heard of a dog that barked at every stranger who approached his master's premises with clothes on, but was easily quieted by a naked thief. It is an interesting question how far men would retain their relative rank if they were divested of their clothes. Could you, in such a case, tell surely of any company of civilized men, which belonged to the most respected class? When Madam Pfeiffer, in her adventurous travels round the world, from east to west, had got so near home as Asiatic Russia, she says that she felt the necessity of wearing other than a travelling dress, when she went to meet the authorities, for she "was now in a civilized country, where ———— people are judged of by their clothes."[8] Even in our democratic New England towns the accidental possession of wealth, and its manifestation in dress and equipage alone, obtain for the possessor almost universal respect. But they who yield such respect, numerous as they are, are so far heathen, and need to have a missionary sent to them. Beside, clothes introduced sewing, a kind of work which you may call endless; a woman's dress, at least, is never done.

A man who has at length found something to do will not need to get a new suit to do it in; for him the old will do, that has lain dusty in the garret for an indeterminate period. Old shoes will serve a hero longer than they have served his valet,—if a hero ever has a valet,—bare feet are older than shoes, and he can make them do. Only they who go to soirées and legislative halls must have new coats, coats to change as often as the man changes in them. But if my jacket and trousers, my hat and shoes, are fit to worship God in, they will do; will they not? Who ever saw his old clothes,—his old coat, actually worn out, resolved into its primitive elements, so that it was not a deed of charity to bestow it on some poor boy, by him perchance to be bestowed on some poorer still, or shall we say richer, who could do with less? I say, beware of all enterprises that require new clothes, and not rather a new wearer of clothes. If there is not a new man, how can the new clothes be made to fit? If you have any enterprise before you, try it in your old clothes. All men want, not something to *do with*, but something to *do*, or rather something to *be*. Perhaps we should never procure a new suit, however ragged or dirty the old, until we have so conducted, so enterprised or sailed in some way, that we feel like new men in the old, and that to retain it would be like keeping new wine in old bottles.[9] Our moulting season, like that of the fowls, must be a crisis in our lives. The loon retires to solitary ponds to spend it. Thus also the snake casts its slough, and the caterpillar its wormy coat, by an internal industry and expansion; for clothes are but our outmost cuticle and mortal coil. Otherwise we shall be found sailing under false colors, and be inevitably cashiered[1] at last by our own opinion, as well as that of mankind.

We don garment after garment, as if we grew like exogenous plants by addition without. Our outside and often thin and fanciful clothes are our

---

8. Ida Pfeiffer (1797–1858), *A Lady's Voyage round the World* (1852).
9. "Neither do men put new wine into old bottles: else the bottles break, and the wine runneth out, and the bottles perish: but they put new wine into new bottles, and both are preserved" (Matthew 9.17).
1. Fired.

epidermis or false skin, which partakes not of our life, and may be stripped off here and there without fatal injury; our thicker garments, constantly worn, are our cellular integument, or cortex; but our shirts are our liber[2] or true bark, which cannot be removed without girdling and so destroying the man. I believe that all races at some seasons wear something equivalent to the shirt. It is desirable that a man be clad so simply that he can lay his hands on himself in the dark, and that he live in all respects so compactly and pre-paredly, that, if an enemy take the town, he can, like the old philosopher, walk out the gate empty-handed without anxiety. While one thick garment is, for most purposes, as good as three thin ones, and cheap clothing can be obtained at prices really to suit customers; while a thick coat can be bought for five dollars, which will last as many years, thick pantaloons for two dol-lars, cowhide boots for a dollar and a half a pair, a summer hat for a quarter of a dollar, and a winter cap for sixty-two and a half cents, or a better be made at home at a nominal cost, where is he so poor that, clad in such a suit, *of his own earning,* there will not be found wise men to do him reverence?

When I ask for a garment of a particular form, my tailoress tells me gravely, "They do not make them so now," not emphasizing the "They" at all, as if she quoted an authority as impersonal as the Fates, and I find it difficult to get made what I want, simply because she cannot believe that I mean what I say, that I am so rash. When I hear this oracular sentence, I am for a moment absorbed in thought, emphasizing to myself each word separately that I may come at the meaning of it, that I may find out by what degree of consanguinity *They* are related to *me,* and what authority they may have in an affair which affects me so nearly; and, finally, I am inclined to answer her with equal mys-tery, and without any more emphasis of the "they,"—"It is true, they did not make them so recently, but they do now." Of what use this measuring of me if she does not measure my character, but only the breadth of my shoulders, as it were a peg to hang the coat on? We worship not the Graces, nor the Parcæ,[3] but Fashion. She spins and weaves and cuts with full authority. The head monkey at Paris puts on a traveller's cap, and all the monkeys in Amer-ica do the same. I sometimes despair of getting any thing quite simple and honest done in this world by the help of men. They would have to be passed through a powerful press first, to squeeze their old notions out of them, so that they would not soon get upon their legs again, and then there would be some one in the company with a maggot in his head, hatched from an egg deposited there nobody knows when, for not even fire kills these things, and you would have lost your labor. Nevertheless, we will not forget that some Egyptian wheat is said to have been handed down to us by a mummy.[4]

On the whole, I think that it cannot be maintained that dressing has in this or any country risen to the dignity of an art. At present men make shift to wear what they can get. Like shipwrecked sailors, they put on what they can find on the beach, and at a little distance, whether of space or time, laugh at each other's masquerade. Every generation laughs at the old fashions, but fol-lows religiously the new. We are amused at beholding the costume of Henry VIII, or Queen Elizabeth, as much as if it was that of the King and Queen of

2. Inner bark. "Integument, or cortex": an envel-oping inner layer.
3. In Roman mythology, the three Fates.

4. Thoreau refers to the popular notion that wheat could be grown from the seeds found in Egyptian tombs.

the Cannibal Islands. All costume off a man is pitiful or grotesque. It is only the serious eye peering from and the sincere life passed within it, which restrain laughter and consecrate the costume of any people. Let Harlequin[5] be taken with a fit of the colic and his trappings will have to serve that mood too. When the soldier is hit by a cannon ball rags are as becoming as purple.

The childish and savage taste of men and women for new patterns keeps how many shaking and squinting through kaleidoscopes that they may discover the particular figure which this generation requires to-day. The manufacturers have learned that this taste is merely whimsical. Of two patterns which differ only by a few threads more or less of a particular color, the one will be sold readily, the other lie on the shelf, though it frequently happens that after the lapse of a season the latter becomes the most fashionable. Comparatively, tattooing is not the hideous custom which it is called. It is not barbarous merely because the printing is skin-deep and unalterable.

I cannot believe that our factory system is the best mode by which men may get clothing. The condition of the operatives is becoming every day more like that of the English; and it cannot be wondered at, since, as far as I have heard or observed, the principal object is, not that mankind may be well and honestly clad, but, unquestionably, that the corporations may be enriched. In the long run men hit only what they aim at. Therefore, though they should fail immediately, they had better aim at something high.

As for a Shelter, I will not deny that this is now a necessary of life, though there are instances of men having done without it for long periods in colder countries than this. Samuel Laing says that "The Laplander in his skin dress, and in a skin bag which he puts over his head and shoulders, will sleep night after night on the snow—in a degree of cold which would extinguish the life of one exposed to it in any woollen clothing." He had seen them asleep thus. Yet he adds, "They are not hardier than other people."[6] But, probably, man did not live long on the earth without discovering the convenience which there is in a house, the domestic comforts, which phrase may have originally signified the satisfactions of the house more than of the family; though these must be extremely partial and occasional in those climates where the house is associated in our thoughts with winter or the rainy season chiefly, and two thirds of the year, except for a parasol, is unnecessary. In our climate, in the summer, it was formerly almost solely a covering at night. In the Indian gazettes a wigwam was the symbol of a day's march, and a row of them cut or painted on the bark of a tree signified that so many times they had camped. Man was not made so large limbed and robust but that he must seek to narrow his world, and wall in a space such as fitted him. He was at first bare and out of doors; but though this was pleasant enough in serene and warm weather, by daylight, the rainy season and the winter, to say nothing of the torrid sun, would perhaps have nipped his race in the bud if he had not made haste to clothe himself with the shelter of a house. Adam and Eve, according to a fable, wore the bower before other clothes. Man wanted a home, a place of warmth, or comfort, first of physical warmth, then the warmth of the affections.

---

5. Comic servant in the Italian *commedia dell'arte*, typically dressed in a mask and many-colored tights.

6. *Journal of a Residence in Norway* (1837), by the English writer Samuel Laing (1780–1868).

We may imagine a time when, in the infancy of the human race, some enterprising mortal crept into a hollow in a rock for shelter. Every child begins the world again, to some extent, and loves to stay out doors, even in wet and cold. It plays house, as well as horse, having an instinct for it. Who does not remember the interest with which when young he looked at shelving rocks, or any approach to a cave? It was the natural yearning of that portion of our most primitive ancestor which still survived in us. From the cave we have advanced to roofs of palm leaves, of bark and boughs, of linen woven and stretched, of grass and straw, of boards and shingles, of stones and tiles. At last, we know not what it is to live in the open air, and our lives are domestic in more senses than we think. From the hearth to the field is a great distance. It would be well perhaps if we were to spend more of our days and nights without any obstruction between us and the celestial bodies, if the poet did not speak so much from under a roof, or the saint dwell there so long. Birds do not sing in caves, nor do doves cherish their innocence in dovecots.

However, if one designs to construct a dwelling house, it behooves him to exercise a little Yankee shrewdness, lest after all he find himself in a work-house, a labyrinth without a clew, a museum, an almshouse, a prison, or a splendid mausoleum instead. Consider first how slight a shelter is absolutely necessary. I have seen Penobscot Indians,[7] in this town, living in tents of thin cotton cloth, while the snow was nearly a foot deep around them, and I thought that they would be glad to have it deeper to keep out the wind. Formerly, when how to get my living honestly, with freedom left for my proper pursuits, was a question which vexed me even more than it does now, for unfortunately I am become somewhat callous, I used to see a large box by the railroad, six feet long by three wide, in which the laborers locked up their tools at night, and it suggested to me that every man who was hard pushed might get such a one for a dollar, and, having bored a few auger holes in it, to admit the air at least, get into it when it rained and at night, and hook down the lid, and so have freedom in his love, and in his soul be free. This did not appear the worst, nor by any means a despicable alternative. You could sit up as late as you pleased, and, whenever you got up, go abroad without any landlord or house-lord dogging you for rent. Many a man is harassed to death to pay the rent of a larger and more luxurious box who would not have frozen to death in such a box as this. I am far from jesting. Economy is a subject which admits of being treated with levity, but it cannot so be disposed of. A comfortable house for a rude and hardy race, that lived mostly out of doors, was once made here almost entirely of such materials as Nature furnished ready to their hands. Gookin, who was superintendent of the Indians subject to the Massachusetts Colony, writing in 1674, says, "The best of their houses are covered very neatly, tight and warm, with barks of trees, slipped from their bodies at those seasons when the sap is up, and made into great flakes, with pressure of weighty timber, when they are green. . . . The meaner sort are covered with mats which they make of a kind of bulrush, and are also indifferently tight and warm, but not so good as the former. . . . Some I have seen, sixty or a hundred feet long and thirty feet broad. . . . I have often lodged in their wigwams, and found them as warm as the best

7. An Algonquin tribe from what is now Maine.

English houses."[8] He adds, that they were commonly carpeted and lined within with well-wrought embroidered mats, and were furnished with various utensils. The Indians had advanced so far as to regulate the effect of the wind by a mat suspended over the hole in the roof and moved by a string. Such a lodge was in the first instance constructed in a day or two at most, and taken down and put up in a few hours; and every family owned one, or its apartment in one.

In the savage state every family owns a shelter as good as the best, and sufficient for its coarser and simpler wants; but I think that I speak within bounds when I say that, though the birds of the air have their nests, and the foxes their holes,[9] and the savages their wigwams, in modern civilized society not more than one half the families own a shelter. In the large towns and cities, where civilization especially prevails, the number of those who own a shelter is a very small fraction of the whole. The rest pay an annual tax for this outside garment of all, become indispensable summer and winter, which would buy a village of Indian wigwams, but now helps to keep them poor as long as they live. I do not mean to insist here on the disadvantage of hiring compared with owning, but it is evident that the savage owns his shelter because it costs so little, while the civilized man hires his commonly because he cannot afford to own it; nor can he, in the long run, any better afford to hire. But, answers one, by merely paying this tax the poor civilized man secures an abode which is a palace compared with the savage's. An annual rent of from twenty-five to a hundred dollars, these are the country rates, entitles him to the benefit of the improvements of centuries, spacious apartments, clean paint and paper, Rumford fireplace,[1] back plastering, Venetian blinds, copper pump, spring lock, a commodious cellar, and many other things. But how happens it that he who is said to enjoy these things is so commonly a *poor* civilized man, while the savage, who has them not, is rich as a savage? If it is asserted that civilization is a real advance in the condition of man,—and I think that it is, though only the wise improve their advantages,—it must be shown that it has produced better dwellings without making them more costly; and the cost of a thing is the amount of what I will call life which is required to be exchanged for it, immediately or in the long run. An average house in this neighborhood costs perhaps eight hundred dollars, and to lay up this sum will take from ten to fifteen years of the laborer's life, even if he is not encumbered with a family;—estimating the pecuniary value of every man's labor at one dollar a day, for if some receive more, others receive less;—so that he must have spent more than half his life commonly before *his* wigwam will be earned. If we suppose him to pay a rent instead, this is but a doubtful choice of evils. Would the savage have been wise to exchange his wigwam for a palace on these terms?

It may be guessed that I reduce almost the whole advantage of holding this superfluous property as a fund in store against the future, so far as the individual is concerned, mainly to the defraying of funeral expenses. But perhaps a man is not required to bury himself. Nevertheless this points to an important distinction between the civilized man and the savage; and, no

8. Daniel Gookin (1612–1687), *Historical Collections of the Indians in New England* (completed in 1674; first published in 1792).
9. "The foxes have holes, and the birds of the air have nests; but the Son of man hath not where to lay his head" (Matthew 8.20).
1. Benjamin Thompson, Count Rumford (1753–1814), devised a shelf inside the chimney to prevent smoke from being carried back into a room by downdrafts.

doubt, they have designs on us for our benefit, in making the life of a civilized people an *institution*, in which the life of the individual is to a great extent absorbed, in order to preserve and perfect that of the race. But I wish to show at what a sacrifice this advantage is at present obtained, and to suggest that we may possibly so live as to secure all the advantage without suffering any of the disadvantage. What mean ye by saying that the poor ye have always with you, or that the fathers have eaten sour grapes, and the children's teeth are set on edge?[2]

"As I live, saith the Lord God, ye shall not have occasion any more to use this proverb in Israel."

"Behold all souls are mine; as the soul of the father, so also the soul of the son is mine: the soul that sinneth it shall die."[3]

When I consider my neighbors, the farmers of Concord, who are at least as well off as the other classes, I find that for the most part they have been toiling twenty, thirty, or forty years, that they may become the real owners of their farms, which commonly they have inherited with encumbrances, or else bought with hired money,—and we may regard one third of that toil as the cost of their houses,—but commonly they have not paid for them yet. It is true, the encumbrances sometimes outweigh the value of the farm, so that the farm itself becomes one great encumbrance, and still a man is found to inherit it, being well acquainted with it, as he says. On applying to the assessors, I am surprised to learn that they cannot at once name a dozen in the town who own their farms free and clear. If you would know the history of these homesteads, inquire at the bank where they are mortgaged. The man who has actually paid for his farm with labor on it is so rare that every neighbor can point to him. I doubt if there are three such men in Concord. What has been said of the merchants, that a very large majority, even ninety-seven in a hundred, are sure to fail, is equally true of the farmers. With regard to the merchants, however, one of them says pertinently that a great part of their failures are not genuine pecuniary failures, but merely failures to fulfil their engagements, because it is inconvenient; that is, it is the moral character that breaks down. But this puts an infinitely worse face on the matter, and suggests, beside, that probably not even the other three succeed in saving their souls, but are perchance bankrupt in a worse sense than they who fail honestly. Bankruptcy and repudiation are the spring-boards from which much of our civilization vaults and turns its somersets,[4] but the savage stands on the unelastic plank of famine. Yet the Middlesex Cattle Show goes off here with *éclat* annually, as if all the joints of the agricultural machine were suent.[5]

The farmer is endeavoring to solve the problem of a livelihood by a formula more complicated than the problem itself. To get his shoestrings he speculates in herds of cattle. With consummate skill he has set his trap with a hair spring to catch comfort and independence, and then, as he turned away, got

2. Thoreau draws on Jesus's words to his disciples: "For ye have the poor always with you; but me ye have not always" (Matthew 26.11) and God's reproof to Ezekiel for employing a self-defeating proverb: "What mean ye, that ye use this proverb concerning the land of Israel, saying, The fathers have eaten sour grapes, and the children's teeth

are set on edge?" (Ezekiel 18.2).
3. Ezekiel 18.3–4, which Thoreau abridges to convey his rejection of the idea that the sins of the fathers must be visited on their children.
4. Somersaults.
5. In good working order; broken in. "*Éclat*": brilliance (French).

his own leg into it. This is the reason he is poor; and for a similar reason we are all poor in respect to a thousand savage comforts, though surrounded by luxuries. As Chapman sings,—

> "The false society of men—
> —for earthly greatness
> All heavenly comforts rarefies to air."[6]

And when the farmer has got his house, he may not be the richer but the poorer for it, and it be the house that has got him. As I understand it, that was a valid objection urged by Momus against the house which Minerva[7] made, that she "had not made it movable, by which means a bad neighborhood might be avoided;" and it may still be urged, for our houses are such unwieldy property that we are often imprisoned rather than housed in them; and the bad neighborhood to be avoided is our own scurvy selves. I know one or two families, at least, in this town, who, for nearly a generation, have been wishing to sell their houses in the outskirts and move into the village, but have not been able to accomplish it, and only death will set them free.

Granted that the *majority* are able at last either to own or hire the modern house with all its improvements. While civilization has been improving our houses, it has not equally improved the men who are to inhabit them. It has created palaces, but it was not so easy to create noblemen and kings. And *if the civilized man's pursuits are no worthier than the savage's, if he is employed the greater part of his life in obtaining gross necessaries and comforts merely, why should he have a better dwelling than the former?*

But how do the poor *minority* fare? Perhaps it will be found, that just in proportion as some have been placed in outward circumstances above the savage, others have been degraded below him. The luxury of one class is counterbalanced by the indigence of another. On the one side is the palace, on the other are the almshouse and "silent poor."[8] The myriads who built the pyramids to be the tombs of the Pharaohs were fed on garlic, and it may be were not decently buried themselves. The mason who finishes the cornice of the palace returns at night perchance to a hut not so good as a wigwam. It is a mistake to suppose that, in a country where the usual evidences of civilization exist, the condition of a very large body of the inhabitants may not be as degraded as that of savages. I refer to the degraded poor, not now to the degraded rich. To know this I should not need to look farther than to the shanties which every where border our railroads, that last improvement in civilization; where I see in my daily walks human beings living in sties, and all winter with an open door, for the sake of light, without any visible, often imaginable, wood pile, and the forms of both old and young are permanently contracted by the long habit of shrinking from cold and misery, and the development of all their limbs and faculties is checked. It certainly is fair to look at that class by whose labor the works which distinguish the generation are accomplished. Such too, to a greater or less extent, is the condition of the operatives of every denomination in England, which is the great workhouse of the world. Or I could refer you to Ireland, which is marked as one

---

6. From the play *Caesar and Pompey* 5.2, by the English writer George Chapman (1559?–1634).
7. In Roman mythology, the goddess of wisdom.

Monus was the Greek god of mockery and blame.
8. Poor people who do not want to be identified as needing public charity.

of the white or enlightened spots on the map.[9] Contrast the physical condition of the Irish with that of the North American Indian, or the South Sea Islander, or any other savage race before it was degraded by contact with the civilized man. Yet I have no doubt that that people's rulers are as wise as the average of civilized rulers. Their condition only proves what squalidness may consist with civilization. I hardly need refer now to the laborers in our Southern States who produce the staple exports of this country, and are themselves a staple production of the South.[1] But to confine myself to those who are said to be in *moderate* circumstances.

Most men appear never to have considered what a house is, and are actually though needlessly poor all their lives because they think that they must have such a one as their neighbors have. As if one were to wear any sort of coat which the tailor might cut out for him, or, gradually leaving off palmleaf hat or cap of woodchuck skin, complain of hard times because he could not afford to buy him a crown! It is possible to invent a house still more convenient and luxurious than we have, which yet all would admit that man could not afford to pay for. Shall we always study to obtain more of these things, and not sometimes to be content with less? Shall the respectable citizen thus gravely teach, by precept and example, the necessity of the young man's providing a certain number of superfluous glow-shoes,[2] and umbrellas, and empty guest chambers for empty guests, before he dies? Why should not our furniture be as simple as the Arab's or the Indian's? When I think of the benefactors of the race, whom we have apotheosized as messengers from heaven, bearers of divine gifts to man, I do not see in my mind any retinue at their heels, any carload of fashionable furniture. Or what if I were to allow—would it not be a singular allowance?—that our furniture should be more complex than the Arab's, in proportion as we are morally and intellectually his superiors! At present our houses are cluttered and defiled with it, and a good housewife would sweep out the greater part into the dust hole, and not leave her morning's work undone. Morning work! By the blushes of Aurora and the music of Memnon,[3] what should be man's *morning work* in this world? I had three pieces of limestone on my desk, but I was terrified to find that they required to be dusted daily, when the furniture of my mind was all undusted still, and I threw them out the window in disgust. How, then, could I have a furnished house? I would rather sit in the open air, for no dust gathers on the grass, unless where man has broken ground.

It is the luxurious and dissipated who set the fashions which the herd so diligently follow. The traveller who stops at the best houses, so called, soon discovers this, for the publicans presume him to be a Sardanapalus,[4] and if he resigned himself to their tender mercies he would soon be completely emasculated. I think that in the railroad car we are inclined to spend more on luxury than on safety and convenience, and it threatens without attaining these to become no better than a modern drawing room, with its divans, and ottomans, and sunshades, and a hundred other oriental things, which we are taking west with us, invented for the ladies of the harem and the effeminate

9. Thoreau refers to the habit some mapmakers had of leaving unexplored terrain in a dark color; other cartographers left unexplored areas white.
1. A reference to the domestic slave trade.
2. Galoshes.

3. In Roman mythology, the goddess of the dawn and her son. Memnon is associated here with the Egyptian colossus near Thebes that was said to emit musical sounds at dawn.
4. Ruler of Assyria (9th century B.C.E.).

natives of the Celestial Empire, which Jonathan[5] should be ashamed to know the names of. I would rather sit on a pumpkin and have it all to myself, than be crowded on a velvet cushion. I would rather ride on earth in an ox cart with a free circulation, than go to heaven in the fancy car of an excursion train and breathe a *malaria* all the way.

The very simplicity and nakedness of man's life in the primitive ages imply this advantage at least, that they left him still but a sojourner in nature. When he was refreshed with food and sleep he contemplated his journey again. He dwelt, as it were, in a tent in this world, and was either threading the valleys, or crossing the plains, or climbing the mountain tops. But lo! men have become the tools of their tools. The man who independently plucked the fruits when he was hungry is become a farmer; and he who stood under a tree for shelter, a housekeeper. We now no longer camp as for a night, but have settled down on earth and forgotten heaven. We have adopted Christianity merely as an improved method of *agri*-culture. We have built for this world a family mansion, and for the next a family tomb. The best works of art are the expression of man's struggle to free himself from this condition, but the effect of our art is merely to make this low state comfortable and that higher state to be forgotten. There is actually no place in this village for a work of *fine* art, if any had come down to us, to stand, for our lives, our houses and streets, furnish no proper pedestal for it. There is not a nail to hang a picture on, nor a shelf to receive the bust of a hero or a saint. When I consider how our houses are built and paid for, or not paid for, and their internal economy managed and sustained, I wonder that the floor does not give way under the visitor while he is admiring the gewgaws upon the mantelpiece, and let him through into the cellar, to some solid and honest though earthy foundation. I cannot but perceive that this so called rich and refined life is a thing jumped at, and I do not get on in the enjoyment of the *fine* arts which adorn it, my attention being wholly occupied with the jump; for I remember that the greatest genuine leap, due to human muscles alone, on record, is that of certain wandering Arabs, who are said to have cleared twenty-five feet on level ground. Without factitious support, man is sure to come to earth again beyond that distance. The first question which I am tempted to put to the proprietor of such great impropriety is, Who bolsters you? Are you one of the ninety-seven who fail? or of the three who succeed? Answer me these questions, and then perhaps I may look at your bawbles and find them ornamental. The cart before the horse is neither beautiful nor useful. Before we can adorn our houses with beautiful objects the walls must be stripped, and our lives must be stripped, and beautiful housekeeping and beautiful living be laid for a foundation: now, a taste for the beautiful is most cultivated out of doors, where there is no house and no housekeeper.

Old Johnson, in his "Wonder-Working Providence," speaking of the first settlers of this town, with whom he was contemporary, tells us that "they burrow themselves in the earth for their first shelter under some hillside, and, casting the soil aloft upon timber, they make a smoky fire against the earth, at the highest side." They did not "provide them houses," says he, "till the earth, by the Lord's blessing, brought forth bread to feed them," and the first year's

---

5. A name at first applied comically to New England farmers; then later (as here, or with the name "Brother Jonathan") to the inhabitants of the entire United States.

crop was so light that "they were forced to cut their bread very thin for a long season."[6] The secretary of the Province of New Netherland, writing in Dutch, in 1650, for the information of those who wished to take up land there, states more particularly, that "those in New Netherland, and especially in New England, who have no means to build farm houses at first according to their wishes, dig a square pit in the ground, cellar fashion, six or seven feet deep, as long and as broad as they think proper, case the earth inside with wood all round the wall, and line the wood with the bark of trees or something else to prevent the caving in of the earth; floor this cellar with plank, and wainscot it overhead for a ceiling, raise a roof of spars clear up, and cover the spars with bark or green sods, so that they can live dry and warm in these houses with their entire families for two, three, and four years, it being understood that partitions are run through those cellars which are adapted to the size of the family. The wealthy and principal men in New England, in the beginning of the colonies, commenced their first dwelling houses in this fashion for two reasons; firstly, in order not to waste time in building, and not to want food the next season; secondly, in order not to discourage poor laboring people whom they brought over in numbers from Fatherland. In the course of three or four years, when the country became adapted to agriculture, they built themselves handsome houses, spending on them several thousands."[7]

In this course which our ancestors took there was a show of prudence at least, as if their principle were to satisfy the more pressing wants first. But are the more pressing wants satisfied now? When I think of acquiring for myself one of our luxurious dwellings, I am deterred, for, so to speak, the country is not yet adapted to *human* culture, and we are still forced to cut our *spiritual* bread far thinner than our forefathers did their wheaten. Not that all architectural ornament is to be neglected even in the rudest periods; but let our houses first be lined with beauty, where they come in contact with our lives, like the tenement of the shellfish, and not overlaid with it. But, alas! I have been inside one or two of them, and know what they are lined with.

Though we are not so degenerate but that we might possibly live in a cave or a wigwam or wear skins to-day, it certainly is better to accept the advantages, though so dearly bought, which the invention and industry of mankind offer. In such a neighborhood as this, boards and shingles, lime and bricks, are cheaper and more easily obtained than suitable caves, or whole logs, or bark in sufficient quantities, or even well-tempered clay or flat stones. I speak understandingly on this subject, for I have made myself acquainted with it both theoretically and practically. With a little more wit we might use these materials so as to become richer than the richest now are, and make our civilization a blessing. The civilized man is a more experienced and wiser savage. But to make haste to my own experiment.

Near the end of March, 1845, I borrowed an axe and went down to the woods by Walden Pond, nearest to where I intended to build my house, and began to cut down some tall arrowy white pines, still in their youth, for timber. It is difficult to begin without borrowing, but perhaps it is the most generous course thus to permit your fellow-men to have an interest in your enterprise. The owner of the axe, as he released his hold on it, said that it was

---

6. Edward Johnson (1598–1672), *Wonder-working Providence of Sion's Saviour in New England* (1654).

7. Edmund Bailey O'Callaghan (1797–1880), *Documentary History of the State of New-York* (1851).

the apple of his eye; but I returned it sharper than I received it. It was a pleasant hillside where I worked, covered with pine woods, through which I looked out on the pond, and a small open field in the woods where pines and hickories were springing up. The ice in the pond was not yet dissolved, though there were some open spaces, and it was all dark colored and saturated with water. There were some slight flurries of snow during the days that I worked there; but for the most part when I came out on to the railroad, on my way home, its yellow sand heap stretched away gleaming in the hazy atmosphere, and the rails shone in the spring sun, and I heard the lark and pewee and other birds already come to commence another year with us. They were pleasant spring days, in which the winter of man's discontent was thawing as well as the earth, and the life that had lain torpid began to stretch itself. One day, when my axe had come off and I had cut a green hickory for a wedge, driving it with a stone, and had placed the whole to soak in a pond hole in order to swell the wood, I saw a striped snake run into the water, and he lay on the bottom, apparently without inconvenience, as long as I staid there, or more than a quarter of an hour; perhaps because he had not yet fairly come out of the torpid state. It appeared to me that for a like reason men remain in their present low and primitive condition; but if they should feel the influence of the spring of springs arousing them, they would of necessity rise to a higher and more ethereal life. I had previously seen the snakes in frosty mornings in my path with portions of their bodies still numb and inflexible, waiting for the sun to thaw them. On the 1st of April it rained and melted the ice, and in the early part of the day, which was very foggy, I heard a stray goose groping about over the pond and cackling as if lost, or like the spirit of the fog.

So I went on for some days cutting and hewing timber, and also studs and rafters, all with my narrow axe, not having many communicable or scholarlike thoughts, singing to myself,—

> Men say they know many things;
> But lo! they have taken wings,—
> The arts and sciences,
> And a thousand appliances;
> The wind that blows
> Is all that any body knows.[8]

I hewed the main timbers six inches square, most of the studs on two sides only, and the rafters and floor timbers on one side, leaving the rest of the bark on, so that they were just as straight and much stronger than sawed ones. Each stick was carefully mortised or tenoned by its stump, for I had borrowed other tools by this time. My days in the woods were not very long ones; yet I usually carried my dinner of bread and butter, and read the newspaper in which it was wrapped, at noon, sitting amid the green pine boughs which I had cut off, and to my bread was imparted some of their fragrance, for my hands were covered with a thick coat of pitch. Before I had done I was more the friend than the foe of the pine tree, though I had cut down some of them, having become better acquainted with it. Sometimes a rambler in the wood was attracted by the sound of my axe, and we chatted pleasantly over the chips which I had made.

---

8. Like other poems in *Walden* not enclosed in quotation marks, this poem is Thoreau's.

By the middle of April, for I made no haste in my work, but rather made the most of it, my house was framed and ready for the raising. I had already bought the shanty of James Collins, an Irishman who worked on the Fitchburg Railroad, for boards. James Collins' shanty was considered an uncommonly fine one. When I called to see it he was not at home. I walked about the outside, at first unobserved from within, the window was so deep and high. It was of small dimensions, with a peaked cottage roof, and not much else to be seen, the dirt being raised five feet all around as if it were a compost heap. The roof was the soundest part, though a good deal warped and made brittle by the sun. Door-sill there was none, but a perennial passage for the hens under the door board. Mrs. C. came to the door and asked me to view it from the inside. The hens were driven in by my approach. It was dark, and had a dirt floor for the most part, dank, clammy, and aguish, only here a board and there a board which would not bear removal. She lighted a lamp to show me the inside of the roof and the walls, and also that the board floor extended under the bed, warning me not to step into the cellar, a sort of dust hole two feet deep. In her own words, they were "good boards overhead, good boards all around, and a good window,"—of two whole squares originally, only the cat had passed out that way lately. There was a stove, a bed, and a place to sit, an infant in the house where it was born, a silk parasol, gilt-framed looking-glass, and a patent new coffee mill nailed to an oak sapling, all told. The bargain was soon concluded, for James had in the mean while returned. I to pay four dollars and twenty-five cents to-night, he to vacate at five to-morrow morning, selling to nobody else meanwhile: I to take possession at six. It were well, he said, to be there early, and anticipate certain indistinct but wholly unjust claims on the score of ground rent and fuel. This he assured me was the only encumbrance. At six I passed him and his family on the road. One large bundle held their all,—bed, coffee-mill, looking-glass, hens,—all but the cat, she took to the woods and became a wild cat, and, as I learned afterward, trod in a trap set for woodchucks, and so became a dead cat at last.

I took down this dwelling the same morning, drawing the nails, and removed it to the pond side by small cartloads, spreading the boards on the grass there to bleach and warp back again in the sun. One early thrush gave me a note or two as I drove along the woodland path. I was informed treacherously by a young Patrick that neighbor Seeley, an Irishman, in the intervals of the carting, transferred the still tolerable, straight, and drivable nails, staples, and spikes to his pocket, and then stood when I came back to pass the time of day, and look freshly up, unconcerned, with spring thoughts, at the devastation; there being a dearth of work, as he said. He was there to represent spectatordom, and help make this seemingly insignificant event one with the removal of the gods of Troy.[9]

I dug my cellar in the side of a hill sloping to the south, where a woodchuck had formerly dug his burrow, down through sumach and blackberry roots, and the lowest stain of vegetation, six feet square by seven deep, to a fine sand where potatoes would not freeze in any winter. The sides were left shelving, and not stoned; but the sun having never shone on them, the sand still keeps its place. It was but two hours' work. I took particular pleasure in

---

9. In Virgil's *Aeneid*, book 2, after the fall of Troy, Aeneas escapes with his father and son and his household gods.

this breaking of ground, for in almost all latitudes men dig into the earth for an equable temperature. Under the most splendid house in the city is still to be found the cellar where they store their roots as of old, and long after the superstructure has disappeared posterity remark its dent in the earth. The house is still but a sort of porch at the entrance of a burrow.

At length, in the beginning of May, with the help of some of my acquaintances, rather to improve so good an occasion for neighborliness than from any necessity, I set up the frame of my house. No man was ever more honored in the character of his raisers[1] than I. They are destined, I trust, to assist at the raising of loftier structures one day. I began to occupy my house on the 4th of July, as soon as it was boarded and roofed, for the boards were carefully feather-edged and lapped, so that it was perfectly impervious to rain; but before boarding I laid the foundation of a chimney at one end, bringing two cartloads of stones up the hill from the pond in my arms. I built the chimney after my hoeing in the fall, before a fire became necessary for warmth, doing my cooking in the mean while out of doors on the ground, early in the morning: which mode I still think is in some respects more convenient and agreeable than the usual one. When it stormed before my bread was baked, I fixed a few boards over the fire, and sat under them to watch my loaf, and passed some pleasant hours in that way. In those days, when my hands were much employed, I read but little, but the least scraps of paper which lay on the ground, my holder, or table-cloth, afforded me as much entertainment, in fact answered the same purpose as the Iliad.[2]

It would be worth the while to build still more deliberately than I did, considering, for instance, what foundation a door, a window, a cellar, a garret, have in the nature of man, and perchance never raising any superstructure until we found a better reason for it than our temporal necessities even. There is some of the same fitness in a man's building his own house that there is in a bird's building its own nest. Who knows but if men constructed their dwellings with their own hands, and provided food for themselves and families simply and honestly enough, the poetic faculty would be universally developed, as birds universally sing when they are so engaged? But alas! we do like cowbirds and cuckoos, which lay their eggs in nests which other birds have built, and cheer no traveller with their chattering and unmusical notes. Shall we forever resign the pleasure of construction to the carpenter? What does architecture amount to in the experience of the mass of men? I never in all my walks came across a man engaged in so simple and natural an occupation as building his house. We belong to the community. It is not the tailor alone who is the ninth part of a man; it is as much the preacher, and the merchant, and the farmer. Where is this division of labor to end? and what object does it finally serve? No doubt another *may* also think for me; but it is not therefore desirable that he should do so to the exclusion of my thinking for myself.

True, there are architects so called in this country, and I have heard of one at least possessed with the idea of making architectural ornaments have a core

---

1. These "raisers" included Emerson; Alcott; Ellery Channing; two young brothers who had participated in the Brook Farm reform community, Burrill and George William Curtis; and the Concord farmer Edmund Hosmer and his three sons.
2. Greek epic traditionally attributed to Homer.

of truth, a necessity, and hence a beauty, as if it were a revelation to him.[3] All very well perhaps from his point of view, but only a little better than the common dilettantism. A sentimental reformer in architecture, he began at the cornice, not at the foundation. It was only how to put a core of truth within the ornaments, that every sugar plum in fact might have an almond or caraway seed in it,—though I hold that almonds are most wholesome without the sugar,—and not how the inhabitant, the indweller, might build truly within and without, and let the ornaments take care of themselves. What reasonable man ever supposed that ornaments were something outward and in the skin merely,—that the tortoise got his spotted shell, or the shellfish its mother-o'-pearl tints, by such a contract as the inhabitants of Broadway their Trinity Church?[4] But a man has no more to do with the style of architecture of his house than a tortoise with that of its shell: nor need the soldier be so idle as to try to paint the precise *color* of his virtue on his standard. The enemy will find it out. He may turn pale when the trial comes. This man seemed to me to lean over the cornice and timidly whisper his half truth to the rude occupants who really knew it better than he. What of architectural beauty I now see, I know has gradually grown from within outward, out of the necessities and character of the indweller, who is the only builder,—out of some unconscious truthfulness, and nobleness, without ever a thought for the appearance; and whatever additional beauty of this kind is destined to be produced will be preceded by a like unconscious beauty of life. The most interesting dwellings in this country, as the painter knows, are the most unpretending, humble log huts and cottages of the poor commonly; it is the life of the inhabitants whose shells they are, and not any peculiarity in their surfaces merely, which makes them *picturesque;* and equally interesting will be the citizen's suburban box, when his life shall be as simple and as agreeable to the imagination, and there is as little straining after effect in the style of his dwelling. A great proportion of architectural ornaments are literally hollow, and a September gale would strip them off, like borrowed plumes, without injury to the substantials. They can do without *architecture* who have no olives nor wines in the cellar. What if an equal ado were made about the ornaments of style in literature, and the architects of our bibles spent as much time about their cornices as the architects of our churches do? So are made the *belles-lettres* and the *beaux-arts*[5] and their professors. Much it concerns a man, forsooth, how a few sticks are slanted over him or under him, and what colors are daubed upon his box. It would signify somewhat, if, in any earnest sense, *he* slanted them and daubed it; but the spirit having departed out of the tenant, it is of a piece with constructing his own coffin,—the architecture of the grave, and "carpenter" is but another name for "coffin-maker." One man says, in his despair or indifference to life, take up a handful of the earth at your feet, and paint your house that color. Is he thinking of his last and narrow house? Toss up a copper for it as well. What an abundance of leisure he must have! Why do you take up a handful of dirt? Better paint your house your own complexion; let it turn pale or blush for you. An enterprise to improve the style of cottage architecture! When you have got my ornaments ready I will wear them.

Before winter I built a chimney, and shingled the sides of my house, which were already impervious to rain, with imperfect and sappy shingles

---

3. The sculptor Horatio Greenough (1805–1852), who insisted on the importance of function in architectural decoration.

4. A New York City church built in a Gothic style during the 1840s.

5. Literature and fine arts (French).

made of the first slice of the log, whose edges I was obliged to straighten with a plane.

I have thus a tight shingled and plastered house, ten feet wide by fifteen long, and eight-feet posts, with a garret and a closet, a large window on each side, two trap doors, one door at the end, and a brick fireplace opposite. The exact cost of my house, paying the usual price for such materials as I used, but not counting the work, all of which was done by myself, was as follows; and I give the details because very few are able to tell exactly what their houses cost, and fewer still, if any, the separate cost of the various materials which compose them:—

Boards,	$8 03½	Mostly shanty boards
Refuse shingles for roof and sides,	4 00	
Laths,	1 25	
Two second-hand windows with glass,	2 43	
One thousand old brick,	4 00	
Two casks of lime,	2 40	That was high
Hair,	0 31	More than I needed
Mantle-tree iron,	0 15	
Nails,	3 90	
Hinges and screws,	0 14	
Latch,	0 10	
Chalk,	0 01	
Transportation,	1 40	I carried a good part on my back
In all,	$28 12½	

These are all the materials excepting the timber stones and sand, which I claimed by squatter's right. I have also a small wood-shed adjoining, made chiefly of the stuff which was left after building the house.

I intend to build me a house which will surpass any on the main street in Concord in grandeur and luxury, as soon as it pleases me as much and will cost me no more than my present one.

I thus found that the student who wishes for a shelter can obtain one for a lifetime at an expense not greater than the rent which he now pays annually. If I seem to boast more than is becoming, my excuse is that I brag for humanity rather than for myself; and my shortcomings and inconsistencies do not affect the truth of my statement. Notwithstanding much cant and hypocrisy,—chaff which I find it difficult to separate from my wheat, but for which I am as sorry as any man,—I will breathe freely and stretch myself in this respect, it is such a relief to both the moral and physical system; and I am resolved that I will not through humility become the devil's attorney. I will endeavor to speak a good word for the truth. At Cambridge College[6] the mere rent of a student's room, which is only a little larger than my own, is thirty dollars each year, though the corporation had the advantage of building thirty-two side by side and under one roof, and the occupant suffers the inconvenience of many and noisy neighbors, and perhaps a residence in the fourth story. I cannot but think that if we had more true wisdom in these

6. Harvard College.

respects, not only less education would be needed, because, forsooth, more would already have been acquired, but the pecuniary expense of getting an education would in a great measure vanish. Those conveniences which the student requires at Cambridge or elsewhere cost him or somebody else ten times as great a sacrifice of life as they would with proper management on both sides. Those things for which the most money is demanded are never the things which the student most wants. Tuition, for instance, is an important item in the term bill, while for the far more valuable education which he gets by associating with the most cultivated of his contemporaries no charge is made. The mode of founding a college is, commonly, to get up a subscription of dollars and cents, and then following blindly the principles of a division of labor to its extreme,—a principle which should never be followed but with circumspection,—to call in a contractor who makes this a subject of speculation, and he employs Irishmen or other operatives actually to lay the foundations, while the students that are to be are said to be fitting themselves for it; and for these oversights successive generations have to pay. I think that it would be *better than this*, for the students, or those who desire to be benefited by it, even to lay the foundation themselves. The student who secures his coveted leisure and retirement by systematically shirking any labor necessary to man obtains but an ignoble and unprofitable leisure, defrauding himself of the experience which alone can make leisure fruitful. "But," says one, "you do not mean that the students should go to work with their hands instead of their heads?" I do not mean that exactly, but I mean something which he might think a good deal like that; I mean that they should not *play* life, or *study* it merely, while the community supports them at this expensive game, but earnestly *live* it from beginning to end. How could youths better learn to live than by at once trying the experiment of living? Methinks this would exercise their minds as much as mathematics. If I wished a boy to know something about the arts and sciences, for instance, I would not pursue the common course, which is merely to send him into the neighborhood of some professor, where any thing is professed and practised but the art of life;—to survey the world through a telescope or a microscope, and never with his natural eye; to study chemistry, and not learn how his bread is made, or mechanics, and not learn how it is earned; to discover new satellites to Neptune, and not detect the motes in his eyes, or to what vagabond he is a satellite himself; or to be devoured by the monsters that swarm all around him, while contemplating the monsters in a drop of vinegar. Which would have advanced the most at the end of the month,—the boy who had made his own jack-knife from the ore which he had dug and smelted, reading as much as would be necessary for this,—or the boy who had attended the lectures on metallurgy at the Institute in the mean while, and had received a Rodgers penknife[7] from his father? Which would be most likely to cut his fingers?—To my astonishment I was informed on leaving college that I had studied navigation!—why, if I had taken one turn down the harbor I should have known more about it. Even the *poor* student studies and is taught only *political* economy, while that economy of living which is synonymous with philosophy is not even sincerely professed in our colleges.

---

7. High-quality knife made by the English firm Joseph Rodgers and Sons.

The consequence is, that while he is reading Adam Smith, Ricardo, and Say,[8] he runs his father in debt irretrievably.

As with our colleges, so with a hundred "modern improvements"; there is an illusion about them; there is not always a positive advance. The devil goes on exacting compound interest to the last for his early share and numerous succeeding investments in them. Our inventions are wont to be pretty toys, which distract our attention from serious things. They are but improved means to an unimproved end, an end which it was already but too easy to arrive at; as railroads lead to Boston or New York. We are in great haste to construct a magnetic telegraph from Maine to Texas; but Maine and Texas, it may be, have nothing important to communicate. Either is in such a predicament as the man who was earnest to be introduced to a distinguished deaf woman, but when he was presented, and one end of her ear trumpet was put into his hand, had nothing to say. As if the main object were to talk fast and not to talk sensibly. We are eager to tunnel under the Atlantic and bring the old world some weeks nearer to the new; but perchance the first news that will leak through into the broad, flapping American ear will be that the Princess Adelaide[9] has the whooping cough. After all, the man whose horse trots a mile in a minute does not carry the most important messages; he is not an evangelist, nor does he come round eating locusts and wild honey. I doubt if Flying Childers[1] ever carried a peck of corn to mill.

One says to me, "I wonder that you do not lay up money; you love to travel; you might take the cars and go to Fitchburg[2] to-day and see the country." But I am wiser than that. I have learned that the swiftest traveller is he that goes afoot. I say to my friend, Suppose we try who will get there first. The distance is thirty miles; the fare ninety cents. That is almost a day's wages. I remember when wages were sixty cents a day for laborers on this very road. Well, I start now on foot, and get there before night; I have travelled at that rate by the week together. You will in the mean while have earned your fare, and arrive there some time to-morrow, or possibly this evening, if you are lucky enough to get a job in season. Instead of going to Fitchburg, you will be working here the greater part of the day. And so, if the railroad reached round the world, I think that I should keep ahead of you; and as for seeing the country and getting experience of that kind, I should have to cut your acquaintance altogether.

Such is the universal law, which no man can ever outwit, and with regard to the railroad even we may say it is as broad as it is long. To make a railroad round the world available to all mankind is equivalent to grading the whole surface of the planet. Men have an indistinct notion that if they keep up this activity of joint stocks and spades long enough all will at length ride somewhere, in next to no time, and for nothing; but though a crowd rushes to the depot, and the conductor shouts "All aboard!" when the smoke is blown away and the vapor condensed, it will be perceived that a few are riding, but the rest are run over,—and it will be called, and will be, "A melancholy accident." No doubt they can ride at last who shall have earned their fare, that is, if they survive so long, but they will probably have lost their elasticity and desire to travel by that time. This spending of the best part of

---

8. Three European economists: Adam Smith (1723–1790), David Ricardo (1772–1823), and Jean Baptiste Say (1767–1832).
9. Adelaide Louisa Theresa Caroline Amelia

(1792–1849), sister of Louis-Philippe, king of France from 1830 to 1848.
1. A famous English racehorse (1714–1741).
2. Village near Concord, Massachusetts.

one's life earning money in order to enjoy a questionable liberty during the least valuable part of it, reminds me of the Englishman who went to India to make a fortune first, in order that he might return to England and live the life of a poet. He should have gone up garret at once. "What!" exclaim a million Irishmen starting up from all the shanties in the land, "is not this railroad which we have built a good thing?" Yes, I answer, *comparatively* good, that is, you might have done worse; but I wish, as you are brothers of mine, that you could have spent your time better than digging in this dirt.

Before I finished my house, wishing to earn ten or twelve dollars by some honest and agreeable method, in order to meet my unusual expenses, I planted about two acres and a half of light and sandy soil near it chiefly with beans, but also a small part with potatoes, corn, peas, and turnips. The whole lot contains eleven acres, mostly growing up to pines and hickories, and was sold the preceding season for eight dollars and eight cents an acre. One farmer said that it was "good for nothing but to raise cheeping squirrels on." I put no manure on this land, not being the owner, but merely a squatter, and not expecting to cultivate so much again, and I did not quite hoe it all once. I got out several cords of stumps in ploughing, which supplied me with fuel for a long time, and left small circles of virgin mould, easily distinguishable through the summer by the greater luxuriance of the beans there. The dead and for the most part unmerchantable wood behind my house, and the driftwood from the pond, have supplied the remainder of my fuel. I was obliged to hire a team and a man for the ploughing, though I held the plough myself. My farm outgoes for the first season were, for implements, seed, work, &c., $14 72½. The seed corn was given me. This never costs any thing to speak of, unless you plant more than enough. I got twelve bushels of beans, and eighteen bushels of potatoes, beside some peas and sweet corn. The yellow corn and turnips were too late to come to any thing. My whole income from the farm was

	$23 44.
Deducting the outgoes,	14 72½
there are left,	$ 8 71½,

beside produce consumed and on hand at the time this estimate was made of the value of $4 50,—the amount on hand much more than balancing a little grass which I did not raise. All things considered, that is, considering the importance of a man's soul and of to-day, notwithstanding the short time occupied by my experiment, nay, partly even because of its transient character, I believe that that was doing better than any farmer in Concord did that year.

The next year I did better still, for I spaded up all the land which I required, about a third of an acre, and I learned from the experience of both years, not being in the least awed by many celebrated works on husbandry, Arthur Young[3] among the rest, that if one would live simply and eat only the crop which he raised, and raise no more than he ate, and not exchange it for an insufficient quantity of more luxurious and expensive things, he would need to cultivate only a few rods of ground, and that it would be cheaper to spade

3. Author of *Rural Oeconomy, or Essays on the Practical Parts of Husbandry* (1773).

up that than to use oxen to plough it, and to select a fresh spot from time to time than to manure the old, and he could do all his necessary farm work as it were with his left hand at odd hours in the summer; and thus he would not be tied to an ox, or horse, or cow, or pig, as at present. I desire to speak impartially on this point, and as one not interested in the success or failure of the present economical and social arrangements. I was more independent than any farmer in Concord, for I was not anchored to a house or farm, but could follow the bent of my genius, which is a very crooked one, every moment. Beside being better off than they already, if my house had been burned or my crops had failed, I should have been nearly as well off as before.

I am wont to think that men are not so much the keepers of herds as herds are the keepers of men, the former are so much the freer. Men and oxen exchange work; but if we consider necessary work only, the oxen will be seen to have greatly the advantage, their farm is so much the larger. Man does some of his part of the exchange work in his six weeks of haying, and it is no boy's play. Certainly no nation that lived simply in all respects, that is, no nation of philosophers, would commit so great a blunder as to use the labor of animals. True, there never was and is not likely soon to be a nation of philosophers, nor am I certain it is desirable that there should be. However, *I* should never have broken a horse or bull and taken him to board for any work he might do for me, for fear I should become a horse-man or a herds-man merely; and if society seems to be the gainer by so doing, are we certain that what is one man's gain is not another's loss, and that the stable-boy has equal cause with his master to be satisfied? Granted that some public works would not have been constructed without this aid, and let man share the glory of such with the ox and horse; does it follow that he could not have accomplished works yet more worthy of himself in that case? When men begin to do, not merely unnecessary or artistic, but luxurious and idle work, with their assistance, it is inevitable that a few do all the exchange work with the oxen, or, in other words, become the slaves of the strongest. Man thus not only works for the animal within him, but, for a symbol of this, he works for the animal without him. Though we have many substantial houses of brick or stone, the prosperity of the farmer is still measured by the degree to which the barn overshadows the house. This town is said to have the largest houses for oxen cows and horses hereabouts, and it is not behindhand in its public buildings; but there are very few halls for free worship or free speech in this county. It should not be by their architecture, but why not even by their power of abstract thought, that nations should seek to commemorate themselves? How much more admirable the Bhagvat-Geeta[4] than all the ruins of the East! Towers and temples are the luxury of princes. A simple and independent mind does not toil at the bidding of any prince. Genius is not a retainer to any emperor, nor is its material silver, or gold, or marble, except to a trifling extent. To what end, pray, is so much stone hammered? In Arcadia,[5] when I was there, I did not see any hammering stone. Nations are possessed with an insane ambition to perpetuate the memory of themselves by the amount of hammered stone they leave. What if equal pains were taken to smooth and polish their manners? One piece of good sense would be more memorable than a monument as high as the moon. I love better to see stones in place. The grandeur of Thebes[6] was

---

4. A sacred Hindu text.
5. Place epitomizing rustic simplicity and contentment, from a region in Greece.
6. City in ancient Egypt.

a vulgar grandeur. More sensible is a rod of stone wall that bounds an honest man's field than a hundred-gated Thebes that has wandered farther from the true end of life. The religion and civilization which are barbaric and heathenish build splendid temples; but what you might call Christianity does not. Most of the stone a nation hammers goes toward its tomb only. It buries itself alive. As for the Pyramids, there is nothing to wonder at in them so much as the fact that so many men could be found degraded enough to spend their lives constructing a tomb for some ambitious booby, whom it would have been wiser and manlier to have drowned in the Nile, and then given his body to the dogs. I might possibly invent some excuse for them and him, but I have no time for it. As for the religion and love of art of the builders, it is much the same all the world over, whether the building be an Egyptian temple or the United States Bank. It costs more than it comes to. The mainspring is vanity, assisted by the love of garlic and bread and butter. Mr. Balcom, a promising young architect, designs it on the back of his Vitruvius,[7] with hard pencil and ruler, and the job is let out to Dobson & Sons, stonecutters. When the thirty centuries begin to look down on it, mankind begin to look up at it. As for your high towers and monuments, there was a crazy fellow once in this town who undertook to dig through to China, and he got so far that, as he said, he heard the Chinese pots and kettles rattle; but I think that I shall not go out of my way to admire the hole which he made. Many are concerned about the monuments of the West and the East,—to know who built them. For my part, I should like to know who in those days did not build them,—who were above such trifling. But to proceed with my statistics.

By surveying, carpentry, and day-labor of various other kinds in the village in the mean while, for I have as many trades as fingers, I had earned $13 34. The expense of food for eight months, namely, from July 4th to March 1st, the time when these estimates were made, though I lived there more than two years,—not counting potatoes, a little green corn, and some peas, which I had raised, nor considering the value of what was on hand at the last date, was

Rice,	01 73½	
Molasses,	1 73	Cheapest form of the saccharine.
Rye meal,	1 04¾	
Indian meal,	0 99¾	Cheaper than rye.
Pork,	0 22	
Flour,	0 88 }	Costs more than Indian meal, both money and trouble.
Sugar,	0 80	
Lard,	0 65	
Apples,	0 25	
Dried apple,	0 22	
Sweet potatoes,	0 10	
One pumpkin,	0 6	
One watermelon,	0 2	
Salt,	0 3	

All experiments which failed. (bracketing Sugar through Salt)

7. Vitruvius Pollio (c. 80–c. 15 B.C.E.), Roman architect during the reigns of Julius Caesar and Augustus, author of *De Architectura*.

Yes, I did eat $8 74, all told; but I should not thus unblushingly publish my guilt, if I did not know that most of my readers were equally guilty with myself, and that their deeds would look no better in print. The next year I sometimes caught a mess of fish for my dinner, and once I went so far as to slaughter a woodchuck which ravaged my bean-field,—effect his transmigration, as a Tartar[8] would say,—and devour him, partly for experiment's sake; but though it afforded me a momentary enjoyment, notwithstanding a musky flavor, I saw that the longest use would not make that a good practice, however it might seem to have your woodchucks ready dressed by the village butcher.

Clothing and some incidental expenses within the same dates, though little can be inferred from this item, amounted to

	$8 40¾
Oil and some household utensils,	$2 00

So that all the pecuniary outgoes, excepting for washing and mending, which for the most part were done out of the house, and their bills have not yet been received,—and these are all and more than all the ways by which money necessarily goes out in this part of the world,—were

House,	$28 12½
Farm one year,	14 72½
Food eight months,	8 74
Clothing, &c., eight months,	8 40¾
Oil, &c., eight months,	2 00
In all,	61 99¾

I address myself now to those of my readers who have a living to get. And to meet this I have for farm produce sold

	$23 44
Earned by day-labor,	13 34
In all,	$36 78,

which subtracted from the sum of the outgoes leaves a balance of $25 21¾ on the one side,—this being very nearly the means with which I started, and the measure of expenses to be incurred,—and on the other, beside the leisure and independence and health thus secured, a comfortable house for me as long as I choose to occupy it.

These statistics, however accidental and therefore uninstructive they may appear, as they have a certain completeness, have a certain value also. Nothing was given me of which I have not rendered some account. It appears from the above estimate, that my food alone cost me in money about twenty-seven cents[9] a week. It was, for nearly two years after this, rye and Indian meal without yeast, potatoes, rice, a very little salt pork, molasses, and salt, and my drink water. It was fit that I should live on rice, mainly, who loved so well the

8. An inhabitant of Tartary, a broad area of Central Asia, and believer in a form of reincarnation called the transmigration of souls (or metempsychosis).

9. Approximately five dollars in today's currency.

philosophy of India. To meet the objections of some inveterate cavillers, I may as well state, that if I dined out occasionally, as I always had done, and I trust shall have opportunities to do again, it was frequently to the detriment of my domestic arrangements. But the dining out, being, as I have stated, a constant element, does not in the least affect a comparative statement like this.

I learned from my two years' experience that it would cost incredibly little trouble to obtain one's necessary food, even in this latitude; that a man may use as simple a diet as the animals, and yet retain health and strength. I have made a satisfactory dinner, satisfactory on several accounts, simply off a dish of purslane[1] (*Portulaca oleracea*) which I gathered in my cornfield, boiled and salted. I give the Latin on account of the savoriness of the trivial name. And pray what more can a reasonable man desire, in peaceful times, in ordinary noons, than a sufficient number of ears of green sweetcorn boiled, with the addition of salt? Even the little variety which I used was a yielding to the demands of appetite, and not of health. Yet men have come to such a pass that they frequently starve, not for want of necessaries, but for want of luxuries; and I know a good woman who thinks that her son lost his life because he took to drinking water only.

The reader will perceive that I am treating the subject rather from an economic than a dietetic point of view, and he will not venture to put my abstemiousness to the test unless he has a well-stocked larder.

Bread I at first made of pure Indian meal and salt, genuine hoe-cakes, which I baked before my fire out of doors on a shingle or the end of a stick of timber sawed off in building my house; but it was wont to get smoked and to have a piny flavor. I tried flour also; but have at last found a mixture of rye and Indian meal most convenient and agreeable. In cold weather it was no little amusement to bake several small loaves of this in succession, tending and turning them as carefully as an Egyptian his hatching eggs.[2] They were a real cereal fruit which I ripened, and they had to my senses a fragrance like that of other noble fruits, which I kept in as long as possible by wrapping them in cloths. I made a study of the ancient and indispensable art of breadmaking, consulting such authorities as offered, going back to the primitive days and first invention of the unleavened kind, when from the wildness of nuts and meats men first reached the mildness and refinement of this diet, and travelling gradually down in my studies through that accidental souring of the dough which, it is supposed, taught the leavening process, and through the various fermentations thereafter, till I came to "good, sweet, wholesome bread," the staff of life. Leaven, which some deem the soul of bread, the *spiritus* which fills its cellular tissue, which is religiously preserved like the vestal fire,—some precious bottle-full, I suppose, first brought over in the Mayflower, did the business for America, and its influence is still rising, swelling, spreading, in cerealian billows over the land,—this seed I regularly and faithfully procured from the village, till at length one morning I forgot the rules, and scalded my yeast; by which accident I discovered that even this was not indispensable,—for my discoveries were not by the synthetic but analytic process,—and I have gladly omitted it since, though most housewives earnestly assured me that safe and wholesome bread without yeast might not be, and elderly people prophesied a speedy decay of the vital forces. Yet I find it

---

1. A type of greens.　　　　2. Egyptians had devised incubators.

not to be an essential ingredient, and after going without it for a year am still in the land of the living; and I am glad to escape the trivialness of carrying a bottle-full in my pocket, which would sometimes pop and discharge its contents to my discomfiture. It is simpler and more respectable to omit it. Man is an animal who more than any other can adapt himself to all climates and circumstances. Neither did I put any sal soda, or other acid or alkali, into my bread. It would seem that I made it according to the recipe which Marcus Porcius Cato gave about two centuries before Christ. "Panem depsticium sic facito. Manus mortariumque bene lavato. Farinam in mortarium indito, aquæ paulatim addito, subigitoque pulchre. Ubi bene subegeris, defingito, coquitoque sub testu."[3] Which I take to mean—"Make kneaded bread thus. Wash your hands and trough well. Put the meal into the trough, add water gradually, and knead it thoroughly. When you have kneaded it well, mould it, and bake it under a cover," that is, in a baking-kettle. Not a word about leaven. But I did not always use this staff of life. At one time, owing to the emptiness of my purse, I saw none of it for more than a month.

Every New Englander might easily raise all his own breadstuffs in this land of rye and Indian corn, and not depend on distant and fluctuating markets for them. Yet so far are we from simplicity and independence that, in Concord, fresh and sweet meal is rarely sold in the shops, and hominy and corn in a still coarser form are hardly used by any. For the most part the farmer gives to his cattle and hogs the grain of his own producing, and buys flour, which is at least no more wholesome, at a greater cost, at the store. I saw that I could easily raise my bushel or two of rye and Indian corn, for the former will grow on the poorest land, and the latter does not require the best, and grind them in a hand-mill, and so do without rice and pork; and if I must have some concentrated sweet, I found by experiment that I could make a very good molasses either of pumpkins or beets, and I knew that I needed only to set out a few maples to obtain it more easily still, and while these were growing I could use various substitutes beside those which I have named, "For," as the Forefathers sang,—

> "we can make liquor to sweeten our lips
> Of pumpkins and parsnips and walnut-tree chips."[4]

Finally, as for salt, that grossest of groceries, to obtain this might be a fit occasion for a visit to the seashore, or, if I did without it altogether, I should probably drink the less water. I do not learn that the Indians ever troubled themselves to go after it.

Thus I could avoid all trade and barter, so far as my food was concerned, and having a shelter already, it would only remain to get clothing and fuel. The pantaloons which I now wear were woven in a farmer's family,—thank Heaven there is so much virtue still in man; for I think the fall from the farmer to the operative as great and memorable as that from the man to the farmer;—and in a new country fuel is an encumbrance. As for a habitat, if I were not permitted still to squat, I might purchase one acre at the same price for which the land I cultivated was sold—namely, eight dollars and eight cents. But as it was, I considered that I enhanced the value of the land by squatting on it.

---

3. From *De Agricultura*, by the Roman political leader Cato (234–149 B.C.E.), who celebrated the simplicity of country life.

4. From the American historian and engraver John Warner Barber's (1798–1885) *Historical Collections of Massachusetts* (1839).

There is a certain class of unbelievers who sometimes ask me such questions as, if I think that I can live on vegetable food alone; and to strike at the root of the matter at once,—for the root is faith,—I am accustomed to answer such, that I can live on board nails. If they cannot understand that, they cannot understand much that I have to say. For my part, I am glad to hear of experiments of this kind being tried; as that a young man tried for a fortnight to live on hard raw corn on the ear, using his teeth for all mortar. The squirrel tribe tried the same and succeeded. The human race is interested in these experiments, though a few old women who are incapacitated for them, or who own their thirds in mills, may be alarmed.

My furniture, part of which I made myself, and the rest cost me nothing of which I have not rendered an account, consisted of a bed, a table, a desk, three chairs, a looking-glass three inches in diameter, a pair of tongs and andirons, a kettle, a skillet, and a frying-pan, a dipper, a wash-bowl, two knives and forks, three plates, one cup, one spoon, a jug for oil, a jug for molasses, and a japanned[5] lamp. None is so poor that he need sit on a pumpkin. That is shiftlessness. There is a plenty of such chairs as I like best in the village garrets to be had for taking them away. Furniture! Thank God, I can sit and I can stand without the aid of a furniture warehouse. What man but a philosopher would not be ashamed to see his furniture packed in a cart and going up country exposed to the light of heaven and the eyes of men, a beggarly account of empty boxes? That is Spaulding's furniture.[6] I could never tell from inspecting such a load whether it belonged to a so called rich man or a poor one; the owner always seemed poverty-stricken. Indeed, the more you have of such things the poorer you are. Each load looks as if it contained the contents of a dozen shanties; and if one shanty is poor, this is a dozen times as poor. Pray, for what do we *move* ever but to get rid of our furniture, our *exuviæ*;[7] at last to go from this world to another newly furnished, and leave this to be burned? It is the same as if all these traps were buckled to a man's belt, and he could not move over the rough country where our lines are cast without dragging them,—dragging his trap. He was a lucky fox that left his tail in the trap. The muskrat will gnaw his third leg off to be free. No wonder man has lost his elasticity. How often he is at a dead set! "Sir, if I may be so bold, what do you mean by a dead set?" If you are a seer, whenever you meet a man you will see all that he owns, ay, and much that he pretends to disown, behind him, even to his kitchen furniture and all the trumpery which he saves and will not burn, and he will appear to be harnessed to it and making what headway he can. I think that the man is at a dead set who has got through a knot hole or gateway where his sledge load of furniture cannot follow him. I cannot but feel compassion when I hear some trig, compact-looking man, seemingly free, all girded and ready, speak of his "furniture," as whether it is insured or not. "But what shall I do with my furniture?" My gay butterfly is entangled in a spider's web then. Even those who seem for a long while not to have any, if you inquire more narrowly you will find have some stored in somebody's barn. I look upon England to-day as an old gentleman who is travelling with a great deal of baggage, trumpery which has

---

5. Lacquered with decorative scenes in the Japanese manner.

6. Unidentified.
7. Discarded objects (Latin).

accumulated from long housekeeping, which he has not the courage to burn; great trunk, little trunk, bandbox and bundle. Throw away the first three at least. It would surpass the powers of a well man nowadays to take up his bed and walk, and I should certainly advise a sick one to lay down his bed and run. When I have met an immigrant tottering under a bundle which contained his all,—looking like an enormous wen which had grown out of the nape of his neck,—I have pitied him, not because that was his all, but because he had all *that* to carry. If I have got to drag my trap, I will take care that it be a light one and do not nip me in a vital part. But perchance it would be wisest never to put one's paw into it.

I would observe, by the way, that it costs me nothing for curtains, for I have no gazers to shut out but the sun and moon, and I am willing that they should look in. The moon will not sour milk nor taint meat of mine, nor will the sun injure my furniture or fade my carpet, and if he is sometimes too warm a friend, I find it still better economy to retreat behind some curtain which nature has provided, than to add a single item to the details of housekeeping. A lady once offered me a mat, but as I had no room to spare within the house, nor time to spare within or without to shake it, I declined it, preferring to wipe my feet on the sod before my door. It is best to avoid the beginnings of evil.

Not long since I was present at the auction of a deacon's effects, for his life had not been ineffectual:—

"The evil that men do lives after them."[8]

As usual, a great proportion was trumpery which had begun to accumulate in his father's day. Among the rest was a dried tapeworm. And now, after lying half a century in his garret and other dust holes, these things were not burned; instead of a *bonfire*, or purifying destruction of them, there was an *auction*, or increasing of them.[9] The neighbors eagerly collected to view them, bought them all, and carefully transported them to their garrets and dust holes, to lie there till their estates are settled, when they will start again. When a man dies he kicks the dust.

The customs of some savage nations might, perchance, be profitably imitated by us, for they at least go through the semblance of casting their slough annually; they have the idea of the thing, whether they have the reality or not. Would it not be well if we were to celebrate such a "busk," or "feast of first fruits," as Bartram[1] describes to have been the custom of the Mucclasse Indians? "When a town celebrates the busk," says he, "having previously provided themselves with new clothes, new pots, pans, and other household utensils and furniture, they collect all their worn out clothes and other despicable things, sweep and cleanse their houses, squares, and the whole town, of their filth, which with all the remaining grain and other old provisions they cast together into one common heap, and consume it with fire. After having taken medicine, and fasted for three days, all the fire in the town is extinguished. During this fast they abstain from the gratification of every appetite and passion whatever. A general amnesty is proclaimed; all malefactors may return to their town.—"

8. From Antony's speech to the citizens, in Shakespeare's *Julius Caesar* 3.2.
9. Thoreau puns on the Latin root of *auction*, which means "to increase."
1. William Bartram (1739–1832), *Travels through North and South Carolina* (1791).

"On the fourth morning, the high priest, by rubbing dry wood together, produces new fire in the public square, from whence every habitation in the town is supplied with the new and pure flame."

They then feast on the new corn and fruits and dance and sing for three days, "and the four following days they receive visits and rejoice with their friends from neighboring towns who have in like manner purified and prepared themselves."

The Mexicans also practised a similar purification at the end of every fifty-two years, in the belief that it was time for the world to come to an end.

I have scarcely heard of a truer sacrament, that is, as the dictionary defines it, "outward and visible sign of an inward and spiritual grace," than this, and I have no doubt that they were originally inspired directly from Heaven to do thus, though they have no biblical record of the revelation.

For more than five years I maintained myself thus solely by the labor of my hands, and I found, that by working about six weeks in a year, I could meet all the expenses of living. The whole of my winters, as well as most of my summers, I had free and clear for study. I have thoroughly tried school-keeping, and found that my expenses were in proportion, or rather out of proportion, to my income, for I was obliged to dress and train, not to say think and believe, accordingly, and I lost my time into the bargain. As I did not teach for the good of my fellow-men, but simply for a livelihood, this was a failure. I have tried trade; but I found that it would take ten years to get under way in that, and that then I should probably be on my way to the devil. I was actually afraid that I might by that time be doing what is called a good business. When formerly I was looking about to see what I could do for a living, some sad experience in conforming to the wishes of friends being fresh in my mind to tax my ingenuity, I thought often and seriously of picking huckleberries; that surely I could do, and its small profits might suffice,—for my greatest skill has been to want but little,—so little capital it required, so little distraction from my wonted moods, I foolishly thought. While my acquaintances went unhesitatingly into trade or the professions, I contemplated this occupation as most like theirs; ranging the hills all summer to pick the berries which came in my way, and thereafter carelessly dispose of them; so, to keep the flocks of Admetus.[2] I also dreamed that I might gather the wild herbs, or carry evergreens to such villagers as loved to be reminded of the woods, even to the city, by hay-cart loads. But I have since learned that trade curses every thing it handles; and though you trade in messages from heaven, the whole curse of trade attaches to the business.

As I preferred some things to others, and especially valued my freedom, as I could fare hard and yet succeed well, I did not wish to spend my time in earning rich carpets or other fine furniture, or delicate cookery, or a house in the Grecian or the Gothic style just yet. If there are any to whom it is no interruption to acquire these things, and who know how to use them when acquired, I relinquish to them the pursuit. Some are "industrious," and appear to love labor for its own sake, or perhaps because it keeps them out of worse mischief; to such I have at present nothing to say. Those who would not know what to do with more leisure than they now enjoy, I might

---

2. Apollo, Greek god of poetry, tended the flocks of Admetus while banished from Olympus.

advise to work twice as hard as they do,—work till they pay for themselves, and get their free papers. For myself I found that the occupation of a day-laborer was the most independent of any, especially as it required only thirty or forty days in a year to support one. The laborer's day ends with the going down of the sun, and he is then free to devote himself to his chosen pursuit, independent of his labor; but his employer, who speculates from month to month, has no respite from one end of the year to the other.

In short, I am convinced, both by faith and experience, that to maintain one's self on this earth is not a hardship but a pastime, if we will live simply and wisely; as the pursuits of the simpler nations are still the sports of the more artificial. It is not necessary that a man should earn his living by the sweat of his brow, unless he sweats easier than I do.

One young man of my acquaintance, who has inherited some acres, told me that he thought he should live as I did, *if he had the means.* I would not have any one adopt *my* mode of living on any account; for, beside that before he has fairly learned it I may have found out another for myself, I desire that there may be as many different persons in the world as possible; but I would have each one be very careful to find out and pursue *his own* way, and not his father's or his mother's or his neighbor's instead. The youth may build or plant or sail, only let him not be hindered from doing that which he tells me he would like to do. It is by a mathematical point only that we are wise, as the sailor or the fugitive slave keeps the polestar in his eye; but that is sufficient guidance for all our life. We may not arrive at our port within a calculable period, but we would preserve the true course.

Undoubtedly, in this case, what is true for one is truer still for a thousand, as a large house is not more expensive than a small one in proportion to its size, since one roof may cover, one cellar underlie, and one wall separate several apartments. But for my part, I preferred the solitary dwelling. More-over, it will commonly be cheaper to build the whole yourself than to con-vince another of the advantage of the common wall; and when you have done this, the common partition, to be much cheaper, must be a thin one, and that other may prove a bad neighbor, and also not keep his side in repair. The only coöperation which is commonly possible is exceedingly partial and superficial; and what little true coöperation there is, is as if it were not, being a harmony inaudible to men. If a man has faith he will coöperate with equal faith every where; if he has not faith, he will continue to live like the rest of the world, whatever company he is joined to. To coöperate, in the highest as well as the lowest sense, means *to get our living together.* I heard it proposed lately that two young men should travel together over the world, the one without money, earning his means as he went, before the mast and behind the plough, the other carrying a bill of exchange in his pocket. It was easy to see that they could not long be companions or coöperate, since one would not *operate* at all. They would part at the first interesting crisis in their adventures. Above all, as I have implied, the man who goes alone can start today; but he who travels with another must wait till that other is ready, and it may be a long time before they get off.

But all this is very selfish, I have heard some of my townsmen say. I confess that I have hitherto indulged very little in philanthropic enterprises. I have made some sacrifices to a sense of duty, and among others have sacrificed this pleasure also. There are those who have used all their arts to persuade me to undertake the support of some poor family in the town; and if I had nothing to do,—for the devil finds employment for the idle,—I might try my hand at some such pastime as that. However, when I have thought to indulge myself in this respect, and lay their Heaven under an obligation by maintaining certain poor persons in all respects as comfortably as I maintain myself, and have even ventured so far as to make them the offer, they have one and all unhesitatingly preferred to remain poor. While my townsmen and women are devoted in so many ways to the good of their fellows, I trust that one at least may be spared to other and less humane pursuits. You must have a genius for charity as well as for any thing else. As for Doing-good, that is one of the professions which are full. Moreover, I have tried it fairly, and, strange as it may seem, am satisfied that it does not agree with my constitution. Probably I should not consciously and deliberately forsake my particular calling to do the good which society demands of me, to save the universe from annihilation; and I believe that a like but infinitely greater steadfastness elsewhere is all that now preserves it. But I would not stand between any man and his genius; and to him who does this work, which I decline, with his whole heart and soul and life, I would say, Persevere, even if the world call it doing evil, as it is most likely they will.

I am far from supposing that my case is a peculiar one; no doubt many of my readers would make a similar defence. At doing something,—I will not engage that my neighbors shall pronounce it good,—I do not hesitate to say that I should be a capital fellow to hire; but what that is, it is for my employer to find out. What *good* I do, in the common sense of that word, must be aside from my main path, and for the most part wholly unintended. Men say, practically, Begin where you are and such as you are, without aiming mainly to become of more worth, and with kindness aforethought go about doing good. If I were to preach at all in this strain, I should say rather, Set about being good. As if the sun should stop when he had kindled his fires up to the splendor of a moon or a star of the sixth magnitude, and go about like a Robin Goodfellow,[3] peeping in at every cottage window, inspiring lunatics, and tainting meats, and making darkness visible, instead of steadily increasing his genial heat and beneficence till he is of such brightness that no mortal can look him in the face, and then, and in the mean while too, going about the world in his own orbit, doing it good, or rather, as a truer philosophy has discovered, the world going about him getting good. When Phaeton,[4] wishing to prove his heavenly birth by his beneficence, had the sun's chariot but one day, and drove out of the beaten track, he burned several blocks of houses in the lower streets of heaven, and scorched the surface of the earth, and dried up every spring, and made the great desert of Sahara, till at length Jupiter hurled him headlong to the earth with a thunderbolt, and the sun, through grief at his death, did not shine for a year.

There is no odor so bad as that which arises from goodness tainted. It is human, it is divine, carrion. If I knew for a certainty that a man was coming to my house with the conscious design of doing me good, I should run for my life, as from that dry and parching wind of the African deserts called the

---

3. Mischievous sprite, known as Puck in Shakespeare's *A Midsummer Night's Dream*.

4. In Greek mythology, the son of Helios. He attempted to drive his father's chariot, the sun.

simoom, which fills the mouth and nose and ears and eyes with dust till you are suffocated, for fear that I should get some of his good done to me,—some of its virus mingled with my blood. No,—in this case I would rather suffer evil the natural way. A man is not a good *man* to me because he will feed me if I should be starving, or warm me if I should be freezing, or pull me out of a ditch if I should ever fall into one. I can find you a Newfoundland dog that will do as much. Philanthropy is not love for one's fellow-man in the broadest sense. Howard[5] was no doubt an exceedingly kind and worthy man in his way, and has his reward; but, comparatively speaking, what are a hundred Howards to *us,* if their philanthropy do not help *us* in our best estate, when we are most worthy to be helped? I never heard of a philanthropic meeting in which it was sincerely proposed to do any good to me, or the like of me.

The Jesuits[6] were quite balked by those Indians who, being burned at the stake, suggested new modes of torture to their tormentors. Being superior to physical suffering, it sometimes chanced that they were superior to any consolation which the missionaries could offer; and the law to do as you would be done by fell with less persuasiveness on the ears of those, who, for their part, did not care how they were done by, who loved their enemies after a new fashion, and came very near freely forgiving them all they did.

Be sure that you give the poor the aid they most need, though it be your example which leaves them far behind. If you give money, spend yourself with it, and do not merely abandon it to them. We make curious mistakes sometimes. Often the poor man is not so cold and hungry as he is dirty and ragged and gross. It is partly his taste, and not merely his misfortune. If you give him money, he will perhaps buy more rags with it. I was wont to pity the clumsy Irish laborers who cut ice on the pond, in such mean and ragged clothes, while I shivered in my more tidy and somewhat more fashionable garments, till, one bitter cold day, one who had slipped into the water came to my house to warm him, and I saw him strip off three pairs of pants and two pairs of stockings ere he got down to the skin, though they were dirty and ragged enough, it is true, and that he could afford to refuse the *extra* garments which I offered him, he had so many *intra* ones. This ducking was the very thing he needed. Then I began to pity myself, and I saw that it would be a greater charity to bestow on me a flannel shirt than a whole slop-shop on him. There are a thousand hacking at the branches of evil to one who is striking at the root, and it may be that he who bestows the largest amount of time and money on the needy is doing the most by his mode of life to produce that misery which he strives in vain to relieve. It is the pious slave-breeder devoting the proceeds of every tenth slave to buy a Sunday's liberty for the rest. Some show their kindness to the poor by employing them in their kitchens. Would they not be kinder if they employed themselves there? You boast of spending a tenth part of your income in charity; may be you should spend the nine tenths so, and done with it. Society recovers only a tenth part of the property then. Is this owing to the generosity of him in whose possession it is found, or to the remissness of the officers of justice?

Philanthropy is almost the only virtue which is sufficiently appreciated by mankind. Nay, it is greatly overrated; and it is our selfishness which

---

5. John Howard (1726?–1790), English prison reformer.
6. Roman Catholic missionaries of the Society

of Jesus who attempted to convert the Indians to Christianity.

overrates it. A robust poor man, one sunny day here in Concord, praised a fellow-townsman to me, because, as he said, he was kind to the poor; meaning himself. The kind uncles and aunts of the race are more esteemed than its true spiritual fathers and mothers. I once heard a reverend lecturer on England, a man of learning and intelligence, after enumerating her scientific, literary, and political worthies, Shakspeare, Bacon, Cromwell, Milton, Newton, and others, speak next of her Christian heroes, whom, as if his profession required it of him, he elevated to a place far above all the rest, as the greatest of the great. They were Penn, Howard, and Mrs. Fry.[7] Every one must feel the falsehood and cant of this. The last were not England's best men and women; only, perhaps, her best philanthropists.

I would not subtract any thing from the praise that is due to philanthropy, but merely demand justice for all who by their lives and works are a blessing to mankind. I do not value chiefly a man's uprightness and benevolence, which are, as it were, his stem and leaves. Those plants of whose greenness withered we make herb tea for the sick, serve but a humble use, and are most employed by quacks. I want the flower and fruit of a man; that some fragrance be wafted over from him to me, and some ripeness flavor our intercourse. His goodness must not be a partial and transitory act, but a constant superfluity, which costs him nothing and of which he is unconscious. This is a charity that hides a multitude of sins. The philanthropist too often surrounds mankind with the remembrance of his own cast-off griefs as an atmosphere, and calls it sympathy. We should impart our courage, and not our despair, our health and ease, and not our disease, and take care that this does not spread by contagion. From what southern plains comes up the voice of wailing? Under what latitudes reside the heathen to whom we would send light? Who is that intemperate and brutal man whom we would redeem? If any thing ail a man, so that he does not perform his functions, if he have a pain in his bowels even,—for that is the seat of sympathy,—he forthwith sets about reforming—the world. Being a microcosm himself, he discovers, and it is a true discovery, and he is the man to make it,—that the world has been eating green apples; to his eyes, in fact, the globe itself is a great green apple, which there is danger awful to think of that the children of men will nibble before it is ripe; and straightway his drastic philanthropy seeks out the Esquimaux and the Patagonian,[8] and embraces the populous Indian and Chinese villages; and thus, by a few years of philanthropic activity, the powers in the mean while using him for their own ends, no doubt, he cures himself of his dyspepsia, the globe acquires a faint blush on one or both of its cheeks, as if it were beginning to be ripe, and life loses its crudity and is once more sweet and wholesome to live. I never dreamed of any enormity greater than I have committed. I never knew, and never shall know, a worse man than myself.

I believe that what so saddens the reformer is not his sympathy with his fellows in distress, but, though he be the holiest son of God, is his private ail. Let this be righted, let the spring come to him, the morning rise over his couch, and he will forsake his generous companions without apology. My excuse for not lecturing against the use of tobacco is, that I never chewed it;

---

7. Elizabeth Fry (1780–1845), English Quaker and prison reformer. William Penn (1644–1718), Quaker leader and proprietor of Pennsylvania.

8. Inhabitant of Patagonia, in southernmost South America.

that is a penalty which reformed tobacco-chewers have to pay; though there are things enough I have chewed, which I could lecture against. If you should ever be betrayed into any of these philanthropies, do not let your left hand know what your right hand does, for it is not worth knowing. Rescue the drowning and tie your shoe-strings. Take your time, and set about some free labor.

Our manners have been corrupted by communication with the saints. Our hymn-books resound with a melodious cursing of God and enduring him forever. One would say that even the prophets and redeemers had rather consoled the fears than confirmed the hopes of man. There is nowhere recorded a simple and irrepressible satisfaction with the gift of life, any memorable praise of God. All health and success does me good, however far off and withdrawn it may appear; all disease and failure helps to make me sad and does me evil, however much sympathy it may have with me or I with it. If, then, we would indeed restore mankind by truly Indian, botanic, magnetic, or natural means, let us first be as simple and well as Nature ourselves, dispel the clouds which hang over our own brows, and take up a little life into our pores. Do not stay to be an overseer of the poor, but endeavor to become one of the worthies of the world.

I read in the Gulistan, or Flower Garden, of Sheik Sadi of Shiraz, that "They asked a wise man, saying; Of the many celebrated trees which the Most High God has created lofty and umbrageous, they call none azad, or free, excepting the cypress, which bears no fruit; what mystery is there in this? He replied; Each has its appropriate produce, and appointed season, during the continuance of which it is fresh and blooming, and during their absence dry and withered; to neither of which states is the cypress exposed, being always flourishing; and of this nature are the azads, or religious independents.—Fix not thy heart on that which is transitory; for the Dijlah, or Tigris, will continue to flow through Bagdad after the race of caliphs is extinct: if thy hand has plenty, be liberal as the date tree; but if it affords nothing to give away, be an azad, or free man, like the cypress."[9]

Complemental Verses[1]

THE PRETENSIONS OF POVERTY

"Thou dost presume too much, poor needy wretch,
To claim a station in the firmament,
Because thy humble cottage, or thy tub,
Nurses some lazy or pedantic virtue
In the cheap sunshine or by shady springs,
With roots and pot-herbs; where thy right hand,
Tearing those humane passions from the mind,
Upon whose stocks fair blooming virtues flourish,
Degradeth nature, and benumbeth sense,
And, Gorgon-like, turns active men to stone.[2]
We not require the dull society

9. Muslih-ud-Din (Saadi) (1184?–1291), *The Gulistan or Rose Garden.*
1. From *Coelum Britannicum* by the English Cavalier poet Thomas Carew (1595?–1645?). The title is Thoreau's invention.
2. In Greek mythology the Gorgons were three sisters, with snakes for hair and eyes, who turned any beholder into stone.

Of your necessitated temperance,
Or that unnatural stupidity
That knows nor joy nor sorrow; nor your forc'd
Falsely exalted passive fortitude
Above the active. This low abject brood,
That fix their seats in mediocrity,
Become your servile minds; but we advance
Such virtues only as admit excess,
Brave, bounteous acts, regal magnificence,
All-seeing prudence, magnanimity
That knows no bound, and that heroic virtue
For which antiquity hath left no name,
But patterns only, such as Hercules,
Achilles, Theseus. Back to thy loath'd cell;
And when thou seest the new enlightened sphere,
Study to know but what those worthies were."

—T. CAREW

2. Where I Lived, and What I Lived For

At a certain season of our life we are accustomed to consider every spot as
the possible site of a house. I have thus surveyed the country on every side
within a dozen miles of where I live. In imagination I have bought all the
farms in succession, for all were to be bought and I knew their price. I
walked over each farmer's premises, tasted his wild apples, discoursed on
husbandry with him, took his farm at his price, at any price, mortgaging it to
him in my mind; even put a higher price on it,—took every thing but a deed
of it,—took his word for his deed, for I dearly love to talk,—cultivated it, and
him too to some extent, I trust, and withdrew when I had enjoyed it long
enough, leaving him to carry it on. This experience entitled me to be
regarded as a sort of real-estate broker by my friends. Wherever I sat, there I
might live, and the landscape radiated from me accordingly. What is a house
but a *sedes*, a seat?—better if a country seat. I discovered many a site for a
house not likely to be soon improved, which some might have thought too
far from the village, but to my eyes the village was too far from it. Well,
there I might live, I said; and there I did live, for an hour, a summer and a
winter life; saw how I could let the years run off, buffet the winter through,
and see the spring come in. The future inhabitants of this region, wherever
they may place their houses, may be sure that they have been anticipated.
An afternoon sufficed to lay out the land into orchard woodlot and pasture,
and to decide what fine oaks or pines should be left to stand before the door,
and whence each blasted tree could be seen to the best advantage; and then
I let it lie, fallow perchance, for a man is rich in proportion to the number of
things which he can afford to let alone.

My imagination carried me so far that I even had the refusal of several
farms,—the refusal was all I wanted,—but I never got my fingers burned by
actual possession. The nearest that I came to actual possession was when I
bought the Hollowell Place, and had begun to sort my seeds, and collected
materials with which to make a wheelbarrow to carry it on or off with; but
before the owner gave me a deed of it, his wife—every man has such a

wife—changed her mind and wished to keep it, and he offered me ten dollars to release him. Now, to speak the truth, I had but ten cents in the world, and it surpassed my arithmetic to tell, if I was that man who had ten cents, or who had a farm, or ten dollars, or all together. However, I let him keep the ten dollars and the farm too, for I had carried it far enough; or rather, to be generous, I sold him the farm for just what I gave for it, and, as he was not a rich man, made him a present of ten dollars, and still had my ten cents, and seeds, and materials for a wheelbarrow left. I found thus that I had been a rich man without any damage to my poverty. But I retained the landscape, and I have since annually carried off what it yielded without a wheelbarrow. With respect to landscapes,—

> "I am monarch of all I *survey*,
> My right there is none to dispute."[3]

I have frequently seen a poet withdraw, having enjoyed the most valuable part of a farm, while the crusty farmer supposed that he had got a few wild apples only. Why, the owner does not know it for many years when a poet has put his farm in rhyme, the most admirable kind of invisible fence, has fairly impounded it, milked it, skimmed it, and got all the cream, and left the farmer only the skimmed milk.

The real attractions of the Hollowell farm, to me, were; its complete retirement, being about two miles from the village, half a mile from the nearest neighbor, and separated from the highway by a broad field; its bounding on the river, which the owner said protected it by its fogs from frosts in the spring, though that was nothing to me; the gray color and ruinous state of the house and barn, and the dilapidated fences, which put such an interval between me and the last occupant; the hollow and lichen-covered apple trees, gnawed by rabbits, showing what kind of neighbors I should have; but above all, the recollection I had of it from my earliest voyages up the river, when the house was concealed behind a dense grove of red maples, through which I heard the house-dog bark. I was in haste to buy it, before the proprietor finished getting out some rocks, cutting down the hollow apple trees, and grubbing up some young birches which had sprung up in the pasture, or, in short, had made any more of his improvements. To enjoy these advantages I was ready to carry it on; like Atlas,[4] to take the world on my shoulders,—I never heard what compensation he received for that,—and do all those things which had no other motive or excuse but that I might pay for it and be unmolested in my possession of it; for I knew all the while that it would yield the most abundant crop of the kind I wanted if I could only afford to let it alone. But it turned out as I have said.

All that I could say, then, with respect to farming on a large scale, (I have always cultivated a garden,) was, that I had had my seeds ready. Many think that seeds improve with age. I have no doubt that time discriminates between the good and the bad; and when at last I shall plant, I shall be less likely to be disappointed. But I would say to my fellows, once for all, As long

---

3. William Cowper (1731–1800), "Verses Supposed to Be Written by Alexander Selkirk," with the pun italicized. Selkirk (1676–1721) was Daniel Defoe's model for Robinson Crusoe.

4. A Titan whom Zeus forced to stand on the earth supporting the heavens as punishment for warring against the Olympian gods.

as possible live free and uncommitted. It makes but little difference whether you are committed to a farm or the county jail.

Old Cato, whose "De Re Rusticâ" is my "Cultivator," says, and the only translation I have seen makes sheer nonsense of the passage, "When you think of getting a farm, turn it thus in your mind, not to buy greedily; nor spare your pains to look at it, and do not think it enough to go round it once. The oftener you go there the more it will please you, if it is good."[5] I think I shall not buy greedily, but go round and round it as long as I live, and be buried in it first, that it may please me the more at last.

The present was my next experiment of this kind, which I purpose to describe more at length; for convenience, putting the experience of two years into one. As I have said, I do not propose to write an ode to dejection, but to brag as lustily as chanticleer in the morning, standing on his roost, if only to wake my neighbors up.

When first I took up my abode in the woods, that is, began to spend my nights as well as days there, which, by accident, was on Independence Day, or the fourth of July, 1845, my house was not finished for winter, but was merely a defence against the rain, without plastering or chimney, the walls being of rough weather-stained boards, with wide chinks, which made it cool at night. The upright white hewn studs and freshly planed door and window casings gave it a clean and airy look, especially in the morning, when its timbers were saturated with dew, so that I fancied that by noon some sweet gum would exude from them. To my imagination it retained throughout the day more or less of this auroral character, reminding me of a certain house on a mountain which I had visited the year before. This was an airy and unplastered cabin, fit to entertain a travelling god, and where a goddess might trail her garments. The winds which passed over my dwelling were such as sweep over the ridges of mountains, bearing the broken strains, or celestial parts only, of terrestrial music. The morning wind forever blows, the poem of creation is uninterrupted; but few are the ears that hear it. Olympus[6] is but the outside of the earth every where.

The only house I had been the owner of before, if I except a boat, was a tent, which I used occasionally when making excursions in the summer, and this is still rolled up in my garret; but the boat, after passing from hand to hand, has gone down the stream of time. With this more substantial shelter about me, I had made some progress toward settling in the world. This frame, so slightly clad, was a sort of crystallization around me, and reacted on the builder. It was suggestive somewhat as a picture in outlines. I did not need to go out doors to take the air, for the atmosphere within had lost none of its freshness. It was not so much within doors as behind a door where I sat, even in the rainiest weather. The Harivansa[7] says, "An abode without birds is like a meat without seasoning." Such was not my abode, for I found myself suddenly neighbor to the birds; not by having imprisoned one, but having caged myself near them. I was not only nearer to some of those which commonly frequent the garden and the orchard, but to those wilder and more thrilling songsters of the forest which never, or rarely, serenade a villager,—the wood-thrush,

5. Cato's *De Agricultura* 1.1.
6. In Greek mythology, home of the gods.

7. A Hindu epic poem.

the veery, the scarlet tanager, the field-sparrow, the whippoorwill, and many others.

I was seated by the shore of a small pond, about a mile and a half south of the village of Concord and somewhat higher than it, in the midst of an extensive wood between that town and Lincoln, and about two miles south of that our only field known to fame, Concord Battle Ground;[8] but I was so low in the woods that the opposite shore, half a mile off, like the rest, covered with wood, was my most distant horizon. For the first week, whenever I looked out on the pond it impressed me like a tarn[9] high up on the side of a mountain, its bottom far above the surface of other lakes, and, as the sun arose, I saw it throwing off its nightly clothing of mist, and here and there, by degrees, its soft ripples or its smooth reflecting surface was revealed, while the mists, like ghosts, were stealthily withdrawing in every direction into the woods, as at the breaking up of some nocturnal conventicle. The very dew seemed to hang upon the trees later into the day than usual, as on the sides of mountains.

This small lake was of most value as a neighbor in the intervals of a gentle rain storm in August, when, both air and water being perfectly still, but the sky overcast, mid-afternoon had all the serenity of evening, and the wood-thrush sang around, and was heard from shore to shore. A lake like this is never smoother than at such a time; and the clear portion of the air above it being shallow and darkened by clouds, the water, full of light and reflections, becomes a lower heaven itself so much the more important. From a hill top near by, where the wood had been recently cut off, there was a pleasing vista southward across the pond, through a wide indentation in the hills which form the shore there, where their opposite sides sloping toward each other suggested a stream flowing out in that direction through a wooded valley, but stream there was none. That way I looked between and over the near green hills to some distant and higher ones in the horizon, tinged with blue. Indeed, by standing on tiptoe I could catch a glimpse of some of the peaks of the still bluer and more distant mountain ranges in the north-west, those true-blue coins from heaven's own mint, and also of some portion of the village. But in other directions, even from this point, I could not see over or beyond the woods which surrounded me. It is well to have some water in your neighborhood, to give buoyancy to and float the earth. One value even of the smallest well is, that when you look into it you see that earth is not continent but insular. This is as important as that it keeps butter cool. When I looked across the pond from this peak toward the Sudbury meadows, which in time of flood I distinguished elevated perhaps by a mirage in their seething valley, like a coin in a basin, all the earth beyond the pond appeared like a thin crust insulated and floated even by this small sheet of intervening water, and I was reminded that this on which I dwelt was but *dry land*.

Though the view from my door was still more contracted, I did not feel crowded or confined in the least. There was pasture enough for my imagination. The low shrub-oak plateau to which the opposite shore arose, stretched away toward the prairies of the West and the steppes of Tartary,[1] affording ample room for all the roving families of men. "There are none happy in the

8. The site of battle on the first day of the American Revolution, April 19, 1775.

9. A small lake.
1. Grasslands and plains of Asiatic Russia.

world but beings who enjoy freely a vast horizon,"—said Damodara,[2] when his herds required new and larger pastures.

Both place and time were changed, and I dwelt nearer to those parts of the universe and to those eras in history which had most attracted me. Where I lived was as far off as many a region viewed nightly by astronomers. We are wont to imagine rare and delectable places in some remote and more celestial corner of the system, behind the constellation of Cassiopeia's Chair, far from noise and disturbance. I discovered that my house actually had its site in such a withdrawn, but forever new and unprofaned, part of the universe. If it were worth the while to settle in those parts near to the Pleiades or the Hyades, to Aldebaran or Altair,[3] then I was really there, or at an equal remoteness from the life which I had left behind, dwindled and twinkling with as fine a ray to my nearest neighbor, and to be seen only in moonless nights by him. Such was that part of creation where I had squatted;—

> "There was a shepherd that did live,
>   And held his thoughts as high
> As were the mounts whereon his flocks
>   Did hourly feed him by."[4]

What should we think of the shepherd's life if his flocks always wandered to higher pastures than his thoughts?

Every morning was a cheerful invitation to make my life of equal simplicity, and I may say innocence, with Nature herself. I have been as sincere a worshipper of Aurora as the Greeks. I got up early and bathed in the pond; that was a religious exercise, and one of the best things which I did. They say that characters were engraven on the bathing tub of king Tching-thang to this effect: "Renew thyself completely each day; do it again, and again, and forever again."[5] I can understand that. Morning brings back the heroic ages. I was as much affected by the faint hum of a mosquito making its invisible and unimaginable tour through my apartment at earliest dawn, when I was sitting with door and windows open, as I could be by any trumpet that ever sang of fame. It was Homer's requiem; itself an Iliad and Odyssey in the air, singing its own wrath and wanderings. There was something cosmical about it; a standing advertisement, till forbidden,[6] of the everlasting vigor and fertility of the world. The morning, which is the most memorable season of the day, is the awakening hour. Then there is least somnolence in us; and for an hour, at least, some part of us awakes which slumbers all the rest of the day and night. Little is to be expected of that day, if it can be called a day, to which we are not awakened by our Genius,[7] but by the mechanical nudgings of some servitor, are not awakened by our own newly-acquired force and aspirations from within, accompanied by the undulations of celestial music, instead of factory bells, and a fragrance filling the air—to a higher life than we fell asleep from; and thus the darkness bear its fruit, and prove itself to be

2. Another name for Krishna, the eighth avatar of Vishnu in Hindu mythology; Thoreau translates from a French edition of *Harivansa*.
3. A star in the constellation Aquila. The Pleiades and the Hyades are constellations. Aldebaran, in the constellation Taurus, is one of the brightest stars.
4. Anonymous Jacobean verse set to music in *The Muses Garden* (1611) and probably found by Thoreau in Thomas Evans's *Old Ballads* (1810).
5. Confucius, *The Great Learning*, ch. 1.
6. In newspaper advertisements "TF" signaled to the compositor that an item was to be repeated daily "till forbidden."
7. Personification of the intellect's insights and perceptions.

good, no less than the light. That man who does not believe that each day contains an earlier, more sacred, and auroral hour than he has yet profaned, has despaired of life, and is pursuing a descending and darkening way. After a partial cessation of his sensuous life, the soul of man, or its organs rather, are reinvigorated each day, and his Genius tries again what noble life it can make. All memorable events, I should say, transpire in morning time and in a morning atmosphere. The Vedas[8] say, "All intelligences awake with the morning." Poetry and art, and the fairest and most memorable of the actions of men, date from such an hour. All poets and heroes, like Memnon, are the children of Aurora, and emit their music at sunrise.[9] To him whose elastic and vigorous thought keeps pace with the sun, the day is a perpetual morning. It matters not what the clocks say or the attitudes and labors of men. Morning is when I am awake and there is a dawn in me. Moral reform is the effort to throw off sleep. Why is it that men give so poor an account of their day if they have not been slumbering? They are not such poor calculators. If they had not been overcome with drowsiness they would have performed something. The millions are awake enough for physical labor; but only one in a million is awake enough for effective intellectual exertion, only one in a hundred millions to a poetic or divine life. To be awake is to be alive. I have never yet met a man who was quite awake. How could I have looked him in the face?

We must learn to reawaken and keep ourselves awake, not by mechanical aids, but by an infinite expectation of the dawn, which does not forsake us in our soundest sleep. I know of no more encouraging fact than the unquestionable ability of man to elevate his life by a conscious endeavor. It is something to be able to paint a particular picture, or to carve a statue, and so to make a few objects beautiful; but it is far more glorious to carve and paint the very atmosphere and medium through which we look, which morally we can do. To affect the quality of the day, that is the highest of arts. Every man is tasked to make his life, even in its details, worthy of the contemplation of his most elevated and critical hour. If we refused, or rather used up, such paltry information as we get, the oracles would distinctly inform us how this might be done.

I went to the woods because I wished to live deliberately, to front only the essential facts of life, and see if I could not learn what it had to teach, and not, when I came to die, discover that I had not lived. I did not wish to live what was not life, living is so dear; nor did I wish to practise resignation, unless it was quite necessary. I wanted to live deep and suck out all the marrow of life, to live so sturdily and Spartan[1]-like as to put to rout all that was not life, to cut a broad swath and shave close, to drive life into a corner, and reduce it to its lowest terms, and, if it proved to be mean, why then to get the whole and genuine meanness of it, and publish its meanness to the world; or if it were sublime, to know it by experience, and be able to give a true account of it in my next excursion. For most men, it appears to me, are in a strange uncertainty about it, whether it is of the devil or of God, and have *somewhat hastily* concluded that it is the chief end of man here to "glorify God and enjoy him forever."[2]

---

8. The Vedas are Hindu scriptures; the quotation has not been located.
9. See p. 938, n. 3.
1. Citizens of Sparta, an ancient Greek city-state, known for their discipline, austerity, and bravery.
2. From the Shorter Catechism in the *New England Primer.*

Still we live meanly, like ants; though the fable tells us that we were long ago changed into men; like pygmies we fight with cranes;[3] it is error upon error, and clout upon clout, and our best virtue has for its occasion a superfluous and evitable wretchedness. Our life is frittered away by detail. An honest man has hardly need to count more than his ten fingers, or in extreme cases he may add his ten toes, and lump the rest. Simplicity, simplicity, simplicity! I say, let your affairs be as two or three, and not a hundred or a thousand; instead of a million count half a dozen, and keep your accounts on your thumb nail. In the midst of this chopping sea of civilized life, such are the clouds and storms and quicksands and thousand-and-one items to be allowed for, that a man has to live, if he would not founder and go to the bottom and not make his port at all, by dead reckoning, and he must be a great calculator indeed who succeeds. Simplify, simplify. Instead of three meals a day, if it be necessary eat but one; instead of a hundred dishes, five; and reduce other things in proportion. Our life is like a German Confederacy,[4] made up of petty states, with its boundary forever fluctuating, so that even a German cannot tell you how it is bounded at any moment. The nation itself, with all its so called internal improvements, which, by the way, are all external and superficial, is just such an unwieldy and overgrown establishment, cluttered with furniture and tripped up by its own traps, ruined by luxury and heedless expense, by want of calculation and a worthy aim, as the million households in the land; and the only cure for it as for them is in a rigid economy, a stern and more than Spartan simplicity of life and elevation of purpose. It lives too fast. Men think that it is essential that the *Nation* have commerce, and export ice, and talk through a telegraph, and ride thirty miles an hour, without a doubt, whether *they* do or not; but whether we should live like baboons or like men, is a little uncertain. If we do not get out sleepers,[5] and forge rails, and devote days and nights to the work, but go to tinkering upon our *lives* to improve *them*, who will build railroads? And if railroads are not built, how shall we get to heaven in season? But if we stay at home and mind our business, who will want railroads? We do not ride on the railroad; it rides upon us. Did you ever think what those sleepers are that underlie the railroad? Each one is a man, an Irish-man, or a Yankee man. The rails are laid on them, and they are covered with sand, and the cars run smoothly over them. They are sound sleepers, I assure you. And every few years a new lot is laid down and run over; so that, if some have the pleasure of riding on a rail, others have the misfortune to be ridden upon. And when they run over a man that is walking in his sleep, a supernumerary sleeper in the wrong position, and wake him up, they suddenly stop the cars, and make a hue and cry about it, as if this were an exception. I am glad to know that it takes a gang of men for every five miles to keep the sleepers down and level in their beds as it is, for this is a sign that they may sometime get up again.

Why should we live with such hurry and waste of life? We are determined to be starved before we are hungry. Men say that a stitch in time saves nine, and so they take a thousand stitches to-day to save nine to-morrow. As for *work*, we haven't any of any consequence. We have the Saint Vitus' dance,[6]

---

3. In book 3 of the *Iliad*, the Trojans are compared to cranes fighting with pygmies. A story in Greek mythology tells of how Aeacus persuaded Zeus to turn ants into men.

4. Germany was not yet a unified nation.
5. Wooden railroad ties (another pun).
6. Chorea, a severe nervous disorder characterized by jerky motions.

and cannot possibly keep our heads still. If I should only give a few pulls at the parish bell-rope, as for a fire, that is, without setting the bell, there is hardly a man on his farm in the outskirts of Concord, notwithstanding that press of engagements which was his excuse so many times this morning, nor a boy, nor a woman, I might almost say, but would forsake all and follow that sound, not mainly to save property from the flames, but, if we will confess the truth, much more to see it burn, since burn it must, and we, be it known, did not set it on fire,—or to see it put out, and have a hand in it, if that is done as handsomely; yes, even if it were the parish church itself. Hardly a man takes a half hour's nap after dinner, but when he wakes he holds up his head and asks, "What's the news?" as if the rest of mankind had stood his sentinels. Some give directions to be waked every half hour, doubtless for no other purpose; and then, to pay for it, they tell what they have dreamed. After a night's sleep the news is as indispensable as the breakfast. "Pray tell me any thing new that has happened to a man any where on this globe",—and he reads it over his coffee and rolls, that a man had had his eyes gouged out this morning on the Wachito River; never dreaming the while that he lives in the dark unfathomed mammoth cave of this world, and has but the rudiment of an eye himself.[7]

For my part, I could easily do without the post-office. I think that there are very few important communications made through it. To speak critically, I never received more than one or two letters in my life—I wrote this some years ago—that were worth the postage. The penny-post is, commonly, an institution through which you seriously offer a man that penny for his thoughts which is so often safely offered in jest. And I am sure that I never read any memorable news in a newspaper. If we read of one man robbed, or murdered, or killed by accident, or one house burned, or one vessel wrecked, or one steamboat blown up, or one cow run over on the Western Railroad, or one mad dog killed, or one lot of grasshoppers in the winter,—we never need read of another. One is enough. If you are acquainted with the principle, what do you care for a myriad instances and applications? To a philosopher all *news*, as it is called, is gossip, and they who edit and read it are old women over their tea. Yet not a few are greedy after this gossip. There was such a rush, as I hear, the other day at one of the offices to learn the foreign news by the last arrival, that several large squares of plate glass belonging to the establishment were broken by the pressure,—news which I seriously think a ready wit might write a twelvemonth or twelve years beforehand with sufficient accuracy. As for Spain, for instance, if you know how to throw in Don Carlos and the Infanta, and Don Pedro and Seville and Granada, from time to time in the right proportions,—they may have changed the names a little since I saw the papers,—and serve up a bull-fight when other entertainments fail, it will be true to the letter, and give us as good an idea of the exact state or ruin of things in Spain as the most succinct and lucid reports under this head in the newspapers: and as for England, almost the last significant scrap of news from that quarter was the revolution of 1649;[8] and if you have learned

7. Sightless fish had been found in Kentucky's Mammoth Cave. "Wachito": also spelled "Ouachita," river flowing from Arkansas into the Red River in Louisiana.
8. The year the Puritan Commonwealth, under Oliver Cromwell (1599–1658), temporarily replaced the British monarchy—the culminating event of the English Civil War of 1642–49. During the 1830s and 1840s, King Ferdinand VII of Spain (1784–1833) and his brother Don Carlos (1788–1855) contested for power, and Ferdinand triumphed when his thirteen-year-old daughter,

the history of her crops for an average year, you never need attend to that thing again, unless your speculations are of a merely pecuniary character. If one may judge who rarely looks into the newspapers, nothing new does ever happen in foreign parts, a French revolution not excepted.

What news! how much more important to know what that is which was never old! "Kieou-pe-yu (great dignitary of the state of Wei) sent a man to Khoung-tseu to know his news. Khoung-tseu caused the messenger to be seated near him, and questioned him in these terms: What is your master doing? The messenger answered with respect: My master desires to diminish the number of his faults, but he cannot accomplish it. The messenger being gone, the philosopher remarked: What a worthy messenger! What a worthy messenger!"[9] The preacher, instead of vexing the ears of drowsy farmers on their day of rest at the end of the week,—for Sunday is the fit conclusion of an ill-spent week, and not the fresh and brave beginning of a new one,— with this one other draggle-tail of a sermon, should shout with thundering voice,—"Pause! Avast! Why so seeming fast, but deadly slow?"

Shams and delusions are esteemed for soundest truths, while reality is fabulous. If men would steadily observe realities only, and not allow themselves to be deluded, life, to compare it with such things as we know, would be like a fairy tale and the Arabian Nights' Entertainments. If we respected only what is inevitable and has a right to be, music and poetry would resound along the streets. When we are unhurried and wise, we perceive that only great and worthy things have any permanent and absolute existence,—that petty fears and petty pleasures are but the shadow of the reality. This is always exhilarating and sublime. By closing the eyes and slumbering, and consenting to be deceived by shows, men establish and confirm their daily life of routine and habit every where, which still is built on purely illusory foundations. Children, who play life, discern its true law and relations more clearly than men, who fail to live it worthily, but who think that they are wiser by experience, that is, by failure. I have read in a Hindoo book, that "there was a king's son, who, being expelled in infancy from his native city, was brought up by a forester, and, growing up to maturity in that state, imagined himself to belong to the barbarous race with which he lived. One of his father's ministers having discovered him, revealed to him what he was, and the misconception of his character was removed, and he knew himself to be a prince. So soul," continues the Hindoo philosopher, "from the circumstances in which it is placed, mistakes its own character, until the truth is revealed to it by some holy teacher, and then it knows itself to be *Brahme*."[1] I perceive that we inhabitants of New England live this mean life that we do because our vision does not penetrate the surface of things. We think that that *is* which *appears* to be. If a man should walk through this town and see only the reality, where, think you, would the "Mill-dam"[2] go to? If he should give us an account of the realities he beheld there, we should not recognize the place in his description. Look at a meeting-house, or a court-house, or a jail, or a shop, or a dwelling-house, and say what that thing really is before a true gaze, and they

the Infanta, or princess (1830–1904), was crowned Queen Isabella II. In 1362, Don Pedro the Cruel of Seville (1334–1369) and his army killed Abu Said Muhammad VI of Granada.
9. Confucius's *Analects* 14.

1. In the Hindu triad, Brahma is the divine reality in the aspect of creator; Vishnu is the preserver; and Siva, the destroyer.
2. The business center of Concord.

would all go to pieces in your account of them. Men esteem truth remote, in the outskirts of the system, behind the farthest star, before Adam and after the last man. In eternity there is indeed something true and sublime. But all these times and places and occasions are now and here. God himself culminates in the present moment, and will never be more divine in the lapse of all the ages. And we are enabled to apprehend at all what is sublime and noble only by the perpetual instilling and drenching of the reality which surrounds us. The universe constantly and obediently answers to our conceptions; whether we travel fast or slow, the track is laid for us. Let us spend our lives in conceiving them. The poet or the artist never yet had so fair and noble a design but some of his posterity at least could accomplish it.

Let us spend one day as deliberately as Nature, and not be thrown off the track by every nutshell and mosquito's wing that falls on the rails. Let us rise early and fast, or break fast, gently and without perturbation; let company come and let company go, let the bells ring and the children cry,—determined to make a day of it. Why should we knock under and go with the stream? Let us not be upset and overwhelmed in that terrible rapid and whirlpool called a dinner, situated in the meridian shallows. Weather this danger and you are safe, for the rest of the way is down hill. With unrelaxed nerves, with morning vigor, sail by it, looking another way, tied to the mast like Ulysses.[3] If the engine whistles, let it whistle till it is hoarse for its pains. If the bell rings, why should we run? We will consider what kind of music they are like. Let us settle ourselves, and work and wedge our feet downward through the mud and slush of opinion, and prejudice, and tradition, and delusion, and appearance, that alluvion[4] which covers the globe, through Paris and London, through New York and Boston and Concord, through church and state, through poetry and philosophy and religion, till we come to a hard bottom and rocks in place, which we can call *reality*, and say, This is, and no mistake; and then begin, having a *point d'appui*, below freshet and frost and fire, a place where you might found a wall or a state, or set a lamp-post safely, or perhaps a gauge, not a Nilometer,[5] but a Realometer, that future ages might know how deep a freshet of shams and appearances had gathered from time to time. If you stand right fronting and face to face to a fact, you will see the sun glimmer on both its surfaces, as if it were a cimeter, and feel its sweet edge dividing you through the heart and marrow, and so you will happily conclude your mortal career. Be it life or death, we crave only reality. If we are really dying, let us hear the rattle in our throats and feel cold in the extremities; if we are alive, let us go about our business.

Time is but the stream I go a-fishing in. I drink at it; but while I drink I see the sandy bottom and detect how shallow it is. Its thin current slides away, but eternity remains. I would drink deeper; fish in the sky, whose bottom is pebbly with stars. I cannot count one. I know not the first letter of the alphabet. I have always been regretting that I was not as wise as the day I was born. The intellect is a cleaver; it discerns and rifts its way into the secret of things. I do not wish to be any more busy with my hands than is necessary. My head

---

3. In Homer's *Odyssey*, Ulysses (Odysseus) took such a precaution to keep himself from yielding to the call of the Sirens—sea nymphs whose singing lured men to destruction.
4. Sediment deposited by flowing water along a shore or bank.
5. Gauge used by the ancient Egyptians for measuring the depth of the Nile. "*Point d'appui*": point of support (French).

is hands and feet. I feel all my best faculties concentrated in it. My instinct tells me that my head is an organ for burrowing, as some creatures use their snout and fore-paws, and with it I would mine and burrow my way through these hills. I think that the richest vein is somewhere hereabouts; so by the divining rod and thin rising vapors I judge; and here I will begin to mine.

5. *Solitude*

This is a delicious evening, when the whole body is one sense, and imbibes delight through every pore. I go and come with a strange liberty in Nature, a part of herself. As I walk along the stony shore of the pond in my shirt sleeves, though it is cool as well as cloudy and windy, and I see nothing special to attract me, all the elements are unusually congenial to me. The bullfrogs trump to usher in the night, and the note of the whippoorwill is borne on the rippling wind from over the water. Sympathy with the fluttering alder and poplar leaves almost takes away my breath; yet, like the lake, my serenity is rippled but not ruffled. These small waves raised by the evening wind are as remote from the storm as the smooth reflecting surface. Though it is now dark, the wind still blows and roars in the wood, the waves still dash, and some creatures lull the rest with their notes. The repose is never complete. The wildest animals do not repose, but seek their prey now; the fox, and skunk, and rabbit, now roam the fields and woods without fear. They are Nature's watchmen,—links which connect the days of animated life.

When I return to my house I find that visitors have been there and left their cards, either a bunch of flowers, or a wreath of evergreen, or a name in pencil on a yellow walnut leaf or a chip. They who come rarely to the woods take some little piece of the forest into their hands to play with by the way, which they leave, either intentionally or accidentally. One has peeled a willow wand, woven it into a ring, and dropped it on my table. I could always tell if visitors had called in my absence, either by the bended twigs or grass, or the print of their shoes, and generally of what sex or age or quality they were by some slight trace left, as a flower dropped, or a bunch of grass plucked and thrown away, even as far off as the railroad, half a mile distant, or by the lingering odor of a cigar or pipe. Nay, I was frequently notified of the passage of a traveller along the highway sixty rods off by the scent of his pipe.

There is commonly sufficient space about us. Our horizon is never quite at our elbows. The thick wood is not just at our door, nor the pond, but somewhat is always clearing, familiar and worn by us, appropriated and fenced in some way, and reclaimed from Nature. For what reason have I this vast range and circuit, some square miles of unfrequented forest, for my privacy, abandoned to me by men? My nearest neighbor is a mile distant, and no house is visible from any place but the hill-tops within half a mile of my own. I have my horizon bounded by woods all to myself; a distant view of the railroad where it touches the pond on the one hand, and of the fence which skirts the woodland road on the other. But for the most part it is as solitary where I live as on the prairies. It is as much Asia or Africa as New England. I have, as it were, my own sun and moon and stars, and a little world all to myself. At night there was never a traveller passed my house, or knocked at my door, more than if I were the first or last man; unless it were in the spring, when at long intervals some came from the village to fish for pouts,—they plainly fished much more in the Walden Pond of their own natures, and baited their hooks with darkness,—but they soon retreated, usually with light baskets, and left "the world to darkness and to me,"[3] and the black kernel of the night was never profaned by any human neighborhood. I believe that men are generally still a little afraid of the dark, though the witches are all hung, and Christianity and candles have been introduced.

Yet I experienced sometimes that the most sweet and tender, the most innocent and encouraging society may be found in any natural object, even for the poor misanthrope and most melancholy man. There can be no very black melancholy to him who lives in the midst of Nature and has his senses still. There was never yet such a storm but it was Æolian[4] music to a healthy and innocent ear. Nothing can rightly compel a simple and brave man to a vulgar sadness. While I enjoy the friendship of the seasons I trust that nothing can make life a burden to me. The gentle rain which waters my beans and keeps me in the house to-day is not drear and melancholy, but good for me too. Though it prevents my hoeing them, it is of far more worth than my hoeing. If it should continue so long as to cause the seeds to rot in the ground and destroy the potatoes in the low lands, it would still be good for the grass on the uplands, and, being good for the grass, it would be good for me. Sometimes, when I compare myself with other men, it seems as if I were more favored by the gods than they, beyond any deserts that I am conscious of; as if I had a warrant and surety at their hands which my fellows have not, and were especially guided and guarded. I do not flatter myself, but if it be possible they flatter me. I have never felt lonesome, or in the least oppressed by a sense of solitude, but once, and that was a few weeks after I came to the woods, when, for an hour, I doubted if the near neighborhood of man was not essential to a serene and healthy life. To be alone was something unpleasant. But I was at the same time conscious of a slight insanity in my mood, and seemed to foresee my recovery. In the midst of a gentle rain while these thoughts prevailed, I was suddenly sensible of such sweet and beneficent society in Nature, in the very pattering of the drops, and in every sound and sight around my house, an infinite and unaccountable friendliness all at once like an atmosphere sustaining me, as made the fancied advantages of human neighborhood insignificant, and I have never thought of them since. Every little pine needle expanded and swelled with sympathy and befriended me. I was so distinctly made aware of the presence of something kindred to me, even in scenes which we are accustomed to call wild and dreary, and also that the nearest of blood to me and humanest was not a person nor a villager, that I thought no place could ever be strange to me again.—

> "Mourning untimely consumes the sad;
> Few are their days in the land of the living,
> Beautiful daughter of Toscar."[5]

---

3. From "Elegy Written in a Country Churchyard" (1751), by the English poet Thomas Gray (1716–1771).
4. The Aeolian harp (named for Aeolus, Greek keeper of the winds) was commonly placed in the open air or near an open window so that the wind could cause it to make musical sounds.
5. From "Croma," in Patrick MacGregor's translation of *The Genuine Remains of Ossian* (1841).

Some of my pleasantest hours were during the long rain storms in the spring or fall, which confined me to the house for the afternoon as well as the forenoon, soothed by their ceaseless roar and pelting; when an early twilight ushered in a long evening in which many thoughts had time to take root and unfold themselves. In those driving north-east rains which tried the village houses so, when the maids stood ready with mop and pail in front entries to keep the deluge out, I sat behind my door in my little house, which was all entry, and thoroughly enjoyed its protection. In one heavy thunder shower the lightning struck a large pitch-pine across the pond, making a very conspicuous and perfectly regular spiral groove from top to bottom, an inch or more deep, and four or five inches wide, as you would groove a walking-stick. I passed it again the other day, and was struck with awe on looking up and beholding that mark, now more distinct than ever, where a terrific and resistless bolt came down out of the harmless sky eight years ago. Men frequently say to me, "I should think you would feel lonesome down there, and want to be nearer to folks, rainy and snowy days and nights especially." I am tempted to reply to such,—This whole earth which we inhabit is but a point in space. How far apart, think you, dwell the two most distant inhabitants of yonder star, the breadth of whose disk cannot be appreciated by our instruments? Why should I feel lonely? is not our planet in the Milky Way? This which you put seems to me not to be the most important question. What sort of space is that which separates a man from his fellows and makes him solitary? I have found that no exertion of the legs can bring two minds much nearer to one another. What do we want most to dwell near to? Not to many men surely, the depot, the post-office, the bar-room, the meeting-house, the school-house, the grocery, Beacon Hill, or the Five Points,[6] where men most congregate, but to the perennial source of our life, whence in all our experience we have found that to issue; as the willow stands near the water and sends out its roots in that direction. This will vary with different natures, but this is the place where a wise man will dig his cellar. . . . I one evening overtook one of my townsmen, who has accumulated what is called "a handsome property",—though I never got a *fair* view of it,—on the Walden road, driving a pair of cattle to market, who inquired of me how I could bring my mind to give up so many of the comforts of life. I answered that I was very sure I liked it passably well; I was not joking. And so I went home to my bed, and left him to pick his way through the darkness and the mud to Brighton,—or Bright-town,—which place he would reach some time in the morning.

Any prospect of awakening or coming to life to a dead man makes indifferent all times and places. The place where that may occur is always the same, and indescribably pleasant to all our senses. For the most part we allow only outlying and transient circumstances to make our occasions. They are, in fact, the cause of our distraction. Nearest to all things is that power which fashions their being. *Next* to us the grandest laws are continually being executed. *Next* to us is not the workman whom we have hired, with whom we love so well to talk, but the workman whose work we are.

---

6. District in lower Manhattan, notorious in Thoreau's time for its poverty and violence. The State House is on Boston's Beacon Hill.

"How vast and profound is the influence of the subtile powers of Heaven and of Earth!"

"We seek to perceive them, and we do not see them; we seek to hear them, and we do not hear them; identified with the substance of things, they cannot be separated from them."

"They cause that in all the universe men purify and sanctify their hearts, and clothe themselves in their holiday garments to offer sacrifices and oblations to their ancestors. It is an ocean of subtile intelligences. They are every where, above us, on our left, on our right; they environ us on all sides."[7]

We are the subjects of an experiment which is not a little interesting to me. Can we not do without the society of our gossips a little while under these circumstances,—have our own thoughts to cheer us? Confucious says truly, "Virtue does not remain as an abandoned orphan; it must of necessity have neighbors."[8]

With thinking we may be beside ourselves in a sane sense. By a conscious effort of the mind we can stand aloof from actions and their consequences; and all things, good and bad, go by us like a torrent. We are not wholly involved in Nature. I may be either the drift-wood in the stream, or Indra[9] in the sky looking down on it. I *may* be affected by a theatrical exhibition; on the other hand, I *may not* be affected by an actual event which appears to concern me much more. I only know myself as a human entity; the scene, so to speak, of thoughts and affections; and am sensible of a certain double-ness by which I can stand as remote from myself as from another. However intense my experience, I am conscious of the presence and criticism of a part of me, which, as it were, is not a part of me, but spectator, sharing no experience, but taking note of it; and that is no more I than it is you. When the play, it may be the tragedy, of life is over, the spectator goes his way. It was a kind of fiction, a work of the imagination only, so far as he was concerned. This doubleness may easily make us poor neighbors and friends sometimes.

I find it wholesome to be alone the greater part of the time. To be in company, even with the best, is soon wearisome and dissipating. I love to be alone. I never found the companion that was so companionable as solitude. We are for the most part more lonely when we go abroad among men than when we stay in our chambers. A man thinking or working is always alone, let him be where he will. Solitude is not measured by the miles of space that intervene between a man and his fellows. The really diligent student in one of the crowded hives of Cambridge College is as solitary as a dervish[1] in the desert. The farmer can work alone in the field or the woods all day, hoeing or chopping, and not feel lonesome, because he is employed; but when he comes home at night he cannot sit down in a room alone, at the mercy of his thoughts, but must be where he can "see the folks," and recreate, and as he thinks remunerate himself for his day's solitude; and hence he wonders how the student can sit alone in the house all night and most of the day without ennui and "the blues;" but he does not realize that the student, though in the house,

---

7. Confucius's *The Doctrine of the Mean* 14.
8. Confucius's *Analects* 4.
9. In the Vedas, the Hindu god of the air,

associated with rain and thunder.
1. Sufi Muslim who takes religious vows of poverty and austerity.

is still at work in *his* field, and chopping in *his* woods, as the farmer in his, and in turn seeks the same recreation and society that the latter does, though it may be a more condensed form of it.

Society is commonly too cheap. We meet at very short intervals, not having had time to acquire any new value for each other. We meet at meals three times a day, and give each other a new taste of that old musty cheese that we are. We have had to agree on a certain set of rules, called etiquette and politeness, to make this frequent meeting tolerable, and that we need not come to open war. We meet at the post-office, and at the sociable, and about the fireside every night; we live thick and are in each other's way, and stumble over one another, and I think that we thus lose some respect for one another. Certainly less frequency would suffice for all important and hearty communications. Consider the girls in a factory,—never alone, hardly in their dreams. It would be better if there were but one inhabitant to a square mile, as where I live. The value of a man is not in his skin, that we should touch him.

I have heard of a man lost in the woods and dying of famine and exhaustion at the foot of a tree, whose loneliness was relieved by the grotesque visions with which, owing to bodily weakness, his diseased imagination surrounded him, and which he believed to be real. So also, owing to bodily and mental health and strength, we may be continually cheered by a like but more normal and natural society, and come to know that we are never alone.

I have a great deal of company in my house; especially in the morning, when nobody calls. Let me suggest a few comparisons, that some one may convey an idea of my situation. I am no more lonely than the loon in the pond that laughs so loud, or than Walden Pond itself. What company has that lonely lake, I pray? And yet it has not the blue devils, but the blue angels in it, in the azure tint of its waters. The sun is alone, except in thick weather, when there sometimes appear to be two, but one is a mock sun. God is alone,—but the devil, he is far from being alone; he sees a great deal of company; he is legion. I am no more lonely than a single mullein or dandelion in a pasture, or a bean leaf, or sorrel, or a horse-fly, or a humble-bee. I am no more lonely than the Mill Brook, or a weathercock, or the northstar, or the south wind, or an April shower, or a January thaw, or the first spider in a new house.

I have occasional visits in the long winter evenings, when the snow falls fast and the wind howls in the wood, from an old settler and original proprietor, who is reported to have dug Walden Pond, and stoned it, and fringed it with pine woods; who tells me stories of old time and of new eternity; and between us we manage to pass a cheerful evening with social mirth and pleasant views of things, even without apples or cider,—a most wise and humorous friend, whom I love much, who keeps himself more secret than ever did Goffe or Whalley;[2] and though he is thought to be dead, none can show where he is buried. An elderly dame,[3] too, dwells in my neighborhood, invisible to most persons, in whose odorous herb garden I love to stroll sometimes, gathering simples and listening to her fables; for she has a genius of unequalled fertility, and her memory runs back farther than mythology, and she can tell me the original of every fable, and on what fact every one is founded, for the incidents occurred when she was young. A ruddy and lusty

2. English Puritans who supported the execution of Charles I of England in 1649 and later, when sought as regicides, hid in Connecticut and Massachusetts settlements. "Old settler": some sort of divine creative power.
3. Mother Nature.

old dame, who delights in all weathers and seasons, and is likely to outlive all her children yet.

The indescribable innocence and beneficence of Nature,—of sun and wind and rain, of summer and winter,—such health, such cheer, they afford forever! and such sympathy have they ever with our race, that all Nature would be affected, and the sun's brightness fade, and the winds would sigh humanely, and the clouds rain tears, and the woods shed their leaves and put on mourning in midsummer, if any man should ever for a just cause grieve. Shall I not have intelligence with the earth? Am I not partly leaves and vegetable mould myself?

What is the pill which will keep us well, serene, contented? Not my or thy great-grandfather's, but our great-grandmother Nature's universal, vegetable, botanic medicines, by which she has kept herself young always, outlived so many old Parrs[4] in her day, and fed her health with their decaying fatness. For my panacea, instead of one of those quack vials of a mixture dipped from Acheron[5] and the Dead Sea, which come out of those long shallow black-schooner looking wagons which we sometimes see made to carry bottles, let me have a draught of undiluted morning air. Morning air! If men will not drink of this at the fountain-head of the day, why, then, we must even bottle up some and sell it in the shops, for the benefit of those who have lost their subscription ticket to morning time in this world. But remember, it will not keep quite till noon-day even in the coolest cellar, but drive out the stopples long ere that and follow westward the steps of Aurora. I am no worshipper of Hygeia, who was the daughter of that old herb-doctor Æsculapius,[6] and who is represented on monuments holding a serpent in one hand, and in the other a cup out of which the serpent sometimes drinks; but rather of Hebe, cupbearer to Jupiter, who was the daughter of Juno and wild lettuce, and who had the power of restoring gods and men to the vigor of youth. She was probably the only thoroughly sound-conditioned, healthy, and robust young lady that ever walked the globe, and wherever she came it was spring.

17. Spring

The opening of large tracts by the ice-cutters commonly causes a pond to break up earlier; for the water, agitated by the wind, even in cold weather, wears away the surrounding ice. But such was not the effect on Walden that year, for she had soon got a thick new garment to take the place of the old. This pond never breaks up so soon as the others in this neighborhood, on account both of its greater depth and its having no stream passing through it to melt or wear away the ice. I never knew it to open in the course of a winter, not excepting that of '52–3, which gave the ponds so severe a trial. It commonly opens about the first of April, a week or ten days later than Flint's Pond and Fair-Haven, beginning to melt on the north side and in the shallower parts where it began to freeze. It indicates better than any water hereabouts the absolute progress of the season, being least affected by transient changes of

---

4. An Englishman known as Old Tom Parr was said to have been alive during three centuries (1483–1635).

5. In Greek mythology, a principal river in Hades.
6. Roman god of medicine. Hygeia was the Greek goddess of health.

temperature. A severe cold of a few days' duration in March may very much retard the opening of the former ponds, while the temperature of Walden increases almost uninterruptedly. A thermometer thrust into the middle of Walden on the 6th of March, 1847, stood at 32°, or freezing point; near the shore at 33°; in the middle of Flint's Pond, the same day, at 32½°; at a dozen rods from the shore, in shallow water, under ice a foot thick, at 36°. This difference of three and a half degrees between the temperature of the deep water and the shallow in the latter pond, and the fact that a great proportion of it is comparatively shallow, show why it should break up so much sooner than Walden. The ice in the shallowest part was at this time several inches thinner than in the middle. In mid-winter the middle had been the warmest and the ice thinnest there. So, also, every one who has waded about the shores of a pond in summer must have perceived how much warmer the water is close to the shore, where only three or four inches deep, than a little distance out, and on the surface where it is deep, than near the bottom. In spring the sun not only exerts an influence through the increased temperature of the air and earth, but its heat passes through ice a foot or more thick, and is reflected from the bottom in shallow water, and so also warms the water and melts the under side of the ice, at the same time that it is melting it more directly above, making it uneven, and causing the air bubbles which it contains to extend themselves upward and downward until it is completely honey-combed, and at last disappears suddenly in a single spring rain. Ice has its grain as well as wood, and when a cake begins to rot or "comb," that is, assume the appearance of honey-comb, whatever may be its position, the air cells are at right angles with what was the water surface. Where there is a rock or a log rising near to the surface the ice over it is much thinner, and is frequently quite dissolved by this reflected heat; and I have been told that in the experiment at Cambridge to freeze water in a shallow wooden pond, though the cold air circulated underneath, and so had access to both sides, the reflection of the sun from the bottom more than counterbalanced this advantage. When a warm rain in the middle of the winter melts off the snow-ice from Walden, and leaves a hard dark or transparent ice on the middle, there will be a strip of rotten though thicker white ice, a rod or more wide, about the shores, created by this reflected heat. Also, as I have said, the bubbles themselves within the ice operate as burning glasses to melt the ice beneath.

The phenomena of the year take place every day in a pond on a small scale. Every morning, generally speaking, the shallow water is being warmed more rapidly than the deep, though it may not be made so warm after all, and every evening it is being cooled more rapidly until the morning. The day is an epitome of the year. The night is the winter, the morning and evening are the spring and fall, and the noon is the summer. The cracking and booming of the ice indicate a change of temperature. One pleasant morning after a cold night, February 24th, 1850, having gone to Flint's Pond to spend the day, I noticed with surprise, that when I struck the ice with the head of my axe, it resounded like a gong for many rods around, or as if I had struck on a tight drum-head. The pond began to boom about an hour after sunrise, when it felt the influence of the sun's rays slanted upon it from the hills; it stretched itself and yawned like a waking man with a gradually increasing tumult, which was kept up three or four hours. It took a short siesta at noon, and boomed once more toward night, as the sun was withdrawing his influence.

In the right stage of the weather a pond fires its evening gun with great regularity. But in the middle of the day, being full of cracks, and the air also being less elastic, it had completely lost its resonance, and probably fishes and muskrats could not then have been stunned by a blow on it. The fishermen say that the "thundering of the pond" scares the fishes and prevents their biting. The pond does not thunder every evening, and I cannot tell surely when to expect its thundering; but though I may perceive no difference in the weather, it does. Who would have suspected so large and cold and thick-skinned a thing to be so sensitive? Yet it has its law to which it thunders obedience when it should as surely as the buds expand in the spring. The earth is all alive and covered with papillæ. The largest pond is as sensitive to atmospheric changes as the globule of mercury in its tube.

One attraction in coming to the woods to live was that I should have leisure and opportunity to see the spring come in. The ice in the pond at length begins to be honey-combed, and I can set my heel in it as I walk. Fogs and rains and warmer suns are gradually melting the snow; the days have grown sensibly longer; and I see how I shall get through the winter without adding to my wood-pile, for large fires are no longer necessary. I am on the alert for the first signs of spring, to hear the chance note of some arriving bird, or the striped squirrel's chirp, for his stores must be now nearly exhausted, or see the woodchuck venture out of his winter quarters. On the 13th of March, after I had heard the bluebird, song-sparrow, and red-wing, the ice was still nearly a foot thick. As the weather grew warmer, it was not sensibly worn away by the water, nor broken up and floated off as in rivers, but, though it was completely melted for half a rod in width about the shore, the middle was merely honey-combed and saturated with water, so that you could put your foot through it when six inches thick; but by the next day evening, perhaps, after a warm rain followed by fog, it would have wholly disappeared, all gone off with the fog, spirited away. One year I went across the middle only five days before it disappeared entirely. In 1845 Walden was first completely open on the 1st of April; in '46, the 25th of March; in '47, the 8th of April; in '51, the 28th of March; in '52, the 18th of April; in '53, the 23rd of March; in '54, about the 7th of April.

Every incident connected with the breaking up of the rivers and ponds and the settling of the weather is particularly interesting to us who live in a climate of so great extremes. When the warmer days come, they who dwell near the river hear the ice crack at night with a startling whoop as loud as artillery, as if its icy fetters were rent from end to end, and within a few days see it rapidly going out. So the alligator comes out of the mud with quakings of the earth. One old man, who has been a close observer of Nature, and seems as thoroughly wise in regard to all her operations as if she had been put upon the stocks when he was a boy, and he had helped to lay her keel,— who has come to his growth, and can hardly acquire more of natural lore if he should live to the age of Methuselah[1]—told me, and I was surprised to hear him express wonder at any of Nature's operations, for I thought that there were no secrets between them, that one spring day he took his gun and boat, and thought that he would have a little sport with the ducks. There

1. "And the days of Methuselah were nine hundred sixty and nine years: and he died" (Genesis 5.27).

was ice still on the meadows, but it was all gone out of the river, and he dropped down without obstruction from Sudbury, where he lived, to Fair-Haven Pond, which he found, unexpectedly, covered for the most part with a firm field of ice. It was a warm day, and he was surprised to see so great a body of ice remaining. Not seeing any ducks, he hid his boat on the north or back side of an island in the pond, and then concealed himself in the bushes on the south side, to await them. The ice was melted for three or four rods from the shore, and there was a smooth and warm sheet of water, with a muddy bottom, such as the ducks love, within, and he thought it likely that some would be along pretty soon. After he had lain still there about an hour he heard a low and seemingly very distant sound, but singularly grand and impressive, unlike any thing he had ever heard, gradually swelling and increasing as if it would have a universal and memorable ending, a sullen rush and roar, which seemed to him all at once like the sound of a vast body of fowl coming in to settle there, and, seizing his gun, he started up in haste and excited; but he found, to his surprise, that the whole body of the ice had started while he lay there, and drifted in to the shore, and the sound he had heard was made by its edge grating on the shore,—at first gently nibbled and crumbled off, but at length heaving up and scattering its wrecks along the island to a considerable height before it came to a stand still.

At length the sun's rays have attained the right angle, and warm winds blow up mist and rain and melt the snow banks, and the sun dispersing the mist smiles on a checkered landscape of russet and white smoking with incense, through which the traveller picks his way from islet to islet, cheered by the music of a thousand tinkling rills and rivulets whose veins are filled with the blood of winter which they are bearing off.

Few phenomena gave me more delight than to observe the forms which thawing sand and clay assume in flowing down the sides of a deep cut on the railroad through which I passed on my way to the village, a phenomenon not very common on so large a scale, though the number of freshly exposed banks of the right material must have been greatly multiplied since railroads were invented. The material was sand of every degree of fineness and of various rich colors, commonly mixed with a little clay. When the frost comes out in the spring, and even in a thawing day in the winter, the sand begins to flow down the slopes like lava, sometimes bursting out through the snow and overflowing it where no sand was to be seen before. Innumerable little streams overlap and interlace one with another, exhibiting a sort of hybrid product, which obeys half way the law of currents, and half way that of vegetation. As it flows it takes the forms of sappy leaves or vines, making heaps of pulpy sprays a foot or more in depth, and resembling, as you look down on them, the laciniated lobed and imbricated thalluses[2] of some lichens; or you are reminded of coral, of leopards' paws or birds' feet, of brains or lungs or bowels, and excrements of all kinds. It is a truly *grotesque* vegetation, whose forms and color we see imitated in bronze, a sort of architectural foliage more ancient and typical than acanthus, chiccory, ivy, vine, or any vegetable leaves; destined perhaps, under some circumstances, to become a puzzle to future geologists. The whole cut impressed me as if it were a cave with its

2. Plant shoots or organisms lapped over in regular order like roof tiles. "Laciniated": deeply, irregularly lobed.

stalactites laid open to the light. The various shades of the sand are singularly rich and agreeable, embracing the different iron colors, brown, gray, yellowish, and reddish. When the flowing mass reaches the drain at the foot of the bank it spreads out flatter into *strands*, the separate streams losing their semi-cylindrical form and gradually becoming more flat and broad, running together as they are more moist, till they form an almost flat *sand*, still variously and beautifully shaded, but in which you can trace the original forms of vegetation; till at length, in the water itself, they are converted into *banks*, like those formed off the mouths of rivers, and the forms of vegetation are lost in the ripple marks on the bottom.

The whole bank, which is from twenty to forty feet high, is sometimes overlaid with a mass of this kind of foliage, or sandy rupture, for a quarter of a mile on one or both sides, the produce of one spring day. What makes this sand foliage remarkable is its springing into existence thus suddenly. When I see on the one side the inert bank,—for the sun acts on one side first,— and on the other this luxuriant foliage, the creation of an hour, I am affected as if in a peculiar sense I stood in the laboratory of the Artist who made the world and me,—had come to where he was still at work, sporting on this bank, and with excess of energy strewing his fresh designs about. I feel as if I were nearer to the vitals of the globe, for this sandy overflow is something such a foliaceous mass as the vitals of the animal body. You find thus in the very sands an anticipation of the vegetable leaf. No wonder that the earth expresses itself outwardly in leaves, it so labors with the idea inwardly. The atoms have already learned this law, and are pregnant by it. The overhanging leaf sees here its prototype. *Internally*, whether in the globe or animal body, it is a moist thick *lobe*, a word especially applicable to the liver and lungs and the *leaves* of fat. (λέιβω, labor, lapsus, to flow or slip downward, a lapsing; λοβος, globus, lobe, globe; also lap, flap, and many other words,) *externally* a dry thin *leaf*, even as the *f* and *v* are a pressed and dried *b*. The radicals of lobe are *lb*, the soft mass of the *b* (single lobed, or B, double lobed,) with a liquid *l* behind it pressing it forward. In globe, *glb*, the guttural *g* adds to the meaning the capacity of the throat. The feathers and wings of birds are still drier and thinner leaves. Thus, also, you pass from the lumpish grub in the earth to the airy and fluttering butterfly. The very globe continually transcends and translates itself, and becomes winged in its orbit. Even ice begins with delicate crystal leaves, as if it had flowed into moulds which the fronds of water plants have impressed on the watery mirror. The whole tree itself is but one leaf, and rivers are still vaster leaves whose pulp is intervening earth, and towns and cities are the ova of insects in their axils.

When the sun withdraws the sand ceases to flow, but in the morning the streams will start once more and branch and branch again into a myriad of others. You here see perchance how blood vessels are formed. If you look closely you observe that first there pushes forward from the thawing mass a stream of softened sand with a drop-like point, like the ball of the finger, feeling its way slowly and blindly downward, until at last with more heat and moisture, as the sun gets higher, the moist fluid portion, in its effort to obey the law to which the most inert also yields, separates from the latter and forms for itself a meandering channel or artery within that, in which is seen a little silvery stream glancing like lightning from one stage of pulpy leaves or branches to another, and ever and anon swallowed up in the sand. It is wonderful how rapidly yet perfectly the sand organizes itself as it flows, using the best material its mass affords to form the sharp edges of its channel. Such are the sources of rivers. In the silicious matter which the water deposits is perhaps the bony system, and in the still finer soil and organic matter the fleshy fibre or cellular tissue. What is man but a mass of thawing clay? The ball of the human finger is but a drop congealed. The fingers and toes flow to their extent from the thawing mass of the body. Who knows what the human body would expand and flow out to under a more genial heaven? Is not the hand a spreading *palm* leaf with its lobes and veins? The ear may be regarded, fancifully, as a lichen, *umbilicaria*, on the side of the head, with its lobe or drop. The lip (*labium* from *labor* (?)) laps or lapses from the sides of the cavernous mouth. The nose is a manifest congealed drop or stalactite. The chin is a still larger drop, the confluent dripping of the face. The cheeks are a slide from the brows into the valley of the face, opposed and diffused by the cheek bones. Each rounded lobe of the vegetable leaf, too, is a thick and now loitering drop, larger or smaller; the lobes are the fingers of the leaf; and as many lobes as it has, in so many directions it tends to flow, and more heat or other genial influences would have caused it to flow yet farther.

Thus it seemed that this one hillside illustrated the principle of all the operations of Nature. The Maker of this earth but patented a leaf. What Champollion[3] will decipher this hieroglyphic for us, that we may turn over a new leaf at last? This phenomenon is more exhilarating to me than the luxuriance and fertility of vineyards. True, it is somewhat excrementitious in its character, and there is no end to the heaps of liver, lights[4] and bowels, as if the globe were turned wrong side outward; but this suggests at least that Nature has some bowels, and there again is mother of humanity. This is the frost coming out of the ground; this is Spring. It precedes the green and flowery spring, as mythology precedes regular poetry. I know of nothing more purgative of winter fumes and indigestions. It convinces me that Earth is still in her swaddling clothes, and stretches forth baby fingers on every side. Fresh curls spring from the baldest brow. There is nothing inorganic. These foliaceous heaps lie along the bank like the slag of a furnace, showing that Nature is "in full blast" within. The earth is not a mere fragment of dead history, stratum upon stratum like the leaves of a book, to be studied by geologists and antiquaries chiefly, but living poetry like the leaves of a tree, which precede flowers and fruit,—not a fossil earth, but a living earth; compared with whose great central life all animal and vegetable life is merely parasitic. Its throes will heave our exuviæ from their graves. You may melt your metals and cast them into the most beautiful moulds you can; they will never excite me like the forms which this molten earth flows out into. And not only it, but the institutions upon it, are plastic like clay in the hands of the potter.

Ere long, not only on these banks, but on every hill and plain and in every hollow, the frost comes out of the ground like a dormant quadruped from its burrow, and seeks the sea with music, or migrates to other climes

3. Jean François Champollion (1790–1832), French archaeologist whose deciphering of the hieroglyphic inscriptions on the Rosetta Stone fueled great popular interest in Egyptology. The stone dates from 196 B.C.E. and was discovered by French soldiers in 1799.
4. Lungs.

in clouds. Thaw with his gentle persuasion is more powerful than Thor with his hammer. The one melts, the other but breaks in pieces.

When the ground was partially bare of snow, and a few warm days had dried its surface somewhat, it was pleasant to compare the first tender signs of the infant year just peeping forth with the stately beauty of the withered vegetation which had withstood the winter,—life-everlasting, golden-rods, pinweeds, and graceful wild grasses, more obvious and interesting frequently than in summer even, as if their beauty was not ripe till then; even cotton-grass, cat-tails, mulleins, johnswort, hard-hack, meadow-sweet, and other strong stemmed plants, those unexhausted granaries which entertain the earliest birds,—decent weeds,[5] at least, which widowed Nature wears. I am particularly attracted by the arching and sheaf-like top of the wool-grass; it brings back the summer to our winter memories, and is among the forms which art loves to copy, and which, in the vegetable kingdom, have the same relation to types already in the mind of man that astronomy has. It is an antique style older than Greek or Egyptian. Many of the phenomena of Winter are suggestive of an inexpressible tenderness and fragile delicacy. We are accustomed to hear this king described as a rude and boisterous tyrant; but with the gentleness of a lover he adorns the tresses of Summer.

At the approach of spring the red-squirrels got under my house, two at a time, directly under my feet as I sat reading or writing, and kept up the queerest chuckling and chirruping and vocal pirouetting and gurgling sounds that ever were heard; and when I stamped they only chirruped the louder, as if past all fear and respect in their mad pranks, defying humanity to stop them. No you don't—chickaree—chickaree. They were wholly deaf to my arguments, or failed to perceive their force, and fell into a strain of invective that was irresistible.

The first sparrow of spring! The year beginning with younger hope than ever! The faint silvery warblings heard over the partially bare and moist fields from the blue-bird, the song-sparrow, and the red-wing, as if the last flakes of winter tinkled as they fell! What at such a time are histories, chronologies, traditions, and all written revelations? The brooks sing carols and glees to the spring. The marsh-hawk sailing low over the meadow is already seeking the first slimy life that awakes. The sinking sound of melting snow is heard in all dells, and the ice dissolves apace in the ponds. The grass flames up on the hillsides like a spring fire,—"et primitus oritur herba imbribus primoribus evocata,"[6]—as if the earth sent forth an inward heat to greet the returning sun; not yellow but green is the color of its flame;—the symbol of perpetual youth, the grass-blade, like a long green ribbon, streams from the sod into the summer, checked indeed by the frost, but anon pushing on again, lifting its spear of last year's hay with the fresh life below. It grows as steadily as the rill oozes out of the ground. It is almost identical with that, for in the growing days of June, when the rills are dry, the grass blades are their channels, and from year to year the herds drink at this perennial green stream, and the mower draws from it betimes their winter supply. So our human life but dies down to its roots, and still puts forth its green blade to eternity.

5. Mourning garments.
6. Varro's *Rerum Rusticarum* 2.2.14; Thoreau goes on to translate.

Walden is melting apace. There is a canal two rods wide along the norther-erly and westerly sides, and wider still at the east end. A great field of ice has cracked off from the main body. I hear a song-sparrow singing from the bushes on the shore,—*olit, olit, olit,—chip, chip, chip, che char,—che wiss, wiss, wiss.* He too is helping to crack it. How handsome the great sweeping curves in the edge of the ice, answering somewhat to those of the shore, but more regular! It is unusually hard, owing to the recent severe but transient cold, and all watered or waved like a palace floor. But the wind slides east-ward over its opaque surface in vain, till it reaches the living surface beyond. It is glorious to behold this ribbon of water sparkling in the sun, the bare face of the pond full of glee and youth, as if it spoke the joy of the fishes within it, and of the sands on its shore,—a silvery sheen as from the scales of a *leuciscus,* as it were all one active fish. Such is the contrast between winter and spring. Walden was dead and is alive again. But this spring it broke up more steadily, as I have said.

The change from storm and winter to serene and mild weather, from dark and sluggish hours to bright and elastic ones, is a memorable crisis which all things proclaim. It is seemingly instantaneous at last. Suddenly an influx of light filled my house, though the evening was at hand, and the clouds of winter still overhung it, and the eaves were dripping with sleety rain. I looked out the window, and lo! where yesterday was cold gray ice there lay the trans-parent pond already calm and full of hope as on a summer evening, reflect-ing a summer evening sky in its bosom, though none was visible overhead, as if it had intelligence with some remote horizon. I heard a robin in the dis-tance, the first I had heard for many a thousand years, methought, whose note I shall not forget for many a thousand more,—the same sweet and powerful song of yore. O the evening robin, at the end of a New England summer day! If I could ever find the twig he sits upon! I mean *he*; I mean *the twig.* This at least is not the *Turdus migratorius.*[7] The pitch-pines and shrub-oaks about my house, which had so long drooped, suddenly resumed their several characters, looked brighter, greener, and more erect and alive, as if effectually cleansed and restored by the rain. I knew that it would not rain any more. You may tell by looking at any twig of the forest, ay, at your very wood-pile, whether its winter is past or not. As it grew darker, I was startled by the *honking* of geese flying low over the woods, like weary travellers get-ting in late from southern lakes, and indulging at last in unrestrained com-plaint and mutual consolation. Standing at my door, I could hear the rush of their wings; when, driving toward my house, they suddenly spied my light, and with hushed clamor wheeled and settled in the pond. So I came in, and shut the door, and passed my first spring night in the woods.

In the morning I watched the geese from the door through the mist, sail-ing in the middle of the pond, fifty rods off, so large and tumultuous that Walden appeared like an aritifical pond for their amusement. But when I stood on the shore they at once rose up with a great flapping of wings at the signal of their commander, and when they had got into rank circled about over my head, twenty-nine of them, and then steered straight to Canada, with a regular *honk* from the leader at intervals, trusting to break their fast

---

7. American robin.

in muddier pools. A "plump" of ducks rose at the same time and took the route to the north in the wake of their noisier cousins.

For a week I heard the circling groping clangor of some solitary goose in the foggy mornings, seeking its companion, and still peopling the woods with the sound of a larger life than they could sustain. In April the pigeons were seen again flying express in small flocks, and in due time I heard the martins twittering over my clearing, though it had not seemed that the township contained so many that it could afford me any, and I fancied that they were peculiarly of the ancient race that dwelt in hollow trees ere white men came. In almost all climes the tortoise and the frog are among the precursors and heralds of this season, and birds fly with song and glancing plumage, and plants spring and bloom, and winds blow, to correct this slight oscillation of the poles and preserve the equilibrium of Nature.

As every season seems best to us in its turn, so the coming in of spring is like the creation of Cosmos out of Chaos and the realization of the Golden Age.—

> "Eurus ad Auroram, Nabathæaque regna recessit,
> Persidaque, et radiis juga subdita matutinis."

> "The East-Wind withdrew to Aurora and the Nabathæan kingdom,
> And the Persian, and the ridges placed under the morning rays.

• • •

> Man was born. Whether that Artificer of things,
> The origin of a better world, made him from the divine seed;
> Or the earth being recent and lately sundered from the high
> Ether, retained some seeds of cognate heaven."[8]

A single gentle rain makes the grass many shades greener. So our prospects brighten on the influx of better thoughts. We should be blessed if we lived in the present always, and took advantage of every accident that befell us, like the grass which confesses the influence of the slightest dew that falls on it; and did not spend our time in atoning for the neglect of past opportunities, which we call doing our duty. We loiter in winter while it is already spring. In a pleasant spring morning all men's sins are forgiven. Such a day is a truce to vice. While such a sun holds out to burn, the vilest sinner may return. Through our own recovered innocence we discern the innocence of our neighbors. You may have known your neighbor yesterday for a thief, a drunkard, or a sensualist, and merely pitied or despised him, and despaired of the world; but the sun shines bright and warm this first spring morning, re-creating the world, and you meet him at some serene work, and see how his exhausted and debauched veins expand with still joy and bless the new day, feel the spring influence with the innocence of infancy, and all his faults are forgotten. There is not only an atmosphere of good will about him, but even a savor of holiness groping for expression, blindly and ineffectually perhaps, like a new-born instinct, and for a short hour the south hill-side echoes to no vulgar jest. You see some innocent fair shoots preparing to burst from his gnarled rind and try another year's life, tender and fresh as

---

8. Ovid's *Metamorphoses* 1.61–62, 78–81.

the youngest plant. Even he has entered into the joy of his Lord. Why the jailer does not leave open his prison doors,—why the judge does not dismiss his case,—why the preacher does not dismiss his congregation! It is because they do not obey the hint which God gives them, nor accept the pardon which he freely offers to all.

"A return to goodness produced each day in the tranquil and beneficent breath of the morning, causes that in respect to the love of virtue and the hatred of vice, one approaches a little the primitive nature of man, as the sprouts of the forest which has been felled. In like manner the evil which one does in the interval of a day prevents the germs of virtues which began to spring up again from developing themselves and destroys them.

"After the germs of virtue have thus been prevented many times from developing themselves, then the beneficent breath of evening does not suffice to preserve them. As soon as the breath of evening does not suffice longer to preserve them, then the nature of man does not differ much from that of the brute. Men seeing the nature of this man like that of the brute, think that he has never possessed the innate faculty of reason. Are those the true and natural sentiments of man?"[9]

> "The Golden Age was first created, which without any avenger
> Spontaneously without law cherished fidelity and rectitude.
> Punishment and fear were not; nor were threatening words read
> On suspended brass; nor did the suppliant crowd fear
> The words of their judge; but were safe without an avenger.
> Not yet the pine felled on its mountains had descended
> To the liquid waves that it might see a foreign world,
> And mortals knew no shore but their own.
>
> • • •
>
> There was eternal spring, and placid zephyrs with warm
> Blasts soothed the flowers born without seed."[1]

On the 29th of April, as I was fishing from the bank of the river near the Nine-Acre-Corner bridge, standing on the quaking grass and willow roots, where the muskrats lurk, I heard a singular rattling sound, somewhat like that of the sticks which boys play with their fingers, when, looking up, I observed a very slight and graceful hawk, like a night-hawk, alternately soaring like a ripple and tumbling a rod or two over and over, showing the underside of its wings, which gleamed like a satin ribbon in the sun, or like the pearly inside of a shell. This sight reminded me of falconry and what nobleness and poetry are associated with that sport. The Merlin[2] it seemed to me it might be called: but I care not for its name. It was the most ethereal flight I had ever witnessed. It did not simply flutter like a butterfly, nor soar like the larger hawks, but it sported with proud reliance in the fields of air; mounting again and again with its strange chuckle, it repeated its free and beautiful fall, turning over and over like a kite, and then recovering from its lofty tumbling, as if it had never set its foot on *terra firma*. It appeared to

---

9. Mencius's (Meng-tzu's) *Works* 6.1.
1. Ovid's *Metamorphoses* 1.89–96, 107–08.

2. Small falcon or pigeon hawk.

have no companion in the universe,—sporting there alone,—and to need none but the morning and the ether with which it played. It was not lonely, but made all the earth lonely beneath it. Where was the parent which hatched it, its kindred, and its father in the heavens? The tenant of the air, it seemed related to the earth but by an egg hatched some time in the crevice of a crag;—or was its native nest made in the angle of a cloud, woven of the rainbow's trimmings and the sunset sky, and lined with some soft midsummer haze caught up from earth? Its eyry[3] now some cliffy cloud.

Beside this I got a rare mess of golden and silver and bright cupreous[4] fishes, which looked like a string of jewels. Ah! I have penetrated to those meadows on the morning of many a first spring day, jumping from hummock to hummock, from willow root to willow root, when the wild river valley and the woods were bathed in so pure and bright a light as would have waked the dead, if they had been slumbering in their graves, as some suppose. There needs no stronger proof of immortality. All things must live in such a light. O Death, where was thy sting? O Grave, where was thy victory, then?[5]

Our village life would stagnate if it were not for the unexplored forests and meadows which surround it. We need the tonic of wildness,—to wade sometimes in marshes where the bittern and the meadow-hen lurk, and hear the booming of the snipe; to smell the whispering sedge where only some wilder and more solitary fowl builds her nest, and the mink crawls with its belly close to the ground. At the same time that we are earnest to explore and learn all things, we require that all things be mysterious and unexplorable, that land and sea be infinitely wild, unsurveyed and unfathomed by us because unfathomable. We can never have enough of Nature. We must be refreshed by the sight of inexhaustible vigor, vast and Titanic features, the sea-coast with its wrecks, the wilderness with its living and its decaying trees, the thunder cloud, and the rain which lasts three weeks and produces freshets. We need to witness our own limits transgressed, and some life pasturing freely where we never wander. We are cheered when we observe the vulture feeding on the carrion which disgusts and disheartens us and deriving health and strength from the repast. There was a dead horse in the hollow by the path to my house, which compelled me sometimes to go out of my way, especially in the night when the air was heavy, but the assurance it gave me of the strong appetite and inviolable health of Nature was my compensation for this. I love to see that Nature is so rife with life that myriads can be afforded to be sacrificed and suffered to prey on one another; that tender organizations can be so serenely squashed out of existence like pulp,—tadpoles which herons gobble up, and tortoises and toads run over in the road; and that sometimes it has rained flesh and blood! With the liability to accident, we must see how little account is to be made of it. The impression made on a wise man is that of universal innocence. Poison is not poisonous after all, nor are any wounds fatal. Compassion is a very untenable ground. It must be expeditious. Its pleadings will not bear to be stereotyped.

Early in May, the oaks, hickories, maples, and other trees, just putting out amidst the pine woods around the pond, imparted a brightness like

---

3. Aerie; bird's nest.
4. Coppery.

5. 1 Corinthians 15.55: "O death, where is thy sting? O grave, where is thy victory?"

sunshine to the landscape, especially in cloudy days, as if the sun were breaking through mists and shining faintly on the hill-sides here and there. On the third or fourth of May I saw a loon in the pond, and during the first week of the month I heard the whippoorwill, the brown-thrasher, the veery, the wood-pewee, the chewink, and other birds. I had heard the woodthrush long before. The phœbe had already come once more and looked in at my door and window, to see if my house was cavern-like enough for her, sustaining herself on humming wings with clinched talons, as if she held by the air, while she surveyed the premises. The sulphur-like pollen of the pitch-pine soon covered the pond and the stones and rotten wood along the shore, so that you could have collected a barrel-ful. This is the "sulphur showers" we hear of. Even in Calidas' drama of Sacontala, we read of "rills dyed yellow with the golden dust of the lotus."[6] And so the seasons went rolling on into summer, as one rambles into higher and higher grass.

Thus was my first year's life in the woods completed; and the second year was similar to it. I finally left Walden September 6th, 1847.

18. Conclusion

To the sick the doctors wisely recommend a change of air and scenery. Thank Heaven, here is not all the world. The buck-eye does not grow in New England, and the mocking-bird is rarely heard here. The wild-goose is more of a cosmopolite than we; he breaks his fast in Canada, takes a luncheon in the Ohio, and plumes himself for the night in a southern bayou. Even the bison, to some extent, keeps pace with the seasons, cropping the pastures of the Colorado only till a greener and sweeter grass awaits him by the Yellowstone. Yet we think that if rail-fences are pulled down, and stone-walls piled up on our farms, bounds are henceforth set to our lives and our fates decided. If you are chosen town-clerk, forsooth, you cannot go to Tierra del Fuego[7] this summer: but you may go to the land of infernal fire nevertheless. The universe is wider than our views of it.

Yet we should oftener look over the tafferel of our craft, like curious passengers, and not make the voyage like stupid sailors picking oakum.[8] The other side of the globe is but the home of our correspondent. Our voyaging is only great-circle sailing, and the doctors prescribe for diseases of the skin merely. One hastens to Southern Africa to chase the giraffe; but surely that is not the game he would be after. How long, pray, would a man hunt giraffes if he could? Snipes and woodcocks also may afford rare sport; but I trust it would be nobler game to shoot one's self.—

> "Direct your eye sight inward, and you'll find
> A thousand regions in your mind
> Yet undiscovered. Travel them, and be
> Expert in home-cosmography."[9]

6. Sir William Jones's 18th-century translation of *Sacontalá*, act 5, by Cálidás (5th century), Hindu writer.
7. Thoreau puns on the meaning of the name of the archipelago at the southern tip of South America: land of fire (Spanish).

8. Picking old rope apart so the pieces of hemp could be tarred and used for caulking. "Tafferel": i.e., taffrail; guardrail at a ship's stern.
9. William Habington (1605–1654), "To My Honoured Friend Sir Ed. P. Knight."

What does Africa,—what does the West stand for? Is not our own interior white on the chart? black though it may prove, like the coast, when discovered. Is it the source of the Nile, or the Niger, or the Mississippi, or a North West Passage around this continent, that we would find? Are these the problems which most concern mankind? Is Franklin[1] the only man who is lost, that his wife should be so earnest to find him? Does Mr. Grinnell[2] know where he himself is? Be rather the Mungo Park, the Lewis and Clarke and Frobisher,[3] of your own streams and oceans; explore your own higher latitudes,—with shiploads of preserved meats to support you, if they be necessary; and pile the empty cans sky-high for a sign. Were preserved meats invented to preserve meat merely? Nay, be a Columbus to whole new continents and worlds within you, opening new channels, not of trade, but of thought. Every man is the lord of a realm beside which the earthly empire of the Czar is but a petty state, a hummock left by the ice. Yet some can be patriotic who have no *self*-respect, and sacrifice the greater to the less. They love the soil which makes their graves, but have no sympathy with the spirit which may still animate their clay. Patriotism is a maggot in their heads. What was the meaning of that South-Sea Exploring Expedition,[4] with all its parade and expense, but an indirect recognition of the fact, that there are continents and seas in the moral world, to which every man is an isthmus or an inlet, yet unexplored by him, but that it is easier to sail many thousand miles through cold and storm and cannibals, in a government ship, with five hundred men and boys to assist one, than it is to explore the private sea, the Atlantic and Pacific Ocean of one's being alone.—

> "Erret, et extremos alter scrutetur Iberos.
> Plus habet hic vitæ, plus habet ille viæ."[5]

> Let them wander and scrutinize the outlandish Australians.
> I have more of God, they more of the road.

It is not worth the while to go round the world to count the cats in Zanzibar.[6] Yet do this even till you can do better, and you may perhaps find some "Symmes' Hole"[7] by which to get at the inside at last. England and France, Spain and Portugal, Gold Coast and Slave Coast, all front on this private sea; but no bark from them has ventured out of sight of land, though it is without doubt the direct way to India. If you would learn to speak all tongues and conform to the customs of all nations, if you would travel farther than all travellers, be naturalized in all climes, and cause the Sphinx

---

1. Sir John Franklin (1785–1847), lost on a British expedition to the Arctic.
2. Henry Grinnell (1799–1874), a rich New York whale-oil merchant from a New Bedford family who sponsored two attempts to rescue Sir Franklin, one in 1850 and another in 1853.
3. I.e., an explorer like Martin Frobisher (1535?–1594), English mariner. Mungo Park (1771–1806), Scottish explorer of Africa. Meriwether Lewis (1774–1809) and William Clark (1770–1838), leaders of the American expedition into the Louisiana Territory (1804–06).
4. The famous expedition to the Pacific Antarctic led by Charles Wilkes (1798–1877) during

1838–1842.
5. Thoreau's journal for May 10, 1841, begins: "A good warning to the restless tourists of these days is contained in the last verses of Claudian's 'Old Man of Verona.'" Claudian (c. 370–404 C.E.) was one of the last of the Latin classic poets and author of *Epigrammata*, where Thoreau found the passage he loosely translates here.
6. Thoreau had read Charles Pickering's *The Races of Man* (1851), which reports on the domestic cats in Zanzibar.
7. In 1818 Captain John Symmes (1780–1829) theorized that the earth was hollow with openings at both the North and South Poles.

to dash her head against a stone,[8] even obey the precept of the old philosopher, and Explore thyself. Herein are demanded the eye and the nerve. Only the defeated and deserters go to the wars, cowards that run away and enlist. Start now on that farthest western way, which does not pause at the Mississippi or the Pacific, nor conduct toward a worn-out China or Japan, but leads on direct a tangent to this sphere, summer and winter, day and night, sun down, moon down, and at last earth down too.

It is said that Mirabeau took to highway robbery "to ascertain what degree of resolution was necessary in order to place one's self in formal opposition to the most sacred laws of society." He declared that "a soldier who fights in the ranks does not require half so much courage as a foot-pad,"—"that honor and religion have never stood in the way of a well-considered and a firm resolve."[9] This was manly, as the world goes; and yet it was idle, if not desperate. A saner man would have found himself often enough "in formal opposition" to what are deemed "the most sacred laws of society," through obedience to yet more sacred laws, and so have tested his resolution without going out of his way. It is not for a man to put himself in such an attitude to society, but to maintain himself in whatever attitude he find himself through obedience to the laws of his being, which will never be one of opposition to a just government, if he should chance to meet with such.

I left the woods for as good a reason as I went there. Perhaps it seemed to me that I had several more lives to live, and could not spare any more time for that one. It is remarkable how easily and insensibly we fall into a particular route, and make a beaten track for ourselves. I had not lived there a week before my feet wore a path from my door to the pond-side; and though it is five or six years since I trod it, it is still quite distinct. It is true, I fear that others may have fallen into it, and so helped to keep it open. The surface of the earth is soft and impressible by the feet of men; and so with the paths which the mind travels. How worn and dusty, then, must be the highways of the world, how deep the ruts of tradition and conformity! I did not wish to take a cabin passage, but rather to go before the mast and on the deck of the world, for there I could best see the moonlight amid the mountains. I do not wish to go below now.

I learned this, at least, by my experiment; that if one advances confidently in the direction of his dreams, and endeavors to live the life which he has imagined, he will meet with a success unexpected in common hours. He will put some things behind, will pass an invisible boundary; new, universal, and more liberal laws will begin to establish themselves around and within him; or the old laws be expanded, and interpreted in his favor in a more liberal sense, and he will live with the license of a higher order of beings. In proportion as he simplifies his life, the laws of the universe will appear less complex, and solitude will not be solitude, nor poverty poverty, nor weakness weakness. If you have built castles in the air, your work need not be lost; that is where they should be. Now put the foundations under them.

---

8. As the Theban Sphinx did when Oedipus guessed her riddle. Thebes here is the ancient Greek city, not the Egyptian city Thoreau previously referred to.

9. Thoreau encountered this passage by the French statesman Comte de Mirabeau (1749–1791) in *Harper's* 1 (1850).

It is a ridiculous demand which England and America make, that you shall speak so that they can understand you. Neither men nor toad-stools grow so. As if that were important, and there were not enough to understand you without them. As if Nature could support but one order of understandings, could not sustain birds as well as quadrupeds, flying as well as creeping things, and *hush* and *who*, which Bright[1] can understand, were the best English. As if there were safety in stupidity alone. I fear chiefly lest my expression may not be *extra-vagant*[2] enough, may not wander far enough beyond the narrow limits of my daily experience, so as to be adequate to the truth of which I have been convinced. *Extra vagance!* it depends on how you are yarded. The migrating buffalo, which seeks new pastures in another latitude, is not extravagant like the cow which kicks over the pail, leaps the cow-yard fence, and runs after her calf, in milking time. I desire to speak somewhere *without* bounds; like a man in a waking moment, to men in their waking moments; for I am convinced that I cannot exaggerate enough even to lay the foundation of a true expression. Who that has heard a strain of music feared then lest he should speak extravagantly any more forever? In view of the future or possible, we should live quite laxly and undefined in front, our outlines dim and misty on that side; as our shadows reveal an insensible perspiration toward the sun. The volatile truth of our words should continually betray the inadequacy of the residual statement. Their truth is instantly *translated*; its literal monument alone remains. The words which express our faith and piety are not definite; yet they are significant and fragrant like frankincense to superior natures.

Why level downward to our dullest perception always, and praise that as common sense? The commonest sense is the sense of men asleep, which they express by snoring. Sometimes we are inclined to class those who are once-and-a-half witted with the half-witted, because we appreciate only a third part of their wit. Some would find fault with the morning-red, if they ever got up early enough. "They pretend," as I hear, "that the verses of Kabir have four different senses; illusion, spirit, intellect, and the exoteric doctrine of the Vedas;"[3] but in this part of the world it is considered a ground for complaint if a man's writings admit of more than one interpretation. While England endeavors to cure the potato-rot, will not any endeavor to cure the brain-rot, which prevails so much more widely and fatally?

I do not suppose that I have attained to obscurity, but I should be proud if no more fatal fault were found with my pages on this score than was found with the Walden ice. Southern customers objected to its blue color, which is the evidence of its purity, as if it were muddy, and preferred the Cambridge ice, which is white, but tastes of weeds. The purity men love is like the mists which envelop the earth, and not like the azure ether beyond.

Some are dinning in our ears that we Americans, and moderns generally, are intellectual dwarfs compared with the ancients, or even the Elizabethan men. But what is that to the purpose? A living dog is better than a dead lion.[4] Shall a man go and hang himself because he belongs to the race of

1. Name for an ox.
2. Thoreau provides the hyphen to emphasize the word's Latin roots (*extra*, "outside"; *vagari*, "to wander").

3. M. Garcin de Tassy's *Histoire de la littérature hindoue* (1839).
4. Ecclesiastes 9.4.

pygmies, and not be the biggest pygmy that he can? Let every one mind his own business, and endeavor to be what he was made.

Why should we be in such desperate haste to succeed, and in such desperate enterprises? If a man does not keep pace with his companions, perhaps it is because he hears a different drummer. Let him step to the music which he hears, however measured or far away. It is not important that he should mature as soon as an apple-tree or an oak. Shall he turn his spring into summer? If the condition of things which we were made for is not yet, what were any reality which we can substitute? We will not be shipwrecked on a vain reality. Shall we with pains erect a heaven of blue glass over ourselves, though when it is done we shall be sure to gaze still at the true ethereal heaven far above, as if the former were not?

There was an artist in the city of Kouroo[5] who was disposed to strive after perfection. One day it came into his mind to make a staff. Having considered that in an imperfect work time is an ingredient, but into a perfect work time does not enter, he said to himself, It shall be perfect in all respects, though I should do nothing else in my life. He proceeded instantly to the forest for wood, being resolved that it should not be made of unsuitable material; and as he searched for and rejected stick after stick, his friends gradually deserted him, for they grew old in their works and died, but he grew not older by a moment. His singleness of purpose and resolution, and his elevated piety, endowed him, without his knowledge, with perennial youth. As he made no compromise with Time, Time kept out of his way, and only sighed at a distance because he could not overcome him. Before he had found a stock in all respects suitable the city of Kouroo was a hoary ruin, and he sat on one of its mounds to peel the stick. Before he had given it the proper shape the dynasty of the Candahars was at an end, and with the point of the stick he wrote the name of the last of that race in the sand, and then resumed his work. By the time he had smoothed and polished the staff Kalpa was no longer the pole-star; and ere he had put on the ferule and the head adorned with precious stones, Brahma had awoke and slumbered many times. But why do I stay to mention these things? When the finishing stroke was put to his work, it suddenly expanded before the eyes of the astonished artist into the fairest of all the creations of Brahma. He had made a new system in making a staff, a world with full and fair proportions; in which, though the old cities and dynasties had passed away, fairer and more glorious ones had taken their places. And now he saw by the heap of shavings still fresh at his feet, that, for him and his work, the former lapse of time had been an illusion, and that no more time had elapsed than is required for a single scintillation from the brain of Brahma to fall on and inflame the tinder of a mortal brain. The material was pure, and his art was pure; how could the result be other than wonderful?

No face which we can give to a matter will stead us so well at last as the truth. This alone wears well. For the most part, we are not where we are, but in a false position. Through an infirmity of our natures, we suppose a case, and put ourselves into it, and hence are in two cases at the same time, and it is doubly difficult to get out. In sane moments we regard only the

---

5. Thoreau in all likelihood invented this fable of artistry, though the reference to "Kouroo" invokes "Kuru," a legendary hero in India.

facts, the case that is. Say what you have to say, not what you ought. Any truth is better than make-believe. Tom Hyde, the tinker, standing on the gallows, was asked if he had any thing to say. "Tell the tailors," said he, "to remember to make a knot in their thread before they take the first stitch."[6] His companion's prayer is forgotten.

However mean your life is, meet it and live it; do not shun it and call it hard names. It is not so bad as you are. It looks poorest when you are richest. The fault-finder will find faults even in paradise. Love your life, poor as it is. You may perhaps have some pleasant, thrilling, glorious hours, even in a poor-house. The setting sun is reflected from the windows of the alms-house as brightly as from the rich man's abode; the snow melts before its door as early in the spring. I do not see but a quiet mind may live as contentedly there, and have as cheering thoughts, as in a palace. The town's poor seem to me often to live the most independent lives of any. May be they are simply great enough to receive without misgiving. Most think that they are above being supported by the town; but it oftener happens that they are not above supporting themselves by dishonest means, which should be more disreputable. Cultivate poverty like a garden herb, like sage. Do not trouble yourself much to get new things, whether clothes or friends. Turn the old; return to them. Things do not change; we change. Sell your clothes and keep your thoughts. God will see that you do not want society. If I were confined to a corner of a garret all my days, like a spider, the world would be just as large to me while I had my thoughts about me. The philosopher said: "From an army of three divisions one can take away its general, and put it in disorder; from the man the most abject and vulgar one cannot take away his thought."[7] Do not seek so anxiously to be developed, to subject yourself to many influences to be played on; it is all dissipation. Humility like darkness reveals the heavenly lights. The shadows of poverty and meanness gather around us, "and lo! creation widens to our view."[8] We are often reminded that if there were bestowed on us the wealth of Crœsus,[9] our aims must still be the same, and our means essentially the same. Moreover, if you are restricted in your range by poverty, if you cannot buy books and newspapers, for instance, you are but confined to the most significant and vital experiences; you are compelled to deal with the material which yields the most sugar and the most starch. It is life near the bone where it is sweetest. You are defended from being a trifler. No man loses ever on a lower level by magnanimity on a higher. Superfluous wealth can buy superfluities only. Money is not required to buy one necessary of the soul.

I live in the angle of a leaden wall, into whose composition was poured a little alloy of bell metal. Often, in the repose of my mid-day, there reaches my ears a confused *tintinnabulum*[1] from without. It is the noise of my contemporaries. My neighbors tell me of their adventures with famous gentlemen and ladies, what notabilities they met at the dinner-table; but I am no more interested in such things than in the contents of the Daily Times. The interest and

6. Presumably a reference to the tailors who will sew Hyde's shroud. Thoreau may have invented this anecdote; scholars have been unable to identify a Tom Hyde who was executed.
7. Confucius's *Analects* 9.25.
8. From the sonnet "To Night" (1828) by the

Spanish-born writer Joseph Blanco White (1775–1841), who emigrated to England in 1810.
9. King of Lydia (d. 546 B.C.E.), fabled as the richest man on earth.
1. Tinkling.

the conversation are about costume and manners chiefly; but a goose is a goose still, dress it as you will. They tell me of California and Texas, of England and the Indies, of the Hon. Mr. ———— of Georgia or of Massachusetts, all transient and fleeting phenomena, till I am ready to leap from their court-yard like the Mameluke bey.[2] I delight to come to my bearings,—not walk in procession with pomp and parade, in a conspicuous place, but to walk even with the Builder of the universe, if I may,—not to live in this restless, nervous, bustling, trivial Nineteenth Century, but stand or sit thoughtfully while it goes by. What are men celebrating? They are all on a committee of arrangements, and hourly expect a speech from somebody. God is only the president of the day, and Webster is his orator.[3] I love to weigh, to settle, to gravitate toward that which most strongly and rightfully attracts me;—not hang by the beam of the scale and try to weigh less,—not suppose a case, but take the case that is; to travel the only path I can, and that on which no power can resist me. It affords me no satisfaction to commence to spring an arch before I have got a solid foundation. Let us not play at kittlybenders.[4] There is a solid bottom every where. We read that the traveller asked the boy if the swamp before him had a hard bottom. The boy replied that it had. But presently the traveller's horse sank in up to the girths, and he observed to the boy, "I thought you said that this bog had a hard bottom." "So it has," answered the latter, "but you have not got half way to it yet." So it is with the bogs and quicksands of society; but he is an old boy that knows it. Only what is thought said or done at a certain rare coincidence is good. I would not be one of those who will foolishly drive a nail into mere lath and plastering; such a deed would keep me awake nights. Give me a hammer, and let me feel for the furring.[5] Do not depend on the putty. Drive a nail home and clinch it so faithfully that you can wake up in the night and think of your work with satisfaction,—a work at which you would not be ashamed to invoke the Muse. So will help you God, and so only. Every nail driven should be as another rivet in the machine of the universe, you carrying on the work.

Rather than love, than money, than fame, give me truth. I sat at a table where were rich food and wine in abundance, and obsequious attendance, but sincerity and truth were not; and I went away hungry from the inhospitable board. The hospitality was as cold as the ices. I thought that there was no need of ice to freeze them. They talked to me of the age of the wine and the fame of the vintage; but I thought of an older, a newer, and purer wine, of a more glorious vintage, which they had not got, and could not buy. The style, the house and grounds and "entertainment" pass for nothing with me. I called on the king, but he made me wait in his hall, and conducted like a man incapacitated for hospitality. There was a man in my neighborhood who lived in a hollow tree. His manners were truly regal. I should have done better had I called on him.

---

2. A famous romantic exploit: in 1811 the Egyptian Mehemet Ali Pasha attempted to massacre the Mameluke caste, but one bey, or officer, escaped by leaping from a wall onto his horse.
3. Political meetings then had "presidents" (because they presided). Thoreau plays on the saying from Islam "There is no other God than Allah, and Mohammed is his prophet." Thoreau again expresses his contempt for Massachusetts senator Daniel Webster.
4. A game of trying to skate or slide over thin ice without breaking through.
5. Narrow lumber nailed as backing for lath. The first edition reads "furrowing," and one manuscript draft reads "stud."

How long shall we sit in our porticoes practising idle and musty virtues, which any work would make impertinent? As if one were to begin the day with long-suffering, and hire a man to hoe his potatoes; and in the afternoon go forth to practise Christian meekness and charity with goodness aforethought! Consider the China[6] pride and stagnant self-complacency of mankind. This generation reclines a little to congratulate itself on being the last of an illustrious line; and in Boston and London and Paris and Rome, thinking of its long descent, it speaks of its progress in art and science and literature with satisfaction. There are the Records of the Philosophical Societies, and the public Eulogies of *Great Men!* It is the good Adam contemplating his own virtue. "Yes, we have done great deeds, and sung divine songs, which shall never die,"—that is, as long as *we* can remember them. The learned societies and great men of Assyria,[7]—where are they? What youthful philosophers and experimentalists we are! There is not one of my readers who has yet lived a whole human life. These may be but the spring months in the life of the race. If we have had the seven-years' itch,[8] we have not seen the seventeen-year locust yet in Concord. We are acquainted with a mere pellicle[9] of the globe on which we live. Most have not delved six feet beneath the surface, nor leaped as many above it. We know not where we are. Beside, we are sound asleep nearly half our time. Yet we esteem ourselves wise, and have an established order on the surface. Truly, we are deep thinkers, we are ambitious spirits! As I stand over the insect crawling amid the pine needles on the forest floor, and endeavoring to conceal itself from my sight, and ask myself why it will cherish those humble thoughts, and hide its head from me who might perhaps be its benefactor, and impart to its race some cheering information, I am reminded of the greater Benefactor and Intelligence that stands over me the human insect.

There is an incessant influx of novelty into the world, and yet we tolerate incredible dulness. I need only suggest what kind of sermons are still listened to in the most enlightened countries. There are such words as joy and sorrow, but they are only the burden of a psalm, sung with a nasal twang, while we believe in the ordinary and mean. We think that we can change our clothes only. It is said that the British Empire is very large and respectable, and that the United States are a first-rate power. We do not believe that a tide rises and falls behind every man which can float the British Empire like a chip, if he should ever harbor it in his mind. Who knows what sort of seventeen-year locust will next come out of the ground? The government of the world I live in was not framed, like that of Britain, in after-dinner conversations over the wine.

The life in us is like the water in the river. It may rise this year higher than man has ever known it, and flood the parched uplands; even this may be the eventful year, which will drown out all our muskrats. It was not always dry land where we dwell. I see far inland the banks which the stream anciently washed, before science began to record its freshets. Every one has heard the story which has gone the rounds of New England, of a strong and beautiful bug which came out of the dry leaf of an old table of apple-tree wood, which

6. Thoreau and others of the time regarded China as complacent in its isolationism.
7. Ancient empire in western Asia.
8. Painful skin irritation caused by mites.
9. Skin.

had stood in a farmer's kitchen for sixty years, first in Connecticut, and afterward in Massachusetts,—from an egg deposited in the living tree many years earlier still, as appeared by counting the annual layers beyond it; which was heard gnawing out for several weeks, hatched perchance by the heat of an urn.[1] Who does not feel his faith in a resurrection and immortality strengthened by hearing of this? Who knows what beautiful and winged life, whose egg has been buried for ages under many concentric layers of woodenness in the dead dry life of society, deposited at first in the alburnum[2] of the green and living tree, which has been gradually converted into the semblance of its well-seasoned tomb,—heard perchance gnawing out now for years by the astonished family of man, as they sat round the festive board,—may unexpectedly come forth from amidst society's most trivial and hand-selled furniture, to enjoy its perfect summer life at last!

I do not say that John or Jonathan[3] will realize all this; but such is the character of that morrow which mere lapse of time can never make to dawn. The light which puts out our eyes is darkness to us. Only that day dawns to which we are awake. There is more day to dawn. The sun is but a morning star.

THE END

1854

---

1. An account of the incident is in Timothy Dwight's *Travels in New England and New York* (1821), vol. 2.

2. Young, soft wood.
3. John Bull or Brother Jonathan, i.e., England or America.

FREDERICK DOUGLASS
1818–1895

In the concluding chapter of his famous autobiography, *Narrative of the Life of Frederick Douglass, An American Slave, Written by Himself* (1845), Douglass describes the moment in 1841 when he first stepped forward to speak at an antislavery convention in Nantucket, Massachusetts. "It was a severe cross," he says, "and I took it up reluctantly." However reluctant he may have been, in the moments following the speech the twenty-three-year-old fugitive slave "felt a degree of freedom" and, just as important, realized he had discovered his vocation. As he states at the end of the *Narrative*: "From that time until now, I have been engaged in pleading the cause of my brethren—with what success, and with what devotion, I leave those acquainted with my labors to decide." Douglass would continue to plead the cause of African Americans for over fifty years. He published three versions of his autobiography—the *Narrative* (1845), *My Bondage and My Freedom* (1855), *Life and Times of Frederick Douglass* (1881; rev. ed. 1892)—as well as a novella, "The Heroic Slave" (1853), and numerous essays and speeches. He also established and edited three African American newspapers—the *North Star* (1847–51), *Frederick Douglass' Paper* (1851–59), and *Douglass' Monthly* (1859–63)—and edited a fourth, the *New*

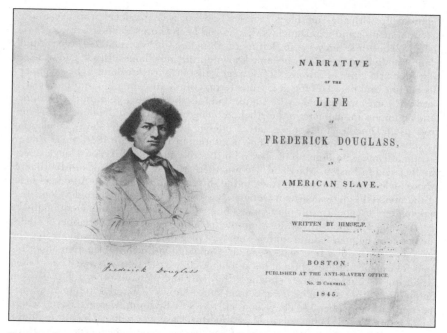

Douglass's *Narrative*. Frontispiece and title page of the first edition (1845).

National Era (1870–73). By the time of his death, Douglass was thought of, in the United States and abroad, as the most influential African American leader of the nineteenth century and as one of the greatest orators of the age. In the manner of Benjamin Franklin, whom he greatly admired, Douglass presented himself as a representative American whose rise to prominence spoke to the promises of the nation's egalitarian ideology. But he also had a clear-eyed understanding of the hurdles that slavery and racism placed in the way of African Americans. Regularly invoking the principles of the Declaration of Independence, Douglass throughout his life challenged the nation to live up to its founding ideals. In "The Lessons of the Hour" (1894), one of his final speeches, Douglass condemned the rise of lynching with the passion and vigor of his early writing, seeing this latest outbreak of violence against black people as a threat to what he had devoted his life to achieving: a multiracial United States offering equal rights and justice for all.

Douglass was born into slavery as Frederick Augustus Washington Bailey in February 1818 at Holme Hill Farm in Talbot County, on the Eastern Shore of Maryland. His mother was Harriet Bailey; his father was a white man whose identity is still not known, although widely assumed to have been his mother's owner, Aaron Anthony. In 1826, about a year after the death of his mother and shortly after the death of Anthony, Douglass became the property of Thomas Auld and was sent to live with Thomas's brother Hugh Auld and his wife, Sophia, in Baltimore. According to the 1845 *Narrative*, Sophia began to teach Douglass how to read, but Hugh forbade her to continue because, he said, learning "would forever unfit him to be a slave." Nevertheless, as the autobiographies recount, Douglass cleverly found ways to learn how to read and write. During this first residence in Baltimore, Douglass acquired and pored over *The Columbian Orator* (1797), a popular school text, finding its many speeches denouncing oppression applicable to his own situation. He read about abolition as an organized movement in the *Baltimore American* and established a close relationship with the free black Charles Lawson, a lay preacher who became his spiritual mentor and told Douglass that he had been chosen to do "great work."

In 1833, after seven years in Baltimore, Douglass was returned to Thomas Auld's plantation, where he quickly became known for his rebellious attitude and was sent to work on the farm of Edward Covey, a specialist in "slave breaking." The account of his decline and reawakening at Covey's farm, culminating in a hand-to-hand battle between Covey and Douglass in August 1834, is the turning point of the *Narrative* (and an important moment in the other autobiographies as well). Following this confrontation, Douglass took on a greater leadership role among the slaves, conducting a Sabbath school at William Freeland's plantation in 1835 and, in 1836, organizing an escape attempt with a group of slaves. For his role in the failed plot, Douglass was briefly jailed in Easton, Maryland. He was then returned to the Aulds in Baltimore, where he learned the caulking trade in the shipyards. Though Hugh Auld kept most of the money Frederick earned, Douglass was able to save enough to develop a feasible plan of escape. In this plan he was helped both financially and emotionally by the free black Anna Murray, to whom he became engaged on September 3, 1838, the very day he boarded a train for New York disguised as a sailor and carrying the borrowed papers of a free black seaman. Douglass withheld information about his mode of escape until the third of his autobiographies, the 1881 *Life and Times*, when disclosing it could no longer endanger the lives and plans of other fugitives from Baltimore. Within days of his escape Anna joined him in New York City, and they were married on September 15. They soon left for New Bedford, Massachusetts, where the likelihood of his being captured as a fugitive slave was reduced by his assuming the name "Douglass," which he took from Sir Walter Scott's poem *Lady of the Lake* (1810).

Though Douglass in the *Narrative* emphasizes the splendor of New Bedford compared to towns under slavery, life in New Bedford was not easy for the newly married couple. Douglass was discriminated against when he sought work as a caulker and had to piece together a living doing odd jobs. In 1839 he became a licensed preacher in the African Methodist Episcopal Zion Church; that same year the Douglasses' first child, Rosetta, was born. A son, Lewis, was born the following year, and the other three Douglass children—Frederick, Charles, and Annie—were born in 1842, 1844, and 1849, respectively. Soon after arriving in New Bedford, Douglass subscribed to the abolitionist William Lloyd Garrison's *Liberator*. Garrison was in the audience when Douglass delivered his first antislavery speech, and shortly thereafter he hired Douglass as a speaker in his Massachusetts Anti-Slavery Society. During 1841–43, Douglass delivered his antislavery message on behalf of Garrison's organization in a number of northern states, and on one occasion in 1843, in Pendleton, Indiana, he was attacked by an anti-abolitionist mob and suffered a broken hand. Douglass began work on his narrative in 1844, and it was published in May 1845 by Garrison's Anti-Slavery Office in Boston. The *Narrative* sold some thirty thousand copies in its first five years, making it a bona fide best-seller for the time and helping to establish Douglass as an international spokesperson for freedom and equality. Some earlier slave narratives had been ghostwritten or composed with the help of white editors, but the *Narrative*'s vivid detail and stylistic distinctiveness, combined with the reputation Douglass had earned as an eloquent speaker, left no doubt that Douglass had in fact written his own story in his own words.

Garrison's abolitionist principles—a commitment to an immediate end to slavery, an advocacy of moral persuasion over violence, and a belief that the Constitution was a proslavery document—inspired Douglass in the early to middle 1840s. When he went on an extended speaking tour in Great Britain during 1845–47 (in part to escape the fugitive-slave hunters that he feared would track him down after the publication of the *Narrative*), he spoke as a Garrisonian abolitionist. But upon his return to the United States as a free man—British antislavery friends had purchased his freedom for $711 in 1846—Douglass became increasingly suspicious of Garrison, particularly when Garrison attempted to bully him into shutting down his newspaper, the *North Star*, which Douglass founded not in New Bedford, but in Rochester, New York, where Douglass resettled in part to escape the influence of Garrison. In the inaugural issue of December 3, 1847, Douglass declared that in the antislavery and antiracism struggle, African Americans "must be our own representatives and advocates, not exclusively, but peculiarly—not distinct from, but in connection with our white friends." Garrison, who wanted absolute loyalty and control of the movement, began to question Douglass's antislavery politics and even published unsubstantiated rumors in the *Liberator* about Douglass's romantic involvement with Julia Griffiths, a white Englishwoman living in the Douglass home and helping with editorial work on the *North Star*. But along with the personality clashes, there were ideological differences between the two. By 1851, after forming a friendship with the New York abolitionist Gerrit Smith, Douglass formally broke with Garrison, announcing his belief in a more pragmatic political abolitionism that regarded the Constitution as an antislavery document, that saw the value in steadily working toward the goals of antislavery, and that defended the strategic use of violence as a response to the violence of slavery.

In 1855 Douglass published *My Bondage and My Freedom*, a revised and substantially longer version of his 1845 autobiography. In covering the ten years of his life since the *Narrative*, Douglass wrote about his encounters with racism in the North, his work as an abolitionist, and his break with Garrison. No longer willing to "leave the philosophy" of abolition to Garrison and other white abolitionists, Douglass asserted his intellectual and interpretive independence and also his deeper connections to black moral reformers and abolitionists. It is significant that the second autobiography was introduced not by white abolitionists (as with the *Narrative*) but by the black physician and abolitionist James McCune Smith (1813–1865), who celebrated Douglass as "a Representative American man—a type of his countrymen." *My Bondage and My Freedom* was widely read, selling eighteen thousand copies during its first two years.

Like all autobiographers, Douglass artistically shaped the facts of his life to underscore the particular truths that he wished to convey at the moment of composition. In the 1845 *Narrative*, he presented himself as relatively isolated from his fellow slaves, describing his fight with Covey as a heroic instance of individual rebellion; in the 1855 *My Bondage and My Freedom*, he depicted the fight as involving several other African Americans who came to his assistance. Similarly, in 1845 Douglass said little about the role of his mother in his life because he wanted to show his white readers how slavery divided mothers and children; in 1855, he celebrated the influence of his grandmother and mother. This new emphasis on the importance of black culture and family to his developing identity as an antislavery leader resonated with the rhetoric of sentiment associated with Harriet Beecher Stowe's *Uncle Tom's Cabin* (1852) and other works by popular mid-nineteenth-century women writers; it testified to Douglass's awareness that women were a powerful force within the abolitionist movement. Stowe's influence can also be felt on Douglass's only work of fiction, the novella "The Heroic Slave," which he published in 1853 in *Frederick Douglass' Paper* and in a fund-raising volume for his newspaper. Like Stowe, he represented sympathetic bonds between whites and blacks that could lead to united action against enslavers. Unlike Stowe in *Uncle Tom's Cabin*, he celebrated a dark-skinned man capable of using violence against whites, and showed blacks moving south to the Caribbean instead of north to Canada.

Following the Supreme Court's 1857 ruling in the *Dred Scott* case, which declared that blacks could never become citizens of the United States, Douglass became more militant in his writing. Though he refused to participate in John Brown's 1859 raid on the federal arsenal at Harpers Ferry, which he regarded as a suicidal action, he was obliged to flee to Canada and thence to England because of his known association with Brown. He returned in May 1860 after receiving news of the death of his daughter Annie. Once the Civil War began, Douglass took an active role in the campaign to make free black men eligible to serve the Union cause; he became a successful recruiter of black soldiers, whose ranks soon included his own sons. Having helped to enlist these men, Douglass subsequently protested directly to President Lincoln over blacks' unequal pay and treatment in the Union army. He met with the president three times during the Civil War; the evidence suggests the men came to greatly admire one another.

After the war, Douglass criticized Lincoln's successors over what he believed was the slow pace of Reconstruction. He was particularly insistent in calling for the swift passage of the Fifteenth Amendment, guaranteeing suffrage to the newly emancipated male slaves. By the 1870s, Douglass was a significant figure in the Republican Party, taking on such positions as president of the Freedman's Bank, federal marshal, and recorder of deeds for the District of Columbia. Never satisfied with the grudging legal concessions the Civil War yielded, Douglass persistently objected to every sign of discrimination against blacks and other disenfranchised people, including women. At times his writings seem to celebrate black manhood, but Douglass had a longstanding interest in women's rights. Though he broke temporarily with women's rights supporters in 1868–69, when he championed the Fifteenth Amendment (which failed to offer suffrage to women), he had attended the first Women's Rights Convention in Seneca Falls, New York, in 1848, and he continued to attend women's rights conventions and to editorialize and lecture in favor of women's rights. His final speech, delivered just hours before he died of a heart attack on February 20, 1895, was at a women's rights rally.

Douglass published the third of his autobiographies, *Life and Times of Frederick Douglass*, in 1881, and he brought out an expanded version in 1892. This last memoir added much to the record of Douglass's post–Civil War years, but did not fare nearly as well in the marketplace as the earlier two autobiographies. Douglass was accused in the black press of betraying his race by marrying his white former secretary Helen Pitts in 1884 (Anna Douglass had died in 1882), and several years later, when he was the U.S. consul general to Haiti, he was accused in newspapers and journals of being overly sympathetic to black Haitians when the United States was attempting to gain a naval port in the island nation. In the final version of his life history, Douglass took on his critics and asserted in the strongest possible terms his commitment to a cosmopolitan vision of a world without invidious racial distinctions and prejudices. It would be difficult to exaggerate the importance for Americans across the color line of Douglass's exemplary career as a champion of human rights.

Narrative of the Life of Frederick Douglass, An American Slave, Written by Himself[1]

Preface[2]

In the month of August, 1841, I attended an anti-slavery convention in Nantucket, at which it was my happiness to become acquainted with FREDERICK DOUGLASS, the writer of the following Narrative. He was a stranger to

1. First printed in May 1845 by the Anti-Slavery Office in Boston, the source of the present text. Punctuation and hyphenation have been slightly regularized and a few typographical emendations have also been made.
2. The preface is by William Lloyd Garrison (1805–1879), the most influential white abolitionist at that time. He edited the antislavery

newspaper the *Liberator*, which he founded in 1831, and headed the American Anti-Slavery Society. Garrison called for immediate emancipation and advocated nonviolent moral persuasion as the best way of achieving social reform. Most slave narratives of the period came with prefaces by white abolitionists attesting to the moral character and literacy of the black author.

nearly every member of that body; but, having recently made his escape from the southern prison-house of bondage, and feeling his curiosity excited to ascertain the principles and measures of the abolitionists,—of whom he had heard a somewhat vague description while he was a slave,—he was induced to give his attendance, on the occasion alluded to, though at that time a resident in New Bedford.[3]

Fortunate, most fortunate occurrence!—fortunate for the millions of his manacled brethren, yet panting for deliverance from their awful thraldom!—fortunate for the cause of negro emancipation, and of universal liberty!—fortunate for the land of his birth, which he has already done so much to save and bless!—fortunate for a large circle of friends and acquaintances, whose sympathy and affection he has strongly secured by the many sufferings he has endured, by his virtuous traits of character, by his ever-abiding remembrance of those who are in bonds, as being bound with them!—fortunate for the multitudes, in various parts of our republic, whose minds he has enlightened on the subject of slavery, and who have been melted to tears by his pathos, or roused to virtuous indignation by his stirring eloquence against the enslavers of men!—fortunate for himself, as it at once brought him into the field of public usefulness, "gave the world assurance of a MAN," quickened the slumbering energies of his soul, and consecrated him to the great work of breaking the rod of the oppressor, and letting the oppressed go free!

I shall never forget his first speech at the convention—the extraordinary emotion it excited in my own mind—the powerful impression it created upon a crowded auditory,[4] completely taken by surprise—the applause which followed from the beginning to the end of his felicitous remarks. I think I never hated slavery so intensely as at that moment; certainly, my perception of the enormous outrage which is inflicted by it, on the godlike nature of its victims, was rendered far more clear than ever. There stood one, in physical proportion and stature commanding and exact—in intellect richly endowed—in natural eloquence a prodigy—in soul manifestly "created but a little lower than the angels"[5]—yet a slave, ay, a fugitive slave,—trembling for his safety, hardly daring to believe that on the American soil, a single white person could be found who would befriend him at all hazards, for the love of God and humanity! Capable of high attainments as an intellectual and moral being—needing nothing but a comparatively small amount of cultivation to make him an ornament to society and a blessing to his race—by the law of the land, by the voice of the people, by the terms of the slave code, he was only a piece of property, a beast of burden, a chattel[6] personal, nevertheless!

A beloved friend[7] from New Bedford prevailed on Mr. DOUGLASS to address the convention. He came forward to the platform with a hesitancy and embarrassment, necessarily the attendants of a sensitive mind in such a novel position. After apologizing for his ignorance, and reminding the audience that slavery was a poor school for the human intellect and heart, he

---

3. Douglass escaped from slavery in Maryland in September 1838 and settled in New Bedford, Massachusetts, where he became active among the New Bedford abolitionists.
4. Auditorium (archaic).
5. God created people "a little lower than the

angels" (Psalms 8.5); Paul declares that Christ was made "a little lower than the angels" (Hebrews 2.7, 9).
6. Property.
7. William C. Coffin (1816–?), a prominent New Bedford abolitionist.

proceeded to narrate some of the facts in his own history as a slave, and in the course of his speech gave utterance to many noble thoughts and thrilling reflections. As soon as he had taken his seat, filled with hope and admiration, I rose, and declared that PATRICK HENRY,[8] of revolutionary fame, never made a speech more eloquent in the cause of liberty, than the one we had just listened to from the lips of that hunted fugitive. So I believed at that time—such is my belief now. I reminded the audience of the peril which surrounded this self-emancipated young man at the North,—even in Massachusetts, on the soil of the Pilgrim Fathers, among the descendants of revolutionary sires; and I appealed to them, whether they would ever allow him to be carried back into slavery,—law or no law, constitution or no constitution. The response was unanimous and in thunder-tones—"NO!" "Will you succor and protect him as a brother-man—a resident of the old Bay State."[9] "YES!" shouted the whole mass, with an energy so startling, that the ruthless tyrants south of Mason and Dixon's line[1] might almost have heard the mighty burst of feeling, and recognized it as the pledge of an invincible determination, on the part of those who gave it, never to betray him that wanders, but to hide the outcast, and firmly to abide the consequences.

It was at once deeply impressed upon my mind, that, if Mr. DOUGLASS could be persuaded to consecrate his time and talents to the promotion of the anti-slavery enterprise, a powerful impetus would be given to it, and a stunning blow at the same time inflicted on northern prejudice against a colored complexion. I therefore endeavored to instill hope and courage into his mind, in order that he might dare to engage in a vocation so anomalous and responsible for a person in his situation; and I was seconded in this effort by warm-hearted friends, especially by the late General Agent of the Massachusetts Anti-Slavery Society, Mr. JOHN A. COLLINS, whose judgment in this instance entirely coincided with my own. At first, he could give no encouragement; with unfeigned diffidence, he expressed his conviction that he was not adequate to the performance of so great a task; the path marked out was wholly an untrodden one; he was sincerely apprehensive that he should do more harm than good. After much deliberation, however, he consented to make a trial; and ever since that period, he has acted as a lecturing agent, under the auspices either of the American or the Massachusetts Anti-Slavery Society. In labors he has been most abundant; and his success in combating prejudice, in gaining proselytes, in agitating the public mind, has far surpassed the most sanguine expectations that were raised at the commencement of his brilliant career. He has borne himself with gentleness and meekness, yet with true manliness of character. As a public speaker, he excels in pathos, wit, comparison, imitation, strength of reasoning, and fluency of language. There is in him that union of head and heart, which is indispensable to an enlightenment of the heads and a winning of the hearts of others. May his strength continue to be equal to his day! May he continue to "grow in grace, and in the knowledge of God," that he may be increasingly serviceable in the cause of bleeding humanity, whether at home or abroad!

---

8. U.S. patriot (1736–1799), famous for the words: "I know not what course others may take, but as for me, give me liberty or give me death."
9. Massachusetts.
1. Established by the British astronomers and surveyors Charles Mason and Jeremiah Dixon during the 1760s, the line separating Pennsylvania and Maryland came to signify the boundary between slave and free states.

It is certainly a very remarkable fact, that one of the most efficient advocates of the slave population, now before the public, is a fugitive slave, in the person of FREDERICK DOUGLASS; and that the free colored population of the United States are as ably represented by one of their own number, in the person of CHARLES LENOX REMOND,[2] whose eloquent appeals have extorted the highest applause of multitudes on both sides of the Atlantic. Let the calumniators of the colored race despise themselves for their baseness and illiberality of spirit, and henceforth cease to talk of the natural inferiority of those who require nothing but time and opportunity to attain to the highest point of human excellence.

It may, perhaps, be fairly questioned, whether any other portion of the population of the earth could have endured the privations, sufferings and horrors of slavery, without having become more degraded in the scale of humanity than the slaves of African descent. Nothing has been left undone to cripple their intellects, darken their minds, debase their moral nature, obliterate all traces of their relationship to mankind; and yet how wonderfully they have sustained the mighty load of a most frightful bondage, under which they have been groaning for centuries! To illustrate the effect of slavery on the white man,—to show that he has no powers of endurance, in such a condition, superior to those of his black brother,—DANIEL O'CONNELL,[3] the distinguished advocate of universal emancipation, and the mightiest champion of prostrate but not conquered Ireland, relates the following anecdote in a speech delivered by him in the Conciliation Hall, Dublin, before the Loyal National Repeal Association, March 31, 1845. "No matter," said Mr. O'CONNELL, "under what specious term it may disguise itself, slavery is still hideous. *It has a natural, an inevitable tendency to brutalize every noble faculty of man.* An American sailor, who was cast away on the shore of Africa, where he was kept in slavery for three years, was, at the expiration of that period, found to be imbruted and stultified—he had lost all reasoning power; and having forgotten his native language, could only utter some savage gibberish between Arabic and English, which nobody could understand, and which even he himself found difficulty in pronouncing. So much for the humanizing influence of THE DOMESTIC INSTITUTION!" Admitting this to have been an extraordinary case of mental deterioration, it proves at least that the white slave can sink as low in the scale of humanity as the black one.

Mr. DOUGLASS has very properly chosen to write his own Narrative, in his own style, and according to the best of his ability, rather than to employ some one else. It is, therefore, entirely his own production; and, considering how long and dark was the career he had to run as a slave,—how few have been his opportunities to improve his mind since he broke his iron fetters,—it is, in my judgment, highly creditable to his head and heart. He who can peruse it without a tearful eye, a heaving breast, an afflicted spirit,—without being filled with an unutterable abhorrence of slavery and all its abettors, and animated with a determination to seek the immediate overthrow of that execrable

---

2. A free-born African American (1810–1873) from Massachusetts who was the first black employed in the United States as an antislavery lecturer. He toured with Douglass for the Massachusetts Anti-Slavery Society in 1842.

3. Irish statesman (1775–1847), called the "Liberator," who advocated Irish independence from England.

system,—without trembling for the fate of this country in the hands of a righteous God, who is ever on the side of the oppressed, and whose arm is not shortened that it cannot save,—must have a flinty heart, and be qualified to act the part of a trafficker "in slaves and the souls of men."[4] I am confident that it is essentially true in all its statements; that nothing has been set down in malice, nothing exaggerated, nothing drawn from the imagination; that it comes short of the reality, rather than overstates a single fact in regard to SLAVERY AS IT IS.[5] The experience of FREDERICK DOUGLASS, as a slave, was not a peculiar one; his lot was not especially a hard one; his case may be regarded as a very fair specimen of the treatment of slaves in Maryland, in which State it is conceded that they are better fed and less cruelly treated than in Georgia, Alabama, or Louisiana. Many have suffered incomparably more, while very few on the plantations have suffered less, than himself. Yet how deplorable was his situation! what terrible chastisements were inflicted upon his person! what still more shocking outrages were perpetrated upon his mind! with all his noble powers and sublime aspirations, how like a brute was he treated, even by those professing to have the same mind in them that was in Christ Jesus! to what dreadful liabilities was he continually subjected! how destitute of friendly counsel and aid, even in his greatest extremities! how heavy was the midnight of woe which shrouded in blackness the last ray of hope, and filled the future with terror and gloom! what longings after freedom took possession of his breast, and how his misery augmented, in proportion as he grew reflective and intelligent,—thus demonstrating that a happy slave is an extinct man! how he thought, reasoned, felt, under the lash of the driver, with the chains upon his limbs! what perils he encountered in his endeavors to escape from his horrible doom! and how signal have been his deliverance and preservation in the midst of a nation of pitiless enemies!

This Narrative contains many affecting incidents, many passages of great eloquence and power; but I think the most thrilling one of them all is the description DOUGLASS gives of his feelings, as he stood soliloquizing respecting his fate, and the chances of his one day being a freeman, on the banks of the Chesapeake Bay—view in the receding vessels as they flew with their white wings before the breeze, and apostrophizing them as animated by the living spirit of freedom. Who can read that passage, and be insensible to its pathos and sublimity? Compressed into it is a whole Alexandrian library[6] of thought, feeling, and sentiment—all that can, all that need be urged, in the form of expostulation, entreaty, rebuke, against that crime of crimes,— making man the property of his fellow-man! O, how accursed is that system, which entombs the godlike mind of man, defaces the divine image, reduces those who by creation were crowned with glory and honor to a level with four-footed beasts, and exalts the dealer in human flesh above all that is called God! Why should its existence be prolonged one hour? Is it not evil, only evil, and that continually? What does its presence imply but the absence of all fear of God, all regard for man, on the part of the people of the United States? Heaven speed its eternal overthrow!

---

4. Revelation 18.13.
5. Probably an allusion to Theodore Weld's widely read antislavery compendium *Slavery as It Is* (1839).

6. Alexandria, in Egypt, home of the greatest library in the Greco-Roman world.

So profoundly ignorant of the nature of slavery are many persons, that they are stubbornly incredulous whenever they read or listen to any recital of the cruelties which are daily inflicted on its victims. They do not deny that the slaves are held as property; but that terrible fact seems to convey to their minds no idea of injustice, exposure to outrage, or savage barbarity. Tell them of cruel scourgings, of mutilations and brandings, of scenes of pollution and blood, of the banishment of all light and knowledge, and they affect to be greatly indignant at such enormous exaggerations, such wholesale misstatements, such abominable libels on the character of the southern planters! As if all these direful outrages were not the natural results of slavery! As if it were less cruel to reduce a human being to the condition of a thing, than to give him a severe flagellation, or to deprive him of necessary food and clothing! As if whips, chains, thumb-screws, paddles, bloodhounds, overseers, drivers, patrols, were not all indispensable to keep the slaves down, and to give protection to their ruthless oppressors! As if, when the marriage institution is abolished, concubinage, adultery, and incest, must not necessarily abound; when all the rights of humanity are annihilated, any barrier remains to protect the victim from the fury of the spoiler; when absolute power is assumed over life and liberty, it will not be wielded with destructive sway! Skeptics of this character abound in society. In some few instances, their incredulity arises from a want of reflection; but, generally, it indicates a hatred of the light, a desire to shield slavery from the assaults of its foes, a contempt of the colored race, whether bond or free. Such will try to discredit the shocking tales of slaveholding cruelty which are recorded in this truthful Narrative; but they will labor in vain. Mr. DOUGLASS has frankly disclosed the place of his birth, the names of those who claimed ownership in his body and soul, and the names also of those who committed the crimes which he has alleged against them. His statements, therefore, may easily be disproved, if they are untrue.

In the course of his Narrative, he relates two instances of murderous cruelty,—in one of which a planter deliberately shot a slave belonging to a neighboring plantation, who had unintentionally gotten within his lordly domain in quest of fish; and in the other, an overseer blew out the brains of a slave who had fled to a stream of water to escape a bloody scourging. Mr. DOUGLASS states that in neither of these instances was any thing done by way of legal arrest or judicial investigation. The Baltimore American, of March 17, 1845, relates a similar case of atrocity, perpetrated with similar impunity—as follows:—"*Shooting a Slave.*—We learn, upon the authority of a letter from Charles county, Maryland, received by a gentleman of this city, that a young man, named Matthews, a nephew of General Matthews, and whose father, it is believed, holds an office at Washington, killed one of the slaves upon his father's farm by shooting him. The letter states that young Matthews had been left in charge of the farm; that he gave an order to the servant, which was disobeyed, when he proceeded to the house, *obtained a gun, and, returning, shot the servant.* He immediately, the letter continues, fled to his father's residence, where he still remains unmolested."—Let it never be forgotten, that no slaveholder or overseer can be convicted of any outrage perpetrated on the person of a slave, however diabolical it may be, on the testimony of colored witnesses, whether bond or free. By the slave code, they are adjudged to be as incompetent to testify against a white man, as though they were indeed a part of the brute creation. Hence, there is no legal protection in fact, whatever there may be in form, for the slave population; and any amount of cruelty may be inflicted on them with impunity. Is it possible for the human mind to conceive of a more horrible state of society?

The effect of a religious profession on the conduct of southern masters is vividly described in the following Narrative, and shown to be any thing but salutary. In the nature of the case, it must be in the highest degree pernicious. The testimony of Mr. DOUGLASS, on this point, is sustained by a cloud of witnesses, whose veracity is unimpeachable. "A slaveholder's profession of Christianity is a palpable imposture. He is a felon of the highest grade. He is a man-stealer. It is of no importance what you put in the other scale."

Reader! are you with the man-stealers in sympathy and purpose, or on the side of their down-trodden victims? If with the former, then are you the foe of God and man. If with the latter, what are you prepared to do and dare in their behalf? Be faithful, be vigilant, be untiring in your efforts to break every yoke, and let the oppressed go free. Come what may—cost what it may—inscribe on the banner which you unfurl to the breeze, as your religious and political motto—"No COMPROMISE WITH SLAVERY! NO UNION WITH SLAVEHOLDERS!"

WM. LLOYD GARRISON

Boston, May 1, 1845.

Letter from Wendell Phillips, Esq.[7]

BOSTON, *April* 22, 1845.

My Dear Friend:

You remember the old fable of "The Man and the Lion" where the lion complained that he should not be so misrepresented "when the lions wrote history."

I am glad the time has come when the "lions write history." We have been left long enough to gather the character of slavery from the involuntary evidence of the masters. One might, indeed, rest sufficiently satisfied with what, it is evident, must be, in general, the results of such a relation, without seeking farther to find whether they have followed in every instance. Indeed, those who stare at the half-peck of corn a week, and love to count the lashes on the slave's back, are seldom the "stuff" out of which reformers and abolitionists are to be made. I remember that, in 1838, many were waiting for the results of the West India experiment,[8] before they could come into our ranks. Those "results" have come long ago; but, alas! few of that number have come with them, as converts. A man must be disposed to judge of emancipation by other tests than whether it has increased the produce of sugar,—and to hate slavery for other reasons than because it starves men and whips women,— before he is ready to lay the first stone of his anti-slavery life.

I was glad to learn, in your story, how early the most neglected of God's children waken to a sense of their rights, and of the injustice done them.

7. A prominent Massachusetts-based abolitionist (1811–1884).
8. On August 1, 1834, England formally abolished

slavery in the West Indies; by 1838 slavery had been abolished throughout the British Empire.

Experience is a keen teacher; and long before you had mastered your A B C, or knew where the "white sails" of the Chesapeake were bound, you began, I see, to gauge the wretchedness of the slave, not by his hunger and want, not by his lashes and toil, but by the cruel and blighting death which gathers over his soul.

In connection with this, there is one circumstance which makes your recollections peculiarly valuable, and renders your early insight the more remarkable. You come from that part of the country where we are told slavery appears with its fairest features. Let us hear, then, what it is at its best estate—gaze on its bright side, if it has one; and then imagination may task her powers to add dark lines to the picture, as she travels southward to that (for the colored man) Valley of the Shadow of Death,[9] where the Mississippi sweeps along.

Again, we have known you long, and can put the most entire confidence in your truth, candor, and sincerity. Every one who has heard you speak has felt, and, I am confident, every one who reads your book will feel, persuaded that you give them a fair specimen of the whole truth. No one-sided portrait,—no wholesale complaints,—but strict justice done, whenever individual kindliness has neutralized, for a moment, the deadly system with which it was strangely allied. You have been with us, too, some years, and can fairly compare the twilight of rights, which your race enjoy at the North, with that "noon of night" under which they labor south of Mason and Dixon's line. Tell us whether, after all, the half-free colored man of Massachusetts is worse off than the pampered slave of the rice swamps!

In reading your life, no one can say that we have unfairly picked out some rare specimens of cruelty. We know that the bitter drops, which even you have drained from the cup, are no incidental aggravations, no individual ills, but such as must mingle always and necessarily in the lot of every slave. They are the essential ingredients, not the occasional results, of the system.

After all, I shall read your book with trembling for you. Some years ago, when you were beginning to tell me your real name and birthplace, you may remember I stopped you, and preferred to remain ignorant of all. With the exception of a vague description, so I continued, till the other day, when you read me your memoirs. I hardly knew, at the time, whether to thank you or not for the sight of them, when I reflected that it was still dangerous, in Massachusetts, for honest men to tell their names! They say the fathers, in 1776, signed the Declaration of Independence with the halter about their necks. You, too, publish your declaration of freedom with danger compassing you around. In all the broad lands which the Constitution of the United States overshadows, there is no single spot,—however narrow or desolate,—where a fugitive slave can plant himself and say, "I am safe." The whole armory of Northern Law has no shield for you. I am free to say that, in your place, I should throw the MS. into the fire.

You, perhaps, may tell your story in safety, endeared as you are to so many warm hearts by rarer gifts, and a still rare devotion of them to the service of others. But it will be owing only to your labors, and the fearless efforts of those who, trampling the laws and Constitution of the country

9. Psalms 23.4.

under their feet, are determined that they will "hide the outcast," and that their hearths shall be, spite of the law, an asylum for the oppressed, if, some time or other, the humblest may stand in our streets, and bear witness in safety against the cruelties which he has been the victim.

Yet it is sad to think, that these very throbbing hearts which welcome your story, and form your best safeguard in telling it, are all beating contrary to the "statute in such case made and provided." Go on, my dear friend, till you, and those who, like you, have been saved, so as by fire, from the dark prison-house, shall stereotype these free, illegal pulses into statutes; and New England, cutting loose from a blood-stained Union, shall glory in being the house of refuge for the oppressed;—till we no longer merely "*hide* the outcast," or make a merit of standing idly by while he is hunted in our midst; but, consecrating anew the soil of the Pilgrims as an asylum for the oppressed, proclaim our *welcome* to the slave so loudly, that the tones shall reach every hut in the Carolinas, and make the broken-hearted bondman leap up at the thought of old Massachusetts.

God speed the day!

Till then, and ever,
Yours truly,
WENDELL PHILLIPS
FREDERICK DOUGLASS.

Chapter I

I was born in Tuckahoe, near Hillsborough, and about twelve miles from Easton, in Talbot county, Maryland. I have no accurate knowledge of my age, never having seen any authentic record containing it. By far the larger part of the slaves know as little of their ages as horses know of theirs, and it is the wish of most masters within my knowledge to keep their slaves thus ignorant. I do not remember to have ever met a slave who could tell of his birthday. They seldom come nearer to it than planting-time, harvest-time, cherry-time, spring-time, or fall-time. A want of information concerning my own was a source of unhappiness to me even during childhood. The white children could tell their ages. I could not tell why I ought to be deprived of the same privilege. I was not allowed to make any inquiries of my master concerning it. He deemed all such inquiries on the part of a slave improper and impertinent, and evidence of a restless spirit. The nearest estimate I can give makes me now between twenty-seven and twenty-eight years of age. I come to this, from hearing my master say, some time during 1835, I was about seventeen years old.

My mother was named Harriet Bailey. She was the daughter of Isaac and Betsey Bailey, both colored, and quite dark. My mother was of a darker complexion than either my grandmother or grandfather.

My father was a white man. He was admitted to be such by all I ever heard speak of my parentage. The opinion was also whispered that my master was my father; but of the correctness of this opinion, I know nothing; the means of knowing was withheld from me. My mother and I were separated when I was but an infant—before I knew her as my mother. It is a common custom, in the part of Maryland from which I ran away, to part children from their mothers at a very early age. Frequently, before the child has reached its twelfth month, its mother is taken from it, and hired out on some farm a considerable distance off, and the child is placed under the care of an old woman, too old for field labor. For what this separation is done, I do not know, unless it be to hinder the development of the child's affection toward its mother, and to blunt and destroy the natural affection of the mother for the child. This is the inevitable result.

I never saw my mother, to know her as such, more than four or five times in my life; and each of these times was very short in duration, and at night. She was hired[1] by a Mr. Stewart, who lived about twelve miles from my home. She made her journeys to see me in the night, travelling the whole distance on foot, after the performance of her day's work. She was a field hand, and a whipping is the penalty of not being in the field at sunrise, unless a slave has special permission from his or her master to the contrary—a permission which they seldom get, and one that gives to him that gives it the proud name of being a kind master. I do not recollect of ever seeing my mother by the light of day. She was with me in the night. She would lie down with me, and get me to sleep, but long before I waked she was gone. Very little communication ever took place between us. Death soon ended what little we could have while she lived, and with it her hardships and suffering. She died when I was about seven years old, on one of my master's farms, near Lee's Mill. I was not allowed to be present during her illness, at her death, or burial. She was gone long before I knew any thing about it. Never having enjoyed, to any considerable extent, her soothing presence, her tender and watchful care, I received the tidings of her death with much the same emotions I should have probably felt at the death of a stranger.

Called thus suddenly away, she left me without the slightest intimation of who my father was. The whisper that my master was my father, may or may not be true; and, true or false, it is of but little consequence to my purpose whilst the fact remains, in all its glaring odiousness, that slaveholders have ordained, and by law established, that the children of slave women shall in all cases follow the condition of their mothers; and this is done too obviously to administer to their own lusts, and make a gratification of their wicked desires profitable as well as pleasurable; for by this cunning arrangement, the slaveholder, in cases not a few, sustains to his slaves the double relation of master and father.

I know of such cases; and it is worthy of remark that such slaves invariably suffer greater hardships, and have more to contend with, than others. They are, in the first place, a constant offence to their mistress. She is ever disposed to find fault with them; they can seldom do any thing to please her; she is never better pleased than when she sees them under the lash, especially when she suspects her husband of showing to his mulatto children favors which he withholds from his black slaves. The master is frequently compelled to sell this class of his slaves, out of deference to the feelings of his white wife; and, cruel as the deed may strike any one to be, for a man to sell his own children to human flesh-mongers, it is often the dictate of humanity for him to do so; for, unless he does this, he must not only whip them himself, but must stand by and see one white son tie up his brother, of but few shades darker complexion than himself, and ply the gory lash to his naked back; and if he lisp one word of disapproval, it is set down

---

1. Slaves who were "hired out" had their wages paid to their owners.

to his parental partiality, and only makes a bad matter worse, both for himself and the slave whom he would protect and defend.

Every year brings with it multitudes of this class of slaves. It was doubtless in consequence of a knowledge of this fact, that one great statesman of the south predicted the downfall of slavery by the inevitable laws of population. Whether this prophecy is ever fulfilled or not, it is nevertheless plain that a very different-looking class of people are springing up at the south, and are now held in slavery, from those originally brought to this country from Africa; and if their increase will do no other good, it will do away the force of the argument, that God cursed Ham, and therefore American slavery is right.[2] If the lineal descendants of Ham are alone to be scripturally enslaved, it is certain that slavery at the south must soon become unscriptural; for thousands are ushered into the world, annually, who, like myself, owe their existence to white fathers, and those fathers most frequently their own masters.

I have had two masters. My first master's name was Anthony. I do not remember his first name. He was generally called Captain Anthony—a title which, I presume, he acquired by sailing a craft on the Chesapeake Bay. He was not considered a rich slaveholder. He owned two or three farms, and about thirty slaves. His farms and slaves were under the care of an overseer. The overseer's name was Plummer. Mr. Plummer was a miserable drunkard, a profane swearer, and a savage monster. He always went armed with a cowskin[3] and a heavy cudgel. I have known him to cut and slash the women's heads so horribly, that even master would be enraged at his cruelty, and would threaten to whip him if he did not mind himself. Master, however, was not a humane slaveholder. It required extraordinary barbarity on the part of an overseer to affect him. He was a cruel man, hardened by a long life of slaveholding. He would at times seem to take great pleasure in whipping a slave. I have often been awakened at the dawn of day by the most heart-rending shrieks of an own aunt of mine, whom he used to tie up to a joist, and whip upon her naked back till she was literally covered with blood. No words, no tears, no prayers, from his gory victim, seemed to move his iron heart from its bloody purpose. The louder she screamed, the harder he whipped; and where the blood ran fastest, there he whipped longest. He would whip her to make her scream, and whip her to make her hush; and not until overcome by fatigue, would he cease to swing the blood-clotted cowskin. I remember the first time I ever witnessed this horrible exhibition. I was quite a child, but I well remember it. I never shall forget it whilst I remember any thing. It was the first of a long series of such outrages, of which I was doomed to be a witness and a participant. It struck me with awful force. It was the blood-stained gate, the entrance to the hell of slavery, through which I was about to pass. It was a most terrible spectacle. I wish I could commit to paper the feelings with which I beheld it.

This occurrence took place very soon after I went to live with my old master, and under the following circumstances. Aunt Hester went out one night,—where or for what I do not know,—and happened to be absent when

2. Some proslavery writers interpreted Genesis 9.20–27, in which Noah curses his son Ham and condemns him to bondage to his brothers, as a biblical justification of slavery.
3. A whip made of raw cowhide.

my master desired her presence. He had ordered her not to go out evenings, and warned her that she must never let him catch her in company with a young man, who was paying attention to her, belonging to Colonel Lloyd. The young man's name was Ned Roberts, generally called Lloyd's Ned. Why master was so careful of her, may be safely left to conjecture. She was a woman of noble form, and of graceful proportions, having very few equals, and fewer superiors, in personal appearance, among the colored or white women of our neighborhood.

Aunt Hester had not only disobeyed his orders in going out, but had been found in company with Lloyd's Ned; which circumstance, I found, from what he said while whipping her, was the chief offence. Had he been a man of pure morals himself, he might have been thought interested in protecting the innocence of my aunt; but those who knew him will not suspect him of any such virtue. Before he commenced whipping Aunt Hester, he took her into the kitchen, and stripped her from neck to waist, leaving her neck, shoulders, and back, entirely naked. He then told her to cross her hands, calling her at the same time a d—d b—h. After crossing her hands, he tied them with a strong rope, and led her to a stool under a large hook in the joist, put in for the purpose. He made her get upon the stool, and tied her hands to the hook. She now stood fair for his infernal purpose. Her arms were stretched up at their full length, so that she stood upon the ends of her toes. He then said to her, "Now, you d—d b—h, I'll learn you how to disobey my orders!" and after rolling up his sleeves, he commenced to lay on the heavy cowskin, and soon the warm, red blood (amid heart-rending shrieks from her, and horrid oaths from him) came dripping to the floor. I was so terrified and horror-stricken at the sight, that I hid myself in a closet, and dared not venture out till long after the bloody transaction was over. I expected it would be my turn next. It was all new to me. I had never seen any thing like it before. I had always lived with my grandmother on the outskirts of the plantation, where she was put to raise the children of the younger women. I had therefore been, until now, out of the way of the bloody scenes that often occurred on the plantation.

Chapter II

My master's family consisted of two sons, Andrew and Richard; one daughter, Lucretia, and her husband, Captain Thomas Auld. They lived in one house, upon the home plantation of Colonel Edward Lloyd. My master was Colonel Lloyd's clerk and superintendent. He was what might be called the overseer of the overseers. I spent two years of childhood on this plantation in my old master's family. It was here that I witnessed the bloody transaction recorded in the first chapter; and as I received my first impressions of slavery on this plantation, I will give some description of it, and of slavery as it there existed. The plantation is about twelve miles north of Easton, in Talbot county, and is situated on the border of Miles River. The principal products raised upon it were tobacco, corn, and wheat. These were raised in great abundance; so that, with the products of this and the other farms belonging to him, he was able to keep in almost constant employment a large sloop, in carrying them to market at Baltimore. This sloop was named Sally Lloyd, in honor of one of the colonel's daughters. My master's son-in-law,

Captain Auld, was master of the vessel; she was otherwise manned by the colonel's own slaves. Their names were Peter, Isaac, Rich, and Jake. These were esteemed very highly by the other slaves, and looked upon as the privileged ones of the plantation; for it was no small affair, in the eyes of the slaves, to be allowed to see Baltimore.

Colonel Lloyd kept from three to four hundred slaves on his home plantation, and owned a large number more on the neighboring farms belonging to him. The names of the farms nearest to the home plantation were Wye Town and New Design. "Wye Town" was under the overseership of a man named Noah Willis. New Design was under the overseership of a Mr. Townsend. The overseers of these, and all the rest of the farms, numbering over twenty, received advice and direction from the managers of the home plantation. This was the great business place. It was the seat of government for the whole twenty farms. All disputes among the overseers were settled here. If a slave was convicted of any high misdemeanor, became unmanageable, or evinced a determination to run away, he was brought immediately here, severely whipped, put on board the sloop, carried to Baltimore, and sold to Austin Woolfolk, or some other slave-trader, as a warning to the slaves remaining.

Here, too, the slaves of all the other farms received their monthly allowance of food, and their yearly clothing. The men and women slaves received, as their monthly allowance of food, eight pounds of pork, or its equivalent in fish, and one bushel of corn meal. Their yearly clothing consisted of two coarse linen shirts, one pair of linen trousers, like the shirts, one jacket, one pair of trousers for winter, made of coarse negro cloth, one pair of stockings, and one pair of shoes; the whole of which could not have cost more than seven dollars. The allowance of the slave children was given to their mothers, or the old women having the care of them. The children unable to work in the field had neither shoes, stockings, jackets, nor trousers, given to them; their clothing consisted of two coarse linen shirts per year. When these failed them, they went naked until the next allowance-day. Children from seven to ten years old, of both sexes, almost naked, might be seen at all seasons of the year.

There were no beds given the slaves, unless one coarse blanket be considered such, and none but the men and women had these. This, however, is not considered a very great privation. They find less difficulty from the want of beds, than from the want of time to sleep; for when their day's work in the field is done, the most of them having their washing, mending, and cooking to do, and having few or none of the ordinary facilities for doing either of these, very many of their sleeping hours are consumed in preparing for the field the coming day; and when this is done, old and young, male and female, married and single, drop down side by side, on one common bed,—the cold, damp floor,—each covering himself or herself with their miserable blankets; and here they sleep till they are summoned to the field by the driver's horn. At the sound of this, all must rise, and be off to the field. There must be no halting; every one must be at his or her post; and woe betides them who hear not this morning summons to the field; for if they are not awakened by the sense of hearing, they are by the sense of feeling: no age nor sex finds any favor. Mr. Severe, the overseer, used to stand by the door of the quarter, armed with a large hickory stick and heavy cowskin, ready to whip any one who was so unfortunate as not to hear, or, from any other cause, was prevented from being ready to start for the field at the sound of the horn.

Mr. Severe was rightly named: he was a cruel man. I have seen him whip a woman, causing the blood to run half an hour at the time; and this, too, in the midst of her crying children, pleading for their mother's release. He seemed to take pleasure in manifesting his fiendish barbarity. Added to his cruelty, he was a profane swearer. It was enough to chill the blood and stiffen the hair of an ordinary man to hear him talk. Scarce a sentence escaped him but that was commenced or concluded by some horrid oath. The field was the place to witness his cruelty and profanity. His presence made it both the field of blood and of blasphemy. From the rising till the going down of the sun, he was cursing, raving, cutting, and slashing among the slaves of the field, in the most frightful manner. His career was short. He died very soon after I went to Colonel Lloyd's; and he died as he lived, uttering, with his dying groans, bitter curses and horrid oaths. His death was regarded by the slaves as the result of a merciful providence.

Mr. Severe's place was filled by a Mr. Hopkins. He was a very different man. He was less cruel, less profane, and made less noise, than Mr. Severe. His course was characterized by no extraordinary demonstrations of cruelty. He whipped, but seemed to take no pleasure in it. He was called by the slaves a good overseer.

The home plantation of Colonel Lloyd wore the appearance of a country village. All the mechanical operations for all the farms were performed here. The shoemaking and mending, the blacksmithing, cartwrighting, coopering, weaving, and grain-grinding, were all performed by the slaves on the home plantation. The whole place wore a business-like aspect very unlike the neighboring farms. The number of houses, too, conspired to give it advantage over the neighboring farms. It was called by the slaves the *Great House Farm*. Few privileges were esteemed higher, by the slaves of the out-farms, than that of being selected to do errands at the Great House Farm. It was associated in their minds with greatness. A representative could not be prouder of his election to a seat in the American Congress, than a slave on one of the out-farms would be of his election to do errands at the Great House Farm. They regarded it as evidence of great confidence reposed in them by their overseers; and it was on this account, as well as a constant desire to be out of the field from under the driver's lash, that they esteemed it a high privilege, one worth careful living for. He was called the smartest and most trusty fellow, who had this honor conferred upon him the most frequently. The competitors for this office sought as diligently to please their overseers, as the office-seekers in the political parties seek to please and deceive the people. The same traits of character might be seen in Colonel Lloyd's slaves, as are seen in the slaves of the political parties.

The slaves selected to go to the Great House Farm, for the monthly allowance for themselves and their fellow-slaves, were peculiarly enthusiastic. While on their way, they would make the dense old woods, for miles around, reverberate with their wild songs, revealing at once the highest joy and the deepest sadness. They would compose and sing as they went along, consulting neither time nor tune. The thought that came up, came out—if not in the word, in the sound;—and as frequently in the one as in the other. They would sometimes sing the most pathetic sentiment in the most rapturous tone, and the most rapturous sentiment in the most pathetic tone. Into all of their songs they would manage to weave something of the Great House Farm. Especially would they do this, when leaving home. They would then sing most exultingly the following words:—

> "I am going away to the Great House Farm!
> O, yea! O, yea! O!"

This they would sing, as a chorus, to words which to many would seem unmeaning jargon, but which, nevertheless, were full of meaning to themselves. I have sometimes thought that the mere hearing of those songs would do more to impress some minds with the horrible character of slavery, than the reading of whole volumes of philosophy on the subject could do.

I did not, when a slave, understand the deep meaning of those rude and apparently incoherent songs. I was myself within the circle; so that I neither saw nor heard as those without might see and hear. They told a tale of woe which was then altogether beyond my feeble comprehension; they were tones loud, long, and deep; they breathed the prayer and complaint of souls boiling over with the bitterest anguish. Every tone was a testimony against slavery, and a prayer to God for deliverance from chains. The hearing of those wild notes always depressed my spirit, and filled me with ineffable sadness. I have frequently found myself in tears while hearing them. The mere recurrence to those songs, even now, afflicts me; and while I am writing these lines, an expression of feeling has already found its way down my cheek. To those songs I trace my first glimmering conception of the dehumanizing character of slavery. I can never get rid of that conception. Those songs still follow me, to deepen my hatred of slavery, and quicken my sympathies for my brethren in bonds. If any one wishes to be impressed with the soul-killing effects of slavery, let him go to Colonel Lloyd's plantation, and, on allowance-day, place himself in the deep pine woods, and there let him, in silence, analyze the sounds that shall pass through the chambers of his soul,—and if he is not thus impressed, it will only be because "there is no flesh in his obdurate heart."[4]

I have often been utterly astonished, since I came to the north, to find persons who could speak of the singing, among slaves, as evidence of their contentment and happiness. It is impossible to conceive of a greater mistake. Slaves sing most when they are most unhappy. The songs of the slave represent the sorrows of his heart; and he is relieved by them, only as an aching heart is relieved by its tears. At least, such is my experience. I have often sung to drown my sorrow, but seldom to express my happiness. Crying for joy, and singing for joy, were alike uncommon to me while in the jaws of slavery. The singing of a man cast away upon a desolate island might be as appropriately considered as evidence of contentment and happiness, as the singing of a slave; the songs of the one and of the other are prompted by the same emotion.

---

4. From William Cowper's popular poem *The Task* (1785).

Chapter III

Colonel Lloyd kept a large and finely cultivated garden, which afforded almost constant employment for four men, besides the chief gardener, (Mr. M'Durmond.) This garden was probably the greatest attraction of the place. During the summer months, people came from far and near—from Baltimore, Easton, and Annapolis—to see it. It abounded in fruits of almost every description, from the hardy apple of the north to the delicate orange of the south. This garden was not the least source of trouble on the plantation. Its excellent fruit was quite a temptation to the hungry swarms of boys, as well as the older slaves, belonging to the colonel, few of whom had the virtue or the vice to resist it. Scarcely a day passed, during the summer, but that some slave had to take the lash for stealing fruit. The colonel had to resort to all kinds of stratagems to keep his slaves out of the garden. The last and most successful one was that of tarring his fence all around, after which, if a slave was caught with any tar upon his person, it was deemed sufficient proof that he had either been into the garden, or had tried to get in. In either case, he was severely whipped by the chief gardener. This plan worked well; the slaves became as fearful of tar as of the lash. They seemed to realize the impossibility of touching *tar* without being defiled.

The colonel also kept a splendid riding equipage. His stable and carriage-house presented the appearance of some of our large city livery establishments. His horses were of the finest form and noblest blood. His carriage-house contained three splendid coaches, three or four gigs, besides dearborns and barouches[5] of the most fashionable style.

This establishment was under the care of two slaves—old Barney and young Barney—father and son. To attend to this establishment was their sole work. But it was by no means an easy employment; for in nothing was Colonel Lloyd more particular than in the management of his horses. The slightest inattention to these was unpardonable, and was visited upon those, under whose care they were placed, with the severest punishment; no excuse could shield them, if the colonel only suspected any want of attention to his horses—a supposition which he frequently indulged, and one which, of course, made the office of old and young Barney a very trying one. They never knew when they were safe from punishment. They were frequently whipped when least deserving, and escaped whipping when most deserving it. Every thing depended upon the looks of the horses, and the state of Colonel Lloyd's own mind when his horses were brought to him for use. If a horse did not move fast enough, or hold his head high enough, it was owing to some fault of his keepers. It was painful to stand near the stable-door, and hear the various complaints against the keepers when a horse was taken out for use. "This horse has not had proper attention. He has not been sufficiently rubbed and curried, or he has not been properly fed; his food was too wet or too dry; he got it too soon or too late; he was too hot or too cold; he had too much hay, and not enough of grain; or he had too much grain, and not enough of hay; instead of old Barney's attending to the horse, he had very improperly left it to his son." To all these complaints, no matter how

5. Different kinds of carriages.

unjust, the slave must answer never a word. Colonel Lloyd could not brook any contradiction from a slave. When he spoke, a slave must stand, listen, and tremble; and such was literally the case. I have seen Colonel Lloyd make old Barney, a man between fifty and sixty years of age, uncover his bald head, kneel down upon the cold, damp ground, and receive upon his naked and toil-worn shoulders more than thirty lashes at the time. Colonel Lloyd had three sons—Edward, Murray, and Daniel,—and three sons-in-law, Mr. Winder, Mr. Nicholson, and Mr. Lowndes. All of these lived at the Great House Farm, and enjoyed the luxury of whipping the servants when they pleased, from old Barney down to William Wilkes, the coach-driver. I have seen Winder make one of the house-servants stand off from him a suitable distance to be touched with the end of his whip, and at every stroke raise great ridges upon his back.

To describe the wealth of Colonel Lloyd would be almost equal to describing the riches of Job.[6] He kept from ten to fifteen house-servants. He was said to own a thousand slaves, and I think this estimate quite within the truth. Colonel Lloyd owned so many that he did not know them when he saw them; nor did all the slaves of the out-farms know him. It is reported of him, that, while riding along the road one day, he met a colored man, and addressed him in the usual manner of speaking to colored people on the public highways of the south: "Well, boy, whom do you belong to?" "To Colonel Lloyd," replied the slave. "Well, does the colonel treat you well?" "No, sir," was the ready reply. "What, does he work you too hard?" "Yes, sir." "Well, don't he give you enough to eat?" "Yes, sir, he gives me enough, such as it is."

The colonel, after ascertaining where the slave belonged, rode on; the man also went on about his business, not dreaming that he had been conversing with his master. He thought, said, and heard nothing more of the matter, until two or three weeks afterwards. The poor man was then informed by his overseer that, for having found fault with his master, he was now to be sold to a Georgia trader. He was immediately chained and handcuffed; and thus, without a moment's warning, he was snatched away, and forever sundered, from his family and friends, by a hand more unrelenting than death. This is the penalty of telling the truth, of telling the simple truth, in answer to a series of plain questions.

It is partly in consequence of such facts, that slaves, when inquired of as to their condition and the character of their masters, almost universally say they are contented, and that their masters are kind. The slaveholders have been known to send in spies among their slaves, to ascertain their views and feelings in regard to their condition. The frequency of this has had the effect to establish among the slaves the maxim, that a still tongue makes a wise head. They suppress the truth rather than take the consequences of telling it, and in so doing prove themselves a part of the human family. If they have any thing to say of their masters, it is generally in their masters' favor, especially when speaking to an untried man. I have been frequently asked, when a slave, if I had a kind master, and do not remember ever to have given a negative answer; nor did I, in pursuing this course, consider myself as uttering what was absolutely false; for I always measured the kindness of my master by the standard of kindness set up among slaveholders around us. Moreover,

6. The biblical figure whose many misfortunes fail to shake his faith in God.

slaves are like other people, and imbibe prejudices quite common to others. They think their own better than that of others. Many, under the influence of this prejudice, think their own masters are better than the masters of other slaves; and this, too, in some cases, when the very reverse is true. Indeed, it is not uncommon for slaves even to fall out and quarrel among themselves about the relative goodness of their masters, each contending for the superior goodness of his own over that of the others. At the very same time, they mutually execrate their masters when viewed separately. It was so on our plantation. When Colonel Lloyd's slaves met the slaves of Jacob Jepson, they seldom parted without a quarrel about their masters; Colonel Lloyd's slaves contending that he was the richest, and Mr. Jepson's slaves that he was the smartest, and most of a man. Colonel Lloyd's slaves would boast his ability to buy and sell Jacob Jepson. Mr. Jepson's slaves would boast his ability to whip Colonel Lloyd. These quarrels would almost always end in a fight between the parties, and those that whipped were supposed to have gained the point at issue. They seemed to think that the greatness of their masters was transferable to themselves. It was considered as being bad enough to be a slave; but to be a poor man's slave was deemed a disgrace indeed!

Chapter IV

Mr. Hopkins remained but a short time in the office of overseer. Why his career was so short, I do not know, but suppose he lacked the necessary severity to suit Colonel Lloyd. Mr. Hopkins was succeeded by Mr. Austin Gore, a man possessing, in an eminent degree, all those traits of character indispensable to what is called a first-rate overseer. Mr. Gore had served Colonel Lloyd, in the capacity of overseer, upon one of the out-farms, and had shown himself worthy of the high station of overseer upon the home or Great House Farm.

Mr. Gore was proud, ambitious, and persevering. He was artful, cruel, and obdurate. He was just the man for such a place, and it was just the place for such a man. It afforded scope for the full exercise of all his powers, and he seemed to be perfectly at home in it. He was one of those who could torture the slightest look, word, or gesture, on the part of the slave, into impudence, and would treat it accordingly. There must be no answering back to him; no explanation was allowed a slave, showing himself to have been wrongfully accused. Mr. Gore acted fully up to the maxim laid down by slaveholders,—"It is better that a dozen slaves suffer under the lash, than that the overseer should be convicted, in the presence of the slaves, of having been at fault." No matter how innocent a slave might be—it availed him nothing, when accused by Mr. Gore of any misdemeanor. To be accused was to be convicted, and to be convicted was to be punished; the one always following the other with immutable certainty. To escape punishment was to escape accusation; and few slaves had the fortune to do either, under the overseership of Mr. Gore. He was just proud enough to demand the most debasing homage of the slave, and quite servile enough to crouch, himself, at the feet of the master. He was ambitious enough to be contented with nothing short of the highest rank of overseers, and persevering enough to reach the height of his ambition. He was cruel enough to inflict the severest punishment, artful enough to descend to the lowest trickery, and obdurate enough to be insensible to the voice of a reproving conscience. He was, of all the overseers, the most dreaded by the slaves. His presence was painful; his eye flashed confusion; and seldom was his sharp, shrill voice heard, without producing horror and trembling in their ranks.

Mr. Gore was a grave man, and, though a young man, he indulged in no jokes, said no funny words, seldom smiled. His words were in perfect keeping with his looks, and his looks were in perfect keeping with his words. Overseers will sometimes indulge in a witty word, even with the slaves; not so with Mr. Gore. He spoke but to command, and commanded but to be obeyed; he dealt sparingly with his words, and bountifully with his whip, never using the former where the latter would answer as well. When he whipped, he seemed to do so from a sense of duty, and feared no consequences. He did nothing reluctantly, no matter how disagreeable; always at his post, never inconsistent. He never promised but to fulfil. He was, in a word, a man of the most inflexible firmness and stone-like coolness.

His savage barbarity was equalled only by the consummate coolness with which he committed the grossest and most savage deeds upon the slaves under his charge. Mr. Gore once undertook to whip one of Colonel Lloyd's slaves, by the name of Demby. He had given Demby but few stripes, when, to get rid of the scourging, he ran and plunged himself into a creek, and stood there at the depth of his shoulders, refusing to come out. Mr. Gore told him that he would give him three calls, and that, if he did not come out at the third call, he would shoot him. The first call was given. Demby made no response, but stood his ground. The second and third calls were given with the same result. Mr. Gore then, without consultation or deliberation with any one, not even giving Demby an additional call, raised his musket to his face, taking deadly aim at his standing victim, and in an instant poor Demby was no more. His mangled body sank out of sight, and blood and brains marked the water where he had stood.

A thrill of horror flashed through every soul upon the plantation, excepting Mr. Gore. He alone seemed cool and collected. He was asked by Colonel Lloyd and my old master, why he resorted to this extraordinary expedient. His reply was, (as well as I can remember,) that Demby had become unmanageable. He was setting a dangerous example to the other slaves,—one which, if suffered to pass without some such demonstration on his part, would finally lead to the total subversion of all rule and order upon the plantation. He argued that if one slave refused to be corrected, and escaped with his life, the other slaves would soon copy the example; the result of which would be, the freedom of the slaves, and the enslavement of the whites. Mr. Gore's defence was satisfactory. He was continued in his station as overseer upon the home plantation. His fame as an overseer went abroad. His horrid crime was not even submitted to judicial investigation. It was committed in the presence of slaves, and they of course could neither institute a suit, nor testify against him; and thus the guilty perpetrator of one of the bloodiest and most foul murders goes unwhipped of justice, and uncensured by the community in which he lives. Mr. Gore lived in St. Michael's, Talbot county, Maryland, when I left there; and if he is still alive, he very probably lives there now; and if so, he is now, as he was then, as highly esteemed and as much respected as though his guilty soul had not been stained with his brother's blood.

I speak advisedly when I say this,—that killing a slave, or any colored person, in Talbot county, Maryland, is not treated as a crime, either by the courts or the community. Mr. Thomas Lanman, of St. Michael's, killed two slaves, one of whom he killed with a hatchet, by knocking his brains out. He used to boast of the commission of the awful and bloody deed. I have heard him do so laughingly, saying, among other things, that he was the only benefactor of his country in the company, and that when others would do as much as he had done, we should be relieved of "the d——d niggers."

The wife of Mr. Giles Hick, living but a short distance from where I used to live, murdered my wife's cousin, a young girl between fifteen and sixteen years of age, mangling her person in the most horrible manner, breaking her nose and breastbone with a stick, so that the poor girl expired in a few hours afterward. She was immediately buried, but had not been in her untimely grave but a few hours before she was taken up and examined by the coroner, who decided that she had come to her death by severe beating. The offence for which this girl was thus murdered was this:—She had been set that night to mind Mrs. Hick's baby, and during the night she fell asleep, and the baby cried. She, having lost her rest for several nights previous, did not hear the crying. They were both in the room with Mrs. Hicks. Mrs. Hicks, finding the girl slow to move, jumped from her bed, seized an oak stick of wood by the fireplace, and with it broke the girl's nose and breastbone, and thus ended her life. I will not say that this most horrid murder produced no sensation in the community. It did produce sensation, but not enough to bring the murderess to punishment. There was a warrant issued for her arrest, but it was never served. Thus she escaped not only punishment, but even the pain of being arraigned before a court for her horrid crime.

Whilst I am detailing bloody deeds which took place during my stay on Colonel Lloyd's plantation, I will briefly narrate another, which occurred about the same time as the murder of Demby by Mr. Gore.

Colonel Lloyd's slaves were in the habit of spending a part of their nights and Sundays in fishing for oysters, and in this way made up the deficiency of their scanty allowance. An old man belonging to Colonel Lloyd, while thus engaged, happened to get beyond the limits of Colonel Lloyd's, and on the premises of Mr. Beal Bondly. At this trespass, Mr. Bondly took offence, and with his musket came down to the shore, and blew its deadly contents into the poor old man.

Mr. Bondly came over to see Colonel Lloyd the next day, whether to pay him for his property, or to justify himself in what he had done, I know not. At any rate, this whole fiendish transaction was soon hushed up. There was very little said about it at all, and nothing done. It was a common saying, even among little white boys, that it was worth a half-cent to kill a "nigger," and a half-cent to bury one.

Chapter V

As to my own treatment while I lived on Colonel Lloyd's plantation, it was very similar to that of the other slave children. I was not old enough to work in the field, and there being little else than field work to do, I had a great deal of leisure time. The most I had to do was to drive up the cows at evening, keep the fowls out of the garden, keep the front yard clean, and run of errands for my old master's daughter, Mrs. Lucretia Auld. The most of my leisure time I spent in helping Master Daniel Lloyd in finding his birds, after he had shot them. My connection with Master Daniel was of some advantage to me. He became quite attached to me, and was a sort of protector of me. He would not allow the older boys to impose upon me, and would divide his cakes with me.

I was seldom whipped by my old master, and suffered little from any thing else than hunger and cold. I suffered much from hunger, but much more from cold. In hottest summer and coldest winter, I was kept almost naked—no shoes, no stockings, no jacket, no trousers, nothing on but a coarse tow linen shirt, reaching only to my knees. I had no bed. I must have perished with cold, but that, the coldest nights, I used to steal a bag which was used for carrying corn to the mill. I would crawl into this bag, and there sleep on the cold, damp, clay floor, with my head in and feet out. My feet have been so cracked with the frost, that the pen with which I am writing might be laid in the gashes.

We were not regularly allowanced. Our food was coarse corn meal boiled. This was called *mush*. It was put into a large wooden tray or trough, and set down upon the ground. The children were then called, like so many pigs, and like so many pigs they would come and devour the mush; some with oyster-shells, others with pieces of shingle, some with naked hands, and none with spoons. He that ate fastest got most; he that was strongest secured the best place; and few left the trough satisfied.

I was probably between seven and eight years old when I left Colonel Lloyd's plantation. I left it with joy. I shall never forget the ecstasy with which I received the intelligence that my old master (Anthony) had determined to let me go to Baltimore, to live with Mr. Hugh Auld, brother to my old master's son-in-law, Captain Thomas Auld. I received this information about three days before my departure. They were three of the happiest days I ever enjoyed. I spent the most part of all these three days in the creek, washing off the plantation scurf, and preparing myself for my departure.

The pride of appearance which this would indicate was not my own. I spent the time in washing, not so much because I wished to, but because Mrs. Lucretia had told me I must get all the dead skin off my feet and knees before I could go to Baltimore; for the people of Baltimore were very cleanly, and would laugh at me if I looked dirty. Besides, she was going to give me a pair of trousers, which I should not put on unless I got all the dirt off me. The thought of owning a pair of trousers was great indeed! It was almost a sufficient motive, not only to make me take off what would be called by pig-drovers the mange, but the skin itself. I went at it in good earnest, working for the first time with the hope of reward.

The ties that ordinarily bind children to their homes were all suspended in my case. I found no severe trial in my departure. My home was charmless; it was not home to me; on parting from it, I could not feel that I was leaving any thing which I could have enjoyed by staying. My mother was dead, my grandmother lived far off, so that I seldom saw her. I had two sisters and one brother, that lived in the same house with me; but the early separation of us from our mother had well nigh blotted the fact of our relationship from our memories. I looked for home elsewhere, and was confident of finding none which I should relish less than the one which I was leaving. If, however, I found in my new home hardship, hunger, whipping, and nakedness, I had the consolation that I should not have escaped any one of them by staying. Having already had more than a taste of them in the house of my old master, and having endured them there, I very naturally inferred my ability to endure them elsewhere, and especially at Baltimore; for I had something of the feeling about Baltimore that is expressed in the proverb, that "being hanged in England is preferable to dying a natural death in Ireland." I had the strongest desire to see Baltimore. Cousin Tom, though not fluent in speech, had inspired me with that desire by his eloquent description of the place. I could never point out any thing at the Great House, no matter how beautiful or powerful, but that he had seen something at Baltimore far exceeding, both in beauty and strength, the object which I pointed out to him. Even the Great House itself, with all its pictures, was far inferior to many buildings in Baltimore. So strong was my desire, that I thought a gratification of it would fully compensate for whatever loss of comforts I should sustain by the exchange. I left without a regret, and with the highest hopes of future happiness.

We sailed out of Miles River for Baltimore on a Saturday morning. I remember only the day of the week, for at that time I had no knowledge of the days of the month, nor the months of the year. On setting sail, I walked aft, and gave to Colonel Lloyd's plantation what I hoped would be the last look. I then placed myself in the bows of the sloop, and there spent the remainder of the day in looking ahead, interesting myself in what was in the distance rather than in things near by or behind.

In the afternoon of that day, we reached Annapolis, the capital of the State. We stopped but a few moments, so that I had no time to go on shore. It was the first large town that I had ever seen, and though it would look small compared with some of our New England factory villages, I thought it a wonderful place for its size—more imposing even than the Great House Farm!

We arrived at Baltimore early on Sunday morning, landing at Smith's Wharf, not far from Bowley's Wharf. We had on board the sloop a large flock of sheep; and after aiding in driving them to the slaughterhouse of Mr. Curtis on Louden Slater's Hill, I was conducted by Rich, one of the hands belonging on board of the sloop, to my new home in Alliciana Street, near Mr. Gardner's ship-yard, on Fells Point.

Mr. and Mrs. Auld were both at home, and met me at the door with their little son Thomas, to take care of whom I had been given. And here I saw what I had never seen before; it was a white face beaming with the most kindly emotions; it was the face of my new mistress, Sophia Auld. I wish I could describe the rapture that flashed through my soul as I beheld it. It was a new and strange sight to me, brightening up my pathway with the light of happiness. Little Thomas was told, there was his Freddy,—and I was told to take care of little Thomas; and thus I entered upon the duties of my new home with the most cheering prospect ahead.

I look upon my departure from Colonel Lloyd's plantation as one of the most interesting events of my life. It is possible, and even quite probable, that but for the mere circumstance of being removed from that plantation to Baltimore, I should have to-day, instead of being here seated by my own table, in the enjoyment of freedom and the happiness of home, writing this Narrative, been confined in the galling chains of slavery. Going to live at Baltimore laid the foundation, and opened the gateway, to all my subsequent prosperity. I have ever regarded it as the first plain manifestation of that kind providence which has ever since attended me, and marked my life with so many favors. I regarded the selection of myself as being somewhat remarkable. There were a number of slave children that might have been sent from the plantation to Baltimore. There were those younger, those older, and those of the same age. I was chosen from among them all, and was the first, last, and only choice.

I may be deemed superstitious, and even egotistical, in regarding this event as a special interposition of divine Providence in my favor. But I should be false to the earliest sentiments of my soul, if I suppressed the opinion. I prefer to be true to myself, even at the hazard of incurring the ridicule of others, rather than to be false, and incur my own abhorrence. From my earliest recollection, I date the entertainment of a deep conviction that slavery would not always be able to hold me within its foul embrace; and in the darkest hours of my career in slavery, this living word of faith and spirit of hope departed not from me, but remained like ministering angels to cheer me through the gloom. This good spirit was from God, and to him I offer thanksgiving and praise.

Chapter VI

My new mistress proved to be all she appeared when I first met her at the door,—a woman of the kindest heart and finest feelings. She had never had a slave under her control previously to myself, and prior to her marriage she had been dependent upon her own industry for a living. She was by trade a weaver; and by constant application to her business, she had been in a good degree preserved from the blighting and dehumanizing effects of slavery. I was utterly astonished at her goodness. I scarcely knew how to behave towards her. She was entirely unlike any other white woman I had ever seen. I could not approach her as I was accustomed to approach other white ladies. My early instruction was all out of place. The crouching servility, usually so acceptable a quality in a slave, did not answer when manifested toward her. Her favor was not gained by it; she seemed to be disturbed by it. She did not deem it impudent or unmannerly for a slave to look her in the face. The meanest slave was put fully at ease in her presence, and none left without feeling better for having seen her. Her face was made of heavenly smiles, and her voice of tranquil music.

But, alas! this kind heart had but a short time to remain such. The fatal poison of irresponsible power was already in her hands, and soon commenced its infernal work. That cheerful eye, under the influence of slavery, soon became red with rage; that voice, made all of sweet accord, changed to one of harsh and horrid discord; and that angelic face gave place to that of a demon.

Very soon after I went to live with Mr. and Mrs. Auld, she very kindly commenced to teach me the A, B, C. After I had learned this, she assisted me in learning to spell words of three or four letters. Just at this point of my progress, Mr. Auld found out what was going on, and at once forbade Mrs. Auld to instruct me further, telling her, among other things, that it was unlawful, as well as unsafe, to teach a slave to read. To use his own words, further, he said, "If you give a nigger an inch, he will take an ell.[7] A nigger should know nothing but to obey his master—to do as he is told to do. Learning would *spoil* the best nigger in the world. Now," said he, "if you teach that nigger (speaking of myself) how to read, there would be no keeping him. It would forever unfit him to be a slave. He would at once become unmanageable, and of no value to his master. As to himself, it could do him no good, but a great deal of harm. It would make him discontented and unhappy." These words sank deep into my heart, stirred up sentiments within that lay slumbering, and called into existence an entirely new train of thought. It was a new and special revelation, explaining dark and mysterious things, with which my youthful understanding had struggled, but struggled in vain. I now understood what had been to me a most perplexing difficulty—to wit, the white man's power to enslave the black man. It was a grand achievement, and I prized it highly. From that moment, I understood the pathway from slavery to freedom. It was just what I wanted, and I got it at a time when I the least expected it. Whilst I was saddened by the thought of losing the aid of my kind mistress, I was gladdened by the invaluable instruction which, by the merest accident, I had gained from my master. Though conscious of the difficulty of learning without a teacher, I set out with high hope, and a fixed purpose, at whatever cost of trouble, to learn how to read. The very decided manner with which he spoke, and strove to impress his wife with the evil consequences of giving me instruction, served to convince me that he was deeply sensible of the truths he was uttering. It gave me the best assurance that I might rely with the utmost confidence on the results which, he said, would flow from teaching me to read. What he most dreaded, that I most desired. What he most loved, that I most hated. That which to him was a great evil, to be carefully shunned, was to me a great good, to be diligently sought; and the argument which he so warmly urged, against my learning to read, only served to inspire me with a desire and determination to learn. In learning to read, I owe almost as much to the bitter opposition of my master, as to the kindly aid of my mistress. I acknowledge the benefit of both.

I had resided but a short time in Baltimore before I observed a marked difference, in the treatment of slaves, from that which I had witnessed in the country. A city slave is almost a freeman, compared with a slave on the plantation. He is much better fed and clothed, and enjoys privileges altogether unknown to the slave on the plantation. There is a vestige of decency, a sense of shame, that does much to curb and check those outbreaks of atrocious cruelty so commonly enacted upon the plantation. He is a desperate slaveholder, who will shock the humanity of his non-slaveholding neighbors with the cries of his lacerated slave. Few are willing to incur the odium attaching to the reputation of being a cruel master; and above all things, they would not be known as not giving a slave enough to eat. Every city slaveholder is anxious to have it known of him, that he feeds his slaves well; and it is due to them to say, that most of them do give their slaves enough to eat. There are, however, some painful exceptions to this rule. Directly opposite to us, on Philpot Street, lived Mr. Thomas Hamilton. He owned two slaves. Their names were Henrietta and Mary. Henrietta was about twenty-two years of age, Mary was about fourteen; and of all the mangled and

---

7. Unit of measurement equal to forty-five inches.

emaciated creatures I ever looked upon, these two were the most so. His heart must be harder than stone, that could look upon these unmoved. The head, neck, and shoulders of Mary were literally cut to pieces. I have frequently felt her head, and found it nearly covered with festering sores, caused by the lash of her cruel mistress. I do not know that her master ever whipped her, but I have been an eye-witness to the cruelty of Mrs. Hamilton. I used to be in Mr. Hamilton's house nearly every day. Mrs. Hamilton used to sit in a large chair in the middle of the room, with a heavy cowskin always by her side, and scarce an hour passed during the day but was marked by the blood of one of these slaves. The girls seldom passed her without her saying, "Move faster, you *black gip!*" at the same time giving them a blow with the cowskin over the head or shoulders, often drawing the blood. She would then say, "Take that, you *black gip!*"—continuing, "If you don't move faster, I'll move you!" Added to the cruel lashings to which these slaves were subjected, they were kept nearly half-starved. They seldom knew what it was to eat a full meal. I have seen Mary contending with the pigs for the offal thrown into the street. So much was Mary kicked and cut to pieces, that she was oftener called *"pecked"* than by her name.

Chapter VII

I lived in Master Hugh's family about seven years. During this time, I succeeded in learning to read and write. In accomplishing this, I was compelled to resort to various stratagems. I had no regular teacher. My mistress, who had kindly commenced to instruct me, had, in compliance with the advice and direction of her husband, not only ceased to instruct, but had set her face against my being instructed by any one else. It is due, however, to my mistress to say of her, that she did not adopt this course of treatment immediately. She at first lacked the depravity indispensable to shutting me up in mental darkness. It was at least necessary for her to have some training in the exercise of irresponsible power, to make her equal to the task of treating me as though I were a brute.

My mistress was, as I have said, a kind and tender-hearted woman; and in the simplicity of her soul she commenced, when I first went to live with her, to treat me as she supposed one human being ought to treat another. In entering upon the duties of a slaveholder, she did not seem to perceive that I sustained to her the relation of a mere chattel, and that for her to treat me as a human being was not only wrong, but dangerously so. Slavery proved as injurious to her as it did to me. When I went there, she was a pious, warm, and tender-hearted woman. There was no sorrow or suffering for which she had not a tear. She had bread for the hungry, clothes for the naked, and comfort for every mourner that came within her reach. Slavery soon proved its ability to divest her of these heavenly qualities. Under its influence, the tender heart became stone, and the lamblike disposition gave way to one of tiger-like fierceness. The first step in her downward course was in her ceasing to instruct me. She now commenced to practise her husband's precepts. She finally became even more violent in her opposition than her husband himself. She was not satisfied with simply doing as well as he had commanded; she seemed anxious to do better. Nothing seemed to make her more angry than to see me with a newspaper. She seemed to think that here lay the danger.

I have had her rush at me with a face made all up of fury, and snatch from me a newspaper, in a manner that fully revealed her apprehension. She was an apt woman; and a little experience soon demonstrated, to her satisfaction, that education and slavery were incompatible with each other.

From this time I was most narrowly watched. If I was in a separate room any considerable length of time, I was sure to be suspected of having a book, and was at once called to give an account of myself. All this, however, was too late. The first step had been taken. Mistress, in teaching me the alphabet, had given me the *inch*, and no precaution could prevent me from taking the *ell*.

The plan which I adopted, and the one by which I was most successful, was that of making friends of all the little white boys whom I met in the street. As many of these as I could, I converted into teachers. With their kindly aid, obtained at different times and in different places, I finally succeeded in learning to read. When I was sent of errands, I always took my book with me, and by going one part of my errand quickly, I found time to get a lesson before my return. I used also to carry bread with me, enough of which was always in the house, and to which I was always welcome; for I was much better off in this regard than many of the poor white children in our neighborhood. This bread I used to bestow upon the hungry little urchins, who, in return, would give me that more valuable bread of knowledge. I am strongly tempted to give the names of two or three of those little boys, as a testimonial of the gratitude and affection I bear them; but prudence forbids;—not that it would injure me, but it might embarrass them; for it is almost an unpardonable offence to teach slaves to read in this Christian country. It is enough to say of the dear little fellows, that they lived on Philpot Street, very near Durgin and Bailey's shipyard. I used to talk this matter of slavery over with them. I would sometimes say to them, I wished I could be as free as they would be when they got to be men. "You will be free as soon as you are twenty-one, *but I am a slave for life!* Have not I as good a right to be free as you have?" These words used to trouble them; they would express for me the liveliest sympathy, and console me with the hope that something would occur by which I might be free.

I was now about twelve years old, and the thought of being *a slave for life* began to bear heavily upon my heart. Just about this time, I got hold of a book entitled "The Columbian Orator."[8] Every opportunity I got, I used to read this book. Among much of other interesting matter, I found in it a dialogue between a master and his slave. The slave was represented as having run away from his master three times. The dialogue represented the conversation which took place between them, when the slave was retaken the third time. In this dialogue, the whole argument in behalf of slavery was brought forward by the master, all of which was disposed of by the slave. The slave was made to say some very smart as well as impressive things in reply to his master—things which had the desired though unexpected effect; for the conversation resulted in the voluntary emancipation of the slave on the part of the master.

In the same book, I met with one of Sheridan's[9] mighty speeches on and in behalf of Catholic emancipation. These were choice documents to me. I read

8. A popular anthology of pieces for recitation (1797) compiled by the Massachusetts teacher and writer Caleb Bingham (1757–1817).

9. Richard Brinsley Sheridan (1751–1816), Irish dramatist and political leader.

them over and over again with unabated interest. They gave tongue to interesting thoughts of my own soul, which had frequently flashed through my
mind, and died away for want of utterance. The moral which I gained from
the dialogue was the power of truth over the conscience of even a slaveholder.
What I got from Sheridan was a bold denunciation of slavery, and a powerful
vindication of human rights. The reading of these documents enabled me to
utter my thoughts, and to meet the arguments brought forward to sustain
slavery; but while they relieved me of one difficulty, they brought on another
even more painful than the one of which I was relieved. The more I read, the
more I was led to abhor and detest my enslavers. I could regard them in no
other light than a band of successful robbers, who had left their homes, and
gone to Africa, and stolen us from our homes, and in a strange land reduced
us to slavery. I loathed them as being the meanest as well as the most wicked
of men. As I read and contemplated the subject, behold! that very discontent-
ment which Master Hugh had predicted would follow my learning to read
had already come, to torment and sting my soul to unutterable anguish. As I
writhed under it, I would at times feel that learning to read had been a curse
rather than a blessing. It had given me a view of my wretched condition, without the remedy. It opened my eyes to the horrible pit, but to no ladder upon
which to get out. In moments of agony, I envied my fellow-slaves for their
stupidity. I have often wished myself a beast. I preferred the condition of the
meanest reptile to my own. Any thing, no matter what, to get rid of thinking!
It was this everlasting thinking of my condition that tormented me. There
was no getting rid of it. It was pressed upon me by every object within sight or
hearing, animate or inanimate. The silver trump of freedom had roused my
soul to eternal wakefulness. Freedom now appeared, to disappear no more
forever. It was heard in every sound, and seen in every thing. It was ever present to torment me with a sense of my wretched condition. I saw nothing
without seeing it, I heard nothing without hearing it, and felt nothing without feeling it. It looked from every star, it smiled in every calm, breathed in
every wind, and moved in every storm.

I often found myself regretting my own existence, and wishing myself
dead; and but for the hope of being free, I have no doubt but that I should
have killed myself, or done something for which I should have been killed.
While in this state of mind, I was eager to hear any one speak of slavery. I was
a ready listener. Every little while, I could hear something about the abolitionists. It was some time before I found what the word meant. It was always
used in such connections as to make it an interesting word to me. If a slave
ran away and succeeded in getting clear, or if a slave killed his master, set fire
to a barn, or did any thing very wrong in the mind of a slaveholder, it was
spoken of as the fruit of *abolition*. Hearing the word in this connection very
often, I set about learning what it meant. The dictionary afforded me little or
no help. I found it was "the act of abolishing;" but then I did not know what
was to be abolished. Here I was perplexed. I did not dare to ask any one about
its meaning, for I was satisfied that it was something they wanted me to know
very little about. After a patient waiting, I got one of our city papers, containing an account of the number of petitions from the north, praying for the
abolition of slavery in the District of Columbia, and of the slave trade between
the States. From this time I understood the words *abolition* and *abolitionist*, and always drew near when that word was spoken, expecting to hear

something of importance to myself and fellow-slaves. The light broke in upon me by degrees. I went one day down on the wharf of Mr. Waters; and seeing two Irishmen unloading a scow of stone, I went, unasked, and helped them. When we had finished, one of them came to me and asked me if I were a slave. I told him I was. He asked, "Are ye a slave for life?" I told him that I was. The good Irishman seemed to be deeply affected by the statement. He said to the other that it was a pity so fine a little fellow as myself should be a slave for life. He said it was a shame to hold me. They both advised me to run away to the north; that I should find friends there, and that I should be free. I pretended not to be interested in what they said, and treated them as if I did not understand them; for I feared they might be treacherous. White men have been known to encourage slaves to escape, and then, to get the reward, catch them and return them to their masters. I was afraid that these seemingly good men might use me so; but I nevertheless remembered their advice, and from that time I resolved to run away. I looked forward to a time at which it would be safe for me to escape. I was too young to think of doing so immediately; besides, I wished to learn how to write, as I might have occasion to write my own pass. I consoled myself with the hope that I should one day find a good chance. Meanwhile, I would learn to write.

The idea as to how I might learn to write was suggested to me by being in Durgin and Bailey's ship-yard, and frequently seeing the ship carpenters, after hewing, and getting a piece of timber ready for use, write on the timber the name of that part of the ship for which it was intended. When a piece of timber was intended for the larboard side, it would be marked thus—"L." When a piece was for the starboard side, it would be marked thus—"S." A piece for the larboard side forward, would be marked thus—"L.F." When a piece was for starboard side forward, it would be marked thus—"S.F." For larboard aft, it would be marked thus—"L.A." For starboard aft, it would be marked thus—"S.A." I soon learned the names of these letters, and for what they were intended when placed upon a piece of timber in the ship-yard. I immediately commenced copying them, and in a short time was able to make the four letters named. After that, when I met with any boy who I knew could write, I would tell him I could write as well as he. The next word would be, "I don't believe you. Let me see you try it." I would then make the letters which I had been so fortunate as to learn, and ask him to beat that. In this way I got a good many lessons in writing, which it is quite possible I should never have gotten in any other way. During this time, my copy-book was the board fence, brick wall, and pavement; my pen and ink was a lump of chalk. With these, I learned mainly how to write. I then commenced and continued copying the Italics in Webster's Spelling Book,[1] until I could make them all without looking on the book. By this time, my little Master Thomas had gone to school, and learned how to write, and had written over a number of copy-books. These had been brought home, and shown to some of our near neighbors, and then laid aside. My mistress used to go to class meeting at the Wilk Street meetinghouse every Monday afternoon, and leave me to take care of the house. When left thus, I used to spend the time in writing in the spaces left in Master Thomas's copy-book, copying what he had written. I continued to do this until I could write a hand very similar

1. *The American Spelling Book* (1783), by Noah Webster (1758–1843).

to that of Master Thomas. Thus, after a long, tedious effort for years, I finally succeeded in learning how to write.

Chapter VIII

In a very short time after I went to live at Baltimore, my old master's youngest son Richard died; and in about three years and six months after his death, my old master, Captain Anthony, died, leaving only his son, Andrew, and daughter, Lucretia, to share his estate. He died while on a visit to see his daughter at Hillsborough. Cut off thus unexpectedly, he left no will as to the disposal of his property. It was therefore necessary to have a valuation of the property, that it might be equally divided between Mrs. Lucretia and Master Andrew. I was immediately sent for, to be valued with the other property. Here again my feelings rose up in detestation of slavery. I had now a new conception of my degraded condition. Prior to this, I had become, if not insensible to my lot, at least partly so. I left Baltimore with a young heart overborne with sadness, and a soul full of apprehension. I took passage with Captain Rowe, in the schooner Wild Cat, and, after a sail of about twenty-four hours, I found myself near the place of my birth. I had now been absent from it almost, if not quite, five years. I, however, remembered the place very well. I was only about five years old when I left it, to go and live with my old master on Colonel Lloyd's plantation; so that I was now between ten and eleven years old.

We were all ranked together at the valuation. Men and women, old and young, married and single, were ranked with horses, sheep, and swine. There were horses and men, cattle and women, pigs and children, all holding the same rank in the scale of being, and were all subjected to the same narrow examination. Silvery-headed age and sprightly youth, maids and matrons, had to undergo the same indelicate inspection. At this moment, I saw more clearly than ever the brutalizing effects of slavery upon both slave and slaveholder.

After the valuation, then came the division. I have no language to express the high excitement and deep anxiety which were felt among us poor slaves during this time. Our fate for life was now to be decided. We had no more voice in that decision than the brutes among whom we were ranked. A single word from the white men was enough—against all our wishes, prayers, and entreaties—to sunder forever the dearest friends, dearest kindred, and strongest ties known to human beings. In addition to the pain of separation, there was the horrid dread of falling into the hands of Master Andrew. He was known to us all as being a most cruel wretch,—a common drunkard, who had, by his reckless mismanagement and profligate dissipation, already wasted a large portion of his father's property. We all felt that we might as well be sold at once to the Georgia traders, as to pass into his hands; for we knew that that would be our inevitable condition,—a condition held by us all in the utmost horror and dread.

I suffered more anxiety than most of my fellow-slaves. I had known what it was to be kindly treated; they had known nothing of the kind. They had seen little or nothing of the world. They were in very deed men and women of sorrow, and acquainted with grief. Their backs had been made familiar with the bloody lash, so that they had become callous; mine was yet tender; for while at Baltimore I got few whippings, and few slaves could boast of a kinder master and mistress than myself; and the thought of passing out of their hands into those of Master Andrew—a man who, but a few days before, to give me a sample of his bloody disposition, took my little brother by the throat, threw him on the ground, and with the heel of his boot stamped upon his head till the blood gushed from his nose and ears—was well calculated to make me anxious as to my fate. After he had committed this savage outrage upon my brother, he turned to me, and said that was the way he meant to serve me one of these days,—meaning, I suppose, when I came into his possession.

Thanks to a kind Providence, I fell to the portion of Mrs. Lucretia, and was sent immediately back to Baltimore, to live again in the family of Master Hugh. Their joy at my return equalled their sorrow at my departure. It was a glad day to me. I had escaped a [fate] worse than lion's jaws. I was absent from Baltimore, for the purpose of valuation and division, just about one month, and it seemed to have been six.

Very soon after my return to Baltimore, my mistress, Lucretia, died, leaving her husband and one child, Amanda; and in a very short time after her death, Master Andrew died. Now all the property of my old master, slaves included, was in the hands of strangers,—strangers who had had nothing to do with accumulating it. Not a slave was left free. All remained slaves, from the youngest to the oldest. If any one thing in my experience, more than another, served to deepen my conviction of the infernal character of slavery, and to fill me with unutterable loathing of slaveholders, it was their base ingratitude to my poor old grandmother. She had served my old master faithfully from youth to old age. She had been the source of all his wealth; she had peopled his plantation with slaves; she had become a great grandmother in his service. She had rocked him in infancy, attended him in childhood, served him through life, and at his death wiped from his icy brow the cold death-sweat, and closed his eyes forever. She was nevertheless left a slave—a slave for life—a slave in the hands of strangers; and in their hands she saw her children, her grandchildren, and her great-grandchildren, divided, like so many sheep, without being gratified with the small privilege of a single word, as to their or her own destiny. And, to cap the climax of their base ingratitude and fiendish barbarity, my grandmother, who was now very old, having outlived my old master and all his children, having seen the beginning and end of all of them, and her present owners finding she was of but little value, her frame already racked with the pains of old age, and complete helplessness fast stealing over her once active limbs, they took her to the woods, built her a little hut, put up a little mud-chimney, and then made her welcome to the privilege of supporting herself there in perfect loneliness; thus virtually turning her out to die! If my poor old grandmother now lives, she lives to suffer in utter loneliness; she lives to remember and mourn over the loss of children, the loss of grandchildren, and the loss of great-grandchildren. They are, in the language of the slave's poet, Whittier,[2]—

> "Gone, gone, sold and gone
> To the rice swamp dank and lone,

---

2. John Greenleaf Whittier (1807–1882), American poet and abolitionist. Douglass quotes from Whittier's antislavery poem "The Farewell: Of a Virginia Slave Mother to Her Daughter Sold into Southern Bondage" (1838).

Where the slave-whip ceaseless swings,
Where the noisome insect stings,
Where the fever-demon strews
Poison with the falling dews,
Where the sickly sunbeams glare
Through the hot and misty air:—
   Gone, gone, sold and gone
   To the rice swamp dank and lone,
   From Virginia hills and waters—
   Woe is me, my stolen daughters!"

The hearth is desolate. The children, the unconscious children, who once sang and danced in her presence, are gone. She gropes her way, in the darkness of age, for a drink of water. Instead of the voices of her children, she hears by day the moans of the dove, and by night the screams of the hideous owl. All is gloom. The grave is at the door. And now, when weighed down by the pains and aches of old age, when the head inclines to the feet, when the beginning and ending of human existence meet, and helpless infancy and painful old age combine together—at this time, this most needful time, the time for the exercise of that tenderness and affection which children only can exercise toward a declining parent—my poor old grandmother, the devoted mother of twelve children, is left all alone, in yonder little hut, before a few dim embers. She stands—she sits—she staggers—she falls—she groans—she dies—and there are none of her children or grandchildren present, to wipe from her wrinkled brow the cold sweat of death, or to place beneath the sod her fallen remains. Will not a righteous God visit for these things?

In about two years after the death of Mrs. Lucretia, Master Thomas married his second wife. Her name was Rowena Hamilton. She was the eldest daughter of Mr. William Hamilton. Master now lived in St. Michael's. Not long after his marriage, a misunderstanding took place between himself and Master Hugh; and as a means of punishing his brother, he took me from him to live with himself at St. Michael's. Here I underwent another most painful separation. It, however, was not so severe as the one I dreaded at the division of property; for, during this interval, a great change had taken place in Master Hugh and his once kind and affectionate wife. The influence of brandy upon him, and of slavery upon her, had effected a disastrous change in the characters of both; so that, as far as they were concerned, I thought I had little to lose by the change. But it was not to them that I was attached. It was to those little Baltimore boys that I felt the strongest attachment. I had received many good lessons from them, and was still receiving them, and the thought of leaving them was painful indeed. I was leaving, too, without the hope of ever being allowed to return. Master Thomas had said he would never let me return again. The barrier betwixt himself and brother he considered impassable.

I then had to regret that I did not at least make the attempt to carry out my resolution to run away; for the chances of success are tenfold greater from the city than from the country.

I sailed from Baltimore for St. Michael's in the sloop Amanda, Captain Edward Dodson. On my passage, I paid particular attention to the direction which the steamboats took to go to Philadelphia. I found, instead of going down, on reaching North Point they went up the bay, in a north-easterly direction. I deemed this knowledge of the utmost importance. My determination to run away was again revived. I resolved to wait only so long as the offering of a favorable opportunity. When that came, I was determined to be off.

Chapter IX

I have now reached a period of my life when I can give dates. I left Baltimore, and went to live with Master Thomas Auld, at St. Michael's, in March, 1832. It was now more than seven years since I lived with him in the family of my old master, on Colonel Lloyd's plantation. We of course were now almost entire strangers to each other. He was to me a new master, and I to him a new slave. I was ignorant of his temper and disposition; he was equally so of mine. A very short time, however brought us into full acquaintance with each other. I was made acquainted with his wife not less than with himself. They were well matched, being equally mean and cruel. I was now, for the first time during a space of more than seven years, made to feel the painful gnawings of hunger—a something which I had not experienced before since I left Colonel Lloyd's plantation. It went hard enough with me then, when I could look back to no period at which I had enjoyed a sufficiency. It was tenfold harder after living in Master Hugh's family, where I had always had enough to eat, and of that which was good. I have said Master Thomas was a mean man. He was so. Not to give a slave enough to eat, is regarded as the most aggravated development of meanness even among slaveholders. The rule is, no matter how coarse the food, only let there be enough of it. This is the theory; and in the part of Maryland from which I came, it is the general practice,—though there are many exceptions. Master Thomas gave us enough of neither coarse nor fine food. There were four slaves of us in the kitchen—my sister Eliza, my aunt Priscilla, Henny, and myself; and we were allowed less than half of a bushel of corn-meal per week, and very little else, either in the shape of meat or vegetables. It was not enough for us to subsist upon. We were therefore reduced to the wretched necessity of living at the expense of our neighbors. This we did by begging and stealing, whichever came handy in the time of need, the one being considered as legitimate as the other. A great many times have we poor creatures been nearly perishing with hunger, when food in abundance lay mouldering in the safe and smoke-house,[3] and our pious mistress was aware of the fact; and yet that mistress and her husband would kneel every morning, and pray that God would bless them in basket and store!

Bad as all slaveholders are, we seldom meet one destitute of every element of character commanding respect. My master was one of this rare sort. I do not know of one single noble act ever performed by him. The leading trait in his character was meanness; and if there were any other element in his nature, it was made subject to this. He was mean; and, like most other mean men, he lacked the ability to conceal his meanness. Captain Auld was not born a slaveholder. He had been a poor man, master only of a Bay craft. He came into possession of all his slaves by marriage; and of all men, adopted

---

3. Used both to cure and to store meat and fish. "Safe": a meat safe is a structure for preserving food.

slaveholders are the worst. He was cruel, but cowardly. He commanded without firmness. In the enforcement of his rules he was at times rigid, and at times lax. At times, he spoke to his slaves with the firmness of Napoleon and the fury of a demon; at other times, he might well be mistaken for an inquirer who had lost his way. He did nothing of himself. He might have passed for a lion, but for his ears.[4] In all things noble which he attempted, his own meanness shone most conspicuous. His airs, words, and actions, were the airs, words, and actions of born slaveholders, and, being assumed, were awkward enough. He was not even a good imitator. He possessed all the disposition to deceive, but wanted the power. Having no resources within himself, he was compelled to be the copyist of many, and being such, he was forever the victim of inconsistency; and of consequence he was an object of contempt, and was held as such even by his slaves. The luxury of having slaves of his own to wait upon him was something new and unprepared for. He was a slaveholder without the ability to hold slaves. He found himself incapable of managing his slaves either by force, fear, or fraud. We seldom called him "master;" we generally called him "Captain Auld," and were hardly disposed to title him at all. I doubt not that our conduct had much to do with making him appear awkward, and of consequence fretful. Our want of reverence for him must have perplexed him greatly. He wished to have us call him master, but lacked the firmness necessary to command us to do so. His wife used to insist upon our calling him so, but to no purpose. In August, 1832, my master attended a Methodist camp-meeting[5] held in the Bay-side, Talbot county, and there experienced religion. I indulged a faint hope that his conversion would lead him to emancipate his slaves, and that, if he did not do this, it would, at any rate, make him more kind and humane. I was disappointed in both these respects. It neither made him to be humane to his slaves, nor to emancipate them. If it had any effect on his character, it made him more cruel and hateful in all his ways; for I believe him to have been a much worse man after his conversion than before. Prior to his conversion, he relied upon his own depravity to shield and sustain him in his savage barbarity; but after his conversion, he found religious sanction and support for his slaveholding cruelty. He made the greatest pretensions to piety. His house was the house of prayer. He prayed morning, noon, and night. He very soon distinguished himself among his brethren, and was soon made a class-leader and exhorter. His activity in revivals was great, and he proved himself an instrument in the hands of the church in converting many souls. His house was the preachers' home. They used to take great pleasure in coming there to put up; for while he starved us, he stuffed them. We have had three or four preachers there at a time. The names of those who used to come most frequently while I lived there, were Mr. Storks, Mr. Ewery, Mr. Humphry, and Mr. Hickey. I have also seen Mr. George Cookman[6] at our house. We slaves loved Mr. Cookman. We believed him to be a good man. We thought him instrumental in getting Mr. Samuel Harrison, a very rich slaveholder, to emancipate his slaves; and by some means got the impression that he was laboring to effect the emancipation of all the slaves. When he was at our

4. The suggestion is that his ears reveal him to be a jackass and thus not as powerful as he pretends.
5. Evangelical religious gathering, usually held outdoors.
6. Prominent English Methodist minister (1800–1841).

house, we were sure to be called in to prayers. When the others were there, we were sometimes called in and sometimes not. Mr. Cookman took more notice of us than either of the other ministers. He could not come among us with betraying his sympathy for us, and, stupid as we were, we had the sagacity to see it.

While I lived with my master in St. Michael's, there was a white young man, a Mr. Wilson, who proposed to keep a Sabbath school for the instruction of such slaves as might be disposed to learn to read the New Testament. We met but three times, when Mr. West and Mr. Fairbanks, both class-leaders, with many others, came upon us with sticks and other missiles, drove us off, and forbade us to meet again. Thus ended our little Sabbath school in the pious town of St. Michael's.

I have said my master found religious sanction for his cruelty. As an example, I will state one of many facts going to prove the charge. I have seen him tie up a lame young woman, and whip her with a heavy cowskin upon her naked shoulders, causing the warm red blood to drip; and, in justification of the bloody deed, he would quote this passage of Scripture—"He that knoweth his master's will, and doeth it not, shall be beaten with many stripes."[7]

Master would keep this lacerated young woman tied up in this horrid situation four or five hours at a time. I have known him to tie her up early in the morning, and whip her before breakfast; leave her, go to his store, return at dinner, and whip her again, cutting her in the places already made raw with his cruel lash. The secret of master's cruelty toward "Henny" is found in the fact of her being almost helpless. When quite a child, she fell into the fire, and burned herself horribly. Her hands were so burnt that she never got the use of them. She could do very little but bear heavy burdens. She was to master a bill of expense; and as he was a mean man, she was a constant offence to him. He seemed desirous of getting the poor girl out of existence. He gave her away once to his sister; but, being a poor gift, she was not disposed to keep her. Finally, my benevolent master, to use his own words, "set her adrift to take care of herself." Here was a recently-converted man, holding on upon the mother, and at the same time turning out her helpless child, to starve and die! Master Thomas was one of the many pious slaveholders who hold slaves for the very charitable purpose of taking care of them.

My master and myself had quite a number of differences. He found me unsuitable to his purpose. My city life, he said, had had a very pernicious effect upon me. It had almost ruined me for every good purpose, and fitted me for every thing which was bad. One of my greatest faults was that of letting his horse run away, and go down to his father-in-law's farm, which was about five miles from St. Michael's. I would then have to go after it. My reason for this kind of carelessness, or carefulness, was, that I could always get something to eat when I went there. Master William Hamilton, my master's father-in-law, always gave his slaves enough to eat. I never left there hungry, no matter how great the need of my speedy return. Master Thomas at length said he would stand it no longer. I had lived with him nine months, during which time he had given me a number of severe whippings, all to no good purpose. He resolved to put me out, as he said, to be broken; and, for

7. Luke 12.47.

this purpose, he let me for one year to a man named Edward Covey. Mr. Covey was a poor man, a farm-renter. He rented the place upon which he lived, as also the hands with which he tilled it. Mr. Covey had acquired a very high reputation for breaking young slaves, and this reputation was of immense value to him. It enabled him to get his farm tilled with much less expense to himself than he could have had it done without such a reputation. Some slaveholders thought it not much loss to allow Mr. Covey to have their slaves one year, for the sake of training to which they were subjected, without any other compensation. He could hire young help with great ease, in consequence of this reputation. Added to the natural good qualities of Mr. Covey, he was a professor of religion—a pious soul—a member and a class-leader in the Methodist church. All of this added weight to his reputation as a "nigger-breaker." I was aware of all the facts, having been made acquainted with them by a young man who had lived there. I nevertheless made the change gladly; for I was sure of getting enough to eat, which is not the smallest consideration to a hungry man.

Chapter X

I left Master Thomas's house, and went to live with Mr. Covey, on the 1st of January, 1833. I was now, for the first time in my life, a field hand. In my new employment, I found myself even more awkward than a country boy appeared to be in a large city. I had been at my new home but one week before Mr. Covey gave me a very severe whipping, cutting my back, causing the blood to run, and raising ridges on my flesh as large as my little finger. The details of this affair are as follows: Mr. Covey sent me, very early in the morning of one of our coldest days in the month of January, to the woods, to get a load of wood. He gave me a team of unbroken oxen. He told me which was the in-hand ox, and which the off-hand one.[8] He then tied the end of a large rope around the horns of the in-hand-ox, and gave me the other end of it, and told me, if the oxen started to run, that I must hold on upon the rope. I had never driven oxen before, and of course I was very awkward. I, however, succeeded in getting to the edge of the woods with little difficulty; but I had got a very few rods into the woods, when the oxen took fright, and started full tilt, carrying the cart against trees, and over stumps, in the most frightful manner. I expected every moment that my brains would be dashed out against the trees. After running thus for a considerable distance, they finally upset the cart, dashing it with great force against a tree, and threw themselves into a dense thicket. How I escaped death, I do not know. There I was, entirely alone, in a thick wood, in a place new to me. My cart was upset and shattered, my oxen were entangled among the young trees, and there was none to help me. After a long spell of effort, I succeeded in getting my cart righted, my oxen disentangled, and again yoked to the cart. I now proceeded with my team to the place where I had, the day before, been chopping wood, and loaded my cart pretty heavily, thinking in this way to tame my oxen. I then proceeded on my way home. I had now consumed one half of the day. I got out of the woods safely, and now felt out of danger. I stopped my oxen to open the woods gate; and just as I did so, before I could

8. The ox on the right of a pair hitched to a wagon. "In-hand ox": the one to the left.

get hold of my ox-rope, the oxen again started, rushed through the gate, catching it between the wheel and the body of the cart, tearing it to pieces, and coming within a few inches of crushing me against the gate-post. Thus twice, in one short day, I escaped death by the merest chance. On my return, I told Mr. Covey what had happened, and how it happened. He ordered me to return to the woods again immediately. I did so, and he followed on after me. Just as I got into the woods, he came up and told me to stop my cart, and that he would teach me how to trifle away my time, and break gates. He then went to a large gum-tree, and with his axe cut three large switches, and, after trimming them up neatly with his pocket-knife, he ordered me to take off my clothes. I made him no answer, but stood with my clothes on. He repeated his order. I still made him no answer, nor did I move to strip myself. Upon this he rushed at me with the fierceness of a tiger, tore off my clothes, and lashed me till he had worn out his switches, cutting me so savagely as to leave the marks visible for a long time after. This whipping was the first of a number just like it, and for similar offences.

I lived with Mr. Covey one year. During the first six months, of that year, scarce a week passed without his whipping me. I was seldom free from a sore back. My awkwardness was almost always his excuse for whipping me. We were worked fully up to the point of endurance. Long before day we were up, our horses fed, and by the first approach of day we were off to the field with our hoes and ploughing teams. Mr. Covey gave us enough to eat, but scarce time to eat it. We were often less than five minutes taking our meals. We were often in the field from the first approach of day till its last lingering ray had left us; and at saving-fodder time, midnight often caught us in the field binding blades.[9]

Covey would be out with us. The way he used to stand it, was this. He would spend the most of his afternoons in bed. He would then come out fresh in the evening, ready to urge us on with his words, example, and frequently with the whip. Mr. Covey was one of the few slaveholders who could and did work with his hands. He was a hard-working man. He knew by himself just what a man or a boy could do. There was no deceiving him. His work went on in his absence almost as well as in his presence; and he had the faculty of making us feel that he was ever present with us. This he did by surprising us. He seldom approached the spot where we were at work openly, if he could do it secretly. He always aimed at taking us by surprise. Such was his cunning, that we used to call him, among ourselves, "the snake." When we were at work in the cornfield, he would sometimes crawl on his hands and knees to avoid detection, and all at once he would rise nearly in our midst, and scream out, "Ha, ha! Come, come! Dash on, dash on!" This being his mode of attack, it was never safe to stop a single minute. His comings were like a thief in the night. He appeared to us as being ever at hand. He was under every tree, behind every stump, in every bush, and at every window, on the plantation. He would sometimes mount his horse, as if bound to St. Michael's, a distance of seven miles, and in half an hour afterwards you would see him coiled up in the corner of the wood-fence, watching every motion of the slaves. He would, for this purpose, leave his horse tied up in the woods. Again, he would sometimes walk up to us, and give us orders as though he was upon the point of

9. I.e., of wheat or other plants. "Saving-fodder time": harvest time.

starting on a long journey, turn his back upon us, and make as though he was going to the house to get ready; and, before he would get half way thither, he would turn short and crawl into a fence-corner, or behind some tree, and there watch us till the going down of the sun.

Mr. Covey's *forte*[1] consisted in his power to deceive. His life was devoted to planning and perpetrating the grossest deceptions. Every thing he possessed in the shape of learning or religion, he made conform to his disposition to deceive. He seemed to think himself equal to deceiving the Almighty. He would make a short prayer in the morning, and a long prayer at night; and, strange as it may seem, few men would at times appear more devotional than he. The exercises of his family devotions were always commenced with singing; and, as he was a very poor singer himself, the duty of raising the hymn generally came upon me. He would read his hymn, and nod at me to commence. I would at times do so; at others, I would not. My non-compliance would almost always produce much confusion. To show himself independent of me, he would start and stagger through with his hymn in the most discordant manner. In this state of mind, he prayed with more than ordinary spirit. Poor man! such was his disposition, and success at deceiving, I do verily believe that he sometimes deceived himself into the solemn belief, that he was a sincere worshiper of the most high God; and this, too, at a time when he may be said to have been guilty of compelling his woman slave to commit the sin of adultery. The facts in the case are these: Mr. Covey was a poor man; he was just commencing in life; he was only able to buy one slave; and, shocking as is the fact, he bought her, as he said, for *a breeder*. This woman was named Caroline. Mr. Covey bought her from Mr. Thomas Lowe, about six miles from St. Michael's. She was a large, able-bodied woman, about twenty years old. She had already given birth to one child, which proved her to be just what he wanted. After buying her, he hired a married man of Mr. Samuel Harrison, to live with him one year; and him he used to fasten up with her every night! The result was, that, at the end of the year, the miserable woman gave birth to twins. At this result Mr. Covey seemed to be highly pleased, both with the man and the wretched woman. Such was his joy, and that of his wife, that nothing they could do for Caroline during her confinement was too good, or too hard, to be done. The children were regarded as being quite an addition to his wealth.

If at any one time of my life more than another, I was made to drink the bitterest dregs of slavery, that time was during the first six months of my stay with Mr. Covey. We were worked in all weathers. It was never too hot or too cold; it could never rain, blow, hail, or snow, too hard for us to work in the field. Work, work, work, was scarcely more the order of the day than of the night. The longest days were too short for him, and the shortest nights too long for him. I was somewhat unmanageable when I first went there, but a few months of this discipline tamed me. Mr. Covey succeeded in breaking me. I was broken in body, soul, and spirit. My natural elasticity was crushed, my intellect languished, the disposition to read departed, the cheerful spark that lingered about my eye died; the dark night of slavery closed in upon me; and behold a man transformed into a brute!

1. Strong point (French).

Sunday was my only leisure time. I spent this in a sort of beast-like stupor, between sleep and wake, under some large tree. At times I would rise up, a flash of energetic freedom would dart through my soul, accompanied with a faint beam of hope, that flickered for a moment, and then vanished. I sank down again, mourning over my wretched condition. I was sometimes prompted to take my life, and that of Covey, but was prevented by a combination of hope and fear. My sufferings on this plantation seem now like a dream rather than a stern reality.

Our house stood within a few rods of the Chesapeake Bay, whose broad bosom was ever white with sails from every quarter of the habitable globe. Those beautiful vessels, robed in purest white, so delightful to the eye of freemen, were to me so many shrouded ghosts, to terrify and torment me with thoughts of my wretched condition. I have often, in the deep stillness of a summer's Sabbath, stood all alone upon the lofty banks of that noble bay, and traced, with saddened heart and tearful eye, the countless number of sails moving off to the mighty ocean. The sight of these always affected me powerfully. My thoughts would compel utterance; and there, with no audience but the Almighty, I would pour out my soul's complaint, in my rude way, with an apostrophe[2] to the moving multitude of ships:—

"You are loosed from your moorings, and are free; I am fast in my chains, and am a slave! You move merrily before the gentle gale, and I sadly before the bloody whip! You are freedom's swift-winged angels, that fly round the world; I am confined in bands of iron! O that I were free! Oh, that I were on one of your gallant decks, and under your protecting wing! Alas! betwixt me and you, the turbid waters roll. Go on, go on. O that I could also go! Could I but swim! If I could fly! O, why was I born a man, of whom to make a brute! The glad ship is gone; she hides in the dim distance. I am left in the hottest hell of unending slavery. O God, save me! God, deliver me! Let me be free! Is there any God? Why am I a slave? I will run away. I will not stand it. Get caught, or get clear, I'll try it. I had as well die with ague as the fever. I have only one life to lose. I had as well be killed running as die standing. Only think of it; one hundred miles straight north, and I am free! Try it? Yes! God helping me, I will. It cannot be that I shall live and die a slave. I will take to the water. This very bay shall yet bear me into freedom. The steamboats steered in a north-east course from North Point. I will do the same; and when I get to the head of the bay, I will turn my canoe adrift, and walk straight through Delaware into Pennsylvania. When I get there, I shall not be required to have a pass; I can travel without being disturbed. Let but the first opportunity offer, and, come what will, I am off. Meanwhile, I will try to bear up under the yoke. I am not the only slave in the world. Why should I fret? I can bear as much as any of them. Besides, I am but a boy, and all boys are bound to some one. It may be that my misery in slavery will only increase my happiness when I get free. There is a better day coming."

Thus I used to think, and thus I used to speak to myself; goaded almost to madness at one moment, and at the next reconciling myself to my wretched lot.

I have already intimated that my condition was much worse, during the first six months of my stay at Mr. Covey's, than in the last six. The circumstances

---

2. Rhetorical term for when a speaker addresses a personified object or thing that could not possibly respond, such as the ships on the Chesapeake Bay.

leading to the change in Mr. Covey's course toward me form an epoch in my humble history. You have seen how a man was made a slave; you shall see how a slave was made a man. On one of the hottest days of the month of August, 1833, Bill Smith, William Hughes, a slave named Eli, and myself, were engaged in fanning wheat.[3] Hughes was clearing the fanned wheat from before the fan, Eli was turning, Smith was feeding, and I was carrying wheat to the fan. The work was simple, requiring strength rather than intellect; yet, to one entirely unused to such work, it came very hard. About three o'clock of that day, I broke down; my strength failed me; I was seized with a violent aching of the head, attended with extreme dizziness; I trembled in every limb. Finding what was coming, I nerved myself up, feeling it would never do to stop work. I stood as long as I could stagger to the hopper with grain. When I could stand no longer, I fell, and felt as if held down by an immense weight. The fan of course stopped; every one had his own work to do; and no one could do the work of the other, and have his own go on at the same time.

Mr. Covey was at the house, about one hundred yards from the treading-yard where we were fanning. On hearing the fan stop, he left immediately, and came to the spot where we were. He hastily inquired what the matter was. Bill answered that I was sick, and there was no one to bring wheat to the fan. I had by this time crawled away under the side of the post and rail-fence by which the yard was enclosed, hoping to find relief by getting out of the sun. He then asked where I was. He was told by one of the hands. He came to the spot, and, after looking at me awhile, asked me what was the matter. I told him as well as I could, for I scarce had strength to speak. He then gave me a savage kick in the side, and told me to get up. I tried to do so, but fell back in the attempt. He gave me another kick, and again told me to rise. I again tried, and succeeded in gaining my feet; but, stooping to get the tub with which I was feeding the fan, I again staggered and fell. While down in this situation, Mr. Covey took up the hickory slat with which Hughes had been striking off the half-bushel measure, and with it gave me a heavy blow upon the head, making a large wound, and the blood ran freely; and with this again told me to get up. I made no effort to comply, having now made up my mind to let him do his worst. In a short time after receiving this blow, my head grew better. Mr. Covey had now left me to my fate. At this moment I resolved, for the first time, to go to my master, enter a complaint, and ask his protection. In order to do this, I must that afternoon walk seven miles; and this, under the circumstances, was truly a severe undertaking. I was exceedingly feeble; made so as much by the kicks and blows which I received, as by the severe fit of sickness to which I had been subjected. I, however, watched my chance, while Covey was looking in an opposite direction, and started for St. Michael's. I succeeded in getting a considerable distance on my way to the woods, when Covey discovered me, and called after me to come back, threatening what he would do if I did not come. I disregarded both his calls and his threats, and made my way to the woods as fast as my feeble state would allow; and thinking I might be overhauled by him if I kept the road, I walked through the woods, keeping far enough from the road to avoid detection, and near enough to prevent

3. Separating the wheat from the chaff.

losing my way. I had not gone far before my little strength again failed me. I could go no farther. I fell down, and lay for a considerable time. The blood was yet oozing from the wound on my head. For a time I thought I should bleed to death; and think now that I should have done so, but that the blood so matted my hair as to stop the wound. After lying there about three quarters of an hour, I nerved myself up again, and started on my way, through bogs and briers, barefooted and bareheaded, tearing my feet sometimes at nearly every step; and after a journey of about seven miles, occupying some five hours to perform it, I arrived at master's store. I then presented an appearance enough to affect any but a heart of iron. From the crown of my head to my feet, I was covered with blood. My hair was all clotted with dust and blood; my shirt was stiff with blood. My legs and feet were torn in sundry places with briers and thorns, and were also covered with blood. I suppose I looked like a man who had escaped a den of wild beasts, and barely escaped them. In this state I appeared before my master, humbly entreating him to interpose his authority for my protection. I told him all the circumstances as well as I could, and it seemed, as I spoke, at times to affect him. He would then walk the floor, and seek to justify Covey by saying he expected I deserved it. He asked me what I wanted. I told him, to let me get a new home; that as sure as I lived with Mr. Covey again, I should live with but to die with him; that Covey would surely kill me; he was in a fair way for it. Master Thomas ridiculed the idea that there was any danger of Mr. Covey's killing me, and said that he knew Mr. Covey; that he was a good man, and that he could not think of taking me from him; that, should he do so, he would lose the whole year's wages; that I belonged to Mr. Covey for one year, and that I must go back to him, come what might; and that I must not trouble him with any more stories, or that he would himself *get hold of me*. After threatening me thus, he gave me a very large dose of salts, telling me that I might remain in St. Michael's that night, (it being quite late,) but that I must be off back to Mr. Covey's early in the morning; and that if I did not, he would *get hold of me*, which meant that he would whip me. I remained all night, and, according to his orders, I started off to Covey's in the morning, (Saturday morning), wearied in body and broken in spirit. I got no supper that night, or breakfast that morning. I reached Covey's about nine o'clock; and just as I was getting over the fence that divided Mrs. Kemp's fields from ours, out ran Covey with his cowskin, to give me another whipping. Before he could reach me, I succeeded in getting to the cornfield; and as the corn was very high, it afforded me the means of hiding. He seemed very angry, and searched for me a long time. My behavior was altogether unaccountable. He finally gave up the chase, thinking, I suppose, that I must come home for something to eat; he would give himself no further trouble in looking for me. I spent that day mostly in the woods, having the alternative before me,—to go home and be whipped to death, or stay in the woods and be starved to death. That night, I fell in with Sandy Jenkins, a slave with whom I was somewhat acquainted. Sandy had a free wife[4] who lived about four miles from Mr. Covey's; and it being Saturday, he was on his way to see her. I told him my circumstances, and he very kindly invited me to go home with him. I went home with him, and talked this whole matter over, and got his advice as to what course it was

4. I.e., his wife had been set free and was not legally a slave.

best for me to pursue. I found Sandy an old adviser. He told me, with great solemnity, I must go back to Covey; but that before I went, I must go with him into another part of the woods, where there was a certain *root*, which, if I would take some of it with me, carrying it *always on my right side*, would render it impossible for Mr. Covey, or any other white man, to whip me. He said he had carried it for years; and since he had done so, he had never received a blow, and never expected to while he carried it. I at first rejected the idea, that the simple carrying of a root in my pocket would have any such effect as he had said, and was not disposed to take it; but Sandy impressed the necessity with much earnestness, telling me it could do no harm, if it did no good. To please him, I at length took the root, and, according to his direction, carried it upon my right side. This was Sunday morning. I immediately started for home; and upon entering the yard gate, out came Mr. Covey on his way to meeting. He spoke to me very kindly, bade me drive the pigs from a lot near by, and passed on towards the church. Now, this singular conduct of Mr. Covey really made me begin to think that there was something in the *root* which Sandy had given me; and had it been on any other day than Sunday, I could have attributed the conduct to no other cause then the influence of that root; and as it was, I was half inclined to think the *root* to be something more than I at first had taken it to be. All went well till Monday morning. On this morning, the virtue of the *root* was fully tested. Long before daylight, I was called to go and rub, curry, and feed, the horses. I obeyed, and was glad to obey. But whilst thus engaged, whilst in the act of throwing down some blades from the loft, Mr. Covey entered the stable with a long rope; and just as I was half out of the loft, he caught hold of my legs, and was about tying me. As soon as I found what he was up to, I gave a sudden spring, and as I did so, he holding to my legs, I was brought sprawling on the stable floor. Mr. Covey seemed now to think he had me, and could do what he pleased; but at this moment—from whence came the spirit I don't know—I resolved to fight; and, suiting my action to the resolution, I seized Covey hard by the throat; and as I did so, I rose. He held on to me, and I to him. My resistance was so entirely unexpected, that Covey seemed taken all aback. He trembled like a leaf. This gave me assurance, and I held him uneasy, causing the blood to run where I touched him with the ends of my fingers. Mr. Covey soon called out to Hughes for help. Hughes came, and, while Covey held me, attempted to tie my right hand. While he was in the act of doing so, I watched my chance, and gave him a heavy kick close under the ribs. This kick fairly sickened Hughes, so that he left me in the hands of Mr. Covey. This kick had the effect of not only weakening Hughes, but Covey also. When he saw Hughes bending over with pain, his courage quailed. He asked me if I meant to persist in my resistance. I told him I did, come what might; that he had used me like a brute for six months, and that I was determined to be used so no longer. With that, he strove to drag me to a stick that was lying just out of the stable door. He meant to knock me down. But just as he was leaning over to get the stick, I seized him with both hands by his collar, and brought him by a sudden snatch to the ground. By this time, Bill came. Covey called upon him for assistance. Bill wanted to know what he could do. Covey said, "Take hold of him, take hold of him!" Bill said his master hired him out to work, and not to help to whip me; so he left Covey and myself to fight our own battle out. We were at it for nearly two hours. Covey at length let me go, puffing and blowing at a great rate, saying that if I had not resisted, he would not have whipped me half so much. The truth was, that he had not whipped me at all. I considered him as getting entirely the worst end of the bargain; for he had drawn no blood from me, but I had from him. The whole six months afterwards, that I spent with Mr. Covey, he never laid the weight of his finger upon me in anger. He would occasionally say, he didn't want to get hold of me again. "No," thought I, "you need not; for you will come off worse than you did before."

This battle with Mr. Covey was the turning-point in my career as a slave. It rekindled the few expiring embers of freedom, and revived within me a sense of my own manhood. It recalled the departed self-confidence, and inspired me again with a determination to be free. The gratification afforded by the triumph was a full compensation for whatever else might follow, even death itself. He only can understand the deep satisfaction which I experienced, who has himself repelled by force the bloody arm of slavery. I felt as I never felt before. It was a glorious resurrection, from the tomb of slavery, to the heaven of freedom. My long-crushed spirit rose, cowardice departed, bold defiance took its place; and I now resolved that, however long I might remain a slave in form, the day had passed forever when I could be a slave in fact. I did not hesitate to let it be known of me, that the white man who expected to succeed in whipping, must also succeed in killing me.

From this time I was never again what might be called fairly whipped, though I remained a slave four years afterwards. I had several fights, but was never whipped.

It was for a long time a matter of surprise to me why Mr. Covey did not immediately have me taken by the constable to the whipping-post, and there regularly whipped for the crime of raising my hand against a white man in defence of myself. And the only explanation I can now think of does not entirely satisfy me; but such as it is, I will give it. Mr. Covey enjoyed the most unbounded reputation for being a first-rate overseer and negro-breaker. It was of considerable importance to him. That reputation was at stake; and had he sent me—a boy about sixteen years old—to the public whipping-post, his reputation would have been lost; so, to save his reputation, he suffered me to go unpunished.

My term of actual service to Mr. Edward Covey ended on Christmas day, 1833. The days between Christmas and New Year's day are allowed as holidays; and, accordingly, we were not required to perform any labor, more than to feed and take care of the stock. This time we regarded as our own, by the grace of our masters; and we therefore used or abused it nearly as we pleased. Those of us who had families at a distance, were generally allowed to spend the whole six days in their society. This time, however, was spent in various ways. The staid, sober, thinking and industrious ones of our number would employ themselves in making corn-brooms, mats, horse-collars, and baskets; and another class of us would spend the time hunting opossums, hares, and coons. But by far the larger part engaged in such sports and merriments as playing ball, wrestling, running foot-races, fiddling, dancing, and drinking whisky; and this latter mode of spending the time was by far the most agreeable to the feelings of our master. A slave who would work during the holidays was considered by our masters as scarcely deserving them. He was regarded as one who rejected the favor of his master. It was deemed a disgrace not to get drunk at Christmas; and he was regarded as lazy indeed, who had not provided himself with the necessary means, during the year, to get whisky enough to last him through Christmas.

From what I know of the effect of these holidays upon the slave, I believe them to be among the most effective means in the hands of the slaveholder in keeping down the spirit of insurrection. Were the slaveholders at once to abandon this practice, I have not the slightest doubt it would lead to an immediate insurrection among the slaves. These holidays serve as conductors, or safety-valves, to carry off the rebellious spirit of enslaved humanity. But for these, the slave would be forced up to the wildest desperation; and woe betide the slaveholder, the day he ventures to remove or hinder the operation of those conductors! I warn him that, in such an event, a spirit will go forth in their midst, more to be dreaded than the most appalling earthquake.

The holidays are part and parcel of the gross fraud, wrong, and inhumanity of slavery. They are professedly a custom established by the benevolence of the slaveholders; but I undertake to say, it is the result of selfishness, and one of the grossest frauds committed upon the down-trodden slave. They do not give the slaves this time because they would not like to have their work during its continuance, but because they know it would be unsafe to deprive them of it. This will be seen by the fact, that the slaveholders like to have their slaves spend those days just in such a manner as to make them as glad of their ending as of their beginning. Their object seems to be, to disgust their slaves with freedom, by plunging them into the lowest depths of dissipation. For instance, the slaveholders not only like to see the slave drink of his own accord, but will adopt various plans to make him drunk. One plan is, to make bets on their slaves, as to who can drink the most whisky without getting drunk; and in this way they succeed in getting whole multitudes to drink to excess. Thus, when the slave asks for virtuous freedom, the cunning slaveholder, knowing his ignorance, cheats him with a dose of vicious dissipation, artfully labelled with the name of liberty. The most of us used to drink it down, and the result was just what might be supposed: many of us were led to think that there was little to choose between liberty and slavery. We felt, and very properly too, that we had almost as well be slaves to man as to rum. So, when the holidays ended, we staggered up from the filth of our wallowing, took a long breath, and marched to the field,—feeling, upon the whole, rather glad to go, from what our master had deceived us into a belief was freedom, back to the arms of slavery.

I have said that this mode of treatment is a part of the whole system of fraud and inhumanity of slavery. It is so. The mode here adopted to disgust the slave with freedom, by allowing him to see only the abuse of it, is carried out in other things. For instance, a slave loves molasses; he steals some. His master, in many cases, goes off to town, and buys a large quantity; he returns, takes his whip, and commands the slave to eat the molasses, until the poor fellow is made sick at the very mention of it. The same mode is sometimes adopted to make the slaves refrain from asking for more food than their regular allowance. A slave runs through his allowance, and applies for more. His master is enraged at him; but, not willing to send him off without food, gives him more than is necessary, and compels him to eat it within a given time. Then, if he complains that he cannot eat it, he is said to be satisfied neither full nor fasting, and is whipped for being hard to please! I have an abundance of such illustrations of the same principle, drawn from my own observation, but think the cases I have cited sufficient. The practice is a very common one.

On the first of January, 1834, I left Mr. Covey, and went to live with Mr. William Freeland, who lived about three miles from St. Michael's. I soon found Mr. Freeland a very different man from Mr. Covey. Though not rich, he was what would be called an educated southern gentleman. Mr. Covey, as I have shown, was a well-trained negro-breaker and slave-driver. The former (slaveholder though he was) seemed to possess some regard for honor, some reverence for justice, and some respect for humanity. The latter seemed totally insensible to all such sentiments. Mr. Freeland had many of the faults peculiar to slaveholders, such as being very passionate and fretful; but I must do him the justice to say, that he was exceedingly free from those degrading vices to which Mr. Covey was constantly addicted. The one was open and frank, and we always knew where to find him. The other was a most artful deceiver, and could be understood only by such as were skilful enough to detect his cunningly-devised frauds. Another advantage I gained in my new master was, he made no pretensions to, or profession of, religion; and this, in my opinion, was truly a great advantage. I assert most unhesitatingly, that the religion of the south is a mere covering for the most horrid crimes,—a justifier of the most appalling barbarity,—a sanctifier of the most hateful frauds,—and a dark shelter under which the darkest, foulest, grossest, and most infernal deeds of slaveholders find the strongest protection. Were I to be again reduced to the chains of slavery, next to that enslavement, I should regard being the slave of a religious master the greatest calamity that could befall me. For of all slaveholders with whom I have ever met, religious slaveholders are the worst. I have ever found them the meanest and basest, the most cruel and cowardly, of all others. It was my unhappy lot not only to belong to a religious slaveholder, but to live in a community of such religionists. Very near Mr. Freeland lived the Rev. Daniel Weeden, and in the same neighborhood lived the Rev. Rigby Hopkins. These were members and ministers in the Reformed Methodist Church. Mr. Weeden owned, among others, a woman slave, whose name I have forgotten. This woman's back, for weeks, was kept literally raw, made so by the lash of this merciless, *religious* wretch. He used to hire hands. His maxim was, Behave well or behave ill, it is the duty of a master occasionally to whip a slave, to remind him of his master's authority. Such was his theory, and such his practice.

Mr. Hopkins was even worse than Mr. Weeden. His chief boast was his ability to manage slaves. The peculiar feature of his government was that of whipping slaves in advance of deserving it. He always managed to have one or more of his slaves to whip every Monday morning. He did this to alarm their fears, and strike terror into those who escaped. His plan was to whip for the smallest offences, to prevent the commission of large ones. Mr. Hopkins could always find some excuse for whipping a slave. It would astonish one, unaccustomed to a slaveholding life, to see with what wonderful ease a slaveholder can find things, of which to make occasion to whip a slave. A mere look, word, or motion,—a mistake, accident, or want of power,—are all matters for which a slave may be whipped at any time. Does a slave look dissatisfied? It is said, he has the devil in him, and it must be whipped out. Does he speak loudly when spoken to by his master? Then he is getting high-minded, and should be taken down a button-hole lower. Does he forget to pull off his hat at the approach of a white person? Then he is wanting in reverence, and should be whipped for it. Does he ever venture to vindicate his conduct, when censured for it? Then he is guilty of impudence,—one of the greatest crimes of which a slave can be guilty. Does he ever venture to suggest a different mode of doing things from that pointed out by his master? He is indeed presumptuous, and getting above himself; and nothing less than a flogging will do for him. Does he, while ploughing, break a plough,—or, while hoeing, break a hoe? It is owing to his carelessness, and for it a slave must always be whipped. Mr. Hopkins could always find something of this sort to justify the use of the lash, and he seldom failed to embrace such opportunities. There was not a man in the whole county, with whom the slaves who had the getting their own home, would not prefer to live, rather than with this Rev. Mr. Hopkins. And yet there was not a man any where round, who made higher professions of religion, or was more active in revivals—more attentive to the class, love-feast, prayer and preaching meetings, or more devotional in his family,—that prayed earlier, later, louder, and longer,—than this same reverend slave-driver, Rigby Hopkins.

But to return to Mr. Freeland, and to my experience while in his employment. He, like Mr. Covey, gave us enough to eat; but unlike Mr. Covey, he also gave us sufficient time to take our meals. He worked us hard, but always between sunrise and sunset. He required a good deal of work to be done, but gave us good tools with which to work. His farm was large, but he employed hands enough to work it, and with ease, compared with many of his neighbors. My treatment, while in his employment, was heavenly, compared with what I experienced at the hands of Mr. Edward Covey.

Mr. Freeland was himself the owner of but two slaves. Their names were Henry Harris and John Harris. The rest of his hands he hired. These consisted of myself, Sandy Jenkins[5] and Handy Caldwell. Henry and John were quite intelligent, and in a very little while after I went there, I succeeded in creating in them a strong desire to learn how to read. This desire soon sprang up in the others also. They very soon mustered up some old spelling-books, and nothing would do but that I must keep a Sabbath school. I agreed to do so, and accordingly devoted my Sundays to teaching these my loved fellow-slaves how to read. Neither of them knew his letters when I went there. Some of the slaves of the neighboring farms found what was going on, and also availed themselves of this little opportunity to learn to read. It was understood, among all who came, that there must be as little display about it as possible. It was necessary to keep our religious masters at St. Michael's unacquainted with the fact, that, instead of spending the Sabbath in wrestling, boxing, and drinking whisky, we were trying to learn how to read the will of God; for they had much rather see us engaged in those degrading sports, than to see us behaving like intellectual, moral, and accountable beings.

5. This is the same man who gave me the roots to prevent my being whipped by Mr. Covey. He was a "clever soul." We used frequently to talk about the fight with Covey, and as often as we did so, he would claim my success as the result of the roots he gave me. This superstition is very common among the more ignorant slaves. A slave seldom dies but that his death is attributed to trickery [Douglass's note].

My blood boils as I think of the bloody manner in which Messrs. Wright Fairbanks and Garrison West, both class-leaders, in connection with many others, rushed in upon us with sticks and stones, and broke up our virtuous little Sabbath school, at St. Michael's—all calling themselves Christians! humble followers of the Lord Jesus Christ! But I am again digressing.

I held my Sabbath school at the house of a free colored man, whose name I deem it imprudent to mention; for should it be known, it might embarrass him greatly, though the crime of holding the school was committed ten years ago. I had at one time over forty scholars, and those of the right sort, ardently desiring to learn. They were of all ages, though mostly men and women. I look back to those Sundays with an amount of pleasure not to be expressed. They were great days to my soul. The work of instructing my dear fellow-slaves was the sweetest engagement with which I was ever blessed. We loved each other, and to leave them at the close of the Sabbath was a severe cross indeed. When I think that those precious souls are to-day shut up in the prison-house of slavery, my feelings overcome me, and I am almost ready to ask, "Does a righteous God govern the universe? and for what does he hold the thunders in his right hand, if not to smite the oppressor, and deliver the spoiled out of the hand of the spoiler?" These dear souls came not to Sabbath school because it was popular to do so, nor did I teach them because it was reputable to be thus engaged. Every moment they spent in that school, they were liable to be taken up, and given thirty-nine lashes. They came because they wished to learn. Their minds had been starved by their cruel masters. They had been shut up in mental darkness. I taught them, because it was the delight of my soul to be doing something that looked like bettering the condition of my race. I kept up my school nearly the whole year I lived with Mr. Freeland; and, beside my Sabbath school, I devoted three evenings in the week, during the winter, to teaching the slaves at home. And I have the happiness to know, that several of those who came to Sabbath school learned how to read; and that one, at least, is now free through my agency.

The year passed off smoothly. It seemed only about half as long as the year which preceded it. I went through it without receiving a single blow. I will give Mr. Freeland the credit of being the best master I ever had, *till I became my own master*. For the ease with which I passed the year, I was, however, somewhat indebted to the society of my fellow-slaves. They were noble souls; they not only possessed loving hearts, but brave ones. We were linked and interlinked with each other. I loved them with a love stronger than any thing I have experienced since. It is sometimes said that we slaves do not love and confide in each other. In answer to this assertion, I can say, I never loved any or confided in any people more than my fellow-slaves, and especially those with whom I lived at Mr. Freeland's. I believe we would have died for each other. We never undertook to do any thing, of any importance, without a mutual consultation. We never moved separately. We were one; and as much so by our tempers and dispositions, as by the mutual hardships to which we were necessarily subjected by our condition as slaves.

At the close of the year 1834, Mr. Freeland again hired me of my master, for the year 1835. But, by this time, I began to want to live *upon free land* as well as *with Freeland*; and I was no longer content, therefore, to live with him or any other slaveholder. I began, with the commencement of the year, to prepare myself for a final struggle, which should decide my fate one way or the other. My tendency was upward. I was fast approaching manhood, and year after year had passed, and I was still a slave. These thoughts roused me—I must do something. I therefore resolved that 1835 should not pass without witnessing an attempt, on my part, to secure my liberty. But I was not willing to cherish this determination alone. My fellow-slaves were dear to me. I was anxious to have them participate with me in this, my life-giving determination. I therefore, though with great prudence, commenced early to ascertain their views and feelings in regard to their condition, and to imbue their minds with thoughts of freedom. I bent myself to devising ways and means for our escape, and meanwhile strove, on all fitting occasions, to impress them with the gross fraud and inhumanity of slavery. I went first to Henry, next to John, then to the others. I found, in them all, warm hearts and noble spirits. They were ready to hear, and ready to act when a feasible plan should be proposed. This was what I wanted. I talked to them of our want of manhood, if we submitted to our enslavement without at least one noble effort to be free. We met often, and consulted frequently, and told our hopes and fears, recounted the difficulties, real and imagined, which we should be called on to meet. At times we were almost disposed to give up, and try to content ourselves with our wretched lot; at others, we were firm and unbending in our determination to go. Whenever we suggested any plan, there was shrinking—the odds were fearful. Our path was beset with the greatest obstacles; and if we succeeded in gaining the end of it, our right to be free was yet questionable—we were yet liable to be returned to bondage. We could see no spot, this side of the ocean, where we could be free. We knew nothing about Canada. Our knowledge of the north did not extend farther than New York; and to go there, and be forever harassed with the frightful liability of being returned to slavery—with the certainty of being treated tenfold worse than before—the thought was truly a horrible one, and one which it was not easy to overcome. The case sometimes stood thus: At every gate through which we were to pass, we saw a watchman—at every ferry a guard—on every bridge a sentinel—and in every wood a patrol. We were hemmed in upon every side. Here were the difficulties, real or imagined—the good to be sought, and the evil to be shunned. On the one hand, there stood slavery, a stern reality, glaring frightfully upon us,—its robes already crimsoned with the blood of millions, and even now feasting itself greedily upon our own flesh. On the other hand, away back in the dim distance, under the flickering light of the north star, behind some craggy hill or snow-covered mountain, stood a doubtful freedom—half frozen—beckoning us to come and share its hospitality. This in itself was sometimes enough to stagger us; but when we permitted ourselves to survey the road, we were frequently appalled. Upon either side we saw grim death, assuming the most horrid shapes. Now it was starvation, causing us to eat our own flesh;—now we were contending with the waves, and were drowned;—now we were overtaken, and torn to pieces by the fangs of the terrible bloodhound. We were stung by scorpions, chased by wild beasts, bitten by snakes, and finally, after having nearly reached the desired spot,—after swimming rivers, encountering wild beasts, sleeping in the woods, suffering hunger and nakedness,—we were overtaken by our pursuers, and in our resistance, we were shot dead upon the spot! I say, this picture sometimes appalled us, and made us

> "rather bear those ills we had,
> Than fly to others, that we knew not of."[6]

In coming to a fixed determination to run away, we did more than Patrick Henry, when he resolved upon liberty or death. With us it was a doubtful liberty at most, and almost certain death if we failed. For my part, I should prefer death to hopeless bondage.

Sandy, one of our number, gave up the notion, but still encouraged us. Our company then consisted of Henry Harris, John Harris, Henry Bailey, Charles Roberts, and myself. Henry Bailey was my uncle, and belonged to my master. Charles married my aunt: he belonged to my master's father-in-law, Mr. William Hamilton.

The plan we finally concluded upon was, to get a large canoe belonging to Mr. Hamilton, and upon the Saturday night previous to Easter holidays, paddle directly up the Chesapeake Bay. On our arrival at the head of the bay, a distance of seventy or eighty miles from where we lived, it was our purpose to turn our canoe adrift, and follow the guidance of the north star till we got beyond the limits of Maryland. Our reason for taking the water route was, that we were less liable to be suspected as runaways; we hoped to be regarded as fishermen; whereas, if we should take the land route, we should be subjected to interruptions of almost every kind. Any one having a white face, and being so disposed, could stop us, and subject us to examination.

The week before our intended start, I wrote several protections, one for each of us. As well as I can remember, they were in the following words, to wit:—

> "This is to certify that I, the undersigned, have given the bearer, my servant, full liberty to go to Baltimore, and spend the Easter holidays. Written with mine own hand, etc., 1835.
>
> "WILLIAM HAMILTON,
> "Near St. Michael's, in Talbot county, Maryland."

We were not going to Baltimore; but, in going up the bay, we went toward Baltimore, and these protections were only intended to protect us while on the bay.

As the time drew near for our departure, our anxiety became more and more intense. It was truly a matter of life and death with us. The strength of our determination was about to be fully tested. At this time, I was very active in explaining every difficulty, removing every doubt, dispelling every fear, and inspiring all with the firmness indispensable to success in our undertaking; assuring them that half was gained the instant we made the move; we had talked long enough; we were now ready to move; if not now, we never should be; and if we did not intend to move now, we had as well fold our arms, sit down, and acknowledge ourselves fit only to be slaves. This, none of us were prepared to acknowledge. Every man stood firm; and at our last meeting, we pledged ourselves afresh, in the most solemn manner, that, at the time appointed, we would certainly start in pursuit of freedom. This was in the middle of the week, at the end of which we were to be off. We went, as usual, to our several fields of labor, but with bosoms highly

6. Shakespeare's *Hamlet* 3.1.81–82.

agitated with thoughts of our truly hazardous undertaking. We tried to conceal our feelings as much as possible; and I think we succeeded very well.

After a painful waiting, the Saturday morning, whose night was to witness our departure, came. I hailed it with joy, bring what of sadness it might. Friday night was a sleepless one for me. I probably felt more anxious than the rest, because I was, by common consent, at the head of the whole affair. The responsibility of success or failure lay heavily upon me. The glory of the one, and the confusion of the other, were alike mine. The first two hours of that morning were such as I never experienced before, and hope never to again. Early in the morning, we went, as usual, to the field. We were spreading manure; and all at once, while thus engaged, I was overwhelmed with an indescribable feeling, in the fulness of which I turned to Sandy, who was near by, and said, "We are betrayed!" "Well," said he, "that thought has this moment struck me." We said no more. I was never more certain of any thing.

The horn was blown as usual, and we went up from the field to the house for breakfast. I went for the form, more than for want of any thing to eat that morning. Just as I got to the house, in looking out at the lane gate, I saw four white men, with two colored men. The white men were on horseback, and the colored ones were walking behind, as if tied. I watched them a few moments till they got up to our lane gate. Here they halted, and tied the colored men to the gate-post. I was not yet certain as to what the matter was. In a few moments, in rode Mr. Hamilton, with a speed betokening great excitement. He came to the door, and inquired if Master William was in. He was told he was at the barn. Mr. Hamilton, without dismounting, rode up to the barn with extraordinary speed. In a few moments, he and Mr. Freeland returned to the house. By this time, the three constables rode up, and in great haste dismounted, tied their horses, and met Master William and Mr. Hamilton returning from the barn; and after talking awhile, they all walked up to the kitchen door. There was no one in the kitchen but myself and John. Henry and Sandy were up at the barn. Mr. Freeland put his head in at the door, and called me by name, saying, there were some gentlemen at the door who wished to see me. I stepped to the door, and inquired what they wanted. They at once seized me, and, without giving me any satisfaction, tied me—lashing my hands closely together. I insisted upon knowing what the matter was. They at length said, that they had learned I had been in a "scrape," and that I was to be examined before my master; and if their information proved false, I should not be hurt.

In a few moments, they succeeded in tying John. They then turned to Henry, who had by this time returned, and commanded him to cross his hands. "I won't!" said Henry, in a firm tone, indicating his readiness to meet the consequences of his refusal. "Won't you?" said Tom Graham, the constable. "No, I won't!" said Henry, in a still stronger tone. With this, two of the constables pulled out their shining pistols, and swore, by their Creator, that they would make him cross his hands or kill him. Each cocked his pistol, and, with fingers on the trigger, walked up to Henry, saying, at the same time, if he did not cross his hands, they would blow his damned heart out. "Shoot me, shoot me!" said Henry; "you can't kill me but once. Shoot, shoot,—and be damned! *I won't be tied!*" This he said in a tone of loud defiance; and at the same time, with a motion as quick as lightning, he with one single stroke dashed the pistols from the hand of each constable. As he did this, all hands fell upon him, and, after beating him some time, they finally overpowered him, and got him tied.

During the scuffle, I managed, I know not how, to get my pass out, and, without being discovered, put it into the fire. We were all now tied; and just as we were to leave for Easton jail, Betsy Freeland, mother of William Freeland, came to the door with her hands full of biscuits, and divided them between Henry and John. She then delivered herself of a speech, to the following effect:—addressing herself to me, she said, "*You devil! You yellow devil!* it was you that put it into the heads of Henry and John to run away. But for you, you long-legged mulatto devil! Henry nor John would never have thought of such a thing." I made no reply, and was immediately hurried off towards St. Michael's. Just a moment previous to the scuffle with Henry, Mr. Hamilton suggested the propriety of making a search for the protections which he had understood Frederick had written for himself and the rest. But, just at the moment he was about carrying his proposal into effect, his aid was needed in helping to tie Henry; and the excitement attending the scuffle caused them either to forget, or to deem it unsafe, under the circumstances, to search. So we were not yet convicted of the intention to run away.

When we got about half way to St. Michael's, while the constables having us in charge were looking ahead, Henry inquired of me what he should do with his pass. I told him to eat it with his biscuit, and own nothing; and we passed the word around, "*Own nothing;*" and "*Own nothing!*" said we all. Our confidence in each other was unshaken. We were resolved to succeed or fail together, after the calamity had befallen us as much as before. We were now prepared for any thing. We were to be dragged that morning fifteen miles behind horses, and then to be placed in the Easton jail. When we reached St. Michael's, we underwent a sort of examination. We all denied that we ever intended to run away. We did this more to bring out the evidence against us, than from any hope of getting clear of being sold; for, as I have said, we were ready for that. The fact was, we cared but little where we went, so we went together. Our greatest concern was about separation. We dreaded that more than any thing this side of death. We found the evidence against us to be the testimony of one person; our master would not tell who it was; but we came to a unanimous decision among ourselves as to who their informant was. We were sent off to the jail at Easton. When we got there, we were delivered up to the sheriff, Mr. Joseph Graham, and by him placed in jail. Henry, John, and myself, were placed in one room together—Charles, and Henry Bailey, in another. Their object in separating us was to hinder concert.

We had been in jail scarcely twenty minutes, when a swarm of slave traders, and agents for slave traders, flocked into jail to look at us, and to ascertain if we were for sale. Such a set of beings I never saw before! I felt myself surrounded by so many fiends from perdition. A band of pirates never looked more like their father, the devil. They laughed and grinned over us, saying, "Ah, my boys! we have got you, haven't we?" And after taunting us in various ways, they one by one went into an examination of us, with intent to ascertain our value. They would impudently ask us if we would not like to have them for our masters. We would make them no answer, and leave them to find out as best they could. Then they would curse and swear at us, telling us that they could take the devil out of us in a very little while, if we were only in their hands.

While in jail, we found ourselves in much more comfortable quarters than we expected when we went there. We did not get much to eat, nor that which was very good; but we had a good clean room, from the windows of which we could see what was going on in the street, which was very much better than though we had been placed in one of the dark, damp cells. Upon the whole, we got along very well, so far as the jail and its keeper were concerned. Immediately after the holidays were over, contrary to all our expectations, Mr. Hamilton and Mr. Freeland came up to Easton, and took Charles, the two Henrys, and John, out of jail, and carried them home, leaving me alone. I regarded this separation as a final one. It caused me more pain than any thing else in the whole transaction. I was ready for any thing rather than separation. I supposed that they had consulted together, and had decided that, as I was the whole cause of the intention of the others to run away, it was hard to make the innocent suffer with the guilty; and that they had, therefore, concluded to take the others home, and sell me, as a warning to the others that remained. It is due to the noble Henry to say, he seemed almost as reluctant at leaving the prison as at leaving home to come to the prison. But we knew we should, in all probability, be separated, if we were sold; and since he was in their hands, he concluded to go peaceably home.

I was now left to my fate. I was all alone, and within the walls of a stone prison. But a few days before, and I was full of hope. I expected to have been safe in a land of freedom; but now I was covered with gloom, sunk down to the utmost despair. I thought the possibility of freedom was gone. I was kept in this way about one week, at the end of which, Captain Auld, my master, to my surprise and utter astonishment, came up, and took me out, with the intention of sending me, with a gentleman of his acquaintance, into Alabama. But, from some cause or other, he did not send me to Alabama, but concluded to send me back to Baltimore, to live again with his brother Hugh, and to learn a trade.

Thus, after an absence of three years and one month, I was once more permitted to return to my old home at Baltimore. My master sent me away, because there existed against me a very great prejudice in the community, and he feared I might be killed.

In a few weeks after I went to Baltimore, Master Hugh hired me to Mr. William Gardner, an extensive ship-builder, on Fell's Point. I was put there to learn how to calk.[7] It, however, proved a very unfavorable place for the accomplishment of this object. Mr. Gardner was engaged that spring in building two large man-of-war brigs, professedly for the Mexican government. The vessels were to be launched in the July of that year, and in failure thereof, Mr. Gardner was to lose a considerable sum; so that when I entered, all was hurry. There was no time to learn any thing. Every man had to do that which he knew how to do. In entering the ship-yard, my orders from Mr. Gardner were, to do whatever the carpenters commanded me to do. This was placing me at the beck and call of about seventy-five men. I was to regard all these as masters. Their word was to be my law. My situation was a most trying one. At times I needed a dozen pair of hands. I was called a dozen ways in the space

---

7. Caulk; to seal a boat's cracks and joints against leakage.

of a single minute. Three or four voices would strike my ear at the same moment. It was—"Fred., come help me to cant this timber here."—"Fred., come carry this timber yonder."—"Fred., bring that roller here."—"Fred., go get a fresh can of water."—"Fred., come help saw off the end of this timber."—"Fred., go quick, and get the crowbar."—"Fred., hold on the end of this fall."[8]—"Fred., go to the blacksmith's shop, and get a new punch."—"Hurra, Fred.! run and bring me a cold chisel."—"I say, Fred., bear a hand, and get up a fire as quick as lightning under that steam-box."—"Halloo, nigger! come, turn this grindstone."—"Come, come! move, move! and *bowse*[9] this timber forward."—"I say, darky, blast your eyes, why don't you heat up some pitch?"—"Halloo! halloo! halloo!" (Three voices at the same time.) "Come here!—Go there!—Hold on where you are! Damn you, if you move, I'll knock your brains out!"

This was my school for eight months; and I might have remained there longer, but for a most horrid fight I had with four of the white apprentices, in which my left eye was nearly knocked out, and I was horribly mangled in other respects. The facts in the case were these: Until a very little while after I went there, white and black ship-carpenters worked side by side, and no one seemed to see any impropriety in it. All hands seemed to be very well satisfied. Many of the black carpenters were freemen. Things seemed to be going on very well. All at once, the white carpenters knocked off, and said they would not work with free colored workmen. Their reason for this, as alleged, was, that if free colored carpenters were encouraged, they would soon take the trade into their own hands, and poor white men would be thrown out of employment. They therefore felt called upon at once to put a stop to it. And, taking advantage of Mr. Gardner's necessities, they broke off, swearing they would work no longer, unless he would discharge his black carpenters. Now, though this did not extend to me in form, it did reach me in fact. My fellow-apprentices very soon began to feel it degrading to them to work with me. They began to put on airs, and talk about the "niggers" taking the country, saying we all ought to be killed; and, being encouraged by the journeymen, they commenced making my condition as hard as they could, by hectoring me around, and sometimes striking me. I, of course, kept the vow I made after the fight with Mr. Covey, and struck back again, regardless of consequences; and while I kept them from combining, I succeeded very well; for I could whip the whole of them, taking them separately. They, however, at length combined, and came upon me, armed with sticks, stones, and heavy handspikes. One came in front with a half brick. There was one at each side of me, and one behind me. While I was attending to those in front, and on either side, the one behind ran up with the handspike, and struck me a heavy blow upon the head. It stunned me. I fell, and with this they all ran upon me, and fell to beating me with their fists. I let them lay on for a while, gathering strength. In an instant, I gave a sudden surge, and rose to my hands and knees. Just as I did that, one of their number gave me, with his heavy boot, a powerful kick in the left eye. My eyeball seemed to have burst.

8. Nautical term for the free end of a rope of a tackle or hoisting device.

9. To haul the timber by pulling on the rope.

When they saw my eye closed, and badly swollen, they left me. With this I seized the handspike, and for a time pursued them. But here the carpenters interfered, and I thought I might as well give it up. It was impossible to stand my hand against so many. All this took place in sight of not less than fifty white ship-carpenters, and not one interposed a friendly word; but some cried, "Kill the damned nigger! Kill him! kill him! He struck a white person." I found my only chance for life was in flight. I succeeded in getting away without an additional blow, and barely so; for to strike a white man is death by Lynch law,[1]—and that was the law in Mr. Gardner's ship-yard; nor is there much of any other out of Mr. Gardner's ship-yard.

I went directly home, and told the story of my wrongs to Master Hugh; and I am happy to say of him, irreligious as he was, his conduct was heavenly, compared with that of his brother Thomas under similar circumstances. He listened attentively to my narration of the circumstances leading to the savage outrage, and gave many proofs of his strong indignation at it. The heart of my once overkind mistress was again melted into pity. My puffed-out eye and blood-covered face moved her to tears. She took a chair by me, washed the blood from my face, and, with a mother's tenderness, bound up my head, covering the wounded eye with a lean piece of fresh beef. It was almost compensation for my suffering to witness, once more, a manifestation of kindness from this, my once affectionate old mistress. Master Hugh was very much enraged. He gave expression to his feelings by pouring out curses upon the heads of those who did the deed. As soon as I got a little the better of my bruises, he took me with him to Esquire Watson's, on Bond Street, to see what could be done about the matter. Mr. Watson inquired who saw the assault committed. Master Hugh told him it was done in Mr. Gardner's ship-yard, at midday, where there were a large company of men at work. "As to that," he said, "the deed was done, and there was no question as to who did it." His answer was, he could do nothing in the case, unless some white man would come forward and testify. He could issue no warrant on my word. If I had been killed in the presence of a thousand colored people, their testimony combined would have been insufficient to have arrested one of the murderers. Master Hugh, for once, was compelled to say this state of things was too bad. Of course, it was impossible to get any white man to volunteer his testimony in my behalf, and against the white young men. Even those who may have sympathized with me were not prepared to do this. It required a degree of courage unknown to them to do so; for just at that time, the slightest manifestation of humanity toward a colored person was denounced as abolitionism, and that name subjected its bearer to frightful liabilities. The watchwords of the bloody-minded in that region, and in those days, were, "Damn the abolitionists!" and "Damn the niggers!" There was nothing done, and probably nothing would have been done if I had been killed. Such was, and such remains, the state of things in the Christian city of Baltimore.

Master Hugh, finding he could get no redress, refused to let me go back again to Mr. Gardner. He kept me himself, and his wife dressed my wound till I was again restored to health. He then took me into the ship-yard of which he was foreman, in the employment of Mr. Walter Price. There I was immediately set to calking, and very soon learned the art of using my mallet

---

1. To be subject to lynching, without benefit of legal procedures.

and irons. In the course of one year from the time I left Mr. Gardner's, I was able to command the highest wages given to the most experienced calkers. I was now of some importance to my master. I was bringing him from six to seven dollars per week. I sometimes brought him nine dollars per week: my wages were a dollar and a half a day. After learning how to calk, I sought my own employment, made my own contracts, and collected the money which I earned. My pathway became much more smooth than before; my condition was now much more comfortable. When I could get no calking to do, I did nothing. During these leisure times, those old notions about freedom would steal over me again. When in Mr. Gardner's employment, I was kept in such a perpetual whirl of excitement, I could think of nothing, scarcely, but my life; and in thinking of my life, I almost forgot my liberty. I have observed this in my experience of slavery,—that whenever my condition was improved, instead of its increasing my contentment, it only increased my desire to be free, and set me to thinking of plans to gain my freedom. I have found that, to make a contented slave, it is necessary to make a thoughtless one. It is necessary to darken his moral and mental vision, and, as far as possible, to annihilate the power of reason. He must be able to detect no inconsistencies in slavery; he must be made to feel that slavery is right; and he can be brought to that only when he ceases to be a man.

I was now getting, as I have said, one dollar and fifty cents per day. I contracted for it; I earned it; it was paid to me; it was rightfully my own; yet, upon each returning Saturday night, I was compelled to deliver every cent of that money to Master Hugh. And why? Not because he earned it,—not because he had any hand in earning it,—not because I owed it to him,—nor because he possessed the slightest shadow of a right to it; but solely because he had the power to compel me to give it up. The right of the grim-visaged pirate upon the high seas is exactly the same.

Chapter XI

I now come to that part of my life during which I planned, and finally succeeded in making, my escape from slavery. But before narrating any of the peculiar circumstances, I deem it proper to make known my intention not to state all the facts connected with the transaction.[2] My reasons for pursuing this course may be understood from the following: First, were I to give a minute statement of all the facts, it is not only possible but quite probable, that others would thereby be involved in the most embarrassing difficulties. Secondly, such a statement would most undoubtedly induce greater vigilance on the part of slaveholders than has existed heretofore among them; which would, of course, be the means of guarding a door whereby some dear brother bondman might escape his galling chains. I deeply regret the necessity that impels me to suppress any thing of importance connected with my experience in slavery. It would afford me great pleasure indeed, as well as materially add to the interest of my narrative, were I at liberty to gratify a

---

2. During this period, many free black men worked as sailors. One of these men loaned Douglass free papers and clothes, enabling Douglass to escape from slavery by train and boat. He described his escape in the third and last of his autobiographies, *Life and Times of Frederick Douglass* (1881; rev. ed. 1892).

curiosity, which I know exists in the minds of many, by an accurate statement of all the facts pertaining to my most fortunate escape. But I must deprive myself of this pleasure, and the curious of the gratification which such a statement would afford. I would allow myself to suffer under the greatest imputations which evil-minded men might suggest, rather than exculpate myself, and thereby run the hazard of closing the slightest avenue by which a brother slave might clear himself of the chains and fetters of slavery.

I have never approved of the very public manner in which some of our western friends have conducted what they call the *underground railroad*,[3] but which, I think, by their own declarations, has been made most emphatically the *upperground railroad*. I honor those good men and women for their noble daring, and applaud them for willingly subjecting themselves to bloody perse-cution, by openly avowing their participation in the escape of slaves. I, how-ever, can see very little good resulting from such a course, either to themselves or the slaves escaping; while, upon the other hand, I see and feel assured that those open declarations are a positive evil to the slaves remaining, who are seeking to escape. They do nothing towards enlightening the slave, whilst they do much towards enlightening the master. They stimulate him to greater watchfulness, and enhance his power to capture his slave. We owe something to the slaves south of the line as well as to those north of it; and in aiding the latter on their way to freedom, we should be careful to do nothing which would be likely to hinder the former from escaping from slavery. I would keep the merciless slaveholder profoundly ignorant of the means of flight adopted by the slave. I would leave him to imagine himself surrounded by myriads of invisible tormentors, ever ready to snatch from his infernal grasp his trem-bling prey. Let him be left to feel his way in the dark; let darkness commen-surate with his crime hover over him; and let him feel that at every step he takes, in pursuit of the flying bondman, he is running the frightful risk of having his hot brains dashed out by an invisible agency. Let us render the tyrant no aid; let us not hold the light by which he can trace the footprints of our flying brother. But enough of this. I will now proceed to the statement of those facts, connected with my escape, for which I am alone responsible, and for which no one can be made to suffer but myself.

In the early part of the year 1838, I became quite restless. I could see no reason why I should, at the end of each week, pour the reward of my toil into the purse of my master. When I carried to him my weekly wages, he would, after counting the money, look me in the face with a robber-like fierceness, and say, "Is this all?" He was satisfied with nothing less than the last cent. He would, however, when I made him six dollars, sometimes give me six cents, to encourage me. It had the opposite effect. I regarded it as a sort of admission of my right to the whole. The fact that he gave me any part of my wages was proof, to my mind, that he believed me entitled to the whole of them. I always felt worse for having received any thing; for I feared that the giving me a few cents would ease his conscience, and make him feel himself to be a pretty honorable sort of robber. My discontent grew upon me. I was ever on the look-out for means of escape; and, finding no direct means,

---

3. The network of routes, guides, and safe houses by which many slaves escaped to the North, moving by night from one known stopping place to the next, often the homes of abolitionists.

I determined to try to hire my time, with a view of getting money with which to make my escape. In the spring of 1838, when Master Thomas came to Baltimore to purchase his spring goods, I got an opportunity, and applied to him to allow me to hire my time. He unhesitatingly refused my request, and told me this was another stratagem by which to escape. He told me I could go nowhere but that he could get me; and that, in the event of my running away, he should spare no pains in his efforts to catch me. He exhorted me to content myself, and be obedient. He told me, if I would be happy, I must lay out no plans for the future. He said, if I behaved myself properly, he would take care of me. Indeed, he advised me to complete thoughtlessness of the future, and taught me to depend solely upon him for happiness. He seemed to see fully the pressing necessity of setting aside my intellectual nature, in order to [insure] contentment in slavery. But in spite of him, and even in spite of myself, I continued to think, and to think about the injustice of my enslavement, and the means of escape.

About two months after this, I applied to Master Hugh for the privilege of hiring my time. He was not acquainted with the fact that I had applied to Master Thomas, and had been refused. He too, at first, seemed disposed to refuse; but, after some reflection, he granted me the privilege, and proposed the following terms: I was to be allowed all my time, make all contracts with those for whom I worked, and find my own employment; and, in return for this liberty, I was to pay him three dollars at the end of each week; find myself in calking tools, and in board and clothing. My board was two dollars and a half per week. This, with the wear and tear of clothing and calking tools, made my regular expenses about six dollars per week. This amount I was compelled to make up, or relinquish the privilege of hiring my time. Rain or shine, work or no work, at the end of each week the money must be forth-coming, or I must give up my privilege. This arrangement, it will be per-ceived, was decidedly in my master's favor. It relieved him of all need of looking after me. His money was sure. He received all the benefits of slave-holding without its evils; while I endured all the evils of a slave, and suffered all the care and anxiety of a freeman. I found it a hard bargain. But, hard as it was, I thought it better than the old mode of getting along. It was a step towards freedom to be allowed to bear the responsibilities of a freeman, and I was determined to hold on upon it. I bent myself to the work of making money. I was ready to work at night as well as day, and by the most untiring perseverance and industry, I made enough to meet my expenses, and lay up a little money every week. I went on thus from May till August. Master Hugh then refused to allow me to hire my time longer. The ground for his refusal was a failure on my part, one Saturday night, to pay him for my week's time. This failure was occasioned by my attending a camp meeting about ten miles from Baltimore. During the week, I had entered into an engagement with a number of young friends to start from Baltimore to the camp ground early Saturday evening; and being detained by my employer, I was unable to get down to Master Hugh's without disappointing the company. I knew that Master Hugh was in no special need of the money that night. I therefore decided to go to camp meeting, and upon my return pay him the three dol-lars. I staid at the camp meeting one day longer than I intended when I left. But as soon as I returned, I called upon him to pay him what he considered his due. I found him very angry; he could scarce restrain his wrath. He said he had a great mind to give me a severe whipping. He wished to know how I dared go out of the city without asking his permission. I told him I hired my time, and while I paid him the price which he asked for it, I did not know that I was bound to ask him when and where I should go. This reply troubled him; and, after reflecting a few moments, he turned to me, and said I should hire my time no longer; that the next thing he should know of, I would be running away. Upon the same plea, he told me to bring my tools and clothing home forthwith. I did so; but instead of seeking work, as I had been accustomed to do previously to hiring my time, I spent the whole week without the perfor-mance of a single stroke of work. I did this in retaliation. Saturday night, he called upon me as usual for my week's wages. I told him I had no wages; I had done no work that week. Here we were upon the point of coming to blows. He raved, and swore his determination to get hold of me. I did not allow myself a single word; but was resolved, if he laid the weight of his hand upon me, it should be blow for blow. He did not strike me, but told me that he would find me in constant employment in future. I thought the matter over during the next day, Sunday, and finally resolved upon the third day of September, as the day upon which I would make a second attempt to secure my freedom. I now had three weeks during which to prepare for my journey. Early on Monday morning, before Master Hugh had time to make any engagement for me, I went out and got employment of Mr. Butler, at his ship-yard near the draw-bridge, upon what is called the City Block, thus making it unnecessary for him to seek employment for me. At the end of the week, I brought him between eight and nine dollars. He seemed very well pleased, and asked me why I did not do the same the week before. He little knew what my plans were. My object in working steadily was to remove any suspicion he might entertain of my intent to run away; and in this I succeeded admirably. I sup-pose he thought I was never better satisfied with my condition than at the very time during which I was planning my escape. The second week passed, and again I carried him my full wages; and so well pleased was he, that he gave me twenty-five cents, (quite a large sum for a slaveholder to give a slave), and bade me to make a good use of it. I told him I would.

Things went on without very smoothly indeed, but within there was trouble. It is impossible for me to describe my feelings as the time of my contemplated start drew near. I had a number of warm-hearted friends in Baltimore,—friends that I loved almost as I did my life,—and the thought of being separated from them forever was painful beyond expression. It is my opinion that thousands would escape from slavery, who now remain, but for the strong cords of affection that bind them to their friends. The thought of leaving my friends was decidedly the most painful thought with which I had to contend. The love of them was my tender point, and shook my decision more than all things else. Besides the pain of separation, the dread and apprehension of a failure exceeded what I had experienced at my first attempt. The appalling defeat I then sustained returned to torment me. I felt assured that, if I failed in this attempt, my case would be a hopeless one—it would seal my fate as a slave forever. I could not hope to get off with any thing less than the severest punishment, and being placed beyond the means of escape. It required no very vivid imagination to depict the most frightful scenes through which I should have to pass, in case I failed. The wretchedness of slavery, and the blessedness of freedom, were perpetually before me. It was life and death with me. But I remained firm, and, according to my resolution, on the third day of September, 1838, I left my chains, and succeeded in reaching New York without the slightest interruption of any kind. How I did so,—what means I adopted,—what direction I travelled, and by what mode of conveyance,—I must leave unexplained, for the reasons before mentioned.

I have been frequently asked how I felt when I found myself in a free State. I have never been able to answer the question with any satisfaction to myself. It was a moment of the highest excitement I ever experienced. I suppose I felt as one may imagine the unarmed mariner to feel when he is rescued by a friendly man-of-war from the pursuit of a pirate. In writing to a dear friend, immediately after my arrival at New York, I said I felt like one who had escaped a den of hungry lions. This state of mind, however, very soon subsided; and I was again seized with a feeling of great insecurity and loneliness. I was yet liable to be taken back, and subjected to all the tortures of slavery. This in itself was enough to damp the ardor of my enthusiasm. But the loneliness overcame me. There I was in the midst of thousands, and yet a perfect stranger; without home and without friends, in the midst of thousands of my own brethren—children of a common Father, and yet I dared not to unfold to any one of them my sad condition. I was afraid to speak to any one for fear of speaking to the wrong one, and thereby falling into the hands of money-loving kidnappers, whose business it was to lie in wait for the panting fugitive, as the ferocious beasts of the forest lie in wait for their prey. The motto which I adopted when I started from slavery was this—"Trust no man!" I saw in every white man an enemy, and in almost every colored man cause for distrust. It was a most painful situation; and, to understand it, one must needs experience it, or imagine himself in similar circumstances. Let him be a fugitive slave in a strange land—a land given up to be the hunting-ground for slaveholders—whose inhabitants are legalized kidnappers—where he is every moment subjected to the terrible liability of being seized upon by his fellowmen, as the hideous crocodile seizes upon his prey!—I say, let him place himself in my situation—without home or friends—without money or credit—wanting shelter, and no one to give it—wanting bread, and no money to buy it,—and at the same time let him feel that he is pursued by merciless men-hunters, and in total darkness as to what to do, where to go, or where to stay,—perfectly helpless both as to the means of defence and means of escape,—in the midst of plenty, yet suffering the terrible gnawings of hunger,—in the midst of houses, yet having no home,—among fellow-men, yet feeling as if in the midst of wild beasts, whose greediness to swallow up the trembling and half-famished fugitive is only equalled by that with which the monsters of the deep swallow up the helpless fish upon which they subsist,—I say, let him be placed in this most trying situation,—the situation in which I was placed,—then, and not till then, will he fully appreciate the hardships of, and know how to sympathize with, the toil-worn and whip-scarred fugitive slave.

Thank Heaven, I remained but a short time in this distressed situation. I was relieved from it by the humane hand of MR. DAVID RUGGLES,[4] whose

---

4. A black journalist and abolitionist (1810–1849) who aided Douglass in his escape from Maryland, and in whose house Douglass stayed on his way to New Bedford in 1838.

vigilance, kindness, and perseverance, I shall never forget. I am glad of an opportunity to express, as far as words can, the love and gratitude I bear him. Mr. Ruggles is now afflicted with blindness, and is himself in need of the same kind offices which he was once so forward in the performance of toward others. I had been in New York but a few days, when Mr. Ruggles sought me out, and very kindly took me to his boarding-house at the corner of Church and Lespenard Streets. Mr. Ruggles was then very deeply engaged in the memorable *Darg* case,[5] as well as attending to a number of other fugitive slaves; devising ways and means for their successful escape; and, though watched and hemmed in on almost every side, he seemed to be more than a match for his enemies.

Very soon after I went to Mr. Ruggles, he wished to know of me where I wanted to go; as he deemed it unsafe for me to remain in New York. I told him I was a calker, and should like to go where I could get work. I thought of going to Canada; but he decided against it, and in favor of my going to New Bedford, thinking I should be able to get work there at my trade. At this time, Anna,[6] my intended wife, came on; for I wrote to her immediately after my arrival at New York, (notwithstanding my homeless, houseless, and helpless condition,) informing her of my successful flight, and wishing her to come on forthwith. In a few days after her arrival, Mr. Ruggles called in the Rev. J.W.C. Pennington,[7] who, in the presence of Mr. Ruggles, Mrs. Michaels, and two or three others, performed the marriage ceremony, and gave us a certificate, of which the following is an exact copy:—

> "This may certify, that I joined together in holy matrimony Frederick Johnson[8] and Anna Murray, as man and wife, in the presence of Mr. David Ruggles and Mrs. Michaels.
>
> "JAMES W. C. PENNINGTON
>
> "*New York, Sept. 15, 1838.*"

Upon receiving this certificate, and a five-dollar bill from Mr. Ruggles, I shouldered one part of our baggage, and Anna took up the other, and we set out forthwith to take passage on board of the steamboat John W. Richmond for Newport, on our way to New Bedford. Mr. Ruggles gave me a letter to a Mr. Shaw in Newport, and told me, in case my money did not serve me to New Bedford, to stop in Newport and obtain further assistance; but upon our arrival at Newport, we were so anxious to get to a place of safety, that, notwithstanding we lacked the necessary money to pay our fare, we decided to take seats in the stage, and promise to pay when we got to New Bedford. We were encouraged to do this by two excellent gentlemen, residents of New Bedford, whose names I afterward ascertained to be Joseph Ricketson and William C. Taber. They seemed at once to understand our circumstances, and gave us such assurance of their friendliness as put us fully at

---

5. In 1839, Ruggles had been arrested for harboring a fugitive slave from the plantation of John P. Darg of Arkansas.
6. She was free [Douglass's note]. Anna Murray Douglass (1813–1882) worked as a domestic in Baltimore and had been a member of the East Baltimore Mental Improvement Society before moving to New York to marry Douglass.

7. Like Douglass, Pennington (1807–1890) escaped from slavery in the Eastern Shore of Maryland. He became an abolitionist and Presbyterian minister, telling his life history in *The Fugitive Blacksmith* (1850).
8. I had changed my name from Frederick *Bailey* to that of *Johnson* [Douglass's note].

ease in their presence. It was good indeed to meet with such friends, at such a time. Upon reaching New Bedford, we were directed to the house of Mr. Nathan Johnson, by whom we were kindly received, and hospitably provided for. Both Mr. and Mrs. Johnson took a deep and lively interest in our welfare. They proved themselves quite worthy of the name of abolitionists. When the stage-driver found us unable to pay our fare, he held on upon our baggage as security for the debt. I had but to mention the fact to Mr. Johnson, and he forthwith advanced the money.

We now began to feel a degree of safety, and to prepare ourselves for the duties and responsibilities of a life of freedom. On the morning after our arrival at New Bedford, while at the breakfast-table, the question arose as to what name I should be called by. The name given me by my mother was, "Frederick Augustus Washington Bailey." I, however, had dispensed with the two middle names long before I left Maryland so that I was generally known by the name of "Frederick Bailey." I started from Baltimore bearing the name of "Stanley." When I got to New York, I again changed my name to "Frederick Johnson," and thought that would be the last change. But when I got to New Bedford, I found it necessary again to change my name. The reason of this necessity was, that there were so many Johnsons in New Bedford, it was already quite difficult to distinguish between them. I gave Mr. Johnson the privilege of choosing me a name, but told him he must not take from me the name of "Frederick." I must hold on to that, to preserve a sense of my identity. Mr. Johnson had just been reading the "Lady of the Lake," and at once suggested that my name be "Douglass."[9] From that time until now I have been called "Frederick Douglass;" and as I am more widely known by that name than by either of the others, I shall continue to use it as my own.

I was quite disappointed at the general appearance of things in New Bedford. The impression which I had received respecting the character and condition of the people of the north, I found to be singularly erroneous. I had very strangely supposed, while in slavery, that few of the comforts, and scarcely any of the luxuries, of life were enjoyed at the north, compared with what were enjoyed by the slaveholders of the south. I probably came to this conclusion from the fact that northern people owned no slaves. I supposed that they were about upon a level with the non-slaveholding population of the south. I knew *they* were exceedingly poor, and I had been accustomed to regard their poverty as the necessary consequence of their being non-slaveholders. I had somehow imbibed the opinion that, in the absence of slaves, there could be no wealth, and very little refinement. And upon coming to the north, I expected to meet with a rough, hard-handed, and uncultivated population, living in the most Spartanlike simplicity, knowing nothing of the ease, luxury, pomp, and grandeur of southern slaveholders. Such being my conjectures, any one acquainted with the appearance of New Bedford may very readily infer how palpably I must have seen my mistake.

In the afternoon of the day when I reached New Bedford, I visited the wharves, to take a view of the shipping. Here I found myself surrounded with the strongest proofs of wealth. Lying at the wharves, and riding in the stream,

9. Sir Walter Scott's (1771–1832) poem *Lady of the Lake* (1810), a historical romance set in the Scottish highlands in the 16th century. The plot involves the banishment and redemption of the Scottish hero James of Douglas.

I saw many ships of the finest model, in the best order, and of the largest size. Upon the right and left, I was walled in by granite warehouses of the widest dimensions, stowed to their utmost capacity with the necessaries and comforts of life. Added to this, almost every body seemed to be at work, but noiselessly so, compared with what I had been accustomed to in Baltimore. There were no loud songs heard from those engaged in loading and unloading ships. I heard no deep oaths or horrid curses on the laborer. I saw no whipping of men; but all seemed to go smoothly on. Every man appeared to understand his work, and went at it with a sober, yet cheerful earnestness, which betokened the deep interest which he felt in what he was doing, as well as a sense of his own dignity as a man. To me this looked exceedingly strange. From the wharves I strolled around and over the town, gazing with wonder and admiration at the splendid churches, beautiful dwellings, and finely-cultivated gardens; evincing an amount of wealth, comfort, taste, and refinement, such as I had never seen in any part of slaveholding Maryland.

Every thing looked clean, new, and beautiful. I saw few or no dilapidated houses, with poverty-stricken inmates; no half-naked children and bare-footed women, such as I had been accustomed to see in Hillsborough, Easton, St. Michael's, and Baltimore. The people looked more able, stronger, healthier, and happier, than those of Maryland. I was for once made glad by a view of extreme wealth, without being saddened by seeing extreme poverty. But the most astonishing as well as the most interesting thing to me was the condition of the colored people, a great many of whom, like myself, had escaped thither as a refuge from the hunters of men. I found many, who had not been seven years out of their chains, living in finer houses, and evidently enjoying more of the comforts of life, than the average of slaveholders in Maryland. I will venture to assert that my friend Mr. Nathan Johnson (of whom I can say with a grateful heart, "I was hungry, and he gave me meat; I was thirsty, and he gave me drink; I was a stranger, and he took me in"[1]) lived in a neater house, dined at a better table; took, paid for, and read, more newspapers; better understood the moral, religious, and political character of the nation,—than nine tenths of the slaveholders in Talbot county Maryland. Yet Mr. Johnson was a working man. His hands were hardened by toil, and not his alone, but those also of Mrs. Johnson. I found the colored people much more spirited than I had supposed they would be. I found among them a determination to protect each other from the blood-thirsty kidnapper, at all hazards. Soon after my arrival, I was told of a circumstance which illustrated their spirit. A colored man and a fugitive slave were on unfriendly terms. The former was heard to threaten the latter with informing his master of his whereabouts. Straightway a meeting was called among the colored people, under the stereotyped notice, "Business of importance!" The betrayer was invited to attend. The people came at the appointed hour, and organized the meeting by appointing a very religious old gentleman as president, who, I believe, made a prayer, after which he addressed the meeting as follows: *Friends, we have got him here, and I would recommend that you young men just take him outside the door, and kill him!* With this, a number

1. Cf. Matthew 25.35.

of them bolted at him; but they were intercepted by some more timid than themselves, and the betrayer escaped their vengeance, and has not been seen in New Bedford since. I believe there have been no more such threats, and should there be hereafter, I doubt not that death would be the consequence.

I found employment, the third day after my arrival, in stowing a sloop with a load of oil. It was new, dirty, and hard work for me; but I went at it with a glad heart and a willing hand. I was now my own master. It was a happy moment, the rapture of which can be understood only by those who have been slaves. It was the first work, the reward of which was to be entirely my own. There was no Master Hugh standing ready, the moment I earned the money, to rob me of it. I worked that day with a pleasure I had never before experienced. I was at work for myself and newly-married wife. It was to me the starting-point of a new existence. When I got through with that job, I went in pursuit of a job of calking; but such was the strength of prejudice against color, among the white calkers, that they refused to work with me, and of course I could get no employment.[2] Finding my trade of no immediate benefit, I threw off my calking habiliments, and prepared myself to do any kind of work I could get to do. Mr. Johnson kindly let me have his wood-horse and saw, and I very soon found myself a plenty of work. There was no work too hard—none too dirty. I was ready to saw wood, shovel coal, carry the hod, sweep the chimney, or roll oil casks,—all of which I did for nearly three years in New Bedford, before I became known to the anti-slavery world.

In about four months after I went to New Bedford, there came a young man to me, and inquired if I did not wish to take the "Liberator."[3] I told him I did; but, just having made my escape from slavery, I remarked that I was unable to pay for it then. I, however, finally became a subscriber to it. The paper came, and I read it from week to week with such feelings as it would be quite idle for me to attempt to describe. The paper became my meat and my drink. My soul was set all on fire. Its sympathy for my brethren in bonds—its scathing denunciations of slaveholders—its faithful exposures of slavery—and its powerful attacks upon the upholders of the institution—sent a thrill of joy through my soul, such as I had never felt before!

I had not long been a reader of the "Liberator," before I got a pretty correct idea of the principles, measures and spirit of the anti-slavery reform. I took right hold of the cause. I could do but little; but what I could, I did with a joyful heart, and never felt happier than when in an anti-slavery meeting. I seldom had much to say at the meetings, because what I wanted to say was said so much better by others. But, while attending an anti-slavery convention at Nantucket, on the 11th of August, 1841, I felt strongly moved to speak, and was at the same time much urged to do so by Mr. William C. Coffin, a gentleman who had heard me speak in the colored people's meeting at New Bedford.[4] It was a severe cross, and I took it up reluctantly. The truth was, I felt

2. I am told that colored persons can now get employment at calking in New Bedford—a result of anti-slavery effort [Douglass's note].
3. The first issue of Garrison's *Liberator* appeared in January 1831. It became the most widely read abolitionist paper during its thirty-five years of publication.
4. Douglass had become a licensed preacher in the African Methodist Episcopal Zion Church in 1839.

myself a slave, and the idea of speaking to white people weighed me down. I spoke but a few moments, when I felt a degree of freedom, and said what I desired with considerable ease. From that time until now, I have been engaged in pleading the cause of my brethren—with what success, and with what devotion, I leave those acquainted with my labors to decide.

Appendix

I find, since reading over the foregoing Narrative, that I have, in several instances, spoken in such a tone and manner, respecting religion, as may possibly lead those unacquainted with my religious views to suppose me an opponent of all religion. To remove the liability of such misapprehension, I deem it proper to append the following brief explanation. What I have said respecting and against religion, I mean strictly to apply to the *slaveholding religion* of this land, and with no possible reference to Christianity proper; for, between the Christianity of this land, and the Christianity of Christ, I recognize the widest possible difference—so wide, that to receive the one as good, pure, and holy, is of necessity to reject the other as bad, corrupt, and wicked. To be the friend of the one, is of necessity to be the enemy of the other. I love the pure, peaceable, and impartial Christianity of Christ: I therefore hate the corrupt, slaveholding, women-whipping, cradle-plundering, partial and hypocritical Christianity of this land. Indeed, I can see no reason, but the most deceitful one, for calling the religion of this land Christianity. I look upon it as the climax of all misnomers, the boldest of all frauds, and the grossest of all libels. Never was there a clearer case of "stealing the livery of the court of heaven to serve the devil in."[5] I am filled with unutterable loathing when I contemplate the religious pomp and show, together with the horrible inconsistencies, which every where surround me. We have men-stealers for ministers, women-whippers for missionaries, and cradle-plunderers for church members. The man who wields the blood-clotted cowskin during the week fills the pulpit on Sunday, and claims to be a minister of the meek and lowly Jesus. The man who robs me of my earnings at the end of each week meets me as a class-leader on Sunday morning, to show me the way of life, and the path of salvation. He who sells my sister, for purposes of prostitution, stands forth as the pious advocate of purity. He who proclaims it a religious duty to read the Bible denies me the right of learning to read the name of the God who made me. He who is the religious advocate of marriage robs whole millions of its sacred influence, and leaves them to the ravages of wholesale pollution. The warm defender of the sacredness of the family relation is the same that scatters whole families,—sundering husbands and wives, parents and children, sisters and brothers,—leaving the hut vacant, and the hearth desolate. We see the thief preaching against theft, and the adulterer against adultery. We have men sold to build churches, women sold to support the gospel, and babes sold to purchase Bibles for the *poor heathen! all for the glory of God and the good of souls!* The slave auctioneer's bell and the church-going bell chime in with each other, and the bitter cries of the heart-broken

---

5. From *The Course of Time* (1827), book 8, 616–18, a popular poem by the Scotsman Robert Pollok (1798–1827).

slave are drowned in the religious shouts of his pious master. Revivals of religion and revivals in the slave-trade go hand in hand together. The slave prison and the church stand near each other. The clanking of fetters and the rattling of chains in the prison, and the pious psalm and solemn prayer in the church, may be heard at the same time. The dealers in the bodies and souls of men erect their stand in the presence of the pulpit, and they mutually help each other. The dealer gives his blood-stained gold to support the pulpit, and the pulpit, in return, covers his infernal business with the garb of Christianity. Here we have religion and robbery the allies of each other—devils dressed in angels' robes, and hell presenting the semblance of paradise.

> "Just God! and these are they,
>   Who minister at thine altar, God of right!
> Men who their hands, with prayer and blessing, lay
>   On Israel's ark of light.[6]
>
> "What! preach, and kidnap men?
>   Give thanks, and rob thy own afflicted poor?
> Talk of thy glorious liberty, and then
>   Bolt hard the captive's door?
>
> "What! servants of thy own
>   Merciful Son, who came to seek and save
> The homeless and the outcast, fettering down
>   The tasked and plundered slave!
>
> "Pilate and Herod[7] friends!
>   Chief priests and rulers, as of old, combine!
> Just God and holy! is that church which lends
>   Strength to the spoiler thine?"[8]

The Christianity of America is a Christianity, of whose votaries it may be as truly said, as it was of the ancient scribes and Pharisees,[9] "They bind heavy burdens, and grievous to be borne, and lay them on men's shoulders, but they themselves will not move them with one of their fingers. All their works they do for to be seen of men.——They love the uppermost rooms at feasts, and the chief seats in the synagogues, ... and to be called of men, Rabbi, Rabbi.——But woe unto you, scribes and Pharisees, hypocrites! for ye shut up the kingdom of heaven against men; for ye neither go in yourselves, neither suffer ye them that are entering to go in. Ye devour widows' houses, and for a pretence make long prayers; therefore ye shall receive the greater damnation. Ye compass sea and land to make one proselyte, and when he is made, ye make him twofold more the child of hell than yourselves.——Woe unto you, scribes and Pharisees, hypocrites! for

---

6. The Holy Ark containing the Torah; by extension, the entire body of law as contained in the Old Testament and Talmud.
7. Herod Antipas, ruler of Galilee, ordered the execution of John the Baptist and participated in the trial of Christ. Pontius Pilate was the Roman authority who condemned Christ to death.
8. From Whittier's antislavery poem "Clerical Oppressors" (1835).
9. Members of a Jewish group that insisted on strict observance of written and oral religious laws. The scribes were the Jewish scholars who taught Jewish law and edited and interpreted the Bible. Christ's denunciation of the scribes and Pharisees is reported in Matthew 23.

ye pay tithe of mint, and anise, and cumin, and have omitted the weightier matters of the law, judgment, mercy, and faith; these ought ye to have done, and not to leave the other undone. Ye blind guides! which strain at a gnat, and swallow a camel. Woe unto you, scribes and Pharisees, hypocrites! for ye make clean the outside of the cup and of the platter; but within, they are full of extortion and excess.——Woe unto you, scribes and Pharisees, hypocrites! for ye are like unto whited sepulchres, which indeed appear beautiful outward, but are within full of dead men's bones, and of all uncleanness. Even so ye also outwardly appear righteous unto men, but within ye are full of hypocrisy and iniquity."[1]

Dark and terrible as is this picture, I hold it to be strictly true of the overwhelming mass of professed Christians in America. They strain at a gnat, and swallow a camel. Could any thing be more true of our churches? They would be shocked at the proposition of fellowshipping a *sheep*-stealer; and at the same time they hug to their communion a *man*-stealer, and brand me with being an infidel, if I find fault with them for it. They attend with Pharisaical strictness to the outward forms of religion, and at the same time neglect the weightier matters of the law, judgment, mercy, and faith. They are always ready to sacrifice, but seldom to show mercy. They are they who are represented as professing to love God whom they have not seen, whilst they hate their brother whom they have seen. They love the heathen on the other side of the globe. They can pray for him, pay money to have the Bible put into his hand, and missionaries to instruct him; while they despise and totally neglect the heathen at their own doors.

Such is, very briefly, my view of the religion of this land; and to avoid any misunderstanding, growing out of the use of general terms, I mean, by the religion of this land, that which is revealed in the words, deeds, and actions, of those bodies, north and south, calling themselves Christian churches, and yet in union with slaveholders. It is against religion, as presented by these bodies, that I have felt it my duty to testify.

I conclude these remarks by copying the following portrait of the religion of the south, (which is, by communion and fellowship, the religion of the north,) which I soberly affirm is "true to the life," and without caricature or the slightest exaggeration. It is said to have been drawn, several years before the present anti-slavery agitation began, by a northern Methodist preacher, who, while residing at the south, had an opportunity to see slaveholding morals, manners, and piety, with his own eyes. "Shall I not visit for these things? saith the Lord. Shall not my soul be avenged on such a nation as this?"[2]

A PARODY[3]

"Come, saints and sinners, hear me tell
How pious priests whip Jack and Nell,
And women buy and children sell,
And preach all sinners down to hell,
    And sing of heavenly union.

---

1. Cf. Matthew 23.4–28.
2. Jeremiah's voicing of God's condemnation of the kingdom of Judah (Jeremiah 5.9).

3. Douglass is parodying "Heavenly Union," a hymn sung in Southern churches at the time.

"They'll bleat and baa, dona like goats,
Gorge down black sheep, and strain at motes,
Array their backs in fine black coats,
Then seize their negroes by their throats,
    And choke, for heavenly union.

"They'll church you if you sip a dram,
And damn you if you steal a lamb;
Yet rob old Tony, Doll, and Sam,
Of human rights, and bread and ham;
    Kidnapper's heavenly union.

"They'll loudly talk of Christ's reward,
And bind his image with a cord,
And scold, and swing the lash abhorred,
And sell their brother in the Lord
    To handcuffed heavenly union.

"They'll read and sing a sacred song,
And make a prayer both loud and long,
And teach the right and do the wrong,
Hailing the brother, sister throng,
    With words of heavenly union.

"We wonder how such saints can sing,
Or praise the Lord upon the wing,
Who roar, and scold, and whip, and sting,
And to their slaves and mammon cling,
    In guilty conscience union.

"They'll raise tobacco, corn, and rye,
And drive, and thieve, and cheat, and lie,
And lay up treasures in the sky,
By making switch and cowskin fly,
    In hope of heavenly union.

"They'll crack old Tony on the skull,
And preach and roar like Bashan[4] bull,
Or braying ass, of mischief full,
Then seize old Jacob by the wool,
    And pull for heavenly union.

"A roaring, ranting, sleek man-thief,
Who lived on mutton, veal, and beef,
Yet never would afford relief
To needy, sable sons of grief,
    Was big with heavenly union.

"'Love not the world,' the preacher said,
And winked his eye, and shook his head;
He seized on Tom, and Dick, and Ned,
Cut short their meat, and clothes, and bread,
    Yet still loved heavenly union.

4. Strong bulls mentioned in the Old Testament.

"Another preacher whining spoke
Of One whose heart for sinners broke:
He tied old Nanny to an oak,
And drew the blood at every stroke,
    And prayed for heavenly union.

"Two others oped their iron jaws,
And waved their children-stealing paws;
There sat their children in gewgaws;
By stinting negroes' backs and maws,
    They kept up heavenly union.

"All good from Jack another takes,
And entertains their flirts and rakes,
Who dress as sleek as glossy snakes,
And cram their mouths with sweetened cakes;
    And this goes down for union."

Sincerely and earnestly hoping that this little book may do something toward throwing light on the American slave system, and hastening the glad day of deliverance to the millions of my brethren in bonds—faithfully relying upon the power of truth, love, and justice, for success in my humble efforts—and solemnly pledging my self anew to the sacred cause,—I subscribe myself,

FREDERICK DOUGLASS.

LYNN, Mass., April 28, 1845.

1845

What to the Slave Is the Fourth of July?

Extract from an Oration, at Rochester, July 5, 1852[1]

Fellow Citizens—Pardon me, and allow me to ask, why am I called upon to speak here to-day? What have I, or those I represent, to do with your national independence? Are the great principles of political freedom and of natural justice, embodied in that Declaration of Independence, extended to us? and am I, therefore, called upon to bring our humble offering to the national altar, and to confess the benefits, and express devout gratitude for the blessings, resulting from your independence to us?

Would to God, both for your sakes and ours, that an affirmative answer could be truthfully returned to these questions! Then would my task be light, and my burden easy and delightful. For who is there so cold that a nation's sympathy could not warm him? Who so obdurate and dead to the claims of gratitude, that would not thankfully acknowledge such priceless benefits? Who so stolid and selfish, that would not give his voice to swell the hallelujahs of a nation's jubilee, when the chains of servitude had been

---

1. Douglass delivered this Fourth of July address on July 5, 1852, in Rochester, New York, before a racially mixed audience of approximately six hundred people. Later that year he published it as a pamphlet. He first published the "Extract" (several key pages from the longer work) in the appendix to *My Bondage and My Freedom* (1855), the source of the present text.

torn from his limbs? I am not that man. In a case like that, the dumb might eloquently speak, and the "lame man leap as an hart."[2]

But, such is not the state of the case. I say it with a sad sense of the disparity between us. I am not included within the pale of this glorious anniversary! Your high independence only reveals the immeasurable distance between us. The blessings in which you this day rejoice, are not enjoyed in common. The rich inheritance of justice, liberty, prosperity, and independence, bequeathed by your fathers, is shared by you, not by me. The sunlight that brought life and healing to you, has brought stripes and death to me. This Fourth of July is *yours*, not *mine*. You may rejoice, *I* must mourn. To drag a man in fetters into the grand illuminated temple of liberty, and call upon him to join you in joyous anthems, were inhuman mockery and sacrilegious irony. Do you mean, citizens, to mock me, by asking me to speak to-day? If so, there is a parallel to your conduct. And let me warn you that it is dangerous to copy the example of a nation whose crimes, towering up to heaven, were thrown down by the breath of the Almighty, burying that nation in irrecoverable ruin! I can to-day take up the plaintive lament of a peeled and woe-smitten people.

"By the rivers of Babylon, there we sat down. Yea! we wept when we remembered Zion. We hanged our harps upon the willows in the midst thereof. For there, they that carried us away captive, required of us a song; and they who wasted us required of us mirth, saying, Sing us one of the songs of Zion. How can we sing the Lord's song in a strange land? If I forget thee, O Jerusalem, let my right hand forget her cunning. If I do not remember thee, let my tongue cleave to the roof of my mouth."[3]

Fellow-citizens, above your national, tumultuous joy, I hear the mournful wail of millions, whose chains, heavy and grievous yesterday, are to-day rendered more intolerable by the jubilant shouts that reach them. If I do forget, if I do not faithfully remember those bleeding children of sorrow this day, "may my right hand forget her cunning, and may my tongue cleave to the roof of my mouth!" To forget them, to pass lightly over their wrongs, and to chime in with the popular theme, would be treason most scandalous and shocking, and would make me a reproach before God and the world. My subject, then, fellow-citizens, is AMERICAN SLAVERY. I shall see this day and its popular characteristics from the slave's point of view. Standing there, identified with the American bondman, making his wrongs mine, I do not hesitate to declare, with all my soul, that the character and conduct of this nation never looked blacker to me than on this Fourth of July. Whether we turn to the declarations of the past, or to the professions of the present, the conduct of the nation seems equally hideous and revolting. America is false to the past, false to the present, and solemnly binds herself to be false to the future. Standing with God and the crushed and bleeding slave on this occasion, I will, in the name of humanity which is outraged, in the name of liberty which is fettered, in the name of the constitution and the bible, which are disregarded and trampled upon, dare to call in question and to denounce, with all the emphasis I can command, everything that serves to perpetuate slavery—the great sin and shame of America! "I will not equivocate; I will not excuse;"[4] I will

2. Deer. The quotation is from Isaiah 35.6.
3. Psalms 137.1–6.
4. From "To the Public," an editorial by William

Lloyd Garrison in the inaugural issue of his antislavery newspaper *The Liberator* (January 1, 1831).

use the severest language I can command; and yet not one word shall escape me that any man, whose judgment is not blinded by prejudice, or who is not at heart a slaveholder, shall not confess to be right and just.

But I fancy I hear some one of my audience say, it is just in this circumstance that you and your brother abolitionists fail to make a favorable impression on the public mind. Would you argue more, and denounce less, would you persuade more and rebuke less, your cause would be much more likely to succeed. But, I submit, where all is plain there is nothing to be argued. What point in the anti-slavery creed would you have me argue? On what branch of the subject do the people of this country need light? Must I undertake to prove that the slave is a man? That point is conceded already. Nobody doubts it. The slaveholders themselves acknowledge it in the enactment of laws for their government. They acknowledge it when they punish disobedience on the part of the slave. There are seventy-two crimes in the state of Virginia, which, if committed by a black man, (no matter how ignorant he be,) subject him to the punishment of death; while only two of these same crimes will subject a white man to the like punishment. What is this but the acknowledgment that the slave is a moral, intellectual, and responsible being. The manhood of the slave is conceded. It is admitted in the fact that southern statute books are covered with enactments forbidding, under severe fines and penalties, the teaching of the slave to read or write. When you can point to any such laws, in reference to the beasts of the field, then I may consent to argue the manhood of the slave. When the dogs in your streets, when the fowls of the air, when the cattle on your hills, when the fish of the sea, and the reptiles that crawl, shall be unable to distinguish the slave from a brute, then will I argue with you that the slave is a man!

For the present, it is enough to affirm the equal manhood of the negro race. Is it not astonishing that, while we are plowing, planting, and reaping, using all kinds of mechanical tools, erecting houses, constructing bridges, building ships, working in metals of brass, iron, copper, silver, and gold; that, while we are reading, writing, and cyphering, acting as clerks, merchants, and secretaries, having among us lawyers, doctors, ministers, poets, authors, editors, orators, and teachers; that, while we are engaged in all manner of enterprises common to other men—digging gold in California, capturing the whale in the Pacific, feeding sheep and cattle on the hillside, living, moving, acting, thinking, planning, living in families as husbands, wives, and children, and, above all, confessing and worshiping the christian's God, and looking hopefully for life and immortality beyond the grave,—we are called upon to prove that we are men![5]

Would you have me argue that man is entitled to liberty? that he is the rightful owner of his own body? You have already declared it. Must I argue the wrongfulness of slavery? Is that a question for republicans? Is it to be settled by the rules of logic and argumentation, as a matter beset with great difficulty, involving a doubtful application of the principle of justice, hard to be understood? How should I look to-day in the presence of Americans, dividing and subdividing a discourse, to show that men have a natural right to freedom, speaking of it relatively and positively, negatively and affirmatively? To do so, would be to make myself ridiculous, and to offer an insult to your

---

5. As suggested by his reference to women and children, Douglass here uses "men" to mean "human."

understanding. There is not a man beneath the canopy of heaven that does not know that slavery is wrong *for him*.

What! am I to argue that it is wrong to make men brutes, to rob them of their liberty, to work them without wages, to keep them ignorant of their relations to their fellow men, to beat them with sticks, to flay their flesh with the lash, to load their limbs with irons, to hunt them with dogs, to sell them at auction, to sunder their families, to knock out their teeth, to burn their flesh, to starve them into obedience and submission to their masters? Must I argue that a system, thus marked with blood and stained with pollution, is wrong? No; I will not. I have better employment for my time and strength than such arguments would imply.

What, then, remains to be argued? Is it that slavery is not divine; that God did not establish it; that our doctors of divinity are mistaken? There is blasphemy in the thought. That which is inhuman cannot be divine. Who can reason on such a proposition! They that can, may; I cannot. The time for such argument is past.

At a time like this, scorching irony, not convincing argument, is needed. Oh! had I the ability, and could I reach the nation's ear, I would to-day pour out a fiery stream of biting ridicule, blasting reproach, withering sarcasm, and stern rebuke. For it is not light that is needed, but fire; it is not the gentle shower, but thunder. We need the storm, the whirlwind, and the earthquake. The feeling of the nation must be quickened; the conscience of the nation must be roused; the propriety of the nation must be startled; the hypocrisy of the nation must be exposed; and its crimes against God and man must be proclaimed and denounced.

What to the American slave is your Fourth of July? I answer, a day that reveals to him, more than all other days in the year, the gross injustice and cruelty to which he is the constant victim. To him, your celebration is a sham; your boasted liberty, an unholy license; your national greatness, swelling vanity; your sounds of rejoicing are empty and heartless; your denunciations of tyrants, brass-fronted impudence; your shouts of liberty and equality, hollow mockery; your prayers and hymns, your sermons and thanksgivings, with all your religious parade and solemnity, are to him mere bombast, fraud, deception, impiety, and hypocrisy—a thin veil to cover up crimes which would disgrace a nation of savages. There is not a nation on the earth guilty of practices more shocking and bloody, than are the people of these United States, at this very hour.

Go where you may, search where you will, roam through all the monarchies and despotisms of the old world, travel through South America, search out every abuse, and when you have found the last, lay your facts by the side of the every-day practices of this nation, and you will say with me, that, for revolting barbarity and shameless hypocrisy, America reigns without a rival.

1852, 1855

WALT WHITMAN
1819–1892

Walt Whitman revolutionized American poetry. Responding to Emerson's call in "The Poet" (1842) for an American bard who would address all "the facts of the animal economy, sex, nutriment, gestation, birth," Whitman put the living, breathing, sexual body at the center of much of his poetry, challenging conventions of the day. Responding to Emerson's call for a "metre-making argument," he rejected traditions of poetic scansion and elevated diction, improvising the form that has come to be known as free verse, while adopting a wide-ranging vocabulary opening new possibilities for poetic expression. A poet of democracy, Whitman celebrated the mystical, divine potential of the individual; a poet of the urban, he wrote about the sights, sounds, and energy of the modern metropolis. In his 1855 preface to *Leaves of Grass*, he declared that "the proof of a poet is that his country absorbs him as affectionately as he has absorbed it." On the evidence of his enormous influence on later poets—Hart Crane, Langston Hughes, Robert Lowell, Allen Ginsberg, Adrienne Rich, Cherrie Moraga, and countless others, including Spain's Federico Garcia Lorca and Chile's Pablo Neruda—Whitman not only was affectionately absorbed by his own country but remains a persistent presence in poetry throughout the world.

Whitman was born on May 31, 1819, in West Hills, Long Island (New York), the second of eight surviving children of the Quakers Louisa Van Velsor and Walter Whitman. In 1823, Whitman's father, a farmer turned carpenter, sought to take advantage of a building boom by moving the family to Brooklyn—then a town at the western and most urbanized part of Long Island. Whitman left school when he was eleven, and was soon employed in the printing office of a newspaper; when his family moved east on Long Island in 1833, he remained in Brooklyn on his own. He began contributing to newspapers in his midteens and spent five years teaching at country and small-town schools on Long Island, interrupting his teaching to start a newspaper of his own in 1838 and to work briefly on another Long Island paper. By early 1840 he had started the series "Sun-Down Papers from the Desk of a School-Master" for the Jamaica, New York, *Democrat* and was writing poems and fiction. One of his stories prophetically culminated with the dream of writing "a wonderful and ponderous book."

Just before he turned twenty-one Whitman stopped teaching, moved to Manhattan, began work at the literary weekly *New World*, and soon became editor of a Manhattan daily, the *Aurora*. He also began a political career by speaking at Democratic rallies and writing for the *Democratic Review*, the foremost magazine of the Democratic Party. He exulted in the extremes of the city, where street-gang violence was countered by the lectures of Emerson and where even a young editor could get to know the poet William Cullen Bryant, editor of the *Evening Post*. Fired from the *Aurora*, which publicly charged him with laziness, he wrote a temperance novel, *Franklin Evans, or the Inebriate*, for a one-issue extra of the *New World* late in 1842. After three years of various literary and political jobs, he returned to Brooklyn in 1845, becoming a special contributor to the *Long Island Star*, assigned to Manhattan events, including theatrical and musical performances. All through the 1840s he attended operas on his journalist's passes and he would later say that without the "emotions, raptures, uplifts" of opera he could never have written *Leaves of Grass*. Just before he was twenty-seven he took over the editorship of the *Brooklyn Eagle*, writing most of the literary reviews, which included books by Carlyle, Emerson, Melville, Fuller, and Goethe, among

Leaves of Grass. Frontispiece and title page of the first edition (1855).

others. Like most Democrats, he was able to justify the Mexican War (1846–48) by hailing the great American mission of "peopling the New World with a noble race." Yet at the beginning of 1848 he was fired from the *Eagle* because, like Bryant, he had become a Free-Soiler, opposed to the acquisition of more territory for slavery. Whitman served as a delegate to the Buffalo Free-Soil convention and helped to found the Free-Soil newspaper the *Brooklyn Freeman.* Around this time he began writing poetry in a serious way, experimenting with form and prosody; he published several topical poems in 1850, including "Europe," which would later appear in *Leaves of Grass.*

Whitman's notebook fragments suggest that he began to invent the overall shape of his first volume of poetry during the period 1853–54. On May 15, 1855, he took out a copyright for *Leaves of Grass,* and he spent the spring and early summer seeing his book through the press, probably setting some of the type himself. Published in Brooklyn, New York, during the first week of July, the volume, bound in dark green cloth with a sprig of grass in gilt on the cover, contained twelve untitled poems (including the initial version of "Song of Myself"), along with an exuberant preface declaring his ambition to be the American bard. In the image of Whitman on the book's frontispiece, which was based on an 1854 daguerreotype, the bearded Whitman—rejecting the conventional suit jacket, buttoned-up shirt, and high collar of the formal studio portrait—stands with one arm akimbo, one hand in a pocket, workingman's hat on slightly cocked head, shirt unbuttoned at the collar, looking directly at the reader. (See the reproduction above.) The image, like the poetry itself, defied convention by aligning the poet with working people. The poems, with their absence of standard verse and stanza patterns (although strongly rhythmic and controlled by numerous poetic devices of repetition and variation), also introduced his use of "catalogs"—journalistic and encyclopedic listings—that were to become a hallmark of his style. Whitman sent out numerous presentation and review copies of his book, receiving an immediate response from Emerson, who greeted him "at the beginning of a great career," but otherwise attracting little notice. As weeks passed, Whitman chose to publish a few anonymous reviews himself, praising *Leaves of Grass* in the *American Phrenological Journal*, for instance, as one of "the most glorious triumphs, in the known history of literature." In October he let Horace Greeley's *New York Tribune* print Emerson's private letter of praise, and he put clippings of the letter in presentation copies to Longfellow, among others. Emerson termed Whitman's appropriation of the letter "a strange, rude thing," but he remained interested in meeting the poet. While Whitman was angling for reviews in England and working on expanding his book, Emerson visited him in December of 1855. Thoreau, who admired *Leaves of Grass* but found several of its poems "simply sensual," visited him later in 1856. That year also saw the appearance of the second edition of *Leaves of Grass*, now with thirty-three poems, including "Crossing Brooklyn Ferry" under its initial title, "Sundown Poem."

Returning to miscellaneous journalism, Whitman edited the *Brooklyn Times* from 1857 to 1859 and published several pieces in the *Times* affirming his Free-Soiler hopes for a continued national expansion into the western territories that would not entail the expansion of slavery. In the third (1860) edition of *Leaves of Grass*, Whitman began to group his poems thematically. For a section called "Enfans d'Adam," later retitled "Children of Adam," he wrote fifteen poems focused on what he termed the "amative" love of man for woman, in contrast to the "adhesive" love of man for man. Adhesive love figured in forty-five poems in a section titled "Calamus." These two sections in the 1860 edition differ from the sections in the final 1891–92 edition, for in the intervening editions (1867, 1871, 1881) Whitman revised and regrouped some of the poems, as he would with numerous other poems in the expanded editions he would go on to publish.

With the outbreak of the Civil War, Whitman began to visit the wounded and eventually offered his services as a nurse. He started at New-York Hospital, but in early 1863, after visiting with his wounded brother George in an army camp in Virginia, he moved to Washington, D.C., and began to work at the huge open-air military hospitals there. Nursing gave Whitman a profound sense of vocation. As he wrote a friend in 1863: "I am very happy . . . I was never so beloved. I am running over with health, fat, red & sunburnt in face. I tell thee I am just the one to go to our sick boys." But ministering to tens of thousands of maimed and dying young men took its toll. He succinctly voiced his anguish in a notebook entry of 1864: "the dead, the dead, the dead, our dead." During this time he worked on a series of poems that conveyed his evolving view of the war from heroic celebration to despair at the horrifying carnage. He later wrote a chapter in his prose work *Specimen Days* (1882) titled "The Real War Will Never Get in the Books," but to incorporate the "real war" into a book of poetry became one of the dominant impulses of the *Drum-Taps* collection, which he published in 1865. After Lincoln's assassination, Whitman reissued the volume with a sequel including "O Captain! My Captain!" and "When Lilacs Last in the Dooryard Bloom'd," his famous elegy for the murdered president.

As he prepared *Drum-Taps and Sequel* for publication in late 1865, Whitman was also revising *Leaves of Grass* at his desk in the Department of the Interior, where he had obtained a position as clerk. The new secretary of the interior, James Harlan, read the annotated copy and fired Whitman for writing an obscene book, objecting to Whitman's frankness about bodily functions and heterosexual love. Whitman's friend William O'Connor, a poet, found him another clerical position in the attorney general's office; and in his rage at the firing, O'Connor wrote *The Good Gray Poet* (1866), identifying Whitman with Jesus and Harlan with the forces of evil. Whitman continued to rework *Leaves of Grass*, incorporating *Drum-Taps* into it in 1867, and with his friends' help continued to propagandize for its recognition as a landmark in the history of poetry. He also published essays in the 1867 and 1868 numbers of the New York periodical *Galaxy*, which he expanded into *Democratic Vistas* (1870), a book conveying his sometimes sharply condemnatory appraisal of postwar democratic culture.

The Washington years came to an abrupt end in 1873 when Whitman suffered a paralytic stroke. His mother died a few months later, and Whitman joined his brother George's household in Camden, New Jersey, to recuperate. During the second year of his illness, the government ceased to hold his clerk job open for him, and he became dependent for a living on occasional publication in newspapers and magazines. The 1867 edition of *Leaves of Grass* had involved much reworking and rearrangement, and the fifth edition (1871) continued that process, adding a new section titled "Passage to India." In 1876 Whitman privately published a prose work, *Memoranda during the War*, and six years later he brought out *Specimen Days*, which has affinities with his early editorial accounts of strolls through the city but is even more intensely personal, the record of representative days in the life of a poet who had lived in the midst of great national events.

During the 1870s and early 1880s, Whitman was increasingly noticed by the leading writers of the time, especially in England. The English poet Algernon Swinburne sent him a poem, the poet laureate Alfred Lord Tennyson sent him an admiring letter, and both Longfellow and Oscar Wilde visited him in Camden. In the United States, writers of a younger generation than Whitman's began to recognize his importance as a poetic voice and organized events to support him. Despite his frail health, Whitman lectured on Thomas Paine in Philadelphia in 1877 and on Abraham Lincoln in New York in 1879 (he would continue to deliver public lectures on Lincoln until 1890). Opposition to his poetry because of its supposed immorality began to dissipate, and readers, having become accustomed over time to Whitman's poetic devices, began to recognize the poet as an artist. Still, in 1881, when the reputable Boston firm of James R. Osgood & Company printed the sixth edition of *Leaves of Grass*, the Boston district attorney threatened to prosecute on the grounds of obscenity. Ironically, when the Philadelphia firm of Rees Welsh and Company reprinted this edition in 1882, the publicity contributed to Whitman's greatest sales in his lifetime: he earned nearly $1,500 in royalties from that edition (around $25,000 in today's value), compared to the $25 he had earned from the Osgood edition before the publisher withdrew it.

In 1884, the still infirm Whitman moved to a cottage at 328 Mickle Street in Camden, which he purchased for $1,750. A year later friends and admirers, including Mark Twain and John Greenleaf Whittier, presented him with a horse and buggy for local travel. He had another stroke in 1888 and in 1890 made preparations for his death by signing a $4,000 contract for the construction in Camden's Harleigh Cemetery of a granite mausoleum, or what he termed a "burial house," suitable for a national bard. In 1891 he did the final editing of *Complete Prose Works* (1892) and oversaw the preparations of the "deathbed" edition of the now more than three hundred poems in *Leaves of Grass* (1891–92), which was in fact a reissue of the 1881 edition with the addition of two later groups of poems, "Sands at Seventy" and "Good-bye My Fancy." Whitman died in Camden on March 26, 1892, and was buried in Harleigh Cemetery in the mausoleum he had helped design.

All the Whitman poems reprinted here, regardless of when they were first composed and printed, are given in their final form: that of the 1891–92 edition of *Leaves of Grass*.

Preface to *Leaves of Grass* (1855)[1]

America does not repel the past or what it has produced under its forms or amid other politics or the idea of castes or the old religions . . . accepts the

---

1. The 1st edition of *Leaves of Grass* contained twelve untitled poems, which were introduced by this manifesto-like preface. The preface was not reprinted in subsequent editions, though some of its ideas were incorporated into future poems. The spellings and ellipses are Whitman's.

lesson with calmness . . . is not so impatient as has been supposed that the slough still sticks to opinions and manners and literature while the life which served its requirements has passed into the new life of the new forms . . . perceives that the corpse is slowly borne from the eating and sleeping rooms of the house . . . perceives that it waits a little while in the door . . . that it was fittest for its days . . . that its action has descended to the stalwart and wellshaped heir who approaches . . . and that he shall be fittest for his days.

The Americans of all nations at any time upon the earth have probably the fullest poetical nature. The United States themselves are essentially the greatest poem. In the history of the earth hitherto the largest and most stirring appear tame and orderly to their ampler largeness and stir. Here at last is something in the doings of man that corresponds with the broadcast doings of the day and night. Here is not merely a nation but a teeming nation of nations. Here is action untied from strings necessarily blind to particulars and details magnificently moving in vast masses. Here is the hospitality which forever indicates heroes. . . . Here are the roughs and beards and space and ruggedness and nonchalance that the soul loves. Here the performance disdaining the trivial unapproached in the tremendous audacity of its crowds and groupings and the push of its perspective spreads with crampless and flowing breadth and showers its prolific and splendid extravagance. One sees it must indeed own the riches of the summer and winter, and need never be bankrupt while corn grows from the ground or the orchards drop apples or the bays contain fish or men beget children upon women.

Other states indicate themselves in their deputies . . . . but the genius of the United States is not best or most in its executives or legislatures, nor in its ambassadors or authors or colleges or churches or parlors, nor even in its newspapers or inventors . . . but always most in the common people. Their manners speech dress friendships—the freshness and candor of their physiognomy—the picturesque looseness of their carriage . . . their deathless attachment to freedom—their aversion to anything indecorous or soft or mean—the practical acknowledgment of the citizens of one state by the citizens of all other states—the fierceness of their roused resentment—their curiosity and welcome of novelty—their self-esteem and wonderful sympathy—their susceptibility to a slight—the air they have of persons who never knew how it felt to stand in the presence of superiors—the fluency of their speech—their delight in music, the sure symptom of manly tenderness and native elegance of soul . . . their good temper and openhandedness—the terrible significance of their elections—the President's taking off his hat to them not they to him—these too are unrhymed poetry. It awaits the gigantic and generous treatment worthy of it.

The largeness of nature or the nation were monstrous without a corresponding largeness and generosity of the spirit of the citizen. Not nature nor swarming states nor streets and steamships nor prosperous business nor farms nor capital nor learning may suffice for the ideal of man . . . nor suffice the poet. No reminiscences may suffice either. A live nation can always cut a deep mark and can have the best authority the cheapest . . . namely from its own soul. This is the sum of the profitable uses of individuals or states and of present action and grandeur and of the subjects of poets.—As if it were necessary to trot back generation after generation to the eastern records! As if the beauty and sacredness of the demonstrable must fall behind that of the mythical! As if men do not make their mark out of any times! As if the opening of the western continent by discovery and what has transpired since in North and South America were less than the small theatre of the antique or the aimless sleepwalking of the middle ages! The pride of the United States leaves the wealth and finesse of the cities and all returns of commerce and agriculture and all the magnitude of geography or shows of exterior victory to enjoy the breed of fullsized men or one fullsized man unconquerable and simple.

The American poets are to enclose old and new for America is the race of races. Of them a bard[2] is to be commensurate with a people. To him the other continents arrive as contributions . . . he gives them reception for their sake and his own sake. His spirit responds to his country's spirit . . . . he incarnates its geography and natural life and rivers and lakes. Mississippi with annual freshets and changing chutes, Missouri and Columbia and Ohio and Saint Lawrence with the falls and beautiful masculine Hudson, do not embouchure[3] where they spend themselves more than they embouchure into him. The blue breadth over the inland sea of Virginia and Maryland and the sea off Massachusetts and Maine and over Manhattan bay and over Champlain and Erie and over Ontario and Huron and Michigan and Superior, and over the Texan and Mexican and Floridian and Cuban seas and over the seas off California and Oregon, is not tallied by the blue breadth of the waters below more than the breadth of above and below is tallied by him. When the long Atlantic coast stretches longer and the Pacific coast stretches longer he easily stretches with them north or south. He spans between them also from east to west and reflects what is between them. On him rise solid growths that offset the growths of pine and cedar and hemlock and liveoak and locust and chestnut and cypress and hickory and limetree and cottonwood and tuliptree and cactus and wildvine and tamarind and persimmon . . . . and tangles as tangled as any canebrake or swamp . . . . and forests coated with transparent ice and icicles hanging from the boughs and crackling in the wind . . . . and sides and peaks of mountains . . . . and pasturage sweet and free as savannah or upland or prairie . . . . with flights and songs and screams that answer those of the wild pigeon and highhold and orchard-oriole and coot and surf-duck and redshouldered-hawk and fish-hawk and white-ibis and indian-hen and cat-owl and water-pheasant and qua-bird and pied-sheldrake and blackbird and mockingbird and buzzard and condor and night-heron and eagle. To him the hereditary countenance descends both mother's and father's. To him enter the essences of the real things and past and present events—of the enormous diversity of temperature and agriculture and mines—the tribes of red aborigines—the weatherbeaten vessels entering new ports or making landings on rocky coasts—the first settlements north or south—the rapid stature and muscle—the haughty defiance of '76, and the war and peace and formation of the constitution . . . . the union always surrounded by blatherers and always calm and impregnable—the perpetual coming of immigrants—the wharf hem'd cities and superior marine—the unsurveyed interior—the loghouses and clearings and wild animals and hunters and trappers . . . . the free commerce—the fisheries and whaling and gold-digging—the endless gestation of new states—the convening of Congress every December, the members duly

---

2. The ideal national poet, usually linked to older heroic or epic traditions.

3. Pour.

coming up from all climates and the uttermost parts . . . . the noble character of the young mechanics and of all free American workmen and workwomen . . . . the general ardor and friendliness and enterprise—the perfect equality of the female with the male . . . . the large amativeness—the fluid movement of the population—the factories and mercantile life and laborsaving machinery—the Yankee swap—the New-York firemen and the target excursion[4]—the southern plantation life—the character of the northeast and of the northwest and southwest—slavery and the tremulous spreading of hands to protect it, and the stern opposition to it which shall never cease till it ceases or the speaking of tongues and the moving of lips cease. For such the expression of the American poet is to be transcendant and new. It is to be indirect and not direct or descriptive or epic. Its quality goes through these to much more. Let the age and wars of other nations be chanted and their eras and characters be illustrated and that finish the verse. Not so the great psalm of the republic. Here the theme is creative and has vista. Here comes one among the wellbeloved stonecutters and plans with decision and science and sees the solid and beautiful forms of the future where there are now no solid forms.

Of all nations the United States with veins full of poetical stuff most need poets and will doubtless have the greatest and use them the greatest. Their Presidents shall not be their common referee so much as their poets shall. Of all mankind the great poet is the equable man. Not in him but off from him things are grotesque or eccentric or fail of their sanity. Nothing out of its place is good and nothing in its place is bad. He bestows on every object or quality its fit proportions neither more nor less. He is the arbiter of the diverse and he is the key. He is the equalizer of his age and land . . . . he supplies what wants supplying and checks what wants checking. If peace is the routine out of him speaks the spirit of peace, large, rich, thrifty, building vast and populous cities, encouraging agriculture and the arts and commerce—lighting the study of man, the soul, immortality—federal, state or municipal government, marriage, health, freetrade, intertravel by land and sea . . . . nothing too close, nothing too far off . . . the stars not too far off. In war he is the most deadly force of the war. Who recruits him recruits horse and foot . . . he fetches parks of artillery[5] the best that engineer ever knew. If the time becomes slothful and heavy he knows how to arouse it . . . he can make every word he speaks draw blood. Whatever stagnates in the flat of custom or obedience or legislation he never stagnates. Obedience does not master him, he masters it. High up out of reach he stands turning a concentrated light . . . he turns the pivot with his finger . . . he baffles the swiftest runners as he stands and easily overtakes and envelops them. The time straying toward infidelity and confections and persiflage[6] he withholds by his steady faith . . . he spreads out his dishes . . . he offers the sweet firmfibred meat that grows men and women. His brain is the ultimate brain. He is no arguer . . . he is judgment. He judges not as the judge judges but as the sun falling around a helpless thing. As he sees the farthest he has the most faith. His thoughts are the hymns of the praise of things. In the talk on the soul and eternity and God off of his equal plane he is silent. He sees eternity less like a play with a prologue and denouement . . . . he sees eternity in

---

4. Shooting contest. "Every December": Before the adoption of the Twentieth Amendment in 1933, Congress convened on the first Monday in December, according to Article 1, Section 4, of the Constitution. "Amativeness": amorousness.
5. I.e., parks full of artillery—from the custom of drilling and parading in civic parks.
6. Bantering talk.

men and women . . . he does not see men and women as dreams or dots. Faith is the antiseptic of the soul . . . it pervades the common people and preserves them . . . they never give up believing and expecting and trusting. There is that indescribable freshness and unconsciousness about an illiterate person that humbles and mocks the power of the noblest expressive genius. The poet sees for a certainty how one not a great artist may be just as sacred and perfect as the greatest artist. . . . . . The power to destroy or remould is freely used by him but never the power of attack. What is past is past. If he does not expose superior models and prove himself by every step he takes he is not what is wanted. The presence of the greatest poet conquers . . . not parleying or struggling or any prepared attempts. Now he has passed that way see after him! there is not left any vestige of despair or misanthropy or cunning or exclusiveness or the ignominy of a nativity or color or delusion of hell or the necessity of hell . . . . . . and no man thenceforward shall be degraded for ignorance or weakness or sin.

The greatest poet hardly knows pettiness or triviality. If he breathes into any thing that was before thought small it dilates with the grandeur and life of the universe. He is a seer . . . . he is individual . . . he is complete in himself . . . . the others are as good as he, only he sees it and they do not. He is not one of the chorus . . . . he does not stop for any regulation . . . he is the president of regulation. What the eyesight does to the rest he does to the rest. Who knows the curious mystery of the eyesight? The other senses corroborate themselves, but this is removed from any proof but its own and foreruns the identities of the spiritual world. A single glance of it mocks all the investigations of man and all the instruments and books of the earth and all reasoning. What is marvellous? what is unlikely? what is impossible or baseless or vague? after you have once just opened the space of a peachpit and given audience to far and near and to the sunset and had all things enter with electric swiftness softly and duly without confusion or jostling or jam.

The land and sea, the animals fishes and birds, the sky of heaven and the orbs, the forests mountains and rivers, are not small themes . . . but folks expect of the poet to indicate more than the beauty and dignity which always attach to dumb real objects . . . . they expect him to indicate the path between reality and their souls. Men and women perceive the beauty well enough . . probably as well as he. The passionate tenacity of hunters, woodmen, early risers, cultivators of gardens and orchards and fields, the love of healthy women for the manly form, sea-faring persons, drivers of horses, the passion for light and the open air, all is an old varied sign of the unfailing perception of beauty and of a residence of the poetic in outdoor people. They can never be assisted by poets to perceive . . . some may but they never can. The poetic quality is not marshalled in rhyme or uniformity or abstract addresses to things nor in melancholy complaints or good precepts, but is the life of these and much else and is in the soul. The profit of rhyme is that it drops seeds of a sweeter and more luxuriant rhyme, and of uniformity that it conveys itself into its own roots in the ground out of sight. The rhyme and uniformity of perfect poems show the free growth of metrical laws and bud from them as unerringly and loosely as lilacs or roses on a bush, and take shapes as compact as the shapes of chestnuts and oranges and melons and pears, and shed the perfume impalpable to form. The fluency and ornaments of the finest poems or music or orations or recitations are not independent but dependent. All beauty comes from beautiful blood and a beautiful brain. If the greatnesses are in conjunction in a

man or woman it is enough . . . . the fact will prevail through the universe
. . . . but the gaggery[7] and gilt of a million years will not prevail. Who troubles
himself about his ornaments or fluency is lost. This is what you shall do: Love
the earth and sun and the animals, despise riches, give alms to every one that
asks, stand up for the stupid and crazy, devote your income and labor to others, hate tyrants, argue not concerning God, have patience and indulgence
toward the people, take off your hat to nothing known or unknown or to any
man or number of men, go freely with powerful uneducated persons and with
the young and with the mothers of families, read these leaves in the open air
every season of every year of your life, reexamine all you have been told at
school or church or in any book, dismiss whatever insults your own soul, and
your very flesh shall be a great poem and have the richest fluency not only in
its words but in the silent lines of its lips and face and between the lashes of
your eyes and in every motion and joint of your body. . . . . The poet shall
not spend his time in unneeded work. He shall know that the ground is
always ready ploughed and manured . . . . others may not know it but he
shall. He shall go directly to the creation. His trust shall master the trust of
everything he touches . . . . and shall master all attachment.

The known universe has one complete lover and that is the greatest poet.
He consumes an eternal passion and is indifferent which chance happens
and which possible contingency of fortune or misfortune and persuades
daily and hourly his delicious pay. What balks or breaks others is fuel for
his burning progress to contact and amorous joy. Other proportions of the
reception of pleasure dwindle to nothing to his proportions. All expected
from heaven or from the highest he is rapport with in the sight of the day-
break or a scene of the winter woods or the presence of children playing or
with his arm round the neck of a man or woman. His love above all love has
leisure and expanse . . . . he leaves room ahead of himself. He is no irresolute or suspicious lover . . . he is sure . . . he scorns intervals. His experience and the showers and thrills are not for nothing. Nothing can jar him
. . . . suffering and darkness cannot—death and fear cannot. To him complaint and jealousy and envy are corpses buried and rotten in the earth . . . .
he saw them buried. The sea is not surer of the shore or the shore of the sea
than he is of the fruition of his love and of all perfection and beauty.

The fruition of beauty is no chance of hit or miss . . . it is inevitable as life
. . . . it is exact and plumb as gravitation. From the eyesight proceeds another
eyesight and from the hearing proceeds another hearing and from the voice
proceeds another voice eternally curious of the harmony of things with man.
To these respond perfections not only in the committees that were supposed to
stand for the rest but in the rest themselves just the same. These understand
the law of perfection in masses and floods . . . that its finish is to each for itself
and onward from itself . . . that it is profuse and impartial . . . that there is not
a minute of the light or dark nor an acre of the earth or sea without it—nor any
direction of the sky nor any trade or employment nor any turn of events. This is
the reason that about the proper expression of beauty there is precision and
balance . . . one part does not need to be thrust above another. The best singer
is not the one who has the most lithe and powerful organ . . . the pleasure of
poems is not in them that take the handsomest measure and similes and sound.

7. Falseness.

Without effort and without exposing in the least how it is done the greatest poet brings the spirit of any or all events and passions and scenes and persons some more and some less to bear on your individual character as you hear or read. To do this well is to compete with the laws that pursue and follow time. What is the purpose must surely be there and the clue of it must be there . . . . and the faintest indication is the indication of the best and then becomes the clearest indication. Past and present and future are not disjoined but joined. The greatest poet forms the consistence of what is to be from what has been and is. He drags the dead out of their coffins and stands them again on their feet . . . . he says to the past, Rise and walk before me that I may realize you. He learns the lesson . . . . he places himself where the future becomes present. The greatest poet does not only dazzle his rays over character and scenes and passions . . . he finally ascends and finishes all . . . he exhibits the pinnacles that no man can tell what they are for or what is beyond . . . . he glows a moment on the extremest verge. He is most wonderful in his last half-hidden smile or frown . . . by that flash of the moment of parting the one that sees it shall be encouraged or terrified afterward for many years. The greatest poet does not moralize or make applications of morals . . . he knows the soul. The soul has that measureless pride which consists in never acknowledging any lessons but its own. But it has sympathy as measureless as its pride and the one balances the other and neither can stretch too far while it stretches in company with the other. The inmost secrets of art sleep with the twain. The greatest poet has lain close betwixt both and they are vital in his style and thoughts.

The art of art, the glory of expression and the sunshine of the light of letters is simplicity. Nothing is better than simplicity . . . . nothing can make up for excess or for the lack of definiteness. To carry on the heave of impulse and pierce intellectual depths and give all subjects their articulations are powers neither common nor very uncommon. But to speak in literature with the perfect rectitude and insousiance of the movements of animals and the unimpeachableness of the sentiment of trees in the woods and grass by the roadside is the flawless triumph of art. If you have looked on him who has achieved it you have looked on one of the masters of the artists of all nations and times. You shall not contemplate the flight of the graygull over the bay or the mettlesome action of the blood horse or the tall leaning of sunflowers on their stalk or the appearance of the sun journeying through heaven or the appearance of the moon afterward with any more satisfaction than you shall contemplate him. The greatest poet has less a marked style and is more the channel of thoughts and things without increase or diminution, and is the free channel of himself. He swears to his art, I will not be meddlesome, I will not have in my writing any elegance or effect or originality to hang in the way between me and the rest like curtains. I will have nothing hang in the way, not the richest curtains. What I tell I tell for precisely what it is. Let who may exalt or startle or fascinate or sooth I will have purposes as health or heat or snow has and be as regardless of observation. What I experience or portray shall go from my composition without a shred of my composition. You shall stand by my side and look in the mirror with me.

The old red blood and stainless gentility of great poets will be proved by their unconstraint. A heroic person walks at his ease through and out of that custom or precedent or authority that suits him not. Of the traits of the brotherhood of writers savans[8] musicians inventors and artists nothing is finer than silent defiance advancing from new free forms. In the need of poems philosophy politics mechanism science behaviour, the craft of art, an appropriate native grand-opera, shipcraft, or any craft, he is greatest forever and forever who contributes the greatest original practical example. The cleanest expression is that which finds no sphere worthy of itself and makes one.

The messages of great poets to each man and woman are, Come to us on equal terms, Only then can you understand us, We are no better than you, What we enclose you enclose, What we enjoy you may enjoy. Did you suppose there could be only one Supreme? We affirm there can be unnumbered Supremes, and that one does not countervail another any more than one eyesight countervails another . . and that men can be good or grand only of the consciousness of their supremacy within them. What do you think is the grandeur of storms and dismemberments and the deadliest battles and wrecks and the wildest fury of the elements and the power of the sea and the motion of nature and of the throes of human desires and dignity and hate and love? It is that something in the soul which says, Rage on, Whirl on, I tread master here and everywhere, Master of the spasms of the sky and of the shatter of the sea, Master of nature and passion and death, And of all terror and all pain.

The American bards shall be marked for generosity and affection and for encouraging competitors . . They shall be kosmos . . without monopoly or secrecy . . glad to pass any thing to any one . . . hungry for equals night and day. They shall not be careful of riches and privilege . . . . they shall be riches and privilege . . . . they shall perceive who the most affluent man is. The most affluent man is he that confronts all the shows he sees by equivalents out of the stronger wealth of himself. The American bard shall delineate no class of persons nor one or two out of the strata of interests nor love most nor truth most nor the soul most nor the body most . . . . and not be for the eastern states more than the western or the northern states more than the southern.

Exact science and its practical movements are no checks on the greatest poet but always his encouragement and support. The outset and remembrance are there . . there the arms that lifted him first and brace him best . . . . there he returns after all his goings and comings. The sailor and traveler . . the anatomist chemist astronomer geologist phrenologist spiritualist mathematician historian and lexicographer are not poets, but they are the lawgivers of poets and their construction underlies the structure of every perfect poem. No matter what rises or is uttered they sent the seed of the conception of it . . . of them and by them stand the visible proofs of souls . . . . . always of their fatherstuff must be begotten the sinewy races of bards. If there shall be love and content between the father and the son and if the greatness of the son is the exuding of the greatness of the father there shall be love between the poet and the man of demonstrable science. In the beauty of poems are the tuft and final applause of science.

Great is the faith of the flush of knowledge and of the investigation of the depths of qualities and things. Cleaving and circling here swells the soul of the poet yet is president of itself always. The depths are fathomless and

8. Learned persons, scientists.

therefore calm. The innocence and nakedness are resumed . . . they are neither modest nor immodest. The whole theory of the special and supernatural and all that was twined with it or educed out of it departs as a dream. What has ever happened . . . . what happens and whatever may or shall happen, the vital laws enclose all . . . . they are sufficient for any case and for all cases . . . none to be hurried or retarded . . . . any miracle of affairs or persons inadmissible in the vast clear scheme where every motion and every spear of grass and the frames and spirits of men and women and all that concerns them are unspeakably perfect miracles all referring to all and each distinct and in its place. It is also not consistent with the reality of the soul to admit that there is anything in the known universe more divine than men and women.

Men and women and the earth and all upon it are simply to be taken as they are, and the investigation of their past and present and future shall be unintermitted and shall be done with perfect candor. Upon this basis philosophy speculates ever looking toward the poet, ever regarding the eternal tendencies of all toward happiness never inconsistent with what is clear to the senses and to the soul. For the eternal tendencies of all toward happiness make the only point of sane philosophy. Whatever comprehends less than that . . . whatever is less than the laws of light and of astronomical motion . . . or less than the laws that follow the thief the liar the glutton and the drunkard through this life and doubtless afterward . . . . . . or less than vast stretches of time or the slow formation of density or the patient upheaving of strata—is of no account. Whatever would put God in a poem or system of philosophy as contending against some being or influence is also of no account. Sanity and ensemble characterise the great master . . . spoilt in one principle all is spoilt. The great master has nothing to do with miracles. He sees health for himself in being one of the mass . . . . he sees the hiatus in singular eminence. To the perfect shape comes common ground. To be under the general law is great for that is to correspond with it. The master knows that he is unspeakably great and that all are unspeakably great . . . . that nothing for instance is greater than to conceive children and bring them up well . . . that to be is just as great as to perceive or tell.

In the make of the great masters the idea of political liberty is indispensible. Liberty takes the adherence of heroes wherever men and women exist . . . . but never takes any adherence or welcome from the rest more than from poets. They are the voice and exposition of liberty. They out of ages are worthy the grand idea . . . . to them it is confided and they must sustain it. Nothing has precedence of it and nothing can warp or degrade it. The attitude of great poets is to cheer up slaves and horrify despots. The turn of their necks, the sound of their feet, the motions of their wrists, are full of hazard to the one and hope to the other. Come nigh them awhile and though they neither speak or advise you shall learn the faithful American lesson. Liberty is poorly served by men whose good intent is quelled from one failure or two failures or any number of failures, or from the casual indifference or ingratitude of the people, or from the sharp show of the tushes of power, or the bringing to bear soldiers and cannon or any penal statutes. Liberty relies upon itself, invites no one, promises nothing, sits in calmness and light, is positive and composed, and knows no discouragement. The battle rages with many a loud alarm and frequent advance and retreat . . . . the enemy triumphs . . . . the prison, the handcuffs, the iron necklace and anklet, the scaffold, garrote and leadballs do their work . . . . the cause is asleep . . . . the strong throats are choked with their own blood . . . . the young men drop their eyelashes toward the ground when they pass each other . . . . and is liberty gone out of that place? No never. When liberty goes it is not the first to go nor the second or third to go . . it waits for all the rest to go . . it is the last. . . When the memories of the old martyrs are faded utterly away . . . . when the large names of patriots are laughed at in the public halls from the lips of the orators . . . . when the boys are no more christened after the same but christened after tyrants and traitors instead . . . . when the laws of the free are grudgingly permitted and laws for informers and bloodmoney are sweet to the taste of the people . . . . when I and you walk abroad upon the earth stung with compassion at the sight of numberless brothers answering our equal friendship and calling no man master—and when we are elated with noble joy at the sight of slaves . . . . when the soul retires in the cool communion of the night and surveys its experience and has much extasy over the word and deed that put back a helpless innocent person into the gripe of the gripers or into any cruel inferiority . . . . when those in all parts of these states who could easier realize the true American character but do not yet—when the swarms of cringers, suckers, doughfaces,[9] lice of politics, planners of sly involutions for their own preferment to city offices or state legislatures of the judiciary or congress or the presidency, obtain a response of love and natural deference from the people whether they get the offices or no . . . . when it is better to be a bound booby and rogue in office at a high salary than the poorest free mechanic or farmer with his hat unmoved from his head and firm eyes and a candid and generous heart . . . . and when servility by town or state or the federal government or any oppression on a large scale or small scale can be tried on without its own punishment following duly after in exact proportion against the smallest chance of escape . . . . or rather when all life and all the souls of men and women are discharged from any part of the earth—then only shall the instinct of liberty be discharged from that part of the earth.

As the attributes of the poets of the kosmos concentre in the real body and soul and in the pleasure of things they possess the superiority of genuineness over all fiction and romance. As they emit themselves facts are showered over with light . . . . the daylight is lit with more volatile light . . . . also the deep between the setting and rising sun goes deeper many fold. Each precise object or condition or combination or process exhibits a beauty . . . . the multiplication table its—old age its—the carpenter's trade its—the grand-opera its . . . . the hugehulled cleanshaped New-York clipper at sea under steam or full sail gleams with unmatched beauty . . . . the American circles and large harmonies of government gleam with theirs . . . . and the commonest definite intentions and actions with theirs. The poets of the kosmos advance through all interpositions and coverings and turmoils and strategems to first principles. They are of use . . . . they dissolve poverty from its need and riches from its conceit. You large proprietor they say shall not realize or perceive more than any one else. The owner of the library is not he who holds a legal title to it having bought and paid for it. Any one and every one is owner of the library who can read the same through all the varieties of tongues and subjects and styles, and in whom they enter with ease and take residence and force

9. Pliable politicians. The term was used at the time to refer to Northern politicians who supported Southern proslavery policies.

toward paternity and maternity, and make supple and powerful and rich and large. . . . . These American states strong and healthy and accomplished shall receive no pleasure from violations of natural models and must not permit them. In paintings or mouldings or carvings in mineral or wood, or in the illustrations of books or newspapers, or in any comic or tragic prints, or in the patterns of woven stuffs or any thing to beautify rooms or furniture or costumes, or to put upon cornices or monuments or on the prows or sterns of ships, or to put anywhere before the human eye indoors or out, that which distorts honest shapes or which creates unearthly beings or places or contingencies is a nuisance and revolt. Of the human form especially it is so great it must never be made ridiculous. Of ornaments to a work nothing outre[1] can be allowed . . but those ornaments can be allowed that conform to the perfect facts of the open air and that flow out of the nature of the work and come irrepressibly from it and are necessary to the completion of the work. Most works are most beautiful without ornament . . . Exaggerations will be revenged in human physiology. Clean and vigorous children are jetted and conceived only in those communities where the models of natural forms are public every day. . . . . Great genius and the people of these states must never be demeaned to romances. As soon as histories are properly told there is no more need of romances.

The great poets are also to be known by the absence in them of tricks and by the justification of perfect personal candor. Then folks echo a new cheap joy and a divine voice leaping from their brains: How beautiful is candor! All faults may be forgiven of him who has perfect candor. Henceforth let no man of us lie, for we have seen that openness wins the inner and outer world and that there is no single exception, and that never since our earth gathered itself in a mass have deceit or subterfuge or prevarication attracted its smallest particle or the faintest tinge of a shade—and that through the enveloping wealth and rank of a state or the whole republic of states a sneak or sly person shall be discovered and despised . . . . and that the soul has never been once fooled and never can be fooled . . . . and thrift without the loving nod of the soul is only a fœtid puff . . . . and there never grew up in any of the continents of the globe nor upon any planet or satellite or star, nor upon the asteroids, nor in any part of ethereal space, nor in the midst of density, nor under the fluid wet of the sea, nor in that condition which precedes the birth of babes, nor at any time during the changes of life, nor in that condition that follows what we term death, nor in any stretch of abeyance or action afterward of vitality, nor in any process of formation or reformation anywhere, a being whose instinct hated the truth.

Extreme caution or prudence, the soundest organic health, large hope and comparison and fondness for women and children, large alimentiveness[2] and destructiveness and causality, with a perfect sense of the oneness of nature and the propriety of the same spirit applied to human affairs . . these are called up of the float of the brain of the world to be parts of the greatest poet from his birth out of his mother's womb and from her birth out of her mother's. Caution seldom goes far enough. It has been thought that the prudent citizen was the citizen who applied himself to solid gains and did well for himself and his family and completed a lawful life without debt or crime. The greatest poet sees

1. Excessive, extravagant; from the French *outré* (outrageous).

2. Love of food.

and admits these economies as he sees the economies of food and sleep, but has higher notions of prudence than to think he gives much when he gives a few slight attentions at the latch of the gate. The premises of the prudence of life are not the hospitality of it or the ripeness and harvest of it. Beyond the independence of a little sum laid aside for burial-money, and of a few clapboards around and shingles overhead on a lot of American soil owned, and the easy dollars that supply the year's plain clothing and meals, the melancholy prudence of the abandonment of such a great being as a man is to the toss and pallor of years of moneymaking with all their scorching days and icy nights and all their stifling deceits and underhanded dodgings, or infinitessimals of parlors, or shameless stuffing while others starve . . and all the loss of the bloom and odor of the earth and of the flowers and atmosphere and of the sea and of the true taste of the women and men you pass or have to do with in youth or middle age, and the issuing sickness and desperate revolt at the close of a life without elevation or naivete, and the ghastly chatter of a death without serenity or majesty, is the great fraud upon modern civilization and forethought, blotching the surface and system which civilization undeniably drafts, and moistening with tears the immense features it spreads and spreads with such velocity before the reached kisses of the soul . . . Still the right explanation remains to be made about prudence. The prudence of the mere wealth and respectability of the most esteemed life appears too faint for the eye to observe at all when little and large alike drop quietly aside at the thought of the prudence suitable for immortality. What is wisdom that fills the thinness of a year or seventy or eighty years to wisdom spaced out by ages and coming back at a certain time with strong reinforcements and rich presents and the clear faces of wedding-guests as far as you can look in every direction running gaily toward you? Only the soul is of itself . . . . all else has reference to what ensues. All that a person does or thinks is of consequence. Not a move can a man or woman make that affects him or her in a day or a month or any part of the direct lifetime or the hour of death but the same affects him or her onward afterward through the indirect lifetime. The indirect is always as great and real as the direct. The spirit receives from the body just as much as it gives to the body. Not one name of word or deed . . not of venereal sores or discolorations . . not the privacy of the onanist[3] . . not of the putrid veins of gluttons or rumdrinkers . . . not peculation or cunning or betrayal or murder . . no serpentine poison of those that seduce women . . not the foolish yielding of women . . not prostitution . . not of any depravity of young men . . not of the attainment of gain by discreditable means . . not any nastiness of appetite . . not any harshness of officers to men or judges to prisoners or fathers to sons or sons to fathers or of husbands to wives or bosses to their boys . . not of greedy looks or malignant wishes . . . nor any of the wiles practised by people upon themselves . . . ever is or ever can be stamped on the programme but it is duly realized and returned, and that returned in further performances . . . and they returned again. Nor can the push of charity or personal force ever be any thing else than the profoundest reason, whether it brings arguments to hand or no. No specification is necessary . . to add or subtract or divide is in vain. Little or big, learned or unlearned, white or black, legal or illegal, sick or well, from the first inspiration down the windpipe to the last expiration out of it, all that a male or female does that is vigorous and benevolent and clean is so much sure profit to him or her in the

---

3. Masturbator; from Onan, son of Judah, who "spilled it [his "seed"] on the ground" (Genesis 38.9).

unshakable order of the universe and through the whole scope of it forever. If the savage or felon is wise it is well . . . . if the greatest poet or savan is wise it is simply the same . . if the President or chief justice is wise it is the same . . . if the young mechanic or farmer is wise it is no more or less . . if the prostitute is wise it is no more nor less. The interest will come round . . all will come round. All the best actions of war and peace . . . all help given to relatives and strangers and the poor and old and sorrowful and young children and widows and the sick, and to all shunned persons . . all furtherance of fugitives and of the escape of slaves . . all the self-denial that stood steady and aloof on wrecks and saw others take the seats of the boats . . . all offering of substance or life for the good old cause, or for a friend's sake or opinion's sake . . . all pains of enthusiasts scoffed at by their neighbors . . all the vast sweet love and precious suffering of mothers . . . all honest men baffled in strifes recorded or unrecorded . . . . all the grandeur and good of the few ancient nations whose fragments of annals we inherit . . and all the good of the hundreds of far mightier and more ancient nations unknown to us by name or date or location . . . . all that was ever manfully begun, whether it succeeded or no . . . . all that has at any time been well suggested out of the divine heart of man or by the divinity of his mouth or by the shaping of his great hands . . and all that is well thought or done this day on any part of the surface of the globe . . or on any of the wandering stars or fixed stars by those there as we are here . . or that is henceforth to be well thought or done by you whoever you are, or by any one—these singly and wholly inured at their time and inure now and will inure always to the identities from which they sprung or shall spring. . . Did you guess any of them lived only its moment? The world does not so exist . . no parts palpable or impalpable so exist . . . no result exists now without being from its long antecedent result, and that from its antecedent, and so backward without the farthest mentionable spot coming a bit nearer the beginning than any other spot. . . . . Whatever satisfies the soul is truth. The prudence of the greatest poet answers at last the craving and glut of the soul, is not contemptuous of less ways of prudence if they conform to its ways, puts off nothing, permits no let-up for its own case or any case, has no particular sabbath or judgment-day, divides not the living from the dead or the righteous from the unrighteous, is satisfied with the present, matches every thought or act by its correlative, knows no possible forgiveness or deputed atonement . . knows that the young man who composedly periled his life and lost it has done exceeding well for himself, while the man who has not periled his life and retains it to old age in riches and ease has perhaps achieved nothing for himself worth mentioning . . and that only that person has no great prudence to learn who has learnt to prefer real longlived things, and favors body and soul the same, and perceives the indirect assuredly following the direct, and what evil or good he does leaping onward and waiting to meet him again—and who in his spirit in any emergency whatever neither hurries or avoids death.

The direct trial of him who would be the greatest poet is today. If he does not flood himself with the immediate age as with vast oceanic tides . . . . . and if he does not attract his own land body and soul to himself and hang on its neck with incomparable love and plunge his semitic[4] muscle into its merits and demerits . . . and if he be not himself the age transfigured . . . . and if to him is not opened the eternity which gives similitude to all periods and

---

4. A coinage for penis, derived from the Latin *semen* (seed).

locations and processes and animate and inanimate forms, and which is the bond of time, and rises up from its inconceivable vagueness and infiniteness in the swimming shape of today, and is held by the ductile anchors of life, and makes the present spot the passage from what was to what shall be, and commits itself to the representation of this wave of an hour and this one of the sixty beautiful children of the wave—let him merge in the general run and wait his development. . . . . Still the final test of poems or any character or work remains. The prescient poet projects himself centuries ahead and judges performer or performance after the changes of time. Does it live through them? Does it still hold on untired? Will the same style and the direction of genius to similar points be satisfactory now? Has no new discovery in science or arrival at superior planes of thought and judgment and behaviour fixed him or his so that either can be looked down upon? Have the marches of tens and hundreds and thousands of years made willing detours to the right hand and the left hand for his sake? Is he beloved long and long after he is buried? Does the young man think often of him? and the young woman think often of him? and do the middleaged and the old think of him?

A great poem is for ages and ages in common and for all degrees and complexions and all departments and sects and for a woman as much as a man and a man as much as a woman. A great poem is no finish to a man or woman but rather a beginning. Has any one fancied he could sit at last under some due authority and rest satisfied with explanations and realize and be content and full? To no such terminus does the greatest poet bring . . . he brings neither cessation or sheltered fatness and ease. The touch of him tells in action. Whom he takes he takes with firm sure grasp into live regions previously unattained . . . . thenceforward is no rest . . . . they see the space and ineffable sheen that turn the old spots and lights into dead vacuums. The companion of him beholds the birth and progress of stars and learns one of the meanings. Now there shall be a man cohered out of tumult and chaos . . . . the elder encourages the younger and shows him how . . . they two shall launch off fearlessly together till the new world fits an orbit for itself and looks unabashed on the lesser orbits of the stars and sweeps through the ceaseless rings and shall never be quiet again.

There will soon be no more priests. Their work is done. They may wait awhile . . perhaps a generation or two . . dropping off by degrees. A superior breed shall take their place . . . . the gangs of kosmos and prophets en masse shall take their place. A new order shall arise and they shall be the priests of man, and every man shall be his own priest. The churches built under their umbrage[5] shall be the churches of men and women. Through the divinity of themselves shall the kosmos and the new breed of poets be interpreters of men and women and of all events and things. They shall find their inspiration in real objects today, symptoms of the past and future . . . . They shall not deign to defend immortality or God or the perfection of things or liberty or the exquisite beauty and reality of the soul. They shall arise in America and be responded to from the remainder of the earth.

The English language befriends the grand American expression . . . . it is brawny enough and limber and full enough. On the tough stock of a race who through all change of circumstance was never without the idea of political liberty, which is the animus of all liberty, it has attracted the terms of daintier and

5. Shadow, protection.

gayer and subtler and more elegant tongues. It is the powerful language of resistance . . . it is the dialect of common sense. It is the speech of the proud and melancholy races and of all who aspire. It is the chosen tongue to express growth faith self-esteem freedom justice equality friendliness amplitude prudence decision and courage. It is the medium that shall well nigh express the inexpressible.

No great literature nor any like style of behaviour or oratory or social intercourse or household arrangements or public institutions or the treatment by bosses of employed people, nor executive detail or detail of the army or navy, nor spirit of legislation or courts or police or tuition or architecture or songs or amusements or the costumes of young men, can long elude the jealous and passionate instinct of American standards. Whether or no the sign appears from the mouths of the people, it throbs a live interrogation in every freeman's and freewoman's heart after that which passes by or this built to remain. Is it uniform with my country? Are its disposals without ignominious distinctions? Is it for the evergrowing communes of brothers and lovers, large, well-united, proud beyond the old models, generous beyond all models? Is it something grown fresh out of the fields or drawn from the sea for use to me today here? I know that what answers for me an American must answer for any individual or nation that serves for a part of my materials. Does this answer? or is it without reference to universal needs? or sprung of the needs of the less developed society of special ranks? or old needs of pleasure overlaid by modern science and forms? Does this acknowledge liberty with audible and absolute acknowledgement, and set slavery at nought for life and death? Will it help breed one goodshaped and wellhung man, and a woman to be his perfect and independent mate? Does it improve manners? Is it for the nursing of the young of the republic? Does it solve[6] readily with the sweet milk of the nipples of the breasts of the mother of many children? Has it too the old ever-fresh forbearance and impartiality? Does it look with the same love on the last born on those hardening toward stature, and on the errant, and on those who disdain all strength of assault outside of their own?

The poems distilled from other poems will probably pass away. The coward will surely pass away. The expectation of the vital and great can only be satisfied by the demeanor of the vital and great. The swarms of the polished deprecating and reflectors and the polite float off and leave no remembrance. America prepares with composure and goodwill for the visitors that have sent word. It is not intellect that is to be their warrant and welcome. The talented, the artist, the ingenious, the editor, the statesman, the erudite . . they are not unappreciated . . they fall in their place and do their work. The soul of the nation also does its work. No disguise can pass on it . . no disguise can conceal from it. It rejects none, it permits all. Only toward as good as itself and toward the like of itself will it advance half-way. An individual is as superb as a nation when he has the qualities which make a superb nation. The soul of the largest and wealthiest and proudest nation may well go half-way to meet that of its poets. The signs are effectual. There is no fear of mistake. If the one is true the other is true. The proof of a poet is that his country absorbs him as affectionately as he has absorbed it.

1855

6. Dissolve.

FROM INSCRIPTIONS[1]

One's-Self I Sing

One's-Self I sing, a simple separate person,
Yet utter the word Democratic, the word En-Masse.

Of physiology from top to toe I sing,
Not physiognomy[2] alone nor brain alone is worthy for the Muse, I
    say the Form complete is worthier far,
The Female equally with the Male I sing.   5

Of Life immense in passion, pulse, and power,
Cheerful, for freest action form'd under the laws divine,
The Modern Man I sing.

                                                                1867, 1871

Shut Not Your Doors

Shut not your doors to me proud libraries,
For that which was lacking on all your well-fill'd shelves, yet
    needed most, I bring,
Forth from the war emerging, a book I have made,
The words of my book nothing, the drift of it every thing,
A book separate, not link'd with the rest nor felt by the intellect,   5
But you ye untold latencies will thrill to every page.

                                                                1865, 1881

————

Song of Myself[1]

1

I celebrate myself, and sing myself,
And what I assume you shall assume,
For every atom belonging to me as good belongs to you.

I loafe and invite my soul,
I lean and loafe at my ease observing a spear of summer grass.   5

1. This title was first used for the opening poems of *Leaves of Grass* in 1871; in 1881 the number of poems was increased from nine to twenty-four.
2. The practice of judging or interpreting human character from facial features.
1. In the 1855 first edition of *Leaves of Grass*, the poem later called "Song of Myself" appeared without a title and without numbered sections or stanzas. For the 1856 edition, Whitman titled it "Poem of Walt Whitman, an American," and in the 1860 edition he titled it "Walt Whitman"; it retained that title in the 1867 and 1871 editions, and in the 1881 edition was named "Song of Myself." Whitman made numerous other changes to the poem from the first 1855 printing to the 1881 final version.

My tongue, every atom of my blood, form'd from this soil, this air,
Born here of parents born here from parents the same, and their parents
    the same,
I, now thirty-seven years old in perfect health begin,
Hoping to cease not till death.

Creeds and schools in abeyance,   10
Retiring back a while sufficed at what they are, but never forgotten,
I harbor for good or bad, I permit to speak at every hazard,
Nature without check with original energy.

2

Houses and rooms are full of perfumes, the shelves are crowded with
    perfumes,
I breathe the fragrance myself and know it and like it,   15
The distillation would intoxicate me also, but I shall not let it.

The atmosphere is not a perfume, it has no taste of the distillation, it is
    odorless,
It is for my mouth forever, I am in love with it,
I will go to the bank by the wood and become undisguised and naked,
I am mad for it to be in contact with me.   20

The smoke of my own breath,
Echoes, ripples, buzz'd whispers, love-root, silk-thread, crotch and vine,
My respiration and inspiration, the beating of my heart, the passing of
    blood and air through my lungs,
The sniff of green leaves and dry leaves, and of the shore and dark-color'd
    sea-rocks, and of hay in the barn,
The sound of the belch'd words of my voice loos'd to the eddies of the
    wind,   25
A few light kisses, a few embraces, a reaching around of arms,
The play of shine and shade on the trees as the supple boughs wag,
The delight alone or in the rush of the streets, or along the fields and hill-
    sides,
The feeling of health, the full-noon trill, the song of me rising from bed
    and meeting the sun.

Have you reckon'd a thousand acres much? have you reckon'd the earth
    much?   30
Have you practis'd so long to learn to read?
Have you felt so proud to get at the meaning of poems?

Stop this day and night with me and you shall possess the origin of all
    poems,
You shall possess the good of the earth and sun, (there are millions of
    suns left,)
You shall no longer take things at second or third hand, nor look through
    the eyes of the dead, nor feed on the spectres in books,   35
You shall not look through my eyes either, nor take things from me,
You shall listen to all sides and filter them from your self.

3

I have heard what the talkers were talking, the talk of the beginning and
    the end,
But I do not talk of the beginning or the end.

There was never any more inception than there is now,   40
Nor any more youth or age than there is now,
And will never be any more perfection than there is now,
Nor any more heaven or hell than there is now.

Urge and urge and urge,
Always the procreant urge of the world.   45

Out of the dimness opposite equals advance, always substance and
    increase, always sex,
Always a knit of identity, always distinction, always a breed of life.

To elaborate is no avail, learn'd and unlearn'd feel that it is so.

Sure as the most certain sure, plumb in the uprights, well entretied,[2]
    braced in the beams,
Stout as a horse, affectionate, haughty, electrical,   50
I and this mystery here we stand.

Clear and sweet is my soul, and clear and sweet is all that is not my soul.

Lack one lacks both, and the unseen is proved by the seen,
Till that becomes unseen and receives proof in its turn.

Showing the best and dividing it from the worst age vexes age,   55
Knowing the perfect fitness and equanimity of things, while they discuss
    I am silent, and go bathe and admire myself.

Welcome is every organ and attribute of me, and of any man hearty and
    clean,
Not an inch nor a particle of an inch is vile, and none shall be less familiar
    than the rest.

I am satisfied—I see, dance, laugh, sing;
As the hugging and loving bed-fellow sleeps at my side through the night,
    and withdraws at the peep of the day with stealthy tread,   60
Leaving me baskets cover'd with white towels swelling the house with
    their plenty,
Shall I postpone my acceptation and realization and scream at my eyes,
That they turn from gazing after and down the road,
And forthwith cipher[3] and show me to a cent,
Exactly the value of one and exactly the value of two, and which is
    ahead?   65

---

2. Cross-braced; reinforced.   3. Calculate.

4

Trippers and askers surround me,
People I meet, the effect upon me of my early life or the ward and city I
    live in, or the nation,
The latest dates, discoveries, inventions, societies, authors old and new,
My dinner, dress, associates, looks, compliments, dues,
The real or fancied indifference of some man or woman I love,   70
The sickness of one of my folks or of myself, or ill-doing or loss or lack
    of money, or depressions or exaltations,
Battles, the horrors of fratricidal war, the fever of doubtful news, the fitful
    events;
These come to me days and nights and go from me again,
But they are not the Me myself.

Apart from the pulling and hauling stands what I am,   75
Stands amused, complacent, compassionating, idle, unitary,
Looks down, is erect, or bends an arm on an impalpable certain rest,
Looking with side-curved head curious what will come next,
Both in and out of the game and watching and wondering at it.

Backward I see in my own days where I sweated through fog with
    linguists and contenders,   80
I have no mockings or arguments, I witness and wait.

5

I believe in you my soul, the other I am must not abase itself to you,
And you must not be abased to the other.

Loafe with me on the grass, loose the stop from your throat,
Not words, not music or rhyme I want, not custom or lecture, not even
    the best,   85
Only the lull I like, the hum of your valvèd voice.

I mind how once we lay such a transparent summer morning,
How you settled your head athwart my hips and gently turn'd over upon
    me,
And parted the shirt from my bosom-bone, and plunged your tongue to
    my bare-stript heart,
And reach'd till you felt my beard, and reach'd till you held my feet.   90

Swiftly arose and spread around me the peace and knowledge that pass
    all the argument of the earth,
And I know that the hand of God is the promise of my own,
And I know that the spirit of God is the brother of my own,
And that all the men ever born are also my brothers, and the women my
    sisters and lovers,
And that a kelson[4] of the creation is love,   95

---

4. A basic structural unit; a reinforcing timber bolted to the keel (backbone) of a ship.

And limitless are leaves stiff or drooping in the fields,
And brown ants in the little wells beneath them,
And mossy scabs of the worm fence,[5] heap'd stones, elder, mullein and
    poke-weed.

6

A child said *What is the grass?* fetching it to me with full hands;
How could I answer the child? I do not know what it is any more than
    he.   100

I guess it must be the flag of my disposition, out of hopeful green stuff
    woven.

Or I guess it is the handkerchief of the Lord,
A scented gift and remembrancer designedly dropt,
Bearing the owner's name someway in the corners, that we may see and
    remark, and say *Whose?*

Or I guess the grass is itself a child, the produced babe of the vegetation. 105

Or I guess it is a uniform hieroglyphic,
And it means, Sprouting alike in broad zones and narrow zones,
Growing among black folks as among white,
Kanuck, Tuckahoe, Congressman, Cuff,[6] I give them the same, I receive
    them the same.

And now it seems to me the beautiful uncut hair of graves.   110

Tenderly will I use you curling grass,
It may be you transpire from the breasts of young men,
It may be if I had known them I would have loved them,
It may be you are from old people, or from offspring taken soon out of
    their mothers' laps,
And here you are the mothers' laps.   115

This grass is very dark to be from the white heads of old mothers,
Darker than the colorless beards of old men,
Dark to come from under the faint red roofs of mouths.

O I perceive after all so many uttering tongues,
And I perceive they do not come from the roofs of mouths for nothing.   120

I wish I could translate the hints about the dead young men and women,
And the hints about old men and mothers, and the offspring taken soon
    out of their laps.

---

5. Fence built of interlocking rails in a zigzag
pattern.
6. From the African word *cuffee* (name for
black male born on a Friday). "Kanuck": French
Canadian (now sometimes considered pejorative).
"Tuckahoe": Virginian, from eaters of the
American Indian food plant tuckahoe.

What do you think has become of the young and old men?
And what do you think has become of the women and children?

They are alive and well somewhere,   125
The smallest sprout shows there is really no death,
And if ever there was it led forward life, and does not wait at the end to
    arrest it,
And ceas'd the moment life appear'd.

All goes onward and outward, nothing collapses,
And to die is different from what any one supposed, and luckier.   130

7

Has any one supposed it lucky to be born?
I hasten to inform him or her it is just as lucky to die, and I know it.

I pass death with the dying and birth with the new-wash'd babe, and
    am not contain'd between my hat and boots,
And peruse manifold objects, no two alike and every one good,
The earth good and the stars good, and their adjuncts all good.   135

I am not an earth nor an adjunct of an earth,
I am the mate and companion of people, all just as immortal and
    fathomless as myself,
(They do not know how immortal, but I know.)

Every kind for itself and its own, for me mine male and female,
For me those that have been boys and that love women,   140
For me the man that is proud and feels how it stings to be slighted,
For me the sweet-heart and the old maid, for me mothers and the mothers
    of mothers,
For me lips that have smiled, eyes that have shed tears,
For me children and the begetters of children.

Undrape! you are not guilty to me, nor stale nor discarded,   145
I see through the broadcloth and gingham whether or no,
And am around, tenacious, acquisitive, tireless, and cannot be shaken
    away.

8

The little one sleeps in its cradle,
I lift the gauze and look a long time, and silently brush away flies with
    my hand.

The youngster and the red-faced girl turn aside up the bushy hill,   150
I peeringly view them from the top.

The suicide sprawls on the bloody floor of the bedroom,
I witness the corpse with its dabbled hair, I note where the pistol has
    fallen.

The blab of the pave, tires of carts, sluff of boot-soles, talk of the
    promenaders,
The heavy omnibus, the driver with his interrogating thumb, the clank
    of the shod horses on the granite floor,   155
The snow-sleighs, clinking, shouted jokes, pelts of snow-balls,
The hurrahs for popular favorites, the fury of rous'd mobs,
The flap of the curtain'd litter, a sick man inside borne to the hospital,
The meeting of enemies, the sudden oath, the blows and fall,
The excited crowd, the policeman with his star quickly working his
    passage to the centre of the crowd,   160
The impassive stones that receive and return so many echoes,
What groans of over-fed or half-starv'd who fall sunstruck or in fits,
What exclamations of women taken suddenly who hurry home and
    give birth to babes,
What living and buried speech is always vibrating here, what howls
    restrain'd by decorum,
Arrests of criminals, slights, adulterous offers made, acceptances,
    rejections with convex lips,   165
I mind them or the show or resonance of them—I come and I depart.

9

The big doors of the country barn stand open and ready,
The dried grass of the harvest-time loads the slow-drawn wagon,
The clear light plays on the brown gray and green intertinged,
The armfuls are pack'd to the sagging mow.   170

I am there, I help, I came stretch'd atop of the load,
I felt its soft jolts, one leg reclined on the other,
I jump from the cross-beams and sieze the clover and timothy,
And roll head over heels and tangle my hair full of wisps.

10

Alone far in the wilds and mountains I hunt,   175
Wandering amazed at my own lightness and glee,
In the late afternoon choosing a safe spot to pass the night,
Kindling a fire and broiling the fresh-kill'd game,
Falling asleep on the gather'd leaves with my dog and gun by my side.

The Yankee clipper is under her sky-sails, she cuts the sparkle and scud, 180
My eyes settle the land, I bend at her prow or shout joyously from the deck.

The boatmen and clam-diggers arose early and stopt for me,
I tuck'd my trowser-ends in my boots and went and had a good time;
You should have been with us that day round the chowder-kettle.

I saw the marriage of the trapper in the open air in the far west, the bride
    was a red girl,   185
Her father and his friends sat near cross-legged and dumbly smoking,
        they had moccasins to their feet and large thick blankets hanging from
        their shoulders,

On a bank lounged the trapper, he was drest mostly in skins, his luxuriant
    beard and curls protected his neck, he held his bride by the hand,
She had long eyelashes, her head was bare, her coarse straight locks
    descended upon her voluptuous limbs and reach'd to her feet.

The runaway slave came to my house and stopt outside,
I heard his motions crackling the twigs of the woodpile,   190
Through the swung half-door of the kitchen I saw him limpsy[7] and weak,
And went where he sat on a log and led him in and assured him,
And brought water and fill'd a tub for his sweated body and bruis'd feet,
And gave him a room that enter'd from my own, and gave him some coarse
    clean clothes,
And remember perfectly well his revolving eyes and his awkwardness,   195
And remember putting plasters on the galls of his neck and ankles;
He staid with me a week before he was recuperated and pass'd north,
I had him sit next me at table, my fire-lock lean'd in the corner.

11

Twenty-eight young men bathe by the shore,
Twenty-eight young men and all so friendly;   200
Twenty-eight years of womanly life and all so lonesome.

She owns the fine house by the rise of the bank,
She hides handsome and richly drest aft the blinds of the window.

Which of the young men does she like the best?
Ah the homeliest of them is beautiful to her.   205

Where are you off to, lady? for I see you,
You splash in the water there, yet stay stock still in your room.

Dancing and laughing along the beach came the twenty-ninth bather,
The rest did not see her, but she saw them and loved them.

The beards of the young men glisten'd with wet, it ran from their long
    hair,
Little streams pass'd over their bodies.   210

An unseen hand also pass'd over their bodies,
It descended tremblingly from their temples and ribs.

The young men float on their backs, their white bellies bulge to the sun,
    they do not ask who seizes fast to them,
They do not know who puffs and declines with pendant and bending
    arch,   215
They do not think whom they souse with spray.

---

7. Limping or swaying.

12

The butcher-boy puts off his killing-clothes, or sharpens his knife
　　at the stall in the market,
I loiter enjoying his repartee and his shuffle and break-down.[8]

Blacksmiths with grimed and hairy chests environ the anvil,
Each has his main-sledge, they are all out, there is a great heat in the
　　fire.　　　　　　　　　　　　　　　　　　　　　　　　　　　　220

From the cinder-strew'd threshold I follow their movements,
The lithe sheer of their waists plays even with their massive arms,
Overhand the hammers swing, overhand so slow, overhand so sure,
They do not hasten, each man hits in his place.

13

The negro holds firmly the reins of his four horses, the block swags
　　underneath on its tied-over chain,　　　　　　　　　　　　　225
The negro that drives the long dray of the stone-yard, steady and tall he
　　stands pois'd on one leg on the string-piece,[9]
His blue shirt exposes his ample neck and breast and loosens over his hip-
　　band,
His glance is calm and commanding, he tosses the slouch of his hat away
　　from his forehead,
The sun falls on his crispy hair and mustache, falls on the black of his
　　polish'd and perfect limbs.

I behold the picturesque giant and love him, and I do not stop there,　230
I go with the team also.

In me the caresser of life wherever moving, backward as well as forward
　　sluing,[1]
To niches aside and junior[2] bending, not a person or object missing,
Absorbing all to myself and for this song.

Oxen that rattle the yoke and chain or halt in the leafy shade, what is
　　that you express in your eyes?　　　　　　　　　　　　　　235
It seems to me more than all the print I have read in my life.

My tread scares the wood-drake and wood-duck on my distant and
　　day-long ramble.
They rise together, they slowly circle around.

I believe in those wing'd purposes,
And acknowledge red, yellow, white, playing within me,　　　　　240
And consider green and violet and the tufted crown intentional,
And do not call the tortoise unworthy because she is not something else,

---

8. Dances familiar in popular entertainment
and minstrelsy. The "shuffle" involves the sliding
of feet across the floor, and the "break-down" is
faster and noisier.

9. Long, heavy timber used to keep a load in
place.
1. Twisting.
2. Smaller.

And the jay in the woods never studied the gamut,[3] yet trills pretty well
  to me,
And the look of the bay mare shames silliness out of me.

14

The wild gander leads his flock through the cool night,   245
Ya-honk he says, and sounds it down to me like an invitation,
The pert may suppose it meaningless, but I listening close,
Find its purpose and place up there toward the wintry sky.

The sharp-hoof'd moose of the north, the cat on the house-sill, the
  chickadee, the prairie-dog,
The litter of the grunting sow as they tug at her teats,   250
The brood of the turkey-hen and she with her half-spread wings,
I see in them and myself the same old law.

The press of my foot to the earth springs a hundred affections,
They scorn the best I can do to relate them.

I am enamour'd of growing out-doors,   255
Of men that live among cattle or taste of the ocean or woods,
Of the builders and steerers of ships and the wielders of axes and mauls,
  and the drivers of horses,
I can eat and sleep with them week in and week out.

What is commonest, cheapest, nearest, easiest, is Me,
Me going in for my chances, spending for vast returns,   260
Adorning myself to bestow myself on the first that will take me,
Not asking the sky to come down to my good will,
Scattering it freely forever.

15

The pure contralto sings in the organ loft,
The carpenter dresses his plank, the tongue of his foreplane whistles
  its wild ascending lisp,   265
The married and unmarried children ride home to their Thanksgiving
  dinner,
The pilot seizes the king-pin,[4] he heaves down with a strong arm,
The mate stands braced in the whale-boat, lance and harpoon are ready,
The duck-shooter walks by silent and cautious stretches,
The deacons are ordain'd with cross'd hands at the altar,   270
The spinning-girl retreats and advances to the hum of the big wheel,
The farmer stops by the bars as he walks on a First-day[5] loafe and looks
  at the oats and rye,
The lunatic is carried at last to the asylum a confirm'd case,
(He will never sleep any more as he did in the cot in his mother's
  bed-room;)

3. Notes of the musical scale.
4. The extended spoke of the pilot wheel, used
to maintain leverage during storms.

5. Sunday. Whitman frequently uses the numer-
ical Quaker designations for the names of days
and months. "Bars": i.e., of a rail fence.

The jour printer[6] with gray head and gaunt jaws works at his case, 275
He turns his quid of tobacco while his eyes blurr with the manuscript;
The malform'd limbs are tied to the surgeon's table,
What is removed drops horribly in a pail;
The quadroon[7] girl is sold at the auction-stand, the drunkard nods by the
 bar-room stove,
The machinist rolls up his sleeves, the policeman travels his beat, the
 gate-keeper marks who pass, 280
The young fellow drives the express-wagon, (I love him, though I do not
 know him;)
The half-breed straps on his light boots to compete in the race,
The western turkey-shooting draws old and young, some lean on their
 rifles, some sit on logs,
Out from the crowd steps the marksman, takes his position, levels his
 piece;
The groups of newly-come immigrants cover the wharf or levee, 285
As the woolly-pates[8] hoe in the sugar-field, the overseer views them
 from his saddle,
The bugle calls in the ball-room, the gentlemen run for their partners,
 the dancers bow to each other,
The youth lies awake in the cedar-roof'd garret and harks to the musical
 rain,
The Wolverine[9] sets traps on the creek that helps fill the Huron,
The squaw wrapt in her yellow-hemm'd cloth is offering moccasins and
 bead-bags for sale, 290
The connoisseur peers along the exhibition-gallery with half-shut eyes
 bent sideways,
As the deck-hands make fast the steamboat the plank is thrown for the
 shore-going passengers,
The young sister holds out the skein while the elder sister winds it off
 in a ball, and stops now and then for the knots,
The one-year wife is recovering and happy having a week ago borne her
 first child,
The clean-hair'd Yankee girl works with her sewing-machine or in the
 factory or mill, 295
The paving-man[1] leans on his two-handed rammer, the reporter's lead
 flies swiftly over the note-book, the sign-painter is lettering with blue
 and gold,
The canal boy trots on the tow-path, the book-keeper counts at his desk,
 the shoemaker waxes his thread,
The conductor beats time for the band and all the performers follow him,
The child is baptized, the convert is making his first professions,
The regatta is spread on the bay, the race is begun, (how the white sails
 sparkle!) 300
The drover watching his drove sings out to them that would stray,
The pedler sweats with his pack on his back, (the purchaser higgling
 about the odd cent;)

---

6. I.e., a journeyman printer, or one who has
passed an apprenticeship and is fully qualified
for all professional work.
7. Term used at the time (often in reference to
slaves) to refer to light-complected people thought

to be one-fourth black.
8. Black slaves (with stereotypical emphasis on
"woolly" hair).
9. Inhabitant of Michigan.
1. Man building or repairing streets.

The bride unrumples her white dress, the minute-hand of the clock
    moves slowly,
The opium-eater reclines with rigid head and just-open'd lips,
The prostitute draggles her shawl, her bonnet bobs on her tipsy and
    pimpled neck,   305
The crowd laugh at her blackguard oaths, the men jeer and wink to each
    other,
(Miserable! I do not laugh at your oaths nor jeer you;)
The President holding a cabinet council is surrounded by the great
    Secretaries,
On the piazza walk three matrons stately and friendly with twined arms,
The crew of the fish-smack pack repeated layers of halibut in the hold,   310
The Missourian crosses the plains toting his wares and his cattle,
As the fare-collector goes through the train he gives notice by the jingling
    of loose change,
The floor-men are laying the floor, the tinners are tinning the roof, the
    masons are calling for mortar,
In single file each shouldering his hod pass onward the laborers;
Seasons pursuing each other the indescribable crowd is gather'd, it is the
    fourth of Seventh-month,[2] (what salutes of cannon and small arms!) 315
Seasons pursuing each other the plougher ploughs, the mower mows,
    and the winter-grain falls in the ground;
Off on the lakes the pike-fisher watches and waits by the hole in the
    frozen surface,
The stumps stand thick round the clearing, the squatter strikes deep
    with his axe,
Flatboatmen make fast towards dusk near the cotton-wood or pecan-trees,
Coon-seekers go through the regions of the Red river or through those
    drain'd by the Tennessee, or through those of the Arkansas,   320
Torches shine in the dark that hangs on the Chattahooch or Altamahaw,[3]
Patriarchs sit at supper with sons and grandsons and great-grandsons
    around them,
In walls of adobie, in canvas tents, rest hunters and trappers after their
    day's sport,
The city sleeps and the country sleeps,
The living sleep for their time, the dead sleep for their time,   325
The old husband sleeps by his wife and the young husband sleeps by his
    wife;
And these tend inward to me, and I tend outward to them,
And such as it is to be of these more or less I am,
And of these one and all I weave the song of myself.

16

I am of old and young, of the foolish as much as the wise,   330
Regardless of others, ever regardful of others,
Maternal as well as paternal, a child as well as a man,
Stuff'd with the stuff that is coarse and stuff'd with the stuff that is fine,
One of the Nation of many nations, the smallest the same and the largest
    the same,

2. I.e., the Fourth of July.   3. Georgia rivers.

A Southerner soon as a Northerner, a planter nonchalant and hospitable
    down by the Oconee[4] I live,   335
A Yankee bound my own way ready for trade, my joints the limberest joints
    on earth and the sternest joints on earth,
A Kentuckian walking the vale of the Elkhorn[5] in my deer-skin leggings, a
    Louisianian or Georgian,
A boatman over lakes or bays or along coasts, a Hoosier, Badger, Buckeye;[6]
At home on Kanadian[7] snow-shoes or up in the bush, or with fishermen
    off Newfoundland,
At home in the fleet of ice-boats, sailing with the rest and tacking,   340
At home on the hills of Vermont or in the woods of Maine, or the Texan
    ranch,
Comrade of Californians, comrade of free North-Westerners, (loving their
    big proportions,)
Comrade of raftsmen and coalmen, comrade of all who shake hands and
    welcome to drink and meat,
A learner with the simplest, a teacher of the thoughtfullest,
A novice beginning yet experient of myriads of seasons,   345
Of every hue and caste am I, of every rank and religion,
A farmer, mechanic, artist, gentleman, sailor, quaker,
Prisoner, fancy-man, rowdy, lawyer, physician, priest.

I resist any thing better than my own diversity,
Breathe the air but leave plenty after me,   350
And am not stuck up, and am in my place.

(The moth and the fish-eggs are in their place,
The bright suns I see and the dark suns I cannot see are in their place,
The palpable is in its place and the impalpable is in its place.)

17

These are really the thoughts of all men in all ages and lands, they are
    not original with me,   355
If they are not yours as much as mine they are nothing, or next to
    nothing,
If they are not the riddle and the untying of the riddle they are nothing,
If they are not just as close as they are distant they are nothing.

This is the grass that grows wherever the land is and the water is,
This the common air that bathes the globe.   360

18

With music strong I come, with my cornets and my drums,
I play not marches for accepted victors only, I play marches for conquer'd
    and slain persons.

---

4. River in central Georgia.
5. River in Nebraska.

6. Inhabitants of Indiana, Wisconsin, and Ohio,
respectively.
7. Canadian.

Have you heard that it was good to gain the day?
I also say it is good to fall, battles are lost in the same spirit in which they
    are won.

I beat and pound for the dead,   365
I blow through my embouchures[8] my loudest and gayest for them.

Vivas to those who have fail'd!
And to those whose war-vessels sank in the sea!
And to those themselves who sank in the sea!
And to all generals that lost engagements, and all overcome heroes!   370
And the numberless unknown heroes equal to the greatest heroes known!

19

This is the meal equally set, this the meat for natural hunger,
It is for the wicked just the same as the righteous, I make appointments
    with all,
I will not have a single person slighted or left away,
The kept-woman, sponger, thief, are hereby invited,   375
The heavy-lipp'd slave is invited, the venerealee[9] is invited;
There shall be no difference between them and the rest.

This is the press of a bashful hand, this the float and odor of hair,
This is the touch of my lips to yours, this the murmur of yearning,
This the far-off depth and height reflecting my own face,   380
This the thoughtful merge of myself, and the outlet again.

Do you guess I have some intricate purpose?
Well I have, for the Fourth-month showers have, and the mica on the
    side of a rock has.

Do you take it I would astonish?
Does the daylight astonish? does the early redstart twittering through
    the woods?   385
Do I astonish more than they?

This hour I tell things in confidence,
I might not tell everybody, but I will tell you.

20

Who goes there? hankering, gross, mystical, nude;
How is it I extract strength from the beef I eat?   390

What is a man anyhow? what am I? what are you?

---

8. Mouthpieces of musical instruments such as
the cornet.

9. Someone afflicted with a venereal (sexually
transmitted) disease.

All I mark as my own you shall offset it with your own,
Else it were time lost listening to me.

I do not snivel that snivel the world over,
That months are vacuums and the ground but wallow and filth.   395

Whimpering and truckling fold with powders for invalids, conformity
    goes to the fourth-remov'd,[1]
I wear my hat as I please indoors or out.

Why should I pray? why should I venerate and be ceremonious?

Having pried through the strata, analyzed to a hair, counsel'd with
    doctors and calculated close,
I find no sweeter fat than sticks to my bones.   400

In all people I see myself, none more and not one a barley-corn[2] less,
And the good or bad I say of myself I say of them.

I know I am solid and sound,
To me the converging objects of the universe perpetually flow,
All are written to me, and I must get what the writing means.   405

I know I am deathless,
I know this orbit of mine cannot be swept by a carpenter's compass,
I know I shall not pass like a child's carlacue[3] cut with a burnt stick at
    night.

I know I am august,
I do not trouble my spirit to vindicate itself or be understood,   410
I see that the elementary laws never apologize,
(I reckon I behave no prouder than the level I plant my house by, after all.)

I exist as I am, that is enough,
If no other in the world be aware I sit content,
And if each and all be aware I sit content.   415

One world is aware and by far the largest to me, and that is myself,
And whether I come to my own to-day or in ten thousand or ten million
    years,
I can cheerfully take it now, or with equal cheerfulness I can wait.

My foothold is tenon'd and mortis'd[4] in granite,
I laugh at what you call dissolution,   420
And I know the amplitude of time.

---

1. Those remote in relationship, such as "third cousin, fourth removed." "Fold with powders": a reference to the custom of wrapping a dose of medicine in a piece of paper.
2. The seed or grain of barley, but also a unit of measure equal to about one-third of an inch.
3. Or *curlicue*, a fancy flourish made with a writing implement, here made in the dark with a lighted stick.
4. Here, mason's terms for a particular way of joining two stones together. A mortise is a cavity in a stone into which is placed the projection (tenon) from another stone.

21

I am the poet of the Body and I am the poet of the Soul,
The pleasures of heaven are with me and the pains of hell are with me,
The first I graft and increase upon myself, the latter I translate into a
    new tongue.

I am the poet of the woman the same as the man,   425
And I say it is as great to be a woman as to be a man,
And I say there is nothing greater than the mother of men.

I chant the chant of dilation or pride,
We have had ducking and deprecating about enough,
I show that size is only development.   430

Have you outstript the rest? are you the President?
It is a trifle, they will more than arrive there every one, and still pass on.

I am he that walks with the tender and growing night,
I call to the earth and sea half-held by the night.

Press close bare-bosom'd night—press close magnetic nourishing night! 435
Night of south winds—night of the large few stars!
Still nodding night—mad naked summer night.

Smile O voluptuous cool-breath'd earth!
Earth of the slumbering and liquid trees!
Earth of departed sunset—earth of the mountains misty-topt!   440
Earth of the vitreous pour of the full moon just tinged with blue!
Earth of shine and dark mottling the tide of the river!
Earth of the limpid gray of clouds brighter and clearer for my sake!
Far-swooping elbow'd earth—rich apple-blossom'd earth!
Smile, for your lover comes.   445

Prodigal, you have given me love—therefore I to you give love!
O unspeakable passionate love.

22

You sea! I resign myself to you also—I guess what you mean,
I behold from the beach your crooked inviting fingers,
I believe you refuse to go back without feeling of me,   450
We must have a turn together, I undress, hurry me out of sight of the
    land,
Cushion me soft, rock me in billowy drowse,
Dash me with amorous wet, I can repay you.

Sea of stretch'd ground-swells,
Sea breathing broad and convulsive breaths,   455
Sea of the brine of life and of unshovell'd yet always-ready graves,
Howler and scooper of storms, capricious and dainty sea,
I am integral with you, I too am of one phase and of all phases.

Partaker of influx and efflux I, extoller of hate and conciliation,
Extoller of amies[5] and those that sleep in each others' arms.　460

I am he attesting sympathy,
(Shall I make my list of things in the house and skip the house that
　　supports them?)

I am not the poet of goodness only, I do not decline to be the poet of
　　wickedness also.

What blurt is this about virtue and about vice?
Evil propels me and reform of evil propels me, I stand indifferent,　465
My gait is no fault-finder's or rejecter's gait,
I moisten the roots of all that has grown.

Did you fear some scrofula[6] out of the unflagging pregnancy?
Did you guess the celestial laws are yet to be work'd over and rectified?

I find one side a balance and the antipodal side a balance,　470
Soft doctrine as steady help as stable doctrine,
Thoughts and deeds of the present our rouse and early start.

This minute that comes to me over the past decillions,[7]
There is no better than it and now.

What behaved well in the past or behaves well to-day is not such a
　　wonder,　475
The wonder is always and always how there can be a mean man or an
　　infidel.

23

Endless unfolding of words of ages!
And mine a word of the modern, the word En-Masse.

A word of the faith that never balks,
Here or henceforward it is all the same to me, I accept Time absolutely. 480

It alone is without flaw, it alone rounds and completes all,
That mystic baffling wonder alone completes all.

I accept Reality and dare not question it.
Materialism first and last imbuing.

Hurrah for positive science! long live exact demonstration!　485
Fetch stonecrop mixt with cedar and branches of lilac,
This is the lexicographer, this the chemist, this made a grammar of the
　　old cartouches,[8]

5. Friends (French).
6. Form of tuberculosis characterized by swelling of the lymph glands.
7. The number one followed by thirty-three zeroes.

8. On tablets of Egyptian hieroglyphics, the ornamental area noting the name of a ruler or deity. "Stonecrop": a fleshy-leafed plant.

These mariners put the ship through dangerous unknown seas,
This is the geologist, this works with the scalpel, and this is a
    mathematician.

Gentlemen, to you the first honors always!   490
Your facts are useful, and yet they are not my dwelling,
I but enter by them to an area of my dwelling.

Less the reminders of properties told my words,
And more the reminders they of life untold, and of freedom and extrication,
And make short account of neuters and geldings, and favor men and
    women fully equipt,   495
And beat the gong of revolt, and stop with fugitives and them that plot and
    conspire.

24

Walt Whitman, a kosmos, of Manhattan the son,
Turbulent, fleshy, sensual, eating, drinking and breeding,
No sentimentalist, no stander above men and women or apart from them,
No more modest than immodest.   500

Unscrew the locks from the doors!
Unscrew the doors themselves from their jambs!

Whoever degrades another degrades me,
And whatever is done or said returns at last to me.

Through me the afflatus[9] surging and surging, through me the current
    and index.   505

I speak the pass-word primeval, I give the sign of democracy,
By God! I will accept nothing which all cannot have their counterpart of
    on the same terms.

Through me many long dumb voices,
Voices of the interminable generations of prisoners and slaves,
Voices of the diseas'd and despairing and of thieves and dwarfs,   510
Voices of cycles of preparation and accretion,
And of the threads that connect the stars, and of wombs and of the
    fatherstuff,
And of the rights of them the others are down upon,
Of the deform'd, trivial, flat, foolish, despised,
Fog in the air, beetles rolling balls of dung.   515

Through me forbidden voices,
Voices of sexes and lusts, voices veil'd and I remove the veil,
Voices indecent by me clarified and transfigur'd.

---

9. Divine wind or spirit.

I do not press my fingers across my mouth,
I keep as delicate around the bowels as around the head and heart,   520
Copulation is no more rank to me than death is.

I believe in the flesh and the appetites,
Seeing, hearing, feeling, are miracles, and each part and tag of me is a
    miracle.

Divine am I inside and out, and I make holy whatever I touch or am
    touch'd from,
The scent of these arm-pits aroma finer than prayer,   525
This head more than churches, bibles, and all the creeds.

If I worship one thing more than another it shall be the spread of my own
    body, or any part of it,
Translucent mould of me it shall be you!
Shaded ledges and rests it shall be you!
Firm masculine colter[1] it shall be you!   530
Whatever goes to the tilth[2] of me it shall be you!
You my rich blood! your milky stream pale strippings of my life!
Breast that presses against other breasts it shall be you!
My brain it shall be your occult convolutions!
Root of wash'd sweet-flag! timorous pond-snipe! nest of guarded duplicate
    eggs! it shall be you!   535
Mix'd tussled hay of head, beard, brawn, it shall be you!
Trickling sap of maple, fibre of manly wheat, it shall be you!
Sun so generous it shall be you!
Vapors lighting and shading my face it shall be you!
You sweaty brooks and dews it shall be you!   540
Winds whose soft-tickling genitals rub against me it shall be you!
Broad muscular fields, branches of live oak, loving lounger in my winding
    paths, it shall be you!
Hands I have taken, face I have kiss'd, mortal I have ever touch'd, it shall
    be you.

I dote on myself, there is that lot of me and all so luscious,
Each moment and whatever happens thrills me with joy,   545
I cannot tell how my ankles bend, nor whence the cause of my faintest
    wish,
Nor the cause of the friendship I emit, nor the cause of the friendship I
    take again.

That I walk up my stoop, I pause to consider if it really be,
A morning-glory at my window satisfies me more than the metaphysics of
    books.

To behold the day-break!   550
The little light fades the immense and diaphanous shadows,
The air tastes good to my palate.

---

1. The blade at the front of a plow.   2. Cultivation or tillage of the soil.

Hefts[3] of the moving world at innocent gambols silently rising freshly
    exuding,
Scooting obliquely high and low.

Something I cannot see puts upward libidinous prongs,   555
Seas of bright juice suffuse heaven.

The earth by the sky staid with, the daily close of their junction,
The heav'd challenge from the east that moment over my head,
The mocking taunt, See then whether you shall be master!

25

Dazzling and tremendous how quick the sun-rise would kill me,   560
If I could not now and always send sun-rise out of me.

We also ascend dazzling and tremendous as the sun,
We found our own O my soul in the calm and cool of the day-break.

My voice goes after what my eyes cannot reach,
With the twirl of my tongue I encompass worlds and volumes of worlds. 565

Speech is the twin of my vision, it is unequal to measure itself,
It provokes me forever, it says sarcastically,
Walt you contain enough, why don't you let it out then?

Come now I will not be tantalized, you conceive too much of articulation,
Do you not know O speech how the buds beneath you are folded?   570
Waiting in gloom, protected by frost,
The dirt receding before my prophetical screams,
I underlying causes to balance them at last,
My knowledge my live parts, it keeping tally with the meaning of all things,
Happiness, (which whoever hears me let him or her set out in search of
    this day.)   575

My final merit I refuse you, I refuse putting from me what I really am,
Encompass worlds, but never try to encompass me.
I crowd your sleekest and best by simply looking toward you.

Writing and talk do not prove me,
I carry the plenum[4] of proof and every thing else in my face,   580
With the hush of my lips I wholly confound the skeptic.

26

Now I will do nothing but listen,
To accrue what I hear into this song, to let sounds contribute toward it.

---

3. Something being heaved or raised upward.   4. Fullness.

I hear bravuras of birds, bustle of growing wheat, gossip of flames, clack
    of sticks cooking my meals,
I hear the sound I love, the sound of the human voice,   585
I hear all sounds running together, combined, fused or following,
Sounds of the city and sounds out of the city, sounds of the day and night,
Talkative young ones to those that like them, the loud laugh of work-people
    at their meals,
The angry base of disjointed friendship, the faint tones of the sick,
The judge with hands tight to the desk, his pallid lips pronouncing a
    death-sentence,   590
The heave'e'yo of stevedores unlading ships by the wharves, the refrain
    of the anchor-lifters,
The ring of alarm-bells, the cry of fire, the whirr of swift-streaking engines
    and hose-carts with premonitory tinkles and color'd lights,
The steam-whistle, the solid roll of the train of approaching cars,
The slow march play'd at the head of the association marching two and
    two,
(They go to guard some corpse, the flag-tops are draped with black
    muslin.)   595

I hear the violoncello ('tis the young man's heart's complaint,)
I hear the key'd cornet, it glides quickly in through my ears,
It shakes mad-sweet pangs through my belly and breast.

I hear the chorus, it is a grand opera,
Ah this indeed is music—this suits me.   600

A tenor large and fresh as the creation fills me,
The orbic flex of his mouth is pouring and filling me full.

I hear the train'd soprano (what work with hers is this?)
The orchestra whirls me wider than Uranus[5] flies,
It wrenches such ardors from me I did not know I possess'd them,   605
It sails me, I dab with bare feet, they are lick'd by the indolent waves,
I am cut by bitter and angry hail, I lose my breath,
Steep'd amid honey'd morphine, my windpipe throttled in fakes[6] of death,
At length let up again to feel the puzzle of puzzles,
And that we call Being.   610

27

To be in any form, what is that?
(Round and round we go, all of us, and ever come back thither,)
If nothing lay more develop'd the quahaug[7] in its callous shell were
    enough.

Mine is no callous shell,
I have instant conductors all over me whether I pass or stop,   615
They seize every object and lead it harmlessly through me.

5. Seventh planet from the sun, thought at the
time to be the outermost limit of the solar system.

6. Coils of rope.
7. Edible clam of the Atlantic coast.

I merely stir, press, feel with my fingers, and am happy,
To touch my person to some one else's is about as much as I can stand.

28

Is this then a touch? quivering me to a new identity,
Flames and ether making a rush for my veins,   620
Treacherous tip of me reaching and crowding to help them,
My flesh and blood playing out lightning to strike what is hardly different
        from myself,
On all sides prurient provokers stiffening my limbs,
Straining the udder of my heart for its withheld drip,
Behaving licentious toward me, taking no denial,   625
Depriving me of my best as for a purpose,
Unbuttoning my clothes, holding me by the bare waist,
Deluding my confusion with the calm of the sunlight and pasture-fields,
Immodestly sliding the fellow-senses away,
They bribed to swap off with touch and go and graze at the edges of me,   630
No consideration, no regard for my draining strength or my anger,
Fetching the rest of the herd around to enjoy them a while,
Then all uniting to stand on a headland and worry me.

The sentries desert every other part of me,
They have left me helpless to a red marauder,   635
They all come to the headland to witness and assist against me.

I am given up by traitors,
I talk wildly, I have lost my wits, I and nobody else am the greatest traitor,
I went myself first to the headland, my own hands carried me there.

You villain touch! what are you doing? my breath is tight in its throat,   640
Unclench your floodgates, you are too much for me.

29

Blind loving wrestling touch, sheath'd hooded sharp-tooth'd touch!
Did it make you ache so, leaving me?

Parting track'd by arriving, perpetual payment of perpetual loan,
Rich showering rain, and recompense richer afterward.   645

Sprouts take and accumulate, stand by the curb prolific and vital,
Landscapes projected masculine, full-sized and golden.

30

All truths wait in all things,
They neither hasten their own delivery nor resist it,
They do not need the obstetric forceps of the surgeon,   650
The insignificant is as big to me as any,
(What is less or more than a touch?)

Logic and sermons never convince,
The damp of the night drives deeper into my soul.

(Only what proves itself to every man and woman is so,   655
Only what nobody denies is so.)

A minute and a drop of me settle my brain,
I believe the soggy clods shall become lovers and lamps,
And a compend[8] of compends is the meat of a man or woman,
And a summit and flower there is the feeling they have for each other,   660
And they are to branch boundlessly out of that lesson until it becomes
        omnific,[9]
And until one and all shall delight us, and we them.

31

I believe a leaf of grass is no less than the journey-work of the stars,
And the pismire[1] is equally perfect, and a grain of sand, and the egg of
        the wren,
And the tree-toad is a chief-d'œuvre for the highest,   665
And the running blackberry would adorn the parlors of heaven,
And the narrowest hinge in my hand puts to scorn all machinery,
And the cow crunching with depress'd head surpasses any statue,
And a mouse is miracle enough to stagger sextillions of infidels.

I find I incorporate gneiss,[2] coal, long-threaded moss, fruits, grains,
        esculent roots,   670
And am stucco'd with quadrupeds and birds all over,
And have distanced what is behind me for good reasons,
But call any thing back again when I desire it.
In vain the speeding or shyness,
In vain the plutonic rocks[3] send their old heat against my approach,   675
In vain the mastodon retreats beneath its own powder'd bones,
In vain objects stand leagues off and assume manifold shapes,
In vain the ocean settling in hollows and the great monsters lying low,
In vain the buzzard houses herself with the sky,
In vain the snake slides through the creepers and logs,   680
In vain the elk takes to the inner passes of the woods,
In vain the razor-bill'd auk sails far north to Labrador,
I follow quickly, I ascend to the nest in the fissure of the cliff.

32

I think I could turn and live with animals, they are so placid and
        self-contain'd,
I stand and look at them long and long.   685

---

8. I.e., a compendium, where something is
reduced to a short, essential summary.
9. All-encompassing.
1. Ant.

2. Metamorphic rock in which minerals are
arranged in layers.
3. Rock of igneous (fire-created) or magmatic (molten) origin; from Pluto, ruler of infernal regions.

They do not sweat and whine about their condition,
They do not lie awake in the dark and weep for their sins,
They do not make me sick discussing their duty to God,
Not one is dissatisfied, not one is demented with the mania of owning
    things,
Not one kneels to another, nor to his kind that lived thousands of
    years ago,   690
Not one is respectable or unhappy over the whole earth.

So they show their relations to me and I accept them,
They bring me tokens of myself, they evince them plainly in their possession.

I wonder where they get those tokens,
Did I pass that way huge times ago and negligently drop them?   695

Myself moving forward then and now and forever,
Gathering and showing more always and with velocity,
Infinite and omnigenous,[4] and the like of these among them,
Not too exclusive toward the reachers of my remembrancers,
Picking out here one that I love, and now go with him on brotherly
    terms.   700

A gigantic beauty of a stallion, fresh and responsive to my caresses,
Head high in the forehead, wide between the ears,
Limbs glossy and supple, tail dusting the ground,
Eyes full of sparkling wickedness, ears finely cut, flexibly moving.

His nostrils dilate as my heels embrace him,   705
His well-built limbs tremble with pleasure as we race around and return.

I but use you a minute, then I resign you, stallion,
Why do I need your paces when I myself out-gallop them?
Even as I stand or sit passing faster than you.

33

Space and Time! now I see it is true, what I guess'd at,   710
What I guess'd when I loaf'd on the grass,
What I guess'd while I lay alone in my bed,
And again as I walk'd the beach under the paling stars of the morning.

My ties and ballasts leave me, my elbows rest in sea-gaps,[5]
I skirt sierras, my palms cover continents,   715
I am afoot with my vision.

By the city's quadrangular houses—in log huts, camping with lumbermen,
Along the ruts of the turnpike, along the dry gulch and rivulet bed,
Weeding my onion-patch or hoeing rows of carrots and parsnips, crossing
    savannas,[6] trailing in forests,

---

4. Belonging to every form of life.   6. Grasslands.
5. Estuaries or bays.

Prospecting, gold-digging, girdling the trees of a new purchase,   720
Scorch'd ankle-deep by the hot sand, hauling my boat down the shallow
    river,
Where the panther walks to and fro on a limb overhead, where the buck
    turns furiously at the hunter,
Where the rattlesnake suns his flabby length on a rock, where the otter is
    feeding on fish,
Where the alligator in his tough pimples sleeps by the bayou,
Where the black bear is searching for roots or honey, where the beaver
    pats the mud with his paddle-shaped tail;   725
Over the growing sugar, over the yellow-flower'd cotton plant, over the rice
    in its low moist field,
Over the sharp-peak'd farm house, with its scallop'd scum and slender
    shoots from the gutters,[7]
Over the western persimmon, over the long-leav'd corn, over the delicate
    blue-flower flax,
Over the white and brown buckwheat, a hummer and buzzer there with
    the rest,
Over the dusky green of the rye as it ripples and shades in the breeze;   730
Scaling mountains, pulling myself cautiously up, holding on by low
    scragged limbs,
Walking the path worn in the grass and beat through the leaves of the
    brush,
Where the quail is whistling betwixt the woods and the wheat-lot,
Where the bat flies in the Seventh-month eve, where the great gold-bug[8]
    drops through the dark,
Where the brook puts out of the roots of the old tree and flows to the
    meadow,   735
Where cattle stand and shake away flies with the tremulous shuddering
    of their hides,
Where the cheese-cloth hangs in the kitchen, where andirons straddle the
    hearth-slab, where cobwebs fall in festoons from the rafters;
Where trip-hammers crash, where the press is whirling its cylinders,
Wherever the human heart beats with terrible throes under its ribs,
Where the pear-shaped balloon is floating aloft, (floating in it myself and
    looking composedly down,)   740
Where the life-car[9] is drawn on the slip-noose, where the heat hatches
    pale-green eggs in the dented sand,
Where the she-whale swims with her calf and never forsakes it,
Where the steam-ship trails hind-ways its long pennant of smoke,
Where the fin of the shark cuts like a black chip out of the water,
Where the half-burn'd brig is riding on unknown currents,   745
Where shells grow to her slimy deck, where the dead are corrupting below;
Where the dense-star'd flag is borne at the head of the regiments,
Approaching Manhattan up by the long-stretching island,
Under Niagara, the cataract falling like a veil over my countenance,

---

7. I.e., plants growing from soil lodged in house gutters and drain pipes. "Scallop'd scum": rain-washed and sometimes weedy sediment on the roofs of old farmhouses.

8. Beetle.

9. Watertight compartment for lowering passengers from a ship when emergency evacuation is required.

Upon a door-step, upon the horse-block of hard wood outside,   750
Upon the race-course, or enjoying picnics or jigs or a good game of
    baseball,
At he-festivals, with blackguard gibes, ironical license, bull-dances,[1]
    drinking, laughter,
At the cider-mill tasting the sweets of the brown mash, sucking the juice
    through a straw,
At apple-peelings wanting kisses for all the red fruit I find,
At musters, beach-parties, friendly bees,[2] huskings, house-raisings;   755
Where the mocking-bird sounds his delicious gurgles, cackles, screams,
    weeps,
Where the hay-rick[3] stands in the barn-yard, where the dry-stalks are
    scatter'd, where the brood-cow waits in the hovel,
Where the bull advances to do his masculine work, where the stud to the
    mare, where the cock is treading the hen,
Where the heifers browse, where geese nip their food with short jerks,
Where sun-down shadows lengthen over the limitless and lonesome
    prairie,   760
Where herds of buffalo make a crawling spread of the square miles far
    and near,
Where the humming-bird shimmers, where the neck of the long-lived
    swan is curving and winding,
Where the laughing-gull scoots by the shore, where she laughs her
    near-human laugh,
Where bee-hives range on a gray bench in the garden half hid by the high
    weeds,
Where band-neck'd partridges roost in a ring on the ground with their
    heads out,   765
Where burial coaches enter the arch'd gates of a cemetery,
Where winter wolves bark amid wastes of snow and icicled trees,
Where the yellow-crown'd heron comes to the edge of the marsh at night
    and feeds upon small crabs,
Where the splash of swimmers and divers cools the warm noon,
Where the katy-did works her chromatic[4] reed on the walnut-tree over
    the well,   770
Through patches of citrons[5] and cucumbers with silver-wired leaves,
Through the salt-lick or orange glade, or under conical firs,
Through the gymnasium, through the curtain'd saloon, through the office
    or public hall;
Pleas'd with the native and pleas'd with the foreign, pleas'd with the new
    and old,
Pleas'd with the homely woman as well as the handsome,   775
Pleas'd with the quakeress as she puts off her bonnet and talks
    melodiously,
Pleas'd with the tune of the choir of the whitewash'd church,
Pleas'd with the earnest words of the sweating Methodist preacher,
    impress'd seriously at the camp-meeting;

---

1. Rowdy backwoods dances for which men took male partners.
2. Gatherings where people work while socializing with their neighbors. "Musters": assemblages of people, particularly gatherings of military troops for drill.
3. Hayrack, from which livestock eat hay.
4. In music, encompassing a full tonal range.
5. Here, small, hard-skinned watermelons.

Looking in at the shop-windows of Broadway the whole forenoon, flatting
    the flesh of my nose on the thick plate glass,
Wandering the same afternoon with my face turn'd up to the clouds, or
    down a lane or along the beach,   780
My right and left arms round the sides of two friends, and I in the
    middle;
Coming home with the silent and dark-cheek'd bush-boy, (behind me he
    rides at the drape of the day,)
Far from the settlements studying the print of animals' feet, or the
    moccasin print,
By the cot in the hospital reaching lemonade to a feverish patient,
Nigh the coffin'd corpse when all is still, examining with a candle;   785
Voyaging to every port to dicker and adventure,
Hurrying with the modern crowd as eager and fickle as any,
Hot toward one I hate, ready in my madness to knife him,
Solitary at midnight in my back yard, my thoughts gone from me a long
    while,
Walking the old hills of Judæa with the beautiful gentle God by my side,   790
Speeding through space, speeding through heaven and the stars,
Speeding amid the seven satellites[6] and the broad ring, and the diameter
    of eighty thousand miles,
Speeding with tail'd meteors, throwing fire-balls like the rest,
Carrying the crescent child that carries its own full mother in its belly,[7]
Storming, enjoying, planning, loving, cautioning,   795
Backing and filling, appearing and disappearing,
I tread day and night such roads.

I visit the orchards of spheres and look at the product,
And look at quintillions ripen'd and look at quintillions green.

I fly those flights of a fluid and swallowing soul,   800
My course runs below the soundings of plummets.

I help myself to material and immaterial,
No guard can shut me off, no law prevent me.

I anchor my ship for a little while only,
My messengers continually cruise away or bring their returns to me.   805

I go hunting polar furs and the seal, leaping chasms with a pike-pointed
    staff, clinging to topples of brittle and blue.[8]

I ascend to the foretruck,[9]
I take my place late at night in the crow's-nest,
We sail the arctic sea, it is plenty light enough,
Through the clear atmosphere I stretch around on the wonderful
    beauty,   810
The enormous masses of ice pass me and I pass them, the scenery is
    plain in all directions,

6. The then known moons of Saturn.   8. Toppled pieces of ice.
7. I.e., a crescent moon, with the full moon also   9. Highest platform of a foremast.
palely visible.

The white-topt mountains show in the distance, I fling out my fancies
    toward them,
We are approaching some great battle-field in which we are soon to be
    engaged,
We pass the colossal outposts of the encampment, we pass with still feet
    and caution,
Or we are entering by the suburbs some vast and ruin'd city,   815
The blocks and fallen architecture more than all the living cities of the globe.

I am a free companion, I bivouac by invading watchfires,
I turn the bridegroom out of bed and stay with the bride myself,
I tighten her all night to my thighs and lips.

My voice is the wife's voice, the screech by the rail of the stairs,   820
They fetch my man's body up dripping and drown'd.

I understand the large hearts of heroes,
The courage of present times and all times,
How the skipper saw the crowded and rudderless wreck of the steam-ship,
    and Death chasing it up and down the storm,
How he knuckled tight and gave not back an inch, and was faithful of days
    and faithful of nights,   825
And chalk'd in large letters on a board, *Be of good cheer, we will not desert you;*
How he follow'd with them and tack'd with them three days and would not
    give it up,
How he saved the drifting company at last,
How the lank loose-gown'd women look'd when boated from the side of
    their prepared graves,
How the silent old-faced infants and the lifted sick, and the sharp-lipp'd
    unshaved men;   830
All this I swallow, it tastes good, I like it well, it becomes mine,
I am the man, I suffer'd, I was there.[1]

The disdain and calmness of martyrs,
The mother of old, condemn'd for a witch, burnt with dry wood, her
    children gazing on,
The hounded slave that flags in the race, leans by the fence, blowing,
    cover'd with sweat,   835
The twinges that sting like needles his legs and neck, the murderous
    buckshot and the bullets,
All these I feel or am.

I am the hounded slave, I wince at the bite of the dogs,
Hell and despair are upon me, crack and again crack the marksmen,
I clutch the rails of the fence, my gore dribs, thinn'd with the ooze of
    my skin,[2]   840
I fall on the weeds and stones,

1. Whitman describes the wreck of the *San Fran-cisco,* which sailed from New York on December 22, 1853, bound for South America, and was caught in a storm a day later. The ship drifted helplessly until early January. Over 150 died in the disaster, which was reported widely in the New York papers.
2. Dribbles down, diluted with sweat.

The riders spur their unwilling horses, haul close,
Taunt my dizzy ears and beat me violently over the head with whip-stocks.

Agonies are one of my changes of garments,
I do not ask the wounded person how he feels, I myself become the
    wounded person,   845
My hurts turn livid upon me as I lean on a cane and observe.

I am the mash'd fireman with breast-bone broken,
Tumbling walls buried me in their debris,
Heat and smoke I inspired, I heard the yelling shouts of my comrades,
I heard the distant click of their picks and shovels,   850
They have clear'd the beams away, they tenderly lift me forth.

I lie in the night air in my red shirt, the pervading hush is for my sake,
Painless after all I lie exhausted but not so unhappy,
White and beautiful are the faces around me, the heads are bared of
    their fire-caps,
The kneeling crowd fades with the light of the torches.   855

Distant and dead resuscitate,
They show as the dial or move as the hands of me, I am the clock myself.

I am an old artillerist, I tell of my fort's bombardment,
I am there again.

Again the long roll of the drummers,   860
Again the attacking cannon, mortars,
Again to my listening ears the cannon responsive.

I take part, I see and hear the whole,
The cries, curses, roar, the plaudits of well-aim'd shots,
The ambulanza slowly passing trailing its red drip,   865
Workmen searching after damages, making indispensable repairs,
The fall of grenades through the rent roof, the fan-shaped explosion,
The whizz of limbs, heads, stone, wood, iron, high in the air.

Again gurgles the mouth of my dying general, he furiously waves with
    his hand,
He gasps through the clot *Mind not me—mind—the entrenchments.*   870

34

Now I tell what I knew in Texas in my early youth,
(I tell not the fall of Alamo,[3]

---

3. During the Texas Revolution of 1835–36, emigrants from the United States to Texas—at the time part of Mexico—attempted to make Texas into an independent republic. Among the battles fought in what is now the state of Texas were the battle of the Alamo (a Spanish mission church compound in San Antonio)—the Alamo fell on March 6, 1836, after a siege by Mexican forces beginning on February 23, when around two hundred men were killed—and the battle of Goliad, when some four hundred secessionist troops were killed after surrendering to the Mexicans on March 19 of the same year.

Not one escaped to tell the fall of Alamo,
The hundred and fifty are dumb yet at Alamo,)
'Tis the tale of the murder in cold blood of four hundred and twelve
    young men.   875

Retreating they had form'd in a hollow square with their baggage for
    breastworks,
Nine hundred lives out of the surrounding enemy's, nine times their
    number, was the price they took in advance,
Their colonel was wounded and their ammunition gone,
They treated for an honorable capitulation, receiv'd writing and seal,
    gave up their arms and march'd back prisoners of war.

They were the glory of the race of rangers,   880
Matchless with horse, rifle, song, supper, courtship,
Large, turbulent, generous, handsome, proud, and affectionate,
Bearded, sunburnt, drest in the free costume of hunters,
Not a single one over thirty years of age.

The second First-day morning they were brought out in squads and
    massacred, it was beautiful early summer,   885
The work commenced about five o'clock and was over by eight.

None obey'd the command to kneel,
Some made a mad and helpless rush, some stood stark and straight,
A few fell at once, shot in the temple or heart, the living and dead lay
    together,
The maim'd and mangled dug in the dirt, the new-comers saw them
    there,   890
Some half-kill'd attempted to crawl away,
These were despatch'd with bayonets or batter'd with the blunts of muskets,
A youth not seventeen years old seiz'd his assassin till two more came to
    release him,
The three were all torn and cover'd with the boy's blood.

At eleven o'clock began the burning of the bodies;   895
That is the tale of the murder of the four hundred and twelve young men.

35

Would you hear of an old-time sea-fight?[4]
Would you learn who won by the light of the moon and stars?
List to the yarn, as my grandmother's father the sailor told it to me.

Our foe was no skulk in his ship I tell you, (said he,)   900
His was the surly English pluck, and there is no tougher or truer, and
    never was, and never will be;
Along the lower'd eve he came horribly raking us.

4. This passage alludes to the famous Revolutionary War sea battle on September 23, 1779, between the American *Bon-Homme Richard*, commanded by John Paul Jones (1747–1792), and the British *Serapis* off the coast of northern England. When Jones was asked to surrender, he famously declared, "I have not yet begun to fight." The American ship eventually defeated the *Serapis*.

We closed with him, the yards entangled, the cannon touch'd,
My captain lash'd fast with his own hands.

We had receiv'd some eighteen pound shots under the water,   905
On our lower-gun-deck two large pieces had burst at the first fire, killing
    all around and blowing up overhead.

Fighting at sun-down, fighting at dark,
Ten o'clock at night, the full moon well up, our leaks on the gain, and five
    feet of water reported,
The master-at-arms loosing the prisoners confined in the after-hold to give
    them a chance for themselves.

The transit to and from the magazine⁵ is now stopt by the sentinels,   910
They see so many strange faces they do not know whom to trust.

Our frigate takes fire,
The other asks if we demand quarter?
If our colors are struck and the fighting done?

Now I laugh content, for I hear the voice of my little captain,   915
We have not struck, he composedly cries, *we have just begun our part of
    the fighting.*

Only three guns are in use,
One is directed by the captain himself against the enemy's mainmast,
Two well serv'd with grape and canister⁶ silence his musketry and clear
    his decks.

The tops⁷ alone second the fire of this little battery, especially the
    main-top,
They hold out bravely during the whole of the action.   920

Not a moment's cease,
The leaks gain fast on the pumps, the fire eats toward the powder-
    magazine.

One of the pumps has been shot away, it is generally thought we are
    sinking.

Serene stands the little captain,   925
He is not hurried, his voice is neither high nor low,
His eyes give more light to us than our battle-lanterns.

Toward twelve there in the beams of the moon they surrender to us.

---

5. Storeroom for ammunition.
6. Grapeshot ("grape"), clusters of small iron balls, was packed inside a metal cylinder ("canis-ter") and fired from a cannon.
7. I.e., the sailors manning the tops—platforms enclosing the heads of each mast.

36

Stretch'd and still lies the midnight,
Two great hulls motionless on the breast of the darkness,   930
Our vessel riddled and slowly sinking, preparations to pass to the one
    we have conquer'd,
The captain on the quarter-deck coldly giving his orders through a
    countenance white as a sheet,
Near by the corpse of the child that serv'd in the cabin,
The dead face of an old salt with long white hair and carefully curl'd
    whiskers,
The flames spite of all that can be done flickering aloft and below,   935
The husky voices of the two or three officers yet fit for duty,
Formless stacks of bodies and bodies by themselves, dabs of flesh upon
    the masts and spars,
Cut of cordage, dangle of rigging, slight shock of the soothe of waves,
Black and impassive guns, litter of powder-parcels, strong scent,
A few large stars overhead, silent and mournful shining,   940
Delicate sniffs of sea-breeze, smells of sedgy grass and fields by the shore,
    death-messages given in charge to survivors,
The hiss of the surgeon's knife, the gnawing teeth of his saw,
Wheeze, cluck, swash of falling blood, short wild scream, and long, dull,
    tapering groan,
These so, these irretrievable.

37

You laggards there on guard! look to your arms!   945
In at the conquer'd doors they crowd! I am possess'd!
Embody all presences outlaw'd or suffering,
See myself in prison shaped like another man,
And feel the dull unintermitted pain.

For me the keepers of convicts shoulder their carbines and keep
    watch,   950
It is I let out in the morning and barr'd at night.

Not a mutineer walks handcuff'd to jail but I am handcuff'd to him and
    walk by his side,
(I am less the jolly one there, and more the silent one with sweat on my
    twitching lips.)

Not a youngster is taken for larceny but I go up too, and am tried and
    sentenced.

Not a cholera patient lies at the last gasp but I also lie at the last
    gasp,   955
My face is ash-color'd, my sinews gnarl, away from me people retreat.

Askers embody themselves in me and I am embodied in them,
I project my hat, sit shame-faced, and beg.

38

Enough! enough! enough!
Somehow I have been stunn'd. Stand back!   960
Give me a little time beyond my cuff'd head, slumbers, dreams, gaping,
I discover myself on the verge of a usual mistake.

That I could forget the mockers and insults!
That I could forget the trickling tears and the blows of the bludgeons
    and hammers!
That I could look with a separate look on my own crucifixion and bloody
    crowning.   965

I remember now,
I resume the overstaid fraction,
The grave of rock multiplies what has been confided to it, or to any
    graves,
Corpses rise, gashes heal, fastenings roll from me.

I troop forth replenish'd with supreme power, one of an average unending
    procession,   970
Inland and sea-coast we go, and pass all boundary lines,
Our swift ordinances on their way over the whole earth,
The blossoms we wear in our hats the growth of thousands of years.

Eleves,[8] I salute you! come forward!
Continue your annotations, continue your questionings.   975

39

The friendly and flowing savage, who is he?
Is he waiting for civilization, or past it and mastering it?

Is he some Southwesterner rais'd out-doors? is he Kanadian?
Is he from the Mississippi country? Iowa, Oregon, California?
The mountains? prairie-life, bush-life? or sailor from the sea?   980

Wherever he goes men and women accept and desire him,
They desire he should like them, touch them, speak to them, stay with
    them.

Behavior lawless as snow-flakes, words simple as grass, uncomb'd head,
    laughter, and naiveté,
Slow-stepping feet, common features, common modes and emanations,
They descend in new forms from the tips of his fingers,   985
They are wafted with the odor of his body or breath, they fly out of the
    glance of his eyes.

8. Students (French).

40

Flaunt of the sunshine I need not your bask—lie over!
You light surfaces only, I force surfaces and depths also.

Earth! you seem to look for something at my hands,
Say, old top-knot,[9] what do you want?   990

Man or woman, I might tell how I like you, but cannot,
And might tell what it is in me and what it is in you, but cannot,
And might tell that pining I have, that pulse of my nights and days.

Behold, I do not give lectures or a little charity,
When I give I give myself.   995

You there, impotent, loose in the knees,
Open your scarf'd chops till I blow grit[1] within you,
Spread your palms and lift the flaps of your pockets,
I am not to be denied, I compel, I have stores plenty and to spare,
And any thing I have I bestow.   1000

I do not ask who you are, that is not important to me,
You can do nothing and be nothing but what I will infold you.

To cotton-field drudge or cleaner of privies I lean,
On his right cheek I put the family kiss,
And in my soul I swear I never will deny him.   1005

On women fit for conception I start bigger and nimbler babes,
(This day I am jetting the stuff of far more arrogant republics.)

To any one dying, thither I speed and twist the knob of the door,
Turn the bed-clothes toward the foot of the bed,
Let the physician and the priest go home.   1010

I seize the descending man and raise him with resistless will,
O despairer, here is my neck,
By God, you shall not go down! hang your whole weight upon me.

I dilate you with tremendous breath, I buoy you up,
Every room of the house do I fill with an arm'd force,   1015
Lovers of me, bafflers of graves.

Sleep—I and they keep guard all night,
Not doubt, not decease shall dare to lay finger upon you,
I have embraced you, and henceforth possess you to myself,
And when you rise in the morning you will find what I tell you is so. 1020

---

9. An epithet common in frontier humor, deriving from the fact that some Native Americans gathered their hair into tufts at the top of the head. The poet seems to be addressing an older Indian, perhaps picking up on the reference to "the friendly and flowing savage" of the previous stanza.

1. Courage. "Scarf'd chops": lined, worn-down jaw or face.

41

I am he bringing help for the sick as they pant on their backs,
And for strong upright men I bring yet more needed help.

I heard what was said of the universe,
Heard it and heard it of several thousand years;
It is middling well as far as it goes—but is that all?   1025

Magnifying and applying come I,
Outbidding at the start the old cautious hucksters,
Taking myself the exact dimensions of Jehovah,[2]
Lithographing Kronos, Zeus his son, and Hercules[3] his grandson,
Buying drafts of Osiris, Isis, Belus, Brahma, Buddha,[4]   1030
In my portfolio placing Manito loose, Allah[5] on a leaf, the crucifix
    engraved,
With Odin and the hideous-faced Mexitli[6] and every idol and image,
Taking them all for what they are worth and not a cent more,
Admitting they were alive and did the work of their days,
(They bore mites as for unfledg'd birds who have now to rise and fly and
    sing for themselves,)   1035
Accepting the rough deific sketches to fill out better in myself, bestowing
    them freely on each man and woman I see,
Discovering as much or more in a framer framing a house,
Putting higher claims for him there with his roll'd-up sleeves driving the
    mallet and chisel,
Not objecting to special revelations, considering a curl of smoke or a hair
    on the back of my hand just as curious as any revelation,
Lads ahold of fire-engines and hook-and-ladder ropes no less to me than
    the gods of the antique wars,   1040
Minding their voices peal through the crash of destruction,
Their brawny limbs passing safe over charr'd laths, their white foreheads
    whole and unhurt out of the flames;
By the mechanic's wife with her babe at her nipple interceding for every
    person born,
Three scythes at harvest whizzing in a row from three lusty angels with
    shirts bagg'd out at their waists,
The snag-tooth'd hostler with red hair redeeming sins past and to
    come,   1045
Selling all he possesses, traveling on foot to fee lawyers for his brother
    and sit by him while he is tried for forgery;
What was strewn in the amplest strewing the square rod about me, and
    not filling the square rod then,

---

2. God of the Jews and Christians.
3. Son of Zeus and the mortal Alcmene, won immortality by performing twelve supposedly impossible feats. Kronos (or Cronus), in Greek mythology, was the Titan who ruled the universe until dethroned by Zeus, his son, the chief of the Olympian gods.
4. The Indian sage Siddhartha Gautama (known as the "Buddha"), founder of Buddhism. Osiris was the Egyptian god who annually died and was reborn, symbolizing the fertility of nature. Isis was the Egyptian goddess of fertility and the sister and wife of Osiris. Belus was a legendary god-king of Assyria. Brahma, in Hinduism, is the divine reality in the role of the creator god.
5. Arabic word for God, the supreme being in Islam. Manito was the nature god of the Algonquian Indians.
6. An Aztec war god. Odin was the chief Norse god.

The bull and the bug never worshipp'd half enough,[7]
Dung and dirt more admirable than was dream'd,
The supernatural of no account, myself waiting my time to be one of the
    supremes,   1050
The day getting ready for me when I shall do as much good as the best,
    and be as prodigious;
By my life-lumps![8] becoming already a creator,
Putting myself here and now to the ambush'd womb of the shadows.

42

A call in the midst of the crowd,
My own voice, orotund sweeping and final.   1055

Come my children,
Come my boys and girls, my women, household and intimates,
Now the performer launches his nerve, he has pass'd his prelude on the
    reeds within.

Easily written loose-finger'd chords—I feel the thrum of your climax
    and close.

My head slues round on my neck,   1060
Music rolls, but not from the organ,
Folks are around me, but they are no household of mine.

Ever the hard unsunk ground,
Ever the eaters and drinkers, ever the upward and downward sun, ever
    the air and the ceaseless tides,
Ever myself and my neighbors, refreshing, wicked, real,   1065
Ever the old inexplicable query, ever that thorn'd thumb, that breath of
    itches and thirsts,
Ever the vexer's *hoot! hoot!* till we find where the sly one hides and bring
    him forth,
Ever love, ever the sobbing liquid of life,
Ever the bandage under the chin, ever the trestles[9] of death.

Here and there with dimes on the eyes[1] walking,   1070
To feed the greed of the belly the brains liberally spooning,
Tickets buying, taking, selling, but in to the feast never once going,
Many sweating, ploughing, thrashing, and then the chaff for payment
    receiving,
A few idly owning, and they the wheat continually claiming.

This is the city and I am one of the citizens,   1075
Whatever interests the rest interests me, politics, wars, markets,
    newspapers, schools,

7. As Whitman implies, the bull and the bug had
been worshiped in earlier religions, the bull in
several, the scarab beetle as an Egyptian symbol
of the soul.
8. Testicles.

9. I.e., sawhorses or similar supports holding up
a coffin.
1. Coins were placed on eyelids of corpses to
hold them closed until burial.

The mayor and councils, banks, tariffs, steamships, factories, stocks,
    stores, real estate and personal estate.

The little plentiful manikins skipping around in collars and tail'd coats,
I am aware who they are, (they are positively not worms or fleas,)
I acknowledge the duplicates of myself, the weakest and shallowest is
    deathless with me,   1080
What I do and say the same waits for them,
Every thought that flounders in me the same flounders in them.

I know perfectly well my own egotism,
Know my omnivorous lines and must not write any less,
And would fetch you whoever you are flush with myself.   1085

Not words of routine this song of mine,
But abruptly to question, to leap beyond yet nearer bring;
This printed and bound book—but the printer and the printing-office boy?
The well-taken photographs—but your wife or friend close and solid in
    your arms?
The black ship mail'd with iron, her mighty guns in her turrets—but the
    pluck of the captain and engineers?   1090
In the houses the dishes and fare and furniture—but the host and
    hostess, and the look out of their eyes?
The sky up there—yet here or next door, or across the way?
The saints and sages in history—but you yourself?
Sermons, creeds, theology—but the fathomless human brain,
And what is reason? and what is love? and what is life?   1095

43

I do not despise you priests, all time, the world over,
My faith is the greatest of faiths and the least of faiths,
Enclosing worship ancient and modern and all between ancient and
    modern,
Believing I shall come again upon the earth after five thousand years,
Waiting responses from oracles, honoring the gods, saluting the sun,   1100
Making a fetich of the first rock or stump, powowing with sticks in the
    circle of obis.[2]
Helping the llama or brahmin[3] as he trims the lamps of the idols,
Dancing yet through the streets in a phallic procession, rapt and austere
    in the woods a gymnosophist,[4]
Drinking mead from the skull-cup, to Shastas and Vedas admirant,
    minding the Koran,[5]
Walking the teokallis,[6] spotted with gore from the stone and knife,
    beating the serpent-skin drum,   1105

2. Magical charms, such as shells, used in African and West Indian religious practices. "Fetich": i.e., fetish; object of worship.
3. Here, also a Buddhist priest. "Llama": i.e., lama; a Buddhist monk of Tibet or Mongolia.
4. Member of an ancient Hindu ascetic sect.
5. The other worshipers include ancient warriors drinking mead (an alcoholic beverage made of fermented honey) from the skulls of defeated enemies; admiring or wondering readers of the sastras (or shastras or shasters, books of Hindu law) or of the Vedas (the oldest sacred writings of Hinduism); and those attentive to the Koran (the sacred book of Islam, containing Allah's revelations to Muhammad).
6. An ancient Central American temple built on a pyramidal mound.

Accepting the Gospels,[7] accepting him that was crucified, knowing
    assuredly that he is divine,
To the mass kneeling or the puritan's prayer rising, or sitting patiently
    in a pew,
Ranting and frothing in my insane crisis, or waiting dead-like till my spirit
    arouses me,
Looking forth on pavement and land, or outside of pavement and land,
Belonging to the winders of the circuit of circuits.   1110

One of that centripetal and centrifugal gang I turn and talk like a man
    leaving charges before a journey.

Down-hearted doubters dull and excluded,
Frivolous, sullen, moping, angry, affected, dishearten'd, atheistical,
I know every one of you, I know the sea of torment, doubt, despair and
    unbelief.

How the flukes[8] splash!   1115
How they contort rapid as lightning, with spasms and spouts of blood!

Be at peace bloody flukes of doubters and sullen mopers,
I take my place among you as much as among any,
The past is the push of you, me, all, precisely the same,
And what is yet untried and afterward is for you, me, all, precisely the
    same.   1120

I do not know what is untried and afterward,
But I know it will in its turn prove sufficient, and cannot fail.

Each who passes is consider'd, each who stops is consider'd, not a single
    one can it fail.

It cannot fail the young man who died and was buried,
Nor the young woman who died and was put by his side,   1125
Nor the little child that peep'd in at the door, and then drew back and
    was never seen again,
Nor the old man who has lived without purpose, and feels it with
    bitterness worse than gall,
Nor him in the poor house tubercled by rum and the bad disorder,[9]
Nor the numberless slaughter'd and wreck'd, nor the brutish koboo[1]
    call'd the ordure of humanity,
Nor the sacs merely floating with open mouths for food to slip in,   1130
Nor any thing in the earth, or down in the oldest graves of the earth,
Nor any thing in the myriads of spheres, nor the myriads of myriads
    that inhabit them,
Nor the present, nor the least wisp that is known.

7. Of the New Testament of the Bible.
8. The flat parts on either side of a whale's tail;
here used figuratively.

9. I.e., syphilis.
1. Native of Sumatra.

44

It is time to explain myself—let us stand up.

What is known I strip away,   1135
I launch all men and women forward with me into the Unknown.

The clock indicates the moment—but what does eternity indicate?

We have thus far exhausted trillions of winters and summers,
There are trillions ahead, and trillions ahead of them.

Births have brought us richness and variety,   1140
And other births will bring us richness and variety.

I do not call one greater and one smaller,
That which fills its period and place is equal to any.

Were mankind murderous or jealous upon you, my brother, my sister?
I am sorry for you, they are not murderous or jealous upon me,   1145
All has been gentle with me, I keep no account with lamentation,
(What have I to do with lamentation?)

I am an acme of things accomplish'd, and I an encloser of things to be.

My feet strike an apex of the apices[2] of the stairs,
On every step bunches of ages, and larger bunches between the steps,   1150
All below duly travel'd, and still I mount and mount.

Rise after rise bow the phantoms behind me,
Afar down I see the huge first Nothing, I know I was even there,
I waited unseen and always, and slept through the lethargic mist,
And took my time, and took no hurt from the fetid carbon.[3]   1155

Long I was hugg'd close—long and long.

Immense have been the preparations for me,
Faithful and friendly the arms that have help'd me.

Cycles[4] ferried my cradle, rowing and rowing like cheerful boatmen,
For room to me stars kept aside in their own rings,   1160
They sent influences to look after what was to hold me.

Before I was born out of my mother generations guided me,
My embryo has never been torpid, nothing could overlay it.

For it the nebula cohered to an orb,
The long slow strata piled to rest it on,   1165
Vast vegetables gave it sustenance,

2. The highest points (variant plural of *apex*).   human beings on earth.
3. The "lethargic mist" (line 1154) and "fetid   4. Centuries.
carbon" suggest a time before the appearance of

Monstrous sauroids[5] transported it in their mouths and deposited it with
    care.

All forces have been steadily employ'd to complete and delight me,
Now on this spot I stand with my robust soul.

45

O span of youth! ever-push'd elasticity!   1170
O manhood, balanced, florid and full.

My lovers suffocate me,
Crowding my lips, thick in the pores of my skin,
Jostling me through streets and public halls, coming naked to me at night,
Crying by day Ahoy! from the rocks of the river, swinging and chirping
    over my head,   1175
Calling my name from flower-beds, vines, tangled underbrush,
Lighting on every moment of my life,
Bussing[6] my body with soft balsamic busses,
Noiselessly passing handfuls out of their hearts and giving them to be mine.

Old age superbly rising! O welcome, ineffable grace of dying days!   1180

Every condition promulges[7] not only itself, it promulges what grows after
    and out of itself,
And the dark hush promulges as much as any.

I open my scuttle[8] at night and see the far-sprinkled systems,
And all I see multiplied as high as I can cipher edge but the rim of the
    farther systems.

Wider and wider they spread, expanding, always expanding,   1185
Outward and outward and forever outward.

My sun has his sun and round him obediently wheels,
He joins with his partners a group of superior circuit,
And greater sets follow, making specks of the greatest inside them.

There is no stoppage and never can be stoppage,   1190
If I, you, and the worlds, and all beneath or upon their surfaces, were
    this moment reduced back to a pallid float,[9] it would not avail in the
    long run,
We should surely bring up again where we now stand,
And surely go as much farther, and then farther and farther.

A few quadrillions of eras, a few octillions of cubic leagues, do not hazard[1]
    the span or make it impatient,
They are but parts, any thing is but a part.   1195

---

5. Prehistoric large reptiles or dinosaurs, thought
to have carried their eggs in their mouths.
6. Kissing.
7. Promulgates, officially announces.

8. Roof hatch (as on a ship).
9. I.e., returned to the era before the formation
of the solar system.
1. Imperil, make hazardous.

See ever so far, there is limitless space outside of that,
Count ever so much, there is limitless time around that.

My rendezvous is appointed, it is certain,
The Lord will be there and wait till I come on perfect terms,
The great Camerado, the lover true for whom I pine will be there.　　1200

46

I know I have the best of time and space, and was never measured and
　　never will be measured.

I tramp a perpetual journey, (come listen all!)
My signs are a rain-proof coat, good shoes, and a staff cut from the woods,
No friend of mine takes his ease in my chair,
I have no chair, no church, no philosophy,　　1205
I lead no man to a dinner-table, library, exchange,[2]
But each man and each woman of you I lead upon a knoll,
My left hand hooking you round the waist,
My right hand pointing to landscapes of continents and the public road.

Not I, not any one else can travel that road for you,　　1210
You must travel it for yourself.

It is not far, it is within reach,
Perhaps you have been on it since you were born and did not know,
Perhaps it is everywhere on water and on land.

Shoulder your duds dear son, and I will mine, and let us hasten forth,　　1215
Wonderful cities and free nations we shall fetch as we go.

If you tire, give me both burdens, and rest the chuff[3] of your hand on
　　my hip,
And in due time you shall repay the same service to me,
For after we start we never lie by again.

This day before dawn I ascended a hill and look'd at the crowded
　　heaven,　　1220
And I said to my spirit *When we become the enfolders of those orbs, and
　　the pleasure and knowledge of every thing in them, shall we be fill'd
　　and satisfied then?*
And my spirit said *No, we but level that lift to pass and continue beyond.*

You are also asking me questions and I hear you,
I answer that I cannot answer, you must find out for yourself.

Sit a while dear son,　　1225
Here are biscuits to eat and here is milk to drink,
But as soon as you sleep and renew yourself in sweet clothes, I kiss you
　　with a good-by kiss and open the gate for your egress hence.

2. Stock exchange, bank.　　　　3. The fleshy part of the palm.

Long enough have you dream'd contemptible dreams,
Now I wash the gum from your eyes,
You must habit yourself to the dazzle of the light and of every moment
    of your life.   1230

Long have you timidly waded holding a plank by the shore,
Now I will you to be a bold swimmer,
To jump off in the midst of the sea, rise again, nod to me, shout, and
    laughingly dash with your hair.

47

I am the teacher of athletes,
He that by me spreads a wider breast than my own proves the width of
    my own,   1235
He most honors my style who learns under it to destroy the teacher.

The boy I love, the same becomes a man not through derived power, but
    in his own right,
Wicked rather than virtuous out of conformity or fear,
Fond of his sweetheart, relishing well his steak,
Unrequited love or a slight cutting him worse than sharp steel cuts,   1240
First-rate to ride, to fight, to hit the bull's eye, to sail a skiff, to sing a
    song or play on the banjo,
Preferring scars and the beard and faces pitted with small-pox over all
    latherers,
And those well-tann'd to those that keep out of the sun.

I teach straying from me, yet who can stray from me?
I follow you whoever you are from the present hour,   1245
My words itch at your ears till you understand them.

I do not say these things for a dollar or to fill up the time while I wait for
    a boat,
(It is you talking just as much as myself, I act as the tongue of you,
Tied in your mouth, in mine it begins to be loosen'd.)

I swear I will never again mention love or death inside a house,   1250
And I swear I will never translate myself at all, only to him or her who
    privately stays with me in the open air.

If you would understand me go to the heights or water-shore,
The nearest gnat is an explanation, and a drop or motion of waves a key,
The maul, the oar, the hand-saw, second my words.

No shutter'd room or school can commune with me,   1255
But roughs and little children better than they.

The young mechanic is closest to me, he knows me well,
The woodman that takes his axe and jug with him shall take me with him
    all day,
The farm-boy ploughing in the field feels good at the sound of my voice,

In vessels that sail my words sail, I go with fishermen and seamen and
    love them.   1260

The soldier camp'd or upon the march is mine,
On the night ere the pending battle many seek me, and I do not fail
    them,
On that solemn night (it may be their last) those that know me seek me.

My face rubs to the hunter's face when he lies down alone in his blanket,
The driver thinking of me does not mind the jolt of his wagon,   1265
The young mother and old mother comprehend me,
The girl and the wife rest the needle a moment and forget where they
    are,
They and all would resume what I have told them.

48

I have said that the soul is not more than the body,
And I have said that the body is not more than the soul,   1270
And nothing, not God, is greater to one than one's self is,
And whoever walks a furlong without sympathy walks to his own funeral
    drest in his shroud,
And I or you pocketless of a dime may purchase the pick of the earth,
And to glance with an eye or show a bean in its pod confounds the
    learning of all times,
And there is no trade or employment but the young man following it
    may become a hero,   1275
And there is no object so soft but it makes a hub for the wheel'd
    universe,
And I say to any man or woman, Let your soul stand cool and composed
    before a million universes.

And I say to mankind, Be not curious about God,
For I who am curious about each am not curious about God,
(No array of terms can say how much I am at peace about God and
    about death.)   1280

I hear and behold God in every object, yet understand God not in the
    least,
Nor do I understand who there can be more wonderful than myself.

Why should I wish to see God better than this day?
I see something of God each hour of the twenty-four, and each moment
    then,
In the faces of men and women I see God, and in my own face in the
    glass,   1285
I find letters from God dropt in the street, and every one is sign'd by
    God's name,
And I leave them where they are, for I know that wheresoe'er I go,
Others will punctually come for ever and ever.

49

And as to you Death, and you bitter hug of mortality, it is idle to try to
    alarm me.

To his work without flinching the accoucheur[4] comes,   1290
I see the elder-hand pressing receiving supporting,
I recline by the sills of the exquisite flexible doors,
And mark the outlet, and mark the relief and escape.

And as to you Corpse I think you are good manure, but that does not
    offend me,
I smell the white roses sweet-scented and growing,   1295
I reach to the leafy lips, I reach to the polish'd breasts of melons.

And as to you Life I reckon you are the leavings of many deaths,
(No doubt I have died myself ten thousand times before.)

I hear you whispering there O stars of heaven,
O suns—O grass of graves—O perpetual transfers and promotions,   1300
If you do not say any thing how can I say any thing?

Of the turbid pool that lies in the autumn forest,
Of the moon that descends the steeps of the soughing twilight,
Toss, sparkles of day and dusk—toss on the black stems that decay in
    the muck,
Toss to the moaning gibberish of the dry limbs.   1305

I ascend from the moon, I ascend from the night,
I perceive that the ghastly glimmer is noonday sunbeams reflected,
And debouch[5] to the steady and central from the offspring great or small.

50

There is that in me—I do not know what it is—but I know it is in me.

Wrench'd and sweaty—calm and cool then my body becomes,   1310
I sleep—I sleep long.

I do not know it—it is without name—it is a word unsaid,
It is not in any dictionary, utterance, symbol.

Something it swings on more than the earth I swing on,
To it the creation is the friend whose embracing awakes me.   1315

Perhaps I might tell more. Outlines! I plead for my brothers and sisters.

Do you see O my brothers and sisters?
It is not chaos or death—it is form, union, plan—it is eternal life—it is
    Happiness.

4. Midwife (French).   5. Pour forth.

51

The past and present wilt—I have fill'd them, emptied them,
And proceed to fill my next fold of the future.   1320

Listener up there! what have you to confide to me?
Look in my face while I snuff the sidle[6] of evening,
(Talk honestly, no one else hears you, and I stay only a minute longer.)

Do I contradict myself?
Very well then I contradict myself,   1325
(I am large, I contain multitudes.)

I concentrate toward them that are nigh, I wait on the door-slab.

Who has done his day's work? who will soonest be through with his supper?
Who wishes to walk with me?

Will you speak before I am gone? will you prove already too late?   1330

52

The spotted hawk swoops by and accuses me, he complains of my gab
    and my loitering.

I too am not a bit tamed, I too am untranslatable.
I sound my barbaric yawp over the roofs of the world.

The last scud of day[7] holds back for me,
It flings my likeness after the rest and true as any on the shadow'd
    wilds,   1335
It coaxes me to the vapor and the dusk.

I depart as air, I shake my white locks at the runaway sun,
I effuse my flesh in eddies,[8] and drift it in lacy jags.

I bequeath myself to the dirt to grow from the grass I love,
If you want me again look for me under your boot-soles.   1340

You will hardly know who I am or what I mean,
But I shall be good health to you nevertheless,
And filter and fibre your blood.

Failing to fetch me at first keep encouraged,
Missing me one place search another,   1345
I stop somewhere waiting for you.

                                                    1855, 1881

---

6. I.e., extinguish the last glimmers of evening.   8. Air currents. "Effuse": pour forth.
7. Wind-driven clouds, or the last rays of the sun.

FROM CHILDREN OF ADAM[1]

Spontaneous Me

Spontaneous me, Nature,
The loving day, the mounting sun, the friend I am happy with,
The arm of my friend hanging idly over my shoulder,
The hillside whiten'd with blossoms of the mountain ash,
The same late in autumn, the hues of red, yellow, drab, purple, and
    light and dark green,   5
The rich coverlet of the grass, animals and birds, the private untrimm'd
    bank, the primitive apples, the pebble-stones,
Beautiful dripping fragments, the negligent list of one after another as I
    happen to call them to me or think of them,
The real poems, (what we call poems being merely pictures,)
The poems of the privacy of the night, and of men like me,
This poem drooping shy and unseen that I always carry, and that all
    men carry,   10
(Know once for all, avow'd on purpose, wherever are men like me, are
    our lusty lurking masculine poems,)
Love-thoughts, love-juice, love-odor, love-yielding, love-climbers, and
    the climbing sap,
Arms and hands of love, lips of love, phallic thumb of love, breasts of love,
    bellies press'd and glued together with love,
Earth of chaste love, life that is only life after love,
The body of my love, the body of the woman I love, the body of the man,
    the body of the earth,   15
Soft forenoon airs that blow from the south-west,
The hairy wild-bee that murmurs and hankers up and down, that gripes
    the full-grown lady-flower, curves upon her with amorous firm legs,
    takes his will of her, and holds himself tremulous and tight till he is
    satisfied;
The wet of woods through the early hours,
Two sleepers at night lying close together as they sleep, one with an arm
    slanting down across and below the waist of the other,
The smell of apples, aromas from crush'd sage-plant, mint, birch-bark,   20
The boy's longings, the glow and pressure as he confides to me what he
    was dreaming,
The dead leaf whirling its spiral whirl and falling still and content to the
    ground,
The no-form'd stings that sights, people, objects, sting me with,
The hubb'd sting of myself, stinging me as much as it ever can any one,
The sensitive, orbic, underlapp'd brothers, that only privileged feelers
    may be intimate where they are,   25

---

1. This group of poems first appeared in the 1860 edition of *Leaves of Grass* as *Enfans d'Adam*; later the contents and order were slightly altered until they reached final form in 1871. In a notebook entry Whitman identifies the relationship of this group to the *Calamus* poems: "Theory of a Cluster of Poems the same *to the passion of Woman-Love* as the 'Calamus-Leaves' are to adhesiveness, manly love. Full of animal-fire, tender, burning, the tremulous ache, delicious, yet such a torment. The swelling elate and vehement, that will not be denied. Adam, as a central figure and type. One piece presenting a vivid picture (in connection with the spirit) of a fully complete, well-developed man, eld, bearded, swart, fiery, as a more than rival of the youthful type-hero of novels and love poems."

The curious roamer the hand roaming all over the body, the bashful
    withdrawing of flesh where the fingers soothingly pause and edge
    themselves,
The limpid liquid within the young man,
The vex'd corrosion so pensive and so painful,
The torment, the irritable tide that will not be at rest,
The like of the same I feel, the like of the same in others,   30
The young man that flushes and flushes, and the young woman that
    flushes and flushes,
The young man that wakes deep at night, the hot hand seeking to repress
    what would master him,
The mystic amorous night, the strange half-welcome pangs, visions, sweats,
The pulse pounding through palms and trembling encircling fingers, the
    young man all color'd, red, ashamed, angry;
The souse upon me of my lover the sea, as I lie willing and naked,   35
The merriment of the twin babes that crawl over the grass in the sun,
    the mother never turning her vigilant eyes from them,
The walnut-trunk, the walnut-husks, and the ripening or ripen'd long-
    round walnuts,
The continence of vegetables, birds, animals,
The consequent meanness of me should I skulk or find myself indecent,
    while birds and animals never once skulk or find themselves indecent,
The great chastity of paternity, to match the great chastity of maternity, 40
The oath of procreation I have sworn, my Adamic and fresh daughters,
The greed that eats me day and night with hungry gnaw, till I saturate
    what shall produce boys to fill my place when I am through,
The wholesome relief, repose, content,
And this bunch pluck'd at random from myself,
It has done its work—I toss it carelessly to fall where it may.   45

1856, 1867

Facing West from California's Shores

Facing west from California's shores,
Inquiring, tireless, seeking what is yet unfound,
I, a child, very old, over waves, towards the house of maternity,[1] the land
    of migrations, look afar,
Look off the shores of my Western sea, the circle almost circled;
For starting westward from Hindustan, from the vales of Kashmere,[2]   5
From Asia, from the north, from the God, the sage, and the hero,
From the south, from the flowery peninsulas and the spice islands,[3]
Long having wander'd since, round the earth having wander'd,
Now I face home again, very pleas'd and joyous,
(But where is what I started for so long ago?   10
And why is it yet unfound?)

1860, 1867

---

1. Asia, at the time believed to be the birthplace of civilization.
2. Mountainous region adjacent to India, Paki-   stan, western China, and Tibet. "Hindustan": India.
3. Indonesia.

Crossing Brooklyn Ferry[1]

1

Flood-tide below me! I see you face to face!
Clouds of the west—sun there half an hour high—I see you also face to
    face.

Crowds of men and women attired in the usual costumes, how curious
    you are to me!
On the ferry-boats the hundreds and hundreds that cross, returning home,
    are more curious to me than you suppose,
And you that shall cross from shore to shore years hence are more to me,
    and more in my meditations, than you might suppose.   5

2

The impalpable sustenance of me from all things at all hours of the day,
The simple, compact, well-join'd scheme, myself disintegrated, every one
    disintegrated yet part of the scheme,
The similitudes of the past and those of the future,
The glories strung like beads on my smallest sights and hearings, on the
    walk in the street and the passage over the river,
The current rushing so swiftly and swimming with me far away,   10
The others that are to follow me, the ties between me and them,
The certainty of others, the life, love, sight, hearing of others.

Others will enter the gates of the ferry and cross from shore to shore,
Others will watch the run of the flood-tide,
Others will see the shipping of Manhattan north and west, and the
    heights of Brooklyn to the south and east,   15
Others will see the islands large and small;
Fifty years hence, others will see them as they cross, the sun half an hour
    high,
A hundred years hence, or ever so many hundred years hence, others will
    see them,
Will enjoy the sunset, the pouring-in of the flood-tide, the falling-back to
    the sea of the ebb-tide.

3

It avails not, time nor place—distance avails not,   20
I am with you, you men and women of a generation, or ever so many
    generations hence,
Just as you feel when you look on the river and sky, so I felt,
Just as any of you is one of a living crowd, I was one of a crowd,

---

1. First published as "Sun-Down Poem" in the 2nd edition of *Leaves of Grass* (1856). "Crossing Brooklyn
Ferry" was given its final title in 1860.

Just as you are refresh'd by the gladness of the river and the bright flow, I
    was refresh'd,
Just as you stand and lean on the rail, yet hurry with the swift current, I
    stood yet was hurried,   25
Just as you look on the numberless masts of ships and the thick-stemm'd
    pipes of steamboats, I look'd.

I too many and many a time cross'd the river of old,
Watched the Twelfth-month[2] sea-gulls, saw them high in the air floating
    with motionless wings, oscillating their bodies,
Saw how the glistening yellow lit up parts of their bodies and left the rest
    in strong shadow,
Saw the slow-wheeling circles and the gradual edging toward the south, 30
Saw the reflection of the summer sky in the water,
Had my eyes dazzled by the shimmering track of beams,
Look'd at the fine centrifugal spokes of light round the shape of my head
    in the sunlit water,
Look'd on the haze on the hills southward and south-westward,
Look'd on the vapor as it flew in fleeces tinged with violet,   35
Look'd toward the lower bay to notice the vessels arriving,
Saw their approach, saw aboard those that were near me,
Saw the white sails of schooners and sloops, saw the ships at anchor,
The sailors at work in the rigging or out astride the spars,
The round masts, the swinging motion of the hulls, the slender
    serpentine pennants,   40
The large and small steamers in motion, the pilots in their pilot-houses,
The white wake left by the passage, the quick tremulous whirl of the
    wheels,
The flags of all nations, the falling of them at sunset.
The scallop-edged waves in the twilight, the ladled cups, the frolicsome
    crests and glistening,
The stretch afar growing dimmer and dimmer, the gray walls of the
    granite storehouses by the docks,   45
On the river the shadowy group, the big steam-tug closely flank'd on
    each side by the barges, the hay-boat, the belated lighter,[3]
On the neighboring shore the fires from the foundry chimneys burning
    high and glaringly into the night,
Casting their flicker of black contrasted with wild red and yellow light
    over the tops of houses, and down into the clefts of streets.

4

These and all else were to me the same as they are to you,
I loved well those cities, loved well the stately and rapid river,   50
The men and women I saw were all near to me,
Others the same—others who looked back on me because I look'd
    forward to them,
(The time will come, though I stop here to-day and to-night.)

---

2. December.   3. Barge used to load or unload a cargo ship.

5

What is it then between us?
What is the count of the scores or hundreds of years between us?   55

Whatever it is, it avails not—distance avails not, and place avails not,
I too lived, Brooklyn of ample hills was mine,
I too walk'd the streets of Manhattan island, and bathed in the waters
    around it,
I too felt the curious abrupt questionings stir within me,
In the day among crowds of people sometimes they came upon me,   60
In my walks home late at night or as I lay in my bed they came upon me,
I too had been struck from the float forever held in solution,
I too had receiv'd identity by my body,
That I was I knew was of my body, and what I should be I knew I should
    be of my body.

6

It is not upon you alone the dark patches fall,   65
The dark threw its patches down upon me also,
The best I had done seem'd to me blank and suspicious,
My great thoughts as I supposed them, were they not in reality meagre?
Nor is it you alone who know what it is to be evil,
I am he who knew what it was to be evil,   70
I too knitted the old knot of contrariety,
Blabb'd, blush'd, resented, lied, stole, grudg'd,
Had guile, anger, lust, hot wishes I dared not speak,
Was wayward, vain, greedy, shallow, sly, cowardly, malignant,
The wolf, the snake, the hog, not wanting in me,   75
The cheating look, the frivolous word, the adulterous wish, not wanting,
Refusals, hates, postponements, meanness, laziness, none of these
    wanting,
Was one with the rest, the days and haps of the rest,
Was call'd by my nighest name by clear loud voices of young men as they
    saw me approaching or passing,
Felt their arms on my neck as I stood, or the negligent leaning of their
    flesh against me as I sat,   80
Saw many I loved in the street or ferry-boat or public assembly, yet never
    told them a word,
Lived the same life with the rest, the same old laughing, gnawing, sleeping,
Play'd the part that still looks back on the actor or actress,
The same old role, the role that is what we make it, as great as we like,
Or as small as we like, or both great and small.   85

7

Closer yet I approach you,
What thought you have of me now, I had as much of you—I laid in my
    stores in advance,
I consider'd long and seriously of you before you were born.

Who was to know what should come home to me?
Who knows but I am enjoying this?   90
Who knows, for all the distance, but I am as good as looking at you now,
    for all you cannot see me?

8

Ah, what can ever be more stately and admirable to me than mast-hemm'd
    Manhattan?
River and sunset and scallop-edg'd waves of flood-tide?
The sea-gulls oscillating their bodies, the hay-boat in the twilight, and
    the belated lighter?
What gods can exceed these that clasp me by the hand, and with voices I
    love call me promptly and loudly by my nighest name as I approach?   95
What is more subtle than this which ties me to the woman or man that
    looks in my face?
Which fuses me into you now, and pours my meaning into you?

We understand then do we not?
What I promis'd without mentioning it, have you not accepted?
What the study could not teach—what the preaching could not
    accomplish is accomplish'd, is it not?   100

9

Flow on, river! flow with the flood-tide, and ebb with the ebb-tide!
Frolic on, crested and scallop-edg'd waves!
Gorgeous clouds of the sunset! drench with your splendor me, or the
    men and women generations after me!
Cross from shore to shore, countless crowds of passengers!
Stand up, tall masts of Mannahatta![4] stand up, beautiful hills of
    Brooklyn!   105
Throb, baffled and curious brain! throw out questions and answers!
Suspend here and everywhere, eternal float of solution!
Gaze, loving and thirsting eyes, in the house or street or public assembly!
Sound out, voices of young men! loudly and musically call me by my
    nighest name!
Live, old life! play the part that looks back on the actor or actress!   110
Play the old role, the role that is great or small according as one makes it!
Consider, you who peruse me, whether I may not in unknown ways be
    looking upon you;
Be firm, rail over the river, to support those who lean idly, yet haste with
    the hasting current;
Fly on, sea-birds! fly sideways, or wheel in large circles high in the air;
Receive the summer sky, you water, and faithfully hold it till all downcast
    eyes have time to take it from you!   115
Diverge, fine spokes of light, from the shape of my head, or any one's
    head, in the sunlit water!

---

4. Variant of Manhattan.

Come on, ships from the lower bay! pass up or down, white-sail'd
    schooners, sloops, lighters!
Flaunt away, flags of all nations! be duly lower'd at sunset!
Burn high your fires, foundry chimneys! cast black shadows at nightfall!
    cast red and yellow light over the tops of the houses!
Appearances, now or henceforth, indicate what you are,   120
You necessary film, continue to envelop the soul,
About my body for me, and your body for you, be hung our divinest aromas,
Thrive, cities—bring your freight, bring your shows, ample and sufficient
    rivers,
Expand, being than which none else is perhaps more spiritual,
Keep your places, objects than which none else is more lasting.   125

You have waited, you always wait, you dumb, beautiful ministers,
We receive you with free sense at last, and are insatiate henceforward,
Not you any more shall be able to foil us, or withhold yourselves from us,
We use you, and do not cast you aside—we plant you permanently within
    us,
We fathom you not—we love you—there is perfection in you also,   130
You furnish your parts toward eternity,
Great or small, you furnish your parts toward the soul.

1856, 1881

FROM SEA-DRIFT[1]

Out of the Cradle Endlessly Rocking[2]

Out of the cradle endlessly rocking,
Out of the mocking-bird's throat, the musical shuttle,
Out of the Ninth-month midnight,
Over the sterile sands and the fields beyond, where the child leaving his
    bed wander'd alone, bareheaded, barefoot,
Down from the shower'd halo,   5
Up from the mystic play of shadows twining and twisting as if they were
    alive,
Out from the patches of briers and blackberries,
From the memories of the bird that chanted to me,
From your memories sad brother, from the fitful risings and fallings I
    heard,
From under that yellow half-moon late-risen and swollen as if with tears,   10
From those beginning notes of yearning and love there in the mist,
From the thousand responses of my heart never to cease,

1. The *Sea-Drift* section of the 1881 edition of
Leaves of Grass was made up of two new poems,
seven poems from *Sea-Shore Memories* in the
1871 *Passage to India* section, and two poems
from the 1876 *Two Rivulets* section.
2. First published as "A Child's Reminiscence" in
the *New York Saturday Press* of December 24,

1859, this poem was incorporated into the 1860
Leaves of Grass as "A Word Out of the Sea." Whitman continued to revise it until it reached the
present form in the *Sea-Drift* section of the 1881
edition. "Out of the Cradle Endlessly Rocking"
had been the first of the "Sea-Shore Memories"
group.

From the myriad thence-arous'd words,
From the word stronger and more delicious than any,
From such as now they start the scene revisiting,   15
As a flock, twittering, rising, or overhead passing,
Borne hither, ere all eludes me, hurriedly,
A man, yet by these tears a little boy again,
Throwing myself on the sand, confronting the waves,
I, chanter of pains and joys, uniter of here and hereafter,   20
Taking all hints to use them, but swiftly leaping beyond them,
A reminiscence sing.

Once Paumanok,[3]
When the lilac-scent was in the air and Fifth-month grass was growing,
Up this seashore in some briers,   25
Two feather'd guests from Alabama, two together,
And their nest, and four light-green eggs spotted with brown,
And every day the he-bird to and fro near at hand,
And every day the she-bird crouch'd on her nest, silent, with bright eyes,
And every day I, a curious boy, never too close, never disturbing them,   30
Cautiously peering, absorbing, translating.

Shine! shine! shine!
Pour down your warmth, great sun!
While we bask, we two together.

Two together!   35
Winds blow south, or winds blow north,
Day come white, or night come black,
Home, or rivers and mountains from home,
Singing all time, minding no time,
While we two keep together.   40

Till of a sudden,
May-be kill'd, unknown to her mate,
One forenoon the she-bird crouch'd not on the nest,
Nor return'd that afternoon, nor the next
Nor ever appear'd again.   45

And thenceforward all summer in the sound of the sea,
And at night under the full of the moon in calmer weather,
Over the hoarse surging of the sea,
Or flitting from brier to brier by day,
I saw, I heard at intervals the remaining one, the he-bird,   50
The solitary guest from Alabama.

Blow! blow! blow!
Blow up sea-winds along Paumanok's shore;
I wait and I wait till you blow my mate to me.

3. Long Island.

Yes, when the stars glisten'd, 55
All night long on the prong of a moss-scallop'd stake,
Down almost amid the slapping waves,
Sat the lone singer wonderful causing tears.

He call'd on his mate,
He pour'd forth the meanings which I of all men know. 60

Yes my brother I know,
The rest might not, but I have treasur'd every note,
For more than once dimly down to the beach gliding,
Silent, avoiding the moonbeams, blending myself with the shadows,
Recalling now the obscure shapes, the echoes, the sounds and sights
after their sorts, 65
The white arms out in the breakers tirelessly tossing,
I, with bare feet, a child, the wind wafting my hair,
Listen'd long and long.

Listen'd to keep, to sing, now translating the notes.
Following you my brother. 70

Soothe! soothe! soothe!
Close on its wave soothes the wave behind,
And again another behind embracing and lapping, every one close,
But my love soothes not me, not me.

Low hangs the moon, it rose late, 75
It is lagging—O I think it is heavy with love, with love.

O madly the sea pushes upon the land,
With love, with love.

O night! do I not see my love fluttering out among the breakers?
What is that little black thing I see there in the white? 80

Loud! loud! loud!
Loud I call to you, my love!

High and clear I shoot my voice over the waves,
Surely you must know who is here, is here,
You must know who I am, my love. 85

Low-hanging moon!
What is that dusky spot in your brown yellow?
O it is the shape, the shape of my mate!
O moon do not keep her from me any longer.

Land! land! O land! 90
Whichever way I turn, O I think you could give me my mate back again
if you only would,
For I am almost sure I see her dimly whichever way I look.

O rising stars!
Perhaps the one I want so much will rise, will rise with some of you.

O throat! O trembling throat!   95
Sound clearer through the atmosphere!
Pierce the woods, the earth,
Somewhere listening to catch you must be the one I want.

Shake out carols!
Solitary here, the night's carols!   100
Carols of lonesome love! death's carols!
Carols under that lagging, yellow, waning moon!
O under that moon where she droops almost down into the sea!
O reckless despairing carols.

But soft! sink low!   105
Soft! let me just murmur,
And do you wait a moment you husky-nois'd sea,
For somewhere I believe I heard my mate responding to me,
So faint, I must be still, be still to listen,
But not altogether still, for then she might not come immediately to me.   110

Hither my love!
Here I am! here!
With this just-sustain'd note I announce myself to you,
This gentle call is for you my love, for you.

Do not be decoy'd elsewhere,   115
That is the whistle of the wind, it is not my voice,
That is the fluttering, the fluttering of the spray,
Those are the shadows of leaves.

O darkness! O in vain!
O I am very sick and sorrowful.   120

O brown halo in the sky near the moon, drooping upon the sea!
O troubled reflection in the sea!
O throat! O throbbing heart!
And I singing uselessly, uselessly all the night.

O past! O happy life! O songs of joy!   125
In the air, in the woods, over fields,
Loved! loved! loved! loved! loved!
But my mate no more, no more with me!
We two together no more.

The aria sinking,   130
All else continuing, the stars shining,
The winds blowing, the notes of the bird continuous echoing,
With angry moans the fierce old mother incessantly moaning,
On the sands of Paumanok's shore gray and rustling,

The yellow half-moon enlarged, sagging down, drooping, the face of the
    sea almost touching,   135
The boy ecstatic, with his bare feet the waves, with his hair the
    atmosphere dallying,
The love in the heart long pent, now loose, now at last tumultuously
    bursting,
The aria's meaning, the ears, the soul, swiftly depositing,
The strange tears down the cheeks coursing,
The colloquy there, the trio, each uttering,   140
The undertone, the savage old mother incessantly crying,
To the boy's soul's questions sullenly timing, some drown'd secret hissing,
To the outsetting bard.

Demon or bird! (said the boy's soul,)
Is it indeed toward your mate you sing? or is it really to me?   145
For I, that was a child, my tongue's use sleeping, now I have heard you,
Now in a moment I know what I am for, I awake,
And already a thousand singers, a thousand songs, clearer, louder and
    more sorrowful than yours,
A thousand warbling echoes have started to life within me, never to die.

O you singer solitary, singing by yourself, projecting me,   150
O solitary me listening, never more shall I cease perpetuating you,
Never more shall I escape, never more the reverberations,
Never more the cries of unsatisfied love be absent from me,
Never again leave me to be the peaceful child I was before what there in
    the night,
By the sea under the yellow and sagging moon,   155
The messenger there arous'd, the fire, the sweet hell within,
The unknown want, the destiny of me.

O give me the clew! (it lurks in the night here somewhere,)
O if I am to have so much, let me have more!

A word then, (for I will conquer it,)   160
The word final, superior to all,
Subtle, sent up—what is it?—I listen;
Are you whispering it, and have been all the time, you sea-waves?
Is that it from your liquid rims and wet sands?

Whereto answering, the sea,   165
Delaying not, hurrying not,
Whisper'd me through the night, and very plainly before daybreak,
Lisp'd to me the low and delicious word death,
And again death, death, death, death,
Hissing melodious, neither like the bird nor like my arous'd
    child's heart,   170
But edging near as privately for me rustling at my feet,
Creeping thence steadily up to my ears and laving me softly all over,
Death, death, death, death, death.

Which I do not forget,
But fuse the song of my dusky demon and brother, 175
That he sang to me in the moonlight on Paumanok's gray beach,
With the thousand responsive songs at random,
My own songs awaked from that hour,
And with them the key, the word up from the waves,
The word of the sweetest song and all songs, 180
That strong and delicious word which, creeping to my feet,
(Or like some old crone rocking the cradle, swathed in sweet garments,
    bending aside,)
The sea whisper'd me.

1859, 1881

FROM BY THE ROADSIDE[1]

When I Heard the Learn'd Astronomer

When I heard the learn'd astronomer,
When the proofs, the figures, were ranged in columns before me,
When I was shown the charts and diagrams, to add, divide, and measure
    them,
When I sitting heard the astronomer where he lectured with much
    applause in the lecture-room,
How soon unaccountable I became tired and sick, 5
Till rising and gliding out I wander'd off by myself,
In the mystical moist night-air, and from time to time,
Look'd up in perfect silence at the stars.

1865

The Dalliance of the Eagles

Skirting the river road, (my forenoon walk, my rest,)
Skyward in air a sudden muffled sound, the dalliance of the eagles,
The rushing amorous contact high in space together,
The clinching interlocking claws, a living, fierce, gyrating wheel,
Four beating wings, two beaks, a swirling mass tight grappling, 5
In tumbling turning clustering loops, straight downward falling,
Till o'er the river pois'd, the twain yet one, a moment's lull,
A motionless still balance in the air, then parting, talons loosing,
Upward again on slow-firm pinions slanting, their separate diverse flight,
She hers, he his, pursuing. 10

1880, 1881

---

1. *By the Roadside* is the 1881 section title for around two dozen short poems of roadside observation, most of which first appeared in the 1860 edition of *Leaves of Grass*.

From Drum-Taps[1]

Beat! Beat! Drums!

Beat! beat! drums!—blow! bugles! blow!
Through the windows—through doors—burst like a ruthless force,
Into the solemn church, and scatter the congregation,
Into the school where the scholar is studying;
Leave not the bridegroom quiet—no happiness must he have now with
    his bride,   5
Nor the peaceful farmer any peace, ploughing his field or gathering his
    grain,
So fierce you whirr and pound you drums—so shrill you bugles blow.

Beat! beat! drums!—blow! bugles! blow!
Over the traffic of cities—over the rumble of wheels in the streets;
Are beds prepared for sleepers at night in the houses? no sleepers must
    sleep in those beds,   10
No bargainers' bargains by day—no brokers or speculators—would they
    continue?
Would the talkers be talking? would the singer attempt to sing?
Would the lawyer rise in the court to state his case before the judge?
Then rattle quicker, heavier drums—you bugles wilder blow.

Beat! beat! drums!—blow! bugles! blow!   15
Make no parley—stop for no expostulation,
Mind not the timid—mind not the weeper or prayer,
Mind not the old man beseeching the young man,
Let not the child's voice be heard, nor the mother's entreaties,
Make even the trestles to shake the dead where they lie awaiting the
    hearses,   20
So strong you thump O terrible drums—so loud you bugles blow.

1861, 1867

Cavalry Crossing a Ford

A line in long array where they wind betwixt green islands,
They take a serpentine course, their arms flash in the sun—hark to the
    musical clank,

1. The contents of the original *Drum-Taps* (first printed in 1865 as a little book) differed considerably from the contents of the *Drum-Taps* section finally arrived at in the 1881 *Leaves of Grass*. In the final arrangement the poetic purpose shifts throughout, roughly reflecting the chronology of the Civil War and the chronology of the composition of the poems. Whitman's initial aim was propagandistic. Indeed, "Beat! Beat! Drums!" served as a kind of recruiting poem when it was first printed in September 1861 issues of *Harper's Weekly* and the *New York Leader*, having been composed after the Southern victory at the first battle of Bull Run. The dominant impulse of most of the later poems is realistic—a determination to record the war the way it was, and in the best of the poems the realism is achieved through elaborate technical subtleties. The stages of Whitman's own attitudes toward the war are well stated in the epigraph he gave the *Drum-Taps* group in 1871 and then inserted parenthetically into "The Wound Dresser" in the 1881 edition: "Arous'd and angry, I'd thought to beat the alarum, and urge relentless war, / But soon my fingers fail'd me, my face droop'd and I resign'd myself / To sit by the wounded and soothe them, or silently watch the dead."

Behold the silvery river, in it the splashing horses loitering stop to drink,
Behold the brown-faced men, each group, each person a picture, the
    negligent rest on the saddles,
Some emerge on the opposite bank, others are just entering the ford—
    while,   5
Scarlet and blue and snowy white,
The guidon flags[1] flutter gayly in the wind.

                                 1865, 1871

The Wound-Dresser

1

An old man bending I come among new faces,
Years looking backward resuming in answer to children,
Come tell us old man, as from young men and maidens that love me,
(Arous'd and angry, I'd thought to beat the alarum, and urge relentless war,
But soon my fingers fail'd me, my face droop'd and I resign'd myself,   5
To sit by the wounded and soothe them, or silently watch the dead;)
Years hence of these scenes, of these furious passions, these chances,
Of unsurpass'd heroes, (was one side so brave? the other was equally
    brave;)
Now be witness again, paint the mightiest armies of earth,
Of those armies so rapid so wondrous what saw you to tell us?   10
What stays with you latest and deepest? of curious panics,
Of hard-fought engagements or sieges tremendous what deepest remains?

2

O maidens and young men I love and that love me,
What you ask of my days those the strangest and sudden your talking
    recalls,
Soldier alert I arrive after a long march cover'd with sweat and dust,   15
In the nick of time I come, plunge in the fight, loudly shout in the rush
    of successful charge,
Enter the captur'd works[1]—yet lo, like a swift-running river they fade,
Pass and are gone they fade—I dwell not on soldiers' perils or soldiers' joys,
(Both I remember well—many the hardships, few the joys, yet I was
    content.)

But in silence in dreams' projections,   20
While the world of gain and appearance and mirth goes on,
So soon what is over forgotten, and waves wash the imprints off the sand,
With hinged knees returning I enter the doors, (while for you up there,
Whoever you are, follow without noise and be of strong heart.)

Bearing the bandages, water and sponge,   25
Straight and swift to my wounded I go,

---

1. Small military flags carried by soldiers for sig-
naling and identification at a distance.

1. Fortified earthworks.

Where they lie on the ground after the battle brought in,
Where their priceless blood reddens the grass the ground,
Or to the rows of the hospital tent, or under the roof'd hospital,
To the long rows of cots up and down each side I return,   30
To each and all one after another I draw near, not one do I miss,
An attendant follows holding a tray, he carries a refuse pail,
Soon to be fill'd with clotted rags and blood, emptied, and fill'd again.

I onward go, I stop,
With hinged knees and steady hand to dress wounds,   35
I am firm with each, the pangs are sharp yet unavoidable,
One turns to me his appealing eyes—poor boy! I never knew you,
Yet I think I could not refuse this moment to die for you, if that would
    save you.

3

On, on I go, (open doors of time! open hospital doors!)
The crush'd head I dress, (poor crazed hand tear not the bandage away,)   40
The neck of the cavalry-man with the bullet through and through I
    examine,
Hard the breathing rattles, quite glazed already the eye, yet life struggles
    hard,
(Come sweet death! be persuaded O beautiful death!
In mercy come quickly.)

From the stump of the arm, the amputated hand,   45
I undo the clotted lint, remove the slough, wash off the matter and blood,
Back on his pillow the soldier bends with curv'd neck and side-falling
    head,
His eyes are closed, his face is pale, he dares not look on the bloody stump,
And has not yet look'd on it.

I dress a wound in the side, deep, deep,   50
But a day or two more, for see the frame all wasted and sinking,
And the yellow-blue countenance see.

I dress the perforated shoulder, the foot with the bullet-wound,
Cleanse the one with a gnawing and putrid gangrene, so sickening, so
    offensive,
While the attendant stands behind aside me holding the tray and pail.   55

I am faithful, I do not give out,
The fractur'd thigh, the knee, the wound in the abdomen,
These and more I dress with impassive hand, (yet deep in my breast a fire,
    a burning flame.)

4

Thus in silence in dreams' projections,
Returning, resuming, I thread my way through the hospitals,   60
The hurt and wounded I pacify with soothing hand,

I sit by the restless all the dark night, some are so young,
Some suffer so much, I recall the experience sweet and sad,
(Many a soldier's loving arms about this neck have cross'd and rested,
Many a soldier's kiss dwells on these bearded lips.)   65

1865, 1881

FROM MEMORIES OF PRESIDENT LINCOLN

When Lilacs Last in the Dooryard Bloom'd[1]

1

When lilacs last in the dooryard bloom'd,
And the great star[2] early droop'd in the western sky in the night,
I mourn'd, and yet shall mourn with ever-returning spring.

Ever-returning spring, trinity sure to me you bring,
Lilac blooming perennial and drooping star in the west,   5
And thought of him I love.

2

O powerful western fallen star!
O shades of night—O moody, tearful night!
O great star disappear'd—O the black murk that hides the star!
O cruel hands that hold me powerless—O helpless soul of me!   10
O harsh surrounding cloud that will not free my soul.

3

In the dooryard fronting an old farm-house near the white-wash'd palings,
Stands the lilac-bush tall-growing with heart-shaped leaves of rich green,
With many a pointed blossom rising delicate, with the perfume strong I love,
With every leaf a miracle—and from this bush in the dooryard,   15
With delicate-color'd blossoms and heart-shaped leaves of rich green,
A sprig with its flower I break.

4

In the swamp in secluded recesses,
A shy and hidden bird is warbling a song.

Solitary the thrush,   20
The hermit withdrawn to himself, avoiding the settlements,
Sings by himself a song.

---

1. Composed in the months following Lincoln's
assassination on April 14, 1865, this elegy was
printed in the fall of that year as an appendix to
the recently published *Drum-Taps* volume. In the
1881 edition of *Leaves of Grass*, it and three shorter
poems were joined to make up the section *Memories of President Lincoln*.
2. Literally Venus, although it becomes associated with Lincoln himself.

Song of the bleeding throat,
Death's outlet song of life, (for well dear brother I know,
If thou wast not granted to sing thou would'st surely die.)   25

5

Over the breast of the spring, the land, amid cities,
Amid lanes and through old woods, where lately the violets peep'd from
     the ground, spotting the gray debris,
Amid the grass in the fields each side of the lanes, passing the endless
     grass,
Passing the yellow-spear'd wheat, every grain from its shroud in the dark-
     brown fields uprisen,
Passing the apple-tree blows[3] of white and pink in the orchards,   30
Carrying a corpse to where it shall rest in the grave,
Night and day journeys a coffin.[4]

6

Coffin that passes through lanes and streets,
Through day and night with the great cloud darkening the land,
With the pomp of the inloop'd flags with the cities draped in black,   35
With the show of the States themselves as of crape-veil'd women standing,
With processions long and winding and the flambeaus[5] of the night,
With the countless torches lit, with the silent sea of faces and the
     unbared heads,
With the waiting depot, the arriving coffin, and the sombre faces,
With dirges through the night, with the thousand voices rising strong
     and solemn,   40
With all the mournful voices of the dirges pour'd around the coffin,
The dim-lit churches and the shuddering organs—where amid these you
     journey,
With the tolling tolling bells' perpetual clang,
Here, coffin that slowly passes,
I give you my sprig of lilac.   45

7

(Nor for you, for one alone,
Blossoms and branches green to coffins all I bring,
For fresh as the morning, thus would I chant a song for you O sane and
     sacred death.

All over bouquets of roses,
O death, I cover you over with roses and early lilies,   50
But mostly and now the lilac that blooms the first,
Copious I break, I break the sprigs from the bushes,
With loaded arms I come, pouring for you,
For you and the coffins all of you O death.)

---

3. Blossoms.
4. The train carrying Lincoln's body traveled from
Washington, D.C., to Springfield, Illinois.
5. Torches.

8

O western orb sailing the heaven,   55
Now I know what you must have meant as a month since I walk'd,
As I walk'd in silence the transparent shadowy night,
As I saw you had something to tell as you bent to me night after night,
As you droop'd from the sky low down as if to my side, (while the other
    stars all look'd on,)
As we wander'd together the solemn night, (for something I know not
    what kept me from sleep,)   60
As the night advanced, and I saw on the rim of the west how full you
    were of woe,
As I stood on the rising ground in the breeze in the cool transparent night,
As I watch'd where you pass'd and was lost in the netherward black of the night,
As my soul in its trouble dissatisfied sank, as where you sad orb,
Concluded, dropt in the night, and was gone.   65

9

Sing on there in the swamp,
O singer bashful and tender, I hear your notes, I hear your call,
I hear, I come presently, I understand you,
But a moment I linger, for the lustrous star has detain'd me,
The star my departing comrade holds and detains me.   70

10

O how shall I warble myself for the dead one there I loved?
And how shall I deck my song for the large sweet soul that has gone?
And what shall my perfume be for the grave of him I love?

Sea-winds blown from east and west,
Blown from the Eastern sea and blown from the Western sea, till there
    on the prairies meeting,   75
These and with these and the breath of my chant,
I'll perfume the grave of him I love.

11

O what shall I hang on the chamber walls?
And what shall the pictures be that I hang on the walls,
To adorn the burial-house of him I love?   80

Pictures of growing spring and farms and homes,
With the Fourth-month[6] eve at sundown, and the gray smoke lucid and
    bright,
With floods of the yellow gold of the gorgeous, indolent, sinking sun,
    burning, expanding the air,

6. April.

With the fresh sweet herbage under foot, and the pale green leaves of the
    trees prolific,
In the distance the flowing glaze, the breast of the river, with a
    wind-dapple here and there, 85
With ranging hills on the banks, with many a line against the sky, and
    shadows,
And the city at hand with dwellings so dense, and stacks of chimneys,
And all the scenes of life and the workshops, and the workmen homeward
    returning.

12

Lo, body and soul—this land,
My own Manhattan with spires, and the sparkling and hurrying tides,
    and the ships, 90
The varied and ample land, the South and the North in the light, Ohio's
    shores and flashing Missouri,
And ever the far-spreading prairies cover'd with grass and corn.

Lo, the most excellent sun so calm and haughty,
The violet and purple morn with just-felt breezes,
The gentle soft-born measureless light, 95
The miracle spreading bathing all, the fulfill'd noon,
The coming eve delicious, the welcome night and the stars,
Over my cities shining all, enveloping man and land.

13

Sing on, sing on you gray-brown bird,
Sing from the swamps, the recesses, pour your chant from the bushes, 100
Limitless out of the dusk, out of the cedars and pines.

Sing on dearest brother, warble your reedy song,
Loud human song, with voice of uttermost woe.

O liquid and free and tender!
O wild and loose to my soul!—O wondrous singer! 105
You only I hear—yet the star holds me, (but will soon depart,)
Yet the lilac with mastering odor holds me.

14

Now while I sat in the day and look'd forth,
In the close of the day with its light and the fields of spring, and the
    farmers preparing their crops,
In the large unconscious scenery of my land with its lakes and forests, 110
In the heavenly aerial beauty, (after the perturb'd winds and the storms,)
Under the arching heavens of the afternoon swift passing, and the voices
    of children and women,
The many-moving sea-tides, and I saw the ships how they sail'd,
And the summer approaching with richness, and the fields all busy with
    labor,

And the infinite separate houses, how they all went on, each with its
    meals and minutia of daily usages,   115
And the streets how their throbbings throbb'd, and the cities pent—lo,
    then and there,
Falling upon them all and among them all, enveloping me with the rest,
Appear'd the cloud, appear'd the long black trail,
And I knew death, its thought, and the sacred knowledge of death.

Then with the knowledge of death as walking one side of me,   120
And the thought of death close-walking the other side of me,
And I in the middle as with companions, and as holding the hands of
    companions,
I fled forth to the hiding receiving night that talks not,
Down to the shores of the water, the path by the swamp in the dimness,
To the solemn shadowy cedars and ghostly pines so still.   125

And the singer so shy to the rest receiv'd me,
The gray-brown bird I know receiv'd us comrades three,
And he sang the carol of death, and a verse for him I love.

From deep secluded recesses,
From the fragrant cedars and the ghostly pines so still,   130
Came the carol of the bird.

And the charm of the carol rapt me,
As I held as if by their hands my comrades in the night,
And the voice of my spirit tallied the song of the bird.

Come lovely and soothing death,   135
Undulate round the world, serenely arriving, arriving,
In the day, in the night, to all, to each,
Sooner or later delicate death.

Prais'd be the fathomless universe,
For life and joy, and for objects and knowledge curious,   140
And for love, sweet love—but praise! praise! praise!
For the sure-enwinding arms of cool-enfolding death.

Dark mother always gliding near with soft feet,
Have none chanted for thee a chant of fullest welcome?
Then I chant it for thee, I glorify thee above all,   145
I bring thee a song that when thou must indeed come, come unfalteringly.

Approach strong deliveress,
When it is so, when thou hast taken them I joyously sing the dead,
Lost in the loving floating ocean of thee,
Laved in the flood of thy bliss O death.   150

From me to thee glad serenades,
Dances for thee I propose saluting thee, adornments and feastings for thee,
And the sights of the open landscape and the high-spread sky are fitting,
And life and the fields, and the huge and thoughtful night.

The night in silence under many a star, 155
The ocean shore and the husky whispering wave whose voice I know,
And the soul turning to thee O vast and well-veil'd death,
And the body gratefully nestling close to thee.

Over the tree-tops I float thee a song,
Over the rising and sinking waves, over the myriad fields and the prairies
    wide, 160
Over the dense-pack'd cities all and the teeming wharves and ways,
I float this carol with joy, with joy to thee O death.

15

To the tally of my soul,
Loud and strong kept up the gray-brown bird,
With pure deliberate notes spreading filling the night. 165

Loud in the pines and cedars dim,
Clear in the freshness moist and the swamp-perfume,
And I with my comrades there in the night.

While my sight that was bound in my eyes unclosed,
As to long panoramas of visions. 170

And I saw askant[7] the armies,
I saw as in noiseless dreams hundreds of battle-flags,
Borne through the smoke of the battles and pierc'd with missiles I saw
    them,
And carried hither and yon through the smoke, and torn and bloody,
And at last but a few shreds left on the staffs, (and all in silence,) 175
And the staffs all splinter'd and broken.

I saw battle-corpses, myriads of them,
And the white skeletons of young men, I saw them,
I saw the debris and debris of all the slain soldiers of the war,
But I saw they were not as was thought, 180
They themselves were fully at rest, they suffer'd not,
The living remain'd and suffer'd, the mother suffer'd,
And the wife and the child and the musing comrade suffer'd,
And the armies that remain'd suffer'd.

16

Passing the visions, passing the night, 185
Passing, unloosing the hold of my comrades' hands,
Passing the song of the hermit bird and the tallying song of my soul,
Victorious song, death's outlet song, yet varying ever-altering song,
As low and wailing, yet clear the notes, rising and falling, flooding the
    night,

7. Sideways, aslant.

Sadly sinking and fainting, as warning and warning, and yet again
    bursting with joy,   190
Covering the earth and filling the spread of the heaven,
As that powerful psalm in the night I heard from recesses,
Passing, I leave thee lilac with heart-shaped leaves,
I leave thee there in the door-yard, blooming, returning with spring.

I cease from my song for thee,   195
From my gaze on thee in the west, fronting the west, communing with
    thee,
O comrade lustrous with silver face in the night.

Yet each to keep and all, retrievements out of the night,
The song, the wondrous chant of the gray-brown bird,
And the tallying chant, the echo arous'd in my soul,   200
With the lustrous and drooping star with the countenance full of woe,
With the holders holding my hand nearing the call of the bird,
Comrades mine and I in the midst, and their memory ever to keep, for
    the dead I loved so well,
For the sweetest, wisest soul of all my days and lands—and this for his
    dear sake,
Lilac and star and bird twined with the chant of my soul,   205
There in the fragrant pines and the cedars dusk and dim.

1865–66, 1881

HERMAN MELVILLE
1819–1891

Herman Melville was born in New York City in 1819, the third of eight children of Allan Melvill, a dry-goods merchant, and Maria Gansevoort, daughter of American Revolutionary hero General Peter Gansevoort. Melville's father incurred massive debt before dying suddenly and in delirium in 1832, and his wife and children, then living in Albany, became dependent on the Gansevoorts. Taken out of school when he was twelve, Melville (the e was added in the 1830s) held a succession of jobs: at a bank, at his brother Gansevoort's fur-cap store in Albany, at his uncle Thomas Melvill's farm in Pittsfield, Massachusetts, and at a country school near Pittsfield. In 1839 he voyaged to and from Liverpool as a cabin boy, but uncertainties about employment continued on his return. At age twenty-one, in January 1841, he sailed on a whaler for the South Seas. After over a year at sea, Melville and a shipmate, Toby Greene, jumped ship at the Marquesas Islands, approximately one thousand miles northeast of Tahiti, and for a few weeks in the summer of 1842 the two lived among the supposedly cannibalistic islanders of Tapai Valley. Picked up by an Australian whaler less than a month after he deserted, Melville signed on as an ordinary seaman with the naval frigate *United States*, cruised the Pacific, and arrived at Boston in October 1844.

Melville was twenty-five; he later said that from that year he dated the beginning of his life. He apparently did not look for a job after his discharge from the navy; he stayed with his brothers in New York City and began writing *Typee*, which drew on his experiences in the Marquesas. The book, published in 1846 in England and the United States, made a great sensation, capturing the imagination of readers with its combination of anthropological novelty and adventure. Shortly after its publication, Melville began writing a second novel, *Omoo*, which also drew on his experiences in the South Sea islands. Published in 1847, it was another best-seller. Three days after his twenty-eighth birthday and in the flush of his success, Melville married Elizabeth Knapp Shaw on August 4, 1847. Her father, Lemuel Shaw, the chief justice of the Massachusetts Supreme Court, had been a school friend of Alan Melvill's. After the marriage Shaw provided several advances against his daughter's inheritance, allowing Melville to establish himself in Manhattan with his bride, his younger brother Allan, Allan's wife, his mother, his four sisters, and his new manuscript. But instead of supplying his publisher with yet another commercially promising tale of a Polynesian adventure, Melville attempted to elevate the travel-narrative genre to the level of spiritual and political allegory. In this third novel, *Mardi*, which was published in April 1849, Melville presented travel (as he would in *Moby-Dick*) as a philosophical journey. It is his longest novel and remains a difficult text for most readers. When first published, it sold poorly and received generally unfavorable reviews. After the birth of his first son, Malcolm, in 1849, Melville, seeking to regain his reputation, rapidly wrote the more accessible *Redburn* (1849), which drew on his travels to Liverpool, and *White-Jacket* (1850), based on his experiences on the man-of-war *United States*. Both novels were received enthusiastically in England and America.

In a buoyant mood, Melville began his whaling novel, *Moby-Dick*. Like *Mardi*, *Moby-Dick* was an enormously ambitious undertaking. There is compelling textual and biographical evidence that Melville wrote the book in stages, radically altering his conception of the novel from a relatively straightforward whaling narrative to something that aspired to be a "Gospels in this century" (as he termed the novel in an 1851 letter to Nathaniel Hawthorne). While composing the novel, Melville came under the spell of Shakespeare, Milton, Emerson, and numerous other writers. Melville was also inspired by his new literary friendship with Hawthorne, whom he had met at an August 1850 picnic in Pittsfield, Massachusetts. Immediately after their meeting, he read Hawthorne's *Mosses from an Old Manse* (1846) and wrote a belated review in which he expressed his thoughts about the challenges facing American writers. Convinced that the day had come when American writers could rival Shakespeare, Melville, in praising Hawthorne's achievements, also honored that which infused the book he was writing: dark "Shakespearean" truths about human nature and the universe that, "in this world of lies," can be told only "covertly" and "by snatches."

As he continued to work on *Moby-Dick* and struggle with his finances, Melville late in 1850 moved his family to a farm near Pittsfield, where he was able to keep up his friendship with Hawthorne, who was living in nearby Lenox. In May 1851, Melville borrowed $2,050 from an old acquaintance, and as he anticipated doing final work on the galleys of *Moby-Dick*, he painfully defined his literary-economic dilemma to Hawthorne: "What I feel most moved to write, that is banned,—it will not pay. Yet, altogether, write the other way I cannot. So the product is a final hash, and all my books are botches." When *Moby-Dick* was published in late 1851, a reviewer for the *London Britannia* declared it "a most extraordinary work"; and a reviewer in the *New York Tribune* proclaimed that it was "the best production which has yet come from that seething brain, and . . . it gives us a higher opinion of the author's originality and power than even the favorite and fragrant first-fruits of his genius, the never-to-be-forgotten *Typee*." Still, there were a number of negative reviews from critics unhappy with the novel's length, philosophical abstractness, and mixing of genres, and the novel quickly vanished from the literary scene without bringing Melville the critical admiration that he had expected.

But Melville was not totally discouraged. Shortly after publishing *Moby-Dick*, he began *Pierre*, thinking he could express the agonies of the growth of a human psyche in a domestic novel focusing on the romantic, ethical, and intellectual perplexities attending Pierre Glendinning's coming into manhood. As he worked on this novel, reviews of *Moby-Dick* continued to appear. Disturbed by the mixed and sometimes hostile responses (the January 1852 *Southern Quarterly Review*, for instance, said a "writ de lunatic" was justified against Melville and his characters), Melville folded into his novel-in-progress a satirical account of the U.S. literary scene in which the timid and genteel succeed and the boldly adventurous fail. With its depictions of clerical hypocrisy, family dishonesty, and seemingly incestuous sexuality, Melville's wildly inventive and parodic novel was greeted—by those who bothered to take notice of it—as the work of a maniac, and it further hurt his chances for a commercially successful literary career. The novel, published in 1852, was widely denounced as immoral, and one *Pierre*-inspired account of the author was captioned: "HERMAN MELVILLE CRAZY." In a panic, family and friends attempted to get Melville a government job, but nothing came of their efforts.

Melville stayed on at the Pittsfield farm with his expanding household (his second son, Stanwix, was born in 1851, and two daughters, Elizabeth and Frances, were born in 1853 and 1855) and began a new career as a writer of short stories and novellas for two major American monthlies, *Harper's* and *Putnam's*. Paid at modest rates for fiction that was published anonymously, Melville, in works like "Bartleby, the Scrivener," "The Paradise of Bachelors and the Tartarus of Maids," and "Benito Cereno," took on such vexing issues of antebellum culture as racial and gender inequities, the social transformations caused by emerging industrial capitalism, and slavery. Some critics regard these works as among Melville's most socially progressive writings; others argue that Melville's choice of topical subjects should not obscure his metaphysical interest in the situation of individuals who exist, as the narrator of "Bartleby" puts it, "alone, absolutely alone in the universe. A bit of wreck in the mid Atlantic." In these enigmatic fictions, Melville seems more intent on exploring and engaging the ideological discourses of his time than on arguing for any particular reforms. For instance, although there may be no shrewder investigation of white racism and the evils of slavery than "Benito Cereno" (1855), which partly entraps readers in the stereotypical racist assumptions of the sea captain Amasa Delano, the novella is not an obvious attack on slavery as such, and it was ignored by the abolitionist press.

In 1855 Melville published *Israel Potter*, a tale of the American Revolution which had been serialized in *Putnam's*; and in 1856 he collected his stories in a volume titled *The Piazza Tales*. One year later he published *The Confidence-Man*, an indictment of the selfishness and duplicities of his contemporary world in the form of a metaphysical satire, allegory, and low comedy set on a Mississippi steamship. The novel went almost unread in the United States; in England the reviews were admiring but sales were disappointing. Deeply depressed by his struggles as a writer, Melville took an extended trip to Europe and the Levant, from October 1856 to May 1857, with funds supplied by his father-in-law, who hoped that the trip would lighten Melville's mood. But in England Melville confessed to Hawthorne (at the time U.S. consul at Liverpool) that he did not expect to enjoy his travels because "the spirit of adventure" had gone out of him. Upon his return he told a Gansevoort relative that he was "not going to write any more at the present." Instead, he lectured for small fees in eastern and midwestern states on "Statues in Rome" (1857), "The South Sea" (1858), and "Travel" (1859).

After the death of Judge Shaw in 1861, the Melvilles inherited funds that eased their economic pressures, and by October 1863 they were living in Manhattan. In 1864 Melville and his brother Allan made a trip to the Virginia battlefields looking for a Gansevoort cousin and (as Allan put it) hoping to "have opportunities to see that they may describe." Some of those opportunities proved fruitful for *Battle-Pieces* (1866), Melville's volume of Civil War poems, which was barely noticed by reviewers.

Highly allusive, tightly formal, and marked by a seemingly Olympian detachment, *Battle-Pieces* is now regarded by many critics, along with Whitman's *Drum-Taps* (1865), as among the best volumes of poetry to have come out of the war. In the same year that he published *Battle-Pieces*, Melville at last obtained a political job as a deputy inspector of customs in New York City. When he had time to write, he worked mostly on his poetry.

These were dreary years for Melville. His job was dull and paid poorly, he had little ability to manage finances, and he was prone to anger and depression. His wife's half-brothers even considered him a danger to their sister, and by early 1867 Elizabeth may have begun to believe that he was insane. Her loyalty to him and her horror of gossip, however, kept her from acting on her minister's suggestion that she seek refuge with her family in Boston. Adding to the misery of the period, Malcolm killed himself late in 1867 at the age of eighteen. In the aftermath of the suicide, Melville began working on a poem about a diverse group of American and European pilgrims—and tourists—who talked their way through some of the same Palestinian scenes he had visited in 1857. This poem, *Clarel*, grew to eighteen thousand lines and appeared in 1876, paid for by a bequest from Elizabeth's uncle Peter Gansevoort. Addressing the conflict between religious faith and Darwinian skepticism that obsessed English contemporaries such as Matthew Arnold, the poem found few readers during the nineteenth century and remains one of Melville's understudied works.

A series of legacies came to the Melvilles in their last years, allowing Melville to retire from the customhouse at the beginning of 1886. During the late 1880s Melville and his wife drew closer together, in part out of their grief at the death of their second son, Stanwix, who was found dead in a San Francisco hotel in 1886. Around that time Melville once again began to devote himself to writing and publishing. He put together two volumes of poems, which he published with his own funds. In the mid-1880s a poem he was working on about a British sailor led him to compose a fictional narrative that was left nearly finished at Melville's death as *Billy Budd, Sailor*, his final study of the tense and ambiguous conflicts between the individual and various forms of authority.

Famously known during the 1840s as the "man who lived among the cannibals," Melville was neglected in the post–Civil War literary world. Shortly before his death in 1891, however, a revival of interest began, especially in England. The true Melville revival, however, took off with essays published on the occasion of Melville's centennial in 1919 and was given added momentum by the posthumous publication of *Billy Budd* in 1924. In one of the most curious phenomena of American literary history, the neglected Melville suddenly came to be regarded in the rarefied company of Shakespeare as a writer who, as Melville said of Shakespeare and Hawthorne, had mastered "the great Art of Telling the Truth" through the dazzling plentitude and sly indirections of his language.

Bartleby, the Scrivener[1]

A Story of Wall-Street

I am a rather elderly man. The nature of my avocations for the last thirty years has brought me into more than ordinary contact with what would seem an interesting and somewhat singular set of men, of whom as yet nothing that I know of has ever been written:—I mean the law-copyists or

---

1. The text of *Bartleby, the Scrivener* is from the first printing in the November and December 1853 issues of *Putnam's Monthly Magazine*.

"Scrivener": copyist or writer; in this story employed to make multiple copies of legal documents with pen and ink.

scriveners. I have known very many of them, professionally and privately, and if I pleased, could relate divers histories, at which good-natured gentlemen might smile, and sentimental souls might weep. But I waive the biographies of all other scriveners for a few passages in the life of Bartleby, who was a scrivener the strangest I ever saw or heard of. While of other law-copyists I might write the complete life, of Bartleby nothing of that sort can be done. I believe that no materials exist for a full and satisfactory biography of this man. It is an irreparable loss to literature. Bartleby was one of those beings of whom nothing is ascertainable, except from the original sources, and in his case those are very small. What my own astonished eyes saw of Bartleby, *that* is all I know of him, except, indeed, one vague report which will appear in the sequel.

Ere introducing the scrivener, as he first appeared to me, it is fit I make some mention of myself, my *employées*, my business, my chambers, and general surroundings; because some such description is indispensable to an adequate understanding of the chief character about to be presented.

Imprimis:[2] I am a man who, from his youth upwards, has been filled with a profound conviction that the easiest way of life is the best. Hence, though I belong to a profession proverbially energetic and nervous, even to turbulence, at times, yet nothing of that sort have I ever suffered to invade my peace. I am one of those unambitious lawyers who never addresses a jury, or in any way draws down public applause; but in the cool tranquillity of a snug retreat, do a snug business among rich men's bonds and mortgages and title-deeds. All who know me, consider me an eminently *safe* man. The late John Jacob Astor,[3] a personage little given to poetic enthusiasm, had no hesitation in pronouncing my first grand point to be prudence; my next, method. I do not speak it in vanity, but simply record the fact, that I was not unemployed in my profession by the late John Jacob Astor; a name which, I admit, I love to repeat, for it hath a rounded and orbicular sound to it, and rings like unto bullion. I will freely add, that I was not insensible to the late John Jacob Astor's good opinion.

Some time prior to the period at which this little history begins, my avocations had been largely increased. The good old office, now extinct in the State of New-York, of a Master in Chancery, had been conferred upon me. It was not a very arduous office, but very pleasantly remunerative. I seldom lose my temper; much more seldom indulge in dangerous indignation at wrongs and outrages; but I must be permitted to be rash here and declare, that I consider the sudden and violent abrogation of the office of Master in Chancery, by the new Constitution,[4] as a——premature act; inasmuch as I had counted upon a life-lease of the profits, whereas I only received those of a few short years. But this is by the way.

My chambers were up stairs at No. — Wall-street. At one end they looked upon the white wall of the interior of a spacious sky-light shaft, penetrating the building from top to bottom. This view might have been considered

---

2. In the first place (Latin).
3. Astor (1763–1848), a New Yorker, had made one of the largest fortunes of his era, first in fur trading and then in real estate and finance.

4. New York had adopted a "new Constitution" in 1846. "Chancery": cases involving equity law that do not require a jury.

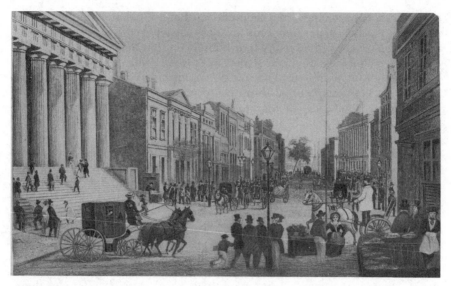

Wall Street, viewed from the corner of Broad Street, New York City, c. 1846.

rather tame than otherwise, deficient in what landscape painters call "life." But if so, the view from the other end of my chambers offered, at least, a contrast, if nothing more. In that direction my windows commanded an unobstructed view of a lofty brick wall, black by age and everlasting shade; which wall required no spy-glass to bring out its lurking beauties, but for the benefit of all near-sighted spectators, was pushed up to within ten feet of my window panes. Owing to the great height of the surrounding buildings, and my chambers being on the second floor, the interval between this wall and mine not a little resembled a huge square cistern.

At the period just preceding the advent of Bartleby, I had two persons as copyists in my employment, and a promising lad as an office-boy. First, Turkey; second, Nippers; third, Ginger Nut. These may seem names, the like of which are not usually found in the Directory. In truth they were nicknames, mutually conferred upon each other by my three clerks, and were deemed expressive of their respective persons or characters. Turkey was a short, pursy[5] Englishman of about my own age, that is, somewhere not far from sixty. In the morning, one might say, his face was of a fine florid hue, but after twelve o'clock, meridian—his dinner hour—it blazed like a grate full of Christmas coals; and continued blazing—but, as it were, with a gradual wane—till 6 o'clock, P.M. or thereabouts, after which I saw no more of the proprietor of the face, which gaining its meridian with the sun, seemed to set with it, to rise, culminate, and decline the following day, with the like regularity and undiminished glory. There are many singular coincidences I have known in the course of my life, not the least among which was the fact, that exactly when Turkey displayed his fullest beams from his red

5. Shortwinded from obesity.

and radiant countenance, just then, too, at that critical moment, began the daily period when I considered his business capacities as seriously disturbed for the remainder of the twenty-four hours. Not that he was absolutely idle, or averse to business then; far from it. The difficulty was, he was apt to be altogether too energetic. There was a strange, inflamed, flurried, flighty recklessness of activity about him. He would be incautious in dipping his pen into his inkstand. All his blots upon my documents, were dropped there after twelve o'clock, meridian. Indeed, not only would he be reckless and sadly given to making blots in the afternoon, but some days he went further, and was rather noisy. At such times, too, his face flamed with augmented blazonry, as if cannel coal had been heaped on anthracite.[6] He made an unpleasant racket with his chair; spilled his sand-box;[7] in mending his pens, impatiently split them all to pieces, and threw them on the floor in a sudden passion; stood up and leaned over his table, boxing his papers about in a most indecorous manner, very sad to behold in an elderly man like him. Nevertheless, as he was in many ways a most valuable person to me, and all the time before twelve o'clock, meridian, was the quickest, steadiest creature too, accomplishing a great deal of work in a style not easy to be matched—for these reasons, I was willing to overlook his eccentricities, though indeed, occasionally, I remonstrated with him. I did this very gently, however, because, though the civilest, nay, the blandest and most reverential of men in the morning, yet in the afternoon he was disposed, upon provocation, to be slightly rash with his tongue, in fact, insolent. Now, valuing his morning services as I did, and resolved not to lose them; yet, at the same time made uncomfortable by his inflamed ways after twelve o'clock; and being a man of peace, unwilling by my admonitions to call forth unseemly retorts from him; I took upon me, one Saturday noon (he was always worse on Saturdays), to hint to him, very kindly, that perhaps now that he was growing old, it might be well to abridge his labors; in short, he need not come to my chambers after twelve o'clock, but, dinner over, had best go home to his lodgings and rest himself till tea-time. But no; he insisted upon his afternoon devotions. His countenance became intolerably fervid, as he oratorically assured me—gesticulating with a long ruler at the other end of the room— that if his services in the morning were useful, how indispensable, then, in the afternoon?

"With submission, sir," said Turkey on this occasion, "I consider myself your right-hand man. In the morning I but marshal and deploy my columns; but in the afternoon I put myself at their head, and gallantly charge the foe, thus!"—and he made a violent thrust with the ruler.

"But the blots, Turkey," intimated I.

"True,—but, with submission, sir, behold these hairs! I am getting old. Surely, sir, a blot or two of a warm afternoon is not to be severely urged against gray hairs. Old age—even if it blot the page—is honorable. With submission, sir, we *both* are getting old."

This appeal to my fellow-feeling was hardly to be resisted. At all events, I saw that go he would not. So I made up my mind to let him stay, resolving,

---

6. The combination of "cannal coal," which burns quickly, and "anthracite," which burns slowly, pro- duces a high, bright flame.
7. Sand for blotting ink.

nevertheless, to see to it, that during the afternoon he had to do with my less important papers.

Nippers, the second on my list, was a whiskered, sallow, and, upon the whole, rather piratical-looking young man of about five and twenty. I always deemed him the victim of two evil powers—ambition and indigestion. The ambition was evinced by a certain impatience of the duties of a mere copyist, an unwarrantable usurpation of strictly professional affairs, such as the original drawing up of legal documents. The indigestion seemed betokened in an occasional nervous testiness and grinning irritability, causing the teeth to audibly grind together over mistakes committed in copying; unnecessary maledictions, hissed, rather than spoken, in the heat of business; and especially by a continual discontent with the height of the table where he worked. Though of a very ingenious mechanical turn, Nippers could never get this table to suit him. He put chips under it, blocks of various sorts, bits of pasteboard, and at last went so far as to attempt an exquisite adjustment by final pieces of folded blotting paper. But no invention would answer. If, for the sake of easing his back, he brought the table lid at a sharp angle well up towards his chin, and wrote there like a man using the steep roof of a Dutch house for his desk:—then he declared that it stopped the circulation in his arms. If now he lowered the table to his waistbands, and stooped over it in writing, then there was a sore aching in his back. In short, the truth of the matter was, Nippers knew not what he wanted. Or, if he wanted any thing, it was to be rid of a scrivener's table altogether. Among the manifestations of his diseased ambition was a fondness he had for receiving visits from certain ambiguous-looking fellows in seedy coats, whom he called his clients. Indeed I was aware that not only was he, at times, considerable of a ward-politician, but he occasionally did a little business at the Justices' courts, and was not unknown on the steps of the Tombs.[8] I have good reason to believe, however, that one individual who called upon him at my chambers, and who, with a grand air, he insisted was his client, was no other than a dun, and the alleged title-deed, a bill. But with all his failings, and the annoyances he caused me, Nippers, like his compatriot Turkey, was a very useful man to me; wrote a neat, swift hand; and, when he chose, was not deficient in a gentlemanly sort of deportment. Added to this, he always dressed in a gentlemanly sort of way; and so, incidentally, reflected credit upon my chambers. Whereas with respect to Turkey, I had much ado to keep him from being a reproach to me. His clothes were apt to look oily and smell of eating-houses. He wore his pantaloons very loose and baggy in summer. His coats were execrable; his hat not to be handled. But while the hat was a thing of indifference to me, inasmuch as his natural civility and deference, as a dependent Englishman, always led him to doff it the moment he entered the room, yet his coat was another matter. Concerning his coats, I reasoned with him; but with no effect. The truth was, I suppose, that a man with so small an income, could not afford to sport such a lustrous face and a lustrous coat at one and the same time. As Nippers once observed, Turkey's money went chiefly for red ink. One winter day I presented Turkey with a highly-respectable looking coat of my own, a padded gray coat, of a most comfortable warmth, and which buttoned straight up from the knee to the neck. I thought Turkey

---

8. The New York City prison, built in 1839 in the spirit of the Egyptian revival architecture of the time.

would appreciate the favor, and abate his rashness and obstreperousness of afternoons. But no. I verily believe that buttoning himself up in so downy and blanket-like a coat had a pernicious effect upon him; upon the same principle that too much oats are bad for horses. In fact, precisely as a rash, restive horse is said to feel his oats, so Turkey felt his coat. It made him insolent. He was a man whom prosperity harmed.

Though concerning the self-indulgent habits of Turkey I had my own private surmises, yet touching Nippers I was well persuaded that whatever might be his faults in other respects, he was, at least, a temperate young man. But indeed, nature herself seemed to have been his vintner, and at his birth charged him so thoroughly with an irritable, brandy-like disposition, that all subsequent potations were needless. When I consider how, amid the stillness of my chambers, Nippers would sometimes impatiently rise from his seat, and stooping over his table, spread his arms wide apart, seize the whole desk, and move it, and jerk it, with a grim, grinding motion on the floor, as if the table were a perverse voluntary agent, intent on thwarting and vexing him; I plainly perceive that for Nippers, brandy and water were altogether superfluous.

It was fortunate for me that, owing to its peculiar cause—indigestion—the irritability and consequent nervousness of Nippers, were mainly observable in the morning, while in the afternoon he was comparatively mild. So that Turkey's paroxysms only coming on about twelve o'clock, I never had to do with their eccentricities at one time. Their fits relieved each other like guards. When Nippers' was on, Turkey's was off; and *vice versa*. This was a good natural arrangement under the circumstances.

Ginger Nut, the third on my list, was a lad some twelve years old. His father was a carman,[9] ambitious of seeing his son on the bench instead of a cart, before he died. So he sent him to my office as student at law, errand boy, and cleaner and sweeper, at the rate of one dollar a week. He had a little desk to himself, but he did not use it much. Upon inspection, the drawer exhibited a great array of the shells of various sorts of nuts. Indeed, to this quick-witted youth the whole noble science of the law was contained in a nut-shell. Not the least among the employments of Ginger Nut, as well as one which he discharged with the most alacrity, was his duty as cake and apple purveyor for Turkey and Nippers. Copying law papers being proverbially a dry, husky sort of business, my two scriveners were fain to moisten their mouths very often with Spitzenbergs[1] to be had at the numerous stalls nigh the Custom House and Post Office. Also, they sent Ginger Nut very frequently for that peculiar cake—small, flat, round, and very spicy—after which he had been named by them. Of a cold morning when business was but dull, Turkey would gobble up scores of these cakes, as if they were mere wafers—indeed they sell them at the rate of six or eight for a penny—the scrape of his pen blending with the crunching of the crisp particles in his mouth. Of all the fiery afternoon blunders and flurried rashnesses of Turkey, was his once moistening a ginger-cake between his lips, and clapping it on to a mortgage for a seal.[2] I came within an ace of dismissing him then. But he mollified me

9. Driver, teamster.
1. Red-and-yellow New York apples.
2. The narrator is playing on the resemblance between thin cookies and wax wafers used for sealing documents.

by making an oriental bow, and saying—"With submission, sir, it was generous of me to find you in stationery on my own account."

Now my original business—that of a conveyancer and title hunter,[3] and drawer-up of recondite documents of all sorts—was considerably increased by receiving the master's office. There was now great work for scriveners. Not only must I push the clerks already with me, but I must have additional help. In answer to my advertisement, a motionless young man one morning, stood upon my office threshold, the door being open, for it was summer. I can see that figure now—pallidly neat, pitiably respectable, incurably forlorn! It was Bartleby.

After a few words touching his qualifications, I engaged him, glad to have among my corps of copyists a man of so singularly sedate an aspect, which I thought might operate beneficially upon the flighty temper of Turkey, and the fiery one of Nippers.

I should have stated before that ground glass folding-doors divided my premises into two parts, one of which was occupied by my scriveners, the other by myself. According to my humor I threw open these doors, or closed them. I resolved to assign Bartleby a corner by the folding-doors, but on my side of them, so as to have this quiet man within easy call, in case any trifling thing was to be done. I placed his desk close up to a small side-window in that part of the room, a window which originally had afforded a lateral view of certain grimy back-yards and bricks, but which, owing to subsequent erections, commanded at present no view at all, though it gave some light. Within three feet of the panes was a wall, and the light came down from far above, between two lofty buildings, as from a very small opening in a dome. Still further to a satisfactory arrangement, I procured a high green folding screen, which might entirely isolate Bartleby from my sight, though not remove him from my voice. And thus, in a manner, privacy and society were conjoined.

At first Bartleby did an extraordinary quantity of writing. As if long famishing for something to copy, he seemed to gorge himself on my documents. There was no pause for digestion. He ran a day and night line, copying by sun-light and by candle-light. I should have been quite delighted with his application, had he been cheerfully industrious. But he wrote on silently, palely, mechanically.

It is, of course, an indispensable part of a scrivener's business to verify the accuracy of his copy, word by word. Where there are two or more scriveners in an office, they assist each other in this examination, one reading from the copy, the other holding the original. It is a very dull, wearisome, and lethargic affair. I can readily imagine that to some sanguine temperaments it would be altogether intolerable. For example, I cannot credit that the mettlesome poet Byron would have contentedly sat down with Bartleby to examine a law document of, say five hundred pages, closely written in a crimpy hand.

Now and then, in the haste of business, it had been my habit to assist in comparing some brief document myself, calling Turkey or Nippers for this purpose. One object I had in placing Bartleby so handy to me behind the screen, was to avail myself of his services on such trivial occasions. It was on

3. Someone who checks records to be sure there are no encumbrances on the title of property to be transferred. "Conveyancer": someone who draws up deeds for transferring title to property.

the third day, I think, of his being with me, and before any necessity had arisen for having his own writing examined, that, being much hurried to complete a small affair I had in hand, I abruptly called to Bartleby. In my haste and natural expectancy of instant compliance, I sat with my head bent over the original on my desk, and my right hand sideways, and somewhat nervously extended with the copy, so that immediately upon emerging from his retreat, Bartleby might snatch it and proceed to business without the least delay.

In this very attitude did I sit when I called to him, rapidly stating what it was I wanted him to do—namely, to examine a small paper with me. Imagine my surprise, nay, my consternation, when without moving from his privacy, Bartleby in a singularly mild, firm voice, replied, "I would prefer not to."

I sat awhile in perfect silence, rallying my stunned faculties. Immediately it occurred to me that my ears had deceived me, or Bartleby had entirely misunderstood my meaning. I repeated my request in the clearest tone I could assume. But in quite as clear a one came the previous reply, "I would prefer not to."

"Prefer not to," echoed I, rising in high excitement, and crossing the room with a stride. "What do you mean? Are you moon-struck? I want you to help me compare this sheet here—take it," and I thrust it towards him.

"I would prefer not to," said he.

I looked at him steadfastly. His face was leanly composed; his gray eye dimly calm. Not a wrinkle of agitation rippled him. Had there been the least uneasiness, anger, impatience or impertinence in his manner; in other words, had there been any thing ordinarily human about him, doubtless I should have violently dismissed him from the premises. But as it was, I should have as soon thought of turning my pale plaster-of-paris bust of Cicero[4] out of doors. I stood gazing at him awhile, as he went on with his own writing, and then reseated myself at my desk. This is very strange, thought I. What had one best do? But my business hurried me. I concluded to forget the matter for the present, reserving it for my future leisure. So calling Nippers from the other room, the paper was speedily examined.

A few days after this, Bartleby concluded four lengthy documents, being quadruplicates of a week's testimony taken before me in my High Court of Chancery. It became necessary to examine them. It was an important suit, and great accuracy was imperative. Having all things arranged I called Turkey, Nippers and Ginger Nut from the next room, meaning to place the four copies in the hands of my four clerks, while I should read from the original. Accordingly Turkey, Nippers and Ginger Nut had taken their seats in a row, each with his document in hand, when I called to Bartleby to join this interesting group.

"Bartleby! quick, I am waiting."

I heard a slow scrape of his chair legs on the uncarpeted floor, and soon he appeared standing at the entrance of his hermitage.

"What is wanted?" said he mildly.

"The copies, the copies," said I hurriedly. "We are going to examine them. There"—and I held towards him the fourth quadruplicate.

"I would prefer not to," he said, and gently disappeared behind the screen.

4. Roman orator and statesman (106–42 B.C.E.).

For a few moments I was turned into a pillar of salt,[5] standing at the head of my seated column of clerks. Recovering myself, I advanced towards the screen, and demanded the reason for such extraordinary conduct.

"*Why* do you refuse?"

"I would prefer not to."

With any other man I should have flown outright into a dreadful passion, scorned all further words, and thrust him ignominiously from my presence. But there was something about Bartleby that not only strangely disarmed me, but in a wonderful manner touched and disconcerted me. I began to reason with him.

"These are your own copies we are about to examine. It is labor saving to you, because one examination will answer for your four papers. It is common usage. Every copyist is bound to help examine his copy. Is it not so? Will you not speak? Answer!"

"I prefer not to," he replied in a flute-like tone. It seemed to me that while I had been addressing him, he carefully revolved every statement that I made; fully comprehended the meaning; could not gainsay the irresistible conclusion; but, at the same time, some paramount consideration prevailed with him to reply as he did.

"You are decided, then, not to comply with my request—a request made according to common usage and common sense?"

He briefly gave me to understand that on that point my judgment was sound. Yes: his decision was irreversible.

It is not seldom the case that when a man is browbeaten in some unprecedented and violently unreasonable way, he begins to stagger in his own plainest faith. He begins, as it were, vaguely to surmise that, wonderful as it may be, all the justice and all the reason is on the other side. Accordingly, if any disinterested persons are present, he turns to them for some reinforcement for his own faltering mind.

"Turkey," said I, "what do you think of this? Am I not right?"

"With submission, sir," said Turkey, with his blandest tone, "I think that you are."

"Nippers," said I, "what do *you* think of it?"

"I think I should kick him out of the office."

(The reader of nice perceptions will here perceive that, it being morning, Turkey's answer is couched in polite and tranquil terms, but Nippers replies in ill-tempered ones. Or, to repeat a previous sentence, Nippers's ugly mood was on duty, and Turkey's off.)

"Ginger Nut," said I, willing to enlist the smallest suffrage in my behalf, "what do *you* think of it?"

"I think, sir, he's a little *luny*," replied Ginger Nut, with a grin.

"You hear what they say," said I, turning towards the screen, "come forth and do your duty."

But he vouchsafed no reply. I pondered a moment in sore perplexity. But once more business hurried me. I determined again to postpone the consideration of this dilemma to my future leisure. With a little trouble we made out to examine the papers without Bartleby, though at every page or two, Turkey deferentially dropped his opinion that this proceeding was quite out

---

5. The punishment of Lot's disobedient wife (Genesis 19.26).

of the common; while Nippers, twitching in his chair with a dyspeptic nervousness, ground out between his set teeth occasional hissing maledictions against the stubborn oaf behind the screen. And for his (Nippers's) part, this was the first and the last time he would do another man's business without pay.

Meanwhile Bartleby sat in his hermitage, oblivious to every thing but his own peculiar business there.

Some days passed, the scrivener being employed upon another lengthy work. His late remarkable conduct led me to regard his ways narrowly. I observed that he never went to dinner; indeed that he never went any where. As yet I had never of my personal knowledge known him to be outside of my office. He was a perpetual sentry in the corner. At about eleven o'clock though, in the morning, I noticed that Ginger Nut would advance toward the opening in Bartleby's screen, as if silently beckoned thither by a gesture invisible to me where I sat. The boy would then leave the office jingling a few pence, and reappear with a handful of ginger-nuts which he delivered in the hermitage, receiving two of the cakes for his trouble.

He lives, then, on ginger-nuts, thought I; never eats a dinner, properly speaking; he must be a vegetarian then; but no; he never eats even vegetables, he eats nothing but ginger-nuts. My mind then ran on in reveries concerning the probable effects upon the human constitution of living entirely on ginger-nuts. Ginger-nuts are so called because they contain ginger as one of their peculiar constituents, and the final flavoring one. Now what was ginger? A hot, spicy thing. Was Bartleby hot and spicy? Not at all. Ginger, then, had no effect upon Bartleby. Probably he preferred it should have none.

Nothing so aggravates an earnest person as a passive resistance. If the individual so resisted be of a not inhumane temper, and the resisting one perfectly harmless in his passivity; then, in the better moods of the former, he will endeavor charitably to construe to his imagination what proves impossible to be solved by his judgment. Even so, for the most part, I regarded Bartleby and his ways. Poor fellow! thought I, he means no mischief; it is plain he intends no insolence; his aspect sufficiently evinces that his eccentricities are involuntary. He is useful to me. I can get along with him. If I turn him away, the chances are he will fall in with some less indulgent employer, and then he will be rudely treated, and perhaps driven forth miserably to starve. Yes. Here I can cheaply purchase a delicious self-approval. To befriend Bartleby; to humor him in his strange wilfulness, will cost me little or nothing, while I lay up in my soul what will eventually prove a sweet morsel for my conscience. But this mood was not invariable with me. The passiveness of Bartleby sometimes irritated me. I felt strangely goaded on to encounter him in new opposition, to elicit some angry spark from him answerable to my own. But indeed I might as well have essayed to strike fire with my knuckles against a bit of Windsor soap.[6] But one afternoon the evil impulse in me mastered me, and the following little scene ensued:

"Bartleby," said I, "when those papers are all copied, I will compare them with you."

"I would prefer not to."

"How? Surely you do not mean to persist in that mulish vagary?"

6. Brown hand soap.

No answer.

I threw open the folding-doors near by, and turning upon Turkey and Nippers, exclaimed in an excited manner—

"He says, a second time, he won't examine his papers. What do you think of it, Turkey?"

It was afternoon, be it remembered. Turkey sat glowing like a brass boiler, his bald head steaming, his hands reeling among his blotted papers.

"Think of it?" roared Turkey; "I think I'll just step behind his screen, and black his eyes for him!"

So saying, Turkey rose to his feet and threw his arms into a pugilistic position. He was hurrying away to make good his promise, when I detained him, alarmed at the effect of incautiously rousing Turkey's combativeness after dinner.

"Sit down, Turkey," said I, "and hear what Nippers has to say. What do you think of it, Nippers? Would I not be justified in immediately dismissing Bartleby?"

"Excuse me, that is for you to decide, sir. I think his conduct quite unusual, and indeed unjust, as regards Turkey and myself. But it may only be a passing whim."

"Ah," exclaimed I, "you have strangely changed your mind then—you speak very gently of him now."

"All beer," cried Turkey; "gentleness is effects of beer—Nippers and I dined together to-day. You see how gentle *I* am, sir. Shall I go and black his eyes?"

"You refer to Bartleby, I suppose. No, not to-day, Turkey," I replied; "pray, put up your fists."

I closed the doors, and again advanced towards Bartleby. I felt additional incentives tempting me to my fate. I burned to be rebelled against again. I remembered that Bartleby never left the office.

"Bartleby," said I, "Ginger Nut is away; just step round to the Post Office, won't you? (it was but a three minutes' walk,) and see if there is any thing for me."

"I would prefer not to."

"You *will* not?"

"I *prefer* not."

I staggered to my desk, and sat there in a deep study. My blind inveteracy returned. Was there any other thing in which I could procure myself to be ignominiously repulsed by this lean, penniless wight?—my hired clerk? What added thing is there, perfectly reasonable, that he will be sure to refuse to do?

"Bartleby!"

No answer.

"Bartleby," in a louder tone.

No answer.

"Bartleby," I roared.

Like a very ghost, agreeably to the laws of magical invocation, at the third summons, he appeared at the entrance of his hermitage.

"Go to the next room, and tell Nippers to come to me."

"I prefer not to," he respectfully and slowly said, and mildly disappeared.

"Very good, Bartleby," said I, in a quiet sort of serenely severe self-possessed tone, intimating the unalterable purpose of some terrible retribution very close at hand. At the moment I half intended something of the kind. But upon the whole, as it was drawing towards my dinner-hour, I thought it best to put on my hat and walk home for the day, suffering much from perplexity and distress of mind.

Shall I acknowledge it? The conclusion of this whole business was, that it soon became a fixed fact of my chambers, that a pale young scrivener, by the name of Bartleby, had a desk there; that he copied for me at the usual rate of four cents a folio (one hundred words); but he was permanently exempt from examining the work done by him, that duty being transferred to Turkey and Nippers, out of compliment doubtless to their superior acuteness; moreover, said Bartleby was never on any account to be dispatched on the most trivial errand of any sort; and that even if entreated to take upon him such a matter, it was generally understood that he would prefer not to—in other words, that he would refuse point-blank.

As days passed on, I became considerably reconciled to Bartleby. His steadiness, his freedom from all dissipation, his incessant industry (except when he chose to throw himself into a standing revery behind his screen), his great stillness, his unalterableness of demeanor under all circumstances, made him a valuable acquisition. One prime thing was this,—*he was always there*;—first in the morning, continually through the day, and the last at night. I had a singular confidence in his honesty. I felt my most precious papers perfectly safe in his hands. Sometimes to be sure I could not, for the very soul of me, avoid falling into sudden spasmodic passions with him. For it was exceeding difficult to bear in mind all the time those strange peculiarities, privileges, and unheard of exemptions, forming the tacit stipulations on Bartleby's part under which he remained in my office. Now and then, in the eagerness of dispatching pressing business, I would inadvertently summon Bartleby, in a short, rapid tone, to put his finger, say, on the incipient tie of a bit of red tape with which I was about compressing some papers. Of course, from behind the screen the usual answer, "I prefer not to," was sure to come; and then, how could a human creature with common infirmities of our nature, refrain from bitterly exclaiming upon such perverseness—such unreasonableness. However, every added repulse of this sort which I received only tended to lessen the probability of my repeating the inadvertence.

Here it must be said, that according to the customs of most legal gentlemen occupying chambers in densely-populated law buildings, there were several keys to my door. One was kept by a woman residing in the attic, which person weekly scrubbed and daily swept and dusted my apartments. Another was kept by Turkey for convenience sake. The third I sometimes carried in my own pocket. The fourth I knew not who had.

Now, one Sunday morning I happened to go to Trinity Church, to hear a celebrated preacher, and finding myself rather early on the ground, I thought I would walk round to my chambers for a while. Luckily I had my key with me; but upon applying it to the lock, I found it resisted by something inserted from the inside. Quite surprised, I called out; when to my consternation a key was turned from within; and thrusting his lean visage at me, and holding the door ajar, the apparition of Bartleby appeared, in his shirt sleeves, and otherwise in a strangely tattered dishabille, saying quietly that he was sorry, but he was deeply engaged just then, and—preferred not admitting me at present. In a brief word or two, he moreover added, that perhaps I had better walk round the block two or three times, and by that time he would probably have concluded his affairs.

Now, the utterly unsurmised appearance of Bartleby, tenanting my law-chambers of a Sunday morning, with his cadaverously gentlemanly *nonchalance*, yet withal firm and self-possessed, had such a strange effect upon me, that incontinently I slunk away from my own door, and did as desired. But not without sundry twinges of impotent rebellion against the mild effrontery of this unaccountable scrivener. Indeed, it was his wonderful mildness chiefly, which not only disarmed me, but unmanned me, as it were. For I consider that one, for the time, is a sort of unmanned when he tranquilly permits his hired clerk to dictate to him, and order him away from his own premises. Furthermore, I was full of uneasiness as to what Bartleby could possibly be doing in my office in his shirt sleeves, and in an otherwise dismantled condition of a Sunday morning. Was any thing amiss going on? Nay, that was out of the question. It was not to be thought of for a moment that Bartleby was an immoral person. But what could he be doing there?—copying? Nay again, whatever might be his eccentricities, Bartleby was an eminently decorous person. He would be the last man to sit down to his desk in any state approaching to nudity. Besides, it was Sunday; and there was something about Bartleby that forbade the supposition that he would by any secular occupation violate the proprieties of the day.

Nevertheless, my mind was not pacified; and full of a restless curiosity, at last I returned to the door. Without hindrance I inserted my key, opened it, and entered. Bartleby was not to be seen. I looked round anxiously, peeped behind his screen; but it was very plain that he was gone. Upon more closely examining the place, I surmised that for an indefinite period Bartleby must have ate, dressed, and slept in my office, and that too without plate, mirror, or bed. The cushioned seat of a rickety old sofa in one corner bore the faint impress of a lean, reclining form. Rolled away under his desk, I found a blanket; under the empty grate, a blacking box and brush; on a chair, a tin basin, with soap and a ragged towel; in a newspaper a few crumbs of ginger-nuts and a morsel of cheese. Yes, thought I, it is evident enough that Bartleby has been making his home here, keeping bachelor's hall all by himself. Immediately then the thought came sweeping across me, What miserable friendlessness and loneliness are here revealed! His poverty is great; but his solitude, how horrible! Think of it. Of a Sunday, Wall-street is deserted as Petra;[7] and every night of every day it is an emptiness. This building too, which of week-days hums with industry and life, at nightfall echoes with sheer vacancy, and all through Sunday is forlorn. And here Bartleby makes his home; sole spectator of a solitude which he has seen all populous—a sort of innocent and transformed Marius[8] brooding among the ruins of Carthage!

For the first time in my life a feeling of overpowering stinging melancholy seized me. Before, I had never experienced aught but a not-unpleasing sadness. The bond of a common humanity now drew me irresistibly to gloom. A fraternal melancholy! For both I and Bartleby were sons of Adam. I remembered the bright silks and sparkling faces I had seen that day, in gala trim,

---

7. Ancient city whose ruins are in Jordan, on a slope of Mount Hor.

8. Gaius Marius (157–86 B.C.E.), Roman general who returned to power after exile.

swan-like sailing down the Mississippi of Broadway; and I contrasted them with the pallid copyist, and thought to myself, Ah, happiness courts the light, so we deem the world is gay; but misery hides aloof, so we deem that misery there is none. These sad fancyings—chimeras, doubtless, of a sick and silly brain—led on to other and more special thoughts, concerning the eccentricities of Bartleby. Presentiments of strange discoveries hovered round me. The scrivener's pale form appeared to me laid out, among uncaring strangers, in its shivering winding sheet.

Suddenly I was attracted by Bartleby's closed desk, the key in open sight left in the lock.

I mean no mischief, seek the gratification of no heartless curiosity, thought I; besides, the desk is mine, and its contents too, so I will make bold to look within. Every thing was methodically arranged, the papers smoothly placed. The pigeon holes were deep, and removing the files of documents, I groped into their recesses. Presently I felt something there, and dragged it out. It was an old bandanna handkerchief, heavy and knotted. I opened it, and saw it was a saving's bank.

I now recalled all the quiet mysteries which I had noted in the man. I remembered that he never spoke but to answer; that though at intervals he had considerable time to himself, yet I had never seen him reading—no, not even a newspaper; that for long periods he would stand looking out, at his pale window behind the screen, upon the dead brick wall; I was quite sure he never visited any refectory or eating house; while his pale face clearly indicated that he never drank beer like Turkey, or tea and coffee even, like other men; that he never went any where in particular that I could learn; never went out for a walk, unless indeed that was the case at present; that he had declined telling who he was, or whence he came, or whether he had any relatives in the world; that though so thin and pale, he never complained of ill health. And more than all, I remembered a certain unconscious air of pallid—how shall I call it?—of pallid haughtiness, say, or rather an austere reserve about him, which had positively awed me into my tame compliance with his eccentricities, when I had feared to ask him to do the slightest incidental thing for me, even though I might know, from his long-continued motionlessness, that behind his screen he must be standing in one of those dead-wall reveries of his.

Revolving all these things, and coupling them with the recently discovered fact that he made my office his constant abiding place and home, and not forgetful of his morbid moodiness; revolving all these things, a prudential feeling began to steal over me. My first emotions had been those of pure melancholy and sincerest pity; but just in proportion as the forlornness of Bartleby grew and grew to my imagination, did that same melancholy merge into fear, that pity into repulsion. So true it is, and so terrible too, that up to a certain point the thought or sight of misery enlists our best affections; but, in certain special cases, beyond that point it does not. They err who would assert that invariably this is owing to the inherent selfishness of the human heart. It rather proceeds from a certain hopelessness of remedying excessive and organic ill. To a sensitive being, pity is not seldom pain. And when at last it is perceived that such pity cannot lead to effectual succor, common sense bids the soul be rid of it. What I saw that morning persuaded me that the scrivener was the victim of innate and incurable disorder. I might give alms to his body; but his body did not pain him; it was his soul that suffered, and his soul I could not reach.

I did not accomplish the purpose of going to Trinity Church that morning. Somehow, the things I had seen disqualified me for the time from church-going. I walked homeward, thinking what I would do with Bartleby. Finally, I resolved upon this;—I would put certain calm questions to him the next morning, touching his history, &c., and if he declined to answer them openly and unreservedly (and I supposed he would prefer not), then to give him a twenty dollar bill over and above whatever I might owe him, and tell him his services were no longer required; but that if in any other way I could assist him, I would be happy to do so, especially if he desired to return to his native place, wherever that might be, I would willingly help to defray the expenses. Moreover, if, after reaching home, he found himself at any time in want of aid, a letter from him would be sure of a reply.

The next morning came.

"Bartleby," said I, gently calling to him behind his screen.

No reply.

"Bartleby," said I, in a still gentler tone, "come here; I am not going to ask you to do any thing you would prefer not to do—I simply wish to speak to you."

Upon this he noiselessly slid into view.

"Will you tell me, Bartleby, where you were born?"

"I would prefer not to."

"Will you tell me *any thing* about yourself?"

"I would prefer not to."

"But what reasonable objection can you have to speak to me? I feel friendly towards you."

He did not look at me while I spoke, but kept his glance fixed upon my bust of Cicero, which as I then sat, was directly behind me, some six inches above my head.

"What is your answer, Bartleby?" said I, after waiting a considerable time for a reply, during which his countenance remained immovable, only there was the faintest conceivable tremor of the white attenuated mouth.

"At present I prefer to give no answer," he said, and retired into his hermitage.

It was rather weak in me I confess, but his manner on this occasion nettled me. Not only did there seem to lurk in it a certain calm disdain, but his perverseness seemed ungrateful, considering the undeniable good usage and indulgence he had received from me.

Again I sat ruminating what I should do. Mortified as I was at his behavior, and resolved as I had been to dismiss him when I entered my office, nevertheless I strangely felt something superstitious knocking at my heart, and forbidding me to carry out my purpose, and denouncing me for a villain if I dared to breathe one bitter word against this forlornest of mankind. At last, familiarly drawing my chair behind his screen, I sat down and said: "Bartleby, never mind then about revealing your history; but let me entreat you, as a friend, to comply as far as may be with the usages of this office. Say now you will help to examine papers to-morrow or next day: in short, say now that in a day or two you will begin to be a little reasonable:—say so, Bartleby."

"At present I would prefer not to be a little reasonable," was his mildly cadaverous reply.

Just then the folding-doors opened, and Nippers approached. He seemed suffering from an unusually bad night's rest, induced by severer indigestion than common. He overheard those final words of Bartleby.

"*Prefer not*, eh?" gritted Nippers—"I'd *prefer* him, if I were you, sir," addressing me—"I'd *prefer* him; I'd give him preferences, the stubborn mule! What is it, sir, pray, that he *prefers* not to do now?"

Bartleby moved not a limb.

"Mr. Nippers," said I, "I'd prefer that you would withdraw for the present."

Somehow, of late I had got into the way of involuntarily using this word "prefer" upon all sorts of not exactly suitable occasions. And I trembled to think that my contact with the scrivener had already and seriously affected me in a mental way. And what further and deeper aberration might it not yet produce? This apprehension had not been without efficacy in determining me to summary means.

As Nippers, looking very sour and sulky, was departing, Turkey blandly and deferentially approached.

"With submission, sir," said he, "yesterday I was thinking about Bartleby here, and I think that if he would but prefer to take a quart of good ale every day, it would do much towards mending him, and enabling him to assist in examining his papers."

"So you have got the word too," said I, slightly excited.

"With submission, what word, sir," asked Turkey, respectfully crowding himself into the contracted space behind the screen, and by so doing, making me jostle the scrivener. "What word, sir?"

"I would prefer to be left alone here," said Bartleby, as if offended at being mobbed in his privacy.

"*That's* the word, Turkey," said I—"*that's* it."

"Oh, *prefer?* oh yes—queer word. I never use it myself. But, sir, as I was saying, if he would but prefer—"

"Turkey," interrupted I, "you will please withdraw."

"Oh certainly, sir, if you prefer that I should."

As he opened the folding-door to retire, Nippers at his desk caught a glimpse of me, and asked whether I would prefer to have a certain paper copied on blue paper or white. He did not in the least roguishly accent the word prefer. It was plain that it involuntarily rolled from his tongue. I thought to myself, surely I must get rid of a demented man, who already has in some degree turned the tongues, if not the heads of myself and clerks. But I thought it prudent not to break the dismission at once.

The next day I noticed that Bartleby did nothing but stand at his window in his dead-wall revery. Upon asking him why he did not write, he said that he had decided upon doing no more writing.

"Why, how now? what next?" exclaimed I, "do no more writing?"

"No more."

"And what is the reason?"

"Do you not see the reason for yourself," he indifferently replied.

I looked steadfastly at him, and perceived that his eyes looked dull and glazed. Instantly it occurred to me, that his unexampled diligence in copying by his dim window for the first few weeks of his stay with me might have temporarily impaired his vision.

I was touched. I said something in condolence with him. I hinted that of course he did wisely in abstaining from writing for a while; and urged him to embrace that opportunity of taking wholesome exercise in the open air. This, however, he did not do. A few days after this, my other clerks being absent, and being in a great hurry to dispatch certain letters by the mail, I thought that, having nothing else earthly to do, Bartleby would surely be less inflexible than usual, and carry these letters to the post-office. But he blankly declined. So, much to my inconvenience, I went myself.

Still added days went by. Whether Bartleby's eyes improved or not, I could not say. To all appearance, I thought they did. But when I asked him if they did, he vouchsafed no answer. At all events, he would do no copying. At last, in reply to my urgings, he informed me that he had permanently given up copying.

"What!" exclaimed I; "suppose your eyes should get entirely well—better than ever before—would you not copy then?"

"I have given up copying," he answered, and slid aside.

He remained as ever, a fixture in my chamber. Nay—if that were possible—he became still more of a fixture than before. What was to be done? He would do nothing in the office: why should he stay there? In plain fact, he had now become a millstone to me, not only useless as a necklace, but afflictive to bear. Yet I was sorry for him. I speak less than truth when I say that, on his own account, he occasioned me uneasiness. If he would but have named a single relative or friend, I would instantly have written, and urged their taking the poor fellow away to some convenient retreat. But he seemed alone, absolutely alone in the universe. A bit of wreck in the mid Atlantic. At length, necessities connected with my business tyrannized over all other considerations. Decently as I could, I told Bartleby that in six days' time he must unconditionally leave the office. I warned him to take measures, in the interval, for procuring some other abode. I offered to assist him in this endeavor, if he himself would but take the first step towards a removal. "And when you finally quit me, Bartleby," added I, "I shall see that you go not away entirely unprovided. Six days from this hour, remember."

At the expiration of that period, I peeped behind the screen, and lo! Bartleby was there.

I buttoned up my coat, balanced myself; advanced slowly towards him, touched his shoulder, and said, "The time has come; you must quit this place; I am sorry for you; here is money; but you must go."

"I would prefer not," he replied, with his back still towards me.

"You *must*."

He remained silent.

Now I had an unbounded confidence in this man's common honesty. He had frequently restored to me sixpences and shillings carelessly dropped upon the floor, for I am apt to be very reckless in such shirt-button affairs. The proceeding then which followed will not be deemed extraordinary.

"Bartleby," said I, "I owe you twelve dollars on account; here are thirty-two; the odd twenty are yours.—Will you take it?" and I handed the bills towards him.

But he made no motion.

"I will leave them here then," putting them under a weight on the table. Then taking my hat and cane and going to the door I tranquilly turned and added—"After you have removed your things from these offices, Bartleby, you will of course lock the door—since every one is now gone for the day but you—and if you please, slip your key underneath the mat, so that I may have it in the morning. I shall not see you again; so good-bye to you. If hereafter in your new place of abode I can be of any service to you, do not fail to advise me by letter. Good-bye, Bartleby, and fare you well."

But he answered not a word; like the last column of some ruined temple, he remained standing mute and solitary in the middle of the otherwise deserted room.

As I walked home in a pensive mood, my vanity got the better of my pity. I could not but highly plume myself on my masterly management in getting rid of Bartleby. Masterly I call it, and such it must appear to any dispassionate thinker. The beauty of my procedure seemed to consist in its perfect quietness. There was no vulgar bullying, no bravado of any sort, no choleric hectoring, and striding to and fro across the apartment, jerking out vehement commands for Bartleby to bundle himself off with his beggarly traps. Nothing of the kind. Without loudly bidding Bartleby depart—as an inferior genius might have done—I *assumed* the ground that depart he must; and upon that assumption built all I had to say. The more I thought over my procedure, the more I was charmed with it. Nevertheless, next morning, upon awakening, I had my doubts,—I had somehow slept off the fumes of vanity. One of the coolest and wisest hours a man has, is just after he awakes in the morning. My procedure seemed as sagacious as ever,—but only in theory. How it would prove in practice—there was the rub. It was truly a beautiful thought to have assumed Bartleby's departure; but, after all, that assumption was simply my own, and none of Bartleby's. The great point was, not whether I had assumed that he would quit me, but whether he would prefer so to do. He was more a man of preferences than assumptions.

After breakfast, I walked down town, arguing the probabilities *pro* and *con*. One moment I thought it would prove a miserable failure, and Bartleby would be found all alive at my office as usual; the next moment it seemed certain that I should see his chair empty. And so I kept veering about. At the corner of Broadway and Canal-street, I saw quite an excited group of people standing in earnest conversation.

"I'll take odds he doesn't," said a voice as I passed.

"Doesn't go?—done!" said I, "put up your money."

I was instinctively putting my hand in my pocket to produce my own, when I remembered that this was an election day. The words I had overheard bore no reference to Bartleby, but to the success or non-success of some candidate for the mayoralty. In my intent frame of mind, I had, as it were, imagined that all Broadway shared in my excitement, and were debating the same question with me. I passed on, very thankful that the uproar of the street screened my momentary absent-mindedness.

As I had intended, I was earlier than usual at my office door. I stood listening for a moment. All was still. He must be gone. I tried the knob. The door was locked. Yes, my procedure had worked to a charm; he indeed must be vanished. Yet a certain melancholy mixed with this: I was almost sorry for my brilliant success. I was fumbling under the door mat for the key, which Bartleby was to have left there for me, when accidentally my knee knocked against a panel, producing a summoning sound, and in response a voice came to me from within—"Not yet; I am occupied."

It was Bartleby.

I was thunderstruck. For an instant I stood like the man who, pipe in mouth, was killed one cloudless afternoon long ago in Virginia, by summer lightning; at his own warm open window he was killed, and remained leaning out there upon the dreamy afternoon, till some one touched him, when he fell.

"Not gone!" I murmured at last. But again obeying that wondrous ascendancy which the inscrutable scrivener had over me, and from which ascendancy, for all my chafing, I could not completely escape, I slowly went down stairs and out into the street, and while walking round the block, considered what I should next do in this unheard-of perplexity. Turn the man out by an actual thrusting I could not; to drive him away by calling him hard names would not do; calling in the police was an unpleasant idea; and yet, permit him to enjoy his cadaverous triumph over me,—this too I could not think of. What was to be done? or, if nothing could be done, was there any thing further that I could *assume* in the matter? Yes, as before I had prospectively assumed that Bartleby would depart, so now I might retrospectively assume that departed he was. In the legitimate carrying out of this assumption, I might enter my office in a great hurry, and pretending not to see Bartleby at all, walk straight against him as if he were air. Such a proceeding would in a singular degree have the appearance of a home-thrust. It was hardly possible that Bartleby could withstand such an application of the doctrine of assumptions. But upon second thoughts the success of the plan seemed rather dubious. I resolved to argue the matter over with him again.

"Bartleby," said I, entering the office, with a quietly severe expression, "I am seriously displeased. I am pained, Bartleby. I had thought better of you. I had imagined you of such a gentlemanly organization, that in any delicate dilemma a slight hint would suffice—in short, an assumption. But it appears I am deceived. Why," I added, unaffectedly starting, "you have not even touched that money yet," pointing to it, just where I had left it the evening previous.

He answered nothing.

"Will you, or will you not, quit me?" I now demanded in a sudden passion, advancing close to him.

"I would prefer *not* to quit you," he replied, gently emphasizing the *not*.

"What earthly right have you to stay here? Do you pay any rent? Do you pay my taxes? Or is this property yours?"

He answered nothing.

"Are you ready to go on and write now? Are your eyes recovered? Could you copy a small paper for me this morning? or help examine a few lines? or step round to the post-office? In a word, will you do any thing at all, to give a coloring to your refusal to depart the premises?"

He silently retired into his hermitage.

I was now in such a state of nervous resentment that I thought it but prudent to check myself at present from further demonstrations. Bartleby and I were alone. I remembered the tragedy of the unfortunate Adams and the still more unfortunate Colt in the solitary office of the latter; and how poor Colt, being dreadfully incensed by Adams,[9] and imprudently permitting himself to get wildly excited, was at unawares hurried into his fatal act—an act which certainly no man could possibly deplore more than the actor himself. Often it had occurred to me in my ponderings upon the subject, that had that altercation taken place in the public street, or at a private residence, it would not have terminated as it did. It was the circumstance of being alone in a solitary office, up stairs, of a building entirely unhallowed by humanizing domestic associations—an uncarpeted office, doubtless, of a dusty, haggard sort of appearance;—this it must have been, which greatly helped to enhance the irritable desperation of the hapless Colt.

But when this old Adam of resentment rose in me and tempted me concerning Bartleby, I grappled him and threw him. How? Why, simply by recalling the divine injunction: "A new commandment give I unto you, that ye love one another."[1] Yes, this it was that saved me. Aside from higher considerations, charity often operates as a vastly wise and prudent principle—a great safeguard to its possessor. Men have committed murder for jealousy's sake, and anger's sake, and hatred's sake, and selfishness' sake, and spiritual pride's sake; but no man that ever I heard of, ever committed a diabolical murder for sweet charity's sake. Mere self-interest, then, if no better motive can be enlisted, should, especially with high-tempered men, prompt all beings to charity and philanthropy. At any rate, upon the occasion in question, I strove to drown my exasperated feelings towards the scrivener by benevolently constructing his conduct. Poor fellow, poor fellow! thought I, he don't mean any thing; and besides, he has seen hard times, and ought to be indulged.

I endeavored also immediately to occupy myself, and at the same time to comfort my despondency. I tried to fancy that in the course of the morning, at such time as might prove agreeable to him, Bartleby, of his own free accord, would emerge from his hermitage, and take up some decided line of march in the direction of the door. But no. Half-past twelve o'clock came; Turkey began to glow in the face, overturn his inkstand, and become generally obstreperous; Nippers abated down into quietude and courtesy; Ginger Nut munched his noon apple; and Bartleby remained standing at his window in one of his profoundest dead-wall reveries. Will it be credited? Ought I to acknowledge it? That afternoon I left the office without saying one further word to him.

Some days now passed, during which, at leisure intervals I looked a little into "Edwards on the Will," and "Priestley on Necessity."[2] Under the

---

9. Notorious murder case that occurred while Melville was in the South Seas. In 1841 Samuel Adams, a printer, called on John C. Colt (brother of the inventor of the revolver) at Broadway and Chambers Street in lower Manhattan to collect a debt. Colt murdered Adams with a hatchet and crated the corpse for shipment to New Orleans. The body was found, and Colt was soon arrested. Despite his pleas of self-defense Colt was convicted the next year, amid continuing newspaper publicity, and stabbed himself to death just before he was to be hanged. The setting of *Bartleby* is not far from the scene of the murder.
1. John 13.34.

2. *Freedom of the Will*, by colonial minister Jonathan Edwards (1703–1754), and *Doctrine of Philosophical Necessity Illustrated*, by English theologian and scientist Joseph Priestley (1733–1804). Both concluded that the will is not free, though from different perspectives. Whereas Edwards believed that God before the beginning of time had decided who should be saved and who should be damned (the Calvinist doctrine of predestination), Priestley rejected Calvinism and believed that benevolent divine forces in the material universe constrained individual free will in order to guide humankind toward a higher perfection.

circumstances, those books induced a salutary feeling. Gradually I slid into the persuasion that these troubles of mine touching the scrivener, had been all predestinated from eternity, and Bartleby was billeted upon me for some mysterious purpose of an all-wise Providence, which it was not for a mere mortal like me to fathom. Yes, Bartleby, stay there behind your screen, thought I; I shall persecute you no more; you are harmless and noiseless as any of these old chairs; in short, I never feel so private as when I know you are here. At last I see it, I feel it; I penetrate to the predestinated purpose of my life. I am content. Others may have loftier parts to enact; but my mission in this world, Bartleby, is to furnish you with office-room for such period as you may see fit to remain.

I believe that this wise and blessed frame of mind would have continued with me, had it not been for the unsolicited and uncharitable remarks obtruded upon me by my professional friends who visited the rooms. But thus it often is, that the constant friction of illiberal minds wears out at last the best resolves of the more generous. Though to be sure, when I reflected upon it, it was not strange that people entering my office should be struck by the peculiar aspect of the unaccountable Bartleby, and so be tempted to throw out some sinister observations concerning him. Sometimes an attorney having business with me, and calling at my office, and finding no one but the scrivener there, would undertake to obtain some sort of precise information from him touching my whereabouts; but without heeding his idle talk, Bartleby would remain standing immovable in the middle of the room. So after contemplating him in that position for a time, the attorney would depart, no wiser than he came.

Also, when a Reference[3] was going on, and the room full of lawyers and witnesses and business was driving fast; some deeply occupied legal gentleman present, seeing Bartleby wholly unemployed, would request him to run round to his (the legal gentleman's) office and fetch some papers for him. Thereupon, Bartleby would tranquilly decline, and yet remain idle as before. Then the lawyer would give a great stare, and turn to me. And what could I say? At last I was made aware that all through the circle of my professional acquaintance, a whisper of wonder was running round, having reference to the strange creature I kept at my office. This worried me very much. And as the idea came upon me of his possibly turning out a long-lived man, and keep occupying my chambers, and denying my authority; and perplexing my visitors; and scandalizing my professional reputation; and casting a general gloom over the premises; keeping soul and body together to the last upon his savings (for doubtless he spent but half a dime a day), and in the end perhaps outlive me, and claim possession of my office by right of his perpetual occupancy: as all these dark anticipations crowded upon me more and more, and my friends continually intruded their relentless remarks upon the apparition in my room; a great change was wrought in me. I resolved to gather all my faculties together, and for ever rid me of this intolerable incubus.

Ere revolving any complicated project, however, adapted to this end, I first simply suggested to Bartleby the propriety of his permanent departure. In a calm and serious tone, I commended the idea to his careful and mature

---

3. The act of referring a disputed matter to referees.

consideration. But having taken three days to meditate upon it, he apprised me that his original determination remained the same; in short, that he still preferred to abide with me.

What shall I do? I now said to myself, buttoning up my coat to the last button. What shall I do? what ought I to do? what does conscience say I *should* do with this man, or rather ghost. Rid myself of him, I must; go, he shall. But how? You will not thrust him, the poor, pale, passive mortal,—you will not thrust such a helpless creature out of your door? you will not dishonor yourself by such cruelty? No, I will not, I cannot do that. Rather would I let him live and die here, and then mason up his remains in the wall. What then will you do? For all your coaxing, he will not budge. Bribes he leaves under your own paper-weight on your table; in short, it is quite plain that he prefers to cling to you.

Then something severe, something unusual must be done. What! surely you will not have him collared by a constable, and commit his innocent pallor to the common jail? And upon what ground could you procure such a thing to be done?—a vagrant, is he? What! he a vagrant, a wanderer, who refuses to budge? It is because he will *not* be a vagrant, then, that you seek to count him *as* a vagrant. That is too absurd. No visible means of support: there I have him. Wrong again: for indubitably he *does* support himself, and that is the only unanswerable proof that any man can show of his possessing the means so to do. No more then. Since he will not quit me, I must quit him. I will change my offices; I will move elsewhere; and give him fair notice, that if I find him on my new premises I will then proceed against him as a common trespasser.

Acting accordingly, next day I thus addressed him: "I find these chambers too far from the City Hall; the air is unwholesome. In a word, I propose to remove my offices next week, and shall no longer require your services. I tell you this now, in order that you may seek another place."

He made no reply, and nothing more was said.

On the appointed day I engaged carts and men, proceeded to my chambers, and having but little furniture, every thing was removed in a few hours. Throughout, the scrivener remained standing behind the screen, which I directed to be removed the last thing. It was withdrawn; and being folded up like a huge folio, left him the motionless occupant of a naked room. I stood in the entry watching him a moment, while something from within me upbraided me.

I re-entered, with my hand in my pocket—and—and my heart in my mouth.

"Good-bye, Bartleby; I am going—good-bye, and God some way bless you; and take that," slipping something in his hand. But it dropped upon the floor, and then,—strange to say—I tore myself from him whom I had so longed to be rid of.

Established in my new quarters, for a day or two I kept the door locked, and started at every footfall in the passages. When I returned to my rooms after any little absence, I would pause at the threshold for an instant, and attentively listen, ere applying my key. But these fears were needless. Bartleby never came nigh me.

I thought all was going well, when a perturbed looking stranger visited me, inquiring whether I was the person who had recently occupied rooms at No. — Wall-street.

Full of forebodings, I replied that I was.

"Then sir," said the stranger, who proved a lawyer, "you are responsible for the man you left there. He refuses to do any copying; he refuses to do any thing; he says he prefers not to; and he refuses to quit the premises."

"I am very sorry, sir," said I, with assumed tranquillity, but an inward tremor, "but, really, the man you allude to is nothing to me—he is no relation or apprentice of mine, that you should hold me responsible for him."

"In mercy's name, who is he?"

"I certainly cannot inform you. I know nothing about him. Formerly I employed him as a copyist; but he has done nothing for me now for some time past."

"I shall settle him then,—good morning, sir."

Several days passed, and I heard nothing more; and though I often felt a charitable prompting to call at the place and see poor Bartleby, yet a certain squeamishness of I know not what withheld me.

All is over with him, by this time, thought I at last, when through another week no further intelligence reached me. But coming to my room the day after, I found several persons waiting at my door in a high state of nervous excitement.

"That's the man—here he comes," cried the foremost one, whom I recognized as the lawyer who had previously called upon me alone.

"You must take him away, sir, at once," cried a portly person among them, advancing upon me, and whom I knew to be the landlord of No.—Wall-street. "These gentlemen, my tenants, cannot stand it any longer; Mr. B——" pointing to the lawyer, "has turned him out of his room, and he now persists in haunting the building generally, sitting upon the banisters of the stairs by day, and sleeping in the entry by night. Every body is concerned; clients are leaving the offices; some fears are entertained of a mob; something you must do, and that without delay."

Aghast at this torrent, I fell back before it, and would fain have locked myself in my new quarters. In vain I persisted that Bartleby was nothing to me—no more than to any one else. In vain:—I was the last person known to have any thing to do with him, and they held me to the terrible account. Fearful then of being exposed in the papers (as one person present obscurely threatened) I considered the matter, and at length said, that if the lawyer would give me a confidential interview with the scrivener, in his (the lawyer's) own room, I would that afternoon strive my best to rid them of the nuisance they complained of.

Going up stairs to my old haunt, there was Bartleby silently sitting upon the banister at the landing.

"What are you doing here, Bartleby?" said I.

"Sitting upon the banister," he mildly replied.

I motioned him into the lawyer's room, who then left us.

"Bartleby," said I, "are you aware that you are the cause of great tribulation to me, by persisting in occupying the entry after being dismissed from the office?"

No answer.

"Now one of two things must take place. Either you must do something, or something must be done to you. Now what sort of business would you like to engage in? Would you like to re-engage in copying for some one?"

"No; I would prefer not to make any change."

"Would you like a clerkship in a dry-goods store?"

"There is too much confinement about that. No, I would not like a clerkship; but I am not particular."

"Too much confinement," I cried, "why you keep yourself confined all the time!"

"I would prefer not to take a clerkship," he rejoined, as if to settle that little item at once.

"How would a bar-tender's business suit you? There is no trying of the eyesight in that."

"I would not like it at all; though, as I said before, I am not particular."

His unwonted wordiness inspirited me. I returned to the charge.

"Well then, would you like to travel through the country collecting bills for the merchants? That would improve your health."

"No, I would prefer to be doing something else."

"How then would going as a companion to Europe, to entertain some young gentleman with your conversation,—how would that suit you?"

"Not at all. It does not strike me that there is any thing definite about that. I like to be stationary. But I am not particular."

"Stationary you shall be then," I cried, now losing all patience, and for the first time in all my exasperating connection with him fairly flying into a passion. "If you do not go away from these premises before night, I shall feel bound—indeed I *am* bound—to—to—to quit the premises myself!" I rather absurdly concluded, knowing not with what possible threat to try to frighten his immobility into compliance. Despairing of all further efforts, I was precipitately leaving him, when a final thought occurred to me—one which had not been wholly unindulged before.

"Bartleby," said I, in the kindest tone I could assume under such exciting circumstances, "will you go home with me now—not to my office, but my dwelling—and remain there till we can conclude upon some convenient arrangement for you at our leisure? Come, let us start now, right away."

"No: at present I would prefer not to make any change at all."

I answered nothing; but effectually dodging every one by the suddenness and rapidity of my flight, rushed from the building, ran up Wall-street towards Broadway, and jumping into the first omnibus was soon removed from pursuit. As soon as tranquillity returned I distinctly perceived that I had now done all that I possibly could, both in respect to the demands of the landlord and his tenants, and with regard to my own desire and sense of duty, to benefit Bartleby, and shield him from rude persecution. I now strove to be entirely care-free and quiescent; and my conscience justified me in the attempt; though indeed it was not so successful as I could have wished. So fearful was I of being again hunted out by the incensed landlord and his exasperated tenants, that, surrendering my business to Nippers, for a few days I drove about the upper part of the town and through the suburbs, in my rockaway; crossed over to Jersey City and Hoboken, and paid fugitive visits to Manhattanville and Astoria.[4] In fact I almost lived in my rockaway for the time.

4. The narrator crossed the Hudson River to Jersey City and Hoboken, then drove far up Manhattan Island to the community of Manhattanville (Grant's Tomb is in what was Manhattanville), and finally crossed the East River to Astoria, on Long Island. "Rockaway": light open-sided carriage.

When again I entered my office, lo, a note from the landlord lay upon the desk. I opened it with trembling hands. It informed me that the writer had sent to the police, and had Bartleby removed to the Tombs as a vagrant. Moreover, since I knew more about him than any one else, he wished me to appear at that place, and make a suitable statement of the facts. These tidings had a conflicting effect upon me. At first I was indignant; but at last almost approved. The landlord's energetic, summary disposition, had led him to adopt a procedure which I do not think I would have decided upon myself; and yet as a last resort, under such peculiar circumstances, it seemed the only plan.

As I afterwards learned, the poor scrivener, when told that he must be conducted to the Tombs, offered not the slightest obstacle, but in his pale unmoving way, silently acquiesced.

Some of the compassionate and curious bystanders joined the party; and headed by one of the constables arm in arm with Bartleby, the silent procession filed its way through all the noise, and heat, and joy of the roaring thoroughfares at noon.

The same day I received the note I went to the Tombs, or to speak more properly, the Halls of Justice. Seeking the right officer, I stated the purpose of my call, and was informed that the individual I described was indeed within. I then assured the functionary that Bartleby was a perfectly honest man, and greatly to be compassionated, however unaccountably eccentric. I narrated all I knew, and closed by suggesting the idea of letting him remain in as indulgent confinement as possible till something less harsh might be done—though indeed I hardly knew what. At all events, if nothing else could be decided upon, the alms-house must receive him. I then begged to have an interview.

Being under no disgraceful charge, and quite serene and harmless in all his ways, they had permitted him freely to wander about the prison, and especially in the inclosed grass-platted yards thereof. And so I found him there, standing all alone in the quietest of the yards, his face towards a high wall, while all around, from the narrow slits of the jail windows, I thought I saw peering out upon him the eyes of murderers and thieves.

"Bartleby!"

"I know you," he said, without looking round,—"and I want nothing to say to you."

"It was not I that brought you here, Bartleby," said I, keenly pained at his implied suspicion. "And to you, this should not be so vile a place. Nothing reproachful attaches to you by being here. And see, it is not so sad a place as one might think. Look, there is the sky, and here is the grass."

"I know where I am," he replied, but would say nothing more, and so I left him.

As I entered the corridor again, a broad meat-like man, in an apron, accosted me, and jerking his thumb over his shoulder said—"Is that your friend?"

"Yes."

"Does he want to starve? If he does, let him live on the prison fare, that's all."

"Who are you?" asked I, not knowing what to make of such an unofficially speaking person in such a place.

"I am the grub-man. Such gentlemen as have friends here, hire me to provide them with something good to eat."

"Is this so?" said I, turning to the turnkey.

He said it was.

"Well then," said I, slipping some silver into the grub-man's hands (for so they called him). "I want you to give particular attention to my friend there; let him have the best dinner you can get. And you must be as polite to him as possible."

"Introduce me, will you?" said the grub-man, looking at me with an expression which seemed to say he was all impatience for an opportunity to give a specimen of his breeding.

Thinking it would prove of benefit to the scrivener, I acquiesced; and asking the grub-man his name, went up with him to Bartleby.

"Bartleby, this is Mr. Cutlets; you will find him very useful to you."

"Your sarvant, sir, your sarvant," said the grub-man, making a low salutation behind his apron. "Hope you find it pleasant here, sir;—spacious grounds—cool apartments, sir—hope you'll stay with us some time—try to make it agreeable. May Mrs. Cutlets and I have the pleasure of your company to dinner, sir, in Mrs. Cutlets' private room?"

"I prefer not to dine to-day," said Bartleby, turning away. "It would disagree with me; I am unused to dinners." So saying he slowly moved to the other side of the inclosure, and took up a position fronting the dead-wall.

"How's this?" said the grub-man, addressing me with a stare of astonishment. "He's odd, aint he?"

"I think he is a little deranged," said I, sadly.

"Deranged? deranged is it? Well now, upon my word, I thought that friend of yourn was a gentleman forger; they are always pale and genteel-like, them forgers. I can't help pity 'em—can't help it, sir. Did you know Monroe Edwards?"[5] he added touchingly, and paused. Then, laying his hand pityingly on my shoulder, sighed, "he died of consumption at Sing-Sing.[6] So you weren't acquainted with Monroe?"

"No, I was never socially acquainted with any forgers. But I cannot stop longer. Look to my friend yonder. You will not lose by it. I will see you again."

Some few days after this, I again obtained admission to the Tombs, and went through the corridors in quest of Bartleby; but without finding him.

"I saw him coming from his cell not long ago," said a turnkey, "may be he's gone to loiter in the yards."

So I went in that direction.

"Are you looking for the silent man?" said another turnkey passing me. "Yonder he lies—sleeping in the yard there. 'Tis not twenty minutes since I saw him lie down."

The yard was entirely quiet. It was not accessible to the common prisoners. The surrounding walls, of amazing thickness, kept off all sounds behind them. The Egyptian character of the masonry weighed upon me with its

---

5. The much-publicized trial of Colonel Edwards (1808–1847), accused of swindling two firms, was held in New York City in 1842 and ended in his conviction.

6. Prison at Ossining, New York, approximately thirty-five miles north of lower Manhattan.

gloom. But a soft imprisoned turf grew under foot. The heart of the eternal pyramids, it seemed, wherein, by some strange magic, through the clefts, grass-seed, dropped by birds, had sprung.

Strangely huddled at the base of the wall, his knees drawn up, and lying on his side, his head touching the cold stones, I saw the wasted Bartleby. But nothing stirred. I paused; then went close up to him; stooped over, and saw that his dim eyes were open; otherwise he seemed profoundly sleeping. Something prompted me to touch him. I felt his hand, when a tingling shiver ran up my arm and down my spine to my feet.

The round face of the grub-man peered upon me now. "His dinner is ready. Won't he dine to-day, either? Or does he live without dining?"

"Lives without dining," said I, and closed the eyes.

"Eh!—He's asleep, aint he?"

"With kings and counsellors,"[7] murmured I.

There would seem little need for proceeding further in this history. Imagination will readily supply the meagre recital of poor Bartleby's interment. But ere parting with the reader, let me say, that if this little narrative has sufficiently interested him, to awaken curiosity as to who Bartleby was, and what manner of life he led prior to the present narrator's making his acquaintance, I can only reply, that in such curiosity I fully share, but am wholly unable to gratify it. Yet here I hardly know whether I should divulge one little item of rumor, which came to my ear a few months after the scrivener's decease. Upon what basis it rested, I could never ascertain; and hence, how true it is I cannot now tell. But inasmuch as this vague report has not been without a certain strange suggestive interest to me, however sad, it may prove the same with some others; and so I will briefly mention it. The report was this: that Bartleby had been a subordinate clerk in the Dead Letter Office at Washington, from which he had been suddenly removed by a change in the administration. When I think over this rumor, I cannot adequately express the emotions which seize me. Dead letters! does it not sound like dead men? Conceive a man by nature and misfortune prone to a pallid hopelessness, can any business seem more fitted to heighten it than that of continually handling these dead letters, and assorting them for the flames? For by the cart-load they are annually burned. Sometimes from out the folded paper the pale clerk takes a ring:—the finger it was meant for, perhaps, moulders in the grave; a bank-note sent in swiftest charity:—he whom it would relieve, nor eats nor hungers any more; pardon for those who died despairing; hope for those who died unhoping; good tidings for those who died stifled by unrelieved calamities. On errands of life, these letters speed to death.

Ah Bartleby! Ah humanity!

1853

---

7. Job 3.14.

Benito Cereno[1]

In the year 1799, Captain Amasa Delano, of Duxbury, in Massachusetts, commanding a large sealer and general trader, lay at anchor, with a valuable cargo, in the harbor of St. Maria—a small, desert, uninhabited island toward the southern extremity of the long coast of Chili. There he had touched for water.

On the second day, not long after dawn, while lying in his berth, his mate came below, informing him that a strange sail was coming into the bay. Ships were then not so plenty in those waters as now. He rose, dressed, and went on deck.

The morning was one peculiar to that coast. Everything was mute and calm; everything gray. The sea, though undulated into long roods of swells, seemed fixed, and was sleeked at the surface like waved lead that has cooled and set in the smelter's mold. The sky seemed a gray surtout.[2] Flights of troubled gray fowl, kith and kin with flights of troubled gray vapors among which they were mixed, skimmed low and fitfully over the waters, as swallows over meadows before storms. Shadows present, foreshadowing deeper shadows to come.

To Captain Delano's surprise, the stranger, viewed through the glass,[3] showed no colors; though to do so upon entering a haven, however uninhabited in its shores, where but a single other ship might be lying, was the custom among peaceful seamen of all nations. Considering the lawlessness and loneliness of the spot, and the sort of stories, at that day, associated with those seas, Captain Delano's surprise might have deepened into some uneasiness had he not been a person of a singularly undistrustful good nature, not liable, except on extraordinary and repeated incentives, and hardly then, to indulge in personal alarms, any way involving the imputation of malign evil in man. Whether, in view of what humanity is capable, such a trait implies, along with a benevolent heart, more than ordinary quickness and accuracy of intellectual perception, may be left to the wise to determine.

But whatever misgivings might have obtruded on first seeing the stranger, would almost, in any seaman's mind, have been dissipated by observing that, the ship, in navigating into the harbor, was drawing too near the land; a sunken reef making out off her bow. This seemed to prove her a stranger, indeed, not only to the sealer, but the island; consequently, she could be no wonted freebooter[4] on that ocean. With no small interest, Captain Delano continued to watch her—a proceeding not much facilitated by the vapors partly mantling the hull, through which the far matin light from her cabin streamed equivocally enough; much like the sun—by this time hemisphered on the rim of the horizon, and apparently, in company with the strange ship, entering the harbor—which, wimpled by the same low, creeping clouds,

1. This text is based on the first printing, in *Putnam's Monthly* for October, November, and December 1855, but it also incorporates the many small revisions Melville made for its 1856 republication in *The Piazza Tales*. Melville based his plot on a few narrative pages in chapter 18 of Captain Amasa Delano's *Narrative of Voyages and Travels in the Northern and Southern Hemispheres* (1817).

Melville's "deposition" near the end of *Benito Cereno* is roughly half from Delano's much longer section of documents, half his own writing. (A later relative of the real Delano [1763–1823] was Franklin Delano Roosevelt.)
2. Long overcoat.
3. Spyglass or telescope.
4. Pirate.

showed not unlike a Lima intriguante's one sinister eye peering across the Plaza from the Indian loop-hole of her dusk *saya-y-manta*.[5]

It might have been but a deception of the vapors, but, the longer the stranger was watched, the more singular appeared her maneuvers. Ere long it seemed hard to decide whether she meant to come in or no—what she wanted, or what she was about. The wind, which had breezed up a little during the night, was now extremely light and baffling, which the more increased the apparent uncertainty of her movements.

Surmising, at last, that it might be a ship in distress, Captain Delano ordered his whale-boat to be dropped, and, much to the wary opposition of his mate, prepared to board her, and, at the least, pilot her in. On the night previous, a fishing-party of the seamen had gone a long distance to some detached rocks out of sight from the sealer, and, an hour or two before daybreak, had returned, having met with no small success. Presuming that the stranger might have been long off soundings, the good captain put several baskets of the fish, for presents, into his boat, and so pulled away. From her continuing too near the sunken reef, deeming her in danger, calling to his men, he made all haste to apprise those on board of their situation. But, some time ere the boat came up, the wind, light though it was, having shifted, had headed the vessel off, as well as partly broken the vapors from about her.

Upon gaining a less remote view, the ship, when made signally visible on the verge of the leaden-hued swells, with the shreds of fog here and there raggedly furring her, appeared like a white-washed monastery after a thunderstorm, seen perched upon some dun cliff among the Pyrenees. But it was no purely fanciful resemblance which now, for a moment, almost led Captain Delano to think that nothing less than a ship-load of monks was before him. Peering over the bulwarks were what really seemed, in the hazy distance, throngs of dark cowls; while, fitfully revealed through the open port-holes, other dark moving figures were dimly descried, as of Black Friars[6] pacing the cloisters.

Upon a still nigher approach, this appearance was modified, and the true character of the vessel was plain—a Spanish merchantman of the first class; carrying negro slaves, amongst other valuable freight, from one colonial port to another. A very large, and, in its time, a very fine vessel, such as in those days were at intervals encountered along that main; sometimes superseded Acapulco treasure-ships, or retired frigates of the Spanish king's navy, which, like superannuated Italian palaces, still, under a decline of masters, preserved signs of former state.

As the whale-boat drew more and more nigh, the cause of the peculiar pipe-clayed[7] aspect of the stranger was seen in the slovenly neglect pervading her. The spars, ropes, and great part of the bulwarks, looked woolly, from long unacquaintance with the scraper, tar, and the brush. Her keel seemed laid, her ribs put together, and she launched, from Ezekiel's Valley of Dry Bones.[8]

5. Skirt-and-cloak combination, the shawl part of which could be drawn about the face so that little more than an eye would show. "Matin": early morning. "Wimpled": veiled.

6. Dominicans; an order of monks who wore black robes, including hoods.
7. Whitened.
8. Ezekiel 37.1.

In the present business in which she was engaged, the ship's general model and rig appeared to have undergone no material change from their original war-like and Froissart pattern.[9] However, no guns were seen.

The tops were large, and were railed about with what had once been octagonal net-work, all now in sad disrepair. These tops hung overhead like three ruinous aviaries, in one of which was seen perched, on a ratlin, a white noddy,[1] strange fowl, so called from its lethargic, somnambulistic character, being frequently caught by hand at sea. Battered and mouldy, the castellated forecastle seemed some ancient turret, long ago taken by assault, and then left to decay. Toward the stern, two high-raised quarter galleries—the balustrades here and there covered with dry, tindery sea-moss—opening out from the unoccupied state-cabin, whose dead lights, for all the mild weather, were hermetically closed and calked—these tenantless balconies hung over the sea as if it were the grand Venetian canal. But the principal relic of faded grandeur was the ample oval of the shield-like stern-piece, intricately carved with the arms of Castile and Leon,[2] medallioned about by groups of mythological or symbolical devices; uppermost and central of which was a dark satyr in a mask, holding his foot on the prostrate neck of a writhing figure, likewise masked.

Whether the ship had a figure-head, or only a plain beak, was not quite certain, owing to canvas wrapped about that part, either to protect it while undergoing a re-furbishing, or else decently to hide its decay. Rudely painted or chalked, as in a sailor freak, along the forward side of a sort of pedestal below the canvas, was the sentence, "*Seguid vuestro jefe,*" (follow your leader); while upon the tarnished head-boards, near by, appeared, in stately capitals, once gilt, the ship's name, "San Dominick," each letter streakingly corroded with tricklings of copper-spike rust; while, like mourning weeds, dark festoons of sea-grass slimily swept to and fro over the name, with every hearse-like roll of the hull.

As at last the boat was hooked from the bow along toward the gangway amidship, its keel, while yet some inches separated from the hull, harshly grated as on a sunken coral reef. It proved a huge bunch of conglobated barnacles adhering below the water to the side like a wen;[3] a token of baffling airs and long calms passed somewhere in those seas.

Climbing the side, the visitor was at once surrounded by a clamorous throng of whites and blacks, but the latter outnumbering the former more than could have been expected, negro transportation-ship as the stranger in port was. But, in one language, and as with one voice, all poured out a common tale of suffering; in which the negresses, of whom there were not a few, exceeded the others in their dolorous vehemence. The scurvy, together with a fever, had swept off a great part of their number, more especially the Spaniards. Off Cape Horn,[4] they had narrowly escaped shipwreck; then, for days together, they had lain tranced without wind; their provisions were low; their water next to none; their lips that moment were baked.

---

9. Medieval; from Sir John Froissart (1337–1410), historian of wars of England and France.
1. Seabird, usually black or brown. "Ratlin": small rope attached to the shrouds of a ship and forming a step of a rope ladder.

2. Old kingdoms of Spain; the arms would include a castle for Castile and a lion for León.
3. Cyst. "Conglobated": ball-like.
4. At the southern tip of South America.

While Captain Delano was thus made the mark of all eager tongues, his one eager glance took in all the faces, with every other object about him.

Always upon first boarding a large and populous ship at sea, especially a foreign one, with a nondescript crew such as Lascars or Manilla men,[5] the impression varies in a peculiar way from that produced by first entering a strange house with strange inmates in a strange land. Both house and ship, the one by its walls and blinds, the other by its high bulwarks like ramparts, hoard from view their interiors till the last moment; but in the case of the ship there is this addition; that the living spectacle it contains, upon its sudden and complete disclosure, has, in contrast with the blank ocean which zones it, something of the effect of enchantment. The ship seems unreal; these strange costumes, gestures, and faces, but a shadowy tableau just emerged from the deep, which directly must receive back what it gave.

Perhaps it was some such influence as above is attempted to be described, which, in Captain Delano's mind, hightened whatever, upon a staid scrutiny, might have seemed unusual; especially the conspicuous figures of four elderly grizzled negroes, their heads like black, doddered willow tops, who, in venerable contrast to the tumult below them, were couched sphynx-like, one on the starboard cat-head,[6] another on the larboard, and the remaining pair face to face on the opposite bulwarks above the main-chains. They each had bits of unstranded old junk in their hands, and, with a sort of stoical self-content, were picking the junk into oakum,[7] a small heap of which lay by their sides. They accompanied the task with a continuous, low, monotonous chant; droning and druling[8] away like so many gray-headed bag-pipers playing a funeral march.

The quarter-deck rose into an ample elevated poop, upon the forward verge of which, lifted, like the oakum-pickers, some eight feet above the general throng, sat along in a row, separated by regular spaces, the cross-legged figures of six other blacks; each with a rusty hatchet in his hand, which, with a bit of brick and a rag, he was engaged like a scullion in scouring; while between each two was a small stack of hatchets, their rusted edges turned forward awaiting a like operation. Though occasionally the four oakum-pickers would briefly address some person or persons in the crowd below, yet the six hatchet-polishers neither spoke to others, nor breathed a whisper among themselves, but sat intent upon their task, except at intervals, when, with the peculiar love in negroes of uniting industry with pastime, two and two they sideways clashed their hatchets together, like cymbals, with a barbarous din. All six, unlike the generality, had the raw aspect of unsophisticated Africans.

But that first comprehensive glance which took in those ten figures, with scores less conspicuous, rested but an instant upon them, as, impatient of the hubbub of voices, the visitor turned in quest of whomsoever it might be that commanded the ship.

But as if not unwilling to let nature make known her own case among his suffering charge, or else in despair of restraining it for the time, the Spanish

---

5. From East India or the Philippines, respectively.
6. Projecting piece of timber near the bow (to which the anchor is hoisted and secured).

7. Loose fiber from pieces of rope, used as waterproof sealant. "Old junk": worn-out rope.
8. Moaning.

captain, a gentlemanly, reserved-looking, and rather young man to a stranger's eye, dressed with singular richness, but bearing plain traces of recent sleepless cares and disquietudes, stood passively by, leaning against the main-mast, at one moment casting a dreary, spiritless look upon his excited people, at the next an unhappy glance toward his visitor. By his side stood a black of small stature, in whose rude face, as occasionally, like a shepherd's dog, he mutely turned it up into the Spaniard's, sorrow and affection were equally blended.

Struggling through the throng, the American advanced to the Spaniard, assuring him of his sympathies, and offering to render whatever assistance might be in his power. To which the Spaniard returned, for the present, but grave and ceremonious acknowledgments, his national formality dusked by the saturnine mood of ill health.

But losing no time in mere compliments, Captain Delano returning to the gangway, had his baskets of fish brought up; and as the wind still continued light, so that some hours at least must elapse ere the ship could be brought to the anchorage, he bade his men return to the sealer, and fetch back as much water as the whale-boat could carry, with whatever soft bread the steward might have, all the remaining pumpkins on board, with a box of sugar, and a dozen of his private bottles of cider.

Not many minutes after the boat's pushing off, to the vexation of all, the wind entirely died away, and the tide turning, began drifting back the ship helplessly seaward. But trusting this would not long last, Captain Delano sought with good hopes to cheer up the strangers, feeling no small satisfaction that, with persons in their condition he could—thanks to his frequent voyages along the Spanish main[9]—converse with some freedom in their native tongue.

While left alone with them, he was not long in observing some things tending to heighten his first impressions; but surprise was lost in pity, both for the Spaniards and blacks, alike evidently reduced from scarcity of water and provisions; while long-continued suffering seemed to have brought out the less good-natured qualities of the negroes, besides, at the same time, impairing the Spaniard's authority over them. But, under the circumstances, precisely this condition of things was to have been anticipated. In armies, navies, cities, or families, in nature herself, nothing more relaxes good order than misery. Still, Captain Delano was not without the idea, that had Benito Cereno been a man of greater energy, misrule would hardly have come to the present pass. But the debility, constitutional or induced by the hardships, bodily and mental, of the Spanish captain, was too obvious to be overlooked. A prey to settled dejection, as if long mocked with hope he would not now indulge it, even when it had ceased to be a mock, the prospect of that day or evening at furthest, lying at anchor, with plenty of water for his people, and a brother captain to counsel and befriend, seemed in no perceptible degree to encourage him. His mind appeared unstrung, if not still more seriously affected. Shut up in these oaken walls, chained to one dull round of command, whose unconditionality cloyed him, like some hypochondriac abbot he moved slowly about, at times suddenly pausing, starting, or staring, biting his

9. Sometimes used for the Caribbean Sea, but here the Atlantic and Pacific coasts of South America (mainland as opposed to islands).

lip, biting his finger-nail, flushing, paling, twitching his beard, with other symptoms of an absent or moody mind. This distempered spirit was lodged, as before hinted, in as distempered a frame. He was rather tall, but seemed never to have been robust, and now with nervous suffering was almost worn to a skeleton. A tendency to some pulmonary complaint appeared to have been lately confirmed. His voice was like that of one with lungs half gone, hoarsely suppressed, a husky whisper. No wonder that, as in this state he tottered about, his private servant apprehensively followed him. Sometimes the negro gave his master his arm, or took his handkerchief out of his pocket for him; performing these and similar offices with that affectionate zeal which transmutes into something filial or fraternal acts in themselves but menial; and which has gained for the negro the repute of making the most pleasing body servant in the world; one, too, whom a master need be on no stiffly superior terms with, but may treat with familiar trust; less a servant than a devoted companion.

Marking the noisy indocility of the blacks in general, as well as what seemed the sullen inefficiency of the whites, it was not without humane satisfaction that Captain Delano witnessed the steady good conduct of Babo.

But the good conduct of Babo, hardly more than the ill-behavior of others, seemed to withdraw the half-lunatic Don Benito from his cloudy langour. Not that such precisely was the impression made by the Spaniard on the mind of his visitor. The Spaniard's individual unrest was, for the present, but noted as a conspicuous feature in the ship's general affliction. Still, Captain Delano was not a little concerned at what he could not help taking for the time to be Don Benito's unfriendly indifference towards himself. The Spaniard's manner, too, conveyed a sort of sour and gloomy disdain, which he seemed at no pains to disguise. But this the American in charity ascribed to the harassing effects of sickness, since, in former instances, he had noted that there are peculiar natures on whom prolonged physical suffering seems to cancel every social instinct of kindness; as if forced to black bread themselves, they deemed it but equity that each person coming nigh them should, indirectly, by some slight or affront, be made to partake of their fare.

But ere long Captain Delano bethought him that, indulgent as he was at the first, in judging the Spaniard, he might not, after all, have exercised charity enough. At bottom it was Don Benito's reserve which displeased him; but the same reserve was shown towards all but his faithful personal attendant. Even the formal reports which, according to sea-usage, were, at stated times, made to him by some petty underling, either a white, mulatto or black, he hardly had patience enough to listen to, without betraying contemptuous aversion. His manner upon such occasions was, in its degree, not unlike that which might be supposed to have been his imperial countryman's, Charles V.,[1] just previous to the anchoritish retirement of that monarch from the throne.

This splenetic disrelish of his place was evinced in almost every function pertaining to it. Proud as he was moody, he condescended to no personal mandate. Whatever special orders were necessary, their delivery was delegated to his body-servant, who in turn transferred them to their ultimate destination, through runners, alert Spanish boys or slave boys, like pages or

---

1. King of Spain and Holy Roman emperor (1500–1558) who spent his last years in a monastery (without, however, relinquishing all political power and material possessions).

pilot-fish[2] within easy call continually hovering round Don Benito. So that to have beheld this undemonstrative invalid gliding about, apathetic and mute, no landsman could have dreamed that in him was lodged a dictator-ship beyond which, while at sea, there was no earthly appeal.

Thus, the Spaniard, regarded in his reserve, seemed as the involuntary victim of mental disorder. But, in fact, his reserve might, in some degree, have proceeded from design. If so, then here was evinced the unhealthy cli-max of that icy though conscientious policy, more or less adopted by all com-manders of large ships, which, except in signal emergencies, obliterates alike the manifestation of sway with every trace of sociality; transforming the man into a block, or rather into a loaded cannon, which, until there is call for thunder, has nothing to say.

Viewing him in this light, it seemed but a natural token of the perverse habit induced by a long course of such hard self-restraint, that, notwithstand-ing the present condition of his ship, the Spaniard should still persist in a demeanor, which, however harmless, or, it may be, appropriate, in a well appointed vessel, such as the San Dominick might have been at the outset of the voyage, was anything but judicious now. But the Spaniard perhaps thought that it was with captains as with gods: reserve, under all events, must still be their cue. But more probably this appearance of slumbering dominion might have been but an attempted disguise to conscious imbecility—not deep policy, but shallow device. But be all this as it might, whether Don Benito's manner was designed or not, the more Captain Delano noted its pervading reserve, the less he felt uneasiness at any particular manifestation of that reserve towards himself.

Neither were his thoughts taken up by the captain alone. Wonted to the quiet orderliness of the sealer's comfortable family of a crew, the noisy confu-sion of the San Dominick's suffering host repeatedly challenged his eye. Some prominent breaches not only of discipline but of decency were observed. These Captain Delano could not but ascribe, in the main, to the absence of those subordinate deck-officers to whom, along with higher duties, is entrusted what may be styled the police department of a populous ship. True, the old oakum-pickers appeared at times to act the part of monitorial constables to their countrymen, the blacks; but though occasionally suc-ceeding in allaying trifling outbreaks now and then between man and man, they could do little or nothing toward establishing general quiet. The San Dominick was in the condition of a transatlantic emigrant ship, among whose multitude of living freight are some individuals, doubtless, as little troublesome as crates and bales; but the friendly remonstrances of such with their ruder companions are of not so much avail as the unfriendly arm of the mate. What the San Dominick wanted was, what the emigrant ship has, stern superior officers. But on these decks not so much as a fourth mate was to be seen.

The visitor's curiosity was roused to learn the particulars of those mis-haps which had brought about such absenteeism, with its consequences; because, though deriving some inkling of the voyage from the wails which at the first moment had greeted him, yet of the details no clear understanding

2. Fish often swimming in the company of a shark, therefore thought to pilot it.

had been had. The best account would, doubtless, be given by the captain. Yet at first the visitor was loth to ask it, unwilling to provoke some distant rebuff. But plucking up courage, he at last accosted Don Benito, renewing the expression of his benevolent interest, adding, that did he (Captain Delano) but know the particulars of the ship's misfortunes, he would, perhaps, be better able in the end to relieve them. Would Don Benito favor him with the whole story?

Don Benito faltered; then, like some somnambulist suddenly interfered with, vacantly stared at his visitor, and ended by looking down on the deck. He maintained this posture so long, that Captain Delano, almost equally disconcerted, and involuntarily almost as rude, turned suddenly from him, walking forward to accost one of the Spanish seamen for the desired information. But he had hardly gone five paces, when with a sort of eagerness Don Benito invited him back, regretting his momentary absence of mind, and professing readiness to gratify him.

While most part of the story was being given, the two captains stood on the after part of the main-deck, a privileged spot, no one being near but the servant.

"It is now a hundred and ninety days," began the Spaniard, in his husky whisper, "that this ship, well officered and well manned, with several cabin passengers—some fifty Spaniards in all—sailed from Buenos Ayres bound to Lima, with a general cargo, hardware, Paraguay tea and the like—and," pointing forward, "that parcel of negroes, now not more than a hundred and fifty, as you see, but then numbering over three hundred souls. Off Cape Horn we had heavy gales. In one moment, by night, three of my best officers, with fifteen sailors, were lost, with the main-yard; the spar snapping under them in the slings, as they sought, with heavers,[3] to beat down the icy sail. To lighten the hull, the heavier sacks of mata were thrown into the sea, with most of the water-pipes[4] lashed on deck at the time. And this last necessity it was, combined with the prolonged detentions afterwards experienced, which eventually brought about our chief causes of suffering. When——"

Here there was a sudden fainting attack of his cough, brought on, no doubt, by his mental distress. His servant sustained him, and drawing a cordial from his pocket placed it to his lips. He a little revived. But unwilling to leave him unsupported while yet imperfectly restored, the black with one arm still encircled his master, at the same time keeping his eye fixed on his face, as if to watch for the first sign of complete restoration, or relapse, as the event might prove.

The Spaniard proceeded, but brokenly and obscurely, as one in a dream.

—"Oh, my God! rather than pass through what I have, with joy I would have hailed the most terrible gales; but——"

His cough returned and with increased violence; this subsiding, with reddened lips and closed eyes he fell heavily against his supporter.

"His mind wanders. He was thinking of the plague that followed the gales," plaintively sighed the servant; "my poor, poor master!" wringing one hand, and with the other wiping the mouth. "But be patient, Señor," again turning to Captain Delano, "these fits do not last long; master will soon be himself."

3. Bars, most often used as levers.   4. Kegs of water. "Mata": Brazilian cotton.

Don Benito reviving, went on; but as this portion of the story was very brokenly delivered, the substance only will here be set down.

It appeared that after the ship had been many days tossed in storms off the Cape, the scurvy broke out, carrying off numbers of the whites and blacks. When at last they had worked round into the Pacific, their spars and sails were so damaged, and so inadequately handled by the surviving mariners, most of whom were become invalids, that, unable to lay her northerly course by the wind, which was powerful, the unmanageable ship for successive days and nights was blown northwestward, where the breeze suddenly deserted her, in unknown waters, to sultry calms. The absence of the water-pipes now proved as fatal to life as before their presence had menaced it. Induced, or at least aggravated, by the less than scanty allowance of water, a malignant fever followed the scurvy; with the excessive heat of the lengthened calm, making such short work of it as to sweep away, as by billows, whole families of the Africans, and a yet larger number, proportionably, of the Spaniards, including, by a luckless fatality, every remaining officer on board. Consequently, in the smart west winds eventually following the calm, the already rent sails having to be simply dropped, not furled, at need, had been gradually reduced to the beggar's rags they were now. To procure substitutes for his lost sailors, as well as supplies of water and sails, the captain at the earliest opportunity had made for Baldivia, the southernmost civilized port of Chili and South America; but upon nearing the coast the thick weather had prevented him from so much as sighting that harbor. Since which period, almost without a crew, and almost without canvas and almost without water, and at intervals giving its added dead to the sea, the San Dominick had been battle-dored[5] about by contrary winds, inveigled by currents, or grown weedy in calms. Like a man lost in woods, more than once she had doubled upon her own track.

"But throughout these calamities," huskily continued Don Benito, painfully turning in the half embrace of his servant, "I have to thank those negroes you see, who, though to your inexperienced eyes appearing unruly, have, indeed, conducted themselves with less of restlessness than even their owner could have thought possible under such circumstances."

Here he again fell faintly back. Again his mind wandered: but he rallied, and less obscurely proceeded.

"Yes, their owner was quite right in assuring me that no fetters would be needed with his blacks; so that while, as is wont in this transportation, those negroes have always remained upon deck—not thrust below, as in the Guineamen[6]—they have, also, from the beginning, been freely permitted to range within given bounds at their pleasure."

Once more the faintness returned—his mind roved—but, recovering, he resumed:

"But it is Babo here to whom, under God, I owe not only my own preservation, but likewise to him, chiefly, the merit is due, of pacifying his more ignorant brethren, when at intervals tempted to murmurings."

"Ah, master," sighed the black, bowing his face, "don't speak of me; Babo is nothing; what Babo has done was but duty."

---

5. Tossed back and forth, as a shuttlecock is hit back and forth by a pair of battledores (or paddles).

6. Ships transporting slaves from Guinea in West Africa.

"Faithful fellow!" cried Capt. Delano. "Don Benito, I envy you such a friend; slave I cannot call him."

As master and man stood before him, the black upholding the white, Captain Delano could not but bethink him of the beauty of that relationship which could present such a spectacle of fidelity on the one hand and confidence on the other. The scene was hightened by the contrast in dress, denoting their relative positions. The Spaniard wore a loose Chili jacket of dark velvet; white small clothes and stockings, with silver buckles at the knee and instep; a high-crowned sombrero, of fine grass; a slender sword, silver mounted, hung from a knot in his sash; the last being an almost invariable adjunct, more for ornament than utility, of a South American gentleman's dress to this hour. Excepting when his occasional nervous contortions brought about disarray, there was a certain precision in his attire, curiously at variance with the unsightly disorder around; especially in the belittered Ghetto, forward of the main-mast, wholly occupied by the blacks.

The servant wore nothing but wide trowsers, apparently, from their coarseness and patches, made out of some old topsail; they were clean, and confined at the waist by a bit of unstranded rope, which, with his composed, deprecatory air at times, made him look something like a begging friar of St. Francis.

However unsuitable for the time and place, at least in the blunt-thinking American's eyes, and however strangely surviving in the midst of all his afflictions, the toilette of Don Benito might not, in fashion at least, have gone beyond the style of the day among South Americans of his class. Though on the present voyage sailing from Buenos Ayres, he had avowed himself a native and resident of Chili, whose inhabitants had not so generally adopted the plain coat and once plebeian pantaloons; but, with a becoming modification, adhered to their provincial costume, picturesque as any in the world. Still, relatively to the pale history of the voyage, and his own pale face, there seemed something so incongruous in the Spaniard's apparel, as almost to suggest the image of an invalid courtier tottering about London streets in the time of the plague.

The portion of the narrative which, perhaps, most excited interest, as well as some surprise, considering the latitudes in question, was the long calms spoken of, and more particularly the ship's so long drifting about. Without communicating the opinion, of course, the American could not but impute at least part of the detentions both to clumsy seamanship and faulty navigation. Eying Don Benito's small, yellow hands, he easily inferred that the young captain had not got into command at the hawse-hole,[7] but the cabin-window; and if so, why wonder at incompetence, in youth, sickness, and gentility united?

But drowning criticism in compassion, after a fresh repetition of his sympathies, Captain Delano having heard out his story, not only engaged, as in the first place, to see Don Benito and his people supplied in their immediate bodily needs, but, also, now further promised to assist him in procuring a large permanent supply of water, as well as some sails and rigging; and, though it would involve no small embarrassment to himself, yet he would spare three of his best seamen for temporary deck officers; so that without

---

7. Metal-lined hole in the bow of a ship, through which a cable passes; the expression here means to begin a career as an ordinary seaman and not as an officer.

delay the ship might proceed to Conception,[8] there fully to refit for Lima, her destined port.

Such generosity was not without its effect, even upon the invalid. His face lighted up; eager and hectic, he met the honest glance of his visitor. With gratitude he seemed overcome.

"This excitement is bad for master," whispered the servant, taking his arm, and with soothing words gently drawing him aside.

When Don Benito returned, the American was pained to observe that his hopefulness, like the sudden kindling in his cheek, was but febrile and transient.

Ere long, with a joyless mien, looking up towards the poop, the host invited his guest to accompany him there, for the benefit of what little breath of wind might be stirring.

As during the telling of the story, Captain Delano had once or twice started at the occasional cymballing of the hatchet-polishers, wondering why such an interruption should be allowed, especially in that part of the ship, and in the ears of an invalid; and moreover, as the hatchets had anything but an attractive look, and the handlers of them still less so, it was, therefore, to tell the truth, not without some lurking reluctance, or even shrinking, it may be, that Captain Delano, with apparent complaisance, acquiesced in his host's invitation. The more so, since with an untimely caprice of punctilio, rendered distressing by his cadaverous aspect, Don Benito, with Castilian bows, solemnly insisted upon his guest's preceding him up the ladder leading to the elevation; where, one on each side of the last step, sat for armorial supporters and sentries two of the ominous file. Gingerly enough stepped good Captain Delano between them, and in the instant of leaving them behind, like one running the gauntlet, he felt an apprehensive twitch in the calves of his legs.

But when, facing about, he saw the whole file, like so many organ-grinders, still stupidly intent on their work, unmindful of everything beside, he could not but smile at his late fidgety panic.

Presently, while standing with his host, looking forward upon the decks below, he was struck by one of those instances of insubordination previously alluded to. Three black boys, with two Spanish boys, were sitting together on the hatches, scraping a rude wooden platter, in which some scanty mess had recently been cooked. Suddenly, one of the black boys, enraged at a word dropped by one of his white companions, seized a knife, and though called to forbear by one of the oakum-pickers, struck the lad over the head, inflicting a gash from which blood flowed.

In amazement, Captain Delano inquired what this meant. To which the pale Don Benito dully muttered, that it was merely the sport of the lad.

"Pretty serious sport, truly," rejoined Captain Delano. "Had such a thing happened on board the Bachelor's Delight, instant punishment would have followed."

At these words the Spaniard turned upon the American one of his sudden, staring, half-lunatic looks; then relapsing into his torpor, answered, "Doubtless, doubtless, Señor."

8. Concepción, Chile.

Is it, thought Captain Delano, that this hapless man is one of those paper captains I've known, who by policy wink at what by power they cannot put down? I know no sadder sight than a commander who has little of command but the name.

"I should think, Don Benito," he now said, glancing towards the oakum-picker who had sought to interfere with the boys, "that you would find it advantageous to keep all your blacks employed, especially the younger ones, no matter at what useless task, and no matter what happens to the ship. Why, even with my little band, I find such a course indispensable. I once kept a crew on my quarter-deck thrumming[9] mats for my cabin, when, for three days, I had given up my ship—mats, men, and all—for a speedy loss, owing to the violence of a gale, in which we could do nothing but helplessly drive before it."

"Doubtless, doubtless," muttered Don Benito.

"But," continued Captain Delano, again glancing upon the oakum-pickers and then at the hatchet-polishers, near by. "I see you keep some at least of your host employed."

"Yes," was again the vacant response.

"Those old men there, shaking their pows[1] from their pulpits," continued Captain Delano, pointing to the oakum-pickers, "seem to act the part of old dominies to the rest, little heeded as their admonitions are at times. Is this voluntary on their part, Don Benito, or have you appointed them shepherds to your flock of black sheep?"

"What posts they fill, I appointed them," rejoined the Spaniard, in an acrid tone, as if resenting some supposed satiric reflection.

"And these others, these Ashantee[2] conjurors here," continued Captain Delano, rather uneasily eying the brandished steel of the hatchet-polishers, where in spots it had been brought to a shine, "this seems a curious business they are at, Don Benito?"

"In the gales we met," answered the Spaniard, "what of our general cargo was not thrown overboard was much damaged by the brine. Since coming into calm weather, I have had several cases of knives and hatchets daily brought up for overhauling and cleaning."

"A prudent idea, Don Benito. You are part owner of ship and cargo, I presume; but not of the slaves, perhaps?"

"I am owner of all you see," impatiently returned Don Benito, "except the main company of blacks, who belonged to my late friend, Alexandro Aranda."

As he mentioned this name, his air was heart-broken; his knees shook: his servant supported him.

Thinking he divined the cause of such unusual emotion, to confirm his surmise, Captain Delano, after a pause, said "And may I ask, Don Benito, whether—since awhile ago you spoke of some cabin passengers—the friend, whose loss so afflicts you at the outset of the voyage accompanied his blacks?"

"Yes."

"But died of the fever?"

"Died of the fever.—Oh, could I but—"

---

9. To "thrum" is to insert pieces of rope yarn into canvas, thus making a rough surface or mat (usually for keeping ropes from chafing against wood or metal).
1. Heads.
2. West African peoples.

gain quivering, the Spaniard paused.

"Pardon me," said Captain Delano lowly, "but I think that, by a sympathetic experience, I conjecture, Don Benito, what it is that gives the keener edge to your grief. It was once my hard fortune to lose at sea a dear friend, my own brother, then supercargo.[3] Assured of the welfare of his spirit, its departure I could have borne like a man; but that honest eye, that honest hand—both of which had so often met mine—and that warm heart; all, all—like scraps to the dogs—to throw all to the sharks! It was then I vowed never to have for fellow-voyager a man I loved, unless, unbeknown to him, I had provided every requisite, in case of a fatality, for embalming his mortal part for interment on shore. Were your friend's remains now on board this ship, Don Benito, not thus strangely would the mention of his name affect you."

"On board this ship?" echoed the Spaniard. Then, with horrified gestures, as directed against some specter, he unconsciously fell into the ready arms of his attendant, who, with a silent appeal toward Captain Delano, seemed beseeching him not again to broach a theme so unspeakably distressing to his master.

This poor fellow now, thought the pained American, is the victim of that sad superstition which associates goblins with the deserted body of man, as ghosts with an abandoned house. How unlike are we made! What to me, in like case, would have been a solemn satisfaction, the bare suggestion, even, terrifies the Spaniard into this trance. Poor Alexandro Aranda! what would you say could you here see your friend—who, on former voyages, when you for months were left behind, has, I dare say, often longed, and longed, for one peep at you—now transported with terror at the least thought of having you anyway nigh him.

At this moment, with a dreary graveyard toll, betokening a flaw, the ship's forecastle bell, smote by one of the grizzled oakum-pickers, proclaimed ten o'clock through the leaden calm; when Captain Delano's attention was caught by the moving figure of a gigantic black, emerging from the general crowd below, and slowly advancing towards the elevated poop. An iron collar was about his neck, from which depended a chain, thrice wound round his body; the terminating links padlocked together at a broad band of iron, his girdle.

"How like a mute Atufal moves," murmured the servant.

The black mounted the steps of the poop, and, like a brave prisoner, brought up to receive sentence, stood in unquailing muteness before Don Benito, now recovered from his attack.

At the first glimpse of his approach, Don Benito had started, a resentful shadow swept over his face; and, as with the sudden memory of bootless rage, his white lips glued together.

This is some mulish mutineer, thought Captain Delano, surveying, not without a mixture of admiration, the colossal form of the negro.

"See, he waits your question, master," said the servant.

Thus reminded, Don Benito, nervously averting his glance, as if shunning, by anticipation, some rebellious response, in a disconcerted voice, thus spoke:—

"Atufal, will you ask my pardon now?"

The black was silent.

---

3. The officer responsible for the commercial affairs of the ship's voyage.

"Again, master," murmured the servant, with bitter upbraiding eying his countryman, "Again, master; he will bend to master yet."

"Answer," said Don Benito, still averting his glance, "say but the one word *pardon*, and your chains shall be off."

Upon this, the black, slowly raising both arms, let them lifelessly fall, his links clanking, his head bowed; as much as to say, "no, I am content."

"Go," said Don Benito, with inkept and unknown emotion.

Deliberately as he had come, the black obeyed.

"Excuse me, Don Benito," said Captain Delano, "but this scene surprises me; what means it, pray?"

"It means that that negro alone, of all the band, has given me peculiar cause of offense. I have put him in chains; I——"

Here he paused; his hand to his head, as if there were a swimming there, or a sudden bewilderment of memory had come over him; but meeting his servant's kindly glance seemed reassured, and proceeded:—

"I could not scourge such a form. But I told him he must ask my pardon. As yet he has not. At my command, every two hours he stands before me."

"And how long has this been?"

"Some sixty days."

"And obedient in all else? And respectful?"

"Yes."

"Upon my conscience, then," exclaimed Captain Delano, impulsively, "he has a royal spirit in him, this fellow."

"He may have some right to it," bitterly returned Don Benito, "he says he was king in his own land."

"Yes," said the servant, entering a word, "those slits in Atufal's ears once held wedges of gold; but poor Babo here, in his own land, was only a poor slave; a black man's slave was Babo, who now is the white's."

Somewhat annoyed by these conversational familiarities, Captain Delano turned curiously upon the attendant, then glanced inquiringly at his master; but, as if long wonted to these little informalities, neither master nor man seemed to understand him.

"What, pray, was Atufal's offense, Don Benito?" asked Captain Delano; "if it was not something very serious, take a fool's advice, and, in view of his general docility, as well as in some natural respect for his spirit, remit him his penalty."

"No, no, master never will do that," here murmured the servant to himself, "proud Atufal must first ask master's pardon. The slave there carries the padlock, but master here carries the key."

His attention thus directed, Captain Delano now noticed for the first time that, suspended by a slender silken cord, from Don Benito's neck hung a key. At once, from the servant's muttered syllables divining the key's purpose, he smiled and said:—"So, Don Benito—padlock and key—significant symbols, truly."

Biting his lip, Don Benito faltered.

Though the remark of Captain Delano, a man of such native simplicity as to be incapable of satire or irony, had been dropped in playful allusion to the Spaniard's singularly evidenced lordship over the black; yet the hypochondriac seemed in some way to have taken it as a malicious reflection upon his confessed inability thus far to break down, at least, on a verbal summons, the entrenched will of the slave. Deploring this supposed misconception, yet despairing of correcting it, Captain Delano shifted the subject; but finding his companion more than ever withdrawn, as if still sourly digesting the lees of the presumed affront above-mentioned, by-and-by Captain Delano likewise became less talkative, oppressed, against his own will, by what seemed the secret vindictiveness of the morbidly sensitive Spaniard. But the good sailor himself, of a quite contrary disposition, refrained, on his part, alike from the appearance as from the feeling of resentment, and if silent, was only so from contagion.

Presently the Spaniard, assisted by his servant, somewhat discourteously crossed over from his guest; a procedure which, sensibly enough, might have been allowed to pass for idle caprice of ill-humor, had not master and man, lingering round the corner of the elevated skylight, began whispering together in low voices. This was unpleasing. And more: the moody air of the Spaniard, which at times had not been without a sort of valetudinarian stateliness, now seemed anything but dignified; while the menial familiarity of the servant lost its original charm of simple-hearted attachment.

In his embarrassment, the visitor turned his face to the other side of the ship. By so doing, his glance accidentally fell on a young Spanish sailor, a coil of rope in his hand, just stepped from the deck to the first round of the mizzen-rigging. Perhaps the man would not have been particularly noticed, were it not that, during his ascent to one of the yards, he, with a sort of covert intentness, kept his eye fixed on Captain Delano, from whom, presently, it passed, as if by a natural sequence, to the two whisperers.

His own attention thus redirected to that quarter, Captain Delano gave a slight start. From something in Don Benito's manner just then, it seemed as if the visitor had, at least partly, been the subject of the withdrawn consultation going on—a conjecture as little agreeable to the guest as it was little flattering to the host.

The singular alternations of courtesy and ill-breeding in the Spanish captain were unaccountable, except on one of two suppositions—innocent lunacy, or wicked imposture.

But the first idea, though it might naturally have occurred to an indifferent observer, and, in some respect, had not hitherto been wholly a stranger to Captain Delano's mind, yet, now that, in an incipient way, he began to regard the stranger's conduct something in the light of an intentional affront, of course the idea of lunacy was virtually vacated. But if not a lunatic, what then? Under the circumstances, would a gentleman, nay, any honest boor, act the part now acted by his host? The man was an impostor. Some low-born adventurer, masquerading as an oceanic grandee; yet so ignorant of the first requisites of mere gentlemanhood as to be betrayed into the present remarkable indecorum. That strange ceremoniousness, too, at other times evinced, seemed not uncharacteristic of one playing a part above his real level. Benito Cereno—Don Benito Cereno—a sounding name. One, too, at that period, not unknown, in the surname, to supercargoes and sea captains trading along the Spanish Main, as belonging to one of the most enterprising and extensive mercantile families in all those provinces; several members of it having titles; a sort of Castilian Rothschild,[4] with a noble brother, or cousin, in every great trading town of South

---

4. Renowned German banking family.

America. The alleged Don Benito was in early manhood, about twenty-nine or thirty. To assume a sort of roving cadetship[5] in the maritime affairs of such a house, what more likely scheme for a young knave of talent and spirit? But the Spaniard was a pale invalid. Never mind. For even to the degree of simulating mortal disease, the craft of some tricksters had been known to attain. To think that, under the aspect of infantile weakness, the most savage energies might be couched—those velvets of the Spaniard but the silky paw to his fangs.

From no train of thought did these fancies come; not from within, but from without; suddenly, too, and in one throng, like hoar frost; yet as soon to vanish as the mild sun of Captain Delano's good-nature regained its meridian.

Glancing over once more towards his host—whose side-face, revealed above the skylight, was now turned towards him—he was struck by the profile, whose clearness of cut was refined by the thinness incident to ill-health, as well as ennobled about the chin by the beard. Away with suspicion. He was a true off-shoot of a true hidalgo[6] Cereno.

Relieved by these and other better thoughts, the visitor, lightly humming a tune, now began indifferently pacing the poop, so as not to betray to Don Benito that he had at all mistrusted incivility, much less duplicity; for such mistrust would yet be proved illusory, and by the event; though, for the present, the circumstance which had provoked that distrust remained unexplained. But when that little mystery should have been cleared up, Captain Delano thought he might extremely regret it, did he allow Don Benito to become aware that he had indulged in ungenerous surmises. In short, to the Spaniard's black-letter text, it was best, for awhile, to leave open margin.[7]

Presently, his pale face twitching and overcast, the Spaniard, still supported by his attendant, moved over towards his guest, when, with even more than his usual embarrassment, and a strange sort of intriguing intonation in his husky whisper, the following conversation began:—

"Señor, may I ask how long you have lain at this isle?"

"Oh, but a day or two, Don Benito."

"And from what port are you last?"

"Canton."[8]

"And there, Señor, you exchanged your seal-skins for teas and silks, I think you said?"

"Yes. Silks, mostly."

"And the balance you took in specie,[9] perhaps?"

Captain Delano, fidgeting a little, answered—

"Yes; some silver; not a very great deal, though."

"Ah—well. May I ask how many men have you, Señor?"

Captain Delano slightly started, but answered—

"About five-and-twenty, all told."

---

5. Position of on-the-job training for a post of authority, appropriate for a younger or youngest son of an aristocratic family.
6. Spanish nobleman.
7. Without the comments then often printed in margins as a gloss on the main text. (Delano is

deciding to reserve judgment.) "Black-letter text": books printed in an early type imitative of medieval script.
8. A port in China.
9. Coin, typically gold or silver.

"And at present, Señor, all on board, I suppose?"

"All on board, Don Benito," replied the Captain, now with satisfaction.

"And will be to-night, Señor?"

At this last question, following so many pertinacious ones, for the soul of him Captain Delano could not but look very earnestly at the questioner, who, instead of meeting the glance, with every token of craven discomposure dropped his eyes to the deck; presenting an unworthy contrast to his servant, who, just then, was kneeling at his feet, adjusting a loose shoe-buckle; his disengaged face meantime, with humble curiosity, turned openly up into his master's downcast one.

The Spaniard, still with a guilty shuffle, repeated his question:—

"And—and will be to-night, Señor?"

"Yes, for aught I know," returned Captain Delano,—"but nay," rallying himself into fearless truth, "some of them talked of going off on another fishing party about midnight."

"Your ships generally go—go more or less armed, I believe, Señor?"

"Oh, a six-pounder or two, in case of emergency," was the intrepidly indifferent reply, "with a small stock of muskets, sealing-spears, and cutlasses, you know."

As he thus responded, Captain Delano again glanced at Don Benito, but the latter's eyes were averted; while abruptly and awkwardly shifting the subject, he made some peevish allusion to the calm, and then, without apology, once more, with his attendant, withdrew to the opposite bulwarks, where the whispering was resumed.

At this moment, and ere Captain Delano could cast a cool thought upon what had just passed, the young Spanish sailor before mentioned was seen descending from the rigging. In act of stooping over to spring inboard to the deck, his voluminous, unconfined frock, or shirt, of coarse woollen, much spotted with tar, opened out far down the chest, revealing a soiled under garment of what seemed the finest linen, edged, about the neck, with a narrow blue ribbon, sadly faded and worn. At this moment the young sailor's eye was again fixed on the whisperers, and Captain Delano thought he observed a lurking significance in it, as if silent signs of some Freemason[1] sort had that instant been interchanged.

This once more impelled his own glance in the direction of Don Benito, and, as before, he could not but infer that himself formed the subject of the conference. He paused. The sound of the hatchet-polishing fell on his ears. He cast another swift side-look at the two. They had the air of conspirators. In connection with the late questionings and the incident of the young sailor, these things now begat such return of involuntary suspicion, that the singular guilelessness of the American could not endure it. Plucking up a gay and humorous expression, he crossed over to the two rapidly, saying:—"Ha, Don Benito, your black here seems high in your trust; a sort of privy-counselor, in fact."

Upon this, the servant looked up with a good-natured grin, but the master started as from a venomous bite. It was a moment or two before the Spaniard

1. A fraternal association founded early in the 18th century in Europe, characterized by local lodges whose members recognized each other by secret signs.

sufficiently recovered himself to reply; which he did, at last, with cold constraint:—"Yes, Señor, I have trust in Babo."

Here Babo, changing his previous grin of mere animal humor into an intelligent smile, not ungratefully eyed his master.

Finding that the Spaniard now stood silent and reserved, as if involuntarily, or purposely giving hint that his guest's proximity was inconvenient just then, Captain Delano, unwilling to appear uncivil even to incivility itself, made some trivial remark and moved off; again and again turning over in his mind the mysterious demeanor of Don Benito Cereno.

He had descended from the poop, and, wrapped in thought, was passing near a dark hatchway, leading down into the steerage, when, perceiving motion there, he looked to see what moved. The same instant there was a sparkle in the shadowy hatchway, and he saw one of the Spanish sailors prowling there hurriedly placing his hand in the bosom of his frock, as if hiding something. Before the man could have been certain who it was that was passing, he slunk below out of sight. But enough was seen of him to make it sure that he was the same young sailor before noticed in the rigging.

What was that which so sparkled? thought Captain Delano. It was no lamp—no match—no live coal. Could it have been a jewel? But how come sailors with jewels?—or with silk-trimmed under-shirts either? Has he been robbing the trunks of the dead cabin passengers? But if so, he would hardly wear one of the stolen articles on board ship here. Ah, ah—if now that was, indeed, a secret sign I saw passing between this suspicious fellow and his captain awhile since; if I could only be certain that in my uneasiness my senses did not deceive me, then—

Here, passing from one suspicious thing to another, his mind revolved the strange questions put to him concerning his ship.

By a curious coincidence, as each point was recalled, the black wizards of Ashantee would strike up with their hatchets, as in ominous comment on the white stranger's thoughts. Pressed by such enigmas and portents, it would have been almost against nature, had not, even into the least distrustful heart, some ugly misgivings obtruded.

Observing the ship now helplessly fallen into a current, with enchanted sails, drifting with increased rapidity seaward; and noting that, from a lately intercepted projection of the land, the sealer was hidden, the stout mariner began to quake at thoughts which he barely durst confess to himself. Above all, he began to feel a ghostly dread of Don Benito. And yet when he roused himself, dilated his chest, felt himself strong on his legs, and coolly considered it—what did all these phantoms amount to?

Had the Spaniard any sinister scheme, it must have reference not so much to him (Captain Delano) as to his ship (the Bachelor's Delight). Hence the present drifting away of the one ship from the other, instead of favoring any such possible scheme, was, for the time at least, opposed to it. Clearly any suspicion, combining such contradictions, must need be delusive. Beside, was it not absurd to think of a vessel in distress—a vessel by sickness almost dismanned of her crew—a vessel whose inmates were parched for water— was it not a thousand times absurd that such a craft should, at present, be of a piratical character; or her commander, either for himself or those under him, cherish any desire but for speedy relief and refreshment? But then, might not general distress, and thirst in particular, be affected? And might not that same undiminished Spanish crew, alleged to have perished off to a remnant, be at that very moment lurking in the hold? On heart-broken pretense of entreating a cup of cold water, fiends in human form had got into lonely dwellings, nor retired until a dark deed had been done. And among the Malay pirates, it was no unusual thing to lure ships after them into their treacherous harbors, or entice boarders from a declared enemy at sea, by the spectacle of thinly manned or vacant decks, beneath which prowled a hundred spears with yellow arms ready to upthrust them through the mats. Not that Captain Delano had entirely credited such things. He had heard of them—and now, as stories, they recurred. The present destination of the ship was the anchorage. There she would be near his own vessel. Upon gaining that vicinity, might not the San Dominick, like a slumbering volcano, suddenly let loose energies now hid?

He recalled the Spaniard's manner while telling his story. There was a gloomy hesitancy and subterfuge about it. It was just the manner of one making up his tale for evil purposes, as he goes. But if that story was not true, what was the truth? That the ship had unlawfully come into the Spaniard's possession? But in many of its details, especially in reference to the more calamitous parts, such as the fatalities among the seamen, the consequent prolonged beating about, the past sufferings from obstinate calms, and still continued suffering from thirst; in all these points, as well as others, Don Benito's story had corroborated not only the wailing ejaculations of the indiscriminate multitude, white and black, but likewise—what seemed impossible to be counterfeit—by the very expression and play of every human feature, which Captain Delano saw. If Don Benito's story was throughout an invention, then every soul on board, down to the youngest negress, was his carefully drilled recruit in the plot: an incredible inference. And yet, if there was ground for mistrusting his veracity, that inference was a legitimate one.

But those questions of the Spaniard. There, indeed, one might pause. Did they not seem put with much the same object with which the burglar or assassin, by day-time, reconnoitres the walls of a house? But, with ill purposes, to solicit such information openly of the chief person endangered, and so, in effect, setting him on his guard; how unlikely a procedure was that? Absurd, then, to suppose that those questions had been prompted by evil designs. Thus, the same conduct, which, in this instance, had raised the alarm, served to dispel it. In short, scarce any suspicion or uneasiness, however apparently reasonable at the time, which was not now, with equal apparent reason, dismissed.

At last he began to laugh at his former forebodings; and laugh at the strange ship for, in its aspect someway siding with them, as it were; and laugh, too, at the odd-looking blacks, particularly those old scissors-grinders, the Ashantees; and those bed-ridden old knitting-women, the oakum-pickers; and almost at the dark Spaniard himself, the central hobglobin of all.

For the rest, whatever in a serious way seemed enigmatical, was now good-naturedly explained away by the thought that, for the most part, the poor invalid scarcely knew what he was about; either sulking in black vapors, or putting idle questions without sense or object. Evidently, for the present, the man was not fit to be entrusted with the ship. On some benevolent plea withdrawing the command from him, Captain Delano would yet have to send her to Conception, in charge of his second mate, a worthy person and good navigator—a plan not more convenient for the San Dominick than for Don Benito; for, relieved from all anxiety, keeping wholly to his cabin, the sick man, under the good nursing of his servant, would probably, by the end of the passage, be in a measure restored to health, and with that he should also be restored to authority.

Such were the American's thoughts. They were tranquilizing. There was a difference between the idea of Don Benito's darkly pre-ordaining Captain Delano's fate, and Captain Delano's lightly arranging Don Benito's. Nevertheless, it was not without something of relief that the good seaman presently perceived his whale-boat in the distance. Its absence had been prolonged by unexpected detention at the sealer's side, as well as its returning trip lengthened by the continual recession of the goal.

The advancing speck was observed by the blacks. Their shouts attracted the attention of Don Benito, who, with a return of courtesy, approaching Captain Delano, expressed satisfaction at the coming of some supplies, slight and temporary as they must necessarily prove.

Captain Delano responded; but while doing so, his attention was drawn to something passing on the deck below: among the crowd climbing the landward bulwarks, anxiously watching the coming boat, two blacks, to all appearances accidentally incommoded by one of the sailors, violently pushed him aside, which the sailor someway resenting, they dashed him to the deck, despite the earnest cries of the oakum-pickers.

"Don Benito," said Captain Delano quickly, "do you see what is going on there? Look!"

But, seized by his cough, the Spaniard staggered, with both hands to his face, on the point of falling. Captain Delano would have supported him, but the servant was more alert, who, with one hand sustaining his master, with the other applied the cordial. Don Benito restored, the black withdrew his support, slipping aside a little, but dutifully remaining within call of a whisper. Such discretion was here evinced as quite wiped away, in the visitor's eyes, any blemish of impropriety which might have attached to the attendant, from the indecorous conferences before mentioned; showing, too, that if the servant were to blame, it might be more the master's fault than his own, since when left to himself he could conduct thus well.

His glance called away from the spectacle of disorder to the more pleasing one before him, Captain Delano could not avoid again congratulating his host upon possessing such a servant, who, though perhaps a little too forward now and then, must upon the whole be invaluable to one in the invalid's situation.

"Tell me, Don Benito," he added, with a smile—"I should like to have your man here myself—what will you take for him? Would fifty doubloons be any object?"

"Master wouldn't part with Babo for a thousand doubloons," murmured the black, overhearing the offer, and taking it in earnest, and, with the strange vanity of a faithful slave appreciated by his master, scorning to hear so paltry a valuation put upon him by a stranger. But Don Benito, apparently hardly yet completely restored, and again interrupted by his cough, made but some broken reply.

Soon his physical distress became so great, affecting his mind, too, apparently, that, as if to screen the sad spectacle, the servant gently conducted his master below.

Left to himself, the American, to while away the time till his boat should arrive, would have pleasantly accosted some one of the few Spanish seamen he saw; but recalling something that Don Benito had said touching their ill conduct, he refrained, as a ship-master indisposed to countenance cowardice or unfaithfulness in seamen.

While, with these thoughts, standing with eye directed forward towards that handful of sailors, suddenly he thought that one or two of them returned the glance and with a sort of meaning. He rubbed his eyes, and looked again; but again seemed to see the same thing. Under a new form, but more obscure than any previous one, the old suspicions recurred, but, in the absence of Don Benito, with less of panic than before. Despite the bad account given of the sailors, Captain Delano resolved forthwith to accost one of them. Descending the poop, he made his way through the blacks, his movement drawing a queer cry from the oakum-pickers, prompted by whom, the negroes, twitching each other aside, divided before him; but, as if curious to see what was the object of this deliberate visit to their Ghetto, closing in behind, in tolerable order, followed the white stranger up. His progress thus proclaimed as by mounted kings-at-arms, and escorted as by a Caffre[2] guard of honor, Captain Delano, assuming a good humored, off-handed air, continued to advance; now and then saying a blithe word to the negroes, and his eye curiously surveying the white faces, here and there sparsely mixed in with the blacks, like stray white pawns venturously involved in the ranks of the chess-men opposed.

While thinking which of them to select for his purpose, he chanced to observe a sailor seated on the deck engaged in tarring the strap of a large block, with a circle of blacks squatted round him inquisitively eying the process.

The mean employment of the man was in contrast with something superior in his figure. His hand, black with continually thrusting it into the tar-pot held for him by a negro, seemed not naturally allied to his face, a face which would have been a very fine one but for its haggardness. Whether this haggardness had aught to do with criminality, could not be determined; since, as intense heat and cold, though unlike, produce like sensations, so innocence and guilt, when, through casual association with mental pain, stamping any visible impress, use one seal—a hacked one.

Not again that this reflection occurred to Captain Delano at the time, charitable man as he was. Rather another idea. Because observing so singular a haggardness combined with a dark eye, averted as in trouble and shame, and then again recalling Don Benito's confessed ill opinion of his crew, insensibly he was operated upon by certain general notions, which, while disconnecting pain and abashment from virtue, invariably link them with vice.

If, indeed, there be any wickedness on board this ship, thought Captain Delano, be sure that man there has fouled his hand in it, even as now he fouls it in the pitch. I don't like to accost him. I will speak to this other, this old Jack here on the windlass.[3]

<hr />

2. Many 19th-century travelers to southern Africa referred admiringly to the Caffre tribe or tribes.

3. Mechanical device used for hoisting heavy objects or hauling up the anchor chain. "Jack": sailor.

He advanced to an old Barcelona tar, in ragged red breeches and dirty night-cap, cheeks trenched and bronzed, whiskers dense as thorn hedges. Seated between two sleepy-looking Africans, this mariner, like his younger shipmate, was employed upon some rigging—splicing a cable—the sleepy-looking blacks performing the inferior function of holding the outer parts of the ropes for him.

Upon Captain Delano's approach, the man at once hung his head below its previous level; the one necessary for business. It appeared as if he desired to be thought absorbed, with more than common fidelity, in his task. Being addressed, he glanced up, but with what seemed a furtive, diffident air, which sat strangely enough on his weather-beaten visage, much as if a grizzly bear, instead of growling and biting, should simper and cast sheep's eyes. He was asked several questions concerning the voyage, questions purposely referring to several particulars in Don Benito's narrative, not previously corroborated by those impulsive cries greeting the visitor on first coming on board. The questions were briefly answered, confirming all that remained to be confirmed of the story. The negroes about the windlass joined in with the old sailor, but, as they became talkative, he by degrees became mute, and at length quite glum, seemed morosely unwilling to answer more questions, and yet, all the while, this ursine air was somehow mixed with his sheepish one.

Despairing of getting into unembarrassed talk with such a centaur, Captain Delano, after glancing round for a more promising countenance, but seeing none, spoke pleasantly to the blacks to make way for him; and so, amid various grins and grimaces, returned to the poop, feeling a little strange at first, he could hardly tell why, but upon the whole with regained confidence in Benito Cereno.

How plainly, thought he, did that old whiskerando yonder betray a consciousness of ill-desert. No doubt, when he saw me coming, he dreaded lest I, apprised by his Captain of the crew's general misbehavior, came with sharp words for him, and so down with his head. And yet—and yet, now that I think of it, that very old fellow, if I err not, was one of those who seemed so earnestly eying me here awhile since. Ah, these currents spin one's head round almost as much as they do the ship. Ha, there now's a pleasant sort of sunny sight; quite sociable, too.

His attention had been drawn to a slumbering negress, partly disclosed through the lace-work of some rigging, lying, with youthful limbs carelessly disposed, under the lee of the bulwarks, like a doe in the shade of a woodland rock. Sprawling at her lapped breasts was her wide-awake fawn, stark naked, its black little body half lifted from the deck, crosswise with its dam's; its hands, like two paws, clambering upon her; its mouth and nose ineffectually rooting to get at the mark; and meantime giving a vexatious half-grunt, blending with the composed snore of the negress.

The uncommon vigor of the child at length roused the mother. She started up, at distance facing Captain Delano. But as if not at all concerned at the attitude in which she had been caught, delightedly she caught the child up, with maternal transports, covering it with kisses.

There's naked nature, now; pure tenderness and love, thought Captain Delano, well pleased.

This incident prompted him to remark the other negresses more particularly than before. He was gratified with their manners; like most uncivilized women, they seemed at once tender of heart and tough of constitution; equally ready to die for their infants or fight for them. Unsophisticated as leopardesses; loving as doves. Ah! thought Captain Delano, these perhaps are some of the very women whom Ledyard[4] saw in Africa, and gave such a noble account of.

These natural sights somehow insensibly deepened his confidence and ease. At last he looked to see how his boat was getting on; but it was still pretty remote. He turned to see if Don Benito had returned; but he had not.

To change the scene, as well as to please himself with a leisurely observation of the coming boat, stepping over into the mizzen-chains he clambered his way into the starboard quarter-gallery;[5] one of those abandoned Venetian-looking water-balconies previously mentioned; retreats cut off from the deck. As his foot pressed the half-damp, half-dry sea-mosses matting the place, and a chance phantom cats-paw[6]—an islet of breeze, unheralded, unfollowed—as this ghostly cats-paw came fanning his cheek, as his glance fell upon the row of small, round dead-lights, all closed like coppered eyes of the coffined, and the state-cabin door, once connecting with the gallery, even as the dead-lights had once looked out upon it, but now calked fast like a sarcophagus lid, to a purple-black, tarred-over panel, threshold, and post; and he bethought him of the time, when that state-cabin and this state-balcony had heard the voices of the Spanish king's officers, and the forms of the Lima viceroy's daughters had perhaps leaned where he stood—as these and other images flitted through his mind, as the cats-paw through the calm, gradually he felt rising a dreamy inquietude, like that of one who alone on the prairie feels unrest from the repose of the noon.

He leaned against the carved balustrade, again looking off toward his boat; but found his eye falling upon the ribboned grass, trailing along the ship's water-line, straight as a border of green box; and parterres[7] of sea-weed, broad ovals and crescents, floating nigh and far, with what seemed long formal alleys between, crossing the terraces of swells, and sweeping round as if leading to the grottoes below. And overhanging all was the balustrade by his arm, which, partly stained with pitch and partly embossed with moss, seemed the charred ruin of some summer-house in a grand garden long running to waste.

Trying to break one charm, he was but becharmed anew. Though upon the wide sea, he seemed in some far inland country; prisoner in some deserted château, left to stare at empty grounds, and peer out at vague roads, where never wagon or wayfarer passed.

But these enchantments were a little disenchanted as his eye fell on the corroded main-chains. Of an ancient style, massy and rusty in link, shackle and bolt, they seemed even more fit for the ship's present business than the one for which she had been built.

Presently he thought something moved nigh the chains. He rubbed his eyes, and looked hard. Groves of rigging were about the chains; and there,

4. John Ledyard (1751–1789), American traveler, whose comment appeared in *Proceedings of the Association for Promoting the Discovery of the Interior Parts of Africa* (1790). In the *Putnam's* serialization, Melville attributed the passage to the Scottish traveler Mungo Park, who quoted it from Ledyard in his *Travels in the Interior of* *Africa* (1799); in *The Piazza Tales* Ledyard's name is properly restored.

5. Balcony or platform projecting from the stern of a ship.

6. Patch of open water visibly stirred by a puff of wind; also, the wind that produces a cat's-paw.

7. Ornamental arrangements, as of flower beds.

peering from behind a great stay, like an Indian from behind a hemlock, a Spanish sailor, a marlingspike[8] in his hand, was seen, who made what seemed an imperfect gesture towards the balcony, but immediately, as if alarmed by some advancing step along the deck within, vanished into the recesses of the hempen forest, like a poacher.

What meant this? Something the man had sought to communicate, unbeknown to any one, even to his captain. Did the secret involve aught unfavorable to his captain? Were those previous misgivings of Captain Delano's about to be verified? Or, in his haunted mood at the moment, had some random, unintentional motion of the man, while busy with the stay, as if repairing it, been mistaken for a significant beckoning?

Not unbewildered, again he gazed off for his boat. But it was temporarily hidden by a rocky spur of the isle. As with some eagerness he bent forward, watching for the first shooting view of its beak, the balustrade gave way before him like charcoal. Had he not clutched an outreaching rope he would have fallen into the sea. The crash, though feeble, and the fall, though hollow, of the rotten fragments, must have been overheard. He glanced up. With sober curiosity peering down upon him was one of the old oakum-pickers, slipped from his perch to an outside boom; while below the old negro, and, invisible to him, reconnoitering from a port-hole like a fox from the mouth of its den, crouched the Spanish sailor again. From something suddenly suggested by the man's air, the mad idea now darted into Captain Delano's mind, that Don Benito's plea of indisposition, in withdrawing below, was but a pretense: that he was engaged there maturing his plot, of which the sailor, by some means gaining an inkling, had a mind to warn the stranger against; incited, it may be, by gratitude for a kind word on first boarding the ship. Was it from foreseeing some possible interference like this, that Don Benito had, beforehand, given such a bad character of his sailors, while praising the negroes; though, indeed, the former seemed as docile as the latter the contrary? The whites, too, by nature, were the shrewder race. A man with some evil design, would he not be likely to speak well of that stupidity which was blind to his depravity, and malign that intelligence from which it might not be hidden? Not unlikely, perhaps. But if the whites had dark secrets concerning Don Benito, could then Don Benito be any way in complicity with the blacks? But they were too stupid. Besides, who ever heard of a white so far a renegade as to apostatize[9] from his very species almost, by leaguing in against it with negroes? These difficulties recalled former ones. Lost in their mazes, Captain Delano, who had now regained the deck, was uneasily advancing along it, when he observed a new face; an aged sailor seated cross-legged near the main hatchway. His skin was shrunk up with wrinkles like a pelican's empty pouch; his hair frosted; his countenance grave and composed. His hands were full of ropes, which he was working into a large knot. Some blacks were about him obligingly dipping the strands for him, here and there, as the exigencies of the operation demanded.

Captain Delano crossed over to him, and stood in silence surveying the knot; his mind, by a not uncongenial transition, passing from its own entanglements to those of the hemp. For intricacy such a knot he had never seen

---

8. Pointed iron tool used to separate and splice strands of rope.

9. To deny or renounce (typically said of religious faith).

in an American ship, or indeed any other. The old man looked like an Egyptian priest, making gordian knots for the temple of Ammon.[1] The knot seemed a combination of double-bowline-knot, treble-crown-knot, back-handed-well-knot, knot-in-and-out-knot, and jamming-knot.

At last, puzzled to comprehend the meaning of such a knot, Captain Delano addressed the knotter:—

"What are you knotting there, my man?"

"The knot," was the brief reply, without looking up.

"So it seems; but what is it for?"

"For some one else to undo," muttered back the old man, plying his fingers harder than ever, the knot being now nearly completed.

While Captain Delano stood watching him, suddenly the old man threw the knot towards him, saying in broken English,—the first heard in the ship,—something to this effect—"Undo it, cut it, quick." It was said lowly, but with such condensation of rapidity, that the long, slow words in Spanish, which had preceded and followed, almost operated as covers to the brief English between.

For a moment, knot in hand, and knot in head, Captain Delano stood mute; while, without further heeding him, the old man was now intent upon other ropes. Presently there was a slight stir behind Captain Delano. Turning, he saw the chained negro, Atufal, standing quietly there. The next moment the old sailor rose, muttering, and, followed by his subordinate negroes, removed to the forward part of the ship, where in the crowd he disappeared.

An elderly negro, in a clout[2] like an infant's, and with a pepper and salt head, and a kind of attorney air, now approached Captain Delano. In tolerable Spanish, and with a good-natured, knowing wink, he informed him that the old knotter was simple-witted, but harmless; often playing his odd tricks. The negro concluded by begging the knot, for of course the stranger would not care to be troubled with it. Unconsciously, it was handed to him. With a sort of congé,[3] the negro received it, and turning his back, ferreted into it like a detective Custom House officer after smuggled laces. Soon, with some African word, equivalent to pshaw, he tossed the knot overboard.

All this is very queer now, thought Captain Delano, with a qualmish sort of emotion; but as one feeling incipient sea-sickness, he strove, by ignoring the symptoms, to get rid of the malady. Once more he looked off for his boat. To his delight, it was now again in view, leaving the rocky spur astern.

The sensation here experienced, after at first relieving his uneasiness, with unforeseen efficacy, soon began to remove it. The less distant sight of that well-known boat—showing it, not as before, half blended with the haze, but with outline defined, so that its individuality, like a man's, was manifest; that boat, Rover by name, which, though now in strange seas, had often pressed the beach of Captain Delano's home, and, brought to its threshold for repairs, had familiarly lain there, as a Newfoundland dog; the sight of that household boat evoked a thousand trustful associations, which, contrasted with previous

---

1. In Egypt the oracle of Jupiter Ammon predicted to Alexander the Great (356–323 B.C.E.) that he would conquer the world. Later in Phrygia (in north-central Asia Minor), where the former King Gordius had foretold that whoever would untie his intricate knot would become master of Asia, Alexander cut the knot with his sword.
2. Diaper; small piece of cloth.
3. Leave taking, signaled by a low bow.

suspicions, filled him not only with lightsome confidence, but somehow with half humorous self-reproaches at his former lack of it.

"What, I, Amasa Delano—Jack of the Beach, as they called me when a lad—I, Amasa; the same that, duck-satchel in hand, used to paddle along the waterside to the school-house made from the old hulk;—I, little Jack of the Beach, that used to go berrying with cousin Nat and the rest; I to be murdered here at the ends of the earth, on board a haunted pirate-ship by a horrible Spaniard?—Too nonsensical to think of! Who would murder Amasa Delano? His conscience is clean. There is some one above. Fie, fie, Jack of the Beach! you are a child indeed; a child of the second childhood, old boy; you are beginning to dote and drule, I'm afraid."

Light of heart and foot, he stepped aft, and there was met by Don Benito's servant, who, with a pleasing expression, responsive to his own present feelings, informed him that his master had recovered from the effects of his coughing fit, and had just ordered him to go present his compliments to his good guest, Don Amasa, and say that he (Don Benito) would soon have the happiness to rejoin him.

There now, do you mark that? again thought Captain Delano, walking the poop. What a donkey I was. This kind gentleman who here sends me his kind compliments, he, but ten minutes ago, dark-lantern in hand, was dodging round some old grind-stone in the hold, sharpening a hatchet for me, I thought. Well, well; these long calms have a morbid effect on the mind, I've often heard, though I never believed it before. Ha! glancing towards the boat; there's Rover; good dog; a white bone in her mouth. A pretty big bone though, seems to me.—What? Yes, she has fallen afoul of the bubbling tide-rip there. It sets her the other way, too, for the time. Patience.

It was now about noon, though, from the grayness of everything, it seemed to be getting towards dusk.

The calm was confirmed. In the far distance, away from the influence of land, the leaden ocean seemed laid out and leaded up, its course finished, soul gone, defunct. But the current from landward, where the ship was, increased; silently sweeping her further and further towards the tranced waters beyond.

Still, from his knowledge of those latitudes, cherishing hopes of a breeze, and a fair and fresh one, at any moment, Captain Delano, despite present prospects, buoyantly counted upon bringing the San Dominick safely to anchor ere night. The distance swept over was nothing; since, with a good wind, ten minutes' sailing would retrace more than sixty minutes' drifting. Meantime, one moment turning to mark "Rover" fighting the tide-rip, and the next to see Don Benito approaching, he continued walking the poop.

Gradually he felt a vexation arising from the delay of his boat; this soon merged into uneasiness; and at last, his eye falling continually, as from a stage-box into the pit, upon the strange crowd before and below him, and by and by recognising there the face—now composed to indifference—of the Spanish sailor who had seemed to beckon from the main chains, something of his old trepidations returned.

Ah, thought he—gravely enough—this is like the ague:[4] because it went off, it follows not that it won't come back.

4. Fever with chills.

Though ashamed of the relapse, he could not altogether subdue it; and so, exerting his good nature to the utmost, insensibly he came to a compromise.

Yes, this is a strange craft; a strange history, too, and strange folks on board. But—nothing more.

By way of keeping his mind out of mischief till the boat should arrive, he tried to occupy it with turning over and over, in a purely speculative sort of way, some lesser peculiarities of the captain and crew. Among others, four curious points recurred.

First, the affair of the Spanish lad assailed with a knife by the slave boy; an act winked at by Don Benito. Second, the tyranny in Don Benito's treatment of Atufal, the black; as if a child should lead a bull of the Nile by the ring in his nose. Third, the trampling of the sailor by the two negroes; a piece of insolence passed over without so much as a reprimand. Fourth, the cringing submission to their master of all the ship's underlings, mostly blacks; as if by the least inadvertence they feared to draw down his despotic displeasure.

Coupling these points, they seemed somewhat contradictory. But what then, thought Captain Delano, glancing towards his now nearing boat,— what then? Why, Don Benito is a very capricious commander. But he is not the first of the sort I have seen; though it's true he rather exceeds any other. But as a nation—continued he in his reveries—these Spaniards are all an odd set; the very word Spaniard has a curious, conspirator, Guy-Fawkish[5] twang to it. And yet, I dare say, Spaniards in the main are as good folks as any in Duxbury, Massachusetts. Ah good! At last "Rover" has come.

As, with its welcome freight, the boat touched the side, the oakum-pickers, with venerable gestures, sought to restrain the blacks, who, at the sight of three gurried[6] water-casks in its bottom, and a pile of wilted pumpkins in its bow, hung over the bulwarks in disorderly raptures.

Don Benito with his servant now appeared; his coming, perhaps, hastened by hearing the noise. Of him Captain Delano sought permission to serve out the water, so that all might share alike, and none injure themselves by unfair excess. But sensible, and, on Don Benito's account, kind as this offer was, it was received with what seemed impatience; as if aware that he lacked energy as a commander, Don Benito, with the true jealousy of weakness, resented as an affront any interference. So, at least, Captain Delano inferred.

In another moment the casks were being hoisted in, when some of the eager negroes accidentally jostled Captain Delano, where he stood by the gangway; so that, unmindful of Don Benito, yielding to the impulse of the moment, with good-natured authority he bade the blacks stand back; to enforce his words making use of a half-mirthful, half-menacing gesture. Instantly the blacks paused, just where they were, each negro and negress suspended in his or her posture, exactly as the word had found them—for a few seconds continuing so—while, as between the responsive posts of a telegraph, an unknown syllable ran from man to man among the perched oakum-pickers. While the visitor's attention was fixed by this scene, suddenly the hatchet-polishers half rose, and a rapid cry came from Don Benito.

Thinking that at the signal of the Spaniard he was about to be massacred, Captain Delano would have sprung for his boat, but paused, as the

---

5. Guy Fawkes (1570–1606), English Catholic conspirator executed for plotting to blow up the House of Lords.

6. Coated with slime, from "gurry," fish offal.

oakum-pickers, dropping down into the crowd with earnest exclamations, forced every white and every negro back, at the same moment, with gestures friendly and familiar, almost jocose, bidding him, in substance, not be a fool. Simultaneously the hatchet-polishers resumed their seats, quietly as so many tailors, and at once, as if nothing had happened, the work of hoisting in the casks was resumed, whites and blacks singing at the tackle.

Captain Delano glanced towards Don Benito. As he saw his meager form in the act of recovering itself from reclining in the servant's arms, into which the agitated invalid had fallen, he could not but marvel at the panic by which himself had been surprised on the darting supposition that such a commander, who upon a legitimate occasion, so trivial, too, as it now appeared, could lose all self-command, was, with energetic iniquity, going to bring about his murder.

The casks being on deck, Captain Delano was handed a number of jars and cups by one of the steward's aids, who, in the name of his captain, entreated him to do as he had proposed: dole out the water. He complied, with republican impartiality as to this republican element, which always seeks one level, serving the oldest white no better than the youngest black; excepting, indeed, poor Don Benito, whose condition, if not rank, demanded an extra allowance. To him, in the first place, Captain Delano presented a fair pitcher of the fluid; but, thirsting as he was for it, the Spaniard quaffed not a drop until after several grave bows and salutes. A reciprocation of courtesies which the sight-loving Africans hailed with clapping of hands.

Two of the less wilted pumpkins being reserved for the cabin table, the residue were minced up on the spot for the general regalement. But the soft bread, sugar, and bottled cider, Captain Delano would have given the whites alone, and in chief Don Benito; but the latter objected; which disinterestedness not a little pleased the American; and so mouthfuls all around were given alike to whites and blacks; excepting one bottle of cider, which Babo insisted upon setting aside for his master.

Here it may be observed that as, on the first visit of the boat, the American had not permitted his men to board the ship, neither did he now; being unwilling to add to the confusion of the decks.

Not uninfluenced by the peculiar good humor at present prevailing, and for the time oblivious of any but benevolent thoughts, Captain Delano, who from recent indications counted upon a breeze within an hour or two at furthest, dispatched the boat back to the sealer with orders for all the hands that could be spared immediately to set about rafting casks to the watering-place and filling them. Likewise he bade word be carried to his chief officer, that if against present expectation the ship was not brought to anchor by sunset, he need be under no concern, for as there was to be a full moon that night, he (Captain Delano) would remain on board ready to play the pilot, come the wind soon or late.

As the two Captains stood together, observing the departing boat—the servant as it happened having just spied a spot on his master's velvet sleeve, and silently engaged rubbing it out—the American expressed his regrets that the San Dominick had no boats; none, at least, but the unseaworthy old hulk of the long-boat,[7] which, warped as a camel's skeleton in the desert, and

7. The largest rowboat stowed on the deck of a large ship.

almost as bleached, lay pot-wise inverted amidships, one side a little tipped, furnishing a subterraneous sort of den for family groups of the blacks, mostly women and small children; who, squatting on old mats below, or perched above in the dark dome, on the elevated seats, were descried, some distance within, like a social circle of bats, sheltering in some friendly cave; at intervals, ebon flights of naked boys and girls, three or four years old, darting in and out of the den's mouth.

"Had you three or four boats now, Don Benito," said Captain Delano, "I think that, by tugging at the oars, your negroes here might help along matters some.—Did you sail from port without boats, Don Benito?"

"They were stove in the gales, Señor."

"That was bad. Many men, too, you lost then. Boats and men.—Those must have been hard gales, Don Benito."

"Past all speech," cringed the Spaniard.

"Tell me, Don Benito," continued his companion with increased interest, "tell me, were these gales immediately off the pitch of Cape Horn?"

"Cape Horn?—who spoke of Cape Horn?"

"Yourself did, when giving me an account of your voyage," answered Captain Delano with almost equal astonishment at this eating of his own words, even as he ever seemed eating his own heart, on the part of the Spaniard. "You yourself, Don Benito, spoke of Cape Horn," he emphatically repeated.

The Spaniard turned, in a sort of stooping posture, pausing an instant, as one about to make a plunging exchange of elements, as from air to water.

At this moment a messenger-boy, a white, hurried by, in the regular performance of his function carrying the last expired half hour forward to the forecastle, from the cabin time-piece, to have it struck at the ship's large bell.

"Master," said the servant, discontinuing his work on the coat sleeve, and addressing the rapt Spaniard with a sort of timid apprehensiveness, as one charged with a duty, the discharge of which, it was foreseen, would prove irksome to the very person who had imposed it, and for whose benefit it was intended, "master told me never mind where he was, or how engaged, always to remind him, to a minute, when shaving-time comes. Miguel has gone to strike the half-hour afternoon. It is *now*, master. Will master go into the cuddy?"[8]

"Ah—yes," answered the Spaniard, starting, somewhat as from dreams into realities; then turning upon Captain Delano, he said that ere long he would resume the conversation.

"Then if master means to talk more to Don Amasa," said the servant, "why not let Don Amasa sit by master in the cuddy, and master can talk, and Don Amasa can listen, while Babo here lathers and strops."

"Yes," said Captain Delano, not unpleased with this sociable plan, "yes, Don Benito, unless you had rather not, I will go with you."

"Be it so, Señor."

As the three passed aft, the American could not but think it another strange instance of his host's capriciousness, this being shaved with such uncommon punctuality in the middle of the day. But he deemed it more than likely that the servant's anxious fidelity had something to do with the matter;

8. Small cabin on the deck of a ship or boat.

inasmuch as the timely interruption served to rally his master from the mood which had evidently been coming upon him.

The place called the cuddy was a light deck-cabin formed by the poop, a sort of attic to the large cabin below. Part of it had formerly been the quarters of the officers; but since their death all the partitionings had been thrown down, and the whole interior converted into one spacious and airy marine hall; for absence of fine furniture and picturesque disarray, of odd appurtenances, somewhat answering to the wide, cluttered hall of some eccentric bachelor-squire in the country, who hangs his shooting-jacket and tobacco-pouch on deer antlers, and keeps his fishing-rod, tongs, and walking-stick in the same corner.

The similitude was hightened, if not originally suggested, by glimpses of the surrounding sea; since, in one aspect, the country and the ocean seem cousins-german.[9]

The floor of the cuddy was matted. Overhead, four or five old muskets were stuck into horizontal holes along the beams. On one side was a claw-footed old table lashed to the deck; a thumbed missal on it, and over it a small, meager crucifix attached to the bulkhead. Under the table lay a dented cutlass or two, with a hacked harpoon, among some melancholy old rigging, like a heap of poor friars' girdles.[1] There were also two long, sharp-ribbed settees of malacca cane, black with age, and uncomfortable to look at as inquisitors' racks, with a large, misshapen arm-chair, which, furnished with a rude barber's crutch[2] at the back, working with a screw, seemed some grotesque engine of torment. A flag locker was in one corner, open, exposing various colored bunting, some rolled up, others half unrolled, still others tumbled. Opposite was a cumbrous washstand, of black mahogany, all of one block, with a pedestal, like a font, and over it a railed shelf, containing combs, brushes, and other implements of the toilet. A torn hammock of stained grass swung near; the sheets tossed, and the pillow wrinkled up like a brow, as if whoever slept here slept but illy, with alternate visitations of sad thoughts and bad dreams.

The further extremity of the cuddy, overhanging the ship's stern, was pierced with three openings, windows or port holes, according as men or cannon might peer, socially or unsocially, out of them. At present neither men nor cannon were seen, though huge ring-bolts and other rusty iron fixtures of the wood-work hinted of twenty-four-pounders.

Glancing towards the hammock as he entered, Captain Delano said, "You sleep here, Don Benito?"

"Yes, Señor, since we got into mild weather."

"This seems a sort of dormitory, sitting-room, sail-loft, chapel, armory, and private closet all together, Don Benito," added Captain Delano, looking round.

"Yes, Señor; events have not been favorable to much order in my arrangements."

Here the servant, napkin on arm, made a motion as if waiting his master's good pleasure. Don Benito signified his readiness, when, seating him in the malacca arm-chair, and for the guest's convenience drawing opposite it one

9. First cousins.
1. Rope belts.

2. Headrest.

of the settees, the servant commenced operations by throwing back his master's collar and loosening his cravat.

There is something in the negro which, in a peculiar way, fits him for avocations about one's person. Most negroes are natural valets and hairdressers; taking to the comb and brush congenially as to the castinets, and flourishing them apparently with almost equal satisfaction. There is, too, a smooth tact about them in this employment, with a marvelous, noiseless, gliding briskness, not ungraceful in its way, singularly pleasing to behold, and still more so to be the manipulated subject of. And above all is the great gift of good humor. Not the mere grin or laugh is here meant. Those were unsuitable. But a certain easy cheerfulness, harmonious in every glance and gesture; as though God had set the whole negro to some pleasant tune.

When to all this is added the docility arising from the unaspiring contentment of a limited mind, and that susceptibility of blind attachment sometimes inhering in indisputable inferiors, one readily perceives why those hypochondriacs, Johnson and Byron—it may be something like the hypochondriac, Benito Cereno—took to their hearts, almost to the exclusion of the entire white race, their serving men, the negroes, Barber and Fletcher.[3] But if there be that in the negro which exempts him from the inflicted sourness of the morbid or cynical mind, how, in his most prepossessing aspects, must he appear to a benevolent one? When at ease with respect to exterior things, Captain Delano's nature was not only benign, but familiarly and humorously so. At home, he had often taken rare satisfaction in sitting in his door, watching some free man of color at his work or play. If on a voyage he chanced to have a black sailor, invariably he was on chatty, and half-gamesome terms with him. In fact, like most men of a good, blithe heart, Captain Delano took to negroes, not philanthropically, but genially, just as other men to Newfoundland dogs.

Hitherto the circumstances in which he found the San Dominick had repressed the tendency. But in the cuddy, relieved from his former uneasiness, and, for various reasons, more sociably inclined than at any previous period of the day, and seeing the colored servant, napkin on arm, so debonair about his master, in a business so familiar as that of shaving, too, all his old weakness for negroes returned.

Among other things, he was amused with an odd instance of the African love of bright colors and fine shows, in the black's informally taking from the flag-locker a great piece of bunting of all hues, and lavishly tucking it under his master's chin for an apron.

The mode of shaving among the Spaniards is a little different from what it is with other nations. They have a basin, specifically called a barber's basin, which on one side is scooped out, so as accurately to receive the chin, against which it is closely held in lathering; which is done, not with a brush, but with soap dipped in the water of the basin and rubbed on the face.

In the present instance salt-water was used for lack of better; and the parts lathered were only the upper lip, and low down under the throat, all the rest being cultivated beard.

3. William Fletcher, valet of Lord Byron (1788–1824), was a white Englishman, here confused with an American black servant of Edward Trelawny who accompanied Byron on some journeys. Frank Barber worked for the English writer Samuel Johnson (1709–1784) for three decades; at his death in 1784 Johnson left Barber a large annuity.

The preliminaries being somewhat novel to Captain Delano, he sat curiously eying them, so that no conversation took place, nor for the present did Don Benito appear disposed to renew any.

Setting down his basin, the negro searched among the razors, as for the sharpest, and having found it, gave it an additional edge by expertly strapping it on the firm, smooth, oily skin of his open palm; he then made a gesture as if to begin, but midway stood suspended for an instant, one hand elevating the razor, the other professionally dabbling among the bubbling suds on the Spaniard's lank neck. Not unaffected by the close sight of the gleaming steel, Don Benito nervously shuddered, his usual ghastliness was hightened by the lather, which lather, again, was intensified in its hue by the contrasting sootiness of the negro's body. Altogether the scene was somewhat peculiar, at least to Captain Delano, nor, as he saw the two thus postured, could he resist the vagary, that in the black he saw a headsman, and in the white, a man at the block. But this was one of those antic conceits, appearing and vanishing in a breath, from which, perhaps, the best regulated mind is not always free.

Meantime the agitation of the Spaniard had a little loosened the bunting from around him, so that one broad fold swept curtain-like over the chair-arm to the floor, revealing, amid a profusion of armorial bars and ground-colors—black, blue, and yellow—a closed castle in a blood-red field diagonal with a lion rampant in a white.

"The castle and the lion," exclaimed Captain Delano—"why, Don Benito, this is the flag of Spain you use here. It's well it's only I, and not the King, that sees this," he added with a smile, "but"—turning towards the black,—"it's all one, I suppose, so the colors be gay;" which playful remark did not fail somewhat to tickle the negro.

"Now, master," he said, readjusting the flag, and pressing the head gently further back into the crotch of the chair; "now master," and the steel glanced nigh the throat.

Again Don Benito faintly shuddered.

"You must not shake so, master.—See, Don Amasa, master always shakes when I shave him. And yet master knows I never yet have drawn blood, though it's true, if master will shake so, I may some of these times. Now master," he continued. "And now, Don Amasa, please go on with your talk about the gale, and all that, master can hear, and between times master can answer."

"Ah yes, these gales," said Captain Delano; "but the more I think of your voyage, Don Benito, the more I wonder, not at the gales, terrible as they must have been, but at the disastrous interval following them. For here, by your account, have you been these two months and more getting from Cape Horn to St. Maria, a distance which I myself, with a good wind, have sailed in a few days. True, you had calms, and long ones, but to be becalmed for two months, that is, at least, unusual. Why, Don Benito, had almost any other gentleman told me such a story, I should have been half disposed to a little incredulity."

Here an involuntary expression came over the Spaniard, similar to that just before on the deck, and whether it was the start he gave, or a sudden gawky roll of the hull in the calm, or a momentary unsteadiness of the servant's hand; however it was, just then the razor drew blood, spots of which stained the creamy lather under the throat; immediately the black barber drew back his steel, and remaining in his professional attitude, back to Captain Delano, and face to Don Benito, held up the trickling razor, saying, with a sort of half humorous sorrow, "See, master,—you shook so—here's Babo's first blood."

No sword drawn before James the First of England, no assassination in that timid King's presence,[4] could have produced a more terrified aspect than was now presented by Don Benito.

Poor fellow, thought Captain Delano, so nervous he can't even bear the sight of barber's blood; and this unstrung, sick man, is it credible that I should have imagined he meant to spill all my blood, who can't endure the sight of one little drop of his own? Surely, Amasa Delano, you have been beside yourself this day. Tell it not when you get home, sappy Amasa. Well, well, he looks like a murderer, doesn't he? More like as if himself were to be done for. Well, well, this day's experience shall be a good lesson.

Meantime, while these things were running through the honest seaman's mind, the servant had taken the napkin from his arm, and to Don Benito had said—"But answer Don Amasa, please, master, while I wipe this ugly stuff off the razor, and strop it again."

As he said the words, his face was turned half round, so as to be alike visible to the Spaniard and the American, and seemed by its expression to hint, that he was desirous, by getting his master to go on with the conversation, considerately to withdraw his attention from the recent annoying accident. As if glad to snatch the offered relief, Don Benito resumed, rehearsing to Captain Delano, that not only were the calms of unusual duration, but the ship had fallen in with obstinate currents; and other things he added, some of which were but repetitions of former statements, to explain how it came to pass that the passage from Cape Horn to St. Maria had been so exceedingly long, now and then mingling with his words, incidental praises, less qualified than before, to the blacks, for their general good conduct.

These particulars were not given consecutively, the servant at convenient times using his razor, and so, between the intervals of shaving, the story and panegyric went on with more than usual huskiness.

To Captain Delano's imagination, now again not wholly at rest, there was something so hollow in the Spaniard's manner, with apparently some reciprocal hollowness in the servant's dusky comment of silence, that the idea flashed across him, that possibly master and man, for some unknown purpose, were acting out, both in word and deed, nay, to the very tremor of Don Benito's limbs, some juggling play before him. Neither did the suspicion of collusion lack apparent support, from the fact of those whispered conferences before mentioned. But then, what could be the object of enacting this play of the barber before him? At last, regarding the notion as a whimsy, insensibly suggested, perhaps, by the theatrical aspect of Don Benito in his harlequin ensign,[5] Captain Delano speedily banished it.

The shaving over, the servant bestirred himself with a small bottle of scented waters, pouring a few drops on the head, and then diligently rubbing; the vehemence of the exercise causing the muscles of his face to twitch rather strangely.

4. James I (1566–1625), king of Great Britain and Ireland (r. 1604–25), who lived in terror of assassination by Catholics, especially after the Gunpowder Plot (1605) and the assassination of King Henry IV of France in 1610.
5. Colorful Spanish flag.

His next operation was with comb, scissors and brush; going round and round, smoothing a curl here, clipping an unruly whisker-hair there, giving a graceful sweep to the temple-lock, with other impromptu touches evincing the hand of a master; while, like any resigned gentleman in barber's hands, Don Benito bore all, much less uneasily, at least, than he had done the razoring; indeed, he sat so pale and rigid now, that the negro seemed a Nubian[6] sculptor finishing off a white statue-head.

All being over at last, the standard of Spain removed, tumbled up, and tossed back into the flag-locker, the negro's warm breath blowing away any stray hair which might have lodged down his master's neck; collar and cravat readjusted; a speck of lint whisked off the velvet lapel; all this being done; backing off a little space, and pausing with an expression of subdued self-complacency, the servant for a moment surveyed his master, as, in toilet at least, the creature of his own tasteful hands.

Captain Delano playfully complimented him upon his achievement; at the same time congratulating Don Benito.

But neither sweet waters, nor shampooing, nor fidelity, nor sociality, delighted the Spaniard. Seeing him relapsing into forbidding gloom, and still remaining seated, Captain Delano, thinking that his presence was undesired just then, withdrew, on pretense of seeing whether, as he had prophecied, any signs of a breeze were visible.

Walking forward to the mainmast, he stood awhile thinking over the scene, and not without some undefined misgivings, when he heard a noise near the cuddy, and turning, saw the negro, his hand to his cheek. Advancing, Captain Delano perceived that the cheek was bleeding. He was about to ask the cause, when the negro's wailing soliloquy enlightened him.

"Ah, when will master get better from his sickness; only the sour heart that sour sickness breeds made him serve Babo so; cutting Babo with the razor, because, only by accident, Babo had given master one little scratch; and for the first time in so many a day, too. Ah, ah, ah," holding his hand to his face.

Is it possible, thought Captain Delano; was it to wreak in private his Spanish spite against this poor friend of his, that Don Benito, by his sullen manner, impelled me to withdraw? Ah, this slavery breeds ugly passions in man—Poor fellow!

He was about to speak in sympathy to the negro, but with a timid reluctance he now reëntered the cuddy.

Presently master and man came forth; Don Benito leaning on his servant as if nothing had happened.

But a sort of love-quarrel, after all, thought Captain Delano.

He accosted Don Benito, and they slowly walked together. They had gone but a few paces, when the steward—a tall, rajah-looking mulatto, orientally set off with a pagoda turban formed by three or four Madras handkerchiefs wound about his head, tier on tier—approaching with a saalam,[7] announced lunch in the cabin.

On their way thither, the two Captains were preceded by the mulatto, who, turning round as he advanced, with continual smiles and bows, ushered them on, a display of elegance which quite completed the insignificance of the small

6. Native of Nubia in East Africa, now part of Sudan.

7. Literally, "health" (Arabic); a Muslim ceremonial greeting.

bare-headed Babo, who, as if not unconscious of inferiority, eyed askance the graceful steward. But in part, Captain Delano imputed his jealous watchfulness to that peculiar feeling which the full-blooded African entertains for the adulterated one. As for the steward, his manner, if not bespeaking much dignity of self-respect, yet evidenced his extreme desire to please; which is doubly meritorious, as at once Christian and Chesterfieldian.[8]

Captain Delano observed with interest that while the complexion of the mulatto was hybrid, his physiognomy was European; classically so.

"Don Benito," whispered he, "I am glad to see this usher-of-the-golden-rod[9] of yours; the sight refutes an ugly remark once made to me by a Barbadoes planter; that when a mulatto has a regular European face, look out for him; he is a devil. But see, your steward here has features more regular than King George's of England; and yet there he nods, and bows, and smiles; a king, indeed—the king of kind hearts and polite fellows. What a pleasant voice he has, too?"

"He has, Señor."

"But, tell me, has he not, so far as you have known him, always proved a good, worthy fellow?" said Captain Delano, pausing, while with a final genuflexion the steward disappeared into the cabin; "come, for the reason just mentioned, I am curious to know."

"Francesco is a good man," a sort of sluggishly responded Don Benito, like a phlegmatic appreciator, who would neither find fault nor flatter.

"Ah, I thought so. For it were strange indeed, and not very creditable to us white-skins, if a little of our blood mixed with the African's, should, far from improving the latter's quality, have the sad effect of pouring vitriolic acid into black broth; improving the hue, perhaps, but not the wholesomeness."

"Doubtless, doubtless, Señor, but"—glancing at Babo—"not to speak of negroes, your planter's remark I have heard applied to the Spanish and Indian intermixtures in our provinces. But I know nothing about the matter," he listlessly added.

And here they entered the cabin.

The lunch was a frugal one. Some of Captain Delano's fresh fish and pumpkins, biscuit and salt beef, the reserved bottle of cider, and the San Dominick's last bottle of Canary.[1]

As they entered, Francesco, with two or three colored aids, was hovering over the table giving the last adjustments. Upon perceiving their master they withdrew, Francesco making a smiling congé, and the Spaniard, without condescending to notice it, fastidiously remarking to his companion that he relished not superfluous attendance.

Without companions, host and guest sat down, like a childless married couple, at opposite ends of the table, Don Benito waving Captain Delano to his place, and, weak as he was, insisting upon that gentleman being seated before himself.

---

8. In his popular *Letters to His Son on the Art of Becoming a Man of the World and a Gentleman* (1747), Philip Stanhope, the fourth earl of Chesterfield (1694–1773), advocated a worldly code at variance with Jesus's absolute morality.
9. In this English usage, "usher" means an attendant charged with walking ceremoniously before a person of rank; certain ushers were known by the color of the rod or scepter they traditionally carried.
1. I.e., wine from the Canary Islands.

The negro placed a rug under Don Benito's feet, and a cushion behind his back, and then stood behind, not his master's chair, but Captain Delano's. At first, this a little surprised the latter. But it was soon evident that, in taking his position, the black was still true to his master; since by facing him he could the more readily anticipate his slightest want.

"This is an uncommonly intelligent fellow of yours, Don Benito," whispered Captain Delano across the table.

"You say true, Señor."

During the repast, the guest again reverted to parts of Don Benito's story, begging further particulars here and there. He inquired how it was that the scurvy and fever should have committed such wholesale havoc upon the whites, while destroying less than half of the blacks. As if this question reproduced the whole scene of plague before the Spaniard's eyes, miserably reminding him of his solitude in a cabin where before he had had so many friends and officers round him, his hand shook, his face became hueless, broken words escaped; but directly the sane memory of the past seemed replaced by insane terrors of the present. With starting eyes he stared before him at vacancy. For nothing was to be seen but the hand of his servant pushing the Canary over towards him. At length a few sips served partially to restore him. He made random reference to the different constitution of races, enabling one to offer more resistance to certain maladies than another. The thought was new to his companion.

Presently Captain Delano, intending to say something to his host concerning the pecuniary part of the business he had undertaken for him, especially—since he was strictly accountable to his owners—with reference to the new suit of sails, and other things of that sort; and naturally preferring to conduct such affairs in private, was desirous that the servant should withdraw; imagining that Don Benito for a few minutes could dispense with his attendance. He, however, waited awhile; thinking that, as the conversation proceeded, Don Benito, without being prompted, would perceive the propriety of the step.

But it was otherwise. At last catching his host's eye, Captain Delano, with a slight backward gesture of his thumb, whispered, "Don Benito, pardon me, but there is an interference with the full expression of what I have to say to you."

Upon this the Spaniard changed countenance; which was imputed to his resenting the hint, as in some way a reflection upon his servant. After a moment's pause, he assured his guest that the black's remaining with them could be of no disservice; because since losing his officers he had made Babo (whose original office, it now appeared, had been captain of the slaves) not only his constant attendant and companion, but in all things his confidant.

After this, nothing more could be said; though, indeed, Captain Delano could hardly avoid some little tinge of irritation upon being left ungratified in so inconsiderable a wish, by one, too, for whom he intended such solid services. But it is only his querulousness, thought he; and so filling his glass he proceeded to business.

The price of the sails and other matters was fixed upon. But while this was being done, the American observed that, though his original offer of assistance had been hailed with hectic animation, yet now when it was reduced to a business transaction, indifference and apathy were betrayed. Don Benito, in fact, appeared to submit to hearing the details more out of regard to common propriety, than from any impression that weighty benefit to himself and his voyage was involved.

Soon, his manner became still more reserved. The effort was vain to seek to draw him into social talk. Gnawed by his splenetic mood, he sat twitching his beard, while to little purpose the hand of his servant, mute as that on the wall, slowly pushed over the Canary.

Lunch being over, they sat down on the cushioned transom; the servant placing a pillow behind his master. The long continuance of the calm had now affected the atmosphere. Don Benito sighed heavily, as if for breath.

"Why not adjourn to the cuddy," said Captain Delano; "there is more air there." But the host sat silent and motionless.

Meantime his servant knelt before him, with a large fan of feathers. And Francesco coming in on tiptoes, handed the negro a little cup of aromatic waters, with which at intervals he chafed his master's brow; smoothing the hair along the temples as a nurse does a child's. He spoke no word. He only rested his eye on his master's, as if, amid all Don Benito's distress, a little to refresh his spirit by the silent sight of fidelity.

Presently the ship's bell sounded two o'clock; and through the cabin-windows a slight rippling of the sea was discerned; and from the desired direction.

"There," exclaimed Captain Delano, "I told you so, Don Benito, look!"

He had risen to his feet, speaking in a very animated tone, with a view the more to rouse his companion. But though the crimson curtain of the stern-window near him that moment fluttered against his pale cheek, Don Benito seemed to have even less welcome for the breeze than the calm.

Poor fellow, thought Captain Delano, bitter experience has taught him that one ripple does not make a wind, any more than one swallow a summer. But he is mistaken for once. I will get his ship in for him, and prove it.

Briefly alluding to his weak condition, he urged his host to remain quietly where he was, since he (Captain Delano) would with pleasure take upon himself the responsibility of making the best use of the wind.

Upon gaining the deck, Captain Delano started at the unexpected figure of Atufal, monumentally fixed at the threshold, like one of those sculptured porters of black marble guarding the porches of Egyptian tombs.

But this time the start was, perhaps, purely physical. Atufal's presence, singularly attesting docility even in sullenness, was contrasted with that of the hatchet-polishers, who in patience evinced their industry; while both spectacles showed, that lax as Don Benito's general authority might be, still, whenever he chose to exert it, no man so savage or colossal but must, more or less, bow.

Snatching a trumpet which hung from the bulwarks, with a free step Captain Delano advanced to the forward edge of the poop, issuing his orders in his best Spanish. The few sailors and many negroes, all equally pleased, obediently set about heading the ship towards the harbor.

While giving some directions about setting a lower stu'n'-sail, suddenly Captain Delano heard a voice faithfully repeating his orders. Turning, he saw Babo, now for the time acting, under the pilot, his original part of captain of the slaves. This assistance proved valuable. Tattered sails and warped yards were soon brought into some trim. And no brace or halyard was pulled but to the blithe songs of the inspirited negroes.

Good fellows, thought Captain Delano, a little training would make fine sailors of them. Why see, the very women pull and sing too. These must be some of those Ashantee negresses that make such capital soldiers, I've heard. But who's at the helm. I must have a good hand there.

He went to see.

The San Dominick steered with a cumbrous tiller, with large horizontal pullies attached. At each pully-end stood a subordinate black, and between them, at the tiller-head, the responsible post, a Spanish seaman, whose countenance evinced his due share in the general hopefulness and confidence at the coming of the breeze.

He proved the same man who had behaved with so shame-faced an air on the windlass.

"Ah—it is you, my man," exclaimed Captain Delano—"well, no more sheep's-eyes now;—look straightforward and keep the ship so. Good hand, I trust? And want to get into the harbor, don't you?"

The man assented with an inward chuckle, grasping the tiller-head firmly. Upon this, unperceived by the American, the two blacks eyed the sailor intently.

Finding all right at the helm, the pilot went forward to the forecastle, to see how matters stood there.

The ship now had way enough to breast the current. With the approach of evening, the breeze would be sure to freshen.

Having done all that was needed for the present, Captain Delano, giving his last orders to the sailors, turned aft to report affairs to Don Benito in the cabin; perhaps additionally incited to rejoin him by the hope of snatching a moment's private chat while the servant was engaged upon deck.

From opposite sides, there were, beneath the poop, two approaches to the cabin; one further forward than the other, and consequently communicating with a longer passage. Marking the servant still above, Captain Delano, taking the nighest entrance—the one last named, and at whose porch Atufal still stood—hurried on his way, till, arrived at the cabin threshold, he paused an instant, a little to recover from his eagerness. Then, with the words of his intended business upon his lips, he entered. As he advanced toward the seated Spaniard, he heard another footstep, keeping time with his. From the opposite door, a salver in hand, the servant was likewise advancing.

"Confound the faithful fellow," thought Captain Delano; "what a vexatious coincidence."

Possibly, the vexation might have been something different, were it not for the brisk confidence inspired by the breeze. But even as it was, he felt a slight twinge, from a sudden indefinite association in his mind of Babo with Atufal.

"Don Benito," said he, "I give you joy; the breeze will hold, and will increase. By the way, your tall man and time-piece, Atufal, stands without. By your order, of course?"

Don Benito recoiled, as if at some bland satirical touch, delivered with such adroit garnish of apparent good-breeding as to present no handle for retort.

He is like one flayed alive, thought Captain Delano; where may one touch him without causing a shrink?

The servant moved before his master, adjusting a cushion; recalled to civility, the Spaniard stiffly replied: "You are right. The slave appears where you saw him, according to my command; which is, that if at the given hour I am below, he must take his stand and abide my coming."

"Ah now, pardon me, but that is treating the poor fellow like an ex-king indeed. Ah, Don Benito," smiling, "for all the license you permit in some things, I fear lest, at bottom, you are a bitter hard master."

Again Don Benito shrank; and this time, as the good sailor thought, from a genuine twinge of his conscience.

Again conversation became constrained. In vain Captain Delano called attention to the now perceptible motion of the keel gently cleaving the sea; with lack-lustre eye, Don Benito returned words few and reserved.

By-and-by, the wind having steadily risen, and still blowing right into the harbor, bore the San Dominick swiftly on. Rounding a point of land, the sealer at distance came into open view.

Meantime Captain Delano had again repaired to the deck, remaining there some time. Having at last altered the ship's course, so as to give the reef a wide berth, he returned for a few moments below.

I will cheer up my poor friend, this time, thought he.

"Better and better, Don Benito," he cried as he blithely reëntered; "there will soon be an end to your cares, at least for awhile. For when, after a long, sad voyage, you know, the anchor drops into the haven, all its vast weight seems lifted from the captain's heart. We are getting on famously, Don Benito. My ship is in sight. Look through this side-light here; there she is; all a-taunt-o! The Bachelor's Delight, my good friend. Ah, how this wind braces one up. Come, you must take a cup of coffee with me this evening. My old steward will give you as fine a cup as ever any sultan tasted. What say you, Don Benito, will you?"

At first, the Spaniard glanced feverishly up, casting a longing look towards the sealer, while with mute concern his servant gazed into his face. Suddenly the old ague of coldness returned, and dropping back to his cushions he was silent.

"You do not answer. Come, all day you have been my host; would you have hospitality all on one side?"

"I cannot go," was the response.

"What? it will not fatigue you. The ships will lie together as near as they can, without swinging foul. It will be little more than stepping from deck to deck; which is but as from room to room. Come, come, you must not refuse me."

"I cannot go," decisively and repulsively repeated Don Benito.

Renouncing all but the last appearance of courtesy, with a sort of cadaverous sullenness, and biting his thin nails to the quick, he glanced, almost glared, at his guest; as if impatient that a stranger's presence should interfere with the full indulgence of his morbid hour. Meantime the sound of the parted waters came more and more gurglingly and merrily in at the windows; as reproaching him for his dark spleen; as telling him that, sulk as he might, and go mad with it, nature cared not a jot; since, whose fault was it, pray?

But the foul mood was now at its depth, as the fair wind at its hight.

There was something in the man so far beyond any mere unsociality or sourness previously evinced, that even the forbearing good-nature of his guest could no longer endure it. Wholly at a loss to account for such demeanor, and deeming sickness with eccentricity, however extreme, no adequate excuse, well satisfied, too, that nothing in his own conduct could justify it, Captain Delano's pride began to be roused. Himself became reserved. But all seemed one to the Spaniard. Quitting him, therefore, Captain Delano once more went to the deck.

The ship was now within less than two miles of the sealer. The whale-boat was seen darting over the interval.

To be brief, the two vessels, thanks to the pilot's skill, ere long in neighborly style lay anchored together.

Before returning to his own vessel, Captain Delano had intended communicating to Don Benito the smaller details of the proposed services to be rendered. But, as it was, unwilling anew to subject himself to rebuffs, he resolved, now that he had seen the San Dominick safely moored, immediately to quit her, without further allusion to hospitality or business. Indefinitely postponing his ulterior plans, he would regulate his future actions according to future circumstances. His boat was ready to receive him; but his host still tarried below. Well, thought Captain Delano, if he has little breeding, the more need to show mine. He descended to the cabin to bid a ceremonious, and, it may be, tacitly rebukeful adieu. But to his great satisfaction, Don Benito, as if he began to feel the weight of that treatment with which his slighted guest had, not indecorously, retaliated upon him, now supported by his servant, rose to his feet, and grasping Captain Delano's hand, stood tremulous; too much agitated to speak. But the good augury hence drawn was suddenly dashed, by his resuming all his previous reserve, with augmented gloom, as, with half-averted eyes, he silently reseated himself on his cushions. With a corresponding return of his own chilled feelings, Captain Delano bowed and withdrew.

He was hardly midway in the narrow corridor, dim as a tunnel, leading from the cabin to the stairs, when a sound, as of the tolling for execution in some jail-yard, fell on his ears. It was the echo of the ship's flawed bell, striking the hour, drearily reverberated in this subterranean vault. Instantly, by a fatality not to be withstood, his mind, responsive to the portent, swarmed with superstitious suspicions. He paused. In images far swifter than these sentences, the minutest details of all his former distrusts swept through him.

Hitherto, credulous good-nature had been too ready to furnish excuses for reasonable fears. Why was the Spaniard, so superfluously punctilious at times, now heedless of common propriety in not accompanying to the side his departing guest? Did indisposition forbid? Indisposition had not forbidden more irksome exertion that day. His last equivocal demeanor recurred. He had risen to his feet, grasped his guest's hand, motioned toward his hat; then, in an instant, all was eclipsed in sinister muteness and gloom. Did this imply one brief, repentent relenting at the final moment, from some iniquitous plot, followed by remorseless return to it? His last glance seemed to express a calamitous, yet acquiescent farewell to Captain Delano forever. Why decline the invitation to visit the sealer that evening? Or was the Spaniard less hardened than the Jew, who refrained not from supping at the board of him whom the same night he meant to betray?[2] What imported all those day-long

---

2. Judas Iscariot, who betrayed Christ after the Last Supper (Matthew 26).

enigmas and contradictions, except they were intended to mystify, preliminary to some stealthy blow? Atufal, the pretended rebel, but punctual shadow, that moment lurked by the threshold without. He seemed a sentry, and more. Who, by his own confession, had stationed him there? Was the negro now lying in wait?

The Spaniard behind—his creature before: to rush from darkness to light was the involuntary choice.

The next moment, with clenched jaw and hand, he passed Atufal, and stood unharmed in the light. As he saw his trim ship lying peacefully at anchor, and almost within ordinary call; as he saw his household boat, with familiar faces in it, patiently rising and falling on the short waves by the San Dominick's side; and then, glancing about the decks where he stood, saw the oakum-pickers still gravely plying their fingers; and heard the low, buzzing whistle and industrious hum of the hatchet-polishers, still bestirring themselves over their endless occupation; and more than all, as he saw the benign aspect of nature, taking her innocent repose in the evening; the screened sun in the quiet camp of the west shining out like the mild light from Abraham's tent,[3] as charmed eye and ear took in all these, with the chained figure of the black, clenched jaw and hand relaxed. Once again he smiled at the phantoms which had mocked him, and felt something like a tinge of remorse, that, by harboring them even for a moment, he should, by implication, have betrayed an atheist doubt of the ever-watchful Providence above.

There was a few minutes' delay, while, in obedience to his orders, the boat was being hooked along to the gangway. During this interval, a sort of saddened satisfaction stole over Captain Delano, at thinking of the kindly offices he had that day discharged for a stranger. Ah, thought he, after good actions one's conscience is never ungrateful, however much so the benefited party may be.

Presently, his foot, in the first act of descent into the boat, pressed the first round of the side-ladder, his face presented inward upon the deck. In the same moment, he heard his name courteously sounded; and, to his pleased surprise, saw Don Benito advancing—an unwonted energy in his air, as if, at the last moment, intent upon making amends for his recent discourtesy. With instinctive good feeling, Captain Delano, withdrawing his foot, turned and reciprocally advanced. As he did so, the Spaniard's nervous eagerness increased, but his vital energy failed; so that, the better to support him, the servant, placing his master's hand on his naked shoulder, and gently holding it there, formed himself into a sort of crutch.

When the two captains met, the Spaniard again fervently took the hand of the American, at the same time casting an earnest glance into his eyes, but, as before, too much overcome to speak.

I have done him wrong, self-reproachfully thought Captain Delano; his apparent coldness has deceived me; in no instance has he meant to offend.

Meantime, as if fearful that the continuance of the scene might too much unstring his master, the servant seemed anxious to terminate it. And so, still presenting himself as a crutch, and walking between the two captains,

---

3. The biblical patriarch Abraham, who pitched his tent in many places during his westward journey from Ur of the Chaldees to Canaan, on to Egypt, and then back to Canaan.

he advanced with them towards the gangway; while still, as if full of kindly contrition, Don Benito would not let go the hand of Captain Delano, but retained it in his, across the black's body.

Soon they were standing by the side, looking over into the boat, whose crew turned up their curious eyes. Waiting a moment for the Spaniard to relinquish his hold, the now embarrassed Captain Delano lifted his foot, to overstep the threshold of the open gangway; but still Don Benito would not let go his hand. And yet, with an agitated tone, he said, "I can go no further; here I must bid you adieu. Adieu, my dear, dear Don Amasa. Go—go!" suddenly tearing his hand loose, "go, and God guard you better than me, my best friend."

Not unaffected, Captain Delano would now have lingered; but catching the meekly admonitory eye of the servant, with a hasty farewell he descended into his boat, followed by the continual adieus of Don Benito, standing rooted in the gangway.

Seating himself in the stern, Captain Delano, making a last salute, ordered the boat shoved off. The crew had their oars on end. The bowsman pushed the boat a sufficient distance for the oars to be lengthwise dropped. The instant that was done, Don Benito sprang over the bulwarks, falling at the feet of Captain Delano; at the same time, calling towards his ship, but in tones so frenzied, that none in the boat could understand him. But, as if not equally obtuse, three sailors, from three different and distant parts of the ship, splashed into the sea, swimming after their captain, as if intent upon his rescue.

The dismayed officer of the boat eagerly asked what this meant. To which, Captain Delano, turning a disdainful smile upon the unaccountable Spaniard, answered that, for his part, he neither knew nor cared; but it seemed as if Don Benito had taken it into his head to produce the impression among his people that the boat wanted to kidnap him. "Or else—give way for your lives," he wildly added, starting at a clattering hubbub in the ship, above which rang the tocsin of the hatchet-polishers; and seizing Don Benito by the throat he added, "this plotting pirate means murder!" Here, in apparent verification of the words, the servant, a dagger in his hand, was seen on the rail overhead, poised in the act of leaping, as if with desperate fidelity to befriend his master to the last; while, seemingly to aid the black, the three white sailors were trying to clamber into the hampered bow. Meantime, the whole host of negroes, as if inflamed at the sight of their jeopardized captain, impended in one sooty avalanche over the bulwarks.

All this, with what preceded, and what followed, occurred with such involutions of rapidity, that past, present, and future seemed one.

Seeing the negro coming, Captain Delano had flung the Spaniard aside, almost in the very act of clutching him, and, by the unconscious recoil, shifting his place, with arms thrown up, so promptly grappled the servant in his descent, that with dagger presented at Captain Delano's heart, the black seemed of purpose to have leaped there as to his mark. But the weapon was wrenched away, and the assailant dashed down into the bottom of the boat, which now, with disentangled oars, began to speed through the sea.

At this juncture, the left hand of Captain Delano, on one side, again clutched the half-reclined Don Benito, heedless that he was in a speechless faint, while his right foot, on the other side, ground the prostrate negro; and his right arm pressed for added speed on the after oar, his eye bent forward, encouraging his men to their utmost.

But here, the officer of the boat, who had at last succeeded in beating off the towing sailors, and was now, with face turned aft, assisting the bowsman at his oar, suddenly called to Captain Delano, to see what the black was about; while a Portuguese oarsman shouted to him to give heed to what the Spaniard was saying.

Glancing down at his feet, Captain Delano saw the freed hand of the servant aiming with a second dagger—a small one, before concealed in his wool—with this he was snakishly writhing up from the boat's bottom, at the heart of his master, his countenance lividly vindictive, expressing the centred purpose of his soul, while the Spaniard, half-choked, was vainly shrinking away, with husky words, incoherent to all but the Portuguese.

That moment, across the long-benighted mind of Captain Delano, a flash of revelation swept, illuminating in unanticipated clearness, his host's whole mysterious demeanor, with every enigmatic event of the day, as well as the entire past voyage of the San Dominick. He smote Babo's hand down, but his own heart smote him harder. With infinite pity he withdrew his hold from Don Benito. Not Captain Delano, but Don Benito, the black, in leaping into the boat, had intended to stab.

Both the black's hands were held, as, glancing up towards the San Dominick, Captain Delano, now with scales dropped from his eyes, saw the negroes, not in misrule, not in tumult, not as if frantically concerned for Don Benito, but with mask torn away, flourishing hatchets and knives, in ferocious piratical revolt. Like delirious black dervishes, the six Ashantees danced on the poop. Prevented by their foes from springing into the water, the Spanish boys were hurrying up to the topmost spars, while such of the few Spanish sailors, not already in the sea, less alert, were descried, helplessly mixed in, on deck, with the blacks.

Meantime Captain Delano hailed his own vessel, ordering the ports up, and the guns run out. But by this time the cable of the San Dominick had been cut; and the fag-end, in lashing out, whipped away the canvas shroud about the beak, suddenly revealing, as the bleached hull swung round towards the open ocean, death for the figure-head, in a human skeleton; chalky comment on the chalked words below, *"Follow your leader."*

At the sight, Don Benito, covering his face, wailed out: "'Tis he, Aranda! my murdered, unburied friend!"

Upon reaching the sealer, calling for ropes, Captain Delano bound the negro, who made no resistance, and had him hoisted to the deck. He would then have assisted the now almost helpless Don Benito up the side; but Don Benito, wan as he was, refused to move, or be moved, until the negro should have been first put below out of view. When, presently assured that it was done, he no more shrank from the ascent.

The boat was immediately dispatched back to pick up the three swimming sailors. Meantime, the guns were in readiness, though, owing to the San Dominick having glided somewhat astern of the sealer, only the aftermost one could be brought to bear. With this, they fired six times; thinking to cripple the fugitive ship by bringing down her spars. But only a few inconsiderable ropes were shot away. Soon the ship was beyond the guns' range, steering broad out of the bay; the blacks thickly clustering round the bowsprit,[4] one moment with taunting cries towards the whites, the next with upthrown gestures hailing the now dusky moors of ocean—cawing crows escaped from the hand of the fowler.

The first impulse was to slip the cables and give chase. But, upon second thoughts, to pursue with whale-boat and yawl seemed more promising.

Upon inquiring of Don Benito what fire arms they had on board the San Dominick, Captain Delano was answered that they had none that could be used; because, in the earlier stages of the mutiny, a cabin-passenger, since dead, had secretly put out of order the locks of what few muskets there were. But with all his remaining strength, Don Benito entreated the American not to give chase, either with ship or boat; for the negroes had already proved themselves such desperadoes, that, in case of a present assault, nothing but a total massacre of the whites could be looked for. But, regarding this warning as coming from one whose spirit had been crushed by misery, the American did not give up his design.

The boats were got ready and armed. Captain Delano ordered his men into them. He was going himself when Don Benito grasped his arm.

"What! have you saved my life, señor, and are you now going to throw away your own?"

The officers also, for reasons connected with their interests and those of the voyage, and a duty owing to the owners, strongly objected against their commander's going. Weighing their remonstrances a moment, Captain Delano felt bound to remain; appointing his chief mate—an athletic and resolute man, who had been a privateer's-man[5]—to head the party. The more to encourage the sailors, they were told, that the Spanish captain considered his ship good as lost; that she and her cargo, including some gold and silver, were worth more than a thousand doubloons. Take her, and no small part should be theirs. The sailors replied with a shout.

The fugitives had now almost gained an offing. It was nearly night; but the moon was rising. After hard, prolonged pulling, the boats came up on the ship's quarters, at a suitable distance laying upon their oars to discharge their muskets. Having no bullets to return, the negroes sent their yells. But, upon the second volley, Indian-like, they hurtled their hatchets. One took off a sailor's fingers. Another struck the whale-boat's bow, cutting off the rope there, and remaining stuck in the gunwale like a woodman's axe. Snatching it, quivering from its lodgment, the mate hurled it back. The returned gauntlet now stuck in the ship's broken quarter-gallery, and so remained.

The negroes giving too hot a reception, the whites kept a more respectful distance. Hovering now just out of reach of the hurtling hatchets, they, with a view to the close encounter which must soon come, sought to decoy the blacks into entirely disarming themselves of their most murderous weapons in a hand-to-hand fight, by foolishly flinging them, as missiles, short of the mark, into the sea. But ere long perceiving the stratagem, the negroes desisted, though not before many of them had to replace their lost hatchets with hand-spikes; an exchange which, as counted upon, proved in the end favorable to the assailants.

---

4. The large spar, such as the pole for a mast, extending from the foremost part of the ship.
5. Had served on a privateer—a ship commissioned by a government to prey on the shipping of other countries.

Meantime, with a strong wind, the ship still clove the water; the boats alternately falling behind, and pulling up, to discharge fresh volleys.

The fire was mostly directed towards the stern, since there, chiefly, the negroes, at present, were clustering. But to kill or maim the negroes was not the object. To take them, with the ship, was the object. To do it, the ship must be boarded; which could not be done by boats while she was sailing so fast.

A thought now struck the mate. Observing the Spanish boys still aloft, high as they could get, he called to them to descend to the yards, and cut adrift the sails. It was done. About this time, owing to causes hereafter to be shown, two Spaniards, in the dress of sailors and conspicuously showing themselves, were killed; not by volleys, but by deliberate marksman's shots; while, as it afterwards appeared, by one of the general discharges, Atufal, the black, and the Spaniard at the helm likewise were killed. What now, with the loss of the sails, and loss of leaders, the ship became unmanageable to the negroes.

With creaking masts, she came heavily round to the wind; the prow slowly swinging, into view of the boats, its skeleton gleaming in the horizontal moon-light, and casting a gigantic ribbed shadow upon the water. One extended arm of the ghost seemed beckoning the whites to avenge it.

"Follow your leader!" cried the mate; and, one on each bow, the boats boarded. Sealing-spears and cutlasses crossed hatchets and hand-spikes. Huddled upon the long-boat amidships, the negresses raised a wailing chant, whose chorus was the clash of the steel.

For a time, the attack wavered; the negroes wedging themselves to beat it back; the half-repelled sailors, as yet unable to gain a footing, fighting as troopers in the saddle, one leg sideways flung over the bulwarks, and one without, plying their cutlasses like carters' whips. But in vain. They were almost overborne, when, rallying themselves into a squad as one man, with a huzza, they sprang inboard; where, entangled, they involuntarily separated again. For a few breaths' space, there was a vague, muffled, inner sound, as of submerged sword-fish rushing hither and thither through shoals of black-fish. Soon, in a reunited band, and joined by the Spanish seamen, the whites came to the surface, irresistibly driving the negroes toward the stern. But a barricade of casks and sacks, from side to side, had been thrown up by the mainmast. Here the negroes faced about, and though scorning peace or truce, yet fain would have had respite. But, without pause, overleaping the barrier, the unflagging sailors again closed. Exhausted, the blacks now fought in despair. Their red tongues lolled, wolf-like, from their black mouths. But the pale sailors' teeth were set; not a word was spoken; and, in five minutes more, the ship was won.

Nearly a score of the negroes were killed. Exclusive of those by the balls,[6] many were mangled; their wounds—mostly inflicted by the long-edged sealing-spears—resembling those shaven ones of the English at Preston Pans, made by the poled scythes of the Highlanders.[7] On the other side, none were killed, though several were wounded; some severely, including

6. Those killed by musketballs.
7. At the battle of Preston Pans (in East Lothian, Scotland) during 1745, Prince Charles Edward, grandson of James II, led Scottish Highlanders armed with scythes fastened to poles to victory over the royal forces.

the mate. The surviving negroes were temporarily secured, and the ship, towed back into the harbor at midnight, once more lay anchored.

Omitting the incidents and arrangements ensuing, suffice it that, after two days spent in refitting, the ships sailed in company for Conception, in Chili, and thence for Lima, in Peru; where, before the vice-regal courts, the whole affair, from the beginning, underwent investigation.

Though, midway on the passage, the ill-fated Spaniard, relaxed from constraint, showed some signs of regaining health with free-will; yet, agreeably to his own foreboding, shortly before arriving at Lima, he relapsed, finally becoming so reduced as to be carried ashore in arms. Hearing of his story and plight, one of the many religious institutions of the City of Kings opened an hospitable refuge to him, where both physician and priest were his nurses, and a member of the order volunteered to be his one special guardian and consoler, by night and by day.

The following extracts, translated from one of the official Spanish documents, will it is hoped, shed light on the preceding narrative, as well as, in the first place, reveal the true port of departure and true history of the San Dominick's voyage, down to the time of her touching at the island of St. Maria.

But, ere the extracts come, it may be well to preface them with a remark.

The document selected, from among many others, for partial translation, contains the deposition of Benito Cereno; the first taken in the case. Some disclosures therein were, at the time, held dubious for both learned and natural reasons. The tribunal inclined to the opinion that the deponent, not undisturbed in his mind by recent events, raved of some things which could never have happened. But subsequent depositions of the surviving sailors, bearing out the revelations of their captain in several of the strangest particulars, gave credence to the rest. So that the tribunal, in its final decision, rested its capital sentences upon statements which, had they lacked confirmation, it would have deemed it but duty to reject.

I, DON JOSE DE ABOS AND PADILLA, His Majesty's Notary for the Royal Revenue, and Register of this Province, and Notary Public of the Holy Crusade of this Bishopric, etc.

Do certify and declare, as much as is requisite in law, that, in the criminal cause commenced the twenty-fourth of the month of September, in the year seventeen hundred and ninety-nine, against the negroes of the ship San Dominick, the following declaration before me was made.

Declaration of the first witness, DON BENITO CERENO

The same day, and month, and year, His Honor, Doctor Juan Martinez de Rozas, Councilor of the Royal Audience of this Kingdom, and learned in the law of this Intendency, ordered the captain of the ship San Dominick, Don Benito Cereno, to appear; which he did in his litter, attended by the monk Infelez; of whom he received the oath, which he took by God, our Lord, and a sign of the Cross; under which he promised to tell the truth of whatever he should know and should be asked;—and being interrogated agreeably to the tenor of the act commencing the process, he said, that on the twentieth of May last, he set sail with his ship from the port of Valparaiso, bound to that of Callao; loaded with the produce of the country beside thirty cases of hardware and one hundred and sixty blacks, of both sexes, mostly belonging to Don Alexandro Aranda, gentleman, of the city of Mendoza;[8] that the crew of the ship consisted of thirty-six men, beside the persons who went as passengers; that the negroes were in part as follows:

[*Here, in the original, follows a list of some fifty names, descriptions, and ages, compiled from certain recovered documents of Aranda's, and also from recollections of the deponent, from which portions only are extracted.*]

—One, from about eighteen to nineteen years, named José, and this was the man that waited upon his master, Don Alexandro, and who speaks well the Spanish, having served him four or five years; * * * a mulatto, named Francisco, the cabin steward, of a good person and voice, having sung in the Valparaiso churches, native of the province of Buenos Ayres, aged about thirty-five years. * * * A smart negro, named Dago, who had been for many years a grave-digger among the Spaniards, aged forty-six years. * * * Four old negroes, born in Africa, from sixty to seventy, but sound, calkers by trade, whose names are as follows:—the first was named Muri, and he was killed (as was also his son named Diamelo); the second, Nacta; the third, Yola, likewise killed; the fourth, Ghofan; and six full-grown negroes, aged from thirty to forty-five, all raw, and born among the Ashantees—Matiluqui, Yan, Lecbe, Mapenda, Yambaio, Akim; four of whom were killed; * * * a powerful negro named Atufal, who, being supposed to have been a chief in Africa, his owners set great store by him. * * * And a small negro of Senegal, but some years among the Spaniards, aged about thirty, which negro's name was Babo; * * * that he does not remember the names of the others, but that still expecting the residue of Don Alexandro's papers will be found, will then take due account of them all, and remit to the court; * * * and thirty-nine women and children of all ages.

[*The catalogue over, the deposition goes on:*]

* * * That all the negroes slept upon deck, as is customary in this navigation, and none wore fetters, because the owner, his friend Aranda, told him that they were all tractable; * * * that on the seventh day after leaving port, at three o'clock in the morning, all the Spaniards being asleep except the two officers on the watch, who were the boatswain, Juan Robles, and the carpenter, Juan Bautista Gayete, and the helmsman and his boy, the negroes revolted suddenly, wounded dangerously the boatswain and the carpenter, and successively killed eighteen men of those who were sleeping upon deck, some with hand-spikes and hatchets, and others by throwing them alive overboard, after tying them; that of the Spaniards upon deck, they left about seven, as he thinks, alive and tied, to manœuvre the ship, and three or four more who hid themselves, remained also alive. Although in the act of revolt the negroes made themselves masters of the hatchway, six or seven wounded went through it to the cockpit, without any hindrance on their part; that

---

8. City in Argentina. "Intendency": court district. "Litter": seat or chair in which a person can be carried. Callao is a city in Peru; Valparaiso is in Chile.

during the act of revolt, the mate and another person, whose name he does not recollect, attempted to come up through the hatchway, but being quickly wounded, were obliged to return to the cabin; that the deponent resolved at break of day to come up the companionway, where the negro Babo was, being the ringleader, and Atufal, who assisted him, and having spoken to them, exhorted them to cease committing such atrocities, asking them, at the same time, what they wanted and intended to do, offering, himself, to obey their commands; that, notwithstanding this, they threw, in his presence, three men, alive and tied, overboard; that they told the deponent to come up, and that they would not kill him; which having done, the negro Babo asked him whether there were in those seas any negro countries where they might be carried, and he answered them, No; that the negro Babo afterwards told him to carry them to Senegal, or to the neighboring islands of St. Nicholas; and he answered, that this was impossible, on account of the great distance, the necessity involved of rounding Cape Horn, the bad condition of the vessel, the want of provisions, sails, and water; but that the negro Babo replied to him he must carry them in any way; that they would do and conform themselves to everything the deponent should require as to eating and drinking; that after a long conference, being absolutely compelled to please them, for they threatened him to kill all the whites if they were not, at all events, carried to Senegal, he told them that what was most wanting for the voyage was water; that they would go near the coast to take it, and thence they would proceed on their course; that the negro Babo agreed to it; and the deponent steered towards the intermediate ports, hoping to meet some Spanish or foreign vessel that would save them; that within ten or eleven days they saw the land, and continued their course by it in the vicinity of Nasca; that the deponent observed that the negroes were now restless and mutinous, because he did not effect the taking in of water, the negro Babo having required, with threats, that it should be done, without fail, the following day; he told him he saw plainly that the coast was steep, and the rivers designated in the maps were not to be found, with other reasons suitable to the circumstances; that the best way would be to go to the island of Santa Maria, where they might water easily, it being a solitary island, as the foreigners did; that the deponent did not go to Pisco, that was near, nor make any other port of the coast, because the negro Babo had intimated to him several times, that he would kill all the whites the very moment he should perceive any city, town, or settlement of any kind on the shores to which they should be carried; that having determined to go to the island of Santa Maria, as the deponent had planned, for the purpose of trying whether, on the passage or near the island itself, they could find any vessel that should favor them, or whether he could escape from it in a boat to the neighboring coast of Arruco;[9] to adopt the necessary means he immediately changed his course, steering for the island; that the negroes Babo and Atufal held daily conferences, in which they discussed what was necessary for their design of returning to Senegal, whether they were to kill all the Spaniards, and particularly the deponent; that eight days after parting from the coast of Nasca, the deponent being on the watch a little after day-break, and soon after the negroes had their meeting, the negro Babo came to the place where the deponent was, and

9. I.e., Arica, Chile. Nasca and Pisco are both in Peru.

told him that he had determined to kill his master, Don Alexandro Aranda, both because he and his companions could not otherwise be sure of their liberty, and that, to keep the seamen in subjection, he wanted to prepare a warning of what road they should be made to take did they or any of them oppose him; and that, by means of the death of Don Alexandro, that warning would best be given; but, that what this last meant, the deponent did not at the time comprehend, nor could not, further than that the death of Don Alexandro was intended; and moreover, the negro Babo proposed to the deponent to call the mate Raneds, who was sleeping in the cabin, before the thing was done, for fear, as the deponent understood it, that the mate, who was a good navigator, should be killed with Don Alexandro and the rest; that the deponent, who was the friend, from youth, of Don Alexandro, prayed and conjured, but all was useless; for the negro Babo answered him that the thing could not be prevented, and that all the Spaniards risked their death if they should attempt to frustrate his will in this matter or any other; that, in this conflict, the deponent called the mate, Raneds, who was forced to go apart, and immediately the negro Babo commanded the Ashantee Martinqui and the Ashantee Lecbe to go and commit the murder; that those two went down with hatchets to the berth of Don Alexandro; that, yet half alive and mangled, they dragged him on deck; that they were going to throw him overboard in that state, but the negro Babo stopped them, bidding the murder be completed on the deck before him, which was done, when, by his orders, the body was carried below, forward; that nothing more was seen of it by the deponent for three days; * * * that Don Alonzo Sidonia, an old man, long resident at Valparaiso, and lately appointed to a civil office in Peru, whither he had taken passage, was at the time sleeping in the berth opposite Don Alexandro's; that, awakening at his cries, surprised by them, and at the sight of the negroes with their bloody hatchets in their hands, he threw himself into the sea through a window which was near him, and was drowned, without it being in the power of the deponent to assist or take him up; * * * that, a short time after killing Aranda, they brought upon deck his germancousin, of middle-age, Don Francisco Masa, of Mendoza, and the young Don Joaquin, Marques de Aramboalaza, then lately from Spain, with his Spanish servant Ponce, and the three young clerks of Aranda, José Morairi, Lorenzo Bargas, and Hermenegildo Gandix, all of Cadiz; that Don Joaquin and Hermenegildo Gandix, the negro Babo for purposes hereafter to appear, preserved alive; but Don Francisco Masa, José Morairi, and Lorenzo Bargas, with Ponce the servant, beside the boatswain, Juan Robles, the boatswain's mates, Manuel Viscaya and Roderigo Hurta, and four of the sailors, the negro Babo ordered to be thrown alive into the sea, although they made no resistance, nor begged for anything else but mercy; that the boatswain, Juan Robles, who knew how to swim, kept the longest above water, making acts of contrition, and, in the last words he uttered, charged this deponent to cause mass to be said for his soul to our Lady of Succor; * * * that, during the three days which followed, the deponent, uncertain what fate had befallen the remains of Don Alexandro, frequently asked the negro Babo where they were, and if still on board, whether they were to be preserved for interment ashore, entreating him so to order it; that the negro Babo answered nothing till the fourth day, when at sunrise, the deponent coming on deck, the negro

Babo showed him a skeleton, which had been substituted for the ship's proper figure-head, the image of Christopher Colon, the discoverer of the New World; that the negro Babo asked him whose skeleton that was, and whether, from its whiteness, he should not think it a white's; that, upon his covering his face, the negro Babo, coming close, said words to this effect: "Keep faith with the blacks from here to Senegal, or you shall in spirit, as now in body, follow your leader," pointing to the prow; * * * that the same morning the negro Babo took by succession each Spaniard forward, and asked him whose skeleton that was, and whether, from its whiteness, he should not think it a white's; that each Spaniard covered his face; that then to each the negro Babo repeated the words in the first place said to the deponent; * * * that they (the Spaniards), being then assembled aft, the negro Babo harangued them, saying that he had now done all; that the deponent (as navigator for the negroes) might pursue his course, warning him and all of them that they should, soul and body, go the way of Don Alexandro if he saw them (the Spaniards) speak or plot anything against them (the negroes)—a threat which was repeated every day; that, before the events last mentioned, they had tied the cook to throw him overboard, for it is not known what thing they heard him speak, but finally the negro Babo spared his life, at the request of the deponent; that a few days after, the deponent, endeavoring not to omit any means to preserve the lives of the remaining whites, spoke to the negroes peace and tranquillity, and agreed to draw up a paper, signed by the deponent and the sailors who could write, as also by the negro Babo, for himself and all the blacks, in which the deponent obliged himself to carry them to Senegal, and they not to kill any more, and he formally to make over to them the ship, with the cargo, with which they were for that time satisfied and quieted. * * * But the next day, the more surely to guard against the sailors' escape, the negro Babo commanded all the boats to be destroyed but the long-boat, which was unseaworthy, and another, a cutter in good condition, which, knowing it would yet be wanted for towing the water casks, he had lowered down into the hold.

✻   ✻   ✻   ✻   ✻

[*Various particulars of the prolonged and perplexed navigation ensuing here follow, with incidents of a calamitous calm, from which portion one passage is extracted, to wit:*]

—That on the fifth day of the calm, all on board suffering much from the heat, and want of water, and five having died in fits, and mad, the negroes became irritable, and for a chance gesture, which they deemed suspicious— though it was harmless—made by the mate, Raneds, to the deponent, in the act of handing a quadrant, they killed him; but that for this they afterwards were sorry, the mate being the only remaining navigator on board, except the deponent.

✻   ✻   ✻   ✻   ✻

—That omitting other events, which daily happened, and which can only serve uselessly to recall past misfortunes and conflicts, after seventy-three days' navigation, reckoned from the time they sailed from Nasca, during which they navigated under a scanty allowance of water, and were afflicted with the calms before mentioned, they at last arrived at the island of Santa Maria, on the seventeenth of the month of August, at about six o'clock in the afternoon, at which hour they cast anchor very near the American ship, Bachelor's Delight, which lay in the same bay, commanded by the generous Captain Amasa Delano; but at six o'clock in the morning, they had already descried the port, and the negroes became uneasy, as soon as at distance they saw the ship, not having expected to see one there; that the negro Babo pacified them, assuring them that no fear need be had; that straightway he ordered the figure on the bow to be covered with canvas, as for repairs, and had the decks a little set in order; that for a time the negro Babo and the negro Atufal conferred; that the negro Atufal was for sailing away, but the negro Babo would not, and, by himself, cast about what to do; that at last he came to the deponent, proposing to him to say and do all that the deponent declares to have said and done to the American captain; * * * * * that the negro Babo warned him that if he varied in the least, or uttered any word, or gave any look that should give the least intimation of the past events or present state, he would instantly kill him, with all his companions, showing a dagger, which he carried hid, saying something which, as he understood it, meant that that dagger would be alert as his eye; that the negro Babo then announced the plan to all his companions, which pleased them; that he then, the better to disguise the truth, devised many expedients, in some of them uniting deceit and defense; that of this sort was the device of the six Ashantees before named, who were his bravoes;[1] that them he stationed on the break of the poop, as if to clean certain hatchets (in cases, which were part of the cargo), but in reality to use them, and distribute them at need, and at a given word he told them that, among other devices, was the device of presenting Atufal, his right-hand man, as chained, though in a moment the chains could be dropped; that in every particular he informed the deponent what part he was expected to enact in every device, and what story he was to tell on every occasion, always threatening him with instant death if he varied in the least; that, conscious that many of the negroes would be turbulent, the negro Babo appointed the four aged negroes, who were calkers, to keep what domestic order they could on the decks; that again and again he harangued the Spaniards and his companions, informing them of his intent, and of his devices, and of the invented story that this deponent was to tell, charging them lest any of them varied from that story; that these arrangements were made and matured during the interval of two or three hours, between their first sighting the ship and the arrival on board of Captain Amasa Delano; that this happened about half-past seven o'clock in the morning, Captain Amasa Delano coming in his boat, and all gladly receiving him; that the deponent, as well as he could force himself, acting then the part of principal owner, and a free captain of the ship, told Captain Amasa Delano, when called upon, that he came from Buenos Ayres, bound to Lima, with three hundred negroes; that off Cape Horn, and in a subsequent fever, many negroes had died; that also, by similar casualties, all the sea officers and the greatest part of the crew had died.

* * * * *

1. Henchmen.

[*And so the deposition goes on, circumstantially recounting the fictitious story dictated to the deponent by Babo, and through the deponent imposed upon Captain Delano; and also recounting the friendly offers of Captain Delano, with other things, but all of which is here omitted. After the fictitious story, etc., the deposition proceeds:*]

—that the generous Captain Amasa Delano remained on board all the day, till he left the ship anchored at six o'clock in the evening, deponent speaking to him always of his pretended misfortunes, under the forementioned principles, without having had it in his power to tell a single word, or give him the least hint, that he might know the truth and state of things; because the negro Babo, performing the office of an officious servant with all the appearance of submission of the humble slave, did not leave the deponent one moment; that this was in order to observe the deponent's actions and words, for the negro Babo understands well the Spanish; and besides, there were thereabout some others who were constantly on the watch, and likewise understood the Spanish; * * * that upon one occasion, while deponent was standing on the deck conversing with Amasa Delano, by a secret sign the negro Babo drew him (the deponent) aside, the act appearing as if originating with the deponent; that then, he being drawn aside, the negro Babo proposed to him to gain from Amasa Delano full particulars about his ship, and crew, and arms; that the deponent asked "For what?" that the negro Babo answered he might conceive; that, grieved at the prospect of what might overtake the generous Captain Amasa Delano, the deponent at first refused to ask the desired questions, and used every argument to induce the negro Babo to give up this new design; that the negro Babo showed the point of his dagger; that, after the information had been obtained, the negro Babo again drew him aside, telling him that that very night he (the deponent) would be captain of two ships, instead of one, for that, great part of the American's ship's crew being to be absent fishing, the six Ashantees, without any one else, would easily take it; that at this time he said other things to the same purpose; that no entreaties availed; that, before Amasa Delano's coming on board, no hint had been given touching the capture of the American ship; that to prevent this project the deponent was powerless; * * * —that in some things his memory is confused, he cannot distinctly recall every event; * * * —that as soon as they had cast anchor at six of the clock in the evening, as has before been stated, the American Captain took leave to return to his vessel; that upon a sudden impulse, which the deponent believes to have come from God and his angels, he, after the farewell had been said, followed the generous Captain Amasa Delano as far as the gunwale, where he stayed, under pretense of taking leave, until Amasa Delano should have been seated in his boat; that on shoving off, the deponent sprang from the gunwale into the boat, and fell into it, he knows not how, God guarding him; that—

* * * * *

[*Here, in the original, follows the account of what further happened at the escape, and how the San Dominick was retaken, and of the passage to the coast; including in the recital many expressions of "eternal gratitude" to the "generous Captain Amasa Delano." The deposition then proceeds with reca-pitulatory remarks, and a partial renumeration of the negroes, making record of their individual part in the past events, with a view to furnishing, according to command of the court, the data whereon to found the criminal sentences to be pronounced. From this portion is the following:*]

—That he believes that all the negroes, though not in the first place know-ing to the design of revolt, when it was accomplished, approved it. * * * That the negro, José, eighteen years old, and in the personal service of Don Alexandro, was the one who communicated the information to the negro Babo, about the state of things in the cabin, before the revolt; that this is known, because, in the preceding midnight, he used to come from his berth, which was under his master's, in the cabin, to the deck where the ringleader and his associates were, and had secret conversations with the negro Babo, in which he was several times seen by the mate; that, one night, the mate drove him away twice; * * that this same negro José, was the one who, with-out being commanded to do so by the negro Babo, as Lecbe and Martinqui were, stabbed his master, Don Alexandro, after he had been dragged half-lifeless to the deck; * * that the mulatto steward, Francisco, was of the first band of revolters, that he was, in all things, the creature and tool of the negro Babo; that, to make his court, he, just before a repast in the cabin, proposed, to the negro Babo, poisoning a dish for the generous Captain Amasa Delano; this is known and believed, because the negroes have said it; but that the negro Babo, having another design, forbade Francisco; * * that the Ashantee Lecbe was one of the worst of them; for that, on the day the ship was retaken, he assisted in the defense of her, with a hatchet in each hand, one of which he wounded, in the breast, the chief mate of Amasa Delano, in the first act of boarding; this all knew; that, in sight of the depo-nent, Lecbe struck, with a hatchet, Don Francisco Masa when, by the negro Babo's orders, he was carrying him to throw him overboard, alive; beside participating in the murder, before mentioned, of Don Alexandro Aranda, and others of the cabin-passengers; that, owing to the fury with which the Ashantees fought in the engagement with the boats, but this Lecbe and Yau survived; that Yau was bad as Lecbe; that Yau was the man who, by Babo's command, willingly prepared the skeleton of Don Alexandro, in a way the negroes afterwards told the deponent, but which he, so long as reason is left him, can never divulge; that Yau and Lecbe were the two who, in a calm by night, riveted the skeleton to the bow; this also the negroes told him; that the negro Babo was he who traced the inscription below it; that the negro Babo was the plotter from first to last; he ordered every murder, and was the helm and keel of the revolt; that Atufal was his lieutenant in all; but Atufal, with his own hand, committed no murder; nor did the negro Babo; * * that Atufal was shot, being killed in the fight with the boats, ere boarding; * * that the negresses, of age, were knowing to the revolt and testified them-selves satisfied at the death of their master, Don Alexandro; that, had the negroes not restrained them, they would have tortured to death, instead of simply killing, the Spaniards slain by command of the negro Babo; that the negresses used their utmost influence to have the deponent made away with; that, in the various acts of murder, they sang songs and danced—not gaily, but solemnly; and before the engagement with the boats, as well as during the action, they sang melancholy songs to the negroes, and that this melancholy tone was more inflaming than a different one would have been, and was so intended; that all this is believed, because the negroes have said it.

—that of the thirty-six men of the crew exclusive of the passengers, (all of whom are now dead), which the deponent had knowledge of, six only remained alive, with four cabin-boys and ship-boys, not included with the crew; * * —that the negroes broke an arm of one of the cabin-boys and gave him strokes with hatchets.

[Then follow various random disclosures referring to various periods of time. The following are extracted:]

—That during the presence of Captain Amasa Delano on board, some attempts were made by the sailors, and one by Hermenegildo Gandix, to convey hints to him of the true state of affairs; but that these attempts were ineffectual, owing to fear of incurring death, and furthermore owing to the devices which offered contradictions to the true state of affairs; as well as owing to the generosity and piety of Amasa Delano incapable of sounding such wickedness; * * * that Luys Galgo, a sailor about sixty years of age, and formerly of the king's navy, was one of those who sought to convey tokens to Captain Amasa Delano; but his intent, though undiscovered, being suspected, he was, on a pretense, made to retire out of sight, and at last into the hold, and there was made away with. This the negroes have since said; * * * that one of the ship-boys feeling, from Captain Amasa Delano's presence, some hopes of release, and not having enough prudence, dropped some chance-word respecting his expectations, which being overheard and understood by a slave-boy with whom he was eating at the time, the latter struck him on the head with a knife, inflicting a bad wound, but of which the boy is now healing; that likewise, not long before the ship was brought to anchor, one of the seamen, steering at the time, endangered himself by letting the blacks remark some expression in his countenance, arising from a cause similar to the above; but this sailor, by his heedful after conduct, escaped; * * * that these statements are made to show the court that from the beginning to the end of the revolt, it was impossible for the deponent and his men to act otherwise than they did; * * * —that the third clerk, Hermenegildo Gandix, who before had been forced to live among the seamen, wearing a seaman's habit, and in all respects appearing to be one for the time; he, Gandix, was killed by a musket-ball fired through a mistake from the boats before boarding; having in his fright run up the mizzen-rigging, calling to the boats—"don't board," lest upon their boarding the negroes should kill him; that this inducing the Americans to believe he some way favored the cause of the negroes, they fired two balls at him, so that he fell wounded from the rigging, and was drowned in the sea; * * * —that the young Don Joaquin, Marques de Arambaolaza, like Hermenegildo Gandix, the third clerk, was degraded to the office and appearance of a common seaman; that upon one occasion when

Don Joaquin shrank, the negro Babo commanded the Ashantee Lecbe to take tar and heat it, and pour it upon Don Joaquin's hands; * * * —that Don Joaquin was killed owing to another mistake of the Americans, but one impossible to be avoided, as upon the approach of the boats, Don Joaquin, with a hatchet tied edge out and upright to his hand, was made by the negroes to appear on the bulwarks; whereupon, seen with arms in his hands and in a questionable attitude, he was shot for a renegade seaman; * * * —that on the person of Don Joaquin was found secreted a jewel, which, by papers that were discovered, proved to have been meant for the shrine of our Lady of Mercy in Lima; a votive offering, beforehand prepared and guarded, to attest his gratitude, when he should have landed in Peru, his last destination, for the safe conclusion of his entire voyage from Spain; * * * —that the jewel, with the other effects of the late Don Joaquin, is in the custody of the brethren of the Hospital de Sacerdotes, awaiting the disposition of the honorable court; * * * —that, owing to the condition of the deponent, as well as the haste in which the boats departed for the attack, the Americans were not forewarned that there were, among the apparent crew, a passenger and one of the clerks disguised by the negro Babo; * * * —that, beside the negroes killed in the action, some were killed after the capture and re-anchoring at night, when shackled to the ring-bolts on deck; that these deaths were committed by the sailors, ere they could be prevented. That so soon as informed of it, Captain Amasa Delano used all his authority, and, in particular with his own hand, struck down Martinez Gola, who, having found a razor in the pocket of an old jacket of his, which one of the shackled negroes had on, was aiming it at the negro's throat; that the noble Captain Amasa Delano also wrenched from the hand of Bartholomew Barlo, a dagger secreted at the time of the massacre of the whites, with which he was in the act of stabbing a shackled negro, who, the same day, with another negro, had thrown him down and jumped upon him; * * * —that, for all the events, befalling through so long a time, during which the ship was in the hands of the negro Babo, he cannot here give account; but that, what he had said is the most substantial of what occurs to him at present, and is the truth under the oath which he has taken; which declaration he affirmed and ratified, after hearing it read to him.

He said that he is twenty-nine years of age, and broken in body and mind; that when finally dismissed by the court, he shall not return home to Chili, but betake himself to the monastery on Mount Agonia without; and signed with his honor, and crossed himself, and, for the time, departed as he came, in his litter, with the monk Infelez, to the Hospital de Sacerdotes.

BENITO CERENO.

DOCTOR ROZAS.

If the Deposition have served as the key to fit into the lock of the complications which precede it, then, as a vault whose door has been flung back, the San Dominick's hull lies open to-day.

Hitherto the nature of this narrative, besides rendering the intricacies in the beginning unavoidable, has more or less required that many things, instead of being set down in the order of occurrence, should be retrospectively, or irregularly given; this last is the case with the following passages, which will conclude the account:

During the long, mild voyage to Lima, there was, as before hinted, a period during which the sufferer a little recovered his health, or, at least in some degree, his tranquillity. Ere the decided relapse which came, the two captains had many cordial conversations—their fraternal unreserve in singular contrast with former withdrawments.

Again and again, it was repeated, how hard it had been to enact the part forced on the Spaniard by Babo.

"Ah, my dear friend," Don Benito once said, "at those very times when you thought me so morose and ungrateful, nay, when, as you now admit, you half thought me plotting your murder, at those very times my heart was frozen; I could not look at you, thinking of what, both on board this ship and your own, hung, from other hands, over my kind benefactor. And as God lives, Don Amasa, I know not whether desire for my own safety alone could have nerved me to that leap into your boat, had it not been for the thought that, did you, unenlightened, return to your ship, you, my best friend, with all who might be with you, stolen upon, that night, in your hammocks, would never in this world have wakened again. Do but think how you walked this deck, how you sat in this cabin, every inch of ground mined into honeycombs under you. Had I dropped the least hint, made the least advance towards an understanding between us, death, explosive death—yours as mine—would have ended the scene."

"True, true," cried Captain Delano, starting, "you saved my life, Don Benito, more than I yours; saved it, too, against my knowledge and will."

"Nay, my friend," rejoined the Spaniard, courteous even to the point of religion, "God charmed your life, but you saved mine. To think of some things you did—those smilings and chattings, rash pointings and gesturings. For less than these, they slew my mate, Raneds; but you had the Prince of Heaven's safe conduct through all ambuscades."

"Yes, all is owing to Providence, I know; but the temper of my mind that morning was more than commonly pleasant, while the sight of so much suffering, more apparent than real, added to my good nature, compassion, and charity, happily interweaving the three. Had it been otherwise, doubtless, as you hint, some of my interferences might have ended unhappily enough. Besides, those feelings I spoke of enabled me to get the better of momentary distrust, at times when acuteness might have cost me my life, without saving another's. Only at the end did my suspicions get the better of me, and you know how wide of the mark they then proved."

"Wide, indeed," said Don Benito, sadly; "you were with me all day; stood with me, sat with me, talked with me, looked at me, ate with me, drank with me; and yet, your last act was to clutch for a monster, not only an innocent man, but the most pitiable of all men. To such degree may malign machinations and deceptions impose. So far may even the best man err, in judging the conduct of one with the recesses of whose condition he is not acquainted. But you were forced to it; and you were in time undeceived. Would that, in both respects, it was so ever, and with all men."

"You generalize, Don Benito; and mournfully enough. But the past is passed; why moralize upon it? Forget it. See, yon bright sun has forgotten it all, and the blue sea, and the blue sky; these have turned over new leaves."

"Because they have no memory," he dejectedly replied; "because they are not human."

"But these mild trades[2] that now fan your cheek, do they not come with a human-like healing to you? Warm friends, steadfast friends are the trades."

"With their steadfastness they but waft me to my tomb, señor," was the foreboding response.

"You are saved," cried Captain Delano, more and more astonished and pained; "you are saved; what has cast such a shadow upon you?"

"The negro."

There was silence, while the moody man sat, slowly and unconsciously gathering his mantle about him, as if it were a pall.

There was no more conversation that day.

But if the Spaniard's melancholy sometimes ended in muteness upon topics like the above, there were others upon which he never spoke at all; on which, indeed, all his old reserves were piled. Pass over the worst, and, only to elucidate, let an item or two of these be cited. The dress so precise and costly, worn by him on the day whose events have been narrated, had not willingly been put on. And that silver-mounted sword, apparent symbol of despotic command, was not, indeed, a sword, but the ghost of one. The scabbard, artificially stiffened, was empty.

As for the black—whose brain, not body, had schemed and led the revolt, with the plot—his slight frame, inadequate to that which it held, had at once yielded to the superior muscular strength of his captor, in the boat. Seeing all was over, he uttered no sound, and could not be forced to. His aspect seemed to say, since I cannot do deeds, I will not speak words. Put in irons in the hold, with the rest, he was carried to Lima. During the passage Don Benito did not visit him. Nor then, nor at any time after, would he look at him. Before the tribunal he refused. When pressed by the judges he fainted. On the testimony of the sailors alone rested the legal identity of Babo.

Some months after, dragged to the gibbet at the tail of a mule, the black met his voiceless end. The body was burned to ashes; but for many days, the head, that hive of subtlety, fixed on a pole in the Plaza, met, unabashed, the gaze of the whites; and across the Plaza looked towards St. Bartholomew's church, in whose vaults slept then, as now, the recovered bones of Aranda; and across the Rimac bridge looked towards the monastery, on Mount Agonia without; where, three months after being dismissed by the court, Benito Cereno, borne on the bier, did, indeed, follow his leader.

1855, 1856

---

2. Trade winds; here, dependable winds blowing from southeast to northwest.

From Battle-Pieces[1]

The Portent

(1859)[2]

Hanging from the beam,
    Slowly swaying (such the law),
Gaunt the shadow on your green,
    Shenandoah!
The cut is on the crown[3]   5
(Lo, John Brown),
And the stabs shall heal no more.

Hidden in the cap[4]
    Is the anguish none can draw;
So your future veils its face,   10
    Shenandoah!
But the streaming beard is shown
(Weird John Brown),
The meteor of the war.

1866

1. *Battle-Pieces and Aspects of the War* was published by the Harpers in 1866, the source of the present texts.
2. On October 16, 1859, John Brown (1800–1859) led twenty-one men, including five African Americans, in an attack on an unguarded federal arsenal at Harpers Ferry in western Virginia in an effort to secure arms for the slave revolt he hoped to inspire. Within two days his group was defeated by a force of American troops. Convicted of treason against the state of Virginia, he was hanged in the Shenandoah Valley, at Charlestown, Virginia, on December 2, 1859. Melville takes Brown's raid as a portent of the Civil War.
3. Brown received a head wound when captured.
4. Hood placed over the head at the time of execution.

FRANCES ELLEN WATKINS HARPER
1825–1911

---

rances Ellen Watkins Harper was the most popular African American poet of the nineteenth century. The author of nine volumes of poetry, four novels, several short stories, and numerous essays and letters, she was also a strikingly effective lecturer, known for her ability to extemporize on such topics as antislavery, temperance, and black uplift. Born in Baltimore, Maryland, then a slave state, to free black parents who died when she was young, Harper was raised by her uncle William J. Watkins, a prominent educator, minister, and abolitionist. She taught school in Ohio and Pennsylvania, writing poetry in her spare time, publishing her first volume of poems, *Forest Leaves*, in 1845. In the early 1850s she left teaching to lecture for the Maine Anti-Slavery Society and other antislavery organizations. She also worked with the African American abolitionist William Still (1821–1902) to help fugitive slaves escape to Canada through the linked networks of sympathizers, known as the Underground Railroad, who offered refuge to fugitives as they traveled north. During this time she began publishing poems in antislavery periodicals and newspapers, bringing out *Poems on Miscellaneous Subjects* in 1854. Prefaced by the abolitionist William Lloyd Garrison, the collection included several poetic responses to Harriet Beecher Stowe's *Uncle Tom's Cabin* (a novel Harper greatly admired), along with poems on temperance, biblical stories, and the black experience in slavery. During its first four years in print, *Poems* sold approximately twelve thousand copies; she revised and enlarged it in 1857, and it was reprinted twenty times thereafter during her lifetime. In her best poems of the antebellum period, such as "Bury Me in a Free Land" (1858), Harper wrote about the slaves' suffering with lyrical intensity; but she also conveyed the sense of blacks' powerful resistance to slavery, along with her hopes for an egalitarian, multiracial America.

With the exception of "Learning to Read," the selections printed here draw from Harper's work during the antebellum period, when she was known as Frances Ellen Watkins, but she remained an actively publishing author and lecturer until around 1900. Though primarily motivated by her literary and political passions, Harper also needed to keep up with her writing and lecturing out of financial necessity. In 1860 she married Fenton Harper, a widower with three children, and when he died in 1864, virtually bankrupt, she took on the responsibility of supporting Fenton Harper's children, along with their own child, Mary. Harper worked as a paid lecturer for several reform organizations, even as she continued to publish her poetry, including *Moses: A Story of the Nile* (1869), a long poem in blank verse; *Poems* (1871), which sold approximately fifty thousand copies over several printings; and *Sketches of Southern Life* (1872), poems that have at their center the feisty former slave Aunt Chloe. That volume, more than any of her other collections published after the Civil War, was informed by Harper's optimism that blacks could rise in the culture and become fully integrated into national life. Between 1869 and 1882, Harper serialized three novels in the *Christian Recorder*, the journal of the African Methodist Episcopal Church—*Minnie's Sacrifice* (1869), *Sowing and Reaping* (1876–77), and *Trial and Triumph* (1888–89). Her best-known work, in addition to her 1854 and 1871 poetry collections, is the 1892 novel *Iola Leroy; or, Shadows Uplifted*, a historical novel tracing the efforts of the light-skinned mulatta Iola Leroy as she attempts to reunite members of her formerly enslaved family after the Civil War. Crucially, at a key point near the end of the novel, Iola rejects the marriage proposal of a white doctor, who wants her to pass as white, choosing to remain close to her family and devote herself to the uplift of her race. After the publication of *Iola Leroy*, Harper published five additional volumes of poetry; she also remained politically active, continuing her work for the Women's Christian Temperance Union and helping to found the National Association of Colored Women in 1896. She died of heart disease in Philadelphia on February 22, 1911.

Eliza Harris[1]

Like a fawn from the arrow, startled and wild,
A woman swept by us, bearing a child;
In her eye was the night of a settled despair,
And her brow was o'ershaded with anguish and care.

---

1. The text is from *Poems on Miscellaneous Subjects* (Boston, 1854). Earlier versions appeared in December 1853 issues of *Frederick Douglass' Paper* and the *Liberator*. In chap. 7 of Harriet Beecher Stowe's *Uncle Tom's Cabin* (1852), the slave Eliza Harris escapes to the North with her son by crossing the icy Ohio River (see p. 848).

She was nearing the river—in reaching the brink,   5
She heeded no danger, she paused not to think!
For she is a mother—her child is a slave—
And she'll give him his freedom, or find him a grave!

'Twas a vision to haunt us, that innocent face—
So pale in its aspect, so fair in its grace;   10
As the tramp of the horse and the bay of the hound,
With the fetters that gall, were trailing the ground!

She was nerved by despair, and strengthen'd by woe,
As she leap'd o'er the chasms that yawn'd from below;
Death howl'd in the tempest, and rav'd in the blast,   15
But she heard not the sound till the danger was past.

Oh! how shall I speak of my proud country's shame?
Of the stains on her glory, how give them their name?
How say that her banner in mockery waves—
Her "star-spangled banner"—o'er millions of slaves?   20

How say that the lawless may torture and chase
A woman whose crime is the hue of her face?
How the depths of the forest may echo around
With the shrieks of despair, and the bay of the hound?

With her step on the ice, and her arm on her child,   25
The danger was fearful, the pathway was wild;
But, aided by Heaven, she gained a free shore,
Where the friends of humanity open'd their door.

So fragile and lovely, so fearfully pale,
Like a lily that bends to the breath of the gale,   30
Save the heave of her breast, and the sway of her hair,
You'd have thought her a statue of fear and despair.

In agony close to her bosom she press'd
The life of her heart, the child of her breast:—
Oh! love from its tenderness gathering might,   35
Had strengthen'd her soul for the dangers of flight.

But she's free!—yes, free from the land where the slave
From the hand of oppression must rest in the grave;
Where bondage and torture, where scourges and chains
Have plac'd on our banner indelible stains.   40

The bloodhounds have miss'd the scent of her way;
The hunter is rifled and foil'd of his prey;
Fierce jargon and cursing, with clanking of chains,
Make sounds of strange discord on Liberty's plains.

With the rapture of love and fullness of bliss,   45
She plac'd on his brow a mother's fond kiss:—
Oh! poverty, danger and death she can brave,
For the child of her love is no longer a slave!

                                        1853, 1854

Bury Me in a Free Land[1]

You may make my grave wherever you will,
    In a lowly vale or a lofty hill;
You may make it among earth's humblest graves,
    But not in a land where men are slaves.

I could not sleep if around my grave   5
    I heard the steps of a trembling slave;
His shadow above my silent tomb
    Would make it a place of fearful gloom.

I could not rest if I heard the tread
    Of a coffle-gang to the shambles[2] led,   10
And the mother's shriek of wild despair
    Rise like a curse on the trembling air.

I could not rest if I heard the lash
    Drinking her blood at each fearful gash,
And I saw her babes torn from her breast   15
    Like trembling doves from their parent nest.

I'd shudder and start, if I heard the bay
    Of the bloodhounds seizing their human prey;
If I heard the captive plead in vain
    As they tightened afresh his galling[3] chain.   20

If I saw young girls, from their mothers' arms
    Bartered and sold for their youthful charms
My eye would flash with a mournful flame,
    My death paled cheek grow red with shame.

I would sleep, dear friends, where bloated might   25
    Can rob no man of his dearest right;
My rest shall be calm in any grave
    Where none calls his brother a slave.

I ask no monument proud and high
    To arrest the gaze of passers by;   30
All that my spirit yearning craves,
    Is—bury me not in the land of slaves.

                                        1858

---

1. The text is from the November 20, 1858, issue
of the *Anti-Slavery Bugle*, published in Salem,
Ohio.

2. Slaughterhouse. "Coffle-gang": chained slaves.
3. Chafing.

Learning to Read[1]

Very soon the Yankee teachers
 Came down and set up school;
But, oh! how the Rebs[2] did hate it,—
 It was agin' their rule.

Our masters always tried to hide   5
 Book learning from our eyes;
Knowledge did'nt agree with slavery—
 'Twould make us all too wise.

But some of us would try to steal
 A little from the book,   10
And put the words together,
 And learn by hook or crook.

I remember Uncle Caldwell,
Who took pot liquor[3] fat
And greased the pages of his book,   15
 And hid it in his hat.

And had his master ever seen
 The leaves upon his head,
He'd have thought them greasy papers,
 But nothing to be read.   20

And there was Mr. Turner's Ben,
 Who heard the children spell,
And picked the words right up by heart,
 And learned to read 'em well.

Well, the Northern folks kept sending 25
 The Yankee teachers down;
And they stood right up and helped us,
 Though Rebs did sneer and frown.

And, I longed to read my Bible,
 For precious words it said;   30
But when I begun to learn it,
 Folks just shook their heads,

And said there is no use trying,
 Oh! Chloe, you're too late;
But as I was rising sixty,   35
 I had no time to wait.

1. The text is from *Sketches from Southern Life* (1872). This is one of six poems in the volume in the voice of the former slave Aunt Chloe.
2. Rebels; Southerners are here linked to the Rebel or Confederate forces that fought during the Civil War.
3. The liquid left after cooking meat and vegetables together.

So I got a pair of glasses,
  And straight to work I went,
And never stopped till I could read
  The hymns and Testament.   40

Then I got a little cabin
  A place to call my own—
And I felt as independent
  As the queen upon her throne.

                                        1872

EMILY DICKINSON
1830–1886

E mily Dickinson is recognized as one of the greatest American poets, a poet who
continues to exert an enormous influence on the way writers think about the
possibilities of poetic craft and vocation. Little known in her own lifetime, she was
first publicized in almost mythic terms as a reclusive, eccentric, death-obsessed
spinster who wrote in fits and starts as the spirit moved her—the image of the
woman poet at her oddest. As with all myths, this one has some truth to it, but the
reality is more interesting and complicated. Though she lived in her parents' homes
for all but a year of her life, she was acutely aware of current events and drew on
them for some of her poetry. Her dazzlingly complex poems—compressed statements abounding in startling imagery and marked by an extraordinary vocabulary—
explore a wide range of subjects: psychic pain and joy, the relationship of self to
nature, the intensely spiritual, and the intensely ordinary. Her poems about death
confront its grim reality with honesty, humor, curiosity, and above all a refusal to
be comforted. In her poems about religion, she expressed piety and hostility, and
she was fully capable of moving within the same poem from religious consolation to
a rejection of doctrinal piety and a querying of God's plans for the universe. Her
many love poems seem to have emerged in part from close relationships with at
least one woman and several men. It is sometimes possible to extract autobiography
from her poems, but she was not a confessional poet; rather, she used personae—
first-person speakers—to dramatize the various situations, moods, and perspectives
she explored in her lyrics. Though each of her poems is individually short, when
collected in one volume her nearly eighteen hundred surviving poems (she probably
wrote hundreds more that were lost) have the feel of an epic produced by a person
who devoted much of her life to her art.

Emily Elizabeth Dickinson was born on December 10, 1830, in Amherst, Massachusetts, the second child of Emily Norcross Dickinson and Edward Dickinson. Economically, politically, and intellectually, the Dickinsons were among Amherst's most
prominent families. Edward Dickinson, a lawyer, served as a state representative and
a state senator. He helped found Amherst College as a Calvinist alternative to the more
liberal Harvard and Yale, and was its treasurer for thirty-six years. During his term
in the U.S. House of Representatives (1853–54), Emily visited him in Washington,
D.C., and stayed briefly in Philadelphia on her way home, but travel of any kind was

unusual for her. She lived most of her life in the spacious Dickinson family house in Amherst called the Homestead. Among her closest friends and lifelong allies were her brother, Austin, a year and a half older than she, and her younger sister, Lavinia. In 1856, when her brother married Emily's close friend Susan Gilbert, the couple moved into what was called the Evergreens, a house next door to the Homestead, built for the newlyweds by Edward Dickinson. Neither Emily nor Lavinia married. The two women stayed with their parents, as was typical of unmarried middle- and upper-class women of the time. New England in this period had many more women than men in these groups, owing to the exodus of the male population during the California gold rush years (1849 and after) and the carnage of the Civil War. For Dickinson, home was a place of "Infinite power."

Dickinson attended Amherst Academy from 1840 through 1846, and then boarded at the Mount Holyoke Female Seminary—located in South Hadley, some ten miles from Amherst—for less than a year, never completing the three-year course of study. The school, presided over by the devoutly Calvinist Mary Lyon, was especially interested in the students' religious development, and hoped that those needing to support themselves or their families would become missionaries. Students were regularly queried as to whether they "professed faith," had "hope," or were resigned to "no hope"; Dickinson remained adamantly among the small group of "no hopes." Arguably, her assertion of no hope was a matter of defiance, a refusal to capitulate to the demands of orthodoxy. A year after leaving Mount Holyoke, Dickinson, in a letter to a friend, described her failure to convert with darkly comic glee: "I am one of the lingering *bad* ones," she said. But she went on to assert that it was her very "failure" to conform to the conventional expectations of her evangelical culture that helped liberate her to think on her own—to "pause," as she put it, "and ponder, and ponder."

Once back at home, Dickinson embarked on a lifelong course of reading. Her deepest literary debts were to the Bible and classic English authors, such as Shakespeare and Milton. Through the national magazines the family subscribed to and books ordered from Boston, she encountered the full range of the English and American literature of her time, including among Americans Longfellow, Holmes, Lowell, Hawthorne, and Emerson. She read the novels of Charles Dickens as they appeared and knew the poems of Robert Browning and the British poet laureate Tennyson. But the English contemporaries who mattered most to her were the Brontë sisters, George Eliot, and above all, as an example of a successful contemporary woman poet, Elizabeth Barrett Browning.

No one has persuasively traced the precise stages of Dickinson's artistic growth from this supposedly "somber Girl" to the young woman who, within a few years of her return from Mount Holyoke, began writing a new kind of poetry, with its distinctive voice, style, and transformation of traditional form. She found a paradoxical poetic freedom within the confines of the meter of the "fourteener"—seven-beat lines usually broken into stanzas alternating four and three beats—familiar to her from earliest childhood. This is the form of nursery rhymes, ballads, church hymns, and some classic English poetry—strongly rhythmical, easy to memorize and recite. But Dickinson veered sharply from this form's expectations. If Walt Whitman at this time was heeding Emerson's call for a "metre-making argument" by turning to an open form—as though rules did not exist—Dickinson made use of this and other familiar forms only to break their rules. She used dashes and syntactical fragments to convey her pursuit of a truth that could best be communicated indirectly; these fragments dispensed with prosy verbiage and went directly to the core. Her use of enjambment (the syntactical technique of running past the conventional stopping place of a line or a stanza break) forced her reader to learn where to pause to collect the sense before reading on, often creating dizzying ambiguities. She multiplied aural possibilities by making use of what later critics termed "off" or "slant" rhymes that, as with her metrical and syntactical experimentations, contributed to the expressive power of her poetry. Poetic forms thought to be simple, predictable, and safe were altered irrevocably by Dickinson's language experiments.

Dickinson wrote approximately half of her extant poems during the Civil War. Unsurprisingly, there has been increasing critical interest in Dickinson as a Civil War poet whose work can be read in relation to the Civil War poetry of Melville and Whitman. This edition of *The Norton Anthology* adds three poems (518, 704, 1212) that appear to have been inspired by the specifics of the Civil War (battles, courage, the enormity of the carnage). There are risks to interpreting any Dickinson poem as only referring to particular events in her life or the world beyond her home, but there are also risks in overemphasizing Dickinson's isolation from current events and popular culture. In her poetry, which at times can appear to be hauntingly private, Dickinson regularly responded to her nineteenth-century world, which she engaged through her reading, conversations, and friendships, epistolary and otherwise.

Writing about religion, science, music, nature, books, and contemporary events both national and local, Dickinson often presented her poetic ideas as terse, striking definitions or propositions, or dramatic narrative scenes, in a highly abstracted moment or setting, often at the boundaries between life and death. The result was a poetry that focused on the speaker's response to a situation rather than the details of the situation itself. Her "nature" poems offer precise observations that are often as much about psychological and spiritual matters as about the specifics of nature. The sight of a familiar bird—the robin—in the poem beginning "A Bird, came down the Walk" leads to a statement about nature's strangeness rather than the expected statement about friendly animals. Whitman generally seems intoxicated by his ability to appropriate nature for his own purposes; Dickinson's nature is much more resistant to human schemes, and the poet's experiences of nature range from a sense of its hostility to an ability to become an "Inebriate of Air" and "Debauchee of Dew." Openly expressive of sexual and romantic longings, her personae reject conventional gender roles. In one of her most famous poems, for instance, she imagines herself as a "Loaded Gun" with "the power to kill."

Dickinson's private letters, in particular three drafts of letters to an unidentified "Master," and dozens of love poems have convinced biographers that she fell in love a number of times; candidates include Benjamin Newton, a law clerk in her father's office; one or more married men; and Susan Gilbert Dickinson, the friend who became her sister-in-law. The exact nature of any of these relationships is hard to determine, in part because Dickinson's letters and poems could just as easily be taken as poetic meditations on desire as writings directed to specific people. On the evidence of the approximately five hundred letters that Dickinson wrote to Susan, many of which contained drafts or copies of her latest poems, that relationship melded love, friendship, intellectual exchange, and art. (See their letters on a Dickinson poem on pp. 1271–73.) One of the men she was involved with was Samuel Bowles, editor of the *Springfield Republican*, whom Dickinson described (in a letter to Bowles himself) as having "the most triumphant face out of paradise"; another was the Reverend Charles Wadsworth, whom she met in Philadelphia in 1855 and who visited her in Amherst in 1860. Evidence suggests that she was upset by his decision to move to San Francisco in 1862, but none of her letters to Wadsworth survive.

Knowing her powers as a poet, Dickinson wanted to be published, but only around a dozen poems appeared during her lifetime. She sent many poems to Bowles, perhaps hoping he would publish them in the *Republican*. Although he did publish a few, he also edited them into more conventional shape. She also sent poems to editor Josiah Holland at *Scribner's*, who chose not to publish her. She sent four poems to Thomas Wentworth Higginson, a contributing editor at the *Atlantic Monthly*, after he printed "Letter to a Young Contributor" in the April 1862 issue. Her cover letter of April 15, 1862, asked him, "Are you too deeply occupied to say if my Verse is alive?"

(See two Dickinson letters to Higginson on pp. 1273–75.) Higginson, like other editors, saw her formal innovations as imperfections. But he remained intrigued by Dickinson and in 1869 invited her to visit him in Boston. When she refused, he visited her in 1870. He would eventually become one of the editors of her posthumously published poetry.

But if Dickinson sought publication, she also regarded it as "the Auction / Of the Mind of Man," as she put it in poem 788; at the very least, she was unwilling to submit to the changes, which she called "surgery," imposed on her poems by editors. Some critics have argued that Dickinson's letters constituted a form of publication, for Dickinson included poems in many of her letters. Even more intriguing, beginning around 1858 Dickinson began to record her poems on white, unlined paper, in some cases marking moments of textual revision, and then folded and stacked the sheets and sewed groups of them together in what are called fascicles. She created thirty such fascicles, ranging in length from sixteen to twenty-four pages; and there is evidence that she worked at the groupings, thinking about chronology, subject matter, and specific thematic orderings within each. These fascicles were left for others to discover after her death, neatly stacked in a drawer. It can be speculated that Dickinson, realizing that her unconventional poetry would not be published in her own lifetime as written, became a sort of self-publisher. Critics remain uncertain, however, about just how self-conscious her arrangements were and argue over what is lost and gained by considering individual poems in the context of their fascicle placement. There is also debate about whether the posthumous publication of Dickinson's manuscript poetry violates the visual look of the poems—their inconsistent dashes and even some of the designs that Dickinson added to particular poems. The selections printed here include a photographic reproduction of poem 269, which can be compared to the now-standard printed version, also included here.

Dickinson's final decades were marked by health problems and a succession of losses. Beginning in the early 1860s she suffered from eye pain. She consulted with an ophthalmologist in Boston in 1864 and remained concerned about losing her vision. In 1874 her father died in a Boston hotel room after taking an injection of morphine for his pain, and one year later her mother had a stroke and would remain bedridden until her death in 1882. Her beloved eight-year-old nephew, Gilbert, died of typhoid fever in 1883, next door at the Evergreens; and in 1885, her close friend from childhood, Helen Hunt Jackson, who had asked to be Dickinson's literary executor, died suddenly in San Francisco. Dickinson's seclusion late in life may have been a response to her grief at these losses or a concern for her own health, but ultimately a focus on the supposed eccentricity of her desire for privacy draws attention away from the huge number of poems she wrote—she may well have secluded herself so that she could follow her vocation. She died on May 15, 1886, perhaps from a kidney disorder called "Bright's Disease," the official diagnosis, but just as likely from hypertension.

In 1881 the astronomer David Todd, with his young wife, Mabel Loomis Todd, arrived in Amherst to direct the Amherst College Observatory. The next year, Austin Dickinson and Mabel Todd began an affair that lasted until Austin's death in 1895. Despite this turn of events, Mabel Todd and Emily Dickinson established a friendship without actually meeting (Todd saw Dickinson once, in her coffin), and Todd decided that the poet was "in many respects a genius." Soon after Dickinson's death, Mabel Todd (at Emily's sister Lavinia's invitation) painstakingly transcribed many of her poems. The subsequent preservation and publication of her poetry and letters was initiated and carried forth by Todd. She persuaded Higginson to help her see a posthumous collection of poems into print in 1890 and a second volume of poems in 1891; she went on to publish a collection of Dickinson's letters in 1894 and a third volume of poems in 1896. Though Dickinson's poetry perplexed some critics, it impressed many others; the three volumes were popular, going through more than ten printings and selling over ten thousand copies. To make Dickinson's violation of the laws of meter more palatable, Todd and Higginson edited some of the poems heavily. This edition of *The Norton Anthology* reprints one of Dickinson's poems, "There's a certain Slant of light" (320), as it was edited by Todd and Higginson so that readers can see Dickinson's poetry as it would have been printed in the late nineteenth century. During the 1890s, Susan Dickinson and her daughter, Martha Dickinson Bianchi, also published a few of Dickinson's poems in journals such as the *Century*.

By 1900 or so, Dickinson's work had fallen out of favor, and had Martha Dickinson Bianchi not resumed publication of her aunt's poetry in 1914 (she published eight volumes of Dickinson's work between 1914 and 1937), Dickinson's writings might never have achieved the audience they have today. Taken together, the editorial labors of Todd, Higginson, Susan Dickinson, and Bianchi set in motion the critical and textual work that would help establish Dickinson as one of the great American poets. They also made her poetry available to the American modernists, poets such as Hart Crane and Marianne Moore; Dickinson and Whitman are the nineteenth-century poets who exerted the greatest influence on American poetry to come.

The texts of the poems, and the numbering, are from R. W. Franklin's one-volume edition, *The Poems of Emily Dickinson: Reading Edition* (1999), which draws on his three-volume variorum, *The Poems of Emily Dickinson* (1998). The dating of Dickinson's poetry remains uncertain. The date following each poem corresponds to Franklin's estimate of Dickinson's first finished draft; if the poem was published in Dickinson's lifetime, that date is supplied as well.

39

I never lost as much but twice -
And that was in the sod.
Twice have I stood a beggar
Before the door of God!

Angels - twice descending   5
Reimbursed my store -
Burglar! Banker - Father!
I am poor once more!

1858

112[1]

Success is counted sweetest
By those who ne'er succeed.
To comprehend a nectar
Requires sorest need.

Not one of all the purple Host   5
Who took the Flag[2] today

---

1. Dickinson published a version of this poem in the *Brooklyn Daily Union*, April 27, 1864, and it was republished in *A Masque of Poets* (1878), edited by her friend Helen Hunt Jackson. When it was printed in *Masque*, most reviewers thought it was by Emerson.
2. I.e., triumphed.

Can tell the definition
So clear of Victory

As he defeated - dying -
On whose forbidden ear   10
The distant strains of triumph
Burst agonized and clear!

1859, 1864

122[1]

These are the days when Birds come back -
A very few - a Bird or two -
To take a backward look.

These are the days when skies resume
The old - old sophistries[2] of June -   5
A blue and gold mistake.

Oh fraud that cannot cheat the Bee.
Almost thy plausibility
Induces my belief,

Till ranks of seeds their witness bear -   10
And softly thro' the altered air
Hurries a timid leaf.

Oh sacrament of summer days,
Oh Last Communion[3] in the Haze -
Permit a child to join -   15

Thy sacred emblems to partake -
Thy consecrated bread to take
And thine immortal wine!

1859, 1864

124[1]

Safe in their Alabaster[2] Chambers -
Untouched by Morning -
And untouched by noon -

1. Dickinson published a version of this poem in
the *Drum Beat*, March 11, 1864.
2. Deceptively subtle reasonings.
3. The end of summer is compared to the death
of Christ commemorated by the Christian sacrament of Communion.
1. Dickinson published a version of this poem in
the *Springfield Daily Republican*, March 1, 1862.
2. Translucent, white chalky material.

Sleep the meek members of the Resurrection,
Rafter of Satin and Roof of Stone -   5

Grand go the Years,
In the Crescent above them -
Worlds scoop their Arcs -
And Firmaments - row -
Diadems - drop -   10
And Doges[3] - surrender -
Soundless as Dots,
On a Disc of Snow.[4]

1859, 1862

● 202

Capilize Fa+L
Gentlemen

"Faith" is a fine invention
For Gentlemen who *see*!
But Microscopes are prudent
In an Emergency!

1861

207

I taste a liquor never brewed -
From Tankards scooped in Pearl -
Not all the Frankfort Berries
Yield such an Alcohol!

Inebriate of air - am I -   5
And Debauchee of Dew -
Reeling - thro' endless summer days -
From inns of molten Blue -

When "Landlords" turn the drunken Bee
Out of the Foxglove's door -   10
When Butterflies - renounce their "drams" -
I shall but drink the more!

Till Seraphs[1] swing their snowy Hats -
And Saints - to windows run -
To see the little Tippler   15
Leaning against the - Sun!

1861

3. Chief magistrates in the republics of Venice and Genoa from the 11th through the 16th centuries.

4. For Dickinson's other versions of this poem, see pp. 1271–73.
1. Angels.

• 236

Some keep the Sabbath going to Church -
I keep it, staying at Home -
With a Bobolink for a Chorister -
And an Orchard, for a Dome -

Some keep the Sabbath in Surplice[1]   5
I, just wear my Wings -
And instead of tolling the Bell, for Church,
Our little Sexton[2] - sings.

God preaches, a noted Clergyman -
And the sermon is never long,   10
So instead of getting to Heaven, at last -
I'm going, all along.

1861

259

A Clock stopped -
Not the Mantel's -
Geneva's[1] farthest skill
Cant put the puppet bowing -
That just now dangled still -   5

An awe came on the Trinket!
The Figures hunched - with pain -
Then quivered out of Decimals -
Into Degreeless noon -

It will not stir for Doctor's -   10
This Pendulum of snow -
The Shopman importunes it -
While cool - concernless No -

Nods from the Gilded pointers -
Nods from the Seconds slim -   15
Decades of Arrogance between
The Dial life -
And Him -

1861

---

1. Open-sleeved ceremonial robe worn by
clergymen.

2. Church custodian.
1. A city in Switzerland famous for its clocks.

260

I'm Nobody! Who are you?
Are you - Nobody - too?
Then there's a pair of us!
Dont tell! they'd advertise - you know!

How dreary - to be - Somebody!   5
How public - like a Frog -
To tell one's name - the livelong June -
To an admiring Bog!

                                    1861

269[1]

Wild nights - Wild nights!
Were I with thee
Wild nights should be
Our luxury!

Futile - the winds -   5
To a Heart in port -
Done with the Compass -
Done with the Chart!

Rowing in Eden -
Ah - the Sea!   10
Might I but moor - tonight -
In thee!

                                    1861

320

There's a certain Slant of light,
Winter Afternoons -
That oppresses, like the Heft
Of Cathedral Tunes -

Heavenly Hurt, it gives us -   5
We can find no scar,
But internal difference -
Where the Meanings, are -

None may teach it - Any -
'Tis the Seal Despair -   10

---

1. See the opposite page for a reproduction of the manuscript of this poem.

Poem 269 of Fascicle 11, from vol. 1 of *The Manuscript Books of Emily Dickinson* (1981), ed. R. W. Franklin, reproduced with the permission of Harvard University Press. Dickinson's handwriting, which changed over the years, can be dated by comparison with her letters.

An imperial affliction
Sent us of the Air -

When it comes, the Landscape listens -
Shadows - hold their breath -
When it goes, 'tis like the Distance   15
On the look of Death -

1862

339

I like a look of Agony,
Because I know it's true -
Men do not sham Convulsion,
Nor simulate, a Throe -

The eyes glaze once - and that is Death -   5
Impossible to feign
The Beads opon the Forehead
By homely Anguish strung.

1862

340

I felt a Funeral, in my Brain,
And Mourners to and fro
Kept treading - treading - till it seemed
That Sense was breaking through -

And when they all were seated,   5
A Service, like a Drum -
Kept beating - beating - till I thought
My mind was going numb -

And then I heard them lift a Box
And creak across my Soul   10
With those same Boots of Lead, again,
Then Space - began to toll,

As all the Heavens were a Bell,
And Being, but an Ear,
And I, and Silence, some strange Race   15
Wrecked, solitary, here -

And then a Plank in Reason, broke,
And I dropped down, and down -
And hit a World, at every plunge,
And Finished knowing - then -   20

1862

353

I'm ceded - I've stopped being Their's -
The name They dropped opon[1] my face
With water, in the country church
Is finished using, now,
And They can put it with my Dolls,   5
My childhood, and the string of spools,
I've finished threading - too -

Baptized, before, without the choice,
But this time, consciously, Of Grace -
Unto supremest name -   10
Called to my Full - The Crescent dropped -
Existence's whole Arc, filled up,
With one - small Diadem -

My second Rank - too small the first -
Crowned - Crowing - on my Father's breast -   15
A half unconscious Queen -
But this time - Adequate - Erect,
With Will to choose,
Or to reject,
And I choose, just a Crown -   20

1862

355

It was not Death, for I stood up,
And all the Dead, lie down -
It was not Night, for all the Bells
Put out their Tongues, for Noon.

It was not Frost, for on my Flesh   5
I felt Siroccos[1] - crawl -
Nor Fire - for just my marble feet
Could keep a Chancel,[2] cool -

And yet, it tasted, like them all,
The Figures I have seen   10
Set orderly, for Burial,
Reminded me, of mine -

As if my life were shaven,
And fitted to a frame,
And could not breathe without a key,   15
And 'twas like Midnight, some -

1. Upon.
1. Hot winds from North Africa.

2. The part of the church that contains the choir and sanctuary.

When everything that ticked - has stopped -
And space stares - all around -
Or Grisly frosts - first Autumn morns,
Repeal the Beating Ground -   20

But, most, like Chaos - Stopless - cool -
Without a Chance, or spar -
Or even a Report of Land -
To justify - Despair.

                                                        1862

359

A Bird, came down the Walk -
He did not know I saw -
He bit an Angle Worm in halves
And ate the fellow, raw,

And then, he drank a Dew   5
From a convenient Grass -
And then hopped sidewise to the Wall
To let a Beetle pass -

He glanced with rapid eyes,
That hurried all abroad -   10
They looked like frightened Beads, I thought,
He stirred his Velvet Head. -

Like one in danger, Cautious,
I offered him a Crumb,
And he unrolled his feathers,   15
And rowed him softer Home -

Than Oars divide the Ocean,
Too silver for a seam,
Or Butterflies, off Banks of Noon,
Leap, plashless[1] as they swim.   20

                                                        1862

365

I know that He exists.
Somewhere - in silence -
He has hid his rare life
From our gross eyes.

---

1. Splashless.

'Tis an instant's play-
'Tis a fond Ambush -
Just to make Bliss
Earn her own surprise!

But - should the play
Prove piercing earnest -
Should the glee - glaze -
In Death's - stiff - stare -

Would not the fun
Look too expensive!
Would not the jest -
Have crawled too far!

1862

372

After great pain, a formal feeling comes -
The Nerves sit ceremonious, like Tombs -
The stiff Heart questions 'was it He, that bore,'
And 'Yesterday, or Centuries before'?

The Feet, mechanical, go round -
A Wooden way
Of Ground, or Air, or Ought -
Regardless grown,
A Quartz contentment, like a stone -

This is the Hour of Lead -
Remembered, if outlived,
As Freezing persons, recollect the Snow -
First - Chill - then Stupor - then the letting go -

1862

373

This World is not conclusion.
A Species stands beyond -
Invisible, as Music -
But positive, as Sound -
It beckons, and it baffles -
Philosophy, dont know -
And through a Riddle, at the last -
Sagacity, must go -
To guess it, puzzles scholars -
To gain it, Men have borne

Contempt of Generations
And Crucifixion, shown -
Faith slips - and laughs, and rallies -
Blushes, if any see -
Plucks at a twig of Evidence -   15
And asks a Vane, the way -
Much Gesture, from the Pulpit -
Strong Hallelujahs roll -
Narcotics cannot still the Tooth
That nibbles at the soul -   20

1862

409

"Dickinson have
copied to past in
her quotes"

The Soul selects her own Society -
Then - shuts the Door -
To her divine Majority -
Present no more -

Unmoved - she notes the Chariots - pausing -   5
At her low Gate -
Unmoved - an Emperor be kneeling
Opon her Mat -

I've known her - from an ample nation -
Choose One -
Then - close the Valves of her attention -   10
Like Stone -

1862

411

Mine - by the Right of the White Election!
Mine - by the Royal Seal!
Mine - by the sign in the Scarlet prison -
Bars - cannot conceal!

Mine - here - in Vision - and in Veto!   5
Mine - by the Grave's Repeal -
Titled - Confirmed -
Delirious Charter!
Mine - long as Ages steal!

1862

446

This was a Poet -
It is That
Distills amazing sense
From Ordinary Meanings -
And Attar[1] so immense   5

From the familiar species
That perished by the Door -
We wonder it was not Ourselves
Arrested it - before -

Of Pictures, the Discloser -   10
The Poet - it is He -
Entitles Us - by Contrast -
To ceaseless Poverty -

Of Portion - so unconscious -
The Robbing - could not harm -   15
Himself - to Him - a Fortune -
Exterior - to Time -

1862

448

I died for Beauty - but was scarce
Adjusted in the Tomb
When One who died for Truth, was lain
In an adjoining Room -

He questioned softly "Why I failed"?   5
"For Beauty", I replied -
"And I - for Truth - Themself are One -
We Bretheren, are", He said -

And so, as Kinsmen, met a Night -
We talked between the Rooms -   10
Until the Moss had reached our lips -
And covered up - Our names -

1862

---

1. Fragrance.

● 479

Because I could not stop for Death -
He kindly stopped for me -
The Carriage held but just Ourselves -
And Immortality.

We slowly drove - He knew no haste   5
And I had put away
My labor and my leisure too,
For His Civility -

We passed the School, where Children strove
At Recess - in the Ring -   10
We passed the Fields of Gazing Grain -
We passed the Setting Sun -

Or rather - He passed Us -
The Dews drew quivering and Chill -
For only Gossamer,[1] my Gown -   15
My Tippet - only Tulle[2] -

We paused before a House that seemed
A Swelling of the Ground -
The Roof was scarcely visible -
The Cornice[3] - in the Ground -   20

Since then - 'tis Centuries - and yet
Feels shorter than the Day
I first surmised the Horses' Heads
Were toward Eternity -

1862

518

When I was small, a Woman died -
Today - her Only Boy
Went up from the Potomac[1]-
His face all Victory

To look at her - How slowly   5
The Seasons must have turned
Till Bullets clipt an Angle
And He passed quickly round -

---

1. Delicate, light fabric.
2. Thin silk. "Tippet": scarf for covering neck
and shoulders.
3. Decorative molding beneath a roof.

1. River along the mid-Atlantic coast, flowing
from Maryland, through Washington, D.C., and
into the Virginias.

If pride shall be in Paradise -
Ourself cannot decide -
Of their imperial conduct -
No person testified -

But, proud in Apparition -
That Woman and her Boy
Pass back and forth, before my Brain
As even in the sky -

I'm confident, that Bravoes -
Perpetual break abroad
For Braveries, remote as this
In Yonder Maryland[2] -

1863

519

This is my letter to the World
That never wrote to Me -
The simple News that Nature told -
With tender Majesty

Her Message is committed
To Hands I cannot see -
For love of Her - Sweet - countrymen -
Judge tenderly - of Me

1863

• 591

I heard a Fly buzz - when I died -
The Stillness in the Room
Was like the Stillness in the Air -
Between the Heaves of Storm -

The Eyes around - had wrung them dry -
And Breaths were gathering firm
For that last Onset - when the King
Be witnessed - in the Room -

I willed my Keepsakes - Signed away
What portion of me be

["She died herself"]
["Jesus is the light"]

2. This reference may have been intended to evoke a specific battle, such as the battle of Antietam near Sharpsburg, Maryland, where over twenty thousand soldiers were killed and injured on a single day (September 17, 1862). Despite the reference to Maryland, some critics believe the poem was inspired by the death of Frazar Stearns (1840–1862), the son of Amherst College's president, who died in March 1862 at the battle of New Bern in North Carolina. Dickinson lamented the death in a letter to her cousins Louise and Frances Norcross, referring to "brave Frazar."

Assignable - and then it was
There interposed a Fly -

With Blue - uncertain - stumbling Buzz -
Between the light - and me -
And then the Windows failed - and then   15
I could not see to see -

1863

598

The Brain - is wider than the Sky -
For - put them side by side -
The one the other will contain
With ease - and You - beside -

The Brain is deeper than the sea -   5
For - hold them - Blue to Blue -
The one the other will absorb -
As Sponges - Buckets - do -

The Brain is just the weight of God -
For - Heft them - Pound for Pound -   10
And they will differ - if they do -
As Syllable from Sound -

1863

620

Much Madness is divinest Sense -
To a discerning Eye -
Much Sense - the starkest Madness -
'Tis the Majority
In this, as all, prevail -   5
Assent - and you are sane -
Demur - you're straightway dangerous -
And handled with a Chain -

1863

656

I started Early - Took my Dog -
And visited the Sea -
The Mermaids in the Basement
Came out to look at me -

And Frigates - in the Upper Floor   5
Extended Hempen Hands -

Presuming Me to be a Mouse -
Aground - opon the Sands -

But no Man moved Me - till the Tide
Went past my simple Shoe -   10
And past my Apron - and my Belt
And past my Boddice - too -

And made as He would eat me up -
As wholly as a Dew
Opon a Dandelion's Sleeve -   15
And then - I started - too -

And He - He followed - close behind -
I felt His Silver Heel
Opon my Ancle[1] - Then My Shoes
Would overflow with Pearl -   20

Until We met the Solid Town -
No One He seemed to know -
And bowing - with a Mighty look -
At me - The Sea withdrew -

                                              1863

704

My Portion is Defeat - today -
A paler luck than Victory -
Less Paeans - fewer Bells -
The Drums dont follow Me - with tunes -
Defeat - a somewhat slower - means -   5
More Arduous than Balls -

'Tis populous with Bone and stain -
And Men too straight to stoop again -
And Piles of solid Moan -
And Chips of Blank - in Boyish Eyes -   10
And scraps of Prayer -
And Death's surprise,
Stamped visible - in stone -

There's somewhat prouder, Over there -
The Trumpets tell it to the Air -   15
How different Victory
To Him who has it - and the One
Who to have had it, would have been
Contenteder - to die -

                                              1863

1. Upon my ankle.

• 706

"poem to Man that try to marry term"

U she love him but not to go with him"

I cannot live with You -
It would be Life -
And Life is over there -
Behind the Shelf

The Sexton keeps the key to -   5
Putting up
Our Life - His Porcelain -
Like a Cup -

Discarded of the Housewife -
Quaint - or Broke -   10
A newer Sevres[1] pleases -
Old Ones crack -

I could not die - with You -
For One must wait
To shut the Other's Gaze down -   15
You - could not -

And I - Could I stand by
And see You - freeze -
Without my Right of Frost -
Death's privilege?   20

Nor could I rise - with You -
Because Your Face
Would put out Jesus' -
That New Grace

Glow plain - and foreign   25
On my homesick eye -
Except that You than He
Shone closer by -

They'd judge Us - How -
For You - served Heaven - You know,   30
Or sought to -
I could not -

Because You saturated sight -
And I had no more eyes
For sordid excellence   35
As Paradise

And were You lost, I would be -
Though my name

---

1. Porcelain china (French), usually elaborately decorated.

Rang loudest
On the Heavenly fame -   40

And were You - saved -
And I - condemned to be
Where You were not
That self - were Hell to me -

So we must meet apart -   45
You there - I - here -
With just the Door ajar
That Oceans are - and Prayer -
And that White Sustenance -
Despair -   50

1863

760

Pain - has an Element of Blank -
It cannot recollect
When it begun - Or if there were
A time when it was not -

It has no Future - but itself -   5
It's Infinite contain
It's Past - enlightened to perceive
New Periods - Of Pain.

1863

764

My Life had stood - a Loaded Gun -
In Corners - till a Day
The Owner passed - identified -
And carried Me away -

And now We roam in Sovreign Woods -   5
And now We hunt the Doe -
And every time I speak for Him
The Mountains straight reply -

And do I smile, such cordial light
Opon the Valley glow -   10
It is as a Vesuvian[1] face
Had let it's pleasure through

---

1. Reference to Mount Vesuvius, the volcano in southern Italy that destroyed Pompeii (79 C.E.).

And when at Night - Our good Day done -
I guard My Master's Head -
'Tis better than the Eider Duck's   15
Deep Pillow - to have shared -

To foe of His - I'm deadly foe -
None stir the second time -
On whom I lay a Yellow Eye -
Or an emphatic Thumb -   20

Though I than He - may longer live
He longer must - than I -
For I have but the power to kill,
Without - the power to die -

                                                    1863

788

Publication - is the Auction
Of the Mind of Man -
Poverty - be justifying
For so foul a thing

Possibly - but We - would rather   5
From Our Garret go
White - unto the White Creator -
Than invest - Our Snow -

Thought belong to Him who gave it -
Then - to Him Who bear   10
It's Corporeal illustration - sell
The Royal Air -

In the Parcel - Be the Merchant
Of the Heavenly Grace -
But reduce no Human Spirit
To Disgrace of Price -

                                                    1863

1096[1]

A narrow Fellow in the Grass
Occasionally rides -
You may have met him? Did you not
His notice instant is -

---

1. Dickinson published a version of this poem in the *Springfield Daily Republican*, February 14, 1866.

The Grass divides as with a Comb -   5
A spotted Shaft is seen,
And then it closes at your Feet
And opens further on -

He likes a Boggy Acre -
A Floor too cool for Corn -   10
But when a Boy and Barefoot
I more than once at Noon

Have passed I thought a Whip Lash
Unbraiding in the Sun
When stooping to secure it   15
It wrinkled And was gone -

Several of Nature's People
I know and they know me
I feel for them a transport
Of Cordiality   20

But never met this Fellow
Attended or alone
Without a tighter Breathing
And Zero at the Bone.

                              1865, 1866

1108

The Bustle in a House
The Morning after Death
Is solemnest of industries
Enacted opon Earth -

The Sweeping up the Heart   5
And putting Love away
We shall not want to use again
Until Eternity -

                                      1865

1212

My Triumph lasted till the Drums
Had left the Dead alone
And then I dropped my Victory
And chastened stole along
To where the finished Faces   5
Conclusion turned on me

And then I hated Glory
And wished myself were They.

What is to be is best descried
When it has also been -   10
Could Prospect taste of Retrospect
The Tyrannies of Men
Were Tenderer, diviner
The Transitive toward -
A Bayonet's contrition   15
Is nothing to the Dead -

                                        1871

1263

Tell all the truth but tell it slant -
Success in Circuit lies
Too bright for our infirm Delight
The Truth's superb surprise
As Lightning to the Children eased   5
With explanation kind
The Truth must dazzle gradually
Or every man be blind -

                                        1872

1577

The Bible is an antique Volume -
Written by faded Men
At the suggestion of Holy Spectres -
Subjects - Bethlehem -
Eden - the ancient Homestead -   5
Satan - the Brigadier -
Judas - the Great Defaulter -
David - the Troubadour -
Sin - a distinguished Precipice
Others must resist -   10
Boys that "believe" are very lonesome -
Other Boys are "lost" -
Had but the Tale a warbling Teller -
All the Boys would come -
Orpheus' Sermon[1] captivated -   15
It did not condemn -

                                        1882

---

1. In Greek mythology, Orpheus played music that would transfix wild beasts and still rivers.

1773[1]

My life closed twice before it's close;
It yet remains to see
If Immortality unveil
A third event to me,

So huge, so hopeless to conceive   5
As these that twice befell.
Parting is all we know of heaven,
And all we need of hell.

Letter Exchange with Susan Gilbert Dickinson on Poem 124[1]

The Sleeping[2]

Safe in their alabaster chambers,
Untouched by morning,
    And untouched by noon,
Sleep the meek members of the Resurrection,
    Rafter of satin, and roof of stone.

Light laughs the breeze
In her castle above them,
    Babbles the bee in a stolid ear,
Pipe the sweet birds in ignorant cadences:
    Ah! What sagacity perished here!
                    Pelham Hill, June, 1861.

Emily Dickinson to Susan Gilbert Dickinson, summer 1861[3]

Safe in their Alabaster Chambers,
Untouched by Morning –
And untouched by Noon –
Lie the meek members of the Resurrection –
Rafter of Satin – and Roof of Stone –
Grand go the Years – in the Crescent – about them –
Worlds scoop their Arcs –
And Firmaments – row –

---

1. Transcribed by Mabel Loomis Todd; there is no surviving manuscript. As with poem 1715, it is hard to determine a probable date of composition.
1. Dickinson exchanged hundreds of letters with her friend and sister-in-law Susan Huntington Gilbert Dickinson (1850–1913), who married Emily's brother, Austin; for the complete exchange, see *Open Me Carefully: Emily Dickinson's Intimate Letters to Susan Huntington Dickinson* (1998), ed. Ellen Louise Hart and Martha Nell

Smith.
2. This version of poem 124 was published in the *Springfield Republican* on March 1, 1862. Dickinson had sent Susan a manuscript version of this poem in spring 1861, but the manuscript is not extant, nor is Susan's initial letter of response, which had criticized the second stanza.
3. This and the next two letters are from *Emily Dickinson: Selected Letters*, ed. Thomas H. Johnson (1971), reprinted by permission of Harvard University Press.

Diadems – drop – and Doges – surrender –
Soundless as dots – on a Disc of Snow –

Perhaps this verse would please you better – Sue –

Emily –

Susan Gilbert Dickinson to Emily Dickinson, summer 1861

I am not suited dear Emily with the second verse – It is remarkable as the chain lightening that blinds us hot nights in the Southern sky but it does not go with the ghostly shimmer of the first verse as well as the other one – It just occurs to me that the first verse is complete in itself it needs no other, and can't be coupled – Strange things always go alone – as there is only one Gabriel and one Sun – You never made a peer for that verse,[4] and I *guess* you[r] kingdom does'nt hold one – I always go to the fire and get warm after thinking of it, but I never *can* again – The flowers are sweet and bright and look as if they would kiss one – ah, they expect a humming-bird – Thanks for them of course – and not thanks only recognition either – Did it ever occur to you that is all there is here after all – "Lord that I may receive my sight"[5] –

Susan is tired making *bibs* for her bird – her ring-dove[6] – he will paint my cheeks when I am old to pay me –

Sue –
Pony Express[7]

Emily Dickinson to Susan Gilbert Dickinson, summer 1861

Is *this frostier?*

Springs – shake the sills –
But – the Echoes – stiffen –
Hoar – is the Window –
And numb – the Door –
Tribes of Eclipse – in Tents of Marble –
Staples of Ages – have buckled – there –[8]

Dear Sue –

Your praise is good – to me – because I *know* it *knows* – and *suppose* – it *means* –

Could I make you and Austin – proud – sometime – a great way off – 'twould give me taller feet –

Here is a crumb – for the "Ring dove" – and a spray for *his Nest,* a little while ago – *just* – "*Sue.*"

Emily.

---

4. Susan refers to Dickinson's poem 285, which calls life on earth "but a filament" of the "diviner thing" that "smites the Tinder in the Sun" and "hinders Gabriel's wing."
5. In Luke 18.41–43, the blind man's faith in Jesus brings him sight.
6. Susan's son, Ned, who was born on July 19,

1861. Susan is imagining her grown son repaying all her attention by caring for her in old age.
7. Here Susan comically emphasizes the speed of her response.
8. Dickinson incorporated this stanza into a new version of the poem, which she bound into Fascicle 10.

From Fascicle 10[9]

Safe in their Alabaster chambers -
Untouched by Morning -
And untouched by Noon -
Lie the meek members of the Resurrection -
Rafter of Satin - and Roof of Stone!

Grand go the Years - in the Crescent - above them -
Worlds scoop their Arcs -
And Firmaments - row -
Diadems - drop - and Doges - surrender -
Soundless as dots - on a Disc of snow -

    Springs - shake the sills -
    But - the Echoes - stiffen -
    Hoar - is the window -
    And - numb - the door -
    Tribes - of Eclipse - in Tents - of Marble -
    Staples - of Ages - have buckled - there -

    Springs - shake the seals -
    But the silence - stiffens -
    Frosts unhook - in the Northern Zones -
    Icicles - crawl from polar Caverns -
    Midnights in Marble -
    Refutes - the Suns -

Letters to Thomas Wentworth Higginson[1]

15 April 1862

Mr Higginson,
    Are you too deeply occupied to say if my Verse is alive?[2]
    The Mind is so near itself – it cannot see, distinctly – and I have none to ask –

---

9. Dickinson wrote out a complete record of her attempts with poem 124, as influenced by her exchanges with Susan Dickinson, and bound it into Fascicle 10. She first wrote a ten-line version of the entire poem and then beneath that version wrote two versions of a six-line stanza that she was considering as a substitution for the five-line second stanza. The fascicle version of poem 124 suggests that many Dickinson poems were always in progress. The source here is *The Poems of Emily Dickinson: Variorum Edition* (1998), ed. R. W. Franklin, reprinted with the permission of Harvard University Press.
1. Dickinson first wrote Higginson (1823–1911) on April 15, 1862, responding to his article "Letter to a Young Contributor," which he published in the *Atlantic Monthly* earlier in the month. A contributing editor at the magazine, Higginson,

who had trained at Harvard Divinity School, had recently resigned his ministry. As an editor, he was intrigued by Dickinson's poetry, but he never offered to publish her work. In her letter of April 25, 1862, Dickinson refers to the editorial "surgery" he did on the poems she sent him. Over the next twenty-four years, she sent him many letters (including one just before she died) and nearly one hundred poems. He visited her twice at her Amherst home, in 1870 and 1873. When he helped to publish the first two volumes of her poems posthumously, Higginson edited the poems, giving them more conventional rhyme and meter. Both letters are taken from *Emily Dickinson: Selected Letters* (1971), ed. Thomas H. Johnson.
2. Dickinson sent four poems with the letter, including 124, "Safe in their Alabaster Chambers."

Should you think it breathed – and had you the leisure to tell me, I should feel quick gratitude –

If I make the mistake – that you dared to tell me – would give me sincerer honor – toward you –

I enclose my name – asking you, if you please – Sir – to tell me what is true?

That you will not betray me – it is needless to ask – since Honor is it's own pawn –[3]

25 April 1862

Mr Higginson,

Your kindness claimed earlier gratitude – but I was ill – and write today, from my pillow:

Thank you for the surgery – it was not so painful as I supposed. I bring you others – as you ask – though they might not differ –

While my thought is undressed – I can make the distinction, but when I put them in the Gown – they look alike, and numb.

You asked how old I was? I made no verse – but one or two – until this winter – Sir –

I had a terror – since September – I could tell to none – and so I sing, as the Boy does by the Burying Ground – because I am afraid – You inquire my Books – For Poets – I have Keats – and Mr and Mrs Browning. For Prose – Mr Ruskin - Sir Thomas Browne – and the Revelations.[4] I went to school – but in your manner of the phrase – had no education. When a little Girl, I had a friend, who taught me Immortality – but venturing too near, himself – he never returned – Soon after, my Tutor, died[5] – and for several years, my Lexicon – was my only companion – Then I found one more – but he was not contented I be his scholar – so he left the Land.[6]

You ask of my Companions Hills – Sir – and the Sundown – and a Dog – large as myself, that my Father bought me – They are better than Beings – because they know – but do not tell – and the noise in the Pool, at Noon – excels my Piano. I have a Brother and Sister – My Mother does not care for thought – and Father, too busy with his Briefs[7] – to notice what we do – He buys me many Books – but begs me not to read them – because he fears they joggle the Mind. They are religious – except me – and address an Eclipse, every morning – whom they call their "Father." But I fear my story fatigues you – I would like to learn – Could you tell me how to grow – or is it unconveyed – like Melody – or Witchcraft?

You speak of Mr Whitman – I never read his Book[8] – but was told that he was disgraceful –

3. Instead of signing the letter, Dickinson enclosed a card with her signature.
4. Revelation is the concluding prophetic book of the New Testament. Dickinson refers to the English poets John Keats (1795–1821), Elizabeth Barrett Browning and Robert Browning; the English art critic and social theorist John Ruskin (1819–1900); and the English physician and writer Sir Thomas Browne (1605–1682).

5. The friend and tutor was probably Benjamin Franklin Newton (1821–1853), who had studied law in her father's office during the 1840s.
6. Dickinson's friend the Reverend Charles Wadsworth (1814–1882) had recently accepted a pastorate in California.
7. Legal documents.
8. The third edition of Whitman's Leaves of Grass was published in 1860.

I read Miss Prescott's "Circumstance,"[9] but it followed me, in the Dark — so I avoided her —

Two Editors of Journals[1] came to my Father's House, this winter — and asked me for my Mind — and when I asked them "Why," they said I was penurious — and they, would use it for the World —

I could not weigh myself — Myself —

My size felt small — to me — I read your Chapters in the Atlantic — and experienced honor for you — I was sure you would not reject a confiding question —

Is this — Sir — what you asked me to tell you?

Your friend,

E – Dickinson.

9. Harriet Prescott Spofford's (1835–1921) short story "Circumstance" had appeared in the May 1860 Atlantic.

1. Possibly Samuel Bowles (1826–1878) and J. G. Holland (1819–1881), who were both associated with the Springfield Daily Republican.

REBECCA HARDING DAVIS
1831–1910

The author of over five hundred published works, including short stories, essays, sketches, novels, and children's writings, Rebecca Harding Davis is best known today for the pioneering realism of her first published story, "Life in the Iron-Mills." The story was a sensation when it appeared in the 1861 *Atlantic Monthly*, and while Davis's subsequent work never equaled it in power, her career was marked by success with both the highbrow readers of the *Atlantic* and the mass audiences that enjoyed her writings in the popular magazines and newspapers of the day.

Rebecca Harding was born in 1831 in Washington, Pennsylvania, her mother's hometown, and then taken to Florence, Alabama, where her father, a book-loving English emigrant, was in business. In 1836 the family moved to Wheeling, Virginia, a jumping-off place for the West as well as a prosperous manufacturing center, located in an anomalous fingerlike part of a slave state that reached far north between the free states of Ohio and Pennsylvania. Rebecca Harding at fourteen returned to her Pennsylvania birthplace, living with an aunt while attending a female seminary. After graduating as valedictorian in 1848, she moved back to be with her family in Wheeling. By her late twenties she had read English reform novels such as those by Charles Kingsley and Elizabeth Gaskell and had begun to publish anonymous reviews of new books in local newspapers. During the election year 1860, she wrote "Life in the Iron-Mills," apparently the first story she completed, and sent it to the *Atlantic Monthly*, the most prestigious magazine in the country, published in Boston under the editorship of James T. Fields. The story appeared anonymously (by custom and by Harding's request) the month the Civil War broke out and Wheeling became capital of the new free state of West Virginia. With the author's name an open secret, the story's strength was recognized by many readers, including Emily Dickinson. Buoyed by Fields's enthusiastic request for additional contributions, Harding began a serialized novel in the October 1861 *Atlantic*—"A Story of Today"—which provided, in one of the characters' words, "a glimpse of the underlife in America." In the voice of her narrator, Harding offered a manifesto of realism before there was a literary movement so identified: "You want something . . . to lift you out of this crowded, tobacco-stained commonplace, to kindle and chafe and glow in you. I want you to dig into this commonplace, this vulgar American life, and see what is in it. Sometimes I think it has a raw and awful significance that we do not see." This work, which Fields published in book form as *Margret Howth* (1862), further explored the dire effects of industrial capitalism, while addressing as well the racial injustice that helped bring about the Civil War.

As a literary celebrity, Harding journeyed to Boston in 1862 and was welcomed by the literary establishment. She met Oliver Wendell Holmes and Nathaniel Hawthorne (whose fiction had inspired her own work), and became good friends with Annie Fields, her hostess. She had received a fan letter from an apprentice lawyer in Philadelphia, L. Clarke Davis, a man literary enough himself to have a connection with *Peterson's Magazine*, one of the leading magazines of the day. She met him on her way home from Boston, and they married in 1863. She continued her career as a magazine writer even after her three children were born, creating an extensive body of work that alternated between romance and social realism. In the best of her later novels, *Waiting for the Verdict* (1868), Davis addressed the continuing injustices facing African Americans in the postemancipation United States. She also addressed questions of gender, and in "The Wife's Story" (1864) and *Earthen Pitchers* (1873–1874) paid particular attention to conflicts between motherhood and career aspirations, as she and many other women of her generation were experiencing them.

In 1892 Davis received favorable critical attention for a collection of short stories, *Silhouettes of American Life*. But well before her death in 1910, she had been overshadowed, first by the success of her husband as an editor and then by the astonishing success of her son, Richard Harding Davis (1864–1916), who became the most glamorous journalist and one of the most popular writers of his generation. Concerned that he might sacrifice his talent for money as perhaps she thought she herself had done, in 1890 she warned him about "beginning to do hack work for money . . . the beginning of decadence both in work and reputation for you. I know by my own and a thousand other people."

"Life in the Iron-Mills" remains a landmark in the development of literary realism in nineteenth-century America. The story achieved a renewed popularity—and brought Rebecca Harding Davis back into a prominent place in literary history—through its re-publication in 1972 in a Feminist Press volume edited by the fiction writer and essayist Tillie Olsen. In "Life in the Iron-Mills," Davis compels her middle-class readers to confront the underside of American industrial prosperity, particularly the exploitation of immigrant laborers, while refusing to provide easy answers to the social problems she so powerfully represents.

Life in the Iron-Mills[1]

"Is this the end?
O Life, as futile, then, as frail!
What hope of answer or redress?"[2]

A cloudy day: do you know what that is in a town of iron-works?[3] The sky sank down before dawn, muddy, flat, immovable. The air is thick, clammy with the breath of crowded human beings. It stifles me. I open the window, and, looking out, can scarcely see through the rain the grocer's shop opposite, where a crowd of drunken Irishmen are puffing Lynchburg tobacco[4] in their pipes. I can detect the scent through all the foul smells ranging loose in the air.

The idiosyncrasy of this town is smoke. It rolls sullenly in slow folds from the great chimneys of the iron-foundries, and settles down in black, slimy pools on the muddy streets. Smoke on the wharves, smoke on the dingy boats, on the yellow river,—clinging in a coating of greasy soot to the house-front, the two faded poplars, the faces of the passers-by. The long train of mules, dragging masses of pig-iron[5] through the narrow street, have a foul vapor hanging to their reeking sides. Here, inside, is a little broken figure of an angel pointing upward from the mantel-shelf; but even its wings are covered with smoke, clotted and black. Smoke everywhere! A dirty canary chirps desolately in a cage beside me. Its dream of green fields and sunshine is a very old dream,—almost worn out, I think.

From the back-window I can see a narrow brick-yard sloping down to the river-side, strewed with rain-butts[6] and tubs. The river, dull and tawny-colored, (*la belle rivière!*)[7] drags itself sluggishly along, tired of the heavy weight of boats and coal-barges. What wonder? When I was a child, I used to fancy a look of weary, dumb appeal upon the face of the negro-like river slavishly bearing its burden day after day. Something of the same idle notion comes to me to-day, when from the street-window I look on the slow stream of human life creeping past, night and morning, to the great mills. Masses of men, with dull, besotted faces bent to the ground, sharpened here and there by pain or cunning; skin and muscle and flesh begrimed with smoke and ashes; stooping all night over boiling caldrons of metal, laired by day in dens of drunkenness and infamy; breathing from infancy to death an air saturated with fog and grease and soot, vileness for soul and body. What do you make of a case like that, amateur psychologist? You call it an altogether serious thing to be alive: to these men it is a drunken jest, a joke,—horrible to angels perhaps, to them commonplace enough. My fancy about the river

---

1. The text is that of the first printing in the *Atlantic Monthly* (April 1861), except for two paragraphs on page 1717, the source of which is *Atlantic Tales* (1865).
2. Adapted from Alfred, Lord Tennyson's *In Memoriam A.H.H.* (1850), 12.4: "'Is this the end of all my care?' . . . 'Is this the end? Is this the end?'" and from 56.7: "O Life as futile, then, as frail / O for thy voice to soothe and bless! / What hope of answer, or redress? / Behind the veil,

behind the veil."
3. The town is not named, but is based on Harding's hometown, Wheeling, Virginia (now West Virginia), on the banks of the Ohio River.
4. A low-cost tobacco from south-central Virginia.
5. Oblong blocks of iron, hardened after being poured from a smelting furnace.
6. Large casks used to catch rainwater for household and industrial use.
7. The beautiful river (French).

was an idle one: it is no type of such a life. What if it be stagnant and slimy here? It knows that beyond there waits for it odorous sunlight,—quaint old gardens, dusky with soft, green foliage of apple-trees, and flushing crimson with roses,—air, and fields, and mountains. The future of the Welsh puddler[8] passing just now is not so pleasant. To be stowed away, after his grimy work is done, in a hole in the muddy graveyard, and after that,——not air, nor green fields, nor curious roses.

Can you see how foggy the day is? As I stand here, idly tapping the window-pane, and looking out through the rain at the dirty back-yard and the coal-boats below, fragments of an old story float up before me,—a story of this house into which I happened to come to-day. You may think it a tiresome story enough, as foggy as the day, sharpened by no sudden flashes of pain or pleasure.—I know: only the outline of a dull life, that long since, with thousands of dull lives like its own, was vainly lived and lost: thousands of them,—massed, vile, slimy lives, like those of the torpid lizards in yonder stagnant water-butt.—Lost? There is a curious point for you to settle, my friend, who study psychology in a lazy, *dilettante* way. Stop a moment. I am going to be honest. This is what I want you to do. I want you to hide your disgust, take no heed to your clean clothes, and come right down with me,— here, into the thickest of the fog and mud and foul effluvia. I want you to hear this story. There is a secret down here, in this nightmare fog, that has lain dumb for centuries: I want to make it a real thing to you. You, Egoist, or Pantheist, or Arminian, busy in making straight paths[9] for your feet on the hills, do not see it clearly,—this terrible question which men here have gone mad and died trying to answer. I dare not put this secret into words. I told you it was dumb. These men, going by with drunken faces and brains full of unawakened power, do not ask it of Society or of God. Their lives ask it; their deaths ask it. There is no reply. I will tell you plainly that I have a great hope; and I bring it to you to be tested. It is this: that this terrible dumb question is its own reply; that it is not the sentence of death we think it, but, from the very extremity of its darkness, the most solemn prophecy which the world has known of the Hope to come. I dare make my meaning no clearer, but will only tell my story. It will, perhaps, seem to you as foul and dark as this thick vapor about us, and as pregnant with death; but if your eyes are free as mine are to look deeper, no perfume-tinted dawn will be so fair with promise of the day that shall surely come.

My story is very simple,—only what I remember of the life of one of these men,—a furnace-tender in one of Kirby & John's rolling-mills,—Hugh Wolfe. You know the mills? They took the great order for the lower Virginia railroads there last winter; run usually with about a thousand men. I cannot tell why I choose the half-forgotten story of this Wolfe more than that of myriads of these furnace-hands. Perhaps because there is a secret, underlying sympathy between that story and this day with its impure fog and thwarted sunshine,—or perhaps simply for the reason that this house is the one where

---

8. Worker who stirs iron oxide into a molten vat of pig iron to make wrought iron or steel.
9. Echoes Hebrews 12.13: "And make straight paths for your feet, lest that which is lame be turned out of the way; but let it rather be healed."

"Egoist": one acting only according to self-interest. "Pantheist": one who identifies the deity with nature. "Arminian": follower of theologian Jacobus Arminius (1560–1607), who argued that salvation was freely available to all through good works.

the Wolfes lived. There were the father and son,—both hands, as I said, in one of Kirby & John's mills for making railroad-iron,—and Deborah, their cousin, a picker[1] in some of the cotton-mills. The house was rented then to half a dozen families. The Wolfes had two of the cellar-rooms. The old man, like many of the puddlers and feeders[2] of the mills, was Welsh,—had spent half of his life in the Cornish tin-mines. You may pick the Welsh emigrants, Cornish miners, out of the throng passing the windows, any day. They are a trifle more filthy; their muscles are not so brawny; they stoop more. When they are drunk, they neither yell, nor shout, nor stagger, but skulk along like beaten hounds. A pure, unmixed blood, I fancy: shows itself in the slight angular bodies and sharply-cut facial lines. It is nearly thirty years since the Wolfes lived here. Their lives were like those of their class: incessant labor, sleeping in kennel-like rooms, eating rank pork and molasses, drinking— God and the distillers only know what; with an occasional night in jail, to atone for some drunken excess. Is that all of their lives?—of the portion given to them and these their duplicates swarming the streets to-day?— nothing beneath?—all? So many a political reformer will tell you,—and many a private reformer, too, who has gone among them with a heart tender with Christ's charity, and come out outraged, hardened.

One rainy night, about eleven o'clock, a crowd of half-clothed women stopped outside of the cellar-door. They were going home from the cotton-mill.

"Good-night, Deb," said one, a mulatto, steadying herself against the gas-post. She needed the post to steady her. So did more than one of them.

"Dah's a ball to Miss Potts' to-night. Ye'd best come."

"Inteet, Deb, if hur'll come, hur'll hef fun," said a shrill Welsh voice in the crowd.

Two or three dirty hands were thrust out to catch the gown of the woman, who was groping for the latch of the door.

"No."

"No? Where's Kit Small, then?"

"Begorra! on the spools.[3] Alleys behint, though we helped her, we dud. An wid ye! Let Deb alone! It's ondacent frettin' a quite body. Be the powers, an' we'll have a night of it! there'll be lashin's o' drink,—the Vargent[4] be blessed and praised for 't!"

They went on, the mulatto inclining for a moment to show fight, and drag the woman Wolfe off with them; but, being pacified, she staggered away.

Deborah groped her way into the cellar, and, after considerable stumbling, kindled a match, and lighted a tallow dip, that sent a yellow glimmer over the room. It was low, damp,—the earthen floor covered with a green, slimy moss,—a fetid air smothering the breath. Old Wolfe lay asleep on a heap of straw, wrapped in a torn horse-blanket. He was a pale, meek little man, with a

1. Worker in a cotton mill who operates the machine that separates cotton fibers.
2. Worker who feeds molten metal into the casting form while the iron is hardening.
3. Spindles in the mill on which the cotton is stretched and wound by the spinning machine.
"Begorra!": a stereotypically Irish form of "By God!"
4. The Virgin Mary.

white face and red rabbit-eyes. The woman Deborah was like him; only her face was even more ghastly, her lips bluer, her eyes more watery. She wore a faded cotton gown and a slouching bonnet. When she walked, one could see that she was deformed, almost a hunchback. She trod softly, so as not to waken him, and went through into the room beyond. There she found by the half-extinguished fire an iron saucepan filled with cold boiled potatoes, which she put upon a broken chair with a pint-cup of ale. Placing the old candlestick beside this dainty repast, she untied her bonnet, which hung limp and wet over her face, and prepared to eat her supper. It was the first food that had touched her lips since morning. There was enough of it, however: there is not always. She was hungry,—one could see that easily enough,—and not drunk, as most of her companions would have been found at this hour. She did not drink, this woman,—her face told that, too,—nothing stronger than ale. Perhaps the weak, flaccid wretch had some stimulant in her pale life to keep her up,—some love or hope, it might be, or urgent need. When that stimulant was gone, she would take to whiskey. Man cannot live by work alone. While she was skinning the potatoes, and munching them, a noise behind her made her stop.

"Janey!" she called, lifting the candle and peering into the darkness. "Janey, are you there?"

A heap of ragged coats was heaved up, and the face of a young girl emerged, staring sleepily at the woman.

"Deborah," she said, at last, "I'm here the night."

"Yes, child. Hur's welcome," she said, quietly eating on.

The girl's face was haggard and sickly; her eyes were heavy with sleep and hunger: real Milesian[5] eyes they were, dark, delicate blue, glooming out from black shadows with a pitiful fright.

"I was alone," she said, timidly.

"Where's the father?" asked Deborah, holding out a potato, which the girl greedily seized.

"He's beyant,—wid Haley,—in the stone house." (Did you ever hear the word *jail* from an Irish mouth?) "I came here. Hugh told me never to stay me-lone."

"Hugh?"

"Yes."

A vexed frown crossed her face. The girl saw it, and added quickly,—

"I have not seen Hugh the day, Deb. The old man says his watch[6] lasts till the mornin'."

The woman sprang up, and hastily began to arrange some bread and flitch[7] in a tin pail, and to pour her own measure of ale into a bottle. Tying on her bonnet, she blew out the candle.

"Lay ye down, Janey dear," she said, gently, covering her with the old rags. "Hur can eat the potatoes, if hur's hungry."

"Where are ye goin', Deb? The rain's sharp."

"To the mill, with Hugh's supper."

"Let him bide till th' morn. Sit ye down."

---

5. Reference to the legendary Miletus, an ancient city on the Aegean whose people were thought by some to be the ancestors of the Irish.

6. Work shift.

7. Salt pork.

"No, no,"—sharply pushing her off. "The boy'll starve."

She hurried from the cellar, while the child wearily coiled herself up for sleep. The rain was falling heavily, as the woman, pail in hand, emerged from the mouth of the alley, and turned down the narrow street, that stretched out, long and black, miles before her. Here and there a flicker of gas lighted an uncertain space of muddy footwalk and gutter; the long rows of houses, except an occasional lager-bier shop, were closed; now and then she met a band of millhands skulking to or from their work.

Not many even of the inhabitants of a manufacturing town know the vast machinery of system by which the bodies of workmen are governed, that goes on unceasingly from year to year. The hands of each mill are divided into watches that relieve each other as regularly as the sentinels of an army. By night and day the work goes on, the unsleeping engines groan and shriek, the fiery pools of metal boil and surge. Only for a day in the week, in half-courtesy to public censure, the fires are partially veiled; but as soon as the clock strikes midnight, the great furnaces break forth with renewed fury, the clamor begins with fresh, breathless vigor, the engines sob and shriek like "gods in pain."

As Deborah hurried down through the heavy rain, the noise of these thousand engines sounded through the sleep and shadow of the city like far-off thunder. The mill to which she was going lay on the river, a mile below the city-limits. It was far, and she was weak, aching from standing twelve hours at the spools. Yet it was her almost nightly walk to take this man his supper, though at every square she sat down to rest, and she knew she should receive small word of thanks.

Perhaps, if she had possessed an artist's eye, the picturesque oddity of the scene might have made her step stagger less, and the path seem shorter; but to her the mills were only "summat deilish[8] to look at by night."

The road leading to the mills had been quarried from the solid rock, which rose abrupt and bare on one side of the cinder-covered road, while the river, sluggish and black, crept past on the other. The mills for rolling[9] iron are simply immense tent-like roofs, covering acres of ground, open on every side. Beneath these roofs Deborah looked in on a city of fires, that burned hot and fiercely in the night. Fire in every horrible form: pits of flame waving in the wind; liquid metal-flames writhing in tortuous streams through the sand; wide caldrons filled with boiling fire, over which bent ghastly wretches stirring the strange brewing; and through all, crowds of half-clad men, looking like revengeful ghosts in the red light, hurried, throwing masses of glittering fire. It was like a street in Hell. Even Deborah muttered, as she crept through, "'T looks like t' Devil's place!" It did,—in more ways than one.

She found the man she was looking for, at last, heaping coal on a furnace. He had not time to eat his supper; so she went behind the furnace, and waited. Only a few men were with him, and they noticed her only by a "Hyur comes t' hunchback, Wolfe."

Deborah was stupid with sleep; her back pained her sharply; and her teeth chattered with cold, with the rain that soaked her clothes and dripped

8. Devilish.   9. Process of producing sheet metal.

from her at every step. She stood, however, patiently holding the pail, and waiting.

"Hout, woman! ye look like a drowned cat. Come near to the fire,"—said one of the men, approaching to scrape away the ashes.

She shook her head. Wolfe had forgotten her. He turned, hearing the man, and came closer.

"I did no' think; gi' me my supper, woman."

She watched him eat with a painful eagerness. With a woman's quick instinct, she saw that he was not hungry,—was eating to please her. Her pale, watery eyes began to gather a strange light.

"Is't good, Hugh? T' ale was a bit sour, I feared."

"No, good enough." He hesitated a moment. "Ye 're tired, poor lass! Bide here till I go. Lay down there on that heap of ash, and go to sleep."

He threw her an old coat for a pillow, and turned to his work. The heap was the refuse of the burnt iron, and was not a hard bed; the half-smothered warmth, too, penetrated her limbs, dulling their pain and cold shiver.

Miserable enough she looked, lying there on the ashes like a limp, dirty rag,—yet not an unfitting figure to crown the scene of hopeless discomfort and veiled crime: more fitting, if one looked deeper into the heart of things,—at her thwarted woman's form, her colorless life, her waking stupor that smothered pain and hunger,—even more fit to be a type of her class. Deeper yet if one could look, was there nothing worth reading in this wet, faded thing, halfcovered with ashes? no story of a soul filled with groping passionate love, heroic unselfishness, fierce jealousy? of years of weary trying to please the one human being whom she loved, to gain one look of real heart-kindness from him? If anything like this were hidden beneath the pale, bleared eyes, and dull, washed-out-looking face, no one had ever taken the trouble to read its faint signs: not the half-clothed furnace-tender, Wolfe, certainly. Yet he was kind to her: it was his nature to be kind, even to the very rats that swarmed in the cellar: kind to her in just the same way. She knew that. And it might be that very knowledge had given to her face its apathy and vacancy more than her low, torpid life. One sees that dead, vacant look steal sometimes over the rarest, finest of women's faces,—in the very midst, it may be, of their warmest summer's day; and then one can guess at the secret of intolerable solitude that lies hid beneath the delicate laces and brilliant smile. There was no warmth, no brilliancy, no summer for this woman; so the stupor and vacancy had time to gnaw into her face perpetually. She was young, too, though no one guessed it; so the gnawing was the fiercer.

She lay quiet in the dark corner, listening, through the monotonous din and uncertain glare of the works, to the dull plash of the rain in the far distance,—shrinking back whenever the man Wolfe happened to look towards her. She knew, in spite of all his kindness, that there was that in her face and form which made him loathe the sight of her. She felt by instinct, although she could not comprehend it, the finer nature of the man, which made him among his fellow-workmen something unique, set apart. She knew, that, down under all the vileness and coarseness of his life, there was a groping passion for whatever was beautiful and pure,—that his soul sickened with disgust at her deformity, even when his words were kindest.

Through this dull consciousness, which never left her, came, like a sting, the recollection of the dark blue eyes and lithe figure of the little Irish girl she had left in the cellar. The recollection struck through even her stupid intellect with a vivid glow of beauty and of grace. Little Janey, timid, helpless, clinging to Hugh as her only friend: that was the sharp thought, the bitter thought, that drove into the glazed eyes a fierce light of pain. You laugh at it? Are pain and jealousy less savage realities down here in this place I am taking you to than in your own house or your own heart,—your heart, which they clutch at sometimes? The note is the same, I fancy, be the octave high or low.

If you could go into this mill where Deborah lay, and drag out from the hearts of these men the terrible tragedy of their lives, taking it as a symptom of the disease of their class, no ghost Horror would terrify you more. A reality of soul-starvation, of living death, that meets you every day under the besotted faces on the street,—I can paint nothing of this, only give you the outside outlines of a night, a crisis in the life of one man: whatever muddy depth of soul-history lies beneath you can read according to the eyes God has given you.

Wolfe, while Deborah watched him as a spaniel its master, bent over the furnace with his iron pole, unconscious of her scrutiny, only stopping to receive orders. Physically, Nature had promised the man but little. He had already lost the strength and instinct vigor of a man, his muscles were thin, his nerves weak, his face (a meek, woman's face) haggard, yellow with consumption. In the mill he was known as one of the girl-men: "Molly Wolfe" was his *sobriquet*.[1] He was never seen in the cockpit, did not own a terrier,[2] drank but seldom; when he did, desperately. He fought sometimes, but was always thrashed, pommelled to a jelly. The man was game enough, when his blood was up: but he was no favorite in the mill; he had the taint of school-learning on him,—not to a dangerous extent, only a quarter or so in the free-school in fact, but enough to ruin him as a good hand in a fight.

For other reasons, too, he was not popular. Not one of themselves, they felt that, though outwardly as filthy and ash-covered; silent, with foreign thoughts and longings breaking out through his quietness in innumerable curious ways: this one, for instance. In the neighboring furnace-buildings lay great heaps of the refuse from the ore after the pig-metal is run. *Korl* we call it here: a light, porous substance, of a delicate, waxen, flesh-colored tinge. Out of the blocks of this korl, Wolfe, in his off-hours from the furnace, had a habit of chipping and moulding figures,—hideous, fantastic enough, but sometimes strangely beautiful: even the mill-men saw that, while they jeered at him. It was a curious fancy in the man, almost a passion. The few hours for rest he spent hewing and hacking with his blunt knife, never speaking, until his watch came again,—working at one figure for months, and, when it was finished, breaking it to pieces perhaps, in a fit of disappointment. A morbid, gloomy man, untaught, unled, left to feed his soul in grossness and crime, and hard, grinding labor.

1. Nickname.
2. Dogs bred to hunt. "Cockpit": where fighting cocks are set against each other until one is severely injured or killed.

I want you to come down and look at this Wolfe, standing there among the lowest of his kind, and see him just as he is, that you may judge him justly when you hear the story of this night. I want you to look back, as he does every day, at his birth in vice, his starved infancy; to remember the heavy years he has groped through as boy and man,—the slow, heavy years of constant, hot work. So long ago he began, that he thinks sometimes he has worked there for ages. There is no hope that it will ever end. Think that God put into this man's soul a fierce thirst for beauty,—to know it, to create it; to *be*—something, he knows not what,—other than he is. There are moments when a passing cloud, the sun glinting on the purple thistles, a kindly smile, a child's face, will rouse him to a passion of pain,—when his nature starts up with a mad cry of rage against God, man, whoever it is that has forced this vile, slimy life upon him. With all this groping, this mad desire, a great blind intellect stumbling through wrong, a loving poet's heart, the man was by habit only a coarse, vulgar laborer, familiar with sights and words you would blush to name. Be just: when I tell you about this night, see him as he is. Be just,—not like man's law, which seizes on one isolated fact, but like God's judging angel, whose clear, sad eye saw all the countless cankering days of this man's life, all the countless nights, when, sick with starving, his soul fainted in him, before it judged him for this night, the saddest of all.

I called this night the crisis of his life. If it was, it stole on him unawares. These great turning-days of life cast no shadow before, slip by unconsciously. Only a trifle, a little turn of the rudder, and the ship goes to heaven or hell.

Wolfe, while Deborah watched him, dug into the furnace of melting iron with his pole, dully thinking only how many rails the lump would yield. It was late,—nearly Sunday morning; another hour, and the heavy work would be done,—only the furnaces to replenish and cover for the next day. The workmen were growing more noisy, shouting, as they had to do, to be heard over the deep clamor of the mills. Suddenly they grew less boisterous,—at the far end, entirely silent. Something unusual had happened. After a moment, the silence came nearer; the men stopped their jeers and drunken choruses. Deborah, stupidly lifting up her head, saw the cause of the quiet. A group of five or six men were slowly approaching, stopping to examine each furnace as they came. Visitors often came to see the mills after night: except by growing less noisy, the men took no notice of them. The furnace where Wolfe worked was near the bounds of the works; they halted there hot and tired: a walk over one of these great foundries is no trifling task. The woman, drawing out of sight, turned over to sleep. Wolfe, seeing them stop, suddenly roused from his indifferent stupor, and watched them keenly. He knew some of them: the overseer, Clarke,—a son of Kirby, one of the mill-owners,—and a Doctor May, one of the town-physicians. The other two were strangers. Wolfe came closer. He seized eagerly every chance that brought him into contact with this mysterious class that shone down on him perpetually with the glamour of another order of being. What made the difference between them? That was the mystery of his life. He had a vague notion that perhaps to-night he could find it out. One of the strangers sat down on a pile of bricks, and beckoned young Kirby to his side.

"This *is* hot, with a vengeance. A match, please?"—lighting his cigar. "But the walk is worth the trouble. If it were not that you must have heard it so often, Kirby, I would tell you that your works look like Dante's Inferno."[3]

Kirby laughed.

"Yes. Yonder is Farinata himself[4] in the burning tomb,"—pointing to some figure in the shimmering shadows.

"Judging from some of the faces of your men," said the other, "they bid fair to try the reality of Dante's vision, some day."

Young Kirby looked curiously around, as if seeing the faces of his hands for the first time.

"They're bad enough, that's true. A desperate set, I fancy. Eh, Clarke?"

The overseer did not hear him. He was talking of net profits just then,— giving, in fact, a schedule of the annual business of the firm to a sharp peering little Yankee, who jotted down notes on a paper laid on the crown of his hat: a reporter for one of the city-papers, getting up a series of reviews of the leading manufactories. The other gentlemen had accompanied them merely for amusement. They were silent until the notes were finished, drying their feet at the furnaces, and sheltering their faces from the intolerable heat. At last the overseer concluded with—

"I believe that is a pretty fair estimate, Captain."

"Here, some of you men!" said Kirby, "bring up those boards. We may as well sit down, gentlemen, until the rain is over. It cannot last much longer at this rate."

"Pig-metal,"—mumbled the reporter,—"um!—coal facilities,—um!— hands employed, twelve hundred,—bitumen,—um!—all right, I believe, Mr. Clarke;—sinking-fund,—what did you say was your sinking-fund?"[5]

"Twelve hundred hands?" said the stranger, the young man who had first spoken. "Do you control their votes, Kirby?"

"Control? No." The young man smiled complacently. "But my father brought seven hundred votes to the polls for his candidate last November. No force-work, you understand,—only a speech or two, a hint to form themselves into a society, and a bit of red and blue bunting to make them a flag. The Invincible Roughs,—I believe that is their name. I forget the motto: 'Our country's hope,' I think."

There was a laugh. The young man talking to Kirby sat with an amused light in his cool gray eye, surveying critically the half-clothed figures of the puddlers, and the slow swing of their brawny muscles. He was a stranger in the city,—spending a couple of months in the borders of a Slave State,[6] to study the institutions of the South,—a brother-in-law of Kirby's,—Mitchell. He was an amateur gymnast,—hence his anatomical eye; a patron, in a *blasé* way, of the prize-ring; a man who sucked the essence out of a science or philosophy in an indifferent, gentlemanly way; who took Kant, Novalis, Humboldt,[7] for what they were worth in his own scales; accepting all,

3. *Hell*, the first part of *The Divine Comedy* by the Italian poet Dante Alighieri (1265–1321).
4. In canto 10 of the *Inferno*, Farinata degli Uberti is one of the heretics, a leader of the Florentine faction opposed to Dante's own family.
5. Fund accumulated to pay off a corporate debt.
6. The story was written and set before the northwest area of the slave state of Virginia broke off to become the free state of West Virginia (1861; admitted to the Union in 1863).
7. Alexander von Humboldt (1769–1859), German naturalist and explorer of South America and Asia. Immanuel Kant (1724–1804), German philosopher. Novalis, pseudonym of the German poet Friedrich von Hardenberg (1772–1801).

despising nothing, in heaven, earth, or hell, but one-idead men; with a temper yielding and brilliant as summer water, until his Self was touched, when it was ice, though brilliant still. Such men are not rare in the States.

As he knocked the ashes from his cigar, Wolfe caught with a quick pleasure the contour of the white hand, the blood-glow of a red ring he wore. His voice, too, and that of Kirby's, touched him like music,—low, even, with chording cadences. About this man Mitchell hung the impalpable atmosphere belonging to the thoroughbred gentleman. Wolfe, scraping away the ashes beside him, was conscious of it, did obeisance to it with his artist sense, unconscious that he did so.

The rain did not cease. Clarke and the reporter left the mills; the others, comfortably seated near the furnace, lingered, smoking and talking in a desultory way. Greek would not have been more unintelligible to the furnace-tenders, whose presence they soon forgot entirely. Kirby drew out a newspaper from his pocket and read aloud some article, which they discussed eagerly. At every sentence, Wolfe listened more and more like a dumb, hopeless animal, with a duller, more stolid look creeping over his face, glancing now and then at Mitchell, marking acutely every smallest sign of refinement, then back to himself, seeing as in a mirror his filthy body, his more stained soul.

Never! He had no words for such a thought, but he knew now, in all the sharpness of the bitter certainty, that between them there was a great gulf[8] never to be passed. Never!

The bell of the mills rang for midnight. Sunday morning had dawned. Whatever hidden message lay in the tolling bells floated past these men unknown. Yet it was there. Veiled in the solemn music ushering the risen Saviour was a key-note to solve the darkest secrets of a world gone wrong,—even this social riddle which the brain of the grimy puddler grappled with madly to-night.

The men began to withdraw the metal from the caldrons. The mills were deserted on Sundays, except by the hands who fed the fires, and those who had no lodgings and slept usually on the ash-heaps. The three strangers sat still during the next hour, watching the men cover the furnaces, laughing now and then at some jest of Kirby's.

"Do you know," said Mitchell, "I like this view of the works better than when the glare was fiercest? These heavy shadows and the amphitheatre of smothered fires are ghostly, unreal. One could fancy these red smouldering lights to be the half-shut eyes of wild beasts, and the spectral figures their victims in the den."

Kirby laughed. "You are fanciful. Come, let us get out of the den. The spectral figures, as you call them, are a little too real for me to fancy a close proximity in the darkness,—unarmed, too."

The others rose, buttoning their overcoats, and lighting cigars.

"Raining, still," said Doctor May, "and hard. Where did we leave the coach, Mitchell?"

---

8. Words Jesus assigns to Abraham in the parable of the beggar Lazarus and the rich man (Luke 16.26): "And beside all this, between us and you there is a great gulf fixed"—the gulf between heaven, where Lazarus has found comfort, and hell, where the rich man is suffering.

"At the other side of the works.—Kirby, what's that?"

Mitchell started back, half-frightened, as, suddenly turning a corner, the white figure of a woman faced him in the darkness,—a woman, white, of giant proportions, crouching on the ground, her arms flung out in some wild gesture of warning.

"Stop! Make that fire burn there!" cried Kirby, stopping short.

The flame burst out, flashing the gaunt figure into bold relief.

Mitchell drew a long breath.

"I thought it was alive," he said, going up curiously.

The others followed.

"Not marble, eh?" asked Kirby, touching it.

One of the lower overseers stopped.

"Korl, Sir."

"Who did it?"

"Can't say. Some of the hands; chipped it out in off-hours."

"Chipped to some purpose, I should say. What a flesh-tint the stuff has! Do you see, Mitchell?"

"I see."

He had stepped aside where the light fell boldest on the figure, looking at it in silence. There was not one line of beauty or grace in it: a nude woman's form, muscular, grown coarse with labor, the powerful limbs instinct with some one poignant longing. One idea: there it was in the tense, rigid muscles, the clutching hands, the wild, eager face, like that of a starving wolf's. Kirby and Doctor May walked around it, critical, curious. Mitchell stood aloof, silent. The figure touched him strangely.

"Not badly done," said Doctor May. "Where did the fellow learn that sweep of the muscles in the arm and hand? Look at them! They are groping,—do you see?—clutching: the peculiar action of a man dying of thirst."

"They have ample facilities for studying anatomy," sneered Kirby, glancing at the half-naked figures.

"Look," continued the Doctor, "at this bony wrist, and the strained sinews of the instep! A working-woman,—the very type of her class."

"God forbid!" muttered Mitchell.

"Why?" demanded May. "What does the fellow intend by the figure? I cannot catch the meaning."

"Ask him," said the other, dryly. "There he stands,"—pointing to Wolfe, who stood with a group of men, leaning on his ash-rake.

The Doctor beckoned him with the affable smile which kind-hearted men put on, when talking to these people.

"Mr. Mitchell has picked you out as the man who did this,—I'm sure I don't know why. But what did you mean by it?"

"She be hungry."

Wolfe's eyes answered Mitchell, not the Doctor.

"Oh-h! But what a mistake you have made, my fine fellow! You have given no sign of starvation to the body. It is strong,—terribly strong. It has the mad, half-despairing gesture of drowning."

Wolfe stammered, glanced appealingly at Mitchell, who saw the soul of the thing, he knew. But the cool, probing eyes were turned on himself now,—mocking, cruel, relentless.

"Not hungry for meat," the furnace-tender said at last.

"What then? Whiskey?" jeered Kirby, with a coarse laugh.

Wolfe was silent a moment, thinking.

"I dunno," he said, with a bewildered look. "It mebbe. Summat to make her live, I think,—like you. Whiskey ull do it, in a way."

The young man laughed again. Mitchell flashed a look of disgust somewhere,—not at Wolfe.

"May," he broke out impatiently, "are you blind? Look at that woman's face! It asks questions of God, and says, 'I have a right to know.' Good God, how hungry it is!"

They looked a moment; then May turned to the mill-owner:—

"Have you many such hands as this? What are you going to do with them? Keep them at puddling iron?"

Kirby shrugged his shoulders. Mitchell's look had irritated him.

"*Ce n'est pas mon affaire.*[9] I have no fancy for nursing infant geniuses. I suppose there are some stray gleams of mind and soul among these wretches. The Lord will take care of his own; or else they can work out their own salvation. I have heard you call our American system a ladder which any man can scale. Do you doubt it? Or perhaps you want to banish all social ladders, and put us all on a flat table-land,—eh, May?"

The Doctor looked vexed, puzzled. Some terrible problem lay hid in this woman's face, and troubled these men. Kirby waited for an answer, and, receiving none, went on, warming with his subject.

"I tell you, there's something wrong that no talk of '*Liberté*' or '*Egalité*'[1] will do away. If I had the making of men, these men who do the lowest part of the world's work should be machines,—nothing more,—hands. It would be kindness. God help them! What are taste, reason, to creatures who must live such lives as that?" He pointed to Deborah, sleeping on the ash-heap. "So many nerves to sting them to pain. What if God had put your brain, with all its agony of touch, into your fingers, and bid you work and strike with that?"

"You think you could govern the world better?" laughed the Doctor.

"I do not think at all."

"That is true philosophy. Drift with the stream, because you cannot dive deep enough to find bottom, eh?"

"Exactly," rejoined Kirby. "I do not think. I wash my hands of all social problems,—slavery, caste, white or black. My duty to my operatives has a narrow limit,—the pay-hour on Saturday night. Outside of that, if they cut korl, or cut each other's throats, (the more popular amusement of the two,) I am not responsible."

The Doctor sighed,—a good honest sigh, from the depths of his stomach.

"God help us! Who is responsible?"

"Not I, I tell you," said Kirby, testily. "What has the man who pays them money to do with their souls' concerns, more than the grocer or butcher who takes it?"

9. It's none of my business (French).
1. "Liberty" and "Equality," slogans of the French Revolution.

"And yet," said Mitchell's cynical voice, "look at her! How hungry she is!"

Kirby tapped his boot with his cane. No one spoke. Only the dumb face of the rough image looking into their faces with the awful question, "What shall we do to be saved?"[2] Only Wolfe's face, with its heavy weight of brain, its weak, uncertain mouth, its desperate eyes, out of which looked the soul of his class,—only Wolfe's face turned towards Kirby's. Mitchell laughed,—a cool, musical laugh.

"Money has spoken!" he said, seating himself lightly on a stone with the air of an amused spectator at a play. "Are you answered?"—turning to Wolfe his clear, magnetic face.

Bright and deep and cold as Arctic air, the soul of the man lay tranquil beneath. He looked at the furnace-tender as he had looked at a rare mosaic in the morning; only the man was the more amusing study of the two.

"Are you answered? Why, May, look at him! 'De profundis clamavi.'[3] Or, to quote in English, 'Hungry and thirsty, his soul faints in him.' And so Money sends back its answer into the depths through you, Kirby! Very clear the answer, too!—I think I remember reading the same words somewhere:— washing your hands in Eau de Cologne, and saying, 'I am innocent of the blood of this man. See ye to it!'"[4]

Kirby flushed angrily.

"You quote Scripture freely."

"Do I not quote correctly? I think I remember another line, which may amend my meaning? 'Inasmuch as ye did it unto one of the least of these, ye did it unto me.' Deist?[5] Bless you, man, I was raised on the milk of the Word. Now, Doctor, the pocket of the world having uttered its voice, what has the heart to say? You are a philanthropist, in a small way,—n'est ce pas?[6] Here, boy, this gentleman can show you how to cut korl better,—or your destiny. Go on, May!"

"I think a mocking devil possesses you to-night," rejoined the Doctor, seriously.

He went to Wolfe and put his hand kindly on his arm. Something of a vague idea possessed the Doctor's brain that much good was to be done here by a friendly word or two: a latent genius to be warmed into life by a waited-for sunbeam. Here it was: he had brought it. So he went on complacently:—

"Do you know, boy, you have it in you to be a great sculptor, a great man?—do you understand?" (talking down to the capacity of his hearer: it is a way people have with children, and men like Wolfe,)—"to live a better,

2. The keeper of the prison in Philippi implored Paul and Silas, after an earthquake had opened the prison doors and released the prisoners' bonds, "Sirs, what must I do to be saved?" (Acts 16.30).
3. The Latin version of Psalm 130.1: "Out of the depths have I cried unto thee, O Lord."
4. The Roman governor Pontius Pilate yielded to the mob's demand that Jesus be crucified but renounced responsibility for it: "When Pilate saw that he could prevail nothing, but that rather a tumult was made, he took water, and washed his hands before the multitude, saying, I am innocent of the blood of this just person: see ye to it" (Matthew 27.24).
5. One who believes in a God who created the world but thereafter leaves it alone. The prior quotation is what Jesus says in Matthew 25.40: "Verily I say unto you, Inasmuch as ye have done it unto one of the least of these my brethren, ye have done it unto me."
6. Aren't you? (French).

stronger life than I, or Mr. Kirby here? A man may make himself anything he chooses. God has given you stronger powers than many men,—me, for instance."

May stopped, heated, glowing with his own magnanimity. And it was magnanimous. The puddler had drunk in every word, looking through the Doctor's flurry, and generous heat, and self-approval, into his will, with those slow, absorbing eyes of his.

"Make yourself what you will. It is your right."

"I know," quietly. "Will you help me?"

Mitchell laughed again. The Doctor turned now, in a passion,—

"You know, Mitchell, I have not the means. You know, if I had, it is in my heart to take this boy and educate him for"—

"The glory of God, and the glory of John May."

May did not speak for a moment; then, controlled, he said,—

"Why should one be raised, when myriads are left?—I have not the money, boy," to Wolfe, shortly.

"Money?" He said it over slowly, as one repeats the guessed answer to a riddle, doubtfully. "That is it? Money?"

"Yes, money,—that is it," said Mitchell, rising, and drawing his furred coat about him. "You've found the cure for all the world's diseases.—Come, May, find your good-humor, and come home. This damp wind chills my very bones. Come and preach your Saint-Simonian doctrines[7] to-morrow to Kirby's hands. Let them have a clear idea of the rights of the soul, and I'll venture next week they'll strike for higher wages. That will be the end of it."

"Will you send the coach-driver to this side of the mills?" asked Kirby, turning to Wolfe.

He spoke kindly: it was his habit to do so. Deborah, seeing the puddler go, crept after him. The three men waited outside. Doctor May walked up and down, chafed. Suddenly he stopped.

"Go back, Mitchell! You say the pocket and the heart of the world speak without meaning to these people. What has its head to say? Taste, culture, refinement? Go!"

Mitchell was leaning against a brick wall. He turned his head indolently, and looked into the mills. There hung about the place a thick, unclean odor. The slightest motion of his hand marked that he perceived it, and his insufferable disgust. That was all. May said nothing, only quickened his angry tramp.

"Besides," added Mitchell, giving a corollary to his answer, "it would be of no use. I am not one of them."

"You do not mean"—said May, facing him.

"Yes, I mean just that. Reform is born of need, not pity. No vital movement of the people's has worked down, for good or evil; fermented, instead, carried up the heaving, cloggy mass. Think back through history, and you will know it. What will this lowest deep—thieves, Magdalens, negroes—do with the light filtered through ponderous Church creeds,

---

7. Doctrines of Henri de Saint-Simon (1760–1825), founder of French socialism.

Baconian theories, Goethe schemes?[8] Some day, out of their bitter need will be thrown up their own light-bringer,—their Jean Paul, their Cromwell,[9] their Messiah."

"Bah!" was the Doctor's inward criticism. However, in practice, he adopted the theory; for, when, night and morning, afterwards, he prayed that power might be given these degraded souls to rise, he glowed at heart, recognizing an accomplished duty.

Wolfe and the woman had stood in the shadow of the works as the coach drove off. The Doctor had held out his hand in a frank, generous way, telling him to "take care of himself, and to remember it was his right to rise." Mitchell had simply touched his hat, as to an equal, with a quiet look of thorough recognition. Kirby had thrown Deborah some money, which she found, and clutched eagerly enough. They were gone now, all of them. The man sat down on the cinder-road, looking up into the murky sky.

"'T be late, Hugh. Wunnot hur come?"

He shook his head doggedly, and the woman crouched out of his sight against the wall. Do you remember rare moments when a sudden light flashed over yourself, your world, God? when you stood on a mountain-peak, seeing your life as it might have been, as it is? one quick instant, when custom lost its force and every-day usage? when your friend, wife, brother, stood in a new light? your soul was bared, and the grave,—a foretaste of the nakedness of the Judgment-Day? So it came before him, his life, that night. The slow tides of pain he had borne gathered themselves up and surged against his soul. His squalid daily life, the brutal coarseness eating into his brain, as the ashes into his skin: before, these things had been a dull aching into his consciousness; to-night, they were reality. He griped the filthy red shirt that clung, stiff with soot, about him, and tore it savagely from his arm. The flesh beneath was muddy with grease and ashes,—and the heart beneath that! And the soul? God knows.

Then flashed before his vivid poetic sense the man who had left him,—the pure face, the delicate, sinewy limbs, in harmony with all he knew of beauty or truth. In his cloudy fancy he had pictured a Something like this. He had found it in this Mitchell, even when he idly scoffed at his pain: a Man all-knowing, all-seeing, crowned by Nature, reigning,—the keen glance of his eye falling like a sceptre on other men. And yet his instinct taught him that he too—He! He looked at himself with sudden loathing, sick, wrung his hands with a cry, and then was silent. With all the phantoms of his heated, ignorant fancy, Wolfe had not been vague in his ambitions. They were practical, slowly built up before him out of his knowledge of what he could do. Through years he had day by day made this hope a real thing to himself,—a clear, projected figure of himself, as he might become.

Able to speak, to know what was best, to raise these men and women working at his side up with him: sometimes he forgot this defined hope in the frantic anguish to escape,—only to escape,—out of the wet, the pain, the ashes,

<hr />

8. Abstract or fanciful theories such as those the English essayist and statesman Francis Bacon (1561–1624) advanced in his *New Atlantis* (1627), or the visionary faith in technological progress revealed by the German writer Johann Wolfgang von Goethe (1749–1832) in *Wilhelm Meister's Travels* (1821–29). "Magdalens": whores; from Mary Magdalene, out of whom Jesus cast seven devils (Mark 16.9).

9. Oliver Cromwell (1599–1658), English military, political, and religious leader. Jean Paul Richter (1763–1825), German novelist, author of *The Titan* (1803).

somewhere, anywhere,—only for one moment of free air on a hillside, to lie down and let his sick soul throb itself out in the sunshine. But to-night he panted for life. The savage strength of his nature was roused; his cry was fierce to God for justice.

"Look at me!" he said to Deborah, with a low, bitter laugh, striking his puny chest savagely. "What am I worth, Deb? Is it my fault that I am no better? My fault? My fault?"

He stopped, stung with a sudden remorse, seeing her hunchback shape writhing with sobs. For Deborah was crying thankless tears, according to the fashion of women.

"God forgi' me, woman! Things go harder wi' you nor me. It's a worse share."

He got up and helped her to rise; and they went doggedly down the muddy street, side by side.

"It's all wrong," he muttered, slowly,—"all wrong! I dunnot understan'. But it'll end some day."

"Come home, Hugh!" she said, coaxingly; for he had stopped, looking around bewildered.

"Home,—and back to the mill!" He went on saying this over to himself, as if he would mutter down every pain in this dull despair.

She followed him through the fog, her blue lips chattering with cold. They reached the cellar at last. Old Wolfe had been drinking since she went out, and had crept nearer the door. The girl Janey slept heavily in the corner. He went up to her, touching softly the worn white arm with his fingers. Some bitterer thought stung him, as he stood there. He wiped the drops from his forehead, and went into the room beyond, livid, trembling. A hope, trifling, perhaps, but very dear, had died just then out of the poor puddler's life, as he looked at the sleeping, innocent girl,—some plan for the future, in which she had borne a part. He gave it up that moment, then and forever. Only a trifle, perhaps, to us: his face grew a shade paler,—that was all. But, somehow, the man's soul, as God and the angels looked down on it, never was the same afterwards.

Deborah followed him into the inner room. She carried a candle, which she placed on the floor, closing the door after her. She had seen the look on his face, as he turned away: her own grew deadly. Yet, as she came up to him, her eyes glowed. He was seated on an old chest, quiet, holding his face in his hands.

"Hugh!" she said, softly.

He did not speak.

"Hugh, did hur hear what the man said,—him with the clear voice? Did hur hear? Money, money,—that it wud do all?"

He pushed her away,—gently, but he was worn out; her rasping tone fretted him.

"Hugh!"

The candle flared a pale yellow light over the cobwebbed brick walls, and the woman standing there. He looked at her. She was young, in deadly earnest; her faded eyes, and wet, ragged figure caught from their frantic eagerness a power akin to beauty.

"Hugh, it is true! Money ull do it! Oh, Hugh, boy, listen till me! He said it true! It is money!"

"I know. Go back! I do not want you here."

"Hugh, it is t' last time. I'll never worrit hur again."

There were tears in her voice now, but she choked them back.

"Hear till me only to-night! If one of t' witch people wud come, them we heard of t' home, and gif hur all hur wants, what then? Say, Hugh!"

"What do you mean?"

"I mean money."

Her whisper shrilled through his brain.

"If one of t' witch dwarfs wud come from t' lane moors to-night, and gif hur money, to go out,—*out*, I say,—out, lad, where t' sun shines, and t' heath grows, and t' ladies walk in silken gownds, and God stays all t' time,—where t' man lives that talked to us to-night,—Hugh knows,—Hugh could walk there like a king!"

He thought the woman mad, tried to check her, but she went on, fierce in her eager haste.

"If *I* were t' witch dwarf, if I had t' money, wud hur thank me? Wud hur take me out o' this place wid hur and Janey? I wud not come into the gran' house hur wud build, to vex hur wid t' hunch,—only at night, when t' shadows were dark, stand far off to see hur."

Mad? Yes! Are many of us mad in this way?

"Poor Deb! poor Deb!" he said, soothingly.

"It is here," she said, suddenly, jerking into his hand a small roll. "I took it! I did it! Me, me!—not hur! I shall be hanged, I shall be burnt in hell, if anybody knows I took it! Out of his pocket, as he leaned against t' bricks. Hur knows?"

She thrust it into his hand, and then, her errand done, began to gather chips together to make a fire, choking down hysteric sobs.

"Has it come to this?"

That was all he said. The Welsh Wolfe blood was honest. The roll was a small green pocket-book containing one or two gold pieces, and a check for an incredible amount, as it seemed to the poor puddler. He laid it down, hiding his face again in his hands.

"Hugh, don't be angry wud me! It's only poor Deb,—hur knows?"

He took the long skinny fingers kindly in his.

"Angry? God help me, no! Let me sleep. I am tired."

He threw himself heavily down on the wooden bench, stunned with pain and weariness. She brought some old rags to cover him.

It was late on Sunday evening before he awoke. I tell God's truth, when I say he had then no thought of keeping this money. Deborah had hid it in his pocket. He found it there. She watched him eagerly, as he took it out.

"I must gif it to him," he said, reading her face.

"Hur knows," she said with a bitter sigh of disappointment. "But it is hur right to keep it."

His right! The word struck him. Doctor May had used the same. He washed himself, and went out to find this man Mitchell. His right! Why did this chance word cling to him so obstinately? Do you hear the fierce devils whisper in his ear, as he went slowly down the darkening street?

The evening came on, slow and calm. He seated himself at the end of an alley leading into one of the larger streets. His brain was clear to-night, keen, intent, mastering. It would not start back, cowardly, from any hellish temptation, but meet it face to face. Therefore the great temptation of his life came to him veiled by no sophistry,[1] but bold, defiant, owning its own vile name, trusting to one bold blow for victory.

He did not deceive himself. Theft! That was it. At first the word sickened him; then he grappled with it. Sitting there on a broken cart-wheel, the fading day, the noisy groups, the church-bells' tolling passed before him like a panorama,[2] while the sharp struggle went on within. This money! He took it out, and looked at it. If he gave it back, what then? He was going to be cool about it.

People going by to church saw only a sickly mill-boy watching them quietly at the alley's mouth. They did not know that he was mad, or they would not have gone by so quietly: mad with hunger; stretching out his hands to the world, that had given so much to them, for leave to live the life God meant him to live. His soul within him was smothering to death; he wanted so much, thought so much, and *knew*—nothing. There was nothing of which he was certain, except the mill and things there. Of God and heaven he had heard so little, that they were to him what fairy-land is to a child: something real, but not here; very far off. His brain, greedy, dwarfed, full of thwarted energy and unused powers, questioned these men and women going by, coldly, bitterly, that night. Was it not his right to live as they,—a pure life, a good, true-hearted life, full of beauty and kind words? He only wanted to know how to use the strength within him. His heart warmed, as he thought of it. He suffered himself to think of it longer. If he took the money?

Then he saw himself as he might be, strong, helpful, kindly. The night crept on, as this one image slowly evolved itself from the crowd of other thoughts and stood triumphant. He looked at it. As he might be! What wonder, if it blinded him to delirium,—the madness that underlies all revolution, all progress, and all fall?

You laugh at the shallow temptation? You see the error underlying its argument so clearly,—that to him a true life was one of full development rather than self-restraint? that he was deaf to the higher tone in a cry of voluntary suffering for truth's sake than in the fullest flow of spontaneous harmony? I do not plead his cause. I only want to show you the mote in my brother's eye: then you can see clearly to take it out.[3]

The money,—there it lay on his knee, a little blotted slip of paper, nothing in itself; used to raise him out of the pit, something straight from God's hand. A thief! Well, what was it to be a thief? He met the question at last, face to face, wiping the clammy drops of sweat from his forehead. God made this money—the fresh air, too—for his children's use. He never made the difference between poor and rich. The Something who looked down on him that moment through the cool gray sky had a kindly face, he knew,— loved his children alike. Oh, he knew that!

1. Subtly deceptive argumentation or reasoning.
2. Continuous scenes painted on a huge canvas and unrolled before audiences; attending a panorama was a popular mid-19th-century recreation.
3. Jesus's words in the Sermon on the Mount (Matthew 7.3–4): "And why beholdest thou the mote that is in thy brother's eye, but considerest not the beam that is in thine own eye? Or how wilt thou say to thy brother, Let me pull out the mote out of thine eye; and behold, a beam is in thine own eye?" (Here a mote is a speck of dust and a beam is the large timber used to support a roof.)

There were times when the soft floods of color in the crimson and purple flames, or the clear depth of amber in the water below the bridge, had somehow given him a glimpse of another world than this,—of an infinite depth of beauty and of quiet somewhere,—somewhere,—a depth of quiet and rest and love. Looking up now, it became strangely real. The sun had sunk quite below the hills, but his last rays struck upward, touching the zenith. The fog had risen, and the town and river were steeped in its thick, gray damp; but overhead, the sun-touched smoke-clouds opened like a cleft ocean,—shifting, rolling seas of crimson mist, waves of billowy silver veined with blood-scarlet, inner depths unfathomable of glancing light. Wolfe's artist-eye grew drunk with color. The gates of that other world! Fading, flashing before him now! What, in that world of Beauty, Content, and Right, were the petty laws, the mine and thine, of mill—owners and mill hands?

A consciousness of power stirred within him. He stood up. A man,—he thought, stretching out his hands,—free to work, to live, to love! Free! His right! He folded the scrap of paper in his hand. As his nervous fingers took it in, limp and blotted, so his soul took in the mean temptation, lapped it in fancied rights, in dreams of improved existences, drifting and endless as the cloud—seas of color. Clutching it, as if the tightness of his hold would strengthen his sense of possession, he went aimlessly down the street. It was his watch at the mill. He need not go, need never go again, thank God!—shaking off the thought with unspeakable loathing.

Shall I go over the history of the hours of that night? how the man wandered from one to another of his old haunts, with a half-consciousness of bidding them farewell,—lanes and alleys and back-yards where the mill-hands lodged,—noting, with a new eagerness, the filth and drunkenness, the pig-pens, the ash-heaps covered with potato-skins, the bloated, pimpled women at the doors,—with a new disgust, a new sense of sudden triumph, and, under all, a new, vague dread, unknown before, smothered down, kept under, but still there? It left him but once during the night, when, for the second time in his life, he entered a church. It was a sombre Gothic pile, where the stained light lost itself in far-retreating arches; built to meet the requirements and sympathies of a far other class than Wolfe's. Yet it touched, moved him uncontrollably. The distances, the shadows, the still, marble figures, the mass of silent kneeling worshippers, the mysterious music, thrilled, lifted his soul with a wonderful pain. Wolfe forgot himself, forgot the new life he was going to live, the mean terror gnawing underneath. The voice of the speaker strengthened the charm; it was clear, feeling, full, strong. An old man, who had lived much, suffered much; whose brain was keenly alive, dominant; whose heart was summer-warm with charity. He taught it to-night. He held up Humanity in its grand total; showed the great world-cancer to his people. Who could show it better? He was a Christian reformer; he had studied the age thoroughly; his outlook at man had been free, world-wide, over all time. His faith stood sublime upon the Rock of Ages; his fiery zeal guided vast schemes by which the Gospel was to be preached to all nations. How did he preach it to-night? In burning, light-laden words he painted Jesus, the incarnate Life, Love, the universal Man: words that became reality in the lives of these people,—that lived again in beautiful words and actions, trifling, but heroic. Sin, as he defined it, was a real foe to them; their trials, temptations, were his. His words passed far over the furnace-tender's grasp, toned to suit another class of culture; they sounded in his ears a very pleasant song in an unknown tongue. He meant to cure this world-cancer with a steady eye that had never glared with hunger, and a hand that neither poverty nor strychnine-whiskey[4] had taught to shake. In this morbid, distorted heart of the Welsh puddler he had failed.

Eighteen centuries ago, the Master of this man tried reform in the streets of a city as crowded and vile as this, and did not fail. His disciple, showing Him to-night to cultured hearers, showing the clearness of the God-power acting through Him, shrank back from one coarse fact; that in birth and habit the man Christ was thrown up from the lowest of the people: his flesh, their flesh; their blood, his blood; tempted like them, to brutalize day by day; to lie, to steal: the actual slime and want of their hourly life, and the wine-press he trod alone.

Yet, is there no meaning in this perpetually covered truth? If the son of the carpenter had stood in the church that night, as he stood with the fishermen and harlots by the sea of Galilee, before His Father and their Father, despised and rejected of men, without a place to lay His head, wounded for their iniquities, bruised for their transgressions, would not that hungry mill-boy at least, in the back seat, have "known the man"? That Jesus did not stand there.[5]

Wolfe rose at last, and turned from the church down the street. He looked up; the night had come on foggy, damp; the golden mists had vanished, and the sky lay dull and ash-colored. He wandered again aimlessly down the street, idly wondering what had become of the cloud-sea of crimson and scarlet. The trial-day of this man's life was over, and he had lost the victory. What followed was mere drifting circumstance,—a quicker walking over the path,—that was all. Do you want to hear the end of it? You wish me to make a tragic story out of it? Why, in the police-reports of the morning paper you can find a dozen such tragedies: hints of shipwrecks unlike any that ever befell on the high seas; hints that here a power was lost to heaven,—that there a soul went down where no tide can ebb or flow. Commonplace enough the hints are,— jocose sometimes, done up in rhyme.

Doctor May, a month after the night I have told you of, was reading to his wife at breakfast from this fourth column of the morning-paper: an unusual thing,—these police-reports not being, in general, choice reading for ladies; but it was only one item he read.

"Oh, my dear! You remember that man I told you of, that we saw at Kirby's mill?—that was arrested for robbing Mitchell? Here he is; just listen:— 'Circuit Court. Judge Day. Hugh Wolfe, operative in Kirby & John's Loudon Mills. Charge, grand larceny. Sentence, nineteen years hard labor in penitentiary.'—Scoundrel! Serves him right! After all our kindness that night! Picking Mitchell's pocket at the very time!"

His wife said something about the ingratitude of that kind of people, and then they began to talk of something else.

---

4. Whiskey full of impurities, sometimes poisonous.
5. This paragraph and the previous one are taken from Davis's 1865 collection, *Atlantic Tales*, where the author inserted this previously censored passage. See Janice Milner Lasseter in the Davis entry in "Selected Bibliographies."

Nineteen years! How easy that was to read! What a simple word for Judge Day to utter! Nineteen years! Half a lifetime!

Hugh Wolfe sat on the window-ledge of his cell, looking out. His ankles were ironed. Not usual in such cases; but he had made two desperate efforts to escape. "Well," as Haley, the jailer, said, "small blame to him! Nineteen years' inprisonment was not a pleasant thing to look forward to." Haley was very good-natured about it, though Wolfe had fought him savagely.

"When he was first caught," the jailer said afterwards, in telling the story, "before the trial, the fellow was cut down at once,—laid there on that pallet like a dead man, with his hands over his eyes. Never saw a man so cut down in my life. Time of the trial, too, came the queerest dodge[6] of any customer I ever had. Would choose no lawyer. Judge gave him one, of course. Gibson it was. He tried to prove the fellow crazy; but it wouldn't go. Thing was plain as daylight: money found on him. 'T was a hard sentence,—all the law allows; but it was for 'xample's sake. These mill-hands are gettin' onbearable. When the sentence was read, he just looked up, and said the money was his by rights, and that all the world had gone wrong. That night, after the trial, a gentleman came to see him here, name of Mitchell,—him as he stole from. Talked to him for an hour. Thought he came for curiosity, like. After he was gone, thought Wolfe was remarkable quiet, and went into his cell. Found him very low; bed all bloody. Doctor said he had been bleeding at the lungs. He was as weak as a cat; yet if ye'll b'lieve me, he tried to get a-past me and get out. I just carried him like a baby, and threw him on the pallet. Three days after, he tried it again: that time reached the wall. Lord help you! he fought like a tiger,—giv' some terrible blows. Fightin' for life, you see; for he can't live long, shut up in the stone crib down yonder. Got a death-cough now. 'T took two of us to bring him down that day; so I just put the irons on his feet. There he sits, in there. Goin' to-morrow, with a batch more of 'em. That woman, hunchback, tried with him,—you remember?—she's only got three years. 'Complice. But *she's* a woman, you know. He's been quiet ever since I put on irons: giv' up, I suppose. Looks white, sick-lookin'. It acts different on 'em, bein' sentenced. Most of 'em gets reckless, devilish—like. Some prays awful, and sings them vile songs of the mills, all in a breath. That woman, now, she's desper't'. Been beggin' to see Hugh, as she calls him, for three days. I'm a-goin' to let her in. She don't go with him. Here she is in this next cell. I'm a-goin' now to let her in."

He let her in. Wolfe did not see her. She crept into a corner of the cell, and stood watching him. He was scratching the iron bars of the window with a piece of tin which he had picked up, with an idle, uncertain, vacant stare, just as a child or idiot would do.

"Tryin' to get out, old boy?" laughed Haley. "Them irons will need a crow-bar beside your tin, before you can open 'em."

Wolfe laughed, too, in a senseless way.

"I think I'll get out," he said.

"I believe his brain's touched," said Haley, when he came out.

---

6. Trick, stratagem.

The puddler scraped away with the tin for half an hour. Still Deborah did not speak. At last she ventured nearer, and touched his arm.

"Blood?" she said, looking at some spots on his coat with a shudder.

He looked up at her. "Why, Deb!" he said, smiling,—such a bright, boyish smile, that it went to poor Deborah's heart directly, and she sobbed and cried out loud.

"Oh, Hugh, lad! Hugh! dunnot look at me, when it wur my fault! To think I brought hur to it! And I loved hur so! Oh lad, I dud!"

The confession, even in this wretch, came with the woman's blush through the sharp cry.

He did not seem to hear her,—scraping away diligently at the bars with the bit of tin.

Was he going mad? She peered closely into his face. Something she saw there made her draw suddenly back,—something which Haley had not seen, that lay beneath the pinched, vacant look it had caught since the trial, or the curious gray shadow that rested on it. That gray shadow,—yes, she knew what that meant. She had often seen it creeping over women's faces for months, who died at last of slow hunger or consumption. That meant death, distant, lingering: but this—Whatever it was the woman saw, or thought she saw, used as she was to crime and misery, seemed to make her sick with a new horror. Forgetting her fear of him, she caught his shoulders, and looked keenly, steadily, into his eyes.

"Hugh!" she cried, in a desperate whisper,—"oh, boy, not that! for God's sake, not *that*!"

The vacant laugh went off his face, and he answered her in a muttered word or two that drove her away. Yet the words were kindly enough. Sitting there on his pallet, she cried silently a hopeless sort of tears, but did not speak again. The man looked up furtively at her now and then. Whatever his own trouble was, her distress vexed him with a momentary sting.

It was market-day. The narrow window of the jail looked down directly on the carts and wagons drawn up in a long line, where they had unloaded. He could see, too, and hear distinctly the clink of money as it changed hands, the busy crowd of whites and blacks shoving, pushing one another, and the chaffering and swearing at the stalls. Somehow, the sound, more than anything else had done, wakened him up,—made the whole real to him. He was done with the world and the business of it. He let the tin fall, and looked out, pressing his face close to the rusty bars. How they crowded and pushed! And he,—he should never walk that pavement again! There came Neff Sanders, one of the feeders at the mill, with a basket on his arm. Sure enough, Neff was married the other week. He whistled, hoping he would look up; but he did not. He wondered if Neff remembered he was there,—if any of the boys thought of him up there, and thought that he never was to go down that old cinder-road again. Never again! He had not quite understood it before; but now he did. Not for days or years, but never!—that was it.

How clear the light fell on that stall in front of the market! and how like a picture it was, the dark-green heaps of corn, and the crimson beets, and golden melons! There was another with game: how the light flickered on that pheasant's breast, with the purplish blood dripping over the brown feathers! He could see the red shining of the drops, it was so near. In one minute he could be down there. It was just a step. So easy, as it seemed, so natural to go! Yet it could never be—not in all the thousands of years to come—that he should put his foot on that street again! He thought of himself with a sorrowful pity, as of some one else. There was a dog down in the market, walking after his master with such a stately, grave look!—only a dog, yet he could go backwards and forwards just as he pleased: he had good luck! Why, the very vilest cur, yelping there in the gutter, had not lived his life, had been free to act out whatever thought God had put into his brain; while he—No, he would not think of that! He tried to put the thought away, and to listen to a dispute between a countryman and a woman about some meat; but it would come back. He, what had he done to bear this?

Then came the sudden picture of what might have been, and now. He knew what it was to be in the penitentiary,—how it went with men there. He knew how in these long years he should slowly die, but not until soul and body had become corrupt and rotten,—how, when he came out, if he lived to come, even the lowest of the mill-hands would jeer him,—how his hands would be weak, and his brain senseless and stupid. He believed he was almost that now. He put his hand to his head, with a puzzled, weary look. It ached, his head, with thinking. He tried to quiet himself. It was only right, perhaps; he had done wrong. But was there right or wrong for such as he? What was right? And who had ever taught him? He thrust the whole matter away. A dark, cold quiet crept through his brain. It was all wrong; but let it be! It was nothing to him more than the others. Let it be!

The door grated, as Haley opened it.

"Come, my woman! Must lock up for t' night. Come, stir yerself!"

She went up and took Hugh's hand.

"Good—night, Deb," he said, carelessly.

She had not hoped he would say more; but the tired pain on her mouth just then was bitterer than death. She took his passive hand and kissed it.

"Hur'll never see Deb again!" she ventured, her lips growing colder and more bloodless.

What did she say that for? Did he not know it? Yet he would not be impatient with poor old Deb. She had trouble of her own, as well as he.

"No, never again," he said, trying to be cheerful.

She stood just a moment, looking at him. Do you laugh at her, standing there, with her hunchback, her rags, her bleared, withered face, and the great despised love tugging at her heart?

"Come, you!" called Haley, impatiently.

She did not move.

"Hugh!" she whispered.

It was to be her last word. What was it?

"Hugh, boy, not THAT!"

He did not answer. She wrung her hands, trying to be silent, looking in his face in an agony of entreaty. He smiled again, kindly.

"It is best, Deb. I cannot bear to be hurted any more."

"Hur knows," she said, humbly.

"Tell my father good-bye; and—and kiss little Janey."

She nodded, saying nothing, looked in his face again, and went out of the door. As she went, she staggered.

"Drinkin' to-day?" broke out Haley, pushing her before him. "Where the Devil did you get it? Here, in with ye!" and he shoved her into her cell, next to Wolfe's, and shut the door.

Along the wall of her cell there was a crack low down by the floor, through which she could see the light from Wolfe's. She had discovered it days before. She hurried in now, and, kneeling down by it, listened, hoping to hear some sound. Nothing but the rasping of the tin on the bars. He was at his old amusement again. Something in the noise jarred on her ear, for she shivered as she heard it. Hugh rasped away at the bars. A dull old bit of tin, not fit to cut korl with.

He looked out of the window again. People were leaving the market now. A tall mulatto girl, following her mistress, her basket on her head, crossed the street just below, and looked up. She was laughing; but, when she caught sight of the haggard face peering out through the bars, suddenly grew grave, and hurried by. A free, firm step, a clear-cut olive face, with a scarlet turban tied on one side, dark, shining eyes, and on the head the basket poised, filled with fruit and flowers, under which the scarlet turban and bright eyes looked out half-shadowed. The picture caught his eye. It was good to see a face like that. He would try to-morrow, and cut one like it. *To-morrow*! He threw down the tin, trembling, and covered his face with his hands. When he looked up again, the daylight was gone.

Deborah, crouching near by on the other side of the wall, heard no noise. He sat on the side of the low pallet, thinking. Whatever was the mystery which the woman had seen on his face, it came out now slowly, in the dark there, and became fixed,—a something never seen on his face before. The evening was darkening fast. The market had been over for an hour; the rumbling of the carts over the pavement grew more infrequent: he listened to each, as it passed, because he thought it was to be for the last time. For the same reason, it was, I suppose, that he strained his eyes to catch a glimpse of each passer-by, wondering who they were, what kind of homes they were going to, if they had children,—listening eagerly to every chance word in the street, as if—(God be merciful to the man! what strange fancy was this?)—as if he never should hear human voices again.

It was quite dark at last. The street was a lonely one. The last passenger, he thought, was gone. No,—there was a quick step: Joe Hill, lighting the lamps. Joe was a good old chap; never passed a fellow without some joke or other. He remembered once seeing the place where he lived with his wife. "Granny Hill" the boys called her. Bedridden she was; but so kind as Joe was to her! kept the room so clean!—and the old woman, when he was there, was laughing at "some of t' lad's foolishness." The step was far down the street; but he could see him place the ladder, run up, and light the gas. A longing seized him to be spoken to once more.

"Joe!" he called, out of the grating. "Good-bye, Joe!"

The old man stopped a moment, listening uncertainly; then hurried on. The prisoner thrust his hand out of the window, and called again, louder; but Joe was too far down the street. It was a little thing; but it hurt him,—this disappointment.

"Good-bye, Joe!" he called, sorrowfully enough.

"Be quiet!" said one of the jailers, passing the door, striking on it with his club.

Oh, that was the last, was it?

There was an inexpressible bitterness on his face, as he lay down on the bed, taking the bit of tin, which he had rasped to a tolerable degree of sharpness, in his hand,—to play with, it may be. He bared his arms, looking intently at their corded veins and sinews. Deborah, listening in the next cell, heard a slight clicking sound, often repeated. She shut her lips tightly, that she might not scream; the cold drops of sweat broke over her, in her dumb agony.

"Hur knows best," she muttered at last, fiercely clutching the boards where she lay.

If she could have seen Wolfe, there was nothing about him to frighten her. He lay quite still, his arms outstretched, looking at the pearly stream of moonlight coming into the window. I think in that one hour that came then he lived back over all the years that had gone before. I think that all the low, vile life, all his wrongs, all his starved hopes, came then, and stung him with a farewell poison that made him sick unto death. He made neither moan nor cry, only turned his worn face now and then to the pure light, that seemed so far off, as one that said, "How long, O Lord? how long?"

The hour was over at last. The moon, passing over her nightly path, slowly came nearer, and threw the light across his bed on his feet. He watched it steadily, as it crept up, inch by inch, slowly. It seemed to him to carry with it a great silence. He had been so hot and tired there always in the mills! The years had been so fierce and cruel! There was coming now quiet and coolness and sleep. His tense limbs relaxed, and settled in a calm languor. The blood ran fainter and slow from his heart. He did not think now with a savage anger of what might be and was not; he was conscious only of deep stillness creeping over him. At first he saw a sea of faces: the mill-men,—women he had known, drunken and bloated,—Janey's timid and pitiful—poor old Debs: then they floated together like a mist, and faded away, leaving only the clear, pearly moonlight.

Whether, as the pure light crept up the stretched-out figure, it brought with it calm and peace, who shall say? His dumb soul was alone with God in judgment. A Voice may have spoken for it from far-off Calvary, "Father, forgive them, for they know not what they do!"[7] Who dare say? Fainter and fainter the heart rose and fell, slower and slower the moon floated from behind a cloud, until, when at last its full tide of white splendor swept over the cell, it seemed to wrap and fold into a deeper stillness the dead figure that never should move again. Silence deeper than the Night! Nothing that moved, save the black, nauseous stream of blood dripping slowly from the pallet to the floor!

There was outcry and crowd enough in the cell the next day. The coroner and his jury, the local editors, Kirby himself, and boys with their hands thrust knowingly into their pockets and heads on one side, jammed into the corners. Coming and going all day. Only one woman. She came late, and outstayed them all. A Quaker, or Friend, as they call themselves. I think this woman was known by that name in heaven. A homely body, coarsely dressed in gray and white. Deborah (for Haley had let her in) took notice of her. She watched them all—sitting on the end of the pallet, holding his head in her

---

7. Luke 23.34: "Father, forgive them: for they know not what they do" (Jesus's words on the cross). Calvary was the site of the Crucifixion.

arms—with the ferocity of a watch-dog, if any of them touched the body. There was no meekness, no sorrow, in her face; the stuff out of which murderers are made, instead. All the time Haley and the woman were laying straight the limbs and cleaning the cell, Deborah sat still, keenly watching the Quaker's face. Of all the crowd there that day, this woman alone had not spoken to her,—only once or twice had put some cordial to her lips. After they all were gone, the woman, in the same still, gentle way, brought a vase of wood-leaves and berries, and placed it by the pallet, then opened the narrow window. The fresh air blew in, and swept the woody fragrance over the dead face. Deborah looked up with a quick wonder.

"Did hur know my boy wud like it? Did hur know Hugh?"

"I know Hugh now."

The white fingers passed in a slow, pitiful way over the dead, worn face. There was a heavy shadow in the quiet eyes.

"Did hur know where they'll bury Hugh?" said Deborah in a shrill tone, catching her arm.

This had been the question hanging on her lips all day.

"In t' town-yard? Under t' mud and ash? T' lad 'll smother, woman! He wur born in t' lane moor, where t' air is frick[8] and strong. Take hur out, for God's sake, take hur out where t' air blows!"

The Quaker hesitated, but only for a moment. She put her strong arm around Deborah and led her to the window.

"Thee sees the hills, friend, over the river? Thee sees how the light lies warm there, and the winds of God blow all the day? I live there,—where the blue smoke is, by the trees. Look at me." She turned Deborah's face to her own, clear and earnest. "Thee will believe me? I will take Hugh and bury him there to-morrow."

Deborah did not doubt her. As the evening wore on, she leaned against the iron bars, looking at the hills that rose far off, through the thick sodden clouds, like a bright, unattainable calm. As she looked, a shadow of their solemn repose fell on her face; its fierce discontent faded into a pitiful, humble quiet. Slow, solemn tears gathered in her eyes: the poor weak eyes turned so hopelessly to the place where Hugh was to rest, the grave heights looking higher and brighter and more solemn than ever before. The Quaker watched her keenly. She came to her at last, and touched her arm.

"When thee comes back," she said, in a low, sorrowful tone, like one who speaks from a strong heart deeply moved with remorse or pity, "thee shall begin thy life again,—there on the hills. I came too late; but not for thee,—by God's help, it may be."

Not too late. Three years after, the Quaker began her work. I end my story here. At evening-time it was light. There is no need to tire you with the long years of sunshine, and fresh air, and slow, patient Christ-love, needed to make healthy and hopeful this impure body and soul. There is a homely pine house, on one of these hills, whose windows overlook broad, wooded slopes and clover-crimsoned meadows,—niched into the very place where the light is warmest, the air freest. It is the Friends'[9] meeting-house. Once a week they sit there, in their grave, earnest way, waiting for the Spirit of Love to

---

8. Fresh.   9. Quakers.

speak, opening their simple hearts to receive His words. There is a woman, old, deformed, who takes a humble place among them: waiting like them: in her gray dress, her worn face, pure and meek, turned now and then to the sky. A woman much loved by these silent, restful people; more silent than they, more humble, more loving. Waiting: with her eyes turned to hills higher and purer than these on which she lives,—dim and far off now, but to be reached some day. There may be in her heart some latent hope to meet there the love denied her here,—that she shall find him whom she lost, and that then she will not be all-unworthy. Who blames her? Something is lost in the passage of every soul from one eternity to the other,—something pure and beautiful, which might have been and was not: a hope, a talent, a love, over which the soul mourns, like Esau deprived of his birthright.[1] What blame to the meek Quaker, if she took her lost hope to make the hills of heaven more fair?

Nothing remains to tell that the poor Welsh puddler once lived, but this figure of the mill-woman cut in korl. I have it here in a corner of my library. I keep it hid behind a curtain,—it is such a rough, ungainly thing. Yet there are about it touches, grand sweeps of outline, that show a master's hand. Sometimes,—to-night, for instance,—the curtain is accidentally drawn back, and I see a bare arm stretched out imploringly in the darkness, and an eager, wolfish face watching mine: a wan, woful face, through which the spirit of the dead korl-cutter looks out, with its thwarted life, its mighty hunger, its unfinished work. Its pale, vague lips seem to tremble with a terrible question. "Is this the End?" they say,—"nothing beyond?—no more?" Why, you tell me you have seen that look in the eyes of dumb brutes,—horses dying under the lash. I know.

The deep of the night is passing while I write. The gas-light wakens from the shadows here and there the objects which lie scattered through the room: only faintly, though; for they belong to the open sunlight. As I glance at them, they each recall some task or pleasure of the coming day. A half-moulded child's head; Aphrodite;[2] a bough of forest-leaves; music; work; homely fragments, in which lie the secrets of all eternal truth and beauty. Prophetic all! Only this dumb, woful face seems to belong to and end with the night. I turn to look at it. Has the power of its desperate need commanded the darkness away? While the room is yet steeped in heavy shadow, a cool, gray light suddenly touches its head like a blessing hand, and its groping arm points through the broken cloud to the far East, where, in the flickering, nebulous crimson, God has set the promise of the Dawn.

1861, 1865

---

1. Genesis 25 and 27 tell the story of Jacob's depriving his elder twin brother, Esau, of his birthright.
2. Venus, the goddess of love.

LOUISA MAY ALCOTT
1832–1888

The author of the perennially popular novel *Little Women* (1868–69), Louisa May Alcott was the second of four daughters of the philosopher-teacher Amos Bronson Alcott and Abigail May Alcott. Born in Germantown, near Philadelphia, on November 29, 1832, she grew up in Boston and Concord and lived among the leading Massachusetts cultural figures of the time. Margaret Fuller taught in her father's school in Boston (which folded in 1839 after controversies over sex education and admitting black children); Ralph Waldo Emerson introduced her to Goethe's writings and encouraged her to borrow books from his library; Thoreau gave her informal lessons about the natural world, and later hosted her and her father while he was living at Walden Pond; Hawthorne for several years lived nearby. Her maternal uncle, Samuel May, was a leading Boston abolitionist, and she came to know William Lloyd Garrison, Theodore Parker, and other prominent abolitionists, joining with them in 1854 when they attempted to prevent the return of the fugitive slave Anthony Burns to Virginia. In "Recollections of My Childhood" (1888), Alcott gloried in having shared in the struggle "which put an end to a great wrong."

During Louisa May Alcott's youth, her father was well known and controversial, regarded by some as a great philosopher but by others as a half-crazed mystic, particularly after the first installment of his abstruse "Orphic Sayings" appeared in the 1840 *Dial*, the journal published by the informal group known as "Transcendentalists." As an educator, he observed his first two daughters closely and took hundreds of pages of notes on their behavior. When Louisa was two years old, he gave her an apple with instructions not to eat it; she ate the apple, while her older sister, to whom Bronson had given the same instructions, dutifully left it alone, an outcome that he interpreted as a sign of his second daughter's overly willful nature. Over time, Louisa, while remaining deeply attached to her father, increasingly resented his efforts to stifle her independence, and much of her writing would deal with young women struggling to express and value their individuality. Her mother more warmly encouraged her reading and writing. With her sisters, she wrote and staged plays for family entertainment. She kept a regular journal, wrote stories from a very early age, and was enamored of Sir Walter Scott's historical novels, John Bunyan's *Pilgrim's Progress*, and Charles Dickens's novels (which she read as they were being serialized), as well as works by Goethe, Hawthorne, the Brontës, and many other writers.

In 1843, when Louisa May Alcott was ten, her father founded Fruitlands, a vegetarian reform community near Concord that banned money and regarded participants as members of one large family. He moved his family there, but after several months of hardship in which, according to his wife's view, the men did nothing but think and the women did all the hard physical work, Abigail threatened to leave with her children, even if that meant severing her ties with her husband. He reluctantly gave up on the project early in 1844 and moved the family back to Concord. (Alcott would later satirize the community in her short story "Transcendental Wild Oats" [1873].) Because Bronson had invested all of his money in Fruitlands, for years afterward the Alcotts lived in poverty. After several years in Concord they moved to Boston, where Abigail tried to support the family by becoming a social worker—one of the earliest practitioners of this profession—and then by running an employment agency, while Bronson attempted to make money by holding "conversations" (symposia in which participants paid a small fee) on various philosophical topics. The family moved constantly in attempts to find rental situations they could afford. Writing about these years of economic struggle in her 1888 "Recollections," Alcott maintained that as a sixteen-year-old she made the following declaration: "I will do something by-and-by. Don't care what, teach, sew, act, write, anything to help the family; I'll be rich and famous and happy before I die, see if I won't."

Alcott did teach and sew; she also worked as a governess and took on other short-term jobs. But mainly she attempted to make money through her writing. Her first story, "The Rival Painters," for which she was paid the modest sum of five dollars, appeared in an 1852 issue of a weekly newspaper called the *Olive Branch*, while a collection of children's stories, *Flower Fables*, originally written for Emerson's daughter Ellen during the 1840s, was published in 1854, earning a total of thirty-five dollars. Although it would be some years before Alcott learned to demand proper payment for her work, she was gaining a reputation with her early publications. In 1860 her story "A Modern Cinderella" appeared in the *Atlantic Monthly*, the most prestigious literary magazine of the time.

Shortly before the Civil War, Alcott's younger sister Lizzie died of the aftereffects of scarlet fever, which Louisa managed to fight off. Her beloved neighbor Henry David Thoreau died in 1862. She was struggling with a novel, *Moods*, which she would eventually publish in 1864, but at this time her chief ambition was to contribute to the Civil War effort. Shortly after writing in her journal, "I long to be a man; but as I can't fight, I will content myself with working for those who can," she volunteered for the nursing corps. Beginning in December 1862, she worked at the unsanitary and poorly run Union Hotel Hospital in Washington, D.C., overseeing amputations and comforting the many men who were dying. The work took its toll, and by late January of 1863 she was suffering from typhoid pneumonia and had to give up nursing. Although she survived the disease, she was badly damaged by the poisonous treatment—huge doses of mercury, at that time the normal therapy for many diseases—which left her with permanent fatigue and neuralgia over the remaining twenty-five years of her life.

Despite her health problems, Alcott began to write again after she recovered from pneumonia. In 1863 she published sketches about her hospital experience in the *Boston Commonwealth*, working with the persona of a feisty, ironic nurse named Tribulation Periwinkle, and the pieces were published as *Hospital Sketches* later in the year. She also published several short stories about the Civil War, including two, "M.L." and "My Contraband," about interracial sexuality. ("M.L." points to the possibility of love across the color line; "My Contraband" offers suggestions about such a possibility, while underscoring the hard truths of the sexual violation of black women on slave plantations.) Eager for money and desirous of experimenting with fiction that would allow her to write unconventionally about such topics as incest, suicide, drug addiction, sexual passion, and the supernatural, she began publishing melodramatic sensation stories under the name of A. M. Barnard, earning $100 (around $1200 in today's currency) for each story. Those stories, discovered by the critic Madeleine Stern during the 1980s and 1990s, helped transform critics' understanding of Alcott, who for over a century was known mainly as the author of *Little Women*.

In 1867 Alcott was offered the editorship of a children's magazine, *Mercury Museum*, and at the same time she was solicited by the editor Thomas Niles of Roberts Brothers to write a novel for girls. She was not initially enthusiastic about the novel, and Niles found the first twelve chapters dull. But his nieces loved what they read. Accordingly, Niles urged Alcott to persevere, and she wrote four hundred manuscript pages during June and July of 1868. Part 1 of *Little Women*, appearing later in the year, quickly sold out its first printing; Part II appeared in 1869, and the novel has never gone out of print. A semiautobiographical story of her girlhood and young womanhood, the novel, which sanitized some of the misery of the Alcotts' poverty, brought together the four differently imperfect but sympathetic March sisters and their adored mother in a family portrait that focused on the girls' struggles and triumphs as three of the four (one dies tragically) grow into young womanhood. More adventurously, the novel explored questions of gender and power, focusing on Jo's dissatisfaction with the constraints of girlhood and her efforts to become a successful writer. There is an appealing neighbor, Laurie, who seems a likely candidate to marry Jo, but she declines his offer. By the end of the novel the successful author Jo chooses to marry the more fatherly Professor Bhaer, temporarily giving up writing to have children and assist her husband in running a school for boys. In Alcott's later novel *Jo's Boys* (1886), however, Jo resumes writing and helps to make the school coeducational.

The novel's success allowed Alcott to pay off her family's debts and support her mother and father. She published *An Old-Fashioned Girl* in 1870, *Little Men* in 1872, and *Work* (one of the finest nineteenth-century novels about women and labor) in 1873. As the physical act of writing became increasingly painful, she tried learning to write with her left hand. In 1874 she confided to her journal: "When I had youth I had no money; now that I have the money I have no time; and when I get the time, if I ever do, I shall have no health to enjoy life." Still, she continued to push on with her writing, returning to the mode of sensation fiction with the novel *A Modern Mephistopheles*, published in 1877 in Roberts Brothers' "No Name Series" (novels published anonymously by famous writers). By the late 1870s Alcott had become almost too ill to write, though she labored on with *Jo's Boys* and several other projects. Her beloved mother, Abigail, died in 1877; two years later, her youngest sister, May (the prototype for Amy in *Little Women*), died in childbirth in Paris, and Louisa adopted the child, Louisa May Nierker, in 1880. Three years later, her father suffered a paralytic stroke, and for a while Alcott was caring for her father and the young Louisa. In 1886, suffering from pain and exhaustion, she was admitted to Dr. Rhoda Lawrence's nursing home in West Roxbury, Massachusetts. She died on March 6, 1888, two days after the death of her father.

In recent decades much of Alcott's writing has been brought back into print, allowing readers to appreciate the wide range of her children's fiction, her realistic novels and short stories, and her slyly comic melodramas and sensation fiction. Jo March's goals were not only to be independent and to help those she loved, but also to produce a literary work of enduring merit that "went to the hearts of those who read it." Alcott achieved that goal as the author of *Little Women* and many other works published during her approximately forty-year career as a writer.

FROM LITTLE WOMEN[1]

From Part Second

Chapter IV

LITERARY LESSONS[2]

Fortune suddenly smiled upon Jo, and dropped a good-luck penny in her path. Not a golden penny, exactly, but I doubt if half a million would have given more real happiness than did the little sum that came to her in this wise.

1. Alcott published *Little Women; or, Meg, Jo, Beth and Amy* in 1868, and a sequel, Part Second, in 1869; the selection here is taken from the 1869 printing. Subsequent printings linked the two parts as one complete novel.
2. At this point in the novel, Jo March, the impetuous and literary second daughter, has decided to devote herself to her writing, as Alcott did, in large part to make money for her impoverished family. In the first part of the novel, Jo at age sixteen had placed tales and sketches at a newspaper, the *Spread Eagle*, but she's initially paid nothing for her work and then earns a dollar a column. Now in her early twenties, she lives with her three sisters, father, and mother (affectionately known as "Marmee") in a town resembling Concord, Massachusetts.

Every few weeks she would shut herself up in her room, put on her scribbling suit, and "fall into a vortex," as she expressed it, writing away at her novel with all her heart and soul, for till that was finished she could find no peace. Her "scribbling suit" consisted of a black pinafore on which she could wipe her pen at will, and a cap of the same material, adorned with a cheerful red bow, into which she bundled her hair when the decks were cleared for action. This cap was a beacon to the inquiring eyes of her family, who, during these periods, kept their distance, merely popping in their heads semi-occasionally, to ask, with interest, "Does genius burn, Jo?" They did not always venture even to ask this question, but took an observation of the cap, and judged accordingly. If this expressive article of dress was drawn low upon the forehead, it was a sign that hard work was going on; in exciting moments it was pushed rakishly askew, and when despair seized the author it was plucked wholly off, and cast upon the floor. At such times the intruder silently withdrew; and not until the red bow was seen gaily erect upon the gifted brow, did any one dare address Jo.

She did not think herself a genius by any means; but when the writing fit came on, she gave herself up to it with entire abandon, and led a blissful life, unconscious of want, care, or bad weather, while she sat safe and happy in an imaginary world, full of friends almost as real and dear to her as any in the flesh. Sleep forsook her eyes, meals stood untasted, day and night were all too short to enjoy the happiness which blessed her only at such times, and made these hours worth living, even if they bore no other fruit. The divine afflatus[3] usually lasted a week or two, and then she emerged from her "vortex" hungry, sleepy, cross, or despondent.

She was just recovering from one of these attacks when she was prevailed upon to escort Miss Crocker[4] to a lecture, and in return for her virtue was rewarded with a new idea. It was a People's Course,[5]—the lecture on the Pyramids,—and Jo rather wondered at the choice of such a subject for such an audience, but took it for granted that some great social evil would be remedied, or some great want supplied by unfolding the glories of the Pharaohs, to an audience whose thoughts were busy with the price of coal and flour, and whose lives were spent in trying to solve harder riddles than that of the Sphinx.[6]

They were early; and while Miss Crocker set the heel of her stocking, Jo amused herself by examining the faces of the people who occupied the seat with them. On her left were two matrons with massive foreheads, and bonnets to match, discussing Woman's Rights and making tatting.[7] Beyond sat a pair of humble lovers artlessly holding each other by the hand, a somber spinster eating peppermints out of a paper bag, and an old gentleman taking his preparatory nap behind a yellow bandanna. On her right, her only neighbor was a studious-looking lad absorbed in a newspaper.

It was a pictorial sheet, and Jo examined the work of art nearest her, idly wondering what unfortuitous concatenation of circumstances needed the melodramatic illustration of an Indian in full war costume, tumbling over a

---

3. Inspiration.
4. A neighbor and minor character.
5. A series of free public lectures.
6. In Greek mythology, a winged monster with a lion's body and head of a woman, who challenged those entering the city of Thebes with a riddle; she

killed those who answered incorrectly. When Oedipus answered correctly, the Sphinx was so distraught that she killed herself, much to the delight of the Theban people, who named Oedipus king.
7. Needlework with handmade lace.

precipice with a wolf at his throat, while two infuriated young gentlemen, with unnaturally small feet and big eyes, were stabbing each other close by, and a dishevelled female was flying away in the background, with her mouth wide open. Pausing to turn a page, the lad saw her looking, and, with boyish good-nature, offered half his paper, saying, bluntly, "Want to read it? That's a first-rate story."

Jo accepted it with a smile, for she had never outgrown her liking for lads, and soon found herself involved in the usual labyrinth of love, mystery, and murder, for the story belonged to that class of light literature in which the passions have a holiday, and when the author's invention fails, a grand catastrophe clears the stage of one-half the *dramatis personæ*,[8] leaving the other half to exult over their downfall.

"Prime, isn't it?" asked the boy, as her eye went down the last paragraph of her portion.

"I guess you and I could do most as well as that if we tried," returned Jo, amused at his admiration of the trash.

"I should think I was a pretty lucky chap if I could. She makes a good living out of such stories, they say;" and he pointed to the name of Mrs. S. L. A. N. G. Northbury,[9] under the title of the tale.

"Do you know her?" asked Jo, with sudden interest.

"No; but I read all her pieces, and I know a fellow that works in the office where this paper is printed."

"Do you say she makes a good living out of stories like this?" and Jo looked more respectfully at the agitated group and thickly-sprinkled exclamation points that adorned the page.

"Guess she does! she knows just what folks like, and gets paid well for writing it."

Here the lecture began, but Jo heard very little of it, for while Professor Sands was prosing away about Belzoni, Cheops, scarabei, and hieroglyphics,[1] she was covertly taking down the address of the paper, and boldly resolving to try for the hundred dollar prize offered in its columns for a sensational story. By the time the lecture ended, and the audience awoke, she had built up a splendid fortune for herself (not the first founded upon paper), and was already deep in the concoction of her story, being unable to decide whether the duel should come before the elopement or after the murder.

She said nothing of her plan at home, but fell to work next day, much to the disquiet of her mother, who always looked a little anxious when "genius took to burning." Jo had never tried this style before, contenting herself with very mild romances for the "Spread Eagle." Her theatrical experience and miscellaneous reading were of service now, for they gave her some idea of dramatic effect, and supplied plot, language, and costumes. Her story was as full of desperation and despair as her limited acquaintance with those uncomfortable emotions enabled her to make it, and, having located it in Lisbon, she wound up with an earthquake, as a striking and appropriate

8. Characters in a dramatic work (Latin).
9. A parodic reworking of the name of the writer Mrs. E. D. E. N. Southworth (1819–1899), author of *The Hidden Hand* (1859) and other popular novels.
1. The Venetian explorer Giovanni Battista

Belzoni (1778–1823) was best known for his study of Egyptology. He explored Cheops, a pyramid built between 2589 and 2566 B.C.E., and studied the Egyptian writing system of hieroglyphics and the use of beetle images (scarabei) for seals and decorations.

denouement.[2] The manuscript was privately dispatched, accompanied by a note, modestly saying that if the tale didn't get the prize, which the writer hardly dared expect, she would be very glad to receive any sum it might be considered worth.

Six weeks is a long time to wait, and a still longer time for a girl to keep a secret; but Jo did both, and was just beginning to give up all hope of ever seeing her manuscript again, when a letter arrived which almost took her breath away; for, on opening it, a check for a hundred dollars fell into her lap.[3] For a minute she stared at it as if it had been a snake, then she read her letter, and began to cry. If the amiable gentleman who wrote that kindly note could have known what intense happiness he was giving a fellow-creature, I think he would devote his leisure hours, if he has any, to that amusement; for Jo valued the letter more than the money, because it was encouraging; and after years of effort it was *so* pleasant to find that she had learned to do *something*, though it was only to write a sensation story.

A prouder young woman was seldom seen than she, when, having composed herself, she electrified the family by appearing before them with the letter in one hand, the check in the other, announcing that she had won the prize! Of course there was a great jubilee, and when the story came every one read and praised it; though after her father had told her that the language was good, the romance fresh and hearty, and the tragedy quite thrilling, he shook his head, and said in his unworldly way,—

"You can do better than this, Jo. Aim at the highest, and never mind the money."

"*I* think the money is the best part of it. What *will* you do with such a fortune?" asked Amy, regarding the magic slip of paper with a reverential eye.

"Send Beth and mother to the sea-side for a month or two," answered Jo promptly.

"Oh, how splendid! No, I can't do it, dear, it would be so selfish," cried Beth, who had clapped her thin hands, and taken a long breath, as if pining for fresh ocean breezes; then stopped herself, and motioned away the check which her sister waved before her.

"Ah, but you shall go, I've set my heart on it; that's what I tried for, and that's why I succeeded. I never get on when I think of myself alone, so it will help me to work for you, don't you see. Besides, Marmee needs the change, and she won't leave you, so you *must* go. Won't it be fun to see you come home plump and rosy again? Hurrah for Dr. Jo, who always cures her patients!"

To the sea-side they went, after much discussion; and though Beth didn't come home as plump and rosy as could be desired, she was much better, while Mrs. March declared she felt ten years younger; so Jo was satisfied with the investment of her prize-money, and fell to work with a cheery spirit, bent on earning more of those delightful checks. She did earn several that year, and began to feel herself a power in the house; for by the magic of a pen, her "rubbish" turned into comforts for them all. "The Duke's Daughter"

2. Final outcome (French). In 1755, an earth-quake had devastated Lisbon, the capital of Portugal, killing over sixty thousand people.

3. In 1863 Alcott won $100 for her own sensation story, "Pauline's Passion and Punishment," which was published in *Frank Leslie's Illustrated Newspaper*. Over the next four years, Alcott published a number of such stories.

"Jo in a vortex." From the 1869 first printing of
Little Women, Part Second.

paid the butcher's bill, "A Phantom Hand" put down a new carpet, and "The
Curse of the Coventrys" proved the blessing of the Marches in the way of
groceries and gowns.

Wealth is certainly a most desirable thing, but poverty has its sunny side,
and one of the sweet uses of adversity, is the genuine satisfaction which
comes from hearty work of head or hand; and to the inspiration of necessity,
we owe half the wise, beautiful, and useful blessings of the world. Jo enjoyed
a taste of this satisfaction, and ceased to envy richer girls, taking great comfort in the knowledge that she could supply her own wants, and need ask no
one for a penny.

Little notice was taken of her stories, but they found a market; and, encouraged by this fact, she resolved to make a bold stroke for fame and fortune.
Having copied her novel for the fourth time, read it to all her confidential
friends, and submitted it with fear and trembling to three publishers, she at
last disposed of it, on condition that she would cut it down one-third, and
omit all the parts which she particularly admired.

"Now I must either bundle it back into my tin-kitchen, to mould, pay for
printing it myself, or chop it up to suit purchasers, and get what I can for it.
Fame is a very good thing to have in the house, but cash is more convenient;
so I wish to take the sense of the meeting on this important subject," said Jo,
calling a family council.

"Don't spoil your book, my girl, for there is more in it than you know, and the idea is well worked out. Let it wait and ripen," was her father's advice; and he practiced as he preached, having waited patiently thirty years for fruit of his own to ripen, and being in no haste to gather it, even now, when it was sweet and mellow.

"It seems to me that Jo will profit more by making the trial than by waiting," said Mrs. March. "Criticism is the best test of such work, for it will show her both unsuspected merits and faults, and help her to do better next time. We are too partial; but the praise and blame of outsiders will prove useful, even if she gets but little money."

"Yes," said Jo, knitting her brows, "that's just it; I've been fussing over the thing so long, I really don't know whether it's good, bad, or indifferent. It will be a great help to have cool, impartial persons take a look at it, and tell me what they think of it."

"I wouldn't leave out a word of it; you'll spoil it if you do, for the interest of the story is more in the minds than in the actions of the people, and it will be all a muddle if you don't explain as you go on," said Meg, who firmly believed that this book was the most remarkable novel ever written.

"But Mr. Allen says, 'Leave out the explanations, make it brief and dramatic, and let the characters tell the story,'" interrupted Jo, turning to the publisher's note.

"Do as he tells you; he knows what will sell, and we don't. Make a good, popular book, and get as much money as you can. By and by, when you've got a name, you can afford to digress, and have philosophical and metaphysical people in your novels," said Amy, who took a strictly practical view of the subject.

"Well," said Jo, laughing, "if my people *are* 'philosophical and metaphysical,' it isn't my fault, for I know nothing about such things, except what I hear father say, sometimes. If I've got some of his wise ideas jumbled up with my romance, so much the better for me. Now, Beth, what do you say?"

"I should so like to see it printed *soon*," was all Beth said, and smiled in saying it; but there was an unconscious emphasis on the last word, and a wistful look in the eyes that never lost their child-like candor, which chilled Jo's heart, for a minute, with a foreboding fear, and decided her to make her little venture "soon."[4]

So, with Spartan firmness, the young authoress laid her first-born on her table, and chopped it up as ruthlessly as any ogre. In the hope of pleasing every one, she took every one's advice; and, like the old man and his donkey in the fable, suited nobody.[5]

Her father liked the metaphysical streak which had unconsciously got into it, so that was allowed to remain, though she had her doubts about it. Her mother thought that there *was* a trifle too much description; out, therefore, it nearly all came, and with it many necessary links in the story. Meg admired the tragedy; so Jo piled up the agony to suit her, while Amy objected to the

4. The third sister, Beth, like Alcott's sister, Lizzie, eventually dies of the lingering effects of scarlet fever.
5. In the fable by the Greek storyteller Aesop, a father and his son are criticized by passers-by for the different ways they ride their donkey; trying to please their critics, they inadvertently drown the donkey. Alcott published her novel *Moods* in 1864, after cutting ten chapters to please her editor. She restored a number of the cut chapters and made other major changes in a revised version that she published in 1881.

fun, and, with the best intentions in life, Jo quenched the sprightly scenes which relieved the sombre character of the story. Then, to complete the ruin, she cut it down one-third, and confidingly sent the poor little romance, like a picked robin, out into the big, busy world, to try its fate.

Well, it was printed, and she got three hundred dollars for it; likewise plenty of praise and blame both so much greater than she expected, that she was thrown into a state of bewilderment, from which it took her some time to recover.

"You said, mother, that criticism would help me; but how can it, when it's so contradictory that I don't know whether I have written a promising book, or broken all the ten commandments," cried poor Jo, turning over a heap of notices, the perusal of which filled her with pride and joy one minute— wrath and dire dismay the next. "This man says 'An exquisite book, full of truth, beauty, and earnestness; all is sweet, pure, and healthy,'" continued the perplexed authoress. "The next, 'The theory of the book is bad,—full of morbid fancies, spiritualistic ideas, and unnatural characters.' Now, as I had no theory of any kind, don't believe in spiritualism,[6] and copied my charac- ters from life, I don't see how this critic *can* be right. Another says, 'It's one of the best American novels which has appeared for years' (I know better than that); and the next asserts that 'though it is original, and written with great force and feeling, it is a dangerous book.' 'Tisn't! Some make fun of it, some over-praise, and nearly all insist that I had a deep theory to expound, when I only wrote it for the pleasure and the money. I wish I'd printed it whole, or not at all, for I do hate to be so horridly misjudged."

Her family and friends administered comfort and commendation liberally; yet it was a hard time for sensitive, high-spirited Jo, who meant so well, and had apparently done so ill. But it did her good, for those whose opinion had real value, gave her the criticism which is an author's best education; and when the first soreness was over, she could laugh at her poor little book, yet believe in it still, and feel herself the wiser and stronger for the buffeting she had received.

"Not being a genius, like Keats,[7] it won't kill me," she said stoutly; "and I've got the joke on my side, after all; for the parts that were taken straight out of real life, are denounced as impossible and absurd, and the scenes that I made up out of my own silly head, are pronounced 'charmingly natural, tender, and true.' So I'll comfort myself with that; and, when I'm ready, I'll up again and take another."

1869

---

6. A belief that the living can communicate with the spirits of the dead, usually through a medium.
7. The English Romantic poet John Keats (1797– 1821), who, according to his poet-friend Percy

Bysshe Shelley (1792–1822), died at a young age in part because of critics' attacks on his poem *Endymion* (1818).

Selected Bibliographies

BEGINNINGS TO 1820

Reference Works

The first volume of Sacvan Bercovitch's *The Cambridge History of American Literature* (1994) serves as a rich guide to the literature of this period. The first two volumes of *A History of the Book in America* (2000; 2010) recount the history of print culture through 1840. The journal *Early American Literature* publishes critical studies of the literature from this period.

The digital *Archive of Americana* has an immense variety of resources, including *Early American Imprints I and II*, which contains virtually every printed work from British North America and the early republic up to 1820. *Early American Imprints* is based on the work of Charles Evans in *American Bibliography: A Chronological Dictionary of All Books, Pamphlets and Periodical Publications Printed in the United States of America . . .* Volume 1: *1639–1729* (1903) for items issued in what became the United States, updated in Clifford K. Shipton and James E. Mooney's two-volume *National Index of American Imprints through 1800* (1969). For items issued elsewhere, consult Joseph Sabin and Wilberforce Eames's twenty-nine volume *Biblioteca Americana: A Dictionary of Books Relating to America* (1868–1936). William Matthews and Roy Harvey Pearce's *American Diaries: An Annotated Bibliography of American Diaries Written Prior to the Year 1861* (1945) lists over three hundred diaries from before 1700; Matthews's *American Diaries in Manuscript, 1580–1954: A Descriptive Bibliography* (1974) adds three dozen others. Harold S. Jantz's *The First Century of New England Verse* (1944) includes a full bibliography. A valuable collection is *Seventeenth-Century American Poetry* (1968), compiled by Harrison T. Meserole. William J. Scheick and JoElla Doggett edited *Seventeenth-Century American Poetry: A Reference Guide* (1977). In 2007 the Library of America published a volume of seventeenth- and eighteenth-century American poetry, edited by David S. Shields.

For background on writings in English, the basic resource is the three-volume *American Writers before 1800: A Biographical and Critical Dictionary* (1983), edited by James A. Levernier and Douglas R. Wilmes, supplemented by *American Prose to 1820: A Guide to Information Sources* (1979), edited by Donald Yannella and John H. Roch. Useful guidance on obscure figures can be found in Evert A. and George L. Duyckinck's two-volume *Cyclopedia of American Literature* (1855).

The texts, introductory materials, and notes in the following volumes of the *Original Narratives of Early American History* series remain useful for non-English (and in some cases English) writers: *Narratives of New Netherland, 1609–1664* (1909), edited by J. Franklin Jameson; *Journal of Jasper Danckaerts* (1913), edited by Jameson and Bartett Burleigh James; *Narratives of Early Pennsylvania, West New Jersey, and Delaware, 1630–1707* (1912), edited by Albert Cook Myers; *The Spanish Explorers in the Southern United States, 1528–1543* (1907), edited by Frederick W. Hodge; *Spanish Exploration in the Southwest, 1542–1706* (1916), edited by Herbert Eugene Bolton; and *Early Narratives of the Northwest, 1634–1699* (1917), edited by Louise P. Kellogg. Henry C. Murphy's *Anthology of New Netherland* (1865) remains the single best source of translated texts (with biographical sketches) of three seventeenth-century writers. John J. Stoudt's *Pennsylvania German Poetry, 1685–1830* (1955) surveys one form of expression in depth.

Histories

Given the involvement of much early American writing in the large-scale expansion of Europe in the first imperial age, considerable insight can be gained from historical studies of that process. For North America, David Beers Quinn's thorough *North America from Earliest Discovery to First Settlements* (1977) and his *England and the Discovery of America, 1481–1620* (1973) give detailed narrative and analysis, as do Gary Nash's *Red, White, and Black: The People of Early America* (1974) and Colin G. Calloway's *New Worlds for All: Indians, Europeans, and the Re-making of Early America* (1997; 2nd ed., 2013). J. H. Elliott provides a comparative history of Spanish and English colonization in *Empires of the Atlantic World: Britain and Spain in America 1492–1830* (2006), while Daniel K. Richter compares European and Native American histories in *Before the Revolution: America's Ancient Pasts* (2011).

The most comprehensive single-volume history of American religion is Sydney E. Ahlstrom's *A Religious History of the American People* (1972). The Great Awakening is covered in Alan Heimert's *Religion and the American Mind* (1966), Jon Butler's *Awash in a Sea of Faith* (1990), and Patricia U. Bonomi's *Under the Cope of Heaven: Religion, Society, and Politics in Colonial America* (1986; rev. ed. 2003). In *The Democratization of American Christianity* (1989), Nathan O. Hatch extends consideration of the relationship between religion and politics into the nineteenth century. David D. Hall explores the complexities of lived religious experience in *Worlds of Wonder, Days of Judgment: Popular Religious Belief in Early New England* (1989). The religious lives of women are addressed in Susan Juster's *Disorderly Women: Sexual Politics and Evangelicalism in Revolutionary New England* (1996) and Catherine Brekus's *Strangers and Pilgrims: Female Preaching in America, 1740–1845* (1998). Albert J. Raboteau addresses the impact of Christianity on enslaved communities in *Slave Religion: The "Invisible Institution" in the Antebellum South* (1978). In *The Indian Great Awakening: Religion and the Shaping of Native Cultures in Early America* (2012), Linford D. Fisher examines how religious transformation reshaped Native societies.

Russel B. Nye's *The Cultural Life of the New Nation* (1960), Neil Harris's *The Artist in American Society: The Formative Years* (1966), Kenneth Silverman's *A Cultural History of the American Revolution* (1976), and Michael Kammen's *A Season of Youth* (1978) offer useful overviews of literary and artistic culture in the early American republic. Henry F. May's *The American Enlightenment* (1976) provides a similar service for philosophical issues, while Bruce Kuklick connects religion to American philosophy in *Churchmen and Philosophers: From Jonathan Edwards to John Dewey* (1987). Foundational histories of American women include Mary Beth Norton's *Liberty's Daughters* (1980) and *Founding Mothers and Daughters* (1996) and Linda Kerber's *Women of the Republic* (1980). Gordon Wood's *The Creation of the American Republic* (1969) and *The Radicalism of the American Revolution* (1996) are the chief guides to revolutionary political history. Wood's *Empire of Liberty: A History of the Early Republic 1789–1815* (2009) and the first part of Sean Wilentz's *The Rise of American Democracy: Jefferson to Lincoln* (2005) provide alternative interpretations of the postrevolutionary United States.

Theory and Criticism

William Carlos Williams's *In the American Grain* (1925) offers evocative discussions of early American writings. Howard Mumford Jones places early American culture in the context of Renaissance Europe in *O Strange New World: American Culture, the Formative Years* (1964), as does Stephen Greenblatt's *Marvelous Possessions: The Wonder of the New World* (1991). Roy Harvey Pearce's *Savagism and Civilization: A Study of the Indian and the American Mind* (1953; 1988) serves as a starting point for a body of criticism exploring the literary impact of the idea of the Indian on "the American mind." This approach is further developed in Richard M. Slotkin's *Regeneration through Violence: The Mythology of the American Frontier, 1600–1860* (1973); Jared Gardner likewise makes race central in *Master Plots: Race and the Founding of an American Literature, 1787–1845* (1998). In *The Machine in the Garden: Technology and the Pastoral Ideal in America* (1964), Leo Marx offers insightful readings of some Renaissance texts (such as Shakespeare's *The Tempest*) that reflect on the sense of lands newly available to the Old World; responses to the New World (and a reading, again, of *The Tempest*) are considered in Eric Cheyfitz's *The Poetics of Imperialism: Translation and Colonization from "The Tempest" to "Tarzan"* (expanded ed., 1997). In *Eloquence Is Power: Oratory and Performance in Early America* (2000), Sandra M. Gustafson emphasizes the verbal art of oratory as a catalyst in the Atlantic world crucible of indigenous American, European, and African cultures. In *A New World of Words: Redefining Early American Literature (1994)*, William C. Spengemann argues for the centrality of early American texts in the transformation of Western writing generally. Paul Giles has several major books that situate early American literature in a variety of transnational contexts.

Important reflections on Native literature appear in Arnold Krupat's *The Voice in the Margin: Native American Literature and the Canon* (1989) and Robert Dale Parker's *The Invention of Native American Literature* (2003). Hilary Wyss's *Writing Indians: Literacy, Christianity, and Native Community in Early America* (2000), Maureen Konkle's *Writing Indian Nations* (2004), and Phillip Round's *Removable Type: Histories of the Book in Indian Country, 1663–1880* (2010) are important studies of early Native writings. In *American Lazarus: Religion and the Rise of African and Native American Literatures* (2003), Joanna Brooks considers the impact of evangelical Protestantism on early African American and Native American writers. A good study of African American authors of the Atlantic Rim is Vincent Carretta and Philip Gould's edited *Genius in Bondage* (1996); Gould has also contributed *Barbaric Traffic: Commerce and Antislavery in the Eighteenth-Century Atlantic World* (2003). Henry Louis Gates Jr. establishes an African background in *The Signifying Monkey: A Theory of African American Literary Criticism* (1989). Dana D. Nelson's *The Word in Black and White: Reading "Race" in American Literature, 1638–1867* (1992) is an important early study; Katy Chiles offers a nuanced approach to race and representation in *Transformable Race: Surprising Metamorphoses in the Literature of Early America* (2014).

Wayne Franklin gives attention to sixteenth-century works in *Discoveries, Explorers, Settlers: The Diligent Writers of Early America* (1979), and Kathleen Donegan offers stylistic analysis of colonization narratives in *Seasons of Misery: Catastrophe and Colonial Settlement in Early America* (2014). A feminist perspective guides Annette Kolodny's *The Lay of the Land: Metaphor as Experience and History in American Life and Letters* (1975). Ralph Bauer considers Spanish and English colonial writings in *The Cultural Geography of Colonial American Literatures: Empire, Travel, Modernity* (2003). Gordon Sayre's *"Les Sauvages Américains": Representations of Native Americans in French and English Colonial Literature* (1997) offers fresh comparative readings of English and French texts and the codes they developed for depicting encounters with Native American peoples. In *A Harmony of the Spirits:*

Translation and the Language of Community in Early Pennsylvania (2013), Patrick E. Erben considers colonial German and English theories of language. Understandings of Asia are the focus of James F. Egan's *Oriental Shadows: The Presence of the East in Early American Literature* (2011).

Perry Miller's foundational studies of the Puritans include *The New England Mind: The Seventeenth Century* (1939) and *The New England Mind: From Colony to Province* (1953), while several important essays (notably "The Marrow of Puritan Divinity" and "From Edwards to Emerson") are collected in *Errand into the Wilderness* (1956). Important correctives to Miller appear in Philip F. Gura's *A Glimpse of Sion's Glory: Puritan Radicalism in New England, 1620–1660* (1986) and Janice Knight's *Orthodoxies in Massachusetts* (1994). Andrew Delbanco's *The Puritan Ordeal* (1989) and Michael J. Colacurcio's *Godly Letters: The Literature of the American Puritans* (2006) provide comprehensive analysis. Sacvan Bercovitch's influential works include *The Puritan Origins of the American Self* (1975). Patricia Caldwell discusses Puritan "relations" in *The Puritan Conversion Narrative* (1983); Teresa Toulouse analyzes the formal dimensions of Puritan sermons in *The Art of Prophesying: New England Sermons and the Shaping of Belief* (1987); and Ivy Schweitzer examines the poetics of gender in *The Work of Self-Representation: Lyric Poetry in Colonial New England* (1991). Lisa M. Gordis looks at Puritan hermeneutics in *Opening Scripture: Bible Reading and Interpretive Authority in Puritan New England* (2002). Puritan missions and their literature are considered in Kristina Bross's *Dry Bones and Indian Sermons: Praying Indians in Colonial America* (2004) and Laura Stevens's *The Poor Indians: British Missionaries, Native Americans, and Colonial Sensibility* (2004). Media-centered studies include Matthew P. Brown's *The Pilgrim and the Bee: Reading Rituals and Book Culture in Early New England* (2007); Matt Cohen's *The Networked Wilderness: Communicating in Early New England* (2009); and Meredith Neuman's *Jeremiah's Scribes: Creating Sermon Literature in Puritan New England* (2013). Sarah Rivett examines the intersections of early modern science and Reformed theology in *The Science of the Soul in Colonial New England* (2011), while Cristobal Silva considers understandings of disease in *Miraculous Plagues: An Epidemiology of Early New England Narrative* (2011). Nan Goodman treats Puritan legal culture in *Banished: Common Law and the Rhetoric of Social Exclusion in Early New England* (2012).

Revolutionary-era rhetoric and political writing are the focus of Emory Elliot's *Revolutionary Writers: Literature and Authority in the New Republic 1725–1810* (1982), Jay Fliegelman's *Prodigals and Pilgrims: The American Revolution Against Patriarchal Authority 1750–1800* (1982), and Robert A. Ferguson's *Reading the Early Republic* (2004). The cultural dynamics shaping political life and the public sphere in the Revolutionary and early national periods are central to Michael Warner's *Letters of the Republic* (1990), Paul Downes's *Democracy, Revolution and Monarchism in Early American Literature* (2002), and Eric Slauter's *The State as a Work of Art: The Cultural Origins of the Constitution* (2009). Stephen Shapiro highlights economic relations in *The Culture and Commerce of the Early American Novel: Reading the Atlantic World-System* (2007). Aesthetics are a leading concern in Christopher Looby's *Voicing America: Language, Literary Form, and the Origins of the United States* (1996) and Edward Cahill's *Liberty of the Imagination: Aesthetic Theory, Literary Form, and Politics in the Early United States* (2012).

David S. Shields's *Oracles of Empire: Poetry, Politics, and Commerce in British America* (1990) addresses transatlantic poetry, while his *Civil Tongues and Polite Letters in America* (1997) examines eighteenth-century club and manuscript culture. Max Cavitch discusses one major poetic form in *American Elegy: The Poetry of Mourning from the Puritans to Whitman* (2006); Christopher N. Phillips examines another in *Epic in American Culture: Settlement to Reconstruction* (2012). On the American novel, Cathy S. Davidson's *Revolution and the Word* (1986) is a foundational study. Shirley Samuels focuses on fiction and gender relations in *Romances of the Republic: Women, the Family, and Violence in the Literature of the Early American Nation* (1996), while Julia Stern analyzes sentiment as a moral and philosophical category that informs the early American novel in *The Plight of Feeling* (1997). Elizabeth Maddock Dillon's *The Gender of Freedom: Fictions of Liberalism and the Literary Public Sphere* (2004) offers an approach anchored in political theory. Marion Rust presents the challenges facing women writers in *Prodigal Daughters: Susanna Rowson's Early American Women* (2008). Walter J. Meserve's *An Emerging Entertainment* (1977); Jeffrey H. Richards's *Theater Enough* (1991) and *Drama, Theatre, and Identity in the New Republic* (2005); Heather Nathans's *Early American Theatre from the Revolution to Thomas Jefferson* (2003) and *Slavery and Sentiment on the American Stage, 1787–1861* (2009); and Dillon's *New World Drama: The Performative Commons in the Atlantic World, 1649–1849* (2014) treat drama in a variety of contexts. In *Democratic Personality: Popular Voice and the Trial of American Authorship* (1998), Nancy Ruttenberg explores the performative and literary creation of "popular voice," spanning from the Salem witchcraft crisis of 1692, through the Great Awakening, to the antebellum era.

Naturalist writings are the focus of Susan Scott Parrish's *American Curiosity: Cultures of Natural History in the Colonial British Atlantic World* (2006) and Christopher P. Iannini's *Fatal Revolutions: Natural History, West Indian Slavery, and the Routes of American Literature* (2012), while Martin Brückner's *Geographic Revolution in Early America: Maps, Literacy, and National Identity* (2006) examines the place of geography in the broader literary culture. Studies of the environment include Timothy Sweet's *American Georgics: Economy and Environment in American Literature, 1580–1864* (2002); Thomas Hallock's *From the Fallen Tree: Frontier Narratives, Environmental Politics, and the Roots of a National Pastoral, 1749–1826* (2003); Monique Allewaert's *Ariel's Ecology: Plantations, Personhood, and Colonialism in the American Tropics* (2013); and Michael Ziser's *Environmental Practice and Early American Literature* (2013). Jennifer Jordan Baker explores economic themes in *Securing the Commonwealth: Debt, Speculation, and Writing in the Making of Early America* (2005), as does Ed White from a different perspective in *The Backcountry and the City: Colonization and Conflict in Early America* (2005). Two treatments of literature and risk are Eric Wertheimer's *Underwriting: The Poetics of Insurance in America, 1722–1872* (2006) and Joseph Fichtelberg's *Risk Culture: Performance and Danger in Early America* (2010).

BEGINNINGS TO 1820

William Bradford

Bradford awaits a new editor of his history and other works, including his poems. Douglas Anderson's *William Bradford's Books: Of Plimmoth Plantation and the Printed Word* (2003) is a major study of Bradford's history. Michelle Burnham has a chapter on Bradford's economic context in *Folded Selves: Colonial New England Writing in the World System* (2007).

Anne Bradstreet

The standard edition is now Jeannine Hensley's *The Works of Anne Bradstreet* (1967), with an introduction by Adrienne Rich. Read-ers interested in textual variants will want to consult *The Complete Works* (1981), edited by J. R. McElrath Jr. and Allen P. Robb. Useful critical discussions may be found in Josephine K. Piercy's *Anne Bradstreet* (1965), Elizabeth W. White's *Anne Bradstreet: The Tenth Muse* (1971), Ann Stanford's *Anne Bradstreet: The Worldly Puritan* (1974), Rosamond Rosenmeier's *Anne Bradstreet* (1991), and Jeffrey Hammond's *Sinful Self, Saintly Self* (1993). Tamara Harvey's *Figuring Modesty in Feminist Discourse Across the Americas, 1633–1700* (2008) includes discussions of both Bradstreet and Sor Juana Inés de la Cruz.

Charles Brockden Brown
The standard edition of Brown's works is from Kent State University Press (1977–87). Useful editions of Brown's novels *Wieland, Ormond, Arthur Mervyn*, and *Edgar Huntly* were edited by Steven Shapiro and Philip Barnard in 2006–09. *Wieland* is available in a Norton Critical Edition, edited by Bryan Waterman in 2010. There is no recent comprehensive biography of Brown. Harry R. Warfel's biography *Charles Brockden Brown: American Gothic Novelist* (1949) can be supplemented with David Lee Clark's *Charles Brockden Brown: Pioneer Voice of America* (1952). Good studies of Brown's complete works include Norman S. Grabo's *The Coincidental Art of Charles Brockden Brown* (1981), Bill Christophersen's *The Apparition in the Glass: Charles Brockden Brown's American Gothic* (1993), and Steven Watts's *The Romance of Real Life: Charles Brockden Brown and the Origins of American Culture* (1994). Thematic studies include Michael Cody's *Charles Brockden Brown and the Literary Magazine: Cultural Journalism in the Early American Republic* (2004), Bryan Waterman's *Republic of Intellect: The Friendly Club of New York City and the Making of American Literature* (2007), and Mark Kamrath's *The Historicism of Charles Brockden Brown: Radical History and the Early Republic* (2010), as well as chapters in Caleb Crain's *American Sympathy: Men, Friendship, and Literature in the New Nation* (2001) and David Kazanjian's *The Colonizing Trick: National Culture and Imperial Citizenship in Early America* (2003). Robert S. Levine includes a chapter on Brown in his *Dislocating Race and Nation: Episodes in Nineteenth-Century American Literary Nationalism* (2008); an opposing view is found in John Carlos Rowe's *Literary Culture and U.S. Imperialism: From the Revolution to World War II* (2000).

Christopher Columbus
The best bilingual edition is Cecil Jane's *Select Documents Illustrating the Four Voyages of Columbus* (1930–33; 1988). Columbus's journal survives only in summaries and unreliable transcriptions by others. The best text is Oliver Dunn and James E. Kelley's bilingual *The Diario of Christopher Columbus's First Voyage to America, 1492–93* (1989); on the problems associated with this text (and others), see David Heninge's *In Search of Columbus: The Sources for the First Voyage* (1991). Biographies include Samuel Eliot Morison's now somewhat dated *Admiral of the Ocean Sea* (1942) and Kirkpatrick Sale's contentious *The Conquest of Paradise: Christopher Columbus and the Columbian Legacy* (1990). James Axtell's *After Columbus* (1988) and *Beyond 1492* (1992) are informative.

J. Hector St. John de Crèvecoeur
Dennis D. Moore has produced a new edition of *Letters from an American Farmer and Other Essays* (2013). The best biographies are by Thomas Philbrick (1970) and Gay Wilson Allen and Roger Asselineau (1987). Important treatments can be found in Ed White's *The Backcountry and the City* (2005) and Wil Verhoeven's *Americomania and the French Revolution Debate in Britain, 1789–1802* (2013).

Jonathan Edwards
Yale University Press has published Edwards's complete works in twenty-six volumes (1957–2008). The best single-volume collection of Edwards's writings is *A Jonathan Edwards Reader* (1995), also from Yale. The best biographies are George Marsden's *Jonathan Edwards: A Life* (2003) and Philip F. Gura's *Jonathan Edwards: America's Evangelical* (2005). Daniel B. Shea Jr. includes a discussion of the *Personal Narrative* in his *Spiritual Autobiography in Early America* (1968). Sandra M. Gustafson highlights Sarah Pierpont Edwards in "Jonathan Edwards and the Reconstruction of 'Feminine' Speech" (*American Literary History*, 1994). Major essay collections are *Jonathan Edwards and the American Experience* (1988), edited by Nathan O. Hatch and Harry S. Stout, and *Jonathan Edwards's Writings* (1996), edited by Stephen J. Stein. See also M. X. Lesser's *Reading Jonathan Edwards: An Annotated Bibliography in Three Parts, 1729–2005* (2008).

Olaudah Equiano
Werner Sollors edited *The Interesting Narrative* in a 2001 Norton Critical Edition. Sidney Kaplan discusses the American publication of Equiano's *Narrative* in *The Black Presence in the Era of the American Revolution, 1770–1800* (1973). Vincent Carretta's *Equiano, the African: Biography of a Self-Made Man* (2005) is a major treatment of the life.

The Federalist
A very useful introduction to *The Federalist* papers is found in Benjamin Fletcher Wright's edition of 1961. On Alexander Hamilton, see Ron Chernow's *Alexander Hamilton* (2004); on James Madison, see Jack N. Rakove's *James Madison and the Creation of the American Republic* (1990); on John Jay, see Walter Stahr's *John Jay: Founding Father* (2005). Several of the works on the Revolutionary period listed in the theory and criticism section include readings of *The Federalist*. For a sustained reading, see Joseph Fichtelberg's "The Aesthetics of the Federalist" in *Early American Literature* (2014).

Benjamin Franklin
The Papers of Benjamin Franklin are being published by Yale University Press. The stan-

dard biography is J. A. Leo Lemay's three-volume *The Life of Benjamin Franklin* (2006). Stacy Schiff focuses on Franklin's French years in *A Great Improvisation: Franklin, France, and the Birth of America* (2006), while Carla J. Mulford situates Franklin in an imperial context in *Benjamin Franklin and the Ends of Empire* (2015). A good selection of Franklin's writings may be found in *Benjamin Franklin: Representative Selection* (1936), edited by F. L. Mott and C. L. Jorgensen. Nian-Sheng Huang surveys two hundred years of American response to Franklin in *Benjamin Franklin in America* (1994). Joyce E. Chaplin assembles D. H. Lawrence's famous attack on Franklin and several other major readings of the *Autobiography* in the 2012 Norton Critical Edition. Douglas Anderson analyzes text and context in *The Unfinished Life of Benjamin Franklin* (2012). Anderson's *The Radical Enlightenments of Benjamin Franklin* (1997) has a different emphasis. Mitchell Robert Breitwieser traces significant continuities in *Cotton Mather and Benjamin Franklin: The Price of Representative Personality* (1984).

Philip Freneau
The standard edition of Freneau's poetry is F. L. Pattee's three-volume *The Poems of Philip Freneau* (1902–07). Lewis Leary, who edited *The Last Poems of Philip Freneau* (1945), wrote the best biography, *That Rascal Freneau: A Study in Literary Failure* (1941). Harry H. Clark provides a useful introduction to Freneau in his edited volume *Poems of Freneau* (1929). Richard C. Vitzhum offers a study of Freneau's lyrics in *Land and Sea* (1978).

Thomas Jefferson
Princeton University Press is publishing the *Papers of Thomas Jefferson*. The most comprehensive biography is Dumas Malone's six-volume *Jefferson and His Time* (1948–81); Malone's concise article on Jefferson in *The Dictionary of American Biography* (1933) is very helpful. Joseph J. Ellis's *American Sphinx: The Character of Thomas Jefferson* (1997) is an important recent biography. Annette Gordon-Reed examines Jefferson's relationship with Sally Hemings and her extended family in *The Hemingses of Monticello: An American Family* (2008). Frank Shuffelton produced two annotated bibliographies of work on Jefferson, extending from 1826 to 1990, as well as an edited collection of critical writings. Other major studies include Garry Wills's *Inventing America: Jefferson's Declaration of Independence* (1978), Jay Fliegelman's *Declaring Independence* (1993), Pauline Maier's *American Scripture* (1997), and Danielle Allen's *Our Declaration* (2014).

Cotton Mather
Kenneth Silverman's *The Life and Times of Cotton Mather* (1984) supersedes earlier biographies. The introduction to Kenneth B. Murdock's *Selections from Cotton Mather* (1926) is still useful, as are David Levin's *Cotton Mather: The Young Life of the Lord's Remembrancer* (1978) and Robert Middlekauff's *The Mathers: Three Generations of Puritan Intellectuals* (1971). Sacvan Bercovich has written about Mather in *Major Writers of Early American Literature* (1972), edited by E. H. Emerson, and in *The Puritan Origins of the American Self* (1975). Mitchell Robert Breitwieser takes a different approach in *Cotton Mather and Benjamin Franklin: The Price of Representative Personality* (1984).

Judith Sargent Murray
The best biographical study is Sheila L. Skemp's *First Lady of Letters: Judith Sargent Murray and the Struggle for Female Independence* (2009). *Selected Writings* (1995), edited by Sharon M. Harris, offers useful commentary on Murray's work. A modern reprint of *The Gleaner* is available with an introduction by Nina Baym (1992).

Native American Oral Traditions
There is an extensive body of scholarship on Native American verbal arts originating in folklore and ethnography, with notable contributions including Dell Hymes's *"In Vain I Tried to Tell You": Essays in Native American Ethnopoetics* (1981) and Dennis Tedlock's *The Spoken Word and the Work of Interpretation* (1983). Barre Toelken's *The Dynamics of Folklore* (rev. ed., 1996) is an excellent survey of oral materials by someone specifically interested in Native American verbal arts. There is also a body of scholarship contrasting oral and written modes of expression, which needs to be approached carefully to avoid reductive characterizations. Walter Ong's *Orality and Literacy: The Technologizing of the Word* (1982) and Eric Havelock's *The Muse Learns to Write* (1986) should be supplemented with Brian V. Street's *Literacy in Theory and Practice* (1984). In *Eloquence Is Power* (2000), Sandra M. Gustafson emphasizes the symbolic dimensions of speech and text in the British colonial setting, with a focus on Native oratory. Two recent analyses of the treaty literature are Andrew Newman's *On Records: Delaware Indians, Colonists, and the Media of History and Memory* (2012) and Jeffrey Glover's *Paper Sovereigns: Anglo-Native Treaties and the Law of Nations, 1604–1664* (2014).

Scholarship on the Iroquois and their creation story begins with Lewis Henry Morgan's *League of the Iroquois* (1972; orig. publ., 1851).

Seneca ethnologist Arthur C. Parker's *Seneca Myths and Folk Tales* (1923) is also useful. Daniel K. Richter's *The Ordeal of the Longhouse: The Peoples of the Iroquois League in the Era of European Colonization* (1992) covers the basic elements of Iroquois language, culture, and history and begins with an overview of Iroquois cosmogonic myths. For David Cusick, see Susan Kalter's "Finding a Place for David Cusick in Native American Literary History" (2002) and Maureen Konkle, *Writing Indian Nations* (2004).

The only book-length treatment of Native American oral trickster tales is Franchot Ballinger's *Living Sideways: Tricksters in American Indian Oral Traditions* (2004). Arnold Krupat revisits trickster tales in chapter 1 of *All That Remains* (2009). In his insightful *Trickster Makes This World: Mischief, Myth, and Art* (1998), Lewis Hyde deals with Native American tricksters, among others. Paul Radin's *The Trickster: A Study in American Indian Mythology* (1956, 1972), with commentaries by Karl Kerenyi and C. G. Jung, has achieved something of a classic status, although Radin's psychological interpretations have not worn well. Barbara Babcock-Abraham's "'A Tolerated Margin of Mess': The Trickster and His Tales Reconsidered," *Journal of the Folklore Institute* (1975), is still fresh.

Samson Occom

Joanna Brooks has edited The *Collected Writings of Samson Occom, Mohegan: Leadership and Literature in Eighteenth-Century Native America* (2006). Occom's "Short Narrative" was first published by Berndt Peyer in *The Elders Wrote: An Anthology of Early Prose by North American Indians, 1768–1931* (1982), and it is still worth consulting. Peyer's *The Tutor'd Mind: Indian Missionary-Writers in Antebellum America* (1997) continues to be useful as well. There are numerous readings of Occom's execution sermon, including a valuable one in Karen A. Weyler's *Empowering Words: Outsiders and Authorship in Early America* (2013).

Thomas Paine

Moncure D. Conway, who edited the four-volume *The Writings of Thomas Paine* (1894–96), wrote a valuable life of Paine (1892). More-recent biographies are by David F. Hawke (1974) and John Keane (1995). H. H. Clark's *Thomas Paine: Representative Selections* (1944) contains a helpful introduction. Eric Foner's *Tom Paine and Revolutionary America* (1976) puts Paine in context. Edward Larkin has written the major critical study *Thomas Paine and the Literature of Revolution* (2005) and edited a helpful critical edition of *Common Sense* (2004).

Mary Rowlandson

The introduction to Neal Salisbury's 1997 edition of the *Narrative* describes the major features of Rowlandson's life and world. Richard Slotkin's *Regeneration through Violence* (1973) contains an influential discussion of Rowlandson's captivity. Mitchell Robert Breitwieser focuses on affect in *American Puritanism and the Defense of Mourning: Religion, Grief, and Ethnology in Mary White Rowlandson's Captivity Narrative* (1990). The transatlantic significance of Rowlandson's narrative is central to Nancy Armstrong and Leonard Tennenhouse's *The Imaginary Puritan: Literature, Intellectual Labor, and the Origins of Personal Life* (1994). Christopher Castiglia explores issues of gender and captivity in *Bound and Determined: Captivity, Culture-Crossing, and White Womanhood from Mary Rowlandson to Patty Hearst* (1996), and, from a different perspective, so does Teresa Toulouse in *The Captive's Position: Female Narrative, Male Identify and Royal Authority in Colonial New England* (2007)

John Smith

Philip L. Barbour produced the definitive three-volume edition of Smith's writings, *The Complete Works of Captain John Smith* (1986). The Library of America has published a volume of his writings (2007). Critical treatments include Barbour's *The Three Worlds of Captain John Smith* (1964), Everett H. Emerson's *Captain John Smith* (1971), and J. A. Leo Lemay's *The American Dream of Captain John Smith* (1991). A useful descriptive bibliography can be found in *American Prose to 1820* (1979), edited by Donald Yanella and John H. Roche.

Edward Taylor

Donald E. Stanford's standard edition, *The Poems of Edward Taylor* (1960), can be supplemented with Daniel Patterson's *Edward Taylor's God Determinations and Preparatory Meditations: A Critical Edition* (2003). Francis Murphy edited Taylor's *Diary* (1964). The best critical biography (1961; rev. ed., 1988) is by Norman S. Grabo, who also edited Taylor's *Christographia* sermons (1962) and *Treatise Concerning the Lord's Supper* (1966). Thomas M. Davis and Virginia L. Davis edited *The Minor Poetry* (1981) with an informative introduction. Thomas Davis also published *A Reading of Edward Taylor* (1992). Other critical studies include William J. Scheick's *The Will and the Word* (1974), Karen E. Rowe's *Saint and Singer* (1986), and Jeffrey Hammond's *Sinful Self, Saintly Self* (1993).

Phillis Wheatley

Julian D. Mason produced the standard edition of Wheatley's poems (1966; rev. ed., 1989).

William H. Robinson's *Phillis Wheatley: A Bio-Bibliography* (1981) establishes the background. Vincent Carretta has written the new standard biography, *Phillis Wheatley: Biography of a Genius in Bondage* (2014). John C. Shields provides critical treatments in *Phillis Wheatley's Poetics of Liberation: Backgrounds and Contexts* (2008) and *Phillis Wheatley and the Romantics* (2010). April Langley considers the African elements of Wheatley's poetry in *The Black Aesthetic Unbound: Theorizing the Dilemma of Eighteenth-Century African American Literature* (2008).

Roger Williams

Major studies of Williams include Perry Miller's *Roger Williams: His Contribution to the American Tradition* (1953), Ola E. Winslow's *Roger Williams* (1957), Edmund S. Morgan's *Roger Williams: The Church and the State* (1967), and Henry Chupack's *Roger Williams* (1969). Perry Miller's introduction to *The Complete Writings of Roger Williams* (1963), Vol. 7, is also valuable. Important readings include Anne G. Myles's "Dissent and the Frontier of Translation: Roger Williams's A Key into the Language of America" in *Possible Pasts: Becoming Colonial in Early America* (2000) and Michelle Burnham's chapter on Williams's economic activities in *Folded Selves: Colonial New England Writing in the World System* (2007).

John Winthrop

The standard edition of *The Journal* was edited by Richard S. Dunn, James Savage, and Laetitia Yeandle (1996), with a valuable introduction by Dunn. Dunn and Yeandle previously prepared an abridged and modernized edition of *The Journal* (1966). *The Winthrop Papers, 1498–1654* (1929–) is in preparation under the auspices of the Massachusetts Historical Society, Boston. Dunn's *Puritans and Yankees: The Winthrop Dynasty of New England* (1962) and Edmund S. Morgan's *The Puritan Dilemma: The Story of John Winthrop* (1958) are among the best critical and biographical studies.

AMERICAN LITERATURE 1820–1865

Reference Works

For scholarship and criticism on writers in this anthology, a good bibliographical resource is the annual *American Literary Scholarship*; many research libraries have access to both the print and the online versions. Also useful is the annual *MLA International Bibliography*, which, like *ALS*, is available in both print and online versions. *American Literature, American Literary History, J19: The Journal of Nineteenth-Century Americanists, ESQ: A Journal of the American Renaissance, Legacy: A Journal of American Women Writers, African American Review, Studies in American Indian Literature*, and *Nineteenth-Century Literature* are among the journals that print essays and reviews on early national and antebellum American writing. For recent developments in the field, see Caroline F. Levander and Robert S. Levine's *Companion to American Literary Studies* (2011); Russ Castronovo's *Oxford Handbook to Nineteenth-Century American Literature* (2011); and Dana Luciano and Ivy G. Wilson's *Unsettled States: Nineteenth-Century American Literary Studies* (2014).

The Web has revolutionized bibliographical, textual, historical, and critical studies in American literature. While it is important to keep in mind that some websites are considerably more reliable than others, and that archives can be short-lived, one can still recognize the crucial importance of digital archives for American literary scholarship in the twenty-first century. The best overview site on American literature is Donna M. Campbell's *American Authors, Timelines, Literary Movements, American Literature Sites*

<wsu.edu/~campbelld/>. This digital archive makes available many of the main websites devoted to American authors, while providing information on chronologies and literary history. Also useful is *PAL: Perspectives in American Literature—A Research and Reference Guide* <www.csustan.edu/english /reuben/pal/table.html>. The Library of Congress's *American Memory* archive <loc.gov/index.html> provides images and rare texts, as does the New York Public Library's Schomburg Center for Research in Black Culture <nypl.org /locations/schomburg>. Other sites worth consulting are Northeastern University's archive on nineteenth-century American women writers <scrib-blingwomen.org/>; the University of North Carolina's archive on slave narratives <docsouth.unc.edu/neh/index.html>; and the Wright American Fiction archive, 1851–75 <letrs.indiana.edu/web/w/wright2/>, which makes available nearly three thousand full texts.

Histories

The *Columbia Literary History of the United States* (1988), under the general editorship of Emory Elliott, is a good one-volume history; see also Sacvan Bercovitch's multivolume *Cambridge History of American Literature* (1994–2005), especially volumes 2 and 4. Greil Marcus and Werner Sollors's provocative *New Literary History of America* (2009) offers short, punchy essays on authors, texts, cultural events, and literary movements. The *Cambridge History of the American Novel* (2011), edited by Leonard Cassuto et al., includes up-to-date essays on antebellum novelists; see also Shirley Samuels's *Companion to American Fiction, 1780–1865* (2004), and J. Gerald Kennedy and Leland S. Person's *The American Novel to 1870* (2014). Also useful are the *Columbia History of the American Novel* (1991), edited by Emory Elliott, and Gregg Crane's *Cambridge Introduction to the Nineteenth-Century American Novel* (2007).

Eric L. Haralson's *Encyclopedia of American Poetry: The Nineteenth Century* (1998) is a companion to John Hollander's two-volume anthology *American Poetry: The Nineteenth Century* (1993). See also Alfred Bendixen and Stephen Burt's *Cambridge History of American Poetry* (2014). On drama, see the *Cambridge History of American Theatre: Beginnings to 1870*, edited by Don B. Wilmeth and Christopher Bigsby (1998). The *Oxford Companion to African American Literature* (1997) is edited by William L. Andrews, Frances Smith Foster, and Trudier Harris; see also Blyden Jackson's *History of Afro-American Literature: The Long Beginnings, 1746–1895* (1989); Audrey A. Fisch's *Cambridge Companion to the African American Slave Narrative* (2007); Gene Andrew Jarrett's *Companion to African American Literature* (2010); and Ezra Tawil's *Cambridge Companion to Slavery in American Literature* (2016). Other useful reference works and collections include Joseph M. Flora and Lucinda H. MacKethan's *Companion to Southern Literature: Themes, Genres, Places, People, Movements, and Motifs* (2002); Cathy Davidson and Linda Wagner-Martin's *Oxford Companion to Women's Writing in the United States* (1995); Denise D. Knight's *Nineteenth-Century American Women Writers: A Bio-Bibliographical Critical Source Book* (1997); and Dale M. Bauer's *Cambridge History of American Women's Literature* (2012). On Transcendentalism, see Joel Myerson's *Transcendental-*

ism: A Reader (2000); Philip F. Gura's *American Transcendentalism: A History* (2007); Myerson, Sandra Harbert Petrulionis, and Laura Dassow Walls's *Oxford Handbook of Transcendentalism* (2010); and Jana L. Argersinger and Phyllis Cole's *Toward a Female Genealogy of Transcendentalism* (2014).

Literary Criticism

For a sampling of classic works in the field, see D. H. Lawrence's *Studies in Classic American Literature* (1923); F. O. Matthiessen's *American Renaissance: Art and Expression in the Age of Emerson and Whitman* (1941); Richard Chase's *The American Novel and Its Tradition* (1957); Leslie A. Fiedler's *Love and Death in the American Novel* (1960); Leo Marx's *The Machine in the Garden: Technology and the Pastoral Ideal in America* (1964); Richard Poirier's *A World Elsewhere: The Place of Style in American Literature* (1966); Lawrence Buell's *Literary Transcendentalism: Style and Vision in the American Renaissance* (1973); and Richard Slotkin's *Regeneration through Violence: The Mythology of the American Frontier, 1600–1860* (1973). Influential works of the past several decades include Annette Kolodny's *The Land before Her: Fantasy and Experience of the American Frontiers, 1630–1860* (1984); Jane Tompkins's *Sensational Designs: The Cultural Work of American Fiction, 1790–1860* (1985); Buell's *New England Literary Culture: From Revolution through Renaissance* (1986); George Dekker's *The American Historical Romance* (1988); Larry J. Reynolds's *European Revolutions and the American Renaissance* (1988); David S. Reynolds's *Beneath the American Renaissance: The Subversive Imagination in the Age of Emerson and Melville* (1989); Robert S. Levine's *Conspiracy and Romance: Studies in Brockden Brown, Cooper, Hawthorne, and Melville* (1989); David Leverenz's *Manhood and the American Renaissance* (1989); Nicholas Bromell's *By the Sweat of the Brow: Literature and Labor in Antebellum America* (1993); Priscilla Wald's *Constituting Americans: Cultural Anxiety and Narrative Form* (1995); Nina Baym's *American Women Writers and the Work of History, 1790–1860* (1995); Teresa A. Goddu's *Gothic America: Narrative, History, and Nation* (1997); Mary Loeffelholz's *From School to Salon: Reading Nineteenth-Century American Women's Poetry* (2004); Max Cavitch's *American Elegy: The Poetry of Mourning from the Puritans to Whitman* (2007); Dana Luciano's *Arranging Grief: Sacred Time and the Body in Nineteenth-Century America* (2007); Christopher Castiglia's *Interior States: Institutional Consciousness and the Inner Life of Democracy in the Antebellum United States* (2008); Lloyd Pratt's *Archives of American Time: Literature and Modernity in the Nineteenth Century* (2009); Justine S. Murison's *The Politics of Anxiety in Nineteenth-Century American Literature* (2011); Marcy J. Dinius's *The Camera and the Press: American Visual and Print Culture in the Age of the Daguerreotype* (2012); Cindy Weinstein and Christopher Looby's *American Literature's Aesthetic Dimensions* (2012); Cody Marrs's *Nineteenth-Century American Literature and the Long Civil War* (2015); and Joel Pfister's *Surveyors of Custom: American Literature as Cultural Analysis* (2016).

Discussions of the early national and antebellum literary marketplace can be found in Susan Coultrap-McQuin's *Doing Literary Business: American Women Writers in the Nineteenth Century* (1990); Michael Winship's

American Literary Publishing in the Mid-Nineteenth Century (1995); Mere-
dith L. McGill's *American Literature and the Culture of Reprinting, 1834–
1853* (2003); Trish Loughran's *The Republic in Print: Print Culture in the
Age of U.S. Nation-Building, 1770–1870* (2007); and James L. Machor's
*Reading Fiction in Antebellum America: Informed Response and Reception
Histories, 1820–1865* (2011). On law and literature, see Gregg D. Crane's
Race, Citizenship, and Law in American Literature (2002); Brook Thomas's
Civic Myths: A Law-and-Literature Approach to Citizenship (2007); and
Hoang Gia Phan's *Bonds of Citizenship: Law and the Labors of Emancipation*
(2013). For discussions of transatlantic and hemispheric perspectives, see
Robert Weisbuch's *Atlantic Double-Cross: American Literature and British
Influence in the Age of Emerson* (1986); Paul Giles's *Transatlantic Insurrections:
British Culture and the Formation of American Literature, 1730–1860*
(2001); Kirsten Silva Gruesz's *Ambassadors of Culture: The Transamerican
Origins of Latino Writing* (2002); Anna Brickhouse's *Transamerican Liter-
ary Relations and the Nineteenth-Century Public Sphere* (2004); Gretchen
Murphy's *Hemispheric Imaginings: The Monroe Doctrine and Narratives
of U.S. Empire* (2005); Leonard Tennenhouse's *The Importance of Feeling
English: American Literature and the British Diaspora, 1750–1850* (2007);
Meredith L. McGill's *The Traffic in Poems: Nineteenth-Century Poetry and
Transatlantic Exchange* (2008); Elisa Tamarkin's *Anglophilia: Deference, Devo-
tion, and Antebellum America* (2008); and Caroline F. Levander and Robert S.
Levine's *Hemispheric American Studies* (2008). Questions of empire and
imperialism have been taken up by a number of critics; see, for example, Amy
Kaplan's *The Anarchy of Empire in the Making of U.S. Culture* (2002); Laura
Doyle's *Freedom's Empire: Race and the Rise of the Novel in Atlantic Modernity, 1640–1940* (2008); and Andy Doolen's *Territories of Empire: U.S. Writing
from the Louisiana Purchase to Mexican Independence* (2013).

Much recent criticism has been inspired by work on gender and race and
the recovery of neglected writings by women, African Americans, and Native
Americans. Nina Baym's *Women's Fiction: A Guide to Novels by and about
Women in America, 1820–1870* (1978; 1993, with a new preface) and Mary
Kelley's *Private Woman, Public Stage: Literary Domesticity in Nineteenth-
Century America* (1984) have been especially influential. On the sometimes
overlapping concerns of domesticity, sentimentalism, and sympathy in
nineteenth-century U.S. writing, see Gillian Brown's *Domestic Individual-
ism: Imagining Self in Nineteenth-Century America* (1990); Baym's *Feminism
and American Literary History* (1992); Lora Romero's *Home Fronts: Domestic-
ity and Its Critics in the Antebellum United States* (1997); Elizabeth Young's
Disarming the Nation: Women's Writing and the American Civil War (1999);
Cindy Weinstein's *Family, Kinship, and Sympathy in Nineteenth-Century
American Literature* (2004); Melissa J. Homestead's *American Women
Authors and Literary Property, 1822–1869* (2005); Elizabeth Barnes's *Love's
Whipping Boy: Violence and Sentimentality in the American Imagination*
(2011); and Peter Coviello's *Tomorrow's Parties: Sex and the Untimely in
Nineteenth-Century America* (2013).

Key works in the study of race and slavery in antebellum writing include
William L. Andrews's *To Tell a Free Story: The First Century of Afro-American
Autobiography, 1760–1865* (1986); Henry Louis Gates Jr.'s *Figures in Black:
Words, Signs, and the "Racial Self"* (1987); Dana D. Nelson's *The Word in*

Black and White: Reading "Race" in American Literature, 1638–1867 (1992); Karen Sánchez-Eppler's *Touching Liberty: Abolition, Feminism, and the Politics of the Body* (1993); Eric J. Sundquist's *To Wake the Nations: Race in the Making of American Literature* (1993); John Ernest's *Resistance and Reformation in Nineteenth-Century American Literature* (1995); Carla L. Peterson's *"Doers of the Word": African-American Women Speakers and Writers in the North (1830–1880)* (1995); Russ Castronovo's *Fathering the Nation: American Genealogies of Slavery and Freedom* (1995); Leonard Cassuto's *The Inhuman Race: The Racial Grotesque in American Literature and Culture* (1997); Rafia Zafar's *African Americans Write American Literature, 1760–1870* (1997); Dana Nelson's *National Manhood: Capitalist Citizenship and the Imagined Fraternity of White Men* (1998); Dickson D. Bruce Jr.'s *The Origins of African American Literature, 1680–1865* (2001); Susan M. Ryan's *The Grammar of Good Intentions: Race and the Antebellum Culture of Benevolence* (2003); Maurice S. Lee's *Slavery, Philosophy, and American Literature, 1830–1860* (2005); Caroline F. Levander's *Cradle of Liberty: Race, the Child, and National Belonging from Thomas Jefferson to W. E. B. Du Bois* (2006); Robert S. Levine's *Dislocating Race and Nation: Episodes in Nineteenth-Century American Literary Nationalism* (2008); Ian Frederick Finseth's *Shades of Green: Visions of Nature in the Literature of American Slavery, 1770–1860* (2009); John Ernest's *Chaotic Justice: Rethinking African American Literary History* (2009); Samuel Otter's *Philadelphia Stories: America's Literature of Race and Freedom* (2010); Yogita Goyal's *Romance, Diaspora, and Black Atlantic Literature* (2010); Celeste-Marie Bernier's *Characters of Blood: Black Heroism in the Transatlantic Imagination* (2012); and Judith Irwin Madera's *Black Atlas: Geography and Flow in Nineteenth-Century African American Literature* (2015).

For important critical work in Native American studies, see Lucy Maddox's *Removals: Nineteenth-Century American Indian Literature and the Politics of Indian Affairs* (1991); Arnold Krupat's *Ethnocriticism: Ethnography, History, Literature* (1992); Helen Carr's *Inventing the American Primitive: Politics, Gender and the Representation of Native American Literary Traditions, 1789–1936* (1996); Cheryl Walker's *Indian Nation: Native American Literature and Nineteenth-Century Nationalisms* (1997); Neil Schmitz's *White Robe's Dilemma: Tribal History in American Literature* (2001); Maureen Konkle's *Writing American Indian Nations: Native Intellectuals and the Politics of Historiography, 1827–1863* (2004); Daniel Justice's *Our Fire Survives the Storm: A Cherokee Literary History* (2006); Krupat's *All That Remains: Varieties of Indigenous Expression* (2009); and Scott Richard Lyons's *X-Marks: Native Signatures of Assent* (2010).

AMERICAN LITERATURE 1820–1865

Louisa May Alcott
Some of Alcott's work never went out of print, and much of the rest has been republished. Madeleine B. Stern has played a pioneering role in the recovery of Alcott's larger canon, including the sensation fiction that Alcott published anonymously. Key editions include Stern's *Behind a Mask: The Unknown Thrillers of Louisa May Alcott* (1975); Elaine Showalter's *Alternative Alcott* (1988); Daniel Shealy, Stern, and Joel Myerson's *Freaks of Genius: Unknown Thrillers of Louisa May Alcott* (1991);

Sarah Elbert's *Louisa May Alcott on Race, Sex, and Slavery* (1997); and Stern's *Louisa May Alcott Unmasked: Collected Thrillers* (1995). Stern's edition of *A Modern Mephistopheles* (1877) appeared in 1987; Joy S. Kasson's edition of *Work* (1873) appeared in 1994; Elbert's edition of *Moods* (1864; revised 1882) appeared in 1991; and Anne K. Phillips and Gregory Eiselein's Norton Critical Edition of *Little Women* appeared in 2003. Myerson and Daniel Shealy, with Stern as associate, edited *The Selected Letters of Louisa May Alcott* (1987) and *The Journals of Louisa May Alcott* (1989); and Shealy edited *Literary Women Abroad: The Alcott Sisters' Letters from Europe, 1870–1871* (2008). Stern's important biography *Louisa May Alcott* (1950, 1978) was republished in 1996 in a revised edition, *Louisa May Alcott: A Biography*. Two excellent recent biographies are John Matteson's *Eden's Outcasts: The Story of Louisa May Alcott and Her Father* (2007) and Harriet Reisen's *Louisa May Alcott: The Woman behind Little Women* (2009). For primary texts bearing on biography, see Shealy's *Alcott in Her Own Time* (2005).

On critical reception, see Beverly Lyon Clark's *Louisa May Alcott: The Contemporary Reviews* (2004). An excellent resource for Alcott's most famous novel is Janice M. Alberghene and Clark's *Little Women and the Feminist Imagination: Criticism, Controversy, Personal Essays* (1999). Also useful is Eiselein and Phillips's *Louisa May Alcott Encyclopedia* (2001). Important critical work includes Stern's *Critical Essays on Louisa May Alcott* (1984); Sarah Elbert's *A Hunger for Home: Louisa May Alcott and "Little Women"* (1987); Keyser's *Whispers in the Dark: The Fiction of Louisa May Alcott* (1993); Anne E. Boyd's *Writing for Immortality: Women and the Emergence of High Literary Culture in America* (2004); Susan S. Williams's *Reclaiming Authorship: Literary Women in America, 1850–1900* (2006); Michelle Ann Abate's *Tomboys: A Literary and Cultural History* (2008); and Clark's *The Afterlife of Little Women* (2014).

William Apess

Barry O'Connell's *On Our Own Ground: The Complete Writings of William Apess, a Pequot* (1992) is the indispensable starting point for a study of Apess. O'Connell's *A Son of the Forest and Other Writings* (1997), a selection from Apess's work, has an updated introduction that provides some new material. An important new work is Philip F. Gura's *The Life of William Apess, Pequot* (2015). Arnold Kruptal discusses Apess in his *The Voice in the Margin* (1989), *Ethnocriticism* (1992), and *All That Remains* (2009). See also Hilary Wyss's

"Captivity and Conversion: William Apess, Mary Jemison, and Narratives of Racial Identity," *American Indian Quarterly* (1999); Maureen Konkle's *Writing Indian Nations* (2004); Robert Warrior's *The People and the Word: Reading Native Nonfiction* (2005); Michael Elliott's "Indians, Incorporated," *American Literary History* (2007); Lisa Brooks's *The Common Pot: The Recovery of Native Space in the Northeast* (2008); and David L. Moore's *The Dream Shall Have a Name: Native Americans Rewriting America* (2013).

William Cullen Bryant

William Cullen Bryant II and Thomas G. Voss edited *The Letters of William Cullen Bryant* (1975–1992) in six volumes. Earlier biographies are superseded by Albert F. McLean's *William Cullen Bryant* (1989). Bryant's poetry has not been edited according to modern standards, but the edition of his *Poetical Works* (1878) published at his death is a useful starting point. His newspaper writing had been buried in the files of the *New York Evening Post* until William Cullen Bryant II republished selected editorials in *Power for Sanity* (1994). For good collections of Bryant's writings, see Frank Gado and Nicholas B. Stevens's *William Cullen Bryant: An American Voice* (2006) and Frank Gado's edition of Bryant's complete stories (2014). An excellent recent study is Gilbert H. Muller's *William Cullen Bryant: Author of America* (2008). Bernard Duffey's *Poetry in America: Expression and Its Values in the Times of Bryant, Whitman, and Pound* (1978) remains provocative.

James Fenimore Cooper

James Franklin Beard was editor-in-chief of a long-planned and, after 1979, fast-appearing edition, *The Writings of James Fenimore Cooper*, published by the State University of New York Press. Excellent volumes of *The Pioneers* and *The Last of the Mohicans*, and many of Cooper's other works, have already appeared as part of an edition with forty-eight proposed volumes. Beard also edited the indispensable six-volume *Letters and Journals of James Fenimore Cooper* (1960–1968). Wayne Franklin's biography should become standard; see the first volume, *James Fenimore Cooper: The Early Years* (2007). Essential background is in Alan Taylor's *William Cooper's Town: Power and Persuasion on the Frontier of the Early American Republic* (1995), a biography of Cooper's father.

Critical reception is surveyed in George Dekker and John P. McWilliams's *Fenimore Cooper: The Critical Heritage* (1973). For collections of essays, see W. M. Verhoeven's *James Fenimore Cooper: New Historical and Literary Contexts* (1993); Leland S. Person's

Historical Guide to James Fenimore Cooper (2006); and Jeffrey Walker's *Leather-Stocking Redux; or, Old Tales, New Essays* (2011). Useful critical work includes McWilliams's *Political Justice in a Republic: James Fenimore Cooper's America* (1972); H. Daniel Peck's *A World by Itself: The Pastoral Moment in Cooper's Fiction* (1977); Wayne Franklin's *The New World of James Fenimore Cooper* (1982); James D. Wallace's *Early Cooper and His Audience* (1986); Charles Hansford Adams's *"The Guardian of the Law": Authority and Identity in James Fenimore Cooper* (1990); Geoffrey Rans's *Cooper's Leatherstocking Series, A Secular Reading* (1991); and Geoffrey Sanborn, *Whipscars and Tattoos: The Last of the Mohicans, Moby-Dick, and the Maori* (2011). See also *Literature in the Early Republic: Annual Studies on Cooper and His Contemporaries* (2009–), edited by Wayne Franklin and Jason Berger.

Rebecca Harding Davis

In 1972, Tillie Olsen's Feminist Press edition of "Life in the Iron-Mills," accompanied by Olsen's "A Biographical Interpretation," helped to revive Davis's critical reputation. Up to that time, Davis had mainly been known through writings about her son, the author-celebrity Richard Harding Davis. Rebecca Harding Davis published an autobiographical volume, *Bits of Gossip*, in 1904. Useful critical studies include Sharon M. Harris's *Rebecca Harding Davis and American Realism* (1991); Jean Pfaelzer's *Parlor Radical: Rebecca Harding Davis and the Origins of American Social Realism* (1996); and William Dow's *Narrating Class in American Fiction* (2009). A groundbreaking article is Janice Milner Lasseter's "The Censored and Uncensored Literary Lives of *Life in the Iron-Mills*," *Legacy* 20 (2003): 175–89. Davis's 1862 novel *Margret Howth* is available in a 1990 edition with an afterword by Jean Fagan Yellin. There are three excellent collections of Davis's writings: Jean Pfaelzer's *A Rebecca Harding Davis Reader* (1995); Janice Milner Lasseter and Sharon M. Harris's *Rebecca Harding Davis: Writing Cultural Autobiography* (2001); and Harris and Robin L. Cadwallader's *Rebecca Harding Davis's Stories of the Civil War Era* (2010).

Emily Dickinson

Three volumes of *The Poems of Emily Dickinson* (1955) were edited by Thomas H. Johnson; and Johnson and Theodora Ward edited three companion volumes of *The Letters of Emily Dickinson* (1958). R. W. Franklin's three-volume *Poems of Emily Dickinson: Variorum Edition* (1998) augments and updates Johnson's three-volume *Poems*. In 1999 Franklin published the one-volume *The Poems of Emily*

Dickinson: Reading Edition. Important biographies include Richard B. Sewall's *The Life of Emily Dickinson* (1974); Cynthia Griffin Wolff's *Emily Dickinson* (1986); Alfred Habegger's *My Wars Are Laid Away in Books: The Life of Emily Dickinson* (2001); Brenda Wineapple's *White Heat: The Friendship of Emily Dickinson and Thomas Wentworth Higginson* (2008); and Lyndall Gordon's *Lives Like Loaded Guns: Emily Dickinson and Her Family's Feuds* (2010). Jay Leyda's *The Years and Hours of Emily Dickinson* (1960) provides two volumes of documents, such as excerpts from family letters. Additional documents can be found in Polly Longsworth's *The World of Emily Dickinson* (1990) and Ellen Louise Hart and Martha Nell Smith's *Open Me Carefully: Emily Dickinson's Intimate Letters to Susan Huntington Dickinson* (1998).

Research tools include Joseph Duchac's *The Poems of Emily Dickinson: An Annotated Guide to Commentary Published in English, 1890–1977* (1979), and the continuation (published in 1993) covering 1978–1989; Karen Dandurand's *Dickinson Scholarship: An Annotated Bibliography 1969–1985* (1988); and Willis J. Buckingham's *Emily Dickinson's Reception in the 1890s* (1989). Also useful are Jane Donahue Eberwein's *An Emily Dickinson Encyclopedia* (1998) and Sharon Leiter's *Critical Companion to Emily Dickinson: A Literary Reference to Her Life and Work* (2007). The *Dickinson Electronic Archives* <emilydickinson.org>, directed by Martha Nell Smith and Marta Werner, offer access to Dickinson's manuscripts, out-of-print volumes about Dickinson, and never-before-published writings by various family members. Other valuable research tools include Martha Nell Smith and Lara Vetter's *Emily Dickinson's Correspondences: A Born-Digital Textual Inquiry* (2008), Amherst College's *Emily Dickinson Collection* <acdc.amherst.edu/browse/collection/ed>, and Harvard University Press and the Houghton Library's *Emily Dickinson Archive* <www.edickinson.org>.

Collections of critical essays provide an excellent introduction to Dickinson studies. See Gudrun Grabher, Roland Hagenbüchle, and Cristanne Miller's *Emily Dickinson Handbook* (1998, 2006); Wendy Martin's *Cambridge Companion to Emily Dickinson* (2002); Vivian R. Pollak's *Historical Guide to Emily Dickinson* (2004); Martha Nell Smith and Mary Loeffelholz's *Companion to Emily Dickinson* (2008); Jane Donahue Eberwein and Cindy MacKenzie's *Reading Emily Dickinson's Letters: Critical Essays* (2009); Eliza Richards's *Emily Dickinson in Context* (2013); Jedd Deppman, Marianne Noble, and Gary Lee Stonum's *Emily Dickinson and Philosophy* (2013); and Eleanor Elson Heginbotham's

Dickinson's Fascicles: A Spectrum of Possibilities (2014). Important studies include Paula Bennett's *Emily Dickinson: Woman Poet* (1990); Martha Nell Smith's *Rowing in Eden: Rereading Emily Dickinson* (1992); Sharon Cameron's *Choosing Not Choosing: Dickinson's Fascicles* (1993); Domhnall Mitchell's *Emily Dickinson: Monarch of Perception* (2000); Eleanor Elson Heginbotham's *Reading the Fascicles of Emily Dickinson* (2003); Virginia Jackson's *Dickinson's Misery: A Theory of Lyric Reading* (2005); Jed Deppman's *Trying to Think with Emily Dickinson* (2008); Cristanne Miller's *Reading in Time: Emily Dickinson In the Nineteenth Century* (2012); and Alexandra Socarides' *Dickinson Unbound: Paper, Process, Poetics* (2012). For a lively engagement with Dickinson's poetry from a celebrated close reader, see Helen Vendler's *Dickinson: Poems and Commentaries* (2010).

Frederick Douglass
The definitive edition of Douglass's writings is under the editorship of John Blassingame and John R. McKivigan; nine volumes of the *Frederick Douglass Papers* have appeared since 1979. Philip S. Foner edited *The Life and Writings of Frederick Douglass* in five volumes (1950–1975). The Library of America's *Frederick Douglass: Autobiographies*, edited by Henry Louis Gates Jr., contains *Narrative of the Life of Frederick Douglass, An American Slave, Written by Himself* (1845), *My Bondage and My Freedom* (1855), and *Life and Times of Frederick Douglass* (1892). For Douglass's one work of fiction, see Robert S. Levine, John Stauffer, and John R. McKivigan's *The Heroic Slave: A Cultural and Critical Edition* (2015).

A good biography is William S. McFeely's *Frederick Douglass* (1991), but it should be supplemented by Dickson J. Preston's *Young Frederick Douglass* (1980); David W. Blight's *Frederick Douglass's Civil War* (1989); Maria Diedrich's *Love Across the Color Lines: Ottilie Assing and Frederick Douglass* (1999); and John Stauffer's *Giants: The Parallel Lives of Frederick Douglass and Abraham Lincoln* (2008). Waldo E. Martin Jr.'s *The Mind of Frederick Douglass* (1984) offers a full-scale intellectual history and remains among the best books in Douglass studies.

Important essays on Douglass can be found in Eric J. Sundquist's *Frederick Douglass: New Literary and Historical Essays* (1990); William L. Andrews's *Critical Essays on Frederick Douglass* (1991); Bill E. Lawson and Frank M. Kirkland's *Frederick Douglass: A Critical Reader* (1999); Alan J. Rice and Martin Crawford's *Liberating Sojourn: Frederick Douglass and Transatlantic Reform* (1999); Robert S. Levine and Samuel Otter's *Frederick Douglass and Herman Melville: Essays in* *Relation* (2008); and Maurice S. Lee's *Cambridge Companion to Frederick Douglass* (2009). For primary materials from memoirs and other nineteenth-century sources, see John Ernest's *Douglass in His Time* (2014). Valuable critical studies include William L. Andrews's *To Tell a Free Story: The First Century of Afro-American Autobiography, 1760–1865* (1986); Eric J. Sundquist's *To Wake the Nations: Race in the Making of American Literature* (1993); Robert S. Levine's *Martin Delany, Frederick Douglass, and the Politics of Representative Identity* (1997); Maggie M. Sale's *The Slumbering Volcano: American Slave Ship Revolts and the Production of Rebellious Masculinity* (1997); Maurice O. Wallace's *Constructing the Black Masculine: Identity and Ideality in African American Men's Literature and Culture, 1775–1995* (2002); James Colaiaco's *Frederick Douglass and the Fourth of July* (2006); Peter C. Myers's *Frederick Douglass: Race and the Rebirth of American Liberalism* (2008); Robert B. Stepto's *A Home Elsewhere: Rereading African American Classics in the Age of Obama* (2010); Celeste-Marie Bernier's *Characters of Blood: Black Heroism in the Transatlantic Imagination* (2012); and Robert S. Levine's *The Lives of Frederick Douglass* (2016).

Ralph Waldo Emerson
An outstanding achievement in Emerson scholarship is the edition of *Journals and Miscellaneous Notebooks*, 16 vols. (1960–1982), edited by William H. Gilman et al. A selection is available in the Library of America's two-volume *Selected Journals* (2010), edited by Lawrence Rosenwald. Stephen E. Whicher, Robert E. Spiller, and Wallace E. Williams edited *The Early Lectures of Ralph Waldo Emerson*, 3 vols. (1959–1972); Ronald A. Bosco and Joel Myerson edited *The Later Lectures of Ralph Waldo Emerson, 1843–1871* (2001). *The Complete Sermons of Ralph Waldo Emerson* (1989) is available in four volumes, under the editorship of Albert J. von Frank. Ralph L. Rusk and Eleanor M. Tilton edited the ten-volume *Letters* (1939, 1990–1995); a welcome distillation is Joel Myerson's *Selected Letters of Ralph Waldo Emerson* (1997). Len Gougeon and Myerson edited *Emerson's Antislavery Writings* (1995); and Kenneth S. Sachs edited *Political Writings: Emerson* (2008).

The most detailed biography is still Ralph L. Rusk's *The Life of Ralph Waldo Emerson* (1949), but see also Gay Wilson Allen's *Waldo Emerson* (1981) and especially Robert D. Richardson's *Emerson: The Mind on Fire* (1995). Phyllis Cole's *Mary Moody Emerson and the Origins of Transcendentalism* (1998) explores the crucial influence of Emerson's aunt on his life and thought. Albert J. von Frank compiled *An Emerson Chronology* (1993); Joel Myerson edited *Emerson and Thoreau: The Contemporary Reviews* (1992); and Robert E. Burkholder edited *Ralph Waldo Emerson: An Annotated Bibliography of Criticism, 1980–1991* (1994). See also David LaRocca, *Estimating Emerson: An Anthology of Criticism from Carlyle to Cavell* (2013).

For critical essays, see Myerson's *Historical Guide to Ralph Waldo Emerson* (1999); Joel Porte and Saundra Morris's *Cambridge Companion to Ralph Waldo Emerson* (1999); Ronald A. Bosco and Myerson's *Emerson Bicentennial Essays* (2006); Arthur S. Lothstein and Michael Brodrick's *New Morning: Emerson in the Twenty-first Century* (2008); John Lysaker and William Rossi's *Emerson and Thoreau: Figures of Friendship* (2010); Branka Arsić and Cary Wolfe's *The Other Emerson* (2010); Alan M. Levine and Daniel S. Malachuk's *A Political Companion to Ralph Waldo Emerson* (2011); and Wesley T. Mott's *Emerson in Context* (2014). Important critical studies include Len Gougeon's *Virtue's Hero: Emerson, Antislavery, and Reform* (1990); Christopher Newfield's *The Emerson Effect: Individualism and Submission in America* (1996); Eduardo Cadava's *Emerson and the Climates of History* (1997); Lawrence Buell's *Emerson* (2003); Kris Fresonke's *West of Emerson: The Design of Manifest Destiny* (2003); Laura Dassow Walls's *Emerson's Life in Science* (2003); Joel Porte's *Consciousness and Culture: Emerson and Thoreau Reviewed* (2004); Randall Fuller's *Emerson's Ghosts: Literature, Politics, and the Making of Americanists* (2007); Neil Dolan's *Emerson's Liberalism* (2009); Branka Arsić's *On Leaving: A Reading in Emerson* (2010); and David Dowling's, *Emerson's Protégés: Mentoring and Marketing Transcendentalism's Future* (2014).

Margaret Fuller

There are substantial collections of Fuller's writings: Bell Gale Chevigny's *The Woman and the Myth: Margaret Fuller's Life and Writings* (1976, 1994); Larry J. Reynolds and Susan Belasco Smith's *"These Sad but Glorious Days": Dispatches from Europe, 1846–1850* (1992); Jeffrey Steele's *The Essential Margaret Fuller* (1992); Mary Kelley's *The Portable Margaret Fuller* (1994); and Judith Mattson Bean and Joel Myerson's *Margaret Fuller, Critic: Writings for the New-York Tribune, 1844–1846* (2000). Robert N. Hudspeth's edition of Fuller's *Letters* is complete in six volumes (1983–1994). Susan Belasco Smith edited *Summer on the Lakes in 1843* (1990), and Larry J. Reynolds edited a Norton Critical Edition of *Woman in the Nineteenth Century* (1997). Madeleine B. Stern's pioneering *The Life of Margaret Fuller* (1942, 1991) should be supplemented by Charles Capper's *Margaret Fuller: An American Romantic Life*, vol. 1: *The Private Years* (1994), and vol. 2: *The Public Years* (2002). Excellent recent biographies include John Matteson's *The Lives of Margaret Fuller* (2012) and Megan Marshall's *Margaret Fuller: A New American Life* (2013). Myerson edited *Fuller in Her Own Time* (2008). For critical approaches, see Jeffrey Steele's *Transfiguring America: Myth, Ideology, Mourning in Margaret Fuller's Writing* (2001); Bruce Mills's *Poe, Fuller, and the Mesmeric Arts* (2006); Charles Capper and Cristina Giorcelli's collection *Margaret Fuller: Transatlantic Crossings in a Revolutionary Age* (2007); and Brigitte Bailey, Katheryn P. Viens, and Conrad Edick Wright's edited collection *Margaret Fuller and Her Circles* (2012).

Frances Ellen Watkins Harper

The best introduction to Harper is Frances Smith Foster's *A Brighter Day Coming: A Frances Watkins Harper Reader* (1990). Maryemma Graham edited Harper's *Complete Poems* (1988), and Foster edited *Three Rediscovered Novels by Frances E. W. Harper* (2000) and Harper's *Iola Leroy* (1988). Good critical commentary on Harper can be found in Hazel V. Carby's *Reconstructing Womanhood: The Emergence of the Afro-American Woman Novelist* (1987); Joan R. Sherman's *Invisible Poets: Afro-Americans of the Nineteenth Century* (1989); Foster's *Written by Herself: Literary Production of Early African-American Women Writers* (1993); Carla L. Peterson's *"Doers of the Word": African-American Women Speakers and Writers in the North (1830–1880)* (1995); John Ernest's *Resistance and Reformation in Nineteenth-Century African-American Literature* (1995); Janet Sinclair Gray's *Race and Time: American Women's Poetics from Antislavery to Racial Modernity* (2004); and Monique-Adelle Callahan's *Between the Lines: Literary Transnationalism and African American Poetics* (2011). For a biographical overview, see Melba Joyce Boyd's *Discovered Legacy: Politics and Poetics in the Life of Frances E. W. Harper, 1825–1911* (1994).

Nathaniel Hawthorne

The Centenary Edition of the Works of Nathaniel Hawthorne (1962–97), published by the Ohio State University Press, offers a comprehensive scholarly edition of Hawthorne's letters, journals, children's writings, romances, stories and sketches, and nonfiction. For selections from the voluminous notebooks, see Robert Milder and Randall Fuller's *The Business of Reflection: Hawthorne in His Notebooks* (2009). A good biography is Brenda Wineapple's *Hawthorne: A Life* (2003); this should be supplemented with James Mellow's *Nathaniel Hawthorne in His Times* (1980) and T. Walter Herbert's *Dearest Beloved: The Hawthornes and the Making of the Middle-Class Family* (1993). Also useful is Ronald A. Bosco and Jillmarie Murphy's *Hawthorne in His Own Time* (2007).

John L. Idol and Buford Jones edited *Hawthorne: The Contemporary Reviews* (1994); see also Gary Scharnhorst's *Nathaniel Hawthorne: An Annotated Bibliography of Comment and Criticism before 1900* (1988). For critical essays, see John L. Idol Jr. and Melissa Ponder's *Hawthorne and Women: Engendering and Expanding the Hawthorne Tradition* (1999); Larry J. Reynolds's *Historical Guide to Nathaniel Hawthorne* (2001); Richard H. Millington's *Cambridge Companion to Nathaniel Hawthorne* (2004); Millicent Bell's *Hawthorne and the Real: Bicentennial Essays* (2005); and Jana L. Argersinger and Leland S. Person's *Hawthorne and Melville: Writing a Relationship* (2008). Person's Norton Critical Edition of *The Scarlet Letter and Other Writings* (2005) collects a wide range of primary and secondary texts; see also Robert S. Levine's Norton Critical Edition of *The House of the Seven Gables* (2006) and Richard Millington's Norton Critical Edition of *The Blithedale Romance* (2011).

The scholarship on Hawthorne is rich and voluminous. A good starting point is Leland S. Person's *Cambridge Introduction to Nathaniel Hawthorne* (2007). Important studies include Nina Baym's *The Shape of Hawthorne's Career* (1976); Michael J. Colacurcio's *The Province of Piety: Moral History in Hawthorne's Early Tales* (1984); Richard Brodhead's *The School of Hawthorne* (1986); Gordon Hutner's *Secrets and Sympathy: Forms of Disclosure in Hawthorne's Novels* (1988); Sacvan Bercovitch's *The Office of the Scarlet Letter* (1991); Joel Pfister's *The Production of Personal Life: Class, Gender, and the Psychological in Hawthorne's Fiction* (1991); Richard H. Millington's *Practicing Romance: Narrative Form and Cultural Engagement in Hawthorne's Fiction* (1992); Samuel Chase Coale's *Mesmerism and Hawthorne* (1998); Clark Davis's *Hawthorne's Shyness: Ethics, Politics, and the Question of Engagement* (2005); Larry J. Reynolds's *Devils and Rebels: The Making of Hawthorne's Damned Politics* (2008); David Greven's *The Fragility of Manhood: Hawthorne, Freud, and the Politics of Gender* (2012); and Robert Milder's *Hawthorne's Habitations: A Literary Life* (2013).

Washington Irving

The Complete Works of Washington Irving (1969–), organized under the editorship of Henry A. Pochmann, was continued by Herbert L. Kleinfield, then by Richard Dilworth Rust. Three volumes of Irving's writings are available in the Library of America series: *History, Tales, and Sketches* (1983); *Bracebridge Hall; Tales of a Traveller; The Alhambra* (1991); and *Three Western Narratives* (2004). The standard biographies are Stanley T. Williams's *Life of Washington Irving* (1935) and William L. Hedges's *Washington Irving: An American Study 1802–1832* (1965), though these need to be supplemented by Andrew Burstein's *The Original Knickerbocker: The Life of Washington Irving* (2007) and Brian Jay Jones's *Washington Irving: An American Original* (2008). On reception and critical debate, see Andrew B. Myers's *A Century of Commentary on the Works of Washington Irving* (1976); Edwin and Ralph M. Aderman's *Critical Essays on Washington Irving* (1990); and James Tuttleton's *Washington Irving: The Critical Reaction* (1993). An influential study is Jeffrey Rubin-Dorsky's *Adrift in the Old World: The Psychological Pilgrimage of Washington Irving* (1988). For recent critical work, see David Schuyler's *Sanctified Landscape: Writers, Artists, and the Hudson River Valley, 1820–1909*; David Dowling's *Literary Partnerships and the Marketplace* (2012); and Walter Hugo's *Sanctuaries in Washington Irving's The Sketch Book* (2014).

Harriet Jacobs

Jean Fagin Yellin's pioneering edition of *Incidents in the Life of a Slave Girl* (1987), with biography, interpretation, and annotation, has been reissued (2000) with Harriet's brother John S. Jacobs's 1861 "A True Tale of Slavery." Frances Smith Foster and Nellie Y. McKay edited a Norton Critical Edition of *Incidents* (2001). Yellin's *Harriet Jacobs: A Life* (2004) should remain the standard biography for some time to come. An essential resource is the two-volume *Harriet Jacobs Family Papers* (2008), edited by Yellin et al. For critical discussions, see Rafia Zafar and Deborah M. Garfield's edited collection *Harriet Jacobs and "Incidents in the Life of a Slave Girl": New Critical Essays* (1996). Additional commentary may be found in Valerie Smith's *Self-Discovery and Authority in Afro-American Narrative* (1987); Karen Sánchez-Eppler's *Touching Liberty: Abolition, Feminism, and the Politics of the Body* (1993); Frances Smith Foster's *Written by Herself: Literary Production by African American Women, 1746–1892* (1993); Jennifer Fleischner's *Mastering Slavery: Memory, Family, and Identity in Women's Slave Narratives* (1996); and Carla Kaplan's *The Erotics of Talk: Women's Writing and Feminist Paradigms* (1996). On Lydia Maria Child's editing of *Incidents*, see Carolyn L. Karcher's *Lydia Maria Child: A Cultural Biography* (1994) and Bruce

Mills's *Cultural Reformations: Lydia Maria Child and the Literature of Reform* (1994).

Abraham Lincoln

The most comprehensive collection is *The Collected Works of Abraham Lincoln* (1953), 9 vols., edited by Roy P. Basler et al. The best introductions to Lincoln as a writer are Andrew Delbanco's *The Portable Abraham Lincoln* (1992) and Fred Kaplan's *Lincoln: The Biography of a Writer* (2008). David S. Reynolds edited a Norton Critical Edition of Lincoln's writings (2015). Books on Lincoln constitute a library in themselves. For a sampling, see James M. McPherson's *Abraham Lincoln and the Second American Revolution* (1990); Garry Wills's *Lincoln at Gettysburg: The Words That Remade America* (1992); Harry V. Jaffa's *A New Birth of Freedom: Abraham Lincoln and the Coming of the Civil War* (2000); John Channing Briggs's *Lincoln's Speeches Reconsidered* (2005); John Stauffer's *Giants: The Parallel Lives of Frederick Douglass and Abraham Lincoln* (2008); and Richard Wrightman Fox's *Lincoln's Body: A Cultural History* (2015). Useful edited collections include Harold Holzer's *The Lincoln Anthology: Great Writers on His Life and Legacy from 1860 to Now* (2008); Eric Foner's *Our Lincoln: New Perspectives on Lincoln and His World* (2008); and Henry Louis Gates Jr.'s *Lincoln on Race and Slavery* (2009).

Henry Wadsworth Longfellow

The fullest biography is still the two-volume *Life of Henry Wadsworth Longfellow* (1886–1887), written and edited by the poet's brother, Samuel Longfellow; this should be supplemented by Charles C. Calhoun's *Longfellow: A Rediscovered Life* (2003). Andrew Hilen's *The Letters of Henry Wadsworth Longfellow* (1966–1982) is invaluable, revealing much that Samuel Longfellow suppressed. J. D. McClatchy edited the Library of America's *Henry Wadsworth Longfellow: Poems and Other Writings* (2000). Important discussions of Longfellow and the literary marketplace may be found in William Charvat's *The Profession of Authorship in America, 1800–1870* (1968) and Christopher Irmscher's provocative *Longfellow Redux* (2006). See also Robert L. Gale's *Henry Wadsworth Longfellow Companion* (2003); Christopher N. Phillips's *Epic and American Culture* (2012); and Irmscher and Robert Arbour's *Reconsidering Longfellow* (2014).

Herman Melville

The Northwestern-Newberry Edition of *The Writings of Herman Melville* (1968–), edited by Harrison Hayford, Hershel Parker, and G. Thomas Tanselle, is the standard scholarly edition. Parker's *Herman Melville: A Biography, 1819–1851* (1996) and *Herman Melville: A Biography, 1851–1891* (2002) provide a wealth of new information about Melville and his family. For a good shorter life, see Andrew Delbanco's *Melville: His World and Work* (2005). Stanton Garner's *The Civil War World of Herman Melville* (1993) offers a fascinating perspective on Melville during the 1860s. Nineteenth-century biographical accounts are reprinted and analyzed in Merton M. Sealts Jr.'s *The Early Lives of Melville* (1974). Sealts's *Melville's Reading* (1988), primarily a list of books known to have been in Melville's possession, should be supplemented by Mary K. Bercaw's *Melville's Sources* (1987). Brian Higgins and Parker compiled *Herman Melville: The Contemporary Reviews* (1995). See also Jay Leyda's monumental compilation of documents *The Melville Log* (1951; repr. 1969, with a supplement), and Steven Olsen-Smith's *Melville in His Own Time* (2015).

Edited collections of critical essays and reviews provide excellent introductions to Melville criticism; see John Bryant's *Companion to Melville Studies* (1986); Robert S. Levine's *Cambridge Companion to Herman Melville* (1998); Donald Yannella's *New Essays on "Billy Budd"* (2002); Giles Gunn's *Historical Guide to Herman Melville* (2005); Wyn Kelly's *Companion to Herman Melville* (2006); John Bryant, Mary K. Bercaw, and Timothy Marr's *Ungraspable Phantom: Essays on Moby-Dick* (2006); Robert S. Levine and Samuel Otter's *Frederick Douglass and Herman Melville: Essays in Relation* (2008); Jana L. Argersinger and Leland S. Person's *Hawthorne and Melville: Writing a Relationship* (2008); Samuel Otter and Geoffrey Sanborn's *Melville and Aesthetics* (2011); Jason Frank's *Political Companion to Herman Melville* (2013); Sanford E. Marowitz's *Melville as Poet* (2013); and Robert S. Levine's *New Cambridge Companion to Herman Melville* (2014). Visually stunning and illuminating are Robert K. Wallace's *Melville and Turner* (1992) and Elizabeth A. Schultz's *Unpainted to the Last: "Moby-Dick" and Twentieth-Century American Art* (1995). Among the most influential recent works in Melville studies are Wai-chee Dimock's *Empire for Liberty: Melville and the Poetics of Individualism* (1989); John Bryant's *Melville and Repose: The Rhetoric of Humor in the American Renaissance* (1993); Wyn Kelley's *Melville's City* (1996); Elizabeth Renker's *Strike through the Mask: Herman Melville and the Scene of Writing* (1996); Samuel Otter's *Melville's Anatomies* (1999); Robert Milder's *Exiled Royalties: Melville and the Life We Imagine* (2006); Branka Arsić's *Passive Constitutions, or, 7½ Times Bartleby* (2007); Hershel Parker's *Melville: The Making of the Poet*

(2008); Geoffrey Sanborn's *Whipscars and Tattoos: The Last of the Mohicans, Moby-Dick, and the Maori* (2011); Christopher Freeburg's *Melville and the Idea of Blackness* (2012); and Greg Grandin's *The Empire of Necessity: Slavery, Freedom, and Deception in the New World* (2014), which provides essential backgrounds on Amasa Delano and "Benito Cereno."

Edgar Allan Poe

There is no complete modern scholarly edition of Poe, although there are a number of facsimile reprints of early editions as well as modern volumes of the poems edited by Floyd Stovall (1965) and Thomas O. Mabbott (1969). Burton R. Pollin continued Mabbott's long-projected edition of the *Collected Writings*; the first volume appeared in 1981. Patrick F. Quinn's Library of America *Edgar Allan Poe: Poetry and Tales* (1984) is an excellent one-volume collection; and G. R. Thompson's Library of America *Edgar Allan Poe: Essays and Revisions* (1984) makes many elusive documents readily available. See also Thompson's Norton Critical Edition of *The Selected Writings of Edgar Allan Poe* (2004); Stuart Levine and Susan F. Levine's *Edgar Allan Poe, Critical Theory: The Major Documents* (2009); and Levine and Levine's 2004 edition of *Eureka* (2004). John W. Ostrom edited *The Letters of Edgar Allan Poe* (1966). The best recent biography is Kenneth Silverman's *Edgar A. Poe* (1991), but that should be supplemented by Dwight Thomas and David K. Jackson's *The Poe Log: A Documentary Life of Edgar Allan Poe, 1809–1849* (1987) and Benjamin Franklin Fisher's *Poe in His Own Time* (2010). Good handbooks include Dawn B. Sova's *Critical Companion to Edgar Allan Poe* (2007) and Kevin Hayes's *Edgar Allan Poe in Context* (2013).

Modern collections of criticism, such as I. M. Walker's *Edgar Allan Poe: The Critical Heritage* (1986), are largely superseded by Graham Clarke's four-volume *Edgar Allan Poe: Critical Assessments* (1991). Useful collections include Shawn Rosenheim and Stephen Rachman's *The American Face of Edgar Allan Poe* (1995); Eric W. Carlson's *Companion to Poe Studies* (1996); J. Gerald Kennedy's *Historical Guide to Edgar Allan Poe* (2001); Kennedy and Liliane Weissberg's *Romancing the Shadow: Poe and Race* (2001); Hayes's *Cambridge Companion to Edgar Allan Poe* (2002); Richard Kopley and Jana Argersinger's *Poe Writing / Writing Poe* (2013); and Kennedy and Jerome McGann's *Poe and the Remapping of Antebellum Print Culture* (2013). Important critical studies include Jonathan Elmer's *Reading at the Social Limit: Affect, Mass Culture, and Edgar Allan Poe* (1995); Terence Whalen's *Edgar Allan Poe and the Masses: The Political*

Economy of Literature in Antebellum America (1999); Meredith L. McGill's *American Literature and the Culture of Reprinting, 1834–1853* (2003); Scott Peeples's *The Afterlife of Edgar Allan Poe* (2004); Eliza Richards's *Gender and the Politics of Reception in Poe's Circle* (2004); Kopley's *Edgar Allan Poe and the Dupin Mysteries* (2008); Douglas Anderson's *Pictures of Ascent in the Fiction of Edgar Allan Poe* (2009); McGann's *The Poet Edgar Allen Poe* (2014); Barbara Cantalupo's *Poe and the Visual Arts* (2014); and Paul Hurh's *American Terror: The Feeling of Thinking in Edwards, Poe, and Melville* (2015). For good short introductions, see Benjamin F. Fisher's *Cambridge Introduction to Edgar Allan Poe* (2008); Hayes's *Edgar Allan Poe* (2009); and Paul Collins's *Edgar Allan Poe: The Fever Called Living* (2014). Daniel Hoffman's *Poe Poe Poe Poe Poe Poe Poe* (1972) continues to entertain and instruct.

Harriet Beecher Stowe

The Writings of Harriet Beecher Stowe (1896, 1967), in sixteen volumes, though not complete, is comprehensive enough to represent Stowe's literary range. The Library of America's volume contains *Uncle Tom's Cabin, The Minister's Wooing,* and *Oldtown Folks* (1982). Elizabeth Ammons edited a Norton Critical Edition of *Uncle Tom's Cabin* (1994; 2nd ed. 2010), and Joan D. Hedrick edited *The Oxford Harriet Beecher Stowe Reader* (1999). Stowe's second antislavery novel, *Dred: A Tale of the Great Dismal Swamp* (1856), is available in a text edited by Robert S. Levine (2006). Bibliographical resources include Margaret Holbrook Hildreth's *Harriet Beecher Stowe: A Bibliography* (1976) and Jean Ashton's *Harriet Beecher Stowe: A Reference Guide* (1977).

Joan D. Hedrick's *Harriet Beecher Stowe: A Life* (1994) is the standard biography. A good family biography is Milton Rugoff's *The Beechers: An American Family* (1981), which should be supplemented by Barbara A. White's *The Beecher Sisters* (2003). See also Susan Belasco's *Stowe in Her Own Time* (2009). Thomas R. Gossett's *"Uncle Tom's Cabin" and American Culture* (1985) is invaluable; see also Sarah Meer's *Uncle Tom Mania: Slavery, Minstrelsy, and Transatlantic Culture in the 1850s* (2005). Useful collections of critical essays include Eric Sundquist's *New Essays on "Uncle Tom's Cabin"* (1986); Mason I. Lowance Jr., Ellen E. Wesbrook, and R. C. De Prospo's *The Stowe Debate: Rhetorical Strategies in "Uncle Tom's Cabin"* (1994); Cindy Weinstein's *Cambridge Companion to Harriet Beecher Stowe* (2004); and Elizabeth Ammons's *Harriet Beecher Stowe's Uncle Tom's Cabin: A Casebook* (2007).

Specialized critical studies dealing wholly or in part with Stowe include Edwin Bruce

Kirkham's *The Building of "Uncle Tom's Cabin"* (1977); Jane Tompkins's *Sensational Designs* (1985); Gillian Brown's *Domestic Individualism: Imagining Self in Nineteenth-Century America* (1992); Marianne Noble's *The Masochistic Pleasures of Sentimental Literature* (2000); Susan M. Ryan's *The Grammar of Good Intentions: Race and the Antebellum Culture of Benevolence* (2003); Barbara Hochman's *Uncle Tom's Cabin and the Reading Revolution* (2011); John W. Frick's *Uncle Tom's Cabin on the American Stage and Screen* (2012); and Martha Schoolman's *Abolitionist Geographies* (2014). Stephen Railton has developed a useful website, *Uncle Tom's Cabin and American Culture* <iath.virginia.edu/utc/>.

Henry David Thoreau
The Princeton Edition of Thoreau's writings (1971–) is standard. Of the volumes published so far, *Walden* (1971), edited by J. Lyndon Shanley, should be supplemented by Shanley's *The Making of "Walden"* (1957, 1966) and Jeffrey S. Cramer's *Walden: A Fully Annotated Edition* (2004). The Princeton Edition of Thoreau's writings includes the journals (1981–); for an excellent selection, see *I to Myself: An Annotated Selection from the Journal of Henry D. Thoreau* (2007), edited by Cramer. Thoreau's letters can be found in Carl Bode and Walter Harding's *Correspondence of Henry David Thoreau* (1958) and Robert N. Hudspeth's, *The Correspondence of Henry D. Thoreau* (2013). Raymond R. Borst compiled *The Thoreau Log: A Documentary Life of Henry David Thoreau, 1817–1862* (1992); see also Richard Schneider's *Henry David Thoreau: A Documentary Volume* (2004) and Sandra Harbert Petrulionis's *Thoreau in His Own Time* (2012). The most reliable narrative biography is still Walter Harding's *The Days of Henry Thoreau: A Biography* (1965); for an excellent intellectual biography, see Robert D. Richardson's *Henry Thoreau: A Life of the Mind* (1986).

Gary Scharnhorst compiled *Henry David Thoreau: An Annotated Bibliography of Comment and Criticism before 1900* (1992). Thoreau's reputation is surveyed in Joel Myerson's *Emerson and Thoreau: The Contemporary Reviews* (1992) and Scharnhorst's *Henry David Thoreau: A Case Study in Canonization* (1993). Good collections of critical essays include William E. Cain's *Historical Guide to Henry David Thoreau* (2000); Sandra Harbert Petrulionis and Laura Dassow Walls's *More Day to Dawn: Thoreau's "Walden" for the Twenty-first Century* (2007); Jack Turner's *Political Companion to Henry David Thoreau* (2009); John T. Lysaker and William Rossi's *Emerson and Thoreau: Figures of Friendship* (2010); and François Specq, Laura Dassow Walls, and Michael Granger's *Thoreauvian*

Modernities: Transatlantic Conversations on an American Icon (2013).

Critical books on Thoreau's compositional process and literary professionalism include Stephen Adams and Donald Ross Jr.'s *Revising Mythologies: The Composition of Thoreau's Major Works* (1988); Steven Fink's *Prophet in the Marketplace: Thoreau's Development as a Professional Writer* (1992); and Robert Milder's *Reimagining Thoreau* (1995). See also Robert Sattelmeyer's *Thoreau's Reading: A Study in Intellectual History with Bibliographical Catalogue* (1988). Lawrence Buell's *The Environmental Imagination* (1995), which has a major section on Thoreau, is a classic in a new field of study; see also Robert F. Sayre's *Thoreau and the American Indians* (1977) and Walls's *Seeing New Worlds: Henry David Thoreau and Nineteenth-Century Natural Science* (1995). Recent critical work includes David M. Robinson's *Natural Life: Thoreau's Worldly Transcendentalism* (2004); Elise Virginia Lemire's *Black Walden: Slavery and Its Aftermath in Concord, Massachusetts* (2009); Sharon Mariotti's *Thoreau's Democratic Withdrawal: Alienation, Participation, and Modernity* (2010); Patrick Chura's *Thoreau the Land Surveyor* (2010); Robert M. Thorson's *Walden's Shore: Henry David Thoreau and Nineteenth-Century Science* (2014); and Patrick J. Chura, *Thoreau the Land Surveyor* (2010).

Walt Whitman
The study of Whitman has been revolutionized by the *Walt Whitman Archive* <whitmanarchive.org>, directed by Kenneth M. Price and Ed Folsom. Before going to the printed sources listed below, students should explore this huge and superbly organized hypertext archive, which includes a biographical essay by Folsom and Price, all the known contemporary reviews, all the known photographs, the various editions of *Leaves of Grass* and other of Whitman's writings, and a current bibliography of scholarship and criticism.

The Collected Writings of Walt Whitman was under the general editorship of Gay Wilson Allen; part of this edition is *Walt Whitman: The Correspondence* (1961–1969), a six-volume set with two supplements (1990–1991), edited by Edwin H. Miller. Essential, in three volumes, is *"Leaves of Grass": A Textual Variorum of the Printed Poems* (1980), edited by Sculley Bradley, Harold W. Blodgett, Arthur Golden, and William White; see also Michael Moon's Norton Critical Edition of *Leaves of Grass* (2002). Key documents can be found in *Notebooks and Unpublished Prose Manuscripts* (1984), edited by Edward P. Grier, and *Walt Whitman's Selected Journalism* (2014), edited by Douglas A. Noverr and Jason Stacy. For Whitman's temperance novel

Franklin Evans, or The Inebriate: A Tale of the Times (1842), see Christopher Castiglia and Glenn Hendler's informative edition (2007); and Ed Folsom has edited a facsimile (2010) of Whitman's 1870 *Democratic Vistas*. For useful documentary materials, see Joel Myerson's *Whitman in His Own Time* (1991; rev. ed. 2000), and Gary Schmidgall's *Intimate with Walt: Selections from Whitman's Conversations with Horace Traubel, 1888–1892* (2001).

There are a number of good biographies; see Gay Wilson Allen's *The Solitary Singer* (1967); Justin Kaplan's *Walt Whitman: A Life* (1980); David S. Reynolds's *Walt Whitman's America: A Cultural Biography* (1995); Gary Schmidgall's *Walt Whitman: A Gay Life* (1998); Jerome Loving's *Walt Whitman: The Song of Himself* (1999); and Ed Folsom and Kenneth M. Price's *Re-scripting Walt Whitman: An Introduction to His Life and Work* (2005). On the Civil War period, see Roy Morris Jr.'s *The Better Angel: Walt Whitman in the Civil War* (2000) and Ted Genoways's *Walt Whitman and the Civil War* (2009); and for a good biographical and critical overview, see M. Jimmie Killingsworth's *Cambridge Introduction to Walt Whitman* (2007).

On Whitman's critical reception, see Graham Clarke's four-volume *Walt Whitman: Critical Assessments* (1996) and Kenneth M. Price's *Walt Whitman: The Contemporary Reviews* (1996). Valuable collections of critical essays include Betsy Erkkila and Jay Grossman's *Breaking Bounds: Whitman and American Cultural Studies* (1996); David S. Reynolds's *A Historical Guide to Walt Whitman* (2000); Donald D. Kummings's *Companion to Walt Whitman* (2006); Susan Belasco, Ed Folsom, and Kenneth M. Price's *Leaves of Grass: The Sesquicentennial Essays* (2007); David Haven Blake and Michael Robertson's *Walt Whitman: Where the Future Becomes Present* (2008); John Evan Seery's *Political Companion to Walt Whitman* (2011); Joanna Levin and Edward Whitley's *Whitman among the Bohemians* (2014); and Ivy G. Wilson's *Whitman Noir: Black America and the Good Gray Poet* (2014). Important critical work includes Betsy Erkkila's *Whitman the Political Poet* (1989); Kenneth M. Price's *Whitman and*

Tradition (1990); Michael Moon's *Disseminating Whitman: Revision and Corporeality in "Leaves of Grass"* (1991); Ezra Greenspan's *Walt Whitman and the American Reader* (1991); Ed Folsom's *Walt Whitman's Native Representations* (1994); Martin Klammer's *Whitman, Slavery, and the Emergence of "Leaves of Grass"* (1995); Vivian R. Pollack's *The Erotic Whitman* (2000); Jay Grossman's *Reconstituting the American Renaissance: Emerson, Whitman, and the Poetics of Representation* (2003); M. Wynn Thomas's *Transatlantic Connections: Whitman U.S., Whitman U.K.* (2005); David Haven Blake's *Walt Whitman and the Culture of American Celebrity* (2006); Michael Robertson's *Worshipping Whitman: The Whitman Disciples* (2008); Edward Whitley's *American Bards: Walt Whitman and Other Unlikely Candidates for National Poet* (2010); Martin T. Buinicki's *Walt Whitman's Reconstruction: Poetry and Publishing Between Memory and History* (2011); and Gary Schmidgall's *Containing Multitudes: Walt Whitman and the British Literary Tradition* (2014)

John Greenleaf Whittier

Brenda Wineapple has edited a collection of Whittier's *Selected Poems* (2004), but see also Robert Penn Warren's *John Greenleaf Whittier's Poetry: An Appraisal and a Selection* (1971). An interesting collection of Whittier's nonfiction is Edwin Harrison Cady and Harry Hayden Clark's *Whittier on Writers and Writing: The Uncollected Critical Writings* (1971). Samuel T. Pickard's *Life and Letters of John Greenleaf Whittier* (1894) was superseded by *John Greenleaf Whittier: Friend of Man* (1949); John B. Pickard's *John Greenleaf Whittier: An Introduction and Interpretation* (1961); Pickard's three-volume *Letters of John Greenleaf Whittier* (1975); and Roland H. Woodwell's *John Greenleaf Whittier: A Biography* (1985). For a bibliographical guide, see Albert J. von Frank's *Whittier: A Comprehensive Annotated Bibliography* (1976). Pickard edited a collection of criticism, *Memorabilia of John Greenleaf Whittier* (1968), but even more useful is Jayne K. Kribbs's *Critical Essays on John Greenleaf Whittier* (1980).

PERMISSIONS ACKNOWLEDGMENTS

IMAGE CREDITS

COLOR INSERT CREDITS

TEXT CREDITS

Paul Radin: From "The Winnebago Trickster Cycle" from THE TRICKSTER: A STUDY IN AMERICAN INDIAN MYTHOLOGY by Paul Radin, copyright © 1956, published by Routledge & Kegan Paul Ltd. Reproduced with permission of Taylor & Francis Books UK.

Edward Taylor: From THE POEMS OF EDWARD TAYLOR, ed. by Donald E. Stanford. Copyright © 1960, renewed 1988 by Donald E. Stanford. Published by University of North Carolina Press in 1989. Reprinted by permission of Don D. Stanford.

Phillis Wheatley: From THE POEMS OF PHILLIS WHEATLEY, ed. and with an introduction by Julian D. Mason, Jr. Copyright © 1966 by The University of North Carolina Press, renewed 1989. Used by permission of the publisher. www.uncpress.unc.edu.

Index